OVERSIZE

ACPL ITEM
DISCARDED

330 F49 1999

Finance, insurance & real
estate USA

S0-BWX-622

ALLEN COUNTY PUBLIC LIBRARY
FORT WAYNE, INDIANA 46802

You may return this book to any agency or branch
of the Allen County Public Library

DEMCO

F·I·N·A·N·C·E,
I·N·S·U·R·A·N·C·E,
&·R·E·A·L·E·S·T·A·T·E
USA

Fourth Edition

Industry Analyses,
Statistics, and Leading Organizations

ISSN 1066-7350

A *Ward's* Business Directory™

F·I·N·A·N·C·E,
I·N·S·U·R·A·N·C·E,
&·R·E·A·L·ES·T·A·T·E
USA

Fourth Edition

Industry Analyses, Statistics, and Leading Organizations

- A comprehensive guide to statistics on the finance, insurance, and real estate industries—covering 36 major sectors and their activities

- Combines diverse federal and private sources of data in a unique, synthesized, analyzed format

- Includes 2,600 corporate participants with addresses, names, and sales or asset performance

- State data, rankings, and maps

- Covers local data on 2,900 counties

Arsen J. Darnay, Editor

GALE™

DETROIT · LONDON

Arsen J. Darnay, Editor

Editorial Code and Data, Inc. Staff

Joyce Piwowarski, *Associate Editor*
Sherae R. Carroll, *Technical Support*

Gale Research Staff

Amanda Quick, *Coordinator*
Mary Beth Trimper, *Production Director*
Carolyn Fischer, *Production Assistant*

Cynthia Baldwin, *Product Design Manager*
Bernadette M. Gornie, *Cover Designer*

Finance, Insurance, and Real Estate, U.S.A. is published by Gale Research under license from Information Access Company. Ward's Business Directory is a trademark of Information Access Company.

Ward's Business Directory™ utilizes an intensive research approach. Information on companies listed in the directory was gathered from annual reports, questionnaires, banks, trade commissions, newsletters, government documents, and telephone interviews. When sales data are unavailable from private companies, Ward's offers an estimate based on several considerations. Estimates are so noted with an asterisk (*).

While an extensive verification and proofing process preceded the printing of this directory, Information Access Company makes no warranties or representation regarding its accuracy or completeness, and each subscriber or user of the directory understands that Information Access Company disclaims any liability for any damages (even if Information Access Company has been advised of such damages) in connection with its use.

This publication is a creative work fully protected by all applicable copyright laws, as well as by misappropriation, trade secret, unfair competition, and other applicable laws. The authors and editors of this work have added value to the underlying factual material herein through one or more of the following: unique and original selection, coordination, expression, arrangement, and classification of the information.

All rights to this publication will be vigorously defended.

Copyright© 1999 by Arsen J. Darnay

All rights reserved including the right of reproduction in whole or in part in any form.

ISBN 0-7876-2684-8
ISSN 1066-7350

Allen County Public Library
900 Webster Street
PO Box 2270
Fort Wayne, IN 46801-2270

Printed in the United States of America
Published in the United States by Gale Research

TABLE OF CONTENTS

Finance, Insurance and Real Estate by State continued:

Finance, Insurance and Real Estate by County 499

Finance, Insurance and Real Estate by County continued:

Highlights

Finance, Insurance, and Real Estate, USA (*FIRE USA*), now in its fourth edition, has been completely updated, with time series extended by two years. *FIRE USA* presents comprehensive information on 36 standard industrial classifications (SICs) of these financially-oriented industries.

- Detailed information on 24 four-digit and 12 three-digit SIC classifications.

- Most current data available on industrial activity at this level of detail covering the span of the F.I.R.E. industries.

- Statistical data series on establishments, employment, and payroll now from 1990 through 1995 for most industries.

- Financial performance data on all but two of the industries. Detailed presentations on selected industries to 1997.

- Consistently presented, Census-based revenue data for the U.S. industry and for states. Data are from the 1992 Census of the F.I.R.E. sector.

- Graphic illustration of trends in establishments, employment, and payroll.

- More than 2,500 company listings, arranged by sales, revenues, or assets. Up to 100 companies are listed for 50 4-digit SIC industries, showing company name, address, telephone, name of the chief executive officer, sales, revenues, or assets, and employment.

- Occupational data for industry groups in 1996 (a two-year update since the last edition), showing major occupations employed by the group and trends in employment to the year 2006.

- New Input-Output tables for the 1992 benchmark year.

- State rankings and detailed state industry data for 1994 and 1995. State tables are provided with each industry and illustrated with maps. In addition, a section in Part II is devoted to state tables by SIC.

- Detailed data for 3,100 counties for 1994 and 1995, arranged by state, county, and SIC.

Introduction

Finance, Insurance, and Real Estate, USA (FIRE USA), in its fourth edition, presents statistics on 36 industries drawn from a variety of federal, industry, and association sources. These data are combined with information on leading public and private corporations obtained from *Ward's Business Directory of U.S. Private and Public Companies*.

FIRE USA is a unique synthesis of relevant data from *County Business Patterns*, the Federal Deposit Insurance Corporation, the Federal Reserve System, industry association sources, *Input-Output Study of the U.S. Economy*, and the Industry-Occupation Matrix, produced by the U.S. Department of Labor. Data on leading private and public corporations are drawn from *Ward's*, as mentioned above. Together, these materials, in preanalyzed presentation, provide a one-stop, well-indexed access to the most recently available data on finance, insurance, and real estate (F.I.R.E.) in the United States.

Features

The fourth edition is a comprehensive update of the book. Two additional years of data have been added. National, state, and county tables have all been updated. 1992 Census data have been retained and a new table featuring state-level data for 1994 and 1995 has been added. New company information is presented. The base year of the occupational data has been moved to 1996. The Input-Output tables have been updated, showing results for the 1992 Census. Data are presented in analyzed format and illustrated by graphics and maps. Specific features include:

- Coverage of 36 industries, including 12 industries at the 3-digit SIC level and 24 at the 4-digit SIC level (1987 SIC classification).

- National, state, and county data. State data include ratios and data for every industry as well as state rankings for all F.I.R.E. categories. County data include data on 2,914 counties.

- Up to 100 leading companies in each 4-digit industry in the F.I.R.E. classifications, complete with addresses, telephone numbers, names of chief executive officers, and sales or asset information to permit ranking of participants.

- Consistent, analytically presented data permitting comparisons across the F.I.R.E. industries.

- Data series from 1990 through 1995 plus selected data series up to and including 1997.

- Input-Output (I-O) data for the U.S. economy showing relationships between industries.

- Occupational data for 1996 with projections to the year 2006.

- Maps and graphics to aid the user in viewing industry locations and trends.

'The Most Current Data Available'

FIRE USA reports the most current data available at the time of the book's preparation. The objective is to present hard information—data based on actual surveys by authoritative bodies— about all F.I.R.E. industries on a comparable basis.

Scope and Coverage

FIRE USA presents statistical data on 36 F.I.R.E. industries nationally, in all 50 states (when the industry is present), and in 3,100 counties. Data are also presented on 68 occupational groupings employed in the F.I.R.E. industries and 2,600 public and private companies.

Data are shown for the years 1990 to 1995. Revenue data, for the U.S. and states, is shown for 1992 from the Economic Census. These data were not collected before by the Bureau of the Census in this consistent format. Occupational data are presented for 1996 and projected (by the Department of Labor) to the year 2006. Input-Output data for 1992 are taken from the latest I-O study (released in 1997). Corporate data are drawn from the 1998 edition of *Ward's Business Directory of U.S. Private and Public Companies.*

FIRE USA follows the 1987 classification conventions published by the Office of Management and Budget (*Standard Industrial Classification Manual: 1987*)[1].

The SIC convention divides economic activity hierarchically into major industry groups (2-digit code), industry groups (3-digit), and industries (4-digit). Most data presented in *FIRE USA* are

---

[1] The transition to North American Industry Classification System (NAICS) codes will not begin until data are published by the Federal Government in that format.

shown at the 4-digit industry level (24 industries). The 3-digit groups are used in those instances where federal sources do not provide detail below the 3-digit level (12 industries). Occupational data are reported at the 3-digit level or in groups of 3-digit industries.

Organization and Content

FIRE USA is in two parts. Part I shows national and state industry profiles; Part II presents state summaries and county data by state.

In Part I, each industry is presented as follows:

1. Introductory text
2. Table of establishments, employment, and payroll
3. Graphic of establishments, employment, and payroll
4. Table of inputs and outputs for the industry
5. Table of occupations employed by the industry
6. U.S. and state data for 1992 from the Economic Census
7. Table of state-by-state data on establishments, employment, and payroll
8. Maps of establishments, employment, and payroll
9. Table of leading companies

In the case of seven industries, additional tables are presented; they are drawn from federal and association sources. The content of these tables varies from industry to industry; they are all listed in the Table of Contents.

Each industry begins on a new page. The order of graphics and tables is invariable. In a few instances, tables are split between pages.

Part II presents state and county data on the F.I.R.E. industries as follows:

1. State Rankings for 1995, drawn from the *County Business Patterns* for 1994-1995. Population data were taken from the Census Bureau's Web site.
2. Finance, Insurance, and Real Estate by State, 1994 and 1995
3. Finance, Insurance, and Real Estate by County, 1994 and 1995

The State Rankings section shows all F.I.R.E. industries by state. Rankings are provided based on establishments, employment, payroll, and payroll per employee. State data are organized alphabetically by state. Within each state, data are shown by SIC. County data are shown alphabetically within each state. Within each county, data are arranged by SIC.

The four indexes are:

- Standard Industrial Classification (SIC) Code Index
- Keyword Index
- Company Index
- Occupation Index

The SIC Index is in two parts. The first part is arranged in SIC code sequence followed by the name of the industry and the page number on which it begins; the second part is arranged alphabetically by industry name.

For detailed information on *FIRE USA*'s industry profiles and indexes, please consult the "Overview of Sources and Contents."

Acknowledgments

FIRE USA includes copyrighted statistical tabulations obtained from the National Association of Realtors. The Association was most forthcoming in its support of this project by generously giving permission to reprint portions of its proprietary database. Also included, with permission and our thanks, is data published by the American Council of Life Insurance.

Comments and Suggestions Are Welcome

Comments on or suggestions for improvement of the usefulness, format, and coverage of *FIRE USA* are always welcome. Although every effort is made to maintain accuracy, errors may occasionally occur; the editor will be grateful if these are called to his attention. To discuss technical matters and content, call (248) 356-6990. For all other matters, please contact:

> Editor
> *FIRE, USA*
> Gale Research
> 27500 Drake Rd.
> Farmington Hills, MI 48331-3535
> Phone:　　　(248) 699-GALE
> 　　　　　　(800) 347-GALE

Commercial Banks means that the state had 0.9 percent of the nation's total establishments (or payroll) for that industry in 1995.

States are shown in alphabetical order. SICs within each state presentation are shown in SIC order. The source of the data is *County Business Patterns* for 1994 and 1995.

Finance, Insurance, and Real Estate by County

This section is organized in the same manner as the state tabulations just described with the exception that entities reported on are counties and the percentile columns show "% of State" rather than "% of U.S." Data are drawn from the *County Business Patterns*.

Counties are shown in alphabetical order; for this reason, no separate index of counties is provided. Within each county, data are presented in SIC order. SIC categories for which data were suppressed or not available for both 1994 and 1995 are not displayed. On average, this means that 10 percent of F.I.R.E. establishments are not shown at the county level. The smaller the state, the larger the number of establishments not shown. In California, for example, establishments not shown because of disclosure problems were 1.8 percent of total. In the state of Delaware, 23.6 percent. In the case of some counties, the only data available were for the F.I.R.E. industries as a whole.

In Alaska, subdivisions are boroughs or areas; in Louisiana, subdivisions are parishes rather than counties. In Virginia, the Department of Commerce provides, in addition to counties, data for independent cities; other independent cities are Baltimore, MD; Carson City, NV; and St. Louis, MO. The District of Columbia is reported as a separate entity.

Indexes

Unlike most government documents, *FIRE USA* is thoroughly indexed. In addition to fulfilling their primary purpose of directing users to the analyzed industries by supplying page numbers, *FIRE USA*'s indexes also provide SIC codes. All page numbers (or ranges) are indicated by the letter "p." All SIC codes (or ranges) are preceded by the letters "SIC."

SIC Index

Part one of the index is ordered numerically using the 1987 SIC sequence beginning with the first F.I.R.E. industry, *SIC 6010, Central Reserve Depository Institutions* and ending with *SIC 6799, Investors, not elsewhere classified*. This part is immediately followed by an alphabetical listing by industry name—from *Accident and Health Insurance (6321)* to *Trusts, nec (6733)*; each industry name is followed by its SIC and then the page number on which it begins.

Keyword Index

The Keyword Index has nearly 800 alphabetically arranged entries identifying services, activities, and agencies related to F.I.R.E. The names were largely but not exclusively obtained from the SIC Manual. Additional keywords have been added as required. Each term is followed by one or more SIC codes indicating the industry or industries in which the term is used. The references following each entry are arranged in SIC order.

Company Index

This index shows 2,600 company names arranged in alphabetical order; company names that begin with a numeral ("1st," etc.) precede company names that begin with the letter A. Company names are followed by page references and a listing of SICs (within brackets). Some company names are abbreviated.

Occupation Index

The Occupation Index shows 68 occupational groups. Where multiple occupations are part of a group, they are shown separately in the index. Alphabetical rotation is also shown (Registered nurses; Nurses, registered). All told, the index has 130 entries. The index does not attempt to refer the user to every industry in which an occupation occurs; that approach would render the index unwieldy. The total number of 3-digit industries employing the occupation is shown, in parentheses, following the name of the occupation; thereafter, the top ten (or fewer) industry groups are shown in their order of importance; the most important group (that which employs the largest number) is shown first.

The user should note that—

- Occupations are reported by 3-digit industry group; a reference to industry 632, for instance, means that the user can find the occupation under *SIC 6321, Accident and Health Insurance* as well as *6324, Hospital and Medical Service Plans.*

- Only those occupations are included which represent at least 1% of employment in a 3-digit industry group. As an example, many "Librarians, professional" are employed by F.I.R.E. industries; but as highly specialized professionals among others, their numbers do not reach the "reporting threshold" used in *FIRE USA.*

User's Guide

Finance, Insurance, and Real Estate, USA (FIRE USA) provides the user with a wealth of data and a framework for doing many kinds of assessments and analyses. The nature of the work, of course, will depend on the user's need and specific context. For this reason, all the possible uses of such a book cannot be fully described. The purpose of this section is to provide examples of use.

By their nature and function, the F.I.R.E. industries play an enabling and supporting role in the economy. They provide funding; underwrite risk; manage properties for use by others; buy, sell, and hold assets; guarantee loans or bond performance; etc. For this reason, sophisticated uses of the book in economic, policy, or planning studies would typically involve using other resources as well, including the five other books in this series, *Manufacturing USA, Service Industries USA, Wholesale and Retail Trade USA, Transportation and Public Utilities USA,* and *Agriculture, Mining and Construction USA*. The examples that follow do not attempt to depict using *FIRE USA* in analytical studies.

Finding an SIC

At the library reference desk, the librarian is receiving a call. The caller begins by saying something like this: "We're a bonding organization. We provide job completion bonds. We have to fill out this form, and they want to know our SIC. Can you help?" A typical way to fulfill such a request is to identify the SIC associated with an activity or company. Under *Bonding* in the Keyword Index, *job completion guarantee* is shown to be *SIC 6350, Surety Insurance*. A quick reading of the introductory text for the SIC confirms that the SIC does, indeed, include "bonding for guaranteeing job completion."

Providing Magnitude Information

FIRE USA is a convenient resource for answering questions on how big an industry is or what the wages in an industry might be. The question "How big is the Savings & Loan industry?" can be answered rapidly by finding Savings and Loan Associations in the Keyword Index; references are to *SIC 6010* and *6030*; looking further in the index, it becomes clear that Savings banks and Savings institutions are both in *SIC 6030*. Examination of tables in that chapter reveals the number of employees in 1992 (341,920), payroll ($8.4 billion), revenues ($92.3 billion) and earnings per employee ($24,700 per year). These data are from the U.S. and State Data table, U.S. total line. State data can also be found in the table. And in the special tables provided, data are given for such categories as total assets, equity, income, expenses, and profits.

Looking for Trends

With more years available in this edition, the user can spot trends more easily by using national or state tabulations or graphs as well as special tables in areas where they are available.

Answering Geographical Questions

The combined use of indexes, maps, the State table, and the Leading Companies table can help the reference librarian respond quickly and effectively to questions about the concentration of the industry at the state and local levels. A look at the maps provided for *Savings Institutions (SIC 6030)* shows that West Coast states have a proportionally high concentration of this industry (among others). The industry is present in all states.

The State Rankings tables, in Part II, can be used to determine the rank of each state among all F.I.R.E. industries in 1995 using number of establishments, employment, payroll, or pay per employee. Arkansas, for instance, ranks 33rd in establishments, 35th in employment, and 39th in payroll per employee. The state ranks 29th in population.

The F.I.R.E. by State or County tables, also in Part II, are useful in pinpointing salient facts about each F.I.R.E. SIC at the state or local level.

Finding Companies

The Keyword Index, used in conjunction with the Leading Companies tables, gives the reference-provider a way to identify one or more companies within an industry or state. A caller, for instance, may be trying to find a mobile home site operator in Nevada. The Keyword Index points to *SIC 6510, Real Estate Operators and Lessors*. A look through the Leading Companies tables shows five entries for *SIC 6515, Mobile Home Site Operators*. None is listed for Nevada; but three entries in neighboring states (two in California and one in Oregon) may be good points of contact for the caller.

Helping Job Seekers

FIRE USA provides a painless means of matching occupations to industries and companies—provided, of course, that the occupations fall into the F.I.R.E. category and are employed in reasonable numbers. A newlywed couple, moving from Missouri to Florida to be nearer the wife's family, attempt to identify potential employers of property managers (she is working in that occupation now). Their desire is to move to the Miami area. The Occupation Index identifies 3-digit SICs 651 and 653 as the two largest employers of this specialty. A look at companies in *SIC 6510, Real Estate Operators and Lessors* produces seven companies in Florida; of these one is in North Miami Beach and one in Hollywood. These can serve as starting points.

Estimating Financial Data

With the availability of 1992 revenue data for all but two of the 36 industries covered in *FIRE USA* (*SICs 6732, 6733*), estimating the financial performance of industries in this sector has become a little easier: at least one year's worth of "hard" census data is available and can be used to estimate other years. For example:

Suppose you want to estimate the size of *SIC 6510 - Real Estate Operators and Lessors* in 1995 as measured in revenues. A single value, revenues for 1992, is available, $74.0695 billion, from the U.S. and State Data table. You would use this value to obtain an industry revenue figure for 1995 as follows:

1. Calculate change in employment between 1992 and 1995 using the Establishments, Employment and Payroll table. The change is 3.6%.

2. Apply this figure to the employment item in the U.S. and State Data table: 462,546 x 1.036 = 479,363.

3. In 1992, revenues per employee were $160,128. Apply this value to the result in 2. above: 479,363 x 160,128 = $76.759 billion. This is one estimate for 1995 revenues.

You can apply a similar approach to developing longer-range projections as well. Using the Establishments, Employment, and Payroll table (*County Business Patterns*), you can develop various growth factors for this industry. Employment has grown 7.76% in the 1991-1995 period; payroll is up 20.8 percent, etc. Using such data, you can estimate 1997 revenues, say, by applying growth factors to the 1992 census datum.

Such analyses are, of course, bound to be imprecise. But in the absence of better numbers, such exercises can sometimes provide enough of an answer to guide research in the right direction. And for many of the larger industries, data from other sources are provided in special tables to profile industry income, assets, and other factors.

Analyzing Occupational Trends

The Occupation table provides occupations within an industry group for 1996 as well as projections of growth or decline to the year 2006. These data can be used effectively in identifying areas of potential problems for the employee or for the employer.

Generally, higher skill levels are growing, lower skills declining. For example, *Typists and word processors* and *Bookkeeping, auditing, and accounting clerks* are declining occupations in most industries; but more so in some than others. *Computer programmers* are growing in fewer and fewer industries to the year 2006—declining more rapidly in some industries than in others. *Book-keeping clerks*, examining *FIRE USA*, can clearly see (in *SIC 6310, Life Insurance*, for example) that employment of *Accountants and auditors* will decline much less rapidly than their own. A little more job security may be obtained by upgrading skills from the clerical to the professional level. But in this industry of generally declining occupations, the safest strategy is to become an underwriter, the only rapidly-growing category in the higher-income range. Employers, plotting human resource strategies, can predict in this same industry that competition for people with higher skills in the data processing area will become sharp. The number of *Computer programmers* will decrease, but demand for *Systems Analysts* will increase dramatically—and much more in other industries than in Life Insurance.

In addition to the examples listed above, the state and county data provide statistics for a variety of geographical analyses. These might involve comparing counties (or groups of counties aggregated into urban areas) with each other, identifying gaps to be filled in services by expansion, etc. Users who wish to see additional examples illustrated in subsequent editions need but to write to the editor.

SIC 6010

CENTRAL RESERVE DEPOSITORY INSTITUTIONS

Central reserve depository institutions are organizations engaged primarily in receiving deposits from banks and providing advances to such institutions. Reserve depositories generally do not take deposits or make advances to other enterprises and individuals. Included in this category are the Federal Reserve Banks and their branches (SIC 6011), which serve as regional reserve and rediscounting institutions for their members, and Central Reserve Depository Institutions, not elsewhere classified (SIC 6019), which include institutions that are not part of the Federal Reserve System but provide analogous services to savings banks, savings and loan associations, or credit unions. SIC 6019 includes the Central Liquidity Facility, the Federal Home Loans Banks, and the National Credit Union Administration (NCUA).

ESTABLISHMENTS, EMPLOYMENT, AND PAYROLL

	1990	1991		1992		1993		1994		1995		% change 90-95
		Value	%	Value	%	Value	%	Value	%	Value	%	
All Establishments	118	142	20.3	150	5.6	75	-50.0	86	14.7	95	10.5	-19.5
Mid-March Employment	30,513	29,074	-4.7	28,706	-1.3	26,448	-7.9	25,191	-4.8	25,026	-0.7	-18.0
1st Quarter Wages (annualized - $ mil.)	894.5	909.1	1.6	951.8	4.7	912.9	-4.1	921.1	0.9	974.3	5.8	8.9
Payroll per Emp. 1st Q. (annualized)	29,315	31,267	6.7	33,158	6.0	34,516	4.1	36,567	5.9	38,932	6.5	32.8
Annual Payroll ($ mil.)	901.9	917.2	1.7	964.0	5.1	902.9	-6.3	933.7	3.4	980.6	5.0	8.7
Establishments - 1-4 Emp. Number	11	18	63.6	15	-16.7	8	-46.7	8	-	(D)	-	-
Mid-March Employment	13	35	169.2	33	-5.7	12	-63.6	9	-25.0	(D)	-	-
1st Quarter Wages (annualized - $ mil.)	0.2	0.6	129.0	0.5	-8.5	0.3	-48.5	0.3	-6.0	(D)	-	-
Payroll per Emp. 1st Q. (annualized)	19,077	16,229	-14.9	15,758	-2.9	22,333	41.7	28,000	25.4	(D)	-	-
Annual Payroll ($ mil.)	0.8	0.9	13.4	0.9	-4.6	1.4	58.4	0.6	-56.7	(D)	-	-
Establishments - 5-9 Emp. Number	8	8	-	22	175.0	(D)	-	7	-	9	28.6	12.5
Mid-March Employment	56	59	5.4	155	162.7	(D)	-	55	-	67	21.8	19.6
1st Quarter Wages (annualized - $ mil.)	2.3	1.3	-41.7	3.3	149.6	(D)	-	1.2	-	1.5	25.1	-34.1
Payroll per Emp. 1st Q. (annualized)	41,071	22,712	-44.7	21,574	-5.0	(D)	-	22,036	-	22,627	2.7	-44.9
Annual Payroll ($ mil.)	2.7	1.1	-58.9	3.4	204.9	(D)	-	1.3	-	1.9	39.9	-30.1
Establishments - 10-19 Emp. Number	13	17	30.8	17	-	(D)	-	(D)	-	11	-	-15.4
Mid-March Employment	189	(D)	-	275	-	(D)	-	(D)	-	154	-	-18.5
1st Quarter Wages (annualized - $ mil.)	4.3	(D)	-	6.7	-	(D)	-	(D)	-	2.4	-	-42.7
Payroll per Emp. 1st Q. (annualized)	22,519	(D)	-	24,305	-	(D)	-	(D)	-	15,844	-	-29.6
Annual Payroll ($ mil.)	4.6	(D)	-	7.5	-	(D)	-	(D)	-	3.4	-	-27.1
Establishments - 20-49 Emp. Number	20	20	-	24	20.0	8	-66.7	(D)	-	12	-	-40.0
Mid-March Employment	599	607	1.3	691	13.8	251	-63.7	(D)	-	435	-	-27.4
1st Quarter Wages (annualized - $ mil.)	18.1	21.4	18.0	29.4	37.5	5.8	-80.2	(D)	-	11.5	-	-36.5
Payroll per Emp. 1st Q. (annualized)	30,264	35,249	16.5	42,576	20.8	23,219	-45.5	(D)	-	26,446	-	-12.6
Annual Payroll ($ mil.)	19.6	23.4	19.3	28.6	22.4	5.8	-79.8	(D)	-	11.0	-	-44.0
Establishments - 50-99 Emp. Number	10	30	200.0	19	-36.7	7	-63.2	9	28.6	7	-22.2	-30.0
Mid-March Employment	702	2,013	186.8	1,321	-34.4	494	-62.6	666	34.8	479	-28.1	-31.8
1st Quarter Wages (annualized - $ mil.)	18.6	60.6	226.8	38.3	-36.9	15.3	-59.9	23.2	51.3	19.0	-18.1	2.5
Payroll per Emp. 1st Q. (annualized)	26,433	30,126	14.0	28,990	-3.8	31,069	7.2	34,865	12.2	39,699	13.9	50.2
Annual Payroll ($ mil.)	18.9	55.9	195.1	35.7	-36.1	15.2	-57.3	21.6	42.1	16.7	-22.8	-11.7
Establishments - 100-249 Emp. Number	25	20	-20.0	25	25.0	24	-4.0	23	-4.2	26	13.0	4.0
Mid-March Employment	4,453	(D)	-	3,838	-	3,550	-7.5	3,590	1.1	4,018	11.9	-9.8
1st Quarter Wages (annualized - $ mil.)	127.6	(D)	-	121.5	-	117.4	-3.4	120.7	2.8	154.4	27.9	21.0
Payroll per Emp. 1st Q. (annualized)	28,646	(D)	-	31,663	-	33,068	4.4	33,619	1.7	38,416	14.3	34.1
Annual Payroll ($ mil.)	121.9	(D)	-	118.5	-	114.9	-3.1	117.0	1.8	144.9	23.8	18.9
Establishments - 250-499 Emp. Number	17	16	-5.9	15	-6.3	12	-20.0	(D)	-	(D)	-	-
Mid-March Employment	6,289	(D)	-	4,851	-	3,961	-18.3	(D)	-	(D)	-	-
1st Quarter Wages (annualized - $ mil.)	165.8	(D)	-	141.4	-	117.6	-16.8	(D)	-	(D)	-	-
Payroll per Emp. 1st Q. (annualized)	26,370	(D)	-	29,147	-	29,689	1.9	(D)	-	(D)	-	-
Annual Payroll ($ mil.)	164.4	(D)	-	149.3	-	115.6	-22.6	(D)	-	(D)	-	-
Establishments - 500-999 Emp. Number	6	4	-33.3	4	-	(D)	-	5	-	4	-20.0	-33.3
Mid-March Employment	(D)	3,372	-	3,225	-4.4	(D)	-	4,166	-	3,216	-22.8	-
1st Quarter Wages (annualized - $ mil.)	(D)	100.7	-	108.9	8.1	(D)	-	156.5	-	120.9	-22.7	-
Payroll per Emp. 1st Q. (annualized)	(D)	29,878	-	33,759	13.0	(D)	-	37,572	-	37,598	0.1	-
Annual Payroll ($ mil.)	(D)	106.4	-	109.1	2.5	(D)	-	158.9	-	121.1	-23.8	-
Estab. - 1000 or More Emp. Number	8	9	12.5	9	-	9	-	(D)	-	9	-	12.5
Mid-March Employment	(D)	13,997	-	14,317	2.3	14,255	-0.4	(D)	-	13,060	-	-
1st Quarter Wages (annualized - $ mil.)	(D)	478.4	-	501.8	4.9	524.1	4.4	(D)	-	555.2	-	-
Payroll per Emp. 1st Q. (annualized)	(D)	34,179	-	35,048	2.5	36,765	4.9	(D)	-	42,511	-	-
Annual Payroll ($ mil.)	(D)	481.2	-	510.9	6.2	528.5	3.4	(D)	-	565.6	-	-

Source: County Business Patterns, U.S. Department of Commerce, Washington, D.C., for 1990 through 1995. Payroll per employee is calculated using mid-March employment and 1st Quarter wages, annualized. Annual payroll, also shown, may not equal the annualized 1st Quarter wages. Columns headed by a percent sign (%) indicate change from the previous year. *na* stands for not available. The symbol (D) indicates that data are withheld by the source to avoid disclosure of competitive information. A dash (-) indicates that data are not available or cannot be calculated.

ESTABLISHMENTS
Number

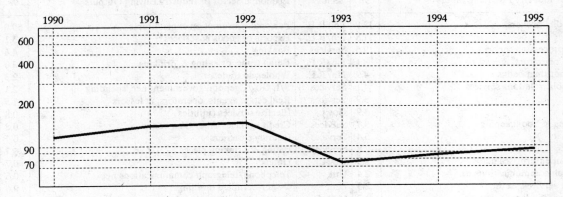

MID-MARCH EMPLOYMENT
Number

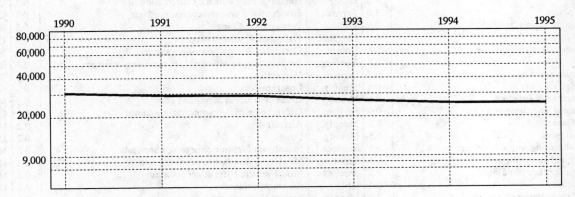

ANNUAL PAYROLL
$ million

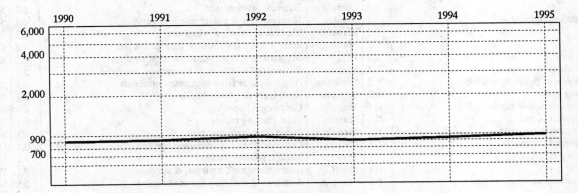

INPUTS AND OUTPUTS FOR ALL BANKING SECTORS - SICs 601, 602, 603, 608, and 609

Economic Sector or Industry Providing Inputs	%	Sector	Economic Sector or Industry Buying Outputs	%	Sector
Security & commodity brokers	12.9	Fin/R.E.	Personal consumption expenditures	59.0	
Banking	11.8	Fin/R.E.	Exports of goods & services	5.1	Foreign
Computer & data processing services	9.5	Services	Banking	4.6	Fin/R.E.
Real estate agents, operators, & lessors	8.1	Fin/R.E.	Retail trade, ex eating & drinking	3.0	Trade
Credit agencies other than banks	4.9	Fin/R.E.	Wholesale trade	2.3	Trade
Management & public relations services	4.1	Services	S/L Govt., general government nec, spending	2.1	S/L Govt
Advertising	3.9	Services	Real estate agents, operators, & lessors	1.5	Fin/R.E.
U.S. Postal Service	3.9	Gov't	Electric services (utilities)	0.8	Util.
Accounting, auditing & bookkeeping	3.7	Services	Credit agencies other than banks	0.8	Fin/R.E.
Business services nec	3.4	Services	Insurance carriers	0.7	Fin/R.E.
Legal services	2.8	Services	Eating & drinking places	0.7	Services
Federal Government enterprises nec	2.5	Gov't	Hotels	0.7	Services
Telephone/telegraph communications nec	2.4	Util.	Telephone/telegraph communications nec	0.6	Util.
Trucking & courier services, ex air	2.3	Util.	Owner-occupied dwellings	0.6	Fin/R.E.
Blankbooks, looseleaf binders & devices	1.7	Manufg.	Doctors & dentists	0.6	Services
Wholesale trade	1.6	Trade	Motor vehicles & passenger car bodies	0.4	Manufg.
Personnel supply services	1.6	Services	Trucking & courier services, ex air	0.4	Util.
Electric services (utilities)	1.5	Util.	Federal Government, nondefense, spending	0.4	Gov't
Warehousing & storage	1.4	Util.	New construction nec	0.3	Constr.
Air transportation	1.0	Util.	Repair & maintenance construction nec	0.3	Constr.
Eating & drinking places	1.0	Services	Residential 1 unit structures, nonfarm	0.3	Constr.
Sanitary services, steam supply, irrigation	0.9	Util.	Petroleum refining	0.3	Manufg.
Insurance carriers	0.9	Fin/R.E.	Railroads & related services	0.3	Util.
Repair & maintenance construction nec	0.8	Constr.	Computer & data processing services	0.3	Services
Hotels	0.8	Services	Engineering, architectural, & surveying services	0.3	Services
Detective & protective services	0.7	Services	Hospitals	0.3	Services
Commercial printing	0.6	Manufg.	Legal services	0.3	Services
Photographic equipment & supplies	0.6	Manufg.	Crude petroleum & natural gas	0.2	Mining
Research, development, & testing services	0.6	Services	Office, industrial/commercial buildings	0.2	Constr.
Manifold business forms	0.5	Manufg.	Aircraft	0.2	Manufg.
Paper & paperboard mills	0.5	Manufg.	Drugs	0.2	Manufg.
Automotive rental & leasing, without drivers	0.5	Services	Industrial inorganic & organic chemicals	0.2	Manufg.
Business & professional associations	0.5	Services	Miscellaneous plastics products, nec	0.2	Manufg.
Services to dwellings & other buildings	0.5	Services	Motor vehicle parts & accessories	0.2	Manufg.
Natural gas distribution	0.4	Util.	Air transportation	0.2	Util.
Magnetic & optical recording media	0.3	Manufg.	Freight forwarders	0.2	Util.
Manufacturing industries, nec	0.3	Manufg.	Water transportation	0.2	Util.
Periodicals	0.3	Manufg.	Security & commodity brokers	0.2	Fin/R.E.
Petroleum refining	0.3	Manufg.	Automotive rental & leasing, without drivers	0.2	Services
Electrical repair shops	0.3	Services	Automotive repair shops & services	0.2	Services
Book publishing	0.2	Manufg.	Business services nec	0.2	Services
Computer peripheral equipment	0.2	Manufg.	Management & public relations services	0.2	Services
Envelopes	0.2	Manufg.	Medical & health services nec	0.2	Services
Textile bags	0.2	Manufg.	State & local government enterprises nec	0.2	Gov't
Local & suburban transit	0.2	Util.	Maintenance/repair of residential structures	0.1	Constr.
Automotive repair shops & services	0.2	Services	Residential additions & alterations, nonfarm	0.1	Constr.
Miscellaneous equipment rental & leasing	0.2	Services	Apparel made from purchased materials	0.1	Manufg.
Miscellaneous repair shops	0.2	Services	Blast furnaces & steel mills	0.1	Manufg.
Die-cut paper & paperboard & cardboard	0.1	Manufg.	Commercial printing	0.1	Manufg.
Fabricated metal products, nec	0.1	Manufg.	Meat packing plants	0.1	Manufg.
Miscellaneous fabricated wire products	0.1	Manufg.	Paper & paperboard mills	0.1	Manufg.
Paperboard containers & boxes	0.1	Manufg.	Cable & other pay television services	0.1	Util.
Retail trade, ex eating & drinking	0.1	Trade	Natural gas distribution	0.1	Util.
Royalties	0.1	Fin/R.E.	Insurance agents, brokers, & services	0.1	Fin/R.E.
State & local government enterprises nec	0.1	Gov't	Accounting, auditing & bookkeeping	0.1	Services
			Motion picture services & theaters	0.1	Services
			Personnel supply services	0.1	Services
			Portrait photographic studios	0.1	Services
			U.S. Postal Service	0.1	Gov't

Source: Benchmark Input-Output Accounts for the U.S. Economy, 1992, U.S. Department of Commerce, Washington, D.C., November 1997. Data, as reported in the source, are organized by the 1987 SIC structure in use in 1992.

OCCUPATIONS EMPLOYED BY BANKING AND CLOSELY RELATED FUNCTIONS, NEC

Occupation	% of Total 1996	Change to 2006	Occupation	% of Total 1996	Change to 2006
Bank tellers	9.0	18.8	Clerical & administrative workers nec	2.6	16.4
General office clerks	7.7	0.1	Computer programmers	2.4	-4.2
Clerical supervisors & managers	6.3	16.4	Loan officers & counselors	2.3	16.4
Adjustment clerks	5.5	57.1	Sales & related workers nec	2.3	28.0
Cashiers	4.7	24.3	Systems analysts	2.3	86.2
Secretaries, except legal & medical	4.4	-7.7	Credit analysts	2.1	16.4
Bookkeeping, accounting, & auditing clerks	4.1	-6.9	Securities & financial sales workers	1.8	74.6
General managers & top executives	3.9	12.8	Data entry keyers, except composing	1.6	-6.9
Financial managers	3.4	16.4	Managers & administrators nec	1.6	15.3
Accountants & auditors	3.2	7.7	Computer operators, ex peripheral equipment	1.5	-30.2
Loan & credit clerks	2.9	17.5	Guards	1.1	4.8
Duplicating, mail, office machine operators	2.8	-24.4	Brokerage clerks	1.1	-2.7

Sources: *Industry-Occupation Matrix*, Bureau of Labor Statistics. These data relate to one or more 3-digit SIC industry groups rather than to a single 4-digit SIC. The change reported for each occupation to the year 2005 is a percent of growth or decline as estimated by the Bureau of Labor Statistics. The abbreviation *nec* stands for not elsewhere classified.

U.S. AND STATE DATA ON INDUSTRY REVENUES AND OTHER ACCOUNTS FOR 1992

State	No. of Estab.	Employ- ment	Payroll ($ mil.)	Revenues ($ mil.)	Empl./ Estab.	Revenue/ Estab. ($)	Payroll/ Estab. ($)	Revenue/ Empl. ($)	Payroll/ Empl. ($)
UNITED STATES	67	26,334	870.4	29,571.7	393	441,369,149	12,991,388	1,122,949	33,053
California	3	2,260	83.2	4,549.0	753	516,321,333	27,740,000	2,012,816	36,823
Colorado	2	392	11.2	18.9	196	9,442,000	5,624,500	48,173	28,696
Florida	2	676	19.3	30.1	338	15,030,000	9,633,000	44,467	28,500
Georgia	2	1,350	49.2	1,780.6	675	890,317,000	24,585,000	1,318,988	36,422
Illinois	2	1,994	73.8	2,449.2	997	224,619,500	36,919,500	1,228,304	37,031
Indiana	1	155	4.8	554.8	155	554,750,000	4,840,000	3,579,032	31,226
Maryland	1	433	11.5	321.3	433	321,307,000	11,537,000	742,048	26,644
Massachusetts	2	1,686	55.1	1,887.6	843	943,789,500	27,527,000	1,119,560	32,654
Michigan	1	426	11.6	440.6	426	440,563,000	11,581,000	1,034,185	27,185
Minnesota	2	1,086	35.9	431.2	543	215,580,000	17,939,000	397,017	33,037
Missouri	4	1,828	60.8	1,100.9	457	275,217,750	15,198,000	602,227	33,256
New Jersey	1	185	5.1	558.0	185	557,951,000	5,087,000	3,015,951	27,497
New York	3	4,167	153.3	8,259.7	1,389	753,224,000	51,108,000	1,982,163	36,795
North Carolina	1	419	10.2	310.9	419	310,917,000	10,230,000	742,045	24,415
Ohio	5	1,342	42.7	1,462.7	268	292,531,200	8,535,200	1,089,908	31,800
Pennsylvania	4	2,244	65.6	1,354.9	561	338,730,750	16,411,000	603,798	29,253
Tennessee	3	419	9.8	76.2	140	25,406,000	3,258,000	181,905	23,327
Texas	5	1,818	59.9	1,516.4	364	303,275,000	11,976,400	834,090	32,938
Virginia	2	1,138	44.5	825.2	569	412,597,000	22,270,000	725,127	39,139
Washington	2	277	9.4	689.6	139	344,815,000	4,701,000	2,489,639	33,942

Source: 1992 Economic Census, U.S. Department of Commerce, Washington, D.C. This is the only table that shows revenue data as collected by the Bureau of the Census in an Economic Census. The symbol (D) indicates that data are withheld by the source to avoid disclosure of competitive information. A dash (-) indicates that data are not available or cannot be calculated.

STATE-BY-STATE DATA ON ESTABLISHMENTS, EMPLOYMENT, AND PAYROLL - 1994 AND 1995

State	1994					1995					% Change Empl.
	No. of Estab.	Employ-ment	Pay / Empl.	Payroll ($ mil.)	Pay / Estab.	No. of Estab.	Employ-ment	Pay / Empl.	Payroll ($ mil.)	Pay / Estab.	
Alabama	8	(D)	-	(D)	-	8	(D)	-	(D)	-	-
Alaska	1	(D)	-	(D)	-	1	(D)	-	(D)	-	-
Arkansas	1	(D)	-	(D)	-	1	(D)	-	(D)	-	-
California	3	(D)	-	(D)	-	3	(D)	-	(D)	-	-
Colorado	2	(D)	-	(D)	-	2	(D)	-	(D)	-	-
Connecticut	1	(D)	-	(D)	-	1	(D)	-	(D)	-	-
District of Columbia	1	(D)	-	(D)	-	1	(D)	-	(D)	-	-
Florida	5	(D)	-	(D)	-	7	861	30,402	26.2	3,741,286	-
Georgia	2	(D)	-	(D)	-	2	(D)	-	(D)	-	-
Illinois	5	(D)	-	(D)	-	3	(D)	-	(D)	-	-
Indiana	1	(D)	-	(D)	-	1	(D)	-	(D)	-	-
Iowa	3	(D)	-	(D)	-	3	(D)	-	(D)	-	-
Kansas	1	(D)	-	(D)	-	1	(D)	-	(D)	-	-
Kentucky	1	(D)	-	(D)	-	1	(D)	-	(D)	-	-
Louisiana	1	(D)	-	(D)	-	1	(D)	-	(D)	-	-
Maine	1	(D)	-	(D)	-	1	(D)	-	(D)	-	-
Maryland	1	(D)	-	(D)	-	2	(D)	-	(D)	-	-
Massachusetts	2	(D)	-	(D)	-	2	(D)	-	(D)	-	-
Michigan	1	(D)	-	(D)	-	1	(D)	-	(D)	-	-
Minnesota	2	(D)	-	(D)	-	2	(D)	-	(D)	-	-
Missouri	4	(D)	-	(D)	-	4	1,848	35,842	66.2	16,538,500	-
Montana	1	(D)	-	(D)	-	2	(D)	-	(D)	-	-
Nebraska	2	(D)	-	(D)	-	2	(D)	-	(D)	-	-
New Jersey	1	(D)	-	(D)	-	1	(D)	-	(D)	-	-
New York	3	(D)	-	(D)	-	3	(D)	-	(D)	-	-
North Carolina	1	(D)	-	(D)	-	1	(D)	-	(D)	-	-
Ohio	6	(D)	-	(D)	-	11	(D)	-	(D)	-	-
Oklahoma	2	(D)	-	(D)	-	2	(D)	-	(D)	-	-
Oregon	2	(D)	-	(D)	-	2	(D)	-	(D)	-	-
Pennsylvania	4	2,067	31,280	65.7	16,425,750	4	1,998	32,270	67.4	16,848,250	-3.3
South Carolina	1	(D)	-	(D)	-	2	(D)	-	(D)	-	-
Tennessee	4	392	26,296	10.6	2,653,750	4	391	28,010	11.0	2,754,000	-0.3
Texas	5	(D)	-	(D)	-	6	(D)	-	(D)	-	-
Utah	1	(D)	-	(D)	-	1	(D)	-	(D)	-	-
Virginia	2	(D)	-	(D)	-	2	(D)	-	(D)	-	-
Washington	3	454	36,308	14.6	4,852,000	3	441	42,630	15.8	5,271,667	-2.9
West Virginia	1	(D)	-	(D)	-	1	(D)	-	(D)	-	-

Source: County Business Patterns, U.S. Department of Commerce, Washington, D.C., for 1994 and 1995. Employment shown is for mid-March of the year shown. Payroll per employee is calculated by annualizing 1st Quarter payroll (not shown) and then dividing that value by mid-March employment. Dividing total annual payroll (columns 5 and 10) by employment, therefore, will *not* yield the payroll per employee figure (columns 4 and 9). The symbol (D) indicates that data are withheld by the source to avoid disclosure of competitive information. A dash (-) indicates that data are not available or cannot be calculated.

ESTABLISHMENTS 1995 - STATE AND REGIONAL CONCENTRATION

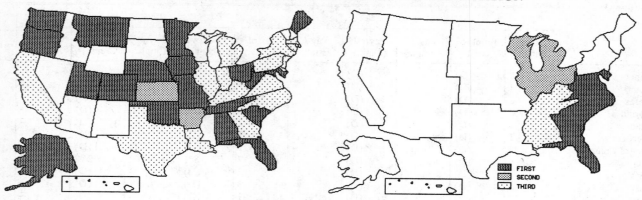

EMPLOYMENT 1995 - STATE AND REGIONAL CONCENTRATION

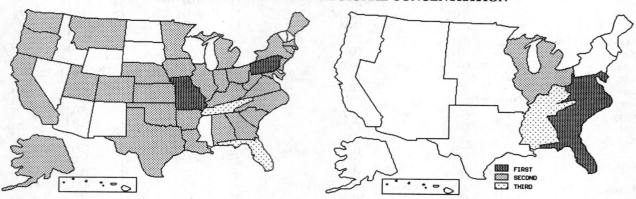

PAYROLL 1995 - STATE AND REGIONAL CONCENTRATION

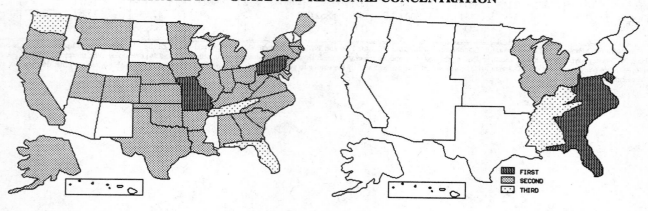

States with the darkest shading indicate those states which have proportionately more establishments, employment, or payrolls than would be indicated by the state's population. States with light shading are states with proportionately fewer establishments, less employment, and lower payrolls than population distribution. States shaded grey are within 15 percent of the state's population proportion in these categories. States for which no data are available are shown as average (grey). *Regions* are shaded to indicate absolute rank in the category. If no data for the category are available, establishment counts are used to shade the regions. Source of the data is the table on the facing page.

LEADING COMPANIES - SIC 6011 - Federal Reserve Banks

Number shown: **11**　　Total sales/assets ($ mil): **490,788**　　Total employment (000): **21.6**

Company Name	Address				CEO Name	Phone	Co. Type	Sales/Assets ($ mil)	Empl. (000)
Federal Reserve Bank of New York	33 Liberty St.	New York	NY	10045	William J. McDonough	212-720-5000	R	186,483 TA	4.0
Federal Reserve Bank of San Francisco	PO Box 7702	San Francisco	CA	94120	Robert T. Parry	415-974-2000	R	63,940 TA	2.5
Federal Reserve Bank of Chicago	PO Box 834	Chicago	IL	60690	Michael Moskow	312-322-5322	R	47,374 TA	1.7
Federal Reserve Bank of Richmond	PO Box 27622	Richmond	VA	23261	J. Alfred Broaddus Jr.	804-697-8000	R	38,077 TA	2.6
Federal Reserve Bank of Atlanta	104 Marietta St. N.W.	Atlanta	GA	30303	Robert P. Forrestal	404-521-8500	R	35,374 TA	2.4
Federal Reserve Bank of Cleveland	PO Box 6387	Cleveland	OH	44101	Jerry L. Jordan	216-579-2000	R	31,680 TA	1.4
Federal Reserve Bank of Boston	600 Atlantic Ave.	Boston	MA	02106	Cathy E. Minehan	617-973-3000	R	28,553 TA	1.5
Federal Reserve Bank of Philadelphia	10 Independence Mall	Philadelphia	PA	19106	Edward G. Boehne	215-574-6000	R	18,797 TA	1.3
Federal Reserve Bank of St. Louis	PO Box 442	St. Louis	MO	63166	William Poole	314-444-8444	R	18,786 TA	1.2
Federal Reserve Bank of Kansas City	925 Grand Blvd.	Kansas City	MO	64198	Thomas M. Hoenig	816-881-2000	R	14,276 TA	1.7
Federal Reserve Bank of Minneapolis	250 Marquette Ave.	Minneapolis	MN	55401	Gary H. Stern	612-340-2345	R	7,448 TA	1.3

*Source: Ward's Business Directory of U.S. Private and Public Companies, 1996. Company type codes: P - Public, R - Private, S - Subsidiary, D - Division, J - Joint Venture, A - Affiliate, G - Group. If the dollar values shown are not sales, the following codes apply: TA - Total Assets; OR - Operating Revenues; GB - Gross Billings. * - estimated dollar value. < - less than; na - not available.*

LEADING COMPANIES - SIC 6019 - Central Reserve Depositories, nec

Number shown: **11**　　Total sales/assets ($ mil): **509,324**　　Total employment (000): **1.7**

Company Name	Address				CEO Name	Phone	Co. Type	Sales/Assets ($ mil)	Empl. (000)
Federal Home Loan Bank of Des Moines	907 Walnut St.	Des Moines	IA	50309	Thurmond C. Connell	515-243-4211	R	260,000 TA	0.1
Federal Home Loan Bank of San Francisco	PO Box 7948	San Francisco	CA	94120	Dean Schultz	415-616-1000	R	50,468 TA	0.2
Federal Home Loan Bank of Atlanta	PO Box 105565	Atlanta	GA	30348	Paul D. Hill	404-888-8000	R	45,000 TA	0.2
Federal Home Loan Bank of New York	7 World Trade Ctr.	New York	NY	10048	Alfred A. Dellibovi	212-441-6600	R	29,300 TA	0.2
Federal Home Loan Bank of Dallas	PO Box 619026	Dallas	TX	75261	George M. Barclay	214-944-8500	R	23,001 TA	0.1
Federal Home Loan Bank of Indianapolis	PO Box 60	Indianapolis	IN	46206	Martin L. Heger	317-465-0200	R	22,000 TA	0.1
Federal Home Loan Bank of Cincinnati	PO Box 598	Cincinnati	OH	45201	Charles L. Thiemann	513-852-7500	R	21,492 TA	0.1

*Company type codes: P - Public, R - Private, S - Subsidiary, D - Division, J - Joint Venture, A - Affiliate, G - Group. If the dollar values shown are not sales, the following codes apply: TA - Total Assets; OR - Operating Revenues; GB - Gross Billings. * - estimated dollar value. < - less than. na - not available.*

Continued on next page.

LEADING COMPANIES - SIC 6019 - Central Reserve Depositories, nec
Continued

Company Name	Address				CEO Name	Phone	Co. Type	Sales/Assets ($ mil)	Empl. (000)
Federal Home Loan Bank of Seattle	1501 4th Ave.	Seattle	WA	98101	James R. Faulstich	206-340-2300	R	20,000 TA	<0.1
Federal Home Loan Bank of Pittsburgh	601 Grant St.	Pittsburgh	PA	15219	James D. Roy	412-288-3400	R	14,120 TA	0.2
Federal Home Loan Bank of Topeka	PO Box 176	Topeka	KS	66601	Frank A. Lowman	913-233-0507	R	13,000 TA	0.3
Federal Home Loan Bank of Chicago	111 E. Wacker Dr.	Chicago	IL	60601	Alex J. Pollock	312-565-5700	R	10,943 TA	0.1

Source: *Ward's Business Directory of U.S. Private and Public Companies*, 1996. Company type codes: P - Public, R - Private, S - Subsidiary, D - Division, J - Joint Venture, A - Affiliate, G - Group. If the dollar values shown are not sales, the following codes apply: TA - Total Assets; OR - Operating Revenues; GB - Gross Billings. * - estimated dollar value. < - less than; *na* - not available.

SIC 6020

COMMERCIAL BANKS

The category of Commercial Banks includes banks and trust companies that accept deposits from the public. SIC 6020 is further subdivided into (1) National Commercial Banks (SIC 6021), which are commercial banks and trust companies that accept deposits and are chartered under the National Bank Act; (2) State Commercial Banks (SIC 6022), which are commercial banks and trust companies that accept deposits and are chartered by states or territories; and (3) Commercial Banks, not elsewhere classified (SIC 6029), which are commercial banks that accept deposits and do not operate under federal or state charter. Trust companies engaged in fiduciary business but not regularly engaged in deposit banking are classified as SIC 6091 and included, in this book, under Functions Closely Related to Banking (SIC 6090).

ESTABLISHMENTS, EMPLOYMENT, AND PAYROLL

	1990	1991		1992		1993		1994		1995		% change 90-95
		Value	%	Value	%	Value	%	Value	%	Value	%	
All Establishments	52,303	61,395	17.4	65,049	6.0	62,629	-3.7	65,791	5.0	66,868	1.6	27.8
Mid-March Employment	1,472,304	1,606,240	9.1	1,576,334	-1.9	1,528,258	-3.0	1,521,226	-0.5	1,532,260	0.7	4.1
1st Quarter Wages (annualized - $ mil.)	37,903.8	42,661.1	12.6	44,325.8	3.9	42,770.8	-3.5	44,961.7	5.1	49,195.2	9.4	29.8
Payroll per Emp. 1st Q. (annualized)	25,745	26,560	3.2	28,120	5.9	27,987	-0.5	29,556	5.6	32,106	8.6	24.7
Annual Payroll ($ mil.)	35,567.3	39,720.3	11.7	42,518.2	7.0	42,099.7	-1.0	43,219.6	2.7	45,656.0	5.6	28.4
Establishments - 1-4 Emp. Number	5,971	6,686	12.0	9,464	41.5	9,220	-2.6	10,516	14.1	10,731	2.0	79.7
Mid-March Employment	(D)	17,647	-	26,404	49.6	24,677	-6.5	24,997	1.3	25,894	3.6	-
1st Quarter Wages (annualized - $ mil.)	(D)	485.5	-	643.7	32.6	584.5	-9.2	635.8	8.8	725.3	14.1	-
Payroll per Emp. 1st Q. (annualized)	(D)	27,513	-	24,380	-11.4	23,687	-2.8	25,435	7.4	28,009	10.1	-
Annual Payroll ($ mil.)	(D)	554.6	-	705.4	27.2	664.6	-5.8	923.5	39.0	850.7	-7.9	-
Establishments - 5-9 Emp. Number	15,871	18,545	16.8	22,048	18.9	20,664	-6.3	21,487	4.0	22,134	3.0	39.5
Mid-March Employment	111,483	131,253	17.7	153,187	16.7	143,829	-6.1	149,860	4.2	153,273	2.3	37.5
1st Quarter Wages (annualized - $ mil.)	2,170.6	2,686.4	23.8	3,165.0	17.8	2,834.9	-10.4	3,069.5	8.3	3,391.7	10.5	56.3
Payroll per Emp. 1st Q. (annualized)	19,470	20,468	5.1	20,661	0.9	19,710	-4.6	20,483	3.9	22,128	8.0	13.7
Annual Payroll ($ mil.)	2,177.0	2,624.9	20.6	3,199.7	21.9	2,913.3	-8.9	3,090.6	6.1	3,365.1	8.9	54.6
Establishments - 10-19 Emp. Number	15,653	21,323	36.2	19,210	-9.9	18,497	-3.7	19,642	6.2	19,936	1.5	27.4
Mid-March Employment	209,283	286,850	37.1	255,785	-10.8	247,056	-3.4	263,283	6.6	263,807	0.2	26.1
1st Quarter Wages (annualized - $ mil.)	4,214.6	5,987.8	42.1	5,530.5	-7.6	5,152.4	-6.8	5,662.0	9.9	5,931.7	4.8	40.7
Payroll per Emp. 1st Q. (annualized)	20,138	20,874	3.7	21,622	3.6	20,855	-3.5	21,505	3.1	22,485	4.6	11.7
Annual Payroll ($ mil.)	4,157.0	5,766.2	38.7	5,504.1	-4.5	5,255.1	-4.5	5,648.0	7.5	5,867.1	3.9	41.1
Establishments - 20-49 Emp. Number	10,034	10,666	6.3	10,112	-5.2	10,096	-0.2	10,028	-0.7	9,995	-0.3	-0.4
Mid-March Employment	301,951	311,243	3.1	297,617	-4.4	298,874	0.4	294,716	-1.4	293,495	-0.4	-2.8
1st Quarter Wages (annualized - $ mil.)	6,144.3	6,720.5	9.4	6,888.8	2.5	6,777.6	-1.6	7,173.5	5.8	7,534.6	5.0	22.6
Payroll per Emp. 1st Q. (annualized)	20,349	21,593	6.1	23,147	7.2	22,677	-2.0	24,341	7.3	25,672	5.5	26.2
Annual Payroll ($ mil.)	6,055.4	6,414.4	5.9	6,841.3	6.7	6,772.7	-1.0	7,034.9	3.9	7,278.1	3.5	20.2
Establishments - 50-99 Emp. Number	2,895	2,376	-17.9	2,408	1.3	2,384	-1.0	2,361	-1.0	2,320	-1.7	-19.9
Mid-March Employment	194,832	158,975	-18.4	161,400	1.5	160,499	-0.6	160,311	-0.1	156,945	-2.1	-19.4
1st Quarter Wages (annualized - $ mil.)	4,216.1	3,820.7	-9.4	4,206.5	10.1	4,148.4	-1.4	4,490.1	8.2	4,730.3	5.3	12.2
Payroll per Emp. 1st Q. (annualized)	21,640	24,033	11.1	26,063	8.4	25,847	-0.8	28,009	8.4	30,140	7.6	39.3
Annual Payroll ($ mil.)	4,081.0	3,597.8	-11.8	4,086.8	13.6	4,110.4	0.6	4,294.1	4.5	4,485.2	4.4	9.9
Establishments - 100-249 Emp. Number	1,288	1,110	-13.8	1,141	2.8	1,131	-0.9	1,103	-2.5	1,096	-0.6	-14.9
Mid-March Employment	190,303	167,159	-12.2	170,084	1.7	169,461	-0.4	164,094	-3.2	164,213	0.1	-13.7
1st Quarter Wages (annualized - $ mil.)	4,771.9	4,602.1	-3.6	4,860.4	5.6	4,830.3	-0.6	5,133.1	6.3	5,663.2	10.3	18.7
Payroll per Emp. 1st Q. (annualized)	25,075	27,531	9.8	28,576	3.8	28,504	-0.3	31,281	9.7	34,487	10.2	37.5
Annual Payroll ($ mil.)	4,508.7	4,232.4	-6.1	4,670.9	10.4	4,755.4	1.8	4,908.1	3.2	5,189.9	5.7	15.1
Establishments - 250-499 Emp. Number	337	388	15.1	367	-5.4	347	-5.4	362	4.3	362	-	7.4
Mid-March Employment	117,946	133,507	13.2	125,541	-6.0	122,838	-2.2	124,710	1.5	125,128	0.3	6.1
1st Quarter Wages (annualized - $ mil.)	3,482.6	4,009.3	15.1	4,121.1	2.8	4,369.2	6.0	4,180.4	-4.3	4,753.8	13.7	36.5
Payroll per Emp. 1st Q. (annualized)	29,527	30,030	1.7	32,827	9.3	35,569	8.4	33,521	-5.8	37,991	13.3	28.7
Annual Payroll ($ mil.)	3,267.5	3,672.8	12.4	3,900.3	6.2	4,266.2	9.4	3,973.1	-6.9	4,350.5	9.5	33.1
Establishments - 500-999 Emp. Number	158	174	10.1	174	-	175	0.6	182	4.0	181	-0.5	14.6
Mid-March Employment	110,948	123,327	11.2	121,128	-1.8	120,841	-0.2	124,191	2.8	123,893	-0.2	11.7
1st Quarter Wages (annualized - $ mil.)	3,600.5	4,012.2	11.4	3,975.8	-0.9	4,266.6	7.3	4,760.0	11.6	5,291.8	11.2	47.0
Payroll per Emp. 1st Q. (annualized)	32,452	32,533	0.3	32,823	0.9	35,307	7.6	38,328	8.6	42,713	11.4	31.6
Annual Payroll ($ mil.)	3,236.9	3,727.6	15.2	3,771.2	1.2	4,089.3	8.4	4,469.5	9.3	4,560.1	2.0	40.9
Estab. - 1000 or More Emp. Number	96	127	32.3	125	-1.6	115	-8.0	110	-4.3	113	2.7	17.7
Mid-March Employment	(D)	276,279	-	265,188	-4.0	240,183	-9.4	215,064	-10.5	225,612	4.9	-
1st Quarter Wages (annualized - $ mil.)	(D)	10,336.6	-	10,933.9	5.8	9,806.8	-10.3	9,857.2	0.5	11,172.9	13.3	-
Payroll per Emp. 1st Q. (annualized)	(D)	37,414	-	41,231	10.2	40,831	-1.0	45,834	12.3	49,523	8.0	-
Annual Payroll ($ mil.)	(D)	9,129.6	-	9,838.6	7.8	9,272.7	-5.8	8,877.7	-4.3	9,709.3	9.4	-

Source: County Business Patterns, U.S. Department of Commerce, Washington, D.C., for 1990 through 1995. Payroll per employee is calculated using mid-March employment and 1st Quarter wages, annualized. Annual payroll, also shown, may not equal the annualized 1st Quarter wages. Columns headed by a percent sign (%) indicate change from the previous year. *na* stands for not available. The symbol (D) indicates that data are withheld by the source to avoid disclosure of competitive information. A dash (-) indicates that data are not available or cannot be calculated.

ESTABLISHMENTS
Number

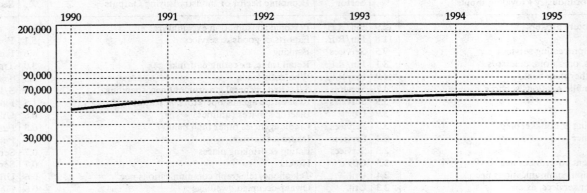

MID-MARCH EMPLOYMENT
Number

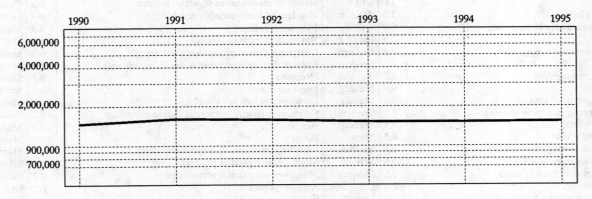

ANNUAL PAYROLL
$ million

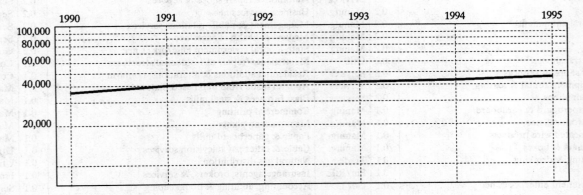

INPUTS AND OUTPUTS FOR ALL BANKING SECTORS - SICs 601, 602, 603, 608, and 609

Economic Sector or Industry Providing Inputs	%	Sector	Economic Sector or Industry Buying Outputs	%	Sector
Security & commodity brokers	12.9	Fin/R.E.	Personal consumption expenditures	59.0	
Banking	11.8	Fin/R.E.	Exports of goods & services	5.1	Foreign
Computer & data processing services	9.5	Services	Banking	4.6	Fin/R.E.
Real estate agents, operators, & lessors	8.1	Fin/R.E.	Retail trade, ex eating & drinking	3.0	Trade
Credit agencies other than banks	4.9	Fin/R.E.	Wholesale trade	2.3	Trade
Management & public relations services	4.1	Services	S/L Govt., general government nec, spending	2.1	S/L Govt
Advertising	3.9	Services	Real estate agents, operators, & lessors	1.5	Fin/R.E.
U.S. Postal Service	3.9	Gov't	Electric services (utilities)	0.8	Util.
Accounting, auditing & bookkeeping	3.7	Services	Credit agencies other than banks	0.8	Fin/R.E.
Business services nec	3.4	Services	Insurance carriers	0.7	Fin/R.E.
Legal services	2.8	Services	Eating & drinking places	0.7	Services
Federal Government enterprises nec	2.5	Gov't	Hotels	0.7	Services
Telephone/telegraph communications nec	2.4	Util.	Telephone/telegraph communications nec	0.6	Util.
Trucking & courier services, ex air	2.3	Util.	Owner-occupied dwellings	0.6	Fin/R.E.
Blankbooks, looseleaf binders & devices	1.7	Manufg.	Doctors & dentists	0.6	Services
Wholesale trade	1.6	Trade	Motor vehicles & passenger car bodies	0.4	Manufg.
Personnel supply services	1.6	Services	Trucking & courier services, ex air	0.4	Util.
Electric services (utilities)	1.5	Util.	Federal Government, nondefense, spending	0.4	Gov't
Warehousing & storage	1.4	Util.	New construction nec	0.3	Constr.
Air transportation	1.0	Util.	Repair & maintenance construction nec	0.3	Constr.
Eating & drinking places	1.0	Services	Residential 1 unit structures, nonfarm	0.3	Constr.
Sanitary services, steam supply, irrigation	0.9	Util.	Petroleum refining	0.3	Manufg.
Insurance carriers	0.9	Fin/R.E.	Railroads & related services	0.3	Util.
Repair & maintenance construction nec	0.8	Constr.	Computer & data processing services	0.3	Services
Hotels	0.8	Services	Engineering, architectural, & surveying services	0.3	Services
Detective & protective services	0.7	Services	Hospitals	0.3	Services
Commercial printing	0.6	Manufg.	Legal services	0.3	Services
Photographic equipment & supplies	0.6	Manufg.	Crude petroleum & natural gas	0.2	Mining
Research, development, & testing services	0.6	Services	Office, industrial/commercial buildings	0.2	Constr.
Manifold business forms	0.5	Manufg.	Aircraft	0.2	Manufg.
Paper & paperboard mills	0.5	Manufg.	Drugs	0.2	Manufg.
Automotive rental & leasing, without drivers	0.5	Services	Industrial inorganic & organic chemicals	0.2	Manufg.
Business & professional associations	0.5	Services	Miscellaneous plastics products, nec	0.2	Manufg.
Services to dwellings & other buildings	0.5	Services	Motor vehicle parts & accessories	0.2	Manufg.
Natural gas distribution	0.4	Util.	Air transportation	0.2	Util.
Magnetic & optical recording media	0.3	Manufg.	Freight forwarders	0.2	Util.
Manufacturing industries, nec	0.3	Manufg.	Water transportation	0.2	Util.
Periodicals	0.3	Manufg.	Security & commodity brokers	0.2	Fin/R.E.
Petroleum refining	0.3	Manufg.	Automotive rental & leasing, without drivers	0.2	Services
Electrical repair shops	0.3	Services	Automotive repair shops & services	0.2	Services
Book publishing	0.2	Manufg.	Business services nec	0.2	Services
Computer peripheral equipment	0.2	Manufg.	Management & public relations services	0.2	Services
Envelopes	0.2	Manufg.	Medical & health services nec	0.2	Services
Textile bags	0.2	Manufg.	State & local government enterprises nec	0.2	Gov't
Local & suburban transit	0.2	Util.	Maintenance/repair of residential structures	0.1	Constr.
Automotive repair shops & services	0.2	Services	Residential additions & alterations, nonfarm	0.1	Constr.
Miscellaneous equipment rental & leasing	0.2	Services	Apparel made from purchased materials	0.1	Manufg.
Miscellaneous repair shops	0.2	Services	Blast furnaces & steel mills	0.1	Manufg.
Die-cut paper & paperboard & cardboard	0.1	Manufg.	Commercial printing	0.1	Manufg.
Fabricated metal products, nec	0.1	Manufg.	Meat packing plants	0.1	Manufg.
Miscellaneous fabricated wire products	0.1	Manufg.	Paper & paperboard mills	0.1	Manufg.
Paperboard containers & boxes	0.1	Manufg.	Cable & other pay television services	0.1	Util.
Retail trade, ex eating & drinking	0.1	Trade	Natural gas distribution	0.1	Util.
Royalties	0.1	Fin/R.E.	Insurance agents, brokers, & services	0.1	Fin/R.E.
State & local government enterprises nec	0.1	Gov't	Accounting, auditing & bookkeeping	0.1	Services
			Motion picture services & theaters	0.1	Services
			Personnel supply services	0.1	Services
			Portrait photographic studios	0.1	Services
			U.S. Postal Service	0.1	Gov't

Source: Benchmark Input-Output Accounts for the U.S. Economy, 1992, U.S. Department of Commerce, Washington, D.C., November 1997. Data, as reported in the source, are organized by the 1987 SIC structure in use in 1992.

OCCUPATIONS EMPLOYED BY COMMERCIAL BANKS, SAVINGS INSTITUTIONS, AND CREDIT UNIONS

Occupation	% of Total 1996	Change to 2006	Occupation	% of Total 1996	Change to 2006
Bank tellers	28.5	0.1	General managers & top executives	3.1	-8.6
Clerical supervisors & managers	6.7	6.7	Clerical & administrative workers nec	1.5	-52.8
Loan officers & counselors	6.6	13.2	Accountants & auditors	1.4	-12.7
Financial managers	6.3	-5.7	Securities & financial sales workers	1.3	41.5
New accounts clerks, banking	5.9	3.8	Adjustment clerks	1.3	27.3
Loan & credit clerks	5.4	-4.8	Statement clerks	1.2	-5.7
General office clerks	4.0	-18.8	Duplicating, mail, office machine operators	1.1	-76.4
Bookkeeping, accounting, & auditing clerks	3.8	-24.5	Managers & administrators nec	1.0	-6.5
Secretaries, except legal & medical	3.7	-25.2			

Sources: Industry-Occupation Matrix, Bureau of Labor Statistics. These data relate to one or more 3-digit SIC industry groups rather than to a single 4-digit SIC. The change reported for each occupation to the year 2005 is a percent of growth or decline as estimated by the Bureau of Labor Statistics. The abbreviation *nec* stands for not elsewhere classified.

U.S. AND STATE DATA ON INDUSTRY REVENUES AND OTHER ACCOUNTS FOR 1992

State	No. of Estab.	Employ- ment	Payroll ($ mil.)	Revenues ($ mil.)	Empl./ Estab.	Revenue/ Estab. ($)	Payroll/ Estab. ($)	Revenue/ Empl. ($)	Payroll/ Empl. ($)
UNITED STATES	62,761	1,506,055	41,206.5	318,076.7	24	5,068,064	656,562	211,199	27,361
Alabama	1,051	23,634	532.8	3,779.9	22	3,596,465	506,909	159,934	22,542
Alaska	127	2,623	72.7	414.8	21	3,265,961	572,252	158,131	27,707
Arizona	828	20,336	576.8	2,517.2	25	3,040,051	696,582	123,779	28,362
Arkansas	831	13,532	285.2	1,978.1	16	2,380,384	343,224	146,179	21,077
California	5,746	145,006	4,224.7	29,229.7	25	5,086,962	735,237	201,576	29,134
Colorado	584	15,977	409.7	2,751.3	27	4,711,146	701,553	172,204	25,644
Connecticut	656	16,568	485.3	2,746.3	25	4,186,502	739,723	165,762	29,289
Delaware	212	22,219	620.2	9,405.4	105	44,365,179	2,925,476	423,305	27,913
District of Columbia	207	4,286	140.3	1,022.1	21	4,937,502	677,657	238,465	32,729
Florida	3,211	74,700	1,763.2	12,904.5	23	4,018,837	549,101	172,751	23,603
Georgia	1,789	41,591	1,066.0	7,205.4	23	4,027,587	595,841	173,243	25,630
Hawaii	251	8,163	237.5	1,619.1	33	6,450,550	946,068	198,345	29,090
Idaho	332	6,523	150.4	864.9	20	2,605,130	453,048	132,593	23,059
Illinois	2,064	82,220	2,471.0	14,489.4	40	7,020,068	1,197,211	176,227	30,054
Indiana	1,765	35,194	759.0	5,490.1	20	3,110,556	430,003	155,996	21,565
Iowa	1,013	18,368	427.2	3,323.4	18	3,280,725	421,751	180,933	23,260
Kansas	901	15,573	363.1	2,567.1	17	2,849,179	402,973	164,844	23,315
Kentucky	1,098	23,445	519.4	4,029.7	21	3,670,024	473,065	171,878	22,155
Louisiana	1,196	23,430	526.0	3,426.1	20	2,864,606	439,807	146,226	22,450
Maine	335	5,030	118.4	810.5	15	2,419,296	353,570	161,126	23,548
Maryland	1,452	30,524	798.2	5,188.4	21	3,573,312	549,751	169,979	26,151
Massachusetts	1,065	40,388	1,263.7	10,537.1	38	9,894,017	1,186,551	260,897	31,288
Michigan	2,559	52,750	1,243.6	8,987.0	21	3,511,922	485,969	170,370	23,575
Minnesota	1,137	25,980	724.5	4,639.4	23	4,080,429	637,224	178,578	27,888
Mississippi	863	13,396	291.7	1,900.2	16	2,201,896	338,044	141,851	21,778
Missouri	1,430	34,060	758.8	5,487.0	24	3,837,034	530,611	161,097	22,278
Montana	199	4,171	94.6	668.1	21	3,357,307	475,422	160,178	22,683
Nebraska	648	11,702	269.8	2,154.9	18	3,325,427	416,381	184,146	23,057
Nevada	337	6,516	149.6	2,049.4	19	6,081,255	443,819	314,516	22,954
New Hampshire	191	3,579	79.9	1,064.1	19	5,570,984	418,356	297,306	22,326
New Jersey	2,147	42,069	1,101.1	7,315.2	20	3,407,166	512,837	173,885	26,173
New Mexico	408	8,157	171.0	1,104.3	20	2,706,728	419,042	135,386	20,960
New York	3,714	155,855	6,889.6	70,480.3	42	18,976,928	1,855,034	452,217	44,205
North Carolina	2,096	40,769	995.4	7,462.1	19	3,560,150	474,903	183,033	24,416
North Dakota	267	4,171	98.9	742.4	16	2,780,438	370,419	177,985	23,712
Ohio	3,079	61,814	1,504.8	13,621.7	20	4,424,073	488,738	220,366	24,344
Oklahoma	737	17,354	417.0	2,544.9	24	3,453,014	565,805	146,645	24,029
Oregon	755	14,781	339.4	2,217.4	20	2,936,903	449,589	150,014	22,965
Pennsylvania	3,774	81,401	1,927.0	14,990.9	22	3,972,162	510,599	184,162	23,673
Rhode Island	172	7,453	184.1	1,769.7	43	10,288,849	1,070,355	237,446	24,702
South Carolina	847	13,929	317.0	2,207.1	16	2,605,765	374,236	158,452	22,757
South Dakota	315	8,104	170.0	3,279.9	26	10,412,508	539,797	404,731	20,982
Tennessee	1,597	28,929	713.2	4,938.4	18	3,092,284	446,587	170,707	24,653
Texas	2,904	87,156	2,308.7	14,406.4	30	4,960,897	795,017	165,295	26,490
Utah	447	8,891	214.6	1,152.7	20	2,578,747	480,107	129,648	24,138
Vermont	220	3,770	79.9	537.0	17	2,440,714	363,000	142,429	21,183
Virginia	2,144	36,348	853.7	6,255.1	17	2,917,480	398,168	172,089	23,486
Washington	1,173	22,941	584.3	3,647.1	20	3,109,171	498,098	158,976	25,468
West Virginia	495	10,842	217.4	1,624.4	22	3,281,600	439,248	149,824	20,054
Wisconsin	1,282	27,393	635.7	4,113.9	21	3,208,966	495,888	150,180	23,208
Wyoming	110	2,444	60.5	415.5	22	3,777,127	550,309	170,002	24,768

Source: 1992 Economic Census, U.S. Department of Commerce, Washington, D.C. This is the only table that shows revenue data as collected by the Bureau of the Census in an Economic Census. The symbol (D) indicates that data are withheld by the source to avoid disclosure of competitive information. A dash (-) indicates that data are not available or cannot be calculated.

STATE-BY-STATE DATA ON ESTABLISHMENTS, EMPLOYMENT, AND PAYROLL - 1994 AND 1995

State	1994					1995					% Change Empl.
	No. of Estab.	Employ-ment	Pay / Empl.	Payroll ($ mil.)	Pay / Estab.	No. of Estab.	Employ-ment	Pay / Empl.	Payroll ($ mil.)	Pay / Estab.	
Alabama	1,077	24,126	24,567	586.9	544,967	1,076	25,780	27,320	678.6	630,641	6.9
Alaska	121	2,959	28,233	85.9	709,826	126	2,868	28,982	82.2	652,056	-3.1
Arizona	873	22,086	30,129	676.8	775,274	827	22,949	32,639	745.0	900,788	3.9
Arkansas	840	13,982	21,810	306.5	364,851	844	13,616	22,131	308.5	365,477	-2.6
California	6,121	158,425	32,717	4,758.6	777,424	6,407	156,558	33,119	4,771.5	744,729	-1.2
Colorado	824	18,040	27,097	463.5	562,522	827	17,979	28,271	474.0	573,206	-0.3
Connecticut	666	14,319	30,767	442.4	664,309	648	13,874	32,735	439.5	678,299	-3.1
Delaware	258	21,153	27,472	650.9	2,522,779	261	21,478	32,181	747.1	2,862,264	1.5
District of Columbia	213	3,730	34,952	128.8	604,549	218	3,588	42,527	138.1	633,697	-3.8
Florida	3,500	74,789	26,847	1,859.7	531,357	3,673	76,663	28,389	2,052.9	558,919	2.5
Georgia	1,846	43,393	28,103	1,133.1	613,790	1,849	44,484	29,056	1,197.6	647,706	2.5
Hawaii	310	8,872	31,998	273.8	883,177	305	8,943	34,535	278.1	911,856	0.8
Idaho	378	7,018	23,798	169.8	449,317	373	7,358	25,147	186.3	499,475	4.8
Illinois	2,211	85,924	32,581	2,712.0	1,226,611	2,385	88,339	36,389	2,866.0	1,201,670	2.8
Indiana	1,805	30,441	21,934	668.6	370,434	1,851	30,275	23,882	721.1	389,548	-0.5
Iowa	1,042	19,406	23,517	452.5	434,300	1,053	19,626	24,414	471.2	447,476	1.1
Kansas	929	15,801	22,815	368.0	396,150	925	15,804	23,382	380.3	411,176	0.0
Kentucky	1,184	22,066	23,365	516.9	436,539	1,222	21,501	24,585	531.7	435,105	-2.6
Louisiana	1,260	23,579	24,881	567.9	450,700	1,274	24,088	26,424	618.1	485,174	2.2
Maine	326	4,433	23,333	106.9	327,837	321	4,420	22,608	98.3	306,181	-0.3
Maryland	1,443	26,821	27,950	760.4	526,936	1,452	27,741	29,802	765.6	527,273	3.4
Massachusetts	1,093	36,861	38,512	1,346.3	1,231,789	1,034	36,595	45,271	1,398.6	1,352,589	-0.7
Michigan	2,584	53,596	23,844	1,283.1	496,566	2,777	52,945	27,127	1,447.0	521,057	-1.2
Minnesota	1,207	28,265	29,129	778.2	644,768	1,265	28,739	31,121	849.7	671,667	1.7
Mississippi	934	14,330	22,201	329.7	353,034	942	14,532	23,248	344.9	366,127	1.4
Missouri	1,470	34,523	23,117	795.8	541,354	1,528	35,169	24,645	850.9	556,853	1.9
Montana	211	4,053	23,772	98.0	464,299	217	4,087	24,771	101.4	467,111	0.8
Nebraska	665	12,933	22,714	296.9	446,420	724	13,578	23,999	335.1	462,787	5.0
Nevada	323	7,775	26,839	196.7	608,864	332	8,055	25,602	196.9	593,175	3.6
New Hampshire	192	3,468	23,659	82.9	431,797	269	4,404	25,385	115.2	428,227	27.0
New Jersey	2,182	40,836	26,817	1,132.8	519,156	2,168	39,651	28,701	1,168.6	539,018	-2.9
New Mexico	429	7,925	22,432	174.5	406,851	430	7,877	24,012	179.5	417,421	-0.6
New York	3,878	132,701	51,744	6,121.3	1,578,464	3,813	130,903	60,717	6,537.5	1,714,531	-1.4
North Carolina	2,284	45,349	30,157	1,342.4	587,720	2,315	49,757	33,156	1,500.4	648,137	9.7
North Dakota	280	4,287	23,749	100.6	359,361	288	4,361	24,482	103.9	360,854	1.7
Ohio	3,105	64,962	25,137	1,593.0	513,034	3,105	67,180	27,464	1,738.7	559,972	3.4
Oklahoma	769	18,020	23,390	424.9	552,559	775	17,721	24,754	431.7	557,017	-1.7
Oregon	923	20,950	27,334	553.4	599,535	899	18,773	27,290	490.3	545,380	-10.4
Pennsylvania	3,821	85,982	25,981	2,232.7	584,328	3,769	80,931	30,160	2,275.7	603,791	-5.9
Rhode Island	167	5,340	29,229	154.4	924,395	172	5,628	29,163	157.9	918,174	5.4
South Carolina	1,015	15,009	22,950	336.0	331,080	1,038	14,513	24,796	366.1	352,688	-3.3
South Dakota	339	8,527	21,806	179.0	528,097	347	8,924	23,779	197.0	567,744	4.7
Tennessee	1,589	28,651	27,203	743.9	468,134	1,624	29,653	27,687	776.7	478,235	3.5
Texas	2,948	87,116	27,414	2,313.5	784,772	3,020	89,624	28,757	2,476.0	819,873	2.9
Utah	456	9,323	24,801	230.0	504,283	478	9,246	26,782	245.6	513,774	-0.8
Vermont	215	3,378	23,693	77.1	358,558	213	3,385	26,860	85.4	400,836	0.2
Virginia	2,208	39,377	26,433	1,031.9	467,327	2,189	42,321	27,607	1,122.0	512,557	7.5
Washington	1,318	23,784	26,736	628.0	476,508	1,301	24,405	28,630	666.5	512,263	2.6
West Virginia	498	11,017	20,348	221.7	445,205	486	10,634	21,494	219.6	451,947	-3.5
Wisconsin	1,343	28,995	22,755	667.1	496,695	1,320	28,362	24,411	668.4	506,369	-2.2
Wyoming	118	2,530	23,562	63.9	541,686	113	2,375	24,724	57.4	507,566	-6.1

Source: County Business Patterns, U.S. Department of Commerce, Washington, D.C., for 1994 and 1995. Employment shown is for mid-March of the year shown. Payroll per employee is calculated by annualizing 1st Quarter payroll (not shown) and then dividing that value by mid-March employment. Dividing total annual payroll (columns 5 and 10) by employment, therefore, will *not* yield the payroll per employee figure (columns 4 and 9). The symbol (D) indicates that data are withheld by the source to avoid disclosure of competitive information. A dash (-) indicates that data are not available or cannot be calculated.

ESTABLISHMENTS 1995 - STATE AND REGIONAL CONCENTRATION

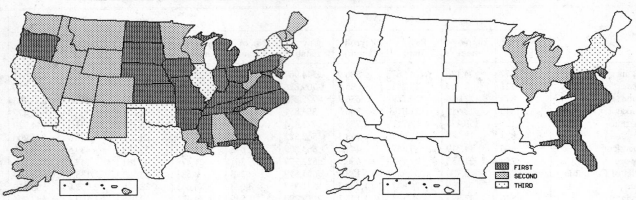

EMPLOYMENT 1995 - STATE AND REGIONAL CONCENTRATION

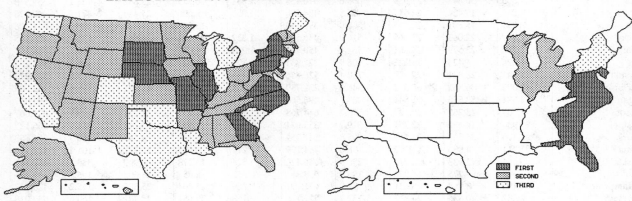

PAYROLL 1995 - STATE AND REGIONAL CONCENTRATION

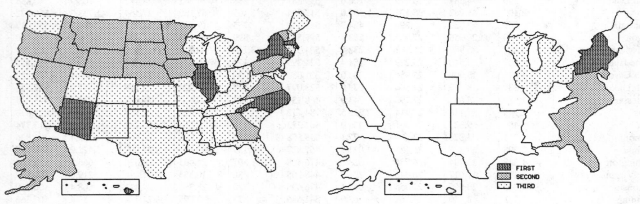

States with the darkest shading indicate those states which have proportionately more establishments, employment, or payrolls than would be indicated by the state's population. States with light shading are states with proportionately fewer establishments, less employment, and lower payrolls than population distribution. States shaded grey are within 15 percent of the state's population proportion in these categories. States for which no data are available are shown as average (grey). *Regions* are shaded to indicate absolute rank in the category. If no data for the category are available, establishment counts are used to shade the regions. Source of the data is the table on the facing page.

LEADING COMPANIES - SIC 6021 - National Commercial Banks

Number shown: **100**   Total sales/assets ($ mil): **3,891,897**   Total employment (000): **1,115.0**

Company Name	Address				CEO Name	Phone	Co. Type	Sales/Assets ($ mil)	Empl. (000)
Chase Manhattan Corp.	1 Chase Manhattan Plaza	New York	NY	10081	Walter V. Shipley	212-552-2222	P	336,099 TA	67.8
BankAmerica Corp.	Dept. 13018	San Francisco	CA	94137	David A. Coulter	415-622-3456	P	255,801 TA	92.1
Citibank N.A.	399 Park Ave.	New York	NY	10043	John S. Reed	212-559-1000	S	250,489 TA	82.6
Bank of America Northwest N.A.	PO Box 3586	Seattle	WA	98124	John Rindlaub	206-358-3000	S	236,982 TA	7.0
Second National Bank of Masontown	110 S. Main St.	Masontown	PA	15461	Patrick Hall	724-583-7701	R	159,000 TA	<0.1
First Tennessee National Corp.	PO Box 84	Memphis	TN	38101	Ralph Horn	901-523-5630	P	144,000 TA	8.2
First Union Corp.	1 First Union Center	Charlotte	NC	28288	Edward E. Crutchfield	704-374-6565	P	134,127 TA	44.3
Banc One Corp.	100 E. Broad St.	Columbus	OH	43271	Richard J. Lehmann	614-248-5800	P	115,901 TA	56.6
First Chicago NBD Corp.	1 First National Plaza	Chicago	IL	60670	Verne G. Istock	312-732-4000	P	104,619 TA	33.4
Wells Fargo and Co.	420 Montgomery St.	San Francisco	CA	94163	Paul Hazen	415-477-1000	P	97,456 TA	36.9
Norwest Bank Minnesota N.A.	6th & Marquette	Minneapolis	MN	55479	Richard M. Kovacevich	612-667-1234	S	88,500 TA	5.4
Fleet Financial Group Inc.	1 Federal St.	Boston	MA	02211	Terrence Murray	617-346-4000	P	85,518 TA	36.0
Norwest Bank Colorado N.A.	1740 Broadway	Denver	CO	80274	David Bailey	303-861-8811	S	85,000 TA	3.0
NationsBank N.A.	101 S. Tryon St.	Charlotte	NC	28255	Michael F. Gooding	704-386-5000	S	79,179 TA	21.5
PNC Bank Corp.	249 5th Ave.	Pittsburgh	PA	15222	Thomas H. O'Brien	412-762-1553	P	73,260 TA	25.4
BankBoston Corp.	PO Box 1987	Boston	MA	02105	Charles K. Gifford	617-434-2200	P	69,268 TA	21.5
Wachovia Corp.	100 N. Main St.	Winston-Salem	NC	27150	L.M. Baker Jr.	910-770-5000	P	65,397 TA	21.7
SunTrust Banks Inc.	PO Box 4418	Atlanta	GA	30302	James B. Williams	404-588-7711	P	57,983 TA	21.2
Republic New York Corp.	452 5th Ave.	New York	NY	10018	Walter H. Weiner	212-525-6100	P	55,638 TA	5.9
NationsBank Texas Corp.	PO Box 831000	Dallas	TX	75283	Hugh L. McColl Jr.	214-508-6262	S	48,368 TA	20.6
PNC Bank N.A.	5th Ave. & Wood St.	Pittsburgh	PA	15222	Bruce E. Robbins	412-762-2000	S	44,566 TA	15.5
Mellon Bank Corp.	1 Mellon Bank Ctr.	Pittsburgh	PA	15258	Frank V. Cahouet	412-234-5000	P	42,013 TA	24.7
First Midwest Bank N.A.	300 Park Blvd. #400	Itasc	IL	60143	Robert P. O'Meara	630-875-7396	S	38,815 TA	1.0
NationsBank National Association	PO Box 4899	Atlanta	GA	30303	James R. Lientz	404-581-2121	S	37,610 TA	9.9
First Bank System Inc.	PO Box 522	Minneapolis	MN	55480	John F. Grundhofer	612-973-1111	P	36,489 TA	12.0
First Fidelity Bancorp.	550 Broad St.	Newark	NJ	07102	Anthony P. Terracciano	201-565-3200	P	36,216 TA	12.0
Republic National Bank of New York	452 5th Ave.	New York	NY	10018	Walter H. Weiner	212-525-5000	S	34,580 TA	2.8
Boatmen's Bancshares Inc.	800 Market St.	St. Louis	MO	63101	Andrew B. Craig III	314-466-6000	P	33,704 TA	17.0
Mellon Bank N.A.	1 Mellon Bank Ctr.	Pittsburgh	PA	15258	Frank V. Cahouet	412-234-4100	S	30,001 TA*	27.5
Union Bank of California N.A.	400 California St.	San Francisco	CA	94104	Kanetaka Yoshida	415-765-0400	S	29,197 TA	9.5
Fleet Bank N.A.	10 Exchange Place Ctr.	Jersey City	NJ	07302	John Tugwell	212-907-5000	S	28,489 TA	6.2

Company type codes: P - Public, R - Private, S - Subsidiary, D - Division, J - Joint Venture, A - Affiliate, G - Group. If the dollar values shown are not sales, the following codes apply: TA - Total Assets; OR - Operating Revenues; GB - Gross Billings. * - estimated dollar value. < - less than. *na* - not available.

Continued on next page.

LEADING COMPANIES - SIC 6021 - National Commercial Banks

Continued

Company Name	Address				CEO Name	Phone	Co. Type	Sales/Assets ($ mil)	Empl. (000)
Marine Midland Bank N.A.	1 Marine Midland Ctr.	Buffalo	NY	14203	Jim Cleave	716-841-2424	S	28,300 TA	9.6
SunTrust Banks of Florida Inc.	PO Box 3833	Orlando	FL	32802	George W. Koehn	407-237-4141	S	27,585 TA	7.9
First Union National Bank of North Carolina	301 S. College St.	Charlotte	NC	28288	Frank H. Dunn Jr.	704-374-6161	S	27,415 TA	9.7
Huntington Bancshares Inc.	41 S. High St.	Columbus	OH	43287	Frank Wobst	614-480-8300	P	26,731 TA	9.5
Society National Bank	127 Public Sq.	Cleveland	OH	44114	Robert B. Heisler Jr.	216-689-3000	S	24,571 TA	4.9
Bank One, Texas N.A.	PO Box 655415	Dallas	TX	75265	Terry Kelley	214-290-2000	S	23,000 TA	7.5
NBD Bank	PO Box 116	Detroit	MI	48226	Thomas H. Jeffs II	313-225-1000	S	22,474 TA	9.2
Harris Bankcorp Inc.	111 W. Monroe St.	Chicago	IL	60603	Alan G. McNally	312-461-2121	S	22,200 TA	6.6
Crestar Financial Corp.	PO Box 26665	Richmond	VA	23261	Richard G. Tilghman	804-782-5000	P	21,810 TA	8.2
Fifth Third Bancorp.	Fifth Third Ctr.	Cincinnati	OH	45263	George A. Schaefer Jr.	513-579-5300	P	21,375 TA	6.8
MBNA Corp.	1100 N. King St.	Wilmington	DE	19884	Charles M. Cawley	302-453-9930	P	21,306 TA	20.0
First of America Bank Corp.	211 S. Rose St.	Kalamazoo	MI	49007	Richard F. Chorman	616-376-9000	P	21,080 TA	10.6
Texas Commerce Bank N.A.	PO Box 2558	Houston	TX	77252	Marc J. Shapiro	713-236-4865	S	19,805 TA	9.2
Popular Inc.	PO Box 362708	San Juan	PR	00936	Richard L. Carrion	787-765-9800	P	19,301 TA	8.9
Mercantile Bancorporation Inc.	PO Box 524	St. Louis	MO	63166	Thomas H. Jacobsen	314-425-2525	P	19,188 TA	7.9
AmSouth Bancorp.	1400 AmSouth-Sonat Twr.	Birmingham	AL	35203	C. Dowd Ritter	205-320-7151	P	18,600 TA	6.4
Northern Trust Corp.	50 S. La Salle St.	Chicago	IL	60675	David W. Fox	312-630-6000	P	18,562 TA	6.6
Union Planters Corp.	PO Box 387	Memphis	TN	38147	Benjamin W. Rawlins Jr.	901-580-6000	P	18,105 TA	5.2
Beneficial Corp.	301 N. Walnut St.	Wilmington	DE	19801	Finn M. Caspersen	302-425-2500	P	17,645 TA	10.2
SunTrust Banks of Georgia Inc.	PO Box 4418	Atlanta	GA	30302	Edward P. Gould	404-827-6510	S	16,854 TA	4.5
First Bank N.A.	601 2nd Ave. S.	Minneapolis	MN	55402	John Grundhofer	612-973-1111	S	16,376 TA	4.2
Simmons First National Corp.	PO Box 7009	Pine Bluff	AR	71611	J. Thomas May	501-541-1000	TA	16,000 TA	0.7
Banc One Arizona Corp.	PO Box 71	Phoenix	AZ	85001	Mike Wellborn	602-221-2900	S	15,257 TA*	5.5
Pacific Century Financial Corp.	PO Box 2900	Honolulu	HI	96846	Lawrence M. Johnson	808-643-3888	P	14,996 TA	5.1
Marshall and Ilsley Corp.	770 N. Water St.	Milwaukee	WI	53202	James B. Wigdale	414-765-7801	P	14,271 TA	11.4
First Maryland Bancorp.	25 S. Charles St.	Baltimore	MD	21201	Frank P. Bramble	410-244-4000	P	14,132 TA	7.1
First Empire State Corp.	PO Box 223	Buffalo	NY	14240	Robert G. Wilmers	716-842-5138	P	14,003 TA	5.1
National City Bank, Pennsylvania	20 Stanwix St.	Pittsburgh	PA	15222	Thomas W. Golonski	412-644-8111	S	13,623 TA	4.5
Compass Bancshares	15 S. 20th St.	Birmingham	AL	35233	D. Paul Jones Jr.	205-933-3000	P	12,602 TA	5.5
United States National Bank of Oregon	PO Box 4412	Portland	OR	97208	John D. Eskildsen	503-275-6111	S	12,126 TA	5.8
Citibank	PO Box 6800	Las Vegas	NV	89163	Wilfried Jackson	702-797-4444	S	12,088 TA	1.7
NBT Bancorp Inc.	52 S. Broad St.	Norwich	NY	13815	Daryl R. Forsythe	607-337-6000	P	12,000 TA	0.5
Huntington National Bank	41 S. High St.	Columbus	OH	43215	W. Lee Hoskins	614-480-8300	S	11,969 TA	3.9
Fleet National Bank	1 Monarch Place	Springfield	MA	01102	Leo Breitman	413-746-1972	S	11,693 TA	3.0

Company type codes: P - Public, R - Private, S - Subsidiary, D - Division, J - Joint Venture, A - Affiliate, G - Group. If the dollar values shown are not sales, the following codes apply: TA - Total Assets; OR - Operating Revenues; GB - Gross Billings. * - estimated dollar value. < - less than. *na* - not available.

Continued on next page.

LEADING COMPANIES - SIC 6021 - National Commercial Banks
Continued

Company Name	Address				CEO Name	Phone	Co. Type	Sales/Assets ($ mil)	Empl. (000)
National City Bank	1900 E. 9th St.	Cleveland	OH	44114	William E. MacDonald III	216-575-2000	S	11,588 TA*	4.7
First Tennessee Bank N.A.	PO Box 84	Memphis	TN	38101	Ralph Horn	901-523-4444	S	11,581 TA	8.0
MainStreet BankGroup Inc.	PO Box 4831	Martinsville	VA	24115	Michael R. Brenan	703-632-2971	P	11,500 TA	0.6
LaSalle National Bank	135 S. LaSalle St.	Chicago	IL	60603	Norman R. Bobins	312-443-2000	S	11,216 TA	0.9
Boatmen's National Bank of St. Louis	800 Market St.	St. Louis	MO	63101	John Morton III	314-554-6000	S	11,131 TA	1.8
SouthTrust Bank of Alabama N.A.	PO Box 2554	Birmingham	AL	35290	Julian W. Banton	205-254-5000	S	11,114 TA	4.5
Star Banc Corp.	425 Walnut St.	Cincinnati	OH	45202	Jerry A. Grundhofer	513-632-4000	P	10,959 TA	0.3
Associated Banc-Corp.	PO Box 13307	Green Bay	WI	54307	Harry B. Conlon	414-433-3166	P	10,700 TA	2.0
Central Fidelity Banks Inc.	PO Box 27602	Richmond	VA	23261	Lewis N. Miller Jr.	804-782-4000	P	10,540 TA	3.5
First American Corp.	1st American Ctr.	Nashville	TN	37237	Dennis C. Bottorff	615-748-2000	P	10,400 TA	3.6
Commerce Bancshares Inc.	PO Box 13686	Kansas City	MO	64199	David W. Kemper	816-234-2000	P	10,307 TA	4.3
First of America Bank-Michigan N.A.	171 Monroe Ave. N.W.	Grand Rapids	MI	49503	William R. Cole	616-771-8800	S	10,145 TA	4.0
First National Bank of Maryland	PO Box 1596	Baltimore	MD	21203	Frank P. Bramble	410-244-4000	S	10,038 TA	3.9
Fleet Bank of New York	69 State St.	Albany	NY	12207	Dean T. Holt	518-447-4119	S	9,966 TA	4.1
NBD Bank N.A.	1 Indiana Sq.	Indianapolis	IN	46266	Andrew J. Paine	317-266-6000	S	9,910 TA	5.8
MBNA America Bank N.A.	400 Christiana Rd.	Newark	DE	19713	Charles M. Cawley	302-456-8588	S	9,672 TA	10.8
FCC National Bank	300 King St.	Wilmington	DE	19801	W.G. Jurgensen	302-594-8600	S	9,650 TA*	3.3
Zions Bancorp.	One Main St.	Salt Lake City	UT	84111	Harris H. Simmons	801-524-4787	P	9,521 TA	4.9
Michigan National Corp.	PO Box 9065	Farmington Hills	MI	48333	Douglas E. Ebert	248-473-3000	S	9,329 TA	4.0
Hibernia Corp.	PO Box 61540	New Orleans	LA	70161	Stephen A. Hansel	504-533-3332	P	9,307 TA	4.5
Michigan National Bank	PO Box 9065	Farmington Hills	MI	48334	Douglas Ebert	248-473-3000	S	9,290 TA	4.0
Synovus Financial Corp.	PO Box 120	Columbus	GA	31902	James H. Blanchard	706-649-2387	P	9,260 TA	8.1
First Commerce Corp.	PO Box 60279	New Orleans	LA	70160	Ian Arnof	504-561-1371	P	9,183 TA	3.8
Hibernia National Bank	PO Box 61540	New Orleans	LA	70161	Stephen Hansel	504-533-3333	S	8,929 TA	4.3
American National Bank and Trust Company of Chicago	120 S. LaSalle St.	Chicago	IL	60690	David P. Bolger	312-661-5000	S	8,750 TA	2.2
Bank One, Indianapolis N.A.	111 Monument Cir.	Indianapolis	IN	46277	Joseph D. Barnette Jr.	317-321-3000	S	8,668 TA	3.6
Norwest Bank Texas N.A.	PO Box 1241	Lubbock	TX	79408	Gary Lawrence	806-765-8861	S	8,645 TA	3.8
Star Bank N.A.	PO Box 1038	Cincinnati	OH	45201	Jerry A. Grundhofer	513-632-4000	S	8,389 TA	3.5
Banc One Wisconsin Corp.	PO Box 481	Milwaukee	WI	53201	William Reed	414-765-3000	S	8,267 TA	2.8
First of America Bank-Illinois N.A.	2595 Waukegan Rd.	Bannockburn	IL	60015	Robert Kinning	708-877-4610	S	7,243 TA	1.9
First Interstate Bank of Arizona N.A.	PO Box 53456	Phoenix	AZ	85072	William S. Randall	602-528-6000	S	7,181 TA	5.1
Firstar Bank Milwaukee N.A.	777 E. Wisconsin Ave.	Milwaukee	WI	53202	Chris M. Bauer	414-765-4321	S	7,130 TA	3.7

Company type codes: P - Public, R - Private, S - Subsidiary, D - Division, J - Joint Venture, A - Affiliate, G - Group. If the dollar values shown are not sales, the following codes apply: TA - Total Assets; OR - Operating Revenues; GB - Gross Billings. * - estimated dollar value. < - less than. *na* - not available.

Continued on next page.

LEADING COMPANIES - SIC 6021 - National Commercial Banks
Continued

Company Name	Address				CEO Name	Phone	Co. Type	Sales/Assets ($ mil)	Empl. (000)
Colorado National Bankshares Inc.	PO Box 5168	Denver	CO	80202	Robert J. Malone	303-585-5000	S	7,076 TA	2.0
Colorado National Bank	PO Box 5168	Denver	CO	80217	Daniel W. Yohannes	303-585-5000	S	7,024 TA	2.0
National City Bank, Kentucky	PO Box 36000	Louisville	KY	40233	James R. Bell III	502-581-4200	S	6,982 TA	2.0

Source: Ward's Business Directory of U.S. Private and Public Companies, 1996. Company type codes: P - Public, R - Private, S - Subsidiary, D - Division, J - Joint Venture, A - Affiliate, G - Group. If the dollar values shown are not sales, the following codes apply: TA - Total Assets; OR - Operating Revenues; GB - Gross Billings. * - estimated dollar value. < - less than; na - not available.

LEADING COMPANIES - SIC 6022 - State Commercial Banks
Number shown: **100**   Total sales/assets ($ mil): **3,219,211**   Total employment (000): **917.7**

Company Name	Address				CEO Name	Phone	Co. Type	Sales/Assets ($ mil)	Empl. (000)
Chase Manhattan Corp.	1 Chase Manhattan Plaza	New York	NY	10081	Walter V. Shipley	212-552-2222	P	336,099 TA	67.8
BankAmerica Corp.	Dept. 13018	San Francisco	CA	94137	David A. Coulter	415-622-3456	P	255,801 TA	92.1
J.P. Morgan and Company Inc.	60 Wall St.	New York	NY	10260	Douglas A. Warner III	212-483-2323	P	252,895 TA	16.9
First Tennessee National Corp.	PO Box 84	Memphis	TN	38101	Ralph Horn	901-523-5630	P	144,000 TA	8.2
Bankers Trust Co.	130 Liberty St.	New York	NY	10006	Frank N. Newman	212-250-2500	S	140,010 TA	17.0
Chemical Bank	270 Park Ave.	New York	NY	10017	Walter V. Shipley	212-270-6000	S	135,742 TA	39.1
Banc One Corp.	100 E. Broad St.	Columbus	OH	43271	Richard J. Lehmann	614-248-5800	P	115,901 TA	56.6
First Chicago NBD Corp.	1 First National Plaza	Chicago	IL	60670	Verne G. Istock	312-732-4000	P	104,619 TA	33.4
Peoples Holding Co.	PO Box 709	Tupelo	MS	38802	John W. Smith	601-680-1001	P	99,161 TA	0.6
Norwest Corp.	Norwest Ctr.	Minneapolis	MN	55479	Richard M. Kovacevich	612-667-1234	P	88,540 TA	57.0
Fleet Financial Group Inc.	1 Federal St.	Boston	MA	02211	Terrence Murray	617-346-4000	P	85,518 TA	36.0
PNC Bank Corp.	249 5th Ave.	Pittsburgh	PA	15222	Thomas H. O'Brien	412-762-1553	P	73,260 TA	25.4
BankBoston Corp.	PO Box 1987	Boston	MA	02105	Charles K. Gifford	617-434-2200	P	69,268 TA	21.5
SunTrust Banks Inc.	PO Box 4418	Atlanta	GA	30302	James B. Williams	404-588-7711	P	57,983 TA	21.2
National City Corp.	1900 E. 9th St.	Cleveland	OH	44114	David A. Daberko	216-575-2000	P	54,684 TA	29.8
Bank of New York Company Inc.	48 Wall St.	New York	NY	10286	J. Carter Bacot	212-495-1784	P	52,891 TA	15.8
Comerica Inc.	500 Woodward Ave.	Detroit	MI	48226	Eugene A. Miller	313-222-4000	P	39,678 TA	13.5
Westamerica Bank	PO Box 600	San Rafael	CA	94902	David L. Payne	415-257-8000	S	37,712 TA	0.7
First Bank System Inc.	PO Box 522	Minneapolis	MN	55480	John F. Grundhofer	612-973-1111	P	36,489 TA	12.0
First Fidelity Bancorp.	550 Broad St.	Newark	NJ	07102	Anthony P. Terracciano	201-565-3200	P	36,216 TA	12.0
Boatmen's Bancshares Inc.	800 Market St.	St. Louis	MO	63101	Andrew B. Craig III	314-466-6000	P	33,704 TA	17.0
U.S. Bancorp	PO Box 4412	Portland	OR	97208	Gerry B. Cameron	503-275-6111	P	33,260 TA	14.1

Company type codes: P - Public, R - Private, S - Subsidiary, D - Division, J - Joint Venture, A - Affiliate, G - Group. If the dollar values shown are not sales, the following codes apply: TA - Total Assets; OR - Operating Revenues; GB - Gross Billings. * - estimated dollar value. < - less than. na - not available.

Continued on next page.

LEADING COMPANIES - SIC 6022 - State Commercial Banks
Continued

Company Name	Address				CEO Name	Phone	Co. Type	Sales/Assets ($ mil)	Empl. (000)
Chase Manhattan Bank	802 Delaware Ave.	Wilmington	DE	19801	Michael S. Barrett	302-575-5000	S	31,846 TA	1.2
SouthTrust Corp.	PO Box 2554	Birmingham	AL	35290	Wallace D. Malone Jr.	205-254-5000	P	30,906 TA	10.3
Summit Bancorp.	PO Box 2066	Princeton	NJ	08543	T. Joseph Semrod	609-987-3200	P	29,964 TA	7.3
Comerica Bank	500 Woodward Ave.	Detroit	MI	48226	Eugene A. Miller	313-222-3300	S	28,936 TA	6.6
SunTrust Banks of Florida Inc.	PO Box 3833	Orlando	FL	32802	George W. Koehn	407-237-4141	S	27,585 TA	7.9
Huntington Bancshares Inc.	41 S. High St.	Columbus	OH	43287	Frank Wobst	614-480-8300	P	26,731 TA	9.5
State Street Bank and Trust Co.	PO Box 351	Boston	MA	02101	Marshall N. Carter	617-786-3000	S	22,778 TA	10.2
Harris Bankcorp Inc.	111 W. Monroe St.	Chicago	IL	60603	Alan G. McNally	312-461-2121	S	22,200 TA	6.6
Fifth Third Bancorp.	Fifth Third Ctr.	Cincinnati	OH	45263	George A. Schaefer Jr.	513-579-5300	P	21,375 TA	6.8
First of America Bank Corp.	211 S. Rose St.	Kalamazoo	MI	49007	Richard F. Chorman	616-376-9000	P	21,080 TA	10.6
Popular Inc.	PO Box 362708	San Juan	PR	00936	Richard L. Carrion	787-765-9800	P	19,301 TA	8.9
Mercantile Bancorporation Inc.	PO Box 524	St. Louis	MO	63166	Thomas H. Jacobsen	314-425-2525	P	19,188 TA	7.9
Northern Trust Corp.	50 S. La Salle St.	Chicago	IL	60675	David W. Fox	312-630-6000	P	18,562 TA	6.6
Union Planters Corp.	PO Box 387	Memphis	TN	38147	Benjamin W. Rawlins Jr.	901-580-6000	P	18,105 TA	5.2
Crestar Bank	PO Box 26665	Richmond	VA	23261	Richard G. Tilghman	804-782-5000	S	17,917 TA	6.7
SunTrust Banks of Georgia Inc.	PO Box 4418	Atlanta	GA	30302	Edward P. Gould	404-827-6510	S	16,854 TA	4.5
Citizens Financial Group Inc.	1 Citizens Plaza	Providence	RI	02903	Lawrence K. Fish	401-456-7000	P	16,221 TA	3.2
Simmons First National Corp.	PO Box 7009	Pine Bluff	AR	71611	J. Thomas May	501-541-1000	P	16,000 TA	0.7
Branch Banking and Trust Co.	PO Box 1260	Winston-Salem	NC	27102	John A. Allison	910-733-2000	S	15,992 TA	6.2
Harris Trust and Savings Bank	PO Box 755	Chicago	IL	60690	Alan G. McNally	312-461-2121	S	15,800 TA	7.0
Norwest Bank Texas, South Central	One O'Connor Plaza	Victoria	TX	77901	Charles Hrdlicka	512-573-5151	S	15,397 TA	1.0
Pacific Century Financial Corp.	PO Box 2900	Honolulu	HI	96846	Lawrence M. Johnson	808-643-3888	P	14,996 TA	5.1
Marshall and Ilsley Corp.	770 N. Water St.	Milwaukee	WI	53202	James B. Wigdale	414-765-7801	P	14,271 TA	11.4
First Maryland Bancorp.	25 S. Charles St.	Baltimore	MD	21201	Frank P. Bramble	410-244-4000	P	14,132 TA	7.1
Old Kent Financial Corp.	111 Lyon St. N.W.	Grand Rapids	MI	49503	David J. Wagner	616-771-5000	P	13,774 TA	6.3
United Jersey Bank	210 Main St.	Hackensack	NJ	07602	T. Joseph Semreo	201-646-5000	S	13,106 TA	1.8
Compass Bancshares	15 S. 20th St.	Birmingham	AL	35233	D. Paul Jones Jr.	205-933-3000	P	12,602 TA	5.5
LaSalle National Corp.	135 S. La Salle St.	Chicago	IL	60603	Ted Roberts	312-443-2000	P	12,385 TA	3.5
M and T Bank	1 M&T Plaza	Buffalo	NY	14240	Robert G. Wilmers	716-842-4200	S	12,009 TA	5.0
Bank of Hawaii	PO Box 2900	Honolulu	HI	96846	Lawrence M. Johnson	808-847-8888	S	11,827 TA	4.2
MainStreet BankGroup Inc.	PO Box 4831	Martinsville	VA	24115	Michael R. Brenan	703-632-2971	P	11,500 TA	0.6
Banco Popular de Puerto Rico	PO Box 362708	San Juan	PR	00936	Richard L. Carrion	809-765-9800	S	11,384 TA	4.5
First Guaranty Bank	PO Box 520	Hammond	LA	70401	Darrell E. Cremeans	504-345-7685	P	11,204 TA	0.1
Central Fidelity National Bank	PO Box 27602	Richmond	VA	23261	Lewis N. Miller Jr.	804-782-4000	S	10,755 TA	3.6
European American Bank	120 Broadway	New York	NY	10271	Edward Travaglianti	516-296-5000	S	10,704 TA	1.8
Associated Banc-Corp.	PO Box 13307	Green Bay	WI	54307	Harry B. Conlon	414-433-3166	P	10,700 TA	2.0

Company type codes: P - Public, R - Private, S - Subsidiary, D - Division, J - Joint Venture, A - Affiliate, G - Group. If the dollar values shown are not sales, the following codes apply: TA - Total Assets; OR - Operating Revenues; GB - Gross Billings. * - estimated dollar value. < - less than. *na* - not available.

Continued on next page.

LEADING COMPANIES - SIC 6022 - State Commercial Banks

Continued

Company Name	Address				CEO Name	Phone	Co. Type	Sales/Assets ($ mil)	Empl. (000)
Commerce Bancshares Inc.	PO Box 13686	Kansas City	MO	64199	David W. Kemper	816-234-2000	P	10,307 TA	4.3
First Alabama Bank	PO Box 10247	Birmingham	AL	35202	J. Stanley Mackin	205-326-7100	S	10,280 TA	4.7
Greenwood Trust Co.	12 Read's Way	New Castle	DE	19720	J. Nathan Hill	302-323-7110	R	10,134 TA	1.6
AmSouth Bank of Alabama	PO Box 11007	Birmingham	AL	35203	John W. Woods	205-326-5120	S	9,826 TA	4.2
Zions Bancorp.	One Main St.	Salt Lake City	UT	84111	Harris H. Simmons	801-524-4787	P	9,521 TA	4.9
Michigan National Corp.	PO Box 9065	Farmington Hills	MI	48333	Douglas E. Ebert	248-473-3000	S	9,329 TA	4.0
Synovus Financial Corp.	PO Box 120	Columbus	GA	31902	James H. Blanchard	706-649-2387	P	9,260 TA	8.1
First Commerce Corp.	PO Box 60279	New Orleans	LA	70160	Ian Arnof	504-561-1371	P	9,183 TA	3.8
First Virginia Bank	6400 Arlington Blvd.	Falls Church	VA	22042	Barry J. Fitzpatrick	703-241-4000	S	9,012 TA	5.1
First Citizens Bank and Trust Co.	PO Box 27131	Raleigh	NC	27611	Lewis R. Holding	919-755-7424	S	9,000 TA	4.1
Bank of America Arizona	PO Box 16290	Phoenix	AZ	85011	David S. Hanna	602-597-5000	S	8,800 TA	2.8
Banc One Wisconsin Corp.	PO Box 481	Milwaukee	WI	53201	William Reed	414-765-3000	S	8,267 TA	2.8
Sanwa Bank California	601 S. Figueroa St.	Los Angeles	CA	90017	Tom Takakura	213-896-7000	S	7,900 TA	3.0
First USA Inc.	1601 Elm St.	Dallas	TX	75201	John C. Tolleson	214-849-2000	P	7,635 TA	2.0
Citibank	99 Garnsey Rd.	Pittsford	NY	14534	Timothy P. McElduff	716-546-0500	S	7,477 TA	1.8
Bank of Tokyo-Mitsubishi Trust Co.	1251 Ave. of the Amer.	New York	NY	10016	Keishi Fujii	212-782-4000	S	7,370 TA	0.2
First USA Bank	PO Box 8600	Wilmington	DE	19886	Richard W. Vague	302-594-4000	S	7,345 TA	1.2
Provident Bancorp Inc.	1 East 4th St.	Cincinnati	OH	45202	Allen L. Davis	513-579-2000	P	6,905 TA	2.5
First Commercial Corp.	400 W. Capitol Ave.	Little Rock	AR	72201	Barnett Grace	501-371-7000	P	6,887 TA	3.3
Colonial BancGroup Inc.	PO Box 1108	Montgomery	AL	36101	Robert E. Lowder	334-240-5000	P	6,851 TA	3.0
AmSouth Bank of Florida	PO Box 17990	Clearwater	FL	32501	E.W. Stephenson Jr.	813-462-1110	S	6,848 TA	1.5
SunTrust Banks of Tennessee Inc.	PO Box 305110	Nashville	TN	37230	John W. Clay Jr.	615-748-4000	S	6,776 TA	2.6
First Hawaiian Bank	PO Box 3200	Honolulu	HI	96847	Walter A. Dods Jr.	808-525-7000	S	6,644 TA	2.7
Mercantile Bankshares Corp.	PO Box 1477	Baltimore	MD	21203	H. Furlong Baldwin	410-237-5900	P	6,643 TA	2.8
Centura Banks Inc.	PO Box 1220	Rocky Mount	NC	27802	Cecil W. Sewell	919-977-4400	P	6,294 TA	2.3
UMB Financial Corp.	PO Box 419226	Kansas City	MO	64141	R. Crosby Kemper	816-860-7000	P	6,281 TA	4.0
Compass Bank	PO Box 10566	Birmingham	AL	35296	D. Paul Jones Jr.	205-933-3000	S	6,264 TA	2.8
Wilmington Trust Corp.	1100 N. Market St.	Wilmington	DE	19890	Robert V. Harra Jr.	302-651-1000	P	6,112 TA	2.4
Bank of Southside Virginia	PO Box 40	Carson	VA	23830	J. Peter Clements	804-246-5211	S	5,763 TA	<0.1
North Fork Bancorporation Inc.	275 Broad Hollow Rd.	Melville	NY	11747	John A. Kanas	516-844-1004	P	5,751 TA	1.3
Old National Bancorp.	PO Box 718	Evansville	IN	47705	John N. Royse	812-464-1434	P	5,686 TA	2.3
Summit Bank	210 Main St.	Hackensack	NJ	07601	T. Joseph Semrod	609-987-3300	S	5,654 TA	1.6
Magna Group Inc.	1401 S. Brentwood Blvd.	St. Louis	MO	63144	G. Thomas Andes	314-963-2500	P	5,458 TA	2.2
ONBANCorp Inc.	PO Box 4983	Syracuse	NY	13221	Robert J. Bennett	315-424-5995	P	5,418 TA	1.3
CCB Financial Corp.	PO Box 931	Durham	NC	27702	Ernest C. Roessler	919-683-7777	P	5,384 TA	2.0

Company type codes: P - Public, R - Private, S - Subsidiary, D - Division, J - Joint Venture, A - Affiliate, G - Group. If the dollar values shown are not sales, the following codes apply: TA - Total Assets; OR - Operating Revenues; GB - Gross Billings. * - estimated dollar value. < - less than. na - not available.

Continued on next page.

LEADING COMPANIES - SIC 6022 - State Commercial Banks
Continued

Company Name	Address				CEO Name	Phone	Co. Type	Sales/Assets ($ mil)	Empl. (000)
Centura Bank	PO Box 1220	Rocky Mount	NC	27804	Cecil W. Sewell	919-977-4400	S	5,327 TA	2.0
Keystone Financial Inc.	PO Box 3660	Harrisburg	PA	17105	Carl L. Campbell	717-233-1555	P	5,231 TA	2.4
Bank of the West	180 Montgomery St.	San Francisco	CA	94104	Don McGrath	415-765-4800	S	5,050 TA	1.8
PNC Bank Kentucky Inc.	500 W. Jefferson St.	Louisville	KY	40202	Michael N. Harreld	502-581-2100	S	5,045 TA	1.6
Sumitomo Bank of California	320 California St.	San Francisco	CA	94104	Tsuneo Onda	415-445-8000	P	4,974 TA	1.6
Magna Bank N.A.	1401 S. Brentwood Blvd.	St. Louis	MO	63141	Dave Harris	314-963-2500	S	4,914 TA	1.5
Cullen/Frost Bankers Inc.	PO Box 1600	San Antonio	TX	78296	T.C. Frost	210-220-4011	P	4,888 TA	2.3

Source: *Ward's Business Directory of U.S. Private and Public Companies*, 1996. Company type codes: P - Public, R - Private, S - Subsidiary, D - Division, J - Joint Venture, A - Affiliate, G - Group. If the dollar values shown are not sales, the following codes apply: TA - Total Assets; OR - Operating Revenues; GB - Gross Billings. * - estimated dollar value. < - less than; *na* - not available.

LEADING COMPANIES - SIC 6029 - Commercial Banks, nec
Number shown: **2**   Total sales/assets ($ mil): **500**   Total employment (000): **0.0**

Company Name	Address				CEO Name	Phone	Co. Type	Sales/Assets ($ mil)	Empl. (000)
Hurley State Bank	811 E. 10th St.	Sioux Falls	SD	57103	Robert L. Wieseneck	605-336-5661	S	470 TA*	<0.1
Treasury Bank Ltd.	1155 15th St.	Washington	DC	20005	Thomas W. Lynn	202-872-8899	R	30 TA	<0.1

Source: *Ward's Business Directory of U.S. Private and Public Companies*, 1996. Company type codes: P - Public, R - Private, S - Subsidiary, D - Division, J - Joint Venture, A - Affiliate, G - Group. If the dollar values shown are not sales, the following codes apply: TA - Total Assets; OR - Operating Revenues; GB - Gross Billings. * - estimated dollar value. < - less than; *na* - not available.

FINANCIAL DATA ON BANKS AND TRUSTS

The following six tables show additional data on banks and trusts obtained from the Federal Deposit Insurance Corporation (FDIC) and the Federal Reserve System as published in the *Statistical Abstract of the United States 1997*. Much more detailed information on banks and trusts is available from the Office of Corporate Communications, FDIC, 550 17th Street, N.W., Washington, D.C. 20429 or from the Federal Reserve System, Publications Services, Mail Stop 128, Board of Governors of the Federal Reserve System, Washington, DC 20551.

BANKING OFFICES, BY TYPE OF BANK: 1980 TO 1996

As of December 31. Include Puerto Rico and outlying areas. Covers all FDIC-insured commercial banks and saving institutions. Data for 1980 include automatic teller machines which were reported by many banks as branches.

ITEM	1980	1985	1990	1991	1992	1993	1994	1995	1996
All banking offices	(NA)	85,083	84,672	84,098	82,002	81,745	82,673	81,893	83,476
Number of banks	(NA)	18,043	15,162	14,488	13,856	13,322	12,602	11,970	11,452
Number of branches	(NA)	67,040	69,510	69,610	68,146	68,423	70,071	69,923	71,024
Commercial banks	53,172	57,710	62,753	63,896	63,401	63,828	65,594	66,454	67,316
Number of banks	14,434	14,417	12,347	11,927	11,466	10,960	10,450	9,941	9,528
Number of branches	38,738	43,293	50,406	51,969	51,935	52,868	55,144	56,513	57,788
Savings institutions	(NA)	27,373	21,919	20,202	18,601	17,917	17,079	15,439	15,160
Number of banks	(NA)	3,626	2,815	2,561	2,390	2,362	2,152	2,029	1,924
Number of branches	(NA)	23,747	19,104	17,641	16,211	15,555	14,927	13,410	13,236

Source: U.S. Federal Deposit Insurance Corporation, *Historical Statistics on Banking, 1934-1995*, 1996 and *Statistics on Banking*, annual. *Note:* NA Not available.

SELECTED FINANCIAL INSTITUTIONS- NUMBER AND ASSETS, BY ASSET SIZE: 1996

As of December. FDIC = Federal Deposit Insurance Corporation.

Asset Size	Number of Institutions			Assets (bil. dol.)		
	F.D.I.C.-insured		Credit unions[1]	F.D.I.C.-insured		Credit unions[1]
	Commercial banks	Savings institutions		Commercial banks[2]	Savings institutions	
Total	9,528	1,924	11,392	4,578.3	1,028.2	326.9
Less than $5.0 million	52	7	5,520	0.2	(Z)	10.0
$5.0 million to $9.9 million	188	31	1,774	1.5	0.3	12.6
$10.0 million to $24.9 million	1,340	120	1,848	24.2	2.2	29.8
$25.0 million to $49.9 million	2,207	268	966	81.0	10.3	34.0
$50.0 million to $99.9 million	2,416	418	619	173.0	31.0	43.0
$100.0 million to $499.9 million	2,650	789	591	523.4	180.8	119.7
$500.0 million to $999.9 million	277	130	51	190.1	89.3	33.5
$1.0 billion to $2.9 billion	207	98	21	342.6	156.8	31.0
$3.0 billion or more	191	63	2	3,242.2	557.5	13.2
			Percent Distribution			
Total	100.0	100.0	100.0	100.0	100.0	100.0
Less than $5.0 million	0.5	0.4	48.5	(Z)	(Z)	3.1
$5.0 million to $9.9 million	2.0	1.6	15.6	(Z)	(Z)	3.9
$10.0 million to $24.9 million	14.1	6.2	16.2	0.5	0.2	9.1
$25.0 million to $49.9 million	23.2	13.9	8.5	1.8	1.0	10.4
$50.0 million to $99.9 million	25.4	21.7	5.4	3.8	3.0	13.2
$100.0 million to $499.9 million	27.8	41.0	5.2	11.4	17.6	36.6
$500.0 million to $999.9 million	2.9	6.8	0.4	4.2	8.7	10.2
$1.0 billion to $2.9 billion	2.2	5.1	0.2	7.5	15.3	9.5
$3.0 billion or more	2.0	3.3	(Z)	70.8	54.2	4.0

Source: Statistical Abstract of the United States, 1997, p. 514. *Primary Source*: Except as noted, U.S. Federal Deposit Insurance Corporation, *Statistics on Banking, 1996. Notes:* Z Less than $50 million or 0.05 percent. 1. Source: National Credit Union Administration, *National Credit Union Administration Yearend Statistics 1996.* Excludes nonfederally insured State chartered credit unions and federally insured corporate credit unions. 2. Includes foreign branches of U.S. banks.

INSURED COMMERCIAL BANKS, ASSETS AND LIABILITIES: 1990 TO 1996

In billions of dollars, except as indicated. As of December 31. Includes outlying areas. Except as noted, includes foreign branches of U.S. banks.

ITEM	1990	1991	1992	1993	1994	1995	1996[1]
Number of banks reporting	12,343	11,921	11,462	10,958	10,450	9,940	9,528
Assets, total	3,389	3,431	3,506	3,706	4,011	4,313	4,578
Net loans and leases	2,055	1,998	1,977	2,097	2,306	2,550	2,757
Real estate loans	830	851	868	923	998	1,080	1,140
Home equity lines of credit[2]	61	70	73	73	76	79	85
Commercial and industrial loans	615	559	536	539	589	661	710
Loan to individuals	404	392	385	419	487	535	561
Farm loans	33	35	35	37	39	40	41
Other loans and leases	242	227	216	239	251	292	364
Less: Reserve for losses	56	55	54	53	52	53	54
Less: Unearned income	14	11	9	7	6	6	5
Investment securities	605	691	773	837	823	811	801
Other	730	742	755	773	882	952	1,020
Domestic office assets	2,999	3,033	3,110	3,258	3,484	3,728	3,906
Foreign office assets	390	398	396	448	527	585	672
Liabilities and capital, total	3,389	3,431	3,506	3,706	4,011	4,313	4,578
Noninterest-bearing deposits[3]	489	480	541	572	572	612	664
Interest-bearing deposits[4]	2,162	2,207	2,158	2,182	2,302	2,416	2,533
Subordinated debt	24	25	34	37	41	44	51
Other liabilities	496	486	510	618	783	892	955
Equity capital	219	232	263	297	312	350	375
Domestic office deposits	2,357	2,383	2,412	2,424	2,442	2,573	2,724
Foreign office deposits	293	305	287	330	432	454	474

Source: U.S. Federal Deposit Insurance Corporation, *The FDIC Quarterly Banking Profile, Annual Report,* and *Statistics on Banking,* annual. *Notes:* NA Not available. 1. Preliminary. 2. For one- to four-family residential properties. 3. Prior to 1985, demand deposits. 4. Prior to 1985, time and saving deposits.

INSURED COMMERCIAL BANKS, INCOME AND MEASURES OF CONDITION: 1990 TO 1996

In billion of dollars, except as indicated. Includes outlying areas. Includes foreign branches of U.S. banks.

ITEM	1990	1991	1992	1993	1994	1995	1996[1]
Interest income	320.4	289.2	255.2	245.1	257.8	302.4	312.8
Interest expense	204.9	167.3	121.8	105.7	111.3	148.2	150.0
Net interest income	115.5	121.9	133.4	139.3	146.3	154.2	62.8
Provisions for loan losses	32.1	34.3	26.0	16.8	10.9	12.6	162.8
Noninterest income	54.9	59.7	65.6	75.0	76.3	82.4	93.6
Noninterest expense	115.7	124.8	130.9	139.7	144.2	149.7	160.7
Income taxes	7.7	8.3	14.5	19.8	22.4	26.1	28.2
Securities gain/loss, net	0.5	3.0	4.0	3.1	-0.6	0.5	1.1
Extraordinary gains, net	0.6	0.7	0.4	2.1	-	-	0.1
Net income	16.0	17.9	32.0	43.1	44.6	48.8	52.4
Ratios of Condition							
Return on assets (percent)[2]	0.48	0.53	0.93	1.20	1.15	1.17	1.19
Return on equity (percent)[3]	7.45	7.94	12.98	15.34	14.61	14.66	14.46
Equity capital to assets (percent)	6.45	6.75	7.51	8.00	7.78	8.11	8.20
Noncurrent assets plus other real estate owned to assets (percent)[4]	2.94	3.02	2.54	1.61	1.01	0.85	0.75
Net charge-offs[5]	29.7	32.9	25.6	17.5	11.2	12.2	15.5
Net charge-offs to loans and leases (percent)	1.43	1.59	1.27	0.85	0.50	0.49	0.58
Net interest margin (percent)[6]	3.94	4.11	4.41	4.40	4.36	4.29	4.27
Percentage of banks losing money	13.4	11.6	6.9	4.9	4.0	3.6	4.1

Source: U.S. Federal Deposit Insurance Corporation, *Annual Report; Statistics on Banking,* annual; and *FDIC Quarterly Banking Profile. Notes:* - Represents or rounds to zero. NA not available. 1. Preliminary. 2. Net income (including securities transactions and nonrecurring items) as a percentage of average total assets. 3. Net income as a percentage of average total equity capital. 4. The sum of loans, leases, debt securities and other assets that are 90 days or more past due, or in nonaccrual status plus foreclosed property. 5. Total loans and leases charged off (removed from balance sheet because of uncollectibility), less amounts recovered on loans and leases previously charged off. 6. Interest income less interest expense as a percentage of average earning assets (i.e. the profit margin a bank earn on its loans and investments).

INSURED COMMERCIAL BANK, BY STATE AND OTHER AREA: 1996

In billion of dollars, except number of banks. As of December 31. Includes foreign branches of U.S. banks.

STATE	Number	Assets	Deposits
Total	9,527	4,578.2	3,197.1
United States	9,507	4,547.4	3,174.9
Northeast	590	1,543.2	986.9
New England	148	197.3	140.9
Maine	20	9.0	6.5
New Hampshire	20	10.7	9.0
Vermont	22	6.2	5.2
Massachusetts	50	154.0	106.6
Rhode Island	8	6.5	5.0
Connecticut	28	10.9	8.6
Middle Atlantic	442	1,345.9	846.1
New York	159	1,032.3	602.5
New Jersey	66	70.0	59.3
Pennsylvania	217	243.7	184.3
Midwest	4,236	961.4	713.4
East North Central	1,835	664.2	485.7
Ohio	257	172.7	117.0
Indiana	204	66.5	52.1
Illinois	833	247.0	181.3
Michigan	176	112.2	84.2
Wisconsin	365	65.7	51.1
West North Central	2,401	297.2	227.7
Minnesota	519	72.1	53.9
Iowa	467	42.5	35.0
Missouri	430	88.3	70.6
North Dakota	123	8.5	7.3
South Dakota	117	29.3	13.2
Nebraska	329	27.8	23.3
Kansas	416	28.6	24.5
South	3,602	1,334.4	959.3
South Atlantic	1,182	795.2	530.5
Delaware	39	115.2	40.1
Maryland	90	38.9	30.2
District of Columbia	8	3.4	2.6
Virginia	154	89.9	64.9
West Virginia	113	22.3	18.0
North Carolina	56	191.4	121.4
South Carolina	79	26.4	21.3
Georgia	354	147.1	101.6
Florida	289	160.7	130.5
East South Central	807	220.4	165.8
Kentucky	275	52.7	39.8
Tennessee	238	75.9	57.2
Alabama	183	63.2	45.5
Mississippi	111	28.5	23.4
West South Central	1,613	318.8	262.9
Arkansas	234	30.7	26.5
Louisiana	172	47.0	38.3
Oklahoma	332	36.1	30.1
Texas	875	205.0	168.1

[Continued]

INSURED COMMERCIAL BANK, BY STATE AND OTHER AREA: 1996
[Continued]

STATE	Number	Assets	Deposits
West	1,079	708.4	515.3
Mountain	570	196.4	122.8
Montana	100	8.7	7.3
Idaho	15	6.6	5.3
Wyoming	54	8.2	7.0
Colorado	223	41.0	34.3
New Mexico	69	15.5	12.0
Arizona	35	48.1	28.2
Utah	48	36.0	18.9
Nevada	26	32.4	9.7
Pacific	509	512.0	392.5
Washington	84	44.7	35.5
Oregon	43	22.2	16.1
California	360	417.2	321.5
Alaska	8	5.8	4.2
Hawaii	14	22.1	15.2
American Samoa	1	0.1	(Z)
Puerto Rico	14	29.9	21.4
Guam	2	0.8	0.7
Pacific Islands	1	(Z)	(Z)
Virgin Islands	2	0.1	0.1

Source: U.S. Federal Deposit Insurance Corporation, *Statistics on Banking,* annual. *Note:* Z Less than $50 million.

INSURED COMMERCIAL BANKS, MEASURES OF CONDITION, BY ASSET SIZE AND REGION: 1996

In percent, except as indicated. Preliminary. Includes outlying areas. Includes foreign branches of U.S. banks.

Asset size and Region	Number of banks	Return on assets	Return on equity	Equity capital to assets	Noncurrent assets plus other real estate owned to total assets	Net charge-offs to loans and leases	Percentage of banks losing money
Total	9,528	1.19	14.46	8.20	0.75	0.58	4.1
Less than $100 million	6,205	1.17	11.02	10.56	0.77	0.26	5.3
$100 million to $1 billion	2,925	1.28	13.56	9.44	0.73	0.42	1.9
$1 billion to $10 billion	325	1.31	14.88	8.77	0.88	0.89	2.5
$10 billion or more	73	1.12	15.12	7.38	0.71	0.52	(NA)
Northeast[1]	743	1.10	14.72	7.36	0.84	0.63	4.8
Southeast[2]	1,577	1.22	14.52	8.48	0.72	0.45	4.9
Central[3]	2,110	1.21	14.30	8.43	0.57	0.44	3.7
Midwest[4]	2,401	1.43	16.18	8.74	0.65	0.70	2.6
Southwest[5]	1,683	1.22	13.98	8.74	0.61	0.34	2.9
West[6]	1,014	1.24	13.53	9.23	0.87	0.79	8.9

Source: U.S. Federal Deposit Insurance Corporation, *The FDIC Quarterly Banking Profile,* Fourth Quarter 1996. *Notes:* NA Not available. 1. Connecticut, Delaware, District of Columbia, Maine, Maryland, Massachuetts, New Hampshire, New Jersey, New York, Pennsylvania, Puerto Rico, Rhode Island and Vermont. 2. Alabama, Florida, Georgia, Mississippi, North Carolina, South Carolina, Tennessee, Virginia and West Virginia. 3. Illinois, Indiana, Kentucky, Missouri, Ohio and Wisconsin. 4. Iowa, Kansas, Minnesota, Missouri, Nebraska, North Dakota and South Dakota. 5. Arkansas, Louisiana, New Mexico, Oklahoma and Texas. 6. Alaska, Arizona, California, Colorado, Hawaii, Idaho, Montana, Nevada, Oregon, Pacific Islands, Utah, Washington and Wyoming.

SIC 6030

SAVINGS INSTITUTIONS

Savings institutions are divided into federally chartered (SIC 6035) and state-chartered (SIC 6036) organizations. Popularly called the Savings & Loans, the S&Ls, or "thrifts", they are institutions that accept deposits and make loans. These institutions may be insured by the Federal Deposit Insurance Corporation's (FDIC) Bank Insurance Fund ("BIF-insured") or by FDIC's Savings Association Insurance Fund ("SAIF-insured"). The FDIC's Deposit Insurance Fund was renamed the Bank Insurance Fund; SAIF has taken over the functions of the Federal Savings and Loan Insurance Corporation (FSLIC). These changes were made upon enactment of the Financial Institutions Reform, Recovery, and Enforcement Act of 1989 (FIRREA), Public Law 101-73, 103 Stat. 183.

ESTABLISHMENTS, EMPLOYMENT, AND PAYROLL

	1990	1991		1992		1993		1994		1995		% change 90-95
		Value	%	Value	%	Value	%	Value	%	Value	%	
All Establishments	21,689	22,211	2.4	21,089	-5.1	19,330	-8.3	17,858	-7.6	16,573	-7.2	-23.6
Mid-March Employment	416,571	393,715	-5.5	355,035	-9.8	318,553	-10.3	299,911	-5.9	267,574	-10.8	-35.8
1st Quarter Wages (annualized - $ mil.)	9,049.6	9,066.6	0.2	8,850.2	-2.4	7,983.4	-9.8	7,984.9	0.0	7,602.2	-4.8	-16.0
Payroll per Emp. 1st Q. (annualized)	21,724	23,028	6.0	24,928	8.2	25,062	0.5	26,624	6.2	28,411	6.7	30.8
Annual Payroll ($ mil.)	8,791.9	8,809.5	0.2	8,758.8	-0.6	8,254.4	-5.8	7,861.0	-4.8	7,367.3	-6.3	-16.2
Establishments - 1-4 Emp. Number	4,146	3,904	-5.8	4,414	13.1	3,863	-12.5	3,449	-10.7	(D)	-	-
Mid-March Employment	(D)	11,271	-	12,843	13.9	10,755	-16.3	9,230	-14.2	(D)	-	-
1st Quarter Wages (annualized - $ mil.)	(D)	231.5	-	270.4	16.8	229.4	-15.2	221.7	-3.4	(D)	-	-
Payroll per Emp. 1st Q. (annualized)	(D)	20,540	-	21,055	2.5	21,328	1.3	24,016	12.6	(D)	-	-
Annual Payroll ($ mil.)	(D)	256.8	-	270.8	5.4	272.3	0.6	254.4	-6.6	(D)	-	-
Establishments - 5-9 Emp. Number	8,562	8,738	2.1	8,610	-1.5	7,935	-7.8	7,068	-10.9	6,519	-7.8	-23.9
Mid-March Employment	57,612	59,939	4.0	57,836	-3.5	53,507	-7.5	47,794	-10.7	44,427	-7.0	-22.9
1st Quarter Wages (annualized - $ mil.)	1,023.6	1,104.1	7.9	1,099.0	-0.5	1,005.6	-8.5	938.0	-6.7	931.5	-0.7	-9.0
Payroll per Emp. 1st Q. (annualized)	17,768	18,421	3.7	19,002	3.2	18,794	-1.1	19,626	4.4	20,966	6.8	18.0
Annual Payroll ($ mil.)	1,010.4	1,103.2	9.2	1,122.0	1.7	1,058.9	-5.6	945.4	-10.7	939.5	-0.6	-7.0
Establishments - 10-19 Emp. Number	5,019	6,238	24.3	4,888	-21.6	4,553	-6.9	4,462	-2.0	4,187	-6.2	-16.6
Mid-March Employment	66,205	82,152	24.1	64,151	-21.9	60,090	-6.3	58,755	-2.2	55,290	-5.9	-16.5
1st Quarter Wages (annualized - $ mil.)	1,208.9	1,569.1	29.8	1,339.2	-14.7	1,205.9	-10.0	1,246.9	3.4	1,227.6	-1.5	1.6
Payroll per Emp. 1st Q. (annualized)	18,259	19,100	4.6	20,876	9.3	20,068	-3.9	21,222	5.7	22,203	4.6	21.6
Annual Payroll ($ mil.)	1,184.6	1,564.8	32.1	1,334.5	-14.7	1,266.0	-5.1	1,227.0	-3.1	1,215.5	-0.9	2.6
Establishments - 20-49 Emp. Number	2,430	2,181	-10.2	2,086	-4.4	1,961	-6.0	1,957	-0.2	1,832	-6.4	-24.6
Mid-March Employment	73,061	63,087	-13.7	61,267	-2.9	58,051	-5.2	58,005	-0.1	53,792	-7.3	-26.4
1st Quarter Wages (annualized - $ mil.)	1,502.6	1,355.1	-9.8	1,497.5	10.5	1,406.3	-6.1	1,524.5	8.4	1,493.1	-2.1	-0.6
Payroll per Emp. 1st Q. (annualized)	20,566	21,481	4.4	24,441	13.8	24,226	-0.9	26,283	8.5	27,757	5.6	35.0
Annual Payroll ($ mil.)	1,439.5	1,325.3	-7.9	1,508.4	13.8	1,464.3	-2.9	1,496.5	2.2	1,473.4	-1.5	2.4
Establishments - 50-99 Emp. Number	876	596	-32.0	623	4.5	615	-1.3	542	-11.9	506	-6.6	-42.2
Mid-March Employment	60,112	40,970	-31.8	42,697	4.2	42,112	-1.4	36,738	-12.8	34,416	-6.3	-42.7
1st Quarter Wages (annualized - $ mil.)	1,360.8	1,012.1	-25.6	1,203.8	18.9	1,151.0	-4.4	1,065.0	-7.5	1,066.4	0.1	-21.6
Payroll per Emp. 1st Q. (annualized)	22,637	24,704	9.1	28,193	14.1	27,331	-3.1	28,990	6.1	30,987	6.9	36.9
Annual Payroll ($ mil.)	1,322.5	989.6	-25.2	1,179.8	19.2	1,190.9	0.9	1,023.2	-14.1	1,045.8	2.2	-20.9
Establishments - 100-249 Emp. Number	502	393	-21.7	330	-16.0	299	-9.4	293	-2.0	233	-20.5	-53.6
Mid-March Employment	75,050	59,990	-20.1	50,183	-16.3	45,871	-8.6	44,812	-2.3	34,543	-22.9	-54.0
1st Quarter Wages (annualized - $ mil.)	1,774.8	1,578.8	-11.0	1,448.8	-8.2	1,371.3	-5.3	1,414.8	3.2	1,175.4	-16.9	-33.8
Payroll per Emp. 1st Q. (annualized)	23,648	26,317	11.3	28,870	9.7	29,896	3.6	31,572	5.6	34,028	7.8	43.9
Annual Payroll ($ mil.)	1,692.4	1,514.9	-10.5	1,436.5	-5.2	1,377.3	-4.1	1,379.1	0.1	1,110.8	-19.5	-34.4
Establishments - 250-499 Emp. Number	107	117	9.3	101	-13.7	76	-24.8	59	-22.4	53	-10.2	-50.5
Mid-March Employment	34,496	39,057	13.2	34,704	-11.1	25,963	-25.2	20,025	-22.9	17,501	-12.6	-49.3
1st Quarter Wages (annualized - $ mil.)	844.2	1,060.3	25.6	981.9	-7.4	836.7	-14.8	710.6	-15.1	720.2	1.3	-14.7
Payroll per Emp. 1st Q. (annualized)	24,472	27,147	10.9	28,294	4.2	32,227	13.9	35,486	10.1	41,152	16.0	68.2
Annual Payroll ($ mil.)	775.0	976.6	26.0	940.5	-3.7	879.3	-6.5	683.4	-22.3	649.6	-4.9	-16.2
Establishments - 500-999 Emp. Number	37	34	-8.1	27	-20.6	22	-18.5	22	-	21	-4.5	-43.2
Mid-March Employment	(D)	21,844	-	17,714	-18.9	14,043	-20.7	14,162	0.8	13,800	-2.6	-
1st Quarter Wages (annualized - $ mil.)	(D)	640.0	-	561.2	-12.3	489.9	-12.7	482.7	-1.5	580.3	20.2	-
Payroll per Emp. 1st Q. (annualized)	(D)	29,298	-	31,682	8.1	34,885	10.1	34,081	-2.3	42,053	23.4	-
Annual Payroll ($ mil.)	(D)	619.1	-	518.6	-16.2	510.8	-1.5	477.4	-6.6	498.0	4.3	-
Estab. - 1000 or More Emp. Number	10	10	-	10	-	6	-40.0	6	-	(D)	-	-
Mid-March Employment	13,453	15,405	14.5	13,640	-11.5	8,161	-40.2	10,390	27.3	(D)	-	-
1st Quarter Wages (annualized - $ mil.)	402.9	515.5	28.0	448.4	-13.0	287.3	-35.9	380.7	32.5	(D)	-	-
Payroll per Emp. 1st Q. (annualized)	29,949	33,464	11.7	32,877	-1.8	35,199	7.1	36,637	4.1	(D)	-	-
Annual Payroll ($ mil.)	399.2	459.2	15.0	447.7	-2.5	234.6	-47.6	374.7	59.7	(D)	-	-

Source: County Business Patterns, U.S. Department of Commerce, Washington, D.C., for 1990 through 1995. Payroll per employee is calculated using mid-March employment and 1st Quarter wages, annualized. Annual payroll, also shown, may not equal the annualized 1st Quarter wages. Columns headed by a percent sign (%) indicate change from the previous year. *na* stands for not available. The symbol (D) indicates that data are withheld by the source to avoid disclosure of competitive information. A dash (-) indicates that data are not available or cannot be calculated.

ESTABLISHMENTS
Number

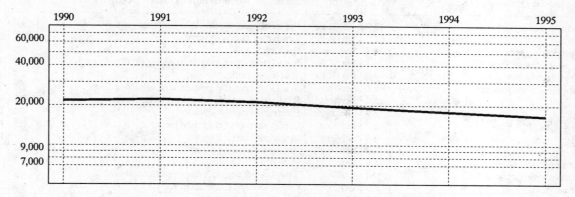

MID-MARCH EMPLOYMENT
Number

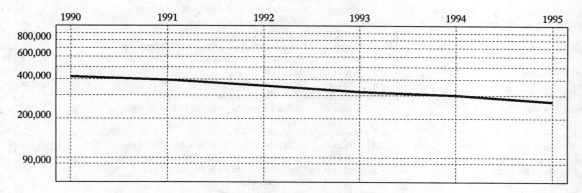

ANNUAL PAYROLL
$ million

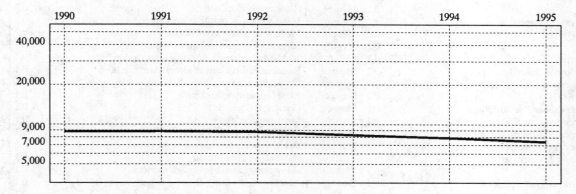

INPUTS AND OUTPUTS FOR ALL BANKING SECTORS - SICs 601, 602, 603, 608, and 609

Economic Sector or Industry Providing Inputs	%	Sector	Economic Sector or Industry Buying Outputs	%	Sector
Security & commodity brokers	12.9	Fin/R.E.	Personal consumption expenditures	59.0	
Banking	11.8	Fin/R.E.	Exports of goods & services	5.1	Foreign
Computer & data processing services	9.5	Services	Banking	4.6	Fin/R.E.
Real estate agents, operators, & lessors	8.1	Fin/R.E.	Retail trade, ex eating & drinking	3.0	Trade
Credit agencies other than banks	4.9	Fin/R.E.	Wholesale trade	2.3	Trade
Management & public relations services	4.1	Services	S/L Govt., general government nec, spending	2.1	S/L Govt
Advertising	3.9	Services	Real estate agents, operators, & lessors	1.5	Fin/R.E.
U.S. Postal Service	3.9	Gov't	Electric services (utilities)	0.8	Util.
Accounting, auditing & bookkeeping	3.7	Services	Credit agencies other than banks	0.8	Fin/R.E.
Business services nec	3.4	Services	Insurance carriers	0.7	Fin/R.E.
Legal services	2.8	Services	Eating & drinking places	0.7	Services
Federal Government enterprises nec	2.5	Gov't	Hotels	0.7	Services
Telephone/telegraph communications nec	2.4	Util.	Telephone/telegraph communications nec	0.6	Util.
Trucking & courier services, ex air	2.3	Util.	Owner-occupied dwellings	0.6	Fin/R.E.
Blankbooks, looseleaf binders & devices	1.7	Manufg.	Doctors & dentists	0.6	Services
Wholesale trade	1.6	Trade	Motor vehicles & passenger car bodies	0.4	Manufg.
Personnel supply services	1.6	Services	Trucking & courier services, ex air	0.4	Util.
Electric services (utilities)	1.5	Util.	Federal Government, nondefense, spending	0.4	Gov't
Warehousing & storage	1.4	Util.	New construction nec	0.3	Constr.
Air transportation	1.0	Util.	Repair & maintenance construction nec	0.3	Constr.
Eating & drinking places	1.0	Services	Residential 1 unit structures, nonfarm	0.3	Constr.
Sanitary services, steam supply, irrigation	0.9	Util.	Petroleum refining	0.3	Manufg.
Insurance carriers	0.9	Fin/R.E.	Railroads & related services	0.3	Util.
Repair & maintenance construction nec	0.8	Constr.	Computer & data processing services	0.3	Services
Hotels	0.8	Services	Engineering, architectural, & surveying services	0.3	Services
Detective & protective services	0.7	Services	Hospitals	0.3	Services
Commercial printing	0.6	Manufg.	Legal services	0.3	Services
Photographic equipment & supplies	0.6	Manufg.	Crude petroleum & natural gas	0.2	Mining
Research, development, & testing services	0.6	Services	Office, industrial/commercial buildings	0.2	Constr.
Manifold business forms	0.5	Manufg.	Aircraft	0.2	Manufg.
Paper & paperboard mills	0.5	Manufg.	Drugs	0.2	Manufg.
Automotive rental & leasing, without drivers	0.5	Services	Industrial inorganic & organic chemicals	0.2	Manufg.
Business & professional associations	0.5	Services	Miscellaneous plastics products, nec	0.2	Manufg.
Services to dwellings & other buildings	0.5	Services	Motor vehicle parts & accessories	0.2	Manufg.
Natural gas distribution	0.4	Util.	Air transportation	0.2	Util.
Magnetic & optical recording media	0.3	Manufg.	Freight forwarders	0.2	Util.
Manufacturing industries, nec	0.3	Manufg.	Water transportation	0.2	Util.
Periodicals	0.3	Manufg.	Security & commodity brokers	0.2	Fin/R.E.
Petroleum refining	0.3	Manufg.	Automotive rental & leasing, without drivers	0.2	Services
Electrical repair shops	0.3	Services	Automotive repair shops & services	0.2	Services
Book publishing	0.2	Manufg.	Business services nec	0.2	Services
Computer peripheral equipment	0.2	Manufg.	Management & public relations services	0.2	Services
Envelopes	0.2	Manufg.	Medical & health services nec	0.2	Services
Textile bags	0.2	Manufg.	State & local government enterprises nec	0.2	Gov't
Local & suburban transit	0.2	Util.	Maintenance/repair of residential structures	0.1	Constr.
Automotive repair shops & services	0.2	Services	Residential additions & alterations, nonfarm	0.1	Constr.
Miscellaneous equipment rental & leasing	0.2	Services	Apparel made from purchased materials	0.1	Manufg.
Miscellaneous repair shops	0.2	Services	Blast furnaces & steel mills	0.1	Manufg.
Die-cut paper & paperboard & cardboard	0.1	Manufg.	Commercial printing	0.1	Manufg.
Fabricated metal products, nec	0.1	Manufg.	Meat packing plants	0.1	Manufg.
Miscellaneous fabricated wire products	0.1	Manufg.	Paper & paperboard mills	0.1	Manufg.
Paperboard containers & boxes	0.1	Manufg.	Cable & other pay television services	0.1	Util.
Retail trade, ex eating & drinking	0.1	Trade	Natural gas distribution	0.1	Util.
Royalties	0.1	Fin/R.E.	Insurance agents, brokers, & services	0.1	Fin/R.E.
State & local government enterprises nec	0.1	Gov't	Accounting, auditing & bookkeeping	0.1	Services
			Motion picture services & theaters	0.1	Services
			Personnel supply services	0.1	Services
			Portrait photographic studios	0.1	Services
			U.S. Postal Service	0.1	Gov't

Source: Benchmark Input-Output Accounts for the U.S. Economy, 1992, U.S. Department of Commerce, Washington, D.C., November 1997. Data, as reported in the source, are organized by the 1987 SIC structure in use in 1992.

OCCUPATIONS EMPLOYED BY COMMERCIAL BANKS, SAVINGS INSTITUTIONS, AND CREDIT UNIONS

Occupation	% of Total 1996	Change to 2006	Occupation	% of Total 1996	Change to 2006
Bank tellers	28.5	0.1	General managers & top executives	3.1	-8.6
Clerical supervisors & managers	6.7	6.7	Clerical & administrative workers nec	1.5	-52.8
Loan officers & counselors	6.6	13.2	Accountants & auditors	1.4	-12.7
Financial managers	6.3	-5.7	Securities & financial sales workers	1.3	41.5
New accounts clerks, banking	5.9	3.8	Adjustment clerks	1.3	27.3
Loan & credit clerks	5.4	-4.8	Statement clerks	1.2	-5.7
General office clerks	4.0	-18.8	Duplicating, mail, office machine operators	1.1	-76.4
Bookkeeping, accounting, & auditing clerks	3.8	-24.5	Managers & administrators nec	1.0	-6.5
Secretaries, except legal & medical	3.7	-25.2			

Sources: Industry-Occupation Matrix, Bureau of Labor Statistics. These data relate to one or more 3-digit SIC industry groups rather than to a single 4-digit SIC. The change reported for each occupation to the year 2005 is a percent of growth or decline as estimated by the Bureau of Labor Statistics. The abbreviation *nec* stands for not elsewhere classified.

U.S. AND STATE DATA ON INDUSTRY REVENUES AND OTHER ACCOUNTS FOR 1992

State	No. of Estab.	Employ-ment	Payroll ($ mil.)	Revenues ($ mil.)	Empl./ Estab.	Revenue/ Estab. ($)	Payroll/ Estab. ($)	Revenue/ Empl. ($)	Payroll/ Empl. ($)
UNITED STATES	20,544	341,920	8,445.6	92,322.2	17	4,493,877	411,097	270,011	24,700
Alabama	192	2,041	41.6	480.3	11	2,501,422	216,667	235,313	20,382
Alaska	3	-	(D)	(D)	(D)	(D)	(D)	(D)	(D)
Arizona	96	909	17.9	166.8	9	1,737,083	185,990	183,454	19,642
Arkansas	129	1,409	30.3	282.1	11	2,186,798	235,225	200,211	21,536
California	2,982	59,775	1,716.2	17,724.2	20	5,943,718	575,515	296,515	28,711
Colorado	189	1,943	40.3	389.7	10	2,062,153	213,492	200,590	20,767
Connecticut	734	15,222	369.7	3,785.6	21	5,157,545	503,668	248,695	24,287
Delaware	39	538	15.3	180.0	14	4,615,564	392,538	334,586	28,455
District of Columbia	79	914	25.7	309.8	12	3,921,278	324,785	338,929	28,072
Florida	1,362	20,084	472.3	5,901.4	15	4,332,899	346,776	293,836	23,517
Georgia	323	5,379	130.2	1,171.4	17	3,626,498	403,111	217,765	24,206
Hawaii	150	2,293	61.4	545.5	15	3,636,460	409,140	237,884	26,765
Idaho	44	343	8.4	116.6	8	2,650,136	191,886	339,959	24,615
Illinois	965	20,126	468.9	5,475.5	21	5,674,110	485,864	272,062	23,296
Indiana	355	5,433	117.8	1,279.5	15	3,604,124	331,856	235,499	21,684
Iowa	206	2,137	46.0	502.6	10	2,440,029	223,291	235,211	21,525
Kansas	189	2,381	52.8	1,100.6	13	5,823,238	279,603	462,239	22,194
Kentucky	239	2,468	57.6	638.7	10	2,672,502	241,134	258,804	23,351
Louisiana	162	2,306	50.3	531.5	14	3,280,765	310,247	230,479	21,795
Maine	165	2,659	59.1	523.5	16	3,172,806	358,473	196,883	22,244
Maryland	435	8,265	210.1	1,990.2	19	4,575,067	483,071	240,793	25,425
Massachusetts	1,075	20,449	534.9	5,013.6	19	4,663,844	497,590	245,177	26,158
Michigan	547	8,305	201.1	2,611.6	15	4,774,373	367,636	314,459	24,214
Minnesota	207	4,444	105.8	1,040.5	21	5,026,763	511,314	234,145	23,817
Mississippi	139	1,704	35.8	306.4	12	2,203,978	257,489	179,785	21,004
Missouri	389	4,929	103.5	1,390.4	13	3,574,270	266,064	282,084	20,998
Montana	62	639	13.9	117.5	10	1,894,387	224,629	183,806	21,795
Nebraska	171	1,970	48.1	659.4	12	3,856,117	281,053	334,719	24,396
Nevada	97	1,366	34.4	318.0	14	3,277,990	354,608	232,771	25,181
New Hampshire	245	4,062	91.7	865.9	17	3,534,469	374,098	213,182	22,564
New Jersey	1,026	15,366	382.2	4,235.4	15	4,128,066	372,490	275,634	24,871
New Mexico	41	-	(D)	(D)	(D)	(D)	(D)	(D)	(D)
New York	1,454	37,325	892.6	10,343.0	26	7,113,488	613,866	277,107	23,913
North Carolina	507	5,750	139.2	1,443.2	11	2,846,586	274,639	250,995	24,216
North Dakota	56	-	(D)	(D)	(D)	(D)	(D)	(D)	(D)
Ohio	1,124	15,082	335.5	3,834.2	13	3,411,228	298,505	254,225	22,246
Oklahoma	177	2,380	46.1	697.8	13	3,942,277	260,226	293,186	19,353
Oregon	229	2,556	64.3	634.0	11	2,768,603	280,860	248,048	25,163
Pennsylvania	957	12,465	279.0	2,979.2	13	3,113,060	291,534	239,005	22,383
Rhode Island	65	1,829	42.0	330.4	28	5,082,523	646,369	180,625	22,971
South Carolina	328	5,001	111.8	954.1	15	2,908,857	340,970	190,783	22,363
South Dakota	64	560	10.2	122.8	9	1,919,156	159,687	219,332	18,250
Tennessee	241	3,157	69.4	706.3	13	2,930,585	287,801	223,716	21,970
Texas	660	10,472	269.7	4,227.6	16	6,405,520	408,615	403,709	25,753
Utah	33	-	(D)	(D)	(D)	(D)	(D)	(D)	(D)
Vermont	49	1,081	26.1	192.2	22	3,921,592	531,939	177,759	24,112
Virginia	525	6,772	159.5	1,754.0	13	3,340,956	303,859	259,008	23,557
Washington	482	7,198	228.7	2,246.8	15	4,661,332	474,546	312,137	31,777
West Virginia	46	609	11.6	138.3	13	3,007,283	252,217	227,151	19,051
Wisconsin	482	7,273	160.0	1,524.7	15	3,163,210	332,017	209,634	22,004
Wyoming	28	-	(D)	(D)	(D)	(D)	(D)	(D)	(D)

Source: 1992 Economic Census, U.S. Department of Commerce, Washington, D.C. This is the only table that shows revenue data as collected by the Bureau of the Census in an Economic Census. The symbol (D) indicates that data are withheld by the source to avoid disclosure of competitive information. A dash (-) indicates that data are not available or cannot be calculated.

STATE-BY-STATE DATA ON ESTABLISHMENTS, EMPLOYMENT, AND PAYROLL - 1994 AND 1995

State	1994					1995					% Change Empl.
	No. of Estab.	Employ-ment	Pay / Empl.	Payroll ($ mil.)	Pay / Estab.	No. of Estab.	Employ-ment	Pay / Empl.	Payroll ($ mil.)	Pay / Estab.	
Alabama	99	1,431	25,549	32.5	328,202	70	1,021	22,535	25.0	356,900	-28.7
Alaska	3	(D)	-	(D)	-	3	(D)	-	(D)	-	-
Arizona	113	639	23,856	12.5	110,487	43	331	26,550	10.3	239,930	-48.2
Arkansas	100	1,398	19,660	28.0	279,840	108	1,462	20,071	30.8	285,176	4.6
California	2,675	51,961	32,191	1,535.0	573,846	2,502	45,102	32,237	1,366.6	546,189	-13.2
Colorado	162	(D)	-	(D)	-	175	(D)	-	(D)	-	-
Connecticut	644	12,416	29,685	361.9	561,970	624	12,070	32,589	376.0	602,548	-2.8
Delaware	38	447	34,416	16.6	435,632	39	648	35,556	21.0	539,077	45.0
District of Columbia	58	721	32,067	21.3	368,017	44	566	34,678	19.8	449,023	-21.5
Florida	1,038	16,550	25,679	418.3	402,985	868	12,580	26,961	341.8	393,832	-24.0
Georgia	210	3,031	25,097	74.3	353,833	192	2,569	24,472	64.1	333,635	-15.2
Hawaii	121	1,784	28,278	50.5	416,950	123	1,834	28,294	50.5	410,935	2.8
Idaho	45	(D)	-	(D)	-	50	(D)	-	(D)	-	-
Illinois	938	19,656	25,551	499.1	532,098	957	18,431	29,196	495.3	517,512	-6.2
Indiana	310	5,328	22,019	120.7	389,448	315	5,450	22,161	122.7	389,610	2.3
Iowa	212	2,567	21,727	58.1	273,887	203	2,345	26,072	61.1	301,158	-8.6
Kansas	186	2,260	26,283	56.4	303,027	175	2,112	30,023	60.2	343,731	-6.5
Kentucky	177	1,802	23,181	43.8	247,480	163	1,651	25,698	45.4	278,301	-8.4
Louisiana	127	1,691	23,525	41.0	322,819	117	1,632	23,034	38.1	325,949	-3.5
Maine	175	2,752	23,840	68.3	390,246	176	2,957	27,858	75.9	431,222	7.4
Maryland	413	7,829	25,566	212.2	513,777	384	8,047	27,564	229.1	596,659	2.8
Massachusetts	976	17,649	26,307	479.5	491,254	909	17,600	27,898	463.3	509,710	-0.3
Michigan	512	8,297	23,615	204.0	398,420	535	8,286	24,107	214.1	400,159	-0.1
Minnesota	205	2,914	24,419	68.6	334,854	142	2,062	25,049	50.9	358,282	-29.2
Mississippi	87	1,365	23,133	29.0	332,989	83	923	23,666	22.1	266,277	-32.4
Missouri	354	5,809	23,608	138.6	391,497	298	4,356	23,225	106.5	357,305	-25.0
Montana	64	706	20,918	16.9	264,734	64	819	21,841	16.6	259,406	16.0
Nebraska	151	1,785	24,007	43.5	288,325	133	1,568	24,487	42.1	316,586	-12.2
Nevada	99	1,436	26,538	40.3	407,222	96	1,467	29,238	41.0	427,604	2.2
New Hampshire	215	3,832	22,830	83.7	389,428	110	2,001	24,256	50.0	454,764	-47.8
New Jersey	847	12,399	26,577	330.8	390,561	799	10,546	29,690	296.3	370,811	-14.9
New Mexico	30	698	23,009	16.1	535,333	28	596	25,255	15.5	554,786	-14.6
New York	1,301	31,462	25,746	836.0	642,607	1,244	28,328	31,198	800.1	643,179	-10.0
North Carolina	332	3,846	26,802	97.7	294,367	306	3,312	25,959	92.8	303,232	-13.9
North Dakota	69	1,027	24,308	24.4	353,159	54	(D)	-	(D)	-	-
Ohio	1,020	14,658	24,612	333.6	327,034	913	12,467	25,728	312.9	342,689	-14.9
Oklahoma	145	1,412	21,802	29.7	204,897	130	1,360	20,694	31.1	239,331	-3.7
Oregon	219	2,171	25,784	53.2	242,817	234	2,420	23,967	63.0	269,385	11.5
Pennsylvania	818	10,432	22,779	247.0	301,949	759	9,822	24,698	248.1	326,859	-5.8
Rhode Island	63	1,235	21,315	21.0	333,302	31	597	28,302	14.3	462,194	-51.7
South Carolina	207	2,978	22,156	69.1	333,676	206	2,946	24,855	73.5	356,811	-1.1
South Dakota	56	509	19,222	10.0	179,161	46	427	21,649	9.2	199,870	-16.1
Tennessee	202	2,885	22,846	69.3	343,074	172	2,427	26,728	69.3	403,128	-15.9
Texas	600	9,648	30,688	301.2	501,943	566	9,993	29,484	308.3	544,763	3.6
Utah	35	665	26,370	17.9	512,400	49	745	27,903	21.8	444,918	12.0
Vermont	35	794	23,859	18.4	525,829	35	945	21,820	19.9	567,857	19.0
Virginia	333	4,110	26,067	102.2	306,781	306	3,351	26,907	81.8	267,392	-18.5
Washington	470	10,191	28,285	289.8	616,674	426	5,928	28,457	193.2	453,430	-41.8
West Virginia	42	535	19,312	10.5	250,143	43	596	19,711	11.6	269,767	11.4
Wisconsin	498	7,593	22,550	171.2	343,765	498	7,087	23,844	168.6	338,637	-6.7
Wyoming	29	410	28,380	11.3	390,414	27	247	35,741	6.9	255,889	-39.8

Source: County Business Patterns, U.S. Department of Commerce, Washington, D.C., for 1994 and 1995. Employment shown is for mid-March of the year shown. Payroll per employee is calculated by annualizing 1st Quarter payroll (not shown) and then dividing that value by mid-March employment. Dividing total annual payroll (columns 5 and 10) by employment, therefore, will *not* yield the payroll per employee figure (columns 4 and 9). The symbol (D) indicates that data are withheld by the source to avoid disclosure of competitive information. A dash (-) indicates that data are not available or cannot be calculated.

ESTABLISHMENTS 1995 - STATE AND REGIONAL CONCENTRATION

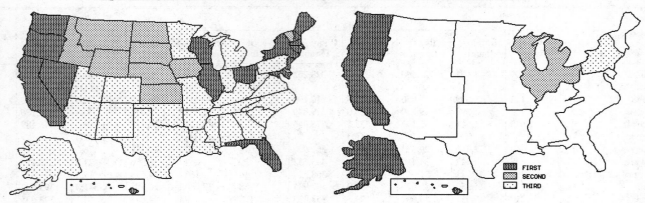

EMPLOYMENT 1995 - STATE AND REGIONAL CONCENTRATION

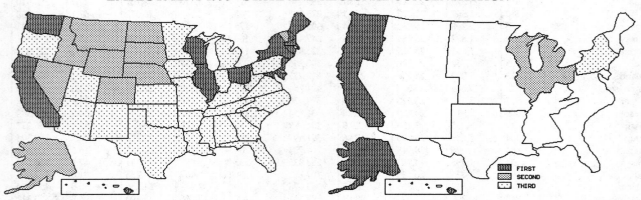

PAYROLL 1995 - STATE AND REGIONAL CONCENTRATION

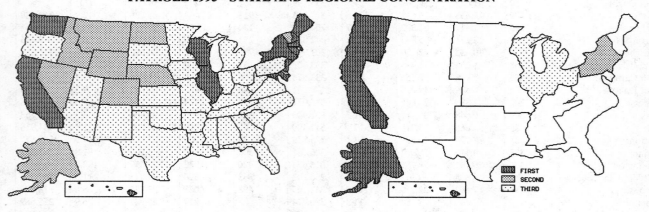

States with the darkest shading indicate those states which have proportionately more establishments, employment, or payrolls than would be indicated by the state's population. States with light shading are states with proportionately fewer establishments, less employment, and lower payrolls than population distribution. States shaded grey are within 15 percent of the state's population proportion in these categories. States for which no data are available are shown as average (grey). *Regions* are shaded to indicate absolute rank in the category. If no data for the category are available, establishment counts are used to shade the regions. Source of the data is the table on the facing page.

LEADING COMPANIES - SIC 6035 - Federal Savings Institutions

Number shown: **93**   Total sales/assets ($ mil): **1,239,576**   Total employment (000): **737.7**

Company Name	Address				CEO Name	Phone	Co. Type	Sales/Assets ($ mil)	Empl. (000)
Citicorp	399 Park Ave.	New York	NY	10043	John S. Reed	212-559-1000	P	281,018 TA	90.0
National City Corp.	1900 E. 9th St.	Cleveland	OH	44114	David A. Daberko	216-575-2000	P	54,684 TA	29.8
Home Savings of America F.S.B.	4900 Rivergrade Rd.	Irwindale	CA	91706	Bruce Willison	626-960-6311	S	49,902 TA	9.5
H.F. Ahmanson and Co.	4900 Rivergrade Rd.	Irwindale	CA	91706	Charles R. Rinehart	818-960-6311	P	49,902 TA	9.5
Great Western Financial Corp.	9200 Oakdale Ave.	Chatsworth	CA	91311	John F. Maher	818-775-3411	P	42,875 TA	13.0
ALBANK F.S.B.	PO Box 70	Albany	NY	12201	Herbert G. Chorbajian	518-445-2100	S	41,000 TA	1.4
World Savings and Loan Association	1901 Harrison St.	Oakland	CA	94612	Herbert M. Sandler	510-446-6000	S	39,590 TA	4.9
Golden West Financial Corp.	1901 Harrison St.	Oakland	CA	94612	Marion O. Sandler	510-446-3420	P	37,731 TA	4.5
Great Western Bank F.S.B.	9200 Oakdale Ave.	Chatsworth	CA	91311	John F. MMaher	818-755-3411	S	37,180 TA	8.3
Household International Inc.	2700 Sanders Rd.	Prospect Heights	IL	60070	William F. Aldinger	847-564-5000	P	30,334 TA	14.7
Huntington Bancshares Inc.	41 S. High St.	Columbus	OH	43287	Frank Wobst	614-480-8300	P	26,731 TA	9.5
Dime Bancorp Inc.	589 5th Ave.	New York	NY	10017	Lawrence J. Total	212-326-6170	P	21,848 TA	3.2
First of America Bank Corp.	211 S. Rose St.	Kalamazoo	MI	49007	Richard F. Chorman	616-376-9000	P	21,080 TA	10.6
Dime Savings Bank of New York F.S.B.	975 Franklin Ave.	Garden City	NY	11530	Richard D. Parsons	516-351-1550	S	20,327 TA	3.2
Popular Inc.	PO Box 362708	San Juan	PR	00936	Richard L. Carrion	787-765-9800	P	19,301 TA	8.9
Regions Financial Corp.	PO Box 10247	Birmingham	AL	35202	J. Stanley Mackin	205-326-7100	P	18,930 TA	8.1
Union Planters Corp.	PO Box 387	Memphis	TN	38147	Benjamin W. Rawlins Jr.	901-580-6000	P	18,105 TA	5.2
Standard Federal Bank	PO Box 3703	Troy	MI	48007	Scott Heitzmann	248-643-9600	S	16,100 TA	4.0
Ford Motor Co.	PO Box 1899	Dearborn	MI	48121	Alex Trotman	313-322-3000	P	15,363	363.9
Pacific Century Financial Corp.	PO Box 2900	Honolulu	HI	96846	Lawrence M. Johnson	808-643-3888	P	14,996 TA	5.1
First Nationwide Holdings Inc.	14651 Dallas Pkwy.	Dallas	TX	75240	Gerald J. Ford	214-770-3700	S	14,600 TA	3.5
Glendale Federal Bank F.S.B.	700 N. Brand Blvd.	Glendale	CA	91203	Stephen J. Trafton	818-500-2210	P	14,457 TA	2.5
Sovereign Bancorp Inc.	PO Box 12646	Reading	PA	19612	Jay S. Sidhu	610-320-8400	P	14,336 TA	2.0
California Federal Bank F.S.B.	5700 Wilshire Blvd.	Los Angeles	CA	90036	Edward G. Harshfield	213-932-4321	S	14,321 TA	2.1
Charter One Bank F.S.B.	1215 Superior Ave.	Cleveland	OH	44114	Charles J. Koch	216-566-5300	S	13,905 TA	2.6
Bank United Corp.	3200 Southwest Fwy.	Houston	TX	77027	Barry C. Burkholder	516-543-6500	P	11,967 TA	1.4
Guaranty Federal Bank F.S.B.	8333 Douglas Ave.	Dallas	TX	75225	Kenny Jastrow	214-360-3360	S	10,000 TA	1.5
Michigan National Corp.	PO Box 9065	Farmington Hills	MI	48333	Douglas E. Ebert	248-473-3000	S	9,329 TA	4.0
Roosevelt Bank	900 Roosevelt Pkwy.	Chesterfield	MO	63017	Stanley J. Bradshaw	314-532-6200	S	9,013 TA	1.2
Coast Federal Bank F.S.B.	1000 Wilshire Blvd.	Los Angeles	CA	90017	Robert L. Hunt II	213-362-2000	S	8,300 TA	1.8
TCF Financial Corp.	801 Marquette Ave.	Minneapolis	MN	55402	William A. Cooper	612-661-6500	P	8,174 TA	4.7
First Hawaiian Inc.	PO Box 3200	Honolulu	HI	96847	Walter A. Dods Jr.	808-525-7000	P	7,918 TA	3.2

Company type codes: P - Public, R - Private, S - Subsidiary, D - Division, J - Joint Venture, A - Affiliate, G - Group. If the dollar values shown are not sales, the following codes apply: TA - Total Assets; OR - Operating Revenues; GB - Gross Billings. * - estimated dollar value. < - less than. *na* - not available.

Continued on next page.

LEADING COMPANIES - SIC 6035 - Federal Savings Institutions
Continued

Company Name	Address				CEO Name	Phone	Co. Type	Sales/Assets ($ mil)	Empl. (000)
Sovereign Bank F.S.B.	1130 Berkshire Blvd.	Wyomissing	PA	19610	Jay S. Sidhu	610-320-8400	S	7,332 TA	1.4
Astoria Federal Savings and Loan Association	1 Astoria Federal Plz.	Lake Success	NY	11042	George L. Engelke Jr.	516-327-3000	S	7,273 TA	1.0
LaSalle Bank F.S.B.	5501 S. Kedzie Ave.	Chicago	IL	60629	Scott K. Heitmann	312-434-3322	S	7,170 TA	1.9
Commercial Federal Corp.	2120 South 72nd St.	Omaha	NE	68124	William A. Fitzgerald	402-554-9200	P	7,097 TA	1.5
Webster Financial Corp.	Webster Plz.	Waterbury	CT	06702	James C. Smith	203-753-2921	P	7,020 TA	1.1
Peoples Heritage Financial Group Inc.	P.O.Box 9540	Portland	ME	04112	William J. Ryan	207-761-8500	P	6,795 TA	2.7
First Bank F.S.B.	PO Box 1980	Fargo	ND	58107	Corry Manning	701-280-3500	S	5,965 TA	1.1
Long Island Savings Bank F.S.B.	201 Old Country Rd.	Melville	NY	11747	John J. Conefry Jr.	516-547-2000	S	5,931 TA	1.5
Downey Financial Corp.	PO Box 6000	Newport Beach	CA	92658	James W. Lokey	714-854-3100	P	5,836 TA	1.3
Washington Federal Inc.	425 Pike St.	Seattle	WA	98101	Guy C. Pinkerton	206-624-7930	P	5,720 TA	0.7
First Financial Bank	1305 Main St.	Stevens Point	WI	54481	John C. Seramur	715-341-0400	P	5,700 TA	1.8
Hawaiian Electric Industries Inc.	PO Box 730	Honolulu	HI	96808	Robert F. Clarke	808-543-5662	P	5,548 TA	3.7
Collective Bank	PO Box 316	Egg Harbor City	NJ	08215	Thomas H. Hamilton	609-965-1234	S	5,499 TA	1.1
Third Federal Savings and Loan Association of Cleveland	7007 Broadway Ave.	Cleveland	OH	44105	Marc A. Stefanski	216-441-6000	R	5,443 TA	0.6
FirstMerit Corp.	III Cascade Plaza	Akron	OH	44308	John R. Cochran	330-996-6300	P	5,308 TA	2.3
Carteret Bancorp Inc.	200 South St.	Morristown	NJ	07960	George M. Gross	201-326-1000	R	5,262 TA	0.9
Collective Bancorp Inc.	PO Box 316	Egg Harbor City	NJ	08215	Thomas H. Hamilton	609-625-1110	P	5,145 TA	1.1
Capitol Federal Savings and Loan Association	700 Kansas Ave.	Topeka	KS	66603	John C. Dicus	913-235-1341	R	5,000 TA	0.7
WestFed Holdings Inc.	13160 Mindanao Way	Marina Del Rey	CA	90292	Preston Martin	310-574-6909	R	4,990 TA	0.8
Chevy Chase Bank F.S.B.	8401 Connecticut Ave.	Chevy Chase	MD	20815	B. Francis Saul II	301-986-7000	R	4,942 TA	2.9
USAA Federal Savings Bank	10750 McDermott Fwy.	San Antonio	TX	78288	Mark H. Wright	210-498-2265	S	4,800 TA	20.0
St. Paul Bancorp Inc.	6700 W. North Ave.	Chicago	IL	60635	Joseph C. Scully	312-622-5000	P	4,557 TA	1.1
CNB Bancshares Inc.	PO Box 778	Evansville	IN	47705	James J. Giancola	812-464-3400	P	4,317 TA	1.9
First Federal Bank of California	401 Wilshire Blvd.	Santa Monica	CA	90401	Babette Heimbuch	310-319-6000	S	4,157 TA	0.5
Brooklyn Bancorp Inc.	211 Montague St.	Brooklyn	NY	11201	Richard A. Kraemer	718-780-0400	P	4,124 TA	0.8
ALBANK Financial Corp.	10 N. Pearl St.	Albany	NY	12207	Herbert G. Chorbajian	518-445-2100	P	4,083 TA	1.5
Webster Bank	First Federal Plz.	Waterbury	CT	06702	James C. Smith	203-578-2230	S	3,918 TA	1.1
Western Financial Savings Bank F.S.B.	16485 Laguna Canyon Rd.	Irvine	CA	92618	Ernest S. Rady	714-727-1000	S	3,729 TA	1.7
Westcorp	PO Box 19733	Irvine	CA	92713	Ernest S. Rady	714-727-1000	P	3,729 TA	3.6
Citadel Holding Corp.	600 N. Brand Blvd.	Glendale	CA	91203	Richard M. Greenwood	818-956-7100	P	3,719 TA	0.9
SFFed Corp.	88 Kearny St.	San Francisco	CA	94108	Roger L. Gordon	415-955-5800	P	3,719 TA	0.7

Company type codes: P - Public, R - Private, S - Subsidiary, D - Division, J - Joint Venture, A - Affiliate, G - Group. If the dollar values shown are not sales, the following codes apply: TA - Total Assets; OR - Operating Revenues; GB - Gross Billings. * - estimated dollar value. < - less than. na - not available.

Continued on next page.

LEADING COMPANIES - SIC 6035 - Federal Savings Institutions
Continued

Company Name	Address				CEO Name	Phone	Co. Type	Sales/Assets ($ mil)	Empl. (000)
Temple-Inland Inc.	303 S. Temple Dr.	Diboll	TX	75941	Clifford J. Grum	409-829-2211	P	3,625	15.6
American Savings Bank F.S.B.	915 Fort Street Mall	Honolulu	HI	96813	Wayne K. Minami	808-627-6900	S	3,600 TA	0.9
American Savings of Florida F.S.B.	17801 Northwest 2nd Ave.	Miami	FL	33169	Stephen D. Taylor	305-653-5353	P	3,561 TA	0.7
MAF Bancorp Inc.	55th St. & Holmes Ave.	Clarendon Hills	IL	60514	Allen H. Koranda	630-325-7300	P	3,458 TA	0.9
New York Bancorp Inc.	241-02 Northern Blvd.	Douglaston	NY	11362	Jr., Michael A. McManus	718-631-8100	P	3,244 TA	0.6
Bluebonnet Savings Bank F.S.B.	PO Box 8400	Dallas	TX	75205	Howard R. Neff	214-443-9000	R	3,201 TA	0.2
Leader Federal Bank for Savings	PO Box 275	Memphis	TN	38101	Ronald W. Stimpson	901-578-2000	S	3,102 TA	0.7
Ocwen Federal Bank F.S.B.	1675 Palm Beach Lakes Blvd.	West Palm Beach	FL	33401	William C. Erbey	561-681-8000	S	3,069 TA	1.2
BankAtlantic Bancorp Inc.	PO Box 8608	Fort Lauderdale	FL	33310	Alan B. Levan	954-760-5000	P	3,065 TA	1.1
Bay View Bank	2121 S. El Camino Real	San Mateo	CA	94403	Edward H. Sondker	415-573-7300	P	3,000 TA	0.4
Citizens Federal Bank F.S.B.	1 Citizens Federal Ctr.	Dayton	OH	45402	Jerry L. Kirby	937-223-4234	S	2,925 TA	0.7
Great Financial Corp.	1 Financial Sq.	Louisville	KY	40202	Paul M. Baker	502-562-6336	P	2,897 TA	0.7
Columbia First Bank F.S.B.	1560 Wilson Blvd.	Arlington	VA	22209	Thomas J. Schaefer	703-247-5000	S	2,849 TA	0.5
Great Lakes Bancorp, A Federal Savings Bank	401 E. Liberty St.	Ann Arbor	MI	48107	Barry N. Winslow	313-769-8300	S	2,777 TA	1.2
Staten Island Bancorp Inc.	15 Beach St.	Staten Island	NY	10304	Harry Doherty	718-447-7900	P	2,650 TA	0.6
Local Federal Bank F.S.B.	PO Box 26020	Oklahoma City	OK	73126	Edward A. Townsand	405-841-2100	S	2,625 TA	0.5
CitFed Bancorp Inc.	1 Citizens Federal Ctr.	Dayton	OH	45402	Jerry L. Kirby	513-223-4234	P	2,598 TA	0.7
PFF Bancorp Inc.	350 S. Garey Ave.	Pomona	CA	91766	Larry M. Rinehart	909-623-2323	P	2,536 TA	0.5
Dollar Bank	340 4th Ave.	Pittsburgh	PA	15222	Stephen C. Hansen	412-261-4900	R	2,535 TA	1.1
Chase Federal Bank F.S.B.	7300 N. Kendall Dr.	Miami	FL	33156	Thomas A. Cooper	305-670-7600	R	2,523 TA	0.5
Leader Financial Corp.	158 Madison Ave.	Memphis	TN	38103	Ronald W. Stimpson	901-578-4300	P	2,448 TA	0.8
Standard Financial Inc.	4192 S. Archer Ave.	Chicago	IL	60632	David H. Mackiewich	312-847-1140	P	2,405 TA	0.5
EurekaBank F.S.B.	950 Tower Ln.	Foster City	CA	94404	Byron A. Scordelis	415-358-6100	S	2,384 TA	0.5
Park National Corp.	PO Box 3500	Newark	OH	43058	C. Daniel DeLawder	614-349-8451	P	2,288 TA	1.0
Commonwealth Bancorp	Commonwealth Bank Plz.	Norristown	PA	19401	Charles H. Meacham	610-313-1600	P	2,269 TA	0.9
First Financial Bancorp.	300 High St.	Hamilton	OH	45011	Stanley N. Pontius	513-867-4700	P	2,262 TA	1.3
CenFed Bank F.S.B.	199 N. Lake Ave.	Pasadena	CA	91101	D. Tad Lowrey	818-585-2400	S	2,189 TA	0.3
BankUnited Financial Corp.	255 Alhambra Cir.	Coral Gables	FL	33134	Alfred R. Camner	305-569-2000	P	2,145 TA	0.2
Trans Financial Inc.	PO Box 90001	Bowling Green	KY	42102	Vince A. Berta	502-793-7717	P	2,115 TA	0.9
Eagle Bank	PO Box 1157	Bristol	CT	06010	Robert J. Britton	860-314-6400	S	2,091 TA	0.5

*Source: Ward's Business Directory of U.S. Private and Public Companies, 1996. Company type codes: P - Public, R - Private, S - Subsidiary, D - Division, J - Joint Venture, A - Affiliate, G - Group. If the dollar values shown are not sales, the following codes apply: TA - Total Assets; OR - Operating Revenues; GB - Gross Billings. * - estimated dollar value. < - less than; na - not available.*

LEADING COMPANIES - SIC 6036 - Savings Institutions, ex Federal

Number shown: **91**   Total sales/assets ($ mil): **342,357**   Total employment (000): **81.3**

Company Name	Address				CEO Name	Phone	Co. Type	Sales/Assets ($ mil)	Empl. (000)
Washington Mutual Inc.	PO Box 834	Seattle	WA	98111	Kerry K. Killinger	206-461-2000	P	97,069 TA	8.3
BankBoston Corp.	PO Box 1987	Boston	MA	02105	Charles K. Gifford	617-434-2200	P	69,268 TA	21.5
Citizens Financial Group Inc.	1 Citizens Plaza	Providence	RI	02903	Lawrence K. Fish	401-456-7000	P	16,221 TA	3.2
GreenPoint Financial Corp.	1981 Marcus Ave.	Lake Success	NY	11419	Thomas S. Johnson	516-327-1100	P	13,083 TA	2.5
People's Bank	850 Main St.	Bridgeport	CT	06604	David E. Carson	203-338-7171	P	7,645 TA	3.0
Hudson City Savings Bank	W. 80 Century Rd.	Paramus	NJ	07652	Leonard Gudelski	201-967-1900	R	6,676 TA	0.9
Emigrant Savings Bank	5 E. 42nd St.	New York	NY	10017	Philip Milstein	212-850-4000	R	6,087 TA	1.3
Citizens Bank of Massachusetts	28 State St.	Boston	MA	02110	Robert M. Mahoney	617-482-2600	S	5,147 TA	0.9
Ohio Savings Bank	1801 East 9th St.	Cleveland	OH	44114	Robert Goldberg	216-696-2222	S	4,060 TA	0.9
Rochester Community Savings Bank	40 Franklin St.	Rochester	NY	14604	Leonard S. Simon	716-258-3000	P	3,900 TA	1.6
Independence Community Bank Corp.	130 Court St.	Brooklyn	NY	11201	Charles J. Hamm	718-722-5300	R	3,672 TA	0.8
OnBank and Trust Co.	PO Box 4950	Syracuse	NY	13221	Robert J. Bennett	315-424-4400	S	3,611 TA	0.9
Center Financial Corp.	60 N. Main St.	Waterbury	CT	06702	Robert J. Narkis	203-578-7000	P	3,583 TA	1.2
Fulton Financial Corp.	PO Box 4887	Lancaster	PA	17604	Rufus A. Fulton Jr.	717-291-2411	P	3,335 TA	1.8
Roosevelt Savings Bank	1122 Franklin Ave.	Garden City	NY	11530	John M. Tsimbinos	516-742-9300	S	3,260 TA	0.5
Adam Corp.	1111 Briarcrest Dr.	Bryan	TX	77802	Don Adam	409-776-1111	R	2,978 TA	0.9
First American Bank S.S.B.	PO Box 8100	Bryan	TX	77805	William Atkinson	409-361-6200	S	2,978 TA	0.9
Coastal Banc SSB	5718 Westheimer Rd.	Houston	TX	77057	Manuel J. Mehos	713-435-5000	P	2,900 TA	0.5
Staten Island Savings Bank	15 Beach St.	Staten Island	NY	10304	Harry P. Doherty	718-447-8880	S	2,650 TA	0.6
Peoples Heritage Bank	PO Box 9540	Portland	ME	04112	William J. Ryan	207-761-8500	S	2,635 TA	1.4
First Republic Bank	388 Market St.	San Francisco	CA	94111	Roger O. Walther	415-392-1400	P	2,423 TA	0.2
Eastern Bank	270 Union St.	Lynn	MA	01901	Stanley J. Lukowski	781-599-2100	S	2,103 TA	1.0
Provident Savings Bank	830 Bergen Ave.	Jersey City	NJ	07306	Paul Pantozzi	201-333-1000	R	2,100 TA	0.6
InterWest Bancorp Inc.	1259 S.E. Pioneer Way	Oak Harbor	WA	98277	Stephen M. Walden	360-679-4181	P	2,047 TA	0.6
River Bank America	145 Huguenot St.	New Rochelle	NY	10801	Jerome R. McDougal	914-654-4500	R	1,998 TA	0.5
New Haven Savings Bank	PO Box 302	New Haven	CT	06502	Charles Terrell	203-787-1111	R	1,910 TA	0.4
Bankers Corp.	210 Smith St.	Perth Amboy	NJ	08861	Joseph P. Gemmell	908-442-4100	P	1,902 TA	0.4
Ridgewood Savings Bank	PO Box 141	Ridgewood	NY	11385	William A. McKenna	718-240-4800	R	1,900 TA	0.6
Boston Bancorp.	460 W. Broadway	South Boston	MA	02127	Robert E. Lee	617-268-2500	P	1,886 TA	0.2
Anchor BanCorp Wisconsin Inc.	25 W. Main St.	Madison	WI	53703	Douglas J. Timmerman	608-252-8700	P	1,885 TA	0.7
Northwest Bancorp M.H.C.	PO Drawer 128	Warren	PA	16365	John O. Hanna	814-726-2140	P	1,878 TA	0.8
Sterling Financial Corp.	111 N. Wall St.	Spokane	WA	99201	Harold B. Gilkey	509-458-3711	P	1,876 TA	0.5
Republic Bancorp Inc.	PO Box 70	Owosso	MI	48867	Jerry D. Campbell	517-725-7337	P	1,873 TA	1.4
Harris Savings Bank	PO Box 1711	Harrisburg	PA	17105	William J. McLaughlin	717-236-4041	P	1,768 TA	0.4
F.N.B. Corp.	Hermitage Sq.	Hermitage	PA	16148	Peter Mortensen	412-981-6000	P	1,727 TA	1.0
North Side Savings Bank	170 Tulip Ave.	Floral Park	NY	11001	John Kanas	516-488-6900	P	1,639 TA	1.5

Company type codes: P - Public, R - Private, S - Subsidiary, D - Division, J - Joint Venture, A - Affiliate, G - Group. If the dollar values shown are not sales, the following codes apply: TA - Total Assets; OR - Operating Revenues; GB - Gross Billings. * - estimated dollar value. < - less than. *na* - not available.

Continued on next page.

LEADING COMPANIES - SIC 6036 - Savings Institutions, ex Federal
Continued

Company Name	Address				CEO Name	Phone	Co. Type	Sales/Assets ($ mil)	Empl. (000)
Republic Savings Bank	23175 Commerce Park Rd.	Beachwood	OH	44122	Frank A. Hawkins	216-765-1100	S	1,490 TA	1.3
CB Bancshares Inc.	PO Box 3709	Honolulu	HI	96811	Ronald K, Migita	808-546-2411	P	1,435 TA	0.5
Franklin First Savings Bank	PO Box 449	Wilkes-Barre	PA	18773	Thomas H. van Arsdale	717-821-7100	S	1,403 TA	0.4
Semperverde Holding Co.	Flourtown Shopping Ctr	Flourtown	PA	19031	Daniel B. Green	215-722-2000	R	1,375 TA	0.2
Queens County Bancorp Inc.	38-25 Main St.	Flushing	NY	11354	Joseph R. Ficalora	718-359-6400	P	1,359 TA	0.3
California Financial Holding Co.	501 W. Weber Ave.	Stockton	CA	95203	David K. Rea	209-948-1675	P	1,337 TA	0.4
Stockton Savings Bank	501 W. Weber Ave.	Stockton	CA	95203	Robert V. Kavanaugh	209-948-6870	S	1,337 TA	0.4
Andover Bancorp Inc.	61 Main St.	Andover	MA	01810	Gerald T. Mulligan	978-749-2000	P	1,323 TA	0.3
Gateway Bank	PO Box 120	Norwalk	CT	06854	Reginald DeKoven III	203-845-7700	S	1,276 TA	0.5
American Savings Bank	PO Box 174	New Britain	CT	06050	Robert T. Kenney	860-225-6431	R	1,165 TA	0.3
Affiliated Community Bancorp Inc.	716 Main St.	Waltham	MA	02254	Timothy J. Hansberry	617-894-6810	P	1,155 TA	0.2
Advest Group Inc.	90 State House Sq.	Hartford	CT	06103	Allen Weintraub	860-509-1000	P	1,077 TA	1.6
Andover Bank	PO Box 2005	Andover	MA	01810	Gerald T. Mulligan	508-749-2000	S	1,058 TA	0.3
Cambridge Savings Bank	PO Box 380206	Cambridge	MA	02238	James P. Ingram	617-864-8700	R	1,053 TA	0.3
First Savings Bank S.L.A.	1000 Woodbridge Center Drive	WoodBridge	NJ	07095	John P. Mulkerin	732-726-9700	P	1,049 TA	0.3
Medford Bank	29 High St.	Medford	MA	02155	Arthur H. Meehan	617-395-7700	P	1,039 TA	0.3
First Savings Bank of Washington	PO Box 907	Walla Walla	WA	99362	Gary L. Sirmon	509-527-3636	S	1,008 TA	0.3
Arvest Bank Group Inc.	PO Box 799	Lowell	AR	72745	Jim Walton	501-750-1400	R	1,000 TA	0.7
Parkvale Financial Corp.	4220 William Penn Hwy.	Monroeville	PA	15146	Robert J. McCarthy Jr.	412-373-7200	P	991 TA	0.2
FCFT Inc.	PO Box 5909	Princeton	WV	24740	James L. Harrison Sr.	304-487-9000	P	949 TA	0.5
First Savings Bancshares M.H.C.	3090 Woodbridge Ave.	Edison	NJ	08837	Joseph S. Yewaisis	908-417-2900	R	945 TA	0.3
Richmond County Savings Bank	1214 Castelton Ave.	Staten Island	NY	10310	Michael Manzulli	718-448-2800	R	940 TA	0.3
Hawthorne Financial Corp.	2381 Rosecrans Ave.	El Segundo	CA	90245	Scott A. Braly	310-725-5000	P	928 TA	0.2
MASSBANK Corp.	123 Haven St.	Reading	MA	01867	Gerard H. Brandi	617-662-0100	P	925 TA	0.2
Metropolitan Financial Corp.	6001 Landerhaven Dr.	Mayfield Heights	OH	44124	Robert M. Kaye	216-646-1111	P	925 TA	0.3
Savings Bank of Utica	233 Genesee St.	Utica	NY	13501	William L. Schrauth	315-768-3000	R	905 TA	0.3
Peoples Bancorp of Worcester Inc.	120 Front St.	Worcester	MA	01608	Woodbury C. Titcomb	508-791-3861	P	891 TA	0.3
Salem Five Cents Savings Bank	210 Essex St.	Salem	MA	01970	William Mitchelson	508-745-5555	R	891 TA	0.3
Progressive Bank Inc.	1301 Rte. 52	Fishkill	NY	12524	Peter Van Kleeck	914-897-7400	P	883 TA	0.3
Pawling Savings Bank	PO Box 2370	Newburgh	NY	12550	Peter Van Kleeck	914-565-1600	S	869 TA	0.3
CFSB Bancorp Inc.	112 E. Allegan St.	Lansing	MI	48933	Robert H. Becker	517-371-2911	P	853 TA	0.3

Company type codes: P - Public, R - Private, S - Subsidiary, D - Division, J - Joint Venture, A - Affiliate, G - Group. If the dollar values shown are not sales, the following codes apply: TA - Total Assets; OR - Operating Revenues; GB - Gross Billings. * - estimated dollar value. < - less than. na - not available.

Continued on next page.

LEADING COMPANIES - SIC 6036 - Savings Institutions, ex Federal
Continued

Company Name	Address				CEO Name	Phone	Co. Type	Sales/Assets ($ mil)	Empl. (000)
Community First Bank	112 E. Allegan St.	Lansing	MI	48933	Robert H. Becker	517-374-3550	S	853 TA	0.3
CFX Bank	PO Box 746	Keene	NH	03431	Peter J. Baxter	603-352-2502	S	808 TA	0.3
Imperial Thrift and Loan Association	700 N. Central Ave.	Glendale	CA	91203	George W. Haligowski	818-551-0600	S	806 TA	0.1
Co-operative Bank of Concord	125 Nagog Park	Acton	MA	01720	Josiah S. Cushing II	508-635-5000	S	783 TA	0.3
Compass Bank for Savings	PO Box 2101	New Bedford	MA	02740	Kevin G. Champagne	508-994-5000	R	773 TA	0.3
Dime Savings Bank of Wallingford	PO Box 700	Wallingford	CT	06492	Richard H. Dionne	203-269-8881	S	749 TA	0.2
Mechanics Savings Bank	100 Pearl St.	Hartford	CT	06103	Edgar C. Gerwig	203-293-4000	P	747 TA	0.2
IBS Financial Corp.	PO Box 5477	Cherry Hill	NJ	08034	Joseph M. Ochman Sr.	609-424-8600	P	735 TA	0.1
Inter-Boro Savings and Loan Association	1909 E. Rte. 70	Cherry Hill	NJ	08003	Joseph M. Ochman Sr.	609-424-1000	S	735 TA	0.1
El Dorado Savings Bank	4040 Eldorado Rd.	Placerville	CA	95667	Thomas C. Meuser	916-622-1492	R	715 TA	0.3
Great Southern Bancorp Inc.	PO Box 9009	Springfield	MO	65808	William V. Turner	417-887-4400	P	708 TA	0.4
Jefferson Savings and Loan Association	PO Box 17	Ballwin	MO	63022	David V. McCay	314-227-3000	S	685 TA	0.1
Norwich Financial Corp.	PO Box 1048	Norwich	CT	06360	Daniel R. Dennis Jr.	860-889-2621	P	683 TA	0.2
Troy Savings Bank	32 2nd St.	Troy	NY	12180	Daniel J. Hogarty Jr.	518-270-3200	R	669 TA	0.3
Brookline Savings Bank	PO Box 470469	Brookline	MA	02147	Richard P. Chapman	617-730-3500	R	666 TA	<0.1
Iberiabank	PO Box 12440	New Iberia	LA	70562	Larrey G. Mouton	318-365-2361	S	663 TA	0.3
Wauwatosa Savings Bank	7500 W. State St.	Wauwatosa	WI	53213	Raymond J. Perry	414-258-5880	R	658 TA	<0.1
International Savings and Loan Association Ltd.	1111 Bishop St.	Honolulu	HI	96813	James Morita	808-547-5110	S	639 TA	0.2
American Bank of Connecticut	2 W. Main St.	Waterbury	CT	06723	Gene C. Guilbert	203-757-9401	P	639 TA	0.1
Statewide Savings Bank S.L.A.	70 Sip Ave.	Jersey City	NJ	07306	William F. Davidson	201-795-7700	R	636 TA	0.2
Beal Bank S.S.B.	15770 Dallas Pkwy.	Dallas	TX	75248	David Meek	972-404-4000	S	635 TA	0.1
Farmers and Mechanics Bank	3 Sunset Rd and 811 Sunset Rd.	Burlington	NJ	08016	Charles Yates	609-386-2400	P	628 TA	0.2
Cape Cod Five Cents Savings Bank	PO Box 10	Orleans	MA	02653	Elliott Carr	508-240-0555	R	620 TA	0.2
First Northern Savings Bank	PO Box 23100	Green Bay	WI	54305	Michael D. Meeuwsen	414-437-7101	S	615 TA	0.2

Source: Ward's Business Directory of U.S. Private and Public Companies, 1996. Company type codes: P - Public, R - Private, S - Subsidiary, D - Division, J - Joint Venture, A - Affiliate, G - Group. If the dollar values shown are not sales, the following codes apply: TA - Total Assets; OR - Operating Revenues; GB - Gross Billings. * - estimated dollar value. < - less than; *na* - not available.

FINANCIAL DATA ON SAVINGS & LOANS

The following table, drawn from the *Statistical Abstract of the United States 1997*, presents additional data on Savings & Loans.

Until 1990, the FDIC insured a subset of all savings and loan institutions; the majority were insured by the Federal Savings and Loan Insurance Corporation (FSLIC). As a consequence of the Financial Institutions Reform, Recovery, and Enforcement Act of 1989 (FIRREA), signed into law on August 9, 1989, the FDIC has taken over insuring all savings and loans under the FDIC Savings Association Insurance Fund (SAIF).

Much more detailed information is available from the Office of Corporate Communications, FDIC, 550 17th Street, N.W., Washington, D.C. 20429.

INSURED SAVINGS INSTITUTION, FINANCIAL SUMMARY: 1990 TO 1996

In billions of dollars, except number of institutions. As of December 31. Includes Puerto Rico, Guam, and Virgin Islands. Covers savings institutions covered by SAIF (Savings Association Insurance Fund) and BIF (Bank Insurance Fund). Exclude institutions in RTC conservatorship and, beginning 1992, excludes one self-liquidating institution. Minus sign (-) indicates loss.

Item	1990	1991	1992	1993	1994	1995	1996 prel.
Number of institutions	2,816	2,561	2,390	2,262	2,152	2,030	1,924
Assets, total	1,267	1,119	1,030	1,001	1,009	1,026	1,028
Loan and leases, net	816	727	648	626	635	648	681
Liabilities, total	1,200	1,051	956	923	929	940	942
Deposits	987	907	828	774	737	742	728
Equity capital	68	69	74	78	80	86	86
Interest and fee income	117	98	78	66	63	71	72
Interest expense	91	70	46	35	33	43	42
Net interest income	26	28	32	32	30	28	30
Net income	-5	1	7	7	6	8	7

Source: U.S. Federal Deposit Insurance Corporation, *Statistic on Banking,* annual and *FDIC Quarterly Banking Profile.*

SIC 6060

CREDIT UNIONS

Credit unions are classified as (1) federally chartered (SIC 6061), also called Federal Credit Unions and (2) not federally chartered (SIC 6062), also called State Credit Unions, not federally charted. These are cooperative thrift and loan associations, accept deposits, and are organized to finance the credit needs of their members. Credit unions are usually associations of employees working for an institution (agency, company) or members of some organization (e.g. a labor union). National Credit Union Administration (NCUA), an independent federal agency, supervises and insures more than 8,500 federal credit unions and insures nearly 4,350 state-chartered credit unions.

ESTABLISHMENTS, EMPLOYMENT, AND PAYROLL

	1990	1991		1992		1993		1994		1995		% change 90-95
		Value	%	Value	%	Value	%	Value	%	Value	%	
All Establishments	3,650	12,356	238.5	13,177	6.6	15,306	16.2	15,142	-1.1	15,063	-0.5	312.7
Mid-March Employment	50,642	114,313	125.7	122,924	7.5	147,359	19.9	151,685	2.9	158,010	4.2	212.0
1st Quarter Wages (annualized - $ mil.)	944.8	2,127.7	125.2	2,448.1	15.1	2,867.4	17.1	3,130.6	9.2	3,463.8	10.6	266.6
Payroll per Emp. 1st Q. (annualized)	18,656	18,613	-0.2	19,915	7.0	19,458	-2.3	20,639	6.1	21,921	6.2	17.5
Annual Payroll ($ mil.)	959.1	2,160.0	125.2	2,516.4	16.5	3,015.0	19.8	3,264.7	8.3	3,532.3	8.2	268.3
Establishments - 1-4 Emp. Number	2,186	5,655	158.7	7,025	24.2	7,998	13.9	7,730	-3.4	7,346	-5.0	236.0
Mid-March Employment	(D)	12,839	-	16,253	26.6	18,466	13.6	17,951	-2.8	17,015	-5.2	-
1st Quarter Wages (annualized - $ mil.)	(D)	180.0	-	247.9	37.7	281.1	13.4	286.9	2.1	292.2	1.9	-
Payroll per Emp. 1st Q. (annualized)	(D)	14,020	-	15,254	8.8	15,221	-0.2	15,983	5.0	17,175	7.5	-
Annual Payroll ($ mil.)	(D)	191.4	-	257.8	34.7	309.2	19.9	313.3	1.3	310.9	-0.8	-
Establishments - 5-9 Emp. Number	638	3,151	393.9	3,011	-4.4	(D)	-	3,510	-	3,616	3.0	466.8
Mid-March Employment	4,158	21,225	410.5	19,889	-6.3	(D)	-	23,190	-	23,690	2.2	469.7
1st Quarter Wages (annualized - $ mil.)	67.4	386.9	473.7	365.4	-5.6	(D)	-	440.4	-	470.6	6.8	597.7
Payroll per Emp. 1st Q. (annualized)	16,221	18,231	12.4	18,373	0.8	(D)	-	18,991	-	19,864	4.6	22.5
Annual Payroll ($ mil.)	69.0	393.9	471.1	375.7	-4.6	(D)	-	461.3	-	480.3	4.1	596.3
Establishments - 10-19 Emp. Number	332	2,296	591.6	1,830	-20.3	2,199	20.2	2,200	0.0	2,293	4.2	590.7
Mid-March Employment	4,487	30,824	587.0	24,831	-19.4	29,814	20.1	29,700	-0.4	30,813	3.7	586.7
1st Quarter Wages (annualized - $ mil.)	76.8	579.7	654.4	486.0	-16.2	558.7	14.9	582.2	4.2	631.9	8.5	722.4
Payroll per Emp. 1st Q. (annualized)	17,124	18,806	9.8	19,573	4.1	18,738	-4.3	19,604	4.6	20,509	4.6	19.8
Annual Payroll ($ mil.)	79.1	584.9	639.7	495.6	-15.3	588.5	18.7	610.7	3.8	646.2	5.8	717.2
Establishments - 20-49 Emp. Number	247	1,081	337.7	964	-10.8	1,200	24.5	1,244	3.7	1,315	5.7	432.4
Mid-March Employment	7,334	30,252	312.5	28,731	-5.0	35,485	23.5	36,975	4.2	38,919	5.3	430.7
1st Quarter Wages (annualized - $ mil.)	134.0	572.7	327.5	591.2	3.2	701.6	18.7	781.4	11.4	865.0	10.7	545.6
Payroll per Emp. 1st Q. (annualized)	18,267	18,930	3.6	20,577	8.7	19,772	-3.9	21,134	6.9	22,225	5.2	21.7
Annual Payroll ($ mil.)	135.3	577.4	326.9	603.1	4.5	738.6	22.5	809.9	9.6	875.4	8.1	547.2
Establishments - 50-99 Emp. Number	134	120	-10.4	255	112.5	324	27.1	336	3.7	364	8.3	171.6
Mid-March Employment	9,240	8,252	-10.7	16,709	102.5	21,619	29.4	22,237	2.9	24,614	10.7	166.4
1st Quarter Wages (annualized - $ mil.)	188.1	173.0	-8.0	371.7	114.9	463.7	24.8	508.8	9.7	600.8	18.1	219.4
Payroll per Emp. 1st Q. (annualized)	20,356	20,959	3.0	22,246	6.1	21,450	-3.6	22,882	6.7	24,409	6.7	19.9
Annual Payroll ($ mil.)	187.6	172.6	-8.0	384.1	122.5	475.2	23.7	516.9	8.8	602.5	16.6	221.1
Establishments - 100-249 Emp. Number	96	43	-55.2	82	90.7	89	8.5	102	14.6	109	6.9	13.5
Mid-March Employment	14,332	(D)	-	11,774	-	12,188	3.5	13,619	11.7	14,704	8.0	2.6
1st Quarter Wages (annualized - $ mil.)	288.7	(D)	-	278.1	-	282.8	1.7	328.7	16.2	387.2	17.8	34.1
Payroll per Emp. 1st Q. (annualized)	20,145	(D)	-	23,619	-	23,199	-1.8	24,135	4.0	26,334	9.1	30.7
Annual Payroll ($ mil.)	282.8	(D)	-	278.9	-	289.6	3.8	337.2	16.4	388.9	15.3	37.5
Establishments - 250-499 Emp. Number	16	9	-43.8	(D)	-	17	-	(D)	-	(D)	-	-
Mid-March Employment	4,968	(D)	-	(D)	-	5,100	-	(D)	-	(D)	-	-
1st Quarter Wages (annualized - $ mil.)	98.5	(D)	-	(D)	-	118.3	-	(D)	-	(D)	-	-
Payroll per Emp. 1st Q. (annualized)	19,826	(D)	-	(D)	-	23,202	-	(D)	-	(D)	-	-
Annual Payroll ($ mil.)	99.5	(D)	-	(D)	-	128.2	-	(D)	-	(D)	-	-
Establishments - 500-999 Emp. Number	-	-	-	-	-	-	-	-	-	-	-	-
Mid-March Employment	-	-	-	-	-	-	-	-	-	-	-	-
1st Quarter Wages (annualized - $ mil.)	-	-	-	-	-	-	-	-	-	-	-	-
Payroll per Emp. 1st Q. (annualized)	(D)	(D)	-	-	-	-	-	-	-	-	-	-
Annual Payroll ($ mil.)	-	-	-	-	-	-	-	-	-	-	-	-
Estab. - 1000 or More Emp. Number	1	1	-	(D)	-	(D)	-	(D)	-	(D)	-	-
Mid-March Employment	(D)	(D)	-	(D)	-	(D)	-	(D)	-	(D)	-	-
1st Quarter Wages (annualized - $ mil.)	(D)	(D)	-	(D)	-	(D)	-	(D)	-	(D)	-	-
Payroll per Emp. 1st Q. (annualized)	(D)	(D)	-	(D)	-	(D)	-	(D)	-	(D)	-	-
Annual Payroll ($ mil.)	(D)	(D)	-	(D)	-	(D)	-	(D)	-	(D)	-	-

Source: County Business Patterns, U.S. Department of Commerce, Washington, D.C., for 1990 through 1995. Payroll per employee is calculated using mid-March employment and 1st Quarter wages, annualized. Annual payroll, also shown, may not equal the annualized 1st Quarter wages. Columns headed by a percent sign (%) indicate change from the previous year. na stands for not available. The symbol (D) indicates that data are withheld by the source to avoid disclosure of competitive information. A dash (-) indicates that data are not available or cannot be calculated.

ESTABLISHMENTS
Number

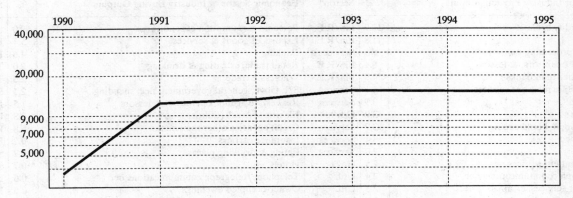

MID-MARCH EMPLOYMENT
Number

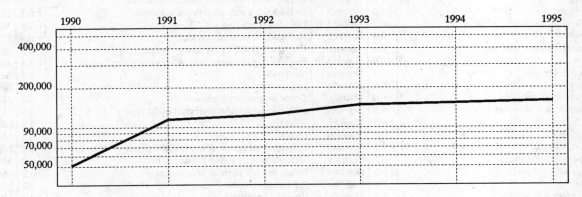

ANNUAL PAYROLL
$ million

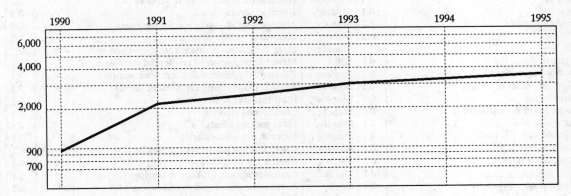

INPUTS AND OUTPUTS FOR ALL BANKING SECTORS - SICs 601, 602, 603, 608, and 609

Economic Sector or Industry Providing Inputs	%	Sector	Economic Sector or Industry Buying Outputs	%	Sector
Security & commodity brokers	12.9	Fin/R.E.	Personal consumption expenditures	59.0	
Banking	11.8	Fin/R.E.	Exports of goods & services	5.1	Foreign
Computer & data processing services	9.5	Services	Banking	4.6	Fin/R.E.
Real estate agents, operators, & lessors	8.1	Fin/R.E.	Retail trade, ex eating & drinking	3.0	Trade
Credit agencies other than banks	4.9	Fin/R.E.	Wholesale trade	2.3	Trade
Management & public relations services	4.1	Services	S/L Govt., general government nec, spending	2.1	S/L Govt
Advertising	3.9	Services	Real estate agents, operators, & lessors	1.5	Fin/R.E.
U.S. Postal Service	3.9	Gov't	Electric services (utilities)	0.8	Util.
Accounting, auditing & bookkeeping	3.7	Services	Credit agencies other than banks	0.8	Fin/R.E.
Business services nec	3.4	Services	Insurance carriers	0.7	Fin/R.E.
Legal services	2.8	Services	Eating & drinking places	0.7	Services
Federal Government enterprises nec	2.5	Gov't	Hotels	0.7	Services
Telephone/telegraph communications nec	2.4	Util.	Telephone/telegraph communications nec	0.6	Util.
Trucking & courier services, ex air	2.3	Util.	Owner-occupied dwellings	0.6	Fin/R.E.
Blankbooks, looseleaf binders & devices	1.7	Manufg.	Doctors & dentists	0.6	Services
Wholesale trade	1.6	Trade	Motor vehicles & passenger car bodies	0.4	Manufg.
Personnel supply services	1.6	Services	Trucking & courier services, ex air	0.4	Util.
Electric services (utilities)	1.5	Util.	Federal Government, nondefense, spending	0.4	Gov't
Warehousing & storage	1.4	Util.	New construction nec	0.3	Constr.
Air transportation	1.0	Util.	Repair & maintenance construction nec	0.3	Constr.
Eating & drinking places	1.0	Services	Residential 1 unit structures, nonfarm	0.3	Constr.
Sanitary services, steam supply, irrigation	0.9	Util.	Petroleum refining	0.3	Manufg.
Insurance carriers	0.9	Fin/R.E.	Railroads & related services	0.3	Util.
Repair & maintenance construction nec	0.8	Constr.	Computer & data processing services	0.3	Services
Hotels	0.8	Services	Engineering, architectural, & surveying services	0.3	Services
Detective & protective services	0.7	Services	Hospitals	0.3	Services
Commercial printing	0.6	Manufg.	Legal services	0.3	Services
Photographic equipment & supplies	0.6	Manufg.	Crude petroleum & natural gas	0.2	Mining
Research, development, & testing services	0.6	Services	Office, industrial/commercial buildings	0.2	Constr.
Manifold business forms	0.5	Manufg.	Aircraft	0.2	Manufg.
Paper & paperboard mills	0.5	Manufg.	Drugs	0.2	Manufg.
Automotive rental & leasing, without drivers	0.5	Services	Industrial inorganic & organic chemicals	0.2	Manufg.
Business & professional associations	0.5	Services	Miscellaneous plastics products, nec	0.2	Manufg.
Services to dwellings & other buildings	0.5	Services	Motor vehicle parts & accessories	0.2	Manufg.
Natural gas distribution	0.4	Util.	Air transportation	0.2	Util.
Magnetic & optical recording media	0.3	Manufg.	Freight forwarders	0.2	Util.
Manufacturing industries, nec	0.3	Manufg.	Water transportation	0.2	Util.
Periodicals	0.3	Manufg.	Security & commodity brokers	0.2	Fin/R.E.
Petroleum refining	0.3	Manufg.	Automotive rental & leasing, without drivers	0.2	Services
Electrical repair shops	0.3	Services	Automotive repair shops & services	0.2	Services
Book publishing	0.2	Manufg.	Business services nec	0.2	Services
Computer peripheral equipment	0.2	Manufg.	Management & public relations services	0.2	Services
Envelopes	0.2	Manufg.	Medical & health services nec	0.2	Services
Textile bags	0.2	Manufg.	State & local government enterprises nec	0.2	Gov't
Local & suburban transit	0.2	Util.	Maintenance/repair of residential structures	0.1	Constr.
Automotive repair shops & services	0.2	Services	Residential additions & alterations, nonfarm	0.1	Constr.
Miscellaneous equipment rental & leasing	0.2	Services	Apparel made from purchased materials	0.1	Manufg.
Miscellaneous repair shops	0.2	Services	Blast furnaces & steel mills	0.1	Manufg.
Die-cut paper & paperboard & cardboard	0.1	Manufg.	Commercial printing	0.1	Manufg.
Fabricated metal products, nec	0.1	Manufg.	Meat packing plants	0.1	Manufg.
Miscellaneous fabricated wire products	0.1	Manufg.	Paper & paperboard mills	0.1	Manufg.
Paperboard containers & boxes	0.1	Manufg.	Cable & other pay television services	0.1	Util.
Retail trade, ex eating & drinking	0.1	Trade	Natural gas distribution	0.1	Util.
Royalties	0.1	Fin/R.E.	Insurance agents, brokers, & services	0.1	Fin/R.E.
State & local government enterprises nec	0.1	Gov't	Accounting, auditing & bookkeeping	0.1	Services
			Motion picture services & theaters	0.1	Services
			Personnel supply services	0.1	Services
			Portrait photographic studios	0.1	Services
			U.S. Postal Service	0.1	Gov't

Source: Benchmark Input-Output Accounts for the U.S. Economy, 1992, U.S. Department of Commerce, Washington, D.C., November 1997. Data, as reported in the source, are organized by the 1987 SIC structure in use in 1992.

OCCUPATIONS EMPLOYED BY COMMERCIAL BANKS, SAVINGS INSTITUTIONS, AND CREDIT UNIONS

Occupation	% of Total 1996	Change to 2006	Occupation	% of Total 1996	Change to 2006
Bank tellers	28.5	0.1	General managers & top executives	3.1	-8.6
Clerical supervisors & managers	6.7	6.7	Clerical & administrative workers nec	1.5	-52.8
Loan officers & counselors	6.6	13.2	Accountants & auditors	1.4	-12.7
Financial managers	6.3	-5.7	Securities & financial sales workers	1.3	41.5
New accounts clerks, banking	5.9	3.8	Adjustment clerks	1.3	27.3
Loan & credit clerks	5.4	-4.8	Statement clerks	1.2	-5.7
General office clerks	4.0	-18.8	Duplicating, mail, office machine operators	1.1	-76.4
Bookkeeping, accounting, & auditing clerks	3.8	-24.5	Managers & administrators nec	1.0	-6.5
Secretaries, except legal & medical	3.7	-25.2			

Sources: Industry-Occupation Matrix, Bureau of Labor Statistics. These data relate to one or more 3-digit SIC industry groups rather than to a single 4-digit SIC. The change reported for each occupation to the year 2005 is a percent of growth or decline as estimated by the Bureau of Labor Statistics. The abbreviation *nec* stands for not elsewhere classified.

LEADING COMPANIES - SIC 6062 - State Credit Unions
Continued

Company Name	Address				CEO Name	Phone	Co. Type	Sales/Assets ($ mil)	Empl. (000)
Gates Credit Union	305 E. Mississippi Ave.	Denver	CO	80210	John Mann	303-744-3535	R	85 TA	<0.1
Nazarene Credit Union	PO Box 4000	Brea	CA	92622	Mendell Thompson	714-671-6963	R	85 TA	<0.1
Oklahoma Employees Credit Union	P.O Box 24027	Oklahoma City	OK	73124	Mark W. Kelly	405-525-8588	R	84 TA	<0.1
Portland Postal Employees Credit Union	12630 S.E. Division St.	Portland	OR	97236	H. Lee Hardiman	503-760-5304	R	81 TA	<0.1
Federal Employees Credit Union	3910 N. College	Bethany	OK	73008	Florence Rogers	405-789-7900	R	76 TA	<0.1
Arsenal Credit Union	8651 Watson Rd.	St. Louis	MO	63119	Linda G. Allen	314-962-6363	R	72 TA*	<0.1
Hawthorne Credit Union	1519 N. Naper Blvd.	Naperville	IL	60563	Carl Sorgatz	708-369-4070	R	72 TA	<0.1
St. Louis Telephone Employees Credit Union	4650 Hampton Ave.	St. Louis	MO	63109	Charles Waalkes	314-832-8500	R	72 TA	<0.1
Hospital and Health Services Credit Union	2100 Commonwealth Blvd	Ann Arbor	MI	48105	Larry Colbert	313-769-4621	R	64 TA*	<0.1
Northeast Catholic Credit Union	16012 E. Seven Mile	Detroit	MI	48205	Roger A. Quitter	313-521-4725	R	64 TA	<0.1
Fort Worth City Credit Union	2309 Montgomery St.	Fort Worth	TX	76107	William B. Gordon	817-732-2803	R	64 TA	<0.1
Jefferson County Teachers Credit Union	PO Box 2385	Birmingham	AL	35201	Joseph Shaw	205-226-3900	R	62 TA	<0.1
Kemba Columbus Credit Union	4220 E. Broad St.	Columbus	OH	43213	Gerald Guy	614-235-2395	R	60 TA	<0.1
Oakland Catholic Credit Union	255 E. Maple Rd.	Troy	MI	48083	Daniel R. Moss	810-689-7400	R	58 TA	<0.1
Weyerhaeuser Community Credit Union	33615 First Way S.	Federal Way	WA	98003	Roger Bulger	206-925-6800	R	58 TA	<0.1
Municipal Employees Credit Union of San Jose	140 Asbury St.	San Jose	CA	95110	Judith A. Larson	408-294-8800	R	54 TA	<0.1
Aerospace Community Credit Union	1550 Country Club Plz.	St. Charles	MO	63303	Nina G. Pilger	314-947-0044	R	54 TA	<0.1
Deere Community Credit Union	PO Box 319	Ankeny	IA	50021	Dennis Skelton	515-289-1822	R	52 TA	<0.1
Coors Credit Union	816 Washington Ave.	Golden	CO	80401	Barbara Cecil	303-279-6414	R	50 TA	<0.1
Greater Cleveland Fire Fighters Credit Union Inc.	2300 St. Clair Ave.	Cleveland	OH	44114	Karen A. McNamara	216-621-4644	R	50 TA	<0.1
Seattle Postal Employees Credit Union	14625 15th Ave. N.E.	Seattle	WA	98155	Roger Gieseke	206-367-7328	R	49 TA	<0.1
Cincinnati Central Credit Union	1717 Western Ave.	Cincinnati	OH	45214	William Herring	513-241-2050	R	44 TA	<0.1
Pinnacle Credit Union	536 North Ave. N.E.	Atlanta	GA	30308	Susan M. Jackson	404-888-1648	R	43 TA	<0.1
Self-Help Credit Union	PO Box 3619	Durham	NC	27702	Martin Eakes	919-956-4400	R	43 TA	<0.1
First Class American Credit Union	PO Box 162539	Fort Worth	TX	76161	Russell Back	817-332-7947	R	43 TA	<0.1
Boulder Valley Credit Union	5505 Arapahoe Rd.	Boulder	CO	80303	Anne Marie Bradford	303-442-8850	R	42 TA	<0.1
T and I Credit Union	600 N. Main	Clawson	MI	48017	Marvin A. Brohl	313-588-6688	R	41 TA	<0.1

Company type codes: P - Public, R - Private, S - Subsidiary, D - Division, J - Joint Venture, A - Affiliate, G - Group. If the dollar values shown are not sales, the following codes apply: TA - Total Assets; OR - Operating Revenues; GB - Gross Billings. * - estimated dollar value. < - less than. *na* - not available.

Continued on next page.

LEADING COMPANIES - SIC 6062 - State Credit Unions

Continued

Company Name	Address				CEO Name	Phone	Co. Type	Sales/Assets ($ mil)	Empl. (000)
Financial Plus Credit Union	1831 25th St.	West Des Moines	IA	50266	Gary Peterson	515-224-1222	R	39 TA	<0.1
Municipal Employees Credit Union of Oklahoma City	101 N. Walker Ave.	Oklahoma City	OK	73102	Agnes C. Berkenbile	405-297-2995	R	39 TA	<0.1
Craftsman Credit Union	2444 Clark St.	Detroit	MI	48209	Mario Maraldo	313-554-9300	R	34 TA	<0.1
Health Services Credit Union	6900 Southpoint Dr. N.	Jacksonville	FL	32216	Maurice Pilver	904-296-1292	R	34 TA	<0.1
Midwest Regional Credit Union	PO Box 12217	Kansas City	KS	66112	Lloyd Nugent	913-334-4200	R	30 TA	<0.1
Trans Air Credit Union	10895 Natural Bridge	Bridgeton	MO	63044	Robert Matteson	314-429-0018	R	30 TA	<0.1
Des Moines Postal Credit Union	303 Euclid Ave.	Des Moines	IA	50313	Kent Strawn	515-282-7363	R	29 TA	<0.1
Laclede Credit Union	3401 E. Broadway	Alton	IL	62002	Janice Callies	618-465-2504	R	29 TA	<0.1
Portland Federal Employees Credit Union	421 S.W. 6th Ave.	Portland	OR	97204	James Lumpkin	503-275-0300	R	28 TA	<0.1
Peoples Credit Union	680 N.E. 124th St.	North Miami	FL	33161	Gail E. Siebe	305-893-4880	R	24 TA	<0.1
Missouri Central Credit Union	825 N.E. Deerbrook St.	Lees Summit	MO	64086	Ray Becker	816-246-0002	R	22 TA	<0.1

Source: *Ward's Business Directory of U.S. Private and Public Companies*, 1996. Company type codes: P - Public, R - Private, S - Subsidiary, D - Division, J - Joint Venture, A - Affiliate, G - Group. If the dollar values shown are not sales, the following codes apply: TA - Total Assets; OR - Operating Revenues; GB - Gross Billings. * - estimated dollar value. < - less than; *na* - not available.

FINANCIAL DATA ON CREDIT UNIONS

The following nine tables present financial data on federal, state, and corporate credit unions, from 1986 or 1990 through 1996.
The data were obtained from the National Credit Union Administration (NCUA), Washington, D.C. 20456.

SELECTED DATA FOR FEDERAL CREDIT UNIONS

December 31, 1935 to 1997.

Year	Charters issued	Charters canceled	Net change	Total outstanding	Inactive credit unions	Active credit unions	Members	($000) Assets[1]	($000) Shares[1]	Loans outstanding
1935	828		828	906	134	772	119,420	2,372	2,228	1,834
1936	956	4	952	1,858	107	1,751	309,700	9,158	8,511	7,344
1937	638	69	569	2,427	114	2,313	483,920	19,265	17,650	15,695
1938	515	83	432	2,859	99	2,760	632,050	29,629	26,876	23,830
1939	529	93	436	3,295	113	3,182	850,770	47,811	43,327	37,673
1940	666	76	590	3,855	129	3,756	1,127,940	72,530	65,806	55,818
1941	583	89	494	4,379	151	4,228	1,408,880	106,052	97,209	69,485
1942	187	89	98	4,477	332	4,145	1,356,940	119,591	109,822	43,053
1943	108	321	-213	4,264	326	3,938	1,311,620	127,329	117,339	35,376
1944	69	285	-216	4,048	233	3,815	1,306,000	144,365	133,677	34,438
1945	96	185	-89	3,959	202	3,757	1,216,625	153,103	140,614	35,155
1946	157	151	6	3,965	204	3,761	1,302,132	173,166	159,718	56,801
1947	207	159	48	4,013	168	3,845	1,445,915	210,376	192,410	91,372
1948	341	130	211	4,224	166	4,058	1,628,339	258,412	235,008	137,642
1949	523	101	422	4,646	151	4,495	1,819,606	316,363	285,001	186,218
1950	565	83	482	5,128	144	4,984	2,126,823	405,835	361,925	263,736
1951	533	75	458	5,586	188	5,398	2,463,898	504,715	457,402	299,756
1952	692	115	577	6,163	238	5,925	2,853,241	662,409	597,374	415,062
1953	825	132	693	6,856	278	6,578	3,255,422	854,232	767,571	573,974
1954	852	122	730	7,586	359	7,227	3,598,790	1,033,179	931,407	681,970
1955	777	188	589	8,175	369	7,806	4,032,220	1,267,427	1,135,165	863,042
1956	741	182	559	8,734	384	8,350	4,502,210	1,529,202	1,366,258	1,049,189
1957	662	194	468	9,202	467	8,735	4,897,689	1,788,768	1,589,191	1,257,319
1958	586	255	331	9,533	503	9,030	5,209,912	2,034,866	1,812,017	1,379,724
1959	700	270	430	9,963	516	9,447	5,643,248	2,352,813	2,075,055	1,666,526
1960	685	274	411	10,374	469	9,905	6,087,378	2,669,734	2,344,337	2,021,463
1961	671	265	406	10,780	509	10,271	6,542,603	3,028,294	2,673,488	2,245,223
1962	601	284	317	11,097	465	10,632	7,007,630	3,429,805	3,020,274	2,560,722
1963	622	312	310	11,407	452	10,955	7,499,747	3,916,541	3,452,615	2,911,159
1964	580	323	257	11,664	386	11,278	8,092,030	4,559,438	4,017,393	3,349,068
1965	584	270	324	11,978	435	11,543	8,640,560	5,165,807	4,538,461	3,864,809
1966	701	318	383	12,361	420	11,941	9,271,967	5,668,941	4,944,033	4,323,943
1967	636	292	344	12,705	495	12,210	9,873,777	6,208,158	5,420,633	4,677,480
1968	662	345	317	13,022	438	12,584	10,508,504	6,902,175	5,986,181	5,398,052
1969	705	323	382	13,404	483	12,921	11,301,805	7,793,573	6,713,385	6,328,720
1970	563	412	151	13,555	578	12,977	11,966,181	8,860,612	7,628,805	6,969,006
1971	400	461	-61	13,494	777	12,717	12,702,135	10,533,740	9,191,182	8,071,201
1972	311	672	-361	13,133	425	12,708	13,572,312	12,513,621	10,956,007	9,424,180
1973	364	523	-159	12,974	286	12,688	14,665,890	14,568,736	12,597,607	11,109,015
1974	367	369	-2	12,972	224	12,748	15,870,434	16,714,673	14,370,744	12,729,653
1975	373	334	39	13,011	274	12,737	17,066,428	20,208,536	17,529,823	14,868,840
1976	354	387	-33	12,978	221	12,757	18,623,862	24,395,896	21,130,293	18,311,204
1977	337	315	22	13,000	250	12,750	20,426,661	29,563,681	25,576,017	22,633,860
1978	348	298	50	13,050	291	12,759	23,259,284	34,760,098	29,802,504	27,686,584
1979	286	336	-50	13,000	262	12,738	24,789,647	36,467,850	31,831,400	28,547,097

[Continued]

SELECTED DATA FOR FEDERAL CREDIT UNIONS

[Continued]

Year	Charters issued	Charters canceled	Net change	Total outstanding	Inactive credit unions	Active credit unions	Members	($000)		
								Assets[1]	Shares[1]	Loans outstanding
1985	55	575	-520	10,247	122	10,125	29,578,808	78,187,651	71,616,202	48,240,770
1986	59	441	-382	9,865	107	9,758	31,041,142	95,483,828	87,953,642	55,304,682
1987	41	460	-419	9,446	45	9,401	32,066,542	105,189,725	96,346,488	64,104,411
1988	45	201	-156	9,290	172	9,118	34,438,304	114,564,579	104,431,487	73,766,200
1989	23	307	-284	9,006	185	8,821	35,612,317	120,666,414	109,652,600	80,272,306
1990	33	410	-377	8,629	118	8,511	36,241,607	130,072,955	117,891,940	83,029,348
1991	14	291	-277	8,352	123	8,229	37,080,854	143,939,504	130,163,749	84,150,334
1992	33	341	-308	8,044	128	7,916	38,205,128	162,543,659	146,078,403	87,632,808
1993	42	258	-216	7,828	132	7,696	39,755,596	172,854,187	153,505,799	94,640,348
1994	39	224	-185	7,643	145	7,498	40,837,392	182,528,895	160,225,678	110,089,530
1995	28	194	-166	7,477	148	7,329	42,162,627	193,781,391	170,300,445	120,514,044
1996	14	189	-175	7,302	150	7,152	43,545,541	206,692,540	180,964,338	134,120,160
1997	17	179	-162	6,994	13	6,981	43,500,553	215,097,395	187,816,918	140,099,926

Source: National Credit Union Administration, *1997 Annual Report*, Alexandria, Va., p. 48. *Note:* 1. Data for 1935-44 are partly estimated.

FEDERAL CREDIT UNIONS - 1990-1997

December 31. Dollar amounts in millions.

	1990	1991	1992	1993	1994	1995	1996	1997
Number of credit unions	8,511	8,229	7,916	7,696	7,498	7,329	7,152	6,981
Number of members	36,241,607	37,080,854	38,205,128	39,755,596	40,837,392	42,162,627	43,545,541	43,500,553
Assets	130,073	143,940	162,544	172,854	182,529	193,781	206,692	215,097
Loans outstanding	83,029	84,150	87,633	94,640	110,090	120,514	134,120	140,100
Shares	117,892	130,164	146,078	153,506	160,226	170,300	180,964	187,817
Reserves[1]	5,158	5,539	6,176	6,976	7,616	8,351	9,092	9,371
Undivided earnings	4,594	5,338	6,793	8,338	9,584	11,445	13,087	14,365
Gross income	13,233	13,559	13,301	12,946	13,496	15,276	16,645	17,404
Operating expenses	4,730	5,068	5,329	5,578	5,964	6,468	7,246	7,793
Dividends	7,372	7,184	5,876	5,038	5,208	6,506	7,087	7,425
Reserve transfers	222	170	191	186	245	262	240	201
Net income	841	1,087	1,897	2,096	1,903	1,886	1,992	1,915

Source: National Credit Union Administration, *1997 Annual Report*, Alexandria, Va., p. 46. *Note:* 1. Does not include the allowance for loan losses.

FEDERAL CREDIT UNIONS - PERCENT CHANGE - 1990-1997

December 31. Dollar amounts in millions.

	1990	1991	1992	1993	1994	1995	1996	1997
Total assets	7.8	10.7	12.9	6.3	5.6	6.2	6.7	4.1
Loans outstanding	3.4	1.3	4.1	8.0	16.3	9.5	11.3	4.5
Savings	7.5	10.4	12.2	5.1	4.4	6.3	6.3	3.8
Reserves	10.0	7.4	11.5	13.0	9.2	9.7	9.3	3.1
Undivided earnings	12.8	16.2	27.3	22.7	14.9	19.4	14.2	9.8
Gross income	6.5	2.5	-1.9	-2.7	4.2	13.2	9.0	4.6
Operating expenses	8.4	7.1	5.1	4.7	6.9	8.5	11.9	7.5
Dividends	6.7	-2.6	-18.2	-14.3	3.4	24.9	8.7	4.8
Net reserve transfers	-16.1	-23.8	12.7	-2.6	31.7	6.9	-8.1	-16.3
Net income	7.6	29.3	74.5	10.5	-9.2	-0.1	6.9	-3.9

Source: National Credit Union Administration, *1997 Annual Report*, Alexandria, Va., p. 46. *Note:* Does not include the allowance for loan losses.

FEDERAL CREDIT UNIONS - SIGNIFICANT RATIOS - 1990-1997

December 31. Dollar amounts in millions.

	1990	1991	1992	1993	1994	1995	1996	1997
Reserves to assets	4.0	3.8	3.8	4.0	4.2	4.3	4.4	4.4
Reserves and undivided earnings to assets	7.3	7.5	7.6	8.0	8.9	10.2	10.7	11.0
Reserves to loans	6.2	6.6	7.0	7.4	6.9	6.9	6.8	6.7
Loans to shares	70.4	64.6	60.0	61.7	68.7	70.8	74.1	74.6
Operating expenses to gross income	35.7	37.4	40.1	43.1	44.2	42.3	39.4	39.4
Salaries and benefits to gross income	15.0	15.7	17.4	19.4	20.2	19.2	19.2	19.3
Dividends to gross income	55.7	53.0	44.2	38.9	38.6	42.6	42.6	42.7
Yield on average assets	10.6	9.9	8.7	7.7	7.6	8.1	8.3	8.3
Cost of funds to average assets	5.9	5.3	3.9	3.1	3.0	3.5	3.6	3.6
Gross spread	4.6	4.6	4.8	4.6	4.6	4.6	4.7	4.7
Net income divided by gross income	6.4	8.0	14.3	16.2	14.1	12.3	12.0	12.2
Yield on average loans	11.4	11.2	10.4	9.4	8.7	8.9	8.5	8.7
Yield on average investments	8.3	7.0	5.5	4.6	5.1	5.6	6.0	5.9

Source: National Credit Union Administration, *1997 Annual Report*, Alexandria, Va., p. 46. *Note:* Does not include the allowance for loan losses.

STATE CHARTERED CREDIT UNIONS - 1990-1997

December 31. Dollar amounts in millions.

	1990	1991	1992	1993	1994	1995	1996	1997
Number of credit unions	4,349	4,731	4,737	4,621	4,493	4,358	4,240	4,257
Number of members	19,453,940	21,619,223	23,859,447	23,996,751	24,294,761	24,926,666	25,665,783	27,921,882
Assets	68,133	83,133	98,767	104,316	106,937	112,861	120,176	136,107
Loans outstanding	44,102	49,268	53,727	57,695	65,769	71,606	79,651	92,117
Shares	62,082	75,626	89,648	93,482	94,797	99,838	105,728	119,359
Reserves[1]	3,047	3,620	4,328	4,754	4,908	5,246	5,689	6,421
Undivided earnings	2,241	2,952	3,910	4,862	5,563	6,645	7,490	8,779
Gross income	6,967	7,878	8,182	7,878	7,955	8,932	9,736	11,124
Operating expenses	2,412	2,860	3,203	3,302	3,473	3,770	4,198	4,939
Dividends	3,908	4,203	3,664	3,109	3,145	3,889	3,367	3,790
Reserve transfers	118	98	121	114	144	147	143	138
Net income	509	711	1,207	1,347	1,146	1,095	1,154	1,237

Source: National Credit Union Administration, *1997 Annual Report*, Alexandria, Va., p. 47. *Note:* 1. Does not include the allowance for loan losses.

STATE-CHARTERED CREDIT UNIONS - PERCENT CHANGE - 1990-1997

December 31. Dollar amounts in millions.

	1990	1991	1992	1993	1994	1995	1996	1997
Total assets	7.8	22.0	18.8	5.6	2.5	5.5	6.5	13.2
Loans outstanding	4.1	11.7	9.1	7.4	14.0	8.9	11.2	15.6
Savings	7.7	21.8	18.5	4.3	1.4	5.3	5.9	12.9
Reserves	6.1	18.8	17.1	12.2	3.2	6.9	8.5	12.9
Undivided earnings	15.2	31.7	32.5	24.3	14.4	19.4	12.4	17.2
Gross income	6.7	13.1	3.9	-3.7	1.0	12.3	9.0	14.3
Operating expenses	8.8	18.6	12.0	3.1	5.2	8.6	11.4	17.7
Dividends	33.4	7.5	-12.8	-15.1	1.2	23.7	-13.4	12.6
Net reserve transfers	-21.3	-16.9	23.5	-5.8	26.3	2.1	-2.7	-3.5
Net income	11.4	39.7	69.8	11.6	-4.5	-4.5	5.7	7.2

Source: National Credit Union Administration, *1997 Annual Report*, Alexandria, Va., p. 47. *Note:* Does not include the allowance for loan losses.

STATE-CHARTERED CREDIT UNIONS - SIGNIFICANT RATIOS - 1990-1997

December 31. Dollar amounts in millions.

	1990	1991	1992	1993	1994	1995	1996	1997
Reserves to assets	4.5	4.4	4.3	4.6	4.6	4.6	4.7	4.7
Reserves and undivided earnings to assets	7.8	7.9	8.2	9.2	9.8	10.5	11.0	11.2
Reserves to loans	6.9	7.3	7.9	8.2	7.5	7.3	7.1	7.0
Loans to shares	71.0	65.1	59.9	61.7	69.4	71.7	75.3	77.2
Operating expenses to gross income	34.6	36.3	39.1	41.9	43.7	42.2	39.1	39.5
Salaries and benefits to gross income	14.7	15.4	16.9	19.0	20.0	19.1	18.8	19.0
Dividends to gross income	56.1	53.4	44.8	39.5	39.5	43.5	35.0	34.1
Yield on average assets	10.6	10.4	9.0	7.8	7.5	8.1	8.4	8.7
Cost of funds to average assets	6.0	5.6	4.1	3.1	3.0	3.5	3.6	3.8
Gross spread	4.6	4.6	4.6	4.7	4.5	4.6	4.7	4.9
Net income divided by gross income	7.3	9.0	14.8	17.1	14.4	12.3	11.9	11.1
Yield on average loans	11.4	11.8	10.8	9.5	8.6	8.9	8.4	9.1
Yield on average investments	8.5	7.4	5.7	4.7	4.9	5.6	6.0	6.1

Source: National Credit Union Administration, *1997 Annual Report*, Alexandria, Va., p. 47. *Note:* Does not include the allowance for loan losses.

CORPORATE CREDIT UNIONS - KEY STATISTICS

December 31, in millions.

	1995	1996	1997
Number	37	36	35
Assets	31,912.6	28,386.5	31,550.1
Loans	293.5	315.7	289.9
Shares	27,537.0	22,742.2	25,477.4
Reserves	602.2	2,026.6[1]	2,088.5[1]
Undivided earnings	253.7	312.8	393.1
Gross income	1,860.3	1,745.3	1,756.4
Operating expenses	118.4	128.5	136.7
Interest on borrowed funds	209.0	153.0	143.8
Dividends and interest	1,469.2	1,375.8	1,425.2
Reserve transfers	16.2	8.2	5.4
Net income	47.5	73.7	45.6

Source: National Credit Union Administration, *1997 Annual Report*, Alexandria, Va., p. 19. *Notes:* Dollar amounts do not include U.S. Central. 1. Includes Membership Capital Share Deposits.

FEDERAL AND STATE-CHARTERED CREDIT UNIONS-SUMMARY: 1980 TO 1996

Except as noted, as of December 31. Federal data include District of Columbia, Puerto Rico, Canal Zone, Guam, and Virgin Islands. Excludes State-insured, privately-insured, and noninsured State-chartered credit unions and corporate central credit unions which have mainly other credit unions as members.

Year	Operating Credit Unions		Number of failed institu- tions[1]	Members (1,000)		Assets (mil. dol.)		Loans Outstanding (mil. dol.)		Savings (mil. dol.)	
	Federal	State		Federal	State	Federal	State	Federal	State	Federal	State
1980	12,440	4,910	239	24,519	12,338	40,092	20,870	26,350	14,582	36,263	18,469
1985	10,125	4,920	94	29,579	15,689	78,188	41,525	48,241	26,168	71,616	37,917
1990	8,511	4,349	164	36,241	19,454	130,073	68,133	83,029	44,102	117,892	62,082
1992	7,908	4,686	114	38,124	23,238	162,066	96,312	87,350	52,192	145,637	87,371
1993	7,696	4,621	37	39,756	23,997	172,854	104,316	94,640	57,695	153,506	93,482
1994	7,498	4,493	33	40,837	24,295	182,529	106,937	110,090	65,769	160,226	94,797
1995	7,329	4,358	26	42,163	24,927	193,781	112,860	120,514	71,606	170,300	99,838
1996	7,152	4,240	19	43,544	25,666	206,685	120,176	134,117	79,651	180,960	105,728

Source: Statistical Abstract of the United States, 1997, p. 517. *Primary Source*: National Credit Union Administration, *Annual Report of the National Credit Union Administration*, and unpublished data. *Notes:* 1. For year ending September 30, except 1995 reflects 15-month period from October 1994 through December 1995 and 1996 reflect calendar year. A failed institution is defined as a credit union which has ceased operation because it was involuntarily liquidated or merged with assistance from the National Credit Union Share Insurance Fund. Assisted mergers were not identified until 1981.

SIC 6080

FOREIGN BANKS & BRANCHES & AGENCIES

Foreign Banks and Branches and Agencies of Foreign Banks are divided into SIC 6081, Branches and Agencies of Foreign Banks and SIC 6082, Foreign Trade and International Banking Institutions.

SIC 6081 represents establishments that specialize in commercial loans, especially to finance trade. They are funded typically by large interbank deposits rather than retail deposits. Federally licensed agencies of foreign banks may not accept deposits; federal branches may accept deposits, but if they accept deposits in denominations of $100,000 or less, federal deposit insurance is required. Foreign-owned banks engaged primarily in accepting retail deposits from the public are classified as SIC 6020.

SIC 6082 includes federally or state-chartered foreign trade companies organized to aid or finance foreign trade. The category also includes banking institutions (federal or state charter) which engage in banking only outside the United States.

ESTABLISHMENTS, EMPLOYMENT, AND PAYROLL

	1990	1991		1992		1993		1994		1995		% change 90-95
		Value	%	Value	%	Value	%	Value	%	Value	%	
All Establishments	235	473	101.3	480	1.5	561	16.9	657	17.1	660	0.5	180.9
Mid-March Employment	13,317	21,627	62.4	23,248	7.5	27,710	19.2	34,998	26.3	35,229	0.7	164.5
1st Quarter Wages (annualized - $ mil.)	661.3	1,114.1	68.5	1,369.6	22.9	1,827.1	33.4	2,996.8	64.0	3,235.6	8.0	389.3
Payroll per Emp. 1st Q. (annualized)	49,659	51,515	3.7	58,912	14.4	65,937	11.9	85,626	29.9	91,846	7.3	85.0
Annual Payroll ($ mil.)	662.7	1,150.7	73.6	1,393.0	21.1	1,810.8	30.0	2,518.4	39.1	2,802.0	11.3	322.8
Establishments - 1-4 Emp. Number	41	73	78.0	42	-42.5	41	-2.4	(D)	-	(D)	-	-
Mid-March Employment	72	(D)	-	98	-	95	-3.1	(D)	-	(D)	-	-
1st Quarter Wages (annualized - $ mil.)	3.8	(D)	-	7.0	-	7.4	5.1	(D)	-	(D)	-	-
Payroll per Emp. 1st Q. (annualized)	52,444	(D)	-	71,837	-	77,853	8.4	(D)	-	(D)	-	-
Annual Payroll ($ mil.)	5.9	(D)	-	7.0	-	8.2	17.4	(D)	-	(D)	-	-
Establishments - 5-9 Emp. Number	20	53	165.0	59	11.3	(D)	-	80	-	87	8.8	335.0
Mid-March Employment	(D)	387	-	400	3.4	(D)	-	582	-	616	5.8	-
1st Quarter Wages (annualized - $ mil.)	(D)	22.0	-	51.4	133.9	(D)	-	41.5	-	46.8	12.8	-
Payroll per Emp. 1st Q. (annualized)	(D)	56,734	-	128,400	126.3	(D)	-	71,292	-	75,968	6.6	-
Annual Payroll ($ mil.)	(D)	26.8	-	32.4	21.1	(D)	-	37.3	-	47.6	27.5	-
Establishments - 10-19 Emp. Number	34	80	135.3	101	26.3	(D)	-	142	-	145	2.1	326.5
Mid-March Employment	(D)	(D)	-	1,435	-	(D)	-	1,996	-	2,064	3.4	-
1st Quarter Wages (annualized - $ mil.)	(D)	(D)	-	74.7	-	(D)	-	139.1	-	141.4	1.6	-
Payroll per Emp. 1st Q. (annualized)	(D)	(D)	-	52,081	-	(D)	-	69,711	-	68,521	-1.7	-
Annual Payroll ($ mil.)	(D)	(D)	-	80.8	-	(D)	-	143.1	-	154.2	7.8	-
Establishments - 20-49 Emp. Number	69	159	130.4	151	-5.0	172	13.9	194	12.8	186	-4.1	169.6
Mid-March Employment	2,166	5,141	137.3	4,630	-9.9	5,260	13.6	5,924	12.6	5,903	-0.4	172.5
1st Quarter Wages (annualized - $ mil.)	99.9	241.8	142.1	226.1	-6.5	280.1	23.9	353.6	26.2	378.6	7.1	279.0
Payroll per Emp. 1st Q. (annualized)	46,122	47,043	2.0	48,838	3.8	53,257	9.0	59,695	12.1	64,144	7.5	39.1
Annual Payroll ($ mil.)	93.0	251.7	170.6	238.4	-5.3	287.3	20.5	346.8	20.7	374.9	8.1	303.2
Establishments - 50-99 Emp. Number	37	60	62.2	74	23.3	87	17.6	91	4.6	82	-9.9	121.6
Mid-March Employment	2,724	4,278	57.0	5,240	22.5	6,113	16.7	6,374	4.3	5,737	-10.0	110.6
1st Quarter Wages (annualized - $ mil.)	130.0	198.4	52.7	274.3	38.2	353.2	28.8	386.9	9.5	367.2	-5.1	182.5
Payroll per Emp. 1st Q. (annualized)	47,724	46,388	-2.8	52,343	12.8	57,784	10.4	60,707	5.1	64,013	5.4	34.1
Annual Payroll ($ mil.)	129.4	209.6	62.0	288.1	37.4	361.3	25.4	406.1	12.4	378.9	-6.7	192.8
Establishments - 100-249 Emp. Number	23	33	43.5	37	12.1	44	18.9	48	9.1	51	6.3	121.7
Mid-March Employment	3,827	4,875	27.4	5,073	4.1	6,749	33.0	7,572	12.2	7,730	2.1	102.0
1st Quarter Wages (annualized - $ mil.)	205.4	260.9	27.0	281.9	8.0	430.2	52.6	512.1	19.1	567.8	10.9	176.4
Payroll per Emp. 1st Q. (annualized)	53,683	53,518	-0.3	55,569	3.8	63,736	14.7	67,633	6.1	73,448	8.6	36.8
Annual Payroll ($ mil.)	205.2	254.4	24.0	300.9	18.3	441.8	46.8	501.0	13.4	550.2	9.8	168.1
Establishments - 250-499 Emp. Number	10	12	20.0	13	8.3	17	30.8	20	17.6	20	-	100.0
Mid-March Employment	3,354	(D)	-	4,582	-	5,971	30.3	7,420	24.3	6,904	-7.0	105.8
1st Quarter Wages (annualized - $ mil.)	166.3	(D)	-	329.3	-	541.0	64.3	831.8	53.8	885.0	6.4	432.1
Payroll per Emp. 1st Q. (annualized)	49,590	(D)	-	71,860	-	90,598	26.1	112,105	23.7	128,191	14.3	158.5
Annual Payroll ($ mil.)	168.7	(D)	-	313.4	-	482.2	53.9	637.9	32.3	677.2	6.2	301.4
Establishments - 500-999 Emp. Number	1	3	200.0	3	-	(D)	-	5	-	7	40.0	600.0
Mid-March Employment	(D)	1,692	-	1,790	5.8	(D)	-	3,311	-	4,563	37.8	-
1st Quarter Wages (annualized - $ mil.)	(D)	77.8	-	124.9	60.6	(D)	-	297.0	-	542.8	82.8	-
Payroll per Emp. 1st Q. (annualized)	(D)	45,953	-	69,777	51.8	(D)	-	89,690	-	118,954	32.6	-
Annual Payroll ($ mil.)	(D)	86.3	-	132.0	52.9	(D)	-	236.1	-	428.4	81.5	-
Estab. - 1000 or More Emp. Number	-	-	-	-	-	-	-	(D)	-	(D)	-	-
Mid-March Employment	-	-	-	-	-	-	-	(D)	-	(D)	-	-
1st Quarter Wages (annualized - $ mil.)	-	-	-	-	-	-	-	(D)	-	(D)	-	-
Payroll per Emp. 1st Q. (annualized)	(D)	(D)	-	-	-	-	-	(D)	-	(D)	-	-
Annual Payroll ($ mil.)	-	-	-	-	-	-	-	(D)	-	(D)	-	-

Source: County Business Patterns, U.S. Department of Commerce, Washington, D.C., for 1990 through 1995. Payroll per employee is calculated using mid-March employment and 1st Quarter wages, annualized. Annual payroll, also shown, may not equal the annualized 1st Quarter wages. Columns headed by a percent sign (%) indicate change from the previous year. na stands for not available. The symbol (D) indicates that data are withheld by the source to avoid disclosure of competitive information. A dash (-) indicates that data are not available or cannot be calculated.

ESTABLISHMENTS
Number

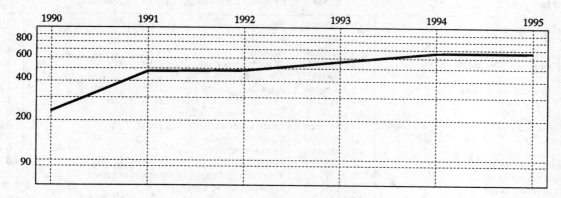

MID-MARCH EMPLOYMENT
Number

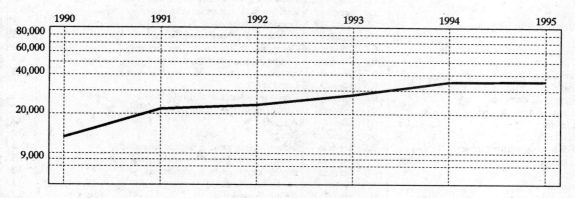

ANNUAL PAYROLL
$ million

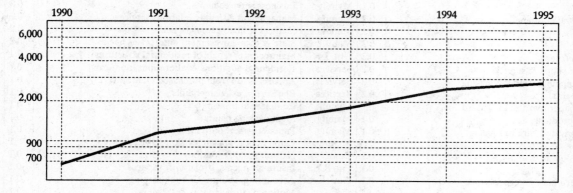

INPUTS AND OUTPUTS FOR ALL BANKING SECTORS - SICs 601, 602, 603, 608, and 609

Economic Sector or Industry Providing Inputs	%	Sector	Economic Sector or Industry Buying Outputs	%	Sector
Security & commodity brokers	12.9	Fin/R.E.	Personal consumption expenditures	59.0	
Banking	11.8	Fin/R.E.	Exports of goods & services	5.1	Foreign
Computer & data processing services	9.5	Services	Banking	4.6	Fin/R.E.
Real estate agents, operators, & lessors	8.1	Fin/R.E.	Retail trade, ex eating & drinking	3.0	Trade
Credit agencies other than banks	4.9	Fin/R.E.	Wholesale trade	2.3	Trade
Management & public relations services	4.1	Services	S/L Govt., general government nec, spending	2.1	S/L Govt
Advertising	3.9	Services	Real estate agents, operators, & lessors	1.5	Fin/R.E.
U.S. Postal Service	3.9	Gov't	Electric services (utilities)	0.8	Util.
Accounting, auditing & bookkeeping	3.7	Services	Credit agencies other than banks	0.8	Fin/R.E.
Business services nec	3.4	Services	Insurance carriers	0.7	Fin/R.E.
Legal services	2.8	Services	Eating & drinking places	0.7	Services
Federal Government enterprises nec	2.5	Gov't	Hotels	0.7	Services
Telephone/telegraph communications nec	2.4	Util.	Telephone/telegraph communications nec	0.6	Util.
Trucking & courier services, ex air	2.3	Util.	Owner-occupied dwellings	0.6	Fin/R.E.
Blankbooks, looseleaf binders & devices	1.7	Manufg.	Doctors & dentists	0.6	Services
Wholesale trade	1.6	Trade	Motor vehicles & passenger car bodies	0.4	Manufg.
Personnel supply services	1.6	Services	Trucking & courier services, ex air	0.4	Util.
Electric services (utilities)	1.5	Util.	Federal Government, nondefense, spending	0.4	Gov't
Warehousing & storage	1.4	Util.	New construction nec	0.3	Constr.
Air transportation	1.0	Util.	Repair & maintenance construction nec	0.3	Constr.
Eating & drinking places	1.0	Services	Residential 1 unit structures, nonfarm	0.3	Constr.
Sanitary services, steam supply, irrigation	0.9	Util.	Petroleum refining	0.3	Manufg.
Insurance carriers	0.9	Fin/R.E.	Railroads & related services	0.3	Util.
Repair & maintenance construction nec	0.8	Constr.	Computer & data processing services	0.3	Services
Hotels	0.8	Services	Engineering, architectural, & surveying services	0.3	Services
Detective & protective services	0.7	Services	Hospitals	0.3	Services
Commercial printing	0.6	Manufg.	Legal services	0.3	Services
Photographic equipment & supplies	0.6	Manufg.	Crude petroleum & natural gas	0.2	Mining
Research, development, & testing services	0.6	Services	Office, industrial/commercial buildings	0.2	Constr.
Manifold business forms	0.5	Manufg.	Aircraft	0.2	Manufg.
Paper & paperboard mills	0.5	Manufg.	Drugs	0.2	Manufg.
Automotive rental & leasing, without drivers	0.5	Services	Industrial inorganic & organic chemicals	0.2	Manufg.
Business & professional associations	0.5	Services	Miscellaneous plastics products, nec	0.2	Manufg.
Services to dwellings & other buildings	0.5	Services	Motor vehicle parts & accessories	0.2	Manufg.
Natural gas distribution	0.4	Util.	Air transportation	0.2	Util.
Magnetic & optical recording media	0.3	Manufg.	Freight forwarders	0.2	Util.
Manufacturing industries, nec	0.3	Manufg.	Water transportation	0.2	Util.
Periodicals	0.3	Manufg.	Security & commodity brokers	0.2	Fin/R.E.
Petroleum refining	0.3	Manufg.	Automotive rental & leasing, without drivers	0.2	Services
Electrical repair shops	0.3	Services	Automotive repair shops & services	0.2	Services
Book publishing	0.2	Manufg.	Business services nec	0.2	Services
Computer peripheral equipment	0.2	Manufg.	Management & public relations services	0.2	Services
Envelopes	0.2	Manufg.	Medical & health services nec	0.2	Services
Textile bags	0.2	Manufg.	State & local government enterprises nec	0.2	Gov't
Local & suburban transit	0.2	Util.	Maintenance/repair of residential structures	0.1	Constr.
Automotive repair shops & services	0.2	Services	Residential additions & alterations, nonfarm	0.1	Constr.
Miscellaneous equipment rental & leasing	0.2	Services	Apparel made from purchased materials	0.1	Manufg.
Miscellaneous repair shops	0.2	Services	Blast furnaces & steel mills	0.1	Manufg.
Die-cut paper & paperboard & cardboard	0.1	Manufg.	Commercial printing	0.1	Manufg.
Fabricated metal products, nec	0.1	Manufg.	Meat packing plants	0.1	Manufg.
Miscellaneous fabricated wire products	0.1	Manufg.	Paper & paperboard mills	0.1	Manufg.
Paperboard containers & boxes	0.1	Manufg.	Cable & other pay television services	0.1	Util.
Retail trade, ex eating & drinking	0.1	Trade	Natural gas distribution	0.1	Util.
Royalties	0.1	Fin/R.E.	Insurance agents, brokers, & services	0.1	Fin/R.E.
State & local government enterprises nec	0.1	Gov't	Accounting, auditing & bookkeeping	0.1	Services
			Motion picture services & theaters	0.1	Services
			Personnel supply services	0.1	Services
			Portrait photographic studios	0.1	Services
			U.S. Postal Service	0.1	Gov't

Source: Benchmark Input-Output Accounts for the U.S. Economy, 1992, U.S. Department of Commerce, Washington, D.C., November 1997. Data, as reported in the source, are organized by the 1987 SIC structure in use in 1992.

OCCUPATIONS EMPLOYED BY BANKING AND CLOSELY RELATED FUNCTIONS, NEC

Occupation	% of Total 1996	Change to 2006	Occupation	% of Total 1996	Change to 2006
Bank tellers	9.0	18.8	Clerical & administrative workers nec	2.6	16.4
General office clerks	7.7	0.1	Computer programmers	2.4	-4.2
Clerical supervisors & managers	6.3	16.4	Loan officers & counselors	2.3	16.4
Adjustment clerks	5.5	57.1	Sales & related workers nec	2.3	28.0
Cashiers	4.7	24.3	Systems analysts	2.3	86.2
Secretaries, except legal & medical	4.4	-7.7	Credit analysts	2.1	16.4
Bookkeeping, accounting, & auditing clerks	4.1	-6.9	Securities & financial sales workers	1.8	74.6
General managers & top executives	3.9	12.8	Data entry keyers, except composing	1.6	-6.9
Financial managers	3.4	16.4	Managers & administrators nec	1.6	15.3
Accountants & auditors	3.2	7.7	Computer operators, ex peripheral equipment	1.5	-30.2
Loan & credit clerks	2.9	17.5	Guards	1.1	4.8
Duplicating, mail, office machine operators	2.8	-24.4	Brokerage clerks	1.1	-2.7

Sources: *Industry-Occupation Matrix*, Bureau of Labor Statistics. These data relate to one or more 3-digit SIC industry groups rather than to a single 4-digit SIC. The change reported for each occupation to the year 2005 is a percent of growth or decline as estimated by the Bureau of Labor Statistics. The abbreviation *nec* stands for not elsewhere classified.

U.S. AND STATE DATA ON INDUSTRY REVENUES AND OTHER ACCOUNTS FOR 1992

State	No. of Estab.	Employ- ment	Payroll ($ mil.)	Revenues ($ mil.)	Empl./ Estab.	Revenue/ Estab. ($)	Payroll/ Estab. ($)	Revenue/ Empl. ($)	Payroll/ Empl. ($)
UNITED STATES	632	34,310	2,263.5	62,689.7	54	99,192,587	3,581,492	1,827,156	65,972
California	126	3,385	211.4	9,869.5	27	78,329,452	1,678,040	2,915,661	62,462
Colorado	1	-	(D)	(D)	(D)	(D)	(D)	(D)	(D)
Florida	58	2,236	89.1	1,206.1	39	20,794,897	1,536,655	539,403	39,860
Georgia	18	337	21.5	922.4	19	51,243,667	1,191,944	2,737,050	63,665
Illinois	55	2,011	122.4	4,296.6	37	78,120,109	2,225,673	2,136,552	60,871
Massachusetts	7	-	(D)	(D)	(D)	(D)	(D)	(D)	(D)
New Jersey	2	-	(D)	(D)	(D)	(D)	(D)	(D)	(D)
New York	307	25,009	1,749.3	45,073.6	81	146,819,577	5,698,036	1,802,296	69,947
North Carolina	1	-	(D)	(D)	(D)	(D)	(D)	(D)	(D)
Pennsylvania	7	303	10.0	153.8	43	21,976,429	1,433,429	507,706	33,116
Texas	25	439	26.1	524.4	18	20,974,880	1,045,120	1,194,469	59,517
Washington	8	154	8.0	181.8	19	22,721,125	999,250	1,180,318	51,909
Wisconsin	1	-	(D)	(D)	(D)	(D)	(D)	(D)	(D)

Source: 1992 Economic Census, U.S. Department of Commerce, Washington, D.C. This is the only table that shows revenue data as collected by the Bureau of the Census in an Economic Census. The symbol (D) indicates that data are withheld by the source to avoid disclosure of competitive information. A dash (-) indicates that data are not available or cannot be calculated.

STATE-BY-STATE DATA ON ESTABLISHMENTS, EMPLOYMENT, AND PAYROLL - 1994 AND 1995

State	1994					1995					% Change Empl.
	No. of Estab.	Employ-ment	Pay / Empl.	Payroll ($ mil.)	Pay / Estab.	No. of Estab.	Employ-ment	Pay / Empl.	Payroll ($ mil.)	Pay / Estab.	
California	125	(D)	-	(D)	-	126	(D)	-	(D)	-	-
Colorado	2	(D)	-	(D)	-	2	(D)	-	(D)	-	-
Connecticut	1	(D)	-	(D)	-	(D)	(D)	(D)	(D)	(D)	-
Delaware	1	(D)	-	(D)	-	1	(D)	-	(D)	-	-
District of Columbia	6	(D)	-	(D)	-	6	(D)	-	(D)	-	-
Florida	62	(D)	-	(D)	-	65	2,277	55,167	115.0	1,769,015	-
Georgia	19	(D)	-	(D)	-	20	406	62,995	26.2	1,308,350	-
Hawaii	3	22	41,455	1.0	344,333	3	23	48,696	1.1	382,000	4.5
Illinois	55	2,182	64,330	137.3	2,496,709	56	2,074	71,090	143.7	2,565,857	-4.9
Iowa	2	(D)	-	(D)	-	2	(D)	-	(D)	-	-
Maryland	6	(D)	-	(D)	-	6	(D)	-	(D)	-	-
Massachusetts	8	(D)	-	(D)	-	6	(D)	-	(D)	-	-
Minnesota	1	(D)	-	(D)	-	1	(D)	-	(D)	-	-
Missouri	2	(D)	-	(D)	-	2	(D)	-	(D)	-	-
Nebraska	1	(D)	-	(D)	-	1	(D)	-	(D)	-	-
Nevada	1	(D)	-	(D)	-	1	(D)	-	(D)	-	-
New Jersey	2	(D)	-	(D)	-	2	(D)	-	(D)	-	-
New York	306	25,019	95,958	1,919.0	6,271,258	304	25,135	103,069	2,161.5	7,110,220	0.5
North Carolina	1	(D)	-	(D)	-	(D)	(D)	(D)	(D)	(D)	-
Ohio	1	(D)	-	(D)	-	1	(D)	-	(D)	-	-
Oregon	3	(D)	-	(D)	-	3	(D)	-	(D)	-	-
Pennsylvania	5	289	35,585	10.4	2,072,600	8	273	45,289	10.5	1,316,250	-5.5
South Carolina	1	(D)	-	(D)	-	1	(D)	-	(D)	-	-
South Dakota	1	(D)	-	(D)	-	1	(D)	-	(D)	-	-
Texas	31	(D)	-	(D)	-	30	(D)	-	(D)	-	-
Virginia	1	(D)	-	(D)	-	2	(D)	-	(D)	-	-
Washington	10	178	50,022	9.2	922,600	10	178	53,281	10.5	1,050,800	0.0

Source: County Business Patterns, U.S. Department of Commerce, Washington, D.C., for 1994 and 1995. Employment shown is for mid-March of the year shown. Payroll per employee is calculated by annualizing 1st Quarter payroll (not shown) and then dividing that value by mid-March employment. Dividing total annual payroll (columns 5 and 10) by employment, therefore, will *not* yield the payroll per employee figure (columns 4 and 9). The symbol (D) indicates that data are withheld by the source to avoid disclosure of competitive information. A dash (-) indicates that data are not available or cannot be calculated.

ESTABLISHMENTS 1995 - STATE AND REGIONAL CONCENTRATION

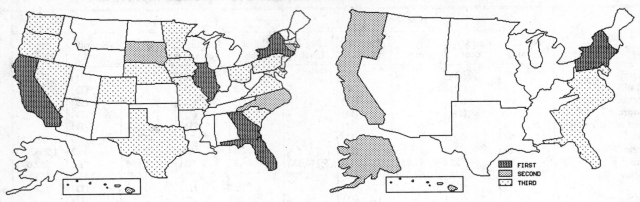

EMPLOYMENT 1995 - STATE AND REGIONAL CONCENTRATION

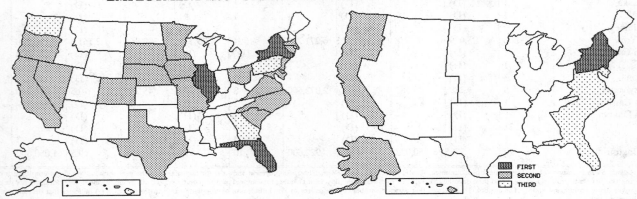

PAYROLL 1995 - STATE AND REGIONAL CONCENTRATION

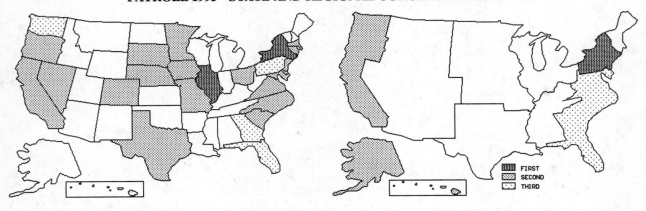

States with the darkest shading indicate those states which have proportionately more establishments, employment, or payrolls than would be indicated by the state's population. States with light shading are states with proportionately fewer establishments, less employment, and lower payrolls than population distribution. States shaded grey are within 15 percent of the state's population proportion in these categories. States for which no data are available are shown as average (grey). *Regions* are shaded to indicate absolute rank in the category. If no data for the category are available, establishment counts are used to shade the regions. Source of the data is the table on the facing page.

LEADING COMPANIES - SIC 6082 - Foreign Trade & International Banks

Number shown: **3**   Total sales/assets ($ mil): **71,011**   Total employment (000): **75.6**

Company Name	Address				CEO Name	Phone	Co. Type	Sales/Assets ($ mil)	Empl. (000)
Inter-American Development Bank	1300 New York Ave. N.W.	Washington	DC	20577	Enrique V. Iglesias	202-623-1000	R	39,361 TA	1.6
American Express Co.	American Express Tower	New York	NY	10285	Harvey Golub	212-640-2000	P	17,760 OR	73.6
French American Banking Corp.	PO Box 127	New York	NY	10008	Pierre Schneider	212-978-5700	S	13,890 TA	0.3

Source: *Ward's Business Directory of U.S. Private and Public Companies*, 1996. Company type codes: P - Public, R - Private, S - Subsidiary, D - Division, J - Joint Venture, A - Affiliate, G - Group. If the dollar values shown are not sales, the following codes apply: TA - Total Assets; OR - Operating Revenues; GB - Gross Billings. * - estimated dollar value. < - less than; *na* - not available.

SIC 6090

FUNCTIONS CLOSELY RELATED TO BANKING

This grouping includes Nondeposit Trust Facilities (SIC 6091) and Functions Related to Depository Banking, not elsewhere classified (SIC 6099).

The trust companies included in SIC 6091 are engaged in fiduciary business (managing funds entrusted to them by others) but not regularly engaged in deposit banking. Some of these establishments hold limited amounts of special types of deposits; their uninvested trust funds are also classified as deposits; but they are not engaged in conventional banking. Trusts may have either national or state charters. Title insurance companies—which operate under charters that limit them to real estate title or mortgage loan activities—are classified as SIC 6361 and are not included here.

SIC 6099 includes a wide range of functions related to deposit banking, including automated clearinghouses, check cashing agencies, check clearinghouse associations, deposit brokers, electronic funds transfer, escrow institutions other than real estate, fiduciary agencies which are not trusts or real estate, foreign currency exchanges, money order issuers, regional clearinghouse associations, representatives of foreign banks that are not agencies or branches, safe deposit companies, tax certificate sale and redemption agencies, and travelers' check issuers.

ESTABLISHMENTS, EMPLOYMENT, AND PAYROLL

	1990	1991		1992		1993		1994		1995		% change 90-95
		Value	%	Value	%	Value	%	Value	%	Value	%	
All Establishments	2,778	3,790	36.4	4,515	19.1	4,692	3.9	5,068	8.0	5,346	5.5	92.4
Mid-March Employment	43,937	48,428	10.2	50,898	5.1	45,967	-9.7	57,977	26.1	60,994	5.2	38.8
1st Quarter Wages (annualized - $ mil.)	1,404.0	1,649.7	17.5	1,801.4	9.2	1,554.6	-13.7	1,883.2	21.1	2,218.2	17.8	58.0
Payroll per Emp. 1st Q. (annualized)	31,956	34,064	6.6	35,393	3.9	33,820	-4.4	32,481	-4.0	36,368	12.0	13.8
Annual Payroll ($ mil.)	1,362.8	1,567.2	15.0	1,735.7	10.7	1,637.2	-5.7	1,935.7	18.2	2,136.3	10.4	56.8
Establishments - 1-4 Emp. Number	1,626	2,392	47.1	2,959	23.7	2,971	0.4	(D)	-	3,402	-	109.2
Mid-March Employment	3,316	5,035	51.8	6,190	22.9	6,681	7.9	(D)	-	6,876	-	107.4
1st Quarter Wages (annualized - $ mil.)	72.9	105.0	44.2	135.9	29.4	142.4	4.8	(D)	-	160.1	-	119.6
Payroll per Emp. 1st Q. (annualized)	21,976	20,864	-5.1	21,956	5.2	21,311	-2.9	(D)	-	23,277	-	5.9
Annual Payroll ($ mil.)	88.9	127.6	43.4	146.0	14.4	164.9	13.0	(D)	-	177.0	-	99.0
Establishments - 5-9 Emp. Number	597	896	50.1	1,026	14.5	1,149	12.0	1,215	5.7	1,179	-3.0	97.5
Mid-March Employment	3,881	5,549	43.0	6,395	15.2	7,333	14.7	7,762	5.9	7,607	-2.0	96.0
1st Quarter Wages (annualized - $ mil.)	86.9	113.8	31.0	134.4	18.1	147.4	9.6	169.8	15.2	179.9	6.0	107.0
Payroll per Emp. 1st Q. (annualized)	22,395	20,513	-8.4	21,023	2.5	20,101	-4.4	21,875	8.8	23,651	8.1	5.6
Annual Payroll ($ mil.)	91.9	116.8	27.1	136.3	16.7	160.3	17.7	174.5	8.9	179.9	3.1	95.9
Establishments - 10-19 Emp. Number	277	250	-9.7	272	8.8	(D)	-	396	-	400	1.0	44.4
Mid-March Employment	3,676	(D)	-	3,458	-	(D)	-	5,127	-	5,196	1.3	41.3
1st Quarter Wages (annualized - $ mil.)	100.3	(D)	-	105.8	-	(D)	-	149.1	-	159.9	7.2	59.5
Payroll per Emp. 1st Q. (annualized)	27,275	(D)	-	30,595	-	(D)	-	29,088	-	30,771	5.8	12.8
Annual Payroll ($ mil.)	98.4	(D)	-	106.9	-	(D)	-	147.1	-	152.1	3.4	54.6
Establishments - 20-49 Emp. Number	151	131	-13.2	138	5.3	169	22.5	(D)	-	206	-	36.4
Mid-March Employment	4,489	4,110	-8.4	4,337	5.5	5,044	16.3	(D)	-	6,228	-	38.7
1st Quarter Wages (annualized - $ mil.)	138.3	152.8	10.5	173.3	13.4	210.8	21.6	(D)	-	271.0	-	95.9
Payroll per Emp. 1st Q. (annualized)	30,812	37,186	20.7	39,970	7.5	41,786	4.5	(D)	-	43,513	-	41.2
Annual Payroll ($ mil.)	131.2	144.5	10.2	161.0	11.4	227.6	41.4	(D)	-	245.0	-	86.8
Establishments - 50-99 Emp. Number	58	45	-22.4	53	17.8	59	11.3	59	-	70	18.6	20.7
Mid-March Employment	3,963	2,943	-25.7	3,724	26.5	3,789	1.7	4,119	8.7	4,794	16.4	21.0
1st Quarter Wages (annualized - $ mil.)	144.3	139.8	-3.2	184.8	32.2	168.1	-9.0	195.5	16.3	220.9	13.0	53.1
Payroll per Emp. 1st Q. (annualized)	36,418	47,486	30.4	49,613	4.5	44,374	-10.6	47,458	7.0	46,083	-2.9	26.5
Annual Payroll ($ mil.)	125.9	126.9	0.8	167.1	31.7	148.7	-11.0	175.5	18.0	184.0	4.8	46.2
Establishments - 100-249 Emp. Number	42	38	-9.5	30	-21.1	35	16.7	44	25.7	52	18.2	23.8
Mid-March Employment	6,382	6,003	-5.9	4,770	-20.5	5,391	13.0	6,889	27.8	7,991	16.0	25.2
1st Quarter Wages (annualized - $ mil.)	214.1	217.9	1.8	170.1	-21.9	236.0	38.7	304.7	29.1	379.4	24.5	77.2
Payroll per Emp. 1st Q. (annualized)	33,555	36,301	8.2	35,670	-1.7	43,784	22.7	44,223	1.0	47,474	7.4	41.5
Annual Payroll ($ mil.)	207.1	188.5	-9.0	170.3	-9.6	276.6	62.4	315.0	13.9	384.6	22.1	85.7
Establishments - 250-499 Emp. Number	13	17	30.8	(D)	-	11	-	19	72.7	21	10.5	61.5
Mid-March Employment	4,985	6,019	20.7	(D)	-	3,913	-	6,281	60.5	7,280	15.9	46.0
1st Quarter Wages (annualized - $ mil.)	133.0	214.9	61.6	(D)	-	105.0	-	225.5	114.7	283.2	25.6	113.0
Payroll per Emp. 1st Q. (annualized)	26,682	35,706	33.8	(D)	-	26,840	-	35,894	33.7	38,907	8.4	45.8
Annual Payroll ($ mil.)	134.1	203.5	51.7	(D)	-	100.1	-	267.7	167.5	300.3	12.1	123.8
Establishments - 500-999 Emp. Number	10	19	90.0	13	-31.6	10	-23.1	10	-	10	-	-
Mid-March Employment	6,923	13,237	91.2	9,874	-25.4	6,939	-29.7	6,771	-2.4	7,005	3.5	1.2
1st Quarter Wages (annualized - $ mil.)	290.8	523.8	80.1	362.6	-30.8	293.2	-19.1	219.1	-25.3	266.7	21.7	-8.3
Payroll per Emp. 1st Q. (annualized)	42,006	39,574	-5.8	36,720	-7.2	42,258	15.1	32,355	-23.4	38,073	17.7	-9.4
Annual Payroll ($ mil.)	257.3	483.9	88.0	349.4	-27.8	273.9	-21.6	214.9	-21.5	246.0	14.5	-4.4
Estab. - 1000 or More Emp. Number	4	2	-50.0	(D)	-	(D)	-	6	-	6	-	50.0
Mid-March Employment	6,322	(D)	-	(D)	-	(D)	-	8,396	-	8,017	-4.5	26.8
1st Quarter Wages (annualized - $ mil.)	223.4	(D)	-	(D)	-	(D)	-	252.6	-	297.2	17.7	33.0
Payroll per Emp. 1st Q. (annualized)	35,335	(D)	-	(D)	-	(D)	-	30,083	-	37,066	23.2	4.9
Annual Payroll ($ mil.)	228.1	(D)	-	(D)	-	(D)	-	259.0	-	267.4	3.3	17.2

Source: County Business Patterns, U.S. Department of Commerce, Washington, D.C., for 1990 through 1995. Payroll per employee is calculated using mid-March employment and 1st Quarter wages, annualized. Annual payroll, also shown, may not equal the annualized 1st Quarter wages. Columns headed by a percent sign (%) indicate change from the previous year. *na* stands for not available. The symbol (D) indicates that data are withheld by the source to avoid disclosure of competitive information. A dash (-) indicates that data are not available or cannot be calculated.

ESTABLISHMENTS
Number

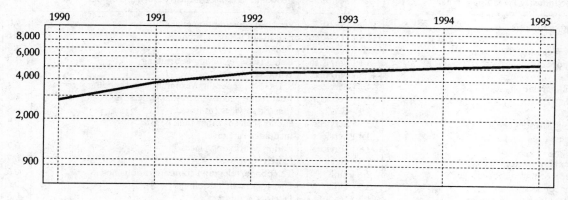

MID-MARCH EMPLOYMENT
Number

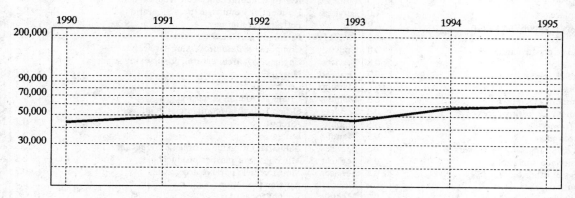

ANNUAL PAYROLL
$ million

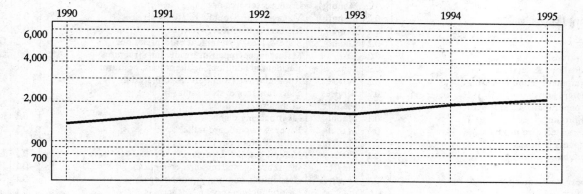

INPUTS AND OUTPUTS FOR ALL BANKING SECTORS - SICs 601, 602, 603, 608, and 609

Economic Sector or Industry Providing Inputs	%	Sector	Economic Sector or Industry Buying Outputs	%	Sector
Security & commodity brokers	12.9	Fin/R.E.	Personal consumption expenditures	59.0	
Banking	11.8	Fin/R.E.	Exports of goods & services	5.1	Foreign
Computer & data processing services	9.5	Services	Banking	4.6	Fin/R.E.
Real estate agents, operators, & lessors	8.1	Fin/R.E.	Retail trade, ex eating & drinking	3.0	Trade
Credit agencies other than banks	4.9	Fin/R.E.	Wholesale trade	2.3	Trade
Management & public relations services	4.1	Services	S/L Govt., general government nec, spending	2.1	S/L Govt
Advertising	3.9	Services	Real estate agents, operators, & lessors	1.5	Fin/R.E.
U.S. Postal Service	3.9	Gov't	Electric services (utilities)	0.8	Util.
Accounting, auditing & bookkeeping	3.7	Services	Credit agencies other than banks	0.8	Fin/R.E.
Business services nec	3.4	Services	Insurance carriers	0.7	Fin/R.E.
Legal services	2.8	Services	Eating & drinking places	0.7	Services
Federal Government enterprises nec	2.5	Gov't	Hotels	0.7	Services
Telephone/telegraph communications nec	2.4	Util.	Telephone/telegraph communications nec	0.6	Util.
Trucking & courier services, ex air	2.3	Util.	Owner-occupied dwellings	0.6	Fin/R.E.
Blankbooks, looseleaf binders & devices	1.7	Manufg.	Doctors & dentists	0.6	Services
Wholesale trade	1.6	Trade	Motor vehicles & passenger car bodies	0.4	Manufg.
Personnel supply services	1.6	Services	Trucking & courier services, ex air	0.4	Util.
Electric services (utilities)	1.5	Util.	Federal Government, nondefense, spending	0.4	Gov't
Warehousing & storage	1.4	Util.	New construction nec	0.3	Constr.
Air transportation	1.0	Util.	Repair & maintenance construction nec	0.3	Constr.
Eating & drinking places	1.0	Services	Residential 1 unit structures, nonfarm	0.3	Constr.
Sanitary services, steam supply, irrigation	0.9	Util.	Petroleum refining	0.3	Manufg.
Insurance carriers	0.9	Fin/R.E.	Railroads & related services	0.3	Util.
Repair & maintenance construction nec	0.8	Constr.	Computer & data processing services	0.3	Services
Hotels	0.8	Services	Engineering, architectural, & surveying services	0.3	Services
Detective & protective services	0.7	Services	Hospitals	0.3	Services
Commercial printing	0.6	Manufg.	Legal services	0.3	Services
Photographic equipment & supplies	0.6	Manufg.	Crude petroleum & natural gas	0.2	Mining
Research, development, & testing services	0.6	Services	Office, industrial/commercial buildings	0.2	Constr.
Manifold business forms	0.5	Manufg.	Aircraft	0.2	Manufg.
Paper & paperboard mills	0.5	Manufg.	Drugs	0.2	Manufg.
Automotive rental & leasing, without drivers	0.5	Services	Industrial inorganic & organic chemicals	0.2	Manufg.
Business & professional associations	0.5	Services	Miscellaneous plastics products, nec	0.2	Manufg.
Services to dwellings & other buildings	0.5	Services	Motor vehicle parts & accessories	0.2	Manufg.
Natural gas distribution	0.4	Util.	Air transportation	0.2	Util.
Magnetic & optical recording media	0.3	Manufg.	Freight forwarders	0.2	Util.
Manufacturing industries, nec	0.3	Manufg.	Water transportation	0.2	Util.
Periodicals	0.3	Manufg.	Security & commodity brokers	0.2	Fin/R.E.
Petroleum refining	0.3	Manufg.	Automotive rental & leasing, without drivers	0.2	Services
Electrical repair shops	0.3	Services	Automotive repair shops & services	0.2	Services
Book publishing	0.2	Manufg.	Business services nec	0.2	Services
Computer peripheral equipment	0.2	Manufg.	Management & public relations services	0.2	Services
Envelopes	0.2	Manufg.	Medical & health services nec	0.2	Services
Textile bags	0.2	Manufg.	State & local government enterprises nec	0.2	Gov't
Local & suburban transit	0.2	Util.	Maintenance/repair of residential structures	0.1	Constr.
Automotive repair shops & services	0.2	Services	Residential additions & alterations, nonfarm	0.1	Constr.
Miscellaneous equipment rental & leasing	0.2	Services	Apparel made from purchased materials	0.1	Manufg.
Miscellaneous repair shops	0.2	Services	Blast furnaces & steel mills	0.1	Manufg.
Die-cut paper & paperboard & cardboard	0.1	Manufg.	Commercial printing	0.1	Manufg.
Fabricated metal products, nec	0.1	Manufg.	Meat packing plants	0.1	Manufg.
Miscellaneous fabricated wire products	0.1	Manufg.	Paper & paperboard mills	0.1	Manufg.
Paperboard containers & boxes	0.1	Manufg.	Cable & other pay television services	0.1	Util.
Retail trade, ex eating & drinking	0.1	Trade	Natural gas distribution	0.1	Util.
Royalties	0.1	Fin/R.E.	Insurance agents, brokers, & services	0.1	Fin/R.E.
State & local government enterprises nec	0.1	Gov't	Accounting, auditing & bookkeeping	0.1	Services
			Motion picture services & theaters	0.1	Services
			Personnel supply services	0.1	Services
			Portrait photographic studios	0.1	Services
			U.S. Postal Service	0.1	Gov't

Source: Benchmark Input-Output Accounts for the U.S. Economy, 1992, U.S. Department of Commerce, Washington, D.C., November 1997. Data, as reported in the source, are organized by the 1987 SIC structure in use in 1992.

OCCUPATIONS EMPLOYED BY BANKING AND CLOSELY RELATED FUNCTIONS, NEC

Occupation	% of Total 1996	Change to 2006	Occupation	% of Total 1996	Change to 2006
Bank tellers	9.0	18.8	Clerical & administrative workers nec	2.6	16.4
General office clerks	7.7	0.1	Computer programmers	2.4	-4.2
Clerical supervisors & managers	6.3	16.4	Loan officers & counselors	2.3	16.4
Adjustment clerks	5.5	57.1	Sales & related workers nec	2.3	28.0
Cashiers	4.7	24.3	Systems analysts	2.3	86.2
Secretaries, except legal & medical	4.4	-7.7	Credit analysts	2.1	16.4
Bookkeeping, accounting, & auditing clerks	4.1	-6.9	Securities & financial sales workers	1.8	74.6
General managers & top executives	3.9	12.8	Data entry keyers, except composing	1.6	-6.9
Financial managers	3.4	16.4	Managers & administrators nec	1.6	15.3
Accountants & auditors	3.2	7.7	Computer operators, ex peripheral equipment	1.5	-30.2
Loan & credit clerks	2.9	17.5	Guards	1.1	4.8
Duplicating, mail, office machine operators	2.8	-24.4	Brokerage clerks	1.1	-2.7

Sources: *Industry-Occupation Matrix*, Bureau of Labor Statistics. These data relate to one or more 3-digit SIC industry groups rather than to a single 4-digit SIC. The change reported for each occupation to the year 2005 is a percent of growth or decline as estimated by the Bureau of Labor Statistics. The abbreviation *nec* stands for not elsewhere classified.

U.S. AND STATE DATA ON INDUSTRY REVENUES AND OTHER ACCOUNTS FOR 1992

State	No. of Estab.	Employ-ment	Payroll ($ mil.)	Revenues ($ mil.)	Empl./ Estab.	Revenue/ Estab. ($)	Payroll/ Estab. ($)	Revenue/ Empl. ($)	Payroll/ Empl. ($)
UNITED STATES	4,836	51,708	1,681.3	8,006.1	11	1,655,527	347,673	154,833	32,516
California	929	7,104	302.7	1,042.8	8	1,122,544	325,864	146,797	42,614
Colorado	83	-	(D)	(D)	(D)	(D)	(D)	(D)	(D)
Florida	310	2,508	76.0	366.1	8	1,180,816	245,187	145,954	30,306
Georgia	136	975	29.1	119.9	7	881,574	214,206	122,968	29,879
Illinois	662	5,152	139.5	442.1	8	667,810	210,745	85,809	27,079
Indiana	25	121	2.7	10.6	5	422,120	107,240	87,215	22,157
Maryland	75	-	(D)	(D)	(D)	(D)	(D)	(D)	(D)
Massachusetts	58	-	(D)	(D)	(D)	(D)	(D)	(D)	(D)
Michigan	59	342	6.3	26.3	6	445,102	107,102	76,787	18,477
Minnesota	49	1,717	51.5	263.7	35	5,382,510	1,050,531	153,607	29,980
Missouri	59	3,082	82.9	282.7	52	4,791,254	1,405,407	91,721	26,904
New Jersey	110	-	(D)	(D)	(D)	(D)	(D)	(D)	(D)
New York	555	9,871	407.5	1,242.8	18	2,239,294	734,229	125,905	41,282
North Carolina	62	-	(D)	(D)	(D)	(D)	(D)	(D)	(D)
Ohio	112	1,051	26.7	145.4	9	1,298,446	238,714	138,369	25,439
Pennsylvania	176	1,476	42.9	157.6	8	895,574	243,835	106,789	29,075
Tennessee	46	-	(D)	(D)	(D)	(D)	(D)	(D)	(D)
Texas	518	2,264	51.3	481.6	4	929,707	98,975	212,716	22,645
Virginia	74	887	27.6	178.7	12	2,415,324	372,527	201,504	31,079
Washington	106	792	25.5	135.5	7	1,278,057	240,528	171,053	32,192
Wisconsin	47	-	(D)	(D)	(D)	(D)	(D)	(D)	(D)

Source: 1992 Economic Census, U.S. Department of Commerce, Washington, D.C. This is the only table that shows revenue data as collected by the Bureau of the Census in an Economic Census. The symbol (D) indicates that data are withheld by the source to avoid disclosure of competitive information. A dash (-) indicates that data are not available or cannot be calculated.

STATE-BY-STATE DATA ON ESTABLISHMENTS, EMPLOYMENT, AND PAYROLL - 1994 AND 1995

State	1994					1995					% Change Empl.
	No. of Estab.	Employ-ment	Pay / Empl.	Payroll ($ mil.)	Pay / Estab.	No. of Estab.	Employ-ment	Pay / Empl.	Payroll ($ mil.)	Pay / Estab.	
Alabama	37	(D)	-	(D)	-	40	(D)	-	(D)	-	-
Alaska	9	(D)	-	(D)	-	8	33	25,697	0.9	110,375	-
Arizona	90	1,862	20,333	35.6	395,444	133	2,206	24,830	44.6	335,000	18.5
Arkansas	25	276	29,754	8.0	319,960	32	185	27,870	5.2	163,688	-33.0
California	969	7,425	36,449	289.2	298,427	977	7,082	37,971	296.8	303,800	-4.6
Colorado	86	1,653	27,284	52.3	608,465	89	1,614	38,208	60.8	682,764	-2.4
Connecticut	36	(D)	-	(D)	-	39	(D)	-	(D)	-	-
Delaware	7	716	31,860	25.0	3,575,714	10	474	37,620	17.6	1,763,700	-33.8
District of Columbia	37	227	42,026	8.8	237,919	42	250	40,656	9.3	220,619	10.1
Florida	298	3,576	40,591	118.9	399,081	304	3,891	43,424	143.9	473,260	8.8
Georgia	144	2,544	24,810	62.2	432,264	153	(D)	-	(D)	-	-
Hawaii	34	633	31,039	19.5	573,794	32	614	31,974	18.1	564,219	-3.0
Idaho	3	(D)	-	(D)	-	5	(D)	-	(D)	-	-
Illinois	613	5,861	29,125	173.2	282,597	629	7,399	32,477	223.9	355,973	26.2
Indiana	36	(D)	-	(D)	-	38	(D)	-	(D)	-	-
Iowa	6	(D)	-	(D)	-	7	(D)	-	(D)	-	-
Kansas	25	(D)	-	(D)	-	22	(D)	-	(D)	-	-
Kentucky	27	(D)	-	(D)	-	28	(D)	-	(D)	-	-
Louisiana	50	(D)	-	(D)	-	56	(D)	-	(D)	-	-
Maine	9	(D)	-	(D)	-	6	(D)	-	(D)	-	-
Maryland	88	(D)	-	(D)	-	96	532	35,526	18.9	196,583	-
Massachusetts	55	520	53,300	30.6	555,455	53	621	94,435	53.5	1,009,208	19.4
Michigan	62	(D)	-	(D)	-	63	(D)	-	(D)	-	-
Minnesota	46	(D)	-	(D)	-	41	(D)	-	(D)	-	-
Mississippi	22	55	13,600	0.8	34,682	26	57	15,509	1.1	43,115	3.6
Missouri	73	2,431	29,455	69.6	952,808	79	2,590	34,908	77.4	979,873	6.5
Montana	10	(D)	-	(D)	-	10	92	29,739	2.9	292,100	-
Nebraska	9	(D)	-	(D)	-	17	(D)	-	(D)	-	-
Nevada	24	(D)	-	(D)	-	29	565	25,678	12.7	438,897	-
New Hampshire	6	84	38,238	3.2	532,000	6	52	51,077	2.5	410,333	-38.1
New Jersey	141	2,918	32,631	106.8	757,298	160	2,217	41,315	82.9	518,219	-24.0
New Mexico	23	173	19,977	3.7	161,435	32	209	21,148	4.4	136,344	20.8
New York	568	8,559	43,859	379.2	667,523	570	9,178	50,394	435.8	764,616	7.2
North Carolina	58	(D)	-	(D)	-	63	(D)	-	(D)	-	-
North Dakota	6	(D)	-	(D)	-	7	(D)	-	(D)	-	-
Ohio	120	(D)	-	(D)	-	127	(D)	-	(D)	-	-
Oklahoma	72	(D)	-	(D)	-	88	(D)	-	(D)	-	-
Oregon	34	342	46,444	24.4	718,088	43	401	47,022	28.4	660,581	17.3
Pennsylvania	182	1,587	31,133	56.5	310,665	202	3,421	24,105	81.1	401,297	115.6
Rhode Island	8	49	58,204	2.6	320,250	8	33	31,758	2.0	249,625	-32.7
South Carolina	43	155	15,613	2.8	65,302	56	208	14,462	3.3	59,571	34.2
South Dakota	3	(D)	-	(D)	-	3	(D)	-	(D)	-	-
Tennessee	50	1,278	27,196	35.5	709,300	89	1,202	30,236	39.3	441,798	-5.9
Texas	572	3,007	18,453	56.4	98,607	574	2,822	22,319	59.3	103,334	-6.2
Utah	18	(D)	-	(D)	-	11	(D)	-	(D)	-	-
Vermont	1	(D)	-	(D)	-	1	(D)	-	(D)	-	-
Virginia	79	(D)	-	(D)	-	91	(D)	-	(D)	-	-
Washington	105	1,001	35,828	32.7	311,152	95	836	39,435	32.6	343,042	-16.5
West Virginia	1	(D)	-	(D)	-	1	(D)	-	(D)	-	-
Wisconsin	43	1,753	30,560	62.8	1,460,209	50	1,757	34,996	57.4	1,148,000	0.2
Wyoming	5	(D)	-	(D)	-	5	21	11,619	0.3	50,800	-

Source: County Business Patterns, U.S. Department of Commerce, Washington, D.C., for 1994 and 1995. Employment shown is for mid-March of the year shown. Payroll per employee is calculated by annualizing 1st Quarter payroll (not shown) and then dividing that value by mid-March employment. Dividing total annual payroll (columns 5 and 10) by employment, therefore, will *not* yield the payroll per employee figure (columns 4 and 9). The symbol (D) indicates that data are withheld by the source to avoid disclosure of competitive information. A dash (-) indicates that data are not available or cannot be calculated.

ESTABLISHMENTS 1995 - STATE AND REGIONAL CONCENTRATION

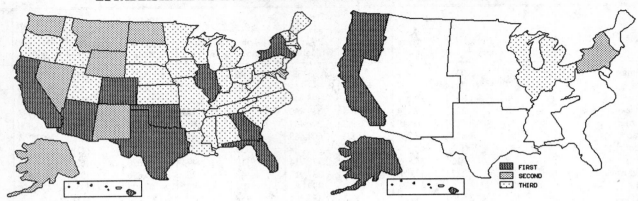

EMPLOYMENT 1995 - STATE AND REGIONAL CONCENTRATION

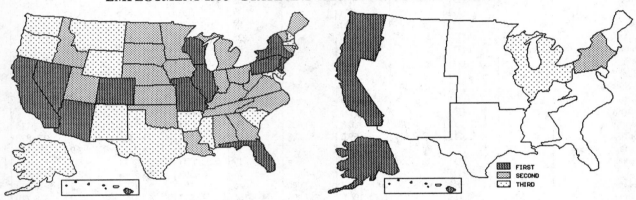

PAYROLL 1995 - STATE AND REGIONAL CONCENTRATION

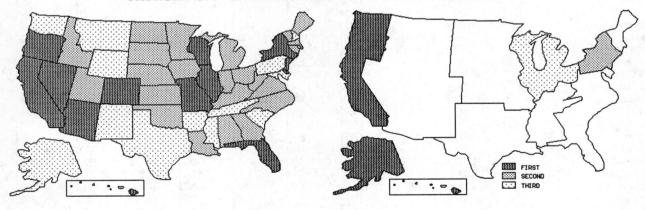

States with the darkest shading indicate those states which have proportionately more establishments, employment, or payrolls than would be indicated by the state's population. States with light shading are states with proportionately fewer establishments, less employment, and lower payrolls than population distribution. States shaded grey are within 15 percent of the state's population proportion in these catego-ries. States for which no data are available are shown as average (grey). *Regions* are shaded to indicate absolute rank in the category. If no data for the category are available, establishment counts are used to shade the regions. Source of the data is the table on the facing page.

LEADING COMPANIES - SIC 6091 - Nondeposit Trust Facilities

Number shown: **46**   Total sales/assets ($ mil): **165,417**   Total employment (000): **45.6**

Company Name	Address				CEO Name	Phone	Co. Type	Sales/Assets ($ mil)	Empl. (000)
PNC Bank Corp.	249 5th Ave.	Pittsburgh	PA	15222	Thomas H. O'Brien	412-762-1553	P	73,260 TA	25.4
Mercantile Trust Company N.A.	PO Box 387	St. Louis	MO	63166	John W. McClure	314-425-2600	S	28,702 TA	0.2
First of America Trust Co.	301 S.W. Adams St.	Peoria	IL	61602	James H. Hawkins	309-655-5895	S	15,638 TA	0.6
New England Trust Co.	144 Westminister St.	Providence	RI	02903	Ralph Fletcher	401-751-4600	S	15,638 TA	0.6
Imperial Trust Co.	201 N. Figueroa St.	Los Angeles	CA	90012	Jai Sondhi	213-627-5600	S	9,300 TA	<0.1
Charles Schwab Trust Co.	101 Montgomery St.	San Francisco	CA	94104	John Coghlan	415-403-5999	S	8,600 TA	<0.1
U.S. Trust Corp.	114 West 47th St.	New York	NY	10036	H. Marshall Schwarz	212-852-1000	P	3,815 TA	1.5
Custodial Trust Co.	101 Carnegie Ctr.	Princeton	NJ	08540	Ronald D. Watson	609-951-2300	S	1,955 TA*	<0.1
Harris Trust Company of California	601 S. Figueroa St.	Los Angeles	CA	90017	Steven R. Rothbloom	213-239-0600	S	1,400*	<0.1
First American Financial Corp.	114 East 5th St.	Santa Ana	CA	92701	Parker S. Kennedy	714-558-3211	P	1,140 TA	11.6
Piper Trust Co.	222 S. 9th St.	Minneapolis	MN	55402	E. Peter Gillette	612-342-6290	S	910 TA	<0.1
Pennsylvania Trust Co.	Five Radnor Corporate Center #B	Radnor	PA	19087	Richardson T. Merriman	610-975-4300	S	750 TA	<0.1
Huntington Trust Company of Florida N.A.	8889 Pelican Bay Blvd.	Naples	FL	33963	Gail S.T. Webster	941-594-1400	S	720 TA	<0.1
Capital Guardian Trust Co.	333 S. Hope St.	Los Angeles	CA	90071	Robert Ronus	213-486-9200	S	700 TA	0.3
Austin Trust Co.	100 Congress Ave.	Austin	TX	78701	William J. Hudspeth Jr.	512-478-2121	R	350 TA	<0.1
Glenwood Investment Corp.	PO Box A3958	Chicago	IL	60690	Frank C. Meyer	312-443-8414	R	350 TA*	<0.1
Participants Trust Co.	55 Water St.	New York	NY	10041	John J. Robinson	212-412-6530	R	300 TA	0.1
Boatmen's Trust Co.	100 N. Broadway	St. Louis	MO	63102	Martin E. Galt III	314-466-6000	S	285 TA	1.2
Firstar Trust Co.	PO Box 2054	Milwaukee	WI	53201	Robert L. Webster	414-765-5000	S	253 TA	0.5
Atlantic Bank and Trust Co.	200 State St.	Boston	MA	02109	Nicholas W. Lazares	617-330-8585	P	231 TA	<0.1
GEMISYS Corp.	3605 S. Teller St.	Lakewood	CO	80235	Darrall E. Robbins	303-969-6000	R	220 TA*	0.1
LaSalle National Trust N.A.	PO Box 729	Chicago	IL	60690	James B. Wynsma	312-904-2017	S	200 TA	0.3
First Commercial Trust Company N.A.	PO Box 1471	Little Rock	AR	72203	Michael A. O'Brien	501-371-7000	S	140 TA*	<0.1
Investors Fiduciary Trust Co.	127 W. 10th St.	Kansas City	MO	64105	Thomas McCrossan	816-474-8786	S	87 TA	0.3
Trust Company of Washington	PO Box 3096	Bellevue	WA	98009	William H. Sperber	206-637-1856	R	85 TA	<0.1
American Stock Transfer and Trust Co.	40 Wall St.	New York	NY	10005	Michael Karfunkel	212-936-5100	R	66 OR*	0.2
Columbian Financial Corp.	4701 W. 110th St.	Overland Park	KS	66211	Sam McCaffree	913-491-1061	R	60 TA	<0.1
Marshall and Ilsley Trust Co.	1000 N. Water St.	Milwaukee	WI	53202	Morry O. Birnbaum	414-765-8200	S	47 TA	0.3
First Trust Corp.	717 17th St.	Denver	CO	80202	Gordon Rockafellow	303-293-2223	S	35 TA	0.6
Bank One Wisconsin Trust Company N.A.	PO Box 1308	Milwaukee	WI	53201	Howard C. Williams	414-765-2800	S	35 TA	0.2
Huntington Trust Company N.A.	41 S. High St.	Columbus	OH	43287	James Buskirk	614-463-4225	S	24 TA	0.3
Key Trust Company of Alaska	101 W. Benson Blvd.	Anchorage	AK	99503	Vernon E. Sayles	907-564-0400	S	24 TA*	<0.1
Fleet Trust Co.	45 East Ave.	Rochester	NY	14604	Sandra M. Democh	716-546-9085	S	24 TA	0.2

Company type codes: P - Public, R - Private, S - Subsidiary, D - Division, J - Joint Venture, A - Affiliate, G - Group. If the dollar values shown are not sales, the following codes apply: TA - Total Assets; OR - Operating Revenues; GB - Gross Billings. * - estimated dollar value. < - less than. *na* - not available.

Continued on next page.

LEADING COMPANIES - SIC 6091 - Nondeposit Trust Facilities

Continued

Company Name	Address				CEO Name	Phone	Co. Type	Sales/Assets ($ mil)	Empl. (000)
Sound Trust Co.	PO Box 1221	Tacoma	WA	98401	R.P. Jones	206-572-5339	S	22 TA*	<0.1
IAA Trust Co.	PO Box 2901	Bloomington	IL	61702	Gary Mede	309-557-3222	S	17 TA	<0.1
Kentucky Home Capital Corp.	450 S. 3rd St.	Louisville	KY	40202	James W. Baxter III	502-585-6104	S	8 TA	<0.1
M and I Marshall and Ilsley Trust Company of Arizona	1 E. Camelback Rd.	Phoenix	AZ	85012	George H. Isbell	602-230-0985	S	5 TA	<0.1
North American Trust Co.	PO Box 84419	San Diego	CA	92138	L. Mark Fingerl	619-237-5378	R	5 TA	0.1
Amcore Trust Co.	501 7th St.	Rockford	IL	61110	Glen Wilson	815-961-7119	S	4 TA	<0.1
AmalgaTrust Company Inc.	1 W. Monroe St.	Chicago	IL	60603	Eugene P. Heytow	312-822-3162	S	3 TA	<0.1
Colonial Trust Co.	5336 N. 19th Ave.	Phoenix	AZ	85015	John Johnson	602-242-3233	P	3 TA*	<0.1
Key Trust Company of the West	600 S. Cherry St.	Denver	CO	80222	James D. Sparks	303-320-5000	S	2 TA	<0.1
First Midwest Trust Company N.A.	121 N. Chicago St.	Joliet	IL	60432	Robert P. O'Meara	815-740-7700	S	2 TA	<0.1
Constitution Trust Co.	PO Box 1049	Dover	NH	03820	John D. Griffiths	603-749-0303	S	1 TA	<0.1
Security Trust Co.	925 B. St.	San Diego	CA	92101	J. Paul Spring	619-239-3091	S	1 TA	<0.1
First Trust of MidAmerica	410 W. 8th St.	Kansas City	MO	64105	Kevin R. Ingrem	816-221-6988	R	1 TA	<0.1

Source: *Ward's Business Directory of U.S. Private and Public Companies*, 1996. Company type codes: P - Public, R - Private, S - Subsidiary, D - Division, J - Joint Venture, A - Affiliate, G - Group. If the dollar values shown are not sales, the following codes apply: TA - Total Assets; OR - Operating Revenues; GB - Gross Billings. * - estimated dollar value. < - less than; *na* - not available.

LEADING COMPANIES - SIC 6099 - Functions Related to Deposit Banking

Number shown: **41**   Total sales/assets ($ mil): **105,205**   Total employment (000): **182.4**

Company Name	Address				CEO Name	Phone	Co. Type	Sales/Assets ($ mil)	Empl. (000)
AT&T Corp.	32 Ave. of the Amer.	New York	NY	10013	C. Michael Armstrong	212-387-5400	P	51,319 OR	130.0
First Bank System Inc.	PO Box 522	Minneapolis	MN	55480	John F. Grundhofer	612-973-1111	P	36,489 TA	12.0
Student Loan Corp.	PO Box 22944	Pittsford	NY	14692	Stephen C. Biklen	716-248-7187	P	5,365 TA	0.8
First Data Merchant Services	265 Broad Hollow Rd.	Melville	NY	11747	Roger Peirce	516-843-6000	S	4,100 TA	3.0
HUBCO Inc.	1000 MacArthur Blvd.	Mahwah	NJ	07430	Kenneth T. Neilson	201-236-2600	P	3,116 TA	1.0
Viad Corp.	1850 N. Central Ave.	Phoenix	AZ	85077	Robert H. Bohannon	602-207-4000	P	2,263	24.8
BTI Services Inc.	6420 S. Point Pkwy.	Jacksonville	FL	32216	David Graham	904-281-7100	S	840 TA	0.5
Prebon Yamane	101 Hudson St.	Jersey City	NJ	07302	Dan Rutter	201-557-5000	R	330 TA*	0.2
Comdata Holdings Corp.	5301 Maryland Way	Brentwood	TN	37027	Tony Holcombe	615-370-7000	S	286 TA*	1.9
Maxcor Financial Group Inc.	2 World Trade Ctr.	New York	NY	10048	Gilbert D. Scharf	212-748-7000	P	179 OR	0.7
ACE Cash Express Inc.	1231 Greenway Dr.	Irving	TX	75038	Donald H. Neustadt	972-550-5000	P	115 TA	1.5
Western Union Financial Services Inc.	1 Mack Centre Dr.	Paramus	NJ	07652	E.J. Fuhrman	201-986-5100	S	100 TA*	2.0

Company type codes: P - Public, R - Private, S - Subsidiary, D - Division, J - Joint Venture, A - Affiliate, G - Group. If the dollar values shown are not sales, the following codes apply: TA - Total Assets; OR - Operating Revenues; GB - Gross Billings. * - estimated dollar value. < - less than. *na* - not available.

Continued on next page.

LEADING COMPANIES - SIC 6099 - Functions Related to Deposit Banking
Continued

Company Name	Address				CEO Name	Phone	Co. Type	Sales/Assets ($ mil)	Empl. (000)
Maestro Latin America Inc.	801 Brickell Ave.	Miami	FL	33131	Richard Child	305-539-2330	S	84 TA*	<0.1
Star System Inc.	401 W. A St.	San Diego	CA	92101	Ronald V. Congemi	619-234-4774	R	70 TA*	<0.1
Ohio Credit Union League	1201 Dublin Rd.	Columbus	OH	43215	Gary B. Gores	614-486-2917	R	59 TA*	<0.1
BHC Securities Inc.	2005 Market St.	Philadelphia	PA	19103	William T. Spane Jr.	215-636-3000	S	56 OR	0.4
Checkfree Corp.	PO Box 897	Columbus	OH	43216	Peter J. Kight	614-898-6000	P	49	0.4
Armored Transport of California Inc.	PO Box 15060	Los Angeles	CA	90015	Gregory W. Irvin	213-383-3611	S	45 OR	0.5
Concord Computing Corp.	2525 Horizon Lake Dr.	Memphis	TN	38133	Dan M. Palmer	901-371-8000	S	45 TA	0.4
Noonan, Astley and Pearce Inc.	10 Exchange Pl.	Jersey City	NJ	07302	Joseph Sciametta	201-200-4500	S	37 TA*	0.3
Pay-O-Matic Corp.	160 Oak Dr.	Syosset	NY	11791	Rayman Mustafa	516-496-4900	P	36 TA	0.6
Electronic Transaction Corp.	19803 N. Creek Pkwy.	Bothell	WA	98011	Timothy C. Birk	425-483-2500	S	30 TA*	0.3
Plus System Inc.	PO Box 5060	Denver	CO	80217	David Brooks	303-486-7587	R	25 TA	<0.1
Telecheck Services Inc.	1099 S.W. Columbia St.	Portland	OR	97201	Steve Shaper	503-222-7222	S	23 TA*	<0.1
HONOR Technologies Inc.	2600 Lake Lucien Dr.	Maitland	FL	32751	Thomas O. Bennion	407-875-2500	R	23 TA*	0.3
American Clearing House Association	2224 W. Northern Ave.	Phoenix	AZ	85021	Holly Merrill	602-995-6900	R	22 TA	<0.1
Game Financial Corp.	PO Box 26008	Minneapolis	MN	55426	Gary A. Dachis	612-544-0062	P	19 TA	0.2
Michigan Safe Deposit Co.	30555 Northwestern Hwy	Farmington Hills	MI	48334	Doug Hexer	810-626-8998	R	16 TA	<0.1
Financial Information Technologies Inc.	201 E. North East Kennedy Blvd.	Tampa	FL	33602	Robert Christensen	813-273-9065	R	12 TA*	<0.1
Foreign Exchange Ltd.	415 Stockton St.	San Francisco	CA	94108	Randy Roberts	415-677-5107	S	11 TA	<0.1
Litton Loan Servicing Inc.	5373 W. Alabama St.	Houston	TX	77056	Larry Litton Sr.	713-960-9676	S	11 TA*	<0.1
National Payment Corp.	100 W. Kennedy Blvd.	Tampa	FL	33602	Jefferson Harkins	813-222-0333	R	9 TA*	<0.1
Cash Station Inc.	225 N. Michigan Ave.	Chicago	IL	60601	Stephen S. Cole	312-977-1150	R	8 TA*	<0.1
GulfNet Inc.	2250 Gause Blvd. E.	Slidell	LA	70461	Del R. Tonguette	504-643-0300	R	4 TA	<0.1
Balfour Investors Inc.	620 5th Ave.	New York	NY	10020	Harry Freund	212-489-7077	R	2	<0.1
Cirrus System Inc.	1 Westbrook Corp. Ctr.	Westchester	IL	60154	G. Henry Mundt III	708-449-4000	S	2 TA*	<0.1
General Credit Corp.	370 Lexington Ave.	New York	NY	10017	Gerald Nimberg	212-697-4441	P	2 TA*	<0.1
TeleCheck Inc.	3500 188th St. S.W.	Lynnwood	WA	98037	Terry Crane	425-775-3220	S	1 TA*	<0.1
Money Access Service Corp.	25209 Country Club Blvd.	North Olmsted	OH	44070	Steven E. Dawe	216-779-2100	S	1 TA	0.1
Zurich Depository Corp.	1165 Northern Blvd.	Manhasset	NY	11030	James Holleran	516-365-4756	R	1 TA	<0.1
Kansas Electronic Transfer System Inc.	1919 N. Amidon St.	Wichita	KS	67203	Richard Schopf	316-838-4411	R	0 TA	<0.1

Source: Ward's Business Directory of U.S. Private and Public Companies, 1996. Company type codes: P - Public, R - Private, S - Subsidiary, D - Division, J - Joint Venture, A - Affiliate, G - Group. If the dollar values shown are not sales, the following codes apply: TA - Total Assets; OR - Operating Revenues; GB - Gross Billings. * - estimated dollar value. < - less than; na - not available.

SIC 6110

FEDERAL & FEDERALLY SPONSORED CREDIT

This SIC groups federal agencies and those sponsored by the federal government engaged in guaranteeing, insuring, or making loans. Federally sponsored credit agencies are established under federal legislation but are not regarded as part of the federal government; they are often owned by their members or borrowers. The category includes banks for cooperatives, the Commodity Credit Corporation, Export-Import Bank, Farmers Home Administration, Federal Home Mortgage Corporation, Federal Intermediate Credit Bank, federal land banks, Federal National Mortgage Association, Government National Mortgage Association, National Consumer Cooperative Bank, Rural Electrification Administration, Student Loan Marketing Association, and the Synthetic Fuels Corporation.

ESTABLISHMENTS, EMPLOYMENT, AND PAYROLL

	1990	1991		1992		1993		1994		1995		% change 90-95
		Value	%	Value	%	Value	%	Value	%	Value	%	
All Establishments	577	787	36.4	828	5.2	1,375	66.1	1,339	-2.6	1,344	0.4	132.9
Mid-March Employment	13,529	16,147	19.4	15,351	-4.9	22,271	45.1	23,498	5.5	23,665	0.7	74.9
1st Quarter Wages (annualized - $ mil.)	422.3	521.6	23.5	507.0	-2.8	1,014.7	100.2	1,150.1	13.3	1,291.7	12.3	205.8
Payroll per Emp. 1st Q. (annualized)	31,218	32,304	3.5	33,025	2.2	45,561	38.0	48,946	7.4	54,583	11.5	74.8
Annual Payroll ($ mil.)	396.7	498.2	25.6	485.0	-2.6	909.9	87.6	1,007.0	10.7	1,103.3	9.6	178.1
Establishments - 1-4 Emp. Number	220	337	53.2	396	17.5	664	67.7	642	-3.3	679	5.8	208.6
Mid-March Employment	588	(D)	-	1,077	-	1,857	72.4	1,831	-1.4	1,840	0.5	212.9
1st Quarter Wages (annualized - $ mil.)	16.8	(D)	-	31.0	-	58.2	87.8	58.0	-0.3	63.6	9.6	278.2
Payroll per Emp. 1st Q. (annualized)	28,592	(D)	-	28,769	-	31,341	8.9	31,688	1.1	34,559	9.1	20.9
Annual Payroll ($ mil.)	19.3	(D)	-	31.0	-	62.1	100.5	59.7	-3.9	125.6	110.5	551.3
Establishments - 5-9 Emp. Number	160	238	48.8	248	4.2	424	71.0	409	-3.5	377	-7.8	135.6
Mid-March Employment	1,050	1,561	48.7	1,600	2.5	2,739	71.2	2,664	-2.7	2,462	-7.6	134.5
1st Quarter Wages (annualized - $ mil.)	28.0	43.1	54.2	47.7	10.7	90.9	90.5	95.9	5.4	98.3	2.6	251.5
Payroll per Emp. 1st Q. (annualized)	26,636	27,621	3.7	29,840	8.0	33,203	11.3	35,983	8.4	39,932	11.0	49.9
Annual Payroll ($ mil.)	27.7	44.1	59.6	48.4	9.6	84.9	75.5	86.4	1.8	85.7	-0.8	209.9
Establishments - 10-19 Emp. Number	83	129	55.4	98	-24.0	167	70.4	165	-1.2	168	1.8	102.4
Mid-March Employment	1,121	1,654	47.5	1,250	-24.4	2,092	67.4	2,098	0.3	2,124	1.2	89.5
1st Quarter Wages (annualized - $ mil.)	32.7	50.2	53.6	37.8	-24.6	80.6	113.1	82.6	2.5	93.7	13.4	186.8
Payroll per Emp. 1st Q. (annualized)	29,128	30,326	4.1	30,250	-0.3	38,512	27.3	39,373	2.2	44,092	12.0	51.4
Annual Payroll ($ mil.)	33.2	48.2	44.9	40.4	-16.1	69.2	71.2	74.6	7.8	80.9	8.4	143.4
Establishments - 20-49 Emp. Number	64	44	-31.3	51	15.9	75	47.1	72	-4.0	71	-1.4	10.9
Mid-March Employment	1,956	1,224	-37.4	1,394	13.9	2,011	44.3	2,002	-0.4	1,999	-0.1	2.2
1st Quarter Wages (annualized - $ mil.)	72.8	49.1	-32.5	61.1	24.3	82.1	34.4	91.8	11.9	98.8	7.6	35.6
Payroll per Emp. 1st Q. (annualized)	37,243	40,150	7.8	43,825	9.2	40,829	-6.8	45,874	12.4	49,421	7.7	32.7
Annual Payroll ($ mil.)	61.4	48.6	-20.8	53.7	10.6	70.4	31.0	77.9	10.6	82.2	5.5	33.9
Establishments - 50-99 Emp. Number	24	14	-41.7	10	-28.6	17	70.0	(D)	-	15	-	-37.5
Mid-March Employment	1,584	(D)	-	675	-	1,190	76.3	(D)	-	1,099	-	-30.6
1st Quarter Wages (annualized - $ mil.)	54.1	(D)	-	22.6	-	54.4	141.3	(D)	-	52.5	-	-3.0
Payroll per Emp. 1st Q. (annualized)	34,167	(D)	-	33,416	-	45,738	36.9	(D)	-	47,782	-	39.8
Annual Payroll ($ mil.)	46.5	(D)	-	20.7	-	51.9	151.0	(D)	-	47.0	-	0.9
Establishments - 100-249 Emp. Number	16	9	-43.8	9	-	13	44.4	18	38.5	18	-	12.5
Mid-March Employment	2,722	1,715	-37.0	1,679	-2.1	2,397	42.8	3,162	31.9	3,050	-3.5	12.0
1st Quarter Wages (annualized - $ mil.)	84.1	66.2	-21.2	56.7	-14.4	119.1	110.1	163.6	37.3	195.7	19.6	132.7
Payroll per Emp. 1st Q. (annualized)	30,892	38,615	25.0	33,768	-12.6	49,695	47.2	51,724	4.1	64,148	24.0	107.7
Annual Payroll ($ mil.)	80.1	64.8	-19.0	51.6	-20.5	113.0	119.2	144.8	28.1	140.2	-3.2	75.1
Establishments - 250-499 Emp. Number	7	9	28.6	10	11.1	5	-50.0	7	40.0	6	-14.3	-14.3
Mid-March Employment	2,452	3,174	29.4	3,818	20.3	1,737	-54.5	2,723	56.8	1,977	-27.4	-19.4
1st Quarter Wages (annualized - $ mil.)	88.2	92.4	4.7	100.8	9.1	96.7	-4.1	153.7	59.0	117.4	-23.6	33.1
Payroll per Emp. 1st Q. (annualized)	35,985	29,105	-19.1	26,410	-9.3	55,650	110.7	56,433	1.4	59,405	5.3	65.1
Annual Payroll ($ mil.)	80.7	94.0	16.4	107.7	14.6	79.9	-25.8	121.9	52.6	78.9	-35.3	-2.3
Establishments - 500-999 Emp. Number	3	6	100.0	6	-	7	16.7	7	-	7	-	133.3
Mid-March Employment	2,056	3,841	86.8	3,858	0.4	4,091	6.0	4,377	7.0	4,511	3.1	119.4
1st Quarter Wages (annualized - $ mil.)	45.6	130.8	186.8	149.2	14.1	142.3	-4.7	210.1	47.7	173.3	-17.5	279.9
Payroll per Emp. 1st Q. (annualized)	22,189	34,063	53.5	38,685	13.6	34,772	-10.1	48,011	38.1	38,415	-20.0	73.1
Annual Payroll ($ mil.)	47.8	115.1	140.6	131.6	14.4	127.0	-3.5	190.9	50.3	143.9	-24.6	200.9
Estab. - 1000 or More Emp. Number	-	1	-	-	-	3	-	(D)	-	3	-	-
Mid-March Employment	-	(D)	-	-	-	4,157	-	(D)	-	4,603	-	-
1st Quarter Wages (annualized - $ mil.)	-	(D)	-	-	-	290.4	-	(D)	-	398.5	-	-
Payroll per Emp. 1st Q. (annualized)	(D)	(D)	-	-	-	69,862	-	(D)	-	86,567	-	-
Annual Payroll ($ mil.)	-	(D)	-	-	-	251.4	-	(D)	-	319.1	-	-

Source: County Business Patterns, U.S. Department of Commerce, Washington, D.C., for 1990 through 1995. Payroll per employee is calculated using mid-March employment and 1st Quarter wages, annualized. Annual payroll, also shown, may not equal the annualized 1st Quarter wages. Columns headed by a percent sign (%) indicate change from the previous year. *na* stands for not available. The symbol (D) indicates that data are withheld by the source to avoid disclosure of competitive information. A dash (-) indicates that data are not available or cannot be calculated.

ESTABLISHMENTS
Number

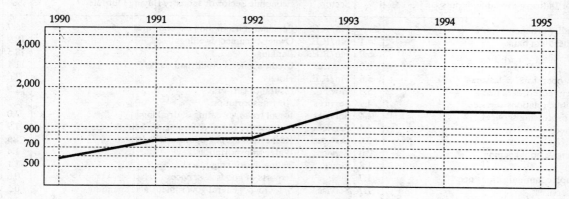

MID-MARCH EMPLOYMENT
Number

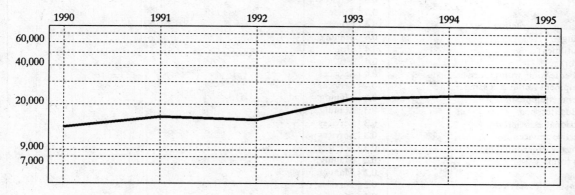

ANNUAL PAYROLL
$ million

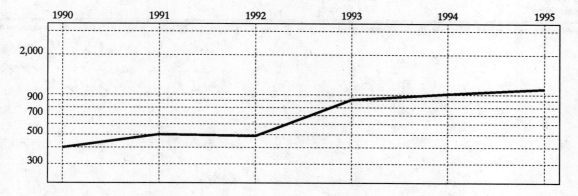

INPUTS AND OUTPUTS FOR CREDIT AGENCIES OTHER THAN BANKS - SICs 606, 611, 614-16

Economic Sector or Industry Providing Inputs	%	Sector	Economic Sector or Industry Buying Outputs	%	Sector
Security & commodity brokers	27.5	Fin/R.E.	Personal consumption expenditures	36.7	
Credit agencies other than banks	14.1	Fin/R.E.	Owner-occupied dwellings	18.9	Fin/R.E.
Banking	6.9	Fin/R.E.	Banking	13.5	Fin/R.E.
Advertising	6.0	Services	Credit agencies other than banks	11.1	Fin/R.E.
Real estate agents, operators, & lessors	5.6	Fin/R.E.	Hotels	3.6	Services
Federal Government enterprises nec	5.3	Gov't	Insurance carriers	2.9	Fin/R.E.
Management & public relations services	4.9	Services	Air transportation	2.1	Util.
Computer & data processing services	4.4	Services	Retail trade, ex eating & drinking	2.0	Trade
Business services nec	3.4	Services	Automotive rental & leasing, without drivers	1.9	Services
Legal services	2.6	Services	Real estate agents, operators, & lessors	1.5	Fin/R.E.
Accounting, auditing & bookkeeping	2.0	Services	Water transportation	1.4	Util.
U.S. Postal Service	1.8	Gov't	Eating & drinking places	1.1	Services
Telephone/telegraph communications nec	1.7	Util.	Exports of goods & services	0.8	Foreign
Personnel supply services	1.7	Services	S/L Govt., general government nec, spending	0.5	S/L Govt
Trucking & courier services, ex air	1.2	Util.	Wholesale trade	0.3	Trade
Research, development, & testing services	0.8	Services	Meat animals	0.2	Agric.
Insurance carriers	0.7	Fin/R.E.	Automotive repair shops & services	0.2	Services
Eating & drinking places	0.7	Services	Feed grains	0.1	Agric.
Air transportation	0.6	Util.			
Hotels	0.6	Services			
Wholesale trade	0.5	Trade			
Repair & maintenance construction nec	0.4	Constr.			
Commercial printing	0.4	Manufg.			
Electric services (utilities)	0.4	Util.			
Warehousing & storage	0.4	Util.			
Automotive rental & leasing, without drivers	0.4	Services			
Miscellaneous equipment rental & leasing	0.4	Services			
Computer peripheral equipment	0.3	Manufg.			
Manufacturing industries, nec	0.3	Manufg.			
Business & professional associations	0.3	Services			
Detective & protective services	0.3	Services			
Services to dwellings & other buildings	0.3	Services			
Manifold business forms	0.2	Manufg.			
Petroleum refining	0.2	Manufg.			
Automotive repair shops & services	0.2	Services			
Book publishing	0.1	Manufg.			
Paper & paperboard mills	0.1	Manufg.			
Periodicals	0.1	Manufg.			
Photographic equipment & supplies	0.1	Manufg.			
Local & suburban transit	0.1	Util.			
Miscellaneous repair shops	0.1	Services			

Source: Benchmark Input-Output Accounts for the U.S. Economy, 1992, U.S. Department of Commerce, Washington, D.C., November 1997. Data, as reported in the source, are organized by the 1987 SIC structure in use in 1992.

OCCUPATIONS EMPLOYED BY FEDERAL AND BUSINESS CREDIT INSTITUTIONS

Occupation	% of Total 1996	Change to 2006	Occupation	% of Total 1996	Change to 2006
Bill & account collectors	11.1	46.3	Credit analysts	3.6	23.7
Adjustment clerks	6.8	67.0	Accountants & auditors	2.9	14.5
Loan officers & counselors	6.8	23.7	Securities & financial sales workers	2.9	85.5
Secretaries, except legal & medical	6.1	-1.9	Correspondence clerks	2.4	23.7
Loan & credit clerks	5.3	24.8	Managers & administrators nec	1.6	22.5
Clerical supervisors & managers	5.0	23.7	Computer programmers	1.6	1.8
General managers & top executives	4.9	19.8	Systems analysts	1.4	97.9
General office clerks	4.9	6.4	Receptionists & information clerks	1.4	23.6
Bookkeeping, accounting, & auditing clerks	4.4	-1.1	Credit checkers	1.3	-19.7
Financial managers	4.4	23.7	Data entry keyers, except composing	1.3	-1.1
Management support workers nec	3.7	23.7	Sales & related workers nec	1.2	36.0

Sources: Industry-Occupation Matrix, Bureau of Labor Statistics. These data relate to one or more 3-digit SIC industry groups rather than to a single 4-digit SIC. The change reported for each occupation to the year 2005 is a percent of growth or decline as estimated by the Bureau of Labor Statistics. The abbreviation *nec* stands for not elsewhere classified.

U.S. AND STATE DATA ON INDUSTRY REVENUES AND OTHER ACCOUNTS FOR 1992

State	No. of Estab.	Employ- ment	Payroll ($ mil.)	Revenues ($ mil.)	Empl./ Estab.	Revenue/ Estab. ($)	Payroll/ Estab. ($)	Revenue/ Empl. ($)	Payroll/ Empl. ($)
UNITED STATES	1,349	21,298	833.1	28,092.0	16	20,824,313	617,532	1,318,997	39,114
Alabama	33	-	(D)	(D)	(D)	(D)	(D)	(D)	(D)
Arizona	5	-	(D)	(D)	(D)	(D)	(D)	(D)	(D)
Arkansas	23	216	4.7	33.3	9	1,446,087	205,609	153,981	21,894
California	64	1,201	48.2	1,791.4	19	27,990,953	753,484	1,491,608	40,152
Colorado	25	-	(D)	(D)	(D)	(D)	(D)	(D)	(D)
Connecticut	3	-	(D)	(D)	(D)	(D)	(D)	(D)	(D)
Delaware	2	-	(D)	(D)	(D)	(D)	(D)	(D)	(D)
District of Columbia	4	-	(D)	(D)	(D)	(D)	(D)	(D)	(D)
Florida	32	-	(D)	(D)	(D)	(D)	(D)	(D)	(D)
Georgia	42	643	26.6	1,452.6	15	34,586,857	634,429	2,259,173	41,440
Hawaii	1	-	(D)	(D)	(D)	(D)	(D)	(D)	(D)
Idaho	19	-	(D)	(D)	(D)	(D)	(D)	(D)	(D)
Illinois	46	-	(D)	(D)	(D)	(D)	(D)	(D)	(D)
Indiana	52	-	(D)	(D)	(D)	(D)	(D)	(D)	(D)
Iowa	34	-	(D)	(D)	(D)	(D)	(D)	(D)	(D)
Kansas	34	-	(D)	(D)	(D)	(D)	(D)	(D)	(D)
Kentucky	54	402	14.4	346.0	7	6,408,111	266,981	860,791	35,863
Louisiana	27	108	3.5	17.4	4	642,593	129,407	160,648	32,352
Maine	5	-	(D)	(D)	(D)	(D)	(D)	(D)	(D)
Maryland	16	-	(D)	(D)	(D)	(D)	(D)	(D)	(D)
Massachusetts	5	-	(D)	(D)	(D)	(D)	(D)	(D)	(D)
Michigan	36	278	8.3	58.2	8	1,616,333	231,028	209,309	29,917
Minnesota	44	940	52.0	837.2	21	19,027,136	1,180,795	890,632	55,271
Mississippi	38	110	3.3	21.9	3	576,079	86,184	199,009	29,773
Missouri	42	510	9.6	178.0	12	4,238,738	227,524	349,073	18,737
Montana	11	-	(D)	(D)	(D)	(D)	(D)	(D)	(D)
Nebraska	34	-	(D)	(D)	(D)	(D)	(D)	(D)	(D)
Nevada	3	-	(D)	(D)	(D)	(D)	(D)	(D)	(D)
New Hampshire	2	-	(D)	(D)	(D)	(D)	(D)	(D)	(D)
New Jersey	6	109	4.0	43.0	18	7,168,333	662,333	394,587	36,459
New Mexico	9	60	1.9	12.5	7	1,388,000	216,333	208,200	32,450
New York	32	364	10.7	128.6	11	4,018,594	333,750	353,283	29,341
North Carolina	84	-	(D)	(D)	(D)	(D)	(D)	(D)	(D)
North Dakota	28	341	9.3	47.7	12	1,704,071	331,107	139,924	27,188
Ohio	53	-	(D)	(D)	(D)	(D)	(D)	(D)	(D)
Oklahoma	24	168	4.8	13.4	7	556,583	201,792	79,512	28,827
Oregon	12	-	(D)	(D)	(D)	(D)	(D)	(D)	(D)
Pennsylvania	39	-	(D)	(D)	(D)	(D)	(D)	(D)	(D)
Rhode Island	1	-	(D)	(D)	(D)	(D)	(D)	(D)	(D)
South Carolina	19	-	(D)	(D)	(D)	(D)	(D)	(D)	(D)
South Dakota	16	-	(D)	(D)	(D)	(D)	(D)	(D)	(D)
Tennessee	54	-	(D)	(D)	(D)	(D)	(D)	(D)	(D)
Texas	119	1,599	48.0	2,084.6	13	17,518,050	403,160	1,303,720	30,004
Utah	1	-	(D)	(D)	(D)	(D)	(D)	(D)	(D)
Vermont	6	-	(D)	(D)	(D)	(D)	(D)	(D)	(D)
Virginia	40	-	(D)	(D)	(D)	(D)	(D)	(D)	(D)
Washington	14	-	(D)	(D)	(D)	(D)	(D)	(D)	(D)
West Virginia	11	45	1.3	14.7	4	1,337,818	119,000	327,022	29,089
Wisconsin	39	414	11.2	65.4	11	1,677,821	286,103	158,056	26,952
Wyoming	6	-	(D)	(D)	(D)	(D)	(D)	(D)	(D)

Source: 1992 Economic Census, U.S. Department of Commerce, Washington, D.C. This is the only table that shows revenue data as collected by the Bureau of the Census in an Economic Census. The symbol (D) indicates that data are withheld by the source to avoid disclosure of competitive information. A dash (-) indicates that data are not available or cannot be calculated.

STATE-BY-STATE DATA ON ESTABLISHMENTS, EMPLOYMENT, AND PAYROLL - 1994 AND 1995

State	1994					1995					% Change Empl.
	No. of Estab.	Employ-ment	Pay / Empl.	Payroll ($ mil.)	Pay / Estab.	No. of Estab.	Employ-ment	Pay / Empl.	Payroll ($ mil.)	Pay / Estab.	
Alabama	34	(D)	-	(D)	-	33	(D)	-	(D)	-	-
Arizona	7	160	33,450	5.9	847,429	8	158	34,127	5.9	733,000	-1.2
Arkansas	24	(D)	-	(D)	-	24	218	43,303	7.4	306,292	-
California	60	1,099	47,574	49.8	830,617	63	1,055	52,246	52.6	835,286	-4.0
Colorado	24	(D)	-	(D)	-	24	(D)	-	(D)	-	-
Connecticut	4	(D)	-	(D)	-	4	(D)	-	(D)	-	-
Delaware	2	(D)	-	(D)	-	2	(D)	-	(D)	-	-
District of Columbia	5	(D)	-	(D)	-	5	(D)	-	(D)	-	-
Florida	34	(D)	-	(D)	-	36	(D)	-	(D)	-	-
Georgia	42	(D)	-	(D)	-	46	354	49,706	17.8	386,543	-
Hawaii	2	(D)	-	(D)	-	2	(D)	-	(D)	-	-
Idaho	19	(D)	-	(D)	-	18	(D)	-	(D)	-	-
Illinois	46	437	68,467	22.5	488,826	49	459	72,305	27.0	551,082	5.0
Indiana	47	(D)	-	(D)	-	45	(D)	-	(D)	-	-
Iowa	31	(D)	-	(D)	-	31	(D)	-	(D)	-	-
Kansas	34	1,034	30,012	30.0	882,206	34	995	32,398	28.3	832,971	-3.8
Kentucky	42	(D)	-	(D)	-	42	302	40,980	11.4	272,405	-
Louisiana	29	104	29,962	3.2	111,000	27	100	28,960	3.0	112,963	-3.8
Maine	6	63	31,365	2.5	413,667	3	(D)	-	(D)	-	-
Maryland	16	291	46,708	12.8	798,875	17	(D)	-	(D)	-	-
Massachusetts	6	(D)	-	(D)	-	5	237	36,068	7.9	1,580,200	-
Michigan	30	249	43,357	8.1	270,533	31	416	66,202	17.5	565,710	67.1
Minnesota	44	1,618	48,845	61.7	1,401,318	50	1,604	45,823	60.3	1,206,540	-0.9
Mississippi	37	143	36,196	5.0	134,892	35	123	34,244	4.4	124,714	-14.0
Missouri	34	237	37,620	7.2	211,941	34	220	43,364	7.5	219,941	-7.2
Montana	11	(D)	-	(D)	-	11	(D)	-	(D)	-	-
Nebraska	32	(D)	-	(D)	-	35	(D)	-	(D)	-	-
Nevada	3	(D)	-	(D)	-	3	(D)	-	(D)	-	-
New Hampshire	1	(D)	-	(D)	-	1	(D)	-	(D)	-	-
New Jersey	4	120	52,000	6.5	1,613,750	2	(D)	-	(D)	-	-
New Mexico	9	(D)	-	(D)	-	9	(D)	-	(D)	-	-
New York	30	325	36,751	12.0	399,800	22	252	50,556	9.8	444,682	-22.5
North Carolina	83	(D)	-	(D)	-	81	(D)	-	(D)	-	-
North Dakota	28	310	47,394	9.9	354,179	29	300	48,893	10.1	349,310	-3.2
Ohio	68	348	31,000	11.4	168,103	65	319	34,708	11.6	178,138	-8.3
Oklahoma	24	169	32,024	5.7	237,667	24	169	40,095	5.8	242,375	0.0
Oregon	12	(D)	-	(D)	-	13	(D)	-	(D)	-	-
Pennsylvania	38	1,111	32,403	35.6	936,079	36	1,202	33,674	38.9	1,081,833	8.2
South Carolina	25	(D)	-	(D)	-	25	(D)	-	(D)	-	-
South Dakota	15	(D)	-	(D)	-	15	(D)	-	(D)	-	-
Tennessee	45	(D)	-	(D)	-	48	176	34,227	6.0	124,313	-
Texas	140	1,656	32,256	53.2	380,357	141	1,851	32,588	57.3	406,170	11.8
Utah	2	(D)	-	(D)	-	2	(D)	-	(D)	-	-
Vermont	5	(D)	-	(D)	-	5	(D)	-	(D)	-	-
Virginia	42	4,158	65,538	235.3	5,602,048	46	4,369	70,007	272.7	5,928,043	5.1
Washington	13	(D)	-	(D)	-	14	(D)	-	(D)	-	-
West Virginia	8	(D)	-	(D)	-	7	(D)	-	(D)	-	-
Wisconsin	37	445	38,274	13.6	368,757	37	440	39,745	14.3	386,595	-1.1
Wyoming	5	(D)	-	(D)	-	5	(D)	-	(D)	-	-

Source: County Business Patterns, U.S. Department of Commerce, Washington, D.C., for 1994 and 1995. Employment shown is for mid-March of the year shown. Payroll per employee is calculated by annualizing 1st Quarter payroll (not shown) and then dividing that value by mid-March employment. Dividing total annual payroll (columns 5 and 10) by employment, therefore, will *not* yield the payroll per employee figure (columns 4 and 9). The symbol (D) indicates that data are withheld by the source to avoid disclosure of competitive information. A dash (-) indicates that data are not available or cannot be calculated.

ESTABLISHMENTS 1995 - STATE AND REGIONAL CONCENTRATION

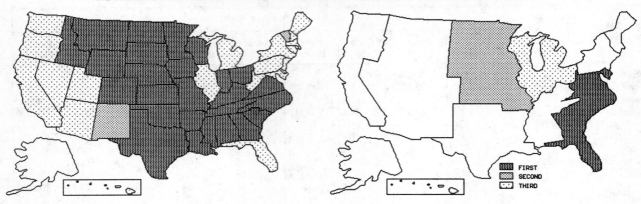

EMPLOYMENT 1995 - STATE AND REGIONAL CONCENTRATION

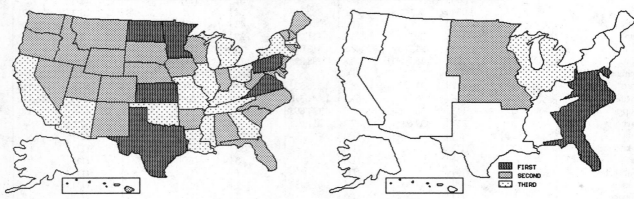

PAYROLL 1995 - STATE AND REGIONAL CONCENTRATION

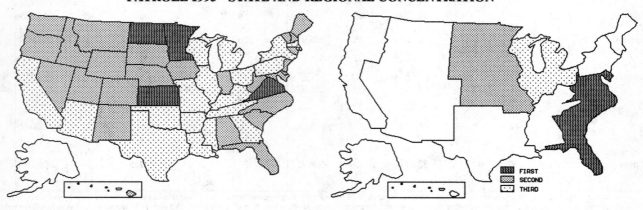

States with the darkest shading indicate those states which have proportionately more establishments, employment, or payrolls than would be indicated by the state's population. States with light shading are states with proportionately fewer establishments, less employment, and lower payrolls than population distribution. States shaded grey are within 15 percent of the state's population proportion in these catego-ries. States for which no data are available are shown as average (grey). *Regions* are shaded to indicate absolute rank in the category. If no data for the category are available, establishment counts are used to shade the regions. Source of the data is the table on the facing page.

LEADING COMPANIES - SIC 6111 - Federal & Federally Sponsored Credit

Number shown: **14**   Total sales/assets ($ mil): **336,879**   Total employment (000): **20.0**

Company Name	Address				CEO Name	Phone	Co. Type	Sales/Assets ($ mil)	Empl. (000)
Federal Home Loan Mortgage Corp.	8200 Jones Branch Dr.	McLean	VA	22102	Leland C. Brendsel	703-903-2000	P	173,866 TA	3.3
Federal Farm Credit Banks Funding Corp.	10 Exchange Pl.	Jersey City	NJ	07302	James A. Brickley	201-200-8000	R	71,000 TA	<0.1
Student Loan Marketing Association	1050 Thomas Jefferson St.	Washington	DC	20007	Albert L. Lord	202-333-8000	P	47,630 TA	4.8
CoBank	PO Box 5110	Denver	CO	80217	Douglas D. Sims	303-740-4000	R	13,000 TA	0.5
AgAmerica FCB	PO Box 13106	Sacremento	CA	95813	James Kirk	916-485-6000	R	7,500 TA	1.2
Farm Credit Bank of Columbia	PO Box 1499	Columbia	SC	29202	Maxey D. Love Jr.	803-799-5000	R	5,608 TA	1.4
Government National Mortgage Association	451 7th St. S.W.	Washington	DC	20410	Kevin G. Chavers	202-708-0926	S	5,042 TA	<0.1
Farm Credit Bank of Texas	PO Box 15919	Austin	TX	78761	Arnold R. Henson	512-465-0400	R	4,512 TA	0.2
Farm Credit Bank of Omaha	206 S. 19th St.	Omaha	NE	68102	James D. Kirk	402-348-3333	R	4,290 TA	0.8
Farm Credit Bank of Wichita	PO Box 2940	Wichita	KS	67201	Jerold L. Harris	316-266-5100	R	3,896 TA	0.9
Federal National Mortgage Association	3900 Wisconsin Ave. N.W.	Washington	DC	20016	James A. Johnson	202-752-7000	P	392 TA	3.3
Great Lakes Higher Education Corp.	2401 International Ln.	Madison	WI	53704	Richard D. George	608-246-1800	R	68 TA*	0.5
Hemar Insurance Corporation of America	3900 W. Technology Corp.	Sioux Falls	SD	57106	Kevin Moehn	605-361-5051	R	55 TA	<0.1
AgriBank F.C.B.	PO Box 64949	St. Paul	MN	55164	C.T. Frederickson	612-282-8800	R	20 TA*	3.0

Source: *Ward's Business Directory of U.S. Private and Public Companies*, 1996. Company type codes: P - Public, R - Private, S - Subsidiary, D - Division, J - Joint Venture, A - Affiliate, G - Group. If the dollar values shown are not sales, the following codes apply: TA - Total Assets; OR - Operating Revenues; GB - Gross Billings. * - estimated dollar value. < - less than; *na* - not available.

SIC 6140

PERSONAL CREDIT INSTITUTIONS

Personal credit institutions are engaged in providing loans to individuals. The SIC also includes organizations engaged primarily in financing retail sales made on the installment plan and those financing automobile loans for individuals. The category includes consumer finance companies, industrial loan "banks" and loan companies not engaged in deposit banking, installment sales finance organizations other than banks, loan companies and societies, Morris plans not engaged in deposit banking, mutual benefit associations, and personal finance companies.

ESTABLISHMENTS, EMPLOYMENT, AND PAYROLL

	1990	1991		1992		1993		1994		1995		% change 90-95
		Value	%	Value	%	Value	%	Value	%	Value	%	
All Establishments	24,960	20,049	*-19.7*	19,887	*-0.8*	17,003	*-14.5*	16,772	*-1.4*	17,945	*7.0*	*-28.1*
Mid-March Employment	236,318	175,823	*-25.6*	158,519	*-9.8*	151,920	*-4.2*	153,102	*0.8*	161,225	*5.3*	*-31.8*
1st Quarter Wages (annualized - $ mil.)	5,735.0	4,627.4	*-19.3*	4,458.7	*-3.6*	3,722.8	*-16.5*	4,628.3	*24.3*	5,505.8	*19.0*	*-4.0*
Payroll per Emp. 1st Q. (annualized)	24,268	26,318	*8.4*	28,127	*6.9*	24,505	*-12.9*	30,230	*23.4*	34,150	*13.0*	*40.7*
Annual Payroll ($ mil.)	5,547.4	4,560.0	*-17.8*	4,487.1	*-1.6*	3,846.8	*-14.3*	4,716.9	*22.6*	5,354.7	*13.5*	*-3.5*
Establishments - 1-4 Emp. Number	13,804	11,240	*-18.6*	12,069	*7.4*	9,766	*-19.1*	10,004	*2.4*	10,553	*5.5*	*-23.6*
Mid-March Employment	35,187	29,789	*-15.3*	32,084	*7.7*	25,079	*-21.8*	26,215	*4.5*	26,988	*2.9*	*-23.3*
1st Quarter Wages (annualized - $ mil.)	655.6	647.6	*-1.2*	732.0	*13.0*	556.8	*-23.9*	627.4	*12.7*	714.2	*13.8*	*8.9*
Payroll per Emp. 1st Q. (annualized)	18,633	21,741	*16.7*	22,816	*4.9*	22,203	*-2.7*	23,933	*7.8*	26,462	*10.6*	*42.0*
Annual Payroll ($ mil.)	697.5	670.4	*-3.9*	768.5	*14.6*	624.9	*-18.7*	727.5	*16.4*	786.4	*8.1*	*12.8*
Establishments - 5-9 Emp. Number	6,760	5,975	*-11.6*	5,560	*-6.9*	4,678	*-15.9*	5,062	*8.2*	5,491	*8.5*	*-18.8*
Mid-March Employment	42,883	37,321	*-13.0*	34,182	*-8.4*	28,871	*-15.5*	31,213	*8.1*	33,730	*8.1*	*-21.3*
1st Quarter Wages (annualized - $ mil.)	853.6	815.0	*-4.5*	814.9	*-0.0*	622.5	*-23.6*	736.0	*18.2*	864.8	*17.5*	*1.3*
Payroll per Emp. 1st Q. (annualized)	19,904	21,838	*9.7*	23,841	*9.2*	21,561	*-9.6*	23,580	*9.4*	25,639	*8.7*	*28.8*
Annual Payroll ($ mil.)	849.1	804.5	*-5.3*	818.1	*1.7*	648.4	*-20.7*	741.2	*14.3*	848.7	*14.5*	*-0.0*
Establishments - 10-19 Emp. Number	2,240	1,552	*-30.7*	1,113	*-28.3*	1,448	*30.1*	882	*-39.1*	1,048	*18.8*	*-53.2*
Mid-March Employment	29,619	20,386	*-31.2*	14,660	*-28.1*	19,639	*34.0*	11,192	*-43.0*	13,176	*17.7*	*-55.5*
1st Quarter Wages (annualized - $ mil.)	635.9	484.5	*-23.8*	406.6	*-16.1*	343.2	*-15.6*	323.8	*-5.7*	435.8	*34.6*	*-31.5*
Payroll per Emp. 1st Q. (annualized)	21,470	23,764	*10.7*	27,736	*16.7*	17,475	*-37.0*	28,927	*65.5*	33,079	*14.4*	*54.1*
Annual Payroll ($ mil.)	626.1	487.7	*-22.1*	402.5	*-17.5*	334.6	*-16.9*	333.1	*-0.4*	406.4	*22.0*	*-35.1*
Establishments - 20-49 Emp. Number	1,383	823	*-40.5*	760	*-7.7*	778	*2.4*	487	*-37.4*	516	*6.0*	*-62.7*
Mid-March Employment	41,615	24,986	*-40.0*	22,899	*-8.4*	22,060	*-3.7*	15,285	*-30.7*	15,799	*3.4*	*-62.0*
1st Quarter Wages (annualized - $ mil.)	1,007.9	688.2	*-31.7*	680.9	*-1.1*	526.0	*-22.7*	495.1	*-5.9*	588.1	*18.8*	*-41.6*
Payroll per Emp. 1st Q. (annualized)	24,220	27,542	*13.7*	29,734	*8.0*	23,844	*-19.8*	32,389	*35.8*	37,227	*14.9*	*53.7*
Annual Payroll ($ mil.)	980.6	688.8	*-29.8*	674.0	*-2.1*	529.5	*-21.4*	484.9	*-8.4*	601.3	*24.0*	*-38.7*
Establishments - 50-99 Emp. Number	558	319	*-42.8*	260	*-18.5*	209	*-19.6*	196	*-6.2*	164	*-16.3*	*-70.6*
Mid-March Employment	38,275	22,075	*-42.3*	17,969	*-18.6*	14,462	*-19.5*	13,482	*-6.8*	11,115	*-17.6*	*-71.0*
1st Quarter Wages (annualized - $ mil.)	1,024.6	727.6	*-29.0*	609.1	*-16.3*	439.2	*-27.9*	457.8	*4.3*	411.3	*-10.2*	*-59.9*
Payroll per Emp. 1st Q. (annualized)	26,770	32,962	*23.1*	33,897	*2.8*	30,366	*-10.4*	33,958	*11.8*	37,007	*9.0*	*38.2*
Annual Payroll ($ mil.)	1,001.1	729.8	*-27.1*	627.7	*-14.0*	450.7	*-28.2*	447.3	*-0.8*	385.4	*-13.8*	*-61.5*
Establishments - 100-249 Emp. Number	170	87	*-48.8*	80	*-8.0*	75	*-6.3*	89	*18.7*	118	*32.6*	*-30.6*
Mid-March Employment	24,023	(D)	-	11,808	-	10,858	*-8.0*	13,208	*21.6*	17,787	*34.7*	*-26.0*
1st Quarter Wages (annualized - $ mil.)	762.1	(D)	-	415.3	-	317.8	*-23.5*	445.1	*40.1*	727.6	*63.5*	*-4.5*
Payroll per Emp. 1st Q. (annualized)	31,726	(D)	-	35,168	-	29,265	*-16.8*	33,699	*15.2*	40,907	*21.4*	*28.9*
Annual Payroll ($ mil.)	679.4	(D)	-	376.8	-	316.6	*-16.0*	437.5	*38.2*	697.0	*59.3*	*2.6*
Establishments - 250-499 Emp. Number	28	34	*21.4*	27	*-20.6*	26	*-3.7*	23	*-11.5*	26	*13.0*	*-7.1*
Mid-March Employment	9,758	11,226	*15.0*	8,888	*-20.8*	9,330	*5.0*	8,143	*-12.7*	8,761	*7.6*	*-10.2*
1st Quarter Wages (annualized - $ mil.)	326.8	363.0	*11.1*	288.8	*-20.4*	269.5	*-6.7*	236.2	*-12.4*	292.6	*23.9*	*-10.5*
Payroll per Emp. 1st Q. (annualized)	33,494	32,332	*-3.5*	32,491	*0.5*	28,887	*-11.1*	29,001	*0.4*	33,395	*15.2*	*-0.3*
Annual Payroll ($ mil.)	299.8	351.1	*17.1*	286.3	*-18.5*	264.8	*-7.5*	219.9	*-17.0*	262.3	*19.3*	*-12.5*
Establishments - 500-999 Emp. Number	15	14	*-6.7*	13	*-7.1*	16	*23.1*	17	*6.3*	17	-	*13.3*
Mid-March Employment	(D)	9,330	-	9,005	*-3.5*	11,533	*28.1*	11,154	*-3.3*	11,527	*3.3*	-
1st Quarter Wages (annualized - $ mil.)	(D)	274.4	-	254.5	*-7.3*	342.4	*34.6*	386.5	*12.9*	432.3	*11.9*	-
Payroll per Emp. 1st Q. (annualized)	(D)	29,407	-	28,257	*-3.9*	29,686	*5.1*	34,653	*16.7*	37,507	*8.2*	-
Annual Payroll ($ mil.)	(D)	262.7	-	276.5	*5.3*	349.9	*26.6*	373.2	*6.6*	364.0	*-2.5*	-
Estab. - 1000 or More Emp. Number	2	5	*150.0*	5	-	7	*40.0*	12	*71.4*	12	-	*500.0*
Mid-March Employment	(D)	(D)	-	7,024	-	10,088	*43.6*	23,210	*130.1*	22,342	*-3.7*	-
1st Quarter Wages (annualized - $ mil.)	(D)	(D)	-	256.6	-	305.5	*19.0*	920.5	*201.3*	1,039.0	*12.9*	-
Payroll per Emp. 1st Q. (annualized)	(D)	(D)	-	36,537	-	30,286	*-17.1*	39,660	*31.0*	46,506	*17.3*	-
Annual Payroll ($ mil.)	(D)	(D)	-	256.7	-	327.4	*27.6*	952.4	*190.9*	1,003.1	*5.3*	-

Source: County Business Patterns, U.S. Department of Commerce, Washington, D.C., for 1990 through 1995. Payroll per employee is calculated using mid-March employment and 1st Quarter wages, annualized. Annual payroll, also shown, may not equal the annualized 1st Quarter wages. Columns headed by a percent sign (%) indicate change from the previous year. *na* stands for not available. The symbol (D) indicates that data are withheld by the source to avoid disclosure of competitive information. A dash (-) indicates that data are not available or cannot be calculated.

ESTABLISHMENTS
Number

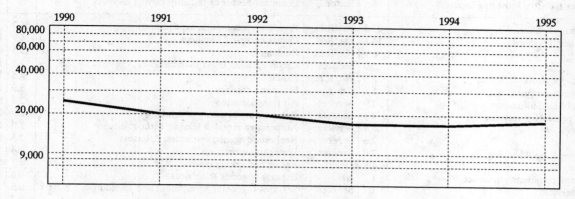

MID-MARCH EMPLOYMENT
Number

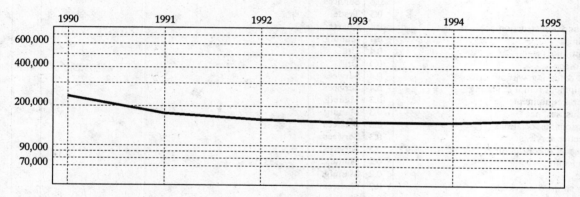

ANNUAL PAYROLL
$ million

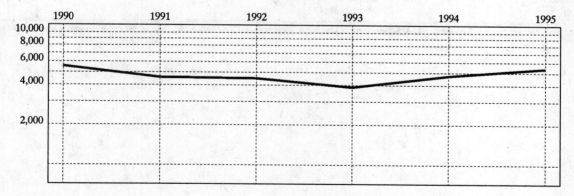

INPUTS AND OUTPUTS FOR CREDIT AGENCIES OTHER THAN BANKS - SICs 606, 611, 614-16

Economic Sector or Industry Providing Inputs	%	Sector	Economic Sector or Industry Buying Outputs	%	Sector
Security & commodity brokers	27.5	Fin/R.E.	Personal consumption expenditures	36.7	
Credit agencies other than banks	14.1	Fin/R.E.	Owner-occupied dwellings	18.9	Fin/R.E.
Banking	6.9	Fin/R.E.	Banking	13.5	Fin/R.E.
Advertising	6.0	Services	Credit agencies other than banks	11.1	Fin/R.E.
Real estate agents, operators, & lessors	5.6	Fin/R.E.	Hotels	3.6	Services
Federal Government enterprises nec	5.3	Gov't	Insurance carriers	2.9	Fin/R.E.
Management & public relations services	4.9	Services	Air transportation	2.1	Util.
Computer & data processing services	4.4	Services	Retail trade, ex eating & drinking	2.0	Trade
Business services nec	3.4	Services	Automotive rental & leasing, without drivers	1.9	Services
Legal services	2.6	Services	Real estate agents, operators, & lessors	1.5	Fin/R.E.
Accounting, auditing & bookkeeping	2.0	Services	Water transportation	1.4	Util.
U.S. Postal Service	1.8	Gov't	Eating & drinking places	1.1	Services
Telephone/telegraph communications nec	1.7	Util.	Exports of goods & services	0.8	Foreign
Personnel supply services	1.7	Services	S/L Govt., general government nec, spending	0.5	S/L Govt
Trucking & courier services, ex air	1.2	Util.	Wholesale trade	0.3	Trade
Research, development, & testing services	0.8	Services	Meat animals	0.2	Agric.
Insurance carriers	0.7	Fin/R.E.	Automotive repair shops & services	0.2	Services
Eating & drinking places	0.7	Services	Feed grains	0.1	Agric.
Air transportation	0.6	Util.			
Hotels	0.6	Services			
Wholesale trade	0.5	Trade			
Repair & maintenance construction nec	0.4	Constr.			
Commercial printing	0.4	Manufg.			
Electric services (utilities)	0.4	Util.			
Warehousing & storage	0.4	Util.			
Automotive rental & leasing, without drivers	0.4	Services			
Miscellaneous equipment rental & leasing	0.4	Services			
Computer peripheral equipment	0.3	Manufg.			
Manufacturing industries, nec	0.3	Manufg.			
Business & professional associations	0.3	Services			
Detective & protective services	0.3	Services			
Services to dwellings & other buildings	0.3	Services			
Manifold business forms	0.2	Manufg.			
Petroleum refining	0.2	Manufg.			
Automotive repair shops & services	0.2	Services			
Book publishing	0.1	Manufg.			
Paper & paperboard mills	0.1	Manufg.			
Periodicals	0.1	Manufg.			
Photographic equipment & supplies	0.1	Manufg.			
Local & suburban transit	0.1	Util.			
Miscellaneous repair shops	0.1	Services			

Source: Benchmark Input-Output Accounts for the U.S. Economy, 1992, U.S. Department of Commerce, Washington, D.C., November 1997. Data, as reported in the source, are organized by the 1987 SIC structure in use in 1992.

OCCUPATIONS EMPLOYED BY PERSONAL CREDIT INSTITUTIONS

Occupation	% of Total 1996	Change to 2006	Occupation	% of Total 1996	Change to 2006
Loan officers & counselors	12.5	45.5	Bank tellers	3.5	23.8
Bill & account collectors	10.7	43.5	Bookkeeping, accounting, & auditing clerks	3.2	-3.0
Loan & credit clerks	10.5	22.4	Management support workers nec	2.4	21.3
Financial managers	9.5	21.3	Credit analysts	2.4	21.3
General office clerks	7.8	4.4	Secretaries, except legal & medical	2.3	-3.8
Adjustment clerks	6.7	63.7	Securities & financial sales workers	1.7	81.9
Clerical supervisors & managers	4.7	21.3	Sales & related workers nec	1.5	33.4
General managers & top executives	4.2	17.5	Accountants & auditors	1.1	12.3
Cashiers	4.0	29.5			

Sources: Industry-Occupation Matrix, Bureau of Labor Statistics. These data relate to one or more 3-digit SIC industry groups rather than to a single 4-digit SIC. The change reported for each occupation to the year 2005 is a percent of growth or decline as estimated by the Bureau of Labor Statistics. The abbreviation *nec* stands for not elsewhere classified.

OCCUPATIONS EMPLOYED BY FEDERAL AND BUSINESS CREDIT INSTITUTIONS

Occupation	% of Total 1996	Change to 2006	Occupation	% of Total 1996	Change to 2006
Bill & account collectors	11.1	46.3	Credit analysts	3.6	23.7
Adjustment clerks	6.8	67.0	Accountants & auditors	2.9	14.5
Loan officers & counselors	6.8	23.7	Securities & financial sales workers	2.9	85.5
Secretaries, except legal & medical	6.1	-1.9	Correspondence clerks	2.4	23.7
Loan & credit clerks	5.3	24.8	Managers & administrators nec	1.6	22.5
Clerical supervisors & managers	5.0	23.7	Computer programmers	1.6	1.8
General managers & top executives	4.9	19.8	Systems analysts	1.4	97.9
General office clerks	4.9	6.4	Receptionists & information clerks	1.4	23.6
Bookkeeping, accounting, & auditing clerks	4.4	-1.1	Credit checkers	1.3	-19.7
Financial managers	4.4	23.7	Data entry keyers, except composing	1.3	-1.1
Management support workers nec	3.7	23.7	Sales & related workers nec	1.2	36.0

Sources: *Industry-Occupation Matrix*, Bureau of Labor Statistics. These data relate to one or more 3-digit SIC industry groups rather than to a single 4-digit SIC. The change reported for each occupation to the year 2005 is a percent of growth or decline as estimated by the Bureau of Labor Statistics. The abbreviation *nec* stands for not elsewhere classified.

U.S. AND STATE DATA ON INDUSTRY REVENUES AND OTHER ACCOUNTS FOR 1992

State	No. of Estab.	Employ-ment	Payroll ($ mil.)	Revenues ($ mil.)	Empl./ Estab.	Revenue/ Estab. ($)	Payroll/ Estab. ($)	Revenue/ Empl. ($)	Payroll/ Empl. ($)
UNITED STATES	5,038	86,526	3,459.2	36,552.8	17	7,255,413	686,623	422,448	39,979
Alabama	36	-	(D)	(D)	(D)	(D)	(D)	(D)	(D)
Alaska	5	-	(D)	(D)	(D)	(D)	(D)	(D)	(D)
Arizona	86	-	(D)	(D)	(D)	(D)	(D)	(D)	(D)
Arkansas	18	33	0.6	3.4	2	187,056	32,778	102,030	17,879
California	755	10,505	452.1	4,562.7	14	6,043,323	598,860	434,337	43,040
Colorado	122	2,202	67.7	453.5	18	3,717,189	555,311	205,948	30,767
Connecticut	86	3,005	199.3	4,106.7	35	47,751,942	2,317,558	1,366,611	66,326
Delaware	53	504	10.9	332.3	10	6,270,094	204,962	659,355	21,554
District of Columbia	24	-	(D)	(D)	(D)	(D)	(D)	(D)	(D)
Florida	270	4,651	158.1	1,526.7	17	5,654,270	585,526	328,242	33,991
Georgia	210	3,863	136.2	1,442.4	18	6,868,629	648,781	373,392	35,269
Hawaii	22	-	(D)	(D)	(D)	(D)	(D)	(D)	(D)
Idaho	12	-	(D)	(D)	(D)	(D)	(D)	(D)	(D)
Illinois	307	8,114	354.0	3,728.0	26	12,143,404	1,152,984	459,456	43,624
Indiana	51	-	(D)	(D)	(D)	(D)	(D)	(D)	(D)
Iowa	41	1,670	48.9	368.4	41	8,986,317	1,193,171	220,622	29,293
Kansas	51	-	(D)	(D)	(D)	(D)	(D)	(D)	(D)
Kentucky	41	762	18.5	134.4	19	3,277,341	451,220	176,340	24,278
Louisiana	57	225	6.5	80.3	4	1,408,158	113,351	356,733	28,716
Maine	10	-	(D)	(D)	(D)	(D)	(D)	(D)	(D)
Maryland	95	-	(D)	(D)	(D)	(D)	(D)	(D)	(D)
Massachusetts	129	1,942	94.3	736.9	15	5,712,465	731,093	379,458	48,564
Michigan	127	2,351	112.1	2,067.7	19	16,281,173	882,709	879,502	47,684
Minnesota	100	1,382	58.8	571.8	14	5,718,270	588,440	413,768	42,579
Mississippi	26	232	4.4	35.5	9	1,367,154	168,538	153,216	18,888
Missouri	85	1,947	64.8	410.3	23	4,826,824	761,847	210,724	33,260
Montana	13	-	(D)	(D)	(D)	(D)	(D)	(D)	(D)
Nebraska	33	-	(D)	(D)	(D)	(D)	(D)	(D)	(D)
Nevada	41	-	(D)	(D)	(D)	(D)	(D)	(D)	(D)
New Hampshire	18	-	(D)	(D)	(D)	(D)	(D)	(D)	(D)
New Jersey	185	4,186	207.7	1,863.9	23	10,075,384	1,122,724	445,281	49,619
New Mexico	26	606	11.5	81.1	23	3,118,269	440,577	133,787	18,903
New York	485	11,727	588.9	4,930.5	24	10,165,889	1,214,282	420,436	50,220
North Carolina	117	1,338	45.9	437.9	11	3,742,915	392,410	327,295	34,314
North Dakota	8	16	0.6	7.4	2	925,125	80,125	462,563	40,063
Ohio	152	2,251	75.6	689.3	15	4,534,829	497,664	306,217	33,605
Oklahoma	43	567	14.6	309.1	13	7,188,279	338,558	545,143	25,675
Oregon	64	1,224	42.1	435.2	19	6,800,266	657,719	355,569	34,391
Pennsylvania	145	2,590	101.4	1,268.2	18	8,745,931	699,241	489,637	39,147
Rhode Island	5	-	(D)	(D)	(D)	(D)	(D)	(D)	(D)
South Carolina	44	-	(D)	(D)	(D)	(D)	(D)	(D)	(D)
South Dakota	16	-	(D)	(D)	(D)	(D)	(D)	(D)	(D)
Tennessee	73	1,695	38.7	293.0	23	4,014,274	530,329	172,886	22,840
Texas	418	5,988	192.7	1,967.8	14	4,707,696	461,100	328,627	32,188
Utah	37	-	(D)	(D)	(D)	(D)	(D)	(D)	(D)
Vermont	6	-	(D)	(D)	(D)	(D)	(D)	(D)	(D)
Virginia	89	1,629	59.3	710.9	18	7,987,157	666,236	436,376	36,400
Washington	112	1,147	44.8	502.9	10	4,490,205	399,670	438,451	39,026
West Virginia	9	15	0.2	1.2	2	131,444	25,556	78,867	15,333
Wisconsin	77	644	22.6	225.7	8	2,930,649	293,065	350,404	35,040
Wyoming	3	-	(D)	(D)	(D)	(D)	(D)	(D)	(D)

Source: 1992 Economic Census, U.S. Department of Commerce, Washington, D.C. This is the only table that shows revenue data as collected by the Bureau of the Census in an Economic Census. The symbol (D) indicates that data are withheld by the source to avoid disclosure of competitive information. A dash (-) indicates that data are not available or cannot be calculated.

STATE-BY-STATE DATA ON ESTABLISHMENTS, EMPLOYMENT, AND PAYROLL - 1994 AND 1995

State	1994					1995					% Change Empl.
	No. of Estab.	Employ- ment	Pay / Empl.	Payroll ($ mil.)	Pay / Estab.	No. of Estab.	Employ- ment	Pay / Empl.	Payroll ($ mil.)	Pay / Estab.	
Alabama	31	323	26,712	8.6	277,839	32	303	26,099	8.2	256,281	-6.2
Alaska	2	(D)	-	(D)	-	1	(D)	-	(D)	-	-
Arizona	113	1,926	38,010	70.2	621,336	128	2,707	30,667	83.9	655,383	40.6
Arkansas	22	(D)	-	(D)	-	20	(D)	-	(D)	-	-
California	666	10,239	55,418	494.8	742,970	628	10,607	57,256	564.9	899,567	3.6
Colorado	121	2,703	30,488	80.4	664,628	132	2,482	34,957	84.4	639,659	-8.2
Connecticut	85	2,313	85,562	168.4	1,980,624	78	2,001	95,784	153.7	1,970,692	-13.5
Delaware	44	1,403	23,809	33.6	762,727	42	1,849	32,491	61.2	1,457,429	31.8
District of Columbia	19	(D)	-	(D)	-	15	137	60,263	12.0	800,133	-
Florida	245	5,655	34,024	190.3	776,849	255	7,036	36,823	230.4	903,439	24.4
Georgia	184	3,158	43,174	125.5	682,304	187	3,119	47,141	132.6	709,214	-1.2
Hawaii	24	(D)	-	(D)	-	24	175	35,863	6.1	256,000	-
Idaho	16	(D)	-	(D)	-	12	(D)	-	(D)	-	-
Illinois	406	6,163	64,793	343.7	846,466	415	6,663	69,895	377.3	909,267	8.1
Indiana	47	294	33,646	12.7	269,447	49	922	26,390	30.4	620,959	213.6
Iowa	45	1,600	38,332	56.1	1,246,133	43	1,612	38,638	57.0	1,324,814	0.8
Kansas	49	1,484	31,555	40.7	830,633	46	1,465	31,121	46.5	1,011,674	-1.3
Kentucky	31	961	24,062	25.3	817,355	33	1,148	20,551	23.6	714,879	19.5
Louisiana	56	255	27,765	7.8	138,393	66	262	27,511	8.5	128,727	2.7
Maine	6	(D)	-	(D)	-	6	17	49,412	0.9	142,833	-
Maryland	79	2,242	36,616	83.7	1,058,987	80	2,355	40,766	93.7	1,171,175	5.0
Massachusetts	100	1,385	59,815	82.6	826,340	97	1,310	73,173	83.3	858,546	-5.4
Michigan	103	1,916	50,643	87.6	850,466	102	2,170	56,024	101.4	994,490	13.3
Minnesota	92	1,368	50,614	59.8	650,380	109	1,503	53,916	64.9	595,688	9.9
Mississippi	21	183	23,956	4.6	218,429	18	172	27,512	4.7	261,833	-6.0
Missouri	82	1,758	32,676	54.5	664,073	80	2,055	26,780	56.4	705,063	16.9
Montana	11	(D)	-	(D)	-	11	(D)	-	(D)	-	-
Nebraska	27	259	28,309	8.9	329,741	26	276	31,551	11.0	423,115	6.6
Nevada	33	269	23,390	7.9	238,273	47	476	25,681	13.1	279,149	77.0
New Hampshire	18	410	42,888	16.0	890,222	17	426	45,737	23.3	1,368,294	3.9
New Jersey	170	4,330	63,878	242.4	1,425,665	154	3,495	74,272	212.6	1,380,630	-19.3
New Mexico	19	(D)	-	(D)	-	22	(D)	-	(D)	-	-
New York	418	13,554	60,384	743.1	1,777,780	420	15,018	68,293	856.7	2,039,755	10.8
North Carolina	95	1,338	45,851	54.5	573,326	97	1,201	54,948	57.2	589,948	-10.2
North Dakota	5	(D)	-	(D)	-	6	(D)	-	(D)	-	-
Ohio	159	4,703	28,191	125.6	790,220	184	5,497	28,214	149.3	811,429	16.9
Oklahoma	40	291	31,326	10.3	256,425	46	381	35,706	20.1	436,565	30.9
Oregon	71	1,608	37,020	51.9	731,577	76	1,422	42,110	55.2	725,697	-11.6
Pennsylvania	118	2,301	37,578	82.2	696,915	118	2,819	40,847	107.8	913,831	22.5
Rhode Island	10	347	56,069	16.2	1,619,800	9	363	53,212	16.4	1,823,444	4.6
South Carolina	42	(D)	-	(D)	-	37	(D)	-	(D)	-	-
South Dakota	16	(D)	-	(D)	-	15	(D)	-	(D)	-	-
Tennessee	68	681	46,150	28.7	421,735	69	886	45,273	42.8	620,565	30.1
Texas	387	6,478	35,217	251.7	650,398	404	7,158	36,764	271.2	671,369	10.5
Utah	53	1,754	20,509	36.0	678,396	51	1,643	23,041	36.3	711,137	-6.3
Vermont	8	(D)	-	(D)	-	8	(D)	-	(D)	-	-
Virginia	95	1,357	41,185	114.8	1,207,989	94	4,602	33,865	151.1	1,607,245	239.1
Washington	111	(D)	-	(D)	-	113	855	40,173	34.2	302,912	-
West Virginia	5	(D)	-	(D)	-	5	25	15,680	0.4	75,400	-
Wisconsin	52	440	33,809	13.7	263,288	57	468	36,342	16.6	291,158	6.4
Wyoming	2	(D)	-	(D)	-	3	(D)	-	(D)	-	-

Source: County Business Patterns, U.S. Department of Commerce, Washington, D.C., for 1994 and 1995. Employment shown is for mid-March of the year shown. Payroll per employee is calculated by annualizing 1st Quarter payroll (not shown) and then dividing that value by mid-March employment. Dividing total annual payroll (columns 5 and 10) by employment, therefore, will *not* yield the payroll per employee figure (columns 4 and 9). The symbol (D) indicates that data are withheld by the source to avoid disclosure of competitive information. A dash (-) indicates that data are not available or cannot be calculated.

ESTABLISHMENTS 1995 - STATE AND REGIONAL CONCENTRATION

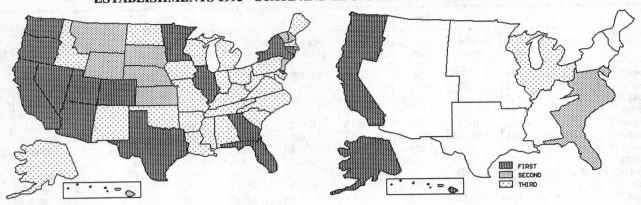

EMPLOYMENT 1995 - STATE AND REGIONAL CONCENTRATION

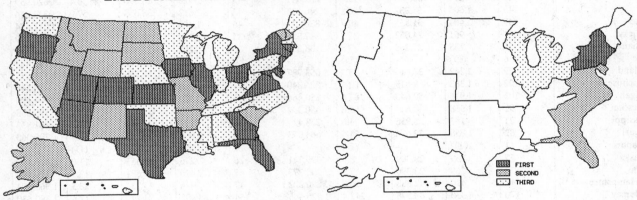

PAYROLL 1995 - STATE AND REGIONAL CONCENTRATION

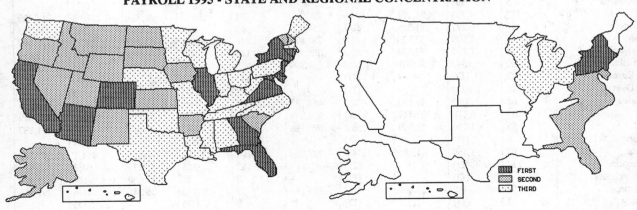

States with the darkest shading indicate those states which have proportionately more establishments, employment, or payrolls than would be indicated by the state's population. States with light shading are states with proportionately fewer establishments, less employment, and lower payrolls than population distribution. States shaded grey are within 15 percent of the state's population proportion in these categories. States for which no data are available are shown as average (grey). *Regions* are shaded to indicate absolute rank in the category. If no data for the category are available, establishment counts are used to shade the regions. Source of the data is the table on the facing page.

LEADING COMPANIES - SIC 6153 - Short-Term Business Credit
Number shown: **62**   Total sales/assets ($ mil): **345,560**   Total employment (000): **150.0**

Company Name	Address				CEO Name	Phone	Co. Type	Sales/Assets ($ mil)	Empl. (000)
General Electric Capital Corp.	260 Long Ridge Rd.	Stamford	CT	06927	Gary C. Wendt	203-357-4000	S	228,777 TA	51.0
CIT Group	650 CIT Dr.	Livingston	NJ	07039	Jr., Albert R. Gamper	201-740-5000	S	18,932 TA	3.0
American Express Co.	American Express Tower	New York	NY	10285	Harvey Golub	212-640-2000	P	17,760 OR	73.6
Heller Financial Inc.	500 W. Monroe St.	Chicago	IL	60661	Richard J. Almeida	312-441-7000	S	12,861 TA	2.3
NationsBank Card Services	PO Box 7029	Dover	DE	19903	Eileen Friars	302-741-1000	D	11,000 TA	3.0
Foothill Capital Corp.	11111 Santa Monica Blvd.	Los Angeles	CA	90025	Peter E. Schwab	310-996-7000	S	10,000 TA	0.2
Sears Roebuck Acceptance Corp.	3711 Kennett Pike	Greenville	DE	19807	Keith E. Trost	302-888-3100	S	7,031 TA	<0.1
American Express Credit Corp.	301 N. Walnut St	Wilmington	DE	19801	Vincent P. Lisanke	302-594-3350	S	6,945 TA*	<0.1
PACCAR Financial Corp.	PO Box 1518	Bellevue	WA	98004	T. Ronald Morton	425-468-7100	S	5,599 TA	0.4
CIT Group/Commercial Services	1211 Ave. of the Amer.	New York	NY	10036	Lawrence A. Marsielllo	212-382-7000	S	4,656 TA*	0.9
First Card Services Inc.	PO Box 2008	Elgin	IL	60121	Scott P. Marks Jr.	847-931-7676	S	4,623 TA*	4.6
ITT Commercial Finance Corp.	655 Maryville Centre Dr.	St. Louis	MO	63141	Melvin F. Brown	314-725-2525	S	4,000 TA	1.5
Ohio Casualty Corp.	136 N. 3rd St.	Hamilton	OH	45025	Lauren N. Patch	513-867-3000	P	3,779 TA	3.4
Credit Acceptance Corp.	25505 W. Twelve Mile Rd.	Southfield	MI	48084	Donald A. Foss	810-353-2700	P	1,074 TA	0.6
Foothill Group Inc.	11111 Santa Monica Blvd.	Los Angeles	CA	90025	John Nikoll	310-478-8383	S	913 TA*	0.2
Finance Enterprises	PO Box 3979	Honolulu	HI	96812	Clifford Yee	808-548-3311	R	860 TA	0.4
Capital Factors Holding Inc.	120 E. Palmetto Park Rd.	Boca Raton	FL	33432	John W. Kiefer	561-368-5011	P	757 TA	0.3
National City Bancorp.	75 S. 5th St.	Minneapolis	MN	55402	David L. Andreas	612-340-3183	P	674 TA	0.3
FirstSpartan Financial Corp.	380 E. Main St.	Spartanburg	SC	29302	Billy L. Painter	864-582-2391	P	665 TA	0.1
Fremont Financial Corp.	2020 Santa Monica Blvd.	Santa Monica	CA	90404	Robert Tenney	310-315-5550	S	600 TA	0.2
Barclays Commercial Corp.	PO Box 31307	Charlotte	NC	28231	Edward L. Boyd	704-339-5000	S	543 TA	0.5
Premium Financing Specialists Inc.	PO Box 13367	Kansas City	MO	64199	Tom Charbonneau	816-391-2350	R	490 TA*	0.2
Capital Factors Inc.	1799 W. Oakland Park Blvd.	Fort Lauderdale	FL	33311	John W. Kiefer	954-730-2900	S	399 TA	0.2
Lomas Financial Corp.	1600 Viceroy Dr.	Dallas	TX	75235	Jess Hay	214-879-4000	P	329 TA	<0.1
Computer Calling Technologies Inc.	135 E. Ortega St.	Santa Barbara	CA	93101	Donald Sledge	805-963-2423	S	310 TA*	0.3
Consumer Portfolio Services Inc.	2 Ada	Irvine	CA	92618	Charles E. Bradley Jr.	714-753-6800	P	226 TA	0.6
Rosenthal and Rosenthal Inc.	1370 Broadway	New York	NY	10018	Stephen J. Rosenthal	212-356-1400	R	190 TA*	0.2
Mesirow Financial Holdings Inc.	350 N. Clark St.	Chicago	IL	60610	Bruce Young	312-670-6000	R	150 TA	0.5
Century Business Credit Corp.	119 W. 40th St.	New York	NY	10018	Stanley Tananbaum	212-703-3500	R	140 TA*	0.1
First Union Energy Group	1001 Fannin St.	Houston	TX	77002	James Kipp	713-650-6344	S	132	<0.1

Company type codes: P - Public, R - Private, S - Subsidiary, D - Division, J - Joint Venture, A - Affiliate, G - Group. If the dollar values shown are not sales, the following codes apply: TA - Total Assets; OR - Operating Revenues; GB - Gross Billings. * - estimated dollar value. < - less than. *na* - not available.

Continued on next page.

LEADING COMPANIES - SIC 6153 - Short-Term Business Credit
Continued

Company Name	Address				CEO Name	Phone	Co. Type	Sales/Assets ($ mil)	Empl. (000)
Working Assets Funding Service	701 Montgomery St.	San Francisco	CA	94111	Laura Scher	415-788-0777	R	117 OR	<0.1
Fidelity Funding Inc.	12770 Merit Dr.	Dallas	TX	75251	Roger D. Marshall	214-687-8000	R	110 TA*	0.1
Arkansas Capital Corp.	225 S. Pulaski St.	Little Rock	AR	72201	Sam Walls	501-374-9247	P	100 TA	<0.1
Prime Rate Premium Finance Corp.	PO Box 100507	Florence	SC	29501	James Lingle	803-669-0937	S	100 TA*	<0.1
Tokai Financial Services Inc.	1055 Westlakes Dr.	Berwyn	PA	19312	Don Campbell	215-651-5000	R	100 TA	0.5
PROMPT Finance Inc.	PO Box 9119	Concord	MA	01742	Eric N. Wickfield	508-369-8078	S	92 TA*	<0.1
Leasing Solutions Receivables Inc.	10 Almaden Blvd.	San Jose	CA	95113	Steven L. Yeffa	408-995-6565	S	63 TA*	<0.1
Systran Financial Service Corp.	PO Box 3289	Portland	OR	97208	Ed Foehl	503-293-6400	R	55 TA	<0.1
Allstate Financial Corp.	2700 S. Quincy St.	Arlington	VA	22206	Craig Fishman	703-931-2274	P	46 TA	<0.1
AMGRO Inc.	100 North Pkwy.	Worcester	MA	01605	Dennis Howard	508-757-1628	S	45 TA	<0.1
Center Capital Corp.	PO Box 10022	Waterbury	CT	06725	Michael D. Weiss	203-674-6888	S	40 TA*	<0.1
Metro Financial Services	PO Box 38604	Dallas	TX	75238	Richard Worthy	214-363-4557	R	40 TA*	<0.1
Creekwood Capital Corp.	1010 Lamar St.	Houston	TX	77002	Steve Rosencranz	713-759-9070	R	37 TA	<0.1
Massachusetts Minority Enterprise Investment Corp.	100 Franklin St.	Boston	MA	02110	Tom Schumpert	617-338-0425	R	29 TA*	<0.1
Chicorp Financial Services Inc.	208 S. La Salle St.	Chicago	IL	60604	Timothy O'Gorman	312-855-5880	S	25 TA*	<0.1
Sitco Corp.	PO Box 5164	San Ramon	CA	94583	Howard T. Goodman	510-830-4777	R	20 TA	<0.1
Xerox Financial Services Inc.	100 1st Stamford Pl.	Stamford	CT	06904	Stuart B. Ross	203-325-6600	S	20 TA*	<0.1
Merchant Factors Corp.	1430 Broadway	New York	NY	10018	Walter Kaye	212-840-7575	R	19 TA	<0.1
Genevieve Holdings of Arizona Ltd.	PO Box 10382	Phoenix	AZ	85064	Arnold Portigal	602-381-0177	R	12 TA	<0.1
Mazon Associates Inc.	1425 Greenway Dr.	Irving	TX	75038	John Mazon	972-550-0111	R	12 TA	<0.1
Global Assurance L.L.C.	2020 Hogback Rd.	Ann Arbor	MI	48105	Gary Crispin	734-971-1570	R	12 TA	<0.1
MTB Bank. Trading Alliance Div.	90 Broad St.	New York	NY	10004	Anthony K. Brown	212-858-3450	D	10 TA*	<0.1
Nissan Capital of America Inc.	399 Park Ave.	New York	NY	10022	Yasuro Osawa	212-572-9100	S	7 TA*	<0.1
LSI Capital L.L.C.	2911 Turtle Creek Blvd.	Dallas	TX	75219	Tom Stephenson Jr.	214-522-8686	R	6 TA	<0.1
Victor Capital Group L.P.	885 Third Ave.	New York	NY	10022	Craig Hatkoff	212-593-5400	R	6 TA	<0.1
DFH Business Consulting Inc.	7261 SW 42nd Court	Davie	FL	33314	Daniel F. Herz	954-370-6200	R	5 OR	<0.1
Command Credit Corp.	100 Garden City Plz.	Garden City	NY	11530	William G. Lucas	516-739-8800	P	4 TA	<0.1
Greater Detroit BIDCO Inc.	645 Griswold St.	Detroit	MI	48226	Dione Alexander-Johnson	313-962-4326	R	4 TA*	<0.1
Caribou Capital Corp.	5350 S. Roslyn St.	Inglewood	CO	80111	Vicki Barone	303-694-6956	R	3 TA	<0.1
Foxmoor Industries Ltd.	3801 E. Florida Ave.	Denver	CO	80210	W. Ross C. Corace	303-759-4626	P	2 TA	<0.1
Capital Trust Co.	4380 Macadam Ave. #450	Portland	OR	97201	Charles Swindell	503-228-2300	R	2 TA*	<0.1

Company type codes: P - Public, R - Private, S - Subsidiary, D - Division, J - Joint Venture, A - Affiliate, G - Group. If the dollar values shown are not sales, the following codes apply: TA - Total Assets; OR - Operating Revenues; GB - Gross Billings. * - estimated dollar value. < - less than. na - not available.

Continued on next page.

LEADING COMPANIES - SIC 6153 - Short-Term Business Credit
Continued

Company Name	Address				CEO Name	Phone	Co. Type	Sales/Assets ($ mil)	Empl. (000)
Chase-Cavett Services Inc.	555 S. Perkins Rd.Extd.	Memphis	TN	38117	Will Chase	901-684-1121	R	2 TA	<0.1

Source: *Ward's Business Directory of U.S. Private and Public Companies*, 1996. Company type codes: P - Public, R - Private, S - Subsidiary, D - Division, J - Joint Venture, A - Affiliate, G - Group. If the dollar values shown are not sales, the following codes apply: TA - Total Assets; OR - Operating Revenues; GB - Gross Billings. * - estimated dollar value. < - less than; *na* - not available.

LEADING COMPANIES - SIC 6159 - Miscellaneous Business Credit Institutions
Number shown: 100   Total sales/assets ($ mil): 761,613   Total employment (000): 1,163.1

Company Name	Address				CEO Name	Phone	Co. Type	Sales/Assets ($ mil)	Empl. (000)
General Electric Capital Corp.	260 Long Ridge Rd.	Stamford	CT	06927	Gary C. Wendt	203-357-4000	S	228,777 TA	51.0
General Motors Corp.	PO Box 431301	Detroit	MI	48265	John F. Smith Jr.	313-556-5000	P	166,445	608.0
Chrysler Corp.	1000 Chrysler Dr.	Highland Park	MI	48326	Robert J. Eaton	248-576-5741	P	61,147	121.0
AT&T Corp.	32 Ave. of the Amer.	New York	NY	10013	C. Michael Armstrong	212-387-5400	P	51,319 OR	130.0
Associates First Capital Corp.	PO Box 660237	Dallas	TX	75266	Keith W. Hughes	972-652-4000	P	41,304 TA	16.6
Ford Holdings Inc.	The American Rd.	Dearborn	MI	48121	Keith W. Hughes	313-322-1639	S	41,304 TA	16.6
Chrysler Financial Corp.	27777 Franklin Rd.	Southfield	MI	48034	Darrell L. Davis	248-948-3058	S	19,321 TA	3.2
IBM Credit Corp.	1133 Westchester Ave.	White Plains	NY	10604	W. Wilson Lowery Jr.	--	S	18,600 TA*	1.3
Textron Inc.	40 Westminster St.	Providence	RI	02903	James F. Hardymon	401-421-2800	P	10,544	57.0
National Rural Utilities Cooperative Finance Corp.	2201 Cooperative Way	Herndon	VA	20171	Sheldon C. Petersen	703-709-6700	R	8,983 TA*	0.2
Dana Corp.	P.O.Box 1000	Toledo	OH	43697	Southwood J. Morcott	419-535-4500	P	8,291	47.9
AT&T Capital Corp.	44 Whippany Rd.	Morristown	NJ	07962	Thomas C. Wajnert	201-397-3000	P	8,092 TA	3.0
Finova Capital Corp.	115 W. Century Rd.	Paramus	NJ	07653	Sam Eichenfield	201-634-3300	S	8,000 TA	0.9
Caterpillar Financial Services Corp.	3322 W. End Ave.	Nashville	TN	37203	James S. Beard	615-386-5800	S	7,426 TA	0.6
FINOVA Group Inc.	PO Box 2209	Phoenix	AZ	85077	Samuel L. Eichenfield	602-207-4900	P	7,037 TA	1.0
John Deere Credit Co.	PO Box 65090	West Des Moines	IA	50265	Michael P. Orr	--	S	6,659 TA	1.0
Westinghouse Electric Corp.	11 Stanwix St.	Pittsburgh	PA	15222	Michael H. Jordan	412-244-2000	P	6,296	77.8
Textron Financial Corp.	PO Box 6687	Providence	RI	02940	Stephen A. Giliotti	401-621-4200	S	5,854 TA*	1.0
Advanta Corp.	PO Box 844	Spring House	PA	19477	Alex W. Hart	215-657-4000	P	5,584 TA	3.5
Farm Credit Services of Mid-America	Hilliard Lyons Center	Louisville	KY	40232	Don Winters	502-566-3700	R	4,210 TA*	0.7
Chrysler Capital Corp.	225 High Ridge Rd.	Stamford	CT	06905	William S. Bishop	203-975-3200	S	2,630 TA	<0.1
Money Store Inc.	2840 Morris Ave.	Union	NJ	07083	Marc Turtletaub	908-686-2000	P	2,612 TA	2.6

Company type codes: P - Public, R - Private, S - Subsidiary, D - Division, J - Joint Venture, A - Affiliate, G - Group. If the dollar values shown are not sales, the following codes apply: TA - Total Assets; OR - Operating Revenues; GB - Gross Billings. * - estimated dollar value. < - less than. *na* - not available.

Continued on next page.

LEADING COMPANIES - SIC 6159 - Miscellaneous Business Credit Institutions
Continued

Company Name	Address				CEO Name	Phone	Co. Type	Sales/Assets ($ mil)	Empl. (000)
Private Export Funding Corp.	280 Park Ave.	New York	NY	10017	Delcour S. Potter	212-286-0520	R	2,488 TA	<0.1
AT&T Capital Leasing Services Inc.	PO Box 9104	Framingham	MA	01701	James Tenner	508-620-0099	S	2,380 TA	0.7
Boeing Capital Corp.	4060 Lakewood Blvd.	Long Beach	CA	90808	Thomas J. Motherway	562-627-3100	S	2,050 TA	<0.1
Associates National Bank	4550 New Linden Hill Rd.	Wilmington	DE	19808	John Hunter	302-636-8000	D	1,920 TA	0.8
Republic Business Credit Corp.	452 5th Ave.	New York	NY	10018	John Heffer	212-525-5200	S	1,895 TA*	0.3
Dana Commercial Credit Corp.	201 W. Big Beaver Rd.	Troy	MI	48084	John Gagne	248-689-7000	S	1,800 TA	0.4
Navistar Financial Corp.	2850 W. Golf Rd.	Rolling Meadows	IL	60008	John J. Bongiorno	847-734-4000	S	1,794 TA*	0.4
Edison Capital	18101 Von Karman Ave.	Irvine	CA	92612	Thomas R. McDaniel	714-757-2400	S	1,777 TA	<0.1
United Carriers Corp.	PO Box 4070	Newark	OH	43055	R.A. Barnes	614-349-8144	R	1,750 TA*	0.3
PacifiCorp Financial Services Inc.	111 S.W. 5th Ave.	Portland	OR	97204	William J. Glasgow	503-797-6330	S	1,686 TA	0.3
GATX Capital Corp.	4 Embarcadero Ctr.	San Francisco	CA	94111	Joseph C. Lane	415-955-3200	S	1,518 TA	0.3
Bankers Leasing and Financial Corp.	989 E. Hillsdale Blvd. #300	Foster City	CA	94404	Robert Keyes	650-573-1200	S	1,422 TA*	<0.1
Norwest Equipment Finance Inc.	733 Marquette Ave.	Minneapolis	MN	55479	James R. Renner	612-667-9876	S	1,321 TA	0.1
Golodetz Trading Corp.	666 5th Ave.	New York	NY	10103	I. Suder	212-581-2400	R	1,300	0.5
Advanta Business Services Corp.	1020 Laurel Oak Rd.	Voorhees	NJ	08043	Charles Podowski	609-782-7300	S	1,020 TA	0.4
Concord Leasing Inc.	40 Richards Ave.	Norwalk	CT	06856	Michael O'Hanlon	203-854-5454	S	1,000 TA	0.3
Clark Credit Corp.	500 Circle Dr.	Buchanan	MI	49107	Dick Goble	616-697-4000	S	800 TA	0.2
Colonial Pacific Leasing Corp.	PO Box 23012	Portland	OR	97281	Michael G. Cingari	503-670-2301	S	750 TA*	0.3
DVI Inc.	500 Hyde Park	Doylestown	PA	18901	Michael A. O'Hanlon	215-345-6600	P	634 TA	0.1
Financial Federal Corp.	400 Park Ave.	New York	NY	10022	Clarence Palitz Jr.	212-888-3344	P	575 TA	0.1
Farm Credit Leasing Services Corp.	5500 Wayzata Blvd.	Minneapolis	MN	55416	James W. Eiler	612-797-7400	R	530 TA	0.1
ASA Investments Inc.	100 Hartsfield Centre Pkwy.	Atlanta	GA	30354	George F. Pickett	404-766-1400		506 TA	2.1
Farm Credit Services of Northern Illinois	PO Box 131	Kaneville	IL	60144	John D. Webb	630-557-2440	R	500 TA	<0.1
American Equipment Leasing Company Inc.	PO Box 13428	Reading	PA	19612	Arthur A. Haberberger	610-775-3134	R	490 TA*	<0.1
First South Production Credit Association	713 S. Pear Orchard Rd.	Ridgeland	MS	39157	Stephen L. Rochelle	601-977-8394	R	480 TA	0.2
Norwest Financial Leasing Inc.	319 7th St.	Des Moines	IA	50309	Greg Janasko	515-282-3993	S	466 TA	0.2
Pentzer Corp.	818 W. Riverside Ave.	Spokane	WA	99201	Richard Davis	509-459-1350	S	420 TA*	1.2
PEC Israel Economic Corp.	511 Fifth Ave.	New York	NY	10017	Frank Klein	212-687-2400	P	408 TA	<0.1

Company type codes: P - Public, R - Private, S - Subsidiary, D - Division, J - Joint Venture, A - Affiliate, G - Group. If the dollar values shown are not sales, the following codes apply: TA - Total Assets; OR - Operating Revenues; GB - Gross Billings. * - estimated dollar value. < - less than. *na* - not available.

Continued on next page.

LEADING COMPANIES - SIC 6159 - Miscellaneous Business Credit Institutions
Continued

Company Name	Address				CEO Name	Phone	Co. Type	Sales/Assets ($ mil)	Empl. (000)
Circle Business Credit Inc.	PO Box 44901	Indianapolis	IN	46244	David McCellan	317-767-0077	S	351 TA*	<0.1
Security Pacific Executive-Professional Services Inc.	14707 E. 2nd Ave.	Aurora	CO	80011	Richard Rushton	303-363-7600	S	350 TA*	<0.1
Rush Enterprises Inc.	PO Box 34630	San Antonio	TX	78265	W. Marvin Rush	210-661-4511	P	344	0.7
Philip Morris Capital Corp.	200 First Stamford Place	Stamford	CT	06902	George R. Lewis	914-335-8155	S	340 TA	<0.1
Mid-North Financial Services Inc.	205 W. Wacker Dr.	Chicago	IL	60606	Al Hanna	312-641-0660	R	318 TA	<0.1
Trans Leasing International Inc.	3000 Dundee Rd.	Northbrook	IL	60062	Larry S. Grossman	847-272-1000	P	311 TA	0.2
Inter-American Investment Corp.	1300 New York Ave. N.W.	Washington	DC	20577	John C. Rahming	202-623-3900	R	306 TA	<0.1
D'Accord Holdings Inc.	1 Embarcadero Ctr.	San Francisco	CA	94111	Christopher W. Gould	415-981-3812	R	300 TA*	<0.1
SNS Investment Co.	36 S. Pennsylvania St.	Indianapolis	IN	46204	Alan B. Gilman	317-633-4100	S	290 TA*	<0.1
Ampal-American Israel Corp.	1177 Ave. of the Amer.	New York	NY	10036	Yehoshua Gleitman	212-782-2100	P	284 TA	<0.1
Gillco Inc.	7611 Bellaire Blvd.	Houston	TX	77036	Ramsay H. Gillman	713-776-7000	R	275	0.9
Potomac Capital Investment Corp.	1801 K St. N.W.	Washington	DC	20006	John D. McCallum	202-775-4620	S	229 TA*	<0.1
Emergent Group Inc.	PO Box 17526	Greenville	SC	29606	John M. Sterling Jr.	864-235-8056	P	224 TA	0.5
Advance Leasing Corp.	7366 N. Lincoln Ave.	Lincolnwood	IL	60646	Edward M. Telman	847-677-3150	R	200 TA*	<0.1
Willis Lease Finance Corp.	180 Harbor Dr.	Sausalito	CA	94965	Charles F. Willis IV	415-331-5281	P	198 TA	<0.1
Capital Associates International Inc.	7175 W. Jefferson Ave.	Lakewood	CO	80235	Dennis J. Lacey	303-980-1000	S	187 OR	0.1
Earnhardt Ford Sales Co.	777 E. Baseline Rd.	Tempe	AZ	85283	Hal Earnhardt	602-838-6000	R	180*	0.5
Ruan Leasing Co.	3200 Ruan Ctr.	Des Moines	IA	50309	Gary Alvord	515-245-2500	R	180 TA	1.8
Ameritech Credit Corp.	2550 W. Golf Rd.	Rolling Meadows	IL	60008	R. Scott Horsley	708-290-5000	S	170 TA	<0.1
Copelco Financial Services Group Inc.	1700 Suckle Plz.	Pennsauken	NJ	08110	Ian J. Berg	609-665-6400	S	165 TA	0.5
NAL Financial Group Inc.	PO Box 8367	Fort Lauderdale	FL	33310	Robert R. Bartolini	305-938-8200	P	150 TA	0.5
Iowa State Bank	PO Box 6100	Des Moines	IA	50309		515-288-0111	S	131 TA	<0.1
First Community Financial Corp.	3550 N. Central Ave.	Phoenix	AZ	85012	James Adamany	602-265-7714	R	131 TA*	<0.1
HPSC Inc.	60 State St.	Boston	MA	02109	John W. Everets	617-720-3600	P	131 TA	<0.1
Hyster Credit Co.	PO Box 4366	Portland	OR	97208	William F. Burke	503-321-5400	D	130 TA	<0.1
Chase Community Development Corp.	2 Chase Manhattan Plz. 12th Fl.	New York	NY	10081	Mark A. Willis	212-552-8519	S	110 TA*	<0.1
Fidelity Funding Inc.	12770 Merit Dr.	Dallas	TX	75251	Roger D. Marshall	214-687-8000	R	110 TA*	0.1
First New England Financial Corp.	1000 Bridgeport Ave.	Shelton	CT	06484	Jim Foley	203-944-2810	S	110 TA*	<0.1

Company type codes: P - Public, R - Private, S - Subsidiary, D - Division, J - Joint Venture, A - Affiliate, G - Group. If the dollar values shown are not sales, the following codes apply: TA - Total Assets; OR - Operating Revenues; GB - Gross Billings. * - estimated dollar value. < - less than. *na* - not available.

Continued on next page.

LEADING COMPANIES - SIC 6159 - Miscellaneous Business Credit Institutions

Continued

Company Name	Address				CEO Name	Phone	Co. Type	Sales/Assets ($ mil)	Empl. (000)
New York Business Development Corp.	PO Box 738	Albany	NY	12201	Robert W. Lazar	518-463-2268	R	100 TA	<0.1
PROMPT Finance Inc.	PO Box 9119	Concord	MA	01742	Eric N. Wickfield	508-369-8078	S	92 TA*	<0.1
Automated Installment Systems	PO Box 66002	Anaheim	CA	92816	Michael Wood	714-978-2268	R	87 TA*	<0.1
Prime Capital Corp.	10275 W. Higgins Rd.	Rosemont	IL	60018	James A. Friedman	847-294-6000	P	81 TA	<0.1
First Sierra Financial Inc.	600 Travis St.	Houston	TX	77002	Thomas J. Depping	713-221-8822	P	79 TA	<0.1
Direct Corp.	905 E. Trinity Ln.	Nashville	TN	37207	Jackie Adair	615-226-2550	R	77 TA	0.8
EnCap Investment L.L.C.	6688 N. Central Expwy.	Dallas	TX	75206	David B. Miller	214-696-6700	R	71 TA*	<0.1
Eagle Finance Corp.	1425 Tri-State Pkwy	Gurnee	IL	60031	Charles F. Wonderlic	847-855-7150	P	64 TA	0.3
Freeman Spogli and Co.	11100 Santa Monica Blvd.	Los Angeles	CA	90025	Bradford Freeman	310-444-1822	R	58 TA*	<0.1
Sovlink Corp.	1221 Ave. of the Amer.	New York	NY	10020	Terrence J. English	212-730-4868	R	58 TA*	<0.1
Domain Energy Corp.	PO Box 2229	Houston	TX	77252	Michael V. Ronca	713-757-5662	P	57	<0.1
Associated Leasing Inc.	PO Box 10	Menomonee Falls	WI	53052	Peter c. Bapes	414-253-2300	S	52 TA*	<0.1
Allied Financial Corp.	1583 Beacon St.	Brookline	MA	02146	Andre Danesh	617-734-7771	R	51 TA	<0.1
Balboa Capital Corp.	2010 Main St.	Irvine	CA	92614	Tommy Romero	714-756-0800	R	51*	0.1
Sterling Industrial Loan Association	5516 Falmouth St.	Richmond	VA	23230	William Bower	804-288-6580	S	49 TA*	<0.1
PDS Financial Corp.	6442 City West Pkwy.	Minneapolis	MN	55344	Johan P. Finley	612-941-9500	P	47 TA	<0.1
Granite Financial Inc.	16100 Table Mountain Pkwy.	Golden	CO	80403	Larry White	303-216-3500	S	46 TA	<0.1
Stratford Capital Partners L.P.	200 Crescent Ct.	Dallas	TX	75201	Michael D. Brown	214-740-7377	S	45 TA	<0.1
Eagle Pacific Industries Inc.	2430 Lincoln Ctr.	Minneapolis	MN	55402	Harry W. Spell	612-371-9650	P	35 TA	0.3
John Hancock Leasing Corp.	PO Box 111	Boston	MA	02117	John M. Butler	617-572-6000	S	34 TA	<0.1
Source Capital Corp.	1825 N. Hutchinson Rd.	Spokane	WA	99212	Michael Jones	509-928-0908	P	31 TA	<0.1
MLC Group Inc.	11150 Sunset Hills Rd.	Reston	VA	20190	Phillip G. Norton	703-834-5710	S	30 TA	<0.1

Source: *Ward's Business Directory of U.S. Private and Public Companies*, 1996. Company type codes: P - Public, R - Private, S - Subsidiary, D - Division, J - Joint Venture, A - Affiliate, G - Group. If the dollar values shown are not sales, the following codes apply: TA - Total Assets; OR - Operating Revenues; GB - Gross Billings. * - estimated dollar value. < - less than; *na* - not available.

SIC 6160

MORTGAGE BANKERS AND BROKERS

The group is divided into SIC 6162, Mortgage Bankers and Loan Correspondents and SIC 6163, Loan Brokers. Mortgage bankers are engaged in originating mortgage loans, selling mortgage loans to permanent investors, and servicing these loans. They may also provide real estate construction loans. Bond and mortgage companies, loan correspondents, mortgage bankers, mortgage brokers using their own money, and urban mortgage companies are included in this category.

SIC 6163 includes establishments engaged in arranging loans for others. These establishments ordinarily operate on a commission or fee basis and do not usually have any continuing relationship with either borrower or lender. Included are agents and brokers for farm or business loans, loan agents and brokers, and mortgage bankers arranging for loans using money of others.

ESTABLISHMENTS, EMPLOYMENT, AND PAYROLL

	1990	1991		1992		1993		1994		1995		% change 90-95
		Value	%	Value	%	Value	%	Value	%	Value	%	
All Establishments	10,867	12,805	17.8	15,098	17.9	18,512	22.6	20,844	12.6	20,490	-1.7	88.6
Mid-March Employment	152,809	149,618	-2.1	180,747	20.8	207,942	15.0	258,006	24.1	202,109	-21.7	32.3
1st Quarter Wages (annualized - $ mil.)	4,823.0	4,684.6	-2.9	6,538.6	39.6	6,934.1	6.0	9,171.7	32.3	7,051.6	-23.1	46.2
Payroll per Emp. 1st Q. (annualized)	31,562	31,310	-0.8	36,176	15.5	33,346	-7.8	35,549	6.6	34,890	-1.9	10.5
Annual Payroll ($ mil.)	4,563.2	5,011.7	9.8	7,100.1	41.7	8,814.7	24.1	7,985.4	-9.4	7,456.6	-6.6	63.4
Establishments - 1-4 Emp. Number	5,797	6,885	18.8	8,237	19.6	10,302	25.1	10,931	6.1	12,099	10.7	108.7
Mid-March Employment	10,579	12,213	15.4	14,165	16.0	16,222	14.5	18,254	12.5	19,667	7.7	85.9
1st Quarter Wages (annualized - $ mil.)	313.3	367.0	17.1	470.6	28.2	518.9	10.3	601.1	15.8	634.0	5.5	102.4
Payroll per Emp. 1st Q. (annualized)	29,614	30,049	1.5	33,225	10.6	31,988	-3.7	32,928	2.9	32,236	-2.1	8.9
Annual Payroll ($ mil.)	373.2	484.9	29.9	652.4	34.6	862.3	32.2	690.4	-19.9	891.0	29.1	138.8
Establishments - 5-9 Emp. Number	2,250	2,791	24.0	3,044	9.1	3,506	15.2	4,180	19.2	4,024	-3.7	78.8
Mid-March Employment	14,911	18,605	24.8	20,202	8.6	23,243	15.1	27,567	18.6	26,403	-4.2	77.1
1st Quarter Wages (annualized - $ mil.)	461.1	566.0	22.8	737.8	30.3	766.7	3.9	955.0	24.6	880.5	-7.8	91.0
Payroll per Emp. 1st Q. (annualized)	30,924	30,424	-1.6	36,523	20.0	32,986	-9.7	34,641	5.0	33,348	-3.7	7.8
Annual Payroll ($ mil.)	447.8	626.6	39.9	834.7	33.2	1,005.2	20.4	826.9	-17.7	963.5	16.5	115.2
Establishments - 10-19 Emp. Number	1,522	1,837	20.7	2,173	18.3	2,704	24.4	3,174	17.4	2,548	-19.7	67.4
Mid-March Employment	20,545	24,569	19.6	29,318	19.3	36,675	25.1	43,212	17.8	34,218	-20.8	66.6
1st Quarter Wages (annualized - $ mil.)	672.3	813.8	21.0	1,139.0	40.0	1,307.7	14.8	1,651.0	26.2	1,234.3	-25.2	83.6
Payroll per Emp. 1st Q. (annualized)	32,723	33,122	1.2	38,851	17.3	35,658	-8.2	38,207	7.1	36,072	-5.6	10.2
Annual Payroll ($ mil.)	632.7	901.7	42.5	1,261.1	39.9	1,721.6	36.5	1,355.8	-21.3	1,272.7	-6.1	101.2
Establishments - 20-49 Emp. Number	809	886	9.5	1,108	25.1	1,461	31.9	1,795	22.9	1,295	-27.9	60.1
Mid-March Employment	24,106	25,366	5.2	32,692	28.9	42,812	31.0	51,782	21.0	37,208	-28.1	54.4
1st Quarter Wages (annualized - $ mil.)	770.8	769.8	-0.1	1,239.2	61.0	1,536.9	24.0	1,970.3	28.2	1,386.9	-29.6	79.9
Payroll per Emp. 1st Q. (annualized)	31,975	30,347	-5.1	37,905	24.9	35,900	-5.3	38,050	6.0	37,275	-2.0	16.6
Annual Payroll ($ mil.)	725.8	839.5	15.7	1,364.7	62.6	1,966.4	44.1	1,632.1	-17.0	1,436.3	-12.0	97.9
Establishments - 50-99 Emp. Number	242	187	-22.7	302	61.5	287	-5.0	439	53.0	282	-35.8	16.5
Mid-March Employment	16,704	13,021	-22.0	20,422	56.8	19,658	-3.7	29,853	51.9	19,183	-35.7	14.8
1st Quarter Wages (annualized - $ mil.)	540.9	381.4	-29.5	715.0	87.5	614.7	-14.0	1,059.1	72.3	650.1	-38.6	20.2
Payroll per Emp. 1st Q. (annualized)	32,382	29,293	-9.5	35,010	19.5	31,270	-10.7	35,477	13.5	33,889	-4.5	4.7
Annual Payroll ($ mil.)	498.8	392.1	-21.4	725.1	84.9	797.8	10.0	898.7	12.7	676.7	-24.7	35.7
Establishments - 100-249 Emp. Number	167	151	-9.6	150	-0.7	157	4.7	216	37.6	160	-25.9	-4.2
Mid-March Employment	25,451	22,761	-10.6	22,716	-0.2	23,884	5.1	33,204	39.0	24,605	-25.9	-3.3
1st Quarter Wages (annualized - $ mil.)	789.3	736.3	-6.7	788.4	7.1	796.1	1.0	1,111.9	39.7	850.4	-23.5	7.7
Payroll per Emp. 1st Q. (annualized)	31,014	32,347	4.3	34,705	7.3	33,330	-4.0	33,486	0.5	34,560	3.2	11.4
Annual Payroll ($ mil.)	781.3	748.9	-4.2	821.7	9.7	910.3	10.8	963.4	5.8	888.7	-7.8	13.7
Establishments - 250-499 Emp. Number	52	43	-17.3	54	25.6	64	18.5	70	9.4	58	-17.1	11.5
Mid-March Employment	17,798	14,494	-18.6	17,677	22.0	21,478	21.5	23,646	10.1	20,241	-14.4	13.7
1st Quarter Wages (annualized - $ mil.)	529.2	441.0	-16.7	569.1	29.1	682.7	20.0	766.4	12.3	728.4	-5.0	37.7
Payroll per Emp. 1st Q. (annualized)	29,731	30,427	2.3	32,196	5.8	31,788	-1.3	32,410	2.0	35,988	11.0	21.0
Annual Payroll ($ mil.)	470.0	413.8	-12.0	586.6	41.7	760.5	29.6	679.1	-10.7	689.6	1.5	46.7
Establishments - 500-999 Emp. Number	21	21	-	25	19.0	26	4.0	31	19.2	18	-41.9	-14.3
Mid-March Employment	(D)	12,814	-	17,121	33.6	17,118	-0.0	20,402	19.2	12,046	-41.0	-
1st Quarter Wages (annualized - $ mil.)	(D)	338.7	-	540.4	59.5	515.3	-4.6	713.9	38.6	449.9	-37.0	-
Payroll per Emp. 1st Q. (annualized)	(D)	26,431	-	31,562	19.4	30,100	-4.6	34,991	16.3	37,350	6.7	-
Annual Payroll ($ mil.)	(D)	351.5	-	573.1	63.1	567.7	-0.9	631.5	11.2	411.3	-34.9	-
Estab. - 1000 or More Emp. Number	7	4	-42.9	5	25.0	5	-	8	60.0	6	-25.0	-14.3
Mid-March Employment	(D)	5,775	-	6,434	11.4	6,852	6.5	10,086	47.2	8,538	-15.3	-
1st Quarter Wages (annualized - $ mil.)	(D)	270.6	-	339.1	25.3	195.1	-42.5	343.2	75.9	237.1	-30.9	-
Payroll per Emp. 1st Q. (annualized)	(D)	46,859	-	52,701	12.5	28,476	-46.0	34,025	19.5	27,768	-18.4	-
Annual Payroll ($ mil.)	(D)	252.8	-	280.6	11.0	222.9	-20.6	307.5	38.0	226.7	-26.3	-

Source: County Business Patterns, U.S. Department of Commerce, Washington, D.C., for 1990 through 1995. Payroll per employee is calculated using mid-March employment and 1st Quarter wages, annualized. Annual payroll, also shown, may not equal the annualized 1st Quarter wages. Columns headed by a percent sign (%) indicate change from the previous year. *na* stands for not available. The symbol (D) indicates that data are withheld by the source to avoid disclosure of competitive information. A dash (-) indicates that data are not available or cannot be calculated.

ESTABLISHMENTS
Number

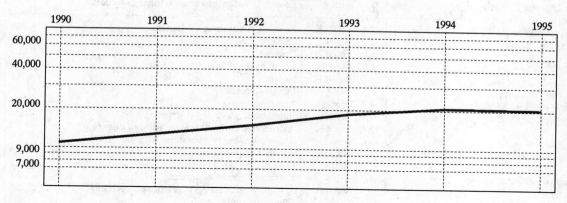

MID-MARCH EMPLOYMENT
Number

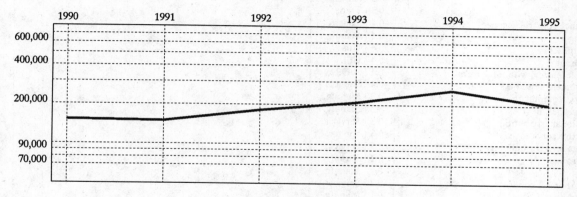

ANNUAL PAYROLL
$ million

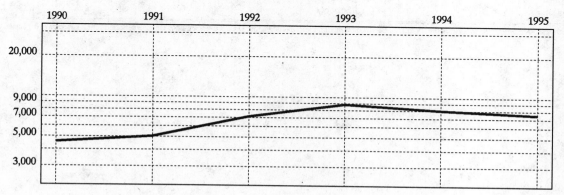

INPUTS AND OUTPUTS FOR CREDIT AGENCIES OTHER THAN BANKS - SICs 606, 611, 614-16

Economic Sector or Industry Providing Inputs	%	Sector	Economic Sector or Industry Buying Outputs	%	Sector
Security & commodity brokers	27.5	Fin/R.E.	Personal consumption expenditures	36.7	
Credit agencies other than banks	14.1	Fin/R.E.	Owner-occupied dwellings	18.9	Fin/R.E.
Banking	6.9	Fin/R.E.	Banking	13.5	Fin/R.E.
Advertising	6.0	Services	Credit agencies other than banks	11.1	Fin/R.E.
Real estate agents, operators, & lessors	5.6	Fin/R.E.	Hotels	3.6	Services
Federal Government enterprises nec	5.3	Gov't	Insurance carriers	2.9	Fin/R.E.
Management & public relations services	4.9	Services	Air transportation	2.1	Util.
Computer & data processing services	4.4	Services	Retail trade, ex eating & drinking	2.0	Trade
Business services nec	3.4	Services	Automotive rental & leasing, without drivers	1.9	Services
Legal services	2.6	Services	Real estate agents, operators, & lessors	1.5	Fin/R.E.
Accounting, auditing & bookkeeping	2.0	Services	Water transportation	1.4	Util.
U.S. Postal Service	1.8	Gov't	Eating & drinking places	1.1	Services
Telephone/telegraph communications nec	1.7	Util.	Exports of goods & services	0.8	Foreign
Personnel supply services	1.7	Services	S/L Govt., general government nec, spending	0.5	S/L Govt
Trucking & courier services, ex air	1.2	Util.	Wholesale trade	0.3	Trade
Research, development, & testing services	0.8	Services	Meat animals	0.2	Agric.
Insurance carriers	0.7	Fin/R.E.	Automotive repair shops & services	0.2	Services
Eating & drinking places	0.7	Services	Feed grains	0.1	Agric.
Air transportation	0.6	Util.			
Hotels	0.6	Services			
Wholesale trade	0.5	Trade			
Repair & maintenance construction nec	0.4	Constr.			
Commercial printing	0.4	Manufg.			
Electric services (utilities)	0.4	Util.			
Warehousing & storage	0.4	Util.			
Automotive rental & leasing, without drivers	0.4	Services			
Miscellaneous equipment rental & leasing	0.4	Services			
Computer peripheral equipment	0.3	Manufg.			
Manufacturing industries, nec	0.3	Manufg.			
Business & professional associations	0.3	Services			
Detective & protective services	0.3	Services			
Services to dwellings & other buildings	0.3	Services			
Manifold business forms	0.2	Manufg.			
Petroleum refining	0.2	Manufg.			
Automotive repair shops & services	0.2	Services			
Book publishing	0.1	Manufg.			
Paper & paperboard mills	0.1	Manufg.			
Periodicals	0.1	Manufg.			
Photographic equipment & supplies	0.1	Manufg.			
Local & suburban transit	0.1	Util.			
Miscellaneous repair shops	0.1	Services			

Source: Benchmark Input-Output Accounts for the U.S. Economy, 1992, U.S. Department of Commerce, Washington, D.C., November 1997. Data, as reported in the source, are organized by the 1987 SIC structure in use in 1992.

OCCUPATIONS EMPLOYED BY MORTGAGE BANKERS AND BROKERS

Occupation	% of Total 1996	Change to 2006	Occupation	% of Total 1996	Change to 2006
Loan officers & counselors	22.3	60.6	Bill & account collectors	1.8	51.9
Loan & credit clerks	20.3	29.6	Management support workers nec	1.6	28.4
General office clerks	7.1	10.5	Clerical & administrative workers nec	1.6	28.5
Clerical supervisors & managers	4.6	28.4	Sales & related workers nec	1.5	41.3
General managers & top executives	4.5	24.5	Securities & financial sales workers	1.5	92.7
Financial managers	4.1	28.4	Accountants & auditors	1.4	18.9
Receptionists & information clerks	3.1	28.5	Adjustment clerks	1.4	73.4
Secretaries, except legal & medical	3.1	1.9	Underwriters	1.3	36.7
Credit analysts	2.8	28.5	Real estate appraisers	1.1	28.5
Bookkeeping, accounting, & auditing clerks	2.7	2.8	Loan interviewers	1.1	28.4

Sources: Industry-Occupation Matrix, Bureau of Labor Statistics. These data relate to one or more 3-digit SIC industry groups rather than to a single 4-digit SIC. The change reported for each occupation to the year 2005 is a percent of growth or decline as estimated by the Bureau of Labor Statistics. The abbreviation nec stands for not elsewhere classified.

U.S. AND STATE DATA ON INDUSTRY REVENUES AND OTHER ACCOUNTS FOR 1992

State	No. of Estab.	Employment	Payroll ($ mil.)	Revenues ($ mil.)	Empl./ Estab.	Revenue/ Estab. ($)	Payroll/ Estab. ($)	Revenue/ Empl. ($)	Payroll/ Empl. ($)
UNITED STATES	16,152	178,976	6,907.7	23,073.7	11	1,428,537	427,669	128,921	38,596
Alabama	196	2,739	80.8	294.0	14	1,499,796	412,122	107,324	29,491
Alaska	22	-	(D)	(D)	(D)	(D)	(D)	(D)	(D)
Arizona	342	3,313	135.0	334.3	10	977,474	394,731	100,904	40,748
Arkansas	65	714	21.6	53.8	11	827,215	332,062	75,307	30,230
California	4,294	37,763	1,561.0	5,527.4	9	1,287,247	363,529	146,372	41,337
Colorado	367	-	(D)	(D)	(D)	(D)	(D)	(D)	(D)
Connecticut	206	-	(D)	(D)	(D)	(D)	(D)	(D)	(D)
Delaware	61	-	(D)	(D)	(D)	(D)	(D)	(D)	(D)
District of Columbia	21	-	(D)	(D)	(D)	(D)	(D)	(D)	(D)
Florida	1,376	-	(D)	(D)	(D)	(D)	(D)	(D)	(D)
Georgia	510	4,701	180.1	596.7	9	1,170,002	353,220	126,931	38,320
Hawaii	96	1,021	48.4	113.7	11	1,183,875	504,656	111,314	47,451
Idaho	55	525	16.7	96.3	10	1,751,382	303,055	183,478	31,749
Illinois	547	-	(D)	(D)	(D)	(D)	(D)	(D)	(D)
Indiana	212	3,626	150.2	371.2	17	1,750,736	708,642	102,360	41,432
Iowa	50	-	(D)	(D)	(D)	(D)	(D)	(D)	(D)
Kansas	91	1,258	40.8	168.9	14	1,855,538	448,187	134,224	32,421
Kentucky	94	1,106	38.7	122.2	12	1,300,149	411,479	110,501	34,972
Louisiana	136	1,301	37.4	108.2	10	795,603	275,088	83,168	28,756
Maine	19	-	(D)	(D)	(D)	(D)	(D)	(D)	(D)
Maryland	422	5,338	265.1	975.1	13	2,310,623	628,268	182,668	49,668
Massachusetts	283	-	(D)	(D)	(D)	(D)	(D)	(D)	(D)
Michigan	354	6,500	233.6	928.5	18	2,622,898	659,831	142,847	35,935
Minnesota	215	4,617	197.6	736.4	21	3,425,316	919,205	159,507	42,805
Mississippi	88	612	14.4	49.6	7	563,386	164,159	81,010	23,605
Missouri	181	4,260	182.1	708.5	24	3,914,641	1,006,326	166,326	42,757
Montana	22	-	(D)	(D)	(D)	(D)	(D)	(D)	(D)
Nebraska	38	518	19.0	80.7	14	2,123,447	498,684	155,774	36,583
Nevada	162	1,319	51.5	183.6	8	1,133,506	317,623	139,218	39,011
New Hampshire	56	650	24.4	72.2	12	1,289,661	435,554	111,109	37,525
New Jersey	480	8,041	312.4	1,054.5	17	2,196,954	650,775	131,145	38,847
New Mexico	62	432	16.7	45.6	7	735,371	269,548	105,539	38,685
New York	774	8,454	325.1	1,289.8	11	1,666,362	420,010	152,563	38,454
North Carolina	340	-	(D)	(D)	(D)	(D)	(D)	(D)	(D)
North Dakota	10	72	1.7	3.8	7	377,800	168,500	52,472	23,403
Ohio	416	-	(D)	(D)	(D)	(D)	(D)	(D)	(D)
Oklahoma	110	1,402	40.4	145.3	13	1,321,182	366,873	103,659	28,785
Oregon	271	-	(D)	(D)	(D)	(D)	(D)	(D)	(D)
Pennsylvania	411	-	(D)	(D)	(D)	(D)	(D)	(D)	(D)
Rhode Island	77	-	(D)	(D)	(D)	(D)	(D)	(D)	(D)
South Carolina	187	1,445	41.3	125.3	8	669,893	220,684	86,692	28,559
South Dakota	14	-	(D)	(D)	(D)	(D)	(D)	(D)	(D)
Tennessee	233	-	(D)	(D)	(D)	(D)	(D)	(D)	(D)
Texas	849	12,394	451.5	1,350.0	15	1,590,151	531,807	108,927	36,429
Utah	133	1,507	63.1	147.8	11	1,111,414	474,241	98,088	41,854
Vermont	24	-	(D)	(D)	(D)	(D)	(D)	(D)	(D)
Virginia	495	-	(D)	(D)	(D)	(D)	(D)	(D)	(D)
Washington	500	-	(D)	(D)	(D)	(D)	(D)	(D)	(D)
West Virginia	15	98	2.7	8.8	7	584,133	177,133	89,408	27,112
Wisconsin	155	1,588	69.4	232.5	10	1,500,290	447,606	146,439	43,690
Wyoming	15	-	(D)	(D)	(D)	(D)	(D)	(D)	(D)

Source: 1992 Economic Census, U.S. Department of Commerce, Washington, D.C. This is the only table that shows revenue data as collected by the Bureau of the Census in an Economic Census. The symbol (D) indicates that data are withheld by the source to avoid disclosure of competitive information. A dash (-) indicates that data are not available or cannot be calculated.

STATE-BY-STATE DATA ON ESTABLISHMENTS, EMPLOYMENT, AND PAYROLL - 1994 AND 1995

State	1994					1995					% Change Empl.
	No. of Estab.	Employ-ment	Pay / Empl.	Payroll ($ mil.)	Pay / Estab.	No. of Estab.	Employ-ment	Pay / Empl.	Payroll ($ mil.)	Pay / Estab.	
Alabama	242	3,468	30,430	101.3	418,401	226	2,269	31,242	74.6	330,049	-34.6
Alaska	29	317	50,562	13.5	464,414	27	235	52,664	13.1	483,519	-25.9
Arizona	439	5,714	36,466	185.8	423,166	473	4,234	35,425	156.0	329,869	-25.9
Arkansas	75	956	30,251	25.7	342,680	87	810	28,998	24.5	281,057	-15.3
California	4,916	51,754	37,442	1,565.9	318,540	4,098	33,135	37,878	1,326.7	323,738	-36.0
Colorado	673	6,573	35,640	192.6	286,227	678	4,965	34,426	188.8	278,400	-24.5
Connecticut	246	(D)	-	(D)	-	252	(D)	-	(D)	-	-
Delaware	83	744	33,613	23.6	284,855	83	581	30,974	20.2	243,880	-21.9
District of Columbia	26	240	60,100	13.6	524,192	26	234	64,684	15.0	578,269	-2.5
Florida	1,693	15,105	30,080	426.8	252,105	1,687	12,416	31,195	406.4	240,884	-17.8
Georgia	674	8,438	33,941	241.3	357,975	696	6,264	32,437	225.3	323,662	-25.8
Hawaii	116	1,411	54,721	50.0	430,828	105	881	44,935	35.8	340,971	-37.6
Idaho	97	583	33,029	17.0	175,464	105	625	28,122	19.0	181,181	7.2
Illinois	791	11,002	35,640	370.9	468,900	897	10,363	35,815	412.0	459,271	-5.8
Indiana	304	5,470	34,336	169.9	559,023	335	5,064	28,818	172.4	514,728	-7.4
Iowa	71	2,089	35,347	62.7	882,803	82	2,324	33,974	69.9	852,402	11.2
Kansas	126	2,030	33,062	58.8	466,556	133	1,648	33,910	54.0	405,759	-18.8
Kentucky	123	1,901	25,953	48.4	393,317	148	1,738	26,115	45.7	308,993	-8.6
Louisiana	199	2,073	28,178	50.0	251,276	213	2,074	30,825	58.8	276,009	0.0
Maine	35	478	30,603	12.1	345,886	38	331	28,218	8.8	232,658	-30.8
Maryland	577	7,717	42,183	283.6	491,503	577	5,580	43,140	242.9	420,974	-27.7
Massachusetts	396	4,887	39,799	154.5	390,030	381	3,290	37,894	139.3	365,669	-32.7
Michigan	447	9,278	29,368	247.9	554,613	522	6,468	32,024	247.5	474,094	-30.3
Minnesota	351	7,277	40,697	231.2	658,715	370	4,905	40,539	180.2	487,127	-32.6
Mississippi	108	811	24,360	17.7	164,046	121	1,058	25,448	25.0	206,628	30.5
Missouri	267	5,791	30,855	162.5	608,498	287	4,672	34,568	170.4	593,568	-19.3
Montana	33	316	25,709	8.1	245,727	42	186	26,538	6.7	159,643	-41.1
Nebraska	59	751	33,598	22.6	382,695	58	712	29,601	27.7	477,103	-5.2
Nevada	205	1,915	40,418	66.9	326,366	228	1,504	36,383	56.2	246,351	-21.5
New Hampshire	72	876	32,050	25.7	356,750	71	854	31,040	30.6	430,803	-2.5
New Jersey	573	9,730	36,549	349.3	609,611	549	8,354	39,552	351.9	640,900	-14.1
New Mexico	103	702	33,829	21.8	211,845	109	634	31,855	19.1	175,596	-9.7
New York	852	11,328	38,861	418.1	490,752	873	12,624	36,937	482.2	552,301	11.4
North Carolina	455	5,509	32,221	159.9	351,534	500	5,578	33,013	168.8	337,504	1.3
North Dakota	11	(D)	-	(D)	-	11	(D)	-	(D)	-	-
Ohio	618	7,230	31,026	207.6	335,947	619	6,293	28,273	204.3	330,099	-13.0
Oklahoma	138	1,635	29,649	43.5	315,435	141	1,417	27,585	39.3	278,745	-13.3
Oregon	363	3,482	37,359	110.1	303,201	387	2,305	34,016	91.3	235,845	-33.8
Pennsylvania	579	7,224	35,068	240.0	414,425	564	5,676	34,700	230.5	408,668	-21.4
Rhode Island	107	1,267	30,870	34.4	321,178	99	1,021	29,587	34.6	349,040	-19.4
South Carolina	225	2,967	29,611	80.5	357,822	253	2,970	31,749	100.6	397,510	0.1
South Dakota	17	113	52,319	4.3	251,765	16	124	50,419	4.7	291,563	9.7
Tennessee	285	3,126	36,223	101.9	357,474	300	2,382	30,294	78.9	263,147	-23.8
Texas	1,157	17,184	37,180	577.9	499,499	1,139	13,893	36,243	502.5	441,220	-19.2
Utah	242	3,673	30,838	90.9	375,682	270	2,274	28,069	75.9	281,248	-38.1
Vermont	27	266	29,158	6.5	239,926	29	226	26,637	6.0	207,552	-15.0
Virginia	620	7,852	39,197	248.3	400,547	613	5,734	36,249	215.5	351,589	-27.0
Washington	749	7,385	34,828	206.9	276,223	691	5,079	35,090	187.9	271,977	-31.2
West Virginia	20	64	27,750	1.9	94,100	24	46	32,087	2.3	94,875	-28.1
Wisconsin	212	3,928	29,280	101.2	477,382	238	3,613	24,498	97.7	410,437	-8.0
Wyoming	18	172	38,860	5.0	279,667	19	135	34,193	4.6	240,316	-21.5

Source: County Business Patterns, U.S. Department of Commerce, Washington, D.C., for 1994 and 1995. Employment shown is for mid-March of the year shown. Payroll per employee is calculated by annualizing 1st Quarter payroll (not shown) and then dividing that value by mid-March employment. Dividing total annual payroll (columns 5 and 10) by employment, therefore, will *not* yield the payroll per employee figure (columns 4 and 9). The symbol (D) indicates that data are withheld by the source to avoid disclosure of competitive information. A dash (-) indicates that data are not available or cannot be calculated.

ESTABLISHMENTS 1995 - STATE AND REGIONAL CONCENTRATION

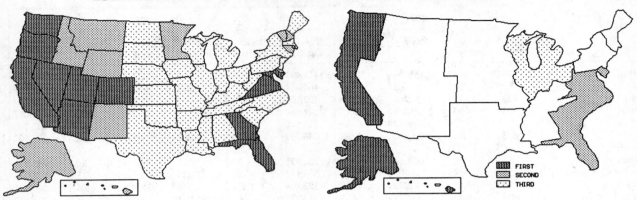

EMPLOYMENT 1995 - STATE AND REGIONAL CONCENTRATION

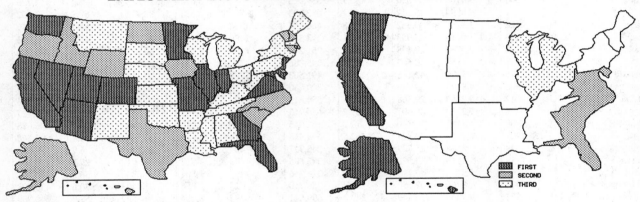

PAYROLL 1995 - STATE AND REGIONAL CONCENTRATION

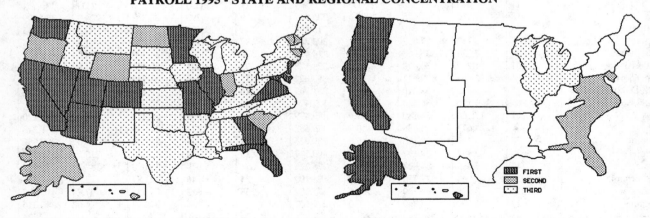

States with the darkest shading indicate those states which have proportionately more establishments, employment, or payrolls than would be indicated by the state's population. States with light shading are states with proportionately fewer establishments, less employment, and lower payrolls than population distribution. States shaded grey are within 15 percent of the state's population proportion in these categories. States for which no data are available are shown as average (grey). *Regions* are shaded to indicate absolute rank in the category. If no data for the category are available, establishment counts are used to shade the regions. Source of the data is the table on the facing page.

LEADING COMPANIES - SIC 6162 - Mortgage Bankers and Correspondents

Number shown: **100**   Total sales/assets ($ mil): **557,119**   Total employment (000): **280.5**

Company Name	Address				CEO Name	Phone	Co. Type	Sales/Assets ($ mil)	Empl. (000)
General Motors Acceptance Corp.	3044 W. Grand Blvd.	Detroit	MI	48202	J.M. Losh	313-556-5000	S	94,573 TA	17.3
Norwest Corp.	Norwest Ctr.	Minneapolis	MN	55479	Richard M. Kovacevich	612-667-1234	P	88,540 TA	57.0
Associates Corporation of North America	PO Box 660237	Dallas	TX	75266	Keith W. Hughes	214-541-4000	S	43,728 TA	15.0
Great Western Financial Corp.	9200 Oakdale Ave.	Chatsworth	CA	91311	John F. Maher	818-775-3411	P	42,875 TA	13.0
Associates First Capital Corp.	PO Box 660237	Dallas	TX	75266	Keith W. Hughes	972-652-4000	P	41,304 TA	16.6
Ford Holdings Inc.	The American Rd.	Dearborn	MI	48121	Keith W. Hughes	313-322-1639	S	41,304 TA	16.6
Crestar Financial Corp.	PO Box 26665	Richmond	VA	23261	Richard G. Tilghman	804-782-5000	P	21,810 TA	8.2
Firstar Corp.	777 E. Wisconsin Ave.	Milwaukee	WI	53202	Roger L. Fitzsimonds	414-765-4321	P	19,323 TA	7.8
Beneficial Corp.	301 N. Walnut St.	Wilmington	DE	19801	Finn M. Caspersen	302-425-2500	P	17,645 TA	10.2
Dominion Resources Inc.	PO Box 26532	Richmond	VA	23261	Thomas E. Capps	804-775-5700	P	14,905 TA	11.2
Central Fidelity Banks Inc.	PO Box 27602	Richmond	VA	23261	Lewis N. Miller Jr.	804-782-4000	P	10,540 TA	3.5
Capstead Mortgage Corp.	2711 N. Haskell Ave.	Dallas	TX	75204	Ronn K. Lytle	214-874-2323	P	10,157 TA	0.2
Countrywide Home Loans Inc.	155 N. Lake Ave.	Pasadena	CA	91101	David S. Loeb	818-304-8400	S	8,658 TA	4.8
First Commercial Corp.	400 W. Capitol Ave.	Little Rock	AR	72201	Barnett Grace	501-371-7000	P	6,887 TA	3.3
Norwest Mortgage Inc.	405 S.W. 5th St.	Des Moines	IA	50309		515-237-7900	S	5,400 TA*	3.5
Green Tree Financial Corp.	1100 Landmark Twr.	St. Paul	MN	55102	Lawrence M. Coss	612-293-3400	P	4,867 TA	5.5
Fleet Mortgage Group Inc.	1333 Main St.	Columbia	SC	29201	A. William Schenck	803-929-7900	S	4,614 TA	3.1
NationsBanc Mortgage Corp.	201 N. Tryon St.	Charlotte	NC	28255	Andrew Woodward	704-386-5000	S	4,600 TA	3.7
Rochester Community Savings Bank	40 Franklin St.	Rochester	NY	14604	Leonard S. Simon	716-258-3000	P	3,900 TA	1.6
Source One Mortgage Services Corp.	27555 Farmington Rd.	Farmington Hills	MI	48334	James A. Conrad	810-488-7000	P	2,650 TA	1.7
Money Store Inc.	2840 Morris Ave.	Union	NJ	07083	Marc Turtletaub	908-686-2000	P	2,612 TA	2.6
Imperial Credit Industries Inc.	20371 Irvine Ave.	Santa Ana Heights	CA	92707	H. Wayne Snavely	714-556-0122	P	2,500 TA	0.6
Pulte Corp.	33 Bloomfield Hills Pkwy.	Bloomfield Hills	MI	48304	William J. Pulte	313-647-2750	P	2,151 TA	4.3
JRMK Company Inc.	7935 E. Prentice Ave.	Englewood	CO	80111	Milton Karavites	303-771-5008	R	2,000 TA	0.1
CRIIMI MAE Inc.	11200 Rockville Pike	Rockville	MD	20852	William B. Dockser	301-816-2300	P	1,873 TA	0.2
Republic Bancorp Inc.	PO Box 70	Owosso	MI	48867	Jerry D. Campbell	517-725-7337	P	1,873 TA	1.4
Fund American Enterprises Holdings Inc.	80 S. Main St.	Hanover	NH	03755	John J. Byrne	603-643-1567	P	1,872 TA	2.1
Sibley Mortgage Corp.	2 State St.	Rochester	NY	14614	Stephen B. Ashley	716-232-1620	R	1,800 TA	0.2
Merrill Lynch Credit Corp.	4802 Deer Lake Dr. E.	Jacksonville	FL	32246	Kevin O'Hanlon	904-928-6000	S	1,722 TA	0.8

Company type codes: P - Public, R - Private, S - Subsidiary, D - Division, J - Joint Venture, A - Affiliate, G - Group. If the dollar values shown are not sales, the following codes apply: TA - Total Assets; OR - Operating Revenues; GB - Gross Billings. * - estimated dollar value. < - less than. *na* - not available.

Continued on next page.

LEADING COMPANIES - SIC 6162 - Mortgage Bankers and Correspondents
Continued

Company Name	Address				CEO Name	Phone	Co. Type	Sales/Assets ($ mil)	Empl. (000)
Countrywide Credit Industries Inc.	PO Box 7137	Pasadena	CA	91109	David S. Loeb	818-304-8400	P	1,718 TA	6.1
Commerce Group Inc.	211 Main St.	Webster	MA	01570	Arthur J. Remillard Jr.	508-943-9000	P	1,712 TA	1.4
IMC Mortgage Co.	3450 Buschwood Park Dr.	Tampa	FL	33618	Thomas G. Middleton	813-932-2211	P	1,707 TA	0.4
Ryland Group Inc.	11000 Broken Land Pkwy.	Columbia	MD	21044	R. Chad Dreier	410-715-7000	P	1,649 OR	2.4
ContiFinancial Corp.	277 Park Ave.	New York	NY	10172	James E Moore	212-207-2800	P	1,546 TA	1.6
Fund American Enterprises Inc.	1820 House Main St.	Norwich	VT	05055	Terry L. Baxter	802-649-3633	S	1,480 TA*	1.7
CB Bancshares Inc.	PO Box 3709	Honolulu	HI	96811	Ronald K, Migita	808-546-2411	P	1,435 TA	0.5
U.S. Home Corp.	PO Box 2863	Houston	TX	77252	Robert J. Strudler	713-877-2311	P	1,320 OR	1.6
General Electric Capital Mortgage Services Inc.	3 Executive Campus	Cherry Hill	NJ	08034	Alan Hainey	609-661-6100	S	1,310 TA*	1.2
Flagstar Bancorp Inc.	2600 Telegraph Rd.	Bloomfield Hills	MI	48302	Mark T. Hammond	810-338-7700	P	1,300 TA	1.3
Margaretten and Company Inc.	PO Box 3014	Edison	NJ	08818	Felix M. Beck	908-205-0500	S	1,203 TA	2.0
Margaretten Financial Corp.	205 Smith St.	Perth Amboy	NJ	08861	Felix M. Beck	908-324-4000	P	1,203 TA	2.0
NVR Inc.	7601 Lewinsville Rd.	McLean	VA	22102	Dwight C. Schar	703-761-2000	P	1,154 OR	2.0
York Financial Corp.	101 S. George St.	York	PA	17401	Robert W. Pullo	717-846-8777	P	1,087 TA	0.4
Resource Bancshares Mortgage Group Inc.	PO Box 7486	Columbia	SC	29202	Edward J. Sebastian	803-741-3000	P	1,078 TA	1.3
Marine Midland Mortgage Corp.	1 Marine Midland Ctr.	Buffalo	NY	14203	James Cleeve	716-841-6183	S	1,000 TA	0.4
M.D.C. Holdings Inc.	3600 S. Yosemite St.	Denver	CO	80237	Larry A. Mizel	303-773-1100	P	970 OR	1.2
Plaza Home Mortgage Corp.	1820 E. 1st St.	Santa Ana	CA	92705	Jack French	714-564-3010	P	953 TA	0.9
Foothill Group Inc.	11111 Santa Monica Blvd.	Los Angeles	CA	90025	John Nikoll	310-478-8383	S	913 TA*	0.2
ContiMortgage Corp.	500 Enterprises Rd.	Horsham	PA	19044	Robert A. Major	215-957-3700	S	893 TA	0.5
George Mason Bankshares Inc.	PO Box 600	Fairfax	VA	22030	Bernard H. Clineburg	703-352-1100	P	873 TA	0.3
Colonial Company Inc.	2000 Interstate Park Dr.	Montgomery	AL	36109	James K. Lowder	205-270-6500	R	870 TA*	0.8
Poughkeepsie Savings Bank F.S.B.	249 Main Mall	Poughkeepsie	NY	12601	Joseph B. Tockarshewsky	914-431-6200	P	859 TA	0.2
North American Mortgage Co.	3883 Airway Dr.	Santa Rosa	CA	95403	John F. Farrell Jr.	707-546-3310	P	854 TA	2.9
Sterling Financial Corp.	PO Box 10608	Lancaster	PA	17605	John E. Stefan	717-295-7551	P	846 TA	0.5
PHH US Mortgage Corp.	6000 Atrium Way	Mount Laurel	NJ	08054	H. Robert Nagel	609-439-6000	S	840 TA	1.1
Household Commercial Financial Services	2700 Sanders Rd.	Prospect Heights	IL	60070	Glenn O. Fick	708-564-5000	S	800 TA	0.2
HomeBanc Mortgage Corp.	5775 N.E. Glenridge Dr.	Atlanta	GA	30328	Patrick S. Flood	404-303-4280	S	732 TA	0.2

Company type codes: P - Public, R - Private, S - Subsidiary, D - Division, J - Joint Venture, A - Affiliate, G - Group. If the dollar values shown are not sales, the following codes apply: TA - Total Assets; OR - Operating Revenues; GB - Gross Billings. * - estimated dollar value. < - less than. *na* - not available.

Continued on next page.

LEADING COMPANIES - SIC 6162 - Mortgage Bankers and Correspondents
Continued

Company Name	Address				CEO Name	Phone	Co. Type	Sales/Assets ($ mil)	Empl. (000)
Continental Homes Holding Corp.	7001 N. Scottsdale Rd.	Scottsdale	AZ	85253	Donald R. Loback	602-483-0006	P	726 OR	0.6
Great Southern Bancorp Inc.	PO Box 9009	Springfield	MO	65808	William V. Turner	417-887-4400	P	708 TA	0.4
Spectrum Home Mortgage	1780 Wehrle Dr.	Williamsville	NY	14221	Robert E. Roth	716-633-6255	D	660 TA*	0.3
Fireside Thrift Co.	5600 Mowry School Rd.	Newark	CA	94560		510-490-6511		660 TA	0.6
PNC Mortgage Corporation of America	75 N. Fairway Dr.	Vernon Hills	IL	60061	Saiyid T. Naqvi	847-549-6500	S	658 TA*	0.6
American Residential Holding Corp.	11119 N. Torrey Pines Rd.	La Jolla	CA	92037	John M. Robbins Jr.	619-535-4900	P	655 TA	1.3
Weyerhaeuser Mortgage Co.	6320 Canoga Ave.	Woodland Hills	CA	91367	Scott McAfee	818-592-2537	S	600 TA*	0.6
AccuBanc Mortgage Corp.	12377 Merit Dr.	Dallas	TX	75251	William R. Starkey Sr.	972-458-9200	S	595 TA	1.5
Advanta Mortgage Corporation USA	16875 W. Bernardo Dr.	San Diego	CA	92127	Milton Riseman	619-674-1800	S	560 TA	0.2
Irwin Mortgage Corp.	9265 Counselors Row	Indianapolis	IN	46240	Rick L. McGuire	317-844-7788	S	503 TA*	1.4
FT Mortgage Co.	2974 Lyndon B. Johnson Fwy.	Dallas	TX	75234	Jim Witherow	214-484-5600	R	500 TA	1.5
Shawmut Mortgage Co.	433 S. Main St.	West Hartford	CT	06110	John J. Spear	203-240-6829	S	500 TA*	0.4
First Franklin Financial Corp.	2150 N. 1st St.	San Jose	CA	95131	William D. Dallas	408-955-9600	R	490 TA*	0.5
AmSouth Mortgage Co.	PO Box 847	Birmingham	AL	35201	Michael Padalino	205-326-5050	S	484 TA	0.8
Castle BancGroup	121 W. Lincoln Hwy.	De Kalb	IL	60115	John W. Castle	815-758-7007	R	475 TA	0.2
CB Commercial Real Estate Group Inc.	533 S. Fremont Ave.	Los Angeles	CA	90071	James J. Didion	213-613-3123	S	468 OR	4.0
Wendover Funding Inc.	725 N. Regional Rd.	Greensboro	NC	27409	Jeffrey S. Taylor	910-668-7000	S	460 TA*	0.4
Centennial Bancorp.	PO Box 1560	Eugene	OR	97440	Richard C. Williams	541-342-3969	P	407 TA	0.2
CrossLand Mortgage Corp.	3902 S. State St.	Salt Lake City	UT	84107	Christopher Sumner	801-269-7600	S	400 TA	1.2
Fleet Real Estate Funding Corp.	PO Box 11988	Columbia	SC	29211	Robert Golitz	803-253-7900	S	400 TA	0.9
PHH Vehicale Management Services	307 International Cir.	Hunt Valley	MD	21031	Mark E. Miller	410-771-3600	S	400 OR*	2.5
New Century Financial Corp.	4910 Birch St.	Newport Beach	CA	92660	Robert K. Cole	714-440-7030	P	398 TA	1.2
Oxford First Corp.	7300 Old York Rd.	Philadelphia	PA	19126	Lewis Collin	215-782-7000	S	390 TA	0.3
Harbourton Financial Services L.P.	7926 Jones Branch Rd.	McLean	VA	22102	David W. Mills	703-761-1490	P	384 TA	0.7
Guild Mortgage Co.	PO Box 85304	San Diego	CA	92186	Martin Gliesch	619-560-6330	R	380 TA*	0.4
Harbor Financial Mortgage Corp.	340 N. Sam Houston Pkwy. E.	Houston	TX	77060	Richard Gillen	713-931-1771	R	380 TA*	0.4
Loan America Financial Corp.	8100 Oak Ln.	Hialeah	FL	33016	Charles B. Stuzin	305-557-9282	P	368 TA	0.4
EQ Services Inc.	235 Peachtree St	Atlanta	GA	30303	Paul S. Klick III	404-654-2000	S	350 TA	0.3
NBD Mortgage Co.	PO Box 331755	Detroit	MI	48232	Thomas McDowell	313-828-2307	S	340 TA*	0.6
Lomas Financial Corp.	1600 Viceroy Dr.	Dallas	TX	75235	Jess Hay	214-879-4000	P	329 TA	<0.1

Company type codes: P - Public, R - Private, S - Subsidiary, D - Division, J - Joint Venture, A - Affiliate, G - Group. If the dollar values shown are not sales, the following codes apply: TA - Total Assets; OR - Operating Revenues; GB - Gross Billings. * - estimated dollar value. < - less than. *na* - not available.

Continued on next page.

LEADING COMPANIES - SIC 6162 - Mortgage Bankers and Correspondents
Continued

Company Name	Address				CEO Name	Phone	Co. Type	Sales/Assets ($ mil)	Empl. (000)
Mission Hills Mortgage Corp.	1403 N. Tustin Ave.	Santa Ana	CA	92705	Jay Ledbetter	714-972-3832	R	320 TA•	0.3
SouthTrust Mortgage Corp.	PO Box 532060	Birmingham	AL	35253	Larry Hamilton	205-254-8308	S	310 TA•	0.3
ICM Mortgage Corp.	6061 S. Willow Dr.	Greenwood Village	CO	80111	Jeffery D. LeClaire	303-740-3323	S	300 TA•	0.2
Arbor National Mortgage Inc.	615 Merrick Ave.	Westbury	NY	11590	Ivan Kaufman	516-832-7200	S	294 TA	0.9
Ampal-American Israel Corp.	1177 Ave. of the Amer.	New York	NY	10036	Yehoshua Gleitman	212-782-2100	P	284 TA	<0.1
SunTrust Mortgage Inc.	PO Box 100100	Atlanta	GA	30348	Robert W. Hearn Jr.	404-955-6000	S	280 TA•	0.3
Aames Financial Corp.	350 S. Grand Ave.	Los Angeles	CA	90071	Cary H. Thompson	213-640-5000	P	273 TA	1.4
Irwin Home Equity Corp.	2400 Camino Ramon	San Ramon	CA	94583	Elena Delgado	510-277-2001	S	270 TA	0.2
Temple-Inland Mortgage Corp.	PO Box 40	Austin	TX	78767	Herb Lloyd	512-477-6561	S	270 TA•	0.3
Delta Financial Corp.	1000 Woodbury Rd.	Woodbury	NY	11797	Hugh I. Miller	516-364-8500	P	233 TA	0.4
First Advantage Mortgage Corp.	8910 Rte. 108	Columbia	MD	21045	Al Kocourek	410-964-4800	R	230 TA	0.3
Emergent Group Inc.	PO Box 17526	Greenville	SC	29606	John M. Sterling Jr.	864-235-8056	P	224 TA	0.5
Kaufman and Broad Mortgage Co.	21650 Oxnord St.	Woodland Hills	CA	91367	Mark Crivelli	818-887-2275	S	218 TA	0.2

*Source: Ward's Business Directory of U.S. Private and Public Companies, 1996. Company type codes: P - Public, R - Private, S - Subsidiary, D - Division, J - Joint Venture, A - Affiliate, G - Group. If the dollar values shown are not sales, the following codes apply: TA - Total Assets; OR - Operating Revenues; GB - Gross Billings. * - estimated dollar value. < - less than; na - not available.*

LEADING COMPANIES - SIC 6162 - Mortgage Bankers and Correspondents
Number shown: **31**   Total sales/assets ($ mil): **986**   Total employment (000): **4.8**

Company Name	Address				CEO Name	Phone	Co. Type	Sales/Assets ($ mil)	Empl. (000)
Delta Financial Corp.	1000 Woodbury Rd.	Woodbury	NY	11797	Hugh I. Miller	516-364-8500	P	233 TA	0.4
LaSalle Partners Inc.	200 E. Randolph Dr.	Chicago	IL	60601	Stuart L. Scott	312-782-5800	P	176 OR	1.1
Trendwest Resorts Inc.	12301 Northeast 10th Place	Bellevue	WA	98005	William F. Peare	425-990-2300	P	117 OR	0.7
DeWolfe Companies Inc.	80 Hayden Ave.	Lexington	MA	02173	Richard B. DeWolfe	617-863-5858	P	83 OR	1.7
Crestview Lending Corp.	9454 Wilshire Blvd 201	Beverly Hills	CA	90212	Gloria Schulman	310-273-9696	R	37 OR•	<0.1
Banyan Mortgage Investors Limited Partnership III Inc.	150 S. Wacker Dr.	Chicago	IL	60606	L. Levine	312-553-9800	R	35 OR•	<0.1
Nationwide Secondary Marketing Inc.	7770 W. Oakland Park Blvd.	Fort Lauderdale	FL	33351	Howard Kaye	305-748-7700	R	31 OR	<0.1
Koenig and Strey Inc.	3201 Old Glenview Rd.	Wilmette	IL	60091	Thomas E. Koenig	708-729-5050	R	30 OR	0.5
HomeVest Financial Group Inc.	580 California St.	San Francisco	CA	94104	C. Earl Corkett	415-397-3278	R	27 OR	<0.1

*Company type codes: P - Public, R - Private, S - Subsidiary, D - Division, J - Joint Venture, A - Affiliate, G - Group. If the dollar values shown are not sales, the following codes apply: TA - Total Assets; OR - Operating Revenues; GB - Gross Billings. * - estimated dollar value. < - less than. na - not available.*

Continued on next page.

LEADING COMPANIES - SIC 6162 - Mortgage Bankers and Correspondents
Continued

Company Name	Address				CEO Name	Phone	Co. Type	Sales/Assets ($ mil)	Empl. (000)
Manhattan Mortgage Co.	425 Park Ave.	New York	NY	10022	Ellen Bitton	212-593-4343	R	27 OR•	<0.1
Fairway Capital Corp.	285 Governors St.	Providence	RI	02906	Arnold Kilberg	401-454-7500	R	21 OR•	<0.1
Homes for South Florida Inc.	1390 Brickell Ave.	Miami	FL	33131	Marie Lee	305-579-3076	R	21 OR	<0.1
NBR Mortgage Company Inc.	PO Box 1987	Santa Rosa	CA	95402	John H. Downey	707-573-4880	S	19 TA•	<0.1
Rio Vista Mortgage Corp.	8880 Rio San Diego Dr.	San Diego	CA	92108	Robert Schuh	619-497-2200	R	19 TA	<0.1
Ashford Financial Corp.	14180 Dallas Pkwy.	Dallas	TX	75240	David Kimichik	214-490-9600	R	16 OR•	<0.1
Meredith and Grew Inc.	160 Federal St.	Boston	MA	02110	Thomas J. Hynes Jr.	617-330-8000	R	16 OR	0.2
USGI Holdings Inc.	PO Box 6003	Norwalk	CT	06852	William C. Gow	203-849-4500	R	14 OR	<0.1
Western Foothill Mortgage Inc.	183 Placerville Dr.	Placerville	CA	95667	Steven Cockerell	916-621-0222	R	14 OR	<0.1
Equivest Finance Inc.	2 Clinton Square	Syracuse	NY	13202		315-422-9088	P	13 OR	<0.1
Randall Mortgage Inc.	1033 Semoran Blvd.	Casselberry	FL	32707	Al Feldman	407-830-9551	R	9 OR•	<0.1
Gallatin Mortgage Co.	409 S. Division	Ann Arbor	MI	48104	Richard H. Hedlund	313-994-1202	R	7 OR	<0.1
Michael V. Coratolo and Associates Inc.	502 Laguardia Pl.	New York	NY	10012	Michael V. Coratolo	212-254-9800	R	4 OR•	<0.1
Banker's Portfolio Exchange Inc.	2200 E. River Rd.	Tucson	AZ	85718	Sherry Neasham	602-299-5399	R	3 OR•	<0.1
DRG Financial Corp.	5125 MacArthur Blvd. N.W.	Washington	DC	20016	Donald M. DeFranceaux	202-965-7000	R	3 OR•	<0.1
LJM Realty Advisors Inc.	18500 Von Karman Ave.	Irvine	CA	92715	Guy K. Johnson	714-660-1999	R	3 OR	<0.1
Baltimore Financial Corp.	PO Box 192011	San Francisco	CA	94119	Joseph Moore	415-435-9621	R	2 OR	<0.1
Elite Financial Group Inc.	2400 W. Cypress Creek Rd.	Fort Lauderdale	FL	33309	Bill C. Stamper	305-938-4366	R	2 OR	<0.1
Federal Services Corp.	3330 Oakwell Ct.	San Antonio	TX	78218	Charles Leone III	210-829-0279	R	2 OR•	<0.1
Mortgage Resource Inc.	14430 S. Outer 40	Chesterfield	MO	63017	Steven Carrico	314-576-5577	R	2 OR	<0.1
Mutual Mortgage Corp.	9200 Glenwood	Overland Park	KS	66212	Thomas J. Rosberg	913-341-3800	R	1 OR	<0.1
Specialty Group	3205 E. McKnight Dr.	Pittsburgh	PA	15237	Ned Sokoloff	412-369-1555	R	1 OR	<0.1

Source: Ward's Business Directory of U.S. Private and Public Companies, 1996. Company type codes: P - Public, R - Private, S - Subsidiary, D - Division, J - Joint Venture, A - Affiliate, G - Group. If the dollar values shown are not sales, the following codes apply: TA - Total Assets; OR - Operating Revenues; GB - Gross Billings. • - estimated dollar value. < - less than; na - not available.

SIC 6210

SECURITY BROKERS AND DEALERS

SIC 6210 includes establishments primarily engaged in the purchase, sale, and brokerage of securities; the SIC also includes investment bankers primarily engaged in originating, underwriting, and distributing issues of securities. Excluded from the SIC are establishments engaged in issuing shares of mutual and money market funds, unit investment trusts, and face-amount certificates; these operations are in SIC 6720, Investment Offices.

The SIC group includes agents for mutual funds; brokers for and dealers in bonds, notes, oil and gas leases, oil royalties, mineral leases and royalties, mortgages (rediscounting), securities, tax certificates, and stock options; distributors of securities; floor traders; investment bankers; investment firms engaged in general brokerage; and sellers of partnership shares in real estate syndicates.

ESTABLISHMENTS, EMPLOYMENT, AND PAYROLL

	1990	1991 Value	%	1992 Value	%	1993 Value	%	1994 Value	%	1995 Value	%	% change 90-95
All Establishments	15,894	17,032	7.2	18,690	9.7	19,616	5.0	22,953	17.0	24,308	5.9	52.9
Mid-March Employment	308,078	295,412	-4.1	310,823	5.2	309,943	-0.3	372,284	20.1	381,459	2.5	23.8
1st Quarter Wages (annualized - $ mil.)	26,669.6	23,152.6	-13.2	30,333.8	31.0	28,631.3	-5.6	36,960.2	29.1	43,274.0	17.1	62.3
Payroll per Emp. 1st Q. (annualized)	86,568	78,374	-9.5	97,592	24.5	92,376	-5.3	99,279	7.5	113,443	14.3	31.0
Annual Payroll ($ mil.)	20,777.4	21,082.3	1.5	26,383.4	25.1	28,896.8	9.5	30,040.7	4.0	34,380.9	14.4	65.5
Establishments - 1-4 Emp. Number	8,144	8,921	9.5	10,322	15.7	11,219	8.7	13,145	17.2	14,117	7.4	73.3
Mid-March Employment	14,882	16,533	11.1	19,055	15.3	18,538	-2.7	21,545	16.2	25,483	18.3	71.2
1st Quarter Wages (annualized - $ mil.)	864.8	917.8	6.1	1,078.0	17.5	1,202.9	11.6	1,496.9	24.4	1,953.2	30.5	125.9
Payroll per Emp. 1st Q. (annualized)	58,108	55,513	-4.5	56,574	1.9	64,890	14.7	69,479	7.1	76,646	10.3	31.9
Annual Payroll ($ mil.)	867.7	936.4	7.9	1,162.8	24.2	1,342.8	15.5	1,405.4	4.7	1,933.5	37.6	122.8
Establishments - 5-9 Emp. Number	2,466	2,648	7.4	2,844	7.4	2,669	-6.2	3,269	22.5	3,383	3.5	37.2
Mid-March Employment	16,485	17,706	7.4	18,810	6.2	17,831	-5.2	21,869	22.6	22,390	2.4	35.8
1st Quarter Wages (annualized - $ mil.)	1,297.0	1,358.7	4.8	1,636.9	20.5	1,560.9	-4.6	2,145.4	37.5	2,732.2	27.3	110.7
Payroll per Emp. 1st Q. (annualized)	78,680	76,735	-2.5	87,025	13.4	87,537	0.6	98,104	12.1	122,028	24.4	55.1
Annual Payroll ($ mil.)	1,041.4	1,138.7	9.3	1,303.6	14.5	1,406.2	7.9	1,596.0	13.5	1,891.4	18.5	81.6
Establishments - 10-19 Emp. Number	2,150	2,279	6.0	2,276	-0.1	2,359	3.6	2,555	8.3	2,812	10.1	30.8
Mid-March Employment	29,621	31,275	5.6	31,343	0.2	32,656	4.2	35,234	7.9	38,843	10.2	31.1
1st Quarter Wages (annualized - $ mil.)	2,100.9	2,286.1	8.8	2,734.5	19.6	2,746.7	0.4	3,301.0	20.2	3,913.8	18.6	86.3
Payroll per Emp. 1st Q. (annualized)	70,927	73,098	3.1	87,246	19.4	84,111	-3.6	93,688	11.4	100,760	7.5	42.1
Annual Payroll ($ mil.)	1,735.5	2,077.5	19.7	2,319.9	11.7	2,581.6	11.3	2,505.4	-3.0	3,040.9	21.4	75.2
Establishments - 20-49 Emp. Number	2,042	2,135	4.6	2,142	0.3	2,235	4.3	2,573	15.1	2,663	3.5	30.4
Mid-March Employment	63,165	65,471	3.7	65,892	0.6	68,734	4.3	79,321	15.4	81,537	2.8	29.1
1st Quarter Wages (annualized - $ mil.)	4,905.7	4,925.8	0.4	5,728.0	16.3	6,204.5	8.3	7,444.8	20.0	7,644.1	2.7	55.8
Payroll per Emp. 1st Q. (annualized)	77,665	75,237	-3.1	86,930	15.5	90,268	3.8	93,857	4.0	93,750	-0.1	20.7
Annual Payroll ($ mil.)	3,949.1	4,459.0	12.9	5,035.5	12.9	5,658.3	12.4	5,625.8	-0.6	6,179.4	9.8	56.5
Establishments - 50-99 Emp. Number	694	669	-3.6	705	5.4	757	7.4	934	23.4	892	-4.5	28.5
Mid-March Employment	46,340	44,942	-3.0	47,492	5.7	50,889	7.2	62,825	23.5	60,640	-3.5	30.9
1st Quarter Wages (annualized - $ mil.)	3,733.8	3,473.5	-7.0	4,447.8	28.1	4,710.6	5.9	5,880.2	24.8	5,718.9	-2.7	53.2
Payroll per Emp. 1st Q. (annualized)	80,575	77,288	-4.1	93,655	21.2	92,567	-1.2	93,596	1.1	94,309	0.8	17.0
Annual Payroll ($ mil.)	2,935.1	3,168.1	7.9	3,998.6	26.2	4,516.2	12.9	4,765.5	5.5	5,003.5	5.0	70.5
Establishments - 100-249 Emp. Number	261	269	3.1	285	5.9	276	-3.2	344	24.6	312	-9.3	19.5
Mid-March Employment	38,612	40,222	4.2	42,556	5.8	41,204	-3.2	49,710	20.6	45,435	-8.6	17.7
1st Quarter Wages (annualized - $ mil.)	3,297.0	2,892.0	-12.3	3,873.9	34.0	3,904.9	0.8	5,308.7	36.0	5,219.6	-1.7	58.3
Payroll per Emp. 1st Q. (annualized)	85,388	71,900	-15.8	91,031	26.6	94,769	4.1	106,793	12.7	114,880	7.6	34.5
Annual Payroll ($ mil.)	2,617.1	2,917.1	11.5	3,585.3	22.9	4,018.5	12.1	4,262.2	6.1	4,244.6	-0.4	62.2
Establishments - 250-499 Emp. Number	82	66	-19.5	65	-1.5	50	-23.1	71	42.0	66	-7.0	-19.5
Mid-March Employment	29,235	22,067	-24.5	22,184	0.5	17,460	-21.3	24,364	39.5	22,799	-6.4	-22.0
1st Quarter Wages (annualized - $ mil.)	2,031.5	1,568.2	-22.8	1,868.4	19.1	1,377.3	-26.3	2,334.3	69.5	2,770.5	18.7	36.4
Payroll per Emp. 1st Q. (annualized)	69,490	71,065	2.3	84,223	18.5	78,882	-6.3	95,811	21.5	121,518	26.8	74.9
Annual Payroll ($ mil.)	1,850.7	1,595.6	-13.8	1,979.5	24.1	1,755.9	-11.3	2,072.3	18.0	2,180.6	5.2	17.8
Establishments - 500-999 Emp. Number	36	28	-22.2	35	25.0	35	-	43	22.9	40	-7.0	11.1
Mid-March Employment	23,575	17,817	-24.4	23,192	30.2	22,879	-1.3	29,400	28.5	28,563	-2.8	21.2
1st Quarter Wages (annualized - $ mil.)	2,708.1	1,697.8	-37.3	2,678.8	57.8	2,045.1	-23.7	3,278.8	60.3	3,793.9	15.7	40.1
Payroll per Emp. 1st Q. (annualized)	114,870	95,292	-17.0	115,507	21.2	89,390	-22.6	111,524	24.8	132,827	19.1	15.6
Annual Payroll ($ mil.)	1,713.9	1,315.0	-23.3	2,262.3	72.0	2,374.0	4.9	2,788.3	17.5	3,172.9	13.8	85.1
Estab. - 1000 or More Emp. Number	19	17	-10.5	16	-5.9	16	-	19	18.8	23	21.1	21.1
Mid-March Employment	46,163	39,379	-14.7	40,299	2.3	39,752	-1.4	48,016	20.8	55,769	16.1	20.8
1st Quarter Wages (annualized - $ mil.)	5,730.8	4,032.7	-29.6	6,287.3	55.9	4,878.4	-22.4	5,770.0	18.3	9,527.8	65.1	66.3
Payroll per Emp. 1st Q. (annualized)	124,142	102,408	-17.5	156,017	52.3	122,720	-21.3	120,168	-2.1	170,844	42.2	37.6
Annual Payroll ($ mil.)	4,066.9	3,475.0	-14.6	4,735.9	36.3	5,243.2	10.7	5,019.7	-4.3	6,734.2	34.2	65.6

Source: County Business Patterns, U.S. Department of Commerce, Washington, D.C., for 1990 through 1995. Payroll per employee is calculated using mid-March employment and 1st Quarter wages, annualized. Annual payroll, also shown, may not equal the annualized 1st Quarter wages. Columns headed by a percent sign (%) indicate change from the previous year. *na* stands for not available. The symbol (D) indicates that data are withheld by the source to avoid disclosure of competitive information. A dash (-) indicates that data are not available or cannot be calculated.

ESTABLISHMENTS
Number

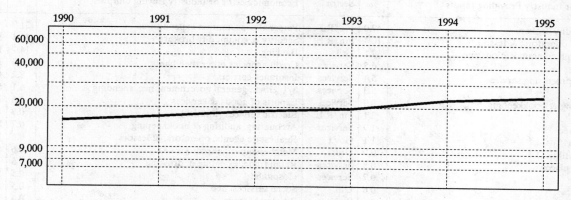

MID-MARCH EMPLOYMENT
Number

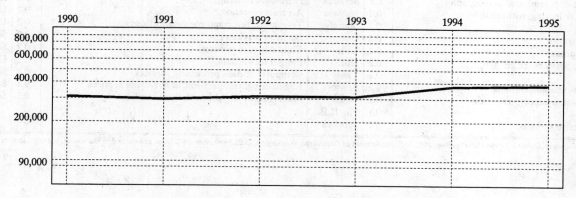

ANNUAL PAYROLL
$ million

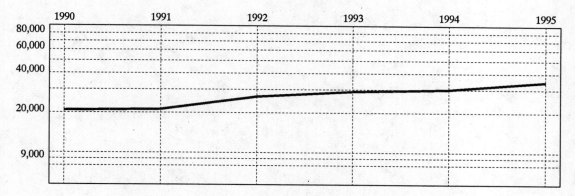

INPUTS AND OUTPUTS FOR SECURITY AND COMMODITY BROKERS - SIC GROUP 62

Economic Sector or Industry Providing Inputs	%	Sector	Economic Sector or Industry Buying Outputs	%	Sector
Security & commodity brokers	47.0	Fin/R.E.	Personal consumption expenditures	31.9	
Real estate agents, operators, & lessors	10.4	Fin/R.E.	Security & commodity brokers	16.4	Fin/R.E.
Telephone/telegraph communications nec	7.1	Util.	Banking	14.7	Fin/R.E.
Legal services	6.5	Services	Credit agencies other than banks	9.0	Fin/R.E.
Computer & data processing services	5.4	Services	Insurance carriers	8.2	Fin/R.E.
Advertising	5.3	Services	S/L Govt., general government nec, spending	6.1	S/L Govt
Accounting, auditing & bookkeeping	3.9	Services	Exports of goods & services	3.6	Foreign
Banking	2.1	Fin/R.E.	Electric services (utilities)	0.9	Util.
Business services nec	1.9	Services	Accounting, auditing & bookkeeping	0.7	Services
U.S. Postal Service	1.1	Gov't	Real estate agents, operators, & lessors	0.6	Fin/R.E.
Electric services (utilities)	0.9	Util.	Membership organizations nec	0.6	Services
Eating & drinking places	0.8	Services	Retail trade, ex eating & drinking	0.5	Trade
Hotels	0.7	Services	Hospitals	0.5	Services
Air transportation	0.6	Util.	Social services, nec	0.5	Services
Management & public relations services	0.6	Services	Wholesale trade	0.4	Trade
Personnel supply services	0.6	Services	Trucking & courier services, ex air	0.3	Util.
Repair & maintenance construction nec	0.5	Constr.	Colleges, universities, & professional schools	0.3	Services
Commercial printing	0.5	Manufg.	Private libraries, vocational schools, nec	0.3	Services
Insurance carriers	0.5	Fin/R.E.	State & local government enterprises nec	0.3	Gov't
Photofinishing labs & commercial photography	0.5	Services	Petroleum refining	0.2	Manufg.
Automotive rental & leasing, without drivers	0.4	Services	Air transportation	0.2	Util.
Petroleum refining	0.2	Manufg.	Telephone/telegraph communications nec	0.2	Util.
Local & suburban transit	0.2	Util.	Business services nec	0.2	Services
Natural gas distribution	0.2	Util.	Child day care services	0.2	Services
Trucking & courier services, ex air	0.2	Util.	Freight forwarders	0.1	Util.
Wholesale trade	0.2	Trade	Computer & data processing services	0.1	Services
Business & professional associations	0.2	Services	Engineering, architectural, & surveying services	0.1	Services
Sanitary services, steam supply, irrigation	0.1	Util.	Management & public relations services	0.1	Services
Royalties	0.1	Fin/R.E.			
Detective & protective services	0.1	Services			

Source: Benchmark Input-Output Accounts for the U.S. Economy, 1992, U.S. Department of Commerce, Washington, D.C., November 1997. Data, as reported in the source, are organized by the 1987 SIC structure in use in 1992.

OCCUPATIONS EMPLOYED BY SECURITY AND COMMODITY BROKERS AND DEALERS

Occupation	% of Total 1996	Change to 2006	Occupation	% of Total 1996	Change to 2006
Securities & financial sales workers	34.8	36.5	Sales & related workers nec	2.2	50.2
Brokerage clerks	13.5	26.9	Computer programmers	1.6	12.4
Management support workers nec	7.7	104.8	Accountants & auditors	1.4	26.4
Secretaries, except legal & medical	7.3	8.3	Receptionists & information clerks	1.3	36.5
General office clerks	3.5	17.5	Marketing & sales worker supervisors	1.3	36.5
General managers & top executives	3.2	32.3	Bookkeeping, accounting, & auditing clerks	1.1	9.2
Clerical supervisors & managers	3.1	36.5	Clerical & administrative workers nec	1.1	36.6
Financial managers	2.7	36.5			

Sources: *Industry-Occupation Matrix*, Bureau of Labor Statistics. These data relate to one or more 3-digit SIC industry groups rather than to a single 4-digit SIC. The change reported for each occupation to the year 2005 is a percent of growth or decline as estimated by the Bureau of Labor Statistics. The abbreviation *nec* stands for not elsewhere classified.

OCCUPATIONS EMPLOYED BY SECURITY AND COMMODITY BROKERS AND DEALERS

Occupation	% of Total 1996	Change to 2006	Occupation	% of Total 1996	Change to 2006
Securities & financial sales workers	34.8	36.5	Sales & related workers nec	2.2	50.2
Brokerage clerks	13.5	26.9	Computer programmers	1.6	12.4
Management support workers nec	7.7	104.8	Accountants & auditors	1.4	26.4
Secretaries, except legal & medical	7.3	8.3	Receptionists & information clerks	1.3	36.5
General office clerks	3.5	17.5	Marketing & sales worker supervisors	1.3	36.5
General managers & top executives	3.2	32.3	Bookkeeping, accounting, & auditing clerks	1.1	9.2
Clerical supervisors & managers	3.1	36.5	Clerical & administrative workers nec	1.1	36.6
Financial managers	2.7	36.5			

Sources: Industry-Occupation Matrix, Bureau of Labor Statistics. These data relate to one or more 3-digit SIC industry groups rather than to a single 4-digit SIC. The change reported for each occupation to the year 2005 is a percent of growth or decline as estimated by the Bureau of Labor Statistics. The abbreviation *nec* stands for not elsewhere classified.

U.S. AND STATE DATA ON INDUSTRY REVENUES AND OTHER ACCOUNTS FOR 1992

State	No. of Estab.	Employ- ment	Payroll ($ mil.)	Revenues ($ mil.)	Empl./ Estab.	Revenue/ Estab. ($)	Payroll/ Estab. ($)	Revenue/ Empl. ($)	Payroll/ Empl. ($)
UNITED STATES	1,450	12,893	706.5	2,558.2	9	1,764,308	487,219	198,421	54,795
Alabama	4	31	0.5	4.1	8	1,029,500	130,000	132,839	16,774
Alaska	1	-	(D)	(D)	(D)	(D)	(D)	(D)	(D)
Arizona	4	7	0.3	0.9	2	232,500	71,500	132,857	40,857
Arkansas	5	19	0.3	0.7	4	132,200	57,600	34,789	15,158
California	62	264	13.3	87.7	4	1,415,129	213,742	332,341	50,197
Colorado	17	-	(D)	(D)	(D)	(D)	(D)	(D)	(D)
Connecticut	18	-	(D)	(D)	(D)	(D)	(D)	(D)	(D)
Delaware	2	-	(D)	(D)	(D)	(D)	(D)	(D)	(D)
District of Columbia	2	-	(D)	(D)	(D)	(D)	(D)	(D)	(D)
Florida	41	388	18.4	39.1	9	954,561	449,780	100,869	47,528
Georgia	14	113	4.9	12.4	8	885,857	352,929	109,752	43,726
Hawaii	2	-	(D)	(D)	(D)	(D)	(D)	(D)	(D)
Idaho	4	-	(D)	(D)	(D)	(D)	(D)	(D)	(D)
Illinois	530	7,284	334.8	1,242.5	14	2,344,332	631,668	170,579	45,962
Indiana	13	-	(D)	(D)	(D)	(D)	(D)	(D)	(D)
Iowa	48	196	8.3	24.1	4	502,021	171,979	122,944	42,117
Kansas	32	-	(D)	(D)	(D)	(D)	(D)	(D)	(D)
Kentucky	5	12	0.3	1.5	2	306,000	66,400	127,500	27,667
Louisiana	4	10	0.3	0.7	3	185,750	77,500	74,300	31,000
Maryland	1	-	(D)	(D)	(D)	(D)	(D)	(D)	(D)
Massachusetts	5	-	(D)	(D)	(D)	(D)	(D)	(D)	(D)
Michigan	5	11	0.6	1.9	2	389,200	127,800	176,909	58,091
Minnesota	32	88	3.5	14.7	3	459,219	110,031	166,989	40,011
Mississippi	5	-	(D)	(D)	(D)	(D)	(D)	(D)	(D)
Missouri	25	-	(D)	(D)	(D)	(D)	(D)	(D)	(D)
Montana	8	-	(D)	(D)	(D)	(D)	(D)	(D)	(D)
Nebraska	17	40	1.4	5.0	2	293,647	81,059	124,800	34,450
Nevada	2	-	(D)	(D)	(D)	(D)	(D)	(D)	(D)
New Hampshire	1	-	(D)	(D)	(D)	(D)	(D)	(D)	(D)
New Jersey	43	228	16.2	50.5	5	1,174,372	376,512	221,482	71,009
New Mexico	3	-	(D)	(D)	(D)	(D)	(D)	(D)	(D)
New York	309	2,776	185.5	533.2	9	1,725,560	600,443	192,074	66,836
North Carolina	5	16	0.2	1.1	3	221,600	46,600	69,250	14,563
North Dakota	5	-	(D)	(D)	(D)	(D)	(D)	(D)	(D)
Ohio	14	39	0.9	1.8	3	130,571	62,714	46,872	22,513
Oklahoma	20	76	2.4	5.2	4	259,850	118,000	68,382	31,053
Oregon	7	12	0.4	1.5	2	208,143	59,714	121,417	34,833
Pennsylvania	11	-	(D)	(D)	(D)	(D)	(D)	(D)	(D)
Rhode Island	2	-	(D)	(D)	(D)	(D)	(D)	(D)	(D)
South Carolina	4	-	(D)	(D)	(D)	(D)	(D)	(D)	(D)
South Dakota	12	-	(D)	(D)	(D)	(D)	(D)	(D)	(D)
Tennessee	20	83	5.8	26.4	4	1,320,600	290,300	318,217	69,952
Texas	48	147	10.2	22.6	3	471,063	212,458	153,816	69,374
Utah	2	-	(D)	(D)	(D)	(D)	(D)	(D)	(D)
Vermont	1	-	(D)	(D)	(D)	(D)	(D)	(D)	(D)
Virginia	7	19	1.0	1.8	3	254,429	145,429	93,737	53,579
Washington	17	28	1.1	3.2	2	187,824	64,765	114,036	39,321
Wisconsin	10	41	1.4	3.1	4	309,500	144,900	75,488	35,341
Wyoming	1	-	(D)	(D)	(D)	(D)	(D)	(D)	(D)

Source: 1992 Economic Census, U.S. Department of Commerce, Washington, D.C. This is the only table that shows revenue data as collected by the Bureau of the Census in an Economic Census. The symbol (D) indicates that data are withheld by the source to avoid disclosure of competitive information. A dash (-) indicates that data are not available or cannot be calculated.

STATE-BY-STATE DATA ON ESTABLISHMENTS, EMPLOYMENT, AND PAYROLL - 1994 AND 1995

State	1994					1995					% Change Empl.
	No. of Estab.	Employ- ment	Pay / Empl.	Payroll ($ mil.)	Pay / Estab.	No. of Estab.	Employ- ment	Pay / Empl.	Payroll ($ mil.)	Pay / Estab.	
Alabama	3	23	18,783	0.6	203,000	2	(D)	-	(D)	-	-
Alaska	1	(D)	-	(D)	-	1	(D)	-	(D)	-	-
Arizona	7	(D)	-	(D)	-	5	(D)	-	(D)	-	-
Arkansas	6	(D)	-	(D)	-	6	(D)	-	(D)	-	-
California	75	358	30,961	15.0	199,880	76	449	35,537	21.0	276,197	25.4
Colorado	21	114	54,386	7.5	358,143	18	87	56,230	5.7	314,000	-23.7
Connecticut	25	150	73,307	18.4	736,080	22	(D)	-	(D)	-	-
Delaware	2	(D)	-	(D)	-	1	(D)	-	(D)	-	-
District of Columbia	4	(D)	-	(D)	-	5	(D)	-	(D)	-	-
Florida	40	326	45,853	15.7	392,675	45	262	53,145	18.3	406,711	-19.6
Georgia	12	30	50,267	1.9	159,167	13	40	67,000	2.8	216,846	33.3
Idaho	5	19	38,947	0.6	129,200	5	20	33,000	0.7	131,200	5.3
Illinois	585	7,065	46,762	367.8	628,711	588	7,876	50,599	392.9	668,148	11.5
Indiana	11	69	33,217	2.8	250,364	12	73	28,767	3.0	251,500	5.8
Iowa	49	226	38,832	9.5	194,878	47	221	36,416	12.1	257,468	-2.2
Kansas	28	(D)	-	(D)	-	31	237	50,852	12.9	417,129	-
Kentucky	4	17	24,471	0.6	147,000	5	30	30,267	1.3	256,000	76.5
Louisiana	5	9	27,556	0.2	48,200	4	12	21,000	0.2	61,750	33.3
Maine	(D)	(D)	(D)	(D)	(D)	1	(D)	-	(D)	-	-
Maryland	4	(D)	-	(D)	-	4	(D)	-	(D)	-	-
Massachusetts	3	(D)	-	(D)	-	3	2	56,000	0.4	144,000	-
Michigan	5	11	96,364	1.1	225,000	8	(D)	-	(D)	-	-
Minnesota	32	(D)	-	(D)	-	36	(D)	-	(D)	-	-
Mississippi	3	(D)	-	(D)	-	4	13	13,846	0.2	46,750	-
Missouri	26	(D)	-	(D)	-	26	148	45,784	6.8	260,077	-
Montana	7	16	21,250	0.4	53,000	8	12	17,667	0.3	43,000	-25.0
Nebraska	20	62	32,387	1.9	93,700	16	57	33,684	1.9	119,500	-8.1
Nevada	1	(D)	-	(D)	-	2	(D)	-	(D)	-	-
New Jersey	53	181	54,541	10.8	202,981	54	200	54,980	12.6	233,463	10.5
New Mexico	1	(D)	-	(D)	-	1	(D)	-	(D)	-	-
New York	298	2,551	64,259	177.2	594,611	303	2,470	74,653	175.8	580,096	-3.2
North Carolina	4	8	23,000	0.2	61,000	7	9	32,000	0.2	35,000	12.5
North Dakota	8	(D)	-	(D)	-	7	14	26,571	0.5	66,286	-
Ohio	12	38	24,737	1.5	126,833	11	61	34,426	3.8	346,727	60.5
Oklahoma	17	79	28,354	2.2	130,941	16	48	38,417	2.1	133,063	-39.2
Oregon	9	40	34,600	2.7	295,333	7	61	39,082	2.6	378,143	52.5
Pennsylvania	15	(D)	-	(D)	-	16	71	66,761	4.7	293,750	-
Rhode Island	3	(D)	-	(D)	-	3	(D)	-	(D)	-	-
South Carolina	4	9	21,778	0.2	54,500	3	(D)	-	(D)	-	-
South Dakota	10	78	16,718	1.0	102,300	10	24	31,167	0.7	65,700	-69.2
Tennessee	18	99	81,697	7.7	427,111	17	86	67,628	7.2	423,588	-13.1
Texas	50	170	58,847	12.4	247,280	55	184	62,848	12.9	233,855	8.2
Utah	3	9	40,444	0.3	108,333	2	(D)	-	(D)	-	-
Vermont	2	(D)	-	(D)	-	3	2	16,000	0.1	22,333	-
Virginia	7	(D)	-	(D)	-	8	14	28,286	0.7	87,125	-
Washington	13	23	39,304	1.1	85,692	14	32	29,000	1.2	83,357	39.1
Wisconsin	9	34	24,118	1.0	110,444	9	41	19,317	1.1	121,333	20.6
Wyoming	1	(D)	-	(D)	-	1	(D)	-	(D)	-	-

Source: County Business Patterns, U.S. Department of Commerce, Washington, D.C., for 1994 and 1995. Employment shown is for mid-March of the year shown. Payroll per employee is calculated by annualizing 1st Quarter payroll (not shown) and then dividing that value by mid-March employment. Dividing total annual payroll (columns 5 and 10) by employment, therefore, will *not* yield the payroll per employee figure (columns 4 and 9). The symbol (D) indicates that data are withheld by the source to avoid disclosure of competitive information. A dash (-) indicates that data are not available or cannot be calculated.

ESTABLISHMENTS 1995 - STATE AND REGIONAL CONCENTRATION

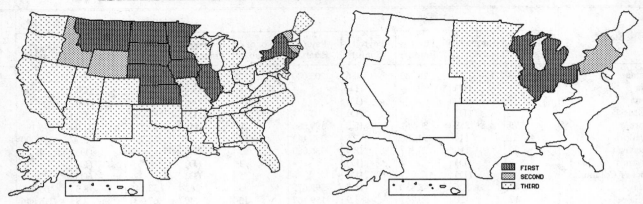

EMPLOYMENT 1995 - STATE AND REGIONAL CONCENTRATION

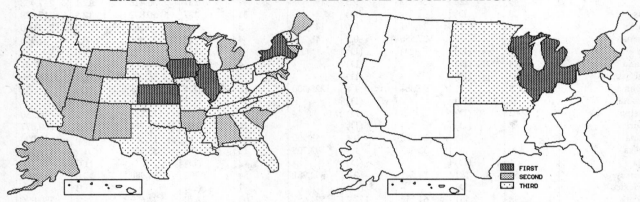

PAYROLL 1995 - STATE AND REGIONAL CONCENTRATION

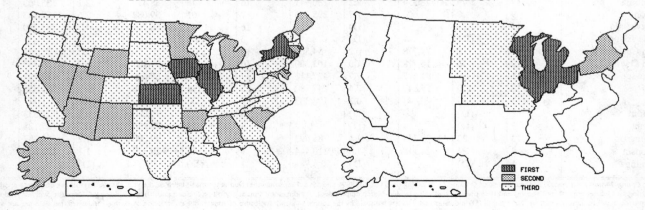

States with the darkest shading indicate those states which have proportionately more establishments, employment, or payrolls than would be indicated by the state's population. States with light shading are states with proportionately fewer establishments, less employment, and lower payrolls than population distribution. States shaded grey are within 15 percent of the state's population proportion in these categories. States for which no data are available are shown as average (grey). *Regions* are shaded to indicate absolute rank in the category. If no data for the category are available, establishment counts are used to shade the regions. Source of the data is the table on the facing page.

LEADING COMPANIES - SIC 6211 - Security Brokers and Dealers

Number shown: **52**   Total sales/assets ($ mil): **3,952**   Total employment (000): **6.0**

Company Name	Address				CEO Name	Phone	Co. Type	Sales/Assets ($ mil)	Empl. (000)
Moccatta Group New York	4 World Trade Center	New York	NY	10048	Tim Jones	212-912-8400	D	1,470 OR	<0.1
Refco Group Ltd.	1 World Financial	New York	NY	10281	Tone Grant	212-693-7000	R	390 OR•	0.5
Geldermann Inc.	440 S. La Salle St.	Chicago	IL	60605	James Curley	312-663-7500	R	310 OR•	0.4
First Options of Chicago Inc.	440 S. La Salle St.	Chicago	IL	60605	Al Salem	312-362-3000	S	273 OR•	0.9
Fimat Futures USA Inc.	181 W. Madison St.	Chicago	IL	60602	L. Brian Kaye	312-578-5200	R	130 OR•	0.2
Carter Marketing Group Inc.	25179 Dequindre Rd.	Madison Heights	MI	48071	Mark Carter	810-740-3900	R	110 OR•	0.2
Gerald Metals Inc.	PO Box 10134	Stamford	CT	06904	Gerald L. Lennard	203-329-4700	R	100 OR	0.7
Auglaize Farmers Cooperative	PO Box 360	Wapakoneta	OH	45895	Larry Hammond	419-738-2137	R	90	0.2
MilBrands Inc.	16415 Addison Rd.	Dallas	TX	75248	Richard K. Ryalls	214-931-2500	S	80 OR	<0.1
Darci International Group Inc.	15400 Knoll Tr.	Dallas	TX	75248	Veni Rastogi	214-490-3893	S	78 OR	<0.1
Sakura Dellsher Inc.	10 S. Wacker Dr.	Chicago	IL	60606	Leo Melamed	312-930-0001	R	78 OR•	0.1
Rosenthal Collins Group L.P.	216 W. Jackson St.	Chicago	IL	60606	Leslie Rosenthal	312-984-5900	R	75 OR	0.2
Klein-Berger Co.	PO Box 609	Stockton	CA	95201	Bob Corkern	209-955-0100	S	64 OR•	0.5
Ore and Chemical Corp.	520 Madison Ave.	New York	NY	10022	Joseph E. Robertson Jr.	212-715-5200	S	64 OR•	<0.1
Brody White and Company Inc.	4 World Trade Ctr.	New York	NY	10048	Steve Bergan	212-504-7500	R	55 OR•	<0.1
McVean Trading and Investments Inc.	850 Ridge Lake Blvd.	Memphis	TN	38120	Charles McVean	901-761-8400	R	55 OR•	<0.1
Siegel Trading Company Inc.	118 N. Clinton Ave.	Chicago	IL	60661	Frank Mazza	312-879-1000	R	47 OR	0.1
Index Futures Group Inc.	200 W. Adams St.	Chicago	IL	60606	Burton J. Meyer	312-419-5800	S	42 OR•	0.3
Jack Carl-312 Futures Inc.	200 W. Adams St.	Chicago	IL	60606	Burton J. Meyer	312-407-5700	P	42 OR	0.3
AIOC Corp.	230 Park Ave.	New York	NY	10169	Alan Clingman	212-949-0600	R	39 OR•	<0.1
Bridgewater Associates Inc.	372 Danbury Rd.	Wilton	CT	06897	Rob Fried	203-762-8511	R	36 OR•	<0.1
Farmers Commodities Corp.	PO Box 4887	Des Moines	IA	50306	Hal Richard	515-223-3788	R	35 OR	0.2
ADM Investors Services Inc.	141 W. Jackson Blvd.	Chicago	IL	60604	Paul Krug	312-435-7000	S	34 OR•	0.2
Alaron Trading Corp.	822 W. Washington Blvd.	Chicago	IL	60607	Steven Greenberg	312-563-8000	R	31 OR•	<0.1
Rand Financial Services Inc.	30 S. Wacker Dr.	Chicago	IL	60606	Jeff Ouinto	312-559-8800	S	30 OR	0.1
General Cocoa Company Inc.	161 Maiden Ln.	New York	NY	10038	Rich Emmanuel	212-422-7520	R	25 OR•	<0.1
Colorado Commodities Management Corp.	1050 Walnut St.	Boulder	CO	80302	Tenny Lode	303-444-8200	R	17 OR•	<0.1
McKeany-Flavell Company Inc.	11 Embarcadero W.	Oakland	CA	94607	Michael Ruffolo	510-832-2866	R	16 OR•	<0.1
Allied Deals Inc.	230 5th Ave.	New York	NY	10001	Viren Rastogi	212-532-7644	R	16 OR•	<0.1
International Marketing Group Inc.	1900 Elm Hill Pike	Nashville	TN	37210	M. Lytle	615-889-8000	R	15 OR	<0.1
MC Baldwin Financial Corp.	209 S. La Salle St.	Chicago	IL	60604	William Taki Jr.	312-553-6100	R	14 OR	<0.1
Johnston Grain and Seed Co.	1133 N. Bowie	Seguin	TX	78155	Art Johnston	210-379-5547	R	13	<0.1
Vincent Commodities Corp.	PO Box 620481	Middleton	WI	53562	Ronald M. Vincent	608-831-4447	R	13 OR	<0.1
Allied Brokerage Group Inc.	1359 Broadway	New York	NY	10018	Alan Miller	212-564-9170	R	8 OR•	<0.1

Company type codes: P - Public, R - Private, S - Subsidiary, D - Division, J - Joint Venture, A - Affiliate, G - Group. If the dollar values shown are not sales, the following codes apply: TA - Total Assets; OR - Operating Revenues; GB - Gross Billings. • - estimated dollar value. < - less than. *na* - not available.

Continued on next page.

LEADING COMPANIES - SIC 6211 - Security Brokers and Dealers

Continued

Company Name	Address				CEO Name	Phone	Co. Type	Sales/Assets ($ mil)	Empl. (000)
DKB Financial Futures Corp.	10 S. Wacker Dr. #1835	Chicago	IL	60606	Shinji Kato	312-466-1700	S	8 OR	<0.1
FSI Futures Inc.	675 Berkmar Ct.	Charlottesville	VA	22901	Robin Rodriguez	804-975-5959	S	6 OR	<0.1
GK Capital Management Inc.	102 S. East St.	Bloomington	IL	61701	Gary Klopfenstein	309-827-5550	R	6 OR	<0.1
Commodity Improvisors Inc.	350 Old Country Rd.	Garden City	NY	11530	Daniel Reddington	516-248-9714	R	5 OR	<0.1
Barex World Trade Corp.	777 W. Putnam Ave.	Greenwich	CT	06830	Steven Rothschild	203-531-1059	R	5 OR	<0.1
Simmons Brothers International Inc.	7110 Pines Rd.	Shreveport	LA	71129	Mitch Simmons	903-935-6071	R	4 OR*	<0.1
Commodities Resource Corp.	PO Box 8700	Incline Village	NV	89452	George Kleinman	702-833-2700	R	3 OR	<0.1
EBCO U.S.A. Inc.	6613 N. Meridian Ave.	Oklahoma City	OK	73116	Paul Smart	405-720-0313	R	3 OR	<0.1
FINEX	4 World Trade Ctr.	New York	NY	10048	Jacqueline Ewing	212-938-2629	D	3 OR	<0.1
I.J. Cohen Company Inc.	PO Box 8378	Shawnee Mission	KS	66208	Phillip L. Gershon	913-648-6668	R	3 OR*	<0.1
RWA Financial Services Inc.	3307 Northland Dr.	Austin	TX	78731	Randall W. Allen	512-459-3911	R	3 OR	<0.1
Midland Inc.	12528 Kirkham Court	Poway	CA	92124	Chris Traios	619-679-3290	P	2	0.1
Keystone Trading Corp.	5420 Milwaukee Ave.	Chicago	IL	60630	Brian McGuire	312-763-8401	R	2 OR	<0.1
Technalloy Inc.	1997 Hartog Dr.	San Jose	CA	95131	Alan Goldberg	408-437-1995	R	2 OR	<0.1
Ingredient Quality Consultants Inc.	4370 S. Tamiami Trail	Sarasota	FL	34231	Wayne Whittaker	813-921-6595	R	1 OR	<0.1
Simonds-Shields-Theis Grain Co.	4800 Main St.	Kansas City	MO	64112	Steven O. Theis	816-561-4155	R	1 OR	<0.1
TW Energy Consulting Inc.	4800 Main St.	Kansas City	MO	64112	Peter Van Cleve	816-531-5455	R	0 OR	<0.1
Phoenixx International Resources Inc.	4955 Steubenville Pike	Pittsburgh	PA	15205	Paul Helsel	412-787-6363	R	0 OR*	<0.1

Source: Ward's Business Directory of U.S. Private and Public Companies, 1996. Company type codes: P - Public, R - Private, S - Subsidiary, D - Division, J - Joint Venture, A - Affiliate, G - Group. If the dollar values shown are not sales, the following codes apply: TA - Total Assets; OR - Operating Revenues; GB - Gross Billings. * - estimated dollar value. < - less than; *na* - not available.

SIC 6230

SECURITY AND COMMODITY EXCHANGES

SIC 6230 includes establishments whose principal activity is to furnish space and other facilities to members for the purpose of buying, selling, or trading in stocks, stock options, bonds, or commodity contracts. Commodity contract exchanges, futures exchanges, security exchanges, stock exchanges, and stock option exchanges are all classified as SIC 6230.

ESTABLISHMENTS, EMPLOYMENT, AND PAYROLL

	1990	1991 Value	%	1992 Value	%	1993 Value	%	1994 Value	%	1995 Value	%	% change 90-95
All Establishments	150	133	-11.3	142	6.8	105	-26.1	88	-16.2	99	12.5	-34.0
Mid-March Employment	9,149	8,268	-9.6	8,624	4.3	7,373	-14.5	7,410	0.5	7,653	3.3	-16.4
1st Quarter Wages (annualized - $ mil.)	485.3	404.1	-16.7	437.1	8.1	407.4	-6.8	421.0	3.3	469.7	11.6	-3.2
Payroll per Emp. 1st Q. (annualized)	53,048	48,881	-7.9	50,682	3.7	55,261	9.0	56,819	2.8	61,378	8.0	15.7
Annual Payroll ($ mil.)	450.3	398.6	-11.5	437.9	9.8	414.2	-5.4	391.7	-5.4	446.8	14.1	-0.8
Establishments - 1-4 Emp. Number	69	60	-13.0	68	13.3	68	-	48	-29.4	56	16.7	-18.8
Mid-March Employment	108	(D)	-	121	-	81	-33.1	70	-13.6	91	30.0	-15.7
1st Quarter Wages (annualized - $ mil.)	5.4	(D)	-	6.3	-	6.0	-5.7	4.1	-31.4	4.9	18.7	-10.0
Payroll per Emp. 1st Q. (annualized)	50,148	(D)	-	52,430	-	73,877	40.9	58,686	-20.6	53,582	-8.7	6.8
Annual Payroll ($ mil.)	8.7	(D)	-	8.4	-	6.5	-21.8	5.6	-14.4	9.7	72.9	11.5
Establishments - 5-9 Emp. Number	18	20	11.1	26	30.0	(D)	-	9	-	(D)	-	-
Mid-March Employment	110	(D)	-	176	-	(D)	-	58	-	(D)	-	-
1st Quarter Wages (annualized - $ mil.)	6.9	(D)	-	12.0	-	(D)	-	2.8	-	(D)	-	-
Payroll per Emp. 1st Q. (annualized)	62,400	(D)	-	68,114	-	(D)	-	47,724	-	(D)	-	-
Annual Payroll ($ mil.)	5.8	(D)	-	11.1	-	(D)	-	2.4	-	(D)	-	-
Establishments - 10-19 Emp. Number	15	13	-13.3	9	-30.8	5	-44.4	(D)	-	5	-	-66.7
Mid-March Employment	212	175	-17.5	123	-29.7	65	-47.2	(D)	-	56	-	-73.6
1st Quarter Wages (annualized - $ mil.)	11.9	10.1	-14.8	6.5	-36.1	2.7	-58.5	(D)	-	5.1	-	-56.6
Payroll per Emp. 1st Q. (annualized)	56,000	57,783	3.2	52,553	-9.1	41,292	-21.4	(D)	-	91,929	-	64.2
Annual Payroll ($ mil.)	13.6	9.6	-29.4	6.2	-35.3	3.0	-52.4	(D)	-	6.3	-	-53.9
Establishments - 20-49 Emp. Number	14	11	-21.4	14	27.3	6	-57.1	4	-33.3	5	25.0	-64.3
Mid-March Employment	408	(D)	-	417	-	204	-51.1	104	-49.0	128	23.1	-68.6
1st Quarter Wages (annualized - $ mil.)	22.0	(D)	-	25.6	-	18.2	-29.2	4.1	-77.2	5.2	25.8	-76.3
Payroll per Emp. 1st Q. (annualized)	53,853	(D)	-	61,477	-	88,980	44.7	39,731	-55.3	40,625	2.3	-24.6
Annual Payroll ($ mil.)	18.8	(D)	-	26.2	-	20.3	-22.4	5.0	-75.2	5.7	13.1	-69.7
Establishments - 50-99 Emp. Number	15	10	-33.3	9	-10.0	5	-44.4	7	40.0	9	28.6	-40.0
Mid-March Employment	1,140	674	-40.9	679	0.7	364	-46.4	480	31.9	653	36.0	-42.7
1st Quarter Wages (annualized - $ mil.)	95.6	42.0	-56.1	47.2	12.5	16.9	-64.1	29.5	74.0	44.8	52.2	-53.1
Payroll per Emp. 1st Q. (annualized)	83,860	62,297	-25.7	69,555	11.7	46,516	-33.1	61,383	32.0	68,674	11.9	-18.1
Annual Payroll ($ mil.)	90.9	61.8	-32.0	64.1	3.7	17.5	-72.7	27.9	59.2	43.0	54.0	-52.8
Establishments - 100-249 Emp. Number	11	12	9.1	8	-33.3	5	-37.5	7	40.0	5	-28.6	-54.5
Mid-March Employment	(D)	(D)	-	1,430	-	752	-47.4	993	32.0	722	-27.3	-
1st Quarter Wages (annualized - $ mil.)	(D)	(D)	-	65.9	-	37.4	-43.2	62.1	65.9	53.6	-13.6	-
Payroll per Emp. 1st Q. (annualized)	(D)	(D)	-	46,081	-	49,787	8.0	62,546	25.6	74,288	18.8	-
Annual Payroll ($ mil.)	(D)	(D)	-	69.6	-	36.7	-47.3	57.8	57.6	44.6	-22.9	-
Establishments - 250-499 Emp. Number	3	2	-33.3	(D)	-	4	-	3	-25.0	(D)	-	-
Mid-March Employment	879	(D)	-	(D)	-	1,601	-	980	-38.8	(D)	-	-
1st Quarter Wages (annualized - $ mil.)	20.2	(D)	-	(D)	-	111.8	-	43.6	-61.0	(D)	-	-
Payroll per Emp. 1st Q. (annualized)	22,999	(D)	-	(D)	-	69,826	-	44,482	-36.3	(D)	-	-
Annual Payroll ($ mil.)	22.5	(D)	-	(D)	-	131.1	-	46.6	-64.5	(D)	-	-
Establishments - 500-999 Emp. Number	4	4	-	(D)	-	(D)	-	(D)	-	(D)	-	-
Mid-March Employment	3,155	(D)	-	(D)	-	(D)	-	(D)	-	(D)	-	-
1st Quarter Wages (annualized - $ mil.)	144.4	(D)	-	(D)	-	(D)	-	(D)	-	(D)	-	-
Payroll per Emp. 1st Q. (annualized)	45,777	(D)	-	(D)	-	(D)	-	(D)	-	(D)	-	-
Annual Payroll ($ mil.)	131.6	(D)	-	(D)	-	(D)	-	(D)	-	(D)	-	-
Estab. - 1000 or More Emp. Number	1	1	-	(D)	-	-	-	-	-	(D)	-	-
Mid-March Employment	(D)	(D)	-	(D)	-	-	-	-	-	(D)	-	-
1st Quarter Wages (annualized - $ mil.)	(D)	(D)	-	(D)	-	-	-	-	-	(D)	-	-
Payroll per Emp. 1st Q. (annualized)	(D)	(D)	-	(D)	-	-	-	-	-	(D)	-	-
Annual Payroll ($ mil.)	(D)	(D)	-	(D)	-	-	-	-	-	(D)	-	-

Source: County Business Patterns, U.S. Department of Commerce, Washington, D.C., for 1990 through 1995. Payroll per employee is calculated using mid-March employment and 1st Quarter wages, annualized. Annual payroll, also shown, may not equal the annualized 1st Quarter wages. Columns headed by a percent sign (%) indicate change from the previous year. *na* stands for not available. The symbol (D) indicates that data are withheld by the source to avoid disclosure of competitive information. A dash (-) indicates that data are not available or cannot be calculated.

ESTABLISHMENTS
Number

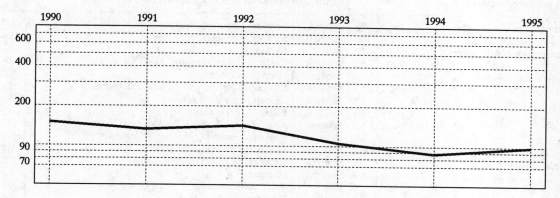

MID-MARCH EMPLOYMENT
Number

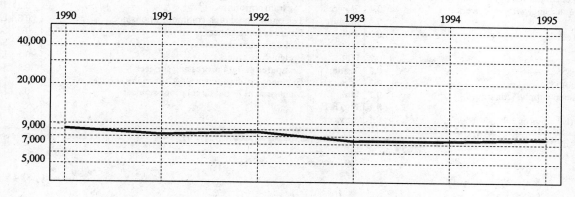

ANNUAL PAYROLL
$ million

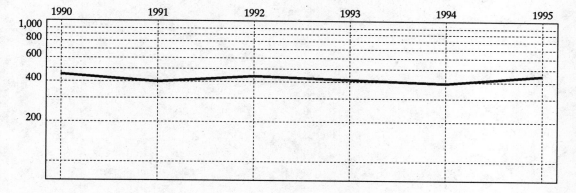

INPUTS AND OUTPUTS FOR SECURITY AND COMMODITY BROKERS - SIC GROUP 62

Economic Sector or Industry Providing Inputs	%	Sector	Economic Sector or Industry Buying Outputs	%	Sector
Security & commodity brokers	47.0	Fin/R.E.	Personal consumption expenditures	31.9	
Real estate agents, operators, & lessors	10.4	Fin/R.E.	Security & commodity brokers	16.4	Fin/R.E.
Telephone/telegraph communications nec	7.1	Util.	Banking	14.7	Fin/R.E.
Legal services	6.5	Services	Credit agencies other than banks	9.0	Fin/R.E.
Computer & data processing services	5.4	Services	Insurance carriers	8.2	Fin/R.E.
Advertising	5.3	Services	S/L Govt., general government nec, spending	6.1	S/L Govt
Accounting, auditing & bookkeeping	3.9	Services	Exports of goods & services	3.6	Foreign
Banking	2.1	Fin/R.E.	Electric services (utilities)	0.9	Util.
Business services nec	1.9	Services	Accounting, auditing & bookkeeping	0.7	Services
U.S. Postal Service	1.1	Gov't	Real estate agents, operators, & lessors	0.6	Fin/R.E.
Electric services (utilities)	0.9	Util.	Membership organizations nec	0.6	Services
Eating & drinking places	0.8	Services	Retail trade, ex eating & drinking	0.5	Trade
Hotels	0.7	Services	Hospitals	0.5	Services
Air transportation	0.6	Util.	Social services, nec	0.5	Services
Management & public relations services	0.6	Services	Wholesale trade	0.4	Trade
Personnel supply services	0.6	Services	Trucking & courier services, ex air	0.3	Util.
Repair & maintenance construction nec	0.5	Constr.	Colleges, universities, & professional schools	0.3	Services
Commercial printing	0.5	Manufg.	Private libraries, vocational schools, nec	0.3	Services
Insurance carriers	0.5	Fin/R.E.	State & local government enterprises nec	0.3	Gov't
Photofinishing labs & commercial photography	0.5	Services	Petroleum refining	0.2	Manufg.
Automotive rental & leasing, without drivers	0.4	Services	Air transportation	0.2	Util.
Petroleum refining	0.2	Manufg.	Telephone/telegraph communications nec	0.2	Util.
Local & suburban transit	0.2	Util.	Business services nec	0.2	Services
Natural gas distribution	0.2	Util.	Child day care services	0.2	Services
Trucking & courier services, ex air	0.2	Util.	Freight forwarders	0.1	Util.
Wholesale trade	0.2	Trade	Computer & data processing services	0.1	Services
Business & professional associations	0.2	Services	Engineering, architectural, & surveying services	0.1	Services
Sanitary services, steam supply, irrigation	0.1	Util.	Management & public relations services	0.1	Services
Royalties	0.1	Fin/R.E.			
Detective & protective services	0.1	Services			

Source: Benchmark Input-Output Accounts for the U.S. Economy, 1992, U.S. Department of Commerce, Washington, D.C., November 1997. Data, as reported in the source, are organized by the 1987 SIC structure in use in 1992.

OCCUPATIONS EMPLOYED BY SECURITY AND COMMODITY EXCHANGES AND SERVICES

Occupation	% of Total 1996	Change to 2006	Occupation	% of Total 1996	Change to 2006
Management support workers nec	12.7	114.1	Computer programmers	2.6	0.7
Securities & financial sales workers	9.1	22.4	Systems analysts	2.6	95.8
Secretaries, except legal & medical	8.7	-2.9	Sales & related workers nec	2.1	34.6
General managers & top executives	7.9	18.6	Data entry keyers, except composing	2.0	-2.1
Brokerage clerks	6.6	2.3	Receptionists & information clerks	1.8	22.3
General office clerks	5.7	5.3	Clerical & administrative workers nec	1.6	22.4
Financial managers	5.2	22.3	Marketing & sales worker supervisors	1.5	22.3
Clerical supervisors & managers	4.4	22.4	Managers & administrators nec	1.3	21.2
Bookkeeping, accounting, & auditing clerks	4.3	-2.1	Professional workers nec	1.2	22.4
Accountants & auditors	2.9	13.3	Computer operators, ex peripheral equipment	1.2	-26.5

Sources: Industry-Occupation Matrix, Bureau of Labor Statistics. These data relate to one or more 3-digit SIC industry groups rather than to a single 4-digit SIC. The change reported for each occupation to the year 2005 is a percent of growth or decline as estimated by the Bureau of Labor Statistics. The abbreviation *nec* stands for not elsewhere classified.

U.S. AND STATE DATA ON INDUSTRY REVENUES AND OTHER ACCOUNTS FOR 1992

State	No. of Estab.	Employ-ment	Payroll ($ mil.)	Revenues ($ mil.)	Empl./ Estab.	Revenue/ Estab. ($)	Payroll/ Estab. ($)	Revenue/ Empl. ($)	Payroll/ Empl. ($)
UNITED STATES	35	6,739	311.8	993.5	193	28,384,743	8,907,514	147,420	46,263
California	7	-	(D)	(D)	(D)	71,101,500	24,435,500	112,681	38,725
Illinois	4	2,524	97.7	284.4	631	71,101,500	24,435,500	112,681	38,725
Massachusetts	1	-	(D)	(D)	(D)	(D)	(D)	(D)	(D)
Minnesota	1	-	(D)	(D)	(D)	(D)	(D)	(D)	(D)
Missouri	2	-	(D)	(D)	(D)	(D)	(D)	(D)	(D)
New York	13	3,436	182.6	621.3	264	47,790,538	14,048,923	180,814	53,154
Ohio	1	-	(D)	(D)	(D)	(D)	(D)	(D)	(D)
Pennsylvania	1	-	(D)	(D)	(D)	(D)	(D)	(D)	(D)
Texas	1	-	(D)	(D)	(D)	(D)	(D)	(D)	(D)

Source: *1992 Economic Census*, U.S. Department of Commerce, Washington, D.C. This is the only table that shows revenue data as collected by the Bureau of the Census in an Economic Census. The symbol (D) indicates that data are withheld by the source to avoid disclosure of competitive information. A dash (-) indicates that data are not available or cannot be calculated.

STATE-BY-STATE DATA ON ESTABLISHMENTS, EMPLOYMENT, AND PAYROLL - 1994 AND 1995

State	1994					1995					% Change Empl.
	No. of Estab.	Employ-ment	Pay / Empl.	Payroll ($ mil.)	Pay / Estab.	No. of Estab.	Employ-ment	Pay / Empl.	Payroll ($ mil.)	Pay / Estab.	
Arizona	1	(D)	-	(D)	-	1	(D)	-	(D)	-	-
Arkansas	(D)	(D)	(D)	(D)	(D)	1	(D)	-	(D)	-	-
California	12	(D)	-	(D)	-	12	445	37,888	17.5	1,461,167	-
Colorado	(D)	(D)	(D)	(D)	(D)	1	(D)	-	(D)	-	-
Connecticut	2	(D)	-	(D)	-	1	(D)	-	(D)	-	-
District of Columbia	4	(D)	-	(D)	-	4	(D)	-	(D)	-	-
Florida	4	(D)	-	(D)	-	2	(D)	-	(D)	-	-
Illinois	16	2,597	43,184	110.8	6,927,250	18	2,694	47,676	121.8	6,766,111	3.7
Iowa	1	(D)	-	(D)	-	1	(D)	-	(D)	-	-
Kansas	2	(D)	-	(D)	-	2	(D)	-	(D)	-	-
Maryland	1	(D)	-	(D)	-	1	(D)	-	(D)	-	-
Massachusetts	2	(D)	-	(D)	-	4	(D)	-	(D)	-	-
Minnesota	2	(D)	-	(D)	-	1	(D)	-	(D)	-	-
Missouri	2	(D)	-	(D)	-	2	(D)	-	(D)	-	-
New Jersey	2	(D)	-	(D)	-	2	(D)	-	(D)	-	-
New York	25	3,365	69,140	209.3	8,372,640	28	3,408	75,860	245.2	8,757,464	1.3
North Dakota	1	(D)	-	(D)	-	1	(D)	-	(D)	-	-
Ohio	1	(D)	-	(D)	-	1	(D)	-	(D)	-	-
Pennsylvania	3	(D)	-	(D)	-	2	(D)	-	(D)	-	-
South Carolina	(D)	(D)	(D)	(D)	(D)	1	(D)	-	(D)	-	-
Texas	7	(D)	-	(D)	-	9	(D)	-	(D)	-	-
Utah	(D)	(D)	(D)	(D)	(D)	2	(D)	-	(D)	-	-
Virginia	(D)	(D)	(D)	(D)	(D)	2	(D)	-	(D)	-	-

Source: County Business Patterns, U.S. Department of Commerce, Washington, D.C., for 1994 and 1995. Employment shown is for mid-March of the year shown. Payroll per employee is calculated by annualizing 1st Quarter payroll (not shown) and then dividing that value by mid-March employment. Dividing total annual payroll (columns 5 and 10) by employment, therefore, will *not* yield the payroll per employee figure (columns 4 and 9). The symbol (D) indicates that data are withheld by the source to avoid disclosure of competitive information. A dash (-) indicates that data are not available or cannot be calculated.

ESTABLISHMENTS 1995 - STATE AND REGIONAL CONCENTRATION

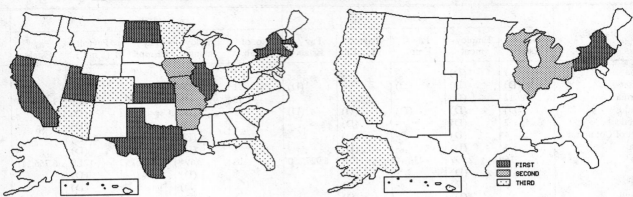

EMPLOYMENT 1995 - STATE AND REGIONAL CONCENTRATION

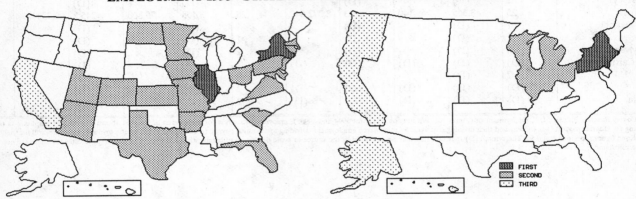

PAYROLL 1995 - STATE AND REGIONAL CONCENTRATION

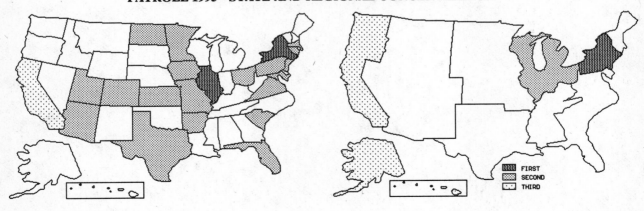

States with the darkest shading indicate those states which have proportionately more establishments, employment, or payrolls than would be indicated by the state's population. States with light shading are states with proportionately fewer establishments, less employment, and lower payrolls than population distribution. States shaded grey are within 15 percent of the state's population proportion in these categories. States for which no data are available are shown as average (grey). *Regions* are shaded to indicate absolute rank in the category. If no data for the category are available, establishment counts are used to shade the regions. Source of the data is the table on the facing page.

LEADING COMPANIES - SIC 6221 - Commodity Contracts Brokers, Dealers

Number shown: **17** Total sales/assets ($ mil): **2,493** Total employment (000): **13.4**

Company Name	Address				CEO Name	Phone	Co. Type	Sales/Assets ($ mil)	Empl. (000)
Nasdaq Stock Market Inc.	1735 K St. N.W.	Washington	DC	20006	Alfred R. Berkeley	202-496-2500	S	634 OR	3.5
National Association of Securities Dealers Inc.	1735 K St. N.W.	Washington	DC	20006	Frank Zarb	202-728-8000	R	634 OR	3.5
New York Stock Exchange Inc.	11 Wall St.	New York	NY	10005	Richard A. Grasso	212-656-3000	R	561 OR	1.5
American Stock Exchange Inc.	86 Trinity Pl.	New York	NY	10006	Richard F. Syron	212-306-1000	R	140 OR*	0.7
Chicago Board of Trade	141 W. Jackson Blvd.	Chicago	IL	60604	Thomas R. Donovan	312-435-3500	R	139 OR*	0.8
Chicago Board Options Exchange Inc.	400 S. LaSalle St.	Chicago	IL	60605	William J. Brodsky	312-786-5600	R	107 OR	0.9
Chicago Mercantile Exchange	30 S. Wacker Dr.	Chicago	IL	60606	Eric Kilcollin	312-930-1000	R	93 OR*	0.9
Pacific Exchange Inc.	301 Pine St.	San Francisco	CA	94104	Robert Greber	415-393-4000	R	59 OR	0.4
Philadelphia Stock Exchange Inc.	1900 Market St.	Philadelphia	PA	19103	Nicholas A. Giordano	215-496-5000	R	38 OR	0.6
Coffee, Sugar and Cocoa Exchange Inc.	4 World Trade Ctr.	New York	NY	10048	James J. Bowe	212-938-2800	R	33 OR*	0.2
Chicago Stock Exchange Inc.	440 S. LaSalle St.	Chicago	IL	60605	Robert H. Forney	312-663-2222	R	21 OR*	0.2
Boston Stock Exchange Inc.	1 Boston Pl.	Boston	MA	02108	William G. Morton Jr.	617-723-9500	R	15 OR	0.1
Citrus Associates of the New York Cotton Exchange Inc.	4 World Trade Ctr.	New York	NY	10048	Joseph J. O'Neill	212-938-2650	R	9 OR	0.1
Minneapolis Grain Exchange	400 S. 4th St.	Minneapolis	MN	55415	James H. Lindau	612-338-6212	R	6 OR	<0.1
IMX Inc.	PO Box 778	San Ramon	CA	94583	Stephen Fraser	510-552-3300	R	3 TA	<0.1
Cincinnati Stock Exchange	400 S. La Salle St.	Chicago	IL	60605	Fred Moss	312-786-8803	R	2 OR*	<0.1
MidAmerica Commodity Exchange	141 W. Jackson Blvd.	Chicago	IL	60604	Thomas R. Donovan	312-341-3000	R	0 OR	<0.1

Source: *Ward's Business Directory of U.S. Private and Public Companies*, 1996. Company type codes: P - Public, R - Private, S - Subsidiary, D - Division, J - Joint Venture, A - Affiliate, G - Group. If the dollar values shown are not sales, the following codes apply: TA - Total Assets; OR - Operating Revenues; GB - Gross Billings. * - estimated dollar value. < - less than; *na* - not available.

SIC 6280

SECURITY AND COMMODITY SERVICES

The group includes SIC 6282, Investment Advice and SIC 6289, Services Allied With the Exchange of Securities or Commodities, not elsewhere classified.

SIC 6282 includes all establishments that furnish investment advice. Investment information is furnished to companies and individuals concerning securities and commodities on a contract or fee basis. Establishments included in SIC 6280 do not act as brokers and dealers; those who furnish investment advice and also sell securities are classified as SIC 6210. Futures and investment advisory services, investment counseling services, investment research organizations, and managers of mutual funds—on a contract or fee basis—are included.

SIC 6289 includes a variety of services to security or commodity holders, brokers, or dealers, including bondholders protective committees, custodians of securities, exchange clearinghouses for commodities and securities, financial reporting services, quotation services for stocks, royalty owners protective associations, security custodian services, security holders protective committees, and stock transfer agents.

ESTABLISHMENTS, EMPLOYMENT, AND PAYROLL

	1990	1991		1992		1993		1994		1995		% change 90-95
		Value	%	Value	%	Value	%	Value	%	Value	%	
All Establishments	7,087	7,954	12.2	11,517	44.8	13,087	13.6	13,880	6.1	14,749	6.3	108.1
Mid-March Employment	75,740	77,674	2.6	91,846	18.2	119,969	30.6	114,526	-4.5	120,115	4.9	58.6
1st Quarter Wages (annualized - $ mil.)	4,813.8	4,897.7	1.7	5,859.0	19.6	7,437.9	26.9	8,586.4	15.4	9,986.3	16.3	107.5
Payroll per Emp. 1st Q. (annualized)	63,557	63,055	-0.8	63,792	1.2	61,998	-2.8	74,973	20.9	83,140	10.9	30.8
Annual Payroll ($ mil.)	4,454.0	5,062.4	13.7	6,488.7	28.2	9,468.3	45.9	8,703.9	-8.1	9,944.9	14.3	123.3
Establishments - 1-4 Emp. Number	5,089	5,738	12.8	8,935	55.7	9,831	10.0	10,525	7.1	11,201	6.4	120.1
Mid-March Employment	8,012	8,527	6.4	13,152	54.2	14,610	11.1	15,804	8.2	16,702	5.7	108.5
1st Quarter Wages (annualized - $ mil.)	308.1	360.2	16.9	515.3	43.1	609.3	18.3	648.0	6.4	721.4	11.3	134.1
Payroll per Emp. 1st Q. (annualized)	38,459	42,237	9.8	39,178	-7.2	41,707	6.5	41,005	-1.7	43,195	5.3	12.3
Annual Payroll ($ mil.)	379.2	490.2	29.3	709.1	44.6	906.1	27.8	859.4	-5.2	996.2	15.9	162.7
Establishments - 5-9 Emp. Number	937	1,116	19.1	1,349	20.9	1,635	21.2	1,723	5.4	1,787	3.7	90.7
Mid-March Employment	6,005	7,267	21.0	8,709	19.8	10,485	20.4	11,127	6.1	11,537	3.7	92.1
1st Quarter Wages (annualized - $ mil.)	352.5	460.6	30.7	593.6	28.9	629.3	6.0	658.9	4.7	735.2	11.6	108.6
Payroll per Emp. 1st Q. (annualized)	58,699	63,387	8.0	68,155	7.5	60,016	-11.9	59,216	-1.3	63,724	7.6	8.6
Annual Payroll ($ mil.)	380.6	511.5	34.4	675.1	32.0	901.2	33.5	759.7	-15.7	850.2	11.9	123.4
Establishments - 10-19 Emp. Number	540	546	1.1	634	16.1	788	24.3	803	1.9	871	8.5	61.3
Mid-March Employment	7,153	7,226	1.0	8,445	16.9	10,652	26.1	10,776	1.2	11,593	7.6	62.1
1st Quarter Wages (annualized - $ mil.)	542.5	521.0	-4.0	602.2	15.6	774.5	28.6	843.9	9.0	981.2	16.3	80.9
Payroll per Emp. 1st Q. (annualized)	75,843	72,095	-4.9	71,311	-1.1	72,709	2.0	78,313	7.7	84,639	8.1	11.6
Annual Payroll ($ mil.)	531.0	575.7	8.4	724.5	25.8	1,061.4	46.5	980.5	-7.6	1,111.1	13.3	109.3
Establishments - 20-49 Emp. Number	293	327	11.6	350	7.0	505	44.3	520	3.0	554	6.5	89.1
Mid-March Employment	8,948	9,647	7.8	10,430	8.1	14,998	43.8	15,536	3.6	16,587	6.8	85.4
1st Quarter Wages (annualized - $ mil.)	723.8	748.4	3.4	842.4	12.5	1,046.4	24.2	1,465.6	40.1	1,772.3	20.9	144.8
Payroll per Emp. 1st Q. (annualized)	80,893	77,583	-4.1	80,762	4.1	69,771	-13.6	94,333	35.2	106,847	13.3	32.1
Annual Payroll ($ mil.)	632.9	849.7	34.3	911.5	7.3	1,357.9	49.0	1,613.0	18.8	1,811.5	12.3	186.2
Establishments - 50-99 Emp. Number	106	119	12.3	119	-	153	28.6	144	-5.9	162	12.5	52.8
Mid-March Employment	7,322	7,791	6.4	8,167	4.8	10,518	28.8	9,823	-6.6	11,166	13.7	52.5
1st Quarter Wages (annualized - $ mil.)	609.3	635.4	4.3	936.0	47.3	764.1	-18.4	1,223.3	60.1	1,112.4	-9.1	82.6
Payroll per Emp. 1st Q. (annualized)	83,212	81,552	-2.0	114,610	40.5	72,649	-36.6	124,530	71.4	99,621	-20.0	19.7
Annual Payroll ($ mil.)	504.1	603.7	19.8	956.5	58.4	840.4	-12.1	1,030.4	22.6	1,086.1	5.4	115.5
Establishments - 100-249 Emp. Number	70	63	-10.0	77	22.2	104	35.1	104	-	115	10.6	64.3
Mid-March Employment	(D)	9,685	-	11,355	17.2	16,176	42.5	16,146	-0.2	17,845	10.5	-
1st Quarter Wages (annualized - $ mil.)	(D)	647.1	-	854.8	32.1	1,426.0	66.8	1,504.0	5.5	1,962.7	30.5	-
Payroll per Emp. 1st Q. (annualized)	(D)	66,818	-	75,282	12.7	88,157	17.1	93,151	5.7	109,988	18.1	-
Annual Payroll ($ mil.)	(D)	637.4	-	959.3	50.5	2,042.6	112.9	1,460.3	-28.5	1,788.1	22.5	-
Establishments - 250-499 Emp. Number	31	25	-19.4	33	32.0	45	36.4	37	-17.8	37	-	19.4
Mid-March Employment	10,682	(D)	-	10,951	-	15,582	42.3	12,670	-18.7	13,302	5.0	24.5
1st Quarter Wages (annualized - $ mil.)	680.0	(D)	-	641.4	-	928.1	44.7	752.9	-18.9	825.9	9.7	21.5
Payroll per Emp. 1st Q. (annualized)	63,658	(D)	-	58,567	-	59,559	1.7	59,423	-0.2	62,086	4.5	-2.5
Annual Payroll ($ mil.)	534.1	(D)	-	609.1	-	875.9	43.8	683.3	-22.0	772.5	13.1	44.6
Establishments - 500-999 Emp. Number	16	14	-12.5	(D)	-	17	-	17	-	(D)	-	-
Mid-March Employment	10,935	(D)	-	(D)	-	11,260	-	11,233	-0.2	(D)	-	-
1st Quarter Wages (annualized - $ mil.)	544.7	(D)	-	(D)	-	608.0	-	696.1	14.5	(D)	-	-
Payroll per Emp. 1st Q. (annualized)	49,810	(D)	-	(D)	-	53,994	-	61,970	14.8	(D)	-	-
Annual Payroll ($ mil.)	527.1	(D)	-	(D)	-	566.8	-	689.5	21.6	(D)	-	-
Estab. - 1000 or More Emp. Number	5	6	20.0	(D)	-	9	-	7	-22.2	(D)	-	-
Mid-March Employment	(D)	(D)	-	(D)	-	15,688	-	11,411	-27.3	(D)	-	-
1st Quarter Wages (annualized - $ mil.)	(D)	(D)	-	(D)	-	652.2	-	793.7	21.7	(D)	-	-
Payroll per Emp. 1st Q. (annualized)	(D)	(D)	-	(D)	-	41,571	-	69,555	67.3	(D)	-	-
Annual Payroll ($ mil.)	(D)	(D)	-	(D)	-	916.0	-	627.9	-31.4	(D)	-	-

Source: County Business Patterns, U.S. Department of Commerce, Washington, D.C., for 1990 through 1995. Payroll per employee is calculated using mid-March employment and 1st Quarter wages, annualized. Annual payroll, also shown, may not equal the annualized 1st Quarter wages. Columns headed by a percent sign (%) indicate change from the previous year. *na* stands for not available. The symbol (D) indicates that data are withheld by the source to avoid disclosure of competitive information. A dash (-) indicates that data are not available or cannot be calculated.

ESTABLISHMENTS
Number

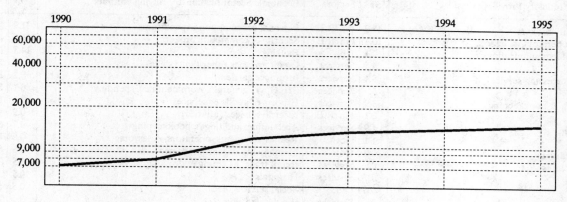

MID-MARCH EMPLOYMENT
Number

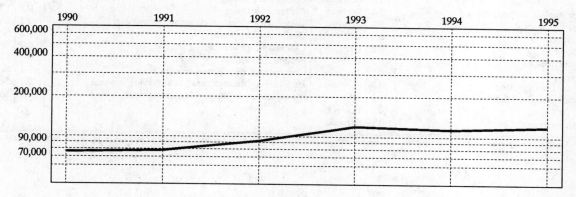

ANNUAL PAYROLL
$ million

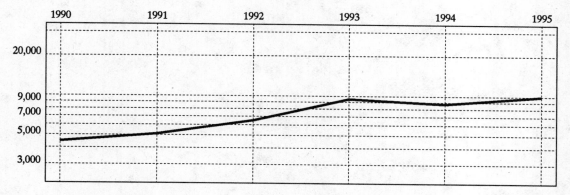

INPUTS AND OUTPUTS FOR SECURITY AND COMMODITY BROKERS - SIC GROUP 62

Economic Sector or Industry Providing Inputs	%	Sector	Economic Sector or Industry Buying Outputs	%	Sector
Security & commodity brokers	47.0	Fin/R.E.	Personal consumption expenditures	31.9	
Real estate agents, operators, & lessors	10.4	Fin/R.E.	Security & commodity brokers	16.4	Fin/R.E.
Telephone/telegraph communications nec	7.1	Util.	Banking	14.7	Fin/R.E.
Legal services	6.5	Services	Credit agencies other than banks	9.0	Fin/R.E.
Computer & data processing services	5.4	Services	Insurance carriers	8.2	Fin/R.E.
Advertising	5.3	Services	S/L Govt., general government nec, spending	6.1	S/L Govt
Accounting, auditing & bookkeeping	3.9	Services	Exports of goods & services	3.6	Foreign
Banking	2.1	Fin/R.E.	Electric services (utilities)	0.9	Util.
Business services nec	1.9	Services	Accounting, auditing & bookkeeping	0.7	Services
U.S. Postal Service	1.1	Gov't	Real estate agents, operators, & lessors	0.6	Fin/R.E.
Electric services (utilities)	0.9	Util.	Membership organizations nec	0.6	Services
Eating & drinking places	0.8	Services	Retail trade, ex eating & drinking	0.5	Trade
Hotels	0.7	Services	Hospitals	0.5	Services
Air transportation	0.6	Util.	Social services, nec	0.5	Services
Management & public relations services	0.6	Services	Wholesale trade	0.4	Trade
Personnel supply services	0.6	Services	Trucking & courier services, ex air	0.3	Util.
Repair & maintenance construction nec	0.5	Constr.	Colleges, universities, & professional schools	0.3	Services
Commercial printing	0.5	Manufg.	Private libraries, vocational schools, nec	0.3	Services
Insurance carriers	0.5	Fin/R.E.	State & local government enterprises nec	0.3	Gov't
Photofinishing labs & commercial photography	0.5	Services	Petroleum refining	0.2	Manufg.
Automotive rental & leasing, without drivers	0.4	Services	Air transportation	0.2	Util.
Petroleum refining	0.2	Manufg.	Telephone/telegraph communications nec	0.2	Util.
Local & suburban transit	0.2	Util.	Business services nec	0.2	Services
Natural gas distribution	0.2	Util.	Child day care services	0.2	Services
Trucking & courier services, ex air	0.2	Util.	Freight forwarders	0.1	Util.
Wholesale trade	0.2	Trade	Computer & data processing services	0.1	Services
Business & professional associations	0.2	Services	Engineering, architectural, & surveying services	0.1	Services
Sanitary services, steam supply, irrigation	0.1	Util.	Management & public relations services	0.1	Services
Royalties	0.1	Fin/R.E.			
Detective & protective services	0.1	Services			

Source: Benchmark Input-Output Accounts for the U.S. Economy, 1992, U.S. Department of Commerce, Washington, D.C., November 1997. Data, as reported in the source, are organized by the 1987 SIC structure in use in 1992.

OCCUPATIONS EMPLOYED BY SECURITY AND COMMODITY EXCHANGES AND SERVICES

Occupation	% of Total 1996	Change to 2006	Occupation	% of Total 1996	Change to 2006
Management support workers nec	12.7	114.1	Computer programmers	2.6	0.7
Securities & financial sales workers	9.1	22.4	Systems analysts	2.6	95.8
Secretaries, except legal & medical	8.7	-2.9	Sales & related workers nec	2.1	34.6
General managers & top executives	7.9	18.6	Data entry keyers, except composing	2.0	-2.1
Brokerage clerks	6.6	2.3	Receptionists & information clerks	1.8	22.3
General office clerks	5.7	5.3	Clerical & administrative workers nec	1.6	22.4
Financial managers	5.2	22.3	Marketing & sales worker supervisors	1.5	22.3
Clerical supervisors & managers	4.4	22.4	Managers & administrators nec	1.3	21.2
Bookkeeping, accounting, & auditing clerks	4.3	-2.1	Professional workers nec	1.2	22.4
Accountants & auditors	2.9	13.3	Computer operators, ex peripheral equipment	1.2	-26.5

Sources: Industry-Occupation Matrix, Bureau of Labor Statistics. These data relate to one or more 3-digit SIC industry groups rather than to a single 4-digit SIC. The change reported for each occupation to the year 2005 is a percent of growth or decline as estimated by the Bureau of Labor Statistics. The abbreviation *nec* stands for not elsewhere classified.

U.S. AND STATE DATA ON INDUSTRY REVENUES AND OTHER ACCOUNTS FOR 1992

State	No. of Estab.	Employ- ment	Payroll ($ mil.)	Revenues ($ mil.)	Empl./ Estab.	Revenue/ Estab. ($)	Payroll/ Estab. ($)	Revenue/ Empl. ($)	Payroll/ Empl. ($)
UNITED STATES	11,905	86,859	6,562.5	17,138.8	7	1,439,629	551,239	197,317	75,553
California	1,741	-	(D)	(D)	(D)	(D)	(D)	(D)	(D)
Colorado	318	3,330	147.6	421.9	10	1,326,780	464,230	126,702	44,332
Florida	697	2,156	131.0	342.7	3	491,742	187,991	158,972	60,775
Georgia	269	1,239	81.9	226.7	5	842,717	304,539	182,963	66,119
Illinois	641	4,528	350.9	1,110.5	7	1,732,505	547,395	245,260	77,491
Indiana	153	756	36.6	89.5	5	584,993	239,092	118,392	48,388
Maryland	239	1,336	82.9	219.2	6	917,285	346,941	164,095	62,065
Massachusetts	498	-	(D)	(D)	(D)	(D)	(D)	(D)	(D)
Michigan	302	986	53.5	129.9	3	430,030	177,036	131,713	54,224
Minnesota	310	-	(D)	(D)	(D)	(D)	(D)	(D)	(D)
Missouri	194	-	(D)	(D)	(D)	(D)	(D)	(D)	(D)
New Jersey	413	7,967	448.9	1,295.9	19	3,137,867	1,086,821	162,663	56,340
New York	1,457	15,855	1,966.7	4,489.5	11	3,081,365	1,349,844	283,163	124,044
North Carolina	174	584	32.7	80.5	3	462,925	187,845	137,926	55,967
Ohio	418	-	(D)	(D)	(D)	(D)	(D)	(D)	(D)
Pennsylvania	476	-	(D)	(D)	(D)	(D)	(D)	(D)	(D)
Tennessee	151	434	37.3	81.5	3	539,728	246,921	187,786	85,910
Texas	691	-	(D)	(D)	(D)	(D)	(D)	(D)	(D)
Virginia	286	1,257	89.7	213.4	4	746,007	313,671	169,736	71,368
Washington	256	1,073	55.2	160.4	4	626,621	215,738	149,501	51,472
Wisconsin	186	1,359	72.3	240.4	7	1,292,366	388,651	176,880	53,193

Source: 1992 Economic Census, U.S. Department of Commerce, Washington, D.C. This is the only table that shows revenue data as collected by the Bureau of the Census in an Economic Census. The symbol (D) indicates that data are withheld by the source to avoid disclosure of competitive information. A dash (-) indicates that data are not available or cannot be calculated.

STATE-BY-STATE DATA ON ESTABLISHMENTS, EMPLOYMENT, AND PAYROLL - 1994 AND 1995

State	1994					1995					% Change Empl.
	No. of Estab.	Employ-ment	Pay / Empl.	Payroll ($ mil.)	Pay / Estab.	No. of Estab.	Employ-ment	Pay / Empl.	Payroll ($ mil.)	Pay / Estab.	
Alabama	64	224	49,375	10.9	170,750	71	230	44,104	11.4	160,338	2.7
Alaska	10	(D)	-	(D)	-	13	(D)	-	(D)	-	-
Arizona	244	621	27,775	20.2	82,832	249	729	56,450	34.3	137,683	17.4
Arkansas	53	(D)	-	(D)	-	51	182	32,154	7.1	139,314	-
California	2,046	15,241	68,777	1,194.4	583,779	2,142	15,648	76,240	1,234.1	576,144	2.7
Colorado	366	3,412	44,720	157.3	429,757	405	4,549	56,638	236.3	583,494	33.3
Connecticut	413	3,040	102,912	305.2	739,010	443	3,446	101,328	370.2	835,580	13.4
Delaware	68	(D)	-	(D)	-	71	373	80,611	50.2	707,127	-
District of Columbia	80	629	72,089	50.6	632,850	92	702	79,487	57.7	627,163	11.6
Florida	786	3,079	56,673	180.8	230,029	844	3,207	51,164	181.8	215,400	4.2
Georgia	325	1,665	44,884	92.1	283,277	336	1,989	45,229	108.1	321,580	19.5
Hawaii	37	131	41,344	6.4	172,243	38	118	42,644	7.4	193,632	-9.9
Idaho	38	87	37,287	4.0	104,447	43	98	34,857	4.1	95,791	12.6
Illinois	791	4,987	78,479	387.7	490,100	850	5,640	100,305	562.6	661,825	13.1
Indiana	195	957	43,122	40.6	208,190	218	1,109	47,859	47.3	216,908	15.9
Iowa	130	452	36,752	16.8	129,000	132	485	54,532	19.8	150,250	7.3
Kansas	139	710	44,169	30.2	217,122	147	679	56,990	34.1	232,116	-4.4
Kentucky	64	239	51,582	14.2	221,844	72	268	80,224	18.4	255,875	12.1
Louisiana	92	550	52,109	27.1	294,261	95	575	44,786	28.3	298,368	4.5
Maine	52	227	52,194	12.0	230,923	50	(D)	-	(D)	-	-
Maryland	264	(D)	-	(D)	-	289	(D)	-	(D)	-	-
Massachusetts	585	15,288	73,137	1,046.3	1,788,496	624	17,546	80,503	1,301.7	2,086,011	14.8
Michigan	312	1,254	46,226	72.0	230,776	334	1,327	47,711	72.1	215,970	5.8
Minnesota	366	1,820	72,376	135.8	371,071	392	2,017	77,896	162.9	415,482	10.8
Mississippi	59	(D)	-	(D)	-	57	153	35,137	5.5	95,860	-
Missouri	202	4,397	37,523	166.4	823,520	213	2,541	39,652	103.6	486,418	-42.2
Montana	34	85	63,247	2.8	82,500	34	94	23,021	2.2	66,059	10.6
Nebraska	90	238	39,176	10.8	119,544	93	295	50,508	13.8	148,796	23.9
Nevada	82	273	31,443	10.0	121,902	87	(D)	-	(D)	-	-
New Hampshire	99	297	50,909	16.9	170,343	109	255	54,322	15.6	142,991	-14.1
New Jersey	550	6,803	58,694	382.4	695,349	591	6,990	55,578	447.0	756,411	2.7
New Mexico	44	(D)	-	(D)	-	51	(D)	-	(D)	-	-
New York	1,664	22,903	125,885	2,784.4	1,673,338	1,750	23,465	140,948	3,187.8	1,821,577	2.5
North Carolina	221	1,051	63,863	53.0	239,778	220	950	98,333	57.5	261,145	-9.6
North Dakota	19	(D)	-	(D)	-	18	(D)	-	(D)	-	-
Ohio	478	2,581	46,810	135.0	282,412	496	2,572	54,599	153.2	308,921	-0.3
Oklahoma	99	380	50,547	21.4	215,788	99	400	42,190	19.6	197,859	5.3
Oregon	133	532	40,737	24.0	180,617	145	698	44,716	33.7	232,538	31.2
Pennsylvania	539	4,101	57,500	282.6	524,232	594	4,423	75,298	329.2	554,246	7.9
Rhode Island	72	(D)	-	(D)	-	71	(D)	-	(D)	-	-
South Carolina	69	161	45,888	6.6	95,304	71	164	37,537	6.5	91,324	1.9
South Dakota	34	165	24,145	3.9	115,941	38	148	23,595	3.7	97,658	-10.3
Tennessee	162	572	60,664	54.4	335,716	184	675	55,775	68.2	370,826	18.0
Texas	716	6,325	69,558	410.5	573,270	734	5,941	74,134	420.1	572,326	-6.1
Utah	84	334	32,323	11.0	130,512	108	(D)	-	(D)	-	-
Vermont	25	(D)	-	(D)	-	27	234	92,393	17.3	640,222	-
Virginia	358	(D)	-	(D)	-	384	1,977	46,341	117.5	306,060	-
Washington	280	1,078	49,495	61.6	220,100	306	1,162	53,780	67.2	219,716	7.8
West Virginia	24	42	21,048	1.0	40,125	26	39	21,641	1.0	38,462	-7.1
Wisconsin	205	1,455	57,317	94.9	462,780	224	1,506	71,296	105.4	470,536	3.5
Wyoming	18	(D)	-	(D)	-	18	(D)	-	(D)	-	-

Source: County Business Patterns, U.S. Department of Commerce, Washington, D.C., for 1994 and 1995. Employment shown is for mid-March of the year shown. Payroll per employee is calculated by annualizing 1st Quarter payroll (not shown) and then dividing that value by mid-March employment. Dividing total annual payroll (columns 5 and 10) by employment, therefore, will *not* yield the payroll per employee figure (columns 4 and 9). The symbol (D) indicates that data are withheld by the source to avoid disclosure of competitive information. A dash (-) indicates that data are not available or cannot be calculated.

ESTABLISHMENTS 1995 - STATE AND REGIONAL CONCENTRATION

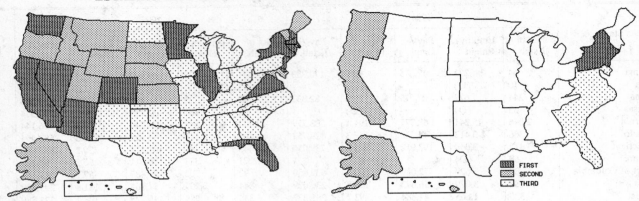

EMPLOYMENT 1995 - STATE AND REGIONAL CONCENTRATION

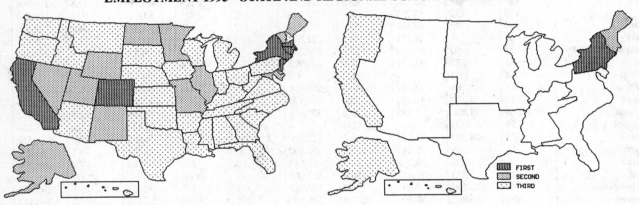

PAYROLL 1995 - STATE AND REGIONAL CONCENTRATION

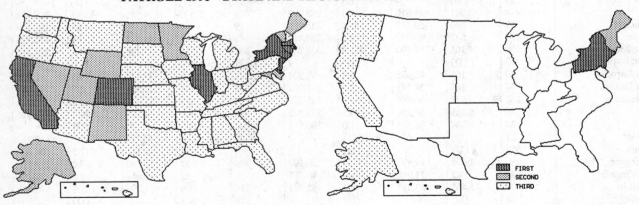

States with the darkest shading indicate those states which have proportionately more establishments, employment, or payrolls than would be indicated by the state's population. States with light shading are states with proportionately fewer establishments, less employment, and lower payrolls than population distribution. States shaded grey are within 15 percent of the state's population proportion in these categories. States for which no data are available are shown as average (grey). *Regions* are shaded to indicate absolute rank in the category. If no data for the category are available, establishment counts are used to shade the regions. Source of the data is the table on the facing page.

LEADING COMPANIES - SIC 6231 - Security and Commodity Exchanges

Number shown: **100**　　Total sales/assets ($ mil): **1,359,647**　　Total employment (000): **620.7**

Company Name	Address				CEO Name	Phone	Co. Type	Sales/Assets ($ mil)	Empl. (000)
J.P. Morgan and Company Inc.	60 Wall St.	New York	NY	10260	Douglas A. Warner III	212-483-2323	P	252,895 TA	16.9
Prudential Insurance Company of America	751 Broad St.	Newark	NJ	07102	Arthur F. Ryan	201-802-6000	R	219,380 TA	100.0
Equitable Companies Inc.	787 7th Ave.	New York	NY	10019	Joseph J. Melone	212-554-1234	P	128,811 TA	14.7
Teachers Insurance and Annuity Association	730 3rd Ave.	New York	NY	10017	John H. Biggs	212-490-9000	R	100,000 TA	4.3
Aetna Inc.	151 Farmington Ave.	Hartford	CT	06156	Richard L. Huber	860-273-0123	P	96,001 TA	38.6
Dreyfus Corp.	200 Park Ave.	New York	NY	10166	Christopher M. Condron	212-922-6000	S	94,000 OR*	2.0
INVESCO Capital Management Inc.	1315 Peachtree St. N.E	Atlanta	GA	30309	Frank Bishop	404-892-0896	S	48,000 TA	0.1
Morgan Stanley, Dean Witter, Discover and Co.	1585 Broadway	New York	NY	10036	Philip J. Purcell	212-761-4000	P	42,414 TA	33.1
State Street Corp.	PO Box 351	Boston	MA	02101	Marshall N. Carter	617-786-3000	P	37,975 TA	14.2
Merrill Lynch and Company Inc.	250 Vesey St.	New York	NY	10281	David H. Komansky	212-449-1000	P	31,731 TA	56.6
Lincoln National Life Insurance Co.	1300 S. Clinton St.	Fort Wayne	IN	46802	Gabriel Shaheen	219-455-2000	S	25,000 TA	3.7
USAA Group Inc.	9800 Fredricksburg Rd.	San Antonio	TX	78288	Robert T. Herres	210-498-2211	R	24,474 TA	18.0
St. Paul Companies Inc.	385 Washington St.	St. Paul	MN	55102	Douglas W. Leatherdale	612-310-7911	P	21,501 TA	10.0
ReliaStar Financial Corp.	20 Washington Ave. S.	Minneapolis	MN	55401	JohnG. Turner	612-372-5432	P	21,001 TA	4.1
Hartford Life Insurance Co.	PO Box 2999	Hartford	CT	06104	Lon A. Smith	203-547-5000	S	16,279 TA	3.2
Liberty Financial Companies Inc.	600 Atlantic Ave.	Boston	MA	02210	Kenneth R. Leibler	--	P	15,852 TA	2.0
LFC Holdings Inc.	175 Berkeley St.	Boston	MA	02117	Kenneth R. Leibler	617-357-9500	S	14,428 TA	2.0
Lehman Brothers Holdings Inc.	3 World Financial Ctr.	New York	NY	10285	Richard S. Fuld Jr.	212-526-7000	P	14,260 OR	8.3
Kemper Corp.	1 Kemper Dr.	Long Grove	IL	60049	David B. Mathis	847-320-2000	P	13,154 TA	6.3
First of America Investment Corp.	303 N. Rose St.	Kalamazoo	MI	49007	Richard A. Wolf	616-385-0200	S	12,901 TA*	<0.1
Mutual Life Insurance Company of New York	1740 Broadway	New York	NY	10019	Michael I. Roth	212-708-2000	R	11,764 TA	4.4
New England Mutual Life Insurance Co.	501 Boylston St.	Boston	MA	02117	James Benson	617-578-2000	S	9,608 TA*	4.0
Boston Company Inc.	1 Boston Place	Boston	MA	02108	W. Keith Smith	617-722-7000	S	9,200 OR*	4.5
USLIFE Corp.	125 Maiden Ln.	New York	NY	10038	Gordon E. Crosby Jr.	212-709-6000	P	7,880 TA	2.2
Principal Financial Group	711 High St.	Des Moines	IA	50309		515-247-5111	S	7,220	18.0
Fortis Inc.	1 Chase Manhattan Plz.	New York	NY	10005	Allen R. Freedman	212-859-7000	P	7,165 TA	6.0
Marsh and McLennan Companies Inc.	1166 Ave. of the Amer.	New York	NY	10036	A.J.C. Smith	212-345-5000	P	6,009	36.0

Company type codes: P - Public, R - Private, S - Subsidiary, D - Division, J - Joint Venture, A - Affiliate, G - Group. If the dollar values shown are not sales, the following codes apply: TA - Total Assets; OR - Operating Revenues; GB - Gross Billings. * - estimated dollar value. < - less than. *na* - not available.

Continued on next page.

LEADING COMPANIES - SIC 6231 - Security and Commodity Exchanges
Continued

Company Name	Address				CEO Name	Phone	Co. Type	Sales/Assets ($ mil)	Empl. (000)
FMR Corp.	82 Devonshire St.	Boston	MA	02109	Edward C. Johnson III	617-563-7000	R	5,800 OR	25.0
PaineWebber Group Inc.	1285 Ave. of the Amer.	New York	NY	10019	Donald B. Marron	212-713-2000	P	5,320 OR	15.9
Associated Group Inc.	120 Monument Cir.	Indianapolis	IN	46204	L. Ben Lytle	317-488-6000	R	4,589 TA	15.0
JMB Realty Corp.	900 N. Michigan Ave.	Chicago	IL	60611	Neil Bluhm	312-440-4800	R	4,570 OR*	15.0
American Express Financial Advisors Inc.	IDS Tower 10	Minneapolis	MN	55440	David R. Hubers	612-671-3131	S	3,942 OR*	8.0
Donaldson, Lufkin and Jenrette Inc.	277 Park Ave.	New York	NY	10172	Joe L. Roby	212-892-3000	P	3,491 OR	5.9
Charles Schwab Corp.	101 Montgomery St.	San Francisco	CA	94104	Charles R. Schwab	415-627-7000	P	2,299 OR	12.7
Franklin Resources Inc.	PO Box 7777	San Mateo	CA	94403	Charles B. Johnson	650-312-2000	P	2,163 OR	6.4
L and B Real Estate Counsel	8750 N. Central Expwy.	Dallas	TX	75231	M. Thoms Lardner	214-989-0800	S	2,000 OR	0.5
Fund American Enterprises Holdings Inc.	80 S. Main St.	Hanover	NH	03755	John J. Byrne	603-643-1567	P	1,872 TA	2.1
Providian Corp.	PO Box 32830	Louisville	KY	40232	Don Shepherd	502-560-2000	S	1,559 TA*	0.5
Primerica Financial Services Inc.	3120 Breckinridge Blvd.	Duluth	GA	30199	Joseph J. Plumeri Jr.	770-381-1000	S	1,360 OR	1.3
Integrated Resources Inc.	10 Union Sq. E.	New York	NY	10003	Frank W. Geller	212-353-7000	P	1,338 TA	0.2
Golodetz Trading Corp.	666 5th Ave.	New York	NY	10103	I. Suder	212-581-2400	R	1,300	0.5
Kemper Financial Companies Inc.	120 S. LaSalle St.	Chicago	IL	60603	Charles M. Kierscht	312-781-1121	S	1,242 OR	2.8
Kansas City Southern Industries Inc.	114 W. 11th St.	Kansas City	MO	64015	Landon H. Rowland	816-556-0303	P	1,058 OR	14.8
Putnam Investments Inc.	1 Post Office Sq.	Boston	MA	02109	Lawrence J. Lasser	617-292-1000	S	1,001 OR*	6.0
M.D.C. Holdings Inc.	3600 S. Yosemite St.	Denver	CO	80237	Larry A. Mizel	303-773-1100	P	970 OR	1.2
United Asset Management Corp.	1 International Pl.	Boston	MA	02110	Charles E. Haldeman	617-330-8900	P	942 OR	2.5
Raymond James Financial Inc.	PO Box 12749	St. Petersburg	FL	33716	Thomas A. James	813-573-3800	P	928 OR	2.9
Capital Group Companies Inc.	333 S. Hope St.	Los Angeles	CA	90071	Larry Clemmensen	213-486-9000	R	915 OR*	3.0
Foothill Group Inc.	11111 Santa Monica Blvd.	Los Angeles	CA	90025	John Nikoll	310-478-8383	S	913 TA*	0.2
SunGard Data Systems Inc.	1285 Drummers Lane	Wayne	PA	19087	James L. Mann	610-341-8700	P	862	4.5
Franklin Advisers Inc.	PO Box 7777	San Mateo	CA	94403	Rupert H. Johnson Jr.	415-312-3200	S	840 OR	4.2
BT Alex. Brown Inc.	135 E. Baltimore St.	Baltimore	MD	21202	Alvin B. Krongard	410-727-1700	S	809 OR	2.3
Alliance Capital Management L.P.	1345 Ave. of the Amer.	New York	NY	10105	Dave H. Williams	212-969-1000	P	788 OR	1.5
T. Rowe Price Associates Inc.	100 E. Pratt St.	Baltimore	MD	21202	George A. Roche	410-345-2000	P	755 OR	3.1
Boston Financial Group Inc.	101 Arch St.	Boston	MA	02110	Fred N. Pratt	617-439-3911	R	690 OR*	2.3

Company type codes: P - Public, R - Private, S - Subsidiary, D - Division, J - Joint Venture, A - Affiliate, G - Group. If the dollar values shown are not sales, the following codes apply: TA - Total Assets; OR - Operating Revenues; GB - Gross Billings. * - estimated dollar value. < - less than. *na* - not available.

Continued on next page.

LEADING COMPANIES - SIC 6231 - Security and Commodity Exchanges
Continued

Company Name	Address				CEO Name	Phone	Co. Type	Sales/Assets ($ mil)	Empl. (000)
Twentieth Century Companies Inc.	PO Box 419200	Kansas City	MO	64141	James E. Stowers Sr.	816-531-5575	R	660 OR*	2.2
Legg Mason Inc.	PO Box 1476	Baltimore	MD	21202	Raymond A. Mason	410-539-0000	P	640 OR	3.5
Van Kampen American Capital Investment Advisory Corp.	1 Parkview Plz.	Oakbrook Terrace	IL	60181	Don G. Powell	708-684-6000	S	633 OR*	0.5
EVEREN Capital Corp.	77 W. Wacker Dr.	Chicago	IL	60601	James R. Boris	312-574-6000	P	630 OR	3.2
NationsBanc Montgomery Securities L.L.C.	600 Montgomery St.	San Francisco	CA	94111	Thomas W. Weisel	415-627-2000	S	618 OR*	2.2
Piper Jaffray Companies Inc.	222 S. 9th St.	Minneapolis	MN	55402	Addison L. Piper	612-342-6000	P	602 OR	3.2
D. George Harris and Associates	399 Park Ave.	New York	NY	10022	D. George Harris	212-480-0650	R	600 OR	3.0
TCW Management Co.	865 S. Figueroa St.	Los Angeles	CA	90017	Marc I. Stern	213-244-0000	S	550 OR*	0.6
Robert W. Baird and Company Inc.	777 E. Wisconsin Ave.	Milwaukee	WI	53202	G. Frederick Kasten Jr.	414-765-3500	S	548 OR*	1.8
Tiger Management Corp.	101 Park Ave.	New York	NY	10178	Julian H. Robertson Jr.	212-867-4350	R	525 OR*	0.2
Physicians Insurance Company of Ohio	13515 Yarmouth Dr.	Pickerington	OH	43147	John R. Hart	614-864-7100	S	510 TA	<0.1
Pax World Management Corp.	224 State St.	Portsmouth	NH	03801	Luther E. Tyson	603-431-8022	R	485 OR	<0.1
Lynch Corp.	8 Sound Shore Dr.	Greenwich	CT	06830	Mario J. Gabelli	203-629-3333	P	468 OR	1.9
Massachusetts Financial Services Co.	500 Boylston St.	Boston	MA	02116	Jeffrey Shames	617-954-5000	S	442 OR*	1.7
AIM Management Group Inc.	11 Greenway Plz.	Houston	TX	77046	Charles T. Bauer	713-626-1919	R	436 OR*	1.6
AMRESCO Inc.	700 N. Pearl St.	Dallas	TX	75201	Robert H. Lutz Jr.	214-953-7700	P	424 OR	1.6
PEC Israel Economic Corp.	511 Fifth Ave.	New York	NY	10017	Frank Klein	212-687-2400	P	408 TA	<0.1
Furman Selz L.L.C.	230 Park Ave.	New York	NY	10169	Edmund A. Hajim	212-309-8200	S	400 OR	0.8
FCCI Investment Group Inc.	2601 Cattlemen Rd.	Sarasota	FL	34232	Ray Neff	941-955-2811	S	396 OR	0.6
Van Kampen American Capital Inc.	1 Parkview Plz.	Oakbrook Terrace	IL	60181	Don G. Powell	630-684-6000	S	378 OR*	1.3
Beneficial Management Corp.	Beneficial Ctr.	Peapack	NJ	07977	David J. Farris	908-781-3000	S	360 OR*	1.2
United Investors Management Co.	2001 3rd Ave. S.	Birmingham	AL	35233	Keith A. Tucker	205-325-4200	P	334 OR	1.5
Lincoln National Investment Management Co.	PO Box 1110	Fort Wayne	IN	46801	Jeffery J. Nick	219-455-3841	S	310 OR*	1.0
Montgomery Asset Management L.P.	101 California St.	San Francisco	CA	94111	Thom Geist	415-627-2400	S	310 OR*	<0.1
Strong Capital Management Inc.	PO Box 2936	Milwaukee	WI	53201	Richard S. Strong	414-359-3400	R	305 OR*	1.0
BankIllinois Trust Co.	100 W. University Ave.	Champaign	IL	61820	Robert J. Cochran	217-351-2741	S	300 OR	<0.1
PIMCO Advisors L.P.	800 Newport Center Dr.	Newport Beach	CA	92660	William D. Cvengros	714-717-7022	P	282 OR	0.5
Siphron Capital Management	280 S. Beverly Dr.	Beverly Hills	CA	90212	David C. Siphron	310-858-7281	R	271 TA	<0.1
Oxford Realty Services Corp.	7200 Wisconsin Ave.	Bethesda	MD	20814	Leo Zickler	301-654-3100	R	270 OR	1.6
Tucker Anthony Inc.	200 Liberty St.	New York	NY	10281	John H. Goldsmith	212-225-8000	R	260 OR*	1.0

Company type codes: P - Public, R - Private, S - Subsidiary, D - Division, J - Joint Venture, A - Affiliate, G - Group. If the dollar values shown are not sales, the following codes apply: TA - Total Assets; OR - Operating Revenues; GB - Gross Billings. * - estimated dollar value. < - less than. *na* - not available.

Continued on next page.

LEADING COMPANIES - SIC 6231 - Security and Commodity Exchanges

Continued

Company Name	Address				CEO Name	Phone	Co. Type	Sales/Assets ($ mil)	Empl. (000)
Heitman Financial	180 N. LaSalle St.	Chicago	IL	60601	Norman Perlmutter	312-855-5700	S	240 OR	1.0
John Nuveen Co.	333 W. Wacker Dr.	Chicago	IL	60606	Timothy R. Schwertfeger	312-917-7700	P	232 OR	0.5
Capital Associates Inc.	175 W. Jefferson Ave.	Lakewood	CO	80235	Dennis J. Lacey	303-980-1000	P	228 OR	0.1
SEI Corp.	680 E. Swedesford Rd.	Wayne	PA	19087	Alfred P. West Jr.	610-254-1000	P	226 OR	1.2
Winrich Capital Management Inc.	23702 Birtcher Dr.	Lake Forest	CA	92630	Kurt Winrich	714-380-0200	R	220 TA	<0.1
Southwest Securities Group Inc.	1201 Elm St.	Dallas	TX	75270	David Glatstein	214-651-1800	P	218 OR	0.7
Wellspring Associates L.L.C.	620 5th Ave.	New York	NY	10020	Martin S. Davis	212-332-7555	R	210 OR*	0.7
Eaton Vance Corp.	24 Federal St.	Boston	MA	02110	James B. Hawkes	617-482-8260	P	201 OR	0.4
Equus Capital Corp.	2929 Allen Pkwy.	Houston	TX	77019	Sam P. Douglass	713-529-0900	R	200 TA	<0.1
Pioneer Group Inc.	60 State St.	Boston	MA	02109	John F. Cogan Jr.	617-742-7825	P	199 OR	1.1
Frank Russell Co.	909 A St.	Tacoma	WA	98402	George Russell Jr.	253-572-9500	R	188 OR	1.3
Pacific Investment Management Co.	840 Newport Center Dr.	Newport Beach	CA	92660	William S. Thompson	714-640-3031	S	188 OR*	0.4
Janus Capital Corp.	100 Fillmore St.	Denver	CO	80206	Thomas H. Bailey	303-333-3863	S	181 OR	0.5
LaSalle Partners Inc.	200 E. Randolph Dr.	Chicago	IL	60601	Stuart L. Scott	312-782-5800	P	176 OR	1.1
Delaware Management Company Inc.	1 Commerce Sq.	Philadelphia	PA	19103	Wayne A. Stork	215-255-1200	S	170 OR*	0.6

Source: *Ward's Business Directory of U.S. Private and Public Companies*, 1996. Company type codes: P - Public, R - Private, S - Subsidiary, D - Division, J - Joint Venture, A - Affiliate, G - Group. If the dollar values shown are not sales, the following codes apply: TA - Total Assets; OR - Operating Revenues; GB - Gross Billings. * - estimated dollar value. < - less than; na - not available.

LEADING COMPANIES - SIC 6282 - Investment Advice

Number shown: **48**   Total sales/assets ($ mil): **12,048**   Total employment (000): **58.6**

Company Name	Address				CEO Name	Phone	Co. Type	Sales/Assets ($ mil)	Empl. (000)
First Data Corp.	401 Hackensack Ave.	Hackensack	NJ	07601	Henry C. Duques	201-525-4700	P	4,938	40.0
Pershing and Co.	1 Pershing Plaza	Jersey City	NJ	07399	Alton C. Jones	201-413-2000	D	3,460 OR	2.8
Rauscher Pierce Refsnes Inc.	2711 N. Haskell Ave. #2400	Dallas	TX	75204	William A. Johnstone	214-989-1000	S	586 OR*	3.0
Priority Investment Services Inc.	230 S. County Rd.	Palm Beach	FL	33480	Leslie C. Quick Jr.	407-655-8000	P	459 OR	1.1
T. Rowe Price Investment Services Inc.	100 E. Pratt St.	Baltimore	MD	21202	George Collins	410-547-2000	S	382 OR	1.9
Instinet Corp.	757 3rd Ave.	New York	NY	10017	Michael Sanderson	212-310-9500	S	220 OR*	0.8
Pioneer Group Inc.	60 State St.	Boston	MA	02109	John F. Cogan Jr.	617-742-7825	P	199 OR	1.1
Concord EFS Inc.	2525 Horizon Lake.	Memphis	TN	38133	Dan M. Palmer	901-371-8000	P	167 OR	0.4

Company type codes: P - Public, R - Private, S - Subsidiary, D - Division, J - Joint Venture, A - Affiliate, G - Group. If the dollar values shown are not sales, the following codes apply: TA - Total Assets; OR - Operating Revenues; GB - Gross Billings. * - estimated dollar value. < - less than. *na* - not available.

Continued on next page.

LEADING COMPANIES - SIC 6282 - Investment Advice
Continued

Company Name	Address				CEO Name	Phone	Co. Type	Sales/Assets ($ mil)	Empl. (000)
Linsco/Private Ledger Corp.	5935 Cornerstone Ct. W.	San Diego	CA	92121	Todd Robinson	619-450-9240	R	165 OR*	0.3
Boston Financial Data Services Inc.	2 Heritage Dr.	North Quincy	MA	02171	Joseph Hooley	617-328-5000	J	158 OR	1.7
Kemper Service Co.	811 Main St.	Kansas City	MO	64105	Frank Diaz	816-421-4100	S	150 OR	1.0
ITG Inc.	380 Madison Ave.	New York	NY	10017	Scott P. Mason	212-588-4000	S	137 OR	0.2
Investment Technology Group Inc.	900 3rd Ave.	New York	NY	10022	Scott P. Mason	212-755-6800	P	112 OR	<0.1
Commodity Exchange Inc.	4 World Trade Ctr.	New York	NY	10048	David Halperin	212-938-7921	R	90 OR*	0.3
BHC Financial Inc.	2005 Market St.	Philadelphia	PA	19103	William T. Spane Jr.	215-636-3000	P	81 OR	0.4
Ragen MacKenzie Inc.	999 3rd Ave.	Seattle	WA	98104	Lesa Sroufe	206-343-5000	R	80 OR	0.3
EVEREN Clearing Corp.	111 E. Kilbourn Ave.	Milwaukee	WI	53202	C. Michael Viviano	414-225-4100	S	75 OR	0.4
American Stock Transfer and Trust Co.	40 Wall St.	New York	NY	10005	Michael Karfunkel	212-936-5100	R	66 OR*	0.2
Options Clearing Corp.	440 S. LaSalle St.	Chicago	IL	60605	Wayne P. Luthringshausen	312-322-6200	R	53 OR	0.3
Benham Financial Services Inc.	1665 Charleston Rd.	Mountain View	CA	94043	James M. Benham	415-965-8300	S	45 OR*	0.2
Shareholder Communications Corp.	17 State St.	New York	NY	10004	Alexander Miller	212-809-3600	R	45 OR*	0.2
EJV Partners L.P.	77 Water St.	New York	NY	10005	Tom Wendel	212-574-1000	R	43 OR*	0.1
Sage Clearing Corp.	220 Bush St.	San Francisco	CA	94104	Douglas J. Engmann	415-781-7430	R	35 OR	0.1
InfoBase Holdings Inc.	11 Penn Plz.	New York	NY	10001	Mark McDonnell	212-967-8800	R	33	0.2
Coast Fed Services Corp.	P.O.Box 10387	West Hills	CA	91307	Bill Moody	818-316-8800	S	30 OR*	0.1
Colson Services Corp.	150 Nassau St.	New York	NY	10038	Peter Del Col	212-266-7800	R	30 OR*	0.1
Georgeson and Company Inc.	Wall St. Plz.	New York	NY	10005	William M. Crane	212-440-9800	R	30 OR*	0.2
M.H. Meyerson and Company Inc.	30 Montgomery St.	Jersey City	NJ	07302	Martin H. Meyerson	201-332-3380	P	25 OR	0.2
R.J. O'Brien and Associates Inc.	555 W. Jackson Blvd.	Chicago	IL	60661	Robert O'Brien	312-408-4700	R	24 OR*	<0.1
United Check Clearing Corp.	14276 23rd Ave. N.	Minneapolis	MN	55447	Elloyd A. Hauser	612-559-2225	R	19 OR*	<0.1
Government Securities Clearing Corp.	55 Water St.	New York	NY	10041	Charles A. Moran	212-412-8400	R	16 OR	<0.1
Loan Pricing Corp.	135 W. 50th St.	New York	NY	10020	Jim Davis	212-489-5455	R	13 OR*	<0.1
MBS Clearing Corp.	55 Water St.	New York	NY	10041	Ronald A. Stewart	212-412-8770	R	13 OR*	<0.1
Philadelphia Depository Trust Co.	2000 Market St.	Philadelphia	PA	19103	Timothy J. Guiheen	215-496-5008	S	11 OR*	0.3
Rodney Square Management Corp.	1105 N. Market St.	Wilmington	DE	19801	Martin L. Klopping	302-651-8280	S	10 OR	0.1
Midwest Clearing Corp.	440 S. LaSalle St.	Chicago	IL	60605	Robert J. McGrail	312-663-2222	R	9 OR	<0.1
Keller Enterprises Inc.	888 S.W. 5th Ave.	Portland	OR	97204	Richard Keller	503-228-6200	R	9 OR	<0.1
Big Sandy Management Company Inc.	18 Tremont St.	Boston	MA	02108	Richard Hull	617-227-0600	R	8 OR	<0.1
National Quotation Bureau Co.	11 Penn Plz.	New York	NY	10001	Carl Giangrasso	212-868-7100	S	5 OR	0.1

Company type codes: P - Public, R - Private, S - Subsidiary, D - Division, J - Joint Venture, A - Affiliate, G - Group. If the dollar values shown are not sales, the following codes apply: TA - Total Assets; OR - Operating Revenues; GB - Gross Billings. * - estimated dollar value. < - less than. *na* - not available.

Continued on next page.

LEADING COMPANIES - SIC 6282 - Investment Advice

Continued

Company Name	Address				CEO Name	Phone	Co. Type	Sales/Assets ($ mil)	Empl. (000)
Illinois Stock Transfer Co.	223 W. Jackson Bvd.	Chicago	IL	60606	George D. Pearson	312-427-2953	R	4 OR*	<0.1
Leland O'Brien Rubenstein Associates Inc.	523 W. 6th St.	Los Angeles	CA	90014	John W. O'Brien	213-488-2700	R	4 OR*	<0.1
American Securities Transfer Inc.	1825 Lawrence St.	Denver	CO	80202	Charles R. Harrison	303-234-5300	R	3 OR	<0.1
Stocktrans Inc.	7 E. Lancaster Ave.	Ardmore	PA	19003	Jonathan E. Miller	610-649-7300	R	2 OR*	<0.1
Western American Exchange Corp.	300 Montgomery St.	San Francisco	CA	94104	Radah Butler	415-392-1031	S	2 OR	<0.1
Fidelity Transfer Co.	1800 S. West Temple	Salt Lake City	UT	84115	Linda Kener	801-484-7222	R	1 OR*	<0.1
Jacoway Financial Corp.	6300 S. Syracuse Way	Inglewood	CO	80111	M. Doak Jacoway	303-793-9395	R	1 OR	<0.1
First Call Licensing Corp.	2 Mill Rd.	Wilmington	DE	19806	James R. Schurr	302-594-4706	S	1 OR*	<0.1
Market Profile Theorems Inc.	1000 2nd Ave.	Seattle	WA	98104	Russell J. Brooks	206-583-0360	R	0 OR	<0.1

Source: Ward's Business Directory of U.S. Private and Public Companies, 1996. Company type codes: P - Public, R - Private, S - Subsidiary, D - Division, J - Joint Venture, A - Affiliate, G - Group. If the dollar values shown are not sales, the following codes apply: TA - Total Assets; OR - Operating Revenues; GB - Gross Billings. * - estimated dollar value. < - less than; *na* - not available.

SIC 6310

LIFE INSURANCE

SIC 6310 includes all establishments primarily engaged in underwriting life insurance. Ownership of these establishments may be by stockholders, policyholders, or other carriers.

The category includes assessment life insurance organizations, benevolent insurance associations, burial insurance societies, cooperative life insurance organizations, fraternal life insurance organizations and protective associations, funeral insurance, legal reserve life insurance companies, life insurance companies and funds, life reinsurance organizations, and reinsurance carriers of life insurance.

ESTABLISHMENTS, EMPLOYMENT, AND PAYROLL

	1990	1991		1992		1993		1994		1995		% change 90-95
		Value	%	Value	%	Value	%	Value	%	Value	%	
All Establishments	14,057	14,461	2.9	14,531	0.5	12,691	-12.7	12,043	-5.1	11,759	-2.4	-16.3
Mid-March Employment	571,775	616,584	7.8	625,841	1.5	618,304	-1.2	574,444	-7.1	556,819	-3.1	-2.6
1st Quarter Wages (annualized - $ mil.)	16,703.5	18,702.3	12.0	20,415.7	9.2	20,282.2	-0.7	20,543.2	1.3	21,359.7	4.0	27.9
Payroll per Emp. 1st Q. (annualized)	29,213	30,332	3.8	32,621	7.5	32,803	0.6	35,762	9.0	38,360	7.3	31.3
Annual Payroll ($ mil.)	16,272.5	17,993.8	10.6	19,507.9	8.4	19,716.8	1.1	19,415.6	-1.5	19,685.4	1.4	21.0
Establishments - 1-4 Emp. Number	4,273	4,817	12.7	4,811	-0.1	3,463	-28.0	3,511	1.4	3,712	5.7	-13.1
Mid-March Employment	8,165	8,698	6.5	9,036	3.9	6,907	-23.6	6,833	-1.1	7,016	2.7	-14.1
1st Quarter Wages (annualized - $ mil.)	318.4	310.3	-2.5	327.1	5.4	323.3	-1.2	319.8	-1.1	352.0	10.1	10.5
Payroll per Emp. 1st Q. (annualized)	38,995	35,677	-8.5	36,201	1.5	46,802	29.3	46,798	-0.0	50,168	7.2	28.7
Annual Payroll ($ mil.)	331.0	301.0	-9.0	303.7	0.9	335.5	10.5	324.9	-3.2	331.8	2.1	0.3
Establishments - 5-9 Emp. Number	2,011	1,833	-8.9	1,898	3.5	1,719	-9.4	1,678	-2.4	1,668	-0.6	-17.1
Mid-March Employment	14,076	12,688	-9.9	13,084	3.1	11,799	-9.8	11,460	-2.9	11,461	0.0	-18.6
1st Quarter Wages (annualized - $ mil.)	435.2	402.8	-7.5	454.0	12.7	430.5	-5.2	484.3	12.5	504.0	4.1	15.8
Payroll per Emp. 1st Q. (annualized)	30,920	31,746	2.7	34,697	9.3	36,489	5.2	42,261	15.8	43,977	4.1	42.2
Annual Payroll ($ mil.)	425.9	407.2	-4.4	426.9	4.9	391.7	-8.3	436.5	11.4	446.1	2.2	4.7
Establishments - 10-19 Emp. Number	3,111	2,992	-3.8	2,985	-0.2	2,779	-6.9	2,368	-14.8	2,268	-4.2	-27.1
Mid-March Employment	43,720	41,964	-4.0	42,147	0.4	39,754	-5.7	33,584	-15.5	32,112	-4.4	-26.6
1st Quarter Wages (annualized - $ mil.)	1,268.7	1,247.9	-1.6	1,343.7	7.7	1,376.9	2.5	1,207.3	-12.3	1,172.6	-2.9	-7.6
Payroll per Emp. 1st Q. (annualized)	29,019	29,737	2.5	31,882	7.2	34,635	8.6	35,949	3.8	36,517	1.6	25.8
Annual Payroll ($ mil.)	1,238.2	1,220.3	-1.4	1,297.1	6.3	1,234.2	-4.9	1,092.6	-11.5	1,017.6	-6.9	-17.8
Establishments - 20-49 Emp. Number	3,020	2,979	-1.4	3,065	2.9	3,014	-1.7	2,867	-4.9	2,592	-9.6	-14.2
Mid-March Employment	88,619	87,430	-1.3	91,183	4.3	89,355	-2.0	85,867	-3.9	78,259	-8.9	-11.7
1st Quarter Wages (annualized - $ mil.)	2,404.9	2,452.6	2.0	2,700.9	10.1	2,816.3	4.3	2,738.5	-2.8	2,637.5	-3.7	9.7
Payroll per Emp. 1st Q. (annualized)	27,138	28,052	3.4	29,621	5.6	31,518	6.4	31,892	1.2	33,702	5.7	24.2
Annual Payroll ($ mil.)	2,378.7	2,393.8	0.6	2,672.9	11.7	2,659.9	-0.5	2,584.9	-2.8	2,430.9	-6.0	2.2
Establishments - 50-99 Emp. Number	922	1,020	10.6	929	-8.9	809	-12.9	830	2.6	756	-8.9	-18.0
Mid-March Employment	62,457	69,867	11.9	63,213	-9.5	56,241	-11.0	57,345	2.0	51,580	-10.1	-17.4
1st Quarter Wages (annualized - $ mil.)	1,650.9	1,922.3	16.4	1,857.2	-3.4	1,692.9	-8.8	1,871.4	10.5	1,780.2	-4.9	7.8
Payroll per Emp. 1st Q. (annualized)	26,432	27,514	4.1	29,381	6.8	30,101	2.5	32,633	8.4	34,513	5.8	30.6
Annual Payroll ($ mil.)	1,617.0	1,873.4	15.9	1,808.2	-3.5	1,615.2	-10.7	1,820.0	12.7	1,695.1	-6.9	4.8
Establishments - 100-249 Emp. Number	395	451	14.2	450	-0.2	525	16.7	441	-16.0	421	-4.5	6.6
Mid-March Employment	60,363	68,294	13.1	68,720	0.6	80,590	17.3	66,563	-17.4	63,553	-4.5	5.3
1st Quarter Wages (annualized - $ mil.)	1,557.7	1,778.9	14.2	2,084.7	17.2	2,337.3	12.1	2,267.3	-3.0	2,303.0	1.6	47.9
Payroll per Emp. 1st Q. (annualized)	25,805	26,048	0.9	30,336	16.5	29,002	-4.4	34,062	17.4	36,238	6.4	40.4
Annual Payroll ($ mil.)	1,512.9	1,716.8	13.5	1,982.9	15.5	2,287.6	15.4	2,189.8	-4.3	2,192.9	0.1	44.9
Establishments - 250-499 Emp. Number	159	184	15.7	206	12.0	202	-1.9	170	-15.8	175	2.9	10.1
Mid-March Employment	55,890	64,615	15.6	73,406	13.6	72,585	-1.1	58,838	-18.9	61,470	4.5	10.0
1st Quarter Wages (annualized - $ mil.)	1,637.8	1,876.0	14.5	2,267.7	20.9	2,177.0	-4.0	1,893.8	-13.0	2,184.7	15.4	33.4
Payroll per Emp. 1st Q. (annualized)	29,304	29,034	-0.9	30,892	6.4	29,993	-2.9	32,187	7.3	35,542	10.4	21.3
Annual Payroll ($ mil.)	1,567.9	1,803.4	15.0	2,173.5	20.5	2,173.0	-0.0	1,871.5	-13.9	2,054.4	9.8	31.0
Establishments - 500-999 Emp. Number	85	101	18.8	110	8.9	105	-4.5	107	1.9	96	-10.3	12.9
Mid-March Employment	58,489	68,735	17.5	76,901	11.9	74,446	-3.2	71,883	-3.4	65,744	-8.5	12.4
1st Quarter Wages (annualized - $ mil.)	1,675.6	2,063.1	23.1	2,346.1	13.7	2,371.4	1.1	2,451.1	3.4	2,516.1	2.7	50.2
Payroll per Emp. 1st Q. (annualized)	28,649	30,015	4.8	30,509	1.6	31,854	4.4	34,098	7.0	38,272	12.2	33.6
Annual Payroll ($ mil.)	1,560.7	1,943.0	24.5	2,262.6	16.4	2,397.3	6.0	2,339.4	-2.4	2,374.6	1.5	52.1
Estab. - 1000 or More Emp. Number	81	84	3.7	77	-8.3	75	-2.6	71	-5.3	71	-	-12.3
Mid-March Employment	179,996	194,293	7.9	188,151	-3.2	186,627	-0.8	182,071	-2.4	185,624	2.0	3.1
1st Quarter Wages (annualized - $ mil.)	5,754.3	6,648.3	15.5	7,034.3	5.8	6,756.5	-3.9	7,309.8	8.2	7,909.4	8.2	37.5
Payroll per Emp. 1st Q. (annualized)	31,969	34,218	7.0	37,386	9.3	36,203	-3.2	40,148	10.9	42,610	6.1	33.3
Annual Payroll ($ mil.)	5,640.3	6,335.0	12.3	6,580.3	3.9	6,622.4	0.6	6,756.0	2.0	7,142.1	5.7	26.6

Source: County Business Patterns, U.S. Department of Commerce, Washington, D.C., for 1990 through 1995. Payroll per employee is calculated using mid-March employment and 1st Quarter wages, annualized. Annual payroll, also shown, may not equal the annualized 1st Quarter wages. Columns headed by a percent sign (%) indicate change from the previous year. *na* stands for not available. The symbol (D) indicates that data are withheld by the source to avoid disclosure of competitive information. A dash (-) indicates that data are not available or cannot be calculated.

ESTABLISHMENTS
Number

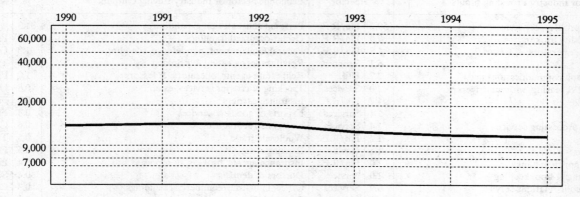

MID-MARCH EMPLOYMENT
Number

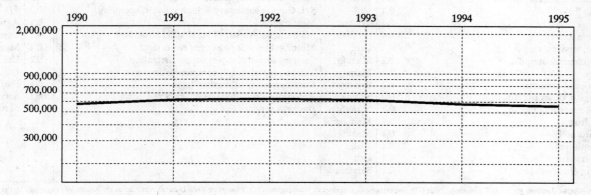

ANNUAL PAYROLL
$ million

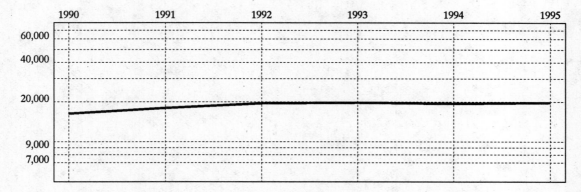

INPUTS AND OUTPUTS FOR INSURANCE CARRIERS - SIC GROUP 63

Economic Sector or Industry Providing Inputs	%	Sector	Economic Sector or Industry Buying Outputs	%	Sector
Insurance agents, brokers, & services	59.2	Fin/R.E.	Personal consumption expenditures	81.3	
Security & commodity brokers	7.0	Fin/R.E.	Owner-occupied dwellings	1.8	Fin/R.E.
Real estate agents, operators, & lessors	5.8	Fin/R.E.	Federal Government, nondefense, spending	1.3	Gov't
Legal services	5.1	Services	Retail trade, ex eating & drinking	1.0	Trade
Telephone/telegraph communications nec	2.7	Util.	Real estate agents, operators, & lessors	1.0	Fin/R.E.
Automotive rental & leasing, without drivers	2.0	Services	Trucking & courier services, ex air	0.8	Util.
Banking	1.7	Fin/R.E.	Insurance carriers	0.8	Fin/R.E.
Advertising	1.4	Services	Exports of goods & services	0.8	Foreign
Computer & data processing services	1.4	Services	New construction nec	0.6	Constr.
Insurance carriers	1.2	Fin/R.E.	Wholesale trade	0.5	Trade
U.S. Postal Service	1.1	Gov't	Banking	0.5	Fin/R.E.
Credit agencies other than banks	1.0	Fin/R.E.	Insurance agents, brokers, & services	0.4	Fin/R.E.
Accounting, auditing & bookkeeping	1.0	Services	Doctors & dentists	0.4	Services
Management & public relations services	0.9	Services	Office, industrial/commercial buildings	0.3	Constr.
Commercial printing	0.8	Manufg.	Repair & maintenance construction nec	0.3	Constr.
Business services nec	0.8	Services	Residential 1 unit structures, nonfarm	0.3	Constr.
Eating & drinking places	0.6	Services	Hospitals	0.3	Services
Hotels	0.5	Services	Highways, bridges, horizontal construction	0.2	Constr.
Miscellaneous equipment rental & leasing	0.5	Services	Electric services (utilities)	0.2	Util.
Repair & maintenance construction nec	0.4	Constr.	Eating & drinking places	0.2	Services
Air transportation	0.4	Util.	S/L Govt., elementary & high schools, spending	0.2	S/L Govt
Wholesale trade	0.4	Trade	Meat animals	0.1	Agric.
Personnel supply services	0.4	Services	Maintenance/repair of residential structures	0.1	Constr.
Trucking & courier services, ex air	0.3	Util.	Motor vehicles & passenger car bodies	0.1	Manufg.
Photographic equipment & supplies	0.2	Manufg.	Sanitary services, steam supply, irrigation	0.1	Util.
Tires & inner tubes	0.2	Manufg.	Telephone/telegraph communications nec	0.1	Util.
Business & professional associations	0.2	Services	Credit agencies other than banks	0.1	Fin/R.E.
Services to dwellings & other buildings	0.2	Services	Automotive repair shops & services	0.1	Services
Magnetic & optical recording media	0.1	Manufg.	Business services nec	0.1	Services
Manifold business forms	0.1	Manufg.			
Paper & paperboard mills	0.1	Manufg.			
Electric services (utilities)	0.1	Util.			
Local & suburban transit	0.1	Util.			
Automobile parking & car washes	0.1	Services			

Source: Benchmark Input-Output Accounts for the U.S. Economy, 1992, U.S. Department of Commerce, Washington, D.C., November 1997. Data, as reported in the source, are organized by the 1987 SIC structure in use in 1992.

OCCUPATIONS EMPLOYED BY LIFE INSURANCE

Occupation	% of Total 1996	Change to 2006	Occupation	% of Total 1996	Change to 2006
Insurance sales workers	19.8	-7.9	Underwriters	2.7	41.7
General office clerks	6.8	-15.1	Managers & administrators nec	2.4	-2.3
Insurance policy processing clerks	5.9	-21.1	Marketing & sales worker supervisors	2.3	-1.4
Insurance claims clerks	4.5	0.8	Bookkeeping, accounting, & auditing clerks	2.1	-21.1
Management support workers nec	4.3	-1.4	Adjustment clerks	1.9	33.2
Clerical supervisors & managers	4.0	-1.4	Accountants & auditors	1.8	-8.7
Secretaries, except legal & medical	3.9	-21.8	Professional workers nec	1.6	-1.4
Insurance adjusters, examiners, investigators	3.7	1.3	Claims examiners, property & casualty	1.5	-0.6
Computer programmers	3.0	-18.8	Sales & related workers nec	1.2	8.5
Systems analysts	2.8	47.3	Typists, including word processing	1.0	-35.9
General managers & top executives	2.8	-4.4	File clerks	1.0	-29.6

Sources: Industry-Occupation Matrix, Bureau of Labor Statistics. These data relate to one or more 3-digit SIC industry groups rather than to a single 4-digit SIC. The change reported for each occupation to the year 2005 is a percent of growth or decline as estimated by the Bureau of Labor Statistics. The abbreviation *nec* stands for not elsewhere classified.

U.S. AND STATE DATA ON INDUSTRY REVENUES AND OTHER ACCOUNTS FOR 1992

State	No. of Estab.	Employ-ment	Payroll ($ mil.)	Revenues ($ mil.)	Empl./ Estab.	Revenue/ Estab. ($)	Payroll/ Estab. ($)	Revenue/ Empl. ($)	Payroll/ Empl. ($)
UNITED STATES	13,424	609,237	19,410.7	378,401.7	45	28,188,449	1,445,970	621,108	31,861
Alabama	306	6,840	200.5	2,736.7	22	8,943,346	655,258	400,097	29,314
Alaska	15	-	(D)	(D)	(D)	(D)	(D)	(D)	(D)
Arizona	199	4,070	114.7	2,045.2	20	10,277,271	576,236	502,500	28,175
Arkansas	123	2,354	58.1	671.3	19	5,457,569	472,195	285,166	24,673
California	1,062	39,186	1,290.6	31,872.8	37	30,012,067	1,215,283	813,373	32,936
Colorado	199	7,551	250.4	5,127.9	38	25,768,337	1,258,327	679,102	33,162
Connecticut	211	46,335	1,856.3	15,173.2	220	71,911,047	8,797,540	327,468	40,062
Delaware	49	1,776	52.7	616.8	36	12,588,020	1,075,367	347,305	29,669
District of Columbia	33	787	31.0	785.8	24	23,812,030	940,788	998,471	39,449
Florida	791	28,311	850.9	12,162.6	36	15,376,182	1,075,748	429,605	30,056
Georgia	479	20,831	592.0	7,984.6	43	16,669,344	1,235,977	383,304	28,421
Hawaii	53	-	(D)	(D)	(D)	(D)	(D)	(D)	(D)
Idaho	42	-	(D)	(D)	(D)	(D)	(D)	(D)	(D)
Illinois	648	30,118	890.1	23,479.2	46	36,233,363	1,373,611	779,574	29,554
Indiana	325	12,608	388.1	13,154.8	39	40,476,458	1,194,191	1,043,373	30,783
Iowa	177	15,184	450.3	5,952.5	86	33,629,983	2,544,124	392,025	29,657
Kansas	169	4,819	141.5	4,417.6	29	26,139,651	837,568	916,705	29,373
Kentucky	220	5,280	161.5	4,434.6	24	20,157,159	734,214	839,882	30,592
Louisiana	345	7,347	202.4	2,958.4	21	8,574,994	586,733	402,664	27,552
Maine	57	4,307	179.4	1,463.2	76	25,670,667	3,148,158	339,733	41,664
Maryland	261	7,323	231.3	5,555.7	28	21,286,387	886,375	758,671	31,591
Massachusetts	296	36,149	1,253.7	21,177.1	122	71,544,105	4,235,314	585,827	34,680
Michigan	337	11,859	351.1	11,524.0	35	34,195,703	1,041,751	971,747	29,604
Minnesota	210	15,157	605.0	11,737.8	72	55,894,276	2,881,014	774,414	39,916
Mississippi	171	3,754	99.8	1,962.3	22	11,475,526	583,713	522,726	26,589
Missouri	294	10,908	330.8	5,666.6	37	19,274,150	1,125,296	519,490	30,330
Montana	36	755	14.8	277.2	21	7,699,750	411,694	367,140	19,630
Nebraska	111	5,307	145.0	2,550.2	48	22,974,829	1,306,261	480,536	27,321
Nevada	39	447	11.0	254.9	11	6,537,026	282,974	570,345	24,689
New Hampshire	65	-	(D)	(D)	(D)	(D)	(D)	(D)	(D)
New Jersey	462	28,172	1,028.1	21,295.1	61	46,093,294	2,225,346	755,896	36,494
New Mexico	61	1,635	34.1	429.6	27	7,043,443	558,475	262,783	20,836
New York	798	63,903	2,070.7	63,992.9	80	80,191,576	2,594,878	1,001,406	32,404
North Carolina	428	12,528	344.2	5,565.8	29	13,004,201	804,157	444,269	27,473
North Dakota	37	612	18.3	373.6	17	10,096,649	494,216	610,418	29,879
Ohio	619	20,260	575.8	15,586.0	33	25,179,309	930,237	769,299	28,421
Oklahoma	149	4,507	115.8	1,649.4	30	11,069,866	777,242	365,966	25,695
Oregon	109	3,199	82.3	1,754.1	29	16,092,413	755,101	548,319	25,729
Pennsylvania	742	40,069	1,239.0	12,881.8	54	17,360,973	1,669,802	321,491	30,921
Rhode Island	53	2,523	60.1	545.5	48	10,292,245	1,133,189	216,207	23,805
South Carolina	242	5,700	155.6	1,410.2	24	5,827,434	643,017	247,410	27,300
South Dakota	40	963	26.0	825.0	24	20,625,975	651,250	856,738	27,051
Tennessee	326	11,906	323.9	6,657.7	37	20,422,503	993,546	559,192	27,204
Texas	1,047	34,862	960.8	19,460.2	33	18,586,625	917,656	558,207	27,560
Utah	75	2,228	49.2	701.7	30	9,356,107	656,653	314,950	22,105
Vermont	43	1,452	48.4	562.5	34	13,081,163	1,126,116	387,390	33,349
Virginia	331	9,922	290.6	7,135.2	30	21,556,541	877,846	719,131	29,285
Washington	203	6,229	183.3	5,921.0	31	29,167,320	903,079	950,548	29,431
West Virginia	90	1,427	34.7	498.0	16	5,532,844	385,378	348,953	24,306
Wisconsin	227	23,092	861.9	13,237.3	102	58,314,247	3,797,048	573,243	37,326
Wyoming	19	-	(D)	(D)	(D)	(D)	(D)	(D)	(D)

Source: 1992 Economic Census, U.S. Department of Commerce, Washington, D.C. This is the only table that shows revenue data as collected by the Bureau of the Census in an Economic Census. The symbol (D) indicates that data are withheld by the source to avoid disclosure of competitive information. A dash (-) indicates that data are not available or cannot be calculated.

STATE-BY-STATE DATA ON ESTABLISHMENTS, EMPLOYMENT, AND PAYROLL - 1994 AND 1995

State	1994					1995					% Change Empl.
	No. of Estab.	Employ- ment	Pay / Empl.	Payroll ($ mil.)	Pay / Estab.	No. of Estab.	Employ- ment	Pay / Empl.	Payroll ($ mil.)	Pay / Estab.	
Alabama	263	6,416	29,254	180.0	684,418	243	5,907	30,353	169.9	699,263	-7.9
Alaska	11	117	45,709	5.7	515,000	10	103	48,233	5.3	527,800	-12.0
Arizona	167	3,766	30,728	112.7	674,743	165	3,760	33,163	114.3	692,491	-0.2
Arkansas	111	2,267	26,597	61.4	552,937	105	2,199	28,338	60.3	574,267	-3.0
California	950	33,665	39,712	1,215.0	1,278,912	936	30,641	42,539	1,164.4	1,244,068	-9.0
Colorado	181	8,382	31,560	274.5	1,516,359	177	9,493	31,529	303.4	1,714,322	13.3
Connecticut	194	37,917	48,636	1,700.8	8,766,954	182	34,081	54,745	1,860.3	10,221,324	-10.1
Delaware	41	1,595	31,456	55.1	1,343,512	42	1,955	32,135	66.6	1,585,262	22.6
District of Columbia	29	1,017	46,328	44.8	1,544,966	28	1,123	45,500	47.9	1,711,286	10.4
Florida	717	26,876	32,441	842.5	1,175,011	727	25,194	34,356	840.4	1,156,028	-6.3
Georgia	438	19,497	31,629	602.2	1,374,790	433	18,628	33,378	586.0	1,353,339	-4.5
Hawaii	50	1,150	39,513	45.7	913,540	51	1,152	37,285	43.1	845,588	0.2
Idaho	32	549	26,251	14.6	457,281	32	528	25,788	13.4	417,500	-3.8
Illinois	544	27,938	32,265	878.1	1,614,132	533	26,191	34,856	852.0	1,598,422	-6.3
Indiana	275	12,066	33,613	378.8	1,377,309	273	11,646	38,645	408.6	1,496,659	-3.5
Iowa	166	15,270	34,984	492.9	2,969,428	161	15,200	38,678	516.0	3,204,988	-0.5
Kansas	158	4,274	34,569	135.7	859,044	161	4,192	37,377	143.5	891,571	-1.9
Kentucky	187	4,456	28,910	128.2	685,578	176	3,967	31,977	121.2	688,364	-11.0
Louisiana	309	6,745	29,986	197.4	638,767	306	6,299	32,211	190.4	622,144	-6.6
Maine	46	4,368	52,223	174.9	3,802,326	42	4,228	38,990	161.7	3,849,286	-3.2
Maryland	238	6,280	37,232	218.2	917,017	223	5,701	37,613	202.2	906,534	-9.2
Massachusetts	291	35,021	42,379	1,439.6	4,947,137	278	37,083	42,760	1,383.9	4,978,072	5.9
Michigan	293	10,826	31,799	321.5	1,097,423	291	9,944	34,499	317.9	1,092,357	-8.1
Minnesota	186	16,113	40,719	601.9	3,236,016	195	18,423	39,252	675.5	3,464,026	14.3
Mississippi	159	3,299	28,366	92.9	583,994	166	3,143	28,501	86.4	520,729	-4.7
Missouri	259	11,444	34,398	354.5	1,368,656	245	10,599	37,338	366.5	1,495,735	-7.4
Montana	28	325	26,203	8.4	300,786	30	277	27,177	7.5	248,533	-14.8
Nebraska	96	5,770	31,778	177.2	1,845,365	92	5,687	32,996	174.8	1,899,989	-1.4
Nevada	34	369	30,190	10.4	305,676	36	327	30,128	9.2	255,694	-11.4
New Hampshire	57	2,385	33,176	74.0	1,298,772	55	2,255	31,943	71.8	1,304,600	-5.5
New Jersey	490	30,436	40,959	1,227.0	2,504,135	493	31,454	44,032	1,337.7	2,713,438	3.3
New Mexico	58	1,676	22,007	36.0	620,431	56	1,383	23,367	30.9	552,018	-17.5
New York	743	54,819	38,810	1,905.2	2,564,175	726	53,308	47,540	2,040.5	2,810,613	-2.8
North Carolina	396	12,413	30,870	376.8	951,556	385	12,310	33,476	386.8	1,004,595	-0.8
North Dakota	33	634	28,189	17.4	525,879	32	411	28,457	11.1	345,562	-35.2
Ohio	531	19,364	31,714	584.4	1,100,573	498	17,838	34,302	553.2	1,110,793	-7.9
Oklahoma	137	4,371	28,866	116.5	850,489	125	4,274	28,419	110.4	883,600	-2.2
Oregon	96	3,171	33,275	98.3	1,023,906	93	2,889	31,376	88.5	952,118	-8.9
Pennsylvania	692	43,064	26,714	1,110.2	1,604,370	690	41,466	26,673	1,079.5	1,564,499	-3.7
Rhode Island	42	2,570	24,121	61.1	1,453,595	42	2,538	22,391	51.7	1,232,119	-1.2
South Carolina	218	5,623	30,002	166.6	764,431	208	5,308	30,557	151.0	726,144	-5.6
South Dakota	38	962	28,141	26.1	686,026	36	995	28,535	30.4	845,444	3.4
Tennessee	294	10,977	32,313	334.3	1,136,986	281	10,407	36,075	304.8	1,084,737	-5.2
Texas	893	31,156	31,518	962.5	1,077,871	847	29,286	33,759	947.2	1,118,295	-6.0
Utah	70	2,174	24,585	51.9	742,114	71	1,810	28,621	50.8	716,141	-16.7
Vermont	32	1,454	38,176	48.0	1,501,344	28	1,351	48,536	63.4	2,263,250	-7.1
Virginia	299	8,761	31,673	279.0	933,070	295	8,656	33,232	270.4	916,776	-1.2
Washington	177	6,177	34,467	195.8	1,106,243	176	5,974	35,359	196.0	1,113,614	-3.3
West Virginia	82	1,245	25,015	32.3	393,902	75	1,201	25,572	29.3	390,400	-3.5
Wisconsin	199	23,035	43,758	941.2	4,729,638	196	23,860	44,520	982.5	5,012,628	3.6
Wyoming	13	199	29,226	5.5	423,231	12	174	29,701	5.0	412,583	-12.6

Source: County Business Patterns, U.S. Department of Commerce, Washington, D.C., for 1994 and 1995. Employment shown is for mid-March of the year shown. Payroll per employee is calculated by annualizing 1st Quarter payroll (not shown) and then dividing that value by mid-March employment. Dividing total annual payroll (columns 5 and 10) by employment, therefore, will *not* yield the payroll per employee figure (columns 4 and 9). The symbol (D) indicates that data are withheld by the source to avoid disclosure of competitive information. A dash (-) indicates that data are not available or cannot be calculated.

ESTABLISHMENTS 1995 - STATE AND REGIONAL CONCENTRATION

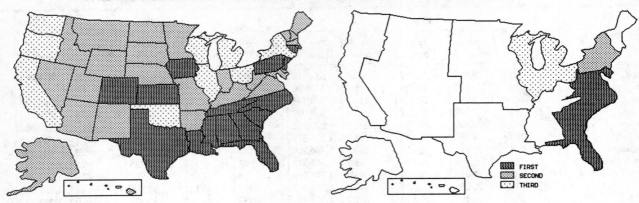

EMPLOYMENT 1995 - STATE AND REGIONAL CONCENTRATION

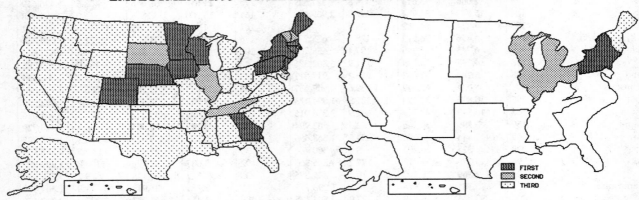

PAYROLL 1995 - STATE AND REGIONAL CONCENTRATION

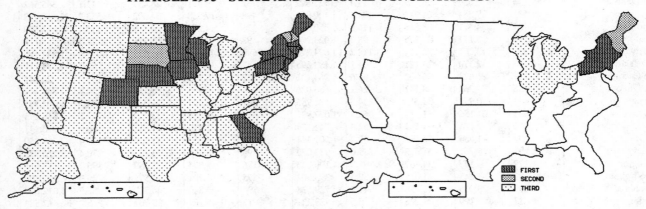

States with the darkest shading indicate those states which have proportionately more establishments, employment, or payrolls than would be indicated by the state's population. States with light shading are states with proportionately fewer establishments, less employment, and lower payrolls than population distribution. States shaded grey are within 15 percent of the state's population proportion in these categories. States for which no data are available are shown as average (grey). *Regions* are shaded to indicate absolute rank in the category. If no data for the category are available, establishment counts are used to shade the regions. Source of the data is the table on the facing page.

PREMIUM RECEIPTS OF U.S. LIFE INSURANCE COMPANIES BY STATE 1996

In millions.

State	Life	Annuity	Health	Deposit-Type funds	Total
Alabama	1,376	304	804	1,031	3,515
Alaska	135	78	267	261	741
Arizona	1,071	743	939	1,660	4,412
Arkansas	708	239	585	462	1,993
California	8,886	5,944	5,928	11,903	32,661
Colorado	1,328	636	1,166	2,160	5,289
Connecticut	1,852	1,196	1,075	2,937	7,060
Delaware	664	588	209	882	2,343
D.C.	442	109	497	1,716	2,764
Florida	4,669	2,632	3,930	5,884	17,114
Georgia	2,758	647	2,318	2,004	7,727
Hawaii	438	244	153	582	1,417
Idaho	332	187	187	368	1,074
Illinois	4,948	2,327	4,224	9,898	21,396
Indiana	2,189	972	1,788	2,052	7,001
Iowa	1,106	775	830	1,399	4,109
Kansas	947	401	745	907	3,001
Kentucky	1,146	417	705	947	3,215
Louisiana	1,453	553	1,051	1,012	4,068
Maine	314	149	344	466	1,272
Maryland	1,912	836	1,042	2,840	6,630
Massachusetts	2,389	1,325	1,375	7,240	12,329
Michigan	3,527	1,889	1,886	5,388	12,689
Minnesota	1,746	1,001	889	2,699	6,335
Mississippi	734	186	695	417	2,031
Missouri	1,925	907	1,611	2,258	6,702
Montana	224	119	228	202	773
Nebraska	671	651	616	803	2,742
Nevada	383	249	422	488	1,542
New Hampshire	412	205	306	418	1,341
New Jersey	3,672	1,782	2,783	5,503	13,740
New Mexico	411	401	336	424	1,573
New York	7,454	3,316	4,987	15,927	31,684
North Carolina	2,951	936	2,138	3,157	9,182
North Dakota	216	117	152	210	694
Ohio	4,731	1,594	2,868	5,537	14,729
Oklahoma	877	385	950	730	2,943
Oregon	859	645	496	1,462	3,462
Pennsylvania	4,522	2,067	2,146	6,332	15,068
Rhode Island	373	261	148	398	1,180
South Carolina	1,274	358	994	921	3,546
South Dakota	263	115	253	222	852
Tennessee	1,780	686	1,667	1,677	5,810
Texas	5,506	2,560	5,435	5,836	19,337
Utah	612	356	505	495	1,968
Vermont	186	102	131	217	636
Virginia	2,540	1,036	1,676	2,284	7,536
Washington	1,403	1,636	845	2,262	6,147
West Virginia	533	223	422	359	1,537
Wisconsin	1,677	936	1,301	2,629	6,542
Wyoming	161	57	131	142	491
Total U.S.	92,684	46,075	67,178	128,007	333,944

Source: American Council of Life Insurance. *Notes:* Data refer to direct premiums collected in each state, without deducting reinsurance ceded, but excluding reinsurance assumed.

MORTGAGES OWNED BY U.S. LIFE INSURANCE COMPANIES BY TYPE AND STATE 1996

In thousands.

State	Farm	Nonfarm	Total
Alabama	26,607	1,371,150	1,397,757
Alaska	-	159,469	159,469
Arizona	135,931	3,401,920	3,537,851
Arkansas	304,845	329,604	634,449
California	3,016,804	34,077,514	37,094,318
Colorado	150,282	3,410,792	3,561,074
Connecticut	-	2,637,144	2,637,144
Delaware	-	572,627	572,627
District of Columbia	-	3,950,291	3,950,291
Florida	1,218,928	11,488,871	12,707,799
Georgia	164,300	6,637,638	6,801,938
Hawaii	12,676	528,293	540,969
Idaho	245,826	328,807	574,633
Illinois	330,907	10,016,194	10,347,101
Indiana	317,015	2,656,839	2,973,854
Iowa	431,417	957,021	1,388,438
Kansas	139,725	1,302,113	1,441,838
Kentucky	52,962	1,505,192	1,558,154
Louisiana	115,127	1,128,711	1,243,838
Maine	46,345	334,937	390,282
Maryland	21,378	5,608,031	5,629,409
Massachusetts	22,522	8,235,040	8,257,562
Michigan	55,237	5,148,486	5,203,723
Minnesota	268,570	3,576,563	3,845,133
Mississippi	269,746	450,087	719,833
Missouri	172,510	3,383,822	3,556,332
Montana	214,073	161,244	375,317
Nebraska	330,576	713,987	1,044,563
Nevada	13,057	2,050,813	2,063,870
New Hampshire	-	563,071	563,071
New Jersey	256	8,667,559	8,667,815
New Mexico	72,324	567,109	639,433
New York	7,739	14,227,546	14,235,285
North Carolina	94,202	4,329,300	4,423,502
North Dakota	33,825	129,924	163,749
Ohio	103,894	6,679,095	6,782,989
Oklahoma	170,248	445,766	616,014
Oregon	234,150	2,519,169	2,753,319
Pennsylvania	743	6,079,458	6,080,201
Rhode Island	-	285,449	285,449
South Carolina	6,361	1,507,439	1,513,800
South Dakota	84,565	79,737	164,302
Tennessee	29,096	2,835,034	2,864,130
Texas	479,447	13,026,735	13,506,182
Utah	10,679	1,170,320	1,180,999
Vermont	18	71,057	71,075
Virginia	37,765	8,243,186	8,280,951
Washington	352,869	5,925,747	6,278,616
West Virginia	70,051	225,071	295,122
Wisconsin	77,640	1,426,005	1,503,645
Wyoming	78,538	34,234	112,772
Puerto Rico	-	194,180	194,180
U.S. Territories and Possessions	-	4,099	4,099
Total U.S.	10,021,776	195,368,487	205,390,263
Canada	1,978	2,212,017	2,213,995
Other Foreign	-	174,856	174,856
Grand Total	10,023,753	197,755,360	207,779,113

Source: American Council of Life Insurance.

CHANGE IN LIFE INSURANCE COMPANIES IN BUSINESS IN THE U.S.

Year	In business year-end			Net changes during year
	Stock	Mutual	Total	
1980	1,823	135	1,958	63
1981	1,855	136	1,991	33
1982	1,926	134	2,060	69
1983	1,985	132	2,117	57
1984	2,062	131	2,193	76
1985	2,133	128	2,261	68
1986	2,128	126	2,254	-7
1987	2,212	125	2,337	83
1988	2,225	118	2,343	6
1989	2,153	117	2,270	-73
1990	2,078	117	2,195	-75
1991	1,947	117	2,064	-131
1992	1,835	109	1,944	-120
1993	1,736	108	1,844	-100
1994	1,639	106	1,745	-99
1995	1,620	95	1,715	-30
1996	1,604	91	1,695	-20

Source: American Council of Life Insurance *Notes:* Data for 1993 are revised. The figure for year-end 1994 is preliminary. A change in domicile is reflected in both new and discontinued operations. N.A. stands for not available. 1. Includes seven companies domiciled in Alaska and Hawaii that were started in earlier years.

NUMBER OF PERSONS EMPLOYED IN INSURANCE IN THE UNITED STATES

Year	Home office personnel				Agents, brokers, service personnel	Total
	Life insurance	Health insurance	Other	Total		
1980	531,900	141,900	550,300	1,224,100	463,800	1,687,900
1981	542,200	142,700	552,000	1,236,900	475,800	1,712,700
1982	546,100	142,100	549,100	1,237,300	485,900	1,723,200
1983	539,900	144,800	544,200	1,228,900	498,900	1,727,800
1984	536,700	153,900	549,100	1,239,700	525,000	1,764,700
1985	559,300	170,700	561,600	1,291,600	548,200	1,839,800
1986	578,200	188,100	598,500	1,364,800	579,400	1,944,200
1987	578,000	202,100	634,900	1,415,000	611,800	2,026,800
1988	570,400	216,500	648,500	1,435,400	639,600	2,075,000
1989	550,200	228,100	660,100	1,438,400	651,800	2,090,200
1990	547,500	241,600	673,100	1,462,200	663,300	2,125,500
1991	560,000	258,700	675,900	1,494,600	666,300	2,160,900
1992	550,300	270,100	675,200	1,495,600	656,600	2,152,200
1993	571,900	280,500	676,600	1,529,000	668,000	2,197,000
1994	581,100	293,300	677,500	1,551,900	683,600	2,235,500
1995	564,400	304,700	660,000	1,529,100	695,500	2,224,600
1996	521,600	322,100	666,300	1,510,000	707,400	2,217,400

Source: U.S. Department of Labor, Bureau of Labor Statistics, *Employment and Earnings*, various issues. *Notes:* Includes only persons on the payroll of insurance establishments that participate in the unemployment insurance program.

SIC 6321

ACCIDENT AND HEALTH INSURANCE

This industry includes organizations that engage in underwriting accident and health insurance. It includes establishments that provide health insurance protection for disability income losses and medical expense coverage on an indemnity basis. Ownership of these establishments may be by stockholders, policyholders, or other carriers. Establishments engaged primarily in providing hospital, medical, and other health services on a service basis or combination of service and indemnity bases are classified under SIC 6324 (see next chapter).

Members of this industry are organizations providing accident and health insurance, assessment associations, disability health insurance providers, fraternal accident and health insurance organizations, health insurance indemnity plans, mutual accident associations, reciprocal interinsurance exchanges for accident and health insurance, mutual sick benefit associations, and reinsurance carriers for these categories.

ESTABLISHMENTS, EMPLOYMENT, AND PAYROLL

	1990	1991 Value	%	1992 Value	%	1993 Value	%	1994 Value	%	1995 Value	%	% change 90-95
All Establishments	1,067	1,385	29.8	1,441	4.0	1,132	-21.4	1,074	-5.1	1,051	-2.1	-1.5
Mid-March Employment	47,878	55,167	15.2	61,291	11.1	53,925	-12.0	51,729	-4.1	52,430	1.4	9.5
1st Quarter Wages (annualized - $ mil.)	1,194.8	1,493.2	25.0	1,621.5	8.6	1,465.4	-9.6	1,527.1	4.2	1,715.8	12.4	43.6
Payroll per Emp. 1st Q. (annualized)	24,954	27,066	8.5	26,455	-2.3	27,174	2.7	29,521	8.6	32,725	10.9	31.1
Annual Payroll ($ mil.)	1,277.6	1,501.9	17.6	1,575.4	4.9	1,486.1	-5.7	1,518.7	2.2	1,666.8	9.8	30.5
Establishments - 1-4 Emp. Number	423	649	53.4	731	12.6	474	-35.2	(D)	-	445	-	5.2
Mid-March Employment	(D)	1,254	-	1,488	18.7	949	-36.2	(D)	-	869	-	-
1st Quarter Wages (annualized - $ mil.)	(D)	38.2	-	51.9	35.9	41.4	-20.2	(D)	-	46.8	-	-
Payroll per Emp. 1st Q. (annualized)	(D)	30,469	-	34,890	14.5	43,646	25.1	(D)	-	53,910	-	-
Annual Payroll ($ mil.)	(D)	41.9	-	55.9	33.2	41.3	-26.0	(D)	-	85.1	-	-
Establishments - 5-9 Emp. Number	272	264	-2.9	259	-1.9	228	-12.0	244	7.0	(D)	-	-
Mid-March Employment	1,786	1,767	-1.1	1,726	-2.3	1,521	-11.9	1,639	7.8	(D)	-	-
1st Quarter Wages (annualized - $ mil.)	61.5	69.9	13.7	70.3	0.5	58.0	-17.4	59.2	2.0	(D)	-	-
Payroll per Emp. 1st Q. (annualized)	34,408	39,554	15.0	40,707	2.9	38,138	-6.3	36,112	-5.3	(D)	-	-
Annual Payroll ($ mil.)	61.3	66.4	8.3	69.9	5.3	56.6	-19.0	56.1	-0.9	(D)	-	-
Establishments - 10-19 Emp. Number	127	146	15.0	149	2.1	151	1.3	134	-11.3	123	-8.2	-3.1
Mid-March Employment	1,638	1,934	18.1	1,976	2.2	2,022	2.3	1,779	-12.0	1,637	-8.0	-0.1
1st Quarter Wages (annualized - $ mil.)	48.0	65.5	36.5	68.2	4.2	74.6	9.3	69.5	-6.8	75.5	8.6	57.4
Payroll per Emp. 1st Q. (annualized)	29,287	33,853	15.6	34,532	2.0	36,892	6.8	39,069	5.9	46,111	18.0	57.4
Annual Payroll ($ mil.)	49.8	62.7	25.9	65.3	4.2	77.3	18.4	69.3	-10.4	74.1	6.9	48.8
Establishments - 20-49 Emp. Number	102	159	55.9	135	-15.1	102	-24.4	100	-2.0	101	1.0	-1.0
Mid-March Employment	3,111	4,939	58.8	4,249	-14.0	3,091	-27.3	3,173	2.7	3,110	-2.0	-0.0
1st Quarter Wages (annualized - $ mil.)	90.5	159.8	76.6	129.3	-19.1	105.5	-18.4	111.8	6.0	106.3	-4.9	17.4
Payroll per Emp. 1st Q. (annualized)	29,093	32,353	11.2	30,422	-6.0	34,118	12.1	35,222	3.2	34,168	-3.0	17.4
Annual Payroll ($ mil.)	89.4	157.5	76.2	127.8	-18.8	107.5	-15.9	112.3	4.4	103.9	-7.4	16.3
Establishments - 50-99 Emp. Number	53	65	22.6	63	-3.1	69	9.5	66	-4.3	62	-6.1	17.0
Mid-March Employment	3,614	4,761	31.7	4,362	-8.4	4,767	9.3	4,641	-2.6	4,520	-2.6	25.1
1st Quarter Wages (annualized - $ mil.)	83.2	113.7	36.7	120.7	6.2	134.8	11.7	133.8	-0.8	148.1	10.7	78.1
Payroll per Emp. 1st Q. (annualized)	23,018	23,884	3.8	27,673	15.9	28,287	2.2	28,834	1.9	32,776	13.7	42.4
Annual Payroll ($ mil.)	85.0	113.7	33.8	113.1	-0.5	138.1	22.1	137.9	-0.2	143.0	3.7	68.3
Establishments - 100-249 Emp. Number	47	58	23.4	(D)	-	57	-	59	3.5	64	8.5	36.2
Mid-March Employment	7,404	9,087	22.7	(D)	-	8,633	-	9,108	5.5	9,757	7.1	31.8
1st Quarter Wages (annualized - $ mil.)	157.5	193.1	22.6	(D)	-	196.7	-	243.3	23.7	312.1	28.3	98.1
Payroll per Emp. 1st Q. (annualized)	21,275	21,253	-0.1	(D)	-	22,786	-	26,713	17.2	31,984	19.7	50.3
Annual Payroll ($ mil.)	157.3	196.8	25.1	(D)	-	200.1	-	251.3	25.6	288.8	14.9	83.6
Establishments - 250-499 Emp. Number	28	28	-	32	14.3	37	15.6	30	-18.9	30	-	7.1
Mid-March Employment	8,983	9,177	2.2	11,108	21.0	13,474	21.3	10,744	-20.3	10,609	-1.3	18.1
1st Quarter Wages (annualized - $ mil.)	199.2	215.8	8.3	263.7	22.2	307.3	16.5	252.3	-17.9	256.2	1.6	28.6
Payroll per Emp. 1st Q. (annualized)	22,179	23,515	6.0	23,741	1.0	22,807	-3.9	23,480	2.9	24,149	2.9	8.9
Annual Payroll ($ mil.)	208.1	214.5	3.1	260.6	21.5	308.5	18.4	249.6	-19.1	262.0	5.0	25.9
Establishments - 500-999 Emp. Number	9	9	-	9	-	(D)	-	7	-	10	42.9	11.1
Mid-March Employment	5,870	5,685	-3.2	6,062	6.6	(D)	-	4,838	-	6,909	42.8	17.7
1st Quarter Wages (annualized - $ mil.)	153.8	143.1	-6.9	239.8	67.5	(D)	-	127.3	-	198.1	55.6	28.8
Payroll per Emp. 1st Q. (annualized)	26,198	25,172	-3.9	39,550	57.1	(D)	-	26,306	-	28,671	9.0	9.4
Annual Payroll ($ mil.)	199.0	149.7	-24.8	206.2	37.8	(D)	-	130.9	-	208.3	59.1	4.7
Estab. - 1000 or More Emp. Number	6	7	16.7	(D)	-	(D)	-	(D)	-	(D)	-	-
Mid-March Employment	(D)	16,563	-	(D)	-	(D)	-	(D)	-	(D)	-	-
1st Quarter Wages (annualized - $ mil.)	(D)	494.1	-	(D)	-	(D)	-	(D)	-	(D)	-	-
Payroll per Emp. 1st Q. (annualized)	(D)	29,829	-	(D)	-	(D)	-	(D)	-	(D)	-	-
Annual Payroll ($ mil.)	(D)	498.6	-	(D)	-	(D)	-	(D)	-	(D)	-	-

Source: County Business Patterns, U.S. Department of Commerce, Washington, D.C., for 1990 through 1995. Payroll per employee is calculated using mid-March employment and 1st Quarter wages, annualized. Annual payroll, also shown, may not equal the annualized 1st Quarter wages. Columns headed by a percent sign (%) indicate change from the previous year. *na* stands for not available. The symbol (D) indicates that data are withheld by the source to avoid disclosure of competitive information. A dash (-) indicates that data are not available or cannot be calculated.

ESTABLISHMENTS
Number

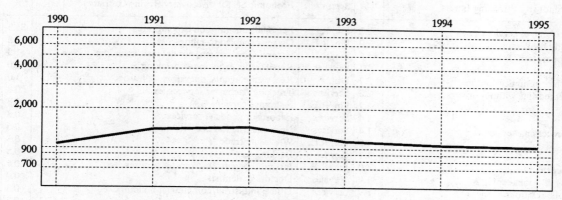

MID-MARCH EMPLOYMENT
Number

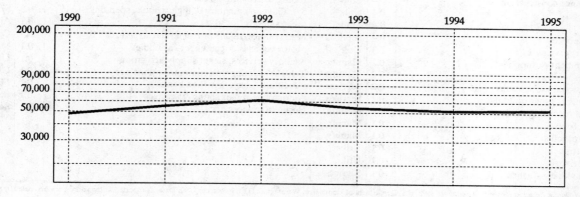

ANNUAL PAYROLL
$ million

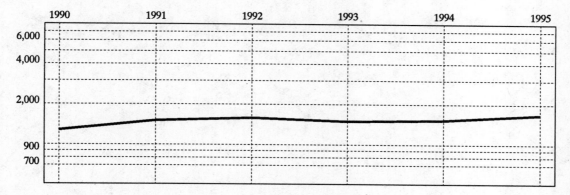

INPUTS AND OUTPUTS FOR INSURANCE CARRIERS - SIC GROUP 63

Economic Sector or Industry Providing Inputs	%	Sector	Economic Sector or Industry Buying Outputs	%	Sector
Insurance agents, brokers, & services	59.2	Fin/R.E.	Personal consumption expenditures	81.3	
Security & commodity brokers	7.0	Fin/R.E.	Owner-occupied dwellings	1.8	Fin/R.E.
Real estate agents, operators, & lessors	5.8	Fin/R.E.	Federal Government, nondefense, spending	1.3	Gov't
Legal services	5.1	Services	Retail trade, ex eating & drinking	1.0	Trade
Telephone/telegraph communications nec	2.7	Util.	Real estate agents, operators, & lessors	1.0	Fin/R.E.
Automotive rental & leasing, without drivers	2.0	Services	Trucking & courier services, ex air	0.8	Util.
Banking	1.7	Fin/R.E.	Insurance carriers	0.8	Fin/R.E.
Advertising	1.4	Services	Exports of goods & services	0.8	Foreign
Computer & data processing services	1.4	Services	New construction nec	0.6	Constr.
Insurance carriers	1.2	Fin/R.E.	Wholesale trade	0.5	Trade
U.S. Postal Service	1.1	Gov't	Banking	0.5	Fin/R.E.
Credit agencies other than banks	1.0	Fin/R.E.	Insurance agents, brokers, & services	0.4	Fin/R.E.
Accounting, auditing & bookkeeping	1.0	Services	Doctors & dentists	0.4	Services
Management & public relations services	0.9	Services	Office, industrial/commercial buildings	0.3	Constr.
Commercial printing	0.8	Manufg.	Repair & maintenance construction nec	0.3	Constr.
Business services nec	0.8	Services	Residential 1 unit structures, nonfarm	0.3	Constr.
Eating & drinking places	0.6	Services	Hospitals	0.3	Services
Hotels	0.5	Services	Highways, bridges, horizontal construction	0.2	Constr.
Miscellaneous equipment rental & leasing	0.5	Services	Electric services (utilities)	0.2	Util.
Repair & maintenance construction nec	0.4	Constr.	Eating & drinking places	0.2	Services
Air transportation	0.4	Util.	S/L Govt., elementary & high schools, spending	0.2	S/L Govt
Wholesale trade	0.4	Trade	Meat animals	0.1	Agric.
Personnel supply services	0.4	Services	Maintenance/repair of residential structures	0.1	Constr.
Trucking & courier services, ex air	0.3	Util.	Motor vehicles & passenger car bodies	0.1	Manufg.
Photographic equipment & supplies	0.2	Manufg.	Sanitary services, steam supply, irrigation	0.1	Util.
Tires & inner tubes	0.2	Manufg.	Telephone/telegraph communications nec	0.1	Util.
Business & professional associations	0.2	Services	Credit agencies other than banks	0.1	Fin/R.E.
Services to dwellings & other buildings	0.2	Services	Automotive repair shops & services	0.1	Services
Magnetic & optical recording media	0.1	Manufg.	Business services nec	0.1	Services
Manifold business forms	0.1	Manufg.			
Paper & paperboard mills	0.1	Manufg.			
Electric services (utilities)	0.1	Util.			
Local & suburban transit	0.1	Util.			
Automobile parking & car washes	0.1	Services			

Source: Benchmark Input-Output Accounts for the U.S. Economy, 1992, U.S. Department of Commerce, Washington, D.C., November 1997. Data, as reported in the source, are organized by the 1987 SIC structure in use in 1992.

OCCUPATIONS EMPLOYED BY MEDICAL SERVICE AND HEALTH INSURANCE

Occupation	% of Total 1996	Change to 2006	Occupation	% of Total 1996	Change to 2006
Insurance adjusters, examiners, investigators	7.9	45.8	Systems analysts	2.7	112.1
Insurance claims clerks	7.5	45.0	Managers & administrators nec	2.1	40.7
General office clerks	5.6	22.2	Accountants & auditors	2.0	31.5
Adjustment clerks	5.6	91.7	Registered nurses	1.9	112.9
Insurance policy processing clerks	4.9	13.6	Bookkeeping, accounting, & auditing clerks	1.9	13.6
Clerical supervisors & managers	4.9	42.0	Sales & related workers nec	1.6	56.2
Secretaries, except legal & medical	4.3	12.6	Receptionists & information clerks	1.5	42.0
Claims examiners, property & casualty	4.0	43.0	Mail clerks	1.2	13.9
Insurance sales workers	3.8	32.5	Health professionals/paraprofessionals nec	1.2	41.9
Clerical & administrative workers nec	3.3	42.0	Computer operators, ex peripheral equipment	1.2	-14.8
Data entry keyers, except composing	3.0	13.6	File clerks	1.2	1.4
Computer programmers	2.9	16.9	Correspondence clerks	1.2	42.0
Management support workers nec	2.9	42.0	Operations research analysts	1.1	13.6
General managers & top executives	2.8	37.6	Underwriters	1.1	51.1

Sources: Industry-Occupation Matrix, Bureau of Labor Statistics. These data relate to one or more 3-digit SIC industry groups rather than to a single 4-digit SIC. The change reported for each occupation to the year 2005 is a percent of growth or decline as estimated by the Bureau of Labor Statistics. The abbreviation *nec* stands for not elsewhere classified.

U.S. AND STATE DATA ON INDUSTRY REVENUES AND OTHER ACCOUNTS FOR 1992

State	No. of Estab.	Employ- ment	Payroll ($ mil.)	Revenues ($ mil.)	Empl./ Estab.	Revenue/ Estab. ($)	Payroll/ Estab. ($)	Revenue/ Empl. ($)	Payroll/ Empl. ($)
UNITED STATES	1,100	53,599	1,466.6	23,446.3	49	21,314,805	1,333,302	437,439	27,363
California	66	1,735	51.1	955.6	26	14,478,515	774,091	550,768	29,447
Colorado	21	183	6.4	87.8	9	4,181,190	305,333	479,809	35,038
Florida	60	1,844	50.1	1,284.4	31	21,405,883	835,200	696,504	27,176
Georgia	19	919	18.8	217.3	48	11,435,895	987,947	236,433	20,425
Illinois	42	6,119	174.5	2,895.9	146	68,949,833	4,155,286	473,262	28,521
Indiana	27	738	22.6	403.3	27	14,938,815	838,704	546,542	30,684
Maryland	17	-	(D)	(D)	(D)	(D)	(D)	(D)	(D)
Massachusetts	23	1,426	46.3	406.8	62	17,687,000	2,012,261	285,274	32,456
Michigan	28	968	24.4	367.0	35	13,105,500	870,607	379,085	25,183
Minnesota	21	872	21.0	240.0	42	11,430,429	1,000,381	275,274	24,092
Missouri	24	530	12.2	272.5	22	11,355,500	508,875	514,211	23,043
New Jersey	19	832	23.0	224.7	44	11,824,579	1,209,947	270,032	27,631
New York	37	1,742	60.1	999.8	47	27,022,595	1,625,595	573,959	34,528
North Carolina	30	1,064	25.9	418.7	35	13,957,767	861,767	393,546	24,298
Ohio	55	4,814	147.5	2,938.1	88	53,419,345	2,681,309	610,317	30,634
Pennsylvania	52	2,417	62.0	706.6	46	13,588,692	1,191,538	292,351	25,635
Tennessee	32	-	(D)	(D)	(D)	(D)	(D)	(D)	(D)
Texas	118	4,466	110.5	2,551.5	38	21,622,695	936,297	571,312	24,739
Virginia	30	580	10.2	267.1	19	8,903,267	340,067	460,514	17,590
Washington	18	218	5.6	128.4	12	7,131,389	313,056	588,830	25,849
Wisconsin	30	4,369	112.3	945.1	146	31,504,367	3,742,167	216,327	25,696

Source: 1992 Economic Census, U.S. Department of Commerce, Washington, D.C. This is the only table that shows revenue data as collected by the Bureau of the Census in an Economic Census. The symbol (D) indicates that data are withheld by the source to avoid disclosure of competitive information. A dash (-) indicates that data are not available or cannot be calculated.

STATE-BY-STATE DATA ON ESTABLISHMENTS, EMPLOYMENT, AND PAYROLL - 1994 AND 1995

State	1994					1995					% Change Empl.
	No. of Estab.	Employ-ment	Pay / Empl.	Payroll ($ mil.)	Pay / Estab.	No. of Estab.	Employ-ment	Pay / Empl.	Payroll ($ mil.)	Pay / Estab.	
Alabama	31	482	22,116	10.2	329,677	31	447	24,922	10.7	344,774	-7.3
Alaska	1	(D)	-	(D)	-	1	(D)	-	(D)	-	-
Arizona	17	209	46,431	9.4	552,118	17	231	44,017	9.8	575,059	10.5
Arkansas	7	216	23,722	5.4	771,714	7	232	23,569	5.7	815,000	7.4
California	64	1,643	40,273	63.9	997,938	60	1,645	46,181	68.3	1,139,150	0.1
Colorado	21	186	32,946	6.0	287,476	21	296	33,919	10.2	486,238	59.1
Connecticut	10	355	21,487	14.3	1,431,800	11	830	21,653	21.7	1,970,000	133.8
Delaware	3	(D)	-	(D)	-	3	(D)	-	(D)	-	-
District of Columbia	4	45	32,444	1.8	449,750	5	96	26,792	2.6	512,400	113.3
Florida	60	1,949	24,813	45.7	761,933	65	1,882	25,269	50.7	780,369	-3.4
Georgia	18	780	17,456	16.9	939,333	16	790	18,496	17.4	1,089,750	1.3
Hawaii	5	(D)	-	(D)	-	7	(D)	-	(D)	-	-
Idaho	4	65	20,615	1.2	290,250	4	61	20,262	1.2	293,250	-6.2
Illinois	42	5,523	24,417	141.2	3,361,405	54	6,535	28,891	189.8	3,515,426	18.3
Indiana	29	812	40,158	30.8	1,062,207	29	885	37,288	29.0	1,001,414	9.0
Iowa	14	(D)	-	(D)	-	15	(D)	-	(D)	-	-
Kansas	17	331	33,221	10.1	596,529	18	322	34,087	10.3	573,833	-2.7
Kentucky	11	278	21,799	6.3	576,636	13	274	21,883	6.1	472,000	-1.4
Louisiana	26	213	26,610	5.9	226,769	23	180	31,311	5.5	238,913	-15.5
Maine	2	(D)	-	(D)	-	2	(D)	-	(D)	-	-
Maryland	15	283	29,357	8.2	548,867	15	251	39,649	9.6	638,867	-11.3
Massachusetts	22	775	34,328	36.3	1,651,091	18	988	35,409	39.4	2,186,667	27.5
Michigan	32	924	30,082	28.8	898,906	29	926	29,577	27.3	941,966	0.2
Minnesota	22	776	25,804	19.0	863,045	19	653	26,383	15.5	813,316	-15.9
Mississippi	16	(D)	-	(D)	-	13	(D)	-	(D)	-	-
Missouri	25	532	25,398	12.8	512,360	23	555	27,805	13.4	584,609	4.3
Montana	6	(D)	-	(D)	-	6	(D)	-	(D)	-	-
Nebraska	19	8,444	36,961	273.8	14,410,263	19	7,830	41,428	252.9	13,312,158	-7.3
Nevada	16	202	33,366	6.9	430,000	13	222	34,000	7.8	599,923	9.9
New Hampshire	7	(D)	-	(D)	-	6	(D)	-	(D)	-	-
New Jersey	20	583	31,252	18.2	911,700	20	519	44,378	21.8	1,088,150	-11.0
New Mexico	4	30	31,333	1.0	255,750	4	27	37,333	1.2	291,500	-10.0
New York	44	1,979	28,661	60.2	1,368,773	44	2,221	34,069	77.2	1,753,909	12.2
North Carolina	30	1,793	24,181	48.0	1,600,233	35	1,906	29,058	53.9	1,539,000	6.3
North Dakota	6	(D)	-	(D)	-	6	107	20,486	2.2	373,667	-
Ohio	56	5,173	30,529	156.9	2,802,429	64	4,722	34,196	193.4	3,022,547	-8.7
Oklahoma	26	1,173	23,355	30.3	1,163,615	20	1,081	27,519	29.9	1,494,650	-7.8
Oregon	10	293	27,741	7.8	782,100	9	296	25,338	7.3	809,333	1.0
Pennsylvania	41	2,235	23,060	56.5	1,378,951	41	2,342	25,959	65.4	1,595,098	4.8
Rhode Island	1	(D)	-	(D)	-	1	(D)	-	(D)	-	-
South Carolina	24	(D)	-	(D)	-	22	(D)	-	(D)	-	-
South Dakota	9	81	24,444	2.0	217,444	9	82	31,171	2.1	236,556	1.2
Tennessee	28	491	29,238	14.4	514,286	32	547	34,347	19.4	606,594	11.4
Texas	109	3,604	30,253	106.8	979,651	81	3,383	33,150	108.1	1,334,173	-6.1
Utah	14	488	27,697	16.5	1,180,643	15	538	30,543	16.5	1,098,267	10.2
Vermont	6	(D)	-	(D)	-	4	(D)	-	(D)	-	-
Virginia	26	480	23,900	12.3	471,308	27	474	26,262	11.9	442,407	-1.2
Washington	17	364	30,066	10.7	629,118	17	401	29,855	10.6	625,706	10.2
West Virginia	7	199	15,196	3.2	457,714	7	(D)	-	(D)	-	-
Wisconsin	29	3,271	28,155	93.6	3,227,138	29	3,135	37,659	115.9	3,994,862	-4.2
Wyoming	1	(D)	-	(D)	-	1	(D)	-	(D)	-	-

Source: County Business Patterns, U.S. Department of Commerce, Washington, D.C., for 1994 and 1995. Employment shown is for mid-March of the year shown. Payroll per employee is calculated by annualizing 1st Quarter payroll (not shown) and then dividing that value by mid-March employment. Dividing total annual payroll (columns 5 and 10) by employment, therefore, will *not* yield the payroll per employee figure (columns 4 and 9). The symbol (D) indicates that data are withheld by the source to avoid disclosure of competitive information. A dash (-) indicates that data are not available or cannot be calculated.

ESTABLISHMENTS 1995 - STATE AND REGIONAL CONCENTRATION

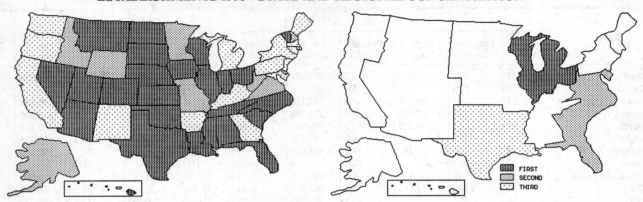

EMPLOYMENT 1995 - STATE AND REGIONAL CONCENTRATION

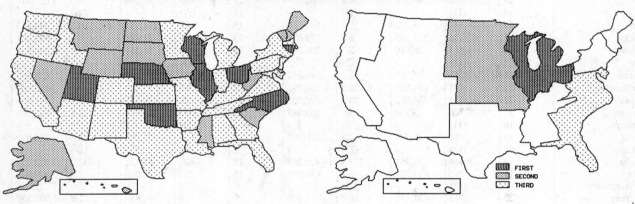

PAYROLL 1995 - STATE AND REGIONAL CONCENTRATION

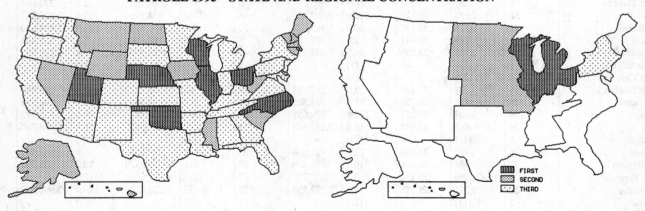

States with the darkest shading indicate those states which have proportionately more establishments, employment, or payrolls than would be indicated by the state's population. States with light shading are states with proportionately fewer establishments, less employment, and lower payrolls than population distribution. States shaded grey are within 15 percent of the state's population proportion in these categories. States for which no data are available are shown as average (grey). *Regions* are shaded to indicate absolute rank in the category. If no data for the category are available, establishment counts are used to shade the regions. Source of the data is the table on the facing page.

OCCUPATIONS EMPLOYED BY MEDICAL SERVICE AND HEALTH INSURANCE

Occupation	% of Total 1996	Change to 2006	Occupation	% of Total 1996	Change to 2006
Insurance adjusters, examiners, investigators	7.9	45.8	Systems analysts	2.7	112.1
Insurance claims clerks	7.5	45.0	Managers & administrators nec	2.1	40.7
General office clerks	5.6	22.2	Accountants & auditors	2.0	31.5
Adjustment clerks	5.6	91.7	Registered nurses	1.9	112.9
Insurance policy processing clerks	4.9	13.6	Bookkeeping, accounting, & auditing clerks	1.9	13.6
Clerical supervisors & managers	4.9	42.0	Sales & related workers nec	1.6	56.2
Secretaries, except legal & medical	4.3	12.6	Receptionists & information clerks	1.5	42.0
Claims examiners, property & casualty	4.0	43.0	Mail clerks	1.2	13.9
Insurance sales workers	3.8	32.5	Health professionals/paraprofessionals nec	1.2	41.9
Clerical & administrative workers nec	3.3	42.0	Computer operators, ex peripheral equipment	1.2	-14.8
Data entry keyers, except composing	3.0	13.6	File clerks	1.2	1.4
Computer programmers	2.9	16.9	Correspondence clerks	1.2	42.0
Management support workers nec	2.9	42.0	Operations research analysts	1.1	13.6
General managers & top executives	2.8	37.6	Underwriters	1.1	51.1

Sources: Industry-Occupation Matrix, Bureau of Labor Statistics. These data relate to one or more 3-digit SIC industry groups rather than to a single 4-digit SIC. The change reported for each occupation to the year 2005 is a percent of growth or decline as estimated by the Bureau of Labor Statistics. The abbreviation *nec* stands for not elsewhere classified.

U.S. AND STATE DATA ON INDUSTRY REVENUES AND OTHER ACCOUNTS FOR 1992

State	No. of Estab.	Employ- ment	Payroll ($ mil.)	Revenues ($ mil.)	Empl./ Estab.	Revenue/ Estab. ($)	Payroll/ Estab. ($)	Revenue/ Empl. ($)	Payroll/ Empl. ($)
UNITED STATES	1,746	196,637	6,078.7	124,813.2	113	71,485,208	3,481,474	634,739	30,913
California	251	23,269	796.6	23,231.0	93	92,553,789	3,173,725	998,367	34,235
Colorado	33	2,762	69.5	898.5	84	27,227,152	2,106,394	325,306	25,167
Florida	96	9,529	296.1	4,077.8	99	42,477,396	3,083,958	427,939	31,069
Georgia	30	1,908	58.0	1,271.5	64	42,382,333	1,933,967	666,389	30,408
Illinois	81	8,897	305.8	4,498.2	110	55,533,877	3,775,235	505,591	34,370
Indiana	19	1,737	58.1	1,150.6	91	60,560,211	3,056,579	662,432	33,434
Maryland	36	-	(D)	(D)	(D)	(D)	(D)	(D)	(D)
Massachusetts	53	8,245	278.0	5,367.1	156	101,266,491	5,244,925	650,955	33,715
Michigan	63	9,980	342.8	7,587.7	158	120,438,889	5,441,016	760,286	34,347
Minnesota	32	3,500	110.9	1,158.5	109	36,203,469	3,466,187	331,003	31,691
Missouri	45	4,654	162.1	2,995.6	103	66,569,556	3,601,444	643,668	34,823
New Jersey	50	4,460	148.6	4,091.2	89	81,823,080	2,971,140	917,299	33,309
New York	83	19,718	590.6	13,667.6	238	164,670,470	7,115,277	693,156	29,951
North Carolina	25	2,442	74.6	1,563.8	98	62,551,680	2,984,360	640,373	30,552
Ohio	59	4,916	151.0	2,832.8	83	48,013,780	2,558,949	576,243	30,712
Pennsylvania	75	17,700	533.3	10,017.0	236	133,559,893	7,111,080	565,932	30,132
Tennessee	25	-	(D)	(D)	(D)	(D)	(D)	(D)	(D)
Texas	82	5,582	175.6	3,724.2	68	45,417,268	2,140,866	667,183	31,449
Virginia	46	4,602	142.2	3,017.5	100	65,597,587	3,090,435	655,691	30,891
Washington	50	5,292	151.2	2,721.9	106	54,438,580	3,023,420	514,348	28,566
Wisconsin	52	6,074	134.6	2,153.9	117	41,421,288	2,589,346	354,611	22,168

Source: 1992 Economic Census, U.S. Department of Commerce, Washington, D.C. This is the only table that shows revenue data as collected by the Bureau of the Census in an Economic Census. The symbol (D) indicates that data are withheld by the source to avoid disclosure of competitive information. A dash (-) indicates that data are not available or cannot be calculated.

STATE-BY-STATE DATA ON ESTABLISHMENTS, EMPLOYMENT, AND PAYROLL - 1994 AND 1995

State	1994					1995					% Change Empl.
	No. of Estab.	Employ-ment	Pay / Empl.	Payroll ($ mil.)	Pay / Estab.	No. of Estab.	Employ-ment	Pay / Empl.	Payroll ($ mil.)	Pay / Estab.	
Alabama	34	3,559	38,406	119.5	3,514,618	34	3,536	43,781	130.4	3,835,118	-0.6
Alaska	1	(D)	-	(D)	-	1	(D)	-	(D)	-	-
Arizona	37	3,567	34,753	131.7	3,559,973	34	3,607	34,241	119.8	3,524,324	1.1
Arkansas	21	1,377	32,183	46.5	2,214,762	24	1,534	35,570	55.8	2,324,167	11.4
California	243	25,081	36,643	896.7	3,690,053	245	25,840	43,216	1,042.8	4,256,139	3.0
Colorado	32	2,378	33,983	85.3	2,664,562	39	2,738	33,674	93.3	2,393,385	15.1
Connecticut	18	4,617	37,021	180.5	10,027,167	19	5,855	41,393	249.9	13,150,105	26.8
Delaware	6	(D)	-	(D)	-	4	(D)	-	(D)	-	-
District of Columbia	14	2,633	36,685	105.7	7,548,786	13	2,317	45,937	104.3	8,021,308	-12.0
Florida	105	10,548	34,847	351.7	3,349,362	147	12,353	36,640	437.9	2,979,218	17.1
Georgia	37	2,284	33,268	79.3	2,142,757	45	2,841	43,068	107.2	2,382,111	24.4
Hawaii	12	(D)	-	(D)	-	11	(D)	-	(D)	-	-
Idaho	16	737	29,422	21.4	1,335,812	16	811	29,761	23.4	1,464,625	10.0
Illinois	86	8,192	37,583	322.7	3,752,523	88	8,723	41,996	369.8	4,202,159	6.5
Indiana	29	2,174	37,869	79.8	2,750,621	29	2,264	40,030	87.5	3,016,379	4.1
Iowa	26	(D)	-	(D)	-	31	(D)	-	(D)	-	-
Kansas	31	2,284	25,513	61.4	1,980,710	27	2,143	31,442	64.1	2,374,963	-6.2
Kentucky	38	3,661	28,380	103.6	2,725,711	50	3,747	28,809	118.5	2,370,020	2.3
Louisiana	24	1,485	30,580	44.4	1,851,750	25	1,767	30,834	52.7	2,109,600	19.0
Maine	5	(D)	-	(D)	-	4	(D)	-	(D)	-	-
Maryland	38	4,174	36,024	151.5	3,987,316	37	4,527	41,028	181.6	4,909,405	8.5
Massachusetts	49	9,180	37,249	361.6	7,380,041	47	9,088	42,373	397.9	8,466,234	-
Michigan	60	9,593	40,444	379.8	6,330,567	62	9,513	42,552	381.2	6,147,935	-0.8
Minnesota	33	5,089	34,060	180.3	5,462,515	33	6,656	38,368	243.4	7,377,273	30.8
Mississippi	8	(D)	-	(D)	-	10	(D)	-	(D)	-	-
Missouri	52	4,952	34,386	175.3	3,371,404	57	5,106	37,818	203.2	3,565,298	3.1
Montana	8	(D)	-	(D)	-	8	(D)	-	(D)	-	-
Nebraska	14	1,053	33,531	33.7	2,404,643	15	1,173	38,213	40.5	2,702,400	11.4
Nevada	21	605	32,423	22.0	1,048,429	25	985	33,706	35.3	1,413,920	62.8
New Hampshire	8	(D)	-	(D)	-	8	(D)	-	(D)	-	-
New Jersey	40	4,214	43,169	145.6	3,640,450	47	4,343	47,201	179.9	3,828,511	3.1
New Mexico	9	1,264	29,481	38.1	4,234,333	11	1,007	33,355	31.9	2,900,364	-20.3
New York	89	20,026	30,836	655.2	7,362,180	94	19,476	33,534	681.3	7,248,074	-2.7
North Carolina	28	2,828	31,676	97.7	3,487,821	29	3,335	33,078	122.0	4,205,655	17.9
North Dakota	9	(D)	-	(D)	-	10	(D)	-	(D)	-	-
Ohio	62	5,193	32,286	177.4	2,861,629	67	4,826	51,872	202.4	3,021,045	-7.1
Oklahoma	23	1,197	29,240	38.9	1,691,391	23	1,221	30,781	39.8	1,732,478	2.0
Oregon	31	3,724	32,879	122.6	3,953,710	28	3,334	34,989	115.6	4,127,036	-10.5
Pennsylvania	65	15,480	32,276	484.2	7,449,308	69	17,108	34,669	577.6	8,370,493	10.5
Rhode Island	6	(D)	-	(D)	-	6	(D)	-	(D)	-	-
South Carolina	13	(D)	-	(D)	-	13	(D)	-	(D)	-	-
South Dakota	12	190	26,126	5.1	425,083	13	243	28,938	8.5	655,462	27.9
Tennessee	32	3,625	28,433	99.6	3,111,750	32	3,789	31,203	115.0	3,595,000	4.5
Texas	93	7,301	31,115	237.2	2,551,054	103	7,938	33,682	275.5	2,676,126	8.7
Utah	16	1,255	25,979	38.3	2,394,250	18	1,431	29,839	44.2	2,454,556	14.0
Vermont	3	(D)	-	(D)	-	4	(D)	-	(D)	-	-
Virginia	38	4,628	33,788	145.8	3,835,816	42	4,005	42,760	156.6	3,727,881	-13.5
Washington	50	4,955	33,069	160.4	3,207,220	43	5,330	33,463	176.8	4,111,070	7.6
West Virginia	8	1,033	21,630	24.2	3,019,750	8	(D)	-	(D)	-	-
Wisconsin	63	6,135	27,985	163.0	2,588,079	68	6,089	28,485	174.1	2,560,588	-0.7
Wyoming	14	(D)	-	(D)	-	14	(D)	-	(D)	-	-

Source: County Business Patterns, U.S. Department of Commerce, Washington, D.C., for 1994 and 1995. Employment shown is for mid-March of the year shown. Payroll per employee is calculated by annualizing 1st Quarter payroll (not shown) and then dividing that value by mid-March employment. Dividing total annual payroll (columns 5 and 10) by employment, therefore, will *not* yield the payroll per employee figure (columns 4 and 9). The symbol (D) indicates that data are withheld by the source to avoid disclosure of competitive information. A dash (-) indicates that data are not available or cannot be calculated.

ESTABLISHMENTS 1995 - STATE AND REGIONAL CONCENTRATION

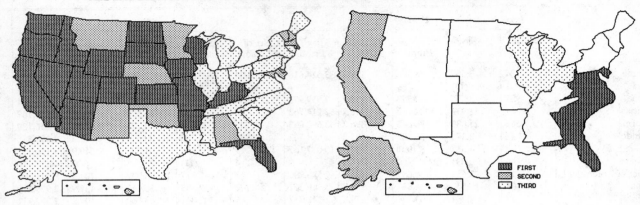

EMPLOYMENT 1995 - STATE AND REGIONAL CONCENTRATION

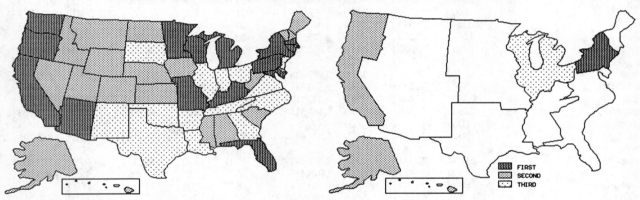

PAYROLL 1995 - STATE AND REGIONAL CONCENTRATION

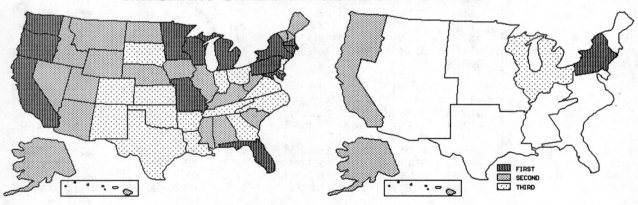

States with the darkest shading indicate those states which have proportionately more establishments, employment, or payrolls than would be indicated by the state's population. States with light shading are states with proportionately fewer establishments, less employment, and lower payrolls than population distribution. States shaded grey are within 15 percent of the state's population proportion in these categories. States for which no data are available are shown as average (grey). *Regions* are shaded to indicate absolute rank in the category. If no data for the category are available, establishment counts are used to shade the regions. Source of the data is the table on the facing page.

LEADING COMPANIES - SIC 6321 - Accident and Health Insurance

Number shown: **100**   Total sales/assets ($ mil): **279,474**   Total employment (000): **447.0**

Company Name	Address				CEO Name	Phone	Co. Type	Sales/Assets ($ mil)	Empl. (000)
Aetna Inc.	151 Farmington Ave.	Hartford	CT	06156	Richard L. Huber	860-273-0123	P	96,001 TA	38.6
Hartford Life Inc.	200 Hopmeadow St.	Weatogue	CT	06089	Lowndes A. Smith	860-843-7716	P	79,933 TA	3.7
Kaiser Foundation Health Plan Inc.	1 Kaiser Plaza	Oakland	CA	94612	David M. Lawrence	510-271-5910	R	11,729 TA	83.9
Principal Financial Group	711 High St.	Des Moines	IA	50309		515-247-5111	S	7,220	18.0
Humana Inc.	PO Box 1438	Louisville	KY	40201	David A. Jones	502-580-1000	P	5,418 TA	18.3
PacifiCare Health Systems Inc.	5995 Plaza Dr.	Cypress	CA	90630	Alan Hoops	714-952-1121	P	4,868 TA	9.8
Standard Insurance Co.	PO Box 711	Portland	OR	97207	Ronald E. Timpe	503-321-7000	R	4,100 TA	1.6
Foundation Health Systems Inc.	21600 Oxnard St.	Woodland Hills	CA	91367	Malik M. Hasan	818-719-6978	P	4,076 TA	15.2
Wellpoint Health Networks Inc.	21555 Oxnard St.	Woodland Hills	CA	91367	Leonard D. Schaeffer	818-703-4000	P	3,406 TA	6.6
Blue Cross and Blue Shield of Florida Inc.	PO Box 1798	Jacksonville	FL	32231	Michael Cascone Jr.	904-791-6111	R	3,000 TA	6.8
Blue Cross and Blue Shield of Michigan	600 Lafayette E.	Detroit	MI	48226	Richard E. Whitmer	313-225-9000	R	2,914 TA*	6.7
Blue Cross of California	PO Box 70000	Van Nuys	CA	91470	Ron Williams	818-703-2711	S	2,679 TA	6.0
Delta Dental Plan of California	PO Box 7736	San Francisco	CA	94120	William T. Ward	415-972-8300	R	2,278 TA*	2.0
Group Health Cooperative of Puget Sound	521 Wall St.	Seattle	WA	98121	Phil Nudelman	206-326-3000	R	2,240 TA*	8.6
Independence Blue Cross	1901 Market St.	Philadelphia	PA	19103	G. Fred DiBona Jr.	215-241-2751	R	2,040 TA*	5.0
FHP International Corp.	PO Box 25186	Santa Ana	CA	92799	Westcott W. Price III	714-550-0684	S	2,014 TA	10.0
Foundation Health Corp.	3400 Data Dr.	Rancho Cordova	CA	95670	Daniel D. Crowley	916-631-5000	P	1,964 TA	8.9
Trigon Healthcare Inc.	PO Box 27401	Richmond	VA	23279	Norwood H. Davis Jr.	804-354-7000	P	1,929 TA	3.6
Health Care Service Corporation	233 N. Michigan Ave.	Chicago	IL	60601	Ray McCaskey	312-938-6000	R	1,740 TA*	4.0
U.S. Healthcare Inc.	PO Box 1109	Blue Bell	PA	19422	Leonard Abramson	215-628-4800	S	1,667 TA	4.3
ValueRx Pharmacy Program Inc.	4700 Nathan Ln. N.	Plymouth	MN	55442	Kevin Roberg	612-509-2500	S	1,590 TA	1.4
Veritus Inc.	120 5th Ave.	Pittsburgh	PA	15222	Eugene J. Barone	412-544-7000	R	1,553 TA	2.8
Mercy Health Services	34605 12 Mile Rd.	Farmington Hills	MI	48331	Judy Pelham	248-489-6000	R	1,500 OR*	36.0
Blue Cross and Blue Shield of Connecticut Inc.	370 Bassett Rd.	North Haven	CT	06473	Harry Torelo	203-239-4911	R	1,477 TA	2.5
UniHealth America	3400 Riverside Dr.	Burbank	CA	91505	David Carpenter	818-238-6000	R	1,420 TA	10.0
Oxford Health Plans Inc.	800 Connecticut Ave.	Norwalk	CT	06854	William M. Sullivan	203-852-1442	P	1,398 TA	7.2
Franciscan Health System	1 MacIntyre Dr.	Aston	PA	19014	William Foley	610-358-3950	D	1,200 OR	12.0
Blue Cross and Blue Shield of Massachusetts Inc.	100 Summer St.	Boston	MA	02110	William C. Van Faasen	617-832-5000	R	1,174 TA*	2.7

Company type codes: P - Public, R - Private, S - Subsidiary, D - Division, J - Joint Venture, A - Affiliate, G - Group. If the dollar values shown are not sales, the following codes apply: TA - Total Assets; OR - Operating Revenues; GB - Gross Billings. * - estimated dollar value. < - less than. *na* - not available.

Continued on next page.

LEADING COMPANIES - SIC 6321 - Accident and Health Insurance

Continued

Company Name	Address				CEO Name	Phone	Co. Type	Sales/Assets ($ mil)	Empl. (000)
Healthsource Inc.	Two College Park Dr.	Hooksett	NH	03106	Norman C. Payson	603-268-7000	P	1,007 TA	5.5
Blue Cross and Blue Shield of New Jersey Inc.	3 Penn Plz.	Newark	NJ	07105	William Marino	973-466-4000	R	993 TA*	3.0
Blue Cross and Blue Shield of Missouri	1831 Chestnut St.	St. Louis	MO	63103	John O'Rourke	314-923-4444	R	925 TA	1.6
Blue Cross and Blue Shield of the National Capital Area	550 12th St. S.W.	Washington	DC	20065	Larry C. Glasscock	202-479-8000	S	917 TA	1.8
Kaiser Foundation Health Plan of the Northwest	3600 N. Interstate Ave.	Portland	OR	97227	Michael Katcher	503-280-2000	S	910 TA*	7.4
Value Health Inc.	22 Waterville Rd.	Avon	CT	06001	Robert E. Patricelli	860-678-3400	P	895 TA	6.0
United Wisconsin Services Inc.	401 W. Michigan St.	Milwaukee	WI	53203	Thomas R. Hefty	414-226-6900	P	796 TA	3.3
Blue Cross and Blue Shield of Oregon	PO Box 1271	Portland	OR	97207	Don Sacco	503-225-5221	S	772 TA	2.3
Blue Cross and Blue Shield of North Carolina	PO Box 2291	Durham	NC	27702	Kenneth C. Otis II	919-489-7431	R	771 TA	2.2
Blue Cross and Blue Shield of Maryland Inc.	10455 Mill Run Cir.	Owings Mills	MD	21117	William L. Jews	410-581-3000	R	736 TA	3.9
Blue Cross and Blue Shield of Ohio	2060 E. 9th St.	Cleveland	OH	44115	John Burry Jr.	216-687-7000	R	736 TA	3.0
IASD Health Services Corp.	636 Grand Ave.	Des Moines	IA	50309	John D. Forsyth	515-245-4500	R	731 TA*	2.7
Sierra Health Services Inc.	PO Box 15645	Las Vegas	NV	89114	Anthony M. Marlon	702-242-7000	P	722 TA	2.6
Crozer Keystone Health System	1400 N. Providence Rd.	Media	PA	19063	John C. McMeekin	215-892-8000	R	700 TA*	4.0
Maxicare Health Plans Inc.	1149 S. Broadway St.	Los Angeles	CA	90015	Peter J. Ratican	213-765-2000	P	664	0.5
Blue Cross and Blue Shield of Kansas City	2301 Main St.	Kansas City	MO	64108	Jake Mascotte	816-395-2222	R	650 TA	1.1
Blue Cross and Blue Shield United of Wisconsin	1515 N. River Ctr. Dr.	Milwaukee	WI	53212	Thomas R. Hefty	414-226-5000	R	600 TA	2.4
United HealthCare of Ohio Inc.	3650 Olentangy River Rd.	Columbus	OH	43214	Robert J. Sheehy	614-442-7100	S	580 TA	0.7
Aware Integrated Inc.	PO Box 64560	St. Paul	MN	55164	Andrew Czajkowski	612-456-8786	R	573 TA	3.0
Comprecare Inc.	6455 S. Yosemite St.	Englewood	CO	80011	Eric Sipf	303-220-5800	S	460 TA*	0.6
Finger Lakes Blue Cross and Blue Shield	150 E. Maine St.	Rochester	NY	14647	Howard Berman	716-454-1700	R	460 TA	2.4
Coventry Corp.	53 Century Blvd.	Nashville	TN	37214	Allen F. Wise	615-391-2440	P	449 TA	3.2
Kaiser Foundation Health Plan of Colorado	10350 E. Dakota Ave.	Denver	CO	80231	R. Michael Alexander	303-344-7200	S	403 TA*	3.3
Blue Cross of Washington and Alaska	PO Box 327	Seattle	WA	98111	Betty Woods	425-670-4000	R	390 TA*	1.2
Community Health Plan	1 CHP Plz.	Latham	NY	12110	John Baackes	518-783-1864	R	379 TA	3.0
Mid Atlantic Medical Services Inc.	4 Taft Ct.	Rockville	MD	20850	George T. Jochum	301-294-5140	P	354 TA	2.4

Company type codes: P - Public, R - Private, S - Subsidiary, D - Division, J - Joint Venture, A - Affiliate, G - Group. If the dollar values shown are not sales, the following codes apply: TA - Total Assets; OR - Operating Revenues; GB - Gross Billings. * - estimated dollar value. < - less than. *na* - not available.

Continued on next page.

LEADING COMPANIES - SIC 6321 - Accident and Health Insurance

Continued

Company Name	Address				CEO Name	Phone	Co. Type	Sales/Assets ($ mil)	Empl. (000)
Kaiser Foundation Health Plan of the Mid-Atlantic States Inc.	2101 E. Jefferson St.	Rockville	MD	20852	Alan J. Silverstone	301-816-2424	S	340 TA*	2.8
TakeCare Inc.	2300 Clayton Rd.	Concord	CA	94520	Larry D. Gray	510-246-1300	S	336 TA	1.1
MVP Health Plan Inc.	111 Liberty St.	Schenectady	NY	12305	David Oliker	518-370-4793	R	335 TA	0.5
Arkansas Blue Cross and Blue Shield	PO Box 2181	Little Rock	AR	72203	Robert L. Shoptaw	501-378-2000	R	333 TA	1.3
ODS Health Plans	315 S.W. 5th Ave.	Portland	OR	97204	A.G. Lindstrand	503-228-6554	S	329 TA*	0.4
PARTNERS National Health Plans of North Carolina Inc.	PO Box 24907	Winston-Salem	NC	27114	John W. Jones	336-760-4822	R	296 TA	0.4
Blue Cross and Blue Shield of Rhode Island	444 Westminster St.	Providence	RI	02903	Douglas J. McIntosh	401-272-8500	R	283 TA	1.5
Blue Cross and Blue Shield of South Carolina	I-20 and Alpine Rd.	Columbia	SC	29219	M. Edward Sellers	803-788-0222	R	278 TA	3.5
Lifeguard HMO Inc.	PO Box 5506	San Jose	CA	95150	Mark G. Hyde	408-943-9400	R	273 TA	0.5
Compcare Health Services Insurance Corp.	PO Box 2947	Milwaukee	WI	53201	Jeffrey J. Nohl	414-226-6744	S	253 TA	0.3
Comprehensive Health Services Inc.	2875 W. Grand Blvd.	Detroit	MI	48202	James W. Patton	313-875-4200	R	250 TA	0.9
Westmoreland Health System	532 W. Pittsburgh St.	Greensburg	PA	15601	Joseph J. Peluso	412-832-5040	R	250 TA*	1.8
Qual-Med Inc.	225 N. Main St.	Pueblo	CO	81003	Michael Pugh	719-542-0500	S	245 TA	0.9
Blue Cross and Blue Shield of Georgia Inc.	PO Box 4445	Atlanta	GA	30302	Richard D. Shirk	404-842-8000	R	239 TA*	1.2
Physicians Health Services Inc.	120 Hawley Ln.	Trumbull	CT	06611	Michael E. Herbert	203-381-6400	P	238 TA	1.0
Louisiana Health Service and Indemnity Co.	PO Box 98029	Baton Rouge	LA	70898	P.J. Mills	504-295-3307	R	225 TA	0.8
Blue Cross and Blue Shield of Mississippi	PO Box 1043	Jackson	MS	39215	Richard J. Hale	601-932-3704	R	225 TA	1.0
EBP HealthPlans Inc.	435 Ford Rd.	Minneapolis	MN	55426	William E. Sagan	612-546-4353	S	215 TA	1.5
CompDent Corp.	100 Mansell Ct. E.	Roswell	GA	30076	David R. Klock	770-998-8936	P	210 TA	0.5
Blue Cross and Blue Shield of Delaware Inc.	PO Box 1991	Wilmington	DE	19899	Robert C. Cole Jr.	302-421-3000	R	206 TA	0.8
Kaiser Foundation Health Plan of Texas	12720 Hillcrest Rd.	Dallas	TX	75230	Sharon Flaherty	214-458-5000	S	205 TA	1.0
Group Health Service of Oklahoma Inc.	PO Box 3283	Tulsa	OK	74102	Ralph S. Rhoades	918-560-3500	R	200 TA*	0.9
HealthPartners of Arizona Inc.	3141 N. 3rd Ave.	Phoenix	AZ	85013	Paul Zucarelli	602-664-2600	R	200 TA	0.7
Constitution HealthCare Inc.	370 Bassett Rd.	North Haven	CT	06473	J.L. Mueller	203-234-2011	R	190 TA	0.2
Nylcare Health Plan of the Southwest Inc.	4500 Fuller Dr.	Irving	TX	75038	Steve P. Yerxa	214-650-5500	S	185 TA	0.3
M.D. Enterprises of Connecticut Inc.	6 Devine St.	North Haven	CT	06473	Barbara Bradow	203-230-1000	S	178 TA	0.3
Good Health Plan of Washington	1501 4th Ave.	Seattle	WA	98101	Lee Hooks	206-622-6111	S	172 TA*	0.4
Gencare Health Systems Inc.	PO Box 419079	St. Louis	MO	63141	Barrett Toan	314-434-6114	S	170 TA*	0.3

Company type codes: P - Public, R - Private, S - Subsidiary, D - Division, J - Joint Venture, A - Affiliate, G - Group. If the dollar values shown are not sales, the following codes apply: TA - Total Assets; OR - Operating Revenues; GB - Gross Billings. * - estimated dollar value. < - less than. *na* - not available.

Continued on next page.

LEADING COMPANIES - SIC 6321 - Accident and Health Insurance
Continued

Company Name	Address				CEO Name	Phone	Co. Type	Sales/Assets ($ mil)	Empl. (000)
United Dental Care Inc.	14755 Preston Rd.	Dallas	TX	75240	William H. Wilcox	972-458-7474	P	166 TA	0.5
Blue Cross and Blue Shield of Arizona Inc.	PO Box 13466	Phoenix	AZ	85002	Robert B. Bulla	602-864-4100	R	163 TA	0.9
HealthPlus of Michigan Inc.	PO Box 1700	Flint	MI	48501	Paul A. Fuhs	313-230-2000	R	160 TA*	0.2
Kaiser Foundation Health Plan of Georgia Inc.	3495 Piedmont Rd.	Atlanta	GA	30305	Christopher Binkley	404-233-0555	S	160 TA*	1.4
Intergroup Healthcare Corp.	1010 N Finance Ctr. Dr.	Tucson	AZ	85710	Charles F. Barrett	602-721-4444	P	156 TA	0.6
New Hampshire-Vermont Health Service	3000 Goffs Falls Rd.	Manchester	NH	03111	Joseph L. Marcille	603-695-7000	R	156 TA	0.8
PCA Health Plans of Florida Inc.	6101 Blue Lagoon Dr.	Miami	FL	33126	Peter Killissanly	305-267-6633	S	150 TA*	1.2
Value Rx Pharmacy Program Inc.	30445 Northwestern Hwy.	Farmington	MI	48334	Barry Smith	810-539-0220	S	150 TA*	0.3
Delta Dental Plan of New Jersey	PO Box 222	Parsippany	NJ	07054	Robert J. Ott	201-334-6300	R	145 TA	0.2
Health Care Plan	900 Guaranty Bldg.	Buffalo	NY	14202	Arthur Goshin	716-847-1480	R	144 TA	1.2
Southeastern Mutual Insurance Co.	9901 Linn Station Rd.	Louisville	KY	40223	James P. Murphy	502-423-2011	R	140 TA*	0.7
Kaiser Foundation Health Plan of North Carolina	3120 Highwoods Blvd.	Raleigh	NC	27604	Theodore M. Carpenter	919-981-6000	S	130 TA*	1.1
CIGNA Healthcare of Florida Inc.	5404 Cypress Center Dr.	Tampa	FL	33609	Betty Gimel	813-281-1000	S	121 TA	0.6
Keystone Health Plan Central	PO Box 898812	Camp Hill	PA	17089	Joseph Pfister	717-975-7458	S	120 TA	0.1
Rocky Mountain HMO Inc.	PO Box 10600	Grand Junction	CO	81502	Michael J. Weber	970-244-7760	R	120 TA*	0.2
Unity Health Plans Insurance Corp.	840 Carolina St.	Sauk City	WI	53583	Nicholas J. Reiland III	608-643-2491	S	115 TA	0.1
HMO America Inc.	540 N. LaSalle St.	Chicago	IL	60610	Robert J. Weinstein	312-751-7500	P	110 TA	0.4
Family Health Plan Cooperative	11524W Theo Trecker Wy	Milwaukee	WI	53214		414-256-0006	R	110 TA	0.9

Source: *Ward's Business Directory of U.S. Private and Public Companies*, 1996. Company type codes: P - Public, R - Private, S - Subsidiary, D - Division, J - Joint Venture, A - Affiliate, G - Group. If the dollar values shown are not sales, the following codes apply: TA - Total Assets; OR - Operating Revenues; GB - Gross Billings. * - estimated dollar value. < - less than; *na* - not available.

SIC 6330

FIRE, MARINE, AND CASUALTY INSURANCE

This industry includes all establishments whose primary activity is the underwriting of fire, marine, and casualty insurance. The establishments may be owned by stockholders, policyholders, or other carriers. Specific categories include agricultural insurance (crop and livestock); assessment associations for fire, marine, and casualty insurance; associated factory mutuals for these categories; automobile, boiler, and burglary and theft insurance; contact lens insurance; the Federal Crop Insurance Corporation; insurance carriers for these categories, including mutual insurance; plate glass insurance; property damage insurance; reciprocal interinsurance exchanges for these categories; and workers' compensation insurance.

ESTABLISHMENTS, EMPLOYMENT, AND PAYROLL

	1990	1991		1992		1993		1994		1995		% change 90-95
		Value	%	Value	%	Value	%	Value	%	Value	%	
All Establishments	18,335	21,737	18.6	21,722	-0.1	19,055	-12.3	19,915	4.5	20,783	4.4	13.4
Mid-March Employment	532,536	569,584	7.0	584,236	2.6	585,278	0.2	610,368	4.3	587,737	-3.7	10.4
1st Quarter Wages (annualized - $ mil.)	17,077.0	19,288.9	13.0	20,813.1	7.9	21,381.0	2.7	23,748.3	11.1	24,893.4	4.8	45.8
Payroll per Emp. 1st Q. (annualized)	32,067	33,865	5.6	35,624	5.2	36,531	2.5	38,908	6.5	42,355	8.9	32.1
Annual Payroll ($ mil.)	16,979.5	19,115.6	12.6	20,642.2	8.0	21,586.8	4.6	23,049.1	6.8	24,246.0	5.2	42.8
Establishments - 1-4 Emp. Number	12,714	15,489	21.8	15,274	-1.4	12,667	-17.1	13,414	5.9	14,449	7.7	13.6
Mid-March Employment	22,025	26,517	20.4	26,150	-1.4	21,072	-19.4	21,666	2.8	22,336	3.1	1.4
1st Quarter Wages (annualized - $ mil.)	1,122.1	1,220.0	8.7	1,306.5	7.1	1,293.1	-1.0	1,367.1	5.7	1,488.0	8.8	32.6
Payroll per Emp. 1st Q. (annualized)	50,944	46,007	-9.7	49,963	8.6	61,368	22.8	63,098	2.8	66,620	5.6	30.8
Annual Payroll ($ mil.)	1,165.0	1,287.6	10.5	1,402.5	8.9	1,361.8	-2.9	1,493.0	9.6	1,594.8	6.8	36.9
Establishments - 5-9 Emp. Number	1,773	1,993	12.4	1,997	0.2	1,810	-9.4	1,795	-0.8	1,762	-1.8	-0.6
Mid-March Employment	11,408	(D)	-	12,958	-	11,898	-8.2	11,787	-0.9	11,524	-2.2	1.0
1st Quarter Wages (annualized - $ mil.)	377.9	(D)	-	441.8	-	444.0	0.5	469.1	5.6	488.0	4.0	29.1
Payroll per Emp. 1st Q. (annualized)	33,123	(D)	-	34,092	-	37,315	9.5	39,794	6.6	42,345	6.4	27.8
Annual Payroll ($ mil.)	367.4	(D)	-	449.8	-	456.1	1.4	459.3	0.7	476.3	3.7	29.6
Establishments - 10-19 Emp. Number	936	1,093	16.8	1,215	11.2	1,244	2.4	1,276	2.6	1,220	-4.4	30.3
Mid-March Employment	12,805	14,818	15.7	16,499	11.3	16,938	2.7	17,423	2.9	16,787	-3.7	31.1
1st Quarter Wages (annualized - $ mil.)	389.2	479.5	23.2	571.7	19.2	604.5	5.7	682.4	12.9	703.8	3.1	80.8
Payroll per Emp. 1st Q. (annualized)	30,392	32,358	6.5	34,649	7.1	35,692	3.0	39,169	9.7	41,926	7.0	37.9
Annual Payroll ($ mil.)	388.7	483.0	24.2	576.2	19.3	624.0	8.3	670.7	7.5	696.7	3.9	79.2
Establishments - 20-49 Emp. Number	1,068	1,224	14.6	1,230	0.5	1,296	5.4	1,371	5.8	1,362	-0.7	27.5
Mid-March Employment	33,592	38,624	15.0	39,105	1.2	41,904	7.2	44,519	6.2	43,924	-1.3	30.8
1st Quarter Wages (annualized - $ mil.)	1,057.0	1,278.7	21.0	1,391.4	8.8	1,482.3	6.5	1,715.7	15.7	1,853.3	8.0	75.3
Payroll per Emp. 1st Q. (annualized)	31,466	33,106	5.2	35,580	7.5	35,374	-0.6	38,539	8.9	42,194	9.5	34.1
Annual Payroll ($ mil.)	1,032.4	1,249.3	21.0	1,344.6	7.6	1,496.5	11.3	1,705.5	14.0	1,795.7	5.3	73.9
Establishments - 50-99 Emp. Number	777	828	6.6	870	5.1	887	2.0	907	2.3	882	-2.8	13.5
Mid-March Employment	56,183	59,729	6.3	62,093	4.0	62,332	0.4	63,349	1.6	62,280	-1.7	10.9
1st Quarter Wages (annualized - $ mil.)	1,718.0	1,938.1	12.8	2,169.4	11.9	2,196.9	1.3	2,435.0	10.8	2,585.3	6.2	50.5
Payroll per Emp. 1st Q. (annualized)	30,578	32,448	6.1	34,937	7.7	35,245	0.9	38,438	9.1	41,512	8.0	35.8
Annual Payroll ($ mil.)	1,696.5	1,895.8	11.7	2,147.5	13.3	2,243.8	4.5	2,432.4	8.4	2,508.6	3.1	47.9
Establishments - 100-249 Emp. Number	649	668	2.9	672	0.6	687	2.2	663	-3.5	650	-2.0	0.2
Mid-March Employment	98,699	101,837	3.2	103,022	1.2	105,291	2.2	101,745	-3.4	100,808	-0.9	2.1
1st Quarter Wages (annualized - $ mil.)	2,993.4	3,268.1	9.2	3,552.1	8.7	3,569.1	0.5	3,706.6	3.9	3,914.8	5.6	30.8
Payroll per Emp. 1st Q. (annualized)	30,328	32,092	5.8	34,479	7.4	33,897	-1.7	36,430	7.5	38,834	6.6	28.0
Annual Payroll ($ mil.)	2,954.6	3,186.9	7.9	3,449.0	8.2	3,606.1	4.6	3,646.9	1.1	3,858.5	5.8	30.6
Establishments - 250-499 Emp. Number	235	236	0.4	252	6.8	257	2.0	275	7.0	253	-8.0	7.7
Mid-March Employment	83,451	83,808	0.4	89,255	6.5	90,422	1.3	97,137	7.4	89,406	-8.0	7.1
1st Quarter Wages (annualized - $ mil.)	2,553.6	2,697.0	5.6	3,052.8	13.2	2,979.6	-2.4	3,403.3	14.2	3,477.1	2.2	36.2
Payroll per Emp. 1st Q. (annualized)	30,600	32,181	5.2	34,203	6.3	32,952	-3.7	35,036	6.3	38,891	11.0	27.1
Annual Payroll ($ mil.)	2,505.3	2,650.9	5.8	2,985.0	12.6	3,049.7	2.2	3,279.6	7.5	3,318.5	1.2	32.5
Establishments - 500-999 Emp. Number	109	130	19.3	132	1.5	125	-5.3	129	3.2	120	-7.0	10.1
Mid-March Employment	75,353	88,326	17.2	87,958	-0.4	81,683	-7.1	83,785	2.6	78,996	-5.7	4.8
1st Quarter Wages (annualized - $ mil.)	2,176.3	2,848.1	30.9	2,978.7	4.6	2,815.0	-5.5	3,009.1	6.9	3,026.7	0.6	39.1
Payroll per Emp. 1st Q. (annualized)	28,881	32,245	11.6	33,866	5.0	34,462	1.8	35,915	4.2	38,314	6.7	32.7
Annual Payroll ($ mil.)	2,150.3	2,833.7	31.8	2,917.2	2.9	2,810.9	-3.6	2,875.3	2.3	2,981.6	3.7	38.7
Estab. - 1000 or More Emp. Number	74	76	2.7	80	5.3	82	2.5	85	3.7	85	-	14.9
Mid-March Employment	139,020	(D)	-	147,196	-	153,738	4.4	168,957	9.9	161,676	-4.3	16.3
1st Quarter Wages (annualized - $ mil.)	4,689.6	(D)	-	5,348.8	-	5,996.5	12.1	6,960.0	16.1	7,356.5	5.7	56.9
Payroll per Emp. 1st Q. (annualized)	33,734	(D)	-	36,338	-	39,005	7.3	41,194	5.6	45,501	10.5	34.9
Annual Payroll ($ mil.)	4,719.2	(D)	-	5,370.4	-	5,937.9	10.6	6,486.3	9.2	7,015.2	8.2	48.7

Source: County Business Patterns, U.S. Department of Commerce, Washington, D.C., for 1990 through 1995. Payroll per employee is calculated using mid-March employment and 1st Quarter wages, annualized. Annual payroll, also shown, may not equal the annualized 1st Quarter wages. Columns headed by a percent sign (%) indicate change from the previous year. *na* stands for not available. The symbol (D) indicates that data are withheld by the source to avoid disclosure of competitive information. A dash (-) indicates that data are not available or cannot be calculated.

ESTABLISHMENTS
Number

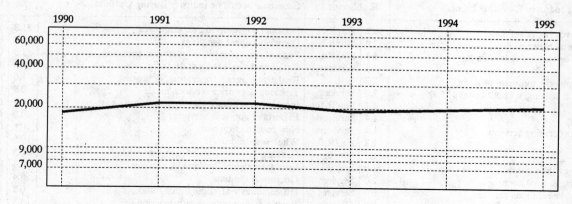

MID-MARCH EMPLOYMENT
Number

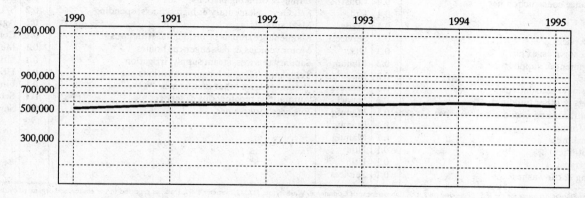

ANNUAL PAYROLL
$ million

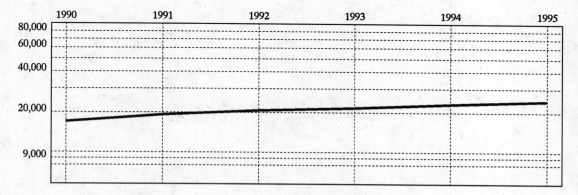

INPUTS AND OUTPUTS FOR INSURANCE CARRIERS - SIC GROUP 63

Economic Sector or Industry Providing Inputs	%	Sector	Economic Sector or Industry Buying Outputs	%	Sector
Insurance agents, brokers, & services	59.2	Fin/R.E.	Personal consumption expenditures	81.3	
Security & commodity brokers	7.0	Fin/R.E.	Owner-occupied dwellings	1.8	Fin/R.E.
Real estate agents, operators, & lessors	5.8	Fin/R.E.	Federal Government, nondefense, spending	1.3	Gov't
Legal services	5.1	Services	Retail trade, ex eating & drinking	1.0	Trade
Telephone/telegraph communications nec	2.7	Util.	Real estate agents, operators, & lessors	1.0	Fin/R.E.
Automotive rental & leasing, without drivers	2.0	Services	Trucking & courier services, ex air	0.8	Util.
Banking	1.7	Fin/R.E.	Insurance carriers	0.8	Fin/R.E.
Advertising	1.4	Services	Exports of goods & services	0.8	Foreign
Computer & data processing services	1.4	Services	New construction nec	0.6	Constr.
Insurance carriers	1.2	Fin/R.E.	Wholesale trade	0.5	Trade
U.S. Postal Service	1.1	Gov't	Banking	0.5	Fin/R.E.
Credit agencies other than banks	1.0	Fin/R.E.	Insurance agents, brokers, & services	0.4	Fin/R.E.
Accounting, auditing & bookkeeping	1.0	Services	Doctors & dentists	0.4	Services
Management & public relations services	0.9	Services	Office, industrial/commercial buildings	0.3	Constr.
Commercial printing	0.8	Manufg.	Repair & maintenance construction nec	0.3	Constr.
Business services nec	0.8	Services	Residential 1 unit structures, nonfarm	0.3	Constr.
Eating & drinking places	0.6	Services	Hospitals	0.3	Services
Hotels	0.5	Services	Highways, bridges, horizontal construction	0.2	Constr.
Miscellaneous equipment rental & leasing	0.5	Services	Electric services (utilities)	0.2	Util.
Repair & maintenance construction nec	0.4	Constr.	Eating & drinking places	0.2	Services
Air transportation	0.4	Util.	S/L Govt., elementary & high schools, spending	0.2	S/L Govt
Wholesale trade	0.4	Trade	Meat animals	0.1	Agric.
Personnel supply services	0.4	Services	Maintenance/repair of residential structures	0.1	Constr.
Trucking & courier services, ex air	0.3	Util.	Motor vehicles & passenger car bodies	0.1	Manufg.
Photographic equipment & supplies	0.2	Manufg.	Sanitary services, steam supply, irrigation	0.1	Util.
Tires & inner tubes	0.2	Manufg.	Telephone/telegraph communications nec	0.1	Util.
Business & professional associations	0.2	Services	Credit agencies other than banks	0.1	Fin/R.E.
Services to dwellings & other buildings	0.2	Services	Automotive repair shops & services	0.1	Services
Magnetic & optical recording media	0.1	Manufg.	Business services nec	0.1	Services
Manifold business forms	0.1	Manufg.			
Paper & paperboard mills	0.1	Manufg.			
Electric services (utilities)	0.1	Util.			
Local & suburban transit	0.1	Util.			
Automobile parking & car washes	0.1	Services			

Source: Benchmark Input-Output Accounts for the U.S. Economy, 1992, U.S. Department of Commerce, Washington, D.C., November 1997. Data, as reported in the source, are organized by the 1987 SIC structure in use in 1992.

OCCUPATIONS EMPLOYED BY FIRE, MARINE, AND CASUALTY INSURANCE

Occupation	% of Total 1996	Change to 2006	Occupation	% of Total 1996	Change to 2006
Insurance adjusters, examiners, investigators	12.7	19.7	Bookkeeping, accounting, & auditing clerks	2.5	-6.7
Insurance policy processing clerks	7.0	-6.7	File clerks	2.3	-16.8
Underwriters	6.9	-0.8	Managers & administrators nec	2.3	15.5
Insurance sales workers	6.7	8.8	Computer programmers	2.2	-4.0
Clerical supervisors & managers	5.2	16.6	Systems analysts	1.7	74.1
General office clerks	4.9	0.3	Accountants & auditors	1.4	7.9
Secretaries, except legal & medical	4.6	-7.5	Data entry keyers, except composing	1.4	-6.7
Claims examiners, property & casualty	4.5	17.4	Professional workers nec	1.3	16.6
Insurance claims clerks	4.3	19.1	Adjusters & investigators nec	1.2	4.9
Clerical & administrative workers nec	3.3	16.6	Lawyers	1.1	16.6
General managers & top executives	2.9	13.0	Billing, cost, & rate clerks	1.1	4.9
Management support workers nec	2.8	16.6			

Sources: Industry-Occupation Matrix, Bureau of Labor Statistics. These data relate to one or more 3-digit SIC industry groups rather than to a single 4-digit SIC. The change reported for each occupation to the year 2005 is a percent of growth or decline as estimated by the Bureau of Labor Statistics. The abbreviation *nec* stands for not elsewhere classified.

U.S. AND STATE DATA ON INDUSTRY REVENUES AND OTHER ACCOUNTS FOR 1992

State	No. of Estab.	Employ-ment	Payroll ($ mil.)	Revenues ($ mil.)	Empl./ Estab.	Revenue/ Estab. ($)	Payroll/ Estab. ($)	Revenue/ Empl. ($)	Payroll/ Empl. ($)
UNITED STATES	19,002	588,333	21,182.6	258,394.7	31	13,598,290	1,114,758	439,198	36,004
Alabama	495	5,261	184.1	2,812.3	11	5,681,459	371,846	534,560	34,987
Alaska	46	409	20.8	310.5	9	6,750,630	452,804	759,240	50,927
Arizona	284	7,537	245.7	3,247.6	27	11,435,387	865,070	430,894	32,597
Arkansas	130	1,153	37.2	797.6	9	6,135,754	286,485	691,802	32,301
California	2,302	73,370	2,815.6	34,173.4	32	14,845,087	1,223,104	465,768	38,375
Colorado	293	8,569	280.6	3,058.4	29	10,438,389	957,560	356,920	32,742
Connecticut	323	22,617	941.5	9,858.5	70	30,521,653	2,915,003	435,889	41,630
Delaware	38	-	(D)	(D)	(D)	(D)	(D)	(D)	(D)
District of Columbia	17	216	9.5	235.5	13	13,854,118	557,294	1,090,370	43,861
Florida	1,227	22,037	781.3	10,558.7	18	8,605,302	636,726	479,135	35,452
Georgia	521	16,916	579.1	6,362.3	32	12,211,737	1,111,568	376,112	34,235
Hawaii	51	1,427	52.2	696.2	28	13,650,431	1,023,647	487,857	36,584
Idaho	94	1,150	32.6	497.1	12	5,288,766	346,894	432,299	28,355
Illinois	1,059	51,554	2,011.6	25,395.6	49	23,980,730	1,899,524	492,602	39,019
Indiana	435	12,039	384.6	4,567.0	28	10,498,961	884,131	379,354	31,946
Iowa	249	7,222	208.8	2,309.3	29	9,274,149	838,739	319,754	28,918
Kansas	201	6,394	195.6	2,307.3	32	11,478,970	973,254	360,850	30,595
Kentucky	238	2,465	85.2	1,407.9	10	5,915,542	358,189	571,156	34,584
Louisiana	339	5,405	192.8	2,966.7	16	8,751,345	568,705	548,882	35,669
Maine	88	1,771	50.9	595.2	20	6,763,989	578,159	336,099	28,728
Maryland	388	12,238	505.8	5,419.7	32	13,968,232	1,303,665	442,856	41,332
Massachusetts	169	16,995	597.3	7,764.5	101	45,943,716	3,534,408	456,869	35,147
Michigan	620	19,489	685.8	9,802.1	31	15,809,882	1,106,106	502,957	35,188
Minnesota	379	13,876	452.8	5,801.6	37	15,307,726	1,194,821	418,105	32,635
Mississippi	126	2,244	71.5	788.2	18	6,255,627	567,714	351,252	31,877
Missouri	433	10,807	357.7	4,387.0	25	10,131,624	826,067	405,940	33,098
Montana	64	310	9.1	222.3	5	3,473,281	141,984	717,065	29,313
Nebraska	132	4,859	144.8	2,334.0	37	17,681,932	1,096,962	480,349	29,800
Nevada	99	748	30.3	472.2	8	4,770,162	305,687	631,345	40,459
New Hampshire	102	6,209	200.7	1,247.6	61	12,230,951	1,967,863	200,927	32,328
New Jersey	384	27,876	1,090.8	9,927.2	73	25,852,174	2,840,625	356,121	39,130
New Mexico	98	616	22.0	394.4	6	4,024,357	224,020	640,239	35,640
New York	1,288	42,784	1,778.6	24,909.9	33	19,339,985	1,380,914	582,225	41,572
North Carolina	466	10,642	359.7	4,643.3	23	9,964,105	771,959	436,316	33,803
North Dakota	59	-	(D)	(D)	(D)	(D)	(D)	(D)	(D)
Ohio	845	32,242	1,090.5	11,893.3	38	14,074,953	1,290,514	368,877	33,822
Oklahoma	216	5,025	161.5	1,775.7	23	8,220,991	747,903	353,380	32,149
Oregon	298	6,504	216.0	1,980.5	22	6,646,044	724,940	304,508	33,215
Pennsylvania	704	29,791	1,011.6	14,237.8	42	20,224,190	1,436,972	477,924	33,958
Rhode Island	67	3,644	126.3	1,508.2	54	22,511,149	1,885,119	413,899	34,661
South Carolina	189	2,373	81.6	1,969.9	13	10,422,624	431,614	830,121	34,376
South Dakota	63	671	15.5	238.1	11	3,779,873	246,508	354,891	23,145
Tennessee	362	7,192	240.7	3,153.8	20	8,712,204	664,870	438,518	33,465
Texas	1,381	39,591	1,386.8	16,221.8	29	11,746,416	1,004,211	409,735	35,029
Utah	137	1,375	43.9	706.4	10	5,156,328	320,679	513,758	31,951
Vermont	36	591	17.7	315.0	16	8,750,500	490,722	533,025	29,892
Virginia	536	13,049	436.2	4,013.8	24	7,488,461	813,879	307,596	33,431
Washington	446	9,952	347.6	3,431.0	22	7,692,787	779,482	344,753	34,933
West Virginia	77	580	21.1	506.8	8	6,582,338	274,052	873,862	36,383
Wisconsin	383	16,789	511.7	5,509.3	44	14,384,543	1,335,914	328,148	30,476
Wyoming	25	-	(D)	(D)	(D)	(D)	(D)	(D)	(D)

Source: 1992 Economic Census, U.S. Department of Commerce, Washington, D.C. This is the only table that shows revenue data as collected by the Bureau of the Census in an Economic Census. The symbol (D) indicates that data are withheld by the source to avoid disclosure of competitive information. A dash (-) indicates that data are not available or cannot be calculated.

STATE-BY-STATE DATA ON ESTABLISHMENTS, EMPLOYMENT, AND PAYROLL - 1994 AND 1995

State	1994					1995					% Change Empl.
	No. of Estab.	Employ-ment	Pay / Empl.	Payroll ($ mil.)	Pay / Estab.	No. of Estab.	Employ-ment	Pay / Empl.	Payroll ($ mil.)	Pay / Estab.	
Alabama	529	5,888	37,635	218.6	413,306	548	5,738	40,273	229.6	419,051	-2.5
Alaska	52	374	62,150	20.2	387,769	51	410	61,366	23.0	450,157	9.6
Arizona	312	8,208	36,353	290.2	930,138	359	7,830	38,293	284.8	793,379	-4.6
Arkansas	132	1,072	34,776	37.8	286,015	135	1,144	34,706	41.0	303,511	6.7
California	2,266	72,849	41,859	2,939.3	1,297,134	2,229	68,264	44,596	2,965.9	1,330,618	-6.3
Colorado	319	9,172	35,371	319.3	1,000,868	349	8,671	39,726	335.5	961,347	-5.5
Connecticut	353	22,970	49,822	1,060.3	3,003,788	371	22,448	53,425	1,115.5	3,006,717	-2.3
Delaware	45	1,728	33,706	60.1	1,336,067	47	2,025	31,251	65.2	1,388,255	17.2
District of Columbia	21	214	66,131	13.0	619,143	18	221	62,842	14.0	778,778	3.3
Florida	1,280	22,981	36,169	826.7	645,871	1,298	21,277	40,330	850.5	655,240	-7.4
Georgia	536	17,180	38,290	645.9	1,204,959	589	17,466	40,688	700.5	1,189,384	1.7
Hawaii	56	961	41,095	38.7	690,768	56	1,125	51,125	48.7	870,250	17.1
Idaho	94	1,202	32,639	38.9	413,564	96	1,178	36,061	39.8	414,302	-2.0
Illinois	1,042	55,102	43,125	2,156.6	2,069,651	1,145	51,942	47,985	2,390.1	2,087,408	-5.7
Indiana	447	11,698	32,944	377.8	845,154	481	11,898	37,979	425.6	884,909	1.7
Iowa	254	7,685	30,576	241.6	951,303	249	7,757	34,265	257.4	1,033,566	0.9
Kansas	202	6,736	34,268	217.1	1,074,713	196	6,087	39,059	222.8	1,136,878	-9.6
Kentucky	237	2,464	34,666	85.6	361,249	241	2,895	35,088	107.3	445,046	17.5
Louisiana	333	5,272	37,554	186.3	559,345	362	4,889	42,654	203.5	562,215	-7.3
Maine	94	2,169	25,846	57.8	614,723	94	2,161	29,323	75.4	802,149	-0.4
Maryland	427	13,905	42,441	567.5	1,329,005	455	13,729	43,087	596.9	1,311,848	-1.3
Massachusetts	189	16,009	37,864	592.8	3,136,571	180	16,659	42,557	665.1	3,694,789	4.1
Michigan	670	21,015	38,149	770.7	1,150,290	721	20,431	42,869	854.0	1,184,449	-2.8
Minnesota	381	13,948	37,169	495.1	1,299,378	390	13,871	40,598	534.3	1,369,941	-0.6
Mississippi	128	2,594	31,392	81.5	636,656	122	2,363	33,898	79.9	654,779	-8.9
Missouri	425	11,246	33,153	384.0	903,572	426	10,951	34,721	386.9	908,131	-2.6
Montana	66	229	34,463	9.2	139,939	70	254	40,079	10.8	154,257	10.9
Nebraska	133	5,446	31,826	170.6	1,282,474	133	5,147	34,938	179.0	1,346,150	-5.5
Nevada	110	609	41,668	27.0	245,318	124	651	43,951	29.6	238,790	6.9
New Hampshire	100	4,667	38,510	181.4	1,814,020	104	5,026	40,778	186.5	1,793,481	7.7
New Jersey	419	25,005	44,800	1,057.8	2,524,542	417	22,713	49,292	1,058.4	2,538,127	-9.2
New Mexico	104	664	34,175	24.7	237,529	116	709	39,199	28.5	245,474	6.8
New York	1,386	45,096	43,453	1,932.7	1,394,473	1,456	43,121	47,569	2,052.6	1,409,742	-4.4
North Carolina	522	10,581	36,294	393.4	753,632	546	10,418	38,536	401.8	735,910	-1.5
North Dakota	59	551	26,127	15.2	257,627	59	554	27,791	16.1	272,593	0.5
Ohio	902	34,598	36,104	1,237.5	1,371,921	965	31,586	40,352	1,228.0	1,272,548	-8.7
Oklahoma	225	4,678	33,997	156.4	695,098	236	4,340	38,627	162.8	689,657	-7.2
Oregon	306	8,085	34,674	265.0	866,098	322	7,650	38,849	281.3	873,540	-5.4
Pennsylvania	803	33,366	38,020	1,286.2	1,601,706	850	32,940	41,025	1,308.9	1,539,935	-1.3
Rhode Island	72	3,712	36,457	139.1	1,932,194	70	3,693	41,566	144.6	2,065,200	-0.5
South Carolina	206	2,193	39,362	87.7	425,524	215	2,257	43,355	96.2	447,474	2.9
South Dakota	56	620	23,594	16.0	285,804	56	627	28,242	17.6	314,946	1.1
Tennessee	387	8,120	33,162	271.0	700,380	403	7,071	39,441	272.6	676,484	-12.9
Texas	1,526	41,696	36,128	1,522.1	997,439	1,654	41,469	38,124	1,628.2	984,425	-0.5
Utah	147	1,223	34,067	43.4	295,027	163	1,757	36,421	65.6	402,374	43.7
Vermont	45	653	30,322	19.7	437,178	47	627	32,951	22.5	478,000	-4.0
Virginia	549	14,140	34,453	484.9	883,215	588	14,067	37,077	520.4	885,105	-0.5
Washington	463	11,105	41,464	390.2	842,773	467	9,894	44,739	406.8	871,047	-10.9
West Virginia	98	652	40,325	28.0	285,867	94	650	45,791	29.5	313,372	-0.3
Wisconsin	385	17,926	32,166	563.2	1,462,795	395	16,971	35,392	580.5	1,469,519	-5.3
Wyoming	22	111	32,288	3.5	161,318	25	115	39,513	4.0	161,120	3.6

Source: County Business Patterns, U.S. Department of Commerce, Washington, D.C., for 1994 and 1995. Employment shown is for mid-March of the year shown. Payroll per employee is calculated by annualizing 1st Quarter payroll (not shown) and then dividing that value by mid-March employment. Dividing total annual payroll (columns 5 and 10) by employment, therefore, will *not* yield the payroll per employee figure (columns 4 and 9). The symbol (D) indicates that data are withheld by the source to avoid disclosure of competitive information. A dash (-) indicates that data are not available or cannot be calculated.

ESTABLISHMENTS 1995 - STATE AND REGIONAL CONCENTRATION

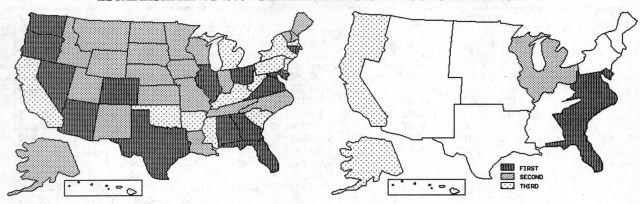

EMPLOYMENT 1995 - STATE AND REGIONAL CONCENTRATION

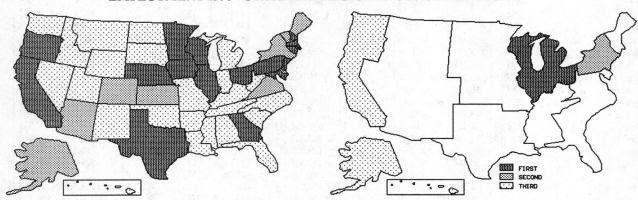

PAYROLL 1995 - STATE AND REGIONAL CONCENTRATION

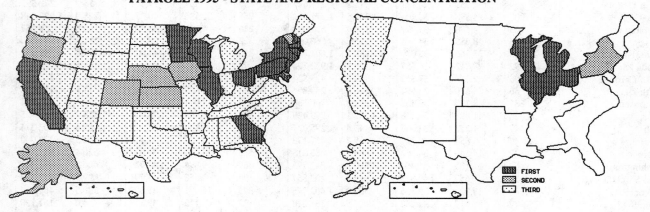

States with the darkest shading indicate those states which have proportionately more establishments, employment, or payrolls than would be indicated by the state's population. States with light shading are states with proportionately fewer establishments, less employment, and lower payrolls than population distribution. States shaded grey are within 15 percent of the state's population proportion in these categories. States for which no data are available are shown as average (grey). *Regions* are shaded to indicate absolute rank in the category. If no data for the category are available, establishment counts are used to shade the regions. Source of the data is the table on the facing page.

LEADING COMPANIES - SIC 6324 - Hospital and Medical Service Plans

Number shown: **97**   Total sales/assets ($ mil): **2,118,491**   Total employment (000): **1,023.9**

Company Name	Address				CEO Name	Phone	Co. Type	Sales/Assets ($ mil)	Empl. (000)
Travelers Group Inc.	388 Greenwich St.	New York	NY	10013	Sanford I. Weill	212-816-8000	P	386,555 TA	68.9
General Electric Capital Services Inc.	260 Long Ridge Rd.	Stamford	CT	06927	Gary C. Wendt	203-357-6978	S	211,730 TA	25.0
American International Group Inc.	70 Pine St.	New York	NY	10270	Maurice R. Greenberg	212-770-7000	P	163,971 TA	40.0
Lincoln National Corp.	PO Box 1110	Fort Wayne	IN	46801	Ian M. Rolland	219-455-2000	P	119,100 TA	10.3
Hartford Financial Services Group Inc.	Hartford Plaza	Hartford	CT	06115	Ramani Ayer	860-547-5000	P	108,840 TA	22.0
General Motors Acceptance Corp.	3044 W. Grand Blvd.	Detroit	MI	48202	J.M. Losh	313-556-5000	S	94,573 TA	17.3
Allstate Insurance Co.	2775 Sanders Rd.	Northbrook	IL	60062	Jerry D. Choate	847-402-5000	S	77,291 TA*	50.0
Loews Corp.	667 Madison Ave.	New York	NY	10021	Laurence A. Tisch	212-545-2000	P	67,683 TA	35.3
American General Corp.	PO Box 3247	Houston	TX	77253	Harold S. Hook	713-522-1111	P.	61,153 TA	12.9
State Farm Mutual Automobile Insurance Co.	1 State Farm Plz.	Bloomington	IL	61710	Edward B. Rust Jr.	309-766-2311	R	54,756 TA	68.0
Liberty Mutual Insurance Co.	175 Berkeley St.	Boston	MA	02117	Gary L. Countryman	617-357-9500	R	50,001 TA	22.0
Transamerica Corp.	600 Montgomery St.	San Francisco	CA	94111	Frank C. Herringer	415-983-4000	P	49,875 TA	10.4
Berkshire Hathaway Inc.	1440 Kiewit Plz.	Omaha	NE	68131	Warren E. Buffett	402-346-1400	P	43,409 TA	24.0
General Re Corp.	PO Box 10351	Stamford	CT	06904	Ronald E. Ferguson	203-328-5000	P	41,459 TA	3.9
SAFECO Corp.	SAFECO Plz.	Seattle	WA	98185	Roger H. Eigsti	206-545-5000	P	29,467 TA	8.0
Employers Reinsurance Corp.	PO Box 2991	Overland Park	KS	66201	Kaj Ahlmann	913-676-5200	S	27,532 TA	2.0
Travelers Property Casualty Corp.	1 Tower Sq.	Hartford	CT	06183	Robert I. Lipp	860-277-0111	P	24,621 TA	24.0
Jefferson-Pilot Corp.	PO Box 21008	Greensboro	NC	27420	David A. Stonecipher	910-691-3691	P	23,131 TA	4.2
National Indemnity Co.	3024 Harney St.	Omaha	NE	68131	Donald F. Wurster	402-536-3000	S	22,045 TA	0.3
St. Paul Companies Inc.	385 Washington St.	St. Paul	MN	55102	Douglas W. Leatherdale	612-310-7911	P	21,501 TA	10.0
Chubb Corp.	PO Box 1615	Warren	NJ	07061	Dean R. O'Hare	908-903-2000	P	19,616 TA	9.7
Allmerica Financial Corp.	440 Lincoln St.	Worcester	MA	01653	John F. O'Brien	508-855-1000	P	18,998 TA	6.8
Xerox Corp.	PO Box 1600	Stamford	CT	06904	Paul A. Allaire	203-968-3000	P	18,200	86.7
Continental Corp.	180 Maiden Ln.	New York	NY	10038	John P. Mascotte	212-440-3980	P	16,221 TA	15.0
Hartford Fire Insurance Co.	Hartford Plz.	Hartford	CT	06115	Donald R. Frahm	203-547-5000	S	15,406 TA	19.7
USF and G Corp.	PO Box 1138	Baltimore	MD	21203	Norman P. Blake Jr.	410-547-3000	P	14,407 TA	6.1
American Financial Corp.	1 E. 4th St.	Cincinnati	OH	45202	Carl H. Lindner	513-579-2121	S	12,414 TA	9.0
Reliance Group Holdings Inc.	55 East 52nd St.	New York	NY	10055	Saul P. Steinberg	212-909-1100	P	11,332 TA	1.2
Deere and Co.	One John Deere Place	Moline	IL	61265	Hans W. Becherer	309-765-8000	P	11,082	34.4
Aetna Casualty and Surety Co.	151 Farmington Ave.	Hartford	CT	06156	Ronald E. Compton	860-273-0123	S	10,489 TA	10.0
Torchmark Corp.	2001 3rd Ave. S.	Birmingham	AL	35233	R.K. Richey	205-325-4200	P	9,800 TA	6.3
Talegen Holdings Inc.	1011 Western Ave.	Seattle	WA	98104	Joseph W. Brown Jr.	206-654-2600	S	8,930 TA*	11.0
Halliburton Co.	500 N. Akard St.	Dallas	TX	75201	Richard B. Cheney	214-978-2600	P	8,819	70.8
American States Financial Corp.	500 N. Meridian St.	Indianapolis	IN	46204	William J. Lawson	317-262-6262	P	8,800 TA	3.5

Company type codes: P - Public, R - Private, S - Subsidiary, D - Division, J - Joint Venture, A - Affiliate, G - Group. If the dollar values shown are not sales, the following codes apply: TA - Total Assets; OR - Operating Revenues; GB - Gross Billings. * - estimated dollar value. < - less than. *na* - not available.

Continued on next page.

LEADING COMPANIES - SIC 6324 - Hospital and Medical Service Plans

Continued

Company Name	Address				CEO Name	Phone	Co. Type	Sales/Assets ($ mil)	Empl. (000)
ING North America Insurance Corp.	5780 Powers Ferry Rd.	Atlanta	GA	30327	Joseph H. Youngs	770-980-3300	S	8,569 TA	3.8
Allianz of America Inc.	777 San Marin Dr.	Novato	CA	94998	Herbert F. Hansmeyer	415-899-2000	S	8,350 TA*	9.0
American National Insurance Co.	1 Moody Plz.	Galveston	TX	77550	Robert L. Moody	409-763-4661	P	7,988 TA	5.0
American Re-Insurance Co.	555 College Rd. E.	Princeton	NJ	08543	Paul H. Inderbitzin	609-243-4200	S	7,814 TA	1.3
Government Employees Insurance Co.	1 Geico Plz.	Washington	DC	20076	Olza M. Nicely	301-986-3000	S	7,700 TA	11.5
Progressive Corp.	6300 Wilson Mills Rd.	Mayfield Village	OH	44143	Peter B. Lewis	440-461-5000	P	7,560 TA	15.0
Mutual of Omaha Insurance Co.	Mutual of Omaha Plz.	Omaha	NE	68175	Thomas J. Skutt	402-342-7600	R	7,543 TA	8.0
Farmers Insurance Exchange	PO Box 2478	Los Angeles	CA	90051	Martin D. Feinstein	213-932-3200	S	7,205 TA*	17.5
State Compensation Insurance Fund	PO Box 420807	San Francisco	CA	94142	Kenneth C. Bollier	415-565-1234	R	7,175 TA*	6.5
Royal and SunAlliance USA Inc.	PO Box 1000	Charlotte	NC	28201	Terry Broderick	704-522-2000	S	7,000 TA	5.0
Old Republic International Corp.	307 N. Michigan Ave.	Chicago	IL	60601	A.C. Zucaro	312-346-8100	P	6,923 TA	5.9
Fremont Compensation Insurance Co.	100 California St.	San Francisco	CA	94111	James Little	415-362-3333	S	6,091 TA	2.8
Fremont General Corp.	2020 Santa Monica Blvd.	Santa Monica	CA	90404	James A. McIntyre	310-315-5500	P	6,091 TA	2.8
Everest Reinsurance Co.	477 Martinsville Rd. PO Box 83	Liberty Corner	NJ	07938	Thomas J. Gallagher	908-604-3000	S	5,538 TA	0.4
Ingram Industries Inc.	PO Box 23049	Nashville	TN	37202	Martha Ingram	615-298-8200	R	5,500	5.0
Utica Mutual Insurance Co.	180 Genesee St.	New Hartford	NY	13413	W. Craig Heston	315-734-2000	R	5,500 TA	1.4
Leucadia National Corp.	315 Park Ave. S.	New York	NY	10010	Joseph S. Steinberg	212-460-1900	P	5,194 TA	3.9
Hanover Insurance Co.	100 North Pkwy.	Worcester	MA	01605	John F. O'Brien	508-853-7200	S	5,100 TA	5.0
Farmers Group Inc.	4680 Wilshire Blvd.	Los Angeles	CA	90010	Martin D. Feinstein	213-932-3200	S	5,050 TA*	16.7
Everest Reinsurance Holdings Inc.	Three Gateway Center	Newark	NJ	07102	Joseph V. Taranto	201-802-8000	P	5,039 TA	0.4
Anthem Insurance Companies Inc.	120 Monument Cir.	Indianapolis	IN	46204	L. Ben Lytle	317-488-6000	R	5,000 TA	14.0
Unitrin Inc.	1 E. Wacker Dr.	Chicago	IL	60601	Richard C. Vie	312-661-4600	P	4,921 TA	6.9
Transatlantic Holdings Inc.	80 Pine St.	New York	NY	10005	Robert F. Orlich	212-770-2162	P	4,835 TA	0.4
PennCorp Financial Group Inc.	2610 Wycliff Rd.	Raleigh	NC	27607	David J. Stone	212-832-0700	P	4,834 TA	1.4
Employers Insurance of Wausau A Mutual Co.	PO Box 8017	Wausau	WI	54402	Dwight Davis	715-845-5211	R	4,700 TA	5.0
W.R. Berkley Corp.	PO Box 2518	Greenwich	CT	06836	William R. Berkley	203-629-3000	P	4,599 TA	3.5
Home Insurance Co.	59 Maiden Ln.	New York	NY	10038	Lars-Goran Nilsson	212-530-7000	S	4,258 TA	5.5
Horace Mann Educators Corp.	1 Horace Mann Plz.	Springfield	IL	62715	Paul J. Kardos	217-789-2500	P	4,131 TA	2.7
American Manufacturers Mutual Insurance Co.	1 Kemper Dr.	Long Grove	IL	60049	David B. Mathis	847-320-2000	S	3,900 TA	10.0

Company type codes: P - Public, R - Private, S - Subsidiary, D - Division, J - Joint Venture, A - Affiliate, G - Group. If the dollar values shown are not sales, the following codes apply: TA - Total Assets; OR - Operating Revenues; GB - Gross Billings. * - estimated dollar value. < - less than. *na* - not available.

Continued on next page.

LEADING COMPANIES - SIC 6324 - Hospital and Medical Service Plans
Continued

Company Name	Address				CEO Name	Phone	Co. Type	Sales/Assets ($ mil)	Empl. (000)
Orion Capital Corp.	9 Farm Springs Rd	Farmington	CT	06032	W. Marston Becker	860-674-6600	P	3,884 TA	3.3
Ohio Casualty Corp.	136 N. 3rd St.	Hamilton	OH	45025	Lauren N. Patch	513-867-3000	P	3,779 TA	3.4
Great American Insurance Co.	580 Walnut St.	Cincinnati	OH	45202	Carl H. Linder III	513-369-5000	S	3,765 TA	3.4
Cuna Mutual Insurance Society	PO Box 391	Madison	WI	53701	Michael Kitchen	608-238-5851	R	3,600 TA	5.0
Cincinnati Financial Corp.	PO Box 145496	Cincinnati	OH	45250	Robert B. Morgan	513-870-2000	P	3,311 TA	2.3
General Accident Insurance Company of America	PO Box 1109	Philadelphia	PA	19105	Walter E. Farnam	215-625-1000	S	3,257 TA	5.6
FBL Financial Group Inc.	5400 University Ave.	West Des Moines	IA	50266	Thomas R. Gibson	515-225-5400	P	3,091 TA	1.0
Sentry Insurance A Mutual Co.	1800 North Point Dr.	Stevens Point	WI	54481	Dale R. Schuh	715-346-6000	R	3,032 TA	4.3
NAC Re Corp.	PO Box 2568	Greenwich	CT	06836	Ronald L. Bornhuetter	203-622-5200	P	3,000 TA	0.3
Prudential Property and Casualty Insurance Co.	23 Main St.	Holmdel	NJ	07733	Tom Crawford	732-946-5000	S	2,747 TA*	5.2
Lumbermens Mutual Casualty Co.	1 Kemper Dr.	Long Grove	IL	60049	Gerald L. Maatman	708-320-2000	R	2,632 TA	7.0
Commercial Union Insurance Cos.	1 Beacon St.	Boston	MA	02108	Ken J. Duffy	617-725-6000	S	2,580 TA	4.0
Continental Insurance Co.	180 Maiden Ln.	New York	NY	10038	John P. Mascotte	212-440-3000	S	2,535 TA	24.7
New Jersey Manufacturers Insurance Co.	301 Sullivan Way	West Trenton	NJ	08628	Anthony G. Dickson	609-883-1300	R	2,489 TA	1.7
Highlands Insurance Group Inc.	10370 Richmond Ave.	Houston	TX	77042	Richard M. Haverland	713-952-9555	P	2,367 TA	1.1
Selective Insurance Group Inc.	40 Wantage Ave.	Branchville	NJ	07890	James W. Entringer	201-948-3000	P	2,306 TA	1.9
Zurich Reinsurance Centre Holdings Inc.	1 Chase Manhattan Plz.	New York	NY	10005	Richard E. Smith	212-898-5000	P	2,243 TA	0.2
Federated Mutual Insurance Co.	121 E. Park Sq.	Owatonna	MN	55060	Charles I. Buxton II	507-455-5200	R	2,194 TA	2.7
Nationwide Corp.	1 Nationwide Plz.	Columbus	OH	43216	D. Richard McFerson	614-249-7111	S	2,140 TA	4.4
Amica Mutual Insurance Co.	PO Box 6008	Providence	RI	02940	Thomas A. Taylor	401-334-6000	R	2,093 TA*	3.0
Allendale Mutual Insurance Co.	PO Box 7500	Johnston	RI	02919	Shivan S. Subramaniam	401-275-3000	R	1,912 TA	1.0
Markel Corp.	PO Box 2009	Glen Allen	VA	23058	Alan I. Kirshner	804-747-0136	P	1,870 TA	0.8
Argonaut Group Inc.	1800 Avenue of the Stars	Los Angeles	CA	90067	Charles E. Rinsch	310-553-0561	P	1,861 TA	0.6
Wesco Financial Corp.	301 E. Colorado Blvd.	Pasadena	CA	91101	Charles T. Munger	818-585-6700	P	1,818 TA	0.3
Harleysville Group Inc.	355 Maple Ave.	Harleysville	PA	19438	Walter R. Bateman II	215-256-5000	P	1,801 TA	2.7
Argonaut Insurance Co.	250 Middlefield Rd.	Menlo Park	CA	94025	Charles Rinsch	650-326-0900	S	1,781 TA*	0.5
Mercury General Corp.	4484 Wilshire Blvd.	Los Angeles	CA	90010	George Joseph	213-937-1060	P	1,726 TA	2.1
National Re Corp.	PO Box 10167	Stamford	CT	06904	William D. Warren	203-329-7700	P	1,725 TA	0.3
Citizens Insurance Company of America	645 W. Grand River Ave.	Howell	MI	48843	James R. McAuliffe	517-546-2160	S	1,715 TA	1.4

Company type codes: P - Public, R - Private, S - Subsidiary, D - Division, J - Joint Venture, A - Affiliate, G - Group. If the dollar values shown are not sales, the following codes apply: TA - Total Assets; OR - Operating Revenues; GB - Gross Billings. * - estimated dollar value. < - less than. na - not available.

Continued on next page.

LEADING COMPANIES - SIC 6324 - Hospital and Medical Service Plans

Continued

Company Name	Address				CEO Name	Phone	Co. Type	Sales/Assets ($ mil)	Empl. (000)
Commerce Group Inc.	211 Main St.	Webster	MA	01570	Arthur J. Remillard Jr.	508-943-9000	P	1,712 TA	1.4
Vesta Insurance Group Inc.	P.O .Box 43360	Birmingham	AL	35243	Robert Y. Huffman	205-970-7000	P	1,676 TA	0.7
Providian Corp.	PO Box 32830	Louisville	KY	40232	Don Shepherd	502-560-2000	S	1,559 TA*	0.5
Underwriters Reinsurance Co.	26050 Mureau Rd.	Calabassass	CA	91302	Steven H. Newman	818-878-9500	S	1,496 TA	0.3
20th Century Insurance Co.	PO Box 2000	Woodland Hills	CA	91367	William L. Mellick	818-704-3700	S	1,483 TA	2.2

Source: Ward's Business Directory of U.S. Private and Public Companies, 1996. Company type codes: P - Public, R - Private, S - Subsidiary, D - Division, J - Joint Venture, A - Affiliate, G - Group. If the dollar values shown are not sales, the following codes apply: TA - Total Assets; OR - Operating Revenues; GB - Gross Billings. * - estimated dollar value. < - less than; na - not available.

SIC 6350

SURETY INSURANCE

SIC 6350 includes organizations that provide insurance for financial responsibility such as bonding, fidelity, liability, and surety insurance. Specific categories include assessment associations for surety and fidelity insurance; bonding for guaranteeing job completion; bonding of employees; bonding for fidelity or surety, credit and other financial responsibility insurance; fidelity insurance; financial responsibility insurance; liability insurance; mortgage guaranty insurance; reciprocal interinsurance exchanges for these categories; surety insurance; and warranty insurance on homes.

ESTABLISHMENTS, EMPLOYMENT, AND PAYROLL

	1990	1991 Value	%	1992 Value	%	1993 Value	%	1994 Value	%	1995 Value	%	% change 90-95
All Establishments	586	777	32.6	801	3.1	594	-25.8	583	-1.9	595	2.1	1.5
Mid-March Employment	14,629	18,636	27.4	17,381	-6.7	11,918	-31.4	11,114	-6.7	10,520	-5.3	-28.1
1st Quarter Wages (annualized - $ mil.)	445.7	716.9	60.9	709.2	-1.1	545.7	-23.1	541.3	-0.8	680.5	25.7	52.7
Payroll per Emp. 1st Q. (annualized)	30,466	38,470	26.3	40,801	6.1	45,785	12.2	48,703	6.4	64,686	32.8	112.3
Annual Payroll ($ mil.)	455.6	628.6	38.0	662.6	5.4	543.4	-18.0	493.2	-9.2	529.7	7.4	16.3
Establishments - 1-4 Emp. Number	251	395	57.4	414	4.8	304	-26.6	(D)	-	324	-	29.1
Mid-March Employment	446	(D)	-	838	-	520	-37.9	(D)	-	495	-	11.0
1st Quarter Wages (annualized - $ mil.)	12.5	(D)	-	28.0	-	19.8	-29.2	(D)	-	27.2	-	117.6
Payroll per Emp. 1st Q. (annualized)	27,973	(D)	-	33,470	-	38,169	14.0	(D)	-	54,853	-	96.1
Annual Payroll ($ mil.)	13.9	(D)	-	34.4	-	23.1	-32.9	(D)	-	23.1	-	66.1
Establishments - 5-9 Emp. Number	103	129	25.2	153	18.6	112	-26.8	122	8.9	117	-4.1	13.6
Mid-March Employment	659	(D)	-	988	-	718	-27.3	774	7.8	759	-1.9	15.2
1st Quarter Wages (annualized - $ mil.)	21.7	(D)	-	35.9	-	26.8	-25.2	31.8	18.6	37.3	17.2	71.8
Payroll per Emp. 1st Q. (annualized)	32,923	(D)	-	36,287	-	37,354	2.9	41,090	10.0	49,123	19.5	49.2
Annual Payroll ($ mil.)	19.8	(D)	-	36.2	-	27.6	-23.7	30.1	8.9	32.8	9.2	66.1
Establishments - 10-19 Emp. Number	81	92	13.6	95	3.3	61	-35.8	70	14.8	55	-21.4	-32.1
Mid-March Employment	1,132	1,254	10.8	1,291	3.0	810	-37.3	961	18.6	740	-23.0	-34.6
1st Quarter Wages (annualized - $ mil.)	34.0	40.2	18.1	44.0	9.4	31.4	-28.5	41.8	32.9	39.1	-6.3	15.0
Payroll per Emp. 1st Q. (annualized)	30,042	32,041	6.7	34,045	6.3	38,810	14.0	43,467	12.0	52,865	21.6	76.0
Annual Payroll ($ mil.)	33.9	42.1	24.1	46.3	10.1	33.4	-27.9	39.6	18.5	34.3	-13.3	1.2
Establishments - 20-49 Emp. Number	85	110	29.4	95	-13.6	75	-21.1	62	-17.3	61	-1.6	-28.2
Mid-March Employment	2,662	3,591	34.9	3,100	-13.7	2,431	-21.6	1,971	-18.9	1,868	-5.2	-29.8
1st Quarter Wages (annualized - $ mil.)	76.5	145.9	90.6	132.3	-9.3	110.1	-16.8	98.1	-10.9	104.5	6.6	36.6
Payroll per Emp. 1st Q. (annualized)	28,739	40,616	41.3	42,679	5.1	45,270	6.1	49,755	9.9	55,951	12.5	94.7
Annual Payroll ($ mil.)	75.1	138.8	84.8	121.0	-12.8	105.3	-13.0	93.5	-11.2	95.7	2.4	27.4
Establishments - 50-99 Emp. Number	34	30	-11.8	23	-23.3	21	-8.7	20	-4.8	16	-20.0	-52.9
Mid-March Employment	2,423	1,989	-17.9	1,515	-23.8	1,396	-7.9	1,317	-5.7	1,069	-18.8	-55.9
1st Quarter Wages (annualized - $ mil.)	75.5	105.2	39.3	79.5	-24.4	56.9	-28.4	56.7	-0.4	43.5	-23.4	-42.5
Payroll per Emp. 1st Q. (annualized)	31,165	52,895	69.7	52,491	-0.8	40,774	-22.3	43,065	5.6	40,651	-5.6	30.4
Annual Payroll ($ mil.)	73.6	92.4	25.5	69.7	-24.5	54.2	-22.3	52.8	-2.5	39.5	-25.1	-46.3
Establishments - 100-249 Emp. Number	23	11	-52.2	14	27.3	12	-14.3	12	-	13	8.3	-43.5
Mid-March Employment	3,248	1,615	-50.3	2,103	30.2	1,925	-8.5	2,072	7.6	2,160	4.2	-33.5
1st Quarter Wages (annualized - $ mil.)	107.8	86.3	-19.9	140.7	63.0	128.4	-8.7	162.5	26.6	273.4	68.2	153.6
Payroll per Emp. 1st Q. (annualized)	33,197	53,446	61.0	66,889	25.2	66,697	-0.3	78,450	17.6	126,581	61.4	281.3
Annual Payroll ($ mil.)	114.7	86.5	-24.6	129.3	49.4	133.7	3.4	130.7	-2.2	166.1	27.1	44.8
Establishments - 250-499 Emp. Number	6	7	16.7	(D)	-	6	-	6	-	9	50.0	50.0
Mid-March Employment	1,908	(D)	-	(D)	-	2,127	-	2,228	4.7	3,429	53.9	79.7
1st Quarter Wages (annualized - $ mil.)	50.8	(D)	-	(D)	-	94.1	-	75.9	-19.3	155.6	105.0	206.5
Payroll per Emp. 1st Q. (annualized)	26,602	(D)	-	(D)	-	44,233	-	34,059	-23.0	45,364	33.2	70.5
Annual Payroll ($ mil.)	53.0	(D)	-	(D)	-	88.6	-	74.7	-15.7	138.1	85.0	160.5
Establishments - 500-999 Emp. Number	3	2	-33.3	(D)	-	3	-	(D)	-	-	-	-
Mid-March Employment	2,151	(D)	-	(D)	-	1,991	-	(D)	-	-	-	-
1st Quarter Wages (annualized - $ mil.)	66.9	(D)	-	(D)	-	78.1	-	(D)	-	-	-	-
Payroll per Emp. 1st Q. (annualized)	31,104	(D)	-	(D)	-	39,231	-	(D)	-	-	-	-
Annual Payroll ($ mil.)	71.5	(D)	-	(D)	-	77.6	-	(D)	-	-	-	-
Estab. - 1000 or More Emp. Number	-	1		(D)	-	-	-	-	-	-	-	-
Mid-March Employment	-	(D)	-	(D)	-	-	-	-	-	-	-	-
1st Quarter Wages (annualized - $ mil.)	-	(D)	-	(D)	-	-	-	-	-	-	-	-
Payroll per Emp. 1st Q. (annualized)	(D)	(D)	-	(D)	-	-	-	-	-	-	-	-
Annual Payroll ($ mil.)	-	(D)	-	(D)	-	-	-	-	-	-	-	-

Source: County Business Patterns, U.S. Department of Commerce, Washington, D.C., for 1990 through 1995. Payroll per employee is calculated using mid-March employment and 1st Quarter wages, annualized. Annual payroll, also shown, may not equal the annualized 1st Quarter wages. Columns headed by a percent sign (%) indicate change from the previous year. *na* stands for not available. The symbol (D) indicates that data are withheld by the source to avoid disclosure of competitive information. A dash (-) indicates that data are not available or cannot be calculated.

ESTABLISHMENTS
Number

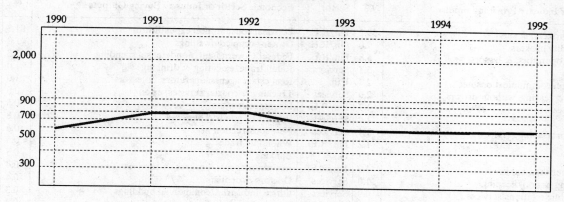

MID-MARCH EMPLOYMENT
Number

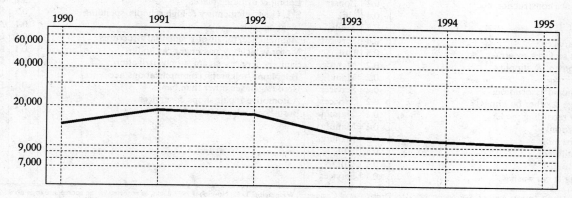

ANNUAL PAYROLL
$ million

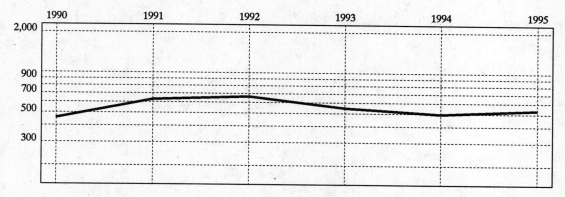

INPUTS AND OUTPUTS FOR INSURANCE CARRIERS - SIC GROUP 63

Economic Sector or Industry Providing Inputs	%	Sector	Economic Sector or Industry Buying Outputs	%	Sector
Insurance agents, brokers, & services	59.2	Fin/R.E.	Personal consumption expenditures	81.3	
Security & commodity brokers	7.0	Fin/R.E.	Owner-occupied dwellings	1.8	Fin/R.E.
Real estate agents, operators, & lessors	5.8	Fin/R.E.	Federal Government, nondefense, spending	1.3	Gov't
Legal services	5.1	Services	Retail trade, ex eating & drinking	1.0	Trade
Telephone/telegraph communications nec	2.7	Util.	Real estate agents, operators, & lessors	1.0	Fin/R.E.
Automotive rental & leasing, without drivers	2.0	Services	Trucking & courier services, ex air	0.8	Util.
Banking	1.7	Fin/R.E.	Insurance carriers	0.8	Fin/R.E.
Advertising	1.4	Services	Exports of goods & services	0.8	Foreign
Computer & data processing services	1.4	Services	New construction nec	0.6	Constr.
Insurance carriers	1.2	Fin/R.E.	Wholesale trade	0.5	Trade
U.S. Postal Service	1.1	Gov't	Banking	0.5	Fin/R.E.
Credit agencies other than banks	1.0	Fin/R.E.	Insurance agents, brokers, & services	0.4	Fin/R.E.
Accounting, auditing & bookkeeping	1.0	Services	Doctors & dentists	0.4	Services
Management & public relations services	0.9	Services	Office, industrial/commercial buildings	0.3	Constr.
Commercial printing	0.8	Manufg.	Repair & maintenance construction nec	0.3	Constr.
Business services nec	0.8	Services	Residential 1 unit structures, nonfarm	0.3	Constr.
Eating & drinking places	0.6	Services	Hospitals	0.3	Services
Hotels	0.5	Services	Highways, bridges, horizontal construction	0.2	Constr.
Miscellaneous equipment rental & leasing	0.5	Services	Electric services (utilities)	0.2	Util.
Repair & maintenance construction nec	0.4	Constr.	Eating & drinking places	0.2	Services
Air transportation	0.4	Util.	S/L Govt., elementary & high schools, spending	0.2	S/L Govt
Wholesale trade	0.4	Trade	Meat animals	0.1	Agric.
Personnel supply services	0.4	Services	Maintenance/repair of residential structures	0.1	Constr.
Trucking & courier services, ex air	0.3	Util.	Motor vehicles & passenger car bodies	0.1	Manufg.
Photographic equipment & supplies	0.2	Manufg.	Sanitary services, steam supply, irrigation	0.1	Util.
Tires & inner tubes	0.2	Manufg.	Telephone/telegraph communications nec	0.1	Util.
Business & professional associations	0.2	Services	Credit agencies other than banks	0.1	Fin/R.E.
Services to dwellings & other buildings	0.2	Services	Automotive repair shops & services	0.1	Services
Magnetic & optical recording media	0.1	Manufg.	Business services nec	0.1	Services
Manifold business forms	0.1	Manufg.			
Paper & paperboard mills	0.1	Manufg.			
Electric services (utilities)	0.1	Util.			
Local & suburban transit	0.1	Util.			
Automobile parking & car washes	0.1	Services			

Source: Benchmark Input-Output Accounts for the U.S. Economy, 1992, U.S. Department of Commerce, Washington, D.C., November 1997. Data, as reported in the source, are organized by the 1987 SIC structure in use in 1992.

OCCUPATIONS EMPLOYED BY PENSION FUNDS AND INSURANCE, NEC

Occupation	% of Total 1996	Change to 2006	Occupation	% of Total 1996	Change to 2006
Title examiners & searchers	10.6	8.8	Underwriters	2.7	44.7
General office clerks	8.4	17.0	Sales & related workers nec	2.7	49.6
Secretaries, except legal & medical	6.9	7.9	Insurance sales workers	2.6	26.9
General managers & top executives	6.3	31.8	Management support workers nec	2.2	36.0
Clerical supervisors & managers	4.9	36.0	Financial managers	2.1	36.0
Bookkeeping, accounting, & auditing clerks	4.6	8.8	File clerks	2.0	-2.9
Legal assistants & clerks nec	4.3	104.0	Accountants & auditors	1.8	25.9
Typists, including word processing	4.0	-11.6	Computer programmers	1.8	12.0
Insurance policy processing clerks	3.2	8.8	Messengers	1.3	8.8
Receptionists & information clerks	3.0	36.0	Marketing & sales worker supervisors	1.3	36.1
Insurance claims clerks	3.0	38.9	Claims examiners, property & casualty	1.3	37.0
Loan & credit clerks	2.9	37.3	Data entry keyers, except composing	1.2	8.8
Insurance adjusters, examiners, investigators	2.8	39.7	Managers & administrators nec	1.0	34.7

Sources: Industry-Occupation Matrix, Bureau of Labor Statistics. These data relate to one or more 3-digit SIC industry groups rather than to a single 4-digit SIC. The change reported for each occupation to the year 2005 is a percent of growth or decline as estimated by the Bureau of Labor Statistics. The abbreviation *nec* stands for not elsewhere classified.

U.S. AND STATE DATA ON INDUSTRY REVENUES AND OTHER ACCOUNTS FOR 1992

State	No. of Estab.	Employ- ment	Payroll ($ mil.)	Revenues ($ mil.)	Empl./ Estab.	Revenue/ Estab. ($)	Payroll/ Estab. ($)	Revenue/ Empl. ($)	Payroll/ Empl. ($)
UNITED STATES	548	11,167	518.9	4,005.4	20	7,309,053	946,883	358,678	46,467
Alabama	7	-	(D)	(D)	(D)	(D)	(D)	(D)	(D)
Alaska	1	-	(D)	(D)	(D)	(D)	(D)	(D)	(D)
Arizona	15	123	5.5	54.3	8	3,621,067	369,933	441,593	45,114
Arkansas	3	-	(D)	(D)	(D)	(D)	(D)	(D)	(D)
California	97	1,857	82.2	574.7	19	5,925,052	846,969	309,494	44,241
Colorado	12	65	2.0	20.3	5	1,690,000	162,667	312,000	30,031
Connecticut	4	-	(D)	(D)	(D)	(D)	(D)	(D)	(D)
District of Columbia	2	-	(D)	(D)	(D)	(D)	(D)	(D)	(D)
Florida	35	414	12.0	200.0	12	5,714,857	343,657	483,140	29,053
Georgia	17	165	6.2	44.9	10	2,641,118	363,882	272,115	37,491
Hawaii	1	-	(D)	(D)	(D)	(D)	(D)	(D)	(D)
Idaho	1	-	(D)	(D)	(D)	(D)	(D)	(D)	(D)
Illinois	22	488	25.1	291.4	22	13,243,182	1,140,273	597,029	51,406
Indiana	8	42	1.4	13.5	5	1,686,375	179,000	321,214	34,095
Iowa	6	-	(D)	(D)	(D)	(D)	(D)	(D)	(D)
Kansas	9	103	3.4	27.2	11	3,024,778	375,333	264,301	32,796
Kentucky	3	55	1.8	8.6	18	2,875,333	591,667	156,836	32,273
Louisiana	5	-	(D)	(D)	(D)	(D)	(D)	(D)	(D)
Maine	1	-	(D)	(D)	(D)	(D)	(D)	(D)	(D)
Maryland	18	887	34.9	153.8	49	8,546,556	1,936,278	173,436	39,293
Massachusetts	17	-	(D)	(D)	(D)	(D)	(D)	(D)	(D)
Michigan	17	74	2.4	38.1	4	2,243,412	140,412	515,378	32,257
Minnesota	12	-	(D)	(D)	(D)	(D)	(D)	(D)	(D)
Mississippi	1	-	(D)	(D)	(D)	(D)	(D)	(D)	(D)
Missouri	7	60	1.9	20.3	9	2,897,714	274,000	338,067	31,967
Montana	1	-	(D)	(D)	(D)	(D)	(D)	(D)	(D)
Nebraska	5	-	(D)	(D)	(D)	(D)	(D)	(D)	(D)
Nevada	3	-	(D)	(D)	(D)	(D)	(D)	(D)	(D)
New Hampshire	1	-	(D)	(D)	(D)	(D)	(D)	(D)	(D)
New Jersey	20	797	35.5	267.4	40	13,369,200	1,777,150	335,488	44,596
New Mexico	1	-	(D)	(D)	(D)	(D)	(D)	(D)	(D)
New York	39	1,089	117.0	805.5	28	20,654,718	3,000,538	739,701	107,457
North Carolina	17	949	42.0	508.2	56	29,895,941	2,470,294	535,544	44,252
Ohio	17	78	2.6	25.9	5	1,522,412	153,588	331,808	33,474
Oklahoma	2	-	(D)	(D)	(D)	(D)	(D)	(D)	(D)
Oregon	4	21	1.1	6.1	5	1,518,500	271,750	289,238	51,762
Pennsylvania	26	223	12.0	213.5	9	8,211,000	463,038	957,336	53,987
South Carolina	4	8	0.1	1.1	2	278,750	24,000	139,375	12,000
South Dakota	2	-	(D)	(D)	(D)	(D)	(D)	(D)	(D)
Tennessee	9	47	1.5	12.4	5	1,377,556	172,222	263,787	32,979
Texas	37	467	15.6	132.5	13	3,580,027	422,108	283,642	33,443
Utah	4	-	(D)	(D)	(D)	(D)	(D)	(D)	(D)
Virginia	11	246	8.8	74.5	22	6,776,000	799,636	302,992	35,756
Washington	9	113	4.8	32.7	13	3,638,222	535,556	289,770	42,655
Wisconsin	13	981	40.5	60.0	75	4,613,000	3,116,846	61,130	41,304
Wyoming	2	-	(D)	(D)	(D)	(D)	(D)	(D)	(D)

Source: 1992 Economic Census, U.S. Department of Commerce, Washington, D.C. This is the only table that shows revenue data as collected by the Bureau of the Census in an Economic Census. The symbol (D) indicates that data are withheld by the source to avoid disclosure of competitive information. A dash (-) indicates that data are not available or cannot be calculated.

STATE-BY-STATE DATA ON ESTABLISHMENTS, EMPLOYMENT, AND PAYROLL - 1994 AND 1995

State	1994					1995					% Change Empl.
	No. of Estab.	Employ-ment	Pay / Empl.	Payroll ($ mil.)	Pay / Estab.	No. of Estab.	Employ-ment	Pay / Empl.	Payroll ($ mil.)	Pay / Estab.	
Alabama	9	(D)	-	(D)	-	10	135	47,556	6.1	605,000	-
Arizona	19	133	44,481	4.7	247,684	16	65	37,969	2.1	129,125	-51.1
Arkansas	2	(D)	-	(D)	-	2	(D)	-	(D)	-	-
California	94	1,698	39,847	68.1	724,298	82	1,570	47,366	69.0	841,073	-7.5
Colorado	17	78	45,282	3.0	173,588	20	125	52,160	5.8	291,650	60.3
Connecticut	6	(D)	-	(D)	-	6	(D)	-	(D)	-	-
Delaware	(D)	(D)	(D)	(D)	(D)	1	(D)	-	(D)	-	-
District of Columbia	3	(D)	-	(D)	-	3	(D)	-	(D)	-	-
Florida	33	321	36,150	11.2	339,970	36	313	38,492	11.7	324,389	-2.5
Georgia	16	157	47,414	7.6	475,437	20	199	53,186	9.5	474,550	26.8
Hawaii	2	(D)	-	(D)	-	2	(D)	-	(D)	-	-
Idaho	(D)	(D)	(D)	(D)	(D)	1	(D)	-	(D)	-	-
Illinois	23	304	53,132	15.5	673,870	28	273	72,908	16.9	602,786	-10.2
Indiana	8	36	40,444	2.0	245,375	7	(D)	-	(D)	-	-
Iowa	8	464	24,000	10.1	1,266,750	8	501	23,257	11.1	1,383,750	8.0
Kansas	9	116	36,552	4.6	513,000	9	96	46,542	3.6	402,222	-17.2
Kentucky	3	68	28,471	2.3	756,333	4	70	32,114	2.5	627,000	2.9
Louisiana	6	121	44,000	5.3	876,000	5	(D)	-	(D)	-	-
Maine	1	(D)	-	(D)	-	2	(D)	-	(D)	-	-
Maryland	20	855	48,122	37.2	1,861,000	22	772	55,891	37.4	1,701,545	-9.7
Massachusetts	12	118	43,424	4.9	410,583	13	103	59,340	5.4	411,692	-12.7
Michigan	17	74	35,568	2.5	148,353	19	66	41,333	3.2	170,105	-10.8
Minnesota	12	51	30,118	1.7	138,750	11	40	45,500	1.9	168,818	-21.6
Mississippi	3	(D)	-	(D)	-	3	(D)	-	(D)	-	-
Missouri	14	109	42,936	3.6	259,500	15	75	42,453	3.0	202,267	-31.2
Montana	1	(D)	-	(D)	-	1	(D)	-	(D)	-	-
Nebraska	4	(D)	-	(D)	-	4	(D)	-	(D)	-	-
Nevada	7	(D)	-	(D)	-	7	(D)	-	(D)	-	-
New Hampshire	1	(D)	-	(D)	-	(D)	(D)	(D)	(D)	(D)	-
New Jersey	18	886	46,144	36.4	2,021,889	17	811	47,970	37.2	2,188,941	-8.5
New Mexico	1	(D)	-	(D)	-	1	(D)	-	(D)	-	-
New York	42	896	120,750	80.6	1,917,976	36	854	254,632	107.9	2,998,028	-4.7
North Carolina	22	1,713	46,183	70.1	3,187,455	24	1,339	62,019	68.7	2,860,667	-21.8
North Dakota	1	(D)	-	(D)	-	1	(D)	-	(D)	-	-
Ohio	12	80	45,900	3.7	307,833	14	58	62,000	3.3	236,571	-27.5
Oklahoma	1	(D)	-	(D)	-	1	(D)	-	(D)	-	-
Oregon	4	(D)	-	(D)	-	5	(D)	-	(D)	-	-
Pennsylvania	29	187	41,904	8.0	276,862	29	151	50,013	7.3	251,207	-19.3
South Carolina	8	(D)	-	(D)	-	5	(D)	-	(D)	-	-
South Dakota	2	(D)	-	(D)	-	2	(D)	-	(D)	-	-
Tennessee	13	237	46,295	11.2	859,769	17	206	54,485	10.7	630,294	-13.1
Texas	39	410	43,063	17.5	447,872	38	462	44,026	18.0	472,579	12.7
Utah	4	(D)	-	(D)	-	6	(D)	-	(D)	-	-
Vermont	(D)	(D)	(D)	(D)	(D)	1	(D)	-	(D)	-	-
Virginia	12	268	45,776	10.7	889,500	13	174	42,736	6.7	512,538	-35.1
Washington	10	149	44,161	6.9	689,500	12	(D)	-	(D)	-	-
West Virginia	1	(D)	-	(D)	-	1	(D)	-	(D)	-	-
Wisconsin	13	680	46,941	33.1	2,547,692	14	657	53,053	34.9	2,492,857	-3.4
Wyoming	1	(D)	-	(D)	-	1	(D)	-	(D)	-	-

Source: County Business Patterns, U.S. Department of Commerce, Washington, D.C., for 1994 and 1995. Employment shown is for mid-March of the year shown. Payroll per employee is calculated by annualizing 1st Quarter payroll (not shown) and then dividing that value by mid-March employment. Dividing total annual payroll (columns 5 and 10) by employment, therefore, will *not* yield the payroll per employee figure (columns 4 and 9). The symbol (D) indicates that data are withheld by the source to avoid disclosure of competitive information. A dash (-) indicates that data are not available or cannot be calculated.

ESTABLISHMENTS 1995 - STATE AND REGIONAL CONCENTRATION

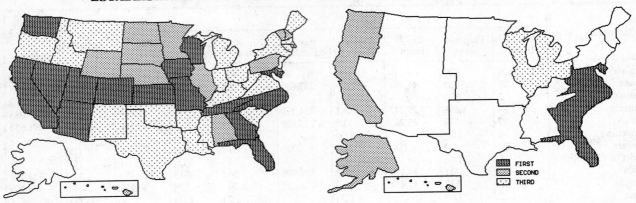

EMPLOYMENT 1995 - STATE AND REGIONAL CONCENTRATION

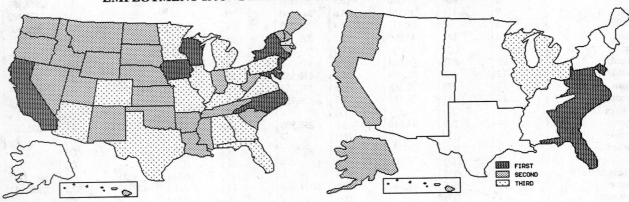

PAYROLL 1995 - STATE AND REGIONAL CONCENTRATION

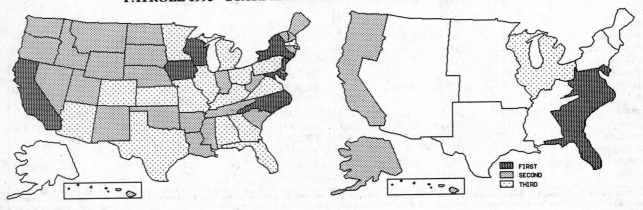

States with the darkest shading indicate those states which have proportionately more establishments, employment, or payrolls than would be indicated by the state's population. States with light shading are states with proportionately fewer establishments, less employment, and lower payrolls than population distribution. States shaded grey are within 15 percent of the state's population proportion in these categories. States for which no data are available are shown as average (grey). *Regions* are shaded to indicate absolute rank in the category. If no data for the category are available, establishment counts are used to shade the regions. Source of the data is the table on the facing page.

LEADING COMPANIES - SIC 6331 - Fire, Marine, and Casualty Insurance

Number shown: **90**   Total sales/assets ($ mil): **326,042**   Total employment (000): **207.9**

Company Name	Address				CEO Name	Phone	Co. Type	Sales/Assets ($ mil)	Empl. (000)
General Electric Capital Corp.	260 Long Ridge Rd.	Stamford	CT	06927	Gary C. Wendt	203-357-4000	S	228,777 TA	51.0
Xerox Corp.	PO Box 1600	Stamford	CT	06904	Paul A. Allaire	203-968-3000	P	18,200	86.7
Aetna Casualty and Surety Co.	151 Farmington Ave.	Hartford	CT	06156	Ronald E. Compton	860-273-0123	S	10,489 TA	10.0
AMBAC Inc.	1 State Street Plz.	New York	NY	10004	Phillip B. Lassiter	212-668-0340	P	8,250 TA	0.3
MBIA Inc.	113 King St.	Armonk	NY	10504	David H. Elliott	914-273-4545	P	7,700 TA	0.6
Old Republic International Corp.	307 N. Michigan Ave.	Chicago	IL	60601	A.C. Zucaro	312-346-8100	P	6,923 TA	5.9
Advanta Corp.	PO Box 844	Spring House	PA	19477	Alex W. Hart	215-657-4000	P	5,584 TA	3.5
Cuna Mutual Insurance Society	PO Box 391	Madison	WI	53701	Michael Kitchen	608-238-5851	R	3,600 TA	5.0
MGIC Investment Corp.	PO Box 488	Milwaukee	WI	53201	William H. Lacy	414-347-6480	P	2,618 TA	1.0
FGIC Corp.	115 Broadway	New York	NY	10006	Ann C. Stern	212-312-3000	S	2,300 TA	0.2
Financial Security Assurance Holdings Ltd.	350 Park Ave.	New York	NY	10022	Robert P. Cochran	212-826-0100	P	1,901 TA	0.2
MMI Companies Inc.	540 Lake Cook Rd.	Deerfield	IL	60015	B. Frederick Becker	847-940-7550	P	1,884 TA	0.8
Markel Corp.	PO Box 2009	Glen Allen	VA	23058	Alan I. Kirshner	804-747-0136	P	1,870 TA	0.8
Executive Risk Inc.	PO Box 2002	Simsbury	CT	06070	Stephen J. Sills	860-408-2000	P	1,486 TA	0.5
United States Fire Insurance Co.	305 Madison Ave.	Morristown	NJ	07034	James A. Stark	--	S	1,394 TA*	1.5
Capital Re Corp.	1325 Ave. of the Amer.	New York	NY	10019	Michael E. Satz	212-974-0100	P	1,388 TA	0.2
General Electric Mortgage Insurance Corp.	6601 Six Forks Rd.	Raleigh	NC	27615	Thomas H. Mann	919-846-4100	S	1,290 TA	0.8
Quaker State Corp.	225 E. John Carpenter Fwy.	Irving	TX	75062	Herbert M. Baum	214-868-0400	P	1,190	6.0
First American Financial Corp.	114 East 5th St.	Santa Ana	CA	92701	Parker S. Kennedy	714-558-3211	P	1,140 TA	11.6
PMI Group Inc.	601 Montgomery St.	San Francisco	CA	94111	W. Roger Haughton	415-788-7878	P	1,130 TA	0.6
Securities Investor Protection Corp.	805 15th St. N.W.	Washington	DC	20005	Michael E. Don	202-371-8300	R	990 TA	<0.1
Enhance Financial Services Group Inc.	335 Madison Ave.	New York	NY	10017	Daniel Gross	212-983-3100	P	983 TA	0.1
Oakwood Homes Corp.	PO Box 27081	Greensboro	NC	27425	Nicholas J. St. George	336-664-2400	P	953	7.6
Frontier Insurance Group Inc.	PO Box 8000	Rock Hill	NY	12775	Walter A. Rhulen	914-796-2100	P	773 TA	0.6
Sedgwick James of Oregon Inc.	111 Columbia St.	Portland	OR	97201	Ronald J. Kutella	503-248-6400	S	770 TA	0.3
Fidelity and Deposit Company of Maryland	PO Box 1227	Baltimore	MD	21203	Richard F. Williams	410-539-0800	S	758 TA	1.0
Physicians' Reciprocal Insurers	111 E. Shore Rd.	Manhasset	NY	11030	Anthony J. Bonomo	516-365-6690	R	757 TA	0.3
GE Capital Mortgage Services Inc.	3 Executive Campus	Cherry Hill	NJ	08002	Gregory T. Barmore	609-661-6100	S	757 TA*	0.4
CMAC Investment Corp.	1601 Market St.	Philadelphia	PA	19103	Frank P. Filipps	215-564-6600	S	752 TA*	0.7
MAIC Holdings Inc.	100 Brookwood Pl.	Birmingham	AL	35209	A.D. Crowe	205-877-4400	P	721 TA	0.1
Seaboard Surety Co.	Burnt Mills Rd.	Bedminster	NJ	07921	George Thompson	908-658-3500	S	690 TA*	0.4

Company type codes: P - Public, R - Private, S - Subsidiary, D - Division, J - Joint Venture, A - Affiliate, G - Group. If the dollar values shown are not sales, the following codes apply: TA - Total Assets; OR - Operating Revenues; GB - Gross Billings. * - estimated dollar value. < - less than. *na* - not available.

Continued on next page.

LEADING COMPANIES - SIC 6331 - Fire, Marine, and Casualty Insurance
Continued

Company Name	Address				CEO Name	Phone	Co. Type	Sales/Assets ($ mil)	Empl. (000)
United Guaranty Residential Insurance Co.	PO Box 21367	Greensboro	NC	27420	Charles M. Reid	910-373-0232	S	510 TA	0.4
Western Insurance Holdings Inc.	PO Box 85563	San Diego	CA	92186	Bernard M. Feldman	619-350-2400	S	500 TA	0.4
Evanston Insurance Co.	1007 Church St.	Evanston	IL	60201	Paul W. Springman	847-866-2800	S	497 TA	<0.1
Medical Mutual Liability Insurance Society of Maryland	225 International Cir.	Hunt Valley	MD	21030	Raymond M. Yow	410-785-0050	R	430 TA	<0.1
Healthcare Underwriters Mutual Insurance Co.	8 British America Blvd.	Latham	NY	12110	Gerald Cassidy	518-786-2700	R	428 TA	<0.1
Manufacturers Alliance Insurance Co.	925 Chestnut St.	Philadelphia	PA	19107	William M. Loftus	215-629-5000	S	411 TA	0.5
Capital Markets Assurance Corp.	885 3rd Ave.	New York	NY	10022	John B. Caouette	212-755-1155	S	391 TA	0.1
Insurance Company of the West	PO Box 85563	San Diego	CA	92186	Bernard M. Feldman	619-546-2400	S	350 TA	0.4
Victor O. Schinnerer and Company Inc.	2 Wisconsin Cir.	Chevy Chase	MD	20815	Vince Santorelli	301-961-9800	S	340 TA	0.2
Capital Guaranty Corp.	Steuart Twr.	San Francisco	CA	94105	Michael Djordjevich	415-995-8000	P	334 TA	<0.1
Meadowbrook Insurance Group Inc.	26600 Telegraph Rd.	Southfield	MI	48034	Merton J. Segal	248-358-1100	P	329 TA	0.6
Florida Physicians Insurance Co.	1000 Riverside Ave.	Jacksonville	FL	32204	William R. Russell	904-354-5910	S	277 TA	0.1
American International Specialty Lines Insurance Co.	401 Plaza 3	Jersey City	NJ	07311	Thomas Tizzo	201-309-1100	S	250 TA	<0.1
Nobel Insurance Ltd.	8001 L.B.J. Fwy.	Dallas	TX	75251	Jeffry K. Amsbaugh	214-644-0434	P	223 TA	0.3
Bertholon-Rowland Corp.	16 J St.	New York	NY	10013	James Caroll	212-966-9400	R	184 TA*	0.1
Amwest Insurance Group Inc.	PO Box 4500	Woodland Hills	CA	91365	John E. Savage	818-871-2000	P	181 TA	0.5
Intercargo Corp.	1450 E. American Ln	Schaumburg	IL	60173	Stanley A. Galinski	847-517-2990	P	165 TA	0.2
Aon Specialty Group Inc.	123 N. Wacker Dr.	Chicago	IL	60606	Michael D. Rice	312-701-4538	S	156*	0.6
Home Buyers Warranty Corp.	1728 Montreal Cir.	Tucker	GA	30084	Gary Mabry	404-496-4969	R	150 TA*	0.3
Midwest Indemnity Corp.	5550 W. Touhy Ave.	Skokie	IL	60077	Marvin Silverman	708-982-9800	R	140 TA	<0.1
P.I.E. Mutual Insurance Co.	1001 Lakeside Ave.	Cleveland	OH	44114	Larry E. Rogers	216-736-8400	R	140 TA	0.1
Triad Guaranty Inc.	101 S. Stratford Rd.	Winston-Salem	NC	27104	Darryl W. Thompson	919-723-1282	P	139 TA	0.1
American Credit Indemnity Co.	100 E. Pratt St.	Baltimore	MD	21202	H. Michael Cushinsky	410-554-0700	S	126 TA	0.3
Amerin Guaranty Corp.	303 E. Wacker Dr.	Chicago	IL	60601	Gerald L. Friedman	312-540-0078	S	107 TA	<0.1
Kentucky Medical Insurance Co.	303 N. Hurstbourne Pkwy.	Louisville	KY	40222	Steven L. Salman	502-339-5700	P	88 TA	<0.1
Triad Guaranty Insurance Corp.	101 S. Stratford Rd.	Winston-Salem	NC	27104	Darryl W. Thompson	910-723-1282	S	86 TA	<0.1
MOMED Holding Co.	8630 Delmar Blvd.	St. Louis	MO	63124	Richard V. Bradley	314-872-8000	P	81 TA	<0.1
Pace American Group Inc.	3567 E. Sunrise Dr.	Tucson	AZ	85718	Don H. Pace	602-745-8855	P	81 TA	0.1
Equisure Inc.	701 4th Ave.	Minneapolis	MN	55415	Barrie Harding	612-337-9507	P	77 TA	<0.1

Company type codes: P - Public, R - Private, S - Subsidiary, D - Division, J - Joint Venture, A - Affiliate, G - Group. If the dollar values shown are not sales, the following codes apply: TA - Total Assets; OR - Operating Revenues; GB - Gross Billings. * - estimated dollar value. < - less than. *na* - not available.

Continued on next page.

LEADING COMPANIES - SIC 6331 - Fire, Marine, and Casualty Insurance
Continued

Company Name	Address				CEO Name	Phone	Co. Type	Sales/Assets ($ mil)	Empl. (000)
Professional Liability Underwriting Managers Inc.	505 Hwy. 169	Plymouth	MN	55451	Paul Mahaffey	612-512-2100	S	76 TA*	<0.1
Premier Inc.	12730 High Bluff Dr.	San Diego	CA	92130	Robert W. O'Leary	619-481-2727	R	75 OR*	1.0
Mahoney Group	PO Box 15001	Casa Grande	AZ	85230	John W. McEvoy	602-836-7483	R	70 TA	0.1
Wilshire Insurance Co.	PO Box 10800	Raleigh	NC	27605	George King	919-833-1600	S	58 TA	<0.1
Roanoke Companies Inc.	1930 Thoreau Dr.	Schaumburg	IL	60173	William D. Sterrett	708-490-9540	R	53 TA*	0.2
American Excess Insurance Association	77 Hartland St.	East Hartford	CT	06108	Clinton N. Greene	860-528-2105	R	52 TA	<0.1
Monumental General Insurance Group	1111 N. Charles St.	Baltimore	MD	21201	Bart Herbert	410-685-5500	S	48 TA*	0.3
R.V.I. Services Company Inc.	177 Broad St.	Stamford	CT	06901	Philip W. Ness Jr.	203-975-2100	R	44 TA*	<0.1
American Bonding Co.	6245 E. Broadway Blvd.	Tucson	AZ	85711	Steve Ramsey	602-747-5555	R	41 TA*	<0.1
Condor Services Inc.	2361 Rosecrans Ave.	El Segundo	CA	90245	Guy A. Main	310-322-7344	P	40 TA*	<0.1
Crusader Insurance Co.	23251 Mulholland Dr.	Woodland Hills	CA	91364	Erwin Cheldin	818-591-9800	S	40 TA	0.1
Texas Lawyers Insurance Exchange	PO Box 13325	Austin	TX	78711	John B. Randolph	512-480-9074	R	38 TA*	<0.1
Homeowners Group Inc.	PO Box 9200	Hollywood	FL	33084	Carl Buccellato	954-845-9100	P	38 TA	0.2
Safe Passage International	410 17th St.	Denver	CO	80202	James A. Irwin	303-893-5680	S	30 TA	<0.1
Property and Casualty Insurance Guaranty Corp.	305 Washington Ave.	Baltimore	MD	21204	Joseph Petr	410-296-1620	R	27 TA*	<0.1
Delta Holding Inc.	PO Box 58665	Renton	WA	98058	David L. Larson	206-251-9192	R	22 TA	0.2
Savers Property and Casualty Insurance Co.	10985 Cody	Overland Park	KS	66210	Karl Koch	913-451-0002	S	22 TA*	<0.1
Credit Card Service Corp.	6860 Commercial Dr.	Springfield	VA	22151	Dave Phillips	703-750-3026	R	15 TA	<0.1
Delta Management Company Inc.	PO Box 7000	Issaquah	WA	98027	David L. Larson	206-391-2000	P	12 TA	0.2
Amerinst Insurance Group Inc.	1751 West 47th St.	Chicago	IL	60609	Norman Batchelder	312-523-4416	R	10 TA	<0.1
Hodge Hart and Associates Inc.	10605 Concord St.	Kensington	MD	20895	David F. Hodge Jr.	301-946-1555	R	10 TA	<0.1
J.P. Everhart and Co.	8350 N. Central Expwy	Dallas	TX	75206	John P. Everhart	214-691-6911	R	8 TA	<0.1
Acstar Holdings Inc.	233 Main St.	New Britain	CT	06050	Henry W. Nozko Jr.	203-224-2000	S	7 TA	<0.1
Securities Guaranty Insurance Services Inc.	2677 N. Main St.	Santa Ana	CA	92701	Jim Brooks	714-647-0400	R	6 TA	<0.1
Far West Insurance Co.	6320 Canoga Ave.	Woodland Hills	CA	91367	John E. Savage	818-704-1111	S	5 TA	0.3
Aaron Richardson Insurance Services Corp.	417 Montgomery St.	San Francisco	CA	94104	Ingrid Merriwether	415-986-3999	R	3	<0.1
Kirk Horse Insurance Inc.	316 W. High St.	Lexington	KY	40507	Ronald K. Kirk	606-231-0838	R	2 TA	<0.1
Commodore Insurance Services Inc.	26300 La Alameda	Mission Viejo	CA	92691	David E. Worden	714-365-0474	R	1 TA*	<0.1

Company type codes: P - Public, R - Private, S - Subsidiary, D - Division, J - Joint Venture, A - Affiliate, G - Group. If the dollar values shown are not sales, the following codes apply: TA - Total Assets; OR - Operating Revenues; GB - Gross Billings. * - estimated dollar value. < - less than. *na* - not available.

Continued on next page.

LEADING COMPANIES - SIC 6331 - Fire, Marine, and Casualty Insurance
Continued

Company Name	Address				CEO Name	Phone	Co. Type	Sales/Assets ($ mil)	Empl. (000)
Freberg Environmental Inc.	1675 Broadway	Denver	CO	80202	Michael J. Hill	303-571-4235	R	1 TA*	<0.1
Municipal Mutual Insurance Co.	1981 N.Broadway	Walnut Creek	CA	94596	Jame J. Gregg	310-515-6800	R	1 TA*	<0.1

Source: Ward's Business Directory of U.S. Private and Public Companies, 1996. Company type codes: P - Public, R - Private, S - Subsidiary, D - Division, J - Joint Venture, A - Affiliate, G - Group. If the dollar values shown are not sales, the following codes apply: TA - Total Assets; OR - Operating Revenues; GB - Gross Billings. * - estimated dollar value. < - less than; *na* - not available.

SIC 6360

TITLE INSURANCE

This industry is made up of establishments engaged primarily in underwriting insurance to protect the owners of real estate and those who lend money on real estate against loss sustained due to a defective title of ownership. Real estate title insurance, title insurance, and title guaranty organizations are included.

ESTABLISHMENTS, EMPLOYMENT, AND PAYROLL

	1990	1991		1992		1993		1994		1995		% change 90-95
		Value	%	Value	%	Value	%	Value	%	Value	%	
All Establishments	3,196	3,496	9.4	3,560	1.8	2,294	-35.6	2,436	6.2	2,520	3.4	-21.2
Mid-March Employment	56,650	49,399	-12.8	54,042	9.4	40,169	-25.7	46,677	16.2	38,927	-16.6	-31.3
1st Quarter Wages (annualized - $ mil.)	1,587.2	1,379.8	-13.1	1,629.2	18.1	1,277.1	-21.6	1,687.2	32.1	1,452.0	-13.9	-8.5
Payroll per Emp. 1st Q. (annualized)	28,018	27,932	-0.3	30,147	7.9	31,793	5.5	36,146	13.7	37,301	3.2	33.1
Annual Payroll ($ mil.)	1,574.3	1,452.8	-7.7	1,749.3	20.4	1,442.0	-17.6	1,437.9	-0.3	1,364.4	-5.1	-13.3
Establishments - 1-4 Emp. Number	1,210	1,350	11.6	1,352	0.1	(D)	-	(D)	-	(D)	-	-
Mid-March Employment	2,782	(D)	-	3,140	-	(D)	-	(D)	-	(D)	-	-
1st Quarter Wages (annualized - $ mil.)	75.4	(D)	-	77.3	-	(D)	-	(D)	-	(D)	-	-
Payroll per Emp. 1st Q. (annualized)	27,104	(D)	-	24,614	-	(D)	-	(D)	-	(D)	-	-
Annual Payroll ($ mil.)	75.5	(D)	-	90.4	-	(D)	-	(D)	-	(D)	-	-
Establishments - 5-9 Emp. Number	798	1,040	30.3	1,022	-1.7	636	-37.8	660	3.8	609	-7.7	-23.7
Mid-March Employment	5,335	7,047	32.1	6,781	-3.8	4,185	-38.3	4,400	5.1	4,035	-8.3	-24.4
1st Quarter Wages (annualized - $ mil.)	132.5	166.7	25.9	176.3	5.7	125.2	-29.0	148.7	18.8	133.0	-10.6	0.4
Payroll per Emp. 1st Q. (annualized)	24,828	23,657	-4.7	25,994	9.9	29,920	15.1	33,795	13.0	32,965	-2.5	32.8
Annual Payroll ($ mil.)	129.5	179.2	38.4	197.3	10.1	139.1	-29.5	126.9	-8.8	126.9	0.0	-2.0
Establishments - 10-19 Emp. Number	479	521	8.8	541	3.8	357	-34.0	401	12.3	373	-7.0	-22.1
Mid-March Employment	6,528	7,062	8.2	7,241	2.5	4,819	-33.4	5,369	11.4	5,064	-5.7	-22.4
1st Quarter Wages (annualized - $ mil.)	160.2	181.5	13.2	191.6	5.6	140.5	-26.7	182.7	30.1	174.6	-4.4	8.9
Payroll per Emp. 1st Q. (annualized)	24,547	25,694	4.7	26,465	3.0	29,148	10.1	34,025	16.7	34,476	1.3	40.4
Annual Payroll ($ mil.)	158.2	190.0	20.1	209.7	10.4	157.4	-25.0	153.7	-2.3	161.2	4.9	1.9
Establishments - 20-49 Emp. Number	451	392	-13.1	420	7.1	322	-23.3	342	6.2	310	-9.4	-31.3
Mid-March Employment	14,014	11,971	-14.6	13,012	8.7	10,110	-22.3	10,592	4.8	9,508	-10.2	-32.2
1st Quarter Wages (annualized - $ mil.)	364.1	320.0	-12.1	366.3	14.5	296.2	-19.1	364.1	22.9	337.8	-7.2	-7.2
Payroll per Emp. 1st Q. (annualized)	25,982	26,729	2.9	28,148	5.3	29,295	4.1	34,372	17.3	35,523	3.3	36.7
Annual Payroll ($ mil.)	366.5	333.3	-9.1	403.6	21.1	328.4	-18.6	300.1	-8.6	305.6	1.8	-16.6
Establishments - 50-99 Emp. Number	172	133	-22.7	152	14.3	127	-16.4	158	24.4	116	-26.6	-32.6
Mid-March Employment	11,710	9,035	-22.8	10,414	15.3	8,434	-19.0	10,736	27.3	7,752	-27.8	-33.8
1st Quarter Wages (annualized - $ mil.)	330.7	255.8	-22.7	323.6	26.5	270.9	-16.3	374.4	38.2	275.6	-26.4	-16.7
Payroll per Emp. 1st Q. (annualized)	28,243	28,312	0.2	31,076	9.8	32,120	3.4	34,878	8.6	35,547	1.9	25.9
Annual Payroll ($ mil.)	323.8	275.6	-14.9	340.7	23.6	294.2	-13.6	308.6	4.9	260.7	-15.5	-19.5
Establishments - 100-249 Emp. Number	72	49	-31.9	61	24.5	55	-9.8	65	18.2	40	-38.5	-44.4
Mid-March Employment	10,294	7,001	-32.0	9,030	29.0	8,158	-9.7	9,345	14.6	5,658	-39.5	-45.0
1st Quarter Wages (annualized - $ mil.)	326.5	228.7	-29.9	315.2	37.8	283.0	-10.2	365.1	29.0	211.1	-42.2	-35.3
Payroll per Emp. 1st Q. (annualized)	31,716	32,668	3.0	34,910	6.9	34,688	-0.6	39,072	12.6	37,317	-4.5	17.7
Annual Payroll ($ mil.)	329.6	235.6	-28.5	333.2	41.5	319.6	-4.1	318.7	-0.3	224.4	-29.6	-31.9
Establishments - 250-499 Emp. Number	9	9	-	(D)	-	6	-	10	66.7	9	-10.0	-
Mid-March Employment	2,973	(D)	-	(D)	-	2,290	-	3,530	54.1	3,058	-13.4	2.9
1st Quarter Wages (annualized - $ mil.)	102.5	(D)	-	(D)	-	87.8	-	153.1	74.4	151.7	-0.9	48.0
Payroll per Emp. 1st Q. (annualized)	34,476	(D)	-	(D)	-	38,323	-	43,362	13.1	49,614	14.4	43.9
Annual Payroll ($ mil.)	96.2	(D)	-	(D)	-	96.6	-	132.0	36.7	123.6	-6.4	28.5
Establishments - 500-999 Emp. Number	5	2	-60.0	(D)	-	(D)	-	(D)	-	(D)	-	-
Mid-March Employment	3,014	(D)	-	(D)	-	(D)	-	(D)	-	(D)	-	-
1st Quarter Wages (annualized - $ mil.)	95.3	(D)	-	(D)	-	(D)	-	(D)	-	(D)	-	-
Payroll per Emp. 1st Q. (annualized)	31,622	(D)	-	(D)	-	(D)	-	(D)	-	(D)	-	-
Annual Payroll ($ mil.)	95.0	(D)	-	(D)	-	(D)	-	(D)	-	(D)	-	-
Estab. - 1000 or More Emp. Number	-	-	-	-	-	-	-	-	-	-	-	-
Mid-March Employment	-	-	-	-	-	-	-	-	-	-	-	-
1st Quarter Wages (annualized - $ mil.)	-	-	-	-	-	-	-	-	-	-	-	-
Payroll per Emp. 1st Q. (annualized)	(D)	(D)	-	-	-	-	-	-	-	-	-	-
Annual Payroll ($ mil.)	-	-	-	-	-	-	-	-	-	-	-	-

Source: County Business Patterns, U.S. Department of Commerce, Washington, D.C., for 1990 through 1995. Payroll per employee is calculated using mid-March employment and 1st Quarter wages, annualized. Annual payroll, also shown, may not equal the annualized 1st Quarter wages. Columns headed by a percent sign (%) indicate change from the previous year. na stands for not available. The symbol (D) indicates that data are withheld by the source to avoid disclosure of competitive information. A dash (-) indicates that data are not available or cannot be calculated.

ESTABLISHMENTS
Number

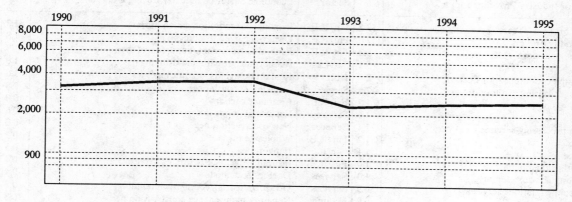

MID-MARCH EMPLOYMENT
Number

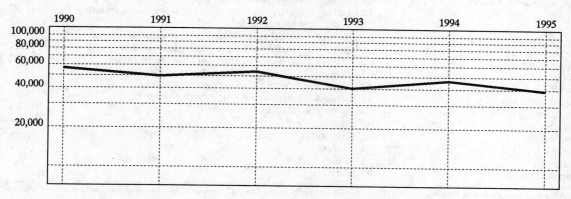

ANNUAL PAYROLL
$ million

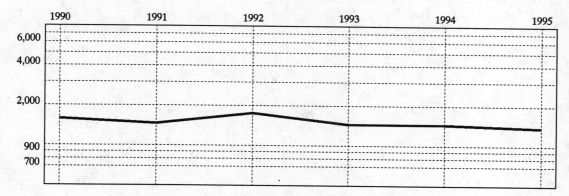

INPUTS AND OUTPUTS FOR INSURANCE CARRIERS - SIC GROUP 63

Economic Sector or Industry Providing Inputs	%	Sector	Economic Sector or Industry Buying Outputs	%	Sector
Insurance agents, brokers, & services	59.2	Fin/R.E.	Personal consumption expenditures	81.3	
Security & commodity brokers	7.0	Fin/R.E.	Owner-occupied dwellings	1.8	Fin/R.E.
Real estate agents, operators, & lessors	5.8	Fin/R.E.	Federal Government, nondefense, spending	1.3	Gov't
Legal services	5.1	Services	Retail trade, ex eating & drinking	1.0	Trade
Telephone/telegraph communications nec	2.7	Util.	Real estate agents, operators, & lessors	1.0	Fin/R.E.
Automotive rental & leasing, without drivers	2.0	Services	Trucking & courier services, ex air	0.8	Util.
Banking	1.7	Fin/R.E.	Insurance carriers	0.8	Fin/R.E.
Advertising	1.4	Services	Exports of goods & services	0.8	Foreign
Computer & data processing services	1.4	Services	New construction nec	0.6	Constr.
Insurance carriers	1.2	Fin/R.E.	Wholesale trade	0.5	Trade
U.S. Postal Service	1.1	Gov't	Banking	0.5	Fin/R.E.
Credit agencies other than banks	1.0	Fin/R.E.	Insurance agents, brokers, & services	0.4	Fin/R.E.
Accounting, auditing & bookkeeping	1.0	Services	Doctors & dentists	0.4	Services
Management & public relations services	0.9	Services	Office, industrial/commercial buildings	0.3	Constr.
Commercial printing	0.8	Manufg.	Repair & maintenance construction nec	0.3	Constr.
Business services nec	0.8	Services	Residential 1 unit structures, nonfarm	0.3	Constr.
Eating & drinking places	0.6	Services	Hospitals	0.3	Services
Hotels	0.5	Services	Highways, bridges, horizontal construction	0.2	Constr.
Miscellaneous equipment rental & leasing	0.5	Services	Electric services (utilities)	0.2	Util.
Repair & maintenance construction nec	0.4	Constr.	Eating & drinking places	0.2	Services
Air transportation	0.4	Util.	S/L Govt., elementary & high schools, spending	0.2	S/L Govt
Wholesale trade	0.4	Trade	Meat animals	0.1	Agric.
Personnel supply services	0.4	Services	Maintenance/repair of residential structures	0.1	Constr.
Trucking & courier services, ex air	0.3	Util.	Motor vehicles & passenger car bodies	0.1	Manufg.
Photographic equipment & supplies	0.2	Manufg.	Sanitary services, steam supply, irrigation	0.1	Util.
Tires & inner tubes	0.2	Manufg.	Telephone/telegraph communications nec	0.1	Util.
Business & professional associations	0.2	Services	Credit agencies other than banks	0.1	Fin/R.E.
Services to dwellings & other buildings	0.2	Services	Automotive repair shops & services	0.1	Services
Magnetic & optical recording media	0.1	Manufg.	Business services nec	0.1	Services
Manifold business forms	0.1	Manufg.			
Paper & paperboard mills	0.1	Manufg.			
Electric services (utilities)	0.1	Util.			
Local & suburban transit	0.1	Util.			
Automobile parking & car washes	0.1	Services			

Source: Benchmark Input-Output Accounts for the U.S. Economy, 1992, U.S. Department of Commerce, Washington, D.C., November 1997. Data, as reported in the source, are organized by the 1987 SIC structure in use in 1992.

OCCUPATIONS EMPLOYED BY PENSION FUNDS AND INSURANCE, NEC

Occupation	% of Total 1996	Change to 2006	Occupation	% of Total 1996	Change to 2006
Title examiners & searchers	10.6	8.8	Underwriters	2.7	44.7
General office clerks	8.4	17.0	Sales & related workers nec	2.7	49.6
Secretaries, except legal & medical	6.9	7.9	Insurance sales workers	2.6	26.9
General managers & top executives	6.3	31.8	Management support workers nec	2.2	36.0
Clerical supervisors & managers	4.9	36.0	Financial managers	2.1	36.0
Bookkeeping, accounting, & auditing clerks	4.6	8.8	File clerks	2.0	-2.9
Legal assistants & clerks nec	4.3	104.0	Accountants & auditors	1.8	25.9
Typists, including word processing	4.0	-11.6	Computer programmers	1.8	12.0
Insurance policy processing clerks	3.2	8.8	Messengers	1.3	8.8
Receptionists & information clerks	3.0	36.0	Marketing & sales worker supervisors	1.3	36.1
Insurance claims clerks	3.0	38.9	Claims examiners, property & casualty	1.3	37.0
Loan & credit clerks	2.9	37.3	Data entry keyers, except composing	1.2	8.8
Insurance adjusters, examiners, investigators	2.8	39.7	Managers & administrators nec	1.0	34.7

Sources: *Industry-Occupation Matrix*, Bureau of Labor Statistics. These data relate to one or more 3-digit SIC industry groups rather than to a single 4-digit SIC. The change reported for each occupation to the year 2005 is a percent of growth or decline as estimated by the Bureau of Labor Statistics. The abbreviation *nec* stands for not elsewhere classified.

STATE-BY-STATE DATA ON ESTABLISHMENTS, EMPLOYMENT, AND PAYROLL - 1994 AND 1995

State	1994					1995					% Change Empl.
	No. of Estab.	Employment	Pay / Empl.	Payroll ($ mil.)	Pay / Estab.	No. of Estab.	Employment	Pay / Empl.	Payroll ($ mil.)	Pay / Estab.	
Alabama	12	(D)	-	(D)	-	9	(D)	-	(D)	-	-
Alaska	7	(D)	-	(D)	-	5	18	33,333	0.7	137,200	-
Arizona	33	434	21,382	9.3	282,152	29	406	23,813	9.8	338,759	-6.5
Arkansas	20	142	24,225	3.0	151,050	11	49	25,469	1.1	102,182	-65.5
California	462	3,842	33,424	131.2	284,056	402	3,839	34,983	143.7	357,418	-0.1
Colorado	45	1,241	28,815	37.0	823,111	39	1,209	34,220	45.8	1,174,179	-2.6
Connecticut	45	661	31,268	25.6	568,378	41	4,221	18,116	72.5	1,767,805	538.6
Delaware	10	94	35,660	3.2	315,200	4	21	30,667	0.8	202,500	-77.7
District of Columbia	19	372	22,011	8.6	451,158	13	312	20,744	6.8	520,308	-16.1
Florida	131	743	25,443	18.7	142,504	98	667	30,795	22.1	225,612	-10.2
Georgia	82	1,438	17,558	30.8	376,134	59	1,991	20,456	44.2	749,915	38.5
Hawaii	12	(D)	-	(D)	-	11	(D)	-	(D)	-	-
Idaho	3	(D)	-	(D)	-	4	(D)	-	(D)	-	-
Illinois	125	1,548	30,514	48.1	384,848	120	1,360	31,474	43.2	359,592	-12.1
Indiana	57	765	27,739	17.7	310,140	46	669	27,540	18.6	403,674	-12.5
Iowa	30	(D)	-	(D)	-	25	(D)	-	(D)	-	-
Kansas	19	234	24,376	5.1	267,474	12	167	28,192	4.9	406,583	-28.6
Kentucky	19	117	15,282	1.9	100,368	18	101	30,099	3.0	168,944	-13.7
Louisiana	37	308	16,948	7.8	211,216	29	218	21,046	4.3	147,552	-29.2
Maine	18	109	20,183	2.0	112,667	14	65	23,200	1.9	134,429	-40.4
Maryland	82	568	24,993	15.1	184,073	53	516	29,124	15.6	293,962	-9.2
Massachusetts	64	1,150	14,838	20.4	318,234	53	845	26,646	25.1	473,943	-26.5
Michigan	103	1,513	22,964	28.3	274,913	79	801	28,739	25.1	317,684	-47.1
Minnesota	45	575	31,687	20.0	444,800	46	714	34,655	24.2	526,304	24.2
Mississippi	23	149	23,436	4.6	201,696	16	122	27,508	4.5	283,062	-18.1
Missouri	46	613	29,135	18.3	398,065	42	716	27,346	18.8	448,119	16.8
Montana	5	(D)	-	(D)	-	5	(D)	-	(D)	-	-
Nebraska	12	88	85,045	6.0	500,250	10	343	34,671	6.7	667,900	289.8
Nevada	21	94	28,085	4.2	200,476	10	89	31,551	3.0	301,400	-5.3
New Hampshire	9	347	29,429	11.0	1,224,333	6	195	30,974	7.1	1,175,667	-43.8
New Jersey	103	826	37,792	28.5	276,806	78	631	45,363	25.6	327,974	-23.6
New Mexico	11	124	6,548	0.8	68,636	8	53	18,491	0.8	105,875	-57.3
New York	214	2,598	29,892	80.6	376,636	185	3,181	29,456	99.1	535,578	22.4
North Carolina	51	656	27,232	20.4	400,569	44	780	29,774	23.8	540,795	18.9
North Dakota	2	(D)	-	(D)	-	2	(D)	-	(D)	-	-
Ohio	126	2,014	24,491	47.0	373,270	104	1,644	30,071	52.3	502,452	-18.4
Oklahoma	29	263	21,582	6.0	207,931	25	246	25,301	6.9	275,040	-6.5
Oregon	44	1,812	15,508	18.4	417,568	31	521	31,455	18.4	594,000	-71.2
Pennsylvania	179	2,160	21,678	50.7	283,117	150	2,234	25,859	59.7	398,127	3.4
Rhode Island	10	124	34,452	5.1	513,800	11	147	39,837	6.2	562,273	18.5
South Carolina	20	100	19,280	2.2	109,850	13	124	18,645	1.9	149,462	24.0
South Dakota	4	(D)	-	(D)	-	3	(D)	-	(D)	-	-
Tennessee	37	337	24,819	9.1	246,730	27	357	26,555	10.8	399,556	5.9
Texas	165	1,512	21,489	33.7	204,000	119	1,865	24,345	57.3	481,412	23.3
Utah	14	386	35,461	12.0	859,714	12	367	32,589	11.3	944,000	-4.9
Vermont	7	32	23,375	0.9	123,571	6	42	20,857	1.1	176,333	31.3
Virginia	67	329	29,435	9.7	145,299	56	356	30,528	22.0	392,393	8.2
Washington	44	852	31,850	26.3	598,523	42	861	32,409	28.3	673,452	1.1
West Virginia	14	(D)	-	(D)	-	13	(D)	-	(D)	-	-
Wisconsin	53	753	27,458	21.4	404,302	46	638	26,520	18.1	394,370	-15.3
Wyoming	1	(D)	-	(D)	-	(D)	(D)	(D)	(D)	(D)	-

Source: County Business Patterns, U.S. Department of Commerce, Washington, D.C., for 1994 and 1995. Employment shown is for mid-March of the year shown. Payroll per employee is calculated by annualizing 1st Quarter payroll (not shown) and then dividing that value by mid-March employment. Dividing total annual payroll (columns 5 and 10) by employment, therefore, will *not* yield the payroll per employee figure (columns 4 and 9). The symbol (D) indicates that data are withheld by the source to avoid disclosure of competitive information. A dash (-) indicates that data are not available or cannot be calculated.

ESTABLISHMENTS 1995 - STATE AND REGIONAL CONCENTRATION

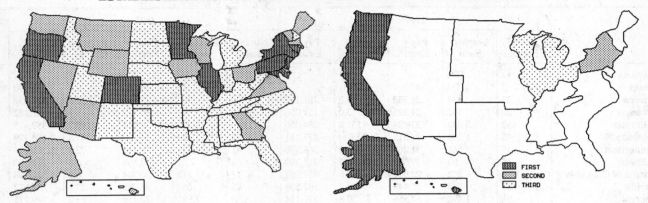

EMPLOYMENT 1995 - STATE AND REGIONAL CONCENTRATION

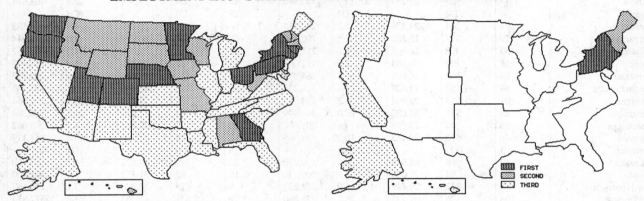

PAYROLL 1995 - STATE AND REGIONAL CONCENTRATION

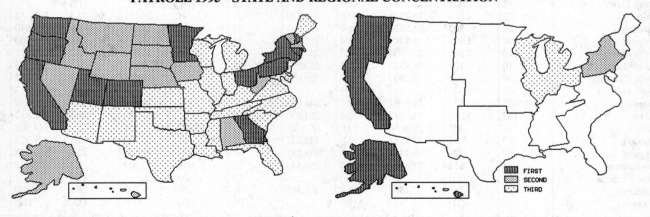

States with the darkest shading indicate those states which have proportionately more establishments, employment, or payrolls than would be indicated by the state's population. States with light shading are states with proportionately fewer establishments, less employment, and lower payrolls than population distribution. States shaded grey are within 15 percent of the state's population proportion in these categories. States for which no data are available are shown as average (grey). *Regions* are shaded to indicate absolute rank in the category. If no data for the category are available, establishment counts are used to shade the regions. Source of the data is the table on the facing page.

LEADING COMPANIES - SIC 6371 - Pension, Health, and Welfare Funds
Number shown: **16**   Total sales/assets ($ mil): **161,821**   Total employment (000): **40.0**

Company Name	Address				CEO Name	Phone	Co. Type	Sales/Assets ($ mil)	Empl. (000)
Aetna Inc.	151 Farmington Ave.	Hartford	CT	06156	Richard L. Huber	860-273-0123	P	96,001 TA	38.6
Trust Company of the West	865 S. Figueroa St.	Los Angeles	CA	90017	Thomas Larkin	213-244-0000	R	50,000 TA	0.6
Public Employees' Retirement System of Mississippi	429 Mississippi St.	Jackson	MS	39201	Milton G. Walker	601-359-3589	3	7,000 TA	<0.1
Orange County Employees Retirement System	2223 Wellington Ave.	Santa Ana	CA	92701	Raymond A. Fleming	714-975-1962	R	3,900 TA	<0.1
Employees' Retirement System of the County of Milwaukee	901 N. 9th St.	Milwaukee	WI	53233	Jac R. Amerell	414-278-4242	R	1,200 TA	<0.1
IPC Pensions Services Company Inc.	PO Box 2389	Seattle	WA	98111	Jeffrey Cashman	206-343-2333	R	1,080 TA*	<0.1
Los Angeles County Employees' Retirement Association	PO Box 7060	Pasadena	CA	91109	Marsha Richter	818-564-6000	3	980 TA	0.2
Metric Realty Inc.	950 Tower Ln.	Foster City	CA	94404	W. Patrick McDowell	415-378-7000	S	720 TA*	0.3
Wyoming Retirement System	1st Fl. East Herschler Bldg.	Cheyenne	WY	82002	Gerald Fox	307-777-7691	R	480 TA*	<0.1
Hialeah City Employees' Retirement System	501 Palm Ave.	Hialeah	FL	33010	Myles Milander	305-883-8050	3	275 TA	<0.1
Oklahoma Police Pension and Retirement System	6600 N. Harvey St.	Oklahoma City	OK	73116	Robert J. Wallace	405-521-2286	3	89 TA	<0.1
Mobile Policemen and Firefighter's Pension	PO Box 1827	Mobile	AL	36633	Bennett Howard	334-434-7360	3	39 TA	<0.1
Colorado Public Funds Investment Trust	717 17th St.	Denver	CO	80202	Robert S. Hullinghorst	303-825-3300	3	30 TA	<0.1
Queen City Insurance Agencies Inc.	4785 Eastern Ave.	Cincinnati	OH	45226	Thomas D. Cassady	513-533-1100	R	23 TA	<0.1
Public School Teachers' Pension Retirement Fund of Chicago	205 W. Wacker Dr.	Chicago	IL	60606	James Ward	312-641-4464	3	4 TA	<0.1
SCI-Tower-Pension Specialists Inc.	PO Box 1326	Cedar Rapids	IA	52406	Jim Anderson	319-368-2626	S	1 TA	<0.1

Source: Ward's Business Directory of U.S. Private and Public Companies, 1996. Company type codes: P - Public, R - Private, S - Subsidiary, D - Division, J - Joint Venture, A - Affiliate, G - Group. If the dollar values shown are not sales, the following codes apply: TA - Total Assets; OR - Operating Revenues; GB - Gross Billings. * - estimated dollar value. < - less than; *na* - not available.

FINANCIAL DATA ON PENSION FUNDS

The following seven tables present information on various aspects of pension funds. Data were obtained from the American Council of Life Insurance, 1001 Pennsylvania Avenue, N.W., Washington, D.C. 20004-2599, and are reproduced by permission.

NUMBER OF PERSONS COVERED BY MAJOR PENSION AND RETIREMENT PROGRAMS

In the United States. In thousands.

Year	Private plans		Government-administered plans			
	With life insurance companies	Other private plans	Railroad retirement	Federal civilian employees[2]	State and local employees	OASI[2]
1940	695	3,565	1,349	745	1,552	24,310
1945	1,470	5,240	1,846	2,928	2,008	34,170
1950	2,755	7,500	1,881	1,872	2,894	61,506
1955	4,105	12,290	1,876	2,333	3,927	73,987
1960	5,475	17,540	1,654	2,703	5,160	90,496
1965	7,040	21,060	1,661	3,114	6,780	102,827
1970	10,580	25,520	1,633	3,624	8,591	118,558
1975	15,190	30,300[1]	1,564	4,171	11,230	134,290
1976	16,965	N.A.	1,572	4,210	12,290	137,200
1977	19,205	N.A.	1,567	4,292	13,124	140,398
1978	21,165	N.A.	1,580	4,380	13,400[1]	140,663
1979	23,310	N.A.	1,567	4,398	13,680[1]	148,686
1980	26,185	N.A.	1,533	4,460	13,950[1]	151,734
1981	27,665	N.A.	1,483	4,566	14,230[1]	154,210
1982	31,010	N.A.	1,404	4,610	14,504	155,833
1983	32,680	N.A.	1,383	4,683	14,464	157,340
1984	35,570	N.A.	1,362	4,791	14,788	159,002
1985	39,620	N.A.	1,309	4,887	15,235	161,575
1986	45,895	N.A.	1,271	4,938	15,426	163,949
1987	51,015	N.A.	1,243	5,065	15,460	166,418
1988	54,000	N.A.	1,229	5,281	15,864	168,972
1989	59,185	N.A.	1,212	5,499	17,086	172,023
1990	61,990	N.A.	1,184	5,447	16,857	174,705
1991	59,255	N.A.	1,157	5,503	17,502	176,690
1992	58,290	N.A.	1,133	5,475	18,320	178,298
1993	60,680	N.A.	1,107	5,330	18,028	179,800
1994	64,385	N.A.	1,084	5,340	18,179	181,314
1995	60,028	N.A.	1,045	5,339	N.A.	183,287
1996	59,174	N.A.	1,013	5,373	N.A.	185,109

Source: Compiled by the American Council of Life Insurance. *Notes:* Some data are revised. It is not possible to obtain a total for number of persons covered by pension plans by adding together the figures shown by the year. Each series has been derived separately and there are differences in amount of duplication within each series and among the various series and also differences in definition of "coverage" among the series. Private plans with life insurance companies include persons covered by Keogh plans, tax-deferred annuities and, after 1974, IRA plans. Data for "Other Private Plans," compiled by the Social Security Administration, exclude plans for the self-employed, those having vested benefits but not presently employed at the firm where benefits were accrued, and also exclude an estimated number who have vested benefits from employment other than from their current employment. These data represent various dates during the year, since the fiscal years of the plans are not necessarily the same. Trends from year to year within each series are not affected. The number of persons covered include survivors or dependents of deceased workers and beneficiaries as well as retired workers. Retirement arrangements for members of the armed forces, and provisions for veterans' pensions, are not included. N.A. stands for not available. 1. Estimated. 2. Includes members of the U.S. Civil Service Retirement System, the Tennessee Valley Authority Retirement System, the Foreign Service Retirement System, and the Federal Reserve Employee Retirement System (Board and Bank plans). 3. Includes living workers insured for retirement and/or survivors benefits, including the self-employed, plus dependents of retired workers and survivors of deceased workers who are receiving periodic benefits.

ASSETS AND RESERVES OF MAJOR PENSION AND RETIREMENT PROGRAMS

In the United States. In millions.

Year	Private plans		Government-administered plans			
	With life insurance companies	Other private means	Railroad retirement	Federal civilian employees[1]	State and local employees	Old-age, survivors and disability insurance[2]
1950	5,600	N.A.	2,553	4,344	5,154	13,721
1960	18,850	40,900	3,740	10,790	19,600	22,613
1965	27,350	80,200	3,946	16,516	33,100	19,841
1970	41,175	123,900	4,398	23,922	58,200	38,068
1975	72,210	244,300	3,100	39,248	103,700	44,342
1976	88,990	275,300	3,065	44,089	117,300	41,133
1977	101,520	297,300	2,584	50,832	130,800	35,861
1978	116,555	351,300	2,787	57,677	142,573	31,746
1979	138,515	413,100	2,611	65,914	161,649	30,291
1980	166,850	504,400	2,086	75,802	185,226	26,453
1981	193,210	530,200	1,126	86,867	209,444	24,539
1982	233,790	658,100	460	99,462	245,252	24,778[3]
1983	269,425	800,700	601	114,219	289,731	24,867[3]
1984	313,215	860,900	3,712	129,787	324,369	31,075[3]
1985	373,475	1,098,000	5,109	148,166	373,932	42,163[3]
1986	441,390	1,103,200	6,365	167,606	437,229	46,861
1987	495,420	1,126,200	6,860	185,946	512,854	68,807
1988	562,155	1,194,100	8,031	205,145	577,621	109,762
1989	624,290	1,424,900	8,906	225,963	634,978	162,968
1990	695,700	1,383,100	9,891	247,513	720,803	225,277
1991	745,950	1,653,800	10,655	272,765	783,405	280,747
1992	768,215	1,760,700	11,746	300,555	866,131	331,473
1993	825,375	1,989,400	12,047	330,701	929,399	378,285
1994	878,460	2,068,000	12,929	358,012	1,025,381	436,385
1995	892,466	2,431,200	14,271	386,852	N.A.	496,068
1996	915,952	2,794,200	14,898	416,651	N.A.	566,950

Source: Compiled by the American Council of Life Insurance. *Notes:* Some data are revised. These data are as of various dates during the year, since the fiscal years of the plans are not necessarily the same. Trends from year to year are not affected. N.A. stands for not available. 1. Includes the U.S. Civil Service Retirement System, the Tennessee Valley Retirement System, the Foreign Service Retirement System, and the Federal Reserve Employee Retirement System (Board and Bank plans). 2. Beginning in 1957, assets of Disability Insurance trust Funds are included. Hospital and Supplementary Medical Insurance is not included. 3. Included funds borrowed from the Hospital Insurance Trust Fund.

PENSION FUNDS - DISTRIBUTION OF ASSETS - 1952-1996

In millions. Data are for Non-insured Private Pension Funds.

Calendar year	U.S. government securities	Corporate and foreign bonds	Corporate equities	Mortgages	Open-market paper[1]	Time deposits	Demand deposits and currency	Miscellaneous	Total
1952	2,500	4,600	1,800	200	-	400	300	900	10,700
1955	3,000	7,900	6,100	300	-	700	400	1,300	19,600
1960	2,700	15,700	16,600	1,300	-	1,400	600	2,800	40,900
1965	3,000	22,700	41,200	3,400	-	2,900	900	6,200	80,200
1970	3,000	29,400	67,900	4,200	-	6,300	1,100	11,900	123,900
1975	17,900	41,900	110,800	2,400	9,100	14,500	4,400	43,500	244,300
1976	24,200	40,200	129,000	2,400	11,000	16,700	4,500	47,400	275,300
1977	29,800	44,600	127,300	2,500	11,400	19,700	4,800	57,200	297,300
1978	31,900	53,000	154,000	2,700	11,600	23,700	5,200	69,400	351,300
1979	38,600	63,700	180,500	3,100	16,600	27,900	5,100	77,700	413,100
1980	50,500	77,700	230,600	3,600	22,100	31,900	4,200	83,800	504,400
1981	66,900	83,300	222,600	3,900	31,100	36,500	3,400	82,600	530,200
1982	107,800	95,200	288,700	7,800	19,900	49,400	2,300	87,000	658,100
1983	132,700	107,900	357,200	10,100	23,100	60,900	2,700	106,000	800,700
1984	153,900	123,400	366,900	9,700	26,500	68,000	3,300	109,100	860,900
1985	201,000	99,400	519,900	14,300	31,000	76,500	3,300	152,600	1,098,000
1986	183,000	124,400	494,100	11,600	36,700	87,000	1,900	164,500	1,103,200
1987	194,300	122,200	509,400	8,300	45,800	76,200	1,600	168,400	1,126,200
1988	210,600	126,400	502,600	16,600	41,700	85,800	4,500	205,600	1,194,100
1989	255,700	133,900	637,200	24,600	44,700	108,200	4,100	216,400	1,424,900
1990	288,900	146,300	591,100	24,900	45,100	99,000	3,300	184,600	1,383,100
1991	310,900	162,500	797,600	18,200	51,500	99,500	3,000	210,700	1,653,800
1992	327,300	185,600	882,700	14,500	54,300	77,400	2,900	216,000	1,760,700
1993	351,100	207,800	1,053,700	14,500	64,400	69,000	3,000	226,000	1,989,400
1994	365,400	230,500	1,091,900	15,700	79,200	62,900	2,900	219,600	2,068,000
1995	393,900	264,300	1,412,100	16,700	85,000	47,200	2,800	209,300	2,431,200
1996	407,300	292,200	1,737,300	18,000	89,600	37,500	2,700	209,600	2,794,200

Source: Federal Reserve System. *Notes:* Some data are revised. Details may not add to totals due to rounding. 1. Includes Money Market Fund shares.

PENSION FUNDS - FEDERAL - 1940-1996

In millions. Data are for Federal Old-Age, Survivors and Disability Insurance Programs.

Year	Persons insured for retirement benefits	Assets[2] (trust funds) (end of year)	Contributions during year[1]			
			Employer	Employee	Self-employed	Total
1940	24.2	2,031	319	319	-	638
1945	33.4	7,121	643	643	-	1,285
1950	59.8	13,721	1,334	1,334	-	2,667
1955	70.5	21,663	2,730	2,664	319	5,713
1960	84.4	22,613	5,632	5,543	701	11,876
1965	94.8	19,841	8,183	7,991	1,032	17,205
1970	108.3	38,068	16,643	16,321	1,774	34,737
1975	123.1	44,342	30,746	30,478	3,036	64,259
1976	126.0	41,133	34,381	34,080	3,133	71,595
1977	129.0	35,861	37,724	37,439	3,548	78,710
1978	133.3	31,746	42,745	42,370	3,768	88,883
1979	137.3	30,291	49,546	49,084	4,404	103,034
1980	140.4	26,453	56,036	55,692	4,983	116,711
1981	142.9	24,539	67,046	66,690	5,628	139,364
1982	144.7	24,778[3]	69,702	69,492	6,473	145,667
1983	146.5	24,867[3]	72,314	72,070	5,879	150,263
1984	148.3	31,075[3]	85,647	81,125	7,372	174,145
1985	150.9	42,163[3]	91,801	91,488	8,497	191,785
1986	153.2	46,861	98,964	98,454	9,611	207,029
1987	155.7	68,807	104,781	104,375	11,104	220,260
1988	158.3	109,762	117,728	117,165	14,317	249,209
1989	161.3	162,968	128,832	127,960	14,799	271,591
1990	164.0	225,277	138,686	137,819	17,508	294,013
1991	165.9	280,747	140,751	140,081	20,380	301,212
1992	167.4	331,473	146,353	145,603	18,962	310,918
1993	168.9	378,285	153,154	152,636	15,917	321,707
1994	170.4	436,385	163,079	162,254	19,019	344,352
1995	172.4	496,068	169,643	168,880	20,247	358,771
1996	174.3	566,950	180,687	179,788	18,096	378,571

Source: Social Security Administration. *Notes:* Some data are revised. Data may not add to totals due to rounding. 1. Figures do not include contributions to the hospital and medical insurance programs. 2. Assets do not reflect solely the contributions paid for Social Security by the private economy, less payments and administration costs. For example, prior to 1940, contributions were paid into the government general funds, and an appropriation was then made to a "reserve account" from the general funds, not necessarily equal to the contributions. The OASI trust fund was established in 1940, and from time to time payments from government general funds have been made to this trust fund to cover special items, such as costs of benefits to survivors of certain World War II servicemen. The DI trust fund was established in 1957, and includes certain payments other than regular contributions, such as reimbursement for non-contributory credit for military service. Other payments from government general funds will be made into these funds in the future to cover costs of such items as the special payments to persons 72 and over provided in the Tax Adjustment Act of 1966. The assets shown above do not include funds in the two newest trust funds - the hospital insurance trust fund, effective January 1, 1966, and the supplementary medical insurance trust fund, effective July, 1966. 3. Includes funds borrowed from the Hospital Insurance Trust Fund.

PENSION PLAN COVERAGE OF WORKERS, BY SELECTED CHARACTERISTICS, 1995

Covers workers as of March 1996 who had earnings in 1995. Based on Current Population Survey.

Sex and age	Number with coverage (1,000)				Percent of total workers			
	Total[1]	White	Black	Hispanic[2]	Total[1]	White	Black	Hispanic[2]
Total	57,837	49,435	6,260	3,191	41.2	41.4	41.2	25.1
Male	32,310	28,050	3,059	1,831	43.3	43.6	42.2	24.5
Under 65 years old	31,633	27,458	2,997	1,807	44.0	44.5	42.3	24.5
15 to 24 years old	1,633	1,368	179	138	13.3	13.1	13.8	8.7
25 to 44 years old	18,217	15,661	1,845	1,189	47.3	47.8	46.1	26.7
45 to 64 years old	11,784	10,430	973	480	55.9	56.4	54.5	36.5
65 years old and over	677	592	62	25	23.7	22.7	35.3	21.0
Female	25,527	21,385	3,202	1,360	38.9	38.9	40.3	26.0
Under 65 years old	25,057	20,967	3,157	1,344	39.4	39.5	40.5	26.1
15 to 24 years old	1,092	903	145	95	9.6	9.6	10.4	8.5
25 to 44 years old	14,672	12,099	2,004	869	43.7	43.8	45.1	29.6
45 to 6 years old	9,293	7,965	1,009	380	49.8	49.8	51.7	34.7
65 years old and over	470	418	44	16	22.3	22.0	27.0	24.5

Source: Statistical Abstract of the United States, 1997, p. 381. *Primary Source*: U.S. Bureau of the Census, unpublished data. *Notes:* 1. Includes other races, not shown separately. 2. Hispanic persons may be of any race.

STATE AND LOCAL GOVERNMENT RETIREMENT SYSTEMS, BENEFICIARIES AND FINANCES: 1980 TO 1994

In billions of dollars, except as indicated. For fiscal years closed during the 12 months ending June 30.

Year and level of government	Number of beneficiaries (1,000)	Receipts					Benefits and withdrawals			Cash and security holdings
		Total	Employee contri-butions	Government contributions		Earnings on investments	Total	Benefits	With-drawals	
				State	Local					
1980:										
All systems	(NA)	37.3	6.5	7.6	10.0	13.3	14.0	12.2	1.8	185
State-administered	(NA)	28.6	5.3	7.4	5.6	10.3	10.3	8.8	1.4	145
Locally administered	(NA)	8.7	1.2	0.2	4.3	3.0	3.8	3.4	0.4	41
1990:										
All systems	4,026	111.3	13.9	14.0	18.6	64.9	38.4	36.0	2.4	721
State-administered	3,232	89.2	11.6	14.0	11.5	52.0	29.6	27.6	2.0	575
Locally administered	794	22.2	2.2	(Z)	7.0	12.9	8.8	8.4	0.4	145
1993:										
All systems	4,562	135.4	16.5	15.2	20.4	83.3	51.6	49.1	2.5	929
State-administered	3,643	109.4	13.8	15.2	12.9	67.6	40.0	37.9	2.1	750
Locally administered	919	26.0	2.7	(Z)	7.5	15.8	11.6		0.4	180
1994:										
All systems	4,889	138.7	17.3	15.5	21.2	84.6	56.4	53.4	3.0	1,025
State-administered	3,979	113.2	14.7	15.5	13.6	69.4	43.8	41.2	2.6	826
Locally administered	910	25.5	2.6	(Z)	7.7	15.2	12.6	12.2	0.5	199

Source: *Statistical Abstract of the United States*, 1997, p. 381. *Primary Source*: U.S. Bureau of the Census, *Finances of Employee-Retirement Systems of State and Local Governments*, series GF, No. 2, annual.

FEDERAL CIVIL SERVICE RETIREMENT: 1980 TO 1996

As of September 30 or for year ending September 30. Covers both Civil Service Retirement System and Federal Employees Retirement System.

Item	Unit	1980	1985	1990	1991	1992	1993	1994	1995	1996
Employees covered[1]	1,000	2,720	2,750	2,945	2,885	2,933	2,843	2,778	2,668	2,629
Annuitants, total	1,000	1,675	1,955	2,143	2,184	2,185	2,242	2,263	2,311	2,333
Age and service	1,000	905	1,122	1,288	1,325	1,322	1,378	1,398	1,441	1,459
Disability	1,000	343	332	297	289	282	274	268	263	260
Survivors	1,000	427	501	558	570	581	589	597	607	614
Receipts, total[2]	Mil. dol.	24,389	40,790	52,689	56,815	59,737	62,878	63,390	65,684	67,535
Employee contributions	Mil. dol.	3,686	4,679	4,501	4,563	4,713	4,703	4,610	4,498	4,398
Federal government contributions	Mil. dol.	15,562	22,301	27,368	29,509	30,785	32,668	32,434	33,130	33,991
Disbursements, total[3]	Mil. dol.	14,977	23,203	31,416	33,209	33,187	35,123	36,532	38,435	39,711
Age and service annuitants[4]	Mil. dol.	12,639	19,414	26,495	27,997	27,684	29,288	30,440	32,070	32,970
Survivors	Mil. dol.	1,912	3,158	4,366	4,716	5,093	5,377	5,607	5,864	6,221
Average monthly benefit:										
Age and service	Dollars	992	1,189	1,369	1,439	1,493	1,537	1,587	1,643	1,698
Disability	Dollars	723	881	1,008	1,059	1,094	1,120	1,141	1,164	1,184
Survivors	Dollars	392	528	653	698	731	760	789	819	849
Cash and security holdings	Bil. dol.	73.7	142.3	238.0	261.6	289.6	317.4	344.3	366.2	394.1

Source: Statistical Abstract of the United States, 1997, p. 380. *Primary Source*: U.S. Office of Personnel Management, *Civil Service Retirement and Disability Trust Fund Annual Report. Notes:* 1. Excludes employees in Leave Without Pay status. 2. Includes interest on investments. 3. Includes refunds, death claims. 4. Includes disability annuitants.

SIC 6390

INSURANCE CARRIERS, NEC

This industry includes all establishments that provide insurance coverage but are not classified under any of the other insurance categories. The types of organizations included under this SIC include bank deposit insurance providers, deposit or share insurance underwriters, the Federal Deposit Insurance Corporation (FDIC), the Federal Savings and Loan Insurance Corporation (FSLIC) and/or its successor organization (after 1989), health insurance for pets, and warranty insurance on automobiles.

ESTABLISHMENTS, EMPLOYMENT, AND PAYROLL

	1990	1991		1992		1993		1994		1995		% change 90-95
		Value	%	Value	%	Value	%	Value	%	Value	%	
All Establishments	262	189	-27.9	211	11.6	162	-23.2	164	1.2	173	5.5	-34.0
Mid-March Employment	7,881	4,161	-47.2	4,903	17.8	2,891	-41.0	2,440	-15.6	2,583	5.9	-67.2
1st Quarter Wages (annualized - $ mil.)	218.5	117.1	-46.4	142.9	22.0	98.9	-30.8	74.6	-24.5	88.7	18.8	-59.4
Payroll per Emp. 1st Q. (annualized)	27,729	28,151	1.5	29,151	3.6	34,193	17.3	30,590	-10.5	34,337	12.2	23.8
Annual Payroll ($ mil.)	226.4	131.8	-41.8	147.9	12.3	95.7	-35.3	84.1	-12.1	91.9	9.3	-59.4
Establishments - 1-4 Emp. Number	114	91	-20.2	100	9.9	(D)	-	86	-	90	4.7	-21.1
Mid-March Employment	205	(D)	-	166	-	(D)	-	142	-	149	4.9	-27.3
1st Quarter Wages (annualized - $ mil.)	6.5	(D)	-	3.8	-	(D)	-	4.8	-	6.3	31.8	-3.0
Payroll per Emp. 1st Q. (annualized)	31,902	(D)	-	22,892	-	(D)	-	33,887	-	42,577	25.6	33.5
Annual Payroll ($ mil.)	7.9	(D)	-	4.5	-	(D)	-	9.2	-	7.2	-22.1	-9.6
Establishments - 5-9 Emp. Number	42	32	-23.8	36	12.5	22	-38.9	(D)	-	(D)	-	-
Mid-March Employment	286	225	-21.3	237	5.3	136	-42.6	(D)	-	(D)	-	-
1st Quarter Wages (annualized - $ mil.)	8.8	7.7	-12.0	8.0	2.8	3.3	-58.3	(D)	-	(D)	-	-
Payroll per Emp. 1st Q. (annualized)	30,797	34,436	11.8	33,620	-2.4	24,412	-27.4	(D)	-	(D)	-	-
Annual Payroll ($ mil.)	9.0	8.8	-1.8	8.6	-2.3	4.2	-51.9	(D)	-	(D)	-	-
Establishments - 10-19 Emp. Number	43	24	-44.2	30	25.0	12	-60.0	18	50.0	21	16.7	-51.2
Mid-March Employment	581	322	-44.6	388	20.5	164	-57.7	260	58.5	298	14.6	-48.7
1st Quarter Wages (annualized - $ mil.)	20.2	9.5	-52.7	10.9	13.8	6.2	-43.0	8.7	40.5	11.6	33.1	-42.7
Payroll per Emp. 1st Q. (annualized)	34,775	29,652	-14.7	28,010	-5.5	37,756	34.8	33,462	-11.4	38,859	16.1	11.7
Annual Payroll ($ mil.)	22.4	9.7	-56.5	11.6	19.0	5.8	-49.6	8.6	46.6	11.8	38.1	-47.1
Establishments - 20-49 Emp. Number	40	20	-50.0	21	5.0	19	-9.5	22	15.8	27	22.7	-32.5
Mid-March Employment	1,279	624	-51.2	685	9.8	580	-15.3	646	11.4	858	32.8	-32.9
1st Quarter Wages (annualized - $ mil.)	46.9	20.4	-56.5	30.0	47.0	20.2	-32.5	21.3	5.1	33.3	56.5	-29.0
Payroll per Emp. 1st Q. (annualized)	36,669	32,699	-10.8	43,790	33.9	34,910	-20.3	32,935	-5.7	38,816	17.9	5.9
Annual Payroll ($ mil.)	45.5	19.4	-57.4	27.3	41.0	19.8	-27.7	23.4	18.4	36.3	55.2	-20.1
Establishments - 50-99 Emp. Number	11	10	-9.1	13	30.0	12	-7.7	10	-16.7	6	-40.0	-45.5
Mid-March Employment	742	(D)	-	899	-	864	-3.9	688	-20.4	426	-38.1	-42.6
1st Quarter Wages (annualized - $ mil.)	22.2	(D)	-	25.8	-	21.9	-15.4	21.7	-0.8	14.7	-32.1	-33.6
Payroll per Emp. 1st Q. (annualized)	29,881	(D)	-	28,752	-	25,310	-12.0	31,517	24.5	34,573	9.7	15.7
Annual Payroll ($ mil.)	19.9	(D)	-	27.3	-	22.9	-16.0	23.9	4.4	13.0	-45.7	-34.7
Establishments - 100-249 Emp. Number	5	9	80.0	7	-22.2	3	-57.1	(D)	-	3	-	-40.0
Mid-March Employment	690	1,111	61.0	988	-11.1	463	-53.1	(D)	-	392	-	-43.2
1st Quarter Wages (annualized - $ mil.)	23.0	21.9	-4.9	23.2	6.1	13.9	-40.0	(D)	-	11.3	-	-50.9
Payroll per Emp. 1st Q. (annualized)	33,380	19,723	-40.9	23,522	19.3	30,108	28.0	(D)	-	28,827	-	-13.6
Annual Payroll ($ mil.)	24.5	23.6	-3.8	23.7	0.6	12.5	-47.4	(D)	-	11.6	-	-52.7
Establishments - 250-499 Emp. Number	4	3	-25.0	4	33.3	-	-	(D)	-	(D)	-	-
Mid-March Employment	1,376	(D)	-	1,540	-	-	-	(D)	-	(D)	-	-
1st Quarter Wages (annualized - $ mil.)	34.0	(D)	-	41.2	-	-	-	(D)	-	(D)	-	-
Payroll per Emp. 1st Q. (annualized)	24,692	(D)	-	26,758	-	-	-	(D)	-	(D)	-	-
Annual Payroll ($ mil.)	38.3	(D)	-	44.9	-	-	-	(D)	-	(D)	-	-
Establishments - 500-999 Emp. Number	2	-	-	-	-	(D)	-	-	-	-	-	-
Mid-March Employment	(D)	-	-	-	-	(D)	-	-	-	-	-	-
1st Quarter Wages (annualized - $ mil.)	(D)	-	-	-	-	(D)	-	-	-	-	-	-
Payroll per Emp. 1st Q. (annualized)	(D)	(D)	-	-	-	(D)	-	-	-	-	-	-
Annual Payroll ($ mil.)	(D)	-	-	-	-	(D)	-	-	-	-	-	-
Estab. - 1000 or More Emp. Number	1	-	-	-	-	-	-	-	-	-	-	-
Mid-March Employment	(D)	-	-	-	-	-	-	-	-	-	-	-
1st Quarter Wages (annualized - $ mil.)	(D)	-	-	-	-	-	-	-	-	-	-	-
Payroll per Emp. 1st Q. (annualized)	(D)	(D)	-	-	-	-	-	-	-	-	-	-
Annual Payroll ($ mil.)	(D)	-	-	-	-	-	-	-	-	-	-	-

Source: County Business Patterns, U.S. Department of Commerce, Washington, D.C., for 1990 through 1995. Payroll per employee is calculated using mid-March employment and 1st Quarter wages, annualized. Annual payroll, also shown, may not equal the annualized 1st Quarter wages. Columns headed by a percent sign (%) indicate change from the previous year. *na* stands for not available. The symbol (D) indicates that data are withheld by the source to avoid disclosure of competitive information. A dash (-) indicates that data are not available or cannot be calculated.

ESTABLISHMENTS
Number

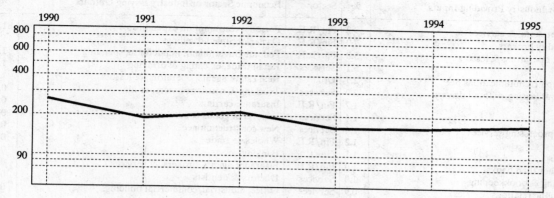

MID-MARCH EMPLOYMENT
Number

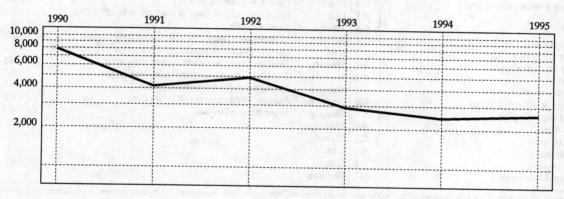

ANNUAL PAYROLL
$ million

INPUTS AND OUTPUTS FOR INSURANCE CARRIERS - SIC GROUP 63

Economic Sector or Industry Providing Inputs	%	Sector	Economic Sector or Industry Buying Outputs	%	Sector
Insurance agents, brokers, & services	59.2	Fin/R.E.	Personal consumption expenditures	81.3	
Security & commodity brokers	7.0	Fin/R.E.	Owner-occupied dwellings	1.8	Fin/R.E.
Real estate agents, operators, & lessors	5.8	Fin/R.E.	Federal Government, nondefense, spending	1.3	Gov't
Legal services	5.1	Services	Retail trade, ex eating & drinking	1.0	Trade
Telephone/telegraph communications nec	2.7	Util.	Real estate agents, operators, & lessors	1.0	Fin/R.E.
Automotive rental & leasing, without drivers	2.0	Services	Trucking & courier services, ex air	0.8	Util.
Banking	1.7	Fin/R.E.	Insurance carriers	0.8	Fin/R.E.
Advertising	1.4	Services	Exports of goods & services	0.8	Foreign
Computer & data processing services	1.4	Services	New construction nec	0.6	Constr.
Insurance carriers	1.2	Fin/R.E.	Wholesale trade	0.5	Trade
U.S. Postal Service	1.1	Gov't	Banking	0.5	Fin/R.E.
Credit agencies other than banks	1.0	Fin/R.E.	Insurance agents, brokers, & services	0.4	Fin/R.E.
Accounting, auditing & bookkeeping	1.0	Services	Doctors & dentists	0.4	Services
Management & public relations services	0.9	Services	Office, industrial/commercial buildings	0.3	Constr.
Commercial printing	0.8	Manufg.	Repair & maintenance construction nec	0.3	Constr.
Business services nec	0.8	Services	Residential 1 unit structures, nonfarm	0.3	Constr.
Eating & drinking places	0.6	Services	Hospitals	0.3	Services
Hotels	0.5	Services	Highways, bridges, horizontal construction	0.2	Constr.
Miscellaneous equipment rental & leasing	0.5	Services	Electric services (utilities)	0.2	Util.
Repair & maintenance construction nec	0.4	Constr.	Eating & drinking places	0.2	Services
Air transportation	0.4	Util.	S/L Govt., elementary & high schools, spending	0.2	S/L Govt
Wholesale trade	0.4	Trade	Meat animals	0.1	Agric.
Personnel supply services	0.4	Services	Maintenance/repair of residential structures	0.1	Constr.
Trucking & courier services, ex air	0.3	Util.	Motor vehicles & passenger car bodies	0.1	Manufg.
Photographic equipment & supplies	0.2	Manufg.	Sanitary services, steam supply, irrigation	0.1	Util.
Tires & inner tubes	0.2	Manufg.	Telephone/telegraph communications nec	0.1	Util.
Business & professional associations	0.2	Services	Credit agencies other than banks	0.1	Fin/R.E.
Services to dwellings & other buildings	0.2	Services	Automotive repair shops & services	0.1	Services
Magnetic & optical recording media	0.1	Manufg.	Business services nec	0.1	Services
Manifold business forms	0.1	Manufg.			
Paper & paperboard mills	0.1	Manufg.			
Electric services (utilities)	0.1	Util.			
Local & suburban transit	0.1	Util.			
Automobile parking & car washes	0.1	Services			

Source: Benchmark Input-Output Accounts for the U.S. Economy, 1992, U.S. Department of Commerce, Washington, D.C., November 1997. Data, as reported in the source, are organized by the 1987 SIC structure in use in 1992.

OCCUPATIONS EMPLOYED BY PENSION FUNDS AND INSURANCE, NEC

Occupation	% of Total 1996	Change to 2006	Occupation	% of Total 1996	Change to 2006
Title examiners & searchers	10.6	8.8	Underwriters	2.7	44.7
General office clerks	8.4	17.0	Sales & related workers nec	2.7	49.6
Secretaries, except legal & medical	6.9	7.9	Insurance sales workers	2.6	26.9
General managers & top executives	6.3	31.8	Management support workers nec	2.2	36.0
Clerical supervisors & managers	4.9	36.0	Financial managers	2.1	36.0
Bookkeeping, accounting, & auditing clerks	4.6	8.8	File clerks	2.0	-2.9
Legal assistants & clerks nec	4.3	104.0	Accountants & auditors	1.8	25.9
Typists, including word processing	4.0	-11.6	Computer programmers	1.8	12.0
Insurance policy processing clerks	3.2	8.8	Messengers	1.3	8.8
Receptionists & information clerks	3.0	36.0	Marketing & sales worker supervisors	1.3	36.1
Insurance claims clerks	3.0	38.9	Claims examiners, property & casualty	1.3	37.0
Loan & credit clerks	2.9	37.3	Data entry keyers, except composing	1.2	8.8
Insurance adjusters, examiners, investigators	2.8	39.7	Managers & administrators nec	1.0	34.7

Sources: *Industry-Occupation Matrix*, Bureau of Labor Statistics. These data relate to one or more 3-digit SIC industry groups rather than to a single 4-digit SIC. The change reported for each occupation to the year 2005 is a percent of growth or decline as estimated by the Bureau of Labor Statistics. The abbreviation *nec* stands for not elsewhere classified.

U.S. AND STATE DATA ON INDUSTRY REVENUES AND OTHER ACCOUNTS FOR 1992

State	No. of Estab.	Employ-ment	Payroll ($ mil.)	Revenues ($ mil.)	Empl./ Estab.	Revenue/ Estab. ($)	Payroll/ Estab. ($)	Revenue/ Empl. ($)	Payroll/ Empl. ($)
UNITED STATES	134	2,823	95.9	700.7	21	5,229,321	715,567	248,221	33,966
California	13	835	35.8	8.8	64	680,615	2,755,769	10,596	42,904
Colorado	4	110	3.8	9.1	28	2,272,000	947,500	82,618	34,455
Florida	7	-	(D)	(D)	(D)	(D)	(D)	(D)	(D)
Georgia	5	-	(D)	(D)	(D)	(D)	(D)	(D)	(D)
Illinois	7	-	(D)	(D)	(D)	(D)	(D)	(D)	(D)
Maryland	4	-	(D)	(D)	(D)	(D)	(D)	(D)	(D)
Massachusetts	3	-	(D)	(D)	(D)	(D)	(D)	(D)	(D)
Michigan	1	-	(D)	(D)	(D)	(D)	(D)	(D)	(D)
Minnesota	1	-	(D)	(D)	(D)	(D)	(D)	(D)	(D)
Missouri	1	-	(D)	(D)	(D)	(D)	(D)	(D)	(D)
New Jersey	8	388	10.7	46.0	49	5,749,250	1,339,250	118,541	27,613
New York	6	23	0.6	2.0	4	339,500	97,833	88,565	25,522
North Carolina	2	-	(D)	(D)	(D)	(D)	(D)	(D)	(D)
Ohio	7	62	2.5	26.8	9	3,825,143	354,857	431,871	40,065
Pennsylvania	6	-	(D)	(D)	(D)	(D)	(D)	(D)	(D)
Tennessee	2	-	(D)	(D)	(D)	(D)	(D)	(D)	(D)
Texas	11	178	5.7	26.0	16	2,366,273	516,909	146,230	31,944
Virginia	2	-	(D)	(D)	(D)	(D)	(D)	(D)	(D)
Washington	1	-	(D)	(D)	(D)	(D)	(D)	(D)	(D)
Wisconsin	3	-	(D)	(D)	(D)	(D)	(D)	(D)	(D)

Source: 1992 Economic Census, U.S. Department of Commerce, Washington, D.C. This is the only table that shows revenue data as collected by the Bureau of the Census in an Economic Census. The symbol (D) indicates that data are withheld by the source to avoid disclosure of competitive information. A dash (-) indicates that data are not available or cannot be calculated.

STATE-BY-STATE DATA ON ESTABLISHMENTS, EMPLOYMENT, AND PAYROLL - 1994 AND 1995

State	1994					1995					% Change Empl.
	No. of Estab.	Employ-ment	Pay / Empl.	Payroll ($ mil.)	Pay / Estab.	No. of Estab.	Employ-ment	Pay / Empl.	Payroll ($ mil.)	Pay / Estab.	
Alabama	3	(D)	-	(D)	-	3	(D)	-	(D)	-	-
Alaska	1	(D)	-	(D)	-	1	(D)	-	(D)	-	-
Arkansas	2	(D)	-	(D)	-	1	(D)	-	(D)	-	-
California	12	170	30,024	6.8	569,750	13	174	46,828	7.2	553,385	2.4
Colorado	7	127	30,425	4.1	592,571	6	34	45,294	1.7	278,833	-73.2
Connecticut	4	(D)	-	(D)	-	4	(D)	-	(D)	-	-
Delaware	1	(D)	-	(D)	-	1	(D)	-	(D)	-	-
District of Columbia	1	(D)	-	(D)	-	1	(D)	-	(D)	-	-
Florida	11	233	31,313	7.7	701,273	13	206	29,320	6.6	507,692	-11.6
Georgia	5	72	50,278	3.9	785,200	4	32	20,375	0.6	159,000	-55.6
Idaho	1	(D)	-	(D)	-	1	(D)	-	(D)	-	-
Illinois	12	175	31,794	5.7	476,333	14	177	33,966	5.4	389,000	1.1
Indiana	3	(D)	-	(D)	-	3	(D)	-	(D)	-	-
Iowa	1	(D)	-	(D)	-	1	(D)	-	(D)	-	-
Kansas	2	(D)	-	(D)	-	2	(D)	-	(D)	-	-
Kentucky	1	(D)	-	(D)	-	2	(D)	-	(D)	-	-
Louisiana	2	(D)	-	(D)	-	2	(D)	-	(D)	-	-
Maryland	4	20	33,600	0.7	168,250	4	20	36,800	0.7	162,500	0.0
Massachusetts	5	27	79,407	2.8	553,400	6	67	57,612	3.6	605,500	148.1
Michigan	3	(D)	-	(D)	-	1	(D)	-	(D)	-	-
Minnesota	2	(D)	-	(D)	-	2	(D)	-	(D)	-	-
Mississippi	1	(D)	-	(D)	-	1	(D)	-	(D)	-	-
Missouri	4	7	18,286	0.2	40,750	5	(D)	-	(D)	-	-
Montana	(D)	(D)	(D)	(D)	(D)	1	(D)	-	(D)	-	-
Nebraska	1	(D)	-	(D)	-	(D)	(D)	(D)	(D)	(D)	-
Nevada	2	(D)	-	(D)	-	2	(D)	-	(D)	-	-
New Hampshire	1	(D)	-	(D)	-	1	(D)	-	(D)	-	-
New Jersey	12	259	37,328	9.1	759,167	6	178	40,202	6.7	1,124,333	-31.3
New Mexico	1	(D)	-	(D)	-	1	(D)	-	(D)	-	-
New York	8	24	22,333	1.2	152,750	9	65	39,446	3.2	354,778	170.8
North Carolina	3	7	11,429	0.3	88,333	3	(D)	-	(D)	-	-
North Dakota	1	(D)	-	(D)	-	1	(D)	-	(D)	-	-
Ohio	6	58	36,000	2.3	384,000	5	53	39,925	2.5	499,600	-8.6
Oklahoma	3	(D)	-	(D)	-	6	402	21,085	8.9	1,478,833	-
Oregon	1	(D)	-	(D)	-	1	(D)	-	(D)	-	-
Pennsylvania	10	89	24,000	2.8	280,000	13	189	24,466	5.1	395,846	112.4
South Carolina	1	(D)	-	(D)	-	1	(D)	-	(D)	-	-
South Dakota	1	(D)	-	(D)	-	1	(D)	-	(D)	-	-
Tennessee	3	9	48,444	0.5	166,000	4	7	63,429	0.4	107,750	-22.2
Texas	10	267	26,532	8.3	828,600	11	250	41,280	12.6	1,146,455	-6.4
Utah	2	(D)	-	(D)	-	2	(D)	-	(D)	-	-
Vermont	1	(D)	-	(D)	-	1	(D)	-	(D)	-	-
Virginia	4	31	27,871	1.4	349,500	6	65	30,031	2.0	337,667	109.7
Washington	(D)	(D)	(D)	(D)	(D)	2	(D)	-	(D)	-	-
Wisconsin	5	55	33,018	1.8	356,400	5	(D)	-	(D)	-	-

Source: County Business Patterns, U.S. Department of Commerce, Washington, D.C., for 1994 and 1995. Employment shown is for mid-March of the year shown. Payroll per employee is calculated by annualizing 1st Quarter payroll (not shown) and then dividing that value by mid-March employment. Dividing total annual payroll (columns 5 and 10) by employment, therefore, will *not* yield the payroll per employee figure (columns 4 and 9). The symbol (D) indicates that data are withheld by the source to avoid disclosure of competitive information. A dash (-) indicates that data are not available or cannot be calculated.

ESTABLISHMENTS 1995 - STATE AND REGIONAL CONCENTRATION

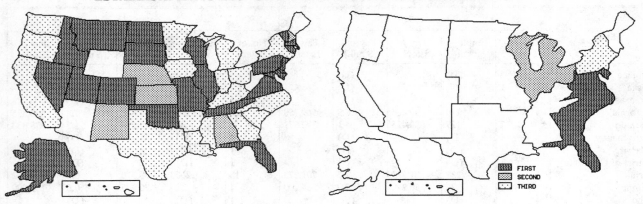

EMPLOYMENT 1995 - STATE AND REGIONAL CONCENTRATION

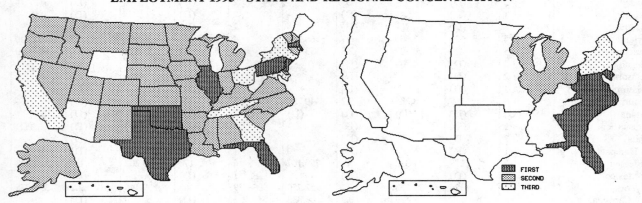

PAYROLL 1995 - STATE AND REGIONAL CONCENTRATION

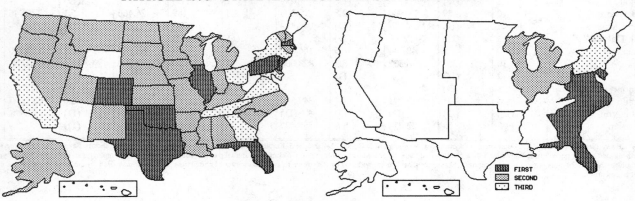

States with the darkest shading indicate those states which have proportionately more establishments, employment, or payrolls than would be indicated by the state's population. States with light shading are states with proportionately fewer establishments, less employment, and lower payrolls than population distribution. States shaded grey are within 15 percent of the state's population proportion in these catego-ries. States for which no data are available are shown as average (grey). *Regions* are shaded to indicate absolute rank in the category. If no data for the category are available, establishment counts are used to shade the regions. Source of the data is the table on the facing page.

LEADING COMPANIES - SIC 6399 - Insurance Carriers, nec

Number shown: **19**   Total sales/assets ($ mil): **38,711**   Total employment (000): **11.5**

Company Name	Address				CEO Name	Phone	Co. Type	Sales/Assets ($ mil)	Empl. (000)
Federal Deposit Insurance Corp.	550 17th St. N.W.	Washington	DC	20429	Dennis F. Geer	202-393-8400	R	27,279 TA	9.2
Pension Benefit Guaranty Corp.	1200 K St. N.W.	Washington	DC	20005	Martin Slate	202-326-4000	R	6,602 TA	0.7
Fidelity and Guaranty Life Insurance Co.	100 E. Pratt St.	Baltimore	MD	21202	Harry N. Stout	410-895-0100	S	2,570 TA*	0.1
Western World Insurance Group Inc.	48 S. Franklin Tpk.	Ramsey	NJ	07446	Andrew Frazier	201-847-8600	R	501 TA	0.2
Mutual Insurance Company of Arizona	2602 E. Thomas Ave.	Phoenix	AZ	85016	Robert Crawford	602-956-5276	R	385 TA	<0.1
General Star Management Co.	PO Box 10354	Stamford	CT	06904	Kevin P. Brooks	203-328-5700	S	360 TA*	0.2
K and K Insurance Group Inc.	PO Box 2338	Fort Wayne	IN	46801	Stephen Lunsford	219-459-5000	S	290 TA*	0.3
Danielson Holding Corp.	767 3rd Ave.	New York	NY	10017	Martin J. Whitman	212-888-0347	P	188 TA	0.2
Travel Guard International Inc.	1145 Clark St.	Stevens Point	WI	54481	John M. Noel	715-345-0505	R	120 TA	0.1
American Mutual Share Insurance Corp.	5656 Frantz Rd.	Dublin	OH	43017	Dennis Adams	614-764-1900	R	85 TA	<0.1
Equisure Inc.	701 4th Ave.	Minneapolis	MN	55415	Barrie Harding	612-337-9507	P	77 TA	<0.1
California Veterinary Services Inc.	4175 E. La Palma Ave.	Anaheim	CA	92807	Jack Stephens	714-996-2311	R	60 TA	<0.1
Kansas Bankers Surety Co.	611 S. Kansas Ave.	Topeka	KS	66603	Don Towel	913-234-2631	R	54 TA	<0.1
Safeware, The Insurance Agency Inc.	2929 N. High St.	Columbus	OH	43202	Sherry Scott	614-262-0559	R	38 TA*	<0.1
Media/Professional Insurance Agency Inc.	2300 Main St.	Kansas City	MO	64108	John Pfannenstiel	816-471-6118	S	34	0.1
Bancinsurance Corp.	PO Box 182138	Columbus	OH	43218	Si Sokol	614-228-2800	P	31 TA	<0.1
Automobile Protection Corp.	15 Dunwood Park Dr.	Atlanta	GA	30338	Larry I. Dorfman	770-394-7070	P	31 TA	0.1
National Capital Management Corp.	520 Madison Ave.	New York	NY	10022	John C. Shaw	212-980-3883	P	4 TA	<0.1
Kirk Horse Insurance Inc.	316 W. High St.	Lexington	KY	40507	Ronald K. Kirk	606-231-0838	R	2 TA	<0.1

Source: Ward's Business Directory of U.S. Private and Public Companies, 1996. Company type codes: P - Public, R - Private, S - Subsidiary, D - Division, J - Joint Venture, A - Affiliate, G - Group. If the dollar values shown are not sales, the following codes apply: TA - Total Assets; OR - Operating Revenues; GB - Gross Billings. * - estimated dollar value. < - less than; *na* - not available.

SIC 6411

INSURANCE AGENTS, BROKERS, & SERVICE

The industry includes agents and brokers dealing in insurance as well as organizations that offer services to insurance companies and to policyholders. The agents and brokers included in SIC 6410 are primarily engaged in representing one or more insurance carriers. They are independent contractors in the sale or placement of insurance contracts with carriers; they are not employed by the insurance carriers that they represent. The service organizations included here provide services to the insurance industry; however, establishments engaged in searching real estate titles are excluded from this SIC; they are included under SIC 6540 (found later in this book).

In addition to insurance agents and brokers, specific categories of activity included in SIC 6410 are fire insurance underwriters' laboratories, fire loss appraisers, insurance adjusters, advisory services, claim adjusters operating independently, educational services, information bureaus, inspection and investigation services, loss prevention services, medical claims processing services on a fee basis, patrol services, pension and retirement plan consulting services, policyholders' consulting services, professional standards organizations for insurance, rate making organizations for insurance, and report and research services.

ESTABLISHMENTS, EMPLOYMENT, AND PAYROLL

	1990	1991		1992		1993		1994		1995		% change 90-95
		Value	%	Value	%	Value	%	Value	%	Value	%	
All Establishments	110,834	112,559	1.6	114,032	1.3	122,292	7.2	123,998	1.4	125,361	1.1	13.1
Mid-March Employment	712,305	678,423	-4.8	641,875	-5.4	656,007	2.2	661,685	0.9	676,602	2.3	-5.0
1st Quarter Wages (annualized - $ mil.)	19,935.0	19,265.0	-3.4	18,976.2	-1.5	18,864.4	-0.6	20,099.7	6.5	22,183.7	10.4	11.3
Payroll per Emp. 1st Q. (annualized)	27,987	28,397	1.5	29,564	4.1	28,756	-2.7	30,377	5.6	32,787	7.9	17.2
Annual Payroll ($ mil.)	20,250.9	19,581.5	-3.3	19,443.6	-0.7	20,259.4	4.2	21,241.8	4.8	22,830.4	7.5	12.7
Establishments - 1-4 Emp. Number	80,038	80,594	0.7	83,835	4.0	90,608	8.1	92,310	1.9	93,437	1.2	16.7
Mid-March Employment	146,650	148,258	1.1	151,890	2.4	163,934	7.9	165,511	1.0	168,505	1.8	14.9
1st Quarter Wages (annualized - $ mil.)	2,679.1	2,801.0	4.5	2,974.1	6.2	3,152.3	6.0	3,346.3	6.2	3,642.0	8.8	35.9
Payroll per Emp. 1st Q. (annualized)	18,269	18,893	3.4	19,580	3.6	19,229	-1.8	20,218	5.1	21,613	6.9	18.3
Annual Payroll ($ mil.)	3,004.9	3,198.1	6.4	3,350.5	4.8	3,663.7	9.3	3,844.5	4.9	4,121.9	7.2	37.2
Establishments - 5-9 Emp. Number	17,666	19,384	9.7	18,107	-6.6	19,247	6.3	19,127	-0.6	19,204	0.4	8.7
Mid-March Employment	113,731	124,790	9.7	115,936	-7.1	123,045	6.1	122,015	-0.8	122,686	0.5	7.9
1st Quarter Wages (annualized - $ mil.)	2,735.6	3,148.7	15.1	3,000.6	-4.7	3,126.5	4.2	3,210.2	2.7	3,437.9	7.1	25.7
Payroll per Emp. 1st Q. (annualized)	24,053	25,232	4.9	25,882	2.6	25,409	-1.8	26,310	3.5	28,022	6.5	16.5
Annual Payroll ($ mil.)	2,853.8	3,290.2	15.3	3,163.1	-3.9	3,406.6	7.7	3,474.4	2.0	3,644.5	4.9	27.7
Establishments - 10-19 Emp. Number	7,478	7,541	0.8	7,177	-4.8	7,608	6.0	7,627	0.2	7,664	0.5	2.5
Mid-March Employment	99,375	99,192	-0.2	94,373	-4.9	100,103	6.1	100,049	-0.1	101,127	1.1	1.8
1st Quarter Wages (annualized - $ mil.)	2,873.4	3,007.3	4.7	3,037.7	1.0	3,052.9	0.5	3,204.8	5.0	3,476.6	8.5	21.0
Payroll per Emp. 1st Q. (annualized)	28,914	30,318	4.9	32,188	6.2	30,498	-5.2	32,033	5.0	34,378	7.3	18.9
Annual Payroll ($ mil.)	2,988.4	3,114.8	4.2	3,083.6	-1.0	3,326.4	7.9	3,431.8	3.2	3,644.6	6.2	22.0
Establishments - 20-49 Emp. Number	3,902	3,527	-9.6	3,482	-1.3	3,432	-1.4	3,534	3.0	3,622	2.5	-7.2
Mid-March Employment	115,595	103,687	-10.3	103,823	0.1	101,794	-2.0	105,031	3.2	107,073	1.9	-7.4
1st Quarter Wages (annualized - $ mil.)	3,729.0	3,471.2	-6.9	3,585.9	3.3	3,442.1	-4.0	3,790.5	10.1	4,166.0	9.9	11.7
Payroll per Emp. 1st Q. (annualized)	32,259	33,478	3.8	34,539	3.2	33,814	-2.1	36,090	6.7	38,908	7.8	20.6
Annual Payroll ($ mil.)	3,768.8	3,484.9	-7.5	3,657.8	5.0	3,701.8	1.2	3,937.2	6.4	4,234.5	7.6	12.4
Establishments - 50-99 Emp. Number	1,043	909	-12.8	866	-4.7	875	1.0	874	-0.1	898	2.7	-13.9
Mid-March Employment	70,611	61,837	-12.4	58,306	-5.7	59,080	1.3	59,157	0.1	61,070	3.2	-13.5
1st Quarter Wages (annualized - $ mil.)	2,363.9	2,088.4	-11.7	2,092.2	0.2	2,129.0	1.8	2,301.3	8.1	2,583.7	12.3	9.3
Payroll per Emp. 1st Q. (annualized)	33,477	33,772	0.9	35,883	6.2	36,036	0.4	38,901	8.0	42,307	8.8	26.4
Annual Payroll ($ mil.)	2,285.3	2,018.7	-11.7	2,073.5	2.7	2,196.8	5.9	2,279.4	3.8	2,501.1	9.7	9.4
Establishments - 100-249 Emp. Number	545	453	-16.9	451	-0.4	422	-6.4	433	2.6	423	-2.3	-22.4
Mid-March Employment	80,761	68,524	-15.2	65,601	-4.3	61,765	-5.8	64,375	4.2	62,038	-3.6	-23.2
1st Quarter Wages (annualized - $ mil.)	2,742.1	2,345.7	-14.5	2,401.5	2.4	2,273.3	-5.3	2,468.7	8.6	2,611.6	5.8	-4.8
Payroll per Emp. 1st Q. (annualized)	33,953	34,232	0.8	36,607	6.9	36,806	0.5	38,349	4.2	42,097	9.8	24.0
Annual Payroll ($ mil.)	2,600.3	2,240.0	-13.9	2,300.6	2.7	2,281.4	-0.8	2,459.3	7.8	2,531.1	2.9	-2.7
Establishments - 250-499 Emp. Number	113	114	0.9	87	-23.7	75	-13.8	70	-6.7	86	22.9	-23.9
Mid-March Employment	37,061	38,867	4.9	28,253	-27.3	24,933	-11.8	23,324	-6.5	28,743	23.2	-22.4
1st Quarter Wages (annualized - $ mil.)	1,238.9	1,287.5	3.9	1,100.6	-14.5	848.0	-23.0	947.3	11.7	1,177.6	24.3	-4.9
Payroll per Emp. 1st Q. (annualized)	33,430	33,125	-0.9	38,956	17.6	34,012	-12.7	40,616	19.4	40,971	0.9	22.6
Annual Payroll ($ mil.)	1,185.3	1,151.8	-2.8	1,012.7	-12.1	826.0	-18.4	942.8	14.1	1,163.9	23.5	-1.8
Establishments - 500-999 Emp. Number	31	23	-25.8	17	-26.1	16	-5.9	15	-6.3	20	33.3	-35.5
Mid-March Employment	20,345	15,324	-24.7	11,176	-27.1	9,507	-14.9	10,173	7.0	13,617	33.9	-33.1
1st Quarter Wages (annualized - $ mil.)	613.3	456.6	-25.5	369.8	-19.0	393.6	6.4	369.3	-6.2	547.3	48.2	-10.8
Payroll per Emp. 1st Q. (annualized)	30,145	29,798	-1.2	33,090	11.0	41,406	25.1	36,305	-12.3	40,191	10.7	33.3
Annual Payroll ($ mil.)	607.1	423.9	-30.2	363.0	-14.4	368.4	1.5	370.3	0.5	531.5	43.6	-12.5
Estab. - 1000 or More Emp. Number	18	14	-22.2	10	-28.6	9	-10.0	8	-11.1	7	-12.5	-61.1
Mid-March Employment	28,176	17,944	-36.3	12,517	-30.2	11,846	-5.4	12,050	1.7	11,743	-2.5	-58.3
1st Quarter Wages (annualized - $ mil.)	959.8	658.5	-31.4	413.8	-37.2	446.6	7.9	461.1	3.2	541.0	17.3	-43.6
Payroll per Emp. 1st Q. (annualized)	34,063	36,698	7.7	33,061	-9.9	37,701	14.0	38,267	1.5	46,068	20.4	35.2
Annual Payroll ($ mil.)	956.9	659.2	-31.1	438.8	-33.4	488.4	11.3	502.3	2.9	457.2	-9.0	-52.2

Source: County Business Patterns, U.S. Department of Commerce, Washington, D.C., for 1990 through 1995. Payroll per employee is calculated using mid-March employment and 1st Quarter wages, annualized. Annual payroll, also shown, may not equal the annualized 1st Quarter wages. Columns headed by a percent sign (%) indicate change from the previous year. *na* stands for not available. The symbol (D) indicates that data are withheld by the source to avoid disclosure of competitive information. A dash (-) indicates that data are not available or cannot be calculated.

ESTABLISHMENTS
Number

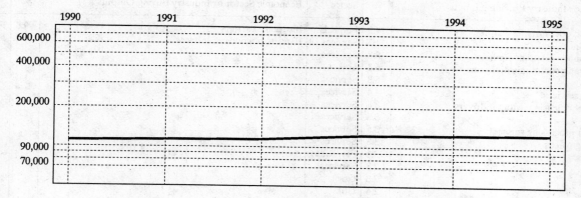

MID-MARCH EMPLOYMENT
Number

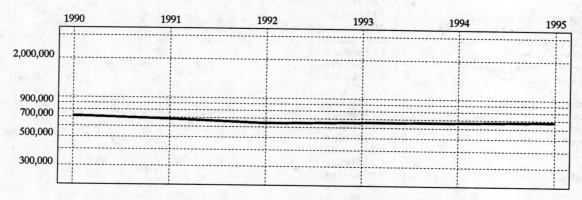

ANNUAL PAYROLL
$ million

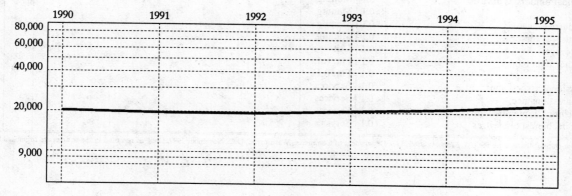

INPUTS AND OUTPUTS FOR INSURANCE AGENTS, BROKERS, & SERVICE - SIC 6411

Economic Sector or Industry Providing Inputs	%	Sector	Economic Sector or Industry Buying Outputs	%	Sector
Real estate agents, operators, & lessors	14.3	Fin/R.E.	Insurance carriers	99.6	Fin/R.E.
Business services nec	11.5	Services	Exports of goods & services	0.4	Foreign
Management & public relations services	8.8	Services			
Telephone/telegraph communications nec	6.3	Util.			
Advertising	5.8	Services			
Personnel supply services	4.4	Services			
Automotive rental & leasing, without drivers	3.8	Services			
Legal services	3.8	Services			
Computer & data processing services	3.5	Services			
Eating & drinking places	3.3	Services			
Insurance carriers	3.1	Fin/R.E.			
Hotels	2.8	Services			
U.S. Postal Service	2.8	Gov't			
Air transportation	2.6	Util.			
Trucking & courier services, ex air	2.4	Util.			
Accounting, auditing & bookkeeping	2.4	Services			
Banking	1.9	Fin/R.E.			
Commercial printing	1.7	Manufg.			
Electric services (utilities)	1.2	Util.			
Wholesale trade	1.2	Trade			
Miscellaneous equipment rental & leasing	1.1	Services			
Repair & maintenance construction nec	0.9	Constr.			
Computer peripheral equipment	0.8	Manufg.			
Automotive repair shops & services	0.8	Services			
Research, development, & testing services	0.8	Services			
Photographic equipment & supplies	0.7	Manufg.			
Local & suburban transit	0.7	Util.			
Magnetic & optical recording media	0.5	Manufg.			
Manifold business forms	0.4	Manufg.			
Tires & inner tubes	0.4	Manufg.			
Automobile parking & car washes	0.4	Services			
Paper & paperboard mills	0.3	Manufg.			
Petroleum refining	0.3	Manufg.			
Miscellaneous repair shops	0.3	Services			
Hardware, nec	0.2	Manufg.			
Natural gas distribution	0.2	Util.			
Sanitary services, steam supply, irrigation	0.2	Util.			
Retail trade, ex eating & drinking	0.2	Trade			
Electrical repair shops	0.2	Services			
Blankbooks, looseleaf binders & devices	0.1	Manufg.			
Envelopes	0.1	Manufg.			
Manufacturing industries, nec	0.1	Manufg.			
Motor vehicle parts & accessories	0.1	Manufg.			
Warehousing & storage	0.1	Util.			
Credit agencies other than banks	0.1	Fin/R.E.			
Royalties	0.1	Fin/R.E.			
Business & professional associations	0.1	Services			
Membership organizations nec	0.1	Services			
Physical fitness facilities & membership clubs	0.1	Services			
Theatrical producers, bands, orchestras	0.1	Services			

Source: Benchmark Input-Output Accounts for the U.S. Economy, 1992, U.S. Department of Commerce, Washington, D.C., November 1997. Data, as reported in the source, are organized by the 1987 SIC structure in use in 1992.

OCCUPATIONS EMPLOYED BY INSURANCE AGENTS, BROKERS, AND SERVICE

Occupation	% of Total 1996	Change to 2006	Occupation	% of Total 1996	Change to 2006
Insurance sales workers	18.5	13.4	Insurance claims clerks	3.1	24.1
Insurance policy processing clerks	13.6	-2.8	Receptionists & information clerks	2.9	21.5
General managers & top executives	7.7	17.7	Marketing & sales worker supervisors	2.1	21.4
Insurance adjusters, examiners, investigators	6.1	24.7	Typists, including word processing	2.0	-21.1
General office clerks	6.1	4.5	File clerks	1.9	-13.3
Secretaries, except legal & medical	5.8	-3.7	Financial managers	1.8	21.4
Clerical supervisors & managers	4.6	21.5	Management support workers nec	1.8	21.5
Underwriters	4.5	-16.0	Accountants & auditors	1.0	12.4
Bookkeeping, accounting, & auditing clerks	4.3	-2.8	Clerical & administrative workers nec	1.0	21.5

Sources: *Industry-Occupation Matrix*, Bureau of Labor Statistics. These data relate to one or more 3-digit SIC industry groups rather than to a single 4-digit SIC. The change reported for each occupation to the year 2005 is a percent of growth or decline as estimated by the Bureau of Labor Statistics. The abbreviation *nec* stands for not elsewhere classified.

U.S. AND STATE DATA ON INDUSTRY REVENUES AND OTHER ACCOUNTS FOR 1992

State	No. of Estab.	Employ- ment	Payroll ($ mil.)	Revenues ($ mil.)	Empl./ Estab.	Revenue/ Estab. ($)	Payroll/ Estab. ($)	Revenue/ Empl. ($)	Payroll/ Empl. ($)
UNITED STATES	121,662	635,536	18,921.1	51,705.1	5	424,989	155,522	81,357	29,772
Alabama	1,562	6,925	176.2	555.7	4	355,783	112,784	80,250	25,439
Alaska	203	1,097	37.1	87.3	5	429,842	182,665	79,542	33,802
Arizona	1,874	9,419	252.0	759.6	5	405,324	134,470	80,643	26,754
Arkansas	1,217	4,242	98.4	284.6	3	233,869	80,859	67,095	23,198
California	12,116	69,979	2,393.4	6,429.8	6	530,690	197,541	91,882	34,202
Colorado	2,227	8,623	223.7	645.7	4	289,951	100,445	74,883	25,941
Connecticut	1,561	10,648	389.9	1,029.1	7	659,275	249,751	96,650	36,614
Delaware	301	1,344	36.6	89.4	4	296,907	121,731	66,495	27,263
District of Columbia	132	1,852	78.9	181.6	14	1,375,992	597,356	98,073	42,576
Florida	7,567	39,067	1,031.1	3,131.9	5	413,890	136,257	80,168	26,392
Georgia	3,174	17,882	531.7	1,330.3	6	419,136	167,517	74,395	29,734
Hawaii	375	2,663	79.9	215.8	7	575,491	213,003	81,040	29,995
Idaho	570	2,414	51.4	155.8	4	273,304	90,167	64,533	21,290
Illinois	6,203	34,855	1,096.9	2,922.8	6	471,195	176,831	83,857	31,470
Indiana	2,857	14,127	369.2	1,031.8	5	361,141	129,224	73,036	26,134
Iowa	2,032	7,703	175.1	517.0	4	254,414	86,150	67,113	22,726
Kansas	1,797	7,341	179.3	502.0	4	279,328	99,784	68,377	24,426
Kentucky	1,648	8,274	191.6	555.2	5	336,900	116,274	67,103	23,159
Louisiana	2,183	10,896	259.6	760.1	5	348,186	118,900	69,759	23,821
Maine	519	3,054	80.9	208.7	6	402,164	155,879	68,344	26,490
Maryland	1,994	12,330	393.0	997.7	6	500,344	197,109	80,915	31,876
Massachusetts	2,886	19,886	679.1	1,751.3	7	606,816	235,319	88,066	34,151
Michigan	3,987	20,968	606.3	1,662.1	5	416,867	152,069	79,266	28,915
Minnesota	2,861	12,407	366.5	1,114.0	4	389,391	128,113	89,792	29,542
Mississippi	1,130	4,209	95.8	273.2	4	241,761	84,793	64,906	22,765
Missouri	3,184	14,019	355.1	1,013.2	4	318,206	111,526	72,271	25,330
Montana	621	2,219	46.4	150.1	4	241,721	74,771	67,647	20,925
Nebraska	1,369	4,845	103.1	334.8	4	244,570	75,278	69,106	21,270
Nevada	627	2,703	69.9	188.8	4	301,078	111,544	69,839	25,874
New Hampshire	497	2,731	76.8	198.2	5	398,779	154,445	72,572	28,107
New Jersey	3,225	22,752	826.3	2,117.0	7	656,449	256,226	93,049	36,319
New Mexico	764	3,345	73.6	213.9	4	279,955	96,385	63,942	22,014
New York	7,000	54,300	2,037.8	5,100.0	8	728,570	291,113	93,922	37,528
North Carolina	3,102	12,955	354.2	1,035.7	4	333,875	114,187	79,944	27,341
North Dakota	563	1,490	29.0	100.7	3	178,821	51,430	67,568	19,433
Ohio	5,344	23,576	635.0	1,799.8	4	336,787	118,820	76,340	26,933
Oklahoma	1,806	6,429	139.9	451.4	4	249,955	77,471	70,216	21,763
Oregon	1,537	7,436	205.0	604.5	5	393,295	133,407	81,293	27,575
Pennsylvania	5,136	29,094	921.3	2,467.4	6	480,410	179,376	84,807	31,665
Rhode Island	396	2,224	69.8	184.6	6	466,263	176,227	83,022	31,379
South Carolina	1,422	7,050	173.4	485.5	5	341,390	121,922	68,859	24,592
South Dakota	629	1,775	34.0	107.6	3	171,114	54,038	60,637	19,149
Tennessee	2,307	10,429	285.5	771.0	5	334,188	123,766	73,926	27,378
Texas	8,780	44,461	1,267.8	3,659.2	5	416,764	144,397	82,301	28,515
Utah	837	4,311	109.3	291.9	5	348,760	130,575	67,713	25,352
Vermont	311	1,498	41.1	96.1	5	309,109	132,199	64,174	27,446
Virginia	2,784	14,220	391.5	1,015.9	5	364,897	140,615	71,440	27,530
Washington	2,364	13,099	407.6	957.4	6	405,011	172,408	73,093	31,115
West Virginia	741	3,085	67.7	188.7	4	254,625	91,368	61,159	21,946
Wisconsin	3,037	12,412	311.0	931.5	4	306,716	102,397	75,048	25,055
Wyoming	303	873	15.6	47.7	3	157,422	51,591	54,638	17,906

Source: 1992 Economic Census, U.S. Department of Commerce, Washington, D.C. This is the only table that shows revenue data as collected by the Bureau of the Census in an Economic Census. The symbol (D) indicates that data are withheld by the source to avoid disclosure of competitive information. A dash (-) indicates that data are not available or cannot be calculated.

STATE-BY-STATE DATA ON ESTABLISHMENTS, EMPLOYMENT, AND PAYROLL - 1994 AND 1995

State	1994					1995					% Change Empl.
	No. of Estab.	Employ- ment	Pay / Empl.	Payroll ($ mil.)	Pay / Estab.	No. of Estab.	Employ- ment	Pay / Empl.	Payroll ($ mil.)	Pay / Estab.	
Alabama	1,581	7,678	26,531	227.9	144,161	1,584	7,854	28,809	241.1	152,213	2.3
Alaska	199	1,156	35,080	41.1	206,618	201	(D)	-	(D)	-	-
Arizona	1,959	11,217	28,197	316.7	161,676	2,040	11,685	29,682	368.3	180,545	4.2
Arkansas	1,300	4,556	23,700	110.1	84,695	1,303	4,600	25,787	117.3	90,005	1.0
California	11,665	66,850	36,068	2,450.5	210,076	11,562	66,975	38,733	2,626.6	227,173	0.2
Colorado	2,355	9,889	27,782	285.5	121,249	2,446	11,971	30,044	329.8	134,821	21.1
Connecticut	1,541	10,140	37,160	396.4	257,216	1,569	10,250	39,266	429.0	273,397	1.1
Delaware	304	1,631	29,135	50.4	165,799	313	(D)	-	(D)	-	-
District of Columbia	119	1,862	43,747	80.6	677,092	117	1,984	45,603	85.1	727,325	6.6
Florida	7,695	42,991	27,264	1,252.3	162,742	7,868	44,043	29,672	1,368.9	173,985	2.4
Georgia	3,335	17,829	32,140	598.7	179,510	3,347	18,937	33,573	664.1	198,408	6.2
Hawaii	347	2,880	32,265	93.2	268,715	351	2,912	33,376	99.4	283,162	1.1
Idaho	587	2,765	22,349	65.2	111,046	604	2,848	22,104	66.7	110,401	3.0
Illinois	6,394	37,280	33,703	1,371.3	214,463	6,458	38,632	37,667	1,458.6	225,864	3.6
Indiana	3,002	15,246	26,830	423.1	140,925	3,017	15,326	28,755	446.4	147,952	0.5
Iowa	2,093	8,281	23,330	206.0	98,420	2,124	8,229	24,458	205.8	96,911	-0.6
Kansas	1,866	7,112	24,843	190.1	101,885	1,911	7,520	26,447	212.9	111,421	5.7
Kentucky	1,660	8,442	23,500	209.9	126,458	1,691	8,955	26,330	236.0	139,539	6.1
Louisiana	2,177	10,921	24,736	285.7	131,237	2,146	10,962	27,176	310.3	144,616	0.4
Maine	522	3,198	27,590	94.2	180,533	543	3,333	29,661	101.3	186,589	4.2
Maryland	1,998	12,500	33,382	436.2	218,333	2,030	13,220	34,385	473.3	233,150	5.8
Massachusetts	2,954	19,771	34,703	732.7	248,023	2,976	20,956	37,618	796.2	267,539	6.0
Michigan	4,064	22,064	27,984	675.5	166,221	4,097	22,006	30,578	719.9	175,715	-0.3
Minnesota	3,089	14,069	30,002	426.2	137,976	3,199	14,412	32,484	471.6	147,427	2.4
Mississippi	1,131	4,310	22,934	110.5	97,682	1,105	4,506	24,972	120.1	108,652	4.5
Missouri	3,279	14,155	26,357	393.1	119,871	3,292	14,393	29,214	432.7	131,453	1.7
Montana	628	2,430	20,046	53.1	84,492	640	2,497	21,938	57.1	89,244	2.8
Nebraska	1,428	5,057	21,701	113.1	79,205	1,434	5,558	23,304	133.1	92,841	9.9
Nevada	672	3,024	24,884	81.8	121,702	701	3,259	27,181	93.2	133,023	7.8
New Hampshire	492	2,732	28,698	83.7	170,100	508	2,719	29,311	84.4	166,094	-0.5
New Jersey	3,148	24,347	36,360	962.4	305,718	3,148	23,894	39,541	1,018.2	323,452	-1.9
New Mexico	786	4,223	20,889	96.3	122,455	781	4,140	21,174	98.4	125,933	-2.0
New York	7,159	53,590	37,932	2,152.6	300,680	7,211	54,208	42,226	2,291.0	317,714	1.2
North Carolina	3,116	13,080	28,027	395.1	126,788	3,217	13,315	30,852	428.5	133,184	1.8
North Dakota	622	1,597	19,609	33.2	53,452	628	1,678	19,926	34.9	55,616	5.1
Ohio	5,435	25,255	27,164	726.0	133,584	5,565	26,575	29,027	809.3	145,434	5.2
Oklahoma	1,877	6,753	21,522	155.4	82,786	1,862	6,595	22,936	161.8	86,918	-2.3
Oregon	1,688	8,209	28,751	240.4	142,439	1,703	8,930	30,658	263.5	154,752	8.8
Pennsylvania	5,082	29,766	30,936	1,030.2	202,706	5,117	31,094	33,478	1,118.3	218,547	4.5
Rhode Island	412	2,180	29,189	71.2	172,738	415	2,141	31,174	70.9	170,795	-1.8
South Carolina	1,427	7,444	25,436	204.1	142,994	1,459	7,723	27,941	222.5	152,515	3.7
South Dakota	652	1,924	19,890	41.6	63,768	642	1,967	21,216	43.9	68,346	2.2
Tennessee	2,354	11,025	29,939	352.9	149,929	2,375	11,840	32,300	397.6	167,393	7.4
Texas	9,055	46,988	28,389	1,396.2	154,195	9,126	47,405	29,636	1,468.1	160,871	0.9
Utah	887	5,125	25,456	142.6	160,806	920	5,353	27,119	152.7	166,007	4.4
Vermont	327	1,486	27,752	43.2	132,183	315	1,506	29,232	45.1	143,117	1.3
Virginia	2,888	14,377	28,978	427.2	147,924	2,930	14,385	31,095	444.8	151,812	0.1
Washington	2,423	13,213	32,537	436.2	180,005	2,513	13,320	34,312	457.1	181,881	0.8
West Virginia	748	3,072	23,661	75.3	100,715	773	3,199	25,200	82.6	106,886	4.1
Wisconsin	3,166	14,814	24,201	384.6	121,469	3,182	13,102	26,686	362.9	114,042	-11.6
Wyoming	310	1,181	19,844	20.4	65,861	302	(D)	-	(D)	-	-

Source: County Business Patterns, U.S. Department of Commerce, Washington, D.C., for 1994 and 1995. Employment shown is for mid-March of the year shown. Payroll per employee is calculated by annualizing 1st Quarter payroll (not shown) and then dividing that value by mid-March employment. Dividing total annual payroll (columns 5 and 10) by employment, therefore, will *not* yield the payroll per employee figure (columns 4 and 9). The symbol (D) indicates that data are withheld by the source to avoid disclosure of competitive information. A dash (-) indicates that data are not available or cannot be calculated.

ESTABLISHMENTS 1995 - STATE AND REGIONAL CONCENTRATION

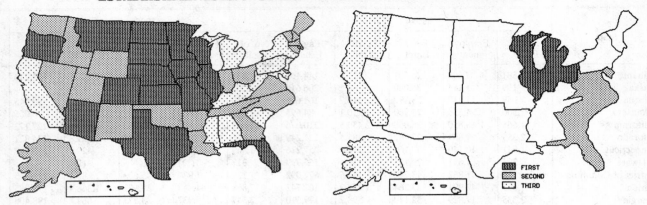

EMPLOYMENT 1995 - STATE AND REGIONAL CONCENTRATION

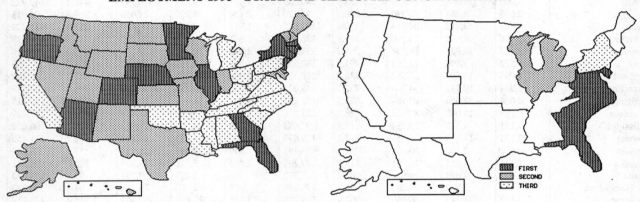

PAYROLL 1995 - STATE AND REGIONAL CONCENTRATION

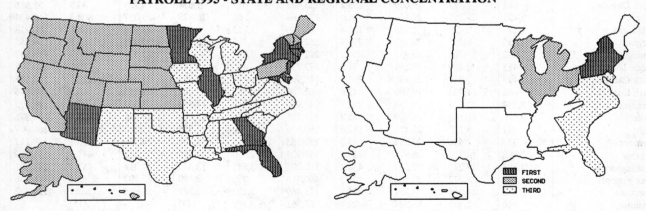

States with the darkest shading indicate those states which have proportionately more establishments, employment, or payrolls than would be indicated by the state's population. States with light shading are states with proportionately fewer establishments, less employment, and lower payrolls than population distribution. States shaded grey are within 15 percent of the state's population proportion in these categories. States for which no data are available are shown as average (grey). *Regions* are shaded to indicate absolute rank in the category. If no data for the category are available, establishment counts are used to shade the regions. Source of the data is the table on the facing page.

LEADING COMPANIES - SIC 6411 - Insurance Agents, Brokers, & Service

Number shown: **100**   Total sales/assets ($ mil): **104,306**   Total employment (000): **217.3**

Company Name	Address				CEO Name	Phone	Co. Type	Sales/Assets ($ mil)	Empl. (000)
Provident Companies Inc.	1 Fountain Sq.	Chattanooga	TN	37402	J. Harold Chandler	423-755-1011	P	23,178 TA	5.3
St. Paul Companies Inc.	385 Washington St.	St. Paul	MN	55102	Douglas W. Leatherdale	612-310-7911	P	21,501 TA	10.0
Aon Group Inc.	125 Wacker Dr.	Chicago	IL	60606	Michael D. O'Halleran	312-701-4800	S	17,000	14.0
AMBAC Inc.	1 State Street Plz.	New York	NY	10004	Phillip B. Lassiter	212-668-0340	P	8,250 TA	0.3
Marsh and McLennan Companies Inc.	1166 Ave. of the Amer.	New York	NY	10036	A.J.C. Smith	212-345-5000	P	6,009	36.0
Anthem Insurance Companies Inc.	120 Monument Cir.	Indianapolis	IN	46204	L. Ben Lytle	317-488-6000	R	5,000 TA	14.0
Caremark International Inc.	2215 Sanders Rd.	Northbrook	IL	60062	C.A. Lance Piccolo	847-559-4700	S	2,374	10.0
U.S. Healthcare Inc.	PO Box 1109	Blue Bell	PA	19422	Leonard Abramson	215-628-4800	S	1,667 TA	4.3
Equifax Inc.	PO Box 4081	Atlanta	GA	30302	Thomas F. Chapman	404-885-8000	P	1,366 OR	10.0
Alexander and Alexander Services Inc.	1185 Ave. of the Amer.	New York	NY	10036	Frank G. Zarb	212-444-4500	S	1,282	11.9
Johnson and Higgins	125 Broad St.	New York	NY	10004	David Olsen	212-574-7000	R	1,080	8.5
Willis Corroon Corp.	26 Century Blvd.	Nashville	TN	37214	Richard M. Miller	615-872-3000	P	900	13.0
Poughkeepsie Savings Bank F.S.B.	249 Main Mall	Poughkeepsie	NY	12601	Joseph B. Tockarshewsky	914-431-6200	P	859 TA	0.2
Scottsdale Insurance Co.	PO Box 4110	Scottsdale	AZ	85261	R. Max Williamson	602-948-0505	S	795•	1.0
Horace Mann Service Corp.	1 Horace Mann Plz.	Springfield	IL	62715	Paul J. Kardos	217-789-2500	S	771	2.7
Great Northern Insured Annuity Corp.	PO Box 490	Seattle	WA	98111	Patrick E. Welch	206-625-1755	S	708	1.0
Crawford and Co.	PO Box 5047	Atlanta	GA	30342	Dennis A. Smith	404-256-0830	P	692	6.8
Acordia Inc.	111 Monument Cir.	Indianapolis	IN	46204	Frank C. Witthun	317-488-2500	R	661	6.9
Wisconsin Physician Service Insurance Corp.	PO Box 8190	Madison	WI	53708	James Riordan	608-221-4711	R	650 TA	2.9
Arthur J. Gallagher and Co.	2 Pierce Place	Itasca	IL	60143	J. Patrick Gallagher Jr.	630-773-3800	P	455	4.8
HSB Industrial Risk Insurers	85 Woodland St.	Hartford	CT	06102	Mike Downs	860-520-7300	J	418 TA•	0.8
Equifax Services Inc.	1000 Alderman Dr.	Alpharetta	GA	30005	Derek V. Smith	770-752-6000	P	417	3.7
American Medical Security Inc.	PO Box 19032	Green Bay	WI	54307	Sam Miller	920-661-2402	S	390•	2.0
Acordia Southeast Inc.	PO Box 31666	Tampa	FL	33631	James R. Harper	813-796-6666	S	350	0.3
Minet Group	1114 Ave. of the Amer.	New York	NY	10036	J. Bernard Friemann	212-782-6000	S	348	3.7
CIGNA RE Corp.	900 Cottage Grove Rd.	Hartford	CT	06152	Francine W. Newman	203-726-6000	S	300	0.1
HealthPlan Services Corp.	PO Box 30098	Tampa	FL	33607	James K. Murray Jr.	813-289-1000	P	283	3.4
MIM Corp.	PO Box 1670	Pearl River	NY	10965	John H. Klein	914-735-3555	P	283	0.1
Burns and Wilcox Ltd.	PO Box 707	Southfield	MI	48037	Herbert W. Kaufman	810-932-9000	S	265	0.6
Guy Carpenter and Company Inc.	2 World Trade Ctr.	New York	NY	10048	Brandon W. Sweitzer	212-323-1000	S	258	1.4
Hilb, Rogal and Hamilton Co.	PO Box 1220	Glen Allen	VA	23060	Andrew L. Rogal	804-747-6500	P	247	1.8

Company type codes: P - Public, R - Private, S - Subsidiary, D - Division, J - Joint Venture, A - Affiliate, G - Group. If the dollar values shown are not sales, the following codes apply: TA - Total Assets; OR - Operating Revenues; GB - Gross Billings. • - estimated dollar value. < - less than. *na* - not available.

Continued on next page.

LEADING COMPANIES - SIC 6411 - Insurance Agents, Brokers, & Service
Continued

Company Name	Address				CEO Name	Phone	Co. Type	Sales/Assets ($ mil)	Empl. (000)
Universal American Financial Corp.	Mount Ebo Corporate Park	Brewster	NY	10509	Richard A. Barasch	914-278-4094	P	242 TA	0.2
Great Western Life Insurance Co.	8515 E. Orchard Rd.	Englewood	CO	80111	William McCallum	303-689-3000	R	200•	1.8
Employee Benefit Plans Inc.	435 Ford Rd.	Minneapolis	MN	55426	William E. Sagan	612-546-4353	P	184 TA	1.3
Seabury and Smith Inc.	1166 Ave. of the Amer.	New York	NY	10036	Claude Y. Mercier	212-345-4418	S	180•	1.5
ESIS Inc.	1601 Chestnut St.	Philadelphia	PA	19192	Ray Hafner	215-761-6779	S	175	2.7
E.W. Blanch Holdings Inc.	4300 Centerview Dr.	San Antonio	TX	78228	Edgar W. Blanch Jr.	210-734-2015	P	167	1.1
Kirke-Van Orsdel Inc.	1776 W. Lakes Pkwy.	West Des Moines	IA	50398	William A. Van Orsdel	515-243-1830	R	160•	1.4
Aon Specialty Group Inc.	123 N. Wacker Dr.	Chicago	IL	60606	Michael D. Rice	312-701-4538	S	156•	0.6
Factory Mutual Engineering Corp.	1151 Boston Prov. Tpk.	Norwood	MA	02062	Paul M. Fitzgerald	617-762-4300	R	155	2.0
GENEX Services Inc.	440 East Swedesford Rd.	Wayne	PA	19087	Peter Madeja	610-964-5100	S	151 TA•	1.3
CoreSource Inc.	630 Dundee Rd.	Northbrook	IL	60062	James Duff	708-559-8321	R	150•	1.3
Kemper Service Co.	811 Main St.	Kansas City	MO	64105	Frank Diaz	816-421-4100	S	150 OR	1.0
Southwestern/Great American Inc.	PO Box 305140	Nashville	TN	37230	Ralph W. Mosley	615-391-2500	R	130	0.6
Mednet MPC Corp.	871-C Grier Dr.	Las Vegas	NV	89119	M.B. Merryman	702-361-3119	P	114	0.4
United American Healthcare Corp.	1155 Brewery Park Blvd.	Detroit	MI	48207	Julius V. Combs	313-393-0200	P	113 OR	0.4
Norcal Mutual Insurance Co.	50 Fremont St.	San Francisco	CA	94105	William Newton	415-777-4200	R	112	0.2
Medical Professional Liability Agency Ltd.	2 Depot Plz.	Bedford Hills	NY	10507	Thomas J. Dietz	914-666-0555	S	110	<0.1
Kemper Risk Management Services	1 Kemper Dr.	Long Grove	IL	60049	E.M. Lindner	708-320-2400	S	107	0.3
Poe and Brown Inc.	PO Box 2412	Daytona Beach	FL	32115	J. Hyatt Brown	904-252-9601	P	106	1.0
National Loss Control Service Corp.	1 Kemper Dr.	Long Grove	IL	60049	C. David Sullivan	708-540-2400	S	100	0.4
Willis Faber North America Inc.	PO Box 2500	Stoney Creek	NC	27377	Horrace M. Johnson	910-584-0166	S	99 TA•	0.2
Jardine Insurance Brokers Inc.	333 Bush St.	San Francisco	CA	94104	George W. Brown	415-391-2600	S	97	1.1
Crop Growers Corp.	201 Crop Growers Dr.	Great Falls	MT	59405	John J. Hemmingson	406-452-8101	P	88	0.5
Brakke-Schafnitz Insurance Brokers Inc.	28202 Cabot Rd.	Laguna Niguel	CA	92677	Jim Brakke	714-365-5100	R	85	<0.1
HCIA Inc.	300 E. Lombard St.	Baltimore	MD	21202	George D. Pillari	410-332-7532	P	83	0.8
AON Re Inc.	123 N. Wacker Dr.	Chicago	IL	60606	Michael G. Bungert	312-781-7900	S	76•	0.3
Gay and Taylor Inc.	6 Concorse Pkwy.	Atlanta	GA	30328	James P. Rippy	404-395-1000	S	72	1.3
First of Michigan Capital Corp.	100 Renaissance Ctr.	Detroit	MI	48243	Conrad W. Koski	313-259-2600	P	72 OR	0.6
Equifax Healthcare Administrative Services Inc.	5001 Spring Valley Rd.	Dallas	TX	75244	C. Page	214-789-6400	S	69•	0.6

Company type codes: P - Public, R - Private, S - Subsidiary, D - Division, J - Joint Venture, A - Affiliate, G - Group. If the dollar values shown are not sales, the following codes apply: TA - Total Assets; OR - Operating Revenues; GB - Gross Billings. • - estimated dollar value. < - less than. *na* - not available.

Continued on next page.

LEADING COMPANIES - SIC 6411 - Insurance Agents, Brokers, & Service
Continued

Company Name	Address				CEO Name	Phone	Co. Type	Sales/Assets ($ mil)	Empl. (000)
Norwest Insurance Inc.	80 S. 8th St.	Minneapolis	MN	55479	Tim King	612-667-0791	S	69•	0.6
National Insurance Group	395 Oyster Point Blvd.	S. San Francisco	CA	94080	Mark A. Speizer	415-872-6772	P	67 TA	0.4
Louisiana Cos.	PO Box 991	Baton Rouge	LA	70821	J.R. Querbes III	504-383-4761	R	60	<0.1
MedView Services Inc.	32991 Hamilton Ct.	Farmington Hills	MI	48334	Robert Marks	313-488-5260	S	59•	0.1
Kaye Group Inc.	122 E. 42nd St.	New York	NY	10168	Bruce D. Guthart	212-338-2100	P	58	0.3
Kaye Insurance Associates L.P.	122 E. 42nd St.	New York	NY	10168	Bruce D. Guthart	212-210-9200	S	55	0.4
Warner Computer Systems Inc.	17-01 Pollitt Dr.	Fair Lawn	NJ	07410	Harvey Krieger	201-794-4800	P	55	0.5
Roanoke Companies Inc.	1930 Thoreau Dr.	Schaumburg	IL	60173	William D. Sterrett	708-490-9540	R	53 TA•	0.2
H.W. Kaufman Financial Group Inc.	30833 Northwestern Hwy.	Farmington Hills	MI	48334	Herbert W. Kaufman	810-932-9000	P	52	0.5
Lovitt and Touche Inc.	PO Box 32702	Tucson	AZ	85751	Charles A. Touche	602-722-3000	R	52•	<0.1
Crop Growers Insurance Inc.	PO Box 5024	Great Falls	MT	59403	John J. Hemmingson	406-452-8101	S	52	0.2
Fox and Lazo Inc.	30 Washington Ave.	Haddonfield	NJ	08033	G. William Fox	609-429-7227	R	51 OR•	0.3
Genelco Inc.	1600 S. Brentwood Blvd.	St. Louis	MO	63144	E. Christopher Simonds	314-963-8114	S	51	0.4
McGriff, Seibels and Williams Inc.	PO Box 10265	Birmingham	AL	35202	Bruce C. Dunbar Jr.	205-252-9871	R	50	<0.1
MetLife Brokerage	214 Carnegie Ctr.	Princeton	NJ	08540	Robert W. Powell	609-243-7100	S	50	0.1
National Insurance Services Inc.	3629 Queen Palm Dr.	Tampa	FL	33619	Carl Giffin	813-626-6111	S	50•	0.4
Norwest Commercial Insurance Services	7401 Metro Blvd.	Minneapolis	MN	55439	David M. Franske	612-921-2701	S	50•	<0.1
Roger Bouchard Insurance Inc.	101 Starcrest Dr.	Clearwater	FL	34625	Richard Bouchard	813-447-6481	R	50	<0.1
Noble Lowndes	3 Becker Farm Rd.	Roseland	NJ	07068	Peter Brew	201-533-4500	S	48	0.6
Financial Pacific Insurance Group Inc.	PO Box 29220	Sacramento	CA	95829	Robert C. Goodell	916-630-5000	R	47	0.1
United Title Agency of Arizona Inc.	3030 N. Central Ave.	Phoenix	AZ	85012	Milt Farrentelli	602-279-9381	R	46	0.4
MMI Risk Management Resources Inc.	540 Lake Cook Rd.	Deerfield	IL	60015	Anne Marie Hajek	708-940-7550	S	46•	0.4
Laub Group Inc.	1555 N. Rivercenter Dr.	Milwaukee	WI	53212	Raymond H. Laub	414-271-4292	R	45	<0.1
Lincoln Insurance Group Inc.	Two Mill Rd.	Wilmington	DE	19806	James R. Schurr	302-594-4706	S	45 TA	<0.1
Walter P. Dolle Insurance Agency Inc.	312 Walnut St.	Cincinnati	OH	45202	Robert D. Lang	513-421-6515	R	45	<0.1
Sedgwick James Inc.	600 Montgomery St.	San Francisco	CA	94111	Donald K. Morford	415-983-5250	S	41•	0.4
American Southern Insurance Co.	PO Box 723030	Atlanta	GA	31139	Roy Jr. Thompson	404-266-9599	S	40	<0.1
National Electronics Warranty Corp.	44873 Falcon Pl.	Sterling	VA	20166	Fred Schaufeld	703-318-7700	R	40	0.2

Company type codes: P - Public, R - Private, S - Subsidiary, D - Division, J - Joint Venture, A - Affiliate, G - Group. If the dollar values shown are not sales, the following codes apply: TA - Total Assets; OR - Operating Revenues; GB - Gross Billings. • - estimated dollar value. < - less than. *na* - not available.

Continued on next page.

LEADING COMPANIES - SIC 6411 - Insurance Agents, Brokers, & Service
Continued

Company Name	Address				CEO Name	Phone	Co. Type	Sales/Assets ($ mil)	Empl. (000)
Proctor Homer Warren Inc.	2100 W. Big Beaver Rd.	Troy	MI	48084	Thomas W. Proctor	810-649-8730	R	40	0.1
Superior National Insurance Co.	26601 Agoura Rd.	Calabasas	CA	91302	William Gentz	818-880-1600	R	39•	0.3
Vantage Computer Systems Inc.	100 Great Meadow Rd.	Wethersfield	CT	06109	Robert S. Maltempo	203-721-0694	S	39	0.5
Transcend Services Inc.	3353 Peachtree Rd. N.E.	Atlanta	GA	30326	Larry G. Gerdes	404-364-8000	P	38	0.7
Florida Employers Insurance Service Corp.	2601 Cattlemen Rd.	Sarasota	FL	34232	Ray Neff	813-955-2811	S	36	0.5
Near North Insurance Brokerage Inc.	875 N. Michigan Ave.	Chicago	IL	60611	Michael Segal	312-280-5600	R	35	<0.1
Media/Professional Insurance Agency Inc.	2300 Main St.	Kansas City	MO	64108	John Pfannenstiel	816-471-6118	S	34	0.1
Group Council Mutual Insurance Co.	230 W. 41st St.	New York	NY	10036	John Grywalski Jr.	212-592-6000	R	32	<0.1
Lockton Cos.	7400 State Line Rd.	Prairie Village	KS	66208	John T. Lockton III	913-676-9000	R	32	0.3
Acordia of California	525 Market St.	San Francisco	CA	94105	Jim Well	415-541-7900	S	31•	0.4
ABR CobraServ Inc.	34125 U.S. Hwy. 19 N.	Palm Harbor	FL	34684	Dennis A. Sweeney	813-785-2819	S	31	0.6
Bland and Co.	12300 Old Tesson Rd.	St. Louis	MO	63128	Steve Mach	314-849-9990	R	30	0.1

Source: *Ward's Business Directory of U.S. Private and Public Companies*, 1996. Company type codes: P - Public, R - Private, S - Subsidiary, D - Division, J - Joint Venture, A - Affiliate, G - Group. If the dollar values shown are not sales, the following codes apply: TA - Total Assets; OR - Operating Revenues; GB - Gross Billings. • - estimated dollar value. < - less than; *na* - not available.

SIC 6510

REAL ESTATE OPERATORS AND LESSORS

The industry is made up of SIC 6512, Operators of Nonresidential Buildings; SIC 6513, Operators of Apartment Buildings; SIC 6514 Operators of Dwellings Other Than Apartment Buildings; SIC 6515, Operators of Residential Mobile Home Sites; SIC 6517 Lessors of Railroad Property; and SIC 6519, Lessors of Real Property, not elsewhere classified.

Real estate operators and lessors exclude developers (classified under Construction and not included in this book). Lessors primarily engaged in development or improvement of unimproved real property are also excluded (see SIC 6552). The group includes operators of apartment hotels and residential mobile home sites but does not include hotels, rooming and boarding houses, camps, and other places of lodging; these activities are classified as Services. "Operators" in this group are owner-operators. Establishments primarily engaged in renting, buying, selling, managing, and appraising real estate for others are in SIC 6530, Real Estate Agents and Managers.

The industry includes operation and leasing of the following types of real property: under SIC 6512: bank buildings; insurance buildings; piers, docks, and associated buildings and facilities; nonresidential buildings; retail establishments; shopping centers; and theaters; under SIC 6513: apartment buildings, apartment hotels, residential hotels, and retirement hotels; under SIC 6514: dwellings and residential buildings with four or fewer housing units; under SIC 6515: residential mobile home sites; under SIC 6517: railroad property; under SIC 6519: airports, landholding offices, all other property except railroad buildings or home sites.

ESTABLISHMENTS, EMPLOYMENT, AND PAYROLL

	1990	1991		1992		1993		1994		1995		% change 90-95
		Value	%	Value	%	Value	%	Value	%	Value	%	
All Establishments	95,676	88,078	-7.9	91,607	4.0	101,779	11.1	99,852	-1.9	100,154	0.3	4.7
Mid-March Employment	509,078	456,568	-10.3	474,751	4.0	490,730	3.4	483,250	-1.5	491,993	1.8	-3.4
1st Quarter Wages (annualized - $ mil.)	8,425.0	7,562.3	-10.2	7,863.1	4.0	8,095.3	3.0	8,465.5	4.6	9,151.0	8.1	8.6
Payroll per Emp. 1st Q. (annualized)	16,549	16,563	0.1	16,563	-0.0	16,496	-0.4	17,518	6.2	18,600	6.2	12.4
Annual Payroll ($ mil.)	8,732.2	7,922.4	-9.3	8,324.1	5.1	8,869.3	6.5	9,149.7	3.2	9,569.2	4.6	9.6
Establishments - 1-4 Emp. Number	72,133	65,978	-8.5	68,629	4.0	77,005	12.2	75,612	-1.8	75,636	0.0	4.9
Mid-March Employment	118,239	108,922	-7.9	113,634	4.3	126,408	11.2	124,005	-1.9	124,153	0.1	5.0
1st Quarter Wages (annualized - $ mil.)	1,615.1	1,493.7	-7.5	1,631.7	9.2	1,821.5	11.6	1,874.0	2.9	2,006.1	7.1	24.2
Payroll per Emp. 1st Q. (annualized)	13,660	13,713	0.4	14,359	4.7	14,410	0.4	15,112	4.9	16,158	6.9	18.3
Annual Payroll ($ mil.)	1,956.6	1,746.7	-10.7	1,900.9	8.8	2,246.2	18.2	2,281.8	1.6	2,337.9	2.5	19.5
Establishments - 5-9 Emp. Number	13,497	13,227	-2.0	13,809	4.4	15,245	10.4	14,707	-3.5	14,837	0.9	9.9
Mid-March Employment	87,349	85,303	-2.3	88,951	4.3	97,975	10.1	94,669	-3.4	95,715	1.1	9.6
1st Quarter Wages (annualized - $ mil.)	1,359.5	1,346.2	-1.0	1,445.2	7.4	1,573.0	8.8	1,609.7	2.3	1,713.7	6.5	26.1
Payroll per Emp. 1st Q. (annualized)	15,564	15,782	1.4	16,247	3.0	16,055	-1.2	17,004	5.9	17,904	5.3	15.0
Annual Payroll ($ mil.)	1,383.2	1,383.6	0.0	1,506.0	8.8	1,670.1	10.9	1,709.3	2.3	1,767.7	3.4	27.8
Establishments - 10-19 Emp. Number	6,044	5,350	-11.5	5,663	5.9	5,981	5.6	5,945	-0.6	5,982	0.6	-1.0
Mid-March Employment	79,622	70,108	-11.9	74,106	5.7	78,056	5.3	78,013	-0.1	78,396	0.5	-1.5
1st Quarter Wages (annualized - $ mil.)	1,357.4	1,207.1	-11.1	1,313.7	8.8	1,346.2	2.5	1,417.8	5.3	1,511.3	6.6	11.3
Payroll per Emp. 1st Q. (annualized)	17,047	17,218	1.0	17,728	3.0	17,247	-2.7	18,174	5.4	19,277	6.1	13.1
Annual Payroll ($ mil.)	1,364.8	1,230.3	-9.9	1,352.6	9.9	1,431.2	5.8	1,494.7	4.4	1,560.2	4.4	14.3
Establishments - 20-49 Emp. Number	2,837	2,492	-12.2	2,475	-0.7	2,544	2.8	2,565	0.8	2,654	3.5	-6.5
Mid-March Employment	83,853	74,466	-11.2	74,041	-0.6	76,254	3.0	76,661	0.5	78,884	2.9	-5.9
1st Quarter Wages (annualized - $ mil.)	1,412.2	1,317.5	-6.7	1,315.4	-0.2	1,311.3	-0.3	1,403.4	7.0	1,548.2	10.3	9.6
Payroll per Emp. 1st Q. (annualized)	16,841	17,693	5.1	17,766	0.4	17,196	-3.2	18,307	6.5	19,626	7.2	16.5
Annual Payroll ($ mil.)	1,429.2	1,333.9	-6.7	1,358.4	1.8	1,378.1	1.5	1,466.7	6.4	1,547.5	5.5	8.3
Establishments - 50-99 Emp. Number	768	694	-9.6	702	1.2	702	-	712	1.4	723	1.5	-5.9
Mid-March Employment	52,587	46,116	-12.3	47,127	2.2	47,131	0.0	47,874	1.6	49,015	2.4	-6.8
1st Quarter Wages (annualized - $ mil.)	881.2	823.7	-6.5	810.5	-1.6	843.3	4.0	908.7	7.8	987.8	8.7	12.1
Payroll per Emp. 1st Q. (annualized)	16,757	17,861	6.6	17,198	-3.7	17,893	4.0	18,981	6.1	20,152	6.2	20.3
Annual Payroll ($ mil.)	897.3	838.3	-6.6	823.5	-1.8	869.9	5.6	921.0	5.9	977.1	6.1	8.9
Establishments - 100-249 Emp. Number	305	267	-12.5	249	-6.7	227	-8.8	255	12.3	261	2.4	-14.4
Mid-March Employment	44,956	38,166	-15.1	35,936	-5.8	32,140	-10.6	36,590	13.8	37,917	3.6	-15.7
1st Quarter Wages (annualized - $ mil.)	1,003.3	727.9	-27.4	709.7	-2.5	598.3	-15.7	729.6	21.9	820.9	12.5	-18.2
Payroll per Emp. 1st Q. (annualized)	22,318	19,073	-14.5	19,749	3.5	18,616	-5.7	19,939	7.1	21,649	8.6	-3.0
Annual Payroll ($ mil.)	925.0	737.1	-20.3	732.1	-0.7	628.0	-14.2	731.4	16.5	832.1	13.8	-10.1
Establishments - 250-499 Emp. Number	65	50	-23.1	(D)	-	58	-	39	-32.8	(D)	-	-
Mid-March Employment	21,952	17,547	-20.1	(D)	-	19,261	-	13,162	-31.7	(D)	-	-
1st Quarter Wages (annualized - $ mil.)	376.6	336.6	-10.6	(D)	-	361.4	-	244.0	-32.5	(D)	-	-
Payroll per Emp. 1st Q. (annualized)	17,155	19,181	11.8	(D)	-	18,764	-	18,541	-1.2	(D)	-	-
Annual Payroll ($ mil.)	377.3	329.4	-12.7	(D)	-	401.7	-	266.4	-33.7	(D)	-	-
Establishments - 500-999 Emp. Number	24	17	-29.2	19	11.8	(D)	-	(D)	-	17	-	-29.2
Mid-March Employment	(D)	(D)	-	12,160	-	(D)	-	(D)	-	10,844	-	-
1st Quarter Wages (annualized - $ mil.)	(D)	(D)	-	193.4	-	(D)	-	(D)	-	272.2	-	-
Payroll per Emp. 1st Q. (annualized)	(D)	(D)	-	15,908	-	(D)	-	(D)	-	25,097	-	-
Annual Payroll ($ mil.)	(D)	(D)	-	183.5	-	(D)	-	(D)	-	258.1	-	-
Estab. - 1000 or More Emp. Number	3	3	-	(D)	-	(D)	-	(D)	-	(D)	-	-
Mid-March Employment	(D)	(D)	-	(D)	-	(D)	-	(D)	-	(D)	-	-
1st Quarter Wages (annualized - $ mil.)	(D)	(D)	-	(D)	-	(D)	-	(D)	-	(D)	-	-
Payroll per Emp. 1st Q. (annualized)	(D)	(D)	-	(D)	-	(D)	-	(D)	-	(D)	-	-
Annual Payroll ($ mil.)	(D)	(D)	-	(D)	-	(D)	-	(D)	-	(D)	-	-

Source: County Business Patterns, U.S. Department of Commerce, Washington, D.C., for 1990 through 1995. Payroll per employee is calculated using mid-March employment and 1st Quarter wages, annualized. Annual payroll, also shown, may not equal the annualized 1st Quarter wages. Columns headed by a percent sign (%) indicate change from the previous year. na stands for not available. The symbol (D) indicates that data are withheld by the source to avoid disclosure of competitive information. A dash (-) indicates that data are not available or cannot be calculated.

ESTABLISHMENTS
Number

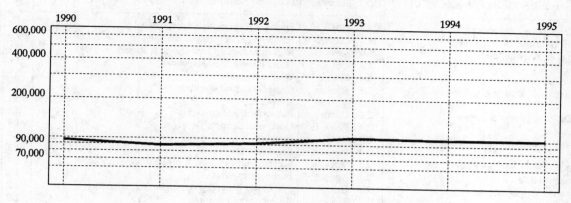

MID-MARCH EMPLOYMENT
Number

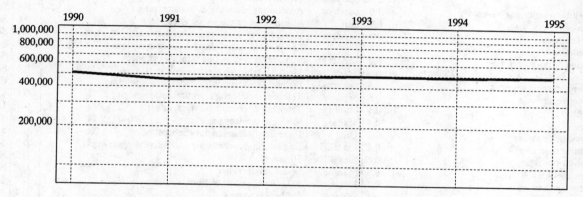

ANNUAL PAYROLL
$ million

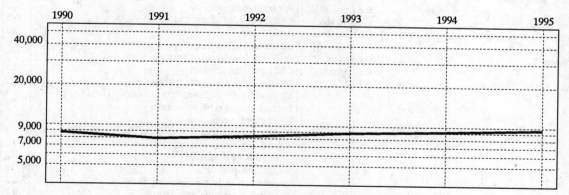

INPUTS AND OUTPUTS FOR ALL REAL ESTATE SECTORS - SIC GROUP 65

Economic Sector or Industry Providing Inputs	%	Sector	Economic Sector or Industry Buying Outputs	%	Sector
Real estate agents, operators, & lessors	25.9	Fin/R.E.	Personal consumption expenditures	32.4	
Maintenance/repair of residential structures	14.1	Constr.	Retail trade, ex eating & drinking	7.9	Trade
Services to dwellings & other buildings	5.9	Services	Real estate agents, operators, & lessors	7.1	Fin/R.E.
Electric services (utilities)	4.8	Util.	Gross private fixed investment	5.6	Cap Inv
Repair & maintenance construction nec	4.4	Constr.	Wholesale trade	3.3	Trade
Engineering, architectural, & surveying services	3.7	Services	Owner-occupied dwellings	3.3	Fin/R.E.
Advertising	3.6	Services	Hospitals	3.1	Services
Maintenance/repair of highways & streets	2.9	Constr.	Eating & drinking places	2.3	Services
Banking	2.9	Fin/R.E.	Doctors & dentists	1.9	Services
Telephone/telegraph communications nec	2.7	Util.	Banking	1.7	Fin/R.E.
Legal services	2.4	Services	Legal services	1.5	Services
Automotive rental & leasing, without drivers	2.3	Services	Colleges, universities, & professional schools	1.4	Services
Landscape & horticultural services	2.1	Agric.	Insurance carriers	1.2	Fin/R.E.
Sanitary services, steam supply, irrigation	2.1	Util.	S/L Govt., general government nec, spending	1.2	S/L Govt
Business services nec	1.8	Services	Religious organizations	1.0	Services
Electrical repair shops	1.4	Services	Feed grains	0.8	Agric.
Insurance carriers	1.2	Fin/R.E.	Nursing & personal care facilities	0.7	Services
Eating & drinking places	1.2	Services	Meat animals	0.6	Agric.
U.S. Postal Service	1.1	Gov't	Insurance agents, brokers, & services	0.6	Fin/R.E.
Hotels	1.0	Services	Security & commodity brokers	0.6	Fin/R.E.
Management & public relations services	1.0	Services	Accounting, auditing & bookkeeping	0.6	Services
Air transportation	0.9	Util.	Automotive repair shops & services	0.6	Services
Personnel supply services	0.8	Services	Computer & data processing services	0.6	Services
Natural gas distribution	0.7	Util.	Labor, civic, social, fraternal organizations	0.6	Services
Accounting, auditing & bookkeeping	0.7	Services	Management & public relations services	0.6	Services
Wholesale trade	0.6	Trade	Medical & health services nec	0.6	Services
Computer & data processing services	0.5	Services	Federal Government, nondefense, spending	0.6	Gov't
Detective & protective services	0.5	Services	Telephone/telegraph communications nec	0.5	Util.
Commercial printing	0.4	Manufg.	Trucking & courier services, ex air	0.5	Util.
Petroleum refining	0.4	Manufg.	Business services nec	0.5	Services
Water supply & sewerage systems	0.4	Util.	Elementary & secondary schools	0.5	Services
Credit agencies other than banks	0.4	Fin/R.E.	Engineering, architectural, & surveying services	0.5	Services
Security & commodity brokers	0.4	Fin/R.E.	Hotels	0.5	Services
Concrete products, ex block & brick	0.3	Manufg.	Social services, nec	0.5	Services
Trucking & courier services, ex air	0.3	Util.	S/L Govt., public welfare, spending	0.5	S/L Govt
Automotive repair shops & services	0.3	Services	Oil bearing crops	0.4	Agric.
Business & professional associations	0.3	Services	Electric services (utilities)	0.4	Util.
State & local government enterprises nec	0.3	Gov't	Membership organizations nec	0.4	Services
Local & suburban transit	0.2	Util.	State & local government enterprises nec	0.4	Gov't
Retail trade, ex eating & drinking	0.2	Trade	Food grains	0.3	Agric.
Royalties	0.2	Fin/R.E.	Air transportation	0.3	Util.
Miscellaneous repair shops	0.2	Services	Credit agencies other than banks	0.3	Fin/R.E.
Research, development, & testing services	0.2	Services	Advertising	0.3	Services
Manifold business forms	0.1	Manufg.	Beauty & barber shops	0.3	Services
Paper & paperboard mills	0.1	Manufg.	Business & professional associations	0.3	Services
Paper coating & glazing	0.1	Manufg.	Child day care services	0.3	Services
Tires & inner tubes	0.1	Manufg.	Motion picture services & theaters	0.3	Services
			Physical fitness facilities & membership clubs	0.3	Services
			Portrait photographic studios	0.3	Services
			Residential care	0.3	Services
			New construction nec	0.2	Constr.
			Repair & maintenance construction nec	0.2	Constr.
			Warehousing & storage	0.2	Util.
			Water transportation	0.2	Util.
			Amusement & recreation services nec	0.2	Services
			Automobile parking & car washes	0.2	Services
			Automotive rental & leasing, without drivers	0.2	Services
			Laundry, cleaning, garment services, shoe repair	0.2	Services

Continued on next page.

INPUTS AND OUTPUTS FOR ALL REAL ESTATE SECTORS - SIC GROUP 65 - Continued

Economic Sector or Industry Providing Inputs	%	Sector	Economic Sector or Industry Buying Outputs	%	Sector
			Private libraries, vocational schools, nec	0.2	Services
			Research, development, & testing services	0.2	Services
			Exports of goods & services	0.2	Foreign
			Dairy farm products	0.1	Agric.
			Vegetables	0.1	Agric.
			Crude petroleum & natural gas	0.1	Mining
			Residential 1 unit structures, nonfarm	0.1	Constr.
			Apparel made from purchased materials	0.1	Manufg.
			Commercial printing	0.1	Manufg.
			Electronic computers	0.1	Manufg.
			Miscellaneous plastics products, nec	0.1	Manufg.
			Job training & related services	0.1	Services
			Miscellaneous equipment rental & leasing	0.1	Services
			Miscellaneous repair shops	0.1	Services
			Personnel supply services	0.1	Services
			Photofinishing labs & commercial photography	0.1	Services
			Theatrical producers, bands, orchestras	0.1	Services
			Video tape rental	0.1	Services
			U.S. Postal Service	0.1	Gov't
			Federal Government, national defense, spending	0.1	Fed Govt

Source: Benchmark Input-Output Accounts for the U.S. Economy, 1992, U.S. Department of Commerce, Washington, D.C., November 1997. Data, as reported in the source, are organized by the 1987 SIC structure in use in 1992.

OCCUPATIONS EMPLOYED BY REAL ESTATE OPERATORS AND LESSORS

Occupation	% of Total 1996	Change to 2006	Occupation	% of Total 1996	Change to 2006
Maintenance repairers, general utility	18.8	16.1	Receptionists & information clerks	2.9	13.2
Janitors & cleaners, maids	17.2	-9.4	Bookkeeping, accounting, & auditing clerks	2.9	-9.4
Property & real estate managers	10.0	1.9	Secretaries, except legal & medical	2.7	-10.2
Guards	7.0	1.9	Sales agents, real estate	2.4	29.8
Gardeners, nursery workers	5.4	1.9	Painters & paperhangers	1.7	18.3
Food preparation workers nec	3.9	24.5	Cleaning & building service workers nec	1.3	13.2
General office clerks	3.8	-2.6	Financial managers	1.3	13.2
General managers & top executives	3.4	9.7	Marketing & sales worker supervisors	1.1	13.2

Sources: Industry-Occupation Matrix, Bureau of Labor Statistics. These data relate to one or more 3-digit SIC industry groups rather than to a single 4-digit SIC. The change reported for each occupation to the year 2005 is a percent of growth or decline as estimated by the Bureau of Labor Statistics. The abbreviation nec stands for not elsewhere classified.

U.S. AND STATE DATA ON INDUSTRY REVENUES AND OTHER ACCOUNTS FOR 1992

State	No. of Estab.	Employ-ment	Payroll ($ mil.)	Revenues ($ mil.)	Empl./ Estab.	Revenue/ Estab. ($)	Payroll/ Estab. ($)	Revenue/ Empl. ($)	Payroll/ Empl. ($)
UNITED STATES	102,887	462,564	8,257.8	74,069.5	4	719,912	80,261	160,128	17,852
Alabama	1,149	5,354	75.1	549.7	5	478,454	65,326	102,679	14,019
Alaska	217	1,205	29.5	232.4	6	1,071,101	135,802	192,887	24,456
Arizona	1,570	6,922	95.8	763.0	4	485,974	61,039	110,225	13,845
Arkansas	622	2,018	26.3	217.4	3	349,540	42,206	107,737	13,009
California	15,443	70,003	1,301.0	12,129.0	5	785,407	84,248	173,264	18,586
Colorado	1,697	7,884	118.7	874.3	5	515,187	69,947	110,892	15,056
Connecticut	1,206	5,201	106.5	1,072.8	4	889,532	88,321	206,263	20,480
Delaware	301	1,529	30.2	225.4	5	748,671	100,309	147,384	19,747
District of Columbia	641	4,083	97.4	887.9	6	1,385,131	151,963	217,455	23,857
Florida	6,627	30,622	466.2	3,873.9	5	584,558	70,345	126,506	15,224
Georgia	2,064	9,299	159.8	1,165.1	5	564,504	77,411	125,297	17,182
Hawaii	729	4,217	96.4	752.7	6	1,032,495	132,236	178,489	22,860
Idaho	281	1,183	13.8	96.8	4	344,395	49,135	81,805	11,671
Illinois	3,832	19,364	389.5	3,244.2	5	846,600	101,646	167,536	20,115
Indiana	1,569	7,379	102.4	785.1	5	500,376	65,287	106,395	13,882
Iowa	938	3,187	46.3	438.5	3	467,463	49,371	137,584	14,531
Kansas	782	2,764	39.9	358.1	4	457,910	51,060	129,554	14,446
Kentucky	1,048	4,266	54.8	421.5	4	402,171	52,322	98,799	12,853
Louisiana	1,314	5,596	70.7	564.1	4	429,295	53,773	100,803	12,627
Maine	349	1,034	16.8	133.2	3	381,607	48,014	128,802	16,206
Maryland	1,573	11,277	214.1	1,801.2	7	1,145,053	136,099	159,720	18,984
Massachusetts	1,846	8,713	198.4	1,658.3	5	898,310	107,485	190,323	22,773
Michigan	2,487	11,909	188.1	1,878.8	5	755,450	75,645	157,763	15,797
Minnesota	1,684	7,839	116.0	1,062.9	5	631,194	68,894	135,595	14,800
Mississippi	1,031	2,684	25.3	246.3	3	238,876	24,547	91,759	9,429
Missouri	1,825	8,803	137.0	1,054.0	5	577,546	75,065	119,734	15,562
Montana	366	1,136	11.6	85.7	3	234,052	31,612	75,408	10,185
Nebraska	540	2,012	26.4	207.0	4	383,374	48,957	102,894	13,140
Nevada	795	3,947	55.1	544.4	5	684,767	69,332	137,925	13,965
New Hampshire	380	1,421	25.8	173.5	4	456,466	67,900	122,067	18,158
New Jersey	3,535	15,376	306.9	3,033.1	4	858,009	86,816	197,259	19,959
New Mexico	613	2,284	28.5	242.3	4	395,192	46,520	106,065	12,486
New York	15,762	64,831	1,568.5	16,154.3	4	1,024,890	99,514	249,176	24,194
North Carolina	1,773	7,080	114.6	889.2	4	501,540	64,632	125,597	16,185
North Dakota	298	1,045	13.2	102.8	4	344,963	44,275	98,372	12,626
Ohio	3,412	17,948	253.7	2,150.9	5	630,393	74,369	119,841	14,138
Oklahoma	1,047	4,378	57.3	370.0	4	353,389	54,698	84,513	13,081
Oregon	1,493	5,447	76.6	671.0	4	449,448	51,299	123,192	14,061
Pennsylvania	2,918	16,703	304.0	2,786.7	6	955,014	104,189	166,840	18,202
Rhode Island	324	1,645	28.7	184.3	5	568,781	88,673	112,027	17,465
South Carolina	758	3,412	48.1	422.0	5	556,737	63,433	123,683	14,092
South Dakota	279	830	9.0	64.1	3	229,789	32,369	77,242	10,881
Tennessee	1,395	6,088	96.4	757.0	4	542,686	69,122	124,351	15,839
Texas	6,499	29,402	500.2	3,967.4	5	610,466	76,971	134,937	17,014
Utah	487	2,281	28.6	243.4	5	499,819	58,628	106,713	12,517
Vermont	166	580	9.7	64.8	3	390,488	58,488	111,760	16,740
Virginia	2,035	10,888	184.3	1,877.4	5	922,532	90,558	172,424	16,926
Washington	2,785	10,217	168.5	1,567.0	4	562,651	60,504	153,370	16,492
West Virginia	617	2,058	32.5	224.8	3	364,345	52,611	109,233	15,773
Wisconsin	1,570	6,713	88.3	763.2	4	486,124	56,245	113,692	13,154
Wyoming	215	507	5.2	36.8	2	171,372	24,112	72,673	10,225

Source: 1992 Economic Census, U.S. Department of Commerce, Washington, D.C. This is the only table that shows revenue data as collected by the Bureau of the Census in an Economic Census. The symbol (D) indicates that data are withheld by the source to avoid disclosure of competitive information. A dash (-) indicates that data are not available or cannot be calculated.

STATE-BY-STATE DATA ON ESTABLISHMENTS, EMPLOYMENT, AND PAYROLL - 1994 AND 1995

State	1994					1995					% Change Empl.
	No. of Estab.	Employ-ment	Pay / Empl.	Payroll ($ mil.)	Pay / Estab.	No. of Estab.	Employ-ment	Pay / Empl.	Payroll ($ mil.)	Pay / Estab.	
Alabama	1,111	5,773	12,734	78.6	70,712	1,116	5,208	15,932	84.7	75,867	-9.8
Alaska	219	1,400	30,254	42.4	193,493	228	1,323	30,080	39.4	172,886	-5.5
Arizona	1,554	7,112	13,289	105.0	67,562	1,558	7,861	14,567	120.6	77,377	10.5
Arkansas	689	2,472	13,451	34.8	50,511	695	2,608	13,505	36.4	52,433	5.5
California	14,380	69,654	17,242	1,275.9	88,727	14,372	70,401	18,557	1,346.5	93,689	1.1
Colorado	1,727	9,407	15,056	155.8	90,230	1,734	8,798	17,086	159.8	92,166	-6.5
Connecticut	1,127	5,805	21,569	136.0	120,640	1,120	6,280	23,241	146.6	130,932	8.2
Delaware	290	1,514	19,427	33.1	114,203	296	1,572	19,595	33.2	112,236	3.8
District of Columbia	545	3,905	23,591	90.4	165,802	524	3,540	23,714	84.3	160,824	-9.3
Florida	6,353	30,209	15,179	498.7	78,503	6,330	32,022	16,390	542.2	85,648	6.0
Georgia	1,948	9,359	18,414	183.2	94,062	1,995	9,133	19,537	190.8	95,659	-2.4
Hawaii	651	4,081	25,196	103.9	159,621	632	3,688	28,606	100.6	159,179	-9.6
Idaho	294	1,291	12,465	16.9	57,456	307	1,325	13,069	19.2	62,534	2.6
Illinois	3,591	19,201	19,862	418.2	116,453	3,503	19,295	20,787	413.3	117,988	0.5
Indiana	1,556	7,381	14,145	118.4	76,064	1,620	7,512	15,586	130.2	80,356	1.8
Iowa	890	3,812	13,635	56.8	63,801	894	3,996	14,356	58.7	65,640	4.8
Kansas	768	3,058	13,704	48.9	63,734	784	3,648	14,320	58.7	74,815	19.3
Kentucky	1,079	4,450	12,327	61.2	56,764	1,071	4,852	13,295	68.9	64,352	9.0
Louisiana	1,335	5,877	12,618	79.5	59,557	1,361	5,803	13,799	84.8	62,289	-1.3
Maine	350	1,025	15,930	18.7	53,549	354	1,011	17,302	19.6	55,367	-1.4
Maryland	1,525	11,513	19,334	239.2	156,839	1,506	11,118	19,615	235.6	156,447	-3.4
Massachusetts	1,627	9,104	26,612	246.6	151,596	1,626	10,078	26,160	260.3	160,115	10.7
Michigan	2,439	13,290	15,230	228.6	93,726	2,477	13,714	16,096	245.2	98,996	3.2
Minnesota	1,659	8,045	16,479	136.2	82,078	1,642	7,949	16,300	134.3	81,769	-1.2
Mississippi	810	2,322	10,550	28.6	35,322	731	2,286	12,462	29.9	40,848	-1.6
Missouri	1,885	9,598	14,581	160.0	84,888	1,889	11,061	14,075	175.2	92,739	15.2
Montana	390	1,244	11,463	16.1	41,390	392	1,265	12,345	17.2	43,793	1.7
Nebraska	527	2,190	13,041	29.0	55,030	538	2,285	12,047	31.4	58,323	4.3
Nevada	849	4,972	16,104	80.8	95,223	842	5,043	17,532	89.2	105,897	1.4
New Hampshire	345	1,636	17,939	33.2	96,159	373	1,762	18,806	38.5	103,335	7.7
New Jersey	3,347	15,529	19,931	343.5	102,618	3,355	15,915	21,325	364.9	108,768	2.5
New Mexico	636	3,025	14,136	36.1	56,690	647	2,477	13,980	36.9	57,019	-18.1
New York	15,451	67,513	22,680	1,620.3	104,865	15,431	68,653	23,887	1,703.5	110,397	1.7
North Carolina	1,779	7,678	16,515	146.1	82,099	1,846	8,060	17,534	156.2	84,612	5.0
North Dakota	297	1,227	12,561	16.6	55,754	289	1,264	12,835	17.5	60,550	3.0
Ohio	3,287	19,653	14,273	313.9	95,501	3,310	19,529	15,995	320.6	96,859	-0.6
Oklahoma	1,030	4,427	14,081	69.1	67,050	1,007	4,466	14,667	66.6	66,139	0.9
Oregon	1,569	6,742	12,971	97.2	61,928	1,582	6,914	14,158	98.2	62,054	2.6
Pennsylvania	2,812	17,518	17,775	356.0	126,608	2,791	17,882	19,277	360.1	129,023	2.1
Rhode Island	294	1,351	18,967	28.4	96,724	291	1,385	21,334	30.4	104,498	2.5
South Carolina	777	3,348	15,453	59.8	76,954	806	3,509	18,776	70.1	86,945	4.8
South Dakota	315	1,054	12,076	13.2	41,822	321	929	11,061	11.4	35,508	-11.9
Tennessee	1,390	6,364	16,027	110.0	79,108	1,419	6,636	17,061	119.7	84,359	4.3
Texas	6,519	32,335	17,248	609.9	93,553	6,565	32,381	17,852	590.2	89,901	0.1
Utah	513	2,797	15,638	48.1	93,696	535	2,935	16,226	52.8	98,669	4.9
Vermont	159	585	17,497	9.7	61,277	160	954	26,197	24.6	153,550	63.1
Virginia	1,877	10,752	16,231	187.6	99,947	1,938	10,172	17,664	191.3	98,693	-5.4
Washington	2,825	11,196	14,721	187.0	66,189	2,845	11,711	15,410	198.5	69,783	4.6
West Virginia	639	2,382	15,563	34.6	54,191	658	2,237	14,997	37.5	56,995	-6.1
Wisconsin	1,546	6,300	13,537	99.0	64,006	1,568	6,789	14,805	113.1	72,136	7.8
Wyoming	277	774	10,853	9.2	33,144	280	758	11,193	9.9	35,471	-2.1

Source: County Business Patterns, U.S. Department of Commerce, Washington, D.C., for 1994 and 1995. Employment shown is for mid-March of the year shown. Payroll per employee is calculated by annualizing 1st Quarter payroll (not shown) and then dividing that value by mid-March employment. Dividing total annual payroll (columns 5 and 10) by employment, therefore, will *not* yield the payroll per employee figure (columns 4 and 9). The symbol (D) indicates that data are withheld by the source to avoid disclosure of competitive information. A dash (-) indicates that data are not available or cannot be calculated.

ESTABLISHMENTS 1995 - STATE AND REGIONAL CONCENTRATION

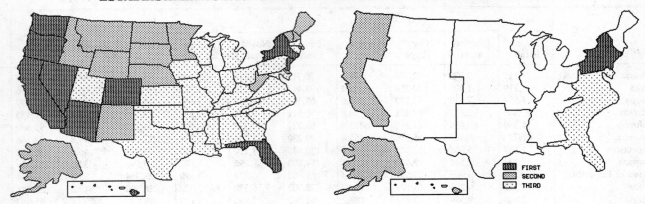

EMPLOYMENT 1995 - STATE AND REGIONAL CONCENTRATION

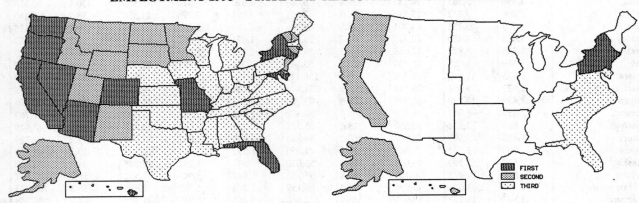

PAYROLL 1995 - STATE AND REGIONAL CONCENTRATION

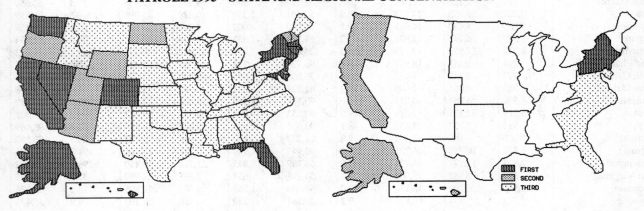

States with the darkest shading indicate those states which have proportionately more establishments, employment, or payrolls than would be indicated by the state's population. States with light shading are states with proportionately fewer establishments, less employment, and lower payrolls than population distribution. States shaded grey are within 15 percent of the state's population proportion in these categories. States for which no data are available are shown as average (grey). *Regions* are shaded to indicate absolute rank in the category. If no data for the category are available, establishment counts are used to shade the regions. Source of the data is the table on the facing page.

LEADING COMPANIES - SIC 6512 - Nonresidential Building Operators

Number shown: **100**   Total sales/assets ($ mil): **21,436**   Total employment (000): **85.2**

Company Name	Address				CEO Name	Phone	Co. Type	Sales/Assets ($ mil)	Empl. (000)
U.S. Steel Group	600 Grant St.	Pittsburgh	PA	15219	Paul J. Wilhelm	412-433-1121	S	6,941	20.7
Equity Office Properties Trust	Two N. Riverside Plaza	Chicago	IL	60606	Timothy H. Callahan	312-466-3300	P	3,913 TA	0.7
Ingles Markets Inc.	PO Box 6676	Asheville	NC	28816	Robert P. Ingle	704-669-2941	P	1,472	11.0
Rouse Co.	10275 Little Patuxent Pkwy.	Columbia	MD	21044	Anothy W. Deering	410-992-6000	P	832 OR	4.3
Forest City Enterprises Inc.	10800 Brookpark Rd.	Cleveland	OH	44130	Charles A. Ratner	216-267-1200	P	610 OR	3.4
Inland Group Inc.	2901 Butterfield Rd.	Oak Brook	IL	60523	Daniel L. Goodwin	630-218-8000	R	570 OR*	0.8
Herrick Company Inc.	PO Box 5010	Boca Raton	FL	33431	Norton Herrick	407-241-9880	R	500 OR*	<0.1
PM Realty Group	1177 W. Loop S.	Houston	TX	77027	Mike Lutton	713-966-3600	R	430 OR	3.0
Carlson Real Estate Co.	111 Cheshire Ln.	Minnetonka	MN	55305	Dean Riesen	612-333-9898	S	350 OR	<0.1
TrizecHahn Centers Inc.	4350 La Jolla Village Dr.	San Diego	CA	92122	Lee Wagman	619-546-1001	D	320 OR*	1.5
Shubert Organization Inc.	225 W. 44th St.	New York	NY	10036	Bernard B. Jacobs	212-944-3700	R	280 OR*	2.0
Pyramid Management Group Inc.	4 Clinton Sq.	Syracuse	NY	13202	Robert Congel	315-422-7000	R	260 OR	1.4
Wisteria Ventures Corp.	750 N St Paul Dr #1280	Dallas	TX	75201	Fumio Hanya	214-740-0090	R	247 TA	0.6
A.G. Spanos Construction Inc.	PO Box 7126	Stockton	CA	95267	Dean Spanos	209-478-7954	R	234 OR	0.5
Taubman Realty Group L.P.	200 E. Long Lake Rd.	Bloomfield Hills	MI	48304	Robert S. Taubman	810-258-6800	R	229 OR	0.4
Charles E. Smith Management Inc.	2345 Crystal Dr.	Arlington	VA	22202	Robert P. Kogod	703-920-8500	R	202 OR*	1.4
Group Financial Partners Inc.	Starks Bldg.	Louisville	KY	40202	Jeffrey T. Gill	502-585-5544	R	200*	1.6
Portman Holdings L.P.	303 Peachtree St.	Atlanta	GA	30308	John C. Portman Jr.	404-614-5555	R	150 OR*	0.2
Rockefeller Group Inc.	1221 Ave. of the Amer.	New York	NY	10020	Lorian Marlantes	212-698-8500	R	145 OR*	1.0
Catellus Development Corp.	201 Mission St.	San Francisco	CA	94105	Nelson C. Rising	415-974-4500	P	144 OR	0.4
First Allied Corp.	270 Commerce Dr.	Rochester	NY	14623	Malcolm Glazer	716-359-3000	R	140 OR*	1.0
Westfield Corp.	11601 Wilshire Blvd.	Los Angeles	CA	90025	Richard E. Green	310-478-4456	R	140 OR*	1.0
Crown American Associates	Pasquerilla Plz.	Johnstown	PA	15907	Frank J. Pasquerilla	814-536-4441	S	134 OR	0.4
Texas Stadium Corp.	2401 E. Airport Fwy.	Irving	TX	75062	Jerry Jones	214-438-7676	R	110 OR	<0.1
Constellation Real Estate Group Inc.	250 W. Pratt St.	Baltimore	MD	21201	Randall M. Griffin	410-783-2800	S	107 OR	0.5
H.G. Hill Co.	PO Box 41503	Nashville	TN	37204	Wentworth Caldwell Jr.	615-244-4520	R	103*	1.1
Gannett Fleming Affiliates Inc.	PO Box 67100	Harrisburg	PA	17106	Maurice A. Wadsworth	717-763-7211	R	103 OR*	1.6
PIER 39 L.P.	PO Box 193730	San Francisco	CA	94119	Fritz Arko	415-705-5500	S	100 OR	0.2
Horizon/Glen Outlet Centers L.P.	500 Hakes Dr.	Norton Shores	MI	49441	Jeffrey A. Kerr	616-798-9100	S	94 OR	0.5

Company type codes: P - Public, R - Private, S - Subsidiary, D - Division, J - Joint Venture, A - Affiliate, G - Group. If the dollar values shown are not sales, the following codes apply: TA - Total Assets; OR - Operating Revenues; GB - Gross Billings. * - estimated dollar value. < - less than. *na* - not available.

Continued on next page.

LEADING COMPANIES - SIC 6512 - Nonresidential Building Operators
Continued

Company Name	Address				CEO Name	Phone	Co. Type	Sales/Assets ($ mil)	Empl. (000)
Kemmons Wilson Inc.	1629 Winchester Rd.	Memphis	TN	38116	Spence Wilson	901-346-8800	R	80 OR*	3.0
Kimco Development Corp.	PO Box C	Roslyn	NY	11576	David Samber	516-484-5858	R	80 OR	0.1
Williard Inc.	PO Box 9002	Jenkintown	PA	19046	Joseph Doody	215-885-5000	S	80 OR	0.8
Goodale and Barbieri Cos.	W. 201 N. River Dr.	Spokane	WA	99201	Donald K. Barbieri	509-459-6100	R	78 OR*	1.3
Brim Inc.	305 N.E. 102nd Ave.	Portland	OR	97220	Armand Brim	503-256-2070	R	74 OR*	0.8
Madison Square Garden Corp.	2 Penn Plz.	New York	NY	10121	David Checketts	212-465-6000	J	72 OR*	0.5
Helmsley-Spear Inc.	60 E. 42nd St.	New York	NY	10165	Harry B. Helmsley	212-687-6400	R	64 OR*	0.3
Turnberry Associates	19495 Biscayne Blvd.	North Miami Beach	FL	33180	Donald Soffer	305-937-6200	R	64 OR*	0.3
Forest City Management Inc.	704 Terminal Twr.	Cleveland	OH	44113	Ron Ratner	216-621-6060	S	60 OR	0.6
C and W Supply and Investment	700 W. Chase St.	Springfield	MO	65803	W.B. White Jr.	417-869-5865	R	58 OR*	<0.1
Midland Properties Inc.	2001 Shawnee Mission Pkwy.	Shawnee Mission	KS	66205	Alan Atterbury	913-677-5300	R	57 OR*	0.4
R.H. White Companies Inc.	41 Central St.	Auburn	MA	01501	L.H. White	508-832-3295	R	56 OR*	0.3
CBS Investment Realty Inc.	3033 N. 44th St.	Phoenix	AZ	85018	James Schlesing	602-952-1900	R	56 OR	0.6
Oppenheimer Companies Inc.	877 W. Main St.	Boise	ID	83702	Arthur F. Oppenheimer	208-343-2602	R	54	0.3
Chelsea G.C.A. Realty Partnership L.P.	103 Eisenhower Pkwy.	Roseland	NJ	07068	David Bloom	201-228-6111	S	53 OR	0.1
Schiavone Corp.	1032 Chapel St.	New Haven	CT	06510	Joel Shiavone	203-777-3071	R	53 OR*	0.3
Rogue Valley Manor	1200 Mira Mar Ave.	Medford	OR	97504	Thomas Becker	503-773-7411	R	51 OR*	0.4
Charan Industries Inc.	PO Box 74	Garden City	NY	11530	Charles P. Ryan	516-747-6500	R	50 OR	2.0
Combined Properties Inc.	1899 L St. N.W.	Washington	DC	20036	Ronald S. Haft	202-293-4500	R	50 OR	<0.1
Daley Hotel Group Inc.	138 St. James Ave.	Boston	MA	02116	James Daley	617-267-5300	R	50 OR	1.2
Aircoa Hotel Partners L.P.	5775 DTC Blvd.	Englewood	CO	80111	Douglas M. Pasquale	303-220-2000	P	48 OR	1.0
First Republic Corporation of America	302 5th Ave.	New York	NY	10001	Norman A. Halper	212-279-6100	P	48	0.4
Cynwyd Investments	725 Conshohocken State	Bala Cynwyd	PA	19004	Herbert Kurtz	215-839-4100	R	45 OR	0.2
Arena Associates Inc.	2 Championship Dr.	Auburn Hills	MI	48326	Tom Wilson	810-377-8200	S	43 OR*	0.3
3900 Corp.	5518 Baltimore National Pike	Baltimore	MD	21228	Nathan Weinberg	410-744-6142	R	40 OR*	0.5
Charles Dunn Co.	1200 Wilshire Blvd.	Los Angeles	CA	90017	Joseph C. Dunn	213-481-1800	R	38 OR*	0.4
Transamerica Realty Services Inc.	600 Montgomery St.	San Francisco	CA	94111	Kent L. Colwell	415-983-5420	S	37 OR	<0.1
Bresler and Reiner Inc.	401 M St. S.W.	Washington	DC	20024	Charles S. Bresler	202-488-8800	P	35 OR	0.1
Lipton Realty Inc.	9100 Overland Plz.	St. Louis	MO	63114	Randall Lipton	314-423-2222	R	32 OR*	0.2
Selig Enterprises Inc.	1100 Spring St. NW	Atlanta	GA	30309	S.S. Selig III	404-876-5511	R	32 OR*	0.3
Sunriver Resort	PO Box 3609	Sunriver	OR	97707	Charles S. Peck	541-593-1000	R	30 OR*	0.6

Company type codes: P - Public, R - Private, S - Subsidiary, D - Division, J - Joint Venture, A - Affiliate, G - Group. If the dollar values shown are not sales, the following codes apply: TA - Total Assets; OR - Operating Revenues; GB - Gross Billings. * - estimated dollar value. < - less than. *na* - not available.

Continued on next page.

INPUTS AND OUTPUTS FOR ALL REAL ESTATE SECTORS - SIC GROUP 65 - Continued

Economic Sector or Industry Providing Inputs	%	Sector	Economic Sector or Industry Buying Outputs	%	Sector
			Private libraries, vocational schools, nec	0.2	Services
			Research, development, & testing services	0.2	Services
			Exports of goods & services	0.2	Foreign
			Dairy farm products	0.1	Agric.
			Vegetables	0.1	Agric.
			Crude petroleum & natural gas	0.1	Mining
			Residential 1 unit structures, nonfarm	0.1	Constr.
			Apparel made from purchased materials	0.1	Manufg.
			Commercial printing	0.1	Manufg.
			Electronic computers	0.1	Manufg.
			Miscellaneous plastics products, nec	0.1	Manufg.
			Job training & related services	0.1	Services
			Miscellaneous equipment rental & leasing	0.1	Services
			Miscellaneous repair shops	0.1	Services
			Personnel supply services	0.1	Services
			Photofinishing labs & commercial photography	0.1	Services
			Theatrical producers, bands, orchestras	0.1	Services
			Video tape rental	0.1	Services
			U.S. Postal Service	0.1	Gov't
			Federal Government, national defense, spending	0.1	Fed Govt

Source: Benchmark Input-Output Accounts for the U.S. Economy, 1992, U.S. Department of Commerce, Washington, D.C., November 1997. Data, as reported in the source, are organized by the 1987 SIC structure in use in 1992.

OCCUPATIONS EMPLOYED BY REAL ESTATE AGENTS AND MANAGERS

Occupation	% of Total 1996	Change to 2006	Occupation	% of Total 1996	Change to 2006
Maintenance repairers, general utility	11.5	41.5	Guards	3.2	13.9
Property & real estate managers	10.2	39.2	Gardeners, nursery workers	3.2	13.9
Janitors & cleaners, maids	9.4	1.2	Brokers, real estate	3.1	18.9
Secretaries, except legal & medical	7.1	0.4	Real estate clerks	2.5	13.5
Sales agents, real estate	5.8	-5.7	Financial managers	2.1	26.5
General office clerks	5.2	8.9	Marketing & sales worker supervisors	1.7	26.5
Bookkeeping, accounting, & auditing clerks	5.0	1.2	Service workers nec	1.4	26.5
Receptionists & information clerks	4.9	26.5	Accountants & auditors	1.3	17.1
General managers & top executives	4.4	22.6	Clerical supervisors & managers	1.3	26.5
Real estate appraisers	3.7	14.1	Typists, including word processing	1.1	-17.8

Sources: Industry-Occupation Matrix, Bureau of Labor Statistics. These data relate to one or more 3-digit SIC industry groups rather than to a single 4-digit SIC. The change reported for each occupation to the year 2005 is a percent of growth or decline as estimated by the Bureau of Labor Statistics. The abbreviation nec stands for not elsewhere classified.

U.S. AND STATE DATA ON INDUSTRY REVENUES AND OTHER ACCOUNTS FOR 1992

State	No. of Estab.	Employ- ment	Payroll ($ mil.)	Revenues ($ mil.)	Empl./ Estab.	Revenue/ Estab. ($)	Payroll/ Estab. ($)	Revenue/ Empl. ($)	Payroll/ Empl. ($)
UNITED STATES	106,552	646,561	14,859.5	53,747.0	6	504,421	139,458	83,128	22,982
Alabama	989	4,960	96.7	363.1	5	367,172	97,762	73,212	19,493
Alaska	237	1,176	25.5	102.4	5	432,030	107,447	87,067	21,654
Arizona	2,049	12,841	271.4	971.4	6	474,109	132,448	75,652	21,134
Arkansas	600	3,088	43.9	192.5	5	320,762	73,215	62,324	14,226
California	15,432	93,153	2,370.3	8,212.6	6	532,179	153,596	88,162	25,445
Colorado	2,733	16,451	318.0	1,166.5	6	426,819	116,355	70,907	19,330
Connecticut	1,487	7,885	243.9	1,170.7	5	787,321	164,032	148,478	30,934
Delaware	285	1,189	27.5	133.7	4	469,165	96,593	112,458	23,153
District of Columbia	544	5,876	168.0	465.2	11	855,090	308,783	79,164	28,587
Florida	10,400	58,634	1,112.6	4,515.3	6	434,166	106,982	77,009	18,976
Georgia	2,386	15,958	432.1	1,400.9	7	587,136	181,082	87,787	27,075
Hawaii	1,591	8,832	193.9	733.7	6	461,181	121,881	83,077	21,956
Idaho	463	1,281	23.8	156.0	3	336,937	51,322	121,781	18,550
Illinois	5,027	35,500	979.2	3,315.5	7	659,541	194,790	93,395	27,583
Indiana	1,560	9,053	180.5	671.7	6	430,556	115,722	74,193	19,941
Iowa	733	2,989	58.9	262.5	4	358,181	80,371	87,838	19,710
Kansas	814	5,038	81.6	307.8	6	378,145	100,270	61,098	16,201
Kentucky	785	3,121	51.0	249.3	4	317,583	64,910	79,879	16,326
Louisiana	908	5,633	94.1	329.2	6	362,541	103,607	58,439	16,701
Maine	557	1,949	36.9	155.7	3	279,616	66,321	79,911	18,954
Maryland	2,220	17,256	407.1	1,330.1	8	599,144	183,370	77,080	23,591
Massachusetts	2,390	18,289	522.9	1,533.0	8	641,422	218,767	83,821	28,588
Michigan	2,896	17,458	348.8	1,176.7	6	406,309	120,435	67,400	19,978
Minnesota	1,624	9,816	189.2	779.8	6	480,166	116,520	79,441	19,278
Mississippi	460	1,760	23.8	101.4	4	220,376	51,685	57,598	13,509
Missouri	1,695	9,522	193.3	701.7	6	413,970	114,018	73,690	20,296
Montana	352	910	12.5	89.4	3	254,085	35,608	98,284	13,774
Nebraska	453	2,407	44.9	184.7	5	407,828	99,117	76,754	18,654
Nevada	784	4,418	83.0	341.2	6	435,224	105,893	77,233	18,791
New Hampshire	581	2,377	50.7	194.7	4	335,072	87,196	81,900	21,313
New Jersey	3,325	18,179	436.9	1,839.9	5	553,359	131,411	101,211	24,036
New Mexico	606	2,322	38.8	198.9	4	328,224	64,035	85,661	16,712
New York	10,157	62,036	1,876.4	6,814.8	6	670,947	184,738	109,853	30,247
North Carolina	2,374	11,090	224.2	923.0	5	388,796	94,426	83,228	20,213
North Dakota	165	680	10.4	47.3	4	286,800	62,958	69,591	15,276
Ohio	2,863	21,434	421.9	1,522.3	7	531,712	147,358	71,022	19,683
Oklahoma	883	4,733	88.9	304.9	5	345,256	100,678	64,412	18,783
Oregon	1,327	7,798	133.7	596.3	6	449,376	100,726	76,471	17,141
Pennsylvania	3,134	20,130	438.9	1,621.5	6	517,383	140,041	80,550	21,803
Rhode Island	354	1,780	36.0	145.8	5	411,723	101,794	81,882	20,244
South Carolina	1,287	7,055	132.9	489.4	5	380,256	103,238	69,368	18,833
South Dakota	206	715	10.2	50.2	3	243,738	49,665	70,224	14,309
Tennessee	1,443	9,032	163.6	636.5	6	441,072	113,378	70,468	18,114
Texas	6,778	52,218	1,168.1	3,413.1	8	503,560	172,331	65,363	22,369
Utah	637	3,876	68.8	309.1	6	485,243	108,050	79,747	17,757
Vermont	343	1,132	20.3	88.7	3	258,612	59,044	78,360	17,890
Virginia	2,779	19,721	427.7	1,456.5	7	524,117	153,900	73,856	21,687
Washington	2,716	15,183	314.3	1,293.3	6	476,195	115,707	85,184	20,698
West Virginia	329	976	14.5	82.5	3	250,866	44,061	84,565	14,852
Wisconsin	1,605	7,017	137.9	553.2	4	344,683	85,899	78,840	19,648
Wyoming	206	634	9.5	51.2	3	248,413	45,893	80,715	14,912

Source: 1992 Economic Census, U.S. Department of Commerce, Washington, D.C. This is the only table that shows revenue data as collected by the Bureau of the Census in an Economic Census. The symbol (D) indicates that data are withheld by the source to avoid disclosure of competitive information. A dash (-) indicates that data are not available or cannot be calculated.

STATE-BY-STATE DATA ON ESTABLISHMENTS, EMPLOYMENT, AND PAYROLL - 1994 AND 1995

State	1994					1995					% Change Empl.
	No. of Estab.	Employ- ment	Pay / Empl.	Payroll ($ mil.)	Pay / Estab.	No. of Estab.	Employ- ment	Pay / Empl.	Payroll ($ mil.)	Pay / Estab.	
Alabama	1,128	6,797	17,896	136.0	120,556	1,164	6,974	19,389	142.6	122,524	2.6
Alaska	245	1,144	20,455	24.5	99,988	242	1,183	20,132	25.0	103,496	3.4
Arizona	2,337	15,359	21,073	361.0	154,481	2,366	15,600	22,194	370.9	156,753	1.6
Arkansas	685	3,139	15,856	54.3	79,266	713	3,341	16,864	60.4	84,696	6.4
California	15,481	105,344	25,771	2,761.6	178,386	14,763	106,138	26,835	2,864.6	194,037	0.8
Colorado	3,264	18,133	19,975	381.2	116,775	3,383	19,019	21,074	417.6	123,430	4.9
Connecticut	1,558	9,516	28,379	285.2	183,069	1,530	9,396	29,931	293.0	191,474	-1.3
Delaware	303	1,368	22,263	33.7	111,106	315	1,435	23,682	35.1	111,371	4.9
District of Columbia	567	6,434	29,641	192.1	338,871	543	6,009	33,113	185.6	341,740	-6.6
Florida	11,018	62,775	19,073	1,299.8	117,971	11,034	66,832	20,058	1,392.6	126,208	6.5
Georgia	2,796	20,864	25,311	582.9	208,494	2,976	22,599	27,531	630.8	211,964	8.3
Hawaii	1,555	9,047	23,408	217.1	139,605	1,497	8,818	23,247	214.2	143,069	-2.5
Idaho	544	1,963	14,174	33.1	60,835	572	1,959	15,806	32.9	57,481	-0.2
Illinois	5,428	36,977	27,370	1,095.6	201,847	5,394	37,804	29,265	1,147.1	212,663	2.2
Indiana	1,822	11,569	21,912	265.4	145,647	1,911	11,647	20,127	244.7	128,063	0.7
Iowa	845	3,975	16,930	74.6	88,227	852	4,249	17,775	79.7	93,558	6.9
Kansas	897	5,649	17,572	104.9	116,972	953	5,392	18,548	107.9	113,252	-4.5
Kentucky	910	3,575	17,028	68.7	75,527	893	3,966	17,832	75.2	84,202	10.9
Louisiana	1,015	6,397	16,711	116.2	114,460	1,026	6,421	17,083	114.8	111,935	0.4
Maine	568	1,969	17,515	39.4	69,280	593	2,014	18,393	39.9	67,224	2.3
Maryland	2,405	19,357	23,291	481.0	200,017	2,466	20,269	24,191	523.5	212,290	4.7
Massachusetts	2,726	20,144	28,226	613.5	225,050	2,695	19,356	30,513	632.4	234,645	-3.9
Michigan	2,967	18,753	20,130	414.8	139,818	2,999	18,646	22,932	440.4	146,843	-0.6
Minnesota	1,905	11,231	19,378	234.8	123,278	1,955	11,544	21,529	261.6	133,828	2.8
Mississippi	515	1,913	15,220	32.3	62,627	528	1,926	15,728	31.8	60,259	0.7
Missouri	1,893	11,056	21,141	257.1	135,808	1,878	11,136	22,543	273.7	145,766	0.7
Montana	427	1,229	13,627	18.4	43,049	438	1,341	13,241	19.4	44,201	9.1
Nebraska	524	2,947	19,790	61.8	117,885	547	2,886	20,981	65.5	119,773	-2.1
Nevada	869	4,514	18,930	99.3	114,219	879	4,862	19,675	103.0	117,154	7.7
New Hampshire	664	2,726	17,925	54.9	82,745	650	2,734	18,854	59.3	91,200	0.3
New Jersey	3,499	17,719	25,714	504.7	144,230	3,439	18,014	27,819	525.1	152,676	1.7
New Mexico	690	2,884	18,171	62.6	90,665	717	3,302	18,618	66.2	92,393	14.5
New York	10,624	66,133	31,590	2,181.2	205,309	10,691	66,686	34,480	2,310.0	216,066	0.8
North Carolina	2,746	14,551	21,043	338.8	123,397	2,827	15,879	22,069	373.1	131,991	9.1
North Dakota	202	981	13,708	13.4	66,371	193	981	12,979	13.3	69,062	0.0
Ohio	3,148	25,611	19,129	543.6	172,689	3,270	25,606	20,685	560.1	171,282	0.0
Oklahoma	1,034	4,899	19,272	100.5	97,169	1,081	4,642	17,450	88.3	81,707	-5.2
Oregon	1,577	9,885	17,433	187.5	118,916	1,632	9,905	17,886	192.5	117,949	0.2
Pennsylvania	3,290	27,039	21,302	607.6	184,686	3,318	27,418	22,373	632.7	190,690	1.4
Rhode Island	402	1,840	18,457	37.9	94,348	394	1,898	20,067	40.3	102,277	3.2
South Carolina	1,419	8,330	18,218	176.0	124,039	1,487	9,038	18,649	191.4	128,744	8.5
South Dakota	227	981	14,275	15.4	67,714	225	1,110	15,506	18.8	83,662	13.1
Tennessee	1,598	10,169	19,026	225.7	141,263	1,648	10,541	21,112	242.4	147,107	3.7
Texas	7,137	60,803	22,199	1,457.4	204,202	7,322	58,194	23,894	1,448.1	197,770	-4.3
Utah	850	4,889	16,277	89.4	105,196	866	5,178	17,359	100.3	115,819	5.9
Vermont	352	1,305	17,232	24.6	69,852	351	1,279	18,549	25.4	72,313	-2.0
Virginia	2,979	20,849	22,841	524.3	176,009	2,952	20,687	24,660	527.7	178,776	-0.8
Washington	2,944	17,887	20,327	380.3	129,169	2,903	16,693	21,101	364.3	125,500	-6.7
West Virginia	367	1,137	14,093	18.7	50,837	377	1,129	15,844	18.9	50,072	-0.7
Wisconsin	1,736	8,174	18,196	165.0	95,022	1,716	8,508	19,040	173.9	101,358	4.1
Wyoming	246	693	13,183	10.3	42,033	245	734	14,120	11.2	45,804	5.9

Source: County Business Patterns, U.S. Department of Commerce, Washington, D.C., for 1994 and 1995. Employment shown is for mid-March of the year shown. Payroll per employee is calculated by annualizing 1st Quarter payroll (not shown) and then dividing that value by mid-March employment. Dividing total annual payroll (columns 5 and 10) by employment, therefore, will *not* yield the payroll per employee figure (columns 4 and 9). The symbol (D) indicates that data are withheld by the source to avoid disclosure of competitive information. A dash (-) indicates that data are not available or cannot be calculated.

ESTABLISHMENTS 1995 - STATE AND REGIONAL CONCENTRATION

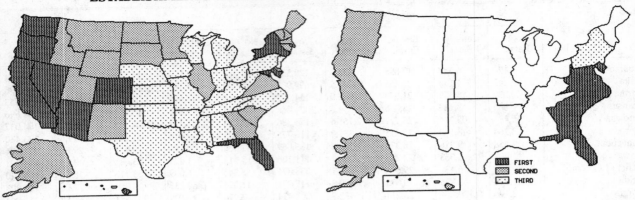

EMPLOYMENT 1995 - STATE AND REGIONAL CONCENTRATION

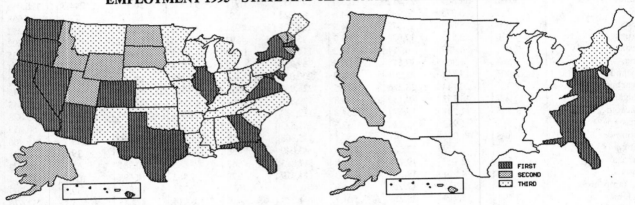

PAYROLL 1995 - STATE AND REGIONAL CONCENTRATION

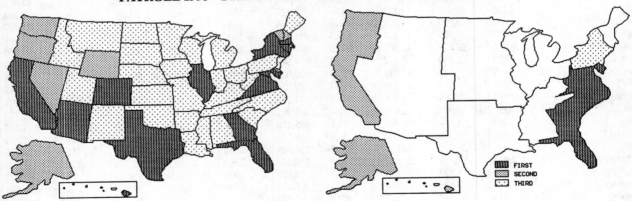

States with the darkest shading indicate those states which have proportionately more establishments, employment, or payrolls than would be indicated by the state's population. States with light shading are states with proportionately fewer establishments, less employment, and lower payrolls than population distribution. States shaded grey are within 15 percent of the state's population proportion in these categories. States for which no data are available are shown as average (grey). *Regions* are shaded to indicate absolute rank in the category. If no data for the category are available, establishment counts are used to shade the regions. Source of the data is the table on the facing page.

LEADING COMPANIES - SIC 6531 - Real Estate Agents and Managers

Number shown: **100**   Total sales/assets ($ mil): **27,636**   Total employment (000): **153.2**

Company Name	Address				CEO Name	Phone	Co. Type	Sales/Assets ($ mil)	Empl. (000)
Alleghany Corp.	375 Park Ave.	New York	NY	10152	John J. Burns Jr.	212-752-1356	P	4,501 TA	9.8
Coldwell Banker Corp.	27271 Las Ramblas	Mission Viejo	CA	92690	Chandler B. Barton	714-367-1800	R	1,700 OR	2.5
Chicago Title and Trust Co.	171 N. Clark St.	Chicago	IL	60601	Richard P. Toft	312-223-2000	S	1,170 TA	7.6
York Financial Corp.	101 S. George St.	York	PA	17401	Robert W. Pullo	717-846-8777	P	1,087 TA	0.4
Simon DeBartolo Group L.P.	PO Box 7033	Indianapolis	IN	46207	David Simon	317-636-1600	S	1,000 OR	6.0
Progressive Bank Inc.	1301 Rte. 52	Fishkill	NY	12524	Peter Van Kleeck	914-897-7400	P	883 TA	0.3
Northland Co.	1285 Northland Dr.	St. Paul	MN	55120	Austin Chapman	612-893-7569	R	810 TA*	0.6
Weichert Realtors Inc.	1625 Rte. 10 E.	Morris Plains	NJ	07960	James Weichert	201-267-7777	R	780 OR*	7.1
CB Commercial Real Estate Services Group Inc.	533 S. Fremont Ave.	Los Angeles	CA	90071	James J. Didion	213-613-3123	P	730 OR	6.7
Lowe Enterprises Inc.	11777 San Vicente Blvd.	Los Angeles	CA	90049	Robert J. Lowe	310-820-6661	R	620 OR	4.5
Inland Group Inc.	2901 Butterfield Rd.	Oak Brook	IL	60523	Daniel L. Goodwin	630-218-8000	R	570 OR*	0.8
Carlsberg Management Co.	2800 28th St.	Santa Monica	CA	90405	William Geary	310-450-9696	R	500 OR*	0.5
Flatley Co.	50 Braintree Hill Park	Braintree	MA	02184	Thomas Flatley	617-848-2000	R	490 OR*	4.5
Host Marriott Corp.	10400 Fernwood Rd.	Bethesda	MD	20817	Terence C. Golden	301-380-9000	P	484 OR	0.8
Starwood Lodging Corp.	2231 E. Camelback Rd.	Phoenix	AZ	85016	Earle F. Jones	602-852-3900	P	429 OR	8.9
Slifer, Smith and Frampton/Vail Associates Real Estate	P.O. Drawer 2820	Avon	CO	81620	Mark Smith	970-845-2000	R	380 OR	0.1
ERE Yarmouth Inc.	787 7th Ave.	New York	NY	10019	Douglas Tibbitts	212-605-0700	S	367 TA	3.3
Fortune International Realty	2666 Brickell Ave.	Miami	FL	33129	Edgardo Defortuna	305-856-2600	R	345 OR	0.3
DeBartolo Realty Partnership L.P.	7655 Market St.	Youngstown	OH	44513	Richard S. Sokolov	216-758-7292	S	333 OR	3.8
Mason-McDuffie Real Estate Inc.	1901 Olympic Blvd. 3rd. Fl.	Walnut Creek	CA	94596	David Cobo	510-279-0555	R	285 OR	0.1
Florida East Coast Industries Inc.	1 Malaga St.	St. Augustine	FL	32084	Carl F. Zellers Jr.	904-829-3421	P	251 OR	1.2
Mendik Co.	330 Madison Ave.	New York	NY	10017	David Greenbaum	212-557-1100	R	250 OR*	1.2
Grubb and Ellis Co.	2215 Senaters Rd.	Northbrook	IL	60062	Neil Young	847-753-9010	P	230 OR	4.0
Taubman Company L.P.	200 E. Long Lake Rd.	Bloomfield Hills	MI	48304	Robert S. Taubman	313-258-6800	S	229 OR	0.4
Bryant and Associates	3350 Peachtree N.E.	Atlanta	GA	30326	Richard Bryant Jr.	404-262-2828	R	228 OR	<0.1
Insignia Financial Group Inc.	PO Box 1089	Greenville	SC	29602	Andrew L. Farkas	864-239-1000	P	227 TA	9.3
Cushman and Wakefield Inc.	51 W. 52nd St.	New York	NY	10019	Arthur Mirante II	212-841-7500	S	220 OR	2.1
N.D.C. Inc.	6312 S. 27th St.	Oak Creek	WI	53154	David Ulrich	414-761-2040	R	220 OR*	2.0
Trammell Crow Co.	2001 Ross Ave.	Dallas	TX	75201	George Lippe	214-863-3000	R	220 OR*	2.0
Sampson Investments	222 E. Erie St.	Milwaukee	WI	53202	Harold Sampson	414-272-4440	R	210 OR*	1.0
A and B Hawaii Inc.	PO Box 3440	Honolulu	HI	96801	John C. Couch	808-525-6611	S	200	1.5

Company type codes: P - Public, R - Private, S - Subsidiary, D - Division, J - Joint Venture, A - Affiliate, G - Group. If the dollar values shown are not sales, the following codes apply: TA - Total Assets; OR - Operating Revenues; GB - Gross Billings. * - estimated dollar value. < - less than. *na* - not available.

Continued on next page.

LEADING COMPANIES - SIC 6531 - Real Estate Agents and Managers
Continued

Company Name	Address				CEO Name	Phone	Co. Type	Sales/Assets ($ mil)	Empl. (000)
Dobson and Johnson Inc.	2209 Crestmoor Rd.	Nasville	TN	37215	Albert W. Johnson	615-292-8800	R	200 OR	<0.1
GFS International Inc.	PO Box 58666	Seattle	WA	98138	John Goodman	206-575-9393	R	200 OR*	2.0
Habitat Co.	350 W. Hubbard	Chicago	IL	60610	Daniel E. Levin	312-527-5400	R	200 OR*	1.0
North American Title Co.	2185 N. California Blvd.	Walnut Creek	CA	94596	Dan Wentzel	925-935-5599	S	200 OR*	1.2
Realty One Inc.	6000 Rockside Woods	Independence	OH	44131	Joseph T. Aveni	216-328-2500	R	200 OR*	2.0
NHP Inc.	1225 Eye St. N.W.	Washington	DC	20005	J. Roderick Heller III	202-347-6247	P	195 OR	5.5
JPI Investments Inc.	600 E. Los Colinas Blvd.. #1800	Irving	TX	75039	J. Frank Miller III	214-556-1700	R	180 OR*	0.9
Mego Financial Corp.	4310 Paradise Rd.	Las Vegas	NV	89109	Robert Nederlander	702-737-3700	P	178 TA	1.3
LaSalle Partners Inc.	200 E. Randolph Dr.	Chicago	IL	60601	Stuart L. Scott	312-782-5800	P	176 OR	1.1
Arthur J. Rogers and Co.	3170 Des Plaines Ave.	Des Plaines	IL	60016	William G. Schmitz	847-297-2200	R	174 OR	0.2
Richard Bowers and Co.	3475 Lenox Rd. N.E.	Atlanta	GA	30326	Richard Bowers	404-816-1600	R	170 OR*	<0.1
Charles E. Smith Residential Realty L.P.	2345 Crystal Dr.	Arlington	VA	22202	Robert P. Kogod	703-920-8500	S	168 OR	1.2
Capital Realty Group Corp.	14160 Dallas Pkwy.	Dallas	TX	75240	Jeffrey L. Beck	214-770-5600	R	160 OR*	1.5
Alper Holdings USA Inc.	800 3rd. Ave.	New York	NY	10022	Nicolas Combele	212-750-0200	R	150 OR*	3.0
Hardaway Group Inc.	615 Main St.	Nashville	TN	37206	L.H. Hardaway Jr.	615-254-5461	R	150 OR	0.9
Maxim Property Management	350 Bridge Pkwy.	Redwood City	CA	94065	John H. Pringle	415-596-5300	R	150 OR*	0.6
Catellus Development Corp.	201 Mission St.	San Francisco	CA	94105	Nelson C. Rising	415-974-4500	P	144 OR	0.4
Starrett Corp.	909 3rd Ave.	New York	NY	10022	Paul Milstein	212-751-3100	P	141 OR	1.1
Keyes Company Realtors	1 S.E. 3rd Ave.	Miami	FL	33131	Michael Pappas	305-371-3592	R	140 OR*	1.3
Abrams Industries Inc.	PO Box 76600	Atlanta	GA	30358	Edward M. Abrams	404-256-9785	P	136 OR	0.4
Peabody Hotel Group	5118 Park Ave.	Memphis	TN	38117	Martin S. Belz	901-762-5400	R	135 OR	2.8
Riverbay Corp.	2049 Bartow Ave.	Bronx	NY	10475	Clarence Powell	718-320-3300	R	130 OR*	0.8
Mills L.P.	3000 K St. N.W.	Washington	DC	20007	Herbert S. Miller	202-965-3600	S	127 OR	0.7
CMT Holding Ltd.	19353 U.S. Hwy. 19 N.	Clearwater	FL	34624	Richard W. Cope	813-538-5468	R	124 OR	0.5
SunCor Development Co.	3838 N. Central Ave.	Phoenix	AZ	85012	John C. Ogden	602-285-6800	S	124 OR	1.2
John L. Scott Real Estate	3380 146th Pl. S.E.	Bellevue	WA	98007	J.L. Scott	206-462-5000	R	120 OR	1.3
Kilroy Industries	2250 E. Imperial Hwy.	El Segundo	CA	90245	John B. Kilroy Jr.	213-772-1193	R	120 OR*	0.1
Trendwest Resorts Inc.	12301 Northeast 10th Place	Bellevue	WA	98005	William F. Peare	425-990-2300	P	117 OR	0.7
Barclay's International Realty Inc.	249 Peruvian Ave.	Palm Beach	FL	33480	Robert Wyner	407-659-0000	R	115 OR	<0.1
Vacation Break U.S.A. Inc.	6400 N. Andrews Ave.	Fort Lauderdale	FL	33009	Ralph Muller	305-351-8500	P	104 OR	0.5
Belz Enterprises	PO Box 171199	Memphis	TN	38187	Jack A. Belz	901-767-4780	R	100 OR*	3.0

Company type codes: P - Public, R - Private, S - Subsidiary, D - Division, J - Joint Venture, A - Affiliate, G - Group. If the dollar values shown are not sales, the following codes apply: TA - Total Assets; OR - Operating Revenues; GB - Gross Billings. * - estimated dollar value. < - less than. *na* - not available.

Continued on next page.

LEADING COMPANIES - SIC 6531 - Real Estate Agents and Managers
Continued

Company Name	Address				CEO Name	Phone	Co. Type	Sales/Assets ($ mil)	Empl. (000)
ConAm Management Corp.	1764 San Diego Ave.	San Diego	CA	92110	Daniel J. Epstein	619-297-6771	R	100 OR*	1.5
Equity Group Investments Inc.	2 N. Riverside Plz.	Chicago	IL	60606	Samuel Zell	312-454-0100	R	100 OR*	0.5
Long and Foster Real Estate Inc.	11351 Random Hills Rd.	Fairfax	VA	22030	P. Wesley Foster Jr.	703-359-1500	R	99 OR*	0.9
PREMISYS Real Estate Services Inc.	2500 City West Blvd.	Houston	TX	77042	Joe Hudec	713-781-1114	S	99 OR*	0.9
Pembrook Management Inc.	305 E. 47th St.	New York	NY	10017	Hans C. Mautner	212-421-8200	R	91 OR*	1.1
Diamond Parking Inc.	3161 Elliot Ave.	Seattle	WA	98121	Joel Diamond	206-284-6303	R	90 OR	0.7
Muselli Commercial Realtors	301 Arizona Ave.	Santa Monica	CA	90401	Vincent C. Muselli	310-458-4100	R	90 OR	<0.1
Wirtz Corp.	680 N. Lakeshore Dr.	Chicago	IL	60611	William Wirtz	312-943-7000	R	90*	0.3
Shorenstein Co.	555 California St.	San Francisco	CA	94104	Douglas Shorenstein	415-772-7000	R	88 OR*	0.8
American Appraisal Associates Inc.	100E Wisconsin Av 2100	Milwaukee	WI	53202	Richard A. Giesen	414-271-7240	R	85 OR*	0.8
United Capital Corp.	9 Park Pl.	Great Neck	NY	11021	A.F. Petrocelli	516-466-6464	P	85 OR	0.6
DeWolfe Companies Inc.	80 Hayden Ave.	Lexington	MA	02173	Richard B. DeWolfe	617-863-5858	P	83 OR	1.7
West Shell Inc.	PO Box 5390	Cincinnati	OH	45201	Mark Rippe	513-721-4200	R	82 OR	0.8
Kimco Development Corp.	PO Box C	Roslyn	NY	11576	David Samber	516-484-5858	R	80 OR	0.1
Robert Martin Co.	100 Clearbrook Rd.	Elmsford	NY	10523	Brad Berger	914-592-4800	R	80 OR	0.1
Slater Realtors	2737 McRae Rd.	Richmond	VA	23235	E.M. Jackson	804-320-1391	R	80 OR	<0.1
Village Resorts Inc.	PO Box 4800	Park City	UT	84060	Barbara Zimonja	435-655-4800	R	80 OR*	2.0
Snyder-Hunt Corp.	800 Hethwood Blvd.	Blacksburg	VA	24060	Harry H. Hunt III	703-552-3515	R	77 OR*	0.7
Carr Realty L.P.	1700 Pennsylvania Ave. N.W.	Washington	DC	20006	Oliver T. Carr Jr.	202-624-7500	S	76 OR	0.5
J.J. Gumberg Co.	1051 Brinton Rd.	Pittsburgh	PA	15221	Ira J. Gumberg	412-244-4000	R	75 OR*	0.4
Justice Corp.	19329 U.S. Hwy. 19 N.	Clearwater	FL	34624	Albert N. Justice	813-531-4600	R	74 OR*	<0.1
Celebrity Properties Inc.	9328 Civic Center Dr.	Beverly Hills	CA	90210	Sherry Sexton	310-657-6000	R	72 OR*	<0.1
American Real Estate Partners L.P.	100 S. Bedford Rd.	Mount Kisco	NY	10549	Carl C. Icahn	914-242-7700	P	72 OR	<0.1
Kevin F. Donohoe Company Inc.	Curtis Ctr.	Philadelphia	PA	19106	Kevin F. Donohoe	215-238-6400	R	71 OR	<0.1
Koplar Enterprises	4935 Lindell Blvd.	St. Louis	MO	63108	Edward J. Koplar	314-454-6455	R	70	0.2
Mahoney Group	PO Box 15001	Casa Grande	AZ	85230	John W. McEvoy	602-836-7483	R	70 TA	0.1
Polinger Shannon and Luchs Inc.	5530 Wisconsin Ave.	Chevy Chase	MD	20815	John Gordon	301-657-3600	R	70 OR*	0.7
FRP Properties Inc.	155 E. 21st St.	Jacksonville	FL	32206	John E. Anderson	904-355-1781	P	69 OR	0.7
Gene B. Glick Company Inc.	PO Box 40177	Indianapolis	IN	46240	Eugene B. Glick	317-469-0400	R	68 OR*	0.6
SUSA Partnership L.P.	10440 Little Patuxent Pkwy.	Columbia	MD	21044	Dean Jernigan	410-730-9500	S	68 OR	0.8
Chicago Capital Consultants Inc.	1919 N. Sheffield	Chicago	IL	60614	Jeffrey B. Gellman	312-296-4900	R	67 OR	<0.1

Company type codes: P - Public, R - Private, S - Subsidiary, D - Division, J - Joint Venture, A - Affiliate, G - Group. If the dollar values shown are not sales, the following codes apply: TA - Total Assets; OR - Operating Revenues; GB - Gross Billings. * - estimated dollar value. < - less than. *na* - not available.

Continued on next page.

LEADING COMPANIES - SIC 6531 - Real Estate Agents and Managers

Continued

Company Name	Address				CEO Name	Phone	Co. Type	Sales/Assets ($ mil)	Empl. (000)
Cohen-Esrey Real Estate Services Inc.	4435 Main St.	Kansas City	MO	64111	Robert E. Esrey	816-531-8100	R	67 OR•	0.7
Amli Residential Properties L.P.	125 S. Wacker Dr.	Chicago	IL	60606	Gregory T. Mutz	312-984-5037	S	66 OR	0.3
Mid Atlantic Asset Management Co.	422 Allegheny St.	Hollidaysburg	PA	16648	P. Jules Patt	814-696-4377	R	66 OR•	0.6
Shapell Industries Inc.	8383 Wilshire Blvd.	Beverly Hills	CA	90211	Nathan Shapell	213-655-7330	R	66 OR•	0.3
Voit Cos.	21600 Oxnard St.	Woodland Hills	CA	91367	Robert D. Voit	818-593-6200	R	66 OR•	0.6
Lexford Properties Inc.	6954 Americana Pkwy.	Reynoldsburg	OH	43068	John B. Bartling	614-759-1566	R	65 OR	2.5
JBG Cos.	1250 Connecticut Ave N.W.	Washington	DC	20036	Lewis Rumford III	202-364-6300	R	64 OR•	0.3

Source: *Ward's Business Directory of U.S. Private and Public Companies*, 1996. Company type codes: P - Public, R - Private, S - Subsidiary, D - Division, J - Joint Venture, A - Affiliate, G - Group. If the dollar values shown are not sales, the following codes apply: TA - Total Assets; OR - Operating Revenues; GB - Gross Billings. • - estimated dollar value. < - less than; *na* - not available.

FINANCIAL DATA ON REAL ESTATE

The following six tables present data on real estate sales and on the employment and structure of real estate companies. Data for the first two tables were obtained from the National Association of Realtors, 777 14th Street, N.W., Washington, D.C. 20005 and are reproduced with permission. Much more detailed data are available from the association. Additional tables, dealing with mortgages, are drawn from the *Statistical Abstract of the United States 1997*.

TOTAL SALES: SINGLE-FAMILY, APARTMENT CONDOS AND CO-OPS

Units in thousands.

State	1995	1996	1997	State	1995	1996	1997	State	1995	1996	1997
Alabama	74.2	76.8	82.2	Kentucky	78.2	78.8	81.1	North Dakota	10.6	12.0	11.9
Alaska	NA	NA	NA	Louisiana	50.4	50.9	52.9	Ohio	182.8	192.7	187.3
Arizona	122.0	128.2	135.1	Maine[2]	13.1	14.2	14.7	Oklahoma	57.7	60.6	64.2
Arkansas	57.5	59.7	58.8	Maryland	58.7	60.3	66.4	Oregon	59.0	58.9	60.1
California[1]	425.6	505.4	555.4	Massachusetts	68.1	81.9	94.3	Pennsylvania	217.2	224.3	233.3
Colorado	76.9	81.6	86.6	Michigan	176.3	179.8	180.3	Rhode Island	11.5	12.9	14.3
Connecticut	51.4	49.2	55.0	Minnesota	76.7	85.8	88.0	South Carolina	68.9	74.2	81.5
Delaware	10.2	NA	NA	Mississippi	46.1	46.7	57.7	South Dakota	13.3	13.9	15.2
District of Columbia	11.6	10.8	14.2	Missouri	108.3	113.7	115.9	Tennessee	133.6	142.9	149.9
Florida	220.3	225.5	234.4	Montana	13.8	14.2	14.9	Texas	256.8	257.0	293.1
Georgia	NA	NA	NA	Nebraska	21.1	20.3	23.4	Utah	31.6	33.8	30.0
Hawaii	10.0	9.8	11.1	Nevada	29.6	31.8	29.7	Vermont	8.8	8.4	8.1
Idaho	20.5	20.2	20.7	New Hampshire	NA	NA	NA	Virginia	92.2	92.2	98.5
Illinois	183.5	191.6	199.7	New Jersey	138.3	147.8	157.3	Washington	95.5	101.5	116.5
Indiana	100.6	103.5	111.5	New Mexico	28.9	26.7	25.5	West Virginia	43.2	43.8	45.2
Iowa	51.6	56.4	57.7	New York	150.4	165.8	171.0	Wisconsin	93.2	101.0	104.6
Kansas	54.4	59.9	61.6	North Carolina	201.0	212.5	228.0	Wyoming	9.4	8.6	9.5

Source: Real Estate Outlook. Market Trends and Insights, Volume 5, Number 6, June 1998, p. 15. Reproduced by permission. *Notes:* NA Not applicable. 1. Provided by the California Association of Realtors. 2. Due to a change in reporting, raw data for 1995 have been estimated by NAR. All Main estimates are preliminary.

APARTMENT CONDOS AND CO-OPS

Year	Unit volume Seasonally adjusted annual rate					Median sales price Not seasonally adjusted				
	United States	Northeast	Midwest	South	West	United States	Northeast	Midwest	South	West
1995	428,000	99,000	73,000	143,000	113,000	$87,400	$94,800	$90,700	$70,600	$105,300
1996	472,000	112,000	81,000	153,000	126,000	91,100	97,400	94,900	73,600	110,700
1997	515,000	126,000	89,000	162,000	139,000	95,500	101,000	99,100	76,300	118,400
1997										
I	484,000	119,000	79,000	156,000	130,000	$91,600	$96,600	$94,800	$74,700	$111,200
II	501,000	126,000	86,000	155,000	133,000	96,500	104,500	98,500	77,200	118,700
III	525,000	128,000	92,000	164,000	142,000	96,900	103,900	101,600	76,000	119,900
IV	549,000	132,000	96,000	171,000	149,000	96,300	99,400	100,300	76,900	122,600
1998										
Ip	558,000	136,000	96,000	173,000	152,000	96,600	98,500	100,600	77,700	122,000

Source: Real Estate Outlook. Market Trends and Insights, Volume 5, Number 6, June 1998, p. 14. Reproduced by permission. *Note:* p Preliminary.

MORTGAGE DEBT OUTSTANDING, BY TYPE OF PROPERTY AND HOLDER: 1990 TO 1996

In billions of dollars. As of December 31. Includes Puerto Rico and Guam.

Type of Property and Holder	1990	1991	1992	1993	1994	1995	1996
Mortgage debt, total	3,804	3,967	4,100	4,275	4,481	4,714	5,054
Residential nonfarm	2,966	3,139	3,319	3,505	3,713	3,922	4,221
One- to four-family homes	2,677	2,855	3,044	3,234	3,438	3,634	3,912
Savings institutions	600	538	490	470	478	482	514
Mortgage pools or trusts[1]	1,046	1,227	1,395	1,514	1,653	1,766	1,925
Government National Mortgage Association	392	416	411	405	441	461	494
Federal Home Loan Mortgage Corp.	308	352	402	443	488	512	552
Commercial banks	456	484	508	557	611	664	696
Individuals and others[2]	408	431	448	456	461	486	542
Federal and related agencies	153	163	192	228	228	229	227
Federal National Mortgage Association	94	100	124	151	162	168	170
Life insurance companies	13	12	11	9	8	7	7
Five or more units	290	284	274	271	276	288	309
Commercial	759	748	701	689	685	710	745
Farm	79	79	81	81	83	84	88
Type of Holder							
Savings institutions	802	705	628	598	596	597	629
Commercial banks	845	876	895	941	1,004	1,080	1,136
Life insurance companies	268	265	247	229	215	212	212
Individuals and others[2]	570	591	604	609	619	650	713
Mortgage pools or trusts[1]	1,081	1,263	1,441	1,571	1,727	1,862	2,055
Government National Mortgage Association	404	425	420	414	451	472	506
Federal Home Loan Mortgage Corp.	316	359	408	447	491	515	554
Federal National Mortgage Association	300	372	445	496	530	583	651
Farmers Home Administration[3]	(Z)	(Z)	(Z)	(Z)	(Z)	(Z)	(Z)
Federal and related agencies	239	266	286	327	319	314	309
Federal National Mortgage Association	105	112	138	167	178	184	184
Farmers Home Administration[3]	41	42	42	41	42	42	42
Federal Land Banks	29	29	29	28	29	28	30
Federal Home Loan Mortgage Corp.	22	27	34	47	42	44	45
Federal Housing and Veterans Administration	7	9	11	11	10	9	6
Government National Mortgage Association	(Z)	(Z)	(Z)	(Z)	(Z)	(Z)	(Z)
Federal Deposit Insurance Corp.	(X)	(X)	(X)	(X)	(X)	(X)	(Z)
Resolution Trust Corporation	33	46	32	17	10	2	(X)

Source: Statistical Abstract of the United States, 1997, p. 518. *Primary Source:* Board of Governors of the Federal Reserve System, *Federal Reserve Bulletin,* monthly. *Notes:* X Not applicable. Z Less than $500 million. 1. Outstanding principal balances of mortgage pool backing securities insured or guaranteed by the agency indicated. Includes other pools not shown separately. 2. Includes mortgage companies, real estate investment trusts, State and local retirement funds, noninsured pension funds, State and local credit agencies, credit unions, and finance companies. 3. FmHA-guaranteed securities sold to the Federal Financing Bank were reallocated from FmHA mortgage pools to FmHA mortgage holding in 1986 because of accounting changes by the Farmers Home Administration.

VOLUME OF LONG-TERM MORTGAGE LOANS ORIGINATED, BY TYPE OF PROPERTY, 1980 TO 1995, AND BY LENDER, 1995

In billion of dollar. Covers credit extended in primary mortgage markets for financing real estate acquisitions.

Type of Property	1980	1985	1990	1991	1992	1993	1994	1995, by Lender				
								Total[1]	Com-mercial banks	Mort-gage companies	Savings and loan	Life insurance companies
Loans, total	197.2	430.0	710.5	793.3	1,124.0	1,241.7	1,019.2	930.0	374.5	364.8	103.6	36.5
1-4 unit family home	133.8	289.8	458.4	562.1	893.7	1,019.9	768.7	639.4	155.4	358.7	95.6	0.7
New units	49.1	59.0	110.7	120.0	132.4	117.3	114.6	110.7	49.3	47.2	12.2	0.2
Existing units	84.6	230.8	347.7	442.1	761.3	902.5	654.2	528.7	106.1	311.5	83.4	0.5
Multifamily residential	12.5	31.9	32.6	25.5	25.7	31.7	32.7	39.2	23.1	6.1	3.9	1.6
New units	8.6	10.6	6.5	6.1	4.9	4.4	4.5	5.4	2.0	1.4	0.2	0.7
Existing units	3.9	21.3	26.0	19.4	20.9	27.3	28.2	33.8	21.1	4.7	3.7	0.9
Nonresidental	35.9	99.4	209.5	194.6	184.4	172.5	190.0	220.8	173.8	-	4.2	33.4
Farm properties	15.0	9.0	10.0	11.1	20.2	17.6	27.8	30.6	22.2	-	-	0.8

Source: Statistical Abstract of the United States, 1997, p. 518. *Primary Source*: U.S. Dept. of Housing and Urban Development, monthly and quarterly press releases based on the Survey of Mortgage Lending Activity. *Notes:* - Represents zero. 1. Includes other lenders not shown separately.

MORTGAGE DELINQUENCY AND FORECLOSURE RATES: 1990 TO 1996

In percent, except as indicated. Covers one- to four-family residential nonfarm mortgage loans.

Item	1990	1991	1992	1993	1994	1995	1996
Number of mortgage loans outstanding (1,000)	40,638	41,586	42,562	45,336	48,625	50,670	51,625
Delinquency rates:[1]							
Total	4.7	5.0	4.6	4.2	4.1	4.3	4.3
Conventional loans	3.0	3.3	2.9	2.7	2.6	2.8	2.8
VA loans	6.4	6.8	6.5	6.3	6.3	6.4	6.7
FHA loans	6.7	7.3	7.1	7.1	7.3	7.6	8.1
Foreclosure rates:[2]							
Total	0.9	1.0	1.0	1.0	0.9	0.9	1.0
Conventional loans	0.7	0.8	0.8	0.8	0.7	0.7	0.7
VA loans	1.2	1.3	1.3	1.3	1.3	1.3	1.6
FHA loans	1.3	1.4	1.4	1.5	1.5	1.4	1.6

Source: Statistical Abstract of the United States, 1997, p. 519. *Primary Source*: Mortgage Bankers Association of America, Washington, D.C., *National Delinquency Survey*, quarterly. *Notes:* 1. Number of loans delinquent 30 days or more as percentage of mortgage loans serviced in survey. Annual average of quarterly figures. 2. Percentage of loans in the foreclosure process at yearend, not seasonally adjusted.

CHARACTERISTICS OF CONVENTIONAL FIRST MORTGAGE LOANS FOR PURCHASE OF SINGLE-FAMILY HOMES: 1990 TO 1996

In percent, except as indicated. Annual averages. Covers fully amortized conventional mortgage loans used to purchase single-family nonfarm homes. Excludes refinancing loans, nonamortized and balloon loans, loans insured by the Federal Housing Administration, and loans guaranteed by the Veterans Administration. Based on a sample of mortgage lenders, including savings and loans associations, savings banks, commercial banks, and mortgage companies.

Loan Characteristics	New Homes						Previously occupied homes					
	1990	1992	1993	1994	1995	1996	1990	1992	1993	1994	1995	1996
Contract interest rate, all loans[1]	9.7	8.0	7.0	7.3	7.7	7.6	9.8	7.8	6.9	7.3	7.7	7.6
Fixed-rate loans	10.1	8.3	7.3	7.9	8.0	7.8	10.1	8.2	7.3	8.0	8.0	7.8
Adjustable-rate loans[2]	8.9	6.6	5.8	6.5	7.2	7.0	8.9	6.3	5.5	6.2	7.0	6.9
Initial fees, charges[3]	1.98	1.59	1.29	1.29	1.20	1.21	1.74	1.58	1.19	1.07	0.93	0.93
Effective interest rate, all loans[4]	10.1	8.2	7.2	7.5	7.9	7.8	10.1	8.1	7.1	7.5	7.8	7.7
Fixed-rate loans	10.4	8.5	7.5	8.1	8.2	8.0	10.4	8.5	7.5	8.2	8.2	8.0
Adjustable-rate loans[2]	9.2	6.9	5.9	6.6	7.4	7.2	9.2	6.5	5.7	6.4	7.1	7.1
Term to maturity (years)	27.3	25.6	26.1	27.5	27.7	27.1	27.0	25.4	25.4	27.1	27.4	26.8
Purchase price ($1,000)	154.1	158.1	163.7	170.7	175.4	182.6	140.3	144.1	139.6	136.4	137.3	150.2
Loan to price ratio	74.9	76.6	78.0	78.7	78.6	78.1	74.9	76.5	77.1	80.1	80.1	79.1
Percent of number of loans with adjustable rates	31	17	18	41	37	26	27	21	20	39	31	27

Source: Statistical Abstract of the United States, 1997, p. 519. *Primary Source*: U.S. Federal Housing Finance Board, *Rates & Terms on Conventional Home Mortgages, Annual Summary*. *Notes:* 1. Initial interest rate paid by the borrower as specified in the loan contract. 2. Loans with a contractual provision for periodic adjustments in the contract interest rate. 3. Includes all fees, commissions, discounts and "points" paid by the borrower, or seller, in order to obtain the loan. Excludes those charges for mortgage, credit, life or property insurance; for property transfer; and for title search and insurance. 4. Contract interest rate plus fees and charges amortized over a 10-year period.

SIC 6540

TITLE ABSTRACT OFFICES

Title abstract offices are establishments engaged primarily in searching real estate titles. This industry does not include title insurance companies (for these, see SIC 6360). The SIC includes title abstract companies, title and trust companies, title reconveyance companies, and title search companies.

ESTABLISHMENTS, EMPLOYMENT, AND PAYROLL

	1990	1991		1992		1993		1994		1995		% change 90-95
		Value	%	Value	%	Value	%	Value	%	Value	%	
All Establishments	3,067	3,529	15.1	4,198	19.0	4,766	13.5	4,881	2.4	4,818	-1.3	57.1
Mid-March Employment	23,880	23,481	-1.7	29,286	24.7	37,536	28.2	42,593	13.5	33,707	-20.9	41.2
1st Quarter Wages (annualized - $ mil.)	499.8	500.9	0.2	654.9	30.7	853.1	30.3	1,048.2	22.9	809.0	-22.8	61.9
Payroll per Emp. 1st Q. (annualized)	20,930	21,334	1.9	22,361	4.8	22,726	1.6	24,610	8.3	24,002	-2.5	14.7
Annual Payroll ($ mil.)	518.0	558.2	7.7	755.0	35.3	1,047.9	38.8	1,020.2	-2.6	864.7	-15.2	66.9
Establishments - 1-4 Emp. Number	1,723	1,872	8.6	2,363	26.2	2,435	3.0	(D)	-	2,668	-	54.8
Mid-March Employment	3,698	3,992	8.0	5,129	28.5	5,034	-1.9	(D)	-	5,560	-	50.4
1st Quarter Wages (annualized - $ mil.)	59.2	64.6	9.1	94.5	46.3	92.6	-2.0	(D)	-	112.5	-	90.0
Payroll per Emp. 1st Q. (annualized)	16,011	16,186	1.1	18,429	13.9	18,394	-0.2	(D)	-	20,234	-	26.4
Annual Payroll ($ mil.)	65.3	80.6	23.4	118.4	46.8	128.2	8.2	(D)	-	132.9	-	103.4
Establishments - 5-9 Emp. Number	765	1,079	41.0	1,124	4.2	1,323	17.7	1,366	3.3	1,216	-11.0	59.0
Mid-March Employment	5,038	7,166	42.2	7,332	2.3	8,646	17.9	9,028	4.4	7,907	-12.4	56.9
1st Quarter Wages (annualized - $ mil.)	93.1	146.6	57.4	152.4	3.9	176.7	15.9	198.6	12.4	172.3	-13.2	85.0
Payroll per Emp. 1st Q. (annualized)	18,489	20,458	10.6	20,783	1.6	20,432	-1.7	22,000	7.7	21,794	-0.9	17.9
Annual Payroll ($ mil.)	95.5	159.7	67.2	176.1	10.3	224.4	27.4	198.0	-11.7	187.4	-5.4	96.2
Establishments - 10-19 Emp. Number	357	403	12.9	461	14.4	648	40.6	723	11.6	610	-15.6	70.9
Mid-March Employment	4,648	5,231	12.5	6,089	16.4	8,579	40.9	9,663	12.6	8,076	-16.4	73.8
1st Quarter Wages (annualized - $ mil.)	99.3	115.6	16.4	137.5	19.0	197.5	43.6	236.5	19.8	194.9	-17.6	96.3
Payroll per Emp. 1st Q. (annualized)	21,360	22,092	3.4	22,581	2.2	23,019	1.9	24,476	6.3	24,131	-1.4	13.0
Annual Payroll ($ mil.)	99.4	126.3	27.0	158.2	25.3	247.3	56.3	227.0	-8.2	206.0	-9.3	107.1
Establishments - 20-49 Emp. Number	165	133	-19.4	195	46.6	283	45.1	355	25.4	274	-22.8	66.1
Mid-March Employment	4,805	3,798	-21.0	5,707	50.3	8,511	49.1	10,429	22.5	8,094	-22.4	68.4
1st Quarter Wages (annualized - $ mil.)	100.1	85.3	-14.8	136.4	59.9	195.9	43.6	268.3	37.0	213.4	-20.5	113.2
Payroll per Emp. 1st Q. (annualized)	20,832	22,453	7.8	23,896	6.4	23,015	-3.7	25,725	11.8	26,360	2.5	26.5
Annual Payroll ($ mil.)	101.9	95.0	-6.8	154.5	62.7	240.7	55.8	260.8	8.4	224.4	-14.0	120.3
Establishments - 50-99 Emp. Number	42	36	-14.3	42	16.7	60	42.9	82	36.7	40	-51.2	-4.8
Mid-March Employment	2,839	2,285	-19.5	2,743	20.0	3,929	43.2	5,281	34.4	2,668	-49.5	-6.0
1st Quarter Wages (annualized - $ mil.)	57.9	59.0	1.9	69.0	16.9	106.3	54.1	140.6	32.2	71.1	-49.4	22.7
Payroll per Emp. 1st Q. (annualized)	20,410	25,836	26.6	25,159	-2.6	27,064	7.6	26,616	-1.7	26,640	0.1	30.5
Annual Payroll ($ mil.)	63.2	61.7	-2.2	75.2	21.8	120.6	60.4	124.2	2.9	72.5	-41.6	14.7
Establishments - 100-249 Emp. Number	13	5	-61.5	(D)	-	(D)	-	18	-	10	-44.4	-23.1
Mid-March Employment	(D)	(D)	-	(D)	-	(D)	-	2,291	-	1,402	-38.8	-
1st Quarter Wages (annualized - $ mil.)	(D)	(D)	-	(D)	-	(D)	-	66.7	-	44.9	-32.6	-
Payroll per Emp. 1st Q. (annualized)	(D)	(D)	-	(D)	-	(D)	-	29,095	-	32,026	10.1	-
Annual Payroll ($ mil.)	(D)	(D)	-	(D)	-	(D)	-	65.1	-	41.6	-36.1	-
Establishments - 250-499 Emp. Number	1	1	-	(D)	-	(D)	-	(D)	-	-	-	-
Mid-March Employment	(D)	(D)	-	(D)	-	(D)	-	(D)	-	-	-	-
1st Quarter Wages (annualized - $ mil.)	(D)	(D)	-	(D)	-	(D)	-	(D)	-	-	-	-
Payroll per Emp. 1st Q. (annualized)	(D)	(D)	-	(D)	-	(D)	-	(D)	-	-	-	-
Annual Payroll ($ mil.)	(D)	(D)	-	(D)	-	(D)	-	(D)	-	-	-	-
Establishments - 500-999 Emp. Number	1	-	-	-	-	(D)	-	(D)	-	-	-	-
Mid-March Employment	(D)	-	-	-	-	(D)	-	(D)	-	-	-	-
1st Quarter Wages (annualized - $ mil.)	(D)	-	-	-	-	(D)	-	(D)	-	-	-	-
Payroll per Emp. 1st Q. (annualized)	(D)	(D)	-	-	-	(D)	-	(D)	-	-	-	-
Annual Payroll ($ mil.)	(D)	-	-	-	-	(D)	-	(D)	-	-	-	-
Estab. - 1000 or More Emp. Number	-	-	-	-	-	-	-	-	-	-	-	-
Mid-March Employment	-	-	-	-	-	-	-	-	-	-	-	-
1st Quarter Wages (annualized - $ mil.)	-	-	-	-	-	-	-	-	-	-	-	-
Payroll per Emp. 1st Q. (annualized)	(D)	(D)	-	-	-	-	-	-	-	-	-	-
Annual Payroll ($ mil.)	-	-	-	-	-	-	-	-	-	-	-	-

Source: County Business Patterns, U.S. Department of Commerce, Washington, D.C., for 1990 through 1995. Payroll per employee is calculated using mid-March employment and 1st Quarter wages, annualized. Annual payroll, also shown, may not equal the annualized 1st Quarter wages. Columns headed by a percent sign (%) indicate change from the previous year. na stands for not available. The symbol (D) indicates that data are withheld by the source to avoid disclosure of competitive information. A dash (-) indicates that data are not available or cannot be calculated.

ESTABLISHMENTS
Number

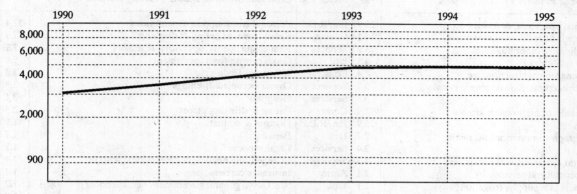

MID-MARCH EMPLOYMENT
Number

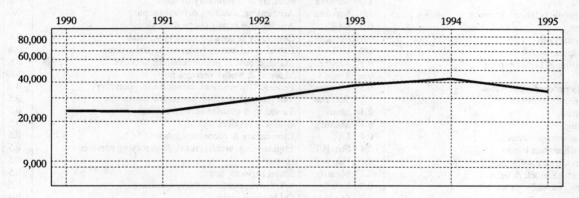

ANNUAL PAYROLL
$ million

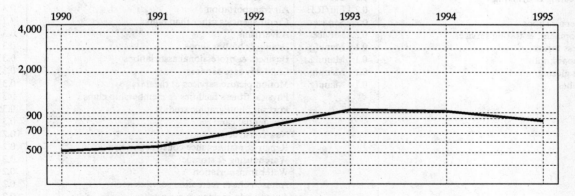

INPUTS AND OUTPUTS FOR ALL REAL ESTATE SECTORS - SIC GROUP 65

Economic Sector or Industry Providing Inputs	%	Sector	Economic Sector or Industry Buying Outputs	%	Sector
Real estate agents, operators, & lessors	25.9	Fin/R.E.	Personal consumption expenditures	32.4	
Maintenance/repair of residential structures	14.1	Constr.	Retail trade, ex eating & drinking	7.9	Trade
Services to dwellings & other buildings	5.9	Services	Real estate agents, operators, & lessors	7.1	Fin/R.E.
Electric services (utilities)	4.8	Util.	Gross private fixed investment	5.6	Cap Inv
Repair & maintenance construction nec	4.4	Constr.	Wholesale trade	3.3	Trade
Engineering, architectural, & surveying services	3.7	Services	Owner-occupied dwellings	3.3	Fin/R.E.
Advertising	3.6	Services	Hospitals	3.1	Services
Maintenance/repair of highways & streets	2.9	Constr.	Eating & drinking places	2.3	Services
Banking	2.9	Fin/R.E.	Doctors & dentists	1.9	Services
Telephone/telegraph communications nec	2.7	Util.	Banking	1.7	Fin/R.E.
Legal services	2.4	Services	Legal services	1.5	Services
Automotive rental & leasing, without drivers	2.3	Services	Colleges, universities, & professional schools	1.4	Services
Landscape & horticultural services	2.1	Agric.	Insurance carriers	1.2	Fin/R.E.
Sanitary services, steam supply, irrigation	2.1	Util.	S/L Govt., general government nec, spending	1.2	S/L Govt
Business services nec	1.8	Services	Religious organizations	1.0	Services
Electrical repair shops	1.4	Services	Feed grains	0.8	Agric.
Insurance carriers	1.2	Fin/R.E.	Nursing & personal care facilities	0.7	Services
Eating & drinking places	1.2	Services	Meat animals	0.6	Agric.
U.S. Postal Service	1.1	Gov't	Insurance agents, brokers, & services	0.6	Fin/R.E.
Hotels	1.0	Services	Security & commodity brokers	0.6	Fin/R.E.
Management & public relations services	1.0	Services	Accounting, auditing & bookkeeping	0.6	Services
Air transportation	0.9	Util.	Automotive repair shops & services	0.6	Services
Personnel supply services	0.8	Services	Computer & data processing services	0.6	Services
Natural gas distribution	0.7	Util.	Labor, civic, social, fraternal organizations	0.6	Services
Accounting, auditing & bookkeeping	0.7	Services	Management & public relations services	0.6	Services
Wholesale trade	0.6	Trade	Medical & health services nec	0.6	Services
Computer & data processing services	0.5	Services	Federal Government, nondefense, spending	0.6	Gov't
Detective & protective services	0.5	Services	Telephone/telegraph communications nec	0.5	Util.
Commercial printing	0.4	Manufg.	Trucking & courier services, ex air	0.5	Util.
Petroleum refining	0.4	Manufg.	Business services nec	0.5	Services
Water supply & sewerage systems	0.4	Util.	Elementary & secondary schools	0.5	Services
Credit agencies other than banks	0.4	Fin/R.E.	Engineering, architectural, & surveying services	0.5	Services
Security & commodity brokers	0.4	Fin/R.E.	Hotels	0.5	Services
Concrete products, ex block & brick	0.3	Manufg.	Social services, nec	0.5	Services
Trucking & courier services, ex air	0.3	Util.	S/L Govt., public welfare, spending	0.5	S/L Govt
Automotive repair shops & services	0.3	Services	Oil bearing crops	0.4	Agric.
Business & professional associations	0.3	Services	Electric services (utilities)	0.4	Util.
State & local government enterprises nec	0.3	Gov't	Membership organizations nec	0.4	Services
Local & suburban transit	0.2	Util.	State & local government enterprises nec	0.4	Gov't
Retail trade, ex eating & drinking	0.2	Trade	Food grains	0.3	Agric.
Royalties	0.2	Fin/R.E.	Air transportation	0.3	Util.
Miscellaneous repair shops	0.2	Services	Credit agencies other than banks	0.3	Fin/R.E.
Research, development, & testing services	0.2	Services	Advertising	0.3	Services
Manifold business forms	0.1	Manufg.	Beauty & barber shops	0.3	Services
Paper & paperboard mills	0.1	Manufg.	Business & professional associations	0.3	Services
Paper coating & glazing	0.1	Manufg.	Child day care services	0.3	Services
Tires & inner tubes	0.1	Manufg.	Motion picture services & theaters	0.3	Services
			Physical fitness facilities & membership clubs	0.3	Services
			Portrait photographic studios	0.3	Services
			Residential care	0.3	Services
			New construction nec	0.2	Constr.
			Repair & maintenance construction nec	0.2	Constr.
			Warehousing & storage	0.2	Util.
			Water transportation	0.2	Util.
			Amusement & recreation services nec	0.2	Services
			Automobile parking & car washes	0.2	Services
			Automotive rental & leasing, without drivers	0.2	Services
			Laundry, cleaning, garment services, shoe repair	0.2	Services

Continued on next page.

INPUTS AND OUTPUTS FOR ALL REAL ESTATE SECTORS - SIC GROUP 65 - Continued

Economic Sector or Industry Providing Inputs	%	Sector	Economic Sector or Industry Buying Outputs	%	Sector
			Private libraries, vocational schools, nec	0.2	Services
			Research, development, & testing services	0.2	Services
			Exports of goods & services	0.2	Foreign
			Dairy farm products	0.1	Agric.
			Vegetables	0.1	Agric.
			Crude petroleum & natural gas	0.1	Mining
			Residential 1 unit structures, nonfarm	0.1	Constr.
			Apparel made from purchased materials	0.1	Manufg.
			Commercial printing	0.1	Manufg.
			Electronic computers	0.1	Manufg.
			Miscellaneous plastics products, nec	0.1	Manufg.
			Job training & related services	0.1	Services
			Miscellaneous equipment rental & leasing	0.1	Services
			Miscellaneous repair shops	0.1	Services
			Personnel supply services	0.1	Services
			Photofinishing labs & commercial photography	0.1	Services
			Theatrical producers, bands, orchestras	0.1	Services
			Video tape rental	0.1	Services
			U.S. Postal Service	0.1	Gov't
			Federal Government, national defense, spending	0.1	Fed Govt

Source: Benchmark Input-Output Accounts for the U.S. Economy, 1992, U.S. Department of Commerce, Washington, D.C., November 1997. Data, as reported in the source, are organized by the 1987 SIC structure in use in 1992.

OCCUPATIONS EMPLOYED BY ALL OTHER REAL ESTATE

Occupation	% of Total 1996	Change to 2006	Occupation	% of Total 1996	Change to 2006
Gardeners, nursery workers	18.5	18.6	Janitors & cleaners, maids	2.3	5.0
General managers & top executives	6.8	24.9	Typists, including word processing	2.0	-20.5
General office clerks	6.7	9.1	Food preparation workers nec	1.8	31.8
Secretaries, except legal & medical	6.5	2.1	Marketing & sales worker supervisors	1.7	29.3
Maintenance repairers, general utility	4.4	22.7	Farming, forestry, agriculture supervisors	1.6	31.8
Sales agents, real estate	4.2	5.6	Accountants & auditors	1.5	21.0
Title examiners & searchers	4.2	20.6	Legal assistants & clerks nec	1.2	20.9
Bookkeeping, accounting, & auditing clerks	4.2	4.0	Guards	1.2	18.5
Sales & related workers nec	3.9	43.5	Carpenters	1.1	6.6
Property & real estate managers	3.6	31.4	Service workers nec	1.1	31.7
Receptionists & information clerks	3.1	28.5	Blue collar worker supervisors	1.0	27.2
Financial managers	2.7	30.1			

Sources: Industry-Occupation Matrix, Bureau of Labor Statistics. These data relate to one or more 3-digit SIC industry groups rather than to a single 4-digit SIC. The change reported for each occupation to the year 2005 is a percent of growth or decline as estimated by the Bureau of Labor Statistics. The abbreviation *nec* stands for not elsewhere classified.

U.S. AND STATE DATA ON INDUSTRY REVENUES AND OTHER ACCOUNTS FOR 1992

State	No. of Estab.	Employment	Payroll ($ mil.)	Revenues ($ mil.)	Empl./ Estab.	Revenue/ Estab. ($)	Payroll/ Estab. ($)	Revenue/ Empl. ($)	Payroll/ Empl. ($)
UNITED STATES	4,716	33,742	880.1	2,337.3	7	495,619	186,622	69,271	26,083
Alabama	62	324	6.3	15.1	5	244,177	100,903	46,725	19,309
Alaska	7	39	1.4	3.2	6	460,857	196,143	82,718	35,205
Arizona	22	148	3.4	7.6	7	347,091	154,045	51,595	22,899
Arkansas	107	607	11.9	26.8	6	250,916	111,402	44,231	19,638
California	284	4,285	137.9	340.4	15	1,198,655	485,736	79,444	32,193
Colorado	61	408	9.3	24.6	7	402,787	152,934	60,221	22,865
Connecticut	25	59	1.6	3.5	2	141,880	65,760	60,119	27,864
Delaware	4	-	(D)	(D)	(D)	(D)	(D)	(D)	(D)
District of Columbia	11	111	2.5	4.6	10	417,636	226,455	41,387	22,441
Florida	305	1,984	47.3	112.9	7	370,134	155,167	56,901	23,854
Georgia	41	212	5.1	12.5	5	304,146	123,512	58,821	23,887
Hawaii	13	532	15.3	25.9	41	1,995,462	1,178,846	48,761	28,806
Idaho	43	413	10.7	26.0	10	605,535	249,791	63,046	26,007
Illinois	232	1,703	40.5	120.2	7	518,198	174,716	70,594	23,802
Indiana	162	1,175	23.6	58.3	7	359,827	145,617	49,610	20,077
Iowa	130	760	14.7	33.0	6	253,554	113,300	43,371	19,380
Kansas	129	635	11.0	29.2	5	226,209	85,163	45,954	17,301
Kentucky	16	80	1.4	5.2	5	325,188	90,125	65,038	18,025
Louisiana	65	381	9.2	21.9	6	336,923	141,231	57,480	24,094
Maine	14	77	2.8	5.9	6	420,643	196,429	76,481	35,714
Maryland	198	1,000	31.8	82.6	5	417,162	160,480	82,598	31,775
Massachusetts	49	233	7.0	17.9	5	364,633	142,143	76,682	29,893
Michigan	103	831	21.4	54.6	8	529,748	207,689	65,661	25,742
Minnesota	162	1,500	38.5	113.0	9	697,469	237,383	75,327	25,637
Mississippi	6	22	0.2	0.8	4	136,000	38,833	37,091	10,591
Missouri	178	1,045	21.4	50.2	6	281,916	120,382	48,020	20,505
Montana	28	183	4.0	10.9	7	387,679	141,107	59,317	21,590
Nebraska	54	177	3.0	8.5	3	157,981	55,926	48,198	17,062
Nevada	25	452	15.3	32.0	18	1,280,640	611,680	70,832	33,832
New Hampshire	20	150	4.8	10.4	8	518,150	242,450	69,087	32,327
New Jersey	146	709	23.4	66.4	5	454,911	160,377	93,677	33,025
New Mexico	44	291	6.9	17.6	7	400,250	156,682	60,519	23,691
New York	385	2,542	74.4	207.3	7	538,569	193,249	81,569	29,269
North Carolina	22	48	1.8	4.9	2	221,273	81,273	101,417	37,250
North Dakota	48	147	2.7	8.1	3	168,604	56,354	55,054	18,401
Ohio	199	1,617	47.7	119.8	8	601,784	239,789	74,060	29,510
Oklahoma	157	1,250	27.9	64.6	8	411,624	178,013	51,700	22,358
Oregon	27	330	8.4	24.6	12	911,222	311,111	74,555	25,455
Pennsylvania	231	1,627	48.7	204.1	7	883,619	211,030	125,455	29,962
Rhode Island	8	42	1.0	3.7	5	458,500	127,250	87,333	24,238
South Carolina	42	119	2.1	5.1	3	122,405	50,381	43,202	17,782
South Dakota	48	157	2.5	7.0	3	145,375	52,688	44,446	16,108
Tennessee	69	304	8.2	18.1	4	262,435	119,029	59,566	27,016
Texas	390	2,633	62.0	181.2	7	464,567	158,992	68,812	23,550
Utah	44	345	9.0	22.4	8	509,000	203,977	64,916	26,014
Vermont	2	-	(D)	(D)	(D)	(D)	(D)	(D)	(D)
Virginia	103	419	12.4	29.8	4	289,019	120,515	71,048	29,625
Washington	46	550	13.5	35.0	12	761,848	293,413	63,718	24,540
West Virginia	3	-	(D)	(D)	(D)	(D)	(D)	(D)	(D)
Wisconsin	137	1,022	22.5	56.3	7	411,197	164,022	55,121	21,987
Wyoming	9	-	(D)	(D)	(D)	(D)	(D)	(D)	(D)

Source: 1992 Economic Census, U.S. Department of Commerce, Washington, D.C. This is the only table that shows revenue data as collected by the Bureau of the Census in an Economic Census. The symbol (D) indicates that data are withheld by the source to avoid disclosure of competitive information. A dash (-) indicates that data are not available or cannot be calculated.

STATE-BY-STATE DATA ON ESTABLISHMENTS, EMPLOYMENT, AND PAYROLL - 1994 AND 1995

State	1994 No. of Estab.	Employ-ment	Pay / Empl.	Payroll ($ mil.)	Pay / Estab.	1995 No. of Estab.	Employ-ment	Pay / Empl.	Payroll ($ mil.)	Pay / Estab.	% Change Empl.
Alabama	65	376	19,191	8.2	125,692	60	319	21,868	7.3	122,433	-15.2
Alaska	6	55	36,218	2.1	342,667	6	43	35,814	1.7	276,667	-21.8
Arizona	21	207	23,188	5.6	264,286	21	181	26,718	4.9	232,952	-12.6
Arkansas	114	904	16,690	17.2	150,851	116	808	17,861	15.9	136,957	-10.6
California	270	3,999	33,724	111.4	412,667	225	2,502	32,569	71.8	319,129	-37.4
Colorado	63	532	23,662	12.5	198,365	59	466	24,086	11.6	196,305	-12.4
Connecticut	29	73	25,151	2.0	67,655	26	56	26,286	1.6	62,923	-23.3
Delaware	5	(D)	-	(D)	-	5	(D)	-	(D)	-	-
District of Columbia	8	78	32,718	2.2	273,375	9	52	29,769	1.6	182,111	-33.3
Florida	325	2,481	23,495	54.7	168,258	311	2,044	23,924	49.4	158,749	-17.6
Georgia	52	215	27,405	5.3	102,712	59	193	27,316	5.0	83,932	-10.2
Hawaii	12	533	27,602	14.5	1,207,917	10	340	30,047	10.3	1,032,000	-36.2
Idaho	43	640	20,913	12.9	301,093	44	528	21,848	12.5	284,750	-17.5
Illinois	239	2,194	21,894	47.2	197,397	242	1,774	20,884	41.6	172,095	-19.1
Indiana	175	1,439	19,575	28.9	165,394	182	1,292	17,817	26.4	145,302	-10.2
Iowa	131	763	17,913	14.7	111,870	128	697	18,812	13.7	106,852	-8.7
Kansas	124	620	21,213	11.5	92,621	124	536	18,784	10.2	82,516	-13.5
Kentucky	17	116	19,931	2.0	118,765	23	74	22,270	2.0	85,870	-36.2
Louisiana	74	548	22,657	11.6	156,784	85	356	19,517	9.6	113,518	-35.0
Maine	12	91	23,824	2.1	172,500	15	66	23,273	1.8	120,200	-27.5
Maryland	238	1,615	29,305	38.8	162,899	230	980	26,367	29.5	128,174	-39.3
Massachusetts	56	316	28,785	8.8	156,839	56	224	29,232	6.9	123,982	-29.1
Michigan	104	1,007	22,677	24.3	233,856	100	809	21,849	20.6	205,660	-19.7
Minnesota	175	2,154	22,527	44.0	251,280	175	1,467	24,202	37.4	213,554	-31.9
Mississippi	4	(D)	-	(D)	-	5	32	20,125	0.7	142,400	-
Missouri	170	1,191	19,369	25.5	150,059	157	1,137	18,512	24.5	155,885	-4.5
Montana	27	239	18,644	4.6	171,778	27	199	19,859	4.4	162,556	-16.7
Nebraska	53	203	16,788	3.7	69,660	51	173	17,618	3.4	67,020	-14.8
Nevada	23	636	28,239	18.4	799,609	23	462	33,212	17.0	740,261	-27.4
New Hampshire	24	230	24,539	5.1	213,417	22	147	25,497	4.1	186,682	-36.1
New Jersey	159	1,000	26,836	30.2	189,874	161	795	28,830	27.1	168,217	-20.5
New Mexico	44	408	27,029	9.6	219,068	43	408	28,775	9.9	230,209	0.0
New York	401	3,178	27,458	92.1	229,566	392	2,739	28,974	86.8	221,383	-13.8
North Carolina	23	66	39,455	2.6	112,087	23	66	47,030	2.8	120,435	0.0
North Dakota	50	192	19,896	3.4	68,040	50	176	16,023	3.1	61,180	-8.3
Ohio	214	2,117	25,039	56.2	262,650	216	1,935	25,013	53.6	248,023	-8.6
Oklahoma	157	1,534	21,836	33.1	210,599	156	1,358	21,688	31.5	201,609	-11.5
Oregon	30	515	23,588	12.2	407,533	41	648	24,395	16.0	389,439	25.8
Pennsylvania	241	2,267	28,628	63.1	261,826	226	1,115	20,929	26.1	115,292	-50.8
Rhode Island	10	105	11,048	1.3	126,800	11	88	13,545	1.3	120,909	-16.2
South Carolina	41	135	21,037	2.9	70,951	40	127	19,622	2.6	63,875	-5.9
South Dakota	49	191	19,267	3.5	72,184	51	186	16,645	3.3	64,804	-2.6
Tennessee	73	450	23,209	11.8	161,986	83	402	23,851	12.3	147,771	-10.7
Texas	375	3,691	23,510	85.7	228,563	373	3,187	22,949	76.5	205,190	-13.7
Utah	51	676	20,367	13.7	269,078	52	466	22,833	13.0	250,154	-31.1
Vermont	2	(D)	-	(D)	-	2	(D)	-	(D)	-	-
Virginia	115	778	25,537	17.6	152,800	110	445	27,479	13.6	123,382	-42.8
Washington	37	602	23,336	14.3	385,297	40	513	24,164	13.2	329,025	-14.8
West Virginia	4	4	10,000	0.1	16,000	4	(D)	-	(D)	-	-
Wisconsin	136	1,143	20,276	24.6	181,066	139	1,024	19,078	22.8	164,000	-10.4
Wyoming	10	44	17,636	1.0	99,000	9	37	19,784	0.9	104,556	-15.9

Source: County Business Patterns, U.S. Department of Commerce, Washington, D.C., for 1994 and 1995. Employment shown is for mid-March of the year shown. Payroll per employee is calculated by annualizing 1st Quarter payroll (not shown) and then dividing that value by mid-March employment. Dividing total annual payroll (columns 5 and 10) by employment, therefore, will *not* yield the payroll per employee figure (columns 4 and 9). The symbol (D) indicates that data are withheld by the source to avoid disclosure of competitive information. A dash (-) indicates that data are not available or cannot be calculated.

ESTABLISHMENTS 1995 - STATE AND REGIONAL CONCENTRATION

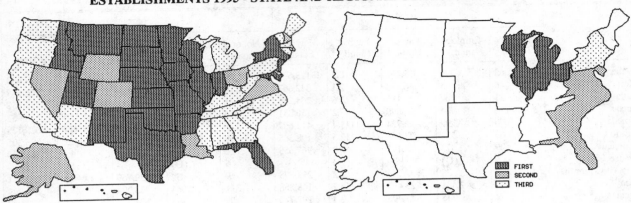

EMPLOYMENT 1995 - STATE AND REGIONAL CONCENTRATION

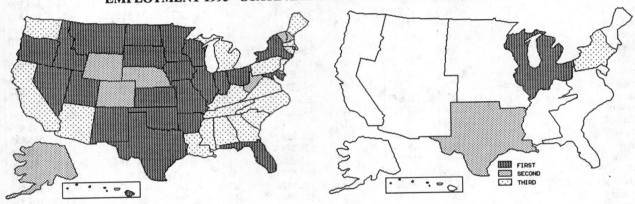

PAYROLL 1995 - STATE AND REGIONAL CONCENTRATION

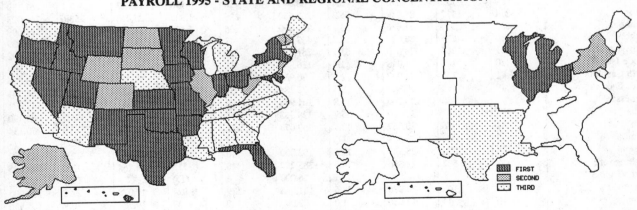

States with the darkest shading indicate those states which have proportionately more establishments, employment, or payrolls than would be indicated by the state's population. States with light shading are states with proportionately fewer establishments, less employment, and lower payrolls than population distribution. States shaded grey are within 15 percent of the state's population proportion in these categories. States for which no data are available are shown as average (grey). *Regions* are shaded to indicate absolute rank in the category. If no data for the category are available, establishment counts are used to shade the regions. Source of the data is the table on the facing page.

LEADING COMPANIES - SIC 6541 - Title Abstract Offices

Number shown: **17**   Total sales/assets ($ mil): **1,908**   Total employment (000): **5.8**

Company Name	Address				CEO Name	Phone	Co. Type	Sales/Assets ($ mil)	Empl. (000)
Lennar Corp.	700 N.W. 107th Ave.	Miami	FL	33172	Stuart A. Miller	305-559-4000	P	1,303 OR	2.2
North American Title Co.	2185 N. California Blvd.	Walnut Creek	CA	94596	Dan Wentzel	925-935-5599	S	200 OR*	1.2
First American Title Company of Alaska Inc.	510 W. Tudor Rd.	Anchorage	AK	99503	Steven Jewett	907-562-0510	S	120 OR	<0.1
American Title Co.	17911 Von Karman Ave.	Irvine	CA	92614	Wayne Diaz	714-257-6300	S	100 OR*	0.6
Old Republic Title	101 E. Glenoaks Blvd.	Glendale	CA	91202	Al Gudel	818-247-2917	R	50 OR*	0.3
Koenig and Strey Inc.	3201 Old Glenview Rd.	Wilmette	IL	60091	Thomas E. Koenig	708-729-5050	R	30 OR	0.5
Guardian Title Co.	27271 Las Ramblas	Mission Viejo	CA	92691	Thomas Rutledge	714-367-2115	R	20 OR*	0.1
Monroe Title Insurance Corp.	47 W. Main St.	Rochester	NY	14614	Dennis W. O'Neill	716-232-2070	R	16 TA	0.3
Southwest Land Title Co.	500 N. Akard St.	Dallas	TX	75201	William G. Moize	214-720-1020	R	16 OR	0.2
Bay Title and Abstract Inc.	PO Box 173	Green Bay	WI	54305	John May	414-431-6100	R	11 TA*	<0.1
Beach Abstract and Guaranty Co.	PO Box 2580	Little Rock	AR	72203	George Pitts Jr.	501-376-3301	R	10 OR*	<0.1
Houston Title Co.	1800 St. James Place Ste. 400	Houston	TX	77056	Mary Chapman	713-626-9220	S	10 OR*	<0.1
Stewart Fidelity Title Co.	4134 Central Ave.	St. Petersburg	FL	33711	Kevin Hussey	813-327-5775	S	8 OR	<0.1
Southwest Title and Trust Co.	PO Box 1234	Oklahoma City	OK	73101	James Kott	405-236-2861	S	7 TA	0.1
Old Republic Title Company of St. Louis	7730 Forsyth Blvd.	Clayton	MO	63105	James Davis	314-863-0022	S	4 OR*	<0.1
Land Records of Texas Inc.	1945 Walnut Hill Ln.	Irving	TX	75038	Jay Jacobs	972-580-8575	S	2 OR*	<0.1
Community Title and Escrow Inc.	112 W. Homer Adams Pkwy.	Alton	IL	62002	Peggy A. Stillwell	618-466-7755	R	1 OR*	<0.1

Source: *Ward's Business Directory of U.S. Private and Public Companies*, 1996. Company type codes: P - Public, R - Private, S - Subsidiary, D - Division, J - Joint Venture, A - Affiliate, G - Group. If the dollar values shown are not sales, the following codes apply: TA - Total Assets; OR - Operating Revenues; GB - Gross Billings. * - estimated dollar value. < - less than; *na* - not available.

SIC 6552

SUBDIVIDERS AND DEVELOPERS, NEC

Land subdividers and developers are establishments primarily engaged in subdividing real property into lots and in developing the property on their own account. Cemetery subdividers have their own classification—SIC 6553—shown in the next chapter. Establishments primarily engaged in developing lots for others are classified as Construction and are not included in this book.

ESTABLISHMENTS, EMPLOYMENT, AND PAYROLL

	1990	1991		1992		1993		1994		1995		% change 90-95
		Value	%	Value	%	Value	%	Value	%	Value	%	
All Establishments	10,750	11,362	5.7	9,172	-19.3	9,400	2.5	9,950	5.9	10,335	3.9	-3.9
Mid-March Employment	87,798	90,033	2.5	75,160	-16.5	57,277	-23.8	61,706	7.7	69,341	12.4	-21.0
1st Quarter Wages (annualized - $ mil.)	2,292.0	2,293.2	0.1	1,886.1	-17.8	1,511.0	-19.9	1,673.5	10.7	2,077.9	24.2	-9.3
Payroll per Emp. 1st Q. (annualized)	26,105	25,470	-2.4	25,095	-1.5	26,381	5.1	27,120	2.8	29,966	10.5	14.8
Annual Payroll ($ mil.)	2,260.1	2,341.8	3.6	1,987.5	-15.1	1,748.8	-12.0	1,916.5	9.6	2,216.3	15.6	-1.9
Establishments - 1-4 Emp. Number	7,351	7,756	5.5	6,389	-17.6	7,165	12.1	7,535	5.2	7,621	1.1	3.7
Mid-March Employment	11,595	12,388	6.8	10,006	-19.2	9,173	-8.3	10,235	11.6	10,290	0.5	-11.3
1st Quarter Wages (annualized - $ mil.)	337.7	337.6	-0.0	278.4	-17.5	245.5	-11.8	277.4	13.0	310.4	11.9	-8.1
Payroll per Emp. 1st Q. (annualized)	29,125	27,253	-6.4	27,826	2.1	26,759	-3.8	27,107	1.3	30,164	11.3	3.6
Annual Payroll ($ mil.)	398.2	419.0	5.2	350.9	-16.2	398.2	13.5	428.4	7.6	450.8	5.2	13.2
Establishments - 5-9 Emp. Number	1,635	1,747	6.9	1,319	-24.5	1,110	-15.8	1,224	10.3	1,379	12.7	-15.7
Mid-March Employment	10,636	11,298	6.2	8,637	-23.6	7,156	-17.1	7,889	10.2	8,932	13.2	-16.0
1st Quarter Wages (annualized - $ mil.)	277.4	302.7	9.1	247.2	-18.3	183.1	-25.9	216.9	18.4	256.6	18.3	-7.5
Payroll per Emp. 1st Q. (annualized)	26,084	26,791	2.7	28,622	6.8	25,585	-10.6	27,488	7.4	28,726	4.5	10.1
Annual Payroll ($ mil.)	263.3	297.9	13.2	250.0	-16.1	200.0	-20.0	237.0	18.5	270.8	14.3	2.9
Establishments - 10-19 Emp. Number	935	1,050	12.3	783	-25.4	606	-22.6	618	2.0	703	13.8	-24.8
Mid-March Employment	12,479	13,853	11.0	10,557	-23.8	8,041	-23.8	8,197	1.9	9,388	14.5	-24.8
1st Quarter Wages (annualized - $ mil.)	332.8	391.7	17.7	297.6	-24.0	208.7	-29.9	228.8	9.6	281.3	23.0	-15.5
Payroll per Emp. 1st Q. (annualized)	26,672	28,276	6.0	28,188	-0.3	25,954	-7.9	27,908	7.5	29,962	7.4	12.3
Annual Payroll ($ mil.)	322.1	400.5	24.4	291.3	-27.3	231.9	-20.4	258.3	11.4	301.2	16.6	-6.5
Establishments - 20-49 Emp. Number	541	536	-0.9	438	-18.3	345	-21.2	368	6.7	405	10.1	-25.1
Mid-March Employment	16,138	16,041	-0.6	12,815	-20.1	10,512	-18.0	10,898	3.7	11,784	8.1	-27.0
1st Quarter Wages (annualized - $ mil.)	442.4	425.3	-3.9	340.3	-20.0	290.1	-14.7	294.5	1.5	333.9	13.4	-24.5
Payroll per Emp. 1st Q. (annualized)	27,416	26,514	-3.3	26,551	0.1	27,602	4.0	27,026	-2.1	28,331	4.8	3.3
Annual Payroll ($ mil.)	418.7	416.8	-0.5	358.1	-14.1	308.2	-13.9	310.6	0.8	341.6	10.0	-18.4
Establishments - 50-99 Emp. Number	167	157	-6.0	141	-10.2	99	-29.8	124	25.3	136	9.7	-18.6
Mid-March Employment	11,378	(D)	-	9,827	-	6,952	-29.3	8,610	23.8	9,313	8.2	-18.1
1st Quarter Wages (annualized - $ mil.)	277.6	(D)	-	202.6	-	176.2	-13.0	246.7	40.0	325.4	31.9	17.2
Payroll per Emp. 1st Q. (annualized)	24,396	(D)	-	20,620	-	25,349	22.9	28,650	13.0	34,937	21.9	43.2
Annual Payroll ($ mil.)	268.3	(D)	-	215.3	-	201.2	-6.6	258.7	28.6	288.6	11.6	7.6
Establishments - 100-249 Emp. Number	92	86	-6.5	77	-10.5	62	-19.5	69	11.3	71	2.9	-22.8
Mid-March Employment	13,566	12,833	-5.4	11,942	-6.9	9,362	-21.6	10,469	11.8	10,079	-3.7	-25.7
1st Quarter Wages (annualized - $ mil.)	324.2	278.5	-14.1	273.9	-1.7	289.5	5.7	276.7	-4.4	333.1	20.4	2.7
Payroll per Emp. 1st Q. (annualized)	23,902	21,702	-9.2	22,935	5.7	30,921	34.8	26,434	-14.5	33,052	25.0	38.3
Annual Payroll ($ mil.)	317.7	280.2	-11.8	269.5	-3.8	285.5	6.0	280.6	-1.7	331.8	18.2	4.4
Establishments - 250-499 Emp. Number	22	23	4.5	(D)	-	9	-	(D)	-	(D)	-	-
Mid-March Employment	7,356	(D)	-	(D)	-	2,849	-	(D)	-	(D)	-	-
1st Quarter Wages (annualized - $ mil.)	189.9	(D)	-	(D)	-	56.6	-	(D)	-	(D)	-	-
Payroll per Emp. 1st Q. (annualized)	25,809	(D)	-	(D)	-	19,867	-	(D)	-	(D)	-	-
Annual Payroll ($ mil.)	164.7	(D)	-	(D)	-	58.1	-	(D)	-	(D)	-	-
Establishments - 500-999 Emp. Number	7	7	-	4	-42.9	(D)	-	(D)	-	6	-	-14.3
Mid-March Employment	4,650	4,498	-3.3	2,748	-38.9	(D)	-	(D)	-	4,448	-	-4.3
1st Quarter Wages (annualized - $ mil.)	109.9	111.3	1.3	46.0	-58.6	(D)	-	(D)	-	116.7	-	6.2
Payroll per Emp. 1st Q. (annualized)	23,628	24,736	4.7	16,757	-32.3	(D)	-	(D)	-	26,238	-	11.0
Annual Payroll ($ mil.)	107.1	111.2	3.8	50.2	-54.9	(D)	-	(D)	-	118.9	-	11.0
Estab. - 1000 or More Emp. Number	-	-	-	(D)	-	(D)	-	-	-	(D)	-	-
Mid-March Employment	-	-	-	(D)	-	(D)	-	-	-	(D)	-	-
1st Quarter Wages (annualized - $ mil.)	-	-	-	(D)	-	(D)	-	-	-	(D)	-	-
Payroll per Emp. 1st Q. (annualized)	(D)	(D)	-	(D)	-	(D)	-	-	-	(D)	-	-
Annual Payroll ($ mil.)	-	-	-	(D)	-	(D)	-	-	-	(D)	-	-

Source: County Business Patterns, U.S. Department of Commerce, Washington, D.C., for 1990 through 1995. Payroll per employee is calculated using mid-March employment and 1st Quarter wages, annualized. Annual payroll, also shown, may not equal the annualized 1st Quarter wages. Columns headed by a percent sign (%) indicate change from the previous year. na stands for not available. The symbol (D) indicates that data are withheld by the source to avoid disclosure of competitive information. A dash (-) indicates that data are not available or cannot be calculated.

ESTABLISHMENTS
Number

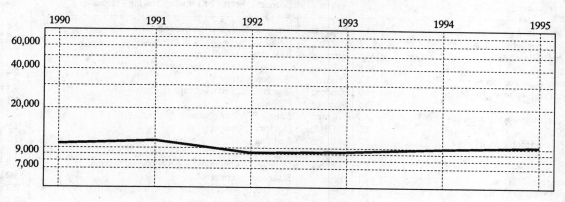

MID-MARCH EMPLOYMENT
Number

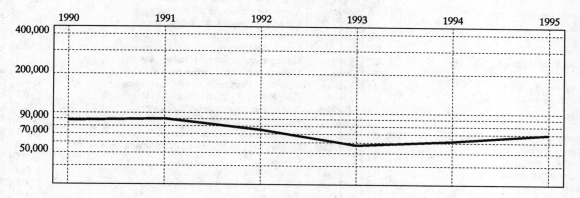

ANNUAL PAYROLL
$ million

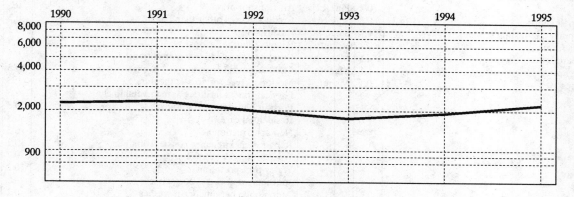

INPUTS AND OUTPUTS FOR ALL REAL ESTATE SECTORS - SIC GROUP 65

Economic Sector or Industry Providing Inputs	%	Sector	Economic Sector or Industry Buying Outputs	%	Sector
Real estate agents, operators, & lessors	25.9	Fin/R.E.	Personal consumption expenditures	32.4	
Maintenance/repair of residential structures	14.1	Constr.	Retail trade, ex eating & drinking	7.9	Trade
Services to dwellings & other buildings	5.9	Services	Real estate agents, operators, & lessors	7.1	Fin/R.E.
Electric services (utilities)	4.8	Util.	Gross private fixed investment	5.6	Cap Inv
Repair & maintenance construction nec	4.4	Constr.	Wholesale trade	3.3	Trade
Engineering, architectural, & surveying services	3.7	Services	Owner-occupied dwellings	3.3	Fin/R.E.
Advertising	3.6	Services	Hospitals	3.1	Services
Maintenance/repair of highways & streets	2.9	Constr.	Eating & drinking places	2.3	Services
Banking	2.9	Fin/R.E.	Doctors & dentists	1.9	Services
Telephone/telegraph communications nec	2.7	Util.	Banking	1.7	Fin/R.E.
Legal services	2.4	Services	Legal services	1.5	Services
Automotive rental & leasing, without drivers	2.3	Services	Colleges, universities, & professional schools	1.4	Services
Landscape & horticultural services	2.1	Agric.	Insurance carriers	1.2	Fin/R.E.
Sanitary services, steam supply, irrigation	2.1	Util.	S/L Govt., general government nec, spending	1.2	S/L Govt
Business services nec	1.8	Services	Religious organizations	1.0	Services
Electrical repair shops	1.4	Services	Feed grains	0.8	Agric.
Insurance carriers	1.2	Fin/R.E.	Nursing & personal care facilities	0.7	Services
Eating & drinking places	1.2	Services	Meat animals	0.6	Agric.
U.S. Postal Service	1.1	Gov't	Insurance agents, brokers, & services	0.6	Fin/R.E.
Hotels	1.0	Services	Security & commodity brokers	0.6	Fin/R.E.
Management & public relations services	1.0	Services	Accounting, auditing & bookkeeping	0.6	Services
Air transportation	0.9	Util.	Automotive repair shops & services	0.6	Services
Personnel supply services	0.8	Services	Computer & data processing services	0.6	Services
Natural gas distribution	0.7	Util.	Labor, civic, social, fraternal organizations	0.6	Services
Accounting, auditing & bookkeeping	0.7	Services	Management & public relations services	0.6	Services
Wholesale trade	0.6	Trade	Medical & health services nec	0.6	Services
Computer & data processing services	0.5	Services	Federal Government, nondefense, spending	0.6	Gov't
Detective & protective services	0.5	Services	Telephone/telegraph communications nec	0.5	Util.
Commercial printing	0.4	Manufg.	Trucking & courier services, ex air	0.5	Util.
Petroleum refining	0.4	Manufg.	Business services nec	0.5	Services
Water supply & sewerage systems	0.4	Util.	Elementary & secondary schools	0.5	Services
Credit agencies other than banks	0.4	Fin/R.E.	Engineering, architectural, & surveying services	0.5	Services
Security & commodity brokers	0.4	Fin/R.E.	Hotels	0.5	Services
Concrete products, ex block & brick	0.3	Manufg.	Social services, nec	0.5	Services
Trucking & courier services, ex air	0.3	Util.	S/L Govt., public welfare, spending	0.5	S/L Govt
Automotive repair shops & services	0.3	Services	Oil bearing crops	0.4	Agric.
Business & professional associations	0.3	Services	Electric services (utilities)	0.4	Util.
State & local government enterprises nec	0.3	Gov't	Membership organizations nec	0.4	Services
Local & suburban transit	0.2	Util.	State & local government enterprises nec	0.4	Gov't
Retail trade, ex eating & drinking	0.2	Trade	Food grains	0.3	Agric.
Royalties	0.2	Fin/R.E.	Air transportation	0.3	Util.
Miscellaneous repair shops	0.2	Services	Credit agencies other than banks	0.3	Fin/R.E.
Research, development, & testing services	0.2	Services	Advertising	0.3	Services
Manifold business forms	0.1	Manufg.	Beauty & barber shops	0.3	Services
Paper & paperboard mills	0.1	Manufg.	Business & professional associations	0.3	Services
Paper coating & glazing	0.1	Manufg.	Child day care services	0.3	Services
Tires & inner tubes	0.1	Manufg.	Motion picture services & theaters	0.3	Services
			Physical fitness facilities & membership clubs	0.3	Services
			Portrait photographic studios	0.3	Services
			Residential care	0.3	Services
			New construction nec	0.2	Constr.
			Repair & maintenance construction nec	0.2	Constr.
			Warehousing & storage	0.2	Util.
			Water transportation	0.2	Util.
			Amusement & recreation services nec	0.2	Services
			Automobile parking & car washes	0.2	Services
			Automotive rental & leasing, without drivers	0.2	Services
			Laundry, cleaning, garment services, shoe repair	0.2	Services

Continued on next page.

INPUTS AND OUTPUTS FOR ALL REAL ESTATE SECTORS - SIC GROUP 65 - Continued

Economic Sector or Industry Providing Inputs	%	Sector	Economic Sector or Industry Buying Outputs	%	Sector
			Private libraries, vocational schools, nec	0.2	Services
			Research, development, & testing services	0.2	Services
			Exports of goods & services	0.2	Foreign
			Dairy farm products	0.1	Agric.
			Vegetables	0.1	Agric.
			Crude petroleum & natural gas	0.1	Mining
			Residential 1 unit structures, nonfarm	0.1	Constr.
			Apparel made from purchased materials	0.1	Manufg.
			Commercial printing	0.1	Manufg.
			Electronic computers	0.1	Manufg.
			Miscellaneous plastics products, nec	0.1	Manufg.
			Job training & related services	0.1	Services
			Miscellaneous equipment rental & leasing	0.1	Services
			Miscellaneous repair shops	0.1	Services
			Personnel supply services	0.1	Services
			Photofinishing labs & commercial photography	0.1	Services
			Theatrical producers, bands, orchestras	0.1	Services
			Video tape rental	0.1	Services
			U.S. Postal Service	0.1	Gov't
			Federal Government, national defense, spending	0.1	Fed Govt

Source: Benchmark Input-Output Accounts for the U.S. Economy, 1992, U.S. Department of Commerce, Washington, D.C., November 1997. Data, as reported in the source, are organized by the 1987 SIC structure in use in 1992.

OCCUPATIONS EMPLOYED BY ALL OTHER REAL ESTATE

Occupation	% of Total 1996	Change to 2006	Occupation	% of Total 1996	Change to 2006
Gardeners, nursery workers	18.5	18.6	Janitors & cleaners, maids	2.3	5.0
General managers & top executives	6.8	24.9	Typists, including word processing	2.0	-20.5
General office clerks	6.7	9.1	Food preparation workers nec	1.8	31.8
Secretaries, except legal & medical	6.5	2.1	Marketing & sales worker supervisors	1.7	29.3
Maintenance repairers, general utility	4.4	22.7	Farming, forestry, agriculture supervisors	1.6	31.8
Sales agents, real estate	4.2	5.6	Accountants & auditors	1.5	21.0
Title examiners & searchers	4.2	20.6	Legal assistants & clerks nec	1.2	20.9
Bookkeeping, accounting, & auditing clerks	4.2	4.0	Guards	1.2	18.5
Sales & related workers nec	3.9	43.5	Carpenters	1.1	6.6
Property & real estate managers	3.6	31.4	Service workers nec	1.1	31.7
Receptionists & information clerks	3.1	28.5	Blue collar worker supervisors	1.0	27.2
Financial managers	2.7	30.1			

Sources: Industry-Occupation Matrix, Bureau of Labor Statistics. These data relate to one or more 3-digit SIC industry groups rather than to a single 4-digit SIC. The change reported for each occupation to the year 2005 is a percent of growth or decline as estimated by the Bureau of Labor Statistics. The abbreviation *nec* stands for not elsewhere classified.

U.S. AND STATE DATA ON INDUSTRY REVENUES AND OTHER ACCOUNTS FOR 1992

State	No. of Estab.	Employ- ment	Payroll ($ mil.)	Revenues ($ mil.)	Empl./ Estab.	Revenue/ Estab. ($)	Payroll/ Estab. ($)	Revenue/ Empl. ($)	Payroll/ Empl. ($)
UNITED STATES	8,848	48,502	1,452.6	9,219.7	5	1,042,009	164,178	190,089	29,950
Alabama	104	355	6.8	44.6	3	428,779	65,750	125,614	19,262
Alaska	19	-	(D)	(D)	(D)	(D)	(D)	(D)	(D)
Arizona	197	1,098	29.3	258.8	6	1,313,761	148,589	235,711	26,659
Arkansas	65	590	12.4	78.9	9	1,213,569	191,231	133,698	21,068
California	1,387	8,763	299.6	1,574.9	6	1,135,440	215,983	179,716	34,186
Colorado	166	676	22.6	158.3	4	953,861	136,006	234,232	33,398
Connecticut	117	265	12.0	73.3	2	626,838	102,308	276,755	45,170
Delaware	33	78	2.0	10.1	2	306,970	61,364	129,872	25,962
District of Columbia	16	46	1.7	18.2	3	1,139,375	104,875	396,304	36,478
Florida	902	6,708	173.2	1,188.8	7	1,317,969	191,979	177,222	25,815
Georgia	317	2,291	68.2	331.3	7	1,045,192	215,101	144,621	29,763
Hawaii	102	877	35.9	306.4	9	3,003,667	351,559	349,343	40,888
Idaho	51	112	3.6	30.7	2	602,784	70,216	274,482	31,973
Illinois	305	1,451	58.8	353.3	5	1,158,354	192,843	243,486	40,535
Indiana	143	616	19.8	143.5	4	1,003,832	138,762	233,032	32,213
Iowa	45	134	3.6	37.3	3	827,911	80,378	278,030	26,993
Kansas	48	198	6.0	66.3	4	1,381,563	125,042	334,924	30,313
Kentucky	82	266	5.9	40.9	3	498,829	71,390	153,774	22,008
Louisiana	89	513	12.4	84.0	6	944,056	139,303	163,784	24,168
Maine	26	30	0.6	7.7	1	296,192	24,692	256,700	21,400
Maryland	206	1,169	39.6	225.7	6	1,095,583	192,136	193,062	33,858
Massachusetts	179	741	19.1	130.9	4	731,324	106,687	176,663	25,772
Michigan	181	800	26.6	109.8	4	606,530	147,133	137,228	33,289
Minnesota	135	501	16.5	104.4	4	773,304	122,333	208,375	32,964
Mississippi	51	373	7.3	33.6	7	658,686	143,549	90,062	19,627
Missouri	188	560	13.8	171.9	3	914,330	73,266	306,954	24,596
Montana	32	200	4.5	20.4	6	638,469	140,063	102,155	22,410
Nebraska	28	45	1.1	13.1	2	467,714	38,571	291,022	24,000
Nevada	113	1,257	44.2	202.0	11	1,787,593	391,062	160,698	35,155
New Hampshire	55	226	7.0	64.4	4	1,170,109	126,764	284,761	30,850
New Jersey	212	1,113	41.3	320.6	5	1,512,448	194,712	288,085	37,088
New Mexico	63	288	8.8	80.7	5	1,281,476	140,063	280,323	30,639
New York	339	1,333	59.5	233.2	4	687,808	175,602	174,919	44,658
North Carolina	319	2,017	45.9	323.9	6	1,015,467	143,824	160,602	22,747
North Dakota	8	-	(D)	(D)	(D)	(D)	(D)	(D)	(D)
Ohio	216	1,539	44.1	309.3	7	1,431,796	204,134	200,954	28,650
Oklahoma	92	264	6.0	38.0	3	412,902	64,967	143,890	22,640
Oregon	117	305	12.4	131.2	3	1,121,726	106,291	430,302	40,774
Pennsylvania	275	1,061	31.1	198.9	4	723,131	112,927	187,428	29,270
Rhode Island	35	90	3.9	18.8	3	537,343	112,486	208,967	43,744
South Carolina	142	1,519	33.2	219.6	11	1,546,718	233,782	144,591	21,855
South Dakota	18	48	1.2	5.0	3	278,056	67,778	104,271	25,417
Tennessee	132	436	11.0	71.2	3	539,742	83,242	163,408	25,202
Texas	645	3,627	92.0	576.4	6	893,611	142,603	158,913	25,360
Utah	64	206	6.5	61.1	3	954,266	100,922	296,471	31,354
Vermont	36	133	3.3	13.0	4	360,611	92,722	97,609	25,098
Virginia	272	1,665	41.8	327.0	6	1,202,272	153,835	196,407	25,131
Washington	295	1,252	37.1	257.7	4	873,712	125,793	205,867	29,640
West Virginia	53	-	(D)	(D)	(D)	(D)	(D)	(D)	(D)
Wisconsin	117	378	11.5	95.7	3	817,684	98,658	253,093	30,537
Wyoming	16	45	0.7	3.4	3	215,250	42,750	76,533	15,200

Source: 1992 Economic Census, U.S. Department of Commerce, Washington, D.C. This is the only table that shows revenue data as collected by the Bureau of the Census in an Economic Census. The symbol (D) indicates that data are withheld by the source to avoid disclosure of competitive information. A dash (-) indicates that data are not available or cannot be calculated.

STATE-BY-STATE DATA ON ESTABLISHMENTS, EMPLOYMENT, AND PAYROLL - 1994 AND 1995

State	1994					1995					% Change Empl.
	No. of Estab.	Employment	Pay / Empl.	Payroll ($ mil.)	Pay / Estab.	No. of Estab.	Employment	Pay / Empl.	Payroll ($ mil.)	Pay / Estab.	
Alabama	123	867	19,322	17.3	140,780	132	821	23,177	19.1	144,424	-5.3
Alaska	15	61	21,902	1.8	117,467	16	(D)	-	(D)	-	-
Arizona	256	1,421	27,662	44.3	173,004	256	1,510	34,021	49.7	194,094	6.3
Arkansas	86	609	24,368	14.9	173,372	97	745	29,664	18.9	194,711	22.3
California	1,291	8,740	31,822	302.5	234,295	1,289	9,810	33,866	349.0	270,790	12.2
Colorado	247	748	33,578	32.7	132,275	288	913	34,309	35.1	121,806	22.1
Connecticut	120	394	34,234	18.6	154,800	123	418	27,923	13.9	113,268	6.1
Delaware	36	104	18,692	2.9	80,083	37	127	20,157	3.1	83,811	22.1
District of Columbia	15	117	40,855	5.3	356,333	18	182	56,286	12.5	695,056	55.6
Florida	982	8,471	25,159	231.5	235,693	994	9,219	26,389	267.2	268,811	8.8
Georgia	371	2,242	24,219	65.2	175,668	393	2,338	28,996	74.8	190,425	4.3
Hawaii	93	2,145	30,545	68.2	733,280	87	2,216	32,895	73.6	845,736	3.3
Idaho	86	241	25,676	7.1	82,651	82	232	24,621	6.7	81,098	-3.7
Illinois	353	1,690	34,907	72.9	206,453	371	1,956	33,679	81.7	220,310	15.7
Indiana	188	910	25,820	27.6	146,936	197	1,204	26,472	37.8	191,883	32.3
Iowa	57	204	21,745	4.9	86,421	60	219	18,027	5.3	88,450	7.4
Kansas	65	541	20,407	11.5	177,323	78	308	27,753	9.8	125,436	-43.1
Kentucky	104	415	20,145	10.2	98,221	108	379	19,694	9.1	84,000	-8.7
Louisiana	90	583	16,501	13.2	146,822	85	519	17,950	12.2	143,553	-11.0
Maine	29	31	21,290	1.1	37,345	32	40	28,300	1.7	54,469	29.0
Maryland	244	1,824	27,693	65.7	269,184	237	1,813	37,739	73.6	310,620	-0.6
Massachusetts	192	746	24,954	24.3	126,609	199	976	27,918	28.7	144,211	30.8
Michigan	217	1,037	25,805	32.9	151,728	248	1,298	26,062	40.1	161,677	25.2
Minnesota	162	591	24,115	21.4	131,790	169	880	21,873	24.5	144,775	48.9
Mississippi	54	363	18,182	8.4	155,704	62	315	21,270	7.5	121,516	-13.2
Missouri	256	1,007	18,677	22.6	88,434	258	1,105	19,569	25.4	98,372	9.7
Montana	45	251	16,749	6.3	139,644	39	166	22,361	4.9	124,795	-33.9
Nebraska	34	122	13,016	1.8	54,235	29	110	14,909	2.2	74,310	-9.8
Nevada	145	2,168	32,792	79.6	549,110	155	2,857	32,886	101.4	654,084	31.8
New Hampshire	68	373	16,815	10.3	151,809	69	361	40,277	18.2	263,290	-3.2
New Jersey	262	1,523	29,560	55.3	211,046	259	1,826	30,620	57.9	223,571	19.9
New Mexico	78	501	27,186	17.2	220,000	79	569	27,192	17.8	225,519	13.6
New York	356	1,663	40,851	79.1	222,222	378	2,004	41,836	94.1	248,894	20.5
North Carolina	354	2,328	25,636	61.8	174,596	364	2,744	36,284	79.5	218,316	17.9
North Dakota	9	(D)	-	(D)	-	11	(D)	-	(D)	-	-
Ohio	273	2,495	26,764	74.4	272,465	308	2,690	29,790	82.6	268,240	7.8
Oklahoma	100	573	17,668	12.0	120,490	101	310	21,806	8.4	83,406	-45.9
Oregon	162	655	24,085	20.6	126,963	188	756	24,788	23.1	123,080	15.4
Pennsylvania	284	1,621	26,041	49.4	173,887	285	1,609	35,632	60.8	213,446	-0.7
Rhode Island	30	85	49,459	5.1	170,167	30	86	45,209	4.9	161,933	1.2
South Carolina	144	1,529	20,484	35.8	248,736	148	1,727	20,718	39.7	267,980	12.9
South Dakota	22	88	10,864	1.8	79,727	24	111	8,216	1.2	51,708	26.1
Tennessee	154	580	18,945	16.5	107,448	157	837	19,589	20.2	128,637	44.3
Texas	670	4,023	27,467	119.0	177,681	698	5,217	28,828	153.1	219,374	29.7
Utah	110	351	26,439	11.4	103,945	138	432	24,944	13.3	96,304	23.1
Vermont	39	116	19,828	2.9	74,923	40	138	18,870	2.8	70,550	19.0
Virginia	291	1,944	24,031	54.8	188,340	291	2,381	27,052	64.3	220,794	22.5
Washington	362	1,654	27,879	49.8	137,583	387	1,783	33,999	54.8	141,716	7.8
West Virginia	64	182	16,571	3.1	49,063	62	184	16,674	3.2	50,839	1.1
Wisconsin	138	533	26,199	17.2	124,775	156	737	25,883	23.3	149,237	38.3
Wyoming	24	(D)	-	(D)	-	23	61	21,180	1.5	67,130	-

Source: County Business Patterns, U.S. Department of Commerce, Washington, D.C., for 1994 and 1995. Employment shown is for mid-March of the year shown. Payroll per employee is calculated by annualizing 1st Quarter payroll (not shown) and then dividing that value by mid-March employment. Dividing total annual payroll (columns 5 and 10) by employment, therefore, will *not* yield the payroll per employee figure (columns 4 and 9). The symbol (D) indicates that data are withheld by the source to avoid disclosure of competitive information. A dash (-) indicates that data are not available or cannot be calculated.

INPUTS AND OUTPUTS FOR ALL REAL ESTATE SECTORS - SIC GROUP 65 - Continued

Economic Sector or Industry Providing Inputs	%	Sector	Economic Sector or Industry Buying Outputs	%	Sector
			Private libraries, vocational schools, nec	0.2	Services
			Research, development, & testing services	0.2	Services
			Exports of goods & services	0.2	Foreign
			Dairy farm products	0.1	Agric.
			Vegetables	0.1	Agric.
			Crude petroleum & natural gas	0.1	Mining
			Residential 1 unit structures, nonfarm	0.1	Constr.
			Apparel made from purchased materials	0.1	Manufg.
			Commercial printing	0.1	Manufg.
			Electronic computers	0.1	Manufg.
			Miscellaneous plastics products, nec	0.1	Manufg.
			Job training & related services	0.1	Services
			Miscellaneous equipment rental & leasing	0.1	Services
			Miscellaneous repair shops	0.1	Services
			Personnel supply services	0.1	Services
			Photofinishing labs & commercial photography	0.1	Services
			Theatrical producers, bands, orchestras	0.1	Services
			Video tape rental	0.1	Services
			U.S. Postal Service	0.1	Gov't
			Federal Government, national defense, spending	0.1	Fed Govt

Source: Benchmark Input-Output Accounts for the U.S. Economy, 1992, U.S. Department of Commerce, Washington, D.C., November 1997. Data, as reported in the source, are organized by the 1987 SIC structure in use in 1992.

OCCUPATIONS EMPLOYED BY ALL OTHER REAL ESTATE

Occupation	% of Total 1996	Change to 2006	Occupation	% of Total 1996	Change to 2006
Gardeners, nursery workers	18.5	18.6	Janitors & cleaners, maids	2.3	5.0
General managers & top executives	6.8	24.9	Typists, including word processing	2.0	-20.5
General office clerks	6.7	9.1	Food preparation workers nec	1.8	31.8
Secretaries, except legal & medical	6.5	2.1	Marketing & sales worker supervisors	1.7	29.3
Maintenance repairers, general utility	4.4	22.7	Farming, forestry, agriculture supervisors	1.6	31.8
Sales agents, real estate	4.2	5.6	Accountants & auditors	1.5	21.0
Title examiners & searchers	4.2	20.6	Legal assistants & clerks nec	1.2	20.9
Bookkeeping, accounting, & auditing clerks	4.2	4.0	Guards	1.2	18.5
Sales & related workers nec	3.9	43.5	Carpenters	1.1	6.6
Property & real estate managers	3.6	31.4	Service workers nec	1.1	31.7
Receptionists & information clerks	3.1	28.5	Blue collar worker supervisors	1.0	27.2
Financial managers	2.7	30.1			

Sources: Industry-Occupation Matrix, Bureau of Labor Statistics. These data relate to one or more 3-digit SIC industry groups rather than to a single 4-digit SIC. The change reported for each occupation to the year 2005 is a percent of growth or decline as estimated by the Bureau of Labor Statistics. The abbreviation *nec* stands for not elsewhere classified.

U.S. AND STATE DATA ON INDUSTRY REVENUES AND OTHER ACCOUNTS FOR 1992

State	No. of Estab.	Employ-ment	Payroll ($ mil.)	Revenues ($ mil.)	Empl./ Estab.	Revenue/ Estab. ($)	Payroll/ Estab. ($)	Revenue/ Empl. ($)	Payroll/ Empl. ($)
UNITED STATES	6,490	40,102	795.0	2,299.6	6	354,336	122,497	57,345	19,825
Alabama	107	691	9.8	33.4	6	312,252	91,402	48,352	14,153
Alaska	3	-	(D)	(D)	(D)	(D)	(D)	(D)	(D)
Arizona	34	552	9.9	27.1	16	796,265	290,676	49,045	17,904
Arkansas	69	190	2.8	10.7	3	155,174	40,348	56,353	14,653
California	267	3,869	92.8	323.0	14	1,209,682	347,509	83,480	23,982
Colorado	50	434	7.4	20.1	9	402,560	148,680	46,378	17,129
Connecticut	98	435	10.0	28.9	4	294,694	102,510	66,391	23,094
Delaware	20	-	(D)	(D)	(D)	(D)	(D)	(D)	(D)
District of Columbia	7	50	0.9	2.4	7	336,429	132,857	47,100	18,600
Florida	201	3,025	59.8	204.0	15	1,015,070	297,627	67,448	19,776
Georgia	133	861	15.2	57.1	6	429,624	114,338	66,365	17,662
Hawaii	17	453	10.5	23.3	27	1,369,588	616,882	51,397	23,150
Idaho	21	33	0.6	2.5	2	121,048	27,000	77,030	17,182
Illinois	369	1,930	47.7	130.5	5	353,661	129,171	67,617	24,696
Indiana	215	1,262	20.1	51.7	6	240,247	93,712	40,929	15,965
Iowa	154	433	6.6	16.2	3	104,916	42,890	37,314	15,254
Kansas	92	344	5.5	15.2	4	165,554	60,228	44,276	16,108
Kentucky	123	639	10.4	25.7	5	208,602	84,325	40,153	16,232
Louisiana	81	708	9.0	29.8	9	368,222	111,704	42,127	12,780
Maine	63	127	2.1	5.5	2	87,905	33,032	43,606	16,386
Maryland	110	1,301	25.8	63.3	12	575,255	234,982	48,638	19,868
Massachusetts	136	767	19.2	42.6	6	313,037	141,449	55,506	25,081
Michigan	158	1,248	28.1	91.8	8	580,930	178,025	73,547	22,538
Minnesota	144	384	6.3	18.6	3	129,097	44,049	48,411	16,518
Mississippi	43	141	1.9	5.5	3	127,767	43,140	38,965	13,156
Missouri	162	683	10.1	28.1	4	173,167	62,228	41,073	14,760
Montana	28	67	0.9	2.3	2	82,750	33,607	34,582	14,045
Nebraska	60	182	2.6	9.7	3	161,767	43,133	53,330	14,220
Nevada	11	111	3.4	7.3	10	662,182	308,273	65,622	30,550
New Hampshire	29	55	1.0	2.1	2	71,690	33,414	37,800	17,618
New Jersey	204	1,463	38.5	94.5	7	463,353	188,529	64,610	26,288
New Mexico	22	130	1.9	6.3	6	287,318	86,364	48,623	14,615
New York	663	3,607	91.5	238.0	5	358,998	137,964	65,987	25,359
North Carolina	155	810	14.4	43.8	5	282,271	92,632	54,015	17,726
North Dakota	37	-	(D)	(D)	(D)	(D)	(D)	(D)	(D)
Ohio	308	1,920	33.5	96.0	6	311,711	108,623	50,004	17,425
Oklahoma	59	378	5.8	16.8	6	285,559	99,051	44,571	15,460
Oregon	58	322	5.2	20.3	6	350,276	88,845	63,093	16,003
Pennsylvania	671	3,143	54.4	153.0	5	228,034	81,077	48,683	17,309
Rhode Island	34	151	3.6	10.8	4	318,353	104,529	71,682	23,536
South Carolina	101	579	9.6	28.9	6	285,802	94,693	49,855	16,518
South Dakota	30	60	0.7	1.7	2	55,767	22,300	27,883	11,150
Tennessee	131	811	12.6	35.5	6	270,634	96,252	43,715	15,547
Texas	330	2,539	46.7	119.4	8	361,788	141,530	47,022	18,395
Utah	15	97	1.7	6.2	6	413,733	113,000	63,979	17,474
Vermont	57	-	(D)	(D)	(D)	(D)	(D)	(D)	(D)
Virginia	146	1,051	19.1	50.4	7	344,993	131,089	47,925	18,210
Washington	98	682	16.2	46.2	7	471,653	165,327	67,774	23,757
West Virginia	114	460	6.2	21.1	4	184,667	54,404	45,765	13,483
Wisconsin	247	732	10.2	24.5	3	99,016	41,381	33,411	13,963
Wyoming	5	-	(D)	(D)	(D)	(D)	(D)	(D)	(D)

Source: 1992 Economic Census, U.S. Department of Commerce, Washington, D.C. This is the only table that shows revenue data as collected by the Bureau of the Census in an Economic Census. The symbol (D) indicates that data are withheld by the source to avoid disclosure of competitive information. A dash (-) indicates that data are not available or cannot be calculated.

STATE-BY-STATE DATA ON ESTABLISHMENTS, EMPLOYMENT, AND PAYROLL - 1994 AND 1995

State	1994					1995					% Change Empl.
	No. of Estab.	Employ-ment	Pay / Empl.	Payroll ($ mil.)	Pay / Estab.	No. of Estab.	Employ-ment	Pay / Empl.	Payroll ($ mil.)	Pay / Estab.	
Alabama	89	856	11,103	10.3	116,191	92	866	12,222	11.2	122,152	1.2
Alaska	3	(D)	-	(D)	-	3	(D)	-	(D)	-	-
Arizona	31	677	15,634	12.1	389,097	28	703	17,183	13.2	470,286	3.8
Arkansas	62	200	12,420	2.7	43,532	59	184	13,413	2.7	45,847	-8.0
California	245	4,256	19,949	91.8	374,661	246	4,836	19,660	98.9	401,931	13.6
Colorado	54	621	15,124	10.0	184,833	49	612	13,556	9.3	189,102	-1.4
Connecticut	93	430	21,888	10.7	115,118	92	439	22,232	11.1	120,728	2.1
Delaware	18	80	18,900	1.7	93,833	18	74	20,703	1.7	92,222	-7.5
District of Columbia	7	41	23,317	1.0	145,429	7	43	22,326	1.1	150,429	4.9
Florida	180	3,560	15,934	59.8	332,456	190	3,504	19,179	74.1	389,821	-1.6
Georgia	133	1,059	19,762	21.7	163,241	122	1,183	16,622	19.8	162,344	11.7
Hawaii	14	350	20,274	7.2	512,000	16	355	19,910	8.5	529,375	1.4
Idaho	22	65	9,908	0.8	38,409	22	(D)	-	(D)	-	-
Illinois	344	1,986	23,376	53.0	154,148	333	2,330	20,795	59.7	179,144	17.3
Indiana	204	1,208	14,719	20.3	99,275	198	1,173	16,089	20.5	103,677	-2.9
Iowa	147	401	13,127	6.6	44,871	137	417	13,151	6.2	45,591	4.0
Kansas	90	316	11,456	4.4	48,733	87	323	12,099	4.5	51,356	2.2
Kentucky	116	784	12,327	11.0	94,914	120	792	14,217	12.3	102,375	1.0
Louisiana	70	802	11,761	10.5	150,300	70	712	13,607	10.5	149,414	-11.2
Maine	59	96	12,792	1.9	32,847	58	87	13,333	1.8	31,397	-9.4
Maryland	102	1,252	16,965	26.2	256,676	101	1,228	19,909	30.6	303,347	-1.9
Massachusetts	129	702	21,989	18.2	141,000	128	679	23,429	18.6	145,656	-3.3
Michigan	161	1,332	21,339	31.9	198,311	159	1,362	21,944	32.4	203,748	2.3
Minnesota	146	378	13,513	6.7	45,664	142	445	12,854	7.0	49,070	17.7
Mississippi	46	153	13,804	2.3	50,457	44	176	13,000	2.3	53,182	15.0
Missouri	160	784	13,857	12.6	78,994	158	803	14,854	13.8	87,241	2.4
Montana	28	53	18,415	1.1	40,286	28	91	12,703	1.2	43,143	71.7
Nebraska	56	175	14,423	2.8	49,839	56	175	14,171	3.0	52,964	0.0
Nevada	11	132	27,455	3.4	304,818	10	155	17,548	2.9	286,500	17.4
New Hampshire	29	43	14,698	1.0	33,310	29	44	15,909	1.0	33,069	2.3
New Jersey	200	1,511	24,296	42.6	212,870	193	1,573	25,788	44.0	227,756	4.1
New Mexico	21	142	13,803	2.5	118,667	20	152	11,684	1.9	94,600	7.0
New York	622	3,075	27,646	98.6	158,489	608	3,162	27,913	101.0	166,064	2.8
North Carolina	160	1,146	18,373	22.6	140,950	154	1,250	17,082	22.6	146,558	9.1
North Dakota	37	37	8,541	0.5	13,432	34	(D)	-	(D)	-	-
Ohio	311	1,985	15,865	37.1	119,431	304	1,949	17,872	38.3	126,007	-1.8
Oklahoma	58	466	12,292	6.4	109,914	57	514	12,125	7.2	125,667	10.3
Oregon	57	391	14,486	6.0	104,544	62	485	15,249	7.8	125,468	24.0
Pennsylvania	629	3,245	15,360	59.7	94,886	617	3,190	17,490	59.7	96,827	-1.7
Rhode Island	35	140	21,400	3.6	104,143	37	152	21,553	3.7	99,703	8.6
South Carolina	103	898	14,503	14.5	141,233	96	777	14,589	11.7	121,979	-13.5
South Dakota	29	53	9,283	0.7	22,931	27	51	11,137	0.7	25,815	-3.8
Tennessee	131	1,046	12,853	15.3	116,977	125	1,250	12,390	16.5	132,032	19.5
Texas	343	3,735	15,284	61.7	179,767	334	4,419	13,791	65.8	196,889	18.3
Utah	15	76	14,632	1.5	98,133	16	77	17,455	2.0	126,188	1.3
Vermont	58	44	7,818	0.8	13,138	55	42	8,000	0.7	12,127	-4.5
Virginia	140	1,235	15,715	22.3	159,143	136	1,119	17,008	21.3	156,794	-9.4
Washington	96	706	21,649	16.3	169,760	98	703	22,521	16.7	170,520	-0.4
West Virginia	115	484	14,711	8.1	70,357	108	505	13,584	7.9	73,120	4.3
Wisconsin	249	707	12,458	10.7	42,940	245	790	12,289	11.2	45,571	11.7
Wyoming	5	(D)	-	(D)	-	5	5	5,600	0.0	8,600	-

Source: County Business Patterns, U.S. Department of Commerce, Washington, D.C., for 1994 and 1995. Employment shown is for mid-March of the year shown. Payroll per employee is calculated by annualizing 1st Quarter payroll (not shown) and then dividing that value by mid-March employment. Dividing total annual payroll (columns 5 and 10) by employment, therefore, will *not* yield the payroll per employee figure (columns 4 and 9). The symbol (D) indicates that data are withheld by the source to avoid disclosure of competitive information. A dash (-) indicates that data are not available or cannot be calculated.

ESTABLISHMENTS 1995 - STATE AND REGIONAL CONCENTRATION

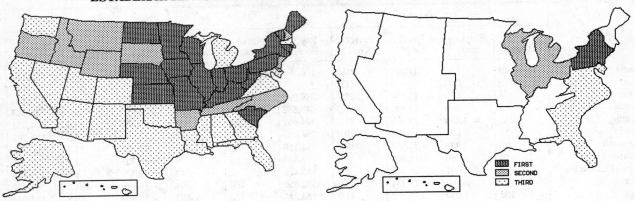

EMPLOYMENT 1995 - STATE AND REGIONAL CONCENTRATION

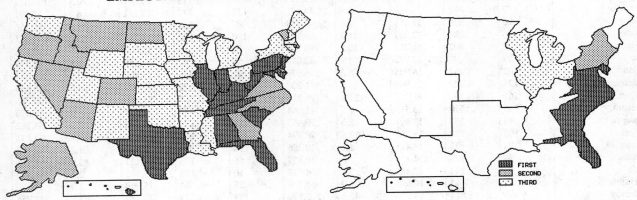

PAYROLL 1995 - STATE AND REGIONAL CONCENTRATION

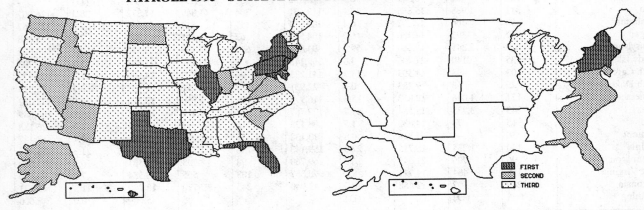

States with the darkest shading indicate those states which have proportionately more establishments, employment, or payrolls than would be indicated by the state's population. States with light shading are states with proportionately fewer establishments, less employment, and lower payrolls than population distribution. States shaded grey are within 15 percent of the state's population proportion in these categories. States for which no data are available are shown as average (grey). *Regions* are shaded to indicate absolute rank in the category. If no data for the category are available, establishment counts are used to shade the regions. Source of the data is the table on the facing page.

LEADING COMPANIES - SIC 6553 - Cemetery Subdividers and Developers

Number shown: **10**   Total sales/assets ($ mil): **3,383**   Total employment (000): **35.4**

Company Name	Address				CEO Name	Phone	Co. Type	Sales/Assets ($ mil)	Empl. (000)
Service Corporation International	PO Box 130548	Houston	TX	77219	Robert L. Waltrip	713-522-5141	P	2,468 OR	22.6
Stewart Enterprises Inc.	PO Box 19925	New Orleans	LA	70179	Joseph P. Henican III	504-837-5880	P	533 OR	9.3
Forest Lawn Memorial Parks	1712 S. Glendale Ave.	Glendale	CA	91205	Fredrick Llewellyn	213-254-7251	R	170 OR*	0.8
Caballero Woodlawn Funeral Homes and Cemeteries Inc.	PO Box 14141A	Miami	FL	33114	Keenan Knopke	305-238-3672	R	53 OR*	0.3
Carriage Services Inc.	1300 Post Oak Blvd.	Houston	TX	77056	Melvin C. Payne	281-556-7400	P	40 OR	0.9
F.I. Management Inc.	7900 Glades Rd.	Boca Raton	FL	33434	Monte Friedkin	407-479-1882	R	40	0.4
Rose Hills Co.	PO Box 110	Whittier	CA	90608	Dennis Poulsen	310-699-0921	R	35 OR*	0.6
MHI Group Inc.	3100 Capital Cir.	Tallahassee	FL	32308	Clifford R. Hinkle	904-385-8883	S	24 OR	0.2
Uniservice Corp.	PO Box 11067	Portland	OR	97211	Ellsworth D. Purdy	503-283-1980	R	14 OR	0.2
Parklawn Inc.	PO Box 725	Rockville	MD	20848	Robert Maclary	301-881-2151	S	6 OR*	<0.1

Source: *Ward's Business Directory of U.S. Private and Public Companies*, 1996. Company type codes: P - Public, R - Private, S - Subsidiary, D - Division, J - Joint Venture, A - Affiliate, G - Group. If the dollar values shown are not sales, the following codes apply: TA - Total Assets; OR - Operating Revenues; GB - Gross Billings. * - estimated dollar value. < - less than; *na* - not available.

SIC 6710

HOLDING OFFICES

Holding Offices includes SIC 6712, Offices of Bank Holding Companies and SIC 6719, Offices of Holding Companies, not elsewhere classified.

SIC 6712 includes establishments engaged in holding or owning the securities of banks for the sole purpose of exercising some degree of control over the activities of bank companies whose securities they hold. Companies holding securities of banks but which are predominantly operating banks, are classified as banks under the SIC that best fits their operations.

SIC 6719 are establishments that hold the securities of companies other than banks for the sole purpose of exercising some degree of control over the companies whose securities they hold. Companies that hold securities but are predominantly operating companies are classified under the SIC that best fits their operations. This SIC includes holding companies, investment holding companies, personal holding companies—all holding securities of companies other than banks—and public utility holding companies.

ESTABLISHMENTS, EMPLOYMENT, AND PAYROLL

	1990	1991 Value	%	1992 Value	%	1993 Value	%	1994 Value	%	1995 Value	%	% change 90-95
All Establishments	6,241	6,950	11.4	7,459	7.3	7,944	6.5	8,011	0.8	8,472	5.8	35.7
Mid-March Employment	123,470	125,745	1.8	137,750	9.5	127,662	-7.3	127,905	0.2	136,850	7.0	10.8
1st Quarter Wages (annualized - $ mil.)	5,785.0	5,869.8	1.5	6,669.7	13.6	6,626.1	-0.7	7,048.2	6.4	8,691.4	23.3	50.2
Payroll per Emp. 1st Q. (annualized)	46,854	46,680	-0.4	48,419	3.7	51,903	7.2	55,105	6.2	63,511	15.3	35.6
Annual Payroll ($ mil.)	5,429.7	5,642.7	3.9	6,635.5	17.6	6,986.0	5.3	6,950.4	-0.5	8,216.2	18.2	51.3
Establishments - 1-4 Emp. Number	3,439	3,937	14.5	4,356	10.6	4,899	12.5	5,000	2.1	5,248	5.0	52.6
Mid-March Employment	5,527	6,050	9.5	6,824	12.8	7,231	6.0	7,221	-0.1	7,596	5.2	37.4
1st Quarter Wages (annualized - $ mil.)	321.7	310.3	-3.5	391.0	26.0	417.5	6.8	425.9	2.0	500.0	17.4	55.5
Payroll per Emp. 1st Q. (annualized)	58,197	51,297	-11.9	57,304	11.7	57,736	0.8	58,980	2.2	65,829	11.6	13.1
Annual Payroll ($ mil.)	415.7	407.8	-1.9	478.7	17.4	571.2	19.3	550.0	-3.7	630.7	14.7	51.7
Establishments - 5-9 Emp. Number	956	1,075	12.4	1,105	2.8	1,098	-0.6	1,087	-1.0	1,146	5.4	19.9
Mid-March Employment	6,492	7,297	12.4	7,465	2.3	7,330	-1.8	7,272	-0.8	7,691	5.8	18.5
1st Quarter Wages (annualized - $ mil.)	361.5	397.5	10.0	437.3	10.0	435.0	-0.5	504.5	16.0	601.3	19.2	66.4
Payroll per Emp. 1st Q. (annualized)	55,677	54,473	-2.2	58,576	7.5	59,342	1.3	69,380	16.9	78,182	12.7	40.4
Annual Payroll ($ mil.)	361.2	394.6	9.3	472.5	19.7	455.0	-3.7	514.2	13.0	596.0	15.9	65.0
Establishments - 10-19 Emp. Number	702	775	10.4	806	4.0	800	-0.7	790	-1.3	839	6.2	19.5
Mid-March Employment	9,680	10,589	9.4	11,020	4.1	11,012	-0.1	10,745	-2.4	11,509	7.1	18.9
1st Quarter Wages (annualized - $ mil.)	613.7	609.5	-0.7	706.1	15.8	710.5	0.6	773.0	8.8	954.0	23.4	55.5
Payroll per Emp. 1st Q. (annualized)	63,396	57,564	-9.2	64,078	11.3	64,517	0.7	71,945	11.5	82,892	15.2	30.8
Annual Payroll ($ mil.)	577.4	586.2	1.5	710.5	21.2	747.4	5.2	778.5	4.2	897.5	15.3	55.4
Establishments - 20-49 Emp. Number	610	627	2.8	634	1.1	621	-2.1	610	-1.8	663	8.7	8.7
Mid-March Employment	18,837	19,049	1.1	19,441	2.1	19,224	-1.1	18,522	-3.7	20,248	9.3	7.5
1st Quarter Wages (annualized - $ mil.)	1,054.6	1,042.0	-1.2	1,110.0	6.5	1,058.0	-4.7	1,176.8	11.2	1,403.0	19.2	33.0
Payroll per Emp. 1st Q. (annualized)	55,984	54,700	-2.3	57,098	4.4	55,036	-3.6	63,536	15.4	69,289	9.1	23.8
Annual Payroll ($ mil.)	946.6	1,016.9	7.4	1,099.4	8.1	1,082.4	-1.5	1,103.6	2.0	1,338.3	21.3	41.4
Establishments - 50-99 Emp. Number	289	284	-1.7	282	-0.7	273	-3.2	282	3.3	306	8.5	5.9
Mid-March Employment	19,784	19,515	-1.4	19,436	-0.4	18,728	-3.6	19,256	2.8	21,503	11.7	8.7
1st Quarter Wages (annualized - $ mil.)	915.2	841.5	-8.1	1,006.0	19.6	1,023.8	1.8	1,034.0	1.0	1,506.8	45.7	64.6
Payroll per Emp. 1st Q. (annualized)	46,260	43,119	-6.8	51,760	20.0	54,666	5.6	53,695	-1.8	70,074	30.5	51.5
Annual Payroll ($ mil.)	787.2	805.7	2.4	962.5	19.5	1,011.8	5.1	1,024.5	1.3	1,321.4	29.0	67.9
Establishments - 100-249 Emp. Number	174	176	1.1	194	10.2	175	-9.8	167	-4.6	187	12.0	7.5
Mid-March Employment	27,216	26,833	-1.4	29,570	10.2	26,718	-9.6	26,093	-2.3	28,203	8.1	3.6
1st Quarter Wages (annualized - $ mil.)	1,154.1	1,151.5	-0.2	1,251.9	8.7	1,334.6	6.6	1,358.9	1.8	1,627.6	19.8	41.0
Payroll per Emp. 1st Q. (annualized)	42,406	42,913	1.2	42,338	-1.3	49,950	18.0	52,078	4.3	57,709	10.8	36.1
Annual Payroll ($ mil.)	1,086.0	1,058.8	-2.5	1,229.9	16.2	1,419.0	15.4	1,283.0	-9.6	1,494.9	16.5	37.7
Establishments - 250-499 Emp. Number	49	52	6.1	52	-	54	3.8	49	-9.3	59	20.4	20.4
Mid-March Employment	17,355	(D)	-	17,089	-	18,864	10.4	17,289	-8.3	20,911	20.9	20.5
1st Quarter Wages (annualized - $ mil.)	714.7	(D)	-	821.4	-	836.2	1.8	920.0	10.0	1,189.0	29.2	66.4
Payroll per Emp. 1st Q. (annualized)	41,183	(D)	-	48,063	-	44,330	-7.8	53,210	20.0	56,861	6.9	38.1
Annual Payroll ($ mil.)	657.5	(D)	-	812.2	-	856.8	5.5	878.6	2.6	1,081.5	23.1	64.5
Establishments - 500-999 Emp. Number	18	20	11.1	22	10.0	(D)	-	20	-	19	-5.0	5.6
Mid-March Employment	12,678	13,304	4.9	15,283	14.9	(D)	-	13,217	-	12,705	-3.9	0.2
1st Quarter Wages (annualized - $ mil.)	431.8	497.6	15.2	689.7	38.6	(D)	-	623.6	-	696.2	11.6	61.2
Payroll per Emp. 1st Q. (annualized)	34,062	37,400	9.8	45,128	20.7	(D)	-	47,181	-	54,799	16.1	60.9
Annual Payroll ($ mil.)	385.0	471.3	22.4	637.8	35.3	(D)	-	558.6	-	617.8	10.6	60.5
Estab. - 1000 or More Emp. Number	4	4	-	8	100.0	(D)	-	6		5	-16.7	25.0
Mid-March Employment	5,901	(D)	-	11,622	-	(D)	-	8,290	-	6,484	-21.8	9.9
1st Quarter Wages (annualized - $ mil.)	217.8	(D)	-	256.2	-	(D)	-	231.5	-	213.5	-7.8	-2.0
Payroll per Emp. 1st Q. (annualized)	36,906	(D)	-	22,043	-	(D)	-	27,931	-	32,931	17.9	-10.8
Annual Payroll ($ mil.)	213.2	(D)	-	231.8	-	(D)	-	259.3	-	238.0	-8.2	11.6

Source: County Business Patterns, U.S. Department of Commerce, Washington, D.C., for 1990 through 1995. Payroll per employee is calculated using mid-March employment and 1st Quarter wages, annualized. Annual payroll, also shown, may not equal the annualized 1st Quarter wages. Columns headed by a percent sign (%) indicate change from the previous year. *na* stands for not available. The symbol (D) indicates that data are withheld by the source to avoid disclosure of competitive information. A dash (-) indicates that data are not available or cannot be calculated.

ESTABLISHMENTS
Number

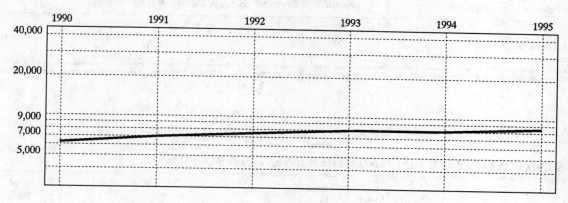

MID-MARCH EMPLOYMENT
Number

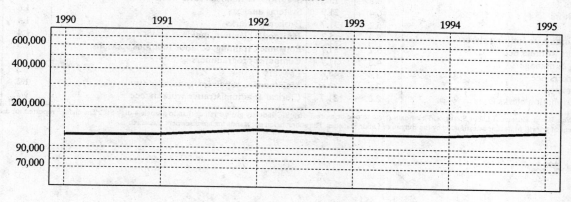

ANNUAL PAYROLL
$ million

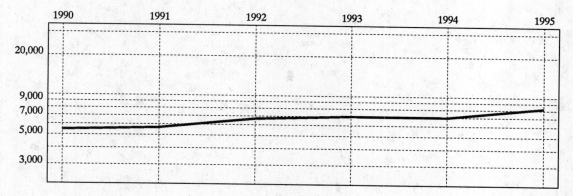

INPUTS AND OUTPUTS FOR HOLDING AND OTHER INVESTMENT OFFICES - SIC GROUP 67

Economic Sector or Industry Providing Inputs	%	Sector	Economic Sector or Industry Buying Outputs	%	Sector
No Input-Output data are available for this industry group.					

Source: Benchmark Input-Output Accounts for the U.S. Economy, 1992, U.S. Department of Commerce, Washington, D.C., November 1997. Data, as reported in the source, are organized by the 1987 SIC structure in use in 1992.

OCCUPATIONS EMPLOYED BY HOLDING AND OTHER INVESTMENT OFFICES

Occupation	% of Total 1996	Change to 2006	Occupation	% of Total 1996	Change to 2006
General managers & top executives	10.4	27.6	Managers & administrators nec	1.9	30.5
Secretaries, except legal & medical	10.4	4.4	Marketing & sales worker supervisors	1.9	31.7
General office clerks	6.8	13.3	Securities & financial sales workers	1.8	31.7
Accountants & auditors	6.4	21.9	Systems analysts	1.6	95.2
Financial managers	6.2	31.7	Brokerage clerks	1.4	10.1
Bookkeeping, accounting, & auditing clerks	5.9	5.3	Janitors & cleaners, maids	1.4	5.3
Management support workers nec	5.1	31.7	Personnel, training, & labor relations specialists	1.3	31.6
Clerical supervisors & managers	4.3	31.7	Computer programmers	1.3	8.4
Sales & related workers nec	3.3	44.8	Lawyers	1.2	31.6
Professional workers nec	2.6	31.6	Maintenance repairers, general utility	1.2	22.7
Receptionists & information clerks	2.0	31.7	Clerical & administrative workers nec	1.2	31.7

Sources: Industry-Occupation Matrix, Bureau of Labor Statistics. These data relate to one or more 3-digit SIC industry groups rather than to a single 4-digit SIC. The change reported for each occupation to the year 2005 is a percent of growth or decline as estimated by the Bureau of Labor Statistics. The abbreviation nec stands for not elsewhere classified.

U.S. AND STATE DATA ON INDUSTRY REVENUES AND OTHER ACCOUNTS FOR 1992

State	No. of Estab.	Employ-ment	Payroll ($ mil.)	Revenues ($ mil.)	Empl./ Estab.	Revenue/ Estab. ($)	Payroll/ Estab. ($)	Revenue/ Empl. ($)	Payroll/ Empl. ($)
UNITED STATES	10,381	108,235	5,934.2	43,634.1	10	4,203,267	571,644	403,142	54,827
Alabama	118	1,265	61.5	319.4	11	2,706,983	521,008	252,509	48,600
Alaska	19	546	12.5	78.4	29	4,124,895	657,000	143,540	22,863
Arizona	100	989	59.8	428.3	10	4,282,810	598,460	433,044	60,512
Arkansas	86	951	44.8	207.1	11	2,408,070	520,802	217,764	47,097
California	807	9,426	543.7	2,473.5	12	3,065,025	673,668	262,410	57,676
Colorado	150	1,840	106.9	756.2	12	5,041,580	712,660	410,998	58,097
Connecticut	216	1,705	130.1	822.1	8	3,806,060	602,116	482,175	76,280
Delaware	970	-	(D)	(D)	(D)	(D)	(D)	(D)	(D)
District of Columbia	30	305	24.6	270.8	10	9,027,033	818,567	887,905	80,515
Florida	499	5,508	249.3	1,144.9	11	2,294,467	499,525	207,868	45,255
Georgia	282	2,376	140.1	531.0	8	1,883,025	496,876	223,490	58,973
Hawaii	51	-	(D)	(D)	(D)	(D)	(D)	(D)	(D)
Idaho	19	-	(D)	(D)	(D)	(D)	(D)	(D)	(D)
Illinois	582	5,688	314.6	3,482.6	10	5,983,763	540,493	612,263	55,304
Indiana	184	1,677	118.2	693.7	9	3,770,228	642,446	413,668	70,489
Iowa	185	587	32.1	260.8	3	1,409,838	173,276	444,327	54,610
Kansas	170	2,175	79.3	547.4	13	3,219,906	466,429	251,671	36,457
Kentucky	116	1,727	93.5	504.3	15	4,347,845	805,784	292,038	54,123
Louisiana	108	917	44.9	631.9	8	5,851,093	415,935	689,115	48,987
Maine	42	237	14.3	46.1	6	1,098,167	340,190	194,612	60,287
Maryland	131	3,018	148.2	426.7	23	3,257,397	1,131,107	141,391	49,097
Massachusetts	221	2,408	115.6	798.4	11	3,612,557	523,213	331,551	48,019
Michigan	264	2,602	124.8	859.0	10	3,253,712	472,754	330,123	47,966
Minnesota	226	1,955	119.7	478.8	9	2,118,730	529,819	244,927	61,248
Mississippi	82	516	20.5	115.1	6	1,403,963	250,500	223,110	39,808
Missouri	275	2,723	141.0	1,433.5	10	5,212,760	512,640	526,445	51,772
Montana	30	169	8.1	57.2	6	1,905,200	268,533	338,201	47,669
Nebraska	124	901	43.1	226.0	7	1,822,266	347,226	250,789	47,787
Nevada	82	498	29.5	237.6	6	2,897,805	359,512	477,149	59,197
New Hampshire	48	1,155	41.9	198.3	24	4,130,708	872,104	171,666	36,243
New Jersey	289	5,474	265.2	1,361.3	19	4,710,381	917,751	248,685	48,453
New Mexico	37	805	36.5	71.7	22	1,937,081	986,568	89,034	45,345
New York	840	9,730	850.1	7,846.5	12	9,341,038	1,011,979	806,421	87,365
North Carolina	139	1,383	81.8	484.9	10	3,488,324	588,230	350,598	59,121
North Dakota	31	83	5.0	31.7	3	1,021,548	161,097	381,542	60,169
Ohio	397	5,821	257.6	1,916.8	15	4,828,277	648,768	329,295	44,247
Oklahoma	119	1,002	43.0	205.2	8	1,724,277	361,756	204,779	42,963
Oregon	80	1,261	54.5	101.5	16	1,268,475	681,662	80,474	43,246
Pennsylvania	398	5,674	336.8	1,493.4	14	3,752,254	846,158	263,200	59,353
Rhode Island	38	194	15.6	81.5	5	2,144,158	411,526	419,990	80,608
South Carolina	92	995	37.1	233.3	11	2,535,565	403,783	234,444	37,335
South Dakota	42	-	(D)	(D)	(D)	(D)	(D)	(D)	(D)
Tennessee	162	1,772	64.3	324.0	11	2,000,056	397,000	182,849	36,295
Texas	750	8,043	486.4	3,005.4	11	4,007,219	648,547	373,668	60,476
Utah	46	241	8.0	60.7	5	1,320,239	173,065	251,996	33,033
Vermont	23	88	4.8	35.5	4	1,544,826	208,261	403,761	54,432
Virginia	215	5,308	227.9	1,901.4	25	8,843,735	1,059,833	358,215	42,928
Washington	138	1,667	107.3	281.4	12	2,039,428	777,188	168,831	64,338
West Virginia	58	260	12.4	100.1	4	1,725,966	213,966	385,023	47,731
Wisconsin	251	2,594	115.5	817.8	10	3,258,259	460,032	315,275	44,513
Wyoming	19	81	1.9	30.9	4	1,627,895	100,842	381,852	23,654

Source: 1992 Economic Census, U.S. Department of Commerce, Washington, D.C. This is the only table that shows revenue data as collected by the Bureau of the Census in an Economic Census. The symbol (D) indicates that data are withheld by the source to avoid disclosure of competitive information. A dash (-) indicates that data are not available or cannot be calculated.

STATE-BY-STATE DATA ON ESTABLISHMENTS, EMPLOYMENT, AND PAYROLL - 1994 AND 1995

State	1994					1995					% Change Empl.
	No. of Estab.	Employ-ment	Pay / Empl.	Payroll ($ mil.)	Pay / Estab.	No. of Estab.	Employ-ment	Pay / Empl.	Payroll ($ mil.)	Pay / Estab.	
Alabama	75	1,089	59,383	68.5	912,933	75	922	88,499	74.1	987,400	-15.3
Alaska	18	313	56,396	15.0	831,278	18	284	54,197	11.6	647,167	-9.3
Arizona	92	1,072	62,041	65.2	708,859	97	1,473	72,519	98.3	1,013,711	37.4
Arkansas	60	1,539	40,153	58.0	966,917	57	1,381	52,672	60.7	1,065,632	-10.3
California	679	9,691	67,219	633.0	932,318	686	12,054	70,790	786.8	1,146,993	24.4
Colorado	128	2,169	83,078	152.1	1,188,109	130	2,360	76,203	179.6	1,381,492	8.8
Connecticut	142	1,994	80,351	156.4	1,101,669	144	2,359	94,292	187.9	1,304,604	18.3
Delaware	1,088	2,672	27,617	74.7	68,647	1,242	2,658	28,825	107.7	86,694	-0.5
District of Columbia	35	714	56,818	43.5	1,241,486	36	444	123,748	43.2	1,200,333	-37.8
Florida	396	4,646	57,908	261.9	661,472	414	4,928	62,093	277.2	669,655	6.1
Georgia	212	4,281	48,543	208.7	984,425	231	4,069	65,741	234.0	1,012,874	-5.0
Hawaii	29	228	62,105	13.6	470,655	32	291	50,213	14.7	458,281	27.6
Idaho	15	49	25,143	1.5	96,800	18	69	22,493	1.6	87,167	40.8
Illinois	395	9,376	60,172	547.5	1,386,048	405	8,692	62,874	529.6	1,307,533	-7.3
Indiana	108	1,164	64,065	71.8	664,870	112	1,567	79,045	114.8	1,024,973	34.6
Iowa	123	2,093	40,545	90.4	734,878	132	2,707	46,032	124.1	940,311	29.3
Kansas	105	1,988	39,143	75.1	714,762	109	2,394	42,814	101.4	930,413	20.4
Kentucky	92	2,506	55,936	126.1	1,370,978	90	2,341	58,474	125.9	1,399,289	-6.6
Louisiana	71	1,469	36,877	56.9	800,831	82	1,882	41,005	85.1	1,037,854	28.1
Maine	27	243	57,235	14.7	544,407	27	319	62,947	16.2	599,926	31.3
Maryland	96	3,862	47,792	182.0	1,895,417	94	3,435	52,157	175.7	1,869,138	-11.1
Massachusetts	155	1,741	64,460	115.6	745,671	158	1,963	75,069	136.4	863,222	12.8
Michigan	176	2,783	51,011	156.2	887,591	195	4,162	49,849	230.4	1,181,467	49.6
Minnesota	136	3,326	63,616	190.8	1,402,603	148	3,257	86,686	226.4	1,529,946	-2.1
Mississippi	34	520	44,015	19.7	580,088	34	418	52,775	20.1	592,471	-19.6
Missouri	194	3,409	46,998	173.9	896,284	205	4,521	56,479	245.4	1,197,122	32.6
Montana	24	290	42,221	12.7	529,083	27	419	30,749	12.6	465,741	44.5
Nebraska	81	1,038	55,002	54.9	677,889	86	1,102	64,490	66.2	770,058	6.2
Nevada	138	645	52,335	39.3	285,051	181	948	51,578	46.3	255,884	47.0
New Hampshire	29	483	45,093	22.2	765,241	30	416	49,375	25.4	845,633	-13.9
New Jersey	221	7,170	48,977	360.5	1,631,217	224	7,183	56,040	424.8	1,896,362	0.2
New Mexico	37	440	41,173	18.4	497,108	39	582	50,199	26.9	689,974	32.3
New York	647	15,764	68,132	1,032.2	1,595,289	676	13,434	102,379	1,213.2	1,794,738	-14.8
North Carolina	97	1,787	52,674	92.7	956,021	108	2,341	53,985	125.8	1,164,630	31.0
North Dakota	18	118	51,695	6.6	367,111	18	146	61,151	12.9	717,611	23.7
Ohio	293	5,480	47,428	244.3	833,942	289	5,579	52,980	281.0	972,145	1.8
Oklahoma	88	1,118	36,254	44.4	504,977	102	1,620	43,533	88.3	865,725	44.9
Oregon	84	1,774	43,436	86.1	1,025,274	90	2,205	45,633	94.9	1,054,044	24.3
Pennsylvania	243	7,494	46,130	354.2	1,457,494	240	7,682	52,619	388.4	1,618,129	2.5
Rhode Island	32	229	139,773	25.0	782,219	32	260	174,185	31.5	984,750	13.5
South Carolina	64	807	41,998	35.5	554,000	66	1,017	35,965	42.3	640,909	26.0
South Dakota	25	133	31,368	4.2	168,720	28	133	36,872	5.0	177,536	0.0
Tennessee	127	2,382	42,002	102.9	810,362	124	2,894	36,554	109.3	881,371	21.5
Texas	561	7,262	52,767	404.8	721,640	600	9,648	58,610	548.0	913,383	32.9
Utah	34	489	31,869	12.8	376,118	40	588	45,442	18.5	462,375	20.2
Vermont	31	487	35,877	17.2	555,032	29	504	37,952	18.8	647,034	3.5
Virginia	161	2,945	61,218	172.9	1,073,950	149	1,971	76,530	155.6	1,044,060	-33.1
Washington	96	1,389	61,898	75.8	789,833	108	1,401	68,674	86.5	800,880	0.9
West Virginia	41	650	47,551	32.8	800,659	43	702	49,396	34.8	809,000	8.0
Wisconsin	145	2,545	46,059	123.1	848,862	158	3,051	51,375	148.0	936,835	19.9
Wyoming	13	49	74,449	2.1	161,385	14	74	49,351	2.4	172,714	51.0

Source: County Business Patterns, U.S. Department of Commerce, Washington, D.C., for 1994 and 1995. Employment shown is for mid-March of the year shown. Payroll per employee is calculated by annualizing 1st Quarter payroll (not shown) and then dividing that value by mid-March employment. Dividing total annual payroll (columns 5 and 10) by employment, therefore, will *not* yield the payroll per employee figure (columns 4 and 9). The symbol (D) indicates that data are withheld by the source to avoid disclosure of competitive information. A dash (-) indicates that data are not available or cannot be calculated.

ESTABLISHMENTS 1995 - STATE AND REGIONAL CONCENTRATION

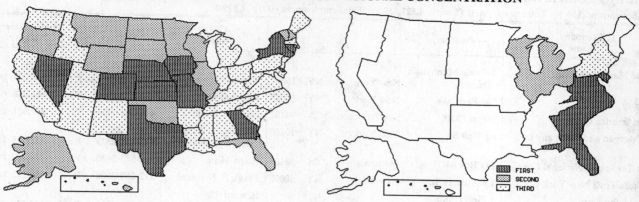

EMPLOYMENT 1995 - STATE AND REGIONAL CONCENTRATION

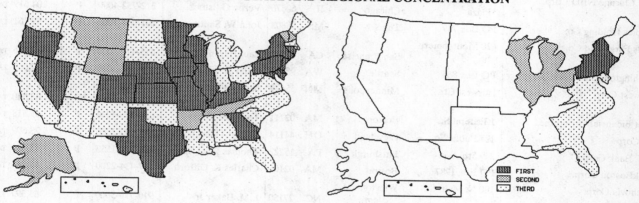

PAYROLL 1995 - STATE AND REGIONAL CONCENTRATION

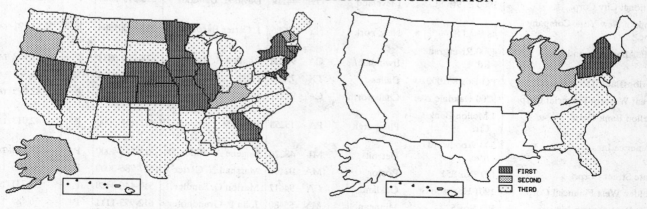

States with the darkest shading indicate those states which have proportionately more establishments, employment, or payrolls than would be indicated by the state's population. States with light shading are states with proportionately fewer establishments, less employment, and lower payrolls than population distribution. States shaded grey are within 15 percent of the state's population proportion in these categories. States for which no data are available are shown as average (grey). *Regions* are shaded to indicate absolute rank in the category. If no data for the category are available, establishment counts are used to shade the regions. Source of the data is the table on the facing page.

LEADING COMPANIES - SIC 6712 - Bank Holding Companies

Number shown: **100**   Total sales/assets ($ mil): **4,127,850**   Total employment (000): **1,579.0**

Company Name	Address				CEO Name	Phone	Co. Type	Sales/Assets ($ mil)	Empl. (000)
Chase Manhattan Corp.	1 Chase Manhattan Plaza	New York	NY	10081	Walter V. Shipley	212-552-2222	P	336,099 TA	67.8
Citicorp	399 Park Ave.	New York	NY	10043	John S. Reed	212-559-1000	P	281,018 TA	90.0
BankAmerica Corp.	Dept. 13018	San Francisco	CA	94137	David A. Coulter	415-622-3456	P	255,801 TA	92.1
J.P. Morgan and Company Inc.	60 Wall St.	New York	NY	10260	Douglas A. Warner III	212-483-2323	P	252,895 TA	16.9
First Tennessee National Corp.	PO Box 84	Memphis	TN	38101	Ralph Horn	901-523-5630	P	144,000 TA	8.2
Bankers Trust New York Corp.	130 Liberty St.	New York	NY	10006	Frank N. Newman	212-250-2500	P	140,102 TA	18.3
First Union Corp.	1 First Union Center	Charlotte	NC	28288	Edward E. Crutchfield	704-374-6565	P	134,127 TA	44.3
Banc One Corp.	100 E. Broad St.	Columbus	OH	43271	Richard J. Lehmann	614-248-5800	P	115,901 TA	56.6
First Chicago NBD Corp.	1 First National Plaza	Chicago	IL	60670	Verne G. Istock	312-732-4000	P	104,619 TA	33.4
Peoples Holding Co.	PO Box 709	Tupelo	MS	38802	John W. Smith	601-680-1001	P	99,161 TA	0.6
Wells Fargo and Co.	420 Montgomery St.	San Francisco	CA	94163	Paul Hazen	415-477-1000	P	97,456 TA	36.9
Washington Mutual Inc.	PO Box 834	Seattle	WA	98111	Kerry K. Killinger	206-461-2000	P	97,069 TA	8.3
Norwest Corp.	Norwest Ctr.	Minneapolis	MN	55479	Richard M. Kovacevich	612-667-1234	P	88,540 TA	57.0
Fleet Financial Group Inc.	1 Federal St.	Boston	MA	02211	Terrence Murray	617-346-4000	P	85,518 TA	36.0
KeyCorp	127 Public Sq.	Cleveland	OH	44114	Robert Gillespie	216-689-3000	P	73,699 TA	27.0
PNC Bank Corp.	249 5th Ave.	Pittsburgh	PA	15222	Thomas H. O'Brien	412-762-1553	P	73,260 TA	25.4
BankBoston Corp.	PO Box 1987	Boston	MA	02105	Charles K. Gifford	617-434-2200	P	69,268 TA	21.5
Wachovia Corp.	100 N. Main St.	Winston-Salem	NC	27150	L.M. Baker Jr.	910-770-5000	P	65,397 TA	21.7
SunTrust Banks Inc.	PO Box 4418	Atlanta	GA	30302	James B. Williams	404-588-7711	P	57,983 TA	21.2
Republic New York Corp.	452 5th Ave.	New York	NY	10018	Walter H. Weiner	212-525-6100	P	55,638 TA	5.9
National City Corp.	1900 E. 9th St.	Cleveland	OH	44114	David A. Daberko	216-575-2000	P	54,684 TA	29.8
Bank of New York Company Inc.	48 Wall St.	New York	NY	10286	J. Carter Bacot	212-495-1784	P	52,891 TA	15.8
H.F. Ahmanson and Co.	4900 Rivergrade Rd.	Irwindale	CA	91706	Charles R. Rinehart	818-960-6311	P	49,902 TA	9.5
NationsBank Texas Corp.	PO Box 831000	Dallas	TX	75283	Hugh L. McColl Jr.	214-508-6262	S	48,368 TA	20.6
Great Western Financial Corp.	9200 Oakdale Ave.	Chatsworth	CA	91311	John F. Maher	818-775-3411	P	42,875 TA	13.0
Mellon Bank Corp.	1 Mellon Bank Ctr.	Pittsburgh	PA	15258	Frank V. Cahouet	412-234-5000	P	42,013 TA	24.7
Comerica Inc.	500 Woodward Ave.	Detroit	MI	48226	Eugene A. Miller	313-222-4000	P	39,678 TA	13.5
State Street Corp.	PO Box 351	Boston	MA	02101	Marshall N. Carter	617-786-3000	P	37,975 TA	14.2
Golden West Financial Corp.	1901 Harrison St.	Oakland	CA	94612	Marion O. Sandler	510-446-3420	P	37,731 TA	4.5
First Bank System Inc.	PO Box 522	Minneapolis	MN	55480	John F. Grundhofer	612-973-1111	P	36,489 TA	12.0
First Fidelity Bancorp.	550 Broad St.	Newark	NJ	07102	Anthony P. Terracciano	201-565-3200	P	36,216 TA	12.0
Boatmen's Bancshares Inc.	800 Market St.	St. Louis	MO	63101	Andrew B. Craig III	314-466-6000	P	33,704 TA	17.0
U.S. Bancorp	PO Box 4412	Portland	OR	97208	Gerry B. Cameron	503-275-6111	P	33,260 TA	14.1

Company type codes: P - Public, R - Private, S - Subsidiary, D - Division, J - Joint Venture, A - Affiliate, G - Group. If the dollar values shown are not sales, the following codes apply: TA - Total Assets; OR - Operating Revenues; GB - Gross Billings. * - estimated dollar value. < - less than. *na* - not available.

Continued on next page.

LEADING COMPANIES - SIC 6712 - Bank Holding Companies
Continued

Company Name	Address				CEO Name	Phone	Co. Type	Sales/Assets ($ mil)	Empl. (000)
SouthTrust Corp.	PO Box 2554	Birmingham	AL	35290	Wallace D. Malone Jr.	205-254-5000	P	30,906 TA	10.3
Summit Bancorp.	PO Box 2066	Princeton	NJ	08543	T. Joseph Semrod	609-987-3200	P	29,964 TA	7.3
UnionBanCal Corp.	PO Box 7104	San Francisco	CA	94119	Takahiro Moriguchi	415-705-7000	P	29,693 TA	9.8
Marine Midland Banks Inc.	1 Marine Midland Ctr.	Buffalo	NY	14240	Jim Cleave	716-841-2424	S	28,300 TA	9.6
SunTrust Banks of Florida Inc.	PO Box 3833	Orlando	FL	32802	George W. Koehn	407-237-4141	S	27,585 TA	7.9
Huntington Bancshares Inc.	41 S. High St.	Columbus	OH	43287	Frank Wobst	614-480-8300	P	26,731 TA	9.5
Harris Bankcorp Inc.	111 W. Monroe St.	Chicago	IL	60603	Alan G. McNally	312-461-2121	S	22,200 TA	6.6
Dime Bancorp Inc.	589 5th Ave.	New York	NY	10017	Lawrence J. Total	212-326-6170	P	21,848 TA	3.2
Crestar Financial Corp.	PO Box 26665	Richmond	VA	23261	Richard G. Tilghman	804-782-5000	P	21,810 TA	8.2
Fifth Third Bancorp.	Fifth Third Ctr.	Cincinnati	OH	45263	George A. Schaefer Jr.	513-579-5300	P	21,375 TA	6.8
MBNA Corp.	1100 N. King St.	Wilmington	DE	19884	Charles M. Cawley	302-453-9930	P	21,306 TA	20.0
First of America Bank Corp.	211 S. Rose St.	Kalamazoo	MI	49007	Richard F. Chorman	616-376-9000	P	21,080 TA	10.6
Firstar Corp.	777 E. Wisconsin Ave.	Milwaukee	WI	53202	Roger L. Fitzsimonds	414-765-4321	P	19,323 TA	7.8
Popular Inc.	PO Box 362708	San Juan	PR	00936	Richard L. Carrion	787-765-9800	P	19,301 TA	8.9
Mercantile Bancorporation Inc.	PO Box 524	St. Louis	MO	63166	Thomas H. Jacobsen	314-425-2525	P	19,188 TA	7.9
Regions Financial Corp.	PO Box 10247	Birmingham	AL	35202	J. Stanley Mackin	205-326-7100	P	18,930 TA	8.1
AmSouth Bancorp.	1400 AmSouth-Sonat Twr.	Birmingham	AL	35203	C. Dowd Ritter	205-320-7151	P	18,600 TA	6.4
Northern Trust Corp.	50 S. La Salle St.	Chicago	IL	60675	David W. Fox	312-630-6000	P	18,562 TA	6.6
Union Planters Corp.	PO Box 387	Memphis	TN	38147	Benjamin W. Rawlins Jr.	901-580-6000	P	18,105 TA	5.2
SunTrust Banks of Georgia Inc.	PO Box 4418	Atlanta	GA	30302	Edward P. Gould	404-827-6510	S	16,854 TA	4.5
Citizens Financial Group Inc.	1 Citizens Plaza	Providence	RI	02903	Lawrence K. Fish	401-456-7000	P	16,221 TA	3.2
Simmons First National Corp.	PO Box 7009	Pine Bluff	AR	71611	J. Thomas May	501-541-1000	P	16,000 TA	0.7
Standard Federal Bancorporation Inc.	PO Box 3703	Troy	MI	48007	Thomas R. Ricketts	810-643-9600	P	15,651 TA	4.0
Ford Motor Co.	PO Box 1899	Dearborn	MI	48121	Alex Trotman	313-322-3000	P	15,363	363.9
Banc One Arizona Corp.	PO Box 71	Phoenix	AZ	85001	Mike Wellborn	602-221-2900	S	15,257 TA*	5.5
Pacific Century Financial Corp.	PO Box 2900	Honolulu	HI	96846	Lawrence M. Johnson	808-643-3888	P	14,996 TA	5.1
First Nationwide Holdings Inc.	14651 Dallas Pkwy.	Dallas	TX	75240	Gerald J. Ford	214-770-3700	S	14,600 TA	3.5
Sovereign Bancorp Inc.	PO Box 12646	Reading	PA	19612	Jay S. Sidhu	610-320-8400	P	14,336 TA	2.0
Marshall and Ilsley Corp.	770 N. Water St.	Milwaukee	WI	53202	James B. Wigdale	414-765-7801	P	14,271 TA	11.4
First Maryland Bancorp.	25 S. Charles St.	Baltimore	MD	21201	Frank P. Bramble	410-244-4000	P	14,132 TA	7.1
First Empire State Corp.	PO Box 223	Buffalo	NY	14240	Robert G. Wilmers	716-842-5138	P	14,003 TA	5.1
Charter One Financial Inc.	1215 Superior Ave.	Cleveland	OH	44114	Charles J. Koch	216-566-5300	P	13,894 TA	2.6
Old Kent Financial Corp.	111 Lyon St. N.W.	Grand Rapids	MI	49503	David J. Wagner	616-771-5000	P	13,774 TA	6.3
GreenPoint Financial Corp.	1981 Marcus Ave.	Lake Success	NY	11419	Thomas S. Johnson	516-327-1100	P	13,083 TA	2.5
Compass Bancshares	15 S. 20th St.	Birmingham	AL	35233	D. Paul Jones Jr.	205-933-3000	P	12,602 TA	5.5

Company type codes: P - Public, R - Private, S - Subsidiary, D - Division, J - Joint Venture, A - Affiliate, G - Group. If the dollar values shown are not sales, the following codes apply: TA - Total Assets; OR - Operating Revenues; GB - Gross Billings. * - estimated dollar value. < - less than. *na* - not available.

Continued on next page.

LEADING COMPANIES - SIC 6712 - Bank Holding Companies
Continued

Company Name	Address				CEO Name	Phone	Co. Type	Sales/Assets ($ mil)	Empl. (000)
LaSalle National Corp.	135 S. La Salle St.	Chicago	IL	60603	Ted Roberts	312-443-2000	S	12,385 TA	3.5
NBT Bancorp Inc.	52 S. Broad St.	Norwich	NY	13815	Daryl R. Forsythe	607-337-6000	P	12,000 TA	0.5
Bank United Corp.	3200 Southwest Fwy.	Houston	TX	77027	Barry C. Burkholder	516-543-6500	P	11,967 TA	1.4
MainStreet BankGroup Inc.	PO Box 4831	Martinsville	VA	24115	Michael R. Brenan	703-632-2971	P	11,500 TA	0.6
Star Banc Corp.	425 Walnut St.	Cincinnati	OH	45202	Jerry A. Grundhofer	513-632-4000	P	10,959 TA	0.3
Associated Banc-Corp.	PO Box 13307	Green Bay	WI	54307	Harry B. Conlon	414-433-3166	P	10,700 TA	2.0
Central Fidelity Banks Inc.	PO Box 27602	Richmond	VA	23261	Lewis N. Miller Jr.	804-782-4000	P	10,540 TA	3.5
First American Corp.	1st American Ctr.	Nashville	TN	37237	Dennis C. Bottorff	615-748-2000	P	10,400 TA	3.6
Commerce Bancshares Inc.	PO Box 13686	Kansas City	MO	64199	David W. Kemper	816-234-2000	P	10,307 TA	4.3
Zions Bancorp.	One Main St.	Salt Lake City	UT	84111	Harris H. Simmons	801-524-4787	P	9,521 TA	4.9
Michigan National Corp.	PO Box 9065	Farmington Hills	MI	48333	Douglas E. Ebert	248-473-3000	S	9,329 TA	4.0
Hibernia Corp.	PO Box 61540	New Orleans	LA	70161	Stephen A. Hansel	504-533-3332	P	9,307 TA	4.5
Synovus Financial Corp.	PO Box 120	Columbus	GA	31902	James H. Blanchard	706-649-2387	P	9,260 TA	8.1
First Commerce Corp.	PO Box 60279	New Orleans	LA	70160	Ian Arnof	504-561-1371	P	9,183 TA	3.8
Roosevelt Financial Group Inc.	900 Roosevelt Pkwy.	Chesterfield	MO	63017	Stanley J. Bradshaw	314-532-6200	P	9,013 TA	1.2
First Citizens BancShares Inc.	PO Box 151	Raleigh	NC	27602	Lewis R. Holding	919-755-7000	P	8,951 TA	4.3
Coast Savings Financial Inc.	1000 Wilshire Blvd.	Los Angeles	CA	90017	Ray Martin	213-362-2000	P	8,705 TA	1.5
First Virginia Banks Inc.	6400 Arlington Blvd.	Falls Church	VA	22042	Barry J. Fitzpatrick	703-241-4000	P	8,660 TA	5.7
Banc One Wisconsin Corp.	PO Box 481	Milwaukee	WI	53201	William Reed	414-765-3000	S	8,267 TA	2.8
TCF Financial Corp.	801 Marquette Ave.	Minneapolis	MN	55402	William A. Cooper	612-661-6500	P	8,174 TA	4.7
First Hawaiian Inc.	PO Box 3200	Honolulu	HI	96847	Walter A. Dods Jr.	808-525-7000	P	7,918 TA	3.2
People's Mutual Holdings	850 Main St.	Bridgeport	CT	06604	David E. Carson	203-338-7171	R	7,645 TA	3.0
First USA Inc.	1601 Elm St.	Dallas	TX	75201	John C. Tolleson	214-849-2000	P	7,635 TA	2.0
Commercial Federal Corp.	2120 South 72nd St.	Omaha	NE	68124	William A. Fitzgerald	402-554-9200	P	7,097 TA	1.5
Colorado National Bankshares Inc.	PO Box 5168	Denver	CO	80202	Robert J. Malone	303-585-5000	S	7,076 TA	2.0
Webster Financial Corp.	Webster Plz.	Waterbury	CT	06702	James C. Smith	203-753-2921	P	7,020 TA	1.1
Deposit Guaranty Corp.	PO Box 1200	Jackson	MS	39215	IV, H. Lawson Hembree	601-354-8564	P	6,940 TA	3.5
Provident Bancorp Inc.	1 East 4th St.	Cincinnati	OH	45202	Allen L. Davis	513-579-2000	P	6,905 TA	2.5
First Commercial Corp.	400 W. Capitol Ave.	Little Rock	AR	72201	Barnett Grace	501-371-7000	P	6,887 TA	3.3
Colonial BancGroup Inc.	PO Box 1108	Montgomery	AL	36101	Robert E. Lowder	334-240-5000	P	6,851 TA	3.0
Peoples Heritage Financial Group Inc.	P.O.Box 9540	Portland	ME	04112	William J. Ryan	207-761-8500	P	6,795 TA	2.7
SunTrust Banks of Tennessee Inc.	PO Box 305110	Nashville	TN	37230	John W. Clay Jr.	615-748-4000	S	6,776 TA	2.6

*Source: Ward's Business Directory of U.S. Private and Public Companies, 1996. Company type codes: P - Public, R - Private, S - Subsidiary, D - Division, J - Joint Venture, A - Affiliate, G - Group. If the dollar values shown are not sales, the following codes apply: TA - Total Assets; OR - Operating Revenues; GB - Gross Billings. * - estimated dollar value. < - less than; na - not available.*

ESTABLISHMENTS 1995 - STATE AND REGIONAL CONCENTRATION

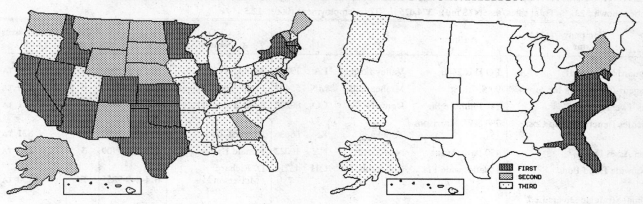

EMPLOYMENT 1995 - STATE AND REGIONAL CONCENTRATION

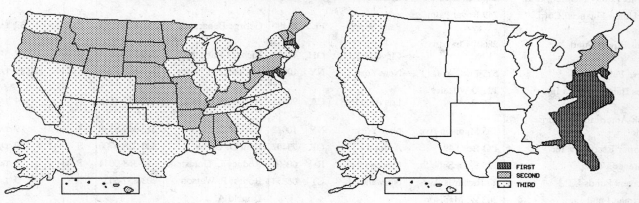

PAYROLL 1995 - STATE AND REGIONAL CONCENTRATION

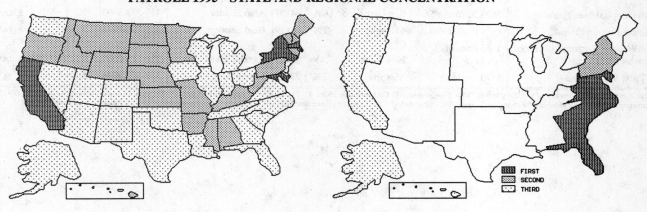

States with the darkest shading indicate those states which have proportionately more establishments, employment, or payrolls than would be indicated by the state's population. States with light shading are states with proportionately fewer establishments, less employment, and lower payrolls than population distribution. States shaded grey are within 15 percent of the state's population proportion in these categories. States for which no data are available are shown as average (grey). *Regions* are shaded to indicate absolute rank in the category. If no data for the category are available, establishment counts are used to shade the regions. Source of the data is the table on the facing page.

LEADING COMPANIES - SIC 6722 - Management Investment, Open-End

Number shown: **23**   Total sales/assets ($ mil): **374,026**   Total employment (000): **12.5**

Company Name	Address				CEO Name	Phone	Co. Type	Sales/Assets ($ mil)	Empl. (000)
Vanguard Windsor II	PO Box 2600	Valley Forge	PA	19482	John C. Bogle	610-669-1000	3	360,000 TA	10.0
Voyageur Companies Inc.	90 S. 7th St.	Minneapolis	MN	55402	Frank Tonnemaker	612-376-7000	S	6,500 TA	<0.1
Janus Twenty Fund	100 Fillmore St.	Denver	CO	80206	Scott Schoelzel	303-333-3863	3	5,871 TA	<0.1
Securities Benefit Group Cos.	700 S.W. Harrison St.	Topeka	KS	66636	Howard Fricke	913-295-3000	R	821 TA	0.6
Baron Asset Fund	450 Park Ave.	New York	NY	10022	Ronald Baron	212-759-7700	3	290 TA	<0.1
Nationwide Bond Fund	1 Nationwide Plz.	Columbus	OH	43216	D. Richard McFerson	614-249-7855	S	130 TA	<0.1
Colonial Strategic Diversified Income Fund	1 Financial Ctr.	Boston	MA	02111	Hal Cogger	617-426-3750	R	130 TA*	0.7
AIM Equity Funds Inc.	11 Greenway Plz.	Houston	TX	77046	Charles T. Bauer	713-626-1919	S	100 TA*	0.6
Phoenix Equity Planning Corp.	PO Box 2200	Enfield	CT	06083	Phillip McLoughlin	203-253-1000	S	40 TA	0.3
InterUnion Financial Corp.	249 Royal Palm Way	Palm Beach	FL	33480	George Benarroch	561-820-0084	P	39 TA	<0.1
Maxus Equity Fund	28601 Chagrin Blvd.	Cleveland	OH	44122	Richard Barone	216-292-3434	P	37	<0.1
Revere Fund Inc.	575 Fifth Ave.	New York	NY	10017	Michael E. Chaney	212-661-5290	3	22 TA	<0.1
James Buchanan Rea Inc.	12100 Wilshire Blvd.	Los Angeles	CA	90025	Jr., James B. Rea	310-442-2660	R	14 TA	<0.1
Polish-American Enterprise Fund	535 Madison Ave.	New York	NY	10022	Robert G. Faris	212-339-8330	3	9 TA*	<0.1
Tripower Resources Inc.	PO Box 849	Ardmore	OK	73402	John D. Gibbs	580-226-6700	S	7 TA*	<0.1
Frontenac VI	135 S. La Salle St.	Chicago	IL	60603	Rodney L. Goldstein	312-368-0044	R	5 TA*	<0.1
Managers Funds L.P.	40 Richards Ave.	Norwalk	CT	06854	Robert P. Watson	203-857-5321	R	3 TA*	<0.1
Yacktman Fund	303 W. Madison St.	Chicago	IL	60606	Donald A. Yacktman	312-201-9400	3	2 TA	<0.1
Mint Investment Management Co.	2 Hudson Pl.	Hoboken	NJ	07030	David Hall	201-216-8820	R	2 TA*	<0.1
Snyder Capital Management	350 California St.	San Francisco	CA	94104	Alan Snyder	415-392-3900	R	1 TA*	<0.1
Longleaf Partners Fund	6075 Poplar Ave.	Memphis	TN	38119	Reid Sanders	901-761-2474	3	1 TA*	<0.1
PaineWebber Regional Financial Growth Fund	1285 Ave. of Amer.	New York	NY	10019	Karen Finkle	212-713-2000	3	1 TA*	<0.1
AmTrust Value Fund	PO Box 3467	Victoria	TX	77903	Jimmy Baker	512-578-7778	3	1 TA	<0.1

Source: *Ward's Business Directory of U.S. Private and Public Companies*, 1996. Company type codes: P - Public, R - Private, S - Subsidiary, D - Division, J - Joint Venture, A - Affiliate, G - Group. If the dollar values shown are not sales, the following codes apply: TA - Total Assets; OR - Operating Revenues; GB - Gross Billings. * - estimated dollar value. < - less than; *na* - not available.

LEADING COMPANIES - SIC 6726 - Investment Offices, nec

Number shown: **22**   Total sales/assets ($ mil): **19,579**   Total employment (000): **3.9**

Company Name	Address				CEO Name	Phone	Co. Type	Sales/Assets ($ mil)	Empl. (000)
Pacific Mutual Life Insurance Co.	700 Newport Center Dr.	Newport Beach	CA	92660	Thomas C. Sutton	714-640-3011	R	11,547 TA*	2.5
Voyageur Companies Inc.	90 S. 7th St.	Minneapolis	MN	55402	Frank Tonnemaker	612-376-7000	S	6,500 TA	<0.1
Sirrom Capital Corp.	500 Church St.	Nashville	TN	37219	George M. Miller II	615-256-0701	P	509 TA	<0.1
Chicago Milwaukee Corp.	547 W. Jackson Blvd.	Chicago	IL	60661	Edwin Jacobson	312-822-0400	3	296 TA	<0.1
Preferred Income Opportunity Fund Inc.	301 E. Colorado Blvd.	Pasadena	CA	91101	Robert T. Flaherty	818-795-7300	3	200 OR	<0.1
PMC Capital Inc.	17290 Preston Rd.	Dallas	TX	75252	Lance B. Rosemore	214-380-0044	3	157 TA	<0.1
Macerich Partnership L.P.	PO Box 2172	Santa Monica	CA	90407	Arthur M. Coppola	310-394-5333	S	155 OR	0.9
First Robinson Financial Corp.	501 E. Main St.	Robinson	IL	62454	Rick L. Catt	618-544-8621	P	68 TA	<0.1
First Carolina Investors Inc.	PO Box 33607	Charlotte	NC	28233	H. Thomas Webb III	704-846-1066	3	58 TA	<0.1
Mitchell Hutchins Asset Management Inc.	1285 Ave. of the Amer	New York	NY	10019	Joyce Fensterstock	212-713-2000	S	34 OR*	0.2
MorAmerica Capital Corp.	101 2nd St. S.E.	Cedar Rapids	IA	52401	Carl Schuettpelz	319-363-8249	3	15 TA	<0.1
Rand Capital Corp.	1300 Rand Bldg.	Buffalo	NY	14203	Allen F. Grum	716-853-0802	3	10 TA	<0.1
Enercorp Inc.	7001 Orchard Lake Rd.	West Bloomfield	MI	48322	Robert R. Hebard	810-851-5654	3	7 TA	<0.1
Harbourton Mortgage Corp.	3800 Greensboro Dr.	McLean	VA	22102	Steven P. Gavula	703-883-2900	3	6 TA*	<0.1
Gold Company of America	1 Seaport Plz. 33rd Fl	New York	NY	10292	James Kelso	212-214-1000	3	5 TA	<0.1
NAIC Growth Fund Inc.	1515 E. 11 Mile Rd.	Royal Oak	MI	48067	Thomas E. O'Hara	313-543-0612	3	5 TA	<0.1
Greenspring Fund Inc.	2330 W. Joppa Rd. #110	Baltimore	MD	21210	Daniel R. Long III	410-823-5353	3	4 TA	<0.1
E.I. Biskind and Associates	1121 E. Main St.	St. Charles	IL	60174	Edward I. Biskind	708-513-0497	R	1 TA*	<0.1
Investad Inc.	200 Jefferson Ave.	Memphis	TN	38103	M. Kirk	901-683-1546	3	1 TA*	<0.1
Venture Capital Fund of New England	160 Federal St.	Boston	MA	02110	Richard Farrell	617-439-4646	R	1 TA	<0.1
Medallion Financial Corp.	205 E. 42nd St.	New York	NY	10017	Alvin Murstein	212-682-3300	3	1 TA	<0.1
Quaestus Partner Fund L.P.	330 E. Kilbourn Ave.	Milwaukee	WI	53202	Richard Weening	414-283-4500	3	0 TA*	<0.1

Source: *Ward's Business Directory of U.S. Private and Public Companies*, 1996. Company type codes: P - Public, R - Private, S - Subsidiary, D - Division, J - Joint Venture, A - Affiliate, G - Group. If the dollar values shown are not sales, the following codes apply: TA - Total Assets; OR - Operating Revenues; GB - Gross Billings. * - estimated dollar value. < - less than; *na* - not available.

SIC 6732

EDUCATIONAL, RELIGIOUS, ETC. TRUSTS

Educational, religious, and charitable trusts are establishments primarily engaged in the management of funds of trusts and foundations organized for religious, educational, charitable, or nonprofit research purposes. The SIC includes charitable trusts, educational trusts, and religious trusts. The trust operations of not-for-profit research institutes are included under this SIC; the operational activities of such institutes are classified under appropriate Service Industry categories (e.g. business, health, educational, social, or engineering services).

ESTABLISHMENTS, EMPLOYMENT, AND PAYROLL

	1990	1991		1992		1993		1994		1995		% change 90-95
		Value	%	Value	%	Value	%	Value	%	Value	%	
All Establishments	3,595	4,391	22.1	4,632	5.5	4,708	1.6	2,197	-53.3	2,477	12.7	-31.1
Mid-March Employment	41,508	37,000	-10.9	37,048	0.1	36,539	-1.4	17,353	-52.5	20,485	18.0	-50.6
1st Quarter Wages (annualized - $ mil.)	845.9	799.2	-5.5	881.4	10.3	874.2	-0.8	431.6	-50.6	504.4	16.9	-40.4
Payroll per Emp. 1st Q. (annualized)	20,379	21,599	6.0	23,791	10.1	23,925	0.6	24,872	4.0	24,621	-1.0	20.8
Annual Payroll ($ mil.)	897.2	836.6	-6.8	909.9	8.8	958.0	5.3	473.4	-50.6	569.6	20.3	-36.5
Establishments - 1-4 Emp. Number	2,360	3,020	28.0	3,238	7.2	3,257	0.6	1,520	-53.3	1,705	12.2	-27.8
Mid-March Employment	4,179	5,105	22.2	5,596	9.6	5,568	-0.5	2,234	-59.9	2,594	16.1	-37.9
1st Quarter Wages (annualized - $ mil.)	92.4	115.7	25.3	133.2	15.1	133.2	0.0	61.6	-53.7	65.5	6.3	-29.1
Payroll per Emp. 1st Q. (annualized)	22,105	22,669	2.6	23,797	5.0	23,917	0.5	27,595	15.4	25,264	-8.4	14.3
Annual Payroll ($ mil.)	111.0	128.6	15.9	147.0	14.3	151.4	2.9	73.4	-51.5	86.6	18.0	-22.0
Establishments - 5-9 Emp. Number	530	629	18.7	667	6.0	702	5.2	310	-55.8	343	10.6	-35.3
Mid-March Employment	3,485	4,094	17.5	4,306	5.2	4,526	5.1	2,096	-53.7	2,241	6.9	-35.7
1st Quarter Wages (annualized - $ mil.)	82.0	100.1	22.1	108.6	8.5	118.9	9.5	57.2	-51.9	58.7	2.7	-28.4
Payroll per Emp. 1st Q. (annualized)	23,527	24,460	4.0	25,227	3.1	26,278	4.2	27,269	3.8	26,185	-4.0	11.3
Annual Payroll ($ mil.)	83.4	101.5	21.8	113.9	12.3	127.3	11.7	57.8	-54.5	61.1	5.6	-26.7
Establishments - 10-19 Emp. Number	345	383	11.0	395	3.1	415	5.1	195	-53.0	229	17.4	-33.6
Mid-March Employment	4,635	5,128	10.6	5,293	3.2	5,589	5.6	2,609	-53.3	3,117	19.5	-32.8
1st Quarter Wages (annualized - $ mil.)	96.9	119.3	23.1	116.0	-2.8	133.5	15.1	64.9	-51.4	76.5	17.8	-21.1
Payroll per Emp. 1st Q. (annualized)	20,909	23,272	11.3	21,919	-5.8	23,883	9.0	24,871	4.1	24,531	-1.4	17.3
Annual Payroll ($ mil.)	103.7	123.2	18.8	123.3	0.1	140.7	14.1	69.9	-50.3	78.0	11.6	-24.8
Establishments - 20-49 Emp. Number	223	255	14.3	234	-8.2	235	0.4	119	-49.4	138	16.0	-38.1
Mid-March Employment	6,718	7,084	5.4	6,823	-3.7	7,030	3.0	3,405	-51.6	3,984	17.0	-40.7
1st Quarter Wages (annualized - $ mil.)	142.7	148.8	4.3	161.4	8.5	173.3	7.4	91.0	-47.5	110.5	21.4	-22.6
Payroll per Emp. 1st Q. (annualized)	21,243	21,005	-1.1	23,651	12.6	24,652	4.2	26,735	8.4	27,742	3.8	30.6
Annual Payroll ($ mil.)	148.7	157.2	5.8	168.3	7.0	183.5	9.0	98.0	-46.6	116.6	19.0	-21.6
Establishments - 50-99 Emp. Number	67	51	-23.9	(D)	-	(D)	-	29	-	(D)	-	-
Mid-March Employment	4,457	3,533	-20.7	(D)	-	(D)	-	2,088	-	(D)	-	-
1st Quarter Wages (annualized - $ mil.)	82.1	62.6	-23.8	(D)	-	(D)	-	50.1	-	(D)	-	-
Payroll per Emp. 1st Q. (annualized)	18,429	17,723	-3.8	(D)	-	(D)	-	24,002	-	(D)	-	-
Annual Payroll ($ mil.)	87.0	61.4	-29.5	(D)	-	(D)	-	56.8	-	(D)	-	-
Establishments - 100-249 Emp. Number	46	39	-15.2	32	-17.9	34	6.3	19	-44.1	24	26.3	-47.8
Mid-March Employment	7,081	6,187	-12.6	4,721	-23.7	5,154	9.2	2,991	-42.0	3,534	18.2	-50.1
1st Quarter Wages (annualized - $ mil.)	118.9	136.4	14.8	118.0	-13.5	134.8	14.2	69.1	-48.8	98.1	42.0	-17.5
Payroll per Emp. 1st Q. (annualized)	16,786	22,047	31.3	24,995	13.4	26,153	4.6	23,092	-11.7	27,757	20.2	65.4
Annual Payroll ($ mil.)	122.4	143.0	16.9	121.8	-14.8	162.6	33.5	73.5	-54.8	125.9	71.3	2.9
Establishments - 250-499 Emp. Number	17	11	-35.3	10	-9.1	10	-	5	-50.0	(D)	-	-
Mid-March Employment	5,621	(D)	-	3,532	-	3,675	4.0	1,930	-47.5	(D)	-	-
1st Quarter Wages (annualized - $ mil.)	129.1	(D)	-	108.3	-	82.3	-23.9	37.7	-54.2	(D)	-	-
Payroll per Emp. 1st Q. (annualized)	22,967	(D)	-	30,651	-	22,408	-26.9	19,534	-12.8	(D)	-	-
Annual Payroll ($ mil.)	134.6	(D)	-	91.7	-	89.0	-2.9	44.0	-50.6	(D)	-	-
Establishments - 500-999 Emp. Number	6	3	-50.0	(D)	-	(D)	-	-	-	(D)	-	-
Mid-March Employment	(D)	(D)	-	(D)	-	(D)	-	-	-	(D)	-	-
1st Quarter Wages (annualized - $ mil.)	(D)	(D)	-	(D)	-	(D)	-	-	-	(D)	-	-
Payroll per Emp. 1st Q. (annualized)	(D)	(D)	-	(D)	-	(D)	-	-	-	(D)	-	-
Annual Payroll ($ mil.)	(D)	(D)	-	(D)	-	(D)	-	-	-	(D)	-	-
Estab. - 1000 or More Emp. Number	1	-	-	-	-	-	-	-	-	-	-	-
Mid-March Employment	(D)	-	-	-	-	-	-	-	-	-	-	-
1st Quarter Wages (annualized - $ mil.)	(D)	-	-	-	-	-	-	-	-	-	-	-
Payroll per Emp. 1st Q. (annualized)	(D)	(D)	-	-	-	-	-	-	-	-	-	-
Annual Payroll ($ mil.)	(D)	-	-	-	-	-	-	-	-	-	-	-

Source: County Business Patterns, U.S. Department of Commerce, Washington, D.C., for 1990 through 1995. Payroll per employee is calculated using mid-March employment and 1st Quarter wages, annualized. Annual payroll, also shown, may not equal the annualized 1st Quarter wages. Columns headed by a percent sign (%) indicate change from the previous year. *na* stands for not available. The symbol (D) indicates that data are withheld by the source to avoid disclosure of competitive information. A dash (-) indicates that data are not available or cannot be calculated.

ESTABLISHMENTS
Number

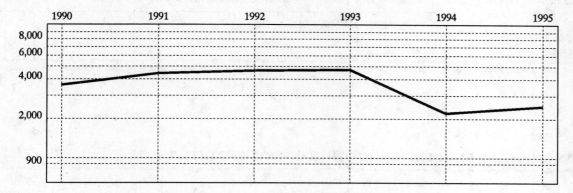

MID-MARCH EMPLOYMENT
Number

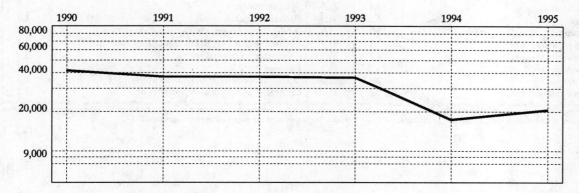

ANNUAL PAYROLL
$ million

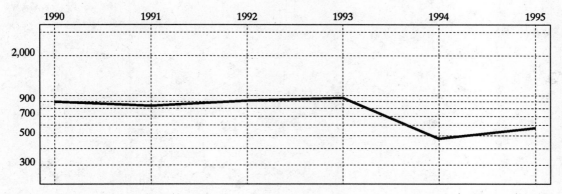

INPUTS AND OUTPUTS FOR HOLDING AND OTHER INVESTMENT OFFICES - SIC GROUP 67

Economic Sector or Industry Providing Inputs	%	Sector	Economic Sector or Industry Buying Outputs	%	Sector
No Input-Output data are available for this industry group.					

Source: Benchmark Input-Output Accounts for the U.S. Economy, 1992, U.S. Department of Commerce, Washington, D.C., November 1997. Data, as reported in the source, are organized by the 1987 SIC structure in use in 1992.

OCCUPATIONS EMPLOYED BY HOLDING AND OTHER INVESTMENT OFFICES

Occupation	% of Total 1996	Change to 2006	Occupation	% of Total 1996	Change to 2006
General managers & top executives	10.4	27.6	Managers & administrators nec	1.9	30.5
Secretaries, except legal & medical	10.4	4.4	Marketing & sales worker supervisors	1.9	31.7
General office clerks	6.8	13.3	Securities & financial sales workers	1.8	31.7
Accountants & auditors	6.4	21.9	Systems analysts	1.6	95.2
Financial managers	6.2	31.7	Brokerage clerks	1.4	10.1
Bookkeeping, accounting, & auditing clerks	5.9	5.3	Janitors & cleaners, maids	1.4	5.3
Management support workers nec	5.1	31.7	Personnel, training, & labor relations specialists	1.3	31.6
Clerical supervisors & managers	4.3	31.7	Computer programmers	1.3	8.4
Sales & related workers nec	3.3	44.8	Lawyers	1.2	31.6
Professional workers nec	2.6	31.6	Maintenance repairers, general utility	1.2	22.7
Receptionists & information clerks	2.0	31.7	Clerical & administrative workers nec	1.2	31.7

Sources: Industry-Occupation Matrix, Bureau of Labor Statistics. These data relate to one or more 3-digit SIC industry groups rather than to a single 4-digit SIC. The change reported for each occupation to the year 2005 is a percent of growth or decline as estimated by the Bureau of Labor Statistics. The abbreviation nec stands for not elsewhere classified.

STATE-BY-STATE DATA ON ESTABLISHMENTS, EMPLOYMENT, AND PAYROLL - 1994 AND 1995

State	1994					1995					% Change Empl.
	No. of Estab.	Employ-ment	Pay / Empl.	Payroll ($ mil.)	Pay / Estab.	No. of Estab.	Employ-ment	Pay / Empl.	Payroll ($ mil.)	Pay / Estab.	
Alabama	21	66	22,424	1.6	76,571	29	81	20,395	2.0	69,414	22.7
Alaska	9	22	36,364	0.9	100,222	14	42	27,619	1.4	102,929	90.9
Arizona	30	160	16,475	2.8	93,400	42	218	15,890	4.0	96,333	36.3
Arkansas	13	(D)	-	(D)	-	18	55	14,327	0.9	50,778	-
California	338	3,828	20,957	88.6	262,086	429	4,832	21,362	108.9	253,821	26.2
Colorado	50	403	23,097	9.4	187,600	59	447	23,025	10.9	184,763	10.9
Connecticut	31	224	38,696	11.1	357,968	37	332	35,771	14.3	387,378	48.2
Delaware	7	9	31,111	0.3	42,571	7	8	28,500	0.3	38,429	-11.1
District of Columbia	69	450	38,009	19.8	286,420	78	542	37,683	23.1	295,513	20.4
Florida	90	656	18,799	13.4	149,178	93	566	20,678	13.5	145,656	-13.7
Georgia	39	334	18,635	6.4	162,872	45	366	19,355	6.9	153,956	9.6
Hawaii	13	(D)	-	(D)	-	14	99	25,899	2.6	182,500	-
Idaho	6	22	9,818	0.2	39,500	8	27	10,074	0.3	40,000	22.7
Illinois	106	450	30,969	11.5	108,613	111	555	23,286	13.3	119,685	23.3
Indiana	47	545	23,486	13.5	288,234	48	555	25,867	14.8	308,646	1.8
Iowa	16	175	20,251	3.8	235,437	18	312	15,705	5.6	309,944	78.3
Kansas	22	215	20,819	6.5	294,318	21	160	18,525	3.5	165,857	-25.6
Kentucky	30	237	25,975	6.3	208,467	28	234	26,889	7.0	249,000	-1.3
Louisiana	24	102	13,569	1.5	60,417	27	168	11,095	2.5	93,370	64.7
Maine	13	66	33,091	3.2	246,615	12	117	34,803	4.2	351,250	77.3
Maryland	42	821	30,699	31.2	743,690	48	1,124	30,025	38.0	791,125	36.9
Massachusetts	66	557	44,223	26.1	395,273	72	636	42,113	51.5	714,861	14.2
Michigan	47	319	22,696	7.4	157,702	45	359	20,724	8.2	181,333	12.5
Minnesota	42	315	24,114	8.0	190,548	46	353	24,691	9.0	196,000	12.1
Mississippi	9	55	13,018	2.1	228,000	10	79	50,076	4.3	433,200	43.6
Missouri	34	318	17,975	6.0	176,765	36	355	17,690	7.0	194,361	11.6
Montana	8	37	21,081	0.9	107,625	10	41	25,073	1.1	108,400	10.8
Nebraska	16	344	16,593	5.8	363,500	19	347	18,029	6.6	348,000	0.9
Nevada	8	16	28,000	0.9	111,875	10	38	40,947	0.7	73,900	137.5
New Hampshire	16	143	25,147	4.0	250,687	16	161	27,130	4.7	296,437	12.6
New Jersey	54	201	29,254	7.0	129,315	58	259	29,483	8.2	141,690	28.9
New Mexico	15	52	24,462	1.5	100,133	18	69	26,493	2.1	115,667	32.7
New York	246	2,049	32,221	69.8	283,577	278	2,288	32,600	77.0	276,957	11.7
North Carolina	35	219	24,183	5.4	154,429	40	202	24,020	5.1	128,550	-7.8
North Dakota	9	20	6,800	0.2	17,444	9	(D)	-	(D)	-	-
Ohio	56	481	16,366	8.4	150,679	57	524	16,702	9.5	165,860	8.9
Oklahoma	28	89	22,067	2.4	87,071	33	139	21,640	3.2	97,242	56.2
Oregon	36	214	19,645	4.4	122,333	49	309	20,505	6.9	140,041	44.4
Pennsylvania	101	657	27,683	21.7	214,861	110	1,028	20,288	28.7	260,609	56.5
Rhode Island	7	38	35,053	1.4	198,000	7	41	37,171	1.6	231,429	7.9
South Carolina	9	(D)	-	(D)	-	9	28	14,143	0.5	53,889	-
South Dakota	5	(D)	-	(D)	-	7	(D)	-	(D)	-	-
Tennessee	33	350	12,023	5.2	156,061	31	273	16,469	4.6	149,613	-22.0
Texas	144	1,105	18,675	22.1	153,632	150	1,238	19,887	25.6	170,453	12.0
Utah	13	58	10,552	0.7	53,231	14	61	12,787	0.9	66,929	5.2
Vermont	8	27	14,222	0.7	83,125	7	30	14,667	0.7	92,857	11.1
Virginia	73	531	33,416	18.8	257,877	83	505	32,222	17.2	207,699	-4.9
Washington	28	161	35,727	5.7	202,536	34	164	23,415	4.3	127,676	1.9
West Virginia	15	(D)	-	(D)	-	14	20	11,600	0.2	16,143	-
Wisconsin	16	44	27,182	1.2	73,000	15	52	23,692	1.5	99,733	18.2
Wyoming	4	(D)	-	(D)	-	4	(D)	-	(D)	-	-

Source: County Business Patterns, U.S. Department of Commerce, Washington, D.C., for 1994 and 1995. Employment shown is for mid-March of the year shown. Payroll per employee is calculated by annualizing 1st Quarter payroll (not shown) and then dividing that value by mid-March employment. Dividing total annual payroll (columns 5 and 10) by employment, therefore, will *not* yield the payroll per employee figure (columns 4 and 9). The symbol (D) indicates that data are withheld by the source to avoid disclosure of competitive information. A dash (-) indicates that data are not available or cannot be calculated.

ESTABLISHMENTS 1995 - STATE AND REGIONAL CONCENTRATION

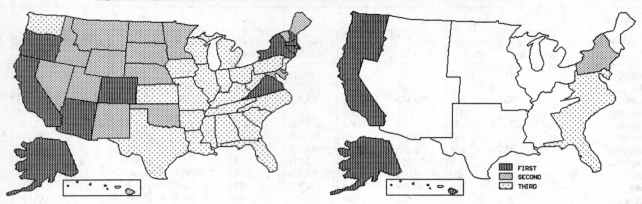

EMPLOYMENT 1995 - STATE AND REGIONAL CONCENTRATION

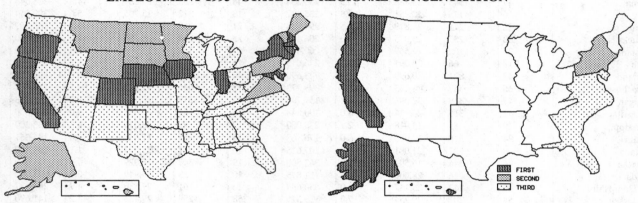

PAYROLL 1995 - STATE AND REGIONAL CONCENTRATION

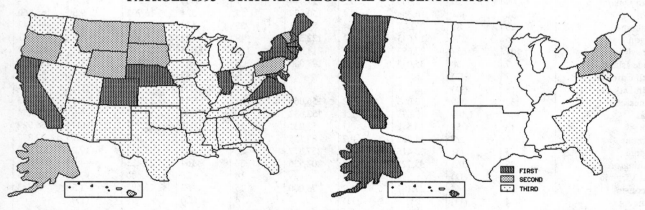

States with the darkest shading indicate those states which have proportionately more establishments, employment, or payrolls than would be indicated by the state's population. States with light shading are states with proportionately fewer establishments, less employment, and lower payrolls than population distribution. States shaded grey are within 15 percent of the state's population proportion in these categories. States for which no data are available are shown as average (grey). *Regions* are shaded to indicate absolute rank in the category. If no data for the category are available, establishment counts are used to shade the regions. Source of the data is the table on the facing page.

LEADING COMPANIES - SIC 6732 - Educational, Religious, etc. Trusts

No company data available for this industry.

SIC 6733

TRUSTS, NEC

The primary activity of establishments classified under SIC 6733 is to manage the funds of trusts and foundations that are organized for purposes other than religious, educational, charitable, or nonprofit research (which are included under SIC 6732, previous chapter). This SIC includes the administration of private estates, personal investment trusts, trusteeships, vacation funds for employees, and other similar trust funds without educational, religious, charitable, or research purposes.

ESTABLISHMENTS, EMPLOYMENT, AND PAYROLL

	1990	1991		1992		1993		1994		1995		% change 90-95
		Value	%	Value	%	Value	%	Value	%	Value	%	
All Establishments	4,234	6,411	51.4	6,060	-5.5	5,648	-6.8	2,678	-52.6	2,691	0.5	-36.4
Mid-March Employment	23,682	25,163	6.3	27,630	9.8	28,135	1.8	13,289	-52.8	14,183	6.7	-40.1
1st Quarter Wages (annualized - $ mil.)	505.9	533.6	5.5	684.4	28.3	625.0	-8.7	327.9	-47.5	367.6	12.1	-27.3
Payroll per Emp. 1st Q. (annualized)	21,363	21,206	-0.7	24,770	16.8	22,215	-10.3	24,678	11.1	25,921	5.0	21.3
Annual Payroll ($ mil.)	532.7	655.8	23.1	752.9	14.8	712.9	-5.3	344.2	-51.7	383.9	11.5	-27.9
Establishments - 1-4 Emp. Number	3,174	5,305	67.1	4,889	-7.8	4,575	-6.4	2,146	-53.1	2,143	-0.1	-32.5
Mid-March Employment	5,094	5,587	9.7	6,130	9.7	5,839	-4.7	2,930	-49.8	2,955	0.9	-42.0
1st Quarter Wages (annualized - $ mil.)	115.1	103.7	-9.9	120.4	16.0	120.1	-0.2	65.2	-45.8	71.9	10.4	-37.5
Payroll per Emp. 1st Q. (annualized)	22,601	18,570	-17.8	19,636	5.7	20,575	4.8	22,236	8.1	24,345	9.5	7.7
Annual Payroll ($ mil.)	130.1	224.4	72.5	183.8	-18.1	198.5	8.0	91.5	-53.9	93.9	2.6	-27.8
Establishments - 5-9 Emp. Number	532	593	11.5	631	6.4	542	-14.1	289	-46.7	276	-4.5	-48.1
Mid-March Employment	3,478	3,887	11.8	4,121	6.0	3,537	-14.2	1,862	-47.4	1,752	-5.9	-49.6
1st Quarter Wages (annualized - $ mil.)	64.3	75.8	18.0	92.4	21.8	83.9	-9.2	43.6	-48.1	45.6	4.8	-29.0
Payroll per Emp. 1st Q. (annualized)	18,483	19,510	5.6	22,421	14.9	23,707	5.7	23,390	-1.3	26,041	11.3	40.9
Annual Payroll ($ mil.)	69.8	76.1	9.0	90.3	18.6	83.1	-8.0	44.2	-46.8	45.1	2.0	-35.4
Establishments - 10-19 Emp. Number	301	289	-4.0	330	14.2	306	-7.3	139	-54.6	158	13.7	-47.5
Mid-March Employment	4,050	3,777	-6.7	4,415	16.9	4,114	-6.8	1,847	-55.1	2,180	18.0	-46.2
1st Quarter Wages (annualized - $ mil.)	80.5	76.6	-4.8	100.6	31.3	104.9	4.3	49.1	-53.2	60.4	22.8	-25.0
Payroll per Emp. 1st Q. (annualized)	19,882	20,286	2.0	22,787	12.3	25,509	11.9	26,607	4.3	27,686	4.1	39.2
Annual Payroll ($ mil.)	83.1	84.2	1.3	109.5	30.0	119.5	9.1	51.5	-56.9	60.4	17.4	-27.3
Establishments - 20-49 Emp. Number	167	184	10.2	168	-8.7	144	-14.3	66	-54.2	71	7.6	-57.5
Mid-March Employment	5,132	5,643	10.0	5,092	-9.8	4,210	-17.3	1,942	-53.9	2,097	8.0	-59.1
1st Quarter Wages (annualized - $ mil.)	106.8	110.0	3.0	111.0	0.9	86.4	-22.2	48.1	-44.3	56.7	18.0	-46.9
Payroll per Emp. 1st Q. (annualized)	20,812	19,494	-6.3	21,790	11.8	20,512	-5.9	24,752	20.7	27,054	9.3	30.0
Annual Payroll ($ mil.)	108.2	99.9	-7.7	112.6	12.8	82.5	-26.7	50.1	-39.3	58.8	17.4	-45.6
Establishments - 50-99 Emp. Number	45	21	-53.3	(D)	-	(D)	-	21	-	25	19.0	-44.4
Mid-March Employment	3,068	1,477	-51.9	(D)	-	(D)	-	1,457	-	1,616	10.9	-47.3
1st Quarter Wages (annualized - $ mil.)	64.2	43.1	-32.8	(D)	-	(D)	-	41.5	-	47.3	13.9	-26.3
Payroll per Emp. 1st Q. (annualized)	20,920	29,197	39.6	(D)	-	(D)	-	28,508	-	29,270	2.7	39.9
Annual Payroll ($ mil.)	67.1	46.0	-31.4	(D)	-	(D)	-	35.2	-	44.8	27.2	-33.2
Establishments - 100-249 Emp. Number	11	13	18.2	12	-7.7	22	83.3	13	-40.9	12	-7.7	9.1
Mid-March Employment	1,446	2,149	48.6	1,903	-11.4	3,730	96.0	1,802	-51.7	1,625	-9.8	12.4
1st Quarter Wages (annualized - $ mil.)	36.9	51.3	38.9	49.4	-3.7	81.4	64.8	44.3	-45.6	38.3	-13.4	3.9
Payroll per Emp. 1st Q. (annualized)	25,535	23,862	-6.6	25,940	8.7	21,810	-15.9	24,570	12.7	23,599	-4.0	-7.6
Annual Payroll ($ mil.)	37.4	53.2	42.1	50.6	-4.9	83.8	65.7	47.0	-43.9	39.7	-15.6	6.0
Establishments - 250-499 Emp. Number	4	4	-	10	150.0	5	-50.0	4	-20.0	6	50.0	50.0
Mid-March Employment	1,414	(D)	-	3,604	-	1,853	-48.6	1,449	-21.8	1,958	35.1	38.5
1st Quarter Wages (annualized - $ mil.)	38.1	(D)	-	138.9	-	37.7	-72.8	36.2	-4.0	47.3	30.7	24.4
Payroll per Emp. 1st Q. (annualized)	26,925	(D)	-	38,528	-	20,356	-47.2	24,997	22.8	24,180	-3.3	-10.2
Annual Payroll ($ mil.)	37.0	(D)	-	143.0	-	37.2	-74.0	24.8	-33.4	41.3	66.6	11.8
Establishments - 500-999 Emp. Number	-	2	-	(D)	-	(D)	-	-	-	-	-	-
Mid-March Employment	-	(D)	-	(D)	-	(D)	-	-	-	-	-	-
1st Quarter Wages (annualized - $ mil.)	-	(D)	-	(D)	-	(D)	-	-	-	-	-	-
Payroll per Emp. 1st Q. (annualized)	(D)	(D)	-	(D)	-	(D)	-	-	-	-	-	-
Annual Payroll ($ mil.)	-	(D)	-	(D)	-	(D)	-	-	-	-	-	-
Estab. - 1000 or More Emp. Number	-	-	-	-	-	-	-	-	-	-	-	-
Mid-March Employment	-	-	-	-	-	-	-	-	-	-	-	-
1st Quarter Wages (annualized - $ mil.)	-	-	-	-	-	-	-	-	-	-	-	-
Payroll per Emp. 1st Q. (annualized)	(D)	(D)	-	-	-	-	-	-	-	-	-	-
Annual Payroll ($ mil.)	-	-	-	-	-	-	-	-	-	-	-	-

Source: County Business Patterns, U.S. Department of Commerce, Washington, D.C., for 1990 through 1995. Payroll per employee is calculated using mid-March employment and 1st Quarter wages, annualized. Annual payroll, also shown, may not equal the annualized 1st Quarter wages. Columns headed by a percent sign (%) indicate change from the previous year. *na* stands for not available. The symbol (D) indicates that data are withheld by the source to avoid disclosure of competitive information. A dash (-) indicates that data are not available or cannot be calculated.

ESTABLISHMENTS
Number

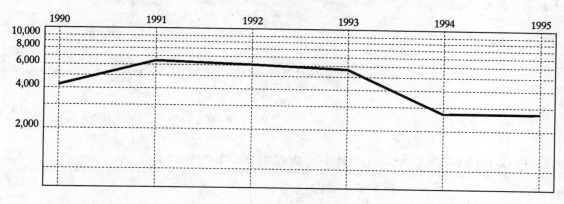

MID-MARCH EMPLOYMENT
Number

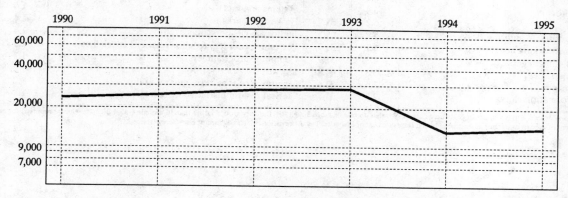

ANNUAL PAYROLL
$ million

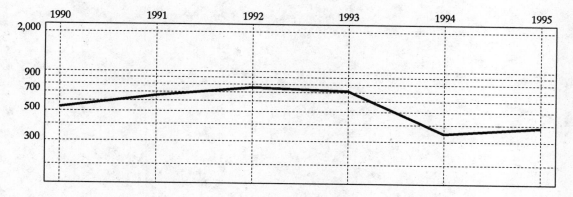

INPUTS AND OUTPUTS FOR HOLDING AND OTHER INVESTMENT OFFICES - SIC GROUP 67

Economic Sector or Industry Providing Inputs	%	Sector	Economic Sector or Industry Buying Outputs	%	Sector
No Input-Output data are available for this industry group.					

Source: Benchmark Input-Output Accounts for the U.S. Economy, 1992, U.S. Department of Commerce, Washington, D.C., November 1997. Data, as reported in the source, are organized by the 1987 SIC structure in use in 1992.

OCCUPATIONS EMPLOYED BY HOLDING AND OTHER INVESTMENT OFFICES

Occupation	% of Total 1996	Change to 2006	Occupation	% of Total 1996	Change to 2006
General managers & top executives	10.4	27.6	Managers & administrators nec	1.9	30.5
Secretaries, except legal & medical	10.4	4.4	Marketing & sales worker supervisors	1.9	31.7
General office clerks	6.8	13.3	Securities & financial sales workers	1.8	31.7
Accountants & auditors	6.4	21.9	Systems analysts	1.6	95.2
Financial managers	6.2	31.7	Brokerage clerks	1.4	10.1
Bookkeeping, accounting, & auditing clerks	5.9	5.3	Janitors & cleaners, maids	1.4	5.3
Management support workers nec	5.1	31.7	Personnel, training, & labor relations specialists	1.3	31.6
Clerical supervisors & managers	4.3	31.7	Computer programmers	1.3	8.4
Sales & related workers nec	3.3	44.8	Lawyers	1.2	31.6
Professional workers nec	2.6	31.6	Maintenance repairers, general utility	1.2	22.7
Receptionists & information clerks	2.0	31.7	Clerical & administrative workers nec	1.2	31.7

Sources: Industry-Occupation Matrix, Bureau of Labor Statistics. These data relate to one or more 3-digit SIC industry groups rather than to a single 4-digit SIC. The change reported for each occupation to the year 2005 is a percent of growth or decline as estimated by the Bureau of Labor Statistics. The abbreviation nec stands for not elsewhere classified.

STATE-BY-STATE DATA ON ESTABLISHMENTS, EMPLOYMENT, AND PAYROLL - 1994 AND 1995

State	1994					1995					% Change Empl.
	No. of Estab.	Employ-ment	Pay / Empl.	Payroll ($ mil.)	Pay / Estab.	No. of Estab.	Employ-ment	Pay / Empl.	Payroll ($ mil.)	Pay / Estab.	
Alabama	21	38	19,368	0.7	34,619	16	73	23,562	1.7	108,375	92.1
Alaska	13	41	22,829	1.1	86,923	12	24	27,833	0.8	70,167	-41.5
Arizona	74	227	21,110	5.0	66,919	68	215	22,307	5.5	81,250	-5.3
Arkansas	16	(D)	-	(D)	-	14	48	10,583	1.0	70,000	-
California	499	2,707	22,939	63.4	126,994	499	2,074	28,299	58.5	117,253	-23.4
Colorado	51	182	16,484	3.8	73,706	53	390	15,631	6.8	127,396	114.3
Connecticut	35	66	34,000	2.7	76,971	32	89	38,966	3.8	119,281	34.8
Delaware	14	98	31,878	3.3	232,286	12	90	31,289	2.8	237,000	-8.2
District of Columbia	28	270	40,237	12.2	436,500	30	308	30,377	10.7	357,967	14.1
Florida	144	557	28,955	16.4	114,194	141	539	31,978	17.0	120,645	-3.2
Georgia	50	172	23,814	5.4	108,800	64	336	30,393	11.0	171,922	95.3
Hawaii	30	206	31,029	6.9	228,433	33	225	30,773	7.1	216,212	9.2
Idaho	14	70	18,914	1.5	107,357	14	73	21,918	1.6	115,357	4.3
Illinois	102	994	29,718	17.5	171,578	96	572	26,175	17.3	180,385	-42.5
Indiana	48	169	31,598	3.2	66,375	42	370	41,741	7.7	183,214	118.9
Iowa	20	63	23,810	1.6	79,500	22	106	5,774	0.6	28,682	68.3
Kansas	30	63	13,841	1.1	35,333	36	84	16,905	1.5	40,500	33.3
Kentucky	18	65	28,800	3.0	167,222	15	57	14,737	0.8	56,467	-12.3
Louisiana	25	84	19,762	1.8	73,480	25	70	30,057	2.2	89,080	-16.7
Maine	16	48	19,167	1.0	62,000	14	22	21,455	0.5	37,500	-54.2
Maryland	40	709	36,260	30.2	755,200	48	919	26,172	25.5	532,208	29.6
Massachusetts	90	241	33,494	8.5	94,233	97	277	52,375	16.2	166,598	14.9
Michigan	66	420	35,895	16.1	244,561	56	444	38,243	17.8	317,196	5.7
Minnesota	35	(D)	-	(D)	-	35	(D)	-	(D)	-	-
Mississippi	19	61	12,590	0.7	38,474	15	45	14,667	0.7	45,200	-26.2
Missouri	34	(D)	-	(D)	-	37	61	26,098	2.3	60,973	-
Montana	9	(D)	-	(D)	-	12	(D)	-	(D)	-	-
Nebraska	10	15	14,400	0.2	24,500	11	15	14,933	0.4	34,455	0.0
Nevada	33	115	15,791	2.3	70,303	38	115	21,635	3.5	91,105	0.0
New Hampshire	10	20	16,600	0.4	42,100	14	32	17,750	0.7	47,143	60.0
New Jersey	46	129	29,271	5.8	126,913	44	150	40,800	5.4	122,364	16.3
New Mexico	15	49	12,816	0.9	62,200	22	99	10,828	1.1	51,455	102.0
New York	188	908	22,198	26.1	138,596	165	831	25,381	22.7	137,442	-8.5
North Carolina	39	86	20,837	1.9	47,744	42	123	20,813	2.5	60,143	43.0
North Dakota	3	(D)	-	(D)	-	3	(D)	-	(D)	-	-
Ohio	43	234	26,769	4.0	94,163	41	251	17,498	4.8	117,854	7.3
Oklahoma	70	271	23,749	6.2	88,857	78	270	27,067	6.9	88,359	-0.4
Oregon	34	172	19,349	3.5	104,088	46	127	17,512	2.6	56,391	-26.2
Pennsylvania	101	497	20,966	11.8	116,782	94	587	20,811	13.9	147,351	18.1
Rhode Island	11	(D)	-	(D)	-	10	18	17,333	0.3	31,800	-
South Carolina	15	33	20,848	0.6	41,067	10	(D)	-	(D)	-	-
South Dakota	6	(D)	-	(D)	-	6	(D)	-	(D)	-	-
Tennessee	39	200	19,820	3.3	85,615	37	150	17,680	3.2	86,270	-25.0
Texas	278	1,506	21,904	38.0	136,608	279	1,879	27,027	53.2	190,652	24.8
Utah	16	52	15,769	1.2	74,063	21	73	20,000	1.7	82,476	40.4
Vermont	6	(D)	-	(D)	-	5	(D)	-	(D)	-	-
Virginia	43	515	10,447	6.2	144,605	45	638	17,404	12.0	266,067	23.9
Washington	73	382	25,183	9.1	124,068	88	471	21,682	14.5	164,307	23.3
West Virginia	18	(D)	-	(D)	-	14	(D)	-	(D)	-	-
Wisconsin	34	126	27,873	4.8	139,853	34	534	13,326	7.1	210,088	323.8
Wyoming	6	110	10,691	1.1	176,833	6	93	9,505	0.9	147,500	-15.5

Source: County Business Patterns, U.S. Department of Commerce, Washington, D.C., for 1994 and 1995. Employment shown is for mid-March of the year shown. Payroll per employee is calculated by annualizing 1st Quarter payroll (not shown) and then dividing that value by mid-March employment. Dividing total annual payroll (columns 5 and 10) by employment, therefore, will *not* yield the payroll per employee figure (columns 4 and 9). The symbol (D) indicates that data are withheld by the source to avoid disclosure of competitive information. A dash (-) indicates that data are not available or cannot be calculated.

ESTABLISHMENTS 1995 - STATE AND REGIONAL CONCENTRATION

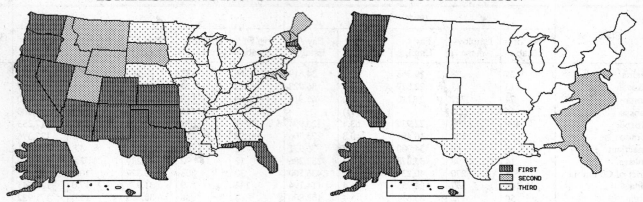

EMPLOYMENT 1995 - STATE AND REGIONAL CONCENTRATION

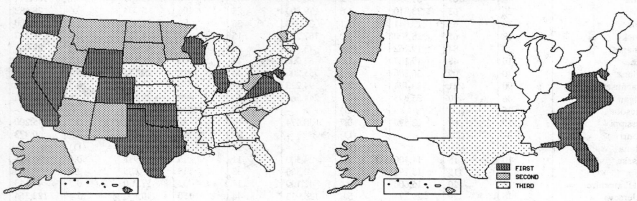

PAYROLL 1995 - STATE AND REGIONAL CONCENTRATION

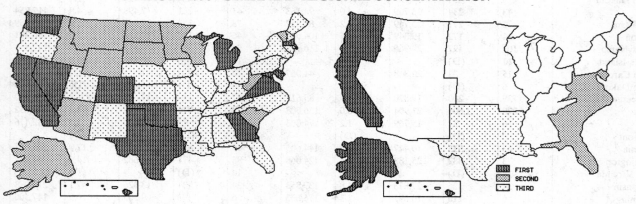

States with the darkest shading indicate those states which have proportionately more establishments, employment, or payrolls than would be indicated by the state's population. States with light shading are states with proportionately fewer establishments, less employment, and lower payrolls than population distribution. States shaded grey are within 15 percent of the state's population proportion in these categories. States for which no data are available are shown as average (grey). *Regions* are shaded to indicate absolute rank in the category. If no data for the category are available, establishment counts are used to shade the regions. Source of the data is the table on the facing page.

LEADING COMPANIES - SIC 6733 - Trusts, nec

Number shown: **4**   Total sales/assets ($ mil): **19,627**   Total employment (000): **8.6**

Company Name	Address				CEO Name	Phone	Co. Type	Sales/Assets ($ mil)	Empl. (000)
Firstar Corp.	777 E. Wisconsin Ave.	Milwaukee	WI	53202	Roger L. Fitzsimonds	414-765-4321	P	19,323 TA	7.8
Sealaska Corp.	One Sealaska Plaza	Juneau	AK	99801	Leo H. Barlow	907-586-1512	R	237	0.5
Gould Investors L.P.	60 Cutter Mill Rd.	Great Neck	NY	11021	Fredric H. Gould	516-466-3100	3	34 TA	<0.1
Kirkpatrick, Pettis, Smith, Polian Inc.	10250 Regency Circle	Omaha	NE	68114	Peter Lahti	402-397-5777	S	33 OR	0.3

Source: *Ward's Business Directory of U.S. Private and Public Companies,* 1996. Company type codes: P - Public, R - Private, S - Subsidiary, D - Division, J - Joint Venture, A - Affiliate, G - Group. If the dollar values shown are not sales, the following codes apply: TA - Total Assets; OR - Operating Revenues; GB - Gross Billings. * - estimated dollar value. < - less than; *na* - not available.

SIC 6792

OIL ROYALTY TRADERS

Establishments in this industry invest in oil and gas royalties or leases; they may own or have only fractional interests in such properties. Activities in this category include buying and selling of oil leases on own account and operation of oil royalty companies.

ESTABLISHMENTS, EMPLOYMENT, AND PAYROLL

	1990	1991		1992		1993		1994		1995		% change 90-95
		Value	%	Value	%	Value	%	Value	%	Value	%	
All Establishments	582	465	-20.1	603	29.7	774	28.4	698	-9.8	698	-	19.9
Mid-March Employment	2,369	1,561	-34.1	2,202	41.1	2,621	19.0	2,436	-7.1	2,375	-2.5	0.3
1st Quarter Wages (annualized - $ mil.)	76.9	55.3	-28.1	86.2	55.8	94.3	9.4	91.3	-3.1	96.4	5.6	25.4
Payroll per Emp. 1st Q. (annualized)	32,449	35,426	9.2	39,128	10.5	35,963	-8.1	37,484	4.2	40,581	8.3	25.1
Annual Payroll ($ mil.)	79.3	59.0	-25.6	94.0	59.4	102.5	9.0	97.8	-4.6	99.5	1.8	25.5
Establishments - 1-4 Emp. Number	469	390	-16.8	488	25.1	634	29.9	569	-10.3	566	-0.5	20.7
Mid-March Employment	831	642	-22.7	796	24.0	993	24.7	916	-7.8	868	-5.2	4.5
1st Quarter Wages (annualized - $ mil.)	26.7	17.7	-33.8	27.8	57.2	30.4	9.6	29.4	-3.4	28.6	-2.7	7.1
Payroll per Emp. 1st Q. (annualized)	32,111	27,502	-14.4	34,864	26.8	30,626	-12.2	32,057	4.7	32,931	2.7	2.6
Annual Payroll ($ mil.)	26.6	18.7	-29.8	28.4	51.9	34.5	21.5	32.3	-6.2	33.9	4.7	27.2
Establishments - 5-9 Emp. Number	72	46	-36.1	70	52.2	(D)	-	83	-	92	10.8	27.8
Mid-March Employment	474	(D)	-	451	-	(D)	-	495	-	565	14.1	19.2
1st Quarter Wages (annualized - $ mil.)	17.1	(D)	-	17.7	-	(D)	-	18.5	-	26.1	41.5	52.8
Payroll per Emp. 1st Q. (annualized)	36,101	(D)	-	39,202	-	(D)	-	37,333	-	46,280	24.0	28.2
Annual Payroll ($ mil.)	16.4	(D)	-	18.9	-	(D)	-	18.6	-	26.8	43.8	63.5
Establishments - 10-19 Emp. Number	26	21	-19.2	30	42.9	31	3.3	(D)	-	25	-	-3.8
Mid-March Employment	320	276	-13.8	405	46.7	433	6.9	(D)	-	342	-	6.9
1st Quarter Wages (annualized - $ mil.)	11.3	12.7	11.7	18.4	45.5	19.5	5.9	(D)	-	11.2	-	-1.4
Payroll per Emp. 1st Q. (annualized)	35,438	45,899	29.5	45,501	-0.9	45,053	-1.0	(D)	-	32,678	-	-7.8
Annual Payroll ($ mil.)	12.5	13.0	3.6	20.2	55.6	20.8	3.2	(D)	-	11.5	-	-8.0
Establishments - 20-49 Emp. Number	11	6	-45.5	(D)	-	(D)	-	13	-	(D)	-	-
Mid-March Employment	328	160	-51.2	(D)	-	(D)	-	444	-	(D)	-	-
1st Quarter Wages (annualized - $ mil.)	10.2	6.6	-35.3	(D)	-	(D)	-	18.3	-	(D)	-	-
Payroll per Emp. 1st Q. (annualized)	31,024	41,125	32.6	(D)	-	(D)	-	41,189	-	(D)	-	-
Annual Payroll ($ mil.)	10.8	8.7	-19.3	(D)	-	(D)	-	19.1	-	(D)	-	-
Establishments - 50-99 Emp. Number	2	2	-	(D)	-	6	-	(D)	-	(D)	-	-
Mid-March Employment	(D)	(D)	-	(D)	-	361	-	(D)	-	(D)	-	-
1st Quarter Wages (annualized - $ mil.)	(D)	(D)	-	(D)	-	13.3	-	(D)	-	(D)	-	-
Payroll per Emp. 1st Q. (annualized)	(D)	(D)	-	(D)	-	36,931	-	(D)	-	(D)	-	-
Annual Payroll ($ mil.)	(D)	(D)	-	(D)	-	14.4	-	(D)	-	(D)	-	-
Establishments - 100-249 Emp. Number	2	-		-		-		-		-		-
Mid-March Employment	(D)	-		-		-		-		-		-
1st Quarter Wages (annualized - $ mil.)	(D)	-		-		-		-		-		-
Payroll per Emp. 1st Q. (annualized)	(D)	(D)	-	-		-		-		-		-
Annual Payroll ($ mil.)	(D)	-		-		-		-		-		-
Establishments - 250-499 Emp. Number	-	-		-		-		-		-		-
Mid-March Employment	-	-		-		-		-		-		-
1st Quarter Wages (annualized - $ mil.)	-	-		-		-		-		-		-
Payroll per Emp. 1st Q. (annualized)	(D)	(D)	-	-		-		-		-		-
Annual Payroll ($ mil.)	-	-		-		-		-		-		-
Establishments - 500-999 Emp. Number	-	-		-		-		-		-		-
Mid-March Employment	-	-		-		-		-		-		-
1st Quarter Wages (annualized - $ mil.)	-	-		-		-		-		-		-
Payroll per Emp. 1st Q. (annualized)	(D)	(D)	-	-		-		-		-		-
Annual Payroll ($ mil.)	-	-		-		-		-		-		-
Estab. - 1000 or More Emp. Number	-	-		-		-		-		-		-
Mid-March Employment	-	-		-		-		-		-		-
1st Quarter Wages (annualized - $ mil.)	-	-		-		-		-		-		-
Payroll per Emp. 1st Q. (annualized)	(D)	(D)	-	-		-		-		-		-
Annual Payroll ($ mil.)	-	-		-		-		-		-		-

Source: County Business Patterns, U.S. Department of Commerce, Washington, D.C., for 1990 through 1995. Payroll per employee is calculated using mid-March employment and 1st Quarter wages, annualized. Annual payroll, also shown, may not equal the annualized 1st Quarter wages. Columns headed by a percent sign (%) indicate change from the previous year. *na* stands for not available. The symbol (D) indicates that data are withheld by the source to avoid disclosure of competitive information. A dash (-) indicates that data are not available or cannot be calculated.

ESTABLISHMENTS
Number

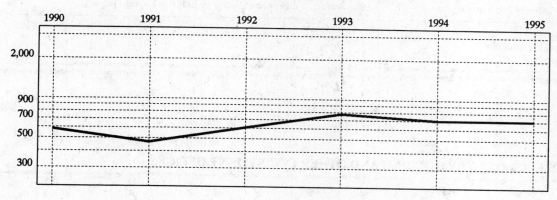

MID-MARCH EMPLOYMENT
Number

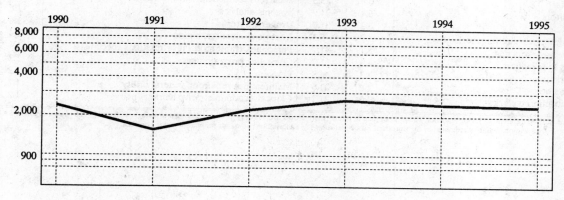

ANNUAL PAYROLL
$ million

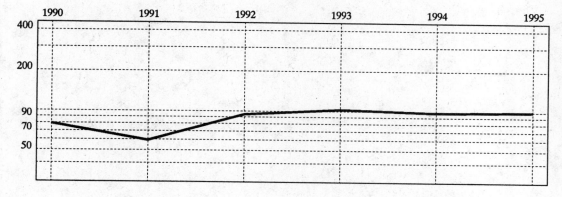

INPUTS AND OUTPUTS FOR HOLDING AND OTHER INVESTMENT OFFICES - SIC GROUP 67

Economic Sector or Industry Providing Inputs	%	Sector	Economic Sector or Industry Buying Outputs	%	Sector
No Input-Output data are available for this industry group.					

Source: *Benchmark Input-Output Accounts for the U.S. Economy, 1992*, U.S. Department of Commerce, Washington, D.C., November 1997. Data, as reported in the source, are organized by the 1987 SIC structure in use in 1992.

OCCUPATIONS EMPLOYED BY HOLDING AND OTHER INVESTMENT OFFICES

Occupation	% of Total 1996	Change to 2006	Occupation	% of Total 1996	Change to 2006
General managers & top executives	10.4	27.6	Managers & administrators nec	1.9	30.5
Secretaries, except legal & medical	10.4	4.4	Marketing & sales worker supervisors	1.9	31.7
General office clerks	6.8	13.3	Securities & financial sales workers	1.8	31.7
Accountants & auditors	6.4	21.9	Systems analysts	1.6	95.2
Financial managers	6.2	31.7	Brokerage clerks	1.4	10.1
Bookkeeping, accounting, & auditing clerks	5.9	5.3	Janitors & cleaners, maids	1.4	5.3
Management support workers nec	5.1	31.7	Personnel, training, & labor relations specialists	1.3	31.6
Clerical supervisors & managers	4.3	31.7	Computer programmers	1.3	8.4
Sales & related workers nec	3.3	44.8	Lawyers	1.2	31.6
Professional workers nec	2.6	31.6	Maintenance repairers, general utility	1.2	22.7
Receptionists & information clerks	2.0	31.7	Clerical & administrative workers nec	1.2	31.7

Sources: *Industry-Occupation Matrix*, Bureau of Labor Statistics. These data relate to one or more 3-digit SIC industry groups rather than to a single 4-digit SIC. The change reported for each occupation to the year 2005 is a percent of growth or decline as estimated by the Bureau of Labor Statistics. The abbreviation *nec* stands for not elsewhere classified.

U.S. AND STATE DATA ON INDUSTRY REVENUES AND OTHER ACCOUNTS FOR 1992

State	No. of Estab.	Employ- ment	Payroll ($ mil.)	Revenues ($ mil.)	Empl./ Estab.	Revenue/ Estab. ($)	Payroll/ Estab. ($)	Revenue/ Empl. ($)	Payroll/ Empl. ($)
UNITED STATES	746	2,228	92.7	686.7	3	920,462	124,311	308,198	41,623
California	38	95	2.6	43.3	3	1,139,079	68,079	455,632	27,232
Colorado	35	94	3.6	37.2	3	1,061,686	103,000	395,309	38,351
Florida	7	14	0.5	2.2	2	315,286	72,857	157,643	36,429
Georgia	5	3	0.2	0.9	1	186,200	32,600	310,333	54,333
Illinois	14	18	1.1	5.7	1	405,857	78,000	315,667	60,667
Indiana	3	-	(D)	(D)	(D)	(D)	(D)	(D)	(D)
Maryland	1	-	(D)	(D)	(D)	(D)	(D)	(D)	(D)
Massachusetts	4	-	(D)	(D)	(D)	(D)	(D)	(D)	(D)
Michigan	11	21	0.6	3.7	2	340,182	52,091	178,190	27,286
Minnesota	4	-	(D)	(D)	(D)	(D)	(D)	(D)	(D)
Missouri	5	-	(D)	(D)	(D)	(D)	(D)	(D)	(D)
New Jersey	2	-	(D)	(D)	(D)	(D)	(D)	(D)	(D)
New York	20	-	(D)	(D)	(D)	(D)	(D)	(D)	(D)
North Carolina	1	-	(D)	(D)	(D)	(D)	(D)	(D)	(D)
Ohio	10	30	1.1	4.1	3	412,300	112,300	137,433	37,433
Pennsylvania	13	-	(D)	(D)	(D)	(D)	(D)	(D)	(D)
Tennessee	1	-	(D)	(D)	(D)	(D)	(D)	(D)	(D)
Texas	307	1,013	46.6	280.5	3	913,697	151,795	276,905	46,003
Virginia	2	-	(D)	(D)	(D)	(D)	(D)	(D)	(D)
Wisconsin	2	-	(D)	(D)	(D)	(D)	(D)	(D)	(D)

Source: *1992 Economic Census*, U.S. Department of Commerce, Washington, D.C. This is the only table that shows revenue data as collected by the Bureau of the Census in an Economic Census. The symbol (D) indicates that data are withheld by the source to avoid disclosure of competitive information. A dash (-) indicates that data are not available or cannot be calculated.

STATE-BY-STATE DATA ON ESTABLISHMENTS, EMPLOYMENT, AND PAYROLL - 1994 AND 1995

State	1994					1995					% Change Empl.
	No. of Estab.	Employ-ment	Pay / Empl.	Payroll ($ mil.)	Pay / Estab.	No. of Estab.	Employ-ment	Pay / Empl.	Payroll ($ mil.)	Pay / Estab.	
Alabama	6	(D)	-	(D)	-	5	(D)	-	(D)	-	-
Arizona	1	(D)	-	(D)	-	(D)	(D)	(D)	(D)	(D)	-
Arkansas	5	(D)	-	(D)	-	6	(D)	-	(D)	-	-
California	41	223	27,193	5.8	142,220	40	160	30,500	5.3	132,800	-28.3
Colorado	33	122	40,033	4.9	147,636	35	156	54,077	7.4	211,171	27.9
Connecticut	3	(D)	-	(D)	-	3	(D)	-	(D)	-	-
Florida	5	10	38,000	0.5	95,400	5	(D)	-	(D)	-	-
Georgia	2	(D)	-	(D)	-	1	(D)	-	(D)	-	-
Idaho	1	(D)	-	(D)	-	1	(D)	-	(D)	-	-
Illinois	12	41	49,659	2.6	212,583	9	24	88,833	1.8	202,000	-41.5
Indiana	3	19	20,211	0.4	135,667	3	(D)	-	(D)	-	-
Iowa	3	(D)	-	(D)	-	3	(D)	-	(D)	-	-
Kansas	16	(D)	-	(D)	-	14	(D)	-	(D)	-	-
Kentucky	6	(D)	-	(D)	-	6	(D)	-	(D)	-	-
Louisiana	50	150	25,867	4.5	89,220	50	159	24,528	4.4	87,720	6.0
Maryland	1	(D)	-	(D)	-	1	(D)	-	(D)	-	-
Massachusetts	5	(D)	-	(D)	-	4	9	23,111	0.2	42,750	-
Michigan	6	13	26,462	0.3	50,333	6	13	27,385	0.4	63,167	0.0
Minnesota	2	(D)	-	(D)	-	5	(D)	-	(D)	-	-
Mississippi	4	5	18,400	0.1	24,500	4	(D)	-	(D)	-	-
Missouri	5	9	20,889	0.2	43,200	6	26	43,846	1.0	172,500	188.9
Montana	7	17	42,118	0.6	87,429	8	20	34,200	0.6	70,875	17.6
Nebraska	1	(D)	-	(D)	-	1	(D)	-	(D)	-	-
Nevada	2	(D)	-	(D)	-	3	(D)	-	(D)	-	-
New Jersey	3	(D)	-	(D)	-	2	(D)	-	(D)	-	-
New Mexico	19	(D)	-	(D)	-	19	(D)	-	(D)	-	-
New York	9	43	75,163	3.5	389,778	8	36	92,667	2.7	340,750	-16.3
North Dakota	4	11	12,727	0.2	53,250	5	22	8,364	0.4	74,600	100.0
Ohio	10	39	34,769	1.5	146,800	10	34	44,235	1.5	146,500	-12.8
Oklahoma	92	372	35,527	13.7	149,163	90	339	36,389	12.4	137,256	-8.9
Oregon	1	(D)	-	(D)	-	1	(D)	-	(D)	-	-
Pennsylvania	8	29	78,069	2.3	291,250	8	27	88,000	2.3	287,750	-6.9
Tennessee	1	(D)	-	(D)	-	1	(D)	-	(D)	-	-
Texas	302	977	37,711	40.2	132,960	310	1,005	40,736	42.9	138,361	2.9
Utah	6	(D)	-	(D)	-	5	(D)	-	(D)	-	-
Virginia	2	(D)	-	(D)	-	2	(D)	-	(D)	-	-
West Virginia	12	102	40,078	4.1	342,000	10	81	39,704	3.2	323,200	-20.6
Wisconsin	2	(D)	-	(D)	-	2	(D)	-	(D)	-	-
Wyoming	7	9	9,778	0.1	13,000	6	(D)	-	(D)	-	-

Source: County Business Patterns, U.S. Department of Commerce, Washington, D.C., for 1994 and 1995. Employment shown is for mid-March of the year shown. Payroll per employee is calculated by annualizing 1st Quarter payroll (not shown) and then dividing that value by mid-March employment. Dividing total annual payroll (columns 5 and 10) by employment, therefore, will *not* yield the payroll per employee figure (columns 4 and 9). The symbol (D) indicates that data are withheld by the source to avoid disclosure of competitive information. A dash (-) indicates that data are not available or cannot be calculated.

ESTABLISHMENTS 1995 - STATE AND REGIONAL CONCENTRATION

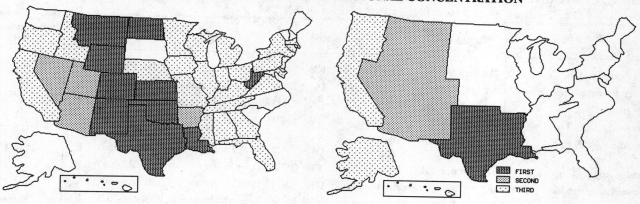

EMPLOYMENT 1995 - STATE AND REGIONAL CONCENTRATION

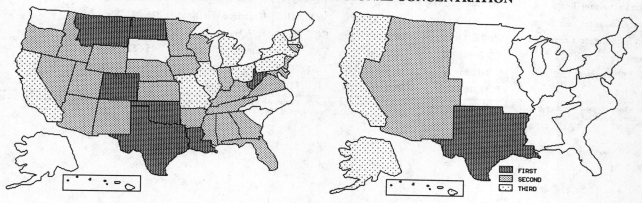

PAYROLL 1995 - STATE AND REGIONAL CONCENTRATION

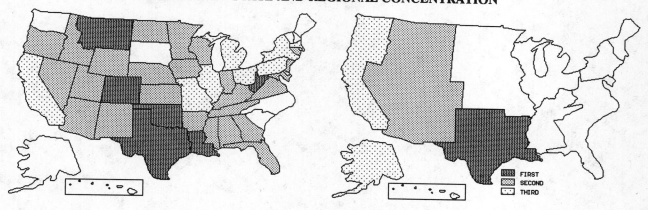

States with the darkest shading indicate those states which have proportionately more establishments, employment, or payrolls than would be indicated by the state's population. States with light shading are states with proportionately fewer establishments, less employment, and lower payrolls than population distribution. States shaded grey are within 15 percent of the state's population proportion in these categories. States for which no data are available are shown as average (grey). *Regions* are shaded to indicate absolute rank in the category. If no data for the category are available, establishment counts are used to shade the regions. Source of the data is the table on the facing page.

LEADING COMPANIES - SIC 6792 - Oil Royalty Traders

Number shown: **15**   Total sales/assets ($ mil): **1,087**   Total employment (000): **3.2**

Company Name	Address				CEO Name	Phone	Co. Type	Sales/Assets ($ mil)	Empl. (000)
Triarc Companies Inc.	280 Park Ave.	New York	NY	10017	Nelson Peltz	212-451-3000	P	861	2.0
National Propane Corp.	200 1st St. SE	Cedar Rapids	IA	52401	Ronald D. Paliughi	319-365-1550	S	149	1.0
Tejon Ranch Co.	PO Box 1000	Lebec	CA	93243	Matt J. Echeverria	805-327-8481	P	20	<0.1
Texas Pacific Land Trust	80 Broad St.	New York	NY	10004	George C. Fraser III	212-269-2266	P	14 TA	<0.1
Panhandle Royalty Co.	5400 N.W. Grand Blvd.	Oklahoma City	OK	73112	H.W. Peace II	405-948-1560	P	12 TA	<0.1
Toreador Royalty Corp.	8117 Preston Rd.	Dallas	TX	75225	Peter R. Vig	214-369-0080	P	7 TA	<0.1
Tripower Resources Inc.	PO Box 849	Ardmore	OK	73402	John D. Gibbs	580-226-6700	S	7 TA	<0.1
Golden Triangle Industries Inc.	PO Box 22010	Albuquerque	NM	87154	Kenneth Owens	505-856-5075	P	7 TA	<0.1
North European Oil Royalty Trust	PO Box 456	Red Bank	NJ	07701	John R. Van Kirk	908-741-4008	3	3 TA	<0.1
Marine Petroleum Trust	PO Box 830241	Dallas	TX	75283	R. Ray Bell	214-508-1796	3	3 TA	<0.1
Central Coal and Coke Corp.	127 W. 10th St.	Kansas City	MO	64105	Beekman Winthrop	816-842-2430	P	2 OR	<0.1
Aspen Exploration Corp.	2050 S. Oneida St.	Denver	CO	80224	R.V. Bailey	303-639-9860	P	1	<0.1
Testamentary Trust	PO Box 3726	Midland	TX	79702	Sam N. McDuffey	915-682-3451	3	1 TA*	<0.1
Seven J Stock Farm Inc.	808 Travis St.	Houston	TX	77002	John R. Parten	713-228-8900	P	1	<0.1
Actron Inc.	PO Box 430	Shreveport	LA	71162	John Butcher	318-221-5555	3	1 TA	<0.1

Source: Ward's Business Directory of U.S. Private and Public Companies, 1996. Company type codes: P - Public, R - Private, S - Subsidiary, D - Division, J - Joint Venture, A - Affiliate, G - Group. If the dollar values shown are not sales, the following codes apply: TA - Total Assets; OR - Operating Revenues; GB - Gross Billings. * - estimated dollar value. < - less than; *na* - not available.

SIC 6794

PATENT OWNERS AND LESSORS

Patent owners and lessors are engaged primarily in owning or leasing franchises, patents, and copyrights which they, in turn, license to others for use. Activities include the buying and licensing of copyrights; the selling or licensing of franchises; the licensing of music to radio stations; music royalties on sheet music or recorded music; the buying, leasing, and licensing of patents; and the publishing and licensing of performance rights.

ESTABLISHMENTS, EMPLOYMENT, AND PAYROLL

	1990	1991 Value	%	1992 Value	%	1993 Value	%	1994 Value	%	1995 Value	%	% change 90-95
All Establishments	861	864	0.3	1,146	32.6	1,606	40.1	1,678	4.5	1,430	-14.8	66.1
Mid-March Employment	15,392	13,246	-13.9	17,538	32.4	18,363	4.7	18,851	2.7	16,059	-14.8	4.3
1st Quarter Wages (annualized - $ mil.)	503.7	426.6	-15.3	586.6	37.5	719.7	22.7	791.0	9.9	656.9	-17.0	30.4
Payroll per Emp. 1st Q. (annualized)	32,726	32,207	-1.6	33,448	3.9	39,191	17.2	41,960	7.1	40,903	-2.5	25.0
Annual Payroll ($ mil.)	439.8	460.7	4.8	636.3	38.1	802.4	26.1	847.0	5.6	692.8	-18.2	57.5
Establishments - 1-4 Emp. Number	484	479	-1.0	693	44.7	971	40.1	976	0.5	841	-13.8	73.8
Mid-March Employment	767	765	-0.3	1,108	44.8	1,393	25.7	1,455	4.5	1,253	-13.9	63.4
1st Quarter Wages (annualized - $ mil.)	24.0	24.5	2.1	103.7	323.8	46.7	-54.9	54.2	16.0	49.5	-8.7	106.6
Payroll per Emp. 1st Q. (annualized)	31,244	31,984	2.4	93,588	192.6	33,556	-64.1	37,273	11.1	39,508	6.0	26.5
Annual Payroll ($ mil.)	42.6	37.6	-11.6	144.9	285.1	94.0	-35.1	80.4	-14.4	90.0	11.9	111.4
Establishments - 5-9 Emp. Number	135	150	11.1	182	21.3	249	36.8	275	10.4	229	-16.7	69.6
Mid-March Employment	885	981	10.8	1,197	22.0	1,623	35.6	1,832	12.9	1,500	-18.1	69.5
1st Quarter Wages (annualized - $ mil.)	33.4	38.4	14.8	36.1	-5.8	56.1	55.1	62.5	11.5	55.7	-10.9	66.6
Payroll per Emp. 1st Q. (annualized)	37,754	39,099	3.6	30,195	-22.8	34,543	14.4	34,120	-1.2	37,115	8.8	-1.7
Annual Payroll ($ mil.)	30.3	37.3	23.0	40.4	8.4	65.0	60.9	69.3	6.6	64.2	-7.5	111.8
Establishments - 10-19 Emp. Number	115	113	-1.7	140	23.9	192	37.1	221	15.1	180	-18.6	56.5
Mid-March Employment	1,529	1,508	-1.4	1,896	25.7	2,503	32.0	2,918	16.6	2,488	-14.7	62.7
1st Quarter Wages (annualized - $ mil.)	67.5	52.6	-22.1	68.4	29.9	90.5	32.3	100.5	11.1	94.6	-5.8	40.1
Payroll per Emp. 1st Q. (annualized)	44,178	34,907	-21.0	36,059	3.3	36,145	0.2	34,450	-4.7	38,040	10.4	-13.9
Annual Payroll ($ mil.)	54.9	57.2	4.3	75.5	31.9	102.1	35.4	113.0	10.6	96.9	-14.2	76.7
Establishments - 20-49 Emp. Number	70	73	4.3	85	16.4	131	54.1	142	8.4	122	-14.1	74.3
Mid-March Employment	2,033	2,076	2.1	2,525	21.6	3,931	55.7	4,329	10.1	3,786	-12.5	86.2
1st Quarter Wages (annualized - $ mil.)	55.5	66.9	20.6	85.6	28.0	138.1	61.4	149.2	8.0	147.5	-1.1	165.9
Payroll per Emp. 1st Q. (annualized)	27,282	32,212	18.1	33,898	5.2	35,138	3.7	34,468	-1.9	38,959	13.0	42.8
Annual Payroll ($ mil.)	58.3	72.3	24.1	89.1	23.2	146.1	64.0	155.8	6.6	153.6	-1.4	163.6
Establishments - 50-99 Emp. Number	37	27	-27.0	(D)	-	36	-	36	-	39	8.3	5.4
Mid-March Employment	(D)	1,739	-	(D)	-	2,334	-	2,444	4.7	2,730	11.7	-
1st Quarter Wages (annualized - $ mil.)	(D)	42.1	-	(D)	-	73.9	-	122.0	65.1	114.5	-6.2	-
Payroll per Emp. 1st Q. (annualized)	(D)	24,235	-	(D)	-	31,650	-	49,913	57.7	41,933	-16.0	-
Annual Payroll ($ mil.)	(D)	48.0	-	(D)	-	78.0	-	126.1	61.7	115.9	-8.0	-
Establishments - 100-249 Emp. Number	12	14	16.7	15	7.1	21	40.0	23	9.5	13	-43.5	8.3
Mid-March Employment	(D)	1,952	-	2,206	13.0	3,374	52.9	3,464	2.7	1,978	-42.9	-
1st Quarter Wages (annualized - $ mil.)	(D)	70.6	-	95.8	35.6	143.4	49.7	164.5	14.7	85.2	-48.2	-
Payroll per Emp. 1st Q. (annualized)	(D)	36,186	-	43,422	20.0	42,497	-2.1	47,475	11.7	43,094	-9.2	-
Annual Payroll ($ mil.)	(D)	72.0	-	94.8	31.7	159.5	68.3	163.4	2.5	82.9	-49.3	-
Establishments - 250-499 Emp. Number	3	4	33.3	(D)	-	(D)	-	(D)	-	(D)	-	-
Mid-March Employment	(D)	(D)	-	(D)	-	(D)	-	(D)	-	(D)	-	-
1st Quarter Wages (annualized - $ mil.)	(D)	(D)	-	(D)	-	(D)	-	(D)	-	(D)	-	-
Payroll per Emp. 1st Q. (annualized)	(D)	(D)	-	(D)	-	(D)	-	(D)	-	(D)	-	-
Annual Payroll ($ mil.)	(D)	(D)	-	(D)	-	(D)	-	(D)	-	(D)	-	-
Establishments - 500-999 Emp. Number	3	4	33.3	(D)	-	(D)	-	(D)	-	(D)	-	-
Mid-March Employment	(D)	(D)	-	(D)	-	(D)	-	(D)	-	(D)	-	-
1st Quarter Wages (annualized - $ mil.)	(D)	(D)	-	(D)	-	(D)	-	(D)	-	(D)	-	-
Payroll per Emp. 1st Q. (annualized)	(D)	(D)	-	(D)	-	(D)	-	(D)	-	(D)	-	-
Annual Payroll ($ mil.)	(D)	(D)	-	(D)	-	(D)	-	(D)	-	(D)	-	-
Estab. - 1000 or More Emp. Number	2	-	-	(D)	-	-	-	-	-	-	-	-
Mid-March Employment	(D)	-	-	(D)	-	-	-	-	-	-	-	-
1st Quarter Wages (annualized - $ mil.)	(D)	-	-	(D)	-	-	-	-	-	-	-	-
Payroll per Emp. 1st Q. (annualized)	(D)	(D)	-	(D)	-	-	-	-	-	-	-	-
Annual Payroll ($ mil.)	(D)	-	-	(D)	-	-	-	-	-	-	-	-

Source: County Business Patterns, U.S. Department of Commerce, Washington, D.C., for 1990 through 1995. Payroll per employee is calculated using mid-March employment and 1st Quarter wages, annualized. Annual payroll, also shown, may not equal the annualized 1st Quarter wages. Columns headed by a percent sign (%) indicate change from the previous year. *na* stands for not available. The symbol (D) indicates that data are withheld by the source to avoid disclosure of competitive information. A dash (-) indicates that data are not available or cannot be calculated.

ESTABLISHMENTS
Number

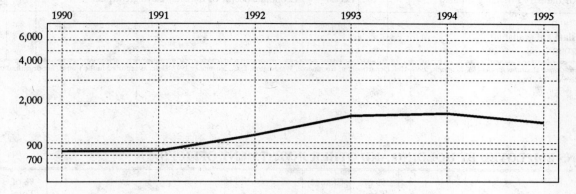

MID-MARCH EMPLOYMENT
Number

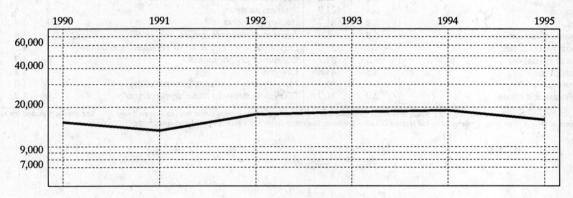

ANNUAL PAYROLL
$ million

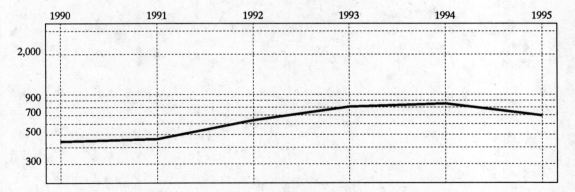

INPUTS AND OUTPUTS FOR HOLDING AND OTHER INVESTMENT OFFICES - SIC GROUP 67

Economic Sector or Industry Providing Inputs	%	Sector	Economic Sector or Industry Buying Outputs	%	Sector
No Input-Output data are available for this industry group.					

Source: Benchmark Input-Output Accounts for the U.S. Economy, 1992, U.S. Department of Commerce, Washington, D.C., November 1997. Data, as reported in the source, are organized by the 1987 SIC structure in use in 1992.

OCCUPATIONS EMPLOYED BY HOLDING AND OTHER INVESTMENT OFFICES

Occupation	% of Total 1996	Change to 2006	Occupation	% of Total 1996	Change to 2006
General managers & top executives	10.4	27.6	Managers & administrators nec	1.9	30.5
Secretaries, except legal & medical	10.4	4.4	Marketing & sales worker supervisors	1.9	31.7
General office clerks	6.8	13.3	Securities & financial sales workers	1.8	31.7
Accountants & auditors	6.4	21.9	Systems analysts	1.6	95.2
Financial managers	6.2	31.7	Brokerage clerks	1.4	10.1
Bookkeeping, accounting, & auditing clerks	5.9	5.3	Janitors & cleaners, maids	1.4	5.3
Management support workers nec	5.1	31.7	Personnel, training, & labor relations specialists	1.3	31.6
Clerical supervisors & managers	4.3	31.7	Computer programmers	1.3	8.4
Sales & related workers nec	3.3	44.8	Lawyers	1.2	31.6
Professional workers nec	2.6	31.6	Maintenance repairers, general utility	1.2	22.7
Receptionists & information clerks	2.0	31.7	Clerical & administrative workers nec	1.2	31.7

Sources: Industry-Occupation Matrix, Bureau of Labor Statistics. These data relate to one or more 3-digit SIC industry groups rather than to a single 4-digit SIC. The change reported for each occupation to the year 2005 is a percent of growth or decline as estimated by the Bureau of Labor Statistics. The abbreviation nec stands for not elsewhere classified.

U.S. AND STATE DATA ON INDUSTRY REVENUES AND OTHER ACCOUNTS FOR 1992

State	No. of Estab.	Employ- ment	Payroll ($ mil.)	Revenues ($ mil.)	Empl./ Estab.	Revenue/ Estab. ($)	Payroll/ Estab. ($)	Revenue/ Empl. ($)	Payroll/ Empl. ($)
UNITED STATES	1,514	17,409	689.3	5,412.5	11	3,574,967	455,264	310,902	39,593
California	231	2,832	134.2	924.4	12	4,001,753	580,835	326,414	47,377
Colorado	26	-	(D)	(D)	(D)	(D)	(D)	(D)	(D)
Florida	88	884	25.3	101.8	10	1,156,500	287,182	115,127	28,588
Georgia	45	1,620	30.1	142.1	36	3,157,800	669,800	87,717	18,606
Illinois	63	443	17.4	110.7	7	1,757,254	275,762	249,903	39,217
Indiana	18	-	(D)	(D)	(D)	(D)	(D)	(D)	(D)
Maryland	31	-	(D)	(D)	(D)	(D)	(D)	(D)	(D)
Massachusetts	21	-	(D)	(D)	(D)	(D)	(D)	(D)	(D)
Michigan	56	322	14.9	68.3	6	1,219,518	265,696	212,090	46,208
Minnesota	42	-	(D)	(D)	(D)	(D)	(D)	(D)	(D)
Missouri	29	362	11.3	63.3	12	2,183,414	388,000	174,914	31,083
New Jersey	40	1,527	93.1	652.4	38	16,310,900	2,328,125	427,267	60,986
New York	160	3,032	146.6	1,155.5	19	7,222,031	916,431	381,110	48,360
North Carolina	18	199	7.0	41.7	11	2,315,333	391,056	209,427	35,372
Ohio	48	380	12.3	42.4	8	883,354	256,479	111,582	32,397
Pennsylvania	49	445	15.9	65.6	9	1,338,755	324,163	147,413	35,694
Tennessee	57	550	17.4	108.0	10	1,894,807	305,912	196,371	31,704
Texas	81	986	36.8	170.8	12	2,108,963	454,506	173,252	37,338
Virginia	25	-	(D)	(D)	(D)	(D)	(D)	(D)	(D)
Washington	28	125	4.8	31.0	4	1,106,286	173,179	247,808	38,792
Wisconsin	20	113	3.8	42.5	6	2,123,450	191,450	375,832	33,885

Source: 1992 Economic Census, U.S. Department of Commerce, Washington, D.C. This is the only table that shows revenue data as collected by the Bureau of the Census in an Economic Census. The symbol (D) indicates that data are withheld by the source to avoid disclosure of competitive information. A dash (-) indicates that data are not available or cannot be calculated.

STATE-BY-STATE DATA ON ESTABLISHMENTS, EMPLOYMENT, AND PAYROLL - 1994 AND 1995

State	1994					1995					% Change Empl.
	No. of Estab.	Employ-ment	Pay / Empl.	Payroll ($ mil.)	Pay / Estab.	No. of Estab.	Employ-ment	Pay / Empl.	Payroll ($ mil.)	Pay / Estab.	
Alabama	15	106	22,340	2.5	164,400	13	114	21,544	2.4	186,538	7.5
Alaska	1	(D)	-	(D)	-	(D)	(D)	(D)	(D)	(D)	-
Arizona	30	259	23,598	6.3	210,000	27	199	26,131	5.7	211,630	-23.2
Arkansas	5	13	22,154	0.7	134,000	5	(D)	-	(D)	-	-
California	227	3,085	48,683	157.3	692,775	190	2,846	47,606	135.5	712,905	-7.7
Colorado	40	417	45,640	19.6	489,600	35	353	61,473	21.2	604,629	-15.3
Connecticut	31	130	31,938	4.8	153,871	27	137	41,022	6.0	220,556	5.4
Delaware	112	271	51,365	24.5	218,589	103	358	55,140	27.4	265,670	32.1
District of Columbia	2	(D)	-	(D)	-	2	(D)	-	(D)	-	-
Florida	103	773	29,847	28.5	276,369	94	780	34,277	50.2	533,574	0.9
Georgia	55	873	46,369	40.7	740,327	47	493	44,389	21.4	455,553	-43.5
Hawaii	5	45	7,911	0.3	63,000	3	24	7,167	0.2	54,333	-46.7
Idaho	4	6	66,000	0.5	121,000	3	(D)	-	(D)	-	-
Illinois	51	536	28,209	15.4	301,588	49	429	39,385	18.3	374,020	-20.0
Indiana	15	128	30,563	4.1	271,467	13	186	20,129	4.1	314,692	45.3
Iowa	11	87	31,402	2.8	252,273	10	112	31,464	3.5	346,200	28.7
Kansas	21	322	32,522	11.9	568,524	20	360	36,189	13.7	684,600	11.8
Kentucky	6	104	29,192	4.1	676,667	6	106	20,566	2.5	413,167	1.9
Louisiana	19	81	20,346	1.8	96,421	14	54	17,926	1.3	90,000	-33.3
Maine	3	32	19,500	0.8	266,000	(D)	(D)	(D)	(D)	(D)	-
Maryland	31	(D)	-	(D)	-	28	(D)	-	(D)	-	-
Massachusetts	23	(D)	-	(D)	-	19	124	51,742	5.0	261,842	-
Michigan	51	375	37,920	16.9	331,078	50	393	38,992	17.8	356,560	4.8
Minnesota	43	417	32,700	15.3	356,163	33	564	35,206	19.7	596,152	35.3
Mississippi	2	(D)	-	(D)	-	4	66	45,030	2.3	575,750	-
Missouri	45	316	37,418	14.7	325,556	32	254	47,449	14.1	440,906	-19.6
Montana	3	(D)	-	(D)	-	3	8	14,000	0.3	85,667	-
Nebraska	6	121	35,570	4.0	667,833	4	26	37,538	0.8	208,500	-78.5
Nevada	27	178	26,944	4.7	175,704	31	170	24,753	5.2	169,129	-4.5
New Hampshire	3	9	20,889	0.2	58,667	3	(D)	-	(D)	-	-
New Jersey	51	1,131	73,577	67.8	1,328,569	40	902	77,494	44.8	1,120,275	-20.2
New Mexico	4	(D)	-	(D)	-	4	(D)	-	(D)	-	-
New York	171	3,548	55,183	206.6	1,208,363	130	2,292	47,454	118.0	907,454	-35.4
North Carolina	26	374	16,332	9.1	351,423	22	157	30,268	4.4	200,318	-58.0
North Dakota	6	48	22,833	1.2	199,500	3	(D)	-	(D)	-	-
Ohio	62	581	24,399	15.4	248,532	44	354	34,000	12.3	280,341	-39.1
Oklahoma	12	36	40,111	1.8	150,833	8	37	18,703	0.8	105,875	2.8
Oregon	17	(D)	-	(D)	-	18	(D)	-	(D)	-	-
Pennsylvania	65	773	34,898	29.3	450,446	55	1,055	23,306	27.8	506,364	36.5
Rhode Island	5	(D)	-	(D)	-	6	(D)	-	(D)	-	-
South Carolina	9	33	30,788	1.1	117,444	10	31	41,161	1.6	164,100	-6.1
South Dakota	4	18	26,222	0.8	189,750	6	28	24,857	0.8	135,667	55.6
Tennessee	65	636	30,497	22.8	350,492	45	682	28,821	18.9	419,000	7.2
Texas	87	903	33,564	36.9	424,632	73	799	35,474	34.1	467,274	-11.5
Utah	13	114	28,491	3.6	274,692	10	117	24,684	3.4	335,600	2.6
Vermont	(D)	(D)	(D)	(D)	(D)	2	(D)	-	(D)	-	-
Virginia	40	317	29,085	10.4	258,825	35	278	39,065	11.2	320,686	-12.3
Washington	29	264	28,348	10.7	369,724	27	277	16,477	5.7	210,296	4.9
West Virginia	2	(D)	-	(D)	-	4	(D)	-	(D)	-	-
Wisconsin	20	109	22,789	2.8	142,300	19	125	20,928	3.1	163,474	14.7
Wyoming	(D)	(D)	(D)	(D)	(D)	1	(D)	-	(D)	-	-

Source: County Business Patterns, U.S. Department of Commerce, Washington, D.C., for 1994 and 1995. Employment shown is for mid-March of the year shown. Payroll per employee is calculated by annualizing 1st Quarter payroll (not shown) and then dividing that value by mid-March employment. Dividing total annual payroll (columns 5 and 10) by employment, therefore, will *not* yield the payroll per employee figure (columns 4 and 9). The symbol (D) indicates that data are withheld by the source to avoid disclosure of competitive information. A dash (-) indicates that data are not available or cannot be calculated.

ESTABLISHMENTS 1995 - STATE AND REGIONAL CONCENTRATION

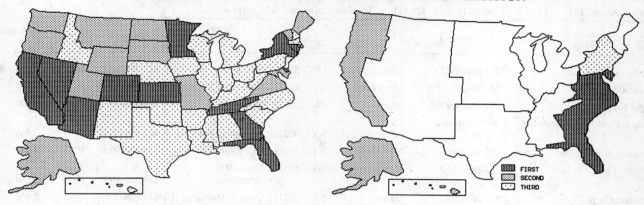

EMPLOYMENT 1995 - STATE AND REGIONAL CONCENTRATION

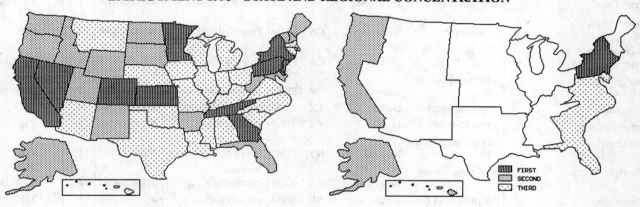

PAYROLL 1995 - STATE AND REGIONAL CONCENTRATION

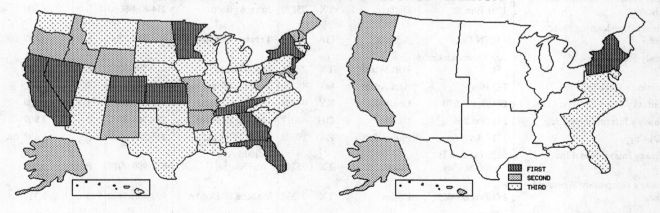

States with the darkest shading indicate those states which have proportionately more establishments, employment, or payrolls than would be indicated by the state's population. States with light shading are states with proportionately fewer establishments, less employment, and lower payrolls than population distribution. States shaded grey are within 15 percent of the state's population proportion in these categories. States for which no data are available are shown as average (grey). *Regions* are shaded to indicate absolute rank in the category. If no data for the category are available, establishment counts are used to shade the regions. Source of the data is the table on the facing page.

LEADING COMPANIES - SIC 6794 - Patent Owners and Lessors

Number shown: **100**   Total sales/assets ($ mil): **180,531**   Total employment (000): **4,914.4**

Company Name	Address				CEO Name	Phone	Co. Type	Sales/Assets ($ mil)	Empl. (000)
Carlson Holdings Inc.	PO Box 59159	Minneapolis	MN	55459	Curtis Carlson	612-449-1000	R	13,040 OR	145.0
McDonald's Corp.	McDonald's Plz.	Oak Brook	IL	60521	James R. Cantalupo	708-575-3000	P	10,686	237.0
Burger King Corp.	PO Box 020783	Miami	FL	33102	Paul Clayton	305-378-7011	S	9,800	300.0
Tricon Global Restaurants Inc.	1441 Gardiner Lane	Louisville	KY	40213	Andrall E. Pearson	502-456-8080	P	9,738	336.0
PolyGram Holding Inc.	825 8th Ave.	New York	NY	10019	Eric Kronfeld	212-333-8000	P	9,488	12.5
Manpower Inc	PO Box 2053	Milwaukee	WI	53201	Mitchell S. Fromstein	414-961-1000	P	8,860 OR	1,610.2
Southland Corp.	PO Box 711	Dallas	TX	75221	Clark J. Matthews II	214-828-7011	P	7,060	29.5
IYG Holding Co.	PO Box 711	Dallas	TX	75221	Clark J. Matthews II	214-828-7587	S	6,746	30.5
ITT Sheraton Corp.	60 State St.	Boston	MA	02109	John Kapioltas	617-367-3600	S	5,572 OR	18.0
Cendant Corp.	6 Sylvan Way	Parsippany	NJ	07054	Henry R. Silverman	973-952-8414	P	5,315 OR	34.0
Taco Bell Corp.	17901 Von Karman	Irvine	CA	92714	Peter C. Waller	949-863-4500	S	5,000	120.0
CFC Franchising Co.	3355 Michaelson Dr.	Irvine	CA	92612	Craig Bushey	714-251-5700	S	4,643 TA•	<0.1
MicroAge Inc.	2400 S. MicroAge Way	Tempe	AZ	85282	Jeffrey D. McKeever	602-804-2000	P	4,446 OR	4.4
Pizza Hut Inc.	14841 Dallas Pkwy.	Dallas	TX	75240	Michael S. Rawlings	972-338-7700	S	4,129	220.0
IT Financial Corp.	13150 Coit Rd.	Dallas	TX	75240	Ron Blaylock	972-671-1100	R	4,125 OR	<0.1
Olsten Corp.	175 Broad Hollow Rd.	Melville	NY	11747	Frank N. Liguori	516-844-7800	P	4,113	591.7
Hilton Hotels Corp.	9336 Civic Center Dr.	Beverly Hills	CA	90210	Stephen F. Bollenbach	310-278-4321	P	3,940 OR	65.0
InaCom Corp.	10810 Farnam Dr.	Omaha	NE	68154	Bill L. Fairfield	402-392-3900	P	3,900	2.9
TW Services Inc.	203 E. Main St.	Spartanburg	SC	29319	Jerome J. Richardson	803-597-8000	S	3,720	116.0
Blockbuster Entertainment Group	1201 Elm St.	Dallas	TX	75270	John Antioco	214-854-3000	S	3,500	70.0
Turner Broadcasting System Inc.	1 CNN Ctr.	Atlanta	GA	30348	Terence McGuirk	404-827-1700	S	3,437 OR	7.0
Tandy-Radio Shack	100 Thorockmorton St.	Fort Worth	TX	76102	Len Roberts	817-390-3011	D	3,260•	35.0
Domino's Pizza Inc.	PO Box 997	Ann Arbor	MI	48106	Thomas Monaghan	313-930-3030	R	2,400•	20.0
Kentucky Fried Chicken Corp.	PO Box 32070	Louisville	KY	40232	Jeffrey A. Moody	502-874-8300	S	2,300	66.0
Wendy's International Inc.	PO Box 256	Dublin	OH	43017	Gordon F. Teter	614-764-3100	P	2,037	50.0
CDI Corp.	1717 Arch St.	Philadelphia	PA	19103	Mitch Wienick	215-569-2200	P	1,497 OR	2.0
Brinker International Inc.	6820 Lyndon B. Johnson Fwy.	Dallas	TX	75240	Ronald A. McDougall	972-980-9917	P	1,335	47.0
Friday's Hospitality Worldwide Inc.	PO Box 809062	Dallas	TX	75380	Wallace B. Doolin	972-450-5400	S	1,317	42.5
America's Favorite Chicken Co.	6 Concourse Pkwy. N.E.	Atlanta	GA	30328	Frank Velatti	770-391-9500	R	1,240•	13.4
Shoney's Inc.	PO Box 1260	Nashville	TN	37202	J. Michael Bodnar	615-391-5201	P	1,203	3.3
Little Caesar Enterprises Inc.	2211 Woodward Ave.	Detroit	MI	48201	Michael Ilitch	313-983-6000	R	1,160	86.0

Company type codes: P - Public, R - Private, S - Subsidiary, D - Division, J - Joint Venture, A - Affiliate, G - Group. If the dollar values shown are not sales, the following codes apply: TA - Total Assets; OR - Operating Revenues; GB - Gross Billings. • - estimated dollar value. < - less than. *na* - not available.

Continued on next page.

LEADING COMPANIES - SIC 6794 - Patent Owners and Lessors
Continued

Company Name	Address				CEO Name	Phone	Co. Type	Sales/Assets ($ mil)	Empl. (000)
Casey's General Stores Inc.	1 Convenience Blvd.	Ankeny	IA	50021	Ronald M. Lamb	515-965-6100	P	1,114	9.5
El Pollo Loco	PO Box 15390	Irvine	CA	92713		714-251-5000	S	1,090	2.8
Jack in the Box Div.	9330 Balboa Ave.	San Diego	CA	92123	Robert J. Nugent	619-571-2121	D	1,026	33.7
Norrell Corp.	3535 Piedmont Rd. N.E.	Atlanta	GA	30305	C. Douglas Miller	404-240-3000	P	1,014 OR	1.3
General Nutrition Companies Inc.	921 Penn Ave.	Pittsburgh	PA	15222	William E. Watts	412-288-4600	P	991	9.6
Outback Steakhouse Inc.	550 N. Reo St.	Tampa	FL	33609	Chris T. Sullivan	813-282-1225	P	937	23.0
Robert Half International Inc.	2884 Sand Hill Rd.	Menlo Park	CA	94025	Harold M. Messmer Jr.	415-854-9700	P	899 OR	2.9
Drug Emporium Inc.	155 Hidden Ravines Dr.	Powell	OH	43065	David L. Kriegel	614-548-7080	P	885	6.5
Triarc Companies Inc.	280 Park Ave.	New York	NY	10017	Nelson Peltz	212-451-3000	P	861	2.0
Pearle Vision Inc.	2534 Royal Ln.	Dallas	TX	75229	David Hardie	214-277-5000	S	850•	4.9
Buffets Inc.	10260 Viking Dr.	Eden Prairie	MN	55344	Roe H. Hatlen	612-942-9760	P	809	24.8
UOP	25 E. Algonquin Rd.	Des Plaines	IL	60017	Michael D. Winfield	847-391-2000	J	770•	4.0
Ruby Tuesday Inc.	4721 Morrison Dr.	Mobile	AL	36609	III, Sandy E. Beall	334-344-3000	P	654	24.4
Long John Silver's Restaurants Inc.	PO Box 11988	Lexington	KY	40579	Rolf Towe	606-263-6000	R	646•	20.0
CFC Holdings Corp.	1000 Corporate Dr.	Fort Lauderdale	FL	33334	John Carson	305-351-5600	S	610•	9.0
Midas International Corp.	225 N. Michigan Ave.	Chicago	IL	60601	John R. Moore	312-565-7500	P	604 OR	3.5
Ryan's Family Steak Houses Inc.	PO Box 100	Greer	SC	29652	Charles D. Way	864-879-1000	P	599	18.0
CKE Restaurants Inc.	PO Box 4349	Anaheim	CA	92803	William P. Foley	714-774-5796	P	588	11.1
Dairy Mart Convenience Stores Inc.	210 Broadway E.	Cuyahoga Falls	OH	44222	Robert B. Stein Jr.	330-923-0421	P	586	4.1
Western Staff Services Inc.	PO Box 9280	Walnut Creek	CA	94598	W. Robert Stover	510-930-5300	P	577 OR	1.1
Applebee's International Inc.	4551 W. 107th St.	Overland Park	KS	66207	Lloyd L. Hill	913-967-4000	P	516 OR	18.1
Staff Builders Inc.	1981 Marcus Ave.	Lake Success	NY	11042	Stephen Savitsky	516-358-1000	P	480 OR	3.3
Personnel Group of America Inc.	6302 Fairview Rd.	Charlotte	NC	28210	Edward P. Drudge Jr.	704-442-5100	P	476 OR	52.9
Boston Chicken Inc.	PO Box 4086	Golden	CO	80401	Saad J. Nadhir	303-278-9500	P	462	1.0
W.S. Badcock Corp.	PO Box 497	Mulberry	FL	33860	Ben Badcock	941-425-4921	R	450 OR•	1.5
Apple South Inc.	Hancock at Washington	Madison	GA	30650	Tom E. DuPree Jr.	706-342-4552	P	440	8.4
Sizzler International Inc.	PO Box 92092	Los Angeles	CA	90066	Kevin W. Perkins	310-827-2300	P	436	8.2
Chi-Chi's Inc.	10200 Linn Station Rd.	Louisville	KY	40223	Roger Chamnes	502-426-3900	S	430•	20.0
Watsco Inc.	2665 S. Bayshore Dr.	Coconut Grove	FL	33133	Albert H. Nahmad	305-858-0828	P	425	1.3
Fred's Inc.	4300 New Getwell Rd.	Memphis	TN	38118	Michael J. Hayes	901-365-8880	P	418	4.2

Company type codes: P - Public, R - Private, S - Subsidiary, D - Division, J - Joint Venture, A - Affiliate, G - Group. If the dollar values shown are not sales, the following codes apply: TA - Total Assets; OR - Operating Revenues; GB - Gross Billings. • - estimated dollar value. < - less than. *na* - not available.

Continued on next page.

LEADING COMPANIES - SIC 6794 - Patent Owners and Lessors

Continued

Company Name	Address				CEO Name	Phone	Co. Type	Sales/Assets ($ mil)	Empl. (000)
International Dairy Queen Inc.	7505 Metro Blvd.	Minneapolis	MN	55439	Michael P. Sullivan	612-830-0200	P	411	0.6
DAKA International Inc.	1 Corporate Pl.	Danvers	MA	01923	William H. Baumhauer	508-774-9115	P	392	13.7
Nautica Enterprises Inc.	40 West 57th St.	New York	NY	10019	Harvey Sanders	212-541-5990	P	387	1.3
Ben Franklin Retail Stores Inc.	PO Box 5938	Chicago	IL	60680	Robert A. Kendig	708-462-6100	P	375 OR	2.0
Gymboree Corp.	700 Airport Blvd.	Burlingame	CA	94010	Nancy J. Pedot	650-579-0600	P	374	6.0
North Central Food Systems Inc.	2901 Metro Dr.	Bloomington	MN	55425	Dave Guckenberg	612-854-7944	R	370 OR•	4.0
Jenny Craig Inc.	11355 N. Torrey Pines Rd.	La Jolla	CA	92037	C. Joseph LaBonte	619-259-7000	P	365 OR	4.2
Papa John's International Inc.	11492 Bluegrass Pkwy.	Louisville	KY	40299	John H. Schnatter	502-266-5200	P	360	9.5
ShowBiz Pizza Time Inc.	PO Box 152077	Irving	TX	75015	Richard M. Frank	972-258-8507	P	350	13.6
Sbarro Inc.	763 Larkfield Rd.	Commack	NY	11725	Mario Sbarro	516-864-0200	P	329	7.8
Jiffy Lube International Inc.	PO Box 2967	Houston	TX	77252	James M. Wheat	713-546-4100	S	329 OR	7.0
VICORP Restaurants Inc.	PO Box 16601	Denver	CO	80216	J. Michael Jenkins	303-296-2121	P	326	12.4
Insituform Technologies Inc.	702 Spirit 40 Park Drive	Chesterfield	MO	63005	Anthony W. Hooper	314-530-8000	P	321 OR	1.4
Maxim Group Inc.	210 TownPark Dr.	Kennesaw	GA	30144	A.J. Nassar	770-590-9369	P	310	2.4
Doubletree Corp.	410 North 44th St.	Phoenix	AZ	85008	Richard M. Kelleher	602-220-6666	P	305 OR	29.0
NPC International Inc.	PO Box 62643	Pittsburg	KS	66762	O. Gene Bicknell	316-231-3390	P	295	12.0
White Hen Pantry Inc.	660 Industrial Dr.	Elmhurst	IL	60126	Robert G. Robertson	708-833-3100	R	290 OR•	0.5
RTM Winners L.P.	5995 Barfield Rd.	Atlanta	GA	30328	Russell V. Umphenour Jr.	404-256-4900	R	289	12.0
TPI Enterprises Inc.	3950 RCA Blvd.	Palm Beach	FL	33410	J. Gary Sharp	407-691-8800	P	287	10.3
Whataburger Inc.	4600 Parkdale Dr.	Corpus Christi	TX	78411	Tom Dobson	512-878-0650	R	264•	8.0
Consolidated Products Inc.	36 S. Pennsylvania St.	Indianapolis	IN	46204	Alan B. Gilman	317-633-4100	P	263	12.0
Perkins Family Restaurants L.P.	6075 Poplar Ave.	Memphis	TN	38119	Richard K. Arras	901-766-6400	P	253	9.2
Ben Franklin Stores Inc.	PO Box 5938	Chicago	IL	60188	Robert A. Kendig	630-462-6100	S	250 OR	0.6
Damon's International Inc.	4645 Executive Dr.	Columbus	OH	43220	Ken Cole	614-442-7900	R	250 OR	<0.1
Krystal Co.	1 Union Sq.	Chattanooga	TN	37402	Carl D. Long	423-757-1550	P	244	9.3
American Speedy Printing Centers Inc.	1800 W. Maple	Troy	MI	48084	William McIntyre	248-614-3700	R	238 OR•	<0.1
Au Bon Pain Company Inc.	19 Fid Kennedy Ave.	Boston	MA	02210	Ronald M. Shaich	617-423-2100	P	237	6.7
Country Kitchen International Inc.	PO Box 59159	Minneapolis	MN	55459	Charles Foster	612-449-1300	S	235 OR	10.8
Playboy Enterprises Inc.	680 N. Lake Shore Dr.	Chicago	IL	60611	Christie Hefner	312-751-8000	P	219	0.6
Ground Round Inc.	PO Box 9078	Braintree	MA	02184	Dan Scoggin	617-380-3100	S	219	9.4
IHOP Corp.	525 N. Brand Blvd.	Glendale	CA	91203	Richard K. Herzer	818-240-6055	P	215 OR	2.6
Arby's Inc.	PO Box 407008	Fort Lauderdale	FL	33340	Roland Smith	954-351-5100	S	215	9.0

Company type codes: P - Public, R - Private, S - Subsidiary, D - Division, J - Joint Venture, A - Affiliate, G - Group. If the dollar values shown are not sales, the following codes apply: TA - Total Assets; OR - Operating Revenues; GB - Gross Billings. • - estimated dollar value. < - less than. *na* - not available.

Continued on next page.

LEADING COMPANIES - SIC 6794 - Patent Owners and Lessors
Continued

Company Name	Address				CEO Name	Phone	Co. Type	Sales/Assets ($ mil)	Empl. (000)
O'Charley's Inc.	3038 Sidco Dr.	Nashville	TN	37204	Gregory L. Burns	615-256-8500	P	200	6.5
Checkers Drive-In Restaurants Inc.	PO Box 1079	Clearwater	FL	34617	Albert J. DiMarco	813-441-3500	P	195	6.5
Choice Hotels Franchising Inc.	10750 Columbia Pike	Silver Spring	MD	20901	William R. Floyd	301-979-5000	S	188 OR	2.4
Valvoline Instant Oil Change Franchising Inc.	PO Box 14046	Lexington	KY	40512	Gerald L. Wipf	606-357-7070	S	185 OR	4.0
Sonic Corp.	101 Park Ave.	Oklahoma City	OK	73102	J. Clifford Hudson	405-280-7654	P	184	8.0
Discovery Zone Inc.	110 E. Broward Blvd.	Ft. Lauderdale	FL	33301	Scott W. Bernstein	305-627-2400	P	182 OR	5.9
Roto-Rooter Inc.	2500 Chemed Ctr.	Cincinnati	OH	45202		513-762-6690	P	180 OR	2.6

Source: Ward's Business Directory of U.S. Private and Public Companies, 1996. Company type codes: P - Public, R - Private, S - Subsidiary, D - Division, J - Joint Venture, A - Affiliate, G - Group. If the dollar values shown are not sales, the following codes apply: TA - Total Assets; OR - Operating Revenues; GB - Gross Billings. * - estimated dollar value. < - less than; *na* - not available.

SIC 6798

REAL ESTATE INVESTMENT TRUSTS

Real estate investment trusts are establishments primarily engaged in closed-end investments in real estate or related mortgage assets. They operate so that they can meet the requirements of the Real Estate Investment Trust Act of 1960 as later amended. This act exempts trusts from corporate income and capital gains taxation, provided that they invest primarily in specified assets, pay out most of their income to shareholders, and meet certain requirements regarding the dispersion of trust ownership. Types of organizations that are included are mortgage trusts and mortgage investment trusts; real estate investment trusts (REITs), realty investment trusts, and realty trusts.

ESTABLISHMENTS, EMPLOYMENT, AND PAYROLL

	1990	1991		1992		1993		1994		1995		% change 90-95
		Value	%	Value	%	Value	%	Value	%	Value	%	
All Establishments	696	969	39.2	1,031	6.4	558	-45.9	610	9.3	604	-1.0	-13.2
Mid-March Employment	7,448	6,734	-9.6	7,800	15.8	5,403	-30.7	6,761	25.1	7,935	17.4	6.5
1st Quarter Wages (annualized - $ mil.)	286.9	257.1	-10.4	286.4	11.4	195.6	-31.7	246.1	25.8	329.1	33.7	14.7
Payroll per Emp. 1st Q. (annualized)	38,523	38,172	-0.9	36,724	-3.8	36,205	-1.4	36,407	0.6	41,472	13.9	7.7
Annual Payroll ($ mil.)	258.6	248.3	-4.0	295.0	18.8	212.8	-27.9	255.9	20.3	416.4	62.7	61.0
Establishments - 1-4 Emp. Number	463	742	60.3	795	7.1	408	-48.7	426	4.4	385	-9.6	-16.8
Mid-March Employment	797	1,133	42.2	1,240	9.4	568	-54.2	643	13.2	516	-19.8	-35.3
1st Quarter Wages (annualized - $ mil.)	29.0	33.5	15.3	39.3	17.3	16.2	-58.6	19.3	19.0	19.1	-1.2	-34.2
Payroll per Emp. 1st Q. (annualized)	36,442	29,546	-18.9	31,668	7.2	28,599	-9.7	30,072	5.2	37,023	23.1	1.6
Annual Payroll ($ mil.)	30.4	36.2	19.1	54.0	49.1	26.3	-51.3	27.7	5.4	31.2	12.4	2.5
Establishments - 5-9 Emp. Number	104	101	-2.9	102	1.0	(D)	-	87	-	109	25.3	4.8
Mid-March Employment	676	647	-4.3	649	0.3	(D)	-	560	-	706	26.1	4.4
1st Quarter Wages (annualized - $ mil.)	26.4	22.5	-14.9	21.8	-3.0	(D)	-	23.9	-	37.7	58.0	43.0
Payroll per Emp. 1st Q. (annualized)	39,036	34,726	-11.0	33,578	-3.3	(D)	-	42,636	-	53,445	25.4	36.9
Annual Payroll ($ mil.)	25.8	21.1	-18.3	22.1	4.9	(D)	-	23.6	-	29.4	24.8	13.9
Establishments - 10-19 Emp. Number	60	68	13.3	68	-	30	-55.9	34	13.3	42	23.5	-30.0
Mid-March Employment	833	914	9.7	900	-1.5	410	-54.4	472	15.1	556	17.8	-33.3
1st Quarter Wages (annualized - $ mil.)	36.1	45.7	26.5	50.8	11.0	21.1	-58.5	27.4	30.1	35.5	29.4	-1.7
Payroll per Emp. 1st Q. (annualized)	43,366	50,013	15.3	56,391	12.8	51,424	-8.8	58,102	13.0	63,835	9.9	47.2
Annual Payroll ($ mil.)	33.0	40.6	23.3	41.8	2.8	23.3	-44.2	25.9	11.2	34.7	33.8	5.1
Establishments - 20-49 Emp. Number	38	32	-15.8	(D)	-	(D)	-	37	-	(D)	-	-
Mid-March Employment	1,158	896	-22.6	(D)	-	(D)	-	1,228	-	(D)	-	-
1st Quarter Wages (annualized - $ mil.)	51.7	33.3	-35.6	(D)	-	(D)	-	46.9	-	(D)	-	-
Payroll per Emp. 1st Q. (annualized)	44,642	37,165	-16.7	(D)	-	(D)	-	38,182	-	(D)	-	-
Annual Payroll ($ mil.)	47.1	32.6	-30.8	(D)	-	(D)	-	51.4	-	(D)	-	-
Establishments - 50-99 Emp. Number	16	15	-6.3	(D)	-	18	-	(D)	-	19	-	18.8
Mid-March Employment	1,038	(D)	-	(D)	-	1,085	-	(D)	-	1,266	-	22.0
1st Quarter Wages (annualized - $ mil.)	38.4	(D)	-	(D)	-	38.8	-	(D)	-	47.2	-	22.7
Payroll per Emp. 1st Q. (annualized)	37,037	(D)	-	(D)	-	35,779	-	(D)	-	37,254	-	0.6
Annual Payroll ($ mil.)	32.0	(D)	-	(D)	-	42.8	-	(D)	-	49.8	-	55.9
Establishments - 100-249 Emp. Number	11	9	-18.2	8	-11.1	9	12.5	9	-	7	-22.2	-36.4
Mid-March Employment	1,593	1,417	-11.0	1,428	0.8	1,466	2.7	1,394	-4.9	942	-32.4	-40.9
1st Quarter Wages (annualized - $ mil.)	58.1	57.9	-0.4	56.5	-2.4	62.3	10.3	69.7	12.0	61.0	-12.6	5.0
Payroll per Emp. 1st Q. (annualized)	36,454	40,833	12.0	39,532	-3.2	42,475	7.4	50,029	17.8	64,735	29.4	77.6
Annual Payroll ($ mil.)	47.8	56.0	17.0	57.4	2.6	57.9	0.9	62.2	7.3	57.5	-7.6	20.2
Establishments - 250-499 Emp. Number	4	2	-50.0	4	100.0	-	-	(D)	-	5	-	25.0
Mid-March Employment	1,353	(D)	-	1,330	-	-	-	(D)	-	1,942	-	43.5
1st Quarter Wages (annualized - $ mil.)	47.2	(D)	-	41.8	-	-	-	(D)	-	66.0	-	39.9
Payroll per Emp. 1st Q. (annualized)	34,850	(D)	-	31,447	-	-	-	(D)	-	33,975	-	-2.5
Annual Payroll ($ mil.)	42.5	(D)	-	42.0	-	-	-	(D)	-	153.9	-	262.0
Establishments - 500-999 Emp. Number	-	-	-	-	-	(D)	-	(D)	-	(D)	-	-
Mid-March Employment	-	-	-	-	-	(D)	-	(D)	-	(D)	-	-
1st Quarter Wages (annualized - $ mil.)	-	-	-	-	-	(D)	-	(D)	-	(D)	-	-
Payroll per Emp. 1st Q. (annualized)	(D)	(D)	-	-	-	(D)	-	(D)	-	(D)	-	-
Annual Payroll ($ mil.)	-	-	-	-	-	(D)	-	(D)	-	(D)	-	-
Estab. - 1000 or More Emp. Number	-	-	-	-	-	-	-	-	-	-	-	-
Mid-March Employment	-	-	-	-	-	-	-	-	-	-	-	-
1st Quarter Wages (annualized - $ mil.)	-	-	-	-	-	-	-	-	-	-	-	-
Payroll per Emp. 1st Q. (annualized)	(D)	(D)	-	-	-	-	-	-	-	-	-	-
Annual Payroll ($ mil.)	-	-	-	-	-	-	-	-	-	-	-	-

Source: County Business Patterns, U.S. Department of Commerce, Washington, D.C., for 1990 through 1995. Payroll per employee is calculated using mid-March employment and 1st Quarter wages, annualized. Annual payroll, also shown, may not equal the annualized 1st Quarter wages. Columns headed by a percent sign (%) indicate change from the previous year. na stands for not available. The symbol (D) indicates that data are withheld by the source to avoid disclosure of competitive information. A dash (-) indicates that data are not available or cannot be calculated.

ESTABLISHMENTS
Number

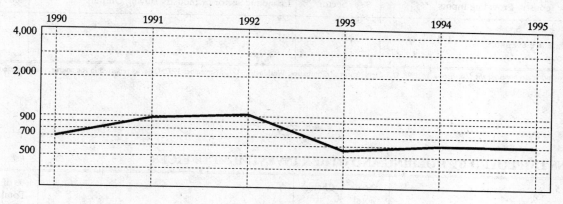

MID-MARCH EMPLOYMENT
Number

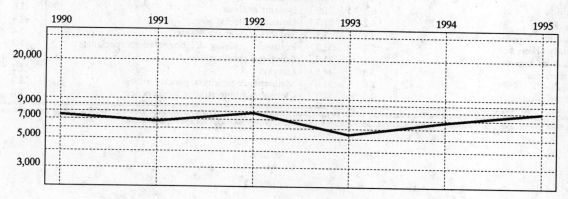

ANNUAL PAYROLL
$ million

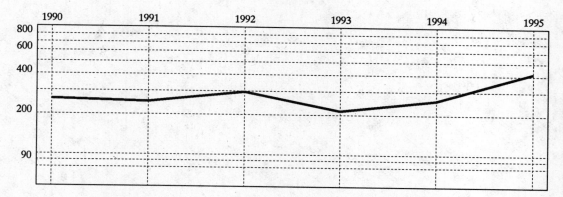

INPUTS AND OUTPUTS FOR HOLDING AND OTHER INVESTMENT OFFICES - SIC GROUP 67

Economic Sector or Industry Providing Inputs	%	Sector	Economic Sector or Industry Buying Outputs	%	Sector
No Input-Output data are available for this industry group.					

Source: *Benchmark Input-Output Accounts for the U.S. Economy, 1992,* U.S. Department of Commerce, Washington, D.C., November 1997. Data, as reported in the source, are organized by the 1987 SIC structure in use in 1992.

OCCUPATIONS EMPLOYED BY HOLDING AND OTHER INVESTMENT OFFICES

Occupation	% of Total 1996	Change to 2006	Occupation	% of Total 1996	Change to 2006
General managers & top executives	10.4	27.6	Managers & administrators nec	1.9	30.5
Secretaries, except legal & medical	10.4	4.4	Marketing & sales worker supervisors	1.9	31.7
General office clerks	6.8	13.3	Securities & financial sales workers	1.8	31.7
Accountants & auditors	6.4	21.9	Systems analysts	1.6	95.2
Financial managers	6.2	31.7	Brokerage clerks	1.4	10.1
Bookkeeping, accounting, & auditing clerks	5.9	5.3	Janitors & cleaners, maids	1.4	5.3
Management support workers nec	5.1	31.7	Personnel, training, & labor relations specialists	1.3	31.6
Clerical supervisors & managers	4.3	31.7	Computer programmers	1.3	8.4
Sales & related workers nec	3.3	44.8	Lawyers	1.2	31.6
Professional workers nec	2.6	31.6	Maintenance repairers, general utility	1.2	22.7
Receptionists & information clerks	2.0	31.7	Clerical & administrative workers nec	1.2	31.7

Sources: *Industry-Occupation Matrix,* Bureau of Labor Statistics. These data relate to one or more 3-digit SIC industry groups rather than to a single 4-digit SIC. The change reported for each occupation to the year 2005 is a percent of growth or decline as estimated by the Bureau of Labor Statistics. The abbreviation *nec* stands for not elsewhere classified.

U.S. AND STATE DATA ON INDUSTRY REVENUES AND OTHER ACCOUNTS FOR 1992

State	No. of Estab.	Employ-ment	Payroll ($ mil.)	Revenues ($ mil.)	Empl./ Estab.	Revenue/ Estab. ($)	Payroll/ Estab. ($)	Revenue/ Empl. ($)	Payroll/ Empl. ($)
UNITED STATES	655	4,771	181.8	2,507.5	7	3,828,263	277,537	525,574	38,102
California	121	830	38.6	434.9	7	3,594,579	319,116	524,029	46,522
Colorado	10	-	(D)	(D)	(D)	(D)	(D)	(D)	(D)
Florida	47	211	6.8	131.1	4	2,789,574	143,872	621,374	32,047
Georgia	17	229	6.7	89.6	13	5,268,882	392,353	391,140	29,127
Illinois	27	720	20.2	123.5	27	4,575,148	746,481	171,568	27,993
Indiana	3	-	(D)	(D)	(D)	(D)	(D)	(D)	(D)
Maryland	17	302	10.4	390.9	18	22,992,000	611,118	1,294,252	34,401
Massachusetts	54	334	14.2	97.8	6	1,811,870	262,463	292,937	42,434
Michigan	15	23	0.6	8.1	2	542,267	38,000	353,652	24,783
Minnesota	6	6	0.2	2.3	1	375,333	34,500	375,333	34,500
Missouri	9	-	(D)	(D)	(D)	(D)	(D)	(D)	(D)
New Jersey	25	49	2.4	41.0	2	1,640,440	95,000	836,959	48,469
New York	42	-	(D)	(D)	(D)	(D)	(D)	(D)	(D)
North Carolina	24	168	2.8	26.9	7	1,120,208	115,625	160,030	16,518
Ohio	15	131	5.9	106.9	9	7,127,800	390,533	816,160	44,718
Pennsylvania	26	-	(D)	(D)	(D)	(D)	(D)	(D)	(D)
Tennessee	4	-	(D)	(D)	(D)	(D)	(D)	(D)	(D)
Texas	48	268	8.7	152.6	6	3,179,188	181,917	569,407	32,582
Virginia	35	-	(D)	(D)	(D)	(D)	(D)	(D)	(D)
Washington	7	20	0.3	2.1	3	302,429	48,571	105,850	17,000
Wisconsin	4	-	(D)	(D)	(D)	(D)	(D)	(D)	(D)

Source: 1992 Economic Census, U.S. Department of Commerce, Washington, D.C. This is the only table that shows revenue data as collected by the Bureau of the Census in an Economic Census. The symbol (D) indicates that data are withheld by the source to avoid disclosure of competitive information. A dash (-) indicates that data are not available or cannot be calculated.

STATE-BY-STATE DATA ON ESTABLISHMENTS, EMPLOYMENT, AND PAYROLL - 1994 AND 1995

State	1994					1995					% Change Empl.
	No. of Estab.	Employ- ment	Pay / Empl.	Payroll ($ mil.)	Pay / Estab.	No. of Estab.	Employ- ment	Pay / Empl.	Payroll ($ mil.)	Pay / Estab.	
Alabama	1	(D)	-	(D)	-	1	(D)	-	(D)	-	-
Alaska	2	(D)	-	(D)	-	1	(D)	-	(D)	-	-
Arizona	14	(D)	-	(D)	-	12	43	35,442	1.5	126,917	-
Arkansas	1	(D)	-	(D)	-	1	(D)	-	(D)	-	-
California	108	881	44,286	41.7	386,472	107	1,334	59,058	168.0	1,569,654	51.4
Colorado	14	69	82,319	5.0	357,714	11	93	68,559	8.5	771,818	34.8
Connecticut	9	(D)	-	(D)	-	6	(D)	-	(D)	-	-
Delaware	1	(D)	-	(D)	-	1	(D)	-	(D)	-	-
District of Columbia	6	(D)	-	(D)	-	6	(D)	-	(D)	-	-
Florida	56	406	20,463	8.3	148,339	52	(D)	-	(D)	-	-
Georgia	21	734	26,371	18.6	885,762	20	(D)	-	(D)	-	-
Hawaii	5	25	63,680	1.6	324,600	5	30	59,067	2.1	412,600	20.0
Idaho	3	(D)	-	(D)	-	4	(D)	-	(D)	-	-
Illinois	30	709	34,324	32.3	1,076,233	37	1,006	55,221	50.6	1,367,135	41.9
Indiana	4	19	34,316	0.8	208,750	6	(D)	-	(D)	-	-
Iowa	7	(D)	-	(D)	-	7	(D)	-	(D)	-	-
Kansas	2	(D)	-	(D)	-	1	(D)	-	(D)	-	-
Kentucky	2	(D)	-	(D)	-	2	(D)	-	(D)	-	-
Louisiana	7	57	8,491	0.6	85,857	6	17	23,765	0.8	138,167	-70.2
Maine	3	(D)	-	(D)	-	3	(D)	-	(D)	-	-
Maryland	11	376	58,851	17.8	1,619,545	11	578	39,543	20.9	1,903,636	53.7
Massachusetts	40	842	24,679	21.3	532,725	34	1,066	23,471	23.1	678,353	26.6
Michigan	12	18	26,222	0.5	41,167	10	42	28,381	1.0	103,900	133.3
Minnesota	5	(D)	-	(D)	-	6	(D)	-	(D)	-	-
Mississippi	3	(D)	-	(D)	-	2	(D)	-	(D)	-	-
Missouri	8	15	55,467	0.7	86,875	7	13	7,385	0.1	20,143	-13.3
Montana	1	(D)	-	(D)	-	1	(D)	-	(D)	-	-
Nevada	4	(D)	-	(D)	-	4	(D)	-	(D)	-	-
New Hampshire	3	80	31,600	2.9	970,667	3	(D)	-	(D)	-	-
New Jersey	13	(D)	-	(D)	-	13	(D)	-	(D)	-	-
New Mexico	3	(D)	-	(D)	-	2	(D)	-	(D)	-	-
New York	38	516	77,876	34.2	899,474	39	464	68,621	33.2	852,436	-10.1
North Carolina	21	102	29,098	2.4	115,238	25	530	16,174	8.7	349,240	419.6
North Dakota	2	(D)	-	(D)	-	2	(D)	-	(D)	-	-
Ohio	17	601	18,669	12.7	746,706	19	709	27,961	21.5	1,130,632	18.0
Oklahoma	8	32	14,375	0.6	69,500	9	24	15,833	0.6	61,333	-25.0
Oregon	2	(D)	-	(D)	-	2	(D)	-	(D)	-	-
Pennsylvania	19	125	44,768	6.3	332,684	16	119	48,908	6.1	379,438	-4.8
Rhode Island	2	(D)	-	(D)	-	3	(D)	-	(D)	-	-
South Carolina	7	25	20,960	1.8	252,571	7	34	18,235	1.1	153,857	36.0
Tennessee	7	(D)	-	(D)	-	6	(D)	-	(D)	-	-
Texas	38	283	22,403	7.1	187,632	43	301	34,365	13.1	304,256	6.4
Utah	3	(D)	-	(D)	-	2	(D)	-	(D)	-	-
Virginia	34	(D)	-	(D)	-	35	(D)	-	(D)	-	-
Washington	9	30	18,400	0.5	58,000	11	109	10,275	1.4	127,727	263.3
Wisconsin	4	(D)	-	(D)	-	3	(D)	-	(D)	-	-

Source: County Business Patterns, U.S. Department of Commerce, Washington, D.C., for 1994 and 1995. Employment shown is for mid-March of the year shown. Payroll per employee is calculated by annualizing 1st Quarter payroll (not shown) and then dividing that value by mid-March employment. Dividing total annual payroll (columns 5 and 10) by employment, therefore, will *not* yield the payroll per employee figure (columns 4 and 9). The symbol (D) indicates that data are withheld by the source to avoid disclosure of competitive information. A dash (-) indicates that data are not available or cannot be calculated.

ESTABLISHMENTS 1995 - STATE AND REGIONAL CONCENTRATION

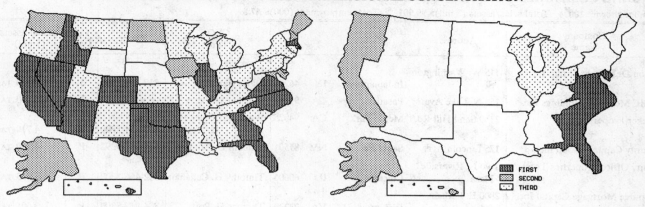

EMPLOYMENT 1995 - STATE AND REGIONAL CONCENTRATION

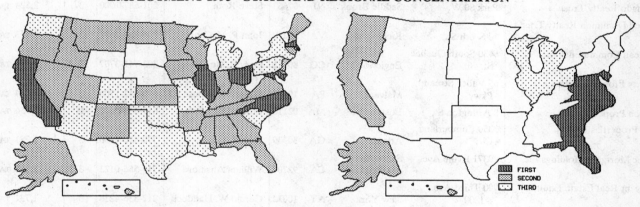

PAYROLL 1995 - STATE AND REGIONAL CONCENTRATION

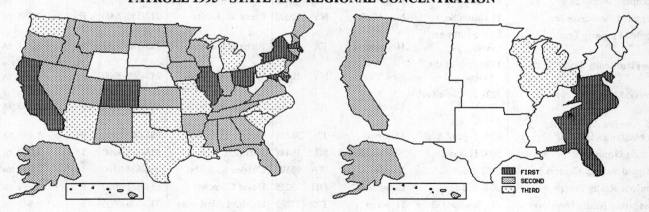

States with the darkest shading indicate those states which have proportionately more establishments, employment, or payrolls than would be indicated by the state's population. States with light shading are states with proportionately fewer establishments, less employment, and lower payrolls than population distribution. States shaded grey are within 15 percent of the state's population proportion in these categories. States for which no data are available are shown as average (grey). *Regions* are shaded to indicate absolute rank in the category. If no data for the category are available, establishment counts are used to shade the regions. Source of the data is the table on the facing page.

LEADING COMPANIES - SIC 6798 - Real Estate Investment Trusts

Number shown: **100**   Total sales/assets ($ mil): **99,901**   Total employment (000): **47.8**

Company Name	Address				CEO Name	Phone	Co. Type	Sales/Assets ($ mil)	Empl. (000)
Simon DeBartolo Group Inc.	115 W. Washington St.	Indianapolis	IN	46204	David Simon	317-636-1600	3	7,663 TA	6.3
INMC Mortgage Holdings Inc.	155 N. Lake Ave.	Pasadena	CA	91101	Michael W. Perry	--	3	6,000 TA	1.0
Spieker Properties Inc.	2180 Sand Hill Rd.	Menlo Park	CA	94025	Warren E. Spieker Jr.	650-854-5600	3	4,700 TA	0.4
Security Capital Group Inc.	125 Lincoln Ave.	Santa Fe	NM	87501	William D. Sanders	505-982-9292	P	4,460 TA	0.3
Equity Office Properties Trust	Two N. Riverside Plaza	Chicago	IL	60606	Timothy H. Callahan	312-466-3300	P	3,913 TA	0.7
Resource Mortgage Capital Inc.	2800 E. Parham Rd.	Richmond	VA	23228	Thomas H. Potts	804-967-5800	P	3,601 TA	0.2
Capstone Capital Corp.	1000 Urban Center Pkwy.	Birmingham	AL	35242	John McRoberts	205-967-2092	P	3,182 TA	<0.1
Vornado Realty Trust	Park 80 W.	Saddle Brook	NJ	07663	Steve Roth	201-587-1000	3	2,524 TA	0.2
United Dominion Realty Trust Inc.	10 S. 6th St.	Richmond	VA	23219	John P. McCann	804-780-2691	3	2,473 TA	1.9
Chateau Communities Inc.	6430 South Quebec St.	Englewood	CO	80111	Gary P. Mc Daniel	303-741-3707	P	2,129 TA*	3.0
Liberty Property Trust	65 Valley Stream Pkwy.	Malvern	PA	19355	Willard G. Rouse III	610-648-1700	3	2,094 TA	0.3
Boston Properties Inc.	8 Arlington St.	Boston	MA	02116	Edward H. Linde	617-859-2600	P	1,954 TA	0.3
Post Properties Inc.	3350 Cumberland Cir.	Atlanta	GA	30339	John T. Glover	770-850-4400	3	1,781 TA	1.6
Impac Mortgage Holdings Inc.	20371 Irvine Ave.	Santa Ana Heights	CA	92707	William Ahsmore	714-556-0122	3	1,752 TA	0.2
Crescent Real Estate Equities Inc.	900 Third Ave. #1800	New York	NY	10022	Gerald W. Haddock	212-836-4216	3	1,731 TA	0.2
DeBartolo Realty Corp.	7655 Market St.	Youngstown	OH	44513	Richard S. Sokolov	330-758-7292	S	1,532 TA	3.8
Merry Land and Investment Company Inc.	PO Box 1417	Augusta	GA	30903	W. Tennent Houston	706-722-6756	3	1,428 TA	0.9
Integrated Resources Inc.	10 Union Sq. E.	New York	NY	10003	Frank W. Geller	212-353-7000	P	1,338 TA	0.2
Camden Property Trust	3200 Southwest Fwy.	Houston	TX	77027	Richard J. Campo	713-964-3555	3	1,324 TA	0.6
New Plan Realty Trust	1120 Ave. of the Amer.	New York	NY	10036	William Newman	212-869-3000	3	1,261 TA	0.6
Starwood Lodging Trust	2231 E. Camelback Rd.	Phoenix	AZ	85016	Barry S. Sternlicht	602-852-3900	3	1,233 TA	<0.1
Mid-America Apartment Communities Inc.	6584 Poplar Ave.	Memphis	TN	38138	George E. Cates	901-682-6600	P	1,199 TA	0.2
Horizon Group Inc.	5000 Hakes Dr.	Norton Shores	MI	49441	Jeffrey A. Kerr	616-798-9100	3	1,059 TA	0.5
Shurgard Storage Centers Inc.	1201 3rd Ave.	Seattle	WA	98101	Charles K. Barbo	206-624-8100	3	956 TA	0.9
Glimcher Realty Trust	20 S. 3rd St.	Columbus	OH	43215	David Glimcher	614-621-9000	P	949 TA	0.5
Weingarten Realty Investors	PO Box 924133	Houston	TX	77292	Stanford Alexander	713-866-6000	3	947 TA	0.2
Kimco Realty Corp.	3333 New Hyde Park Rd.	New Hyde Park	NY	11042	Milton Cooper	516-869-9000	3	932 TA	<0.1
Prime Retail Inc.	100 E. Pratt St.	Baltimore	MD	21202	Abraham Rosenthal	410-234-0782	3	904 TA	0.6
Federal Realty Investment Trust	4800 Hampden Ln.	Bethesda	MD	20814	Steven J. Guttman	301-652-3360	3	886 TA	0.1

Company type codes: P - Public, R - Private, S - Subsidiary, D - Division, J - Joint Venture, A - Affiliate, G - Group. If the dollar values shown are not sales, the following codes apply: TA - Total Assets; OR - Operating Revenues; GB - Gross Billings. * - estimated dollar value. < - less than. *na* - not available.

Continued on next page.

LEADING COMPANIES - SIC 6798 - Real Estate Investment Trusts
Continued

Company Name	Address				CEO Name	Phone	Co. Type	Sales/Assets ($ mil)	Empl. (000)
Glenborough Realty Trust Inc.	400 S. El Camino Real	San Mateo	CA	94402	Robert Batinovich	650-343-9300	3	866 TA	0.5
Charles E. Smith Residential Realty Inc.	2345 Crystal Dr.	Crystal City	VA	22202	Robert H. Smith	703-920-8500	P	865 TA	1.3
Weeks Corp.	4497 Park Dr.	Norcross	GA	30093	Jr., A. Ray Weeks	770-923-4076	3	852 TA	0.4
Developers Diversified Realty Corp.	34555 Charigan Blvd.	Moreland Hills	OH	44022	Scott A. Wolstein	216-247-4700	3	830 TA	<0.1
Regency Realty Corp.	121 W. Forsyth St.	Jacksonville	FL	32202	Martin E. Stein Jr.	904-356-7000	3	827 TA	0.3
Mills Corp.	1300 Wilson Blvd.	Arlington	VA	22209	Lawrence Siegel	703-526-5000	3	827 TA	0.9
Crown American Realty Trust	Pasquerilla Plaza	Johnstown	PA	15907	Frank J. Pasquerilla	814-536-4441	3	786 TA	0.4
Macerich Co.	PO Box 2172	Santa Monica	CA	90407	Arthur M. Coppola	310-394-5333	3	763 TA	0.8
Highwoods Properties Inc.	3100 Smoketree Ct.	Raleigh	NC	27604	Ronald P. Gibson	919-872-4924	3	750 TA	0.5
Sunstone Hotel Investors Inc.	115 Calle de Industrias	San Clemente	CA	92672	Robert A. Alter	714-361-3900	3	740 TA	<0.1
Evans Withycombe Residential Inc.	6991 E. Camelback Rd.	Scottsdale	AZ	85251	Stephen O. Evans	602-840-1040	3	736 TA	0.6
Health Care REIT Inc.	PO Box 1475	Toledo	OH	43603	George L. Chapman	419-247-2800	3	734 TA	<0.1
Franchise Finance Corporation of America	17207 N. Perimeter Dr.	Scottsdale	AZ	85255	M.H. Fleischer	602-585-4500	3	724 TA*	<0.1
American Health Properties Inc.	6400 S. Fiddlers Green Cir.	Englewood	CO	80111	Joseph P. Sullivan	303-796-9793	3	691 TA	<0.1
Walden Residential Properties Inc.	5400 LBJ Frwy.	Dallas	TX	75240	Marshall B. Edwards	972-788-0510	3	690 TA	0.6
Bradley Real Estate Inc.	699 Boylston St.	Boston	MA	02116	Thomas P. D'Arcy	617-867-4200	P	669 TA	<0.1
Health Care Property Investors Inc.	10990 Wilshire Blvd.	Los Angeles	CA	90024	Kenneth B. Roath	310-473-1990	3	668 TA	<0.1
Price REIT Inc.	7979 Ivanhoe Ave.	La Jolla	CA	92037	Joseph Kornwasser	619-551-2320	3	637 TA	<0.1
Omega Healthcare Investors Inc.	905 W. Eisenhower Circle	Ann Arbor	MI	48103	Essel W. Bailey Jr.	313-747-9790	3	635 TA	<0.1
RFS Hotel Investors Inc.	850 Ridge Lake Blvd.	Memphis	TN	38120	Minor Perkins	901-767-7005	3	617 TA	<0.1
Urban Shopping Centers Inc.	900 N. Michigan Ave.	Chicago	IL	60611	Matthew S. Dominski	312-915-2000	3	599 TA	2.4
CenterPoint Properties Corp.	401 N. Michigan Ave.	Chicago	IL	60611	John S. Gates Jr.	312-346-5600	3	597 TA	0.1
Koger Equity Inc.	3986 Boulevard Center Dr.	Jacksonville	FL	32207	Victor A. Hughes Jr.	904-398-3403	3	585 TA	0.2
Berkshire Realty Company Inc.	470 Atlantic Ave.	Boston	MA	02210	Laurence Gerber	617-423-2233	3	570 TA	0.7
Gables Residential Trust	2859 Paces Ferry Rd.	Atlanta	GA	30339	Marcus E. Bromley	404-436-4600	3	563 TA	0.9
FelCor Suite Hotels Inc.	545 E. John Carpenter Fwy.	Irving	TX	75062	Thomas J. Corcoran Jr.	214-869-0013	3	548 TA	<0.1
Commercial Net Lease Realty Inc.	400 E. South St.	Orlando	FL	32801	Jr., James M. Seneff	407-422-1574	3	537 TA	<0.1
National Golf Properties Inc.	2828 Donald Douglas Loop N.	Santa Monica	CA	90405	James M. Stenich	310-664-4100	3	535 TA	<0.1

Company type codes: P - Public, R - Private, S - Subsidiary, D - Division, J - Joint Venture, A - Affiliate, G - Group. If the dollar values shown are not sales, the following codes apply: TA - Total Assets; OR - Operating Revenues; GB - Gross Billings. * - estimated dollar value. < - less than. *na* - not available.

Continued on next page.

LEADING COMPANIES - SIC 6798 - Real Estate Investment Trusts
Continued

Company Name	Address				CEO Name	Phone	Co. Type	Sales/Assets ($ mil)	Empl. (000)
Storage USA Inc.	10440 Little Patuxent Pkwy.	Columbia	MD	21044	Dean Jernigan	410-730-9500	3	510 TA	0.6
LTC Properties Inc.	300 Esplanade Dr #1260	Oxnard	CA	93030	Andre C. Dimitriadis	805-981-8655	3	504 TA	<0.1
Meditrust Inc.	197 1st Ave.	Needham Heights	MA	02194	Abraham D. Gosman	781-433-6000	P	500 TA	<0.1
IRT Property Co.	200 Galleria Pkwy.	Atlanta	GA	30339	Thomas H. McAuley	770-955-4406	3	498 TA	<0.1
Ambassador Apartments Inc.	77 W. Wacker Dr.	Chicago	IL	60601	David M. Glickman	312-917-1600	3	489 TA*	0.5
Bay Apartment Communities Inc.	4340 Stevens Creek Blvd.	San Jose	CA	95129	Gilbert M. Meyer	408-983-1500	3	477 TA	0.2
First Union Real Estate Equity and Mortgage Investments	55 Public Sq.	Cleveland	OH	44113	James C. Mastandrea	216-781-4030	3	440 TA	<0.1
Mortgage and Realty Trust	8380 Old York Rd. #300	Elkins Park	PA	19117	C.W. Strong Jr.	215-881-1525	3	427 TA	<0.1
Bedford Property Investors Inc.	270 Lafayette Cir.	Lafayette	CA	94549	Peter B. Bedford	510-283-8910	3	423 TA	<0.1
Cousins Properties Inc.	2500 Windy Ridge Pkwy.	Atlanta	GA	30339	Thomas G. Cousins	770-955-2200	3	418 TA	0.1
Associated Estates Realty Corp.	5025 Swetland Ct.	Richmond Heights	OH	44143	Jeffrey I. Friedman	216-261-5000	3	418 TA	0.8
Essex Property Trust Inc.	777 California Ave.	Palo Alto	CA	94304	Keith R. Guericke	415-494-3700	3	417 TA	0.3
Tanger Factory Outlet Centers Inc.	PO Box 29168	Greensboro	NC	27429	Stanley K. Tanger	919-274-1666	3	416 TA	<0.1
JP Realty Inc.	35 Century Park-Way	Salt Lake City	UT	84115	John Price	801-486-3911	3	412 TA*	0.4
Columbus Realty Trust	15851 Dallas Pkwy.	Dallas	TX	75248	Robert L. Shaw	972-387-1492	P	375 TA	0.2
Pacific Gulf Properties Inc.	363 San Miguel Dr.	Newport Beach	CA	92660	Glenn L. Carpenter	714-721-2700	P	365 TA	0.1
MGI Properties	1 Winthrope Sq.	Boston	MA	02110	W. Pearce Coues	617-442-6000	3	362 TA	<0.1
FAC Realty Inc.	230 N. Equity Dr.	Smithfield	NC	27577	J. Dixon Fleming Jr.	919-934-9446	3	355 TA	<0.1
BRE Properties Inc.	1 Montgomery St.	San Francisco	CA	94104	Frank C. McDowell	415-445-6530	3	348 TA	<0.1
Lomas and Nettleton Mortgage Investors	PO Box 655644	Dallas	TX	75265	Robert T. Enloe III	214-879-5800	3	338 TA	<0.1
Meridian Industrial Trust Inc.	455 Market St.	San Francisco	CA	94105	Allen J. Anderson	415-281-3900	3	333 TA	<0.1
Burnham Pacific Properties Inc.	610 W. Ash St.	San Diego	CA	92101	J. David Martin	619-652-4700	3	328 TA	<0.1
Equity Inns Inc.	4735 Spottswood	Memphis	TN	38117	Sr., Phillip H. McNeill	901-761-9651	3	318 TA	<0.1
First Washington Realty Trust Inc.	4350 East-West Hwy.	Bethesda	MD	20814	William J. Wolfe	301-907-7800	P	314 TA	<0.1
Summit Properties Inc.	212 S. Tryon St.	Charlotte	NC	28281	William F. Paulsen	704-334-9905	3	309 TA	0.7
Lexington Corporate Properties Inc.	355 Lexington Ave. 14th Fl.	New York	NY	10017	Robert Roskind	212-692-7260	3	309 TA	<0.1
Storage Trust Realty	PO Box 459	Columbia	MO	65202	Michael G. Burnam	573-499-4799	3	309 TA	0.5
Sentinel Real Estate Corp.	1290 Ave. of the Amer	New York	NY	10104	John Streicker	212-408-2910	3	300 TA*	1.3
Winston Hotels Inc.	2209 Century Dr.	Raleigh	NC	27612	Robert W. Winston III	919-510-6010	3	288 TA	<0.1

Company type codes: P - Public, R - Private, S - Subsidiary, D - Division, J - Joint Venture, A - Affiliate, G - Group. If the dollar values shown are not sales, the following codes apply: TA - Total Assets; OR - Operating Revenues; GB - Gross Billings. * - estimated dollar value. < - less than. *na* - not available.

Continued on next page.

LEADING COMPANIES - SIC 6798 - Real Estate Investment Trusts
Continued

Company Name	Address				CEO Name	Phone	Co. Type	Sales/Assets ($ mil)	Empl. (000)
Carr Realty Corp.	1700 Pennsylvania Ave. N.W.	Washington	DC	20006	Oliver T. Carr Jr.	202-624-1700	3	287 TA	0.5
Washington Real Estate Investment Trust	4936 Fairmont Ave.	Bethesda	MD	20814	Edmund B. Cronin	301-652-4300	3	283 TA	<0.1
Crocker Realty Trust Inc.	433 Plaza Real	Boca Raton	FL	33432	Thomas J. Crocker	407-395-9666	S	278 TA	<0.1
Paragon Group Inc.	7557 Rambler Rd.	Dallas	TX	75231	William R. Cooper	214-891-2000	3	263 TA	1.8
Saul Centers Inc.	8401 Connecticut Ave.	Chevy Chase	MD	20815	Philip D. Caraci	301-986-6000	P	261 TA	0.1
Nationwide Health Properties Inc.	4675 MacArthur Ct.	Newport Beach	CA	92660	R. Bruce Andrews	714-251-1211	3	254 TA	<0.1
Amli Residential Properties Trust	125 S. Wacker Dr.	Chicago	IL	60606	Allan J. Sweet	312-984-5037	3	243 TA	0.3
RPS Realty Trust	733 3rd Ave.	New York	NY	10017	Herbert Liechtung	212-370-8585	3	242 TA	<0.1
Southwestern Property Trust Inc.	5949 Sherry Ln.	Dallas	TX	75225	John S. Schneider	214-369-1995	3	229 TA	0.3
Malan Realty Investors Inc.	30200 Telegraph Rd.	Birmingham	MI	48025	Anthony S. Gramer	248-644-7110	3	216 TA	<0.1
Centennial Group Inc.	282 S. Anita Dr.	Orange	CA	92668	Ronald R. White	714-634-9200	3	191 TA	<0.1
Irvine Apartment Communities Inc.	550 Newport Center Dr.	Newport Beach	CA	92660	T. Patrick Smith	714-720-2400	3	186 TA	<0.1
Pennsylvania Real Estate Investment Trust	455 Pennsylvania Ave.	Fort Washington	PA	19034	Sylvan M. Cohen	215-542-9250	3	166 TA	1.1
Sovran Self Storage Inc.	5166 Main St.	Williamsville	NY	14221	Kenneth F. Myszka	716-633-1850	3	160 TA	0.2

Source: Ward's Business Directory of U.S. Private and Public Companies, 1996. Company type codes: P - Public, R - Private, S - Subsidiary, D - Division, J - Joint Venture, A - Affiliate, G - Group. If the dollar values shown are not sales, the following codes apply: TA - Total Assets; OR - Operating Revenues; GB - Gross Billings. * - estimated dollar value. < - less than; *na* - not available.

SIC 6799

INVESTORS, NEC

SIC 6799 includes establishments engaged in investment activities not already classified under a specific category. Included under this SIC are commodity contract pool operators; commodity contract trading companies; holders, buyers, and sellers of tax liens; investment clubs; security speculators for their own account; and venture capital companies.

ESTABLISHMENTS, EMPLOYMENT, AND PAYROLL

	1990	1991		1992		1993		1994		1995		% change 90-95
		Value	%	Value	%	Value	%	Value	%	Value	%	
All Establishments	2,795	3,542	26.7	3,784	6.8	5,133	35.7	4,975	-3.1	4,811	-3.3	72.1
Mid-March Employment	18,028	15,721	-12.8	16,089	2.3	23,006	43.0	23,261	1.1	23,590	1.4	30.9
1st Quarter Wages (annualized - $ mil.)	786.0	658.5	-16.2	761.4	15.6	1,068.1	40.3	1,238.9	16.0	1,413.3	14.1	79.8
Payroll per Emp. 1st Q. (annualized)	43,598	41,889	-3.9	47,322	13.0	46,429	-1.9	53,260	14.7	59,910	12.5	37.4
Annual Payroll ($ mil.)	710.4	709.5	-0.1	846.2	19.3	1,259.6	48.9	1,342.0	6.5	1,480.0	10.3	108.3
Establishments - 1-4 Emp. Number	2,129	2,896	36.0	3,049	5.3	4,096	34.3	3,959	-3.3	3,764	-4.9	76.8
Mid-March Employment	3,390	4,042	19.2	4,620	14.3	6,100	32.0	6,040	-1.0	5,608	-7.2	65.4
1st Quarter Wages (annualized - $ mil.)	113.4	150.7	32.9	167.0	10.8	232.6	39.2	259.2	11.4	247.4	-4.6	118.2
Payroll per Emp. 1st Q. (annualized)	33,441	37,285	11.5	36,156	-3.0	38,130	5.5	42,913	12.5	44,112	2.8	31.9
Annual Payroll ($ mil.)	131.8	166.1	26.0	205.3	23.6	299.4	45.8	292.1	-2.5	298.6	2.3	126.5
Establishments - 5-9 Emp. Number	339	374	10.3	433	15.8	603	39.3	583	-3.3	592	1.5	74.6
Mid-March Employment	2,233	2,427	8.7	2,760	13.7	3,913	41.8	3,785	-3.3	3,851	1.7	72.5
1st Quarter Wages (annualized - $ mil.)	95.4	118.1	23.7	143.0	21.1	219.2	53.2	235.1	7.3	311.2	32.4	226.1
Payroll per Emp. 1st Q. (annualized)	42,735	48,648	13.8	51,820	6.5	56,006	8.1	62,103	10.9	80,808	30.1	89.1
Annual Payroll ($ mil.)	99.2	125.5	26.5	153.1	21.9	277.8	81.5	238.3	-14.2	275.0	15.4	177.2
Establishments - 10-19 Emp. Number	184	153	-16.8	184	20.3	255	38.6	252	-1.2	254	0.8	38.0
Mid-March Employment	2,457	2,001	-18.6	2,454	22.6	3,491	42.3	3,384	-3.1	3,416	0.9	39.0
1st Quarter Wages (annualized - $ mil.)	102.8	105.8	2.9	119.7	13.1	189.2	58.1	221.1	16.8	242.7	9.8	136.1
Payroll per Emp. 1st Q. (annualized)	41,846	52,886	26.4	48,776	-7.8	54,195	11.1	65,326	20.5	71,055	8.8	69.8
Annual Payroll ($ mil.)	106.6	113.5	6.5	131.8	16.1	230.6	74.9	252.1	9.4	264.5	4.9	148.1
Establishments - 20-49 Emp. Number	97	84	-13.4	82	-2.4	130	58.5	123	-5.4	(D)	-	-
Mid-March Employment	3,074	2,654	-13.7	2,529	-4.7	3,825	51.2	3,496	-8.6	(D)	-	-
1st Quarter Wages (annualized - $ mil.)	139.3	123.9	-11.1	127.1	2.6	186.0	46.3	210.4	13.1	(D)	-	-
Payroll per Emp. 1st Q. (annualized)	45,330	46,674	3.0	50,267	7.7	48,620	-3.3	60,178	23.8	(D)	-	-
Annual Payroll ($ mil.)	144.9	139.1	-4.0	146.2	5.1	210.6	44.1	215.1	2.1	(D)	-	-
Establishments - 50-99 Emp. Number	29	23	-20.7	(D)	-	32	-	34	6.3	44	29.4	51.7
Mid-March Employment	1,960	(D)	-	(D)	-	2,229	-	2,321	4.1	3,085	32.9	57.4
1st Quarter Wages (annualized - $ mil.)	173.6	(D)	-	(D)	-	109.7	-	123.5	12.6	154.2	24.9	-11.2
Payroll per Emp. 1st Q. (annualized)	88,576	(D)	-	(D)	-	49,201	-	53,205	8.1	49,982	-6.1	-43.6
Annual Payroll ($ mil.)	101.3	(D)	-	(D)	-	116.3	-	133.5	14.8	150.2	12.5	48.3
Establishments - 100-249 Emp. Number	11	10	-9.1	10	-	13	30.0	20	53.8	18	-10.0	63.6
Mid-March Employment	2,016	1,816	-9.9	1,715	-5.6	1,853	8.0	3,049	64.5	2,883	-5.4	43.0
1st Quarter Wages (annualized - $ mil.)	60.9	83.9	37.9	99.3	18.4	76.4	-23.1	147.3	92.7	176.3	19.7	189.7
Payroll per Emp. 1st Q. (annualized)	30,190	46,207	53.1	57,924	25.4	41,241	-28.8	48,298	17.1	61,154	26.6	102.6
Annual Payroll ($ mil.)	58.1	93.4	60.7	109.3	17.1	67.9	-37.9	159.9	135.5	216.7	35.5	272.9
Establishments - 250-499 Emp. Number	3	-	-	(D)	-	(D)	-	4	-	(D)	-	-
Mid-March Employment	(D)	-	-	(D)	-	(D)	-	1,186	-	(D)	-	-
1st Quarter Wages (annualized - $ mil.)	(D)	-	-	(D)	-	(D)	-	42.4	-	(D)	-	-
Payroll per Emp. 1st Q. (annualized)	(D)	(D)	-	(D)	-	(D)	-	35,774	-	(D)	-	-
Annual Payroll ($ mil.)	(D)	-	-	(D)	-	(D)	-	51.1	-	(D)	-	-
Establishments - 500-999 Emp. Number	3	2	-33.3	-	-	(D)	-	-	-	-	-	-
Mid-March Employment	(D)	(D)	-	-	-	(D)	-	-	-	-	-	-
1st Quarter Wages (annualized - $ mil.)	(D)	(D)	-	-	-	(D)	-	-	-	-	-	-
Payroll per Emp. 1st Q. (annualized)	(D)	(D)	-	-	-	(D)	-	-	-	-	-	-
Annual Payroll ($ mil.)	(D)	(D)	-	-	-	(D)	-	-	-	-	-	-
Estab. - 1000 or More Emp. Number	-	-	-	-	-	-	-	-	-	-	-	-
Mid-March Employment	-	-	-	-	-	-	-	-	-	-	-	-
1st Quarter Wages (annualized - $ mil.)	-	-	-	-	-	-	-	-	-	-	-	-
Payroll per Emp. 1st Q. (annualized)	(D)	(D)	-	-	-	-	-	-	-	-	-	-
Annual Payroll ($ mil.)	-	-	-	-	-	-	-	-	-	-	-	-

Source: County Business Patterns, U.S. Department of Commerce, Washington, D.C., for 1990 through 1995. Payroll per employee is calculated using mid-March employment and 1st Quarter wages, annualized. Annual payroll, also shown, may not equal the annualized 1st Quarter wages. Columns headed by a percent sign (%) indicate change from the previous year. *na* stands for not available. The symbol (D) indicates that data are withheld by the source to avoid disclosure of competitive information. A dash (-) indicates that data are not available or cannot be calculated.

ESTABLISHMENTS
Number

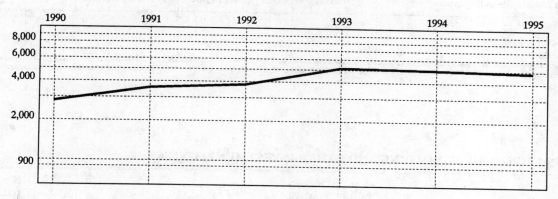

MID-MARCH EMPLOYMENT
Number

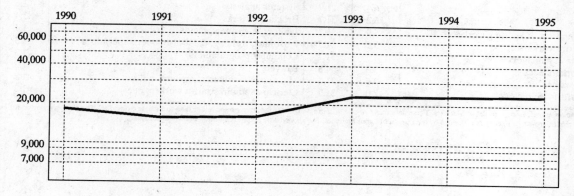

ANNUAL PAYROLL
$ million

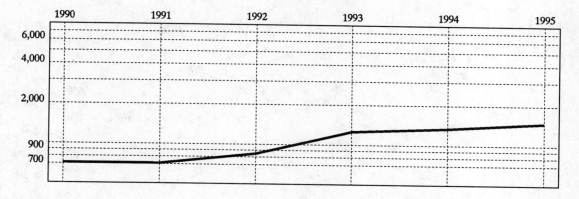

INPUTS AND OUTPUTS FOR HOLDING AND OTHER INVESTMENT OFFICES - SIC GROUP 67

Economic Sector or Industry Providing Inputs	%	Sector	Economic Sector or Industry Buying Outputs	%	Sector
No Input-Output data are available for this industry group.					

Source: Benchmark Input-Output Accounts for the U.S. Economy, 1992, U.S. Department of Commerce, Washington, D.C., November 1997. Data, as reported in the source, are organized by the 1987 SIC structure in use in 1992.

OCCUPATIONS EMPLOYED BY HOLDING AND OTHER INVESTMENT OFFICES

Occupation	% of Total 1996	Change to 2006	Occupation	% of Total 1996	Change to 2006
General managers & top executives	10.4	27.6	Managers & administrators nec	1.9	30.5
Secretaries, except legal & medical	10.4	4.4	Marketing & sales worker supervisors	1.9	31.7
General office clerks	6.8	13.3	Securities & financial sales workers	1.8	31.7
Accountants & auditors	6.4	21.9	Systems analysts	1.6	95.2
Financial managers	6.2	31.7	Brokerage clerks	1.4	10.1
Bookkeeping, accounting, & auditing clerks	5.9	5.3	Janitors & cleaners, maids	1.4	5.3
Management support workers nec	5.1	31.7	Personnel, training, & labor relations specialists	1.3	31.6
Clerical supervisors & managers	4.3	31.7	Computer programmers	1.3	8.4
Sales & related workers nec	3.3	44.8	Lawyers	1.2	31.6
Professional workers nec	2.6	31.6	Maintenance repairers, general utility	1.2	22.7
Receptionists & information clerks	2.0	31.7	Clerical & administrative workers nec	1.2	31.7

Sources: Industry-Occupation Matrix, Bureau of Labor Statistics. These data relate to one or more 3-digit SIC industry groups rather than to a single 4-digit SIC. The change reported for each occupation to the year 2005 is a percent of growth or decline as estimated by the Bureau of Labor Statistics. The abbreviation nec stands for not elsewhere classified.

U.S. AND STATE DATA ON INDUSTRY REVENUES AND OTHER ACCOUNTS FOR 1992

State	No. of Estab.	Employ-ment	Payroll ($ mil.)	Revenues ($ mil.)	Empl./ Estab.	Revenue/ Estab. ($)	Payroll/ Estab. ($)	Revenue/ Empl. ($)	Payroll/ Empl. ($)
UNITED STATES	6,202	24,423	1,225.1	9,750.1	4	1,572,088	197,534	399,217	50,162
California	989	3,545	180.6	942.0	4	952,467	182,646	265,724	50,955
Colorado	128	293	11.5	77.7	2	607,273	90,070	265,294	39,348
Florida	480	1,464	64.6	450.5	3	938,548	134,667	307,721	44,153
Georgia	114	388	12.6	59.0	3	517,325	110,781	151,997	32,549
Illinois	303	1,654	97.2	689.1	5	2,274,376	320,713	416,648	58,752
Indiana	51	188	7.7	40.9	4	802,627	151,353	217,734	41,059
Maryland	106	718	37.2	223.3	7	2,106,283	351,368	310,955	51,873
Massachusetts	176	694	61.6	361.6	4	2,054,653	350,000	521,065	88,761
Michigan	104	362	13.1	103.4	3	994,308	126,163	285,657	36,246
Minnesota	79	-	(D)	(D)	(D)	(D)	(D)	(D)	(D)
Missouri	104	-	(D)	(D)	(D)	(D)	(D)	(D)	(D)
New Jersey	142	537	45.5	174.5	4	1,229,211	320,521	325,043	84,756
New York	600	4,040	250.1	2,056.2	7	3,427,062	416,818	508,970	61,904
North Carolina	101	237	8.9	42.2	2	417,366	87,891	177,865	37,456
Ohio	129	913	31.8	110.3	7	854,806	246,155	120,778	34,780
Pennsylvania	115	515	24.9	81.6	4	709,878	216,313	158,517	48,303
Tennessee	73	-	(D)	(D)	(D)	(D)	(D)	(D)	(D)
Texas	756	2,650	118.8	876.9	4	1,159,970	157,127	330,920	44,826
Virginia	105	366	21.8	152.0	3	1,447,505	207,200	415,268	59,443
Washington	124	336	16.2	60.9	3	491,444	131,000	181,366	48,345
Wisconsin	73	296	6.9	45.7	4	626,096	95,123	154,409	23,459

Source: 1992 Economic Census, U.S. Department of Commerce, Washington, D.C. This is the only table that shows revenue data as collected by the Bureau of the Census in an Economic Census. The symbol (D) indicates that data are withheld by the source to avoid disclosure of competitive information. A dash (-) indicates that data are not available or cannot be calculated.

STATE-BY-STATE DATA ON ESTABLISHMENTS, EMPLOYMENT, AND PAYROLL - 1994 AND 1995

State	1994					1995					% Change Empl.
	No. of Estab.	Employ-ment	Pay / Empl.	Payroll ($ mil.)	Pay / Estab.	No. of Estab.	Employ-ment	Pay / Empl.	Payroll ($ mil.)	Pay / Estab.	
Alabama	50	153	45,516	7.0	140,620	49	191	40,314	8.4	172,163	24.8
Alaska	20	93	28,989	2.5	123,950	17	(D)	-	(D)	-	-
Arizona	86	382	29,990	12.0	139,372	75	363	32,287	12.0	160,293	-5.0
Arkansas	37	95	23,326	2.3	62,243	35	107	22,991	2.4	68,229	12.6
California	770	3,693	43,912	183.0	237,675	729	4,062	44,824	202.9	278,355	10.0
Colorado	112	311	32,540	12.3	110,196	110	387	37,881	17.9	162,636	24.4
Connecticut	62	287	189,199	48.9	788,629	60	293	323,604	62.8	1,047,250	2.1
Delaware	109	(D)	-	(D)	-	96	(D)	-	(D)	-	-
District of Columbia	23	119	71,765	7.2	311,261	22	111	66,919	7.4	336,818	-6.7
Florida	360	1,388	45,960	61.5	170,742	337	1,319	38,829	59.7	177,045	-5.0
Georgia	99	(D)	-	(D)	-	95	533	31,947	17.4	183,368	-
Hawaii	31	136	31,118	6.2	200,516	28	119	49,042	5.1	180,536	-12.5
Idaho	21	68	21,882	1:6	77,667	17	68	20,176	1.5	90,765	0.0
Illinois	254	1,395	55,710	84.2	331,528	247	1,287	72,777	92.6	374,789	-7.7
Indiana	32	126	25,397	3.7	116,656	32	150	35,973	5.6	174,313	19.0
Iowa	33	162	28,444	6.3	189,697	36	146	36,877	6.9	192,639	-9.9
Kansas	35	121	20,959	2.0	57,429	37	104	23,577	2.1	56,108	-14.0
Kentucky	35	222	20,270	5.6	160,343	32	190	24,947	6.1	191,469	-14.4
Louisiana	63	264	40,530	9.8	156,032	68	242	38,215	9.6	140,824	-8.3
Maine	8	(D)	-	(D)	-	8	19	11,158	0.6	74,750	-
Maryland	65	562	50,420	29.7	457,292	63	411	59,007	24.3	385,127	-26.9
Massachusetts	105	664	100,530	72.1	687,076	112	697	128,293	87.0	776,607	5.0
Michigan	73	416	27,731	12.9	177,137	71	511	32,337	20.4	286,648	22.8
Minnesota	68	264	73,924	17.3	254,235	65	208	104,538	19.2	295,585	-21.2
Mississippi	21	74	35,189	2.7	126,381	20	61	38,557	1.6	79,750	-17.6
Missouri	78	227	89,533	16.0	205,577	82	302	47,748	17.7	215,817	33.0
Montana	12	(D)	-	(D)	-	12	(D)	-	(D)	-	-
Nebraska	12	(D)	-	(D)	-	12	(D)	-	(D)	-	-
Nevada	77	217	35,687	9.5	123,727	80	285	33,137	9.7	121,300	31.3
New Hampshire	17	46	75,043	3.8	224,824	18	69	55,826	5.0	279,889	50.0
New Jersey	143	915	82,474	75.6	528,874	137	740	69,681	53.8	392,883	-19.1
New Mexico	27	(D)	-	(D)	-	25	83	14,602	1.3	53,200	-
New York	483	3,178	77,854	311.0	643,917	466	3,718	86,013	387.7	831,940	17.0
North Carolina	73	279	51,599	14.4	197,767	69	312	63,769	15.3	221,261	11.8
North Dakota	3	(D)	-	(D)	-	4	10	8,800	0.1	28,250	-
Ohio	98	906	31,046	34.1	347,622	97	790	35,620	29.8	307,082	-12.8
Oklahoma	88	289	32,346	9.9	112,091	82	223	36,574	10.2	124,439	-22.8
Oregon	57	247	33,279	10.1	177,947	49	260	27,908	8.6	174,796	5.3
Pennsylvania	84	503	46,712	27.8	331,369	88	518	61,861	29.9	339,307	3.0
Rhode Island	16	37	53,838	2.0	122,125	17	31	54,452	1.9	111,824	-16.2
South Carolina	35	223	14,709	3.3	95,457	34	203	15,704	3.5	102,441	-9.0
South Dakota	12	27	44,593	0.8	62,583	13	33	41,333	0.9	71,385	22.2
Tennessee	55	231	43,082	10.0	182,145	63	238	53,193	12.0	190,381	3.0
Texas	732	2,968	47,148	140.4	191,806	706	2,782	49,859	141.6	200,530	-6.3
Utah	42	123	30,407	4.0	94,548	39	163	33,669	5.8	147,769	32.5
Vermont	5	(D)	-	(D)	-	4	15	41,067	0.7	182,750	-
Virginia	69	328	64,561	20.0	290,464	70	261	85,349	21.4	305,700	-20.4
Washington	97	266	45,579	12.4	127,619	100	289	49,785	13.1	131,170	8.6
West Virginia	21	56	28,143	2.0	96,000	17	78	33,846	2.6	151,882	39.3
Wisconsin	57	260	34,046	9.7	170,351	53	212	46,962	8.2	154,604	-18.5
Wyoming	10	13	101,538	1.1	108,900	13	(D)	-	(D)	-	-

Source: County Business Patterns, U.S. Department of Commerce, Washington, D.C., for 1994 and 1995. Employment shown is for mid-March of the year shown. Payroll per employee is calculated by annualizing 1st Quarter payroll (not shown) and then dividing that value by mid-March employment. Dividing total annual payroll (columns 5 and 10) by employment, therefore, will *not* yield the payroll per employee figure (columns 4 and 9). The symbol (D) indicates that data are withheld by the source to avoid disclosure of competitive information. A dash (-) indicates that data are not available or cannot be calculated.

ESTABLISHMENTS 1995 - STATE AND REGIONAL CONCENTRATION

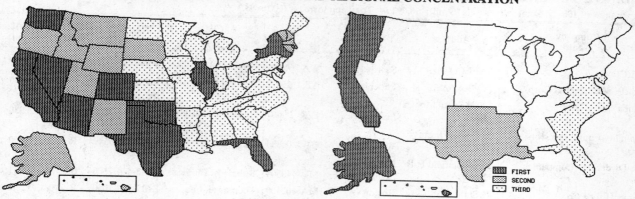

EMPLOYMENT 1995 - STATE AND REGIONAL CONCENTRATION

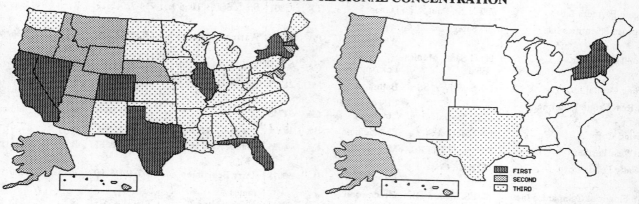

PAYROLL 1995 - STATE AND REGIONAL CONCENTRATION

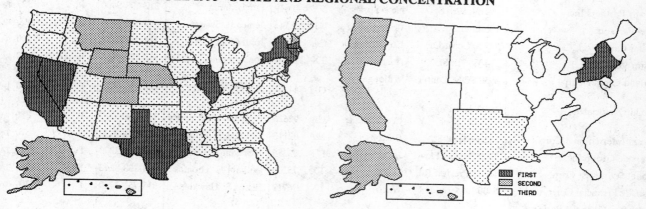

States with the darkest shading indicate those states which have proportionately more establishments, employment, or payrolls than would be indicated by the state's population. States with light shading are states with proportionately fewer establishments, less employment, and lower payrolls than population distribution. States shaded grey are within 15 percent of the state's population proportion in these categories. States for which no data are available are shown as average (grey). *Regions* are shaded to indicate absolute rank in the category. If no data for the category are available, establishment counts are used to shade the regions. Source of the data is the table on the facing page.

LEADING COMPANIES - SIC 6799 - Investors, nec

Number shown: **100**   Total sales/assets ($ mil): **68,097**   Total employment (000): **93.3**

Company Name	Address				CEO Name	Phone	Co. Type	Sales/Assets ($ mil)	Empl. (000)
SAFECO Corp.	SAFECO Plz.	Seattle	WA	98185	Roger H. Eigsti	206-545-5000	P	29,467 TA	8.0
Pinnacle West Capital Corp.	PO Box 52132	Phoenix	AZ	85072	Richard Snell	602-379-2500	P	6,850 TA	7.1
Yucaipa Cos.	10000 Santa Monica Blvd.	Los Angeles	CA	90067	Ronald W. Burkle	310-789-7200	R	3,930•	30.0
Hospitality Equity Investors Inc.	55 Greens Farms Rd.	Westport	CT	06880	Gary Mendell	203-226-9540	R	2,460 TA•	1.0
Pulte Diversified Companies Inc.	33 Bloomfield Hill Pkwy.	Bloomfield Hills	MI	48304	Robert K. Burgess	248-644-7300	S	1,851 OR•	3.0
Thomas H. Lee Co.	75 State St.	Boston	MA	02109	Thomas H. Lee	617-227-1050	R	1,500 TA	0.1
Centre Capital Investors L.P.	30 Rockefeller Plz.	New York	NY	10020	Lester Pollack	212-332-5800	R	1,480 TA•	<0.1
Golder, Thoma, Cressey, Rauner Inc.	233 S. Wacker Dr.	Chicago	IL	60606	Carl Thoma	312-382-2200	R	1,200 TA	<0.1
Wingate Partners L.P.	750 N. St. Paul St.	Dallas	TX	75201	Frederick B. Hegi Jr.	214-720-1313	R	1,200 TA	<0.1
Safeguard Scientifics Inc.	800 Safeguard Bldg.	Wayne	PA	19087	Warren V. Musser	610-293-0600	P	936 TA	4.6
Foothill Group Inc.	11111 Santa Monica Blvd.	Los Angeles	CA	90025	John Nikoll	310-478-8383	S	913 TA•	0.2
Sterling Capital Ltd.	111 S. Calvert St.	Baltimore	MD	21202	Eric Becker	410-385-2200	R	800 TA	<0.1
AIB Real Estate Investment Inc.	18605 E. Gale Ave.	City of Industry	CA	91748	Huey Yu	818-854-8604	S	740 TA•	0.3
Berwind Corp.	1500 Market St.	Philadelphia	PA	19102	Graham Berwind Jr.	215-563-2800	R	726•	4.0
InterWest Partners	3000 Sand Hill Rd.	Menlo Park	CA	94025	Robert Momsen	650-854-8585	R	615 TA•	<0.1
Specialty Foods Corp.	520 Lake Cook Rd.	Deerfield	IL	60015	Larry Benjamin	847-405-5300	R	560 TA•	15.0
Pulte Financial Companies Inc.	6061 S. Willow Dr.	Greenwood Village	CO	80111	James A. Weissenborn	303-740-3323	S	548 TA	<0.1
TL Ventures	435 Devon Park Dr.	Wayne	PA	19087	Robert E. Keith Jr.	610-975-9770	R	542 TA	<0.1
Fenway Partners Inc.	152 W. 57th St.	New York	NY	10019	Peter Lamm	212-698-9400	R	527 TA	<0.1
Accel Partners	1 Palmer Sq.	Princeton	NJ	08542	James R. Swartz	609-683-4500	R	500 TA	<0.1
Westar Capital L.L.C.	949 S. Coast Dr.	Costa Mesa	CA	92626	John Clark	714-481-5160	R	500 TA	<0.1
Austin Ventures L.P.	114 W. 7th St.	Austin	TX	78701	Joe Aragona	512-479-0055	R	448 TA	<0.1
Kirtland Capital Corp.	2550 SOM Center Rd.	Willoughby Hills	OH	44094	John F. Turben	440-585-9010	R	400 TA	<0.1
Domain Associates	650 Town Center Dr.	Costa Mesa	CA	92626	Richard S. Schneider	714-434-6227	R	380 TA•	<0.1
Advent International Corp.	101 Federal St.	Boston	MA	02110	Douglas R. Brown	617-951-9400	R	370 TA•	0.2
Riverside Group Inc.	7800 Belfort Pkwy.	Jacksonville	FL	32256	J. Steven Wilson	904-281-2200	P	314 TA	<0.1
Capital Southwest Corp.	12900 Preston Rd.	Dallas	TX	75230	William R. Thomas	214-233-8242	P	311 TA	<0.1
FirstCity Financial Corp.	6400 Imperial Dr.	Waco	TX	76712	James R. Hawkins	817-751-1750	P	309 TA	0.2
Healthcare Financial Partners Inc.	2 Wisconsin Cir.	Chevy Chase	MD	20815	John K. Delaney	301-961-1640	P	272 TA	<0.1
Signalert Corp.	150 Great Neck Rd.	Great Neck	NY	11021	Gerald Appel	516-466-3125	R	260 TA	<0.1
Circle Investors Inc.	251 N. Illinois St.	Indianapolis	IN	46204	R. Matthew Neff	317-237-3374	R	257 TA	<0.1

Company type codes: P - Public, R - Private, S - Subsidiary, D - Division, J - Joint Venture, A - Affiliate, G - Group. If the dollar values shown are not sales, the following codes apply: TA - Total Assets; OR - Operating Revenues; GB - Gross Billings. • - estimated dollar value. < - less than. *na* - not available.

Continued on next page.

LEADING COMPANIES - SIC 6799 - Investors, nec
Continued

Company Name	Address				CEO Name	Phone	Co. Type	Sales/Assets ($ mil)	Empl. (000)
Code, Hennessy and Simmons Inc.	10 S. Wacker Dr.	Chicago	IL	60606	Andrew Code	312-876-1840	R	237 TA	6.0
PNC Equity Management Corp.	5th Ave. & Wood St.	Pittsburgh	PA	15222	Gary Zentner	412-762-2666	S	220 TA	<0.1
Florida Capital Partners	100 N. Tampa St.	Tampa	FL	33602	John Kirtley	813-222-8000	R	216	<0.1
CRL Inc.	6300 S. Syracuse Way	Englewood	CO	80111	Jonathan P. Johnson	303-773-2800	R	210•	1.6
Hicks, Muse, Tate and Furst Inc.	200 Crescent Ct.	Dallas	TX	75201	Thomas O. Hicks	214-740-7300	R	210 OR	1.0
IIC Industries Inc.	420 Lexington Ave.	New York	NY	10170	Bernard Schreier	212-297-6132	P	204	4.5
Ampersand Ventures	55 William St.	Wellesley	MA	02181	Richard Charpie	617-239-0700	R	200 TA	0.1
Grotech Capital Group Inc.	9690 Deereco Rd.	Lutherville	MD	21093	Frank A. Adams	410-560-2000	R	200 TA	<0.1
Morgenthaler Ventures	629 Euclid Ave.	Cleveland	OH	44114	David T. Morgenthaler	216-621-3070	R	200 TA	<0.1
Resource America Inc.	1521 Locust St.	Philadelphia	PA	19102	Edward E. Cohen	215-546-5005	P	195 TA	0.1
Saugatuck Capital Company L.P.	1 Canterbury Green	Stamford	CT	06901	Frank J. Hawley Jr.	203-348-6669	R	190 TA	<0.1
Dartfort Partnership	801 Montgomery St.	San Francisco	CA	94133	Ian R. Wilson	415-982-3019	R	180 TA	<0.1
Riverton Investment Corp.	1855 Front Royal Rd.	Winchester	VA	22602	Toby Mercuro	703-722-4333	R	170 TA•	0.4
Galen Associates	666 3rd Ave.	New York	NY	10017	Bruce F. Wesson	212-818-0240	R	160 TA	<0.1
Sierra Ventures	3000 Sandhill Rd.	Menlo Park	CA	94025	J.M. Drazan	415-854-1000	R	160 TA	<0.1
Heller Investments Inc.	500 W. Monroe St.	Chicago	IL	60661	William C. Morro	312-441-7340	S	150 TA	<0.1
Mesirow Financial Holdings Inc.	350 N. Clark St.	Chicago	IL	60610	Bruce Young	312-670-6000	R	150 TA	0.5
Triumph Capital L.P.	237 Park Ave.	New York	NY	10017	Melanie A. Okun	212-551-3636	R	150 TA	<0.1
Mesirow Financial Inc.	350 N. Clark St.	Chicago	IL	60610	Bruce Young	312-595-6000	S	132 OR	0.8
Jupiter National Inc.	39 W. Montgomery Ave.	Rockville	MD	20850	David L. Chandler	301-738-3939	S	127 TA	1.5
Apex Investment Partners	233 S. Wacker Dr.	Chicago	IL	60606	James A. Johnson	312-258-0320	R	120 TA	<0.1
CID Equity Partners	PO Box 82074	Indianapolis	IN	46282	John T. Hackett	317-269-2350	R	106 TA	<0.1
E.M. Warburg, Pincus and Company Inc.	466 Lexington Ave.	New York	NY	10017	Lionel Pincus	212-878-0600	R	102 TA•	0.3
Lubar and Co.	777 E. Wisconsin Ave.	Milwaukee	WI	53202	David J. Lubar	414-291-9000	R	100 TA	<0.1
Pioneer Capital Corp.	60 State St.	Boston	MA	02109	Frank M. Polestra	617-742-7825	S	100 TA	<0.1
Thompson Clive Inc.	3000 Sand Hill Rd.	Menlo Park	CA	94025	Peter Ziebelman	415-854-0314	S	100 TA	<0.1
Wilshire Oil Company of Texas	921 Bergen Ave.	Jersey City	NJ	07306	S. Wilzig Izak	201-420-2796	P	98 TA	<0.1
Burr, Egan, Deleage and Co.	1 Post Office Sq.	Boston	MA	02109	Bill Egan	617-482-8020	R	98 TA	<0.1
Hambro International Venture Fund	650 Madison Ave.	New York	NY	10022	Edwin Goodman	212-223-7400	R	98 TA•	<0.1
Hyperion Partners L.P.	520 Madison Ave.	New York	NY	10022	Lewis S. Ranieri	212-980-8400	R	86 TA•	<0.1
Ranieri and Company Inc.	50 Charles Lindbergh Blvd.	Uniondale	NY	11553	Lewis Ranieri	516-745-6644	R	86 TA•	<0.1

Company type codes: P - Public, R - Private, S - Subsidiary, D - Division, J - Joint Venture, A - Affiliate, G - Group. If the dollar values shown are not sales, the following codes apply: TA - Total Assets; OR - Operating Revenues; GB - Gross Billings. • - estimated dollar value. < - less than. *na* - not available.

Continued on next page.

LEADING COMPANIES - SIC 6799 - Investors, nec

Continued

Company Name	Address				CEO Name	Phone	Co. Type	Sales/Assets ($ mil)	Empl. (000)
Fleet Equity Partners	50 Kennedy Plaza	Providence	RI	02903	Robert M. Van Degna	401-278-6770	S	81 TA	<0.1
Technology Management and Funding L.P.	707 State Rd.	Princeton	NJ	08540	Anthony C. Warren	609-921-2001	R	81 TA	<0.1
Edelson Technology Partners	300 Tice Blvd.	Woodcliff Lake	NJ	07675	Harry Edelson	201-930-9898	R	80 TA	<0.1
Bando McGlocklin Capital Corp.	13555 Bishops Ct.	Brookfield	WI	53005	George R. Schonath	414-523-4300	P	79 TA	<0.1
Premier Inc.	12730 High Bluff Dr.	San Diego	CA	92130	Robert W. O'Leary	619-481-2727	R	75 OR*	1.0
Boston Ventures Management Inc.	1 Federal St.	Boston	MA	02110	William F. Thompson	617-350-1500		72 TA*	<0.1
EnCap Investment L.L.C.	6688 N. Central Expwy.	Dallas	TX	75206	David B. Miller	214-696-6700	R	71 TA*	<0.1
Paul Revere Investment Management Co.	18 Chestnut St.	Worcester	MA	01608	John Lemery	508-799-4441	S	69 TA	<0.1
M and I Capital Markets Group Inc.	770 N. Water St.	Milwaukee	WI	53202	John T. Byrnes	414-765-7800	S	67 TA	<0.1
Sprout Group	140 Broadway	New York	NY	10005	Richard E. Kroon	212-504-3000	S	66 TA*	<0.1
Cooper Life Sciences Inc.	160 Broadway	New York	NY	10038		212-791-5362	P	65 TA	<0.1
Berkeley International Capital Corp.	650 California St.	San Francisco	CA	94108	Michael Mayer	415-391-4790	S	61 TA*	<0.1
Canaan Partners	2884 Sand Hill Rd.	Menlo Park	CA	94025	Eric A. Young	415-854-8092	R	61 TA*	<0.1
EnCompass Group Inc.	4040 Lake Washington Blvd. NE	Kirkland	WA	98033	Yasuki Matsumoto	206-828-1030	R	61 TA*	<0.1
Equitable Investment Services Inc.	604 Locust St.	Des Moines	IA	50306	Paul R. Schlaak	515-245-6911	S	61 TA*	<0.1
CIT Group/Venture Capital Inc.	650 CIT Dr.	Livingston	NJ	07039	Paul J. Laud	973-740-5570	S	60 TA	<0.1
Madison Dearborn Partners Inc.	31st National Plaza	Chicago	IL	60602	John A. Canning Jr.	312-732-5400	R	59 TA*	<0.1
Freeman Spogli and Co.	11100 Santa Monica Blvd.	Los Angeles	CA	90025	Bradford Freeman	310-444-1822	R	58 TA*	<0.1
Kitty Hawk Capital Inc.	2700 Coltsgate Rd.	Charlotte	NC	28211	Walter Wilkinson Jr.	704-362-3909	R	55 TA*	<0.1
Greylock Management Corp.	1 Federal St.	Boston	MA	02110	Henry McCance	617-423-5525	R	54 TA*	<0.1
New Enterprise Associates	2490 Sand Hill Rd.	Menlo Park	CA	94025	C. Richard Kramlich	650-854-9499	R	54 TA*	<0.1
Texas Pacific Group	201 Main St.	Fort Worth	TX	76102	David Bonderman	817-871-4000	R	52 TA*	<0.1
Centennial Funds	1999 Broadway	Denver	CO	80202	Jack Tankersley	303-298-9066	R	51 TA*	<0.1
Vietnam Investment Fund Inc.	PO Box 150148	San Rafael	CA	94915	Dennis D. Powell	415-455-8500	R	50 TA	<0.1
Carlyle Real Estate L.P.	900 N. Michigan Ave.	Chicago	IL	60611	H. Rigel Barber	312-915-1987	R	50 TA	<0.1
Abrams, Rothman and Company Inc.	9719 Conway Rd.	St. Louis	MO	63124	Lloyd R. Abrams	314-993-3686	R	49 TA	<0.1
Institutional Venture Partners	3000 Sand Hill Rd.	Menlo Park	CA	94025		650-854-0132	R	49 TA	<0.1
Starwood Capital Group L.P.	3 Pickwick Plz.	Greenwich	CT	06830	Barry Sternlicht	203-861-2100	R	49 TA	<0.1
Venture America Services L.P.	8230 Leesburg Pike	Vienna	VA	22182	James Ball	703-442-4500	R	49 TA*	<0.1

Company type codes: P - Public, R - Private, S - Subsidiary, D - Division, J - Joint Venture, A - Affiliate, G - Group. If the dollar values shown are not sales, the following codes apply: TA - Total Assets; OR - Operating Revenues; GB - Gross Billings. * - estimated dollar value. < - less than. *na* - not available.

Continued on next page.

LEADING COMPANIES - SIC 6799 - Investors, nec
Continued

Company Name	Address				CEO Name	Phone	Co. Type	Sales/Assets ($ mil)	Empl. (000)
VIP Global Capital Inc.	1360 S. Clarkson St.	Denver	CO	80210	T. Vasko	303-777-0554	R	49 TA*	<0.1
Pfingsten Partners L.P.	520 Lake Cook Rd.	Deerfield	IL	60015	Thomas S. Bagley	847-374-9140	R	48 TA	<0.1
Churchill Capital Inc.	333 S. 7th St.	Minneapolis	MN	55402	Mike Hahn	612-673-6633	R	44 TA*	<0.1
Elfman Venture Partners	650 Dundee Rd.	Northbrook	IL	60062	Rick Elfman	708-571-0606	R	43 TA	<0.1
Hillman Co.	1900 Grant Bldg.	Pittsburgh	PA	15219	Henry L. Hillman	412-281-2620	R	43 OR	0.2
Citizens Lumber and Supply Co.	747 E. 7th St.	Lexington	KY	40505	Frank Sadler	606-254-1151	R	41 TA*	<0.1
Alpha Capital Partners Ltd.	3 First National Plz.	Chicago	IL	60602	Andrew Kalnow	312-214-3440	R	40	<0.1
Massey Burch Capital Corp.	310 25th Ave. N. # 103	Nashville	TN	37203	Donald M. Johnston	615-329-9448	R	40 TA	<0.1
Discus Acquisition Corp.	2430 Metropolitan Ctr.	Minneapolis	MN	55402	William H. Spell	612-305-0339	P	39 TA	0.3

Source: *Ward's Business Directory of U.S. Private and Public Companies*, 1996. Company type codes: P - Public, R - Private, S - Subsidiary, D - Division, J - Joint Venture, A - Affiliate, G - Group. If the dollar values shown are not sales, the following codes apply: TA - Total Assets; OR - Operating Revenues; GB - Gross Billings. * - estimated dollar value. < - less than; *na* - not available.

STATE AND COUNTY SUMMARIES

STATE AND COUNTY SUMMARIES

STATE RANKINGS
FINANCE, INSURANCE, AND REAL ESTATE, 1995
Ordered by Population Rank

State	Popul. Rank	Establishments			Employment			Payroll			Pay / Employee	
		Number	Rank	Per Capita Rank	Number	Rank	Per Capita Rank	($ 000)	Rank	Per Capita Rank	$	Rank
California	1	73,484	1	49	792,727	1	37	29,740,916	2	28	38,306	8
Texas	2	41,528	4	50	440,607	3	39	14,240,133	4	34	32,290	17
New York	3	55,394	2	18	758,802	2	9	46,480,158	1	3	74,738	1
Illinois	4	29,524	5	48	404,604	4	24	16,231,759	3	16	42,271	6
Ohio	5	23,339	7	43	270,106	7	31	8,107,899	9	31	30,472	27
Florida	6	42,659	3	8	395,150	5	13	11,938,724	5	15	30,284	30
Pennsylvania	7	23,695	6	25	328,988	6	12	10,649,988	6	13	32,632	13
Michigan	8	18,193	9	37	200,997	10	29	6,421,160	11	27	31,358	21
New Jersey	9	19,143	8	15	241,289	8	11	10,244,894	7	7	44,598	5
Indiana	10	12,597	17	36	128,762	19	36	3,709,445	20	33	29,169	33
Minnesota	11	11,888	18	41	142,981	17	27	5,149,344	14	20	38,605	7
Wisconsin	12	11,776	19	40	141,858	18	25	4,355,796	18	25	31,573	19
Missouri	13	12,771	16	31	143,687	16	23	4,391,490	17	23	30,900	23
Arizona	14	10,223	22	46	104,917	23	38	3,254,155	23	37	30,764	25
North Carolina	15	15,366	11	19	156,581	13	18	4,917,894	16	18	33,179	11
Tennessee	16	10,882	21	34	109,083	22	34	3,345,102	22	30	30,571	26
Massachusetts	17	13,219	14	20	231,300	9	6	9,993,487	8	5	46,653	4
Virginia	18	15,202	12	11	165,377	12	14	5,361,563	13	14	32,606	14
Washington	19	14,405	13	12	123,342	20	19	3,847,357	19	22	31,451	20
Georgia	20	16,578	10	10	181,778	11	10	6,040,880	12	11	34,443	10
Colorado	21	12,848	15	17	116,929	21	20	3,677,799	21	21	31,675	18
Alabama	22	7,968	26	44	77,948	27	42	2,238,944	26	39	29,111	35
Oklahoma	23	7,648	28	45	61,190	31	49	1,607,914	31	50	25,647	44
Louisiana	24	9,325	23	24	79,825	25	33	2,179,393	27	35	27,322	37
Iowa	25	7,286	29	39	80,838	24	30	2,291,670	25	32	29,668	31
Kansas	26	6,803	31	38	61,252	30	43	1,739,266	30	41	28,377	36
Oregon	27	8,691	24	22	79,553	26	26	2,315,981	24	29	29,163	34
Kentucky	28	7,215	30	28	65,840	29	35	1,785,359	29	36	26,643	40
Arkansas	29	4,964	33	42	39,092	35	48	1,027,324	38	49	26,984	39
Utah	30	4,532	35	47	44,958	33	44	1,227,551	35	42	26,284	43
Maryland	31	11,687	20	4	143,694	15	3	4,983,998	15	4	35,523	9
Mississippi	32	5,090	32	32	37,925	37	46	954,988	39	47	24,740	45
Connecticut	33	8,420	25	7	144,114	14	2	6,901,248	10	2	51,433	2
South Carolina	34	7,864	27	9	68,741	28	16	1,864,111	28	19	26,469	41
Nebraska	35	4,566	34	33	53,709	32	22	1,553,691	32	24	30,351	28
New Mexico	36	3,784	38	35	29,031	40	47	720,927	43	48	24,525	46
Nevada	37	4,479	36	13	37,577	38	21	1,036,822	37	26	27,167	38
Idaho	38	2,801	41	29	20,449	45	45	511,240	45	45	24,438	47
West Virginia	39	3,224	40	16	24,571	44	32	573,787	44	40	23,428	50
D.C.	40	2,203	45	26	30,373	39	15	1,407,935	34	8	49,754	3
Rhode Island	41	1,983	47	30	25,405	43	17	806,206	41	17	32,482	15
Montana	42	2,458	44	14	14,840	47	40	356,737	48	43	22,891	51
South Dakota	43	2,183	46	21	18,418	46	28	429,975	46	38	23,589	49
North Dakota	44	1,976	48	23	13,929	48	41	334,949	49	44	26,352	42
Alaska	45	1,151	51	51	9,695	50	50	311,365	50	46	32,465	16
Hawaii	46	3,845	37	3	38,917	36	4	1,191,584	36	6	31,156	22
New Hampshire	47	2,734	42	6	28,108	41	8	883,147	40	10	30,306	29
Maine	48	2,666	43	5	25,568	42	7	751,974	42	12	29,296	32
Wyoming	49	1,318	50	27	7,028	51	51	168,427	51	51	23,918	48
Delaware	50	3,405	39	1	42,809	34	1	1,514,793	33	1	32,999	12
Vermont	51	1,516	49	2	12,894	49	5	390,874	47	9	30,882	24

Source: County Business Patterns 1994/95, CBP-94/95, U.S. Department of Commerce, Washington DC, November 1997. The employment column represents mid-March employment in the year. Pay per employee is calculated by dividing 1st Quarter payroll, annualized, by mid-March employment. Data represent totals for all SIC categories in agriculture, construction, and mining in the corresponding state. States with the highest number or ratio in a data field (e.g., number of establishments have a rank of (1). Per capita ratio is calculated by dividing a data field of a state by the population of that state in 1995. The ranking by which the table is ordered is shown in bold.

State Rankings, Finance, Insurance, and Real Estate, 1995

Ordered by Establishment Rank

State	Popul. Rank	Establishments			Employment			Payroll			Pay / Employee	
		Number	Rank	Per Capita Rank	Number	Rank	Per Capita Rank	($ 000)	Rank	Per Capita Rank	$	Rank
California	1	73,484	1	49	792,727	1	37	29,740,916	2	28	38,306	8
New York	3	55,394	2	18	758,802	2	9	46,480,158	1	3	74,738	1
Florida	6	42,659	3	8	395,150	5	13	11,938,724	5	15	30,284	30
Texas	2	41,528	4	50	440,607	3	39	14,240,133	4	34	32,290	17
Illinois	4	29,524	5	48	404,604	4	24	16,231,759	3	16	42,271	6
Pennsylvania	7	23,695	6	25	328,988	6	12	10,649,988	6	13	32,632	13
Ohio	5	23,339	7	43	270,106	7	31	8,107,899	9	31	30,472	27
New Jersey	9	19,143	8	15	241,289	8	11	10,244,894	7	7	44,598	5
Michigan	8	18,193	9	37	200,997	10	29	6,421,160	11	27	31,358	21
Georgia	20	16,578	10	10	181,778	11	10	6,040,880	12	11	34,443	10
North Carolina	15	15,366	11	19	156,581	13	18	4,917,894	16	18	33,179	11
Virginia	18	15,202	12	11	165,377	12	14	5,361,563	13	14	32,606	14
Washington	19	14,405	13	12	123,342	20	19	3,847,357	19	22	31,451	20
Massachusetts	17	13,219	14	20	231,300	9	6	9,993,487	8	5	46,653	4
Colorado	21	12,848	15	17	116,929	21	20	3,677,799	21	21	31,675	18
Missouri	13	12,771	16	31	143,687	16	23	4,391,490	17	23	30,900	23
Indiana	10	12,597	17	36	128,762	19	36	3,709,445	20	33	29,169	33
Minnesota	11	11,888	18	41	142,981	17	27	5,149,344	14	20	38,605	7
Wisconsin	12	11,776	19	40	141,858	18	25	4,355,796	18	25	31,573	19
Maryland	31	11,687	20	4	143,694	15	3	4,983,998	15	4	35,523	9
Tennessee	16	10,882	21	34	109,083	22	34	3,345,102	22	30	30,571	26
Arizona	14	10,223	22	46	104,917	23	38	3,254,155	23	37	30,764	25
Louisiana	24	9,325	23	24	79,825	25	33	2,179,393	27	35	27,322	37
Oregon	27	8,691	24	22	79,553	26	26	2,315,981	24	29	29,163	34
Connecticut	33	8,420	25	7	144,114	14	2	6,901,248	10	2	51,433	2
Alabama	22	7,968	26	44	77,948	27	42	2,238,944	26	39	29,111	35
South Carolina	34	7,864	27	9	68,741	28	16	1,864,111	28	19	26,469	41
Oklahoma	23	7,648	28	45	61,190	31	49	1,607,914	31	50	25,647	44
Iowa	25	7,286	29	39	80,838	24	30	2,291,670	25	32	29,668	31
Kentucky	28	7,215	30	28	65,840	29	35	1,785,359	29	36	26,643	40
Kansas	26	6,803	31	38	61,252	30	43	1,739,266	30	41	28,377	36
Mississippi	32	5,090	32	32	37,925	37	46	954,988	39	47	24,740	45
Arkansas	29	4,964	33	42	39,092	35	48	1,027,324	38	49	26,984	39
Nebraska	35	4,566	34	33	53,709	32	22	1,553,691	32	24	30,351	28
Utah	30	4,532	35	47	44,958	33	44	1,227,551	35	42	26,284	43
Nevada	37	4,479	36	13	37,577	38	21	1,036,822	37	26	27,167	38
Hawaii	46	3,845	37	3	38,917	36	4	1,191,584	36	6	31,156	22
New Mexico	36	3,784	38	35	29,031	40	47	720,927	43	48	24,525	46
Delaware	50	3,405	39	1	42,809	34	1	1,514,793	33	1	32,999	12
West Virginia	39	3,224	40	16	24,571	44	32	573,787	44	40	23,428	50
Idaho	38	2,801	41	29	20,449	45	45	511,240	45	45	24,438	47
New Hampshire	47	2,734	42	6	28,108	41	8	883,147	40	10	30,306	29
Maine	48	2,666	43	5	25,568	42	7	751,974	42	12	29,296	32
Montana	42	2,458	44	14	14,840	47	40	356,737	48	43	22,891	51
D.C.	40	2,203	45	26	30,373	39	15	1,407,935	34	8	49,754	3
South Dakota	43	2,183	46	21	18,418	46	28	429,975	46	38	23,589	49
Rhode Island	41	1,983	47	30	25,405	43	17	806,206	41	17	32,482	15
North Dakota	44	1,976	48	23	13,929	48	41	334,949	49	44	26,352	42
Vermont	51	1,516	49	2	12,894	49	5	390,874	47	9	30,882	24
Wyoming	49	1,318	50	27	7,028	51	51	168,427	51	51	23,918	48
Alaska	45	1,151	51	51	9,695	50	50	311,365	50	46	32,465	16

Source: County Business Patterns 1994/95, CBP-94/95, U.S. Department of Commerce, Washington DC, November 1997. The employment column represents mid-March employment in the year. Pay per employee is calculated by dividing 1st Quarter payroll, annualized, by mid-March employment. Data represent totals for all SIC categories in agriculture, construction, and mining in the corresponding state. States with the highest number or ratio in a data field (e.g., number of establishments have a rank of (1). Per capita ratio is calculated by dividing a data field of a state by the population of that state in 1995. The ranking by which the table is ordered is shown in bold.

State Rankings, Finance, Insurance, and Real Estate, 1995

Ordered by Employment Rank

State	Popul. Rank	Establishments			Employment			Payroll			Pay / Employee	
		Number	Rank	Per Capita Rank	Number	Rank	Per Capita Rank	($ 000)	Rank	Per Capita Rank	$	Rank
California	1	73,484	1	49	792,727	1	37	29,740,916	2	28	38,306	8
New York	3	55,394	2	18	758,802	2	9	46,480,158	1	3	74,738	1
Texas	2	41,528	4	50	440,607	3	39	14,240,133	4	34	32,290	17
Illinois	4	29,524	5	48	404,604	4	24	16,231,759	3	16	42,271	6
Florida	6	42,659	3	8	395,150	5	13	11,938,724	5	15	30,284	30
Pennsylvania	7	23,695	6	25	328,988	6	12	10,649,988	6	13	32,632	13
Ohio	5	23,339	7	43	270,106	7	31	8,107,899	9	31	30,472	27
New Jersey	9	19,143	8	15	241,289	8	11	10,244,894	7	7	44,598	5
Massachusetts	17	13,219	14	20	231,300	9	6	9,993,487	8	5	46,653	4
Michigan	8	18,193	9	37	200,997	10	29	6,421,160	11	27	31,358	21
Georgia	20	16,578	10	10	181,778	11	10	6,040,880	12	11	34,443	10
Virginia	18	15,202	12	11	165,377	12	14	5,361,563	13	14	32,606	14
North Carolina	15	15,366	11	19	156,581	13	18	4,917,894	16	18	33,179	11
Connecticut	33	8,420	25	7	144,114	14	2	6,901,248	10	2	51,433	2
Maryland	31	11,687	20	4	143,694	15	3	4,983,998	15	4	35,523	9
Missouri	13	12,771	16	31	143,687	16	23	4,391,490	17	23	30,900	23
Minnesota	11	11,888	18	41	142,981	17	27	5,149,344	14	20	38,605	7
Wisconsin	12	11,776	19	40	141,858	18	25	4,355,796	18	25	31,573	19
Indiana	10	12,597	17	36	128,762	19	36	3,709,445	20	33	29,169	33
Washington	19	14,405	13	12	123,342	20	19	3,847,357	19	22	31,451	20
Colorado	21	12,848	15	17	116,929	21	20	3,677,799	21	21	31,675	18
Tennessee	16	10,882	21	34	109,083	22	34	3,345,102	22	30	30,571	26
Arizona	14	10,223	22	46	104,917	23	38	3,254,155	23	37	30,764	25
Iowa	25	7,286	29	39	80,838	24	30	2,291,670	25	32	29,668	31
Louisiana	24	9,325	23	24	79,825	25	33	2,179,393	27	35	27,322	37
Oregon	27	8,691	24	22	79,553	26	26	2,315,981	24	29	29,163	34
Alabama	22	7,968	26	44	77,948	27	42	2,238,944	26	39	29,111	35
South Carolina	34	7,864	27	9	68,741	28	16	1,864,111	28	19	26,469	41
Kentucky	28	7,215	30	28	65,840	29	35	1,785,359	29	36	26,643	40
Kansas	26	6,803	31	38	61,252	30	43	1,739,266	30	41	28,377	36
Oklahoma	23	7,648	28	45	61,190	31	49	1,607,914	31	50	25,647	44
Nebraska	35	4,566	34	33	53,709	32	22	1,553,691	32	24	30,351	28
Utah	30	4,532	35	47	44,958	33	44	1,227,551	35	42	26,284	43
Delaware	50	3,405	39	1	42,809	34	1	1,514,793	33	1	32,999	12
Arkansas	29	4,964	33	42	39,092	35	48	1,027,324	38	49	26,984	39
Hawaii	46	3,845	37	3	38,917	36	4	1,191,584	36	6	31,156	22
Mississippi	32	5,090	32	32	37,925	37	46	954,988	39	47	24,740	45
Nevada	37	4,479	36	13	37,577	38	21	1,036,822	37	26	27,167	38
D.C.	40	2,203	45	26	30,373	39	15	1,407,935	34	8	49,754	3
New Mexico	36	3,784	38	35	29,031	40	47	720,927	43	48	24,525	46
New Hampshire	47	2,734	42	6	28,108	41	8	883,147	40	10	30,306	29
Maine	48	2,666	43	5	25,568	42	7	751,974	42	12	29,296	32
Rhode Island	41	1,983	47	30	25,405	43	17	806,206	41	17	32,482	15
West Virginia	39	3,224	40	16	24,571	44	32	573,787	44	40	23,428	50
Idaho	38	2,801	41	29	20,449	45	45	511,240	45	45	24,438	47
South Dakota	43	2,183	46	21	18,418	46	28	429,975	46	38	23,589	49
Montana	42	2,458	44	14	14,840	47	40	356,737	48	43	22,891	51
North Dakota	44	1,976	48	23	13,929	48	41	334,949	49	44	26,352	42
Vermont	51	1,516	49	2	12,894	49	5	390,874	47	9	30,882	24
Alaska	45	1,151	51	51	9,695	50	50	311,365	50	46	32,465	16
Wyoming	49	1,318	50	27	7,028	51	51	168,427	51	51	23,918	48

Source: County Business Patterns 1994/95, CBP-94/95, U.S. Department of Commerce, Washington DC, November 1997. The employment column represents mid-March employment in the year. Pay per employee is calculated by dividing 1st Quarter payroll, annualized, by mid-March employment. Data represent totals for all SIC categories in agriculture, construction, and mining in the corresponding state. States with the highest number or ratio in a data field (e.g., number of establishments have a rank of (1). Per capita ratio is calculated by dividing a data field of a state by the population of that state in 1995. The ranking by which the table is ordered is shown in bold.

SIC	Industry	No. Establishments			Employment		Pay / Employee		Annual Payroll ($ 000)		
		1994	1995	% US	1994	1995	1994	1995	1994	1995	% US
FLORIDA - [continued]											
6300	Insurance carriers	2,599	2,660	6.4	66,738	64,711	33,727	36,326	2,181,058	2,300,289	4.1
6310	Life insurance	717	727	6.2	26,876	25,194	32,441	34,356	842,483	840,432	4.3
6320	Medical service and health insurance	165	213	7.1	12,497	14,235	33,282	35,137	397,399	488,704	5.1
6321	Accident and health insurance	60	65	6.2	1,949	1,882	24,813	25,269	45,716	50,724	3.0
6324	Hospital and medical service plans	105	147	7.6	10,548	12,353	34,847	36,640	351,683	437,945	5.5
6330	Fire, marine, and casualty insurance	1,280	1,298	6.2	22,981	21,277	36,169	40,330	826,715	850,501	3.5
6350	Surety insurance	33	36	6.1	321	313	36,150	38,492	11,219	11,678	2.2
6360	Title insurance	245	246	9.8	3,020	2,525	30,734	32,190	75,879	72,272	5.3
6370	Pension, health, and welfare funds	131	98	4.3	743	667	25,443	30,795	18,668	22,110	2.2
6390	Insurance carriers, n.e.c.	11	13	7.5	233	206	31,313	29,320	7,714	6,600	7.2
6400	Insurance agents, brokers, and service	7,695	7,868	6.3	42,991	44,043	27,264	29,672	1,252,297	1,368,915	6.0
6500	Real estate	19,459	19,883	8.1	108,035	115,330	18,449	19,570	2,164,135	2,371,430	7.2
6510	Real estate operators and lessors	6,353	6,330	6.3	30,209	32,022	15,179	16,390	498,729	542,154	5.7
6530	Real estate agents and managers	11,018	11,034	9.6	62,775	66,832	19,073	20,058	1,299,801	1,392,580	7.4
6540	Title abstract offices	325	311	6.5	2,481	2,044	23,495	23,924	54,684	49,371	5.7
6550	Subdividers and developers	1,224	1,291	7.3	12,069	13,046	22,458	24,391	294,473	351,871	10.8
6552	Subdividers and developers, n.e.c.	982	994	9.6	8,471	9,219	25,159	26,389	231,451	267,198	12.1
6553	Cemetery subdividers and developers	180	190	3.1	3,560	3,504	15,934	19,179	59,842	74,066	8.0
6700	Holding and other investment offices	1,268	1,287	5.5	8,645	8,758	46,461	50,871	408,098	457,965	3.3
6710	Holding offices	396	414	4.9	4,646	4,928	57,908	62,093	261,943	277,237	3.4
6720	Investment offices	37	36	4.2	113	173	50,726	96,370	13,014	17,420	1.1
6730	Trusts	234	236	4.5	1,213	1,108	23,462	26,502	29,870	30,970	3.2
6732	Educational, religious, etc. trusts	90	93	3.8	656	566	18,799	20,678	13,426	13,546	2.4
6733	Trusts, n.e.c.	144	141	5.2	557	539	28,955	31,978	16,444	17,011	4.4
6790	Miscellaneous investing	524	488	6.5	2,577	2,376	37,079	36,328	98,717	118,688	4.4
6794	Patent owners and lessors	103	94	6.6	773	780	29,847	34,277	28,466	50,156	7.2
6799	Investors, n.e.c.	360	337	7.0	1,388	1,319	45,960	38,829	61,467	59,664	4.0
GEORGIA											
60 –	**Finance, insurance, and real estate**	15,962	16,578	2.6	180,955	181,778	32,301	34,443	5,711,795	6,040,880	2.4
6000	Depository institutions	2,527	2,524	2.4	53,176	52,334	27,945	28,973	1,399,335	1,421,709	2.3
6020	Commercial banks	1,846	1,849	2.8	43,393	44,484	28,103	29,056	1,133,056	1,197,608	2.6
6030	Savings institutions	210	192	1.2	3,031	2,569	25,097	24,472	74,305	64,058	0.9
6060	Credit unions	304	306	2.0	2,479	2,598	21,125	21,945	54,138	58,484	1.7
6100	Nondepository institutions	2,061	2,164	4.8	18,327	16,602	33,840	36,824	566,858	581,772	3.2
6140	Personal credit institutions	1,115	1,167	6.5	6,313	6,705	28,492	35,686	182,310	200,361	3.7
6150	Business credit institutions	184	187	3.9	3,158	3,119	43,174	47,141	125,544	132,623	3.0
6160	Mortgage bankers and brokers	674	696	3.4	8,438	6,264	33,941	32,437	241,275	225,269	3.0
6200	Security and commodity brokers	859	923	2.3	6,862	7,757	82,490	81,358	488,412	565,256	1.2
6210	Security brokers and dealers	521	568	2.3	5,167	5,719	94,795	94,112	394,390	454,121	1.3
6220	Commodity contracts brokers, dealers	12	13	0.8	30	40	50,267	67,000	1,910	2,819	0.4
6280	Security and commodity services	325	336	2.3	1,665	1,989	44,884	45,229	92,065	108,051	1.1
6300	Insurance carriers	1,150	1,188	2.9	41,541	42,104	33,892	36,351	1,392,758	1,472,575	2.6
6310	Life insurance	438	433	3.7	19,497	18,628	31,629	33,378	602,158	585,996	3.0
6320	Medical service and health insurance	55	61	2.0	3,064	3,631	29,243	37,722	96,190	124,631	1.3
6321	Accident and health insurance	18	16	1.5	780	790	17,456	18,496	16,908	17,436	1.0
6324	Hospital and medical service plans	37	45	2.3	2,284	2,841	33,268	43,068	79,282	107,195	1.3
6330	Fire, marine, and casualty insurance	536	589	2.8	17,180	17,466	38,290	40,688	645,858	700,547	2.9
6350	Surety insurance	16	20	3.4	157	199	47,414	53,186	7,607	9,491	1.8
6360	Title insurance	15	16	0.6	132	148	56,636	60,838	6,141	6,776	0.5
6370	Pension, health, and welfare funds	82	59	2.6	1,438	1,991	17,558	20,456	30,843	44,245	4.4
6390	Insurance carriers, n.e.c.	5	4	2.3	72	32	50,278	20,375	3,926	636	0.7
6400	Insurance agents, brokers, and service	3,335	3,347	2.7	17,829	18,937	32,140	33,573	598,666	664,071	2.9
6500	Real estate	5,472	5,844	2.4	33,951	36,038	23,122	25,134	866,127	940,307	2.9
6510	Real estate operators and lessors	1,948	1,995	2.0	9,359	9,133	18,414	19,537	183,233	190,840	2.0
6530	Real estate agents and managers	2,796	2,976	2.6	20,864	22,599	25,311	27,531	582,950	630,806	3.4
6540	Title abstract offices	52	59	1.2	215	193	27,405	27,316	5,341	4,952	0.6
6550	Subdividers and developers	521	554	3.1	3,305	3,625	22,798	24,867	87,920	99,552	3.1

Source: County Business Patterns, 1994/95, CBP-94/95, U.S. Department of Commerce, Washington, D.C., November 1997. SIC categories for which data were suppressed or not available for both 1994 and 1995 are not displayed. The employment columns represent mid-March employment in the year. Pay per employee is calculated by dividing 1st Quarter payroll, annualized, by mid-March employment. The columns headed "% US" show the state's percentage of the national total for the SIC in 1995; for example, 1.4% for SIC 6000 means that the state had 1.4 percent of the national total establishments (or payroll) in SIC 6000 in 1995. A dash (-) is used to indicate that data are not available or cannot be calculated; nec means not elsewhere classified.

Continued on next page.

SIC	Industry	No. Establishments			Employment		Pay / Employee		Annual Payroll ($ 000)		
		1994	1995	% US	1994	1995	1994	1995	1994	1995	% US
GEORGIA - [continued]											
6552	Subdividers and developers, n.e.c.	371	393	3.8	2,242	2,338	24,219	28,996	65,173	74,837	3.4
6553	Cemetery subdividers and developers	133	122	2.0	1,059	1,183	19,762	16,622	21,711	19,806	2.1
6700	Holding and other investment offices	521	546	2.4	7,068	6,271	43,344	54,767	304,093	312,215	2.3
6710	Holding offices	212	231	2.7	4,281	4,069	48,543	65,741	208,698	233,974	2.8
6720	Investment offices	27	21	2.4	185	127	40,238	45,417	7,476	8,497	0.5
6730	Trusts	89	110	2.1	506	702	20,395	24,638	11,792	17,944	1.9
6732	Educational, religious, etc. trusts	39	45	1.8	334	366	18,635	19,355	6,352	6,928	1.2
6733	Trusts, n.e.c.	50	64	2.4	172	336	23,814	30,393	5,440	11,003	2.9
6790	Miscellaneous investing	177	163	2.2	2,088	1,319	38,628	38,329	75,358	48,546	1.8
6794	Patent owners and lessors	55	47	3.3	873	493	46,369	44,389	40,718	21,411	3.1
HAWAII											
60 –	**Finance, insurance, and real estate**	3,897	3,845	0.6	39,811	38,917	30,136	31,156	1,178,984	1,191,584	0.5
6000	Depository institutions	599	594	0.6	12,608	12,747	30,872	32,591	378,021	382,197	0.6
6020	Commercial banks	310	305	0.5	8,872	8,943	31,998	34,535	273,785	278,116	0.6
6030	Savings institutions	121	123	0.7	1,784	1,834	28,278	28,294	50,451	50,545	0.7
6060	Credit unions	131	131	0.9	1,297	1,333	26,476	25,461	33,243	34,335	1.0
6080	Foreign bank and branches and agencies	3	3	0.5	22	23	41,455	48,696	1,033	1,146	0.0
6090	Functions closely related to banking	34	32	0.6	633	614	31,039	31,974	19,509	18,055	0.8
6100	Nondepository institutions	240	231	0.5	1,991	1,496	47,484	39,382	67,398	55,873	0.3
6140	Personal credit institutions	98	99	0.6	440	426	28,645	29,474	12,656	13,255	0.2
6160	Mortgage bankers and brokers	116	105	0.5	1,411	881	54,721	44,935	49,976	35,802	0.5
6200	Security and commodity brokers	87	100	0.2	844	803	53,555	50,062	41,603	42,991	0.1
6210	Security brokers and dealers	50	61	0.3	713	685	55,798	51,340	35,230	35,555	0.1
6280	Security and commodity services	37	38	0.3	131	118	41,344	42,644	6,373	7,358	0.1
6300	Insurance carriers	151	152	0.4	4,412	4,445	31,343	35,570	148,213	160,191	0.3
6310	Life insurance	50	51	0.4	1,150	1,152	39,513	37,285	45,677	43,125	0.2
6320	Medical service and health insurance	17	18	0.6	1,783	1,820	24,509	26,429	53,531	57,817	0.6
6330	Fire, marine, and casualty insurance	56	56	0.3	961	1,125	41,095	51,125	38,683	48,734	0.2
6360	Title insurance	14	13	0.5	366	221	19,508	26,389	7,087	6,850	0.5
6400	Insurance agents, brokers, and service	347	351	0.3	2,880	2,912	32,265	33,376	93,244	99,390	0.4
6500	Real estate	2,345	2,281	0.9	16,181	15,480	24,881	25,979	411,918	410,670	1.2
6510	Real estate operators and lessors	651	632	0.6	4,081	3,688	25,196	28,606	103,913	100,601	1.1
6530	Real estate agents and managers	1,555	1,497	1.3	9,047	8,818	23,408	23,247	217,085	214,174	1.1
6540	Title abstract offices	12	10	0.2	533	340	27,602	30,047	14,495	10,320	1.2
6550	Subdividers and developers	107	104	0.6	2,495	2,574	29,105	31,176	75,363	82,183	2.5
6552	Subdividers and developers, n.e.c.	93	87	0.8	2,145	2,216	30,545	32,895	68,195	73,579	3.3
6553	Cemetery subdividers and developers	14	16	0.3	350	355	20,274	19,910	7,168	8,470	0.9
6700	Holding and other investment offices	117	126	0.5	732	821	39,574	39,737	31,115	32,626	0.2
6710	Holding offices	29	32	0.4	228	291	62,105	50,213	13,649	14,665	0.2
6733	Trusts, n.e.c.	30	33	1.2	206	225	31,029	30,773	6,853	7,135	1.9
6790	Miscellaneous investing	41	36	0.5	206	173	30,000	44,971	8,154	7,281	0.3
6794	Patent owners and lessors	5	3	0.2	45	24	7,911	7,167	315	163	0.0
6798	Real estate investment trusts	5	5	0.8	25	30	63,680	59,067	1,623	2,063	0.5
6799	Investors, n.e.c.	31	28	0.6	136	119	31,118	49,042	6,216	5,055	0.3
IDAHO											
60 –	**Finance, insurance, and real estate**	2,706	2,801	0.4	19,959	20,449	23,559	24,438	480,715	511,240	0.2
6000	Depository institutions	542	547	0.5	8,311	8,744	23,224	24,416	195,329	214,435	0.3
6020	Commercial banks	378	373	0.6	7,018	7,358	23,798	25,147	169,842	186,304	0.4
6060	Credit unions	115	118	0.8	887	940	16,812	17,740	14,646	15,919	0.5
6100	Nondepository institutions	211	217	0.5	1,088	1,156	30,779	30,166	31,890	35,981	0.2
6140	Personal credit institutions	77	77	0.4	327	349	23,682	27,186	7,893	9,014	0.2
6160	Mortgage bankers and brokers	97	105	0.5	583	625	33,029	28,122	17,020	19,024	0.3
6200	Security and commodity brokers	122	127	0.3	581	629	51,587	50,811	28,638	34,689	0.1
6210	Security brokers and dealers	79	79	0.3	475	511	54,712	54,568	24,023	29,914	0.1
6220	Commodity contracts brokers, dealers	5	5	0.3	19	20	38,947	33,000	646	656	0.1
6280	Security and commodity services	38	43	0.3	87	98	37,287	34,857	3,969	4,119	0.0

Source: County Business Patterns, 1994/95, CBP-94/95, U.S. Department of Commerce, Washington, D.C., November 1997. SIC categories for which data were suppressed or not available for both 1994 and 1995 are not displayed. The employment columns represent mid-March employment in the year. Pay per employee is calculated by dividing 1st Quarter payroll, annualized, by mid-March employment. The columns headed "% US" show the state's percentage of the national total for the SIC in 1995; for example, 1.4% for SIC 6000 means that the state had 1.4 percent of the national total establishments (or payroll) in SIC 6000 in 1995. A dash (-) is used to indicate that data are not available or cannot be calculated; nec means not elsewhere classified.

Continued on next page.

SIC	Industry	No. Establishments			Employment		Pay / Employee		Annual Payroll ($ 000)		
		1994	1995	% US	1994	1995	1994	1995	1994	1995	% US
IDAHO - [continued]											
6300	Insurance carriers	157	165	0.4	2,718	2,650	29,333	31,657	79,204	80,296	0.1
6310	Life insurance	32	32	0.3	549	528	26,251	25,788	14,633	13,360	0.1
6320	Medical service and health insurance	20	20	0.7	802	872	28,708	29,096	22,534	24,607	0.3
6321	Accident and health insurance	4	4	0.4	65	61	20,615	20,262	1,161	1,173	0.1
6324	Hospital and medical service plans	16	16	0.8	737	811	29,422	29,761	21,373	23,434	0.3
6330	Fire, marine, and casualty insurance	94	96	0.5	1,202	1,178	32,639	36,061	38,875	39,773	0.2
6400	Insurance agents, brokers, and service	587	604	0.5	2,765	2,848	22,349	22,104	65,184	66,682	0.3
6500	Real estate	1,014	1,066	0.4	4,213	4,160	15,257	16,039	71,623	72,928	0.2
6510	Real estate operators and lessors	294	307	0.3	1,291	1,325	12,465	13,069	16,892	19,198	0.2
6530	Real estate agents and managers	544	572	0.5	1,963	1,959	14,174	15,806	33,094	32,879	0.2
6540	Title abstract offices	43	44	0.9	640	528	20,913	21,848	12,947	12,529	1.4
6550	Subdividers and developers	111	109	0.6	306	306	22,327	20,902	8,221	7,459	0.2
6552	Subdividers and developers, n.e.c.	86	82	0.8	241	232	25,676	24,621	7,108	6,650	0.3
6710	Holding offices	15	18	0.2	49	69	25,143	22,493	1,452	1,569	0.0
6730	Trusts	20	22	0.4	92	100	16,739	18,720	1,740	1,935	0.2
6732	Educational, religious, etc. trusts	6	8	0.3	22	27	9,818	10,074	237	320	0.1
6733	Trusts, n.e.c.	14	14	0.5	70	73	18,914	21,918	1,503	1,615	0.4
6790	Miscellaneous investing	29	25	0.3	89	80	29,528	23,950	2,791	2,083	0.1
6799	Investors, n.e.c.	21	17	0.4	68	68	21,882	20,176	1,631	1,543	0.1
ILLINOIS											
60 –	**Finance, insurance, and real estate**	28,693	29,524	4.7	404,811	404,604	37,979	42,271	15,061,973	16,231,759	6.3
6000	Depository institutions	4,537	4,726	4.5	120,830	123,197	31,328	35,062	3,702,899	3,914,447	6.3
6020	Commercial banks	2,211	2,385	3.6	85,924	88,339	32,581	36,389	2,712,038	2,865,982	6.3
6030	Savings institutions	938	957	5.8	19,656	18,431	25,551	29,196	499,108	495,259	6.7
6080	Foreign bank and branches and agencies	55	56	8.5	2,182	2,074	64,330	71,090	137,319	143,688	5.1
6090	Functions closely related to banking	613	629	11.8	5,861	7,399	29,125	32,477	173,232	223,907	10.5
6100	Nondepository institutions	1,848	2,049	4.5	26,553	24,019	41,252	46,568	1,011,890	1,073,497	5.8
6110	Federal and Federally-sponsored credit	46	49	3.6	437	459	68,467	72,305	22,486	27,003	2.4
6140	Personal credit institutions	584	666	3.7	8,934	6,507	30,639	38,026	273,972	255,751	4.8
6150	Business credit institutions	406	415	8.7	6,163	6,663	64,793	69,895	343,665	377,346	8.6
6160	Mortgage bankers and brokers	791	897	4.4	11,002	10,363	35,640	35,815	370,900	411,966	5.5
6200	Security and commodity brokers	2,726	2,882	7.0	34,744	36,998	76,988	84,836	2,513,050	2,894,578	6.4
6210	Security brokers and dealers	1,312	1,380	5.7	20,082	20,713	91,655	98,671	1,645,703	1,811,634	5.3
6220	Commodity contracts brokers, dealers	585	588	38.2	7,065	7,876	46,762	50,599	367,796	392,871	52.7
6230	Security and commodity exchanges	16	18	18.2	2,597	2,694	43,184	47,676	110,836	121,790	27.3
6280	Security and commodity services	791	850	5.8	4,987	5,640	78,479	100,305	387,669	562,551	5.7
6300	Insurance carriers	1,961	2,091	5.1	101,120	97,442	38,500	42,679	3,650,529	3,958,816	7.0
6310	Life insurance	544	533	4.5	27,938	26,191	32,265	34,856	878,088	851,959	4.3
6320	Medical service and health insurance	128	142	4.8	13,715	15,258	32,281	36,383	463,896	559,623	5.8
6321	Accident and health insurance	42	54	5.1	5,523	6,535	24,417	28,891	141,179	189,833	11.4
6324	Hospital and medical service plans	86	88	4.6	8,192	8,723	37,583	41,996	322,717	369,790	4.6
6330	Fire, marine, and casualty insurance	1,042	1,145	5.5	55,102	51,942	43,125	47,985	2,156,576	2,390,082	9.9
6350	Surety insurance	23	28	4.7	304	273	53,132	72,908	15,499	16,878	3.2
6360	Title insurance	80	100	4.0	2,336	2,213	44,394	57,967	82,381	90,357	6.6
6370	Pension, health, and welfare funds	125	120	5.3	1,548	1,360	30,514	31,474	48,106	43,151	4.2
6390	Insurance carriers, n.e.c.	12	14	8.1	175	177	31,794	33,966	5,716	5,446	5.9
6400	Insurance agents, brokers, and service	6,394	6,458	5.2	37,280	38,632	33,703	37,667	1,371,275	1,458,629	6.4
6500	Real estate	10,166	10,182	4.1	62,346	63,915	24,943	26,167	1,700,452	1,764,525	5.4
6510	Real estate operators and lessors	3,591	3,503	3.5	19,201	19,295	19,862	20,787	418,183	413,312	4.3
6530	Real estate agents and managers	5,428	5,394	4.7	36,977	37,804	27,370	29,265	1,095,624	1,147,104	6.1
6540	Title abstract offices	239	242	5.0	2,194	1,774	21,894	20,884	47,178	41,647	4.8
6550	Subdividers and developers	717	737	4.2	3,706	4,429	28,749	26,637	127,522	145,532	4.5
6552	Subdividers and developers, n.e.c.	353	371	3.6	1,690	1,956	34,907	33,679	72,878	81,735	3.7
6553	Cemetery subdividers and developers	344	333	5.4	1,986	2,330	23,376	20,795	53,027	59,655	6.5
6700	Holding and other investment offices	1,014	1,074	4.6	13,909	13,140	53,552	58,613	730,436	753,197	5.5
6710	Holding offices	395	405	4.8	9,376	8,692	60,172	62,874	547,489	529,551	6.4
6720	Investment offices	40	80	9.3	346	490	48,775	50,294	17,179	25,767	1.6

Source: County Business Patterns, 1994/95, CBP-94/95, U.S. Department of Commerce, Washington, D.C., November 1997. SIC categories for which data were suppressed or not available for both 1994 and 1995 are *not* displayed. The employment columns represent mid-March employment in the year. Pay per employee is calculated by dividing 1st Quarter payroll, annualized, by mid-March employment. The columns headed "% US" show the state's percentage of the national total for the SIC in 1995; for example, 1.4% for SIC 6000 means that the state had 1.4 percent of the national total establishments (or payroll) in SIC 6000 in 1995. A dash (-) is used to indicate that data are not available or cannot be calculated; *nec* means not elsewhere classified.

Continued on next page.

SIC	Industry	No. Establishments			Employment		Pay / Employee		Annual Payroll ($ 000)		
		1994	1995	% US	1994	1995	1994	1995	1994	1995	% US
ILLINOIS - [continued]											
6730	Trusts	209	208	4.0	1,450	1,133	30,008	24,657	29,055	30,649	3.2
6732	Educational, religious, etc. trusts	106	111	4.5	450	555	30,969	23,286	11,513	13,285	2.3
6733	Trusts, n.e.c.	102	96	3.6	994	572	29,718	26,175	17,501	17,317	4.5
6790	Miscellaneous investing	347	343	4.5	2,681	2,747	44,464	61,262	134,427	163,343	6.1
6792	Oil royalty traders	12	9	1.3	41	24	49,659	88,833	2,551	1,818	1.8
6794	Patent owners and lessors	51	49	3.4	536	429	28,209	39,385	15,381	18,327	2.6
6798	Real estate investment trusts	30	37	6.1	709	1,006	34,324	55,221	32,287	50,584	12.1
6799	Investors, n.e.c.	254	247	5.1	1,395	1,287	55,710	72,777	84,208	92,573	6.3
INDIANA											
60 –	**Finance, insurance, and real estate**	12,153	12,597	2.0	124,996	128,762	27,331	29,169	3,392,210	3,709,445	1.4
6000	Depository institutions	2,598	2,649	2.5	40,575	40,772	21,687	23,439	887,908	953,052	1.5
6020	Commercial banks	1,805	1,851	2.8	30,441	30,275	21,934	23,882	668,634	721,054	1.6
6030	Savings institutions	310	315	1.9	5,328	5,450	22,019	22,161	120,729	122,727	1.7
6060	Credit unions	444	442	2.9	4,478	4,604	19,361	21,255	89,429	95,561	2.7
6100	Nondepository institutions	781	835	1.8	11,463	13,063	33,147	30,026	368,863	415,719	2.3
6140	Personal credit institutions	373	394	2.2	5,443	6,861	32,002	31,167	177,889	204,656	3.8
6150	Business credit institutions	47	49	1.0	294	922	33,646	26,390	12,664	30,427	0.7
6160	Mortgage bankers and brokers	304	335	1.6	5,470	5,064	34,336	28,818	169,943	172,434	2.3
6200	Security and commodity brokers	562	622	1.5	4,066	4,323	58,140	59,254	211,491	235,858	0.5
6210	Security brokers and dealers	354	390	1.6	3,038	3,138	63,464	64,022	168,054	185,431	0.5
6220	Commodity contracts brokers, dealers	11	12	0.8	69	73	33,217	28,767	2,754	3,018	0.4
6280	Security and commodity services	195	218	1.5	957	1,109	43,122	47,859	40,597	47,286	0.5
6300	Insurance carriers	883	909	2.2	28,094	27,885	33,715	38,060	901,214	985,203	1.7
6310	Life insurance	275	273	2.3	12,066	11,646	33,613	38,645	378,760	408,588	2.1
6320	Medical service and health insurance	58	58	1.9	2,986	3,149	38,492	39,259	110,572	116,516	1.2
6321	Accident and health insurance	29	29	2.8	812	885	40,158	37,288	30,804	29,041	1.7
6324	Hospital and medical service plans	29	29	1.5	2,174	2,264	37,869	40,030	79,768	87,475	1.1
6330	Fire, marine, and casualty insurance	447	481	2.3	11,698	11,898	32,944	37,979	377,784	425,641	1.8
6360	Title insurance	34	39	1.5	529	459	33,414	30,937	13,399	12,819	0.9
6370	Pension, health, and welfare funds	57	46	2.0	765	669	27,739	27,540	17,678	18,569	1.8
6400	Insurance agents, brokers, and service	3,002	3,017	2.4	15,246	15,326	26,830	28,755	423,056	446,370	2.0
6500	Real estate	4,035	4,270	1.7	22,732	23,181	18,997	18,526	467,481	465,376	1.4
6510	Real estate operators and lessors	1,556	1,620	1.6	7,381	7,512	14,145	15,586	118,355	130,177	1.4
6530	Real estate agents and managers	1,822	1,911	1.7	11,569	11,647	21,912	20,127	265,368	244,728	1.3
6540	Title abstract offices	175	182	3.8	1,439	1,292	19,575	17,817	28,944	26,445	3.1
6550	Subdividers and developers	406	424	2.4	2,137	2,462	19,467	20,996	48,539	59,674	1.8
6552	Subdividers and developers, n.e.c.	188	197	1.9	910	1,204	25,820	26,472	27,624	37,801	1.7
6553	Cemetery subdividers and developers	204	198	3.2	1,208	1,173	14,719	16,089	20,252	20,528	2.2
6700	Holding and other investment offices	274	276	1.2	2,307	2,965	48,125	60,747	110,188	164,768	1.2
6710	Holding offices	108	112	1.3	1,164	1,567	64,065	79,045	71,806	114,797	1.4
6720	Investment offices	13	10	1.2	123	74	80,846	206,595	12,347	14,996	0.9
6730	Trusts	95	90	1.7	714	925	25,406	32,216	16,733	22,510	2.4
6732	Educational, religious, etc. trusts	47	48	1.9	545	555	23,486	25,867	13,547	14,815	2.6
6733	Trusts, n.e.c.	48	42	1.6	169	370	31,598	41,741	3,186	7,695	2.0
6790	Miscellaneous investing	54	54	0.7	292	380	27,904	27,126	9,047	11,461	0.4
6794	Patent owners and lessors	15	13	0.9	128	186	30,563	20,129	4,072	4,091	0.6
6799	Investors, n.e.c.	32	32	0.7	126	150	25,397	35,973	3,733	5,578	0.4
IOWA											
60 –	**Finance, insurance, and real estate**	7,185	7,286	1.2	78,719	80,838	27,946	29,668	2,155,717	2,291,670	0.9
6000	Depository institutions	1,527	1,532	1.5	24,131	24,178	22,898	24,158	552,027	576,531	0.9
6020	Commercial banks	1,042	1,053	1.6	19,406	19,626	23,517	24,414	452,541	471,192	1.0
6030	Savings institutions	212	203	1.2	2,567	2,345	21,727	26,072	58,064	61,135	0.8
6060	Credit unions	262	264	1.8	1,961	2,000	17,006	18,040	34,513	36,700	1.0
6100	Nondepository institutions	272	290	0.6	5,080	5,734	40,122	38,071	173,748	188,198	1.0
6150	Business credit institutions	45	43	0.9	1,600	1,612	38,333	38,638	56,076	56,967	1.3
6160	Mortgage bankers and brokers	71	82	0.4	2,089	2,324	35,347	33,974	62,679	69,897	0.9

Source: County Business Patterns, 1994/95, CBP-94/95, U.S. Department of Commerce, Washington, D.C., November 1997. SIC categories for which data were suppressed or not available for both 1994 and 1995 are *not* displayed. The employment columns represent mid-March employment in the year. Pay per employee is calculated by dividing 1st Quarter payroll, annualized, by mid-March employment. The columns headed "% US" show the state's percentage of the national total for the SIC in 1995; for example, 1.4% for SIC 6000 means that the state had 1.4 percent of the national total establishments (or payroll) in SIC 6000 in 1995. A dash (-) is used to indicate that data are not available or cannot be calculated; *nec* means not elsewhere classified.

Continued on next page.

SIC	Industry	No. Establishments			Employment		Pay / Employee		Annual Payroll ($ 000)		
		1994	1995	% US	1994	1995	1994	1995	1994	1995	% US
IOWA - [continued]											
6200	Security and commodity brokers	457	470	1.1	2,351	2,420	52,556	49,164	110,353	116,616	0.3
6210	Security brokers and dealers	276	284	1.2	1,673	1,688	58,680	49,678	83,854	83,683	0.2
6220	Commodity contracts brokers, dealers	49	47	3.0	226	221	38,832	36,416	9,549	12,101	1.6
6280	Security and commodity services	130	132	0.9	452	485	36,752	54,532	16,770	19,833	0.2
6300	Insurance carriers	507	498	1.2	26,776	26,976	32,649	35,980	838,063	888,830	1.6
6310	Life insurance	166	161	1.4	15,270	15,200	34,984	38,678	492,925	516,003	2.6
6320	Medical service and health insurance	40	46	1.5	2,566	2,786	27,944	29,236	71,511	81,585	0.8
6330	Fire, marine, and casualty insurance	254	249	1.2	7,685	7,757	30,576	34,265	241,631	257,358	1.1
6350	Surety insurance	8	8	1.3	464	501	24,000	23,257	10,134	11,070	2.1
6400	Insurance agents, brokers, and service	2,093	2,124	1.7	8,281	8,229	23,330	24,458	205,994	205,838	0.9
6500	Real estate	2,099	2,128	0.9	9,176	9,653	15,592	16,248	158,435	165,756	0.5
6510	Real estate operators and lessors	890	894	0.9	3,812	3,996	13,635	14,356	56,783	58,682	0.6
6530	Real estate agents and managers	845	852	0.7	3,975	4,249	16,930	17,775	74,552	79,711	0.4
6540	Title abstract offices	131	128	2.7	763	697	17,913	18,812	14,655	13,677	1.6
6550	Subdividers and developers	210	211	1.2	612	662	16,346	15,372	12,135	12,441	0.4
6552	Subdividers and developers, n.e.c.	57	60	0.6	204	219	21,745	18,027	4,926	5,307	0.2
6553	Cemetery subdividers and developers	147	137	2.2	401	417	13,127	13,151	6,596	6,246	0.7
6710	Holding offices	123	132	1.6	2,093	2,707	40,545	46,032	90,390	124,121	1.5
6730	Trusts	36	40	0.8	238	418	21,193	13,187	5,357	6,210	0.7
6732	Educational, religious, etc. trusts	16	18	0.7	175	312	20,251	15,705	3,767	5,579	1.0
6733	Trusts, n.e.c.	20	22	0.8	63	106	23,810	5,774	1,590	631	0.2
6790	Miscellaneous investing	54	56	0.7	306	309	33,895	35,081	12,220	12,308	0.5
6794	Patent owners and lessors	11	10	0.7	87	112	31,402	31,464	2,775	3,462	0.5
6799	Investors, n.e.c.	33	36	0.7	162	146	28,444	36,877	6,260	6,935	0.5
KANSAS											
60 –	**Finance, insurance, and real estate**	6,636	6,803	1.1	61,905	61,252	26,728	28,377	1,636,950	1,739,266	0.7
6000	Depository institutions	1,320	1,299	1.2	19,702	19,581	23,216	24,165	463,011	480,983	0.8
6020	Commercial banks	929	925	1.4	15,801	15,804	22,815	23,382	368,023	380,338	0.8
6030	Savings institutions	186	175	1.1	2,260	2,112	26,283	30,023	56,363	60,153	0.8
6060	Credit unions	179	176	1.2	1,213	1,229	18,038	19,079	22,701	23,788	0.7
6100	Nondepository institutions	348	364	0.8	5,499	5,170	30,961	31,406	154,262	158,033	0.9
6110	Federal and Federally-sponsored credit	34	34	2.5	1,034	995	30,012	32,398	29,995	28,321	2.6
6140	Personal credit institutions	138	148	0.8	951	1,061	26,578	26,993	24,775	29,188	0.5
6150	Business credit institutions	49	46	1.0	1,484	1,465	31,555	31,121	40,701	46,537	1.1
6160	Mortgage bankers and brokers	126	133	0.6	2,030	1,648	33,062	33,910	58,786	53,966	0.7
6200	Security and commodity brokers	402	426	1.0	2,257	2,277	50,501	49,723	106,010	113,302	0.2
6210	Security brokers and dealers	231	242	1.0	1,327	1,352	54,957	45,976	64,383	65,817	0.2
6280	Security and commodity services	139	147	1.0	710	679	44,169	56,990	30,180	34,121	0.3
6300	Insurance carriers	457	444	1.1	14,205	13,139	32,702	36,993	439,413	453,429	0.8
6310	Life insurance	158	161	1.4	4,274	4,192	34,569	37,377	135,729	143,543	0.7
6320	Medical service and health insurance	48	45	1.5	2,615	2,465	26,489	31,787	71,543	74,453	0.8
6321	Accident and health insurance	17	18	1.7	331	322	33,221	34,087	10,141	10,329	0.6
6324	Hospital and medical service plans	31	27	1.4	2,284	2,143	25,513	31,442	61,402	64,124	0.8
6330	Fire, marine, and casualty insurance	202	196	0.9	6,736	6,087	34,268	39,059	217,092	222,828	0.9
6350	Surety insurance	9	9	1.5	116	96	36,552	46,542	4,617	3,620	0.7
6360	Title insurance	18	17	0.7	222	98	27,550	26,490	4,756	2,556	0.2
6370	Pension, health, and welfare funds	19	12	0.5	234	167	24,376	28,192	5,082	4,879	0.5
6400	Insurance agents, brokers, and service	1,866	1,911	1.5	7,112	7,520	24,843	26,447	190,117	212,926	0.9
6500	Real estate	1,979	2,086	0.8	10,250	10,304	16,536	17,047	182,110	192,516	0.6
6510	Real estate operators and lessors	768	784	0.8	3,058	3,648	13,704	14,320	48,948	58,655	0.6
6530	Real estate agents and managers	897	953	0.8	5,649	5,392	17,572	18,548	104,924	107,929	0.6
6540	Title abstract offices	124	124	2.6	620	536	21,213	18,784	11,485	10,232	1.2
6550	Subdividers and developers	164	171	1.0	863	645	17,010	19,460	15,990	14,369	0.4
6552	Subdividers and developers, n.e.c.	65	78	0.8	541	308	20,407	27,753	11,526	9,784	0.4
6553	Cemetery subdividers and developers	90	87	1.4	316	323	11,456	12,099	4,386	4,468	0.5
6700	Holding and other investment offices	250	260	1.1	2,771	3,168	35,388	39,312	98,905	124,894	0.9
6710	Holding offices	105	109	1.3	1,988	2,394	39,143	42,814	75,050	101,415	1.2

Source: County Business Patterns, 1994/95, CBP-94/95, U.S. Department of Commerce, Washington, D.C., November 1997. SIC categories for which data were suppressed or not available for both 1994 and 1995 are not displayed. The employment columns represent mid-March employment in the year. Pay per employee is calculated by dividing 1st Quarter payroll, annualized, by mid-March employment. The columns headed "% US" show the state's percentage of the national total for the SIC in 1995; for example, 1.4% for SIC 6000 means that the state had 1.4 percent of the national total establishments (or payroll) in SIC 6000 in 1995. A dash (-) is used to indicate that data are not available or cannot be calculated; nec means not elsewhere classified.

Continued on next page.

SIC	Industry	No. Establishments			Employment		Pay / Employee		Annual Payroll ($ 000)		
		1994	1995	% US	1994	1995	1994	1995	1994	1995	% US
KANSAS - [continued]											
6730	Trusts	52	57	1.1	278	244	19,237	17,967	7,535	4,941	0.5
6732	Educational, religious, etc. trusts	22	21	0.8	215	160	20,819	18,525	6,475	3,483	0.6
6733	Trusts, n.e.c.	30	36	1.3	63	84	13,841	16,905	1,060	1,458	0.4
6790	Miscellaneous investing	74	72	1.0	475	495	28,994	33,212	14,929	16,743	0.6
6794	Patent owners and lessors	21	20	1.4	322	360	32,522	36,189	11,939	13,692	2.0
6799	Investors, n.e.c.	35	37	0.8	121	104	20,959	23,577	2,010	2,076	0.1
KENTUCKY											
60 –	**Finance, insurance, and real estate**	6,997	7,215	1.1	64,714	65,840	25,480	26,643	1,680,155	1,785,359	0.7
6000	Depository institutions	1,552	1,575	1.5	25,432	24,822	23,102	24,406	592,830	612,671	1.0
6020	Commercial banks	1,184	1,222	1.8	22,066	21,501	23,365	24,585	516,862	531,698	1.2
6030	Savings institutions	177	163	1.0	1,802	1,651	23,181	25,698	43,804	45,363	0.6
6060	Credit unions	163	160	1.1	1,269	1,332	18,389	19,664	24,489	26,703	0.8
6100	Nondepository institutions	549	656	1.4	4,993	5,350	24,254	24,651	126,937	131,564	0.7
6140	Personal credit institutions	349	425	2.4	1,834	2,153	20,521	23,355	41,706	50,365	0.9
6150	Business credit institutions	31	33	0.7	961	1,148	24,062	20,551	25,338	23,591	0.5
6160	Mortgage bankers and brokers	123	148	0.7	1,901	1,738	25,953	26,115	48,378	45,731	0.6
6200	Security and commodity brokers	245	269	0.7	1,865	1,963	58,312	55,081	106,320	117,120	0.3
6210	Security brokers and dealers	177	192	0.8	1,609	1,665	59,669	51,481	91,534	97,417	0.3
6220	Commodity contracts brokers, dealers	4	5	0.3	17	30	24,471	30,267	588	1,280	0.2
6280	Security and commodity services	64	72	0.5	239	268	51,582	80,224	14,198	18,423	0.2
6300	Insurance carriers	503	513	1.2	11,121	11,164	29,721	31,357	330,559	360,295	0.6
6310	Life insurance	187	176	1.5	4,456	3,967	28,910	31,977	128,203	121,152	0.6
6320	Medical service and health insurance	49	63	2.1	3,939	4,021	27,916	28,337	109,920	124,637	1.3
6321	Accident and health insurance	11	13	1.2	278	274	21,799	21,883	6,343	6,136	0.4
6324	Hospital and medical service plans	38	50	2.6	3,661	3,747	28,380	28,809	103,577	118,501	1.5
6330	Fire, marine, and casualty insurance	237	241	1.2	2,464	2,895	34,666	35,088	85,616	107,256	0.4
6350	Surety insurance	3	4	0.7	68	70	28,471	32,114	2,269	2,508	0.5
6370	Pension, health, and welfare funds	19	18	0.8	117	101	15,282	30,099	1,907	3,041	0.3
6400	Insurance agents, brokers, and service	1,660	1,691	1.3	8,442	8,955	23,500	26,330	209,921	235,961	1.0
6500	Real estate	2,280	2,305	0.9	9,379	10,187	14,552	15,457	154,607	169,693	0.5
6510	Real estate operators and lessors	1,079	1,071	1.1	4,450	4,852	12,327	13,295	61,248	68,921	0.7
6530	Real estate agents and managers	910	893	0.8	3,575	3,966	17,028	17,832	68,730	75,192	0.4
6540	Title abstract offices	17	23	0.5	116	74	19,931	22,270	2,019	1,975	0.2
6550	Subdividers and developers	228	247	1.4	1,200	1,185	15,023	15,990	21,545	21,763	0.7
6552	Subdividers and developers, n.e.c.	104	108	1.0	415	379	20,145	19,694	10,215	9,072	0.4
6553	Cemetery subdividers and developers	116	120	2.0	784	792	12,327	14,217	11,010	12,285	1.3
6700	Holding and other investment offices	196	194	0.8	3,181	2,986	49,423	51,058	146,575	144,009	1.0
6710	Holding offices	92	90	1.1	2,506	2,341	55,936	58,474	126,130	125,936	1.5
6730	Trusts	48	43	0.8	302	291	26,583	24,509	9,264	7,819	0.8
6732	Educational, religious, etc. trusts	30	28	1.1	237	234	25,975	26,889	6,254	6,972	1.2
6733	Trusts, n.e.c.	18	15	0.6	65	57	28,800	14,737	3,010	847	0.2
6790	Miscellaneous investing	49	46	0.6	362	322	24,464	24,571	10,921	9,454	0.4
6794	Patent owners and lessors	6	6	0.4	104	106	29,192	20,566	4,060	2,479	0.4
6799	Investors, n.e.c.	35	32	0.7	222	190	20,270	24,947	5,612	6,127	0.4
LOUISIANA											
60 –	**Finance, insurance, and real estate**	9,135	9,325	1.5	79,600	79,825	25,717	27,322	2,031,969	2,179,393	0.9
6000	Depository institutions	1,775	1,779	1.7	28,047	28,590	24,172	25,561	662,098	714,098	1.1
6020	Commercial banks	1,260	1,274	1.9	23,579	24,088	24,881	26,424	567,882	618,112	1.4
6030	Savings institutions	127	117	0.7	1,691	1,632	23,525	23,034	40,998	38,136	0.5
6060	Credit unions	337	330	2.2	2,224	2,267	17,550	18,998	40,500	44,606	1.3
6100	Nondepository institutions	1,176	1,262	2.8	6,267	6,661	24,347	25,003	149,178	168,482	0.9
6110	Federal and Federally-sponsored credit	29	27	2.0	104	100	29,962	28,960	3,219	3,050	0.3
6140	Personal credit institutions	866	917	5.1	3,811	4,120	21,733	21,833	86,635	95,847	1.8
6150	Business credit institutions	56	66	1.4	255	262	27,765	27,511	7,750	8,496	0.2
6160	Mortgage bankers and brokers	199	213	1.0	2,073	2,074	28,178	30,825	50,004	58,790	0.8
6200	Security and commodity brokers	324	329	0.8	2,645	2,627	62,737	60,033	149,267	154,431	0.3

Source: County Business Patterns, 1994/95, CBP-94/95, U.S. Department of Commerce, Washington, D.C., November 1997. SIC categories for which data were suppressed or not available for both 1994 and 1995 are *not* displayed. The employment columns represent mid-March employment in the year. Pay per employee is calculated by dividing 1st Quarter payroll, annualized, by mid-March employment. The columns headed "% US" show the state's percentage of the national total for the SIC in 1995; for example, 1.4% for SIC 6000 means that the state had 1.4 percent of the national total establishments (or payroll) in SIC 6000 in 1995. A dash (-) is used to indicate that data are not available or cannot be calculated; *nec* means not elsewhere classified.

Continued on next page.

SIC	Industry	No. Establishments			Employment		Pay / Employee		Annual Payroll ($ 000)		
		1994	1995	% US	1994	1995	1994	1995	1994	1995	% US
LOUISIANA - [continued]											
6210	Security brokers and dealers	225	229	0.9	2,085	2,036	65,719	64,583	121,727	125,784	0.4
6220	Commodity contracts brokers, dealers	5	4	0.3	9	12	27,556	21,000	241	247	0.0
6280	Security and commodity services	92	95	0.6	550	575	52,109	44,786	27,072	28,345	0.3
6300	Insurance carriers	754	773	1.9	14,442	13,716	32,681	35,666	455,804	469,634	0.8
6310	Life insurance	309	306	2.6	6,745	6,299	29,986	32,211	197,379	190,376	1.0
6320	Medical service and health insurance	50	48	1.6	1,698	1,947	30,082	30,878	50,338	58,235	0.6
6321	Accident and health insurance	26	23	2.2	213	180	26,610	31,311	5,896	5,495	0.3
6324	Hospital and medical service plans	24	25	1.3	1,485	1,767	30,580	30,834	44,442	52,740	0.7
6330	Fire, marine, and casualty insurance	333	362	1.7	5,272	4,889	37,554	42,654	186,262	203,522	0.8
6360	Title insurance	13	15	0.6	232	177	35,397	30,712	7,020	5,041	0.4
6370	Pension, health, and welfare funds	37	29	1.3	308	218	16,948	21,046	7,815	4,279	0.4
6400	Insurance agents, brokers, and service	2,177	2,146	1.7	10,921	10,962	24,736	27,176	285,702	310,347	1.4
6500	Real estate	2,636	2,726	1.1	14,231	14,011	14,958	15,568	232,477	236,225	0.7
6510	Real estate operators and lessors	1,335	1,361	1.4	5,877	5,803	12,618	13,799	79,509	84,775	0.9
6530	Real estate agents and managers	1,015	1,026	0.9	6,397	6,421	16,711	17,083	116,177	114,845	0.6
6540	Title abstract offices	74	85	1.8	548	356	22,657	19,517	11,602	9,649	1.1
6550	Subdividers and developers	167	170	1.0	1,386	1,243	13,752	15,434	24,000	23,599	0.7
6552	Subdividers and developers, n.e.c.	90	85	0.8	583	519	16,501	17,950	13,214	12,202	0.6
6553	Cemetery subdividers and developers	70	70	1.1	802	712	11,761	13,607	10,521	10,459	1.1
6700	Holding and other investment offices	277	295	1.3	2,235	2,676	33,332	36,274	77,408	107,253	0.8
6710	Holding offices	71	82	1.0	1,469	1,882	36,877	41,005	56,859	85,104	1.0
6720	Investment offices	11	9	1.0	25	18	22,080	22,000	419	424	0.0
6730	Trusts	49	52	1.0	186	238	16,366	16,672	3,287	4,748	0.5
6732	Educational, religious, etc. trusts	24	27	1.1	102	168	13,569	11,095	1,450	2,521	0.4
6733	Trusts, n.e.c.	25	25	0.9	84	70	19,762	30,057	1,837	2,227	0.6
6790	Miscellaneous investing	139	139	1.8	552	473	30,275	30,706	16,724	16,055	0.6
6792	Oil royalty traders	50	50	7.2	150	159	25,867	24,528	4,461	4,386	4.4
6794	Patent owners and lessors	19	14	1.0	81	54	20,346	17,926	1,832	1,260	0.2
6798	Real estate investment trusts	7	6	1.0	57	17	8,491	23,765	601	829	0.2
6799	Investors, n.e.c.	63	68	1.4	264	242	40,530	38,215	9,830	9,576	0.6
MAINE											
60 –	**Finance, insurance, and real estate**	2,618	2,666	0.4	25,533	25,568	30,116	29,296	735,160	751,974	0.3
6000	Depository institutions	638	631	0.6	8,714	9,013	22,806	23,672	206,458	206,383	0.3
6020	Commercial banks	326	321	0.5	4,433	4,420	23,333	22,608	106,875	98,284	0.2
6030	Savings institutions	175	176	1.1	2,752	2,957	23,840	27,858	68,293	75,895	1.0
6060	Credit unions	127	127	0.8	1,318	1,452	18,583	19,102	25,770	28,809	0.8
6160	Mortgage bankers and brokers	35	38	0.2	478	331	30,603	28,218	12,106	8,841	0.1
6200	Security and commodity brokers	109	107	0.3	796	813	62,482	59,754	43,628	45,878	0.1
6210	Security brokers and dealers	56	55	0.2	566	574	66,933	64,021	31,616	34,342	0.1
6300	Insurance carriers	170	165	0.4	8,529	8,119	39,688	35,347	288,127	295,091	0.5
6310	Life insurance	46	42	0.4	4,368	4,228	52,223	38,990	174,907	161,670	0.8
6320	Medical service and health insurance	7	6	0.2	1,861	1,648	27,499	34,345	52,513	55,416	0.6
6330	Fire, marine, and casualty insurance	94	94	0.5	2,169	2,161	25,846	29,323	57,784	75,402	0.3
6370	Pension, health, and welfare funds	18	14	0.6	109	65	20,183	23,200	2,028	1,882	0.2
6400	Insurance agents, brokers, and service	522	543	0.4	3,198	3,333	27,590	29,661	94,238	101,318	0.4
6500	Real estate	1,047	1,093	0.4	3,220	3,288	17,061	18,038	64,057	66,261	0.2
6510	Real estate operators and lessors	350	354	0.4	1,025	1,011	15,930	17,302	18,742	19,600	0.2
6530	Real estate agents and managers	568	593	0.5	1,969	2,014	17,515	18,393	39,351	39,864	0.2
6540	Title abstract offices	12	15	0.3	91	66	23,824	23,273	2,070	1,803	0.2
6550	Subdividers and developers	90	95	0.5	127	128	14,866	18,125	3,059	3,617	0.1
6552	Subdividers and developers, n.e.c.	29	32	0.3	31	40	21,290	28,300	1,083	1,743	0.1
6553	Cemetery subdividers and developers	59	58	0.9	96	87	12,792	13,333	1,938	1,821	0.2
6700	Holding and other investment offices	75	70	0.3	413	493	43,981	51,124	20,186	21,809	0.2
6710	Holding offices	27	27	0.3	243	319	57,235	62,947	14,699	16,198	0.2

Source: County Business Patterns, 1994/95, CBP-94/95, U.S. Department of Commerce, Washington, D.C., November 1997. SIC categories for which data were suppressed or not available for both 1994 and 1995 are not displayed. The employment columns represent mid-March employment in the year. Pay per employee is calculated by dividing 1st Quarter payroll, annualized, by mid-March employment. The columns headed "% US" show the state's percentage of the national total for the SIC in 1995; for example, 1.4% for SIC 6000 means that the state had 1.4 percent of the national total establishments (or payroll) in SIC 6000 in 1995. A dash (-) is used to indicate that data are not available or cannot be calculated; nec means not elsewhere classified.

Continued on next page.

SIC	Industry	No. Establishments			Employment		Pay / Employee		Annual Payroll ($ 000)		
		1994	1995	% US	1994	1995	1994	1995	1994	1995	% US
MAINE - [continued]											
6730	Trusts	29	26	0.5	114	139	27,228	32,691	4,198	4,740	0.5
6732	Educational, religious, etc. trusts	13	12	0.5	66	117	33,091	34,803	3,206	4,215	0.7
6733	Trusts, n.e.c.	16	14	0.5	48	22	19,167	21,455	992	525	0.1
MARYLAND											
60 –	**Finance, insurance, and real estate**	11,485	11,687	1.9	144,073	143,694	33,699	35,523	4,760,460	4,983,998	1.9
6000	Depository institutions	2,171	2,172	2.1	38,888	40,003	26,889	29,100	1,073,559	1,108,660	1.8
6020	Commercial banks	1,443	1,452	2.2	26,821	27,741	27,950	29,802	760,368	765,601	1.7
6030	Savings institutions	413	384	2.3	7,829	8,047	25,566	27,564	212,190	229,117	3.1
6060	Credit unions	220	230	1.5	2,965	3,163	21,812	24,991	69,021	77,451	2.2
6100	Nondepository institutions	960	984	2.2	13,964	11,903	37,889	41,567	480,849	460,020	2.5
6140	Personal credit institutions	281	300	1.7	3,710	3,680	29,063	34,435	100,706	112,100	2.1
6150	Business credit institutions	79	80	1.7	2,242	2,355	36,616	40,766	83,660	93,694	2.1
6160	Mortgage bankers and brokers	577	577	2.8	7,717	5,580	42,183	43,140	283,597	242,902	3.3
6200	Security and commodity brokers	533	560	1.4	5,619	5,775	88,253	92,449	401,988	435,379	1.0
6210	Security brokers and dealers	261	261	1.1	3,515	3,663	111,679	117,760	291,656	319,234	0.9
6300	Insurance carriers	859	854	2.1	26,371	25,800	39,820	41,626	1,008,450	1,054,422	1.9
6310	Life insurance	238	223	1.9	6,280	5,701	37,232	37,613	218,250	202,157	1.0
6320	Medical service and health insurance	53	52	1.7	4,457	4,778	35,601	40,956	159,751	191,231	2.0
6321	Accident and health insurance	15	15	1.4	283	251	29,357	39,649	8,233	9,583	0.6
6324	Hospital and medical service plans	38	37	1.9	4,174	4,527	36,024	41,028	151,518	181,648	2.3
6330	Fire, marine, and casualty insurance	427	455	2.2	13,905	13,729	42,441	43,087	567,485	596,891	2.5
6350	Surety insurance	20	22	3.7	855	772	48,122	55,891	37,220	37,434	7.1
6360	Title insurance	34	38	1.5	286	282	40,014	47,149	9,974	10,163	0.7
6370	Pension, health, and welfare funds	82	53	2.3	568	516	24,993	29,124	15,094	15,580	1.5
6390	Insurance carriers, n.e.c.	4	4	2.3	20	20	33,600	36,800	673	650	0.7
6400	Insurance agents, brokers, and service	1,998	2,030	1.6	12,500	13,220	33,382	34,385	436,229	473,294	2.1
6500	Real estate	4,621	4,712	1.9	35,666	35,668	22,280	23,337	854,691	901,549	2.7
6510	Real estate operators and lessors	1,525	1,506	1.5	11,513	11,118	19,334	19,615	239,180	235,609	2.5
6530	Real estate agents and managers	2,405	2,466	2.1	19,357	20,269	23,291	24,191	481,042	523,507	2.8
6540	Title abstract offices	238	230	4.8	1,615	980	29,305	26,367	38,770	29,480	3.4
6550	Subdividers and developers	359	365	2.1	3,085	3,064	23,326	30,482	92,445	106,333	3.3
6552	Subdividers and developers, n.e.c.	244	237	2.3	1,824	1,813	27,693	37,739	65,681	73,617	3.3
6553	Cemetery subdividers and developers	102	101	1.6	1,252	1,228	16,965	19,909	26,181	30,638	3.3
6700	Holding and other investment offices	307	327	1.4	7,670	7,942	45,064	45,826	363,805	386,874	2.8
6710	Holding offices	96	94	1.1	3,862	3,435	47,792	52,157	181,960	175,699	2.1
6720	Investment offices	13	15	1.7	919	977	51,604	67,153	58,673	86,168	5.2
6730	Trusts	82	97	1.9	1,530	2,043	33,276	28,292	61,443	63,536	6.7
6732	Educational, religious, etc. trusts	42	48	1.9	821	1,124	30,699	30,025	31,235	37,974	6.7
6733	Trusts, n.e.c.	40	48	1.8	709	919	36,260	26,172	30,208	25,546	6.7
6790	Miscellaneous investing	108	103	1.4	1,352	1,423	45,799	42,510	61,412	60,033	2.2
6798	Real estate investment trusts	11	11	1.8	376	578	58,851	39,543	17,815	20,940	5.0
6799	Investors, n.e.c.	65	63	1.3	562	411	50,420	59,007	29,724	24,263	1.6
MASSACHUSETTS											
60 –	**Finance, insurance, and real estate**	13,208	13,219	2.1	224,257	231,300	42,085	46,653	9,267,187	9,993,487	3.9
6000	Depository institutions	2,536	2,401	2.3	60,679	60,608	34,073	39,145	2,010,489	2,079,944	3.3
6020	Commercial banks	1,093	1,034	1.5	36,861	36,595	38,512	45,271	1,346,345	1,398,577	3.1
6030	Savings institutions	976	909	5.5	17,649	17,600	26,307	27,898	479,464	463,326	6.3
6060	Credit unions	402	395	2.6	3,994	4,149	21,583	23,180	89,955	99,335	2.8
6090	Functions closely related to banking	55	53	1.0	520	621	53,300	94,435	30,550	53,488	2.5
6100	Nondepository institutions	670	653	1.4	9,052	7,341	39,757	42,298	322,192	305,318	1.7
6140	Personal credit institutions	160	161	0.9	2,438	2,470	28,212	32,010	71,163	73,198	1.4
6150	Business credit institutions	100	97	2.0	1,385	1,310	59,815	73,173	82,634	83,279	1.9
6160	Mortgage bankers and brokers	396	381	1.9	4,887	3,290	39,799	37,894	154,452	139,320	1.9
6200	Security and commodity brokers	998	1,083	2.6	29,612	31,850	74,897	81,169	1,999,769	2,361,486	5.2
6210	Security brokers and dealers	406	447	1.8	14,250	14,231	76,941	82,166	949,397	1,054,946	3.1
6280	Security and commodity services	585	624	4.2	15,288	17,546	73,137	80,503	1,046,270	1,301,671	13.1

Source: County Business Patterns, 1994/95, CBP-94/95, U.S. Department of Commerce, Washington, D.C., November 1997. SIC categories for which data were suppressed or not available for both 1994 and 1995 are not displayed. The employment columns represent mid-March employment in the year. Pay per employee is calculated by dividing 1st Quarter payroll, annualized, by mid-March employment. The columns headed "% US" show the state's percentage of the national total for the SIC in 1995; for example, 1.4% for SIC 6000 means that the state had 1.4 percent of the national total establishments (or payroll) in SIC 6000 in 1995. A dash (-) is used to indicate that data are not available or cannot be calculated; nec means not elsewhere classified.

Continued on next page.

SIC	Industry	No. Establishments			Employment		Pay / Employee		Annual Payroll ($ 000)		
		1994	1995	% US	1994	1995	1994	1995	1994	1995	% US
MASSACHUSETTS - [continued]											
6300	Insurance carriers	650	613	1.5	62,446	65,021	39,939	42,413	2,467,317	2,536,966	4.5
6310	Life insurance	291	278	2.4	35,021	37,083	42,379	42,760	1,439,617	1,383,904	7.0
6320	Medical service and health insurance	71	65	2.2	9,955	10,076	37,022	41,690	397,946	437,273	4.5
6321	Accident and health insurance	22	18	1.7	775	988	34,328	35,409	36,324	39,360	2.4
6324	Hospital and medical service plans	49	47	2.4	9,180	9,088	37,249	42,373	361,622	397,913	5.0
6330	Fire, marine, and casualty insurance	189	180	0.9	16,009	16,659	37,864	42,557	592,812	665,062	2.7
6350	Surety insurance	12	13	2.2	118	103	43,424	59,340	4,927	5,352	1.0
6360	Title insurance	16	15	0.6	166	187	65,398	56,150	8,408	8,639	0.6
6370	Pension, health, and welfare funds	64	53	2.3	1,150	845	14,838	26,646	20,367	25,119	2.5
6390	Insurance carriers, n.e.c.	5	6	3.5	27	67	79,407	57,612	2,767	3,633	4.0
6400	Insurance agents, brokers, and service	2,954	2,976	2.4	19,771	20,956	34,703	37,618	732,661	796,197	3.5
6500	Real estate	4,838	4,910	2.0	31,109	32,080	27,516	28,774	919,557	976,733	3.0
6510	Real estate operators and lessors	1,627	1,626	1.6	9,104	10,078	26,612	26,160	246,646	260,347	2.7
6530	Real estate agents and managers	2,726	2,695	2.3	20,144	19,356	28,226	30,513	613,486	632,369	3.4
6540	Title abstract offices	56	56	1.2	316	224	28,785	29,232	8,783	6,943	0.8
6550	Subdividers and developers	340	363	2.1	1,451	1,689	23,520	26,347	43,357	49,983	1.5
6552	Subdividers and developers, n.e.c.	192	199	1.9	746	976	24,954	27,918	24,309	28,698	1.3
6553	Cemetery subdividers and developers	129	128	2.1	702	679	21,989	23,429	18,189	18,644	2.0
6700	Holding and other investment offices	535	557	2.4	10,039	11,812	67,720	83,270	738,504	865,825	6.3
6710	Holding offices	155	158	1.9	1,741	1,963	64,460	75,069	115,579	136,389	1.7
6720	Investment offices	39	35	4.1	5,513	7,006	77,003	95,954	471,671	542,425	32.8
6730	Trusts	156	170	3.3	798	913	40,982	45,227	34,569	67,708	7.1
6732	Educational, religious, etc. trusts	66	72	2.9	557	636	44,223	42,113	26,088	51,470	9.0
6733	Trusts, n.e.c.	90	97	3.6	241	277	33,494	52,375	8,481	16,160	4.2
6790	Miscellaneous investing	173	169	2.2	1,909	1,896	55,996	63,852	114,300	115,190	4.3
6798	Real estate investment trusts	40	34	5.6	842	1,066	24,679	23,471	21,309	23,064	5.5
6799	Investors, n.e.c.	105	112	2.3	664	697	100,530	128,293	72,143	86,980	5.9
MICHIGAN											
60 –	**Finance, insurance, and real estate**	17,552	18,193	2.9	205,415	200,997	28,697	31,358	5,943,277	6,421,160	2.5
6000	Depository institutions	3,907	4,125	3.9	71,516	71,276	23,415	26,015	1,694,293	1,885,287	3.0
6020	Commercial banks	2,584	2,777	4.2	53,596	52,945	23,844	27,127	1,283,127	1,446,975	3.2
6030	Savings institutions	512	535	3.2	8,297	8,286	23,615	24,107	203,991	214,085	2.9
6060	Credit unions	748	747	5.0	8,892	9,280	20,391	21,220	187,975	202,764	5.7
6100	Nondepository institutions	764	857	1.9	15,135	12,566	32,700	38,302	460,491	499,075	2.7
6110	Federal and Federally-sponsored credit	30	31	2.3	249	416	43,357	66,202	8,116	17,537	1.6
6140	Personal credit institutions	167	182	1.0	3,653	3,476	31,217	35,751	116,035	131,223	2.5
6150	Business credit institutions	103	102	2.1	1,916	2,170	50,643	56,024	87,598	101,438	2.3
6160	Mortgage bankers and brokers	447	522	2.5	9,278	6,468	29,368	32,024	247,912	247,477	3.3
6200	Security and commodity brokers	893	955	2.3	7,345	7,085	61,269	60,875	414,792	437,709	1.0
6210	Security brokers and dealers	566	602	2.5	6,065	5,714	64,432	64,194	341,268	363,976	1.1
6280	Security and commodity services	312	334	2.3	1,254	1,327	46,226	47,711	72,002	72,134	0.7
6300	Insurance carriers	1,249	1,280	3.1	45,374	42,911	36,200	39,807	1,566,775	1,641,347	2.9
6310	Life insurance	293	291	2.5	10,826	9,944	31,799	34,499	321,545	317,876	1.6
6320	Medical service and health insurance	92	91	3.0	10,517	10,439	39,534	41,401	408,599	408,489	4.2
6321	Accident and health insurance	32	29	2.8	924	926	30,082	29,577	28,765	27,317	1.6
6324	Hospital and medical service plans	60	62	3.2	9,593	9,513	40,444	42,552	379,834	381,172	4.8
6330	Fire, marine, and casualty insurance	670	721	3.5	21,015	20,431	38,149	42,869	770,694	853,988	3.5
6350	Surety insurance	17	19	3.2	74	66	35,568	41,333	2,522	3,232	0.6
6360	Title insurance	63	66	2.6	1,350	1,177	30,759	25,315	33,366	30,920	2.3
6370	Pension, health, and welfare funds	103	79	3.5	1,513	801	22,964	28,739	28,316	25,097	2.5
6400	Insurance agents, brokers, and service	4,064	4,097	3.3	22,064	22,006	27,984	30,578	675,523	719,903	3.2
6500	Real estate	6,171	6,357	2.6	35,916	36,644	18,547	20,394	747,257	805,235	2.4
6510	Real estate operators and lessors	2,439	2,477	2.5	13,290	13,714	15,230	16,096	228,597	245,212	2.6
6530	Real estate agents and managers	2,967	2,999	2.6	18,753	18,646	20,130	22,932	414,841	440,383	2.3
6540	Title abstract offices	104	100	2.1	1,007	809	22,677	21,849	24,321	20,566	2.4
6550	Subdividers and developers	420	460	2.6	2,487	2,867	23,230	24,480	69,500	81,166	2.5
6552	Subdividers and developers, n.e.c.	217	248	2.4	1,037	1,298	25,805	26,062	32,925	40,096	1.8

Source: County Business Patterns, 1994/95, CBP-94/95, U.S. Department of Commerce, Washington, D.C., November 1997. SIC categories for which data were suppressed or not available for both 1994 and 1995 are not displayed. The employment columns represent mid-March employment in the year. Pay per employee is calculated by dividing 1st Quarter payroll, annualized, by mid-March employment. The columns headed "% US" show the state's percentage of the national total for the SIC in 1995; for example, 1.4% for SIC 6000 means that the state had 1.4 percent of the national total establishments (or payroll) in SIC 6000 in 1995. A dash (-) is used to indicate that data are not available or cannot be calculated; nec means not elsewhere classified.

Continued on next page.

SIC	Industry	No. Establishments			Employment		Pay / Employee		Annual Payroll ($ 000)		
		1994	1995	% US	1994	1995	1994	1995	1994	1995	% US
MICHIGAN - [continued]											
6553	Cemetery subdividers and developers	161	159	2.6	1,332	1,362	21,339	21,944	31,928	32,396	3.5
6700	Holding and other investment offices	480	500	2.2	4,647	6,304	44,323	45,145	233,012	319,706	2.3
6710	Holding offices	176	195	2.3	2,783	4,162	51,011	49,849	156,216	230,386	2.8
6720	Investment offices	15	16	1.9	78	54	24,000	19,630	1,602	1,461	0.1
6730	Trusts	114	102	2.0	746	805	29,973	30,385	23,597	25,965	2.7
6732	Educational, religious, etc. trusts	47	45	1.8	319	359	22,696	20,724	7,412	8,160	1.4
6733	Trusts, n.e.c.	66	56	2.1	420	444	35,895	38,243	16,141	17,763	4.6
6790	Miscellaneous investing	142	137	1.8	822	959	32,326	34,824	30,612	39,598	1.5
6792	Oil royalty traders	6	6	0.9	13	13	26,462	27,385	302	379	0.4
6794	Patent owners and lessors	51	50	3.5	375	393	37,920	38,992	16,885	17,828	2.6
6798	Real estate investment trusts	12	10	1.7	18	42	26,222	28,381	494	1,039	0.2
6799	Investors, n.e.c.	73	71	1.5	416	511	27,731	32,337	12,931	20,352	1.4
MINNESOTA											
60 –	**Finance, insurance, and real estate**	11,549	11,888	1.9	140,295	142,981	36,117	38,605	4,684,286	5,149,344	2.0
6000	Depository institutions	1,745	1,736	1.7	35,614	35,729	28,520	30,662	970,663	1,033,947	1.7
6020	Commercial banks	1,207	1,265	1.9	28,265	28,739	29,129	31,121	778,235	849,659	1.9
6030	Savings institutions	205	142	0.9	2,914	2,062	24,419	25,049	68,645	50,876	0.7
6060	Credit unions	284	285	1.9	2,544	2,613	19,558	21,047	51,036	55,232	1.6
6100	Nondepository institutions	672	732	1.6	12,381	10,532	41,392	42,063	419,945	404,537	2.2
6110	Federal and Federally-sponsored credit	44	50	3.7	1,618	1,604	48,845	45,823	61,658	60,327	5.5
6140	Personal credit institutions	179	188	1.0	2,096	2,378	31,800	35,233	64,354	91,077	1.7
6150	Business credit institutions	92	109	2.3	1,368	1,503	50,614	53,916	59,835	64,930	1.5
6160	Mortgage bankers and brokers	351	370	1.8	7,277	4,905	40,697	40,539	231,209	180,237	2.4
6200	Security and commodity brokers	801	836	2.0	9,829	9,938	74,990	72,346	635,997	711,146	1.6
6210	Security brokers and dealers	398	404	1.7	7,815	7,697	76,597	71,957	493,259	539,228	1.6
6280	Security and commodity services	366	392	2.7	1,820	2,017	72,376	77,896	135,812	162,869	1.6
6300	Insurance carriers	732	762	1.8	37,502	41,167	37,732	39,204	1,344,178	1,520,198	2.7
6310	Life insurance	186	195	1.7	16,113	18,423	40,719	39,252	601,899	675,485	3.4
6320	Medical service and health insurance	55	52	1.7	5,865	7,309	32,968	37,297	199,250	258,903	2.7
6321	Accident and health insurance	22	19	1.8	776	653	25,804	26,383	18,987	15,453	0.9
6324	Hospital and medical service plans	33	33	1.7	5,089	6,656	34,060	38,368	180,263	243,450	3.1
6330	Fire, marine, and casualty insurance	381	390	1.9	13,948	13,871	37,169	40,598	495,063	534,277	2.2
6350	Surety insurance	12	11	1.8	51	40	30,118	45,500	1,665	1,857	0.4
6360	Title insurance	47	59	2.3	930	712	28,766	33,371	24,041	21,471	1.6
6370	Pension, health, and welfare funds	45	46	2.0	575	714	31,687	34,655	20,016	24,210	2.4
6400	Insurance agents, brokers, and service	3,089	3,199	2.6	14,069	14,412	30,002	32,484	426,207	471,618	2.1
6500	Real estate	4,129	4,231	1.7	22,464	22,495	18,675	19,674	445,560	470,599	1.4
6510	Real estate operators and lessors	1,659	1,642	1.6	8,045	7,949	16,479	16,300	136,167	134,264	1.4
6530	Real estate agents and managers	1,905	1,955	1.7	11,231	11,544	19,378	21,529	234,844	261,634	1.4
6540	Title abstract offices	175	175	3.6	2,154	1,467	22,527	24,202	43,974	37,372	4.3
6550	Subdividers and developers	319	329	1.9	969	1,425	19,979	19,130	28,319	33,659	1.0
6552	Subdividers and developers, n.e.c.	162	169	1.6	591	880	24,115	21,873	21,350	24,467	1.1
6553	Cemetery subdividers and developers	146	142	2.3	378	445	13,513	12,854	6,667	6,968	0.8
6700	Holding and other investment offices	359	369	1.6	7,374	7,622	61,900	75,023	386,831	455,108	3.3
6710	Holding offices	136	148	1.7	3,326	3,257	63,616	86,686	190,754	226,432	2.8
6732	Educational, religious, etc. trusts	42	46	1.9	315	353	24,114	24,691	8,003	9,016	1.6
6790	Miscellaneous investing	118	109	1.4	693	798	48,583	52,727	33,414	39,472	1.5
6794	Patent owners and lessors	43	33	2.3	417	564	32,700	35,206	15,315	19,673	2.8
6799	Investors, n.e.c.	68	65	1.4	264	208	73,924	104,538	17,288	19,213	1.3
MISSISSIPPI											
60 –	**Finance, insurance, and real estate**	5,113	5,090	0.8	38,216	37,925	23,786	24,740	925,504	954,988	0.4
6000	Depository institutions	1,191	1,197	1.1	16,568	16,348	21,994	22,968	374,680	384,173	0.6
6020	Commercial banks	934	942	1.4	14,330	14,532	22,201	23,248	329,734	344,892	0.8
6030	Savings institutions	87	83	0.5	1,365	923	23,133	23,666	28,970	22,101	0.3
6060	Credit unions	148	146	1.0	818	836	17,046	17,828	15,213	16,059	0.5
6090	Functions closely related to banking	22	26	0.5	55	57	13,600	15,509	763	1,121	0.1

Source: County Business Patterns, 1994/95, CBP-94/95, U.S. Department of Commerce, Washington, D.C., November 1997. SIC categories for which data were suppressed or not available for both 1994 and 1995 are not displayed. The employment columns represent mid-March employment in the year. Pay per employee is calculated by dividing 1st Quarter payroll, annualized, by mid-March employment. The columns headed "% US" show the state's percentage of the national total for the SIC in 1995; for example, 1.4% for SIC 6000 means that the state had 1.4 percent of the national total establishments (or payroll) in SIC 6000 in 1995. A dash (-) is used to indicate that data are not available or cannot be calculated; nec means not elsewhere classified.

Continued on next page.

SIC	Industry	No. Establishments			Employment		Pay / Employee		Annual Payroll ($ 000)		
		1994	1995	% US	1994	1995	1994	1995	1994	1995	% US
MISSISSIPPI - [continued]											
6100	Nondepository institutions	728	756	1.7	3,520	3,811	23,031	24,191	79,755	93,177	0.5
6110	Federal and Federally-sponsored credit	37	35	2.6	143	123	36,196	34,244	4,991	4,365	0.4
6140	Personal credit institutions	556	572	3.2	2,378	2,446	21,712	22,932	52,304	58,710	1.1
6150	Business credit institutions	21	18	0.4	183	172	23,956	27,512	4,587	4,713	0.1
6160	Mortgage bankers and brokers	108	121	0.6	811	1,058	24,360	25,448	17,717	25,002	0.3
6200	Security and commodity brokers	165	176	0.4	821	860	52,760	48,609	39,019	43,119	0.1
6210	Security brokers and dealers	102	114	0.5	671	689	58,188	52,395	34,515	37,299	0.1
6300	Insurance carriers	342	338	0.8	7,289	6,763	29,113	30,828	212,586	205,610	0.4
6310	Life insurance	159	166	1.4	3,299	3,143	28,366	28,501	92,855	86,441	0.4
6320	Medical service and health insurance	24	23	0.8	1,167	1,015	26,862	31,417	31,339	31,039	0.3
6330	Fire, marine, and casualty insurance	128	122	0.6	2,594	2,363	31,392	33,898	81,492	79,883	0.3
6360	Title insurance	4	4	0.2	74	78	29,243	32,718	2,059	2,541	0.2
6370	Pension, health, and welfare funds	23	16	0.7	149	122	23,436	27,508	4,639	4,529	0.2
6400	Insurance agents, brokers, and service	1,131	1,105	0.9	4,310	4,506	22,934	24,972	110,478	120,060	0.5
6500	Real estate	1,455	1,418	0.6	4,774	4,788	13,143	14,425	72,433	73,774	0.2
6510	Real estate operators and lessors	810	731	0.7	2,322	2,286	10,550	12,462	28,611	29,860	0.3
6530	Real estate agents and managers	515	528	0.5	1,913	1,926	15,220	15,728	32,253	31,817	0.2
6550	Subdividers and developers	104	116	0.7	517	509	16,859	18,287	10,768	10,422	0.3
6552	Subdividers and developers, n.e.c.	54	62	0.6	363	315	18,182	21,270	8,408	7,534	0.3
6553	Cemetery subdividers and developers	46	44	0.7	153	176	13,804	13,000	2,321	2,340	0.3
6710	Holding offices	34	34	0.4	520	418	44,015	52,775	19,723	20,144	0.2
6730	Trusts	28	25	0.5	116	124	12,793	37,226	2,783	5,010	0.5
6732	Educational, religious, etc. trusts	9	10	0.4	55	79	13,018	50,076	2,052	4,332	0.8
6733	Trusts, n.e.c.	19	15	0.6	61	45	12,590	14,667	731	678	0.2
6790	Miscellaneous investing	30	30	0.4	157	137	41,121	39,854	6,762	4,052	0.2
6799	Investors, n.e.c.	21	20	0.4	74	61	35,189	38,557	2,654	1,595	0.1
MISSOURI											
60 –	**Finance, insurance, and real estate**	12,563	12,771	2.0	144,258	143,687	29,574	30,900	4,169,150	4,391,490	1.7
6000	Depository institutions	2,130	2,137	2.0	46,712	46,147	23,831	25,334	1,112,498	1,146,526	1.8
6020	Commercial banks	1,470	1,528	2.3	34,523	35,169	23,117	24,645	795,791	850,871	1.9
6030	Savings institutions	354	298	1.8	5,809	4,356	23,608	23,225	138,590	106,477	1.4
6090	Functions closely related to banking	73	79	1.5	2,431	2,590	29,455	34,908	69,555	77,410	3.6
6100	Nondepository institutions	685	758	1.7	9,804	9,276	30,650	31,598	281,605	307,677	1.7
6110	Federal and Federally-sponsored credit	34	34	2.5	237	220	37,620	43,364	7,206	7,478	0.7
6140	Personal credit institutions	300	346	1.9	1,992	2,297	27,452	28,946	56,837	72,691	1.4
6150	Business credit institutions	82	80	1.7	1,758	2,055	32,676	26,780	54,454	56,405	1.3
6160	Mortgage bankers and brokers	267	287	1.4	5,791	4,672	30,855	34,568	162,469	170,354	2.3
6200	Security and commodity brokers	697	761	1.9	12,685	11,054	56,919	55,738	586,422	543,599	1.2
6210	Security brokers and dealers	465	517	2.1	8,135	8,334	67,455	60,930	413,403	432,266	1.3
6280	Security and commodity services	202	213	1.4	4,397	2,541	37,523	39,652	166,351	103,607	1.0
6300	Insurance carriers	872	861	2.1	29,708	28,660	33,408	35,798	968,590	1,010,034	1.8
6310	Life insurance	259	245	2.1	11,444	10,599	34,398	37,338	354,482	366,455	1.9
6320	Medical service and health insurance	77	80	2.7	5,484	5,661	33,514	36,837	188,122	216,668	2.2
6321	Accident and health insurance	25	23	2.2	532	555	25,398	27,805	12,809	13,446	0.8
6324	Hospital and medical service plans	52	57	3.0	4,952	5,106	34,386	37,818	175,313	203,222	2.5
6330	Fire, marine, and casualty insurance	425	426	2.0	11,246	10,951	33,153	34,721	384,018	386,864	1.6
6350	Surety insurance	14	15	2.5	109	75	42,936	42,453	3,633	3,034	0.6
6360	Title insurance	42	42	1.7	738	566	24,634	27,816	17,539	15,163	1.1
6370	Pension, health, and welfare funds	46	42	1.8	613	716	29,135	27,346	18,311	18,821	1.9
6400	Insurance agents, brokers, and service	3,279	3,292	2.6	14,155	14,393	26,357	29,214	393,058	432,742	1.9
6500	Real estate	4,463	4,514	1.8	23,884	25,576	18,001	18,245	483,389	519,984	1.6
6510	Real estate operators and lessors	1,885	1,889	1.9	9,598	11,061	14,581	14,075	160,014	175,184	1.8
6530	Real estate agents and managers	1,893	1,878	1.6	11,056	11,136	21,141	22,543	257,085	273,749	1.5
6540	Title abstract offices	170	157	3.3	1,191	1,137	19,369	18,512	25,510	24,474	2.8
6550	Subdividers and developers	438	440	2.5	1,851	1,957	16,577	17,619	37,089	40,511	1.2
6552	Subdividers and developers, n.e.c.	256	258	2.5	1,007	1,105	18,677	19,569	22,639	25,380	1.1
6553	Cemetery subdividers and developers	160	158	2.6	784	803	13,857	14,854	12,639	13,784	1.5

Source: County Business Patterns, 1994/95, CBP-94/95, U.S. Department of Commerce, Washington, D.C., November 1997. SIC categories for which data were suppressed or not available for both 1994 and 1995 are not displayed. The employment columns represent mid-March employment in the year. Pay per employee is calculated by dividing 1st Quarter payroll, annualized, by mid-March employment. The columns headed "% US" show the state's percentage of the national total for the SIC in 1995; for example, 1.4% for SIC 6000 means that the state had 1.4 percent of the national total establishments (or payroll) in SIC 6000 in 1995. A dash (-) is used to indicate that data are not available or cannot be calculated; nec means not elsewhere classified.

Continued on next page.

SIC	Industry	No. Establishments			Employment		Pay / Employee		Annual Payroll ($ 000)		
		1994	1995	% US	1994	1995	1994	1995	1994	1995	% US
MISSOURI - [continued]											
6700	Holding and other investment offices	419	432	1.9	6,421	7,709	41,007	49,441	289,932	374,445	2.7
6710	Holding offices	194	205	2.4	3,409	4,521	46,998	56,479	173,879	245,410	3.0
6732	Educational, religious, etc. trusts	34	36	1.5	318	355	17,975	17,690	6,010	6,997	1.2
6790	Miscellaneous investing	136	127	1.7	567	595	58,497	46,568	31,596	32,982	1.2
6792	Oil royalty traders	5	6	0.9	9	26	20,889	43,846	216	1,035	1.0
6794	Patent owners and lessors	45	32	2.2	316	254	37,418	47,449	14,650	14,109	2.0
6798	Real estate investment trusts	8	7	1.2	15	13	55,467	7,385	695	141	0.0
6799	Investors, n.e.c.	78	82	1.7	227	302	89,533	47,748	16,035	17,697	1.2
MONTANA											
60 –	**Finance, insurance, and real estate**	2,371	2,458	0.4	14,683	14,840	22,449	22,891	345,047	356,737	0.1
6000	Depository institutions	389	397	0.4	5,857	5,920	22,084	23,499	134,078	138,768	0.2
6020	Commercial banks	211	217	0.3	4,053	4,087	23,772	24,771	97,967	101,363	0.2
6030	Savings institutions	64	64	0.4	706	819	20,918	21,841	16,943	16,602	0.2
6100	Nondepository institutions	91	105	0.2	728	601	26,000	28,632	19,173	18,603	0.1
6140	Personal credit institutions	35	40	0.2	247	260	24,405	26,354	6,326	6,728	0.1
6160	Mortgage bankers and brokers	33	42	0.2	316	186	25,709	26,538	8,109	6,705	0.1
6200	Security and commodity brokers	138	148	0.4	705	710	52,868	41,352	34,007	35,550	0.1
6210	Security brokers and dealers	97	106	0.4	604	604	52,245	44,675	30,831	32,960	0.1
6220	Commodity contracts brokers, dealers	7	8	0.5	16	12	21,250	17,667	371	344	0.0
6280	Security and commodity services	34	34	0.2	85	94	63,247	23,021	2,805	2,246	0.0
6300	Insurance carriers	123	130	0.3	1,475	1,408	26,221	28,241	41,117	41,755	0.1
6310	Life insurance	28	30	0.3	325	277	26,203	27,177	8,422	7,456	0.0
6320	Medical service and health insurance	14	14	0.5	803	735	24,134	25,698	20,704	19,933	0.2
6330	Fire, marine, and casualty insurance	66	70	0.3	229	254	34,463	40,079	9,236	10,798	0.0
6360	Title insurance	9	8	0.3	66	61	21,576	21,443	1,180	1,152	0.1
6400	Insurance agents, brokers, and service	628	640	0.5	2,430	2,497	20,046	21,938	53,061	57,116	0.3
6500	Real estate	933	960	0.4	3,025	3,109	13,473	13,736	46,801	48,022	0.1
6510	Real estate operators and lessors	390	392	0.4	1,244	1,265	11,463	12,345	16,142	17,167	0.2
6530	Real estate agents and managers	427	438	0.4	1,229	1,341	13,627	13,241	18,382	19,360	0.1
6540	Title abstract offices	27	27	0.6	239	199	18,644	19,859	4,638	4,389	0.5
6550	Subdividers and developers	74	74	0.4	304	257	17,039	18,942	7,420	6,500	0.2
6552	Subdividers and developers, n.e.c.	45	39	0.4	251	166	16,749	22,361	6,284	4,867	0.2
6553	Cemetery subdividers and developers	28	28	0.5	53	91	18,415	12,703	1,128	1,208	0.1
6710	Holding offices	24	27	0.3	290	419	42,221	30,749	12,698	12,575	0.2
6732	Educational, religious, etc. trusts	8	10	0.4	37	41	21,081	25,073	861	1,084	0.2
6790	Miscellaneous investing	23	24	0.3	59	52	21,017	24,385	1,195	1,241	0.0
6792	Oil royalty traders	7	8	1.1	17	20	42,118	34,200	612	567	0.6
NEBRASKA											
60 –	**Finance, insurance, and real estate**	4,457	4,566	0.7	53,040	53,709	28,699	30,351	1,458,131	1,553,691	0.6
6000	Depository institutions	942	990	0.9	15,968	16,452	22,611	23,753	365,494	404,340	0.6
6020	Commercial banks	665	724	1.1	12,933	13,578	22,714	23,999	296,869	335,058	0.7
6030	Savings institutions	151	133	0.8	1,785	1,568	24,007	24,487	43,537	42,106	0.6
6060	Credit unions	114	113	0.8	931	1,005	18,462	19,546	17,898	19,810	0.6
6140	Personal credit institutions	56	64	0.4	340	322	26,882	29,453	8,871	9,229	0.2
6150	Business credit institutions	27	26	0.5	259	276	28,309	31,551	8,903	11,001	0.2
6160	Mortgage bankers and brokers	59	58	0.3	751	712	33,598	29,601	22,579	27,672	0.4
6200	Security and commodity brokers	266	273	0.7	1,712	1,757	62,911	58,559	86,751	89,547	0.2
6210	Security brokers and dealers	156	163	0.7	1,412	1,404	68,252	61,293	74,118	73,782	0.2
6220	Commodity contracts brokers, dealers	20	16	1.0	62	57	32,387	33,684	1,874	1,912	0.3
6280	Security and commodity services	90	93	0.6	238	295	39,176	50,508	10,759	13,838	0.1
6300	Insurance carriers	292	286	0.7	20,950	20,655	34,217	36,942	665,001	666,944	1.2
6310	Life insurance	96	92	0.8	5,770	5,687	31,778	32,996	177,155	174,799	0.9
6320	Medical service and health insurance	33	34	1.1	9,497	9,003	36,580	41,009	307,460	293,467	3.0
6321	Accident and health insurance	19	19	1.8	8,444	7,830	36,961	41,428	273,795	252,931	15.2
6324	Hospital and medical service plans	14	15	0.8	1,053	1,173	33,531	38,213	33,665	40,536	0.5
6330	Fire, marine, and casualty insurance	133	133	0.6	5,446	5,147	31,826	34,938	170,569	179,038	0.7

Source: County Business Patterns, 1994/95, CBP-94/95, U.S. Department of Commerce, Washington, D.C., November 1997. SIC categories for which data were suppressed or not available for both 1994 and 1995 are not displayed. The employment columns represent mid-March employment in the year. Pay per employee is calculated by dividing 1st Quarter payroll, annualized, by mid-March employment. The columns headed "% US" show the state's percentage of the national total for the SIC in 1995; for example, 1.4% for SIC 6000 means that the state had 1.4 percent of the national total establishments (or payroll) in SIC 6000 in 1995. A dash (-) is used to indicate that data are not available or cannot be calculated; nec means not elsewhere classified.

Continued on next page.

SIC	Industry	No. Establishments			Employment		Pay / Employee		Annual Payroll ($ 000)		
		1994	1995	% US	1994	1995	1994	1995	1994	1995	% US
NEBRASKA - [continued]											
6370	Pension, health, and welfare funds	12	10	0.4	88	343	85,045	34,671	6,003	6,679	0.7
6400	Insurance agents, brokers, and service	1,428	1,434	1.1	5,057	5,558	21,701	23,304	113,105	133,134	0.6
6500	Real estate	1,213	1,248	0.5	5,647	5,759	16,741	16,742	99,456	107,111	0.3
6510	Real estate operators and lessors	527	538	0.5	2,190	2,285	13,041	12,047	29,001	31,378	0.3
6530	Real estate agents and managers	524	547	0.5	2,947	2,886	19,790	20,981	61,772	65,516	0.3
6540	Title abstract offices	53	51	1.1	203	173	16,788	17,618	3,692	3,418	0.4
6550	Subdividers and developers	91	86	0.5	299	287	13,900	14,523	4,679	5,169	0.2
6552	Subdividers and developers, n.e.c.	34	29	0.3	122	110	13,016	14,909	1,844	2,155	0.1
6553	Cemetery subdividers and developers	56	56	0.9	175	175	14,423	14,171	2,791	2,966	0.3
6700	Holding and other investment offices	139	150	0.6	2,000	1,853	36,384	45,651	70,429	80,793	0.6
6710	Holding offices	81	86	1.0	1,038	1,102	55,002	64,490	54,909	66,225	0.8
6730	Trusts	26	30	0.6	359	362	16,501	17,901	6,061	6,991	0.7
6732	Educational, religious, etc. trusts	16	19	0.8	344	347	16,593	18,029	5,816	6,612	1.2
6733	Trusts, n.e.c.	10	11	0.4	15	15	14,400	14,933	245	379	0.1
6790	Miscellaneous investing	19	17	0.2	139	51	35,453	36,863	4,640	1,638	0.1
6794	Patent owners and lessors	6	4	0.3	121	26	35,570	37,538	4,007	834	0.1
NEVADA											
60 –	**Finance, insurance, and real estate**	4,204	4,479	0.7	34,094	37,577	26,832	27,167	942,384	1,036,822	0.4
6000	Depository institutions	506	522	0.5	10,675	11,152	26,186	25,666	270,543	275,197	0.4
6020	Commercial banks	323	332	0.5	7,775	8,055	26,839	25,602	196,663	196,934	0.4
6030	Savings institutions	99	96	0.6	1,436	1,467	26,538	29,238	40,315	41,050	0.6
6060	Credit unions	59	62	0.4	902	1,060	21,783	21,083	21,181	24,041	0.7
6100	Nondepository institutions	332	394	0.9	3,032	3,530	33,968	28,992	96,800	98,817	0.5
6140	Personal credit institutions	84	100	0.6	791	1,475	22,008	22,552	20,403	27,528	0.5
6150	Business credit institutions	33	47	1.0	269	476	23,390	25,681	7,863	13,120	0.3
6160	Mortgage bankers and brokers	205	228	1.1	1,915	1,504	40,418	36,383	66,905	56,168	0.8
6200	Security and commodity brokers	171	185	0.5	1,000	1,117	58,620	57,816	55,724	65,935	0.1
6210	Security brokers and dealers	87	96	0.4	727	791	68,825	65,451	45,671	50,731	0.1
6300	Insurance carriers	234	248	0.6	2,546	2,900	33,560	34,850	91,548	106,850	0.2
6310	Life insurance	34	36	0.3	369	327	30,190	30,128	10,393	9,205	0.0
6320	Medical service and health insurance	37	38	1.3	807	1,207	32,659	33,760	28,897	43,147	0.4
6321	Accident and health insurance	16	13	1.2	202	222	33,366	34,000	6,880	7,799	0.5
6324	Hospital and medical service plans	21	25	1.3	605	985	32,423	33,706	22,017	35,348	0.4
6330	Fire, marine, and casualty insurance	110	124	0.6	609	651	41,668	43,951	26,985	29,610	0.1
6360	Title insurance	22	30	1.2	588	487	28,694	30,784	16,812	18,686	1.4
6370	Pension, health, and welfare funds	21	10	0.4	94	89	28,085	31,551	4,210	3,014	0.3
6400	Insurance agents, brokers, and service	672	701	0.6	3,024	3,259	24,884	27,181	81,784	93,249	0.4
6500	Real estate	1,956	2,029	0.8	12,482	13,901	20,728	22,003	282,991	324,924	1.0
6510	Real estate operators and lessors	849	842	0.8	4,972	5,043	16,104	17,532	80,844	89,165	0.9
6530	Real estate agents and managers	869	879	0.8	4,514	4,862	18,930	19,675	99,256	102,978	0.5
6540	Title abstract offices	23	23	0.5	636	462	28,239	33,212	18,391	17,026	2.0
6550	Subdividers and developers	165	182	1.0	2,302	3,268	32,575	31,460	83,147	109,953	3.4
6552	Subdividers and developers, n.e.c.	145	155	1.5	2,168	2,857	32,792	32,886	79,621	101,383	4.6
6553	Cemetery subdividers and developers	11	10	0.2	132	155	27,455	17,548	3,353	2,865	0.3
6700	Holding and other investment offices	325	392	1.7	1,270	1,655	41,244	42,821	61,356	70,636	0.5
6710	Holding offices	138	181	2.1	645	948	52,335	51,578	39,337	46,315	0.6
6720	Investment offices	20	20	2.3	47	50	61,021	67,440	3,153	3,032	0.2
6730	Trusts	41	48	0.9	131	153	17,282	26,431	3,215	4,201	0.4
6732	Educational, religious, etc. trusts	8	10	0.4	16	38	28,000	40,947	895	739	0.1
6733	Trusts, n.e.c.	33	38	1.4	115	115	15,791	21,635	2,320	3,462	0.9
6790	Miscellaneous investing	110	118	1.6	412	472	31,583	29,941	14,777	15,415	0.6
6794	Patent owners and lessors	27	31	2.2	178	170	26,944	24,753	4,744	5,243	0.8
6799	Investors, n.e.c.	77	80	1.7	217	285	35,687	33,137	9,527	9,704	0.7
NEW HAMPSHIRE											
60 –	**Finance, insurance, and real estate**	2,686	2,734	0.4	28,327	28,108	28,776	30,306	832,244	883,147	0.3
6000	Depository institutions	463	434	0.4	8,164	7,237	23,133	24,892	188,812	185,838	0.3

Source: County Business Patterns, 1994/95, CBP-94/95, U.S. Department of Commerce, Washington, D.C., November 1997. SIC categories for which data were suppressed or not available for both 1994 and 1995 are not displayed. The employment columns represent mid-March employment in the year. Pay per employee is calculated by dividing 1st Quarter payroll, annualized, by mid-March employment. The columns headed "% US" show the state's percentage of the national total for the SIC in 1995; for example, 1.4% for SIC 6000 means that the state had 1.4 percent of the national total establishments (or payroll) in SIC 6000 in 1995. A dash (-) is used to indicate that data are not available or cannot be calculated; nec means not elsewhere classified.

Continued on next page.

SIC	Industry	No. Establishments			Employment		Pay / Employee		Annual Payroll ($ 000)		
		1994	1995	% US	1994	1995	1994	1995	1994	1995	% US
NEW HAMPSHIRE - [continued]											
6020	Commercial banks	192	269	0.4	3,468	4,404	23,659	25,385	82,905	115,193	0.3
6030	Savings institutions	215	110	0.7	3,832	2,001	22,830	24,256	83,727	50,024	0.7
6060	Credit unions	50	49	0.3	780	780	20,662	21,990	18,988	18,159	0.5
6090	Functions closely related to banking	6	6	0.1	84	52	38,238	51,077	3,192	2,462	0.1
6100	Nondepository institutions	132	135	0.3	1,570	1,636	34,673	35,892	50,605	66,123	0.4
6150	Business credit institutions	18	17	0.4	410	426	42,888	45,737	16,024	23,261	0.5
6160	Mortgage bankers and brokers	72	71	0.3	876	854	32,050	31,040	25,686	30,587	0.4
6200	Security and commodity brokers	166	187	0.5	849	886	57,908	50,673	47,412	47,283	0.1
6210	Security brokers and dealers	66	78	0.3	552	631	61,674	49,198	30,547	31,697	0.1
6280	Security and commodity services	99	109	0.7	297	255	50,909	54,322	16,864	15,586	0.2
6300	Insurance carriers	187	185	0.4	9,174	9,770	34,763	35,928	319,262	336,075	0.6
6310	Life insurance	57	55	0.5	2,385	2,255	33,176	31,943	74,030	71,753	0.4
6320	Medical service and health insurance	15	14	0.5	1,754	2,272	27,767	29,548	51,901	69,873	0.7
6330	Fire, marine, and casualty insurance	100	104	0.5	4,667	5,026	38,510	40,778	181,402	186,522	0.8
6370	Pension, health, and welfare funds	9	6	0.3	347	195	29,429	30,974	11,019	7,054	0.7
6400	Insurance agents, brokers, and service	492	508	0.4	2,732	2,719	28,698	29,311	83,689	84,376	0.4
6500	Real estate	1,156	1,192	0.5	5,013	5,115	18,119	20,583	105,102	123,252	0.4
6510	Real estate operators and lessors	345	373	0.4	1,636	1,762	17,939	18,806	33,175	38,544	0.4
6530	Real estate agents and managers	664	650	0.6	2,726	2,734	17,925	18,854	54,943	59,280	0.3
6540	Title abstract offices	24	22	0.5	230	147	24,539	25,497	5,122	4,107	0.5
6550	Subdividers and developers	100	103	0.6	416	418	16,596	37,158	11,318	19,532	0.6
6552	Subdividers and developers, n.e.c.	68	69	0.7	373	361	16,815	40,277	10,323	18,167	0.8
6553	Cemetery subdividers and developers	29	29	0.5	43	44	14,698	15,909	966	959	0.1
6710	Holding offices	29	30	0.4	483	416	45,093	49,375	22,192	25,369	0.3
6730	Trusts	26	30	0.6	163	193	24,098	25,575	4,432	5,403	0.6
6732	Educational, religious, etc. trusts	16	16	0.6	143	161	25,147	27,130	4,011	4,743	0.8
6733	Trusts, n.e.c.	10	14	0.5	20	32	16,600	17,750	421	660	0.2
6790	Miscellaneous investing	23	24	0.3	135	116	45,689	40,483	6,910	6,242	0.2
6799	Investors, n.e.c.	17	18	0.4	46	69	75,043	55,826	3,822	5,038	0.3
NEW JERSEY											
60 –	**Finance, insurance, and real estate**	18,966	19,143	3.0	247,786	241,289	39,955	44,598	9,595,368	10,244,894	4.0
6000	Depository institutions	3,542	3,490	3.3	58,466	54,867	26,950	29,244	1,627,767	1,608,033	2.6
6020	Commercial banks	2,182	2,168	3.2	40,836	39,651	26,817	28,701	1,132,798	1,168,592	2.6
6030	Savings institutions	847	799	4.8	12,399	10,546	26,577	29,690	330,805	296,278	4.0
6060	Credit unions	367	357	2.4	2,119	2,248	21,616	22,651	47,937	50,896	1.4
6090	Functions closely related to banking	141	160	3.0	2,918	2,217	32,631	41,315	106,779	82,915	3.9
6100	Nondepository institutions	1,017	1,019	2.2	16,310	14,004	43,561	48,068	670,421	650,543	3.5
6140	Personal credit institutions	259	290	1.6	2,119	2,044	33,912	37,748	71,925	76,918	1.4
6150	Business credit institutions	170	154	3.2	4,330	3,495	63,878	74,272	242,363	212,617	4.8
6160	Mortgage bankers and brokers	573	549	2.7	9,730	8,354	36,549	39,552	349,307	351,854	4.7
6200	Security and commodity brokers	1,845	2,047	5.0	31,202	32,885	70,759	83,333	1,874,637	2,303,007	5.1
6210	Security brokers and dealers	1,229	1,385	5.7	24,203	25,678	74,303	91,145	1,481,026	1,842,304	5.4
6220	Commodity contracts brokers, dealers	53	54	3.5	181	200	54,541	54,980	10,758	12,607	1.7
6280	Security and commodity services	550	591	4.0	6,803	6,990	58,694	55,578	382,442	447,039	4.5
6300	Insurance carriers	1,155	1,131	2.7	62,710	61,013	42,554	46,279	2,539,117	2,681,285	4.7
6310	Life insurance	490	493	4.2	30,436	31,454	40,959	44,032	1,227,026	1,337,725	6.8
6320	Medical service and health insurance	60	67	2.2	4,797	4,862	41,721	46,900	163,852	201,703	2.1
6321	Accident and health insurance	20	20	1.9	583	519	31,252	44,378	18,234	21,763	1.3
6324	Hospital and medical service plans	40	47	2.4	4,214	4,343	43,169	47,201	145,618	179,940	2.3
6330	Fire, marine, and casualty insurance	419	417	2.0	25,005	22,713	44,800	49,292	1,057,783	1,058,399	4.4
6350	Surety insurance	18	17	2.9	886	811	46,144	47,970	36,394	37,212	7.0
6360	Title insurance	50	45	1.8	501	339	39,449	45,062	16,251	12,623	0.9
6370	Pension, health, and welfare funds	103	78	3.4	826	631	37,792	45,363	28,511	25,582	2.5
6390	Insurance carriers, n.e.c.	12	6	3.5	259	178	37,328	40,202	9,110	6,746	7.3
6400	Insurance agents, brokers, and service	3,148	3,148	2.5	24,347	23,894	36,360	39,541	962,400	1,018,227	4.5
6500	Real estate	7,616	7,669	3.1	37,551	38,907	23,414	25,096	985,805	1,041,741	3.2
6510	Real estate operators and lessors	3,347	3,355	3.3	15,529	15,915	19,931	21,325	343,461	364,916	3.8

Source: County Business Patterns, 1994/95, CBP-94/95, U.S. Department of Commerce, Washington, D.C., November 1997. SIC categories for which data were suppressed or not available for both 1994 and 1995 are not displayed. The employment columns represent mid-March employment in the year. Pay per employee is calculated by dividing 1st Quarter payroll, annualized, by mid-March employment. The columns headed "% US" show the state's percentage of the national total for the SIC in 1995; for example, 1.4% for SIC 6000 means that the state had 1.4 percent of the national total establishments (or payroll) in SIC 6000 in 1995. A dash (-) is used to indicate that data are not available or cannot be calculated; nec means not elsewhere classified.

Continued on next page.

SIC	Industry	No. Establishments			Employment		Pay / Employee		Annual Payroll ($ 000)		
		1994	1995	% US	1994	1995	1994	1995	1994	1995	% US
NEW JERSEY - [continued]											
6530	Real estate agents and managers	3,499	3,439	3.0	17,719	18,014	25,714	27,819	504,662	525,053	2.8
6540	Title abstract offices	159	161	3.3	1,000	795	26,836	28,830	30,190	27,083	3.1
6550	Subdividers and developers	485	493	2.8	3,045	3,586	26,911	28,904	98,792	109,680	3.4
6552	Subdividers and developers, n.e.c.	262	259	2.5	1,523	1,826	29,560	30,620	55,294	57,905	2.6
6553	Cemetery subdividers and developers	200	193	3.1	1,511	1,573	24,296	25,788	42,574	43,957	4.8
6700	Holding and other investment offices	562	561	2.4	9,700	9,471	55,161	58,876	538,558	569,386	4.1
6710	Holding offices	221	224	2.6	7,170	7,183	48,977	56,040	360,499	424,785	5.2
6720	Investment offices	19	21	2.4	102	109	125,059	141,211	18,699	27,995	1.7
6730	Trusts	100	104	2.0	330	413	29,261	33,317	12,821	13,637	1.4
6732	Educational, religious, etc. trusts	54	58	2.3	201	259	29,254	29,483	12,821	13,637	1.4
6733	Trusts, n.e.c.	46	44	1.6	129	150	29,271	40,800	6,983	8,218	1.4
6790	Miscellaneous investing	210	192	2.5	2,078	1,694	76,735	72,857	5,838	5,384	1.4
6794	Patent owners and lessors	51	40	2.8	1,131	902	73,577	77,494	144,311	100,775	3.7
6799	Investors, n.e.c.	143	137	2.8	915	740	82,474	69,681	67,757	44,811	6.5
									75,629	53,825	3.6
NEW MEXICO											
60 –	**Finance, insurance, and real estate**	3,651	3,784	0.6	29,246	29,031	23,162	24,525	694,913	720,927	0.3
6000	Depository institutions	569	577	0.6	10,002	9,987	22,094	23,640	219,102	227,524	0.3
6020	Commercial banks	429	430	0.6	7,925	7,877	22,432	24,012	174,539	179,491	0.4
6030	Savings institutions	30	28	0.2	698	596	23,009	25,255	16,060	15,534	0.4
6060	Credit unions	87	87	0.6	1,206	1,305	19,642	21,051	24,790	28,136	0.2
6090	Functions closely related to banking	23	32	0.6	173	209	19,977	21,148	3,713	4,363	0.8
6100	Nondepository institutions	300	317	0.7	2,264	2,516	25,012	23,677	59,439	59,062	0.2
6140	Personal credit institutions	168	174	1.0	912	995	22,759	23,755	21,893	24,463	0.3
6160	Mortgage bankers and brokers	103	109	0.5	702	634	33,829	31,855	21,820	19,140	0.5
6200	Security and commodity brokers	141	163	0.4	927	977	54,438	55,844	49,149	56,007	0.3
6210	Security brokers and dealers	95	111	0.5	709	732	56,305	56,743	36,712	41,234	0.1
6300	Insurance carriers	200	213	0.5	3,988	3,409	26,614	30,144	108,151	102,396	0.1
6310	Life insurance	58	56	0.5	1,676	1,383	22,007	23,367	35,985	30,913	0.2
6320	Medical service and health insurance	13	15	0.5	1,294	1,034	29,524	33,458	39,132	33,070	0.2
6321	Accident and health insurance	4	4	0.4	30	27	31,333	37,333	1,023	1,166	0.3
6324	Hospital and medical service plans	9	11	0.6	1,264	1,007	29,481	33,355	38,109	31,904	0.1
6330	Fire, marine, and casualty insurance	104	116	0.6	664	709	34,175	39,199	24,703	28,475	0.4
6360	Title insurance	9	12	0.5	220	223	33,364	30,386	7,383	8,751	0.1
6370	Pension, health, and welfare funds	11	8	0.4	124	53	6,548	18,491	755	847	0.6
6400	Insurance agents, brokers, and service	786	781	0.6	4,223	4,140	20,889	21,174	96,250	98,354	0.1
6500	Real estate	1,521	1,586	0.6	7,031	7,009	17,502	18,068	129,390	135,498	0.4
6510	Real estate operators and lessors	636	647	0.6	3,025	2,477	14,136	13,980	36,055	36,891	0.4
6530	Real estate agents and managers	690	717	0.6	2,884	3,302	18,171	18,618	62,559	66,246	0.4
6540	Title abstract offices	44	43	0.9	408	408	27,029	28,775	9,639	9,899	0.4
6550	Subdividers and developers	104	110	0.6	650	738	24,991	23,886	20,014	20,715	1.1
6552	Subdividers and developers, n.e.c.	78	79	0.8	501	569	27,186	27,192	17,160	17,816	0.6
6553	Cemetery subdividers and developers	21	20	0.3	142	152	13,803	11,684	2,492	1,892	0.8
6710	Holding offices	37	39	0.5	440	582	41,173	50,199	18,393	26,909	0.2
6720	Investment offices	4	5	0.6	7	6	10,286	15,333	41	73	0.3
6730	Trusts	30	40	0.8	101	168	18,812	17,262	2,435	3,214	0.0
6732	Educational, religious, etc. trusts	15	18	0.7	52	69	24,462	26,493	1,502	2,082	0.3
6733	Trusts, n.e.c.	15	22	0.8	49	99	12,816	10,828	933	1,132	0.4
6790	Miscellaneous investing	53	50	0.7	240	206	44,600	54,388	11,365	10,787	0.3
											0.4
NEW YORK											
60 –	**Finance, insurance, and real estate**	54,599	55,394	8.8	754,049	758,802	62,866	74,738	41,597,250	46,480,158	18.1
6000	Depository institutions	6,766	6,635	6.3	207,776	203,562	51,727	59,946	9,571,569	10,270,727	16.4
6020	Commercial banks	3,878	3,813	5.7	132,701	130,903	51,744	60,717	6,121,282	6,537,505	14.3
6030	Savings institutions	1,301	1,244	7.5	31,462	28,328	25,746	31,198	836,032	800,115	10.9
6080	Foreign bank and branches and agencies	306	304	46.1	25,019	25,135	95,958	103,069	1,919,005	2,161,507	77.1
6090	Functions closely related to banking	568	570	10.7	8,559	9,178	43,859	50,394	379,153	435,831	20.4
6100	Nondepository institutions	1,758	1,804	4.0	33,028	36,183	51,270	56,137	1,606,372	1,880,101	10.2

Source: *County Business Patterns, 1994/95,* CBP-94/95, U.S. Department of Commerce, Washington, D.C., November 1997. SIC categories for which data were suppressed or not available for both 1994 and 1995 are *not* displayed. The employment columns represent mid-March employment in the year. Pay per employee is calculated by dividing 1st Quarter payroll, annualized, by mid-March employment. The columns headed "% US" show the state's percentage of the national total for the SIC in 1995; for example, 1.4% for SIC 6000 means that the state had 1.4 percent of the national total establishments (or payroll) in SIC 6000 in 1995. A dash (-) is used to indicate that data are not available or cannot be calculated; *nec* means not elsewhere classified.

Continued on next page.

SIC	Industry	No. Establishments			Employment		Pay / Employee		Annual Payroll ($ 000)		
		1994	1995	% US	1994	1995	1994	1995	1994	1995	% US
NEW YORK - [continued]											
6110	Federal and Federally-sponsored credit	30	22	1.6	325	252	36,751	50,556	11,994	9,783	0.9
6140	Personal credit institutions	434	451	2.5	7,759	8,168	54,336	64,016	431,414	524,978	9.8
6150	Business credit institutions	418	420	8.8	13,554	15,018	60,384	68,293	743,112	856,697	19.5
6160	Mortgage bankers and brokers	852	873	4.3	11,328	12,624	38,861	36,937	418,121	482,159	6.5
6200	Security and commodity brokers	6,335	6,663	16.3	156,695	160,693	138,554	169,538	17,132,308	20,020,217	44.0
6210	Security brokers and dealers	4,332	4,547	18.7	127,851	131,294	144,156	178,917	13,959,285	16,405,829	47.7
6220	Commodity contracts brokers, dealers	298	303	19.7	2,551	2,470	64,259	74,653	177,194	175,769	23.6
6230	Security and commodity exchanges	25	28	28.3	3,365	3,408	69,140	75,860	209,316	245,209	54.9
6280	Security and commodity services	1,664	1,750	11.9	22,903	23,465	125,885	140,948	2,784,435	3,187,760	32.1
6300	Insurance carriers	2,606	2,644	6.4	126,842	123,473	39,581	46,084	4,773,078	5,118,239	9.0
6310	Life insurance	743	726	6.2	54,819	53,308	38,810	47,540	1,905,182	2,040,505	10.4
6320	Medical service and health insurance	133	138	4.6	22,005	21,697	30,640	33,589	715,460	758,491	7.9
6321	Accident and health insurance	44	44	4.2	1,979	2,221	28,661	34,069	60,226	77,172	4.6
6324	Hospital and medical service plans	89	94	4.9	20,026	19,476	30,836	33,534	655,234	681,319	8.5
6330	Fire, marine, and casualty insurance	1,386	1,456	7.0	45,096	43,121	43,453	47,569	1,932,739	2,052,585	8.5
6350	Surety insurance	42	36	6.1	896	854	120,750	254,632	80,555	107,929	20.4
6360	Title insurance	71	77	3.1	1,395	1,205	52,054	50,709	57,011	54,953	4.0
6370	Pension, health, and welfare funds	214	185	8.1	2,598	3,181	29,892	29,456	80,600	99,082	9.7
6390	Insurance carriers, n.e.c.	8	9	5.2	24	65	22,333	39,446	1,222	3,193	3.5
6400	Insurance agents, brokers, and service	7,159	7,211	5.8	53,590	54,208	37,932	42,226	2,152,569	2,291,033	10.0
6500	Real estate	27,825	28,257	11.5	141,900	144,518	27,250	29,199	4,086,285	4,342,226	13.2
6510	Real estate operators and lessors	15,451	15,431	15.4	67,513	68,653	22,680	23,887	1,620,262	1,703,530	17.8
6530	Real estate agents and managers	10,624	10,691	9.3	66,133	66,686	31,590	34,480	2,181,204	2,309,962	12.3
6540	Title abstract offices	401	392	8.1	3,178	2,739	27,458	28,974	92,056	86,782	10.0
6550	Subdividers and developers	1,009	1,033	5.9	4,764	5,231	32,196	33,227	178,793	197,795	6.1
6552	Subdividers and developers, n.e.c.	356	378	3.7	1,663	2,004	40,851	41,836	79,111	94,082	4.2
6553	Cemetery subdividers and developers	622	608	9.9	3,075	3,162	27,646	27,913	98,580	100,967	11.0
6700	Holding and other investment offices	1,911	1,949	8.4	27,169	30,163	65,995	76,415	1,817,427	2,092,087	15.2
6710	Holding offices	647	676	8.0	15,764	13,434	68,132	102,379	1,032,152	1,213,243	14.8
6720	Investment offices	82	95	11.1	1,073	1,228	116,887	124,459	120,231	143,988	8.7
6730	Trusts	434	443	8.5	2,957	3,119	29,143	30,676	95,816	99,672	10.4
6732	Educational, religious, etc. trusts	246	278	11.2	2,049	2,288	32,221	32,600	69,760	76,994	13.5
6733	Trusts, n.e.c.	188	165	6.1	908	831	22,198	25,381	26,056	22,678	5.9
6790	Miscellaneous investing	701	644	8.5	7,285	6,510	66,798	71,234	555,330	541,643	20.1
6792	Oil royalty traders	9	8	1.1	43	36	75,163	92,667	3,508	2,726	2.7
6794	Patent owners and lessors	171	130	9.1	3,548	2,292	55,183	47,454	206,630	117,969	17.0
6798	Real estate investment trusts	38	39	6.5	516	464	77,876	68,621	34,180	33,245	8.0
6799	Investors, n.e.c.	483	466	9.7	3,178	3,718	77,854	86,013	311,012	387,684	26.2
NORTH CAROLINA											
60 –	**Finance, insurance, and real estate**	14,840	15,366	2.4	147,636	156,581	30,178	33,179	4,435,171	4,917,894	1.9
6000	Depository institutions	3,010	3,025	2.9	53,381	58,395	29,115	31,761	1,527,381	1,715,045	2.7
6020	Commercial banks	2,284	2,315	3.5	45,349	49,757	30,157	33,156	1,342,353	1,500,437	3.3
6030	Savings institutions	332	306	1.8	3,846	3,312	26,802	25,959	97,730	92,789	1.3
6060	Credit unions	334	338	2.2	3,500	3,850	18,979	19,182	69,495	74,294	2.1
6100	Nondepository institutions	1,376	1,467	3.2	14,947	15,006	29,875	32,243	423,535	452,401	2.5
6140	Personal credit institutions	732	763	4.3	7,112	7,397	25,406	28,424	183,567	203,879	3.8
6150	Business credit institutions	95	97	2.0	1,338	1,201	45,851	54,948	54,466	57,225	1.3
6160	Mortgage bankers and brokers	455	500	2.4	5,509	5,578	32,221	33,013	159,948	168,752	2.3
6200	Security and commodity brokers	704	730	1.8	5,269	5,787	72,562	87,251	314,748	387,952	0.9
6210	Security brokers and dealers	478	502	2.1	4,209	4,828	74,842	85,173	261,504	330,249	1.0
6220	Commodity contracts brokers, dealers	4	7	0.5	8	9	23,000	32,000	244	245	0.0
6280	Security and commodity services	221	220	1.5	1,051	950	63,863	98,333	52,991	57,452	0.6
6300	Insurance carriers	1,110	1,126	2.7	30,464	30,430	33,116	36,068	1,015,062	1,066,982	1.9
6310	Life insurance	396	385	3.3	12,413	12,310	30,870	33,476	376,816	386,769	2.0
6320	Medical service and health insurance	58	64	2.1	4,621	5,241	28,768	31,616	145,666	175,829	1.8
6321	Accident and health insurance	30	35	3.3	1,793	1,906	24,181	29,058	48,007	53,865	3.2
6324	Hospital and medical service plans	28	29	1.5	2,828	3,335	31,676	33,078	97,659	121,964	1.5

Source: County Business Patterns, 1994/95, CBP-94/95, U.S. Department of Commerce, Washington, D.C., November 1997. SIC categories for which data were suppressed or not available for both 1994 and 1995 are not displayed. The employment columns represent mid-March employment in the year. Pay per employee is calculated by dividing 1st Quarter payroll, annualized, by mid-March employment. The columns headed "% US" show the state's percentage of the national total for the SIC in 1995; for example, 1.4% for SIC 6000 means that the state had 1.4 percent of the national total establishments (or payroll) in SIC 6000 in 1995. A dash (-) is used to indicate that data are not available or cannot be calculated; nec means not elsewhere classified.

Continued on next page.

SIC	Industry	No. Establishments			Employment		Pay / Employee		Annual Payroll ($ 000)		
		1994	1995	% US	1994	1995	1994	1995	1994	1995	% US
NORTH CAROLINA - [continued]											
6330	Fire, marine, and casualty insurance	522	546	2.6	10,581	10,418	36,294	38,536	393,396	401,807	1.7
6350	Surety insurance	22	24	4.0	1,713	1,339	46,183	62,019	70,124	68,656	13.0
6360	Title insurance	55	58	2.3	267	321	36,240	35,352	7,835	9,116	0.7
6370	Pension, health, and welfare funds	51	44	1.9	656	780	27,232	29,774	20,429	23,795	2.3
6400	Insurance agents, brokers, and service	3,116	3,217	2.6	13,080	13,315	28,027	30,852	395,071	428,452	1.9
6500	Real estate	5,201	5,451	2.2	25,911	28,465	19,997	21,946	576,822	647,578	2.0
6510	Real estate operators and lessors	1,779	1,846	1.8	7,678	8,060	16,515	17,534	146,055	156,193	1.6
6530	Real estate agents and managers	2,746	2,827	2.4	14,551	15,879	21,043	22,069	338,847	373,139	2.0
6540	Title abstract offices	23	23	0.5	66	66	39,455	47,030	2,578	2,770	0.3
6550	Subdividers and developers	535	554	3.1	3,478	4,044	23,255	30,188	85,279	104,236	3.2
6552	Subdividers and developers, n.e.c.	354	364	3.5	2,328	2,744	25,636	36,284	61,807	79,467	3.6
6553	Cemetery subdividers and developers	160	154	2.5	1,146	1,250	18,373	17,082	22,552	22,570	2.4
6700	Holding and other investment offices	306	329	1.4	2,922	3,764	43,441	45,153	128,614	164,847	1.2
6710	Holding offices	97	108	1.3	1,787	2,341	52,674	53,985	92,734	125,780	1.5
6720	Investment offices	8	10	1.2	44	78	40,273	21,897	2,262	2,026	0.1
6730	Trusts	74	84	1.6	305	326	23,239	22,761	7,267	7,877	0.8
6732	Educational, religious, etc. trusts	35	40	1.6	219	202	24,183	24,020	5,405	5,142	0.9
6733	Trusts, n.e.c.	39	42	1.6	86	123	20,837	20,813	1,862	2,526	0.7
6790	Miscellaneous investing	120	116	1.5	755	999	31,089	33,253	25,994	28,405	1.1
6794	Patent owners and lessors	26	22	1.5	374	157	16,332	30,268	9,137	4,407	0.6
6798	Real estate investment trusts	21	25	4.1	102	530	29,098	16,174	2,420	8,731	2.1
6799	Investors, n.e.c.	73	69	1.4	279	312	51,599	63,769	14,437	15,267	1.0
NORTH DAKOTA											
60 –	**Finance, insurance, and real estate**	1,985	1,976	0.3	13,472	13,929	23,360	26,352	311,288	334,949	0.1
6000	Depository institutions	444	437	0.4	5,886	6,450	23,267	29,549	135,407	153,758	0.2
6020	Commercial banks	280	288	0.4	4,287	4,361	23,749	24,482	100,621	103,926	0.2
6110	Federal and Federally-sponsored credit	28	29	2.2	310	300	47,394	48,893	9,917	10,130	0.9
6140	Personal credit institutions	18	18	0.1	159	112	23,346	29,964	3,517	3,172	0.1
6200	Security and commodity brokers	94	99	0.2	430	436	49,833	42,339	20,184	19,658	0.0
6210	Security brokers and dealers	66	73	0.3	364	379	55,022	46,153	19,129	18,568	0.1
6300	Insurance carriers	112	112	0.3	2,334	2,106	27,013	28,965	63,403	61,166	0.1
6310	Life insurance	33	32	0.3	634	411	28,189	28,457	17,354	11,058	0.1
6330	Fire, marine, and casualty insurance	59	59	0.3	551	554	26,127	27,791	15,200	16,083	0.1
6400	Insurance agents, brokers, and service	622	628	0.5	1,597	1,678	19,609	19,926	33,247	34,927	0.2
6500	Real estate	600	586	0.2	2,461	2,505	13,562	13,046	34,326	35,002	0.1
6510	Real estate operators and lessors	297	289	0.3	1,227	1,264	12,561	12,835	16,559	17,499	0.2
6530	Real estate agents and managers	202	193	0.2	981	981	13,708	12,979	13,407	13,329	0.1
6540	Title abstract offices	50	50	1.0	192	176	19,896	16,023	3,402	3,059	0.4
6550	Subdividers and developers	47	45	0.3	48	55	12,000	12,145	785	822	0.0
6700	Holding and other investment offices	49	49	0.2	223	284	36,359	38,620	9,092	15,408	0.1
6710	Holding offices	18	18	0.2	118	146	51,695	61,151	6,608	12,917	0.2
6792	Oil royalty traders	4	5	0.7	11	22	12,727	8,364	213	373	0.4
OHIO											
60 –	**Finance, insurance, and real estate**	22,898	23,339	3.7	272,730	270,106	28,190	30,472	7,653,792	8,107,899	3.2
6000	Depository institutions	5,016	4,904	4.7	87,509	87,924	24,799	26,800	2,106,375	2,246,489	3.6
6020	Commercial banks	3,105	3,105	4.6	64,962	67,180	25,137	27,464	1,592,972	1,738,714	3.8
6030	Savings institutions	1,020	913	5.5	14,658	12,467	24,612	25,728	333,575	312,875	4.2
6060	Credit unions	762	745	4.9	5,476	5,585	18,355	19,603	103,363	110,833	3.1
6100	Nondepository institutions	1,480	1,553	3.4	18,688	18,656	28,190	28,294	505,621	540,792	2.9
6110	Federal and Federally-sponsored credit	68	65	4.8	348	319	31,000	34,708	11,431	11,579	1.0
6140	Personal credit institutions	624	668	3.7	6,403	6,501	24,838	28,155	160,590	173,902	3.2
6150	Business credit institutions	159	184	3.8	4,703	5,497	28,191	28,214	125,645	149,303	3.4
6160	Mortgage bankers and brokers	618	619	3.0	7,230	6,293	31,026	28,273	207,615	204,331	2.7
6200	Security and commodity brokers	1,153	1,216	3.0	10,611	10,593	63,111	61,892	626,077	673,133	1.5
6210	Security brokers and dealers	659	706	2.9	7,986	7,953	68,576	64,487	489,304	515,811	1.5
6220	Commodity contracts brokers, dealers	12	11	0.7	38	61	24,737	34,426	1,522	3,814	0.5

Source: County Business Patterns, 1994/95, CBP-94/95, U.S. Department of Commerce, Washington, D.C., November 1997. SIC categories for which data were suppressed or not available for both 1994 and 1995 are not displayed. The employment columns represent mid-March employment in the year. Pay per employee is calculated by dividing 1st Quarter payroll, annualized, by mid-March employment. The columns headed "% US" show the state's percentage of the national total for the SIC in 1995; for example, 1.4% for SIC 6000 means that the state had 1.4 percent of the national total establishments (or payroll) in SIC 6000 in 1995. A dash (-) is used to indicate that data are not available or cannot be calculated; nec means not elsewhere classified.

Continued on next page.

SIC	Industry	No. Establishments			Employment		Pay / Employee		Annual Payroll ($ 000)		
		1994	1995	% US	1994	1995	1994	1995	1994	1995	% US
OHIO - [continued]											
6280	Security and commodity services	478	496	3.4	2,581	2,572	46,810	54,599	134,993	153,225	1.5
6300	Insurance carriers	1,774	1,809	4.4	67,935	61,994	33,672	38,558	2,246,740	2,269,423	4.0
6310	Life insurance	531	498	4.2	19,364	17,838	31,714	34,302	584,404	553,175	2.8
6320	Medical service and health insurance	119	132	4.4	10,367	9,549	31,411	43,131	334,405	395,897	4.1
6321	Accident and health insurance	56	64	6.1	5,173	4,722	30,529	34,196	156,936	193,443	11.6
6324	Hospital and medical service plans	62	67	3.5	5,193	4,826	32,286	51,872	177,421	202,410	2.5
6330	Fire, marine, and casualty insurance	902	965	4.6	34,598	31,586	36,104	40,352	1,237,473	1,228,009	5.1
6350	Surety insurance	12	14	2.4	80	58	45,900	62,000	3,694	3,312	0.6
6360	Title insurance	71	83	3.3	1,451	1,246	30,012	29,406	37,265	33,817	2.5
6370	Pension, health, and welfare funds	126	104	4.6	2,014	1,644	24,491	30,071	47,032	52,255	5.1
6390	Insurance carriers, n.e.c.	6	5	2.9	58	53	36,000	39,925	2,304	2,498	2.7
6400	Insurance agents, brokers, and service	5,435	5,565	4.4	25,255	26,575	27,164	29,027	726,027	809,341	3.5
6500	Real estate	7,384	7,645	3.1	52,046	52,174	17,772	19,413	1,031,685	1,067,085	3.2
6510	Real estate operators and lessors	3,287	3,310	3.3	19,653	19,529	14,273	15,995	313,913	320,604	3.4
6530	Real estate agents and managers	3,148	3,270	2.8	25,611	25,606	19,129	20,685	543,625	560,091	3.0
6540	Title abstract offices	214	216	4.5	2,117	1,935	25,039	25,013	56,207	53,573	6.2
6550	Subdividers and developers	607	656	3.7	4,491	4,715	21,906	24,644	112,847	123,303	3.8
6552	Subdividers and developers, n.e.c.	273	308	3.0	2,495	2,690	26,764	29,790	74,383	82,618	3.7
6553	Cemetery subdividers and developers	311	304	5.0	1,985	1,949	15,865	17,872	37,143	38,306	4.2
6700	Holding and other investment offices	609	601	2.6	8,395	8,566	39,947	44,527	324,533	372,180	2.7
6710	Holding offices	293	289	3.4	5,480	5,579	47,428	52,980	244,345	280,950	3.4
6720	Investment offices	15	14	1.6	67	70	94,985	81,829	3,389	3,317	0.2
6730	Trusts	99	98	1.9	715	775	19,771	16,960	12,487	14,286	1.5
6732	Educational, religious, etc. trusts	56	57	2.3	481	524	16,366	16,702	8,438	9,454	1.7
6733	Trusts, n.e.c.	43	41	1.5	234	251	26,769	17,498	4,049	4,832	1.3
6790	Miscellaneous investing	187	170	2.3	2,127	1,887	25,802	32,594	63,638	65,069	2.4
6792	Oil royalty traders	10	10	1.4	39	34	34,769	44,235	1,468	1,465	1.5
6794	Patent owners and lessors	62	44	3.1	581	354	24,399	34,000	15,409	12,335	1.8
6798	Real estate investment trusts	17	19	3.1	601	709	18,669	27,961	12,694	21,482	5.2
6799	Investors, n.e.c.	98	97	2.0	906	790	31,046	35,620	34,067	29,787	2.0
OKLAHOMA											
60 –	**Finance, insurance, and real estate**	7,530	7,648	1.2	62,413	61,190	24,677	25,647	1,568,922	1,607,914	0.6
6000	Depository institutions	1,136	1,143	1.1	21,969	21,827	23,075	24,239	512,352	525,809	0.8
6020	Commercial banks	769	775	1.2	18,020	17,721	23,390	24,754	424,918	431,688	0.9
6030	Savings institutions	145	130	0.8	1,412	1,360	21,802	20,694	29,710	31,113	0.4
6060	Credit unions	148	148	1.0	1,904	2,032	20,307	22,061	41,530	45,213	1.3
6100	Nondepository institutions	810	855	1.9	4,663	4,637	24,061	24,411	110,116	121,060	0.7
6110	Federal and Federally-sponsored credit	24	24	1.8	169	169	32,024	40,095	5,704	5,817	0.5
6140	Personal credit institutions	596	620	3.5	2,560	2,642	19,178	20,223	50,442	55,424	1.0
6150	Business credit institutions	40	46	1.0	291	381	31,326	35,706	10,257	20,082	0.5
6160	Mortgage bankers and brokers	138	141	0.7	1,635	1,417	29,649	27,585	43,530	39,303	0.5
6200	Security and commodity brokers	386	396	1.0	1,946	2,001	57,155	49,683	101,673	104,103	0.2
6210	Security brokers and dealers	270	280	1.2	1,487	1,553	60,374	51,961	78,084	82,356	0.2
6220	Commodity contracts brokers, dealers	17	16	1.0	79	48	28,354	38,417	2,226	2,129	0.3
6280	Security and commodity services	99	99	0.7	380	400	50,547	42,190	21,363	19,588	0.2
6300	Insurance carriers	455	447	1.1	12,081	11,639	29,892	32,055	356,816	360,834	0.6
6310	Life insurance	137	125	1.1	4,371	4,274	28,866	28,419	116,517	110,450	0.6
6320	Medical service and health insurance	49	43	1.4	2,370	2,302	26,327	29,249	69,156	69,740	0.7
6321	Accident and health insurance	26	20	1.9	1,173	1,081	23,355	27,519	30,254	29,893	1.8
6324	Hospital and medical service plans	23	23	1.2	1,197	1,221	29,240	30,781	38,902	39,847	0.5
6330	Fire, marine, and casualty insurance	225	236	1.1	4,678	4,340	33,997	38,627	156,397	162,759	0.7
6370	Pension, health, and welfare funds	29	25	1.1	263	246	21,582	25,301	6,030	6,876	0.7
6400	Insurance agents, brokers, and service	1,877	1,862	1.5	6,753	6,595	21,522	22,936	155,389	161,842	0.7
6500	Real estate	2,442	2,503	1.0	11,931	11,611	17,307	16,606	222,618	206,933	0.6
6510	Real estate operators and lessors	1,030	1,007	1.0	4,427	4,466	14,081	14,667	69,061	66,602	0.7
6530	Real estate agents and managers	1,034	1,081	0.9	4,899	4,642	19,272	17,450	100,473	88,325	0.5
6540	Title abstract offices	157	156	3.2	1,534	1,358	21,836	21,688	33,064	31,451	3.6

Source: County Business Patterns, 1994/95, CBP-94/95, U.S. Department of Commerce, Washington, D.C., November 1997. SIC categories for which data were suppressed or not available for both 1994 and 1995 are not displayed. The employment columns represent mid-March employment in the year. Pay per employee is calculated by dividing 1st Quarter payroll, annualized, by mid-March employment. The columns headed "% US" show the state's percentage of the national total for the SIC in 1995; for example, 1.4% for SIC 6000 means that the state had 1.4 percent of the national total establishments (or payroll) in SIC 6000 in 1995. A dash (-) is used to indicate that data are not available or cannot be calculated; nec means not elsewhere classified.

Continued on next page.

SIC	Industry	No. Establishments			Employment		Pay / Employee		Annual Payroll ($ 000)		
		1994	1995	% US	1994	1995	1994	1995	1994	1995	% US
OKLAHOMA - [continued]											
6550	Subdividers and developers	168	174	1.0	1,040	897	15,262	15,608	18,865	16,616	0.5
6552	Subdividers and developers, n.e.c.	100	101	1.0	573	310	17,668	21,806	12,049	8,424	0.4
6553	Cemetery subdividers and developers	58	57	0.9	466	514	12,292	12,125	6,375	7,163	0.8
6710	Holding offices	88	102	1.2	1,118	1,620	36,254	43,533	44,438	88,304	1.1
6720	Investment offices	19	18	2.1	39	55	12,103	11,345	569	752	0.0
6730	Trusts	99	111	2.1	361	409	23,280	25,222	8,659	10,101	1.1
6732	Educational, religious, etc. trusts	28	33	1.3	89	139	22,067	21,640	2,438	3,209	0.6
6733	Trusts, n.e.c.	70	78	2.9	271	270	23,749	27,067	6,220	6,892	1.8
6790	Miscellaneous investing	200	189	2.5	729	623	33,564	34,613	25,953	23,956	0.9
6792	Oil royalty traders	92	90	12.9	372	339	35,527	36,389	13,723	12,353	12.4
6794	Patent owners and lessors	12	8	0.6	36	37	40,111	18,703	1,810	847	0.1
6798	Real estate investment trusts	8	9	1.5	32	24	14,375	15,833	556	552	0.1
6799	Investors, n.e.c.	88	82	1.7	289	223	32,346	36,574	9,864	10,204	0.7
OREGON											
60 –	**Finance, insurance, and real estate**	8,410	8,691	1.4	83,710	79,553	27,975	29,163	2,301,581	2,315,981	0.9
6000	Depository institutions	1,382	1,385	1.3	26,253	24,386	26,937	26,954	693,993	649,378	1.0
6020	Commercial banks	923	899	1.3	20,950	18,773	27,334	27,290	553,371	490,297	1.1
6030	Savings institutions	219	234	1.4	2,171	2,420	25,784	23,967	53,177	63,036	0.9
6060	Credit unions	201	204	1.4	2,587	2,603	21,727	23,734	56,603	60,739	1.7
6090	Functions closely related to banking	34	43	0.8	342	401	46,444	47,022	24,415	28,405	1.3
6100	Nondepository institutions	619	655	1.4	6,208	4,879	35,599	35,379	195,506	182,338	1.0
6150	Business credit institutions	71	76	1.6	1,608	1,422	37,020	42,110	51,942	55,153	1.3
6160	Mortgage bankers and brokers	363	387	1.9	3,482	2,305	37,359	34,016	110,062	91,272	1.2
6200	Security and commodity brokers	386	412	1.0	2,910	3,227	61,076	61,869	167,612	196,079	0.4
6210	Security brokers and dealers	243	258	1.1	2,338	2,461	66,157	67,283	140,874	158,923	0.5
6220	Commodity contracts brokers, dealers	9	7	0.5	40	61	34,600	39,082	2,658	2,647	0.4
6280	Security and commodity services	133	145	1.0	532	698	40,737	44,716	24,022	33,718	0.3
6300	Insurance carriers	592	589	1.4	18,993	16,036	31,609	35,507	559,989	555,962	1.0
6310	Life insurance	96	93	0.8	3,171	2,889	33,275	31,376	98,295	88,547	0.4
6320	Medical service and health insurance	41	37	1.2	4,017	3,630	32,504	34,202	130,386	122,841	1.3
6321	Accident and health insurance	10	9	0.9	293	296	27,741	25,338	7,821	7,284	0.4
6324	Hospital and medical service plans	31	28	1.5	3,724	3,334	32,879	34,989	122,565	115,557	1.4
6330	Fire, marine, and casualty insurance	306	322	1.5	8,085	7,650	34,674	38,849	265,026	281,280	1.2
6360	Title insurance	100	98	3.9	1,864	1,319	29,041	30,290	46,668	43,850	3.2
6370	Pension, health, and welfare funds	44	31	1.4	1,812	521	15,508	31,455	18,373	18,414	1.8
6400	Insurance agents, brokers, and service	1,688	1,703	1.4	8,209	8,930	28,751	30,658	240,437	263,542	1.2
6500	Real estate	3,490	3,663	1.5	18,220	18,847	16,132	16,934	324,949	341,500	1.0
6510	Real estate operators and lessors	1,569	1,582	1.6	6,742	6,914	12,971	14,158	97,165	98,170	1.0
6530	Real estate agents and managers	1,577	1,632	1.4	9,885	9,905	17,433	17,886	187,530	192,492	1.0
6540	Title abstract offices	30	41	0.9	515	648	23,588	24,395	12,226	15,967	1.8
6550	Subdividers and developers	226	265	1.5	1,047	1,252	20,481	20,978	26,655	31,359	1.0
6552	Subdividers and developers, n.e.c.	162	188	1.8	655	756	24,085	24,788	20,568	23,139	1.0
6553	Cemetery subdividers and developers	57	62	1.0	391	485	14,486	15,249	5,959	7,779	0.8
6700	Holding and other investment offices	246	271	1.2	2,718	3,133	36,908	39,465	112,172	121,751	0.9
6710	Holding offices	84	90	1.1	1,774	2,205	43,436	45,633	86,123	94,864	1.2
6730	Trusts	71	96	1.8	386	445	19,513	19,739	7,998	9,693	1.0
6732	Educational, religious, etc. trusts	36	49	2.0	214	309	19,645	20,505	4,404	6,862	1.2
6733	Trusts, n.e.c.	34	46	1.7	172	127	19,349	17,512	3,539	2,594	0.7
6790	Miscellaneous investing	77	70	0.9	530	439	27,804	30,150	16,830	16,286	0.6
6799	Investors, n.e.c.	57	49	1.0	247	260	33,279	27,908	10,143	8,565	0.6
PENNSYLVANIA											
60 –	**Finance, insurance, and real estate**	23,496	23,695	3.8	330,953	328,988	29,986	32,632	10,106,376	10,649,988	4.2
6000	Depository institutions	5,678	5,571	5.3	105,823	102,100	25,501	28,961	2,721,573	2,801,451	4.5
6010	Central reserve depository	4	4	4.2	2,067	1,998	31,280	32,270	65,703	67,393	6.9
6020	Commercial banks	3,821	3,769	5.6	85,982	80,931	25,981	30,160	2,232,717	2,275,689	5.0
6030	Savings institutions	818	759	4.6	10,432	9,822	22,779	24,698	246,994	248,086	3.4

Source: County Business Patterns, 1994/95, CBP-94/95, U.S. Department of Commerce, Washington, D.C., November 1997. SIC categories for which data were suppressed or not available for both 1994 and 1995 are *not* displayed. The employment columns represent mid-March employment in the year. Pay per employee is calculated by dividing 1st Quarter payroll, annualized, by mid-March employment. The columns headed "% US" show the state's percentage of the national total for the SIC in 1995; for example, 1.4% for SIC 6000 means that the state had 1.4 percent of the national total establishments (or payroll) in SIC 6000 in 1995. A dash (-) is used to indicate that data are not available or cannot be calculated; *nec* means not elsewhere classified.

Continued on next page.

SIC	Industry	No. Establishments			Employment		Pay / Employee		Annual Payroll ($ 000)		
		1994	1995	% US	1994	1995	1994	1995	1994	1995	% US
PENNSYLVANIA - [continued]											
6060	Credit unions	848	827	5.5	5,466	5,655	18,793	20,192	109,255	118,641	3.4
6080	Foreign bank and branches and agencies	5	8	1.2	289	273	35,585	45,289	10,363	10,530	0.4
6090	Functions closely related to banking	182	202	3.8	1,587	3,421	31,133	24,105	56,541	81,062	3.8
6100	Nondepository institutions	1,388	1,445	3.2	15,262	14,537	33,786	38,063	495,749	550,850	3.0
6110	Federal and Federally-sponsored credit	38	36	2.7	1,111	1,202	32,403	33,674	35,571	38,946	3.5
6140	Personal credit institutions	646	712	4.0	4,623	4,788	30,209	41,641	137,347	171,386	3.2
6150	Business credit institutions	118	118	2.5	2,301	2,819	37,578	40,847	82,236	107,832	2.4
6160	Mortgage bankers and brokers	579	564	2.8	7,224	5,676	35,068	34,700	239,952	230,489	3.1
6200	Security and commodity brokers	1,362	1,455	3.6	14,300	15,004	69,192	71,680	956,715	1,069,499	2.3
6210	Security brokers and dealers	801	834	3.4	9,686	10,177	74,487	71,382	649,687	723,568	2.1
6280	Security and commodity services	539	594	4.0	4,101	4,423	57,500	75,298	282,561	329,222	3.3
6300	Insurance carriers	1,913	1,943	4.7	97,836	97,801	31,488	33,134	3,048,679	3,157,043	5.6
6310	Life insurance	692	690	5.9	43,064	41,466	26,714	26,673	1,110,224	1,079,504	5.5
6320	Medical service and health insurance	106	110	3.7	17,715	19,450	31,113	33,620	540,742	642,963	6.7
6321	Accident and health insurance	41	41	3.9	2,235	2,342	23,060	25,959	56,537	65,399	3.9
6324	Hospital and medical service plans	65	69	3.6	15,480	17,108	32,276	34,669	484,205	577,564	7.2
6330	Fire, marine, and casualty insurance	803	850	4.1	33,366	32,940	38,020	41,025	1,286,170	1,308,945	5.4
6350	Surety insurance	29	29	4.9	187	151	41,904	50,013	8,029	7,285	1.4
6360	Title insurance	86	85	3.4	1,243	1,351	43,025	43,571	49,840	52,932	3.9
6370	Pension, health, and welfare funds	179	150	6.6	2,160	2,234	21,678	25,859	50,678	59,719	5.9
6390	Insurance carriers, n.e.c.	10	13	7.5	89	189	24,000	24,466	2,800	5,146	5.6
6400	Insurance agents, brokers, and service	5,082	5,117	4.1	29,766	31,094	30,936	33,478	1,030,153	1,118,303	4.9
6500	Real estate	7,357	7,434	3.0	51,922	51,597	20,193	21,381	1,142,691	1,154,962	3.5
6510	Real estate operators and lessors	2,812	2,791	2.8	17,518	17,882	17,775	19,277	356,023	360,104	3.8
6530	Real estate agents and managers	3,290	3,318	2.9	27,039	27,418	21,302	22,373	607,616	632,709	3.4
6540	Title abstract offices	241	226	4.7	2,267	1,115	28,628	20,929	63,100	26,056	3.0
6550	Subdividers and developers	926	928	5.3	4,875	4,824	19,079	23,627	109,872	121,752	3.7
6552	Subdividers and developers, n.e.c.	284	285	2.8	1,621	1,609	26,041	35,632	49,384	60,832	2.7
6553	Cemetery subdividers and developers	629	617	10.1	3,245	3,190	15,360	17,490	59,683	59,742	6.5
6700	Holding and other investment offices	657	668	2.9	13,891	14,926	39,822	43,017	609,176	691,295	5.0
6710	Holding offices	243	240	2.8	7,494	7,682	46,130	52,619	354,171	388,351	4.7
6730	Trusts	202	204	3.9	1,154	1,615	24,790	20,478	33,496	42,518	4.5
6732	Educational, religious, etc. trusts	101	110	4.4	657	1,028	27,683	20,288	21,701	28,667	5.0
6733	Trusts, n.e.c.	101	94	3.5	497	587	20,966	20,811	11,795	13,851	3.6
6790	Miscellaneous investing	176	167	2.2	1,430	1,719	40,792	37,713	65,765	66,082	2.5
6792	Oil royalty traders	8	8	1.1	29	27	78,069	88,000	2,330	2,302	2.3
6794	Patent owners and lessors	65	55	3.8	773	1,055	34,898	23,306	29,279	27,850	4.0
6798	Real estate investment trusts	19	16	2.6	125	119	44,768	48,908	6,321	6,071	1.5
6799	Investors, n.e.c.	84	88	1.8	503	518	46,712	61,861	27,835	29,859	2.0
RHODE ISLAND											
60 –	**Finance, insurance, and real estate**	2,014	1,983	0.3	25,614	25,405	31,075	32,482	792,669	806,206	0.3
6000	Depository institutions	309	275	0.3	7,514	7,165	27,035	28,153	197,408	194,802	0.3
6020	Commercial banks	167	172	0.3	5,340	5,628	29,229	29,163	154,374	157,926	0.3
6030	Savings institutions	63	31	0.2	1,235	597	21,315	28,302	20,998	14,328	0.2
6060	Credit unions	71	64	0.4	890	907	20,090	21,658	19,474	20,551	0.6
6090	Functions closely related to banking	8	8	0.1	49	33	58,204	31,758	2,562	1,997	0.1
6100	Nondepository institutions	152	143	0.3	1,903	1,573	33,595	34,500	56,404	55,868	0.3
6140	Personal credit institutions	35	34	0.2	289	188	18,561	25,085	5,840	4,876	0.1
6150	Business credit institutions	10	9	0.2	347	363	56,069	53,212	16,198	16,411	0.4
6160	Mortgage bankers and brokers	107	99	0.5	1,267	1,021	30,870	29,587	34,366	34,555	0.5
6200	Security and commodity brokers	129	132	0.3	1,939	1,940	48,736	45,784	85,138	86,869	0.2
6210	Security brokers and dealers	53	56	0.2	757	709	61,358	61,427	40,816	43,431	0.1
6300	Insurance carriers	137	139	0.3	8,136	8,455	32,475	33,478	274,143	275,404	0.5
6310	Life insurance	42	42	0.4	2,570	2,538	24,121	22,391	61,051	51,749	0.3
6320	Medical service and health insurance	7	7	0.2	1,659	2,001	36,176	32,108	66,571	70,616	0.7
6330	Fire, marine, and casualty insurance	72	70	0.3	3,712	3,693	36,457	41,566	139,118	144,564	0.6
6360	Title insurance	6	7	0.3	71	67	36,789	35,940	2,265	2,083	0.2

Source: County Business Patterns, 1994/95, CBP-94/95, U.S. Department of Commerce, Washington, D.C., November 1997. SIC categories for which data were suppressed or not available for both 1994 and 1995 are *not* displayed. The employment columns represent mid-March employment in the year. Pay per employee is calculated by dividing 1st Quarter payroll, annualized, by mid-March employment. The columns headed "% US" show the state's percentage of the national total for the SIC in 1995; for example, 1.4% for SIC 6000 means that the state had 1.4 percent of the national total establishments (or payroll) in SIC 6000 in 1995. A dash (-) is used to indicate that data are not available or cannot be calculated; *nec* means not elsewhere classified.

Continued on next page.

SIC	Industry	No. Establishments			Employment		Pay / Employee		Annual Payroll ($ 000)		
		1994	1995	% US	1994	1995	1994	1995	1994	1995	% US
RHODE ISLAND - [continued]											
6370	Pension, health, and welfare funds	10	11	0.5	124	147	34,452	39,837	5,138	6,185	0.6
6400	Insurance agents, brokers, and service	412	415	0.3	2,180	2,141	29,189	31,174	71,168	70,880	0.3
6500	Real estate	797	796	0.3	3,554	3,715	19,347	21,138	77,646	83,674	0.3
6510	Real estate operators and lessors	294	291	0.3	1,351	1,385	18,967	21,334	28,437	30,409	0.3
6530	Real estate agents and managers	402	394	0.3	1,840	1,898	18,457	20,067	37,928	40,297	0.2
6540	Title abstract offices	10	11	0.2	105	88	11,048	13,545	1,268	1,330	0.2
6550	Subdividers and developers	67	71	0.4	225	244	32,000	29,672	8,802	8,829	0.3
6552	Subdividers and developers, n.e.c.	30	30	0.3	85	86	49,459	45,209	5,105	4,858	0.2
6553	Cemetery subdividers and developers	35	37	0.6	140	152	21,400	21,553	3,645	3,689	0.4
6710	Holding offices	32	32	0.4	229	260	139,773	174,185	25,031	31,512	0.4
6732	Educational, religious, etc. trusts	7	7	0.3	38	41	35,053	37,171	1,386	1,620	0.3
6790	Miscellaneous investing	23	26	0.3	92	75	42,522	50,987	3,771	4,018	0.1
6799	Investors, n.e.c.	16	17	0.4	37	31	53,838	54,452	1,954	1,901	0.1
SOUTH CAROLINA											
60 –	**Finance, insurance, and real estate**	7,557	7,864	1.3	67,117	68,741	24,678	26,469	1,717,361	1,864,111	0.7
6000	Depository institutions	1,452	1,491	1.4	20,092	19,705	22,560	24,502	449,752	493,834	0.8
6020	Commercial banks	1,015	1,038	1.6	15,009	14,513	22,950	24,796	336,046	366,090	0.8
6030	Savings institutions	207	206	1.2	2,978	2,946	22,156	24,855	69,071	73,503	1.0
6060	Credit unions	184	185	1.2	1,856	1,943	20,485	22,612	39,353	43,601	1.2
6090	Functions closely related to banking	43	56	1.0	155	208	15,613	14,462	2,808	3,336	0.2
6100	Nondepository institutions	1,176	1,236	2.7	7,566	7,922	25,278	27,440	189,811	228,910	1.2
6140	Personal credit institutions	873	904	5.0	3,847	4,265	21,419	23,761	86,655	103,495	1.9
6160	Mortgage bankers and brokers	225	253	1.2	2,967	2,970	29,611	31,749	80,510	100,570	1.3
6200	Security and commodity brokers	280	308	0.8	1,819	1,933	58,911	58,516	101,611	110,694	0.2
6210	Security brokers and dealers	206	229	0.9	1,648	1,758	60,417	60,721	94,804	103,883	0.3
6280	Security and commodity services	69	71	0.5	161	164	45,888	37,537	6,576	6,484	0.1
6300	Insurance carriers	499	494	1.2	13,511	13,673	29,475	31,268	401,254	403,684	0.7
6310	Life insurance	218	208	1.8	5,623	5,308	30,002	30,557	166,646	151,038	0.8
6320	Medical service and health insurance	37	36	1.2	5,529	5,911	25,181	27,518	142,829	152,205	1.6
6330	Fire, marine, and casualty insurance	206	215	1.0	2,193	2,257	39,362	43,355	87,658	96,207	0.4
6360	Title insurance	9	15	0.6	48	58	38,667	40,000	1,681	2,057	0.2
6370	Pension, health, and welfare funds	20	13	0.6	100	124	19,280	18,645	2,197	1,943	0.2
6400	Insurance agents, brokers, and service	1,427	1,459	1.2	7,444	7,723	25,436	27,941	204,053	222,519	1.0
6500	Real estate	2,562	2,709	1.1	14,383	15,588	17,542	18,581	291,671	322,908	1.0
6510	Real estate operators and lessors	777	806	0.8	3,348	3,509	15,453	18,776	59,793	70,078	0.7
6530	Real estate agents and managers	1,419	1,487	1.3	8,330	9,038	18,218	18,649	176,011	191,443	1.0
6540	Title abstract offices	41	40	0.8	135	127	21,037	19,622	2,909	2,555	0.3
6550	Subdividers and developers	261	263	1.5	2,433	2,568	18,257	18,726	50,634	52,999	1.6
6552	Subdividers and developers, n.e.c.	144	148	1.4	1,529	1,727	20,484	20,718	35,818	39,661	1.8
6553	Cemetery subdividers and developers	103	96	1.6	898	777	14,503	14,589	14,547	11,710	1.3
6700	Holding and other investment offices	149	154	0.7	1,157	1,410	34,769	32,443	43,345	52,498	0.4
6710	Holding offices	64	66	0.8	807	1,017	41,998	35,965	35,456	42,300	0.5
6790	Miscellaneous investing	51	51	0.7	281	268	17,153	18,970	6,166	6,201	0.2
6794	Patent owners and lessors	9	10	0.7	33	31	30,788	41,161	1,057	1,641	0.2
6798	Real estate investment trusts	7	7	1.2	25	34	20,960	18,235	1,768	1,077	0.3
6799	Investors, n.e.c.	35	34	0.7	223	203	14,709	15,704	3,341	3,483	0.2
SOUTH DAKOTA											
60 –	**Finance, insurance, and real estate**	2,155	2,183	0.3	17,844	18,418	22,143	23,589	389,543	429,975	0.2
6000	Depository institutions	476	474	0.5	9,574	9,912	21,446	23,410	198,885	216,816	0.3
6020	Commercial banks	339	347	0.5	8,527	8,924	21,806	23,779	179,025	197,007	0.4
6030	Savings institutions	56	46	0.3	509	427	19,222	21,649	10,033	9,194	0.1
6100	Nondepository institutions	75	82	0.2	796	879	31,543	32,542	22,623	30,498	0.2
6140	Personal credit institutions	26	35	0.2	445	515	20,773	21,786	10,280	17,748	0.3
6160	Mortgage bankers and brokers	17	16	0.1	113	124	52,319	50,419	4,280	4,665	0.1
6200	Security and commodity brokers	118	126	0.3	605	537	42,817	37,073	22,695	21,364	0.0
6210	Security brokers and dealers	74	77	0.3	362	365	56,950	42,926	17,730	16,991	0.0

Source: County Business Patterns, 1994/95, CBP-94/95, U.S. Department of Commerce, Washington, D.C., November 1997. SIC categories for which data were suppressed or not available for both 1994 and 1995 are *not* displayed. The employment columns represent mid-March employment in the year. Pay per employee is calculated by dividing 1st Quarter payroll, annualized, by mid-March employment. The columns headed "% US" show the state's percentage of the national total for the SIC in 1995; for example, 1.4% for SIC 6000 means that the state had 1.4 percent of the national total establishments (or payroll) in SIC 6000 in 1995. A dash (-) is used to indicate that data are not available or cannot be calculated; *nec* means not elsewhere classified.

Continued on next page.

SIC	Industry	No. Establishments			Employment		Pay / Employee		Annual Payroll ($ 000)		
		1994	1995	% US	1994	1995	1994	1995	1994	1995	% US
SOUTH DAKOTA - [continued]											
6220	Commodity contracts brokers, dealers	10	10	0.6	78	24	16,718	31,167	1,023	657	0.1
6280	Security and commodity services	34	38	0.3	165	148	24,145	23,595	3,942	3,711	0.0
6300	Insurance carriers	124	125	0.3	2,342	2,470	26,273	28,923	62,261	72,969	0.1
6310	Life insurance	38	36	0.3	962	995	28,141	28,535	26,069	30,436	0.2
6320	Medical service and health insurance	21	22	0.7	271	325	25,624	29,502	7,058	10,650	0.1
6321	Accident and health insurance	9	9	0.9	81	82	24,444	31,171	1,957	2,129	0.1
6324	Hospital and medical service plans	12	13	0.7	190	243	26,126	28,938	5,101	8,521	0.1
6330	Fire, marine, and casualty insurance	56	56	0.3	620	627	23,594	28,242	16,005	17,637	0.1
6400	Insurance agents, brokers, and service	652	642	0.5	1,924	1,967	19,890	21,216	41,577	43,878	0.2
6500	Real estate	652	666	0.3	2,373	2,398	13,441	13,396	34,553	36,088	0.1
6510	Real estate operators and lessors	315	321	0.3	1,054	929	12,076	11,061	13,174	11,398	0.1
6530	Real estate agents and managers	227	225	0.2	981	1,110	14,275	15,506	15,371	18,824	0.1
6540	Title abstract offices	49	51	1.1	191	186	19,267	16,645	3,537	3,305	0.4
6550	Subdividers and developers	52	53	0.3	142	165	10,225	9,042	2,423	1,950	0.1
6552	Subdividers and developers, n.e.c.	22	24	0.2	88	111	10,864	8,216	1,754	1,241	0.1
6553	Cemetery subdividers and developers	29	27	0.4	53	51	9,283	11,137	665	697	0.1
6710	Holding offices	25	28	0.3	133	133	31,368	36,872	4,218	4,971	0.1
6790	Miscellaneous investing	16	19	0.3	45	61	37,244	33,770	1,510	1,742	0.1
6794	Patent owners and lessors	4	6	0.4	18	28	26,222	24,857	759	814	0.1
6799	Investors, n.e.c.	12	13	0.3	27	33	44,593	41,333	751	928	0.1
TENNESSEE											
60 –	**Finance, insurance, and real estate**	10,567	10,882	1.7	108,497	109,083	29,750	30,571	3,224,662	3,345,102	1.3
6000	Depository institutions	2,216	2,252	2.2	36,287	36,888	26,410	27,417	932,237	974,833	1.6
6010	Central reserve depository	4	4	4.2	392	391	26,296	28,010	10,615	11,016	1.1
6020	Commercial banks	1,589	1,624	2.4	28,651	29,653	27,203	27,687	743,865	776,654	1.7
6030	Savings institutions	202	172	1.0	2,885	2,427	22,846	26,728	69,301	69,338	0.9
6060	Credit unions	371	362	2.4	3,081	3,211	22,056	24,331	72,991	78,195	2.2
6090	Functions closely related to banking	50	89	1.7	1,278	1,202	27,196	30,236	35,465	39,320	1.8
6100	Nondepository institutions	958	1,058	2.3	7,037	8,033	32,588	31,158	218,369	263,413	1.4
6140	Personal credit institutions	549	616	3.4	3,021	4,553	25,887	28,833	81,368	134,577	2.5
6150	Business credit institutions	68	69	1.4	681	886	46,150	45,273	28,678	42,819	1.0
6160	Mortgage bankers and brokers	285	300	1.5	3,126	2,382	36,223	30,294	101,880	78,944	1.1
6200	Security and commodity brokers	464	489	1.2	4,620	4,668	80,579	65,081	339,616	362,747	0.8
6210	Security brokers and dealers	283	287	1.2	3,949	3,907	83,436	66,632	277,508	287,304	0.8
6220	Commodity contracts brokers, dealers	18	17	1.1	99	86	81,697	67,628	7,688	7,201	1.0
6280	Security and commodity services	162	184	1.2	572	675	60,664	55,775	54,386	68,232	0.7
6300	Insurance carriers	813	821	2.0	24,032	22,637	32,011	36,244	747,042	741,230	1.3
6310	Life insurance	294	281	2.4	10,977	10,407	32,313	36,075	334,274	304,811	1.5
6320	Medical service and health insurance	60	64	2.1	4,116	4,336	28,529	31,600	113,976	134,451	1.4
6321	Accident and health insurance	28	32	3.0	491	547	29,238	34,347	14,400	19,411	1.2
6324	Hospital and medical service plans	32	32	1.7	3,625	3,789	28,433	31,203	99,576	115,040	1.4
6330	Fire, marine, and casualty insurance	387	403	1.9	8,120	7,071	33,162	39,441	271,047	272,623	1.1
6350	Surety insurance	13	17	2.9	237	206	46,295	54,485	11,177	10,715	2.0
6360	Title insurance	18	21	0.8	236	226	34,407	32,885	6,815	6,654	0.5
6370	Pension, health, and welfare funds	37	27	1.2	337	357	24,819	26,555	9,129	10,788	1.1
6390	Insurance carriers, n.e.c.	3	4	2.3	9	7	48,444	63,429	498	431	0.5
6400	Insurance agents, brokers, and service	2,354	2,375	1.9	11,025	11,840	29,939	32,300	352,933	397,559	1.7
6500	Real estate	3,402	3,540	1.4	18,640	19,833	17,748	19,212	381,046	416,648	1.3
6510	Real estate operators and lessors	1,390	1,419	1.4	6,364	6,636	16,027	17,061	109,960	119,706	1.3
6530	Real estate agents and managers	1,598	1,648	1.4	10,169	10,541	19,026	21,112	225,738	242,432	1.3
6540	Title abstract offices	73	83	1.7	450	402	23,209	23,851	11,825	12,265	1.4
6550	Subdividers and developers	295	296	1.7	1,631	2,101	15,142	15,417	32,286	37,169	1.1
6552	Subdividers and developers, n.e.c.	154	157	1.5	580	837	18,945	19,589	16,547	20,196	0.9
6553	Cemetery subdividers and developers	131	125	2.0	1,046	1,250	12,853	12,390	15,324	16,504	1.8
6700	Holding and other investment offices	347	335	1.4	6,360	4,466	32,309	34,594	224,793	157,293	1.1
6710	Holding offices	127	124	1.5	2,382	2,894	42,002	36,554	102,916	109,290	1.3
6720	Investment offices	12	13	1.5	44	75	45,455	52,107	3,657	4,180	0.3

Source: County Business Patterns, 1994/95, CBP-94/95, U.S. Department of Commerce, Washington, D.C., November 1997. SIC categories for which data were suppressed or not available for both 1994 and 1995 are *not* displayed. The employment columns represent mid-March employment in the year. Pay per employee is calculated by dividing 1st Quarter payroll, annualized, by mid-March employment. The columns headed "% US" show the state's percentage of the national total for the SIC in 1995; for example, 1.4% for SIC 6000 means that the state had 1.4 percent of the national total establishments (or payroll) in SIC 6000 in 1995. A dash (-) is used to indicate that data are not available or cannot be calculated; *nec* means not elsewhere classified.

Continued on next page.

SIC	Industry	No. Establishments			Employment		Pay / Employee		Annual Payroll ($ 000)		
		1994	1995	% US	1994	1995	1994	1995	1994	1995	% US
TENNESSEE - [continued]											
6730	Trusts	72	69	1.3	550	424	14,858	16,877	8,489	7,850	0.8
6732	Educational, religious, etc. trusts	33	31	1.3	350	273	12,023	16,469	5,150	4,638	0.8
6733	Trusts, n.e.c.	39	37	1.4	200	150	19,820	17,680	3,339	3,192	0.8
6790	Miscellaneous investing	128	115	1.5	898	1,005	34,904	35,323	34,717	33,494	1.2
6794	Patent owners and lessors	65	45	3.1	636	682	30,497	28,821	22,782	18,855	2.7
6799	Investors, n.e.c.	55	63	1.3	231	238	43,082	53,193	10,018	11,994	0.8
TEXAS											
60 –	**Finance, insurance, and real estate**	40,454	41,528	6.6	438,017	440,607	31,118	32,290	13,547,901	14,240,133	5.6
6000	Depository institutions	5,165	5,210	5.0	113,192	116,605	27,034	28,193	3,003,640	3,203,951	5.1
6020	Commercial banks	2,948	3,020	4.5	87,116	89,624	27,414	28,757	2,313,508	2,476,017	5.4
6030	Savings institutions	600	566	3.4	9,648	9,993	30,688	29,484	301,166	308,336	4.2
6060	Credit unions	1,007	1,009	6.7	11,227	11,958	20,394	21,353	238,163	263,665	7.5
6090	Functions closely related to banking	572	574	10.7	3,007	2,822	18,453	22,319	56,403	59,314	2.8
6100	Nondepository institutions	3,201	3,354	7.4	38,225	37,991	33,829	33,170	1,270,293	1,292,486	7.0
6110	Federal and Federally-sponsored credit	140	141	10.5	1,656	1,851	32,256	32,588	53,250	57,270	5.2
6140	Personal credit institutions	1,480	1,585	8.8	12,799	14,748	28,914	28,816	382,641	451,493	8.4
6150	Business credit institutions	387	404	8.4	6,478	7,158	35,217	36,764	251,704	271,233	6.2
6160	Mortgage bankers and brokers	1,157	1,139	5.6	17,184	13,893	37,180	36,243	577,920	502,550	6.7
6200	Security and commodity brokers	2,181	2,339	5.7	21,645	21,705	78,046	73,868	1,456,601	1,519,825	3.3
6210	Security brokers and dealers	1,399	1,527	6.3	15,040	15,446	81,798	74,067	1,025,727	1,078,714	3.1
6220	Commodity contracts brokers, dealers	50	55	3.6	170	184	58,847	62,848	12,364	12,862	1.7
6280	Security and commodity services	716	734	5.0	6,325	5,941	69,558	74,134	410,461	420,087	4.2
6300	Insurance carriers	3,023	3,060	7.4	89,813	87,950	33,822	36,010	3,024,040	3,169,374	5.6
6310	Life insurance	893	847	7.2	31,156	29,286	31,518	33,759	962,539	947,196	4.8
6320	Medical service and health insurance	202	185	6.2	10,905	11,322	30,830	33,521	344,030	383,750	4.0
6321	Accident and health insurance	109	81	7.7	3,604	3,383	30,253	33,150	106,782	108,068	6.5
6324	Hospital and medical service plans	93	103	5.3	7,301	7,938	31,115	33,682	237,248	275,641	3.5
6330	Fire, marine, and casualty insurance	1,526	1,654	8.0	41,696	41,469	36,128	38,124	1,522,092	1,628,239	6.7
6350	Surety insurance	39	38	6.4	410	462	43,063	44,026	17,467	17,958	3.4
6360	Title insurance	182	189	7.5	3,851	3,228	40,407	43,201	135,698	120,306	8.8
6370	Pension, health, and welfare funds	165	119	5.2	1,512	1,865	21,489	24,345	33,660	57,288	5.6
6390	Insurance carriers, n.e.c.	10	11	6.4	267	250	26,532	41,280	8,286	12,611	13.7
6400	Insurance agents, brokers, and service	9,055	9,126	7.3	46,988	47,405	28,389	29,636	1,396,237	1,468,109	6.4
6500	Real estate	15,457	15,993	6.5	105,092	105,155	20,668	21,798	2,353,560	2,382,616	7.2
6510	Real estate operators and lessors	6,519	6,565	6.6	32,335	32,381	17,248	17,852	609,870	590,198	6.2
6530	Real estate agents and managers	7,137	7,322	6.3	60,803	58,194	22,199	23,894	1,457,391	1,448,075	7.7
6540	Title abstract offices	375	373	7.7	3,691	3,187	23,510	22,949	85,711	76,536	8.9
6550	Subdividers and developers	1,065	1,110	6.3	7,805	9,772	21,574	22,091	182,324	225,462	6.9
6552	Subdividers and developers, n.e.c.	670	698	6.8	4,023	5,217	27,467	28,828	119,046	153,123	6.9
6553	Cemetery subdividers and developers	343	334	5.4	3,735	4,419	15,284	13,791	61,660	65,761	7.1
6700	Holding and other investment offices	2,280	2,350	10.1	15,984	18,367	41,898	48,243	712,143	889,698	6.4
6710	Holding offices	561	600	7.1	7,262	9,648	52,767	58,610	404,840	548,030	6.7
6720	Investment offices	68	63	7.3	309	250	57,463	45,952	18,226	12,476	0.8
6730	Trusts	422	431	8.3	2,611	3,119	20,538	24,205	60,100	78,932	8.3
6732	Educational, religious, etc. trusts	144	150	6.1	1,105	1,238	18,675	19,887	22,123	25,568	4.5
6733	Trusts, n.e.c.	278	279	10.4	1,506	1,879	21,904	27,027	37,977	53,192	13.9
6790	Miscellaneous investing	1,159	1,132	15.0	5,131	4,887	41,596	44,677	224,629	231,660	8.6
6792	Oil royalty traders	302	310	44.4	977	1,005	37,711	40,736	40,154	42,892	43.1
6794	Patent owners and lessors	87	73	5.1	903	799	33,564	35,474	36,943	34,111	4.9
6798	Real estate investment trusts	38	43	7.1	283	301	22,403	34,365	7,130	13,083	3.1
6799	Investors, n.e.c.	732	706	14.7	2,968	2,782	47,148	49,859	140,402	141,574	9.6
UTAH											
60 –	**Finance, insurance, and real estate**	4,242	4,532	0.7	44,084	44,958	24,943	26,284	1,113,665	1,227,551	0.5
6000	Depository institutions	740	776	0.7	14,362	14,481	24,031	25,716	349,083	375,484	0.6
6020	Commercial banks	456	478	0.7	9,323	9,246	24,801	26,782	229,953	245,584	0.5
6030	Savings institutions	35	49	0.3	665	745	26,370	27,903	17,934	21,801	0.3

*Source: County Business Patterns, 1994/95, CBP-94/95, U.S. Department of Commerce, Washington, D.C., November 1997. SIC categories for which data were suppressed or not available for both 1994 and 1995 are *not* displayed. The employment columns represent mid-March employment in the year. Pay per employee is calculated by dividing 1st Quarter payroll, annualized, by mid-March employment. The columns headed "% US" show the state's percentage of the national total for the SIC in 1995; for example, 1.4% for SIC 6000 means that the state had 1.4 percent of the national total establishments (or payroll) in SIC 6000 in 1995. A dash (-) is used to indicate that data are not available or cannot be calculated; nec means not elsewhere classified.*

Continued on next page.

SIC	Industry	No. Establishments			Employment		Pay / Employee		Annual Payroll ($ 000)		
		1994	1995	% US	1994	1995	1994	1995	1994	1995	% US
UTAH - [continued]											
6060	Credit unions	230	237	1.6	2,469	2,585	17,431	18,072	47,280	51,237	1.5
6100	Nondepository institutions	430	473	1.0	6,797	5,711	26,755	26,198	160,441	161,139	0.9
6140	Personal credit institutions	129	143	0.8	1,145	1,556	24,409	27,488	28,782	44,038	0.8
6150	Business credit institutions	53	51	1.1	1,754	1,643	20,509	23,041	35,955	36,268	0.8
6160	Mortgage bankers and brokers	242	270	1.3	3,673	2,274	30,838	28,069	90,915	75,937	1.0
6200	Security and commodity brokers	175	202	0.5	1,391	1,482	53,104	54,391	67,361	83,698	0.2
6210	Security brokers and dealers	88	90	0.4	1,048	1,138	59,836	60,243	56,073	66,971	0.2
6300	Insurance carriers	281	306	0.7	5,822	6,199	27,856	31,361	170,585	196,651	0.3
6310	Life insurance	70	71	0.6	2,174	1,810	24,585	28,621	51,948	50,846	0.3
6320	Medical service and health insurance	30	33	1.1	1,743	1,969	26,460	30,031	54,837	60,656	0.6
6321	Accident and health insurance	14	15	1.4	488	538	27,697	30,543	16,529	16,474	1.0
6324	Hospital and medical service plans	16	18	0.9	1,255	1,431	25,979	29,839	38,308	44,182	0.6
6330	Fire, marine, and casualty insurance	147	163	0.8	1,223	1,757	34,067	36,421	43,369	65,587	0.3
6360	Title insurance	14	18	0.7	254	241	24,079	27,270	7,392	7,172	0.5
6370	Pension, health, and welfare funds	14	12	0.5	386	367	35,461	32,589	12,036	11,328	1.1
6400	Insurance agents, brokers, and service	887	920	0.7	5,125	5,353	25,456	27,119	142,635	152,726	0.7
6500	Real estate	1,588	1,704	0.7	8,844	9,223	17,437	17,667	167,397	185,620	0.6
6510	Real estate operators and lessors	513	535	0.5	2,797	2,935	15,638	16,226	48,066	52,788	0.6
6530	Real estate agents and managers	850	866	0.8	4,889	5,178	16,277	17,359	89,417	100,299	0.5
6540	Title abstract offices	51	52	1.1	676	466	20,367	22,833	13,723	13,008	1.5
6550	Subdividers and developers	138	173	1.0	446	525	36,493	23,703	14,789	15,800	0.5
6552	Subdividers and developers, n.e.c.	110	138	1.3	351	432	26,439	24,944	11,434	13,290	0.6
6553	Cemetery subdividers and developers	15	16	0.3	76	77	14,632	17,455	1,472	2,019	0.2
6700	Holding and other investment offices	132	143	0.6	857	1,028	28,331	36,669	22,512	30,803	0.2
6710	Holding offices	34	40	0.5	489	588	31,869	45,442	12,788	18,495	0.2
6730	Trusts	29	35	0.7	110	134	13,018	16,716	1,877	2,669	0.3
6732	Educational, religious, etc. trusts	13	14	0.6	58	61	10,552	12,787	692	937	0.2
6733	Trusts, n.e.c.	16	21	0.8	52	73	15,769	20,000	1,185	1,732	0.5
6790	Miscellaneous investing	64	56	0.7	249	298	28,321	29,060	7,731	9,330	0.3
6794	Patent owners and lessors	13	10	0.7	114	117	28,491	24,684	3,571	3,356	0.5
6799	Investors, n.e.c.	42	39	0.8	123	163	30,407	33,669	3,971	5,763	0.4
VERMONT											
60 –	**Finance, insurance, and real estate**	1,513	1,516	0.2	12,261	12,894	27,548	30,882	332,097	390,874	0.2
6000	Depository institutions	309	305	0.3	4,551	4,734	23,510	25,444	103,595	114,078	0.2
6020	Commercial banks	215	213	0.3	3,378	3,385	23,693	26,860	77,090	85,378	0.2
6030	Savings institutions	35	35	0.2	794	945	23,859	21,820	18,404	19,875	0.3
6160	Mortgage bankers and brokers	27	29	0.1	266	226	29,158	26,637	6,478	6,019	0.1
6200	Security and commodity brokers	59	70	0.2	407	557	63,744	68,855	24,924	34,199	0.1
6210	Security brokers and dealers	32	40	0.2	274	321	67,620	52,025	16,562	16,846	0.0
6300	Insurance carriers	98	96	0.2	2,582	2,461	34,098	40,538	80,774	99,775	0.2
6310	Life insurance	32	28	0.2	1,454	1,351	38,176	48,536	48,043	63,371	0.3
6320	Medical service and health insurance	9	8	0.3	433	428	26,762	28,533	11,779	12,408	0.1
6330	Fire, marine, and casualty insurance	45	47	0.2	653	627	30,322	32,951	19,673	22,466	0.1
6370	Pension, health, and welfare funds	7	6	0.3	32	42	23,375	20,857	865	1,058	0.1
6400	Insurance agents, brokers, and service	327	315	0.3	1,486	1,506	27,752	29,232	43,224	45,082	0.2
6500	Real estate	622	631	0.3	2,055	2,438	17,242	21,293	38,191	53,863	0.2
6510	Real estate operators and lessors	159	160	0.2	585	954	17,497	26,197	9,743	24,568	0.3
6530	Real estate agents and managers	352	351	0.3	1,305	1,279	17,232	18,549	24,588	25,382	0.1
6550	Subdividers and developers	98	96	0.5	160	180	16,525	16,333	3,729	3,494	0.1
6552	Subdividers and developers, n.e.c.	39	40	0.4	116	138	19,828	18,870	2,922	2,822	0.1
6553	Cemetery subdividers and developers	58	55	0.9	44	42	7,818	8,000	762	667	0.1
6700	Holding and other investment offices	52	52	0.2	587	623	35,434	38,626	21,821	24,286	0.2
6710	Holding offices	31	29	0.3	487	504	35,877	37,952	17,206	18,764	0.2
6732	Educational, religious, etc. trusts	8	7	0.3	27	30	14,222	14,667	665	650	0.1
VIRGINIA											
60 –	**Finance, insurance, and real estate**	14,927	15,202	2.4	164,064	165,377	31,724	32,606	5,250,275	5,361,563	2.1

Source: County Business Patterns, 1994/95, CBP-94/95, U.S. Department of Commerce, Washington, D.C., November 1997. SIC categories for which data were suppressed or not available for both 1994 and 1995 are *not* displayed. The employment columns represent mid-March employment in the year. Pay per employee is calculated by dividing 1st Quarter payroll, annualized, by mid-March employment. The columns headed "% US" show the state's percentage of the national total for the SIC in 1995; for example, 1.4% for SIC 6000 means that the state had 1.4 percent of the national total establishments (or payroll) in SIC 6000 in 1995. A dash (-) is used to indicate that data are not available or cannot be calculated; *nec* means not elsewhere classified.

Continued on next page.

SIC	Industry	No. Establishments			Employment		Pay / Employee		Annual Payroll ($ 000)		
		1994	1995	% US	1994	1995	1994	1995	1994	1995	% US
VIRGINIA - [continued]											
6000	Depository institutions	3,002	2,971	2.8	52,228	54,945	26,427	27,696	1,389,355	1,479,338	2.4
6020	Commercial banks	2,208	2,189	3.3	39,377	42,321	26,433	27,607	1,031,858	1,121,987	2.5
6030	Savings institutions	333	306	1.8	4,110	3,351	26,067	26,907	102,158	81,822	1.1
6060	Credit unions	377	378	2.5	6,325	6,548	22,194	23,502	154,886	165,093	4.7
6100	Nondepository institutions	1,149	1,198	2.6	16,019	17,256	44,663	43,079	674,457	714,882	3.9
6110	Federal and Federally-sponsored credit	42	46	3.4	4,158	4,369	65,538	70,007	235,286	272,690	24.7
6140	Personal credit institutions	388	427	2.4	2,651	2,540	29,904	28,935	75,901	74,935	1.4
6150	Business credit institutions	95	94	2.0	1,357	4,602	41,185	33,865	114,759	151,081	3.4
6160	Mortgage bankers and brokers	620	613	3.0	7,852	5,734	39,197	36,249	248,339	215,524	2.9
6200	Security and commodity brokers	767	800	2.0	6,723	7,329	65,677	54,223	453,408	454,761	1.0
6210	Security brokers and dealers	401	402	1.7	4,892	5,335	67,411	57,236	321,272	336,173	1.0
6300	Insurance carriers	1,096	1,149	2.8	29,497	28,508	33,333	36,426	968,218	1,013,066	1.8
6310	Life insurance	299	295	2.5	8,761	8,656	31,673	33,232	278,988	270,449	1.4
6320	Medical service and health insurance	64	69	2.3	5,108	4,479	32,859	41,014	158,015	168,516	1.7
6321	Accident and health insurance	26	27	2.6	480	474	23,900	26,262	12,254	11,945	0.7
6324	Hospital and medical service plans	38	42	2.2	4,628	4,005	33,788	42,760	145,761	156,571	2.0
6330	Fire, marine, and casualty insurance	549	588	2.8	14,140	14,067	34,453	37,077	484,885	520,442	2.1
6350	Surety insurance	12	13	2.2	268	174	45,776	42,736	10,674	6,663	1.3
6360	Title insurance	99	114	4.5	860	700	32,474	35,914	24,489	22,841	1.7
6370	Pension, health, and welfare funds	67	56	2.5	329	356	29,435	30,528	9,735	21,974	2.2
6390	Insurance carriers, n.e.c.	4	6	3.5	31	65	27,871	30,031	1,398	2,026	2.2
6400	Insurance agents, brokers, and service	2,888	2,930	2.3	14,377	14,385	28,978	31,095	427,204	444,808	1.9
6500	Real estate	5,545	5,662	2.3	35,673	35,216	20,703	22,600	811,459	830,762	2.5
6510	Real estate operators and lessors	1,877	1,938	1.9	10,752	10,172	16,231	17,664	187,601	191,268	2.0
6530	Real estate agents and managers	2,979	2,952	2.6	20,849	20,687	22,841	24,660	524,330	527,748	2.8
6540	Title abstract offices	115	110	2.3	778	445	25,537	27,479	17,572	13,572	1.6
6550	Subdividers and developers	449	456	2.6	3,181	3,572	20,795	23,890	77,616	87,682	2.7
6552	Subdividers and developers, n.e.c.	291	291	2.8	1,944	2,381	24,031	27,052	54,807	64,251	2.9
6553	Cemetery subdividers and developers	140	136	2.2	1,235	1,119	15,715	17,008	22,280	21,324	2.3
6700	Holding and other investment offices	444	455	2.0	4,942	4,128	48,761	54,989	237,740	236,228	1.7
6710	Holding offices	161	149	1.8	2,945	1,971	61,218	76,530	172,906	155,565	1.9
6720	Investment offices	11	13	1.5	26	81	36,769	60,889	1,195	6,739	0.4
6730	Trusts	116	129	2.5	1,046	1,144	22,107	23,948	25,043	29,222	3.1
6732	Educational, religious, etc. trusts	73	83	3.4	531	505	33,416	32,222	18,825	17,239	3.0
6733	Trusts, n.e.c.	43	45	1.7	515	638	10,447	17,404	6,218	11,973	3.1
6790	Miscellaneous investing	145	142	1.9	909	895	40,180	48,483	38,251	43,057	1.6
6794	Patent owners and lessors	40	35	2.4	317	278	29,085	39,065	10,353	11,224	1.6
6799	Investors, n.e.c.	69	70	1.5	328	261	64,561	85,349	20,042	21,399	1.4
WASHINGTON											
60 –	**Finance, insurance, and real estate**	14,189	14,405	2.3	130,341	123,342	30,282	31,451	3,814,422	3,847,357	1.5
6000	Depository institutions	2,229	2,163	2.1	40,582	36,823	27,041	28,462	1,085,958	1,040,052	1.7
6010	Central reserve depository	3	3	3.2	454	441	36,308	42,630	14,556	15,815	1.6
6020	Commercial banks	1,318	1,301	1.9	23,784	24,405	26,736	28,630	628,038	666,454	1.5
6030	Savings institutions	470	426	2.6	10,191	5,928	28,285	28,457	289,837	193,161	2.6
6060	Credit unions	323	326	2.2	4,974	5,033	22,514	23,717	111,630	121,304	3.4
6080	Foreign bank and branches and agencies	10	10	1.5	178	178	50,022	53,281	9,226	10,508	0.4
6090	Functions closely related to banking	105	95	1.8	1,001	836	35,828	39,435	32,671	32,589	1.5
6100	Nondepository institutions	1,128	1,101	2.4	9,974	7,777	34,754	35,555	294,845	285,921	1.6
6140	Personal credit institutions	245	268	1.5	1,491	1,611	30,573	33,460	46,241	53,942	1.0
6160	Mortgage bankers and brokers	749	691	3.4	7,385	5,079	34,828	35,090	206,891	187,936	2.5
6200	Security and commodity brokers	761	822	2.0	5,761	5,921	63,731	64,994	359,108	386,684	0.8
6210	Security brokers and dealers	465	496	2.0	4,659	4,722	67,154	68,050	296,317	317,985	0.9
6220	Commodity contracts brokers, dealers	13	14	0.9	23	32	39,304	29,000	1,114	1,167	0.2
6280	Security and commodity services	280	306	2.1	1,078	1,162	49,495	53,780	61,628	67,233	0.7
6300	Insurance carriers	820	824	2.0	25,662	24,035	37,302	38,679	847,598	871,918	1.5
6310	Life insurance	177	176	1.5	6,177	5,974	34,467	35,359	195,805	195,996	1.0
6320	Medical service and health insurance	67	60	2.0	5,319	5,731	32,863	33,210	171,056	187,413	1.9

Source: County Business Patterns, 1994/95, CBP-94/95, U.S. Department of Commerce, Washington, D.C., November 1997. SIC categories for which data were suppressed or not available for both 1994 and 1995 are *not* displayed. The employment columns represent mid-March employment in the year. Pay per employee is calculated by dividing 1st Quarter payroll, annualized, by mid-March employment. The columns headed "% US" show the state's percentage of the national total for the SIC in 1995; for example, 1.4% for SIC 6000 means that the state had 1.4 percent of the national total establishments (or payroll) in SIC 6000 in 1995. A dash (-) is used to indicate that data are not available or cannot be calculated; *nec* means not elsewhere classified.

Continued on next page.

SIC	Industry	No. Establishments			Employment		Pay / Employee		Annual Payroll ($ 000)		
		1994	1995	% US	1994	1995	1994	1995	1994	1995	% US
WASHINGTON - [continued]											
6321	Accident and health insurance	17	17	1.6	364	401	30,066	29,855	10,695	10,637	0.6
6324	Hospital and medical service plans	50	43	2.2	4,955	5,330	33,069	33,463	160,361	176,776	2.2
6330	Fire, marine, and casualty insurance	463	467	2.2	11,105	9,894	41,464	44,739	390,204	406,779	1.7
6360	Title insurance	58	63	2.5	2,059	1,418	36,606	35,599	57,295	46,045	3.4
6370	Pension, health, and welfare funds	44	42	1.8	852	861	31,850	32,409	26,335	28,285	2.8
6400	Insurance agents, brokers, and service	2,423	2,513	2.0	13,213	13,320	32,537	34,312	436,153	457,066	2.0
6500	Real estate	6,440	6,550	2.7	32,190	32,077	18,838	19,754	653,636	661,778	2.0
6510	Real estate operators and lessors	2,825	2,845	2.8	11,196	11,711	14,721	15,410	186,984	198,534	2.1
6530	Real estate agents and managers	2,944	2,903	2.5	17,887	16,693	20,327	21,101	380,275	364,327	1.9
6540	Title abstract offices	37	40	0.8	602	513	23,336	24,164	14,256	13,161	1.5
6550	Subdividers and developers	486	525	3.0	2,382	2,716	25,914	29,097	67,418	75,018	2.3
6552	Subdividers and developers, n.e.c.	362	387	3.7	1,654	1,783	27,879	33,999	49,805	54,844	2.5
6553	Cemetery subdividers and developers	96	98	1.6	706	703	21,649	22,521	16,297	16,711	1.8
6700	Holding and other investment offices	364	411	1.8	2,560	3,071	48,302	44,556	118,439	132,263	1.0
6710	Holding offices	96	108	1.3	1,389	1,401	61,898	68,674	75,824	86,495	1.1
6720	Investment offices	17	16	1.9	49	165	34,776	24,558	3,332	4,042	0.2
6730	Trusts	101	123	2.4	543	635	28,309	22,129	14,728	18,801	2.0
6732	Educational, religious, etc. trusts	28	34	1.4	161	164	35,727	23,415	5,671	4,341	0.8
6733	Trusts, n.e.c.	73	88	3.3	382	471	25,183	21,682	9,057	14,459	3.8
6790	Miscellaneous investing	135	138	1.8	560	675	36,000	29,736	23,623	20,200	0.8
6794	Patent owners and lessors	29	27	1.9	264	277	28,348	16,477	10,722	5,678	0.8
6798	Real estate investment trusts	9	11	1.8	30	109	18,400	10,275	522	1,405	0.3
6799	Investors, n.e.c.	97	100	2.1	266	289	45,579	49,785	12,379	13,117	0.9
WEST VIRGINIA											
60 –	**Finance, insurance, and real estate**	3,176	3,224	0.5	24,776	24,571	22,331	23,428	557,938	573,787	0.2
6000	Depository institutions	679	666	0.6	12,261	11,914	19,989	21,155	243,365	243,539	0.4
6020	Commercial banks	498	486	0.7	11,017	10,634	20,348	21,494	221,712	219,646	0.5
6030	Savings institutions	42	43	0.3	535	596	19,312	19,711	10,506	11,600	0.2
6140	Personal credit institutions	94	101	0.6	451	487	23,557	25,552	11,036	12,820	0.2
6160	Mortgage bankers and brokers	20	24	0.1	64	46	27,750	32,087	1,882	2,277	0.0
6200	Security and commodity brokers	95	97	0.2	550	528	63,891	61,098	29,594	29,318	0.1
6210	Security brokers and dealers	71	71	0.3	508	489	67,433	64,245	28,631	28,318	0.1
6280	Security and commodity services	24	26	0.2	42	39	21,048	21,641	963	1,000	0.0
6300	Insurance carriers	211	199	0.5	3,226	3,194	26,326	28,339	89,982	90,430	0.2
6310	Life insurance	82	75	0.6	1,245	1,201	25,015	25,572	32,300	29,280	0.1
6320	Medical service and health insurance	15	15	0.5	1,232	1,209	20,591	22,581	27,362	28,859	0.3
6330	Fire, marine, and casualty insurance	98	94	0.5	652	650	40,325	45,791	28,015	29,457	0.1
6400	Insurance agents, brokers, and service	748	773	0.6	3,072	3,199	23,661	25,200	75,335	82,623	0.4
6500	Real estate	1,204	1,247	0.5	4,191	4,166	15,107	14,979	64,870	68,881	0.2
6510	Real estate operators and lessors	639	658	0.7	2,382	2,237	15,563	14,997	34,628	37,503	0.4
6530	Real estate agents and managers	367	377	0.3	1,137	1,129	14,093	15,844	18,657	18,877	0.1
6550	Subdividers and developers	182	178	1.0	667	694	15,250	14,380	11,312	11,220	0.3
6552	Subdividers and developers, n.e.c.	64	62	0.6	182	184	16,571	16,674	3,140	3,152	0.1
6553	Cemetery subdividers and developers	115	108	1.8	484	505	14,711	13,584	8,091	7,897	0.9
6700	Holding and other investment offices	110	103	0.4	903	972	41,980	43,366	40,274	42,292	0.3
6710	Holding offices	41	43	0.5	650	702	47,551	49,396	32,827	34,787	0.4
6792	Oil royalty traders	12	10	1.4	102	81	40,078	39,704	4,104	3,232	3.2
6799	Investors, n.e.c.	21	17	0.4	56	78	28,143	33,846	2,016	2,582	0.2
WISCONSIN											
60 –	**Finance, insurance, and real estate**	11,618	11,776	1.9	142,881	141,858	29,497	31,573	4,172,605	4,355,796	1.7
6000	Depository institutions	2,383	2,360	2.3	43,054	42,076	22,364	24,015	982,593	982,922	1.6
6020	Commercial banks	1,343	1,320	2.0	28,995	28,362	22,755	24,411	667,061	668,407	1.5
6030	Savings institutions	498	498	3.0	7,593	7,087	22,550	23,844	171,195	168,641	2.3
6060	Credit unions	499	491	3.3	4,713	4,870	16,607	17,993	81,548	88,315	2.5
6090	Functions closely related to banking	43	50	0.9	1,753	1,757	30,560	34,996	62,789	57,400	2.7
6100	Nondepository institutions	516	567	1.2	6,711	6,515	29,947	28,318	180,569	186,216	1.0

Source: County Business Patterns, 1994/95, CBP-94/95, U.S. Department of Commerce, Washington, D.C., November 1997. SIC categories for which data were suppressed or not available for both 1994 and 1995 are not displayed. The employment columns represent mid-March employment in the year. Pay per employee is calculated by dividing 1st Quarter payroll, annualized, by mid-March employment. The columns headed "% US" show the state's percentage of the national total for the SIC in 1995; for example, 1.4% for SIC 6000 means that the state had 1.4 percent of the national total establishments (or payroll) in SIC 6000 in 1995. A dash (-) is used to indicate that data are not available or cannot be calculated; nec means not elsewhere classified.

Continued on next page.

SIC	Industry	No. Establishments			Employment		Pay / Employee		Annual Payroll ($ 000)		
		1994	1995	% US	1994	1995	1994	1995	1994	1995	% US
WISCONSIN - [continued]											
6110	Federal and Federally-sponsored credit	37	37	2.8	445	440	38,274	39,745	13,644	14,304	1.3
6140	Personal credit institutions	213	232	1.3	1,896	1,992	28,496	30,845	52,020	57,610	1.1
6150	Business credit institutions	52	57	1.2	440	468	33,809	36,342	13,691	16,596	0.4
6160	Mortgage bankers and brokers	212	238	1.2	3,928	3,613	29,280	24,498	101,205	97,684	1.3
6200	Security and commodity brokers	621	639	1.6	5,522	5,710	61,263	69,394	310,354	360,142	0.8
6210	Security brokers and dealers	406	402	1.7	4,033	4,151	63,000	69,363	214,451	253,393	0.7
6220	Commodity contracts brokers, dealers	9	9	0.6	34	41	24,118	19,317	994	1,092	0.1
6280	Security and commodity services	205	224	1.5	1,455	1,506	57,317	71,296	94,870	105,400	1.1
6300	Insurance carriers	755	768	1.9	52,013	51,554	36,688	39,057	1,822,617	1,912,919	3.4
6310	Life insurance	199	196	1.7	23,035	23,860	43,758	44,520	941,198	982,475	5.0
6320	Medical service and health insurance	92	98	3.3	9,406	9,225	28,044	31,602	256,636	289,996	3.0
6321	Accident and health insurance	29	29	2.8	3,271	3,135	28,155	37,659	93,587	115,851	7.0
6324	Hospital and medical service plans	63	68	3.5	6,135	6,089	27,985	28,485	163,049	174,120	2.2
6330	Fire, marine, and casualty insurance	385	395	1.9	17,926	16,971	32,166	35,392	563,176	580,460	2.4
6350	Surety insurance	13	14	2.4	680	657	46,941	53,053	33,120	34,900	6.6
6370	Pension, health, and welfare funds	53	46	2.0	753	638	27,458	26,520	21,428	18,141	1.8
6400	Insurance agents, brokers, and service	3,166	3,182	2.5	14,814	13,102	24,201	26,686	384,571	362,882	1.6
6500	Real estate	3,870	3,942	1.6	16,906	18,062	16,649	17,344	318,779	348,856	1.1
6510	Real estate operators and lessors	1,546	1,568	1.6	6,300	6,789	13,537	14,805	98,954	113,109	1.2
6530	Real estate agents and managers	1,736	1,716	1.5	8,174	8,508	18,196	19,040	164,958	173,931	0.9
6540	Title abstract offices	136	139	2.9	1,143	1,024	20,276	19,078	24,625	22,796	2.6
6550	Subdividers and developers	400	419	2.4	1,252	1,568	18,511	18,699	28,245	35,511	1.1
6552	Subdividers and developers, n.e.c.	138	156	1.5	533	737	26,199	25,883	17,219	23,281	1.1
6553	Cemetery subdividers and developers	249	245	4.0	707	790	12,458	12,289	10,692	11,165	1.2
6700	Holding and other investment offices	296	308	1.3	3,122	4,059	42,980	44,735	143,129	171,032	1.2
6710	Holding offices	145	158	1.9	2,545	3,051	46,059	51,375	123,085	148,020	1.8
6720	Investment offices	8	9	1.0	25	24	13,760	23,667	407	676	0.0
6730	Trusts	51	50	1.0	170	586	27,694	14,246	5,925	8,642	0.9
6732	Educational, religious, etc. trusts	16	15	0.6	44	52	27,182	23,692	1,168	1,496	0.3
6733	Trusts, n.e.c.	34	34	1.3	126	534	27,873	13,326	4,755	7,143	1.9
6790	Miscellaneous investing	83	77	1.0	382	348	31,183	41,103	13,301	12,506	0.5
6794	Patent owners and lessors	20	19	1.3	109	125	22,789	20,928	2,846	3,106	0.4
6799	Investors, n.e.c.	57	53	1.1	260	212	34,046	46,962	9,710	8,194	0.6
WYOMING											
60 –	**Finance, insurance, and real estate**	1,315	1,318	0.2	7,737	7,028	22,471	23,918	171,381	168,427	0.1
6000	Depository institutions	195	188	0.2	3,278	2,986	23,555	24,703	81,496	70,649	0.1
6020	Commercial banks	118	113	0.2	2,530	2,375	23,562	24,724	63,919	57,355	0.1
6030	Savings institutions	29	27	0.2	410	247	28,380	35,741	11,322	6,909	0.1
6160	Mortgage bankers and brokers	18	19	0.1	172	135	38,860	34,193	5,034	4,566	0.1
6200	Security and commodity brokers	71	74	0.2	269	262	56,461	58,397	14,105	16,118	0.0
6300	Insurance carriers	71	73	0.2	700	656	26,074	31,457	18,180	19,179	0.0
6310	Life insurance	13	12	0.1	199	174	29,226	29,701	5,502	4,951	0.0
6330	Fire, marine, and casualty insurance	22	25	0.1	111	115	32,288	39,513	3,549	4,028	0.0
6500	Real estate	580	584	0.2	1,782	1,639	11,969	13,096	22,908	24,492	0.1
6510	Real estate operators and lessors	277	280	0.3	774	758	10,853	11,193	9,181	9,932	0.1
6530	Real estate agents and managers	246	245	0.2	693	734	13,183	14,120	10,340	11,222	0.1
6540	Title abstract offices	10	9	0.2	44	37	17,636	19,784	990	941	0.1
6550	Subdividers and developers	30	29	0.2	241	67	10,871	19,761	1,956	1,592	0.0
6710	Holding offices	13	14	0.2	49	74	74,449	49,351	2,098	2,418	0.0
6733	Trusts, n.e.c.	6	6	0.2	110	93	10,691	9,505	1,061	885	0.2
6790	Miscellaneous investing	17	20	0.3	22	29	64,000	68,552	1,180	4,569	0.2

Source: County Business Patterns, 1994/95, CBP-94/95, U.S. Department of Commerce, Washington, D.C., November 1997. SIC categories for which data were suppressed or not available for both 1994 and 1995 are *not* displayed. The employment columns represent mid-March employment in the year. Pay per employee is calculated by dividing 1st Quarter payroll, annualized, by mid-March employment. The columns headed "% US" show the state's percentage of the national total for the SIC in 1995; for example, 1.4% for SIC 6000 means that the state had 1.4 percent of the national total establishments (or payroll) in SIC 6000 in 1995. A dash (-) is used to indicate that data are not available or cannot be calculated; *nec* means not elsewhere classified.

FINANCE, INSURANCE, AND REAL ESTATE BY COUNTY

ALABAMA

SIC	Industry	No. Establishments			Employment		Pay / Employee		Annual Payroll ($ 000)		
		1994	1995	% State	1994	1995	1994	1995	1994	1995	% State
AUTAUGA, AL											
60 –	**Finance, insurance, and real estate**	53	57	0.7	295	295	20,705	22,495	6,595	7,006	0.3
6000	Depository institutions	12	13	0.9	167	174	20,862	22,437	3,680	3,774	0.5
6020	Commercial banks	9	10	0.9	144	156	22,389	23,026	3,435	3,506	0.5
6100	Nondepository institutions	8	8	1.0	27	27	24,593	25,185	724	956	0.6
6300	Insurance carriers	5	5	0.6	52	44	23,154	28,455	1,383	1,218	0.2
6400	Insurance agents, brokers, and service	9	9	0.6	12	8	12,000	12,500	150	153	0.1
6500	Real estate	16	19	0.7	31	36	16,129	15,333	537	742	0.3
6530	Real estate agents and managers	6	7	0.6	12	13	22,000	18,462	283	204	0.1
BALDWIN, AL											
60 –	**Finance, insurance, and real estate**	304	312	3.9	1,756	2,029	19,478	18,835	37,413	41,742	1.9
6000	Depository institutions	32	32	2.1	481	498	20,757	21,574	9,900	10,115	1.3
6020	Commercial banks	26	28	2.6	469	480	20,785	21,750	9,669	9,772	1.4
6100	Nondepository institutions	21	23	2.8	56	66	20,500	18,182	1,253	1,444	0.9
6140	Personal credit institutions	9	9	1.8	30	32	19,600	20,375	672	687	1.0
6160	Mortgage bankers and brokers	6	9	4.0	14	22	25,143	14,545	361	527	0.7
6200	Security and commodity brokers	12	12	4.5	38	38	40,842	36,947	1,395	1,692	1.3
6210	Security brokers and dealers	9	9	4.7	31	30	48,000	42,000	1,287	1,511	1.2
6280	Security and commodity services	3	3	4.2	7	8	9,143	18,000	108	181	1.6
6300	Insurance carriers	19	20	2.2	133	127	35,278	36,535	4,902	4,844	0.9
6330	Fire, marine, and casualty insurance	14	15	2.7	73	81	38,849	41,333	3,252	3,535	1.5
6400	Insurance agents, brokers, and service	42	47	3.0	129	142	22,109	23,352	2,973	3,454	1.4
6500	Real estate	174	173	6.4	911	1,151	15,205	14,586	16,861	20,070	7.4
6510	Real estate operators and lessors	30	27	2.4	193	293	15,150	12,669	3,079	4,389	5.2
6530	Real estate agents and managers	111	114	9.8	521	685	14,726	14,920	10,332	12,107	8.5
6540	Title abstract offices	7	7	11.7	50	46	17,040	17,304	913	952	13.0
6550	Subdividers and developers	22	21	8.4	145	127	16,524	16,220	2,512	2,552	8.1
6552	Subdividers and developers, n.e.c.	16	16	12.1	134	106	15,701	16,566	2,221	2,064	10.8
6553	Cemetery subdividers and developers	4	4	4.3	11	19	26,545	15,368	289	393	3.5
6700	Holding and other investment offices	4	5	2.5	8	7	15,500	17,714	129	123	0.1
BARBOUR, AL											
60 –	**Finance, insurance, and real estate**	44	42	0.5	308	305	20,597	21,298	6,442	6,503	0.3
6000	Depository institutions	14	13	0.9	170	173	21,671	21,827	3,522	3,560	0.5
6300	Insurance carriers	9	9	1.0	80	82	22,000	24,341	1,869	2,080	0.4
6400	Insurance agents, brokers, and service	8	8	0.5	27	27	16,593	17,185	537	550	0.2
6500	Real estate	7	8	0.3	14	13	5,143	3,692	64	98	0.0
BIBB, AL											
60 –	**Finance, insurance, and real estate**	14	15	0.2	99	104	14,465	15,615	1,657	1,711	0.1
6000	Depository institutions	3	3	0.2	49	53	15,429	15,472	812	910	0.1
BLOUNT, AL											
60 –	**Finance, insurance, and real estate**	43	43	0.5	263	274	32,228	34,774	7,087	7,281	0.3
6000	Depository institutions	7	8	0.5	154	159	28,208	29,308	3,529	3,596	0.5
6400	Insurance agents, brokers, and service	10	10	0.6	25	26	16,640	21,538	487	491	0.2
6530	Real estate agents and managers	5	3	0.3	9	5	26,222	21,600	213	99	0.1
6550	Subdividers and developers	4	4	1.6	10	11	12,000	18,909	194	198	0.6
BUTLER, AL											
60 –	**Finance, insurance, and real estate**	30	31	0.4	207	192	17,101	21,896	3,869	4,276	0.2

Source: County Business Patterns, 1994/95, CBP-94/95, U.S. Department of Commerce, Washington, D.C., November 1997. SIC categories for which data were suppressed or not available for both 1994 and 1995 are *not* displayed. The employment columns represent mid-March employment in the year. Pay per employee is calculated by dividing 1st Quarter payroll, annualized, by mid-March employment. The columns headed "% State" show the county's percentage of the state total for the SIC in 1995; for example, 1.4% for SIC 6000 means that the county had 1.4 percent of the state's total establishments (or payroll) in SIC 6000 in 1995. A dash (-) is used to indicate that data are not available or cannot be calculated; *nec* means not elsewhere classified.

Continued on next page.

SIC	Industry	No. Establishments			Employment		Pay / Employee		Annual Payroll ($ 000)		
		1994	1995	% State	1994	1995	1994	1995	1994	1995	% State
BUTLER, AL - [continued]											
6000	Depository institutions	9	9	0.6	117	117	17,265	20,239	2,268	2,519	0.3
6400	Insurance agents, brokers, and service	7	8	0.5	10	13	18,800	18,154	206	283	0.1
6500	Real estate	7	7	0.3	14	14	8,571	9,429	129	150	0.1
CALHOUN, AL											
60 –	**Finance, insurance, and real estate**	207	215	2.7	1,228	1,261	21,127	22,354	26,393	28,313	1.3
6000	Depository institutions	49	50	3.3	575	579	21,016	21,927	12,072	12,081	1.6
6020	Commercial banks	31	33	3.1	482	479	22,149	23,065	10,376	10,186	1.5
6100	Nondepository institutions	27	28	3.4	92	92	26,565	24,000	2,074	2,237	1.4
6140	Personal credit institutions	17	17	3.4	63	67	25,524	24,836	1,367	1,501	2.1
6300	Insurance carriers	32	30	3.4	228	248	25,667	30,194	6,216	7,047	1.3
6310	Life insurance	9	9	3.7	156	159	23,718	23,874	3,712	3,619	2.1
6400	Insurance agents, brokers, and service	34	36	2.3	110	106	15,164	14,981	2,057	2,362	1.0
6500	Real estate	58	62	2.3	189	199	11,894	13,286	2,534	2,936	1.1
6510	Real estate operators and lessors	26	26	2.3	93	98	9,548	10,776	1,003	1,127	1.3
6530	Real estate agents and managers	28	28	2.4	82	84	14,537	14,571	1,349	1,413	1.0
CHAMBERS, AL											
60 –	**Finance, insurance, and real estate**	35	39	0.5	208	234	21,808	25,487	4,564	5,483	0.2
6000	Depository institutions	11	11	0.7	143	153	23,273	26,013	3,198	3,442	0.4
6400	Insurance agents, brokers, and service	11	13	0.8	35	53	21,029	27,170	827	1,416	0.6
6510	Real estate operators and lessors	6	6	0.5	6	7	11,333	12,571	81	89	0.1
CHEROKEE, AL											
60 –	**Finance, insurance, and real estate**	24	24	0.3	126	156	16,635	19,615	2,246	3,200	0.1
6000	Depository institutions	7	6	0.4	83	80	16,771	17,950	1,381	1,467	0.2
6400	Insurance agents, brokers, and service	5	3	0.2	9	13	12,444	15,077	151	200	0.1
6500	Real estate	6	8	0.3	10	12	10,400	9,000	120	151	0.1
6510	Real estate operators and lessors	3	3	0.3	5	5	8,800	8,800	51	63	0.1
CHILTON, AL											
60 –	**Finance, insurance, and real estate**	42	45	0.6	273	274	20,469	22,788	6,035	6,384	0.3
6000	Depository institutions	9	9	0.6	147	148	18,748	20,297	3,032	3,128	0.4
6100	Nondepository institutions	9	9	1.1	37	37	16,216	20,541	637	748	0.5
6140	Personal credit institutions	9	9	1.8	37	37	16,216	20,541	637	748	1.1
6400	Insurance agents, brokers, and service	12	11	0.7	23	21	11,652	12,571	278	270	0.1
6500	Real estate	7	9	0.3	14	12	10,000	14,667	156	197	0.1
CHOCTAW, AL											
60 –	**Finance, insurance, and real estate**	18	14	0.2	94	85	20,681	22,682	1,780	1,829	0.1
6000	Depository institutions	5	5	0.3	63	60	22,286	24,400	1,205	1,299	0.2
6400	Insurance agents, brokers, and service	7	3	0.2	16	7	16,000	14,857	222	130	0.1
CLARKE, AL											
60 –	**Finance, insurance, and real estate**	50	51	0.6	363	423	23,747	22,903	7,838	9,188	0.4
6000	Depository institutions	14	14	0.9	197	244	26,457	22,443	4,246	4,943	0.6
6020	Commercial banks	11	11	1.0	191	234	26,702	22,769	4,123	4,793	0.7
6100	Nondepository institutions	4	5	0.6	18	14	22,444	26,000	288	355	0.2
6300	Insurance carriers	8	7	0.8	78	91	26,205	27,209	2,267	2,420	0.4
6400	Insurance agents, brokers, and service	13	12	0.8	52	55	15,000	21,018	839	1,183	0.5
6500	Real estate	8	10	0.4	15	14	9,067	11,143	152	222	0.1
CLAY, AL											
60 –	**Finance, insurance, and real estate**	16	15	0.2	96	94	16,750	17,362	1,714	1,713	0.1
6000	Depository institutions	6	7	0.5	70	71	18,343	18,761	1,315	1,341	0.2
6020	Commercial banks	6	7	0.7	70	71	18,343	18,761	1,315	1,341	0.2
CLEBURNE, AL											
60 –	**Finance, insurance, and real estate**	6	7	0.1	59	54	21,492	24,519	1,275	1,276	0.1

Source: County Business Patterns, 1994/95, CBP-94/95, U.S. Department of Commerce, Washington, D.C., November 1997. SIC categories for which data were suppressed or not available for both 1994 and 1995 are not displayed. The employment columns represent mid-March employment in the year. Pay per employee is calculated by dividing 1st Quarter payroll, annualized, by mid-March employment. The columns headed "% State" show the county's percentage of the state total for the SIC in 1995; for example, 1.4% for SIC 6000 means that the county had 1.4 percent of the state's total establishments (or payroll) in SIC 6000 in 1995. A dash (-) is used to indicate that data are not available or cannot be calculated; nec means not elsewhere classified.

SIC	Industry	No. Establishments			Employment		Pay / Employee		Annual Payroll ($ 000)		
		1994	1995	% State	1994	1995	1994	1995	1994	1995	% State
COFFEE, AL											
60 –	**Finance, insurance, and real estate**	91	81	*1.0*	609	559	18,837	21,245	12,391	11,742	*0.5*
6000	Depository institutions	24	21	*1.4*	309	246	19,340	21,301	6,824	5,401	*0.7*
6020	Commercial banks	19	15	*1.4*	267	200	18,757	21,580	6,068	4,597	*0.7*
6100	Nondepository institutions	11	10	*1.2*	49	55	23,755	27,418	1,162	1,507	*1.0*
6300	Insurance carriers	7	7	*0.8*	120	125	22,700	26,624	2,589	3,015	*0.5*
6500	Real estate	22	18	*0.7*	78	69	10,462	12,232	893	869	*0.3*
6510	Real estate operators and lessors	8	7	*0.6*	18	16	10,222	13,000	209	239	*0.3*
6530	Real estate agents and managers	9	7	*0.6*	43	41	11,814	11,610	535	515	*0.4*
COLBERT, AL											
60 –	**Finance, insurance, and real estate**	107	105	*1.3*	696	659	19,621	20,486	13,689	13,671	*0.6*
6000	Depository institutions	39	38	*2.5*	426	424	20,798	21,632	8,851	8,978	*1.2*
6020	Commercial banks	21	20	*1.9*	256	245	21,828	22,743	5,306	5,151	*0.8*
6400	Insurance agents, brokers, and service	21	19	*1.2*	66	74	24,485	21,351	1,780	1,616	*0.7*
6500	Real estate	33	32	*1.2*	157	119	12,790	13,546	1,889	1,813	*0.7*
6510	Real estate operators and lessors	11	10	*0.9*	27	19	10,519	12,000	236	248	*0.3*
6530	Real estate agents and managers	14	12	*1.0*	69	43	12,348	9,953	705	491	*0.3*
6540	Title abstract offices	3	3	*5.0*	10	10	25,600	26,000	285	281	*3.8*
6550	Subdividers and developers	5	6	*2.4*	51	46	12,078	14,957	663	762	*2.4*
CONECUH, AL											
60 –	**Finance, insurance, and real estate**	14	14	*0.2*	72	75	21,000	20,213	1,617	1,563	*0.1*
6000	Depository institutions	5	5	*0.3*	55	58	22,982	21,586	1,356	1,285	*0.2*
6020	Commercial banks	5	5	*0.5*	55	58	22,982	21,586	1,356	1,285	*0.2*
6510	Real estate operators and lessors	3	3	*0.3*	6	7	10,667	11,429	75	79	*0.1*
COVINGTON, AL											
60 –	**Finance, insurance, and real estate**	62	64	*0.8*	419	404	22,558	23,040	8,900	9,323	*0.4*
6000	Depository institutions	14	13	*0.9*	251	227	21,657	21,956	4,835	4,799	*0.6*
6020	Commercial banks	11	10	*0.9*	243	218	21,597	21,927	4,627	4,583	*0.7*
6060	Credit unions	3	3	*1.0*	8	9	23,500	22,667	208	216	*0.4*
6100	Nondepository institutions	5	7	*0.8*	12	12	16,667	17,000	186	291	*0.2*
6300	Insurance carriers	9	9	*1.0*	88	84	32,818	35,476	2,773	2,788	*0.5*
6310	Life insurance	3	3	*1.2*	57	56	36,702	37,214	1,879	1,784	*1.0*
6500	Real estate	16	16	*0.6*	29	32	8,828	9,500	270	328	*0.1*
6510	Real estate operators and lessors	5	5	*0.4*	11	10	3,273	3,600	33	38	*0.0*
6530	Real estate agents and managers	10	10	*0.9*	18	21	12,222	12,000	233	270	*0.2*
CRENSHAW, AL											
60 –	**Finance, insurance, and real estate**	14	13	*0.2*	91	161	17,802	12,373	1,887	2,185	*0.1*
6000	Depository institutions	4	4	*0.3*	60	118	20,000	11,458	1,436	1,502	*0.2*
6020	Commercial banks	4	4	*0.4*	60	118	20,000	11,458	1,436	1,502	*0.2*
6500	Real estate	5	4	*0.1*	16	14	6,250	6,571	105	93	*0.0*
CULLMAN, AL											
60 –	**Finance, insurance, and real estate**	116	123	*1.5*	617	707	20,512	25,748	13,035	17,160	*0.8*
6000	Depository institutions	29	29	*1.9*	356	347	19,427	20,945	6,868	7,348	*0.9*
6020	Commercial banks	21	22	*2.0*	291	290	19,203	20,828	5,440	5,984	*0.9*
6100	Nondepository institutions	18	19	*2.3*	67	60	25,254	27,600	1,776	2,013	*1.3*
6140	Personal credit institutions	12	13	*2.6*	50	46	22,320	26,174	1,182	1,323	*1.9*
6300	Insurance carriers	13	13	*1.5*	65	84	27,446	25,667	1,855	2,345	*0.4*
6500	Real estate	30	35	*1.3*	64	145	13,563	39,972	1,170	4,146	*1.5*
6510	Real estate operators and lessors	9	10	*0.9*	30	111	16,267	48,577	603	3,568	*4.2*
6530	Real estate agents and managers	13	15	*1.3*	22	21	12,182	11,619	344	255	*0.2*
6550	Subdividers and developers	6	7	*2.8*	10	11	10,800	10,909	186	257	*0.8*
DALE, AL											
60 –	**Finance, insurance, and real estate**	63	61	*0.8*	440	431	16,027	18,005	7,465	7,850	*0.4*

Source: County Business Patterns, 1994/95, CBP-94/95, U.S. Department of Commerce, Washington, D.C., November 1997. SIC categories for which data were suppressed or not available for both 1994 and 1995 are not displayed. The employment columns represent mid-March employment in the year. Pay per employee is calculated by dividing 1st Quarter payroll, annualized, by mid-March employment. The columns headed "% State" show the county's percentage of the state total for the SIC in 1995; for example, 1.4% for SIC 6000 means that the county had 1.4 percent of the state's total establishments (or payroll) in SIC 6000 in 1995. A dash (-) is used to indicate that data are not available or cannot be calculated; nec means not elsewhere classified.

Continued on next page.

SIC	Industry	No. Establishments			Employment		Pay / Employee		Annual Payroll ($ 000)		
		1994	1995	% State	1994	1995	1994	1995	1994	1995	% State
DALE, AL - [continued]											
6000	Depository institutions	20	18	*1.2*	278	280	15,871	17,929	4,536	4,948	*0.6*
6100	Nondepository institutions	5	4	*0.5*	23	21	21,043	22,857	509	529	*0.3*
6400	Insurance agents, brokers, and service	8	10	*0.6*	26	24	15,538	15,500	403	394	*0.2*
6500	Real estate	22	21	*0.8*	90	83	12,622	15,133	1,306	1,261	*0.5*
6510	Real estate operators and lessors	14	13	*1.2*	44	39	11,636	13,744	561	480	*0.6*
6530	Real estate agents and managers	8	8	*0.7*	46	44	13,565	16,364	745	781	*0.5*
DALLAS, AL											
60 –	**Finance, insurance, and real estate**	75	77	*1.0*	552	519	19,297	23,507	11,323	12,483	*0.6*
6000	Depository institutions	15	15	*1.0*	277	249	18,484	24,691	5,561	6,275	*0.8*
6020	Commercial banks	12	12	*1.1*	254	229	18,693	25,432	5,226	5,945	*0.9*
6100	Nondepository institutions	8	8	*1.0*	29	28	18,621	20,286	512	564	*0.4*
6300	Insurance carriers	9	9	*1.0*	109	110	25,798	29,345	2,883	3,094	*0.6*
6310	Life insurance	5	5	*2.1*	95	94	23,916	27,617	2,371	2,412	*1.4*
6400	Insurance agents, brokers, and service	14	14	*0.9*	49	46	19,510	22,870	1,041	1,132	*0.5*
6500	Real estate	25	28	*1.0*	82	80	10,293	11,150	994	1,113	*0.4*
6510	Real estate operators and lessors	14	15	*1.3*	21	24	8,190	9,333	242	298	*0.4*
DE KALB, AL											
60 –	**Finance, insurance, and real estate**	78	75	*0.9*	481	448	19,842	21,759	9,908	10,496	*0.5*
6000	Depository institutions	22	21	*1.4*	211	245	21,915	22,318	5,158	5,769	*0.7*
6300	Insurance carriers	11	11	*1.2*	62	60	34,129	35,267	2,409	2,453	*0.4*
6400	Insurance agents, brokers, and service	14	14	*0.9*	42	41	10,286	11,512	387	444	*0.2*
6500	Real estate	17	16	*0.6*	126	54	11,873	12,444	1,027	736	*0.3*
6510	Real estate operators and lessors	9	8	*0.7*	113	42	12,248	12,952	900	570	*0.7*
6530	Real estate agents and managers	5	5	*0.4*	10	10	8,800	11,200	102	143	*0.1*
6550	Subdividers and developers	3	3	*1.2*	3	2	8,000	8,000	25	23	*0.1*
6553	Cemetery subdividers and developers	3	3	*3.3*	3	2	8,000	8,000	25	23	*0.2*
ELMORE, AL											
60 –	**Finance, insurance, and real estate**	58	60	*0.8*	293	305	19,713	21,233	6,403	6,809	*0.3*
6000	Depository institutions	14	15	*1.0*	197	213	21,259	22,347	4,702	4,911	*0.6*
6140	Personal credit institutions	3	3	*0.6*	5	7	19,200	16,000	85	119	*0.2*
6400	Insurance agents, brokers, and service	9	8	*0.5*	26	22	18,462	21,818	483	495	*0.2*
6500	Real estate	26	26	*1.0*	52	44	10,077	10,818	541	515	*0.2*
6510	Real estate operators and lessors	9	11	*1.0*	17	12	8,000	10,000	142	128	*0.2*
ESCAMBIA, AL											
60 –	**Finance, insurance, and real estate**	57	56	*0.7*	507	550	23,282	23,324	11,261	14,447	*0.6*
6000	Depository institutions	17	15	*1.0*	287	285	23,401	23,060	6,099	7,202	*0.9*
6100	Nondepository institutions	6	6	*0.7*	21	21	21,143	22,667	500	527	*0.3*
6200	Security and commodity brokers	4	4	*1.5*	5	9	16,800	24,000	90	231	*0.2*
6300	Insurance carriers	4	4	*0.4*	59	56	31,593	29,071	1,794	1,717	*0.3*
6400	Insurance agents, brokers, and service	10	10	*0.6*	50	56	19,840	22,500	1,191	1,511	*0.6*
6500	Real estate	13	12	*0.4*	56	56	11,357	14,071	770	860	*0.3*
6510	Real estate operators and lessors	9	7	*0.6*	49	48	12,082	14,750	714	714	*0.8*
6700	Holding and other investment offices	3	5	*2.5*	29	67	36,828	28,179	817	2,399	*2.6*
ETOWAH, AL											
60 –	**Finance, insurance, and real estate**	159	157	*2.0*	1,158	1,085	25,320	25,644	29,280	27,712	*1.2*
6000	Depository institutions	23	26	*1.7*	473	477	23,197	25,149	10,667	11,221	*1.4*
6020	Commercial banks	17	20	*1.9*	351	339	22,746	24,944	7,433	7,689	*1.1*
6140	Personal credit institutions	13	12	*2.4*	55	49	29,891	32,490	1,603	1,428	*2.0*
6300	Insurance carriers	27	25	*2.8*	263	209	28,837	27,675	7,378	6,129	*1.1*
6400	Insurance agents, brokers, and service	39	36	*2.3*	129	135	21,116	23,733	2,996	3,393	*1.4*

Source: County Business Patterns, 1994/95, CBP-94/95, U.S. Department of Commerce, Washington, D.C., November 1997. SIC categories for which data were suppressed or not available for both 1994 and 1995 are *not* displayed. The employment columns represent mid-March employment in the year. Pay per employee is calculated by dividing 1st Quarter payroll, annualized, by mid-March employment. The columns headed "% State" show the county's percentage of the state total for the SIC in 1995; for example, 1.4% for SIC 6000 means that the county had 1.4 percent of the state's total establishments (or payroll) in SIC 6000 in 1995. A dash (-) is used to indicate that data are not available or cannot be calculated; *nec* means not elsewhere classified.

Continued on next page.

SIC	Industry	No. Establishments			Employment		Pay / Employee		Annual Payroll ($ 000)		
		1994	1995	% State	1994	1995	1994	1995	1994	1995	% State
ETOWAH, AL - [continued]											
6500	Real estate	43	46	1.7	135	143	12,859	12,364	1,921	1,937	0.7
6510	Real estate operators and lessors	20	19	1.7	71	73	9,070	8,329	609	696	0.8
6530	Real estate agents and managers	19	22	1.9	33	37	17,576	15,459	774	611	0.4
FAYETTE, AL											
60–	**Finance, insurance, and real estate**	19	16	0.2	99	103	22,465	24,117	2,397	2,659	0.1
6000	Depository institutions	6	6	0.4	61	71	28,197	28,056	1,952	2,119	0.3
6020	Commercial banks	6	6	0.6	61	71	28,197	28,056	1,952	2,119	0.3
6400	Insurance agents, brokers, and service	6	4	0.3	16	14	12,000	13,714	194	200	0.1
FRANKLIN, AL											
60–	**Finance, insurance, and real estate**	47	53	0.7	285	295	20,842	21,722	5,836	5,997	0.3
6000	Depository institutions	19	19	1.3	204	205	20,510	21,990	3,863	4,010	0.5
6020	Commercial banks	16	16	1.5	192	191	20,875	22,325	3,679	3,774	0.6
6060	Credit unions	3	3	1.0	12	14	14,667	17,429	184	236	0.4
6100	Nondepository institutions	3	4	0.5	6	7	20,000	21,143	124	165	0.1
6140	Personal credit institutions	3	3	0.6	6	7	20,000	21,143	124	141	0.2
6300	Insurance carriers	4	4	0.4	36	37	29,000	29,622	1,061	1,066	0.2
6500	Real estate	7	11	0.4	16	22	15,250	10,727	244	284	0.1
6510	Real estate operators and lessors	4	4	0.4	6	10	12,667	8,000	54	73	0.1
GENEVA, AL											
60–	**Finance, insurance, and real estate**	33	35	0.4	219	239	16,110	15,933	3,978	4,080	0.2
6000	Depository institutions	9	8	0.5	142	161	18,282	17,391	2,983	3,033	0.4
6400	Insurance agents, brokers, and service	10	10	0.6	29	31	11,310	11,742	350	362	0.2
6510	Real estate operators and lessors	5	6	0.5	23	25	6,957	6,880	163	172	0.2
HALE, AL											
60–	**Finance, insurance, and real estate**	11	11	0.1	80	86	19,450	19,860	1,821	1,923	0.1
6000	Depository institutions	4	4	0.3	60	64	19,200	20,313	1,376	1,470	0.2
6020	Commercial banks	4	4	0.4	60	64	19,200	20,313	1,376	1,470	0.2
HENRY, AL											
60–	**Finance, insurance, and real estate**	23	20	0.3	105	91	17,371	18,418	1,930	1,830	0.1
6000	Depository institutions	8	6	0.4	64	54	20,125	21,481	1,343	1,285	0.2
6400	Insurance agents, brokers, and service	6	5	0.3	13	12	9,231	8,333	108	105	0.0
6500	Real estate	3	3	0.1	14	12	8,286	5,667	135	42	0.0
HOUSTON, AL											
60–	**Finance, insurance, and real estate**	212	214	2.7	1,519	1,499	25,253	25,534	36,901	35,725	1.6
6000	Depository institutions	39	38	2.5	601	616	23,108	24,253	13,722	14,534	1.9
6020	Commercial banks	27	27	2.5	513	535	24,031	25,211	12,223	13,032	1.9
6100	Nondepository institutions	32	35	4.2	153	127	27,137	28,063	3,884	3,603	2.3
6140	Personal credit institutions	21	24	4.7	107	108	26,243	28,815	2,665	2,962	4.2
6280	Security and commodity services	3	3	4.2	3	2	18,667	26,000	59	91	0.8
6300	Insurance carriers	27	26	2.9	229	214	27,214	29,682	6,128	6,082	1.1
6310	Life insurance	9	7	2.9	174	159	23,448	25,610	4,004	3,731	2.2
6400	Insurance agents, brokers, and service	41	39	2.5	156	128	24,256	22,875	4,037	3,085	1.3
6500	Real estate	59	60	2.2	270	286	12,993	14,224	3,996	4,487	1.7
6510	Real estate operators and lessors	27	24	2.2	174	184	10,621	12,283	2,173	2,413	2.8
6530	Real estate agents and managers	27	30	2.6	81	89	17,531	17,933	1,602	1,865	1.3
6730	Trusts	4	3	6.5	2	3	8,000	9,333	30	31	0.8
JACKSON, AL											
60–	**Finance, insurance, and real estate**	69	66	0.8	426	442	20,479	21,050	9,261	9,534	0.4
6000	Depository institutions	22	21	1.4	278	302	17,799	17,722	5,283	5,484	0.7
6020	Commercial banks	17	16	1.5	258	279	17,876	17,864	4,918	5,080	0.7
6060	Credit unions	5	5	1.6	20	23	16,800	16,000	365	404	0.7

Source: County Business Patterns, 1994/95, CBP-94/95, U.S. Department of Commerce, Washington, D.C., November 1997. SIC categories for which data were suppressed or not available for both 1994 and 1995 are not displayed. The employment columns represent mid-March employment in the year. Pay per employee is calculated by dividing 1st Quarter payroll, annualized, by mid-March employment. The columns headed "% State" show the county's percentage of the state total for the SIC in 1995; for example, 1.4% for SIC 6000 means that the county had 1.4 percent of the state's total establishments (or payroll) in SIC 6000 in 1995. A dash (-) is used to indicate that data are not available or cannot be calculated; nec means not elsewhere classified.

Continued on next page.

SIC	Industry	No. Establishments			Employment		Pay / Employee		Annual Payroll ($ 000)		
		1994	1995	% State	1994	1995	1994	1995	1994	1995	% State
JACKSON, AL - [continued]											
6300	Insurance carriers	12	12	*1.3*	73	72	33,534	35,222	2,593	2,559	*0.5*
6400	Insurance agents, brokers, and service	8	9	*0.6*	26	24	21,692	25,667	556	607	*0.3*
6500	Real estate	19	16	*0.6*	26	19	8,923	13,053	293	279	*0.1*
JEFFERSON, AL											
60 –	**Finance, insurance, and real estate**	1,689	1,701	*21.3*	30,019	29,511	32,178	36,300	928,631	1,021,944	*45.6*
6000	Depository institutions	253	247	*16.5*	9,240	10,387	29,083	33,357	262,353	335,938	*43.4*
6020	Commercial banks	156	155	*14.4*	7,831	9,167	29,466	34,562	225,801	305,020	*45.0*
6030	Savings institutions	14	9	*12.9*	471	251	36,059	26,964	14,586	7,453	*29.8*
6060	Credit unions	73	74	*24.1*	662	651	19,353	20,805	13,884	14,071	*23.8*
6100	Nondepository institutions	179	186	*22.5*	2,560	1,965	31,808	34,768	76,962	61,658	*38.9*
6140	Personal credit institutions	81	88	*17.4*	743	864	28,016	30,880	19,920	24,329	*34.3*
6150	Business credit institutions	12	13	*40.6*	143	130	30,294	24,154	3,600	3,007	*36.7*
6160	Mortgage bankers and brokers	81	80	*35.4*	1,668	939	33,705	40,430	53,247	33,835	*45.4*
6200	Security and commodity brokers	61	63	*23.5*	839	853	64,458	65,210	50,076	55,973	*41.9*
6210	Security brokers and dealers	43	42	*21.9*	780	793	65,513	66,926	47,423	53,417	*43.8*
6300	Insurance carriers	229	228	*25.5*	9,268	8,961	37,481	40,527	313,880	328,772	*59.3*
6310	Life insurance	79	71	*29.2*	2,605	2,397	33,310	35,151	80,570	78,583	*46.2*
6320	Medical service and health insurance	19	21	*32.3*	3,265	3,255	38,173	42,798	107,592	116,129	*82.3*
6321	Accident and health insurance	9	9	*29.0*	173	159	23,445	25,333	3,675	3,673	*34.4*
6324	Hospital and medical service plans	10	12	*35.3*	3,092	3,096	38,997	43,695	103,917	112,456	*86.2*
6330	Fire, marine, and casualty insurance	112	117	*21.4*	3,174	3,078	39,761	42,390	117,398	125,222	*54.5*
6350	Surety insurance	5	6	*60.0*	123	126	56,195	48,286	5,045	5,731	*94.7*
6360	Title insurance	6	6	*46.2*	60	60	30,533	31,667	1,800	1,853	*61.5*
6400	Insurance agents, brokers, and service	379	381	*24.1*	2,357	2,548	32,014	33,670	81,506	92,019	*38.2*
6500	Real estate	520	532	*19.8*	4,920	4,155	17,397	22,171	93,094	93,184	*34.5*
6510	Real estate operators and lessors	218	227	*20.3*	2,393	1,491	14,081	21,282	35,243	29,825	*35.2*
6530	Real estate agents and managers	235	228	*19.6*	2,007	2,106	21,887	23,947	48,485	52,615	*36.9*
6540	Title abstract offices	8	9	*15.0*	60	50	23,267	26,240	1,678	1,437	*19.6*
6550	Subdividers and developers	50	52	*20.9*	457	474	14,092	17,046	7,524	8,458	*26.8*
6552	Subdividers and developers, n.e.c.	24	25	*18.9*	120	145	26,400	30,814	3,790	4,357	*22.9*
6553	Cemetery subdividers and developers	22	21	*22.8*	337	324	9,709	10,889	3,644	3,747	*33.3*
6700	Holding and other investment offices	62	58	*29.0*	722	511	66,720	103,319	46,730	49,483	*53.0*
6710	Holding offices	28	27	*36.0*	642	423	71,414	117,995	44,344	46,550	*62.9*
6730	Trusts	13	12	*26.1*	28	26	24,714	25,385	744	884	*23.3*
6790	Miscellaneous investing	20	18	*26.5*	52	32	31,385	36,625	1,356	1,101	*9.1*
6794	Patent owners and lessors	6	5	*38.5*	33	15	36,970	57,867	968	810	*33.4*
LAMAR, AL											
60 –	**Finance, insurance, and real estate**	16	15	*0.2*	168	171	23,262	25,006	5,019	4,988	*0.2*
6000	Depository institutions	9	9	*0.6*	101	107	21,069	20,112	2,207	2,405	*0.3*
6020	Commercial banks	9	9	*0.8*	101	107	21,069	20,112	2,207	2,405	*0.4*
LAUDERDALE, AL											
60 –	**Finance, insurance, and real estate**	185	179	*2.2*	1,150	1,096	27,784	24,810	30,408	27,714	*1.2*
6000	Depository institutions	38	37	*2.5*	598	555	27,920	22,350	15,111	12,161	*1.6*
6020	Commercial banks	25	24	*2.2*	486	434	29,119	23,115	12,795	9,635	*1.4*
6100	Nondepository institutions	15	14	*1.7*	65	54	21,046	25,037	1,278	1,276	*0.8*
6140	Personal credit institutions	11	11	*2.2*	51	48	20,157	24,250	994	1,107	*1.6*
6160	Mortgage bankers and brokers	4	3	*1.3*	14	6	24,286	31,333	284	169	*0.2*
6300	Insurance carriers	20	20	*2.2*	171	153	33,942	36,314	5,323	5,052	*0.9*
6310	Life insurance	7	7	*2.9*	126	109	33,079	35,927	3,594	3,352	*2.0*
6400	Insurance agents, brokers, and service	40	39	*2.5*	156	158	24,564	25,241	4,045	4,342	*1.8*
6500	Real estate	64	63	*2.3*	125	138	14,464	13,681	1,954	2,341	*0.9*
6510	Real estate operators and lessors	33	31	*2.8*	46	58	11,478	10,483	555	660	*0.8*
6530	Real estate agents and managers	25	25	*2.1*	57	55	12,912	12,582	791	942	*0.7*
LAWRENCE, AL											
60 –	**Finance, insurance, and real estate**	19	19	*0.2*	109	116	16,587	19,310	2,025	2,314	*0.1*

Source: County Business Patterns, 1994/95, CBP-94/95, U.S. Department of Commerce, Washington, D.C., November 1997. SIC categories for which data were suppressed or not available for both 1994 and 1995 are not displayed. The employment columns represent mid-March employment in the year. Pay per employee is calculated by dividing 1st Quarter payroll, annualized, by mid-March employment. The columns headed "% State" show the county's percentage of the state total for the SIC in 1995; for example, 1.4% for SIC 6000 means that the county had 1.4 percent of the state's total establishments (or payroll) in SIC 6000 in 1995. A dash (-) is used to indicate that data are not available or cannot be calculated; nec means not elsewhere classified.

Continued on next page.

SIC	Industry	No. Establishments			Employment		Pay / Employee		Annual Payroll ($ 000)		
		1994	1995	% State	1994	1995	1994	1995	1994	1995	% State
LAWRENCE, AL - [continued]											
6000	Depository institutions	8	8	0.5	83	90	14,699	17,244	1,318	1,510	0.2
6400	Insurance agents, brokers, and service	4	3	0.2	6	6	11,333	13,333	78	74	0.0
6500	Real estate	3	4	0.1	5	5	13,600	14,400	69	101	0.0
LEE, AL											
60 –	**Finance, insurance, and real estate**	180	172	2.2	1,278	1,333	18,664	19,811	25,166	27,077	1.2
6000	Depository institutions	27	30	2.0	508	530	21,614	22,430	11,215	12,109	1.6
6100	Nondepository institutions	20	17	2.1	60	57	21,067	19,439	1,222	1,084	0.7
6210	Security brokers and dealers	4	4	2.1	16	19	52,250	65,053	867	1,207	1.0
6300	Insurance carriers	12	12	1.3	146	133	25,699	28,000	3,936	3,638	0.7
6310	Life insurance	3	3	1.2	104	94	25,308	27,362	2,716	2,309	1.4
6400	Insurance agents, brokers, and service	28	23	1.5	77	106	20,000	18,642	1,777	2,044	0.8
6500	Real estate	86	83	3.1	466	483	11,313	12,928	5,869	6,690	2.5
6530	Real estate agents and managers	31	32	2.7	305	338	12,590	13,953	4,315	5,095	3.6
LIMESTONE, AL											
60 –	**Finance, insurance, and real estate**	80	85	1.1	333	345	18,883	19,907	6,766	7,255	0.3
6000	Depository institutions	14	14	0.9	126	137	19,810	23,796	2,868	3,146	0.4
6020	Commercial banks	9	9	0.8	112	106	20,250	24,000	2,540	2,441	0.4
6100	Nondepository institutions	12	12	1.4	36	39	19,778	19,897	738	783	0.5
6400	Insurance agents, brokers, and service	17	16	1.0	44	44	20,182	20,636	1,019	983	0.4
6500	Real estate	27	31	1.2	97	95	12,041	9,221	1,058	1,117	0.4
6510	Real estate operators and lessors	13	13	1.2	39	42	11,385	10,857	465	478	0.6
6530	Real estate agents and managers	10	13	1.1	50	49	9,680	8,245	441	418	0.3
6550	Subdividers and developers	4	4	1.6	8	3	30,000	4,000	152	211	0.7
LOWNDES, AL											
60 –	**Finance, insurance, and real estate**	10	12	0.2	60	71	24,867	24,394	1,373	1,587	0.1
6500	Real estate	4	5	0.2	10	10	6,000	6,400	62	83	0.0
MACON, AL											
60 –	**Finance, insurance, and real estate**	14	15	0.2	146	132	17,945	19,333	2,486	2,494	0.1
6000	Depository institutions	5	5	0.3	99	95	21,091	20,968	1,904	1,951	0.3
6510	Real estate operators and lessors	5	6	0.5	34	21	8,235	10,667	262	219	0.3
MADISON, AL											
60 –	**Finance, insurance, and real estate**	591	577	7.2	4,149	4,026	23,444	25,407	98,543	105,611	4.7
6000	Depository institutions	91	87	5.8	1,538	1,559	21,202	23,800	33,910	36,840	4.8
6020	Commercial banks	68	65	6.0	1,027	1,042	22,388	26,518	23,969	25,308	3.7
6100	Nondepository institutions	58	62	7.5	339	256	27,139	25,016	8,267	6,231	3.9
6140	Personal credit institutions	29	32	6.3	138	131	23,739	25,679	3,283	3,211	4.5
6160	Mortgage bankers and brokers	26	25	11.1	189	112	29,333	23,929	4,565	2,622	3.5
6200	Security and commodity brokers	23	22	8.2	204	214	64,118	68,822	12,463	14,615	10.9
6300	Insurance carriers	62	64	7.2	573	541	30,848	34,270	17,639	17,779	3.2
6310	Life insurance	16	13	5.3	315	266	24,635	28,165	7,395	6,944	4.1
6330	Fire, marine, and casualty insurance	40	45	8.2	177	186	36,927	37,763	7,134	7,311	3.2
6400	Insurance agents, brokers, and service	104	101	6.4	343	345	21,738	21,704	7,505	7,869	3.3
6500	Real estate	244	230	8.6	1,074	1,018	14,570	16,000	16,930	18,272	6.8
6510	Real estate operators and lessors	105	96	8.6	487	436	12,591	14,138	6,615	6,798	8.0
6530	Real estate agents and managers	107	102	8.8	510	515	16,957	17,274	8,621	9,252	6.5
6540	Title abstract offices	4	3	5.0	15	9	11,200	12,889	138	99	1.3
6550	Subdividers and developers	18	19	7.6	59	40	11,390	19,500	1,348	1,567	5.0
6552	Subdividers and developers, n.e.c.	12	10	7.6	46	26	11,391	20,769	814	755	4.0
6553	Cemetery subdividers and developers	4	6	6.5	12	10	10,667	20,400	189	459	4.1
6700	Holding and other investment offices	9	11	5.5	78	93	20,513	18,667	1,829	4,005	4.3
6790	Miscellaneous investing	5	6	8.8	64	83	19,938	18,747	1,523	1,674	13.9
MARENGO, AL											
60 –	**Finance, insurance, and real estate**	31	32	0.4	254	282	22,142	21,929	5,995	6,367	0.3

Source: County Business Patterns, 1994/95, CBP-94/95, U.S. Department of Commerce, Washington, D.C., November 1997. SIC categories for which data were suppressed or not available for both 1994 and 1995 are not displayed. The employment columns represent mid-March employment in the year. Pay per employee is calculated by dividing 1st Quarter payroll, annualized, by mid-March employment. The columns headed "% State" show the county's percentage of the state total for the SIC in 1995; for example, 1.4% for SIC 6000 means that the county had 1.4 percent of the state's total establishments (or payroll) in SIC 6000 in 1995. A dash (-) is used to indicate that data are not available or cannot be calculated; nec means not elsewhere classified.

Continued on next page.

SIC	Industry	No. Establishments			Employment		Pay / Employee		Annual Payroll ($ 000)		
		1994	1995	% State	1994	1995	1994	1995	1994	1995	% State
CRAIGHEAD, AR - [continued]											
6300	Insurance carriers	19	18	6.0	109	104	29,578	32,385	3,445	3,186	1.9
6310	Life insurance	8	7	6.7	69	61	25,449	29,836	1,917	1,513	2.5
6400	Insurance agents, brokers, and service	44	44	3.4	106	115	21,962	23,026	2,656	2,864	2.4
6500	Real estate	59	63	3.6	246	297	14,293	13,441	3,966	4,188	3.1
6510	Real estate operators and lessors	32	30	4.3	94	109	13,574	13,101	1,464	1,386	3.8
6530	Real estate agents and managers	15	19	2.7	68	106	15,235	13,132	1,232	1,515	2.5
6550	Subdividers and developers	8	10	6.0	35	39	11,771	12,103	465	605	2.8
6700	Holding and other investment offices	4	5	3.4	13	27	31,385	35,407	419	1,176	1.8
CRAWFORD, AR											
60 –	**Finance, insurance, and real estate**	55	58	1.2	280	291	19,957	21,017	6,188	6,187	0.6
6000	Depository institutions	14	16	1.5	188	192	21,298	22,688	4,390	4,339	1.2
6400	Insurance agents, brokers, and service	10	10	0.8	23	25	13,217	14,080	317	370	0.3
6500	Real estate	25	27	1.5	60	65	13,667	14,338	1,060	1,004	0.7
6530	Real estate agents and managers	10	11	1.5	19	25	14,316	14,080	405	386	0.6
6550	Subdividers and developers	4	4	2.4	7	9	15,429	19,556	189	262	1.2
CRITTENDEN, AR											
60 –	**Finance, insurance, and real estate**	70	66	1.3	536	517	22,821	23,582	11,591	12,104	1.2
6000	Depository institutions	19	19	1.8	304	304	22,539	22,500	6,591	6,958	1.9
6020	Commercial banks	15	15	1.8	218	212	21,890	22,094	4,669	4,533	1.5
6300	Insurance carriers	4	3	1.0	45	37	22,933	23,676	934	843	0.5
6400	Insurance agents, brokers, and service	14	14	1.1	33	34	19,636	19,294	661	631	0.5
6500	Real estate	29	26	1.5	133	125	23,549	26,944	2,946	3,088	2.3
6510	Real estate operators and lessors	16	15	2.2	91	91	26,330	29,978	1,832	2,196	6.0
CROSS, AR											
60 –	**Finance, insurance, and real estate**	30	31	0.6	194	188	18,227	19,000	3,501	3,701	0.4
6000	Depository institutions	11	10	0.9	160	151	19,375	20,503	3,083	3,213	0.9
6530	Real estate agents and managers	3	4	0.6	2	4	10,000	6,000	21	17	0.0
DALLAS, AR											
60 –	**Finance, insurance, and real estate**	12	13	0.3	94	95	17,277	16,800	1,909	1,757	0.2
6000	Depository institutions	6	6	0.6	74	81	17,514	17,580	1,509	1,562	0.4
DESHA, AR											
60 –	**Finance, insurance, and real estate**	37	39	0.8	201	203	16,657	17,655	3,658	3,752	0.4
6000	Depository institutions	10	10	0.9	111	109	21,117	21,982	2,502	2,497	0.7
6020	Commercial banks	10	10	1.2	111	109	21,117	21,982	2,502	2,497	0.8
6500	Real estate	17	19	1.1	57	58	7,930	8,966	531	566	0.4
6530	Real estate agents and managers	5	5	0.7	24	24	10,833	12,833	315	354	0.6
DREW, AR											
60 –	**Finance, insurance, and real estate**	22	21	0.4	154	181	22,208	19,470	3,089	3,455	0.3
6530	Real estate agents and managers	4	4	0.6	11	36	19,273	7,778	307	509	0.8
FAULKNER, AR											
60 –	**Finance, insurance, and real estate**	109	115	2.3	599	572	19,907	22,510	12,296	13,723	1.3
6000	Depository institutions	23	21	2.0	326	301	19,632	22,724	6,450	7,069	2.0
6300	Insurance carriers	8	9	3.0	38	44	26,526	30,000	913	1,155	0.7
6400	Insurance agents, brokers, and service	26	25	1.9	104	88	16,462	19,000	1,822	1,803	1.5
6500	Real estate	38	43	2.5	87	90	14,805	15,733	1,449	1,805	1.3
6510	Real estate operators and lessors	15	19	2.7	24	30	13,167	10,933	375	535	1.5
6530	Real estate agents and managers	16	16	2.2	35	37	15,314	18,811	647	839	1.4

Source: County Business Patterns, 1994/95, CBP-94/95, U.S. Department of Commerce, Washington, D.C., November 1997. SIC categories for which data were suppressed or not available for both 1994 and 1995 are not displayed. The employment columns represent mid-March employment in the year. Pay per employee is calculated by dividing 1st Quarter payroll, annualized, by mid-March employment. The columns headed "% State" show the county's percentage of the state total for the SIC in 1995; for example, 1.4% for SIC 6000 means that the county had 1.4 percent of the state's total establishments (or payroll) in SIC 6000 in 1995. A dash (-) is used to indicate that data are not available or cannot be calculated; nec means not elsewhere classified.

Continued on next page.

SIC	Industry	No. Establishments			Employment		Pay / Employee		Annual Payroll ($ 000)		
		1994	1995	% State	1994	1995	1994	1995	1994	1995	% State
FRANKLIN, AR - [continued]											
60 –	**Finance, insurance, and real estate**	18	22	*0.4*	127	227	21,323	24,952	2,987	5,994	*0.6*
6000	Depository institutions	6	7	*0.7*	106	118	23,321	22,339	2,748	2,935	*0.8*
FULTON, AR											
60 –	**Finance, insurance, and real estate**	13	10	*0.2*	83	63	18,265	18,857	1,511	1,153	*0.1*
6400	Insurance agents, brokers, and service	4	3	*0.2*	9	10	14,667	14,000	138	127	*0.1*
GARLAND, AR											
60 –	**Finance, insurance, and real estate**	190	195	*3.9*	1,535	1,524	20,060	21,281	31,627	33,051	*3.2*
6000	Depository institutions	31	33	*3.1*	486	431	19,646	23,629	9,904	10,409	*2.9*
6020	Commercial banks	22	23	*2.7*	444	391	19,946	24,041	9,196	9,599	*3.1*
6200	Security and commodity brokers	9	10	*4.2*	51	65	79,373	49,415	3,540	3,321	*2.6*
6300	Insurance carriers	9	10	*3.3*	64	55	31,188	36,364	2,014	1,865	*1.1*
6310	Life insurance	3	3	*2.9*	57	45	26,246	28,178	1,459	1,116	*1.9*
6400	Insurance agents, brokers, and service	45	47	*3.6*	135	166	21,600	21,904	3,324	3,835	*3.3*
6500	Real estate	83	84	*4.8*	782	787	15,223	16,483	12,425	13,197	*9.6*
6510	Real estate operators and lessors	24	20	*2.9*	116	117	12,552	14,427	1,828	1,533	*4.2*
6530	Real estate agents and managers	49	49	*6.9*	533	513	13,666	14,113	7,495	7,928	*13.1*
6550	Subdividers and developers	7	8	*4.8*	110	124	24,691	27,774	2,668	2,985	*13.6*
6730	Trusts	3	3	*9.4*	4	7	22,000	14,857	88	103	*5.4*
6790	Miscellaneous investing	4	3	*6.4*	5	7	32,800	31,429	167	208	*6.8*
GRANT, AR											
60 –	**Finance, insurance, and real estate**	14	12	*0.2*	87	97	19,632	19,505	1,854	1,827	*0.2*
6000	Depository institutions	5	5	*0.5*	69	79	20,696	20,304	1,462	1,536	*0.4*
6400	Insurance agents, brokers, and service	4	4	*0.3*	13 ·	12	15,692	16,333	201	203	*0.2*
GREENE, AR											
60 –	**Finance, insurance, and real estate**	54	56	*1.1*	275	295	23,855	22,264	6,657	6,866	*0.7*
6000	Depository institutions	10	11	*1.0*	169	172	24,615	21,093	4,007	4,027	*1.1*
6500	Real estate	19	20	*1.1*	34	35	13,882	12,229	550	446	*0.3*
6510	Real estate operators and lessors	7	8	*1.2*	9	7	16,000	11,429	163	84	*0.2*
6530	Real estate agents and managers	9	9	*1.3*	12	12	10,667	8,667	128	122	*0.2*
HEMPSTEAD, AR											
60 –	**Finance, insurance, and real estate**	27	25	*0.5*	206	212	19,417	20,943	4,265	4,412	*0.4*
6000	Depository institutions	8	8	*0.7*	145	149	20,966	23,060	3,310	3,377	*0.9*
HOT SPRING, AR											
60 –	**Finance, insurance, and real estate**	33	31	*0.6*	232	215	18,190	19,144	4,519	3,880	*0.4*
6000	Depository institutions	9	10	*0.9*	145	141	18,179	18,213	2,957	2,521	*0.7*
6400	Insurance agents, brokers, and service	11	10	*0.8*	22	22	11,091	12,727	345	305	*0.3*
HOWARD, AR											
60 –	**Finance, insurance, and real estate**	22	22	*0.4*	106	87	20,151	19,402	2,198	1,704	*0.2*
6000	Depository institutions	9	7	*0.7*	83	62	21,012	20,194	1,794	1,271	*0.4*
6500	Real estate	4	5	*0.3*	5	6	12,000	10,667	65	84	*0.1*
INDEPENDENCE, AR											
60 –	**Finance, insurance, and real estate**	55	57	*1.1*	291	281	18,694	21,082	5,869	6,325	*0.6*
6000	Depository institutions	18	18	*1.7*	190	177	18,968	21,672	3,736	3,896	*1.1*
6400	Insurance agents, brokers, and service	14	14	*1.1*	45	45	18,578	19,111	922	1,003	*0.9*
IZARD, AR											
60 –	**Finance, insurance, and real estate**	24	29	*0.6*	137	149	14,102	16,107	2,244	2,519	*0.2*
6000	Depository institutions	7	7	*0.7*	67	68	18,269	21,353	1,299	1,416	*0.4*

Source: County Business Patterns, 1994/95, CBP-94/95, U.S. Department of Commerce, Washington, D.C., November 1997. SIC categories for which data were suppressed or not available for both 1994 and 1995 are *not* displayed. The employment columns represent mid-March employment in the year. Pay per employee is calculated by dividing 1st Quarter payroll, annualized, by mid-March employment. The columns headed "% State" show the county's percentage of the state total for the SIC in 1995; for example, 1.4% for SIC 6000 means that the county had 1.4 percent of the state's total establishments (or payroll) in SIC 6000 in 1995. A dash (-) is used to indicate that data are not available or cannot be calculated; *nec* means not elsewhere classified.

Continued on next page.

SIC	Industry	No. Establishments			Employment		Pay / Employee		Annual Payroll ($ 000)		
		1994	1995	% State	1994	1995	1994	1995	1994	1995	% State
IZARD, AR - [continued]											
6020	Commercial banks	7	7	0.8	67	68	18,269	21,353	1,299	1,416	0.5
6500	Real estate	12	13	0.7	45	49	6,133	6,776	373	425	0.3
6530	Real estate agents and managers	9	9	1.3	36	38	6,000	6,842	312	356	0.6
JACKSON, AR											
60–	**Finance, insurance, and real estate**	35	35	0.7	168	169	22,214	19,787	3,490	3,423	0.3
6000	Depository institutions	10	10	0.9	104	100	20,615	19,880	2,178	2,125	0.6
6400	Insurance agents, brokers, and service	10	10	0.8	24	30	20,333	16,800	434	464	0.4
6500	Real estate	11	10	0.6	29	28	23,310	18,857	604	537	0.4
6510	Real estate operators and lessors	6	5	0.7	14	12	34,000	21,667	290	244	0.7
JEFFERSON, AR											
60–	**Finance, insurance, and real estate**	147	150	3.0	1,330	1,362	20,953	21,495	29,286	30,946	3.0
6000	Depository institutions	36	32	3.0	654	644	22,147	22,901	15,742	16,299	4.5
6020	Commercial banks	27	22	2.6	593	586	22,314	23,113	14,420	15,077	4.9
6300	Insurance carriers	13	15	5.0	72	65	26,778	32,062	1,941	1,768	1.1
6310	Life insurance	6	8	7.6	60	51	24,200	28,941	1,445	1,121	1.9
6400	Insurance agents, brokers, and service	41	41	3.1	136	143	23,529	25,566	3,249	3,523	3.0
6500	Real estate	46	48	2.7	386	430	11,337	11,237	4,701	5,236	3.8
6510	Real estate operators and lessors	19	19	2.7	212	269	10,434	8,996	2,227	2,535	7.0
6530	Real estate agents and managers	20	21	2.9	137	129	11,650	14,171	1,754	2,019	3.3
JOHNSON, AR											
60–	**Finance, insurance, and real estate**	33	35	0.7	161	210	17,963	18,552	3,190	3,997	0.4
6000	Depository institutions	8	11	1.0	88	123	20,091	18,667	1,882	2,361	0.7
6500	Real estate	15	14	0.8	46	50	15,739	17,280	864	961	0.7
6510	Real estate operators and lessors	8	7	1.0	28	32	16,857	18,000	528	580	1.6
LAFAYETTE, AR											
60–	**Finance, insurance, and real estate**	10	10	0.2	71	71	20,901	21,521	1,571	1,947	0.2
6000	Depository institutions	4	4	0.4	48	44	24,167	25,909	1,142	1,359	0.4
6020	Commercial banks	4	4	0.5	48	44	24,167	25,909	1,142	1,359	0.4
LAWRENCE, AR											
60–	**Finance, insurance, and real estate**	26	24	0.5	150	144	17,307	16,250	2,561	2,394	0.2
6000	Depository institutions	11	10	0.9	109	104	20,330	19,038	2,183	2,008	0.6
6400	Insurance agents, brokers, and service	8	8	0.6	18	19	12,000	12,632	221	253	0.2
LEE, AR											
60–	**Finance, insurance, and real estate**	13	13	0.3	62	62	16,645	17,484	1,144	1,209	0.1
6400	Insurance agents, brokers, and service	3	3	0.2	12	12	13,000	20,333	194	248	0.2
LINCOLN, AR											
60–	**Finance, insurance, and real estate**	9	14	0.3	63	70	19,238	20,800	1,167	1,176	0.1
LITTLE RIVER, AR											
60–	**Finance, insurance, and real estate**	23	22	0.4	119	123	18,689	19,317	2,149	2,244	0.2
6000	Depository institutions	7	7	0.7	66	67	22,121	22,925	1,394	1,271	0.4
LOGAN, AR											
60–	**Finance, insurance, and real estate**	36	36	0.7	188	185	18,234	19,135	3,578	3,591	0.3
6000	Depository institutions	11	11	1.0	128	132	20,063	20,091	2,709	2,702	0.8
6020	Commercial banks	8	8	0.9	121	123	20,430	20,650	2,597	2,597	0.8
6500	Real estate	8	9	0.5	15	14	10,133	11,429	160	179	0.1
6530	Real estate agents and managers	4	4	0.6	7	6	8,571	10,667	66	71	0.1
LONOKE, AR											
60–	**Finance, insurance, and real estate**	53	55	1.1	268	287	19,493	18,899	5,703	5,884	0.6

Source: County Business Patterns, 1994/95, CBP-94/95, U.S. Department of Commerce, Washington, D.C., November 1997. SIC categories for which data were suppressed or not available for both 1994 and 1995 are not displayed. The employment columns represent mid-March employment in the year. Pay per employee is calculated by dividing 1st Quarter payroll, annualized, by mid-March employment. The columns headed "% State" show the county's percentage of the state total for the SIC in 1995; for example, 1.4% for SIC 6000 means that the county had 1.4 percent of the state's total establishments (or payroll) in SIC 6000 in 1995. A dash (-) is used to indicate that data are not available or cannot be calculated; nec means not elsewhere classified.

Continued on next page.

SIC	Industry	No. Establishments			Employment		Pay / Employee		Annual Payroll ($ 000)		
		1994	1995	% State	1994	1995	1994	1995	1994	1995	% State
LONOKE, AR - [continued]											
6000	Depository institutions	15	15	1.4	185	182	19,914	20,418	4,180	4,181	1.2
6400	Insurance agents, brokers, and service	15	13	1.0	32	35	17,875	16,457	586	590	0.5
6500	Real estate	19	21	1.2	39	46	13,846	10,522	621	535	0.4
6510	Real estate operators and lessors	3	5	0.7	4	4	6,000	6,000	24	32	0.1
6550	Subdividers and developers	6	6	3.6	7	14	14,286	8,857	180	79	0.4
6552	Subdividers and developers, n.e.c.	5	5	5.2	7	8	14,286	11,000	144	43	0.2
MADISON, AR											
60 –	**Finance, insurance, and real estate**	14	14	0.3	68	79	17,294	16,405	1,278	1,408	0.1
6000	Depository institutions	5	5	0.5	56	60	18,000	18,267	1,074	1,156	0.3
6020	Commercial banks	5	5	0.6	56	60	18,000	18,267	1,074	1,156	0.4
6400	Insurance agents, brokers, and service	4	4	0.3	7	11	14,857	10,182	112	118	0.1
6500	Real estate	5	5	0.3	5	8	12,800	11,000	92	134	0.1
MARION, AR											
60 –	**Finance, insurance, and real estate**	22	23	0.5	109	120	15,817	15,833	1,943	1,970	0.2
6000	Depository institutions	7	8	0.7	72	79	18,000	17,873	1,366	1,402	0.4
MILLER, AR											
60 –	**Finance, insurance, and real estate**	45	46	0.9	502	405	21,307	22,647	11,363	10,214	1.0
6000	Depository institutions	12	11	1.0	307	222	21,459	24,090	6,869	5,638	1.6
6300	Insurance carriers	5	5	1.7	82	75	27,659	28,320	2,289	2,636	1.6
6500	Real estate	11	15	0.9	61	67	8,459	10,687	680	890	0.6
6510	Real estate operators and lessors	5	6	0.9	13	15	8,923	8,000	140	152	0.4
6530	Real estate agents and managers	3	6	0.8	9	25	11,556	12,320	213	443	0.7
MISSISSIPPI, AR											
60 –	**Finance, insurance, and real estate**	91	87	1.8	529	471	23,297	28,442	11,607	12,268	1.2
6000	Depository institutions	23	23	2.1	301	288	18,578	20,056	5,829	5,864	1.6
6400	Insurance agents, brokers, and service	29	26	2.0	69	64	17,333	17,688	1,215	1,234	1.1
6500	Real estate	27	25	1.4	89	61	12,539	16,328	1,031	926	0.7
6510	Real estate operators and lessors	14	16	2.3	64	47	9,188	12,000	565	562	1.5
MONROE, AR											
60 –	**Finance, insurance, and real estate**	16	17	0.3	126	120	19,587	20,633	2,612	2,593	0.3
6000	Depository institutions	5	5	0.5	76	77	20,211	20,623	1,696	1,717	0.5
6400	Insurance agents, brokers, and service	5	6	0.5	14	9	15,143	20,444	207	201	0.2
MONTGOMERY, AR											
60 –	**Finance, insurance, and real estate**	8	9	0.2	33	40	14,667	16,600	619	709	0.1
NEVADA, AR											
60 –	**Finance, insurance, and real estate**	8	8	0.2	50	45	19,840	20,089	1,013	966	0.1
NEWTON, AR											
60 –	**Finance, insurance, and real estate**	3	3	0.1	-	-	-	-	-	-	-
OUACHITA, AR											
60 –	**Finance, insurance, and real estate**	50	41	0.8	330	296	19,673	22,297	6,472	7,186	0.7
6000	Depository institutions	18	13	1.2	159	149	19,019	22,416	3,044	3,388	0.9
6400	Insurance agents, brokers, and service	15	12	0.9	46	46	17,043	17,652	922	1,039	0.9
6500	Real estate	10	12	0.7	91	93	22,374	23,914	2,134	2,523	1.8
PERRY, AR											
60 –	**Finance, insurance, and real estate**	3	4	0.1	-	-	-	-	-	-	-
PHILLIPS, AR											
60 –	**Finance, insurance, and real estate**	43	39	0.8	268	281	18,194	19,687	5,162	5,668	0.6

Source: County Business Patterns, 1994/95, CBP-94/95, U.S. Department of Commerce, Washington, D.C., November 1997. SIC categories for which data were suppressed or not available for both 1994 and 1995 are *not* displayed. The employment columns represent mid-March employment in the year. Pay per employee is calculated by dividing 1st Quarter payroll, annualized, by mid-March employment. The columns headed "% State" show the county's percentage of the state total for the SIC in 1995; for example, 1.4% for SIC 6000 means that the county had 1.4 percent of the state's total establishments (or payroll) in SIC 6000 in 1995. A dash (-) is used to indicate that data are not available or cannot be calculated; *nec* means not elsewhere classified.

Continued on next page.

SIC	Industry	No. Establishments			Employment		Pay / Employee		Annual Payroll ($ 000)		
		1994	1995	% State	1994	1995	1994	1995	1994	1995	% State
PHILLIPS, AR - [continued]											
6000	Depository institutions	7	7	0.7	160	167	20,850	22,108	3,439	3,639	1.0
6020	Commercial banks	7	7	0.8	160	167	20,850	22,108	3,439	3,639	1.2
6500	Real estate	23	20	1.1	71	70	9,859	11,429	842	1,000	0.7
6510	Real estate operators and lessors	13	10	1.4	47	36	9,702	13,000	522	557	1.5
6530	Real estate agents and managers	5	4	0.6	13	9	7,385	11,556	125	120	0.2
PIKE, AR											
60 –	**Finance, insurance, and real estate**	15	17	0.3	106	124	18,151	16,871	2,051	2,185	0.2
6000	Depository institutions	5	5	0.5	89	92	18,831	18,261	1,732	1,773	0.5
6020	Commercial banks	5	5	0.6	89	92	18,831	18,261	1,732	1,773	0.6
POINSETT, AR											
60 –	**Finance, insurance, and real estate**	34	35	0.7	247	237	18,364	21,080	4,946	5,276	0.5
6000	Depository institutions	11	11	1.0	142	136	18,479	20,794	2,936	3,006	0.8
6400	Insurance agents, brokers, and service	8	8	0.6	16	15	11,500	12,000	196	176	0.2
6510	Real estate operators and lessors	7	8	1.2	34	26	15,059	20,308	589	589	1.6
POLK, AR											
60 –	**Finance, insurance, and real estate**	28	29	0.6	163	172	17,080	17,256	2,925	2,901	0.3
6000	Depository institutions	8	8	0.7	115	118	20,174	20,881	2,349	2,320	0.6
6510	Real estate operators and lessors	4	3	0.4	11	10	4,364	3,200	44	31	0.1
6530	Real estate agents and managers	6	8	1.1	7	13	11,429	6,462	107	115	0.2
POPE, AR											
60 –	**Finance, insurance, and real estate**	101	104	2.1	595	570	21,513	23,951	12,976	12,155	1.2
6000	Depository institutions	23	23	2.1	278	259	18,360	22,471	5,190	4,866	1.4
6400	Insurance agents, brokers, and service	28	32	2.5	89	92	18,427	16,522	1,596	1,636	1.4
6500	Real estate	36	33	1.9	87	98	11,586	10,816	1,197	1,218	0.9
6530	Real estate agents and managers	17	17	2.4	42	55	13,048	13,091	713	864	1.4
6550	Subdividers and developers	5	3	1.8	12	15	3,667	4,000	84	66	0.3
PRAIRIE, AR											
60 –	**Finance, insurance, and real estate**	11	12	0.2	49	50	16,082	17,600	915	932	0.1
6400	Insurance agents, brokers, and service	3	3	0.2	6	6	12,000	12,667	114	101	0.1
PULASKI, AR											
60 –	**Finance, insurance, and real estate**	1,180	1,182	23.8	14,690	14,447	31,325	35,003	445,698	468,349	45.6
6000	Depository institutions	188	190	17.7	3,093	2,821	25,937	23,970	72,173	70,233	19.6
6020	Commercial banks	136	135	16.0	2,360	2,136	26,210	24,245	54,861	53,654	17.4
6030	Savings institutions	11	12	11.1	215	245	26,065	20,441	5,070	5,532	18.0
6140	Personal credit institutions	8	7	33.3	267	270	29,483	39,067	7,543	9,737	73.8
6160	Mortgage bankers and brokers	37	40	46.0	788	626	31,391	30,038	21,209	19,586	80.1
6200	Security and commodity brokers	74	75	31.8	1,531	1,496	59,046	77,222	85,923	91,279	71.6
6210	Security brokers and dealers	46	48	27.1	1,400	1,381	61,346	80,353	79,234	86,043	71.8
6300	Insurance carriers	140	132	44.1	4,056	4,230	29,982	31,887	125,685	135,661	81.7
6310	Life insurance	60	53	50.5	1,632	1,611	26,723	28,775	45,347	45,476	75.4
6321	Accident and health insurance	7	7	100.0	216	232	23,722	23,569	5,402	5,705	100.0
6330	Fire, marine, and casualty insurance	51	48	35.6	811	836	35,004	34,483	28,446	29,853	72.9
6400	Insurance agents, brokers, and service	328	327	25.1	1,653	1,617	32,939	37,452	50,869	55,739	47.5
6500	Real estate	354	356	20.3	2,155	2,269	18,983	19,085	41,992	42,751	31.2
6510	Real estate operators and lessors	146	136	19.6	667	668	16,204	13,976	10,714	9,409	25.8
6530	Real estate agents and managers	158	163	22.9	1,172	1,195	19,877	20,994	23,542	24,228	40.1
6540	Title abstract offices	19	20	17.2	216	155	19,685	23,561	5,201	4,156	26.2
6550	Subdividers and developers	25	26	15.5	76	211	28,474	21,517	2,091	4,241	19.3
6552	Subdividers and developers, n.e.c.	16	16	16.5	27	154	41,778	23,299	1,031	3,133	16.6
6553	Cemetery subdividers and developers	9	8	13.6	49	56	21,143	16,786	1,060	1,012	37.4
6700	Holding and other investment offices	39	45	30.8	894	889	35,857	50,686	31,063	34,921	52.9

Source: County Business Patterns, 1994/95, CBP-94/95, U.S. Department of Commerce, Washington, D.C., November 1997. SIC categories for which data were suppressed or not available for both 1994 and 1995 are *not* displayed. The employment columns represent mid-March employment in the year. Pay per employee is calculated by dividing 1st Quarter payroll, annualized, by mid-March employment. The columns headed "% State" show the county's percentage of the state total for the SIC in 1995; for example, 1.4% for SIC 6000 means that the county had 1.4 percent of the state's total establishments (or payroll) in SIC 6000 in 1995. A dash (-) is used to indicate that data are not available or cannot be calculated; *nec* means not elsewhere classified.

Continued on next page.

SIC	Industry	No. Establishments			Employment		Pay / Employee		Annual Payroll ($ 000)		
		1994	1995	% State	1994	1995	1994	1995	1994	1995	% State
PULASKI, AR - [continued]											
6710	Holding offices	20	19	33.3	833	780	36,927	55,031	28,868	32,221	53.0
6730	Trusts	9	12	37.5	31	67	12,774	10,627	476	1,265	66.8
6790	Miscellaneous investing	9	9	19.1	30	39	30,000	35,077	1,616	1,241	40.7
RANDOLPH, AR											
60 –	**Finance, insurance, and real estate**	25	24	0.5	135	147	20,444	20,980	3,139	3,365	0.3
6000	Depository institutions	7	6	0.6	88	94	22,682	23,404	2,355	2,541	0.7
6510	Real estate operators and lessors	4	3	0.4	4	6	6,000	18,000	81	53	0.1
ST. FRANCIS, AR											
60 –	**Finance, insurance, and real estate**	43	42	0.8	280	291	19,771	20,866	5,740	5,868	0.6
6000	Depository institutions	12	14	1.3	157	171	18,369	19,883	3,011	3,177	0.9
6400	Insurance agents, brokers, and service	11	12	0.9	27	26	12,000	14,000	395	406	0.3
6510	Real estate operators and lessors	5	3	0.4	9	8	7,111	7,500	65	61	0.2
6530	Real estate agents and managers	5	5	0.7	6	8	8,000	8,000	68	77	0.1
SALINE, AR											
60 –	**Finance, insurance, and real estate**	86	104	2.1	468	459	17,650	19,974	8,990	10,226	1.0
6000	Depository institutions	14	18	1.7	226	235	19,699	19,472	4,585	4,732	1.3
6300	Insurance carriers	4	6	2.0	19	23	21,474	23,478	517	621	0.4
6400	Insurance agents, brokers, and service	23	27	2.1	71	75	17,634	17,813	1,459	1,600	1.4
6500	Real estate	40	48	2.7	147	114	12,898	20,772	2,206	2,829	2.1
6510	Real estate operators and lessors	17	16	2.3	36	26	10,222	13,231	360	319	0.9
6530	Real estate agents and managers	15	19	2.7	85	72	14,024	24,056	1,456	2,074	3.4
6540	Title abstract offices	3	5	4.3	13	11	12,923	22,545	166	254	1.6
6550	Subdividers and developers	5	7	4.2	13	5	12,923	8,800	224	172	0.8
SCOTT, AR											
60 –	**Finance, insurance, and real estate**	13	13	0.3	93	105	17,935	17,105	1,687	1,750	0.2
6000	Depository institutions	5	5	0.5	77	85	19,273	18,541	1,481	1,543	0.4
6500	Real estate	4	4	0.2	8	10	10,000	11,200	94	101	0.1
SEARCY, AR											
60 –	**Finance, insurance, and real estate**	6	5	0.1	32	27	19,125	17,333	608	480	0.0
SEBASTIAN, AR											
60 –	**Finance, insurance, and real estate**	294	309	6.2	2,421	2,285	23,554	22,899	57,857	53,497	5.2
6000	Depository institutions	50	55	5.1	1,054	1,103	19,787	20,272	21,548	23,076	6.4
6020	Commercial banks	34	34	4.0	761	792	20,131	20,298	16,085	16,788	5.4
6060	Credit unions	8	7	8.0	54	53	19,407	19,547	1,041	1,050	-
6200	Security and commodity brokers	16	19	8.1	91	92	47,297	39,217	3,503	3,748	2.9
6210	Security brokers and dealers	11	14	7.9	71	76	57,408	45,263	3,339	3,217	2.7
6280	Security and commodity services	5	5	9.8	20	16	11,400	10,500	164	531	7.5
6300	Insurance carriers	20	24	8.0	101	102	28,277	36,863	2,696	3,545	2.1
6400	Insurance agents, brokers, and service	88	90	6.9	275	282	20,655	22,184	6,574	6,671	5.7
6500	Real estate	97	100	5.7	399	418	14,586	15,301	6,291	7,057	5.2
6510	Real estate operators and lessors	52	48	6.9	248	223	13,935	14,978	3,514	3,557	9.8
6530	Real estate agents and managers	33	36	5.0	81	123	16,247	15,317	1,589	2,132	3.5
6540	Title abstract offices	4	5	4.3	47	43	15,234	16,372	787	816	5.1
6550	Subdividers and developers	7	8	4.8	23	28	14,435	14,857	370	506	2.3
SEVIER, AR											
60 –	**Finance, insurance, and real estate**	18	20	0.4	111	119	21,550	21,244	2,371	2,512	0.2
6000	Depository institutions	8	8	0.7	85	86	23,106	23,442	1,862	1,929	0.5

Source: County Business Patterns, 1994/95, CBP-94/95, U.S. Department of Commerce, Washington, D.C., November 1997. SIC categories for which data were suppressed or not available for both 1994 and 1995 are *not* displayed. The employment columns represent mid-March employment in the year. Pay per employee is calculated by dividing 1st Quarter payroll, annualized, by mid-March employment. The columns headed "% State" show the county's percentage of the state total for the SIC in 1995; for example, 1.4% for SIC 6000 means that the county had 1.4 percent of the state's total establishments (or payroll) in SIC 6000 in 1995. A dash (-) is used to indicate that data are not available or cannot be calculated; *nec* means not elsewhere classified.

SIC	Industry	No. Establishments			Employment		Pay / Employee		Annual Payroll ($ 000)		
		1994	1995	% State	1994	1995	1994	1995	1994	1995	% State
SHARP, AR											
60–	**Finance, insurance, and real estate**	35	37	*0.7*	187	199	15,016	16,824	3,034	3,707	*0.4*
6000	Depository institutions	11	12	*1.1*	121	129	16,860	19,752	2,165	2,492	*0.7*
6530	Real estate agents and managers	11	11	*1.5*	31	35	11,742	9,943	457	448	*0.7*
STONE, AR											
60–	**Finance, insurance, and real estate**	11	12	*0.2*	64	64	17,688	17,750	1,163	1,236	*0.1*
UNION, AR											
60–	**Finance, insurance, and real estate**	91	99	*2.0*	766	726	22,219	23,328	16,684	16,560	*1.6*
6000	Depository institutions	19	22	*2.1*	445	411	21,582	21,830	9,593	8,911	*2.5*
6300	Insurance carriers	8	7	*2.3*	87	74	27,632	31,892	2,261	2,174	*1.3*
6400	Insurance agents, brokers, and service	21	24	*1.8*	75	72	19,520	20,111	1,603	1,614	*1.4*
6500	Real estate	28	28	*1.6*	92	90	12,348	14,133	1,182	1,277	*0.9*
6510	Real estate operators and lessors	14	16	*2.3*	45	46	8,267	9,739	416	442	*1.2*
6790	Miscellaneous investing	6	7	*14.9*	22	23	22,364	17,565	409	409	*13.4*
VAN BUREN, AR											
60–	**Finance, insurance, and real estate**	27	24	*0.5*	188	118	16,702	19,051	3,435	2,612	*0.3*
6000	Depository institutions	9	7	*0.7*	81	46	18,765	16,783	1,528	797	*0.2*
6020	Commercial banks	9	7	*0.8*	81	46	18,765	16,783	1,528	797	*0.3*
6500	Real estate	9	10	*0.6*	85	57	13,600	19,719	1,468	1,470	*1.1*
6530	Real estate agents and managers	6	7	*1.0*	78	50	13,487	19,920	1,297	1,280	*2.1*
WASHINGTON, AR											
60–	**Finance, insurance, and real estate**	319	343	*6.9*	2,080	2,095	28,458	29,321	55,790	60,473	*5.9*
6000	Depository institutions	53	52	*4.9*	923	782	21,473	23,018	20,345	18,304	*5.1*
6020	Commercial banks	41	38	*4.5*	815	659	21,070	23,053	18,181	15,716	*5.1*
6030	Savings institutions	6	9	*8.3*	84	104	17,762	20,308	1,396	2,022	*6.6*
6100	Nondepository institutions	12	13	*8.5*	91	112	21,670	27,393	2,273	3,303	*-*
6200	Security and commodity brokers	19	21	*8.9*	189	208	84,910	78,962	11,435	13,389	*10.5*
6210	Security brokers and dealers	13	14	*7.9*	165	187	92,921	84,492	10,716	12,490	*10.4*
6280	Security and commodity services	6	7	*13.7*	24	21	29,833	29,714	719	899	*12.7*
6300	Insurance carriers	18	19	*6.4*	105	107	38,743	36,935	3,724	3,739	*2.3*
6330	Fire, marine, and casualty insurance	13	15	*11.1*	59	90	38,915	37,911	2,257	3,187	*7.8*
6400	Insurance agents, brokers, and service	71	70	*5.4*	295	285	21,085	23,719	6,728	7,087	*6.0*
6500	Real estate	139	161	*9.2*	392	519	15,316	16,408	6,939	9,869	*7.2*
6510	Real estate operators and lessors	69	75	*10.8*	127	175	12,472	12,023	1,778	2,409	*6.6*
6530	Real estate agents and managers	52	59	*8.3*	207	256	17,082	19,344	4,039	5,717	*9.5*
6550	Subdividers and developers	10	14	*8.3*	7	16	11,429	21,000	165	371	*1.7*
6552	Subdividers and developers, n.e.c.	7	10	*10.3*	5	12	12,000	19,333	137	241	*1.3*
6700	Holding and other investment offices	7	7	*4.8*	85	82	59,529	57,415	4,346	4,782	*7.2*
WHITE, AR											
60–	**Finance, insurance, and real estate**	101	105	*2.1*	548	555	16,197	16,850	9,654	9,999	*1.0*
6000	Depository institutions	26	26	*2.4*	311	316	18,431	18,899	6,089	6,366	*1.8*
6020	Commercial banks	22	22	*2.6*	301	306	18,671	19,137	5,979	6,248	*2.0*
6060	Credit unions	4	4	*4.6*	10	10	11,200	11,600	110	118	*-*
6400	Insurance agents, brokers, and service	36	34	*2.6*	110	107	12,836	13,533	1,531	1,643	*1.4*
6500	Real estate	32	36	*2.1*	102	105	8,941	11,390	1,301	1,304	*1.0*
6510	Real estate operators and lessors	17	17	*2.4*	49	52	8,000	10,769	570	567	*1.6*
6530	Real estate agents and managers	10	13	*1.8*	20	25	11,800	11,840	368	296	*0.5*
WOODRUFF, AR											
60–	**Finance, insurance, and real estate**	9	11	*0.2*	64	67	19,500	20,119	1,446	1,514	*0.1*
6500	Real estate	4	4	*0.2*	14	16	10,000	9,250	138	132	*0.1*

Source: County Business Patterns, 1994/95, CBP-94/95, U.S. Department of Commerce, Washington, D.C., November 1997. SIC categories for which data were suppressed or not available for both 1994 and 1995 are not displayed. The employment columns represent mid-March employment in the year. Pay per employee is calculated by dividing 1st Quarter payroll, annualized, by mid-March employment. The columns headed "% State" show the county's percentage of the state total for the SIC in 1995; for example, 1.4% for SIC 6000 means that the county had 1.4 percent of the state's total establishments (or payroll) in SIC 6000 in 1995. A dash (-) is used to indicate that data are not available or cannot be calculated; nec means not elsewhere classified.

SIC	Industry	No. Establishments			Employment		Pay / Employee		Annual Payroll ($ 000)		
		1994	1995	% State	1994	1995	1994	1995	1994	1995	% State
YELL, AR											
60 –	**Finance, insurance, and real estate**	26	25	0.5	126	157	19,111	18,166	2,827	3,388	0.3
6000	Depository institutions	7	8	0.7	89	109	18,876	18,128	2,043	2,393	0.7
6530	Real estate agents and managers	5	6	0.8	5	18	11,200	15,556	161	379	0.6

Source: County Business Patterns, 1994/95, CBP-94/95, U.S. Department of Commerce, Washington, D.C., November 1997. SIC categories for which data were suppressed or not available for both 1994 and 1995 are *not* displayed. The employment columns represent mid-March employment in the year. Pay per employee is calculated by dividing 1st Quarter payroll, annualized, by mid-March employment. The columns headed "% State" show the county's percentage of the state total for the SIC in 1995; for example, 1.4% for SIC 6000 means that the county had 1.4 percent of the state's total establishments (or payroll) in SIC 6000 in 1995. A dash (-) is used to indicate that data are not available or cannot be calculated; *nec* means not elsewhere classified.

CALIFORNIA

SIC	Industry	No. Establishments			Employment		Pay / Employee		Annual Payroll ($ 000)		
		1994	1995	% State	1994	1995	1994	1995	1994	1995	% State
ALAMEDA, CA											
60–	**Finance, insurance, and real estate**	3,067	2,966	4.0	28,830	26,870	30,281	30,990	852,629	825,513	2.8
6000	Depository institutions	444	443	3.9	10,009	9,499	27,978	27,305	266,091	247,759	3.4
6020	Commercial banks	201	212	3.3	5,982	6,134	25,631	25,536	147,552	146,703	3.1
6030	Savings institutions	125	113	4.5	3,023	2,336	33,661	32,844	93,127	74,834	5.5
6060	Credit unions	73	71	5.7	730	749	26,822	27,359	19,519	20,419	4.2
6090	Functions closely related to banking	45	47	4.8	274	280	19,591	19,714	5,893	5,803	2.0
6100	Nondepository institutions	263	231	3.6	2,229	2,139	39,404	39,690	77,453	83,775	3.2
6140	Personal credit institutions	66	67	4.3	760	889	38,547	35,154	26,303	32,299	4.7
6150	Business credit institutions	24	22	3.5	287	352	50,997	58,114	12,592	16,742	3.0
6160	Mortgage bankers and brokers	169	139	3.4	1,152	861	38,021	38,239	38,337	34,402	2.6
6200	Security and commodity brokers	131	131	2.8	984	1,019	55,159	54,563	59,021	62,340	1.5
6210	Security brokers and dealers	64	68	2.9	668	644	63,413	62,273	40,667	40,155	1.3
6300	Insurance carriers	213	197	4.3	4,726	4,349	37,835	39,420	175,223	165,217	2.8
6310	Life insurance	30	33	3.5	416	387	32,971	36,031	12,890	11,554	1.0
6320	Medical service and health insurance	18	16	5.2	638	433	45,429	50,882	29,165	20,883	1.9
6330	Fire, marine, and casualty insurance	87	82	3.7	2,606	2,497	37,434	40,851	96,233	96,419	3.3
6360	Title insurance	44	38	6.6	622	570	37,010	29,789	19,806	17,929	3.8
6370	Pension, health, and welfare funds	29	24	6.0	401	431	33,875	35,369	14,661	16,880	11.7
6400	Insurance agents, brokers, and service	460	446	3.9	2,083	2,194	34,635	36,660	74,298	84,739	3.2
6500	Real estate	1,443	1,406	4.4	7,657	6,631	19,495	20,651	152,470	141,081	2.9
6510	Real estate operators and lessors	726	708	4.9	3,764	2,877	14,948	17,661	60,718	53,145	3.9
6530	Real estate agents and managers	618	587	4.0	3,301	3,181	22,722	21,909	75,316	71,630	2.5
6540	Title abstract offices	22	16	7.1	182	73	32,242	36,493	3,587	2,587	3.6
6550	Subdividers and developers	55	58	3.5	399	437	29,935	28,998	12,520	12,082	2.6
6552	Subdividers and developers, n.e.c.	42	42	3.3	205	158	32,956	43,949	6,682	5,919	1.7
6553	Cemetery subdividers and developers	10	10	4.1	194	275	26,742	20,669	5,320	5,699	5.8
6700	Holding and other investment offices	95	96	3.3	658	673	43,988	39,572	29,423	26,685	1.5
6710	Holding offices	23	15	2.2	338	265	51,858	46,219	17,214	11,515	1.5
6720	Investment offices	3	3	3.0	4	5	17,000	14,400	68	76	0.0
6730	Trusts	35	43	4.6	202	277	37,386	36,029	7,681	10,239	6.1
6732	Educational, religious, etc. trusts	17	25	5.8	48	56	18,917	20,357	1,000	1,249	1.1
6733	Trusts, n.e.c.	18	18	3.6	154	221	43,143	40,000	6,681	8,990	15.4
6790	Miscellaneous investing	33	34	3.2	114	124	33,298	34,419	4,453	4,798	0.9
6799	Investors, n.e.c.	23	23	3.2	58	64	29,448	32,438	2,259	2,211	1.1
ALPINE, CA											
60–	**Finance, insurance, and real estate**	4	5	0.0	-	-	-	-	-	-	-
AMADOR, CA											
60–	**Finance, insurance, and real estate**	71	67	0.1	388	317	18,515	19,836	6,456	5,932	0.0
6000	Depository institutions	16	16	0.1	148	137	19,649	24,204	2,817	3,000	0.0
6020	Commercial banks	9	9	0.1	113	100	19,717	26,160	2,176	2,283	0.0
6300	Insurance carriers	5	4	0.1	72	15	27,222	31,200	1,215	472	0.0
6400	Insurance agents, brokers, and service	13	10	0.1	62	53	19,613	19,547	1,192	1,019	0.0
6500	Real estate	29	30	0.1	94	96	9,915	10,917	912	994	0.0
6510	Real estate operators and lessors	15	16	0.1	55	57	8,800	8,842	496	522	0.0
6530	Real estate agents and managers	9	9	0.1	21	30	12,381	12,933	315	402	0.0
6550	Subdividers and developers	5	5	0.3	18	9	10,444	17,333	101	70	0.0
BUTTE, CA											
60–	**Finance, insurance, and real estate**	401	400	0.5	2,836	2,761	21,474	21,224	58,822	57,956	0.2

Source: County Business Patterns, 1994/95, CBP-94/95, U.S. Department of Commerce, Washington, D.C., November 1997. SIC categories for which data were suppressed or not available for both 1994 and 1995 are not displayed. The employment columns represent mid-March employment in the year. Pay per employee is calculated by dividing 1st Quarter payroll, annualized, by mid-March employment. The columns headed "% State" show the county's percentage of the state total for the SIC in 1995; for example, 1.4% for SIC 6000 means that the county had 1.4 percent of the state's total establishments (or payroll) in SIC 6000 in 1995. A dash (-) is used to indicate that data are not available or cannot be calculated; nec means not elsewhere classified.

Continued on next page.

SIC	Industry	No. Establishments			Employment		Pay / Employee		Annual Payroll ($ 000)		
		1994	1995	% State	1994	1995	1994	1995	1994	1995	% State
BUTTE, CA - [continued]											
6000	Depository institutions	67	69	0.6	947	888	22,817	22,117	19,944	18,609	0.3
6020	Commercial banks	44	47	0.7	722	701	23,745	23,041	15,840	15,312	0.3
6030	Savings institutions	11	11	0.4	149	129	20,564	19,690	2,784	2,480	0.2
6100	Nondepository institutions	29	27	0.4	140	115	30,400	34,017	3,993	3,542	0.1
6200	Security and commodity brokers	25	27	0.6	120	130	44,333	42,462	5,197	5,880	0.1
6210	Security brokers and dealers	18	17	0.7	79	86	57,215	51,581	4,145	4,594	0.2
6280	Security and commodity services	7	10	0.5	41	44	19,512	24,636	1,052	1,286	0.1
6300	Insurance carriers	27	26	0.6	344	345	28,860	26,899	8,938	8,248	0.1
6400	Insurance agents, brokers, and service	82	87	0.8	296	291	25,189	25,320	7,767	7,364	0.3
6500	Real estate	162	155	0.5	954	970	12,486	13,031	12,473	13,896	0.3
6510	Real estate operators and lessors	71	71	0.5	352	338	9,068	9,751	3,633	3,681	0.3
6530	Real estate agents and managers	80	71	0.5	508	470	14,047	14,145	7,040	7,108	0.2
6552	Subdividers and developers, n.e.c.	8	7	0.5	37	107	12,865	16,150	779	2,065	0.6
6730	Trusts	4	4	0.4	20	5	9,600	8,000	266	110	0.1
CALAVERAS, CA											
60 –	**Finance, insurance, and real estate**	70	66	0.1	365	345	20,921	18,249	7,168	7,565	0.0
6000	Depository institutions	11	11	0.1	154	149	20,675	19,275	2,968	2,820	0.0
6300	Insurance carriers	7	7	0.2	27	24	21,926	20,833	558	604	0.0
6400	Insurance agents, brokers, and service	12	10	0.1	57	47	21,614	22,638	1,249	1,032	0.0
6500	Real estate	35	34	0.1	109	109	19,486	15,266	2,044	2,833	0.1
6510	Real estate operators and lessors	6	7	0.0	14	15	29,714	28,267	433	505	0.0
6530	Real estate agents and managers	25	23	0.2	48	47	15,417	11,660	643	587	0.0
6550	Subdividers and developers	4	4	0.2	47	47	20,596	14,723	968	1,741	0.4
6552	Subdividers and developers, n.e.c.	4	4	0.3	47	47	20,596	14,723	968	1,741	0.5
COLUSA, CA											
60 –	**Finance, insurance, and real estate**	29	31	0.0	389	168	23,280	25,786	7,988	3,762	0.0
6000	Depository institutions	8	8	0.1	70	67	15,486	15,224	1,123	971	0.0
6020	Commercial banks	8	8	0.1	70	67	15,486	15,224	1,123	971	0.0
6500	Real estate	11	10	0.0	271	38	25,461	16,105	5,692	651	0.0
CONTRA COSTA, CA											
60 –	**Finance, insurance, and real estate**	2,758	2,690	3.7	33,187	31,256	36,534	36,768	1,161,450	1,098,992	3.7
6000	Depository institutions	494	490	4.3	14,040	13,409	37,883	36,734	511,280	451,508	6.2
6020	Commercial banks	336	339	5.3	12,125	12,010	39,076	37,853	459,109	415,483	8.7
6030	Savings institutions	93	85	3.4	1,474	996	30,999	28,900	40,405	26,598	1.9
6060	Credit unions	41	38	3.0	346	293	31,214	24,587	9,875	7,121	1.5
6090	Functions closely related to banking	24	28	2.9	95	110	16,758	17,927	1,891	2,306	0.8
6100	Nondepository institutions	328	284	4.4	3,506	2,151	39,075	40,067	110,671	88,290	3.3
6140	Personal credit institutions	49	50	3.2	393	379	27,878	32,443	10,988	14,050	2.0
6150	Business credit institutions	23	31	4.9	207	234	45,179	51,983	9,034	10,897	1.9
6160	Mortgage bankers and brokers	256	203	5.0	2,906	1,538	40,154	40,133	90,649	63,343	4.8
6200	Security and commodity brokers	175	189	4.1	1,083	1,190	65,647	60,387	64,375	72,686	1.7
6210	Security brokers and dealers	82	84	3.5	665	747	76,102	68,011	42,930	48,772	1.6
6280	Security and commodity services	90	101	4.7	415	437	49,330	47,945	21,392	23,708	1.9
6300	Insurance carriers	227	220	4.8	4,905	4,577	40,445	40,912	196,265	175,902	3.0
6310	Life insurance	56	60	6.4	1,985	1,905	41,961	43,108	77,838	76,480	6.6
6320	Medical service and health insurance	9	11	3.6	541	580	36,924	40,172	27,760	15,346	1.4
6330	Fire, marine, and casualty insurance	90	85	3.8	1,319	1,138	41,625	42,320	54,007	49,386	1.7
6350	Surety insurance	8	6	7.3	156	135	36,128	38,370	5,915	4,785	6.9
6360	Title insurance	49	44	7.6	724	636	39,823	35,019	24,671	23,169	4.9
6370	Pension, health, and welfare funds	15	13	3.2	180	183	31,911	33,989	6,074	6,697	4.7
6400	Insurance agents, brokers, and service	428	412	3.6	2,575	2,572	35,045	38,409	90,889	101,179	3.9
6500	Real estate	1,036	1,017	3.2	6,212	6,330	23,395	24,715	149,135	156,692	3.3
6510	Real estate operators and lessors	382	387	2.7	1,673	1,681	15,782	19,141	27,779	31,179	2.3
6530	Real estate agents and managers	556	521	3.5	4,005	4,071	24,907	25,076	100,744	103,597	3.6
6550	Subdividers and developers	66	75	4.5	409	463	33,046	39,991	15,260	17,772	3.8

Source: County Business Patterns, 1994/95, CBP-94/95, U.S. Department of Commerce, Washington, D.C., November 1997. SIC categories for which data were suppressed or not available for both 1994 and 1995 are *not* displayed. The employment columns represent mid-March employment in the year. Pay per employee is calculated by dividing 1st Quarter payroll, annualized, by mid-March employment. The columns headed "% State" show the county's percentage of the state total for the SIC in 1995; for example, 1.4% for SIC 6000 means that the county had 1.4 percent of the state's total establishments (or payroll) in SIC 6000 in 1995. A dash (-) is used to indicate that data are not available or cannot be calculated; *nec* means not elsewhere classified.

Continued on next page.

SIC	Industry	No. Establishments			Employment		Pay / Employee		Annual Payroll ($ 000)		
		1994	1995	% State	1994	1995	1994	1995	1994	1995	% State
CONTRA COSTA, CA - [continued]											
6552	Subdividers and developers, n.e.c.	51	58	4.5	250	283	34,880	43,675	10,349	11,844	3.4
6553	Cemetery subdividers and developers	13	12	4.9	159	172	30,164	32,488	4,866	5,426	5.5
6700	Holding and other investment offices	63	70	2.4	539	688	46,397	56,477	25,858	36,164	2.1
6710	Holding offices	15	18	2.6	326	449	52,196	70,646	17,534	27,825	3.5
6733	Trusts, n.e.c.	10	8	1.6	47	47	30,553	33,957	1,427	1,517	2.6
6790	Miscellaneous investing	29	26	2.4	137	114	42,832	33,263	5,618	4,436	0.9
6799	Investors, n.e.c.	21	18	2.5	59	50	49,898	44,720	2,955	2,686	1.3
DEL NORTE, CA											
60 –	**Finance, insurance, and real estate**	36	36	0.0	161	192	17,342	16,354	2,849	3,345	0.0
6000	Depository institutions	9	9	0.1	82	79	17,220	17,924	1,413	1,317	0.0
6020	Commercial banks	5	5	0.1	65	60	16,923	17,800	1,099	964	0.0
6400	Insurance agents, brokers, and service	7	8	0.1	38	60	24,737	20,333	946	1,482	0.1
EL DORADO, CA											
60 –	**Finance, insurance, and real estate**	327	305	0.4	2,092	1,911	20,151	21,229	43,483	40,522	0.1
6000	Depository institutions	43	44	0.4	487	502	20,320	19,267	10,027	10,369	0.1
6020	Commercial banks	18	21	0.3	275	317	19,651	18,095	5,450	6,170	0.1
6030	Savings institutions	19	17	0.7	173	146	22,497	22,795	3,913	3,564	0.3
6100	Nondepository institutions	29	21	0.3	109	62	26,275	26,258	2,765	2,317	0.1
6160	Mortgage bankers and brokers	25	17	0.4	97	53	26,887	24,528	2,489	2,018	0.2
6300	Insurance carriers	20	19	0.4	412	287	25,553	29,826	9,645	5,978	0.1
6360	Title insurance	8	8	1.4	63	51	29,460	26,824	1,591	1,464	0.3
6400	Insurance agents, brokers, and service	56	53	0.5	217	207	20,424	24,792	5,013	5,238	0.2
6500	Real estate	159	148	0.5	804	774	16,507	17,835	14,714	14,658	0.3
6510	Real estate operators and lessors	56	56	0.4	228	230	11,842	12,591	3,542	3,177	0.2
6530	Real estate agents and managers	78	69	0.5	439	419	15,189	15,857	7,347	7,829	0.3
6552	Subdividers and developers, n.e.c.	14	12	0.9	48	54	26,833	23,111	1,646	1,387	0.4
FRESNO, CA											
60 –	**Finance, insurance, and real estate**	1,410	1,402	1.9	13,680	13,495	27,162	27,552	358,232	362,687	1.2
6000	Depository institutions	211	212	1.9	3,433	3,774	24,886	24,843	79,679	88,195	1.2
6020	Commercial banks	127	128	2.0	2,479	2,789	25,399	25,781	57,978	66,847	1.4
6030	Savings institutions	41	41	1.6	448	441	26,304	23,193	10,652	9,618	0.7
6060	Credit unions	27	26	2.1	438	462	22,192	22,390	10,012	10,456	2.1
6090	Functions closely related to banking	16	17	1.7	68	82	14,176	15,610	1,037	1,274	0.4
6100	Nondepository institutions	148	143	2.2	1,087	820	33,509	32,546	31,321	26,439	1.0
6140	Personal credit institutions	41	44	2.8	293	272	31,577	33,750	8,106	7,734	1.1
6150	Business credit institutions	19	17	2.7	69	68	36,986	33,882	2,778	2,675	0.5
6160	Mortgage bankers and brokers	81	74	1.8	685	440	33,834	31,155	18,919	14,316	1.1
6200	Security and commodity brokers	51	56	1.2	471	451	73,945	72,426	27,802	28,678	0.7
6210	Security brokers and dealers	27	29	1.2	425	394	79,595	79,320	26,686	26,933	0.9
6300	Insurance carriers	143	133	2.9	3,413	3,300	29,558	30,125	101,034	95,900	1.6
6310	Life insurance	33	32	3.4	1,071	995	25,587	25,705	26,520	23,557	2.0
6320	Medical service and health insurance	11	9	3.0	251	182	34,454	49,560	11,792	9,310	0.8
6330	Fire, marine, and casualty insurance	63	56	2.5	1,375	1,479	31,718	32,143	44,445	45,723	1.5
6360	Title insurance	15	15	2.6	377	292	34,928	32,027	10,756	9,699	2.0
6370	Pension, health, and welfare funds	21	21	5.2	339	352	23,740	22,511	7,521	7,611	5.3
6400	Insurance agents, brokers, and service	328	331	2.9	1,858	1,735	28,263	32,475	53,917	57,316	2.2
6500	Real estate	478	480	1.5	2,784	2,819	17,055	17,908	48,900	51,978	1.1
6510	Real estate operators and lessors	232	223	1.6	1,251	1,314	14,257	13,562	17,727	17,237	1.3
6530	Real estate agents and managers	202	196	1.3	1,268	1,280	19,013	21,553	25,503	27,756	1.0
6550	Subdividers and developers	34	45	2.7	197	208	20,690	23,231	4,540	6,419	1.4
6552	Subdividers and developers, n.e.c.	26	35	2.7	116	120	20,724	22,500	2,622	3,749	1.1
6553	Cemetery subdividers and developers	5	5	2.0	81	83	20,642	24,819	1,885	2,106	2.1

Source: County Business Patterns, 1994/95, CBP-94/95, U.S. Department of Commerce, Washington, D.C., November 1997. SIC categories for which data were suppressed or not available for both 1994 and 1995 are not displayed. The employment columns represent mid-March employment in the year. Pay per employee is calculated by dividing 1st Quarter payroll, annualized, by mid-March employment. The columns headed "% State" show the county's percentage of the state total for the SIC in 1995; for example, 1.4% for SIC 6000 means that the county had 1.4 percent of the state's total establishments (or payroll) in SIC 6000 in 1995. A dash (-) is used to indicate that data are not available or cannot be calculated; nec means not elsewhere classified.

Continued on next page.

SIC	Industry	No. Establishments			Employment		Pay / Employee		Annual Payroll ($ 000)		
		1994	1995	% State	1994	1995	1994	1995	1994	1995	% State
FRESNO, CA - [continued]											
6700	Holding and other investment offices	47	42	1.4	564	544	20,333	18,478	12,912	11,741	0.7
6730	Trusts	17	19	2.0	458	437	14,594	14,920	7,249	7,353	4.4
6799	Investors, n.e.c.	8	8	1.1	8	15	26,500	26,133	461	652	0.3
GLENN, CA											
60 –	**Finance, insurance, and real estate**	40	36	0.0	167	160	22,419	17,800	3,264	3,022	0.0
6000	Depository institutions	9	9	0.1	78	77	19,744	17,299	1,435	1,351	0.0
6400	Insurance agents, brokers, and service	14	12	0.1	49	45	19,510	19,467	966	962	0.0
6500	Real estate	12	11	0.0	15	16	6,133	5,750	127	118	0.0
6530	Real estate agents and managers	7	6	0.0	7	8	9,714	8,000	102	59	0.0
HUMBOLDT, CA											
60 –	**Finance, insurance, and real estate**	267	268	0.4	1,717	1,740	19,180	19,595	34,838	36,011	0.1
6000	Depository institutions	45	41	0.4	649	709	18,687	19,306	12,759	13,446	0.2
6020	Commercial banks	29	25	0.4	471	524	18,446	18,893	9,068	9,653	0.2
6160	Mortgage bankers and brokers	7	6	0.1	34	29	30,353	11,862	734	384	0.0
6200	Security and commodity brokers	7	9	0.2	51	57	52,941	49,404	2,692	2,921	0.1
6300	Insurance carriers	8	10	0.2	74	66	33,514	34,545	2,536	2,591	0.0
6400	Insurance agents, brokers, and service	53	55	0.5	200	205	20,640	22,888	4,704	5,099	0.2
6500	Real estate	132	131	0.4	435	390	14,860	14,718	6,599	6,199	0.1
6510	Real estate operators and lessors	60	65	0.5	215	203	14,772	16,177	3,214	3,334	0.2
6530	Real estate agents and managers	57	45	0.3	144	134	10,528	9,672	1,618	1,429	0.0
IMPERIAL, CA											
60 –	**Finance, insurance, and real estate**	158	169	0.2	1,201	1,143	20,070	21,319	24,103	24,198	0.1
6000	Depository institutions	29	34	0.3	517	513	22,499	22,394	10,949	11,064	0.2
6020	Commercial banks	17	18	0.3	382	361	24,314	24,166	8,271	8,003	0.2
6090	Functions closely related to banking	4	6	0.6	13	24	13,231	13,167	256	336	0.1
6100	Nondepository institutions	11	13	0.2	39	40	22,462	38,800	792	1,585	0.1
6140	Personal credit institutions	6	7	0.4	29	24	24,828	32,500	679	749	0.1
6400	Insurance agents, brokers, and service	36	37	0.3	121	130	22,744	22,769	2,969	2,917	0.1
6500	Real estate	65	67	0.2	429	376	15,571	16,883	7,322	6,468	0.1
6510	Real estate operators and lessors	37	38	0.3	230	200	13,339	14,380	3,283	2,915	0.2
INYO, CA											
60 –	**Finance, insurance, and real estate**	37	35	0.0	166	146	17,928	17,342	3,163	2,923	0.0
6000	Depository institutions	7	7	0.1	85	86	17,224	16,047	1,418	1,361	0.0
6020	Commercial banks	4	4	0.1	67	68	17,433	15,882	1,121	1,050	0.0
6400	Insurance agents, brokers, and service	7	7	0.1	18	18	17,111	14,889	310	267	0.0
6500	Real estate	17	15	0.0	47	28	14,894	19,571	936	854	0.0
6510	Real estate operators and lessors	7	7	0.0	16	11	15,500	18,545	309	352	0.0
KERN, CA											
60 –	**Finance, insurance, and real estate**	855	834	1.1	9,481	8,905	29,988	31,561	269,883	278,590	0.9
6000	Depository institutions	148	134	1.2	2,230	2,179	21,783	22,021	49,437	45,413	0.6
6020	Commercial banks	94	81	1.3	1,403	1,318	20,895	21,399	30,827	27,014	0.6
6060	Credit unions	32	31	2.5	550	600	22,313	22,367	12,117	12,424	2.5
6100	Nondepository institutions	84	85	1.3	575	478	33,864	33,548	16,429	15,015	0.6
6140	Personal credit institutions	31	31	2.0	157	143	28,280	29,650	4,218	4,078	0.6
6160	Mortgage bankers and brokers	46	44	1.1	393	312	36,112	35,295	11,482	9,918	0.7
6200	Security and commodity brokers	27	27	0.6	175	258	49,166	53,690	7,935	14,471	0.3
6210	Security brokers and dealers	16	17	0.7	156	235	53,564	57,804	7,687	14,169	0.5
6280	Security and commodity services	11	10	0.5	19	23	13,053	11,652	248	302	0.0
6300	Insurance carriers	53	57	1.3	4,144	3,634	37,873	42,334	144,954	154,536	2.6
6360	Title insurance	8	8	1.4	263	180	32,867	35,556	7,844	7,038	1.5
6400	Insurance agents, brokers, and service	189	182	1.6	596	606	27,141	28,112	14,421	15,869	0.6
6500	Real estate	328	326	1.0	1,696	1,678	18,302	17,783	32,997	29,428	0.6
6510	Real estate operators and lessors	136	138	1.0	604	632	13,861	13,816	9,692	9,398	0.7

Source: County Business Patterns, 1994/95, CBP-94/95, U.S. Department of Commerce, Washington, D.C., November 1997. SIC categories for which data were suppressed or not available for both 1994 and 1995 are not displayed. The employment columns represent mid-March employment in the year. Pay per employee is calculated by dividing 1st Quarter payroll, annualized, by mid-March employment. The columns headed "% State" show the county's percentage of the state total for the SIC in 1995; for example, 1.4% for SIC 6000 means that the county had 1.4 percent of the state's total establishments (or payroll) in SIC 6000 in 1995. A dash (-) is used to indicate that data are not available or cannot be calculated; nec means not elsewhere classified.

Continued on next page.

SIC	Industry	No. Establishments			Employment		Pay / Employee		Annual Payroll ($ 000)		
		1994	1995	% State	1994	1995	1994	1995	1994	1995	% State
KERN, CA - [continued]											
6530	Real estate agents and managers	164	158	1.1	830	819	16,819	17,495	15,142	14,431	0.5
6552	Subdividers and developers, n.e.c.	16	16	1.2	106	66	50,000	46,788	4,209	3,177	0.9
6553	Cemetery subdividers and developers	5	5	2.0	87	84	14,345	18,048	1,348	1,548	1.6
6732	Educational, religious, etc. trusts	3	3	0.7	5	3	36,800	49,333	188	146	0.1
6790	Miscellaneous investing	12	9	0.8	22	16	71,091	18,750	774	314	0.1
6799	Investors, n.e.c.	6	3	0.4	10	4	125,600	21,000	401	37	0.0
KINGS, CA											
60 –	**Finance, insurance, and real estate**	114	114	0.2	721	702	21,221	22,171	15,567	17,038	0.1
6000	Depository institutions	21	21	0.2	266	281	17,759	17,879	4,741	5,061	0.1
6020	Commercial banks	11	11	0.2	168	176	17,310	17,523	2,903	3,065	0.1
6060	Credit unions	6	6	0.5	73	76	19,836	19,684	1,443	1,533	0.3
6100	Nondepository institutions	13	14	0.2	76	75	33,368	31,733	2,144	2,582	0.1
6400	Insurance agents, brokers, and service	22	24	0.2	128	120	27,563	28,767	3,940	3,960	0.2
6500	Real estate	48	44	0.1	181	142	13,193	13,775	2,450	1,994	0.0
6510	Real estate operators and lessors	26	24	0.2	86	71	10,233	12,000	887	795	0.1
LAKE, CA											
60 –	**Finance, insurance, and real estate**	102	94	0.1	684	586	21,766	23,959	13,617	12,667	0.0
6000	Depository institutions	20	18	0.2	209	222	24,976	25,495	5,044	5,211	0.1
6020	Commercial banks	14	13	0.2	172	199	26,163	26,291	4,365	4,750	0.1
6400	Insurance agents, brokers, and service	13	16	0.1	51	53	20,863	17,208	916	929	0.0
6500	Real estate	50	44	0.1	180	131	13,889	14,870	1,901	1,925	0.0
6530	Real estate agents and managers	19	16	0.1	83	56	14,699	15,286	695	916	0.0
6700	Holding and other investment offices	4	3	0.1	12	11	17,667	21,818	247	271	0.0
LASSEN, CA											
60 –	**Finance, insurance, and real estate**	42	39	0.1	187	186	24,620	24,323	4,346	4,391	0.0
6000	Depository institutions	8	9	0.1	97	98	17,278	17,388	1,686	1,694	0.0
6020	Commercial banks	5	6	0.1	78	86	17,333	16,837	1,380	1,420	0.0
6510	Real estate operators and lessors	5	4	0.0	9	9	7,556	7,111	72	50	0.0
LOS ANGELES, CA											
60 –	**Finance, insurance, and real estate**	20,240	20,108	27.4	248,138	244,987	38,744	41,064	9,445,268	9,892,890	33.3
6000	Depository institutions	2,753	2,741	24.3	79,036	76,594	34,467	35,291	2,597,984	2,586,330	35.5
6020	Commercial banks	1,264	1,282	20.0	47,005	46,040	33,061	33,971	1,434,547	1,439,008	30.2
6030	Savings institutions	747	702	28.1	20,380	18,739	34,200	34,056	637,341	595,070	43.5
6060	Credit unions	295	301	24.0	4,478	4,831	27,524	29,509	125,157	142,272	29.2
6080	Foreign bank and branches and agencies	90	91	72.2	3,091	3,099	64,691	65,881	219,139	224,785	-
6090	Functions closely related to banking	353	362	37.1	3,344	3,194	37,239	39,762	156,680	158,541	53.4
6100	Nondepository institutions	1,752	1,717	26.6	19,026	17,472	41,161	43,119	679,628	752,152	28.5
6140	Personal credit institutions	358	351	22.3	4,139	4,434	33,166	36,128	141,446	156,663	22.7
6150	Business credit institutions	216	196	31.2	3,841	3,951	54,800	53,968	175,663	192,768	34.1
6160	Mortgage bankers and brokers	1,157	1,136	27.7	10,745	8,764	39,044	41,115	347,213	384,167	29.0
6200	Security and commodity brokers	1,174	1,222	26.4	15,509	15,787	86,565	97,489	1,402,204	1,442,422	33.8
6210	Security brokers and dealers	597	630	26.6	11,070	10,629	87,996	99,388	927,374	974,538	32.5
6220	Commodity contracts brokers, dealers	26	26	34.2	98	115	41,592	44,800	5,545	5,540	26.4
6280	Security and commodity services	542	553	25.8	4,250	4,886	84,931	96,824	465,671	457,196	37.0
6300	Insurance carriers	1,079	1,055	23.2	46,817	43,732	42,710	45,774	1,892,836	1,912,594	32.2
6310	Life insurance	278	266	28.4	12,840	11,076	41,789	43,943	485,606	448,553	38.5
6320	Medical service and health insurance	69	70	23.0	8,288	9,721	38,406	44,766	315,994	412,788	37.2
6321	Accident and health insurance	18	17	28.3	852	887	34,948	40,108	31,132	33,019	48.3
6324	Hospital and medical service plans	50	53	21.6	7,427	8,834	38,824	45,233	284,729	379,769	36.4
6330	Fire, marine, and casualty insurance	523	518	23.2	20,658	18,410	45,838	48,417	904,039	869,374	29.3
6350	Surety insurance	24	19	23.2	849	811	36,137	47,374	30,951	35,679	51.7
6360	Title insurance	48	49	8.5	3,025	2,440	42,002	41,857	112,703	96,963	20.4
6370	Pension, health, and welfare funds	131	125	31.1	1,079	1,125	34,714	36,786	39,526	42,843	29.8
6390	Insurance carriers, n.e.c.	5	6	46.2	78	98	33,026	49,837	4,016	4,625	64.3

Source: County Business Patterns, 1994/95, CBP-94/95, U.S. Department of Commerce, Washington, D.C., November 1997. SIC categories for which data were suppressed or not available for both 1994 and 1995 are not displayed. The employment columns represent mid-March employment in the year. Pay per employee is calculated by dividing 1st Quarter payroll, annualized, by mid-March employment. The columns headed "% State" show the county's percentage of the state total for the SIC in 1995; for example, 1.4% for SIC 6000 means that the county had 1.4 percent of the state's total establishments (or payroll) in SIC 6000 in 1995. A dash (-) is used to indicate that data are not available or cannot be calculated; nec means not elsewhere classified.

Continued on next page.

SIC	Industry	No. Establishments			Employment		Pay / Employee		Annual Payroll ($ 000)		
		1994	1995	% State	1994	1995	1994	1995	1994	1995	% State
LOS ANGELES, CA - [continued]											
6400	Insurance agents, brokers, and service	2,968	2,912	25.2	19,921	20,694	39,601	42,335	818,895	896,064	34.1
6500	Real estate	9,471	9,402	29.6	55,196	56,035	24,236	25,047	1,357,273	1,400,553	29.2
6510	Real estate operators and lessors	4,735	4,707	32.8	22,401	22,695	18,650	19,671	448,087	462,314	34.3
6530	Real estate agents and managers	4,167	4,006	27.1	28,467	28,452	27,996	29,163	787,397	805,664	28.1
6540	Title abstract offices	34	28	12.4	1,185	783	37,293	35,060	36,050	21,893	30.5
6550	Subdividers and developers	385	402	24.4	2,986	3,468	25,147	25,419	79,989	95,218	20.5
6552	Subdividers and developers, n.e.c.	303	315	24.4	1,606	1,864	27,375	28,234	46,668	60,588	17.4
6553	Cemetery subdividers and developers	61	54	22.0	1,346	1,464	22,582	21,656	31,692	32,119	32.5
6700	Holding and other investment offices	962	981	33.6	9,413	11,515	50,162	52,590	520,948	726,244	41.3
6710	Holding offices	236	244	35.6	2,876	4,332	77,743	69,009	206,033	284,475	36.2
6720	Investment offices	29	29	29.0	504	696	70,278	78,167	78,404	101,461	43.1
6730	Trusts	255	291	31.3	2,754	2,776	20,899	22,713	61,111	62,224	37.1
6732	Educational, religious, etc. trusts	96	116	27.0	1,588	2,010	20,516	19,475	35,726	39,507	36.3
6733	Trusts, n.e.c.	159	175	35.1	1,166	766	21,420	31,211	25,385	22,717	38.8
6790	Miscellaneous investing	412	359	33.7	3,243	3,469	47,546	52,322	166,903	267,977	52.4
6792	Oil royalty traders	13	13	32.5	69	70	27,594	28,057	1,911	2,036	38.3
6794	Patent owners and lessors	98	63	33.2	1,523	1,224	56,068	54,984	89,234	66,436	49.0
6798	Real estate investment trusts	46	42	39.3	389	826	55,270	71,317	24,215	142,611	84.9
6799	Investors, n.e.c.	255	241	33.1	1,262	1,349	35,971	39,534	51,543	56,894	28.0
MADERA, CA											
60 –	**Finance, insurance, and real estate**	131	135	0.2	633	653	21,049	19,718	14,168	13,670	0.0
6000	Depository institutions	24	22	0.2	246	279	22,358	20,659	5,243	5,569	0.1
6020	Commercial banks	13	13	0.2	181	216	24,199	21,685	4,115	4,529	0.1
6100	Nondepository institutions	7	8	0.1	33	27	29,212	33,926	833	879	0.0
6300	Insurance carriers	10	10	0.2	68	62	31,882	32,323	1,892	2,079	0.0
6360	Title insurance	5	5	0.9	59	51	29,627	30,510	1,476	1,651	0.3
6400	Insurance agents, brokers, and service	25	25	0.2	54	50	20,667	22,720	1,210	1,241	0.0
6500	Real estate	57	62	0.2	196	214	12,633	11,981	2,938	3,276	0.1
6530	Real estate agents and managers	44	45	0.3	129	147	11,349	9,823	1,599	2,099	0.1
MARIN, CA											
60 –	**Finance, insurance, and real estate**	1,112	1,096	1.5	9,389	9,675	40,094	43,248	357,051	436,253	1.5
6000	Depository institutions	106	108	1.0	1,557	1,584	29,590	29,311	44,889	47,275	0.6
6020	Commercial banks	62	64	1.0	1,142	1,194	29,737	29,260	33,423	36,111	0.8
6030	Savings institutions	34	34	1.4	378	354	29,820	29,966	10,569	10,216	0.7
6100	Nondepository institutions	87	78	1.2	678	627	40,560	35,789	20,321	25,711	1.0
6140	Personal credit institutions	11	9	0.6	70	51	30,686	39,451	1,937	2,144	0.3
6150	Business credit institutions	14	15	2.4	67	69	48,776	38,841	3,392	4,040	0.7
6160	Mortgage bankers and brokers	61	52	1.3	540	496	40,874	35,597	14,989	19,439	1.5
6200	Security and commodity brokers	106	113	2.4	759	628	70,672	84,955	61,820	65,003	1.5
6210	Security brokers and dealers	30	34	1.4	270	272	68,207	64,971	17,589	21,105	0.7
6280	Security and commodity services	76	79	3.7	489	356	72,033	100,225	44,231	43,898	3.6
6300	Insurance carriers	54	51	1.1	2,818	3,015	52,379	59,128	118,778	179,093	3.0
6310	Life insurance	10	9	1.0	587	520	56,968	65,962	32,175	27,059	2.3
6330	Fire, marine, and casualty insurance	28	28	1.3	2,108	2,340	51,241	58,928	81,601	147,062	5.0
6370	Pension, health, and welfare funds	5	3	0.7	26	23	56,923	87,304	1,714	1,866	1.3
6400	Insurance agents, brokers, and service	188	183	1.6	883	880	36,897	41,573	34,218	37,098	1.4
6500	Real estate	492	478	1.5	2,216	2,539	21,742	20,619	52,124	55,527	1.2
6510	Real estate operators and lessors	220	219	1.5	941	1,004	15,005	16,570	15,302	17,698	1.3
6530	Real estate agents and managers	244	231	1.6	1,075	1,323	25,310	23,332	29,816	32,081	1.1
6552	Subdividers and developers, n.e.c.	17	17	1.3	73	137	26,904	15,796	3,112	2,910	0.8
6700	Holding and other investment offices	72	78	2.7	374	317	33,754	56,240	16,013	16,770	1.0
6710	Holding offices	12	15	2.2	152	94	19,947	88,979	2,905	6,411	0.8
6720	Investment offices	4	7	7.0	3	5	64,000	54,400	228	285	0.1
6730	Trusts	18	23	2.5	80	102	33,900	33,882	2,910	3,653	2.2
6732	Educational, religious, etc. trusts	9	11	2.6	62	86	38,710	35,860	2,484	3,137	2.9
6733	Trusts, n.e.c.	9	12	2.4	18	16	17,333	23,250	426	516	0.9

Source: County Business Patterns, 1994/95, CBP-94/95, U.S. Department of Commerce, Washington, D.C., November 1997. SIC categories for which data were suppressed or not available for both 1994 and 1995 are *not* displayed. The employment columns represent mid-March employment in the year. Pay per employee is calculated by dividing 1st Quarter payroll, annualized, by mid-March employment. The columns headed "% State" show the county's percentage of the state total for the SIC in 1995; for example, 1.4% for SIC 6000 means that the county had 1.4 percent of the state's total establishments (or payroll) in SIC 6000 in 1995. A dash (-) is used to indicate that data are not available or cannot be calculated; *nec* means not elsewhere classified.

Continued on next page.

SIC	Industry	No. Establishments			Employment		Pay / Employee		Annual Payroll ($ 000)		
		1994	1995	% State	1994	1995	1994	1995	1994	1995	% State
MARIN, CA - [continued]											
6790	Miscellaneous investing	35	30	2.8	132	112	49,303	50,536	9,730	6,298	1.2
6794	Patent owners and lessors	8	5	2.6	46	32	60,870	47,250	2,813	1,035	0.8
6798	Real estate investment trusts	4	3	2.8	11	11	65,818	46,909	739	528	0.3
6799	Investors, n.e.c.	23	22	3.0	75	69	39,787	52,638	6,178	4,735	2.3
MARIPOSA, CA											
60 –	**Finance, insurance, and real estate**	24	24	0.0	218	223	14,312	13,865	3,166	3,129	0.0
6500	Real estate	10	10	0.0	55	68	11,782	9,294	735	742	0.0
6530	Real estate agents and managers	6	7	0.0	50	57	12,480	9,965	674	665	0.0
MENDOCINO, CA											
60 –	**Finance, insurance, and real estate**	165	169	0.2	978	949	19,636	19,452	19,356	18,883	0.1
6000	Depository institutions	31	32	0.3	421	412	21,349	21,680	9,453	9,452	0.1
6020	Commercial banks	22	23	0.4	322	326	21,689	22,000	7,524	7,654	0.2
6030	Savings institutions	5	5	0.2	57	42	21,614	21,810	1,133	929	0.1
6060	Credit unions	4	4	0.3	42	44	18,381	19,182	796	869	0.2
6100	Nondepository institutions	9	9	0.1	27	20	23,704	31,800	569	575	0.0
6300	Insurance carriers	10	11	0.2	119	101	29,479	29,426	3,104	2,635	0.0
6400	Insurance agents, brokers, and service	33	32	0.3	100	96	22,760	21,292	2,056	1,972	0.1
6500	Real estate	75	76	0.2	301	308	11,375	10,961	3,819	3,704	0.1
6510	Real estate operators and lessors	31	31	0.2	124	118	10,226	11,186	1,439	1,403	0.1
6530	Real estate agents and managers	38	42	0.3	165	184	11,806	10,609	2,246	2,197	0.1
MERCED, CA											
60 –	**Finance, insurance, and real estate**	242	248	0.3	2,304	2,281	27,528	26,951	58,812	56,846	0.2
6000	Depository institutions	42	43	0.4	571	572	22,543	21,776	11,577	11,071	0.2
6020	Commercial banks	28	29	0.5	389	395	20,679	20,294	7,311	7,247	0.2
6060	Credit unions	6	6	0.5	108	99	29,667	27,798	2,789	2,216	0.5
6100	Nondepository institutions	18	15	0.2	113	83	30,938	34,169	3,122	2,572	0.1
6200	Security and commodity brokers	7	8	0.2	26	30	94,000	64,533	1,766	1,685	0.0
6300	Insurance carriers	17	18	0.4	969	920	34,576	35,448	29,944	29,165	0.5
6400	Insurance agents, brokers, and service	47	47	0.4	218	216	23,193	25,574	5,511	6,105	0.2
6500	Real estate	107	112	0.4	400	407	14,650	12,079	5,873	5,548	0.1
6510	Real estate operators and lessors	60	63	0.4	159	164	10,063	9,146	1,645	1,651	0.1
6530	Real estate agents and managers	39	38	0.3	150	133	16,240	13,955	2,461	1,527	0.1
6552	Subdividers and developers, n.e.c.	3	4	0.3	38	64	6,526	5,188	289	1,037	0.3
6700	Holding and other investment offices	4	5	0.2	7	53	27,429	22,566	1,019	700	0.0
MODOC, CA											
60 –	**Finance, insurance, and real estate**	15	12	0.0	57	70	17,474	18,686	1,142	1,369	0.0
6400	Insurance agents, brokers, and service	3	3	0.0	7	6	21,143	19,333	154	125	0.0
6500	Real estate	5	4	0.0	16	19	18,250	13,263	284	281	0.0
MONO, CA											
60 –	**Finance, insurance, and real estate**	62	62	0.1	389	515	15,959	13,693	5,769	6,058	0.0
6400	Insurance agents, brokers, and service	5	5	0.0	9	10	13,778	12,000	127	107	0.0
6500	Real estate	51	52	0.2	331	460	15,094	13,574	4,800	5,312	0.1
6530	Real estate agents and managers	44	44	0.3	268	397	14,388	13,128	3,579	4,157	0.1
MONTEREY, CA											
60 –	**Finance, insurance, and real estate**	735	734	1.0	7,302	6,389	25,454	29,121	186,377	183,879	0.6
6000	Depository institutions	108	106	0.9	1,547	1,529	24,975	24,568	36,172	35,730	0.5
6020	Commercial banks	55	53	0.8	1,034	1,006	24,727	24,306	23,778	23,054	0.5
6030	Savings institutions	33	33	1.3	335	337	26,925	25,804	8,296	8,350	0.6
6060	Credit unions	16	16	1.3	172	175	22,977	24,594	3,961	4,157	0.9
6090	Functions closely related to banking	4	4	0.4	6	11	16,000	10,182	137	169	0.1
6100	Nondepository institutions	59	53	0.8	2,739	1,847	21,084	33,971	59,575	61,112	2.3
6200	Security and commodity brokers	45	48	1.0	296	297	74,824	63,138	20,596	19,572	0.5

Source: County Business Patterns, 1994/95, CBP-94/95, U.S. Department of Commerce, Washington, D.C., November 1997. SIC categories for which data were suppressed or not available for both 1994 and 1995 are not displayed. The employment columns represent mid-March employment in the year. Pay per employee is calculated by dividing 1st Quarter payroll, annualized, by mid-March employment. The columns headed "% State" show the county's percentage of the state total for the SIC in 1995; for example, 1.4% for SIC 6000 means that the county had 1.4 percent of the state's total establishments (or payroll) in SIC 6000 in 1995. A dash (-) is used to indicate that data are not available or cannot be calculated; nec means not elsewhere classified.

Continued on next page.

SIC	Industry	No. Establishments			Employment		Pay / Employee		Annual Payroll ($ 000)		
		1994	1995	% State	1994	1995	1994	1995	1994	1995	% State
MONTEREY, CA - [continued]											
6210	Security brokers and dealers	24	24	1.0	256	255	78,000	67,467	18,068	16,946	0.6
6280	Security and commodity services	21	24	1.1	40	42	54,500	36,857	2,528	2,626	0.2
6300	Insurance carriers	41	39	0.9	746	667	36,000	37,025	26,439	24,632	0.4
6310	Life insurance	3	3	0.3	119	123	36,941	36,520	4,037	4,051	0.3
6330	Fire, marine, and casualty insurance	14	16	0.7	313	288	36,460	37,778	12,393	12,201	0.4
6360	Title insurance	15	13	2.2	267	208	35,191	35,712	8,381	6,466	1.4
6400	Insurance agents, brokers, and service	122	111	1.0	425	397	30,616	31,718	13,827	12,239	0.5
6500	Real estate	328	346	1.1	1,426	1,565	16,351	17,408	26,272	28,068	0.6
6510	Real estate operators and lessors	149	163	1.1	822	859	14,686	15,674	12,752	13,083	1.0
6530	Real estate agents and managers	157	157	1.1	550	639	18,444	19,800	11,263	13,027	0.5
6550	Subdividers and developers	19	18	1.1	50	57	21,360	17,333	2,208	1,666	0.4
6552	Subdividers and developers, n.e.c.	15	15	1.2	28	43	22,714	17,581	1,781	1,534	0.4
6730	Trusts	14	15	1.6	40	29	24,700	23,862	533	677	0.4
6732	Educational, religious, etc. trusts	3	7	1.6	3	14	34,667	33,143	95	446	0.4
6733	Trusts, n.e.c.	11	8	1.6	37	15	23,892	15,200	438	231	0.4
NAPA, CA											
60 –	**Finance, insurance, and real estate**	290	282	0.4	1,924	1,998	31,297	32,008	58,530	63,457	0.2
6000	Depository institutions	47	47	0.4	518	527	26,023	24,395	12,743	12,109	0.2
6020	Commercial banks	29	30	0.5	396	417	26,758	25,017	10,230	9,657	0.2
6030	Savings institutions	10	9	0.4	80	65	25,250	22,646	1,650	1,498	0.1
6060	Credit unions	8	8	0.6	42	45	20,571	21,156	863	954	0.2
6100	Nondepository institutions	23	20	0.3	98	78	33,959	30,923	2,493	2,447	0.1
6160	Mortgage bankers and brokers	14	10	0.2	65	32	36,000	31,750	1,526	1,111	0.1
6200	Security and commodity brokers	15	14	0.3	76	83	68,158	60,578	4,925	6,059	0.1
6210	Security brokers and dealers	9	8	0.3	67	71	72,119	61,972	4,500	5,343	0.2
6280	Security and commodity services	6	6	0.3	9	12	38,667	52,333	425	716	0.1
6300	Insurance carriers	13	15	0.3	76	109	37,053	32,073	2,552	3,427	0.1
6400	Insurance agents, brokers, and service	42	35	0.3	514	496	46,685	55,597	23,863	24,885	0.9
6500	Real estate	137	139	0.4	580	652	16,241	16,767	10,227	12,817	0.3
6510	Real estate operators and lessors	66	67	0.5	353	430	10,595	12,028	4,284	6,504	0.5
6530	Real estate agents and managers	59	56	0.4	171	166	25,029	25,494	4,048	4,535	0.2
6550	Subdividers and developers	12	14	0.8	56	55	25,000	27,491	1,895	1,534	0.3
6552	Subdividers and developers, n.e.c.	9	10	0.8	29	28	19,448	21,286	876	519	0.1
6553	Cemetery subdividers and developers	3	3	1.2	27	27	30,963	33,926	1,019	994	1.0
NEVADA, CA											
60 –	**Finance, insurance, and real estate**	196	200	0.3	1,349	1,272	24,510	23,434	31,189	28,761	0.1
6000	Depository institutions	31	30	0.3	447	403	27,034	25,538	10,869	9,815	0.1
6020	Commercial banks	16	17	0.3	342	317	29,509	27,760	8,903	8,333	0.2
6100	Nondepository institutions	16	19	0.3	71	62	27,887	20,065	1,835	1,555	0.1
6140	Personal credit institutions	4	4	0.3	22	17	24,000	27,294	512	529	0.1
6160	Mortgage bankers and brokers	12	15	0.4	49	45	29,633	17,333	1,323	1,026	0.1
6200	Security and commodity brokers	10	12	0.3	31	39	59,097	40,103	1,660	1,761	0.0
6210	Security brokers and dealers	6	5	0.2	20	27	79,600	47,556	1,415	1,467	0.0
6280	Security and commodity services	4	7	0.3	11	12	21,818	23,333	245	294	0.0
6300	Insurance carriers	11	10	0.2	313	229	24,550	24,734	7,051	4,246	0.1
6400	Insurance agents, brokers, and service	23	25	0.2	96	111	29,792	32,036	2,894	3,479	0.1
6500	Real estate	102	97	0.3	387	397	17,085	17,864	6,843	7,701	0.2
6510	Real estate operators and lessors	31	27	0.2	73	66	10,192	13,212	922	909	0.1
6530	Real estate agents and managers	55	58	0.4	211	219	15,299	14,521	3,441	3,377	0.1
6540	Title abstract offices	6	8	3.6	89	106	27,596	27,811	2,286	3,280	4.6
6550	Subdividers and developers	9	4	0.2	14	6	13,143	15,333	188	135	0.0
6700	Holding and other investment offices	3	7	0.2	4	31	3,000	12,774	37	204	0.0
ORANGE, CA											
60 –	**Finance, insurance, and real estate**	7,928	7,693	10.5	105,337	99,450	36,182	37,925	3,696,925	3,778,838	12.7
6000	Depository institutions	890	874	7.8	22,101	19,710	30,326	29,964	622,205	559,024	7.7

Source: County Business Patterns, 1994/95, CBP-94/95, U.S. Department of Commerce, Washington, D.C., November 1997. SIC categories for which data were suppressed or not available for both 1994 and 1995 are not displayed. The employment columns represent mid-March employment in the year. Pay per employee is calculated by dividing 1st Quarter payroll, annualized, by mid-March employment. The columns headed "% State" show the county's percentage of the state total for the SIC in 1995; for example, 1.4% for SIC 6000 means that the county had 1.4 percent of the state's total establishments (or payroll) in SIC 6000 in 1995. A dash (-) is used to indicate that data are not available or cannot be calculated; nec means not elsewhere classified.

Continued on next page.

SIC	Industry	No. Establishments			Employment		Pay / Employee		Annual Payroll ($ 000)		
		1994	1995	% State	1994	1995	1994	1995	1994	1995	% State
ORANGE, CA - [continued]											
6020	Commercial banks	430	433	6.8	12,851	12,254	28,645	28,015	339,484	328,854	6.9
6030	Savings institutions	274	259	10.4	6,670	4,909	34,208	35,276	210,496	160,502	11.7
6060	Credit unions	107	104	8.3	1,772	1,849	25,406	27,472	46,898	48,282	9.9
6100	Nondepository institutions	1,100	950	14.7	15,041	11,431	38,790	41,310	516,260	503,245	19.0
6140	Personal credit institutions	210	235	15.0	3,154	3,224	34,091	42,278	117,732	137,203	19.8
6150	Business credit institutions	118	111	17.7	1,409	1,531	49,547	53,056	65,310	78,673	13.9
6160	Mortgage bankers and brokers	756	589	14.4	10,391	6,631	38,857	38,258	328,135	286,051	21.6
6200	Security and commodity brokers	499	510	11.0	5,734	4,141	58,566	65,413	326,114	281,306	6.6
6210	Security brokers and dealers	248	248	10.5	3,337	2,766	64,903	74,701	193,367	201,981	6.7
6280	Security and commodity services	238	243	11.3	2,333	1,256	50,289	48,245	129,876	72,279	5.9
6300	Insurance carriers	567	532	11.7	21,871	20,925	41,476	46,217	869,096	889,471	15.0
6310	Life insurance	120	112	12.0	5,835	5,295	48,557	56,450	239,035	238,478	20.5
6320	Medical service and health insurance	38	39	12.8	3,747	4,026	35,352	45,502	142,971	171,417	15.4
6321	Accident and health insurance	10	9	15.0	334	400	55,317	62,800	15,455	19,975	29.2
6324	Hospital and medical service plans	28	30	12.2	3,413	3,626	33,398	43,594	127,516	151,442	14.5
6330	Fire, marine, and casualty insurance	309	295	13.2	9,892	9,559	39,021	41,875	389,145	385,058	13.0
6350	Surety insurance	17	15	18.3	273	273	45,216	49,788	12,648	12,997	18.8
6360	Title insurance	24	25	4.3	1,696	1,327	46,200	42,011	69,959	65,498	13.8
6370	Pension, health, and welfare funds	54	39	9.7	337	358	36,677	35,095	12,761	12,682	8.8
6400	Insurance agents, brokers, and service	1,367	1,349	11.7	8,813	8,590	37,048	39,985	323,717	351,697	13.4
6500	Real estate	3,125	3,100	9.7	26,579	28,948	28,167	29,010	789,692	853,537	17.8
6510	Real estate operators and lessors	1,179	1,209	8.4	6,556	7,012	20,415	22,471	145,689	156,726	11.6
6530	Real estate agents and managers	1,664	1,568	10.6	17,213	18,831	29,260	29,254	531,674	571,001	19.9
6540	Title abstract offices	20	19	8.4	457	278	36,945	37,295	14,709	8,994	12.5
6550	Subdividers and developers	196	201	12.2	2,300	2,677	40,290	44,072	94,369	110,129	23.7
6552	Subdividers and developers, n.e.c.	174	170	13.2	2,094	2,234	41,775	46,972	85,011	94,928	27.2
6553	Cemetery subdividers and developers	13	15	6.1	190	299	24,147	21,177	5,208	7,146	7.2
6700	Holding and other investment offices	314	309	10.6	4,379	4,620	45,737	51,765	213,138	288,039	16.4
6710	Holding offices	86	96	14.0	2,461	2,536	50,731	56,640	133,034	145,799	18.5
6730	Trusts	76	63	6.8	459	278	29,098	29,827	12,345	8,343	5.0
6732	Educational, religious, etc. trusts	16	22	5.1	149	111	26,631	23,279	3,116	2,790	2.6
6733	Trusts, n.e.c.	60	41	8.2	310	167	30,284	34,180	9,229	5,553	9.5
6790	Miscellaneous investing	129	126	11.8	1,124	1,041	41,413	43,585	46,841	46,711	9.1
6792	Oil royalty traders	7	8	20.0	41	32	27,220	41,000	1,198	1,337	25.2
6794	Patent owners and lessors	31	31	16.3	499	466	46,413	51,863	22,013	22,431	16.6
6798	Real estate investment trusts	13	15	14.0	52	75	95,769	70,880	3,960	4,844	2.9
6799	Investors, n.e.c.	78	72	9.9	532	468	32,504	31,145	19,670	18,099	8.9
PLACER, CA											
60 –	**Finance, insurance, and real estate**	608	588	0.8	4,751	4,514	25,392	25,174	115,685	113,271	0.4
6000	Depository institutions	111	103	0.9	1,341	1,176	22,297	23,337	32,355	26,530	0.4
6020	Commercial banks	75	69	1.1	925	851	21,557	23,093	22,586	18,017	0.4
6030	Savings institutions	27	25	1.0	349	259	24,986	24,880	8,383	7,153	0.5
6100	Nondepository institutions	67	60	0.9	493	413	39,797	34,140	14,446	13,323	0.5
6160	Mortgage bankers and brokers	47	39	1.0	321	251	44,137	33,992	9,768	8,096	0.6
6200	Security and commodity brokers	26	26	0.6	88	126	52,909	45,524	4,534	6,168	0.1
6210	Security brokers and dealers	17	16	0.7	76	111	56,895	48,685	4,171	5,814	0.2
6300	Insurance carriers	45	42	0.9	603	597	33,924	33,843	19,695	20,132	0.3
6310	Life insurance	7	7	0.7	135	177	27,585	28,339	3,737	5,241	0.5
6330	Fire, marine, and casualty insurance	21	17	0.8	272	212	39,897	39,906	11,168	8,805	0.3
6360	Title insurance	13	13	2.2	169	92	29,515	30,957	3,902	2,981	0.6
6400	Insurance agents, brokers, and service	81	87	0.8	333	291	25,550	26,543	7,216	7,986	0.3
6500	Real estate	256	242	0.8	1,707	1,702	18,978	18,653	31,793	32,721	0.7
6510	Real estate operators and lessors	90	83	0.6	747	760	14,576	11,100	10,497	10,288	0.8

Source: County Business Patterns, 1994/95, CBP-94/95, U.S. Department of Commerce, Washington, D.C., November 1997. SIC categories for which data were suppressed or not available for both 1994 and 1995 are not displayed. The employment columns represent mid-March employment in the year. Pay per employee is calculated by dividing 1st Quarter payroll, annualized, by mid-March employment. The columns headed "% State" show the county's percentage of the state total for the SIC in 1995; for example, 1.4% for SIC 6000 means that the county had 1.4 percent of the state's total establishments (or payroll) in SIC 6000 in 1995. A dash (-) is used to indicate that data are not available or cannot be calculated; nec means not elsewhere classified.

Continued on next page.

SIC	Industry	No. Establishments			Employment		Pay / Employee		Annual Payroll ($ 000)		
		1994	1995	% State	1994	1995	1994	1995	1994	1995	% State
PLACER, CA - [continued]											
6530	Real estate agents and managers	143	134	0.9	827	856	19,995	23,192	16,975	19,362	0.7
6710	Holding offices	9	9	1.3	61	81	28,721	37,679	2,135	2,556	0.3
6799	Investors, n.e.c.	5	5	0.7	40	36	8,300	18,333	469	772	0.4
PLUMAS, CA											
60 –	**Finance, insurance, and real estate**	55	56	0.1	253	247	20,253	22,640	5,505	5,472	0.0
6000	Depository institutions	10	11	0.1	114	110	22,386	21,091	2,428	2,306	0.0
6400	Insurance agents, brokers, and service	10	10	0.1	22	21	23,636	48,762	534	493	0.0
6500	Real estate	29	28	0.1	99	96	16,768	19,083	2,139	2,199	0.0
6510	Real estate operators and lessors	6	6	0.0	26	23	15,231	17,217	454	499	0.0
6530	Real estate agents and managers	16	15	0.1	32	28	11,875	12,571	634	548	0.0
RIVERSIDE, CA											
60 –	**Finance, insurance, and real estate**	2,132	2,079	2.8	17,383	15,673	25,747	27,286	439,618	439,410	1.5
6000	Depository institutions	312	311	2.8	4,986	4,566	22,154	22,039	105,710	106,608	1.5
6020	Commercial banks	152	152	2.4	3,054	2,853	21,840	21,566	63,195	64,731	1.4
6030	Savings institutions	105	103	4.1	1,495	1,306	22,518	22,619	32,303	32,149	2.4
6060	Credit unions	19	22	1.8	280	280	23,157	24,143	6,613	6,901	1.4
6100	Nondepository institutions	239	212	3.3	2,917	1,865	33,386	37,716	81,270	63,383	2.4
6140	Personal credit institutions	52	52	3.3	244	268	23,623	26,313	5,739	7,130	1.0
6150	Business credit institutions	15	17	2.7	127	130	30,929	34,277	5,211	4,939	0.9
6160	Mortgage bankers and brokers	169	138	3.4	2,515	1,447	34,365	39,997	69,305	50,322	3.8
6200	Security and commodity brokers	94	105	2.3	596	646	66,289	56,080	34,857	37,195	0.9
6210	Security brokers and dealers	56	62	2.6	508	504	72,827	65,611	31,397	32,019	1.1
6280	Security and commodity services	38	42	2.0	88	142	28,545	22,254	3,460	5,175	0.4
6300	Insurance carriers	110	110	2.4	1,536	1,659	34,247	42,020	54,098	63,684	1.1
6330	Fire, marine, and casualty insurance	67	66	3.0	432	557	46,787	43,153	27,680	24,434	0.8
6360	Title insurance	9	9	1.6	743	568	30,859	32,880	17,128	18,014	3.8
6400	Insurance agents, brokers, and service	297	303	2.6	1,117	1,068	26,861	28,944	33,085	31,360	1.2
6500	Real estate	1,028	986	3.1	5,928	5,117	18,318	19,251	119,500	114,230	2.4
6510	Real estate operators and lessors	378	378	2.6	1,841	1,780	15,383	16,454	31,628	30,589	2.3
6530	Real estate agents and managers	559	519	3.5	3,722	2,950	19,070	20,633	73,982	60,626	2.1
6550	Subdividers and developers	68	61	3.7	306	336	25,895	21,726	12,671	20,047	4.3
6552	Subdividers and developers, n.e.c.	56	48	3.7	208	193	32,769	27,710	11,255	17,972	5.1
6553	Cemetery subdividers and developers	7	7	2.8	96	123	11,167	10,862	1,257	1,593	1.6
6710	Holding offices	11	11	1.6	58	80	69,034	52,850	4,814	4,985	0.6
6733	Trusts, n.e.c.	11	12	2.4	22	47	19,818	13,021	485	644	1.1
6790	Miscellaneous investing	18	16	1.5	177	564	17,401	26,007	4,282	15,406	3.0
6799	Investors, n.e.c.	11	10	1.4	46	437	23,391	28,421	1,526	12,372	6.1
SACRAMENTO, CA											
60 –	**Finance, insurance, and real estate**	2,710	2,626	3.6	35,019	34,728	30,155	31,374	1,058,781	1,111,571	3.7
6000	Depository institutions	379	377	3.3	8,868	8,064	25,997	26,563	224,261	206,431	2.8
6020	Commercial banks	187	207	3.2	5,916	5,712	26,462	27,315	155,169	149,976	3.1
6030	Savings institutions	85	70	2.8	1,326	776	28,646	26,490	33,405	20,207	1.5
6060	Credit unions	74	75	6.0	1,465	1,485	23,080	24,366	33,683	34,867	7.2
6090	Functions closely related to banking	33	25	2.6	161	91	13,640	15,868	2,004	1,381	0.5
6100	Nondepository institutions	323	265	4.1	3,834	3,180	33,398	35,599	111,134	117,333	4.4
6110	Federal and Federally-sponsored credit	4	4	6.3	306	228	45,595	49,070	12,148	11,053	21.0
6140	Personal credit institutions	73	78	5.0	807	844	23,549	27,938	19,524	23,206	3.4
6150	Business credit institutions	22	16	2.5	250	307	40,672	50,293	10,891	16,107	2.9
6160	Mortgage bankers and brokers	224	165	4.0	2,471	1,801	34,368	34,978	68,571	66,064	5.0
6200	Security and commodity brokers	135	125	2.7	973	941	53,805	51,838	49,561	49,923	1.2
6210	Security brokers and dealers	70	65	2.7	724	699	60,602	57,144	41,201	41,648	1.4
6300	Insurance carriers	272	266	5.8	10,393	10,807	36,567	37,724	373,690	398,939	6.7
6310	Life insurance	56	56	6.0	868	870	31,304	33,540	26,643	28,761	2.5
6320	Medical service and health insurance	37	39	12.8	3,538	3,631	35,822	39,870	122,959	138,570	12.5
6321	Accident and health insurance	6	8	13.3	64	78	19,375	26,000	1,263	2,140	3.1

Source: County Business Patterns, 1994/95, CBP-94/95, U.S. Department of Commerce, Washington, D.C., November 1997. SIC categories for which data were suppressed or not available for both 1994 and 1995 are not displayed. The employment columns represent mid-March employment in the year. Pay per employee is calculated by dividing 1st Quarter payroll, annualized, by mid-March employment. The columns headed "% State" show the county's percentage of the state total for the SIC in 1995; for example, 1.4% for SIC 6000 means that the county had 1.4 percent of the state's total establishments (or payroll) in SIC 6000 in 1995. A dash (-) is used to indicate that data are not available or cannot be calculated; nec means not elsewhere classified.

Continued on next page.

SIC	Industry	No. Establishments			Employment		Pay / Employee		Annual Payroll ($ 000)		
		1994	1995	% State	1994	1995	1994	1995	1994	1995	% State

SACRAMENTO, CA - [continued]

SIC	Industry	1994	1995	% State	1994	1995	1994	1995	1994	1995	% State
6324	Hospital and medical service plans	31	31	12.7	3,474	3,553	36,126	40,175	121,696	136,430	13.1
6330	Fire, marine, and casualty insurance	126	127	5.7	5,464	5,897	38,208	37,391	209,008	216,991	7.3
6360	Title insurance	25	22	3.8	377	289	34,249	32,055	9,894	9,718	2.0
6370	Pension, health, and welfare funds	22	17	4.2	120	103	29,533	31,379	4,172	4,259	3.0
6400	Insurance agents, brokers, and service	529	544	4.7	3,178	3,424	32,069	33,812	103,871	117,882	4.5
6500	Real estate	999	976	3.1	6,739	6,944	19,998	20,743	143,819	154,536	3.2
6510	Real estate operators and lessors	394	405	2.8	1,534	1,803	14,683	16,222	25,499	31,638	2.3
6530	Real estate agents and managers	514	478	3.2	4,478	4,433	20,298	21,319	95,564	102,255	3.6
6550	Subdividers and developers	58	52	3.2	476	565	25,185	27,214	13,948	15,272	3.3
6552	Subdividers and developers, n.e.c.	41	35	2.7	270	324	30,874	33,556	9,972	10,786	3.1
6553	Cemetery subdividers and developers	15	15	6.1	206	227	17,728	18,678	3,898	4,347	4.4
6700	Holding and other investment offices	65	67	2.3	920	1,204	25,409	30,458	46,501	57,711	3.3
6710	Holding offices	13	10	1.5	257	347	11,938	22,190	21,111	25,165	3.2
6733	Trusts, n.e.c.	13	15	3.0	127	109	18,268	13,761	2,536	1,630	2.8
6799	Investors, n.e.c.	18	19	2.6	29	46	27,034	32,087	1,597	1,447	0.7

SAN BENITO, CA

SIC	Industry	1994	1995	% State	1994	1995	1994	1995	1994	1995	% State
60 –	**Finance, insurance, and real estate**	56	51	0.1	285	297	21,881	21,185	6,767	7,301	0.0
6000	Depository institutions	9	9	0.1	112	128	24,000	20,938	2,554	2,899	0.0
6300	Insurance carriers	4	4	0.1	34	35	31,294	30,057	1,080	1,310	0.0
6400	Insurance agents, brokers, and service	10	10	0.1	54	56	25,926	27,286	1,810	1,835	0.1
6500	Real estate	26	23	0.1	71	66	12,338	13,091	1,127	1,041	0.0

SAN BERNARDINO, CA

SIC	Industry	1994	1995	% State	1994	1995	1994	1995	1994	1995	% State
60 –	**Finance, insurance, and real estate**	2,058	1,976	2.7	19,285	16,711	26,179	25,835	472,222	434,770	1.5
6000	Depository institutions	333	329	2.9	5,795	5,390	23,393	22,538	128,159	117,888	1.6
6020	Commercial banks	137	139	2.2	3,378	3,264	21,878	21,357	70,502	66,130	1.4
6030	Savings institutions	90	83	3.3	1,591	1,322	27,857	25,867	40,463	34,233	2.5
6060	Credit unions	53	53	4.2	555	547	21,391	24,110	12,125	13,062	2.7
6090	Functions closely related to banking	53	54	5.5	271	257	20,177	17,074	5,069	4,463	1.5
6100	Nondepository institutions	290	244	3.8	3,410	2,097	28,869	31,880	79,940	71,696	2.7
6140	Personal credit institutions	82	80	5.1	600	548	26,733	27,854	16,179	15,929	2.3
6160	Mortgage bankers and brokers	186	140	3.4	2,609	1,373	28,376	32,466	55,769	48,288	3.6
6200	Security and commodity brokers	62	60	1.3	342	293	44,456	43,577	13,283	14,891	0.3
6210	Security brokers and dealers	36	33	1.4	272	224	46,265	43,857	11,559	11,995	0.4
6300	Insurance carriers	142	136	3.0	3,338	2,350	34,374	35,762	101,638	84,183	1.4
6310	Life insurance	27	24	2.6	513	459	26,955	26,876	12,927	11,935	1.0
6320	Medical service and health insurance	7	6	2.0	99	56	40,202	46,357	2,963	2,789	0.3
6330	Fire, marine, and casualty insurance	88	85	3.8	1,877	1,265	37,590	41,072	62,692	51,539	1.7
6360	Title insurance	14	13	2.2	810	558	30,835	29,871	22,183	17,435	3.7
6400	Insurance agents, brokers, and service	383	371	3.2	1,709	1,730	27,979	27,457	50,678	47,877	1.8
6500	Real estate	795	784	2.5	4,101	4,296	19,191	19,654	84,147	84,120	1.8
6510	Real estate operators and lessors	334	322	2.2	1,378	1,567	13,533	15,056	19,657	23,744	1.8
6530	Real estate agents and managers	416	400	2.7	1,826	1,736	19,908	19,044	36,834	33,185	1.2
6540	Title abstract offices	5	5	2.2	135	93	24,237	34,108	2,782	1,228	1.7
6550	Subdividers and developers	31	36	2.2	757	861	26,906	27,963	24,744	25,511	5.5
6552	Subdividers and developers, n.e.c.	22	24	1.9	502	552	34,367	37,442	21,350	21,917	6.3
6553	Cemetery subdividers and developers	9	10	4.1	255	308	12,220	11,026	3,394	3,573	3.6
6700	Holding and other investment offices	45	42	1.4	512	490	19,898	24,253	10,994	12,155	0.7
6710	Holding offices	12	11	1.6	262	215	21,893	31,051	5,989	6,716	0.9
6730	Trusts	18	21	2.3	73	96	13,534	13,750	1,165	1,411	0.8
6732	Educational, religious, etc. trusts	10	10	2.3	67	76	12,955	13,842	958	1,155	1.1
6733	Trusts, n.e.c.	8	11	2.2	6	20	20,000	13,400	207	256	0.4
6790	Miscellaneous investing	13	9	0.8	174	143	19,011	22,545	3,430	3,335	0.7
6794	Patent owners and lessors	3	3	1.6	57	37	33,614	48,541	1,951	1,805	1.3
6799	Investors, n.e.c.	10	6	0.8	117	106	11,897	13,472	1,479	1,530	0.8

SAN DIEGO, CA

SIC	Industry	1994	1995	% State	1994	1995	1994	1995	1994	1995	% State
60 –	**Finance, insurance, and real estate**	6,993	6,836	9.3	66,320	61,889	30,979	31,905	1,974,629	1,966,129	6.6

Source: *County Business Patterns, 1994/95,* CBP-94/95, U.S. Department of Commerce, Washington, D.C., November 1997. SIC categories for which data were suppressed or not available for both 1994 and 1995 are *not* displayed. The employment columns represent mid-March employment in the year. Pay per employee is calculated by dividing 1st Quarter payroll, annualized, by mid-March employment. The columns headed "% State" show the county's percentage of the state total for the SIC in 1995; for example, 1.4% for SIC 6000 means that the county had 1.4 percent of the state's total establishments (or payroll) in SIC 6000 in 1995. A dash (-) is used to indicate that data are not available or cannot be calculated; *nec* means not elsewhere classified.

Continued on next page.

SIC	Industry	No. Establishments			Employment		Pay / Employee		Annual Payroll ($ 000)		
		1994	1995	% State	1994	1995	1994	1995	1994	1995	% State
SAN DIEGO, CA - [continued]											
6000	Depository institutions	951	867	7.7	16,964	15,449	27,757	26,908	453,850	397,338	5.4
6020	Commercial banks	508	448	7.0	11,475	10,408	27,815	26,586	312,226	264,066	5.5
6030	Savings institutions	227	198	7.9	2,698	2,234	30,179	28,879	73,001	60,005	4.4
6060	Credit unions	119	120	9.6	2,176	2,236	25,669	26,678	54,856	58,621	12.0
6100	Nondepository institutions	673	579	9.0	7,934	5,562	36,048	38,985	259,144	231,596	8.8
6140	Personal credit institutions	148	137	8.7	1,180	1,346	32,990	34,264	54,524	44,486	6.4
6150	Business credit institutions	41	40	6.4	382	676	34,052	52,166	13,109	41,490	7.3
6160	Mortgage bankers and brokers	480	392	9.6	6,363	3,504	36,716	38,346	191,003	144,487	10.9
6200	Security and commodity brokers	426	467	10.1	3,729	4,101	67,769	70,547	242,364	286,011	6.7
6210	Security brokers and dealers	228	253	10.7	2,767	2,876	66,314	61,697	156,103	169,919	5.7
6280	Security and commodity services	188	205	9.6	941	1,198	73,233	92,417	85,906	114,893	9.3
6300	Insurance carriers	354	358	7.9	9,268	8,815	36,149	37,922	316,544	324,140	5.5
6310	Life insurance	88	93	9.9	2,444	2,389	34,385	34,744	77,659	78,745	6.8
6320	Medical service and health insurance	25	24	7.9	1,109	1,027	32,779	33,496	36,743	34,148	3.1
6321	Accident and health insurance	5	3	5.0	51	24	31,529	52,833	1,588	1,570	2.3
6324	Hospital and medical service plans	20	21	8.6	1,058	1,003	32,839	33,033	35,155	32,578	3.1
6330	Fire, marine, and casualty insurance	176	177	7.9	4,330	4,459	37,222	40,536	157,978	174,919	5.9
6350	Surety insurance	12	12	14.6	151	54	34,808	37,185	4,662	1,439	2.1
6360	Title insurance	17	18	3.1	1,048	705	41,225	41,169	34,574	29,824	6.3
6370	Pension, health, and welfare funds	36	34	8.5	186	181	26,946	28,177	4,928	5,065	3.5
6400	Insurance agents, brokers, and service	962	958	8.3	5,089	4,750	33,684	35,252	174,042	170,455	6.5
6500	Real estate	3,305	3,317	10.4	21,134	20,843	21,048	22,064	436,875	462,475	9.7
6510	Real estate operators and lessors	1,415	1,415	9.8	7,662	7,418	15,742	17,460	120,811	132,213	9.8
6530	Real estate agents and managers	1,633	1,593	10.8	11,530	11,128	23,662	23,864	257,993	264,869	9.2
6540	Title abstract offices	10	14	6.2	100	84	28,320	18,429	2,184	1,693	2.4
6550	Subdividers and developers	177	188	11.4	1,739	2,012	27,160	28,592	51,571	57,351	12.4
6552	Subdividers and developers, n.e.c.	151	157	12.2	1,249	1,487	31,872	33,178	44,370	48,810	14.0
6553	Cemetery subdividers and developers	17	17	6.9	471	498	14,854	15,269	6,777	7,357	7.4
6700	Holding and other investment offices	274	277	9.5	1,689	2,094	31,768	34,884	62,110	79,627	4.5
6710	Holding offices	78	71	10.3	367	647	50,027	49,156	21,483	31,337	4.0
6730	Trusts	89	95	10.2	489	446	15,493	18,843	8,651	9,178	5.5
6732	Educational, religious, etc. trusts	46	52	12.1	283	313	15,463	15,502	4,990	5,644	5.2
6733	Trusts, n.e.c.	43	42	8.4	206	131	15,534	26,473	3,661	3,444	5.9
6790	Miscellaneous investing	94	90	8.4	827	939	33,451	32,780	29,617	34,651	6.8
6794	Patent owners and lessors	27	25	13.2	517	591	28,395	30,132	16,523	20,142	14.9
6799	Investors, n.e.c.	61	57	7.8	248	259	38,613	31,876	9,875	10,256	5.1
SAN FRANCISCO, CA											
60 –	**Finance, insurance, and real estate**	4,635	4,891	6.7	74,547	77,537	59,095	64,586	3,919,710	4,554,011	15.3
6000	Depository institutions	1,376	1,656	14.7	28,288	28,723	52,470	54,804	1,246,198	1,392,175	19.1
6020	Commercial banks	1,100	1,381	21.6	22,432	22,888	52,988	55,242	983,454	1,106,115	23.2
6030	Savings institutions	136	138	5.5	2,291	2,265	39,104	41,805	78,483	84,878	6.2
6080	Foreign bank and branches and agencies	31	31	24.6	518	535	89,714	84,426	36,456	36,299	-
6090	Functions closely related to banking	69	69	7.1	930	962	75,243	76,129	59,755	70,425	23.7
6100	Nondepository institutions	209	176	2.7	2,668	2,281	70,756	75,784	151,625	149,930	5.7
6140	Personal credit institutions	28	23	1.5	238	96	54,437	46,500	11,241	3,881	0.6
6150	Business credit institutions	49	50	8.0	1,495	1,512	89,506	86,180	101,224	108,322	19.2
6160	Mortgage bankers and brokers	130	96	2.3	935	649	44,928	56,462	39,129	35,509	2.7
6200	Security and commodity brokers	554	606	13.1	11,488	13,219	106,473	118,106	1,088,111	1,444,993	33.8
6210	Security brokers and dealers	309	340	14.3	8,893	9,953	107,135	125,628	829,057	1,131,673	37.8
6300	Insurance carriers	264	242	5.3	11,538	11,871	46,993	49,459	522,675	543,275	9.1
6310	Life insurance	63	62	6.6	2,251	2,410	40,682	43,811	87,980	96,348	8.3
6320	Medical service and health insurance	14	12	3.9	1,923	1,705	51,624	62,780	84,753	80,971	7.3
6330	Fire, marine, and casualty insurance	105	100	4.5	6,301	5,992	48,324	48,362	307,608	277,597	9.4
6350	Surety insurance	6	6	7.3	94	93	50,085	85,978	5,375	8,015	11.6
6360	Title insurance	39	37	6.4	509	1,237	43,623	44,918	17,654	54,011	11.4
6370	Pension, health, and welfare funds	35	23	5.7	460	427	43,374	49,199	19,152	26,105	18.2
6400	Insurance agents, brokers, and service	436	418	3.6	5,054	4,924	50,848	55,111	248,692	261,484	10.0

Source: County Business Patterns, 1994/95, CBP-94/95, U.S. Department of Commerce, Washington, D.C., November 1997. SIC categories for which data were suppressed or not available for both 1994 and 1995 are not displayed. The employment columns represent mid-March employment in the year. Pay per employee is calculated by dividing 1st Quarter payroll, annualized, by mid-March employment. The columns headed "% State" show the county's percentage of the state total for the SIC in 1995; for example, 1.4% for SIC 6000 means that the county had 1.4 percent of the state's total establishments (or payroll) in SIC 6000 in 1995. A dash (-) is used to indicate that data are not available or cannot be calculated; nec means not elsewhere classified.

Continued on next page.

SIC	Industry	No. Establishments			Employment		Pay / Employee		Annual Payroll ($ 000)		
		1994	1995	% State	1994	1995	1994	1995	1994	1995	% State
SAN FRANCISCO, CA - [continued]											
6500	Real estate	1,545	1,531	4.8	11,590	12,214	30,398	33,943	358,353	411,027	8.6
6510	Real estate operators and lessors	792	791	5.5	4,125	4,253	22,019	24,695	89,752	103,280	7.7
6530	Real estate agents and managers	679	653	4.4	7,238	7,639	35,173	39,295	260,279	297,072	10.4
6550	Subdividers and developers	52	53	3.2	200	246	26,240	27,967	6,467	7,471	1.6
6552	Subdividers and developers, n.e.c.	45	42	3.3	155	195	28,465	29,990	5,310	6,101	1.7
6553	Cemetery subdividers and developers	6	7	2.8	45	49	18,578	20,163	1,037	1,046	1.1
6700	Holding and other investment offices	231	237	8.1	2,968	3,550	85,650	98,861	230,860	292,947	16.7
6710	Holding offices	57	55	8.0	1,667	1,541	109,346	147,888	149,775	166,107	21.1
6720	Investment offices	19	20	20.0	136	127	94,147	92,535	16,727	18,308	7.8
6730	Trusts	78	78	8.4	583	637	32,357	35,152	19,680	22,860	13.6
6732	Educational, religious, etc. trusts	43	49	11.4	470	536	34,085	35,381	16,927	19,487	17.9
6733	Trusts, n.e.c.	35	29	5.8	113	101	25,168	33,941	2,753	3,373	5.8
6790	Miscellaneous investing	73	71	6.7	582	560	69,175	84,243	42,811	48,440	9.5
6794	Patent owners and lessors	7	8	4.2	99	101	94,586	99,921	9,762	8,985	6.6
6798	Real estate investment trusts	7	6	5.6	47	60	45,447	59,733	2,805	4,528	2.7
6799	Investors, n.e.c.	59	57	7.8	436	399	65,963	83,960	30,244	34,927	17.2
SAN JOAQUIN, CA											
60 –	**Finance, insurance, and real estate**	913	889	1.2	8,825	8,017	26,577	26,158	227,395	212,033	0.7
6000	Depository institutions	145	138	1.2	3,495	3,314	25,942	25,870	87,647	83,689	1.1
6020	Commercial banks	70	70	1.1	1,747	1,747	23,242	23,244	41,200	41,623	0.9
6030	Savings institutions	37	34	1.4	1,475	1,333	29,901	29,581	41,114	36,747	2.7
6060	Credit unions	25	25	2.0	209	208	23,560	25,635	4,720	5,003	1.0
6090	Functions closely related to banking	13	9	0.9	64	26	16,188	13,846	613	316	0.1
6100	Nondepository institutions	95	85	1.3	606	483	32,238	29,159	15,788	13,639	0.5
6160	Mortgage bankers and brokers	57	43	1.0	355	227	35,268	28,828	7,947	6,073	0.5
6200	Security and commodity brokers	33	32	0.7	213	173	51,023	54,566	10,494	9,843	0.2
6210	Security brokers and dealers	18	15	0.6	173	134	56,116	53,970	9,138	8,210	0.3
6300	Insurance carriers	73	66	1.4	1,712	1,268	28,400	29,606	47,684	38,640	0.7
6310	Life insurance	12	11	1.2	632	491	22,158	25,279	13,362	11,522	1.0
6320	Medical service and health insurance	10	9	3.0	612	335	28,235	29,803	18,079	12,115	1.1
6330	Fire, marine, and casualty insurance	31	32	1.4	154	185	46,312	35,459	7,329	6,615	0.2
6400	Insurance agents, brokers, and service	176	187	1.6	757	762	27,736	29,265	21,385	23,415	0.9
6500	Real estate	372	363	1.1	1,917	1,903	21,486	19,514	41,973	39,978	0.8
6510	Real estate operators and lessors	162	169	1.2	539	553	13,699	14,684	8,101	8,415	0.6
6530	Real estate agents and managers	177	160	1.1	1,158	1,158	24,100	21,136	28,628	26,096	0.9
6550	Subdividers and developers	25	21	1.3	106	115	26,038	21,426	2,800	3,483	0.8
6552	Subdividers and developers, n.e.c.	14	10	0.8	36	20	20,000	21,800	725	403	0.1
6553	Cemetery subdividers and developers	10	11	4.5	70	95	29,143	21,347	2,050	3,080	3.1
6710	Holding offices	3	4	0.6	6	5	28,667	221,600	109	525	0.1
6730	Trusts	5	4	0.4	90	88	15,289	17,227	1,429	1,467	0.9
SAN LUIS OBISPO, CA											
60 –	**Finance, insurance, and real estate**	523	519	0.7	3,034	3,113	24,523	23,829	72,044	70,957	0.2
6000	Depository institutions	85	82	0.7	1,320	1,372	23,497	22,857	30,553	30,112	0.4
6020	Commercial banks	52	53	0.8	982	1,032	23,263	23,236	22,836	23,325	0.5
6030	Savings institutions	23	19	0.8	221	200	26,950	24,200	5,368	4,235	0.3
6060	Credit unions	10	10	0.8	117	140	18,940	18,143	2,349	2,552	0.5
6100	Nondepository institutions	41	41	0.6	248	222	31,952	31,658	6,845	6,331	0.2
6160	Mortgage bankers and brokers	32	29	0.7	199	161	29,487	28,994	4,969	4,257	0.3
6200	Security and commodity brokers	34	39	0.8	122	140	51,672	38,057	5,978	5,873	0.1
6210	Security brokers and dealers	20	22	0.9	94	109	59,745	44,183	5,316	5,371	0.2
6300	Insurance carriers	25	24	0.5	239	223	34,962	37,883	7,220	7,542	0.1
6310	Life insurance	5	4	0.4	68	53	28,118	29,208	1,925	1,486	0.1
6400	Insurance agents, brokers, and service	86	84	0.7	325	330	27,729	26,521	8,857	9,103	0.3
6500	Real estate	241	238	0.7	744	738	15,151	14,943	11,749	10,790	0.2
6510	Real estate operators and lessors	94	100	0.7	277	337	10,498	11,442	3,398	3,881	0.3

Source: County Business Patterns, 1994/95, CBP-94/95, U.S. Department of Commerce, Washington, D.C., November 1997. SIC categories for which data were suppressed or not available for both 1994 and 1995 are *not* displayed. The employment columns represent mid-March employment in the year. Pay per employee is calculated by dividing 1st Quarter payroll, annualized, by mid-March employment. The columns headed "% State" show the county's percentage of the state total for the SIC in 1995; for example, 1.4% for SIC 6000 means that the county had 1.4 percent of the state's total establishments (or payroll) in SIC 6000 in 1995. A dash (-) is used to indicate that data are not available or cannot be calculated; *nec* means not elsewhere classified.

Continued on next page.

SIC	Industry	No. Establishments			Employment		Pay / Employee		Annual Payroll ($ 000)		
		1994	1995	% State	1994	1995	1994	1995	1994	1995	% State
SAN LUIS OBISPO, CA - [continued]											
6530	Real estate agents and managers	126	118	0.8	408	326	17,225	17,031	6,788	5,369	0.2
6550	Subdividers and developers	13	15	0.9	36	68	21,556	21,471	1,190	1,405	0.3
6700	Holding and other investment offices	11	11	0.4	36	88	14,444	25,409	842	1,206	0.1
SAN MATEO, CA											
60 –	**Finance, insurance, and real estate**	2,138	2,126	2.9	24,559	25,166	38,543	40,723	979,721	1,052,911	3.5
6000	Depository institutions	247	246	2.2	4,095	4,067	28,352	29,453	114,745	114,759	1.6
6020	Commercial banks	106	103	1.6	1,972	2,025	22,949	22,929	44,561	45,585	1.0
6030	Savings institutions	89	86	3.4	1,590	1,472	34,906	38,454	54,185	51,355	3.8
6060	Credit unions	35	39	3.1	437	438	28,549	29,352	12,490	13,466	2.8
6090	Functions closely related to banking	17	18	1.8	96	132	29,875	29,485	3,509	4,353	1.5
6100	Nondepository institutions	181	149	2.3	3,140	3,008	55,437	58,170	193,067	193,293	7.3
6150	Business credit institutions	23	23	3.7	1,196	1,101	55,826	55,212	65,102	58,183	10.3
6200	Security and commodity brokers	175	189	4.1	2,643	2,883	50,135	53,919	137,899	163,227	3.8
6210	Security brokers and dealers	64	72	3.0	601	723	77,378	83,463	41,234	57,273	1.9
6220	Commodity contracts brokers, dealers	6	6	7.9	23	19	38,435	64,421	1,244	1,268	6.0
6280	Security and commodity services	105	111	5.2	2,019	2,141	42,159	43,849	95,421	104,686	8.5
6300	Insurance carriers	142	144	3.2	4,508	4,054	40,100	41,195	173,524	164,086	2.8
6310	Life insurance	26	28	3.0	781	768	27,928	31,729	21,935	21,920	1.9
6320	Medical service and health insurance	5	7	2.3	643	668	40,193	36,892	24,258	24,634	2.2
6330	Fire, marine, and casualty insurance	58	61	2.7	2,207	2,052	44,265	48,347	97,463	99,870	3.4
6360	Title insurance	36	34	5.9	642	402	40,872	33,174	22,243	12,299	2.6
6400	Insurance agents, brokers, and service	343	332	2.9	2,131	1,998	37,117	46,128	80,733	88,155	3.4
6500	Real estate	893	887	2.8	6,313	7,054	26,845	28,038	178,040	200,094	4.2
6510	Real estate operators and lessors	410	423	2.9	2,335	2,567	20,365	22,861	50,123	60,439	4.5
6530	Real estate agents and managers	426	399	2.7	3,428	3,812	30,222	29,815	107,165	114,333	4.0
6550	Subdividers and developers	45	44	2.7	517	613	34,275	39,700	19,990	23,809	5.1
6552	Subdividers and developers, n.e.c.	32	33	2.6	231	289	45,022	54,436	10,828	14,371	4.1
6553	Cemetery subdividers and developers	10	10	4.1	286	323	25,594	26,526	9,136	9,361	9.5
6700	Holding and other investment offices	145	167	5.7	1,034	1,364	65,671	64,815	70,340	96,333	5.5
6710	Holding offices	29	37	5.4	238	526	95,042	71,483	17,788	34,432	4.4
6720	Investment offices	9	8	8.0	172	185	35,070	37,189	6,775	7,848	3.3
6730	Trusts	24	34	3.7	172	172	20,651	35,674	3,830	6,650	4.0
6732	Educational, religious, etc. trusts	8	15	3.5	140	130	21,171	36,800	3,125	5,200	4.8
6733	Trusts, n.e.c.	16	19	3.8	32	42	18,375	32,190	705	1,450	2.5
6790	Miscellaneous investing	77	80	7.5	449	449	79,323	82,414	41,753	46,710	9.1
6794	Patent owners and lessors	6	4	2.1	58	77	32,483	37,299	2,144	2,735	2.0
6799	Investors, n.e.c.	65	69	9.5	360	341	89,878	96,645	38,167	42,563	21.0
SANTA BARBARA, CA											
60 –	**Finance, insurance, and real estate**	1,025	1,008	1.4	8,226	7,759	27,935	29,034	224,365	228,269	0.8
6000	Depository institutions	137	133	1.2	2,387	2,302	26,457	27,440	59,267	62,199	0.9
6020	Commercial banks	86	86	1.3	1,816	1,772	26,566	27,526	45,247	48,316	1.0
6030	Savings institutions	30	27	1.1	363	340	29,576	29,365	9,722	9,708	0.7
6100	Nondepository institutions	80	68	1.1	688	570	30,669	36,253	19,422	18,436	0.7
6140	Personal credit institutions	24	22	1.4	396	377	29,758	39,088	11,710	12,837	1.9
6200	Security and commodity brokers	89	86	1.9	629	618	58,130	54,816	35,757	37,380	0.9
6210	Security brokers and dealers	43	48	2.0	447	435	64,814	61,315	26,358	28,197	0.9
6300	Insurance carriers	67	66	1.4	722	567	38,947	39,965	23,170	21,574	0.4
6310	Life insurance	8	7	0.7	262	243	40,366	35,951	8,786	8,271	0.7
6320	Medical service and health insurance	5	5	1.6	56	66	38,357	39,394	2,443	2,763	0.2
6324	Hospital and medical service plans	5	5	2.0	56	66	38,357	39,394	2,443	2,763	0.3
6330	Fire, marine, and casualty insurance	34	35	1.6	91	90	43,516	48,444	3,787	3,698	0.1
6360	Title insurance	13	13	2.2	284	141	36,803	41,050	7,183	5,710	1.2
6400	Insurance agents, brokers, and service	133	136	1.2	810	849	34,494	35,746	28,075	29,274	1.1
6500	Real estate	468	465	1.5	2,702	2,580	16,761	17,910	50,754	50,270	1.0
6510	Real estate operators and lessors	226	236	1.6	906	851	13,170	14,444	13,538	13,792	1.0
6530	Real estate agents and managers	219	204	1.4	1,655	1,542	17,752	18,895	32,741	32,078	1.1

Source: County Business Patterns, 1994/95, CBP-94/95, U.S. Department of Commerce, Washington, D.C., November 1997. SIC categories for which data were suppressed or not available for both 1994 and 1995 are not displayed. The employment columns represent mid-March employment in the year. Pay per employee is calculated by dividing 1st Quarter payroll, annualized, by mid-March employment. The columns headed "% State" show the county's percentage of the state total for the SIC in 1995; for example, 1.4% for SIC 6000 means that the county had 1.4 percent of the state's total establishments (or payroll) in SIC 6000 in 1995. A dash (-) is used to indicate that data are not available or cannot be calculated; nec means not elsewhere classified.

Continued on next page.

SIC	Industry	No. Establishments			Employment		Pay / Employee		Annual Payroll ($ 000)		
		1994	1995	% State	1994	1995	1994	1995	1994	1995	% State
SANTA BARBARA, CA - [continued]											
6550	Subdividers and developers	15	16	1.0	114	133	26,456	26,346	3,373	3,417	0.7
6552	Subdividers and developers, n.e.c.	13	13	1.0	101	112	26,020	26,536	2,889	2,818	0.8
6730	Trusts	18	20	2.2	197	192	18,721	21,188	4,060	4,118	2.5
6732	Educational, religious, etc. trusts	3	5	1.2	5	22	8,000	16,000	67	429	0.4
6733	Trusts, n.e.c.	15	15	3.0	192	170	19,000	21,859	3,993	3,689	6.3
6799	Investors, n.e.c.	14	11	1.5	61	29	29,639	25,103	1,162	809	0.4
SANTA CLARA, CA											
60 –	**Finance, insurance, and real estate**	3,904	3,769	5.1	32,448	29,836	32,678	31,986	1,010,432	969,000	3.3
6000	Depository institutions	534	533	4.7	9,277	9,815	27,016	27,386	238,672	246,369	3.4
6020	Commercial banks	269	273	4.3	6,345	6,822	27,000	26,811	159,995	160,854	3.4
6030	Savings institutions	137	129	5.2	1,672	1,618	26,923	27,869	42,519	43,585	3.2
6060	Credit unions	76	76	6.1	1,068	1,169	27,831	30,382	30,661	35,906	7.4
6100	Nondepository institutions	444	335	5.2	4,886	2,101	37,538	37,386	152,746	83,230	3.1
6150	Business credit institutions	35	24	3.8	272	210	48,382	59,924	14,237	13,877	2.5
6160	Mortgage bankers and brokers	340	249	6.1	4,125	1,454	37,854	36,259	121,785	55,980	4.2
6200	Security and commodity brokers	206	223	4.8	2,322	1,907	62,972	64,571	130,794	130,105	3.0
6210	Security brokers and dealers	90	98	4.1	1,356	1,155	70,330	69,018	85,536	80,378	2.7
6300	Insurance carriers	274	250	5.5	3,937	3,689	41,304	40,773	153,500	152,077	2.6
6310	Life insurance	38	39	4.2	780	749	38,538	37,768	28,251	25,339	2.2
6320	Medical service and health insurance	9	7	2.3	295	388	46,536	49,330	13,994	19,002	1.7
6330	Fire, marine, and casualty insurance	126	126	5.7	1,519	1,563	44,790	44,732	67,697	71,766	2.4
6360	Title insurance	70	54	9.3	1,132	811	39,830	34,727	38,034	31,098	6.5
6400	Insurance agents, brokers, and service	608	612	5.3	2,564	2,465	32,952	35,122	81,825	86,784	3.3
6500	Real estate	1,706	1,671	5.3	8,791	8,835	22,757	23,199	213,496	219,300	4.6
6510	Real estate operators and lessors	725	714	5.0	3,380	3,562	18,214	18,191	66,793	68,742	5.1
6530	Real estate agents and managers	880	844	5.7	4,575	4,471	25,841	27,319	126,058	129,813	4.5
6550	Subdividers and developers	52	65	3.9	518	646	19,653	20,533	12,479	15,207	3.3
6552	Subdividers and developers, n.e.c.	44	56	4.3	171	239	35,860	31,314	7,235	9,365	2.7
6553	Cemetery subdividers and developers	6	5	2.0	346	401	11,642	13,137	5,089	5,656	5.7
6700	Holding and other investment offices	123	135	4.6	501	728	51,824	41,027	30,956	37,044	2.1
6710	Holding offices	22	24	3.5	196	340	52,510	43,141	13,772	17,704	2.3
6720	Investment offices	6	5	5.0	15	16	63,200	42,500	889	670	0.3
6730	Trusts	31	40	4.3	84	98	25,810	20,735	2,170	2,507	1.5
6732	Educational, religious, etc. trusts	13	17	4.0	54	65	26,963	19,938	1,515	1,596	1.5
6733	Trusts, n.e.c.	18	23	4.6	30	33	23,733	22,303	655	911	1.6
6790	Miscellaneous investing	58	62	5.8	205	268	61,093	45,970	13,087	15,903	3.1
6799	Investors, n.e.c.	46	47	6.4	156	175	67,333	60,091	11,179	8,975	4.4
SANTA CRUZ, CA											
60 –	**Finance, insurance, and real estate**	580	570	0.8	3,646	3,621	23,798	21,107	83,345	78,658	0.3
6000	Depository institutions	78	78	0.7	1,190	1,254	24,934	20,679	28,333	25,540	0.4
6020	Commercial banks	41	41	0.6	749	863	25,244	18,753	18,282	15,709	0.3
6030	Savings institutions	26	26	1.0	307	260	25,173	24,862	7,093	6,592	0.5
6060	Credit unions	8	8	0.6	123	118	21,691	23,763	2,626	2,820	0.6
6090	Functions closely related to banking	3	3	0.3	11	13	33,455	36,923	332	419	0.1
6100	Nondepository institutions	48	39	0.6	232	138	35,517	29,594	5,561	4,086	0.2
6160	Mortgage bankers and brokers	37	26	0.6	187	101	36,984	26,297	4,478	2,946	0.2
6200	Security and commodity brokers	21	21	0.5	110	102	39,236	38,314	4,829	4,827	0.1
6210	Security brokers and dealers	15	16	0.7	101	98	40,396	38,367	4,609	4,615	0.2
6280	Security and commodity services	6	5	0.2	9	4	26,222	37,000	220	212	0.0
6300	Insurance carriers	29	30	0.7	239	177	34,979	33,989	7,380	6,272	0.1
6400	Insurance agents, brokers, and service	86	90	0.8	418	376	29,722	28,096	11,796	10,842	0.4
6500	Real estate	296	285	0.9	1,336	1,402	15,982	15,912	22,582	23,767	0.5
6510	Real estate operators and lessors	120	113	0.8	585	679	14,058	13,325	8,784	9,323	0.7
6530	Real estate agents and managers	147	146	1.0	562	501	17,502	18,978	10,211	10,074	0.4
6550	Subdividers and developers	21	17	1.0	172	194	16,442	16,041	3,073	3,713	0.8
6552	Subdividers and developers, n.e.c.	16	12	0.9	143	159	16,615	15,522	2,552	3,146	0.9

Source: County Business Patterns, 1994/95, CBP-94/95, U.S. Department of Commerce, Washington, D.C., November 1997. SIC categories for which data were suppressed or not available for both 1994 and 1995 are *not* displayed. The employment columns represent mid-March employment in the year. Pay per employee is calculated by dividing 1st Quarter payroll, annualized, by mid-March employment. The columns headed "% State" show the county's percentage of the state total for the SIC in 1995; for example, 1.4% for SIC 6000 means that the county had 1.4 percent of the state's total establishments (or payroll) in SIC 6000 in 1995. A dash (-) is used to indicate that data are not available or cannot be calculated; *nec* means not elsewhere classified.

Continued on next page.

SIC	Industry	No. Establishments			Employment		Pay / Employee		Annual Payroll ($ 000)		
		1994	1995	% State	1994	1995	1994	1995	1994	1995	% State
SANTA CRUZ, CA - [continued]											
6553	Cemetery subdividers and developers	4	4	1.6	29	31	15,586	19,355	505	552	0.6
6700	Holding and other investment offices	22	27	0.9	121	172	19,868	21,023	2,864	3,324	0.2
6710	Holding offices	5	5	0.7	65	54	23,385	33,630	1,699	1,605	0.2
6733	Trusts, n.e.c.	3	5	1.0	7	12	18,857	12,333	140	158	0.3
SHASTA, CA											
60 –	**Finance, insurance, and real estate**	350	339	0.5	2,124	1,820	20,974	21,156	42,209	39,212	0.1
6000	Depository institutions	53	46	0.4	755	680	22,299	22,282	16,521	14,788	0.2
6020	Commercial banks	36	33	0.5	632	583	22,816	22,731	14,163	12,904	0.3
6100	Nondepository institutions	33	32	0.5	187	137	30,417	26,686	4,301	3,699	0.2
6160	Mortgage bankers and brokers	24	21	0.5	144	88	31,028	24,000	3,070	2,090	0.2
6200	Security and commodity brokers	12	13	0.3	54	64	51,111	40,813	2,855	3,176	0.1
6300	Insurance carriers	22	21	0.5	199	150	28,523	28,293	4,737	4,388	0.1
6360	Title insurance	6	6	1.0	122	93	25,508	25,118	2,512	2,347	0.5
6400	Insurance agents, brokers, and service	74	75	0.6	209	214	20,689	22,000	4,307	4,740	0.2
6500	Real estate	150	148	0.5	683	537	12,433	13,728	8,478	7,434	0.2
6510	Real estate operators and lessors	72	77	0.5	279	228	7,885	10,737	2,337	2,653	0.2
6530	Real estate agents and managers	54	51	0.3	212	174	14,396	15,724	3,129	2,598	0.1
6552	Subdividers and developers, n.e.c.	15	12	0.9	91	52	14,989	14,077	1,198	759	0.2
6700	Holding and other investment offices	6	4	0.1	37	38	20,865	20,000	1,010	987	0.1
SIERRA, CA											
60 –	**Finance, insurance, and real estate**	4	4	0.0	-	-	-	-	-	-	-
SOLANO, CA											
60 –	**Finance, insurance, and real estate**	583	569	0.8	3,779	3,527	22,795	23,392	83,528	80,597	0.3
6000	Depository institutions	95	92	0.8	1,351	1,362	19,772	20,558	27,752	27,822	0.4
6020	Commercial banks	54	51	0.8	769	857	20,765	20,499	16,687	16,954	0.4
6030	Savings institutions	15	13	0.5	174	109	17,885	21,138	3,179	2,250	0.2
6060	Credit unions	19	19	1.5	369	354	19,425	21,525	7,422	8,274	1.7
6090	Functions closely related to banking	7	9	0.9	39	42	11,897	12,095	464	344	0.1
6100	Nondepository institutions	63	54	0.8	359	278	37,003	33,094	9,795	7,822	0.3
6160	Mortgage bankers and brokers	39	27	0.7	252	136	42,825	39,500	7,281	3,901	0.3
6300	Insurance carriers	39	39	0.9	656	402	30,848	34,279	19,662	13,172	0.2
6330	Fire, marine, and casualty insurance	17	17	0.8	232	168	39,138	36,548	9,643	6,022	0.2
6360	Title insurance	13	12	2.1	198	151	33,980	29,483	5,608	4,427	0.9
6400	Insurance agents, brokers, and service	85	87	0.8	231	232	23,342	24,586	5,586	5,893	0.2
6500	Real estate	278	269	0.8	1,100	1,045	16,276	17,213	17,910	17,913	0.4
6510	Real estate operators and lessors	115	114	0.8	440	481	12,664	14,578	6,352	6,716	0.5
6530	Real estate agents and managers	145	138	0.9	569	492	17,336	18,504	9,278	8,899	0.3
6552	Subdividers and developers, n.e.c.	9	7	0.5	26	18	22,000	22,222	608	412	0.1
SONOMA, CA											
60 –	**Finance, insurance, and real estate**	1,113	1,075	1.5	12,926	11,371	32,872	34,637	386,286	371,880	1.3
6000	Depository institutions	149	150	1.3	2,311	2,373	28,324	27,486	61,068	62,552	0.9
6020	Commercial banks	77	79	1.2	1,430	1,434	26,445	26,787	35,752	35,772	0.7
6030	Savings institutions	50	51	2.0	668	675	33,760	31,401	20,062	21,007	1.5
6060	Credit unions	16	15	1.2	188	248	24,766	21,742	4,856	5,536	1.1
6090	Functions closely related to banking	6	5	0.5	25	16	17,280	14,000	398	237	0.1
6100	Nondepository institutions	119	104	1.6	1,717	1,273	40,137	25,998	61,128	33,615	1.3
6140	Personal credit institutions	20	19	1.2	82	74	22,976	29,027	2,021	2,267	0.3
6160	Mortgage bankers and brokers	90	75	1.8	1,581	1,145	41,270	25,425	57,231	29,515	2.2
6200	Security and commodity brokers	73	69	1.5	335	349	55,546	57,249	18,904	20,627	0.5
6210	Security brokers and dealers	41	39	1.6	276	282	60,652	61,106	15,914	17,645	0.6
6280	Security and commodity services	32	30	1.4	59	67	31,661	41,015	2,990	2,982	0.2
6300	Insurance carriers	78	75	1.6	5,398	4,205	36,158	46,645	167,458	178,022	3.0
6310	Life insurance	14	12	1.3	524	330	36,092	31,879	17,352	9,157	0.8
6330	Fire, marine, and casualty insurance	37	36	1.6	4,390	3,490	36,908	49,901	138,222	157,103	5.3

Source: County Business Patterns, 1994/95, CBP-94/95, U.S. Department of Commerce, Washington, D.C., November 1997. SIC categories for which data were suppressed or not available for both 1994 and 1995 are not displayed. The employment columns represent mid-March employment in the year. Pay per employee is calculated by dividing 1st Quarter payroll, annualized, by mid-March employment. The columns headed "% State" show the county's percentage of the state total for the SIC in 1995; for example, 1.4% for SIC 6000 means that the county had 1.4 percent of the state's total establishments (or payroll) in SIC 6000 in 1995. A dash (-) is used to indicate that data are not available or cannot be calculated; nec means not elsewhere classified.

Continued on next page.

SIC	Industry	No. Establishments			Employment		Pay / Employee		Annual Payroll ($ 000)		
		1994	1995	% State	1994	1995	1994	1995	1994	1995	% State
SONOMA, CA - [continued]											
6400	Insurance agents, brokers, and service	188	187	1.6	1,112	1,148	29,335	28,557	33,070	33,329	1.3
6500	Real estate	477	460	1.4	1,677	1,711	19,203	18,672	33,421	33,855	0.7
6510	Real estate operators and lessors	190	181	1.3	541	654	16,244	14,147	9,745	10,521	0.8
6530	Real estate agents and managers	247	243	1.6	973	923	19,881	21,096	19,403	19,125	0.7
6550	Subdividers and developers	30	24	1.5	84	69	21,667	25,507	2,139	2,338	0.5
6552	Subdividers and developers, n.e.c.	24	17	1.3	43	33	20,651	22,788	1,104	1,068	0.3
6710	Holding offices	6	6	0.9	20	156	93,600	61,513	1,794	5,856	0.7
6733	Trusts, n.e.c.	5	5	1.0	8	9	13,000	13,778	139	139	0.2
STANISLAUS, CA											
60–	**Finance, insurance, and real estate**	694	681	0.9	5,526	5,245	25,023	24,949	129,366	126,482	0.4
6000	Depository institutions	109	114	1.0	1,686	1,660	21,779	22,542	35,364	35,417	0.5
6020	Commercial banks	58	64	1.0	1,196	1,148	21,000	22,341	24,460	23,994	0.5
6030	Savings institutions	26	25	1.0	281	278	25,808	24,791	6,448	6,516	0.5
6060	Credit unions	13	13	1.0	159	177	21,585	21,627	3,505	3,784	0.8
6090	Functions closely related to banking	12	11	1.1	50	53	18,400	19,623	951	1,065	0.4
6100	Nondepository institutions	88	78	1.2	776	484	31,959	33,248	18,923	15,335	0.6
6140	Personal credit institutions	22	24	1.5	109	127	28,257	30,394	2,795	3,378	0.5
6160	Mortgage bankers and brokers	57	45	1.1	571	258	29,520	27,969	12,079	7,605	0.6
6200	Security and commodity brokers	24	21	0.5	193	217	53,078	45,032	8,866	9,308	0.2
6210	Security brokers and dealers	15	14	0.6	183	206	55,432	46,971	8,709	9,181	0.3
6280	Security and commodity services	9	7	0.3	10	11	10,000	8,727	157	127	0.0
6300	Insurance carriers	50	54	1.2	1,045	897	28,896	29,784	27,256	26,189	0.4
6330	Fire, marine, and casualty insurance	24	27	1.2	99	115	42,545	39,409	4,209	4,610	0.2
6360	Title insurance	13	11	1.9	265	156	34,989	32,359	7,476	5,453	1.1
6400	Insurance agents, brokers, and service	128	133	1.2	552	604	26,319	27,940	15,019	16,921	0.6
6500	Real estate	276	265	0.8	1,147	1,321	15,766	17,142	19,697	21,635	0.5
6510	Real estate operators and lessors	119	122	0.8	591	547	13,604	14,018	8,104	8,116	0.6
6530	Real estate agents and managers	132	115	0.8	376	372	17,660	27,129	7,552	8,810	0.3
6550	Subdividers and developers	21	20	1.2	170	386	19,506	12,280	3,923	4,562	1.0
6552	Subdividers and developers, n.e.c.	12	12	0.9	142	353	19,887	11,830	3,339	3,968	1.1
6553	Cemetery subdividers and developers	9	8	3.3	28	33	17,571	17,091	584	594	0.6
6700	Holding and other investment offices	19	16	0.5	127	62	29,165	21,613	4,241	1,677	0.1
6733	Trusts, n.e.c.	8	6	1.2	17	15	14,824	17,067	330	322	0.6
6790	Miscellaneous investing	5	5	0.5	4	4	40,000	27,000	184	137	0.0
SUTTER, CA											
60–	**Finance, insurance, and real estate**	149	141	0.2	971	907	22,505	22,783	20,666	20,648	0.1
6000	Depository institutions	21	21	0.2	386	376	24,207	23,543	9,202	9,265	0.1
6020	Commercial banks	11	12	0.2	242	254	24,298	22,016	6,028	5,981	0.1
6030	Savings institutions	6	5	0.2	75	68	23,253	21,824	1,565	1,510	0.1
6100	Nondepository institutions	20	19	0.3	104	89	42,731	45,034	3,307	3,186	0.1
6160	Mortgage bankers and brokers	8	7	0.2	51	36	55,451	57,667	1,617	1,397	0.1
6300	Insurance carriers	9	8	0.2	57	42	32,702	34,952	1,797	1,487	0.0
6400	Insurance agents, brokers, and service	23	23	0.2	89	83	19,461	20,627	1,744	1,749	0.1
6500	Real estate	70	64	0.2	318	299	12,981	14,234	4,213	4,506	0.1
6530	Real estate agents and managers	35	30	0.2	225	212	12,764	13,849	2,999	3,168	0.1
TEHAMA, CA											
60–	**Finance, insurance, and real estate**	85	84	0.1	567	603	20,282	19,595	10,443	9,939	0.0
6000	Depository institutions	13	13	0.1	219	252	21,169	21,984	3,921	4,561	0.1
6020	Commercial banks	10	10	0.2	204	235	21,275	22,281	3,651	4,265	0.1
6200	Security and commodity brokers	4	5	0.1	6	13	26,000	14,769	170	228	0.0
6300	Insurance carriers	8	8	0.2	184	157	25,457	25,834	4,306	3,023	0.1
6500	Real estate	35	35	0.1	96	116	8,250	7,517	832	893	0.0
6510	Real estate operators and lessors	20	20	0.1	69	85	8,058	7,435	580	639	0.0

Source: County Business Patterns, 1994/95, CBP-94/95, U.S. Department of Commerce, Washington, D.C., November 1997. SIC categories for which data were suppressed or not available for both 1994 and 1995 are *not* displayed. The employment columns represent mid-March employment in the year. Pay per employee is calculated by dividing 1st Quarter payroll, annualized, by mid-March employment. The columns headed "% State" show the county's percentage of the state total for the SIC in 1995; for example, 1.4% for SIC 6000 means that the county had 1.4 percent of the state's total establishments (or payroll) in SIC 6000 in 1995. A dash (-) is used to indicate that data are not available or cannot be calculated; *nec* means not elsewhere classified.

Continued on next page.

SIC	Industry	No. Establishments			Employment		Pay / Employee		Annual Payroll ($ 000)		
		1994	1995	% State	1994	1995	1994	1995	1994	1995	% State
TRINITY, CA - [continued]											
60 –	**Finance, insurance, and real estate**	16	16	0.0	68	61	15,824	14,295	1,128	932	0.0
6400	Insurance agents, brokers, and service	3	4	0.0	10	13	11,600	8,000	126	107	0.0
TULARE, CA											
60 –	**Finance, insurance, and real estate**	423	446	0.6	3,787	3,457	24,466	23,970	92,228	83,198	0.3
6000	Depository institutions	70	71	0.6	1,217	1,174	23,504	23,901	27,550	26,068	0.4
6020	Commercial banks	44	46	0.7	947	882	25,187	25,388	22,564	20,388	0.4
6060	Credit unions	9	9	0.7	124	166	21,452	20,892	2,888	3,568	0.7
6100	Nondepository institutions	50	56	0.9	317	277	32,997	30,989	10,117	9,089	0.3
6200	Security and commodity brokers	9	14	0.3	58	85	56,414	35,435	3,243	3,862	0.1
6300	Insurance carriers	37	35	0.8	1,143	819	27,885	28,039	30,355	22,961	0.4
6330	Fire, marine, and casualty insurance	19	19	0.9	478	244	33,950	38,311	14,977	8,593	0.3
6360	Title insurance	12	10	1.7	199	120	28,382	33,900	4,683	4,057	0.9
6400	Insurance agents, brokers, and service	98	107	0.9	429	434	22,107	23,696	10,796	10,883	0.4
6500	Real estate	146	148	0.5	575	583	12,814	13,976	9,063	9,052	0.2
6510	Real estate operators and lessors	54	60	0.4	258	269	9,364	8,877	3,272	3,082	0.2
6530	Real estate agents and managers	77	75	0.5	232	224	16,793	17,107	4,245	3,657	0.1
6550	Subdividers and developers	15	12	0.7	85	78	12,424	18,410	1,546	1,736	0.4
6552	Subdividers and developers, n.e.c.	14	11	0.9	80	73	13,050	19,507	1,530	1,718	0.5
6710	Holding offices	4	4	0.6	30	64	8,533	4,750	277	344	0.0
6730	Trusts	6	7	0.8	7	9	22,857	19,556	168	180	0.1
TUOLUMNE, CA											
60 –	**Finance, insurance, and real estate**	121	110	0.1	629	557	20,502	20,618	13,113	10,606	0.0
6000	Depository institutions	19	20	0.2	240	252	20,367	18,254	4,840	4,761	0.1
6020	Commercial banks	12	12	0.2	176	185	19,500	18,011	3,543	3,358	0.1
6030	Savings institutions	7	8	0.3	64	67	22,750	18,925	1,297	1,403	0.1
6300	Insurance carriers	8	7	0.2	120	69	25,433	39,710	3,400	1,446	0.0
6400	Insurance agents, brokers, and service	15	13	0.1	68	61	26,412	28,131	1,853	1,735	0.1
6500	Real estate	67	59	0.2	170	151	13,341	13,192	2,282	2,150	0.0
6510	Real estate operators and lessors	24	21	0.1	75	65	8,213	9,908	688	721	0.1
6530	Real estate agents and managers	34	29	0.2	55	53	13,745	14,717	741	736	0.0
VENTURA, CA											
60 –	**Finance, insurance, and real estate**	1,336	1,290	1.8	12,442	11,680	28,846	30,830	327,744	359,649	1.2
6000	Depository institutions	195	199	1.8	3,299	2,991	23,935	22,268	69,460	61,286	0.8
6020	Commercial banks	101	109	1.7	2,317	2,009	23,650	22,142	46,179	39,589	0.8
6030	Savings institutions	57	53	2.1	602	609	25,694	23,113	14,653	13,580	1.0
6060	Credit unions	23	24	1.9	298	305	21,503	22,492	6,587	6,848	1.4
6090	Functions closely related to banking	14	13	1.3	82	68	27,902	17,412	2,041	1,269	0.4
6100	Nondepository institutions	146	119	1.8	786	661	30,819	34,312	21,063	21,980	0.8
6140	Personal credit institutions	33	37	2.4	238	223	24,387	27,283	5,779	6,033	0.9
6160	Mortgage bankers and brokers	104	74	1.8	442	338	34,226	38,249	12,145	12,430	0.9
6200	Security and commodity brokers	72	72	1.6	671	650	44,715	43,169	29,108	30,835	0.7
6210	Security brokers and dealers	36	37	1.6	409	366	54,758	51,432	20,802	20,793	0.7
6300	Insurance carriers	82	83	1.8	3,810	3,641	37,717	42,281	119,033	151,832	2.6
6330	Fire, marine, and casualty insurance	44	47	2.1	1,800	1,837	36,849	38,254	61,931	66,250	2.2
6360	Title insurance	8	9	1.6	367	321	41,112	39,776	13,715	11,819	2.5
6400	Insurance agents, brokers, and service	261	268	2.3	827	887	29,664	30,422	26,565	30,142	1.1
6500	Real estate	540	514	1.6	2,775	2,585	18,175	21,430	54,685	56,513	1.2
6510	Real estate operators and lessors	195	193	1.3	1,149	1,155	14,437	14,604	18,381	19,400	1.4
6530	Real estate agents and managers	309	280	1.9	1,374	1,242	21,077	25,890	31,488	30,110	1.1
6540	Title abstract offices	4	4	1.8	8	10	19,500	22,400	241	234	0.3
6550	Subdividers and developers	22	20	1.2	234	141	16,581	33,617	3,780	5,191	1.1
6552	Subdividers and developers, n.e.c.	18	15	1.2	198	103	15,495	38,563	2,888	4,517	1.3
6553	Cemetery subdividers and developers	4	4	1.6	36	38	22,556	20,211	892	656	0.7
6710	Holding offices	11	10	1.5	50	59	42,720	34,712	2,456	2,293	0.3

Source: County Business Patterns, 1994/95, CBP-94/95, U.S. Department of Commerce, Washington, D.C., November 1997. SIC categories for which data were suppressed or not available for both 1994 and 1995 are *not* displayed. The employment columns represent mid-March employment in the year. Pay per employee is calculated by dividing 1st Quarter payroll, annualized, by mid-March employment. The columns headed "% State" show the county's percentage of the state total for the SIC in 1995; for example, 1.4% for SIC 6000 means that the county had 1.4 percent of the state's total establishments (or payroll) in SIC 6000 in 1995. A dash (-) is used to indicate that data are not available or cannot be calculated; *nec* means not elsewhere classified.

Continued on next page.

SIC	Industry	No. Establishments			Employment		Pay / Employee		Annual Payroll ($ 000)		
		1994	1995	% State	1994	1995	1994	1995	1994	1995	% State
VENTURA, CA - [continued]											
6730	Trusts	12	12	1.3	75	118	20,960	16,407	1,841	2,127	1.3
6790	Miscellaneous investing	13	11	1.0	141	85	21,021	27,294	3,200	2,464	0.5
6799	Investors, n.e.c.	7	6	0.8	9	5	16,000	11,200	164	79	0.0
YOLO, CA											
60 –	**Finance, insurance, and real estate**	274	262	0.4	3,915	4,032	26,901	26,167	105,132	105,558	0.4
6000	Depository institutions	42	42	0.4	1,327	1,474	26,806	24,502	36,413	33,282	0.5
6020	Commercial banks	23	26	0.4	612	779	19,353	15,117	11,684	12,501	0.3
6100	Nondepository institutions	9	9	0.1	82	72	49,317	42,722	2,793	3,070	0.1
6140	Personal credit institutions	3	3	0.2	13	10	20,308	28,000	260	327	0.0
6200	Security and commodity brokers	8	11	0.2	44	55	30,455	30,909	1,495	1,825	0.0
6300	Insurance carriers	23	19	0.4	1,325	1,209	31,004	32,867	39,677	41,251	0.7
6400	Insurance agents, brokers, and service	34	29	0.3	134	145	27,612	30,841	3,907	5,057	0.2
6500	Real estate	150	145	0.5	981	1,056	19,458	19,004	20,333	20,635	0.4
6510	Real estate operators and lessors	79	74	0.5	387	439	14,326	13,613	5,785	6,446	0.5
6530	Real estate agents and managers	54	55	0.4	508	515	22,071	22,548	12,257	11,588	0.4
YUBA, CA											
60 –	**Finance, insurance, and real estate**	70	67	0.1	581	536	19,855	18,612	10,560	10,269	0.0
6000	Depository institutions	12	11	0.1	156	145	20,564	17,683	2,842	2,744	0.0
6020	Commercial banks	6	6	0.1	118	107	20,881	17,757	2,087	2,017	0.0
6300	Insurance carriers	5	5	0.1	239	214	23,029	22,449	4,422	4,707	0.1
6400	Insurance agents, brokers, and service	20	20	0.2	65	66	22,892	21,394	1,642	1,573	0.1
6500	Real estate	29	27	0.1	102	103	11,647	10,252	1,229	1,035	0.0
6510	Real estate operators and lessors	15	13	0.1	49	51	10,612	10,118	539	516	0.0
6530	Real estate agents and managers	7	9	0.1	8	14	11,000	12,000	113	126	0.0

Source: County Business Patterns, 1994/95, CBP-94/95, U.S. Department of Commerce, Washington, D.C., November 1997. SIC categories for which data were suppressed or not available for both 1994 and 1995 are *not* displayed. The employment columns represent mid-March employment in the year. Pay per employee is calculated by dividing 1st Quarter payroll, annualized, by mid-March employment. The columns headed "% State" show the county's percentage of the state total for the SIC in 1995; for example, 1.4% for SIC 6000 means that the county had 1.4 percent of the state's total establishments (or payroll) in SIC 6000 in 1995. A dash (-) is used to indicate that data are not available or cannot be calculated; *nec* means not elsewhere classified.

COLORADO

SIC	Industry	No. Establishments			Employment		Pay / Employee		Annual Payroll ($ 000)		
		1994	1995	% State	1994	1995	1994	1995	1994	1995	% State
ADAMS, CO											
60 –	**Finance, insurance, and real estate**	504	526	4.1	3,245	3,328	22,119	23,060	72,226	80,434	2.2
6000	Depository institutions	66	71	5.2	1,016	1,047	22,606	23,798	23,240	26,264	4.1
6020	Commercial banks	32	31	3.7	730	738	24,214	26,401	18,261	20,020	4.2
6060	Credit unions	17	17	6.5	177	201	20,023	18,328	3,443	3,764	5.8
6100	Nondepository institutions	48	41	3.7	376	399	33,500	34,276	11,315	11,927	3.1
6140	Personal credit institutions	20	16	6.6	189	230	30,074	33,461	5,612	5,929	6.9
6160	Mortgage bankers and brokers	26	22	3.2	186	167	37,140	35,665	5,693	5,951	3.2
6200	Security and commodity brokers	16	13	1.5	23	34	22,087	17,882	685	733	0.1
6300	Insurance carriers	31	30	4.1	244	225	29,262	32,693	7,315	7,626	0.9
6320	Medical service and health insurance	3	4	6.7	50	52	27,840	31,308	1,430	1,971	1.9
6400	Insurance agents, brokers, and service	129	136	5.6	328	331	21,878	22,755	7,756	8,500	2.6
6500	Real estate	204	226	3.9	1,143	1,176	12,423	15,207	16,114	20,390	3.2
6510	Real estate operators and lessors	74	81	4.7	642	592	9,788	11,669	7,557	7,833	4.9
6530	Real estate agents and managers	118	130	3.8	445	451	16,548	17,854	7,887	9,239	2.2
6550	Subdividers and developers	9	11	3.0	54	133	9,852	21,985	635	3,212	7.0
6553	Cemetery subdividers and developers	6	6	12.2	51	51	9,647	11,216	592	652	7.0
6700	Holding and other investment offices	10	9	1.9	115	116	62,504	41,138	5,801	4,994	1.9
6790	Miscellaneous investing	3	4	2.1	18	9	7,556	15,556	173	188	0.3
ALAMOSA, CO											
60 –	**Finance, insurance, and real estate**	31	35	0.3	204	203	22,314	23,764	4,348	4,836	0.1
6000	Depository institutions	6	6	0.4	125	120	21,504	24,300	2,530	2,889	0.4
6400	Insurance agents, brokers, and service	12	13	0.5	53	50	27,170	28,160	1,218	1,300	0.4
6500	Real estate	9	12	0.2	18	23	14,000	14,261	355	408	0.1
6510	Real estate operators and lessors	5	5	0.3	8	12	16,000	12,000	195	215	0.1
6530	Real estate agents and managers	4	7	0.2	10	11	12,400	16,727	160	193	0.0
ARAPAHOE, CO											
60 –	**Finance, insurance, and real estate**	1,987	2,132	16.6	27,214	29,362	32,571	34,051	871,221	981,137	26.7
6000	Depository institutions	190	204	15.0	3,306	3,283	25,342	31,604	89,611	101,067	15.6
6020	Commercial banks	124	131	15.8	1,470	1,486	24,732	26,961	35,262	37,829	8.0
6060	Credit unions	29	28	10.8	421	419	21,368	20,592	8,717	9,266	14.3
6100	Nondepository institutions	246	272	24.7	5,343	4,539	33,536	32,902	152,559	151,145	39.6
6160	Mortgage bankers and brokers	152	164	24.2	2,139	1,223	34,809	34,129	55,496	49,631	26.3
6200	Security and commodity brokers	149	163	18.5	2,529	2,014	40,346	47,932	87,759	97,599	17.9
6210	Security brokers and dealers	81	81	17.8	1,622	1,177	43,546	51,283	56,713	62,488	20.7
6300	Insurance carriers	196	211	29.1	8,544	9,762	32,007	32,649	298,123	327,047	39.3
6310	Life insurance	53	52	29.4	4,600	5,711	27,766	28,289	146,580	169,781	56.0
6320	Medical service and health insurance	14	17	28.3	520	811	37,708	28,977	25,305	28,593	27.6
6330	Fire, marine, and casualty insurance	95	103	29.5	2,757	2,561	38,807	43,519	105,683	103,752	30.9
6370	Pension, health, and welfare funds	13	17	43.6	464	506	25,198	28,356	13,352	16,896	36.9
6500	Real estate	724	773	13.3	4,469	4,646	20,326	23,284	99,957	117,432	18.2
6510	Real estate operators and lessors	219	218	12.6	1,286	1,194	19,076	29,052	24,307	36,350	22.7
6530	Real estate agents and managers	445	469	13.9	2,902	3,183	20,229	20,819	64,436	72,738	17.4
6550	Subdividers and developers	36	42	11.6	239	191	27,230	30,513	9,403	6,479	14.1
6552	Subdividers and developers, n.e.c.	30	35	12.2	165	141	35,370	37,816	8,872	5,876	16.8
6700	Holding and other investment offices	96	100	20.6	924	925	94,238	81,691	73,446	88,459	33.0
6710	Holding offices	25	28	21.5	513	491	122,511	96,692	49,749	59,312	33.0
6720	Investment offices	6	5	20.0	13	13	29,538	32,308	354	649	4.7
6730	Trusts	11	14	12.3	22	53	21,273	21,887	530	1,405	7.9
6732	Educational, religious, etc. trusts	5	7	11.9	2	8	24,000	16,000	114	256	2.3

Source: County Business Patterns, 1994/95, CBP-94/95, U.S. Department of Commerce, Washington, D.C., November 1997. SIC categories for which data were suppressed or not available for both 1994 and 1995 are *not* displayed. The employment columns represent mid-March employment in the year. Pay per employee is calculated by dividing 1st Quarter payroll, annualized, by mid-March employment. The columns headed "% State" show the county's percentage of the state total for the SIC in 1995; for example, 1.4% for SIC 6000 means that the county had 1.4 percent of the state's total establishments (or payroll) in SIC 6000 in 1995. A dash (-) is used to indicate that data are not available or cannot be calculated; *nec* means not elsewhere classified.

Continued on next page.

SIC	Industry	No. Establishments			Employment		Pay / Employee		Annual Payroll ($ 000)		
		1994	1995	% State	1994	1995	1994	1995	1994	1995	% State
ARAPAHOE, CO - [continued]											
6733	Trusts, n.e.c.	6	7	13.2	20	45	21,000	22,933	416	1,149	17.0
6790	Miscellaneous investing	52	49	25.7	376	364	62,170	72,385	22,798	26,805	48.8
6794	Patent owners and lessors	20	18	51.4	277	250	57,978	73,824	16,297	17,693	83.6
6799	Investors, n.e.c.	23	22	20.0	61	72	37,049	41,278	2,798	5,524	30.9
ARCHULETA, CO											
60 –	**Finance, insurance, and real estate**	27	33	0.3	192	215	16,208	19,088	4,114	4,798	0.1
6000	Depository institutions	4	4	0.3	57	62	18,456	18,903	1,144	1,263	0.2
6400	Insurance agents, brokers, and service	6	7	0.3	20	32	11,800	12,500	251	403	0.1
6500	Real estate	17	22	0.4	115	121	15,861	20,926	2,719	3,132	0.5
6530	Real estate agents and managers	11	15	0.4	81	89	14,025	20,404	1,973	2,181	0.5
BACA, CO											
60 –	**Finance, insurance, and real estate**	10	10	0.1	45	45	15,733	16,978	765	846	0.0
6500	Real estate	4	4	0.1	7	7	9,714	9,714	68	72	0.0
BENT, CO											
60 –	**Finance, insurance, and real estate**	7	7	0.1	52	48	17,385	18,833	1,034	1,085	0.0
6000	Depository institutions	3	3	0.2	46	41	18,435	20,390	973	996	0.2
BOULDER, CO											
60 –	**Finance, insurance, and real estate**	928	964	7.5	5,622	5,432	26,935	27,280	153,301	156,281	4.2
6000	Depository institutions	89	87	6.4	1,667	1,652	24,322	25,610	37,681	37,136	5.7
6020	Commercial banks	56	56	6.8	1,289	1,299	25,803	27,652	30,395	30,289	6.4
6060	Credit unions	17	17	6.5	248	270	19,323	18,681	4,928	5,447	8.4
6100	Nondepository institutions	83	83	7.5	673	548	34,134	32,102	22,440	22,086	5.8
6140	Personal credit institutions	10	10	4.1	76	78	20,105	25,897	1,769	2,244	2.6
6150	Business credit institutions	11	10	7.6	115	114	24,661	28,772	3,188	4,178	4.9
6160	Mortgage bankers and brokers	62	60	8.8	482	349	38,606	35,095	17,483	15,529	8.2
6200	Security and commodity brokers	89	90	10.2	423	366	61,267	55,421	25,844	22,950	4.2
6210	Security brokers and dealers	41	39	8.6	313	249	70,415	59,036	19,503	15,551	5.2
6280	Security and commodity services	42	45	11.1	102	107	34,588	41,121	4,834	5,338	2.3
6300	Insurance carriers	31	36	5.0	289	140	30,671	38,943	6,889	5,159	0.6
6400	Insurance agents, brokers, and service	162	172	7.0	534	527	22,142	21,176	13,075	13,315	4.0
6500	Real estate	445	464	8.0	1,712	1,891	17,437	19,353	34,573	38,907	6.0
6510	Real estate operators and lessors	145	153	8.8	738	819	13,707	15,629	12,420	14,538	9.1
6530	Real estate agents and managers	262	253	7.5	866	945	19,150	21,960	18,208	20,440	4.9
6550	Subdividers and developers	28	31	8.6	79	86	31,595	27,116	3,289	2,809	6.1
6552	Subdividers and developers, n.e.c.	23	26	9.0	43	55	33,023	25,091	2,119	1,887	5.4
6553	Cemetery subdividers and developers	5	5	10.2	36	31	29,889	30,710	1,170	922	10.0
6700	Holding and other investment offices	29	32	6.6	324	308	35,358	48,026	12,799	16,728	6.2
6790	Miscellaneous investing	11	11	5.8	67	74	32,597	49,892	2,541	6,770	12.3
CHAFFEE, CO											
60 –	**Finance, insurance, and real estate**	42	45	0.4	198	220	21,374	20,855	4,259	4,656	0.1
6000	Depository institutions	7	8	0.6	116	119	26,379	26,286	2,914	3,026	0.5
6020	Commercial banks	4	4	0.5	80	80	31,850	31,150	2,362	2,325	0.5
6500	Real estate	21	23	0.4	47	63	10,043	10,476	615	781	0.1
6510	Real estate operators and lessors	6	6	0.3	13	28	8,000	7,571	193	243	0.2
6530	Real estate agents and managers	10	10	0.3	21	22	11,048	13,091	278	339	0.1
CHEYENNE, CO											
60 –	**Finance, insurance, and real estate**	4	4	0.0	41	47	20,390	18,213	933	984	0.0
CLEAR CREEK, CO											
60 –	**Finance, insurance, and real estate**	20	21	0.2	62	73	19,806	19,945	1,329	1,559	0.0
6500	Real estate	11	12	0.2	21	22	10,857	11,091	249	250	0.0
6530	Real estate agents and managers	6	6	0.2	7	7	4,571	6,286	45	40	0.0

Source: County Business Patterns, 1994/95, CBP-94/95, U.S. Department of Commerce, Washington, D.C., November 1997. SIC categories for which data were suppressed or not available for both 1994 and 1995 are *not* displayed. The employment columns represent mid-March employment in the year. Pay per employee is calculated by dividing 1st Quarter payroll, annualized, by mid-March employment. The columns headed "% State" show the county's percentage of the state total for the SIC in 1995; for example, 1.4% for SIC 6000 means that the county had 1.4 percent of the state's total establishments (or payroll) in SIC 6000 in 1995. A dash (-) is used to indicate that data are not available or cannot be calculated; *nec* means not elsewhere classified.

SIC	Industry	No. Establishments			Employment		Pay / Employee		Annual Payroll ($ 000)		
		1994	1995	% State	1994	1995	1994	1995	1994	1995	% State
CUSTER, CO											
60 –	**Finance, insurance, and real estate**	11	13	0.1	63	58	14,413	14,966	1,160	954	0.0
6500	Real estate	7	9	0.2	21	19	12,762	9,684	474	254	0.0
6530	Real estate agents and managers	7	8	0.2	21	18	12,762	9,778	474	246	0.1
DELTA, CO											
60 –	**Finance, insurance, and real estate**	53	58	0.5	278	276	17,223	18,652	4,749	5,338	0.1
6000	Depository institutions	14	15	1.1	134	153	20,776	21,229	2,608	3,141	0.5
6020	Commercial banks	8	9	1.1	106	124	20,943	21,516	2,016	2,510	0.5
6100	Nondepository institutions	3	3	0.3	28	13	16,571	19,692	416	372	0.1
6500	Real estate	21	23	0.4	64	58	10,750	14,552	823	872	0.1
6510	Real estate operators and lessors	3	5	0.3	5	6	5,600	5,333	36	75	0.0
DENVER, CO											
60 –	**Finance, insurance, and real estate**	2,570	2,612	20.3	34,609	34,405	35,317	38,671	1,196,130	1,305,744	35.5
6000	Depository institutions	272	269	19.8	7,095	6,815	29,271	30,240	202,803	196,903	30.4
6020	Commercial banks	157	157	19.0	5,772	5,495	30,649	31,881	171,678	162,992	34.4
6030	Savings institutions	30	30	17.1	263	258	20,259	20,419	5,106	6,164	-
6060	Credit unions	57	53	20.4	605	602	21,098	23,229	13,290	14,056	21.7
6100	Nondepository institutions	207	224	20.3	3,231	2,789	34,679	34,824	99,107	94,640	24.8
6140	Personal credit institutions	25	29	11.9	404	458	28,416	25,100	12,119	11,279	13.1
6150	Business credit institutions	43	43	32.6	865	655	31,477	42,186	24,821	22,121	26.2
6160	Mortgage bankers and brokers	135	149	22.0	1,952	1,667	37,393	34,534	61,534	60,801	32.2
6200	Security and commodity brokers	247	251	28.5	4,731	5,702	58,459	63,609	267,296	347,378	63.7
6210	Security brokers and dealers	126	125	27.5	2,660	2,460	62,847	63,398	154,489	161,263	53.4
6300	Insurance carriers	174	163	22.5	6,956	6,859	36,717	38,495	243,682	262,639	31.5
6310	Life insurance	65	59	33.3	2,583	2,518	39,167	40,531	93,750	100,402	33.1
6320	Medical service and health insurance	17	18	30.0	1,767	1,783	33,974	37,900	57,343	62,305	60.2
6321	Accident and health insurance	4	5	23.8	107	216	23,589	26,037	2,456	5,713	55.9
6324	Hospital and medical service plans	13	13	33.3	1,660	1,567	34,643	39,535	54,887	56,592	60.6
6330	Fire, marine, and casualty insurance	55	59	16.9	1,292	1,309	36,402	36,425	48,396	50,497	15.1
6360	Title insurance	11	9	12.3	669	601	35,426	31,940	21,495	21,019	56.6
6500	Real estate	1,118	1,139	19.6	8,417	8,045	22,377	23,512	206,179	200,399	31.0
6510	Real estate operators and lessors	464	444	25.6	3,407	2,516	17,444	19,366	66,009	49,464	31.0
6530	Real estate agents and managers	573	584	17.3	4,643	5,012	25,602	25,427	126,714	135,321	32.4
6540	Title abstract offices	9	7	11.9	168	130	24,262	27,877	3,945	3,408	29.4
6550	Subdividers and developers	41	47	13.0	171	208	31,368	33,058	8,154	8,181	17.8
6552	Subdividers and developers, n.e.c.	35	42	14.6	70	97	54,286	48,990	3,814	5,708	16.3
6700	Holding and other investment offices	173	167	34.4	1,672	1,772	53,809	64,174	88,050	106,153	39.5
6710	Holding offices	47	41	31.5	973	994	70,578	82,137	59,850	70,689	39.4
6720	Investment offices	6	9	36.0	111	136	49,514	78,382	9,662	11,211	81.5
6730	Trusts	40	41	36.0	260	257	19,246	21,292	5,414	7,017	39.4
6732	Educational, religious, etc. trusts	19	21	35.6	170	182	22,494	23,143	3,828	4,702	43.1
6733	Trusts, n.e.c.	21	20	37.7	90	75	13,111	16,800	1,586	2,315	34.3
6790	Miscellaneous investing	76	70	36.6	299	381	32,254	41,449	11,738	16,153	29.4
6792	Oil royalty traders	16	18	51.4	84	118	44,381	58,915	3,721	6,187	83.7
6794	Patent owners and lessors	12	10	28.6	80	78	25,700	33,538	2,513	2,798	13.2
6798	Real estate investment trusts	3	3	27.3	10	14	20,400	18,857	219	270	3.2
6799	Investors, n.e.c.	45	39	35.5	125	171	29,248	34,854	5,285	6,898	38.6
DOLORES, CO											
60 –	**Finance, insurance, and real estate**	3	4	0.0	-	-	-	-	-	-	-
DOUGLAS, CO											
60 –	**Finance, insurance, and real estate**	214	233	1.8	774	839	24,300	24,591	19,507	21,506	0.6
6000	Depository institutions	20	18	1.3	235	222	28,323	26,162	5,862	5,623	0.9
6020	Commercial banks	16	14	1.7	213	198	28,770	25,960	5,300	4,935	1.0
6100	Nondepository institutions	16	17	1.5	29	25	19,586	24,480	665	866	0.2
6150	Business credit institutions	3	4	3.0	3	4	28,000	35,000	148	245	0.3

Source: County Business Patterns, 1994/95, CBP-94/95, U.S. Department of Commerce, Washington, D.C., November 1997. SIC categories for which data were suppressed or not available for both 1994 and 1995 are *not* displayed. The employment columns represent mid-March employment in the year. Pay per employee is calculated by dividing 1st Quarter payroll, annualized, by mid-March employment. The columns headed "% State" show the county's percentage of the state total for the SIC in 1995; for example, 1.4% for SIC 6000 means that the county had 1.4 percent of the state's total establishments (or payroll) in SIC 6000 in 1995. A dash (-) is used to indicate that data are not available or cannot be calculated; *nec* means not elsewhere classified.

Continued on next page.

SIC	Industry	No. Establishments			Employment		Pay / Employee		Annual Payroll ($ 000)		
		1994	1995	% State	1994	1995	1994	1995	1994	1995	% State
DOUGLAS, CO - [continued]											
6200	Security and commodity brokers	12	14	1.6	27	25	33,481	24,160	755	751	0.1
6210	Security brokers and dealers	5	6	1.3	10	15	46,000	32,000	510	595	0.2
6280	Security and commodity services	7	8	2.0	17	10	26,118	12,400	245	156	0.1
6300	Insurance carriers	11	15	2.1	87	131	31,494	35,878	2,484	4,583	0.6
6400	Insurance agents, brokers, and service	44	43	1.8	124	97	28,419	22,021	3,489	2,548	0.8
6500	Real estate	107	120	2.1	268	331	16,433	20,073	6,211	6,969	1.1
6510	Real estate operators and lessors	22	22	1.3	47	37	7,660	9,838	402	471	0.3
6530	Real estate agents and managers	74	84	2.5	217	282	18,304	21,532	5,548	6,247	1.5
6550	Subdividers and developers	5	8	2.2	4	5	18,000	19,200	111	127	0.3
6700	Holding and other investment offices	4	6	1.2	4	8	3,000	16,000	41	166	0.1
EAGLE, CO											
60 –	**Finance, insurance, and real estate**	222	236	1.8	1,628	1,852	22,106	22,793	35,850	40,919	1.1
6000	Depository institutions	12	13	1.0	228	268	31,105	33,403	6,596	8,477	1.3
6500	Real estate	170	183	3.1	1,285	1,470	18,677	19,823	24,797	27,743	4.3
6510	Real estate operators and lessors	21	23	1.3	135	141	15,496	17,929	2,045	2,349	1.5
6530	Real estate agents and managers	126	126	3.7	1,045	1,204	17,780	18,967	18,682	21,213	5.1
6550	Subdividers and developers	13	21	5.8	84	91	34,476	35,033	3,526	3,468	7.5
6552	Subdividers and developers, n.e.c.	12	19	6.6	84	90	34,476	35,333	3,521	3,422	9.8
ELBERT, CO											
60 –	**Finance, insurance, and real estate**	12	13	0.1	45	48	18,400	23,833	938	1,291	0.0
6400	Insurance agents, brokers, and service	3	4	0.2	5	9	17,600	19,111	131	168	0.1
EL PASO, CO											
60 –	**Finance, insurance, and real estate**	1,261	1,309	10.2	9,566	9,771	25,532	26,220	242,233	267,483	7.3
6000	Depository institutions	119	122	9.0	1,978	1,992	23,137	23,488	42,108	44,338	6.9
6020	Commercial banks	59	58	7.0	1,181	1,117	27,251	27,918	27,812	27,914	5.9
6060	Credit unions	32	33	12.7	629	716	16,197	17,682	11,365	13,069	20.1
6100	Nondepository institutions	119	119	10.8	927	826	36,992	39,661	30,671	31,892	8.4
6140	Personal credit institutions	32	37	15.2	204	200	24,804	25,860	5,177	4,859	5.7
6160	Mortgage bankers and brokers	76	73	10.8	558	496	39,305	40,645	17,814	19,949	10.6
6200	Security and commodity brokers	84	85	9.6	536	461	50,806	49,007	23,832	23,717	4.3
6210	Security brokers and dealers	50	46	10.1	435	357	56,395	53,714	20,735	20,417	6.8
6280	Security and commodity services	33	39	9.6	100	104	26,960	32,846	3,093	3,300	1.4
6300	Insurance carriers	74	82	11.3	2,798	3,002	27,983	30,080	81,484	93,875	11.3
6310	Life insurance	20	23	13.0	502	678	23,984	20,997	13,945	13,619	4.5
6330	Fire, marine, and casualty insurance	38	41	11.7	2,084	2,027	28,624	34,094	61,832	71,880	21.4
6360	Title insurance	7	9	12.3	167	116	32,766	30,276	4,268	3,577	9.6
6400	Insurance agents, brokers, and service	233	240	9.8	904	837	20,106	21,553	18,708	19,850	6.0
6500	Real estate	601	622	10.7	2,262	2,373	16,340	16,425	40,553	46,150	7.1
6510	Real estate operators and lessors	165	168	9.7	643	683	12,566	12,849	8,799	10,089	6.3
6530	Real estate agents and managers	384	383	11.3	1,502	1,497	17,411	17,860	27,779	31,200	7.5
6550	Subdividers and developers	33	38	10.5	108	154	23,556	17,818	3,292	3,867	8.4
6552	Subdividers and developers, n.e.c.	29	32	11.1	60	100	35,467	21,920	2,762	3,202	9.1
6700	Holding and other investment offices	31	39	8.0	161	280	21,839	24,057	4,877	7,661	2.9
6710	Holding offices	10	11	8.5	74	168	19,189	23,786	2,570	4,654	2.6
6730	Trusts	8	11	9.6	48	66	23,333	21,030	1,185	1,614	9.1
6790	Miscellaneous investing	8	12	6.3	21	24	32,952	33,500	753	896	1.6
FREMONT, CO											
60 –	**Finance, insurance, and real estate**	44	49	0.4	314	316	22,013	22,582	6,651	7,464	0.2
6000	Depository institutions	9	10	0.7	188	180	23,936	24,067	3,926	4,170	0.6
6020	Commercial banks	6	7	0.8	173	168	24,717	24,738	3,741	4,011	0.8
6500	Real estate	17	20	0.3	70	65	11,714	12,862	1,056	1,158	0.2
6530	Real estate agents and managers	9	11	0.3	25	35	11,680	10,171	391	528	0.1
GARFIELD, CO											
60 –	**Finance, insurance, and real estate**	118	132	1.0	817	819	22,453	24,503	17,449	19,158	0.5

Source: County Business Patterns, 1994/95, CBP-94/95, U.S. Department of Commerce, Washington, D.C., November 1997. SIC categories for which data were suppressed or not available for both 1994 and 1995 are not displayed. The employment columns represent mid-March employment in the year. Pay per employee is calculated by dividing 1st Quarter payroll, annualized, by mid-March employment. The columns headed "% State" show the county's percentage of the state total for the SIC in 1995; for example, 1.4% for SIC 6000 means that the county had 1.4 percent of the state's total establishments (or payroll) in SIC 6000 in 1995. A dash (-) is used to indicate that data are not available or cannot be calculated; nec means not elsewhere classified.

Continued on next page.

SIC	Industry	No. Establishments			Employment		Pay / Employee		Annual Payroll ($ 000)		
		1994	1995	% State	1994	1995	1994	1995	1994	1995	% State
GARFIELD, CO - [continued]											
6000	Depository institutions	15	15	1.1	236	228	24,458	28,018	5,462	6,009	0.9
6400	Insurance agents, brokers, and service	28	28	1.1	100	101	20,720	24,554	2,497	2,494	0.8
6500	Real estate	61	74	1.3	340	345	14,376	15,513	5,156	6,026	0.9
6510	Real estate operators and lessors	17	20	1.2	134	196	13,910	14,224	2,049	2,675	1.7
6530	Real estate agents and managers	35	40	1.2	183	124	13,814	17,129	2,532	2,644	0.6
6550	Subdividers and developers	7	9	2.5	22	21	22,000	16,571	530	620	1.3
6552	Subdividers and developers, n.e.c.	6	7	2.4	22	21	22,000	16,571	505	519	1.5
GILPIN, CO											
60 –	**Finance, insurance, and real estate**	4	3	0.0	8	6	15,000	26,667	179	171	0.0
GRAND, CO											
60 –	**Finance, insurance, and real estate**	56	63	0.5	394	384	15,777	16,094	6,142	6,286	0.2
6000	Depository institutions	6	5	0.4	63	51	21,841	21,490	1,150	994	0.2
6500	Real estate	42	48	0.8	297	296	14,128	14,703	4,238	4,456	0.7
6510	Real estate operators and lessors	9	10	0.6	52	50	11,462	12,160	528	637	0.4
6530	Real estate agents and managers	28	33	1.0	226	228	13,912	14,789	3,120	3,246	0.8
GUNNISON, CO											
60 –	**Finance, insurance, and real estate**	65	60	0.5	500	547	16,048	15,561	8,082	7,976	0.2
6000	Depository institutions	5	4	0.3	91	124	22,989	18,968	2,071	2,353	0.4
6500	Real estate	49	47	0.8	372	380	14,129	14,116	4,999	4,800	0.7
6510	Real estate operators and lessors	6	4	0.2	24	11	16,500	18,182	457	399	0.2
6530	Real estate agents and managers	38	39	1.2	335	346	13,946	13,954	4,269	4,112	1.0
HINSDALE, CO											
60 –	**Finance, insurance, and real estate**	6	7	0.1	20	27	19,200	19,556	579	612	0.0
HUERFANO, CO											
60 –	**Finance, insurance, and real estate**	18	18	0.1	53	47	14,642	14,809	863	810	0.0
6400	Insurance agents, brokers, and service	4	5	0.2	7	8	16,571	22,500	110	142	0.0
6530	Real estate agents and managers	3	3	0.1	4	5	5,000	11,200	30	86	0.0
6540	Title abstract offices	3	3	5.1	15	8	17,333	11,500	292	120	1.0
JACKSON, CO											
60 –	**Finance, insurance, and real estate**	2	1	0.0	-	-	-	-	-	-	-
JEFFERSON, CO											
60 –	**Finance, insurance, and real estate**	1,417	1,509	11.7	9,578	9,862	27,049	28,067	253,254	277,397	7.5
6000	Depository institutions	137	135	9.9	2,429	2,443	25,578	27,874	57,143	64,345	9.9
6020	Commercial banks	82	82	9.9	1,581	1,578	27,304	30,292	38,206	42,755	9.0
6030	Savings institutions	21	21	12.0	348	321	20,885	24,087	7,135	8,256	-
6060	Credit unions	26	25	9.6	333	336	19,544	19,405	6,653	7,110	11.0
6090	Functions closely related to banking	8	7	7.9	167	208	31,042	29,058	5,149	6,224	10.2
6100	Nondepository institutions	135	137	12.4	986	943	31,091	30,995	29,687	33,809	8.9
6140	Personal credit institutions	27	32	13.2	286	235	36,196	37,736	8,698	7,419	8.6
6150	Business credit institutions	15	19	14.4	101	158	27,168	28,886	3,403	5,732	6.8
6160	Mortgage bankers and brokers	89	76	11.2	586	499	29,645	29,467	17,238	18,906	10.0
6200	Security and commodity brokers	95	117	13.3	662	912	33,468	29,961	20,087	25,653	4.7
6210	Security brokers and dealers	48	65	14.3	547	800	32,709	29,230	15,564	21,576	7.1
6220	Commodity contracts brokers, dealers	5	4	22.2	12	12	23,667	27,667	241	253	4.5
6280	Security and commodity services	42	48	11.9	103	100	38,641	36,080	4,282	3,824	1.6
6300	Insurance carriers	83	87	12.0	1,036	808	34,405	41,807	30,929	29,339	3.5
6310	Life insurance	14	16	9.0	325	241	36,505	40,614	9,266	8,587	2.8
6400	Insurance agents, brokers, and service	346	362	14.8	1,366	1,475	28,366	27,761	45,858	49,406	15.0
6500	Real estate	559	606	10.4	2,420	2,563	16,686	18,666	44,368	51,367	7.9
6510	Real estate operators and lessors	172	175	10.1	831	837	11,658	13,749	10,526	12,361	7.7
6530	Real estate agents and managers	338	365	10.8	1,292	1,414	19,502	21,109	27,418	32,414	7.8

Source: County Business Patterns, 1994/95, CBP-94/95, U.S. Department of Commerce, Washington, D.C., November 1997. SIC categories for which data were suppressed or not available for both 1994 and 1995 are not displayed. The employment columns represent mid-March employment in the year. Pay per employee is calculated by dividing 1st Quarter payroll, annualized, by mid-March employment. The columns headed "% State" show the county's percentage of the state total for the SIC in 1995; for example, 1.4% for SIC 6000 means that the county had 1.4 percent of the state's total establishments (or payroll) in SIC 6000 in 1995. A dash (-) is used to indicate that data are not available or cannot be calculated; nec means not elsewhere classified.

Continued on next page.

SIC	Industry	No. Establishments			Employment		Pay / Employee		Annual Payroll ($ 000)		
		1994	1995	% State	1994	1995	1994	1995	1994	1995	% State
JEFFERSON, CO - [continued]											
6550	Subdividers and developers	34	37	10.2	286	267	18,462	21,948	5,832	5,569	12.1
6710	Holding offices	10	12	9.2	94	92	82,979	82,000	7,517	6,129	3.4
6790	Miscellaneous investing	21	23	12.0	58	85	42,621	40,518	2,484	3,208	5.8
KIOWA, CO											
60 –	**Finance, insurance, and real estate**	2	2	0.0	-	-	-	-	-	-	-
KIT CARSON, CO											
60 –	**Finance, insurance, and real estate**	24	27	0.2	128	125	18,188	20,256	2,557	2,647	0.1
6000	Depository institutions	5	6	0.4	63	75	23,873	23,467	1,580	1,868	0.3
6500	Real estate	3	4	0.1	10	11	16,800	17,818	209	175	0.0
LAKE, CO											
60 –	**Finance, insurance, and real estate**	17	16	0.1	61	60	15,607	15,867	1,063	1,098	0.0
6500	Real estate	8	7	0.1	18	18	6,000	6,889	106	124	0.0
6530	Real estate agents and managers	5	4	0.1	13	14	4,615	7,429	59	93	0.0
LA PLATA, CO											
60 –	**Finance, insurance, and real estate**	146	150	1.2	753	766	21,726	24,773	17,710	19,940	0.5
6000	Depository institutions	11	11	0.8	297	285	21,737	24,618	6,810	7,140	1.1
6100	Nondepository institutions	7	9	0.8	23	40	50,609	34,100	805	1,094	0.3
6160	Mortgage bankers and brokers	4	5	0.7	14	30	65,143	35,067	510	745	0.4
6200	Security and commodity brokers	6	6	0.7	50	56	52,720	75,714	2,999	4,399	0.8
6400	Insurance agents, brokers, and service	24	26	1.1	74	70	18,000	16,057	1,662	1,547	0.5
6500	Real estate	95	95	1.6	306	311	15,490	16,630	5,397	5,710	0.9
6510	Real estate operators and lessors	26	26	1.5	73	83	13,973	13,398	1,191	1,226	0.8
6530	Real estate agents and managers	59	56	1.7	188	182	14,511	17,033	2,923	3,112	0.7
6700	Holding and other investment offices	3	3	0.6	3	4	10,667	15,000	37	50	0.0
LARIMER, CO											
60 –	**Finance, insurance, and real estate**	612	640	5.0	3,366	3,543	24,410	25,175	77,922	85,877	2.3
6000	Depository institutions	55	56	4.1	1,166	1,186	25,787	25,848	26,369	27,876	4.3
6020	Commercial banks	42	42	5.1	922	1,017	27,540	26,918	22,745	24,254	5.1
6060	Credit unions	6	6	2.3	109	107	17,394	17,981	2,019	2,207	3.4
6100	Nondepository institutions	55	57	5.2	332	294	33,771	33,605	8,575	10,116	2.7
6140	Personal credit institutions	12	11	4.5	53	53	24,377	26,868	1,307	1,340	1.6
6160	Mortgage bankers and brokers	37	39	5.8	258	218	35,829	34,459	6,503	7,487	4.0
6200	Security and commodity brokers	39	43	4.9	123	125	48,033	45,280	5,027	5,563	1.0
6210	Security brokers and dealers	22	25	5.5	85	86	55,388	56,744	4,131	4,690	1.6
6300	Insurance carriers	29	31	4.3	264	240	35,273	37,183	9,081	8,223	1.0
6310	Life insurance	7	6	3.4	124	101	39,161	42,455	4,605	3,896	1.3
6360	Title insurance	6	6	8.2	61	52	26,426	25,000	1,397	1,434	3.9
6400	Insurance agents, brokers, and service	140	145	5.9	421	408	18,081	18,559	8,101	8,638	2.6
6500	Real estate	282	295	5.1	1,027	1,242	16,849	16,560	20,013	22,913	3.5
6510	Real estate operators and lessors	100	95	5.5	412	530	11,816	10,551	5,686	6,424	4.0
6530	Real estate agents and managers	161	166	4.9	525	606	19,512	21,406	11,638	13,455	3.2
6550	Subdividers and developers	16	20	5.5	88	97	20,227	19,794	2,489	2,597	5.6
6700	Holding and other investment offices	12	13	2.7	33	48	22,667	123,667	756	2,548	0.9
LAS ANIMAS, CO											
60 –	**Finance, insurance, and real estate**	25	23	0.2	130	128	18,400	21,344	2,565	2,836	0.1
6000	Depository institutions	5	5	0.4	80	80	22,550	24,100	1,880	2,029	0.3
6400	Insurance agents, brokers, and service	9	9	0.4	22	18	13,273	17,556	303	309	0.1
LINCOLN, CO											
60 –	**Finance, insurance, and real estate**	10	11	0.1	60	58	20,533	21,793	1,372	1,395	0.0
LOGAN, CO											
60 –	**Finance, insurance, and real estate**	55	53	0.4	328	272	31,915	25,250	7,655	6,571	0.2

Source: County Business Patterns, 1994/95, CBP-94/95, U.S. Department of Commerce, Washington, D.C., November 1997. SIC categories for which data were suppressed or not available for both 1994 and 1995 are *not* displayed. The employment columns represent mid-March employment in the year. Pay per employee is calculated by dividing 1st Quarter payroll, annualized, by mid-March employment. The columns headed "% State" show the county's percentage of the state total for the SIC in 1995; for example, 1.4% for SIC 6000 means that the county had 1.4 percent of the state's total establishments (or payroll) in SIC 6000 in 1995. A dash (-) is used to indicate that data are not available or cannot be calculated; *nec* means not elsewhere classified.

Continued on next page.

SIC	Industry	No. Establishments			Employment		Pay / Employee		Annual Payroll ($ 000)		
		1994	1995	% State	1994	1995	1994	1995	1994	1995	% State
LOGAN, CO - [continued]											
6000	Depository institutions	10	9	0.7	204	139	29,510	21,525	3,994	3,001	0.5
6020	Commercial banks	6	5	0.6	115	76	29,078	23,263	1,997	1,682	0.4
6400	Insurance agents, brokers, and service	18	17	0.7	65	75	47,754	32,267	2,171	2,075	0.6
6500	Real estate	17	17	0.3	24	24	9,000	8,833	240	253	0.0
6530	Real estate agents and managers	7	8	0.2	6	8	10,000	8,000	64	74	0.0
MESA, CO											
60 –	**Finance, insurance, and real estate**	253	251	2.0	1,511	1,511	23,118	23,714	33,175	34,198	0.9
6000	Depository institutions	41	41	3.0	580	553	23,600	24,998	12,302	12,560	1.9
6020	Commercial banks	24	25	3.0	438	428	24,731	25,925	9,608	9,787	2.1
6060	Credit unions	11	11	4.2	84	84	19,000	20,952	1,675	1,763	2.7
6100	Nondepository institutions	19	23	2.1	114	117	31,018	31,214	3,385	3,249	0.9
6160	Mortgage bankers and brokers	10	11	1.6	69	70	34,493	31,943	2,181	1,904	1.0
6200	Security and commodity brokers	14	14	1.6	47	56	64,681	53,429	2,824	2,924	0.5
6210	Security brokers and dealers	10	8	1.8	41	49	70,634	58,449	2,681	2,778	0.9
6280	Security and commodity services	4	6	1.5	6	7	24,000	18,286	143	146	0.1
6300	Insurance carriers	11	12	1.7	54	52	29,556	27,308	1,640	1,492	0.2
6310	Life insurance	3	3	1.7	35	27	26,057	18,370	825	428	0.1
6400	Insurance agents, brokers, and service	61	55	2.2	244	258	21,574	22,419	5,002	5,572	1.7
6500	Real estate	99	98	1.7	419	404	14,854	14,881	6,002	5,936	0.9
6510	Real estate operators and lessors	27	28	1.6	141	143	11,121	10,294	1,659	1,571	1.0
6530	Real estate agents and managers	63	60	1.8	215	196	13,581	14,367	3,039	2,944	0.7
6700	Holding and other investment offices	8	8	1.6	53	71	29,887	30,254	2,020	2,465	0.9
MOFFAT, CO											
60 –	**Finance, insurance, and real estate**	21	20	0.2	98	87	23,959	18,851	2,290	1,620	0.0
6000	Depository institutions	5	4	0.3	61	51	24,918	21,569	1,397	1,031	0.2
6500	Real estate	7	9	0.2	17	19	14,588	12,842	295	276	0.0
MONTEZUMA, CO											
60 –	**Finance, insurance, and real estate**	44	48	0.4	288	337	17,069	16,997	5,851	6,467	0.2
6000	Depository institutions	8	7	0.5	153	150	18,797	19,733	3,478	3,698	0.6
6100	Nondepository institutions	3	3	0.3	9	9	25,333	28,000	228	235	0.1
6400	Insurance agents, brokers, and service	12	12	0.5	41	42	17,561	18,476	884	827	0.3
6500	Real estate	17	22	0.4	77	126	10,805	7,778	956	1,129	0.2
6510	Real estate operators and lessors	6	7	0.4	53	97	8,604	5,691	531	648	0.4
MONTROSE, CO											
60 –	**Finance, insurance, and real estate**	74	76	0.6	439	487	23,308	23,277	10,387	12,415	0.3
6000	Depository institutions	12	12	0.9	165	165	26,739	27,976	4,074	4,029	0.6
6020	Commercial banks	8	8	1.0	142	141	27,972	29,475	3,636	3,558	0.8
6160	Mortgage bankers and brokers	5	6	0.9	24	20	13,667	18,200	343	402	0.2
6400	Insurance agents, brokers, and service	18	21	0.9	56	65	16,357	15,077	1,017	1,445	0.4
6500	Real estate	32	31	0.5	110	121	15,927	14,116	1,837	1,897	0.3
6510	Real estate operators and lessors	13	9	0.5	48	64	10,917	9,438	567	629	0.4
MORGAN, CO											
60 –	**Finance, insurance, and real estate**	59	65	0.5	282	330	22,270	21,927	6,510	7,646	0.2
6000	Depository institutions	14	14	1.0	158	180	24,405	23,356	3,722	4,366	0.7
6020	Commercial banks	7	7	0.8	125	148	24,768	23,703	3,050	3,772	0.8
6100	Nondepository institutions	4	4	0.4	14	19	26,286	23,158	392	391	0.1
6400	Insurance agents, brokers, and service	17	19	0.8	60	65	20,600	23,815	1,495	1,661	0.5
6500	Real estate	17	20	0.3	35	45	11,200	10,489	425	570	0.1
6510	Real estate operators and lessors	5	7	0.4	12	19	6,333	11,368	91	246	0.2
OTERO, CO											
60 –	**Finance, insurance, and real estate**	38	37	0.3	231	252	17,766	18,794	4,695	5,265	0.1
6000	Depository institutions	14	13	1.0	147	163	20,653	21,153	3,483	3,905	0.6

Source: County Business Patterns, 1994/95, CBP-94/95, U.S. Department of Commerce, Washington, D.C., November 1997. SIC categories for which data were suppressed or not available for both 1994 and 1995 are *not* displayed. The employment columns represent mid-March employment in the year. Pay per employee is calculated by dividing 1st Quarter payroll, annualized, by mid-March employment. The columns headed "% State" show the county's percentage of the state total for the SIC in 1995; for example, 1.4% for SIC 6000 means that the county had 1.4 percent of the state's total establishments (or payroll) in SIC 6000 in 1995. A dash (-) is used to indicate that data are not available or cannot be calculated; *nec* means not elsewhere classified.

Continued on next page.

SIC	Industry	No. Establishments			Employment		Pay / Employee		Annual Payroll ($ 000)		
		1994	1995	% State	1994	1995	1994	1995	1994	1995	% State
OTERO, CO - [continued]											
6020	Commercial banks	10	9	1.1	135	151	21,333	21,748	3,294	3,704	0.8
6500	Real estate	7	8	0.1	31	34	10,452	10,000	357	404	0.1
6510	Real estate operators and lessors	3	3	0.2	19	20	11,158	10,800	226	240	0.2
6530	Real estate agents and managers	4	5	0.1	12	14	9,333	8,857	131	164	0.0
OURAY, CO											
60 –	**Finance, insurance, and real estate**	14	21	0.2	46	51	14,696	17,020	917	1,050	0.0
6530	Real estate agents and managers	8	10	0.3	14	13	8,000	14,154	168	187	0.0
PARK, CO											
60 –	**Finance, insurance, and real estate**	15	16	0.1	31	37	15,613	18,595	634	·1,017	0.0
6500	Real estate	11	13	0.2	11	12	11,273	15,667	222	494	0.1
6530	Real estate agents and managers	4	6	0.2	6	7	16,667	20,000	143	242	0.1
PHILLIPS, CO											
60 –	**Finance, insurance, and real estate**	16	20	0.2	77	73	18,494	18,466	1,493	1,366	0.0
6000	Depository institutions	6	7	0.5	59	54	19,525	19,333	1,197	1,062	0.2
6500	Real estate	3	3	0.1	5	5	7,200	9,600	41	45	0.0
PITKIN, CO											
60 –	**Finance, insurance, and real estate**	176	188	1.5	1,198	1,226	23,409	24,352	26,946	29,227	0.8
6000	Depository institutions	8	8	0.6	149	132	35,463	35,576	4,483	4,264	0.7
6100	Nondepository institutions	11	12	1.1	22	30	36,727	45,467	1,059	1,191	0.3
6280	Security and commodity services	7	7	1.7	5	7	26,400	20,000	172	176	0.1
6500	Real estate	126	133	2.3	930	952	20,151	21,366	18,111	19,455	3.0
6510	Real estate operators and lessors	26	30	1.7	89	91	17,438	19,253	1,884	1,983	1.2
6530	Real estate agents and managers	85	88	2.6	816	846	20,221	21,560	15,331	16,787	4.0
6550	Subdividers and developers	7	9	2.5	18	8	27,333	14,500	501	393	0.9
PROWERS, CO											
60 –	**Finance, insurance, and real estate**	44	44	0.3	208	214	21,442	21,383	4,424	4,560	0.1
6000	Depository institutions	11	10	0.7	127	140	24,598	23,429	3,104	3,136	0.5
6020	Commercial banks	7	6	0.7	113	128	24,106	24,313	2,705	2,976	0.6
6060	Credit unions	4	4	1.5	14	12	28,571	14,000	399	160	0.2
6400	Insurance agents, brokers, and service	14	14	0.6	37	34	15,135	16,118	603	610	0.2
6500	Real estate	15	16	0.3	27	23	9,185	11,478	223	336	0.1
6530	Real estate agents and managers	7	8	0.2	6	6	17,333	21,333	67	118	0.0
PUEBLO, CO											
60 –	**Finance, insurance, and real estate**	241	250	1.9	1,634	1,852	32,355	28,060	47,942	54,156	1.5
6000	Depository institutions	38	39	2.9	664	674	21,114	22,255	14,461	15,436	2.4
6020	Commercial banks	16	17	2.1	438	449	22,658	24,356	10,478	11,194	2.4
6140	Personal credit institutions	8	10	4.1	29	163	24,552	36,908	811	6,089	7.1
6300	Insurance carriers	15	15	2.1	183	206	23,738	25,748	4,943	5,520	0.7
6310	Life insurance	4	4	2.3	66	81	18,485	22,914	1,140	1,840	0.6
6400	Insurance agents, brokers, and service	67	73	3.0	229	229	18,044	18,218	4,312	4,495	1.4
6500	Real estate	92	92	1.6	263	319	16,608	15,147	4,820	5,028	0.8
6510	Real estate operators and lessors	38	38	2.2	145	148	10,703	10,973	1,702	1,710	1.1
6530	Real estate agents and managers	44	43	1.3	79	95	15,646	15,453	1,360	1,485	0.4
6550	Subdividers and developers	5	7	1.9	23	61	54,609	22,820	1,322	1,474	3.2
RIO BLANCO, CO											
60 –	**Finance, insurance, and real estate**	13	13	0.1	60	73	20,667	19,014	1,385	1,426	0.0
6000	Depository institutions	4	4	0.3	44	50	20,727	20,080	983	1,011	0.2
6400	Insurance agents, brokers, and service	3	3	0.1	9	9	16,889	18,222	160	175	0.1
6500	Real estate	6	6	0.1	7	14	25,143	15,714	242	240	0.0
RIO GRANDE, CO											
60 –	**Finance, insurance, and real estate**	34	31	0.2	143	148	17,287	20,351	2,986	3,294	0.1

Source: County Business Patterns, 1994/95, CBP-94/95, U.S. Department of Commerce, Washington, D.C., November 1997. SIC categories for which data were suppressed or not available for both 1994 and 1995 are not displayed. The employment columns represent mid-March employment in the year. Pay per employee is calculated by dividing 1st Quarter payroll, annualized, by mid-March employment. The columns headed "% State" show the county's percentage of the state total for the SIC in 1995; for example, 1.4% for SIC 6000 means that the county had 1.4 percent of the state's total establishments (or payroll) in SIC 6000 in 1995. A dash (-) is used to indicate that data are not available or cannot be calculated; nec means not elsewhere classified.

Continued on next page.

SIC	Industry	No. Establishments			Employment		Pay / Employee		Annual Payroll ($ 000)		
		1994	1995	% State	1994	1995	1994	1995	1994	1995	% State
RIO GRANDE, CO - [continued]											
6000	Depository institutions	7	7	0.5	77	79	20,831	21,165	1,751	1,867	0.3
6400	Insurance agents, brokers, and service	6	5	0.2	13	14	11,692	17,714	190	283	0.1
6500	Real estate	17	15	0.3	29	29	10,345	15,034	404	481	0.1
6530	Real estate agents and managers	6	5	0.1	8	8	7,000	17,000	112	130	0.0
ROUTT, CO											
60–	**Finance, insurance, and real estate**	85	96	0.7	885	903	19,693	20,089	15,095	15,959	0.4
6000	Depository institutions	5	5	0.4	113	125	26,265	26,400	2,637	2,964	0.5
6100	Nondepository institutions	5	6	0.5	20	16	28,600	28,250	571	640	0.2
6160	Mortgage bankers and brokers	5	6	0.9	20	16	28,600	28,250	571	640	0.3
6400	Insurance agents, brokers, and service	16	15	0.6	57	65	25,895	24,985	1,596	1,967	0.6
6500	Real estate	52	63	1.1	643	647	14,669	15,116	8,041	8,200	1.3
6510	Real estate operators and lessors	4	5	0.3	5	10	6,400	10,800	56	134	0.1
6530	Real estate agents and managers	42	51	1.5	634	634	14,776	15,205	7,869	7,972	1.9
6550	Subdividers and developers	4	4	1.1	2	2	14,000	10,000	96	27	0.1
SAGUACHE, CO											
60–	**Finance, insurance, and real estate**	5	6	0.0	26	27	21,077	23,111	487	445	0.0
SAN JUAN, CO											
60–	**Finance, insurance, and real estate**	2	2	0.0	-	-	-	-	-	-	-
SAN MIGUEL, CO											
60–	**Finance, insurance, and real estate**	71	66	0.5	620	511	20,355	23,429	11,197	11,731	0.3
6000	Depository institutions	4	4	0.3	64	80	21,500	21,750	1,538	2,060	0.3
6020	Commercial banks	4	4	0.5	64	80	21,500	21,750	1,538	2,060	0.4
6500	Real estate	58	53	0.9	512	396	20,016	23,162	8,742	8,661	1.3
6530	Real estate agents and managers	39	31	0.9	451	313	15,858	16,869	5,555	4,930	1.2
6550	Subdividers and developers	9	10	2.8	23	31	75,826	72,774	1,809	2,138	4.6
SEDGWICK, CO											
60–	**Finance, insurance, and real estate**	8	7	0.1	32	32	16,875	16,500	609	595	0.0
SUMMIT, CO											
60–	**Finance, insurance, and real estate**	176	173	1.3	1,250	1,123	22,688	27,288	26,633	26,656	0.7
6000	Depository institutions	6	6	0.4	130	136	29,138	30,206	3,586	3,023	0.5
6100	Nondepository institutions	4	5	0.5	33	23	32,970	38,783	865	683	0.2
6160	Mortgage bankers and brokers	4	5	0.7	33	23	32,970	38,783	865	683	0.4
6400	Insurance agents, brokers, and service	11	11	0.4	74	56	24,703	29,857	1,756	1,736	0.5
6500	Real estate	147	142	2.4	989	883	20,987	26,206	19,615	20,402	3.2
6510	Real estate operators and lessors	16	15	0.9	85	79	20,282	22,025	1,832	1,643	1.0
6530	Real estate agents and managers	111	108	3.2	847	732	20,477	25,071	15,327	15,991	3.8
6550	Subdividers and developers	11	10	2.8	32	42	33,000	43,714	1,519	1,534	3.3
6552	Subdividers and developers, n.e.c.	11	10	3.5	32	42	33,000	43,714	1,519	1,534	4.4
6700	Holding and other investment offices	5	5	1.0	21	23	40,952	34,609	777	756	0.3
TELLER, CO											
60–	**Finance, insurance, and real estate**	57	57	0.4	310	306	14,129	15,686	4,820	5,206	0.1
6000	Depository institutions	4	4	0.3	73	85	20,493	20,988	1,462	1,746	0.3
6400	Insurance agents, brokers, and service	5	6	0.2	40	38	16,900	17,263	711	860	0.3
6500	Real estate	41	42	0.7	183	172	9,399	11,395	2,255	2,205	0.3
6510	Real estate operators and lessors	11	12	0.7	15	23	11,467	10,087	292	357	0.2
6530	Real estate agents and managers	23	23	0.7	159	132	9,308	11,939	1,850	1,716	0.4
6550	Subdividers and developers	5	5	1.4	8	16	8,000	9,250	109	126	0.3
6552	Subdividers and developers, n.e.c.	3	3	1.0	6	9	7,333	7,556	87	91	0.3

Source: County Business Patterns, 1994/95, CBP-94/95, U.S. Department of Commerce, Washington, D.C., November 1997. SIC categories for which data were suppressed or not available for both 1994 and 1995 are *not* displayed. The employment columns represent mid-March employment in the year. Pay per employee is calculated by dividing 1st Quarter payroll, annualized, by mid-March employment. The columns headed "% State" show the county's percentage of the state total for the SIC in 1995; for example, 1.4% for SIC 6000 means that the county had 1.4 percent of the state's total establishments (or payroll) in SIC 6000 in 1995. A dash (-) is used to indicate that data are not available or cannot be calculated; *nec* means not elsewhere classified.

SIC	Industry	No. Establishments			Employment		Pay / Employee		Annual Payroll ($ 000)		
		1994	1995	% State	1994	1995	1994	1995	1994	1995	% State
WASHINGTON, CO											
60 –	**Finance, insurance, and real estate**	10	10	0.1	54	59	21,926	19,119	1,121	1,081	0.0
6000	Depository institutions	6	6	0.4	42	47	25,524	21,702	1,016	985	0.2
6020	Commercial banks	3	3	0.4	34	38	28,824	25,158	933	934	0.2
WELD, CO											
60 –	**Finance, insurance, and real estate**	281	284	2.2	4,039	3,835	31,251	33,207	119,353	125,407	3.4
6000	Depository institutions	40	40	2.9	698	732	24,332	25,279	15,998	17,426	2.7
6020	Commercial banks	28	27	3.3	607	640	24,936	25,844	14,184	15,453	3.3
6060	Credit unions	6	6	2.3	65	66	20,985	21,697	1,356	1,455	2.2
6160	Mortgage bankers and brokers	11	9	1.3	64	42	31,000	34,286	1,531	1,233	0.7
6400	Insurance agents, brokers, and service	64	62	2.5	219	215	18,740	20,967	5,699	5,887	1.8
6500	Real estate	117	126	2.2	427	462	14,520	14,468	6,941	7,353	1.1
6510	Real estate operators and lessors	59	57	3.3	205	213	10,380	11,155	2,338	2,621	1.6
6530	Real estate agents and managers	49	56	1.7	161	164	15,776	16,707	2,998	2,933	0.7
6550	Subdividers and developers	4	6	1.7	25	31	16,960	25,290	520	705	1.5
6790	Miscellaneous investing	3	5	2.6	4	5	14,000	12,800	65	100	0.2
YUMA, CO											
60 –	**Finance, insurance, and real estate**	24	25	0.2	122	140	21,836	22,886	2,618	3,302	0.1
6000	Depository institutions	9	9	0.7	79	95	23,696	23,453	1,747	2,284	0.4

Source: County Business Patterns, 1994/95, CBP-94/95, U.S. Department of Commerce, Washington, D.C., November 1997. SIC categories for which data were suppressed or not available for both 1994 and 1995 are not displayed. The employment columns represent mid-March employment in the year. Pay per employee is calculated by dividing 1st Quarter payroll, annualized, by mid-March employment. The columns headed "% State" show the county's percentage of the state total for the SIC in 1995; for example, 1.4% for SIC 6000 means that the county had 1.4 percent of the state's total establishments (or payroll) in SIC 6000 in 1995. A dash (-) is used to indicate that data are not available or cannot be calculated; nec means not elsewhere classified.

CONNECTICUT

SIC	Industry	No. Establishments			Employment		Pay / Employee		Annual Payroll ($ 000)		
		1994	1995	% State	1994	1995	1994	1995	1994	1995	% State

FAIRFIELD, CT

SIC	Industry	1994	1995	% State	1994	1995	1994	1995	1994	1995	% State
60 –	**Finance, insurance, and real estate**	2,860	2,946	35.0	35,040	35,823	61,822	80,085	2,013,134	2,398,853	34.8
6000	Depository institutions	451	443	27.8	7,990	7,727	32,967	37,333	256,860	283,926	32.1
6020	Commercial banks	220	216	33.3	3,670	3,428	30,002	36,173	104,098	120,217	27.4
6030	Savings institutions	149	145	23.2	3,846	3,717	35,625	37,464	133,033	136,118	36.2
6100	Nondepository institutions	187	192	44.0	5,832	5,248	68,912	90,637	346,094	342,359	75.0
6140	Personal credit institutions	32	36	36.0	2,578	2,874	58,335	91,150	144,564	166,697	85.9
6150	Business credit institutions	59	57	73.1	2,035	1,609	88,863	104,527	148,893	132,522	86.2
6200	Security and commodity brokers	447	488	58.9	5,040	5,198	119,238	184,073	530,363	699,120	69.9
6210	Security brokers and dealers	173	185	52.1	2,732	2,800	128,041	253,196	285,067	419,068	71.4
6280	Security and commodity services	248	275	62.1	1,861	1,991	117,352	108,992	209,323	236,996	64.0
6300	Insurance carriers	173	178	27.4	6,187	6,270	65,084	75,603	353,277	464,942	13.9
6330	Fire, marine, and casualty insurance	82	90	24.3	3,062	2,730	85,514	107,026	214,895	260,390	23.3
6400	Insurance agents, brokers, and service	411	410	26.1	2,721	2,653	45,727	52,927	131,032	139,215	32.5
6500	Real estate	984	1,026	34.4	5,384	6,064	32,353	33,340	191,915	208,620	44.1
6510	Real estate operators and lessors	342	354	31.6	1,744	2,152	24,028	27,216	47,791	57,419	39.2
6530	Real estate agents and managers	565	567	37.1	3,330	3,586	36,553	36,992	128,726	138,723	47.4
6540	Title abstract offices	13	14	53.8	46	42	28,348	26,952	1,399	1,220	74.6
6550	Subdividers and developers	49	57	24.5	255	238	35,106	36,857	13,223	9,911	38.2
6552	Subdividers and developers, n.e.c.	29	35	28.5	113	97	48,673	52,454	9,375	5,895	42.3
6553	Cemetery subdividers and developers	18	18	19.6	142	141	24,310	26,128	3,810	3,862	34.8
6700	Holding and other investment offices	198	199	58.2	1,732	2,512	108,062	123,556	192,284	246,192	80.3
6710	Holding offices	92	90	62.5	1,182	1,789	97,993	105,509	118,576	154,815	82.4
6720	Investment offices	12	11	57.9	62	201	136,452	82,468	11,820	11,990	51.2
6730	Trusts	26	27	39.1	175	191	48,183	52,503	10,779	12,318	67.9
6732	Educational, religious, etc. trusts	11	13	35.1	147	163	47,102	52,613	9,177	10,626	74.1
6733	Trusts, n.e.c.	15	14	43.8	28	28	53,857	51,857	1,602	1,692	44.3
6790	Miscellaneous investing	67	61	63.5	312	328	174,051	287,622	50,993	65,216	86.9
6799	Investors, n.e.c.	47	47	78.3	244	253	200,213	350,767	42,818	57,390	91.3

HARTFORD, CT

SIC	Industry	1994	1995	% State	1994	1995	1994	1995	1994	1995	% State
60 –	**Finance, insurance, and real estate**	2,357	2,320	27.6	73,198	74,039	43,972	45,748	3,084,951	3,347,930	48.5
6000	Depository institutions	447	429	26.9	10,511	10,572	31,750	34,004	344,864	334,125	37.8
6020	Commercial banks	179	174	26.9	6,831	6,927	34,401	34,175	242,219	229,717	52.3
6030	Savings institutions	158	149	23.9	2,860	2,827	27,404	35,628	82,046	83,651	22.2
6060	Credit unions	99	95	33.7	749	760	23,685	26,205	17,913	18,973	39.9
6100	Nondepository institutions	107	111	25.5	1,220	1,377	45,607	50,521	57,544	66,987	14.7
6150	Business credit institutions	15	14	17.9	232	333	65,138	62,246	17,285	18,082	11.8
6160	Mortgage bankers and brokers	71	74	29.4	815	670	42,930	38,346	34,385	29,978	-
6200	Security and commodity brokers	166	177	21.4	2,600	3,145	73,180	73,587	183,925	240,858	24.1
6210	Security brokers and dealers	76	83	23.4	1,591	1,895	65,139	56,802	97,718	117,121	20.0
6280	Security and commodity services	89	93	21.0	1,008	1,249	85,929	99,103	86,191	123,727	33.4
6300	Insurance carriers	264	257	39.6	49,067	49,105	47,394	49,116	2,171,441	2,362,103	70.8
6310	Life insurance	81	75	41.2	28,758	25,394	50,358	57,539	1,316,907	1,469,011	79.0
6330	Fire, marine, and casualty insurance	141	145	39.1	18,153	18,035	44,681	46,205	774,104	783,601	70.2
6370	Pension, health, and welfare funds	19	16	39.0	405	4,005	20,365	16,148	13,116	58,904	81.3
6400	Insurance agents, brokers, and service	505	510	32.5	3,936	4,084	36,661	36,891	151,443	172,117	40.1
6500	Real estate	800	769	25.8	5,197	5,206	24,910	25,442	135,897	138,103	29.2
6510	Real estate operators and lessors	330	320	28.6	1,709	1,783	24,644	24,597	42,238	43,258	29.5
6530	Real estate agents and managers	392	370	24.2	3,161	3,022	24,895	26,700	83,652	85,361	29.1
6540	Title abstract offices	6	5	19.2	8	6	25,500	21,333	218	160	9.8
6550	Subdividers and developers	60	58	24.9	254	273	27,354	16,571	7,398	5,719	22.1

Source: County Business Patterns, 1994/95, CBP-94/95, U.S. Department of Commerce, Washington, D.C., November 1997. SIC categories for which data were suppressed or not available for both 1994 and 1995 are not displayed. The employment columns represent mid-March employment in the year. Pay per employee is calculated by dividing 1st Quarter payroll, annualized, by mid-March employment. The columns headed "% State" show the county's percentage of the state total for the SIC in 1995; for example, 1.4% for SIC 6000 means that the county had 1.4 percent of the state's total establishments (or payroll) in SIC 6000 in 1995. A dash (-) is used to indicate that data are not available or cannot be calculated; nec means not elsewhere classified.

Continued on next page.

SIC	Industry	No. Establishments			Employment		Pay / Employee		Annual Payroll ($ 000)		
		1994	1995	% State	1994	1995	1994	1995	1994	1995	% State
HARTFORD, CT - [continued]											
6552	Subdividers and developers, n.e.c.	40	36	29.3	178	181	28,876	14,586	5,252	3,285	23.6
6553	Cemetery subdividers and developers	16	17	18.5	66	83	24,667	20,819	1,871	2,158	19.4
6710	Holding offices	27	27	18.8	421	279	60,029	58,022	22,214	17,493	9.3
6790	Miscellaneous investing	21	17	17.7	97	83	78,845	106,458	8,401	8,035	10.7
LITCHFIELD, CT											
60 –	**Finance, insurance, and real estate**	301	303	3.6	2,031	1,942	26,338	28,107	56,179	58,001	0.8
6000	Depository institutions	86	85	5.3	1,169	1,144	23,884	24,860	28,123	29,230	3.3
6020	Commercial banks	40	39	6.0	522	502	24,567	25,363	12,913	13,055	3.0
6030	Savings institutions	39	39	6.3	614	606	23,375	24,554	14,427	15,339	4.1
6060	Credit unions	7	7	2.5	33	36	22,545	23,000	783	836	1.8
6400	Insurance agents, brokers, and service	64	68	4.3	334	313	30,623	33,585	10,750	11,283	2.6
6500	Real estate	108	105	3.5	294	272	21,211	20,721	7,045	6,620	1.4
6510	Real estate operators and lessors	30	31	2.8	78	79	12,974	14,987	1,215	1,419	1.0
6530	Real estate agents and managers	58	54	3.5	166	141	25,663	24,823	4,665	3,911	1.3
6552	Subdividers and developers, n.e.c.	5	5	4.1	5	6	26,400	20,667	160	226	1.6
6553	Cemetery subdividers and developers	11	11	12.0	42	42	19,333	18,952	957	963	8.7
6790	Miscellaneous investing	3	4	4.2	8	10	9,000	15,200	94	500	0.7
MIDDLESEX, CT											
60 –	**Finance, insurance, and real estate**	300	301	3.6	7,850	7,433	41,564	42,572	321,031	316,949	4.6
6000	Depository institutions	74	72	4.5	934	945	28,882	31,666	24,063	26,275	3.0
6020	Commercial banks	25	24	3.7	258	250	21,969	19,952	5,307	4,711	1.1
6030	Savings institutions	42	41	6.6	639	660	32,163	36,558	17,973	20,748	5.5
6060	Credit unions	7	7	2.5	37	35	20,432	23,086	783	816	1.7
6500	Real estate	115	114	3.8	517	577	18,213	19,182	11,455	12,793	2.7
6510	Real estate operators and lessors	45	45	4.0	339	355	18,761	19,966	7,705	8,147	5.6
6530	Real estate agents and managers	56	57	3.7	167	203	17,269	17,872	3,294	4,002	1.4
6550	Subdividers and developers	13	11	4.7	11	19	15,636	18,526	432	620	2.4
6552	Subdividers and developers, n.e.c.	5	5	4.1	3	10	12,000	21,600	143	435	3.1
6553	Cemetery subdividers and developers	7	6	6.5	8	9	17,000	15,111	194	185	1.7
NEW HAVEN, CT											
60 –	**Finance, insurance, and real estate**	1,786	1,784	21.2	19,666	20,064	30,501	32,722	599,969	649,541	9.4
6000	Depository institutions	375	367	23.0	5,873	5,419	27,162	28,407	156,309	155,070	17.5
6020	Commercial banks	138	131	20.2	2,251	2,011	26,735	29,766	60,522	56,219	12.8
6030	Savings institutions	149	153	24.5	3,172	2,971	27,702	27,919	85,366	88,441	23.5
6100	Nondepository institutions	84	88	20.2	1,327	1,069	33,218	32,131	42,186	37,948	8.3
6160	Mortgage bankers and brokers	49	54	21.4	1,008	762	34,421	32,588	32,559	28,006	-
6200	Security and commodity brokers	95	95	11.5	627	718	62,699	58,000	36,417	41,499	4.1
6210	Security brokers and dealers	51	55	15.5	559	619	65,445	61,325	32,548	37,341	6.4
6280	Security and commodity services	41	39	8.8	67	98	40,657	37,469	3,821	4,146	1.1
6300	Insurance carriers	116	123	19.0	5,421	6,566	34,802	38,395	188,513	228,021	6.8
6400	Insurance agents, brokers, and service	361	367	23.4	2,092	2,186	31,359	31,751	70,068	73,867	17.2
6500	Real estate	709	696	23.3	3,976	3,770	21,403	22,901	90,987	87,724	18.5
6510	Real estate operators and lessors	273	258	23.0	1,452	1,428	17,928	19,109	28,641	27,948	19.1
6530	Real estate agents and managers	368	358	23.4	2,321	2,091	23,428	25,406	56,103	52,659	18.0
6540	Title abstract offices	3	4	15.4	8	6	29,000	32,000	233	207	12.7
6550	Subdividers and developers	59	58	24.9	194	213	22,969	24,357	5,718	5,926	22.9
6552	Subdividers and developers, n.e.c.	28	27	22.0	70	87	26,800	29,287	2,604	2,632	18.9
6553	Cemetery subdividers and developers	27	26	28.3	124	123	20,806	20,715	2,935	2,957	26.6
6710	Holding offices	16	18	12.5	275	251	57,324	62,406	13,288	13,269	7.1
6733	Trusts, n.e.c.	11	11	34.4	24	47	22,167	39,149	842	1,946	51.0
6790	Miscellaneous investing	6	7	7.3	25	12	16,160	32,333	414	439	0.6
NEW LONDON, CT											
60 –	**Finance, insurance, and real estate**	428	434	5.2	2,932	2,864	27,207	27,420	79,263	79,242	1.1
6000	Depository institutions	119	112	7.0	1,510	1,444	22,485	22,742	33,591	33,496	3.8

Source: County Business Patterns, 1994/95, CBP-94/95, U.S. Department of Commerce, Washington, D.C., November 1997. SIC categories for which data were suppressed or not available for both 1994 and 1995 are not displayed. The employment columns represent mid-March employment in the year. Pay per employee is calculated by dividing 1st Quarter payroll, annualized, by mid-March employment. The columns headed "% State" show the county's percentage of the state total for the SIC in 1995; for example, 1.4% for SIC 6000 means that the county had 1.4 percent of the state's total establishments (or payroll) in SIC 6000 in 1995. A dash (-) is used to indicate that data are not available or cannot be calculated; nec means not elsewhere classified.

Continued on next page.

SIC	Industry	No. Establishments			Employment		Pay / Employee		Annual Payroll ($ 000)		
		1994	1995	% State	1994	1995	1994	1995	1994	1995	% State
NEW LONDON, CT - [continued]											
6020	Commercial banks	38	38	5.9	498	473	21,341	21,784	11,186	9,747	2.2
6030	Savings institutions	54	46	7.4	707	642	23,802	24,717	15,713	16,829	4.5
6160	Mortgage bankers and brokers	13	13	5.2	66	39	37,212	36,410	1,620	1,090	-
6200	Security and commodity brokers	25	26	3.1	116	143	82,103	71,469	7,829	9,266	0.9
6330	Fire, marine, and casualty insurance	21	20	5.4	165	166	40,776	41,639	6,483	6,943	0.6
6400	Insurance agents, brokers, and service	74	80	5.1	327	356	28,122	27,393	10,886	10,108	2.4
6500	Real estate	154	158	5.3	561	543	19,337	20,059	12,583	11,999	2.5
6510	Real estate operators and lessors	56	57	5.1	221	227	14,136	15,577	3,908	4,074	2.8
6530	Real estate agents and managers	75	77	5.0	279	254	22,581	22,378	6,867	5,931	2.0
6550	Subdividers and developers	16	18	7.7	55	58	25,018	28,345	1,670	1,832	7.1
6552	Subdividers and developers, n.e.c.	10	11	8.9	21	30	35,238	31,867	938	1,033	7.4
6553	Cemetery subdividers and developers	6	6	6.5	34	28	18,706	24,571	732	759	6.8
TOLLAND, CT											
60 –	**Finance, insurance, and real estate**	183	191	2.3	1,013	1,115	25,481	25,424	26,173	28,123	0.4
6000	Depository institutions	47	46	2.9	476	535	23,630	23,948	11,229	12,211	1.4
6030	Savings institutions	33	31	5.0	343	405	24,292	25,077	8,343	9,424	2.5
6500	Real estate	66	71	2.4	227	233	19,471	20,446	4,807	5,360	1.1
6510	Real estate operators and lessors	31	32	2.9	154	157	18,442	19,516	3,045	3,057	2.1
6530	Real estate agents and managers	29	33	2.2	64	68	23,125	23,353	1,585	1,840	0.6
WINDHAM, CT											
60 –	**Finance, insurance, and real estate**	140	141	1.7	793	834	26,018	26,120	19,320	22,609	0.3
6000	Depository institutions	43	41	2.6	425	428	21,544	21,047	9,007	9,274	1.0
6030	Savings institutions	20	20	3.2	235	242	22,332	22,298	5,008	5,440	1.4
6400	Insurance agents, brokers, and service	30	33	2.1	151	150	39,126	37,360	5,141	5,775	1.3
6500	Real estate	44	46	1.5	149	146	15,651	13,671	1,965	2,101	0.4
6510	Real estate operators and lessors	20	23	2.1	108	99	16,852	13,859	1,418	1,322	0.9
6530	Real estate agents and managers	15	14	0.9	28	31	12,286	11,742	329	528	0.2
6550	Subdividers and developers	9	9	3.9	13	16	12,923	16,250	218	251	1.0

Source: County Business Patterns, 1994/95, CBP-94/95, U.S. Department of Commerce, Washington, D.C., November 1997. SIC categories for which data were suppressed or not available for both 1994 and 1995 are not displayed. The employment columns represent mid-March employment in the year. Pay per employee is calculated by dividing 1st Quarter payroll, annualized, by mid-March employment. The columns headed "% State" show the county's percentage of the state total for the SIC in 1995; for example, 1.4% for SIC 6000 means that the county had 1.4 percent of the state's total establishments (or payroll) in SIC 6000 in 1995. A dash (-) is used to indicate that data are not available or cannot be calculated; nec means not elsewhere classified.

DELAWARE

SIC	Industry	No. Establishments			Employment		Pay / Employee		Annual Payroll ($ 000)		
		1994	1995	% State	1994	1995	1994	1995	1994	1995	% State
KENT, DE											
60–	**Finance, insurance, and real estate**	249	252	7.4	2,900	2,814	22,578	29,798	69,144	76,470	5.0
6000	Depository institutions	41	43	11.8	1,365	1,036	14,453	17,432	20,176	18,792	2.4
6020	Commercial banks	31	33	12.6	1,269	937	14,247	17,306	18,384	16,777	2.2
6100	Nondepository institutions	23	22	10.9	320	348	21,625	20,897	6,775	8,055	7.6
6140	Personal credit institutions	13	13	18.6	55	53	25,600	25,132	1,302	1,353	5.8
6310	Life insurance	8	8	19.0	124	126	24,387	25,651	3,058	3,124	4.7
6400	Insurance agents, brokers, and service	58	61	19.5	231	250	25,403	25,664	6,936	7,214	-
6500	Real estate	86	85	12.0	241	232	15,087	15,966	4,019	4,064	5.4
6510	Real estate operators and lessors	40	43	14.5	129	120	14,357	15,500	2,075	2,114	6.4
6530	Real estate agents and managers	36	33	10.5	100	98	16,720	17,224	1,741	1,768	5.0
6552	Subdividers and developers, n.e.c.	5	3	8.1	4	4	8,000	13,000	74	47	1.5
6553	Cemetery subdividers and developers	3	3	16.7	6	6	8,667	8,000	64	55	3.3
NEW CASTLE, DE											
60–	**Finance, insurance, and real estate**	2,636	2,805	82.4	34,678	37,663	30,083	33,799	1,157,435	1,377,297	90.9
6000	Depository institutions	265	264	72.3	20,021	20,649	28,755	33,342	648,943	739,769	93.2
6020	Commercial banks	180	176	67.4	18,641	19,297	28,569	33,292	602,396	695,900	93.2
6030	Savings institutions	34	35	89.7	438	641	34,895	35,782	16,451	20,887	99.3
6090	Functions closely related to banking	7	10	100.0	716	474	31,860	37,620	25,030	17,637	100.0
6100	Nondepository institutions	165	160	79.2	2,435	2,864	28,371	33,258	66,504	95,987	90.6
6200	Security and commodity brokers	132	133	89.3	929	1,061	73,339	75,977	87,197	93,770	95.2
6300	Insurance carriers	88	84	78.5	4,263	4,627	32,596	32,083	145,459	159,309	89.6
6310	Life insurance	33	34	81.0	1,471	1,829	32,052	32,582	52,026	63,457	95.3
6320	Medical service and health insurance	9	7	100.0	1,461	1,355	31,526	29,482	45,506	43,630	100.0
6500	Real estate	400	425	60.0	2,328	2,390	22,136	22,904	57,469	56,706	74.8
6510	Real estate operators and lessors	175	181	61.1	1,117	1,163	20,741	20,822	25,264	24,782	74.6
6530	Real estate agents and managers	178	186	59.0	1,049	1,004	23,859	25,259	27,229	25,505	72.7
6550	Subdividers and developers	30	34	54.8	129	177	19,845	22,780	3,671	4,885	83.9
6552	Subdividers and developers, n.e.c.	16	18	48.6	63	77	18,095	22,234	2,051	2,315	74.7
6553	Cemetery subdividers and developers	11	11	61.1	66	60	21,515	23,867	1,566	1,543	93.0
6700	Holding and other investment offices	1,377	1,527	98.3	3,442	3,434	29,269	29,825	111,847	140,200	88.8
SUSSEX, DE											
60–	**Finance, insurance, and real estate**	327	348	10.2	2,144	2,332	23,334	23,937	52,681	61,026	4.0
6000	Depository institutions	53	58	15.9	1,283	1,284	24,412	26,037	30,958	35,341	4.5
6020	Commercial banks	47	52	19.9	1,243	1,244	24,525	26,141	30,097	34,374	4.6
6100	Nondepository institutions	18	20	9.9	66	66	30,667	27,030	1,764	1,852	1.7
6500	Real estate	189	198	28.0	535	685	16,860	18,429	11,367	15,083	19.9
6510	Real estate operators and lessors	75	72	24.3	268	289	16,388	16,360	5,780	6,326	19.0
6530	Real estate agents and managers	89	96	30.5	219	333	17,151	20,829	4,695	7,809	22.3
6552	Subdividers and developers, n.e.c.	15	16	43.2	37	46	20,865	17,304	758	739	23.8
6553	Cemetery subdividers and developers	4	4	22.2	8	8	5,000	6,500	59	62	3.7

Source: County Business Patterns, 1994/95, CBP-94/95, U.S. Department of Commerce, Washington, D.C., November 1997. SIC categories for which data were suppressed or not available for both 1994 and 1995 are *not* displayed. The employment columns represent mid-March employment in the year. Pay per employee is calculated by dividing 1st Quarter payroll, annualized, by mid-March employment. The columns headed "% State" show the county's percentage of the state total for the SIC in 1995; for example, 1.4% for SIC 6000 means that the county had 1.4 percent of the state's total establishments (or payroll) in SIC 6000 in 1995. A dash (-) is used to indicate that data are not available or cannot be calculated; *nec* means not elsewhere classified.

WASHINGTON, D.C.

SIC	Industry	No. Establishments			Employment		Pay / Employee		Annual Payroll ($ 000)		
		1994	1995	% State	1994	1995	1994	1995	1994	1995	% State
WASHINGTON, D.C.											
60 –	**Finance, insurance, and real estate**	2,223	2,203	100.0	31,124	30,373	44,243	49,754	1,342,826	1,407,935	100.0
6000	Depository institutions	409	404	100.0	5,769	5,472	33,424	39,100	190,340	199,969	100.0
6020	Commercial banks	213	218	100.0	3,730	3,588	34,952	42,527	128,769	138,146	100.0
6030	Savings institutions	58	44	100.0	721	566	32,067	34,678	21,345	19,757	100.0
6060	Credit unions	94	93	100.0	1,015	992	25,297	26,891	27,554	28,058	100.0
6090	Functions closely related to banking	37	42	100.0	227	250	42,026	40,656	8,803	9,266	100.0
6100	Nondepository institutions	57	55	100.0	3,615	3,760	78,807	90,861	235,216	282,823	100.0
6160	Mortgage bankers and brokers	26	26	100.0	240	234	60,100	64,684	13,629	15,035	100.0
6200	Security and commodity brokers	202	213	100.0	3,011	2,921	86,080	87,878	264,742	256,755	100.0
6210	Security brokers and dealers	113	110	100.0	2,236	2,068	88,079	87,979	201,817	184,398	100.0
6280	Security and commodity services	80	92	100.0	629	702	72,089	79,487	50,628	57,699	100.0
6300	Insurance carriers	96	86	100.0	4,420	4,201	39,360	44,556	179,484	181,466	100.0
6310	Life insurance	29	28	100.0	1,017	1,123	46,328	45,500	44,804	47,916	100.0
6320	Medical service and health insurance	18	18	100.0	2,678	2,413	36,614	45,175	107,482	106,839	100.0
6321	Accident and health insurance	4	5	100.0	45	96	32,444	26,792	1,799	2,562	100.0
6324	Hospital and medical service plans	14	13	100.0	2,633	2,317	36,685	45,937	105,683	104,277	100.0
6330	Fire, marine, and casualty insurance	21	18	100.0	214	221	66,131	62,842	13,002	14,018	100.0
6370	Pension, health, and welfare funds	19	13	100.0	372	312	22,011	20,744	8,572	6,764	100.0
6400	Insurance agents, brokers, and service	119	117	100.0	1,862	1,984	43,747	45,603	80,574	85,097	100.0
6500	Real estate	1,153	1,129	100.0	10,575	9,893	27,529	30,054	291,384	287,050	100.0
6510	Real estate operators and lessors	545	524	100.0	3,905	3,540	23,591	23,714	90,362	84,272	100.0
6530	Real estate agents and managers	567	543	100.0	6,434	6,009	29,641	33,113	192,140	185,565	100.0
6540	Title abstract offices	8	9	100.0	78	52	32,718	29,769	2,187	1,639	100.0
6550	Subdividers and developers	23	27	100.0	158	225	36,304	49,796	6,381	13,688	100.0
6552	Subdividers and developers, n.e.c.	15	18	100.0	117	182	40,855	56,286	5,345	12,511	100.0
6553	Cemetery subdividers and developers	7	7	100.0	41	43	23,317	22,326	1,018	1,053	100.0
6700	Holding and other investment offices	175	188	100.0	1,711	1,609	49,798	69,263	94,663	102,743	100.0
6710	Holding offices	35	36	100.0	714	444	56,818	123,748	43,452	43,212	100.0
6720	Investment offices	7	8	100.0	43	99	51,349	122,465	5,978	11,486	100.0
6730	Trusts	97	108	100.0	720	850	38,844	35,035	31,985	33,789	100.0
6732	Educational, religious, etc. trusts	69	78	100.0	450	542	38,009	37,683	19,763	23,050	100.0
6733	Trusts, n.e.c.	28	30	100.0	270	308	40,237	30,377	12,222	10,739	100.0
6790	Miscellaneous investing	31	30	100.0	232	211	62,259	68,512	13,171	13,963	100.0
6799	Investors, n.e.c.	23	22	100.0	119	111	71,765	66,919	7,159	7,410	100.0

Source: County Business Patterns, 1994/95, CBP-94/95, U.S. Department of Commerce, Washington, D.C., November 1997. SIC categories for which data were suppressed or not available for both 1994 and 1995 are *not* displayed. The employment columns represent mid-March employment in the year. Pay per employee is calculated by dividing 1st Quarter payroll, annualized, by mid-March employment. The columns headed "% State" show the county's percentage of the state total for the SIC in 1995; for example, 1.4% for SIC 6000 means that the county had 1.4 percent of the state's total establishments (or payroll) in SIC 6000 in 1995. A dash (-) is used to indicate that data are not available or cannot be calculated; nec means not elsewhere classified.

FLORIDA

SIC	Industry	No. Establishments			Employment		Pay / Employee		Annual Payroll ($ 000)		
		1994	1995	% State	1994	1995	1994	1995	1994	1995	% State
ALACHUA, FL											
60 –	**Finance, insurance, and real estate**	481	495	1.2	4,329	4,271	22,268	24,465	98,586	103,706	0.9
6000	Depository institutions	48	49	0.9	873	869	22,025	21,804	17,931	18,036	0.6
6020	Commercial banks	33	35	1.0	623	599	23,249	22,558	13,268	12,895	0.6
6060	Credit unions	10	10	1.8	219	238	18,466	19,714	4,383	4,893	2.7
6100	Nondepository institutions	33	37	1.2	177	191	29,311	25,529	4,851	5,508	0.6
6140	Personal credit institutions	11	13	1.4	60	65	24,933	23,262	1,408	1,483	0.5
6160	Mortgage bankers and brokers	17	18	1.1	81	77	29,086	22,545	2,117	2,419	0.6
6210	Security brokers and dealers	11	9	0.6	57	42	62,386	52,286	3,188	2,249	0.2
6300	Insurance carriers	41	42	1.6	1,255	1,214	30,075	33,987	38,362	37,756	1.6
6330	Fire, marine, and casualty insurance	20	24	1.8	977	975	30,391	34,658	30,999	31,053	3.7
6400	Insurance agents, brokers, and service	81	86	1.1	374	416	24,150	29,231	10,052	13,117	1.0
6500	Real estate	248	245	1.2	1,426	1,367	13,332	15,424	21,436	23,419	1.0
6510	Real estate operators and lessors	107	105	1.7	627	482	11,413	14,656	8,073	7,717	1.4
6530	Real estate agents and managers	113	109	1.0	676	684	14,065	15,111	10,094	11,249	0.8
6540	Title abstract offices	3	4	1.3	52	49	21,385	22,286	1,160	1,167	2.4
6550	Subdividers and developers	23	22	1.7	71	129	17,408	16,775	1,948	2,762	0.8
6552	Subdividers and developers, n.e.c.	21	19	1.9	71	109	17,408	15,156	1,429	1,812	0.7
6730	Trusts	6	7	3.0	24	20	17,000	32,400	493	713	2.3
BAKER, FL											
60 –	**Finance, insurance, and real estate**	12	12	0.0	100	105	16,200	17,105	1,845	1,925	0.0
6500	Real estate	4	4	0.0	6	7	6,000	6,857	37	43	0.0
BAY, FL											
60 –	**Finance, insurance, and real estate**	390	400	0.9	4,352	4,897	18,373	19,018	84,722	96,652	0.8
6000	Depository institutions	55	57	1.0	839	1,091	21,716	20,708	17,490	23,332	0.8
6020	Commercial banks	28	29	0.8	401	402	25,157	21,114	9,476	8,558	0.4
6100	Nondepository institutions	18	21	0.7	683	935	21,429	21,784	14,444	19,346	1.9
6210	Security brokers and dealers	12	11	0.7	76	76	54,316	44,684	3,531	3,125	0.2
6300	Insurance carriers	20	24	0.9	177	183	28,655	29,945	5,298	5,310	0.2
6400	Insurance agents, brokers, and service	74	79	1.0	413	379	19,196	22,406	9,060	9,348	0.7
6500	Real estate	202	201	1.0	2,146	2,165	13,797	14,627	34,166	35,091	1.5
6530	Real estate agents and managers	118	117	1.1	1,106	1,147	11,049	11,414	14,895	15,563	1.1
BRADFORD, FL											
60 –	**Finance, insurance, and real estate**	25	27	0.1	113	100	19,363	20,360	1,951	2,052	0.0
6000	Depository institutions	5	4	0.1	68	57	21,235	20,982	1,227	1,169	0.0
6500	Real estate	6	9	0.0	10	10	12,000	10,400	100	145	0.0
6510	Real estate operators and lessors	3	5	0.1	3	2	10,667	8,000	26	36	0.0
BREVARD, FL											
60 –	**Finance, insurance, and real estate**	1,072	1,079	2.5	5,783	6,053	23,250	22,967	134,957	145,813	1.2
6000	Depository institutions	141	143	2.6	1,790	1,685	19,759	21,082	34,504	35,163	1.2
6020	Commercial banks	94	96	2.6	1,117	1,049	20,344	20,759	20,716	20,991	1.0
6060	Credit unions	20	23	4.2	438	443	18,301	22,149	9,223	10,181	5.6
6100	Nondepository institutions	67	73	2.5	313	270	30,939	28,356	8,652	7,694	0.8
6160	Mortgage bankers and brokers	43	44	2.6	225	164	33,440	29,829	6,357	4,898	1.2
6200	Security and commodity brokers	54	62	2.5	383	436	57,640	47,688	20,079	22,322	1.5
6210	Security brokers and dealers	42	48	3.1	364	419	59,868	48,955	19,556	21,608	1.7
6280	Security and commodity services	12	13	1.5	19	17	14,947	16,471	523	706	0.4
6300	Insurance carriers	68	64	2.4	444	440	34,631	36,964	15,163	15,975	0.7

Source: *County Business Patterns, 1994/95*, CBP-94/95, U.S. Department of Commerce, Washington, D.C., November 1997. SIC categories for which data were suppressed or not available for both 1994 and 1995 are *not* displayed. The employment columns represent mid-March employment in the year. Pay per employee is calculated by dividing 1st Quarter payroll, annualized, by mid-March employment. The columns headed "% State" show the county's percentage of the state total for the SIC in 1995; for example, 1.4% for SIC 6000 means that the county had 1.4 percent of the state's total establishments (or payroll) in SIC 6000 in 1995. A dash (-) is used to indicate that data are not available or cannot be calculated; *nec* means not elsewhere classified.

Continued on next page.

SIC	Industry	No. Establishments			Employment		Pay / Employee		Annual Payroll ($ 000)		
		1994	1995	% State	1994	1995	1994	1995	1994	1995	% State

BREVARD, FL - [continued]

SIC	Industry	1994	1995	% State	1994	1995	1994	1995	1994	1995	% State
6310	Life insurance	9	11	1.5	167	158	30,946	29,013	4,991	4,188	0.5
6360	Title insurance	16	14	5.7	142	111	25,493	25,333	2,937	2,474	3.4
6400	Insurance agents, brokers, and service	181	186	2.4	724	667	20,608	20,882	15,194	16,291	1.2
6500	Real estate	538	532	2.7	2,078	2,502	16,539	16,919	38,871	46,128	1.9
6510	Real estate operators and lessors	155	145	2.3	527	642	14,095	14,704	7,775	9,622	1.8
6530	Real estate agents and managers	332	327	3.0	1,235	1,506	16,645	16,916	23,906	27,098	1.9
6540	Title abstract offices	8	8	2.6	32	24	22,250	22,667	671	579	1.2
6550	Subdividers and developers	36	39	3.0	279	312	20,115	21,103	6,367	8,495	2.4
6730	Trusts	8	5	2.1	8	20	18,000	8,400	239	180	0.6
6790	Miscellaneous investing	10	8	1.6	17	11	20,235	21,091	370	161	0.1

BROWARD, FL

SIC	Industry	1994	1995	% State	1994	1995	1994	1995	1994	1995	% State
60 –	**Finance, insurance, and real estate**	4,871	5,008	11.7	42,309	42,199	30,325	31,911	1,266,928	1,378,963	11.6
6000	Depository institutions	541	541	9.9	10,138	9,940	30,092	33,682	281,258	310,846	10.9
6020	Commercial banks	307	331	9.0	5,783	5,741	31,202	34,479	159,089	171,631	8.4
6030	Savings institutions	164	148	17.1	3,131	2,863	25,344	25,943	80,089	77,510	22.7
6090	Functions closely related to banking	33	27	8.9	874	949	41,689	47,933	31,593	40,234	28.0
6100	Nondepository institutions	376	385	12.9	6,418	6,250	30,630	32,681	196,325	212,642	21.3
6140	Personal credit institutions	101	98	10.7	4,252	4,405	30,933	31,888	133,568	140,515	42.9
6150	Business credit institutions	45	50	19.6	271	332	31,365	40,554	10,023	14,753	6.4
6160	Mortgage bankers and brokers	221	228	13.5	1,890	1,502	29,862	33,406	52,643	57,129	14.1
6200	Security and commodity brokers	226	247	10.1	2,656	2,249	68,108	71,031	171,277	166,969	11.5
6210	Security brokers and dealers	152	156	10.1	2,251	1,851	70,529	71,200	143,797	132,409	10.6
6280	Security and commodity services	64	80	9.5	287	310	59,652	73,665	21,429	28,008	15.4
6300	Insurance carriers	258	283	10.6	4,580	4,575	37,878	36,867	167,278	174,739	7.6
6310	Life insurance	51	53	7.3	1,237	1,040	37,614	38,708	43,573	39,283	4.7
6320	Medical service and health insurance	26	40	18.8	1,516	1,934	35,003	32,184	52,288	67,917	13.9
6330	Fire, marine, and casualty insurance	141	146	11.2	1,547	1,380	41,210	41,997	62,710	58,962	6.9
6350	Surety insurance	6	6	16.7	22	21	50,000	51,619	914	995	8.5
6360	Title insurance	18	23	9.3	163	144	35,534	36,972	4,416	5,099	7.1
6400	Insurance agents, brokers, and service	965	993	12.6	4,971	4,987	25,642	27,649	136,675	148,929	10.9
6500	Real estate	2,351	2,397	12.1	12,453	13,303	19,461	21,506	262,568	292,902	12.4
6510	Real estate operators and lessors	714	730	11.5	3,013	3,738	16,824	18,553	55,051	73,096	13.5
6530	Real estate agents and managers	1,444	1,400	12.7	8,448	8,246	18,949	21,397	174,882	176,743	12.7
6540	Title abstract offices	29	34	10.9	247	194	26,899	25,134	5,528	5,151	10.4
6550	Subdividers and developers	98	111	8.6	689	978	34,218	33,579	25,112	33,890	9.6
6552	Subdividers and developers, n.e.c.	87	92	9.3	629	744	34,296	37,624	22,875	28,339	10.6
6553	Cemetery subdividers and developers	7	11	5.8	59	211	33,695	19,280	2,109	4,123	5.6
6710	Holding offices	48	49	11.8	510	371	78,071	106,458	31,637	32,962	11.9
6730	Trusts	21	28	11.9	97	134	31,052	31,672	3,384	4,429	14.3
6732	Educational, religious, etc. trusts	5	9	9.7	10	19	34,400	31,368	494	826	6.1
6733	Trusts, n.e.c.	16	19	13.5	87	115	30,667	31,722	2,890	3,603	21.2
6790	Miscellaneous investing	68	62	12.7	410	350	27,337	28,937	13,166	32,270	27.2
6794	Patent owners and lessors	25	21	22.3	227	182	34,767	38,615	9,083	28,684	57.2
6798	Real estate investment trusts	6	7	13.5	94	103	5,447	9,631	773	1,150	-
6799	Investors, n.e.c.	37	34	10.1	89	65	31,506	32,431	3,310	2,436	4.1

CALHOUN, FL

SIC	Industry	1994	1995	% State	1994	1995	1994	1995	1994	1995	% State
60 –	**Finance, insurance, and real estate**	13	13	0.0	66	71	15,697	16,451	1,499	1,189	0.0
6000	Depository institutions	4	4	0.1	47	53	15,404	16,075	1,183	866	0.0
6500	Real estate	3	3	0.0	6	6	12,667	12,667	84	80	0.0

CHARLOTTE, FL

SIC	Industry	1994	1995	% State	1994	1995	1994	1995	1994	1995	% State
60 –	**Finance, insurance, and real estate**	299	297	0.7	1,579	1,413	24,147	22,681	37,230	33,863	0.3
6000	Depository institutions	43	41	0.7	573	438	22,464	22,493	13,472	10,540	0.4
6020	Commercial banks	27	25	0.7	384	353	22,615	23,048	8,151	7,385	0.4
6030	Savings institutions	13	13	1.5	175	68	22,629	22,000	5,093	2,902	0.8
6200	Security and commodity brokers	17	23	0.9	88	83	52,182	42,506	4,133	4,006	0.3

Source: County Business Patterns, 1994/95, CBP-94/95, U.S. Department of Commerce, Washington, D.C., November 1997. SIC categories for which data were suppressed or not available for both 1994 and 1995 are not displayed. The employment columns represent mid-March employment in the year. Pay per employee is calculated by dividing 1st Quarter payroll, annualized, by mid-March employment. The columns headed "% State" show the county's percentage of the state total for the SIC in 1995; for example, 1.4% for SIC 6000 means that the county had 1.4 percent of the state's total establishments (or payroll) in SIC 6000 in 1995. A dash (-) is used to indicate that data are not available or cannot be calculated; nec means not elsewhere classified.

Continued on next page.

SIC	Industry	No. Establishments			Employment		Pay / Employee		Annual Payroll ($ 000)		
		1994	1995	% State	1994	1995	1994	1995	1994	1995	% State
CHARLOTTE, FL - [continued]											
6210	Security brokers and dealers	10	13	0.8	77	71	57,610	46,873	3,971	3,716	0.3
6280	Security and commodity services	7	10	1.2	11	12	14,182	16,667	162	290	0.2
6300	Insurance carriers	12	12	0.5	42	35	50,857	54,057	2,133	1,905	0.1
6400	Insurance agents, brokers, and service	47	46	0.6	150	159	18,880	20,302	3,013	3,577	0.3
6500	Real estate	157	150	0.8	624	603	19,712	16,318	11,375	9,976	0.4
6510	Real estate operators and lessors	37	36	0.6	173	178	13,757	14,247	2,557	2,519	0.5
6530	Real estate agents and managers	103	98	0.9	343	337	21,889	17,733	7,034	6,199	0.4
6540	Title abstract offices	3	3	1.0	6	5	25,333	28,000	172	167	0.3
6550	Subdividers and developers	12	10	0.8	101	82	22,337	14,439	1,602	1,075	0.3
6552	Subdividers and developers, n.e.c.	8	6	0.6	33	20	26,909	26,400	590	528	0.2
6553	Cemetery subdividers and developers	4	3	1.6	68	62	20,118	10,581	1,012	542	0.7
CITRUS, FL											
60 –	**Finance, insurance, and real estate**	217	218	0.5	1,039	1,092	19,553	20,286	22,473	23,305	0.2
6000	Depository institutions	43	39	0.7	465	425	17,901	20,932	8,744	8,499	0.3
6020	Commercial banks	34	30	0.8	375	330	18,251	21,612	6,949	6,675	0.3
6030	Savings institutions	6	6	0.7	78	81	16,103	18,617	1,572	1,576	0.5
6060	Credit unions	3	3	0.5	12	14	18,667	18,286	223	248	0.1
6100	Nondepository institutions	8	10	0.3	35	39	20,000	26,667	940	1,072	0.1
6200	Security and commodity brokers	9	10	0.4	46	37	44,696	47,135	2,029	1,873	0.1
6210	Security brokers and dealers	6	7	0.5	41	32	48,976	53,250	1,972	1,825	0.1
6280	Security and commodity services	3	3	0.4	5	5	9,600	8,000	57	48	0.0
6300	Insurance carriers	8	8	0.3	18	20	46,444	52,000	871	1,025	0.0
6400	Insurance agents, brokers, and service	44	45	0.6	168	174	19,143	18,897	3,444	3,455	0.3
6500	Real estate	100	99	0.5	296	351	15,378	13,436	5,134	4,909	0.2
6510	Real estate operators and lessors	27	25	0.4	60	68	10,867	8,765	730	749	0.1
6530	Real estate agents and managers	51	51	0.5	99	131	13,697	10,260	1,617	1,517	0.1
6540	Title abstract offices	4	3	1.0	17	18	18,353	14,889	315	204	0.4
6550	Subdividers and developers	12	11	0.9	118	120	18,780	19,333	2,320	2,141	0.6
6700	Holding and other investment offices	5	7	0.5	11	46	57,455	31,043	1,311	2,472	0.5
CLAY, FL											
60 –	**Finance, insurance, and real estate**	194	196	0.5	895	989	20,031	20,659	18,907	22,094	0.2
6000	Depository institutions	24	26	0.5	257	272	19,409	20,574	5,073	5,395	0.2
6020	Commercial banks	15	17	0.5	185	200	19,178	20,040	3,542	3,866	0.2
6100	Nondepository institutions	21	21	0.7	99	93	22,424	25,376	2,045	3,101	0.3
6160	Mortgage bankers and brokers	12	9	0.5	62	39	22,323	27,692	1,235	1,003	0.2
6300	Insurance carriers	16	14	0.5	65	53	33,785	39,170	2,185	2,273	0.1
6400	Insurance agents, brokers, and service	47	48	0.6	117	112	14,120	16,107	1,856	1,984	0.1
6500	Real estate	79	81	0.4	339	433	18,454	18,088	7,134	8,656	0.4
6510	Real estate operators and lessors	23	28	0.4	105	192	16,838	15,813	1,937	2,915	0.5
6530	Real estate agents and managers	45	43	0.4	151	154	20,556	21,455	3,624	4,081	0.3
COLLIER, FL											
60 –	**Finance, insurance, and real estate**	927	957	2.2	5,588	6,167	29,485	29,051	160,039	193,221	1.6
6000	Depository institutions	100	91	1.7	1,675	1,316	28,193	32,927	46,606	37,687	1.3
6020	Commercial banks	77	72	2.0	1,541	1,206	28,195	33,012	43,149	34,695	1.7
6030	Savings institutions	13	8	0.9	86	52	26,140	31,077	2,052	1,404	0.4
6160	Mortgage bankers and brokers	21	21	1.2	70	64	32,229	29,188	1,903	2,153	0.5
6200	Security and commodity brokers	46	45	1.8	373	377	73,984	69,931	24,887	27,450	1.9
6210	Security brokers and dealers	36	33	2.1	341	345	72,563	66,238	22,010	24,280	1.9
6280	Security and commodity services	10	12	1.4	32	32	89,125	109,750	2,877	3,170	1.7
6300	Insurance carriers	27	27	1.0	108	91	45,037	48,967	4,323	4,931	0.2
6400	Insurance agents, brokers, and service	101	106	1.3	454	482	28,749	33,436	13,358	15,338	1.1
6500	Real estate	591	625	3.1	2,364	3,502	20,283	20,589	49,513	80,393	3.4
6510	Real estate operators and lessors	96	92	1.5	322	677	18,112	17,849	6,417	12,226	2.3
6530	Real estate agents and managers	418	433	3.9	1,666	2,346	17,729	18,474	30,920	43,185	3.1
6540	Title abstract offices	10	12	3.9	94	75	15,830	18,880	1,475	1,483	3.0

Source: County Business Patterns, 1994/95, CBP-94/95, U.S. Department of Commerce, Washington, D.C., November 1997. SIC categories for which data were suppressed or not available for both 1994 and 1995 are not displayed. The employment columns represent mid-March employment in the year. Pay per employee is calculated by dividing 1st Quarter payroll, annualized, by mid-March employment. The columns headed "% State" show the county's percentage of the state total for the SIC in 1995; for example, 1.4% for SIC 6000 means that the county had 1.4 percent of the state's total establishments (or payroll) in SIC 6000 in 1995. A dash (-) is used to indicate that data are not available or cannot be calculated; nec means not elsewhere classified.

Continued on next page.

SIC	Industry	No. Establishments			Employment		Pay / Employee		Annual Payroll ($ 000)		
		1994	1995	% State	1994	1995	1994	1995	1994	1995	% State
COLLIER, FL - [continued]											
6550	Subdividers and developers	45	50	3.9	255	342	42,133	41,614	10,023	22,112	6.3
6552	Subdividers and developers, n.e.c.	39	44	4.4	253	263	39,652	45,643	9,189	19,920	7.5
6700	Holding and other investment offices	29	30	2.3	483	270	37,797	40,459	17,045	22,520	4.9
6790	Miscellaneous investing	16	16	3.3	363	228	43,559	40,018	15,107	9,824	8.3
COLUMBIA, FL											
60 –	**Finance, insurance, and real estate**	74	80	0.2	541	557	19,512	20,876	11,147	11,640	0.1
6000	Depository institutions	12	13	0.2	256	259	22,266	25,035	5,547	5,910	0.2
6020	Commercial banks	8	9	0.2	230	233	22,939	25,768	5,056	5,379	0.3
6060	Credit unions	4	4	0.7	26	26	16,308	18,462	491	531	0.3
6300	Insurance carriers	6	6	0.2	102	107	20,824	20,486	2,178	2,315	0.1
6400	Insurance agents, brokers, and service	16	20	0.3	59	74	17,153	15,568	1,082	1,177	0.1
6500	Real estate	32	32	0.2	99	83	11,556	13,494	1,402	1,099	0.0
6530	Real estate agents and managers	14	16	0.1	31	33	10,194	14,909	378	458	0.0
6550	Subdividers and developers	6	6	0.5	31	14	13,677	20,000	589	278	0.1
6552	Subdividers and developers, n.e.c.	4	3	0.3	31	9	13,677	22,222	585	198	0.1
DADE, FL											
60 –	**Finance, insurance, and real estate**	6,647	6,806	16.0	65,026	65,832	31,641	32,792	2,016,707	2,184,135	18.3
6000	Depository institutions	763	804	14.7	20,880	20,419	30,170	33,481	615,030	668,298	23.4
6020	Commercial banks	415	465	12.7	12,955	13,700	28,720	32,425	365,489	443,460	21.6
6030	Savings institutions	142	129	14.9	3,744	2,457	27,791	26,810	103,506	65,624	19.2
6060	Credit unions	64	64	11.6	1,145	1,212	23,853	26,201	27,263	31,160	17.3
6100	Nondepository institutions	479	499	16.8	4,850	4,149	30,361	30,505	150,116	130,381	13.0
6110	Federal and Federally-sponsored credit	4	3	8.3	17	14	32,941	32,857	371	427	-
6140	Personal credit institutions	108	111	12.1	1,167	1,167	32,356	35,424	41,117	42,460	12.9
6150	Business credit institutions	52	53	20.8	288	328	28,750	29,561	9,241	9,862	4.3
6160	Mortgage bankers and brokers	306	318	18.9	3,376	2,616	29,809	27,394	99,169	76,280	18.8
6200	Security and commodity brokers	369	394	16.1	3,179	3,132	103,126	79,254	253,042	242,919	16.7
6210	Security brokers and dealers	221	238	15.5	2,624	2,551	107,390	82,307	214,150	202,362	16.2
6220	Commodity contracts brokers, dealers	14	16	35.6	112	93	49,857	52,946	6,317	7,857	42.9
6280	Security and commodity services	129	136	16.1	441	474	91,737	69,367	32,334	32,197	17.7
6300	Insurance carriers	298	301	11.3	9,337	9,271	33,465	39,391	313,325	386,778	16.8
6310	Life insurance	74	74	10.2	4,817	4,508	34,325	42,714	160,410	212,367	25.3
6320	Medical service and health insurance	25	25	11.7	1,990	2,424	29,616	34,837	64,996	83,604	17.1
6321	Accident and health insurance	8	7	10.8	203	112	25,419	27,071	5,114	3,775	7.4
6324	Hospital and medical service plans	17	18	12.2	1,787	2,312	30,093	35,213	59,882	79,829	18.2
6330	Fire, marine, and casualty insurance	126	126	9.7	1,703	1,532	37,536	40,676	65,945	65,703	7.7
6350	Surety insurance	8	10	27.8	157	158	33,707	35,722	5,125	5,474	46.9
6360	Title insurance	23	29	11.8	362	320	30,807	31,575	8,905	8,724	12.1
6370	Pension, health, and welfare funds	34	24	24.5	263	231	25,262	31,896	6,535	7,687	34.8
6400	Insurance agents, brokers, and service	1,126	1,144	14.5	5,932	5,988	29,573	32,027	178,823	193,947	14.2
6500	Real estate	3,333	3,390	17.0	18,767	20,294	19,736	21,159	414,593	442,951	18.7
6510	Real estate operators and lessors	1,429	1,436	22.7	6,000	6,275	16,892	17,892	115,842	113,677	21.0
6530	Real estate agents and managers	1,560	1,543	14.0	10,682	11,541	20,852	22,020	249,257	260,281	18.7
6540	Title abstract offices	46	40	12.9	470	404	24,204	25,020	11,088	9,621	19.5
6550	Subdividers and developers	201	217	16.8	1,534	1,838	21,713	25,985	34,695	51,863	14.7
6552	Subdividers and developers, n.e.c.	171	176	17.7	1,176	1,051	21,929	25,968	26,358	30,162	11.3
6553	Cemetery subdividers and developers	21	24	12.6	350	743	20,229	25,594	7,803	19,547	26.4
6700	Holding and other investment offices	273	268	20.8	1,939	2,410	44,895	43,227	85,558	109,742	24.0
6710	Holding offices	79	79	19.1	1,044	1,446	49,755	46,360	50,566	71,388	25.7
6720	Investment offices	11	8	22.2	47	48	61,872	152,000	2,871	3,989	22.9
6730	Trusts	44	43	18.2	414	434	20,222	23,668	9,367	11,399	36.8
6732	Educational, religious, etc. trusts	20	17	18.3	323	308	18,910	20,286	6,099	7,601	56.1

Source: County Business Patterns, 1994/95, CBP-94/95, U.S. Department of Commerce, Washington, D.C., November 1997. SIC categories for which data were suppressed or not available for both 1994 and 1995 are not displayed. The employment columns represent mid-March employment in the year. Pay per employee is calculated by dividing 1st Quarter payroll, annualized, by mid-March employment. The columns headed "% State" show the county's percentage of the state total for the SIC in 1995; for example, 1.4% for SIC 6000 means that the county had 1.4 percent of the state's total establishments (or payroll) in SIC 6000 in 1995. A dash (-) is used to indicate that data are not available or cannot be calculated; nec means not elsewhere classified.

Continued on next page.

SIC	Industry	No. Establishments			Employment		Pay / Employee		Annual Payroll ($ 000)		
		1994	1995	% State	1994	1995	1994	1995	1994	1995	% State
DADE, FL - [continued]											
6733	Trusts, n.e.c.	24	26	18.4	91	126	24,879	31,937	3,268	3,798	22.3
6790	Miscellaneous investing	122	115	23.6	425	456	55,605	41,491	22,041	21,546	18.2
6799	Investors, n.e.c.	91	88	26.1	291	265	65,663	40,166	16,270	12,786	21.4
DE SOTO, FL											
60 –	**Finance, insurance, and real estate**	39	36	0.1	168	174	16,786	18,115	3,094	3,498	0.0
6000	Depository institutions	7	6	0.1	93	100	17,419	19,760	1,866	2,000	0.1
6400	Insurance agents, brokers, and service	11	9	0.1	30	36	16,533	15,111	543	569	0.0
6500	Real estate	17	16	0.1	39	33	12,718	14,424	471	450	0.0
6510	Real estate operators and lessors	7	6	0.1	20	16	11,000	12,750	189	162	0.0
6530	Real estate agents and managers	7	6	0.1	8	8	13,000	13,500	110	107	0.0
DUVAL, FL											
60 –	**Finance, insurance, and real estate**	2,080	2,174	5.1	47,236	50,391	32,167	33,903	1,425,303	1,611,655	13.5
6000	Depository institutions	266	275	5.0	11,273	11,976	30,524	31,512	311,737	367,810	12.9
6020	Commercial banks	157	177	4.8	9,412	10,152	31,331	32,149	266,099	318,643	15.5
6060	Credit unions	66	68	12.3	938	974	21,352	23,400	20,674	22,353	12.4
6100	Nondepository institutions	185	203	6.8	6,181	6,959	33,488	35,803	194,174	224,800	22.5
6160	Mortgage bankers and brokers	108	111	6.6	2,572	2,861	28,714	33,679	72,513	88,189	21.7
6200	Security and commodity brokers	156	196	8.0	2,052	2,271	48,119	47,672	80,542	89,008	6.1
6210	Security brokers and dealers	113	132	8.6	1,672	1,896	46,797	49,530	67,327	76,894	6.1
6300	Insurance carriers	228	235	8.8	18,337	18,889	34,004	35,521	586,708	632,180	27.5
6310	Life insurance	108	115	15.8	7,602	7,490	32,417	33,317	242,537	245,717	29.2
6320	Medical service and health insurance	18	20	9.4	6,550	6,814	34,253	37,243	201,984	229,523	47.0
6330	Fire, marine, and casualty insurance	79	80	6.2	3,765	4,176	37,737	37,514	132,379	147,308	17.3
6360	Title insurance	10	10	4.1	202	207	28,000	28,792	4,617	4,911	6.8
6400	Insurance agents, brokers, and service	432	427	5.4	2,809	2,744	30,928	36,657	88,107	97,162	7.1
6500	Real estate	716	743	3.7	4,576	4,707	20,483	22,339	95,668	104,482	4.4
6510	Real estate operators and lessors	278	283	4.5	1,777	1,807	13,506	14,634	25,285	27,620	5.1
6530	Real estate agents and managers	360	374	3.4	2,116	2,221	27,234	29,030	56,842	61,766	4.4
6540	Title abstract offices	10	11	3.5	93	107	23,140	27,327	2,044	2,862	5.8
6550	Subdividers and developers	54	51	4.0	579	549	17,022	19,730	10,937	11,502	3.3
6552	Subdividers and developers, n.e.c.	38	33	3.3	256	255	22,922	25,396	6,244	7,358	2.8
6553	Cemetery subdividers and developers	13	11	5.8	323	269	12,347	14,290	4,575	3,485	4.7
6700	Holding and other investment offices	85	82	6.4	623	1,173	40,295	35,823	30,157	43,358	9.5
6710	Holding offices	32	31	7.5	379	896	44,992	34,670	21,434	33,320	12.0
6720	Investment offices	3	3	8.3	12	5	30,333	28,000	294	137	0.8
6730	Trusts	16	17	7.2	54	53	25,630	30,189	1,592	1,567	5.1
6732	Educational, religious, etc. trusts	7	8	8.6	25	25	26,880	33,600	786	816	6.0
6733	Trusts, n.e.c.	9	9	6.4	29	28	24,552	27,143	806	751	4.4
6790	Miscellaneous investing	28	27	5.5	178	219	35,416	42,082	6,711	8,214	6.9
ESCAMBIA, FL											
60 –	**Finance, insurance, and real estate**	589	601	1.4	4,098	4,009	24,670	25,054	100,757	100,256	0.8
6000	Depository institutions	100	105	1.9	1,473	1,477	22,664	23,399	32,345	32,301	1.1
6020	Commercial banks	66	71	1.9	1,027	1,015	24,888	25,281	23,922	23,437	1.1
6060	Credit unions	27	27	4.9	419	432	17,375	19,083	7,833	8,175	4.5
6090	Functions closely related to banking	7	7	2.3	27	30	20,148	21,867	590	689	0.5
6100	Nondepository institutions	48	52	1.7	278	302	29,338	27,801	7,962	8,509	0.9
6160	Mortgage bankers and brokers	21	22	1.3	127	108	31,717	29,370	3,797	3,304	0.8
6200	Security and commodity brokers	24	23	0.9	219	215	48,219	55,628	10,884	11,863	0.8
6210	Security brokers and dealers	15	14	0.9	196	192	51,714	56,771	10,396	10,956	0.9
6280	Security and commodity services	9	9	1.1	23	23	18,435	46,087	488	907	0.5
6300	Insurance carriers	51	51	1.9	580	461	32,869	34,568	17,487	16,189	0.7
6310	Life insurance	22	21	2.9	316	240	29,392	27,383	8,213	6,221	0.7
6400	Insurance agents, brokers, and service	115	121	1.5	538	512	24,364	25,938	13,165	13,453	1.0
6500	Real estate	235	236	1.2	896	1,019	15,446	15,109	15,875	17,129	0.7
6510	Real estate operators and lessors	73	79	1.2	226	287	14,690	13,659	3,769	4,171	0.8

Source: County Business Patterns, 1994/95, CBP-94/95, U.S. Department of Commerce, Washington, D.C., November 1997. SIC categories for which data were suppressed or not available for both 1994 and 1995 are not displayed. The employment columns represent mid-March employment in the year. Pay per employee is calculated by dividing 1st Quarter payroll, annualized, by mid-March employment. The columns headed "% State" show the county's percentage of the state total for the SIC in 1995; for example, 1.4% for SIC 6000 means that the county had 1.4 percent of the state's total establishments (or payroll) in SIC 6000 in 1995. A dash (-) is used to indicate that data are not available or cannot be calculated; nec means not elsewhere classified.

Continued on next page.

SIC	Industry	No. Establishments			Employment		Pay / Employee		Annual Payroll ($ 000)		
		1994	1995	% State	1994	1995	1994	1995	1994	1995	% State
ESCAMBIA, FL - [continued]											
6530	Real estate agents and managers	141	136	1.2	516	590	14,682	14,847	8,937	10,014	0.7
6540	Title abstract offices	4	4	1.3	31	25	26,065	27,200	705	677	1.4
6550	Subdividers and developers	12	10	0.8	120	85	17,400	21,318	2,402	1,828	0.5
6552	Subdividers and developers, n.e.c.	4	3	0.3	21	3	17,333	26,667	452	94	0.0
6553	Cemetery subdividers and developers	7	5	2.6	99	81	17,414	21,333	1,945	1,720	2.3
6700	Holding and other investment offices	16	13	1.0	114	23	26,175	39,652	3,039	812	0.2
FLAGLER, FL											
60 –	**Finance, insurance, and real estate**	66	76	0.2	524	415	23,924	26,159	12,631	10,094	0.1
6000	Depository institutions	9	10	0.2	104	100	22,000	23,280	2,167	2,256	0.1
6500	Real estate	44	47	0.2	350	244	24,754	28,262	8,839	6,254	0.3
6530	Real estate agents and managers	32	35	0.3	315	222	25,130	28,613	8,107	5,533	0.4
FRANKLIN, FL											
60 –	**Finance, insurance, and real estate**	27	27	0.1	175	203	15,360	16,473	3,041	3,595	0.0
6000	Depository institutions	8	8	0.1	60	66	17,133	18,727	1,085	1,373	0.0
6500	Real estate	15	15	0.1	100	117	13,400	13,744	1,525	1,737	0.1
6530	Real estate agents and managers	9	10	0.1	63	75	13,651	15,413	1,001	1,270	0.1
GADSDEN, FL											
60 –	**Finance, insurance, and real estate**	41	42	0.1	265	309	21,087	18,641	5,364	5,251	0.0
6000	Depository institutions	11	11	0.2	133	134	23,820	24,537	2,915	2,871	0.1
6500	Real estate	20	19	0.1	79	122	11,899	7,738	1,039	887	0.0
6510	Real estate operators and lessors	12	12	0.2	60	102	9,600	5,608	600	464	0.1
GILCHRIST, FL											
60 –	**Finance, insurance, and real estate**	11	11	0.0	53	63	19,623	22,667	1,091	1,296	0.0
6000	Depository institutions	5	5	0.1	36	38	21,444	28,316	803	916	0.0
GLADES, FL											
60 –	**Finance, insurance, and real estate**	9	21	0.0	24	124	14,500	18,161	349	2,165	0.0
GULF, FL											
60 –	**Finance, insurance, and real estate**	24	24	0.1	138	142	15,478	16,000	2,324	2,554	0.0
6000	Depository institutions	7	7	0.1	90	89	14,978	16,045	1,501	1,641	0.1
6530	Real estate agents and managers	4	5	0.0	6	9	10,000	10,667	75	104	0.0
HAMILTON, FL											
60 –	**Finance, insurance, and real estate**	4	5	0.0	-	-	-	-	-	-	-
HARDEE, FL											
60 –	**Finance, insurance, and real estate**	29	28	0.1	225	227	17,884	19,313	4,824	5,084	0.0
6000	Depository institutions	6	5	0.1	136	144	20,206	20,500	3,241	3,413	0.1
6020	Commercial banks	6	5	0.1	136	144	20,206	20,500	3,241	3,413	0.2
6500	Real estate	13	13	0.1	49	44	11,837	12,182	676	590	0.0
6530	Real estate agents and managers	5	4	0.0	9	6	12,444	14,667	181	159	0.0
HENDRY, FL											
60 –	**Finance, insurance, and real estate**	43	30	0.1	258	177	18,357	18,463	4,897	3,305	0.0
6000	Depository institutions	10	7	0.1	180	125	19,933	20,448	3,861	2,519	0.1
6500	Real estate	17	13	0.1	42	31	11,333	12,129	431	343	0.0
HERNANDO, FL											
60 –	**Finance, insurance, and real estate**	200	198	0.5	1,355	1,415	22,173	21,953	28,980	30,923	0.3
6000	Depository institutions	49	42	0.8	659	608	25,141	26,901	14,751	15,542	0.5
6020	Commercial banks	42	36	1.0	621	579	25,630	27,337	14,076	14,995	0.7
6100	Nondepository institutions	10	9	0.3	23	21	20,000	23,429	467	578	0.1
6200	Security and commodity brokers	14	16	0.7	55	52	60,218	42,846	3,067	2,344	0.2

Source: County Business Patterns, 1994/95, CBP-94/95, U.S. Department of Commerce, Washington, D.C., November 1997. SIC categories for which data were suppressed or not available for both 1994 and 1995 are not displayed. The employment columns represent mid-March employment in the year. Pay per employee is calculated by dividing 1st Quarter payroll, annualized, by mid-March employment. The columns headed "% State" show the county's percentage of the state total for the SIC in 1995; for example, 1.4% for SIC 6000 means that the county had 1.4 percent of the state's total establishments (or payroll) in SIC 6000 in 1995. A dash (-) is used to indicate that data are not available or cannot be calculated; nec means not elsewhere classified.

Continued on next page.

SIC	Industry	No. Establishments			Employment		Pay / Employee		Annual Payroll ($ 000)		
		1994	1995	% State	1994	1995	1994	1995	1994	1995	% State
HERNANDO, FL - [continued]											
6400	Insurance agents, brokers, and service	37	39	0.5	152	145	16,658	18,428	2,688	2,843	0.2
6500	Real estate	77	77	0.4	422	553	12,796	14,373	6,272	8,222	0.3
6510	Real estate operators and lessors	21	19	0.3	58	151	10,483	15,576	578	2,393	0.4
6530	Real estate agents and managers	44	47	0.4	278	290	12,086	12,703	4,072	3,749	0.3
6540	Title abstract offices	6	5	1.6	38	34	19,474	23,176	794	927	1.9
6550	Subdividers and developers	4	4	0.3	47	77	14,553	14,442	816	1,137	0.3
HIGHLANDS, FL											
60 –	**Finance, insurance, and real estate**	168	152	0.4	964	864	20,004	20,755	19,058	16,952	0.1
6000	Depository institutions	33	31	0.6	423	409	22,894	23,599	9,568	8,623	0.3
6020	Commercial banks	27	24	0.7	384	372	23,073	23,634	8,604	7,604	0.4
6200	Security and commodity brokers	8	7	0.3	27	24	63,704	44,667	1,411	1,013	0.1
6400	Insurance agents, brokers, and service	25	24	0.3	123	119	18,634	19,966	2,413	2,444	0.2
6500	Real estate	88	74	0.4	303	261	12,634	14,130	4,213	3,692	0.2
6530	Real estate agents and managers	50	43	0.4	112	109	12,286	13,358	1,566	1,528	0.1
6550	Subdividers and developers	7	6	0.5	106	72	12,981	16,556	1,536	1,172	0.3
HILLSBOROUGH, FL											
60 –	**Finance, insurance, and real estate**	2,610	2,693	6.3	38,231	37,790	29,037	31,022	1,084,441	1,126,592	9.4
6000	Depository institutions	322	324	5.9	9,475	9,894	24,341	25,664	212,824	227,798	8.0
6020	Commercial banks	212	216	5.9	7,245	7,473	24,745	25,994	159,873	162,823	7.9
6060	Credit unions	44	45	8.1	1,056	1,131	19,962	21,705	22,990	25,678	14.2
6090	Functions closely related to banking	30	30	9.9	876	1,028	26,128	27,759	22,386	31,272	21.7
6100	Nondepository institutions	251	259	8.7	4,997	4,493	29,624	34,495	135,286	135,350	13.5
6140	Personal credit institutions	68	75	8.2	1,215	876	28,589	33,511	35,302	30,121	9.2
6150	Business credit institutions	35	35	13.7	1,723	2,676	27,886	35,617	51,595	73,738	32.0
6160	Mortgage bankers and brokers	141	140	8.3	1,070	755	34,157	33,923	32,109	25,961	6.4
6200	Security and commodity brokers	155	163	6.6	1,945	1,971	60,590	60,940	103,246	108,488	7.5
6210	Security brokers and dealers	93	97	6.3	1,667	1,753	60,612	61,659	89,869	99,166	7.9
6280	Security and commodity services	59	62	7.3	257	199	62,895	57,045	13,044	8,315	4.6
6300	Insurance carriers	292	301	11.3	10,899	9,474	31,649	33,531	345,038	315,297	13.7
6310	Life insurance	107	109	15.0	4,456	3,590	30,977	32,700	135,281	103,765	12.3
6320	Medical service and health insurance	23	32	15.0	924	1,132	32,130	30,799	28,334	39,031	8.0
6321	Accident and health insurance	10	7	10.8	197	106	25,827	21,019	3,196	2,224	4.4
6324	Hospital and medical service plans	13	25	17.0	727	1,026	33,838	31,809	25,138	36,807	8.4
6330	Fire, marine, and casualty insurance	118	111	8.6	5,020	4,349	32,062	34,665	168,454	158,654	18.7
6350	Surety insurance	6	6	16.7	45	42	48,533	50,952	2,002	1,881	16.1
6360	Title insurance	25	26	10.6	342	257	30,725	31,097	8,337	7,886	10.9
6370	Pension, health, and welfare funds	12	14	14.3	107	99	32,000	44,202	2,478	3,902	17.6
6400	Insurance agents, brokers, and service	547	563	7.2	4,475	5,490	26,405	28,540	129,959	163,096	11.9
6500	Real estate	966	998	5.0	5,850	5,827	21,223	22,669	128,223	134,976	5.7
6510	Real estate operators and lessors	357	349	5.5	1,981	2,086	16,287	17,264	35,043	36,825	6.8
6530	Real estate agents and managers	498	519	4.7	2,859	2,762	23,719	25,762	69,255	72,836	5.2
6540	Title abstract offices	32	26	8.4	219	127	28,055	25,732	4,477	3,438	7.0
6550	Subdividers and developers	49	49	3.8	754	750	23,029	26,549	18,279	18,742	5.3
6552	Subdividers and developers, n.e.c.	39	34	3.4	460	655	27,043	25,808	13,428	15,709	5.9
6553	Cemetery subdividers and developers	9	9	4.7	286	87	15,930	33,011	4,631	2,888	3.9
6710	Holding offices	24	28	6.8	195	235	33,703	42,860	9,198	10,431	3.8
6730	Trusts	14	14	5.9	37	34	15,892	19,765	614	644	2.1
6732	Educational, religious, etc. trusts	8	10	10.8	28	25	16,286	20,800	470	499	3.7
6733	Trusts, n.e.c.	6	4	2.8	9	9	14,667	16,889	144	145	0.9
6790	Miscellaneous investing	29	29	5.9	105	94	44,000	53,745	5,240	5,670	4.8
6799	Investors, n.e.c.	14	17	5.0	54	59	56,889	63,390	3,004	3,717	6.2
HOLMES, FL											
60 –	**Finance, insurance, and real estate**	10	11	0.0	59	61	20,136	19,869	1,225	1,294	0.0

Source: County Business Patterns, 1994/95, CBP-94/95, U.S. Department of Commerce, Washington, D.C., November 1997. SIC categories for which data were suppressed or not available for both 1994 and 1995 are not displayed. The employment columns represent mid-March employment in the year. Pay per employee is calculated by dividing 1st Quarter payroll, annualized, by mid-March employment. The columns headed "% State" show the county's percentage of the state total for the SIC in 1995; for example, 1.4% for SIC 6000 means that the county had 1.4 percent of the state's total establishments (or payroll) in SIC 6000 in 1995. A dash (-) is used to indicate that data are not available or cannot be calculated; nec means not elsewhere classified.

Continued on next page.

SIC	Industry	No. Establishments			Employment		Pay / Employee		Annual Payroll ($ 000)		
		1994	1995	% State	1994	1995	1994	1995	1994	1995	% State
HOLMES, FL - [continued]											
6000	Depository institutions	4	4	0.1	45	41	21,956	22,829	993	1,004	0.0
6400	Insurance agents, brokers, and service	3	3	0.0	10	11	16,000	16,364	173	178	0.0
6500	Real estate	3	4	0.0	4	9	10,000	10,667	59	112	0.0
INDIAN RIVER, FL											
60 –	**Finance, insurance, and real estate**	326	342	0.8	2,188	2,238	23,545	24,347	52,871	53,732	0.5
6000	Depository institutions	45	50	0.9	652	614	21,485	24,834	14,527	15,514	0.5
6020	Commercial banks	31	33	0.9	531	508	20,798	25,331	11,531	12,847	0.6
6030	Savings institutions	10	12	1.4	91	79	20,835	24,456	1,956	2,210	0.6
6160	Mortgage bankers and brokers	6	5	0.3	16	6	16,000	19,333	171	129	0.0
6200	Security and commodity brokers	24	24	1.0	184	197	64,087	52,467	10,719	10,211	0.7
6210	Security brokers and dealers	19	17	1.1	161	173	63,950	52,855	9,195	8,888	0.7
6300	Insurance carriers	12	11	0.4	36	30	54,778	64,400	1,942	1,931	0.1
6400	Insurance agents, brokers, and service	53	65	0.8	233	259	24,738	21,189	5,796	6,227	0.5
6500	Real estate	168	168	0.8	962	1,021	16,333	18,402	17,412	17,066	0.7
6510	Real estate operators and lessors	52	52	0.8	248	254	13,274	14,598	3,729	2,793	0.5
6530	Real estate agents and managers	99	93	0.8	576	595	17,021	18,454	10,532	10,349	0.7
6550	Subdividers and developers	10	12	0.9	117	149	18,838	24,107	2,674	3,269	0.9
6700	Holding and other investment offices	10	10	0.8	89	86	19,146	23,721	1,946	2,071	0.5
JACKSON, FL											
60 –	**Finance, insurance, and real estate**	74	69	0.2	486	489	22,247	22,748	10,741	10,800	0.1
6000	Depository institutions	19	19	0.3	236	227	22,712	24,300	5,198	5,179	0.2
6020	Commercial banks	15	15	0.4	223	213	22,996	24,582	4,987	4,937	0.2
6060	Credit unions	4	4	0.7	13	14	17,846	20,000	211	242	0.1
6300	Insurance carriers	8	7	0.3	77	75	28,779	27,520	2,051	1,972	0.1
6400	Insurance agents, brokers, and service	20	17	0.2	68	76	15,529	15,632	1,194	1,373	0.1
6500	Real estate	21	19	0.1	65	68	12,123	13,294	892	885	0.0
JEFFERSON, FL											
60 –	**Finance, insurance, and real estate**	17	16	0.0	112	115	18,893	20,870	2,301	2,550	0.0
6000	Depository institutions	3	3	0.1	68	67	20,118	22,866	1,339	1,504	0.1
LAFAYETTE, FL											
60 –	**Finance, insurance, and real estate**	2	3	0.0	-	-	-	-	-	-	-
LAKE, FL											
60 –	**Finance, insurance, and real estate**	368	363	0.9	2,346	2,378	20,191	20,669	49,451	51,775	0.4
6000	Depository institutions	63	66	1.2	1,038	1,035	21,291	22,643	22,255	22,951	0.8
6020	Commercial banks	48	50	1.4	861	859	21,347	22,882	18,281	18,686	0.9
6160	Mortgage bankers and brokers	6	5	0.3	24	14	16,500	13,143	314	214	0.1
6200	Security and commodity brokers	18	19	0.8	82	85	57,317	45,976	4,705	4,514	0.3
6210	Security brokers and dealers	11	12	0.8	70	71	59,829	49,634	4,268	4,137	0.3
6280	Security and commodity services	7	7	0.8	12	14	42,667	27,429	437	377	0.2
6300	Insurance carriers	17	17	0.6	105	122	43,010	40,426	4,618	4,285	0.2
6400	Insurance agents, brokers, and service	56	57	0.7	233	257	21,219	20,218	5,758	5,843	0.4
6500	Real estate	193	188	0.9	833	838	12,053	12,921	11,136	13,309	0.6
6510	Real estate operators and lessors	73	68	1.1	515	429	11,441	13,408	6,259	6,209	1.1
6530	Real estate agents and managers	94	94	0.9	220	317	14,327	13,426	3,745	5,917	0.4
6550	Subdividers and developers	14	11	0.9	82	72	8,341	6,389	719	644	0.2
6552	Subdividers and developers, n.e.c.	10	7	0.7	25	17	13,120	14,824	302	407	0.2
6553	Cemetery subdividers and developers	4	4	2.1	57	55	6,246	3,782	417	237	0.3
LEE, FL											
60 –	**Finance, insurance, and real estate**	1,286	1,282	3.0	9,062	8,231	25,108	26,480	222,390	218,941	1.8
6000	Depository institutions	185	161	2.9	2,794	2,435	26,902	27,441	68,343	60,409	2.1
6020	Commercial banks	145	143	3.9	2,265	2,256	25,551	26,881	51,080	54,780	2.7
6030	Savings institutions	35	12	1.4	488	109	33,844	30,862	16,483	3,130	0.9

Source: County Business Patterns, 1994/95, CBP-94/95, U.S. Department of Commerce, Washington, D.C., November 1997. SIC categories for which data were suppressed or not available for both 1994 and 1995 are not displayed. The employment columns represent mid-March employment in the year. Pay per employee is calculated by dividing 1st Quarter payroll, annualized, by mid-March employment. The columns headed "% State" show the county's percentage of the state total for the SIC in 1995; for example, 1.4% for SIC 6000 means that the county had 1.4 percent of the state's total establishments (or payroll) in SIC 6000 in 1995. A dash (-) is used to indicate that data are not available or cannot be calculated; nec means not elsewhere classified.

Continued on next page.

SIC	Industry	No. Establishments			Employment		Pay / Employee		Annual Payroll ($ 000)		
		1994	1995	% State	1994	1995	1994	1995	1994	1995	% State
LEE, FL - [continued]											
6100	Nondepository institutions	81	83	2.8	397	379	26,035	25,119	9,902	10,153	1.0
6140	Personal credit institutions	20	23	2.5	123	121	24,715	28,529	2,968	3,274	1.0
6160	Mortgage bankers and brokers	55	54	3.2	268	251	26,746	23,602	6,815	6,572	1.6
6200	Security and commodity brokers	48	52	2.1	433	410	55,834	48,673	22,435	21,757	1.5
6210	Security brokers and dealers	32	32	2.1	395	358	58,066	48,402	20,897	19,191	1.5
6300	Insurance carriers	67	70	2.6	463	422	36,717	41,488	16,585	15,916	0.7
6310	Life insurance	21	22	3.0	244	216	30,574	31,778	6,823	5,824	0.7
6330	Fire, marine, and casualty insurance	36	36	2.8	140	146	53,629	59,671	7,885	8,430	1.0
6360	Title insurance	7	8	3.3	58	44	23,793	28,636	1,236	1,130	1.6
6400	Insurance agents, brokers, and service	223	233	3.0	1,101	921	23,615	26,463	28,944	27,205	2.0
6500	Real estate	661	660	3.3	3,656	3,601	19,125	21,531	71,692	80,965	3.4
6510	Real estate operators and lessors	157	146	2.3	905	660	13,666	17,279	12,359	11,738	2.2
6530	Real estate agents and managers	428	416	3.8	1,771	1,842	19,191	22,117	37,443	41,214	3.0
6540	Title abstract offices	12	11	3.5	104	72	20,769	25,944	2,096	1,758	3.6
6550	Subdividers and developers	46	51	4.0	864	955	24,583	23,359	19,405	24,714	7.0
LEON, FL											
60 –	**Finance, insurance, and real estate**	605	623	1.5	5,064	5,165	25,365	26,679	127,410	141,384	1.2
6000	Depository institutions	80	83	1.5	1,312	1,434	23,530	25,821	28,684	35,050	1.2
6020	Commercial banks	49	51	1.4	959	915	24,275	26,470	20,843	21,774	1.1
6060	Credit unions	22	22	4.0	321	327	20,474	22,471	6,613	7,960	4.4
6100	Nondepository institutions	40	44	1.5	313	280	31,144	28,300	9,159	8,805	0.9
6140	Personal credit institutions	18	21	2.3	117	136	26,120	27,794	3,292	4,395	1.3
6200	Security and commodity brokers	26	27	1.1	157	169	66,854	55,527	10,670	10,382	0.7
6210	Security brokers and dealers	16	17	1.1	121	123	72,959	61,333	8,813	8,217	0.7
6280	Security and commodity services	10	10	1.2	36	46	46,333	40,000	1,857	2,165	1.2
6300	Insurance carriers	63	63	2.4	916	878	29,913	32,469	28,149	28,052	1.2
6310	Life insurance	18	17	2.3	301	250	28,173	32,672	8,292	7,644	0.9
6330	Fire, marine, and casualty insurance	33	31	2.4	247	179	34,834	40,670	8,965	7,569	0.9
6400	Insurance agents, brokers, and service	133	127	1.6	929	1,056	27,268	29,492	26,805	35,055	2.6
6500	Real estate	245	261	1.3	1,216	1,278	14,714	15,183	20,165	20,881	0.9
6510	Real estate operators and lessors	85	92	1.5	449	516	11,474	11,519	5,873	6,107	1.1
6530	Real estate agents and managers	135	133	1.2	635	653	16,094	17,109	11,541	12,285	0.9
6540	Title abstract offices	5	5	1.6	62	23	19,290	25,043	1,066	473	1.0
6550	Subdividers and developers	17	21	1.6	70	73	18,914	19,726	1,539	1,678	0.5
6710	Holding offices	4	7	1.7	29	39	101,517	91,487	1,901	2,234	0.8
LEVY, FL											
60 –	**Finance, insurance, and real estate**	45	47	0.1	270	272	18,148	17,500	4,948	5,180	0.0
6000	Depository institutions	13	12	0.2	154	158	21,117	19,772	3,345	3,464	0.1
6400	Insurance agents, brokers, and service	15	13	0.2	48	45	16,833	17,778	763	798	0.1
6500	Real estate	14	17	0.1	58	56	12,414	11,786	721	742	0.0
6530	Real estate agents and managers	5	6	0.1	22	16	10,364	10,000	200	187	0.0
6550	Subdividers and developers	4	6	0.5	8	9	16,000	14,222	125	174	0.0
6552	Subdividers and developers, n.e.c.	4	6	0.6	8	9	16,000	14,222	125	174	0.1
LIBERTY, FL											
60 –	**Finance, insurance, and real estate**	4	4	0.0	-	-	-	-	-	-	-
MADISON, FL											
60 –	**Finance, insurance, and real estate**	22	20	0.0	97	98	17,608	18,980	1,769	1,941	0.0
6000	Depository institutions	6	5	0.1	59	56	20,814	22,000	1,197	1,190	0.0
6500	Real estate	8	7	0.0	17	19	10,588	15,789	226	396	0.0
MANATEE, FL											
60 –	**Finance, insurance, and real estate**	559	583	1.4	3,442	3,536	22,221	23,321	78,300	83,467	0.7
6000	Depository institutions	79	89	1.6	987	1,008	21,730	23,258	21,632	22,252	0.8
6020	Commercial banks	52	60	1.6	763	833	22,364	23,505	17,230	18,213	0.9

Source: County Business Patterns, 1994/95, CBP-94/95, U.S. Department of Commerce, Washington, D.C., November 1997. SIC categories for which data were suppressed or not available for both 1994 and 1995 are not displayed. The employment columns represent mid-March employment in the year. Pay per employee is calculated by dividing 1st Quarter payroll, annualized, by mid-March employment. The columns headed "% State" show the county's percentage of the state total for the SIC in 1995; for example, 1.4% for SIC 6000 means that the county had 1.4 percent of the state's total establishments (or payroll) in SIC 6000 in 1995. A dash (-) is used to indicate that data are not available or cannot be calculated; nec means not elsewhere classified.

Continued on next page.

SIC	Industry	No. Establishments			Employment		Pay / Employee		Annual Payroll ($ 000)		
		1994	1995	% State	1994	1995	1994	1995	1994	1995	% State
MANATEE, FL - [continued]											
6030	Savings institutions	20	21	2.4	182	131	20,066	22,992	3,664	3,198	0.9
6100	Nondepository institutions	30	34	1.1	232	243	24,879	24,214	6,298	6,094	0.6
6160	Mortgage bankers and brokers	18	18	1.1	135	134	31,230	25,015	4,498	3,840	0.9
6200	Security and commodity brokers	24	27	1.1	159	170	57,811	52,800	8,897	9,878	0.7
6210	Security brokers and dealers	17	17	1.1	146	147	59,616	56,544	8,388	9,205	0.7
6300	Insurance carriers	23	23	0.9	162	152	36,420	37,368	4,847	5,122	0.2
6400	Insurance agents, brokers, and service	97	102	1.3	386	385	22,021	23,719	9,319	9,956	0.7
6500	Real estate	291	293	1.5	1,414	1,460	16,122	17,551	24,016	25,399	1.1
6510	Real estate operators and lessors	106	107	1.7	570	521	14,372	16,507	8,750	8,702	1.6
6530	Real estate agents and managers	162	158	1.4	702	721	17,436	17,931	12,131	12,320	0.9
6550	Subdividers and developers	14	14	1.1	132	150	16,576	22,480	2,862	3,796	1.1
6552	Subdividers and developers, n.e.c.	10	10	1.0	58	73	16,414	28,000	1,327	2,569	1.0
6553	Cemetery subdividers and developers	4	4	2.1	74	77	16,703	17,247	1,535	1,227	1.7
6700	Holding and other investment offices	15	15	1.2	102	118	28,196	31,559	3,291	4,766	1.0
6710	Holding offices	5	5	1.2	86	94	29,395	33,957	2,891	3,459	1.2
6730	Trusts	4	4	1.7	4	4	21,000	20,000	82	82	0.3
6790	Miscellaneous investing	4	3	0.6	12	17	22,000	25,412	313	503	0.4
MARION, FL											
60 –	**Finance, insurance, and real estate**	453	480	1.1	2,677	2,932	23,426	22,847	61,947	65,335	0.5
6000	Depository institutions	78	89	1.6	1,137	1,189	23,370	23,374	25,626	24,868	0.9
6020	Commercial banks	69	79	2.2	1,093	1,136	23,510	23,500	24,721	23,757	1.2
6100	Nondepository institutions	25	29	1.0	140	133	23,943	25,895	3,269	3,574	0.4
6140	Personal credit institutions	14	17	1.9	72	89	24,611	28,135	1,921	2,691	0.8
6200	Security and commodity brokers	19	16	0.7	123	113	56,683	58,513	6,078	6,200	0.4
6210	Security brokers and dealers	14	12	0.8	111	107	61,369	60,299	5,922	6,052	0.5
6280	Security and commodity services	5	4	0.5	12	6	13,333	26,667	156	148	0.1
6300	Insurance carriers	25	26	1.0	147	155	35,429	31,535	5,077	4,809	0.2
6400	Insurance agents, brokers, and service	104	106	1.3	402	402	21,502	24,060	9,029	10,320	0.8
6500	Real estate	194	207	1.0	676	884	15,047	14,656	11,137	13,745	0.6
6510	Real estate operators and lessors	55	56	0.9	218	219	12,569	13,059	2,823	3,320	0.6
6530	Real estate agents and managers	107	118	1.1	281	385	16,712	14,899	5,137	5,886	0.4
6540	Title abstract offices	7	7	2.3	74	65	21,081	20,554	1,671	1,696	3.4
6550	Subdividers and developers	18	18	1.4	97	211	11,505	14,123	1,393	2,757	0.8
6552	Subdividers and developers, n.e.c.	14	14	1.4	35	132	19,771	17,000	861	1,990	0.7
6553	Cemetery subdividers and developers	3	3	1.6	62	78	6,839	9,333	530	759	1.0
6700	Holding and other investment offices	8	7	0.5	52	56	34,462	29,000	1,731	1,819	0.4
MARTIN, FL											
60 –	**Finance, insurance, and real estate**	454	470	1.1	2,906	2,944	29,001	28,493	81,926	85,303	0.7
6000	Depository institutions	68	68	1.2	851	818	30,754	28,900	20,030	22,565	0.8
6020	Commercial banks	43	44	1.2	647	645	32,717	29,557	15,854	17,814	0.9
6100	Nondepository institutions	14	14	0.5	53	39	29,434	31,179	1,200	875	0.1
6160	Mortgage bankers and brokers	10	8	0.5	44	25	30,364	33,920	968	534	0.1
6200	Security and commodity brokers	40	38	1.5	284	298	76,704	66,564	19,729	20,185	1.4
6210	Security brokers and dealers	23	21	1.4	248	261	74,726	58,927	16,445	16,808	1.3
6300	Insurance carriers	16	19	0.7	67	71	58,746	50,817	3,420	4,633	0.2
6400	Insurance agents, brokers, and service	66	72	0.9	279	290	22,581	27,214	7,079	7,384	0.5
6500	Real estate	237	244	1.2	1,335	1,369	16,977	18,504	23,625	26,517	1.1
6510	Real estate operators and lessors	68	64	1.0	348	347	16,586	19,066	6,167	7,238	1.3
6530	Real estate agents and managers	149	150	1.4	881	856	15,968	17,350	14,114	15,096	1.1
6550	Subdividers and developers	16	21	1.6	100	152	27,160	24,474	3,230	3,998	1.1
6700	Holding and other investment offices	13	15	1.2	37	59	50,270	40,000	6,843	3,144	0.7
MONROE, FL											
60 –	**Finance, insurance, and real estate**	330	343	0.8	1,863	2,165	22,149	20,015	42,691	44,583	0.4
6000	Depository institutions	48	47	0.9	597	613	24,945	25,873	14,970	15,223	0.5
6020	Commercial banks	40	40	1.1	519	536	25,272	26,291	13,052	13,407	0.7

Source: County Business Patterns, 1994/95, CBP-94/95, U.S. Department of Commerce, Washington, D.C., November 1997. SIC categories for which data were suppressed or not available for both 1994 and 1995 are not displayed. The employment columns represent mid-March employment in the year. Pay per employee is calculated by dividing 1st Quarter payroll, annualized, by mid-March employment. The columns headed "% State" show the county's percentage of the state total for the SIC in 1995; for example, 1.4% for SIC 6000 means that the county had 1.4 percent of the state's total establishments (or payroll) in SIC 6000 in 1995. A dash (-) is used to indicate that data are not available or cannot be calculated; nec means not elsewhere classified.

Continued on next page.

SIC	Industry	No. Establishments			Employment		Pay / Employee		Annual Payroll ($ 000)		
		1994	1995	% State	1994	1995	1994	1995	1994	1995	% State
MONROE, FL - [continued]											
6400	Insurance agents, brokers, and service	39	35	0.4	181	172	28,442	27,744	5,682	5,575	0.4
6500	Real estate	213	225	1.1	923	1,038	15,597	16,435	16,332	18,547	0.8
6510	Real estate operators and lessors	52	62	1.0	152	143	15,974	16,308	2,327	2,598	0.5
6530	Real estate agents and managers	142	140	1.3	699	729	14,604	15,561	11,396	11,790	0.8
6540	Title abstract offices	6	6	1.9	36	33	22,000	20,727	833	778	1.6
6552	Subdividers and developers, n.e.c.	7	9	0.9	19	43	30,526	25,209	638	2,124	0.8
6700	Holding and other investment offices	8	10	0.8	5	9	22,400	22,222	180	307	0.1
6790	Miscellaneous investing	3	3	0.6	2	5	16,000	20,800	44	104	0.1
NASSAU, FL											
60 –	**Finance, insurance, and real estate**	77	81	0.2	379	442	25,446	24,299	9,212	11,168	0.1
6000	Depository institutions	18	20	0.4	177	181	21,989	22,232	3,405	3,624	0.1
6020	Commercial banks	11	14	0.4	152	162	22,526	22,519	2,917	3,238	0.2
6300	Insurance carriers	5	5	0.2	14	14	26,857	35,429	415	466	0.0
6400	Insurance agents, brokers, and service	12	13	0.2	68	68	18,529	19,471	1,293	1,295	0.1
6500	Real estate	32	30	0.2	75	129	21,653	16,775	1,559	2,272	0.1
6510	Real estate operators and lessors	7	7	0.1	15	45	9,333	11,022	208	650	0.1
6530	Real estate agents and managers	22	20	0.2	54	81	25,630	20,148	1,286	1,588	0.1
OKALOOSA, FL											
60 –	**Finance, insurance, and real estate**	447	471	1.1	3,537	3,701	19,067	19,444	74,415	76,436	0.6
6000	Depository institutions	61	69	1.3	1,198	1,241	19,917	19,758	26,066	24,838	0.9
6020	Commercial banks	44	57	1.6	772	968	20,959	20,211	17,300	19,945	1.0
6100	Nondepository institutions	25	25	0.8	140	143	24,657	27,608	4,304	4,026	0.4
6160	Mortgage bankers and brokers	10	7	0.4	64	64	25,438	25,438	1,772	1,806	0.4
6200	Security and commodity brokers	18	20	0.8	101	98	61,584	54,612	5,057	5,079	0.3
6210	Security brokers and dealers	11	13	0.8	87	82	69,379	62,488	4,851	4,810	0.4
6280	Security and commodity services	7	7	0.8	14	16	13,143	14,250	206	269	0.1
6300	Insurance carriers	24	24	0.9	189	185	30,899	32,324	5,849	5,735	0.2
6310	Life insurance	6	7	1.0	92	111	28,348	23,964	2,522	2,294	0.3
6400	Insurance agents, brokers, and service	77	78	1.0	374	353	17,401	21,530	7,448	8,216	0.6
6500	Real estate	232	247	1.2	1,454	1,605	14,160	14,495	24,696	27,091	1.1
6510	Real estate operators and lessors	54	59	0.9	249	245	11,839	13,763	3,343	3,870	0.7
6530	Real estate agents and managers	151	160	1.5	1,074	1,215	14,089	13,505	17,004	19,165	1.4
6550	Subdividers and developers	13	13	1.0	82	98	22,390	25,510	3,556	3,072	0.9
OKEECHOBEE, FL											
60 –	**Finance, insurance, and real estate**	53	50	0.1	274	261	19,985	23,448	5,455	5,470	0.0
6000	Depository institutions	8	8	0.1	145	129	20,800	27,938	2,864	2,978	0.1
6400	Insurance agents, brokers, and service	16	14	0.2	62	66	20,839	19,758	1,361	1,413	0.1
6500	Real estate	25	23	0.1	56	55	15,286	16,509	953	810	0.0
6530	Real estate agents and managers	13	12	0.1	18	21	20,000	17,905	384	314	0.0
ORANGE, FL											
60 –	**Finance, insurance, and real estate**	2,432	2,495	5.8	30,524	30,790	29,345	31,349	872,980	954,163	8.0
6000	Depository institutions	297	290	5.3	7,202	7,219	30,852	30,342	180,812	190,724	6.7
6020	Commercial banks	186	186	5.1	5,684	5,809	28,123	26,432	137,766	146,744	7.1
6060	Credit unions	37	40	7.2	664	694	18,633	20,219	12,930	14,472	8.0
6090	Functions closely related to banking	30	34	11.2	307	341	125,042	123,191	19,129	20,810	14.5
6100	Nondepository institutions	207	199	6.7	1,864	1,673	31,056	35,123	55,349	60,532	6.1
6140	Personal credit institutions	57	65	7.1	436	569	26,404	30,636	12,237	18,461	5.6
6150	Business credit institutions	14	13	5.1	98	102	37,673	54,667	4,240	4,877	2.1
6160	Mortgage bankers and brokers	133	118	7.0	1,315	995	32,058	35,719	38,376	36,896	9.1
6200	Security and commodity brokers	131	139	5.7	1,645	1,613	57,170	58,574	81,862	94,449	6.5
6210	Security brokers and dealers	82	87	5.6	1,395	1,340	59,951	62,155	69,974	80,789	6.5
6300	Insurance carriers	218	213	8.0	7,061	6,573	30,903	35,708	218,368	218,773	9.5
6310	Life insurance	67	64	8.8	3,217	3,261	30,975	33,285	99,761	96,086	11.4
6320	Medical service and health insurance	17	18	8.5	624	666	32,417	33,574	20,170	22,734	4.7

Source: County Business Patterns, 1994/95, CBP-94/95, U.S. Department of Commerce, Washington, D.C., November 1997. SIC categories for which data were suppressed or not available for both 1994 and 1995 are not displayed. The employment columns represent mid-March employment in the year. Pay per employee is calculated by dividing 1st Quarter payroll, annualized, by mid-March employment. The columns headed "% State" show the county's percentage of the state total for the SIC in 1995; for example, 1.4% for SIC 6000 means that the county had 1.4 percent of the state's total establishments (or payroll) in SIC 6000 in 1995. A dash (-) is used to indicate that data are not available or cannot be calculated; nec means not elsewhere classified.

Continued on next page.

SIC	Industry	No. Establishments			Employment		Pay / Employee		Annual Payroll ($ 000)		
		1994	1995	% State	1994	1995	1994	1995	1994	1995	% State
ORANGE, FL - [continued]											
6321	Accident and health insurance	7	7	10.8	96	93	27,708	31,828	2,881	2,900	5.7
6324	Hospital and medical service plans	10	10	6.8	528	573	33,273	33,857	17,289	19,799	4.5
6330	Fire, marine, and casualty insurance	96	96	7.4	2,606	2,069	28,421	38,556	78,010	79,221	9.3
6360	Title insurance	27	24	9.8	547	518	41,397	43,490	18,384	19,037	26.3
6370	Pension, health, and welfare funds	7	8	8.2	41	41	22,049	22,146	1,257	1,139	5.2
6400	Insurance agents, brokers, and service	474	479	6.1	3,614	3,500	28,806	29,574	116,104	114,279	8.3
6500	Real estate	1,037	1,104	5.6	8,674	9,539	20,393	21,738	197,995	230,932	9.7
6510	Real estate operators and lessors	321	329	5.2	1,759	2,005	16,464	17,404	31,272	33,601	6.2
6530	Real estate agents and managers	586	604	5.5	5,348	6,008	20,555	20,830	122,947	144,433	10.4
6540	Title abstract offices	21	18	5.8	227	199	23,119	26,050	5,226	4,685	9.5
6550	Subdividers and developers	76	88	6.8	1,304	1,218	24,794	32,016	37,472	44,280	12.6
6552	Subdividers and developers, n.e.c.	57	70	7.0	739	945	30,885	35,890	28,869	38,509	14.4
6553	Cemetery subdividers and developers	12	12	6.3	559	255	16,859	18,275	8,377	5,442	7.3
6710	Holding offices	26	25	6.0	300	260	58,613	78,785	16,686	15,852	5.7
6730	Trusts	10	10	4.2	17	29	18,118	26,759	367	712	2.3
6732	Educational, religious, etc. trusts	3	4	4.3	2	5	12,000	16,000	24	85	0.6
6733	Trusts, n.e.c.	7	6	4.3	15	24	18,933	29,000	343	627	3.7
6790	Miscellaneous investing	20	22	4.5	70	74	36,171	32,054	2,675	2,899	2.4
6794	Patent owners and lessors	4	6	6.4	34	35	33,412	14,857	1,281	557	1.1
6799	Investors, n.e.c.	13	12	3.6	27	29	43,111	54,759	1,092	1,985	3.3
OSCEOLA, FL											
60 –	**Finance, insurance, and real estate**	300	303	0.7	2,860	3,388	20,165	18,516	57,901	60,780	0.5
6000	Depository institutions	32	30	0.5	499	431	20,289	20,798	9,576	9,464	0.3
6160	Mortgage bankers and brokers	7	7	0.4	16	22	21,250	20,727	312	388	0.1
6300	Insurance carriers	18	17	0.6	96	85	37,583	44,188	3,559	3,418	0.1
6310	Life insurance	3	3	0.4	42	39	38,190	45,128	1,475	1,543	0.2
6400	Insurance agents, brokers, and service	41	43	0.5	172	167	27,256	29,198	4,787	4,932	0.4
6500	Real estate	181	183	0.9	1,969	2,561	18,637	16,675	37,665	40,468	1.7
6510	Real estate operators and lessors	46	43	0.7	143	148	13,063	16,405	2,112	3,406	0.6
6530	Real estate agents and managers	118	116	1.1	1,721	2,301	18,931	16,431	33,294	32,913	2.4
6550	Subdividers and developers	9	7	0.5	101	96	21,861	23,458	2,135	3,767	1.1
6790	Miscellaneous investing	4	4	0.8	6	6	15,333	14,000	91	95	0.1
6799	Investors, n.e.c.	4	4	1.2	6	6	15,333	14,000	91	95	0.2
PALM BEACH, FL											
60 –	**Finance, insurance, and real estate**	4,075	4,153	9.7	31,809	31,492	35,034	35,030	1,078,637	1,129,426	9.5
6000	Depository institutions	467	468	8.6	7,166	6,969	28,573	31,050	191,225	203,752	7.1
6020	Commercial banks	239	249	6.8	3,473	3,521	28,873	30,908	93,602	102,517	5.0
6030	Savings institutions	195	185	21.3	3,223	2,992	28,201	30,662	82,848	85,701	25.1
6060	Credit unions	22	22	4.0	317	307	19,256	24,495	7,201	7,874	4.4
6100	Nondepository institutions	229	230	7.7	1,550	1,191	32,826	35,893	47,793	45,838	4.6
6140	Personal credit institutions	43	46	5.0	293	267	34,225	38,682	8,968	9,433	2.9
6150	Business credit institutions	26	32	12.5	184	218	31,152	35,945	6,293	9,340	4.1
6160	Mortgage bankers and brokers	150	140	8.3	1,046	668	32,669	34,617	31,430	25,350	6.2
6200	Security and commodity brokers	382	389	15.9	3,910	4,179	72,057	66,304	260,338	300,375	20.7
6210	Security brokers and dealers	235	241	15.6	3,265	3,430	77,072	70,290	214,616	251,611	20.1
6220	Commodity contracts brokers, dealers	7	7	15.6	40	38	36,500	27,684	1,551	1,383	7.6
6280	Security and commodity services	137	133	15.8	605	704	47,345	49,381	44,129	46,991	25.8
6300	Insurance carriers	186	203	7.6	2,225	2,205	43,060	45,255	86,759	93,658	4.1
6310	Life insurance	52	50	6.9	1,047	949	41,158	42,891	37,947	34,848	4.1
6320	Medical service and health insurance	6	20	9.4	122	312	23,508	31,295	2,747	11,420	2.3
6330	Fire, marine, and casualty insurance	97	99	7.6	802	727	49,965	54,960	37,748	38,371	4.5
6360	Title insurance	20	18	7.3	200	159	38,680	43,321	5,972	5,367	7.4
6400	Insurance agents, brokers, and service	676	692	8.8	3,558	3,549	37,641	36,612	131,804	133,274	9.7
6500	Real estate	1,934	1,971	9.9	11,757	12,184	20,680	21,532	268,617	283,362	11.9
6510	Real estate operators and lessors	491	488	7.7	2,314	2,333	18,209	20,048	47,621	50,075	9.2
6530	Real estate agents and managers	1,234	1,246	11.3	8,189	8,545	19,708	21,449	174,230	195,675	14.1

Source: County Business Patterns, 1994/95, CBP-94/95, U.S. Department of Commerce, Washington, D.C., November 1997. SIC categories for which data were suppressed or not available for both 1994 and 1995 are not displayed. The employment columns represent mid-March employment in the year. Pay per employee is calculated by dividing 1st Quarter payroll, annualized, by mid-March employment. The columns headed "% State" show the county's percentage of the state total for the SIC in 1995; for example, 1.4% for SIC 6000 means that the county had 1.4 percent of the state's total establishments (or payroll) in SIC 6000 in 1995. A dash (-) is used to indicate that data are not available or cannot be calculated; nec means not elsewhere classified.

Continued on next page.

SIC	Industry	No. Establishments			Employment		Pay / Employee		Annual Payroll ($ 000)		
		1994	1995	% State	1994	1995	1994	1995	1994	1995	% State
PALM BEACH, FL - [continued]											
6540	Title abstract offices	28	25	8.0	167	123	29,796	26,634	4,462	3,551	7.2
6550	Subdividers and developers	114	111	8.6	991	1,051	33,401	25,819	39,326	30,539	8.7
6552	Subdividers and developers, n.e.c.	100	95	9.6	763	796	39,371	30,070	35,360	26,779	10.0
6553	Cemetery subdividers and developers	10	11	5.8	226	249	13,451	12,707	3,828	3,528	4.8
6700	Holding and other investment offices	193	191	14.8	1,280	902	71,503	63,996	81,132	52,369	11.4
6710	Holding offices	55	56	13.5	737	468	94,828	83,675	57,061	30,844	11.1
6720	Investment offices	7	8	22.2	16	37	34,750	40,757	1,617	2,328	13.4
6730	Trusts	37	35	14.8	221	115	35,710	38,783	7,421	3,870	12.5
6732	Educational, religious, etc. trusts	16	13	14.0	138	55	20,725	20,291	3,174	1,101	8.1
6733	Trusts, n.e.c.	21	21	14.9	83	57	60,627	51,228	4,247	2,390	14.0
6790	Miscellaneous investing	79	76	15.6	278	256	45,439	43,688	13,637	13,490	11.4
6794	Patent owners and lessors	14	14	14.9	107	86	24,336	30,000	2,996	2,641	5.3
6799	Investors, n.e.c.	57	54	16.0	158	156	59,519	50,718	9,925	10,032	16.8
PASCO, FL											
60 –	**Finance, insurance, and real estate**	528	554	1.3	2,903	2,811	21,831	22,171	63,320	62,791	0.5
6000	Depository institutions	109	106	1.9	1,111	1,066	21,239	22,394	22,776	22,680	0.8
6020	Commercial banks	85	85	2.3	939	922	21,896	23,015	19,632	19,443	0.9
6030	Savings institutions	21	17	2.0	145	114	17,545	17,825	2,588	2,557	0.7
6060	Credit unions	3	4	0.7	27	30	18,222	20,667	556	680	0.4
6100	Nondepository institutions	24	28	0.9	93	87	26,796	25,103	2,910	2,660	0.3
6140	Personal credit institutions	9	13	1.4	38	50	22,316	23,680	980	1,230	0.4
6160	Mortgage bankers and brokers	13	13	0.8	51	32	30,431	28,250	1,836	1,312	0.3
6200	Security and commodity brokers	26	27	1.1	185	180	54,724	49,111	9,738	8,578	0.6
6210	Security brokers and dealers	21	20	1.3	175	168	57,234	51,786	9,443	8,357	0.7
6280	Security and commodity services	5	7	0.8	10	12	10,800	11,667	295	221	0.1
6300	Insurance carriers	26	27	1.0	150	150	45,547	45,120	6,341	6,617	0.3
6400	Insurance agents, brokers, and service	102	101	1.3	345	343	19,270	20,222	6,997	8,055	0.6
6500	Real estate	232	256	1.3	997	959	13,380	13,898	14,169	13,854	0.6
6510	Real estate operators and lessors	96	103	1.6	403	374	11,831	12,310	5,243	4,842	0.9
6530	Real estate agents and managers	105	110	1.0	352	341	14,091	14,592	5,127	4,910	0.4
6540	Title abstract offices	5	9	2.9	30	36	19,200	16,444	647	645	1.3
6550	Subdividers and developers	22	24	1.9	209	197	14,431	15,289	3,109	3,225	0.9
6552	Subdividers and developers, n.e.c.	17	19	1.9	69	88	19,536	14,864	1,313	1,271	0.5
6553	Cemetery subdividers and developers	4	4	2.1	140	109	11,914	15,633	1,773	1,946	2.6
6700	Holding and other investment offices	9	9	0.7	22	26	15,636	15,231	389	347	0.1
6790	Miscellaneous investing	6	5	1.0	19	22	14,947	16,182	331	311	0.3
PINELLAS, FL											
60 –	**Finance, insurance, and real estate**	2,859	2,870	6.7	26,377	25,195	26,606	29,879	718,853	756,525	6.3
6000	Depository institutions	390	393	7.2	5,481	5,221	23,732	24,418	125,625	126,602	4.4
6020	Commercial banks	263	295	8.0	3,852	4,272	23,753	24,753	86,346	103,830	5.1
6030	Savings institutions	85	54	6.2	1,286	516	24,678	24,000	31,697	13,015	3.8
6060	Credit unions	29	28	5.1	256	255	18,063	21,882	5,082	5,441	3.0
6100	Nondepository institutions	187	193	6.5	2,154	1,404	22,669	30,726	47,759	49,921	5.0
6140	Personal credit institutions	54	57	6.2	828	381	9,116	25,113	8,496	10,313	3.1
6150	Business credit institutions	15	15	5.9	89	121	32,180	37,587	4,484	5,309	2.3
6160	Mortgage bankers and brokers	114	113	6.7	1,235	897	31,087	32,205	34,701	34,106	8.4
6200	Security and commodity brokers	177	175	7.1	3,249	3,542	52,751	51,818	170,457	191,067	13.1
6210	Security brokers and dealers	108	112	7.3	2,921	3,249	51,360	52,553	148,061	176,745	14.1
6280	Security and commodity services	67	60	7.1	324	288	65,346	43,694	22,038	13,785	7.6
6300	Insurance carriers	187	178	6.7	3,150	3,205	30,530	30,182	93,331	96,365	4.2
6310	Life insurance	29	28	3.9	923	975	29,521	23,569	25,141	22,232	2.6
6320	Medical service and health insurance	7	7	3.3	76	91	30,789	27,341	2,366	3,459	0.7
6330	Fire, marine, and casualty insurance	111	116	8.9	1,737	1,869	31,691	34,440	55,825	63,993	7.5
6360	Title insurance	19	15	6.1	287	195	26,997	23,610	6,466	4,301	6.0
6400	Insurance agents, brokers, and service	577	577	7.3	3,715	3,205	22,892	28,351	93,510	98,474	7.2
6500	Real estate	1,254	1,265	6.4	7,645	7,537	15,745	16,714	126,426	132,498	5.6

Source: County Business Patterns, 1994/95, CBP-94/95, U.S. Department of Commerce, Washington, D.C., November 1997. SIC categories for which data were suppressed or not available for both 1994 and 1995 are not displayed. The employment columns represent mid-March employment in the year. Pay per employee is calculated by dividing 1st Quarter payroll, annualized, by mid-March employment. The columns headed "% State" show the county's percentage of the state total for the SIC in 1995; for example, 1.4% for SIC 6000 means that the county had 1.4 percent of the state's total establishments (or payroll) in SIC 6000 in 1995. A dash (-) is used to indicate that data are not available or cannot be calculated; nec means not elsewhere classified.

Continued on next page.

SIC	Industry	No. Establishments			Employment		Pay / Employee		Annual Payroll ($ 000)		
		1994	1995	% State	1994	1995	1994	1995	1994	1995	% State
PINELLAS, FL - [continued]											
6510	Real estate operators and lessors	471	447	7.1	2,866	2,924	13,839	14,858	40,476	43,962	8.1
6530	Real estate agents and managers	683	691	6.3	3,780	3,822	17,335	17,371	70,607	70,581	5.1
6540	Title abstract offices	14	8	2.6	57	38	18,596	15,684	995	633	1.3
6550	Subdividers and developers	53	61	4.7	915	682	15,025	20,804	13,783	15,352	4.4
6552	Subdividers and developers, n.e.c.	36	40	4.0	503	331	15,523	20,036	7,685	6,547	2.5
6553	Cemetery subdividers and developers	14	15	7.9	412	349	14,417	21,444	6,055	8,457	11.4
6700	Holding and other investment offices	81	84	6.5	807	961	57,710	85,249	58,208	58,763	12.8
6710	Holding offices	37	32	7.7	522	497	74,207	139,034	49,092	41,769	15.1
6733	Trusts, n.e.c.	14	12	8.5	79	75	26,734	30,400	2,158	2,321	13.6
6790	Miscellaneous investing	25	30	6.1	198	374	27,960	26,791	6,713	13,647	11.5
6799	Investors, n.e.c.	14	16	4.7	101	229	37,386	30,183	4,222	10,171	17.0
POLK, FL											
60 –	**Finance, insurance, and real estate**	885	905	2.1	9,385	8,974	26,974	30,217	244,700	267,305	2.2
6000	Depository institutions	146	142	2.6	2,163	2,050	20,401	23,709	44,374	45,620	1.6
6020	Commercial banks	104	103	2.8	1,616	1,675	21,032	23,833	33,622	36,865	1.8
6030	Savings institutions	19	9	1.0	381	187	18,068	24,749	7,239	4,988	1.5
6060	Credit unions	17	25	4.5	148	176	20,649	21,909	3,336	3,586	2.0
6090	Functions closely related to banking	6	5	1.6	18	12	11,111	16,667	177	181	0.1
6100	Nondepository institutions	60	69	2.3	288	246	24,778	26,683	6,927	6,984	0.7
6140	Personal credit institutions	31	38	4.1	121	151	24,793	25,033	3,283	3,913	1.2
6160	Mortgage bankers and brokers	23	25	1.5	137	69	23,241	25,043	2,546	2,009	0.5
6200	Security and commodity brokers	35	39	1.6	208	202	69,673	71,050	11,633	11,661	0.8
6210	Security brokers and dealers	24	25	1.6	189	179	75,175	77,296	11,245	11,044	0.9
6280	Security and commodity services	11	14	1.7	19	23	14,947	22,435	388	617	0.3
6300	Insurance carriers	68	68	2.6	3,481	3,021	35,759	43,636	114,870	124,271	5.4
6310	Life insurance	21	21	2.9	410	407	28,029	27,361	10,763	10,077	1.2
6400	Insurance agents, brokers, and service	192	194	2.5	1,358	1,431	23,853	26,460	34,721	45,369	3.3
6500	Real estate	368	374	1.9	1,867	1,960	15,916	15,755	31,446	31,475	1.3
6510	Real estate operators and lessors	181	178	2.8	858	934	14,895	14,330	13,281	13,774	2.5
6530	Real estate agents and managers	143	144	1.3	479	454	17,002	17,154	8,941	8,168	0.6
6540	Title abstract offices	7	6	1.9	44	32	27,364	28,250	1,075	806	1.6
6550	Subdividers and developers	29	29	2.2	480	534	15,658	16,307	8,048	8,518	2.4
6552	Subdividers and developers, n.e.c.	24	23	2.3	413	470	15,603	15,523	6,875	7,059	2.6
6553	Cemetery subdividers and developers	3	3	1.6	63	60	15,619	22,267	1,087	1,384	1.9
6730	Trusts	5	6	2.5	4	32	32,000	15,375	141	1,171	3.8
6790	Miscellaneous investing	6	6	1.2	14	11	41,429	13,818	401	174	0.1
6799	Investors, n.e.c.	6	6	1.8	14	11	41,429	13,818	401	174	0.3
PUTNAM, FL											
60 –	**Finance, insurance, and real estate**	99	96	0.2	473	487	17,548	20,263	9,110	10,341	0.1
6000	Depository institutions	20	19	0.3	261	247	19,372	21,409	5,306	5,272	0.2
6020	Commercial banks	13	12	0.3	133	121	19,519	22,942	2,613	2,553	0.1
6100	Nondepository institutions	10	7	0.2	27	27	26,074	25,333	600	633	0.1
6400	Insurance agents, brokers, and service	29	31	0.4	99	115	13,657	19,409	1,641	3,002	0.2
6500	Real estate	35	36	0.2	76	89	9,895	14,966	1,161	1,059	0.0
6530	Real estate agents and managers	16	15	0.1	26	41	8,154	8,585	456	343	0.0
6550	Subdividers and developers	4	4	0.3	10	10	9,600	48,400	223	220	0.1
ST. JOHNS, FL											
60 –	**Finance, insurance, and real estate**	264	287	0.7	1,345	1,513	25,448	27,551	33,593	40,692	0.3
6000	Depository institutions	29	29	0.5	402	395	22,010	23,514	8,604	8,918	0.3
6100	Nondepository institutions	10	11	0.4	19	24	16,632	22,333	286	894	0.1
6200	Security and commodity brokers	14	19	0.8	98	111	92,286	83,820	8,035	9,790	0.7
6300	Insurance carriers	13	12	0.5	81	42	26,568	36,952	1,808	1,690	0.1
6310	Life insurance	4	3	0.4	25	18	16,000	19,556	408	427	0.1
6400	Insurance agents, brokers, and service	40	43	0.5	123	188	28,911	28,936	3,476	4,701	0.3
6500	Real estate	150	165	0.8	612	733	16,359	15,825	11,073	12,426	0.5

Source: County Business Patterns, 1994/95, CBP-94/95, U.S. Department of Commerce, Washington, D.C., November 1997. SIC categories for which data were suppressed or not available for both 1994 and 1995 are not displayed. The employment columns represent mid-March employment in the year. Pay per employee is calculated by dividing 1st Quarter payroll, annualized, by mid-March employment. The columns headed "% State" show the county's percentage of the state total for the SIC in 1995; for example, 1.4% for SIC 6000 means that the county had 1.4 percent of the state's total establishments (or payroll) in SIC 6000 in 1995. A dash (-) is used to indicate that data are not available or cannot be calculated; nec means not elsewhere classified.

Continued on next page.

SIC	Industry	No. Establishments			Employment		Pay / Employee		Annual Payroll ($ 000)		
		1994	1995	% State	1994	1995	1994	1995	1994	1995	% State
ST. JOHNS, FL - [continued]											
6510	Real estate operators and lessors	32	36	0.6	148	196	15,378	13,980	2,487	2,813	0.5
6530	Real estate agents and managers	100	107	1.0	375	426	16,256	15,878	6,743	7,332	0.5
6550	Subdividers and developers	10	13	1.0	81	90	18,716	19,467	1,586	1,904	0.5
6700	Holding and other investment offices	8	8	0.6	10	20	30,000	198,200	311	2,273	0.5
ST. LUCIE, FL											
60 –	**Finance, insurance, and real estate**	324	324	0.8	2,468	2,309	22,579	25,072	56,264	55,221	0.5
6000	Depository institutions	50	50	0.9	1,079	935	22,943	27,470	24,255	23,707	0.8
6020	Commercial banks	31	32	0.9	728	690	24,016	27,559	16,748	17,080	0.8
6030	Savings institutions	15	15	1.7	326	224	21,387	28,339	7,181	6,278	1.8
6100	Nondepository institutions	24	27	0.9	150	141	20,933	23,348	3,187	3,819	0.4
6160	Mortgage bankers and brokers	12	13	0.8	104	89	20,192	22,831	2,150	2,538	0.6
6200	Security and commodity brokers	7	8	0.3	27	31	65,185	46,452	1,425	1,388	0.1
6300	Insurance carriers	26	26	1.0	172	116	33,372	47,069	5,779	4,730	0.2
6310	Life insurance	6	8	1.1	84	73	33,238	36,548	2,700	2,121	0.3
6400	Insurance agents, brokers, and service	74	72	0.9	215	281	20,316	21,751	4,736	5,961	0.4
6500	Real estate	134	133	0.7	783	766	17,997	18,601	14,303	13,313	0.6
6510	Real estate operators and lessors	40	37	0.6	319	352	14,834	17,170	5,342	5,910	1.1
6530	Real estate agents and managers	83	84	0.8	390	364	19,149	18,791	7,481	6,170	0.4
6700	Holding and other investment offices	9	8	0.6	42	39	44,476	42,462	2,579	2,303	0.5
SANTA ROSA, FL											
60 –	**Finance, insurance, and real estate**	157	154	0.4	635	683	17,480	17,757	11,861	12,685	0.1
6000	Depository institutions	26	28	0.5	263	285	18,160	19,565	5,100	5,750	0.2
6020	Commercial banks	22	22	0.6	240	252	17,983	19,635	4,618	4,944	0.2
6060	Credit unions	4	6	1.1	23	33	20,000	19,030	482	806	0.4
6300	Insurance carriers	8	10	0.4	9	10	51,556	97,600	637	832	0.0
6400	Insurance agents, brokers, and service	28	24	0.3	82	70	19,512	18,629	1,679	1,448	0.1
6500	Real estate	83	80	0.4	249	287	14,297	12,613	3,833	3,977	0.2
6530	Real estate agents and managers	46	43	0.4	133	114	14,466	12,246	1,683	1,562	0.1
6550	Subdividers and developers	13	12	0.9	66	76	13,091	14,526	1,098	1,166	0.3
6552	Subdividers and developers, n.e.c.	10	10	1.0	65	73	13,169	13,918	1,066	1,110	0.4
SARASOTA, FL											
60 –	**Finance, insurance, and real estate**	1,258	1,290	3.0	8,026	7,992	29,987	31,695	232,561	246,355	2.1
6000	Depository institutions	179	176	3.2	2,551	2,416	27,923	29,801	63,426	68,447	2.4
6020	Commercial banks	124	123	3.3	2,075	2,032	28,767	29,929	51,667	55,505	2.7
6030	Savings institutions	43	39	4.5	371	273	25,574	31,018	9,540	10,187	3.0
6060	Credit unions	6	7	1.3	85	92	19,059	22,696	1,794	2,136	1.2
6090	Functions closely related to banking	6	7	2.3	20	19	21,600	33,053	425	619	0.4
6100	Nondepository institutions	68	68	2.3	268	201	24,866	24,100	6,600	5,794	0.6
6160	Mortgage bankers and brokers	49	44	2.6	175	135	28,000	24,652	4,680	4,183	1.0
6200	Security and commodity brokers	101	101	4.1	882	795	63,955	62,636	49,722	44,951	3.1
6210	Security brokers and dealers	63	62	4.0	782	705	67,673	66,270	45,922	41,975	3.4
6280	Security and commodity services	38	37	4.4	100	90	34,880	34,178	3,800	2,935	1.6
6300	Insurance carriers	74	74	2.8	619	474	36,407	41,899	22,026	19,397	0.8
6310	Life insurance	14	12	1.7	294	217	31,946	33,401	8,742	6,819	0.8
6330	Fire, marine, and casualty insurance	41	43	3.3	184	148	51,087	60,811	9,668	9,118	1.1
6360	Title insurance	9	10	4.1	97	61	24,165	28,000	1,990	1,632	2.3
6400	Insurance agents, brokers, and service	188	201	2.6	1,072	1,303	34,907	41,455	41,106	53,254	3.9
6500	Real estate	605	624	3.1	2,554	2,718	17,532	18,502	47,386	50,985	2.1
6510	Real estate operators and lessors	136	134	2.1	749	705	14,959	14,423	10,601	10,939	2.0
6530	Real estate agents and managers	405	407	3.7	1,526	1,602	17,785	18,944	29,835	29,877	2.1
6540	Title abstract offices	8	8	2.6	33	32	26,061	26,875	855	820	1.7
6550	Subdividers and developers	38	45	3.5	243	329	22,831	24,912	5,780	8,448	2.4
6552	Subdividers and developers, n.e.c.	31	33	3.3	138	223	27,246	26,404	3,820	5,977	2.2
6553	Cemetery subdividers and developers	5	5	2.6	105	104	17,029	21,885	1,940	2,080	2.8
6710	Holding offices	10	13	3.1	18	24	23,556	51,167	407	1,494	0.5

Source: County Business Patterns, 1994/95, CBP-94/95, U.S. Department of Commerce, Washington, D.C., November 1997. SIC categories for which data were suppressed or not available for both 1994 and 1995 are not displayed. The employment columns represent mid-March employment in the year. Pay per employee is calculated by dividing 1st Quarter payroll, annualized, by mid-March employment. The columns headed "% State" show the county's percentage of the state total for the SIC in 1995; for example, 1.4% for SIC 6000 means that the county had 1.4 percent of the state's total establishments (or payroll) in SIC 6000 in 1995. A dash (-) is used to indicate that data are not available or cannot be calculated; nec means not elsewhere classified.

Continued on next page.

SIC	Industry	No. Establishments			Employment		Pay / Employee		Annual Payroll ($ 000)		
		1994	1995	% State	1994	1995	1994	1995	1994	1995	% State
SARASOTA, FL - [continued]											
6730	Trusts	11	12	5.1	20	24	24,600	21,333	721	864	2.8
6733	Trusts, n.e.c.	11	12	8.5	20	24	24,600	21,333	721	864	5.1
6790	Miscellaneous investing	14	9	1.8	38	24	15,368	17,500	873	537	0.5
SEMINOLE, FL											
60 –	**Finance, insurance, and real estate**	923	972	2.3	5,994	6,352	25,937	27,193	169,867	181,314	1.5
6000	Depository institutions	102	103	1.9	1,227	1,310	23,123	23,304	28,701	31,368	1.1
6020	Commercial banks	64	72	2.0	853	912	23,489	22,390	18,848	20,805	1.0
6030	Savings institutions	19	14	1.6	282	303	23,773	27,459	8,069	8,617	2.5
6060	Credit unions	10	10	1.8	70	75	18,343	20,000	1,492	1,657	0.9
6090	Functions closely related to banking	9	7	2.3	22	20	15,818	14,400	292	289	0.2
6100	Nondepository institutions	110	120	4.0	651	565	29,382	31,802	16,971	18,771	1.9
6140	Personal credit institutions	25	27	2.9	144	146	30,000	32,247	3,778	4,297	1.3
6160	Mortgage bankers and brokers	80	86	5.1	497	413	28,877	31,496	12,710	14,098	3.5
6280	Security and commodity services	21	24	2.8	73	76	15,781	20,632	1,634	3,320	1.8
6300	Insurance carriers	82	84	3.2	792	933	38,641	35,871	28,708	33,720	1.5
6310	Life insurance	19	24	3.3	228	232	32,632	33,793	7,161	7,773	0.9
6330	Fire, marine, and casualty insurance	42	39	3.0	420	344	45,686	48,826	17,999	16,128	1.9
6360	Title insurance	12	9	3.7	76	43	25,842	26,791	1,725	1,308	1.8
6400	Insurance agents, brokers, and service	207	228	2.9	1,460	1,716	27,118	29,807	55,533	53,076	3.9
6500	Real estate	361	370	1.9	1,553	1,539	18,689	18,984	30,546	32,171	1.4
6510	Real estate operators and lessors	92	88	1.4	495	408	11,814	12,216	6,079	6,361	1.2
6530	Real estate agents and managers	216	227	2.1	855	940	21,464	20,813	19,371	20,300	1.5
6540	Title abstract offices	10	8	2.6	46	43	23,565	23,628	1,075	1,106	2.2
6550	Subdividers and developers	26	26	2.0	138	94	24,783	31,234	3,596	3,483	1.0
6700	Holding and other investment offices	22	19	1.5	167	101	21,389	39,960	4,709	4,255	0.9
6710	Holding offices	5	4	1.0	80	58	11,200	11,310	746	522	0.2
6790	Miscellaneous investing	13	10	2.0	54	38	42,963	87,158	3,506	3,636	3.1
SUMTER, FL											
60 –	**Finance, insurance, and real estate**	34	28	0.1	136	129	15,353	16,930	2,159	2,354	0.0
6000	Depository institutions	6	6	0.1	56	54	16,643	17,407	960	954	0.0
6500	Real estate	17	14	0.1	45	39	9,778	12,000	444	569	0.0
6510	Real estate operators and lessors	10	10	0.2	33	31	9,939	11,226	315	432	0.1
SUWANNEE, FL											
60 –	**Finance, insurance, and real estate**	37	45	0.1	230	255	20,870	21,553	4,397	5,046	0.0
6000	Depository institutions	6	6	0.1	107	114	26,206	29,193	2,257	2,664	0.1
6400	Insurance agents, brokers, and service	11	14	0.2	42	49	18,381	16,571	914	1,018	0.1
6500	Real estate	15	19	0.1	50	64	10,000	9,063	518	551	0.0
6510	Real estate operators and lessors	5	5	0.1	31	43	6,194	4,744	191	212	0.0
6530	Real estate agents and managers	6	10	0.1	12	14	16,333	18,286	214	230	0.0
TAYLOR, FL											
60 –	**Finance, insurance, and real estate**	24	24	0.1	194	204	15,918	17,804	3,703	3,763	0.0
6000	Depository institutions	6	6	0.1	138	143	17,536	20,028	2,704	2,990	0.1
6500	Real estate	8	8	0.0	27	28	12,741	13,857	576	416	0.0
6530	Real estate agents and managers	4	4	0.0	10	12	13,600	12,000	183	156	0.0
VOLUSIA, FL											
60 –	**Finance, insurance, and real estate**	1,044	1,062	2.5	6,442	6,532	22,873	22,773	145,535	150,205	1.3
6000	Depository institutions	139	144	2.6	1,830	1,834	26,264	25,511	44,793	45,006	1.6
6020	Commercial banks	120	119	3.2	1,699	1,648	25,782	24,893	39,749	39,182	1.9
6030	Savings institutions	14	13	1.5	121	132	34,050	35,606	4,842	4,681	1.4
6100	Nondepository institutions	62	62	2.1	363	321	24,595	22,268	8,198	7,938	0.8
6160	Mortgage bankers and brokers	32	30	1.8	214	136	27,271	21,971	4,518	3,687	0.9
6200	Security and commodity brokers	36	37	1.5	223	230	50,135	46,157	10,524	11,354	0.8
6210	Security brokers and dealers	21	24	1.6	197	199	53,706	50,171	9,946	10,330	0.8

Source: County Business Patterns, 1994/95, CBP-94/95, U.S. Department of Commerce, Washington, D.C., November 1997. SIC categories for which data were suppressed or not available for both 1994 and 1995 are *not* displayed. The employment columns represent mid-March employment in the year. Pay per employee is calculated by dividing 1st Quarter payroll, annualized, by mid-March employment. The columns headed "% State" show the county's percentage of the state total for the SIC in 1995; for example, 1.4% for SIC 6000 means that the county had 1.4 percent of the state's total establishments (or payroll) in SIC 6000 in 1995. A dash (-) is used to indicate that data are not available or cannot be calculated; *nec* means not elsewhere classified.

Continued on next page.

SIC	Industry	No. Establishments			Employment		Pay / Employee		Annual Payroll ($ 000)		
		1994	1995	% State	1994	1995	1994	1995	1994	1995	% State
VOLUSIA, FL - [continued]											
6280	Security and commodity services	15	13	1.5	26	31	23,077	20,387	578	1,024	0.6
6300	Insurance carriers	67	71	2.7	511	559	34,387	34,605	17,626	19,960	0.9
6310	Life insurance	14	14	1.9	186	173	27,333	28,023	4,615	4,267	0.5
6320	Medical service and health insurance	10	13	6.1	126	162	39,937	34,790	5,178	6,612	1.4
6330	Fire, marine, and casualty insurance	33	34	2.6	167	182	39,808	44,593	7,148	8,229	1.0
6360	Title insurance	10	10	4.1	32	42	25,250	17,714	685	852	1.2
6400	Insurance agents, brokers, and service	178	180	2.3	877	888	31,818	31,653	27,815	26,406	1.9
6500	Real estate	551	558	2.8	2,592	2,658	12,801	13,691	36,089	39,151	1.7
6510	Real estate operators and lessors	172	172	2.7	923	866	11,276	12,000	10,909	10,969	2.0
6530	Real estate agents and managers	333	328	3.0	1,437	1,447	12,699	13,932	20,211	21,616	1.6
6540	Title abstract offices	5	6	1.9	51	46	25,725	27,217	1,247	1,218	2.5
6550	Subdividers and developers	33	38	2.9	174	275	17,540	15,156	3,468	4,860	1.4
6552	Subdividers and developers, n.e.c.	20	21	2.1	52	127	25,231	15,591	1,576	1,898	0.7
6553	Cemetery subdividers and developers	12	15	7.9	122	147	14,262	14,667	1,877	2,920	3.9
6700	Holding and other investment offices	11	10	0.8	46	42	11,304	8,571	490	390	0.1
WAKULLA, FL											
60 –	**Finance, insurance, and real estate**	21	20	0.0	114	116	17,263	18,966	2,041	2,309	0.0
6000	Depository institutions	4	4	0.1	66	76	20,485	20,842	1,382	1,662	0.1
6500	Real estate	11	9	0.0	36	27	11,667	13,778	447	396	0.0
WALTON, FL											
60 –	**Finance, insurance, and real estate**	71	73	0.2	526	645	14,981	15,560	8,931	11,966	0.1
6000	Depository institutions	9	10	0.2	93	99	17,419	19,232	1,547	1,927	0.1
6400	Insurance agents, brokers, and service	6	6	0.1	22	18	14,545	17,778	354	323	0.0
6500	Real estate	51	52	0.3	399	517	12,441	14,190	5,890	9,013	0.4
6510	Real estate operators and lessors	10	8	0.1	20	23	12,000	13,043	298	321	0.1
6530	Real estate agents and managers	37	37	0.3	358	443	12,201	13,535	5,181	7,134	0.5
6550	Subdividers and developers	4	6	0.5	21	51	16,952	20,392	411	1,537	0.4
6552	Subdividers and developers, n.e.c.	4	5	0.5	21	49	16,952	20,898	411	1,523	0.6
WASHINGTON, FL											
60 –	**Finance, insurance, and real estate**	19	23	0.1	71	68	18,197	20,765	1,432	1,611	0.0
6000	Depository institutions	4	4	0.1	31	32	18,839	20,125	596	615	0.0
6500	Real estate	7	10	0.1	18	14	13,333	14,000	332	445	0.0

Source: County Business Patterns, 1994/95, CBP-94/95, U.S. Department of Commerce, Washington, D.C., November 1997. SIC categories for which data were suppressed or not available for both 1994 and 1995 are *not* displayed. The employment columns represent mid-March employment in the year. Pay per employee is calculated by dividing 1st Quarter payroll, annualized, by mid-March employment. The columns headed "% State" show the county's percentage of the state total for the SIC in 1995; for example, 1.4% for SIC 6000 means that the county had 1.4 percent of the state's total establishments (or payroll) in SIC 6000 in 1995. A dash (-) is used to indicate that data are not available or cannot be calculated; nec means not elsewhere classified.

GEORGIA

SIC	Industry	No. Establishments			Employment		Pay / Employee		Annual Payroll ($ 000)		
		1994	1995	% State	1994	1995	1994	1995	1994	1995	% State
APPLING, GA											
60 –	**Finance, insurance, and real estate**	18	19	0.1	111	123	21,514	21,626	2,428	2,627	0.0
6000	Depository institutions	3	3	0.1	72	87	24,111	21,011	1,774	1,851	0.1
6400	Insurance agents, brokers, and service	7	8	0.2	18	14	10,222	13,429	214	192	0.0
BACON, GA											
60 –	**Finance, insurance, and real estate**	15	13	0.1	99	112	20,646	20,607	2,122	2,265	0.0
6000	Depository institutions	3	3	0.1	69	87	22,667	21,011	1,656	1,811	0.1
6400	Insurance agents, brokers, and service	5	4	0.1	13	10	11,692	17,200	171	173	0.0
BAKER, GA											
60 –	**Finance, insurance, and real estate**	1	1	0.0	-	-	-	-	-	-	-
BALDWIN, GA											
60 –	**Finance, insurance, and real estate**	61	63	0.4	394	368	21,340	23,337	8,446	8,464	0.1
6000	Depository institutions	12	12	0.5	248	228	22,532	25,263	5,635	5,553	0.4
6020	Commercial banks	8	8	0.4	228	207	22,842	25,874	5,225	5,095	0.4
6100	Nondepository institutions	15	13	0.6	51	49	20,471	22,694	1,040	1,093	0.2
6400	Insurance agents, brokers, and service	12	14	0.4	42	43	14,952	15,349	689	694	0.1
6500	Real estate	14	15	0.3	40	31	12,600	13,935	512	513	0.1
6530	Real estate agents and managers	5	5	0.2	16	14	12,250	11,714	207	224	0.0
BANKS, GA											
60 –	**Finance, insurance, and real estate**	3	3	0.0	-	-	-	-	-	-	-
BARROW, GA											
60 –	**Finance, insurance, and real estate**	41	43	0.3	275	268	22,415	21,821	6,185	6,183	0.1
6000	Depository institutions	7	6	0.2	184	174	19,370	21,264	3,704	3,989	0.3
6100	Nondepository institutions	9	9	0.4	36	28	37,778	25,286	1,127	728	0.1
6400	Insurance agents, brokers, and service	9	8	0.2	28	31	22,143	23,613	651	682	0.1
6500	Real estate	13	17	0.3	23	30	15,130	14,000	414	463	0.0
6550	Subdividers and developers	3	5	0.9	3	7	29,333	15,429	100	96	0.1
BARTOW, GA											
60 –	**Finance, insurance, and real estate**	99	105	0.6	459	508	21,935	21,283	10,985	11,525	0.2
6000	Depository institutions	15	15	0.6	226	223	20,991	22,135	5,037	5,222	0.4
6020	Commercial banks	10	10	0.5	208	208	20,808	22,404	4,645	4,850	0.4
6100	Nondepository institutions	18	18	0.8	64	51	26,688	26,196	1,833	1,231	0.2
6300	Insurance carriers	8	7	0.6	18	32	46,000	40,500	1,002	1,206	0.1
6400	Insurance agents, brokers, and service	23	21	0.6	58	63	21,034	22,159	1,358	1,461	0.2
6500	Real estate	29	36	0.6	65	66	16,554	14,970	1,161	1,329	0.1
6510	Real estate operators and lessors	9	9	0.5	22	17	15,273	17,882	382	405	0.2
6550	Subdividers and developers	3	5	0.9	7	8	11,429	8,500	97	284	0.3
BEN HILL, GA											
60 –	**Finance, insurance, and real estate**	40	45	0.3	246	253	19,984	21,787	5,427	5,704	0.1
6000	Depository institutions	6	6	0.2	83	87	23,133	25,195	1,947	2,148	0.2
6100	Nondepository institutions	8	8	0.4	33	34	16,606	18,118	609	630	0.1
6400	Insurance agents, brokers, and service	11	15	0.4	26	33	14,462	21,939	511	721	0.1
6500	Real estate	10	11	0.2	48	40	15,000	12,400	849	519	0.1
BERRIEN, GA											
60 –	**Finance, insurance, and real estate**	28	28	0.2	186	210	23,914	24,629	4,869	5,338	0.1

Source: County Business Patterns, 1994/95, CBP-94/95, U.S. Department of Commerce, Washington, D.C., November 1997. SIC categories for which data were suppressed or not available for both 1994 and 1995 are not displayed. The employment columns represent mid-March employment in the year. Pay per employee is calculated by dividing 1st Quarter payroll, annualized, by mid-March employment. The columns headed "% State" show the county's percentage of the state total for the SIC in 1995; for example, 1.4% for SIC 6000 means that the county had 1.4 percent of the state's total establishments (or payroll) in SIC 6000 in 1995. A dash (-) is used to indicate that data are not available or cannot be calculated; nec means not elsewhere classified.

Continued on next page.

SIC	Industry	No. Establishments			Employment		Pay / Employee		Annual Payroll ($ 000)		
		1994	1995	% State	1994	1995	1994	1995	1994	1995	% State
BERRIEN, GA - [continued]											
6000	Depository institutions	10	10	0.4	88	87	18,500	18,345	1,825	1,791	0.1
6020	Commercial banks	7	7	0.4	79	77	19,139	18,701	1,688	1,587	0.1
6400	Insurance agents, brokers, and service	5	5	0.1	12	15	24,333	32,533	392	453	0.1
6500	Real estate	3	3	0.1	3	3	8,000	16,000	46	42	0.0
BIBB, GA											
60 –	**Finance, insurance, and real estate**	446	462	2.8	7,186	7,394	28,611	29,878	199,130	211,052	3.5
6000	Depository institutions	74	73	2.9	1,279	1,258	24,500	27,288	28,049	29,448	2.1
6020	Commercial banks	49	47	2.5	1,038	1,019	24,740	27,949	22,123	23,013	1.9
6100	Nondepository institutions	62	71	3.3	767	783	26,060	26,529	20,803	23,709	4.1
6140	Personal credit institutions	48	51	4.4	220	233	23,709	25,717	5,443	5,958	3.0
6200	Security and commodity brokers	17	17	1.8	137	158	79,942	79,570	8,417	9,356	1.7
6210	Security brokers and dealers	13	13	2.3	130	143	83,292	86,881	8,302	9,186	2.0
6280	Security and commodity services	4	4	1.2	7	15	17,714	9,867	115	170	0.2
6300	Insurance carriers	49	49	4.1	3,779	3,900	31,276	32,515	114,452	119,824	8.1
6330	Fire, marine, and casualty insurance	22	23	3.9	3,204	3,374	31,287	32,567	97,212	104,476	14.9
6400	Insurance agents, brokers, and service	94	95	2.8	345	350	23,490	25,097	8,300	8,980	1.4
6500	Real estate	141	150	2.6	862	927	19,485	18,697	18,797	19,384	2.1
6510	Real estate operators and lessors	53	58	2.9	202	213	11,941	13,146	2,684	2,778	1.5
6530	Real estate agents and managers	68	69	2.3	571	595	20,862	21,089	12,461	13,280	2.1
6540	Title abstract offices	3	4	6.8	12	9	16,000	17,778	218	188	3.8
6550	Subdividers and developers	16	18	3.2	76	110	29,947	16,582	3,430	3,077	3.1
6552	Subdividers and developers, n.e.c.	11	14	3.6	42	53	22,000	18,642	1,930	1,937	2.6
6553	Cemetery subdividers and developers	5	4	3.3	34	57	39,765	14,667	1,500	1,140	5.8
6700	Holding and other investment offices	9	7	1.3	17	18	13,412	18,000	312	351	0.1
BLECKLEY, GA											
60 –	**Finance, insurance, and real estate**	13	13	0.1	79	80	20,000	20,750	1,551	1,581	0.0
6000	Depository institutions	3	3	0.1	56	56	21,786	23,214	1,183	1,225	0.1
6400	Insurance agents, brokers, and service	5	5	0.1	10	9	12,800	14,222	146	135	0.0
BRANTLEY, GA											
60 –	**Finance, insurance, and real estate**	5	5	0.0	32	28	17,250	18,000	504	459	0.0
BROOKS, GA											
60 –	**Finance, insurance, and real estate**	17	16	0.1	92	99	20,913	19,879	2,026	2,107	0.0
6000	Depository institutions	8	8	0.3	65	71	22,215	20,901	1,497	1,535	0.1
BRYAN, GA											
60 –	**Finance, insurance, and real estate**	23	22	0.1	120	146	21,667	28,658	2,781	3,667	0.1
6000	Depository institutions	4	4	0.2	79	99	19,291	20,364	1,667	2,007	0.1
6020	Commercial banks	4	4	0.2	79	99	19,291	20,364	1,667	2,007	0.2
BULLOCH, GA											
60 –	**Finance, insurance, and real estate**	81	83	0.5	636	624	22,050	24,423	14,241	14,790	0.2
6000	Depository institutions	16	16	0.6	244	299	22,443	23,264	5,248	6,707	0.5
6100	Nondepository institutions	15	15	0.7	86	85	21,907	27,388	2,039	2,296	0.4
6300	Insurance carriers	6	6	0.5	111	109	31,171	32,220	3,370	3,119	0.2
6500	Real estate	27	29	0.5	87	70	10,483	12,686	1,017	1,023	0.1
6530	Real estate agents and managers	19	18	0.6	52	62	13,385	13,548	781	911	0.1
BUTTS, GA											
60 –	**Finance, insurance, and real estate**	25	27	0.2	125	137	20,032	19,679	2,563	2,898	0.0
6500	Real estate	12	12	0.2	39	50	20,000	17,520	870	976	0.1
6510	Real estate operators and lessors	9	9	0.5	34	44	21,294	18,364	805	916	0.5
6530	Real estate agents and managers	3	3	0.1	5	6	11,200	11,333	65	60	0.0
CALHOUN, GA											
60 –	**Finance, insurance, and real estate**	8	7	0.0	54	36	21,481	28,222	1,005	863	0.0

Source: County Business Patterns, 1994/95, CBP-94/95, U.S. Department of Commerce, Washington, D.C., November 1997. SIC categories for which data were suppressed or not available for both 1994 and 1995 are not displayed. The employment columns represent mid-March employment in the year. Pay per employee is calculated by dividing 1st Quarter payroll, annualized, by mid-March employment. The columns headed "% State" show the county's percentage of the state total for the SIC in 1995; for example, 1.4% for SIC 6000 means that the county had 1.4 percent of the state's total establishments (or payroll) in SIC 6000 in 1995. A dash (-) is used to indicate that data are not available or cannot be calculated; nec means not elsewhere classified.

SIC	Industry	No. Establishments			Employment		Pay / Employee		Annual Payroll ($ 000)		
		1994	1995	% State	1994	1995	1994	1995	1994	1995	% State
CAMDEN, GA											
60–	**Finance, insurance, and real estate**	55	55	0.3	256	311	22,391	21,453	5,288	6,234	0.1
6000	Depository institutions	13	13	0.5	136	170	18,324	17,553	2,551	2,877	0.2
6400	Insurance agents, brokers, and service	10	11	0.3	25	27	12,320	11,111	310	336	0.1
6500	Real estate	25	22	0.4	65	53	12,308	12,981	798	858	0.1
6530	Real estate agents and managers	12	10	0.3	27	23	11,111	10,087	276	233	0.0
CANDLER, GA											
60–	**Finance, insurance, and real estate**	12	14	0.1	63	81	16,698	19,753	1,118	1,730	0.0
6400	Insurance agents, brokers, and service	4	4	0.1	12	13	13,667	14,154	150	153	0.0
CARROLL, GA											
60–	**Finance, insurance, and real estate**	133	142	0.9	993	1,017	21,539	23,088	22,293	23,432	0.4
6000	Depository institutions	31	32	1.3	565	580	20,949	22,828	12,001	13,209	0.9
6100	Nondepository institutions	24	29	1.3	85	86	21,647	22,791	2,091	2,121	0.4
6140	Personal credit institutions	19	22	1.9	73	77	20,712	21,766	1,792	1,797	0.9
6160	Mortgage bankers and brokers	3	4	0.6	9	5	25,333	27,200	202	201	0.1
6200	Security and commodity brokers	6	5	0.5	8	10	28,000	26,800	297	405	0.1
6300	Insurance carriers	8	10	0.8	99	86	32,848	34,651	3,391	2,810	0.2
6400	Insurance agents, brokers, and service	23	24	0.7	93	88	26,065	30,909	2,437	2,510	0.4
6500	Real estate	41	42	0.7	143	167	12,671	13,844	2,076	2,377	0.3
6510	Real estate operators and lessors	14	15	0.8	45	49	11,556	11,102	546	536	0.3
6530	Real estate agents and managers	23	21	0.7	76	97	14,105	15,093	1,277	1,454	0.2
6550	Subdividers and developers	4	4	0.7	22	21	10,000	14,476	253	361	0.4
CATOOSA, GA											
60–	**Finance, insurance, and real estate**	41	42	0.3	334	358	23,425	27,430	7,558	8,812	0.1
6000	Depository institutions	12	13	0.5	185	197	28,670	32,426	4,471	5,256	0.4
6400	Insurance agents, brokers, and service	9	9	0.3	32	27	15,750	18,815	507	513	0.1
6500	Real estate	15	16	0.3	77	69	10,286	12,464	892	932	0.1
6530	Real estate agents and managers	9	8	0.3	61	53	10,689	12,604	750	754	0.1
CHARLTON, GA											
60–	**Finance, insurance, and real estate**	8	7	0.0	48	42	16,583	17,143	824	683	0.0
6500	Real estate	3	3	0.1	9	10	6,222	9,600	107	72	0.0
CHATHAM, GA											
60–	**Finance, insurance, and real estate**	566	564	3.4	4,943	4,619	26,679	26,812	137,118	127,350	2.1
6000	Depository institutions	100	96	3.8	1,197	1,151	22,804	23,944	25,986	26,872	1.9
6020	Commercial banks	66	64	3.5	1,060	1,009	23,623	24,971	23,528	24,258	2.0
6100	Nondepository institutions	61	60	2.8	271	277	26,273	26,181	7,121	7,135	1.2
6140	Personal credit institutions	39	40	3.4	171	186	26,550	26,860	4,369	4,580	2.3
6200	Security and commodity brokers	31	31	3.4	254	260	57,039	57,369	15,787	15,793	2.8
6210	Security brokers and dealers	19	20	3.5	225	226	58,524	59,699	14,332	14,158	3.1
6280	Security and commodity services	12	11	3.3	29	34	45,517	41,882	1,455	1,635	1.5
6300	Insurance carriers	52	54	4.5	902	872	29,942	29,858	26,120	26,253	1.8
6310	Life insurance	20	21	4.8	439	390	28,118	29,754	12,428	11,747	2.0
6330	Fire, marine, and casualty insurance	23	24	4.1	428	429	31,103	29,212	12,270	12,562	1.8
6370	Pension, health, and welfare funds	4	5	8.5	6	11	15,333	20,000	97	217	0.5
6400	Insurance agents, brokers, and service	109	105	3.1	580	591	27,483	26,985	16,137	16,203	2.4
6500	Real estate	191	199	3.4	1,310	1,292	20,238	20,721	29,094	29,337	3.1
6510	Real estate operators and lessors	89	95	4.8	475	429	17,120	16,382	8,754	7,843	4.1
6530	Real estate agents and managers	85	83	2.8	648	678	18,451	19,705	14,251	15,499	2.5
6550	Subdividers and developers	13	14	2.5	184	180	34,609	35,067	6,024	5,878	5.9
6700	Holding and other investment offices	22	19	3.5	429	176	31,497	30,455	16,873	5,757	1.8

Source: County Business Patterns, 1994/95, CBP-94/95, U.S. Department of Commerce, Washington, D.C., November 1997. SIC categories for which data were suppressed or not available for both 1994 and 1995 are not displayed. The employment columns represent mid-March employment in the year. Pay per employee is calculated by dividing 1st Quarter payroll, annualized, by mid-March employment. The columns headed "% State" show the county's percentage of the state total for the SIC in 1995; for example, 1.4% for SIC 6000 means that the county had 1.4 percent of the state's total establishments (or payroll) in SIC 6000 in 1995. A dash (-) is used to indicate that data are not available or cannot be calculated; nec means not elsewhere classified.

Continued on next page.

SIC	Industry	No. Establishments			Employment		Pay / Employee		Annual Payroll ($ 000)		
		1994	1995	% State	1994	1995	1994	1995	1994	1995	% State
CHATHAM, GA - [continued]											
6710	Holding offices	12	9	3.9	385	102	32,623	40,706	15,829	4,594	2.0
6730	Trusts	5	5	4.5	16	21	13,500	11,619	235	284	1.6
6790	Miscellaneous investing	5	5	3.1	28	53	26,286	18,189	809	879	1.8
CHATTOOGA, GA											
60 –	**Finance, insurance, and real estate**	16	17	0.1	141	136	19,149	17,824	2,859	2,746	0.0
6000	Depository institutions	5	5	0.2	110	105	18,291	16,267	2,155	2,100	0.1
6020	Commercial banks	5	5	0.3	110	105	18,291	16,267	2,155	2,100	0.2
6400	Insurance agents, brokers, and service	6	7	0.2	18	18	22,000	26,222	378	390	0.1
CHEROKEE, GA											
60 –	**Finance, insurance, and real estate**	140	148	0.9	808	781	24,213	24,645	20,068	20,626	0.3
6000	Depository institutions	22	22	0.9	505	480	23,976	24,883	11,769	12,201	0.9
6100	Nondepository institutions	15	15	0.7	63	46	34,730	24,435	1,367	1,523	0.3
6160	Mortgage bankers and brokers	6	7	1.0	29	24	26,345	22,833	670	1,000	0.4
6200	Security and commodity brokers	4	6	0.7	7	7	17,714	21,714	127	234	0.0
6400	Insurance agents, brokers, and service	36	33	1.0	84	78	19,952	22,154	2,018	2,521	0.4
6500	Real estate	55	60	1.0	110	105	17,055	18,400	3,329	2,085	0.2
6510	Real estate operators and lessors	10	9	0.5	32	11	8,000	6,909	300	147	0.1
6530	Real estate agents and managers	31	35	1.2	48	46	17,583	16,000	895	944	0.1
6550	Subdividers and developers	14	14	2.5	30	48	25,867	23,333	2,134	961	1.0
6552	Subdividers and developers, n.e.c.	8	8	2.0	21	19	24,571	28,421	1,540	479	0.6
6553	Cemetery subdividers and developers	4	4	3.3	9	22	28,889	21,273	398	357	1.8
CLARKE, GA											
60 –	**Finance, insurance, and real estate**	274	298	1.8	1,793	1,778	25,836	26,531	44,346	46,306	0.8
6000	Depository institutions	39	42	1.7	575	605	23,910	25,269	13,119	13,829	1.0
6020	Commercial banks	30	31	1.7	529	557	24,439	25,975	12,217	12,878	1.1
6100	Nondepository institutions	30	34	1.6	152	166	29,132	26,699	3,699	4,222	0.7
6140	Personal credit institutions	18	20	1.7	103	123	24,466	25,984	2,463	2,998	1.5
6160	Mortgage bankers and brokers	12	13	1.9	49	43	38,939	28,744	1,236	1,213	0.5
6200	Security and commodity brokers	20	22	2.4	115	128	70,643	57,531	7,048	7,554	1.3
6210	Security brokers and dealers	10	12	2.1	89	99	84,809	68,687	6,466	6,956	1.5
6280	Security and commodity services	10	10	3.0	26	29	22,154	19,448	582	598	0.6
6300	Insurance carriers	22	23	1.9	285	271	32,786	34,834	8,989	8,789	0.6
6310	Life insurance	12	13	3.0	242	229	31,901	33,834	7,328	6,975	1.2
6400	Insurance agents, brokers, and service	48	47	1.4	210	216	22,076	21,981	5,035	5,203	0.8
6500	Real estate	109	125	2.1	352	367	13,125	14,474	5,080	6,102	0.6
6510	Real estate operators and lessors	46	53	2.7	160	174	11,625	12,000	2,040	2,446	1.3
6530	Real estate agents and managers	50	55	1.8	134	135	16,000	17,659	2,291	2,544	0.4
6550	Subdividers and developers	9	10	1.8	52	47	7,692	10,043	509	625	0.6
6700	Holding and other investment offices	6	5	0.9	104	25	13,692	23,520	1,376	607	0.2
CLAY, GA											
60 –	**Finance, insurance, and real estate**	2	2	0.0	-	-	-	-	-	-	-
CLAYTON, GA											
60 –	**Finance, insurance, and real estate**	291	304	1.8	1,694	1,752	24,989	23,943	46,125	43,458	0.7
6000	Depository institutions	58	58	2.3	648	637	24,827	24,063	15,347	14,603	1.0
6020	Commercial banks	40	41	2.2	480	467	26,533	26,321	11,772	11,505	1.0
6060	Credit unions	8	8	2.6	99	118	18,990	17,356	2,216	2,005	3.4
6100	Nondepository institutions	27	30	1.4	176	234	25,273	24,393	4,283	6,354	1.1
6200	Security and commodity brokers	6	8	0.9	16	10	25,250	27,600	453	303	0.1
6300	Insurance carriers	17	20	1.7	116	121	42,552	45,223	4,872	5,420	0.4
6400	Insurance agents, brokers, and service	69	69	2.1	243	212	25,728	22,585	6,531	5,896	0.9
6500	Real estate	105	110	1.9	421	496	18,014	18,194	9,038	9,299	1.0
6510	Real estate operators and lessors	51	54	2.7	189	238	14,963	16,437	3,623	4,287	2.2
6530	Real estate agents and managers	41	45	1.5	192	199	16,250	17,367	3,446	3,186	0.5

Source: County Business Patterns, 1994/95, CBP-94/95, U.S. Department of Commerce, Washington, D.C., November 1997. SIC categories for which data were suppressed or not available for both 1994 and 1995 are not displayed. The employment columns represent mid-March employment in the year. Pay per employee is calculated by dividing 1st Quarter payroll, annualized, by mid-March employment. The columns headed "% State" show the county's percentage of the state total for the SIC in 1995; for example, 1.4% for SIC 6000 means that the county had 1.4 percent of the state's total establishments (or payroll) in SIC 6000 in 1995. A dash (-) is used to indicate that data are not available or cannot be calculated; nec means not elsewhere classified.

Continued on next page.

SIC	Industry	No. Establishments			Employment		Pay / Employee		Annual Payroll ($ 000)		
		1994	1995	% State	1994	1995	1994	1995	1994	1995	% State
CLAYTON, GA - [continued]											
6550	Subdividers and developers	10	8	1.4	30	37	50,533	38,919	1,783	1,521	1.5
6552	Subdividers and developers, n.e.c.	7	6	1.5	24	30	37,667	40,533	1,230	1,243	1.7
6700	Holding and other investment offices	9	9	1.6	74	42	35,405	32,190	5,601	1,583	0.5
6710	Holding offices	3	3	1.3	52	18	38,462	37,556	4,912	888	0.4
COBB, GA											
60 –	**Finance, insurance, and real estate**	1,453	1,532	9.2	15,419	15,820	32,206	34,860	501,949	552,057	9.1
6000	Depository institutions	164	158	6.3	2,780	2,273	26,787	27,567	68,557	57,737	4.1
6020	Commercial banks	126	122	6.6	2,048	1,801	25,789	28,664	47,540	50,332	4.2
6090	Functions closely related to banking	17	18	11.8	497	271	29,296	22,878	14,850	3,668	-
6100	Nondepository institutions	202	200	9.2	2,617	2,117	36,576	40,382	88,162	89,129	15.3
6140	Personal credit institutions	66	72	6.2	345	379	35,270	46,565	11,708	14,757	7.4
6150	Business credit institutions	29	29	15.5	716	784	36,134	42,005	24,997	29,988	22.6
6160	Mortgage bankers and brokers	103	94	13.5	1,443	862	34,625	31,573	44,915	36,021	16.0
6200	Security and commodity brokers	85	91	9.9	570	597	55,930	59,055	32,713	35,007	6.2
6210	Security brokers and dealers	33	36	6.3	348	334	50,506	53,677	16,603	17,959	4.0
6300	Insurance carriers	105	136	11.4	2,581	2,819	33,615	37,447	86,870	99,085	6.7
6310	Life insurance	42	48	11.1	1,572	1,792	30,178	32,703	47,739	53,948	9.2
6330	Fire, marine, and casualty insurance	55	77	13.1	994	864	38,777	46,616	38,268	38,126	5.4
6400	Insurance agents, brokers, and service	302	315	9.4	1,603	1,700	31,276	32,508	55,617	59,909	9.0
6500	Real estate	532	565	9.7	4,119	5,019	27,401	28,060	121,057	149,246	15.9
6510	Real estate operators and lessors	163	155	7.8	1,384	1,182	20,335	22,443	27,889	28,571	15.0
6530	Real estate agents and managers	297	325	10.9	2,457	3,330	30,799	28,613	81,954	99,670	15.8
6550	Subdividers and developers	49	48	8.7	188	393	33,149	41,578	8,483	17,976	18.1
6552	Subdividers and developers, n.e.c.	39	40	10.2	159	338	27,673	45,834	6,587	16,854	22.5
6700	Holding and other investment offices	57	60	11.0	980	1,113	36,433	50,925	40,709	52,674	16.9
6710	Holding offices	23	27	11.7	687	816	36,047	51,627	29,044	37,605	16.1
6730	Trusts	5	6	5.5	8	11	37,000	11,636	225	201	1.1
6790	Miscellaneous investing	24	21	12.9	273	275	37,802	50,502	11,062	14,256	29.4
6794	Patent owners and lessors	14	12	25.5	194	151	32,763	42,358	6,669	7,089	33.1
COFFEE, GA											
60 –	**Finance, insurance, and real estate**	57	56	0.3	381	376	20,220	22,340	8,283	8,023	0.1
6000	Depository institutions	16	16	0.6	183	191	23,672	27,518	4,573	4,905	0.3
6020	Commercial banks	13	12	0.6	176	176	24,114	28,227	4,387	4,561	0.4
6100	Nondepository institutions	11	11	0.5	42	51	22,762	22,980	996	1,107	0.2
6400	Insurance agents, brokers, and service	13	13	0.4	47	49	14,979	16,082	875	919	0.1
6500	Real estate	10	10	0.2	41	39	8,390	11,590	364	465	0.0
6510	Real estate operators and lessors	5	5	0.3	31	28	8,903	10,143	279	309	0.2
6530	Real estate agents and managers	5	5	0.2	10	11	6,800	15,273	85	156	0.0
COLQUITT, GA											
60 –	**Finance, insurance, and real estate**	69	68	0.4	365	385	24,537	23,751	8,647	8,807	0.1
6000	Depository institutions	9	9	0.4	157	164	28,611	27,073	4,039	3,999	0.3
6100	Nondepository institutions	13	13	0.6	49	54	26,531	24,815	1,153	1,195	0.2
6400	Insurance agents, brokers, and service	17	16	0.5	69	67	17,565	19,224	1,255	1,341	0.2
6500	Real estate	19	19	0.3	48	53	12,167	12,981	671	754	0.1
6510	Real estate operators and lessors	10	10	0.5	21	24	9,905	11,167	229	251	0.1
COLUMBIA, GA											
60 –	**Finance, insurance, and real estate**	136	141	0.9	684	688	23,327	21,128	16,901	15,891	0.3
6000	Depository institutions	19	20	0.8	188	205	21,468	20,507	4,107	4,238	0.3
6020	Commercial banks	13	14	0.8	153	161	22,327	21,640	3,416	3,512	0.3
6100	Nondepository institutions	23	21	1.0	166	131	25,060	20,947	3,648	3,052	0.5
6160	Mortgage bankers and brokers	14	11	1.6	139	97	27,281	22,268	3,223	2,406	1.1
6300	Insurance carriers	10	10	0.8	102	93	32,824	36,688	3,405	3,134	0.2
6400	Insurance agents, brokers, and service	33	32	1.0	74	84	18,054	18,095	1,582	1,876	0.3
6500	Real estate	46	53	0.9	146	167	18,575	15,138	3,382	3,192	0.3

Source: County Business Patterns, 1994/95, CBP-94/95, U.S. Department of Commerce, Washington, D.C., November 1997. SIC categories for which data were suppressed or not available for both 1994 and 1995 are *not* displayed. The employment columns represent mid-March employment in the year. Pay per employee is calculated by dividing 1st Quarter payroll, annualized, by mid-March employment. The columns headed "% State" show the county's percentage of the state total for the SIC in 1995; for example, 1.4% for SIC 6000 means that the county had 1.4 percent of the state's total establishments (or payroll) in SIC 6000 in 1995. A dash (-) is used to indicate that data are not available or cannot be calculated; *nec* means not elsewhere classified.

Continued on next page.

SIC	Industry	No. Establishments			Employment		Pay / Employee		Annual Payroll ($ 000)		
		1994	1995	% State	1994	1995	1994	1995	1994	1995	% State
COLUMBIA, GA - [continued]											
6510	Real estate operators and lessors	7	7	0.4	24	38	18,667	13,263	496	425	0.2
6530	Real estate agents and managers	29	36	1.2	93	106	19,226	15,358	2,230	2,279	0.4
6550	Subdividers and developers	9	8	1.4	29	17	16,414	18,353	639	395	0.4
6552	Subdividers and developers, n.e.c.	5	6	1.5	15	14	18,933	20,857	420	370	0.5
COOK, GA											
60 –	**Finance, insurance, and real estate**	18	21	0.1	197	262	15,492	14,870	3,433	4,053	0.1
6000	Depository institutions	6	6	0.2	76	72	18,947	21,778	1,643	1,624	0.1
COWETA, GA											
60 –	**Finance, insurance, and real estate**	95	96	0.6	535	532	22,064	22,767	12,518	12,831	0.2
6000	Depository institutions	24	22	0.9	319	309	20,727	21,735	6,962	7,019	0.5
6100	Nondepository institutions	14	14	0.6	59	53	17,220	18,717	1,101	1,125	0.2
6160	Mortgage bankers and brokers	5	6	0.9	28	23	15,000	18,261	513	539	0.2
6200	Security and commodity brokers	4	5	0.5	5	9	42,400	31,556	277	340	0.1
6300	Insurance carriers	4	6	0.5	7	8	46,857	44,500	343	361	0.0
6400	Insurance agents, brokers, and service	17	15	0.4	68	66	30,647	29,576	2,091	1,978	0.3
6500	Real estate	32	34	0.6	77	87	20,156	20,828	1,744	2,008	0.2
6510	Real estate operators and lessors	7	9	0.5	23	35	18,261	14,971	456	559	0.3
6530	Real estate agents and managers	18	16	0.5	43	36	23,070	30,556	1,144	1,210	0.2
6550	Subdividers and developers	3	5	0.9	9	11	14,667	16,364	107	182	0.2
CRISP, GA											
60 –	**Finance, insurance, and real estate**	48	50	0.3	290	295	18,938	19,797	5,744	6,020	0.1
6000	Depository institutions	9	9	0.4	139	135	20,691	24,326	3,040	3,215	0.2
6400	Insurance agents, brokers, and service	12	13	0.4	30	29	14,533	16,414	494	535	0.1
6500	Real estate	18	17	0.3	58	67	10,345	9,910	659	726	0.1
6510	Real estate operators and lessors	13	12	0.6	52	57	10,308	9,965	570	604	0.3
DADE, GA											
60 –	**Finance, insurance, and real estate**	10	7	0.0	84	71	18,667	19,775	1,557	1,585	0.0
6400	Insurance agents, brokers, and service	4	4	0.1	8	7	11,500	14,286	107	115	0.0
DAWSON, GA											
60 –	**Finance, insurance, and real estate**	10	13	0.1	67	70	17,851	22,743	1,310	1,635	0.0
6500	Real estate	3	6	0.1	3	5	9,333	19,200	55	113	0.0
DECATUR, GA											
60 –	**Finance, insurance, and real estate**	49	55	0.3	349	337	20,940	24,546	7,232	8,125	0.1
6000	Depository institutions	7	7	0.3	124	109	20,258	24,587	2,550	2,677	0.2
6020	Commercial banks	4	4	0.2	88	83	21,864	23,422	1,813	1,832	0.2
6100	Nondepository institutions	11	13	0.6	96	91	27,042	36,571	2,362	2,830	0.5
6400	Insurance agents, brokers, and service	15	16	0.5	30	35	15,600	15,200	553	589	0.1
6500	Real estate	10	13	0.2	28	40	9,143	12,700	311	543	0.1
6510	Real estate operators and lessors	4	6	0.3	16	14	4,250	6,286	86	94	0.0
6530	Real estate agents and managers	5	6	0.2	12	25	15,667	16,320	221	435	0.1
DE KALB, GA											
60 –	**Finance, insurance, and real estate**	1,806	1,843	11.1	22,522	22,335	32,829	35,094	746,099	778,354	12.9
6000	Depository institutions	231	232	9.2	3,219	3,101	27,319	29,696	91,000	88,812	6.2
6020	Commercial banks	148	150	8.1	2,282	2,171	27,171	30,030	64,688	60,645	5.1
6030	Savings institutions	17	13	6.8	288	233	27,653	26,901	8,477	6,871	10.7
6060	Credit unions	34	33	10.8	388	407	23,515	24,924	9,602	10,588	18.1
6100	Nondepository institutions	230	241	11.1	3,424	2,706	39,035	38,381	119,961	106,933	18.4
6140	Personal credit institutions	69	76	6.5	848	868	38,024	38,134	32,338	33,063	16.5
6150	Business credit institutions	44	41	21.9	863	793	53,122	50,280	39,437	35,546	26.8
6160	Mortgage bankers and brokers	115	111	15.9	1,704	1,029	32,545	29,846	48,070	37,495	16.6
6200	Security and commodity brokers	82	88	9.5	559	777	50,039	47,310	26,637	37,557	6.6

Source: County Business Patterns, 1994/95, CBP-94/95, U.S. Department of Commerce, Washington, D.C., November 1997. SIC categories for which data were suppressed or not available for both 1994 and 1995 are not displayed. The employment columns represent mid-March employment in the year. Pay per employee is calculated by dividing 1st Quarter payroll, annualized, by mid-March employment. The columns headed "% State" show the county's percentage of the state total for the SIC in 1995; for example, 1.4% for SIC 6000 means that the county had 1.4 percent of the state's total establishments (or payroll) in SIC 6000 in 1995. A dash (-) is used to indicate that data are not available or cannot be calculated; nec means not elsewhere classified.

Continued on next page.

SIC	Industry	No. Establishments			Employment		Pay / Employee		Annual Payroll ($ 000)		
		1994	1995	% State	1994	1995	1994	1995	1994	1995	% State
DE KALB, GA - [continued]											
6210	Security brokers and dealers	42	45	7.9	331	381	56,810	53,081	15,853	19,902	4.4
6280	Security and commodity services	37	39	11.6	219	385	39,178	39,969	9,937	16,628	15.4
6300	Insurance carriers	185	169	14.2	6,835	6,672	36,327	39,554	259,436	259,875	17.6
6310	Life insurance	69	60	13.9	3,123	3,085	36,565	38,632	119,291	112,127	19.1
6320	Medical service and health insurance	7	11	18.0	115	193	31,965	38,487	4,140	7,532	6.0
6330	Fire, marine, and casualty insurance	82	79	13.4	3,399	3,198	36,280	40,857	128,117	133,437	19.0
6350	Surety insurance	3	4	20.0	67	129	30,388	36,124	2,438	4,682	49.3
6400	Insurance agents, brokers, and service	357	348	10.4	2,862	2,921	34,507	35,184	102,259	102,286	15.4
6500	Real estate	661	700	12.0	4,982	5,321	22,926	25,294	120,612	140,276	14.9
6510	Real estate operators and lessors	222	219	11.0	1,266	1,344	19,033	21,524	26,222	29,788	15.6
6530	Real estate agents and managers	367	396	13.3	3,316	3,585	24,428	26,174	85,043	97,115	15.4
6540	Title abstract offices	8	8	13.6	37	38	30,703	37,053	1,262	1,218	24.6
6550	Subdividers and developers	45	46	8.3	357	329	21,770	30,371	7,621	11,315	11.4
6552	Subdividers and developers, n.e.c.	35	34	8.7	190	116	22,358	35,897	4,264	5,495	7.3
6553	Cemetery subdividers and developers	9	9	7.4	167	136	21,102	27,176	3,047	3,426	17.3
6710	Holding offices	24	28	12.1	230	450	69,496	86,142	13,520	31,125	13.3
6730	Trusts	13	13	11.8	49	56	20,490	19,286	1,213	1,376	7.7
6732	Educational, religious, etc. trusts	5	6	13.3	11	13	14,545	19,077	210	271	3.9
6733	Trusts, n.e.c.	8	7	10.9	38	43	22,211	19,349	1,003	1,105	10.0
6790	Miscellaneous investing	16	16	9.8	126	104	19,968	21,885	2,641	2,179	4.5
6794	Patent owners and lessors	6	5	10.6	82	56	18,878	21,214	1,680	954	4.5
DODGE, GA											
60 –	**Finance, insurance, and real estate**	28	28	0.2	209	227	18,488	18,485	3,921	4,353	0.1
6000	Depository institutions	8	8	0.3	98	119	21,265	22,387	2,363	2,721	0.2
6400	Insurance agents, brokers, and service	10	10	0.3	21	23	16,762	16,870	403	440	0.1
DOOLY, GA											
60 –	**Finance, insurance, and real estate**	14	14	0.1	94	97	21,021	28,536	2,117	2,595	0.0
DOUGHERTY, GA											
60 –	**Finance, insurance, and real estate**	264	274	1.7	1,752	1,789	27,662	27,168	44,750	45,973	0.8
6000	Depository institutions	36	37	1.5	694	694	23,297	24,905	14,484	14,869	1.0
6020	Commercial banks	26	27	1.5	552	543	23,348	26,343	11,522	11,787	1.0
6100	Nondepository institutions	34	35	1.6	212	201	38,792	24,139	6,051	5,219	0.9
6200	Security and commodity brokers	10	12	1.3	56	65	61,357	53,292	3,256	3,286	0.6
6300	Insurance carriers	26	29	2.4	304	298	31,947	34,255	9,554	9,426	0.6
6310	Life insurance	11	12	2.8	246	238	27,772	29,176	6,683	6,330	1.1
6400	Insurance agents, brokers, and service	63	62	1.9	220	251	23,691	23,060	5,898	6,563	1.0
6500	Real estate	91	92	1.6	248	256	15,726	16,328	4,068	4,746	0.5
6510	Real estate operators and lessors	46	42	2.1	115	108	11,687	15,111	1,414	1,831	1.0
6530	Real estate agents and managers	39	40	1.3	107	114	20,486	18,351	2,245	2,377	0.4
6550	Subdividers and developers	4	6	1.1	23	26	13,391	12,923	341	409	0.4
6700	Holding and other investment offices	4	7	1.3	18	24	100,667	117,833	1,439	1,864	0.6
DOUGLAS, GA											
60 –	**Finance, insurance, and real estate**	114	114	0.7	921	614	27,944	22,879	20,326	14,611	0.2
6000	Depository institutions	28	27	1.1	315	321	21,029	21,981	6,743	7,059	0.5
6020	Commercial banks	21	21	1.1	258	267	20,589	22,292	5,451	5,596	0.5
6400	Insurance agents, brokers, and service	20	22	0.7	96	90	20,125	20,133	1,917	2,211	0.3
6500	Real estate	40	39	0.7	115	126	17,148	18,254	2,190	2,559	0.3
6510	Real estate operators and lessors	14	12	0.6	48	49	13,500	10,776	651	573	0.3
6530	Real estate agents and managers	16	18	0.6	25	39	22,240	24,923	652	1,150	0.2
6550	Subdividers and developers	5	4	0.7	23	19	16,696	18,105	398	261	0.3
EARLY, GA											
60 –	**Finance, insurance, and real estate**	17	19	0.1	132	149	18,939	21,181	2,567	2,974	0.0

Source: County Business Patterns, 1994/95, CBP-94/95, U.S. Department of Commerce, Washington, D.C., November 1997. SIC categories for which data were suppressed or not available for both 1994 and 1995 are *not* displayed. The employment columns represent mid-March employment in the year. Pay per employee is calculated by dividing 1st Quarter payroll, annualized, by mid-March employment. The columns headed "% State" show the county's percentage of the state total for the SIC in 1995; for example, 1.4% for SIC 6000 means that the county had 1.4 percent of the state's total establishments (or payroll) in SIC 6000 in 1995. A dash (-) is used to indicate that data are not available or cannot be calculated; *nec* means not elsewhere classified.

Continued on next page.

SIC	Industry	No. Establishments			Employment		Pay / Employee		Annual Payroll ($ 000)		
		1994	1995	% State	1994	1995	1994	1995	1994	1995	% State
PICKENS, GA - [continued]											
6000	Depository institutions	6	5	0.2	146	148	26,548	26,027	3,730	4,402	0.3
6500	Real estate	16	21	0.4	146	126	14,932	20,571	2,757	1,499	0.2
6530	Real estate agents and managers	9	11	0.4	102	99	16,314	20,081	2,003	701	0.1
PIERCE, GA											
60 –	**Finance, insurance, and real estate**	16	17	0.1	88	93	19,091	20,129	1,801	1,975	0.0
6000	Depository institutions	4	4	0.2	53	58	19,623	21,379	1,155	1,324	0.1
6100	Nondepository institutions	4	3	0.1	14	13	22,000	23,692	317	304	0.1
6400	Insurance agents, brokers, and service	5	5	0.1	15	14	17,867	18,000	258	271	0.0
6500	Real estate	3	5	0.1	6	8	10,667	9,000	71	76	0.0
PIKE, GA											
60 –	**Finance, insurance, and real estate**	9	9	0.1	57	59	15,509	17,763	1,083	1,216	0.0
POLK, GA											
60 –	**Finance, insurance, and real estate**	54	55	0.3	252	256	18,222	20,297	4,857	5,489	0.1
6000	Depository institutions	13	13	0.5	156	160	21,923	22,100	3,491	3,988	0.3
6100	Nondepository institutions	9	9	0.4	23	20	15,826	34,400	352	513	0.1
6140	Personal credit institutions	6	6	0.5	18	16	18,000	39,500	314	426	0.2
6400	Insurance agents, brokers, and service	15	13	0.4	29	28	14,759	16,714	554	474	0.1
6500	Real estate	14	16	0.3	34	36	10,000	12,667	424	428	0.0
6510	Real estate operators and lessors	6	7	0.4	9	9	9,333	12,000	95	113	0.1
PULASKI, GA											
60 –	**Finance, insurance, and real estate**	16	16	0.1	114	110	16,000	17,164	2,000	2,124	0.0
6400	Insurance agents, brokers, and service	6	6	0.2	15	12	14,400	18,667	221	251	0.0
PUTNAM, GA											
60 –	**Finance, insurance, and real estate**	17	18	0.1	110	112	20,436	24,857	2,700	3,205	0.1
6100	Nondepository institutions	4	3	0.1	12	12	36,667	35,667	416	494	0.1
6530	Real estate agents and managers	3	3	0.1	14	13	11,143	12,308	138	171	0.0
RABUN, GA											
60 –	**Finance, insurance, and real estate**	32	32	0.2	160	168	20,425	20,238	3,242	3,677	0.1
6000	Depository institutions	4	4	0.2	92	102	25,870	24,392	2,259	2,545	0.2
6400	Insurance agents, brokers, and service	4	5	0.1	10	11	20,400	20,364	228	318	0.0
6500	Real estate	21	20	0.3	53	50	10,113	10,640	635	702	0.1
6510	Real estate operators and lessors	4	5	0.3	17	17	8,471	8,000	161	130	0.1
6530	Real estate agents and managers	13	10	0.3	28	25	11,286	11,680	349	426	0.1
6550	Subdividers and developers	3	3	0.5	5	4	8,800	10,000	52	46	0.0
6552	Subdividers and developers, n.e.c.	3	3	0.8	5	4	8,800	10,000	52	46	0.1
RANDOLPH, GA											
60 –	**Finance, insurance, and real estate**	12	11	0.1	56	56	18,000	16,857	1,094	970	0.0
6400	Insurance agents, brokers, and service	4	4	0.1	8	8	11,500	12,500	101	100	0.0
RICHMOND, GA											
60 –	**Finance, insurance, and real estate**	435	458	2.8	3,769	3,565	23,822	24,726	91,086	88,463	1.5
6000	Depository institutions	67	68	2.7	852	855	22,728	21,764	18,265	17,864	1.3
6020	Commercial banks	40	38	2.1	656	633	24,159	23,014	14,620	13,570	1.1
6060	Credit unions	14	16	5.2	96	118	19,750	18,780	1,977	2,370	4.1
6140	Personal credit institutions	39	42	3.6	141	154	20,312	23,091	2,981	3,472	1.7
6200	Security and commodity brokers	18	21	2.3	173	172	59,676	66,395	8,448	10,874	1.9
6210	Security brokers and dealers	12	14	2.5	160	157	62,550	68,866	7,882	10,054	2.2
6280	Security and commodity services	6	7	2.1	13	15	24,308	40,533	566	820	0.8
6300	Insurance carriers	31	31	2.6	699	680	21,196	21,482	17,019	17,081	1.2
6310	Life insurance	13	14	3.2	255	233	27,169	28,996	6,406	6,170	1.1
6320	Medical service and health insurance	3	3	4.9	412	422	13,670	14,834	8,852	9,276	7.4

Source: County Business Patterns, 1994/95, CBP-94/95, U.S. Department of Commerce, Washington, D.C., November 1997. SIC categories for which data were suppressed or not available for both 1994 and 1995 are *not* displayed. The employment columns represent mid-March employment in the year. Pay per employee is calculated by dividing 1st Quarter payroll, annualized, by mid-March employment. The columns headed "% State" show the county's percentage of the state total for the SIC in 1995; for example, 1.4% for SIC 6000 means that the county had 1.4 percent of the state's total establishments (or payroll) in SIC 6000 in 1995. A dash (-) is used to indicate that data are not available or cannot be calculated; *nec* means not elsewhere classified.

Continued on next page.

SIC	Industry	No. Establishments			Employment		Pay / Employee		Annual Payroll ($ 000)		
		1994	1995	% State	1994	1995	1994	1995	1994	1995	% State
RICHMOND, GA - [continued]											
6400	Insurance agents, brokers, and service	85	95	2.8	363	418	22,887	21,502	10,210	10,687	1.6
6500	Real estate	164	166	2.8	673	716	18,383	17,486	14,566	12,875	1.4
6510	Real estate operators and lessors	79	83	4.2	315	338	13,486	14,367	4,793	5,201	2.7
6530	Real estate agents and managers	72	71	2.4	324	343	20,296	19,837	8,113	6,872	1.1
6550	Subdividers and developers	8	8	1.4	26	32	49,692	23,750	1,415	682	0.7
ROCKDALE, GA											
60 –	**Finance, insurance, and real estate**	122	119	0.7	536	558	23,709	24,158	13,079	15,253	0.3
6000	Depository institutions	24	23	0.9	223	226	28,556	28,389	6,193	6,705	0.5
6020	Commercial banks	15	14	0.8	189	182	28,804	28,945	5,178	5,488	0.5
6100	Nondepository institutions	12	11	0.5	72	62	17,500	18,258	1,202	1,264	0.2
6140	Personal credit institutions	8	8	0.7	48	52	14,333	16,538	775	878	0.4
6300	Insurance carriers	6	6	0.5	38	37	36,105	38,811	1,462	1,510	0.1
6400	Insurance agents, brokers, and service	27	26	0.8	82	84	21,024	22,429	1,984	2,122	0.3
6500	Real estate	44	44	0.8	108	127	15,444	16,535	1,839	3,069	0.3
6510	Real estate operators and lessors	14	17	0.9	38	54	13,789	18,370	536	1,544	0.8
6530	Real estate agents and managers	25	23	0.8	62	62	16,387	15,613	1,126	1,335	0.2
6550	Subdividers and developers	5	3	0.5	8	11	16,000	12,727	177	173	0.2
SCHLEY, GA											
60 –	**Finance, insurance, and real estate**	3	3	0.0	-	-	-	-	-	-	-
SCREVEN, GA											
60 –	**Finance, insurance, and real estate**	20	19	0.1	97	105	17,196	19,429	1,794	2,394	0.0
6000	Depository institutions	4	4	0.2	59	58	18,712	20,000	1,214	1,481	0.1
6100	Nondepository institutions	6	6	0.3	16	14	21,500	25,429	323	325	0.1
6500	Real estate	4	3	0.1	4	5	6,000	6,400	28	29	0.0
SEMINOLE, GA											
60 –	**Finance, insurance, and real estate**	13	13	0.1	89	97	18,022	17,526	1,837	2,021	0.0
6000	Depository institutions	3	3	0.1	66	74	19,212	18,432	1,491	1,649	0.1
6400	Insurance agents, brokers, and service	5	4	0.1	13	11	11,385	11,636	160	146	0.0
SPALDING, GA											
60 –	**Finance, insurance, and real estate**	108	106	0.6	886	799	26,059	24,416	22,360	21,278	0.4
6000	Depository institutions	15	15	0.6	301	298	20,944	23,584	7,126	7,571	0.5
6020	Commercial banks	11	11	0.6	227	236	22,009	23,373	6,387	6,079	0.5
6100	Nondepository institutions	17	17	0.8	240	158	33,600	23,797	6,553	5,512	0.9
6300	Insurance carriers	14	14	1.2	175	158	29,349	31,266	4,904	4,157	0.3
6400	Insurance agents, brokers, and service	19	18	0.5	50	52	19,760	18,538	1,013	1,034	0.2
6500	Real estate	39	36	0.6	114	105	15,789	15,543	1,978	1,682	0.2
6510	Real estate operators and lessors	16	15	0.8	50	47	13,440	13,787	802	662	0.3
6530	Real estate agents and managers	20	18	0.6	49	48	18,857	17,833	985	895	0.1
STEPHENS, GA											
60 –	**Finance, insurance, and real estate**	35	33	0.2	269	268	49,606	57,104	9,824	11,016	0.2
6000	Depository institutions	8	8	0.3	134	133	23,045	22,256	3,150	3,151	0.2
6020	Commercial banks	4	4	0.2	107	104	23,850	22,538	2,529	2,452	0.2
6510	Real estate operators and lessors	5	4	0.2	8	12	16,500	15,333	137	213	0.1
STEWART, GA											
60 –	**Finance, insurance, and real estate**	7	7	0.0	36	34	16,556	18,118	639	667	0.0
SUMTER, GA											
60 –	**Finance, insurance, and real estate**	45	48	0.3	401	347	20,279	22,732	7,776	7,857	0.1
6000	Depository institutions	7	7	0.3	184	170	20,478	19,788	3,607	3,510	0.2
6020	Commercial banks	7	7	0.4	184	170	20,478	19,788	3,607	3,510	0.3
6100	Nondepository institutions	9	9	0.4	33	28	20,242	25,857	602	656	0.1

Source: County Business Patterns, 1994/95, CBP-94/95, U.S. Department of Commerce, Washington, D.C., November 1997. SIC categories for which data were suppressed or not available for both 1994 and 1995 are *not* displayed. The employment columns represent mid-March employment in the year. Pay per employee is calculated by dividing 1st Quarter payroll, annualized, by mid-March employment. The columns headed "*% State*" show the county's percentage of the state total for the SIC in 1995; for example, 1.4% for SIC 6000 means that the county had 1.4 percent of the state's total establishments (or payroll) in SIC 6000 in 1995. A dash (-) is used to indicate that data are not available or cannot be calculated; *nec* means not elsewhere classified.

Continued on next page.

SIC	Industry	No. Establishments			Employment		Pay / Employee		Annual Payroll ($ 000)		
		1994	1995	% State	1994	1995	1994	1995	1994	1995	% State
SUMTER, GA - [continued]											
6400	Insurance agents, brokers, and service	11	12	0.4	42	44	16,952	18,545	772	830	0.1
6500	Real estate	13	14	0.2	66	27	9,273	13,630	415	400	0.0
6510	Real estate operators and lessors	10	11	0.6	63	22	9,206	14,545	374	352	0.2
TALBOT, GA											
60 –	**Finance, insurance, and real estate**	2	2	0.0	-	-	-	-	-	-	-
TATTNALL, GA											
60 –	**Finance, insurance, and real estate**	22	23	0.1	146	150	17,918	19,120	2,980	3,285	0.1
6000	Depository institutions	8	8	0.3	117	120	19,316	20,733	2,576	2,851	0.2
6100	Nondepository institutions	3	3	0.1	8	6	14,500	20,000	114	124	0.0
6140	Personal credit institutions	3	3	0.3	8	6	14,500	20,000	114	124	0.1
6400	Insurance agents, brokers, and service	7	8	0.2	15	19	13,067	12,000	244	257	0.0
6500	Real estate	4	4	0.1	6	5	7,333	6,400	46	53	0.0
TAYLOR, GA											
60 –	**Finance, insurance, and real estate**	15	15	0.1	62	60	18,323	20,267	1,221	1,289	0.0
6400	Insurance agents, brokers, and service	4	3	0.1	8	5	9,500	15,200	83	84	0.0
6500	Real estate	4	4	0.1	4	5	9,000	6,400	34	32	0.0
TELFAIR, GA											
60 –	**Finance, insurance, and real estate**	18	19	0.1	131	130	17,710	19,785	2,468	2,757	0.0
6000	Depository institutions	6	7	0.3	64	80	19,063	19,500	1,458	1,775	0.1
6400	Insurance agents, brokers, and service	4	4	0.1	16	11	15,250	22,909	214	225	0.0
6500	Real estate	3	3	0.1	8	7	6,500	5,714	49	38	0.0
6510	Real estate operators and lessors	3	3	0.2	8	7	6,500	5,714	49	38	0.0
TERRELL, GA											
60 –	**Finance, insurance, and real estate**	10	11	0.1	82	80	20,927	23,000	1,945	1,915	0.0
6000	Depository institutions	3	3	0.1	56	56	20,643	22,929	1,359	1,412	0.1
6020	Commercial banks	3	3	0.2	56	56	20,643	22,929	1,359	1,412	0.1
THOMAS, GA											
60 –	**Finance, insurance, and real estate**	100	107	0.6	708	750	27,345	19,712	20,502	15,095	0.2
6000	Depository institutions	18	19	0.8	235	237	25,106	25,603	5,619	5,555	0.4
6020	Commercial banks	15	16	0.9	187	186	26,353	26,839	4,534	4,377	0.4
6100	Nondepository institutions	9	9	0.4	34	37	18,353	18,486	664	656	0.1
6140	Personal credit institutions	9	9	0.8	34	37	18,353	18,486	664	656	0.3
6200	Security and commodity brokers	7	7	0.8	37	29	154,811	36,138	5,841	1,184	0.2
6300	Insurance carriers	6	6	0.5	139	116	26,561	22,483	3,839	2,513	0.2
6400	Insurance agents, brokers, and service	24	25	0.7	151	177	14,914	14,938	2,748	3,265	0.5
6500	Real estate	27	31	0.5	94	127	9,362	9,638	1,473	1,375	0.1
6510	Real estate operators and lessors	17	15	0.8	70	96	8,286	8,833	842	797	0.4
6530	Real estate agents and managers	10	13	0.4	24	31	12,500	12,129	631	564	0.1
6700	Holding and other investment offices	9	10	1.8	18	27	15,778	18,815	318	547	0.2
TIFT, GA											
60 –	**Finance, insurance, and real estate**	91	89	0.5	520	524	20,692	22,244	11,034	11,403	0.2
6000	Depository institutions	16	17	0.7	262	266	22,794	23,865	5,744	5,885	0.4
6100	Nondepository institutions	12	12	0.6	82	77	24,244	29,662	2,200	2,306	0.4
6140	Personal credit institutions	9	9	0.8	38	35	23,474	28,343	928	893	0.4
6300	Insurance carriers	4	4	0.3	38	42	19,579	20,762	800	804	0.1
6400	Insurance agents, brokers, and service	28	27	0.8	75	74	14,720	16,757	1,234	1,325	0.2
6500	Real estate	26	24	0.4	48	51	10,583	10,039	623	649	0.1
6530	Real estate agents and managers	11	11	0.4	26	31	12,462	12,000	414	390	0.1
TOOMBS, GA											
60 –	**Finance, insurance, and real estate**	49	49	0.3	269	295	22,439	22,007	6,421	7,323	0.1

Source: County Business Patterns, 1994/95, CBP-94/95, U.S. Department of Commerce, Washington, D.C., November 1997. SIC categories for which data were suppressed or not available for both 1994 and 1995 are not displayed. The employment columns represent mid-March employment in the year. Pay per employee is calculated by dividing 1st Quarter payroll, annualized, by mid-March employment. The columns headed "% State" show the county's percentage of the state total for the SIC in 1995; for example, 1.4% for SIC 6000 means that the county had 1.4 percent of the state's total establishments (or payroll) in SIC 6000 in 1995. A dash (-) is used to indicate that data are not available or cannot be calculated; nec means not elsewhere classified.

Continued on next page.

SIC	Industry	No. Establishments			Employment		Pay / Employee		Annual Payroll ($ 000)		
		1994	1995	% State	1994	1995	1994	1995	1994	1995	% State
TOOMBS, GA - [continued]											
6000	Depository institutions	10	11	0.4	142	156	20,479	22,077	3,245	3,747	0.3
6400	Insurance agents, brokers, and service	16	15	0.4	44	48	19,182	19,750	862	1,157	0.2
6500	Real estate	13	14	0.2	62	68	29,871	24,059	1,837	1,930	0.2
6510	Real estate operators and lessors	6	7	0.4	18	18	12,667	14,000	259	275	0.1
TOWNS, GA											
60 –	**Finance, insurance, and real estate**	17	21	0.1	77	101	16,519	17,347	1,538	1,755	0.0
6530	Real estate agents and managers	5	6	0.2	8	7	10,500	16,000	124	127	0.0
TROUP, GA											
60 –	**Finance, insurance, and real estate**	103	101	0.6	807	783	27,544	29,727	20,714	21,601	0.4
6000	Depository institutions	17	16	0.6	396	400	25,030	24,950	9,189	9,793	0.7
6100	Nondepository institutions	20	19	0.9	69	54	25,565	27,852	1,556	1,203	0.2
6210	Security brokers and dealers	3	3	0.5	23	21	42,087	41,143	851	856	0.2
6300	Insurance carriers	7	7	0.6	106	107	28,642	24,972	2,976	2,899	0.2
6400	Insurance agents, brokers, and service	20	21	0.6	103	93	28,427	32,301	2,819	3,098	0.5
6500	Real estate	32	30	0.5	75	83	17,067	15,759	1,415	1,798	0.2
TURNER, GA											
60 –	**Finance, insurance, and real estate**	13	14	0.1	77	80	16,623	18,150	1,596	1,735	0.0
6400	Insurance agents, brokers, and service	5	6	0.2	13	14	7,692	11,429	155	228	0.0
6500	Real estate	4	4	0.1	4	6	9,000	7,333	46	52	0.0
6510	Real estate operators and lessors	4	4	0.2	4	6	9,000	7,333	46	52	0.0
TWIGGS, GA											
60 –	**Finance, insurance, and real estate**	4	4	0.0	14	16	17,714	19,000	288	308	0.0
UNION, GA											
60 –	**Finance, insurance, and real estate**	26	30	0.2	169	209	18,462	19,789	4,089	5,027	0.1
UPSON, GA											
60 –	**Finance, insurance, and real estate**	36	34	0.2	220	220	24,200	22,527	4,942	4,768	0.1
6000	Depository institutions	7	7	0.3	128	132	24,219	20,818	2,987	2,808	0.2
WALKER, GA											
60 –	**Finance, insurance, and real estate**	63	61	0.4	388	420	20,649	20,924	8,710	9,136	0.2
6000	Depository institutions	16	17	0.7	212	218	21,906	23,119	4,820	4,994	0.4
6020	Commercial banks	10	11	0.6	169	181	22,107	22,807	3,928	4,140	0.3
6400	Insurance agents, brokers, and service	17	17	0.5	79	86	20,101	23,767	2,139	2,370	0.4
6500	Real estate	17	14	0.2	61	82	14,098	11,122	825	945	0.1
6510	Real estate operators and lessors	7	5	0.3	19	13	14,316	13,846	301	190	0.1
6530	Real estate agents and managers	5	5	0.2	15	17	9,333	10,353	146	190	0.0
6550	Subdividers and developers	5	4	0.7	27	52	16,593	10,692	378	565	0.6
6553	Cemetery subdividers and developers	5	4	3.3	27	52	16,593	10,692	378	565	2.9
WALTON, GA											
60 –	**Finance, insurance, and real estate**	59	65	0.4	376	390	21,138	20,933	8,373	8,600	0.1
6000	Depository institutions	12	13	0.5	198	203	22,202	20,847	4,461	4,324	0.3
6400	Insurance agents, brokers, and service	15	15	0.4	43	42	16,651	22,667	936	1,112	0.2
6500	Real estate	19	20	0.3	59	61	10,712	11,541	763	927	0.1
6510	Real estate operators and lessors	8	8	0.4	39	43	10,872	11,349	477	518	0.3
6530	Real estate agents and managers	7	8	0.3	13	10	8,615	12,000	174	301	0.0
6550	Subdividers and developers	4	3	0.5	7	8	13,714	12,000	112	105	0.1
WARE, GA											
60 –	**Finance, insurance, and real estate**	76	75	0.5	509	511	20,472	22,051	10,182	11,243	0.2
6000	Depository institutions	16	16	0.6	235	254	21,923	23,559	5,002	5,922	0.4
6100	Nondepository institutions	10	9	0.4	35	33	19,429	20,970	586	663	0.1

Source: County Business Patterns, 1994/95, CBP-94/95, U.S. Department of Commerce, Washington, D.C., November 1997. SIC categories for which data were suppressed or not available for both 1994 and 1995 are not displayed. The employment columns represent mid-March employment in the year. Pay per employee is calculated by dividing 1st Quarter payroll, annualized, by mid-March employment. The columns headed "% State" show the county's percentage of the state total for the SIC in 1995; for example, 1.4% for SIC 6000 means that the county had 1.4 percent of the state's total establishments (or payroll) in SIC 6000 in 1995. A dash (-) is used to indicate that data are not available or cannot be calculated; nec means not elsewhere classified.

Continued on next page.

SIC	Industry	No. Establishments			Employment		Pay / Employee		Annual Payroll ($ 000)		
		1994	1995	% State	1994	1995	1994	1995	1994	1995	% State
WARE, GA - [continued]											
6300	Insurance carriers	6	5	0.4	96	80	20,833	26,450	2,049	1,955	0.1
6400	Insurance agents, brokers, and service	20	21	0.6	74	78	20,919	17,846	1,508	1,557	0.2
6500	Real estate	21	21	0.4	58	56	12,759	15,000	742	898	0.1
6510	Real estate operators and lessors	9	8	0.4	18	23	12,667	12,696	249	324	0.2
6530	Real estate agents and managers	9	10	0.3	32	26	13,875	18,462	424	506	0.1
6550	Subdividers and developers	3	3	0.5	8	7	8,500	9,714	69	68	0.1
WARREN, GA											
60 –	**Finance, insurance, and real estate**	4	4	0.0	17	19	15,529	17,895	335	326	0.0
WASHINGTON, GA											
60 –	**Finance, insurance, and real estate**	29	30	0.2	157	166	20,153	20,530	3,399	3,665	0.1
6000	Depository institutions	6	6	0.2	104	111	19,846	21,045	2,229	2,376	0.2
6400	Insurance agents, brokers, and service	6	6	0.2	23	24	19,652	21,500	485	558	0.1
6510	Real estate operators and lessors	5	5	0.3	6	6	7,333	6,000	95	84	0.0
WAYNE, GA											
60 –	**Finance, insurance, and real estate**	26	25	0.2	133	129	22,376	22,357	2,775	2,604	0.0
6000	Depository institutions	7	7	0.3	83	86	23,518	23,442	1,709	1,755	0.1
6400	Insurance agents, brokers, and service	8	6	0.2	26	17	14,154	12,235	443	217	0.0
6500	Real estate	4	4	0.1	4	5	24,000	19,200	97	93	0.0
WEBSTER, GA											
60 –	**Finance, insurance, and real estate**	1	1	0.0	-	-	-	-	-	-	-
WHITE, GA											
60 –	**Finance, insurance, and real estate**	27	31	0.2	189	188	20,910	21,532	4,027	4,091	0.1
6000	Depository institutions	6	6	0.2	99	91	28,202	29,275	2,667	2,615	0.2
6020	Commercial banks	6	6	0.3	99	91	28,202	29,275	2,667	2,615	0.2
6500	Real estate	15	19	0.3	75	84	12,320	13,810	1,133	1,255	0.1
WHITFIELD, GA											
60 –	**Finance, insurance, and real estate**	153	162	1.0	1,167	1,105	24,089	26,943	28,872	30,513	0.5
6000	Depository institutions	18	19	0.8	476	488	25,118	26,844	11,789	12,847	0.9
6100	Nondepository institutions	28	35	1.6	130	148	23,508	25,946	3,146	3,656	0.6
6140	Personal credit institutions	19	23	2.0	87	89	19,310	23,326	1,753	1,891	0.9
6160	Mortgage bankers and brokers	6	9	1.3	34	48	28,000	27,750	1,037	1,370	0.6
6200	Security and commodity brokers	5	5	0.5	25	22	68,640	51,636	1,130	1,237	0.2
6210	Security brokers and dealers	5	5	0.9	25	22	68,640	51,636	1,130	1,237	0.3
6300	Insurance carriers	10	9	0.8	65	59	37,785	52,339	2,428	3,154	0.2
6400	Insurance agents, brokers, and service	38	39	1.2	131	134	25,649	29,104	4,006	4,332	0.7
6500	Real estate	47	47	0.8	158	213	14,861	16,432	3,064	3,759	0.4
6510	Real estate operators and lessors	22	23	1.2	61	99	13,836	18,020	1,103	1,785	0.9
6530	Real estate agents and managers	17	15	0.5	47	39	17,191	15,077	924	718	0.1
6550	Subdividers and developers	5	7	1.3	49	65	14,041	15,262	960	1,114	1.1
6700	Holding and other investment offices	7	8	1.5	182	41	17,692	29,463	3,309	1,528	0.5
WILKES, GA											
60 –	**Finance, insurance, and real estate**	22	18	0.1	98	88	20,082	21,455	2,272	2,064	0.0
6400	Insurance agents, brokers, and service	6	6	0.2	15	18	24,000	20,667	449	453	0.1
6500	Real estate	5	3	0.1	5	5	13,600	17,600	80	98	0.0
WILKINSON, GA											
60 –	**Finance, insurance, and real estate**	9	8	0.0	58	66	18,207	18,667	1,257	1,412	0.0
6000	Depository institutions	5	5	0.2	47	57	19,319	19,088	1,097	1,256	0.1
WORTH, GA											
60 –	**Finance, insurance, and real estate**	20	21	0.1	122	125	20,951	21,760	2,722	2,862	0.0

Source: County Business Patterns, 1994/95, CBP-94/95, U.S. Department of Commerce, Washington, D.C., November 1997. SIC categories for which data were suppressed or not available for both 1994 and 1995 are *not* displayed. The employment columns represent mid-March employment in the year. Pay per employee is calculated by dividing 1st Quarter payroll, annualized, by mid-March employment. The columns headed "% State" show the county's percentage of the state total for the SIC in 1995; for example, 1.4% for SIC 6000 means that the county had 1.4 percent of the state's total establishments (or payroll) in SIC 6000 in 1995. A dash (-) is used to indicate that data are not available or cannot be calculated; *nec* means not elsewhere classified.

Continued on next page.

SIC	Industry	No. Establishments			Employment		Pay / Employee		Annual Payroll ($ 000)		
		1994	1995	% State	1994	1995	1994	1995	1994	1995	% State
WORTH, GA - [continued]											
6000	Depository institutions	4	4	0.2	71	70	22,817	24,114	1,649	1,709	0.1
6020	Commercial banks	4	4	0.2	71	70	22,817	24,114	1,649	1,709	0.1
6100	Nondepository institutions	4	4	0.2	12	12	18,333	18,667	175	196	0.0
6140	Personal credit institutions	4	4	0.3	12	12	18,333	18,667	175	196	0.1
6400	Insurance agents, brokers, and service	6	6	0.2	33	31	20,242	22,839	842	820	0.1
6500	Real estate	6	7	0.1	6	12	8,000	8,333	56	137	0.0
6510	Real estate operators and lessors	3	3	0.2	3	3	5,333	5,333	17	16	0.0
6550	Subdividers and developers	3	3	0.5	3	8	10,667	10,000	39	108	0.1

Source: County Business Patterns, 1994/95, CBP-94/95, U.S. Department of Commerce, Washington, D.C., November 1997. SIC categories for which data were suppressed or not available for both 1994 and 1995 are *not* displayed. The employment columns represent mid-March employment in the year. Pay per employee is calculated by dividing 1st Quarter payroll, annualized, by mid-March employment. The columns headed "% State" show the county's percentage of the state total for the SIC in 1995; for example, 1.4% for SIC 6000 means that the county had 1.4 percent of the state's total establishments (or payroll) in SIC 6000 in 1995. A dash (-) is used to indicate that data are not available or cannot be calculated; *nec* means not elsewhere classified.

HAWAII

SIC	Industry	No. Establishments			Employment		Pay / Employee		Annual Payroll ($ 000)		
		1994	1995	% State	1994	1995	1994	1995	1994	1995	% State
HAWAII, HI											
60 –	**Finance, insurance, and real estate**	383	371	*9.6*	3,096	3,044	26,698	26,127	79,446	82,960	*7.0*
6000	Depository institutions	65	68	*11.4*	679	685	29,131	25,606	17,499	17,238	*4.5*
6020	Commercial banks	33	36	*11.8*	354	354	27,740	27,311	9,250	9,244	*3.3*
6060	Credit unions	16	16	*12.2*	224	226	33,143	23,310	5,737	5,394	*15.7*
6100	Nondepository institutions	21	20	*8.7*	116	102	52,552	33,059	3,856	3,883	*6.9*
6160	Mortgage bankers and brokers	9	8	*7.6*	78	61	64,154	35,475	2,769	2,702	*7.5*
6300	Insurance carriers	11	9	*5.9*	109	87	25,174	28,552	2,850	2,605	*1.6*
6400	Insurance agents, brokers, and service	31	30	*8.5*	138	140	29,652	26,371	4,146	3,996	*4.0*
6500	Real estate	240	227	*10.0*	1,975	1,944	23,449	24,479	47,508	50,651	*12.3*
6530	Real estate agents and managers	149	135	*9.0*	653	684	21,292	21,848	14,426	16,175	*7.6*
6550	Subdividers and developers	19	20	*19.2*	744	703	27,285	28,370	20,198	20,454	*24.9*
HONOLULU, HI											
60 –	**Finance, insurance, and real estate**	2,894	2,881	*74.9*	32,334	31,582	31,103	32,458	988,347	998,862	*83.8*
6000	Depository institutions	433	423	*71.2*	11,060	11,158	31,359	33,608	338,882	343,378	*89.8*
6020	Commercial banks	227	218	*71.5*	8,014	8,076	32,438	35,356	251,735	256,396	*92.2*
6030	Savings institutions	86	88	*71.5*	1,524	1,546	29,018	29,278	44,122	43,985	*87.0*
6060	Credit unions	90	89	*67.9*	892	923	25,350	26,041	23,034	24,262	*70.7*
6080	Foreign bank and branches and agencies	3	3	*100.0*	22	23	41,455	48,696	1,033	1,146	*100.0*
6090	Functions closely related to banking	27	25	*78.1*	608	590	31,461	32,278	18,958	17,589	*97.4*
6100	Nondepository institutions	180	176	*76.2*	1,694	1,271	47,244	40,554	56,708	47,605	*85.2*
6160	Mortgage bankers and brokers	86	80	*76.2*	1,211	751	54,111	46,738	42,028	30,435	*85.0*
6200	Security and commodity brokers	70	83	*83.0*	772	722	52,523	49,407	36,994	38,447	*89.4*
6300	Insurance carriers	126	132	*86.8*	4,224	4,291	31,358	35,627	142,465	154,757	*96.6*
6400	Insurance agents, brokers, and service	279	285	*81.2*	2,625	2,642	32,792	34,133	86,368	92,114	*92.7*
6500	Real estate	1,706	1,676	*73.5*	11,228	10,654	25,534	26,728	292,539	287,721	*70.1*
6510	Real estate operators and lessors	512	501	*79.3*	2,709	2,489	27,290	30,378	73,464	70,545	*70.1*
6530	Real estate agents and managers	1,105	1,080	*72.1*	6,575	6,224	23,668	23,617	158,429	153,088	*71.5*
6550	Subdividers and developers	69	67	*64.4*	1,434	1,602	29,914	32,355	46,138	52,035	*63.3*
6552	Subdividers and developers, n.e.c.	60	56	*64.4*	1,257	1,404	31,889	34,678	43,401	48,492	*65.9*
6553	Cemetery subdividers and developers	9	10	*62.5*	177	195	15,887	14,667	2,737	3,409	*40.2*
6700	Holding and other investment offices	92	99	*78.6*	594	656	43,145	42,262	27,514	27,773	*85.1*
6733	Trusts, n.e.c.	17	19	*57.6*	120	132	32,700	31,333	4,166	4,317	*60.5*
6790	Miscellaneous investing	33	29	*80.6*	185	149	31,784	44,591	7,816	6,079	*83.5*
6794	Patent owners and lessors	5	3	*100.0*	45	24	7,911	7,167	315	163	*100.0*
KAUAI, HI											
60 –	**Finance, insurance, and real estate**	187	177	*4.6*	1,303	1,251	24,031	24,125	30,868	30,768	*2.6*
6000	Depository institutions	37	38	*6.4*	321	335	26,492	25,803	7,908	8,319	*2.2*
6020	Commercial banks	19	19	*6.2*	165	175	29,624	26,263	4,200	4,360	*1.6*
6030	Savings institutions	6	6	*4.9*	41	41	22,439	26,829	975	1,046	*2.1*
6060	Credit unions	12	13	*9.9*	115	119	23,443	24,773	2,733	2,913	*8.5*
6100	Nondepository institutions	14	12	*5.2*	47	31	28,511	28,645	1,155	991	*1.8*
6160	Mortgage bankers and brokers	7	5	*4.8*	22	11	35,091	31,636	596	360	*1.0*
6400	Insurance agents, brokers, and service	17	17	*4.8*	40	49	24,300	27,755	942	1,258	*1.3*
6500	Real estate	104	96	*4.2*	833	770	22,679	23,044	19,086	18,594	*4.5*
6530	Real estate agents and managers	75	69	*4.6*	383	408	20,125	19,667	8,587	9,382	*4.4*
MAUI, HI											
60 –	**Finance, insurance, and real estate**	433	416	*10.8*	3,078	3,040	26,019	25,567	80,323	78,994	*6.6*
6000	Depository institutions	64	65	*10.9*	548	569	25,766	25,040	13,732	13,262	*3.5*

Source: County Business Patterns, 1994/95, CBP-94/95, U.S. Department of Commerce, Washington, D.C., November 1997. SIC categories for which data were suppressed or not available for both 1994 and 1995 are not displayed. The employment columns represent mid-March employment in the year. Pay per employee is calculated by dividing 1st Quarter payroll, annualized, by mid-March employment. The columns headed "% State" show the county's percentage of the state total for the SIC in 1995; for example, 1.4% for SIC 6000 means that the county had 1.4 percent of the state's total establishments (or payroll) in SIC 6000 in 1995. A dash (-) is used to indicate that data are not available or cannot be calculated; nec means not elsewhere classified.

Continued on next page.

SIC	Industry	No. Establishments			Employment		Pay / Employee		Annual Payroll ($ 000)		
		1994	1995	% State	1994	1995	1994	1995	1994	1995	% State
MAUI, HI - [continued]											
6020	Commercial banks	31	32	10.5	339	338	27,209	26,769	8,600	8,116	2.9
6060	Credit unions	13	13	9.9	66	65	24,364	25,969	1,739	1,766	5.1
6100	Nondepository institutions	25	23	10.0	134	92	52,776	33,826	5,679	3,394	6.1
6160	Mortgage bankers and brokers	14	12	11.4	100	58	59,080	34,069	4,583	2,305	6.4
6400	Insurance agents, brokers, and service	20	19	5.4	77	81	23,117	24,198	1,788	2,022	2.0
6500	Real estate	295	282	12.4	2,145	2,112	23,636	24,653	52,785	53,704	13.1
6510	Real estate operators and lessors	53	52	8.2	644	548	22,161	27,869	15,295	14,554	14.5
6530	Real estate agents and managers	226	213	14.2	1,436	1,502	24,058	23,321	35,643	35,529	16.6
6700	Holding and other investment offices	12	12	9.5	68	78	24,529	25,692	1,721	1,943	6.0

Source: County Business Patterns, 1994/95, CBP-94/95, U.S. Department of Commerce, Washington, D.C., November 1997. SIC categories for which data were suppressed or not available for both 1994 and 1995 are *not* displayed. The employment columns represent mid-March employment in the year. Pay per employee is calculated by dividing 1st Quarter payroll, annualized, by mid-March employment. The columns headed "% State" show the county's percentage of the state total for the SIC in 1995; for example, 1.4% for SIC 6000 means that the county had 1.4 percent of the state's total establishments (or payroll) in SIC 6000 in 1995. A dash (-) is used to indicate that data are not available or cannot be calculated; *nec* means not elsewhere classified.

IDAHO

SIC	Industry	No. Establishments			Employment		Pay / Employee		Annual Payroll ($ 000)		
		1994	1995	% State	1994	1995	1994	1995	1994	1995	% State
ADA, ID											
60 –	**Finance, insurance, and real estate**	850	880	31.4	8,857	9,425	26,261	27,068	236,035	259,668	50.8
6000	Depository institutions	145	152	27.8	4,126	4,622	25,414	27,178	105,422	123,363	57.5
6020	Commercial banks	105	107	28.7	3,711	4,190	26,039	27,814	98,140	115,234	61.9
6060	Credit unions	26	26	22.0	305	305	17,980	19,266	4,536	4,720	29.7
6100	Nondepository institutions	85	88	40.6	539	583	33,833	32,659	17,584	19,889	55.3
6140	Personal credit institutions	26	26	33.8	108	123	23,074	29,398	2,556	3,359	37.3
6160	Mortgage bankers and brokers	49	54	51.4	395	415	36,051	31,865	12,806	13,748	72.3
6200	Security and commodity brokers	42	41	32.3	296	302	54,068	54,609	15,006	17,957	51.8
6210	Security brokers and dealers	25	23	29.1	251	253	54,789	56,379	12,452	15,252	51.0
6300	Insurance carriers	77	81	49.1	1,232	1,248	29,172	30,231	36,443	37,575	46.8
6310	Life insurance	22	22	68.8	331	330	23,940	24,352	8,404	7,771	58.2
6330	Fire, marine, and casualty insurance	42	42	43.8	355	335	34,220	39,749	12,888	13,053	32.8
6400	Insurance agents, brokers, and service	178	188	31.1	883	911	27,094	25,989	23,925	24,499	36.7
6500	Real estate	293	303	28.4	1,629	1,656	17,272	17,761	31,533	33,125	45.4
6510	Real estate operators and lessors	80	90	29.3	434	491	15,198	14,998	6,688	8,627	44.9
6530	Real estate agents and managers	151	151	26.4	830	810	15,229	16,395	15,145	14,452	44.0
6540	Title abstract offices	10	10	22.7	229	228	22,812	24,211	5,078	6,005	47.9
6550	Subdividers and developers	41	40	36.7	125	107	28,384	28,150	4,331	3,737	50.1
6552	Subdividers and developers, n.e.c.	38	36	43.9	118	94	29,458	30,766	4,108	3,490	52.5
6733	Trusts, n.e.c.	7	5	35.7	29	27	16,828	22,519	531	586	36.3
ADAMS, ID											
60 –	**Finance, insurance, and real estate**	7	6	0.2	20	18	15,600	17,111	352	380	0.1
6500	Real estate	4	3	0.3	9	7	12,444	17,143	146	167	0.2
BANNOCK, ID											
60 –	**Finance, insurance, and real estate**	153	153	5.5	1,804	1,687	25,239	26,957	44,320	44,051	8.6
6000	Depository institutions	35	29	5.3	389	316	21,954	23,013	8,875	7,532	3.5
6020	Commercial banks	21	16	4.3	257	184	23,128	24,739	6,158	4,684	2.5
6100	Nondepository institutions	12	11	5.1	58	50	25,931	27,920	1,300	1,427	4.0
6200	Security and commodity brokers	7	9	7.1	40	41	41,600	39,512	1,545	1,721	5.0
6300	Insurance carriers	18	17	10.3	864	858	30,181	32,317	24,679	25,249	31.4
6400	Insurance agents, brokers, and service	25	26	4.3	97	109	21,938	22,495	1,945	2,594	3.9
6500	Real estate	50	54	5.1	337	286	15,727	16,126	5,596	5,162	7.1
6510	Real estate operators and lessors	17	18	5.9	90	88	9,867	10,773	988	1,059	5.5
6530	Real estate agents and managers	27	30	5.2	87	67	12,552	14,866	1,241	1,253	3.8
6700	Holding and other investment offices	6	7	9.5	19	27	16,842	14,667	380	366	-
BEAR LAKE, ID											
60 –	**Finance, insurance, and real estate**	10	10	0.4	85	82	10,353	10,829	1,033	914	0.2
6400	Insurance agents, brokers, and service	3	3	0.5	9	8	10,667	12,500	106	114	0.2
BENEWAH, ID											
60 –	**Finance, insurance, and real estate**	16	14	0.5	74	71	13,514	15,324	1,079	1,068	0.2
6000	Depository institutions	4	4	0.7	32	33	16,625	18,182	575	605	0.3
6400	Insurance agents, brokers, and service	6	5	0.8	21	18	8,381	9,778	195	173	0.3
6500	Real estate	6	5	0.5	21	20	13,905	15,600	309	290	0.4
BINGHAM, ID											
60 –	**Finance, insurance, and real estate**	45	47	1.7	183	200	20,175	24,140	4,010	4,837	0.9

Source: County Business Patterns, 1994/95, CBP-94/95, U.S. Department of Commerce, Washington, D.C., November 1997. SIC categories for which data were suppressed or not available for both 1994 and 1995 are *not* displayed. The employment columns represent mid-March employment in the year. Pay per employee is calculated by dividing 1st Quarter payroll, annualized, by mid-March employment. The columns headed "% State" show the county's percentage of the state total for the SIC in 1995; for example, 1.4% for SIC 6000 means that the county had 1.4 percent of the state's total establishments (or payroll) in SIC 6000 in 1995. A dash (-) is used to indicate that data are not available or cannot be calculated; *nec* means not elsewhere classified.

Continued on next page.

SIC	Industry	No. Establishments			Employment		Pay / Employee		Annual Payroll ($ 000)		
		1994	1995	% State	1994	1995	1994	1995	1994	1995	% State
BINGHAM, ID - [continued]											
6000	Depository institutions	16	16	2.9	112	118	17,464	20,508	2,152	2,486	1.2
6020	Commercial banks	8	8	2.1	78	84	17,333	20,714	1,465	1,741	0.9
6530	Real estate agents and managers	8	8	1.4	9	10	16,000	12,800	147	149	0.5
BLAINE, ID											
60–	**Finance, insurance, and real estate**	115	121	4.3	445	514	21,924	25,634	11,446	13,271	2.6
6000	Depository institutions	10	10	1.8	97	79	20,660	23,190	2,003	2,027	0.9
6100	Nondepository institutions	10	9	4.1	23	62	26,609	11,226	663	734	2.0
6400	Insurance agents, brokers, and service	11	9	1.5	40	38	25,600	24,842	1,087	1,056	1.6
6500	Real estate	67	75	7.0	244	282	15,607	19,858	5,007	4,889	6.7
6510	Real estate operators and lessors	17	19	6.2	35	43	11,657	9,581	439	464	2.4
6530	Real estate agents and managers	41	46	8.0	191	212	15,832	21,075	3,837	3,477	10.6
6799	Investors, n.e.c.	4	4	23.5	6	6	18,000	18,667	132	134	8.7
BOISE, ID											
60–	**Finance, insurance, and real estate**	3	3	0.1	5	3	7,200	12,000	46	31	0.0
6500	Real estate	3	3	0.3	5	3	7,200	12,000	46	31	0.0
BONNER, ID											
60–	**Finance, insurance, and real estate**	84	90	3.2	479	492	18,489	20,138	9,043	10,096	2.0
6000	Depository institutions	10	9	1.6	127	133	24,346	25,143	2,765	3,114	1.5
6100	Nondepository institutions	7	6	2.8	11	16	33,091	23,000	357	508	1.4
6160	Mortgage bankers and brokers	7	6	5.7	11	16	33,091	23,000	357	508	2.7
6400	Insurance agents, brokers, and service	8	9	1.5	60	50	19,600	25,760	1,247	1,380	2.1
6500	Real estate	49	56	5.3	263	272	14,084	14,926	4,108	4,258	5.8
6510	Real estate operators and lessors	12	14	4.6	70	77	21,257	20,831	1,604	1,589	8.3
6530	Real estate agents and managers	28	32	5.6	170	169	10,776	11,905	1,954	2,032	6.2
6550	Subdividers and developers	6	6	5.5	12	21	14,667	16,000	362	511	6.9
6552	Subdividers and developers, n.e.c.	5	6	7.3	12	21	14,667	16,000	332	511	7.7
BONNEVILLE, ID											
60–	**Finance, insurance, and real estate**	185	196	7.0	1,188	1,159	23,229	23,085	27,830	28,055	5.5
6000	Depository institutions	39	39	7.1	575	535	21,482	20,508	12,605	11,240	5.2
6020	Commercial banks	27	26	7.0	416	359	23,346	22,139	9,803	8,189	4.4
6100	Nondepository institutions	18	20	9.2	117	124	27,829	27,194	2,729	3,061	8.5
6140	Personal credit institutions	11	11	14.3	66	65	25,394	26,277	1,510	1,529	17.0
6200	Security and commodity brokers	10	10	7.9	63	73	57,841	44,603	3,242	3,442	9.9
6400	Insurance agents, brokers, and service	47	48	7.9	220	225	22,218	23,769	5,367	6,055	9.1
6500	Real estate	59	65	6.1	158	146	13,848	15,288	2,580	2,618	3.6
6530	Real estate agents and managers	34	38	6.6	89	91	15,685	16,703	1,727	1,758	5.3
6550	Subdividers and developers	4	3	2.8	4	3	20,000	12,000	60	25	0.3
6552	Subdividers and developers, n.e.c.	4	3	3.7	4	3	20,000	12,000	60	25	0.4
BOUNDARY, ID											
60–	**Finance, insurance, and real estate**	17	19	0.7	63	59	15,302	14,441	917	874	0.2
6530	Real estate agents and managers	6	7	1.2	12	12	11,000	8,333	128	112	0.3
BUTTE, ID											
60–	**Finance, insurance, and real estate**	5	6	0.2	20	23	16,000	14,087	311	355	0.1
CAMAS, ID											
60–	**Finance, insurance, and real estate**	2	2	0.1	-	-	-	-	-	-	-
CANYON, ID											
60–	**Finance, insurance, and real estate**	178	178	6.4	1,068	1,110	20,918	21,002	23,071	24,987	4.9
6000	Depository institutions	37	38	6.9	390	396	21,210	21,808	8,612	9,253	4.3
6020	Commercial banks	18	18	4.8	266	258	21,188	22,140	5,544	5,912	3.2
6030	Savings institutions	6	6	12.0	71	78	25,070	24,667	2,186	2,290	

Source: *County Business Patterns, 1994/95, CBP-94/95*, U.S. Department of Commerce, Washington, D.C., November 1997. SIC categories for which data were suppressed or not available for both 1994 and 1995 are *not* displayed. The employment columns represent mid-March employment in the year. Pay per employee is calculated by dividing 1st Quarter payroll, annualized, by mid-March employment. The columns headed "% State" show the county's percentage of the state total for the SIC in 1995; for example, 1.4% for SIC 6000 means that the county had 1.4 percent of the state's total establishments (or payroll) in SIC 6000 in 1995. A dash (-) is used to indicate that data are not available or cannot be calculated; *nec* means not elsewhere classified.

Continued on next page.

SIC	Industry	No. Establishments			Employment		Pay / Employee		Annual Payroll ($ 000)		
		1994	1995	% State	1994	1995	1994	1995	1994	1995	% State
CANYON, ID - [continued]											
6100	Nondepository institutions	14	13	6.0	91	80	29,582	32,500	2,477	2,852	7.9
6300	Insurance carriers	8	8	4.8	110	133	32,618	29,113	3,467	3,894	4.8
6400	Insurance agents, brokers, and service	44	46	7.6	170	197	15,953	16,812	3,600	3,790	5.7
6500	Real estate	66	64	6.0	286	289	14,294	14,201	4,041	4,368	6.0
6510	Real estate operators and lessors	24	22	7.2	194	202	12,639	12,673	2,373	2,554	13.3
6530	Real estate agents and managers	38	36	6.3	54	59	14,519	14,983	914	1,142	3.5
CARIBOU, ID											
60 –	**Finance, insurance, and real estate**	11	15	0.5	-	-	-	-	-	-	-
6500	Real estate	5	6	0.6	10	12	11,600	10,667	161	202	0.3
CASSIA, ID											
60 –	**Finance, insurance, and real estate**	39	47	1.7	246	237	18,293	19,156	5,077	5,247	1.0
6000	Depository institutions	14	14	2.6	133	127	17,895	18,142	2,711	2,736	1.3
6020	Commercial banks	9	9	2.4	118	113	17,119	17,310	2,432	2,459	1.3
6400	Insurance agents, brokers, and service	7	9	1.5	59	61	16,678	15,672	1,203	1,168	1.8
6500	Real estate	11	16	1.5	32	30	9,625	12,800	291	406	0.6
CLARK, ID											
60 –	**Finance, insurance, and real estate**	3	3	0.1	-	-	-	-	-	-	-
CLEARWATER, ID											
60 –	**Finance, insurance, and real estate**	17	15	0.5	65	62	13,723	15,613	973	984	0.2
6000	Depository institutions	6	6	1.1	37	37	17,189	19,027	672	696	0.3
6400	Insurance agents, brokers, and service	5	5	0.8	22	21	10,182	11,238	258	246	0.4
6500	Real estate	6	4	0.4	6	4	5,333	7,000	43	42	0.1
CUSTER, ID											
60 –	**Finance, insurance, and real estate**	7	7	0.2	29	30	15,862	15,867	469	494	0.1
6000	Depository institutions	3	3	0.5	19	19	18,737	19,789	360	387	0.2
ELMORE, ID											
60 –	**Finance, insurance, and real estate**	34	35	1.2	196	185	13,796	14,811	2,977	2,937	0.6
6000	Depository institutions	9	9	1.6	85	86	17,271	18,558	1,620	1,706	0.8
6100	Nondepository institutions	3	3	1.4	5	4	22,400	27,000	132	127	0.4
6400	Insurance agents, brokers, and service	10	13	2.2	37	38	12,865	13,368	561	545	0.8
6500	Real estate	8	7	0.7	59	46	7,390	8,261	423	421	0.6
FREMONT, ID											
60 –	**Finance, insurance, and real estate**	11	12	0.4	67	69	15,343	13,333	1,168	982	0.2
6400	Insurance agents, brokers, and service	4	6	1.0	9	14	14,222	10,857	147	187	0.3
GEM, ID											
60 –	**Finance, insurance, and real estate**	14	17	0.6	67	61	15,881	17,574	1,063	1,124	0.2
GOODING, ID											
60 –	**Finance, insurance, and real estate**	22	24	0.9	83	96	16,048	15,542	1,541	1,524	0.3
6000	Depository institutions	6	6	1.1	47	47	18,894	18,213	974	995	0.5
6020	Commercial banks	6	6	1.6	47	47	18,894	18,213	974	995	0.5
6400	Insurance agents, brokers, and service	7	7	1.2	19	18	12,632	14,889	251	266	0.4
6500	Real estate	6	7	0.7	10	14	6,400	6,857	147	166	0.2
IDAHO, ID											
60 –	**Finance, insurance, and real estate**	23	24	0.9	108	143	14,370	13,427	1,761	1,928	0.4
6000	Depository institutions	9	9	1.6	63	67	15,556	15,761	1,076	1,096	0.5
6500	Real estate	7	7	0.7	17	45	13,412	10,044	324	414	0.6

Source: County Business Patterns, 1994/95, CBP-94/95, U.S. Department of Commerce, Washington, D.C., November 1997. SIC categories for which data were suppressed or not available for both 1994 and 1995 are not displayed. The employment columns represent mid-March employment in the year. Pay per employee is calculated by dividing 1st Quarter payroll, annualized, by mid-March employment. The columns headed "% State" show the county's percentage of the state total for the SIC in 1995; for example, 1.4% for SIC 6000 means that the county had 1.4 percent of the state's total establishments (or payroll) in SIC 6000 in 1995. A dash (-) is used to indicate that data are not available or cannot be calculated; nec means not elsewhere classified.

SIC	Industry	No. Establishments			Employment		Pay / Employee		Annual Payroll ($ 000)		
		1994	1995	% State	1994	1995	1994	1995	1994	1995	% State
JEFFERSON, ID											
60 –	**Finance, insurance, and real estate**	17	18	0.6	65	65	18,338	20,492	1,240	1,334	0.3
6000	Depository institutions	5	5	0.9	41	42	21,366	23,619	911	1,000	0.5
6500	Real estate	7	7	0.7	12	10	8,667	8,800	107	105	0.1
KOOTENAI, ID											
60 –	**Finance, insurance, and real estate**	259	267	9.5	1,310	1,283	22,995	22,316	30,350	31,013	6.1
6000	Depository institutions	38	39	7.1	479	465	24,351	23,372	11,020	11,329	5.3
6020	Commercial banks	30	30	8.0	429	409	23,981	23,071	9,554	9,768	5.2
6100	Nondepository institutions	21	23	10.6	75	69	24,640	24,406	1,641	2,040	5.7
6160	Mortgage bankers and brokers	13	14	13.3	47	39	24,851	22,051	992	1,266	6.7
6200	Security and commodity brokers	13	13	10.2	51	63	54,824	46,222	2,617	3,081	8.9
6210	Security brokers and dealers	8	9	11.4	43	50	60,558	53,040	2,435	2,861	9.6
6280	Security and commodity services	5	4	9.3	8	13	24,000	20,000	182	220	5.3
6400	Insurance agents, brokers, and service	46	41	6.8	193	215	24,021	21,153	5,312	5,295	7.9
6500	Real estate	124	134	12.6	454	420	16,361	17,171	7,893	7,729	10.6
6530	Real estate agents and managers	72	75	13.1	200	193	13,700	16,021	3,211	3,404	10.4
6550	Subdividers and developers	18	21	19.3	105	90	22,362	21,244	2,122	1,875	25.1
LATAH, ID											
60 –	**Finance, insurance, and real estate**	72	76	2.7	315	339	16,622	16,861	5,756	6,302	1.2
6000	Depository institutions	15	18	3.3	151	163	18,305	17,939	2,761	3,050	1.4
6400	Insurance agents, brokers, and service	16	15	2.5	63	66	13,206	15,394	992	1,201	1.8
6500	Real estate	32	31	2.9	88	96	14,091	14,375	1,464	1,601	2.2
LEMHI, ID											
60 –	**Finance, insurance, and real estate**	10	12	0.4	46	52	16,696	16,462	883	919	0.2
6400	Insurance agents, brokers, and service	4	5	0.8	10	10	10,400	12,000	129	124	0.2
LEWIS, ID											
60 –	**Finance, insurance, and real estate**	10	8	0.3	-	-	-	-	-	-	-
6000	Depository institutions	5	5	0.9	28	30	14,857	15,200	442	462	0.2
MADISON, ID											
60 –	**Finance, insurance, and real estate**	42	42	1.5	160	166	16,150	17,422	2,953	3,136	0.6
6000	Depository institutions	9	9	1.6	88	95	16,909	17,600	1,695	1,791	0.8
6020	Commercial banks	5	5	1.3	66	67	17,394	18,209	1,309	1,319	0.7
6100	Nondepository institutions	4	4	1.8	14	12	27,714	35,000	390	357	1.0
6400	Insurance agents, brokers, and service	8	7	1.2	21	24	19,048	16,667	471	468	0.7
6500	Real estate	17	16	1.5	30	28	6,400	7,857	237	261	0.4
6510	Real estate operators and lessors	11	11	3.6	24	22	5,500	6,727	169	170	0.9
6530	Real estate agents and managers	6	5	0.9	6	6	10,000	12,000	68	91	0.3
MINIDOKA, ID											
60 –	**Finance, insurance, and real estate**	15	17	0.6	76	86	18,105	17,814	1,382	1,579	0.3
6000	Depository institutions	6	6	1.1	52	54	21,385	22,815	1,099	1,225	0.6
NEZ PERCE, ID											
60 –	**Finance, insurance, and real estate**	104	111	4.0	1,050	1,055	24,621	26,730	26,311	26,366	5.2
6000	Depository institutions	21	22	4.0	255	280	23,059	22,886	6,096	6,450	3.0
6020	Commercial banks	11	11	2.9	144	150	24,972	24,693	3,573	3,515	1.9
6200	Security and commodity brokers	7	8	6.3	24	27	46,833	39,259	1,106	1,278	3.7
6400	Insurance agents, brokers, and service	30	31	5.1	370	351	23,989	24,798	8,781	7,593	11.4
6500	Real estate	32	35	3.3	86	75	16,605	17,867	1,551	1,427	2.0
6530	Real estate agents and managers	16	18	3.1	54	49	18,667	20,980	1,158	1,100	3.3
6550	Subdividers and developers	3	4	3.7	4	5	8,000	9,600	42	59	0.8
ONEIDA, ID											
60 –	**Finance, insurance, and real estate**	5	5	0.2	80	83	15,700	15,614	1,368	1,472	0.3

Source: County Business Patterns, 1994/95, CBP-94/95,,U.S. Department of Commerce, Washington, D.C., November 1997. SIC categories for which data were suppressed or not available for both 1994 and 1995 are *not* displayed. The employment columns represent mid-March employment in the year. Pay per employee is calculated by dividing 1st Quarter payroll, annualized, by mid-March employment. The columns headed "% State" show the county's percentage of the state total for the SIC in 1995; for example, 1.4% for SIC 6000 means that the county had 1.4 percent of the state's total establishments (or payroll) in SIC 6000 in 1995. A dash (-) is used to indicate that data are not available or cannot be calculated; *nec* means not elsewhere classified.

SIC	Industry	No. Establishments			Employment		Pay / Employee		Annual Payroll ($ 000)		
		1994	1995	% State	1994	1995	1994	1995	1994	1995	% State
OWYHEE, ID											
60 –	**Finance, insurance, and real estate**	9	9	0.3	37	33	16,541	20,364	606	665	0.1
PAYETTE, ID											
60 –	**Finance, insurance, and real estate**	28	25	0.9	189	113	18,815	20,000	3,930	2,526	0.5
6000	Depository institutions	5	5	0.9	52	55	21,538	21,164	1,188	1,281	0.6
6020	Commercial banks	5	5	1.3	52	55	21,538	21,164	1,188	1,281	0.7
6400	Insurance agents, brokers, and service	7	6	1.0	30	29	23,867	20,276	861	609	0.9
6500	Real estate	11	9	0.8	20	18	9,000	6,667	184	150	0.2
POWER, ID											
60 –	**Finance, insurance, and real estate**	12	11	0.4	-	-	-	-	-	-	-
6400	Insurance agents, brokers, and service	4	4	0.7	5	6	6,400	5,333	31	31	0.0
SHOSHONE, ID											
60 –	**Finance, insurance, and real estate**	30	30	1.1	154	130	16,312	17,446	2,422	2,229	0.4
6000	Depository institutions	8	8	1.5	58	56	19,241	19,357	1,110	1,111	0.5
6500	Real estate	13	14	1.3	68	39	10,824	11,179	698	434	0.6
TETON, ID											
60 –	**Finance, insurance, and real estate**	8	8	0.3	27	33	13,185	12,364	452	475	0.1
TWIN FALLS, ID											
60 –	**Finance, insurance, and real estate**	152	152	5.4	868	845	23,885	24,066	21,243	21,728	4.3
6000	Depository institutions	31	30	5.5	373	381	25,834	26,530	9,402	10,044	4.7
6020	Commercial banks	21	20	5.4	296	307	24,095	25,238	7,625	8,134	4.4
6030	Savings institutions	5	5	10.0	61	57	38,098	38,175	1,591	1,712	-
6060	Credit unions	5	5	4.2	16	17	11,250	10,824	186	198	1.2
6100	Nondepository institutions	13	13	6.0	74	64	27,135	31,625	1,978	2,008	5.6
6210	Security brokers and dealers	6	7	8.9	15	21	41,333	30,667	759	891	3.0
6400	Insurance agents, brokers, and service	37	36	6.0	185	185	23,676	22,119	4,800	4,987	7.5
6500	Real estate	48	46	4.3	138	137	12,580	12,409	2,000	2,053	2.8
6510	Real estate operators and lessors	19	19	6.2	66	65	12,242	12,985	883	947	4.9
6530	Real estate agents and managers	23	23	4.0	53	54	12,151	11,704	804	844	2.6
VALLEY, ID											
60 –	**Finance, insurance, and real estate**	36	39	1.4	103	105	15,456	15,429	1,861	1,939	0.4
6400	Insurance agents, brokers, and service	5	6	1.0	14	13	16,571	19,692	242	283	0.4
6500	Real estate	24	26	2.4	51	48	12,549	13,083	794	867	1.2
6540	Title abstract offices	3	4	9.1	28	18	13,143	12,444	420	402	3.2
WASHINGTON, ID											
60 –	**Finance, insurance, and real estate**	17	18	0.6	80	79	13,500	15,392	1,211	1,276	0.2
6500	Real estate	5	6	0.6	23	18	5,565	7,333	148	132	0.2
6530	Real estate agents and managers	5	6	1.0	23	18	5,565	7,333	148	132	0.4

Source: County Business Patterns, 1994/95, CBP-94/95, U.S. Department of Commerce, Washington, D.C., November 1997. SIC categories for which data were suppressed or not available for both 1994 and 1995 are not displayed. The employment columns represent mid-March employment in the year. Pay per employee is calculated by dividing 1st Quarter payroll, annualized, by mid-March employment. The columns headed "% State" show the county's percentage of the state total for the SIC in 1995; for example, 1.4% for SIC 6000 means that the county had 1.4 percent of the state's total establishments (or payroll) in SIC 6000 in 1995. A dash (-) is used to indicate that data are not available or cannot be calculated; nec means not elsewhere classified.

ILLINOIS

SIC	Industry	No. Establishments			Employment		Pay / Employee		Annual Payroll ($ 000)		
		1994	1995	% State	1994	1995	1994	1995	1994	1995	% State
ADAMS, IL											
60 –	**Finance, insurance, and real estate**	180	180	0.6	1,369	1,359	19,173	21,242	27,813	28,614	0.2
6000	Depository institutions	40	41	0.9	513	614	19,025	19,681	10,902	11,951	0.3
6020	Commercial banks	24	25	1.0	414	510	19,082	20,769	9,257	10,450	0.4
6030	Savings institutions	5	5	0.5	59	59	22,983	15,797	1,126	933	0.2
6060	Credit unions	11	11	1.6	40	45	12,600	12,444	519	568	-
6300	Insurance carriers	13	14	0.7	318	333	19,660	24,048	6,525	7,506	0.2
6310	Life insurance	3	3	0.6	65	63	28,062	34,095	1,792	1,776	0.2
6400	Insurance agents, brokers, and service	47	48	0.7	113	119	19,504	20,370	2,403	2,460	0.2
6500	Real estate	57	58	0.6	141	162	9,362	11,556	1,643	2,375	0.1
6510	Real estate operators and lessors	31	32	0.9	76	92	7,789	11,435	765	1,430	0.3
6540	Title abstract offices	3	3	1.2	14	12	15,143	17,333	237	218	0.5
6700	Holding and other investment offices	4	3	0.3	206	56	11,417	19,571	2,645	1,318	0.2
BOND, IL											
60 –	**Finance, insurance, and real estate**	35	45	0.2	169	190	17,444	17,958	3,273	3,842	0.0
6000	Depository institutions	7	7	0.1	97	96	17,072	17,917	1,802	1,779	0.0
BOONE, IL											
60 –	**Finance, insurance, and real estate**	64	69	0.2	358	351	19,028	20,422	7,257	7,687	0.0
6000	Depository institutions	15	15	0.3	241	220	20,332	23,055	5,290	5,225	0.1
6020	Commercial banks	9	9	0.4	166	155	22,458	24,568	3,948	3,819	0.1
6500	Real estate	26	30	0.3	60	72	15,467	16,556	1,090	1,434	0.1
6550	Subdividers and developers	8	9	1.2	20	24	15,000	19,167	313	525	0.4
BROWN, IL											
60 –	**Finance, insurance, and real estate**	15	16	0.1	72	68	16,944	17,000	1,444	1,287	0.0
6000	Depository institutions	5	5	0.1	52	48	19,462	19,750	1,035	1,024	0.0
BUREAU, IL											
60 –	**Finance, insurance, and real estate**	75	80	0.3	483	522	21,607	21,441	11,113	11,884	0.1
6000	Depository institutions	22	25	0.5	344	379	21,570	21,351	7,967	8,416	0.2
6020	Commercial banks	18	21	0.9	337	370	21,697	21,351	7,835	8,231	0.3
6400	Insurance agents, brokers, and service	25	27	0.4	86	88	21,349	21,591	1,838	2,051	0.1
6530	Real estate agents and managers	6	5	0.1	10	6	17,600	15,333	191	128	0.0
CALHOUN, IL											
60 –	**Finance, insurance, and real estate**	10	9	0.0	56	63	19,857	20,381	1,354	1,467	0.0
CARROLL, IL											
60 –	**Finance, insurance, and real estate**	38	37	0.1	263	243	18,190	19,078	4,948	4,870	0.0
6000	Depository institutions	15	15	0.3	178	167	20,225	20,455	3,599	3,471	0.1
6020	Commercial banks	11	11	0.5	152	140	20,737	21,114	3,153	3,005	0.1
CASS, IL											
60 –	**Finance, insurance, and real estate**	24	23	0.1	177	175	18,395	20,114	3,622	3,786	0.0
6000	Depository institutions	8	8	0.2	123	124	19,382	20,419	2,581	2,874	0.1
CHAMPAIGN, IL											
60 –	**Finance, insurance, and real estate**	393	394	1.3	3,489	3,413	24,009	24,800	84,234	90,152	0.6
6000	Depository institutions	71	71	1.5	1,627	1,381	23,058	23,809	37,034	34,024	0.9
6020	Commercial banks	38	39	1.6	1,349	1,093	23,861	24,930	31,140	28,059	1.0

Source: County Business Patterns, 1994/95, CBP-94/95, U.S. Department of Commerce, Washington, D.C., November 1997. SIC categories for which data were suppressed or not available for both 1994 and 1995 are not displayed. The employment columns represent mid-March employment in the year. Pay per employee is calculated by dividing 1st Quarter payroll, annualized, by mid-March employment. The columns headed "% State" show the county's percentage of the state total for the SIC in 1995; for example, 1.4% for SIC 6000 means that the county had 1.4 percent of the state's total establishments (or payroll) in SIC 6000 in 1995. A dash (-) is used to indicate that data are not available or cannot be calculated; nec means not elsewhere classified.

Continued on next page.

SIC	Industry	No. Establishments			Employment		Pay / Employee		Annual Payroll ($ 000)		
		1994	1995	% State	1994	1995	1994	1995	1994	1995	% State
CHAMPAIGN, IL - [continued]											
6030	Savings institutions	9	8	0.8	94	96	19,957	20,375	1,978	2,001	0.4
6060	Credit unions	21	21	3.0	162	161	16,370	17,143	2,998	2,977	-
6090	Functions closely related to banking	3	3	0.5	22	31	36,364	29,548	918	987	0.4
6100	Nondepository institutions	17	19	0.9	98	109	42,939	40,954	2,997	3,640	0.3
6160	Mortgage bankers and brokers	5	6	0.7	35	29	30,743	25,103	904	911	0.2
6200	Security and commodity brokers	31	30	1.0	154	161	43,195	45,416	6,446	8,891	0.3
6210	Security brokers and dealers	13	14	1.0	94	97	44,553	44,825	3,559	5,475	0.3
6220	Commodity contracts brokers, dealers	5	4	0.7	18	26	31,333	39,538	663	1,012	0.3
6280	Security and commodity services	13	12	1.4	42	38	45,238	50,947	2,224	2,404	0.4
6300	Insurance carriers	23	24	1.1	404	457	27,426	28,683	10,288	12,439	0.3
6310	Life insurance	7	7	1.3	100	89	33,240	24,225	2,879	2,023	0.2
6400	Insurance agents, brokers, and service	99	95	1.5	328	359	28,232	25,348	9,398	9,960	0.7
6500	Real estate	147	147	1.4	841	905	16,623	17,640	16,477	17,418	1.0
6510	Real estate operators and lessors	57	57	1.6	369	371	15,783	17,768	6,252	6,950	1.7
6530	Real estate agents and managers	71	76	1.4	429	478	17,548	18,025	9,493	9,756	0.9
CHRISTIAN, IL											
60 –	**Finance, insurance, and real estate**	69	75	0.3	529	554	15,856	20,029	10,394	10,408	0.1
6000	Depository institutions	21	21	0.4	295	310	14,292	20,813	5,974	5,914	0.2
6020	Commercial banks	16	17	0.7	269	283	14,097	21,300	5,517	5,485	0.2
CLARK, IL											
60 –	**Finance, insurance, and real estate**	30	30	0.1	190	205	17,958	17,854	3,688	3,765	0.0
6000	Depository institutions	8	8	0.2	120	133	18,400	18,105	2,445	2,504	0.1
CLAY, IL											
60 –	**Finance, insurance, and real estate**	27	29	0.1	273	272	16,689	17,721	4,806	5,010	0.0
6000	Depository institutions	7	7	0.1	118	117	20,237	21,778	2,485	2,619	0.1
6500	Real estate	6	8	0.1	124	126	12,742	13,079	1,653	1,733	0.1
CLINTON, IL											
60 –	**Finance, insurance, and real estate**	64	61	0.2	414	427	15,333	15,785	7,190	7,302	0.0
6000	Depository institutions	20	20	0.4	235	236	18,128	18,814	4,952	4,924	0.1
6020	Commercial banks	15	15	0.6	206	208	18,447	19,250	4,450	4,440	0.2
6500	Real estate	16	14	0.1	114	121	9,158	9,289	1,144	1,168	0.1
6510	Real estate operators and lessors	8	6	0.2	98	103	8,816	9,204	924	971	0.2
COLES, IL											
60 –	**Finance, insurance, and real estate**	108	114	0.4	713	713	20,208	25,105	14,241	16,153	0.1
6000	Depository institutions	32	30	0.6	430	422	21,256	22,493	8,732	9,130	0.2
6020	Commercial banks	20	19	0.8	331	328	19,795	21,183	6,162	6,845	0.2
6030	Savings institutions	6	6	0.6	75	72	30,720	31,333	2,259	1,982	0.4
6060	Credit unions	6	5	0.7	24	22	11,833	13,091	311	303	-
6100	Nondepository institutions	6	7	0.3	16	20	19,000	15,400	295	315	0.0
6300	Insurance carriers	6	7	0.3	104	100	20,077	23,440	2,036	2,235	0.1
6400	Insurance agents, brokers, and service	32	33	0.5	90	90	15,289	48,311	1,683	2,669	0.2
6500	Real estate	26	29	0.3	61	68	14,098	13,706	929	1,146	0.1
6510	Real estate operators and lessors	10	10	0.3	20	20	11,200	10,800	253	268	0.1
6540	Title abstract offices	3	3	1.2	13	15	22,154	19,733	297	316	0.8
COOK, IL											
60 –	**Finance, insurance, and real estate**	14,029	14,232	48.2	239,627	241,447	43,671	49,065	10,216,532	11,038,702	68.0
6000	Depository institutions	1,747	1,817	38.4	68,924	70,630	38,040	42,887	2,513,484	2,646,833	67.6
6020	Commercial banks	507	577	24.2	46,707	49,290	41,066	46,431	1,816,004	1,931,969	67.4
6030	Savings institutions	454	453	47.3	11,689	10,134	26,766	28,661	301,864	277,922	56.1
6090	Functions closely related to banking	508	520	82.7	5,137	6,183	29,816	33,217	155,662	190,201	84.9
6100	Nondepository institutions	874	932	45.5	13,718	12,984	46,430	52,205	576,446	626,818	58.4
6150	Business credit institutions	171	170	41.0	3,259	3,579	77,925	85,541	205,152	231,636	61.4

Source: County Business Patterns, 1994/95, CBP-94/95, U.S. Department of Commerce, Washington, D.C., November 1997. SIC categories for which data were suppressed or not available for both 1994 and 1995 are not displayed. The employment columns represent mid-March employment in the year. Pay per employee is calculated by dividing 1st Quarter payroll, annualized, by mid-March employment. The columns headed "% State" show the county's percentage of the state total for the SIC in 1995; for example, 1.4% for SIC 6000 means that the county had 1.4 percent of the state's total establishments (or payroll) in SIC 6000 in 1995. A dash (-) is used to indicate that data are not available or cannot be calculated; nec means not elsewhere classified.

Continued on next page.

SIC	Industry	No. Establishments			Employment		Pay / Employee		Annual Payroll ($ 000)		
		1994	1995	% State	1994	1995	1994	1995	1994	1995	% State

COOK, IL - [continued]

SIC	Industry	1994	1995	% State	1994	1995	1994	1995	1994	1995	% State
6160	Mortgage bankers and brokers	455	495	55.2	6,860	6,241	35,994	36,552	234,782	241,255	58.6
6200	Security and commodity brokers	1,739	1,833	63.6	29,972	31,710	79,508	88,740	2,231,802	2,567,486	88.7
6210	Security brokers and dealers	783	835	60.5	16,592	17,045	96,994	106,068	1,433,182	1,573,937	86.9
6220	Commodity contracts brokers, dealers	451	450	76.5	6,721	7,432	46,388	50,647	345,283	370,081	94.2
6280	Security and commodity services	475	501	58.9	4,056	4,483	86,196	111,403	341,732	497,078	88.4
6300	Insurance carriers	903	953	45.6	50,097	47,537	42,656	46,264	2,023,050	2,136,053	54.0
6310	Life insurance	254	246	46.2	13,158	12,645	33,131	35,745	428,934	431,784	50.7
6320	Medical service and health insurance	73	72	50.7	9,644	10,437	34,561	36,605	351,932	401,684	71.8
6321	Accident and health insurance	19	19	35.2	3,552	3,875	21,939	22,902	83,765	100,130	52.7
6324	Hospital and medical service plans	54	53	60.2	6,092	6,562	41,920	44,697	268,167	301,554	81.5
6330	Fire, marine, and casualty insurance	449	509	44.5	24,464	21,952	50,751	55,442	1,131,241	1,190,673	49.8
6350	Surety insurance	11	13	46.4	200	157	54,700	80,484	10,669	10,730	63.6
6360	Title insurance	38	43	43.0	1,522	1,433	50,347	71,874	60,998	69,677	77.1
6370	Pension, health, and welfare funds	68	59	49.2	936	728	35,282	35,159	33,444	25,297	58.6
6390	Insurance carriers, n.e.c.	9	8	57.1	173	163	32,000	35,656	5,692	5,118	94.0
6400	Insurance agents, brokers, and service	2,383	2,390	37.0	19,448	20,703	39,843	44,922	851,457	910,351	62.4
6500	Real estate	5,727	5,608	55.1	42,161	42,704	27,630	29,335	1,256,762	1,293,087	73.3
6510	Real estate operators and lessors	2,168	2,072	59.1	12,324	12,323	22,296	23,553	297,895	289,528	70.1
6530	Real estate agents and managers	3,169	3,078	57.1	26,762	26,892	29,627	32,162	849,933	882,136	76.9
6540	Title abstract offices	57	56	23.1	733	614	25,926	24,287	18,657	17,449	41.9
6550	Subdividers and developers	238	247	33.5	2,149	2,537	33,761	30,439	81,127	93,550	64.3
6552	Subdividers and developers, n.e.c.	160	167	45.0	1,140	1,269	36,260	36,117	46,699	53,290	65.2
6553	Cemetery subdividers and developers	71	69	20.7	1,009	1,222	30,938	24,759	34,199	38,915	65.2
6700	Holding and other investment offices	622	653	60.8	9,599	9,187	49,788	58,216	496,741	512,406	68.0
6710	Holding offices	233	229	56.5	6,260	5,744	51,577	60,276	342,314	327,062	61.8
6720	Investment offices	22	55	68.8	251	396	52,335	48,768	12,860	20,570	79.8
6730	Trusts	113	120	57.7	1,123	821	34,518	25,101	23,402	23,287	76.0
6732	Educational, religious, etc. trusts	65	71	64.0	252	395	44,317	21,610	8,470	9,154	68.9
6733	Trusts, n.e.c.	48	49	51.0	871	426	31,683	28,338	14,932	14,133	81.6
6790	Miscellaneous investing	238	226	65.9	1,911	2,174	53,417	67,516	116,088	139,402	85.3
6794	Patent owners and lessors	27	22	44.9	291	250	36,000	42,848	10,068	11,149	60.8
6799	Investors, n.e.c.	184	173	70.0	1,098	1,098	64,291	75,574	77,383	81,427	88.0

CRAWFORD, IL

SIC	Industry	1994	1995	% State	1994	1995	1994	1995	1994	1995	% State
60 –	**Finance, insurance, and real estate**	46	42	0.1	350	354	19,040	19,819	6,788	7,150	0.0
6000	Depository institutions	12	12	0.3	237	242	19,662	20,066	4,514	4,791	0.1
6400	Insurance agents, brokers, and service	11	10	0.2	56	65	15,643	17,662	1,144	1,272	0.1
6540	Title abstract offices	3	3	1.2	19	13	14,526	15,692	293	244	0.6

CUMBERLAND, IL

SIC	Industry	1994	1995	% State	1994	1995	1994	1995	1994	1995	% State
60 –	**Finance, insurance, and real estate**	11	10	0.0	68	59	18,824	19,322	1,469	1,323	0.0

DE KALB, IL

SIC	Industry	1994	1995	% State	1994	1995	1994	1995	1994	1995	% State
60 –	**Finance, insurance, and real estate**	152	158	0.5	1,131	1,208	22,073	24,596	25,111	29,686	0.2
6000	Depository institutions	29	32	0.7	696	711	24,218	27,302	15,966	18,497	0.5
6020	Commercial banks	22	25	1.0	638	649	24,627	28,062	14,878	17,361	0.6
6030	Savings institutions	4	4	0.4	33	32	16,485	18,875	585	575	0.1
6140	Personal credit institutions	4	5	0.8	13	16	21,846	24,000	282	458	0.2
6280	Security and commodity services	3	4	0.5	7	8	5,714	5,000	44	99	0.0
6400	Insurance agents, brokers, and service	39	37	0.6	116	123	22,931	24,488	2,810	3,015	0.2
6500	Real estate	57	57	0.6	214	230	12,056	13,357	3,104	3,803	0.2
6510	Real estate operators and lessors	21	20	0.6	123	137	12,650	13,022	1,631	1,977	0.5
6530	Real estate agents and managers	25	26	0.5	69	73	12,174	13,096	1,064	1,398	0.1
6550	Subdividers and developers	11	11	1.5	22	20	8,364	16,600	409	428	0.3
6552	Subdividers and developers, n.e.c.	5	5	1.3	9	8	5,333	18,500	220	209	0.3
6553	Cemetery subdividers and developers	6	6	1.8	13	12	10,462	15,333	189	219	0.4

Source: County Business Patterns, 1994/95, CBP-94/95, U.S. Department of Commerce, Washington, D.C., November 1997. SIC categories for which data were suppressed or not available for both 1994 and 1995 are *not* displayed. The employment columns represent mid-March employment in the year. Pay per employee is calculated by dividing 1st Quarter payroll, annualized, by mid-March employment. The columns headed "% State" show the county's percentage of the state total for the SIC in 1995; for example, 1.4% for SIC 6000 means that the county had 1.4 percent of the state's total establishments (or payroll) in SIC 6000 in 1995. A dash '(-) is used to indicate that data are not available or cannot be calculated; *nec* means not elsewhere classified.

SIC	Industry	No. Establishments			Employment		Pay / Employee		Annual Payroll ($ 000)		
		1994	1995	% State	1994	1995	1994	1995	1994	1995	% State
DE WITT, IL											
60 –	**Finance, insurance, and real estate**	28	28	0.1	159	155	20,226	22,348	3,326	3,828	0.0
6000	Depository institutions	8	8	0.2	105	105	22,743	23,543	2,498	2,801	0.1
6020	Commercial banks	5	5	0.2	86	85	23,163	24,000	2,075	2,348	0.1
DOUGLAS, IL											
60 –	**Finance, insurance, and real estate**	33	34	0.1	201	235	23,303	22,128	4,684	5,268	0.0
6000	Depository institutions	10	10	0.2	116	134	25,828	24,597	2,816	3,191	0.1
6020	Commercial banks	7	7	0.3	103	124	27,262	24,839	2,630	2,966	0.1
6400	Insurance agents, brokers, and service	12	13	0.2	53	52	22,189	24,308	1,308	1,407	0.1
6530	Real estate agents and managers	4	4	0.1	10	16	8,400	7,750	111	136	0.0
DU PAGE, IL											
60 –	**Finance, insurance, and real estate**	2,620	2,768	9.4	35,023	35,022	33,277	37,523	1,177,648	1,278,640	7.9
6000	Depository institutions	275	298	6.3	7,093	7,900	26,028	30,948	184,539	224,795	5.7
6020	Commercial banks	120	129	5.4	3,625	3,604	24,973	28,088	88,628	98,549	3.4
6030	Savings institutions	107	119	12.4	2,850	3,212	27,878	34,442	80,338	95,333	19.2
6100	Nondepository institutions	262	280	13.7	4,402	4,093	35,681	37,683	153,238	159,592	14.9
6150	Business credit institutions	40	39	9.4	980	1,118	44,984	47,556	41,935	47,481	12.6
6160	Mortgage bankers and brokers	157	169	18.8	2,013	1,705	34,609	34,571	68,116	75,137	18.2
6200	Security and commodity brokers	253	276	9.6	1,851	2,029	64,512	76,720	112,385	140,194	4.8
6210	Security brokers and dealers	111	112	8.1	1,397	1,340	67,462	76,693	84,635	93,899	5.2
6220	Commodity contracts brokers, dealers	53	55	9.4	103	179	59,146	58,034	7,878	8,968	2.3
6280	Security and commodity services	88	102	12.0	351	502	54,348	84,303	19,828	36,701	6.5
6300	Insurance carriers	275	296	14.2	8,548	7,999	33,054	40,385	275,583	299,509	7.6
6310	Life insurance	93	88	16.5	3,256	2,539	37,584	44,510	111,595	99,072	11.6
6320	Medical service and health insurance	14	15	10.6	661	757	28,635	35,271	19,841	25,148	4.5
6321	Accident and health insurance	5	6	11.1	304	403	19,026	17,926	4,448	7,943	4.2
6324	Hospital and medical service plans	9	9	10.2	357	354	36,818	55,017	15,393	17,205	4.7
6330	Fire, marine, and casualty insurance	129	151	13.2	4,058	4,113	29,694	38,830	126,001	154,991	6.5
6360	Title insurance	13	16	16.0	259	300	36,680	34,133	7,152	7,854	8.7
6370	Pension, health, and welfare funds	15	13	10.8	213	181	28,488	35,978	6,196	6,539	15.2
6400	Insurance agents, brokers, and service	576	618	9.6	4,746	4,663	36,824	40,049	185,824	190,904	13.1
6500	Real estate	885	893	8.8	6,132	6,587	25,504	26,264	176,933	188,102	10.7
6510	Real estate operators and lessors	215	212	6.1	1,587	1,432	21,560	22,989	39,300	37,359	9.0
6530	Real estate agents and managers	587	593	11.0	4,061	4,573	26,979	27,529	120,939	131,603	11.5
6540	Title abstract offices	13	11	4.5	199	134	25,206	22,866	4,342	3,150	7.6
6550	Subdividers and developers	48	52	7.1	254	339	27,228	26,714	11,086	13,486	9.3
6552	Subdividers and developers, n.e.c.	35	39	10.5	126	166	34,698	32,361	7,964	8,897	10.9
6553	Cemetery subdividers and developers	8	8	2.4	120	119	19,167	20,908	2,783	3,157	5.3
6710	Holding offices	31	38	9.4	666	414	64,120	51,681	37,759	21,827	4.1
6720	Investment offices	7	13	16.3	39	49	45,846	54,612	2,386	2,806	10.9
6790	Miscellaneous investing	31	31	9.0	265	155	27,200	49,187	6,532	7,351	4.5
EDGAR, IL											
60 –	**Finance, insurance, and real estate**	33	32	0.1	253	281	19,146	20,071	5,255	5,543	0.0
6000	Depository institutions	12	12	0.3	207	232	20,116	21,172	4,503	4,797	0.1
6510	Real estate operators and lessors	3	4	0.1	2	5	10,000	8,000	36	35	0.0
6530	Real estate agents and managers	3	3	0.1	3	3	10,667	12,000	34	35	0.0
EDWARDS, IL											
60 –	**Finance, insurance, and real estate**	16	16	0.1	126	124	13,556	14,387	2,003	2,020	0.0
6500	Real estate	6	6	0.1	61	57	8,000	8,070	582	586	0.0
EFFINGHAM, IL											
60 –	**Finance, insurance, and real estate**	75	81	0.3	521	437	16,230	19,936	8,738	8,445	0.1
6000	Depository institutions	15	14	0.3	299	271	18,635	20,782	5,753	5,112	0.1

Source: County Business Patterns, 1994/95, CBP-94/95, U.S. Department of Commerce, Washington, D.C., November 1997. SIC categories for which data were suppressed or not available for both 1994 and 1995 are not displayed. The employment columns represent mid-March employment in the year. Pay per employee is calculated by dividing 1st Quarter payroll, annualized, by mid-March employment. The columns headed "% State" show the county's percentage of the state total for the SIC in 1995; for example, 1.4% for SIC 6000 means that the county had 1.4 percent of the state's total establishments (or payroll) in SIC 6000 in 1995. A dash (-) is used to indicate that data are not available or cannot be calculated; nec means not elsewhere classified.

Continued on next page.

SIC	Industry	No. Establishments			Employment		Pay / Employee		Annual Payroll ($ 000)		
		1994	1995	% State	1994	1995	1994	1995	1994	1995	% State
EFFINGHAM, IL - [continued]											
6020	Commercial banks	10	10	0.4	255	232	18,886	20,862	4,940	4,228	0.1
6400	Insurance agents, brokers, and service	29	30	0.5	64	72	19,500	19,000	1,314	1,442	0.1
6510	Real estate operators and lessors	5	8	0.2	14	19	10,286	11,368	178	228	0.1
FAYETTE, IL											
60 –	**Finance, insurance, and real estate**	30	31	0.1	172	193	19,372	19,378	3,853	3,847	0.0
6000	Depository institutions	8	8	0.2	121	131	18,843	19,084	2,726	2,677	0.1
6020	Commercial banks	8	8	0.3	121	131	18,843	19,084	2,726	2,677	0.1
6510	Real estate operators and lessors	6	5	0.1	8	10	9,000	7,200	84	82	0.0
FORD, IL											
60 –	**Finance, insurance, and real estate**	38	33	0.1	172	162	18,070	20,790	3,347	3,399	0.0
6000	Depository institutions	12	12	0.3	132	123	19,121	22,732	2,681	2,775	0.1
6530	Real estate agents and managers	6	4	0.1	6	5	6,000	7,200	50	43	0.0
FULTON, IL											
60 –	**Finance, insurance, and real estate**	71	72	0.2	354	372	19,480	18,656	6,642	6,900	0.0
6000	Depository institutions	24	25	0.5	235	249	22,945	21,510	5,007	5,247	0.1
6400	Insurance agents, brokers, and service	24	26	0.4	57	53	12,702	15,094	833	845	0.1
6500	Real estate	19	17	0.2	54	61	8,074	8,131	467	482	0.0
GALLATIN, IL											
60 –	**Finance, insurance, and real estate**	9	8	0.0	56	55	17,357	23,345	1,233	1,198	0.0
GREENE, IL											
60 –	**Finance, insurance, and real estate**	26	26	0.1	138	147	15,101	18,721	2,107	2,507	0.0
6000	Depository institutions	7	8	0.2	102	111	17,529	21,982	1,786	2,185	0.1
GRUNDY, IL											
60 –	**Finance, insurance, and real estate**	74	77	0.3	471	526	17,834	17,658	8,936	12,337	0.1
6000	Depository institutions	16	18	0.4	266	301	19,353	19,282	5,452	6,748	0.2
6020	Commercial banks	9	11	0.5	205	239	20,215	19,849	4,435	5,702	0.2
6500	Real estate	26	24	0.2	126	114	12,571	11,018	1,690	1,466	0.1
HAMILTON, IL											
60 –	**Finance, insurance, and real estate**	15	15	0.1	97	103	17,691	17,981	1,749	2,291	0.0
HANCOCK, IL											
60 –	**Finance, insurance, and real estate**	38	39	0.1	233	240	18,833	20,400	4,488	4,618	0.0
6000	Depository institutions	14	14	0.3	181	185	19,204	21,103	3,641	3,713	0.1
HARDIN, IL											
60 –	**Finance, insurance, and real estate**	5	5	0.0	45	40	9,956	11,900	439	547	0.0
HENDERSON, IL											
60 –	**Finance, insurance, and real estate**	12	13	0.0	91	90	16,747	17,822	1,644	1,617	0.0
6000	Depository institutions	6	6	0.1	70	70	19,371	20,400	1,471	1,427	0.0
HENRY, IL											
60 –	**Finance, insurance, and real estate**	97	94	0.3	618	618	21,327	22,058	12,758	13,998	0.1
6000	Depository institutions	26	26	0.6	382	383	21,518	22,538	7,342	8,302	0.2
6020	Commercial banks	18	18	0.8	328	329	21,366	22,723	6,144	7,132	0.2
6400	Insurance agents, brokers, and service	34	34	0.5	119	117	20,000	21,983	2,644	2,858	0.2
6510	Real estate operators and lessors	5	5	0.1	6	7	6,000	10,286	63	84	0.0
6530	Real estate agents and managers	13	11	0.2	49	49	16,816	17,143	997	1,012	0.1
IROQUOIS, IL											
60 –	**Finance, insurance, and real estate**	68	69	0.2	368	377	19,663	20,233	8,050	8,595	0.1

Source: County Business Patterns, 1994/95, CBP-94/95,.U.S. Department of Commerce, Washington, D.C., November 1997. SIC categories for which data were suppressed or not available for both 1994 and 1995 are not displayed. The employment columns represent mid-March employment in the year. Pay per employee is calculated by dividing 1st Quarter payroll, annualized, by mid-March employment. The columns headed "% State" show the county's percentage of the state total for the SIC in 1995; for example, 1.4% for SIC 6000 means that the county had 1.4 percent of the state's total establishments (or payroll) in SIC 6000 in 1995. A dash (-) is used to indicate that data are not available or cannot be calculated; nec means not elsewhere classified.

Continued on next page.

SIC	Industry	No. Establishments			Employment		Pay / Employee		Annual Payroll ($ 000)		
		1994	1995	% State	1994	1995	1994	1995	1994	1995	% State
IROQUOIS, IL - [continued]											
6000	Depository institutions	21	21	0.4	243	250	20,626	21,104	5,711	6,007	0.2
6020	Commercial banks	15	15	0.6	197	202	20,365	20,297	4,628	4,862	0.2
6400	Insurance agents, brokers, and service	28	30	0.5	76	80	15,053	16,150	1,348	1,638	0.1
JACKSON, IL											
60 –	**Finance, insurance, and real estate**	142	141	0.5	1,031	999	21,556	24,156	20,493	22,386	0.1
6000	Depository institutions	24	21	0.4	379	361	17,573	19,036	6,535	7,203	0.2
6020	Commercial banks	15	11	0.5	281	272	18,064	19,000	5,180	5,475	0.2
6030	Savings institutions	4	4	0.4	57	52	15,579	18,000	637	975	0.2
6100	Nondepository institutions	6	7	0.3	28	34	28,429	27,294	750	789	0.1
6140	Personal credit institutions	6	7	1.1	28	34	28,429	27,294	750	789	0.3
6200	Security and commodity brokers	11	9	0.3	55	57	45,891	46,105	2,272	2,657	0.1
6300	Insurance carriers	7	7	0.3	137	133	30,394	35,579	4,022	4,097	0.1
6400	Insurance agents, brokers, and service	35	33	0.5	97	97	24,000	25,320	2,537	2,617	0.2
6500	Real estate	49	59	0.6	247	294	10,089	10,422	2,761	3,362	0.2
6510	Real estate operators and lessors	28	30	0.9	113	154	10,301	9,922	1,336	1,559	0.4
6530	Real estate agents and managers	16	22	0.4	110	112	9,200	11,179	999	1,328	0.1
6700	Holding and other investment offices	10	5	0.5	88	23	37,045	150,087	1,616	1,661	0.2
JASPER, IL											
60 –	**Finance, insurance, and real estate**	21	24	0.1	131	127	18,779	20,094	2,491	2,592	0.0
6000	Depository institutions	4	4	0.1	84	86	21,333	23,023	1,906	2,000	0.1
JEFFERSON, IL											
60 –	**Finance, insurance, and real estate**	86	87	0.3	590	587	25,614	26,685	14,181	15,173	0.1
6000	Depository institutions	14	16	0.3	284	284	20,141	23,282	5,675	6,567	0.2
6020	Commercial banks	11	13	0.5	270	268	20,859	24,269	5,584	6,460	0.2
6300	Insurance carriers	10	10	0.5	71	70	34,930	35,029	2,340	2,273	0.1
6400	Insurance agents, brokers, and service	26	26	0.4	55	62	22,255	19,097	1,236	1,403	0.1
6500	Real estate	22	19	0.2	64	55	15,375	11,491	968	666	0.0
6510	Real estate operators and lessors	10	9	0.3	29	29	12,276	11,586	383	354	0.1
6530	Real estate agents and managers	9	7	0.1	22	14	23,273	11,429	458	182	0.0
6700	Holding and other investment offices	5	5	0.5	17	20	21,412	24,000	436	491	0.1
6710	Holding offices	5	5	1.2	17	20	21,412	24,000	436	491	0.1
JERSEY, IL											
60 –	**Finance, insurance, and real estate**	19	20	0.1	144	155	20,667	21,342	2,748	3,003	0.0
6000	Depository institutions	4	4	0.1	104	114	21,192	21,649	1,943	2,140	0.1
6020	Commercial banks	4	4	0.2	104	114	21,192	21,649	1,943	2,140	0.1
JO DAVIESS, IL											
60 –	**Finance, insurance, and real estate**	61	67	0.2	366	363	19,333	20,871	7,885	8,078	0.0
6000	Depository institutions	17	17	0.4	203	203	21,714	22,680	4,552	4,458	0.1
6500	Real estate	24	29	0.3	109	103	17,578	19,922	2,529	2,679	0.2
6530	Real estate agents and managers	11	15	0.3	89	81	19,191	22,765	2,248	2,383	0.2
6540	Title abstract offices	3	3	1.2	9	7	13,778	12,000	109	96	0.2
JOHNSON, IL											
60 –	**Finance, insurance, and real estate**	14	13	0.0	65	55	18,462	17,091	1,266	985	0.0
6000	Depository institutions	4	3	0.1	46	35	21,391	20,457	1,042	790	0.0
KANE, IL											
60 –	**Finance, insurance, and real estate**	701	717	2.4	10,483	11,277	25,642	24,979	281,698	302,664	1.9
6000	Depository institutions	117	125	2.6	4,413	4,708	23,022	22,574	115,177	129,040	3.3
6020	Commercial banks	61	64	2.7	3,705	4,008	23,713	22,643	101,124	112,684	3.9
6030	Savings institutions	23	26	2.7	498	513	18,827	22,667	10,100	12,330	2.5
6060	Credit unions	29	29	4.2	147	154	21,333	21,766	3,338	3,437	-
6090	Functions closely related to banking	4	6	1.0	63	33	19,492	16,606	615	589	0.3

Source: County Business Patterns, 1994/95, CBP-94/95, U.S. Department of Commerce, Washington, D.C., November 1997. SIC categories for which data were suppressed or not available for both 1994 and 1995 are not displayed. The employment columns represent mid-March employment in the year. Pay per employee is calculated by dividing 1st Quarter payroll, annualized, by mid-March employment. The columns headed "% State" show the county's percentage of the state total for the SIC in 1995; for example, 1.4% for SIC 6000 means that the county had 1.4 percent of the state's total establishments (or payroll) in SIC 6000 in 1995. A dash (-) is used to indicate that data are not available or cannot be calculated; nec means not elsewhere classified.

Continued on next page.

SIC	Industry	No. Establishments			Employment		Pay / Employee		Annual Payroll ($ 000)		
		1994	1995	% State	1994	1995	1994	1995	1994	1995	% State
KANE, IL - [continued]											
6100	Nondepository institutions	37	51	2.5	314	275	37,121	38,167	10,920	10,853	1.0
6140	Personal credit institutions	21	27	4.1	123	132	29,431	31,394	3,698	4,184	1.6
6160	Mortgage bankers and brokers	12	19	2.1	151	99	36,026	38,343	5,129	4,211	1.0
6210	Security brokers and dealers	19	21	1.5	59	79	46,847	70,633	2,689	5,859	0.3
6300	Insurance carriers	53	56	2.7	3,311	3,824	26,358	25,173	88,362	89,723	2.3
6310	Life insurance	14	15	2.8	1,908	2,343	20,778	19,049	42,372	41,911	4.9
6330	Fire, marine, and casualty insurance	29	27	2.4	1,204	1,275	34,252	35,376	39,812	41,250	1.7
6370	Pension, health, and welfare funds	4	6	5.0	69	89	26,145	22,337	1,819	2,084	4.8
6400	Insurance agents, brokers, and service	173	173	2.7	932	963	29,884	27,954	28,099	28,224	1.9
6500	Real estate	265	253	2.5	1,146	1,132	19,480	19,346	24,381	25,165	1.4
6510	Real estate operators and lessors	75	70	2.0	519	497	15,769	14,704	9,391	8,379	2.0
6530	Real estate agents and managers	152	141	2.6	453	450	19,267	20,480	9,501	11,075	1.0
6540	Title abstract offices	7	8	3.3	79	56	23,494	20,714	1,600	1,254	3.0
6550	Subdividers and developers	29	27	3.7	94	124	37,787	33,484	3,879	4,306	3.0
6552	Subdividers and developers, n.e.c.	19	18	4.9	44	64	47,818	39,688	2,153	2,493	3.1
6553	Cemetery subdividers and developers	9	8	2.4	28	31	20,143	18,323	748	939	1.6
6700	Holding and other investment offices	20	17	1.6	282	259	50,085	46,981	9,962	11,419	1.5
6710	Holding offices	7	7	1.7	58	58	160,138	127,655	4,551	5,953	1.1
6790	Miscellaneous investing	6	6	1.7	202	190	21,663	23,263	4,808	5,261	3.2
KANKAKEE, IL											
60 –	**Finance, insurance, and real estate**	218	216	0.7	1,726	1,635	20,392	22,420	35,595	37,070	0.2
6000	Depository institutions	67	65	1.4	764	639	20,932	23,524	16,514	14,754	0.4
6020	Commercial banks	34	31	1.3	537	400	20,924	25,000	11,260	9,455	0.3
6060	Credit unions	22	22	3.2	90	101	17,778	17,426	1,615	1,686	-
6140	Personal credit institutions	5	7	1.1	21	22	19,619	23,818	428	505	0.2
6210	Security brokers and dealers	6	6	0.4	37	41	80,757	71,220	2,361	2,320	0.1
6280	Security and commodity services	3	4	0.5	3	5	8,000	8,800	24	41	0.0
6300	Insurance carriers	9	9	0.4	433	438	20,582	20,758	9,042	10,006	0.3
6400	Insurance agents, brokers, and service	55	52	0.8	168	151	16,048	16,503	2,730	2,682	0.2
6500	Real estate	64	62	0.6	267	238	12,554	14,807	3,686	3,797	0.2
6510	Real estate operators and lessors	27	24	0.7	175	144	11,429	13,444	2,067	2,076	0.5
6530	Real estate agents and managers	28	27	0.5	54	57	12,889	14,175	850	835	0.1
KENDALL, IL											
60 –	**Finance, insurance, and real estate**	48	54	0.2	329	350	20,438	20,594	7,049	7,506	0.0
6000	Depository institutions	10	11	0.2	224	224	19,857	22,125	4,705	5,040	0.1
KNOX, IL											
60 –	**Finance, insurance, and real estate**	109	113	0.4	581	593	20,151	19,373	11,454	11,715	0.1
6000	Depository institutions	30	30	0.6	328	323	21,671	20,087	6,758	6,508	0.2
6020	Commercial banks	15	15	0.6	219	212	21,826	21,943	4,796	4,642	0.2
6400	Insurance agents, brokers, and service	26	28	0.4	84	88	17,857	18,227	1,586	1,705	0.1
6500	Real estate	31	31	0.3	101	107	9,030	9,533	1,034	1,130	0.1
6510	Real estate operators and lessors	12	12	0.3	56	57	8,500	8,842	531	565	0.1
6530	Real estate agents and managers	12	11	0.2	28	24	8,429	10,667	270	280	0.0
LAKE, IL											
60 –	**Finance, insurance, and real estate**	1,595	1,724	5.8	21,006	19,813	41,453	44,793	843,434	856,996	5.3
6000	Depository institutions	175	204	4.3	3,478	3,535	26,331	28,544	92,950	94,932	2.4
6020	Commercial banks	90	112	4.7	2,558	2,492	26,869	29,266	68,982	66,761	2.3
6030	Savings institutions	31	38	4.0	466	577	30,730	32,929	14,960	18,439	3.7
6060	Credit unions	26	27	3.9	364	369	19,319	20,054	7,294	7,997	-
6100	Nondepository institutions	254	283	13.8	5,334	3,767	38,204	50,142	191,265	185,792	17.3
6140	Personal credit institutions	35	50	7.5	3,020	997	27,615	47,679	79,452	48,751	19.1
6150	Business credit institutions	172	176	42.4	1,766	1,774	54,399	56,090	91,475	91,075	24.1
6160	Mortgage bankers and brokers	47	56	6.2	548	996	44,372	42,012	20,338	45,955	11.2
6200	Security and commodity brokers	184	199	6.9	870	979	62,634	57,973	63,107	67,723	2.3

Source: County Business Patterns, 1994/95, CBP-94/95, U.S. Department of Commerce, Washington, D.C., November 1997. SIC categories for which data were suppressed or not available for both 1994 and 1995 are not displayed. The employment columns represent mid-March employment in the year. Pay per employee is calculated by dividing 1st Quarter payroll, annualized, by mid-March employment. The columns headed "% State" show the county's percentage of the state total for the SIC in 1995; for example, 1.4% for SIC 6000 means that the county had 1.4 percent of the state's total establishments (or payroll) in SIC 6000 in 1995. A dash (-) is used to indicate that data are not available or cannot be calculated; nec means not elsewhere classified.

Continued on next page.

SIC	Industry	No. Establishments			Employment		Pay / Employee		Annual Payroll ($ 000)		
		1994	1995	% State	1994	1995	1994	1995	1994	1995	% State
LAKE, IL - [continued]											
6210	Security brokers and dealers	81	83	6.0	544	596	67,838	62,993	41,179	44,515	2.5
6220	Commodity contracts brokers, dealers	38	42	7.1	92	117	42,174	40,274	6,735	5,922	1.5
6280	Security and commodity services	62	68	8.0	231	263	58,840	54,692	15,044	17,095	3.0
6300	Insurance carriers	110	122	5.8	6,984	7,425	38,882	46,632	262,287	287,776	7.3
6310	Life insurance	16	16	3.0	1,300	1,100	47,548	53,884	52,990	50,858	6.0
6330	Fire, marine, and casualty insurance	77	87	7.6	4,345	4,986	37,716	46,376	165,950	189,376	7.9
6500	Real estate	537	552	5.4	2,174	2,173	24,937	24,926	60,618	63,489	3.6
6510	Real estate operators and lessors	169	167	4.8	764	745	18,571	20,870	15,767	16,407	4.0
6530	Real estate agents and managers	312	314	5.8	1,146	1,160	26,764	26,266	34,295	36,342	3.2
6540	Title abstract offices	8	8	3.3	114	62	25,544	20,065	2,339	1,367	3.3
6550	Subdividers and developers	36	40	5.4	145	185	43,614	33,146	7,630	7,998	5.5
6552	Subdividers and developers, n.e.c.	25	28	7.5	97	133	55,134	38,887	6,495	6,775	8.3
6553	Cemetery subdividers and developers	9	9	2.7	48	52	20,333	18,462	1,104	1,153	1.9
6700	Holding and other investment offices	51	65	6.1	782	835	152,951	114,218	89,842	100,586	13.4
6710	Holding offices	23	28	6.9	745	724	158,668	121,536	88,113	93,951	17.7
6720	Investment offices	5	4	5.0	18	9	18,889	100,889	459	952	3.7
6730	Trusts	8	5	2.4	6	5	22,000	16,800	169	75	0.2
6790	Miscellaneous investing	15	24	7.0	13	92	71,385	67,000	1,101	5,137	3.1
6799	Investors, n.e.c.	12	19	7.7	10	60	69,200	89,467	825	4,142	4.5
LA SALLE, IL											
60 –	**Finance, insurance, and real estate**	250	248	0.8	1,550	1,662	20,385	21,083	32,490	36,014	0.2
6000	Depository institutions	82	77	1.6	998	1,038	19,671	22,902	20,786	23,679	0.6
6020	Commercial banks	44	41	1.7	689	711	19,623	23,826	14,451	16,791	0.6
6030	Savings institutions	13	13	1.4	185	190	23,741	25,474	4,516	4,850	1.0
6060	Credit unions	22	20	2.9	117	125	14,085	14,656	1,716	1,883	-
6090	Functions closely related to banking	3	3	0.5	7	12	10,286	13,333	103	155	0.1
6140	Personal credit institutions	6	8	1.2	18	23	20,667	22,783	378	545	0.2
6400	Insurance agents, brokers, and service	74	71	1.1	235	219	18,621	19,763	4,415	4,578	0.3
6500	Real estate	57	61	0.6	163	247	13,571	10,057	2,714	3,228	0.2
6530	Real estate agents and managers	21	25	0.5	80	133	12,300	8,030	1,263	1,466	0.1
6553	Cemetery subdividers and developers	14	13	3.9	25	24	10,400	10,500	311	320	0.5
LAWRENCE, IL											
60 –	**Finance, insurance, and real estate**	24	23	0.1	1,002	402	21,058	26,488	27,955	12,988	0.1
6020	Commercial banks	6	6	0.3	68	70	22,000	22,057	1,593	1,707	0.1
LEE, IL											
60 –	**Finance, insurance, and real estate**	71	74	0.3	490	536	19,592	17,455	10,462	10,707	0.1
6000	Depository institutions	15	17	0.4	204	232	21,392	16,310	4,515	4,864	0.1
6020	Commercial banks	10	11	0.5	173	203	22,104	16,020	3,978	4,337	0.2
6500	Real estate	27	26	0.3	151	156	11,338	12,051	2,079	2,237	0.1
6530	Real estate agents and managers	17	16	0.3	104	112	11,423	11,929	1,549	1,679	0.1
LIVINGSTON, IL											
60 –	**Finance, insurance, and real estate**	92	90	0.3	461	488	20,954	21,689	10,285	11,039	0.1
6000	Depository institutions	19	20	0.4	319	336	22,031	22,631	7,186	7,609	0.2
6020	Commercial banks	14	15	0.6	289	305	22,145	22,807	6,543	7,244	0.3
6100	Nondepository institutions	3	4	0.2	8	7	39,000	46,857	212	239	0.0
6400	Insurance agents, brokers, and service	39	36	0.6	90	100	17,689	18,640	2,139	2,360	0.2
6530	Real estate agents and managers	11	9	0.2	15	13	9,067	6,769	153	130	0.0
LOGAN, IL											
60 –	**Finance, insurance, and real estate**	90	89	0.3	589	543	19,355	21,783	11,787	11,952	0.1
6000	Depository institutions	23	24	0.5	251	210	19,602	23,790	5,000	5,099	0.1
6300	Insurance carriers	4	5	0.2	183	174	21,574	23,816	4,237	4,075	0.1

Source: County Business Patterns, 1994/95, CBP-94/95, U.S. Department of Commerce, Washington, D.C., November 1997. SIC categories for which data were suppressed or not available for both 1994 and 1995 are not displayed. The employment columns represent mid-March employment in the year. Pay per employee is calculated by dividing 1st Quarter payroll, annualized, by mid-March employment. The columns headed "% State" show the county's percentage of the state total for the SIC in 1995; for example, 1.4% for SIC 6000 means that the county had 1.4 percent of the state's total establishments (or payroll) in SIC 6000 in 1995. A dash (-) is used to indicate that data are not available or cannot be calculated; nec means not elsewhere classified.

Continued on next page.

SIC	Industry	No. Establishments			Employment		Pay / Employee		Annual Payroll ($ 000)		
		1994	1995	% State	1994	1995	1994	1995	1994	1995	% State
LOGAN, IL - [continued]											
6400	Insurance agents, brokers, and service	34	30	0.5	97	97	16,577	18,392	1,713	1,902	0.1
6500	Real estate	25	26	0.3	50	54	10,000	9,852	508	550	0.0
6530	Real estate agents and managers	9	10	0.2	14	16	8,571	8,250	117	144	0.0
MCDONOUGH, IL											
60 –	**Finance, insurance, and real estate**	70	69	0.2	519	486	17,133	18,362	9,444	9,315	0.1
6000	Depository institutions	17	15	0.3	259	224	19,166	20,393	5,057	4,561	0.1
6400	Insurance agents, brokers, and service	21	21	0.3	60	57	17,733	21,825	1,296	1,436	0.1
6500	Real estate	20	19	0.2	151	157	9,325	10,166	1,677	1,830	0.1
6510	Real estate operators and lessors	9	8	0.2	125	131	9,632	10,473	1,406	1,538	0.4
MCHENRY, IL											
60 –	**Finance, insurance, and real estate**	384	415	1.4	2,513	2,569	25,335	25,179	65,241	68,624	0.4
6000	Depository institutions	69	74	1.6	1,206	1,251	22,040	21,848	27,308	29,629	0.8
6020	Commercial banks	36	44	1.8	836	939	23,876	23,186	20,583	23,434	0.8
6100	Nondepository institutions	27	35	1.7	143	152	27,357	23,921	3,726	3,956	0.4
6160	Mortgage bankers and brokers	14	16	1.8	101	91	28,198	22,066	2,548	2,398	0.6
6200	Security and commodity brokers	21	24	0.8	71	85	84,056	53,082	5,444	4,937	0.2
6280	Security and commodity services	10	11	1.3	19	22	14,737	16,000	307	367	0.1
6300	Insurance carriers	16	23	1.1	79	86	31,949	34,558	2,359	2,946	0.1
6400	Insurance agents, brokers, and service	107	109	1.7	439	416	23,936	25,462	11,479	12,076	0.8
6500	Real estate	134	139	1.4	473	472	17,040	18,653	9,922	9,697	0.5
6510	Real estate operators and lessors	25	29	0.8	89	113	14,247	13,699	1,627	1,804	0.4
6530	Real estate agents and managers	78	81	1.5	265	262	16,121	20,137	5,520	5,827	0.5
6540	Title abstract offices	4	4	1.7	28	16	16,000	17,250	323	282	0.7
6550	Subdividers and developers	24	18	2.4	78	69	23,077	21,507	2,119	1,497	1.0
6552	Subdividers and developers, n.e.c.	13	10	2.7	36	26	30,333	23,846	1,169	578	0.7
6553	Cemetery subdividers and developers	9	8	2.4	42	43	16,857	20,093	928	919	1.5
6700	Holding and other investment offices	10	11	1.0	102	107	59,961	63,888	5,003	5,383	0.7
MCLEAN, IL											
60 –	**Finance, insurance, and real estate**	316	353	1.2	19,717	18,367	38,742	42,937	668,681	780,708	4.8
6000	Depository institutions	63	80	1.7	1,269	1,361	23,051	24,658	28,445	35,106	0.9
6020	Commercial banks	38	55	2.3	1,042	1,116	23,117	24,018	23,279	28,111	1.0
6030	Savings institutions	8	8	0.8	140	137	22,029	25,489	2,935	3,525	0.7
6160	Mortgage bankers and brokers	7	14	1.6	177	142	26,486	30,113	4,530	4,476	1.1
6210	Security brokers and dealers	15	18	1.3	63	77	119,619	64,779	5,944	5,104	0.3
6310	Life insurance	11	8	1.5	1,260	866	32,375	39,113	47,132	32,865	3.9
6400	Insurance agents, brokers, and service	90	93	1.4	2,090	2,062	33,133	37,759	74,486	79,681	5.5
6530	Real estate agents and managers	34	40	0.7	203	210	16,355	16,495	3,489	3,472	0.3
MACON, IL											
60 –	**Finance, insurance, and real estate**	259	273	0.9	2,041	2,043	21,631	22,960	44,551	47,289	0.3
6000	Depository institutions	70	66	1.4	1,094	1,043	20,431	22,596	23,133	22,934	0.6
6020	Commercial banks	33	30	1.3	757	704	21,522	24,449	16,992	16,560	0.6
6060	Credit unions	23	22	3.2	191	193	18,010	19,067	3,480	3,597	-
6100	Nondepository institutions	9	10	0.5	63	55	35,111	35,200	1,964	1,640	0.2
6200	Security and commodity brokers	14	19	0.7	83	115	60,193	50,400	4,312	6,617	0.2
6400	Insurance agents, brokers, and service	95	95	1.5	257	246	20,467	22,374	5,036	5,129	0.4
6500	Real estate	54	62	0.6	411	443	11,221	11,567	5,375	6,036	0.3
6510	Real estate operators and lessors	25	28	0.8	278	320	7,367	7,888	2,575	2,895	0.7
6530	Real estate agents and managers	22	24	0.4	113	102	19,327	21,608	2,358	2,456	0.2
MADISON, IL											
60 –	**Finance, insurance, and real estate**	509	542	1.8	3,592	3,753	21,833	21,752	78,750	81,528	0.5
6000	Depository institutions	112	117	2.5	1,606	1,760	21,537	19,057	34,551	34,123	0.9
6020	Commercial banks	64	70	2.9	1,208	1,387	22,103	18,789	26,631	26,316	0.9
6060	Credit unions	32	32	4.6	229	240	16,996	17,933	4,139	4,520	-

Source: County Business Patterns, 1994/95, CBP-94/95., U.S. Department of Commerce, Washington, D.C., November 1997. SIC categories for which data were suppressed or not available for both 1994 and 1995 are *not* displayed. The employment columns represent mid-March employment in the year. Pay per employee is calculated by dividing 1st Quarter payroll, annualized, by mid-March employment. The columns headed "% State" show the county's percentage of the state total for the SIC in 1995; for example, 1.4% for SIC 6000 means that the county had 1.4 percent of the state's total establishments (or payroll) in SIC 6000 in 1995. A dash (-) is used to indicate that data are not available or cannot be calculated; *nec* means not elsewhere classified.

Continued on next page.

SIC	Industry	No. Establishments			Employment		Pay / Employee		Annual Payroll ($ 000)		
		1994	1995	% State	1994	1995	1994	1995	1994	1995	% State
MADISON, IL - [continued]											
6100	Nondepository institutions	18	20	1.0	83	86	24,289	23,442	2,113	2,012	0.2
6140	Personal credit institutions	14	15	2.3	59	62	19,797	25,290	1,400	1,510	0.6
6160	Mortgage bankers and brokers	4	5	0.6	24	24	35,333	18,667	713	502	0.1
6200	Security and commodity brokers	30	33	1.1	72	87	39,278	32,460	2,548	3,079	0.1
6210	Security brokers and dealers	19	20	1.4	54	61	46,741	38,885	2,137	2,424	0.1
6300	Insurance carriers	35	41	2.0	744	718	28,726	34,323	19,919	21,348	0.5
6310	Life insurance	3	3	0.6	55	75	31,127	29,547	1,193	1,676	0.2
6330	Fire, marine, and casualty insurance	28	31	2.7	654	606	28,214	34,990	17,801	18,662	0.8
6400	Insurance agents, brokers, and service	160	162	2.5	377	370	15,480	16,973	6,925	7,225	0.5
6500	Real estate	143	158	1.6	612	625	13,386	14,918	9,491	10,920	0.6
6510	Real estate operators and lessors	47	50	1.4	212	197	11,887	12,041	2,883	2,965	0.7
6530	Real estate agents and managers	64	74	1.4	201	210	14,030	15,352	3,132	3,634	0.3
6540	Title abstract offices	8	8	3.3	128	116	15,781	18,241	2,275	2,051	4.9
6550	Subdividers and developers	20	22	3.0	71	95	11,718	13,979	1,170	2,003	1.4
6552	Subdividers and developers, n.e.c.	6	7	1.9	18	23	13,111	16,522	363	755	0.9
6553	Cemetery subdividers and developers	14	15	4.5	53	72	11,245	13,167	807	1,248	2.1
6700	Holding and other investment offices	11	11	1.0	98	107	36,653	28,112	3,203	2,821	0.4
MARION, IL											
60 –	**Finance, insurance, and real estate**	91	97	0.3	646	623	21,486	21,149	13,978	13,418	0.1
6000	Depository institutions	24	26	0.6	301	278	19,482	19,986	5,839	5,819	0.1
6020	Commercial banks	19	21	0.9	270	244	19,674	20,098	5,220	5,110	0.2
6400	Insurance agents, brokers, and service	30	30	0.5	83	84	18,024	20,952	1,611	1,680	0.1
6500	Real estate	17	19	0.2	53	71	13,660	11,437	832	910	0.1
6510	Real estate operators and lessors	4	4	0.1	9	15	11,556	7,467	118	141	0.0
6530	Real estate agents and managers	9	10	0.2	24	28	14,167	11,571	342	366	0.0
MARSHALL, IL											
60 –	**Finance, insurance, and real estate**	29	31	0.1	137	149	20,000	19,248	3,065	3,067	0.0
6000	Depository institutions	7	8	0.2	86	89	25,209	24,225	2,403	2,239	0.1
MASON, IL											
60 –	**Finance, insurance, and real estate**	33	33	0.1	165	174	16,339	17,057	2,883	2,932	0.0
6000	Depository institutions	9	9	0.2	114	124	19,860	19,548	2,384	2,421	0.1
MASSAC, IL											
60 –	**Finance, insurance, and real estate**	18	18	0.1	117	136	18,838	17,618	2,268	2,635	0.0
6000	Depository institutions	6	6	0.1	79	103	20,354	18,214	1,572	1,995	0.1
MENARD, IL											
60 –	**Finance, insurance, and real estate**	26	24	0.1	115	104	17,530	20,500	2,059	2,201	0.0
6000	Depository institutions	7	7	0.1	74	67	21,405	25,433	1,596	1,682	0.0
6020	Commercial banks	7	7	0.3	74	67	21,405	25,433	1,596	1,682	0.1
MERCER, IL											
60 –	**Finance, insurance, and real estate**	35	30	0.1	145	149	16,469	17,128	2,630	2,627	0.0
6000	Depository institutions	12	12	0.3	103	107	16,000	17,607	1,830	2,019	0.1
6020	Commercial banks	8	8	0.3	91	94	16,659	18,468	1,683	1,880	0.1
MONROE, IL											
60 –	**Finance, insurance, and real estate**	57	55	0.2	317	318	17,338	18,000	5,630	6,130	0.0
6000	Depository institutions	13	11	0.2	177	166	18,237	19,349	3,255	3,383	0.1
6400	Insurance agents, brokers, and service	19	17	0.3	53	53	14,264	15,094	805	764	0.1
6500	Real estate	14	16	0.2	59	68	9,831	12,529	765	1,068	0.1
6530	Real estate agents and managers	6	8	0.1	13	24	14,154	16,500	197	526	0.0
MONTGOMERY, IL											
60 –	**Finance, insurance, and real estate**	69	70	0.2	430	417	18,326	20,393	7,909	8,275	0.1

Source: County Business Patterns, 1994/95, CBP-94/95, U.S. Department of Commerce, Washington, D.C., November 1997. SIC categories for which data were suppressed or not available for both 1994 and 1995 are not displayed. The employment columns represent mid-March employment in the year. Pay per employee is calculated by dividing 1st Quarter payroll, annualized, by mid-March employment. The columns headed "% State" show the county's percentage of the state total for the SIC in 1995; for example, 1.4% for SIC 6000 means that the county had 1.4 percent of the state's total establishments (or payroll) in SIC 6000 in 1995. A dash (-) is used to indicate that data are not available or cannot be calculated; nec means not elsewhere classified.

Continued on next page.

SIC	Industry	No. Establishments			Employment		Pay / Employee		Annual Payroll ($ 000)		
		1994	1995	% State	1994	1995	1994	1995	1994	1995	% State
MONTGOMERY, IL - [continued]											
6000	Depository institutions	22	23	0.5	325	313	19,409	20,792	6,194	6,327	0.2
6020	Commercial banks	17	18	0.8	299	285	19,639	21,249	5,757	5,864	0.2
6510	Real estate operators and lessors	5	5	0.1	4	6	9,000	9,333	52	58	0.0
6530	Real estate agents and managers	9	7	0.1	18	13	9,333	9,846	172	115	0.0
MORGAN, IL											
60 –	**Finance, insurance, and real estate**	75	78	0.3	863	815	23,314	24,933	20,214	19,608	0.1
6000	Depository institutions	19	20	0.4	303	307	22,284	23,726	6,766	6,846	0.2
6400	Insurance agents, brokers, and service	20	22	0.3	84	78	22,190	18,410	1,797	1,821	0.1
MOULTRIE, IL											
60 –	**Finance, insurance, and real estate**	20	19	0.1	122	141	19,869	21,021	2,512	2,754	0.0
6000	Depository institutions	6	7	0.1	86	109	22,605	21,174	2,015	2,221	0.1
6020	Commercial banks	6	7	0.3	86	109	22,605	21,174	2,015	2,221	0.1
OGLE, IL											
60 –	**Finance, insurance, and real estate**	99	97	0.3	504	508	19,778	19,780	10,287	10,891	0.1
6000	Depository institutions	23	24	0.5	345	352	21,171	21,398	7,537	8,125	0.2
6020	Commercial banks	13	14	0.6	277	278	22,325	21,871	6,347	6,735	0.2
6030	Savings institutions	5	5	0.5	50	53	16,880	21,585	910	1,108	0.2
6060	Credit unions	5	5	0.7	18	21	15,333	14,667	280	282	-
6400	Insurance agents, brokers, and service	34	34	0.5	83	81	16,482	16,198	1,430	1,416	0.1
6500	Real estate	31	30	0.3	50	53	11,600	11,245	683	720	0.0
6510	Real estate operators and lessors	6	6	0.2	14	15	7,714	8,800	136	150	0.0
6530	Real estate agents and managers	12	11	0.2	20	18	13,200	11,778	269	215	0.0
6553	Cemetery subdividers and developers	6	6	1.8	4	2	5,000	2,000	34	13	0.0
PEORIA, IL											
60 –	**Finance, insurance, and real estate**	519	542	1.8	5,621	5,564	30,269	31,807	162,397	173,397	1.1
6000	Depository institutions	84	84	1.8	2,005	1,807	23,986	26,444	47,637	44,518	1.1
6020	Commercial banks	44	45	1.9	1,259	1,121	24,861	28,321	30,640	28,410	1.0
6060	Credit unions	19	20	2.9	514	539	23,704	25,351	12,597	13,626	-
6140	Personal credit institutions	14	20	3.0	118	216	21,051	26,741	2,779	5,801	2.3
6200	Security and commodity brokers	34	31	1.1	237	245	68,338	68,931	13,763	17,262	0.6
6210	Security brokers and dealers	21	18	1.3	208	217	73,058	73,530	12,475	15,718	0.9
6300	Insurance carriers	53	58	2.8	1,632	1,693	39,858	39,497	56,494	59,639	1.5
6310	Life insurance	24	24	4.5	810	801	34,607	33,663	24,735	25,036	2.9
6330	Fire, marine, and casualty insurance	23	25	2.2	661	676	50,899	49,101	28,409	27,936	1.2
6400	Insurance agents, brokers, and service	177	177	2.7	748	724	22,037	22,713	17,898	17,596	1.2
6500	Real estate	131	141	1.4	675	692	18,578	18,983	13,277	15,252	0.9
6510	Real estate operators and lessors	56	58	1.7	217	203	20,203	21,399	4,399	5,089	1.2
6530	Real estate agents and managers	58	67	1.2	376	400	17,755	17,780	7,230	8,415	0.7
6550	Subdividers and developers	12	12	1.6	80	80	18,050	19,750	1,582	1,659	1.1
6700	Holding and other investment offices	14	15	1.4	124	114	50,935	63,684	8,318	9,742	1.3
6710	Holding offices	5	5	1.2	112	100	53,571	69,280	7,847	9,277	1.8
6730	Trusts	4	4	1.9	4	6	19,000	16,667	107	87	0.3
6790	Miscellaneous investing	5	5	1.5	8	8	30,000	29,000	364	339	0.2
6799	Investors, n.e.c.	5	5	2.0	8	8	30,000	29,000	364	339	0.4
PERRY, IL											
60 –	**Finance, insurance, and real estate**	36	35	0.1	236	184	15,864	19,217	3,951	3,772	0.0
6000	Depository institutions	8	9	0.2	181	140	16,331	20,600	3,062	3,053	0.1
PIATT, IL											
60 –	**Finance, insurance, and real estate**	28	29	0.1	206	208	16,854	17,808	3,842	4,123	0.0
6000	Depository institutions	10	9	0.2	135	134	17,067	17,761	2,475	2,574	0.1

Source: County Business Patterns, 1994/95, CBP-94/95, U.S. Department of Commerce, Washington, D.C., November 1997. SIC categories for which data were suppressed or not available for both 1994 and 1995 are *not* displayed. The employment columns represent mid-March employment in the year. Pay per employee is calculated by dividing 1st Quarter payroll, annualized, by mid-March employment. The columns headed "% State" show the county's percentage of the state total for the SIC in 1995; for example, 1.4% for SIC 6000 means that the county had 1.4 percent of the state's total establishments (or payroll) in SIC 6000 in 1995. A dash (-) is used to indicate that data are not available or cannot be calculated; *nec* means not elsewhere classified.

Continued on next page.

SIC	Industry	No. Establishments			Employment		Pay / Employee		Annual Payroll ($ 000)		
		1994	1995	% State	1994	1995	1994	1995	1994	1995	% State
PIKE, IL - [continued]											
60 –	**Finance, insurance, and real estate**	39	36	*0.1*	182	177	19,824	18,712	3,711	3,436	*0.0*
6000	Depository institutions	12	10	*0.2*	124	115	18,065	18,087	2,559	2,281	*0.1*
PUTNAM, IL											
60 –	**Finance, insurance, and real estate**	10	10	*0.0*	54	53	21,407	22,415	1,206	1,296	*0.0*
6000	Depository institutions	4	4	*0.1*	36	37	25,333	25,946	953	1,050	*0.0*
RANDOLPH, IL											
60 –	**Finance, insurance, and real estate**	59	58	*0.2*	397	402	20,433	21,075	7,541	8,267	*0.1*
6000	Depository institutions	21	21	*0.4*	271	267	21,668	23,431	5,123	5,917	*0.2*
6020	Commercial banks	12	12	*0.5*	185	179	19,395	21,006	3,747	3,786	*0.1*
6510	Real estate operators and lessors	5	5	*0.1*	5	6	4,000	4,000	26	27	*0.0*
RICHLAND, IL											
60 –	**Finance, insurance, and real estate**	29	32	*0.1*	197	197	28,954	31,208	4,817	5,308	*0.0*
6000	Depository institutions	7	7	*0.1*	124	122	31,419	35,836	2,869	3,176	*0.1*
ROCK ISLAND, IL											
60 –	**Finance, insurance, and real estate**	289	311	*1.1*	4,408	4,521	25,534	30,067	110,676	133,415	*0.8*
6000	Depository institutions	70	75	*1.6*	1,408	1,299	20,807	22,386	29,369	29,855	*0.8*
6020	Commercial banks	43	47	*2.0*	1,027	957	21,951	23,156	22,550	23,280	*0.8*
6060	Credit unions	21	21	*3.0*	335	295	17,182	19,932	5,790	5,864	*-*
6100	Nondepository institutions	15	18	*0.9*	69	85	31,594	30,918	3,267	3,591	*0.3*
6140	Personal credit institutions	10	11	*1.7*	53	59	33,509	33,288	1,818	1,887	*0.7*
6200	Security and commodity brokers	14	12	*0.4*	55	66	97,091	46,000	3,317	3,070	*0.1*
6300	Insurance carriers	22	29	*1.4*	2,210	2,401	29,019	37,218	61,806	82,950	*2.1*
6310	Life insurance	9	9	*1.7*	1,882	1,685	29,016	32,961	51,318	51,506	*6.0*
6400	Insurance agents, brokers, and service	63	66	*1.0*	217	204	21,972	24,157	5,175	5,554	*0.4*
6500	Real estate	99	105	*1.0*	422	431	14,085	13,652	6,738	7,048	*0.4*
6510	Real estate operators and lessors	49	48	*1.4*	237	260	13,283	13,169	3,688	3,713	*0.9*
6530	Real estate agents and managers	37	41	*0.8*	87	86	16,000	14,651	1,504	1,643	*0.1*
6700	Holding and other investment offices	6	6	*0.6*	27	35	33,185	29,029	1,004	1,347	*0.2*
ST. CLAIR, IL											
60 –	**Finance, insurance, and real estate**	465	468	*1.6*	3,433	3,468	22,545	24,176	80,910	82,024	*0.5*
6000	Depository institutions	96	94	*2.0*	1,839	1,847	20,672	21,971	38,573	38,882	*1.0*
6020	Commercial banks	61	62	*2.6*	1,463	1,484	21,173	21,895	31,417	31,089	*1.1*
6030	Savings institutions	10	10	*1.0*	122	121	18,328	18,545	2,166	2,442	*0.5*
6060	Credit unions	18	15	*2.2*	155	144	15,071	18,333	2,544	2,551	*-*
6090	Functions closely related to banking	7	7	*1.1*	99	98	24,929	32,694	2,446	2,800	*1.3*
6100	Nondepository institutions	31	32	*1.6*	218	200	30,073	26,740	6,364	5,447	*0.5*
6140	Personal credit institutions	21	23	*3.5*	92	101	23,870	23,762	2,327	2,232	*0.9*
6160	Mortgage bankers and brokers	9	9	*1.0*	126	99	34,603	29,778	3,977	3,215	*0.8*
6200	Security and commodity brokers	29	30	*1.0*	139	151	40,863	38,252	5,438	6,384	*0.2*
6210	Security brokers and dealers	16	17	*1.2*	78	91	63,949	53,407	4,551	5,542	*0.3*
6280	Security and commodity services	13	13	*1.5*	61	60	11,344	15,267	887	842	*0.1*
6300	Insurance carriers	28	28	*1.3*	241	174	28,365	43,356	7,060	6,579	*0.2*
6310	Life insurance	8	7	*1.3*	175	111	26,354	35,279	4,792	3,504	*0.4*
6400	Insurance agents, brokers, and service	126	121	*1.9*	364	364	17,659	17,901	6,875	7,225	*0.5*
6500	Real estate	143	153	*1.5*	527	609	15,651	15,567	10,194	10,539	*0.6*
6510	Real estate operators and lessors	51	56	*1.6*	204	246	13,961	12,488	3,135	3,535	*0.9*
6530	Real estate agents and managers	68	70	*1.3*	229	222	15,424	17,838	4,330	4,130	*0.4*
6552	Subdividers and developers, n.e.c.	8	11	*3.0*	20	25	26,600	20,640	738	717	*0.9*
6553	Cemetery subdividers and developers	8	7	*2.1*	40	78	20,700	16,718	1,360	1,427	*2.4*
6700	Holding and other investment offices	12	10	*0.9*	105	123	53,638	69,919	6,406	6,968	*0.9*
SALINE, IL											
60 –	**Finance, insurance, and real estate**	57	58	*0.2*	370	372	18,962	19,753	7,144	7,491	*0.0*

Source: County Business Patterns, 1994/95, CBP-94/95, U.S. Department of Commerce, Washington, D.C., November 1997. SIC categories for which data were suppressed or not available for both 1994 and 1995 are not *displayed. The employment columns represent mid-March employment in the year. Pay per employee is calculated by dividing 1st Quarter payroll, annualized, by mid-March employment. The columns headed "% State" show the county's percentage of the state total for the SIC in 1995; for example, 1.4% for SIC 6000 means that the county had 1.4 percent of the state's total establishments (or payroll) in SIC 6000 in 1995. A dash (-) is used to indicate that data are not available or cannot be calculated; nec means not elsewhere classified.*

Continued on next page.

SIC	Industry	No. Establishments			Employment		Pay / Employee		Annual Payroll ($ 000)		
		1994	1995	% State	1994	1995	1994	1995	1994	1995	% State
SALINE, IL - [continued]											
6000	Depository institutions	16	18	0.4	235	232	17,515	19,276	4,142	4,387	0.1
6100	Nondepository institutions	4	4	0.2	17	18	22,588	21,556	369	397	0.0
6530	Real estate agents and managers	5	4	0.1	13	8	6,462	15,000	107	117	0.0
SANGAMON, IL											
60 –	**Finance, insurance, and real estate**	483	513	1.7	7,977	7,782	27,803	31,590	217,058	231,819	1.4
6000	Depository institutions	88	88	1.9	2,136	1,942	22,925	24,908	46,965	46,634	1.2
6020	Commercial banks	65	66	2.8	1,936	1,749	23,242	25,342	43,010	42,563	1.5
6060	Credit unions	14	14	2.0	127	127	17,323	19,717	2,347	2,447	-
6100	Nondepository institutions	24	31	1.5	540	552	35,044	32,210	17,408	19,504	1.8
6160	Mortgage bankers and brokers	11	13	1.4	469	491	36,017	32,432	15,576	17,670	4.3
6200	Security and commodity brokers	25	26	0.9	122	140	65,115	58,857	6,888	8,054	0.3
6210	Security brokers and dealers	14	17	1.2	100	116	73,280	66,897	6,505	7,629	0.4
6300	Insurance carriers	58	64	3.1	3,879	3,740	29,638	36,452	110,972	120,961	3.1
6310	Life insurance	16	18	3.4	1,789	1,748	26,473	33,876	50,071	53,338	6.3
6320	Medical service and health insurance	7	7	4.9	395	408	23,656	30,755	9,322	11,516	2.1
6330	Fire, marine, and casualty insurance	28	30	2.6	1,642	1,539	34,697	41,227	50,279	54,945	2.3
6400	Insurance agents, brokers, and service	128	124	1.9	618	636	22,401	23,673	16,560	16,031	1.1
6500	Real estate	144	160	1.6	512	555	16,859	17,686	9,966	11,218	0.6
6510	Real estate operators and lessors	62	63	1.8	202	203	15,208	14,700	3,244	3,167	0.8
6530	Real estate agents and managers	59	67	1.2	232	239	17,138	19,833	4,848	5,513	0.5
6540	Title abstract offices	4	6	2.5	54	51	20,593	20,784	1,195	1,142	2.7
6553	Cemetery subdividers and developers	5	4	1.2	14	14	16,857	17,714	255	252	0.4
6700	Holding and other investment offices	16	20	1.9	170	217	50,047	47,189	8,299	9,417	1.3
6710	Holding offices	10	11	2.7	165	171	51,006	48,538	8,128	7,737	1.5
SCHUYLER, IL											
60 –	**Finance, insurance, and real estate**	9	12	0.0	55	62	16,509	15,484	1,024	1,081	0.0
SHELBY, IL											
60 –	**Finance, insurance, and real estate**	43	47	0.2	230	238	19,496	18,874	4,743	5,407	0.0
6000	Depository institutions	15	17	0.4	148	148	20,973	20,378	3,248	3,575	0.1
6020	Commercial banks	12	14	0.6	134	134	20,866	20,060	2,930	3,245	0.1
6030	Savings institutions	3	3	0.3	14	14	22,000	23,429	318	330	0.1
6530	Real estate agents and managers	4	4	0.1	5	5	16,000	14,400	81	78	0.0
STARK, IL											
60 –	**Finance, insurance, and real estate**	16	15	0.1	78	74	13,590	14,757	1,224	1,280	0.0
STEPHENSON, IL											
60 –	**Finance, insurance, and real estate**	121	126	0.4	2,130	2,139	25,852	26,876	55,845	59,075	0.4
6000	Depository institutions	22	24	0.5	354	367	22,689	21,886	7,999	7,520	0.2
6020	Commercial banks	16	17	0.7	283	297	23,901	22,801	6,684	6,132	0.2
6140	Personal credit institutions	3	3	0.5	9	16	30,222	28,250	208	645	0.3
6300	Insurance carriers	17	17	0.8	1,340	1,180	26,934	27,942	35,815	35,321	0.9
6400	Insurance agents, brokers, and service	38	39	0.6	101	220	18,416	26,400	1,995	5,565	0.4
6500	Real estate	24	27	0.3	112	113	15,393	14,867	1,703	1,863	0.1
6510	Real estate operators and lessors	4	6	0.2	20	26	16,400	14,154	404	449	0.1
6530	Real estate agents and managers	14	15	0.3	42	48	13,524	13,167	503	664	0.1
6700	Holding and other investment offices	8	8	0.7	192	220	30,938	33,691	7,114	7,053	0.9
TAZEWELL, IL											
60 –	**Finance, insurance, and real estate**	219	224	0.8	1,859	1,807	20,671	22,240	41,019	42,330	0.3
6000	Depository institutions	53	53	1.1	710	685	19,273	20,572	14,281	14,797	0.4
6020	Commercial banks	31	31	1.3	497	447	19,284	21,915	9,924	10,042	0.4
6330	Fire, marine, and casualty insurance	9	8	0.7	463	450	23,931	26,338	11,962	11,934	0.5
6400	Insurance agents, brokers, and service	75	80	1.2	225	234	20,018	20,872	5,140	5,438	0.4
6500	Real estate	59	58	0.6	254	212	13,984	15,698	4,141	3,715	0.2

Source: County Business Patterns, 1994/95, CBP-94/95, U.S. Department of Commerce, Washington, D.C., November 1997. SIC categories for which data were suppressed or not available for both 1994 and 1995 are not displayed. The employment columns represent mid-March employment in the year. Pay per employee is calculated by dividing 1st Quarter payroll, annualized, by mid-March employment. The columns headed "% State" show the county's percentage of the state total for the SIC in 1995; for example, 1.4% for SIC 6000 means that the county had 1.4 percent of the state's total establishments (or payroll) in SIC 6000 in 1995. A dash (-) is used to indicate that data are not available or cannot be calculated; nec means not elsewhere classified.

Continued on next page.

SIC	Industry	No. Establishments			Employment		Pay / Employee		Annual Payroll ($ 000)		
		1994	1995	% State	1994	1995	1994	1995	1994	1995	% State
TAZEWELL, IL - [continued]											
6510	Real estate operators and lessors	14	12	0.3	47	46	11,660	13,391	622	723	0.2
6530	Real estate agents and managers	36	33	0.6	177	133	14,576	16,692	2,941	2,392	0.2
6550	Subdividers and developers	4	8	1.1	5	7	4,000	7,429	46	92	0.1
6553	Cemetery subdividers and developers	4	4	1.2	5	5	4,000	4,000	46	44	0.1
UNION, IL											
60 –	**Finance, insurance, and real estate**	27	30	0.1	156	155	17,385	17,600	2,951	2,928	0.0
6000	Depository institutions	9	9	0.2	122	120	16,557	16,067	2,012	2,089	0.1
6020	Commercial banks	6	6	0.3	114	113	16,561	15,858	1,921	1,947	0.1
VERMILION, IL											
60 –	**Finance, insurance, and real estate**	169	178	0.6	1,563	1,548	20,673	23,049	33,793	35,391	0.2
6000	Depository institutions	45	50	1.1	664	626	18,247	19,342	12,617	11,698	0.3
6020	Commercial banks	22	27	1.1	507	467	18,706	19,760	9,834	8,762	0.3
6060	Credit unions	17	17	2.4	102	103	15,569	16,583	1,646	1,748	-
6100	Nondepository institutions	6	6	0.3	25	23	24,160	24,174	585	541	0.1
6200	Security and commodity brokers	4	6	0.2	17	16	52,706	50,250	785	874	0.0
6300	Insurance carriers	10	12	0.6	319	307	21,367	24,625	6,537	6,890	0.2
6400	Insurance agents, brokers, and service	47	47	0.7	314	337	23,822	28,451	8,559	10,381	0.7
6500	Real estate	50	50	0.5	215	229	18,698	20,437	4,217	4,518	0.3
6510	Real estate operators and lessors	21	20	0.6	51	49	9,098	9,959	515	480	0.1
6530	Real estate agents and managers	14	15	0.3	41	40	16,585	19,600	649	753	0.1
6540	Title abstract offices	4	5	2.1	24	28	16,667	13,571	401	397	1.0
6550	Subdividers and developers	9	8	1.1	90	109	26,133	27,523	2,554	2,865	2.0
6553	Cemetery subdividers and developers	9	8	2.4	90	109	26,133	27,523	2,554	2,865	4.8
6700	Holding and other investment offices	7	7	0.7	9	10	42,222	38,400	493	489	0.1
6710	Holding offices	4	4	1.0	5	5	68,000	68,000	448	429	0.1
WABASH, IL											
60 –	**Finance, insurance, and real estate**	22	26	0.1	167	184	20,814	22,478	4,004	4,266	0.0
6000	Depository institutions	9	11	0.2	125	142	20,064	21,268	2,755	3,148	0.1
6020	Commercial banks	6	7	0.3	113	113	20,531	21,487	2,543	2,562	0.1
WARREN, IL											
60 –	**Finance, insurance, and real estate**	31	32	0.1	249	258	17,671	18,233	4,803	4,943	0.0
6000	Depository institutions	8	10	0.2	179	193	17,877	17,865	3,552	3,659	0.1
6200	Security and commodity brokers	5	4	0.1	9	7	11,556	15,429	104	115	0.0
WASHINGTON, IL											
60 –	**Finance, insurance, and real estate**	32	32	0.1	170	180	20,047	20,422	3,537	3,604	0.0
6000	Depository institutions	11	11	0.2	123	125	19,935	19,840	2,607	2,657	0.1
WAYNE, IL											
60 –	**Finance, insurance, and real estate**	27	24	0.1	193	126	20,808	17,492	4,047	2,334	0.0
6000	Depository institutions	5	4	0.1	99	78	20,121	20,974	1,948	1,732	0.0
WHITE, IL											
60 –	**Finance, insurance, and real estate**	36	36	0.1	194	192	23,113	22,875	4,309	4,351	0.0
6000	Depository institutions	6	7	0.1	108	105	23,889	25,029	2,438	2,437	0.1
6020	Commercial banks	6	7	0.3	108	105	23,889	25,029	2,438	2,437	0.1
6400	Insurance agents, brokers, and service	13	12	0.2	26	26	21,385	20,615	598	578	0.0
6510	Real estate operators and lessors	4	5	0.1	10	9	5,200	5,778	52	66	0.0
WHITESIDE, IL											
60 –	**Finance, insurance, and real estate**	125	132	0.4	793	803	21,776	22,994	16,785	18,016	0.1
6000	Depository institutions	22	22	0.5	483	463	22,410	25,495	10,510	11,184	0.3
6020	Commercial banks	12	12	0.5	362	347	22,619	26,432	8,044	8,524	0.3

Source: County Business Patterns, 1994/95, CBP-94/95, U.S. Department of Commerce, Washington, D.C., November 1997. SIC categories for which data were suppressed or not available for both 1994 and 1995 are *not* displayed. The employment columns represent mid-March employment in the year. Pay per employee is calculated by dividing 1st Quarter payroll, annualized, by mid-March employment. The columns headed "% State" show the county's percentage of the state total for the SIC in 1995; for example, 1.4% for SIC 6000 means that the county had 1.4 percent of the state's total establishments (or payroll) in SIC 6000 in 1995. A dash (-) is used to indicate that data are not available or cannot be calculated; *nec* means not elsewhere classified.

Continued on next page.

SIC	Industry	No. Establishments			Employment		Pay / Employee		Annual Payroll ($ 000)		
		1994	1995	% State	1994	1995	1994	1995	1994	1995	% State
WHITESIDE, IL - [continued]											
6400	Insurance agents, brokers, and service	37	39	0.6	124	132	17,194	17,394	2,281	2,391	0.2
6500	Real estate	40	42	0.4	93	108	11,656	10,889	1,260	1,377	0.1
6530	Real estate agents and managers	20	19	0.4	37	43	7,892	7,628	432	444	0.0
WILL, IL											
60 –	**Finance, insurance, and real estate**	563	608	2.1	4,369	4,364	24,527	26,363	118,346	120,078	0.7
6000	Depository institutions	104	113	2.4	2,098	2,105	21,817	24,264	52,456	50,686	1.3
6020	Commercial banks	59	68	2.9	1,506	1,508	22,223	24,324	32,828	35,118	1.2
6030	Savings institutions	19	21	2.2	427	432	19,981	25,750	16,030	12,089	2.4
6060	Credit unions	18	17	2.4	93	97	17,204	17,402	1,772	1,870	-
6090	Functions closely related to banking	8	7	1.1	72	68	30,167	23,294	1,826	1,609	0.7
6100	Nondepository institutions	40	48	2.3	270	188	25,141	25,234	6,475	6,039	0.6
6160	Mortgage bankers and brokers	17	23	2.6	180	96	25,444	24,458	4,151	3,597	0.9
6210	Security brokers and dealers	19	19	1.4	57	73	43,649	32,055	2,363	2,391	0.1
6280	Security and commodity services	10	9	1.1	16	21	45,750	29,524	742	594	0.1
6300	Insurance carriers	30	35	1.7	688	706	32,006	33,807	21,886	23,675	0.6
6310	Life insurance	7	8	1.5	260	261	27,138	29,134	7,114	7,340	0.9
6330	Fire, marine, and casualty insurance	18	19	1.7	310	330	36,465	38,109	11,422	13,054	0.5
6400	Insurance agents, brokers, and service	160	166	2.6	547	539	26,764	30,108	17,428	17,934	1.2
6500	Real estate	184	199	2.0	639	651	19,023	19,551	13,305	13,551	0.8
6510	Real estate operators and lessors	38	44	1.3	132	144	13,061	13,667	1,986	2,454	0.6
6530	Real estate agents and managers	107	113	2.1	382	381	19,424	20,462	7,753	7,947	0.7
6540	Title abstract offices	6	6	2.5	52	34	28,462	22,000	1,334	784	1.9
6550	Subdividers and developers	28	30	4.1	70	86	21,771	25,163	2,207	2,201	1.5
6552	Subdividers and developers, n.e.c.	20	20	5.4	42	40	24,952	32,700	1,506	1,550	1.9
6553	Cemetery subdividers and developers	8	9	2.7	28	46	17,000	18,609	701	643	1.1
6730	Trusts	5	4	1.9	3	25	14,667	6,560	151	183	0.6
6790	Miscellaneous investing	4	4	1.2	34	28	27,412	30,429	1,050	1,010	0.6
WILLIAMSON, IL											
60 –	**Finance, insurance, and real estate**	118	123	0.4	998	1,006	20,990	21,861	22,116	22,185	0.1
6000	Depository institutions	22	24	0.5	321	355	18,717	16,203	6,179	6,329	0.2
6020	Commercial banks	15	17	0.7	282	315	18,865	15,568	5,413	5,451	0.2
6300	Insurance carriers	8	8	0.4	404	383	23,109	29,326	9,689	10,781	0.3
6400	Insurance agents, brokers, and service	46	48	0.7	123	122	15,675	19,410	2,080	2,323	0.2
6500	Real estate	25	26	0.3	111	110	12,036	12,945	1,693	1,746	0.1
6510	Real estate operators and lessors	9	8	0.2	71	65	10,986	10,400	832	703	0.2
6540	Title abstract offices	4	4	1.7	18	20	17,778	22,200	517	675	1.6
WINNEBAGO, IL											
60 –	**Finance, insurance, and real estate**	594	594	2.0	5,904	6,128	27,230	31,737	161,793	173,541	1.1
6000	Depository institutions	96	97	2.1	2,162	2,166	24,833	35,897	50,135	55,350	1.4
6020	Commercial banks	43	45	1.9	1,388	1,438	27,190	29,185	34,086	36,482	1.3
6030	Savings institutions	17	18	1.9	499	443	19,639	64,542	9,641	12,154	2.5
6060	Credit unions	28	26	3.7	165	161	13,988	16,447	2,468	2,605	-
6090	Functions closely related to banking	8	8	1.3	110	124	34,909	36,645	3,940	4,109	1.8
6100	Nondepository institutions	36	43	2.1	264	298	32,333	26,738	8,218	8,992	0.8
6160	Mortgage bankers and brokers	19	20	2.2	192	192	34,083	26,479	5,888	6,181	1.5
6200	Security and commodity brokers	47	44	1.5	256	255	57,797	49,773	13,656	12,813	0.4
6210	Security brokers and dealers	28	24	1.7	222	215	62,505	55,572	12,620	11,846	0.7
6280	Security and commodity services	19	20	2.4	34	40	27,059	18,600	1,036	967	0.2
6300	Insurance carriers	48	49	2.3	958	1,157	28,635	28,356	28,334	33,083	0.8
6310	Life insurance	18	17	3.2	436	508	29,982	26,512	12,872	13,269	1.6
6320	Medical service and health insurance	6	6	4.2	230	337	26,783	31,632	7,398	11,177	2.0
6330	Fire, marine, and casualty insurance	19	21	1.8	253	275	29,881	28,960	7,407	7,699	0.3
6370	Pension, health, and welfare funds	5	5	4.2	39	37	16,410	19,351	657	938	2.2
6400	Insurance agents, brokers, and service	152	153	2.4	600	629	23,993	27,866	15,591	17,911	1.2
6500	Real estate	195	186	1.8	1,018	1,043	16,833	16,314	19,684	19,804	1.1

Source: County Business Patterns, 1994/95, CBP-94/95, U.S. Department of Commerce, Washington, D.C., November 1997. SIC categories for which data were suppressed or not available for both 1994 and 1995 are not displayed. The employment columns represent mid-March employment in the year. Pay per employee is calculated by dividing 1st Quarter payroll, annualized, by mid-March employment. The columns headed "% State" show the county's percentage of the state total for the SIC in 1995; for example, 1.4% for SIC 6000 means that the county had 1.4 percent of the state's total establishments (or payroll) in SIC 6000 in 1995. A dash (-) is used to indicate that data are not available or cannot be calculated; nec means not elsewhere classified.

Continued on next page.

SIC	Industry	No. Establishments			Employment		Pay / Employee		Annual Payroll ($ 000)		
		1994	1995	% State	1994	1995	1994	1995	1994	1995	% State
WINNEBAGO, IL - [continued]											
6510	Real estate operators and lessors	83	75	2.1	248	261	13,161	13,793	3,784	4,097	1.0
6530	Real estate agents and managers	83	79	1.5	542	574	15,956	14,983	9,538	9,528	0.8
6540	Title abstract offices	6	5	2.1	135	97	25,363	25,361	3,226	2,742	6.6
6550	Subdividers and developers	20	20	2.7	93	102	19,355	22,235	3,117	3,251	2.2
6552	Subdividers and developers, n.e.c.	10	9	2.4	22	23	26,000	30,783	1,555	1,347	1.6
6553	Cemetery subdividers and developers	10	10	3.0	71	78	17,296	19,949	1,562	1,879	3.1
6700	Holding and other investment offices	20	22	2.0	646	580	38,359	49,517	26,175	25,588	3.4
6710	Holding offices	7	6	1.5	593	532	39,467	51,083	24,636	23,785	4.5
WOODFORD, IL											
60 –	**Finance, insurance, and real estate**	48	50	0.2	245	231	18,563	23,255	5,014	5,828	0.0
6000	Depository institutions	15	16	0.3	161	143	19,354	25,231	3,367	3,756	0.1
6020	Commercial banks	10	10	0.4	135	111	20,681	29,225	3,013	3,319	0.1
6400	Insurance agents, brokers, and service	19	17	0.3	46	45	13,391	15,111	791	771	0.1

Source: County Business Patterns, 1994/95, CBP-94/95, U.S. Department of Commerce, Washington, D.C., November 1997. SIC categories for which data were suppressed or not available for both 1994 and 1995 are not displayed. The employment columns represent mid-March employment in the year. Pay per employee is calculated by dividing 1st Quarter payroll, annualized, by mid-March employment. The columns headed "% State" show the county's percentage of the state total for the SIC in 1995; for example, 1.4% for SIC 6000 means that the county had 1.4 percent of the state's total establishments (or payroll) in SIC 6000 in 1995. A dash (-) is used to indicate that data are not available or cannot be calculated; nec means not elsewhere classified.

INDIANA

SIC	Industry	No. Establishments			Employment		Pay / Employee		Annual Payroll ($ 000)		
		1994	1995	% State	1994	1995	1994	1995	1994	1995	% State
ADAMS, IN											
60 –	**Finance, insurance, and real estate**	58	58	0.5	306	326	17,974	18,650	6,037	6,525	0.2
6000	Depository institutions	18	18	0.7	187	190	20,278	21,137	3,961	4,197	0.4
6020	Commercial banks	12	12	0.6	168	171	20,714	21,497	3,604	3,824	0.5
6400	Insurance agents, brokers, and service	19	17	0.6	51	61	16,235	15,869	1,035	1,091	0.2
6500	Real estate	15	15	0.4	54	60	12,815	14,667	860	1,003	0.2
6530	Real estate agents and managers	7	8	0.4	8	9	10,000	10,667	91	109	0.0
ALLEN, IN											
60 –	**Finance, insurance, and real estate**	801	827	6.6	12,538	11,917	33,143	36,590	371,479	407,844	11.0
6000	Depository institutions	146	148	5.6	3,040	3,013	23,203	24,020	67,700	71,527	7.5
6020	Commercial banks	84	89	4.8	2,283	2,255	25,069	25,614	53,150	56,335	7.8
6030	Savings institutions	17	17	5.4	200	180	18,320	19,289	3,849	3,752	3.1
6060	Credit unions	40	38	8.6	545	564	17,233	19,000	10,318	11,053	11.6
6100	Nondepository institutions	62	69	8.3	1,542	1,277	35,326	31,850	51,076	52,567	12.6
6160	Mortgage bankers and brokers	28	33	9.9	1,404	1,144	36,735	32,357	48,321	49,147	28.5
6200	Security and commodity brokers	56	63	10.1	701	587	50,636	80,082	28,383	37,411	15.9
6280	Security and commodity services	25	26	11.9	450	261	45,084	105,732	15,025	18,565	39.3
6300	Insurance carriers	64	69	7.6	4,339	4,441	37,746	44,084	142,045	165,018	16.7
6320	Medical service and health insurance	5	5	8.6	180	196	35,911	45,408	6,588	7,776	6.7
6330	Fire, marine, and casualty insurance	36	37	7.7	475	482	42,644	47,311	18,605	20,977	4.9
6400	Insurance agents, brokers, and service	218	216	7.2	1,365	1,080	35,484	29,652	41,076	32,989	7.4
6510	Real estate operators and lessors	92	97	6.0	448	438	14,670	16,192	7,189	8,059	6.2
6530	Real estate agents and managers	120	118	6.2	634	617	17,110	19,105	12,393	12,723	5.2
6550	Subdividers and developers	23	26	6.1	127	147	18,299	19,048	3,069	3,830	6.4
6552	Subdividers and developers, n.e.c.	11	13	6.6	28	39	32,714	30,154	1,407	1,975	5.2
6553	Cemetery subdividers and developers	11	11	5.6	99	108	14,222	15,037	1,657	1,830	8.9
BARTHOLOMEW, IN											
60 –	**Finance, insurance, and real estate**	173	184	1.5	2,251	2,318	31,977	38,892	69,934	89,713	2.4
6000	Depository institutions	30	32	1.2	540	557	29,185	44,323	13,394	23,221	2.4
6020	Commercial banks	20	21	1.1	285	339	37,558	56,519	8,203	17,823	2.5
6100	Nondepository institutions	14	15	1.8	44	57	24,000	23,368	1,212	1,615	0.4
6200	Security and commodity brokers	9	10	1.6	105	80	80,229	70,700	9,239	4,941	2.1
6300	Insurance carriers	12	14	1.5	655	657	33,307	35,653	21,327	22,996	2.3
6400	Insurance agents, brokers, and service	43	44	1.5	552	561	24,507	27,586	13,449	15,510	3.5
6500	Real estate	57	63	1.5	293	325	18,853	19,335	6,208	7,214	1.6
6510	Real estate operators and lessors	28	32	2.0	114	133	18,386	18,496	2,548	3,026	2.3
6530	Real estate agents and managers	20	21	1.1	88	96	23,000	20,917	2,070	2,124	0.9
6540	Title abstract offices	3	3	1.6	24	17	14,167	19,059	374	361	1.4
6550	Subdividers and developers	6	6	1.4	67	79	15,881	18,886	1,216	1,623	2.7
6700	Holding and other investment offices	8	6	2.2	62	81	94,710	164,099	5,105	14,216	8.6
BENTON, IN											
60 –	**Finance, insurance, and real estate**	22	21	0.2	145	138	18,041	19,884	2,709	2,698	0.1
6000	Depository institutions	7	7	0.3	95	99	18,737	20,202	1,830	1,958	0.2
6020	Commercial banks	7	7	0.4	95	99	18,737	20,202	1,830	1,958	0.3
6500	Real estate	4	4	0.1	17	13	15,059	18,462	318	285	0.1

Source: County Business Patterns, 1994/95, CBP-94/95, U.S. Department of Commerce, Washington, D.C., November 1997. SIC categories for which data were suppressed or not available for both 1994 and 1995 are not displayed. The employment columns represent mid-March employment in the year. Pay per employee is calculated by dividing 1st Quarter payroll, annualized, by mid-March employment. The columns headed "% State" show the county's percentage of the state total for the SIC in 1995; for example, 1.4% for SIC 6000 means that the county had 1.4 percent of the state's total establishments (or payroll) in SIC 6000 in 1995. A dash (-) is used to indicate that data are not available or cannot be calculated; nec means not elsewhere classified.

Continued on next page.

SIC	Industry	No. Establishments			Employment		Pay / Employee		Annual Payroll ($ 000)		
		1994	1995	% State	1994	1995	1994	1995	1994	1995	% State
BLACKFORD, IN - [continued]											
60 –	**Finance, insurance, and real estate**	19	20	0.2	151	161	18,066	17,689	2,590	2,811	0.1
6000	Depository institutions	9	9	0.3	98	108	17,143	16,778	1,667	1,799	0.2
BOONE, IN											
60 –	**Finance, insurance, and real estate**	85	91	0.7	500	566	20,080	19,965	10,911	11,522	0.3
6000	Depository institutions	20	19	0.7	194	169	21,072	20,142	3,947	3,461	0.4
6200	Security and commodity brokers	5	6	1.0	12	22	42,000	27,455	492	716	0.3
6400	Insurance agents, brokers, and service	31	30	1.0	80	90	17,950	18,311	1,652	1,766	0.4
6500	Real estate	23	28	0.7	69	151	13,391	16,901	1,251	2,247	0.5
6510	Real estate operators and lessors	4	6	0.4	5	45	12,000	18,933	78	292	0.2
6530	Real estate agents and managers	11	13	0.7	36	65	10,889	15,631	565	1,112	0.5
6540	Title abstract offices	3	3	1.6	17	18	17,647	14,889	313	285	1.1
6550	Subdividers and developers	4	4	0.9	11	21	15,636	18,667	291	542	0.9
BROWN, IN											
60 –	**Finance, insurance, and real estate**	18	23	0.2	81	82	15,802	17,317	1,357	1,396	0.0
6000	Depository institutions	4	6	0.2	33	30	16,727	20,933	552	584	0.1
6020	Commercial banks	4	6	0.3	33	30	16,727	20,933	552	584	0.1
6400	Insurance agents, brokers, and service	3	3	0.1	16	15	19,750	22,133	335	309	0.1
6500	Real estate	11	14	0.3	32	37	12,875	12,432	470	503	0.1
6510	Real estate operators and lessors	5	4	0.2	14	23	14,286	11,826	244	285	0.2
CARROLL, IN											
60 –	**Finance, insurance, and real estate**	31	32	0.3	195	202	16,164	17,307	3,527	3,642	0.1
6000	Depository institutions	9	10	0.4	128	125	15,469	17,408	2,199	2,281	0.2
6400	Insurance agents, brokers, and service	9	10	0.3	39	42	18,564	20,190	816	860	0.2
6530	Real estate agents and managers	5	5	0.3	11	16	15,636	12,000	230	233	0.1
CASS, IN											
60 –	**Finance, insurance, and real estate**	61	60	0.5	402	382	20,856	22,942	8,218	8,706	0.2
6000	Depository institutions	19	18	0.7	241	229	20,299	20,751	4,360	4,613	0.5
6020	Commercial banks	12	11	0.6	180	166	18,733	19,422	2,937	3,158	0.4
6200	Security and commodity brokers	3	3	0.5	18	17	52,667	53,882	1,001	1,073	0.5
6400	Insurance agents, brokers, and service	18	21	0.7	72	78	19,333	24,410	1,553	1,778	0.4
6510	Real estate operators and lessors	6	4	0.2	7	5	6,286	8,000	45	42	0.0
6540	Title abstract offices	3	3	1.6	9	12	18,222	17,333	217	123	0.5
CLARK, IN											
60 –	**Finance, insurance, and real estate**	155	169	1.3	1,015	1,052	19,602	18,897	21,701	21,654	0.6
6000	Depository institutions	39	43	1.6	469	511	22,397	20,932	11,660	11,593	1.2
6020	Commercial banks	28	32	1.7	386	425	22,373	20,828	9,568	9,465	1.3
6100	Nondepository institutions	10	10	1.2	50	50	29,120	31,920	1,629	1,664	0.4
6400	Insurance agents, brokers, and service	29	33	1.1	77	86	15,013	14,465	1,265	1,345	0.3
6500	Real estate	60	66	1.5	337	351	11,300	12,695	4,363	4,888	1.1
6510	Real estate operators and lessors	31	34	2.1	210	218	9,905	11,046	2,269	2,630	2.0
6530	Real estate agents and managers	17	19	1.0	95	103	14,105	15,495	1,588	1,770	0.7
6550	Subdividers and developers	7	6	1.4	20	16	10,800	14,500	259	251	0.4
CLAY, IN											
60 –	**Finance, insurance, and real estate**	40	39	0.3	253	228	18,972	19,596	4,938	4,582	0.1
6000	Depository institutions	13	11	0.4	192	160	18,750	20,550	3,652	3,286	0.3
6400	Insurance agents, brokers, and service	10	12	0.4	30	36	18,800	16,667	621	681	0.2
6500	Real estate	10	10	0.2	15	15	14,400	13,867	227	237	0.1
CLINTON, IN ✦											
60 –	**Finance, insurance, and real estate**	58	58	0.5	310	326	18,310	18,012	5,841	6,678	0.2
6000	Depository institutions	12	15	0.6	209	222	16,689	18,414	3,733	4,649	0.5

Source: County Business Patterns, 1994/95, CBP-94/95, U.S. Department of Commerce, Washington, D.C., November 1997. SIC categories for which data were suppressed or not available for both 1994 and 1995 are not displayed. The employment columns represent mid-March employment in the year. Pay per employee is calculated by dividing 1st Quarter payroll, annualized, by mid-March employment. The columns headed "% State" show the county's percentage of the state total for the SIC in 1995; for example, 1.4% for SIC 6000 means that the county had 1.4 percent of the state's total establishments (or payroll) in SIC 6000 in 1995. A dash (-) is used to indicate that data are not available or cannot be calculated; nec means not elsewhere classified.

Continued on next page.

SIC	Industry	No. Establishments			Employment		Pay / Employee		Annual Payroll ($ 000)		
		1994	1995	% State	1994	1995	1994	1995	1994	1995	% State
CLINTON, IN - [continued]											
6500	Real estate	21	20	0.5	48	51	10,667	10,431	636	588	0.1
6510	Real estate operators and lessors	10	9	0.6	22	24	7,091	6,500	169	153	0.1
6530	Real estate agents and managers	6	6	0.3	7	5	20,000	28,000	196	174	0.1
CRAWFORD, IN											
60 –	**Finance, insurance, and real estate**	15	15	0.1	60	74	22,200	23,297	1,359	1,577	0.0
DAVIESS, IN											
60 –	**Finance, insurance, and real estate**	57	55	0.4	268	274	20,194	21,533	5,681	5,818	0.2
6000	Depository institutions	18	17	0.6	184	188	22,957	24,255	4,396	4,402	0.5
6400	Insurance agents, brokers, and service	11	14	0.5	27	31	13,185	15,484	424	530	0.1
6530	Real estate agents and managers	11	8	0.4	16	16	7,750	7,500	163	148	0.1
6550	Subdividers and developers	4	5	1.2	12	11	12,333	12,364	180	153	0.3
6553	Cemetery subdividers and developers	4	5	2.5	12	11	12,333	12,364	180	153	0.7
DEARBORN, IN											
60 –	**Finance, insurance, and real estate**	82	87	0.7	502	539	17,976	18,835	9,977	11,173	0.3
6000	Depository institutions	23	23	0.9	294	309	17,265	17,579	5,400	5,468	0.6
6020	Commercial banks	15	15	0.8	173	176	17,665	19,295	3,272	3,256	0.5
6030	Savings institutions	4	4	1.3	112	124	17,250	15,548	2,028	2,103	1.7
6060	Credit unions	4	4	0.9	9	9	9,778	12,000	100	109	0.1
6100	Nondepository institutions	4	4	0.5	7	11	18,857	19,273	153	234	0.1
6400	Insurance agents, brokers, and service	16	16	0.5	63	65	27,683	30,462	1,895	1,938	0.4
6500	Real estate	31	35	0.8	115	128	12,870	14,938	1,924	2,907	0.6
6510	Real estate operators and lessors	8	9	0.6	27	32	6,815	10,750	257	374	0.3
6530	Real estate agents and managers	15	17	0.9	45	50	12,444	11,440	601	637	0.3
6540	Title abstract offices	3	3	1.6	13	13	14,769	17,846	203	232	0.9
6550	Subdividers and developers	5	6	1.4	30	33	18,133	23,152	863	1,664	2.8
DECATUR, IN											
60 –	**Finance, insurance, and real estate**	42	42	0.3	272	249	21,015	24,562	6,113	5,852	0.2
6000	Depository institutions	8	9	0.3	160	136	19,500	23,353	3,189	2,788	0.3
6100	Nondepository institutions	3	4	0.5	15	12	24,267	31,333	384	381	0.1
6400	Insurance agents, brokers, and service	10	10	0.3	27	27	14,519	14,519	425	421	0.1
6500	Real estate	14	12	0.3	38	32	12,105	14,250	539	521	0.1
6510	Real estate operators and lessors	5	4	0.2	11	12	14,182	15,333	169	183	0.1
6530	Real estate agents and managers	5	4	0.2	16	10	13,000	16,400	227	221	0.1
DE KALB, IN											
60 –	**Finance, insurance, and real estate**	53	54	0.4	283	307	22,869	20,651	6,569	6,927	0.2
6000	Depository institutions	17	17	0.6	173	174	22,173	20,230	3,893	3,993	0.4
6020	Commercial banks	9	9	0.5	99	94	24,485	20,979	2,273	2,244	0.3
6500	Real estate	14	16	0.4	49	58	12,571	13,379	706	894	0.2
6530	Real estate agents and managers	7	9	0.5	27	32	12,889	14,125	366	495	0.2
DELAWARE, IN											
60 –	**Finance, insurance, and real estate**	235	243	1.9	1,944	1,872	20,979	22,128	41,289	41,834	1.1
6000	Depository institutions	63	66	2.5	956	950	21,502	22,611	20,743	21,808	2.3
6020	Commercial banks	41	44	2.4	665	648	21,149	22,531	14,507	15,156	2.1
6100	Nondepository institutions	15	14	1.7	79	90	20,405	26,844	1,862	2,393	0.6
6200	Security and commodity brokers	10	10	1.6	28	33	43,143	38,182	1,183	1,281	0.5
6210	Security brokers and dealers	6	6	1.5	19	20	51,789	52,000	972	1,035	0.6
6280	Security and commodity services	4	4	1.8	9	13	24,889	16,923	211	246	0.5
6300	Insurance carriers	13	14	1.5	197	162	29,543	29,309	5,847	4,612	0.5
6400	Insurance agents, brokers, and service	55	53	1.8	179	167	21,095	24,958	4,013	4,015	0.9
6500	Real estate	73	80	1.9	480	444	14,600	14,432	6,828	6,895	1.5
6510	Real estate operators and lessors	29	31	1.9	190	134	18,463	18,657	2,887	2,749	2.1
6530	Real estate agents and managers	34	35	1.8	157	131	11,771	14,351	2,098	2,049	0.8

Source: County Business Patterns, 1994/95, CBP-94/95, U.S. Department of Commerce, Washington, D.C., November 1997. SIC categories for which data were suppressed or not available for both 1994 and 1995 are *not* displayed. The employment columns represent mid-March employment in the year. Pay per employee is calculated by dividing 1st Quarter payroll, annualized, by mid-March employment. The columns headed "% State" show the county's percentage of the state total for the SIC in 1995; for example, 1.4% for SIC 6000 means that the county had 1.4 percent of the state's total establishments (or payroll) in SIC 6000 in 1995. A dash (-) is used to indicate that data are not available or cannot be calculated; *nec* means not elsewhere classified.

Continued on next page.

SIC	Industry	No. Establishments			Employment		Pay / Employee		Annual Payroll ($ 000)		
		1994	1995	% State	1994	1995	1994	1995	1994	1995	% State
DELAWARE, IN - [continued]											
6540	Title abstract offices	3	3	1.6	38	37	16,105	18,486	738	700	2.6
6550	Subdividers and developers	7	9	2.1	95	142	10,947	9,465	1,105	1,364	2.3
6700	Holding and other investment offices	6	6	2.2	25	26	32,160	36,308	813	830	0.5
DUBOIS, IN											
60 –	**Finance, insurance, and real estate**	95	93	0.7	669	684	19,528	21,281	14,514	15,471	0.4
6000	Depository institutions	34	34	1.3	447	449	19,964	23,572	9,775	10,999	1.2
6020	Commercial banks	30	30	1.6	428	429	20,336	24,075	9,502	10,739	1.5
6300	Insurance carriers	5	6	0.7	40	33	33,000	25,939	1,185	814	0.1
6400	Insurance agents, brokers, and service	25	23	0.8	62	63	15,419	17,714	1,351	1,405	0.3
6500	Real estate	23	22	0.5	101	108	11,129	10,519	1,386	1,361	0.3
6510	Real estate operators and lessors	12	11	0.7	23	25	14,783	14,720	436	411	0.3
6530	Real estate agents and managers	8	7	0.4	70	76	9,829	8,947	855	858	0.4
ELKHART, IN											
60 –	**Finance, insurance, and real estate**	352	370	2.9	2,518	2,776	23,959	23,924	60,627	68,891	1.9
6000	Depository institutions	73	79	3.0	1,225	1,427	21,567	22,778	27,234	33,222	3.5
6020	Commercial banks	54	60	3.2	982	1,179	22,688	23,542	22,858	28,317	3.9
6100	Nondepository institutions	18	19	2.3	67	68	29,851	28,294	2,191	2,047	0.5
6200	Security and commodity brokers	19	18	2.9	55	55	57,455	53,818	2,717	2,922	1.2
6210	Security brokers and dealers	11	11	2.8	43	45	62,977	58,400	2,318	2,513	1.4
6280	Security and commodity services	8	7	3.2	12	10	37,667	33,200	399	409	0.9
6300	Insurance carriers	14	16	1.8	276	281	31,609	32,142	8,668	8,966	0.9
6400	Insurance agents, brokers, and service	79	82	2.7	289	307	20,180	22,436	5,995	7,123	1.6
6500	Real estate	137	144	3.4	557	601	17,645	18,176	10,691	12,145	2.6
6510	Real estate operators and lessors	51	58	3.6	241	253	20,116	22,704	4,695	6,603	5.1
6530	Real estate agents and managers	70	69	3.6	241	263	16,149	14,160	4,195	3,937	1.6
6550	Subdividers and developers	8	10	2.4	16	24	6,250	14,167	289	366	0.6
6552	Subdividers and developers, n.e.c.	7	8	4.1	16	23	6,250	14,261	270	356	0.9
6700	Holding and other investment offices	12	12	4.3	49	37	89,061	58,919	3,131	2,466	1.5
FAYETTE, IN											
60 –	**Finance, insurance, and real estate**	49	53	0.4	278	256	17,468	18,594	5,617	4,712	0.1
6000	Depository institutions	16	16	0.6	173	127	17,410	18,803	2,981	2,363	0.2
6020	Commercial banks	12	12	0.6	120	76	16,567	17,526	1,874	1,255	0.2
6400	Insurance agents, brokers, and service	12	13	0.4	28	33	16,000	17,212	473	590	0.1
6500	Real estate	15	18	0.4	45	49	11,822	12,490	594	642	0.1
FLOYD, IN											
60 –	**Finance, insurance, and real estate**	142	151	1.2	859	974	22,673	23,060	21,423	22,946	0.6
6000	Depository institutions	37	39	1.5	347	409	22,421	23,892	8,818	9,893	1.0
6020	Commercial banks	23	25	1.4	207	272	21,256	23,897	5,815	6,523	0.9
6030	Savings institutions	10	10	3.2	113	111	26,407	25,369	2,611	2,915	2.4
6060	Credit unions	4	4	0.9	27	26	14,667	17,538	392	455	0.5
6100	Nondepository institutions	5	7	0.8	22	27	33,455	31,704	905	855	0.2
6300	Insurance carriers	8	7	0.8	96	62	33,333	34,516	3,153	2,195	0.2
6400	Insurance agents, brokers, and service	43	41	1.4	172	178	23,256	27,573	4,399	5,153	1.2
6500	Real estate	41	46	1.1	196	205	14,837	18,283	3,259	3,770	0.8
6510	Real estate operators and lessors	12	16	1.0	95	100	12,253	18,280	1,288	1,644	1.3
6530	Real estate agents and managers	22	23	1.2	72	73	14,389	15,288	1,219	1,310	0.5
6550	Subdividers and developers	5	4	0.9	27	26	24,148	28,308	652	715	1.2
FOUNTAIN, IN											
60 –	**Finance, insurance, and real estate**	32	27	0.2	177	148	15,910	15,459	2,865	2,397	0.1
6000	Depository institutions	18	13	0.5	148	119	17,568	16,908	2,616	2,066	0.2
6020	Commercial banks	15	10	0.5	140	110	17,829	17,091	2,505	1,960	0.3

Source: County Business Patterns, 1994/95, CBP-94/95, U.S. Department of Commerce, Washington, D.C., November 1997. SIC categories for which data were suppressed or not available for both 1994 and 1995 are not displayed. The employment columns represent mid-March employment in the year. Pay per employee is calculated by dividing 1st Quarter payroll, annualized, by mid-March employment. The columns headed "% State" show the county's percentage of the state total for the SIC in 1995; for example, 1.4% for SIC 6000 means that the county had 1.4 percent of the state's total establishments (or payroll) in SIC 6000 in 1995. A dash (-) is used to indicate that data are not available or cannot be calculated; nec means not elsewhere classified.

Continued on next page.

SIC	Industry	No. Establishments			Employment		Pay / Employee		Annual Payroll ($ 000)		
		1994	1995	% State	1994	1995	1994	1995	1994	1995	% State
FOUNTAIN, IN - [continued]											
6400	Insurance agents, brokers, and service	6	6	0.2	9	9	8,000	8,444	76	86	0.0
6500	Real estate	8	8	0.2	20	20	7,200	10,000	173	245	0.1
6510	Real estate operators and lessors	4	3	0.2	11	4	2,545	5,000	22	20	0.0
FRANKLIN, IN											
60 –	**Finance, insurance, and real estate**	21	23	0.2	142	148	23,831	23,811	3,804	3,801	0.1
6000	Depository institutions	6	6	0.2	109	104	25,358	27,269	3,204	3,050	0.3
FULTON, IN											
60 –	**Finance, insurance, and real estate**	37	38	0.3	203	207	30,660	26,203	5,288	5,547	0.1
6000	Depository institutions	12	13	0.5	131	131	31,664	24,000	3,296	3,393	0.4
6020	Commercial banks	9	10	0.5	81	80	22,469	24,600	1,856	1,927	0.3
6300	Insurance carriers	3	3	0.3	8	10	27,500	25,600	243	272	0.0
6330	Fire, marine, and casualty insurance	3	3	0.6	8	10	27,500	25,600	243	272	0.1
6500	Real estate	12	12	0.3	35	34	17,829	20,000	772	807	0.2
GIBSON, IN											
60 –	**Finance, insurance, and real estate**	56	56	0.4	290	284	18,966	19,845	5,657	5,639	0.2
6000	Depository institutions	17	17	0.6	180	171	20,067	21,801	3,736	3,573	0.4
6020	Commercial banks	12	12	0.6	144	136	21,389	22,647	3,176	3,103	0.4
6030	Savings institutions	5	5	1.6	36	35	14,778	18,514	560	470	0.4
6100	Nondepository institutions	3	4	0.5	10	14	16,400	18,571	185	275	0.1
6510	Real estate operators and lessors	7	4	0.2	24	19	9,167	12,000	238	238	0.2
6550	Subdividers and developers	3	4	0.9	4	15	3,000	10,400	48	157	0.3
GRANT, IN											
60 –	**Finance, insurance, and real estate**	142	147	1.2	1,058	1,099	20,514	22,118	23,623	26,686	0.7
6000	Depository institutions	39	40	1.5	421	422	19,192	21,602	9,014	9,926	1.0
6020	Commercial banks	21	21	1.1	283	270	16,989	20,296	5,327	5,910	0.8
6060	Credit unions	12	12	2.7	81	82	15,753	17,268	1,368	1,456	1.5
6100	Nondepository institutions	9	12	1.4	60	76	18,333	23,526	1,366	2,051	0.5
6300	Insurance carriers	10	12	1.3	94	87	32,085	32,230	2,999	2,875	0.3
6400	Insurance agents, brokers, and service	29	27	0.9	114	103	17,649	20,816	2,286	2,452	0.5
6500	Real estate	43	44	1.0	269	273	13,561	14,535	4,471	4,576	1.0
6510	Real estate operators and lessors	23	20	1.2	197	129	14,457	12,279	3,478	1,710	1.3
6530	Real estate agents and managers	12	16	0.8	46	122	10,957	16,689	590	2,553	1.0
6550	Subdividers and developers	5	5	1.2	15	10	10,133	11,600	211	81	0.1
GREENE, IN											
60 –	**Finance, insurance, and real estate**	55	57	0.5	310	309	18,465	17,502	5,518	5,292	0.1
6000	Depository institutions	15	15	0.6	186	188	19,742	17,851	3,425	3,265	0.3
6400	Insurance agents, brokers, and service	17	17	0.6	47	47	12,936	13,787	674	663	0.1
6500	Real estate	19	21	0.5	52	48	9,846	10,500	520	520	0.1
6510	Real estate operators and lessors	5	6	0.4	12	18	2,333	3,556	33	67	0.1
6530	Real estate agents and managers	5	6	0.3	7	8	10,857	11,000	81	89	0.0
6540	Title abstract offices	4	4	2.2	11	10	16,000	16,000	187	173	0.7
6550	Subdividers and developers	5	5	1.2	22	12	10,545	16,000	219	191	0.3
HAMILTON, IN											
60 –	**Finance, insurance, and real estate**	459	483	3.8	7,334	7,613	31,887	38,507	240,878	286,683	7.7
6020	Commercial banks	46	48	2.6	386	425	22,155	24,311	8,345	10,384	1.4
6060	Credit unions	5	5	1.1	95	92	16,589	31,652	1,715	2,346	2.5
6100	Nondepository institutions	46	45	5.4	1,794	2,005	34,488	35,783	60,385	70,418	16.9
6200	Security and commodity brokers	28	29	4.7	753	670	47,517	63,242	34,121	36,937	15.7
6210	Security brokers and dealers	16	16	4.1	692	590	48,329	66,983	30,824	33,215	17.9
6300	Insurance carriers	60	64	7.0	2,491	2,532	31,634	36,221	79,053	93,189	9.5
6310	Life insurance	23	24	8.8	1,561	1,660	28,853	35,723	48,856	64,473	15.8
6330	Fire, marine, and casualty insurance	27	30	6.2	847	754	36,628	37,533	26,918	24,764	5.8

Source: County Business Patterns, 1994/95, CBP-94/95, U.S. Department of Commerce, Washington, D.C., November 1997. SIC categories for which data were suppressed or not available for both 1994 and 1995 are not displayed. The employment columns represent mid-March employment in the year. Pay per employee is calculated by dividing 1st Quarter payroll, annualized, by mid-March employment. The columns headed "% State" show the county's percentage of the state total for the SIC in 1995; for example, 1.4% for SIC 6000 means that the county had 1.4 percent of the state's total establishments (or payroll) in SIC 6000 in 1995. A dash (-) is used to indicate that data are not available or cannot be calculated; nec means not elsewhere classified.

Continued on next page.

SIC	Industry	No. Establishments			Employment		Pay / Employee		Annual Payroll ($ 000)		
		1994	1995	% State	1994	1995	1994	1995	1994	1995	% State
HAMILTON, IN - [continued]											
6370	Pension, health, and welfare funds	5	6	13.0	66	92	31,030	31,478	2,329	2,737	14.7
6400	Insurance agents, brokers, and service	116	125	4.1	476	526	29,118	28,266	15,206	16,128	3.6
6500	Real estate	141	149	3.5	1,091	1,064	22,944	26,526	28,985	29,999	6.4
6510	Real estate operators and lessors	36	41	2.5	203	260	15,409	22,169	4,864	6,312	4.8
6530	Real estate agents and managers	75	79	4.1	670	611	18,752	21,336	14,276	14,355	5.9
6550	Subdividers and developers	19	17	4.0	175	154	47,726	56,182	8,789	8,340	14.0
6552	Subdividers and developers, n.e.c.	16	14	7.1	168	149	49,357	57,638	8,680	8,211	21.7
6700	Holding and other investment offices	11	12	4.3	198	238	34,909	122,941	11,268	25,635	15.6
HANCOCK, IN											
60 –	**Finance, insurance, and real estate**	70	76	0.6	369	397	20,369	19,627	7,721	7,912	0.2
6000	Depository institutions	14	14	0.5	169	160	20,331	20,850	3,114	3,245	0.3
6300	Insurance carriers	5	5	0.6	28	29	29,286	27,724	820	823	0.1
6400	Insurance agents, brokers, and service	23	23	0.8	67	69	22,090	22,551	1,525	1,691	0.4
6500	Real estate	21	24	0.6	92	126	10,130	11,143	1,487	1,462	0.3
6510	Real estate operators and lessors	8	9	0.6	13	18	13,231	12,222	224	241	0.2
6530	Real estate agents and managers	8	9	0.5	18	20	12,222	14,000	323	304	0.1
6550	Subdividers and developers	3	4	0.9	10	14	23,200	26,000	380	353	0.6
HARRISON, IN											
60 –	**Finance, insurance, and real estate**	35	42	0.3	194	244	19,938	22,672	4,083	5,969	0.2
6000	Depository institutions	12	12	0.5	143	166	19,189	22,795	2,836	4,028	0.4
6400	Insurance agents, brokers, and service	9	10	0.3	25	31	22,560	23,742	646	802	0.2
6510	Real estate operators and lessors	5	5	0.3	7	8	8,000	10,500	60	93	0.1
HENDRICKS, IN											
60 –	**Finance, insurance, and real estate**	146	161	1.3	717	683	21,874	23,116	15,539	16,970	0.5
6000	Depository institutions	25	26	1.0	258	254	19,736	22,157	5,149	6,177	0.6
6020	Commercial banks	20	21	1.1	212	202	19,981	22,990	4,090	5,000	0.7
6100	Nondepository institutions	7	6	0.7	68	50	26,647	28,960	1,578	1,130	0.3
6160	Mortgage bankers and brokers	3	3	0.9	59	37	26,915	31,027	1,353	812	0.5
6400	Insurance agents, brokers, and service	34	40	1.3	145	145	21,076	22,979	3,351	3,368	0.8
6500	Real estate	67	74	1.7	201	186	14,289	14,258	3,333	3,608	0.8
6510	Real estate operators and lessors	23	23	1.4	64	55	10,500	13,236	897	1,103	0.8
6530	Real estate agents and managers	33	34	1.8	94	80	12,681	12,650	1,298	1,213	0.5
6552	Subdividers and developers, n.e.c.	6	8	4.1	9	27	35,111	20,889	429	698	1.8
6553	Cemetery subdividers and developers	3	3	1.5	6	7	14,000	11,429	92	107	0.5
HENRY, IN											
60 –	**Finance, insurance, and real estate**	73	77	0.6	486	530	22,700	22,611	11,150	12,158	0.3
6000	Depository institutions	23	23	0.9	299	316	21,043	21,823	6,373	6,751	0.7
6100	Nondepository institutions	4	4	0.5	13	19	31,692	30,737	483	535	0.1
6300	Insurance carriers	3	3	0.3	14	13	30,571	29,846	450	407	0.0
6400	Insurance agents, brokers, and service	19	19	0.6	57	57	20,070	21,333	1,216	1,224	0.3
6500	Real estate	20	24	0.6	87	106	12,184	12,981	1,286	1,488	0.3
6510	Real estate operators and lessors	12	13	0.8	48	54	11,167	11,704	630	716	0.6
6530	Real estate agents and managers	3	5	0.3	6	18	9,333	8,222	70	152	0.1
HOWARD, IN											
60 –	**Finance, insurance, and real estate**	176	186	1.5	1,429	1,350	24,910	26,498	34,298	34,252	0.9
6000	Depository institutions	39	39	1.5	645	485	20,434	22,416	13,353	11,281	1.2
6020	Commercial banks	26	27	1.5	435	364	19,283	20,956	8,417	7,963	1.1
6030	Savings institutions	4	3	1.0	113	20	18,124	14,200	2,170	302	0.2
6060	Credit unions	9	9	2.0	97	101	28,289	29,307	2,766	3,016	3.2
6100	Nondepository institutions	13	14	1.7	48	52	21,000	18,769	925	1,092	0.3
6200	Security and commodity brokers	14	17	2.7	38	51	43,368	39,373	1,820	2,136	0.9
6210	Security brokers and dealers	7	10	2.6	26	34	52,615	45,765	1,369	1,618	0.9
6280	Security and commodity services	7	7	3.2	12	17	23,333	26,588	451	518	1.1

Source: County Business Patterns, 1994/95, CBP-94/95, U.S. Department of Commerce, Washington, D.C., November 1997. SIC categories for which data were suppressed or not available for both 1994 and 1995 are *not* displayed. The employment columns represent mid-March employment in the year. Pay per employee is calculated by dividing 1st Quarter payroll, annualized, by mid-March employment. The columns headed "% State" show the county's percentage of the state total for the SIC in 1995; for example, 1.4% for SIC 6000 means that the county had 1.4 percent of the state's total establishments (or payroll) in SIC 6000 in 1995. A dash (-) is used to indicate that data are not available or cannot be calculated; *nec* means not elsewhere classified.

Continued on next page.

SIC	Industry	No. Establishments			Employment		Pay / Employee		Annual Payroll ($ 000)		
		1994	1995	% State	1994	1995	1994	1995	1994	1995	% State
HOWARD, IN - [continued]											
6300	Insurance carriers	11	11	*1.2*	237	257	44,253	44,358	8,060	8,970	*0.9*
6310	Life insurance	7	7	*2.6*	231	251	44,537	44,478	7,858	8,679	*2.1*
6400	Insurance agents, brokers, and service	42	44	*1.5*	206	213	25,883	27,099	5,372	5,667	*1.3*
6500	Real estate	57	61	*1.4*	255	292	15,451	16,247	4,768	5,106	*1.1*
6510	Real estate operators and lessors	26	29	*1.8*	79	85	12,203	14,071	1,159	1,377	*1.1*
6530	Real estate agents and managers	25	24	*1.3*	87	82	15,126	15,268	1,357	1,406	*0.6*
HUNTINGTON, IN											
60 –	**Finance, insurance, and real estate**	70	79	*0.6*	402	411	20,259	22,599	8,424	9,057	*0.2*
6000	Depository institutions	21	22	*0.8*	223	211	18,278	21,877	4,220	4,441	*0.5*
6020	Commercial banks	12	12	*0.6*	153	146	19,660	21,479	3,000	3,021	*0.4*
6100	Nondepository institutions	4	5	*0.6*	8	9	26,500	42,667	241	364	*0.1*
6400	Insurance agents, brokers, and service	16	18	*0.6*	81	83	28,593	30,651	2,266	2,502	*0.6*
6500	Real estate	23	27	*0.6*	69	78	11,884	13,538	1,076	1,066	*0.2*
6510	Real estate operators and lessors	8	10	*0.6*	21	26	9,905	12,462	316	255	*0.2*
JACKSON, IN											
60 –	**Finance, insurance, and real estate**	82	86	*0.7*	516	499	19,279	20,641	10,575	11,044	*0.3*
6000	Depository institutions	23	23	*0.9*	330	324	18,958	21,185	6,657	7,024	*0.7*
6400	Insurance agents, brokers, and service	20	21	*0.7*	74	73	18,649	20,712	1,755	1,751	*0.4*
6500	Real estate	29	30	*0.7*	60	64	11,067	12,000	851	1,057	*0.2*
6510	Real estate operators and lessors	13	12	*0.7*	26	22	5,538	7,455	219	264	*0.2*
6530	Real estate agents and managers	11	11	*0.6*	17	20	15,765	14,400	354	477	*0.2*
JASPER, IN											
60 –	**Finance, insurance, and real estate**	59	62	*0.5*	293	326	15,386	20,466	5,176	7,845	*0.2*
6000	Depository institutions	17	15	*0.6*	181	165	16,575	19,782	3,375	3,662	*0.4*
6400	Insurance agents, brokers, and service	20	19	*0.6*	42	41	15,143	16,390	703	688	*0.2*
6500	Real estate	19	22	*0.5*	58	60	8,966	10,533	751	1,037	*0.2*
6510	Real estate operators and lessors	7	6	*0.4*	10	9	8,000	7,111	90	92	*0.1*
6530	Real estate agents and managers	8	8	*0.4*	14	14	12,571	15,429	231	320	*0.1*
JAY, IN											
60 –	**Finance, insurance, and real estate**	40	40	*0.3*	203	208	19,094	20,385	4,119	4,676	*0.1*
6000	Depository institutions	14	14	*0.5*	139	134	17,065	18,507	2,502	2,600	*0.3*
6400	Insurance agents, brokers, and service	12	12	*0.4*	30	38	16,133	14,737	519	570	*0.1*
6500	Real estate	7	7	*0.2*	13	13	7,385	7,385	118	109	*0.0*
6550	Subdividers and developers	4	4	*0.9*	5	5	5,600	5,600	34	33	*0.1*
6553	Cemetery subdividers and developers	4	4	*2.0*	5	5	5,600	5,600	34	33	*0.2*
JEFFERSON, IN											
60 –	**Finance, insurance, and real estate**	53	55	*0.4*	259	264	19,336	20,894	5,131	5,863	*0.2*
6000	Depository institutions	17	18	*0.7*	151	161	21,775	22,360	3,323	3,727	*0.4*
6020	Commercial banks	9	9	*0.5*	108	118	22,593	22,712	2,381	2,662	*0.4*
6500	Real estate	17	19	*0.4*	59	50	8,814	14,880	634	907	*0.2*
6510	Real estate operators and lessors	8	7	*0.4*	17	25	5,412	9,600	198	290	*0.2*
JENNINGS, IN											
60 –	**Finance, insurance, and real estate**	31	36	*0.3*	162	198	15,679	14,727	2,922	3,310	*0.1*
6000	Depository institutions	7	10	*0.4*	97	103	17,320	17,864	1,736	2,033	*0.2*
6500	Real estate	13	16	*0.4*	38	62	12,316	9,226	648	723	*0.2*
JOHNSON, IN											
60 –	**Finance, insurance, and real estate**	228	238	*1.9*	1,539	1,544	23,498	24,513	35,976	39,120	*1.1*
6000	Depository institutions	34	41	*1.5*	432	464	20,546	22,621	9,187	10,243	*1.1*
6020	Commercial banks	28	33	*1.8*	376	401	20,798	23,092	8,047	8,967	*1.2*
6100	Nondepository institutions	24	27	*3.2*	210	159	28,400	31,296	5,369	5,615	*1.4*
6160	Mortgage bankers and brokers	14	16	*4.8*	164	114	30,610	33,965	4,510	4,590	*2.7*

Source: County Business Patterns, 1994/95, CBP-94/95,, U.S. Department of Commerce, Washington, D.C., November 1997. SIC categories for which data were suppressed or not available for both 1994 and 1995 are not displayed. The employment columns represent mid-March employment in the year. Pay per employee is calculated by dividing 1st Quarter payroll, annualized, by mid-March employment. The columns headed "% State" show the county's percentage of the state total for the SIC in 1995; for example, 1.4% for SIC 6000 means that the county had 1.4 percent of the state's total establishments (or payroll) in SIC 6000 in 1995. A dash (-) is used to indicate that data are not available or cannot be calculated; nec means not elsewhere classified.

Continued on next page.

SIC	Industry	No. Establishments			Employment		Pay / Employee		Annual Payroll ($ 000)		
		1994	1995	% State	1994	1995	1994	1995	1994	1995	% State
JOHNSON, IN - [continued]											
6280	Security and commodity services	4	5	2.3	11	16	19,636	18,250	266	319	0.7
6300	Insurance carriers	18	21	2.3	146	125	30,658	36,736	3,907	4,156	0.4
6310	Life insurance	5	5	1.8	97	80	32,454	38,800	2,704	2,658	0.7
6400	Insurance agents, brokers, and service	50	53	1.8	313	279	26,735	32,473	8,162	8,886	2.0
6500	Real estate	89	84	2.0	389	465	16,751	14,761	7,199	8,043	1.7
6510	Real estate operators and lessors	23	20	1.2	71	68	20,113	21,824	1,575	1,644	1.3
6530	Real estate agents and managers	44	42	2.2	198	253	15,333	13,075	3,446	3,564	1.5
6540	Title abstract offices	3	3	1.6	27	10	34,370	23,200	431	350	1.3
6550	Subdividers and developers	16	16	3.8	92	132	12,174	13,758	1,720	2,441	4.1
6552	Subdividers and developers, n.e.c.	9	11	5.6	21	49	19,429	20,735	888	1,522	4.0
KNOX, IN											
60–	**Finance, insurance, and real estate**	84	82	0.7	635	607	20,926	21,819	14,331	13,029	0.4
6000	Depository institutions	23	22	0.8	416	381	21,317	21,669	9,568	7,877	0.8
6020	Commercial banks	17	16	0.9	251	225	24,924	25,973	6,727	5,107	0.7
6100	Nondepository institutions	4	4	0.5	16	13	25,750	30,462	441	319	0.1
6300	Insurance carriers	6	6	0.7	63	52	22,540	20,538	1,489	1,161	0.1
6310	Life insurance	3	3	1.1	57	46	22,667	20,348	1,355	1,012	0.2
6330	Fire, marine, and casualty insurance	3	3	0.6	6	6	21,333	22,000	134	149	0.0
6400	Insurance agents, brokers, and service	18	17	0.6	58	64	20,000	21,750	1,279	1,448	0.3
6500	Real estate	26	25	0.6	62	57	10,065	10,386	759	636	0.1
6510	Real estate operators and lessors	12	11	0.7	28	30	9,857	10,000	405	335	0.3
6530	Real estate agents and managers	10	10	0.5	18	12	11,111	12,000	195	150	0.1
KOSCIUSKO, IN											
60–	**Finance, insurance, and real estate**	129	131	1.0	790	803	21,585	23,965	16,961	18,383	0.5
6000	Depository institutions	40	40	1.5	512	535	21,289	23,806	10,358	11,443	1.2
6020	Commercial banks	32	32	1.7	439	458	22,387	25,144	9,276	10,272	1.4
6030	Savings institutions	5	5	1.6	50	53	14,400	14,491	704	762	0.6
6060	Credit unions	3	3	0.7	23	24	15,304	18,833	378	409	0.4
6100	Nondepository institutions	4	3	0.4	12	10	27,667	30,800	355	362	0.1
6300	Insurance carriers	5	5	0.6	25	23	23,200	24,000	632	595	0.1
6400	Insurance agents, brokers, and service	31	32	1.1	82	82	21,610	23,220	1,820	2,057	0.5
6500	Real estate	41	42	1.0	106	106	16,377	15,660	2,103	2,081	0.4
LAGRANGE, IN											
60–	**Finance, insurance, and real estate**	35	36	0.3	271	263	17,417	18,981	4,984	5,451	0.1
6000	Depository institutions	14	14	0.5	203	198	18,187	19,434	3,904	4,282	0.4
6400	Insurance agents, brokers, and service	8	8	0.3	30	31	16,267	19,226	503	591	0.1
6500	Real estate	10	9	0.2	31	26	11,226	13,538	395	399	0.1
LAKE, IN											
60–	**Finance, insurance, and real estate**	857	851	6.8	7,287	6,730	23,458	24,527	168,382	167,074	4.5
6000	Depository institutions	195	201	7.6	3,432	3,213	21,019	22,577	69,300	72,194	7.6
6020	Commercial banks	96	101	5.5	2,326	2,069	20,270	22,254	44,840	46,566	6.5
6030	Savings institutions	45	48	15.2	715	744	23,720	24,145	16,093	16,957	13.8
6060	Credit unions	50	48	10.9	368	379	20,565	21,266	7,913	8,133	8.5
6090	Functions closely related to banking	4	4	10.5	23	21	20,000	22,476	454	538	-
6100	Nondepository institutions	49	48	5.7	480	418	29,708	29,799	13,340	13,102	3.2
6160	Mortgage bankers and brokers	29	25	7.5	377	320	30,080	29,525	10,278	10,267	6.0
6200	Security and commodity brokers	32	32	5.1	209	217	69,531	56,903	11,822	11,934	5.1
6210	Security brokers and dealers	19	19	4.9	180	185	71,933	60,757	10,833	10,928	5.9
6280	Security and commodity services	13	13	6.0	29	32	54,621	34,625	989	1,006	2.1
6300	Insurance carriers	61	65	7.2	859	616	30,417	40,500	24,704	20,202	2.1
6310	Life insurance	19	18	6.6	581	325	25,473	42,978	14,467	9,286	2.3
6330	Fire, marine, and casualty insurance	31	35	7.3	164	162	42,829	42,543	7,024	7,350	1.7
6400	Insurance agents, brokers, and service	215	209	6.9	1,026	949	20,172	22,588	23,606	24,617	5.5
6500	Real estate	285	278	6.5	1,227	1,259	17,320	15,193	23,427	22,632	4.9

Source: County Business Patterns, 1994/95, CBP-94/95, U.S. Department of Commerce, Washington, D.C., November 1997. SIC categories for which data were suppressed or not available for both 1994 and 1995 are *not* displayed. The employment columns represent mid-March employment in the year. Pay per employee is calculated by dividing 1st Quarter payroll, annualized, by mid-March employment. The columns headed "% State" show the county's percentage of the state total for the SIC in 1995; for example, 1.4% for SIC 6000 means that the county had 1.4 percent of the state's total establishments (or payroll) in SIC 6000 in 1995. A dash (-) is used to indicate that data are not available or cannot be calculated; *nec* means not elsewhere classified.

Continued on next page.

SIC	Industry	No. Establishments			Employment		Pay / Employee		Annual Payroll ($ 000)		
		1994	1995	% State	1994	1995	1994	1995	1994	1995	% State
LAKE, IN - [continued]											
6510	Real estate operators and lessors	107	101	6.2	526	514	14,776	13,743	8,114	7,790	6.0
6530	Real estate agents and managers	148	146	7.6	464	519	16,862	15,461	9,381	9,502	3.9
6540	Title abstract offices	4	5	2.7	98	74	29,837	16,649	2,832	1,810	6.8
6550	Subdividers and developers	19	19	4.5	137	146	19,912	18,877	3,066	3,423	5.7
6552	Subdividers and developers, n.e.c.	9	8	4.1	22	22	26,909	17,636	549	781	2.1
6553	Cemetery subdividers and developers	8	8	4.0	115	118	18,574	19,492	2,512	2,544	12.4
6730	Trusts	5	4	4.4	10	6	22,800	31,333	222	229	1.0
6790	Miscellaneous investing	5	5	9.3	18	23	36,000	34,957	645	820	7.2
LA PORTE, IN											
60 –	**Finance, insurance, and real estate**	184	192	1.5	1,205	1,067	19,907	22,017	24,738	24,111	0.6
6000	Depository institutions	50	53	2.0	817	661	20,431	23,661	16,252	15,285	1.6
6020	Commercial banks	30	33	1.8	561	405	21,911	27,032	11,717	10,288	1.4
6030	Savings institutions	6	6	1.9	155	155	18,297	19,484	2,981	3,338	2.7
6060	Credit unions	14	14	3.2	101	101	15,485	16,554	1,554	1,659	1.7
6200	Security and commodity brokers	7	7	1.1	10	8	32,400	33,500	360	277	0.1
6400	Insurance agents, brokers, and service	35	41	1.4	139	150	23,568	22,693	4,107	3,925	0.9
6500	Real estate	64	64	1.5	156	162	11,897	13,012	2,173	2,389	0.5
6510	Real estate operators and lessors	34	38	2.3	102	112	12,431	13,000	1,479	1,569	1.2
6530	Real estate agents and managers	25	21	1.1	42	38	12,286	14,842	575	686	0.3
6550	Subdividers and developers	4	3	0.7	11	10	5,818	6,800	112	112	0.2
LAWRENCE, IN											
60 –	**Finance, insurance, and real estate**	69	71	0.6	397	408	17,169	18,118	7,033	7,780	0.2
6000	Depository institutions	14	13	0.5	236	232	15,864	17,517	3,954	4,196	0.4
6100	Nondepository institutions	4	3	0.4	10	10	21,600	22,000	180	260	0.1
6140	Personal credit institutions	4	3	0.8	10	10	21,600	22,000	180	260	0.1
6400	Insurance agents, brokers, and service	21	24	0.8	66	65	19,273	18,708	1,331	1,409	0.3
6500	Real estate	24	24	0.6	72	72	14,778	14,833	1,142	1,180	0.3
6510	Real estate operators and lessors	7	8	0.5	21	25	10,857	10,720	242	293	0.2
6550	Subdividers and developers	6	4	0.9	15	6	15,200	19,333	227	136	0.2
MADISON, IN											
60 –	**Finance, insurance, and real estate**	240	251	2.0	1,412	1,334	22,660	22,189	29,660	29,827	0.8
6000	Depository institutions	64	64	2.4	732	607	22,027	23,025	14,411	13,261	1.4
6020	Commercial banks	50	49	2.6	593	460	19,494	20,157	10,330	8,872	1.2
6100	Nondepository institutions	16	18	2.2	128	125	28,250	29,536	3,395	4,222	1.0
6160	Mortgage bankers and brokers	5	6	1.8	70	57	29,143	32,702	1,824	2,243	1.3
6200	Security and commodity brokers	9	10	1.6	35	40	73,600	51,200	1,978	2,004	0.8
6300	Insurance carriers	8	9	1.0	46	46	25,739	30,870	1,257	1,448	0.1
6400	Insurance agents, brokers, and service	57	60	2.0	137	145	17,664	17,986	2,527	2,622	0.6
6500	Real estate	83	87	2.0	323	358	18,427	15,978	5,965	6,168	1.3
6510	Real estate operators and lessors	36	32	2.0	127	119	11,024	12,941	1,678	1,797	1.4
6530	Real estate agents and managers	36	39	2.0	94	135	26,809	16,859	2,162	2,285	0.9
6540	Title abstract offices	3	3	1.6	64	61	21,438	20,459	1,390	1,234	4.7
6550	Subdividers and developers	6	9	2.1	38	42	17,368	15,048	724	787	1.3
6553	Cemetery subdividers and developers	6	7	3.5	38	42	17,368	15,048	724	728	3.5
6700	Holding and other investment offices	3	3	1.1	11	13	11,273	10,462	127	102	0.1
MARION, IN											
60 –	**Finance, insurance, and real estate**	2,423	2,544	20.2	40,132	43,742	31,494	32,647	1,255,629	1,392,812	37.5
6000	Depository institutions	337	346	13.1	7,290	7,854	24,431	25,836	185,599	201,718	21.2
6020	Commercial banks	229	240	13.0	5,309	5,826	24,800	26,426	136,914	153,722	21.3
6030	Savings institutions	18	17	5.4	927	991	24,872	22,959	24,836	22,705	18.5
6060	Credit unions	69	66	14.9	805	778	21,511	22,797	17,135	17,346	18.2
6100	Nondepository institutions	220	239	28.6	3,958	4,873	33,124	27,188	122,594	145,638	35.0
6140	Personal credit institutions	76	84	21.3	1,257	1,465	28,853	29,917	35,760	40,854	20.0
6150	Business credit institutions	22	25	51.0	173	767	34,775	24,083	8,738	23,549	77.4

Source: County Business Patterns, 1994/95, CBP-94/95,.U.S. Department of Commerce, Washington, D.C., November 1997. SIC categories for which data were suppressed or not available for both 1994 and 1995 are not displayed. The employment columns represent mid-March employment in the year. Pay per employee is calculated by dividing 1st Quarter payroll, annualized, by mid-March employment. The columns headed "% State" show the county's percentage of the state total for the SIC in 1995; for example, 1.4% for SIC 6000 means that the county had 1.4 percent of the state's total establishments (or payroll) in SIC 6000 in 1995. A dash (-) is used to indicate that data are not available or cannot be calculated; nec means not elsewhere classified.

Continued on next page.

SIC	Industry	No. Establishments			Employment		Pay / Employee		Annual Payroll ($ 000)		
		1994	1995	% State	1994	1995	1994	1995	1994	1995	% State
MARION, IN - [continued]											
6160	Mortgage bankers and brokers	116	126	37.6	2,523	2,635	35,152	26,585	77,848	80,954	46.9
6200	Security and commodity brokers	119	137	22.0	1,089	1,426	69,469	58,163	67,369	79,032	33.5
6210	Security brokers and dealers	67	76	19.5	853	879	76,858	76,314	54,887	60,143	32.4
6220	Commodity contracts brokers, dealers	3	3	25.0	42	40	39,333	38,500	2,046	2,029	67.2
6280	Security and commodity services	49	58	26.6	194	507	43,505	28,245	10,436	16,860	35.7
6300	Insurance carriers	286	289	31.8	12,897	13,282	34,605	38,827	433,425	483,590	49.1
6310	Life insurance	86	82	30.0	3,455	3,464	36,072	39,898	120,720	126,739	31.0
6320	Medical service and health insurance	28	28	48.3	1,580	1,663	42,154	41,032	62,443	63,414	54.4
6330	Fire, marine, and casualty insurance	129	140	29.1	7,029	7,485	32,466	38,499	229,195	272,857	64.1
6360	Title insurance	10	12	30.8	237	183	36,996	34,951	6,480	5,683	44.3
6370	Pension, health, and welfare funds	26	20	43.5	558	436	29,419	28,321	12,351	12,542	67.5
6400	Insurance agents, brokers, and service	558	562	18.6	5,168	5,477	32,302	36,453	174,837	194,761	43.6
6500	Real estate	811	873	20.4	8,678	8,639	24,438	22,404	218,658	198,910	42.7
6510	Real estate operators and lessors	334	335	20.7	2,146	2,182	15,968	18,189	39,720	43,826	33.7
6530	Real estate agents and managers	387	427	22.3	5,884	5,678	27,354	23,730	160,640	132,579	54.2
6540	Title abstract offices	16	19	10.4	172	166	25,860	19,108	4,008	4,012	15.2
6550	Subdividers and developers	57	58	13.7	339	581	25,805	26,059	9,787	17,342	29.1
6552	Subdividers and developers, n.e.c.	39	40	20.3	147	374	26,748	26,278	4,411	11,914	31.5
6553	Cemetery subdividers and developers	16	16	8.1	191	201	25,131	25,930	5,195	5,296	25.8
6700	Holding and other investment offices	82	85	30.8	589	989	58,703	63,292	33,087	47,999	29.1
6710	Holding offices	35	39	34.8	306	483	77,098	82,890	23,921	34,205	29.8
6720	Investment offices	5	4	40.0	24	23	81,333	115,130	1,569	1,685	11.2
6730	Trusts	26	24	26.7	173	394	33,827	40,629	3,923	8,164	36.3
6732	Educational, religious, etc. trusts	15	14	29.2	92	112	27,261	27,357	2,655	3,109	21.0
6733	Trusts, n.e.c.	11	10	23.8	81	282	41,284	45,901	1,268	5,055	65.7
6790	Miscellaneous investing	16	17	31.5	86	89	36,977	43,865	3,674	3,927	34.3
MARSHALL, IN											
60 –	**Finance, insurance, and real estate**	81	79	0.6	459	438	21,359	26,977	10,318	11,554	0.3
6000	Depository institutions	16	17	0.6	202	190	21,683	26,253	4,148	4,117	0.4
6020	Commercial banks	11	11	0.6	145	120	21,379	30,700	3,187	2,796	0.4
6100	Nondepository institutions	3	4	0.5	10	10	28,400	26,800	263	306	0.1
6400	Insurance agents, brokers, and service	28	23	0.8	104	109	25,769	32,954	3,308	3,865	0.9
6500	Real estate	28	28	0.7	116	97	14,000	15,918	1,624	1,509	0.3
6510	Real estate operators and lessors	9	7	0.4	31	23	8,516	7,304	301	215	0.2
6530	Real estate agents and managers	15	17	0.9	70	58	15,714	19,379	1,041	1,032	0.4
6540	Title abstract offices	3	3	1.6	15	15	17,333	16,267	279	253	1.0
MARTIN, IN											
60 –	**Finance, insurance, and real estate**	18	16	0.1	106	105	17,245	18,057	1,962	2,038	0.1
6000	Depository institutions	7	7	0.3	90	92	18,622	18,739	1,807	1,836	0.2
6020	Commercial banks	4	4	0.2	57	59	19,649	18,441	1,148	1,144	0.2
MIAMI, IN											
60 –	**Finance, insurance, and real estate**	56	57	0.5	288	274	18,861	19,825	5,390	5,531	0.1
6000	Depository institutions	22	21	0.8	192	184	21,208	21,804	3,806	3,961	0.4
6020	Commercial banks	16	16	0.9	118	115	23,356	24,139	2,550	2,684	0.4
6100	Nondepository institutions	3	4	0.5	9	7	25,333	27,429	218	212	0.1
6400	Insurance agents, brokers, and service	13	13	0.4	48	45	15,500	16,444	923	868	0.2
MONROE, IN											
60 –	**Finance, insurance, and real estate**	268	274	2.2	1,965	2,163	19,463	20,168	40,840	46,069	1.2
6000	Depository institutions	48	46	1.7	639	677	19,931	20,414	12,064	13,275	1.4
6020	Commercial banks	33	33	1.8	427	433	19,166	20,194	7,268	7,956	1.1
6100	Nondepository institutions	11	9	1.1	97	207	20,784	19,536	2,859	5,602	1.3
6280	Security and commodity services	7	8	3.7	13	14	21,538	20,571	292	261	0.6
6300	Insurance carriers	16	14	1.5	93	82	35,828	36,976	3,292	2,907	0.3
6310	Life insurance	6	5	1.8	74	60	34,324	34,067	2,483	1,964	0.5

Source: County Business Patterns, 1994/95, CBP-94/95, U.S. Department of Commerce, Washington, D.C., November 1997. SIC categories for which data were suppressed or not available for both 1994 and 1995 are not displayed. The employment columns represent mid-March employment in the year. Pay per employee is calculated by dividing 1st Quarter payroll, annualized, by mid-March employment. The columns headed "% State" show the county's percentage of the state total for the SIC in 1995; for example, 1.4% for SIC 6000 means that the county had 1.4 percent of the state's total establishments (or payroll) in SIC 6000 in 1995. A dash (-) is used to indicate that data are not available or cannot be calculated; nec means not elsewhere classified.

Continued on next page.

SIC	Industry	No. Establishments			Employment		Pay / Employee		Annual Payroll ($ 000)		
		1994	1995	% State	1994	1995	1994	1995	1994	1995	% State
MONROE, IN - [continued]											
6400	Insurance agents, brokers, and service	59	58	1.9	174	176	17,287	17,477	3,322	3,292	0.7
6500	Real estate	115	124	2.9	608	678	14,941	15,782	10,787	11,850	2.5
6510	Real estate operators and lessors	45	51	3.1	225	264	13,120	14,939	3,556	4,433	3.4
6530	Real estate agents and managers	55	60	3.1	253	266	17,628	17,368	5,256	5,228	2.1
6540	Title abstract offices	3	3	1.6	22	26	14,727	15,692	412	399	1.5
6550	Subdividers and developers	9	7	1.7	103	52	12,466	21,769	1,223	1,291	2.2
MONTGOMERY, IN											
60 –	**Finance, insurance, and real estate**	75	74	0.6	404	366	20,465	21,388	8,230	8,131	0.2
6000	Depository institutions	20	18	0.7	191	179	22,534	23,441	4,045	3,949	0.4
6020	Commercial banks	15	13	0.7	127	112	22,142	22,929	2,525	2,606	0.4
6300	Insurance carriers	6	5	0.6	65	36	28,862	33,556	1,603	1,199	0.1
6400	Insurance agents, brokers, and service	21	17	0.6	79	79	15,291	17,570	1,530	1,605	0.4
6500	Real estate	22	25	0.6	54	52	11,481	11,692	795	848	0.2
6530	Real estate agents and managers	9	8	0.4	17	15	8,706	9,067	181	183	0.1
MORGAN, IN											
60 –	**Finance, insurance, and real estate**	97	95	0.8	518	485	20,471	20,437	10,224	9,915	0.3
6000	Depository institutions	21	22	0.8	308	272	21,143	22,118	6,163	5,704	0.6
6100	Nondepository institutions	5	4	0.5	15	11	22,400	21,091	303	251	0.1
6400	Insurance agents, brokers, and service	27	26	0.9	80	75	17,300	19,200	1,436	1,584	0.4
6500	Real estate	36	35	0.8	97	110	17,072	14,036	1,567	1,668	0.4
6510	Real estate operators and lessors	15	14	0.9	38	59	15,263	14,576	653	856	0.7
6530	Real estate agents and managers	15	14	0.7	22	28	10,545	11,571	281	391	0.2
6540	Title abstract offices	3	3	1.6	26	19	16,154	17,263	468	343	1.3
NEWTON, IN											
60 –	**Finance, insurance, and real estate**	19	19	0.2	105	103	20,952	21,204	2,434	2,468	0.1
6000	Depository institutions	9	9	0.3	91	90	21,538	21,778	2,179	2,135	0.2
6400	Insurance agents, brokers, and service	6	7	0.2	8	9	18,500	19,556	165	287	0.1
NOBLE, IN											
60 –	**Finance, insurance, and real estate**	62	62	0.5	278	253	19,871	21,834	5,525	5,340	0.1
6000	Depository institutions	17	19	0.7	173	166	21,249	24,145	3,636	3,816	0.4
6400	Insurance agents, brokers, and service	19	18	0.6	40	40	17,100	16,900	696	648	0.1
6500	Real estate	18	16	0.4	32	24	10,125	10,000	338	292	0.1
6510	Real estate operators and lessors	5	4	0.2	9	5	8,444	6,400	72	49	0.0
6530	Real estate agents and managers	8	8	0.4	13	10	10,462	10,800	152	135	0.1
6700	Holding and other investment offices	3	3	1.1	13	11	27,385	27,636	352	284	0.2
OHIO, IN											
60 –	**Finance, insurance, and real estate**	4	5	0.0	19	21	11,368	11,238	231	237	0.0
ORANGE, IN											
60 –	**Finance, insurance, and real estate**	27	28	0.2	200	204	18,940	18,471	3,971	3,846	0.1
6000	Depository institutions	8	9	0.3	137	140	20,409	20,371	2,958	2,901	0.3
6500	Real estate	8	7	0.2	29	26	11,724	10,769	320	290	0.1
6530	Real estate agents and managers	5	4	0.2	22	18	13,636	12,889	270	242	0.1
OWEN, IN											
60 –	**Finance, insurance, and real estate**	17	17	0.1	125	124	16,224	17,129	2,259	2,366	0.1
6000	Depository institutions	6	6	0.2	95	92	16,632	18,000	1,771	1,868	0.2
6400	Insurance agents, brokers, and service	4	4	0.1	16	16	18,000	18,750	330	321	0.1
6500	Real estate	4	4	0.1	9	10	6,222	6,000	72	74	0.0

Source: County Business Patterns, 1994/95, CBP-94/95, U.S. Department of Commerce, Washington, D.C., November 1997. SIC categories for which data were suppressed or not available for both 1994 and 1995 are *not* displayed. The employment columns represent mid-March employment in the year. Pay per employee is calculated by dividing 1st Quarter payroll, annualized, by mid-March employment. The columns headed "% State" show the county's percentage of the state total for the SIC in 1995; for example, 1.4% for SIC 6000 means that the county had 1.4 percent of the state's total establishments (or payroll) in SIC 6000 in 1995. A dash (-) is used to indicate that data are not available or cannot be calculated; *nec* means not elsewhere classified.

SIC	Industry	No. Establishments			Employment		Pay / Employee		Annual Payroll ($ 000)		
		1994	1995	% State	1994	1995	1994	1995	1994	1995	% State
PARKE, IN											
60 –	**Finance, insurance, and real estate**	24	25	0.2	122	124	14,951	17,387	1,986	2,209	0.1
6000	Depository institutions	8	9	0.3	76	73	17,684	19,342	1,371	1,443	0.2
6020	Commercial banks	8	9	0.5	76	73	17,684	19,342	1,371	1,443	0.2
PERRY, IN											
60 –	**Finance, insurance, and real estate**	31	28	0.2	263	274	17,658	19,343	4,742	5,410	0.1
6000	Depository institutions	6	5	0.2	189	190	17,122	18,842	3,288	3,661	0.4
6300	Insurance carriers	3	3	0.3	18	27	15,333	19,852	295	558	0.1
6500	Real estate	6	6	0.1	15	18	22,400	21,778	346	404	0.1
PIKE, IN											
60 –	**Finance, insurance, and real estate**	16	16	0.1	124	120	16,484	20,533	2,112	2,475	0.1
6000	Depository institutions	9	9	0.3	94	91	16,511	21,319	1,596	1,916	0.2
PORTER, IN											
60 –	**Finance, insurance, and real estate**	238	242	1.9	1,574	1,581	21,611	23,190	33,509	37,318	1.0
6000	Depository institutions	51	56	2.1	776	809	21,149	23,698	15,673	19,569	2.1
6020	Commercial banks	33	38	2.1	429	460	19,179	22,078	7,971	10,882	1.5
6200	Security and commodity brokers	14	14	2.3	54	64	64,519	51,063	3,268	3,096	1.3
6210	Security brokers and dealers	7	7	1.8	48	56	69,167	54,643	2,981	2,785	1.5
6300	Insurance carriers	12	13	1.4	129	96	33,643	33,042	3,572	2,921	0.3
6400	Insurance agents, brokers, and service	54	48	1.6	167	181	18,323	20,044	3,503	3,824	0.9
6500	Real estate	94	97	2.3	393	393	14,158	16,417	6,421	6,868	1.5
6510	Real estate operators and lessors	36	41	2.5	206	224	13,340	14,839	2,924	3,458	2.7
6530	Real estate agents and managers	46	42	2.2	135	125	14,904	17,984	2,390	2,547	1.0
6550	Subdividers and developers	9	10	2.4	51	42	15,608	20,667	1,096	809	1.4
6552	Subdividers and developers, n.e.c.	5	6	3.0	25	16	16,640	26,000	622	312	0.8
6553	Cemetery subdividers and developers	4	4	2.0	26	26	14,615	17,385	474	497	2.4
POSEY, IN											
60 –	**Finance, insurance, and real estate**	29	31	0.2	181	209	17,370	19,177	3,480	4,326	0.1
6000	Depository institutions	12	13	0.5	133	161	16,872	19,205	2,464	3,300	0.3
6020	Commercial banks	9	10	0.5	118	145	17,390	19,917	2,278	3,111	0.4
6030	Savings institutions	3	3	1.0	15	16	12,800	12,750	186	189	0.2
6400	Insurance agents, brokers, and service	6	6	0.2	20	19	25,000	23,579	596	555	0.1
6500	Real estate	8	8	0.2	21	20	11,619	13,200	259	282	0.1
PULASKI, IN											
60 –	**Finance, insurance, and real estate**	29	31	0.2	192	176	17,479	17,068	3,100	3,174	0.1
6000	Depository institutions	6	6	0.2	106	108	18,415	17,444	1,824	1,949	0.2
6510	Real estate operators and lessors	4	4	0.2	10	8	8,000	10,000	92	96	0.1
PUTNAM, IN											
60 –	**Finance, insurance, and real estate**	50	47	0.4	288	294	18,917	19,565	6,293	6,400	0.2
6000	Depository institutions	9	9	0.3	165	166	19,055	19,060	3,398	3,333	0.3
6400	Insurance agents, brokers, and service	11	11	0.4	54	57	19,481	20,912	1,499	1,554	0.3
6500	Real estate	24	22	0.5	45	47	11,733	13,532	640	791	0.2
6510	Real estate operators and lessors	8	8	0.5	10	14	11,200	14,286	148	265	0.2
RANDOLPH, IN											
60 –	**Finance, insurance, and real estate**	40	40	0.3	244	233	17,262	19,416	4,404	4,665	0.1
6000	Depository institutions	16	16	0.6	162	157	19,037	21,146	3,186	3,237	0.3
6020	Commercial banks	12	12	0.6	147	142	19,075	21,296	2,926	2,963	0.4
6400	Insurance agents, brokers, and service	13	13	0.4	60	56	14,933	17,571	994	1,117	0.3
6530	Real estate agents and managers	3	3	0.2	3	2	4,000	6,000	15	71	0.0
RIPLEY, IN											
60 –	**Finance, insurance, and real estate**	44	53	0.4	634	594	35,117	31,697	20,271	19,714	0.5

Source: County Business Patterns, 1994/95, CBP-94/95, U.S. Department of Commerce, Washington, D.C., November 1997. SIC categories for which data were suppressed or not available for both 1994 and 1995 are not displayed. The employment columns represent mid-March employment in the year. Pay per employee is calculated by dividing 1st Quarter payroll, annualized, by mid-March employment. The columns headed "% State" show the county's percentage of the state total for the SIC in 1995; for example, 1.4% for SIC 6000 means that the county had 1.4 percent of the state's total establishments (or payroll) in SIC 6000 in 1995. A dash (-) is used to indicate that data are not available or cannot be calculated; nec means not elsewhere classified.

Continued on next page.

SIC	Industry	No. Establishments			Employment		Pay / Employee		Annual Payroll ($ 000)		
		1994	1995	% State	1994	1995	1994	1995	1994	1995	% State
RIPLEY, IN - [continued]											
6000	Depository institutions	11	12	0.5	153	173	18,484	20,532	2,994	3,552	0.4
6500	Real estate	16	21	0.5	55	54	9,600	13,407	672	756	0.2
6530	Real estate agents and managers	6	9	0.5	29	37	11,034	14,486	474	552	0.2
RUSH, IN											
60 –	**Finance, insurance, and real estate**	34	35	0.3	175	174	18,903	19,954	3,199	3,213	0.1
6000	Depository institutions	11	11	0.4	111	113	19,928	20,673	2,153	2,144	0.2
6400	Insurance agents, brokers, and service	7	7	0.2	25	25	9,920	11,200	259	262	0.1
6500	Real estate	12	12	0.3	21	20	10,476	12,600	251	274	0.1
6530	Real estate agents and managers	6	7	0.4	10	11	10,800	11,636	121	144	0.1
ST. JOSEPH, IN											
60 –	**Finance, insurance, and real estate**	549	578	4.6	6,152	6,251	25,525	27,312	162,530	173,049	4.7
6000	Depository institutions	102	102	3.9	2,090	2,147	23,426	26,662	50,520	54,773	5.7
6020	Commercial banks	68	65	3.5	1,472	1,485	24,932	28,399	37,259	40,785	5.7
6030	Savings institutions	10	11	3.5	151	151	21,881	22,199	3,539	3,706	3.0
6060	Credit unions	24	26	5.9	467	511	19,178	22,935	9,722	10,282	10.8
6100	Nondepository institutions	47	49	5.9	960	945	34,375	34,971	34,786	32,249	7.8
6140	Personal credit institutions	21	24	6.1	710	697	37,228	38,422	28,072	25,327	12.4
6200	Security and commodity brokers	29	28	4.5	190	207	55,032	49,179	8,773	9,250	3.9
6210	Security brokers and dealers	20	20	5.1	183	190	56,087	51,642	8,486	8,854	4.8
6280	Security and commodity services	9	8	3.7	7	17	27,429	21,647	287	396	0.8
6300	Insurance carriers	52	58	6.4	1,400	1,342	21,900	24,516	30,439	32,308	3.3
6310	Life insurance	18	18	6.6	590	511	16,780	16,838	9,449	9,175	2.2
6330	Fire, marine, and casualty insurance	28	33	6.9	622	591	23,215	27,492	14,405	15,667	3.7
6400	Insurance agents, brokers, and service	156	161	5.3	593	624	23,892	24,115	16,012	16,747	3.8
6500	Real estate	148	165	3.9	860	897	17,698	17,298	16,232	18,493	4.0
6510	Real estate operators and lessors	52	54	3.3	260	231	11,862	13,177	3,145	3,961	3.0
6530	Real estate agents and managers	71	79	4.1	374	414	20,770	19,237	8,105	8,899	3.6
6540	Title abstract offices	3	3	1.6	113	115	21,097	20,452	2,523	3,002	11.4
6550	Subdividers and developers	20	21	5.0	111	132	17,153	16,061	2,403	2,511	4.2
6552	Subdividers and developers, n.e.c.	10	9	4.6	25	28	24,160	22,429	909	816	2.2
6553	Cemetery subdividers and developers	9	9	4.5	79	92	15,544	15,130	1,412	1,528	7.4
SCOTT, IN											
60 –	**Finance, insurance, and real estate**	28	30	0.2	144	146	19,028	21,315	3,007	3,261	0.1
6000	Depository institutions	8	9	0.3	79	87	18,228	18,989	1,615	1,768	0.2
6400	Insurance agents, brokers, and service	9	8	0.3	23	23	15,130	15,652	376	458	0.1
6500	Real estate	8	8	0.2	23	21	11,826	16,000	345	383	0.1
6510	Real estate operators and lessors	4	4	0.2	15	11	8,800	11,636	146	137	0.1
SHELBY, IN											
60 –	**Finance, insurance, and real estate**	86	81	0.6	302	293	18,358	21,775	5,840	6,362	0.2
6000	Depository institutions	21	18	0.7	146	127	19,479	24,945	2,706	2,828	0.3
6020	Commercial banks	17	14	0.8	113	83	20,389	28,337	2,057	1,973	0.3
6100	Nondepository institutions	5	4	0.5	17	16	21,647	27,500	421	461	0.1
6400	Insurance agents, brokers, and service	21	17	0.6	49	58	19,102	21,724	1,040	1,316	0.3
6500	Real estate	34	36	0.8	84	84	13,524	14,381	1,338	1,374	0.3
6530	Real estate agents and managers	17	18	0.9	57	59	13,825	14,712	947	972	0.4
6540	Title abstract offices	3	4	2.2	5	5	15,200	20,800	86	97	0.4
SPENCER, IN											
60 –	**Finance, insurance, and real estate**	29	31	0.2	187	182	16,791	16,879	3,298	3,144	0.1
6400	Insurance agents, brokers, and service	8	8	0.3	31	31	14,710	19,097	567	605	0.1
6500	Real estate	9	11	0.3	59	59	10,712	11,525	664	698	0.1
6530	Real estate agents and managers	6	8	0.4	55	55	10,982	11,855	633	665	0.3

Source: County Business Patterns, 1994/95, CBP-94/95, U.S. Department of Commerce, Washington, D.C., November 1997. SIC categories for which data were suppressed or not available for both 1994 and 1995 are not displayed. The employment columns represent mid-March employment in the year. Pay per employee is calculated by dividing 1st Quarter payroll, annualized, by mid-March employment. The columns headed "% State" show the county's percentage of the state total for the SIC in 1995; for example, 1.4% for SIC 6000 means that the county had 1.4 percent of the state's total establishments (or payroll) in SIC 6000 in 1995. A dash·(-) is used to indicate that data are not available or cannot be calculated; nec means not elsewhere classified.

SIC	Industry	No. Establishments			Employment		Pay / Employee		Annual Payroll ($ 000)		
		1994	1995	% State	1994	1995	1994	1995	1994	1995	% State
STARKE, IN											
60 –	**Finance, insurance, and real estate**	22	21	0.2	120	83	17,167	19,663	2,177	1,685	0.0
6000	Depository institutions	9	8	0.3	82	51	18,537	22,824	1,602	1,187	0.1
6400	Insurance agents, brokers, and service	5	5	0.2	16	17	19,250	19,294	342	334	0.1
STEUBEN, IN											
60 –	**Finance, insurance, and real estate**	48	52	0.4	256	270	22,063	22,785	5,678	7,399	0.2
6000	Depository institutions	16	16	0.6	154	153	22,909	22,248	3,461	3,692	0.4
6020	Commercial banks	11	11	0.6	118	118	25,186	23,356	2,781	2,965	0.4
6200	Security and commodity brokers	3	3	0.5	20	10	32,400	41,600	618	845	0.4
6500	Real estate	16	21	0.5	51	74	18,431	22,973	1,005	2,245	0.5
6510	Real estate operators and lessors	6	6	0.4	23	37	18,261	13,189	478	596	0.5
SULLIVAN, IN											
60 –	**Finance, insurance, and real estate**	38	40	0.3	227	226	17,110	17,947	3,954	4,374	0.1
6000	Depository institutions	12	12	0.5	135	136	18,993	18,471	2,424	2,629	0.3
6020	Commercial banks	12	12	0.6	135	136	18,993	18,471	2,424	2,629	0.4
6400	Insurance agents, brokers, and service	10	11	0.4	36	37	11,556	13,081	477	496	0.1
6500	Real estate	12	13	0.3	23	23	10,261	10,609	266	266	0.1
6530	Real estate agents and managers	7	7	0.4	11	10	10,182	10,000	121	111	0.0
SWITZERLAND, IN											
60 –	**Finance, insurance, and real estate**	10	9	0.1	55	51	16,291	16,784	941	884	0.0
TIPPECANOE, IN											
60 –	**Finance, insurance, and real estate**	301	305	2.4	4,369	4,125	28,037	31,020	120,531	124,059	3.3
6000	Depository institutions	57	57	2.2	1,144	1,112	21,706	23,633	25,595	26,065	2.7
6020	Commercial banks	44	44	2.4	972	921	21,930	24,122	22,023	21,951	3.0
6200	Security and commodity brokers	18	19	3.1	72	75	52,722	62,187	3,530	3,822	1.6
6210	Security brokers and dealers	10	10	2.6	56	54	63,000	81,185	3,257	3,567	1.9
6300	Insurance carriers	18	19	2.1	2,196	2,059	34,692	38,963	71,757	74,827	7.6
6400	Insurance agents, brokers, and service	69	67	2.2	272	268	22,662	24,015	7,335	7,507	1.7
6500	Real estate	122	126	3.0	582	548	14,674	15,131	9,740	9,838	2.1
6510	Real estate operators and lessors	56	56	3.5	234	213	11,949	12,225	3,197	3,034	2.3
6530	Real estate agents and managers	48	52	2.7	207	238	14,802	14,387	3,430	4,199	1.7
6552	Subdividers and developers, n.e.c.	9	9	4.6	98	58	19,143	24,690	2,176	1,741	4.6
TIPTON, IN											
60 –	**Finance, insurance, and real estate**	24	26	0.2	157	156	15,006	18,718	2,552	3,022	0.1
6000	Depository institutions	4	5	0.2	101	101	14,020	18,812	1,529	2,072	0.2
6400	Insurance agents, brokers, and service	7	6	0.2	24	21	15,667	17,333	395	385	0.1
6500	Real estate	8	10	0.2	17	17	6,824	7,059	146	121	0.0
6530	Real estate agents and managers	3	5	0.3	4	6	7,000	8,000	59	56	0.0
UNION, IN											
60 –	**Finance, insurance, and real estate**	16	12	0.1	91	96	18,022	19,083	1,805	1,969	0.1
VANDERBURGH, IN											
60 –	**Finance, insurance, and real estate**	465	485	3.9	5,709	6,548	27,827	27,459	163,611	180,907	4.9
6000	Depository institutions	78	77	2.9	1,973	2,005	21,841	23,162	44,432	48,029	5.0
6020	Commercial banks	46	44	2.4	1,483	1,400	22,274	23,320	33,605	34,531	4.8
6030	Savings institutions	17	16	5.1	354	356	20,282	20,213	7,955	7,046	5.7
6100	Nondepository institutions	45	50	6.0	1,165	1,937	39,011	30,239	46,152	55,702	13.4
6210	Security brokers and dealers	15	15	3.8	201	202	67,602	62,812	11,848	12,725	6.9
6300	Insurance carriers	44	42	4.6	378	348	33,640	40,793	12,785	13,502	1.4
6310	Life insurance	14	14	5.1	187	167	29,476	37,198	5,308	6,115	1.5
6330	Fire, marine, and casualty insurance	24	22	4.6	92	85	36,391	42,776	3,606	3,456	0.8
6400	Insurance agents, brokers, and service	108	110	3.6	658	623	28,438	28,013	20,291	18,745	4.2
6500	Real estate	155	169	4.0	1,029	1,058	14,126	14,397	15,998	16,776	3.6

Source: County Business Patterns, 1994/95, CBP-94/95, U.S. Department of Commerce, Washington, D.C., November 1997. SIC categories for which data were suppressed or not available for both 1994 and 1995 are not displayed. The employment columns represent mid-March employment in the year. Pay per employee is calculated by dividing 1st Quarter payroll, annualized, by mid-March employment. The columns headed "% State" show the county's percentage of the state total for the SIC in 1995; for example, 1.4% for SIC 6000 means that the county had 1.4 percent of the state's total establishments (or payroll) in SIC 6000 in 1995. A dash (-) is used to indicate that data are not available or cannot be calculated; nec means not elsewhere classified.

Continued on next page.

SIC	Industry	No. Establishments			Employment		Pay / Employee		Annual Payroll ($ 000)		
		1994	1995	% State	1994	1995	1994	1995	1994	1995	% State
VANDERBURGH, IN - [continued]											
6510	Real estate operators and lessors	75	79	4.9	509	531	11,269	12,256	6,424	7,063	5.4
6530	Real estate agents and managers	61	68	3.6	406	409	16,808	16,763	7,432	7,632	3.1
6540	Title abstract offices	5	5	2.7	61	55	17,836	17,309	1,094	935	3.5
6550	Subdividers and developers	13	14	3.3	53	63	16,755	14,540	1,040	1,125	1.9
6552	Subdividers and developers, n.e.c.	6	6	3.0	7	10	21,714	17,200	256	351	0.9
6553	Cemetery subdividers and developers	7	7	3.5	46	51	16,000	14,431	784	765	3.7
6710	Holding offices	8	7	6.3	276	347	37,203	42,444	11,550	14,628	12.7
VERMILLION, IN											
60 –	**Finance, insurance, and real estate**	21	22	0.2	130	132	16,769	16,879	2,336	2,387	0.1
6000	Depository institutions	7	7	0.3	93	94	17,763	17,957	1,749	1,777	0.2
6020	Commercial banks	7	7	0.4	93	94	17,763	17,957	1,749	1,777	0.2
6500	Real es8U	6	7	0.2	12	16	9,667	7,500	125	174	0.0
VIGO, IN											
60 –	**Finance, insurance, and real estate**	212	207	1.6	1,833	1,706	23,127	25,754	40,882	40,877	1.1
6000	Depository institutions	42	42	1.6	967	910	19,735	21,358	19,583	19,725	2.1
6020	Commercial banks	31	32	1.7	858	809	20,047	21,523	17,617	17,737	2.5
6100	Nondepository institutions	12	12	1.4	67	70	25,493	36,229	1,789	2,367	0.6
6140	Personal credit institutions	12	12	3.0	67	70	25,493	36,229	1,789	2,367	1.2
6200	Security and commodity brokers	7	10	1.6	59	56	61,966	58,357	3,316	3,369	1.4
6300	Insurance carriers	16	14	1.5	99	75	23,111	24,960	2,341	1,870	0.2
6310	Life insurance	3	3	1.1	79	61	21,722	21,049	1,738	1,273	0.3
6400	Insurance agents, brokers, and service	49	48	1.6	217	209	41,972	49,397	5,831	6,201	1.4
6500	Real estate	76	73	1.7	381	365	14,688	16,241	7,071	6,773	1.5
6510	Real estate operators and lessors	35	34	2.1	163	140	14,994	16,429	2,825	2,575	2.0
6530	Real estate agents and managers	29	28	1.5	149	145	14,792	18,152	3,032	3,001	1.2
6540	Title abstract offices	4	4	2.2	40	47	15,700	12,766	774	746	2.8
6550	Subdividers and developers	7	5	1.2	29	31	11,034	11,742	410	419	0.7
WABASH, IN											
60 –	**Finance, insurance, and real estate**	99	117	0.9	436	448	18,532	18,786	8,084	8,351	0.2
6000	Depository institutions	24	24	0.9	245	240	20,359	21,817	4,700	4,956	0.5
6020	Commercial banks	16	16	0.9	165	155	22,133	24,284	3,277	3,412	0.5
6400	Insurance agents, brokers, and service	17	16	0.5	69	65	21,043	22,954	1,505	1,522	0.3
6500	Real estate	48	69	1.6	105	129	9,448	9,209	1,234	1,426	0.3
6510	Real estate operators and lessors	21	48	3.0	33	64	9,818	7,125	422	613	0.5
6530	Real estate agents and managers	19	14	0.7	49	45	8,735	11,200	534	579	0.2
6540	Title abstract offices	3	3	1.6	19	16	10,737	11,250	221	171	0.6
6550	Subdividers and developers	3	3	0.7	4	3	9,000	12,000	53	51	0.1
WARREN, IN											
60 –	**Finance, insurance, and real estate**	13	14	0.1	76	119	14,263	16,336	1,171	2,214	0.1
6500	Real estate	5	6	0.1	29	33	11,172	15,152	387	574	0.1
WARRICK, IN											
60 –	**Finance, insurance, and real estate**	72	77	0.6	351	376	20,752	18,574	7,634	7,941	0.2
6000	Depository institutions	22	21	0.8	211	226	21,934	19,929	4,768	4,896	0.5
6020	Commercial banks	11	10	0.5	119	121	20,739	21,058	2,699	2,837	0.4
6500	Real estate	23	30	0.7	57	76	14,807	13,895	1,097	1,399	0.3
6510	Real estate operators and lessors	6	8	0.5	10	14	29,600	23,714	379	301	0.2
6530	Real estate agents and managers	11	13	0.7	32	39	11,875	11,692	498	506	0.2
WASHINGTON, IN											
60 –	**Finance, insurance, and real estate**	34	35	0.3	167	164	18,228	18,927	3,299	3,234	0.1
6000	Depository institutions	9	9	0.3	87	81	19,080	20,593	1,546	1,680	0.2
6400	Insurance agents, brokers, and service	11	11	0.4	35	36	16,114	15,111	582	636	0.1
WAYNE, IN											
60 –	**Finance, insurance, and real estate**	151	157	1.2	1,158	1,149	19,623	21,946	24,620	24,267	0.7

Source: County Business Patterns, 1994/95, CBP-94/95, U.S. Department of Commerce, Washington, D.C., November 1997. SIC categories for which data were suppressed or not available for both 1994 and 1995 are not displayed. The employment columns represent mid-March employment in the year. Pay per employee is calculated by dividing 1st Quarter payroll, annualized, by mid-March employment. The columns headed "% State" show the county's percentage of the state total for the SIC in 1995; for example, 1.4% for SIC 6000 means that the county had 1.4 percent of the state's total establishments (or payroll) in SIC 6000 in 1995. A dash (-) is used to indicate that data are not available or cannot be calculated; nec means not elsewhere classified.

Continued on next page.

SIC	Industry	No. Establishments			Employment		Pay / Employee		Annual Payroll ($ 000)		
		1994	1995	% State	1994	1995	1994	1995	1994	1995	% State
WAYNE, IN - [continued]											
6000	Depository institutions	44	44	1.7	442	446	18,525	22,888	9,138	9,695	1.0
6020	Commercial banks	25	25	1.4	256	233	18,109	25,013	5,062	4,950	0.7
6030	Savings institutions	7	7	2.2	122	148	21,639	22,946	3,133	3,695	3.0
6060	Credit unions	12	12	2.7	64	65	14,250	15,138	943	1,050	1.1
6100	Nondepository institutions	10	10	1.2	33	49	20,606	22,041	858	998	0.2
6200	Security and commodity brokers	8	9	1.4	23	28	50,261	45,571	1,055	1,327	0.6
6300	Insurance carriers	11	10	1.1	285	261	22,414	24,307	6,722	5,575	0.6
6400	Insurance agents, brokers, and service	31	31	1.0	118	117	20,237	22,769	2,530	2,663	0.6
6500	Real estate	44	49	1.1	247	237	15,012	14,211	4,036	3,762	0.8
6510	Real estate operators and lessors	17	19	1.2	162	152	13,185	12,895	2,280	2,212	1.7
6530	Real estate agents and managers	15	18	0.9	34	36	26,000	20,778	955	812	0.3
6550	Subdividers and developers	9	9	2.1	27	21	15,259	13,714	423	332	0.6
6700	Holding and other investment offices	3	4	1.4	10	11	21,600	25,091	281	247	0.1
WELLS, IN											
60 –	**Finance, insurance, and real estate**	48	51	0.4	249	240	21,847	22,583	4,985	5,119	0.1
6000	Depository institutions	10	10	0.4	156	156	22,000	21,256	3,131	3,153	0.3
6020	Commercial banks	7	7	0.4	142	142	21,944	21,155	2,818	2,854	0.4
6400	Insurance agents, brokers, and service	10	10	0.3	28	32	19,857	24,875	613	739	0.2
6500	Real estate	23	26	0.6	56	43	19,786	23,070	909	910	0.2
6510	Real estate operators and lessors	8	12	0.7	20	20	19,800	19,400	276	323	0.2
6530	Real estate agents and managers	11	10	0.5	24	13	22,000	36,615	460	412	0.2
WHITE, IN											
60 –	**Finance, insurance, and real estate**	52	52	0.4	272	263	21,471	22,525	6,304	6,343	0.2
6000	Depository institutions	14	14	0.5	161	160	21,168	21,975	3,490	3,663	0.4
6400	Insurance agents, brokers, and service	18	19	0.6	61	49	16,000	20,653	1,108	1,119	0.3
6500	Real estate	12	12	0.3	22	25	24,182	26,080	811	817	0.2
WHITLEY, IN											
60 –	**Finance, insurance, and real estate**	47	49	0.4	279	304	20,975	20,645	5,615	6,538	0.2
6000	Depository institutions	12	14	0.5	161	178	22,112	20,382	3,090	3,479	0.4
6020	Commercial banks	7	9	0.5	137	152	23,562	21,395	2,729	3,084	0.4
6400	Insurance agents, brokers, and service	14	14	0.5	57	67	21,193	21,194	1,195	1,633	0.4
6500	Real estate	15	15	0.4	51	48	15,608	18,000	943	1,105	0.2
6530	Real estate agents and managers	8	9	0.5	32	35	19,375	20,686	747	941	0.4

Source: County Business Patterns, 1994/95, CBP-94/95, U.S. Department of Commerce, Washington, D.C., November 1997. SIC categories for which data were suppressed or not available for both 1994 and 1995 are *not* displayed. The employment columns represent mid-March employment in the year. Pay per employee is calculated by dividing 1st Quarter payroll, annualized, by mid-March employment. The columns headed "% State" show the county's percentage of the state total for the SIC in 1995; for example, 1.4% for SIC 6000 means that the county had 1.4 percent of the state's total establishments (or payroll) in SIC 6000 in 1995. A dash (-) is used to indicate that data are not available or cannot be calculated; *nec* means not elsewhere classified.

IOWA

SIC	Industry	No. Establishments			Employment		Pay / Employee		Annual Payroll ($ 000)		
		1994	1995	% State	1994	1995	1994	1995	1994	1995	% State
ADAMS, IA											
60 –	**Finance, insurance, and real estate**	12	11	0.2	51	54	17,255	14,444	935	868	0.0
6500	Real estate	4	3	0.1	4	3	5,000	5,333	18	16	0.0
ALLAMAKEE, IA											
60 –	**Finance, insurance, and real estate**	34	33	0.5	168	158	18,762	20,253	3,540	3,562	0.2
6000	Depository institutions	7	7	0.5	103	104	23,650	22,654	2,619	2,608	0.5
6020	Commercial banks	7	7	0.7	103	104	23,650	22,654	2,619	2,608	0.6
6400	Insurance agents, brokers, and service	10	11	0.5	20	22	10,000	14,909	227	334	0.2
APPANOOSE, IA											
60 –	**Finance, insurance, and real estate**	23	20	0.3	163	146	24,564	23,096	3,658	3,185	0.1
6400	Insurance agents, brokers, and service	7	7	0.3	23	26	13,565	12,000	314	310	0.2
AUDUBON, IA											
60 –	**Finance, insurance, and real estate**	19	19	0.3	82	79	18,488	19,392	1,487	1,515	0.1
6000Y6020	Depository institutions	5	5	0.3	55	54	21,455	22,519	1,172	1,160	0.2
	Commercial banks	5	5	0.5	55	54	21,455	22,519	1,172	1,160	0.2
6400	Insurance agents, brokers, and service	6	5	0.2	11	9	17,091	18,667	172	204	0.1
6510	Real estate operators and lessors	3	3	0.3	3	3	4,000	4,000	12	12	0.0
BENTON, IA											
60 –	**Finance, insurance, and real estate**	50	54	0.7	-	-	-	-	-	-	-
6000	Depository institutions	16	16	1.0	156	153	22,077	22,954	3,542	3,698	0.6
6400	Insurance agents, brokers, and service	20	20	0.9	45	44	15,644	19,818	764	846	0.4
6500	Real estate	9	13	0.6	25	33	12,480	10,545	354	424	0.3
6530	Real estate agents and managers	3	5	0.6	8	9	9,500	12,000	85	105	0.1
BLACK HAWK, IA											
60 –	**Finance, insurance, and real estate**	302	316	4.3	2,522	2,746	23,889	24,380	62,726	68,339	3.0
6000	Depository institutions	60	64	4.2	977	1,010	23,279	22,515	22,921	22,662	3.9
6020	Commercial banks	34	34	3.2	640	645	23,856	22,710	15,445	14,776	3.1
6100	Nondepository institutions	15	17	5.9	562	582	26,164	27,443	15,443	16,421	8.7
6200	Security and commodity brokers	20	21	4.5	135	153	34,756	31,216	4,099	5,167	4.4
6210	Security brokers and dealers	11	9	3.2	82	73	47,659	43,288	3,250	3,361	4.0
6300	Insurance carriers	16	18	3.6	204	274	25,255	28,657	4,796	7,517	0.8
6310	Life insurance	8	9	5.6	132	172	27,364	25,488	3,619	4,858	0.9
6330	Fire, marine, and casualty insurance	5	5	2.0	52	51	19,769	20,314	585	603	0.2
6400	Insurance agents, brokers, and service	80	82	3.9	272	326	24,441	26,896	7,577	9,209	4.5
6500	Real estate	101	103	4.8	336	352	15,155	15,932	5,864	5,908	3.6
6510	Real estate operators and lessors	48	46	5.1	141	136	12,284	15,294	1,965	1,929	3.3
6530	Real estate agents and managers	44	48	5.6	136	184	18,235	16,870	2,928	3,571	4.5
6700	Holding and other investment offices	10	11	4.6	36	49	33,778	25,143	2,026	1,455	1.0
BOONE, IA											
60 –	**Finance, insurance, and real estate**	53	46	0.6	246	215	18,504	20,670	4,441	4,513	0.2
6000	Depository institutions	11	10	0.7	150	133	21,680	24,722	3,196	3,267	0.6
6400	Insurance agents, brokers, and service	22	20	0.9	55	55	15,709	15,345	829	916	0.4
6500	Real estate	14	9	0.4	31	17	8,258	7,765	242	127	0.1
BREMER, IA											
60 –	**Finance, insurance, and real estate**	65	68	0.9	1,249	1,142	25,640	23,968	28,629	26,796	1.2

Source: County Business Patterns, 1994/95, CBP-94/95, U.S. Department of Commerce, Washington, D.C., November 1997. SIC categories for which data were suppressed or not available for both 1994 and 1995 are not displayed. The employment columns represent mid-March employment in the year. Pay per employee is calculated by dividing 1st Quarter payroll, annualized, by mid-March employment. The columns headed "% State" show the county's percentage of the state total for the SIC in 1995; for example, 1.4% for SIC 6000 means that the county had 1.4 percent of the state's total establishments (or payroll) in SIC 6000 in 1995. A dash (-) is used to indicate that data are not available or cannot be calculated; nec means not elsewhere classified.

Continued on next page.

SIC	Industry	No. Establishments			Employment		Pay / Employee		Annual Payroll ($ 000)		
		1994	1995	% State	1994	1995	1994	1995	1994	1995	% State
BREMER, IA - [continued]											
6000	Depository institutions	15	15	1.0	181	182	19,912	21,099	3,982	4,254	0.7
6400	Insurance agents, brokers, and service	24	28	1.3	56	62	18,786	18,903	1,086	1,187	0.6
6530	Real estate agents and managers	6	6	0.7	22	20	18,000	17,600	434	526	0.7
BUCHANAN, IA											
60 –	**Finance, insurance, and real estate**	53	53	0.7	254	242	15,606	24,512	4,133	5,413	0.2
6000	Depository institutions	15	15	1.0	148	143	16,027	29,035	2,415	3,728	0.6
6020	Commercial banks	10	10	0.9	132	126	16,485	30,984	2,206	3,470	0.7
6400	Insurance agents, brokers, and service	18	18	0.8	51	47	11,451	14,213	647	664	0.3
6500	Real estate	12	14	0.7	23	24	7,304	8,500	206	225	0.1
6510	Real estate operators and lessors	5	6	0.7	9	9	4,889	4,444	54	53	0.1
6530	Real estate agents and managers	4	5	0.6	8	8	3,000	6,500	40	54	0.1
BUENA VISTA, IA											
60 –	**Finance, insurance, and real estate**	71	69	0.9	384	366	21,823	23,716	9,025	9,397	0.4
6000	Depository institutions	18	18	1.2	233	225	21,871	25,511	6,090	6,522	1.1
6200	Security and commodity brokers	8	7	1.5	33	28	30,424	25,429	858	743	0.6
6210	Security brokers and dealers	4	4	1.4	22	21	37,818	31,238	740	662	0.8
6400	Insurance agents, brokers, and service	20	21	1.0	51	57	16,392	16,281	870	979	0.5
6500	Real estate	18	18	0.8	40	32	11,800	14,250	473	487	0.3
6510	Real estate operators and lessors	7	8	0.9	13	13	8,923	8,308	95	115	0.2
6530	Real estate agents and managers	7	7	0.8	17	10	13,176	21,200	240	236	0.3
BUTLER, IA											
60 –	**Finance, insurance, and real estate**	26	28	0.4	136	143	20,382	20,811	2,734	2,957	0.1
6000	Depository institutions	9	9	0.6	92	96	23,565	25,250	2,091	2,320	0.4
6020	Commercial banks	9	9	0.9	92	96	23,565	25,250	2,091	2,320	0.5
6400	Insurance agents, brokers, and service	13	15	0.7	30	31	14,267	11,742	432	426	0.2
CALHOUN, IA											
60 –	**Finance, insurance, and real estate**	32	30	0.4	155	159	18,503	18,918	2,966	3,040	0.1
6000	Depository institutions	8	8	0.5	98	98	21,388	22,122	2,180	2,225	0.4
6400	Insurance agents, brokers, and service	15	12	0.6	37	30	12,865	14,667	414	365	0.2
CARROLL, IA											
60 –	**Finance, insurance, and real estate**	65	69	0.9	689	723	19,628	19,635	13,644	14,526	0.6
6000	Depository institutions	15	15	1.0	194	198	25,773	25,394	5,334	5,351	0.9
6200	Security and commodity brokers	5	5	1.1	18	17	39,556	36,471	649	616	0.5
6400	Insurance agents, brokers, and service	23	23	1.1	59	66	16,203	16,606	1,149	1,220	0.6
6500	Real estate	12	15	0.7	24	25	11,167	11,040	316	308	0.2
CASS, IA											
60 –	**Finance, insurance, and real estate**	50	49	0.7	223	231	17,740	19,152	4,228	4,741	0.2
6000	Depository institutions	10	10	0.7	117	117	22,803	22,940	2,635	2,800	0.5
6200	Security and commodity brokers	5	5	1.1	5	10	23,200	30,800	203	391	0.3
6400	Insurance agents, brokers, and service	21	21	1.0	67	71	11,642	14,085	895	1,093	0.5
6500	Real estate	10	9	0.4	19	18	10,526	10,444	216	201	0.1
6510	Real estate operators and lessors	3	3	0.3	5	5	11,200	8,800	67	45	0.1
CEDAR, IA											
60 –	**Finance, insurance, and real estate**	35	34	0.5	195	200	21,149	22,240	4,510	4,762	0.2
6000	Depository institutions	10	9	0.6	133	136	20,962	21,647	3,013	3,269	0.6
CERRO GORDO, IA											
60 –	**Finance, insurance, and real estate**	149	141	1.9	1,091	1,194	22,988	23,916	25,802	28,738	1.3
6000	Depository institutions	34	31	2.0	313	318	23,246	27,950	7,242	7,817	1.4
6020	Commercial banks	19	17	1.6	246	246	25,138	27,496	6,105	6,104	1.3
6100	Nondepository institutions	5	4	1.4	27	18	14,667	36,222	676	514	0.3

Source: County Business Patterns, 1994/95, CBP-94/95, U.S. Department of Commerce, Washington, D.C., November 1997. SIC categories for which data were suppressed or not available for both 1994 and 1995 are not displayed. The employment columns represent mid-March employment in the year. Pay per employee is calculated by dividing 1st Quarter payroll, annualized, by mid-March employment. The columns headed "% State" show the county's percentage of the state total for the SIC in 1995; for example, 1.4% for SIC 6000 means that the county had 1.4 percent of the state's total establishments (or payroll) in SIC 6000 in 1995. A dash (-) is used to indicate that data are not available or cannot be calculated; nec means not elsewhere classified.

Continued on next page.

SIC	Industry	No. Establishments			Employment		Pay / Employee		Annual Payroll ($ 000)		
		1994	1995	% State	1994	1995	1994	1995	1994	1995	% State
CERRO GORDO, IA - [continued]											
6200	Security and commodity brokers	11	11	2.3	36	39	45,111	36,308	1,579	1,624	1.4
6210	Security brokers and dealers	5	6	2.1	30	35	49,333	37,714	1,394	1,453	1.7
6400	Insurance agents, brokers, and service	47	45	2.1	106	104	23,962	25,500	2,442	2,431	1.2
6500	Real estate	42	38	1.8	102	95	9,020	11,032	1,144	1,165	0.7
6510	Real estate operators and lessors	21	17	1.9	49	49	6,694	8,898	395	388	0.7
6530	Real estate agents and managers	14	13	1.5	39	33	9,744	11,758	520	496	0.6
6550	Subdividers and developers	4	4	1.9	5	4	10,400	17,000	58	89	0.7
CHEROKEE, IA											
60-	**Finance, insurance, and real estate**	37	38	0.5	182	170	19,099	21,600	3,551	3,665	0.2
6000	Depository institutions	13	13	0.8	116	116	21,966	23,690	2,609	2,676	0.5
6400	Insurance agents, brokers, and service	15	15	0.7	50	42	15,040	17,429	742	729	0.4
6500	Real estate	6	6	0.3	8	8	12,500	13,500	113	119	0.1
CHICKASAW, IA											
60-	**Finance, insurance, and real estate**	31	29	0.4	148	149	18,486	20,403	3,076	3,458	0.2
6000	Depository institutions	9	9	0.6	98	99	20,612	22,869	2,312	2,499	0.4
6400	Insurance agents, brokers, and service	9	9	0.4	33	33	15,152	16,485	529	710	0.3
6500	Real estate	9	7	0.3	10	8	8,800	10,500	96	101	0.1
6550	Subdividers and developers	3	3	1.4	3	3	12,000	12,000	38	51	0.4
CLARKE, IA											
60-	**Finance, insurance, and real estate**	19	19	0.3	97	94	21,320	21,447	1,984	1,949	0.1
6500	Real estate	6	6	0.3	9	8	13,778	14,000	132	111	0.1
6510	Real estate operators and lessors	3	3	0.3	4	3	11,000	13,333	51	42	0.1
6530	Real estate agents and managers	3	3	0.4	5	5	16,000	14,400	81	69	0.1
CLAY, IA											
60-	**Finance, insurance, and real estate**	56	53	0.7	336	299	20,619	23,197	6,438	6,883	0.3
6000	Depository institutions	11	10	0.7	209	181	23,445	26,564	4,605	4,748	0.8
6200	Security and commodity brokers	6	6	1.3	12	13	29,000	37,231	275	523	0.4
6400	Insurance agents, brokers, and service	17	17	0.8	40	42	15,800	16,190	605	661	0.3
6500	Real estate	17	16	0.8	33	41	11,030	12,683	463	539	0.3
CLAYTON, IA											
60-	**Finance, insurance, and real estate**	53	53	0.7	242	241	20,198	20,880	5,378	5,669	0.2
6000	Depository institutions	13	13	0.8	161	163	23,602	23,902	4,301	4,476	0.8
6400	Insurance agents, brokers, and service	21	21	1.0	42	40	13,714	12,000	546	506	0.2
6500	Real estate	14	15	0.7	22	22	12,182	13,091	295	314	0.2
CLINTON, IA											
60-	**Finance, insurance, and real estate**	126	120	1.6	795	782	19,240	19,693	15,806	15,670	0.7
6000	Depository institutions	25	25	1.6	396	361	19,424	20,266	7,728	7,440	1.3
6020	Commercial banks	13	13	1.2	303	277	20,924	21,603	6,309	5,986	1.3
6210	Security brokers and dealers	6	7	2.5	12	14	35,667	22,286	529	370	0.4
6300	Insurance carriers	5	5	1.0	164	174	24,341	24,138	4,005	4,222	0.5
6400	Insurance agents, brokers, and service	37	34	1.6	89	88	16,584	20,136	1,524	1,697	0.8
6500	Real estate	48	41	1.9	118	131	11,424	10,870	1,596	1,567	0.9
6510	Real estate operators and lessors	17	19	2.1	40	56	9,800	7,071	429	455	0.8
6530	Real estate agents and managers	19	14	1.6	46	48	12,435	14,250	714	716	0.9
6550	Subdividers and developers	7	4	1.9	16	8	10,500	5,000	149	63	0.5
6553	Cemetery subdividers and developers	7	4	2.9	16	8	10,500	5,000	149	63	1.0
CRAWFORD, IA											
60-	**Finance, insurance, and real estate**	44	45	0.6	201	195	20,935	21,497	4,161	4,174	0.2
6000	Depository institutions	14	14	0.9	124	118	24,419	25,797	2,884	2,895	0.5
6400	Insurance agents, brokers, and service	15	16	0.8	47	50	14,979	14,560	782	833	0.4

Source: County Business Patterns, 1994/95, CBP-94/95, U.S. Department of Commerce, Washington, D.C., November 1997. SIC categories for which data were suppressed or not available for both 1994 and 1995 are *not* displayed. The employment columns represent mid-March employment in the year. Pay per employee is calculated by dividing 1st Quarter payroll, annualized, by mid-March employment. The columns headed "% State" show the county's percentage of the state total for the SIC in 1995; for example, 1.4% for SIC 6000 means that the county had 1.4 percent of the state's total establishments (or payroll) in SIC 6000 in 1995. A dash (-) is used to indicate that data are not available or cannot be calculated; *nec* means not elsewhere classified.

Continued on next page.

SIC	Industry	No. Establishments			Employment		Pay / Employee		Annual Payroll ($ 000)		
		1994	1995	% State	1994	1995	1994	1995	1994	1995	% State
CRAWFORD, IA - [continued]											
6500	Real estate	12	11	0.5	16	13	7,000	7,385	151	111	0.1
6510	Real estate operators and lessors	6	5	0.6	10	7	7,200	7,429	82	64	0.1
6530	Real estate agents and managers	3	3	0.4	3	3	6,667	8,000	44	21	0.0
DALLAS, IA											
60 –	**Finance, insurance, and real estate**	55	60	0.8	342	348	24,947	25,414	8,073	8,184	0.4
6000	Depository institutions	16	16	1.0	180	177	23,422	22,350	3,817	3,468	0.6
6100	Nondepository institutions	3	3	1.0	31	31	45,935	54,452	1,138	1,250	0.7
6200	Security and commodity brokers	5	5	1.1	21	27	47,238	39,556	910	1,142	1.0
6400	Insurance agents, brokers, and service	19	21	1.0	75	73	18,507	18,137	1,479	1,430	0.7
6500	Real estate	12	15	0.7	35	40	14,629	20,200	729	894	0.5
6510	Real estate operators and lessors	5	7	0.8	10	19	16,800	25,474	329	489	0.8
DAVIS, IA											
60 –	**Finance, insurance, and real estate**	10	8	0.1	70	75	21,657	18,507	1,498	1,364	0.1
6000	Depository institutions	4	3	0.2	56	54	22,000	20,667	1,197	1,085	0.2
DECATUR, IA											
60 –	**Finance, insurance, and real estate**	12	11	0.2	55	53	13,236	16,075	800	849	0.0
6500	Real estate	4	3	0.1	7	4	2,857	3,000	19	12	0.0
DELAWARE, IA											
60 –	**Finance, insurance, and real estate**	29	26	0.4	149	143	19,436	20,727	3,223	3,275	0.1
6000	Depository institutions	6	6	0.4	94	88	18,681	21,091	2,073	2,115	0.4
6020	Commercial banks	6	6	0.6	94	88	18,681	21,091	2,073	2,115	0.4
6400	Insurance agents, brokers, and service	12	11	0.5	28	27	15,143	16,741	491	501	0.2
DES MOINES, IA											
60 –	**Finance, insurance, and real estate**	102	102	1.4	667	667	20,204	20,384	14,641	14,982	0.7
6000	Depository institutions	22	21	1.4	336	333	23,083	23,159	7,474	7,496	1.3
6020	Commercial banks	9	9	0.9	245	247	24,082	23,385	5,734	5,745	1.2
6330	Fire, marine, and casualty insurance	3	3	1.2	9	9	26,667	27,111	282	258	0.1
6400	Insurance agents, brokers, and service	28	29	1.4	77	76	19,429	20,474	1,566	1,589	0.8
6500	Real estate	34	34	1.6	132	170	11,091	12,635	1,708	2,445	1.5
6510	Real estate operators and lessors	17	17	1.9	65	58	10,462	9,034	775	575	1.0
6530	Real estate agents and managers	10	8	0.9	32	67	10,875	14,448	364	674	0.8
DICKINSON, IA											
60 –	**Finance, insurance, and real estate**	69	71	1.0	390	419	16,379	17,652	7,466	7,893	0.3
6000	Depository institutions	13	13	0.8	138	148	23,652	25,081	3,287	3,606	0.6
6400	Insurance agents, brokers, and service	16	17	0.8	35	44	16,914	15,727	574	587	0.3
6500	Real estate	33	34	1.6	195	214	10,646	12,299	3,096	3,277	2.0
6530	Real estate agents and managers	19	21	2.5	165	189	10,764	12,593	2,635	2,778	3.5
DUBUQUE, IA											
60 –	**Finance, insurance, and real estate**	221	234	3.2	1,772	1,838	21,235	24,992	39,825	44,539	1.9
6000	Depository institutions	51	51	3.3	938	982	21,497	23,914	21,073	23,020	4.0
6020	Commercial banks	26	26	2.5	647	705	24,043	25,679	15,536	17,222	3.7
6200	Security and commodity brokers	15	15	3.2	109	82	31,193	32,732	2,833	2,696	2.3
6300	Insurance carriers	15	17	3.4	172	196	20,744	22,796	3,814	4,461	0.5
6330	Fire, marine, and casualty insurance	6	6	2.4	16	18	20,000	20,889	366	368	0.1
6400	Insurance agents, brokers, and service	58	63	3.0	206	211	24,350	24,929	5,727	5,868	2.9
6500	Real estate	71	75	3.5	300	312	12,280	13,179	4,434	4,523	2.7
6510	Real estate operators and lessors	37	36	4.0	218	228	10,697	11,754	2,703	2,806	4.8
6530	Real estate agents and managers	25	29	3.4	54	54	14,074	14,519	853	925	1.2
6553	Cemetery subdividers and developers	4	4	2.9	13	14	17,538	18,000	292	298	4.8

Source: County Business Patterns, 1994/95, CBP-94/95, U.S. Department of Commerce, Washington, D.C., November 1997. SIC categories for which data were suppressed or not available for both 1994 and 1995 are not displayed. The employment columns represent mid-March employment in the year. Pay per employee is calculated by dividing 1st Quarter payroll, annualized, by mid-March employment. The columns headed "% State" show the county's percentage of the state total for the SIC in 1995; for example, 1.4% for SIC 6000 means that the county had 1.4 percent of the state's total establishments (or payroll) in SIC 6000 in 1995. A dash (-) is used to indicate that data are not available or cannot be calculated; nec means not elsewhere classified.

SIC	Industry	No. Establishments			Employment		Pay / Employee		Annual Payroll ($ 000)		
		1994	1995	% State	1994	1995	1994	1995	1994	1995	% State
EMMET, IA											
60 –	**Finance, insurance, and real estate**	25	28	0.4	119	123	17,681	18,016	2,075	2,362	0.1
6000	Depository institutions	7	7	0.5	75	72	19,467	19,667	1,507	1,554	0.3
6020	Commercial banks	4	4	0.4	57	55	20,491	20,655	1,226	1,274	0.3
FAYETTE, IA											
60 –	**Finance, insurance, and real estate**	48	50	0.7	268	234	18,060	18,120	5,135	4,552	0.2
6000	Depository institutions	13	12	0.8	184	144	18,870	20,056	3,712	3,095	0.5
6400	Insurance agents, brokers, and service	21	23	1.1	47	54	13,191	11,704	685	709	0.3
6500	Real estate	9	10	0.5	21	21	9,524	10,286	214	232	0.1
FLOYD, IA											
60 –	**Finance, insurance, and real estate**	38	46	0.6	230	235	20,661	21,123	4,667	4,945	0.2
6000	Depository institutions	8	8	0.5	139	140	22,187	23,257	2,904	3,109	0.5
6400	Insurance agents, brokers, and service	17	19	0.9	48	49	16,333	16,163	823	810	0.4
6500	Real estate	9	14	0.7	28	29	6,857	8,138	241	266	0.2
FRANKLIN, IA											
60 –	**Finance, insurance, and real estate**	39	40	0.5	134	136	19,254	21,941	2,704	3,150	0.1
6000	Depository institutions	9	9	0.6	83	81	18,506	24,346	1,567	1,866	0.3
6500	Real estate	13	13	0.6	15	15	8,267	8,800	184	191	0.1
6530	Real estate agents and managers	4	4	0.5	4	3	5,000	6,667	18	20	0.0
FREMONT, IA											
60 –	**Finance, insurance, and real estate**	15	15	0.2	79	86	23,089	23,814	1,848	2,007	0.1
6000	Depository institutions	7	7	0.5	62	67	24,065	25,433	1,518	1,663	0.3
6400	Insurance agents, brokers, and service	8	8	0.4	17	19	19,529	18,105	330	344	0.2
GREENE, IA											
60 –	**Finance, insurance, and real estate**	28	30	0.4	169	163	23,882	26,675	4,163	4,375	0.2
6000	Depository institutions	8	7	0.5	107	99	24,636	25,374	2,693	2,403	0.4
6400	Insurance agents, brokers, and service	13	14	0.7	44	42	19,364	33,905	836	1,406	0.7
6500	Real estate	4	5	0.2	8	13	12,500	12,923	151	232	0.1
GRUNDY, IA											
60 –	**Finance, insurance, and real estate**	29	28	0.4	129	148	27,163	26,270	3,260	3,789	0.2
6000	Depository institutions	9	8	0.5	102	109	31,137	31,229	2,862	3,228	0.6
6400	Insurance agents, brokers, and service	10	9	0.4	9	12	8,000	9,000	90	117	0.1
GUTHRIE, IA											
60 –	**Finance, insurance, and real estate**	34	32	0.4	174	230	15,839	14,278	3,135	3,713	0.2
6000	Depository institutions	7	6	0.4	73	71	20,877	21,972	1,589	1,705	0.3
6400	Insurance agents, brokers, and service	13	14	0.7	48	56	15,167	15,714	752	895	0.4
6500	Real estate	9	8	0.4	43	93	7,442	6,710	605	899	0.5
6530	Real estate agents and managers	6	5	0.6	37	88	7,459	6,636	558	846	1.1
HAMILTON, IA											
60 –	**Finance, insurance, and real estate**	33	32	0.4	210	199	23,257	25,166	5,386	5,039	0.2
6000	Depository institutions	11	11	0.7	156	148	21,000	22,865	3,721	3,399	0.6
6020	Commercial banks	8	8	0.8	119	112	22,017	21,214	3,020	2,558	0.5
6400	Insurance agents, brokers, and service	9	9	0.4	28	30	16,857	18,800	682	699	0.3
6510	Real estate operators and lessors	4	4	0.4	3	4	8,000	7,000	31	31	0.1
HANCOCK, IA											
60 –	**Finance, insurance, and real estate**	36	36	0.5	147	153	17,442	19,451	2,661	2,913	0.1
6000	Depository institutions	10	10	0.7	88	87	18,636	19,034	1,776	1,865	0.3
6020	Commercial banks	10	10	0.9	88	87	18,636	19,034	1,776	1,865	0.4

Source: County Business Patterns, 1994/95, CBP-94/95, U.S. Department of Commerce, Washington, D.C., November 1997. SIC categories for which data were suppressed or not available for both 1994 and 1995 are *not* displayed. The employment columns represent mid-March employment in the year. Pay per employee is calculated by dividing 1st Quarter payroll, annualized, by mid-March employment. The columns headed "% State" show the county's percentage of the state total for the SIC in 1995; for example, 1.4% for SIC 6000 means that the county had 1.4 percent of the state's total establishments (or payroll) in SIC 6000 in 1995. A dash (-) is used to indicate that data are not available or cannot be calculated; *nec* means not elsewhere classified.

Continued on next page.

SIC	Industry	No. Establishments			Employment		Pay / Employee		Annual Payroll ($ 000)		
		1994	1995	% State	1994	1995	1994	1995	1994	1995	% State
HANCOCK, IA - [continued]											
6400	Insurance agents, brokers, and service	13	12	0.6	22	27	12,364	12,444	299	331	0.2
6500	Real estate	10	10	0.5	31	33	17,032	25,818	452	498	0.3
6510	Real estate operators and lessors	5	5	0.6	17	18	8,706	8,889	158	155	0.3
HARDIN, IA											
60 –	**Finance, insurance, and real estate**	63	59	0.8	297	293	20,458	22,389	6,318	6,665	0.3
6000	Depository institutions	17	16	1.0	185	185	22,962	23,741	4,321	4,437	0.8
6300	Insurance carriers	3	3	0.6	5	7	28,800	28,000	141	208	0.0
6400	Insurance agents, brokers, and service	19	16	0.8	54	51	15,630	19,137	992	1,034	0.5
6500	Real estate	18	18	0.8	35	32	8,114	11,375	367	383	0.2
6530	Real estate agents and managers	9	9	1.1	16	17	8,500	12,706	201	224	0.3
6550	Subdividers and developers	5	5	2.4	7	5	4,571	5,600	35	35	0.3
6553	Cemetery subdividers and developers	5	5	3.6	7	5	4,571	5,600	35	35	0.6
HARRISON, IA											
60 –	**Finance, insurance, and real estate**	37	35	0.5	161	161	16,224	16,348	2,623	2,728	0.1
6000	Depository institutions	8	7	0.5	86	81	20,140	21,481	1,697	1,786	0.3
6510	Real estate operators and lessors	6	6	0.7	27	26	8,148	5,692	206	183	0.3
HENRY, IA											
60 –	**Finance, insurance, and real estate**	43	42	0.6	251	274	18,183	16,540	4,559	4,887	0.2
6000	Depository institutions	9	9	0.6	114	116	21,053	20,552	2,374	2,381	0.4
6400	Insurance agents, brokers, and service	12	11	0.5	32	32	14,375	14,625	458	494	0.2
6500	Real estate	17	17	0.8	82	103	9,707	8,466	1,005	991	0.6
6510	Real estate operators and lessors	7	6	0.7	34	39	8,706	8,513	337	406	0.7
HOWARD, IA											
60 –	**Finance, insurance, and real estate**	26	28	0.4	124	121	19,935	22,281	2,519	2,910	0.1
6000	Depository institutions	3	3	0.2	77	74	23,013	24,054	1,759	1,901	0.3
6020	Commercial banks	3	3	0.3	77	74	23,013	24,054	1,759	1,901	0.4
6400	Insurance agents, brokers, and service	9	10	0.5	17	18	18,118	23,778	308	454	0.2
6500	Real estate	9	10	0.5	14	13	14,571	19,385	237	292	0.2
6510	Real estate operators and lessors	4	4	0.4	3	3	4,000	4,000	21	18	0.0
HUMBOLDT, IA											
60 –	**Finance, insurance, and real estate**	20	23	0.3	132	124	21,545	24,613	2,690	2,886	0.1
6000	Depository institutions	5	5	0.3	74	69	24,703	26,957	1,599	1,677	0.3
IDA, IA											
60 –	**Finance, insurance, and real estate**	23	24	0.3	122	126	24,361	26,063	2,759	3,058	0.1
6000	Depository institutions	6	7	0.5	89	95	28,809	29,853	2,278	2,602	0.5
6020	Commercial banks	6	7	0.7	89	95	28,809	29,853	2,278	2,602	0.6
6400	Insurance agents, brokers, and service	6	6	0.3	10	10	8,400	8,000	92	79	0.0
6500	Real estate	8	7	0.3	18	12	13,333	16,000	279	217	0.1
6510	Real estate operators and lessors	4	4	0.4	9	5	7,556	5,600	77	30	0.1
IOWA, IA											
60 –	**Finance, insurance, and real estate**	32	32	0.4	147	166	26,286	27,494	3,935	4,231	0.2
6000	Depository institutions	7	7	0.5	74	84	26,378	28,190	1,912	1,987	0.3
6400	Insurance agents, brokers, and service	14	14	0.7	30	36	13,867	13,667	525	557	0.3
6500	Real estate	6	6	0.3	19	20	17,263	12,200	310	238	0.1
JACKSON, IA											
60 –	**Finance, insurance, and real estate**	43	44	0.6	248	253	19,242	20,822	4,691	5,025	0.2
6000	Depository institutions	11	11	0.7	171	167	21,450	23,641	3,468	3,730	0.6
6020	Commercial banks	11	11	1.0	171	167	21,450	23,641	3,468	3,730	0.8

Source: County Business Patterns, 1994/95, CBP-94/95, U.S. Department of Commerce, Washington, D.C., November 1997. SIC categories for which data were suppressed or not available for both 1994 and 1995 are *not* displayed. The employment columns represent mid-March employment in the year. Pay per employee is calculated by dividing 1st Quarter payroll, annualized, by mid-March employment. The columns headed "% State" show the county's percentage of the state total for the SIC in 1995; for example, 1.4% for SIC 6000 means that the county had 1.4 percent of the state's total establishments (or payroll) in SIC 6000 in 1995. A dash (-) is used to indicate that data are not available or cannot be calculated; *nec* means not elsewhere classified.

Continued on next page.

SIC	Industry	No. Establishments			Employment		Pay / Employee		Annual Payroll ($ 000)		
		1994	1995	% State	1994	1995	1994	1995	1994	1995	% State
JACKSON, IA - [continued]											
6400	Insurance agents, brokers, and service	16	17	0.8	42	48	12,095	14,083	621	669	0.3
6500	Real estate	11	10	0.5	18	18	9,333	13,333	187	205	0.1
6510	Real estate operators and lessors	4	4	0.4	4	3	4,000	2,667	12	12	0.0
JASPER, IA											
60 –	**Finance, insurance, and real estate**	77	75	1.0	406	392	24,512	23,980	8,854	8,729	0.4
6000	Depository institutions	19	20	1.3	235	233	20,664	21,803	4,793	5,139	0.9
6400	Insurance agents, brokers, and service	26	23	1.1	52	52	37,154	36,077	1,262	1,186	0.6
6500	Real estate	22	22	1.0	49	45	11,265	11,022	605	543	0.3
6530	Real estate agents and managers	9	9	1.1	14	11	18,571	21,455	303	284	0.4
JEFFERSON, IA											
60 –	**Finance, insurance, and real estate**	67	69	0.9	305	325	31,318	26,671	8,834	8,460	0.4
6000	Depository institutions	8	7	0.5	133	120	27,098	30,133	3,106	3,147	0.5
6020	Commercial banks	4	4	0.4	120	111	28,333	31,423	2,938	3,036	0.6
6200	Security and commodity brokers	26	25	5.3	86	108	50,279	32,407	4,003	3,674	3.2
6210	Security brokers and dealers	11	10	3.5	29	37	87,172	44,541	2,029	1,622	1.9
6220	Commodity contracts brokers, dealers	8	9	19.1	30	40	37,333	27,300	1,128	1,244	10.3
6280	Security and commodity services	7	6	4.5	27	31	25,037	24,516	846	808	4.1
6400	Insurance agents, brokers, and service	11	13	0.6	20	26	19,200	17,385	455	550	0.3
6500	Real estate	16	17	0.8	42	50	10,381	8,960	440	437	0.3
6530	Real estate agents and managers	10	7	0.8	12	19	8,667	5,263	98	103	0.1
JOHNSON, IA											
60 –	**Finance, insurance, and real estate**	204	205	2.8	1,758	1,700	25,600	25,807	41,244	42,091	1.8
6000	Depository institutions	28	33	2.2	850	795	24,221	25,374	18,717	19,115	3.3
6020	Commercial banks	21	23	2.2	734	661	24,921	26,566	16,306	16,317	3.5
6100	Nondepository institutions	6	5	1.7	20	13	27,800	35,077	505	545	0.3
6200	Security and commodity brokers	13	11	2.3	43	48	75,535	49,583	2,296	1,808	1.6
6210	Security brokers and dealers	7	7	2.5	39	41	82,256	56,195	2,227	1,730	2.1
6280	Security and commodity services	6	4	3.0	4	7	10,000	10,857	69	78	0.4
6300	Insurance carriers	9	9	1.8	32	29	25,250	26,483	716	748	0.1
6400	Insurance agents, brokers, and service	48	50	2.4	344	338	26,581	25,799	8,221	8,256	4.0
6500	Real estate	95	92	4.3	338	337	22,746	23,703	7,468	7,596	4.6
6510	Real estate operators and lessors	40	39	4.4	134	133	32,149	32,962	3,339	3,440	5.9
6530	Real estate agents and managers	38	39	4.6	142	160	15,465	15,875	2,717	3,064	3.8
6540	Title abstract offices	3	3	2.3	31	17	28,516	42,588	725	587	4.3
6550	Subdividers and developers	14	10	4.7	31	26	9,677	12,923	687	503	4.0
6552	Subdividers and developers, n.e.c.	10	6	10.0	18	15	10,222	10,400	492	306	5.8
6700	Holding and other investment offices	5	5	2.1	131	140	22,687	24,200	3,321	4,023	2.8
JONES, IA											
60 –	**Finance, insurance, and real estate**	34	35	0.5	197	203	16,569	17,202	3,623	3,751	0.2
6000	Depository institutions	12	11	0.7	148	153	18,000	18,719	2,952	3,031	0.5
6500	Real estate	6	9	0.4	11	14	13,818	9,714	174	224	0.1
KEOKUK, IA											
60 –	**Finance, insurance, and real estate**	24	23	0.3	127	121	20,346	22,545	2,928	2,981	0.1
6000	Depository institutions	9	8	0.5	83	74	24,627	28,000	2,190	2,147	0.4
6400	Insurance agents, brokers, and service	9	9	0.4	28	31	13,143	14,968	549	635	0.3
KOSSUTH, IA											
60 –	**Finance, insurance, and real estate**	52	50	0.7	402	396	24,050	27,222	9,392	10,020	0.4
6000	Depository institutions	16	17	1.1	174	159	19,379	21,585	3,727	3,802	0.7
6510	Real estate operators and lessors	7	6	0.7	6	6	5,333	4,667	36	35	0.1
6530	Real estate agents and managers	7	7	0.8	20	24	4,600	4,000	93	107	0.1
LEE, IA											
60 –	**Finance, insurance, and real estate**	81	87	1.2	482	480	21,286	21,425	10,485	10,330	0.5

Source: County Business Patterns, 1994/95, CBP-94/95, U.S. Department of Commerce, Washington, D.C., November 1997. SIC categories for which data were suppressed or not available for both 1994 and 1995 are *not* displayed. The employment columns represent mid-March employment in the year. Pay per employee is calculated by dividing 1st Quarter payroll, annualized, by mid-March employment. The columns headed "% State" show the county's percentage of the state total for the SIC in 1995; for example, 1.4% for SIC 6000 means that the county had 1.4 percent of the state's total establishments (or payroll) in SIC 6000 in 1995. A dash (-) is used to indicate that data are not available or cannot be calculated; *nec* means not elsewhere classified.

Continued on next page.

SIC	Industry	No. Establishments			Employment		Pay / Employee		Annual Payroll ($ 000)		
		1994	1995	% State	1994	1995	1994	1995	1994	1995	% State
LEE, IA - [continued]											
6000	Depository institutions	24	24	1.6	294	288	23,687	24,083	7,071	6,684	1.2
6020	Commercial banks	11	11	1.0	241	235	20,846	24,102	5,142	5,610	1.2
6200	Security and commodity brokers	6	7	1.5	17	15	37,176	32,533	591	621	0.5
6400	Insurance agents, brokers, and service	25	29	1.4	75	79	18,187	17,671	1,580	1,703	0.8
6500	Real estate	23	23	1.1	84	85	13,429	14,306	1,009	1,037	0.6
6510	Real estate operators and lessors	10	11	1.2	54	50	8,667	8,880	466	452	0.8
6530	Real estate agents and managers	10	9	1.1	12	20	33,000	24,800	278	314	0.4
6540	Title abstract offices	3	3	2.3	18	15	14,667	18,400	265	271	2.0
LINN, IA											
60 –	**Finance, insurance, and real estate**	505	531	7.3	6,222	6,622	29,695	31,163	181,955	202,009	8.8
6000	Depository institutions	80	82	5.4	1,600	1,626	21,448	21,451	34,020	34,791	6.0
6020	Commercial banks	42	42	4.0	1,184	1,197	22,503	22,195	26,000	25,771	5.5
6060	Credit unions	24	23	8.7	252	253	17,333	17,597	4,432	4,647	12.7
6100	Nondepository institutions	22	20	6.9	293	354	41,133	45,209	10,717	10,750	5.7
6160	Mortgage bankers and brokers	9	9	11.0	66	77	55,697	48,935	2,607	2,649	3.8
6200	Security and commodity brokers	38	38	8.1	347	318	51,043	46,642	13,748	13,994	12.0
6210	Security brokers and dealers	22	24	8.5	277	256	55,206	50,813	11,607	12,089	14.4
6300	Insurance carriers	58	58	11.6	1,369	1,482	29,861	32,478	41,988	46,249	5.2
6310	Life insurance	21	22	13.7	736	857	28,533	32,243	22,019	25,781	5.0
6330	Fire, marine, and casualty insurance	23	21	8.4	549	526	31,220	31,772	17,166	17,061	6.6
6400	Insurance agents, brokers, and service	123	135	6.4	409	473	24,186	25,235	11,222	13,091	6.4
6500	Real estate	153	168	7.9	799	872	20,796	18,991	18,204	17,169	10.4
6510	Real estate operators and lessors	66	71	7.9	306	331	22,340	21,281	7,101	6,572	11.2
6530	Real estate agents and managers	71	75	8.8	402	412	17,602	15,388	7,490	6,997	8.8
6552	Subdividers and developers, n.e.c.	6	8	13.3	5	32	74,400	18,750	628	659	12.4
6700	Holding and other investment offices	31	30	12.7	1,405	1,497	37,933	42,763	52,056	65,965	45.7
6710	Holding offices	16	15	11.4	1,373	1,455	37,827	42,898	50,433	63,714	51.3
LOUISA, IA											
60 –	**Finance, insurance, and real estate**	23	24	0.3	94	96	20,638	22,167	1,930	2,099	0.1
6000	Depository institutions	6	6	0.4	67	69	24,657	26,145	1,608	1,747	0.3
6400	Insurance agents, brokers, and service	9	10	0.5	17	17	10,588	12,941	203	230	0.1
6510	Real estate operators and lessors	3	3	0.3	3	3	8,000	8,000	24	24	0.0
LUCAS, IA											
60 –	**Finance, insurance, and real estate**	15	15	0.2	102	107	28,118	27,551	2,524	2,685	0.1
6400	Insurance agents, brokers, and service	7	5	0.2	26	25	43,077	42,240	828	812	0.4
LYON, IA											
60 –	**Finance, insurance, and real estate**	27	29	0.4	125	114	19,776	21,684	2,485	2,477	0.1
6000	Depository institutions	11	10	0.7	93	86	21,763	23,721	2,034	1,936	0.3
6400	Insurance agents, brokers, and service	11	13	0.6	24	14	15,333	19,714	343	375	0.2
MADISON, IA											
60 –	**Finance, insurance, and real estate**	26	28	0.4	139	145	18,446	18,869	2,876	3,043	0.1
6000	Depository institutions	7	6	0.4	93	91	19,828	21,055	2,020	2,139	0.4
6400	Insurance agents, brokers, and service	8	9	0.4	18	20	14,444	17,200	343	396	0.2
6500	Real estate	6	8	0.4	14	21	12,000	14,476	259	290	0.2
MAHASKA, IA											
60 –	**Finance, insurance, and real estate**	53	44	0.6	288	255	19,750	21,129	6,059	5,460	0.2
6000	Depository institutions	9	8	0.5	173	162	21,202	21,753	3,687	3,526	0.6
6400	Insurance agents, brokers, and service	20	16	0.8	39	31	12,000	15,226	675	505	0.2
6500	Real estate	17	15	0.7	55	43	8,873	8,744	590	435	0.3
6530	Real estate agents and managers	5	4	0.5	11	8	13,818	9,000	203	78	0.1
MARION, IA											
60 –	**Finance, insurance, and real estate**	53	53	0.7	289	308	21,481	24,117	7,150	8,103	0.4

Source: County Business Patterns, 1994/95, CBP-94/95, U.S. Department of Commerce, Washington, D.C., November 1997. SIC categories for which data were suppressed or not available for both 1994 and 1995 are not displayed. The employment columns represent mid-March employment in the year. Pay per employee is calculated by dividing 1st Quarter payroll, annualized, by mid-March employment. The columns headed "% State" show the county's percentage of the state total for the SIC in 1995; for example, 1.4% for SIC 6000 means that the county had 1.4 percent of the state's total establishments (or payroll) in SIC 6000 in 1995. A dash (-) is used to indicate that data are not available or cannot be calculated; nec means not elsewhere classified.

Continued on next page.

SIC	Industry	No. Establishments			Employment		Pay / Employee		Annual Payroll ($ 000)		
		1994	1995	% State	1994	1995	1994	1995	1994	1995	% State
MARION, IA - [continued]											
6000	Depository institutions	12	12	0.8	177	183	22,260	26,645	4,214	4,787	0.8
6400	Insurance agents, brokers, and service	20	18	0.8	62	63	15,742	17,841	1,163	1,329	0.6
6500	Real estate	13	14	0.7	34	39	12,118	10,564	622	609	0.4
6510	Real estate operators and lessors	6	4	0.4	11	12	6,545	9,000	209	202	0.3
MARSHALL, IA											
60 –	**Finance, insurance, and real estate**	98	92	1.3	555	565	20,404	21,048	11,853	12,182	0.5
6000	Depository institutions	24	24	1.6	324	362	21,716	21,912	7,234	7,954	1.4
6020	Commercial banks	14	14	1.3	238	266	22,840	22,346	5,534	5,907	1.3
6100	Nondepository institutions	4	4	1.4	17	17	24,471	31,294	471	516	0.3
6300	Insurance carriers	7	7	1.4	15	15	22,667	24,533	390	381	0.0
6400	Insurance agents, brokers, and service	23	19	0.9	65	56	19,815	23,571	1,404	1,372	0.7
6500	Real estate	32	30	1.4	116	94	11,621	10,426	1,603	1,122	0.7
6510	Real estate operators and lessors	12	10	1.1	43	35	8,651	9,143	406	314	0.5
6530	Real estate agents and managers	13	12	1.4	39	26	15,179	10,308	754	303	0.4
6540	Title abstract offices	3	3	2.3	14	14	10,571	10,000	157	143	1.0
6550	Subdividers and developers	3	3	1.4	19	18	12,211	13,778	282	289	2.3
MILLS, IA											
60 –	**Finance, insurance, and real estate**	18	18	0.2	106	107	21,132	22,654	2,316	2,435	0.1
6000	Depository institutions	5	5	0.3	79	80	24,152	25,650	1,932	2,048	0.4
6530	Real estate agents and managers	4	4	0.5	8	9	9,500	13,778	95	105	0.1
MITCHELL, IA											
60 –	**Finance, insurance, and real estate**	29	27	0.4	149	143	19,114	21,259	3,108	3,645	0.2
6000	Depository institutions	6	6	0.4	104	101	19,769	22,257	2,349	2,454	0.4
6400	Insurance agents, brokers, and service	13	13	0.6	25	26	13,760	13,538	386	817	0.4
6500	Real estate	5	4	0.2	5	5	8,800	9,600	56	50	0.0
MONONA, IA											
60 –	**Finance, insurance, and real estate**	20	20	0.3	128	127	20,094	19,339	2,434	2,618	0.1
6000	Depository institutions	9	9	0.6	88	87	23,636	22,483	1,904	2,057	0.4
6400	Insurance agents, brokers, and service	4	4	0.2	23	22	14,957	14,909	347	337	0.2
MONROE, IA											
60 –	**Finance, insurance, and real estate**	10	9	0.1	57	64	18,035	22,875	1,093	1,545	0.1
MONTGOMERY, IA											
60 –	**Finance, insurance, and real estate**	28	26	0.4	148	149	24,541	27,195	3,271	3,465	0.2
6000	Depository institutions	7	7	0.5	84	86	26,429	29,442	1,864	1,927	0.3
6200	Security and commodity brokers	4	4	0.9	7	9	21,143	17,778	181	165	0.1
6210	Security brokers and dealers	4	4	1.4	7	9	21,143	17,778	181	165	0.2
6400	Insurance agents, brokers, and service	9	7	0.3	21	23	17,143	22,435	476	622	0.3
6500	Real estate	5	5	0.2	19	14	6,947	10,000	163	156	0.1
MUSCATINE, IA											
60 –	**Finance, insurance, and real estate**	81	86	1.2	492	504	23,098	24,960	11,755	12,275	0.5
6000	Depository institutions	21	21	1.4	280	275	21,200	22,778	6,251	6,479	1.1
6020	Commercial banks	14	14	1.3	244	241	22,033	23,502	5,581	5,823	1.2
6300	Insurance carriers	3	3	0.6	22	21	22,727	24,571	478	488	0.1
6330	Fire, marine, and casualty insurance	3	3	1.2	22	21	22,727	24,571	478	488	0.2
6400	Insurance agents, brokers, and service	25	25	1.2	80	81	28,800	29,333	2,018	2,021	1.0
6500	Real estate	24	24	1.1	73	86	18,192	23,953	1,694	1,949	1.2
6700	Holding and other investment offices	4	6	2.5	30	26	33,867	38,769	994	982	0.7
O'BRIEN, IA											
60 –	**Finance, insurance, and real estate**	41	40	0.5	256	278	22,094	22,115	5,949	6,298	0.3
6000	Depository institutions	13	13	0.8	127	141	25,102	25,135	3,428	3,580	0.6

Source: County Business Patterns, 1994/95, CBP-94/95, U.S. Department of Commerce, Washington, D.C., November 1997. SIC categories for which data were suppressed or not available for both 1994 and 1995 are not displayed. The employment columns represent mid-March employment in the year. Pay per employee is calculated by dividing 1st Quarter payroll, annualized, by mid-March employment. The columns headed "% State" show the county's percentage of the state total for the SIC in 1995; for example, 1.4% for SIC 6000 means that the county had 1.4 percent of the state's total establishments (or payroll) in SIC 6000 in 1995. A dash (-) is used to indicate that data are not available or cannot be calculated; nec means not elsewhere classified.

Continued on next page.

SIC	Industry	No. Establishments			Employment		Pay / Employee		Annual Payroll ($ 000)		
		1994	1995	% State	1994	1995	1994	1995	1994	1995	% State
O'BRIEN, IA - [continued]											
6400	Insurance agents, brokers, and service	17	15	0.7	77	86	17,455	17,488	1,555	1,685	0.8
6500	Real estate	7	8	0.4	33	31	9,697	11,355	330	360	0.2
6530	Real estate agents and managers	4	4	0.5	21	19	8,762	7,368	183	162	0.2
OSCEOLA, IA											
60 –	**Finance, insurance, and real estate**	22	23	0.3	107	107	17,533	17,645	1,883	1,871	0.1
6000	Depository institutions	7	6	0.4	69	66	20,928	20,424	1,432	1,370	0.2
6400	Insurance agents, brokers, and service	8	9	0.4	21	23	11,238	13,217	250	274	0.1
PAGE, IA											
60 –	**Finance, insurance, and real estate**	35	36	0.5	207	199	25,913	26,533	5,212	5,028	0.2
6000	Depository institutions	12	10	0.7	142	143	25,972	25,566	3,893	3,818	0.7
6400	Insurance agents, brokers, and service	9	11	0.5	29	22	17,793	19,091	523	451	0.2
6500	Real estate	8	9	0.4	22	19	7,273	8,000	180	149	0.1
6510	Real estate operators and lessors	4	5	0.6	11	9	2,545	4,000	38	38	0.1
PALO ALTO, IA											
60 –	**Finance, insurance, and real estate**	31	33	0.5	135	132	23,644	25,818	3,187	3,191	0.1
6000	Depository institutions	9	8	0.5	91	85	25,802	28,424	2,403	2,353	0.4
6020	Commercial banks	9	8	0.8	91	85	25,802	28,424	2,403	2,353	0.5
6400	Insurance agents, brokers, and service	10	11	0.5	20	22	16,400	20,545	320	351	0.2
6500	Real estate	9	10	0.5	12	12	11,667	13,333	158	156	0.1
PLYMOUTH, IA											
60 –	**Finance, insurance, and real estate**	50	52	0.7	347	336	21,476	22,381	8,460	8,781	0.4
6000	Depository institutions	14	13	0.8	171	162	24,070	26,370	4,910	5,163	0.9
6400	Insurance agents, brokers, and service	16	18	0.8	41	43	12,195	14,233	537	623	0.3
6530	Real estate agents and managers	7	6	0.7	13	16	8,615	8,500	138	148	0.2
6553	Cemetery subdividers and developers	3	3	2.2	3	4	2,667	2,000	11	10	0.2
POCAHONTAS, IA											
60 –	**Finance, insurance, and real estate**	23	23	0.3	134	130	20,478	20,862	2,704	2,720	0.1
6000	Depository institutions	6	6	0.4	98	92	23,184	23,696	2,195	2,194	0.4
6400	Insurance agents, brokers, and service	10	10	0.5	20	21	15,600	16,571	330	341	0.2
6500	Real estate	4	4	0.2	7	9	9,714	9,333	78	83	0.1
POLK, IA											
60 –	**Finance, insurance, and real estate**	1,234	1,277	17.5	35,996	37,258	33,287	35,693	1,146,313	1,226,488	53.5
6000	Depository institutions	173	190	12.4	5,010	5,046	24,744	26,161	120,830	129,362	22.4
6020	Commercial banks	86	95	9.0	3,709	3,852	24,690	25,578	88,905	96,379	20.5
6030	Savings institutions	40	46	22.7	804	699	24,592	29,190	19,440	19,907	32.6
6100	Nondepository institutions	107	118	40.7	3,582	4,181	43,210	39,465	128,371	142,223	75.6
6150	Business credit institutions	28	29	67.4	1,387	1,363	38,803	37,576	48,579	49,789	87.4
6160	Mortgage bankers and brokers	37	43	52.4	1,396	1,618	37,862	36,049	43,163	50,015	71.6
6200	Security and commodity brokers	98	98	20.9	841	866	59,990	62,383	47,534	51,231	43.9
6210	Security brokers and dealers	53	53	18.7	529	532	66,949	55,752	31,604	30,865	36.9
6280	Security and commodity services	37	38	28.8	232	264	48,914	80,515	11,419	14,396	72.6
6300	Insurance carriers	166	169	33.9	20,300	20,443	34,774	38,853	674,921	716,779	80.6
6310	Life insurance	69	65	40.4	12,162	12,103	37,136	41,764	415,961	435,951	84.5
6330	Fire, marine, and casualty insurance	71	73	29.3	5,353	5,470	32,322	36,759	179,210	194,526	75.6
6400	Insurance agents, brokers, and service	283	281	13.2	2,718	2,732	29,664	31,313	87,104	84,897	41.2
6500	Real estate	350	360	16.9	2,866	2,902	18,081	20,096	56,384	60,573	36.5
6510	Real estate operators and lessors	172	175	19.6	1,035	1,064	16,873	18,508	19,445	20,704	35.3
6530	Real estate agents and managers	150	151	17.7	1,540	1,537	18,621	20,942	31,153	33,183	41.6
6540	Title abstract offices	3	3	2.3	119	102	22,521	27,922	2,675	2,817	20.6
6550	Subdividers and developers	22	26	12.3	166	185	17,783	17,708	3,038	3,331	26.8
6552	Subdividers and developers, n.e.c.	13	16	26.7	117	107	20,752	20,673	2,292	2,362	44.5
6553	Cemetery subdividers and developers	7	7	5.1	49	70	10,694	9,771	665	729	11.7

Source: County Business Patterns, 1994/95, CBP-94/95, U.S. Department of Commerce, Washington, D.C., November 1997. SIC categories for which data were suppressed or not available for both 1994 and 1995 are *not* displayed. The employment columns represent mid-March employment in the year. Pay per employee is calculated by dividing 1st Quarter payroll, annualized, by mid-March employment. The columns headed "% State" show the county's percentage of the state total for the SIC in 1995; for example, 1.4% for SIC 6000 means that the county had 1.4 percent of the state's total establishments (or payroll) in SIC 6000 in 1995. A dash (-) is used to indicate that data are not available or cannot be calculated; *nec* means not elsewhere classified.

Continued on next page.

SIC	Industry	No. Establishments			Employment		Pay / Employee		Annual Payroll ($ 000)		
		1994	1995	% State	1994	1995	1994	1995	1994	1995	% State
POLK, IA - [continued]											
6710	Holding offices	25	28	21.2	286	519	56,154	52,355	16,338	28,106	22.6
6790	Miscellaneous investing	14	15	26.8	166	184	46,145	40,587	7,825	7,143	58.0
6799	Investors, n.e.c.	7	9	25.0	65	81	45,108	42,519	3,016	3,283	47.3
POTTAWATTAMIE, IA											
60 –	**Finance, insurance, and real estate**	137	133	1.8	1,267	1,229	21,490	25,605	27,278	30,053	1.3
6000	Depository institutions	35	34	2.2	468	476	20,752	21,697	9,528	9,783	1.7
6020	Commercial banks	24	25	2.4	415	443	21,484	21,571	8,643	8,964	1.9
6300	Insurance carriers	8	4	0.8	112	12	24,036	31,000	2,697	404	0.0
6400	Insurance agents, brokers, and service	32	29	1.4	358	95	24,592	16,211	8,969	1,668	0.8
6500	Real estate	41	45	2.1	196	208	13,531	14,577	3,023	3,445	2.1
6510	Real estate operators and lessors	14	15	1.7	58	55	11,517	11,127	620	815	1.4
6530	Real estate agents and managers	19	20	2.3	102	115	13,490	15,965	1,731	1,865	2.3
6790	Miscellaneous investing	4	4	7.1	10	4	9,600	13,000	81	79	0.6
POWESHIEK, IA											
60 –	**Finance, insurance, and real estate**	47	48	0.7	887	855	24,374	27,415	28,364	23,476	1.0
6000	Depository institutions	11	11	0.7	136	139	27,059	28,058	4,392	4,132	0.7
6530	Real estate agents and managers	7	6	0.7	8	7	4,500	5,714	42	45	0.1
RINGGOLD, IA											
60 –	**Finance, insurance, and real estate**	10	10	0.1	-	-	-	-	-	-	-
6400	Insurance agents, brokers, and service	5	5	0.2	10	10	10,400	10,000	111	117	0.1
SAC, IA											
60 –	**Finance, insurance, and real estate**	34	31	0.4	166	145	17,108	19,062	2,865	2,758	0.1
6000	Depository institutions	12	11	0.7	105	93	19,429	22,409	2,196	2,117	0.4
6510	Real estate operators and lessors	6	4	0.4	14	9	2,000	1,778	25	14	0.0
SCOTT, IA											
60 –	**Finance, insurance, and real estate**	388	406	5.6	3,462	3,629	26,155	25,990	90,212	93,569	4.1
6000	Depository institutions	59	62	4.0	1,183	1,168	23,202	24,264	26,721	27,546	4.8
6020	Commercial banks	32	33	3.1	778	787	24,895	25,479	17,883	18,346	3.9
6030	Savings institutions	10	12	5.9	212	200	24,377	25,540	5,775	5,981	9.8
6060	Credit unions	17	17	6.4	193	181	15,088	17,569	3,063	3,219	8.8
6100	Nondepository institutions	24	27	9.3	161	179	34,360	28,872	4,709	4,858	2.6
6140	Personal credit institutions	12	13	9.9	83	91	25,880	26,637	2,330	2,441	-
6200	Security and commodity brokers	23	27	5.7	227	252	67,912	59,000	13,207	13,255	11.4
6210	Security brokers and dealers	19	22	7.7	209	228	69,608	60,754	12,304	12,101	14.5
6300	Insurance carriers	35	34	6.8	494	517	25,352	27,304	12,237	14,091	1.6
6310	Life insurance	13	13	8.1	259	268	17,205	17,269	4,110	4,472	0.9
6330	Fire, marine, and casualty insurance	15	14	5.6	165	172	33,358	38,860	5,906	6,323	2.5
6400	Insurance agents, brokers, and service	106	112	5.3	419	421	26,568	29,216	12,050	12,815	6.2
6500	Real estate	127	127	6.0	925	1,037	16,947	15,499	17,060	17,674	10.7
6510	Real estate operators and lessors	58	58	6.5	518	639	8,641	7,543	5,691	5,818	9.9
6530	Real estate agents and managers	53	54	6.3	337	339	28,795	29,994	9,673	10,395	13.0
6550	Subdividers and developers	12	10	4.7	59	48	21,966	18,000	1,462	1,249	10.0
6552	Subdividers and developers, n.e.c.	7	5	8.3	24	14	24,000	14,000	678	459	8.6
6553	Cemetery subdividers and developers	4	4	2.9	35	34	20,571	19,647	772	730	11.7
6700	Holding and other investment offices	14	17	7.2	53	55	53,208	62,764	4,228	3,330	2.3
6710	Holding offices	9	10	7.6	48	45	54,583	63,111	3,715	2,694	2.2
6790	Miscellaneous investing	5	4	7.1	5	8	40,000	73,000	513	588	4.8
SHELBY, IA											
60 –	**Finance, insurance, and real estate**	34	34	0.5	181	183	20,464	21,639	3,735	3,972	0.2
6000	Depository institutions	11	11	0.7	117	120	20,547	21,833	2,440	2,701	0.5
6400	Insurance agents, brokers, and service	12	12	0.6	27	29	15,111	15,586	472	462	0.2
SIOUX, IA											
60 –	**Finance, insurance, and real estate**	78	77	1.1	432	462	18,333	18,632	8,127	8,851	0.4

Source: County Business Patterns, 1994/95, CBP-94/95, U.S. Department of Commerce, Washington, D.C., November 1997. SIC categories for which data were suppressed or not available for both 1994 and 1995 are not displayed. The employment columns represent mid-March employment in the year. Pay per employee is calculated by dividing 1st Quarter payroll, annualized, by mid-March employment. The columns headed "% State" show the county's percentage of the state total for the SIC in 1995; for example, 1.4% for SIC 6000 means that the county had 1.4 percent of the state's total establishments (or payroll) in SIC 6000 in 1995. A dash (-) is used to indicate that data are not available or cannot be calculated; nec means not elsewhere classified.

Continued on next page.

SIC	Industry	No. Establishments			Employment		Pay / Employee		Annual Payroll ($ 000)		
		1994	1995	% State	1994	1995	1994	1995	1994	1995	% State
SIOUX, IA - [continued]											
6000	Depository institutions	19	18	1.2	274	300	20,832	20,600	5,760	6,332	1.1
6200	Security and commodity brokers	8	6	1.3	14	12	15,429	19,667	213	222	0.2
6400	Insurance agents, brokers, and service	29	30	1.4	76	85	13,947	14,682	1,114	1,250	0.6
6500	Real estate	17	18	0.8	29	29	9,241	10,897	328	348	0.2
6530	Real estate agents and managers	10	9	1.1	11	14	11,273	10,286	151	157	0.2
6550	Subdividers and developers	3	3	1.4	3	3	2,667	2,667	12	11	0.1
6553	Cemetery subdividers and developers	3	3	2.2	3	3	2,667	2,667	12	11	0.2
STORY, IA											
60 –	**Finance, insurance, and real estate**	153	158	2.2	1,064	1,153	21,718	22,716	23,698	26,156	1.1
6000	Depository institutions	34	35	2.3	478	498	20,527	22,667	9,975	11,092	1.9
6020	Commercial banks	25	25	2.4	339	349	21,133	23,037	7,374	8,140	1.7
6300	Insurance carriers	11	8	1.6	153	160	28,758	32,475	4,516	4,700	0.5
6310	Life insurance	4	3	1.9	103	107	28,233	33,047	2,834	3,038	0.6
6400	Insurance agents, brokers, and service	39	42	2.0	116	115	19,207	19,826	2,374	2,347	1.1
6500	Real estate	58	58	2.7	290	347	15,766	14,963	4,791	5,384	3.2
6510	Real estate operators and lessors	22	24	2.7	109	133	14,422	13,263	1,736	1,876	3.2
6530	Real estate agents and managers	30	26	3.1	148	180	14,216	14,933	2,213	2,761	3.5
TAMA, IA											
60 –	**Finance, insurance, and real estate**	36	35	0.5	236	262	21,576	21,389	5,214	5,579	0.2
6000	Depository institutions	13	13	0.8	98	108	28,531	27,259	2,536	2,812	0.5
6400	Insurance agents, brokers, and service	11	12	0.6	27	27	13,037	13,481	429	442	0.2
TAYLOR, IA											
60 –	**Finance, insurance, and real estate**	17	19	0.3	65	66	20,308	19,455	1,226	1,242	0.1
6000	Depository institutions	5	5	0.3	43	42	25,953	25,429	1,023	973	0.2
6400	Insurance agents, brokers, and service	7	8	0.4	13	15	9,846	9,600	129	147	0.1
6500	Real estate	5	6	0.3	9	9	8,444	8,000	74	122	0.1
UNION, IA											
60 –	**Finance, insurance, and real estate**	31	29	0.4	156	151	21,487	20,265	3,334	3,234	0.1
6000	Depository institutions	6	5	0.3	102	104	24,314	21,923	2,534	2,523	0.4
6400	Insurance agents, brokers, and service	6	5	0.2	18	17	13,556	12,471	253	226	0.1
6530	Real estate agents and managers	9	9	1.1	11	8	8,727	10,000	98	92	0.1
VAN BUREN, IA											
60 –	**Finance, insurance, and real estate**	20	21	0.3	72	81	18,944	20,198	1,456	1,644	0.1
6000	Depository institutions	8	8	0.5	51	55	21,882	23,273	1,162	1,276	0.2
6020	Commercial banks	8	8	0.8	51	55	21,882	23,273	1,162	1,276	0.3
WAPELLO, IA											
60 –	**Finance, insurance, and real estate**	82	77	1.1	412	416	20,777	20,990	8,914	9,029	0.4
6000	Depository institutions	19	19	1.2	238	255	21,143	21,114	5,179	5,606	1.0
6020	Commercial banks	9	9	0.9	176	169	22,500	22,982	4,017	3,997	0.8
6100	Nondepository institutions	5	5	1.7	18	17	33,333	37,176	477	495	0.3
6310	Life insurance	4	3	1.9	22	17	23,455	25,882	510	368	0.1
6400	Insurance agents, brokers, and service	17	15	0.7	47	48	17,532	19,000	1,007	1,077	0.5
6500	Real estate	26	25	1.2	58	56	8,552	9,000	598	556	0.3
WARREN, IA											
60 –	**Finance, insurance, and real estate**	57	54	0.7	263	267	18,798	20,000	5,479	5,606	0.2
6000	Depository institutions	13	14	0.9	161	166	18,509	20,193	3,168	3,327	0.6
6400	Insurance agents, brokers, and service	18	15	0.7	51	49	18,196	16,980	1,172	1,188	0.6

Source: County Business Patterns, 1994/95, CBP-94/95, U.S. Department of Commerce, Washington, D.C., November 1997. SIC categories for which data were suppressed or not available for both 1994 and 1995 are *not* displayed. The employment columns represent mid-March employment in the year. Pay per employee is calculated by dividing 1st Quarter payroll, annualized, by mid-March employment. The columns headed "% State" show the county's percentage of the state total for the SIC in 1995; for example, 1.4% for SIC 6000 means that the county had 1.4 percent of the state's total establishments (or payroll) in SIC 6000 in 1995. A dash (-) is used to indicate that data are not available or cannot be calculated; *nec* means not elsewhere classified.

Continued on next page.

SIC	Industry	No. Establishments			Employment		Pay / Employee		Annual Payroll ($ 000)		
		1994	1995	% State	1994	1995	1994	1995	1994	1995	% State
WARREN, IA - [continued]											
6500	Real estate	22	21	1.0	43	44	16,093	16,273	778	702	0.4
6510	Real estate operators and lessors	8	8	0.9	11	11	12,364	12,364	175	154	0.3
6530	Real estate agents and managers	9	7	0.8	19	17	15,579	18,824	363	266	0.3
WASHINGTON, IA											
60 –	**Finance, insurance, and real estate**	52	50	0.7	217	225	23,207	23,129	4,910	5,185	0.2
6000	Depository institutions	12	12	0.8	131	136	27,206	27,294	3,384	3,541	0.6
6200	Security and commodity brokers	6	4	0.9	8	8	30,000	30,000	230	297	0.3
6400	Insurance agents, brokers, and service	17	18	0.8	36	37	15,222	16,757	624	677	0.3
6500	Real estate	13	12	0.6	27	29	7,852	9,103	264	273	0.2
6510	Real estate operators and lessors	6	6	0.7	8	11	4,000	2,909	55	58	0.1
6530	Real estate agents and managers	4	3	0.4	3	3	8,000	29,333	36	64	0.1
6540	Title abstract offices	3	3	2.3	16	15	9,750	9,600	173	151	1.1
WAYNE, IA											
60 –	**Finance, insurance, and real estate**	15	17	0.2	62	77	17,935	19,896	1,136	1,341	0.1
WEBSTER, IA											
60 –	**Finance, insurance, and real estate**	120	124	1.7	594	596	22,519	25,074	12,750	13,949	0.6
6000	Depository institutions	22	22	1.4	323	335	22,328	23,773	6,657	6,836	1.2
6020	Commercial banks	15	16	1.5	222	217	23,495	25,548	4,737	4,587	1.0
6200	Security and commodity brokers	11	13	2.8	26	27	62,154	77,926	1,560	2,324	2.0
6400	Insurance agents, brokers, and service	39	40	1.9	97	90	18,598	22,844	1,845	1,863	0.9
6500	Real estate	36	36	1.7	96	90	11,917	11,822	1,129	1,176	0.7
6510	Real estate operators and lessors	14	15	1.7	45	41	8,622	11,220	417	525	0.9
6530	Real estate agents and managers	18	17	2.0	31	33	13,935	14,303	438	504	0.6
WINNEBAGO, IA											
60 –	**Finance, insurance, and real estate**	39	36	0.5	182	179	20,462	21,453	3,832	3,942	0.2
6000	Depository institutions	9	9	0.6	123	121	22,862	22,545	2,902	2,894	0.5
6400	Insurance agents, brokers, and service	12	11	0.5	26	25	13,385	16,000	389	437	0.2
6500	Real estate	9	7	0.3	14	13	12,571	14,769	177	177	0.1
6510	Real estate operators and lessors	4	3	0.3	3	1	2,667	4,000	11	6	0.0
6700	Holding and other investment offices	5	5	2.1	6	10	18,667	30,400	139	224	0.2
WINNESHIEK, IA											
60 –	**Finance, insurance, and real estate**	43	40	0.5	229	301	22,690	27,123	4,998	6,257	0.3
6000	Depository institutions	7	8	0.5	146	226	25,808	29,363	3,665	4,721	0.8
6400	Insurance agents, brokers, and service	15	14	0.7	27	35	13,926	18,400	423	691	0.3
6500	Real estate	14	12	0.6	26	14	6,154	7,429	163	149	0.1
6550	Subdividers and developers	4	4	1.9	2	2	12,000	14,000	54	52	0.4
6553	Cemetery subdividers and developers	4	4	2.9	2	2	12,000	14,000	54	52	0.8
WOODBURY, IA											
60 –	**Finance, insurance, and real estate**	238	245	3.4	2,148	2,036	25,097	25,065	51,141	52,895	2.3
6000	Depository institutions	43	44	2.9	810	772	23,348	25,927	19,072	19,952	3.5
6020	Commercial banks	27	28	2.7	597	584	25,213	26,411	14,924	15,575	3.3
6100	Nondepository institutions	12	14	4.8	50	62	34,800	34,968	1,599	1,978	1.1
6200	Security and commodity brokers	15	15	3.2	106	93	64,906	50,796	5,731	5,533	4.7
6210	Security brokers and dealers	12	12	4.2	100	89	67,680	52,135	5,607	5,398	6.5
6280	Security and commodity services	3	3	2.3	6	4	18,667	21,000	124	135	0.7
6300	Insurance carriers	22	21	4.2	554	427	28,614	29,780	13,665	13,080	1.5
6310	Life insurance	12	12	7.5	287	158	30,913	36,253	6,670	5,827	1.1
6400	Insurance agents, brokers, and service	65	64	3.0	173	177	26,012	27,051	4,520	5,100	2.5
6500	Real estate	75	82	3.9	448	494	12,786	12,559	6,195	6,905	4.2
6510	Real estate operators and lessors	40	44	4.9	238	245	11,983	12,669	2,826	2,928	5.0

Source: County Business Patterns, 1994/95, CBP-94/95, U.S. Department of Commerce, Washington, D.C., November 1997. SIC categories for which data were suppressed or not available for both 1994 and 1995 are not displayed. The employment columns represent mid-March employment in the year. Pay per employee is calculated by dividing 1st Quarter payroll, annualized, by mid-March employment. The columns headed "% State" show the county's percentage of the state total for the SIC in 1995; for example, 1.4% for SIC 6000 means that the county had 1.4 percent of the state's total establishments (or payroll) in SIC 6000 in 1995. A dash (-) is used to indicate that data are not available or cannot be calculated; nec means not elsewhere classified.

Continued on next page.

SIC	Industry	No. Establishments			Employment		Pay / Employee		Annual Payroll ($ 000)		
		1994	1995	% State	1994	1995	1994	1995	1994	1995	% State
WOODBURY, IA - [continued]											
6530	Real estate agents and managers	27	30	3.5	147	182	11,810	11,846	2,103	2,785	3.5
6540	Title abstract offices	3	3	2.3	28	23	22,571	22,783	768	710	5.2
6700	Holding and other investment offices	6	5	2.1	7	11	42,286	37,818	359	347	0.2
WORTH, IA											
60 –	**Finance, insurance, and real estate**	20	21	0.3	85	68	19,576	22,412	1,520	1,486	0.1
6000	Depository institutions	7	7	0.5	52	33	25,692	22,909	1,180	653	0.1
WRIGHT, IA											
60 –	**Finance, insurance, and real estate**	43	41	0.6	218	226	20,642	21,133	4,377	4,397	0.2
6000	Depository institutions	11	10	0.7	113	118	28,460	28,712	2,969	2,970	0.5
6400	Insurance agents, brokers, and service	16	16	0.8	71	76	13,239	13,842	1,016	1,093	0.5
6510	Real estate operators and lessors	9	8	0.9	17	18	7,765	8,222	149	147	0.3

Source: County Business Patterns, 1994/95, CBP-94/95, U.S. Department of Commerce, Washington, D.C., November 1997. SIC categories for which data were suppressed or not available for both 1994 and 1995 are *not* displayed. The employment columns represent mid-March employment in the year. Pay per employee is calculated by dividing 1st Quarter payroll, annualized, by mid-March employment. The columns headed "% State" show the county's percentage of the state total for the SIC in 1995; for example, 1.4% for SIC 6000 means that the county had 1.4 percent of the state's total establishments (or payroll) in SIC 6000 in 1995. A dash (-) is used to indicate that data are not available or cannot be calculated; *nec* means not elsewhere classified.

KANSAS

SIC	Industry	No. Establishments			Employment		Pay / Employee		Annual Payroll ($ 000)		
		1994	1995	% State	1994	1995	1994	1995	1994	1995	% State
ALLEN, KS											
60 –	**Finance, insurance, and real estate**	34	32	0.5	176	169	19,091	22,178	3,285	3,598	0.2
6000	Depository institutions	10	8	0.6	115	106	23,304	27,811	2,569	2,744	0.6
6500	Real estate	7	6	0.3	16	15	7,000	7,200	116	108	0.1
ANDERSON, KS											
60 –	**Finance, insurance, and real estate**	16	17	0.2	103	100	15,379	15,080	1,747	1,659	0.1
6000	Depository institutions	7	6	0.5	79	73	17,063	16,493	1,497	1,361	0.3
6020	Commercial banks	7	6	0.6	79	73	17,063	16,493	1,497	1,361	0.4
6400	Insurance agents, brokers, and service	5	5	0.3	20	21	10,800	11,048	227	246	0.1
ATCHISON, KS											
60 –	**Finance, insurance, and real estate**	40	39	0.6	188	179	20,021	19,866	3,601	3,505	0.2
6000	Depository institutions	9	8	0.6	110	112	20,327	21,786	2,314	2,473	0.5
6020	Commercial banks	6	5	0.5	103	105	20,738	22,362	2,222	2,375	0.6
6400	Insurance agents, brokers, and service	12	12	0.6	25	25	14,720	15,680	394	417	0.2
6500	Real estate	12	12	0.6	33	32	10,182	9,375	311	342	0.2
6510	Real estate operators and lessors	5	6	0.8	11	11	8,000	8,000	81	103	0.2
6530	Real estate agents and managers	3	3	0.3	13	14	9,846	9,143	123	133	0.1
6700	Holding and other investment offices	3	3	1.2	4	4	20,000	24,000	78	75	0.1
BARBER, KS											
60 –	**Finance, insurance, and real estate**	19	19	0.3	92	89	18,522	19,011	1,844	1,925	0.1
6000	Depository institutions	9	9	0.7	71	66	20,620	21,758	1,579	1,653	0.3
6020	Commercial banks	9	9	1.0	71	66	20,620	21,758	1,579	1,653	0.4
6400	Insurance agents, brokers, and service	5	5	0.3	11	14	16,727	14,000	199	205	0.1
6500	Real estate	5	5	0.2	10	9	5,600	6,667	66	67	0.0
BARTON, KS											
60 –	**Finance, insurance, and real estate**	82	76	1.1	404	431	26,554	25,244	9,965	10,268	0.6
6000	Depository institutions	19	19	1.5	240	251	22,867	22,550	5,627	5,769	1.2
6300	Insurance carriers	5	5	1.1	23	26	24,870	23,077	577	602	0.1
6400	Insurance agents, brokers, and service	35	32	1.7	87	98	18,391	18,408	1,962	2,115	1.0
6530	Real estate agents and managers	8	7	0.7	18	15	8,444	11,467	308	269	0.2
BOURBON, KS											
60 –	**Finance, insurance, and real estate**	41	38	0.6	582	561	25,601	27,779	13,301	16,846	1.0
6000	Depository institutions	7	7	0.5	108	110	22,815	24,000	2,271	2,615	0.5
6300	Insurance carriers	5	4	0.9	376	342	28,702	32,058	9,102	11,953	2.6
6400	Insurance agents, brokers, and service	11	10	0.5	41	77	14,732	16,312	1,002	1,351	0.6
6500	Real estate	11	10	0.5	22	23	13,455	13,565	364	400	0.2
6530	Real estate agents and managers	3	3	0.3	5	4	8,800	11,000	54	58	0.1
6700	Holding and other investment offices	3	3	1.2	31	4	19,097	63,000	387	351	0.3
BROWN, KS											
60 –	**Finance, insurance, and real estate**	27	29	0.4	140	135	24,686	18,430	3,690	2,617	0.2
6000	Depository institutions	5	5	0.4	101	105	18,693	19,467	2,101	2,145	0.4
6020	Commercial banks	5	5	0.5	101	105	18,693	19,467	2,101	2,145	0.6
6500	Real estate	5	7	0.3	8	9	8,500	7,111	77	97	0.1
BUTLER, KS											
60 –	**Finance, insurance, and real estate**	94	100	1.5	590	589	22,936	21,236	13,226	13,291	0.8

Source: County Business Patterns, 1994/95, CBP-94/95, U.S. Department of Commerce, Washington, D.C., November 1997. SIC categories for which data were suppressed or not available for both 1994 and 1995 are not displayed. The employment columns represent mid-March employment in the year. Pay per employee is calculated by dividing 1st Quarter payroll, annualized, by mid-March employment. The columns headed "% State" show the county's percentage of the state total for the SIC in 1995; for example, 1.4% for SIC 6000 means that the county had 1.4 percent of the state's total establishments (or payroll) in SIC 6000 in 1995. A dash (-) is used to indicate that data are not available or cannot be calculated; nec means not elsewhere classified.

Continued on next page.

SIC	Industry	No. Establishments			Employment		Pay / Employee		Annual Payroll ($ 000)		
		1994	1995	% State	1994	1995	1994	1995	1994	1995	% State
BUTLER, KS - [continued]											
6000	Depository institutions	31	29	2.2	386	388	25,689	23,155	9,142	9,310	1.9
6020	Commercial banks	20	20	2.2	287	296	26,049	21,622	6,931	6,680	1.8
6400	Insurance agents, brokers, and service	30	32	1.7	90	87	16,844	18,437	1,779	1,788	0.8
6500	Real estate	24	28	1.3	81	84	12,988	13,143	1,194	1,258	0.7
6510	Real estate operators and lessors	8	11	1.4	18	35	10,000	10,743	203	428	0.7
6530	Real estate agents and managers	11	13	1.4	27	25	15,852	12,320	443	410	0.4
6540	Title abstract offices	3	3	2.4	23	21	16,348	17,905	427	387	3.8
6700	Holding and other investment offices	3	3	1.2	6	2	18,000	6,000	85	27	0.0
CHASE, KS											
60 –	**Finance, insurance, and real estate**	6	6	0.1	25	23	20,640	24,174	581	571	0.0
CHEROKEE, KS											
60 –	**Finance, insurance, and real estate**	27	26	0.4	148	152	22,054	22,474	3,017	3,253	0.2
6000	Depository institutions	9	9	0.7	103	100	25,398	26,480	2,353	2,453	0.5
6020	Commercial banks	9	9	1.0	103	100	25,398	26,480	2,353	2,453	0.6
6500	Real estate	8	7	0.3	14	15	6,857	11,200	123	185	0.1
CHEYENNE, KS											
60 –	**Finance, insurance, and real estate**	8	10	0.1	43	42	22,512	23,048	1,071	979	0.1
6400	Insurance agents, brokers, and service	4	6	0.3	4	3	7,000	8,000	29	36	0.0
CLARK, KS											
60 –	**Finance, insurance, and real estate**	8	8	0.1	46	49	20,087	20,408	1,213	1,306	0.1
6000	Depository institutions	4	4	0.3	35	38	22,514	22,947	1,062	1,157	0.2
CLAY, KS											
60 –	**Finance, insurance, and real estate**	21	20	0.3	89	64	17,348	20,188	1,713	1,322	0.1
6500	Real estate	5	6	0.3	7	7	10,857	10,286	102	121	0.1
CLOUD, KS											
60 –	**Finance, insurance, and real estate**	31	31	0.5	170	179	19,812	19,061	3,561	3,515	0.2
6000	Depository institutions	11	11	0.8	111	114	20,505	20,877	2,494	2,508	0.5
6400	Insurance agents, brokers, and service	9	9	0.5	31	43	13,806	11,535	472	480	0.2
6510	Real estate operators and lessors	3	3	0.4	4	3	2,000	4,000	11	16	0.0
COWLEY, KS											
60 –	**Finance, insurance, and real estate**	69	66	1.0	406	374	21,764	22,449	9,032	8,716	0.5
6000	Depository institutions	23	23	1.8	271	241	24,310	24,929	6,628	6,271	1.3
6020	Commercial banks	15	15	1.6	252	220	25,111	25,582	6,328	5,858	1.5
6200	Security and commodity brokers	6	5	1.2	11	10	25,455	28,400	266	325	0.3
6400	Insurance agents, brokers, and service	20	17	0.9	60	54	16,867	17,852	1,019	987	0.5
6500	Real estate	13	14	0.7	44	43	12,818	13,302	590	599	0.3
CRAWFORD, KS											
60 –	**Finance, insurance, and real estate**	86	83	1.2	457	496	19,501	20,500	9,493	10,666	0.6
6000	Depository institutions	20	20	1.5	251	277	21,052	22,108	5,726	6,438	1.3
6020	Commercial banks	14	14	1.5	193	219	21,223	21,826	4,483	5,091	1.3
6400	Insurance agents, brokers, and service	28	25	1.3	77	71	14,286	14,761	1,158	1,229	0.6
6500	Real estate	27	26	1.2	63	54	10,095	10,444	686	662	0.3
6510	Real estate operators and lessors	12	11	1.4	25	16	12,320	13,750	302	292	0.5
6530	Real estate agents and managers	12	12	1.3	21	19	8,000	9,263	213	183	0.2
DECATUR, KS											
60 –	**Finance, insurance, and real estate**	14	13	0.2	50	53	17,680	20,755	1,129	1,296	0.1
6500	Real estate	4	5	0.2	7	4	5,143	9,000	77	91	0.0
DICKINSON, KS											
60 –	**Finance, insurance, and real estate**	52	53	0.8	262	239	18,931	19,699	4,860	4,881	0.3

Source: County Business Patterns, 1994/95, CBP-94/95, U.S. Department of Commerce, Washington, D.C., November 1997. SIC categories for which data were suppressed or not available for both 1994 and 1995 are not displayed. The employment columns represent mid-March employment in the year. Pay per employee is calculated by dividing 1st Quarter payroll, annualized, by mid-March employment. The columns headed "% State" show the county's percentage of the state total for the SIC in 1995; for example, 1.4% for SIC 6000 means that the county had 1.4 percent of the state's total establishments (or payroll) in SIC 6000 in 1995. A dash (-) is used to indicate that data are not available or cannot be calculated; nec means not elsewhere classified.

Continued on next page.

SIC	Industry	No. Establishments			Employment		Pay / Employee		Annual Payroll ($ 000)		
		1994	1995	% State	1994	1995	1994	1995	1994	1995	% State
DICKINSON, KS - [continued]											
6000	Depository institutions	17	15	1.2	171	150	20,023	20,987	3,321	3,294	0.7
6400	Insurance agents, brokers, and service	13	14	0.7	31	33	14,581	15,152	455	480	0.2
6500	Real estate	14	17	0.8	26	27	8,308	8,889	235	266	0.1
6530	Real estate agents and managers	3	5	0.5	7	9	8,571	8,000	65	64	0.1
DONIPHAN, KS											
60 –	**Finance, insurance, and real estate**	15	16	0.2	86	79	17,349	19,899	1,825	1,856	0.1
6000	Depository institutions	9	9	0.7	74	71	19,459	21,352	1,760	1,786	0.4
DOUGLAS, KS											
60 –	**Finance, insurance, and real estate**	191	201	3.0	1,620	1,743	21,533	21,542	36,356	40,221	2.3
6000	Depository institutions	31	32	2.5	454	525	24,934	25,623	11,423	14,011	2.9
6020	Commercial banks	15	16	1.7	265	337	22,385	22,457	6,322	8,316	2.2
6100	Nondepository institutions	8	9	2.5	617	589	21,420	21,134	12,217	11,881	7.5
6200	Security and commodity brokers	12	14	3.3	41	48	34,146	27,833	1,375	1,788	1.6
6210	Security brokers and dealers	8	9	3.7	31	36	40,000	32,667	1,229	1,599	2.4
6280	Security and commodity services	4	5	3.4	10	12	16,000	13,333	146	189	0.6
6300	Insurance carriers	9	7	1.6	70	17	22,686	29,412	1,696	490	0.1
6400	Insurance agents, brokers, and service	38	38	2.0	117	120	22,496	25,333	3,358	3,887	1.8
6500	Real estate	87	95	4.6	300	372	14,427	14,290	5,732	6,624	3.4
6510	Real estate operators and lessors	42	42	5.4	138	181	13,594	12,376	2,437	2,473	4.2
6530	Real estate agents and managers	38	43	4.5	143	148	13,483	14,865	2,721	3,004	2.8
6550	Subdividers and developers	5	7	4.1	16	19	29,750	21,263	557	661	4.6
6700	Holding and other investment offices	6	6	2.3	21	72	19,048	20,222	555	1,540	1.2
EDWARDS, KS											
60 –	**Finance, insurance, and real estate**	8	7	0.1	58	52	18,621	18,769	1,085	1,009	0.1
6000	Depository institutions	5	4	0.3	50	44	19,760	19,909	997	917	0.2
ELK, KS											
60 –	**Finance, insurance, and real estate**	8	8	0.1	30	37	20,533	20,108	632	737	0.0
ELLIS, KS											
60 –	**Finance, insurance, and real estate**	79	84	1.2	429	419	19,720	21,585	8,757	8,964	0.5
6000	Depository institutions	15	16	1.2	207	198	21,449	23,091	4,457	4,428	0.9
6200	Security and commodity brokers	5	6	1.4	10	14	36,000	36,857	231	444	0.4
6400	Insurance agents, brokers, and service	24	26	1.4	105	96	18,476	21,500	2,164	2,224	1.0
6500	Real estate	26	26	1.2	66	71	12,424	11,718	969	933	0.5
ELLSWORTH, KS											
60 –	**Finance, insurance, and real estate**	18	18	0.3	78	76	17,795	18,316	1,466	1,458	0.1
6000	Depository institutions	7	7	0.5	59	56	20,203	20,500	1,246	1,203	0.3
6500	Real estate	4	4	0.2	3	4	6,667	7,000	29	30	0.0
FINNEY, KS											
60 –	**Finance, insurance, and real estate**	78	86	1.3	559	526	24,687	24,555	14,015	13,713	0.8
6000	Depository institutions	16	14	1.1	290	300	23,007	23,293	7,001	7,190	1.5
6020	Commercial banks	11	9	1.0	192	189	26,688	27,026	5,071	4,896	1.3
6300	Insurance carriers	4	4	0.9	33	36	37,455	31,333	1,230	1,085	0.2
6400	Insurance agents, brokers, and service	16	21	1.1	64	58	25,500	27,931	1,473	1,649	0.8
6500	Real estate	30	34	1.6	88	79	16,818	19,443	1,571	1,778	0.9
6510	Real estate operators and lessors	11	12	1.5	49	39	14,531	21,026	753	877	1.5
6530	Real estate agents and managers	15	17	1.8	30	30	20,267	18,533	672	736	0.7
6540	Title abstract offices	3	3	2.4	9	9	17,778	17,333	144	157	1.5
FORD, KS											
60 –	**Finance, insurance, and real estate**	73	76	1.1	396	371	24,010	23,515	9,917	9,541	0.5
6000	Depository institutions	19	18	1.4	238	205	24,353	24,468	6,118	5,450	1.1

Source: County Business Patterns, 1994/95, CBP-94/95, U.S. Department of Commerce, Washington, D.C., November 1997. SIC categories for which data were suppressed or not available for both 1994 and 1995 are not displayed. The employment columns represent mid-March employment in the year. Pay per employee is calculated by dividing 1st Quarter payroll, annualized, by mid-March employment. The columns headed "% State" show the county's percentage of the state total for the SIC in 1995; for example, 1.4% for SIC 6000 means that the county had 1.4 percent of the state's total establishments (or payroll) in SIC 6000 in 1995. A dash (-) is used to indicate that data are not available or cannot be calculated; nec means not elsewhere classified.

Continued on next page.

SIC	Industry	No. Establishments			Employment		Pay / Employee		Annual Payroll ($ 000)		
		1994	1995	% State	1994	1995	1994	1995	1994	1995	% State
FORD, KS - [continued]											
6020	Commercial banks	13	12	1.3	184	149	24,696	24,698	4,762	3,946	1.0
6400	Insurance agents, brokers, and service	23	23	1.2	67	75	16,060	16,587	1,234	1,345	0.6
6500	Real estate	19	23	1.1	52	53	17,308	18,113	971	1,108	0.6
6530	Real estate agents and managers	8	8	0.8	16	13	16,250	23,385	303	366	0.3
6700	Holding and other investment offices	3	3	1.2	2	4	10,000	7,000	40	54	0.0
FRANKLIN, KS											
60 –	**Finance, insurance, and real estate**	37	37	0.5	250	193	20,896	21,368	5,384	4,732	0.3
6000	Depository institutions	10	9	0.7	193	133	21,865	22,075	4,147	3,251	0.7
6400	Insurance agents, brokers, and service	15	14	0.7	26	25	16,000	18,720	594	742	0.3
6530	Real estate agents and managers	6	6	0.6	7	7	4,571	5,714	35	40	0.0
GEARY, KS											
60 –	**Finance, insurance, and real estate**	63	67	1.0	367	365	16,763	18,038	6,561	7,051	0.4
6000	Depository institutions	12	15	1.2	187	186	16,920	18,753	3,295	3,598	0.7
6020	Commercial banks	6	10	1.1	159	166	17,862	19,205	2,976	3,306	0.9
6400	Insurance agents, brokers, and service	12	11	0.6	40	37	14,800	15,568	636	608	0.3
6500	Real estate	28	28	1.3	71	75	11,437	12,853	936	1,118	0.6
6530	Real estate agents and managers	9	9	0.9	17	20	11,059	12,600	185	262	0.2
6700	Holding and other investment offices	4	3	1.2	43	35	17,488	15,086	870	744	0.6
GRAHAM, KS											
60 –	**Finance, insurance, and real estate**	11	11	0.2	69	64	17,913	19,813	1,368	1,367	0.1
6000	Depository institutions	5	5	0.4	57	52	19,298	21,923	1,232	1,230	0.3
GRANT, KS											
60 –	**Finance, insurance, and real estate**	14	14	0.2	99	96	19,758	20,792	2,092	2,246	0.1
6000	Depository institutions	5	5	0.4	70	76	23,143	22,368	1,722	1,893	0.4
GRAY, KS											
60 –	**Finance, insurance, and real estate**	14	12	0.2	173	143	26,266	23,552	4,367	3,780	0.2
GREELEY, KS											
60 –	**Finance, insurance, and real estate**	6	5	0.1	17	17	23,294	24,706	401	428	0.0
GREENWOOD, KS											
60 –	**Finance, insurance, and real estate**	18	19	0.3	66	70	19,515	24,457	1,302	1,561	0.1
6000	Depository institutions	6	6	0.5	39	43	21,538	29,581	856	1,121	0.2
6500	Real estate	4	5	0.2	7	8	9,714	11,500	69	82	0.0
HARPER, KS											
60 –	**Finance, insurance, and real estate**	23	24	0.4	112	89	18,250	19,506	2,151	1,975	0.1
6000	Depository institutions	7	6	0.5	83	61	20,000	22,820	1,742	1,554	0.3
6020	Commercial banks	7	6	0.6	83	61	20,000	22,820	1,742	1,554	0.4
6500	Real estate	5	5	0.2	8	7	10,000	4,571	63	48	0.0
HARVEY, KS											
60 –	**Finance, insurance, and real estate**	57	55	0.8	338	338	22,959	21,278	7,786	7,759	0.4
6000	Depository institutions	17	17	1.3	220	228	23,182	21,684	4,908	5,022	1.0
6020	Commercial banks	13	13	1.4	196	199	24,224	22,693	4,559	4,553	1.2
6400	Insurance agents, brokers, and service	21	18	0.9	65	63	20,062	18,476	1,456	1,596	0.7
6510	Real estate operators and lessors	5	3	0.4	8	5	9,500	10,400	81	46	0.1
HASKELL, KS											
60 –	**Finance, insurance, and real estate**	9	9	0.1	43	51	23,163	21,176	1,143	1,210	0.1
HODGEMAN, KS											
60 –	**Finance, insurance, and real estate**	4	4	0.1	-	-	-	-	-	-	-

Source: County Business Patterns, 1994/95, CBP-94/95, U.S. Department of Commerce, Washington, D.C., November 1997. SIC categories for which data were suppressed or not available for both 1994 and 1995 are *not* displayed. The employment columns represent mid-March employment in the year. Pay per employee is calculated by dividing 1st Quarter payroll, annualized, by mid-March employment. The columns headed "% State" show the county's percentage of the state total for the SIC in 1995; for example, 1.4% for SIC 6000 means that the county had 1.4 percent of the state's total establishments (or payroll) in SIC 6000 in 1995. A dash (-) is used to indicate that data are not available or cannot be calculated; *nec* means not elsewhere classified.

SIC	Industry	No. Establishments			Employment		Pay / Employee		Annual Payroll ($ 000)		
		1994	1995	% State	1994	1995	1994	1995	1994	1995	% State
JACKSON, KS											
60 –	**Finance, insurance, and real estate**	20	23	0.3	120	123	16,967	21,366	2,386	2,784	0.2
6000	Depository institutions	8	8	0.6	91	90	19,253	25,200	2,052	2,321	0.5
6500	Real estate	6	8	0.4	13	16	9,538	9,250	149	214	0.1
JEFFERSON, KS											
60 –	**Finance, insurance, and real estate**	22	21	0.3	108	104	16,222	18,231	2,201	2,500	0.1
6000	Depository institutions	8	8	0.6	78	76	19,846	21,579	1,933	2,112	0.4
6400	Insurance agents, brokers, and service	6	6	0.3	13	16	9,846	9,500	141	157	0.1
6500	Real estate	8	7	0.3	17	12	4,471	8,667	127	231	0.1
JEWELL, KS											
60 –	**Finance, insurance, and real estate**	13	12	0.2	67	68	16,657	15,588	1,305	1,424	0.1
6000	Depository institutions	8	8	0.6	63	64	16,762	16,313	1,277	1,404	0.3
JOHNSON, KS											
60 –	**Finance, insurance, and real estate**	1,634	1,699	25.0	23,039	22,290	32,633	35,839	717,060	779,938	44.8
6000	Depository institutions	150	147	11.3	2,767	2,797	25,321	26,804	68,018	74,594	15.5
6020	Commercial banks	87	94	10.2	1,902	2,103	23,836	25,105	43,834	53,374	14.0
6030	Savings institutions	42	34	19.4	584	424	27,575	30,330	14,709	11,752	19.5
6100	Nondepository institutions	164	169	46.4	3,576	3,336	31,934	31,657	99,539	104,774	66.3
6140	Personal credit institutions	52	51	34.5	499	558	27,944	27,333	13,390	15,309	52.4
6150	Business credit institutions	31	30	65.2	1,369	1,345	31,121	30,070	35,475	41,762	89.7
6160	Mortgage bankers and brokers	81	88	66.2	1,708	1,433	33,752	34,830	50,674	47,703	88.4
6200	Security and commodity brokers	115	116	27.2	1,085	1,103	53,187	60,947	56,230	64,165	56.6
6280	Security and commodity services	55	56	38.1	484	477	52,901	69,761	24,507	28,796	84.4
6300	Insurance carriers	204	197	44.4	7,988	7,077	37,851	43,892	276,267	280,997	62.0
6310	Life insurance	72	79	49.1	2,335	2,218	41,310	47,576	85,952	94,315	65.7
6320	Medical service and health insurance	19	16	35.6	363	299	38,171	38,863	12,716	11,403	15.3
6330	Fire, marine, and casualty insurance	85	79	40.3	4,878	4,304	36,610	42,669	165,597	166,433	74.7
6400	Insurance agents, brokers, and service	455	483	25.3	2,684	3,009	32,352	34,072	94,610	111,307	52.3
6500	Real estate	468	502	24.1	3,978	3,678	21,129	21,516	84,434	85,636	44.5
6510	Real estate operators and lessors	166	165	21.0	960	1,099	14,867	15,086	17,861	19,970	34.0
6530	Real estate agents and managers	256	277	29.1	2,723	2,369	21,253	23,404	57,503	59,022	54.7
6540	Title abstract offices	5	5	4.0	131	50	41,405	44,080	2,513	1,714	16.8
6550	Subdividers and developers	33	34	19.9	162	134	39,728	34,627	6,374	4,520	31.5
6552	Subdividers and developers, n.e.c.	23	25	32.1	140	107	42,114	36,636	5,622	3,716	38.0
6553	Cemetery subdividers and developers	7	7	8.0	21	26	25,524	27,538	735	780	17.5
6700	Holding and other investment offices	69	76	29.2	873	1,211	37,956	45,414	35,467	55,694	44.6
6710	Holding offices	30	36	33.0	470	760	43,643	51,637	21,477	39,486	38.9
6720	Investment offices	5	5	41.7	7	6	73,714	66,667	613	592	-
6730	Trusts	6	6	10.5	28	30	13,000	18,267	485	680	13.8
6790	Miscellaneous investing	27	27	37.5	356	402	31,854	35,751	12,395	14,374	85.9
6794	Patent owners and lessors	15	14	70.0	314	352	32,000	35,523	11,428	13,051	95.3
KEARNY, KS											
60 –	**Finance, insurance, and real estate**	3	3	0.0	-	-	-	-	-	-	-
KINGMAN, KS											
60 –	**Finance, insurance, and real estate**	18	17	0.2	123	129	19,967	19,659	2,843	2,983	0.2
6000	Depository institutions	4	4	0.3	80	82	21,300	21,415	1,966	2,127	0.4
6020	Commercial banks	4	4	0.4	80	82	21,300	21,415	1,966	2,127	0.6
6500	Real estate	5	3	0.1	12	8	15,000	16,500	173	137	0.1
KIOWA, KS											
60 –	**Finance, insurance, and real estate**	9	10	0.1	47	47	17,447	18,298	886	857	0.0
LABETTE, KS											
60 –	**Finance, insurance, and real estate**	47	44	0.6	305	308	18,780	18,870	6,110	6,411	0.4

Source: County Business Patterns, 1994/95, CBP-94/95, U.S. Department of Commerce, Washington, D.C., November 1997. SIC categories for which data were suppressed or not available for both 1994 and 1995 are *not* displayed. The employment columns represent mid-March employment in the year. Pay per employee is calculated by dividing 1st Quarter payroll, annualized, by mid-March employment. The columns headed "% State" show the county's percentage of the state total for the SIC in 1995; for example, 1.4% for SIC 6000 means that the county had 1.4 percent of the state's total establishments (or payroll) in SIC 6000 in 1995. A dash (-) is used to indicate that data are not available or cannot be calculated; *nec* means not elsewhere classified.

Continued on next page.

SIC	Industry	No. Establishments			Employment		Pay / Employee		Annual Payroll ($ 000)		
		1994	1995	% State	1994	1995	1994	1995	1994	1995	% State
LABETTE, KS - [continued]											
6000	Depository institutions	14	14	1.1	191	189	17,780	18,540	3,562	3,837	0.8
6400	Insurance agents, brokers, and service	18	17	0.9	64	66	17,563	17,212	1,281	1,307	0.6
6550	Subdividers and developers	5	5	2.9	9	10	8,444	8,000	97	116	0.8
6553	Cemetery subdividers and developers	5	5	5.7	9	10	8,444	8,000	97	116	2.6
LANE, KS											
60 –	**Finance, insurance, and real estate**	7	8	0.1	28	31	31,143	29,806	1,086	1,138	0.1
LEAVENWORTH, KS											
60 –	**Finance, insurance, and real estate**	91	85	1.2	772	788	20,244	21,863	16,938	18,188	1.0
6000	Depository institutions	24	24	1.8	371	381	21,919	23,769	8,099	8,726	1.8
6020	Commercial banks	12	12	1.3	256	261	21,109	22,759	5,402	5,747	1.5
6500	Real estate	28	26	1.2	108	118	17,815	17,424	2,560	2,841	1.5
6530	Real estate agents and managers	13	12	1.3	59	49	19,390	21,469	1,855	1,491	1.4
LINCOLN, KS											
60 –	**Finance, insurance, and real estate**	13	13	0.2	57	60	16,211	16,400	1,045	901	0.1
6000	Depository institutions	5	5	0.4	39	43	18,051	18,233	808	660	0.1
LINN, KS											
60 –	**Finance, insurance, and real estate**	21	21	0.3	90	94	18,622	19,191	2,222	2,048	0.1
6000	Depository institutions	7	7	0.5	49	55	21,388	21,091	1,465	1,312	0.3
6020	Commercial banks	7	7	0.8	49	55	21,388	21,091	1,465	1,312	0.3
6400	Insurance agents, brokers, and service	10	10	0.5	16	14	12,250	14,286	193	202	0.1
6500	Real estate	4	4	0.2	25	25	17,280	17,760	564	534	0.3
LOGAN, KS											
60 –	**Finance, insurance, and real estate**	15	15	0.2	52	62	17,846	16,065	944	1,061	0.1
6400	Insurance agents, brokers, and service	7	7	0.4	15	17	11,467	10,588	188	207	0.1
LYON, KS											
60 –	**Finance, insurance, and real estate**	64	67	1.0	349	372	21,009	21,688	7,250	7,716	0.4
6000	Depository institutions	18	18	1.4	202	207	23,168	25,507	4,549	4,894	1.0
6020	Commercial banks	13	13	1.4	159	162	24,579	23,901	3,830	3,757	1.0
6100	Nondepository institutions	3	3	0.8	20	20	32,600	34,400	658	705	0.4
6400	Insurance agents, brokers, and service	20	21	1.1	51	55	15,608	15,127	938	784	0.4
6500	Real estate	14	16	0.8	64	71	9,438	9,521	607	727	0.4
6510	Real estate operators and lessors	8	9	1.1	33	34	8,121	9,412	292	381	0.6
MCPHERSON, KS											
60 –	**Finance, insurance, and real estate**	71	71	1.0	679	703	21,155	22,526	14,607	17,491	1.0
6000	Depository institutions	22	21	1.6	246	266	20,081	20,722	5,259	5,688	1.2
6020	Commercial banks	17	17	1.8	216	235	20,722	21,294	4,807	5,172	1.4
6500	Real estate	16	16	0.8	59	51	10,169	13,490	637	678	0.4
6700	Holding and other investment offices	4	4	1.5	7	7	64,571	64,571	580	593	0.5
MARION, KS											
60 –	**Finance, insurance, and real estate**	28	29	0.4	150	136	17,147	19,588	2,752	2,887	0.2
6000	Depository institutions	13	12	0.9	122	110	19,344	22,218	2,537	2,632	0.5
6500	Real estate	4	5	0.2	10	9	8,400	10,222	88	115	0.1
MARSHALL, KS											
60 –	**Finance, insurance, and real estate**	35	34	0.5	215	233	21,637	22,524	5,100	5,523	0.3
6000	Depository institutions	11	10	0.8	129	144	22,202	24,722	3,278	3,805	0.8

Source: County Business Patterns, 1994/95, CBP-94/95, U.S. Department of Commerce, Washington, D.C., November 1997. SIC categories for which data were suppressed or not available for both 1994 and 1995 are not displayed. The employment columns represent mid-March employment in the year. Pay per employee is calculated by dividing 1st Quarter payroll, annualized, by mid-March employment. The columns headed "% State" show the county's percentage of the state total for the SIC in 1995; for example, 1.4% for SIC 6000 means that the county had 1.4 percent of the state's total establishments (or payroll) in SIC 6000 in 1995. A dash (-) is used to indicate that data are not available or cannot be calculated; nec means not elsewhere classified.

Continued on next page.

SIC	Industry	No. Establishments			Employment		Pay / Employee		Annual Payroll ($ 000)		
		1994	1995	% State	1994	1995	1994	1995	1994	1995	% State
MARSHALL, KS - [continued]											
6200	Security and commodity brokers	5	5	1.2	11	13	37,455	21,538	394	299	0.3
6400	Insurance agents, brokers, and service	9	9	0.5	25	24	19,360	19,667	483	473	0.2
6500	Real estate	6	6	0.3	5	5	7,200	7,200	81	61	0.0
MEADE, KS											
60 –	**Finance, insurance, and real estate**	9	8	0.1	47	41	20,851	24,390	1,014	997	0.1
MIAMI, KS											
60 –	**Finance, insurance, and real estate**	35	36	0.5	312	299	20,282	21,538	6,382	6,728	0.4
6000	Depository institutions	9	9	0.7	223	216	20,448	21,778	4,721	4,883	1.0
6400	Insurance agents, brokers, and service	11	9	0.5	35	28	14,514	19,857	518	565	0.3
6500	Real estate	11	12	0.6	44	43	11,182	12,651	521	613	0.3
MITCHELL, KS											
60 –	**Finance, insurance, and real estate**	19	20	0.3	97	100	19,794	18,760	2,099	1,934	0.1
6000	Depository institutions	8	7	0.5	76	75	21,368	21,227	1,751	1,638	0.3
MONTGOMERY, KS											
60 –	**Finance, insurance, and real estate**	89	91	1.3	423	432	20,974	21,778	8,938	9,440	0.5
6000	Depository institutions	27	27	2.1	263	289	21,049	22,768	5,958	6,652	1.4
6020	Commercial banks	16	16	1.7	217	242	21,512	23,025	4,942	5,522	1.5
6400	Insurance agents, brokers, and service	31	30	1.6	81	70	16,296	21,486	1,298	1,355	0.6
6500	Real estate	19	23	1.1	46	52	10,435	9,846	572	655	0.3
6510	Real estate operators and lessors	9	12	1.5	13	19	8,615	6,947	146	222	0.4
6700	Holding and other investment offices	4	3	1.2	6	7	108,000	12,000	259	77	0.1
MORRIS, KS											
60 –	**Finance, insurance, and real estate**	16	14	0.2	58	59	15,655	16,339	1,154	1,245	0.1
6000	Depository institutions	6	6	0.5	47	48	17,617	17,917	1,068	1,133	0.2
6020	Commercial banks	6	6	0.6	47	48	17,617	17,917	1,068	1,133	0.3
MORTON, KS											
60 –	**Finance, insurance, and real estate**	7	7	0.1	50	49	23,360	24,571	1,145	1,497	0.1
NEMAHA, KS											
60 –	**Finance, insurance, and real estate**	31	31	0.5	148	161	20,730	21,590	3,114	3,626	0.2
6000	Depository institutions	15	15	1.2	122	139	22,885	22,964	2,797	3,285	0.7
6400	Insurance agents, brokers, and service	8	7	0.4	19	14	12,421	15,714	251	217	0.1
6500	Real estate	5	5	0.2	6	3	6,000	6,667	35	30	0.0
NEOSHO, KS											
60 –	**Finance, insurance, and real estate**	49	43	0.6	225	224	19,876	20,536	4,569	4,628	0.3
6000	Depository institutions	12	12	0.9	125	134	21,472	21,493	2,723	2,910	0.6
6300	Insurance carriers	5	3	0.7	28	19	24,571	29,263	630	521	0.1
6400	Insurance agents, brokers, and service	15	13	0.7	31	29	11,355	13,103	381	432	0.2
6500	Real estate	10	8	0.4	21	22	7,429	9,091	245	192	0.1
6510	Real estate operators and lessors	4	3	0.4	9	10	5,778	6,800	60	58	0.1
NESS, KS											
60 –	**Finance, insurance, and real estate**	13	12	0.2	60	53	19,733	24,302	1,378	1,442	0.1
6000	Depository institutions	5	5	0.4	36	36	21,222	22,889	931	986	0.2
NORTON, KS											
60 –	**Finance, insurance, and real estate**	19	20	0.3	90	98	21,022	21,469	2,250	2,298	0.1
6000	Depository institutions	6	6	0.5	70	75	21,714	22,667	1,792	1,803	0.4
6500	Real estate	5	5	0.2	5	8	9,600	6,500	62	65	0.0

Source: County Business Patterns, 1994/95, CBP-94/95, U.S. Department of Commerce, Washington, D.C., November 1997. SIC categories for which data were suppressed or not available for both 1994 and 1995 are not displayed. The employment columns represent mid-March employment in the year. Pay per employee is calculated by dividing 1st Quarter payroll, annualized, by mid-March employment. The columns headed "% State" show the county's percentage of the state total for the SIC in 1995; for example, 1.4% for SIC 6000 means that the county had 1.4 percent of the state's total establishments (or payroll) in SIC 6000 in 1995. A dash (-) is used to indicate that data are not available or cannot be calculated; nec means not elsewhere classified.

Continued on next page.

SIC	Industry	No. Establishments			Employment		Pay / Employee		Annual Payroll ($ 000)		
		1994	1995	% State	1994	1995	1994	1995	1994	1995	% State
OSAGE, KS - [continued]											
60 –	**Finance, insurance, and real estate**	24	25	0.4	120	128	19,733	19,781	2,722	2,982	0.2
6000	Depository institutions	12	11	0.8	94	99	22,340	21,697	2,401	2,538	0.5
OSBORNE, KS											
60 –	**Finance, insurance, and real estate**	13	12	0.2	81	82	18,914	19,024	1,674	1,736	0.1
6000	Depository institutions	6	6	0.5	68	69	19,412	19,362	1,432	1,480	0.3
6020	Commercial banks	6	6	0.6	68	69	19,412	19,362	1,432	1,480	0.4
OTTAWA, KS											
60 –	**Finance, insurance, and real estate**	10	10	0.1	89	95	21,079	19,747	2,131	2,318	0.1
6000	Depository institutions	4	4	0.3	78	84	20,974	20,333	1,895	2,119	0.4
6020	Commercial banks	4	4	0.4	78	84	20,974	20,333	1,895	2,119	0.6
PAWNEE, KS											
60 –	**Finance, insurance, and real estate**	23	22	0.3	139	124	19,338	20,645	2,900	2,823	0.2
6000	Depository institutions	5	6	0.5	65	74	24,923	21,568	1,788	1,865	0.4
6500	Real estate	6	5	0.2	31	9	8,903	8,444	262	78	0.0
PHILLIPS, KS											
60 –	**Finance, insurance, and real estate**	24	24	0.4	113	135	22,726	21,215	2,653	2,840	0.2
6000	Depository institutions	7	7	0.5	80	99	24,250	22,465	2,130	2,288	0.5
6400	Insurance agents, brokers, and service	11	11	0.6	14	17	12,000	11,294	170	193	0.1
POTTAWATOMIE, KS											
60 –	**Finance, insurance, and real estate**	32	31	0.5	270	210	19,185	17,238	6,907	3,765	0.2
6000	Depository institutions	9	9	0.7	172	184	17,558	17,913	3,005	3,382	0.7
PRATT, KS											
60 –	**Finance, insurance, and real estate**	28	32	0.5	150	152	24,853	25,605	3,908	4,046	0.2
6000	Depository institutions	7	7	0.5	103	99	28,000	29,980	3,034	3,114	0.6
6400	Insurance agents, brokers, and service	8	8	0.4	19	21	18,526	17,333	366	389	0.2
6500	Real estate	7	8	0.4	10	15	8,800	8,000	114	121	0.1
6510	Real estate operators and lessors	4	5	0.6	7	10	5,714	6,000	43	54	0.1
RAWLINS, KS											
60 –	**Finance, insurance, and real estate**	11	9	0.1	52	58	19,923	14,828	1,113	967	0.1
6400	Insurance agents, brokers, and service	3	4	0.2	4	19	24,000	5,474	121	122	0.1
RENO, KS											
60 –	**Finance, insurance, and real estate**	152	148	2.2	1,035	965	22,195	22,591	23,557	22,683	1.3
6000	Depository institutions	33	31	2.4	540	463	22,489	23,559	12,264	11,235	2.3
6020	Commercial banks	22	20	2.2	465	387	23,295	24,496	10,975	9,771	2.6
6100	Nondepository institutions	8	8	2.2	32	60	19,125	23,200	620	1,438	0.9
6140	Personal credit institutions	4	5	3.4	11	46	24,364	23,217	265	1,096	3.8
6200	Security and commodity brokers	13	15	3.5	58	56	42,897	33,214	1,931	2,111	1.9
6210	Security brokers and dealers	6	8	3.3	37	39	48,108	38,359	1,341	1,751	2.7
6280	Security and commodity services	7	7	4.8	21	17	33,714	21,412	590	360	1.1
6300	Insurance carriers	10	10	2.3	76	71	24,632	27,042	2,091	1,827	0.4
6310	Life insurance	3	3	1.9	29	15	22,897	31,467	674	478	0.3
6330	Fire, marine, and casualty insurance	4	4	2.0	25	22	27,680	36,364	838	723	0.3
6400	Insurance agents, brokers, and service	37	40	2.1	131	138	20,885	22,638	3,396	3,564	1.7
6500	Real estate	42	35	1.7	168	163	12,262	13,448	2,166	2,211	1.1
6510	Real estate operators and lessors	18	14	1.8	60	52	9,667	11,077	583	609	1.0
6530	Real estate agents and managers	20	17	1.8	75	75	12,907	13,813	979	982	0.9
6700	Holding and other investment offices	9	9	3.5	30	14	35,333	28,857	1,089	297	0.2

Source: County Business Patterns, 1994/95, CBP-94/95, U.S. Department of Commerce, Washington, D.C., November 1997. SIC categories for which data were suppressed or not available for both 1994 and 1995 are not displayed. The employment columns represent mid-March employment in the year. Pay per employee is calculated by dividing 1st Quarter payroll, annualized, by mid-March employment. The columns headed "% State" show the county's percentage of the state total for the SIC in 1995; for example, 1.4% for SIC 6000 means that the county had 1.4 percent of the state's total establishments (or payroll) in SIC 6000 in 1995. A dash (-) is used to indicate that data are not available or cannot be calculated; nec means not elsewhere classified.

SIC	Industry	No. Establishments			Employment		Pay / Employee		Annual Payroll ($ 000)		
		1994	1995	% State	1994	1995	1994	1995	1994	1995	% State
REPUBLIC, KS											
60–	**Finance, insurance, and real estate**	14	13	0.2	110	101	16,364	17,465	1,877	1,802	0.1
6000	Depository institutions	6	6	0.5	73	76	21,151	21,000	1,611	1,658	0.3
6020	Commercial banks	6	6	0.6	73	76	21,151	21,000	1,611	1,658	0.4
RICE, KS											
60–	**Finance, insurance, and real estate**	26	26	0.4	157	154	17,248	17,351	2,730	2,549	0.1
6000	Depository institutions	11	11	0.8	133	134	18,647	18,537	2,510	2,327	0.5
RILEY, KS											
60–	**Finance, insurance, and real estate**	165	166	2.4	1,323	1,484	24,408	24,809	31,866	35,833	2.1
6000	Depository institutions	17	17	1.3	405	389	20,563	20,802	8,054	8,065	1.7
6020	Commercial banks	9	10	1.1	272	268	21,853	20,716	5,684	5,503	1.4
6100	Nondepository institutions	9	7	1.9	58	50	26,690	34,720	1,720	1,780	1.1
6300	Insurance carriers	12	12	2.7	336	337	28,798	31,015	9,350	9,262	2.0
6400	Insurance agents, brokers, and service	39	38	2.0	104	91	16,462	21,890	1,720	1,837	0.9
6500	Real estate	72	75	3.6	199	411	12,523	15,679	2,969	6,859	3.6
6510	Real estate operators and lessors	33	34	4.3	101	299	10,455	17,043	1,276	4,986	8.5
6530	Real estate agents and managers	34	35	3.7	80	87	9,000	9,149	917	918	0.9
ROOKS, KS											
60–	**Finance, insurance, and real estate**	18	18	0.3	79	85	17,570	18,400	1,634	1,697	0.1
6000	Depository institutions	5	5	0.4	53	57	22,717	24,140	1,425	1,506	0.3
6400	Insurance agents, brokers, and service	6	6	0.3	9	9	6,222	5,778	68	44	0.0
6500	Real estate	4	4	0.2	11	10	1,455	1,600	18	18	0.0
RUSH, KS											
60–	**Finance, insurance, and real estate**	10	11	0.2	43	46	17,860	16,957	785	745	0.0
6000	Depository institutions	5	5	0.4	35	37	19,200	18,486	675	628	0.1
6400	Insurance agents, brokers, and service	5	6	0.3	8	9	12,000	10,667	110	117	0.1
RUSSELL, KS											
60–	**Finance, insurance, and real estate**	22	22	0.3	122	113	20,393	19,150	2,341	2,235	0.1
6000	Depository institutions	6	6	0.5	54	49	15,704	15,918	867	824	0.2
6400	Insurance agents, brokers, and service	6	6	0.3	19	20	18,737	20,000	418	412	0.2
6500	Real estate	4	4	0.2	10	10	9,600	10,000	104	96	0.0
SALINE, KS											
60–	**Finance, insurance, and real estate**	153	150	2.2	797	846	21,084	20,350	17,303	17,715	1.0
6000	Depository institutions	21	20	1.5	379	406	22,248	22,315	8,614	9,017	1.9
6020	Commercial banks	12	12	1.3	343	368	22,519	22,522	7,881	8,318	2.2
6160	Mortgage bankers and brokers	3	3	2.3	11	6	15,273	19,333	232	116	0.2
6200	Security and commodity brokers	14	15	3.5	59	72	44,203	26,667	2,120	1,962	1.7
6300	Insurance carriers	7	9	2.0	21	27	24,190	25,333	513	649	0.1
6400	Insurance agents, brokers, and service	33	38	2.0	103	114	19,845	19,684	2,480	2,618	1.2
6500	Real estate	62	53	2.5	190	190	12,358	13,158	2,606	2,614	1.4
6510	Real estate operators and lessors	35	26	3.3	125	108	11,008	12,889	1,369	1,260	2.1
6530	Real estate agents and managers	19	19	2.0	41	45	14,146	13,422	704	785	0.7
6540	Title abstract offices	3	3	2.4	17	17	17,176	18,353	380	387	3.8
SCOTT, KS											
60–	**Finance, insurance, and real estate**	15	17	0.2	71	75	20,225	20,747	1,710	1,833	0.1
6400	Insurance agents, brokers, and service	4	7	0.4	13	14	8,923	11,714	131	178	0.1
6500	Real estate	4	4	0.2	7	9	8,571	7,111	60	68	0.0
SEDGWICK, KS											
60–	**Finance, insurance, and real estate**	1,058	1,125	16.5	10,824	10,828	25,754	26,979	278,751	291,445	16.8
6000	Depository institutions	143	151	11.6	3,184	3,203	23,499	25,291	76,778	79,528	16.5
6020	Commercial banks	85	87	9.4	2,382	2,305	22,977	24,449	56,532	55,209	14.5

Source: County Business Patterns, 1994/95, CBP-94/95, U.S. Department of Commerce, Washington, D.C., November 1997. SIC categories for which data were suppressed or not available for both 1994 and 1995 are not displayed. The employment columns represent mid-March employment in the year. Pay per employee is calculated by dividing 1st Quarter payroll, annualized, by mid-March employment. The columns headed "% State" show the county's percentage of the state total for the SIC in 1995; for example, 1.4% for SIC 6000 means that the county had 1.4 percent of the state's total establishments (or payroll) in SIC 6000 in 1995. A dash (-) is used to indicate that data are not available or cannot be calculated; nec means not elsewhere classified.

Continued on next page.

SIC	Industry	No. Establishments			Employment		Pay / Employee		Annual Payroll ($ 000)		
		1994	1995	% State	1994	1995	1994	1995	1994	1995	% State
SEDGWICK, KS - [continued]											
6030	Savings institutions	28	35	20.0	486	576	27,737	30,625	13,543	17,232	28.6
6060	Credit unions	24	23	13.1	289	284	20,249	21,408	5,953	6,160	25.9
6090	Functions closely related to banking	6	6	27.3	27	38	28,000	24,526	750	927	-
6100	Nondepository institutions	56	61	16.8	669	641	38,798	41,254	24,768	23,720	15.0
6140	Personal credit institutions	28	31	20.9	209	215	28,555	29,377	5,847	6,270	21.5
6150	Business credit institutions	9	10	21.7	80	95	38,350	42,189	3,859	3,755	8.1
6210	Security brokers and dealers	47	50	20.7	424	403	57,764	47,494	20,497	19,540	29.7
6280	Security and commodity services	22	26	17.7	77	57	16,623	27,298	1,500	1,663	4.9
6300	Insurance carriers	87	90	20.3	1,435	1,381	28,329	30,453	41,059	40,334	8.9
6310	Life insurance	33	32	19.9	621	598	28,554	30,408	17,777	16,357	11.4
6400	Insurance agents, brokers, and service	284	291	15.2	1,298	1,357	27,331	28,383	35,622	38,868	18.3
6500	Real estate	369	404	19.4	2,541	2,471	14,391	15,786	40,635	42,768	22.2
6510	Real estate operators and lessors	145	154	19.6	697	780	16,534	16,518	12,460	13,948	23.8
6530	Real estate agents and managers	189	202	21.2	1,327	1,398	14,454	14,847	21,371	22,200	20.6
6540	Title abstract offices	5	5	4.0	69	45	16,928	17,156	1,110	840	8.2
6550	Subdividers and developers	25	30	17.5	436	227	10,431	18,943	5,480	5,127	35.7
6552	Subdividers and developers, n.e.c.	18	23	29.5	342	135	11,930	27,970	4,885	4,433	45.3
6553	Cemetery subdividers and developers	6	6	6.9	94	92	4,979	5,696	583	682	15.3
6700	Holding and other investment offices	45	47	18.1	1,173	1,297	32,931	33,709	37,071	44,423	35.6
6710	Holding offices	19	19	17.4	1,115	1,239	33,094	33,853	35,173	42,254	41.7
6790	Miscellaneous investing	13	12	16.7	30	23	34,133	39,304	1,071	1,055	6.3
SEWARD, KS											
60 –	**Finance, insurance, and real estate**	59	59	0.9	277	288	23,480	22,153	6,268	7,727	0.4
6000	Depository institutions	8	7	0.5	141	138	25,532	26,522	3,514	4,766	1.0
6100	Nondepository institutions	4	4	1.1	17	14	15,059	19,143	280	392	0.2
6400	Insurance agents, brokers, and service	18	16	0.8	55	53	14,400	16,377	859	889	0.4
6500	Real estate	21	24	1.2	47	61	14,128	12,590	655	769	0.4
6510	Real estate operators and lessors	8	9	1.1	13	24	12,000	10,667	220	321	0.5
6530	Real estate agents and managers	10	12	1.3	28	30	13,571	13,733	325	363	0.3
SHAWNEE, KS											
60 –	**Finance, insurance, and real estate**	476	503	7.4	5,716	5,785	26,501	29,009	153,141	164,128	9.4
6000	Depository institutions	82	83	6.4	1,511	1,492	26,496	27,777	37,258	38,884	8.1
6020	Commercial banks	53	54	5.8	941	919	23,095	23,826	20,992	21,734	5.7
6060	Credit unions	18	18	10.2	191	181	18,262	20,641	3,602	3,713	15.6
6140	Personal credit institutions	15	13	8.8	74	81	26,216	28,444	2,153	2,463	8.4
6200	Security and commodity brokers	34	34	8.0	203	197	52,631	45,685	10,058	9,402	8.3
6210	Security brokers and dealers	18	18	7.4	130	125	57,692	48,576	7,091	6,696	10.2
6280	Security and commodity services	16	16	10.9	73	72	43,616	40,667	2,967	2,706	7.9
6300	Insurance carriers	40	39	8.8	2,509	2,501	27,346	31,696	70,623	76,696	16.9
6310	Life insurance	18	18	11.2	460	516	36,322	30,860	15,051	15,742	11.0
6400	Insurance agents, brokers, and service	118	126	6.6	490	465	23,690	24,998	11,842	11,997	5.6
6500	Real estate	155	172	8.2	806	898	15,533	15,506	14,813	15,253	7.9
6510	Real estate operators and lessors	81	87	11.1	329	416	11,757	11,500	4,911	5,422	9.2
6530	Real estate agents and managers	63	70	7.3	407	410	18,182	18,985	8,409	8,252	7.6
6553	Cemetery subdividers and developers	4	5	5.7	31	35	18,839	19,200	679	760	17.0
6710	Holding offices	8	9	8.3	35	53	107,314	137,283	3,749	6,611	6.5
6790	Miscellaneous investing	4	4	5.6	3	8	22,667	27,000	167	222	1.3
SHERIDAN, KS											
60 –	**Finance, insurance, and real estate**	9	9	0.1	58	56	26,345	27,071	1,715	1,598	0.1
SHERMAN, KS											
60 –	**Finance, insurance, and real estate**	19	18	0.3	117	132	23,761	22,424	2,939	2,907	0.2

Source: County Business Patterns, 1994/95, CBP-94/95, U.S. Department of Commerce, Washington, D.C., November 1997. SIC categories for which data were suppressed or not available for both 1994 and 1995 are not displayed. The employment columns represent mid-March employment in the year. Pay per employee is calculated by dividing 1st Quarter payroll, annualized, by mid-March employment. The columns headed "% State" show the county's percentage of the state total for the SIC in 1995; for example, 1.4% for SIC 6000 means that the county had 1.4 percent of the state's total establishments (or payroll) in SIC 6000 in 1995. A dash (-) is used to indicate that data are not available or cannot be calculated; nec means not elsewhere classified.

Continued on next page.

SIC	Industry	No. Establishments			Employment		Pay / Employee		Annual Payroll ($ 000)		
		1994	1995	% State	1994	1995	1994	1995	1994	1995	% State
SHERMAN, KS - [continued]											
6000	Depository institutions	3	3	0.2	91	99	24,879	24,889	2,362	2,300	0.5
6020	Commercial banks	3	3	0.3	91	99	24,879	24,889	2,362	2,300	0.6
6530	Real estate agents and managers	3	3	0.3	4	4	7,000	7,000	32	29	0.0
SMITH, KS											
60 –	**Finance, insurance, and real estate**	11	13	0.2	76	71	17,895	18,085	1,578	1,595	0.1
6000	Depository institutions	5	4	0.3	69	59	18,435	19,932	1,471	1,448	0.3
6020	Commercial banks	5	4	0.4	69	59	18,435	19,932	1,471	1,448	0.4
6500	Real estate	3	4	0.2	4	6	12,000	6,000	58	51	0.0
STAFFORD, KS											
60 –	**Finance, insurance, and real estate**	15	16	0.2	71	95	21,239	17,600	1,663	1,829	0.1
6000	Depository institutions	6	6	0.5	56	61	24,286	22,951	1,452	1,519	0.3
6020	Commercial banks	6	6	0.6	56	61	24,286	22,951	1,452	1,519	0.4
6500	Real estate	3	3	0.1	4	22	12,000	6,182	91	143	0.1
STANTON, KS											
60 –	**Finance, insurance, and real estate**	1	2	0.0	-	-	-	-	-	-	-
STEVENS, KS											
60 –	**Finance, insurance, and real estate**	9	11	0.2	68	62	19,353	21,161	1,348	1,430	0.1
SUMNER, KS											
60 –	**Finance, insurance, and real estate**	46	49	0.7	272	275	21,103	22,749	6,061	6,466	0.4
6000	Depository institutions	15	15	1.2	190	198	24,611	26,061	4,903	5,232	1.1
6400	Insurance agents, brokers, and service	22	21	1.1	59	51	11,661	13,333	712	749	0.4
6530	Real estate agents and managers	3	5	0.5	5	8	10,400	12,500	56	105	0.1
THOMAS, KS											
60 –	**Finance, insurance, and real estate**	29	31	0.5	150	155	22,613	22,710	3,462	3,583	0.2
6000	Depository institutions	5	4	0.3	66	64	20,788	21,625	1,365	1,396	0.3
6200	Security and commodity brokers	6	6	1.4	9	9	32,444	22,667	254	230	0.2
6400	Insurance agents, brokers, and service	8	10	0.5	25	31	17,600	19,871	603	686	0.3
6500	Real estate	6	7	0.3	21	21	15,619	11,048	274	271	0.1
TREGO, KS											
60 –	**Finance, insurance, and real estate**	10	10	0.1	44	44	18,818	20,727	847	1,006	0.1
6000	Depository institutions	3	3	0.2	27	29	24,444	25,931	685	844	0.2
6400	Insurance agents, brokers, and service	4	4	0.2	13	10	10,462	10,800	133	122	0.1
6500	Real estate	3	3	0.1	4	5	8,000	10,400	29	40	0.0
WABAUNSEE, KS											
60 –	**Finance, insurance, and real estate**	12	12	0.2	54	44	17,407	20,000	1,071	1,019	0.1
6400	Insurance agents, brokers, and service	3	4	0.2	7	5	11,429	8,000	104	52	0.0
WASHINGTON, KS											
60 –	**Finance, insurance, and real estate**	26	24	0.4	99	101	19,192	20,317	2,277	2,294	0.1
6000	Depository institutions	9	8	0.6	77	78	21,195	22,410	1,891	1,883	0.4
6020	Commercial banks	9	8	0.9	77	78	21,195	22,410	1,891	1,883	0.5
6500	Real estate	8	8	0.4	4	4	8,000	6,000	43	35	0.0
6550	Subdividers and developers	4	4	2.3	1	1	4,000	4,000	11	10	0.1
6553	Cemetery subdividers and developers	4	4	4.6	1	1	4,000	4,000	11	10	0.2
WILSON, KS											
60 –	**Finance, insurance, and real estate**	17	17	0.2	81	87	21,580	22,529	2,026	2,234	0.1
6000	Depository institutions	5	5	0.4	59	62	24,610	25,677	1,638	1,816	0.4
WYANDOTTE, KS											
60 –	**Finance, insurance, and real estate**	225	226	3.3	2,341	2,225	20,195	19,560	47,299	43,880	2.5

Source: County Business Patterns, 1994/95, CBP-94/95, U.S. Department of Commerce, Washington, D.C., November 1997. SIC categories for which data were suppressed or not available for both 1994 and 1995 are not displayed. The employment columns represent mid-March employment in the year. Pay per employee is calculated by dividing 1st Quarter payroll, annualized, by mid-March employment. The columns headed "% State" show the county's percentage of the state total for the SIC in 1995; for example, 1.4% for SIC 6000 means that the county had 1.4 percent of the state's total establishments (or payroll) in SIC 6000 in 1995. A dash (-) is used to indicate that data are not available or cannot be calculated; nec means not elsewhere classified.

Continued on next page.

SIC	Industry	No. Establishments			Employment		Pay / Employee		Annual Payroll ($ 000)		
		1994	1995	% State	1994	1995	1994	1995	1994	1995	% State
WYANDOTTE, KS - [continued]											
6000	Depository institutions	67	64	4.9	1,141	986	25,437	24,024	27,360	23,099	4.8
6020	Commercial banks	36	34	3.7	984	830	26,134	23,923	23,885	18,894	5.0
6030	Savings institutions	5	5	2.9	56	56	24,071	30,571	1,429	2,034	3.4
6100	Nondepository institutions	11	12	3.3	71	52	26,648	26,154	1,905	1,489	0.9
6140	Personal credit institutions	7	9	6.1	30	34	21,733	25,765	648	864	3.0
6200	Security and commodity brokers	4	6	1.4	4	10	44,000	48,000	217	446	0.4
6300	Insurance carriers	7	7	1.6	426	415	12,629	14,169	5,754	6,254	1.4
6400	Insurance agents, brokers, and service	38	38	2.0	106	108	17,849	15,778	1,775	1,667	0.8
6500	Real estate	93	94	4.5	531	588	13,868	14,619	8,506	8,969	4.7
6510	Real estate operators and lessors	44	44	5.6	169	177	10,935	12,090	2,108	2,276	3.9
6530	Real estate agents and managers	33	36	3.8	269	314	14,022	15,312	4,242	4,921	4.6
6540	Title abstract offices	5	4	3.2	27	26	21,333	22,462	875	653	6.4
6550	Subdividers and developers	10	9	5.3	66	67	17,697	15,761	1,268	1,092	7.6
6700	Holding and other investment offices	5	5	1.9	62	66	24,968	27,455	1,782	1,956	1.6

Source: County Business Patterns, 1994/95, CBP-94/95, U.S. Department of Commerce, Washington, D.C., November 1997. SIC categories for which data were suppressed or not available for both 1994 and 1995 are *not* displayed. The employment columns represent mid-March employment in the year. Pay per employee is calculated by dividing 1st Quarter payroll, annualized, by mid-March employment. The columns headed "% State" show the county's percentage of the state total for the SIC in 1995; for example, 1.4% for SIC 6000 means that the county had 1.4 percent of the state's total establishments (or payroll) in SIC 6000 in 1995. A dash (-) is used to indicate that data are not available or cannot be calculated; *nec* means not elsewhere classified.

KENTUCKY

SIC	Industry	No. Establishments			Employment		Pay / Employee		Annual Payroll ($ 000)		
		1994	1995	% State	1994	1995	1994	1995	1994	1995	% State
ADAIR, KY											
60 –	**Finance, insurance, and real estate**	21	21	0.3	97	104	17,237	18,038	1,937	2,089	0.1
6000	Depository institutions	7	7	0.4	68	70	19,706	20,114	1,500	1,586	0.3
6400	Insurance agents, brokers, and service	5	5	0.3	13	12	14,154	23,000	194	253	0.1
6500	Real estate	6	6	0.3	9	15	7,556	7,467	156	159	0.1
ALLEN, KY											
60 –	**Finance, insurance, and real estate**	13	13	0.2	114	112	23,684	28,464	2,747	3,045	0.2
6400	Insurance agents, brokers, and service	5	5	0.3	25	21	41,600	56,190	992	1,021	0.4
ANDERSON, KY											
60 –	**Finance, insurance, and real estate**	14	15	0.2	94	99	29,702	29,697	2,818	3,012	0.2
6000	Depository institutions	3	3	0.2	62	70	27,742	27,314	1,757	1,814	0.3
BALLARD, KY											
60 –	**Finance, insurance, and real estate**	12	12	0.2	80	88	20,200	20,136	1,693	1,788	0.1
6000	Depository institutions	6	6	0.4	57	61	23,088	22,492	1,365	1,459	0.2
BARREN, KY											
60 –	**Finance, insurance, and real estate**	61	55	0.8	350	313	19,086	20,562	6,737	7,044	0.4
6000	Depository institutions	15	15	1.0	215	192	18,586	21,021	4,211	4,356	0.7
6020	Commercial banks	12	12	1.0	203	180	18,739	21,378	4,026	4,142	0.8
6100	Nondepository institutions	4	5	0.8	20	22	19,600	24,182	413	511	0.4
6400	Insurance agents, brokers, and service	13	13	0.8	48	51	19,167	19,294	1,031	1,105	0.5
6500	Real estate	22	17	0.7	35	37	13,143	10,486	371	469	0.3
6510	Real estate operators and lessors	10	9	0.8	20	21	15,800	7,619	196	157	0.2
6530	Real estate agents and managers	8	5	0.6	11	8	9,818	12,000	99	81	0.1
BATH, KY											
60 –	**Finance, insurance, and real estate**	17	17	0.2	77	85	21,818	20,376	1,551	1,622	0.1
6000	Depository institutions	6	6	0.4	55	61	22,182	20,918	1,122	1,175	0.2
6020	Commercial banks	6	6	0.5	55	61	22,182	20,918	1,122	1,175	0.2
BELL, KY											
60 –	**Finance, insurance, and real estate**	39	34	0.5	323	301	20,136	22,086	6,687	6,797	0.4
6000	Depository institutions	17	15	1.0	220	202	18,036	20,673	4,281	4,383	0.7
6300	Insurance carriers	3	3	0.6	54	55	30,222	30,182	1,515	1,553	0.4
6500	Real estate	6	5	0.2	19	18	11,368	10,444	227	210	0.1
BOONE, KY											
60 –	**Finance, insurance, and real estate**	128	141	2.0	708	830	23,898	23,788	18,226	20,898	1.2
6000	Depository institutions	33	36	2.3	335	360	21,528	21,633	7,329	7,984	1.3
6020	Commercial banks	28	31	2.5	315	341	22,019	22,123	7,005	7,709	1.4
6030	Savings institutions	5	5	3.1	20	19	13,800	12,842	324	275	0.6
6160	Mortgage bankers and brokers	3	3	2.0	28	27	13,714	12,000	281	447	1.0
6300	Insurance carriers	14	17	3.3	64	85	38,438	41,741	2,726	3,685	1.0
6400	Insurance agents, brokers, and service	22	26	1.5	89	98	31,865	33,592	3,221	3,357	1.4
6500	Real estate	44	48	2.1	141	169	18,099	19,834	3,125	3,828	2.3

Source: County Business Patterns, 1994/95, CBP-94/95, U.S. Department of Commerce, Washington, D.C., November 1997. SIC categories for which data were suppressed or not available for both 1994 and 1995 are *not* displayed. The employment columns represent mid-March employment in the year. Pay per employee is calculated by dividing 1st Quarter payroll, annualized, by mid-March employment. The columns headed "% State" show the county's percentage of the state total for the SIC in 1995; for example, 1.4% for SIC 6000 means that the county had 1.4 percent of the state's total establishments (or payroll) in SIC 6000 in 1995. A dash (-) is used to indicate that data are not available or cannot be calculated; *nec* means not elsewhere classified.

Continued on next page.

SIC	Industry	No. Establishments			Employment		Pay / Employee		Annual Payroll ($ 000)		
		1994	1995	% State	1994	1995	1994	1995	1994	1995	% State
BOONE, KY - [continued]											
6510	Real estate operators and lessors	22	26	2.4	78	85	13,795	16,941	1,254	1,434	2.1
6530	Real estate agents and managers	15	15	1.7	59	75	23,525	22,720	1,604	2,069	2.8
6550	Subdividers and developers	6	5	2.0	4	8	22,000	25,000	264	315	1.4
BOURBON, KY											
60 –	**Finance, insurance, and real estate**	28	32	0.4	145	177	18,483	18,689	3,197	4,034	0.2
6100	Nondepository institutions	5	6	0.9	12	15	18,000	19,467	278	328	0.2
BOYD, KY											
60 –	**Finance, insurance, and real estate**	122	114	1.6	899	771	22,363	24,410	20,184	19,220	1.1
6000	Depository institutions	33	32	2.0	505	465	20,634	22,770	9,974	10,490	1.7
6020	Commercial banks	20	19	1.6	407	366	20,059	22,251	7,472	7,791	1.5
6030	Savings institutions	6	6	3.7	54	55	24,444	26,109	1,496	1,620	3.6
6060	Credit unions	7	7	4.4	44	44	21,273	22,909	1,006	1,079	4.0
6100	Nondepository institutions	6	9	1.4	61	36	19,148	20,222	896	818	0.6
6400	Insurance agents, brokers, and service	23	22	1.3	86	89	32,233	34,831	3,056	3,159	1.3
6500	Real estate	45	39	1.7	151	96	8,238	12,833	1,458	1,394	0.8
6510	Real estate operators and lessors	21	17	1.6	73	25	5,260	12,640	388	403	0.6
6530	Real estate agents and managers	17	16	1.8	42	42	11,905	14,190	631	653	0.9
6550	Subdividers and developers	7	6	2.4	36	29	10,000	11,034	439	338	1.6
BOYLE, KY											
60 –	**Finance, insurance, and real estate**	54	54	0.7	368	386	24,924	25,523	9,647	10,194	0.6
6000	Depository institutions	14	14	0.9	210	207	25,543	24,657	4,829	5,036	0.8
6020	Commercial banks	10	10	0.8	189	184	25,608	24,913	4,302	4,477	0.8
6100	Nondepository institutions	6	8	1.2	25	33	24,320	26,545	698	859	0.7
6400	Insurance agents, brokers, and service	16	16	0.9	39	37	15,487	18,378	777	797	0.3
6500	Real estate	14	12	0.5	35	34	12,571	12,706	498	483	0.3
6510	Real estate operators and lessors	4	3	0.3	12	12	14,333	12,000	170	146	0.2
6530	Real estate agents and managers	6	5	0.6	10	9	15,200	16,444	162	153	0.2
BRACKEN, KY											
60 –	**Finance, insurance, and real estate**	8	7	0.1	49	39	20,000	18,359	827	800	0.0
6400	Insurance agents, brokers, and service	3	3	0.2	5	5	9,600	10,400	62	60	0.0
BREATHITT, KY											
60 –	**Finance, insurance, and real estate**	12	13	0.2	129	181	22,295	15,823	3,214	3,186	0.2
6500	Real estate	3	3	0.1	7	3	6,857	13,333	50	30	0.0
BRECKINRIDGE, KY											
60 –	**Finance, insurance, and real estate**	21	24	0.3	205	222	10,127	10,036	2,644	2,751	0.2
6000	Depository institutions	9	9	0.6	172	186	10,163	9,828	2,270	2,375	0.4
6500	Real estate	4	7	0.3	8	12	7,500	9,333	95	81	0.0
BULLITT, KY											
60 –	**Finance, insurance, and real estate**	55	59	0.8	278	286	17,856	17,846	5,492	5,619	0.3
6000	Depository institutions	6	4	0.3	169	151	18,201	19,258	3,442	3,324	0.5
6100	Nondepository institutions	3	4	0.6	8	9	19,000	21,778	164	203	0.2
6500	Real estate	29	32	1.4	68	88	15,824	13,909	1,108	1,218	0.7
6510	Real estate operators and lessors	10	12	1.1	21	42	11,429	10,095	254	471	0.7
6530	Real estate agents and managers	12	11	1.2	24	23	14,833	14,261	446	326	0.4
6550	Subdividers and developers	7	9	3.6	23	23	20,870	20,522	408	421	1.9
6553	Cemetery subdividers and developers	5	6	5.0	23	20	20,870	22,200	393	370	3.0
BUTLER, KY											
60 –	**Finance, insurance, and real estate**	15	16	0.2	83	93	17,735	17,419	1,621	1,720	0.1
6000	Depository institutions	6	7	0.4	67	66	15,403	16,545	1,075	1,219	0.2

Source: County Business Patterns, 1994/95, CBP-94/95, U.S. Department of Commerce, Washington, D.C., November 1997. SIC categories for which data were suppressed or not available for both 1994 and 1995 are not displayed. The employment columns represent mid-March employment in the year. Pay per employee is calculated by dividing 1st Quarter payroll, annualized, by mid-March employment. The columns headed "% State" show the county's percentage of the state total for the SIC in 1995; for example, 1.4% for SIC 6000 means that the county had 1.4 percent of the state's total establishments (or payroll) in SIC 6000 in 1995. A dash (-) is used to indicate that data are not available or cannot be calculated; nec means not elsewhere classified.

Continued on next page.

SIC	Industry	No. Establishments			Employment		Pay / Employee		Annual Payroll ($ 000)		
		1994	1995	% State	1994	1995	1994	1995	1994	1995	% State
BUTLER, KY - [continued]											
6020	Commercial banks	6	7	0.6	67	66	15,403	16,545	1,075	1,219	0.2
6400	Insurance agents, brokers, and service	3	3	0.2	11	9	15,636	20,889	203	197	0.1
6500	Real estate	6	6	0.3	5	18	53,600	18,889	343	304	0.2
CALDWELL, KY											
60 –	**Finance, insurance, and real estate**	18	19	0.3	144	140	19,694	21,771	3,181	3,087	0.2
6000	Depository institutions	5	5	0.3	98	97	20,000	22,268	2,292	2,274	0.4
6100	Nondepository institutions	5	5	0.8	19	19	22,947	21,263	408	395	0.3
6140	Personal credit institutions	5	5	1.2	19	19	22,947	21,263	408	395	0.8
6400	Insurance agents, brokers, and service	5	6	0.4	22	18	13,455	17,778	341	289	0.1
CALLOWAY, KY											
60 –	**Finance, insurance, and real estate**	62	62	0.9	361	378	20,698	22,042	7,699	7,873	0.4
6000	Depository institutions	13	12	0.8	218	224	21,505	25,089	4,733	4,737	0.8
6100	Nondepository institutions	3	5	0.8	15	17	21,867	24,941	318	410	0.3
6400	Insurance agents, brokers, and service	22	22	1.3	62	66	19,806	18,303	1,289	1,430	0.6
6500	Real estate	19	18	0.8	41	47	6,244	7,404	357	444	0.3
6510	Real estate operators and lessors	10	10	0.9	27	25	4,741	5,440	183	262	0.4
6530	Real estate agents and managers	6	5	0.6	9	16	9,333	9,750	115	151	0.2
6550	Subdividers and developers	3	3	1.2	5	6	8,800	9,333	59	31	0.1
CAMPBELL, KY											
60 –	**Finance, insurance, and real estate**	126	133	1.8	731	799	26,555	28,005	22,022	26,043	1.5
6000	Depository institutions	32	41	2.6	286	324	21,413	22,963	7,126	9,113	1.5
6300	Insurance carriers	9	8	1.6	68	59	30,882	37,424	2,441	2,451	0.7
6400	Insurance agents, brokers, and service	21	24	1.4	112	173	23,607	24,092	2,853	4,687	2.0
6500	Real estate	55	50	2.2	146	147	14,055	14,776	2,835	2,901	1.7
6510	Real estate operators and lessors	23	22	2.1	70	73	13,257	13,753	1,050	1,129	1.6
6530	Real estate agents and managers	24	19	2.1	51	44	14,745	15,273	1,263	1,207	1.6
6550	Subdividers and developers	5	6	2.4	24	27	15,167	17,778	479	534	2.5
CARTER, KY											
60 –	**Finance, insurance, and real estate**	31	30	0.4	198	191	16,566	17,885	3,541	3,821	0.2
6000	Depository institutions	8	8	0.5	136	131	18,059	19,115	2,684	2,828	0.5
6530	Real estate agents and managers	6	6	0.7	11	12	13,818	14,333	181	229	0.3
CASEY, KY											
60 –	**Finance, insurance, and real estate**	13	13	0.2	65	65	18,892	19,754	1,387	1,464	0.1
6000	Depository institutions	7	7	0.4	50	50	19,440	20,160	1,107	1,181	0.2
CHRISTIAN, KY											
60 –	**Finance, insurance, and real estate**	125	124	1.7	881	840	21,821	22,210	19,021	19,029	1.1
6000	Depository institutions	26	26	1.7	523	467	21,468	21,396	10,009	9,392	1.5
6020	Commercial banks	15	16	1.3	364	309	23,264	23,184	7,179	6,378	1.2
6100	Nondepository institutions	15	18	2.7	75	98	20,480	21,265	1,688	2,062	1.6
6300	Insurance carriers	6	4	0.8	66	64	27,333	25,125	2,059	1,881	0.5
6400	Insurance agents, brokers, and service	23	22	1.3	84	83	21,238	22,988	2,158	2,306	1.0
6500	Real estate	49	48	2.1	105	99	11,276	18,303	1,392	1,733	1.0
6510	Real estate operators and lessors	36	34	3.2	70	65	11,086	11,754	817	886	1.3
CLARK, KY											
60 –	**Finance, insurance, and real estate**	47	48	0.7	255	260	20,784	29,800	5,027	6,054	0.3
6000	Depository institutions	8	9	0.6	132	143	23,091	37,091	2,823	3,704	0.6
6400	Insurance agents, brokers, and service	10	12	0.7	30	31	9,067	11,613	307	398	0.2

Source: County Business Patterns, 1994/95, CBP-94/95, U.S. Department of Commerce, Washington, D.C., November 1997. SIC categories for which data were suppressed or not available for both 1994 and 1995 are *not* displayed. The employment columns represent mid-March employment in the year. Pay per employee is calculated by dividing 1st Quarter payroll, annualized, by mid-March employment. The columns headed "% State" show the county's percentage of the state total for the SIC in 1995; for example, 1.4% for SIC 6000 means that the county had 1.4 percent of the state's total establishments (or payroll) in SIC 6000 in 1995. A dash (-) is used to indicate that data are not available or cannot be calculated; *nec* means not elsewhere classified.

Continued on next page.

SIC	Industry	No. Establishments			Employment		Pay / Employee		Annual Payroll ($ 000)		
		1994	1995	% State	1994	1995	1994	1995	1994	1995	% State
CLARK, KY - [continued]											
6500	Real estate	20	16	0.7	49	32	9,061	11,375	440	380	0.2
6510	Real estate operators and lessors	10	6	0.6	21	10	9,524	8,800	153	106	0.2
6530	Real estate agents and managers	7	7	0.8	13	12	10,769	13,667	155	162	0.2
CLAY, KY											
60 –	**Finance, insurance, and real estate**	17	21	0.3	153	153	15,529	18,275	2,789	2,967	0.2
6100	Nondepository institutions	3	4	0.6	27	29	15,704	14,897	523	449	0.3
6140	Personal credit institutions	3	4	0.9	27	29	15,704	14,897	523	449	0.9
6400	Insurance agents, brokers, and service	4	5	0.3	11	11	11,636	18,182	171	237	0.1
6500	Real estate	5	7	0.3	12	11	4,333	5,818	62	85	0.1
CLINTON, KY											
60 –	**Finance, insurance, and real estate**	10	10	0.1	58	61	18,138	18,426	1,152	1,276	0.1
6400	Insurance agents, brokers, and service	6	6	0.4	16	17	22,750	19,294	390	408	0.2
CRITTENDEN, KY											
60 –	**Finance, insurance, and real estate**	14	15	0.2	65	66	16,554	17,273	1,157	1,248	0.1
6500	Real estate	4	5	0.2	5	6	5,600	4,667	36	36	0.0
CUMBERLAND, KY											
60 –	**Finance, insurance, and real estate**	10	11	0.2	59	67	19,458	20,000	1,207	1,330	0.1
6400	Insurance agents, brokers, and service	3	3	0.2	6	6	16,000	18,000	106	107	0.0
DAVIESS, KY											
60 –	**Finance, insurance, and real estate**	199	200	2.8	2,093	1,798	25,047	24,409	48,310	41,573	2.3
6000	Depository institutions	49	51	3.2	700	650	20,629	22,000	13,605	12,954	2.1
6020	Commercial banks	28	29	2.4	531	501	21,484	23,345	10,620	10,181	1.9
6100	Nondepository institutions	15	19	2.9	739	329	28,736	33,860	16,679	9,474	7.2
6200	Security and commodity brokers	7	7	2.6	27	31	72,148	57,419	2,143	2,156	1.8
6210	Security brokers and dealers	7	7	3.6	27	31	72,148	57,419	2,143	2,156	2.2
6300	Insurance carriers	21	21	4.1	208	184	33,038	33,152	6,557	6,225	1.7
6310	Life insurance	8	6	3.4	138	113	27,246	27,186	3,606	3,157	2.6
6400	Insurance agents, brokers, and service	43	40	2.4	147	158	19,837	22,633	3,445	3,611	1.5
6500	Real estate	58	56	2.4	257	411	16,389	13,528	4,941	5,770	3.4
6510	Real estate operators and lessors	34	33	3.1	154	142	15,818	15,718	2,440	2,316	3.4
6530	Real estate agents and managers	18	16	1.8	66	223	17,879	11,749	1,684	2,635	3.5
6550	Subdividers and developers	5	6	2.4	36	45	16,222	15,022	785	778	3.6
6700	Holding and other investment offices	6	6	3.1	15	35	53,333	40,914	940	1,383	1.0
EDMONSON, KY											
60 –	**Finance, insurance, and real estate**	6	6	0.1	55	52	14,836	16,077	931	965	0.1
ESTILL, KY											
60 –	**Finance, insurance, and real estate**	12	14	0.2	102	107	19,333	19,065	1,942	1,999	0.1
6000	Depository institutions	4	5	0.3	74	76	19,730	19,947	1,449	1,481	0.2
6500	Real estate	3	4	0.2	4	8	17,000	14,500	28	76	0.0
FAYETTE, KY											
60 –	**Finance, insurance, and real estate**	789	814	11.3	7,205	7,126	28,079	30,319	205,789	210,194	11.8
6000	Depository institutions	106	116	7.4	1,898	1,767	26,712	26,802	50,505	48,626	7.9
6020	Commercial banks	75	87	7.1	1,609	1,474	27,585	27,517	43,465	40,382	7.6
6060	Credit unions	15	16	10.0	169	179	20,047	20,693	3,616	4,210	15.8
6140	Personal credit institutions	31	37	8.7	178	205	24,764	36,917	4,856	6,117	12.1
6160	Mortgage bankers and brokers	29	30	20.3	128	157	33,750	34,624	4,434	5,714	12.5
6200	Security and commodity brokers	37	38	14.1	308	302	63,234	59,828	18,306	17,885	15.3
6210	Security brokers and dealers	27	26	13.5	269	262	63,420	59,924	15,449	14,954	15.4
6300	Insurance carriers	85	85	16.6	1,611	1,476	28,606	31,791	47,055	46,191	12.8
6310	Life insurance	25	24	13.6	754	512	25,316	29,656	19,850	11,968	9.9

Source: County Business Patterns, 1994/95, CBP-94/95, U.S. Department of Commerce, Washington, D.C., November 1997. SIC categories for which data were suppressed or not available for both 1994 and 1995 are not displayed. The employment columns represent mid-March employment in the year. Pay per employee is calculated by dividing 1st Quarter payroll, annualized, by mid-March employment. The columns headed "% State" show the county's percentage of the state total for the SIC in 1995; for example, 1.4% for SIC 6000 means that the county had 1.4 percent of the state's total establishments (or payroll) in SIC 6000 in 1995. A dash (-) is used to indicate that data are not available or cannot be calculated; nec means not elsewhere classified.

Continued on next page.

SIC	Industry	No. Establishments			Employment		Pay / Employee		Annual Payroll ($ 000)		
		1994	1995	% State	1994	1995	1994	1995	1994	1995	% State
BIENVILLE, LA - [continued]											
6400	Insurance agents, brokers, and service	7	7	0.3	32	33	22,375	26,909	781	892	0.3
6500	Real estate	6	6	0.2	7	9	7,429	7,556	52	71	0.0
6510	Real estate operators and lessors	3	3	0.2	3	4	9,333	8,000	28	37	0.0
BOSSIER, LA											
60 –	**Finance, insurance, and real estate**	131	142	1.5	1,086	1,146	20,435	21,134	22,931	24,813	1.1
6000	Depository institutions	27	26	1.5	412	464	24,553	25,121	10,382	11,360	1.6
6100	Nondepository institutions	20	22	1.7	66	77	25,455	20,675	1,515	1,703	1.0
6140	Personal credit institutions	15	16	1.7	48	59	18,500	19,458	917	1,250	1.3
6160	Mortgage bankers and brokers	4	5	2.3	15	13	51,467	32,308	574	423	0.7
6400	Insurance agents, brokers, and service	24	30	1.4	129	138	17,395	19,739	2,398	2,924	0.9
6500	Real estate	41	44	1.6	190	217	16,526	15,668	3,295	3,788	1.6
6510	Real estate operators and lessors	21	19	1.4	130	132	11,785	11,970	1,755	1,826	2.2
6530	Real estate agents and managers	17	20	1.9	50	70	20,560	18,343	965	1,277	1.1
CADDO, LA											
60 –	**Finance, insurance, and real estate**	638	667	7.2	5,263	5,416	24,920	26,677	123,779	142,331	6.5
6000	Depository institutions	108	111	6.2	1,567	1,653	26,512	28,007	35,555	40,050	5.6
6020	Commercial banks	69	71	5.6	1,277	1,373	28,608	29,637	30,045	33,934	5.5
6060	Credit unions	34	34	10.3	248	223	15,790	19,444	4,285	4,725	10.6
6100	Nondepository institutions	70	79	6.3	462	451	25,584	26,971	11,619	12,330	7.3
6140	Personal credit institutions	50	57	6.2	314	317	24,242	25,868	7,519	8,130	8.5
6200	Security and commodity brokers	28	32	9.7	184	204	52,413	43,373	8,812	8,983	5.8
6210	Security brokers and dealers	20	22	9.6	176	179	53,932	47,419	8,582	8,565	6.8
6280	Security and commodity services	8	10	10.5	8	25	19,000	14,400	230	418	1.5
6300	Insurance carriers	66	68	8.8	1,223	1,010	25,956	26,166	30,154	26,215	5.6
6310	Life insurance	39	39	12.7	1,036	826	24,205	24,736	24,035	19,433	10.2
6330	Fire, marine, and casualty insurance	16	16	4.4	89	76	48,135	44,737	3,668	3,767	1.9
6370	Pension, health, and welfare funds	4	4	13.8	68	79	19,706	17,975	1,513	1,888	44.1
6400	Insurance agents, brokers, and service	151	150	7.0	733	724	26,041	26,680	20,098	21,843	7.0
6500	Real estate	181	187	6.9	1,001	886	14,442	15,449	14,483	14,539	6.2
6510	Real estate operators and lessors	85	83	6.1	406	329	9,103	11,149	4,063	3,700	4.4
6530	Real estate agents and managers	64	73	7.1	441	459	15,873	16,654	7,259	7,851	6.8
6540	Title abstract offices	9	10	11.8	60	42	39,733	21,048	1,575	1,123	11.6
6550	Subdividers and developers	17	13	7.6	92	51	14,565	28,157	1,532	1,735	7.4
6700	Holding and other investment offices	34	40	13.6	93	488	30,710	36,352	3,058	18,371	17.1
CALCASIEU, LA											
60 –	**Finance, insurance, and real estate**	389	397	4.3	2,780	2,786	22,420	23,101	65,111	69,402	3.2
6000	Depository institutions	79	79	4.4	1,169	1,201	21,098	21,968	26,779	29,001	4.1
6020	Commercial banks	55	56	4.4	961	987	21,894	22,614	22,716	24,339	3.9
6140	Personal credit institutions	31	36	3.9	129	144	22,233	22,111	3,041	3,299	3.4
6160	Mortgage bankers and brokers	8	8	3.8	23	24	25,565	26,167	534	551	0.9
6200	Security and commodity brokers	14	16	4.9	79	86	75,392	59,023	5,215	4,882	3.2
6300	Insurance carriers	30	32	4.1	195	215	34,523	28,670	6,531	6,488	1.4
6310	Life insurance	7	6	2.0	122	110	28,066	27,382	3,373	3,044	1.6
6400	Insurance agents, brokers, and service	79	75	3.5	370	337	21,957	25,911	8,963	10,093	3.3
6500	Real estate	137	140	5.1	660	639	12,230	13,577	8,660	9,541	4.0
6510	Real estate operators and lessors	67	67	4.9	281	265	13,537	15,321	3,898	4,164	4.9
6530	Real estate agents and managers	54	55	5.4	233	241	12,584	13,112	3,224	3,583	3.1
6540	Title abstract offices	3	4	4.7	39	41	15,590	16,976	715	715	7.4
6550	Subdividers and developers	11	12	7.1	106	89	6,755	8,360	818	970	4.1
6552	Subdividers and developers, n.e.c.	6	5	5.9	11	12	14,545	13,333	218	197	1.6
6553	Cemetery subdividers and developers	5	5	7.1	95	75	5,853	7,467	600	739	7.1
6700	Holding and other investment offices	9	9	3.1	147	133	34,939	38,977	5,149	5,210	4.9

Source: County Business Patterns, 1994/95, CBP-94/95, U.S. Department of Commerce, Washington, D.C., November 1997. SIC categories for which data were suppressed or not available for both 1994 and 1995 are *not* displayed. The employment columns represent mid-March employment in the year. Pay per employee is calculated by dividing 1st Quarter payroll, annualized, by mid-March employment. The columns headed "% State" show the county's percentage of the state total for the SIC in 1995; for example, 1.4% for SIC 6000 means that the county had 1.4 percent of the state's total establishments (or payroll) in SIC 6000 in 1995. A dash (-) is used to indicate that data are not available or cannot be calculated; *nec* means not elsewhere classified.

Continued on next page.

SIC	Industry	No. Establishments			Employment		Pay / Employee		Annual Payroll ($ 000)		
		1994	1995	% State	1994	1995	1994	1995	1994	1995	% State
CALDWELL, LA - [continued]											
60 –	**Finance, insurance, and real estate**	13	13	0.1	89	96	18,607	18,333	1,893	2,039	0.1
6000	Depository institutions	4	4	0.2	68	74	19,412	19,189	1,527	1,660	0.2
CAMERON, LA											
60 –	**Finance, insurance, and real estate**	11	12	0.1	-	-	-	-	-	-	-
6400	Insurance agents, brokers, and service	3	3	0.1	7	8	11,429	11,000	75	78	0.0
CATAHOULA, LA											
60 –	**Finance, insurance, and real estate**	15	15	0.2	87	85	19,080	19,812	1,681	1,818	0.1
6000	Depository institutions	6	6	0.3	61	61	20,656	20,328	1,262	1,364	0.2
6020	Commercial banks	6	6	0.5	61	61	20,656	20,328	1,262	1,364	0.2
6400	Insurance agents, brokers, and service	4	4	0.2	11	10	14,182	16,000	158	161	0.1
CLAIBORNE, LA											
60 –	**Finance, insurance, and real estate**	20	20	0.2	129	135	15,876	16,948	2,444	3,144	0.1
6000	Depository institutions	5	5	0.3	79	83	17,063	17,976	1,642	2,286	0.3
6400	Insurance agents, brokers, and service	5	5	0.2	24	25	16,167	17,600	495	486	0.2
CONCORDIA, LA											
60 –	**Finance, insurance, and real estate**	20	23	0.2	172	179	19,907	21,006	3,953	4,209	0.2
6100	Nondepository institutions	5	6	0.5	11	13	16,000	21,538	188	305	0.2
6400	Insurance agents, brokers, and service	7	7	0.3	22	23	18,182	19,304	405	442	0.1
DE SOTO, LA											
60 –	**Finance, insurance, and real estate**	63	76	0.8	239	255	17,808	17,192	4,763	4,831	0.2
6000	Depository institutions	14	14	0.8	131	139	18,260	17,669	2,581	2,751	0.4
6100	Nondepository institutions	7	9	0.7	17	18	18,118	18,667	331	397	0.2
6400	Insurance agents, brokers, and service	11	8	0.4	17	19	15,765	15,579	268	273	0.1
6500	Real estate	25	40	1.5	52	55	16,231	12,873	1,080	831	0.4
6510	Real estate operators and lessors	19	33	2.4	16	25	9,250	10,240	199	297	0.4
6530	Real estate agents and managers	6	7	0.7	36	30	19,333	15,067	881	534	0.5
EAST BATON ROUGE, LA											
60 –	**Finance, insurance, and real estate**	1,200	1,239	13.3	13,370	13,316	27,190	29,425	359,402	382,417	17.5
6000	Depository institutions	183	186	10.5	3,834	3,822	27,292	28,397	95,690	100,987	14.1
6020	Commercial banks	138	137	10.8	3,189	3,160	28,696	29,976	82,419	86,578	14.0
6060	Credit unions	34	34	10.3	452	473	19,071	19,899	8,841	9,875	22.1
6100	Nondepository institutions	177	193	15.3	1,219	1,227	26,579	28,443	32,999	36,539	21.7
6140	Personal credit institutions	121	127	13.8	646	660	26,365	23,006	18,321	17,940	18.7
6150	Business credit institutions	9	13	19.7	31	37	27,355	33,622	1,012	1,371	16.1
6160	Mortgage bankers and brokers	36	37	17.4	525	453	25,531	35,823	12,285	15,511	26.4
6200	Security and commodity brokers	53	53	16.1	389	456	62,057	54,482	22,543	24,549	15.9
6210	Security brokers and dealers	30	30	13.1	310	320	67,084	61,838	18,673	19,111	15.2
6280	Security and commodity services	23	23	24.2	79	136	42,329	37,176	3,870	5,438	19.2
6300	Insurance carriers	116	114	14.7	2,980	2,997	31,906	34,613	91,944	97,906	20.8
6310	Life insurance	41	38	12.4	918	805	30,092	36,229	27,178	26,097	13.7
6320	Medical service and health insurance	14	13	27.1	1,368	1,541	29,994	31,406	39,741	45,929	78.9
6321	Accident and health insurance	7	6	26.1	32	27	30,875	43,556	1,085	1,238	22.5
6324	Hospital and medical service plans	7	7	28.0	1,336	1,514	29,973	31,189	38,656	44,691	84.7
6330	Fire, marine, and casualty insurance	52	53	14.6	555	535	39,186	41,839	21,110	21,909	10.8
6400	Insurance agents, brokers, and service	287	286	13.3	1,909	1,970	26,860	29,198	52,881	60,671	19.5
6500	Real estate	344	367	13.5	2,265	1,986	15,315	16,183	39,273	33,809	14.3
6510	Real estate operators and lessors	153	164	12.0	883	822	13,065	14,774	12,187	12,651	14.9
6530	Real estate agents and managers	159	161	15.7	1,112	862	17,529	17,893	22,150	14,783	12.9
6540	Title abstract offices	7	8	9.4	31	30	27,097	24,533	893	1,144	11.9
6550	Subdividers and developers	21	21	12.4	233	260	11,880	13,277	3,892	4,491	19.0
6552	Subdividers and developers, n.e.c.	15	13	15.3	95	104	13,684	14,269	2,141	2,309	18.9
6553	Cemetery subdividers and developers	4	4	5.7	138	150	10,638	12,587	1,653	1,918	18.3

Source: *County Business Patterns, 1994/95,* CBP-94/95, U.S. Department of Commerce, Washington, D.C., November 1997. SIC categories for which data were suppressed or not available for both 1994 and 1995 are *not* displayed. The employment columns represent mid-March employment in the year. Pay per employee is calculated by dividing 1st Quarter payroll, annualized, by mid-March employment. The columns headed "% State" show the county's percentage of the state total for the SIC in 1995; for example, 1.4% for SIC 6000 means that the county had 1.4 percent of the state's total establishments (or payroll) in SIC 6000 in 1995. A dash (-) is used to indicate that data are not available or cannot be calculated; *nec* means not elsewhere classified.

Continued on next page.

SIC	Industry	No. Establishments			Employment		Pay / Employee		Annual Payroll ($ 000)		
		1994	1995	% State	1994	1995	1994	1995	1994	1995	% State
EAST BATON ROUGE, LA - [continued]											
6700	Holding and other investment offices	33	34	11.5	289	350	26,311	28,549	10,058	11,543	10.8
6710	Holding offices	12	14	17.1	216	252	26,074	27,587	7,995	9,115	10.7
6730	Trusts	6	5	9.6	24	16	11,500	17,000	269	310	6.5
6790	Miscellaneous investing	14	12	8.6	49	47	34,612	48,000	1,780	1,771	11.0
EAST CARROLL, LA											
60 –	**Finance, insurance, and real estate**	14	14	0.2	108	66	17,370	22,848	1,626	1,564	0.1
6100	Nondepository institutions	4	5	0.4	7	9	14,857	13,333	99	138	0.1
EAST FELICIANA, LA											
60 –	**Finance, insurance, and real estate**	21	24	0.3	124	127	17,774	19,339	2,482	2,895	0.1
6000	Depository institutions	7	7	0.4	90	87	17,511	19,126	1,739	1,899	0.3
6400	Insurance agents, brokers, and service	7	8	0.4	19	19	15,789	19,158	317	333	0.1
EVANGELINE, LA											
60 –	**Finance, insurance, and real estate**	56	53	0.6	357	386	15,216	16,860	5,819	6,584	0.3
6000	Depository institutions	14	13	0.7	235	267	17,889	18,966	4,456	5,126	0.7
6020	Commercial banks	11	10	0.8	224	247	18,054	19,579	4,271	4,892	0.8
6400	Insurance agents, brokers, and service	16	16	0.7	35	35	10,514	10,971	399	390	0.1
6510	Real estate operators and lessors	10	10	0.7	27	29	7,556	7,448	245	251	0.3
FRANKLIN, LA											
60 –	**Finance, insurance, and real estate**	38	36	0.4	218	208	17,211	18,327	4,006	4,180	0.2
6000	Depository institutions	9	9	0.5	109	112	19,119	19,964	2,396	2,625	0.4
6510	Real estate operators and lessors	3	3	0.2	17	14	9,647	10,286	144	138	0.2
GRANT, LA											
60 –	**Finance, insurance, and real estate**	14	12	0.1	-	-	-	-	-	-	-
6400	Insurance agents, brokers, and service	3	3	0.1	4	4	13,000	14,000	53	55	0.0
6500	Real estate	5	4	0.1	4	4	10,000	20,000	41	72	0.0
IBERIA, LA											
60 –	**Finance, insurance, and real estate**	149	157	1.7	969	1,031	20,871	21,408	20,498	21,262	1.0
6000	Depository institutions	36	36	2.0	523	534	20,772	19,978	9,920	8,979	1.3
6060	Credit unions	6	6	1.8	10	12	8,000	7,333	81	86	0.2
6100	Nondepository institutions	27	26	2.1	81	101	19,802	21,426	1,846	2,573	1.5
6300	Insurance carriers	11	12	1.6	111	112	31,135	31,714	3,678	3,674	0.8
6400	Insurance agents, brokers, and service	33	34	1.6	135	151	17,393	21,616	3,177	3,875	1.2
6500	Real estate	38	43	1.6	95	106	13,305	12,566	1,272	1,381	0.6
6510	Real estate operators and lessors	22	23	1.7	55	60	12,218	13,533	725	825	1.0
6530	Real estate agents and managers	7	7	0.7	11	12	15,273	12,333	155	149	0.1
IBERVILLE, LA											
60 –	**Finance, insurance, and real estate**	52	47	0.5	307	302	20,104	22,344	6,304	7,038	0.3
6000	Depository institutions	17	17	1.0	222	227	21,586	23,066	4,853	5,497	0.8
6020	Commercial banks	12	12	0.9	188	196	21,894	23,653	4,247	4,845	0.8
6100	Nondepository institutions	11	10	0.8	35	31	15,886	16,516	596	568	0.3
6400	Insurance agents, brokers, and service	8	5	0.2	19	17	11,789	25,412	220	269	0.1
6500	Real estate	10	10	0.4	23	19	9,739	13,895	291	361	0.2
6510	Real estate operators and lessors	7	6	0.4	18	14	8,444	14,286	226	284	0.3
6530	Real estate agents and managers	3	3	0.3	5	5	14,400	12,800	65	76	0.1
JACKSON, LA											
60 –	**Finance, insurance, and real estate**	26	29	0.3	145	161	17,297	16,994	2,779	3,046	0.1

Source: County Business Patterns, 1994/95, CBP-94/95, U.S. Department of Commerce, Washington, D.C., November 1997. SIC categories for which data were suppressed or not available for both 1994 and 1995 are not displayed. The employment columns represent mid-March employment in the year. Pay per employee is calculated by dividing 1st Quarter payroll, annualized, by mid-March employment. The columns headed "% State" show the county's percentage of the state total for the SIC in 1995; for example, 1.4% for SIC 6000 means that the county had 1.4 percent of the state's total establishments (or payroll) in SIC 6000 in 1995. A dash (-) is used to indicate that data are not available or cannot be calculated; nec means not elsewhere classified.

Continued on next page.

SIC	Industry	No. Establishments			Employment		Pay / Employee		Annual Payroll ($ 000)		
		1994	1995	% State	1994	1995	1994	1995	1994	1995	% State
JACKSON, LA - [continued]											
6000	Depository institutions	6	6	0.3	76	76	20,211	20,579	1,793	1,863	0.3
6400	Insurance agents, brokers, and service	6	6	0.3	33	39	11,758	11,795	411	391	0.1
6500	Real estate	7	8	0.3	8	17	7,500	8,000	66	140	0.1
JEFFERSON, LA											
60 –	**Finance, insurance, and real estate**	1,255	1,288	13.8	11,313	11,564	26,804	28,627	307,534	341,003	15.6
6000	Depository institutions	160	160	9.0	2,545	2,715	22,584	23,194	57,571	62,836	8.8
6020	Commercial banks	88	92	7.2	2,027	2,185	23,256	23,995	46,668	51,887	8.4
6030	Savings institutions	27	22	18.8	319	278	23,235	22,158	7,486	6,317	16.6
6060	Credit unions	33	33	10.0	163	180	15,411	19,622	2,804	3,663	8.2
6090	Functions closely related to banking	12	13	23.2	36	72	11,444	11,833	613	969	-
6100	Nondepository institutions	125	139	11.0	823	895	27,431	28,693	22,770	25,952	15.4
6140	Personal credit institutions	65	73	8.0	497	544	23,581	26,096	11,917	14,382	15.0
6150	Business credit institutions	11	12	18.2	34	34	30,588	30,235	1,182	1,096	12.9
6160	Mortgage bankers and brokers	49	52	24.4	292	317	33,616	32,984	9,671	10,452	17.8
6210	Security brokers and dealers	22	18	7.9	176	169	43,091	56,095	7,474	8,223	6.5
6300	Insurance carriers	145	153	19.8	2,304	2,457	37,906	39,759	81,829	93,619	19.9
6310	Life insurance	48	48	15.7	961	902	33,765	36,084	32,576	30,473	16.0
6320	Medical service and health insurance	9	10	20.8	102	198	35,137	26,121	3,691	5,819	10.0
6330	Fire, marine, and casualty insurance	76	84	23.2	1,115	1,226	41,543	44,587	40,675	51,765	25.4
6400	Insurance agents, brokers, and service	367	368	17.1	2,123	2,046	27,282	30,274	61,652	62,860	20.3
6500	Real estate	369	387	14.2	2,844	2,834	17,653	18,114	55,135	54,539	23.1
6510	Real estate operators and lessors	171	176	12.9	872	842	16,050	17,986	15,253	15,450	18.2
6530	Real estate agents and managers	161	162	15.8	1,551	1,568	17,656	18,344	29,666	30,521	26.6
6540	Title abstract offices	16	19	22.4	236	122	19,356	20,000	4,475	3,020	31.3
6550	Subdividers and developers	12	12	7.1	180	199	22,844	20,040	5,006	4,175	17.7
6552	Subdividers and developers, n.e.c.	8	8	9.4	60	66	29,733	22,970	1,982	1,649	13.5
6553	Cemetery subdividers and developers	4	4	5.7	120	133	19,400	18,586	3,024	2,526	24.2
6700	Holding and other investment offices	44	43	14.6	434	391	41,880	50,660	19,245	31,137	29.0
6710	Holding offices	10	11	13.4	287	282	50,648	60,142	15,603	27,828	32.7
6730	Trusts	6	6	11.5	28	8	17,286	42,500	276	271	5.7
6790	Miscellaneous investing	25	23	16.5	117	99	26,632	24,970	3,323	3,000	18.7
6794	Patent owners and lessors	12	9	64.3	73	50	21,041	17,520	1,649	1,134	90.0
JEFFERSON DAVIS, LA											
60 –	**Finance, insurance, and real estate**	57	59	0.6	319	328	18,583	19,390	5,807	6,473	0.3
6000	Depository institutions	18	20	1.1	190	202	19,179	21,010	3,906	4,472	0.6
6020	Commercial banks	15	17	1.3	182	195	19,648	21,436	3,832	4,392	0.7
6060	Credit unions	3	3	0.9	8	7	8,500	9,143	74	80	0.2
6100	Nondepository institutions	10	11	0.9	29	35	25,103	21,714	540	651	0.4
6400	Insurance agents, brokers, and service	13	12	0.6	55	51	14,909	16,941	783	804	0.3
6500	Real estate	12	11	0.4	32	26	7,625	8,308	254	229	0.1
LAFAYETTE, LA											
60 –	**Finance, insurance, and real estate**	524	522	5.6	3,599	3,614	27,113	26,744	94,533	97,135	4.5
6000	Depository institutions	79	81	4.6	1,099	1,062	24,673	24,746	25,111	25,781	3.6
6020	Commercial banks	54	55	4.3	842	796	25,777	26,015	19,798	20,011	3.2
6030	Savings institutions	7	8	6.8	165	175	24,703	23,291	3,918	4,262	11.2
6060	Credit unions	14	14	4.2	59	59	17,153	19,661	1,089	1,174	2.6
6090	Functions closely related to banking	4	4	7.1	33	32	9,818	10,500	306	334	-
6100	Nondepository institutions	58	63	5.0	332	317	23,916	24,252	7,988	8,366	5.0
6140	Personal credit institutions	41	45	4.9	229	237	23,581	24,641	5,525	5,986	6.2
6150	Business credit institutions	4	4	6.1	61	35	23,344	19,086	1,341	956	11.3
6200	Security and commodity brokers	32	32	9.7	175	179	62,103	59,061	9,843	10,025	6.5
6210	Security brokers and dealers	29	26	11.4	171	167	62,807	61,198	9,675	9,575	7.6
6280	Security and commodity services	3	6	6.3	4	12	32,000	29,333	168	450	1.6
6300	Insurance carriers	50	53	6.9	570	578	35,179	34,713	20,786	20,768	4.4
6310	Life insurance	19	20	6.5	400	393	34,930	34,860	14,364	14,037	7.4

Source: County Business Patterns, 1994/95, CBP-94/95, U.S. Department of Commerce, Washington, D.C., November 1997. SIC categories for which data were suppressed or not available for both 1994 and 1995 are not displayed. The employment columns represent mid-March employment in the year. Pay per employee is calculated by dividing 1st Quarter payroll, annualized, by mid-March employment. The columns headed "% State" show the county's percentage of the state total for the SIC in 1995; for example, 1.4% for SIC 6000 means that the county had 1.4 percent of the state's total establishments (or payroll) in SIC 6000 in 1995. A dash (-) is used to indicate that data are not available or cannot be calculated; nec means not elsewhere classified.

Continued on next page.

SIC	Industry	No. Establishments			Employment		Pay / Employee		Annual Payroll ($ 000)		
		1994	1995	% State	1994	1995	1994	1995	1994	1995	% State
LAFAYETTE, LA - [continued]											
6320	Medical service and health insurance	8	8	16.7	46	38	30,696	36,632	1,576	1,435	2.5
6330	Fire, marine, and casualty insurance	18	20	5.5	109	126	40,404	36,317	4,456	4,846	2.4
6370	Pension, health, and welfare funds	3	3	10.3	12	19	21,333	18,947	364	420	9.8
6400	Insurance agents, brokers, and service	136	126	5.9	501	502	28,567	31,968	13,783	15,787	5.1
6500	Real estate	155	155	5.7	826	890	12,508	12,544	11,676	12,671	5.4
6510	Real estate operators and lessors	85	89	6.5	544	597	9,581	9,615	6,111	7,042	8.3
6530	Real estate agents and managers	63	56	5.5	261	254	18,238	19,354	5,168	5,081	4.4
6540	Title abstract offices	3	3	3.5	6	5	26,667	20,800	146	90	0.9
6550	Subdividers and developers	3	4	2.4	15	20	13,333	12,000	243	282	1.2
6700	Holding and other investment offices	14	12	4.1	96	86	72,500	56,233	5,346	3,737	3.5
LAFOURCHE, LA											
60 –	**Finance, insurance, and real estate**	148	157	1.7	877	972	20,087	20,852	17,475	19,801	0.9
6000	Depository institutions	48	51	2.9	477	546	17,987	19,136	8,701	10,153	1.4
6100	Nondepository institutions	21	22	1.7	87	88	23,356	24,000	1,899	2,080	1.2
6140	Personal credit institutions	19	19	2.1	80	81	23,350	23,654	1,706	1,827	1.9
6300	Insurance carriers	7	8	1.0	81	82	30,321	31,610	2,450	2,570	0.5
6400	Insurance agents, brokers, and service	40	39	1.8	150	162	23,733	25,457	3,386	3,788	1.2
6500	Real estate	26	30	1.1	67	79	7,940	7,899	582	725	0.3
6530	Real estate agents and managers	9	10	1.0	33	37	4,242	3,892	145	147	0.1
LA SALLE, LA											
60 –	**Finance, insurance, and real estate**	21	21	0.2	152	152	16,447	17,316	2,673	2,899	0.1
6000	Depository institutions	8	8	0.4	93	93	15,269	16,129	1,547	1,767	0.2
6020	Commercial banks	8	8	0.6	93	93	15,269	16,129	1,547	1,767	0.3
6400	Insurance agents, brokers, and service	7	6	0.3	28	28	17,000	20,429	562	579	0.2
LINCOLN, LA											
60 –	**Finance, insurance, and real estate**	111	113	1.2	960	899	20,767	22,278	20,004	21,324	1.0
6000	Depository institutions	24	23	1.3	295	265	21,871	23,653	6,355	6,694	0.9
6020	Commercial banks	19	18	1.4	247	207	22,089	24,000	5,230	5,193	0.8
6140	Personal credit institutions	11	12	1.3	33	41	18,667	18,829	661	882	0.9
6300	Insurance carriers	8	9	1.2	257	253	24,872	27,494	6,561	7,038	1.5
6400	Insurance agents, brokers, and service	26	26	1.2	142	132	19,042	19,606	2,677	2,576	0.8
6500	Real estate	30	32	1.2	113	121	10,973	12,264	1,410	1,430	0.6
6510	Real estate operators and lessors	14	15	1.1	90	85	10,533	12,800	1,060	1,012	1.2
LIVINGSTON, LA											
60 –	**Finance, insurance, and real estate**	63	77	0.8	402	410	24,209	21,649	8,034	8,209	0.4
6000	Depository institutions	15	17	1.0	276	261	23,551	24,061	5,366	5,543	0.8
6100	Nondepository institutions	10	14	1.1	37	39	45,297	21,538	1,107	1,041	0.6
6140	Personal credit institutions	10	12	1.3	37	38	45,297	22,000	1,107	1,028	1.1
6400	Insurance agents, brokers, and service	19	21	1.0	52	55	12,462	13,891	743	790	0.3
6500	Real estate	14	19	0.7	24	40	11,167	8,300	284	288	0.1
6510	Real estate operators and lessors	4	6	0.4	2	7	10,000	6,857	46	60	0.1
6530	Real estate agents and managers	7	8	0.8	19	28	12,000	9,286	215	172	0.1
6550	Subdividers and developers	3	4	2.4	3	3	6,667	6,667	23	49	0.2
MADISON, LA											
60 –	**Finance, insurance, and real estate**	25	24	0.3	103	105	19,029	17,676	2,017	1,936	0.1
6000	Depository institutions	4	4	0.2	62	55	21,548	21,236	1,381	1,240	0.2
6020	Commercial banks	4	4	0.3	62	55	21,548	21,236	1,381	1,240	0.2
6100	Nondepository institutions	5	4	0.3	15	12	24,267	24,667	364	281	0.2
MOREHOUSE, LA											
60 –	**Finance, insurance, and real estate**	59	55	0.6	217	263	23,226	22,464	5,450	6,060	0.3
6000	Depository institutions	13	13	0.7	126	146	26,508	26,137	3,529	3,748	0.5
6100	Nondepository institutions	16	15	1.2	36	55	16,333	16,509	637	964	0.6

Source: County Business Patterns, 1994/95, CBP-94/95, U.S. Department of Commerce, Washington, D.C., November 1997. SIC categories for which data were suppressed or not available for both 1994 and 1995 are not displayed. The employment columns represent mid-March employment in the year. Pay per employee is calculated by dividing 1st Quarter payroll, annualized, by mid-March employment. The columns headed "% State" show the county's percentage of the state total for the SIC in 1995; for example, 1.4% for SIC 6000 means that the county had 1.4 percent of the state's total establishments (or payroll) in SIC 6000 in 1995. A dash (-) is used to indicate that data are not available or cannot be calculated; nec means not elsewhere classified.

Continued on next page.

SIC	Industry	No. Establishments			Employment		Pay / Employee		Annual Payroll ($ 000)		
		1994	1995	% State	1994	1995	1994	1995	1994	1995	% State
MOREHOUSE, LA - [continued]											
6140	Personal credit institutions	13	13	1.4	35	51	15,657	16,863	588	912	1.0
6400	Insurance agents, brokers, and service	13	10	0.5	20	18	13,200	14,222	325	319	0.1
6530	Real estate agents and managers	3	3	0.3	2	3	8,000	9,333	22	25	0.0
NATCHITOCHES, LA											
60 –	**Finance, insurance, and real estate**	85	84	0.9	393	436	19,664	18,954	8,727	9,057	0.4
6000	Depository institutions	15	15	0.8	191	228	22,429	20,667	4,509	4,904	0.7
6020	Commercial banks	12	12	0.9	158	193	23,291	20,788	3,821	4,116	0.7
6100	Nondepository institutions	15	16	1.3	43	46	13,581	15,826	731	770	0.5
6500	Real estate	33	33	1.2	57	77	8,702	7,221	539	528	0.2
6510	Real estate operators and lessors	21	22	1.6	38	61	8,526	6,689	369	407	0.5
6530	Real estate agents and managers	9	8	0.8	16	13	9,750	10,154	153	104	0.1
ORLEANS, LA											
60 –	**Finance, insurance, and real estate**	1,061	1,062	11.4	14,004	14,184	31,524	33,147	426,848	459,778	21.1
6000	Depository institutions	201	197	11.1	5,354	5,446	30,258	33,723	153,538	174,122	24.4
6020	Commercial banks	97	100	7.8	4,339	4,533	31,945	35,741	128,231	152,548	24.7
6030	Savings institutions	25	20	17.1	360	272	24,300	23,603	10,404	6,897	18.1
6060	Credit unions	60	58	17.6	347	340	18,075	19,047	6,635	6,582	14.8
6140	Personal credit institutions	42	41	4.5	208	201	20,404	21,413	4,701	5,378	5.6
6160	Mortgage bankers and brokers	18	23	10.8	277	259	35,856	26,008	8,121	8,231	14.0
6200	Security and commodity brokers	52	50	15.2	1,282	1,167	69,214	69,484	78,832	79,579	51.5
6210	Security brokers and dealers	34	34	14.8	904	852	72,195	73,643	57,919	59,639	47.4
6300	Insurance carriers	96	97	12.5	2,204	2,012	33,973	36,940	73,014	67,704	14.4
6310	Life insurance	45	47	15.4	1,459	1,469	34,646	37,214	47,826	49,213	25.9
6330	Fire, marine, and casualty insurance	31	33	9.1	326	258	41,325	43,240	12,243	11,117	5.5
6360	Title insurance	3	4	26.7	156	96	31,615	34,083	4,759	2,776	55.1
6400	Insurance agents, brokers, and service	192	191	8.9	1,212	1,327	31,343	36,169	40,847	47,876	15.4
6500	Real estate	389	387	14.2	3,129	3,304	15,945	16,707	53,726	60,373	25.6
6510	Real estate operators and lessors	176	171	12.6	1,135	1,142	13,008	14,116	15,684	16,487	19.4
6530	Real estate agents and managers	170	171	16.7	1,639	1,862	17,764	17,991	30,484	36,244	31.6
6540	Title abstract offices	5	5	5.9	83	24	23,711	18,333	1,967	1,253	13.0
6550	Subdividers and developers	28	29	17.1	269	249	14,781	19,149	5,475	6,026	25.5
6552	Subdividers and developers, n.e.c.	17	17	20.0	43	75	25,116	24,907	2,244	2,735	22.4
6553	Cemetery subdividers and developers	11	12	17.1	226	174	12,814	16,667	3,231	3,291	31.5
6710	Holding offices	14	18	22.0	122	173	46,230	56,902	5,999	7,940	9.3
6730	Trusts	11	12	23.1	30	114	24,400	14,526	1,138	2,237	47.1
6732	Educational, religious, etc. trusts	6	6	22.2	21	105	22,857	9,410	567	1,536	60.9
6733	Trusts, n.e.c.	5	6	24.0	9	9	28,000	74,222	571	701	31.5
6790	Miscellaneous investing	30	30	21.6	134	102	47,313	36,745	5,764	4,207	26.2
6799	Investors, n.e.c.	16	16	23.5	91	59	57,275	45,356	4,115	2,748	28.7
OUACHITA, LA											
60 –	**Finance, insurance, and real estate**	429	436	4.7	5,768	5,345	27,693	31,374	151,172	159,616	7.3
6000	Depository institutions	77	73	4.1	1,126	1,109	25,854	25,446	29,459	29,408	4.1
6020	Commercial banks	60	57	4.5	1,029	1,005	26,422	26,018	27,402	27,319	4.4
6100	Nondepository institutions	72	74	5.9	826	966	22,557	26,675	14,823	19,853	11.8
6140	Personal credit institutions	52	57	6.2	193	238	18,031	19,193	3,938	4,903	5.1
6200	Security and commodity brokers	15	18	5.5	97	89	63,299	58,966	4,187	4,171	2.7
6210	Security brokers and dealers	10	12	5.2	84	64	69,476	75,500	3,845	3,718	3.0
6300	Insurance carriers	31	31	4.0	2,862	2,336	31,992	40,087	88,239	90,186	19.2
6400	Insurance agents, brokers, and service	86	86	4.0	317	293	23,634	24,000	7,076	6,955	2.2
6500	Real estate	141	146	5.4	522	528	12,123	13,955	6,983	8,084	3.4
6510	Real estate operators and lessors	95	90	6.6	309	294	13,320	14,544	4,213	4,561	5.4
6530	Real estate agents and managers	37	43	4.2	176	181	10,045	13,657	2,153	2,836	2.5

Source: County Business Patterns, 1994/95, CBP-94/95, U.S. Department of Commerce, Washington, D.C., November 1997. SIC categories for which data were suppressed or not available for both 1994 and 1995 are *not* displayed. The employment columns represent mid-March employment in the year. Pay per employee is calculated by dividing 1st Quarter payroll, annualized, by mid-March employment. The columns headed "% State" show the county's percentage of the state total for the SIC in 1995; for example, 1.4% for SIC 6000 means that the county had 1.4 percent of the state's total establishments (or payroll) in SIC 6000 in 1995. A dash (-) is used to indicate that data are not available or cannot be calculated; *nec* means not elsewhere classified.

Continued on next page.

SIC	Industry	No. Establishments			Employment		Pay / Employee		Annual Payroll ($ 000)		
		1994	1995	% State	1994	1995	1994	1995	1994	1995	% State
OUACHITA, LA - [continued]											
6550	Subdividers and developers	7	7	4.1	37	47	12,000	11,319	599	588	2.5
6552	Subdividers and developers, n.e.c.	4	3	3.5	20	28	11,400	11,143	373	347	2.8
6553	Cemetery subdividers and developers	3	3	4.3	17	19	12,706	11,579	226	235	2.2
PLAQUEMINES, LA											
60 –	**Finance, insurance, and real estate**	44	44	0.5	271	280	20,812	21,214	5,969	6,615	0.3
6000	Depository institutions	10	10	0.6	134	128	19,493	21,313	2,798	2,834	0.4
6100	Nondepository institutions	5	5	0.4	21	24	11,048	12,167	254	309	0.2
6140	Personal credit institutions	5	5	0.5	21	24	11,048	12,167	254	309	0.3
6400	Insurance agents, brokers, and service	9	8	0.4	30	28	18,133	20,000	714	656	0.2
6500	Real estate	15	17	0.6	30	58	12,533	14,552	443	1,113	0.5
6530	Real estate agents and managers	5	4	0.4	12	10	13,667	13,600	166	134	0.1
POINTE COUPEE, LA											
60 –	**Finance, insurance, and real estate**	37	38	0.4	195	179	20,185	20,760	3,987	3,800	0.2
6000	Depository institutions	11	11	0.6	121	118	25,554	24,271	3,021	2,977	0.4
6400	Insurance agents, brokers, and service	9	9	0.4	26	26	17,231	16,769	467	442	0.1
6500	Real estate	11	11	0.4	34	21	6,000	10,476	296	176	0.1
6530	Real estate agents and managers	6	6	0.6	27	15	5,926	11,200	243	122	0.1
RAPIDES, LA											
60 –	**Finance, insurance, and real estate**	290	289	3.1	2,002	1,998	23,469	23,748	46,467	47,427	2.2
6000	Depository institutions	65	64	3.6	741	715	21,781	22,999	15,658	16,105	2.3
6020	Commercial banks	43	44	3.5	597	585	23,471	24,383	13,353	13,758	2.2
6100	Nondepository institutions	40	41	3.2	161	177	19,578	19,774	3,288	3,648	2.2
6140	Personal credit institutions	29	30	3.3	127	142	17,512	18,394	2,335	2,684	2.8
6200	Security and commodity brokers	9	11	3.3	30	35	69,200	46,743	1,805	1,727	1.1
6300	Insurance carriers	35	34	4.4	310	305	30,013	31,095	9,483	9,325	2.0
6310	Life insurance	15	14	4.6	252	247	27,619	27,935	7,194	6,743	3.5
6400	Insurance agents, brokers, and service	71	68	3.2	417	436	26,715	24,321	10,854	10,489	3.4
6500	Real estate	63	62	2.3	308	293	12,649	15,099	4,074	4,712	2.0
6510	Real estate operators and lessors	27	27	2.0	115	134	14,261	15,761	1,597	2,254	2.7
6530	Real estate agents and managers	27	28	2.7	116	104	14,069	16,077	1,794	1,766	1.5
6700	Holding and other investment offices	7	9	3.1	35	37	36,457	36,649	1,305	1,421	1.3
RED RIVER, LA											
60 –	**Finance, insurance, and real estate**	14	15	0.2	85	89	22,541	21,618	2,180	1,966	0.1
6400	Insurance agents, brokers, and service	5	5	0.2	20	20	24,400	21,200	429	435	0.1
RICHLAND, LA											
60 –	**Finance, insurance, and real estate**	33	32	0.3	195	233	21,128	19,880	4,103	5,289	0.2
6000	Depository institutions	7	7	0.4	129	163	22,853	19,583	3,003	3,806	0.5
6100	Nondepository institutions	8	9	0.7	18	26	13,333	22,769	257	641	0.4
6400	Insurance agents, brokers, and service	10	9	0.4	32	30	21,750	20,267	640	630	0.2
6500	Real estate	8	7	0.3	16	14	14,750	17,143	203	212	0.1
SABINE, LA											
60 –	**Finance, insurance, and real estate**	29	32	0.3	209	241	20,746	21,610	4,011	4,648	0.2
6100	Nondepository institutions	11	11	0.9	23	34	15,478	15,176	388	462	0.3
6400	Insurance agents, brokers, and service	4	4	0.2	15	15	20,533	21,333	322	339	0.1
ST. BERNARD, LA											
60 –	**Finance, insurance, and real estate**	70	71	0.8	523	536	20,765	20,119	11,463	10,420	0.5
6000	Depository institutions	29	29	1.6	373	381	22,241	21,239	8,589	7,371	1.0
6020	Commercial banks	23	24	1.9	344	360	22,302	20,978	7,926	6,813	1.1
6400	Insurance agents, brokers, and service	17	16	0.7	64	61	13,500	15,672	1,022	1,170	0.4

Source: County Business Patterns, 1994/95, CBP-94/95, U.S. Department of Commerce, Washington, D.C., November 1997. SIC categories for which data were suppressed or not available for both 1994 and 1995 are *not* displayed. The employment columns represent mid-March employment in the year. Pay per employee is calculated by dividing 1st Quarter payroll, annualized, by mid-March employment. The columns headed "% State" show the county's percentage of the state total for the SIC in 1995; for example, 1.4% for SIC 6000 means that the county had 1.4 percent of the state's total establishments (or payroll) in SIC 6000 in 1995. A dash (-) is used to indicate that data are not available or cannot be calculated; *nec* means not elsewhere classified.

Continued on next page.

SIC	Industry	No. Establishments			Employment		Pay / Employee		Annual Payroll ($ 000)		
		1994	1995	% State	1994	1995	1994	1995	1994	1995	% State
ST. BERNARD, LA - [continued]											
6500	Real estate	19	19	0.7	72	75	16,167	14,507	1,267	1,223	0.5
6530	Real estate agents and managers	4	4	0.4	14	12	9,429	12,000	146	147	0.1
6550	Subdividers and developers	3	3	1.8	15	18	17,600	10,667	265	226	1.0
ST. CHARLES, LA											
60 –	**Finance, insurance, and real estate**	57	62	0.7	352	310	21,920	23,845	7,931	7,762	0.4
6000	Depository institutions	22	23	1.3	224	191	18,071	21,780	4,060	4,337	0.6
6020	Commercial banks	14	14	1.1	168	130	18,476	22,738	3,049	3,102	0.5
6100	Nondepository institutions	3	3	0.2	10	9	15,200	15,556	156	138	0.1
6140	Personal credit institutions	3	3	0.3	10	9	15,200	15,556	156	138	0.1
6400	Insurance agents, brokers, and service	10	11	0.5	22	20	21,091	23,800	720	587	0.2
6500	Real estate	16	18	0.7	51	46	13,804	15,391	721	844	0.4
6510	Real estate operators and lessors	4	4	0.3	13	12	12,615	11,667	157	142	0.2
6530	Real estate agents and managers	9	10	1.0	34	26	14,941	17,385	484	455	0.4
ST. HELENA, LA											
60 –	**Finance, insurance, and real estate**	12	10	0.1	46	54	19,739	18,222	1,009	1,083	0.0
6400	Insurance agents, brokers, and service	5	3	0.1	5	8	13,600	10,500	89	82	0.0
ST. JAMES, LA											
60 –	**Finance, insurance, and real estate**	33	34	0.4	225	236	17,796	19,712	4,547	5,022	0.2
6000	Depository institutions	15	16	0.9	161	167	17,590	20,048	3,265	3,633	0.5
6100	Nondepository institutions	5	5	0.4	26	28	17,077	18,000	450	507	0.3
6140	Personal credit institutions	5	5	0.5	26	28	17,077	18,000	450	507	0.5
6400	Insurance agents, brokers, and service	9	8	0.4	32	34	21,125	22,000	782	830	0.3
6500	Real estate	4	5	0.2	6	7	8,667	7,429	50	52	0.0
ST. JOHN THE BAPTIST, LA											
60 –	**Finance, insurance, and real estate**	52	51	0.5	486	342	20,749	23,380	11,153	8,139	0.4
6000	Depository institutions	15	16	0.9	213	203	18,986	21,458	3,999	4,165	0.6
6020	Commercial banks	11	12	0.9	186	172	20,043	22,884	3,647	3,733	0.6
6060	Credit unions	4	4	1.2	27	31	11,704	13,548	352	432	1.0
6100	Nondepository institutions	5	5	0.4	18	20	29,111	27,200	551	593	0.4
6140	Personal credit institutions	5	5	0.5	18	20	29,111	27,200	551	593	0.6
6400	Insurance agents, brokers, and service	13	12	0.6	46	46	16,435	18,348	833	890	0.3
6500	Real estate	15	13	0.5	186	49	18,860	17,469	4,341	974	0.4
6530	Real estate agents and managers	6	4	0.4	81	10	18,568	12,400	1,897	133	0.1
ST. LANDRY, LA											
60 –	**Finance, insurance, and real estate**	146	136	1.5	936	947	17,423	17,859	18,181	20,791	1.0
6000	Depository institutions	33	33	1.9	362	390	20,409	19,682	7,881	9,081	1.3
6020	Commercial banks	25	25	2.0	293	315	20,328	19,467	6,298	7,498	1.2
6100	Nondepository institutions	20	20	1.6	125	128	18,624	19,125	2,558	2,503	1.5
6300	Insurance carriers	7	9	1.2	91	96	19,121	19,333	1,848	2,255	0.5
6400	Insurance agents, brokers, and service	44	38	1.8	229	237	14,568	16,135	4,470	5,421	1.7
6510	Real estate operators and lessors	27	22	1.6	101	74	9,743	10,541	938	872	1.0
6530	Real estate agents and managers	10	7	0.7	15	10	10,933	10,000	140	112	0.1
ST. MARTIN, LA											
60 –	**Finance, insurance, and real estate**	53	52	0.6	335	341	20,609	19,062	7,391	6,984	0.3
6000	Depository institutions	16	16	0.9	180	195	20,022	20,062	3,959	4,295	0.6
6020	Commercial banks	13	13	1.0	167	181	19,737	19,823	3,745	4,071	0.7
6500	Real estate	11	11	0.4	58	60	14,138	12,867	739	789	0.3
ST. MARY, LA											
60 –	**Finance, insurance, and real estate**	122	125	1.3	705	709	19,626	21,862	15,315	16,578	0.8
6000	Depository institutions	31	34	1.9	366	376	19,508	20,628	8,284	8,454	1.2
6020	Commercial banks	22	23	1.8	294	283	19,361	20,127	6,764	6,548	1.1

Source: County Business Patterns, 1994/95, CBP-94/95, U.S. Department of Commerce, Washington, D.C., November 1997. SIC categories for which data were suppressed or not available for both 1994 and 1995 are not displayed. The employment columns represent mid-March employment in the year. Pay per employee is calculated by dividing 1st Quarter payroll, annualized, by mid-March employment. The columns headed "% State" show the county's percentage of the state total for the SIC in 1995; for example, 1.4% for SIC 6000 means that the county had 1.4 percent of the state's total establishments (or payroll) in SIC 6000 in 1995. A dash (-) is used to indicate that data are not available or cannot be calculated; nec means not elsewhere classified.

Continued on next page.

SIC	Industry	No. Establishments			Employment		Pay / Employee		Annual Payroll ($ 000)		
		1994	1995	% State	1994	1995	1994	1995	1994	1995	% State
ST. MARY, LA - [continued]											
6400	Insurance agents, brokers, and service	23	23	1.1	116	107	21,897	22,243	2,916	3,148	1.0
6500	Real estate	44	42	1.5	125	117	11,936	12,444	1,501	1,483	0.6
6510	Real estate operators and lessors	28	27	2.0	70	64	14,000	14,938	927	939	1.1
6700	Holding and other investment offices	4	5	1.7	41	44	20,976	19,091	877	875	0.8
ST. TAMMANY, LA											
60 –	**Finance, insurance, and real estate**	301	320	3.4	2,045	2,058	25,625	26,517	53,432	54,508	2.5
6000	Depository institutions	55	54	3.0	698	649	20,825	27,618	14,242	14,687	2.1
6020	Commercial banks	45	46	3.6	632	596	21,063	28,523	12,860	13,745	2.2
6100	Nondepository institutions	31	39	3.1	121	138	30,446	30,174	3,022	3,903	2.3
6140	Personal credit institutions	19	22	2.4	65	73	20,923	19,836	1,419	1,643	1.7
6160	Mortgage bankers and brokers	9	13	6.1	50	52	44,000	48,846	1,373	1,796	3.1
6200	Security and commodity brokers	16	16	4.9	58	54	42,966	43,630	2,463	2,660	1.7
6300	Insurance carriers	23	23	3.0	148	155	39,838	46,348	6,165	7,028	1.5
6310	Life insurance	5	6	2.0	79	88	31,949	41,091	2,628	3,290	1.7
6400	Insurance agents, brokers, and service	81	81	3.8	522	536	24,774	25,813	14,399	15,442	5.0
6500	Real estate	86	98	3.6	420	490	17,438	16,620	8,508	9,916	4.2
6530	Real estate agents and managers	47	50	4.9	184	250	21,413	17,760	4,286	4,426	3.9
6550	Subdividers and developers	9	11	6.5	148	163	13,649	14,601	2,707	3,283	13.9
6552	Subdividers and developers, n.e.c.	8	7	8.2	148	162	13,649	14,420	2,696	2,822	23.1
6700	Holding and other investment offices	9	9	3.1	78	36	71,026	26,778	4,633	872	0.8
TANGIPAHOA, LA											
60 –	**Finance, insurance, and real estate**	171	165	1.8	947	992	20,097	21,343	21,098	22,368	1.0
6000	Depository institutions	34	31	1.7	467	456	19,820	22,035	9,803	10,572	1.5
6020	Commercial banks	27	26	2.0	408	400	19,608	21,910	8,611	9,312	1.5
6100	Nondepository institutions	33	35	2.8	93	134	25,204	22,239	3,286	3,282	1.9
6140	Personal credit institutions	24	23	2.5	71	96	21,127	21,042	1,844	2,090	2.2
6300	Insurance carriers	14	11	1.4	93	84	36,645	43,333	3,383	3,719	0.8
6400	Insurance agents, brokers, and service	37	33	1.5	130	127	16,062	16,882	2,226	2,189	0.7
6500	Real estate	43	44	1.6	76	96	10,368	10,750	946	1,283	0.5
6510	Real estate operators and lessors	21	21	1.5	34	42	10,471	12,286	470	741	0.9
6530	Real estate agents and managers	16	15	1.5	31	40	9,548	9,000	317	360	0.3
6540	Title abstract offices	3	3	3.5	5	7	20,800	16,000	125	131	1.4
6730	Trusts	3	3	5.8	13	6	13,538	6,667	77	42	0.9
TENSAS, LA											
60 –	**Finance, insurance, and real estate**	11	9	0.1	71	65	17,465	20,862	1,556	1,415	0.1
TERREBONNE, LA											
60 –	**Finance, insurance, and real estate**	209	220	2.4	1,337	1,321	21,505	23,512	29,587	31,344	1.4
6000	Depository institutions	45	48	2.7	615	609	19,122	21,655	11,785	12,896	1.8
6020	Commercial banks	37	39	3.1	585	571	19,323	22,011	11,298	12,278	2.0
6100	Nondepository institutions	20	22	1.7	82	91	21,317	22,242	1,962	2,198	1.3
6200	Security and commodity brokers	5	4	1.2	12	10	51,667	31,600	523	412	0.3
6300	Insurance carriers	19	16	2.1	180	172	33,378	33,558	6,156	5,978	1.3
6400	Insurance agents, brokers, and service	46	54	2.5	229	209	26,201	32,861	6,277	6,907	2.2
6500	Real estate	69	71	2.6	203	212	11,291	11,849	2,493	2,536	1.1
6510	Real estate operators and lessors	42	43	3.2	146	147	10,055	10,912	1,472	1,537	1.8
6530	Real estate agents and managers	19	19	1.9	49	51	14,857	13,490	881	763	0.7
6550	Subdividers and developers	5	5	2.9	5	7	11,200	12,571	97	93	0.4
6553	Cemetery subdividers and developers	3	3	4.3	4	4	10,000	12,000	49	52	0.5
6700	Holding and other investment offices	5	5	1.7	16	18	20,250	21,111	391	417	0.4
UNION, LA											
60 –	**Finance, insurance, and real estate**	22	23	0.2	209	146	13,703	16,384	2,704	2,563	0.1
6000	Depository institutions	6	6	0.3	101	99	17,624	19,071	1,879	2,001	0.3

Source: County Business Patterns, 1994/95, CBP-94/95, U.S. Department of Commerce, Washington, D.C., November 1997. SIC categories for which data were suppressed or not available for both 1994 and 1995 are not displayed. The employment columns represent mid-March employment in the year. Pay per employee is calculated by dividing 1st Quarter payroll, annualized, by mid-March employment. The columns headed "% State" show the county's percentage of the state total for the SIC in 1995; for example, 1.4% for SIC 6000 means that the county had 1.4 percent of the state's total establishments (or payroll) in SIC 6000 in 1995. A dash (-) is used to indicate that data are not available or cannot be calculated; nec means not elsewhere classified.

Continued on next page.

SIC	Industry	No. Establishments			Employment		Pay / Employee		Annual Payroll ($ 000)		
		1994	1995	% State	1994	1995	1994	1995	1994	1995	% State
UNION, LA - [continued]											
6020	Commercial banks	6	6	0.5	101	99	17,624	19,071	1,879	2,001	0.3
6400	Insurance agents, brokers, and service	4	5	0.2	22	21	6,182	5,143	145	131	0.0
6500	Real estate	7	6	0.2	69	9	9,449	12,000	352	112	0.0
VERMILION, LA											
60 –	**Finance, insurance, and real estate**	80	77	0.8	444	466	20,387	19,562	9,980	9,838	0.5
6000	Depository institutions	25	24	1.3	268	301	20,851	20,306	6,406	6,591	0.9
6020	Commercial banks	21	20	1.6	247	282	20,972	20,213	6,043	6,235	1.0
6300	Insurance carriers	4	4	0.5	33	33	29,939	27,879	967	952	0.2
6400	Insurance agents, brokers, and service	21	21	1.0	58	54	12,483	14,148	752	793	0.3
6500	Real estate	13	12	0.4	28	30	8,571	8,800	316	307	0.1
6530	Real estate agents and managers	6	5	0.5	9	11	8,444	6,182	93	79	0.1
VERNON, LA											
60 –	**Finance, insurance, and real estate**	70	72	0.8	399	411	16,281	18,054	6,955	7,402	0.3
6000	Depository institutions	8	9	0.5	175	175	16,709	17,120	2,853	3,014	0.4
6100	Nondepository institutions	18	20	1.6	77	96	21,247	25,833	1,947	2,313	1.4
6400	Insurance agents, brokers, and service	13	14	0.7	51	50	15,765	17,840	916	929	0.3
6500	Real estate	28	25	0.9	85	79	11,388	10,177	1,044	870	0.4
6510	Real estate operators and lessors	16	15	1.1	64	57	11,875	9,684	778	593	0.7
6530	Real estate agents and managers	9	7	0.7	17	14	9,176	10,571	174	172	0.1
WASHINGTON, LA											
60 –	**Finance, insurance, and real estate**	61	63	0.7	429	477	17,995	18,717	8,868	9,838	0.5
6000	Depository institutions	20	20	1.1	220	226	17,382	18,159	4,510	4,551	0.6
6100	Nondepository institutions	12	13	1.0	72	71	19,444	21,296	1,700	1,712	1.0
6300	Insurance carriers	3	4	0.5	59	69	22,373	21,217	1,449	1,746	0.4
6400	Insurance agents, brokers, and service	20	19	0.9	69	68	16,000	15,294	1,145	1,038	0.3
6510	Real estate operators and lessors	3	3	0.2	6	3	4,667	6,667	20	21	0.0
WEBSTER, LA											
60 –	**Finance, insurance, and real estate**	82	77	0.8	430	412	19,423	20,204	8,607	8,517	0.4
6000	Depository institutions	19	15	0.8	200	170	22,380	23,388	4,507	4,095	0.6
6020	Commercial banks	14	11	0.9	165	143	22,230	23,329	3,731	3,448	0.6
6100	Nondepository institutions	19	18	1.4	40	45	15,300	15,556	797	769	0.5
6300	Insurance carriers	5	5	0.6	32	38	30,750	32,632	1,027	1,280	0.3
6400	Insurance agents, brokers, and service	20	18	0.8	105	89	16,381	18,382	1,646	1,524	0.5
6500	Real estate	14	16	0.6	45	61	9,511	10,426	502	721	0.3
WEST BATON ROUGE, LA											
60 –	**Finance, insurance, and real estate**	15	16	0.2	112	120	22,214	23,567	2,716	3,089	0.1
6400	Insurance agents, brokers, and service	4	5	0.2	15	14	16,800	16,857	315	313	0.1
6500	Real estate	3	3	0.1	10	15	12,400	13,333	198	204	0.1
6510	Real estate operators and lessors	3	3	0.2	10	15	12,400	13,333	198	204	0.2
WEST CARROLL, LA											
60 –	**Finance, insurance, and real estate**	16	16	0.2	78	93	17,487	19,957	1,186	1,444	0.1
6500	Real estate	6	6	0.2	10	10	5,600	6,000	53	65	0.0
6510	Real estate operators and lessors	4	4	0.3	8	8	5,000	5,500	38	49	0.1
WEST FELICIANA, LA											
60 –	**Finance, insurance, and real estate**	7	7	0.1	62	61	19,226	16,852	1,151	1,144	0.1
6000	Depository institutions	3	3	0.2	57	58	19,649	17,103	1,083	1,088	0.2
WINN, LA											
60 –	**Finance, insurance, and real estate**	19	20	0.2	142	124	17,690	20,161	2,491	2,775	0.1
6400	Insurance agents, brokers, and service	7	7	0.3	34	30	15,647	18,133	567	582	0.2
6500	Real estate	5	5	0.2	15	12	8,267	9,333	113	113	0.0

Source: County Business Patterns, 1994/95, CBP-94/95, U.S. Department of Commerce, Washington, D.C., November 1997. SIC categories for which data were suppressed or not available for both 1994 and 1995 are *not* displayed. The employment columns represent mid-March employment in the year. Pay per employee is calculated by dividing 1st Quarter payroll, annualized, by mid-March employment. The columns headed "% State" show the county's percentage of the state total for the SIC in 1995; for example, 1.4% for SIC 6000 means that the county had 1.4 percent of the state's total establishments (or payroll) in SIC 6000 in 1995. A dash (-) is used to indicate that data are not available or cannot be calculated; *nec* means not elsewhere classified.

SIC	Industry	No. Establishments			Employment		Pay / Employee		Annual Payroll ($ 000)		
		1994	1995	% State	1994	1995	1994	1995	1994	1995	% State

BALTIMORE CITY, MD - [continued]

SIC	Industry	1994	1995	% State	1994	1995	1994	1995	1994	1995	% State
6100	Nondepository institutions	91	87	8.8	2,182	1,470	39,461	61,241	79,985	62,410	13.6
6140	Personal credit institutions	43	46	15.3	683	694	38,758	62,974	25,421	35,038	31.3
6160	Mortgage bankers and brokers	32	29	5.0	1,253	556	38,538	31,719	42,565	18,183	7.5
6200	Security and commodity brokers	88	91	16.3	1,951	1,999	149,259	170,121	205,942	223,942	51.4
6210	Security brokers and dealers	43	42	16.1	1,684	1,663	161,226	186,001	179,723	190,010	59.5
6280	Security and commodity services	44	49	17.0	267	336	73,783	91,524	26,200	33,932	-
6300	Insurance carriers	95	92	10.8	6,911	7,043	48,416	46,731	311,622	349,216	33.1
6310	Life insurance	30	30	13.5	1,876	1,612	42,028	38,124	74,353	62,710	31.0
6320	Medical service and health insurance	6	7	13.5	457	506	41,926	42,909	20,083	22,047	11.5
6330	Fire, marine, and casualty insurance	37	35	7.7	3,627	4,045	53,847	50,340	177,980	225,596	37.8
6360	Title insurance	6	5	13.2	132	108	43,303	58,444	4,746	4,047	39.8
6400	Insurance agents, brokers, and service	167	176	8.7	1,626	1,934	39,528	33,032	63,920	66,449	14.0
6500	Real estate	574	590	12.5	5,302	5,392	21,401	22,611	121,735	130,160	14.4
6510	Real estate operators and lessors	279	266	17.7	2,315	2,161	19,452	17,423	46,357	40,410	17.2
6530	Real estate agents and managers	232	249	10.1	2,477	2,590	23,696	25,004	59,293	66,491	12.7
6540	Title abstract offices	15	13	5.7	96	56	27,250	25,000	2,245	1,716	5.8
6550	Subdividers and developers	36	41	11.2	392	548	17,265	31,759	13,355	20,671	19.4
6552	Subdividers and developers, n.e.c.	23	27	11.4	201	358	19,204	39,050	9,644	16,478	22.4
6553	Cemetery subdividers and developers	12	11	10.9	191	187	15,225	17,476	3,702	4,017	13.1
6700	Holding and other investment offices	54	59	18.0	2,350	2,257	40,373	48,362	110,753	132,095	34.1
6710	Holding offices	16	15	16.0	714	325	34,711	36,775	24,673	12,477	7.1
6730	Trusts	18	22	22.7	694	927	30,513	30,658	25,914	31,915	50.2
6732	Educational, religious, etc. trusts	10	12	25.0	632	868	30,785	31,129	24,594	30,428	80.1
6733	Trusts, n.e.c.	8	10	20.8	62	59	27,742	23,729	1,320	1,487	5.8

Source: County Business Patterns, 1994/95, CBP-94/95, U.S. Department of Commerce, Washington, D.C., November 1997. SIC categories for which data were suppressed or not available for both 1994 and 1995 are not displayed. The employment columns represent mid-March employment in the year. Pay per employee is calculated by dividing 1st Quarter payroll, annualized, by mid-March employment. The columns headed "% State" show the county's percentage of the state total for the SIC in 1995; for example, 1.4% for SIC 6000 means that the county had 1.4 percent of the state's total establishments (or payroll) in SIC 6000 in 1995. A dash (-) is used to indicate that data are not available or cannot be calculated; nec means not elsewhere classified.

MASSACHUSETTS

SIC	Industry	No. Establishments			Employment		Pay / Employee		Annual Payroll ($ 000)		
		1994	1995	% State	1994	1995	1994	1995	1994	1995	% State
BARNSTABLE, MA											
60 –	**Finance, insurance, and real estate**	572	567	*4.3*	3,812	3,778	27,105	27,593	100,637	103,931	*1.0*
6000	Depository institutions	113	114	*4.7*	1,370	1,392	26,523	28,563	33,329	33,636	*1.6*
6020	Commercial banks	50	55	*5.3*	676	640	27,243	29,631	16,405	17,080	*1.2*
6030	Savings institutions	58	54	*5.9*	667	723	26,159	28,011	16,400	16,049	*3.5*
6100	Nondepository institutions	25	28	*4.3*	195	112	29,087	27,429	4,107	4,105	*1.3*
6160	Mortgage bankers and brokers	17	18	*4.7*	177	96	29,582	27,250	3,592	3,566	*2.6*
6200	Security and commodity brokers	40	41	*3.8*	214	224	65,645	54,232	11,649	12,378	*0.5*
6210	Security brokers and dealers	20	26	*5.8*	187	199	70,781	56,985	10,733	11,304	*1.1*
6300	Insurance carriers	10	11	*1.8*	186	185	44,086	35,741	6,842	5,696	*0.2*
6400	Insurance agents, brokers, and service	115	110	*3.7*	578	604	28,304	29,523	18,002	19,971	*2.5*
6500	Real estate	252	245	*5.0*	1,147	1,165	17,496	19,255	23,872	25,484	*2.6*
6510	Real estate operators and lessors	56	59	*3.6*	292	307	16,219	15,974	5,146	5,178	*2.0*
6530	Real estate agents and managers	168	161	*6.0*	776	781	18,021	20,517	17,115	18,546	*2.9*
6550	Subdividers and developers	13	12	*3.3*	29	28	23,172	28,286	755	931	*1.9*
6700	Holding and other investment offices	17	18	*3.2*	122	96	21,639	24,917	2,836	2,661	*0.3*
6710	Holding offices	3	3	*1.9*	8	6	23,000	22,667	177	77	*0.1*
6730	Trusts	9	11	*6.5*	81	81	23,753	26,420	2,115	2,432	*3.6*
6790	Miscellaneous investing	5	4	*2.4*	33	9	16,121	12,889	544	152	*0.1*
BERKSHIRE, MA											
60 –	**Finance, insurance, and real estate**	242	256	*1.9*	2,495	2,872	26,105	33,730	66,090	102,426	*1.0*
6000	Depository institutions	66	68	*2.8*	1,026	1,122	26,577	30,774	26,346	31,268	*1.5*
6020	Commercial banks	21	23	*2.2*	349	419	25,903	32,955	7,380	11,171	*0.8*
6030	Savings institutions	27	27	*3.0*	555	581	28,252	30,816	16,230	17,015	*3.7*
6060	Credit unions	18	18	*4.6*	122	122	20,885	23,082	2,736	3,082	*3.1*
6200	Security and commodity brokers	12	11	*1.0*	60	59	56,133	61,085	3,172	3,382	*0.1*
6300	Insurance carriers	6	6	*1.0*	578	747	26,311	48,080	15,575	43,845	*1.7*
6400	Insurance agents, brokers, and service	52	54	*1.8*	344	354	32,512	30,644	11,194	11,501	*1.4*
6500	Real estate	93	101	*2.1*	387	419	14,646	16,516	7,194	7,616	*0.8*
6510	Real estate operators and lessors	38	40	*2.5*	81	97	15,407	16,289	1,647	2,049	*0.8*
6530	Real estate agents and managers	49	53	*2.0*	292	303	14,288	16,092	4,806	4,982	*0.8*
6550	Subdividers and developers	5	4	*1.1*	14	17	17,714	25,882	728	424	*0.8*
BRISTOL, MA											
60 –	**Finance, insurance, and real estate**	831	817	*6.2*	6,799	6,943	24,128	25,719	165,978	158,269	*1.6*
6000	Depository institutions	209	205	*8.5*	2,958	3,370	22,751	25,437	68,487	64,449	*3.1*
6020	Commercial banks	59	55	*5.3*	721	648	22,302	24,049	15,811	14,856	*1.1*
6030	Savings institutions	98	100	*11.0*	1,674	2,167	24,789	27,601	42,563	38,960	*8.4*
6100	Nondepository institutions	32	36	*5.5*	251	182	36,303	36,132	6,740	5,896	*1.9*
6140	Personal credit institutions	13	15	*9.3*	96	82	26,250	31,073	2,405	2,289	*3.1*
6160	Mortgage bankers and brokers	16	18	*4.7*	141	61	44,397	32,197	3,321	2,037	*1.5*
6200	Security and commodity brokers	22	22	*2.0*	88	88	53,909	53,591	4,489	4,611	*0.2*
6210	Security brokers and dealers	11	10	*2.2*	68	64	65,000	65,813	4,052	4,002	*0.4*
6280	Security and commodity services	11	12	*1.9*	20	24	16,200	21,000	437	609	*0.0*
6300	Insurance carriers	31	26	*4.2*	1,189	1,006	27,566	29,006	32,447	27,668	*1.1*
6400	Insurance agents, brokers, and service	233	230	*7.7*	1,088	1,155	26,206	27,065	30,650	33,096	*4.2*
6500	Real estate	285	277	*5.6*	1,128	1,037	16,787	17,003	20,372	19,403	*2.0*
6510	Real estate operators and lessors	113	105	*6.5*	477	469	14,138	14,098	7,202	7,282	*2.8*
6530	Real estate agents and managers	134	136	*5.0*	449	405	20,347	20,306	9,578	8,944	*1.4*
6550	Subdividers and developers	34	31	*8.5*	193	150	14,736	17,040	3,379	2,874	*5.7*

Source: County Business Patterns, 1994/95, CBP-94/95, U.S. Department of Commerce, Washington, D.C., November 1997. SIC categories for which data were suppressed or not available for both 1994 and 1995 are not displayed. The employment columns represent mid-March employment in the year. Pay per employee is calculated by dividing 1st Quarter payroll, annualized, by mid-March employment. The columns headed "% State" show the county's percentage of the state total for the SIC in 1995; for example, 1.4% for SIC 6000 means that the county had 1.4 percent of the state's total establishments (or payroll) in SIC 6000 in 1995. A dash (-) is used to indicate that data are not available or cannot be calculated; nec means not elsewhere classified.

Continued on next page.

SIC	Industry	No. Establishments			Employment		Pay / Employee		Annual Payroll ($ 000)		
		1994	1995	% State	1994	1995	1994	1995	1994	1995	% State
BRISTOL, MA - [continued]											
6552	Subdividers and developers, n.e.c.	18	13	6.5	121	78	15,306	19,641	2,266	1,726	6.0
6553	Cemetery subdividers and developers	15	15	11.7	72	72	13,778	14,222	1,103	1,132	6.1
6710	Holding offices	7	7	4.4	68	70	30,294	37,371	2,161	2,203	1.6
DUKES, MA											
60 –	**Finance, insurance, and real estate**	51	57	0.4	257	369	27,907	26,092	9,861	10,750	0.1
6510	Real estate operators and lessors	5	7	0.4	11	20	22,909	21,800	567	613	0.2
6530	Real estate agents and managers	20	23	0.9	31	109	20,258	26,789	2,120	3,398	0.5
ESSEX, MA											
60 –	**Finance, insurance, and real estate**	1,263	1,292	9.8	11,628	11,320	30,363	31,491	349,848	355,288	3.6
6000	Depository institutions	282	272	11.3	4,433	4,513	25,654	25,750	116,742	115,174	5.5
6020	Commercial banks	100	92	8.9	1,304	1,255	22,724	22,907	30,204	27,477	2.0
6030	Savings institutions	125	124	13.6	2,759	2,896	27,597	27,445	78,418	79,134	17.1
6060	Credit unions	53	51	12.9	355	352	20,665	21,716	7,731	8,183	8.2
6100	Nondepository institutions	78	73	11.2	1,118	628	38,025	43,057	34,090	25,759	8.4
6140	Personal credit institutions	15	18	11.2	146	155	27,370	26,529	3,923	3,736	5.1
6150	Business credit institutions	7	6	6.2	58	61	94,207	123,016	5,437	4,449	5.3
6160	Mortgage bankers and brokers	54	47	12.3	914	411	36,162	37,470	24,698	17,503	12.6
6200	Security and commodity brokers	60	74	6.8	301	384	58,658	57,052	17,525	22,769	1.0
6210	Security brokers and dealers	25	28	6.3	207	243	64,638	56,642	11,655	15,128	1.4
6300	Insurance carriers	43	41	6.7	2,156	2,064	35,417	37,783	71,432	70,294	2.8
6310	Life insurance	17	17	6.1	691	734	27,155	26,627	17,210	18,029	1.3
6330	Fire, marine, and casualty insurance	11	10	5.6	992	953	42,427	46,409	38,770	34,555	5.2
6400	Insurance agents, brokers, and service	304	316	10.6	1,596	1,697	32,429	32,780	56,013	60,010	7.5
6500	Real estate	461	479	9.8	1,721	1,711	21,862	21,873	39,582	40,216	4.1
6510	Real estate operators and lessors	155	151	9.3	470	452	19,779	20,195	9,436	9,663	3.7
6530	Real estate agents and managers	269	274	10.2	1,141	1,121	22,643	22,459	26,640	26,651	4.2
6540	Title abstract offices	5	8	14.3	32	26	31,375	32,769	959	1,019	14.7
6550	Subdividers and developers	29	33	9.1	78	92	19,077	20,478	2,433	2,580	5.2
6552	Subdividers and developers, n.e.c.	13	16	8.0	25	37	16,640	18,378	817	889	3.1
6553	Cemetery subdividers and developers	14	14	10.9	53	54	20,226	21,185	1,359	1,385	7.4
6710	Holding offices	9	13	8.2	56	172	36,143	72,186	2,272	12,970	9.5
6790	Miscellaneous investing	11	10	5.9	115	30	63,270	133,067	7,400	3,609	3.1
FRANKLIN, MA											
60 –	**Finance, insurance, and real estate**	92	92	0.7	1,058	1,018	22,064	22,633	25,342	24,798	0.2
6000	Depository institutions	24	23	1.0	329	316	21,994	22,646	7,221	7,653	0.4
6060	Credit unions	3	3	0.8	12	12	42,000	47,333	422	499	0.5
6400	Insurance agents, brokers, and service	22	21	0.7	120	127	25,833	25,953	3,223	3,548	0.4
6530	Real estate agents and managers	16	14	0.5	30	21	16,267	15,619	434	374	0.1
HAMPDEN, MA											
60 –	**Finance, insurance, and real estate**	859	845	6.4	18,240	20,557	35,772	36,223	726,957	694,607	7.0
6000	Depository institutions	182	174	7.2	2,737	2,515	24,905	27,307	65,637	64,924	3.1
6020	Commercial banks	74	71	6.9	1,162	1,033	24,998	26,788	26,900	25,236	1.8
6030	Savings institutions	76	73	8.0	1,346	1,249	25,551	28,657	33,752	34,399	7.4
6100	Nondepository institutions	38	32	4.9	420	192	34,790	28,979	15,264	6,303	2.1
6200	Security and commodity brokers	36	36	3.3	389	395	69,306	65,884	23,382	24,361	1.0
6210	Security brokers and dealers	19	20	4.5	319	320	61,868	57,288	18,228	18,691	1.8
6280	Security and commodity services	17	16	2.6	70	75	103,200	102,560	5,154	5,670	0.4
6300	Insurance carriers	64	60	9.8	11,687	14,469	39,870	39,181	541,152	517,858	20.4
6400	Insurance agents, brokers, and service	241	237	8.0	1,368	1,371	29,702	30,950	43,285	45,088	5.7
6500	Real estate	281	288	5.9	1,540	1,314	20,556	21,482	33,863	29,509	3.0
6510	Real estate operators and lessors	112	112	6.9	564	496	18,745	18,137	11,208	9,298	3.6

Source: County Business Patterns, 1994/95, CBP-94/95, U.S. Department of Commerce, Washington, D.C., November 1997. SIC categories for which data were suppressed or not available for both 1994 and 1995 are not displayed. The employment columns represent mid-March employment in the year. Pay per employee is calculated by dividing 1st Quarter payroll, annualized, by mid-March employment. The columns headed "% State" show the county's percentage of the state total for the SIC in 1995; for example, 1.4% for SIC 6000 means that the county had 1.4 percent of the state's total establishments (or payroll) in SIC 6000 in 1995. A dash (-) is used to indicate that data are not available or cannot be calculated; nec means not elsewhere classified.

Continued on next page.

SIC	Industry	No. Establishments			Employment		Pay / Employee		Annual Payroll ($ 000)		
		1994	1995	% State	1994	1995	1994	1995	1994	1995	% State
HAMPDEN, MA - [continued]											
6530	Real estate agents and managers	147	152	5.6	859	708	20,661	21,966	19,014	16,393	2.6
6553	Cemetery subdividers and developers	12	13	10.2	66	62	20,303	20,903	1,413	1,448	7.8
6710	Holding offices	5	4	2.5	67	255	52,478	22,118	3,157	5,110	3.7
HAMPSHIRE, MA											
60 –	**Finance, insurance, and real estate**	233	229	1.7	1,382	1,389	23,421	25,063	36,048	36,801	0.4
6000	Depository institutions	49	50	2.1	700	719	20,989	21,446	14,685	15,901	0.8
6020	Commercial banks	21	20	1.9	274	251	20,467	19,267	4,740	3,730	0.3
6030	Savings institutions	21	23	2.5	370	402	21,989	23,393	8,952	11,044	2.4
6060	Credit unions	7	7	1.8	56	66	16,929	17,879	993	1,127	1.1
6400	Insurance agents, brokers, and service	50	53	1.8	244	259	29,000	29,961	8,247	8,673	1.1
6500	Real estate	108	101	2.1	306	278	17,412	18,072	6,148	5,524	0.6
6510	Real estate operators and lessors	39	38	2.3	147	134	17,388	19,075	2,644	2,336	0.9
6530	Real estate agents and managers	54	48	1.8	136	124	16,529	17,484	2,705	2,621	0.4
6550	Subdividers and developers	15	13	3.6	23	18	22,783	15,111	799	506	1.0
MIDDLESEX, MA											
60 –	**Finance, insurance, and real estate**	3,033	3,039	23.0	33,529	33,308	32,403	35,104	1,118,549	1,197,844	12.0
6000	Depository institutions	567	527	21.9	10,486	9,734	27,377	28,781	280,097	268,368	12.9
6020	Commercial banks	258	242	23.4	5,887	4,742	28,353	29,601	153,643	128,660	9.2
6030	Savings institutions	207	183	20.1	3,764	4,030	26,874	27,845	107,691	112,178	24.2
6060	Credit unions	92	91	23.0	794	810	22,605	24,711	17,599	20,522	20.7
6100	Nondepository institutions	175	169	25.9	2,296	1,654	41,812	45,279	81,422	76,655	25.1
6150	Business credit institutions	31	28	28.9	257	288	67,844	79,042	15,866	17,879	21.5
6160	Mortgage bankers and brokers	108	104	27.3	1,699	966	39,477	41,470	54,666	46,679	33.5
6200	Security and commodity brokers	169	186	17.2	1,275	1,461	48,113	54,344	71,929	96,594	4.1
6210	Security brokers and dealers	54	59	13.2	449	608	59,136	57,783	23,807	32,035	3.0
6280	Security and commodity services	115	126	20.2	826	852	42,121	51,883	48,122	64,424	4.9
6300	Insurance carriers	133	137	22.3	6,736	6,940	35,377	40,764	232,682	279,610	11.0
6310	Life insurance	64	63	22.7	1,663	1,591	36,753	41,395	56,258	58,849	4.3
6320	Medical service and health insurance	13	14	21.5	2,033	1,950	34,007	47,436	75,578	95,513	21.8
6330	Fire, marine, and casualty insurance	39	42	23.3	2,963	3,256	35,314	36,338	96,233	119,075	17.9
6400	Insurance agents, brokers, and service	691	685	23.0	4,951	5,538	32,988	34,449	183,571	193,009	24.2
6500	Real estate	1,145	1,172	23.9	6,477	6,706	26,134	26,784	192,327	205,940	21.1
6510	Real estate operators and lessors	397	398	24.5	2,235	2,311	20,564	21,719	51,203	54,125	20.8
6530	Real estate agents and managers	655	651	24.2	3,808	3,707	29,544	30,592	127,399	131,421	20.8
6540	Title abstract offices	7	7	12.5	42	18	27,810	25,333	907	587	8.5
6550	Subdividers and developers	65	71	19.6	387	510	24,713	25,475	12,167	15,285	30.6
6552	Subdividers and developers, n.e.c.	50	50	25.1	233	341	22,798	23,390	6,542	8,301	28.9
6553	Cemetery subdividers and developers	12	12	9.4	153	147	27,686	29,959	5,458	5,632	30.2
6710	Holding offices	44	45	28.5	491	682	70,965	79,026	36,457	48,276	35.4
6730	Trusts	47	53	31.2	185	202	27,719	26,535	5,335	5,687	8.4
6732	Educational, religious, etc. trusts	24	28	38.9	118	130	29,017	27,908	3,585	3,749	7.3
6733	Trusts, n.e.c.	23	25	25.8	67	72	25,433	24,056	1,750	1,938	12.0
6790	Miscellaneous investing	48	50	29.6	371	227	50,253	58,626	22,830	12,796	11.1
6799	Investors, n.e.c.	26	29	25.9	65	92	72,369	79,087	6,612	7,204	8.3
NANTUCKET, MA											
60 –	**Finance, insurance, and real estate**	34	35	0.3	226	337	27,628	28,166	8,390	11,016	0.1
6500	Real estate	24	25	0.5	106	205	24,000	27,785	4,681	6,724	0.7
6530	Real estate agents and managers	17	17	0.6	92	186	26,565	29,462	4,459	6,340	1.0
NORFOLK, MA											
60 –	**Finance, insurance, and real estate**	1,582	1,582	12.0	31,712	33,005	33,907	35,710	1,089,018	1,197,468	12.0
6000	Depository institutions	260	242	10.1	11,282	11,575	33,210	35,556	372,383	397,688	19.1
6020	Commercial banks	133	123	11.9	8,889	9,618	34,908	37,126	307,079	343,148	24.5
6030	Savings institutions	94	87	9.6	2,165	1,719	26,794	27,800	59,256	47,493	10.3
6100	Nondepository institutions	109	105	16.1	2,284	1,910	31,396	32,174	68,208	61,641	20.2

Source: County Business Patterns, 1994/95, CBP-94/95, U.S. Department of Commerce, Washington, D.C., November 1997. SIC categories for which data were suppressed or not available for both 1994 and 1995 are not displayed. The employment columns represent mid-March employment in the year. Pay per employee is calculated by dividing 1st Quarter payroll, annualized, by mid-March employment. The columns headed "% State" show the county's percentage of the state total for the SIC in 1995; for example, 1.4% for SIC 6000 means that the county had 1.4 percent of the state's total establishments (or payroll) in SIC 6000 in 1995. A dash (-) is used to indicate that data are not available or cannot be calculated; nec means not elsewhere classified.

Continued on next page.

SIC	Industry	No. Establishments			Employment		Pay / Employee		Annual Payroll ($ 000)		
		1994	1995	% State	1994	1995	1994	1995	1994	1995	% State
NORFOLK, MA - [continued]											
6140	Personal credit institutions	29	27	16.8	1,209	1,166	27,825	29,173	34,061	31,262	42.7
6150	Business credit institutions	10	11	11.3	113	89	42,549	53,708	4,480	3,680	4.4
6160	Mortgage bankers and brokers	68	66	17.3	962	652	34,574	34,681	29,637	26,623	19.1
6200	Security and commodity brokers	100	111	10.2	837	825	64,502	64,761	53,711	58,273	2.5
6210	Security brokers and dealers	38	41	9.2	551	514	69,619	71,051	37,086	35,301	3.3
6300	Insurance carriers	107	99	16.2	8,964	9,383	35,426	39,001	320,440	376,401	14.8
6310	Life insurance	41	38	13.7	3,468	3,215	31,744	34,834	116,440	118,029	8.5
6320	Medical service and health insurance	12	12	18.5	1,945	2,796	43,574	41,734	77,658	121,388	27.8
6330	Fire, marine, and casualty insurance	35	33	18.3	3,412	3,235	34,370	40,523	120,834	130,799	19.7
6350	Surety insurance	6	6	46.2	81	71	44,790	56,789	3,597	3,659	68.4
6400	Insurance agents, brokers, and service	385	387	13.0	2,227	2,351	34,335	38,043	84,509	90,715	11.4
6500	Real estate	558	579	11.8	3,940	4,237	25,897	26,950	112,356	131,205	13.4
6510	Real estate operators and lessors	170	179	11.0	1,082	1,235	30,244	27,964	31,486	40,235	15.5
6530	Real estate agents and managers	333	328	12.2	2,618	2,431	24,047	26,063	69,784	71,529	11.3
6540	Title abstract offices	6	6	10.7	73	35	29,534	34,857	1,976	1,192	17.2
6550	Subdividers and developers	38	47	12.9	164	211	25,244	26,028	5,599	7,094	14.2
6552	Subdividers and developers, n.e.c.	19	28	14.1	60	107	34,200	28,935	3,090	4,399	15.3
6553	Cemetery subdividers and developers	15	14	10.9	104	99	20,077	23,434	2,385	2,443	13.1
6710	Holding offices	18	17	10.8	51	85	67,216	67,953	3,409	5,068	3.7
6733	Trusts, n.e.c.	8	8	8.2	30	15	65,467	23,200	891	428	2.6
6790	Miscellaneous investing	20	16	9.5	87	65	63,586	57,477	6,034	4,532	3.9
6798	Real estate investment trusts	6	4	11.8	11	12	6,182	6,667	100	88	0.4
PLYMOUTH, MA											
60–	**Finance, insurance, and real estate**	775	788	6.0	8,657	7,690	27,764	28,733	260,047	234,046	2.3
6000	Depository institutions	164	165	6.9	2,413	2,388	24,071	24,482	61,244	58,311	2.8
6020	Commercial banks	57	65	6.3	837	942	24,822	24,204	21,676	22,133	1.6
6030	Savings institutions	81	72	7.9	1,127	966	24,742	25,495	29,348	24,801	5.4
6060	Credit unions	26	27	6.8	449	480	20,989	22,992	10,220	11,169	11.2
6160	Mortgage bankers and brokers	30	30	7.9	266	195	31,053	34,749	7,043	8,775	6.3
6200	Security and commodity brokers	35	42	3.9	689	614	40,464	35,850	24,974	25,611	1.1
6210	Security brokers and dealers	15	17	3.8	162	147	95,086	66,476	11,183	9,911	0.9
6280	Security and commodity services	19	23	3.7	526	466	23,696	26,240	13,779	15,641	1.2
6300	Insurance carriers	37	31	5.1	3,292	2,415	28,899	31,853	108,462	79,548	3.1
6400	Insurance agents, brokers, and service	219	218	7.3	989	1,021	29,327	30,770	32,195	33,318	4.2
6500	Real estate	267	272	5.5	908	946	20,987	21,290	23,121	23,747	2.4
6510	Real estate operators and lessors	63	65	4.0	256	315	22,781	21,816	7,624	8,103	3.1
6530	Real estate agents and managers	165	166	6.2	540	494	19,948	19,603	12,204	11,824	1.9
6540	Title abstract offices	6	6	10.7	32	36	25,000	13,778	663	518	7.5
6550	Subdividers and developers	23	24	6.6	71	76	20,282	28,947	1,985	1,942	3.9
6552	Subdividers and developers, n.e.c.	12	11	5.5	41	40	23,707	28,700	1,416	1,153	4.0
6553	Cemetery subdividers and developers	10	10	7.8	28	31	14,571	14,839	503	548	2.9
SUFFOLK, MA											
60–	**Finance, insurance, and real estate**	2,410	2,431	18.4	85,270	90,327	58,797	67,144	4,699,451	5,301,320	53.0
6000	Depository institutions	318	302	12.6	18,315	18,659	49,272	61,315	846,195	917,429	44.1
6020	Commercial banks	175	168	16.2	14,305	14,819	52,653	65,265	696,625	750,723	53.7
6030	Savings institutions	68	63	6.9	1,458	1,242	28,903	34,071	43,930	41,558	9.0
6090	Functions closely related to banking	30	29	54.7	432	429	56,954	115,347	27,553	44,851	83.9
6100	Nondepository institutions	88	88	13.5	1,262	1,467	62,913	57,816	75,086	80,531	26.4
6140	Personal credit institutions	14	10	6.2	185	171	26,595	32,912	5,360	4,859	6.6
6150	Business credit institutions	34	32	33.0	723	646	62,539	77,864	47,677	48,075	57.7
6160	Mortgage bankers and brokers	39	43	11.3	349	626	82,590	42,575	21,598	26,204	18.8
6200	Security and commodity brokers	456	487	45.0	25,312	27,359	78,351	85,513	1,765,397	2,089,646	88.5
6280	Security and commodity services	258	268	42.9	13,294	15,491	77,976	84,855	947,635	1,176,247	90.4
6300	Insurance carriers	146	133	21.7	17,218	17,904	50,837	54,666	790,933	833,450	32.9
6310	Life insurance	63	57	20.5	10,663	10,423	54,241	56,834	489,718	480,355	34.7
6330	Fire, marine, and casualty insurance	46	44	24.4	4,363	5,299	47,328	53,339	200,517	248,470	37.4

Source: County Business Patterns, 1994/95, CBP-94/95, U.S. Department of Commerce, Washington, D.C., November 1997. SIC categories for which data were suppressed or not available for both 1994 and 1995 are not displayed. The employment columns represent mid-March employment in the year. Pay per employee is calculated by dividing 1st Quarter payroll, annualized, by mid-March employment. The columns headed "% State" show the county's percentage of the state total for the SIC in 1995; for example, 1.4% for SIC 6000 means that the county had 1.4 percent of the state's total establishments (or payroll) in SIC 6000 in 1995. A dash (-) is used to indicate that data are not available or cannot be calculated; nec means not elsewhere classified.

Continued on next page.

SIC	Industry	No. Establishments			Employment		Pay / Employee		Annual Payroll ($ 000)		
		1994	1995	% State	1994	1995	1994	1995	1994	1995	% State
SUFFOLK, MA - [continued]											
6360	Title insurance	11	10	66.7	144	159	66,194	57,761	7,348	7,445	86.2
6400	Insurance agents, brokers, and service	343	364	12.2	4,357	4,333	45,896	54,810	193,372	221,770	27.9
6500	Real estate	867	860	17.5	11,697	12,412	35,063	36,328	418,437	442,995	45.4
6510	Real estate operators and lessors	315	308	18.9	2,833	3,631	39,009	34,714	106,120	109,567	42.1
6530	Real estate agents and managers	480	453	16.8	8,563	8,301	33,886	37,339	301,420	314,232	49.7
6550	Subdividers and developers	50	57	15.7	254	342	30,504	31,029	8,626	10,394	20.8
6552	Subdividers and developers, n.e.c.	35	41	20.6	135	230	31,111	30,887	4,773	6,446	22.5
6553	Cemetery subdividers and developers	14	14	10.9	119	112	29,815	31,321	3,844	3,912	21.0
6700	Holding and other investment offices	182	186	33.4	6,597	7,793	80,887	103,782	583,464	694,132	80.2
6710	Holding offices	45	44	27.8	789	455	67,579	101,046	49,270	41,770	30.6
6720	Investment offices	25	23	65.7	4,240	5,438	92,094	117,075	440,118	506,482	93.4
6730	Trusts	44	47	27.6	357	424	58,476	69,255	23,019	54,196	80.0
6732	Educational, religious, etc. trusts	17	17	23.6	264	293	65,652	61,625	18,279	42,142	81.9
6733	Trusts, n.e.c.	27	30	30.9	93	131	38,108	86,321	4,740	12,054	74.6
6790	Miscellaneous investing	68	66	39.1	1,211	1,459	56,925	65,689	71,057	89,241	77.5
6799	Investors, n.e.c.	53	54	48.2	460	484	113,087	155,000	53,745	70,235	80.7
WORCESTER, MA											
60 -	**Finance, insurance, and real estate**	1,231	1,189	9.0	19,192	18,387	32,048	32,598	610,971	564,923	5.7
6000	Depository institutions	284	242	10.1	4,388	4,011	23,669	25,805	110,766	97,537	4.7
6020	Commercial banks	127	108	10.4	2,227	2,041	24,713	27,669	60,009	51,001	3.6
6030	Savings institutions	100	78	8.6	1,435	1,214	23,640	25,334	34,641	29,297	6.3
6100	Nondepository institutions	70	64	9.8	826	825	34,741	41,251	26,480	30,176	9.9
6140	Personal credit institutions	23	24	14.9	383	438	31,363	42,986	13,191	17,563	24.0
6150	Business credit institutions	9	8	8.2	216	197	43,389	46,457	8,050	7,867	9.4
6160	Mortgage bankers and brokers	36	30	7.9	225	185	32,409	32,432	5,206	4,700	3.4
6210	Security brokers and dealers	16	19	4.3	288	266	60,750	53,398	14,720	15,356	1.5
6300	Insurance carriers	65	62	10.1	9,893	9,397	36,098	34,541	333,242	289,583	11.4
6310	Life insurance	33	33	11.9	7,206	6,660	38,264	34,444	246,291	186,480	13.5
6330	Fire, marine, and casualty insurance	21	18	10.0	2,017	1,994	30,356	35,715	65,317	71,028	10.7
6400	Insurance agents, brokers, and service	289	291	9.8	1,836	2,080	30,606	32,548	65,543	72,507	9.1
6500	Real estate	432	439	8.9	1,633	1,447	19,346	21,006	33,671	33,149	3.4
6510	Real estate operators and lessors	143	141	8.7	612	556	18,288	19,741	11,627	10,948	4.2
6530	Real estate agents and managers	219	219	8.1	809	665	19,155	20,259	15,808	15,114	2.4
6540	Title abstract offices	15	15	26.8	78	63	29,795	27,365	2,388	1,823	26.3
6550	Subdividers and developers	44	45	12.4	125	139	19,264	27,770	3,507	4,499	9.0
6552	Subdividers and developers, n.e.c.	21	21	10.6	55	72	20,655	36,500	1,845	2,795	9.7
6553	Cemetery subdividers and developers	21	21	16.4	70	67	18,171	18,388	1,498	1,531	8.2
6700	Holding and other investment offices	37	32	5.7	229	245	69,240	83,853	22,097	21,965	2.5
6710	Holding offices	19	18	11.4	185	201	62,768	90,249	17,296	18,831	13.8
6733	Trusts, n.e.c.	4	4	4.1	3	4	9,333	7,000	45	62	0.4
6790	Miscellaneous investing	6	5	3.0	20	19	182,200	84,842	3,994	2,190	1.9

Source: County Business Patterns, 1994/95, CBP-94/95, U.S. Department of Commerce, Washington, D.C., November 1997. SIC categories for which data were suppressed or not available for both 1994 and 1995 are *not* displayed. The employment columns represent mid-March employment in the year. Pay per employee is calculated by dividing 1st Quarter payroll, annualized, by mid-March employment. The columns headed "% State" show the county's percentage of the state total for the SIC in 1995; for example, 1.4% for SIC 6000 means that the county had 1.4 percent of the state's total establishments (or payroll) in SIC 6000 in 1995. A dash (-) is used to indicate that data are not available or cannot be calculated; *nec* means not elsewhere classified.

SIC	Industry	No. Establishments			Employment		Pay / Employee		Annual Payroll ($ 000)		
		1994	1995	% State	1994	1995	1994	1995	1994	1995	% State
MONTCALM, MI - [continued]											
6000	Depository institutions	28	28	0.7	281	280	18,149	20,114	5,630	5,692	0.3
6020	Commercial banks	22	22	0.8	238	234	18,773	20,991	4,955	4,987	0.3
6060	Credit unions	6	6	0.8	43	46	14,698	15,652	675	705	0.3
6400	Insurance agents, brokers, and service	29	27	0.7	98	105	18,000	17,448	1,931	2,086	0.3
6500	Real estate	15	16	0.3	32	32	11,125	13,000	455	494	0.1
6510	Real estate operators and lessors	7	7	0.3	17	16	7,059	8,750	162	173	0.1
6530	Real estate agents and managers	8	9	0.3	15	16	15,733	17,250	293	321	0.1
MONTMORENCY, MI											
60 –	**Finance, insurance, and real estate**	19	22	0.1	92	88	13,087	14,818	1,334	1,350	0.0
6400	Insurance agents, brokers, and service	6	6	0.1	18	13	12,667	13,231	236	191	0.0
6530	Real estate agents and managers	4	6	0.2	26	31	9,538	6,839	235	224	0.1
MUSKEGON, MI											
60 –	**Finance, insurance, and real estate**	246	257	1.4	1,722	2,224	26,771	23,980	46,468	55,765	0.9
6000	Depository institutions	63	71	1.7	703	709	19,249	22,922	13,470	16,583	0.9
6020	Commercial banks	36	44	1.6	488	491	19,377	23,943	9,170	12,013	0.8
6100	Nondepository institutions	4	7	0.8	17	17	20,706	16,235	302	593	0.1
6200	Security and commodity brokers	13	14	1.5	128	61	90,094	67,803	8,759	3,295	0.8
6210	Security brokers and dealers	9	10	1.7	116	51	98,172	78,118	8,605	3,168	0.9
6280	Security and commodity services	3	3	0.9	10	8	13,200	17,500	134	118	0.2
6300	Insurance carriers	18	20	1.6	182	176	37,275	33,636	6,195	6,183	0.4
6310	Life insurance	3	4	1.4	56	52	26,429	24,231	1,390	1,274	0.4
6360	Title insurance	3	3	4.5	29	33	29,793	15,758	823	732	2.4
6400	Insurance agents, brokers, and service	63	65	1.6	254	243	20,992	23,654	6,304	6,444	0.9
6500	Real estate	80	73	1.1	427	646	18,576	16,885	10,484	10,604	1.3
6510	Real estate operators and lessors	37	32	1.3	288	470	18,792	16,740	6,636	5,804	2.4
6530	Real estate agents and managers	36	34	1.1	109	133	17,101	16,211	2,393	2,411	0.5
6550	Subdividers and developers	6	5	1.1	29	42	22,345	20,857	1,447	2,357	2.9
6700	Holding and other investment offices	5	7	1.4	11	372	57,818	27,129	954	12,063	3.8
NEWAYGO, MI											
60 –	**Finance, insurance, and real estate**	48	49	0.3	304	328	18,079	19,963	6,696	7,002	0.1
6000	Depository institutions	13	13	0.3	121	152	18,116	20,605	3,051	3,144	0.2
6400	Insurance agents, brokers, and service	15	15	0.4	64	52	16,375	17,923	1,045	1,065	0.1
OAKLAND, MI											
60 –	**Finance, insurance, and real estate**	3,816	4,015	22.1	59,740	55,601	31,702	35,244	1,910,208	2,011,664	31.3
6000	Depository institutions	446	522	12.7	13,302	12,471	25,863	29,014	356,444	373,618	19.8
6020	Commercial banks	294	346	12.5	9,322	8,450	26,796	30,925	255,471	278,539	19.2
6030	Savings institutions	64	83	15.5	2,694	2,655	24,878	26,219	72,747	62,698	29.3
6060	Credit unions	75	80	10.7	1,217	1,292	21,423	22,746	26,741	30,643	15.1
6100	Nondepository institutions	291	324	37.8	9,748	7,426	33,696	38,953	299,473	304,526	61.0
6140	Personal credit institutions	52	53	29.1	2,244	1,895	31,424	37,575	71,520	76,238	58.1
6150	Business credit institutions	41	41	40.2	1,154	1,358	60,596	59,844	59,285	68,575	67.6
6160	Mortgage bankers and brokers	193	222	42.5	6,330	4,156	29,659	32,800	168,180	159,070	64.3
6200	Security and commodity brokers	248	263	27.5	2,716	2,494	63,389	70,055	161,224	180,214	41.2
6210	Security brokers and dealers	125	126	20.9	2,152	1,869	66,046	75,692	122,402	138,403	38.0
6280	Security and commodity services	121	132	39.5	557	617	53,759	53,712	38,717	41,678	57.8
6300	Insurance carriers	347	365	28.5	14,390	13,616	35,656	39,641	504,085	516,446	31.5
6310	Life insurance	100	107	36.8	4,777	4,571	34,729	40,160	157,047	171,262	53.9
6320	Medical service and health insurance	21	24	26.4	4,079	4,015	37,841	39,438	155,641	149,421	36.6
6330	Fire, marine, and casualty insurance	169	179	24.8	4,376	4,126	36,050	41,188	160,428	167,597	19.6
6350	Surety insurance	12	12	63.2	58	49	36,828	44,082	2,086	2,693	83.3
6360	Title insurance	16	17	25.8	609	535	29,589	29,151	15,198	14,017	45.3
6370	Pension, health, and welfare funds	26	25	31.6	462	318	30,909	31,811	13,374	11,436	45.6
6400	Insurance agents, brokers, and service	824	834	20.4	5,937	6,056	31,668	34,818	208,855	232,749	32.3
6500	Real estate	1,510	1,559	24.5	11,883	11,651	22,869	25,395	295,584	313,487	38.9

Source: County Business Patterns, 1994/95, CBP-94/95, U.S. Department of Commerce, Washington, D.C., November 1997. SIC categories for which data were suppressed or not available for both 1994 and 1995 are *not* displayed. The employment columns represent mid-March employment in the year. Pay per employee is calculated by dividing 1st Quarter payroll, annualized, by mid-March employment. The columns headed "% State" show the county's percentage of the state total for the SIC in 1995; for example, 1.4% for SIC 6000 means that the county had 1.4 percent of the state's total establishments (or payroll) in SIC 6000 in 1995. A dash (-) is used to indicate that data are not available or cannot be calculated; *nec* means not elsewhere classified.

Continued on next page.

SIC	Industry	No. Establishments			Employment		Pay / Employee		Annual Payroll ($ 000)		
		1994	1995	% State	1994	1995	1994	1995	1994	1995	% State
OAKLAND, MI - [continued]											
6510	Real estate operators and lessors	575	598	24.1	3,481	3,493	16,203	16,447	66,720	69,002	28.1
6530	Real estate agents and managers	750	741	24.7	7,436	6,996	24,958	29,241	194,819	204,020	46.3
6540	Title abstract offices	13	10	10.0	258	135	25,302	26,459	6,298	3,749	18.2
6550	Subdividers and developers	94	115	25.0	603	848	35,476	30,722	23,928	29,866	36.8
6552	Subdividers and developers, n.e.c.	69	85	34.3	366	535	39,585	32,082	15,615	19,314	48.2
6553	Cemetery subdividers and developers	17	17	10.7	221	244	29,376	30,557	7,880	8,719	26.9
6700	Holding and other investment offices	140	138	27.6	1,273	1,635	44,927	46,850	66,975	80,260	25.1
6710	Holding offices	58	56	28.7	900	1,241	50,556	50,050	53,475	63,177	27.4
6720	Investment offices	4	5	31.3	8	16	45,500	30,000	354	575	39.4
6730	Trusts	22	19	18.6	64	70	17,938	16,114	1,296	1,224	4.7
6732	Educational, religious, etc. trusts	8	8	17.8	24	25	29,333	28,000	712	658	8.1
6733	Trusts, n.e.c.	14	11	19.6	40	45	11,100	9,511	584	566	3.2
6790	Miscellaneous investing	44	42	30.7	254	255	35,591	44,204	10,717	13,140	33.2
6794	Patent owners and lessors	14	13	26.0	157	148	36,255	42,378	7,347	7,203	40.4
OCEANA, MI											
60 –	**Finance, insurance, and real estate**	37	35	0.2	165	160	16,776	17,775	2,984	3,169	0.0
6000	Depository institutions	10	10	0.2	100	98	17,920	19,510	1,869	2,015	0.1
6400	Insurance agents, brokers, and service	11	11	0.3	38	40	17,684	15,300	596	601	0.1
6500	Real estate	12	11	0.2	19	15	9,053	11,200	383	382	0.0
6510	Real estate operators and lessors	5	5	0.2	2	2	4,000	6,000	158	202	0.1
6550	Subdividers and developers	4	3	0.7	8	4	7,000	10,000	82	46	0.1
OGEMAW, MI											
60 –	**Finance, insurance, and real estate**	37	39	0.2	165	175	17,842	17,097	3,496	3,677	0.1
6000	Depository institutions	11	11	0.3	108	110	20,111	19,709	2,352	2,404	0.1
6400	Insurance agents, brokers, and service	9	9	0.2	26	27	17,077	17,333	727	815	0.1
6530	Real estate agents and managers	10	9	0.3	14	17	4,857	5,412	119	120	0.0
OSCEOLA, MI											
60 –	**Finance, insurance, and real estate**	29	28	0.2	136	145	16,235	20,855	2,399	3,231	0.1
6000	Depository institutions	13	13	0.3	102	109	16,588	22,128	1,777	2,600	0.1
6020	Commercial banks	10	10	0.4	98	105	16,898	22,552	1,739	2,557	0.2
6060	Credit unions	3	3	0.4	4	4	9,000	11,000	38	43	0.0
6400	Insurance agents, brokers, and service	11	10	0.2	25	25	15,840	21,120	478	521	0.1
OSCODA, MI											
60 –	**Finance, insurance, and real estate**	14	14	0.1	55	54	11,782	14,889	714	888	0.0
6530	Real estate agents and managers	4	4	0.1	4	7	7,000	7,429	45	48	0.0
OTSEGO, MI											
60 –	**Finance, insurance, and real estate**	50	50	0.3	285	282	20,561	24,780	6,287	7,424	0.1
6000	Depository institutions	11	11	0.3	135	138	20,770	21,884	2,739	2,995	0.2
6300	Insurance carriers	5	5	0.4	55	61	24,582	37,836	1,550	2,292	0.1
6510	Real estate operators and lessors	6	7	0.3	10	10	12,000	16,800	180	203	0.1
6530	Real estate agents and managers	12	11	0.4	30	24	14,400	14,833	460	413	0.1
OTTAWA, MI											
60 –	**Finance, insurance, and real estate**	334	355	2.0	2,700	2,556	25,141	27,700	69,840	74,491	1.2
6000	Depository institutions	78	84	2.0	1,506	1,355	24,231	28,298	34,558	36,506	1.9
6020	Commercial banks	56	63	2.3	1,355	1,201	25,045	29,675	32,175	33,890	2.3
6030	Savings institutions	8	8	1.5	79	79	17,722	18,430	1,145	1,250	0.6
6060	Credit unions	14	13	1.7	72	75	16,056	16,640	1,238	1,366	0.7
6100	Nondepository institutions	7	9	1.1	64	67	23,750	20,060	1,343	2,091	0.4
6140	Personal credit institutions	3	3	1.6	42	43	20,190	17,953	776	760	0.6
6160	Mortgage bankers and brokers	4	6	1.1	22	24	30,545	23,833	567	1,331	0.5
6200	Security and commodity brokers	27	28	2.9	156	114	51,795	51,088	7,618	6,139	1.4
6210	Security brokers and dealers	19	20	3.3	89	96	59,056	52,375	4,756	5,190	1.4

Source: County Business Patterns, 1994/95, CBP-94/95, U.S. Department of Commerce, Washington, D.C., November 1997. SIC categories for which data were suppressed or not available for both 1994 and 1995 are *not* displayed. The employment columns represent mid-March employment in the year. Pay per employee is calculated by dividing 1st Quarter payroll, annualized, by mid-March employment. The columns headed "% State" show the county's percentage of the state total for the SIC in 1995; for example, 1.4% for SIC 6000 means that the county had 1.4 percent of the state's total establishments (or payroll) in SIC 6000 in 1995. A dash (-) is used to indicate that data are not available or cannot be calculated; *nec* means not elsewhere classified.

Continued on next page.

SIC	Industry	No. Establishments			Employment		Pay / Employee		Annual Payroll ($ 000)		
		1994	1995	% State	1994	1995	1994	1995	1994	1995	% State
OTTAWA, MI - [continued]											
6300	Insurance carriers	16	18	1.4	63	62	40,444	41,484	2,549	2,428	0.1
6400	Insurance agents, brokers, and service	72	73	1.8	363	345	24,419	29,055	10,753	10,520	1.5
6500	Real estate	124	133	2.1	472	523	16,593	19,075	9,822	10,962	1.4
6510	Real estate operators and lessors	42	42	1.7	120	138	18,400	19,826	2,776	2,864	1.2
6530	Real estate agents and managers	63	68	2.3	282	318	16,128	18,214	5,671	6,380	1.4
6550	Subdividers and developers	13	16	3.5	61	59	14,754	21,831	1,207	1,520	1.9
6700	Holding and other investment offices	10	10	2.0	76	90	33,474	30,178	3,197	5,845	1.8
PRESQUE ISLE, MI											
60 –	**Finance, insurance, and real estate**	23	24	0.1	122	131	17,508	17,618	2,260	2,424	0.0
6000	Depository institutions	9	9	0.2	75	84	16,960	16,667	1,281	1,445	0.1
6020	Commercial banks	4	4	0.1	34	38	16,235	18,421	574	726	0.1
6500	Real estate	3	4	0.1	7	7	12,571	13,714	122	138	0.0
6530	Real estate agents and managers	3	3	0.1	7	7	12,571	13,714	122	128	0.0
ROSCOMMON, MI											
60 –	**Finance, insurance, and real estate**	48	50	0.3	223	206	13,883	17,612	3,371	4,377	0.1
6000	Depository institutions	11	10	0.2	121	107	15,140	21,720	1,864	2,634	0.1
6400	Insurance agents, brokers, and service	15	14	0.3	52	48	13,231	15,917	871	973	0.1
6500	Real estate	18	22	0.3	31	35	11,613	9,486	368	456	0.1
6530	Real estate agents and managers	14	15	0.5	25	27	11,520	8,741	283	279	0.1
SAGINAW, MI											
60 –	**Finance, insurance, and real estate**	369	370	2.0	3,698	3,736	25,025	27,441	93,088	102,223	1.6
6000	Depository institutions	112	108	2.6	1,607	1,651	19,925	24,162	34,022	40,904	2.2
6020	Commercial banks	60	59	2.1	1,009	1,060	19,306	25,336	20,859	26,984	1.9
6030	Savings institutions	21	18	3.4	230	204	18,504	17,784	4,551	4,568	2.1
6060	Credit unions	31	31	4.1	368	387	22,511	24,310	8,612	9,352	4.6
6100	Nondepository institutions	11	12	1.4	123	78	31,350	36,821	3,530	2,896	0.6
6140	Personal credit institutions	6	6	3.3	86	67	34,186	37,970	2,814	2,389	1.8
6200	Security and commodity brokers	20	21	2.2	169	167	67,787	54,707	9,092	8,567	2.0
6210	Security brokers and dealers	12	13	2.2	150	141	72,933	60,823	8,654	8,089	2.2
6300	Insurance carriers	34	34	2.7	935	946	31,889	33,818	28,914	30,068	1.8
6310	Life insurance	9	9	3.1	386	359	32,829	36,401	11,678	10,609	3.3
6330	Fire, marine, and casualty insurance	16	16	2.2	418	458	32,344	32,978	13,603	15,523	1.8
6400	Insurance agents, brokers, and service	91	92	2.2	385	403	23,553	29,102	9,982	11,417	1.6
6500	Real estate	97	98	1.5	447	454	12,617	13,269	6,843	7,239	0.9
6510	Real estate operators and lessors	41	41	1.7	265	280	10,068	11,329	3,610	3,914	1.6
6530	Real estate agents and managers	48	47	1.6	116	117	12,517	12,239	1,647	1,611	0.4
6700	Holding and other investment offices	4	5	1.0	32	37	21,500	23,676	705	1,132	0.4
ST. CLAIR, MI											
60 –	**Finance, insurance, and real estate**	220	229	1.3	1,872	1,747	23,594	24,959	44,621	45,753	0.7
6000	Depository institutions	56	56	1.4	971	900	21,248	21,178	19,459	20,136	1.1
6020	Commercial banks	39	41	1.5	716	644	22,369	22,323	14,457	15,131	1.0
6100	Nondepository institutions	5	6	0.7	12	23	29,333	35,826	303	1,061	0.2
6200	Security and commodity brokers	5	7	0.7	27	37	53,037	39,459	1,557	1,830	0.4
6210	Security brokers and dealers	5	7	1.2	27	37	53,037	39,459	1,557	1,830	0.5
6300	Insurance carriers	17	17	1.3	197	183	35,391	36,940	7,180	6,879	0.4
6310	Life insurance	4	4	1.4	114	109	28,140	30,239	3,304	3,234	1.0
6400	Insurance agents, brokers, and service	49	50	1.2	210	209	18,952	21,014	4,566	4,734	0.7
6500	Real estate	78	83	1.3	334	283	14,671	17,569	6,159	6,033	0.7
6510	Real estate operators and lessors	33	30	1.2	138	95	11,217	15,663	1,826	1,640	0.7
6530	Real estate agents and managers	36	41	1.4	144	138	16,528	17,246	3,083	2,892	0.7

Source: County Business Patterns, 1994/95, CBP-94/95, U.S. Department of Commerce, Washington, D.C., November 1997. SIC categories for which data were suppressed or not available for both 1994 and 1995 are not displayed. The employment columns represent mid-March employment in the year. Pay per employee is calculated by dividing 1st Quarter payroll, annualized, by mid-March employment. The columns headed "% State" show the county's percentage of the state total for the SIC in 1995; for example, 1.4% for SIC 6000 means that the county had 1.4 percent of the state's total establishments (or payroll) in SIC 6000 in 1995. A dash (-) is used to indicate that data are not available or cannot be calculated; nec means not elsewhere classified.

Continued on next page.

SIC	Industry	No. Establishments			Employment		Pay / Employee		Annual Payroll ($ 000)		
		1994	1995	% State	1994	1995	1994	1995	1994	1995	% State
ST. CLAIR, MI - [continued]											
6540	Title abstract offices	3	3	3.0	41	33	17,854	21,091	862	846	4.1
6700	Holding and other investment offices	10	10	2.0	121	112	48,760	54,786	5,397	5,080	1.6
6710	Holding offices	7	7	3.6	112	100	50,786	57,920	5,196	4,724	2.1
ST. JOSEPH, MI											
60 –	**Finance, insurance, and real estate**	105	104	0.6	520	502	19,192	21,538	9,981	10,607	0.2
6000	Depository institutions	37	35	0.8	340	295	19,024	22,698	5,990	6,137	0.3
6020	Commercial banks	24	22	0.8	244	203	18,082	21,970	4,081	4,068	0.3
6400	Insurance agents, brokers, and service	28	29	0.7	85	99	18,165	18,667	1,761	2,074	0.3
6500	Real estate	28	32	0.5	78	91	16,667	17,407	1,553	1,724	0.2
6530	Real estate agents and managers	18	22	0.7	42	52	10,571	11,692	460	616	0.1
SANILAC, MI											
60 –	**Finance, insurance, and real estate**	76	75	0.4	409	393	18,660	20,132	7,744	8,577	0.1
6000	Depository institutions	19	19	0.5	268	248	17,254	20,419	5,001	5,523	0.3
6400	Insurance agents, brokers, and service	25	24	0.6	71	70	17,239	17,600	1,306	1,434	0.2
6500	Real estate	19	20	0.3	36	39	11,778	12,821	505	576	0.1
6510	Real estate operators and lessors	5	5	0.2	8	9	7,500	8,000	66	77	0.0
6530	Real estate agents and managers	11	12	0.4	26	27	13,231	14,963	415	460	0.1
6550	Subdividers and developers	3	3	0.7	2	3	10,000	8,000	24	39	0.0
SCHOOLCRAFT, MI											
60 –	**Finance, insurance, and real estate**	17	19	0.1	121	121	20,231	25,322	2,376	2,963	0.0
6000	Depository institutions	5	5	0.1	83	82	21,590	28,341	1,674	2,134	0.1
6400	Insurance agents, brokers, and service	3	3	0.1	12	12	28,333	27,000	346	347	0.0
6530	Real estate agents and managers	3	3	0.1	7	6	9,143	13,333	79	73	0.0
SHIAWASSEE, MI											
60 –	**Finance, insurance, and real estate**	90	89	0.5	587	564	23,680	23,206	14,777	14,110	0.2
6000	Depository institutions	28	27	0.7	339	334	18,702	21,150	6,635	7,166	0.4
6020	Commercial banks	20	19	0.7	270	268	19,541	22,418	5,532	6,057	0.4
6400	Insurance agents, brokers, and service	28	30	0.7	111	113	17,802	19,965	2,456	2,804	0.4
6500	Real estate	23	23	0.4	55	62	11,564	12,129	1,010	1,056	0.1
6530	Real estate agents and managers	13	14	0.5	33	37	12,727	11,784	744	745	0.2
TUSCOLA, MI											
60 –	**Finance, insurance, and real estate**	80	80	0.4	419	396	17,012	20,162	7,354	7,599	0.1
6000	Depository institutions	31	32	0.8	308	284	15,597	19,352	5,025	5,017	0.3
6020	Commercial banks	23	24	0.9	269	244	15,480	19,934	4,349	4,298	0.3
6030	Savings institutions	3	3	0.6	16	16	18,500	15,750	311	325	0.2
6060	Credit unions	5	5	0.7	23	24	14,957	15,833	365	394	0.2
6400	Insurance agents, brokers, and service	31	32	0.8	70	76	20,171	20,526	1,424	1,559	0.2
6500	Real estate	13	10	0.2	26	20	12,462	15,000	427	499	0.1
VAN BUREN, MI											
60 –	**Finance, insurance, and real estate**	95	91	0.5	472	418	17,627	18,067	7,795	7,999	0.1
6000	Depository institutions	27	27	0.7	268	239	21,299	19,682	4,918	4,912	0.3
6020	Commercial banks	20	20	0.7	230	200	21,617	19,880	4,117	4,080	0.3
6030	Savings institutions	4	4	0.7	22	21	20,727	18,857	481	436	0.2
6060	Credit unions	3	3	0.4	16	18	17,500	18,444	320	396	0.2
6400	Insurance agents, brokers, and service	31	30	0.7	90	88	15,422	16,591	1,471	1,512	0.2
6500	Real estate	29	29	0.5	91	74	8,615	13,351	964	1,104	0.1
6510	Real estate operators and lessors	12	11	0.4	50	32	5,840	11,750	337	394	0.2
6530	Real estate agents and managers	14	14	0.5	31	32	12,129	13,625	476	506	0.1
WASHTENAW, MI											
60 –	**Finance, insurance, and real estate**	606	647	3.6	5,922	5,750	25,916	28,593	161,835	180,000	2.8
6000	Depository institutions	127	139	3.4	2,103	1,844	23,576	26,996	48,782	53,819	2.9

Source: County Business Patterns, 1994/95, CBP-94/95, U.S. Department of Commerce, Washington, D.C., November 1997. SIC categories for which data were suppressed or not available for both 1994 and 1995 are not displayed. The employment columns represent mid-March employment in the year. Pay per employee is calculated by dividing 1st Quarter payroll, annualized, by mid-March employment. The columns headed "% State" show the county's percentage of the state total for the SIC in 1995; for example, 1.4% for SIC 6000 means that the county had 1.4 percent of the state's total establishments (or payroll) in SIC 6000 in 1995. A dash (-) is used to indicate that data are not available or cannot be calculated; nec means not elsewhere classified.

Continued on next page.

SIC	Industry	No. Establishments			Employment		Pay / Employee		Annual Payroll ($ 000)		
		1994	1995	% State	1994	1995	1994	1995	1994	1995	% State
WASHTENAW, MI - [continued]											
6020	Commercial banks	87	97	3.5	1,304	1,071	21,028	28,575	27,195	30,784	2.1
6030	Savings institutions	26	27	5.0	552	532	31,101	26,451	16,477	17,760	8.3
6100	Nondepository institutions	34	36	4.2	455	401	32,651	37,067	14,507	15,853	3.2
6140	Personal credit institutions	7	8	4.4	147	162	34,231	45,062	5,128	7,394	5.6
6150	Business credit institutions	4	4	3.9	36	38	54,444	50,737	1,614	1,586	1.6
6160	Mortgage bankers and brokers	19	21	4.0	253	188	28,427	27,957	7,240	6,374	2.6
6200	Security and commodity brokers	39	38	4.0	242	247	68,711	66,089	17,364	17,392	4.0
6210	Security brokers and dealers	19	20	3.3	192	187	73,458	63,936	13,518	12,531	3.4
6300	Insurance carriers	35	37	2.9	291	267	34,460	36,434	9,633	9,722	0.6
6310	Life insurance	5	5	1.7	72	61	26,000	33,377	1,774	1,675	0.5
6330	Fire, marine, and casualty insurance	23	25	3.5	125	117	43,904	45,128	5,341	5,345	0.6
6360	Title insurance	3	3	4.5	58	44	28,483	18,727	1,459	1,179	3.8
6400	Insurance agents, brokers, and service	100	108	2.6	473	604	23,290	27,199	13,915	19,363	2.7
6500	Real estate	256	273	4.3	1,866	1,912	18,433	19,824	37,821	41,847	5.2
6510	Real estate operators and lessors	95	102	4.1	503	483	14,417	15,834	7,555	7,621	3.1
6530	Real estate agents and managers	131	130	4.3	1,219	1,202	20,020	21,524	26,823	28,995	6.6
6540	Title abstract offices	5	5	5.0	24	20	19,000	17,000	350	347	1.7
6550	Subdividers and developers	18	23	5.0	93	146	18,581	19,123	2,347	3,268	4.0
6552	Subdividers and developers, n.e.c.	9	12	4.8	49	93	20,327	19,441	1,376	2,183	5.4
6553	Cemetery subdividers and developers	8	8	5.0	44	46	16,636	18,957	862	898	2.8
6790	Miscellaneous investing	5	6	4.4	59	52	19,119	20,538	1,038	1,205	3.0
WAYNE, MI											
60 –	**Finance, insurance, and real estate**	2,364	2,417	13.3	43,087	42,875	33,582	35,507	1,417,020	1,536,298	23.9
6000	Depository institutions	652	664	16.1	16,691	17,766	25,572	26,172	430,566	495,747	26.3
6020	Commercial banks	378	395	14.2	12,919	13,976	25,923	26,414	336,376	384,626	26.6
6030	Savings institutions	96	96	17.9	1,364	1,282	24,868	25,629	35,030	47,224	22.1
6060	Credit unions	138	133	17.8	1,819	1,893	22,540	23,520	42,722	45,762	22.6
6100	Nondepository institutions	89	103	12.0	953	1,136	34,455	44,894	31,401	47,345	9.5
6140	Personal credit institutions	23	28	15.4	355	405	32,530	35,121	11,763	14,340	10.9
6160	Mortgage bankers and brokers	51	60	11.5	432	356	35,315	35,978	13,261	16,835	6.8
6200	Security and commodity brokers	119	133	13.9	1,487	1,572	64,264	62,170	88,938	94,493	21.6
6210	Security brokers and dealers	76	85	14.1	1,258	1,317	68,127	66,970	74,914	85,115	23.4
6280	Security and commodity services	42	47	14.1	229	253	43,039	37,628	14,018	9,366	13.0
6300	Insurance carriers	190	186	14.5	12,677	11,524	41,032	43,201	476,575	494,855	30.1
6310	Life insurance	42	38	13.1	1,662	1,520	27,526	25,187	44,130	36,560	11.5
6330	Fire, marine, and casualty insurance	115	123	17.1	6,244	5,498	43,745	48,951	242,895	271,039	31.7
6400	Insurance agents, brokers, and service	367	370	9.0	2,933	2,815	34,243	37,620	100,704	106,014	14.7
6500	Real estate	855	864	13.6	5,278	5,392	20,067	24,019	113,544	133,841	16.6
6510	Real estate operators and lessors	420	416	16.8	2,288	2,366	18,170	19,657	42,955	52,317	21.3
6530	Real estate agents and managers	358	354	11.8	2,352	2,401	21,077	28,213	53,778	63,596	14.4
6540	Title abstract offices	11	11	11.0	143	139	25,483	23,655	4,085	3,796	18.5
6550	Subdividers and developers	42	42	9.1	444	431	23,586	25,606	11,831	11,507	14.2
6552	Subdividers and developers, n.e.c.	14	17	6.9	124	105	10,613	24,838	2,630	3,072	7.7
6553	Cemetery subdividers and developers	26	23	14.5	318	324	28,629	25,852	9,146	8,297	25.6
6700	Holding and other investment offices	86	92	18.4	941	1,326	63,507	59,557	64,605	81,320	25.4
6710	Holding offices	35	42	21.5	538	788	79,554	69,756	44,554	53,095	23.0
6730	Trusts	15	14	13.7	50	49	20,320	22,857	1,082	1,198	4.6
6732	Educational, religious, etc. trusts	10	10	22.2	38	35	22,737	24,800	867	909	11.1
6733	Trusts, n.e.c.	5	4	7.1	12	14	12,667	18,000	215	289	1.6
6790	Miscellaneous investing	27	23	16.8	221	297	36,579	32,444	9,313	10,631	26.8
6794	Patent owners and lessors	10	10	20.0	85	90	58,071	61,822	5,595	6,281	35.2
6798	Real estate investment trusts	4	3	30.0	5	6	31,200	40,667	102	131	12.6
6799	Investors, n.e.c.	13	10	14.1	131	201	22,840	19,045	3,616	4,219	20.7
WEXFORD, MI											
60 –	**Finance, insurance, and real estate**	60	64	0.4	329	323	17,702	23,653	6,828	8,906	0.1
6000	Depository institutions	16	17	0.4	204	200	18,059	26,180	3,733	5,830	0.3

Source: County Business Patterns, 1994/95, CBP-94/95, U.S. Department of Commerce, Washington, D.C., November 1997. SIC categories for which data were suppressed or not available for both 1994 and 1995 are *not* displayed. The employment columns represent mid-March employment in the year. Pay per employee is calculated by dividing 1st Quarter payroll, annualized, by mid-March employment. The columns headed "% State" show the county's percentage of the state total for the SIC in 1995; for example, 1.4% for SIC 6000 means that the county had 1.4 percent of the state's total establishments (or payroll) in SIC 6000 in 1995. A dash (-) is used to indicate that data are not available or cannot be calculated; *nec* means not elsewhere classified.

Continued on next page.

SIC	Industry	No. Establishments			Employment		Pay / Employee		Annual Payroll ($ 000)		
		1994	1995	% State	1994	1995	1994	1995	1994	1995	% State
WEXFORD, MI - [continued]											
6020	Commercial banks	13	14	0.5	176	172	18,500	27,791	3,298	5,357	0.4
6400	Insurance agents, brokers, and service	21	22	0.5	74	68	17,514	21,529	1,930	1,810	0.3
6500	Real estate	17	21	0.3	35	41	13,257	12,683	786	836	0.1
6510	Real estate operators and lessors	5	5	0.2	7	11	9,714	8,364	83	122	0.0
6530	Real estate agents and managers	8	10	0.3	23	23	14,783	13,043	504	545	0.1

Source: County Business Patterns, 1994/95, CBP-94/95, U.S. Department of Commerce, Washington, D.C., November 1997. SIC categories for which data were suppressed or not available for both 1994 and 1995 are *not* displayed. The employment columns represent mid-March employment in the year. Pay per employee is calculated by dividing 1st Quarter payroll, annualized, by mid-March employment. The columns headed "% State" show the county's percentage of the state total for the SIC in 1995; for example, 1.4% for SIC 6000 means that the county had 1.4 percent of the state's total establishments (or payroll) in SIC 6000 in 1995. A dash (-) is used to indicate that data are not available or cannot be calculated; *nec* means not elsewhere classified.

MINNESOTA

SIC	Industry	No. Establishments			Employment		Pay / Employee		Annual Payroll ($ 000)		
		1994	1995	% State	1994	1995	1994	1995	1994	1995	% State
AITKIN, MN											
60 –	**Finance, insurance, and real estate**	25	21	0.2	144	125	13,972	19,680	2,435	2,618	0.1
6000	Depository institutions	5	5	0.3	78	68	15,538	26,118	1,488	1,757	0.2
6500	Real estate	11	9	0.2	36	36	10,333	10,667	486	554	0.1
ANOKA, MN											
60 –	**Finance, insurance, and real estate**	415	428	3.6	2,173	2,127	21,189	21,715	49,747	49,257	1.0
6000	Depository institutions	53	51	2.9	671	658	22,045	24,213	15,232	15,446	1.5
6020	Commercial banks	31	32	2.5	464	460	24,276	26,452	11,590	11,941	1.4
6100	Nondepository institutions	45	44	6.0	263	220	30,540	29,764	8,141	6,508	1.6
6140	Personal credit institutions	19	20	10.6	93	105	22,581	26,667	2,299	2,885	3.2
6160	Mortgage bankers and brokers	23	20	5.4	163	108	35,117	33,407	5,603	3,480	1.9
6400	Insurance agents, brokers, and service	126	128	4.0	437	448	22,581	24,063	10,424	11,648	2.5
6500	Real estate	155	164	3.9	725	728	15,117	14,582	13,762	13,043	2.8
6510	Real estate operators and lessors	57	59	3.6	248	233	13,194	12,824	3,560	3,335	2.5
6530	Real estate agents and managers	77	77	3.9	276	299	12,333	14,194	4,023	4,617	1.8
6540	Title abstract offices	9	8	4.6	95	59	25,768	20,339	2,091	1,370	3.7
6550	Subdividers and developers	10	13	4.0	105	132	17,410	15,636	3,991	3,508	10.4
BECKER, MN											
60 –	**Finance, insurance, and real estate**	64	63	0.5	345	343	28,499	28,431	6,520	6,874	0.1
6000	Depository institutions	9	8	0.5	169	156	40,095	42,051	3,487	3,415	0.3
6020	Commercial banks	9	8	0.6	169	156	40,095	42,051	3,487	3,415	0.4
6500	Real estate	23	24	0.6	102	107	14,196	12,748	1,436	1,642	0.3
6530	Real estate agents and managers	14	15	0.8	44	47	9,636	6,979	379	372	0.1
BELTRAMI, MN											
60 –	**Finance, insurance, and real estate**	52	52	0.4	362	382	18,210	20,168	7,017	7,241	0.1
6000	Depository institutions	13	13	0.7	219	229	19,963	21,852	4,411	4,538	0.4
6200	Security and commodity brokers	3	3	0.4	6	6	14,000	32,667	105	146	0.0
6400	Insurance agents, brokers, and service	16	16	0.5	60	63	15,467	19,238	1,077	1,182	0.3
6500	Real estate	16	16	0.4	57	60	13,053	12,067	905	863	0.2
6530	Real estate agents and managers	10	10	0.5	38	35	11,474	10,971	529	487	0.2
BENTON, MN											
60 –	**Finance, insurance, and real estate**	29	29	0.2	142	132	17,972	23,121	2,477	2,830	0.1
BIG STONE, MN											
60 –	**Finance, insurance, and real estate**	22	19	0.2	80	70	21,550	23,257	1,754	1,788	0.0
BLUE EARTH, MN											
60 –	**Finance, insurance, and real estate**	199	200	1.7	1,176	1,153	22,772	22,435	25,350	25,525	0.5
6000	Depository institutions	30	29	1.7	397	375	24,332	24,021	9,121	8,701	0.8
6020	Commercial banks	19	19	1.5	272	264	27,956	27,061	7,188	6,710	0.8
6100	Nondepository institutions	12	12	1.6	76	74	48,211	52,541	3,010	3,160	0.8
6200	Security and commodity brokers	15	15	1.8	80	64	44,050	35,188	2,219	1,940	0.3
6300	Insurance carriers	16	16	2.1	105	114	28,686	28,877	3,245	3,355	0.2
6310	Life insurance	6	6	3.1	73	71	31,014	29,465	2,175	2,041	0.3
6400	Insurance agents, brokers, and service	70	70	2.2	154	155	16,831	17,006	2,746	2,917	0.6
6500	Real estate	52	53	1.3	304	312	12,224	12,910	4,294	4,678	1.0
6510	Real estate operators and lessors	28	28	1.7	127	132	7,654	10,091	1,202	1,457	1.1

Source: County Business Patterns, 1994/95, CBP-94/95, U.S. Department of Commerce, Washington, D.C., November 1997. SIC categories for which data were suppressed or not available for both 1994 and 1995 are *not* displayed. The employment columns represent mid-March employment in the year. Pay per employee is calculated by dividing 1st Quarter payroll, annualized, by mid-March employment. The columns headed "% State" show the county's percentage of the state total for the SIC in 1995; for example, 1.4% for SIC 6000 means that the county had 1.4 percent of the state's total establishments (or payroll) in SIC 6000 in 1995. A dash (-) is used to indicate that data are not available or cannot be calculated; *nec* means not elsewhere classified.

Continued on next page.

SIC	Industry	No. Establishments			Employment		Pay / Employee		Annual Payroll ($ 000)		
		1994	1995	% State	1994	1995	1994	1995	1994	1995	% State
BLUE EARTH, MN - [continued]											
6530	Real estate agents and managers	17	18	0.9	142	141	17,042	16,879	2,713	2,754	1.1
6550	Subdividers and developers	5	5	1.5	19	16	14,105	16,500	327	408	1.2
6700	Holding and other investment offices	4	5	1.4	60	59	10,200	12,949	715	774	0.2
BROWN, MN											
60 –	**Finance, insurance, and real estate**	73	76	0.6	512	517	19,945	22,747	10,572	11,278	0.2
6000	Depository institutions	14	16	0.9	302	248	17,086	24,113	5,420	6,081	0.6
6200	Security and commodity brokers	4	6	0.7	37	39	46,919	45,641	1,774	1,467	0.2
6400	Insurance agents, brokers, and service	26	24	0.8	50	53	17,120	18,264	907	966	0.2
6500	Real estate	24	25	0.6	56	110	12,071	10,727	862	1,382	0.3
6510	Real estate operators and lessors	15	14	0.9	26	79	9,692	8,810	328	747	0.6
CARLTON, MN											
60 –	**Finance, insurance, and real estate**	43	44	0.4	312	331	23,359	22,514	6,921	7,446	0.1
6000	Depository institutions	10	10	0.6	183	189	24,525	26,159	4,243	4,564	0.4
6060	Credit unions	4	4	1.4	105	108	20,457	21,963	2,143	2,262	4.1
6400	Insurance agents, brokers, and service	18	17	0.5	41	45	18,634	17,689	834	873	0.2
6500	Real estate	9	11	0.3	30	30	10,400	8,933	304	369	0.1
6530	Real estate agents and managers	5	4	0.2	8	8	7,000	4,500	48	53	0.0
CARVER, MN											
60 –	**Finance, insurance, and real estate**	104	117	1.0	818	809	20,778	22,032	15,544	17,129	0.3
6000	Depository institutions	16	16	0.9	285	274	28,744	31,577	7,135	7,363	0.7
6200	Security and commodity brokers	9	7	0.8	17	18	57,647	40,222	477	499	0.1
6210	Security brokers and dealers	5	3	0.7	12	11	77,333	60,364	417	438	0.1
6400	Insurance agents, brokers, and service	32	34	1.1	81	85	21,481	18,776	1,816	1,748	0.4
6500	Real estate	39	45	1.1	382	371	7,916	9,423	3,290	4,178	0.9
6510	Real estate operators and lessors	17	18	1.1	61	66	7,410	8,000	490	639	0.5
6530	Real estate agents and managers	18	23	1.2	315	299	7,619	9,204	2,611	3,305	1.3
CASS, MN											
60 –	**Finance, insurance, and real estate**	40	41	0.3	196	207	18,816	19,517	3,991	4,537	0.1
6000	Depository institutions	10	10	0.6	116	124	22,310	22,226	2,819	3,106	0.3
6500	Real estate	19	21	0.5	57	56	12,281	12,357	791	982	0.2
6510	Real estate operators and lessors	4	4	0.2	22	24	13,091	14,167	314	528	0.4
6530	Real estate agents and managers	7	9	0.5	4	5	13,000	8,800	70	77	0.0
6540	Title abstract offices	5	5	2.9	29	26	12,276	11,692	383	351	0.9
6550	Subdividers and developers	3	3	0.9	2	1	2,000	4,000	24	26	0.1
CHIPPEWA, MN											
60 –	**Finance, insurance, and real estate**	39	42	0.4	192	190	25,854	27,705	4,275	4,835	0.1
6000	Depository institutions	10	11	0.6	132	130	31,242	33,108	3,470	3,935	0.4
6500	Real estate	8	9	0.2	12	13	5,333	6,154	69	84	0.0
CHISAGO, MN											
60 –	**Finance, insurance, and real estate**	51	55	0.5	304	334	17,474	17,413	5,660	6,359	0.1
6000	Depository institutions	13	13	0.7	176	193	21,045	20,953	3,838	4,221	0.4
6500	Real estate	25	28	0.7	86	101	11,535	11,208	1,125	1,428	0.3
6510	Real estate operators and lessors	13	14	0.9	59	59	9,492	9,695	598	645	0.5
CLAY, MN											
60 –	**Finance, insurance, and real estate**	98	106	0.9	465	491	20,542	21,084	9,177	9,889	0.2
6000	Depository institutions	17	17	1.0	235	232	22,281	24,328	5,141	5,335	0.5
6020	Commercial banks	13	13	1.0	208	205	22,673	23,883	4,608	4,647	0.5
6400	Insurance agents, brokers, and service	40	40	1.3	104	99	14,769	15,515	1,571	1,588	0.3
6500	Real estate	30	37	0.9	80	108	13,450	11,185	969	1,322	0.3

Source: County Business Patterns, 1994/95, CBP-94/95, U.S. Department of Commerce, Washington, D.C., November 1997. SIC categories for which data were suppressed or not available for both 1994 and 1995 are not displayed. The employment columns represent mid-March employment in the year. Pay per employee is calculated by dividing 1st Quarter payroll, annualized, by mid-March employment. The columns headed "% State" show the county's percentage of the state total for the SIC in 1995; for example, 1.4% for SIC 6000 means that the county had 1.4 percent of the state's total establishments (or payroll) in SIC 6000 in 1995. A dash (-) is used to indicate that data are not available or cannot be calculated; nec means not elsewhere classified.

Continued on next page.

SIC	Industry	No. Establishments			Employment		Pay / Employee		Annual Payroll ($ 000)		
		1994	1995	% State	1994	1995	1994	1995	1994	1995	% State
CLEARWATER, MN - [continued]											
60 –	**Finance, insurance, and real estate**	9	10	0.1	81	93	25,778	25,505	2,976	3,708	0.1
6020	Commercial banks	3	3	0.2	61	65	22,951	21,354	1,441	1,443	0.2
COOK, MN											
60 –	**Finance, insurance, and real estate**	14	16	0.1	38	58	16,737	15,655	801	952	0.0
COTTONWOOD, MN											
60 –	**Finance, insurance, and real estate**	36	39	0.3	171	204	20,772	20,882	3,676	4,505	0.1
6000	Depository institutions	6	6	0.3	105	111	20,914	22,342	2,305	2,768	0.3
6020	Commercial banks	6	6	0.5	105	111	20,914	22,342	2,305	2,768	0.3
6530	Real estate agents and managers	3	4	0.2	3	15	8,000	24,800	25	273	0.1
CROW WING, MN											
60 –	**Finance, insurance, and real estate**	131	135	1.1	724	848	19,448	18,943	15,774	17,771	0.3
6000	Depository institutions	24	25	1.4	350	343	21,989	22,601	8,139	7,915	0.8
6020	Commercial banks	17	20	1.6	272	273	22,471	23,018	6,468	6,400	0.8
6200	Security and commodity brokers	5	5	0.6	16	9	28,500	64,000	535	590	0.1
6400	Insurance agents, brokers, and service	35	38	1.2	85	97	17,553	17,237	1,664	1,868	0.4
6500	Real estate	56	56	1.3	223	339	13,794	13,180	3,766	5,804	1.2
6510	Real estate operators and lessors	16	16	1.0	37	31	6,378	9,161	389	419	0.3
6530	Real estate agents and managers	30	30	1.5	90	92	10,311	11,783	1,254	1,390	0.5
DAKOTA, MN											
60 –	**Finance, insurance, and real estate**	631	657	5.5	6,690	6,138	30,340	30,656	185,314	191,526	3.7
6000	Depository institutions	73	75	4.3	1,266	1,223	23,599	26,666	30,263	31,461	3.0
6020	Commercial banks	50	55	4.3	1,081	1,051	24,636	28,285	27,090	28,449	3.3
6100	Nondepository institutions	46	47	6.4	295	251	48,420	38,279	10,244	16,582	4.1
6140	Personal credit institutions	20	19	10.1	71	69	27,831	31,478	1,929	2,078	2.3
6160	Mortgage bankers and brokers	22	21	5.7	199	150	57,407	40,933	7,372	13,290	7.4
6200	Security and commodity brokers	33	32	3.8	102	118	32,824	31,661	3,718	4,754	0.7
6210	Security brokers and dealers	14	14	3.5	53	76	40,830	32,842	2,463	3,441	0.6
6300	Insurance carriers	50	50	6.6	3,322	3,042	36,340	35,199	105,480	99,452	6.5
6330	Fire, marine, and casualty insurance	23	21	5.4	565	579	38,294	44,263	19,025	22,185	4.2
6400	Insurance agents, brokers, and service	162	170	5.3	418	393	22,555	23,990	9,781	10,128	2.1
6500	Real estate	255	272	6.4	1,192	1,046	17,711	20,593	22,104	25,750	5.5
6510	Real estate operators and lessors	94	88	5.4	446	331	12,583	19,287	6,135	8,054	6.0
6530	Real estate agents and managers	123	136	7.0	488	546	19,000	20,989	10,225	12,848	4.9
6540	Title abstract offices	15	17	9.7	213	104	23,343	25,000	3,954	3,066	8.2
6550	Subdividers and developers	14	15	4.6	36	57	30,889	17,404	1,633	1,462	4.3
6700	Holding and other investment offices	12	11	3.0	95	65	44,295	64,062	3,724	3,399	0.7
DODGE, MN											
60 –	**Finance, insurance, and real estate**	33	31	0.3	128	130	23,688	26,215	3,080	3,232	0.1
6000	Depository institutions	6	6	0.3	76	74	23,684	25,405	1,865	1,922	0.2
6020	Commercial banks	6	6	0.5	76	74	23,684	25,405	1,865	1,922	0.2
6510	Real estate operators and lessors	4	5	0.3	6	7	18,667	16,571	112	111	0.1
DOUGLAS, MN											
60 –	**Finance, insurance, and real estate**	102	97	0.8	421	414	20,409	22,300	8,469	8,683	0.2
6000	Depository institutions	14	13	0.7	202	205	22,733	24,546	4,930	4,730	0.5
6020	Commercial banks	9	10	0.8	175	188	23,771	25,191	4,469	4,407	0.5
6400	Insurance agents, brokers, and service	24	24	0.8	64	64	17,250	18,938	1,114	1,246	0.3
6500	Real estate	51	47	1.1	113	105	13,841	16,114	1,418	1,609	0.3
6510	Real estate operators and lessors	24	23	1.4	39	41	9,641	9,073	408	397	0.3
6540	Title abstract offices	4	3	1.7	24	19	29,667	36,421	446	495	1.3

Source: County Business Patterns, 1994/95, CBP-94/95, U.S. Department of Commerce, Washington, D.C., November 1997. SIC categories for which data were suppressed or not available for both 1994 and 1995 are not displayed. The employment columns represent mid-March employment in the year. Pay per employee is calculated by dividing 1st Quarter payroll, annualized, by mid-March employment. The columns headed "% State" show the county's percentage of the state total for the SIC in 1995; for example, 1.4% for SIC 6000 means that the county had 1.4 percent of the state's total establishments (or payroll) in SIC 6000 in 1995. A dash (-) is used to indicate that data are not available or cannot be calculated; nec means not elsewhere classified.

Continued on next page.

SIC	Industry	No. Establishments			Employment		Pay / Employee		Annual Payroll ($ 000)		
		1994	1995	% State	1994	1995	1994	1995	1994	1995	% State
FARIBAULT, MN - [continued]											
60 –	**Finance, insurance, and real estate**	51	48	0.4	249	246	20,980	20,065	5,385	5,428	0.1
6000	Depository institutions	16	14	0.8	167	167	23,090	21,892	3,959	4,017	0.4
FILLMORE, MN											
60 –	**Finance, insurance, and real estate**	54	56	0.5	270	279	20,770	21,663	5,768	6,075	0.1
6000	Depository institutions	14	15	0.9	181	189	24,972	25,757	4,658	4,849	0.5
6500	Real estate	8	8	0.2	9	9	9,333	7,556	85	76	0.0
6510	Real estate operators and lessors	3	3	0.2	4	4	4,000	4,000	16	14	0.0
FREEBORN, MN											
60 –	**Finance, insurance, and real estate**	85	83	0.7	406	397	23,291	22,700	9,745	9,165	0.2
6000	Depository institutions	25	24	1.4	221	210	22,624	23,981	5,364	5,204	0.5
6020	Commercial banks	16	16	1.3	173	168	23,769	25,690	4,516	4,479	0.5
6400	Insurance agents, brokers, and service	25	24	0.8	75	85	21,653	21,553	1,740	1,929	0.4
6500	Real estate	22	22	0.5	48	48	12,750	9,833	647	510	0.1
6510	Real estate operators and lessors	9	9	0.5	12	21	7,000	8,381	124	179	0.1
6530	Real estate agents and managers	7	7	0.4	13	10	17,231	10,000	226	113	0.0
GOODHUE, MN											
60 –	**Finance, insurance, and real estate**	102	100	0.8	629	618	21,793	25,023	14,811	15,795	0.3
6000	Depository institutions	18	18	1.0	306	291	19,686	24,357	6,794	7,224	0.7
6200	Security and commodity brokers	3	3	0.4	15	14	41,333	38,000	555	541	0.1
6400	Insurance agents, brokers, and service	33	35	1.1	77	89	15,532	17,438	1,368	1,724	0.4
6500	Real estate	32	30	0.7	68	60	13,118	12,667	1,259	1,258	0.3
6550	Subdividers and developers	5	3	0.9	4	2	1,000	2,000	94	14	0.0
6700	Holding and other investment offices	6	4	1.1	28	24	15,286	16,833	436	442	0.1
GRANT, MN											
60 –	**Finance, insurance, and real estate**	27	28	0.2	91	74	18,374	18,108	1,894	1,690	0.0
HENNEPIN, MN											
60 –	**Finance, insurance, and real estate**	4,022	4,202	35.3	75,351	77,040	42,055	44,712	2,897,673	3,195,160	62.0
6000	Depository institutions	379	384	22.1	12,907	13,071	35,511	38,853	423,437	457,243	44.2
6020	Commercial banks	227	244	19.3	9,544	9,669	36,316	39,271	311,690	347,708	40.9
6090	Functions closely related to banking	32	28	68.3	735	836	42,079	48,512	27,113	29,286	-
6150	Business credit institutions	65	78	71.6	1,044	1,095	56,008	59,839	49,309	51,798	79.8
6160	Mortgage bankers and brokers	196	208	56.2	6,109	4,067	39,098	39,635	190,597	140,854	78.1
6200	Security and commodity brokers	400	425	50.8	7,651	7,728	81,671	79,692	540,808	608,137	85.5
6210	Security brokers and dealers	174	181	44.8	6,280	6,188	81,600	77,761	422,461	466,924	86.6
6280	Security and commodity services	204	223	56.9	1,199	1,345	88,530	94,647	111,985	132,945	81.6
6300	Insurance carriers	351	356	46.7	21,860	24,795	37,429	38,420	789,113	910,089	59.9
6310	Life insurance	104	111	56.9	12,021	14,104	41,785	39,842	461,517	531,172	78.6
6330	Fire, marine, and casualty insurance	151	146	37.4	5,630	5,058	33,182	35,118	187,636	176,716	33.1
6500	Real estate	1,517	1,555	36.8	11,282	11,229	21,933	23,897	258,057	273,473	58.1
6510	Real estate operators and lessors	615	604	36.8	4,136	3,967	20,457	19,272	82,742	74,303	55.3
6530	Real estate agents and managers	745	760	38.9	5,857	6,026	22,506	26,506	141,906	162,130	62.0
6540	Title abstract offices	33	36	20.6	857	535	24,289	30,475	18,384	17,592	47.1
6550	Subdividers and developers	92	97	29.5	394	640	23,147	23,125	13,341	17,035	50.6
6552	Subdividers and developers, n.e.c.	73	75	44.4	279	381	25,448	26,688	10,361	11,818	48.3
6553	Cemetery subdividers and developers	15	15	10.6	115	166	17,565	14,627	2,794	3,167	45.5
6700	Holding and other investment offices	181	198	53.7	5,959	6,007	65,633	82,197	326,725	384,363	84.5
6710	Holding offices	63	71	48.0	2,545	2,344	64,099	95,956	149,570	175,319	77.4
6790	Miscellaneous investing	69	72	66.1	486	583	59,136	60,261	27,193	33,551	85.0
6799	Investors, n.e.c.	44	46	70.8	171	165	107,135	126,230	16,062	18,524	96.4

Source: County Business Patterns, 1994/95, CBP-94/95, U.S. Department of Commerce, Washington, D.C., November 1997. SIC categories for which data were suppressed or not available for both 1994 and 1995 are *not* displayed. The employment columns represent mid-March employment in the year. Pay per employee is calculated by dividing 1st Quarter payroll, annualized, by mid-March employment. The columns headed "% State" show the county's percentage of the state total for the SIC in 1995; for example, 1.4% for SIC 6000 means that the county had 1.4 percent of the state's total establishments (or payroll) in SIC 6000 in 1995. A dash (-) is used to indicate that data are not available or cannot be calculated; *nec* means not elsewhere classified.

Continued on next page.

SIC	Industry	No. Establishments			Employment		Pay / Employee		Annual Payroll ($ 000)		
		1994	1995	% State	1994	1995	1994	1995	1994	1995	% State
HOUSTON, MN - [continued]											
60 –	**Finance, insurance, and real estate**	36	33	*0.3*	157	171	16,153	20,211	2,698	3,180	*0.1*
6000	Depository institutions	7	8	*0.5*	111	128	18,486	23,344	2,170	2,587	*0.3*
HUBBARD, MN											
60 –	**Finance, insurance, and real estate**	28	26	*0.2*	130	136	18,554	18,647	2,784	2,904	*0.1*
6000	Depository institutions	6	6	*0.3*	78	78	20,205	22,256	1,730	1,887	*0.2*
6020	Commercial banks	6	6	*0.5*	78	78	20,205	22,256	1,730	1,887	*0.2*
6400	Insurance agents, brokers, and service	7	8	*0.3*	20	24	14,400	14,833	388	424	*0.1*
6530	Real estate agents and managers	6	6	*0.3*	6	7	10,667	7,429	63	114	*0.0*
ISANTI, MN											
60 –	**Finance, insurance, and real estate**	37	42	*0.4*	160	186	22,200	21,785	3,758	4,513	*0.1*
6000	Depository institutions	6	6	*0.3*	100	110	26,160	25,491	2,747	3,153	*0.3*
6530	Real estate agents and managers	6	5	*0.3*	9	14	15,556	11,143	139	169	*0.1*
ITASCA, MN											
60 –	**Finance, insurance, and real estate**	80	80	*0.7*	436	423	19,018	21,626	8,980	10,421	*0.2*
6000	Depository institutions	21	20	*1.2*	261	285	21,747	23,060	6,036	7,187	*0.7*
6020	Commercial banks	14	15	*1.2*	217	249	23,115	24,241	5,343	6,633	*0.8*
6100	Nondepository institutions	3	4	*0.5*	9	9	29,333	30,222	252	541	*0.1*
6400	Insurance agents, brokers, and service	23	27	*0.8*	70	61	15,029	19,934	1,239	1,292	*0.3*
6500	Real estate	27	22	*0.5*	85	52	12,000	14,154	1,163	929	*0.2*
6510	Real estate operators and lessors	8	7	*0.4*	49	19	8,653	9,684	417	186	*0.1*
KANABEC, MN											
60 –	**Finance, insurance, and real estate**	18	17	*0.1*	110	120	18,218	18,933	2,275	2,804	*0.1*
6000	Depository institutions	5	5	*0.3*	89	95	19,191	20,758	1,940	2,293	*0.2*
KANDIYOHI, MN											
60 –	**Finance, insurance, and real estate**	112	119	*1.0*	624	710	21,731	21,408	14,212	15,586	*0.3*
6000	Depository institutions	19	19	*1.1*	336	391	22,750	22,056	8,217	8,642	*0.8*
6100	Nondepository institutions	4	6	*0.8*	68	75	33,765	30,987	2,061	2,337	*0.6*
6400	Insurance agents, brokers, and service	41	41	*1.3*	89	96	16,944	17,958	1,666	1,797	*0.4*
6500	Real estate	39	42	*1.0*	104	98	12,577	14,449	1,404	1,607	*0.3*
6510	Real estate operators and lessors	20	21	*1.3*	64	55	9,000	11,855	639	649	*0.5*
KITTSON, MN											
60 –	**Finance, insurance, and real estate**	22	22	*0.2*	87	84	16,092	16,476	1,443	1,452	*0.0*
6500	Real estate	8	8	*0.2*	10	13	2,800	3,077	37	42	*0.0*
6510	Real estate operators and lessors	5	5	*0.3*	9	11	2,667	2,909	28	33	*0.0*
KOOCHICHING, MN											
60 –	**Finance, insurance, and real estate**	28	28	*0.2*	136	131	19,794	21,710	2,666	2,639	*0.1*
6000	Depository institutions	8	8	*0.5*	106	100	21,736	24,120	2,228	2,188	*0.2*
6530	Real estate agents and managers	4	4	*0.2*	5	4	12,800	15,000	63	60	*0.0*
LAC QUI PARLE, MN											
60 –	**Finance, insurance, and real estate**	27	27	*0.2*	113	120	20,920	20,267	2,022	2,140	*0.0*
6000	Depository institutions	9	9	*0.5*	70	72	25,143	26,056	1,574	1,686	*0.2*
LE SUEUR, MN											
60 –	**Finance, insurance, and real estate**	40	43	*0.4*	221	246	22,480	21,398	4,844	5,396	*0.1*
6000	Depository institutions	11	11	*0.6*	147	147	24,680	25,361	3,542	3,857	*0.4*
6500	Real estate	12	11	*0.3*	30	37	11,467	8,432	331	331	*0.1*
6510	Real estate operators and lessors	5	5	*0.3*	6	10	10,667	9,200	83	92	*0.1*

Source: County Business Patterns, 1994/95, CBP-94/95, U.S. Department of Commerce, Washington, D.C., November 1997. SIC categories for which data were suppressed or not available for both 1994 and 1995 are *not* displayed. The employment columns represent mid-March employment in the year. Pay per employee is calculated by dividing 1st Quarter payroll, annualized, by mid-March employment. The columns headed "% State" show the county's percentage of the state total for the SIC in 1995; for example, 1.4% for SIC 6000 means that the county had 1.4 percent of the state's total establishments (or payroll) in SIC 6000 in 1995. A dash (-) is used to indicate that data are not available or cannot be calculated; *nec* means not elsewhere classified.

SIC	Industry	No. Establishments			Employment		Pay / Employee		Annual Payroll ($ 000)		
		1994	1995	% State	1994	1995	1994	1995	1994	1995	% State
LINCOLN, MN											
60 –	**Finance, insurance, and real estate**	16	17	0.1	55	54	14,618	15,259	973	959	0.0
6500	Real estate	4	5	0.1	6	6	3,333	3,333	21	25	0.0
6510	Real estate operators and lessors	4	5	0.3	6	6	3,333	3,333	21	25	0.0
LYON, MN											
60 –	**Finance, insurance, and real estate**	70	71	0.6	657	700	23,604	27,434	14,996	17,222	0.3
6000	Depository institutions	12	12	0.7	216	207	22,185	25,585	4,776	4,677	0.5
6400	Insurance agents, brokers, and service	27	28	0.9	54	57	16,889	16,140	1,032	990	0.2
6500	Real estate	19	18	0.4	66	67	7,030	6,507	462	477	0.1
6510	Real estate operators and lessors	13	13	0.8	55	57	7,055	6,386	384	412	0.3
MCLEOD, MN											
60 –	**Finance, insurance, and real estate**	81	84	0.7	387	409	21,189	20,372	8,843	9,243	0.2
6000	Depository institutions	16	16	0.9	250	254	24,288	24,236	6,384	6,695	0.6
6200	Security and commodity brokers	6	7	0.8	8	8	17,500	12,500	164	112	0.0
6400	Insurance agents, brokers, and service	22	22	0.7	62	70	17,484	16,457	1,227	1,329	0.3
6500	Real estate	31	33	0.8	51	58	11,922	10,069	802	803	0.2
6510	Real estate operators and lessors	13	15	0.9	24	29	6,333	5,793	153	191	0.1
6530	Real estate agents and managers	11	12	0.6	21	25	16,000	12,800	509	494	0.2
MAHNOMEN, MN											
60 –	**Finance, insurance, and real estate**	8	8	0.1	59	73	18,102	16,822	1,170	1,242	0.0
6000	Depository institutions	3	3	0.2	51	64	16,784	16,875	1,032	1,100	0.1
MARSHALL, MN											
60 –	**Finance, insurance, and real estate**	23	22	0.2	133	135	20,722	20,948	3,186	3,396	0.1
6000	Depository institutions	9	9	0.5	91	96	22,945	22,500	2,486	2,557	0.2
MARTIN, MN											
60 –	**Finance, insurance, and real estate**	64	66	0.6	373	380	24,568	27,632	10,399	11,053	0.2
6000	Depository institutions	14	14	0.8	199	200	21,950	22,480	4,781	5,027	0.5
6200	Security and commodity brokers	6	6	0.7	22	23	26,364	25,217	549	504	0.1
6400	Insurance agents, brokers, and service	21	21	0.7	68	68	23,353	25,471	1,741	1,643	0.3
6510	Real estate operators and lessors	8	8	0.5	22	20	6,909	11,600	173	192	0.1
MEEKER, MN											
60 –	**Finance, insurance, and real estate**	46	47	0.4	174	172	19,609	20,860	3,853	3,758	0.1
6000	Depository institutions	9	9	0.5	102	98	23,059	24,694	2,528	2,532	0.2
6500	Real estate	15	14	0.3	23	21	8,348	9,333	217	219	0.0
6510	Real estate operators and lessors	6	6	0.4	9	11	6,222	5,818	64	69	0.1
MILLE LACS, MN											
60 –	**Finance, insurance, and real estate**	39	38	0.3	245	271	22,547	25,181	6,556	6,511	0.1
6000	Depository institutions	11	10	0.6	178	186	24,584	30,151	5,149	5,085	0.5
6020	Commercial banks	6	6	0.5	124	122	27,903	32,033	3,355	3,301	0.4
6500	Real estate	17	15	0.4	28	37	11,429	8,108	444	380	0.1
6510	Real estate operators and lessors	7	6	0.4	13	10	5,538	7,600	172	142	0.1
MORRISON, MN											
60 –	**Finance, insurance, and real estate**	50	50	0.4	277	267	19,466	20,225	5,466	5,793	0.1
6000	Depository institutions	10	10	0.6	141	145	21,078	22,455	3,157	3,407	0.3
6020	Commercial banks	7	7	0.6	110	114	21,964	23,368	2,503	2,723	0.3
6400	Insurance agents, brokers, and service	19	21	0.7	68	64	15,824	17,375	1,259	1,385	0.3
6530	Real estate agents and managers	4	3	0.2	5	4	4,800	5,000	21	21	0.0
MOWER, MN											
60 –	**Finance, insurance, and real estate**	77	75	0.6	375	409	21,397	21,868	8,127	8,680	0.2
6000	Depository institutions	22	22	1.3	243	237	23,802	25,097	5,654	5,610	0.5

Source: County Business Patterns, 1994/95, CBP-94/95, U.S. Department of Commerce, Washington, D.C., November 1997. SIC categories for which data were suppressed or not available for both 1994 and 1995 are not displayed. The employment columns represent mid-March employment in the year. Pay per employee is calculated by dividing 1st Quarter payroll, annualized, by mid-March employment. The columns headed "% State" show the county's percentage of the state total for the SIC in 1995; for example, 1.4% for SIC 6000 means that the county had 1.4 percent of the state's total establishments (or payroll) in SIC 6000 in 1995. A dash (-) is used to indicate that data are not available or cannot be calculated; nec means not elsewhere classified.

Continued on next page.

SIC	Industry	No. Establishments			Employment		Pay / Employee		Annual Payroll ($ 000)		
		1994	1995	% State	1994	1995	1994	1995	1994	1995	% State
FORREST, MS - [continued]											
6300	Insurance carriers	22	17	*5.0*	169	146	24,734	27,096	4,218	3,810	*1.9*
6310	Life insurance	8	7	*4.2*	121	110	21,884	24,727	2,669	2,463	*2.8*
6400	Insurance agents, brokers, and service	48	44	*4.0*	162	189	18,741	21,481	3,913	4,699	*3.9*
6500	Real estate	79	85	*6.0*	294	235	14,993	15,166	4,409	4,192	*5.7*
6510	Real estate operators and lessors	41	41	*5.6*	87	82	12,598	12,098	1,068	1,176	*3.9*
6530	Real estate agents and managers	32	37	*7.0*	202	140	15,980	17,343	2,838	2,687	*8.4*
FRANKLIN, MS											
60 –	**Finance, insurance, and real estate**	9	8	*0.2*	-	-	-	-	-	-	-
GEORGE, MS											
60 –	**Finance, insurance, and real estate**	21	20	*0.4*	120	112	17,667	19,393	2,375	2,273	*0.2*
6000	Depository institutions	6	6	*0.5*	91	83	18,725	21,157	1,912	1,827	*0.5*
6400	Insurance agents, brokers, and service	8	8	*0.7*	12	13	13,000	12,615	164	173	*0.1*
GREENE, MS											
60 –	**Finance, insurance, and real estate**	8	7	*0.1*	32	34	19,375	19,294	663	682	*0.1*
6000	Depository institutions	4	4	*0.3*	29	28	20,690	19,571	601	590	*0.2*
GRENADA, MS											
60 –	**Finance, insurance, and real estate**	53	50	*1.0*	477	454	26,474	23,313	12,868	10,264	*1.1*
6000	Depository institutions	15	16	*1.3*	378	341	27,439	24,235	10,446	8,034	*2.1*
6400	Insurance agents, brokers, and service	5	5	*0.5*	16	18	19,500	17,556	322	305	*0.3*
6500	Real estate	13	10	*0.7*	19	35	8,421	11,543	368	439	*0.6*
6530	Real estate agents and managers	6	6	*1.1*	8	26	9,000	12,462	275	349	*1.1*
HANCOCK, MS											
60 –	**Finance, insurance, and real estate**	61	67	*1.3*	255	266	17,098	18,256	4,788	4,960	*0.5*
6000	Depository institutions	15	16	*1.3*	98	108	17,102	19,222	1,931	2,126	*0.6*
6100	Nondepository institutions	6	7	*0.9*	13	19	23,077	20,211	321	376	*0.4*
6400	Insurance agents, brokers, and service	8	10	*0.9*	26	34	20,154	21,176	662	768	*0.6*
6500	Real estate	27	28	*2.0*	108	95	15,556	16,126	1,703	1,538	*2.1*
6530	Real estate agents and managers	14	13	*2.5*	50	35	12,960	13,486	656	480	*1.5*
HARRISON, MS											
60 –	**Finance, insurance, and real estate**	394	414	*8.1*	2,613	2,774	20,739	22,095	62,636	66,501	*7.0*
6000	Depository institutions	75	81	*6.8*	1,400	1,399	19,280	21,981	31,305	33,596	*8.7*
6020	Commercial banks	48	53	*5.6*	1,052	1,087	19,878	22,859	24,450	26,998	*7.8*
6100	Nondepository institutions	40	49	*6.5*	160	190	25,375	23,937	3,693	4,410	*4.7*
6140	Personal credit institutions	28	31	*5.4*	119	130	23,395	24,185	2,644	2,935	*5.0*
6200	Security and commodity brokers	16	13	*7.4*	73	87	52,055	49,057	3,929	4,460	*10.3*
6210	Security brokers and dealers	9	10	*8.8*	61	77	59,803	50,494	3,688	4,166	*11.2*
6280	Security and commodity services	7	3	*5.3*	12	10	12,667	38,000	241	294	*5.4*
6300	Insurance carriers	29	27	*8.0*	207	181	32,522	35,271	6,560	5,987	*2.9*
6310	Life insurance	12	13	*7.8*	108	104	27,370	29,500	2,970	2,958	*3.4*
6400	Insurance agents, brokers, and service	83	81	*7.3*	273	324	22,505	23,951	8,639	8,908	*7.4*
6500	Real estate	148	160	*11.3*	490	583	12,971	12,844	8,393	9,029	*12.2*
6510	Real estate operators and lessors	76	79	*10.8*	274	326	10,380	12,025	3,996	4,296	*14.4*
6530	Real estate agents and managers	59	65	*12.3*	201	226	15,642	13,894	3,571	3,946	*12.4*
6550	Subdividers and developers	9	12	*10.3*	14	16	25,714	18,250	619	534	*5.1*
6552	Subdividers and developers, n.e.c.	6	9	*14.5*	6	8	26,667	13,000	426	331	*4.4*
6700	Holding and other investment offices	3	3	*3.2*	10	10	10,800	9,200	117	111	*0.4*
HINDS, MS											
60 –	**Finance, insurance, and real estate**	897	899	*17.7*	11,017	10,766	29,319	29,454	313,550	319,114	*33.4*
6000	Depository institutions	132	129	*10.8*	2,810	2,758	25,156	26,283	71,009	74,606	*19.4*
6020	Commercial banks	90	90	*9.6*	2,565	2,527	25,616	26,594	66,226	69,205	*20.1*
6100	Nondepository institutions	100	90	*11.9*	947	806	26,332	26,402	23,409	21,604	*23.2*

Source: County Business Patterns, 1994/95, CBP-94/95, U.S. Department of Commerce, Washington, D.C., November 1997. SIC categories for which data were suppressed or not available for both 1994 and 1995 are not displayed. The employment columns represent mid-March employment in the year. Pay per employee is calculated by dividing 1st Quarter payroll, annualized, by mid-March employment. The columns headed "% State" show the county's percentage of the state total for the SIC in 1995; for example, 1.4% for SIC 6000 means that the county had 1.4 percent of the state's total establishments (or payroll) in SIC 6000 in 1995. A dash (-) is used to indicate that data are not available or cannot be calculated; nec means not elsewhere classified.

Continued on next page.

SIC	Industry	No. Establishments			Employment		Pay / Employee		Annual Payroll ($ 000)		
		1994	1995	% State	1994	1995	1994	1995	1994	1995	% State
HINDS, MS - [continued]											
6140	Personal credit institutions	53	49	8.6	360	344	27,467	28,837	10,195	9,936	16.9
6150	Business credit institutions	6	4	22.2	22	19	44,182	41,263	870	796	16.9
6160	Mortgage bankers and brokers	34	31	25.6	517	412	22,979	22,243	10,409	9,496	38.0
6200	Security and commodity brokers	51	55	31.3	477	498	60,881	55,574	24,357	28,020	65.0
6210	Security brokers and dealers	31	32	28.1	413	415	63,283	57,427	21,604	24,351	65.3
6280	Security and commodity services	20	23	40.4	64	83	45,375	46,313	2,753	3,669	67.1
6300	Insurance carriers	99	101	29.9	3,817	3,732	29,005	29,785	110,689	110,723	53.9
6310	Life insurance	44	45	27.1	1,481	1,503	29,226	28,487	43,455	41,776	48.3
6320	Medical service and health insurance	7	9	39.1	209	232	21,990	23,586	4,528	5,535	17.8
6330	Fire, marine, and casualty insurance	34	31	25.4	1,978	1,819	29,658	31,617	57,918	57,134	71.5
6400	Insurance agents, brokers, and service	227	222	20.1	1,335	1,382	29,483	32,397	42,491	46,580	38.8
6500	Real estate	256	271	19.1	1,149	1,176	13,814	16,578	19,616	20,478	27.8
6510	Real estate operators and lessors	151	152	20.8	599	600	11,132	14,173	8,880	8,906	29.8
6530	Real estate agents and managers	87	90	17.0	412	421	16,602	19,268	8,192	8,385	26.4
6552	Subdividers and developers, n.e.c.	12	12	19.4	86	64	14,140	18,125	1,256	1,290	17.1
6790	Miscellaneous investing	11	9	30.0	94	18	36,000	25,556	4,082	595	14.7
HOLMES, MS											
60 –	**Finance, insurance, and real estate**	29	30	0.6	138	144	20,609	21,917	2,549	2,718	0.3
6000	Depository institutions	10	10	0.8	99	96	24,687	27,125	2,075	2,098	0.5
6020	Commercial banks	10	10	1.1	99	96	24,687	27,125	2,075	2,098	0.6
6510	Real estate operators and lessors	9	10	1.4	13	22	5,538	8,545	108	221	0.7
HUMPHREYS, MS											
60 –	**Finance, insurance, and real estate**	15	17	0.3	89	87	25,618	27,264	2,141	2,200	0.2
6000	Depository institutions	7	7	0.6	69	69	29,507	29,855	1,860	1,866	0.5
6400	Insurance agents, brokers, and service	3	5	0.5	8	9	15,000	17,778	130	188	0.2
ISSAQUENA, MS											
60 –	**Finance, insurance, and real estate**	2	2	0.0	-	-	-	-	-	-	-
ITAWAMBA, MS											
60 –	**Finance, insurance, and real estate**	21	17	0.3	72	72	18,111	18,389	1,322	1,380	0.1
6000	Depository institutions	6	6	0.5	43	44	19,070	19,455	854	907	0.2
6020	Commercial banks	6	6	0.6	43	44	19,070	19,455	854	907	0.3
JACKSON, MS											
60 –	**Finance, insurance, and real estate**	182	194	3.8	1,119	1,110	17,980	19,550	23,408	23,058	2.4
6000	Depository institutions	50	52	4.3	513	537	17,903	19,799	10,984	11,528	3.0
6020	Commercial banks	29	30	3.2	369	361	16,997	19,867	7,535	7,274	2.1
6100	Nondepository institutions	16	24	3.2	58	69	20,621	19,710	1,218	1,531	1.6
6300	Insurance carriers	9	9	2.7	51	60	30,431	26,733	2,101	1,738	0.8
6400	Insurance agents, brokers, and service	38	36	3.3	142	155	17,972	18,890	2,856	3,157	2.6
6500	Real estate	63	67	4.7	334	277	16,383	17,718	5,980	4,769	6.5
6530	Real estate agents and managers	36	39	7.4	76	83	18,474	18,458	1,199	1,335	4.2
JASPER, MS											
60 –	**Finance, insurance, and real estate**	16	15	0.3	89	92	17,708	17,609	1,517	1,698	0.2
6000	Depository institutions	7	7	0.6	61	67	19,148	17,970	1,118	1,259	0.3
6400	Insurance agents, brokers, and service	3	3	0.3	13	10	11,077	14,400	155	151	0.1
JEFFERSON DAVIS, MS											
60 –	**Finance, insurance, and real estate**	16	15	0.3	54	52	17,111	20,462	961	1,074	0.1
6400	Insurance agents, brokers, and service	5	4	0.4	8	6	13,000	14,667	107	85	0.1
JONES, MS											
60 –	**Finance, insurance, and real estate**	108	107	2.1	597	553	19,497	21,237	12,200	12,690	1.3
6000	Depository institutions	30	30	2.5	308	295	20,468	22,536	6,669	7,165	1.9

Source: County Business Patterns, 1994/95, CBP-94/95, U.S. Department of Commerce, Washington, D.C., November 1997. SIC categories for which data were suppressed or not available for both 1994 and 1995 are not displayed. The employment columns represent mid-March employment in the year. Pay per employee is calculated by dividing 1st Quarter payroll, annualized, by mid-March employment. The columns headed "% State" show the county's percentage of the state total for the SIC in 1995; for example, 1.4% for SIC 6000 means that the county had 1.4 percent of the state's total establishments (or payroll) in SIC 6000 in 1995. A dash (-) is used to indicate that data are not available or cannot be calculated; nec means not elsewhere classified.

Continued on next page.

SIC	Industry	No. Establishments			Employment		Pay / Employee		Annual Payroll ($ 000)		
		1994	1995	% State	1994	1995	1994	1995	1994	1995	% State
JONES, MS - [continued]											
6100	Nondepository institutions	20	19	2.5	101	72	19,129	20,444	1,862	1,636	1.8
6140	Personal credit institutions	12	13	2.3	54	51	17,852	21,569	977	1,177	2.0
6160	Mortgage bankers and brokers	5	3	2.5	45	14	20,356	18,000	805	300	1.2
6200	Security and commodity brokers	4	4	2.3	4	8	17,000	15,500	111	170	0.4
6400	Insurance agents, brokers, and service	27	26	2.4	76	79	18,053	18,127	1,599	1,770	1.5
6500	Real estate	20	21	1.5	56	55	13,357	14,909	712	801	1.1
6530	Real estate agents and managers	7	7	1.3	13	12	10,154	11,667	139	144	0.5
KEMPER, MS											
60 –	**Finance, insurance, and real estate**	8	8	0.2	54	56	15,333	15,214	854	924	0.1
6000	Depository institutions	5	5	0.4	41	49	17,073	15,347	726	754	0.2
6020	Commercial banks	5	5	0.5	41	49	17,073	15,347	726	754	0.2
LAFAYETTE, MS											
60 –	**Finance, insurance, and real estate**	67	63	1.2	344	316	16,616	18,013	6,115	5,974	0.6
6000	Depository institutions	14	14	1.2	144	138	19,472	20,232	3,010	2,950	0.8
6140	Personal credit institutions	8	9	1.6	29	28	18,483	24,000	504	527	0.9
6400	Insurance agents, brokers, and service	15	13	1.2	30	30	20,667	22,267	648	754	0.6
6500	Real estate	23	20	1.4	77	78	7,584	8,000	713	698	0.9
6510	Real estate operators and lessors	16	15	2.1	71	73	7,831	8,055	668	640	2.1
6530	Real estate agents and managers	6	4	0.8	6	4	4,667	7,000	43	48	0.2
LAMAR, MS											
60 –	**Finance, insurance, and real estate**	21	18	0.4	123	132	16,195	25,000	2,346	3,385	0.4
6400	Insurance agents, brokers, and service	5	6	0.5	14	17	12,000	14,118	189	243	0.2
6500	Real estate	9	4	0.3	19	13	10,316	11,385	236	140	0.2
LAUDERDALE, MS											
60 –	**Finance, insurance, and real estate**	192	185	3.6	1,268	1,307	23,274	27,988	32,945	35,447	3.7
6000	Depository institutions	41	39	3.3	461	462	21,518	22,528	9,919	10,328	2.7
6020	Commercial banks	32	31	3.3	400	397	21,860	22,660	8,616	8,805	2.6
6100	Nondepository institutions	28	32	4.2	229	251	19,878	21,785	4,920	5,558	6.0
6140	Personal credit institutions	22	23	4.0	109	128	22,862	22,969	2,607	2,946	5.0
6200	Security and commodity brokers	7	7	4.0	26	25	56,923	51,840	1,459	1,487	3.4
6300	Insurance carriers	16	14	4.1	236	275	26,102	29,396	7,012	7,482	3.6
6400	Insurance agents, brokers, and service	34	33	3.0	123	122	25,333	32,689	3,321	3,649	3.0
6500	Real estate	59	53	3.7	128	109	13,031	16,550	2,084	1,810	2.5
6510	Real estate operators and lessors	35	32	4.4	76	65	12,947	18,585	1,098	1,158	3.9
6530	Real estate agents and managers	19	15	2.8	39	30	13,333	14,000	796	451	1.4
6550	Subdividers and developers	3	3	2.6	13	13	12,615	12,615	168	155	1.5
6700	Holding and other investment offices	7	7	7.4	65	63	40,246	87,810	4,230	5,133	17.0
LAWRENCE, MS											
60 –	**Finance, insurance, and real estate**	11	12	0.2	65	62	18,892	20,194	1,172	1,231	0.1
6400	Insurance agents, brokers, and service	4	4	0.4	14	12	13,429	13,667	198	177	0.1
LEAKE, MS											
60 –	**Finance, insurance, and real estate**	22	19	0.4	157	168	28,484	24,024	3,320	3,747	0.4
6000	Depository institutions	8	7	0.6	114	118	31,825	27,559	2,609	3,005	0.8
6100	Nondepository institutions	6	5	0.7	22	20	22,727	21,000	380	379	0.4
6140	Personal credit institutions	6	5	0.9	22	20	22,727	21,000	380	379	0.6
6400	Insurance agents, brokers, and service	5	4	0.4	12	20	13,667	9,800	183	189	0.2
LEE, MS											
60 –	**Finance, insurance, and real estate**	177	174	3.4	1,688	1,708	24,919	25,220	44,958	43,549	4.6
6000	Depository institutions	29	28	2.3	904	1,012	24,712	24,206	25,658	25,560	6.7
6020	Commercial banks	22	22	2.3	876	982	24,594	24,020	25,017	24,831	7.2
6100	Nondepository institutions	31	35	4.6	158	149	27,342	29,020	4,166	4,222	4.5

Source: County Business Patterns, 1994/95, CBP-94/95, U.S. Department of Commerce, Washington, D.C., November 1997. SIC categories for which data were suppressed or not available for both 1994 and 1995 are not displayed. The employment columns represent mid-March employment in the year. Pay per employee is calculated by dividing 1st Quarter payroll, annualized, by mid-March employment. The columns headed "% State" show the county's percentage of the state total for the SIC in 1995; for example, 1.4% for SIC 6000 means that the county had 1.4 percent of the state's total establishments (or payroll) in SIC 6000 in 1995. A dash (-) is used to indicate that data are not available or cannot be calculated; nec means not elsewhere classified.

Continued on next page.

SIC	Industry	No. Establishments			Employment		Pay / Employee		Annual Payroll ($ 000)		
		1994	1995	% State	1994	1995	1994	1995	1994	1995	% State
LEE, MS - [continued]											
6140	Personal credit institutions	24	26	4.5	141	130	25,674	27,846	3,554	3,598	6.1
6210	Security brokers and dealers	5	5	4.4	22	24	51,091	41,000	994	1,158	3.1
6300	Insurance carriers	25	23	6.8	302	199	29,629	36,724	8,740	6,469	3.1
6310	Life insurance	14	13	7.8	273	177	28,791	34,757	7,556	5,388	6.2
6400	Insurance agents, brokers, and service	42	40	3.6	118	109	23,424	27,046	2,911	3,013	2.5
6500	Real estate	42	40	2.8	180	210	13,267	13,657	2,368	2,996	4.1
6510	Real estate operators and lessors	24	23	3.1	124	140	12,194	12,943	1,352	1,880	6.3
LEFLORE, MS											
60 –	**Finance, insurance, and real estate**	83	82	1.6	456	441	22,737	22,358	10,663	10,258	1.1
6000	Depository institutions	17	17	1.4	173	179	23,006	23,531	4,059	4,356	1.1
6100	Nondepository institutions	14	14	1.9	60	64	22,200	22,750	1,451	1,523	1.6
6140	Personal credit institutions	8	8	1.4	35	38	17,943	19,579	568	693	1.2
6300	Insurance carriers	6	7	2.1	129	103	26,822	25,282	3,386	2,684	1.3
6400	Insurance agents, brokers, and service	16	16	1.4	51	50	21,255	21,920	1,282	1,161	1.0
6500	Real estate	26	25	1.8	38	40	12,421	11,100	436	472	0.6
6510	Real estate operators and lessors	19	17	2.3	30	29	8,933	10,069	303	304	1.0
LINCOLN, MS											
60 –	**Finance, insurance, and real estate**	57	54	1.1	285	283	20,716	20,961	5,965	6,339	0.7
6000	Depository institutions	10	10	0.8	141	145	20,794	22,124	3,192	3,357	0.9
6100	Nondepository institutions	14	13	1.7	52	47	21,615	23,234	1,003	1,088	1.2
6400	Insurance agents, brokers, and service	12	10	0.9	38	38	23,474	19,474	824	855	0.7
6500	Real estate	12	11	0.8	23	23	11,652	12,522	301	283	0.4
LOWNDES, MS											
60 –	**Finance, insurance, and real estate**	144	136	2.7	829	791	24,207	25,102	17,996	18,877	2.0
6000	Depository institutions	39	37	3.1	374	378	25,209	26,032	8,600	9,088	2.4
6020	Commercial banks	25	25	2.7	306	308	26,222	27,247	7,044	7,430	2.2
6100	Nondepository institutions	13	16	2.1	62	67	21,806	19,701	1,162	1,352	1.5
6200	Security and commodity brokers	6	6	3.4	23	25	24,522	45,920	925	1,011	2.3
6300	Insurance carriers	13	11	3.3	97	97	32,412	29,113	2,736	2,710	1.3
6310	Life insurance	5	5	3.0	67	74	24,657	20,054	1,509	1,481	1.7
6400	Insurance agents, brokers, and service	35	31	2.8	100	109	19,280	27,596	2,292	2,805	2.3
6500	Real estate	34	32	2.3	92	106	12,435	12,491	1,328	1,508	2.0
6510	Real estate operators and lessors	13	11	1.5	44	41	10,455	11,610	491	519	1.7
6530	Real estate agents and managers	18	18	3.4	47	61	14,468	13,180	813	960	3.0
6700	Holding and other investment offices	4	3	3.2	81	9	30,963	43,556	953	403	1.3
MADISON, MS											
60 –	**Finance, insurance, and real estate**	149	156	3.1	1,261	1,233	28,121	31,471	37,371	41,437	4.3
6000	Depository institutions	24	24	2.0	225	261	22,898	23,387	5,376	6,601	1.7
6100	Nondepository institutions	11	14	1.9	63	62	27,111	27,806	1,679	1,922	2.1
6300	Insurance carriers	28	28	8.3	601	495	33,265	41,131	20,915	20,621	10.0
6310	Life insurance	10	13	7.8	253	171	35,636	44,725	8,778	8,274	9.6
6330	Fire, marine, and casualty insurance	13	10	8.2	337	295	31,834	36,963	11,653	10,972	13.7
6400	Insurance agents, brokers, and service	35	36	3.3	164	185	30,268	32,000	5,490	7,308	6.1
6500	Real estate	43	45	3.2	176	154	13,341	15,974	2,627	2,647	3.6
6510	Real estate operators and lessors	14	12	1.6	67	45	11,403	11,200	769	523	1.8
6530	Real estate agents and managers	25	27	5.1	104	102	14,462	17,294	1,746	1,722	5.4
6550	Subdividers and developers	3	4	3.4	5	6	16,000	31,333	109	225	2.2
MARION, MS											
60 –	**Finance, insurance, and real estate**	39	39	0.8	219	214	18,941	19,364	4,436	4,563	0.5
6000	Depository institutions	11	12	1.0	151	151	20,291	21,139	3,410	3,544	0.9
6100	Nondepository institutions	7	7	0.9	27	25	18,815	20,160	499	540	0.6
6140	Personal credit institutions	7	7	1.2	27	25	18,815	20,160	499	540	0.9

Source: County Business Patterns, 1994/95, CBP-94/95, U.S. Department of Commerce, Washington, D.C., November 1997. SIC categories for which data were suppressed or not available for both 1994 and 1995 are not displayed. The employment columns represent mid-March employment in the year. Pay per employee is calculated by dividing 1st Quarter payroll, annualized, by mid-March employment. The columns headed "% State" show the county's percentage of the state total for the SIC in 1995; for example, 1.4% for SIC 6000 means that the county had 1.4 percent of the state's total establishments (or payroll) in SIC 6000 in 1995. A dash (-) is used to indicate that data are not available or cannot be calculated; nec means not elsewhere classified.

Continued on next page.

SIC	Industry	No. Establishments			Employment		Pay / Employee		Annual Payroll ($ 000)		
		1994	1995	% State	1994	1995	1994	1995	1994	1995	% State
MARION, MS - [continued]											
6400	Insurance agents, brokers, and service	11	11	1.0	22	26	13,455	13,231	338	358	0.3
6500	Real estate	10	9	0.6	19	12	14,737	8,667	189	121	0.2
6530	Real estate agents and managers	3	3	0.6	2	1	4,000	8,000	23	22	0.1
MARSHALL, MS											
60 –	**Finance, insurance, and real estate**	24	25	0.5	172	165	21,558	22,861	3,995	4,395	0.5
6000	Depository institutions	8	8	0.7	121	116	21,421	22,621	2,718	3,000	0.8
6020	Commercial banks	8	8	0.8	121	116	21,421	22,621	2,718	3,000	0.9
6400	Insurance agents, brokers, and service	5	5	0.5	26	24	20,769	23,333	644	649	0.5
6500	Real estate	6	6	0.4	9	11	29,778	29,455	370	434	0.6
MONROE, MS											
60 –	**Finance, insurance, and real estate**	70	66	1.3	385	371	22,514	22,221	8,537	7,862	0.8
6000	Depository institutions	24	23	1.9	180	185	22,156	23,416	4,037	4,191	1.1
6020	Commercial banks	18	18	1.9	158	161	22,785	24,422	3,631	3,758	1.1
6100	Nondepository institutions	16	15	2.0	55	52	16,291	19,462	930	1,049	1.1
6400	Insurance agents, brokers, and service	17	15	1.4	49	47	15,265	14,809	781	708	0.6
6500	Real estate	7	7	0.5	13	9	14,769	18,667	191	247	0.3
MONTGOMERY, MS											
60 –	**Finance, insurance, and real estate**	22	20	0.4	128	120	17,813	20,433	2,615	2,646	0.3
6000	Depository institutions	7	7	0.6	80	76	19,850	23,316	1,888	1,948	0.5
6100	Nondepository institutions	10	8	1.1	30	25	18,000	18,720	544	493	0.5
6140	Personal credit institutions	7	5	0.9	23	19	18,783	19,579	400	369	0.6
6400	Insurance agents, brokers, and service	5	5	0.5	18	19	8,444	11,158	183	205	0.2
NESHOBA, MS											
60 –	**Finance, insurance, and real estate**	40	38	0.7	343	346	16,898	19,376	6,427	6,726	0.7
6000	Depository institutions	19	19	1.6	174	195	18,621	19,918	3,338	3,820	1.0
6400	Insurance agents, brokers, and service	5	5	0.5	11	12	16,364	15,667	182	196	0.2
NEWTON, MS											
60 –	**Finance, insurance, and real estate**	26	28	0.6	142	137	26,789	29,226	3,269	3,220	0.3
6000	Depository institutions	7	7	0.6	88	74	23,818	24,919	2,115	1,865	0.5
6400	Insurance agents, brokers, and service	5	5	0.5	19	18	15,789	17,111	321	319	0.3
6500	Real estate	6	7	0.5	10	15	6,400	10,667	84	132	0.2
NOXUBEE, MS											
60 –	**Finance, insurance, and real estate**	14	13	0.3	76	115	19,526	16,139	1,661	1,875	0.2
6000	Depository institutions	5	5	0.4	58	94	19,724	16,085	1,260	1,444	0.4
6020	Commercial banks	5	5	0.5	58	94	19,724	16,085	1,260	1,444	0.4
6400	Insurance agents, brokers, and service	4	4	0.4	7	9	11,429	10,222	85	91	0.1
OKTIBBEHA, MS											
60 –	**Finance, insurance, and real estate**	77	78	1.5	423	452	23,385	24,761	8,886	9,811	1.0
6000	Depository institutions	19	17	1.4	252	279	28,857	29,921	6,210	6,937	1.8
6100	Nondepository institutions	9	11	1.5	33	42	21,576	24,952	696	935	1.0
6400	Insurance agents, brokers, and service	13	12	1.1	29	29	15,586	15,586	464	470	0.4
6500	Real estate	29	30	2.1	96	91	11,167	11,560	1,115	1,157	1.6
6510	Real estate operators and lessors	15	16	2.2	53	44	9,811	10,273	528	531	1.8
6530	Real estate agents and managers	11	11	2.1	38	42	13,474	13,048	537	536	1.7
6550	Subdividers and developers	3	3	2.6	5	5	8,000	10,400	50	90	0.9
PANOLA, MS											
60 –	**Finance, insurance, and real estate**	42	42	0.8	290	291	21,628	22,983	6,565	7,109	0.7

Source: County Business Patterns, 1994/95, CBP-94/95, U.S. Department of Commerce, Washington, D.C., November 1997. SIC categories for which data were suppressed or not available for both 1994 and 1995 are not displayed. The employment columns represent mid-March employment in the year. Pay per employee is calculated by dividing 1st Quarter payroll, annualized, by mid-March employment. The columns headed "% State" show the county's percentage of the state total for the SIC in 1995; for example, 1.4% for SIC 6000 means that the county had 1.4 percent of the state's total establishments (or payroll) in SIC 6000 in 1995. A dash (-) is used to indicate that data are not available or cannot be calculated; nec means not elsewhere classified.

Continued on next page.

SIC	Industry	No. Establishments			Employment		Pay / Employee		Annual Payroll ($ 000)		
		1994	1995	% State	1994	1995	1994	1995	1994	1995	% State
PANOLA, MS - [continued]											
6000	Depository institutions	10	10	0.8	154	151	19,870	21,510	3,316	3,510	0.9
6400	Insurance agents, brokers, and service	10	10	0.9	38	38	17,368	19,368	703	757	0.6
6510	Real estate operators and lessors	8	5	0.7	9	6	5,778	6,667	43	94	0.3
PEARL RIVER, MS											
60–	**Finance, insurance, and real estate**	57	57	1.1	202	237	18,099	20,523	4,115	5,343	0.6
6000	Depository institutions	12	13	1.1	106	129	17,736	20,093	2,199	2,941	0.8
6400	Insurance agents, brokers, and service	11	10	0.9	29	31	17,931	22,452	570	726	0.6
6500	Real estate	19	19	1.3	23	28	6,609	9,857	212	404	0.5
6510	Real estate operators and lessors	8	5	0.7	8	5	4,000	7,200	47	62	0.2
6530	Real estate agents and managers	8	11	2.1	15	21	8,000	11,238	117	328	1.0
PERRY, MS											
60–	**Finance, insurance, and real estate**	10	8	0.2	64	64	18,125	19,750	1,420	1,429	0.1
PIKE, MS											
60–	**Finance, insurance, and real estate**	81	78	1.5	417	437	17,976	19,973	7,939	8,620	0.9
6000	Depository institutions	18	18	1.5	229	222	20,384	23,459	4,812	5,200	1.4
6100	Nondepository institutions	16	16	2.1	44	57	20,636	20,491	987	1,199	1.3
6140	Personal credit institutions	12	12	2.1	38	48	21,684	21,750	881	1,062	1.8
6200	Security and commodity brokers	3	3	1.7	4	5	23,000	16,000	107	98	0.2
6300	Insurance carriers	6	6	1.8	24	33	21,500	16,848	551	560	0.3
6400	Insurance agents, brokers, and service	13	15	1.4	34	34	15,059	17,059	553	584	0.5
6500	Real estate	22	17	1.2	79	83	9,468	13,060	879	926	1.3
6510	Real estate operators and lessors	14	9	1.2	49	55	6,694	12,364	422	506	1.7
6700	Holding and other investment offices	3	3	3.2	3	3	17,333	17,333	50	53	0.2
PONTOTOC, MS											
60–	**Finance, insurance, and real estate**	26	26	0.5	141	151	17,957	18,305	2,939	2,947	0.3
6000	Depository institutions	6	6	0.5	99	100	19,071	20,160	2,047	2,102	0.5
6020	Commercial banks	6	6	0.6	99	100	19,071	20,160	2,047	2,102	0.6
6100	Nondepository institutions	6	7	0.9	16	19	17,500	17,053	305	457	0.5
6140	Personal credit institutions	6	7	1.2	16	19	17,500	17,053	305	457	0.8
6400	Insurance agents, brokers, and service	8	8	0.7	18	21	18,667	16,571	349	331	0.3
6500	Real estate	6	5	0.4	8	11	3,500	6,909	238	57	0.1
PRENTISS, MS											
60–	**Finance, insurance, and real estate**	34	35	0.7	214	203	15,140	16,690	3,649	3,741	0.4
6000	Depository institutions	10	10	0.8	135	123	16,356	18,569	2,570	2,573	0.7
6020	Commercial banks	10	10	1.1	135	123	16,356	18,569	2,570	2,573	0.7
6400	Insurance agents, brokers, and service	10	10	0.9	35	32	13,829	16,000	532	532	0.4
6500	Real estate	10	10	0.7	31	35	9,161	9,486	314	354	0.5
6510	Real estate operators and lessors	6	5	0.7	27	30	7,852	8,533	246	264	0.9
6530	Real estate agents and managers	3	3	0.6	4	4	18,000	16,000	66	69	0.2
QUITMAN, MS											
60–	**Finance, insurance, and real estate**	15	15	0.3	86	91	18,651	16,923	1,997	1,573	0.2
6000	Depository institutions	6	6	0.5	49	54	20,082	18,444	1,048	1,029	0.3
6020	Commercial banks	6	6	0.6	49	54	20,082	18,444	1,048	1,029	0.3
6400	Insurance agents, brokers, and service	4	5	0.5	21	25	21,333	16,800	800	416	0.3
RANKIN, MS											
60–	**Finance, insurance, and real estate**	193	192	3.8	1,931	1,784	25,384	28,016	50,069	51,070	5.3
6000	Depository institutions	34	36	3.0	376	365	20,266	23,638	8,149	9,042	2.4
6020	Commercial banks	28	29	3.1	360	350	20,456	23,909	7,885	8,707	2.5
6100	Nondepository institutions	25	23	3.0	133	152	25,654	27,395	3,591	5,224	5.6
6300	Insurance carriers	21	23	6.8	964	796	30,037	34,362	28,258	26,544	12.9
6400	Insurance agents, brokers, and service	45	47	4.3	223	233	23,749	26,489	6,083	6,752	5.6

Source: County Business Patterns, 1994/95, CBP-94/95, U.S. Department of Commerce, Washington, D.C., November 1997. SIC categories for which data were suppressed or not available for both 1994 and 1995 are not displayed. The employment columns represent mid-March employment in the year. Pay per employee is calculated by dividing 1st Quarter payroll, annualized, by mid-March employment. The columns headed "% State" show the county's percentage of the state total for the SIC in 1995; for example, 1.4% for SIC 6000 means that the county had 1.4 percent of the state's total establishments (or payroll) in SIC 6000 in 1995. A dash (-) is used to indicate that data are not available or cannot be calculated; nec means not elsewhere classified.

Continued on next page.

SIC	Industry	No. Establishments			Employment		Pay / Employee		Annual Payroll ($ 000)		
		1994	1995	% State	1994	1995	1994	1995	1994	1995	% State
RANKIN, MS - [continued]											
6500	Real estate	63	57	4.0	208	209	15,923	14,545	3,346	2,760	3.7
6510	Real estate operators and lessors	28	23	3.1	69	64	13,217	12,563	913	798	2.7
6530	Real estate agents and managers	24	22	4.2	117	117	15,966	13,846	1,829	1,174	3.7
6550	Subdividers and developers	9	10	8.6	19	22	23,368	24,182	515	672	6.4
6552	Subdividers and developers, n.e.c.	9	9	14.5	19	22	23,368	24,182	515	638	8.5
SCOTT, MS											
60 –	**Finance, insurance, and real estate**	39	36	0.7	261	268	20,751	21,642	5,602	6,104	0.6
6000	Depository institutions	10	10	0.8	171	182	22,526	23,582	3,986	4,411	1.1
6140	Personal credit institutions	8	7	1.2	34	31	19,529	20,129	637	648	1.1
6400	Insurance agents, brokers, and service	13	12	1.1	38	34	15,158	16,235	579	580	0.5
6500	Real estate	6	4	0.3	12	14	11,667	8,571	105	116	0.2
SHARKEY, MS											
60 –	**Finance, insurance, and real estate**	11	11	0.2	45	50	18,311	18,400	951	1,027	0.1
SIMPSON, MS											
60 –	**Finance, insurance, and real estate**	35	32	0.6	164	167	19,561	20,695	3,741	3,686	0.4
6000	Depository institutions	12	11	0.9	116	119	20,862	22,353	2,952	2,895	0.8
6500	Real estate	6	6	0.4	7	5	12,000	5,600	63	32	0.0
SMITH, MS											
60 –	**Finance, insurance, and real estate**	12	9	0.2	90	69	14,711	18,261	1,306	1,193	0.1
STONE, MS											
60 –	**Finance, insurance, and real estate**	14	13	0.3	96	99	16,083	17,616	1,827	1,891	0.2
6000	Depository institutions	5	5	0.4	78	82	17,179	19,024	1,608	1,695	0.4
SUNFLOWER, MS											
60 –	**Finance, insurance, and real estate**	44	42	0.8	290	277	19,807	22,253	5,530	5,937	0.6
6000	Depository institutions	15	15	1.3	188	189	22,128	24,974	4,030	4,449	1.2
6020	Commercial banks	12	12	1.3	178	180	22,652	25,444	3,901	4,286	1.2
6100	Nondepository institutions	7	5	0.7	20	17	21,600	19,529	362	312	0.3
6510	Real estate operators and lessors	7	7	1.0	25	21	12,640	15,619	275	355	1.2
TALLAHATCHIE, MS											
60 –	**Finance, insurance, and real estate**	14	13	0.3	64	60	18,375	18,800	1,156	1,104	0.1
6000	Depository institutions	5	5	0.4	44	45	19,909	19,733	903	866	0.2
6020	Commercial banks	5	5	0.5	44	45	19,909	19,733	903	866	0.3
6400	Insurance agents, brokers, and service	5	4	0.4	16	10	14,250	16,400	175	157	0.1
TATE, MS											
60 –	**Finance, insurance, and real estate**	29	29	0.6	164	182	24,317	23,143	4,014	4,479	0.5
6000	Depository institutions	6	6	0.5	93	101	21,978	25,782	2,356	2,756	0.7
6020	Commercial banks	6	6	0.6	93	101	21,978	25,782	2,356	2,756	0.8
6100	Nondepository institutions	8	9	1.2	34	35	27,647	27,543	823	996	1.1
6400	Insurance agents, brokers, and service	10	10	0.9	33	41	29,333	14,244	787	666	0.6
6500	Real estate	5	4	0.3	4	5	9,000	12,000	48	61	0.1
TIPPAH, MS											
60 –	**Finance, insurance, and real estate**	27	24	0.5	224	207	14,357	15,671	3,562	3,707	0.4
6000	Depository institutions	9	7	0.6	144	139	17,417	18,101	2,811	2,889	0.8
6020	Commercial banks	9	7	0.7	144	139	17,417	18,101	2,811	2,889	0.8
6400	Insurance agents, brokers, and service	6	6	0.5	15	14	14,667	15,429	225	217	0.2

Source: County Business Patterns, 1994/95, CBP-94/95, U.S. Department of Commerce, Washington, D.C., November 1997. SIC categories for which data were suppressed or not available for both 1994 and 1995 are *not* displayed. The employment columns represent mid-March employment in the year. Pay per employee is calculated by dividing 1st Quarter payroll, annualized, by mid-March employment. The columns headed "% State" show the county's percentage of the state total for the SIC in 1995; for example, 1.4% for SIC 6000 means that the county had 1.4 percent of the state's total establishments (or payroll) in SIC 6000 in 1995. A dash (-) is used to indicate that data are not available or cannot be calculated; *nec* means not elsewhere classified.

SIC	Industry	No. Establishments			Employment		Pay / Employee		Annual Payroll ($ 000)		
		1994	1995	% State	1994	1995	1994	1995	1994	1995	% State
TISHOMINGO, MS											
60–	**Finance, insurance, and real estate**	26	26	0.5	162	179	17,654	15,620	2,838	2,994	0.3
6000	Depository institutions	14	14	1.2	133	140	18,677	17,200	2,512	2,612	0.7
6400	Insurance agents, brokers, and service	4	6	0.5	8	13	12,500	9,846	122	149	0.1
TUNICA, MS											
60–	**Finance, insurance, and real estate**	12	11	0.2	86	71	21,581	20,338	1,981	1,447	0.2
UNION, MS											
60–	**Finance, insurance, and real estate**	27	25	0.5	177	166	22,056	21,807	3,538	3,979	0.4
6400	Insurance agents, brokers, and service	8	6	0.5	22	21	19,273	21,524	456	475	0.4
6510	Real estate operators and lessors	5	5	0.7	8	8	8,000	7,500	82	67	0.2
WALTHALL, MS											
60–	**Finance, insurance, and real estate**	12	10	0.2	81	88	15,852	18,409	1,432	1,652	0.2
6000	Depository institutions	4	4	0.3	60	68	16,867	19,941	1,164	1,362	0.4
6400	Insurance agents, brokers, and service	3	3	0.3	13	13	10,769	10,154	141	140	0.1
WARREN, MS											
60–	**Finance, insurance, and real estate**	103	101	2.0	559	539	21,145	21,291	11,572	11,690	1.2
6000	Depository institutions	28	26	2.2	355	345	22,569	21,959	7,653	7,582	2.0
6020	Commercial banks	18	18	1.9	306	281	23,320	23,559	6,664	6,516	1.9
6100	Nondepository institutions	10	13	1.7	32	36	16,875	17,778	579	684	0.7
6300	Insurance carriers	5	5	1.5	11	6	25,091	31,333	285	158	0.1
6400	Insurance agents, brokers, and service	21	18	1.6	75	75	19,307	21,120	1,532	1,627	1.4
6500	Real estate	30	32	2.3	66	63	11,212	13,397	818	914	1.2
6510	Real estate operators and lessors	17	17	2.3	44	40	10,545	12,200	470	576	1.9
6530	Real estate agents and managers	10	11	2.1	21	20	12,381	16,200	326	290	0.9
WASHINGTON, MS											
60–	**Finance, insurance, and real estate**	145	139	2.7	710	718	19,662	20,279	14,238	14,769	1.5
6000	Depository institutions	31	31	2.6	283	276	21,173	23,029	5,858	6,380	1.7
6100	Nondepository institutions	16	15	2.0	57	58	22,456	21,862	1,260	1,361	1.5
6140	Personal credit institutions	11	10	1.7	46	46	20,348	19,652	946	992	1.7
6300	Insurance carriers	9	9	2.7	107	103	23,290	20,155	2,240	2,067	1.0
6400	Insurance agents, brokers, and service	28	25	2.3	102	98	19,647	21,020	2,378	2,112	1.8
6500	Real estate	52	50	3.5	138	154	12,638	14,935	2,138	2,344	3.2
6510	Real estate operators and lessors	36	33	4.5	88	90	14,545	17,733	1,545	1,591	5.3
6530	Real estate agents and managers	11	10	1.9	36	47	10,444	12,766	486	622	2.0
6550	Subdividers and developers	3	4	3.4	13	16	6,462	6,250	99	111	1.1
6553	Cemetery subdividers and developers	3	4	9.1	13	16	6,462	6,250	99	111	4.7
WAYNE, MS											
60–	**Finance, insurance, and real estate**	25	26	0.5	151	161	18,252	20,671	3,079	3,803	0.4
6000	Depository institutions	6	6	0.5	82	98	18,927	19,592	1,704	1,982	0.5
6400	Insurance agents, brokers, and service	7	8	0.7	30	30	15,467	17,467	547	674	0.6
WEBSTER, MS											
60–	**Finance, insurance, and real estate**	12	13	0.3	61	62	18,689	20,710	1,243	1,262	0.1
6000	Depository institutions	5	5	0.4	43	39	19,070	20,923	829	834	0.2
6020	Commercial banks	5	5	0.5	43	39	19,070	20,923	829	834	0.2
6400	Insurance agents, brokers, and service	3	3	0.3	9	13	14,222	20,923	219	179	0.1
WILKINSON, MS											
60–	**Finance, insurance, and real estate**	12	11	0.2	57	63	19,088	19,175	1,240	1,341	0.1
6400	Insurance agents, brokers, and service	3	3	0.3	11	9	13,455	16,889	150	149	0.1

Source: County Business Patterns, 1994/95, CBP-94/95, U.S. Department of Commerce, Washington, D.C., November 1997. SIC categories for which data were suppressed or not available for both 1994 and 1995 are not displayed. The employment columns represent mid-March employment in the year. Pay per employee is calculated by dividing 1st Quarter payroll, annualized, by mid-March employment. The columns headed "% State" show the county's percentage of the state total for the SIC in 1995; for example, 1.4% for SIC 6000 means that the county had 1.4 percent of the state's total establishments (or payroll) in SIC 6000 in 1995. A dash (-) is used to indicate that data are not available or cannot be calculated; nec means not elsewhere classified.

Continued on next page.

SIC	Industry	No. Establishments			Employment		Pay / Employee		Annual Payroll ($ 000)		
		1994	1995	% State	1994	1995	1994	1995	1994	1995	% State
WINSTON, MS - [continued]											
60 –	**Finance, insurance, and real estate**	37	33	*0.6*	352	332	20,148	22,313	7,973	7,798	*0.8*
6000	Depository institutions	13	12	*1.0*	123	113	19,837	21,451	2,604	2,426	*0.6*
YALOBUSHA, MS											
60 –	**Finance, insurance, and real estate**	22	21	*0.4*	105	107	16,000	19,477	1,826	2,037	*0.2*
6000	Depository institutions	7	7	*0.6*	79	72	17,519	20,944	1,464	1,525	*0.4*
6020	Commercial banks	7	7	*0.7*	79	72	17,519	20,944	1,464	1,525	*0.4*
6400	Insurance agents, brokers, and service	5	5	*0.5*	13	14	10,462	10,857	160	160	*0.1*
YAZOO, MS											
60 –	**Finance, insurance, and real estate**	32	34	*0.7*	182	181	26,681	27,072	4,120	4,210	*0.4*
6000	Depository institutions	12	12	*1.0*	122	126	31,246	31,079	3,177	3,204	*0.8*
6400	Insurance agents, brokers, and service	4	4	*0.4*	16	16	27,250	26,750	405	445	*0.4*
6530	Real estate agents and managers	3	3	*0.6*	5	6	13,600	13,333	81	89	*0.3*

Source: *County Business Patterns, 1994/95*, CBP-94/95, U.S. Department of Commerce, Washington, D.C., November 1997. SIC categories for which data were suppressed or not available for both 1994 and 1995 are *not* displayed. The employment columns represent mid-March employment in the year. Pay per employee is calculated by dividing 1st Quarter payroll, annualized, by mid-March employment. The columns headed "% State" show the county's percentage of the state total for the SIC in 1995; for example, 1.4% for SIC 6000 means that the county had 1.4 percent of the state's total establishments (or payroll) in SIC 6000 in 1995. A dash (-) is used to indicate that data are not available or cannot be calculated; *nec* means not elsewhere classified.

MISSOURI

SIC	Industry	No. Establishments			Employment		Pay / Employee		Annual Payroll ($ 000)		
		1994	1995	% State	1994	1995	1994	1995	1994	1995	% State
ADAIR, MO											
60 –	**Finance, insurance, and real estate**	52	49	0.4	275	261	17,076	18,406	4,999	5,010	0.1
6000	Depository institutions	9	9	0.4	168	156	16,310	18,256	2,924	2,940	0.3
6510	Real estate operators and lessors	6	4	0.2	8	6	6,000	7,333	57	50	0.0
6530	Real estate agents and managers	9	9	0.5	23	24	8,174	9,000	225	211	0.1
ANDREW, MO											
60 –	**Finance, insurance, and real estate**	22	21	0.2	78	74	14,103	14,324	1,196	1,237	0.0
6500	Real estate	10	9	0.2	26	23	12,769	11,826	356	343	0.1
6510	Real estate operators and lessors	4	4	0.2	12	11	4,667	5,091	67	67	0.0
ATCHISON, MO											
60 –	**Finance, insurance, and real estate**	22	25	0.2	102	98	15,137	14,980	1,647	1,703	0.0
6000	Depository institutions	5	5	0.2	54	50	18,593	18,400	1,072	1,096	0.1
6020	Commercial banks	5	5	0.3	54	50	18,593	18,400	1,072	1,096	0.1
6400	Insurance agents, brokers, and service	11	13	0.4	31	31	11,355	12,129	396	409	0.1
AUDRAIN, MO											
60 –	**Finance, insurance, and real estate**	63	67	0.5	324	302	17,025	18,689	5,594	5,711	0.1
6000	Depository institutions	17	16	0.7	204	177	18,627	20,565	3,761	3,673	0.3
6020	Commercial banks	13	12	0.8	165	133	19,297	21,925	3,096	2,879	0.3
6100	Nondepository institutions	3	3	0.4	13	13	30,462	34,154	371	376	0.1
6400	Insurance agents, brokers, and service	21	22	0.7	49	52	11,510	11,769	605	639	0.1
6500	Real estate	17	19	0.4	36	36	11,111	12,333	475	555	0.1
BARRY, MO											
60 –	**Finance, insurance, and real estate**	59	56	0.4	318	330	17,119	17,818	5,387	6,336	0.1
6000	Depository institutions	16	16	0.7	215	239	19,126	20,636	4,278	5,281	0.5
6300	Insurance carriers	3	3	0.3	10	11	28,400	9,091	147	98	0.0
6330	Fire, marine, and casualty insurance	3	3	0.7	10	11	28,400	9,091	147	98	0.0
6400	Insurance agents, brokers, and service	17	17	0.5	31	38	12,645	11,789	451	500	0.1
6500	Real estate	18	16	0.4	54	34	8,370	6,471	340	268	0.1
BARTON, MO											
60 –	**Finance, insurance, and real estate**	27	28	0.2	186	184	18,624	22,630	3,497	4,132	0.1
6000	Depository institutions	9	9	0.4	80	80	20,300	22,300	1,830	2,183	0.2
6400	Insurance agents, brokers, and service	7	7	0.2	15	16	12,533	14,250	209	235	0.1
6500	Real estate	7	9	0.2	28	29	5,143	14,483	239	463	0.1
BATES, MO											
60 –	**Finance, insurance, and real estate**	32	34	0.3	170	174	15,882	17,540	2,943	3,090	0.1
6000	Depository institutions	11	12	0.6	114	110	17,018	18,982	2,138	2,167	0.2
6020	Commercial banks	11	12	0.8	114	110	17,018	18,982	2,138	2,167	0.3
6400	Insurance agents, brokers, and service	11	12	0.4	34	36	15,294	16,667	558	592	0.1
6500	Real estate	4	5	0.1	11	16	9,091	10,750	104	188	0.0
BENTON, MO											
60 –	**Finance, insurance, and real estate**	36	39	0.3	132	146	18,788	19,096	2,732	3,073	0.1
6000	Depository institutions	5	5	0.2	75	87	21,973	21,885	1,812	2,053	0.2
6020	Commercial banks	5	5	0.3	75	87	21,973	21,885	1,812	2,053	0.2

Source: County Business Patterns, 1994/95, CBP-94/95, U.S. Department of Commerce, Washington, D.C., November 1997. SIC categories for which data were suppressed or not available for both 1994 and 1995 are *not* displayed. The employment columns represent mid-March employment in the year. Pay per employee is calculated by dividing 1st Quarter payroll, annualized, by mid-March employment. The columns headed "% State" show the county's percentage of the state total for the SIC in 1995; for example, 1.4% for SIC 6000 means that the county had 1.4 percent of the state's total establishments (or payroll) in SIC 6000 in 1995. A dash (-) is used to indicate that data are not available or cannot be calculated; *nec* means not elsewhere classified.

Continued on next page.

SIC	Industry	No. Establishments			Employment		Pay / Employee		Annual Payroll ($ 000)		
		1994	1995	% State	1994	1995	1994	1995	1994	1995	% State
BENTON, MO - [continued]											
6400	Insurance agents, brokers, and service	9	9	0.3	17	13	10,118	12,308	234	240	0.1
6500	Real estate	18	20	0.4	34	38	16,118	17,053	587	707	0.1
6550	Subdividers and developers	5	5	1.1	11	10	29,091	27,200	308	258	0.6
BOLLINGER, MO											
60 –	**Finance, insurance, and real estate**	12	12	0.1	-	-	-	-	-	-	-
6500	Real estate	3	3	0.1	6	6	12,000	12,000	78	81	0.0
BOONE, MO											
60 –	**Finance, insurance, and real estate**	331	329	2.6	5,611	5,475	29,042	31,798	169,522	178,898	4.1
6000	Depository institutions	47	47	2.2	980	929	19,257	22,738	19,641	20,895	1.8
6020	Commercial banks	37	40	2.6	852	824	19,474	23,024	17,169	18,184	2.1
6100	Nondepository institutions	17	20	2.6	62	80	28,129	25,350	1,940	2,259	0.7
6200	Security and commodity brokers	12	14	1.8	46	54	40,174	31,556	1,676	1,980	0.4
6300	Insurance carriers	28	25	2.9	3,431	3,208	35,236	38,783	123,129	125,631	12.4
6310	Life insurance	10	8	3.3	240	222	29,750	31,550	7,205	7,034	1.9
6330	Fire, marine, and casualty insurance	14	13	3.1	3,176	2,947	35,693	39,530	115,448	117,615	30.4
6400	Insurance agents, brokers, and service	79	78	2.4	535	597	22,415	27,558	13,380	17,685	4.1
6500	Real estate	138	134	3.0	506	572	12,941	13,587	8,168	9,159	1.8
6510	Real estate operators and lessors	60	56	3.0	227	245	9,498	10,302	2,696	3,010	1.7
6530	Real estate agents and managers	54	53	2.8	182	211	13,275	13,232	2,816	3,150	1.2
6552	Subdividers and developers, n.e.c.	16	15	5.8	55	64	21,818	25,375	1,773	1,769	7.0
6700	Holding and other investment offices	10	11	2.5	51	35	20,706	17,143	1,588	1,289	0.3
BUCHANAN, MO											
60 –	**Finance, insurance, and real estate**	185	183	1.4	1,860	1,852	21,320	22,717	41,241	43,481	1.0
6000	Depository institutions	38	37	1.7	579	553	21,444	21,447	12,321	12,671	1.1
6020	Commercial banks	20	19	1.2	464	416	21,922	22,500	9,776	9,525	1.1
6030	Savings institutions	4	4	1.3	54	59	20,000	21,627	1,313	1,620	1.5
6100	Nondepository institutions	13	14	1.8	58	53	22,207	30,491	1,349	1,434	0.5
6140	Personal credit institutions	10	10	2.9	31	35	22,839	27,200	778	881	1.2
6300	Insurance carriers	15	13	1.5	711	689	24,214	25,759	18,727	18,709	1.9
6310	Life insurance	6	4	1.6	80	72	22,350	19,944	1,757	1,386	0.4
6330	Fire, marine, and casualty insurance	9	9	2.1	631	617	24,450	26,438	16,970	17,323	4.5
6400	Insurance agents, brokers, and service	52	53	1.6	115	123	22,783	25,333	2,717	3,006	0.7
6500	Real estate	59	57	1.3	364	350	11,418	11,486	4,369	4,394	0.8
6510	Real estate operators and lessors	24	23	1.2	154	150	9,714	9,573	1,577	1,508	0.9
6530	Real estate agents and managers	27	26	1.4	116	119	13,724	12,706	1,576	1,676	0.6
BUTLER, MO											
60 –	**Finance, insurance, and real estate**	79	75	0.6	449	453	19,136	20,574	9,139	9,535	0.2
6000	Depository institutions	17	18	0.8	257	248	19,907	20,968	5,219	5,450	0.5
6020	Commercial banks	13	14	0.9	217	206	20,166	21,456	4,402	4,520	0.5
6100	Nondepository institutions	4	4	0.5	27	25	18,222	22,080	497	540	0.2
6300	Insurance carriers	6	6	0.7	46	52	28,261	28,846	1,312	1,437	0.1
6400	Insurance agents, brokers, and service	27	25	0.8	70	66	15,314	17,394	1,267	1,151	0.3
6500	Real estate	19	16	0.4	40	47	9,200	10,723	493	574	0.1
6510	Real estate operators and lessors	4	4	0.2	7	7	9,143	9,714	68	64	0.0
6530	Real estate agents and managers	8	6	0.3	9	10	8,889	10,400	92	112	0.0
6540	Title abstract offices	4	3	1.9	21	22	9,714	11,455	298	325	1.3
CALDWELL, MO											
60 –	**Finance, insurance, and real estate**	15	16	0.1	91	94	14,154	14,596	1,520	1,546	0.0
6000	Depository institutions	5	5	0.2	66	70	16,182	16,229	1,265	1,293	0.1
CALLAWAY, MO											
60 –	**Finance, insurance, and real estate**	46	45	0.4	311	321	18,058	18,779	6,221	6,412	0.1
6000	Depository institutions	16	16	0.7	188	195	18,447	18,974	3,871	3,937	0.3

Source: County Business Patterns, 1994/95, CBP-94/95, U.S. Department of Commerce, Washington, D.C., November 1997. SIC categories for which data were suppressed or not available for both 1994 and 1995 are not displayed. The employment columns represent mid-March employment in the year. Pay per employee is calculated by dividing 1st Quarter payroll, annualized, by mid-March employment. The columns headed "% State" show the county's percentage of the state total for the SIC in 1995; for example, 1.4% for SIC 6000 means that the county had 1.4 percent of the state's total establishments (or payroll) in SIC 6000 in 1995. A dash (-) is used to indicate that data are not available or cannot be calculated; nec means not elsewhere classified.

Continued on next page.

SIC	Industry	No. Establishments			Employment		Pay / Employee		Annual Payroll ($ 000)		
		1994	1995	% State	1994	1995	1994	1995	1994	1995	% State
CALLAWAY, MO - [continued]											
6020	Commercial banks	12	12	0.8	140	144	18,629	20,444	2,945	3,034	0.4
6030	Savings institutions	4	4	1.3	48	51	17,917	14,824	926	903	0.8
6400	Insurance agents, brokers, and service	12	12	0.4	27	28	10,963	11,714	331	333	0.1
6500	Real estate	12	11	0.2	81	82	17,432	19,415	1,600	1,705	0.3
6530	Real estate agents and managers	5	5	0.3	62	65	18,581	20,308	1,146	1,275	0.5
CAMDEN, MO											
60 –	**Finance, insurance, and real estate**	109	116	0.9	578	552	16,830	18,254	11,443	11,369	0.3
6000	Depository institutions	16	16	0.7	260	248	18,308	20,742	5,531	4,774	0.4
6200	Security and commodity brokers	5	5	0.7	9	10	80,889	48,800	582	573	0.1
6400	Insurance agents, brokers, and service	22	23	0.7	63	70	15,683	16,000	1,118	1,260	0.3
6500	Real estate	63	69	1.5	241	222	13,411	14,937	4,184	4,749	0.9
6510	Real estate operators and lessors	13	15	0.8	16	28	10,250	14,429	266	553	0.3
6530	Real estate agents and managers	32	35	1.9	169	128	12,734	13,313	2,811	2,509	0.9
6540	Title abstract offices	5	4	2.5	35	35	15,200	14,743	582	625	2.6
6550	Subdividers and developers	9	9	2.0	18	27	20,667	24,741	472	995	2.5
6552	Subdividers and developers, n.e.c.	9	9	3.5	18	27	20,667	24,741	472	995	3.9
CAPE GIRARDEAU, MO											
60 –	**Finance, insurance, and real estate**	186	190	1.5	1,372	1,306	21,624	23,149	33,076	31,073	0.7
6000	Depository institutions	22	23	1.1	571	559	18,648	20,408	10,226	11,306	1.0
6300	Insurance carriers	10	8	0.9	68	47	30,941	31,149	1,902	1,561	0.2
6400	Insurance agents, brokers, and service	68	61	1.9	336	299	26,833	30,100	12,156	9,624	2.2
6500	Real estate	67	74	1.6	198	227	12,990	11,841	3,322	2,912	0.6
6510	Real estate operators and lessors	25	31	1.6	98	85	11,429	8,753	1,212	801	0.5
6530	Real estate agents and managers	29	30	1.6	73	90	15,178	14,489	1,503	1,419	0.5
6552	Subdividers and developers, n.e.c.	8	7	2.7	15	40	7,200	9,700	360	419	1.7
6700	Holding and other investment offices	6	6	1.4	75	68	33,280	35,824	2,371	2,435	0.7
6710	Holding offices	3	3	1.5	57	64	38,877	37,813	2,223	2,417	1.0
CARROLL, MO											
60 –	**Finance, insurance, and real estate**	26	24	0.2	116	109	17,724	18,936	2,144	2,202	0.1
6000	Depository institutions	10	9	0.4	87	80	19,862	21,650	1,799	1,850	0.2
6500	Real estate	8	7	0.2	15	14	7,467	8,571	130	126	0.0
6530	Real estate agents and managers	4	3	0.2	4	3	5,000	8,000	24	25	0.0
CASS, MO											
60 –	**Finance, insurance, and real estate**	112	119	0.9	674	668	19,472	20,323	13,570	14,487	0.3
6000	Depository institutions	23	23	1.1	307	301	19,114	19,455	5,972	6,185	0.5
6100	Nondepository institutions	6	6	0.8	24	17	23,833	24,235	434	543	0.2
6400	Insurance agents, brokers, and service	30	31	0.9	84	74	23,381	21,676	1,643	1,642	0.4
6500	Real estate	44	50	1.1	236	258	17,305	20,124	4,938	5,626	1.1
6510	Real estate operators and lessors	20	21	1.1	78	95	14,000	16,632	1,577	1,827	1.0
6530	Real estate agents and managers	17	18	1.0	41	50	22,244	23,200	795	1,022	0.4
CEDAR, MO											
60 –	**Finance, insurance, and real estate**	22	22	0.2	114	118	15,018	15,966	1,959	2,231	0.1
6000	Depository institutions	5	5	0.2	74	76	17,730	17,895	1,485	1,716	0.1
CHARITON, MO											
60 –	**Finance, insurance, and real estate**	30	29	0.2	122	117	14,328	14,598	1,900	1,980	0.0
6000	Depository institutions	7	7	0.3	73	66	16,986	18,121	1,388	1,457	0.1
6020	Commercial banks	7	7	0.5	73	66	16,986	18,121	1,388	1,457	0.2
6400	Insurance agents, brokers, and service	11	9	0.3	17	14	6,588	7,143	118	111	0.0
6500	Real estate	8	9	0.2	18	24	10,000	8,000	200	206	0.0
CHRISTIAN, MO											
60 –	**Finance, insurance, and real estate**	79	79	0.6	327	347	15,682	17,867	5,971	6,783	0.2

Source: County Business Patterns, 1994/95, CBP-94/95, U.S. Department of Commerce, Washington, D.C., November 1997. SIC categories for which data were suppressed or not available for both 1994 and 1995 are not displayed. The employment columns represent mid-March employment in the year. Pay per employee is calculated by dividing 1st Quarter payroll, annualized, by mid-March employment. The columns headed "% State" show the county's percentage of the state total for the SIC in 1995; for example, 1.4% for SIC 6000 means that the county had 1.4 percent of the state's total establishments (or payroll) in SIC 6000 in 1995. A dash (-) is used to indicate that data are not available or cannot be calculated; nec means not elsewhere classified.

Continued on next page.

SIC	Industry	No. Establishments			Employment		Pay / Employee		Annual Payroll ($ 000)		
		1994	1995	% State	1994	1995	1994	1995	1994	1995	% State
CHRISTIAN, MO - [continued]											
6000	Depository institutions	16	17	0.8	191	207	19,435	19,787	4,034	4,457	0.4
6500	Real estate	37	34	0.8	68	80	7,471	14,400	935	1,323	0.3
6510	Real estate operators and lessors	14	12	0.6	32	23	5,000	8,348	180	193	0.1
6530	Real estate agents and managers	17	13	0.7	21	31	8,762	20,000	516	567	0.2
CLARK, MO											
60 –	**Finance, insurance, and real estate**	14	15	0.1	72	79	15,444	16,304	1,171	1,370	0.0
6000	Depository institutions	5	5	0.2	50	57	17,840	18,456	908	1,042	0.1
6500	Real estate	5	5	0.1	11	11	4,727	5,818	66	60	0.0
CLAY, MO											
60 –	**Finance, insurance, and real estate**	367	375	2.9	2,201	2,285	21,465	21,884	50,751	55,049	1.3
6000	Depository institutions	60	63	2.9	878	868	19,640	20,470	17,792	18,091	1.6
6020	Commercial banks	40	39	2.6	640	615	19,619	20,403	12,577	12,387	1.5
6030	Savings institutions	11	14	4.7	160	173	19,800	20,717	3,466	3,886	3.6
6100	Nondepository institutions	32	40	5.3	194	216	31,237	29,148	5,708	6,922	2.2
6160	Mortgage bankers and brokers	17	24	8.4	122	83	31,213	27,036	3,367	2,795	1.6
6280	Security and commodity services	3	3	1.4	6	4	24,000	57,000	200	274	0.3
6300	Insurance carriers	22	25	2.9	144	134	29,389	26,597	4,026	3,616	0.4
6310	Life insurance	4	5	2.0	88	84	22,636	17,333	1,682	1,555	0.4
6330	Fire, marine, and casualty insurance	14	16	3.8	39	37	47,385	44,541	1,882	1,570	0.4
6400	Insurance agents, brokers, and service	90	91	2.8	242	255	18,843	20,439	5,635	6,224	1.4
6500	Real estate	133	126	2.8	637	665	17,871	17,359	12,698	13,668	2.6
6510	Real estate operators and lessors	46	44	2.3	335	344	16,203	17,826	6,724	7,655	4.4
6530	Real estate agents and managers	66	64	3.4	194	182	20,701	18,242	3,955	3,913	1.4
6540	Title abstract offices	6	6	3.8	32	26	19,125	17,846	645	507	2.1
6550	Subdividers and developers	15	11	2.5	76	112	17,474	14,429	1,374	1,589	3.9
6552	Subdividers and developers, n.e.c.	10	7	2.7	60	88	18,667	15,227	1,119	1,261	5.0
6700	Holding and other investment offices	14	13	3.0	59	81	38,576	40,790	3,345	4,129	1.1
CLINTON, MO											
60 –	**Finance, insurance, and real estate**	33	34	0.3	190	231	17,895	17,247	3,907	4,434	0.1
6000	Depository institutions	8	9	0.4	131	138	20,153	21,942	3,024	3,382	0.3
6400	Insurance agents, brokers, and service	8	11	0.3	29	38	13,931	12,632	438	502	0.1
6500	Real estate	12	10	0.2	19	45	7,368	5,244	152	284	0.1
6510	Real estate operators and lessors	5	6	0.3	5	38	6,400	4,421	49	209	0.1
COLE, MO											
60 –	**Finance, insurance, and real estate**	184	195	1.5	2,335	2,322	25,972	27,211	62,282	65,539	1.5
6000	Depository institutions	38	36	1.7	781	767	21,332	23,150	18,475	19,463	1.7
6020	Commercial banks	19	18	1.2	606	601	21,650	23,374	14,627	15,718	1.8
6030	Savings institutions	8	7	2.3	90	76	21,511	25,474	2,128	1,881	1.8
6060	Credit unions	11	11	4.9	85	90	18,871	19,689	1,720	1,864	-
6100	Nondepository institutions	9	10	1.3	105	101	35,848	39,644	3,133	3,288	1.1
6300	Insurance carriers	23	22	2.6	308	267	28,701	31,745	8,929	8,553	0.8
6310	Life insurance	8	7	2.9	128	111	26,313	29,514	3,466	3,020	0.8
6330	Fire, marine, and casualty insurance	8	8	1.9	113	101	31,044	34,970	3,623	3,841	1.0
6400	Insurance agents, brokers, and service	48	53	1.6	488	538	34,672	34,446	17,710	19,808	4.6
6500	Real estate	53	60	1.3	199	168	14,352	16,048	3,025	3,170	0.6
6510	Real estate operators and lessors	28	31	1.6	85	78	11,482	12,821	1,070	1,264	0.7
6530	Real estate agents and managers	14	18	1.0	61	50	14,951	18,080	977	957	0.3
6552	Subdividers and developers, n.e.c.	6	5	1.9	18	9	16,000	15,111	261	158	0.6
COOPER, MO											
60 –	**Finance, insurance, and real estate**	25	25	0.2	123	131	20,065	20,336	2,525	2,574	0.1

Source: County Business Patterns, 1994/95, CBP-94/95, U.S. Department of Commerce, Washington, D.C., November 1997. SIC categories for which data were suppressed or not available for both 1994 and 1995 are not displayed. The employment columns represent mid-March employment in the year. Pay per employee is calculated by dividing 1st Quarter payroll, annualized, by mid-March employment. The columns headed "% State" show the county's percentage of the state total for the SIC in 1995; for example, 1.4% for SIC 6000 means that the county had 1.4 percent of the state's total establishments (or payroll) in SIC 6000 in 1995. A dash (-) is used to indicate that data are not available or cannot be calculated; nec means not elsewhere classified.

Continued on next page.

SIC	Industry	No. Establishments			Employment		Pay / Employee		Annual Payroll ($ 000)		
		1994	1995	% State	1994	1995	1994	1995	1994	1995	% State
COOPER, MO - [continued]											
6000	Depository institutions	8	8	0.4	95	99	20,968	22,020	1,988	2,034	0.2
6400	Insurance agents, brokers, and service	7	8	0.2	13	15	12,308	12,533	171	193	0.0
6500	Real estate	7	6	0.1	10	10	13,600	8,800	169	137	0.0
CRAWFORD, MO											
60 –	**Finance, insurance, and real estate**	30	34	0.3	160	174	16,475	16,644	2,868	3,191	0.1
6000	Depository institutions	7	7	0.3	105	115	18,781	18,574	2,074	2,385	0.2
6020	Commercial banks	7	7	0.5	105	115	18,781	18,574	2,074	2,385	0.3
6510	Real estate operators and lessors	6	7	0.4	12	17	11,667	12,235	175	208	0.1
DADE, MO											
60 –	**Finance, insurance, and real estate**	14	15	0.1	54	55	13,778	13,455	817	838	0.0
6400	Insurance agents, brokers, and service	4	5	0.2	11	13	8,727	7,077	100	107	0.0
6500	Real estate	6	6	0.1	7	7	7,429	9,143	57	69	0.0
DALLAS, MO											
60 –	**Finance, insurance, and real estate**	21	22	0.2	96	106	16,000	16,868	1,755	2,126	0.0
6000	Depository institutions	5	5	0.2	64	74	20,000	19,135	1,394	1,647	0.1
6500	Real estate	8	9	0.2	10	11	4,800	7,636	95	103	0.0
6510	Real estate operators and lessors	4	4	0.2	6	7	2,667	2,857	19	20	0.0
6530	Real estate agents and managers	3	3	0.2	4	3	8,000	10,667	65	45	0.0
DAVIESS, MO											
60 –	**Finance, insurance, and real estate**	15	16	0.1	93	97	12,946	14,021	1,386	1,493	0.0
6000	Depository institutions	5	5	0.2	61	63	14,885	16,317	1,043	1,107	0.1
DE KALB, MO											
60 –	**Finance, insurance, and real estate**	16	13	0.1	285	250	22,695	24,656	6,438	6,383	0.1
DENT, MO											
60 –	**Finance, insurance, and real estate**	27	27	0.2	157	160	21,987	20,100	3,295	3,212	0.1
6000	Depository institutions	6	6	0.3	110	111	23,855	22,054	2,511	2,447	0.2
6400	Insurance agents, brokers, and service	6	6	0.2	17	18	18,588	17,333	310	321	0.1
6500	Real estate	12	12	0.3	24	26	18,667	14,769	400	364	0.1
6510	Real estate operators and lessors	3	3	0.2	3	3	81,333	57,333	177	126	0.1
DOUGLAS, MO											
60 –	**Finance, insurance, and real estate**	13	12	0.1	75	78	15,093	17,231	1,215	1,280	0.0
6000	Depository institutions	5	5	0.2	62	64	16,452	17,875	1,042	1,096	0.1
DUNKLIN, MO											
60 –	**Finance, insurance, and real estate**	75	77	0.6	405	424	15,457	16,094	6,891	7,631	0.2
6000	Depository institutions	18	18	0.8	232	239	17,672	18,159	4,463	4,952	0.4
6020	Commercial banks	14	14	0.9	217	223	17,880	18,386	4,236	4,704	0.6
6400	Insurance agents, brokers, and service	25	23	0.7	51	52	16,471	18,000	901	993	0.2
6500	Real estate	24	28	0.6	90	103	8,356	9,165	911	1,044	0.2
6530	Real estate agents and managers	7	7	0.4	62	64	7,613	9,063	508	614	0.2
FRANKLIN, MO											
60 –	**Finance, insurance, and real estate**	159	168	1.3	876	896	18,977	20,571	18,699	21,103	0.5
6000	Depository institutions	31	31	1.5	517	526	17,911	19,065	11,104	12,116	1.1
6020	Commercial banks	24	24	1.6	444	455	18,009	18,936	9,815	10,549	1.2
6030	Savings institutions	7	7	2.3	73	71	17,315	19,887	1,289	1,567	1.5
6100	Nondepository institutions	5	6	0.8	10	9	16,800	27,111	231	272	0.1
6300	Insurance carriers	9	9	1.0	58	59	26,414	26,441	1,600	1,403	0.1
6400	Insurance agents, brokers, and service	39	41	1.2	108	109	18,111	19,853	2,104	2,121	0.5
6500	Real estate	65	65	1.4	147	157	13,469	15,261	2,134	3,066	0.6

Source: County Business Patterns, 1994/95, CBP-94/95, U.S. Department of Commerce, Washington, D.C., November 1997. SIC categories for which data were suppressed or not available for both 1994 and 1995 are not displayed. The employment columns represent mid-March employment in the year. Pay per employee is calculated by dividing 1st Quarter payroll, annualized, by mid-March employment. The columns headed "% State" show the county's percentage of the state total for the SIC in 1995; for example, 1.4% for SIC 6000 means that the county had 1.4 percent of the state's total establishments (or payroll) in SIC 6000 in 1995. A dash (-) is used to indicate that data are not available or cannot be calculated; nec means not elsewhere classified.

Continued on next page.

SIC	Industry	No. Establishments			Employment		Pay / Employee		Annual Payroll ($ 000)		
		1994	1995	% State	1994	1995	1994	1995	1994	1995	% State
FRANKLIN, MO - [continued]											
6510	Real estate operators and lessors	18	17	0.9	21	22	6,667	6,545	187	277	0.2
6530	Real estate agents and managers	36	36	1.9	96	77	11,792	13,195	1,207	1,294	0.5
6553	Cemetery subdividers and developers	3	3	1.9	1	1	4,000	8,000	6	14	0.1
GASCONADE, MO											
60 –	**Finance, insurance, and real estate**	29	30	0.2	133	150	13,263	11,707	1,980	1,956	0.0
6000	Depository institutions	8	8	0.4	81	95	13,432	10,611	1,134	1,050	0.1
6400	Insurance agents, brokers, and service	8	8	0.2	24	26	17,333	15,385	469	498	0.1
6500	Real estate	8	9	0.2	18	16	8,222	9,500	201	212	0.0
GENTRY, MO											
60 –	**Finance, insurance, and real estate**	19	19	0.1	61	62	15,934	16,452	1,210	1,255	0.0
GREENE, MO											
60 –	**Finance, insurance, and real estate**	718	732	5.7	5,697	6,091	21,662	22,778	125,885	139,012	3.2
6000	Depository institutions	93	101	4.7	1,940	2,111	21,192	22,694	40,546	43,841	3.8
6020	Commercial banks	46	55	3.6	1,348	1,529	22,769	24,154	30,210	32,530	3.8
6030	Savings institutions	30	28	9.4	450	430	17,556	18,651	7,733	8,419	7.9
6100	Nondepository institutions	49	53	7.0	351	366	27,544	27,934	9,399	10,599	3.4
6160	Mortgage bankers and brokers	23	26	9.1	185	184	29,362	31,609	4,931	6,067	3.6
6200	Security and commodity brokers	33	39	5.1	215	228	41,860	36,789	7,598	8,227	1.5
6210	Security brokers and dealers	23	28	5.4	179	189	43,687	37,926	6,624	7,172	1.7
6280	Security and commodity services	10	11	5.2	36	39	32,778	31,282	974	1,055	1.0
6300	Insurance carriers	46	46	5.3	1,027	1,097	24,448	26,669	25,827	28,295	2.8
6310	Life insurance	18	16	6.5	339	370	22,997	26,259	7,186	7,756	2.1
6330	Fire, marine, and casualty insurance	20	21	4.9	540	581	25,704	27,429	14,689	16,785	4.3
6400	Insurance agents, brokers, and service	220	216	6.6	880	899	22,618	24,343	20,608	22,181	5.1
6500	Real estate	266	266	5.9	1,264	1,370	14,307	14,885	21,249	24,791	4.8
6510	Real estate operators and lessors	138	131	6.9	497	508	10,873	10,882	6,102	6,379	3.6
6530	Real estate agents and managers	95	97	5.2	683	747	16,685	17,264	13,124	15,647	5.7
6550	Subdividers and developers	28	31	7.0	60	90	16,000	17,244	1,631	2,332	5.8
6552	Subdividers and developers, n.e.c.	18	22	8.5	31	40	21,161	22,400	933	1,528	6.0
6553	Cemetery subdividers and developers	8	8	5.1	29	48	10,483	12,917	648	768	5.6
6700	Holding and other investment offices	11	11	2.5	20	20	26,600	34,400	658	1,078	0.3
GRUNDY, MO											
60 –	**Finance, insurance, and real estate**	29	31	0.2	128	153	16,188	19,425	2,446	3,292	0.1
6000	Depository institutions	7	7	0.3	83	95	18,410	20,505	1,724	2,133	0.2
6530	Real estate agents and managers	5	4	0.2	14	20	15,143	25,600	374	504	0.2
HARRISON, MO											
60 –	**Finance, insurance, and real estate**	22	21	0.2	105	91	14,133	14,154	1,376	1,410	0.0
6000	Depository institutions	7	6	0.3	67	58	17,552	16,759	1,027	1,055	0.1
6020	Commercial banks	7	6	0.4	67	58	17,552	16,759	1,027	1,055	0.1
6400	Insurance agents, brokers, and service	5	5	0.2	10	10	13,600	12,400	155	147	0.0
6510	Real estate operators and lessors	3	3	0.2	6	7	2,667	2,286	14	16	0.0
6530	Real estate agents and managers	3	3	0.2	12	7	5,000	8,571	63	66	0.0
HENRY, MO											
60 –	**Finance, insurance, and real estate**	52	52	0.4	245	248	19,069	20,839	4,904	5,137	0.1
6000	Depository institutions	15	15	0.7	142	144	18,169	18,972	2,647	2,682	0.2
6400	Insurance agents, brokers, and service	16	16	0.5	65	65	22,892	27,754	1,584	1,777	0.4
6500	Real estate	14	14	0.3	21	23	9,333	9,217	244	247	0.0
6530	Real estate agents and managers	6	5	0.3	11	10	9,818	12,000	143	143	0.1
HICKORY, MO											
60 –	**Finance, insurance, and real estate**	15	15	0.1	33	36	10,303	13,667	393	541	0.0

Source: County Business Patterns, 1994/95, CBP-94/95, U.S. Department of Commerce, Washington, D.C., November 1997. SIC categories for which data were suppressed or not available for both 1994 and 1995 are not displayed. The employment columns represent mid-March employment in the year. Pay per employee is calculated by dividing 1st Quarter payroll, annualized, by mid-March employment. The columns headed "% State" show the county's percentage of the state total for the SIC in 1995; for example, 1.4% for SIC 6000 means that the county had 1.4 percent of the state's total establishments (or payroll) in SIC 6000 in 1995. A dash (-) is used to indicate that data are not available or cannot be calculated; nec means not elsewhere classified.

Continued on next page.

SIC	Industry	No. Establishments			Employment		Pay / Employee		Annual Payroll ($ 000)		
		1994	1995	% State	1994	1995	1994	1995	1994	1995	% State
HICKORY, MO - [continued]											
6500	Real estate	9	8	0.2	11	12	4,000	4,000	50	47	0.0
6550	Subdividers and developers	4	4	0.9	4	4	4,000	4,000	16	14	0.0
6552	Subdividers and developers, n.e.c.	4	4	1.6	4	4	4,000	4,000	16	14	0.1
HOLT, MO											
60 –	**Finance, insurance, and real estate**	14	14	0.1	70	68	15,714	16,529	1,334	1,419	0.0
6000	Depository institutions	6	6	0.3	47	46	17,021	17,304	1,052	1,113	0.1
6020	Commercial banks	6	6	0.4	47	46	17,021	17,304	1,052	1,113	0.1
6400	Insurance agents, brokers, and service	4	4	0.1	7	6	15,429	20,000	116	125	0.0
HOWARD, MO											
60 –	**Finance, insurance, and real estate**	15	15	0.1	84	89	16,476	16,809	1,603	1,656	0.0
6000	Depository institutions	5	5	0.2	64	67	18,688	19,104	1,389	1,469	0.1
6020	Commercial banks	5	5	0.3	64	67	18,688	19,104	1,389	1,469	0.2
6500	Real estate	3	3	0.1	4	4	15,000	13,000	56	53	0.0
HOWELL, MO											
60 –	**Finance, insurance, and real estate**	70	80	0.6	376	367	18,000	20,022	6,891	7,560	0.2
6000	Depository institutions	11	12	0.6	201	197	20,299	22,518	3,943	4,379	0.4
6400	Insurance agents, brokers, and service	25	26	0.8	54	58	16,000	18,000	882	1,028	0.2
6500	Real estate	27	33	0.7	97	85	10,887	10,965	1,224	1,205	0.2
6510	Real estate operators and lessors	11	14	0.7	57	35	9,754	9,257	467	432	0.2
6530	Real estate agents and managers	9	11	0.6	13	14	13,231	12,286	214	205	0.1
6540	Title abstract offices	3	3	1.9	16	23	12,000	11,130	285	272	1.1
IRON, MO											
60 –	**Finance, insurance, and real estate**	19	18	0.1	87	96	15,448	16,083	1,627	1,752	0.0
6000	Depository institutions	7	7	0.3	67	67	17,313	17,970	1,235	1,379	0.1
6500	Real estate	7	7	0.2	12	15	8,667	8,267	134	138	0.0
6510	Real estate operators and lessors	3	3	0.2	4	4	6,000	8,000	30	32	0.0
JACKSON, MO											
60 –	**Finance, insurance, and real estate**	1,698	1,762	13.8	33,278	31,419	31,861	35,145	1,060,313	1,109,847	25.3
6000	Depository institutions	244	249	11.7	9,051	9,200	26,692	27,869	243,767	246,496	21.5
6020	Commercial banks	148	159	10.4	6,832	6,984	25,765	26,959	175,800	177,289	20.8
6030	Savings institutions	25	20	6.7	454	382	23,075	25,602	10,668	10,314	9.7
6090	Functions closely related to banking	18	19	24.1	438	438	27,607	29,470	14,207	15,232	19.7
6100	Nondepository institutions	133	147	19.4	2,003	1,749	31,083	39,353	62,369	83,887	27.3
6140	Personal credit institutions	63	74	21.4	351	416	28,125	29,000	10,118	13,094	18.0
6160	Mortgage bankers and brokers	46	49	17.1	1,522	1,236	31,887	42,670	48,356	66,636	39.1
6200	Security and commodity brokers	106	124	16.3	4,396	2,476	44,847	51,294	188,761	129,658	23.9
6210	Security brokers and dealers	66	83	16.1	1,061	1,099	73,632	75,425	72,786	84,061	19.4
6280	Security and commodity services	26	25	11.7	3,260	1,292	35,553	31,901	112,628	41,328	39.9
6300	Insurance carriers	173	171	19.9	8,329	7,913	35,088	39,272	273,247	298,464	29.5
6310	Life insurance	45	41	16.7	4,268	3,622	36,053	42,180	130,237	139,589	38.1
6320	Medical service and health insurance	29	30	37.5	2,399	2,682	35,000	37,304	86,043	104,056	48.0
6321	Accident and health insurance	5	4	17.4	36	55	55,333	37,818	1,669	1,710	12.7
6324	Hospital and medical service plans	24	26	45.6	2,363	2,627	34,690	37,293	84,374	102,346	50.4
6330	Fire, marine, and casualty insurance	72	73	17.1	1,290	1,181	34,701	39,201	46,374	44,847	11.6
6360	Title insurance	11	11	26.2	148	122	29,081	32,951	3,748	3,628	23.9
6370	Pension, health, and welfare funds	11	10	23.8	155	218	25,239	21,798	4,468	3,672	19.5
6400	Insurance agents, brokers, and service	382	388	11.8	2,750	2,878	29,769	32,042	84,697	95,591	22.1
6500	Real estate	587	602	13.3	3,787	3,908	20,206	21,489	81,535	86,999	16.7
6510	Real estate operators and lessors	287	286	15.1	1,413	1,479	19,830	19,895	29,185	29,704	17.0
6530	Real estate agents and managers	238	238	12.7	1,811	1,877	21,553	23,945	41,869	45,612	16.7
6540	Title abstract offices	7	7	4.5	178	162	24,809	22,988	4,477	4,136	16.9
6550	Subdividers and developers	42	49	11.1	376	361	13,245	14,681	5,864	6,837	16.9
6552	Subdividers and developers, n.e.c.	29	34	13.2	134	116	13,970	14,931	2,342	2,610	10.3

Source: County Business Patterns, 1994/95, CBP-94/95, U.S. Department of Commerce, Washington, D.C., November 1997. SIC categories for which data were suppressed or not available for both 1994 and 1995 are not displayed. The employment columns represent mid-March employment in the year. Pay per employee is calculated by dividing 1st Quarter payroll, annualized, by mid-March employment. The columns headed "% State" show the county's percentage of the state total for the SIC in 1995; for example, 1.4% for SIC 6000 means that the county had 1.4 percent of the state's total establishments (or payroll) in SIC 6000 in 1995. A dash (-) is used to indicate that data are not available or cannot be calculated; nec means not elsewhere classified.

Continued on next page.

SIC	Industry	No. Establishments			Employment		Pay / Employee		Annual Payroll ($ 000)		
		1994	1995	% State	1994	1995	1994	1995	1994	1995	% State
JACKSON, MO - [continued]											
6553	Cemetery subdividers and developers	13	14	8.9	242	245	12,843	14,563	3,522	4,191	30.4
6700	Holding and other investment offices	70	78	18.1	2,907	3,227	36,586	50,101	123,290	165,693	44.3
6710	Holding offices	29	35	17.1	794	999	54,307	69,926	47,580	76,818	31.3
JASPER, MO											
60 –	**Finance, insurance, and real estate**	216	215	1.7	1,334	1,309	19,883	20,862	26,117	27,465	0.6
6000	Depository institutions	36	41	1.9	649	651	20,407	22,138	13,152	14,069	1.2
6020	Commercial banks	28	32	2.1	611	600	20,740	22,493	12,548	13,154	1.5
6200	Security and commodity brokers	12	13	1.7	53	51	45,585	44,314	2,232	2,357	0.4
6300	Insurance carriers	13	11	1.3	97	77	29,608	31,221	2,397	2,204	0.2
6310	Life insurance	4	3	1.2	53	43	26,868	30,419	1,163	1,084	0.3
6400	Insurance agents, brokers, and service	63	60	1.8	206	220	17,398	19,109	3,782	4,419	1.0
6500	Real estate	79	73	1.6	286	262	12,168	12,183	3,746	3,466	0.7
6510	Real estate operators and lessors	37	29	1.5	139	92	10,964	12,609	1,538	1,319	0.8
6530	Real estate agents and managers	30	31	1.7	88	84	12,136	12,333	1,193	1,137	0.4
6552	Subdividers and developers, n.e.c.	5	4	1.6	7	3	5,714	8,000	47	48	0.2
JEFFERSON, MO											
60 –	**Finance, insurance, and real estate**	216	214	1.7	1,108	1,103	18,509	18,727	21,800	22,989	0.5
6000	Depository institutions	38	39	1.8	482	512	18,224	18,930	8,622	10,087	0.9
6020	Commercial banks	29	31	2.0	410	476	18,039	19,017	7,456	9,360	1.1
6030	Savings institutions	5	3	1.0	59	25	21,695	20,640	1,048	567	0.5
6100	Nondepository institutions	8	10	1.3	31	38	19,613	23,684	795	1,060	0.3
6300	Insurance carriers	11	9	1.0	53	38	31,925	31,368	1,509	1,256	0.1
6400	Insurance agents, brokers, and service	54	52	1.6	151	149	15,497	15,651	2,538	2,652	0.6
6500	Real estate	96	96	2.1	376	348	16,543	16,816	7,537	7,244	1.4
6510	Real estate operators and lessors	36	39	2.1	148	142	14,405	14,113	2,076	1,911	1.1
6530	Real estate agents and managers	36	37	2.0	86	78	14,698	14,667	1,507	1,430	0.5
6552	Subdividers and developers, n.e.c.	10	7	2.7	47	38	20,000	23,368	1,026	690	2.7
6553	Cemetery subdividers and developers	6	6	3.8	21	12	6,667	11,000	148	158	1.1
JOHNSON, MO											
60 –	**Finance, insurance, and real estate**	79	77	0.6	349	360	18,441	18,389	7,054	7,378	0.2
6000	Depository institutions	16	16	0.7	204	209	21,098	20,287	4,620	4,855	0.4
6020	Commercial banks	13	13	0.9	173	176	21,757	21,227	4,027	4,209	0.5
6100	Nondepository institutions	3	4	0.5	8	11	18,000	23,636	182	207	0.1
6140	Personal credit institutions	3	4	1.2	8	11	18,000	23,636	182	207	0.3
6200	Security and commodity brokers	4	5	0.7	8	10	18,000	15,200	149	195	0.0
6400	Insurance agents, brokers, and service	26	25	0.8	62	63	12,774	15,111	838	884	0.2
6500	Real estate	26	24	0.5	57	51	11,860	11,059	671	521	0.1
6510	Real estate operators and lessors	12	11	0.6	33	30	7,152	8,000	248	215	0.1
6550	Subdividers and developers	6	4	0.9	8	6	9,500	15,333	95	77	0.2
KNOX, MO											
60 –	**Finance, insurance, and real estate**	9	10	0.1	53	49	31,547	17,714	893	1,132	0.0
LACLEDE, MO											
60 –	**Finance, insurance, and real estate**	60	58	0.5	345	386	16,777	16,984	7,367	6,877	0.2
6000	Depository institutions	11	10	0.5	226	194	19,097	20,784	4,676	4,298	0.4
6400	Insurance agents, brokers, and service	19	19	0.6	58	70	11,172	12,800	671	932	0.2
6500	Real estate	23	23	0.5	46	107	8,348	11,626	424	1,163	0.2
6510	Real estate operators and lessors	11	13	0.7	25	90	8,160	12,667	243	1,044	0.6
LAFAYETTE, MO											
60 –	**Finance, insurance, and real estate**	66	67	0.5	359	373	17,515	17,823	6,813	7,058	0.2
6000	Depository institutions	18	18	0.8	198	197	19,051	19,675	3,984	4,182	0.4

Source: County Business Patterns, 1994/95, CBP-94/95, U.S. Department of Commerce, Washington, D.C., November 1997. SIC categories for which data were suppressed or not available for both 1994 and 1995 are *not* displayed. The employment columns represent mid-March employment in the year. Pay per employee is calculated by dividing 1st Quarter payroll, annualized, by mid-March employment. The columns headed "% State" show the county's percentage of the state total for the SIC in 1995; for example, 1.4% for SIC 6000 means that the county had 1.4 percent of the state's total establishments (or payroll) in SIC 6000 in 1995. A dash (-) is used to indicate that data are not available or cannot be calculated; *nec* means not elsewhere classified.

Continued on next page.

SIC	Industry	No. Establishments			Employment		Pay / Employee		Annual Payroll ($ 000)		
		1994	1995	% State	1994	1995	1994	1995	1994	1995	% State
LAFAYETTE, MO - [continued]											
6400	Insurance agents, brokers, and service	31	30	0.9	82	89	15,317	15,416	1,368	1,376	0.3
6500	Real estate	11	12	0.3	48	54	10,667	10,296	707	653	0.1
6510	Real estate operators and lessors	4	5	0.3	10	9	7,600	8,444	89	92	0.1
LAWRENCE, MO											
60 –	**Finance, insurance, and real estate**	41	42	0.3	222	218	16,685	17,817	3,882	4,072	0.1
6000	Depository institutions	10	11	0.5	139	142	16,863	17,831	2,468	2,764	0.2
6400	Insurance agents, brokers, and service	13	13	0.4	38	37	15,684	16,216	626	633	0.1
6500	Real estate	15	15	0.3	32	26	7,875	8,923	346	281	0.1
6510	Real estate operators and lessors	5	5	0.3	8	5	5,000	8,800	45	46	0.0
6530	Real estate agents and managers	7	7	0.4	18	15	10,000	10,400	223	199	0.1
LEWIS, MO											
60 –	**Finance, insurance, and real estate**	26	29	0.2	132	136	13,485	16,382	2,108	2,411	0.1
6000	Depository institutions	8	8	0.4	81	89	14,765	14,831	1,376	1,462	0.1
6500	Real estate	11	12	0.3	14	15	4,286	4,267	60	67	0.0
LINCOLN, MO											
60 –	**Finance, insurance, and real estate**	47	51	0.4	228	229	19,246	20,087	4,964	5,134	0.1
6000	Depository institutions	12	12	0.6	147	155	20,082	20,258	3,483	3,695	0.3
6400	Insurance agents, brokers, and service	12	13	0.4	33	28	23,394	29,429	715	667	0.2
6500	Real estate	19	23	0.5	36	35	13,778	13,943	591	607	0.1
6530	Real estate agents and managers	10	11	0.6	19	20	15,789	14,000	342	357	0.1
LINN, MO											
60 –	**Finance, insurance, and real estate**	33	31	0.2	159	154	16,428	17,195	2,697	2,646	0.1
6000	Depository institutions	10	10	0.5	106	113	18,377	18,903	2,004	2,074	0.2
6500	Real estate	8	8	0.2	14	14	7,143	8,000	112	114	0.0
6530	Real estate agents and managers	3	3	0.2	3	5	4,000	4,000	17	20	0.0
LIVINGSTON, MO											
60 –	**Finance, insurance, and real estate**	37	41	0.3	245	247	20,555	21,490	5,075	5,247	0.1
6000	Depository institutions	6	6	0.3	157	160	20,484	21,900	3,274	3,425	0.3
6400	Insurance agents, brokers, and service	15	17	0.5	36	36	17,000	17,667	621	657	0.2
6500	Real estate	7	9	0.2	20	16	7,200	12,250	157	194	0.0
MCDONALD, MO											
60 –	**Finance, insurance, and real estate**	17	17	0.1	114	98	17,579	17,878	2,069	1,905	0.0
6000	Depository institutions	7	6	0.3	85	72	20,706	19,556	1,741	1,475	0.1
6020	Commercial banks	7	6	0.4	85	72	20,706	19,556	1,741	1,475	0.2
MACON, MO											
60 –	**Finance, insurance, and real estate**	36	38	0.3	179	187	19,888	20,599	3,675	4,028	0.1
6000	Depository institutions	9	9	0.4	124	122	24,323	26,098	3,059	3,259	0.3
6400	Insurance agents, brokers, and service	10	12	0.4	19	22	9,684	9,636	187	236	0.1
6510	Real estate operators and lessors	5	5	0.3	12	14	7,333	7,143	86	109	0.1
6530	Real estate agents and managers	3	3	0.2	7	8	5,714	7,000	49	51	0.0
MADISON, MO											
60 –	**Finance, insurance, and real estate**	17	16	0.1	92	73	15,826	19,890	1,502	1,322	0.0
6000	Depository institutions	6	6	0.3	60	55	17,000	18,182	969	977	0.1
MARIES, MO											
60 –	**Finance, insurance, and real estate**	14	13	0.1	70	80	21,086	18,150	1,445	1,437	0.0
MARION, MO											
60 –	**Finance, insurance, and real estate**	81	75	0.6	343	349	17,096	17,421	6,298	6,584	0.1
6000	Depository institutions	18	18	0.8	149	158	17,799	17,873	2,677	2,862	0.2

Source: County Business Patterns, 1994/95, CBP-94/95, U.S. Department of Commerce, Washington, D.C., November 1997. SIC categories for which data were suppressed or not available for both 1994 and 1995 are *not* displayed. The employment columns represent mid-March employment in the year. Pay per employee is calculated by dividing 1st Quarter payroll, annualized, by mid-March employment. The columns headed "% State" show the county's percentage of the state total for the SIC in 1995; for example, 1.4% for SIC 6000 means that the county had 1.4 percent of the state's total establishments (or payroll) in SIC 6000 in 1995. A dash (-) is used to indicate that data are not available or cannot be calculated; *nec* means not elsewhere classified.

Continued on next page.

SIC	Industry	No. Establishments			Employment		Pay / Employee		Annual Payroll ($ 000)		
		1994	1995	% State	1994	1995	1994	1995	1994	1995	% State
MARION, MO - [continued]											
6020	Commercial banks	7	7	0.5	93	98	17,161	17,714	1,673	1,810	0.2
6030	Savings institutions	7	7	2.3	51	53	19,843	19,698	957	1,007	0.9
6060	Credit unions	4	4	1.8	5	7	8,800	6,286	47	45	-
6100	Nondepository institutions	3	4	0.5	11	14	33,818	38,571	380	480	0.2
6400	Insurance agents, brokers, and service	31	26	0.8	67	55	12,418	12,800	1,102	1,075	0.2
6500	Real estate	22	20	0.4	35	36	9,943	11,111	423	453	0.1
6510	Real estate operators and lessors	6	5	0.3	10	10	10,000	10,800	101	111	0.1
6530	Real estate agents and managers	12	12	0.6	17	21	9,412	11,238	211	260	0.1
MERCER, MO											
60 –	**Finance, insurance, and real estate**	9	9	0.1	41	82	15,317	17,512	715	1,500	0.0
6000	Depository institutions	3	3	0.1	31	72	16,903	18,444	585	1,370	0.1
6020	Commercial banks	3	3	0.2	31	72	16,903	18,444	585	1,370	0.2
MILLER, MO											
60 –	**Finance, insurance, and real estate**	68	72	0.6	351	347	17,903	19,343	7,545	6,944	0.2
6000	Depository institutions	11	11	0.5	119	114	20,773	24,421	2,656	3,015	0.3
6400	Insurance agents, brokers, and service	10	10	0.3	31	27	12,258	12,593	423	347	0.1
6500	Real estate	39	44	1.0	163	185	15,951	15,351	3,513	3,042	0.6
6530	Real estate agents and managers	25	26	1.4	126	144	17,111	16,306	2,870	2,297	0.8
6550	Subdividers and developers	6	8	1.8	13	12	13,538	17,667	331	394	1.0
6552	Subdividers and developers, n.e.c.	6	7	2.7	13	12	13,538	17,667	331	368	1.4
MISSISSIPPI, MO											
60 –	**Finance, insurance, and real estate**	17	18	0.1	100	107	21,000	21,907	2,050	2,199	0.1
6000	Depository institutions	5	5	0.2	79	80	22,177	24,900	1,668	1,810	0.2
6400	Insurance agents, brokers, and service	9	9	0.3	19	24	17,263	13,833	352	376	0.1
6500	Real estate	3	4	0.1	2	3	10,000	6,667	30	13	0.0
MONITEAU, MO											
60 –	**Finance, insurance, and real estate**	27	29	0.2	112	116	18,286	18,483	2,166	2,274	0.1
6000	Depository institutions	10	9	0.4	82	81	21,463	22,519	1,831	1,925	0.2
6400	Insurance agents, brokers, and service	8	10	0.3	18	17	8,000	9,176	167	180	0.0
6500	Real estate	6	7	0.2	8	12	8,000	7,000	82	85	0.0
MONROE, MO											
60 –	**Finance, insurance, and real estate**	17	19	0.1	74	76	18,378	19,105	1,405	1,507	0.0
6000	Depository institutions	5	5	0.2	55	54	19,273	20,222	1,083	1,090	0.1
MONTGOMERY, MO											
60 –	**Finance, insurance, and real estate**	26	26	0.2	131	146	17,832	20,082	2,513	3,206	0.1
6000	Depository institutions	7	7	0.3	86	104	19,535	20,654	1,715	2,233	0.2
6020	Commercial banks	7	7	0.5	86	104	19,535	20,654	1,715	2,233	0.3
6530	Real estate agents and managers	4	3	0.2	7	5	11,429	16,000	101	84	0.0
MORGAN, MO											
60 –	**Finance, insurance, and real estate**	33	41	0.3	120	150	13,700	14,907	2,013	3,002	0.1
6000	Depository institutions	7	11	0.5	70	94	16,743	17,319	1,474	2,293	0.2
6400	Insurance agents, brokers, and service	7	8	0.2	7	10	13,143	14,800	104	142	0.0
6510	Real estate operators and lessors	5	6	0.3	5	6	4,800	6,000	25	33	0.0
6530	Real estate agents and managers	8	8	0.4	20	22	10,600	11,091	239	300	0.1
NEW MADRID, MO											
60 –	**Finance, insurance, and real estate**	31	31	0.2	167	178	17,653	19,258	3,400	3,663	0.1

Source: County Business Patterns, 1994/95, CBP-94/95, U.S. Department of Commerce, Washington, D.C., November 1997. SIC categories for which data were suppressed or not available for both 1994 and 1995 are not displayed. The employment columns represent mid-March employment in the year. Pay per employee is calculated by dividing 1st Quarter payroll, annualized, by mid-March employment. The columns headed "% State" show the county's percentage of the state total for the SIC in 1995; for example, 1.4% for SIC 6000 means that the county had 1.4 percent of the state's total establishments (or payroll) in SIC 6000 in 1995. A dash (-) is used to indicate that data are not available or cannot be calculated; nec means not elsewhere classified.

Continued on next page.

SIC	Industry	No. Establishments			Employment		Pay / Employee		Annual Payroll ($ 000)		
		1994	1995	% State	1994	1995	1994	1995	1994	1995	% State
NEW MADRID, MO - [continued]											
6000	Depository institutions	11	11	0.5	117	119	18,974	20,303	2,427	2,652	0.2
6400	Insurance agents, brokers, and service	11	11	0.3	27	29	13,926	14,897	384	410	0.1
6510	Real estate operators and lessors	3	3	0.2	2	2	4,000	4,000	10	11	0.0
NEWTON, MO											
60 –	**Finance, insurance, and real estate**	77	76	0.6	391	345	19,959	20,742	7,231	6,915	0.2
6000	Depository institutions	17	17	0.8	187	193	22,310	21,637	3,790	3,938	0.3
6400	Insurance agents, brokers, and service	25	24	0.7	77	66	14,909	20,182	1,233	1,328	0.3
6500	Real estate	25	24	0.5	69	55	15,246	12,800	849	748	0.1
6530	Real estate agents and managers	7	7	0.4	17	21	12,000	12,381	222	250	0.1
NODAWAY, MO											
60 –	**Finance, insurance, and real estate**	41	43	0.3	234	262	20,017	19,679	4,612	5,044	0.1
6000	Depository institutions	10	10	0.5	170	172	21,647	23,233	3,618	3,896	0.3
6500	Real estate	15	17	0.4	31	55	6,452	6,764	244	349	0.1
6510	Real estate operators and lessors	9	10	0.5	17	42	5,882	6,286	112	206	0.1
OREGON, MO											
60 –	**Finance, insurance, and real estate**	17	14	0.1	68	64	15,882	18,375	1,171	1,215	0.0
6000	Depository institutions	4	4	0.2	48	43	18,417	22,233	928	1,001	0.1
6400	Insurance agents, brokers, and service	6	5	0.2	8	6	10,000	8,667	75	55	0.0
6500	Real estate	7	5	0.1	12	15	9,667	11,200	168	159	0.0
OSAGE, MO											
60 –	**Finance, insurance, and real estate**	17	18	0.1	88	93	20,909	20,817	1,980	2,014	0.0
6000	Depository institutions	7	7	0.3	73	79	23,068	22,228	1,825	1,791	0.2
6020	Commercial banks	7	7	0.5	73	79	23,068	22,228	1,825	1,791	0.2
OZARK, MO											
60 –	**Finance, insurance, and real estate**	13	12	0.1	107	122	17,308	16,623	1,988	2,070	0.0
PEMISCOT, MO											
60 –	**Finance, insurance, and real estate**	25	24	0.2	160	156	16,975	17,333	2,981	3,135	0.1
6000	Depository institutions	9	8	0.4	114	114	17,825	19,088	2,389	2,591	0.2
PERRY, MO											
60 –	**Finance, insurance, and real estate**	34	33	0.3	212	250	25,547	24,928	4,758	5,517	0.1
6000	Depository institutions	8	8	0.4	135	136	22,756	23,118	2,910	3,144	0.3
6400	Insurance agents, brokers, and service	8	9	0.3	35	34	16,686	16,588	729	706	0.2
6500	Real estate	11	10	0.2	22	22	9,091	9,273	218	219	0.0
6510	Real estate operators and lessors	4	3	0.2	8	7	6,000	5,143	53	38	0.0
6530	Real estate agents and managers	4	4	0.2	6	6	10,000	8,667	61	63	0.0
PETTIS, MO											
60 –	**Finance, insurance, and real estate**	99	103	0.8	576	575	18,944	20,369	11,445	12,886	0.3
6000	Depository institutions	22	23	1.1	328	311	18,549	21,158	6,065	6,612	0.6
6020	Commercial banks	18	19	1.2	315	296	18,717	21,392	5,873	6,338	0.7
6100	Nondepository institutions	3	4	0.5	14	17	25,429	27,529	337	405	0.1
6400	Insurance agents, brokers, and service	24	26	0.8	69	87	21,391	16,506	1,422	1,475	0.3
6500	Real estate	38	38	0.8	86	83	8,186	9,060	803	891	0.2
6510	Real estate operators and lessors	22	21	1.1	56	52	6,143	7,000	367	477	0.3
PHELPS, MO											
60 –	**Finance, insurance, and real estate**	75	73	0.6	365	376	18,181	20,319	7,323	8,332	0.2
6000	Depository institutions	16	15	0.7	221	217	19,131	21,124	4,523	4,926	0.4
6020	Commercial banks	11	11	0.7	175	180	19,726	21,489	3,627	4,189	0.5
6100	Nondepository institutions	3	4	0.5	10	15	18,800	17,600	233	296	0.1
6300	Insurance carriers	4	3	0.3	22	21	16,909	21,333	383	459	0.0

Source: County Business Patterns, 1994/95, CBP-94/95, U.S. Department of Commerce, Washington, D.C., November 1997. SIC categories for which data were suppressed or not available for both 1994 and 1995 are not displayed. The employment columns represent mid-March employment in the year. Pay per employee is calculated by dividing 1st Quarter payroll, annualized, by mid-March employment. The columns headed "% State" show the county's percentage of the state total for the SIC in 1995; for example, 1.4% for SIC 6000 means that the county had 1.4 percent of the state's total establishments (or payroll) in SIC 6000 in 1995. A dash (-) is used to indicate that data are not available or cannot be calculated; nec means not elsewhere classified.

Continued on next page.

SIC	Industry	No. Establishments			Employment		Pay / Employee		Annual Payroll ($ 000)		
		1994	1995	% State	1994	1995	1994	1995	1994	1995	% State
PHELPS, MO - [continued]											
6400	Insurance agents, brokers, and service	24	25	0.8	54	51	15,037	18,118	926	1,006	0.2
6500	Real estate	22	22	0.5	44	59	14,000	15,186	853	1,047	0.2
6530	Real estate agents and managers	11	11	0.6	21	22	9,333	12,727	270	321	0.1
PIKE, MO											
60 –	**Finance, insurance, and real estate**	29	29	0.2	163	176	19,853	20,795	3,423	3,826	0.1
6000	Depository institutions	9	9	0.4	108	119	21,259	22,487	2,383	2,734	0.2
6400	Insurance agents, brokers, and service	9	9	0.3	25	25	15,040	16,640	369	401	0.1
6500	Real estate	6	6	0.1	17	17	13,647	16,941	352	373	0.1
PLATTE, MO											
60 –	**Finance, insurance, and real estate**	150	157	1.2	2,286	2,618	19,843	20,382	60,052	55,772	1.3
6000	Depository institutions	28	30	1.4	600	452	17,807	21,531	25,286	10,461	0.9
6020	Commercial banks	22	26	1.7	239	287	18,828	23,178	4,778	6,965	0.8
6200	Security and commodity brokers	10	11	1.4	247	260	30,364	37,523	6,560	9,145	1.7
6400	Insurance agents, brokers, and service	33	33	1.0	94	103	23,234	25,320	2,504	3,086	0.7
6500	Real estate	64	66	1.5	169	148	12,947	14,027	2,460	2,696	0.5
6510	Real estate operators and lessors	29	25	1.3	76	74	12,053	11,027	916	890	0.5
6530	Real estate agents and managers	24	26	1.4	67	53	14,507	18,189	1,176	1,216	0.4
6550	Subdividers and developers	8	10	2.3	16	16	15,000	16,250	311	499	1.2
POLK, MO											
60 –	**Finance, insurance, and real estate**	37	40	0.3	321	295	11,950	14,319	4,178	4,842	0.1
6000	Depository institutions	9	10	0.5	140	154	19,857	18,364	2,965	3,302	0.3
6400	Insurance agents, brokers, and service	11	12	0.4	28	31	10,571	12,774	321	407	0.1
6500	Real estate	13	12	0.3	128	69	3,063	7,710	470	538	0.1
PULASKI, MO											
60 –	**Finance, insurance, and real estate**	59	60	0.5	342	318	18,737	18,151	5,859	5,820	0.1
6000	Depository institutions	16	16	0.7	228	230	18,439	18,974	3,794	4,322	0.4
6020	Commercial banks	9	10	0.7	154	159	20,416	20,704	2,617	3,192	0.4
6200	Security and commodity brokers	5	4	0.5	5	4	12,800	15,000	64	52	0.0
6400	Insurance agents, brokers, and service	13	15	0.5	31	30	13,161	14,933	433	479	0.1
6500	Real estate	17	19	0.4	46	39	20,348	13,744	800	601	0.1
PUTNAM, MO											
60 –	**Finance, insurance, and real estate**	13	14	0.1	82	88	14,683	18,091	1,552	1,653	0.0
6400	Insurance agents, brokers, and service	4	4	0.1	7	7	8,000	9,714	64	67	0.0
6530	Real estate agents and managers	3	3	0.2	7	9	8,571	7,556	89	102	0.0
RALLS, MO											
60 –	**Finance, insurance, and real estate**	8	9	0.1	37	35	25,946	29,943	1,114	1,188	0.0
RANDOLPH, MO											
60 –	**Finance, insurance, and real estate**	52	53	0.4*	318	388	22,604	23,062	6,797	7,520	0.2
6000	Depository institutions	14	15	0.7	148	152	21,432	20,079	2,868	3,036	0.3
6400	Insurance agents, brokers, and service	16	15	0.5	43	37	15,163	13,622	694	499	0.1
6500	Real estate	14	13	0.3	47	44	13,191	13,545	664	671	0.1
6530	Real estate agents and managers	9	8	0.4	25	21	8,160	7,238	207	165	0.1
RAY, MO											
60 –	**Finance, insurance, and real estate**	25	25	0.2	134	136	20,567	21,412	2,726	3,218	0.1
6000	Depository institutions	9	9	0.4	97	100	22,928	24,400	2,242	2,649	0.2
6500	Real estate	10	10	0.2	22	21	9,636	8,762	207	263	0.1
6510	Real estate operators and lessors	5	4	0.2	13	12	3,692	4,667	57	56	0.0
REYNOLDS, MO											
60 –	**Finance, insurance, and real estate**	10	8	0.1	29	34	12,552	13,529	401	497	0.0

Source: County Business Patterns, 1994/95, CBP-94/95, U.S. Department of Commerce, Washington, D.C., November 1997. SIC categories for which data were suppressed or not available for both 1994 and 1995 are *not* displayed. The employment columns represent mid-March employment in the year. Pay per employee is calculated by dividing 1st Quarter payroll, annualized, by mid-March employment. The columns headed "% State" show the county's percentage of the state total for the SIC in 1995; for example, 1.4% for SIC 6000 means that the county had 1.4 percent of the state's total establishments (or payroll) in SIC 6000 in 1995. A dash (-) is used to indicate that data are not available or cannot be calculated; *nec* means not elsewhere classified.

SIC	Industry	No. Establishments			Employment		Pay / Employee		Annual Payroll ($ 000)		
		1994	1995	% State	1994	1995	1994	1995	1994	1995	% State
RIPLEY, MO											
60 –	**Finance, insurance, and real estate**	14	14	*0.1*	85	80	17,082	17,350	1,484	1,466	*0.0*
6000	Depository institutions	7	7	*0.3*	68	62	19,235	19,419	1,335	1,282	*0.1*
6400	Insurance agents, brokers, and service	3	3	*0.1*	10	9	8,800	12,444	92	110	*0.0*
ST. CHARLES, MO											
60 –	**Finance, insurance, and real estate**	404	422	*3.3*	2,226	2,211	21,768	23,562	50,616	54,212	*1.2*
6000	Depository institutions	51	52	*2.4*	644	632	20,025	21,222	12,676	13,128	*1.1*
6020	Commercial banks	37	38	*2.5*	523	498	19,755	21,382	10,276	10,346	*1.2*
6030	Savings institutions	9	8	*2.7*	93	104	22,022	21,346	1,879	2,178	*2.0*
6100	Nondepository institutions	28	38	*5.0*	144	161	25,056	27,578	3,358	4,502	*1.5*
6140	Personal credit institutions	17	20	*5.8*	63	87	25,206	27,586	1,924	2,306	*3.2*
6200	Security and commodity brokers	23	28	*3.7*	70	81	42,514	37,481	3,156	3,558	*0.7*
6210	Security brokers and dealers	16	19	*3.7*	54	65	48,148	41,723	2,722	3,134	*0.7*
6280	Security and commodity services	7	9	*4.2*	16	16	23,500	20,250	434	424	*0.4*
6300	Insurance carriers	36	39	*4.5*	282	270	34,468	39,141	9,448	9,925	*1.0*
6310	Life insurance	8	9	*3.7*	131	127	43,634	45,890	5,007	4,863	*1.3*
6330	Fire, marine, and casualty insurance	24	26	*6.1*	99	109	28,364	34,239	3,210	4,023	*1.0*
6400	Insurance agents, brokers, and service	115	118	*3.6*	378	401	19,534	20,738	7,775	9,075	*2.1*
6500	Real estate	146	142	*3.1*	678	613	16,094	16,790	12,466	11,863	*2.3*
6510	Real estate operators and lessors	60	62	*3.3*	255	285	12,204	12,084	3,973	4,564	*2.6*
6530	Real estate agents and managers	63	57	*3.0*	261	173	16,705	22,058	4,470	4,482	*1.6*
6540	Title abstract offices	5	5	*3.2*	41	40	23,512	21,900	992	893	*3.6*
6550	Subdividers and developers	14	10	*2.3*	116	98	20,138	19,143	2,855	1,669	*4.1*
6552	Subdividers and developers, n.e.c.	11	7	*2.7*	56	64	22,571	19,938	1,367	1,008	*4.0*
ST. CLAIR, MO											
60 –	**Finance, insurance, and real estate**	16	17	*0.1*	81	75	10,617	12,427	914	963	*0.0*
6000	Depository institutions	4	4	*0.2*	49	47	12,327	14,043	635	678	*0.1*
6020	Commercial banks	4	4	*0.3*	49	47	12,327	14,043	635	678	*0.1*
6500	Real estate	5	5	*0.1*	15	17	8,533	8,000	150	149	*0.0*
ST. FRANCOIS, MO											
60 –	**Finance, insurance, and real estate**	88	90	*0.7*	559	562	17,145	18,199	10,682	11,221	*0.3*
6000	Depository institutions	20	20	*0.9*	288	290	17,014	18,759	5,232	5,720	*0.5*
6020	Commercial banks	15	15	*1.0*	232	235	15,500	17,464	3,906	4,304	*0.5*
6100	Nondepository institutions	5	5	*0.7*	15	16	24,533	22,750	342	355	*0.1*
6300	Insurance carriers	4	4	*0.5*	46	44	20,783	21,727	1,012	948	*0.1*
6400	Insurance agents, brokers, and service	23	22	*0.7*	64	71	15,563	15,718	1,077	1,269	*0.3*
6500	Real estate	31	34	*0.8*	119	118	13,647	13,424	2,209	2,111	*0.4*
6510	Real estate operators and lessors	15	15	*0.8*	22	31	10,364	10,581	325	419	*0.2*
6530	Real estate agents and managers	9	13	*0.7*	52	64	13,846	12,375	801	943	*0.3*
6550	Subdividers and developers	4	4	*0.9*	9	7	9,333	11,429	91	90	*0.2*
ST. LOUIS, MO											
60 –	**Finance, insurance, and real estate**	3,180	3,211	*25.1*	41,324	40,378	32,334	33,342	1,298,075	1,356,871	*30.9*
6000	Depository institutions	352	333	*15.6*	8,794	7,936	25,783	26,576	209,999	202,289	*17.6*
6020	Commercial banks	198	199	*13.0*	4,646	4,457	25,380	28,401	113,334	117,322	*13.8*
6030	Savings institutions	88	67	*22.5*	2,448	1,779	29,286	25,819	61,526	48,075	*45.2*
6100	Nondepository institutions	231	239	*31.5*	4,724	4,023	33,530	34,373	141,412	137,641	*44.7*
6140	Personal credit institutions	84	99	*28.6*	805	837	28,735	31,345	22,556	31,847	*43.8*
6150	Business credit institutions	32	34	*42.5*	543	470	54,976	52,170	28,173	25,190	*44.7*
6160	Mortgage bankers and brokers	113	102	*35.5*	3,351	2,700	31,216	32,237	89,998	80,002	*47.0*
6200	Security and commodity brokers	259	279	*36.7*	3,821	3,883	47,665	44,033	177,240	180,253	*33.2*
6210	Security brokers and dealers	149	161	*31.1*	3,148	3,129	48,839	43,276	142,237	141,620	*32.8*
6300	Insurance carriers	258	260	*30.2*	9,620	9,571	34,097	34,750	322,107	334,335	*33.1*
6310	Life insurance	95	96	*39.2*	4,680	4,450	35,053	37,088	153,870	155,621	*42.5*
6320	Medical service and health insurance	18	19	*23.8*	583	611	30,058	32,596	18,317	25,965	*12.0*
6330	Fire, marine, and casualty insurance	107	108	*25.4*	3,603	3,825	34,612	33,222	129,128	132,664	*34.3*

Source: County Business Patterns, 1994/95, CBP-94/95, U.S. Department of Commerce, Washington, D.C., November 1997. SIC categories for which data were suppressed or not available for both 1994 and 1995 are not displayed. The employment columns represent mid-March employment in the year. Pay per employee is calculated by dividing 1st Quarter payroll, annualized, by mid-March employment. The columns headed "% State" show the county's percentage of the state total for the SIC in 1995; for example, 1.4% for SIC 6000 means that the county had 1.4 percent of the state's total establishments (or payroll) in SIC 6000 in 1995. A dash (-) is used to indicate that data are not available or cannot be calculated; nec means not elsewhere classified.

Continued on next page.

SIC	Industry	No. Establishments			Employment		Pay / Employee		Annual Payroll ($ 000)		
		1994	1995	% State	1994	1995	1994	1995	1994	1995	% State
ST. LOUIS, MO - [continued]											
6350	Surety insurance	5	6	40.0	31	52	38,968	43,846	1,193	1,988	65.5
6360	Title insurance	17	16	38.1	468	330	24,650	28,194	11,297	9,118	60.1
6370	Pension, health, and welfare funds	16	15	35.7	255	303	35,263	29,611	8,302	8,979	47.7
6400	Insurance agents, brokers, and service	810	818	24.8	3,575	3,619	32,060	36,230	120,946	131,337	30.3
6500	Real estate	1,106	1,109	24.6	8,432	8,267	20,204	21,761	184,955	205,339	39.5
6510	Real estate operators and lessors	454	437	23.1	3,670	3,565	15,717	15,184	63,130	69,072	39.4
6530	Real estate agents and managers	557	551	29.3	4,098	3,984	24,126	27,702	106,417	118,810	43.4
6540	Title abstract offices	7	7	4.5	117	117	26,427	24,786	2,904	3,136	12.8
6550	Subdividers and developers	65	69	15.7	411	475	21,499	21,777	10,066	11,694	28.9
6552	Subdividers and developers, n.e.c.	39	41	15.9	199	241	23,156	23,585	5,344	6,581	25.9
6553	Cemetery subdividers and developers	23	23	14.6	212	220	19,943	19,600	4,685	4,765	34.6
6700	Holding and other investment offices	157	166	38.4	1,655	2,428	56,677	53,751	99,524	123,696	33.0
6710	Holding offices	78	84	41.0	1,224	1,962	52,003	54,691	71,743	95,009	38.7
6790	Miscellaneous investing	56	53	41.7	334	357	79,677	55,854	23,979	24,434	74.1
SALINE, MO											
60 –	**Finance, insurance, and real estate**	45	42	0.3	238	226	16,084	18,726	3,996	4,268	0.1
6000	Depository institutions	9	9	0.4	132	137	19,030	20,496	2,629	2,856	0.2
6400	Insurance agents, brokers, and service	15	13	0.4	44	33	11,636	15,152	474	502	0.1
6500	Real estate	16	16	0.4	51	46	8,627	13,130	501	598	0.1
6510	Real estate operators and lessors	8	8	0.4	7	10	6,857	6,000	55	57	0.0
6530	Real estate agents and managers	4	3	0.2	36	26	8,222	16,308	352	384	0.1
SCOTLAND, MO											
60 –	**Finance, insurance, and real estate**	19	18	0.1	68	69	14,941	17,681	940	1,197	0.0
6000	Depository institutions	4	4	0.2	40	44	17,000	20,273	645	918	0.1
6400	Insurance agents, brokers, and service	8	8	0.2	15	14	8,533	9,714	130	137	0.0
6500	Real estate	4	3	0.1	5	4	5,600	6,000	25	25	0.0
SCOTT, MO											
60 –	**Finance, insurance, and real estate**	73	72	0.6	487	502	21,971	23,753	11,083	11,354	0.3
6000	Depository institutions	17	18	0.8	287	283	19,136	21,187	5,792	6,040	0.5
6300	Insurance carriers	5	5	0.6	54	55	30,296	31,345	1,696	1,656	0.2
6400	Insurance agents, brokers, and service	18	17	0.5	68	78	22,471	27,897	1,593	1,770	0.4
6510	Real estate operators and lessors	13	13	0.7	18	24	5,778	6,167	90	125	0.1
6530	Real estate agents and managers	7	7	0.4	9	12	12,889	8,000	112	106	0.0
SHANNON, MO											
60 –	**Finance, insurance, and real estate**	5	6	0.0	40	39	15,600	16,410	910	968	0.0
SHELBY, MO											
60 –	**Finance, insurance, and real estate**	20	21	0.2	86	91	16,047	15,033	1,448	1,498	0.0
6000	Depository institutions	5	5	0.2	50	50	18,160	17,520	966	1,000	0.1
6400	Insurance agents, brokers, and service	7	8	0.2	16	19	10,750	9,895	190	194	0.0
6500	Real estate	5	5	0.1	10	12	4,800	5,000	59	63	0.0
STODDARD, MO											
60 –	**Finance, insurance, and real estate**	61	58	0.5	242	253	19,636	20,190	4,711	5,135	0.1
6000	Depository institutions	16	15	0.7	146	159	22,000	22,969	3,102	3,310	0.3
6200	Security and commodity brokers	4	3	0.4	5	8	34,400	26,000	165	244	0.0
6400	Insurance agents, brokers, and service	21	20	0.6	42	44	17,524	15,909	773	864	0.2
6500	Real estate	14	16	0.4	29	29	11,448	12,966	364	417	0.1
STONE, MO											
60 –	**Finance, insurance, and real estate**	55	54	0.4	193	229	15,585	16,070	3,378	3,852	0.1

Source: County Business Patterns, 1994/95, CBP-94/95, U.S. Department of Commerce, Washington, D.C., November 1997. SIC categories for which data were suppressed or not available for both 1994 and 1995 are not displayed. The employment columns represent mid-March employment in the year. Pay per employee is calculated by dividing 1st Quarter payroll, annualized, by mid-March employment. The columns headed "% State" show the county's percentage of the state total for the SIC in 1995; for example, 1.4% for SIC 6000 means that the county had 1.4 percent of the state's total establishments (or payroll) in SIC 6000 in 1995. A dash (-) is used to indicate that data are not available or cannot be calculated; nec means not elsewhere classified.

Continued on next page.

SIC	Industry	No. Establishments			Employment		Pay / Employee		Annual Payroll ($ 000)		
		1994	1995	% State	1994	1995	1994	1995	1994	1995	% State
STONE, MO - [continued]											
6000	Depository institutions	9	10	0.5	71	87	17,239	19,310	1,375	1,876	0.2
6500	Real estate	29	29	0.6	90	105	13,556	12,267	1,381	1,230	0.2
6530	Real estate agents and managers	20	17	0.9	65	58	13,785	13,931	1,026	728	0.3
TANEY, MO											
60 –	**Finance, insurance, and real estate**	162	158	1.2	977	1,215	15,844	15,641	20,325	23,040	0.5
6000	Depository institutions	24	26	1.2	261	268	18,299	21,881	4,720	5,422	0.5
6020	Commercial banks	15	19	1.2	216	247	19,185	22,559	3,922	5,043	0.6
6200	Security and commodity brokers	5	4	0.5	15	9	30,400	42,667	480	418	0.1
6210	Security brokers and dealers	5	4	0.8	15	9	30,400	42,667	480	418	0.1
6400	Insurance agents, brokers, and service	17	18	0.5	81	75	16,543	20,747	1,517	1,571	0.4
6500	Real estate	113	105	2.3	598	842	14,268	12,893	13,195	15,135	2.9
6510	Real estate operators and lessors	27	29	1.5	158	283	9,899	9,286	3,379	3,875	2.2
6530	Real estate agents and managers	54	47	2.5	349	448	12,951	13,063	6,991	8,538	3.1
6550	Subdividers and developers	27	23	5.2	87	98	27,448	21,918	2,671	2,430	6.0
6552	Subdividers and developers, n.e.c.	27	23	8.9	87	98	27,448	21,918	2,671	2,430	9.6
TEXAS, MO											
60 –	**Finance, insurance, and real estate**	37	34	0.3	207	212	14,126	14,208	3,426	3,651	0.1
6000	Depository institutions	10	10	0.5	148	150	15,892	15,920	2,820	3,009	0.3
6400	Insurance agents, brokers, and service	15	13	0.4	35	33	10,400	13,697	396	444	0.1
VERNON, MO											
60 –	**Finance, insurance, and real estate**	39	39	0.3	554	319	19,718	24,038	7,490	7,687	0.2
6000	Depository institutions	11	10	0.5	375	244	23,232	25,361	5,543	6,069	0.5
6200	Security and commodity brokers	3	3	0.4	8	8	23,000	25,500	217	205	0.0
6400	Insurance agents, brokers, and service	11	10	0.3	134	31	9,134	15,613	881	573	0.1
6500	Real estate	9	10	0.2	24	21	10,833	12,381	317	335	0.1
6530	Real estate agents and managers	6	5	0.3	11	10	6,909	8,000	122	106	0.0
WARREN, MO											
60 –	**Finance, insurance, and real estate**	35	38	0.3	351	363	15,920	16,209	5,662	6,084	0.1
6000	Depository institutions	6	6	0.3	78	83	20,256	21,446	1,539	1,722	0.2
6510	Real estate operators and lessors	4	5	0.3	11	17	5,455	6,353	73	88	0.1
6530	Real estate agents and managers	4	5	0.3	24	23	12,167	13,565	323	348	0.1
WASHINGTON, MO											
60 –	**Finance, insurance, and real estate**	18	15	0.1	89	87	17,483	20,414	1,626	1,987	0.0
6000	Depository institutions	7	7	0.3	74	78	19,514	21,692	1,526	1,714	0.1
6500	Real estate	4	3	0.1	4	3	10,000	9,333	38	30	0.0
WAYNE, MO											
60 –	**Finance, insurance, and real estate**	15	16	0.1	74	80	14,811	16,100	1,128	1,060	0.0
6400	Insurance agents, brokers, and service	8	8	0.2	23	20	9,739	10,400	220	230	0.1
WEBSTER, MO											
60 –	**Finance, insurance, and real estate**	38	40	0.3	191	224	16,126	16,232	3,703	4,169	0.1
6000	Depository institutions	8	8	0.4	135	146	16,978	16,986	2,659	2,911	0.3
6400	Insurance agents, brokers, and service	9	9	0.3	19	21	13,474	14,476	292	317	0.1
6500	Real estate	18	20	0.4	29	49	12,414	13,714	549	725	0.1
6530	Real estate agents and managers	10	10	0.5	15	23	8,800	17,565	272	396	0.1
WORTH, MO											
60 –	**Finance, insurance, and real estate**	9	9	0.1	20	20	12,200	12,800	248	255	0.0
6500	Real estate	3	3	0.1	4	3	4,000	6,667	20	21	0.0
WRIGHT, MO											
60 –	**Finance, insurance, and real estate**	33	35	0.3	156	153	16,513	17,569	2,634	2,922	0.1

Source: County Business Patterns, 1994/95, CBP-94/95, U.S. Department of Commerce, Washington, D.C., November 1997. SIC categories for which data were suppressed or not available for both 1994 and 1995 are not displayed. The employment columns represent mid-March employment in the year. Pay per employee is calculated by dividing 1st Quarter payroll, annualized, by mid-March employment. The columns headed "% State" show the county's percentage of the state total for the SIC in 1995; for example, 1.4% for SIC 6000 means that the county had 1.4 percent of the state's total establishments (or payroll) in SIC 6000 in 1995. A dash (-) is used to indicate that data are not available or cannot be calculated; nec means not elsewhere classified.

Continued on next page.

SIC	Industry	No. Establishments			Employment		Pay / Employee		Annual Payroll ($ 000)		
		1994	1995	% State	1994	1995	1994	1995	1994	1995	% State
WRIGHT, MO - [continued]											
6000	Depository institutions	9	9	0.4	104	96	17,423	19,708	1,853	2,093	0.2
6400	Insurance agents, brokers, and service	11	12	0.4	24	25	14,333	16,000	364	395	0.1
6500	Real estate	9	11	0.2	15	20	6,933	6,600	125	151	0.0
6510	Real estate operators and lessors	5	5	0.3	11	12	6,545	6,333	79	83	0.0
6530	Real estate agents and managers	4	5	0.3	4	7	8,000	7,429	46	61	0.0
ST. LOUIS CITY, MO											
60 –	**Finance, insurance, and real estate**	904	904	7.1	22,737	23,980	39,339	39,187	774,511	826,485	18.8
6000	Depository institutions	154	151	7.1	8,826	8,972	28,838	31,844	243,477	268,402	23.4
6020	Commercial banks	68	72	4.7	6,398	6,609	27,650	29,210	168,040	188,227	22.1
6060	Credit unions	34	34	15.0	386	385	19,824	23,034	8,196	8,932	-
6140	Personal credit institutions	20	27	7.8	163	185	26,675	28,930	5,617	6,352	8.7
6160	Mortgage bankers and brokers	23	26	9.1	354	273	32,249	33,568	11,629	9,546	5.6
6200	Security and commodity brokers	74	74	9.7	3,408	3,537	88,481	77,967	182,174	189,816	34.9
6210	Security brokers and dealers	47	49	9.5	3,220	3,325	88,588	77,826	168,772	174,024	40.3
6300	Insurance carriers	77	74	8.6	4,620	4,366	33,999	36,847	154,527	154,571	15.3
6310	Life insurance	24	24	9.8	995	1,126	36,261	34,348	32,962	35,825	9.8
6320	Medical service and health insurance	15	15	18.8	2,335	2,179	33,040	38,298	78,635	81,054	37.4
6330	Fire, marine, and casualty insurance	26	22	5.2	1,104	931	34,286	37,139	37,699	32,834	8.5
6370	Pension, health, and welfare funds	8	9	21.4	109	120	27,339	32,267	3,322	4,418	23.5
6400	Insurance agents, brokers, and service	163	157	4.8	1,534	1,556	34,289	38,830	53,516	60,964	14.1
6500	Real estate	326	333	7.4	3,058	4,316	22,269	17,989	78,857	78,943	15.2
6510	Real estate operators and lessors	179	186	9.8	1,291	2,580	15,253	13,109	26,737	31,276	17.9
6530	Real estate agents and managers	126	127	6.8	1,608	1,634	28,216	25,420	49,175	45,128	16.5
6550	Subdividers and developers	13	10	2.3	99	56	16,444	22,429	1,677	1,367	3.4
6552	Subdividers and developers, n.e.c.	10	7	2.7	70	24	12,686	19,833	843	533	2.1
6553	Cemetery subdividers and developers	3	3	1.9	29	32	25,517	24,375	834	834	6.1
6700	Holding and other investment offices	47	45	10.4	512	548	61,711	91,365	31,043	43,569	11.6
6710	Holding offices	24	21	10.2	396	433	69,253	105,848	24,519	38,761	15.8
6799	Investors, n.e.c.	9	9	11.0	79	75	37,013	41,013	3,106	3,292	18.6

Source: County Business Patterns, 1994/95, CBP-94/95, U.S. Department of Commerce, Washington, D.C., November 1997. SIC categories for which data were suppressed or not available for both 1994 and 1995 are *not* displayed. The employment columns represent mid-March employment in the year. Pay per employee is calculated by dividing 1st Quarter payroll, annualized, by mid-March employment. The columns headed "% State" show the county's percentage of the state total for the SIC in 1995; for example, 1.4% for SIC 6000 means that the county had 1.4 percent of the state's total establishments (or payroll) in SIC 6000 in 1995. A dash (-) is used to indicate that data are not available or cannot be calculated; *nec* means not elsewhere classified.

MONTANA

SIC	Industry	No. Establishments			Employment		Pay / Employee		Annual Payroll ($ 000)		
		1994	1995	% State	1994	1995	1994	1995	1994	1995	% State
BEAVERHEAD, MT											
60 –	**Finance, insurance, and real estate**	26	26	1.1	118	114	19,220	20,105	2,457	2,613	0.7
6000	Depository institutions	4	4	1.0	64	64	21,688	22,938	1,546	1,716	1.2
6400	Insurance agents, brokers, and service	10	9	1.4	22	22	13,091	15,273	322	354	0.6
6500	Real estate	9	10	1.0	25	22	12,800	12,000	349	325	0.7
BIG HORN, MT											
60 –	**Finance, insurance, and real estate**	16	15	0.6	81	106	18,222	16,038	1,466	1,458	0.4
6000	Depository institutions	3	3	0.8	46	42	22,087	24,286	958	929	0.7
6400	Insurance agents, brokers, and service	6	6	0.9	20	18	12,600	15,778	297	285	0.5
6500	Real estate	7	6	0.6	15	46	13,867	8,609	211	244	0.5
BLAINE, MT											
60 –	**Finance, insurance, and real estate**	11	12	0.5	117	102	16,821	17,961	2,061	2,000	0.6
6400	Insurance agents, brokers, and service	5	5	0.8	18	16	14,000	15,500	288	290	0.5
CARBON, MT											
60 –	**Finance, insurance, and real estate**	18	18	0.7	72	68	19,722	22,588	1,374	1,514	0.4
6400	Insurance agents, brokers, and service	3	3	0.5	13	13	32,000	32,308	332	378	0.7
CARTER, MT											
60 –	**Finance, insurance, and real estate**	3	3	0.1	-	-	-	-	-	-	-
CASCADE, MT											
60 –	**Finance, insurance, and real estate**	234	240	9.8	1,653	1,555	22,911	24,183	42,217	43,293	12.1
6000	Depository institutions	37	39	9.8	423	423	23,915	23,981	9,974	10,164	7.3
6020	Commercial banks	19	20	9.2	194	201	26,268	26,786	5,184	5,297	5.2
6060	Credit unions	10	10	10.0	132	124	16,545	17,839	2,246	2,291	-
6100	Nondepository institutions	13	13	12.4	173	63	19,029	29,079	3,211	1,762	9.5
6160	Mortgage bankers and brokers	4	5	11.9	112	15	16,821	25,067	1,694	326	4.9
6200	Security and commodity brokers	14	12	8.1	126	126	54,603	47,841	9,143	9,795	27.6
6210	Security brokers and dealers	8	7	6.6	106	109	60,151	51,339	8,514	9,207	27.9
6300	Insurance carriers	20	21	16.2	243	212	22,091	24,811	6,525	6,331	15.2
6330	Fire, marine, and casualty insurance	13	13	18.6	70	65	26,000	33,723	2,953	3,127	29.0
6400	Insurance agents, brokers, and service	65	63	9.8	392	371	20,673	26,933	8,716	9,681	16.9
6500	Real estate	77	83	8.6	230	291	11,461	10,158	2,898	3,791	7.9
6510	Real estate operators and lessors	39	39	9.9	103	108	11,340	11,481	1,339	1,438	8.4
6530	Real estate agents and managers	33	38	8.7	108	163	9,630	8,172	1,062	1,854	9.6
CHOUTEAU, MT											
60 –	**Finance, insurance, and real estate**	15	16	0.7	78	75	20,974	24,213	1,506	1,615	0.5
6400	Insurance agents, brokers, and service	7	8	1.3	21	20	20,381	22,000	479	497	0.9
CUSTER, MT											
60 –	**Finance, insurance, and real estate**	35	32	1.3	192	184	21,521	24,152	4,338	4,717	1.3
6000	Depository institutions	6	7	1.8	96	80	21,792	26,400	2,174	2,115	1.5
6020	Commercial banks	3	4	1.8	84	70	22,952	27,714	1,999	1,947	1.9
6400	Insurance agents, brokers, and service	12	11	1.7	34	37	20,588	20,757	801	852	1.5
6500	Real estate	8	5	0.5	13	6	4,615	6,667	69	49	0.1
DANIELS, MT											
60 –	**Finance, insurance, and real estate**	5	6	0.2	41	40	16,780	18,400	745	793	0.2

Source: County Business Patterns, 1994/95, CBP-94/95, U.S. Department of Commerce, Washington, D.C., November 1997. SIC categories for which data were suppressed or not available for both 1994 and 1995 are not displayed. The employment columns represent mid-March employment in the year. Pay per employee is calculated by dividing 1st Quarter payroll, annualized, by mid-March employment. The columns headed "% State" show the county's percentage of the state total for the SIC in 1995; for example, 1.4% for SIC 6000 means that the county had 1.4 percent of the state's total establishments (or payroll) in SIC 6000 in 1995. A dash (-) is used to indicate that data are not available or cannot be calculated; nec means not elsewhere classified.

SIC	Industry	No. Establishments			Employment		Pay / Employee		Annual Payroll ($ 000)		
		1994	1995	% State	1994	1995	1994	1995	1994	1995	% State
DAWSON, MT											
60 –	**Finance, insurance, and real estate**	21	21	0.9	114	101	17,298	18,099	2,084	2,100	0.6
6000	Depository institutions	7	7	1.8	74	67	17,892	18,328	1,398	1,405	1.0
6060	Credit unions	4	4	4.0	14	14	9,143	11,714	146	170	-
6500	Real estate	6	6	0.6	17	13	6,824	9,538	154	147	0.3
FERGUS, MT											
60 –	**Finance, insurance, and real estate**	26	28	1.1	179	179	20,134	20,782	3,782	3,732	1.0
6000	Depository institutions	6	6	1.5	112	112	22,071	22,250	2,610	2,422	1.7
6400	Insurance agents, brokers, and service	10	11	1.7	21	25	16,571	14,560	391	431	0.8
FLATHEAD, MT											
60 –	**Finance, insurance, and real estate**	243	255	10.4	1,457	1,436	19,058	21,872	30,341	31,744	8.9
6000	Depository institutions	27	27	6.8	490	544	20,204	21,890	9,835	10,334	7.4
6020	Commercial banks	11	11	5.1	345	326	20,684	23,215	6,884	7,053	7.0
6100	Nondepository institutions	10	12	11.4	71	70	30,930	24,971	1,853	2,178	11.7
6140	Personal credit institutions	3	4	10.0	11	15	25,091	22,933	264	368	5.5
6150	Business credit institutions	3	4	36.4	10	11	14,400	20,000	236	227	-
6160	Mortgage bankers and brokers	4	4	9.5	50	44	35,520	26,909	1,353	1,583	23.6
6400	Insurance agents, brokers, and service	54	52	8.1	219	222	19,178	25,495	4,833	5,861	10.3
6500	Real estate	118	122	12.7	559	444	13,123	15,622	9,259	8,313	17.3
6510	Real estate operators and lessors	33	37	9.4	76	74	9,684	8,865	735	780	4.5
6530	Real estate agents and managers	65	62	14.2	236	211	12,119	14,938	3,347	3,050	15.8
6540	Title abstract offices	4	4	14.8	75	51	17,920	19,843	1,281	1,079	24.6
6550	Subdividers and developers	15	15	20.3	172	99	13,930	20,081	3,883	3,276	50.4
6552	Subdividers and developers, n.e.c.	12	10	25.6	167	93	13,868	20,516	3,781	2,804	57.6
6553	Cemetery subdividers and developers	3	3	10.7	5	6	16,000	13,333	102	90	7.5
GALLATIN, MT											
60 –	**Finance, insurance, and real estate**	209	213	8.7	963	1,165	29,047	22,173	26,572	26,429	7.4
6000	Depository institutions	19	18	4.5	280	323	21,343	24,483	7,184	7,969	5.7
6020	Commercial banks	12	12	5.5	228	272	22,439	25,735	6,261	7,065	7.0
6200	Security and commodity brokers	17	16	10.8	101	70	76,792	61,314	4,435	3,875	10.9
6210	Security brokers and dealers	10	10	9.4	65	64	56,123	59,500	3,337	3,507	10.6
6300	Insurance carriers	9	11	8.5	37	39	25,946	26,974	1,003	1,083	2.6
6330	Fire, marine, and casualty insurance	4	5	7.1	4	6	31,000	30,667	120	168	1.6
6400	Insurance agents, brokers, and service	46	49	7.7	138	138	20,029	20,841	2,917	3,129	5.5
6500	Real estate	105	106	11.0	273	380	16,718	13,463	5,526	6,067	12.6
6510	Real estate operators and lessors	33	34	8.7	85	79	10,118	11,089	998	1,286	7.5
6530	Real estate agents and managers	59	59	13.5	131	252	14,076	10,746	2,251	2,952	15.2
GARFIELD, MT											
60 –	**Finance, insurance, and real estate**	1	1	0.0	-	-	-	-	-	-	-
GLACIER, MT											
60 –	**Finance, insurance, and real estate**	16	21	0.9	161	185	19,429	19,719	3,660	3,502	1.0
6000	Depository institutions	5	5	1.3	54	55	18,296	18,982	984	996	0.7
GRANITE, MT											
60 –	**Finance, insurance, and real estate**	5	5	0.2	-	-	-	-	-	-	-
HILL, MT											
60 –	**Finance, insurance, and real estate**	44	40	1.6	192	193	18,958	18,902	3,718	3,835	1.1
6000	Depository institutions	9	9	2.3	87	92	22,207	22,304	1,961	2,008	1.4
6020	Commercial banks	4	4	1.8	53	51	26,642	27,765	1,377	1,365	1.3
6400	Insurance agents, brokers, and service	13	13	2.0	44	39	15,091	17,436	668	716	1.3

Source: County Business Patterns, 1994/95, CBP-94/95, U.S. Department of Commerce, Washington, D.C., November 1997. SIC categories for which data were suppressed or not available for both 1994 and 1995 are not displayed. The employment columns represent mid-March employment in the year. Pay per employee is calculated by dividing 1st Quarter payroll, annualized, by mid-March employment. The columns headed "% State" show the county's percentage of the state total for the SIC in 1995; for example, 1.4% for SIC 6000 means that the county had 1.4 percent of the state's total establishments (or payroll) in SIC 6000 in 1995. A dash (-) is used to indicate that data are not available or cannot be calculated; nec means not elsewhere classified.

Continued on next page.

SIC	Industry	No. Establishments			Employment		Pay / Employee		Annual Payroll ($ 000)		
		1994	1995	% State	1994	1995	1994	1995	1994	1995	% State
HILL, MT - [continued]											
6500	Real estate	18	14	*1.5*	43	44	8,372	8,636	416	410	*0.9*
6510	Real estate operators and lessors	11	9	*2.3*	35	36	8,114	8,000	305	310	*1.8*
6530	Real estate agents and managers	7	5	*1.1*	8	8	9,500	11,500	111	100	*0.5*
JEFFERSON, MT											
60 –	**Finance, insurance, and real estate**	10	12	*0.5*	-	-	-	-	434	484	*0.3*
6000	Depository institutions	3	3	*0.8*	23	24	18,957	19,333	-	-	
6500	Real estate	5	6	*0.6*	7	7	8,571	6,857	203	48	*0.1*
LAKE, MT											
60 –	**Finance, insurance, and real estate**	48	50	*2.0*	267	234	18,697	23,299	5,282	5,641	*1.6*
6000	Depository institutions	9	8	*2.0*	158	128	21,114	28,594	3,554	3,765	*2.7*
6400	Insurance agents, brokers, and service	9	10	*1.6*	45	49	19,378	19,673	929	968	*1.7*
6500	Real estate	22	24	*2.5*	43	37	12,651	13,730	573	580	*1.2*
6530	Real estate agents and managers	12	13	*3.0*	22	20	10,000	8,800	237	198	*1.0*
LEWIS AND CLARK, MT											
60 –	**Finance, insurance, and real estate**	173	176	*7.2*	1,675	1,590	23,238	25,318	42,134	41,773	*11.7*
6000	Depository institutions	31	32	*8.1*	544	499	19,309	24,184	11,137	12,012	*8.7*
6020	Commercial banks	14	14	*6.5*	179	203	23,486	24,571	4,404	5,092	*5.0*
6060	Credit unions	9	9	*9.0*	61	70	16,984	16,229	1,142	1,223	-
6100	Nondepository institutions	9	10	*9.5*	96	114	24,417	25,684	2,496	2,645	*14.2*
6200	Security and commodity brokers	8	8	*5.4*	29	25	48,690	36,160	1,269	1,212	*3.4*
6300	Insurance carriers	16	15	*11.5*	676	577	27,331	28,513	19,938	17,438	*41.8*
6400	Insurance agents, brokers, and service	36	39	*6.1*	171	187	22,830	24,856	4,298	5,025	*8.8*
6500	Real estate	68	67	*7.0*	151	165	13,483	14,206	2,432	2,482	*5.2*
6510	Real estate operators and lessors	34	34	*8.7*	88	88	11,182	12,409	1,048	1,088	*6.3*
6550	Subdividers and developers	5	5	*6.8*	13	15	20,000	18,667	288	290	*4.5*
6700	Holding and other investment offices	5	5	*6.7*	8	23	31,000	39,652	564	959	-
LIBERTY, MT											
60 –	**Finance, insurance, and real estate**	5	6	*0.2*	14	14	19,714	20,857	364	375	*0.1*
LINCOLN, MT											
60 –	**Finance, insurance, and real estate**	33	35	*1.4*	145	175	16,414	18,583	2,665	2,967	*0.8*
6000	Depository institutions	7	7	*1.8*	77	97	19,792	21,897	1,584	1,678	*1.2*
6500	Real estate	18	19	*2.0*	40	46	9,700	10,087	565	575	*1.2*
6510	Real estate operators and lessors	8	8	*2.0*	17	20	6,353	5,600	125	118	*0.7*
6530	Real estate agents and managers	7	7	*1.6*	10	15	12,800	11,200	197	239	*1.2*
MCCONE, MT											
60 –	**Finance, insurance, and real estate**	5	5	*0.2*	17	18	15,059	15,111	265	279	*0.1*
MADISON, MT											
60 –	**Finance, insurance, and real estate**	13	17	*0.7*	69	71	19,188	18,930	1,211	1,269	*0.4*
6500	Real estate	5	9	*0.9*	5	9	12,800	10,222	74	105	*0.2*
6530	Real estate agents and managers	3	3	*0.7*	4	5	15,000	12,800	63	59	*0.3*
MINERAL, MT											
60 –	**Finance, insurance, and real estate**	6	5	*0.2*	-	-	-	-	-	-	
MISSOULA, MT											
60 –	**Finance, insurance, and real estate**	280	291	*11.8*	1,661	1,711	21,515	21,763	38,465	40,517	*11.4*
6000	Depository institutions	33	34	*8.6*	550	568	21,615	23,070	13,630	13,354	*9.6*
6020	Commercial banks	15	15	*6.9*	285	302	24,211	25,497	7,214	7,446	*7.3*
6060	Credit unions	9	9	*9.0*	112	111	15,143	16,577	1,797	1,892	-
6100	Nondepository institutions	15	16	*15.2*	82	87	29,659	29,149	2,273	2,648	*14.2*
6160	Mortgage bankers and brokers	6	7	*16.7*	21	26	41,143	23,538	603	651	*9.7*

Source: County Business Patterns, 1994/95, CBP-94/95, U.S. Department of Commerce, Washington, D.C., November 1997. SIC categories for which data were suppressed or not available for both 1994 and 1995 are not displayed. The employment columns represent mid-March employment in the year. Pay per employee is calculated by dividing 1st Quarter payroll, annualized, by mid-March employment. The columns headed "% State" show the county's percentage of the state total for the SIC in 1995; for example, 1.4% for SIC 6000 means that the county had 1.4 percent of the state's total establishments (or payroll) in SIC 6000 in 1995. A dash (-) is used to indicate that data are not available or cannot be calculated; nec means not elsewhere classified.

Continued on next page.

SIC	Industry	No. Establishments			Employment		Pay / Employee		Annual Payroll ($ 000)		
		1994	1995	% State	1994	1995	1994	1995	1994	1995	% State
MISSOULA, MT - [continued]											
6200	Security and commodity brokers	12	18	12.2	104	117	35,462	28,957	3,246	4,061	11.4
6300	Insurance carriers	18	20	15.4	139	174	27,914	27,379	3,788	5,253	12.6
6400	Insurance agents, brokers, and service	76	73	11.4	320	302	22,638	23,457	8,028	7,712	13.5
6500	Real estate	118	122	12.7	450	437	14,089	13,675	7,156	7,086	14.8
6510	Real estate operators and lessors	43	47	12.0	144	151	10,389	10,596	1,879	2,061	12.0
6530	Real estate agents and managers	58	57	13.0	258	215	15,442	15,721	4,188	3,780	19.5
6790	Miscellaneous investing	4	4	16.7	3	7	21,333	13,714	58	92	7.4
PARK, MT											
60 –	**Finance, insurance, and real estate**	37	44	1.8	113	118	19,327	19,831	2,328	3,142	0.9
6000	Depository institutions	3	6	1.5	47	46	23,234	24,348	1,169	1,697	1.2
6400	Insurance agents, brokers, and service	6	6	0.9	20	19	14,600	16,211	314	322	0.6
6500	Real estate	21	24	2.5	26	26	8,154	8,769	260	403	0.8
6510	Real estate operators and lessors	11	10	2.6	13	10	4,000	5,200	67	153	0.9
6530	Real estate agents and managers	8	10	2.3	7	11	8,000	7,273	62	110	0.6
PETROLEUM, MT											
60 –	**Finance, insurance, and real estate**	1	1	0.0	-	-	-	-	-	-	-
PHILLIPS, MT											
60 –	**Finance, insurance, and real estate**	8	8	0.3	60	63	21,000	22,159	1,360	1,378	0.4
PONDERA, MT											
60 –	**Finance, insurance, and real estate**	15	18	0.7	69	73	21,565	22,301	1,508	1,649	0.5
6000	Depository institutions	4	4	1.0	39	39	24,615	25,333	992	1,011	0.7
6500	Real estate	5	7	0.7	8	14	9,000	10,571	68	141	0.3
POWDER RIVER, MT											
60 –	**Finance, insurance, and real estate**	4	5	0.2	17	15	17,412	20,000	325	336	0.1
POWELL, MT											
60 –	**Finance, insurance, and real estate**	12	14	0.6	51	51	15,843	18,824	1,069	1,252	0.4
6000	Depository institutions	3	3	0.8	36	37	17,556	20,108	870	1,030	0.7
6400	Insurance agents, brokers, and service	3	4	0.6	7	6	13,714	18,667	101	112	0.2
6500	Real estate	6	7	0.7	8	8	10,000	13,000	98	110	0.2
6510	Real estate operators and lessors	3	4	1.0	4	3	4,000	5,333	16	20	0.1
RAVALLI, MT											
60 –	**Finance, insurance, and real estate**	77	83	3.4	353	374	18,085	18,374	6,747	6,973	2.0
6000	Depository institutions	10	10	2.5	171	171	20,421	21,053	3,666	3,778	2.7
6020	Commercial banks	6	6	2.8	138	145	20,348	20,248	2,949	3,127	3.1
6400	Insurance agents, brokers, and service	20	17	2.7	69	76	16,000	18,474	1,233	1,281	2.2
6500	Real estate	38	44	4.6	87	98	12,276	12,163	1,117	1,184	2.5
6510	Real estate operators and lessors	7	9	2.3	23	40	12,348	8,900	324	417	2.4
6530	Real estate agents and managers	26	29	6.6	55	47	12,145	11,745	705	639	3.3
RICHLAND, MT											
60 –	**Finance, insurance, and real estate**	24	24	1.0	128	123	21,094	20,520	2,817	2,738	0.8
6000	Depository institutions	6	6	1.5	78	74	23,231	20,811	1,810	1,766	1.3
6210	Security brokers and dealers	3	3	2.8	5	5	37,600	43,200	203	218	0.7
6400	Insurance agents, brokers, and service	7	7	1.1	22	25	15,455	14,880	388	412	0.7
6500	Real estate	4	4	0.4	10	9	10,000	13,333	113	151	0.3
ROOSEVELT, MT											
60 –	**Finance, insurance, and real estate**	16	17	0.7	93	89	18,065	17,483	1,805	1,770	0.5
6000	Depository institutions	7	7	1.8	76	69	18,947	18,899	1,555	1,484	1.1
ROSEBUD, MT											
60 –	**Finance, insurance, and real estate**	14	15	0.6	123	122	22,276	22,885	2,792	2,929	0.8

Source: County Business Patterns, 1994/95, CBP-94/95, U.S. Department of Commerce, Washington, D.C., November 1997. SIC categories for which data were suppressed or not available for both 1994 and 1995 are not displayed. The employment columns represent mid-March employment in the year. Pay per employee is calculated by dividing 1st Quarter payroll, annualized, by mid-March employment. The columns headed "% State" show the county's percentage of the state total for the SIC in 1995; for example, 1.4% for SIC 6000 means that the county had 1.4 percent of the state's total establishments (or payroll) in SIC 6000 in 1995. A dash (-) is used to indicate that data are not available or cannot be calculated; nec means not elsewhere classified.

Continued on next page.

SIC	Industry	No. Establishments			Employment		Pay / Employee		Annual Payroll ($ 000)		
		1994	1995	% State	1994	1995	1994	1995	1994	1995	% State
CARSON CITY CITY, NV - [continued]											
6500	Real estate	89	95	*4.7*	211	463	21,422	13,417	5,550	7,696	*2.4*
6510	Real estate operators and lessors	42	43	*5.1*	87	330	10,989	7,479	1,099	3,056	*3.4*
6530	Real estate agents and managers	39	44	*5.0*	108	125	28,889	27,712	3,892	4,348	*4.2*

Source: County Business Patterns, 1994/95, CBP-94/95, U.S. Department of Commerce, Washington, D.C., November 1997. SIC categories for which data were suppressed or not available for both 1994 and 1995 are not displayed. The employment columns represent mid-March employment in the year. Pay per employee is calculated by dividing 1st Quarter payroll, annualized, by mid-March employment. The columns headed "% State" show the county's percentage of the state total for the SIC in 1995; for example, 1.4% for SIC 6000 means that the county had 1.4 percent of the state's total establishments (or payroll) in SIC 6000 in 1995. A dash (-) is used to indicate that data are not available or cannot be calculated; nec means not elsewhere classified.

NEW HAMPSHIRE

SIC	Industry	No. Establishments			Employment		Pay / Employee		Annual Payroll ($ 000)		
		1994	1995	% State	1994	1995	1994	1995	1994	1995	% State
BELKNAP, NH											
60 –	**Finance, insurance, and real estate**	139	130	4.8	860	739	23,205	22,057	18,485	18,058	2.0
6000	Depository institutions	20	15	3.5	346	295	21,572	23,390	7,730	8,060	4.3
6030	Savings institutions	15	6	5.5	284	185	21,423	23,330	6,160	5,194	10.4
6400	Insurance agents, brokers, and service	27	24	4.7	125	137	25,024	25,080	3,451	3,863	4.6
6500	Real estate	74	71	6.0	269	243	14,498	15,276	4,029	4,178	3.4
6530	Real estate agents and managers	48	41	6.3	191	164	14,262	15,659	2,771	2,654	4.5
6553	Cemetery subdividers and developers	5	5	17.2	3	4	9,333	17,000	72	86	9.0
CARROLL, NH											
60 –	**Finance, insurance, and real estate**	118	119	4.4	722	767	20,249	20,610	15,385	15,216	1.7
6000	Depository institutions	20	20	4.6	241	251	25,228	22,582	5,666	4,795	2.6
6400	Insurance agents, brokers, and service	20	20	3.9	127	126	26,740	28,095	3,455	3,475	4.1
6500	Real estate	70	71	6.0	344	380	14,140	16,663	5,617	6,400	5.2
6510	Real estate operators and lessors	16	17	4.6	115	122	13,113	12,492	1,324	1,273	3.3
6530	Real estate agents and managers	46	43	6.6	214	240	14,766	17,983	3,906	4,680	7.9
CHESHIRE, NH											
60 –	**Finance, insurance, and real estate**	135	142	5.2	1,991	2,043	30,154	31,499	59,728	64,004	7.2
6000	Depository institutions	29	28	6.5	435	447	20,671	22,604	9,879	10,413	5.6
6020	Commercial banks	11	8	3.0	189	144	22,222	23,028	4,390	3,564	3.1
6100	Nondepository institutions	6	7	5.2	43	24	21,209	24,500	644	672	1.0
6160	Mortgage bankers and brokers	3	3	4.2	35	8	20,457	14,500	350	84	0.3
6200	Security and commodity brokers	11	10	5.3	49	32	45,306	38,875	2,230	1,264	2.7
6300	Insurance carriers	10	9	4.9	1,114	1,130	36,151	38,297	38,692	41,562	12.4
6400	Insurance agents, brokers, and service	26	29	5.7	156	131	25,923	25,160	3,925	3,636	4.3
6500	Real estate	48	51	4.3	179	213	16,536	15,737	3,487	3,855	3.1
6510	Real estate operators and lessors	15	18	4.8	83	101	19,133	17,228	1,609	1,872	4.9
6530	Real estate agents and managers	26	26	4.0	76	92	14,632	14,870	1,481	1,722	2.9
6550	Subdividers and developers	5	5	4.9	19	19	11,789	12,421	254	240	1.2
6700	Holding and other investment offices	5	8	8.7	15	66	42,400	37,758	871	2,602	-
COOS, NH											
60 –	**Finance, insurance, and real estate**	55	51	1.9	445	432	18,220	19,046	8,360	8,634	1.0
6000	Depository institutions	20	17	3.9	265	260	18,808	19,092	5,165	5,284	2.8
6020	Commercial banks	9	12	4.5	160	194	19,000	19,608	3,310	4,062	3.5
6400	Insurance agents, brokers, and service	13	12	2.4	64	51	21,188	24,863	1,392	1,270	1.5
6500	Real estate	19	16	1.3	67	68	11,284	10,529	762	762	0.6
6510	Real estate operators and lessors	8	5	1.3	18	11	12,444	12,727	227	151	0.4
6530	Real estate agents and managers	11	11	1.7	49	57	10,857	10,105	535	611	1.0
GRAFTON, NH											
60 –	**Finance, insurance, and real estate**	226	231	8.4	1,365	1,368	22,637	23,439	34,360	34,772	3.9
6000	Depository institutions	50	46	10.6	549	540	23,658	24,704	12,893	13,623	7.3
6020	Commercial banks	19	26	9.7	213	283	22,930	22,883	5,174	6,810	5.9
6030	Savings institutions	27	15	13.6	321	240	23,340	24,817	7,103	6,094	12.2
6100	Nondepository institutions	4	4	3.0	7	7	17,714	18,857	163	219	0.3
6200	Security and commodity brokers	16	18	9.6	65	63	61,169	62,032	5,334	4,702	9.9
6210	Security brokers and dealers	6	6	7.7	31	30	76,387	81,733	2,050	2,150	6.8
6280	Security and commodity services	10	12	11.0	34	33	47,294	44,121	3,284	2,552	16.4
6400	Insurance agents, brokers, and service	36	35	6.9	173	168	25,549	28,095	5,356	5,264	6.2
6500	Real estate	108	115	9.6	533	557	14,852	15,727	8,894	9,632	7.8

Source: County Business Patterns, 1994/95, CBP-94/95, U.S. Department of Commerce, Washington, D.C., November 1997. SIC categories for which data were suppressed or not available for both 1994 and 1995 are *not* displayed. The employment columns represent mid-March employment in the year. Pay per employee is calculated by dividing 1st Quarter payroll, annualized, by mid-March employment. The columns headed "% State" show the county's percentage of the state total for the SIC in 1995; for example, 1.4% for SIC 6000 means that the county had 1.4 percent of the state's total establishments (or payroll) in SIC 6000 in 1995. A dash (-) is used to indicate that data are not available or cannot be calculated; *nec* means not elsewhere classified.

Continued on next page.

SIC	Industry	No. Establishments			Employment		Pay / Employee		Annual Payroll ($ 000)		
		1994	1995	% State	1994	1995	1994	1995	1994	1995	% State
GRAFTON, NH - [continued]											
6510	Real estate operators and lessors	28	33	8.8	99	128	20,242	19,844	2,153	2,725	7.1
6530	Real estate agents and managers	66	68	10.5	373	388	14,070	14,113	5,701	5,867	9.9
6552	Subdividers and developers, n.e.c.	8	7	10.1	56	36	10,571	18,667	931	914	5.0
HILLSBOROUGH, NH											
60 –	**Finance, insurance, and real estate**	908	899	32.9	10,540	10,368	30,757	31,400	324,383	352,231	39.9
6000	Depository institutions	133	124	28.6	2,711	2,241	26,008	26,053	71,059	62,854	33.8
6020	Commercial banks	60	80	29.7	1,230	1,546	26,000	26,942	32,575	44,925	39.0
6100	Nondepository institutions	62	59	43.7	1,029	1,262	34,507	36,079	33,048	51,721	78.2
6150	Business credit institutions	7	7	41.2	377	392	43,066	45,745	14,631	21,605	92.9
6160	Mortgage bankers and brokers	37	36	50.7	465	628	28,705	29,408	12,544	21,220	69.4
6200	Security and commodity brokers	52	57	30.5	365	347	61,863	58,075	19,143	18,739	39.6
6210	Security brokers and dealers	19	24	30.8	268	265	64,388	55,864	15,071	14,641	46.2
6280	Security and commodity services	33	33	30.3	97	82	54,887	65,220	4,072	4,098	26.3
6300	Insurance carriers	92	94	50.8	3,048	3,280	34,008	33,973	101,283	112,336	33.4
6310	Life insurance	27	27	49.1	606	473	32,983	38,495	18,910	16,141	22.5
6330	Fire, marine, and casualty insurance	51	53	51.0	1,258	1,200	38,242	37,877	46,439	44,394	23.8
6400	Insurance agents, brokers, and service	177	181	35.6	1,147	1,122	29,873	29,743	36,436	36,407	43.1
6500	Real estate	367	357	29.9	1,797	1,746	20,545	21,468	40,800	44,001	35.7
6510	Real estate operators and lessors	102	102	27.3	641	628	18,340	18,739	13,058	13,895	36.0
6530	Real estate agents and managers	219	206	31.7	952	912	21,210	22,798	22,629	24,333	41.0
6540	Title abstract offices	13	10	45.5	148	97	25,595	26,969	3,437	3,147	76.6
6550	Subdividers and developers	22	25	24.3	54	80	21,556	19,050	1,428	1,726	8.8
6553	Cemetery subdividers and developers	6	6	20.7	22	22	18,364	20,364	481	498	51.9
6700	Holding and other investment offices	25	27	29.3	443	370	46,826	51,881	22,614	26,173	-
6710	Holding offices	13	12	40.0	386	318	45,554	51,799	18,553	21,309	84.0
MERRIMACK, NH											
60 –	**Finance, insurance, and real estate**	307	309	11.3	4,399	4,174	29,867	30,472	131,551	132,936	15.1
6000	Depository institutions	53	46	10.6	1,529	1,228	21,300	25,322	30,500	31,199	16.8
6020	Commercial banks	21	28	10.4	683	784	22,272	26,005	15,162	19,707	17.1
6030	Savings institutions	26	13	11.8	758	359	19,847	22,763	13,003	8,886	17.8
6100	Nondepository institutions	12	13	9.6	209	135	33,091	33,659	6,891	5,281	8.0
6200	Security and commodity brokers	23	26	13.9	113	137	67,363	48,818	7,536	7,684	16.3
6210	Security brokers and dealers	14	13	16.7	72	100	67,222	44,840	4,397	4,759	15.0
6280	Security and commodity services	9	13	11.9	41	37	67,610	59,568	3,139	2,925	18.8
6300	Insurance carriers	25	24	13.0	1,717	1,827	36,934	34,323	63,488	64,943	19.3
6310	Life insurance	7	7	12.7	890	933	45,721	37,479	37,301	37,667	52.5
6400	Insurance agents, brokers, and service	60	63	12.4	261	284	31,218	33,662	9,051	9,432	11.2
6500	Real estate	117	117	9.8	415	422	18,622	20,066	8,586	9,664	7.8
6510	Real estate operators and lessors	44	44	11.8	197	221	20,244	20,941	4,440	5,120	13.3
6530	Real estate agents and managers	59	56	8.6	200	183	16,860	18,842	3,662	3,970	6.7
6550	Subdividers and developers	12	12	11.7	18	17	20,444	22,353	477	508	2.6
6553	Cemetery subdividers and developers	5	5	17.2	5	5	8,000	7,200	80	73	7.6
6730	Trusts	9	11	36.7	80	96	25,800	27,750	2,345	3,021	55.9
ROCKINGHAM, NH											
60 –	**Finance, insurance, and real estate**	573	613	22.4	5,319	5,013	28,543	34,068	166,107	176,695	20.0
6000	Depository institutions	89	87	20.0	1,285	1,119	21,921	25,837	28,198	28,747	15.5
6020	Commercial banks	41	59	21.9	546	626	21,832	26,217	11,804	16,715	14.5
6100	Nondepository institutions	32	35	25.9	177	163	36,542	41,939	7,477	7,204	10.9
6150	Business credit institutions	5	5	29.4	15	20	48,800	58,800	703	1,033	4.4
6160	Mortgage bankers and brokers	18	18	25.4	130	106	38,185	43,472	5,894	5,198	17.0
6200	Security and commodity brokers	48	54	28.9	224	256	51,250	44,266	11,557	13,096	27.7
6210	Security brokers and dealers	15	19	24.4	150	178	54,933	42,607	7,594	8,383	26.4
6280	Security and commodity services	32	35	32.1	74	78	43,784	48,051	3,962	4,713	30.2
6300	Insurance carriers	34	28	15.1	1,984	1,780	34,343	43,099	74,352	72,449	21.6
6400	Insurance agents, brokers, and service	88	98	19.3	368	407	26,489	26,762	10,836	11,403	13.5

Source: County Business Patterns, 1994/95, CBP-94/95, U.S. Department of Commerce, Washington, D.C., November 1997. SIC categories for which data were suppressed or not available for both 1994 and 1995 are not displayed. The employment columns represent mid-March employment in the year. Pay per employee is calculated by dividing 1st Quarter payroll, annualized, by mid-March employment. The columns headed "% State" show the county's percentage of the state total for the SIC in 1995; for example, 1.4% for SIC 6000 means that the county had 1.4 percent of the state's total establishments (or payroll) in SIC 6000 in 1995. A dash (-) is used to indicate that data are not available or cannot be calculated; nec means not elsewhere classified.

Continued on next page.

SIC	Industry	No. Establishments			Employment		Pay / Employee		Annual Payroll ($ 000)		
		1994	1995	% State	1994	1995	1994	1995	1994	1995	% State
ROCKINGHAM, NH - [continued]											
6500	Real estate	257	291	24.4	1,131	1,184	18,921	26,807	27,423	38,986	31.6
6510	Real estate operators and lessors	81	93	24.9	337	415	18,718	21,147	8,258	10,552	27.4
6530	Real estate agents and managers	139	152	23.4	505	513	19,255	19,673	10,549	12,195	20.6
6540	Title abstract offices	6	7	31.8	64	31	22,563	25,548	1,276	569	13.9
6550	Subdividers and developers	25	24	23.3	222	212	17,441	55,943	7,237	15,119	77.4
6710	Holding offices	5	4	13.3	52	10	49,538	27,200	1,535	201	0.8
6730	Trusts	4	4	13.3	5	4	22,400	26,000	113	103	1.9
6790	Miscellaneous investing	10	9	37.5	57	76	23,930	30,211	1,799	2,138	34.3
STRAFFORD, NH											
60 –	**Finance, insurance, and real estate**	159	167	6.1	2,167	2,664	29,087	29,784	61,336	68,128	7.7
6000	Depository institutions	35	37	8.5	517	565	22,104	24,297	11,290	14,117	7.6
6020	Commercial banks	12	25	9.3	157	405	24,102	25,304	3,643	10,468	9.1
6030	Savings institutions	17	6	5.5	309	103	21,256	21,981	6,494	2,387	4.8
6100	Nondepository institutions	5	5	3.7	15	14	29,333	32,286	381	455	0.7
6400	Insurance agents, brokers, and service	30	30	5.9	235	214	32,868	34,972	7,389	7,272	8.6
6500	Real estate	67	71	6.0	164	169	15,951	16,544	3,085	3,593	2.9
6510	Real estate operators and lessors	24	29	7.8	69	60	14,203	17,667	1,012	1,635	4.2
6530	Real estate agents and managers	34	31	4.8	78	82	18,103	17,317	1,760	1,570	2.6
6550	Subdividers and developers	7	7	6.8	17	21	13,176	12,000	299	256	1.3
SULLIVAN, NH											
60 –	**Finance, insurance, and real estate**	66	73	2.7	519	540	21,395	22,600	12,549	12,473	1.4
6000	Depository institutions	14	14	3.2	286	291	19,860	24,206	6,432	6,746	3.6
6030	Savings institutions	10	8	7.3	219	207	20,402	26,010	5,144	4,964	9.9
6400	Insurance agents, brokers, and service	15	16	3.1	76	79	28,632	26,937	2,398	2,354	2.8
6500	Real estate	29	32	2.7	114	133	15,544	14,466	2,419	2,181	1.8
6530	Real estate agents and managers	16	16	2.5	88	103	15,773	14,485	1,949	1,678	2.8

Source: County Business Patterns, 1994/95, CBP-94/95, U.S. Department of Commerce, Washington, D.C., November 1997. SIC categories for which data were suppressed or not available for both 1994 and 1995 are *not* displayed. The employment columns represent mid-March employment in the year. Pay per employee is calculated by dividing 1st Quarter payroll, annualized, by mid-March employment. The columns headed "% State" show the county's percentage of the state total for the SIC in 1995; for example, 1.4% for SIC 6000 means that the county had 1.4 percent of the state's total establishments (or payroll) in SIC 6000 in 1995. A dash (-) is used to indicate that data are not available or cannot be calculated; *nec* means not elsewhere classified.

NEW JERSEY

SIC	Industry	No. Establishments			Employment		Pay / Employee		Annual Payroll ($ 000)		
		1994	1995	% State	1994	1995	1994	1995	1994	1995	% State
ATLANTIC, NJ											
60 –	**Finance, insurance, and real estate**	460	473	2.5	4,173	4,163	27,222	29,163	114,026	127,242	1.2
6000	Depository institutions	106	110	3.2	1,325	1,397	23,469	26,133	30,101	33,508	2.1
6020	Commercial banks	58	64	3.0	685	722	25,693	25,291	16,520	16,185	1.4
6030	Savings institutions	29	28	3.5	517	529	22,522	29,928	11,423	14,706	5.0
6100	Nondepository institutions	18	21	2.1	164	106	19,049	19,585	2,596	2,250	0.3
6160	Mortgage bankers and brokers	10	11	2.0	93	51	25,419	14,745	1,748	972	0.3
6200	Security and commodity brokers	14	18	0.9	193	187	84,995	78,118	14,066	13,916	0.6
6300	Insurance carriers	22	24	2.1	850	725	30,212	32,508	25,668	23,890	0.9
6400	Insurance agents, brokers, and service	74	75	2.4	581	594	28,688	31,811	17,997	19,725	1.9
6500	Real estate	219	213	2.8	1,025	1,028	18,142	18,992	21,650	21,583	2.1
6510	Real estate operators and lessors	79	77	2.3	336	328	18,357	19,220	6,673	6,773	1.9
6530	Real estate agents and managers	122	118	3.4	637	641	18,210	18,983	13,878	13,596	2.6
6540	Title abstract offices	4	4	2.5	20	17	18,000	18,353	354	326	1.2
6550	Subdividers and developers	9	7	1.4	32	33	14,625	16,970	542	639	0.6
6700	Holding and other investment offices	7	12	2.1	35	126	57,943	49,397	1,948	12,370	2.2
BERGEN, NJ											
60 –	**Finance, insurance, and real estate**	2,769	2,765	14.4	28,804	25,365	38,129	40,983	1,137,324	1,098,738	10.7
6000	Depository institutions	442	421	12.1	8,853	6,860	28,702	29,689	262,057	200,611	12.5
6020	Commercial banks	298	284	13.1	6,625	5,384	28,632	28,107	195,737	147,569	12.6
6030	Savings institutions	119	112	14.0	2,001	1,234	28,686	35,514	58,315	44,225	14.9
6060	Credit unions	20	19	5.3	161	173	26,236	27,931	4,522	4,880	9.6
6090	Functions closely related to banking	5	6	3.8	66	69	42,182	53,391	3,483	3,937	4.7
6100	Nondepository institutions	153	143	14.0	2,792	1,676	44,205	44,418	128,738	78,030	12.0
6140	Personal credit institutions	30	30	10.3	175	172	39,154	37,186	6,484	6,353	8.3
6150	Business credit institutions	43	36	23.4	1,402	598	57,027	56,876	87,576	39,164	18.4
6160	Mortgage bankers and brokers	79	72	13.1	1,215	899	30,137	37,633	34,659	31,828	9.0
6200	Security and commodity brokers	181	193	9.4	2,262	2,295	67,954	65,234	146,011	174,940	7.6
6210	Security brokers and dealers	90	90	6.5	1,485	1,438	76,935	72,896	95,074	104,419	5.7
6220	Commodity contracts brokers, dealers	13	14	25.9	55	60	64,727	63,467	4,523	5,002	39.7
6280	Security and commodity services	75	86	14.6	718	793	49,900	51,707	46,330	65,428	14.6
6300	Insurance carriers	130	124	11.0	2,946	2,741	47,470	43,800	128,300	125,742	4.7
6310	Life insurance	46	47	9.5	1,884	1,888	47,495	39,706	77,852	79,709	6.0
6320	Medical service and health insurance	7	8	11.9	48	50	65,167	55,680	2,769	2,801	1.4
6330	Fire, marine, and casualty insurance	42	43	10.3	699	541	50,409	57,804	36,417	31,768	3.0
6370	Pension, health, and welfare funds	20	16	20.5	142	131	28,197	33,710	4,660	5,534	21.6
6400	Insurance agents, brokers, and service	437	437	13.9	3,362	3,184	39,440	42,126	142,336	142,991	14.0
6500	Real estate	1,310	1,325	17.3	6,111	6,016	26,573	30,547	183,922	193,694	18.6
6510	Real estate operators and lessors	638	651	19.4	2,500	2,263	21,424	25,020	58,124	57,572	15.8
6530	Real estate agents and managers	580	568	16.5	3,070	3,073	29,395	34,180	103,609	110,393	21.0
6540	Title abstract offices	19	18	11.2	77	63	40,052	40,571	3,427	2,903	10.7
6550	Subdividers and developers	51	53	10.8	437	514	34,114	35,144	17,768	20,015	18.2
6552	Subdividers and developers, n.e.c.	25	25	9.7	95	125	23,032	25,920	3,032	3,693	6.4
6553	Cemetery subdividers and developers	22	21	10.9	342	370	37,193	38,962	14,676	15,590	35.5
6700	Holding and other investment offices	110	115	20.5	1,034	1,057	56,259	88,295	63,114	97,035	17.0
6710	Holding offices	46	48	21.4	787	827	55,405	89,170	48,288	77,112	18.2
6790	Miscellaneous investing	48	44	22.9	201	178	66,109	99,551	13,088	16,965	16.8
6794	Patent owners and lessors	12	11	27.5	52	29	37,615	46,483	2,597	1,904	4.2
6799	Investors, n.e.c.	31	29	21.2	146	142	76,904	114,028	10,317	14,870	27.6
BURLINGTON, NJ											
60 –	**Finance, insurance, and real estate**	845	839	4.4	10,015	10,337	33,072	35,755	322,458	371,704	3.6

Source: County Business Patterns, 1994/95, CBP-94/95, U.S. Department of Commerce, Washington, D.C., November 1997. SIC categories for which data were suppressed or not available for both 1994 and 1995 are *not* displayed. The employment columns represent mid-March employment in the year. Pay per employee is calculated by dividing 1st Quarter payroll, annualized, by mid-March employment. The columns headed "% State" show the county's percentage of the state total for the SIC in 1995; for example, 1.4% for SIC 6000 means that the county had 1.4 percent of the state's total establishments (or payroll) in SIC 6000 in 1995. A dash (-) is used to indicate that data are not available or cannot be calculated; *nec* means not elsewhere classified.

Continued on next page.

SIC	Industry	No. Establishments			Employment		Pay / Employee		Annual Payroll ($ 000)		
		1994	1995	% State	1994	1995	1994	1995	1994	1995	% State
BURLINGTON, NJ - [continued]											
6000	Depository institutions	173	168	4.8	2,791	2,968	21,106	21,438	59,982	63,630	4.0
6020	Commercial banks	119	113	5.2	2,246	2,453	21,907	21,451	49,505	52,334	4.5
6030	Savings institutions	38	38	4.8	404	398	19,614	22,141	8,462	9,031	3.0
6060	Credit unions	12	12	3.4	122	98	12,951	19,347	1,632	1,846	3.6
6090	Functions closely related to banking	4	5	3.1	19	19	10,526	15,789	383	419	0.5
6100	Nondepository institutions	97	95	9.3	1,701	1,730	37,206	45,998	58,541	75,619	11.6
6140	Personal credit institutions	25	27	9.3	169	201	31,929	36,219	5,435	7,080	9.2
6150	Business credit institutions	13	14	9.1	265	680	43,109	51,776	11,408	33,438	15.7
6160	Mortgage bankers and brokers	59	53	9.7	1,267	849	36,676	43,684	41,698	35,086	10.0
6200	Security and commodity brokers	46	52	2.5	515	591	99,666	85,293	35,787	44,080	1.9
6210	Security brokers and dealers	30	33	2.4	477	542	105,853	90,007	34,714	42,096	2.3
6300	Insurance carriers	79	76	6.7	2,119	2,298	36,166	38,292	77,194	94,033	3.5
6310	Life insurance	21	21	4.3	404	375	38,683	40,320	13,630	19,908	1.5
6320	Medical service and health insurance	5	6	9.0	88	149	41,227	48,617	3,665	7,466	3.7
6330	Fire, marine, and casualty insurance	39	40	9.6	1,449	1,678	35,619	37,378	54,321	64,307	6.1
6360	Title insurance	4	3	6.7	29	7	34,483	40,000	588	240	1.9
6370	Pension, health, and welfare funds	8	5	6.4	149	85	31,758	29,882	4,955	1,980	7.7
6400	Insurance agents, brokers, and service	175	179	5.7	1,294	1,293	36,108	38,348	51,070	53,396	5.2
6500	Real estate	255	253	3.3	1,236	1,235	19,942	22,186	27,953	28,225	2.7
6510	Real estate operators and lessors	84	82	2.4	496	462	19,169	21,905	10,452	10,066	2.8
6530	Real estate agents and managers	139	135	3.9	561	574	20,891	23,206	13,574	13,856	2.6
6540	Title abstract offices	11	11	6.8	54	50	30,074	32,480	1,771	1,649	6.1
6550	Subdividers and developers	17	18	3.7	63	88	22,349	20,636	1,789	2,089	1.9
6552	Subdividers and developers, n.e.c.	10	11	4.2	36	48	25,000	26,583	1,233	1,537	2.7
6553	Cemetery subdividers and developers	7	7	3.6	27	40	18,815	13,500	556	552	1.3
CAMDEN, NJ											
60 –	**Finance, insurance, and real estate**	957	959	5.0	11,009	10,635	29,835	33,516	351,418	354,857	3.5
6000	Depository institutions	166	174	5.0	2,404	2,738	21,361	23,582	52,052	64,076	4.0
6020	Commercial banks	118	124	5.7	1,931	2,182	20,878	21,967	40,111	48,426	4.1
6030	Savings institutions	29	29	3.6	419	468	24,315	26,966	11,066	12,585	4.2
6100	Nondepository institutions	88	94	9.2	2,262	2,247	34,207	44,799	80,641	83,512	12.8
6140	Personal credit institutions	20	22	7.6	104	88	52,115	34,318	3,850	2,905	3.8
6150	Business credit institutions	11	13	8.4	406	290	36,493	65,117	17,971	14,398	6.8
6160	Mortgage bankers and brokers	56	57	10.4	1,752	1,868	32,614	42,148	58,807	66,175	18.8
6210	Security brokers and dealers	18	22	1.6	226	226	55,451	52,142	11,972	11,978	0.7
6280	Security and commodity services	19	18	3.0	52	54	27,077	29,481	1,744	1,873	0.4
6300	Insurance carriers	61	55	4.9	2,059	1,511	36,519	43,465	83,946	70,392	2.6
6310	Life insurance	17	18	3.7	432	336	33,269	37,452	14,368	11,771	0.9
6330	Fire, marine, and casualty insurance	22	21	5.0	962	896	42,216	47,487	52,246	47,995	4.5
6350	Surety insurance	3	4	23.5	53	60	38,038	32,200	1,306	2,276	6.1
6400	Insurance agents, brokers, and service	229	232	7.4	1,536	1,373	28,885	31,557	48,290	47,901	4.7
6500	Real estate	346	340	4.4	2,190	2,216	23,872	25,534	58,455	61,972	5.9
6510	Real estate operators and lessors	127	123	3.7	1,118	1,170	23,263	25,292	29,978	31,007	8.5
6530	Real estate agents and managers	184	175	5.1	818	792	25,961	28,308	22,635	25,707	4.9
6540	Title abstract offices	16	16	9.9	138	98	22,203	23,592	3,018	2,645	9.8
6550	Subdividers and developers	17	21	4.3	116	147	17,000	14,830	2,730	2,428	2.2
6552	Subdividers and developers, n.e.c.	7	8	3.1	64	88	17,063	14,182	1,721	1,203	2.1
6553	Cemetery subdividers and developers	9	9	4.7	52	55	16,923	15,782	997	968	2.2
6710	Holding offices	13	12	5.4	211	231	54,389	45,749	11,866	11,219	2.6
CAPE MAY, NJ											
60 –	**Finance, insurance, and real estate**	305	312	1.6	1,599	1,522	22,597	24,657	40,225	41,544	0.4
6000	Depository institutions	75	75	2.1	662	644	22,888	25,161	15,767	16,291	1.0
6020	Commercial banks	41	43	2.0	329	298	22,553	21,651	7,027	6,628	0.6
6400	Insurance agents, brokers, and service	39	41	1.3	293	268	30,539	34,254	9,546	9,988	1.0
6500	Real estate	172	179	2.3	575	562	16,077	17,851	12,436	13,158	1.3

Source: County Business Patterns, 1994/95, CBP-94/95, U.S. Department of Commerce, Washington, D.C., November 1997. SIC categories for which data were suppressed or not available for both 1994 and 1995 are *not* displayed. The employment columns represent mid-March employment in the year. Pay per employee is calculated by dividing 1st Quarter payroll, annualized, by mid-March employment. The columns headed "% State" show the county's percentage of the state total for the SIC in 1995; for example, 1.4% for SIC 6000 means that the county had 1.4 percent of the state's total establishments (or payroll) in SIC 6000 in 1995. A dash (-) is used to indicate that data are not available or cannot be calculated; *nec* means not elsewhere classified.

Continued on next page.

SIC	Industry	No. Establishments			Employment		Pay / Employee		Annual Payroll ($ 000)		
		1994	1995	% State	1994	1995	1994	1995	1994	1995	% State
CAPE MAY, NJ - [continued]											
6510	Real estate operators and lessors	47	48	1.4	88	101	15,136	14,257	2,336	2,567	0.7
6530	Real estate agents and managers	115	116	3.4	452	431	16,115	18,367	9,461	9,658	1.8
6552	Subdividers and developers, n.e.c.	4	6	2.3	18	17	14,667	25,412	292	483	0.8
CUMBERLAND, NJ											
60 –	**Finance, insurance, and real estate**	259	253	1.3	3,443	3,058	26,279	26,900	92,695	87,799	0.9
6000	Depository institutions	69	61	1.7	822	758	21,319	22,011	17,742	16,846	1.0
6020	Commercial banks	41	43	2.0	541	584	22,743	22,240	13,026	13,066	1.1
6030	Savings institutions	20	11	1.4	238	130	18,941	22,062	3,870	2,864	1.0
6140	Personal credit institutions	7	9	3.1	55	65	28,873	31,938	3,519	4,331	5.6
6200	Security and commodity brokers	15	16	0.8	94	114	61,064	52,351	5,807	6,381	0.3
6210	Security brokers and dealers	6	7	0.5	65	76	76,738	63,526	4,609	4,775	0.3
6280	Security and commodity services	9	9	1.5	29	38	25,931	30,000	1,198	1,606	0.4
6330	Fire, marine, and casualty insurance	4	4	1.0	98	98	27,429	29,918	2,752	3,155	0.3
6400	Insurance agents, brokers, and service	49	52	1.7	231	226	25,541	26,814	6,638	7,228	0.7
6500	Real estate	94	95	1.2	279	270	22,050	22,993	7,000	7,863	0.8
6510	Real estate operators and lessors	48	49	1.5	154	138	16,078	17,536	3,044	3,687	1.0
6530	Real estate agents and managers	34	33	1.0	77	84	33,662	34,190	3,023	3,255	0.6
6540	Title abstract offices	4	4	2.5	28	22	27,714	24,909	602	571	2.1
6550	Subdividers and developers	7	7	1.4	20	24	15,400	14,500	328	329	0.3
6790	Miscellaneous investing	3	3	1.6	2	3	10,000	13,333	27	21	0.0
6799	Investors, n.e.c.	3	3	2.2	2	3	10,000	13,333	27	21	0.0
ESSEX, NJ											
60 –	**Finance, insurance, and real estate**	2,109	2,087	10.9	38,838	40,376	42,754	44,479	1,632,199	1,821,626	17.8
6000	Depository institutions	317	317	9.1	6,172	5,704	30,423	33,430	194,953	246,737	15.3
6020	Commercial banks	179	175	8.1	4,090	4,372	28,282	31,893	120,420	195,966	16.8
6030	Savings institutions	74	77	9.6	1,094	1,027	39,565	42,886	41,196	43,198	14.6
6060	Credit unions	40	40	11.2	156	164	18,769	19,829	3,178	3,262	6.4
6090	Functions closely related to banking	24	25	15.6	832	141	31,111	28,028	30,159	4,311	5.2
6150	Business credit institutions	24	20	13.0	702	621	65,140	89,965	37,097	42,477	20.0
6160	Mortgage bankers and brokers	58	51	9.3	684	494	33,620	35,822	22,618	20,819	5.9
6200	Security and commodity brokers	156	162	7.9	4,080	4,065	60,375	57,007	235,201	243,968	10.6
6210	Security brokers and dealers	74	76	5.5	2,078	2.219	66,021	65,127	134,305	145,191	7.9
6280	Security and commodity services	77	82	13.9	1,989	1,832	54,733	47,432	100,682	98,434	22.0
6300	Insurance carriers	196	212	18.7	16,376	18,069	46,140	48,474	720,561	835,280	31.2
6330	Fire, marine, and casualty insurance	39	38	9.1	2,089	1,972	45,225	53,351	93,725	94,670	8.9
6400	Insurance agents, brokers, and service	320	305	9.7	2,427	2,251	36,941	38,756	101,048	107,570	10.6
6500	Real estate	938	924	12.0	5,238	5,720	21,898	22,194	124,351	131,384	12.6
6510	Real estate operators and lessors	534	520	15.5	2,929	2,926	17,027	17,053	51,167	51,123	14.0
6530	Real estate agents and managers	347	342	9.9	2,123	2,385	28,205	28,320	65,362	69,384	13.2
6540	Title abstract offices	8	8	5.0	19	17	21,053	20,706	357	375	1.4
6550	Subdividers and developers	36	34	6.9	149	259	28,027	31,042	6,682	9,301	8.5
6552	Subdividers and developers, n.e.c.	20	17	6.6	62	165	28,968	32,024	3,772	6,078	10.5
6553	Cemetery subdividers and developers	13	13	6.7	87	89	27,356	30,382	2,854	3,041	6.9
6700	Holding and other investment offices	79	72	12.8	2,673	2,907	65,981	62,012	176,793	166,659	29.3
6710	Holding offices	32	28	12.5	1,471	1,965	51,736	49,073	78,896	97,888	23.0
6790	Miscellaneous investing	23	20	10.4	1,085	817	80,387	85,944	78,647	44,779	44.4
GLOUCESTER, NJ											
60 –	**Finance, insurance, and real estate**	295	312	1.6	2,129	2,134	23,438	24,941	53,950	59,609	0.6
6000	Depository institutions	88	91	2.6	1,131	1,148	18,196	19,916	20,102	23,788	1.5
6020	Commercial banks	57	58	2.7	802	837	17,042	18,824	13,766	17,187	1.5
6030	Savings institutions	23	22	2.8	253	225	22,277	24,764	4,953	4,940	1.7
6300	Insurance carriers	14	17	1.5	240	219	41,567	46,612	10,343	10,081	0.4
6400	Insurance agents, brokers, and service	74	75	2.4	316	305	29,203	31,528	12,189	12,368	1.2
6500	Real estate	96	99	1.3	365	359	19,375	18,351	7,693	8,703	0.8
6510	Real estate operators and lessors	39	33	1.0	166	153	20,386	19,712	3,537	3,368	0.9

Source: County Business Patterns, 1994/95, CBP-94/95, U.S. Department of Commerce, Washington, D.C., November 1997. SIC categories for which data were suppressed or not available for both 1994 and 1995 are not displayed. The employment columns represent mid-March employment in the year. Pay per employee is calculated by dividing 1st Quarter payroll, annualized, by mid-March employment. The columns headed "% State" show the county's percentage of the state total for the SIC in 1995; for example, 1.4% for SIC 6000 means that the county had 1.4 percent of the state's total establishments (or payroll) in SIC 6000 in 1995. A dash (-) is used to indicate that data are not available or cannot be calculated; nec means not elsewhere classified.

Continued on next page.

SIC	Industry	No. Establishments			Employment		Pay / Employee		Annual Payroll ($ 000)		
		1994	1995	% State	1994	1995	1994	1995	1994	1995	% State
GLOUCESTER, NJ - [continued]											
6530	Real estate agents and managers	39	44	1.3	102	108	20,353	18,926	2,373	3,645	0.7
6540	Title abstract offices	6	6	3.7	43	38	23,349	24,000	1,093	907	3.3
6550	Subdividers and developers	10	11	2.2	53	60	11,170	10,267	678	722	0.7
HUDSON, NJ											
60 –	**Finance, insurance, and real estate**	1,431	1,474	7.7	25,176	24,637	52,318	62,136	1,214,977	1,407,177	13.7
6000	Depository institutions	237	227	6.5	4,121	4,388	30,273	36,540	139,020	149,854	9.3
6020	Commercial banks	117	109	5.0	2,539	2,824	30,598	37,703	86,331	97,477	8.3
6030	Savings institutions	62	58	7.3	1,176	1,094	26,568	29,082	33,129	31,007	10.5
6090	Functions closely related to banking	25	27	16.9	183	245	47,628	59,102	12,417	14,214	17.1
6100	Nondepository institutions	39	38	3.7	697	707	62,215	61,618	51,803	58,761	9.0
6160	Mortgage bankers and brokers	20	17	3.1	479	560	70,138	65,143	41,842	50,848	14.5
6200	Security and commodity brokers	381	447	21.8	10,806	12,067	66,152	81,335	633,342	862,528	37.5
6210	Security brokers and dealers	306	366	26.4	8,285	9,458	73,301	91,236	520,358	726,393	39.4
6300	Insurance carriers	33	33	2.9	1,344	1,159	39,473	43,821	46,665	46,867	1.7
6310	Life insurance	11	10	2.0	827	724	37,030	43,691	29,642	27,770	2.1
6330	Fire, marine, and casualty insurance	10	6	1.4	350	244	49,223	51,279	11,602	12,647	1.2
6370	Pension, health, and welfare funds	7	11	14.1	140	142	25,800	26,028	3,947	3,806	14.9
6400	Insurance agents, brokers, and service	160	155	4.9	1,216	1,112	38,063	41,406	51,112	52,202	5.1
6500	Real estate	542	532	6.9	3,132	3,005	22,751	23,641	77,014	80,966	7.8
6510	Real estate operators and lessors	304	297	8.9	1,876	1,786	23,559	24,405	46,942	52,261	14.3
6530	Real estate agents and managers	207	204	5.9	1,072	1,067	20,720	21,567	24,409	24,288	4.6
6550	Subdividers and developers	19	16	3.2	120	121	24,800	29,983	3,205	3,521	3.2
6552	Subdividers and developers, n.e.c.	10	7	2.7	60	58	29,267	39,034	1,854	2,054	3.5
6553	Cemetery subdividers and developers	9	9	4.7	60	63	20,333	21,651	1,351	1,467	3.3
6700	Holding and other investment offices	31	35	6.2	579	687	57,810	40,571	34,461	52,143	9.2
6710	Holding offices	15	17	7.6	453	536	37,554	36,373	24,313	40,980	9.6
6790	Miscellaneous investing	11	11	5.7	97	109	156,619	40,661	8,686	6,713	6.7
HUNTERDON, NJ											
60 –	**Finance, insurance, and real estate**	218	218	1.1	1,601	1,648	29,172	31,223	44,911	47,485	0.5
6000	Depository institutions	59	57	1.6	546	537	23,062	27,374	13,223	14,037	0.9
6020	Commercial banks	44	42	1.9	455	447	23,982	28,519	11,346	12,125	1.0
6030	Savings institutions	10	10	1.3	67	69	17,970	20,580	1,388	1,374	0.5
6060	Credit unions	5	5	1.4	24	21	19,833	25,333	489	538	1.1
6300	Insurance carriers	8	11	1.0	552	584	38,674	40,548	17,441	19,680	0.7
6400	Insurance agents, brokers, and service	41	45	1.4	181	182	31,006	32,505	6,043	6,607	0.6
6500	Real estate	89	82	1.1	225	283	17,244	16,594	4,534	4,997	0.5
6510	Real estate operators and lessors	29	30	0.9	84	120	13,714	11,633	1,469	1,506	0.4
6530	Real estate agents and managers	43	36	1.0	118	137	21,864	22,628	2,849	3,267	0.6
6700	Holding and other investment offices	7	6	1.1	5	8	32,000	18,500	122	96	0.0
6790	Miscellaneous investing	7	6	3.1	5	8	32,000	18,500	122	96	0.1
MERCER, NJ											
60 –	**Finance, insurance, and real estate**	980	968	5.1	12,732	12,340	41,863	50,204	506,226	547,850	5.3
6000	Depository institutions	168	164	4.7	2,872	2,581	28,625	29,833	80,589	65,026	4.0
6020	Commercial banks	96	95	4.4	1,987	1,713	27,674	29,684	53,299	41,221	3.5
6030	Savings institutions	34	33	4.1	563	685	26,536	29,139	15,153	18,712	6.3
6140	Personal credit institutions	16	20	6.9	91	95	34,593	36,168	2,908	3,267	4.2
6160	Mortgage bankers and brokers	21	25	4.6	235	181	39,336	40,044	8,630	9,958	2.8
6200	Security and commodity brokers	212	207	10.1	2,519	2,358	71,487	97,559	150,413	171,930	7.5
6210	Security brokers and dealers	159	156	11.3	1,990	1,797	75,218	104,145	111,853	121,331	6.6
6280	Security and commodity services	50	49	8.3	524	560	57,863	76,514	38,482	50,331	11.3
6300	Insurance carriers	78	73	6.5	3,088	3,128	34,184	39,074	106,042	118,652	4.4
6310	Life insurance	38	32	6.5	660	598	39,685	53,057	24,191	23,987	1.8
6330	Fire, marine, and casualty insurance	27	28	6.7	2,191	2,263	32,299	34,657	73,076	81,912	7.7
6400	Insurance agents, brokers, and service	124	129	4.1	965	994	47,328	49,549	47,491	49,676	4.9
6500	Real estate	287	279	3.6	1,836	1,560	24,721	27,536	51,730	48,307	4.6

Source: County Business Patterns, 1994/95, CBP-94/95, U.S. Department of Commerce, Washington, D.C., November 1997. SIC categories for which data were suppressed or not available for both 1994 and 1995 are *not* displayed. The employment columns represent mid-March employment in the year. Pay per employee is calculated by dividing 1st Quarter payroll, annualized, by mid-March employment. The columns headed "% State" show the county's percentage of the state total for the SIC in 1995; for example, 1.4% for SIC 6000 means that the county had 1.4 percent of the state's total establishments (or payroll) in SIC 6000 in 1995. A dash (-) is used to indicate that data are not available or cannot be calculated; *nec* means not elsewhere classified.

Continued on next page.

SIC	Industry	No. Establishments			Employment		Pay / Employee		Annual Payroll ($ 000)		
		1994	1995	% State	1994	1995	1994	1995	1994	1995	% State
MERCER, NJ - [continued]											
6510	Real estate operators and lessors	106	103	3.1	799	672	15,359	17,470	12,903	12,503	3.4
6530	Real estate agents and managers	139	135	3.9	643	575	31,558	38,330	22,895	24,055	4.6
6540	Title abstract offices	11	8	5.0	172	157	24,535	31,618	6,773	6,879	25.4
6550	Subdividers and developers	23	22	4.5	221	143	38,860	28,168	9,023	4,583	4.2
6552	Subdividers and developers, n.e.c.	10	9	3.5	155	76	49,006	38,105	7,880	3,395	5.9
6553	Cemetery subdividers and developers	13	12	6.2	66	67	15,030	16,896	1,143	1,177	2.7
6700	Holding and other investment offices	44	41	7.3	737	1,221	58,752	52,432	43,882	67,234	11.8
6710	Holding offices	10	10	4.5	605	1,047	56,324	50,930	31,751	56,548	13.3
6730	Trusts	24	21	20.2	66	101	34,364	34,139	3,387	2,472	18.1
6732	Educational, religious, etc. trusts	17	15	25.9	38	68	40,632	25,941	2,102	1,958	23.8
6733	Trusts, n.e.c.	7	6	13.6	28	33	25,857	51,030	1,285	514	9.5
6790	Miscellaneous investing	7	7	3.6	65	68	106,031	103,882	8,420	7,809	7.7
MIDDLESEX, NJ											
60–	**Finance, insurance, and real estate**	1,485	1,566	8.2	25,408	25,213	45,795	57,000	1,044,623	1,153,456	11.3
6000	Depository institutions	282	280	8.0	7,212	6,968	29,450	33,027	234,199	228,075	14.2
6020	Commercial banks	157	156	7.2	4,649	4,564	30,240	31,993	161,046	154,615	13.2
6030	Savings institutions	64	61	7.6	1,101	1,021	26,020	31,608	26,994	26,900	9.1
6100	Nondepository institutions	89	83	8.1	1,247	907	38,964	42,871	48,307	41,927	6.4
6140	Personal credit institutions	28	30	10.3	381	294	34,992	42,544	16,285	14,494	18.8
6160	Mortgage bankers and brokers	46	41	7.5	772	543	37,746	39,904	26,403	23,270	6.6
6200	Security and commodity brokers	221	285	13.9	3,744	3,958	91,636	146,269	218,664	304,663	13.2
6210	Security brokers and dealers	188	253	18.3	3,562	3,738	77,163	143,341	192,367	282,327	15.3
6280	Security and commodity services	27	29	4.9	163	208	412,245	203,135	25,003	21,147	4.7
6300	Insurance carriers	105	106	9.4	6,663	6,575	48,685	50,883	293,988	321,634	12.0
6310	Life insurance	45	47	9.5	4,381	4,262	42,693	49,004	183,612	198,779	14.9
6320	Medical service and health insurance	9	11	16.4	125	607	37,280	29,529	4,798	23,036	11.4
6330	Fire, marine, and casualty insurance	36	38	9.1	2,011	1,666	62,518	63,330	99,340	98,028	9.3
6360	Title insurance	6	5	11.1	35	29	45,257	65,517	1,634	1,438	11.4
6400	Insurance agents, brokers, and service	184	189	6.0	1,376	1,326	31,480	33,318	47,390	50,073	4.9
6500	Real estate	543	556	7.2	3,517	3,691	24,813	28,041	96,191	102,875	9.9
6510	Real estate operators and lessors	227	226	6.7	1,344	1,351	20,110	21,845	32,310	31,928	8.7
6530	Real estate agents and managers	241	245	7.1	1,591	1,741	27,573	33,151	45,117	52,580	10.0
6540	Title abstract offices	11	11	6.8	43	34	31,070	27,765	1,283	1,144	4.2
6550	Subdividers and developers	52	54	11.0	493	479	28,227	27,749	16,105	13,579	12.4
6552	Subdividers and developers, n.e.c.	29	29	11.2	303	259	32,515	32,927	10,811	8,047	13.9
6553	Cemetery subdividers and developers	17	16	8.3	184	190	21,696	22,526	5,014	4,852	11.0
6700	Holding and other investment offices	42	44	7.8	829	864	72,362	69,875	67,280	61,402	10.8
6710	Holding offices	22	24	10.7	698	702	73,450	72,644	58,601	53,021	12.5
6790	Miscellaneous investing	14	14	7.3	114	107	73,719	72,860	8,293	7,569	7.5
6799	Investors, n.e.c.	8	8	5.8	83	65	93,542	93,415	7,667	5,755	10.7
MONMOUTH, NJ											
60–	**Finance, insurance, and real estate**	1,415	1,429	7.5	12,521	12,088	33,109	35,085	415,120	444,193	4.3
6000	Depository institutions	245	241	6.9	3,108	3,012	21,408	22,958	68,950	68,919	4.3
6020	Commercial banks	162	158	7.3	2,288	2,174	22,857	24,644	53,663	53,323	4.6
6030	Savings institutions	58	57	7.1	670	672	16,227	16,845	11,212	11,155	3.8
6100	Nondepository institutions	94	91	8.9	968	617	32,281	31,384	26,541	23,590	3.6
6140	Personal credit institutions	22	23	7.9	129	114	29,147	31,333	3,896	3,429	4.5
6160	Mortgage bankers and brokers	60	57	10.4	600	470	35,700	30,834	19,465	18,675	5.3
6200	Security and commodity brokers	137	141	6.9	1,097	1,196	70,410	72,070	74,535	91,766	4.0
6210	Security brokers and dealers	86	85	6.1	974	1,048	71,741	73,126	65,257	78,212	4.2
6220	Commodity contracts brokers, dealers	11	14	25.9	17	26	48,471	44,923	1,117	1,911	15.2
6280	Security and commodity services	40	40	6.8	106	122	61,698	68,787	8,161	11,494	2.6
6300	Insurance carriers	72	76	6.7	3,143	2,846	40,527	42,257	121,512	119,943	4.5
6310	Life insurance	24	31	6.3	1,025	1,193	34,158	39,728	35,755	47,053	3.5
6330	Fire, marine, and casualty insurance	34	31	7.4	1,869	1,277	46,414	47,721	78,099	60,094	5.7
6400	Insurance agents, brokers, and service	259	264	8.4	1,593	1,643	29,828	31,187	51,977	59,417	5.8

Source: County Business Patterns, 1994/95, CBP-94/95, U.S. Department of Commerce, Washington, D.C., November 1997. SIC categories for which data were suppressed or not available for both 1994 and 1995 are not displayed. The employment columns represent mid-March employment in the year. Pay per employee is calculated by dividing 1st Quarter payroll, annualized, by mid-March employment. The columns headed "% State" show the county's percentage of the state total for the SIC in 1995; for example, 1.4% for SIC 6000 means that the county had 1.4 percent of the state's total establishments (or payroll) in SIC 6000 in 1995. A dash (-) is used to indicate that data are not available or cannot be calculated; nec means not elsewhere classified.

Continued on next page.

SIC	Industry	No. Establishments			Employment		Pay / Employee		Annual Payroll ($ 000)		
		1994	1995	% State	1994	1995	1994	1995	1994	1995	% State
MONMOUTH, NJ - [continued]											
6500	Real estate	574	581	7.6	2,227	2,293	22,114	23,105	54,831	57,918	5.6
6510	Real estate operators and lessors	218	219	6.5	736	822	19,283	19,280	15,508	17,608	4.8
6530	Real estate agents and managers	298	294	8.5	1,249	1,231	22,229	23,006	31,015	31,513	6.0
6540	Title abstract offices	14	16	9.9	64	41	31,250	26,537	2,075	1,332	4.9
6550	Subdividers and developers	35	33	6.7	169	178	30,296	40,135	5,619	6,676	6.1
6552	Subdividers and developers, n.e.c.	20	18	6.9	91	99	39,297	50,788	3,604	4,318	7.5
6553	Cemetery subdividers and developers	12	10	5.2	78	71	19,795	24,394	1,771	1,909	4.3
6710	Holding offices	13	15	6.7	217	315	51,742	65,206	12,146	17,849	4.2
6790	Miscellaneous investing	16	12	6.3	156	134	22,923	23,254	3,902	3,339	3.3
MORRIS, NJ											
60 –	**Finance, insurance, and real estate**	1,366	1,380	7.2	22,531	20,584	45,537	49,431	985,478	975,298	9.5
6000	Depository institutions	239	234	6.7	3,158	2,835	31,203	32,020	100,825	92,521	5.8
6020	Commercial banks	150	159	7.3	2,090	2,187	32,425	33,244	68,548	75,249	6.4
6030	Savings institutions	60	48	6.0	864	413	27,921	24,649	25,718	10,203	3.4
6060	Credit unions	25	23	6.4	160	176	22,375	23,432	3,893	4,176	8.2
6100	Nondepository institutions	72	72	7.1	1,926	1,849	73,302	71,366	106,779	109,499	16.8
6160	Mortgage bankers and brokers	44	43	7.8	846	845	44,681	39,759	37,375	41,904	11.9
6200	Security and commodity brokers	123	139	6.8	1,961	1,966	87,676	87,152	157,389	175,041	7.6
6210	Security brokers and dealers	56	67	4.8	1,594	1,613	91,621	88,553	127,507	137,171	7.4
6280	Security and commodity services	61	65	11.0	343	334	73,120	83,174	29,113	37,027	8.3
6300	Insurance carriers	133	138	12.2	7,724	7,219	40,781	45,022	294,084	305,785	11.4
6310	Life insurance	51	57	11.6	3,203	3,139	36,121	41,083	117,544	123,388	9.2
6320	Medical service and health insurance	9	8	11.9	474	470	30,937	37,243	15,350	17,246	8.6
6330	Fire, marine, and casualty insurance	52	56	13.4	3,789	3,445	46,535	49,759	153,159	158,854	15.0
6370	Pension, health, and welfare funds	11	10	12.8	72	54	22,611	31,037	1,877	1,840	7.2
6400	Insurance agents, brokers, and service	262	267	8.5	3,377	3,387	42,551	50,408	154,464	162,203	15.9
6500	Real estate	480	476	6.2	2,361	2,459	27,426	29,619	70,889	71,241	6.8
6510	Real estate operators and lessors	185	189	5.6	517	659	19,420	25,566	12,230	15,359	4.2
6530	Real estate agents and managers	238	227	6.6	1,566	1,504	29,579	30,936	47,818	45,316	8.6
6540	Title abstract offices	9	10	6.2	81	56	25,926	31,000	2,214	1,928	7.1
6550	Subdividers and developers	35	32	6.5	190	217	30,674	33,180	7,945	7,681	7.0
6552	Subdividers and developers, n.e.c.	22	19	7.3	123	147	32,683	36,272	5,954	5,735	9.9
6553	Cemetery subdividers and developers	13	13	6.7	67	70	26,985	26,686	1,991	1,946	4.4
6710	Holding offices	21	16	7.1	1,305	159	39,323	88,050	49,701	9,342	2.2
OCEAN, NJ											
60 –	**Finance, insurance, and real estate**	774	780	4.1	5,777	6,108	25,728	27,821	153,565	162,386	1.6
6000	Depository institutions	205	199	5.7	2,200	2,358	23,571	27,286	51,901	57,631	3.6
6020	Commercial banks	135	129	6.0	1,430	1,488	21,617	26,285	33,398	37,888	3.2
6030	Savings institutions	62	62	7.8	706	800	27,456	29,465	16,830	17,992	6.1
6100	Nondepository institutions	34	36	3.5	407	380	25,612	24,811	10,167	10,296	1.6
6160	Mortgage bankers and brokers	21	21	3.8	323	299	24,929	22,622	7,903	7,764	2.2
6200	Security and commodity brokers	31	30	1.5	171	245	52,538	45,698	8,529	11,254	0.5
6210	Security brokers and dealers	14	15	1.1	151	224	55,762	47,911	7,836	10,699	0.6
6300	Insurance carriers	26	26	2.3	1,062	917	30,806	39,324	32,880	30,152	1.1
6400	Insurance agents, brokers, and service	117	119	3.8	556	568	26,201	27,352	16,506	16,803	1.7
6500	Real estate	351	360	4.7	1,363	1,630	21,145	20,358	32,686	36,052	3.5
6510	Real estate operators and lessors	96	103	3.1	269	465	22,766	17,978	6,229	9,143	2.5
6530	Real estate agents and managers	221	214	6.2	944	1,017	19,691	20,330	21,391	22,322	4.3
6540	Title abstract offices	7	8	5.0	34	25	29,882	28,800	942	797	2.9
6550	Subdividers and developers	24	24	4.9	116	117	26,655	28,410	3,962	3,450	3.1
6552	Subdividers and developers, n.e.c.	19	17	6.6	89	84	29,124	32,190	3,347	2,801	4.8
6553	Cemetery subdividers and developers	4	5	2.6	24	27	16,333	17,333	482	504	1.1
6700	Holding and other investment offices	10	10	1.8	18	10	70,222	18,800	896	198	0.0
PASSAIC, NJ											
60 –	**Finance, insurance, and real estate**	798	804	4.2	11,871	10,909	31,615	35,155	385,833	384,972	3.8

Source: County Business Patterns, 1994/95, CBP-94/95, U.S. Department of Commerce, Washington, D.C., November 1997. SIC categories for which data were suppressed or not available for both 1994 and 1995 are not displayed. The employment columns represent mid-March employment in the year. Pay per employee is calculated by dividing 1st Quarter payroll, annualized, by mid-March employment. The columns headed "% State" show the county's percentage of the state total for the SIC in 1995; for example, 1.4% for SIC 6000 means that the county had 1.4 percent of the state's total establishments (or payroll) in SIC 6000 in 1995. A dash (-) is used to indicate that data are not available or cannot be calculated; nec means not elsewhere classified.

Continued on next page.

SIC	Industry	No. Establishments			Employment		Pay / Employee		Annual Payroll ($ 000)		
		1994	1995	% State	1994	1995	1994	1995	1994	1995	% State
PASSAIC, NJ - [continued]											
6000	Depository institutions	160	160	4.6	3,496	3,162	26,070	27,942	85,671	79,828	5.0
6020	Commercial banks	107	107	4.9	2,680	2,564	26,260	28,807	64,528	64,682	5.5
6030	Savings institutions	26	24	3.0	655	353	27,029	28,544	17,635	10,125	3.4
6090	Functions closely related to banking	12	13	8.1	54	130	17,259	15,815	1,238	2,642	3.2
6140	Personal credit institutions	8	9	3.1	91	84	32,308	37,143	2,412	2,924	3.8
6150	Business credit institutions	8	8	5.2	85	87	47,153	49,195	3,439	3,921	1.8
6160	Mortgage bankers and brokers	23	21	3.8	417	299	29,305	28,201	12,653	8,646	2.5
6200	Security and commodity brokers	30	37	1.8	467	480	82,638	69,825	35,098	35,714	1.6
6210	Security brokers and dealers	17	18	1.3	423	400	87,915	73,650	33,048	31,587	1.7
6300	Insurance carriers	35	30	2.7	3,193	2,567	30,836	39,883	108,648	101,215	3.8
6400	Insurance agents, brokers, and service	161	149	4.7	2,084	2,159	36,182	41,013	81,768	96,588	9.5
6500	Real estate	345	366	4.8	1,487	1,602	22,644	22,310	36,710	37,766	3.6
6510	Real estate operators and lessors	170	171	5.1	552	651	18,435	18,704	11,792	12,369	3.4
6530	Real estate agents and managers	152	158	4.6	802	805	24,833	24,398	20,847	20,931	4.0
6540	Title abstract offices	4	5	3.1	21	18	30,667	26,444	632	491	1.8
6550	Subdividers and developers	14	18	3.7	106	111	27,283	27,712	3,389	3,350	3.1
6552	Subdividers and developers, n.e.c.	7	9	3.5	14	13	31,429	33,538	453	373	0.6
6553	Cemetery subdividers and developers	7	7	3.6	92	97	26,652	27,093	2,936	2,917	6.6
6700	Holding and other investment offices	25	23	4.1	540	468	34,037	40,855	19,024	18,294	3.2
6710	Holding offices	9	8	3.6	514	419	34,374	39,666	16,733	16,476	3.9
SALEM, NJ											
60 –	**Finance, insurance, and real estate**	97	96	0.5	669	677	21,674	23,232	15,624	16,353	0.2
6000	Depository institutions	32	31	0.9	359	402	23,265	23,741	8,612	9,211	0.6
6020	Commercial banks	19	18	0.8	250	265	19,808	20,543	5,287	5,234	0.4
6030	Savings institutions	8	8	1.0	91	118	32,352	30,441	2,840	3,420	1.2
6060	Credit unions	5	5	1.4	18	19	25,333	26,737	485	557	1.1
6400	Insurance agents, brokers, and service	23	23	0.7	114	102	22,737	23,647	2,944	2,884	0.3
6500	Real estate	32	32	0.4	135	114	13,600	16,421	2,404	2,420	0.2
6510	Real estate operators and lessors	16	17	0.5	80	82	15,150	16,537	1,756	1,828	0.5
6530	Real estate agents and managers	10	10	0.3	34	19	8,235	15,789	341	356	0.1
SOMERSET, NJ											
60 –	**Finance, insurance, and real estate**	806	809	4.2	14,713	14,553	46,170	52,208	606,743	649,820	6.3
6000	Depository institutions	154	153	4.4	2,671	2,294	29,038	35,362	77,918	73,416	4.6
6020	Commercial banks	86	83	3.8	1,721	1,463	29,134	35,582	50,476	49,649	4.2
6030	Savings institutions	29	29	3.6	533	373	24,735	29,094	14,313	9,075	3.1
6140	Personal credit institutions	9	12	4.1	59	87	29,017	30,805	1,852	2,471	3.2
6160	Mortgage bankers and brokers	25	28	5.1	217	179	36,829	34,659	7,055	6,415	1.8
6200	Security and commodity brokers	169	176	8.6	2,490	2,454	59,096	59,979	111,113	115,693	5.0
6210	Security brokers and dealers	131	136	9.8	2,362	2,316	57,934	60,016	100,898	104,637	5.7
6220	Commodity contracts brokers, dealers	4	5	9.3	10	34	172,000	70,235	1,379	1,955	15.5
6280	Security and commodity services	32	33	5.6	118	99	72,780	56,606	8,700	8,898	2.0
6300	Insurance carriers	75	48	4.2	6,773	5.978	49,757	56,231	303,996	285,295	10.6
6330	Fire, marine, and casualty insurance	32	28	6.7	4,210	3,711	54,913	61,278	198,380	194,624	18.4
6400	Insurance agents, brokers, and service	120	117	3.7	857	920	39,767	42,348	36,546	41,899	4.1
6500	Real estate	220	234	3.1	1,078	1,269	25,425	30,197	31,882	40,861	3.9
6510	Real estate operators and lessors	68	71	2.1	331	382	23,045	23,215	8,137	9,298	2.5
6530	Real estate agents and managers	123	123	3.6	635	582	25,991	28,131	20,107	18,103	3.4
6540	Title abstract offices	7	7	4.3	42	24	28,476	35,667	1,064	824	3.0
6550	Subdividers and developers	17	22	4.5	69	274	30,029	44,263	2,470	12,250	11.2
6552	Subdividers and developers, n.e.c.	12	16	6.2	46	145	32,261	42,593	1,751	6,608	11.4
6553	Cemetery subdividers and developers	5	5	2.6	23	29	25,565	23,724	719	782	1.8
6710	Holding offices	9	11	4.9	86	82	153,814	147,707	8,517	8,280	1.9
6790	Miscellaneous investing	8	10	5.2	.151	82	112,053	55,902	11,877	4,891	4.9
SUSSEX, NJ											
60 –	**Finance, insurance, and real estate**	194	199	1.0	2,193	2,135	30,466	38,334	72,009	72,778	0.7

Source: County Business Patterns, 1994/95, CBP-94/95, U.S. Department of Commerce, Washington, D.C., November 1997. SIC categories for which data were suppressed or not available for both 1994 and 1995 are *not* displayed. The employment columns represent mid-March employment in the year. Pay per employee is calculated by dividing 1st Quarter payroll, annualized, by mid-March employment. The columns headed "% State" show the county's percentage of the state total for the SIC in 1995; for example, 1.4% for SIC 6000 means that the county had 1.4 percent of the state's total establishments (or payroll) in SIC 6000 in 1995. A dash (-) is used to indicate that data are not available or cannot be calculated; *nec* means not elsewhere classified.

Continued on next page.

SIC	Industry	No. Establishments			Employment		Pay / Employee		Annual Payroll ($ 000)		
		1994	1995	% State	1994	1995	1994	1995	1994	1995	% State
SUSSEX, NJ - [continued]											
6000	Depository institutions	56	57	1.6	542	517	22,052	23,397	11,371	11,439	0.7
6020	Commercial banks	50	52	2.4	501	492	22,228	23,423	10,484	10,854	0.9
6030	Savings institutions	6	5	0.6	41	25	19,902	22,880	887	585	0.2
6280	Security and commodity services	4	3	0.5	3	6	22,667	11,333	127	66	0.0
6400	Insurance agents, brokers, and service	39	37	1.2	216	180	34,148	37,378	8,280	7,152	0.7
6500	Real estate	78	85	1.1	341	345	18,628	20,278	9,105	8,444	0.8
6510	Real estate operators and lessors	19	20	0.6	49	71	25,388	23,718	2,813	2,668	0.7
6530	Real estate agents and managers	43	47	1.4	223	211	16,843	18,711	4,711	4,304	0.8
6553	Cemetery subdividers and developers	7	5	2.6	16	17	12,750	13,176	241	244	0.6
UNION, NJ											
60 –	**Finance, insurance, and real estate**	1,255	1,272	6.6	11,677	11,896	32,979	32,985	384,196	397,094	3.9
6000	Depository institutions	220	220	6.3	3,517	3,098	25,844	26,163	91,777	80,578	5.0
6020	Commercial banks	110	117	5.4	2,586	2,219	26,571	26,688	69,178	58,487	5.0
6030	Savings institutions	57	51	6.4	626	541	24,288	25,316	15,614	13,992	4.7
6060	Credit unions	44	41	11.5	276	299	23,232	24,709	6,370	7,000	13.8
6100	Nondepository institutions	65	66	6.5	940	1,020	36,532	33,651	32,986	36,831	5.7
6140	Personal credit institutions	15	17	5.9	91	126	26,066	28,984	2,830	3,666	4.8
6150	Business credit institutions	14	8	5.2	73	97	44,055	43,629	3,300	3,890	1.8
6160	Mortgage bankers and brokers	36	40	7.3	776	778	37,052	33,537	26,856	28,227	8.0
6200	Security and commodity brokers	64	71	3.5	417	506	77,420	57,130	28,507	30,814	1.3
6210	Security brokers and dealers	31	31	2.2	285	339	98,989	68,236	23,084	23,502	1.3
6300	Insurance carriers	57	51	4.5	1,814	1,787	45,804	50,220	78,188	83,831	3.1
6310	Life insurance	19	19	3.9	609	550	40,782	45,593	22,209	22,469	1.7
6330	Fire, marine, and casualty insurance	20	17	4.1	1,099	1,131	42,846	45,517	49,259	52,627	5.0
6370	Pension, health, and welfare funds	13	8	10.3	89	82	117,258	143,756	6,013	7,522	29.4
6400	Insurance agents, brokers, and service	228	227	7.2	1,587	1,637	37,119	37,354	63,127	65,585	6.4
6500	Real estate	586	599	7.8	2,666	3,071	23,148	23,474	70,963	79,688	7.6
6510	Real estate operators and lessors	296	308	9.2	1,052	1,240	20,019	21,942	24,765	30,709	8.4
6530	Real estate agents and managers	198	192	5.6	921	960	27,813	25,871	27,577	26,984	5.1
6540	Title abstract offices	9	11	6.8	68	69	28,941	29,507	2,536	2,677	9.9
6550	Subdividers and developers	73	74	15.0	601	730	21,032	23,216	15,319	17,559	16.0
6552	Subdividers and developers, n.e.c.	58	59	22.8	333	453	21,489	23,453	9,182	11,007	19.0
6553	Cemetery subdividers and developers	13	13	6.7	268	267	20,463	22,697	6,089	6,250	14.2
6710	Holding offices	13	13	5.8	606	687	27,505	31,563	11,995	16,438	3.9
6733	Trusts, n.e.c.	3	3	6.8	6	7	18,667	21,714	113	127	2.4
WARREN, NJ											
60 –	**Finance, insurance, and real estate**	148	148	0.8	907	911	23,219	23,605	21,768	22,913	0.2
6000	Depository institutions	49	50	1.4	504	498	20,619	22,353	10,955	12,011	0.7
6020	Commercial banks	38	39	1.8	411	419	21,333	23,064	9,102	10,427	0.9
6400	Insurance agents, brokers, and service	33	31	1.0	185	190	33,211	31,895	5,638	5,971	0.6
6500	Real estate	59	59	0.8	164	179	15,439	17,542	3,406	3,624	0.3
6510	Real estate operators and lessors	17	18	0.5	53	73	16,453	19,123	1,296	1,573	0.4
6530	Real estate agents and managers	26	23	0.7	81	77	16,049	17,195	1,670	1,540	0.3
6540	Title abstract offices	4	4	2.5	12	9	17,667	19,556	198	178	0.7
6550	Subdividers and developers	12	13	2.6	18	17	8,222	9,647	242	260	0.2
6553	Cemetery subdividers and developers	11	12	6.2	18	16	8,222	8,750	219	215	0.5

Source: County Business Patterns, 1994/95, CBP-94/95, U.S. Department of Commerce, Washington, D.C., November 1997. SIC categories for which data were suppressed or not available for both 1994 and 1995 are *not* displayed. The employment columns represent mid-March employment in the year. Pay per employee is calculated by dividing 1st Quarter payroll, annualized, by mid-March employment. The columns headed "% State" show the county's percentage of the state total for the SIC in 1995; for example, 1.4% for SIC 6000 means that the county had 1.4 percent of the state's total establishments (or payroll) in SIC 6000 in 1995. A dash (-) is used to indicate that data are not available or cannot be calculated; *nec* means not elsewhere classified.

NEW MEXICO

SIC	Industry	No. Establishments			Employment		Pay / Employee		Annual Payroll ($ 000)		
		1994	1995	% State	1994	1995	1994	1995	1994	1995	% State
BERNALILLO, NM											
60 –	**Finance, insurance, and real estate**	1,516	1,604	42.4	16,061	15,546	24,280	25,598	394,267	403,125	55.9
6000	Depository institutions	189	205	35.5	4,226	4,358	23,641	25,029	98,567	103,614	45.5
6020	Commercial banks	151	158	36.7	3,233	3,277	23,790	25,322	74,580	76,426	42.6
6060	Credit unions	23	24	27.6	643	717	21,897	23,202	14,632	17,045	60.6
6100	Nondepository institutions	126	142	44.8	1,651	1,820	26,103	24,062	44,979	42,587	72.1
6160	Mortgage bankers and brokers	61	71	65.1	580	496	35,538	33,815	18,657	15,631	81.7
6200	Security and commodity brokers	68	79	48.5	530	545	54,174	51,985	25,658	28,711	51.3
6210	Security brokers and dealers	44	50	45.0	434	429	55,014	55,301	21,542	23,756	57.6
6280	Security and commodity services	23	29	56.9	96	116	50,375	39,724	4,104	4,955	-
6300	Insurance carriers	125	133	62.4	3,605	2,984	26,452	30,137	96,335	89,431	87.3
6321	Accident and health insurance	4	4	100.0	30	27	31,333	37,333	1,023	1,166	100.0
6330	Fire, marine, and casualty insurance	53	61	52.6	519	568	31,823	36,866	18,136	21,363	75.0
6360	Title insurance	5	6	50.0	182	154	35,824	33,247	6,093	7,089	81.0
6400	Insurance agents, brokers, and service	353	354	45.3	2,265	2,167	21,098	21,146	52,018	53,523	54.4
6500	Real estate	603	629	39.7	3,428	3,121	17,055	17,230	59,769	59,538	43.9
6510	Real estate operators and lessors	284	287	44.4	1,812	1,232	15,260	14,188	19,866	18,485	50.1
6530	Real estate agents and managers	268	281	39.2	1,391	1,657	18,246	18,576	32,788	33,412	50.4
6550	Subdividers and developers	30	31	28.2	146	145	24,247	23,862	4,806	4,985	24.1
6552	Subdividers and developers, n.e.c.	24	25	31.6	90	101	28,444	27,089	3,643	3,525	19.8
6710	Holding offices	22	24	61.5	276	462	53,623	53,827	15,200	23,249	86.4
6733	Trusts, n.e.c.	5	8	36.4	5	7	4,000	14,286	24	169	14.9
CATRON, NM											
60 –	**Finance, insurance, and real estate**	2	4	0.1	-	-	-	-	-	-	-
CHAVES, NM											
60 –	**Finance, insurance, and real estate**	163	167	4.4	723	702	22,750	22,006	16,321	15,353	2.1
6000	Depository institutions	27	26	4.5	338	324	22,485	23,580	7,030	7,379	3.2
6020	Commercial banks	15	15	3.5	178	172	23,775	24,419	4,044	4,076	2.3
6060	Credit unions	6	5	5.7	22	19	14,909	14,947	335	309	1.1
6100	Nondepository institutions	14	15	4.7	41	41	21,463	28,000	878	1,010	1.7
6200	Security and commodity brokers	10	11	6.7	36	28	63,333	43,714	2,436	1,202	2.1
6400	Insurance agents, brokers, and service	31	30	3.8	82	90	18,146	18,844	1,627	1,783	1.8
6500	Real estate	60	65	4.1	138	137	13,014	12,818	1,865	1,999	1.5
6510	Real estate operators and lessors	28	35	5.4	68	69	10,765	11,246	784	873	2.4
6530	Real estate agents and managers	29	27	3.8	60	66	15,200	14,121	996	1,073	1.6
6550	Subdividers and developers	3	3	2.7	10	2	15,200	24,000	85	53	0.3
6792	Oil royalty traders	10	10	52.6	22	20	21,273	20,200	505	430	-
CIBOLA, NM											
60 –	**Finance, insurance, and real estate**	27	28	0.7	152	168	18,737	19,643	3,139	3,634	0.5
6000	Depository institutions	8	8	1.4	85	82	17,129	19,171	1,524	1,622	0.7
6500	Real estate	8	9	0.6	25	42	15,360	14,095	442	747	0.6
COLFAX, NM											
60 –	**Finance, insurance, and real estate**	33	36	1.0	210	222	18,400	17,964	3,792	3,817	0.5
6000	Depository institutions	13	13	2.3	126	127	19,492	21,008	2,393	2,560	1.1
6500	Real estate	9	12	0.8	36	39	9,333	11,282	302	334	0.2
CURRY, NM											
60 –	**Finance, insurance, and real estate**	92	102	2.7	723	727	18,124	19,147	13,537	13,819	1.9

Source: County Business Patterns, 1994/95, CBP-94/95, U.S. Department of Commerce, Washington, D.C., November 1997. SIC categories for which data were suppressed or not available for both 1994 and 1995 are *not* displayed. The employment columns represent mid-March employment in the year. Pay per employee is calculated by dividing 1st Quarter payroll, annualized, by mid-March employment. The columns headed "% State" show the county's percentage of the state total for the SIC in 1995; for example, 1.4% for SIC 6000 means that the county had 1.4 percent of the state's total establishments (or payroll) in SIC 6000 in 1995. A dash (-) is used to indicate that data are not available or cannot be calculated; *nec* means not elsewhere classified.

Continued on next page.

SIC	Industry	No. Establishments			Employment		Pay / Employee		Annual Payroll ($ 000)		
		1994	1995	% State	1994	1995	1994	1995	1994	1995	% State
CURRY, NM - [continued]											
6000	Depository institutions	21	21	3.6	419	384	17,212	19,188	7,410	7,245	3.2
6020	Commercial banks	16	16	3.7	306	278	17,712	19,971	5,612	5,524	3.1
6400	Insurance agents, brokers, and service	19	21	2.7	83	88	22,024	21,773	1,684	1,809	1.8
6500	Real estate	32	37	2.3	131	149	15,725	13,289	2,128	2,229	1.6
6510	Real estate operators and lessors	14	15	2.3	84	93	16,286	13,290	1,371	1,409	3.8
DE BACA, NM											
60 –	**Finance, insurance, and real estate**	4	4	0.1	-	-	-	-	-	-	-
DONA ANA, NM											
60 –	**Finance, insurance, and real estate**	321	325	8.6	1,794	1,869	21,208	21,487	38,499	41,585	5.8
6000	Depository institutions	44	42	7.3	786	771	22,601	23,414	17,078	17,622	7.7
6020	Commercial banks	37	36	8.4	610	617	24,813	25,186	14,523	15,119	8.4
6100	Nondepository institutions	25	25	7.9	118	133	24,644	24,180	2,883	3,065	5.2
6140	Personal credit institutions	18	18	10.3	81	92	22,667	20,870	2,042	2,124	8.7
6200	Security and commodity brokers	7	10	6.1	59	60	55,254	51,933	2,944	3,047	5.4
6300	Insurance carriers	16	17	8.0	98	99	26,857	29,212	2,697	3,103	3.0
6400	Insurance agents, brokers, and service	67	60	7.7	257	276	17,992	18,188	5,050	5,793	5.9
6500	Real estate	156	164	10.3	428	485	12,841	13,204	6,443	7,417	5.5
6510	Real estate operators and lessors	73	72	11.1	199	217	10,553	11,705	2,318	2,600	7.0
6530	Real estate agents and managers	64	68	9.5	176	203	14,568	13,892	2,905	3,533	5.3
6550	Subdividers and developers	11	13	11.8	24	24	14,167	15,833	373	377	1.8
6552	Subdividers and developers, n.e.c.	7	8	10.1	8	11	12,500	13,091	127	177	1.0
EDDY, NM											
60 –	**Finance, insurance, and real estate**	102	107	2.8	661	663	22,408	22,166	14,853	14,950	2.1
6000	Depository institutions	19	19	3.3	295	304	24,217	24,816	6,848	7,062	3.1
6020	Commercial banks	12	12	2.8	265	274	25,268	25,810	6,398	6,596	3.7
6140	Personal credit institutions	8	8	4.6	21	26	22,286	18,000	485	518	2.1
6400	Insurance agents, brokers, and service	26	28	3.6	147	155	17,442	17,677	3,283	3,394	3.5
6500	Real estate	32	32	2.0	122	101	17,377	13,624	1,911	1,397	1.0
6510	Real estate operators and lessors	19	20	3.1	63	63	9,524	11,238	698	768	2.1
6700	Holding and other investment offices	8	9	6.3	39	38	29,641	34,000	1,203	1,373	-
6792	Oil royalty traders	4	4	21.1	15	13	34,933	41,231	573	645	-
GUADALUPE, NM											
60 –	**Finance, insurance, and real estate**	5	5	0.1	-	-	-	-	-	-	-
HARDING, NM											
60 –	**Finance, insurance, and real estate**	2	3	0.1	-	-	-	-	-	-	-
HIDALGO, NM											
60 –	**Finance, insurance, and real estate**	7	6	0.2	-	-	-	-	-	-	-
LEA, NM											
60 –	**Finance, insurance, and real estate**	102	104	2.7	494	505	19,911	21,513	10,376	11,086	1.5
6000	Depository institutions	25	24	4.2	234	247	20,838	21,247	5,083	5,190	2.3
6020	Commercial banks	18	16	3.7	211	219	21,081	21,205	4,593	4,600	2.6
6060	Credit unions	4	4	4.6	12	13	19,333	19,077	240	251	0.9
6100	Nondepository institutions	10	11	3.5	27	44	12,889	18,273	494	968	1.6
6400	Insurance agents, brokers, and service	26	26	3.3	108	102	18,704	19,451	2,152	2,163	2.2
6500	Real estate	24	27	1.7	58	49	11,655	17,061	729	785	0.6
6510	Real estate operators and lessors	12	12	1.9	28	21	8,857	9,524	244	199	0.5
6700	Holding and other investment offices	8	7	4.9	33	31	26,182	28,258	764	786	-
LINCOLN, NM											
60 –	**Finance, insurance, and real estate**	69	77	2.0	347	330	17,856	17,358	6,068	5,900	0.8
6000	Depository institutions	12	13	2.3	124	113	19,968	19,540	2,377	2,257	1.0

Source: County Business Patterns, 1994/95, CBP-94/95, U.S. Department of Commerce, Washington, D.C., November 1997. SIC categories for which data were suppressed or not available for both 1994 and 1995 are not displayed. The employment columns represent mid-March employment in the year. Pay per employee is calculated by dividing 1st Quarter payroll, annualized, by mid-March employment. The columns headed "% State" show the county's percentage of the state total for the SIC in 1995; for example, 1.4% for SIC 6000 means that the county had 1.4 percent of the state's total establishments (or payroll) in SIC 6000 in 1995. A dash (-) is used to indicate that data are not available or cannot be calculated; nec means not elsewhere classified.

Continued on next page.

SIC	Industry	No. Establishments			Employment		Pay / Employee		Annual Payroll ($ 000)		
		1994	1995	% State	1994	1995	1994	1995	1994	1995	% State
LINCOLN, NM - [continued]											
6020	Commercial banks	8	8	*1.9*	102	95	19,882	19,579	1,986	1,916	*1.1*
6500	Real estate	42	48	*3.0*	150	154	12,853	13,325	2,089	2,055	*1.5*
6510	Real estate operators and lessors	9	12	*1.9*	17	17	9,412	11,294	202	199	*0.5*
6530	Real estate agents and managers	29	33	*4.6*	98	108	12,490	11,889	1,260	1,225	*1.8*
LOS ALAMOS, NM											
60 –	**Finance, insurance, and real estate**	32	32	*0.8*	400	387	23,820	29,013	9,148	9,857	*1.4*
6000	Depository institutions	8	8	*1.4*	295	312	25,275	29,718	7,036	7,890	*3.5*
6500	Real estate	12	12	*0.8*	49	25	13,878	24,640	580	599	*0.4*
6510	Real estate operators and lessors	6	5	*0.8*	15	14	13,600	17,429	234	264	*0.7*
6530	Real estate agents and managers	5	5	*0.7*	34	11	14,000	33,818	338	326	*0.5*
LUNA, NM											
60 –	**Finance, insurance, and real estate**	22	23	*0.6*	142	108	20,845	21,852	2,804	2,172	*0.3*
6500	Real estate	11	11	*0.7*	22	26	12,364	12,769	291	301	*0.2*
6510	Real estate operators and lessors	3	4	*0.6*	8	13	12,000	11,692	105	119	*0.3*
6530	Real estate agents and managers	7	6	*0.8*	13	12	12,923	14,333	178	164	*0.2*
MCKINLEY, NM											
60 –	**Finance, insurance, and real estate**	59	66	*1.7*	-	-	-	-	-	-	-
6000	Depository institutions	15	17	*2.9*	186	178	20,323	21,213	3,557	3,406	*1.5*
6020	Commercial banks	12	14	*3.3*	170	159	19,600	20,478	3,100	2,890	*1.6*
6500	Real estate	23	27	*1.7*	100	91	11,240	13,363	1,201	1,424	*1.1*
6510	Real estate operators and lessors	11	12	*1.9*	29	32	10,207	11,125	298	406	*1.1*
6530	Real estate agents and managers	7	10	*1.4*	57	44	10,667	14,273	669	758	*1.1*
6550	Subdividers and developers	3	3	*2.7*	7	8	9,714	11,000	73	99	*0.5*
OTERO, NM											
60 –	**Finance, insurance, and real estate**	96	94	*2.5*	559	589	16,436	17,806	10,227	11,294	*1.6*
6000	Depository institutions	16	15	*2.6*	270	247	18,133	20,372	5,381	5,580	*2.5*
6020	Commercial banks	6	6	*1.4*	167	142	18,251	20,845	3,474	3,431	*1.9*
6100	Nondepository institutions	13	13	*4.1*	35	41	20,343	23,415	702	958	*1.6*
6400	Insurance agents, brokers, and service	24	24	*3.1*	90	97	13,467	15,175	1,547	1,638	*1.7*
6500	Real estate	36	35	*2.2*	147	170	12,707	12,424	2,130	2,162	*1.6*
6510	Real estate operators and lessors	16	16	*2.5*	77	92	11,221	11,000	921	983	*2.7*
6530	Real estate agents and managers	16	15	*2.1*	47	56	12,596	11,714	721	667	*1.0*
QUAY, NM											
60 –	**Finance, insurance, and real estate**	30	23	*0.6*	157	151	18,930	20,344	3,373	3,145	*0.4*
6000	Depository institutions	8	8	*1.4*	89	91	24,629	25,495	2,513	2,388	*1.0*
6020	Commercial banks	4	4	*0.9*	71	72	25,972	26,833	2,132	1,970	*1.1*
6500	Real estate	12	10	*0.6*	48	44	9,250	8,000	491	420	*0.3*
6510	Real estate operators and lessors	6	5	*0.8*	41	36	9,366	8,000	359	338	*0.9*
6530	Real estate agents and managers	3	3	*0.4*	5	4	7,200	7,000	33	29	*0.0*
RIO ARRIBA, NM											
60 –	**Finance, insurance, and real estate**	36	36	*1.0*	240	242	19,150	21,884	4,555	5,123	*0.7*
6000	Depository institutions	8	9	*1.6*	164	157	18,512	22,777	2,847	3,174	*1.4*
6400	Insurance agents, brokers, and service	10	10	*1.3*	28	32	24,286	23,625	800	914	*0.9*
6500	Real estate	13	12	*0.8*	31	32	14,065	14,625	470	543	*0.4*
6510	Real estate operators and lessors	3	4	*0.6*	2	3	8,000	6,667	17	53	*0.1*
6530	Real estate agents and managers	5	4	*0.6*	6	3	6,667	6,667	36	39	*0.1*
SANDOVAL, NM											
60 –	**Finance, insurance, and real estate**	72	77	*2.0*	419	496	22,654	22,476	9,737	10,729	*1.5*
6000	Depository institutions	11	14	*2.4*	114	158	20,105	19,899	2,168	2,706	*1.2*
6100	Nondepository institutions	6	5	*1.6*	30	28	23,467	23,571	418	493	*0.8*
6400	Insurance agents, brokers, and service	14	14	*1.8*	60	43	24,467	24,837	1,558	1,195	*1.2*

Source: County Business Patterns, 1994/95, CBP-94/95, U.S. Department of Commerce, Washington, D.C., November 1997. SIC categories for which data were suppressed or not available for both 1994 and 1995 are not displayed. The employment columns represent mid-March employment in the year. Pay per employee is calculated by dividing 1st Quarter payroll, annualized, by mid-March employment. The columns headed "% State" show the county's percentage of the state total for the SIC in 1995; for example, 1.4% for SIC 6000 means that the county had 1.4 percent of the state's total establishments (or payroll) in SIC 6000 in 1995. A dash (-) is used to indicate that data are not available or cannot be calculated; nec means not elsewhere classified.

Continued on next page.

SIC	Industry	No. Establishments			Employment		Pay / Employee		Annual Payroll ($ 000)		
		1994	1995	% State	1994	1995	1994	1995	1994	1995	% State
SANDOVAL, NM - [continued]											
6500	Real estate	36	37	2.3	210	230	22,629	22,017	4,741	5,017	3.7
6530	Real estate agents and managers	15	19	2.6	41	49	20,683	21,714	803	1,108	1.7
6550	Subdividers and developers	9	9	8.2	110	153	29,927	23,346	3,295	3,430	16.6
SAN JUAN, NM											
60 –	**Finance, insurance, and real estate**	144	149	3.9	1,139	1,173	21,082	21,449	24,526	25,396	3.5
6000	Depository institutions	29	29	5.0	468	477	18,632	20,528	9,934	10,746	4.7
6020	Commercial banks	20	20	4.7	412	417	18,544	20,537	8,743	9,326	5.2
6100	Nondepository institutions	16	14	4.4	76	66	20,789	20,788	1,620	1,567	2.7
6140	Personal credit institutions	11	11	6.3	56	60	18,643	20,000	1,161	1,432	5.9
6400	Insurance agents, brokers, and service	32	31	4.0	126	136	22,317	25,529	3,576	3,753	3.8
6500	Real estate	55	63	4.0	422	444	22,009	20,090	7,561	7,225	5.3
6510	Real estate operators and lessors	28	29	4.5	159	121	9,836	10,545	1,620	1,453	3.9
6530	Real estate agents and managers	18	21	2.9	120	166	11,767	10,747	1,635	1,813	2.7
6540	Title abstract offices	3	3	7.0	40	35	102,400	111,429	1,656	1,594	16.1
6550	Subdividers and developers	5	5	4.5	103	120	21,515	16,233	2,648	2,303	11.1
6700	Holding and other investment offices	3	4	2.8	4	7	14,000	15,429	71	114	-
SAN MIGUEL, NM											
60 –	**Finance, insurance, and real estate**	40	41	1.1	244	270	19,066	19,807	5,525	5,893	0.8
6000	Depository institutions	9	9	1.6	104	122	21,885	20,951	2,510	2,787	1.2
6100	Nondepository institutions	4	4	1.3	18	19	22,889	22,737	388	412	0.7
6140	Personal credit institutions	4	4	2.3	18	19	22,889	22,737	388	412	1.7
6500	Real estate	16	16	1.0	36	56	9,222	10,571	755	768	0.6
6510	Real estate operators and lessors	5	5	0.8	5	8	5,600	8,000	54	67	0.2
6530	Real estate agents and managers	5	6	0.8	21	26	9,143	8,769	512	486	0.7
SANTA FE, NM											
60 –	**Finance, insurance, and real estate**	389	396	10.5	2,670	2,922	29,703	33,455	86,861	98,121	13.6
6000	Depository institutions	35	36	6.2	685	759	23,393	25,808	15,016	18,222	8.0
6020	Commercial banks	25	26	6.0	552	617	22,848	25,673	11,342	14,625	8.1
6160	Mortgage bankers and brokers	18	12	11.0	48	66	28,917	23,455	2,008	2,140	11.2
6200	Security and commodity brokers	28	33	20.2	207	235	62,860	79,438	14,861	19,237	34.3
6210	Security brokers and dealers	15	19	17.1	109	131	69,835	81,924	6,937	9,983	24.2
6280	Security and commodity services	13	14	27.5	98	104	55,102	76,308	7,924	9,254	-
6400	Insurance agents, brokers, and service	59	61	7.8	445	427	25,600	27,681	11,890	11,156	11.3
6500	Real estate	195	199	12.5	944	1,101	26,280	28,356	29,301	33,756	24.9
6510	Real estate operators and lessors	63	63	9.7	255	296	20,204	22,284	5,657	6,863	18.6
6530	Real estate agents and managers	103	97	13.5	479	553	27,975	29,779	15,262	17,384	26.2
6540	Title abstract offices	5	5	11.6	27	54	15,556	14,370	694	763	7.7
6550	Subdividers and developers	20	25	22.7	172	184	32,837	38,239	7,477	8,333	40.2
6552	Subdividers and developers, n.e.c.	16	20	25.3	166	182	33,614	37,692	7,189	8,070	45.3
6700	Holding and other investment offices	25	24	16.9	245	213	40,800	55,362	11,076	10,537	-
6733	Trusts, n.e.c.	5	6	27.3	26	65	12,923	8,985	597	634	56.0
SIERRA, NM											
60 –	**Finance, insurance, and real estate**	22	26	0.7	161	158	18,311	19,367	3,078	3,190	0.4
6500	Real estate	10	14	0.9	31	35	8,516	8,686	273	319	0.2
6530	Real estate agents and managers	5	8	1.1	8	11	11,000	9,455	83	110	0.2
SOCORRO, NM											
60 –	**Finance, insurance, and real estate**	27	28	0.7	124	137	15,516	15,737	1,974	2,065	0.3
6000	Depository institutions	5	5	0.9	71	77	19,549	19,117	1,333	1,407	0.6
6020	Commercial banks	5	5	1.2	71	77	19,549	19,117	1,333	1,407	0.8
6500	Real estate	12	13	0.8	29	31	9,655	10,065	310	319	0.2
6510	Real estate operators and lessors	7	8	1.2	11	12	3,636	3,333	56	49	0.1
TAOS, NM											
60 –	**Finance, insurance, and real estate**	70	63	1.7	411	453	15,348	15,868	6,793	7,528	1.0

Source: County Business Patterns, 1994/95, CBP-94/95, U.S. Department of Commerce, Washington, D.C., November 1997. SIC categories for which data were suppressed or not available for both 1994 and 1995 are not displayed. The employment columns represent mid-March employment in the year. Pay per employee is calculated by dividing 1st Quarter payroll, annualized, by mid-March employment. The columns headed "% State" show the county's percentage of the state total for the SIC in 1995; for example, 1.4% for SIC 6000 means that the county had 1.4 percent of the state's total establishments (or payroll) in SIC 6000 in 1995. A dash (-) is used to indicate that data are not available or cannot be calculated; nec means not elsewhere classified.

Continued on next page.

SIC	Industry	No. Establishments			Employment		Pay / Employee		Annual Payroll ($ 000)		
		1994	1995	% State	1994	1995	1994	1995	1994	1995	% State
TAOS, NM - [continued]											
6000	Depository institutions	8	8	*1.4*	129	143	20,434	19,133	2,861	2,954	*1.3*
6500	Real estate	49	43	*2.7*	231	240	11,429	12,467	2,662	2,956	*2.2*
6510	Real estate operators and lessors	13	12	*1.9*	46	48	10,348	11,583	384	618	*1.7*
6530	Real estate agents and managers	30	27	*3.8*	137	136	11,358	12,676	1,375	1,433	*2.2*
UNION, NM											
60 –	**Finance, insurance, and real estate**	12	10	*0.3*	80	76	16,450	18,421	1,377	1,678	*0.2*
6000	Depository institutions	3	3	*0.5*	58	57	16,897	19,649	1,093	1,252	*0.6*
6020	Commercial banks	3	3	*0.7*	58	57	16,897	19,649	1,093	1,252	*0.7*
6400	Insurance agents, brokers, and service	5	3	*0.4*	13	9	20,923	22,667	220	258	*0.3*
VALENCIA, NM											
60 –	**Finance, insurance, and real estate**	62	58	*1.5*	410	279	17,278	18,050	7,175	5,394	*0.7*
6000	Depository institutions	14	11	*1.9*	223	126	19,049	16,667	4,258	2,373	*1.0*
6400	Insurance agents, brokers, and service	12	16	*2.0*	38	39	15,158	13,333	507	712	*0.7*
6500	Real estate	25	22	*1.4*	127	89	13,260	19,506	1,757	1,583	*1.2*
6510	Real estate operators and lessors	6	4	*0.6*	33	8	3,879	6,500	164	55	*0.1*
6530	Real estate agents and managers	11	11	*1.5*	23	24	10,783	10,833	379	337	*0.5*
6540	Title abstract offices	3	3	*7.0*	55	35	19,491	32,000	880	887	*9.0*
6550	Subdividers and developers	4	3	*2.7*	16	21	14,750	13,714	323	294	*1.4*
6552	Subdividers and developers, n.e.c.	4	3	*3.8*	16	21	14,750	13,714	323	294	*1.7*

Source: County Business Patterns, 1994/95, CBP-94/95, U.S. Department of Commerce, Washington, D.C., November 1997. SIC categories for which data were suppressed or not available for both 1994 and 1995 are *not* displayed. The employment columns represent mid-March employment in the year. Pay per employee is calculated by dividing 1st Quarter payroll, annualized, by mid-March employment. The columns headed "% State" show the county's percentage of the state total for the SIC in 1995; for example, 1.4% for SIC 6000 means that the county had 1.4 percent of the state's total establishments (or payroll) in SIC 6000 in 1995. A dash (-) is used to indicate that data are not available or cannot be calculated; *nec* means not elsewhere classified.

NEW YORK

SIC	Industry	No. Establishments			Employment		Pay / Employee		Annual Payroll ($ 000)		
		1994	1995	% State	1994	1995	1994	1995	1994	1995	% State
ALBANY, NY											
60 –	**Finance, insurance, and real estate**	990	975	1.8	17,525	17,964	29,797	31,739	551,282	582,479	1.3
6000	Depository institutions	197	192	2.9	4,113	5,449	27,602	30,035	132,998	168,782	1.6
6020	Commercial banks	141	130	3.4	2,731	3,687	29,274	27,882	97,272	109,606	1.7
6030	Savings institutions	32	38	3.1	928	880	22,716	28,409	22,484	24,632	3.1
6100	Nondepository institutions	66	58	3.2	895	537	33,457	31,762	28,503	18,032	1.0
6160	Mortgage bankers and brokers	36	31	3.6	469	339	31,795	30,796	13,223	11,120	2.3
6200	Security and commodity brokers	63	68	1.0	1,023	1,010	71,977	73,933	72,267	72,423	0.4
6210	Security brokers and dealers	36	39	0.9	882	869	73,429	77,409	62,340	65,598	0.4
6300	Insurance carriers	106	106	4.0	7,511	7,057	27,040	29,985	207,625	208,260	4.1
6310	Life insurance	29	28	3.9	1,820	1,168	30,462	37,993	51,113	41,680	2.0
6320	Medical service and health insurance	9	12	8.7	3,421	3,643	21,156	24,942	80,835	90,308	11.9
6330	Fire, marine, and casualty insurance	55	55	3.8	2,209	2,204	32,809	33,808	73,043	74,700	3.6
6400	Insurance agents, brokers, and service	209	220	3.1	1,686	1,710	29,888	30,451	52,162	58,882	2.6
6500	Real estate	328	311	1.1	2,042	1,934	17,677	18,290	38,814	36,150	0.8
6510	Real estate operators and lessors	175	166	1.1	1,198	1,171	13,890	15,105	18,494	17,642	1.0
6530	Real estate agents and managers	126	112	1.0	703	646	21,917	22,161	15,757	14,505	0.6
6540	Title abstract offices	8	10	2.6	67	41	36,299	45,561	2,628	1,933	2.2
6550	Subdividers and developers	16	17	1.6	67	64	23,343	22,063	1,860	1,671	0.8
6552	Subdividers and developers, n.e.c.	6	7	1.9	19	11	26,947	19,636	512	328	0.3
6553	Cemetery subdividers and developers	9	10	1.6	48	53	21,917	22,566	1,273	1,343	1.3
6700	Holding and other investment offices	21	20	1.0	255	267	60,753	58,891	18,913	19,950	1.0
6730	Trusts	7	9	2.0	18	32	13,556	9,500	239	292	0.3
6732	Educational, religious, etc. trusts	4	6	2.2	7	12	21,714	17,667	136	185	0.2
6733	Trusts, n.e.c.	3	3	1.8	11	20	8,364	4,600	103	107	0.5
ALLEGANY, NY											
60 –	**Finance, insurance, and real estate**	62	56	0.1	271	261	16,945	18,682	5,092	4,922	0.0
6000	Depository institutions	23	22	0.3	158	159	15,722	16,403	2,670	2,509	0.0
6020	Commercial banks	19	19	0.5	135	141	15,704	16,284	2,323	2,268	0.0
6400	Insurance agents, brokers, and service	11	11	0.2	50	50	21,680	26,240	1,255	1,288	0.1
6550	Subdividers and developers	8	8	0.8	8	8	11,000	12,000	146	155	0.1
BRONX, NY											
60 –	**Finance, insurance, and real estate**	2,574	2,554	4.6	11,143	11,205	21,816	22,827	258,839	271,869	0.6
6000	Depository institutions	181	182	2.7	2,171	2,003	21,865	23,635	48,940	49,951	0.5
6020	Commercial banks	78	78	2.0	1,182	1,043	22,829	24,560	26,257	26,825	0.4
6030	Savings institutions	37	36	2.9	691	660	18,194	19,952	13,173	12,645	1.6
6100	Nondepository institutions	17	17	0.9	52	72	34,538	36,833	2,363	2,961	0.2
6200	Security and commodity brokers	9	10	0.2	33	37	55,515	21,514	1,779	1,359	0.0
6300	Insurance carriers	34	40	1.5	281	323	45,395	49,065	13,848	16,302	0.3
6400	Insurance agents, brokers, and service	102	106	1.5	280	315	20,814	23,086	6,641	7,362	0.3
6500	Real estate	2,205	2,178	7.7	7,956	8,080	21,167	21,853	179,642	188,614	4.3
6510	Real estate operators and lessors	1,630	1,563	10.1	5,110	4,966	19,501	20,431	105,087	106,426	6.2
6530	Real estate agents and managers	524	530	5.0	2,545	2,746	23,054	23,291	62,980	69,539	3.0
6540	Title abstract offices	6	6	1.5	25	25	31,520	28,000	859	761	0.9
6550	Subdividers and developers	19	20	1.9	268	289	34,418	33,426	10,408	10,669	5.4
6552	Subdividers and developers, n.e.c.	15	16	4.2	30	39	20,667	20,513	771	948	1.0

Source: County Business Patterns, 1994/95, CBP-94/95, U.S. Department of Commerce, Washington, D.C., November 1997. SIC categories for which data were suppressed or not available for both 1994 and 1995 are *not* displayed. The employment columns represent mid-March employment in the year. Pay per employee is calculated by dividing 1st Quarter payroll, annualized, by mid-March employment. The columns headed "% State" show the county's percentage of the state total for the SIC in 1995; for example, 1.4% for SIC 6000 means that the county had 1.4 percent of the state's total establishments (or payroll) in SIC 6000 in 1995. A dash (-) is used to indicate that data are not available or cannot be calculated; *nec* means not elsewhere classified.

Continued on next page.

SIC	Industry	No. Establishments			Employment		Pay / Employee		Annual Payroll ($ 000)		
		1994	1995	% State	1994	1995	1994	1995	1994	1995	% State
RENSSELAER, NY - [continued]											
6530	Real estate agents and managers	20	21	0.2	106	103	14,981	15,029	1,725	1,662	0.1
6540	Title abstract offices	4	4	1.0	29	25	38,621	31,360	890	607	0.7
6550	Subdividers and developers	12	13	1.3	28	29	15,714	16,552	516	567	0.3
RICHMOND, NY											
60 –	**Finance, insurance, and real estate**	551	540	1.0	4,190	3,619	35,094	28,896	147,782	104,875	0.2
6000	Depository institutions	91	93	1.4	1,571	1,419	19,967	23,893	33,112	34,110	0.3
6020	Commercial banks	31	31	0.8	570	451	20,681	25,171	12,251	11,635	0.2
6030	Savings institutions	49	52	4.2	962	931	19,538	23,424	20,120	21,711	2.7
6160	Mortgage bankers and brokers	13	12	1.4	73	83	36,712	31,373	2,402	1,731	0.4
6200	Security and commodity brokers	45	47	0.7	188	176	52,149	49,500	9,437	9,092	0.0
6210	Security brokers and dealers	32	34	0.7	154	136	57,740	53,618	8,280	7,190	0.0
6220	Commodity contracts brokers, dealers	8	6	2.0	26	28	31,538	39,000	943	1,007	0.6
6280	Security and commodity services	5	7	0.4	8	12	11,500	27,333	214	895	0.0
6300	Insurance carriers	33	36	1.4	521	500	50,157	50,904	23,864	22,788	0.4
6400	Insurance agents, brokers, and service	92	87	1.2	346	342	30,301	31,661	11,587	11,672	0.5
6500	Real estate	256	249	0.9	1,005	1,018	22,416	21,096	22,881	23,804	0.5
6510	Real estate operators and lessors	105	99	0.6	444	443	19,991	19,512	8,870	9,131	0.5
6530	Real estate agents and managers	108	106	1.0	351	355	22,872	19,966	7,977	7,700	0.3
6540	Title abstract offices	17	16	4.1	55	44	26,036	30,091	1,391	1,335	1.5
6550	Subdividers and developers	21	19	1.8	154	157	27,195	27,363	4,587	4,918	2.5
6552	Subdividers and developers, n.e.c.	11	9	2.4	25	32	25,120	18,875	750	791	0.8
6553	Cemetery subdividers and developers	9	9	1.5	129	125	27,597	29,536	3,834	3,927	3.9
ROCKLAND, NY											
60 –	**Finance, insurance, and real estate**	755	766	1.4	4,382	4,746	30,809	31,606	142,518	157,273	0.3
6000	Depository institutions	117	115	1.7	1,208	1,202	26,421	29,295	32,761	35,290	0.3
6020	Commercial banks	78	80	2.1	784	854	26,918	30,066	22,360	25,423	0.4
6030	Savings institutions	26	22	1.8	360	278	24,967	27,108	8,441	7,928	1.0
6100	Nondepository institutions	43	37	2.1	260	203	31,600	35,567	7,681	6,793	0.4
6200	Security and commodity brokers	49	53	0.8	261	239	61,640	52,837	17,810	16,386	0.1
6210	Security brokers and dealers	27	27	0.6	224	197	66,875	57,360	13,318	12,959	0.1
6300	Insurance carriers	50	54	2.0	1,050	1,222	37,665	38,678	40,095	47,657	0.9
6310	Life insurance	16	16	2.2	781	732	31,344	35,235	25,062	24,953	1.2
6330	Fire, marine, and casualty insurance	27	32	2.2	259	281	56,973	56,043	14,614	16,089	0.8
6400	Insurance agents, brokers, and service	129	134	1.9	534	555	30,449	33,290	17,301	18,631	0.8
6500	Real estate	352	355	1.3	1,006	1,250	20,036	19,139	23,900	28,187	0.6
6510	Real estate operators and lessors	172	175	1.1	408	556	18,520	18,288	8,676	11,272	0.7
6530	Real estate agents and managers	148	147	1.4	474	564	20,726	19,830	11,923	14,021	0.6
6540	Title abstract offices	8	8	2.0	75	70	24,480	24,057	2,000	1,951	2.2
6550	Subdividers and developers	17	13	1.3	41	42	20,683	19,524	1,111	793	0.4
6552	Subdividers and developers, n.e.c.	11	7	1.9	17	22	23,294	21,455	739	429	0.5
6553	Cemetery subdividers and developers	6	6	1.0	24	20	18,833	17,400	372	364	0.4
6700	Holding and other investment offices	15	18	0.9	63	75	44,762	70,400	2,970	4,329	0.2
6710	Holding offices	6	7	1.0	41	49	38,537	64,408	1,582	2,246	0.2
ST. LAWRENCE, NY											
60 –	**Finance, insurance, and real estate**	162	162	0.3	962	950	18,857	21,183	19,203	20,438	0.0
6000	Depository institutions	58	53	0.8	612	592	17,366	18,791	11,273	11,553	0.1
6020	Commercial banks	38	33	0.9	421	398	16,627	18,724	7,293	7,523	0.1
6030	Savings institutions	7	7	0.6	95	97	20,716	21,773	2,208	2,352	0.3
6300	Insurance carriers	6	5	0.2	65	57	26,769	27,930	1,638	1,368	0.0
6400	Insurance agents, brokers, and service	42	46	0.6	134	139	18,836	19,626	2,927	3,099	0.1
6500	Real estate	49	51	0.2	120	112	14,033	16,107	1,918	1,954	0.0
6510	Real estate operators and lessors	20	22	0.1	63	56	10,540	11,214	741	755	0.0

Source: County Business Patterns, 1994/95, CBP-94/95, U.S. Department of Commerce, Washington, D.C., November 1997. SIC categories for which data were suppressed or not available for both 1994 and 1995 are not displayed. The employment columns represent mid-March employment in the year. Pay per employee is calculated by dividing 1st Quarter payroll, annualized, by mid-March employment. The columns headed "% State" show the county's percentage of the state total for the SIC in 1995; for example, 1.4% for SIC 6000 means that the county had 1.4 percent of the state's total establishments (or payroll) in SIC 6000 in 1995. A dash (-) is used to indicate that data are not available or cannot be calculated; nec means not elsewhere classified.

Continued on next page.

SIC	Industry	No. Establishments			Employment		Pay / Employee		Annual Payroll ($ 000)		
		1994	1995	% State	1994	1995	1994	1995	1994	1995	% State
ST. LAWRENCE, NY - [continued]											
6530	Real estate agents and managers	12	13	0.1	32	28	12,500	13,857	443	397	0.0
6540	Title abstract offices	3	3	0.8	10	11	19,200	21,455	232	239	0.3
6550	Subdividers and developers	14	12	1.2	15	15	28,533	35,467	502	542	0.3
SARATOGA, NY											
60 –	**Finance, insurance, and real estate**	287	302	0.5	4,020	3,794	28,729	32,313	109,728	120,059	0.3
6000	Depository institutions	56	61	0.9	653	661	18,469	20,018	12,444	13,563	0.1
6020	Commercial banks	36	41	1.1	455	469	20,070	20,162	9,265	10,125	0.2
6030	Savings institutions	12	13	1.0	145	143	14,097	19,888	2,255	2,476	0.3
6060	Credit unions	8	7	1.0	53	49	16,679	19,020	924	962	-
6100	Nondepository institutions	13	21	1.2	389	498	31,188	28,112	10,315	13,935	0.7
6160	Mortgage bankers and brokers	8	11	1.3	375	472	31,509	28,237	9,975	13,286	2.8
6310	Life insurance	8	7	1.0	116	82	34,000	42,000	3,257	2,574	0.1
6400	Insurance agents, brokers, and service	66	69	1.0	294	279	25,469	29,520	7,497	7,196	0.3
6500	Real estate	106	108	0.4	451	447	22,244	20,036	10,775	9,804	0.2
6510	Real estate operators and lessors	50	48	0.3	282	293	22,582	19,563	7,081	6,445	0.4
6530	Real estate agents and managers	39	43	0.4	99	96	20,646	20,625	2,240	2,007	0.1
6540	Title abstract offices	4	3	0.8	41	21	29,951	37,524	897	643	0.7
6550	Subdividers and developers	11	11	1.1	29	33	13,517	12,606	533	668	0.3
6553	Cemetery subdividers and developers	7	6	1.0	9	8	7,556	10,000	144	132	0.1
SCHENECTADY, NY											
60 –	**Finance, insurance, and real estate**	243	234	0.4	2,668	2,414	25,276	27,804	72,612	64,607	0.1
6000	Depository institutions	67	64	1.0	946	894	21,552	24,282	22,619	21,121	0.2
6020	Commercial banks	40	36	0.9	651	615	23,404	23,779	17,153	15,374	0.2
6030	Savings institutions	10	12	1.0	164	158	17,707	28,937	3,177	3,262	0.4
6060	Credit unions	17	16	2.3	131	121	17,160	20,760	2,289	2,485	-
6100	Nondepository institutions	8	8	0.4	79	67	15,291	25,313	1,416	1,671	0.1
6140	Personal credit institutions	4	5	1.1	21	25	15,810	39,840	561	920	0.2
6200	Security and commodity brokers	7	9	0.1	41	38	79,415	81,263	2,616	2,398	0.0
6300	Insurance carriers	16	16	0.6	563	569	23,972	28,872	14,401	15,570	0.3
6330	Fire, marine, and casualty insurance	7	8	0.5	84	50	32,048	38,960	2,348	1,703	0.1
6400	Insurance agents, brokers, and service	61	59	0.8	562	393	31,395	31,542	17,761	12,070	0.5
6500	Real estate	80	74	0.3	438	423	24,338	26,667	12,949	11,232	0.3
6510	Real estate operators and lessors	37	37	0.2	194	197	30,351	32,061	7,476	6,787	0.4
6530	Real estate agents and managers	31	27	0.3	203	190	19,212	22,968	4,568	3,803	0.2
SCHOHARIE, NY											
60 –	**Finance, insurance, and real estate**	58	58	0.1	296	382	22,108	22,911	6,982	9,803	0.0
6000	Depository institutions	10	10	0.2	95	93	19,074	19,355	1,808	1,794	0.0
6400	Insurance agents, brokers, and service	13	12	0.2	65	54	16,985	17,185	1,317	966	0.0
6500	Real estate	27	25	0.1	43	58	15,256	16,207	818	874	0.0
6510	Real estate operators and lessors	9	9	0.1	14	30	15,714	15,733	288	437	0.0
6530	Real estate agents and managers	8	7	0.1	25	24	16,480	17,833	455	355	0.0
6550	Subdividers and developers	10	9	0.9	4	4	6,000	10,000	75	82	0.0
6553	Cemetery subdividers and developers	10	9	1.5	4	4	6,000	10,000	75	82	0.1
SENECA, NY											
60 –	**Finance, insurance, and real estate**	41	40	0.1	178	167	21,618	23,186	3,980	4,106	0.0
6000	Depository institutions	14	14	0.2	99	96	18,505	19,583	1,864	1,883	0.0
6020	Commercial banks	8	9	0.2	55	60	17,236	17,933	951	1,010	0.0
6500	Real estate	11	10	0.0	28	22	12,857	12,182	380	312	0.0
6530	Real estate agents and managers	6	6	0.1	14	12	11,429	12,333	165	182	0.0
STEUBEN, NY											
60 –	**Finance, insurance, and real estate**	155	146	0.3	1,129	1,074	22,742	24,838	26,927	27,286	0.1
6000	Depository institutions	54	51	0.8	625	613	22,944	25,096	15,497	15,646	0.2
6020	Commercial banks	33	33	0.9	370	373	18,800	21,716	8,006	7,913	0.1

Source: County Business Patterns, 1994/95, CBP-94/95, U.S. Department of Commerce, Washington, D.C., November 1997. SIC categories for which data were suppressed or not available for both 1994 and 1995 are not displayed. The employment columns represent mid-March employment in the year. Pay per employee is calculated by dividing 1st Quarter payroll, annualized, by mid-March employment. The columns headed "% State" show the county's percentage of the state total for the SIC in 1995; for example, 1.4% for SIC 6000 means that the county had 1.4 percent of the state's total establishments (or payroll) in SIC 6000 in 1995. A dash (-) is used to indicate that data are not available or cannot be calculated; nec means not elsewhere classified.

Continued on next page.

SIC	Industry	No. Establishments			Employment		Pay / Employee		Annual Payroll ($ 000)		
		1994	1995	% State	1994	1995	1994	1995	1994	1995	% State
STEUBEN, NY - [continued]											
6060	Credit unions	15	15	2.2	205	216	29,151	28,481	6,283	6,685	-
6300	Insurance carriers	9	9	0.3	110	87	25,382	27,724	2,529	2,289	0.0
6400	Insurance agents, brokers, and service	35	35	0.5	171	167	22,550	23,210	3,928	4,188	0.2
6500	Real estate	48	45	0.2	164	158	13,854	14,658	2,524	2,480	0.1
6510	Real estate operators and lessors	17	17	0.1	55	50	12,291	12,400	772	674	0.0
6530	Real estate agents and managers	20	18	0.2	79	76	14,228	16,263	1,226	1,264	0.1
6553	Cemetery subdividers and developers	9	8	1.3	17	18	6,118	5,111	151	149	0.1
SUFFOLK, NY											
60 –	**Finance, insurance, and real estate**	2,793	2,869	5.2	29,654	28,971	35,876	36,673	1,081,007	1,094,912	2.4
6000	Depository institutions	446	445	6.7	9,033	8,943	35,581	39,583	331,386	351,962	3.4
6020	Commercial banks	318	324	8.5	6,196	6,378	40,145	43,971	254,520	279,424	4.3
6030	Savings institutions	97	89	7.2	2,140	1,813	24,022	26,822	56,542	50,074	6.3
6090	Functions closely related to banking	12	13	2.3	302	318	39,179	40,164	10,240		2.5
6100	Nondepository institutions	174	190	10.5	2,786	2,754	34,793	36,430	92,482	103,498	5.5
6140	Personal credit institutions	39	45	10.0	691	730	33,991	30,164	19,840	20,623	3.9
6150	Business credit institutions	32	28	6.7	755	601	39,481	61,285	29,728	35,072	4.1
6160	Mortgage bankers and brokers	100	111	12.7	1,333	1,406	32,612	28,970	42,641	46,982	9.7
6200	Security and commodity brokers	174	176	2.6	1,812	1,623	89,585	67,842	134,568	117,471	0.6
6210	Security brokers and dealers	81	81	1.8	1,563	1,375	97,321	73,673	124,545	107,254	0.7
6220	Commodity contracts brokers, dealers	11	11	3.6	30	28	41,467	41,429	1,792	1,593	0.9
6280	Security and commodity services	80	80	4.6	218	219	41,119	34,667	8,219	8,509	0.3
6300	Insurance carriers	213	223	8.4	7,344	7,061	32,745	35,176	250,646	246,318	4.8
6310	Life insurance	51	51	7.0	2,951	3,246	26,594	28,158	77,641	85,381	4.2
6320	Medical service and health insurance	6	10	7.2	750	667	31,008	35,076	28,010	26,960	3.6
6324	Hospital and medical service plans	6	7	7.4	750	635	31,008	34,494	28,010	25,455	3.7
6330	Fire, marine, and casualty insurance	135	141	9.7	3,369	2,918	38,857	43,260	138,886	127,051	6.2
6360	Title insurance	8	8	10.4	134	132	43,463	41,091	4,331	4,935	9.0
6370	Pension, health, and welfare funds	11	10	5.4	133	91	13,774	18,813	1,686	1,711	1.7
6400	Insurance agents, brokers, and service	651	665	9.2	3,370	3,657	31,278	32,120	114,486	124,985	5.5
6500	Real estate	1,049	1,083	3.8	4,266	4,123	21,907	24,779	109,028	114,244	2.6
6510	Real estate operators and lessors	372	365	2.4	1,451	1,377	20,733	21,641	33,837	33,223	2.0
6530	Real estate agents and managers	548	569	5.3	2,093	2,006	21,068	25,362	52,677	55,819	2.4
6540	Title abstract offices	44	40	10.2	239	177	23,381	25,898	5,547	4,793	5.5
6550	Subdividers and developers	60	64	6.2	422	457	30,654	31,877	15,438	16,935	8.6
6552	Subdividers and developers, n.e.c.	26	26	6.9	62	67	25,226	28,418	1,744	2,009	2.1
6553	Cemetery subdividers and developers	29	29	4.8	360	372	31,589	33,387	13,516	14,373	14.2
6710	Holding offices	40	35	5.2	810	503	46,114	43,229	40,164	26,637	2.2
6790	Miscellaneous investing	29	32	5.0	116	135	34,241	36,593	4,971	5,625	1.0
6794	Patent owners and lessors	9	9	6.9	60	63	32,733	40,381	2,633	2,861	2.4
SULLIVAN, NY											
60 –	**Finance, insurance, and real estate**	189	193	0.3	1,742	1,710	27,171	53,273	57,918	68,961	0.1
6000	Depository institutions	38	35	0.5	391	342	18,650	21,509	7,815	7,506	0.1
6020	Commercial banks	29	27	0.7	335	290	18,937	22,028	6,754	6,505	0.1
6200	Security and commodity brokers	7	9	0.1	10	24	16,800	15,167	256	358	0.0
6210	Security brokers and dealers	3	4	0.1	3	8	20,000	11,000	81	80	0.0
6280	Security and commodity services	4	5	0.3	7	16	15,429	17,250	175	278	0.0
6330	Fire, marine, and casualty insurance	4	6	0.4	36	46	36,889	37,304	1,392	1,697	0.1
6400	Insurance agents, brokers, and service	38	38	0.5	244	247	24,623	32,632	7,922	7,865	0.3
6500	Real estate	88	95	0.3	261	290	13,579	14,621	4,369	5,036	0.1
6510	Real estate operators and lessors	41	45	0.3	112	127	16,000	16,945	2,157	2,566	0.2
6530	Real estate agents and managers	36	36	0.3	115	129	10,678	13,085	1,692	1,942	0.1
6540	Title abstract offices	4	4	1.0	25	24	16,320	13,500	400	312	0.4
6550	Subdividers and developers	7	7	0.7	9	9	12,889	7,556	120	194	0.1
TIOGA, NY											
60 –	**Finance, insurance, and real estate**	52	47	0.1	285	264	18,414	20,076	5,541	5,350	0.0

Source: County Business Patterns, 1994/95, CBP-94/95, U.S. Department of Commerce, Washington, D.C., November 1997. SIC categories for which data were suppressed or not available for both 1994 and 1995 are *not* displayed. The employment columns represent mid-March employment in the year. Pay per employee is calculated by dividing 1st Quarter payroll, annualized, by mid-March employment. The columns headed "% State" show the county's percentage of the state total for the SIC in 1995; for example, 1.4% for SIC 6000 means that the county had 1.4 percent of the state's total establishments (or payroll) in SIC 6000 in 1995. A dash (-) is used to indicate that data are not available or cannot be calculated; *nec* means not elsewhere classified.

Continued on next page.

SIC	Industry	No. Establishments			Employment		Pay / Employee		Annual Payroll ($ 000)		
		1994	1995	% State	1994	1995	1994	1995	1994	1995	% State
TIOGA, NY - [continued]											
6000	Depository institutions	16	16	0.2	171	150	18,807	20,933	3,402	3,013	0.0
6400	Insurance agents, brokers, and service	14	14	0.2	55	55	20,145	23,636	1,138	1,351	0.1
6500	Real estate	15	11	0.0	42	47	13,810	13,106	699	736	0.0
6510	Real estate operators and lessors	5	3	0.0	13	11	10,462	12,364	127	123	0.0
6550	Subdividers and developers	8	6	0.6	4	4	9,000	5,000	65	52	0.0
TOMPKINS, NY											
60 –	**Finance, insurance, and real estate**	169	173	0.3	1,312	1,322	24,165	22,974	34,743	31,885	0.1
6000	Depository institutions	35	35	0.5	636	570	21,730	20,414	15,878	12,339	0.1
6020	Commercial banks	19	19	0.5	345	349	19,559	22,384	7,358	7,946	0.1
6140	Personal credit institutions	3	4	0.9	10	9	31,200	36,889	252	335	0.1
6200	Security and commodity brokers	14	14	0.2	68	66	65,824	60,364	3,683	3,756	0.0
6210	Security brokers and dealers	6	7	0.2	59	55	70,305	67,709	3,332	3,399	0.0
6280	Security and commodity services	8	7	0.4	9	11	36,444	23,636	351	357	0.0
6300	Insurance carriers	10	8	0.3	75	74	30,453	28,865	2,150	2,163	0.0
6400	Insurance agents, brokers, and service	28	25	0.3	138	143	25,072	27,916	4,170	4,545	0.2
6500	Real estate	72	77	0.3	368	436	17,804	16,743	7,653	7,565	0.2
6510	Real estate operators and lessors	35	36	0.2	180	253	15,689	13,439	3,261	3,441	0.2
6530	Real estate agents and managers	23	27	0.3	163	162	20,933	22,395	3,776	3,816	0.2
6540	Title abstract offices	3	3	0.8	15	11	15,467	17,455	250	177	0.2
6550	Subdividers and developers	11	10	1.0	10	10	8,400	8,000	366	128	0.1
ULSTER, NY											
60 –	**Finance, insurance, and real estate**	314	285	0.5	3,139	2,594	21,242	21,772	69,430	60,099	0.1
6000	Depository institutions	68	59	0.9	987	813	20,138	20,394	19,783	16,931	0.2
6020	Commercial banks	42	39	1.0	400	328	17,120	19,512	7,109	6,268	0.1
6030	Savings institutions	15	10	0.8	442	331	23,167	20,991	9,190	7,314	0.9
6060	Credit unions	11	10	1.4	145	154	19,228	20,987	3,484	3,349	-
6140	Personal credit institutions	5	4	0.9	19	16	20,632	23,250	348	332	0.1
6400	Insurance agents, brokers, and service	62	61	0.8	318	308	23,874	27,169	8,432	8,165	0.4
6500	Real estate	129	119	0.4	317	260	14,233	15,431	4,929	4,296	0.1
6510	Real estate operators and lessors	53	50	0.3	171	135	13,567	16,237	2,512	2,354	0.1
6530	Real estate agents and managers	51	46	0.4	98	77	16,286	16,416	1,661	1,268	0.1
6540	Title abstract offices	6	4	1.0	18	13	18,444	20,000	342	293	0.3
6550	Subdividers and developers	16	16	1.5	30	33	8,800	8,121	348	342	0.2
WARREN, NY											
60 –	**Finance, insurance, and real estate**	144	143	0.3	2,208	2,060	28,935	31,870	61,445	63,341	0.1
6000	Depository institutions	28	27	0.4	384	549	21,156	24,656	8,618	14,172	0.1
6020	Commercial banks	20	18	0.5	314	467	22,369	25,345	7,356	12,653	0.2
6030	Savings institutions	5	6	0.5	58	69	15,241	20,870	1,040	1,290	0.2
6060	Credit unions	3	3	0.4	12	13	18,000	20,000	222	229	-
6300	Insurance carriers	10	10	0.4	1,023	944	32,594	34,275	30,361	31,025	0.6
6400	Insurance agents, brokers, and service	36	35	0.5	221	203	35,113	40,059	7,525	7,100	0.3
6500	Real estate	54	53	0.2	174	123	18,069	21,593	2,979	2,685	0.1
6510	Real estate operators and lessors	29	29	0.2	101	72	15,644	19,444	1,590	1,578	0.1
6550	Subdividers and developers	7	8	0.8	16	16	13,500	17,000	279	309	0.2
6700	Holding and other investment offices	6	6	0.3	345	177	22,423	30,282	9,048	5,289	0.3
WASHINGTON, NY											
60 –	**Finance, insurance, and real estate**	61	63	0.1	256	274	22,125	21,854	6,253	6,740	0.0
6000	Depository institutions	17	17	0.3	120	134	17,100	17,463	2,054	2,605	0.0
6400	Insurance agents, brokers, and service	18	19	0.3	77	76	21,870	21,684	2,045	1,977	0.1
6510	Real estate operators and lessors	6	5	0.0	8	5	7,500	4,800	74	28	0.0
6530	Real estate agents and managers	6	6	0.1	16	20	9,250	8,000	187	191	0.0
6550	Subdividers and developers	9	9	0.9	12	13	11,333	11,385	240	229	0.1
WAYNE, NY											
60 –	**Finance, insurance, and real estate**	114	110	0.2	545	551	21,189	20,799	11,712	11,627	0.0

Source: County Business Patterns, 1994/95, CBP-94/95, U.S. Department of Commerce, Washington, D.C., November 1997. SIC categories for which data were suppressed or not available for both 1994 and 1995 are not displayed. The employment columns represent mid-March employment in the year. Pay per employee is calculated by dividing 1st Quarter payroll, annualized, by mid-March employment. The columns headed "% State" show the county's percentage of the state total for the SIC in 1995; for example, 1.4% for SIC 6000 means that the county had 1.4 percent of the state's total establishments (or payroll) in SIC 6000 in 1995. A dash (-) is used to indicate that data are not available or cannot be calculated; nec means not elsewhere classified.

Continued on next page.

SIC	Industry	No. Establishments			Employment		Pay / Employee		Annual Payroll ($ 000)		
		1994	1995	% State	1994	1995	1994	1995	1994	1995	% State
WAYNE, NY - [continued]											
6000	Depository institutions	24	23	0.3	267	287	20,075	18,983	5,345	5,510	0.1
6020	Commercial banks	18	17	0.4	172	174	20,186	20,920	3,448	3,636	0.1
6400	Insurance agents, brokers, and service	32	30	0.4	124	117	24,258	27,009	3,044	3,182	0.1
6500	Real estate	48	46	0.2	91	81	13,978	14,815	1,564	1,405	0.0
6510	Real estate operators and lessors	24	21	0.1	65	56	13,538	14,000	875	766	0.0
WESTCHESTER, NY											
60 –	**Finance, insurance, and real estate**	3,700	3,730	6.7	28,086	32,338	37,913	42,226	1,130,341	1,336,509	2.9
6000	Depository institutions	383	377	5.7	6,489	5,978	30,579	34,120	175,214	179,974	1.8
6020	Commercial banks	267	271	7.1	5,132	4,886	30,963	34,599	134,002	144,838	2.2
6030	Savings institutions	65	54	4.3	1,000	782	30,532	33,887	31,405	26,059	3.3
6060	Credit unions	27	27	3.9	239	190	26,025	29,158	6,872	5,803	-
6100	Nondepository institutions	151	150	8.3	2,013	3,530	47,573	44,806	85,228	139,627	7.4
6140	Personal credit institutions	27	28	6.2	343	335	32,455	39,212	11,393	12,059	2.3
6150	Business credit institutions	36	28	6.7	590	2,171	70,285	49,063	32,501	84,654	9.9
6160	Mortgage bankers and brokers	86	91	10.4	1,078	1,019	40,022	37,751	41,308	42,840	8.9
6200	Security and commodity brokers	230	240	3.6	2,365	2,431	71,978	77,290	225,852	277,143	1.4
6210	Security brokers and dealers	96	102	2.2	1,560	1,756	73,700	81,991	130,800	165,721	1.0
6220	Commodity contracts brokers, dealers	10	11	3.6	30	32	50,667	62,250	1,855	1,817	1.0
6280	Security and commodity services	121	123	7.0	769	635	68,801	63,975	92,523	108,778	3.4
6300	Insurance carriers	205	213	8.1	5,006	4,689	41,020	48,534	211,217	235,513	4.6
6310	Life insurance	55	65	9.0	2,137	2,149	37,247	47,899	75,562	89,415	4.4
6320	Medical service and health insurance	10	12	8.7	511	476	30,857	29,504	14,418	14,371	1.9
6330	Fire, marine, and casualty insurance	111	111	7.6	2,144	1,890	46,336	53,820	112,368	123,412	6.0
6360	Title insurance	11	12	15.6	117	106	55,385	56,906	5,314	4,901	8.9
6400	Insurance agents, brokers, and service	494	493	6.8	3,211	3,224	35,826	46,988	130,038	144,087	6.3
6500	Real estate	2,088	2,106	7.5	8,121	8,023	28,063	29,638	251,573	253,346	5.8
6510	Real estate operators and lessors	921	935	6.1	2,768	2,529	23,035	23,932	69,698	65,425	3.8
6530	Real estate agents and managers	1,034	999	9.3	4,605	4,572	30,628	32,430	154,057	154,481	6.7
6540	Title abstract offices	29	31	7.9	200	193	33,700	33,824	7,766	7,216	8.3
6550	Subdividers and developers	71	73	7.1	528	622	30,295	33,498	18,861	23,277	11.8
6552	Subdividers and developers, n.e.c.	47	51	13.5	177	266	24,181	31,308	6,819	10,542	11.2
6553	Cemetery subdividers and developers	20	20	3.3	351	354	33,379	35,266	12,008	12,695	12.6
6700	Holding and other investment offices	145	148	7.6	648	4,358	67,142	44,855	42,468	103,140	4.9
6710	Holding offices	56	51	7.5	419	304	78,158	92,974	29,471	27,147	2.2
6720	Investment offices	5	8	8.4	11	17	50,545	41,647	456	694	0.5
6730	Trusts	26	33	7.4	55	100	29,527	30,320	1,555	2,447	2.5
6732	Educational, religious, etc. trusts	13	21	7.6	27	54	23,259	22,296	578	1,251	1.6
6733	Trusts, n.e.c.	13	12	7.3	28	46	35,571	39,739	977	1,196	5.3
6790	Miscellaneous investing	54	47	7.3	161	232	52,770	67,086	10,873	12,794	2.4
6799	Investors, n.e.c.	40	33	7.1	101	176	50,535	68,000	7,171	9,284	2.4
WYOMING, NY											
60 –	**Finance, insurance, and real estate**	47	47	0.1	375	423	23,040	23,924	8,971	9,541	0.0
6000	Depository institutions	17	17	0.3	237	238	22,127	25,160	5,326	5,379	0.1
6400	Insurance agents, brokers, and service	12	11	0.2	80	88	25,800	25,045	2,332	2,369	0.1
6500	Real estate	13	14	0.0	26	24	9,538	11,667	283	297	0.0
6510	Real estate operators and lessors	5	6	0.0	8	10	5,000	5,600	47	48	0.0
6530	Real estate agents and managers	4	4	0.0	10	6	7,600	16,000	86	99	0.0
YATES, NY											
60 –	**Finance, insurance, and real estate**	30	29	0.1	149	143	18,443	19,049	2,889	2,850	0.0
6500	Real estate	12	15	0.1	50	56	19,600	15,643	984	978	0.0

Source: County Business Patterns, 1994/95, CBP-94/95, U.S. Department of Commerce, Washington, D.C., November 1997. SIC categories for which data were suppressed or not available for both 1994 and 1995 are not displayed. The employment columns represent mid-March employment in the year. Pay per employee is calculated by dividing 1st Quarter payroll, annualized, by mid-March employment. The columns headed "% State" show the county's percentage of the state total for the SIC in 1995; for example, 1.4% for SIC 6000 means that the county had 1.4 percent of the state's total establishments (or payroll) in SIC 6000 in 1995. A dash (-) is used to indicate that data are not available or cannot be calculated; nec means not elsewhere classified.

NORTH CAROLINA

SIC	Industry	No. Establishments			Employment		Pay / Employee		Annual Payroll ($ 000)		
		1994	1995	% State	1994	1995	1994	1995	1994	1995	% State
ALAMANCE, NC											
60 –	**Finance, insurance, and real estate**	212	224	*1.5*	2,091	2,068	30,363	35,427	71,375	75,073	*1.5*
6000	Depository institutions	46	45	*1.5*	533	531	24,833	24,678	13,056	13,691	*0.8*
6020	Commercial banks	29	28	*1.2*	351	353	23,510	23,195	7,935	7,872	*0.5*
6030	Savings institutions	12	12	*3.9*	144	132	29,194	31,394	4,313	4,963	*5.3*
6100	Nondepository institutions	28	31	*2.1*	128	138	23,156	23,913	3,311	3,855	*0.9*
6140	Personal credit institutions	19	19	*2.5*	94	103	23,362	23,806	2,457	2,637	*1.3*
6300	Insurance carriers	18	16	*1.4*	790	778	26,370	26,514	20,577	20,783	*1.9*
6400	Insurance agents, brokers, and service	56	60	*1.9*	458	390	48,314	82,359	30,326	32,056	*7.5*
6500	Real estate	57	63	*1.2*	141	204	14,014	12,314	2,354	3,057	*0.5*
6510	Real estate operators and lessors	22	27	*1.5*	46	107	9,913	9,047	476	1,197	*0.8*
6530	Real estate agents and managers	27	27	*1.0*	61	69	15,279	16,348	1,129	1,346	*0.4*
6550	Subdividers and developers	6	6	*1.1*	31	25	18,452	12,960	693	420	*0.4*
ALEXANDER, NC											
60 –	**Finance, insurance, and real estate**	28	29	*0.2*	125	132	19,712	18,273	2,465	2,564	*0.1*
6000	Depository institutions	12	12	*0.4*	96	97	20,250	19,216	1,941	1,998	*0.1*
6400	Insurance agents, brokers, and service	10	11	*0.3*	20	24	14,000	12,167	289	330	*0.1*
6500	Real estate	3	3	*0.1*	1	2	8,000	10,000	17	20	*0.0*
ALLEGHANY, NC											
60 –	**Finance, insurance, and real estate**	14	15	*0.1*	89	86	17,573	20,093	1,760	2,049	*0.0*
6000	Depository institutions	4	4	*0.1*	49	49	21,224	23,020	1,077	1,257	*0.1*
6020	Commercial banks	4	4	*0.2*	49	49	21,224	23,020	1,077	1,257	*0.1*
ANSON, NC											
60 –	**Finance, insurance, and real estate**	26	29	*0.2*	112	139	20,250	17,842	2,207	2,485	*0.1*
6000	Depository institutions	8	11	*0.4*	71	77	22,085	21,714	1,402	1,635	*0.1*
6500	Real estate	6	6	*0.1*	10	10	14,000	16,800	248	185	*0.0*
ASHE, NC											
60 –	**Finance, insurance, and real estate**	30	33	*0.2*	149	146	17,745	19,671	3,127	3,262	*0.1*
6000	Depository institutions	7	7	*0.2*	61	61	19,475	21,246	1,295	1,398	*0.1*
6400	Insurance agents, brokers, and service	5	5	*0.2*	19	19	23,789	22,526	475	447	*0.1*
6500	Real estate	13	16	*0.3*	51	48	10,824	13,750	868	907	*0.1*
6550	Subdividers and developers	5	5	*0.9*	36	32	8,667	14,875	575	652	*0.6*
AVERY, NC											
60 –	**Finance, insurance, and real estate**	53	54	*0.4*	300	315	16,293	15,975	5,145	5,574	*0.1*
6500	Real estate	43	42	*0.8*	239	249	14,996	14,394	3,873	4,007	*0.6*
6510	Real estate operators and lessors	7	5	*0.3*	6	5	10,000	10,400	63	68	*0.0*
6530	Real estate agents and managers	29	31	*1.1*	220	232	15,127	14,500	3,558	3,705	*1.0*
6550	Subdividers and developers	6	5	*0.9*	13	9	15,077	16,000	230	187	*0.2*
BEAUFORT, NC											
60 –	**Finance, insurance, and real estate**	72	77	*0.5*	385	394	22,036	21,939	8,366	8,622	*0.2*
6000	Depository institutions	19	20	*0.7*	201	211	20,159	20,398	4,085	4,360	*0.3*
6020	Commercial banks	13	13	*0.6*	114	120	19,158	18,867	2,105	2,173	*0.1*
6100	Nondepository institutions	7	9	*0.6*	30	34	24,933	24,706	671	927	*0.2*
6400	Insurance agents, brokers, and service	17	17	*0.5*	50	43	18,080	16,186	821	711	*0.2*
6500	Real estate	26	26	*0.5*	65	66	11,077	10,242	976	867	*0.1*

Source: County Business Patterns, 1994/95, CBP-94/95, U.S. Department of Commerce, Washington, D.C., November 1997. SIC categories for which data were suppressed or not available for both 1994 and 1995 are *not* displayed. The employment columns represent mid-March employment in the year. Pay per employee is calculated by dividing 1st Quarter payroll, annualized, by mid-March employment. The columns headed "% State" show the county's percentage of the state total for the SIC in 1995; for example, 1.4% for SIC 6000 means that the county had 1.4 percent of the state's total establishments (or payroll) in SIC 6000 in 1995. A dash (-) is used to indicate that data are not available or cannot be calculated; *nec* means not elsewhere classified.

Continued on next page.

SIC	Industry	No. Establishments			Employment		Pay / Employee		Annual Payroll ($ 000)		
		1994	1995	% State	1994	1995	1994	1995	1994	1995	% State
BEAUFORT, NC - [continued]											
6510	Real estate operators and lessors	4	4	0.2	9	13	9,333	6,154	87	83	0.1
6530	Real estate agents and managers	15	16	0.6	29	26	13,379	14,154	397	575	0.2
6550	Subdividers and developers	7	6	1.1	27	27	9,185	8,444	492	209	0.2
BERTIE, NC											
60 –	**Finance, insurance, and real estate**	24	24	0.2	82	91	20,829	21,451	1,803	1,847	0.0
6000	Depository institutions	9	9	0.3	50	59	20,320	19,661	1,099	1,134	0.1
BLADEN, NC											
60 –	**Finance, insurance, and real estate**	41	38	0.2	162	167	19,383	20,240	3,270	3,399	0.1
6000	Depository institutions	14	13	0.4	99	92	21,535	22,261	2,087	2,030	0.1
6020	Commercial banks	11	10	0.4	85	77	22,353	23,688	1,850	1,796	0.1
6510	Real estate operators and lessors	4	3	0.2	6	9	16,000	25,333	102	175	0.1
BRUNSWICK, NC											
60 –	**Finance, insurance, and real estate**	148	143	0.9	1,085	1,169	15,207	15,518	18,450	21,550	0.4
6000	Depository institutions	29	28	0.9	201	177	23,443	23,073	4,207	4,481	0.3
6020	Commercial banks	19	18	0.8	149	114	23,114	23,298	2,814	2,864	0.2
6400	Insurance agents, brokers, and service	16	18	0.6	69	74	21,855	20,811	1,554	1,647	0.4
6500	Real estate	90	84	1.5	772	883	12,725	13,454	12,169	14,683	2.3
6510	Real estate operators and lessors	10	10	0.5	23	13	14,087	13,231	387	378	0.2
6530	Real estate agents and managers	58	52	1.8	586	691	12,846	13,800	9,561	11,621	3.1
6550	Subdividers and developers	18	18	3.2	150	173	12,453	11,769	2,113	2,512	2.4
BUNCOMBE, NC											
60 –	**Finance, insurance, and real estate**	424	432	2.8	2,539	2,648	26,056	26,094	69,090	73,377	1.5
6000	Depository institutions	76	74	2.4	964	1,006	25,004	24,231	24,285	24,836	1.4
6020	Commercial banks	47	48	2.1	697	743	25,980	25,093	18,183	18,618	1.2
6100	Nondepository institutions	38	38	2.6	240	188	26,950	33,787	6,083	6,200	1.4
6140	Personal credit institutions	22	21	2.8	119	111	24,067	27,315	3,019	2,935	1.4
6200	Security and commodity brokers	30	30	4.1	164	174	63,512	60,230	10,704	10,531	2.7
6210	Security brokers and dealers	21	22	4.4	134	150	59,075	57,573	7,759	7,939	2.4
6280	Security and commodity services	9	8	3.6	30	24	83,333	76,833	2,945	2,592	4.5
6300	Insurance carriers	34	38	3.4	269	268	31,494	34,134	7,787	8,836	0.8
6310	Life insurance	14	15	3.9	179	170	24,514	26,965	3,907	4,039	1.0
6330	Fire, marine, and casualty insurance	15	16	2.9	58	56	50,414	57,714	2,691	3,115	0.8
6400	Insurance agents, brokers, and service	81	87	2.7	297	301	25,791	25,953	8,861	9,874	2.3
6500	Real estate	155	155	2.8	585	684	13,538	13,936	10,089	11,755	1.8
6510	Real estate operators and lessors	58	58	3.1	182	174	11,934	13,678	2,590	2,748	1.8
6530	Real estate agents and managers	77	78	2.8	325	437	15,458	14,362	6,344	7,947	2.1
6550	Subdividers and developers	18	16	2.9	78	72	9,282	12,056	1,150	1,049	1.0
6552	Subdividers and developers, n.e.c.	8	6	1.6	26	24	14,308	18,000	522	545	0.7
6553	Cemetery subdividers and developers	9	9	5.8	52	48	6,769	9,083	626	497	2.2
6700	Holding and other investment offices	10	10	3.0	20	27	55,800	51,704	1,281	1,345	0.8
BURKE, NC											
60 –	**Finance, insurance, and real estate**	95	96	0.6	440	437	22,564	22,883	10,087	10,445	0.2
6000	Depository institutions	25	26	0.9	233	226	22,901	21,646	5,239	5,201	0.3
6020	Commercial banks	13	17	0.7	145	158	23,807	22,835	3,242	3,781	0.3
6200	Security and commodity brokers	5	6	0.8	16	17	65,000	66,118	972	1,219	0.3
6400	Insurance agents, brokers, and service	21	23	0.7	77	75	21,714	23,200	1,725	1,759	0.4
6500	Real estate	26	25	0.5	57	67	12,421	13,194	738	783	0.1
CABARRUS, NC											
60 –	**Finance, insurance, and real estate**	173	185	1.2	1,147	1,188	25,133	23,306	28,491	26,956	0.5
6000	Depository institutions	36	37	1.2	509	497	27,914	26,761	12,707	10,815	0.6
6020	Commercial banks	31	32	1.4	452	441	27,920	27,519	11,455	10,152	0.7
6140	Personal credit institutions	15	19	2.5	71	76	23,268	24,579	1,680	1,843	0.9

Source: County Business Patterns, 1994/95, CBP-94/95, U.S. Department of Commerce, Washington, D.C., November 1997. SIC categories for which data were suppressed or not available for both 1994 and 1995 are not displayed. The employment columns represent mid-March employment in the year. Pay per employee is calculated by dividing 1st Quarter payroll, annualized, by mid-March employment. The columns headed "% State" show the county's percentage of the state total for the SIC in 1995; for example, 1.4% for SIC 6000 means that the county had 1.4 percent of the state's total establishments (or payroll) in SIC 6000 in 1995. A dash (-) is used to indicate that data are not available or cannot be calculated; nec means not elsewhere classified.

Continued on next page.

SIC	Industry	No. Establishments			Employment		Pay / Employee		Annual Payroll ($ 000)		
		1994	1995	% State	1994	1995	1994	1995	1994	1995	% State
CABARRUS, NC - [continued]											
6300	Insurance carriers	12	12	1.1	94	67	35,660	34,448	3,306	2,408	0.2
6400	Insurance agents, brokers, and service	37	40	1.2	108	125	22,556	21,280	2,627	2,910	0.7
6500	Real estate	62	64	1.2	336	394	19,583	17,584	7,485	8,150	1.3
6510	Real estate operators and lessors	25	25	1.4	235	281	20,051	17,552	5,006	5,402	3.5
6530	Real estate agents and managers	28	28	1.0	67	72	17,254	17,889	1,474	1,709	0.5
6550	Subdividers and developers	6	6	1.1	31	37	20,774	17,297	704	848	0.8
CALDWELL, NC											
60 –	**Finance, insurance, and real estate**	90	92	0.6	473	485	21,285	24,322	9,966	12,372	0.3
6000	Depository institutions	19	19	0.6	222	234	18,955	21,726	4,288	6,294	0.4
6400	Insurance agents, brokers, and service	28	29	0.9	83	81	22,795	25,926	1,709	1,687	0.4
6500	Real estate	25	24	0.4	62	61	14,581	15,475	1,030	1,119	0.2
CAMDEN, NC											
60 –	**Finance, insurance, and real estate**	4	3	0.0	9	28	12,000	8,857	159	164	0.0
CARTERET, NC											
60 –	**Finance, insurance, and real estate**	153	159	1.0	765	781	19,561	20,594	15,967	17,577	0.4
6000	Depository institutions	30	31	1.0	226	237	21,876	23,257	4,858	5,219	0.3
6020	Commercial banks	24	25	1.1	194	201	22,722	24,478	4,293	4,643	0.3
6100	Nondepository institutions	8	12	0.8	43	55	28,279	24,218	1,272	1,644	0.4
6400	Insurance agents, brokers, and service	14	15	0.5	115	128	27,165	24,844	3,630	3,799	0.9
6500	Real estate	90	91	1.7	348	340	12,977	14,729	5,251	5,846	0.9
6510	Real estate operators and lessors	26	23	1.2	75	58	11,147	12,690	895	839	0.5
6530	Real estate agents and managers	55	56	2.0	249	261	13,333	15,464	4,048	4,543	1.2
6550	Subdividers and developers	7	9	1.6	23	18	15,304	11,778	294	410	0.4
CATAWBA, NC											
60 –	**Finance, insurance, and real estate**	269	270	1.8	1,646	1,605	23,852	25,538	39,280	41,198	0.8
6000	Depository institutions	62	63	2.1	734	749	24,082	24,336	18,053	18,193	1.1
6020	Commercial banks	40	42	1.8	471	544	26,429	25,890	12,057	14,257	1.0
6100	Nondepository institutions	23	25	1.7	89	95	26,202	29,516	2,196	2,668	0.6
6140	Personal credit institutions	16	18	2.4	68	70	23,882	27,029	1,617	1,932	0.9
6160	Mortgage bankers and brokers	4	4	0.8	14	15	30,857	30,667	434	533	0.3
6200	Security and commodity brokers	13	10	1.4	142	42	28,338	55,143	2,607	2,519	0.6
6300	Insurance carriers	18	19	1.7	155	180	32,568	37,889	5,020	6,138	0.6
6310	Life insurance	6	7	1.8	108	121	26,704	31,769	2,742	3,240	0.8
6400	Insurance agents, brokers, and service	66	68	2.1	241	235	23,071	24,443	6,001	6,065	1.4
6500	Real estate	82	80	1.5	271	290	16,177	16,662	5,303	5,522	0.9
6510	Real estate operators and lessors	28	26	1.4	120	107	12,900	15,327	1,829	1,706	1.1
6530	Real estate agents and managers	45	44	1.6	127	152	19,843	17,974	2,998	3,135	0.8
6550	Subdividers and developers	6	6	1.1	21	27	13,905	15,111	440	605	0.6
6700	Holding and other investment offices	5	5	1.5	14	14	16,857	17,429	100	93	0.1
CHATHAM, NC											
60 –	**Finance, insurance, and real estate**	46	49	0.3	287	304	20,711	21,750	6,606	8,006	0.2
6000	Depository institutions	16	16	0.5	111	100	20,685	22,280	2,202	2,255	0.1
6020	Commercial banks	12	12	0.5	83	73	21,205	23,068	1,612	1,643	0.1
6400	Insurance agents, brokers, and service	13	14	0.4	34	35	18,118	21,829	750	870	0.2
CHEROKEE, NC											
60 –	**Finance, insurance, and real estate**	43	37	0.2	201	200	19,622	17,860	3,928	3,629	0.1
6000	Depository institutions	12	13	0.4	111	120	19,676	19,833	2,259	2,185	0.1
6020	Commercial banks	8	8	0.3	86	91	18,372	18,725	1,690	1,538	0.1
6400	Insurance agents, brokers, and service	10	6	0.2	38	18	25,895	20,222	564	371	0.1

Source: County Business Patterns, 1994/95, CBP-94/95, U.S. Department of Commerce, Washington, D.C., November 1997. SIC categories for which data were suppressed or not available for both 1994 and 1995 are *not* displayed. The employment columns represent mid-March employment in the year. Pay per employee is calculated by dividing 1st Quarter payroll, annualized, by mid-March employment. The columns headed "% State" show the county's percentage of the state total for the SIC in 1995; for example, 1.4% for SIC 6000 means that the county had 1.4 percent of the state's total establishments (or payroll) in SIC 6000 in 1995. A dash (-) is used to indicate that data are not available or cannot be calculated; *nec* means not elsewhere classified.

Continued on next page.

SIC	Industry	No. Establishments			Employment		Pay / Employee		Annual Payroll ($ 000)		
		1994	1995	% State	1994	1995	1994	1995	1994	1995	% State
CHEROKEE, NC - [continued]											
6500	Real estate	16	13	0.2	34	41	9,765	9,854	629	635	0.1
6510	Real estate operators and lessors	6	5	0.3	20	24	10,000	10,833	332	350	0.2
6530	Real estate agents and managers	7	6	0.2	12	12	10,333	10,667	272	255	0.1
CHOWAN, NC											
60 –	**Finance, insurance, and real estate**	24	26	0.2	118	135	23,153	22,519	2,974	3,403	0.1
6000	Depository institutions	6	7	0.2	49	57	26,449	23,439	1,285	1,506	0.1
6400	Insurance agents, brokers, and service	6	5	0.2	17	17	22,118	20,471	393	314	0.1
6500	Real estate	6	7	0.1	8	14	12,500	11,143	134	229	0.0
CLAY, NC											
60 –	**Finance, insurance, and real estate**	16	19	0.1	63	66	19,429	15,212	1,531	1,487	0.0
6000	Depository institutions	4	4	0.1	25	30	19,520	17,733	512	520	0.0
6020	Commercial banks	4	4	0.2	25	30	19,520	17,733	512	520	0.0
6400	Insurance agents, brokers, and service	3	3	0.1	16	6	23,250	7,333	157	70	0.0
6500	Real estate	9	12	0.2	22	30	16,545	14,267	862	897	0.1
6530	Real estate agents and managers	6	7	0.2	21	21	17,143	17,333	514	503	0.1
CLEVELAND, NC											
60 –	**Finance, insurance, and real estate**	128	139	0.9	893	874	22,020	23,954	19,956	21,600	0.4
6000	Depository institutions	37	40	1.3	441	429	20,082	22,284	9,133	9,852	0.6
6020	Commercial banks	23	27	1.2	285	291	19,733	22,323	5,813	7,374	0.5
6030	Savings institutions	9	8	2.6	123	101	21,626	24,356	2,762	1,891	2.0
6060	Credit unions	5	5	1.5	33	37	17,333	16,324	558	587	0.8
6100	Nondepository institutions	14	14	1.0	54	56	24,963	24,714	1,276	1,368	0.3
6300	Insurance carriers	8	10	0.9	81	79	37,728	39,848	2,795	2,861	0.3
6400	Insurance agents, brokers, and service	21	22	0.7	107	101	28,935	26,574	2,965	2,951	0.7
6500	Real estate	41	43	0.8	185	181	11,589	14,807	2,617	2,951	0.5
6510	Real estate operators and lessors	19	21	1.1	108	98	10,222	15,102	1,254	1,693	1.1
COLUMBUS, NC											
60 –	**Finance, insurance, and real estate**	78	83	0.5	731	830	28,596	30,675	21,070	21,723	0.4
6000	Depository institutions	25	29	1.0	470	508	25,166	25,874	11,736	12,154	0.7
6100	Nondepository institutions	5	6	0.4	21	22	25,714	30,182	583	596	0.1
6400	Insurance agents, brokers, and service	24	24	0.7	80	80	19,200	18,700	1,738	1,444	0.3
6500	Real estate	17	17	0.3	31	35	13,032	14,057	703	779	0.1
6510	Real estate operators and lessors	7	7	0.4	11	12	13,091	14,333	227	252	0.2
CRAVEN, NC											
60 –	**Finance, insurance, and real estate**	157	167	1.1	865	861	23,084	23,289	20,297	20,920	0.4
6000	Depository institutions	35	32	1.1	399	400	21,163	22,210	8,482	8,458	0.5
6020	Commercial banks	25	22	1.0	255	255	24,063	24,580	5,978	5,805	0.4
6100	Nondepository institutions	16	20	1.4	102	77	27,216	28,260	1,993	2,182	0.5
6140	Personal credit institutions	11	12	1.6	57	52	18,035	23,154	1,078	1,215	0.6
6280	Security and commodity services	6	6	2.7	3	7	13,333	7,429	69	55	0.1
6400	Insurance agents, brokers, and service	34	36	1.1	118	132	20,441	23,091	3,112	3,710	0.9
6500	Real estate	49	55	1.0	181	175	15,757	16,503	3,416	3,067	0.5
6510	Real estate operators and lessors	13	15	0.8	43	45	11,070	12,711	543	587	0.4
6530	Real estate agents and managers	28	28	1.0	79	81	24,304	23,654	2,194	1,833	0.5
6550	Subdividers and developers	8	9	1.6	59	48	7,729	8,167	679	548	0.5
CUMBERLAND, NC											
60 –	**Finance, insurance, and real estate**	541	572	3.7	3,302	3,370	22,435	22,884	78,641	83,106	1.7
6000	Depository institutions	84	87	2.9	1,053	1,026	20,517	20,612	20,449	21,955	1.3
6020	Commercial banks	59	64	2.8	767	733	21,721	21,714	15,433	16,768	1.1
6060	Credit unions	13	13	3.8	190	198	17,789	19,354	3,406	3,686	5.0
6100	Nondepository institutions	60	72	4.9	404	488	29,525	30,426	12,147	16,633	3.7
6140	Personal credit institutions	26	31	4.1	189	217	26,709	27,908	4,840	5,754	2.8

Source: County Business Patterns, 1994/95, CBP-94/95, U.S. Department of Commerce, Washington, D.C., November 1997. SIC categories for which data were suppressed or not available for both 1994 and 1995 are not displayed. The employment columns represent mid-March employment in the year. Pay per employee is calculated by dividing 1st Quarter payroll, annualized, by mid-March employment. The columns headed "% State" show the county's percentage of the state total for the SIC in 1995; for example, 1.4% for SIC 6000 means that the county had 1.4 percent of the state's total establishments (or payroll) in SIC 6000 in 1995. A dash (-) is used to indicate that data are not available or cannot be calculated; nec means not elsewhere classified.

Continued on next page.

SIC	Industry	No. Establishments			Employment		Pay / Employee		Annual Payroll ($ 000)		
		1994	1995	% State	1994	1995	1994	1995	1994	1995	% State
CUMBERLAND, NC - [continued]											
6160	Mortgage bankers and brokers	24	31	6.2	171	233	31,906	31,622	6,030	9,585	5.7
6200	Security and commodity brokers	20	24	3.3	112	116	42,214	37,000	4,094	4,351	1.1
6210	Security brokers and dealers	9	11	2.2	80	77	53,450	49,818	3,670	3,683	1.1
6300	Insurance carriers	40	41	3.6	464	452	30,078	29,124	13,538	13,296	1.2
6310	Life insurance	19	20	5.2	337	329	26,362	24,960	8,302	7,726	2.0
6400	Insurance agents, brokers, and service	114	117	3.6	354	358	18,271	20,201	7,068	7,583	1.8
6500	Real estate	217	222	4.1	897	901	16,491	17,168	20,533	18,181	2.8
6510	Real estate operators and lessors	92	94	5.1	460	479	16,043	16,559	11,964	10,193	6.5
6530	Real estate agents and managers	101	103	3.6	338	321	17,728	19,078	6,334	6,192	1.7
6550	Subdividers and developers	19	15	2.7	91	94	14,374	13,617	2,115	1,622	1.6
6552	Subdividers and developers, n.e.c.	13	10	2.7	46	51	14,609	13,961	1,349	898	1.1
6553	Cemetery subdividers and developers	6	5	3.2	45	43	14,133	13,209	766	724	3.2
CURRITUCK, NC											
60 –	**Finance, insurance, and real estate**	21	25	0.2	112	125	19,821	21,408	2,538	3,063	0.1
6530	Real estate agents and managers	10	10	0.4	58	67	18,897	18,806	1,396	1,722	0.5
DARE, NC											
60 –	**Finance, insurance, and real estate**	127	137	0.9	928	948	17,043	18,215	17,976	20,350	0.4
6000	Depository institutions	21	24	0.8	157	156	23,592	24,359	3,396	3,687	0.2
6400	Insurance agents, brokers, and service	13	13	0.4	55	56	20,727	24,357	1,392	1,539	0.4
6500	Real estate	79	86	1.6	675	695	13,760	15,401	11,700	13,504	2.1
6510	Real estate operators and lessors	9	11	0.6	25	18	13,600	15,556	446	452	0.3
6530	Real estate agents and managers	65	70	2.5	643	672	13,723	15,327	11,117	12,949	3.5
DAVIDSON, NC											
60 –	**Finance, insurance, and real estate**	170	173	1.1	1,037	1,061	22,862	23,378	24,404	25,947	0.5
6000	Depository institutions	40	38	1.3	581	558	23,931	24,100	14,102	13,847	0.8
6020	Commercial banks	35	33	1.4	527	501	23,848	24,072	12,680	12,040	0.8
6400	Insurance agents, brokers, and service	35	34	1.1	140	155	25,886	27,381	3,700	4,338	1.0
6500	Real estate	70	71	1.3	258	279	17,426	17,907	4,865	5,335	0.8
6510	Real estate operators and lessors	39	36	2.0	80	66	10,450	11,394	961	882	0.6
6530	Real estate agents and managers	24	29	1.0	146	180	19,178	19,822	3,127	3,820	1.0
6550	Subdividers and developers	5	4	0.7	31	31	26,968	21,032	745	598	0.6
DAVIE, NC											
60 –	**Finance, insurance, and real estate**	30	31	0.2	130	126	24,431	25,651	3,080	3,309	0.1
6000	Depository institutions	11	11	0.4	88	83	23,591	23,952	2,018	2,068	0.1
6400	Insurance agents, brokers, and service	5	5	0.2	20	19	27,800	33,684	517	551	0.1
6500	Real estate	6	6	0.1	8	9	20,000	15,111	182	171	0.0
DUPLIN, NC											
60 –	**Finance, insurance, and real estate**	54	56	0.4	230	217	20,365	20,516	5,050	4,492	0.1
6000	Depository institutions	22	21	0.7	139	125	20,892	20,576	2,630	2,440	0.1
6020	Commercial banks	18	17	0.7	124	108	21,258	21,185	2,341	2,148	0.1
6400	Insurance agents, brokers, and service	15	17	0.5	50	50	19,840	20,160	1,553	1,141	0.3
6550	Subdividers and developers	4	4	0.7	4	5	11,000	12,800	53	73	0.1
DURHAM, NC											
60 –	**Finance, insurance, and real estate**	447	471	3.1	4,028	4,136	31,722	32,490	125,389	132,987	2.7
6000	Depository institutions	88	90	3.0	1,636	1,520	29,663	28,711	45,120	41,895	2.4
6020	Commercial banks	62	63	2.7	1,401	1,299	28,942	29,604	37,272	36,434	2.4
6030	Savings institutions	15	15	4.9	148	105	43,486	31,695	5,930	3,354	3.6
6060	Credit unions	6	7	2.1	72	89	17,722	16,899	1,558	1,727	2.3
6090	Functions closely related to banking	5	5	7.9	15	27	17,867	13,037	360	380	-
6100	Nondepository institutions	33	33	2.2	164	168	31,561	36,476	4,804	5,715	1.3
6160	Mortgage bankers and brokers	13	13	2.6	85	85	42,729	49,506	3,080	3,771	2.2
6200	Security and commodity brokers	25	28	3.8	202	241	64,040	66,058	11,524	13,881	3.6

Source: County Business Patterns, 1994/95, CBP-94/95, U.S. Department of Commerce, Washington, D.C., November 1997. SIC categories for which data were suppressed or not available for both 1994 and 1995 are not displayed. The employment columns represent mid-March employment in the year. Pay per employee is calculated by dividing 1st Quarter payroll, annualized, by mid-March employment. The columns headed "% State" show the county's percentage of the state total for the SIC in 1995; for example, 1.4% for SIC 6000 means that the county had 1.4 percent of the state's total establishments (or payroll) in SIC 6000 in 1995. A dash (-) is used to indicate that data are not available or cannot be calculated; nec means not elsewhere classified.

Continued on next page.

SIC	Industry	No. Establishments			Employment		Pay / Employee		Annual Payroll ($ 000)		
		1994	1995	% State	1994	1995	1994	1995	1994	1995	% State
DURHAM, NC - [continued]											
6210	Security brokers and dealers	16	20	4.0	182	210	67,077	70,057	10,552	12,553	3.8
6280	Security and commodity services	9	8	3.6	20	31	36,400	38,968	972	1,328	2.3
6300	Insurance carriers	33	39	3.5	894	908	36,528	37,789	30,685	33,056	3.1
6310	Life insurance	15	17	4.4	521	556	35,094	35,683	17,247	19,396	5.0
6400	Insurance agents, brokers, and service	78	81	2.5	364	362	30,681	32,873	12,268	12,688	3.0
6500	Real estate	180	188	3.4	729	790	20,093	21,737	17,750	19,749	3.0
6510	Real estate operators and lessors	56	57	3.1	243	264	18,058	19,500	5,122	5,581	3.6
6530	Real estate agents and managers	103	108	3.8	380	438	23,411	23,790	10,818	12,041	3.2
6550	Subdividers and developers	13	14	2.5	89	68	10,787	15,824	1,272	1,387	1.3
6552	Subdividers and developers, n.e.c.	7	7	1.9	25	24	11,200	12,333	553	562	0.7
6553	Cemetery subdividers and developers	6	6	3.9	64	43	10,625	17,581	719	813	3.6
6700	Holding and other investment offices	10	12	3.6	39	147	68,308	36,109	3,238	6,003	3.6
EDGECOMBE, NC											
60 –	**Finance, insurance, and real estate**	116	102	0.7	710	754	26,017	33,050	18,481	24,252	0.5
6000	Depository institutions	24	24	0.8	214	284	22,037	24,155	5,280	6,137	0.4
6020	Commercial banks	16	17	0.7	172	244	22,116	25,066	4,397	5,399	0.4
6030	Savings institutions	4	3	1.0	28	19	25,143	27,789	665	513	0.6
6140	Personal credit institutions	8	7	0.9	23	22	28,348	40,545	625	751	0.4
6400	Insurance agents, brokers, and service	25	22	0.7	132	92	24,848	26,043	3,048	2,526	0.6
6500	Real estate	42	35	0.6	214	176	12,449	14,000	1,894	2,542	0.4
6510	Real estate operators and lessors	20	20	1.1	148	148	11,432	12,541	869	1,983	1.3
6530	Real estate agents and managers	16	9	0.3	45	11	15,111	29,818	732	229	0.1
6550	Subdividers and developers	6	6	1.1	21	17	13,905	16,471	293	330	0.3
FORSYTH, NC											
60 –	**Finance, insurance, and real estate**	760	787	5.1	10,204	12,715	30,777	31,591	325,426	401,463	8.2
6000	Depository institutions	139	141	4.7	4,353	5,910	32,142	32,201	142,842	190,893	11.1
6020	Commercial banks	103	108	4.7	3,976	5,516	32,991	32,830	133,511	181,018	12.1
6060	Credit unions	19	19	5.6	256	280	22,297	21,986	5,559	6,199	8.3
6100	Nondepository institutions	63	65	4.4	1,160	1,116	23,193	23,674	26,941	26,629	5.9
6140	Personal credit institutions	30	33	4.3	182	219	26,418	28,566	5,122	6,701	3.3
6160	Mortgage bankers and brokers	24	24	4.8	454	489	25,383	23,501	11,950	11,739	7.0
6200	Security and commodity brokers	45	45	6.2	354	416	63,525	61,577	23,083	26,002	6.7
6210	Security brokers and dealers	26	28	5.6	307	365	64,300	60,559	19,913	22,170	6.7
6300	Insurance carriers	64	67	6.0	1,945	2,352	35,395	37,687	68,976	87,289	8.2
6310	Life insurance	23	22	5.7	1,199	1,553	27,773	33,888	35,581	50,694	13.1
6330	Fire, marine, and casualty insurance	27	28	5.1	164	149	34,268	39,302	5,538	5,537	1.4
6400	Insurance agents, brokers, and service	163	175	5.4	776	847	35,284	35,547	26,599	31,601	7.4
6500	Real estate	270	279	5.1	1,278	1,898	17,258	16,544	27,946	32,014	4.9
6510	Real estate operators and lessors	118	120	6.5	377	363	19,374	21,311	9,235	7,780	5.0
6530	Real estate agents and managers	128	132	4.7	860	1,373	15,121	14,147	16,679	20,120	5.4
6550	Subdividers and developers	16	21	3.8	36	117	46,889	32,205	1,867	3,651	3.5
6552	Subdividers and developers, n.e.c.	9	10	2.7	5	13	15,200	23,692	210	375	0.5
6553	Cemetery subdividers and developers	6	9	5.8	31	102	52,000	33,333	1,618	3,189	14.1
6700	Holding and other investment offices	16	15	4.6	338	176	19,101	52,227	9,039	7,035	4.3
6710	Holding offices	5	5	4.6	31	52	113,548	70,077	2,768	3,496	2.8
6790	Miscellaneous investing	8	4	3.4	285	93	8,758	52,129	5,845	3,018	10.6
FRANKLIN, NC											
60 –	**Finance, insurance, and real estate**	25	22	0.1	157	147	20,866	24,327	3,579	3,575	0.1
6000	Depository institutions	9	7	0.2	85	68	21,647	22,176	1,968	1,493	0.1
GASTON, NC											
60 –	**Finance, insurance, and real estate**	252	264	1.7	1,862	1,800	24,296	24,671	45,860	45,754	0.9
6000	Depository institutions	64	65	2.1	796	687	23,387	23,528	17,514	17,043	1.0
6020	Commercial banks	47	49	2.1	656	551	23,622	23,521	14,240	13,671	0.9
6030	Savings institutions	11	9	2.9	96	94	25,583	27,319	2,591	2,630	2.8

Source: County Business Patterns, 1994/95, CBP-94/95, U.S. Department of Commerce, Washington, D.C., November 1997. SIC categories for which data were suppressed or not available for both 1994 and 1995 are not displayed. The employment columns represent mid-March employment in the year. Pay per employee is calculated by dividing 1st Quarter payroll, annualized, by mid-March employment. The columns headed "% State" show the county's percentage of the state total for the SIC in 1995; for example, 1.4% for SIC 6000 means that the county had 1.4 percent of the state's total establishments (or payroll) in SIC 6000 in 1995. A dash (-) is used to indicate that data are not available or cannot be calculated; nec means not elsewhere classified.

Continued on next page.

SIC	Industry	No. Establishments			Employment		Pay / Employee		Annual Payroll ($ 000)		
		1994	1995	% State	1994	1995	1994	1995	1994	1995	% State
GASTON, NC - [continued]											
6060	Credit unions	6	7	2.1	44	42	15,091	15,143	683	742	1.0
6100	Nondepository institutions	29	30	2.0	156	140	22,282	25,857	3,400	3,610	0.8
6140	Personal credit institutions	18	18	2.4	98	89	21,388	24,180	1,985	2,115	1.0
6150	Business credit institutions	3	3	3.1	14	15	37,429	46,133	526	595	1.0
6160	Mortgage bankers and brokers	8	9	1.8	44	36	19,455	21,556	889	900	0.5
6200	Security and commodity brokers	9	9	1.2	28	33	29,143	37,697	1,187	1,563	0.4
6300	Insurance carriers	21	21	1.9	296	318	29,216	30,390	8,594	9,115	0.9
6310	Life insurance	6	6	1.6	92	81	33,783	34,716	2,810	2,542	0.7
6400	Insurance agents, brokers, and service	53	56	1.7	228	229	24,561	26,061	5,674	6,147	1.4
6500	Real estate	71	77	1.4	306	346	21,908	18,197	8,260	7,125	1.1
6510	Real estate operators and lessors	22	26	1.4	118	151	16,644	16,132	2,381	2,718	1.7
6530	Real estate agents and managers	39	40	1.4	167	103	14,515	15,845	3,194	1,956	0.5
6550	Subdividers and developers	8	9	1.6	21	87	110,286	24,966	2,639	2,388	2.3
6700	Holding and other investment offices	5	6	1.8	52	47	26,538	30,894	1,231	1,151	0.7
GATES, NC											
60 –	**Finance, insurance, and real estate**	5	6	0.0	-	-	-	-	-	-	-
GRANVILLE, NC											
60 –	**Finance, insurance, and real estate**	53	53	0.3	212	199	23,491	26,030	4,664	4,696	0.1
6000	Depository institutions	15	15	0.5	130	111	24,615	24,324	2,918	2,492	0.1
6020	Commercial banks	11	11	0.5	110	90	25,455	25,378	2,498	2,064	0.1
6400	Insurance agents, brokers, and service	10	10	0.3	33	36	14,788	13,556	513	499	0.1
6500	Real estate	23	21	0.4	35	36	10,971	11,111	456	465	0.1
6510	Real estate operators and lessors	9	8	0.4	14	16	11,143	10,500	177	168	0.1
6530	Real estate agents and managers	9	8	0.3	11	9	12,364	12,444	155	161	0.0
6550	Subdividers and developers	5	5	0.9	10	11	9,200	10,909	124	136	0.1
GREENE, NC											
60 –	**Finance, insurance, and real estate**	11	11	0.1	38	35	19,684	19,086	738	705	0.0
6400	Insurance agents, brokers, and service	4	4	0.1	9	9	17,333	20,000	188	172	0.0
GUILFORD, NC											
60 –	**Finance, insurance, and real estate**	1,164	1,197	7.8	17,427	17,936	28,882	29,823	531,733	536,948	10.9
6000	Depository institutions	179	168	5.6	3,179	3,657	25,081	25,227	107,925	87,463	5.1
6020	Commercial banks	143	133	5.7	2,851	3,254	25,417	25,274	99,947	76,266	5.1
6060	Credit unions	26	25	7.4	224	260	18,161	18,877	4,460	5,023	6.8
6100	Nondepository institutions	115	115	7.8	3,977	3,916	28,120	29,266	109,641	113,014	25.0
6140	Personal credit institutions	50	52	6.8	2,813	2,910	26,847	27,497	76,266	80,225	39.3
6160	Mortgage bankers and brokers	53	50	10.0	908	743	28,573	29,814	24,062	23,107	13.7
6200	Security and commodity brokers	66	63	8.6	481	530	65,289	57,102	27,311	29,237	7.5
6210	Security brokers and dealers	37	37	7.4	378	414	70,254	62,976	23,098	24,346	7.4
6280	Security and commodity services	29	26	11.8	103	116	47,068	36,138	4,213	4,891	8.5
6300	Insurance carriers	120	122	10.8	5,788	5,625	31,411	33,577	182,962	187,712	17.6
6310	Life insurance	46	46	11.9	3,518	3,394	29,185	32,185	102,614	103,724	26.8
6320	Medical service and health insurance	4	4	6.3	485	545	27,810	29,079	13,928	17,496	10.0
6330	Fire, marine, and casualty insurance	50	53	9.7	939	884	32,119	34,285	30,611	31,273	7.8
6400	Insurance agents, brokers, and service	281	286	8.9	1,053	1,194	32,745	33,709	33,886	41,141	9.6
6500	Real estate	372	406	7.4	2,667	2,638	20,628	21,222	59,756	63,286	9.8
6510	Real estate operators and lessors	152	151	8.2	1,116	1,249	19,545	19,062	22,819	25,878	16.6
6530	Real estate agents and managers	188	207	7.3	1,345	1,127	20,803	22,506	30,344	27,626	7.4
6540	Title abstract offices	3	3	13.0	3	4	8,000	7,000	33	30	1.1
6550	Subdividers and developers	23	28	5.1	203	246	25,616	26,927	6,482	9,323	8.9
6552	Subdividers and developers, n.e.c.	15	19	5.2	105	136	27,733	34,294	4,057	7,136	9.0
6553	Cemetery subdividers and developers	6	6	3.9	98	110	23,347	17,818	2,409	2,154	9.5

Source: County Business Patterns, 1994/95, CBP-94/95, U.S. Department of Commerce, Washington, D.C., November 1997. SIC categories for which data were suppressed or not available for both 1994 and 1995 are *not* displayed. The employment columns represent mid-March employment in the year. Pay per employee is calculated by dividing 1st Quarter payroll, annualized, by mid-March employment. The columns headed "% State" show the county's percentage of the state total for the SIC in 1995; for example, 1.4% for SIC 6000 means that the county had 1.4 percent of the state's total establishments (or payroll) in SIC 6000 in 1995. A dash (-) is used to indicate that data are not available or cannot be calculated; *nec* means not elsewhere classified.

Continued on next page.

SIC	Industry	No. Establishments			Employment		Pay / Employee		Annual Payroll ($ 000)		
		1994	1995	% State	1994	1995	1994	1995	1994	1995	% State
GUILFORD, NC - [continued]											
6710	Holding offices	8	8	7.4	172	189	40,140	44,254	7,809	9,481	7.5
6730	Trusts	12	9	10.7	98	21	20,082	30,857	1,894	654	8.3
6790	Miscellaneous investing	7	11	9.5	9	17	15,556	37,882	332	653	2.3
HALIFAX, NC											
60 –	**Finance, insurance, and real estate**	93	96	0.6	528	508	21,705	23,220	11,754	11,375	0.2
6000	Depository institutions	25	25	0.8	258	229	23,287	23,790	6,276	5,302	0.3
6020	Commercial banks	19	18	0.8	158	168	24,152	24,762	3,610	3,861	0.3
6100	Nondepository institutions	12	12	0.8	47	51	20,426	24,314	994	1,220	0.3
6200	Security and commodity brokers	3	3	0.4	8	7	30,500	50,286	245	316	0.1
6210	Security brokers and dealers	3	3	0.6	8	7	30,500	50,286	245	316	0.1
6400	Insurance agents, brokers, and service	24	25	0.8	105	116	22,057	23,517	2,499	2,695	0.6
6500	Real estate	24	26	0.5	76	71	10,105	11,268	828	872	0.1
6510	Real estate operators and lessors	7	7	0.4	38	36	8,632	10,000	363	402	0.3
6530	Real estate agents and managers	13	13	0.5	31	30	11,355	13,467	405	423	0.1
6550	Subdividers and developers	4	5	0.9	7	5	12,571	7,200	60	45	0.0
HARNETT, NC											
60 –	**Finance, insurance, and real estate**	86	88	0.6	589	555	18,370	19,892	11,071	11,848	0.2
6000	Depository institutions	24	25	0.8	274	256	21,168	23,156	5,614	6,107	0.4
6020	Commercial banks	18	19	0.8	196	181	21,653	24,199	4,055	4,442	0.3
6100	Nondepository institutions	7	7	0.5	30	21	20,533	31,238	583	609	0.1
6400	Insurance agents, brokers, and service	20	21	0.7	88	89	23,000	23,191	2,277	2,287	0.5
6500	Real estate	26	27	0.5	144	147	10,917	11,510	1,817	2,075	0.3
6510	Real estate operators and lessors	12	15	0.8	115	107	10,261	11,065	1,331	1,395	0.9
6530	Real estate agents and managers	7	8	0.3	20	32	15,600	14,000	334	601	0.2
6550	Subdividers and developers	7	4	0.7	9	8	8,889	7,500	152	79	0.1
HAYWOOD, NC											
60 –	**Finance, insurance, and real estate**	90	96	0.6	520	507	23,162	20,300	13,116	11,392	0.2
6000	Depository institutions	18	18	0.6	268	251	26,806	21,992	7,701	5,998	0.3
6020	Commercial banks	13	13	0.6	118	106	33,492	22,151	3,949	2,045	0.1
6100	Nondepository institutions	9	9	0.6	37	34	19,784	20,706	689	819	0.2
6400	Insurance agents, brokers, and service	19	19	0.6	69	67	16,870	18,269	1,464	1,373	0.3
6500	Real estate	36	41	0.8	96	104	13,083	11,654	1,589	1,570	0.2
6510	Real estate operators and lessors	10	11	0.6	22	31	9,818	9,032	337	346	0.2
6530	Real estate agents and managers	20	24	0.8	55	60	12,582	12,133	911	970	0.3
6550	Subdividers and developers	6	6	1.1	19	13	18,316	15,692	341	254	0.2
HENDERSON, NC											
60 –	**Finance, insurance, and real estate**	137	144	0.9	805	780	24,080	25,774	19,758	20,005	0.4
6000	Depository institutions	29	26	0.9	290	247	20,952	21,555	6,092	5,088	0.3
6020	Commercial banks	22	20	0.9	245	209	21,600	22,794	5,223	4,467	0.3
6100	Nondepository institutions	16	16	1.1	148	150	23,838	27,333	3,568	4,049	0.9
6400	Insurance agents, brokers, and service	30	33	1.0	134	122	19,403	22,197	2,901	3,004	0.7
6500	Real estate	41	47	0.9	141	174	15,830	14,897	2,621	2,870	0.4
6510	Real estate operators and lessors	16	16	0.9	74	81	11,622	9,679	1,014	915	0.6
6530	Real estate agents and managers	22	26	0.9	56	80	18,929	19,500	1,399	1,736	0.5
6550	Subdividers and developers	3	4	0.7	11	13	28,364	19,077	208	203	0.2
6700	Holding and other investment offices	3	3	0.9	2	8	50,000	117,500	240	523	0.3
HERTFORD, NC											
60 –	**Finance, insurance, and real estate**	39	41	0.3	171	178	18,667	19,753	3,182	3,570	0.1
6000	Depository institutions	9	9	0.3	99	101	20,848	21,703	1,923	2,186	0.1
6140	Personal credit institutions	7	7	0.9	27	29	17,926	21,241	561	667	0.3
6400	Insurance agents, brokers, and service	8	8	0.2	25	26	15,520	16,154	427	423	0.1
6500	Real estate	13	14	0.3	17	19	10,588	11,579	240	251	0.0

Source: County Business Patterns, 1994/95, CBP-94/95, U.S. Department of Commerce, Washington, D.C., November 1997. SIC categories for which data were suppressed or not available for both 1994 and 1995 are *not* displayed. The employment columns represent mid-March employment in the year. Pay per employee is calculated by dividing 1st Quarter payroll, annualized, by mid-March employment. The columns headed "% State" show the county's percentage of the state total for the SIC in 1995; for example, 1.4% for SIC 6000 means that the county had 1.4 percent of the state's total establishments (or payroll) in SIC 6000 in 1995. A dash (-) is used to indicate that data are not available or cannot be calculated; *nec* means not elsewhere classified.

Continued on next page.

SIC	Industry	No. Establishments			Employment		Pay / Employee		Annual Payroll ($ 000)		
		1994	1995	% State	1994	1995	1994	1995	1994	1995	% State
HERTFORD, NC - [continued]											
6510	Real estate operators and lessors	3	4	0.2	6	6	13,333	12,667	92	94	0.1
6530	Real estate agents and managers	6	6	0.2	9	10	9,778	11,200	118	116	0.0
6550	Subdividers and developers	4	4	0.7	2	3	6,000	10,667	30	41	0.0
HOKE, NC											
60 –	**Finance, insurance, and real estate**	24	25	0.2	110	114	20,509	20,281	2,173	2,192	0.0
6000	Depository institutions	6	5	0.2	51	50	19,216	18,160	933	838	0.0
6400	Insurance agents, brokers, and service	7	7	0.2	16	14	17,750	20,857	298	301	0.1
6500	Real estate	7	8	0.1	11	11	5,818	9,818	72	116	0.0
6510	Real estate operators and lessors	4	4	0.2	5	7	3,200	8,571	24	71	0.0
HYDE, NC											
60 –	**Finance, insurance, and real estate**	9	9	0.1	88	71	17,636	21,577	1,655	1,422	0.0
IREDELL, NC											
60 –	**Finance, insurance, and real estate**	176	180	1.2	885	862	25,415	25,657	21,902	21,767	0.4
6000	Depository institutions	42	41	1.4	441	396	24,662	24,010	9,884	9,046	0.5
6020	Commercial banks	35	37	1.6	349	343	26,223	24,082	8,342	7,791	0.5
6100	Nondepository institutions	18	20	1.4	96	100	29,708	30,720	2,889	2,962	0.7
6140	Personal credit institutions	12	13	1.7	59	65	22,780	26,585	1,567	1,673	0.8
6400	Insurance agents, brokers, and service	40	39	1.2	135	130	29,926	33,231	4,005	3,940	0.9
6500	Real estate	54	56	1.0	144	166	14,944	13,952	2,501	2,826	0.4
6510	Real estate operators and lessors	22	24	1.3	51	70	17,961	14,457	1,076	1,219	0.8
6530	Real estate agents and managers	28	27	1.0	67	70	12,358	14,743	1,047	1,247	0.3
JACKSON, NC											
60 –	**Finance, insurance, and real estate**	61	60	0.4	263	273	19,163	18,608	5,331	5,794	0.1
6000	Depository institutions	12	12	0.4	90	90	21,289	20,222	1,846	1,764	0.1
6020	Commercial banks	9	9	0.4	61	61	21,902	20,131	1,244	1,161	0.1
6400	Insurance agents, brokers, and service	10	10	0.3	53	36	22,566	23,444	1,023	1,065	0.2
6500	Real estate	33	31	0.6	100	122	14,800	14,361	1,917	2,262	0.3
6510	Real estate operators and lessors	10	9	0.5	16	25	11,750	10,240	324	433	0.3
6530	Real estate agents and managers	20	18	0.6	79	91	15,696	15,385	1,484	1,636	0.4
JOHNSTON, NC											
60 –	**Finance, insurance, and real estate**	141	150	1.0	780	836	23,077	24,120	17,201	22,692	0.5
6000	Depository institutions	42	41	1.4	398	392	26,623	24,061	9,545	10,539	0.6
6020	Commercial banks	32	32	1.4	337	325	25,911	24,849	8,057	9,046	0.6
6140	Personal credit institutions	10	10	1.3	29	34	21,241	19,294	589	738	0.4
6300	Insurance carriers	6	7	0.6	47	50	35,234	33,440	1,820	1,929	0.2
6400	Insurance agents, brokers, and service	32	34	1.1	119	112	17,983	19,000	2,263	2,371	0.6
6500	Real estate	44	51	0.9	165	227	12,097	24,775	2,253	6,472	1.0
6510	Real estate operators and lessors	14	15	0.8	26	31	10,462	15,097	309	459	0.3
6530	Real estate agents and managers	19	21	0.7	99	33	10,424	14,788	1,157	598	0.2
6550	Subdividers and developers	11	12	2.2	40	44	17,300	21,909	787	1,283	1.2
6552	Subdividers and developers, n.e.c.	5	7	1.9	28	38	21,571	22,211	676	1,101	1.4
6553	Cemetery subdividers and developers	5	4	2.6	12	6	7,333	20,000	86	142	0.6
LEE, NC											
60 –	**Finance, insurance, and real estate**	108	103	0.7	498	572	25,470	24,937	13,441	16,019	0.3
6000	Depository institutions	21	21	0.7	265	256	27,925	27,250	6,752	7,686	0.4
6020	Commercial banks	13	13	0.6	180	172	30,489	29,419	4,811	5,555	0.4
6400	Insurance agents, brokers, and service	24	23	0.7	74	76	23,027	23,211	1,734	1,826	0.4
6500	Real estate	48	46	0.8	112	183	13,036	18,842	2,896	4,151	0.6

Source: County Business Patterns, 1994/95, CBP-94/95, U.S. Department of Commerce, Washington, D.C., November 1997. SIC categories for which data were suppressed or not available for both 1994 and 1995 are *not* displayed. The employment columns represent mid-March employment in the year. Pay per employee is calculated by dividing 1st Quarter payroll, annualized, by mid-March employment. The columns headed "% State" show the county's percentage of the state total for the SIC in 1995; for example, 1.4% for SIC 6000 means that the county had 1.4 percent of the state's total establishments (or payroll) in SIC 6000 in 1995. A dash (-) is used to indicate that data are not available or cannot be calculated; nec means not elsewhere classified.

Continued on next page.

SIC	Industry	No. Establishments			Employment		Pay / Employee		Annual Payroll ($ 000)		
		1994	1995	% State	1994	1995	1994	1995	1994	1995	% State
LEE, NC - [continued]											
6510	Real estate operators and lessors	20	19	1.0	47	49	10,213	10,939	532	610	0.4
6530	Real estate agents and managers	21	19	0.7	43	105	18,233	24,229	2,117	3,064	0.8
6550	Subdividers and developers	7	7	1.3	22	24	8,909	11,167	247	377	0.4
LENOIR, NC											
60 –	**Finance, insurance, and real estate**	127	132	0.9	709	742	25,298	25,693	17,280	17,872	0.4
6000	Depository institutions	28	28	0.9	331	346	22,296	22,786	6,711	6,284	0.4
6020	Commercial banks	24	23	1.0	289	313	23,073	22,607	5,982	5,439	0.4
6100	Nondepository institutions	15	17	1.2	69	70	24,928	27,886	1,654	2,011	0.4
6140	Personal credit institutions	10	11	1.4	60	60	25,467	28,867	1,484	1,789	0.9
6210	Security brokers and dealers	5	6	1.2	22	26	95,455	76,769	1,752	1,892	0.6
6300	Insurance carriers	10	9	0.8	76	79	33,053	34,633	3,007	2,914	0.3
6310	Life insurance	4	4	1.0	64	68	32,688	35,294	2,612	2,517	0.7
6400	Insurance agents, brokers, and service	38	40	1.2	124	133	25,742	25,654	2,992	3,499	0.8
6500	Real estate	28	29	0.5	84	84	12,048	12,476	1,153	1,248	0.2
LINCOLN, NC											
60 –	**Finance, insurance, and real estate**	77	78	0.5	381	386	23,696	26,373	9,159	10,098	0.2
6000	Depository institutions	21	21	0.7	227	231	22,996	24,398	4,949	5,394	0.3
6020	Commercial banks	16	16	0.7	185	188	22,962	24,702	3,863	4,360	0.3
6100	Nondepository institutions	6	5	0.3	21	17	19,429	23,529	419	400	0.1
6500	Real estate	25	27	0.5	71	81	24,845	32,444	2,142	2,728	0.4
6530	Real estate agents and managers	14	11	0.4	55	63	28,291	37,143	1,830	2,293	0.6
MCDOWELL, NC											
60 –	**Finance, insurance, and real estate**	41	38	0.2	189	225	20,508	18,116	4,050	4,761	0.1
6000	Depository institutions	8	8	0.3	101	101	21,901	20,000	2,052	2,259	0.1
6020	Commercial banks	5	5	0.2	71	69	23,944	22,725	1,510	1,719	0.1
6400	Insurance agents, brokers, and service	10	10	0.3	35	50	20,800	15,920	793	914	0.2
6500	Real estate	14	12	0.2	21	44	9,333	9,182	384	546	0.1
MACON, NC											
60 –	**Finance, insurance, and real estate**	55	53	0.3	242	257	20,198	20,187	5,307	5,947	0.1
6000	Depository institutions	15	14	0.5	156	157	19,718	20,764	3,066	3,487	0.2
6400	Insurance agents, brokers, and service	12	11	0.3	47	47	22,043	22,383	1,409	1,419	0.3
6500	Real estate	22	22	0.4	31	40	16,516	14,300	531	705	0.1
6530	Real estate agents and managers	17	16	0.6	27	32	13,778	13,375	423	513	0.1
MADISON, NC											
60 –	**Finance, insurance, and real estate**	18	22	0.1	51	56	19,059	18,143	1,092	1,172	0.0
6000	Depository institutions	6	7	0.2	32	35	19,375	17,029	608	614	0.0
6530	Real estate agents and managers	5	6	0.2	5	8	8,000	10,500	190	116	0.0
MECKLENBURG, NC											
60 –	**Finance, insurance, and real estate**	2,211	2,315	15.1	41,031	46,219	39,568	45,628	1,536,172	1,801,796	36.6
6000	Depository institutions	328	341	11.3	14,538	18,778	38,448	43,574	526,324	694,803	40.5
6020	Commercial banks	251	267	11.5	13,489	17,041	39,491	44,938	500,070	641,758	42.8
6060	Credit unions	36	34	10.1	302	301	21,576	24,040	6,557	7,093	9.5
6100	Nondepository institutions	236	254	17.3	4,376	4,592	35,134	37,730	137,006	144,364	31.9
6140	Personal credit institutions	73	81	10.6	1,242	1,150	26,490	37,353	32,511	36,590	17.9
6150	Business credit institutions	38	40	41.2	769	714	50,044	58,303	34,240	35,661	62.3
6160	Mortgage bankers and brokers	123	126	25.2	2,327	2,719	34,786	32,544	68,194	71,608	42.4
6200	Security and commodity brokers	136	138	18.9	2,075	2,260	98,246	137,818	148,035	193,670	49.9
6210	Security brokers and dealers	91	96	19.1	1,543	1,948	100,913	123,423	115,218	161,718	49.0
6300	Insurance carriers	266	271	24.1	9,722	9,795	36,221	38,335	356,917	363,260	34.0
6310	Life insurance	104	108	28.1	3,217	3,393	37,150	37,034	117,995	118,732	30.7
6320	Medical service and health insurance	13	16	25.0	702	811	23,322	32,947	20,724	22,170	12.6
6321	Accident and health insurance	8	11	31.4	534	626	21,371	33,329	15,482	15,868	29.5

Source: County Business Patterns, 1994/95, CBP-94/95, U.S. Department of Commerce, Washington, D.C., November 1997. SIC categories for which data were suppressed or not available for both 1994 and 1995 are not displayed. The employment columns represent mid-March employment in the year. Pay per employee is calculated by dividing 1st Quarter payroll, annualized, by mid-March employment. The columns headed "% State" show the county's percentage of the state total for the SIC in 1995; for example, 1.4% for SIC 6000 means that the county had 1.4 percent of the state's total establishments (or payroll) in SIC 6000 in 1995. A dash (-) is used to indicate that data are not available or cannot be calculated; nec means not elsewhere classified.

Continued on next page.

SIC	Industry	No. Establishments			Employment		Pay / Employee		Annual Payroll ($ 000)		
		1994	1995	% State	1994	1995	1994	1995	1994	1995	% State
MECKLENBURG, NC - [continued]											
6324	Hospital and medical service plans	5	5	17.2	168	185	29,524	31,654	5,242	6,302	5.2
6330	Fire, marine, and casualty insurance	111	112	20.5	5,375	5,267	38,415	39,885	210,416	211,577	52.7
6370	Pension, health, and welfare funds	16	15	34.1	94	195	27,702	25,374	2,699	4,938	20.8
6400	Insurance agents, brokers, and service	409	439	13.6	2,515	2,550	36,052	39,732	95,456	99,800	23.3
6500	Real estate	742	768	14.1	5,736	6,286	29,680	36,262	172,282	197,793	30.5
6510	Real estate operators and lessors	241	247	13.4	1,410	1,470	22,011	24,283	35,643	38,322	24.5
6530	Real estate agents and managers	410	410	14.5	3,650	3,696	29,086	32,826	107,456	117,316	31.4
6540	Title abstract offices	5	5	21.7	30	29	48,000	46,759	1,207	1,222	44.1
6550	Subdividers and developers	58	61	11.0	590	1,007	52,325	67,837	26,508	38,659	37.1
6552	Subdividers and developers, n.e.c.	43	43	11.8	474	811	59,662	80,173	23,301	35,311	44.4
6553	Cemetery subdividers and developers	11	12	7.8	114	182	21,649	15,582	2,780	2,827	12.5
6710	Holding offices	31	37	34.3	996	1,149	47,972	55,154	51,567	67,304	53.5
6730	Trusts	13	14	16.7	54	70	40,000	38,686	2,127	2,836	36.0
6732	Educational, religious, etc. trusts	6	5	12.5	34	46	51,882	44,087	1,759	2,043	39.7
6790	Miscellaneous investing	33	34	29.3	188	214	50,979	49,551	9,468	9,076	32.0
6799	Investors, n.e.c.	19	19	27.5	62	70	72,452	79,200	4,844	4,739	31.0
MITCHELL, NC											
60 –	**Finance, insurance, and real estate**	22	20	0.1	114	111	22,491	23,640	2,455	2,581	0.1
6000	Depository institutions	6	6	0.2	53	56	21,132	21,286	1,105	1,078	0.1
MONTGOMERY, NC											
60 –	**Finance, insurance, and real estate**	31	33	0.2	193	202	24,041	25,347	4,163	4,564	0.1
6000	Depository institutions	17	17	0.6	143	157	27,049	28,561	3,347	3,897	0.2
6020	Commercial banks	14	14	0.6	131	143	27,634	29,035	3,086	3,645	0.2
6500	Real estate	6	6	0.1	22	13	9,455	9,846	216	147	0.0
MOORE, NC											
60 –	**Finance, insurance, and real estate**	137	145	0.9	820	828	30,083	25,227	21,374	20,644	0.4
6000	Depository institutions	37	37	1.2	335	327	39,833	25,639	9,071	8,283	0.5
6020	Commercial banks	32	32	1.4	273	261	23,853	25,333	6,028	6,315	0.4
6200	Security and commodity brokers	13	12	1.6	53	51	55,547	62,667	3,125	3,410	0.9
6210	Security brokers and dealers	9	8	1.6	44	43	63,000	70,791	2,965	3,217	1.0
6280	Security and commodity services	4	4	1.8	9	8	19,111	19,000	160	193	0.3
6400	Insurance agents, brokers, and service	27	28	0.9	97	116	24,784	24,448	2,602	2,680	0.6
6500	Real estate	50	57	1.0	309	308	15,663	16,909	5,406	5,318	0.8
6510	Real estate operators and lessors	5	6	0.3	9	12	6,667	5,667	68	78	0.0
6530	Real estate agents and managers	35	35	1.2	116	130	22,000	20,492	2,771	2,820	0.8
6550	Subdividers and developers	7	11	2.0	180	159	12,111	14,642	2,500	2,281	2.2
NASH, NC											
60 –	**Finance, insurance, and real estate**	163	171	1.1	1,786	1,810	26,934	29,030	45,512	46,025	0.9
6000	Depository institutions	43	41	1.4	1,116	1,116	27,767	32,588	29,052	30,078	1.8
6020	Commercial banks	36	34	1.5	971	981	28,601	33,884	25,571	26,890	1.8
6200	Security and commodity brokers	11	10	1.4	90	133	44,978	24,602	3,162	2,770	0.7
6210	Security brokers and dealers	6	5	1.0	56	33	63,786	55,152	2,721	2,094	0.6
6280	Security and commodity services	5	5	2.3	34	100	14,000	14,520	441	676	1.2
6300	Insurance carriers	15	14	1.2	220	146	31,200	33,863	6,701	4,547	0.4
6400	Insurance agents, brokers, and service	35	40	1.2	107	123	20,336	23,154	2,286	3,186	0.7
6500	Real estate	47	51	0.9	191	225	12,880	14,756	2,792	3,709	0.6
6530	Real estate agents and managers	25	28	1.0	77	114	14,909	15,684	1,328	2,163	0.6
NEW HANOVER, NC											
60 –	**Finance, insurance, and real estate**	443	454	3.0	3,354	3,127	21,685	24,468	75,730	81,064	1.6
6000	Depository institutions	76	77	2.5	803	843	23,781	26,894	20,558	23,324	1.4
6020	Commercial banks	52	53	2.3	541	579	22,499	26,453	13,486	15,995	1.1
6030	Savings institutions	11	11	3.6	176	181	30,727	31,669	5,466	5,623	6.1
6100	Nondepository institutions	44	46	3.1	356	238	21,270	22,454	7,458	6,319	1.4

Source: County Business Patterns, 1994/95, CBP-94/95, U.S. Department of Commerce, Washington, D.C., November 1997. SIC categories for which data were suppressed or not available for both 1994 and 1995 are not displayed. The employment columns represent mid-March employment in the year. Pay per employee is calculated by dividing 1st Quarter payroll, annualized, by mid-March employment. The columns headed "% State" show the county's percentage of the state total for the SIC in 1995; for example, 1.4% for SIC 6000 means that the county had 1.4 percent of the state's total establishments (or payroll) in SIC 6000 in 1995. A dash (-) is used to indicate that data are not available or cannot be calculated; nec means not elsewhere classified.

Continued on next page.

SIC	Industry	No. Establishments			Employment		Pay / Employee		Annual Payroll ($ 000)		
		1994	1995	% State	1994	1995	1994	1995	1994	1995	% State
NEW HANOVER, NC - [continued]											
6160	Mortgage bankers and brokers	22	22	4.4	265	123	20,392	21,203	5,307	3,341	2.0
6200	Security and commodity brokers	20	25	3.4	131	153	46,382	47,216	6,868	8,408	2.2
6210	Security brokers and dealers	15	18	3.6	114	131	49,895	45,863	5,692	6,722	2.0
6300	Insurance carriers	28	29	2.6	218	215	33,119	35,870	7,084	7,380	0.7
6310	Life insurance	11	12	3.1	166	161	28,651	28,820	4,378	4,466	1.2
6400	Insurance agents, brokers, and service	81	77	2.4	344	347	24,372	25,441	9,329	9,464	2.2
6500	Real estate	185	192	3.5	1,245	1,183	15,643	17,971	19,827	23,035	3.6
6510	Real estate operators and lessors	43	48	2.6	274	258	12,131	13,116	3,965	3,864	2.5
6530	Real estate agents and managers	108	106	3.7	374	445	16,941	19,973	7,143	9,898	2.7
6550	Subdividers and developers	28	30	5.4	581	461	16,021	18,100	8,146	8,747	8.4
6552	Subdividers and developers, n.e.c.	21	23	6.3	506	387	16,917	19,349	7,233	7,896	9.9
6553	Cemetery subdividers and developers	6	5	3.2	75	73	9,973	11,616	912	838	3.7
NORTHAMPTON, NC											
60 –	**Finance, insurance, and real estate**	13	14	0.1	49	53	14,939	19,321	748	981	0.0
6000	Depository institutions	6	6	0.2	35	33	14,857	22,424	503	703	0.0
6020	Commercial banks	6	6	0.3	35	33	14,857	22,424	503	703	0.0
6500	Real estate	4	4	0.1	3	6	10,667	11,333	45	73	0.0
ONSLOW, NC											
60 –	**Finance, insurance, and real estate**	219	215	1.4	1,125	1,123	17,390	18,379	20,157	21,503	0.4
6000	Depository institutions	38	37	1.2	450	459	18,347	19,573	8,342	8,762	0.5
6020	Commercial banks	25	24	1.0	244	240	20,656	21,350	4,769	4,917	0.3
6060	Credit unions	9	9	2.7	189	202	15,640	17,822	3,307	3,529	4.8
6100	Nondepository institutions	17	18	1.2	76	89	27,000	25,708	1,720	1,996	0.4
6140	Personal credit institutions	9	10	1.3	41	61	23,317	21,574	940	1,372	0.7
6400	Insurance agents, brokers, and service	39	40	1.2	171	156	18,292	18,641	3,422	3,704	0.9
6500	Real estate	101	99	1.8	365	369	12,866	13,799	5,308	5,305	0.8
6510	Real estate operators and lessors	37	36	2.0	121	126	14,083	15,683	1,670	1,803	1.2
6530	Real estate agents and managers	52	53	1.9	206	219	11,709	12,055	2,933	2,967	0.8
6550	Subdividers and developers	12	10	1.8	38	24	15,263	19,833	705	535	0.5
ORANGE, NC											
60 –	**Finance, insurance, and real estate**	200	214	1.4	2,988	3,132	29,080	31,589	91,444	106,777	2.2
6000	Depository institutions	43	43	1.4	485	433	23,192	22,448	10,121	9,725	0.6
6020	Commercial banks	36	34	1.5	372	299	24,430	23,157	7,893	6,800	0.5
6400	Insurance agents, brokers, and service	28	31	1.0	130	157	28,462	40,866	5,404	7,624	1.8
6500	Real estate	98	103	1.9	281	307	18,932	20,378	5,661	6,804	1.1
6510	Real estate operators and lessors	27	30	1.6	101	90	15,564	15,511	1,617	1,494	1.0
6530	Real estate agents and managers	59	59	2.1	160	179	21,950	23,307	3,317	4,136	1.1
6550	Subdividers and developers	8	7	1.3	18	35	11,333	18,743	480	584	0.6
6552	Subdividers and developers, n.e.c.	7	7	1.9	18	35	11,333	18,743	473	584	0.7
PAMLICO, NC											
60 –	**Finance, insurance, and real estate**	13	13	0.1	45	55	18,756	17,091	875	890	0.0
6500	Real estate	7	7	0.1	10	23	12,400	11,130	188	217	0.0
PASQUOTANK, NC											
60 –	**Finance, insurance, and real estate**	74	76	0.5	395	409	22,522	21,888	8,889	9,436	0.2
6000	Depository institutions	15	15	0.5	176	177	22,205	22,576	4,073	4,281	0.2
6020	Commercial banks	10	10	0.4	124	129	24,871	24,744	3,258	3,468	0.2
6100	Nondepository institutions	8	10	0.7	29	30	24,414	23,067	623	766	0.2
6400	Insurance agents, brokers, and service	16	16	0.5	55	57	28,000	24,491	1,453	1,380	0.3
6500	Real estate	27	27	0.5	81	92	13,580	11,696	1,165	1,118	0.2
6510	Real estate operators and lessors	16	15	0.8	59	71	11,458	10,704	718	691	0.4
PENDER, NC											
60 –	**Finance, insurance, and real estate**	46	53	0.3	176	168	16,432	17,881	3,278	3,774	0.1

Source: County Business Patterns, 1994/95, CBP-94/95, U.S. Department of Commerce, Washington, D.C., November 1997. SIC categories for which data were suppressed or not available for both 1994 and 1995 are not displayed. The employment columns represent mid-March employment in the year. Pay per employee is calculated by dividing 1st Quarter payroll, annualized, by mid-March employment. The columns headed "% State" show the county's percentage of the state total for the SIC in 1995; for example, 1.4% for SIC 6000 means that the county had 1.4 percent of the state's total establishments (or payroll) in SIC 6000 in 1995. A dash (-) is used to indicate that data are not available or cannot be calculated; nec means not elsewhere classified.

Continued on next page.

SIC	Industry	No. Establishments			Employment		Pay / Employee		Annual Payroll ($ 000)		
		1994	1995	% State	1994	1995	1994	1995	1994	1995	% State
PENDER, NC - [continued]											
6000	Depository institutions	8	9	0.3	66	66	22,121	22,364	1,450	1,722	0.1
6400	Insurance agents, brokers, and service	4	5	0.2	10	9	11,600	13,333	131	180	0.0
6500	Real estate	30	34	0.6	93	84	12,043	14,381	1,537	1,648	0.3
6530	Real estate agents and managers	19	18	0.6	56	58	12,643	14,345	962	1,040	0.3
PERQUIMANS, NC											
60 –	**Finance, insurance, and real estate**	11	10	0.1	68	113	12,059	9,062	1,015	995	0.0
PERSON, NC											
60 –	**Finance, insurance, and real estate**	42	41	0.3	187	189	19,273	21,101	4,012	4,221	0.1
6000	Depository institutions	10	9	0.3	98	96	19,796	21,125	2,063	2,008	0.1
6100	Nondepository institutions	6	6	0.4	24	28	18,667	19,857	509	584	0.1
6400	Insurance agents, brokers, and service	11	11	0.3	34	34	18,471	21,647	754	826	0.2
6500	Real estate	9	9	0.2	27	19	16,741	20,211	444	410	0.1
6530	Real estate agents and managers	5	5	0.2	17	8	18,118	29,000	328	229	0.1
PITT, NC											
60 –	**Finance, insurance, and real estate**	260	274	1.8	1,579	1,622	24,643	25,581	39,488	42,794	0.9
6000	Depository institutions	54	54	1.8	724	783	24,144	24,674	17,233	18,935	1.1
6020	Commercial banks	46	44	1.9	675	733	24,504	25,037	16,186	17,760	1.2
6100	Nondepository institutions	27	27	1.8	185	166	30,357	32,675	5,503	5,780	1.3
6140	Personal credit institutions	17	18	2.4	97	105	26,021	30,590	2,862	3,616	1.8
6200	Security and commodity brokers	13	16	2.2	51	53	45,020	48,226	2,413	3,237	0.8
6210	Security brokers and dealers	10	12	2.4	49	51	46,612	49,804	2,395	3,211	1.0
6280	Security and commodity services	3	4	1.8	2	2	6,000	8,000	18	26	0.0
6300	Insurance carriers	15	17	1.5	133	130	31,789	34,338	4,299	4,225	0.4
6310	Life insurance	4	4	1.0	60	56	27,533	29,571	1,654	1,710	0.4
6400	Insurance agents, brokers, and service	51	55	1.7	156	163	22,385	25,374	3,849	4,192	1.0
6500	Real estate	96	100	1.8	292	292	16,466	16,041	5,231	5,308	0.8
6510	Real estate operators and lessors	30	33	1.8	107	92	11,252	13,174	1,308	1,445	0.9
6530	Real estate agents and managers	49	49	1.7	147	156	17,333	17,359	2,936	2,814	0.8
6550	Subdividers and developers	16	16	2.9	38	43	27,789	17,674	985	1,025	1.0
6552	Subdividers and developers, n.e.c.	13	12	3.3	34	39	27,765	17,333	887	827	1.0
6553	Cemetery subdividers and developers	3	3	1.9	4	4	28,000	21,000	98	67	0.3
6700	Holding and other investment offices	4	5	1.5	38	35	26,105	25,943	960	1,117	0.7
POLK, NC											
60 –	**Finance, insurance, and real estate**	38	39	0.3	136	119	23,824	27,966	3,123	3,820	0.1
6000	Depository institutions	7	7	0.2	60	56	25,067	27,143	1,349	1,299	0.1
6200	Security and commodity brokers	5	5	0.7	32	19	32,000	57,053	746	904	0.2
6500	Real estate	18	20	0.4	24	24	15,500	13,167	380	469	0.1
RANDOLPH, NC											
60 –	**Finance, insurance, and real estate**	138	137	0.9	856	861	22,117	22,922	19,972	18,494	0.4
6000	Depository institutions	42	41	1.4	524	495	22,336	23,038	11,898	10,024	0.6
6020	Commercial banks	33	33	1.4	392	367	20,888	21,787	8,569	8,067	0.5
6100	Nondepository institutions	10	12	0.8	46	53	22,696	20,981	1,096	1,209	0.3
6300	Insurance carriers	9	9	0.8	29	33	40,414	37,333	1,242	1,388	0.1
6400	Insurance agents, brokers, and service	35	35	1.1	91	107	20,440	27,140	2,054	2,488	0.6
6500	Real estate	34	34	0.6	153	162	18,824	17,062	3,377	3,045	0.5
6510	Real estate operators and lessors	13	13	0.7	101	95	21,861	20,589	2,349	1,935	1.2
6530	Real estate agents and managers	15	17	0.6	32	40	17,625	14,200	698	803	0.2
6550	Subdividers and developers	5	4	0.7	19	27	5,474	8,889	327	307	0.3
RICHMOND, NC											
60 –	**Finance, insurance, and real estate**	65	67	0.4	329	330	20,815	20,982	6,683	7,030	0.1
6000	Depository institutions	18	19	0.6	156	160	20,436	21,775	3,131	3,562	0.2
6020	Commercial banks	12	13	0.6	92	98	21,478	23,102	1,909	2,309	0.2

Source: County Business Patterns, 1994/95, CBP-94/95, U.S. Department of Commerce, Washington, D.C., November 1997. SIC categories for which data were suppressed or not available for both 1994 and 1995 are *not* displayed. The employment columns represent mid-March employment in the year. Pay per employee is calculated by dividing 1st Quarter payroll, annualized, by mid-March employment. The columns headed "% State" show the county's percentage of the state total for the SIC in 1995; for example, 1.4% for SIC 6000 means that the county had 1.4 percent of the state's total establishments (or payroll) in SIC 6000 in 1995. A dash (-) is used to indicate that data are not available or cannot be calculated; *nec* means not elsewhere classified.

Continued on next page.

SIC	Industry	No. Establishments			Employment		Pay / Employee		Annual Payroll ($ 000)		
		1994	1995	% State	1994	1995	1994	1995	1994	1995	% State
RICHMOND, NC - [continued]											
6300	Insurance carriers	3	4	0.4	41	34	34,537	37,294	1,268	1,228	0.1
6400	Insurance agents, brokers, and service	14	14	0.4	37	39	12,541	14,564	529	583	0.1
6500	Real estate	18	20	0.4	40	50	10,800	9,920	569	533	0.1
6510	Real estate operators and lessors	7	9	0.5	21	27	9,714	10,815	226	298	0.2
6530	Real estate agents and managers	9	9	0.3	12	12	11,000	11,000	251	170	0.0
ROBESON, NC											
60 –	**Finance, insurance, and real estate**	130	136	0.9	1,137	1,097	24,000	25,790	26,833	27,165	0.6
6000	Depository institutions	33	41	1.4	747	725	25,542	27,432	17,988	18,391	1.1
6020	Commercial banks	27	35	1.5	677	661	26,157	27,776	16,644	16,961	1.1
6100	Nondepository institutions	16	16	1.1	73	70	21,205	22,857	1,584	1,615	0.4
6140	Personal credit institutions	13	13	1.7	57	55	17,754	18,691	1,094	1,091	0.5
6300	Insurance carriers	9	8	0.7	119	111	30,521	34,378	3,566	3,685	0.3
6400	Insurance agents, brokers, and service	39	37	1.2	112	103	19,036	19,534	2,684	2,419	0.6
6500	Real estate	29	30	0.6	78	78	9,949	10,923	864	919	0.1
6510	Real estate operators and lessors	16	16	0.9	43	47	7,628	6,979	335	355	0.2
6530	Real estate agents and managers	10	11	0.4	30	26	12,400	16,462	428	464	0.1
ROCKINGHAM, NC											
60 –	**Finance, insurance, and real estate**	123	126	0.8	597	684	23,504	21,965	14,706	15,157	0.3
6000	Depository institutions	36	34	1.1	320	355	25,125	23,290	8,629	8,536	0.5
6020	Commercial banks	26	27	1.2	242	289	24,099	23,626	6,786	6,974	0.5
6100	Nondepository institutions	12	14	1.0	56	69	26,857	28,406	1,550	1,940	0.4
6400	Insurance agents, brokers, and service	24	27	0.8	74	78	21,946	21,744	1,612	1,360	0.3
6500	Real estate	39	41	0.8	104	112	10,500	11,821	1,186	1,389	0.2
6510	Real estate operators and lessors	13	13	0.7	29	30	11,172	12,667	363	385	0.2
6530	Real estate agents and managers	20	21	0.7	57	62	9,053	10,065	581	636	0.2
6550	Subdividers and developers	5	6	1.1	18	13	14,000	12,923	188	196	0.2
ROWAN, NC											
60 –	**Finance, insurance, and real estate**	173	168	1.1	1,169	1,087	24,729	25,667	28,324	24,902	0.5
6000	Depository institutions	46	44	1.5	448	453	28,188	27,461	11,111	9,901	0.6
6020	Commercial banks	32	30	1.3	334	318	27,150	28,252	8,024	7,212	0.5
6030	Savings institutions	8	8	2.6	79	81	37,519	31,160	2,487	1,914	2.1
6060	Credit unions	6	6	1.8	35	54	17,029	17,259	600	775	1.0
6100	Nondepository institutions	13	13	0.9	81	83	25,383	24,867	2,162	2,155	0.5
6140	Personal credit institutions	9	9	1.2	39	37	21,026	22,486	864	848	0.4
6300	Insurance carriers	12	10	0.9	142	93	27,127	29,290	3,592	3,012	0.3
6310	Life insurance	5	3	0.8	112	56	24,071	22,857	2,321	1,459	0.4
6400	Insurance agents, brokers, and service	45	43	1.3	144	140	18,500	20,400	2,682	2,975	0.7
6500	Real estate	42	43	0.8	156	143	16,179	22,126	2,966	3,306	0.5
6510	Real estate operators and lessors	20	18	1.0	55	55	10,982	13,091	670	793	0.5
6530	Real estate agents and managers	16	19	0.7	49	46	25,551	36,435	1,522	1,740	0.5
6550	Subdividers and developers	5	5	0.9	51	41	12,863	18,341	761	757	0.7
RUTHERFORD, NC											
60 –	**Finance, insurance, and real estate**	84	88	0.6	425	423	20,113	21,957	8,884	9,779	0.2
6000	Depository institutions	24	23	0.8	201	202	22,468	23,050	4,461	4,556	0.3
6100	Nondepository institutions	6	9	0.6	22	29	23,273	25,931	566	807	0.2
6400	Insurance agents, brokers, and service	24	24	0.7	79	78	15,949	17,179	1,343	1,411	0.3
6500	Real estate	26	28	0.5	93	81	13,376	16,148	1,375	1,864	0.3
6510	Real estate operators and lessors	7	8	0.4	13	11	5,538	9,818	99	117	0.1
6530	Real estate agents and managers	15	16	0.6	71	62	15,099	17,613	1,162	1,619	0.4
6550	Subdividers and developers	4	4	0.7	9	8	11,111	13,500	114	128	0.1
SAMPSON, NC											
60 –	**Finance, insurance, and real estate**	74	76	0.5	304	274	20,697	22,263	6,288	6,444	0.1
6000	Depository institutions	21	22	0.7	141	125	20,936	23,104	2,706	2,972	0.2

Source: County Business Patterns, 1994/95, CBP-94/95, U.S. Department of Commerce, Washington, D.C., November 1997. SIC categories for which data were suppressed or not available for both 1994 and 1995 are not displayed. The employment columns represent mid-March employment in the year. Pay per employee is calculated by dividing 1st Quarter payroll, annualized, by mid-March employment. The columns headed "% State" show the county's percentage of the state total for the SIC in 1995; for example, 1.4% for SIC 6000 means that the county had 1.4 percent of the state's total establishments (or payroll) in SIC 6000 in 1995. A dash (-) is used to indicate that data are not available or cannot be calculated; nec means not elsewhere classified.

Continued on next page.

SIC	Industry	No. Establishments			Employment		Pay / Employee		Annual Payroll ($ 000)		
		1994	1995	% State	1994	1995	1994	1995	1994	1995	% State
SAMPSON, NC - [continued]											
6100	Nondepository institutions	10	10	0.7	54	54	24,148	28,815	1,285	1,677	0.4
6140	Personal credit institutions	7	7	0.9	30	30	22,000	23,333	625	778	0.4
6400	Insurance agents, brokers, and service	24	25	0.8	61	63	15,475	16,063	1,114	1,020	0.2
6500	Real estate	16	16	0.3	40	23	15,600	9,913	722	298	0.0
6510	Real estate operators and lessors	5	5	0.3	30	11	17,067	11,273	594	128	0.1
6530	Real estate agents and managers	8	8	0.3	9	9	11,556	9,333	107	122	0.0
SCOTLAND, NC											
60 –	**Finance, insurance, and real estate**	63	66	0.4	306	295	21,686	24,108	7,238	7,350	0.1
6000	Depository institutions	15	16	0.5	110	105	22,436	23,429	2,447	2,315	0.1
6020	Commercial banks	10	11	0.5	81	75	21,333	22,187	1,758	1,689	0.1
6100	Nondepository institutions	7	8	0.5	30	33	22,533	25,455	727	843	0.2
6400	Insurance agents, brokers, and service	16	14	0.4	84	64	16,905	24,188	1,567	1,645	0.4
6500	Real estate	19	22	0.4	57	68	12,561	12,118	843	1,041	0.2
6510	Real estate operators and lessors	9	9	0.5	33	36	14,061	13,111	564	603	0.4
6530	Real estate agents and managers	7	10	0.4	19	25	8,211	9,920	175	327	0.1
STANLY, NC											
60 –	**Finance, insurance, and real estate**	76	80	0.5	445	478	20,836	21,741	9,751	10,236	0.2
6000	Depository institutions	23	23	0.8	246	251	22,341	20,845	5,273	5,221	0.3
6100	Nondepository institutions	10	10	0.7	31	32	17,161	25,000	614	780	0.2
6140	Personal credit institutions	7	7	0.9	24	27	15,333	24,444	460	634	0.3
6400	Insurance agents, brokers, and service	17	19	0.6	66	60	19,152	21,467	1,500	1,536	0.4
6500	Real estate	19	20	0.4	90	106	16,267	19,887	1,840	1,678	0.3
STOKES, NC											
60 –	**Finance, insurance, and real estate**	24	26	0.2	109	114	21,725	22,386	2,400	2,583	0.1
6000	Depository institutions	9	9	0.3	78	83	21,846	22,554	1,694	1,852	0.1
6020	Commercial banks	9	9	0.4	78	83	21,846	22,554	1,694	1,852	0.1
SURRY, NC											
60 –	**Finance, insurance, and real estate**	101	113	0.7	640	637	22,525	25,137	14,117	16,196	0.3
6000	Depository institutions	25	25	0.8	392	379	24,224	27,947	8,650	9,994	0.6
6100	Nondepository institutions	11	14	1.0	50	55	21,360	22,618	1,320	1,543	0.3
6400	Insurance agents, brokers, and service	30	29	0.9	108	106	22,111	21,585	2,555	2,753	0.6
6500	Real estate	30	39	0.7	72	80	10,278	12,850	950	1,211	0.2
6510	Real estate operators and lessors	15	19	1.0	37	45	6,703	11,467	361	502	0.3
6530	Real estate agents and managers	12	16	0.6	25	27	16,160	16,444	466	495	0.1
SWAIN, NC											
60 –	**Finance, insurance, and real estate**	10	10	0.1	42	40	17,333	19,700	826	787	0.0
6500	Real estate	3	3	0.1	2	2	8,000	6,000	29	30	0.0
TRANSYLVANIA, NC											
60 –	**Finance, insurance, and real estate**	47	55	0.4	277	291	24,462	21,649	6,562	6,606	0.1
6000	Depository institutions	11	11	0.4	107	113	22,916	20,000	2,394	2,228	0.1
6020	Commercial banks	7	7	0.3	79	81	24,253	20,938	1,855	1,647	0.1
6400	Insurance agents, brokers, and service	7	8	0.2	41	32	13,854	19,750	655	672	0.2
6500	Real estate	24	30	0.6	113	130	22,938	19,292	2,607	2,829	0.4
6510	Real estate operators and lessors	4	4	0.2	11	11	14,545	13,455	194	203	0.1
6530	Real estate agents and managers	15	18	0.6	68	74	14,765	18,324	1,287	1,481	0.4
6550	Subdividers and developers	4	4	0.7	34	39	42,000	23,282	1,125	811	0.8
TYRRELL, NC											
60 –	**Finance, insurance, and real estate**	5	5	0.0	12	17	13,000	14,118	198	235	0.0
UNION, NC											
60 –	**Finance, insurance, and real estate**	145	143	0.9	1,052	1,033	24,954	26,443	24,928	25,551	0.5

Source: County Business Patterns, 1994/95, CBP-94/95, U.S. Department of Commerce, Washington, D.C., November 1997. SIC categories for which data were suppressed or not available for both 1994 and 1995 are not displayed. The employment columns represent mid-March employment in the year. Pay per employee is calculated by dividing 1st Quarter payroll, annualized, by mid-March employment. The columns headed "% State" show the county's percentage of the state total for the SIC in 1995; for example, 1.4% for SIC 6000 means that the county had 1.4 percent of the state's total establishments (or payroll) in SIC 6000 in 1995. A dash (-) is used to indicate that data are not available or cannot be calculated; nec means not elsewhere classified.

Continued on next page.

SIC	Industry	No. Establishments			Employment		Pay / Employee		Annual Payroll ($ 000)		
		1994	1995	% State	1994	1995	1994	1995	1994	1995	% State
UNION, NC - [continued]											
6000	Depository institutions	36	30	1.0	675	693	23,822	25,553	14,749	15,208	0.9
6100	Nondepository institutions	15	17	1.2	84	63	23,810	29,079	1,872	1,920	0.4
6140	Personal credit institutions	11	11	1.4	30	35	28,400	33,257	995	1,032	0.5
6210	Security brokers and dealers	3	3	0.6	4	6	16,000	40,667	63	225	0.1
6300	Insurance carriers	10	11	1.0	82	79	43,317	42,127	3,584	3,357	0.3
6400	Insurance agents, brokers, and service	35	34	1.1	70	74	20,629	21,189	1,523	1,918	0.4
6500	Real estate	41	43	0.8	114	100	16,807	16,000	1,967	1,755	0.3
6510	Real estate operators and lessors	17	16	0.9	47	31	17,362	16,774	776	466	0.3
6530	Real estate agents and managers	15	17	0.6	34	29	15,647	19,448	620	678	0.2
6550	Subdividers and developers	6	6	1.1	33	39	17,212	13,128	551	591	0.6
VANCE, NC											
60 –	**Finance, insurance, and real estate**	76	78	0.5	317	351	22,486	21,869	7,707	8,890	0.2
6000	Depository institutions	12	13	0.4	114	127	24,211	21,449	2,593	3,338	0.2
6020	Commercial banks	7	8	0.3	100	110	24,960	21,782	2,311	3,037	0.2
6060	Credit unions	5	5	1.5	14	17	18,857	19,294	282	301	0.4
6100	Nondepository institutions	10	11	0.7	44	52	22,909	24,615	1,092	1,282	0.3
6400	Insurance agents, brokers, and service	15	15	0.5	49	49	23,429	24,245	1,489	1,467	0.3
6500	Real estate	34	32	0.6	98	106	15,878	16,604	1,835	2,040	0.3
6510	Real estate operators and lessors	16	15	0.8	43	42	13,116	16,952	765	940	0.6
6530	Real estate agents and managers	14	12	0.4	35	39	22,171	20,615	821	815	0.2
6550	Subdividers and developers	3	3	0.5	20	25	10,800	9,760	242	275	0.3
WAKE, NC											
60 –	**Finance, insurance, and real estate**	1,537	1,612	10.5	18,368	18,869	30,072	32,662	547,240	605,473	12.3
6000	Depository institutions	240	249	8.2	5,100	4,661	26,727	26,896	135,030	129,095	7.5
6020	Commercial banks	178	183	7.9	4,099	3,573	27,683	28,124	111,572	100,455	6.7
6030	Savings institutions	23	26	8.5	238	227	25,042	27,401	6,118	10,356	11.2
6060	Credit unions	36	36	10.7	747	839	21,960	21,340	16,866	17,555	23.6
6090	Functions closely related to banking	3	4	6.3	16	22	29,500	34,000	474	729	-
6100	Nondepository institutions	135	137	9.3	1,251	1,181	39,047	46,174	45,788	50,157	11.1
6140	Personal credit institutions	41	44	5.8	324	375	30,432	31,872	9,758	11,895	5.8
6160	Mortgage bankers and brokers	86	83	16.6	768	679	37,760	47,929	27,453	28,014	16.6
6200	Security and commodity brokers	86	92	12.6	700	715	56,177	62,931	35,335	45,085	11.6
6210	Security brokers and dealers	48	49	9.8	565	599	64,304	69,643	32,535	41,056	12.4
6280	Security and commodity services	38	42	19.1	135	116	22,163	28,276	2,800	4,023	7.0
6300	Insurance carriers	167	161	14.3	5,799	5,530	31,127	37,442	178,204	187,455	17.6
6310	Life insurance	56	49	12.7	1,471	1,261	26,722	32,752	35,908	33,504	8.7
6320	Medical service and health insurance	14	13	20.3	800	1,064	32,015	31,327	27,299	38,640	22.0
6321	Accident and health insurance	8	7	20.0	613	618	27,772	29,301	17,207	22,627	42.0
6324	Hospital and medical service plans	6	6	20.7	187	446	45,925	34,135	10,092	16,013	13.1
6330	Fire, marine, and casualty insurance	78	80	14.7	2,462	2,439	32,567	36,213	83,854	85,593	21.3
6400	Insurance agents, brokers, and service	311	321	10.0	1,386	1,424	27,374	30,037	40,870	44,672	10.4
6500	Real estate	554	608	11.2	3,292	3,757	22,691	22,990	83,743	96,587	14.9
6510	Real estate operators and lessors	176	201	10.9	761	812	16,373	18,961	14,172	17,641	11.3
6530	Real estate agents and managers	313	329	11.6	2,301	2,703	24,741	24,110	62,072	70,840	19.0
6550	Subdividers and developers	51	55	9.9	220	214	22,145	22,037	6,430	6,974	6.7
6552	Subdividers and developers, n.e.c.	39	40	11.0	135	125	22,163	20,352	4,464	4,160	5.2
6553	Cemetery subdividers and developers	10	8	5.2	85	67	22,118	25,254	1,885	1,881	8.3
6710	Holding offices	10	12	11.1	83	425	166,940	58,221	8,760	21,822	17.3
6732	Educational, religious, etc. trusts	10	12	30.0	43	56	21,023	20,786	978	1,258	24.5
6790	Miscellaneous investing	16	14	12.1	85	453	71,624	22,790	4,626	9,261	32.6
WARREN, NC											
60 –	**Finance, insurance, and real estate**	16	12	0.1	52	49	20,000	20,735	1,044	977	0.0
6000	Depository institutions	4	4	0.1	31	31	22,452	21,935	662	617	0.0
6400	Insurance agents, brokers, and service	5	3	0.1	12	11	14,000	16,000	191	185	0.0
WASHINGTON, NC											
60 –	**Finance, insurance, and real estate**	21	22	0.1	112	107	18,929	22,131	2,169	2,110	0.0

Source: County Business Patterns, 1994/95, CBP-94/95, U.S. Department of Commerce, Washington, D.C., November 1997. SIC categories for which data were suppressed or not available for both 1994 and 1995 are *not* displayed. The employment columns represent mid-March employment in the year. Pay per employee is calculated by dividing 1st Quarter payroll, annualized, by mid-March employment. The columns headed "% State" show the county's percentage of the state total for the SIC in 1995; for example, 1.4% for SIC 6000 means that the county had 1.4 percent of the state's total establishments (or payroll) in SIC 6000 in 1995. A dash (-) is used to indicate that data are not available or cannot be calculated; *nec* means not elsewhere classified.

Continued on next page.

SIC	Industry	No. Establishments			Employment		Pay / Employee		Annual Payroll ($ 000)		
		1994	1995	% State	1994	1995	1994	1995	1994	1995	% State
WASHINGTON, NC - [continued]											
6000	Depository institutions	9	9	0.3	81	76	19,901	23,579	1,649	1,500	0.1
6100	Nondepository institutions	4	4	0.3	15	15	14,133	15,200	225	261	0.1
6400	Insurance agents, brokers, and service	3	4	0.1	13	13	20,615	25,231	262	264	0.1
6500	Real estate	5	5	0.1	3	3	9,333	6,667	33	85	0.0
WATAUGA, NC											
60 –	**Finance, insurance, and real estate**	97	101	0.7	596	568	16,584	17,056	10,808	10,796	0.2
6000	Depository institutions	13	12	0.4	163	155	22,479	22,581	3,598	3,484	0.2
6100	Nondepository institutions	9	9	0.6	20	16	18,200	23,750	381	457	0.1
6400	Insurance agents, brokers, and service	16	17	0.5	78	75	19,282	21,867	1,779	2,012	0.5
6500	Real estate	52	57	1.0	313	314	11,080	11,987	4,063	4,374	0.7
6510	Real estate operators and lessors	13	12	0.7	69	74	10,319	11,838	809	978	0.6
6530	Real estate agents and managers	34	39	1.4	199	204	12,342	13,000	2,873	3,094	0.8
6550	Subdividers and developers	5	5	0.9	45	36	6,667	6,556	381	284	0.3
WAYNE, NC											
60 –	**Finance, insurance, and real estate**	177	180	1.2	1,183	1,220	23,750	24,049	31,655	31,009	0.6
6000	Depository institutions	43	42	1.4	483	469	25,665	25,510	12,482	12,368	0.7
6020	Commercial banks	33	32	1.4	425	408	26,560	26,412	11,329	11,080	0.7
6140	Personal credit institutions	13	13	1.7	71	81	21,972	22,519	1,607	1,778	0.9
6300	Insurance carriers	10	8	0.7	289	303	25,606	30,574	9,483	9,547	0.9
6400	Insurance agents, brokers, and service	50	46	1.4	194	152	17,711	18,605	4,443	3,083	0.7
6500	Real estate	51	56	1.0	120	173	19,200	13,965	2,641	2,795	0.4
6530	Real estate agents and managers	26	25	0.9	69	76	21,449	18,684	1,485	1,403	0.4
WILKES, NC											
60 –	**Finance, insurance, and real estate**	77	85	0.6	957	690	21,864	24,730	21,754	16,687	0.3
6000	Depository institutions	20	22	0.7	699	422	19,754	21,156	13,733	8,663	0.5
6100	Nondepository institutions	6	9	0.6	31	75	25,419	41,760	711	1,919	0.4
6200	Security and commodity brokers	7	6	0.8	13	13	32,923	30,462	403	535	0.1
6300	Insurance carriers	8	7	0.6	90	40	31,422	26,700	3,185	1,676	0.2
6400	Insurance agents, brokers, and service	15	17	0.5	59	67	27,051	28,418	2,069	2,230	0.5
6500	Real estate	21	24	0.4	65	73	22,708	22,411	1,653	1,664	0.3
6510	Real estate operators and lessors	6	8	0.4	13	11	9,846	11,636	134	141	0.1
6530	Real estate agents and managers	10	9	0.3	23	33	23,130	21,455	610	666	0.2
6550	Subdividers and developers	4	5	0.9	29	28	28,138	28,429	908	847	0.8
WILSON, NC											
60 –	**Finance, insurance, and real estate**	145	141	0.9	1,826	1,552	30,458	31,887	53,585	52,162	1.1
6000	Depository institutions	36	34	1.1	1,376	1,138	31,262	32,699	41,157	37,983	2.2
6020	Commercial banks	28	27	1.2	1,238	1,094	32,233	33,203	39,752	37,051	2.5
6030	Savings institutions	5	4	1.3	112	18	23,321	19,778	905	379	0.4
6060	Credit unions	3	3	0.9	26	26	19,231	20,462	500	553	0.7
6100	Nondepository institutions	13	14	1.0	97	99	22,557	24,525	2,371	2,335	0.5
6300	Insurance carriers	8	8	0.7	78	69	33,590	36,000	2,575	2,331	0.2
6400	Insurance agents, brokers, and service	34	36	1.1	104	104	27,423	30,731	2,675	5,032	1.2
6500	Real estate	44	40	0.7	128	98	15,625	15,592	2,177	1,840	0.3
6510	Real estate operators and lessors	10	8	0.4	39	30	12,205	13,467	498	408	0.3
6530	Real estate agents and managers	28	28	1.0	59	57	14,712	15,719	1,036	1,115	0.3
YADKIN, NC											
60 –	**Finance, insurance, and real estate**	25	25	0.2	122	131	19,148	19,481	2,551	2,710	0.1
6000	Depository institutions	8	8	0.3	66	65	21,394	21,785	1,461	1,475	0.1
6400	Insurance agents, brokers, and service	8	8	0.2	29	29	19,448	20,000	649	635	0.1
6500	Real estate	4	5	0.1	16	25	9,250	9,600	187	263	0.0

Source: County Business Patterns, 1994/95, CBP-94/95, U.S. Department of Commerce, Washington, D.C., November 1997. SIC categories for which data were suppressed or not available for both 1994 and 1995 are *not* displayed. The employment columns represent mid-March employment in the year. Pay per employee is calculated by dividing 1st Quarter payroll, annualized, by mid-March employment. The columns headed "% State" show the county's percentage of the state total for the SIC in 1995; for example, 1.4% for SIC 6000 means that the county had 1.4 percent of the state's total establishments (or payroll) in SIC 6000 in 1995. A dash (-) is used to indicate that data are not available or cannot be calculated; *nec* means not elsewhere classified.

SIC	Industry	No. Establishments			Employment		Pay / Employee		Annual Payroll ($ 000)		
		1994	1995	% State	1994	1995	1994	1995	1994	1995	% State
YANCEY, NC											
60 –	**Finance, insurance, and real estate**	25	26	0.2	97	148	16,454	14,405	1,950	2,735	0.1
6400	Insurance agents, brokers, and service	7	6	0.2	19	54	15,789	11,852	370	882	0.2
6500	Real estate	10	12	0.2	32	55	11,375	11,564	719	1,080	0.2

Source: County Business Patterns, 1994/95, CBP-94/95, U.S. Department of Commerce, Washington, D.C., November 1997. SIC categories for which data were suppressed or not available for both 1994 and 1995 are not displayed. The employment columns represent mid-March employment in the year. Pay per employee is calculated by dividing 1st Quarter payroll, annualized, by mid-March employment. The columns headed "% State" show the county's percentage of the state total for the SIC in 1995; for example, 1.4% for SIC 6000 means that the county had 1.4 percent of the state's total establishments (or payroll) in SIC 6000 in 1995. A dash (-) is used to indicate that data are not available or cannot be calculated; nec means not elsewhere classified.

NORTH DAKOTA

SIC	Industry	No. Establishments			Employment		Pay / Employee		Annual Payroll ($ 000)		
		1994	1995	% State	1994	1995	1994	1995	1994	1995	% State
ADAMS, ND											
60 –	**Finance, insurance, and real estate**	12	12	*0.6*	-	-	-	-	-	-	-
BARNES, ND											
60 –	**Finance, insurance, and real estate**	31	30	*1.5*	149	165	25,289	25,236	3,634	3,934	*1.2*
6000	Depository institutions	7	7	*1.6*	94	106	26,766	27,170	2,494	2,717	*1.8*
6550	Subdividers and developers	4	4	*8.9*	1	1	12,000	12,000	30	26	*3.2*
6553	Cemetery subdividers and developers	4	4	*11.8*	1	1	12,000	12,000	30	26	-
BENSON, ND											
60 –	**Finance, insurance, and real estate**	12	11	*0.6*	61	56	20,066	22,000	1,265	1,350	*0.4*
6400	Insurance agents, brokers, and service	5	4	*0.6*	7	5	8,000	10,400	54	55	*0.2*
BILLINGS, ND											
60 –	**Finance, insurance, and real estate**	1	1	*0.1*	-	-	-	-	-	-	-
BOTTINEAU, ND											
60 –	**Finance, insurance, and real estate**	31	32	*1.6*	116	103	21,517	21,553	2,332	2,111	*0.6*
6000	Depository institutions	10	10	*2.3*	78	67	25,231	26,925	1,810	1,646	*1.1*
6400	Insurance agents, brokers, and service	8	8	*1.3*	14	13	12,571	12,000	192	190	*0.5*
6500	Real estate	9	10	*1.7*	16	16	7,000	5,500	136	131	*0.4*
BURKE, ND											
60 –	**Finance, insurance, and real estate**	13	13	*0.7*	42	43	14,095	15,349	671	742	*0.2*
6000	Depository institutions	4	4	*0.9*	26	27	19,385	19,556	566	603	*0.4*
6020	Commercial banks	4	4	*1.4*	26	27	19,385	19,556	566	603	*0.6*
6500	Real estate	6	6	*1.0*	10	7	3,200	5,143	35	37	*0.1*
BURLEIGH, ND											
60 –	**Finance, insurance, and real estate**	239	241	*12.2*	1,517	1,404	24,327	28,094	37,376	39,184	*11.7*
6000	Depository institutions	37	35	*8.0*	567	588	25,961	30,823	13,235	15,668	*10.2*
6020	Commercial banks	19	18	*6.3*	410	425	28,371	29,920	10,184	11,538	*11.1*
6100	Nondepository institutions	8	9	*13.8*	76	32	15,000	30,125	952	617	*4.1*
6140	Personal credit institutions	3	3	*16.7*	51	14	8,863	29,714	415	397	*12.5*
6200	Security and commodity brokers	19	20	*20.2*	134	133	43,313	41,805	6,178	5,849	*29.8*
6210	Security brokers and dealers	15	16	*21.9*	131	130	43,695	41,908	6,090	5,720	*30.8*
6300	Insurance carriers	19	18	*16.1*	236	177	28,678	35,706	6,999	6,248	*10.2*
6400	Insurance agents, brokers, and service	71	72	*11.5*	174	182	19,379	19,407	4,321	5,412	*15.5*
6500	Real estate	74	76	*13.0*	286	248	13,720	14,565	4,119	3,680	*10.5*
6510	Real estate operators and lessors	37	39	*13.5*	118	119	9,627	10,084	1,246	1,291	*7.4*
6530	Real estate agents and managers	29	28	*14.5*	130	97	17,662	20,412	2,332	1,850	*13.9*
6700	Holding and other investment offices	11	11	*22.4*	44	44	26,727	30,273	1,572	1,710	*11.1*
CASS, ND											
60 –	**Finance, insurance, and real estate**	434	440	*22.3*	5,219	5,734	25,843	30,827	133,186	149,636	*44.7*
6000	Depository institutions	74	72	*16.5*	1,553	2,067	25,666	39,232	38,563	49,624	*32.3*
6020	Commercial banks	43	44	*15.3*	818	835	25,237	24,872	19,759	19,426	*18.7*
6090	Functions closely related to banking	3	3	*42.9*	60	48	24,467	32,667	1,464	1,422	-
6100	Nondepository institutions	18	18	*27.7*	156	149	43,308	45,235	5,590	5,640	*37.5*
6140	Personal credit institutions	7	7	*38.9*	78	67	33,385	32,836	2,423	2,042	*64.4*
6160	Mortgage bankers and brokers	6	6	*54.5*	16	18	35,000	31,778	535	659	-
6200	Security and commodity brokers	23	26	*26.3*	170	160	56,494	48,625	8,331	7,981	*40.6*

Source: County Business Patterns, 1994/95, CBP-94/95, U.S. Department of Commerce, Washington, D.C., November 1997. SIC categories for which data were suppressed or not available for both 1994 and 1995 are not *displayed. The employment columns represent mid-March employment in the year. Pay per employee is calculated by dividing 1st Quarter payroll, annualized, by mid-March employment. The columns headed "% State" show the county's percentage of the state total for the SIC in 1995; for example, 1.4% for SIC 6000 means that the county had 1.4 percent of the state's total establishments (or payroll) in SIC 6000 in 1995. A dash (-) is used to indicate that data are not available or cannot be calculated;* nec *means not elsewhere classified.*

Continued on next page.

SIC	Industry	No. Establishments			Employment		Pay / Employee		Annual Payroll ($ 000)		
		1994	1995	% State	1994	1995	1994	1995	1994	1995	% State
CASS, ND - [continued]											
6210	Security brokers and dealers	15	18	24.7	132	129	67,182	57,395	7,873	7,589	40.9
6280	Security and commodity services	8	8	44.4	38	31	19,368	12,129	458	392	-
6300	Insurance carriers	40	42	37.5	1,725	1,567	26,841	28,699	46,512	45,097	73.7
6400	Insurance agents, brokers, and service	127	131	20.9	493	549	27,181	26,251	14,016	13,789	39.5
6500	Real estate	137	138	23.5	1,005	1,134	14,229	13,072	15,168	16,595	47.4
6510	Real estate operators and lessors	58	61	21.1	407	482	16,177	15,369	7,201	8,424	48.1
6530	Real estate agents and managers	61	59	30.6	530	565	12,264	10,726	6,659	6,879	51.6
6550	Subdividers and developers	13	13	28.9	22	29	17,455	16,552	443	452	55.0
6552	Subdividers and developers, n.e.c.	7	8	72.7	8	14	31,500	23,143	226	302	-
6710	Holding offices	6	6	33.3	58	86	56,414	72,605	3,492	10,053	77.8
6730	Trusts	3	4	33.3	6	6	9,333	12,000	65	140	45.8
CAVALIER, ND											
60 –	**Finance, insurance, and real estate**	23	22	1.1	83	90	21,301	22,400	1,986	2,255	0.7
6000	Depository institutions	5	5	1.1	49	53	26,776	27,698	1,415	1,529	1.0
6400	Insurance agents, brokers, and service	10	10	1.6	21	19	13,905	15,579	421	475	1.4
6500	Real estate	4	3	0.5	5	5	6,400	6,400	31	29	0.1
DICKEY, ND											
60 –	**Finance, insurance, and real estate**	15	14	0.7	68	70	19,000	20,000	1,521	1,275	0.4
6000	Depository institutions	5	5	1.1	53	55	21,358	22,109	1,352	1,099	0.7
6400	Insurance agents, brokers, and service	6	5	0.8	10	9	12,800	14,667	125	131	0.4
6500	Real estate	4	4	0.7	5	6	6,400	8,667	44	45	0.1
DUNN, ND											
60 –	**Finance, insurance, and real estate**	8	8	0.4	-	-	-	-	-	-	-
EDDY, ND											
60 –	**Finance, insurance, and real estate**	6	7	0.4	22	28	16,000	14,857	361	419	0.1
EMMONS, ND											
60 –	**Finance, insurance, and real estate**	12	11	0.6	56	58	20,357	22,897	1,236	1,362	0.4
6400	Insurance agents, brokers, and service	4	4	0.6	6	8	9,333	8,500	60	72	0.2
GRAND FORKS, ND											
60 –	**Finance, insurance, and real estate**	172	164	8.3	1,219	1,195	23,734	25,466	27,672	27,981	8.4
6000	Depository institutions	34	35	8.0	521	519	21,359	27,114	10,931	11,964	7.8
6020	Commercial banks	16	16	5.6	403	393	22,223	25,130	8,815	8,964	8.6
6100	Nondepository institutions	6	6	9.2	68	67	39,471	41,015	1,993	1,940	12.9
6200	Security and commodity brokers	10	11	11.1	39	48	60,718	36,333	2,059	2,042	10.4
6300	Insurance carriers	12	12	10.7	142	138	29,634	30,696	4,270	4,266	7.0
6330	Fire, marine, and casualty insurance	7	7	11.9	82	85	27,756	29,082	2,248	2,492	15.5
6400	Insurance agents, brokers, and service	45	46	7.3	157	161	21,529	22,435	3,469	3,651	10.5
6500	Real estate	59	50	8.5	275	247	15,622	14,316	4,072	3,652	10.4
6510	Real estate operators and lessors	29	22	7.6	142	105	11,183	12,343	1,710	1,335	7.6
6530	Real estate agents and managers	24	22	11.4	113	121	14,655	16,099	1,813	1,915	14.4
6700	Holding and other investment offices	6	4	8.2	17	15	51,059	32,267	878	466	3.0
GRANT, ND											
60 –	**Finance, insurance, and real estate**	8	10	0.5	42	51	18,857	17,020	863	1,012	0.3
6500	Real estate	3	4	0.7	3	5	6,667	12,000	48	64	0.2
HETTINGER, ND											
60 –	**Finance, insurance, and real estate**	15	13	0.7	51	52	18,196	17,846	907	966	0.3
6500	Real estate	3	3	0.5	6	5	6,667	6,400	46	32	0.1
LA MOURE, ND											
60 –	**Finance, insurance, and real estate**	17	17	0.9	90	89	21,422	22,202	1,854	1,924	0.6

Source: County Business Patterns, 1994/95, CBP-94/95, U.S. Department of Commerce, Washington, D.C., November 1997. SIC categories for which data were suppressed or not available for both 1994 and 1995 are *not* displayed. The employment columns represent mid-March employment in the year. Pay per employee is calculated by dividing 1st Quarter payroll, annualized, by mid-March employment. The columns headed "% State" show the county's percentage of the state total for the SIC in 1995; for example, 1.4% for SIC 6000 means that the county had 1.4 percent of the state's total establishments (or payroll) in SIC 6000 in 1995. A dash (-) is used to indicate that data are not available or cannot be calculated; *nec* means not elsewhere classified.

Continued on next page.

SIC	Industry	No. Establishments			Employment		Pay / Employee		Annual Payroll ($ 000)		
		1994	1995	% State	1994	1995	1994	1995	1994	1995	% State
LA MOURE, ND - [continued]											
6000	Depository institutions	8	8	*1.8*	67	68	20,955	21,706	1,466	1,544	*1.0*
6020	Commercial banks	5	5	*1.7*	46	46	22,348	23,217	1,082	1,146	*1.1*
6060	Credit unions	3	3	*3.4*	21	22	17,905	18,545	384	398	*-*
LOGAN, ND											
60 –	**Finance, insurance, and real estate**	6	7	*0.4*	-	-	-	-	-	-	*-*
6000	Depository institutions	3	3	*0.7*	26	25	17,692	19,680	719	751	*0.5*
MCHENRY, ND											
60 –	**Finance, insurance, and real estate**	19	19	*1.0*	65	79	15,938	14,987	1,199	1,287	*0.4*
6000	Depository institutions	8	8	*1.8*	47	59	18,043	16,881	1,035	1,110	*0.7*
6400	Insurance agents, brokers, and service	4	4	*0.6*	7	9	19,429	14,667	99	106	*0.3*
6500	Real estate	7	7	*1.2*	11	11	4,727	5,091	65	71	*0.2*
MCINTOSH, ND											
60 –	**Finance, insurance, and real estate**	14	14	*0.7*	56	57	16,929	17,404	979	1,021	*0.3*
6400	Insurance agents, brokers, and service	5	5	*0.8*	6	6	6,667	8,000	37	38	*0.1*
6500	Real estate	3	3	*0.5*	4	4	6,000	8,000	27	30	*0.1*
MCKENZIE, ND											
60 –	**Finance, insurance, and real estate**	9	10	*0.5*	100	121	21,640	23,769	2,088	2,705	*0.8*
6000	Depository institutions	5	6	*1.4*	93	113	22,065	24,000	1,946	2,558	*1.7*
MCLEAN, ND											
60 –	**Finance, insurance, and real estate**	27	26	*1.3*	135	134	16,711	15,940	2,540	2,440	*0.7*
6000	Depository institutions	10	10	*2.3*	101	93	19,406	19,613	2,218	2,101	*1.4*
6400	Insurance agents, brokers, and service	10	9	*1.4*	16	16	9,250	9,750	156	156	*0.4*
MERCER, ND											
60 –	**Finance, insurance, and real estate**	21	20	*1.0*	100	103	16,560	18,563	1,730	1,909	*0.6*
6000	Depository institutions	8	7	*1.6*	80	79	17,150	20,354	1,454	1,623	*1.1*
6500	Real estate	5	4	*0.7*	7	8	7,429	6,000	59	50	*0.1*
MORTON, ND											
60 –	**Finance, insurance, and real estate**	42	42	*2.1*	253	244	23,953	27,984	5,261	5,435	*1.6*
6000	Depository institutions	12	12	*2.7*	130	124	22,277	29,548	2,962	3,025	*2.0*
6020	Commercial banks	7	7	*2.4*	112	107	22,679	29,084	2,612	2,561	*2.5*
6510	Real estate operators and lessors	7	6	*2.1*	15	10	9,067	6,800	109	66	*0.4*
MOUNTRAIL, ND											
60 –	**Finance, insurance, and real estate**	20	19	*1.0*	127	119	19,528	21,445	2,455	2,811	*0.8*
6400	Insurance agents, brokers, and service	10	9	*1.4*	17	16	9,647	13,750	217	316	*0.9*
NELSON, ND											
60 –	**Finance, insurance, and real estate**	22	21	*1.1*	68	76	17,529	19,474	1,628	1,915	*0.6*
6000	Depository institutions	8	8	*1.8*	52	56	20,846	23,000	1,497	1,726	*1.1*
6500	Real estate	8	8	*1.4*	7	9	4,571	4,889	45	44	*0.1*
6510	Real estate operators and lessors	5	5	*1.7*	6	7	4,000	4,571	29	28	*0.2*
OLIVER, ND											
60 –	**Finance, insurance, and real estate**	4	4	*0.2*	-	-	-	-	-	-	*-*
PEMBINA, ND											
60 –	**Finance, insurance, and real estate**	30	29	*1.5*	129	126	22,078	22,603	2,886	2,791	*0.8*
6000	Depository institutions	10	10	*2.3*	96	88	23,292	24,364	2,296	2,195	*1.4*
6500	Real estate	8	8	*1.4*	7	14	9,143	10,286	84	97	*0.3*
PIERCE, ND											
60 –	**Finance, insurance, and real estate**	16	18	*0.9*	84	88	18,857	18,909	1,644	1,802	*0.5*

Source: County Business Patterns, 1994/95, CBP-94/95, U.S. Department of Commerce, Washington, D.C., November 1997. SIC categories for which data were suppressed or not available for both 1994 and 1995 are *not* displayed. The employment columns represent mid-March employment in the year. Pay per employee is calculated by dividing 1st Quarter payroll, annualized, by mid-March employment. The columns headed "% State" show the county's percentage of the state total for the SIC in 1995; for example, 1.4% for SIC 6000 means that the county had 1.4 percent of the state's total establishments (or payroll) in SIC 6000 in 1995. A dash (-) is used to indicate that data are not available or cannot be calculated; *nec* means not elsewhere classified.

Continued on next page.

SIC	Industry	No. Establishments			Employment		Pay / Employee		Annual Payroll ($ 000)		
		1994	1995	% State	1994	1995	1994	1995	1994	1995	% State
PIERCE, ND - [continued]											
6000	Depository institutions	3	3	0.7	32	34	19,625	20,118	653	711	0.5
6400	Insurance agents, brokers, and service	5	6	1.0	10	10	10,400	13,200	113	116	0.3
6500	Real estate	5	5	0.9	4	5	11,000	11,200	49	58	0.2
RAMSEY, ND											
60 –	**Finance, insurance, and real estate**	40	37	1.9	253	270	16,933	17,185	4,584	4,807	1.4
6000	Depository institutions	11	11	2.5	151	162	20,026	20,691	3,214	3,481	2.3
6020	Commercial banks	8	8	2.8	120	129	20,633	20,186	2,649	2,775	2.7
6400	Insurance agents, brokers, and service	13	13	2.1	31	29	15,484	16,690	542	462	1.3
6500	Real estate	11	9	1.5	63	69	6,857	7,014	495	564	1.6
RANSOM, ND											
60 –	**Finance, insurance, and real estate**	21	19	1.0	90	77	20,444	25,714	1,653	1,587	0.5
6500	Real estate	6	6	1.0	5	7	10,400	8,571	63	70	0.2
RENVILLE, ND											
60 –	**Finance, insurance, and real estate**	13	13	0.7	30	32	12,933	12,500	421	403	0.1
6000	Depository institutions	5	5	1.1	20	22	14,600	14,182	309	308	0.2
6400	Insurance agents, brokers, and service	5	5	0.8	5	6	14,400	10,667	86	70	0.2
6500	Real estate	3	3	0.5	5	4	4,800	6,000	26	25	0.1
RICHLAND, ND											
60 –	**Finance, insurance, and real estate**	42	42	2.1	188	193	23,596	23,440	4,050	4,006	1.2
6000	Depository institutions	13	13	3.0	108	109	24,741	27,009	2,479	2,598	1.7
6020	Commercial banks	8	8	2.8	82	85	26,146	25,318	1,964	1,976	1.9
6400	Insurance agents, brokers, and service	11	11	1.8	18	18	19,778	21,556	348	377	1.1
6500	Real estate	14	14	2.4	43	46	11,070	9,913	573	513	1.5
ROLETTE, ND											
60 –	**Finance, insurance, and real estate**	17	17	0.9	83	87	16,530	17,103	1,499	1,641	0.5
6000	Depository institutions	5	5	1.1	63	64	17,905	18,875	1,227	1,327	0.9
6400	Insurance agents, brokers, and service	7	6	1.0	13	14	15,692	16,571	223	257	0.7
SIOUX, ND											
60 –	**Finance, insurance, and real estate**	1	1	0.1	-	-	-	-	-	-	-
STARK, ND											
60 –	**Finance, insurance, and real estate**	71	74	3.7	261	295	19,801	19,986	5,392	5,301	1.6
6000	Depository institutions	10	10	2.3	138	154	18,928	19,844	2,943	2,665	1.7
6020	Commercial banks	6	6	2.1	104	118	19,154	19,017	2,343	1,896	1.8
6400	Insurance agents, brokers, and service	30	31	4.9	54	55	12,963	14,691	759	825	2.4
6500	Real estate	21	22	3.8	35	39	9,257	9,744	398	446	1.3
6700	Holding and other investment offices	3	4	8.2	10	22	21,200	13,818	222	311	2.0
STEELE, ND											
60 –	**Finance, insurance, and real estate**	9	7	0.4	32	34	17,250	17,647	818	853	0.3
6000	Depository institutions	3	3	0.7	23	24	19,130	20,500	641	686	0.4
6020	Commercial banks	3	3	1.0	23	24	19,130	20,500	641	686	0.7
STUTSMAN, ND											
60 –	**Finance, insurance, and real estate**	64	63	3.2	412	379	21,951	24,433	9,081	9,386	2.8
6000	Depository institutions	11	10	2.3	159	150	21,006	25,653	3,333	3,721	2.4
6020	Commercial banks	6	6	2.1	76	73	20,947	21,096	1,582	1,746	1.7
6300	Insurance carriers	6	6	5.4	83	87	29,446	25,839	2,360	2,251	3.7
6400	Insurance agents, brokers, and service	16	18	2.9	52	55	17,308	17,818	999	1,062	3.0

Source: County Business Patterns, 1994/95, CBP-94/95, U.S. Department of Commerce, Washington, D.C., November 1997. SIC categories for which data were suppressed or not available for both 1994 and 1995 are not displayed. The employment columns represent mid-March employment in the year. Pay per employee is calculated by dividing 1st Quarter payroll, annualized, by mid-March employment. The columns headed "% State" show the county's percentage of the state total for the SIC in 1995; for example, 1.4% for SIC 6000 means that the county had 1.4 percent of the state's total establishments (or payroll) in SIC 6000 in 1995. A dash (-) is used to indicate that data are not available or cannot be calculated; nec means not elsewhere classified.

Continued on next page.

SIC	Industry	No. Establishments			Employment		Pay / Employee		Annual Payroll ($ 000)		
		1994	1995	% State	1994	1995	1994	1995	1994	1995	% State
STUTSMAN, ND - [continued]											
6500	Real estate	21	20	3.4	79	51	7,342	10,353	753	670	1.9
6510	Real estate operators and lessors	11	8	2.8	48	21	4,917	8,762	334	243	1.4
6530	Real estate agents and managers	7	7	3.6	23	22	10,087	9,818	261	247	1.9
TOWNER, ND											
60 –	**Finance, insurance, and real estate**	20	18	0.9	74	69	16,595	18,203	1,201	1,277	0.4
6400	Insurance agents, brokers, and service	7	6	1.0	9	8	12,000	14,000	107	116	0.3
6500	Real estate	4	4	0.7	12	12	5,333	6,333	67	79	0.2
TRAILL, ND											
60 –	**Finance, insurance, and real estate**	33	33	1.7	135	133	21,689	24,301	2,535	2,829	0.8
6000	Depository institutions	8	8	1.8	86	87	22,000	24,552	1,887	2,107	1.4
6400	Insurance agents, brokers, and service	13	13	2.1	29	28	21,517	25,000	391	448	1.3
6500	Real estate	9	9	1.5	10	8	8,800	7,000	80	72	0.2
6510	Real estate operators and lessors	5	4	1.4	6	4	11,333	9,000	53	42	0.2
WALSH, ND											
60 –	**Finance, insurance, and real estate**	47	47	2.4	182	191	24,132	22,723	3,999	3,894	1.2
6000	Depository institutions	11	11	2.5	109	102	26,642	26,392	2,568	2,466	1.6
6400	Insurance agents, brokers, and service	18	18	2.9	27	34	18,222	16,588	389	442	1.3
6500	Real estate	12	12	2.0	18	28	9,556	8,143	163	168	0.5
WARD, ND											
60 –	**Finance, insurance, and real estate**	165	160	8.1	891	926	22,218	22,423	19,202	19,984	6.0
6000	Depository institutions	27	25	5.7	441	454	22,041	23,762	9,560	10,244	6.7
6020	Commercial banks	12	12	4.2	312	328	23,821	23,366	7,269	7,436	7.2
6100	Nondepository institutions	4	4	6.2	42	38	40,857	40,105	1,400	1,259	8.4
6200	Security and commodity brokers	13	13	13.1	31	31	29,548	26,194	991	1,070	5.4
6300	Insurance carriers	10	11	9.8	53	47	29,132	32,511	1,458	1,465	2.4
6400	Insurance agents, brokers, and service	45	45	7.2	111	112	18,883	19,536	2,045	2,131	6.1
6500	Real estate	59	55	9.4	199	190	16,663	16,421	3,047	2,989	8.5
6530	Real estate agents and managers	32	28	14.5	113	100	14,195	14,200	1,474	1,484	11.1
6700	Holding and other investment offices	7	7	14.3	14	54	34,857	14,889	701	826	5.4
WELLS, ND											
60 –	**Finance, insurance, and real estate**	20	23	1.2	69	67	18,957	20,836	1,234	1,336	0.4
WILLIAMS, ND											
60 –	**Finance, insurance, and real estate**	65	66	3.3	368	359	22,022	23,398	7,336	8,078	2.4
6000	Depository institutions	11	11	2.5	227	224	22,714	25,036	4,820	5,295	3.4
6020	Commercial banks	6	6	2.1	178	172	23,685	25,698	3,853	4,138	4.0
6200	Security and commodity brokers	7	7	7.1	12	16	31,667	30,750	474	753	3.8
6210	Security brokers and dealers	7	7	9.6	12	16	31,667	30,750	474	753	4.1
6400	Insurance agents, brokers, and service	21	23	3.7	61	54	15,803	15,852	885	779	2.2
6500	Real estate	22	20	3.4	52	50	22,538	21,200	808	823	2.4
6530	Real estate agents and managers	7	6	3.1	14	13	52,286	51,385	355	407	3.1

Source: County Business Patterns, 1994/95, CBP-94/95, U.S. Department of Commerce, Washington, D.C., November 1997. SIC categories for which data were suppressed or not available for both 1994 and 1995 are *not* displayed. The employment columns represent mid-March employment in the year. Pay per employee is calculated by dividing 1st Quarter payroll, annualized, by mid-March employment. The columns headed "% State" show the county's percentage of the state total for the SIC in 1995; for example, 1.4% for SIC 6000 means that the county had 1.4 percent of the state's total establishments (or payroll) in SIC 6000 in 1995. A dash (-) is used to indicate that data are not available or cannot be calculated; *nec* means not elsewhere classified.

OHIO

SIC	Industry	No. Establishments			Employment		Pay / Employee		Annual Payroll ($ 000)		
		1994	1995	% State	1994	1995	1994	1995	1994	1995	% State
ADAMS, OH											
60 –	**Finance, insurance, and real estate**	34	36	0.2	161	149	16,000	17,584	2,666	2,752	0.0
6000	Depository institutions	10	10	0.2	102	101	17,647	19,287	1,967	1,980	0.1
6400	Insurance agents, brokers, and service	12	13	0.2	23	33	23,304	15,879	521	476	0.1
6530	Real estate agents and managers	4	3	0.1	4	3	7,000	10,667	37	24	0.0
ALLEN, OH											
60 –	**Finance, insurance, and real estate**	242	247	1.1	1,696	1,785	20,413	20,943	34,296	36,438	0.4
6000	Depository institutions	56	53	1.1	805	809	21,317	24,030	16,485	17,626	0.8
6020	Commercial banks	38	37	1.2	630	666	21,321	25,111	12,754	14,916	0.9
6100	Nondepository institutions	16	17	1.1	61	70	29,246	24,857	1,546	1,664	0.3
6140	Personal credit institutions	11	11	1.6	49	53	28,000	25,585	1,119	1,205	0.7
6160	Mortgage bankers and brokers	5	6	1.0	12	17	34,333	22,588	427	459	0.2
6200	Security and commodity brokers	11	16	1.3	48	62	43,917	34,581	1,663	1,984	0.3
6210	Security brokers and dealers	6	9	1.3	43	49	46,791	38,531	1,568	1,767	0.3
6280	Security and commodity services	5	7	1.4	5	13	19,200	19,692	95	217	0.1
6300	Insurance carriers	16	12	0.7	206	164	23,922	26,390	4,569	4,352	0.2
6330	Fire, marine, and casualty insurance	10	8	0.8	108	98	25,333	29,510	2,705	2,942	0.2
6400	Insurance agents, brokers, and service	64	67	1.2	232	235	18,776	19,847	4,962	5,132	0.6
6500	Real estate	73	78	1.0	315	429	11,594	10,713	4,218	5,025	0.5
6510	Real estate operators and lessors	35	36	1.1	188	154	10,021	10,857	2,032	1,748	0.5
6530	Real estate agents and managers	30	32	1.0	89	245	14,337	9,502	1,600	2,629	0.5
6700	Holding and other investment offices	6	4	0.7	29	16	21,793	29,500	853	655	0.2
ASHLAND, OH											
60 –	**Finance, insurance, and real estate**	79	81	0.3	436	445	20,312	20,953	8,664	9,531	0.1
6000	Depository institutions	25	26	0.5	238	231	19,261	21,437	4,475	4,942	0.2
6020	Commercial banks	14	14	0.5	162	153	22,840	25,359	3,541	3,748	0.2
6030	Savings institutions	5	6	0.7	59	58	12,271	14,828	752	990	0.3
6060	Credit unions	6	6	0.8	17	20	9,412	10,600	182	204	0.2
6100	Nondepository institutions	4	5	0.3	16	15	38,500	34,133	533	487	0.1
6400	Insurance agents, brokers, and service	21	22	0.4	69	80	21,565	19,950	1,688	1,803	0.2
6500	Real estate	24	22	0.3	88	88	12,455	11,182	933	964	0.1
6510	Real estate operators and lessors	11	10	0.3	55	50	4,800	5,440	336	340	0.1
6530	Real estate agents and managers	10	9	0.3	22	24	34,182	23,667	460	438	0.1
6550	Subdividers and developers	3	3	0.5	11	14	7,273	10,286	137	186	0.2
6553	Cemetery subdividers and developers	3	3	1.0	11	14	7,273	10,286	137	186	0.5
ASHTABULA, OH											
60 –	**Finance, insurance, and real estate**	166	169	0.7	879	908	18,385	20,661	16,725	18,871	0.2
6000	Depository institutions	51	52	1.1	522	544	18,674	21,529	9,524	10,583	0.5
6020	Commercial banks	24	31	1.0	236	432	21,966	22,611	4,738	8,594	0.5
6030	Savings institutions	15	9	1.0	233	59	16,069	17,898	3,923	1,084	0.3
6060	Credit unions	12	12	1.6	53	53	15,472	16,755	863	905	0.8
6210	Security brokers and dealers	4	4	0.6	11	12	66,182	47,667	658	625	0.1
6400	Insurance agents, brokers, and service	49	43	0.8	137	136	21,927	24,147	3,462	3,695	0.5
6500	Real estate	48	55	0.7	147	141	10,612	11,518	1,812	2,298	0.2
6510	Real estate operators and lessors	25	28	0.8	70	51	6,800	7,451	494	513	0.2
6530	Real estate agents and managers	17	23	0.7	55	59	12,800	12,136	836	1,133	0.2
ATHENS, OH											
60 –	**Finance, insurance, and real estate**	100	103	0.4	543	568	18,144	18,430	10,836	11,461	0.1

Source: County Business Patterns, 1994/95, CBP-94/95, U.S. Department of Commerce, Washington, D.C., November 1997. SIC categories for which data were suppressed or not available for both 1994 and 1995 are not displayed. The employment columns represent mid-March employment in the year. Pay per employee is calculated by dividing 1st Quarter payroll, annualized, by mid-March employment. The columns headed "% State" show the county's percentage of the state total for the SIC in 1995; for example, 1.4% for SIC 6000 means that the county had 1.4 percent of the state's total establishments (or payroll) in SIC 6000 in 1995. A dash (-) is used to indicate that data are not available or cannot be calculated; nec means not elsewhere classified.

Continued on next page.

SIC	Industry	No. Establishments			Employment		Pay / Employee		Annual Payroll ($ 000)		
		1994	1995	% State	1994	1995	1994	1995	1994	1995	% State
ATHENS, OH - [continued]											
6000	Depository institutions	25	25	0.5	321	316	19,514	20,734	6,374	6,599	0.3
6020	Commercial banks	21	21	0.7	276	261	19,159	20,736	5,351	5,505	0.3
6400	Insurance agents, brokers, and service	19	19	0.3	79	89	22,177	20,809	2,106	2,350	0.3
6500	Real estate	42	44	0.6	99	118	9,010	9,898	1,302	1,590	0.1
6510	Real estate operators and lessors	28	28	0.8	78	77	8,615	9,351	809	865	0.3
6530	Real estate agents and managers	7	10	0.3	5	17	11,200	11,529	298	477	0.1
6550	Subdividers and developers	5	4	0.6	16	21	10,250	8,952	167	178	0.1
6700	Holding and other investment offices	4	4	0.7	11	10	7,636	9,600	120	96	0.0
AUGLAIZE, OH											
60 –	**Finance, insurance, and real estate**	81	80	0.3	470	450	18,613	19,716	9,034	8,945	0.1
6000	Depository institutions	23	19	0.4	235	222	20,579	20,721	4,357	4,204	0.2
6020	Commercial banks	20	16	0.5	224	207	20,286	20,502	4,086	3,896	0.2
6100	Nondepository institutions	6	5	0.3	25	24	25,120	28,833	617	565	0.1
6400	Insurance agents, brokers, and service	21	21	0.4	87	90	16,644	18,978	1,956	2,175	0.3
6500	Real estate	21	23	0.3	54	48	9,111	13,417	569	686	0.1
6510	Real estate operators and lessors	5	6	0.2	14	8	6,571	11,000	99	123	0.0
6530	Real estate agents and managers	10	10	0.3	29	24	11,310	17,000	338	359	0.1
6550	Subdividers and developers	4	5	0.8	10	13	6,800	8,308	105	150	0.1
BELMONT, OH											
60 –	**Finance, insurance, and real estate**	136	134	0.6	1,029	918	18,655	20,776	18,759	18,639	0.2
6000	Depository institutions	40	36	0.7	503	438	19,746	21,982	9,000	9,116	0.4
6020	Commercial banks	27	24	0.8	366	352	19,596	22,977	6,154	7,463	0.4
6300	Insurance carriers	11	11	0.6	190	191	25,011	28,293	4,694	5,127	0.2
6400	Insurance agents, brokers, and service	42	43	0.8	107	104	16,710	18,192	2,096	2,151	0.3
6500	Real estate	36	37	0.5	211	167	11,526	10,323	2,649	1,873	0.2
6510	Real estate operators and lessors	17	17	0.5	110	75	13,709	11,893	1,657	921	0.3
6530	Real estate agents and managers	12	14	0.4	75	72	7,360	8,167	590	639	0.1
6550	Subdividers and developers	7	6	0.9	26	20	14,308	12,200	402	313	0.3
6553	Cemetery subdividers and developers	5	5	1.6	26	20	14,308	12,200	374	293	0.8
BROWN, OH											
60 –	**Finance, insurance, and real estate**	40	43	0.2	318	428	20,314	24,243	6,821	8,322	0.1
6000	Depository institutions	15	15	0.3	220	340	23,418	25,565	5,104	6,296	0.3
6400	Insurance agents, brokers, and service	9	9	0.2	29	35	16,000	20,914	718	932	0.1
6500	Real estate	13	14	0.2	55	46	12,073	15,565	797	886	0.1
6510	Real estate operators and lessors	5	6	0.2	18	8	8,222	18,000	153	168	0.1
BUTLER, OH											
60 –	**Finance, insurance, and real estate**	466	472	2.0	6,592	6,761	26,146	28,320	192,360	201,767	2.5
6000	Depository institutions	111	115	2.3	1,337	1,344	20,550	21,765	27,507	29,608	1.3
6020	Commercial banks	68	68	2.2	918	914	21,699	23,037	19,913	20,767	1.2
6030	Savings institutions	21	26	2.8	250	251	19,312	21,227	5,012	5,627	1.8
6100	Nondepository institutions	25	26	1.7	228	217	22,895	24,350	5,850	5,847	1.1
6150	Business credit institutions	5	5	2.7	75	81	19,947	21,630	1,902	2,293	1.5
6160	Mortgage bankers and brokers	5	6	1.0	84	63	26,619	29,333	2,387	1,882	0.9
6200	Security and commodity brokers	15	17	1.4	23	29	16,696	18,069	519	711	0.1
6210	Security brokers and dealers	7	9	1.3	13	18	21,231	22,444	346	526	0.1
6280	Security and commodity services	8	8	1.6	10	11	10,800	10,909	173	185	0.1
6300	Insurance carriers	28	28	1.5	3,846	3,925	29,882	33,074	130,549	136,161	6.0
6400	Insurance agents, brokers, and service	118	112	2.0	366	401	23,552	24,459	9,847	10,569	1.3
6500	Real estate	155	164	2.1	609	682	19,396	19,267	13,524	15,089	1.4
6510	Real estate operators and lessors	59	58	1.8	281	290	15,915	16,979	5,079	5,621	1.8
6530	Real estate agents and managers	72	75	2.3	251	313	18,884	17,035	5,773	6,344	1.1
6550	Subdividers and developers	20	25	3.8	50	63	39,120	41,143	2,127	2,590	2.1
6552	Subdividers and developers, n.e.c.	13	15	4.9	11	16	121,455	113,000	1,399	1,691	2.0

Source: County Business Patterns, 1994/95, CBP-94/95, U.S. Department of Commerce, Washington, D.C., November 1997. SIC categories for which data were suppressed or not available for both 1994 and 1995 are *not* displayed. The employment columns represent mid-March employment in the year. Pay per employee is calculated by dividing 1st Quarter payroll, annualized, by mid-March employment. The columns headed "% State" show the county's percentage of the state total for the SIC in 1995; for example, 1.4% for SIC 6000 means that the county had 1.4 percent of the state's total establishments (or payroll) in SIC 6000 in 1995. A dash (-) is used to indicate that data are not available or cannot be calculated; *nec* means not elsewhere classified.

Continued on next page.

SIC	Industry	No. Establishments			Employment		Pay / Employee		Annual Payroll ($ 000)		
		1994	1995	% State	1994	1995	1994	1995	1994	1995	% State
BUTLER, OH - [continued]											
6553	Cemetery subdividers and developers	6	6	2.0	39	41	15,897	15,220	726	773	2.0
6700	Holding and other investment offices	14	10	1.7	183	163	21,399	22,380	4,564	3,782	1.0
6710	Holding offices	8	7	2.4	166	152	21,855	22,842	3,972	3,537	1.3
CARROLL, OH											
60 –	**Finance, insurance, and real estate**	24	23	0.1	106	120	14,377	15,067	1,597	1,946	0.0
6000	Depository institutions	8	9	0.2	52	70	16,846	15,257	863	1,196	0.1
6400	Insurance agents, brokers, and service	6	7	0.1	12	14	16,000	24,571	232	293	0.0
CHAMPAIGN, OH											
60 –	**Finance, insurance, and real estate**	53	52	0.2	369	365	19,198	21,468	6,776	7,340	0.1
6000	Depository institutions	23	19	0.4	263	244	21,977	26,574	5,312	5,801	0.3
6400	Insurance agents, brokers, and service	13	15	0.3	53	53	13,358	13,811	820	842	0.1
6500	Real estate	14	15	0.2	36	51	4,000	3,843	185	235	0.0
6530	Real estate agents and managers	4	5	0.2	5	11	7,200	3,636	41	52	0.0
CLARK, OH											
60 –	**Finance, insurance, and real estate**	211	214	0.9	1,530	1,539	21,318	22,264	32,524	33,651	0.4
6000	Depository institutions	51	52	1.1	595	608	19,045	20,349	11,712	12,717	0.6
6020	Commercial banks	33	34	1.1	448	440	18,357	19,618	8,560	9,037	0.5
6030	Savings institutions	5	5	0.5	61	72	20,459	22,556	1,453	1,840	0.6
6060	Credit unions	13	13	1.7	86	96	21,628	22,042	1,699	1,840	1.7
6100	Nondepository institutions	14	14	0.9	285	301	21,305	19,495	4,985	5,212	1.0
6200	Security and commodity brokers	7	6	0.5	15	18	51,733	48,444	854	1,012	0.2
6300	Insurance carriers	12	14	0.8	144	128	33,722	43,406	4,678	4,699	0.2
6400	Insurance agents, brokers, and service	56	57	1.0	219	213	25,954	26,573	5,868	5,935	0.7
6500	Real estate	65	65	0.9	253	258	13,897	13,860	4,041	3,853	0.4
6510	Real estate operators and lessors	29	28	0.8	121	126	10,545	10,762	1,332	1,404	0.4
6530	Real estate agents and managers	24	24	0.7	69	66	15,710	18,667	1,399	1,319	0.2
6550	Subdividers and developers	10	10	1.5	59	62	18,237	14,839	1,217	1,061	0.9
CLERMONT, OH											
60 –	**Finance, insurance, and real estate**	181	189	0.8	2,423	2,383	26,849	30,249	67,464	71,418	0.9
6000	Depository institutions	45	46	0.9	509	489	22,554	24,303	11,123	11,390	0.5
6020	Commercial banks	31	31	1.0	378	378	23,270	24,783	8,233	8,468	0.5
6100	Nondepository institutions	10	10	0.6	904	877	27,810	32,160	27,148	28,837	5.3
6400	Insurance agents, brokers, and service	36	38	0.7	111	113	19,495	19,434	2,242	2,236	0.3
6500	Real estate	70	73	1.0	328	314	15,061	16,854	5,268	5,362	0.5
6510	Real estate operators and lessors	32	32	1.0	219	209	12,037	14,067	2,990	3,183	1.0
6530	Real estate agents and managers	28	31	0.9	64	64	17,813	17,688	1,281	1,252	0.2
6540	Title abstract offices	3	4	1.9	14	16	20,286	20,750	233	537	1.0
6550	Subdividers and developers	6	5	0.8	30	25	28,800	35,520	746	384	0.3
CLINTON, OH											
60 –	**Finance, insurance, and real estate**	68	71	0.3	606	633	20,825	26,370	13,886	16,261	0.2
6000	Depository institutions	18	18	0.4	326	316	23,092	25,139	7,078	7,827	0.3
6020	Commercial banks	12	12	0.4	228	221	23,789	25,014	4,719	4,779	0.3
6100	Nondepository institutions	4	4	0.3	145	139	16,634	22,590	2,968	3,019	0.6
6400	Insurance agents, brokers, and service	14	14	0.3	58	61	25,034	25,836	1,412	1,509	0.2
6500	Real estate	25	26	0.3	56	46	12,143	16,957	760	751	0.1
6510	Real estate operators and lessors	7	7	0.2	21	15	8,952	13,600	210	210	0.1
6530	Real estate agents and managers	10	11	0.3	15	18	21,333	24,444	349	376	0.1
6550	Subdividers and developers	8	8	1.2	20	13	8,600	10,462	201	165	0.1
COLUMBIANA, OH											
60 –	**Finance, insurance, and real estate**	174	181	0.8	1,144	1,101	18,636	18,910	22,486	22,217	0.3
6000	Depository institutions	57	53	1.1	675	611	17,908	17,872	12,453	11,530	0.5
6020	Commercial banks	40	34	1.1	504	409	18,310	19,120	9,422	8,238	0.5

Source: County Business Patterns, 1994/95, CBP-94/95, U.S. Department of Commerce, Washington, D.C., November 1997. SIC categories for which data were suppressed or not available for both 1994 and 1995 are *not* displayed. The employment columns represent mid-March employment in the year. Pay per employee is calculated by dividing 1st Quarter payroll, annualized, by mid-March employment. The columns headed "% State" show the county's percentage of the state total for the SIC in 1995; for example, 1.4% for SIC 6000 means that the county had 1.4 percent of the state's total establishments (or payroll) in SIC 6000 in 1995. A dash (-) is used to indicate that data are not available or cannot be calculated; *nec* means not elsewhere classified.

Continued on next page.

SIC	Industry	No. Establishments			Employment		Pay / Employee		Annual Payroll ($ 000)		
		1994	1995	% State	1994	1995	1994	1995	1994	1995	% State
COLUMBIANA, OH - [continued]											
6200	Security and commodity brokers	4	5	0.4	18	20	58,667	56,400	992	1,184	0.2
6300	Insurance carriers	12	15	0.8	132	136	26,848	25,853	3,893	3,734	0.2
6310	Life insurance	5	5	1.0	105	104	28,381	26,385	3,218	2,872	0.5
6330	Fire, marine, and casualty insurance	7	10	1.0	27	32	20,889	24,125	675	862	0.1
6400	Insurance agents, brokers, and service	49	50	0.9	156	159	17,205	17,912	2,928	3,183	0.4
6500	Real estate	45	48	0.6	133	147	8,962	11,156	1,544	1,842	0.2
6510	Real estate operators and lessors	16	16	0.5	74	65	6,216	7,262	568	602	0.2
6530	Real estate agents and managers	20	21	0.6	29	52	11,448	12,692	545	672	0.1
6550	Subdividers and developers	9	11	1.7	30	30	13,333	16,933	431	568	0.5
COSHOCTON, OH											
60 –	**Finance, insurance, and real estate**	46	46	0.2	269	253	18,067	20,870	5,123	5,655	0.1
6000	Depository institutions	13	13	0.3	160	151	18,175	20,503	2,941	3,150	0.1
6100	Nondepository institutions	6	6	0.4	17	17	27,529	32,471	528	595	0.1
6500	Real estate	9	10	0.1	14	13	7,429	9,538	125	181	0.0
CRAWFORD, OH											
60 –	**Finance, insurance, and real estate**	87	81	0.3	576	563	19,694	19,858	11,870	11,971	0.1
6000	Depository institutions	24	22	0.4	294	289	19,279	19,668	5,910	5,943	0.3
6020	Commercial banks	13	11	0.4	184	181	19,217	19,182	3,646	3,556	0.2
6400	Insurance agents, brokers, and service	31	31	0.6	72	74	17,333	19,189	1,434	1,653	0.2
6500	Real estate	22	19	0.2	47	44	9,872	10,273	603	623	0.1
6510	Real estate operators and lessors	12	10	0.3	20	15	10,200	13,600	212	220	0.1
6530	Real estate agents and managers	6	5	0.2	15	12	9,333	9,667	143	144	0.0
6550	Subdividers and developers	3	3	0.5	11	12	9,091	8,667	121	132	0.1
6553	Cemetery subdividers and developers	3	3	1.0	11	12	9,091	8,667	121	132	0.3
CUYAHOGA, OH											
60 –	**Finance, insurance, and real estate**	3,787	3,826	16.4	60,158	59,562	30,372	32,778	1,804,238	1,916,125	23.6
6000	Depository institutions	723	694	14.2	15,997	16,306	28,229	29,598	433,909	465,913	20.7
6020	Commercial banks	319	316	10.2	10,502	11,267	28,487	30,097	298,588	327,623	18.8
6030	Savings institutions	203	178	19.5	3,653	3,175	28,443	29,703	86,842	87,796	28.1
6060	Credit unions	143	138	18.5	727	746	16,204	16,676	12,371	12,674	11.4
6100	Nondepository institutions	231	247	15.9	3,047	2,575	32,299	33,410	92,114	88,254	16.3
6140	Personal credit institutions	78	86	12.9	793	771	26,179	30,112	20,267	22,500	12.9
6150	Business credit institutions	35	34	18.5	645	395	42,468	55,008	25,019	17,780	11.9
6160	Mortgage bankers and brokers	116	123	19.9	1,608	1,408	31,244	29,153	46,772	47,582	23.3
6200	Security and commodity brokers	234	255	21.0	2,906	2,881	70,087	65,470	194,475	212,050	31.5
6210	Security brokers and dealers	118	136	19.3	2,383	2,277	74,095	66,122	164,013	169,359	32.8
6220	Commodity contracts brokers, dealers	3	3	27.3	4	32	32,000	34,750	334	2,070	54.3
6280	Security and commodity services	113	116	23.4	519	572	51,977	64,594	30,128	40,621	26.5
6300	Insurance carriers	343	351	19.4	14,371	10,864	35,785	43,668	491,160	436,238	19.2
6310	Life insurance	118	115	23.1	3,300	2,920	28,588	31,827	92,722	86,494	15.6
6320	Medical service and health insurance	20	26	19.7	2,939	2,649	31,608	51,129	99,346	107,696	27.2
6330	Fire, marine, and casualty insurance	161	163	16.9	6,962	4,213	41,751	50,496	267,230	210,619	17.2
6360	Title insurance	14	14	16.9	773	665	30,272	29,287	19,841	17,941	53.1
6370	Pension, health, and welfare funds	25	23	22.1	379	390	32,728	33,456	11,225	12,322	23.6
6400	Insurance agents, brokers, and service	797	807	14.5	5,627	6,759	33,078	33,561	191,738	231,478	28.6
6500	Real estate	1,319	1,328	17.4	15,724	15,969	18,415	20,743	323,669	327,596	30.7
6510	Real estate operators and lessors	617	596	18.0	6,600	6,911	15,278	17,375	116,343	112,084	35.0
6530	Real estate agents and managers	578	585	17.9	7,716	7,476	19,480	22,249	162,613	166,986	29.8
6540	Title abstract offices	28	32	14.8	527	539	28,744	28,935	16,222	16,281	30.4
6550	Subdividers and developers	67	71	10.8	847	945	26,451	29,278	27,036	29,967	24.3
6552	Subdividers and developers, n.e.c.	39	43	14.0	529	601	29,535	31,967	18,654	20,702	25.1
6553	Cemetery subdividers and developers	24	21	6.9	318	324	21,321	24,901	8,066	8,747	22.8
6700	Holding and other investment offices	131	134	22.3	1,604	1,326	34,800	46,905	50,845	60,000	16.1
6710	Holding offices	63	60	20.8	985	701	36,313	58,322	34,127	37,213	13.2
6730	Trusts	21	23	23.5	343	290	22,845	18,069	5,713	5,895	41.3

Source: County Business Patterns, 1994/95, CBP-94/95, U.S. Department of Commerce, Washington, D.C., November 1997. SIC categories for which data were suppressed or not available for both 1994 and 1995 are *not* displayed. The employment columns represent mid-March employment in the year. Pay per employee is calculated by dividing 1st Quarter payroll, annualized, by mid-March employment. The columns headed "% State" show the county's percentage of the state total for the SIC in 1995; for example, 1.4% for SIC 6000 means that the county had 1.4 percent of the state's total establishments (or payroll) in SIC 6000 in 1995. A dash (-) is used to indicate that data are not available or cannot be calculated; *nec* means not elsewhere classified.

Continued on next page.

SIC	Industry	No. Establishments			Employment		Pay / Employee		Annual Payroll ($ 000)		
		1994	1995	% State	1994	1995	1994	1995	1994	1995	% State
CUYAHOGA, OH - [continued]											
6732	Educational, religious, etc. trusts	13	13	22.8	256	282	16,328	18,028	4,614	5,550	58.7
6733	Trusts, n.e.c.	8	10	24.4	87	8	42,023	19,500	1,099	345	7.1
6790	Miscellaneous investing	40	37	21.8	266	229	32,677	39,249	9,753	8,857	13.6
6798	Real estate investment trusts	5	6	31.6	114	127	26,947	48,126	3,376	5,337	24.8
6799	Investors, n.e.c.	26	24	24.7	80	61	40,000	27,082	4,746	1,945	6.5
DARKE, OH											
60 –	**Finance, insurance, and real estate**	94	94	0.4	573	594	20,803	22,923	12,280	13,035	0.2
6000	Depository institutions	30	29	0.6	351	360	20,889	22,722	7,291	7,509	0.3
6020	Commercial banks	25	24	0.8	300	307	21,280	22,971	6,263	6,416	0.4
6400	Insurance agents, brokers, and service	31	31	0.6	125	125	21,600	24,256	2,912	2,964	0.4
6500	Real estate	19	21	0.3	54	64	17,556	21,625	1,048	1,498	0.1
DEFIANCE, OH											
60 –	**Finance, insurance, and real estate**	68	64	0.3	533	492	24,720	26,577	13,222	13,054	0.2
6000	Depository institutions	20	18	0.4	345	298	24,545	26,577	7,793	7,068	0.3
6020	Commercial banks	13	12	0.4	173	172	21,942	23,070	3,674	3,535	0.2
6100	Nondepository institutions	3	3	0.2	12	12	37,000	35,000	335	421	0.1
6300	Insurance carriers	5	5	0.3	33	34	21,455	22,400	724	798	0.0
6400	Insurance agents, brokers, and service	19	17	0.3	80	83	22,800	23,663	2,329	2,489	0.3
6530	Real estate agents and managers	10	9	0.3	27	26	14,222	15,077	428	545	0.1
6550	Subdividers and developers	3	3	0.5	8	9	9,000	8,444	89	78	0.1
DELAWARE, OH											
60 –	**Finance, insurance, and real estate**	138	152	0.7	1,290	1,236	25,718	26,871	34,946	34,476	0.4
6000	Depository institutions	26	25	0.5	859	797	27,213	28,959	24,506	23,654	1.1
6020	Commercial banks	20	18	0.6	833	770	27,443	29,319	23,941	23,093	1.3
6100	Nondepository institutions	7	8	0.5	61	48	30,557	19,167	1,631	936	0.2
6200	Security and commodity brokers	5	7	0.6	15	11	22,133	38,182	378	544	0.1
6300	Insurance carriers	9	9	0.5	49	52	26,776	28,154	1,343	1,411	0.1
6400	Insurance agents, brokers, and service	33	36	0.6	93	106	26,538	27,736	2,921	3,014	0.4
6500	Real estate	55	64	0.8	205	212	17,873	19,755	3,957	4,723	0.4
6510	Real estate operators and lessors	27	34	1.0	122	123	18,426	20,390	2,411	2,690	0.8
6530	Real estate agents and managers	22	23	0.7	69	66	16,232	16,727	1,200	1,383	0.2
6550	Subdividers and developers	3	3	0.5	8	9	16,000	17,778	147	170	0.1
6700	Holding and other investment offices	3	3	0.5	8	10	20,000	20,000	210	194	0.1
ERIE, OH											
60 –	**Finance, insurance, and real estate**	179	183	0.8	970	979	20,812	20,114	21,425	21,860	0.3
6000	Depository institutions	34	35	0.7	401	440	19,531	19,973	7,941	8,851	0.4
6020	Commercial banks	24	25	0.8	320	353	19,750	19,875	6,423	7,082	0.4
6030	Savings institutions	5	5	0.5	37	42	19,135	18,952	671	731	0.2
6060	Credit unions	5	5	0.7	44	45	18,273	21,689	847	1,038	0.9
6100	Nondepository institutions	6	7	0.5	23	22	15,130	21,455	505	643	0.1
6200	Security and commodity brokers	10	12	1.0	43	42	36,837	30,286	1,613	2,153	0.3
6300	Insurance carriers	15	15	0.8	125	81	30,720	25,926	3,578	2,042	0.1
6400	Insurance agents, brokers, and service	46	47	0.8	122	128	25,410	24,750	3,444	3,446	0.4
6500	Real estate	60	59	0.8	201	207	14,687	15,865	3,681	3,962	0.4
6510	Real estate operators and lessors	25	24	0.7	88	83	11,182	13,012	1,319	1,345	0.4
6530	Real estate agents and managers	26	23	0.7	92	97	17,913	18,268	1,874	2,093	0.4
6540	Title abstract offices	3	3	1.4	15	16	14,933	17,000	242	229	0.4
6550	Subdividers and developers	5	5	0.8	6	9	16,000	15,111	228	245	0.2
6700	Holding and other investment offices	8	8	1.3	55	59	9,673	10,305	663	763	0.2
FAIRFIELD, OH											
60 –	**Finance, insurance, and real estate**	176	184	0.8	1,060	929	22,660	20,977	23,484	21,371	0.3
6000	Depository institutions	32	34	0.7	380	385	23,211	23,460	8,451	8,918	0.4
6020	Commercial banks	22	24	0.8	297	300	21,104	21,440	5,945	6,269	0.4

Source: County Business Patterns, 1994/95, CBP-94/95, U.S. Department of Commerce, Washington, D.C., November 1997. SIC categories for which data were suppressed or not available for both 1994 and 1995 are not displayed. The employment columns represent mid-March employment in the year. Pay per employee is calculated by dividing 1st Quarter payroll, annualized, by mid-March employment. The columns headed "% State" show the county's percentage of the state total for the SIC in 1995; for example, 1.4% for SIC 6000 means that the county had 1.4 percent of the state's total establishments (or payroll) in SIC 6000 in 1995. A dash (-) is used to indicate that data are not available or cannot be calculated; nec means not elsewhere classified.

Continued on next page.

SIC	Industry	No. Establishments			Employment		Pay / Employee		Annual Payroll ($ 000)		
		1994	1995	% State	1994	1995	1994	1995	1994	1995	% State
FAIRFIELD, OH - [continued]											
6100	Nondepository institutions	12	13	0.8	73	83	30,192	29,253	2,843	3,688	0.7
6200	Security and commodity brokers	7	8	0.7	20	22	71,800	55,091	1,115	1,168	0.2
6300	Insurance carriers	12	12	0.7	163	55	37,350	24,000	5,137	1,332	0.1
6400	Insurance agents, brokers, and service	42	45	0.8	98	114	18,367	16,772	1,941	2,007	0.2
6500	Real estate	67	67	0.9	302	239	10,026	11,347	3,294	3,419	0.3
6510	Real estate operators and lessors	23	24	0.7	149	79	6,040	9,924	873	960	0.3
6530	Real estate agents and managers	30	30	0.9	95	100	18,568	15,360	1,821	1,729	0.3
6540	Title abstract offices	4	3	1.4	39	39	6,154	6,256	448	489	0.9
6550	Subdividers and developers	9	9	1.4	19	19	6,526	6,947	144	225	0.2
6700	Holding and other investment offices	4	5	0.8	24	31	26,833	28,129	703	839	0.2
FAYETTE, OH											
60 –	**Finance, insurance, and real estate**	43	43	0.2	224	219	21,875	22,630	5,174	5,241	0.1
6000	Depository institutions	9	8	0.2	103	92	21,087	24,435	2,194	2,243	0.1
6400	Insurance agents, brokers, and service	12	12	0.2	37	47	17,730	16,255	833	894	0.1
6500	Real estate	10	11	0.1	22	19	7,091	9,895	191	217	0.0
FRANKLIN, OH											
60 –	**Finance, insurance, and real estate**	3,021	3,096	13.3	58,775	57,934	32,441	34,855	1,866,927	1,934,077	23.9
6000	Depository institutions	481	473	9.6	13,934	13,508	31,174	33,142	425,194	426,959	19.0
6020	Commercial banks	333	344	11.1	11,627	11,369	31,610	33,554	364,596	363,698	20.9
6030	Savings institutions	80	58	6.4	1,052	731	30,175	35,787	24,910	21,719	6.9
6090	Functions closely related to banking	17	19	15.0	701	795	31,178	32,352	22,181	26,623	-
6100	Nondepository institutions	300	319	20.5	7,301	7,936	26,067	25,338	185,295	209,515	38.7
6140	Personal credit institutions	92	99	14.8	2,035	2,118	25,085	26,635	54,172	59,954	34.5
6150	Business credit institutions	62	87	47.3	2,696	3,746	21,553	22,426	56,206	82,212	55.1
6160	Mortgage bankers and brokers	143	129	20.8	2,569	2,058	31,586	29,429	74,746	67,099	32.8
6200	Security and commodity brokers	176	169	13.9	2,301	2,202	66,686	69,490	137,778	145,304	21.6
6210	Security brokers and dealers	103	97	13.7	1,877	1,747	71,197	74,374	115,585	121,127	23.5
6300	Insurance carriers	324	332	18.4	20,224	19,354	36,199	40,252	710,296	715,987	31.5
6310	Life insurance	88	82	16.5	5,996	5,667	36,692	40,269	208,129	199,804	36.1
6320	Medical service and health insurance	35	34	25.8	2,748	2,502	31,734	34,568	83,823	86,487	21.8
6321	Accident and health insurance	16	16	25.0	1,815	1,628	32,921	33,349	57,224	53,589	27.7
6324	Hospital and medical service plans	18	17	25.4	932	873	29,403	36,825	26,551	32,854	16.2
6330	Fire, marine, and casualty insurance	143	155	16.1	10,616	10,498	37,493	41,864	392,471	405,613	33.0
6360	Title insurance	24	25	30.1	276	191	33,493	37,277	7,879	6,028	17.8
6370	Pension, health, and welfare funds	25	26	25.0	478	408	26,561	32,314	13,062	13,483	25.8
6400	Insurance agents, brokers, and service	602	620	11.1	4,116	3,861	30,660	36,334	122,358	137,298	17.0
6500	Real estate	1,030	1,077	14.1	8,887	8,833	19,224	21,454	184,631	197,814	18.5
6510	Real estate operators and lessors	439	447	13.5	2,416	2,337	14,657	17,053	38,363	40,456	12.6
6530	Real estate agents and managers	478	507	15.5	5,437	5,508	20,352	22,006	118,296	127,800	22.8
6540	Title abstract offices	34	36	16.7	321	297	27,414	27,596	8,826	8,440	15.8
6550	Subdividers and developers	57	59	9.0	667	639	22,063	30,435	17,346	19,300	15.7
6552	Subdividers and developers, n.e.c.	38	40	13.0	532	499	21,714	32,369	13,853	15,668	19.0
6553	Cemetery subdividers and developers	17	16	5.3	135	138	23,437	23,768	3,487	3,606	9.4
6700	Holding and other investment offices	90	87	14.5	1,809	1,809	50,306	51,920	93,093	86,373	23.2
6710	Holding offices	34	32	11.1	1,127	1,056	61,661	65,314	68,862	63,871	22.7
6730	Trusts	18	14	14.3	77	144	17,403	16,528	1,290	2,268	15.9
6732	Educational, religious, etc. trusts	8	6	10.5	20	57	22,000	11,509	421	699	7.4
6733	Trusts, n.e.c.	10	8	19.5	57	87	15,789	19,816	869	1,569	32.5
6790	Miscellaneous investing	32	34	20.0	591	466	33,645	45,185	22,554	18,551	28.5
6799	Investors, n.e.c.	21	22	22.7	483	352	31,255	38,977	17,615	12,320	41.4
FULTON, OH											
60 –	**Finance, insurance, and real estate**	72	75	0.3	879	888	18,184	19,383	17,301	17,928	0.2

Source: County Business Patterns, 1994/95, CBP-94/95, U.S. Department of Commerce, Washington, D.C., November 1997. SIC categories for which data were suppressed or not available for both 1994 and 1995 are *not* displayed. The employment columns represent mid-March employment in the year. Pay per employee is calculated by dividing 1st Quarter payroll, annualized, by mid-March employment. The columns headed "% State" show the county's percentage of the state total for the SIC in 1995; for example, 1.4% for SIC 6000 means that the county had 1.4 percent of the state's total establishments (or payroll) in SIC 6000 in 1995. A dash (-) is used to indicate that data are not available or cannot be calculated; *nec* means not elsewhere classified.

Continued on next page.

SIC	Industry	No. Establishments			Employment		Pay / Employee		Annual Payroll ($ 000)		
		1994	1995	% State	1994	1995	1994	1995	1994	1995	% State
FULTON, OH - [continued]											
6000	Depository institutions	23	22	0.4	309	264	19,482	19,348	5,904	5,130	0.2
6400	Insurance agents, brokers, and service	25	25	0.4	73	78	19,781	21,590	1,670	1,784	0.2
6510	Real estate operators and lessors	4	4	0.1	9	11	7,111	9,091	90	97	0.0
GALLIA, OH											
60 –	**Finance, insurance, and real estate**	49	50	0.2	312	320	17,936	19,863	6,930	7,376	0.1
6000	Depository institutions	9	9	0.2	182	193	17,363	19,772	4,328	4,532	0.2
6400	Insurance agents, brokers, and service	10	10	0.2	48	47	24,083	25,787	1,199	1,340	0.2
6500	Real estate	22	24	0.3	50	49	11,520	12,571	628	638	0.1
6510	Real estate operators and lessors	11	11	0.3	25	25	12,800	13,600	345	344	0.1
6530	Real estate agents and managers	7	8	0.2	11	14	17,818	12,857	210	190	0.0
GEAUGA, OH											
60 –	**Finance, insurance, and real estate**	135	143	0.6	694	657	21,176	20,925	14,938	14,919	0.2
6000	Depository institutions	30	29	0.6	298	286	21,463	22,182	6,244	6,248	0.3
6020	Commercial banks	18	20	0.6	203	210	21,990	22,762	4,423	4,546	0.3
6200	Security and commodity brokers	4	5	0.4	21	14	42,476	23,714	900	354	0.1
6400	Insurance agents, brokers, and service	38	44	0.8	97	101	17,979	19,921	2,017	2,307	0.3
6500	Real estate	47	49	0.6	210	194	18,724	18,186	4,060	4,058	0.4
6510	Real estate operators and lessors	13	16	0.5	41	42	11,317	12,476	574	618	0.2
6530	Real estate agents and managers	24	25	0.8	81	82	17,037	16,732	1,769	1,731	0.3
6540	Title abstract offices	3	3	1.4	20	17	50,600	24,471	561	458	0.9
6550	Subdividers and developers	6	5	0.8	67	53	16,000	22,943	1,155	1,251	1.0
GREENE, OH											
60 –	**Finance, insurance, and real estate**	219	228	1.0	1,784	1,828	21,744	23,241	44,018	46,878	0.6
6000	Depository institutions	51	52	1.1	682	675	19,273	20,344	14,159	14,195	0.6
6020	Commercial banks	29	33	1.1	252	311	18,794	21,891	5,040	6,437	0.4
6100	Nondepository institutions	12	15	1.0	79	127	35,190	35,528	3,367	4,184	0.8
6160	Mortgage bankers and brokers	6	9	1.5	48	91	41,333	37,231	2,423	3,127	1.5
6200	Security and commodity brokers	17	18	1.5	44	52	46,545	53,923	4,802	5,815	0.9
6300	Insurance carriers	9	13	0.7	425	440	24,922	22,709	9,968	10,116	0.4
6400	Insurance agents, brokers, and service	45	45	0.8	123	123	21,984	27,122	3,095	3,342	0.4
6500	Real estate	80	81	1.1	413	393	16,368	18,422	7,452	7,494	0.7
6510	Real estate operators and lessors	32	32	1.0	171	175	17,146	19,680	3,167	3,339	1.0
6550	Subdividers and developers	10	10	1.5	115	113	14,226	17,982	2,212	2,145	1.7
6552	Subdividers and developers, n.e.c.	5	4	1.3	99	98	15,111	19,020	2,042	1,953	2.4
6553	Cemetery subdividers and developers	4	4	1.3	8	7	7,000	8,000	73	71	0.2
6700	Holding and other investment offices	5	4	0.7	18	18	42,444	48,222	1,175	1,732	0.5
GUERNSEY, OH											
60 –	**Finance, insurance, and real estate**	56	58	0.2	410	499	17,951	21,098	7,869	10,564	0.1
6000	Depository institutions	13	12	0.2	196	199	19,633	21,789	4,073	4,228	0.2
6020	Commercial banks	8	7	0.2	73	68	20,055	25,059	1,494	1,569	0.1
6100	Nondepository institutions	4	4	0.3	19	13	26,105	27,385	427	324	0.1
6300	Insurance carriers	4	4	0.2	32	28	25,250	28,429	822	899	0.0
6500	Real estate	17	20	0.3	117	127	10,222	10,457	1,378	1,533	0.1
6550	Subdividers and developers	4	4	0.6	80	79	9,250	9,013	767	795	0.6
HAMILTON, OH											
60 –	**Finance, insurance, and real estate**	2,494	2,542	10.9	34,604	34,476	31,066	34,281	1,078,601	1,187,497	14.6
6000	Depository institutions	471	469	9.6	9,656	10,414	26,108	30,658	242,068	299,105	13.3
6020	Commercial banks	277	275	8.9	7,365	8,161	26,416	31,994	183,676	240,205	13.8
6030	Savings institutions	117	117	12.8	1,286	1,217	24,547	25,137	32,019	31,852	10.2
6060	Credit unions	64	65	8.7	602	577	20,963	23,875	12,370	13,160	11.9
6100	Nondepository institutions	165	168	10.8	1,383	1,458	38,525	33,717	48,806	53,449	9.9
6140	Personal credit institutions	53	58	8.7	386	450	29,358	31,227	11,835	14,783	8.5
6160	Mortgage bankers and brokers	93	91	14.7	803	802	37,469	30,963	27,641	29,125	14.3

Source: County Business Patterns, 1994/95, CBP-94/95, U.S. Department of Commerce, Washington, D.C., November 1997. SIC categories for which data were suppressed or not available for both 1994 and 1995 are not displayed. The employment columns represent mid-March employment in the year. Pay per employee is calculated by dividing 1st Quarter payroll, annualized, by mid-March employment. The columns headed "% State" show the county's percentage of the state total for the SIC in 1995; for example, 1.4% for SIC 6000 means that the county had 1.4 percent of the state's total establishments (or payroll) in SIC 6000 in 1995. A dash (-) is used to indicate that data are not available or cannot be calculated; nec means not elsewhere classified.

Continued on next page.

SIC	Industry	No. Establishments			Employment		Pay / Employee		Annual Payroll ($ 000)		
		1994	1995	% State	1994	1995	1994	1995	1994	1995	% State

HAMILTON, OH - [continued]

SIC	Industry	1994	1995	% State	1994	1995	1994	1995	1994	1995	% State
6200	Security and commodity brokers	152	162	13.3	1,751	1,842	64,628	63,646	108,687	120,268	17.9
6210	Security brokers and dealers	84	96	13.6	1,223	1,320	65,730	63,545	72,111	80,509	15.6
6280	Security and commodity services	66	64	12.9	523	516	62,164	64,202	36,323	39,480	25.8
6300	Insurance carriers	236	236	13.0	10,265	10,139	33,796	38,861	337,667	394,498	17.4
6310	Life insurance	85	82	16.5	5,334	5,259	32,367	35,128	161,791	166,475	30.1
6320	Medical service and health insurance	20	21	15.9	2,279	2,229	33,825	43,363	79,057	122,771	31.0
6330	Fire, marine, and casualty insurance	102	107	11.1	2,393	2,451	37,717	43,290	90,639	98,494	8.0
6370	Pension, health, and welfare funds	20	15	14.4	215	140	26,102	31,343	4,771	4,764	9.1
6400	Insurance agents, brokers, and service	522	540	9.7	2,991	3,203	29,044	30,553	94,967	105,561	13.0
6500	Real estate	862	888	11.6	6,571	6,493	20,035	21,852	148,217	152,455	14.3
6510	Real estate operators and lessors	372	373	11.3	2,169	1,972	14,296	16,424	34,299	36,612	11.4
6530	Real estate agents and managers	393	402	12.3	3,513	3,601	21,455	22,121	85,725	84,089	15.0
6540	Title abstract offices	13	13	6.0	163	123	28,515	28,780	5,779	5,085	9.5
6550	Subdividers and developers	73	79	12.0	716	745	28,709	33,541	22,077	25,039	20.3
6552	Subdividers and developers, n.e.c.	45	47	15.3	496	511	32,250	38,372	16,216	18,823	22.8
6553	Cemetery subdividers and developers	26	24	7.9	220	223	20,727	23,390	5,693	5,854	15.3
6700	Holding and other investment offices	78	74	12.3	828	660	49,792	67,576	48,103	44,123	11.9
6710	Holding offices	43	39	13.5	601	453	56,639	77,651	38,789	33,560	11.9
6730	Trusts	17	16	16.3	133	100	19,188	27,720	3,155	3,145	22.0
6732	Educational, religious, etc. trusts	11	10	17.5	97	44	16,206	19,364	1,636	994	10.5
6733	Trusts, n.e.c.	6	6	14.6	36	56	27,222	34,286	1,519	2,151	44.5
6790	Miscellaneous investing	16	15	8.8	94	103	49,319	62,874	5,840	7,234	11.1
6799	Investors, n.e.c.	10	9	9.3	68	76	56,294	68,474	4,979	6,051	20.3

HANCOCK, OH

SIC	Industry	1994	1995	% State	1994	1995	1994	1995	1994	1995	% State
60 –	**Finance, insurance, and real estate**	159	159	0.7	1,152	1,055	22,149	23,147	25,555	26,033	0.3
6000	Depository institutions	36	32	0.7	419	400	21,632	22,330	8,468	8,377	0.4
6020	Commercial banks	28	24	0.8	366	350	22,175	23,143	7,444	7,489	0.4
6100	Nondepository institutions	8	10	0.6	77	84	25,662	26,857	2,390	2,999	0.6
6210	Security brokers and dealers	4	5	0.7	19	24	117,684	79,333	1,724	1,788	0.3
6300	Insurance carriers	15	15	0.8	153	136	22,222	22,588	3,504	3,150	0.1
6310	Life insurance	4	4	0.8	87	72	23,954	24,111	2,129	1,689	0.3
6400	Insurance agents, brokers, and service	38	37	0.7	124	124	22,806	25,355	3,446	3,844	0.5
6500	Real estate	49	53	0.7	340	268	14,529	15,418	4,859	4,769	0.4
6510	Real estate operators and lessors	26	28	0.8	118	112	12,136	12,750	1,447	1,835	0.6
6530	Real estate agents and managers	17	17	0.5	207	141	15,401	17,362	3,075	2,502	0.4

HARDIN, OH

SIC	Industry	1994	1995	% State	1994	1995	1994	1995	1994	1995	% State
60 –	**Finance, insurance, and real estate**	42	39	0.2	219	210	18,301	20,952	4,014	4,215	0.1
6000	Depository institutions	16	15	0.3	153	144	18,379	21,556	2,751	2,849	0.1
6020	Commercial banks	12	11	0.4	127	116	16,693	21,414	2,162	2,250	0.1
6400	Insurance agents, brokers, and service	13	11	0.2	39	34	16,923	21,647	749	784	0.1
6500	Real estate	9	8	0.1	10	14	6,400	7,143	105	117	0.0
6510	Real estate operators and lessors	4	4	0.1	3	7	9,333	6,286	52	42	0.0
6530	Real estate agents and managers	5	4	0.1	7	7	5,143	8,000	53	75	0.0

HARRISON, OH

SIC	Industry	1994	1995	% State	1994	1995	1994	1995	1994	1995	% State
60 –	**Finance, insurance, and real estate**	19	18	0.1	154	150	23,506	11,013	2,137	1,694	0.0
6500	Real estate	7	6	0.1	99	99	27,596	7,717	1,272	797	0.1

HENRY, OH

SIC	Industry	1994	1995	% State	1994	1995	1994	1995	1994	1995	% State
60 –	**Finance, insurance, and real estate**	50	55	0.2	266	274	21,699	20,248	5,930	5,510	0.1
6000	Depository institutions	14	17	0.3	138	143	18,580	17,902	2,669	2,792	0.1
6100	Nondepository institutions	3	4	0.3	9	12	29,333	18,333	294	235	0.0
6400	Insurance agents, brokers, and service	17	19	0.3	50	54	25,520	25,481	1,094	1,130	0.1
6500	Real estate	9	10	0.1	26	34	7,231	8,706	226	334	0.0

HIGHLAND, OH

SIC	Industry	1994	1995	% State	1994	1995	1994	1995	1994	1995	% State
60 –	**Finance, insurance, and real estate**	63	66	0.3	373	400	19,560	25,000	7,556	9,257	0.1

Source: County Business Patterns, 1994/95, CBP-94/95, U.S. Department of Commerce, Washington, D.C., November 1997. SIC categories for which data were suppressed or not available for both 1994 and 1995 are not displayed. The employment columns represent mid-March employment in the year. Pay per employee is calculated by dividing 1st Quarter payroll, annualized, by mid-March employment. The columns headed "% State" show the county's percentage of the state total for the SIC in 1995; for example, 1.4% for SIC 6000 means that the county had 1.4 percent of the state's total establishments (or payroll) in SIC 6000 in 1995. A dash (-) is used to indicate that data are not available or cannot be calculated; nec means not elsewhere classified.

Continued on next page.

SIC	Industry	No. Establishments			Employment		Pay / Employee		Annual Payroll ($ 000)		
		1994	1995	% State	1994	1995	1994	1995	1994	1995	% State
HIGHLAND, OH - [continued]											
6000	Depository institutions	19	19	0.4	223	240	21,973	28,883	5,024	6,531	0.3
6020	Commercial banks	10	10	0.3	162	171	20,642	30,035	3,387	4,728	0.3
6500	Real estate	21	22	0.3	66	71	10,364	11,831	865	891	0.1
6530	Real estate agents and managers	9	10	0.3	22	30	16,909	17,333	501	595	0.1
HOCKING, OH											
60 –	**Finance, insurance, and real estate**	27	31	0.1	153	160	16,392	16,875	2,824	3,084	0.0
6000	Depository institutions	7	7	0.1	101	98	16,554	18,204	1,745	1,898	0.1
6400	Insurance agents, brokers, and service	8	8	0.1	25	25	16,000	16,480	597	639	0.1
6500	Real estate	8	11	0.1	8	15	7,000	4,533	66	120	0.0
6510	Real estate operators and lessors	3	5	0.2	2	5	6,000	3,200	13	47	0.0
HOLMES, OH											
60 –	**Finance, insurance, and real estate**	32	33	0.1	263	276	22,707	21,116	5,685	6,380	0.1
6000	Depository institutions	14	15	0.3	196	203	19,878	21,754	3,760	4,192	0.2
6500	Real estate	3	4	0.1	11	13	5,091	4,615	67	70	0.0
HURON, OH											
60 –	**Finance, insurance, and real estate**	99	98	0.4	559	518	25,503	26,286	13,407	13,439	0.2
6000	Depository institutions	26	25	0.5	321	323	23,065	24,557	6,903	7,380	0.3
6020	Commercial banks	18	17	0.5	224	224	21,089	22,625	4,765	5,070	0.3
6100	Nondepository institutions	5	5	0.3	20	22	25,600	27,818	551	595	0.1
6400	Insurance agents, brokers, and service	27	26	0.5	82	83	18,634	20,434	1,789	1,844	0.2
6500	Real estate	29	29	0.4	62	59	54,129	37,898	2,768	2,412	0.2
6510	Real estate operators and lessors	15	13	0.4	27	20	6,519	10,200	219	300	0.1
JACKSON, OH											
60 –	**Finance, insurance, and real estate**	52	55	0.2	1,048	1,075	21,122	27,658	21,018	21,172	0.3
6000	Depository institutions	17	16	0.3	232	218	21,741	26,514	5,334	5,073	0.2
6020	Commercial banks	11	10	0.3	144	155	19,028	20,645	3,321	4,117	0.2
6400	Insurance agents, brokers, and service	16	17	0.3	56	54	19,786	22,444	1,258	1,350	0.2
JEFFERSON, OH											
60 –	**Finance, insurance, and real estate**	139	139	0.6	1,212	1,097	17,535	18,655	20,658	20,796	0.3
6000	Depository institutions	44	38	0.8	627	558	16,740	18,638	10,002	9,578	0.4
6020	Commercial banks	33	29	0.9	570	508	16,933	19,118	9,200	8,858	0.5
6300	Insurance carriers	9	8	0.4	115	98	28,417	27,184	2,913	2,336	0.1
6310	Life insurance	4	4	0.8	97	87	27,216	24,506	2,425	1,959	0.4
6330	Fire, marine, and casualty insurance	5	4	0.4	18	11	34,889	48,364	488	377	0.0
6400	Insurance agents, brokers, and service	36	37	0.7	97	104	18,268	17,923	2,143	2,272	0.3
6500	Real estate	37	37	0.5	249	260	10,892	11,662	3,042	3,770	0.4
6510	Real estate operators and lessors	16	15	0.5	196	197	9,898	11,269	2,181	2,881	0.9
6550	Subdividers and developers	7	8	1.2	34	36	15,294	15,000	597	589	0.5
6700	Holding and other investment offices	5	6	1.0	60	25	27,400	36,320	1,093	920	0.2
KNOX, OH											
60 –	**Finance, insurance, and real estate**	83	81	0.3	512	504	19,328	19,468	10,115	10,403	0.1
6000	Depository institutions	17	17	0.3	297	304	21,306	20,632	6,065	6,365	0.3
6020	Commercial banks	10	10	0.3	234	239	22,872	21,607	4,998	5,137	0.3
6100	Nondepository institutions	5	4	0.3	17	18	28,706	28,889	602	572	0.1
6400	Insurance agents, brokers, and service	19	20	0.4	57	54	21,544	19,556	1,311	1,341	0.2
6500	Real estate	36	35	0.5	124	113	11,129	12,673	1,612	1,577	0.1
6510	Real estate operators and lessors	15	14	0.4	51	40	10,039	10,100	560	461	0.1
6530	Real estate agents and managers	15	17	0.5	62	65	13,097	14,523	952	1,038	0.2
6550	Subdividers and developers	4	4	0.6	9	8	5,778	10,500	91	78	0.1
6553	Cemetery subdividers and developers	4	4	1.3	9	8	5,778	10,500	91	78	0.2
LAKE, OH											
60 –	**Finance, insurance, and real estate**	442	454	1.9	3,022	3,039	23,122	23,754	66,876	71,198	0.9

Source: County Business Patterns, 1994/95, CBP-94/95, U.S. Department of Commerce, Washington, D.C., November 1997. SIC categories for which data were suppressed or not available for both 1994 and 1995 are not displayed. The employment columns represent mid-March employment in the year. Pay per employee is calculated by dividing 1st Quarter payroll, annualized, by mid-March employment. The columns headed "% State" show the county's percentage of the state total for the SIC in 1995; for example, 1.4% for SIC 6000 means that the county had 1.4 percent of the state's total establishments (or payroll) in SIC 6000 in 1995. A dash (-) is used to indicate that data are not available or cannot be calculated; nec means not elsewhere classified.

Continued on next page.

SIC	Industry	No. Establishments			Employment		Pay / Employee		Annual Payroll ($ 000)		
		1994	1995	% State	1994	1995	1994	1995	1994	1995	% State
LAKE, OH - [continued]											
6000	Depository institutions	108	108	2.2	1,311	1,263	20,098	22,321	25,067	26,011	1.2
6020	Commercial banks	50	58	1.9	868	938	21,710	22,934	17,565	19,560	1.1
6030	Savings institutions	34	26	2.8	355	238	17,487	21,933	6,223	5,035	1.6
6140	Personal credit institutions	13	16	2.4	66	71	29,515	38,366	1,853	2,677	1.5
6160	Mortgage bankers and brokers	10	11	1.8	85	72	23,059	21,722	1,760	1,983	1.0
6210	Security brokers and dealers	11	10	1.4	78	77	66,923	53,195	4,699	4,218	0.8
6300	Insurance carriers	28	29	1.6	236	275	29,051	30,822	6,786	8,072	0.4
6330	Fire, marine, and casualty insurance	18	20	2.1	89	110	36,180	38,364	3,255	4,259	0.3
6400	Insurance agents, brokers, and service	101	105	1.9	314	317	24,599	24,580	7,056	7,510	0.9
6500	Real estate	149	152	2.0	714	735	14,017	14,884	10,834	12,054	1.1
6510	Real estate operators and lessors	68	68	2.1	319	310	10,771	13,445	3,744	4,651	1.5
6530	Real estate agents and managers	61	61	1.9	220	254	17,836	16,567	4,318	4,534	0.8
6540	Title abstract offices	11	11	5.1	75	73	23,573	20,658	1,750	1,599	3.0
6550	Subdividers and developers	5	8	1.2	95	95	9,011	10,568	989	1,162	0.9
6552	Subdividers and developers, n.e.c.	4	6	1.9	95	90	9,011	10,622	949	1,099	1.3
LAWRENCE, OH											
60 –	**Finance, insurance, and real estate**	60	62	0.3	632	832	25,848	39,024	17,929	21,273	0.3
6000	Depository institutions	21	21	0.4	427	663	24,600	38,902	11,123	16,474	0.7
6030	Savings institutions	7	7	0.8	59	69	14,847	13,913	919	986	0.3
6100	Nondepository institutions	7	7	0.5	118	75	36,068	65,120	4,841	2,658	0.5
6400	Insurance agents, brokers, and service	19	20	0.4	64	67	17,188	18,925	1,310	1,326	0.2
6530	Real estate agents and managers	3	3	0.1	6	7	13,333	12,000	86	82	0.0
LICKING, OH											
60 –	**Finance, insurance, and real estate**	216	231	1.0	4,116	3,703	31,292	36,535	119,559	123,013	1.5
6000	Depository institutions	53	53	1.1	700	682	26,011	28,059	15,321	15,359	0.7
6020	Commercial banks	36	35	1.1	558	541	26,817	29,102	12,276	12,230	0.7
6030	Savings institutions	11	11	1.2	92	91	25,696	26,681	2,078	2,076	0.7
6160	Mortgage bankers and brokers	6	4	0.6	23	32	42,087	34,000	1,036	1,425	0.7
6310	Life insurance	6	6	1.2	135	136	28,978	29,971	3,289	3,700	0.7
6400	Insurance agents, brokers, and service	59	66	1.2	175	179	20,457	21,162	3,745	3,895	0.5
6500	Real estate	59	66	0.9	387	321	13,736	16,997	5,912	6,087	0.6
6530	Real estate agents and managers	37	39	1.2	285	267	14,667	16,689	4,689	4,729	0.8
LOGAN, OH											
60 –	**Finance, insurance, and real estate**	79	79	0.3	479	409	18,981	19,980	8,955	7,791	0.1
6000	Depository institutions	26	23	0.5	314	239	19,631	19,013	5,844	4,558	0.2
6020	Commercial banks	19	18	0.6	224	161	19,804	17,317	3,905	2,700	0.2
6400	Insurance agents, brokers, and service	20	23	0.4	64	72	16,750	16,389	1,112	1,164	0.1
6500	Real estate	23	23	0.3	58	54	12,069	11,704	769	689	0.1
6510	Real estate operators and lessors	12	12	0.4	40	34	11,300	12,118	482	425	0.1
LORAIN, OH											
60 –	**Finance, insurance, and real estate**	471	485	2.1	3,672	3,688	20,920	23,315	80,912	86,933	1.1
6000	Depository institutions	133	134	2.7	1,956	1,831	20,726	23,211	40,585	41,599	1.9
6020	Commercial banks	87	88	2.8	1,127	1,055	19,666	20,971	22,059	22,187	1.3
6030	Savings institutions	19	19	2.1	702	644	23,350	28,627	16,460	17,363	5.5
6100	Nondepository institutions	20	20	1.3	118	113	27,153	26,796	3,232	3,563	0.7
6140	Personal credit institutions	12	11	1.6	71	66	25,634	25,576	1,692	1,666	1.0
6200	Security and commodity brokers	19	21	1.7	70	72	38,400	35,111	2,480	2,482	0.4
6210	Security brokers and dealers	14	15	2.1	62	63	41,935	37,333	2,398	2,284	0.4
6280	Security and commodity services	5	6	1.2	8	9	11,000	19,556	82	198	0.1
6300	Insurance carriers	20	26	1.4	156	332	32,641	33,410	5,271	10,363	0.5
6330	Fire, marine, and casualty insurance	15	20	2.1	51	162	43,216	40,395	2,163	6,586	0.5
6400	Insurance agents, brokers, and service	95	98	1.8	347	324	19,043	20,296	7,761	7,180	0.9
6500	Real estate	171	175	2.3	956	973	16,038	19,161	17,818	19,473	1.8
6510	Real estate operators and lessors	84	82	2.5	236	237	10,847	13,350	3,090	3,342	1.0

Source: County Business Patterns, 1994/95, CBP-94/95, U.S. Department of Commerce, Washington, D.C., November 1997. SIC categories for which data were suppressed or not available for both 1994 and 1995 are *not* displayed. The employment columns represent mid-March employment in the year. Pay per employee is calculated by dividing 1st Quarter payroll, annualized, by mid-March employment. The columns headed "% State" show the county's percentage of the state total for the SIC in 1995; for example, 1.4% for SIC 6000 means that the county had 1.4 percent of the state's total establishments (or payroll) in SIC 6000 in 1995. A dash (-) is used to indicate that data are not available or cannot be calculated; *nec* means not elsewhere classified.

Continued on next page.

SIC	Industry	No. Establishments			Employment		Pay / Employee		Annual Payroll ($ 000)		
		1994	1995	% State	1994	1995	1994	1995	1994	1995	% State
LORAIN, OH - [continued]											
6530	Real estate agents and managers	64	63	1.9	494	483	13,830	17,896	7,944	8,632	1.5
6540	Title abstract offices	8	8	3.7	87	90	22,207	23,111	2,091	2,404	4.5
6550	Subdividers and developers	14	21	3.2	136	162	29,294	29,210	4,683	5,060	4.1
6700	Holding and other investment offices	13	11	1.8	69	43	48,638	37,581	3,765	2,273	0.6
LUCAS, OH											
60 –	**Finance, insurance, and real estate**	948	1,000	4.3	10,093	10,062	26,093	30,067	268,094	291,801	3.6
6000	Depository institutions	205	204	4.2	3,710	3,632	23,513	25,431	85,215	88,123	3.9
6020	Commercial banks	122	122	3.9	3,013	2,988	24,187	26,602	70,693	74,330	4.3
6100	Nondepository institutions	52	53	3.4	389	286	21,882	28,112	7,962	9,804	1.8
6160	Mortgage bankers and brokers	26	26	4.2	246	140	18,309	26,200	4,311	6,018	2.9
6200	Security and commodity brokers	50	56	4.6	531	500	55,872	59,400	26,887	29,046	4.3
6210	Security brokers and dealers	27	29	4.1	449	421	62,129	65,026	24,589	26,286	5.1
6300	Insurance carriers	75	82	4.5	1,928	1,860	29,338	42,211	57,900	62,832	2.8
6310	Life insurance	20	21	4.2	587	364	27,135	26,868	15,469	8,964	1.6
6320	Medical service and health insurance	10	10	7.6	1,033	931	29,235	55,553	32,322	35,989	9.1
6330	Fire, marine, and casualty insurance	38	42	4.4	222	481	37,477	30,644	7,832	15,186	1.2
6400	Insurance agents, brokers, and service	268	278	5.0	1,287	1,354	25,641	26,733	36,808	40,536	5.0
6500	Real estate	260	284	3.7	1,811	1,908	17,175	18,920	37,462	41,588	3.9
6510	Real estate operators and lessors	119	130	3.9	610	633	13,980	15,836	9,367	11,102	3.5
6530	Real estate agents and managers	116	126	3.9	992	1,039	18,661	20,231	22,403	23,834	4.3
6540	Title abstract offices	4	4	1.9	53	49	21,811	29,469	1,441	1,536	2.9
6550	Subdividers and developers	15	17	2.6	155	160	18,735	19,625	4,120	4,379	3.6
6552	Subdividers and developers, n.e.c.	8	10	3.2	77	81	15,532	15,556	1,709	1,754	2.1
6553	Cemetery subdividers and developers	6	6	2.0	78	76	21,897	23,632	1,906	2,012	5.3
6700	Holding and other investment offices	38	43	7.2	437	522	39,524	41,425	15,860	19,872	5.3
6710	Holding offices	14	15	5.2	169	269	60,426	50,662	8,987	11,856	4.2
6790	Miscellaneous investing	15	15	8.8	177	146	28,542	36,685	5,094	5,795	8.9
MADISON, OH											
60 –	**Finance, insurance, and real estate**	56	54	0.2	206	214	16,466	17,757	3,690	4,041	0.0
6000	Depository institutions	12	11	0.2	85	82	18,494	19,415	1,702	1,603	0.1
6400	Insurance agents, brokers, and service	17	17	0.3	43	48	20,279	21,250	963	1,068	0.1
6500	Real estate	23	21	0.3	66	69	10,121	11,014	713	970	0.1
6510	Real estate operators and lessors	12	9	0.3	35	35	7,429	8,229	307	308	0.1
MAHONING, OH											
60 –	**Finance, insurance, and real estate**	529	526	2.3	4,943	4,716	24,740	24,968	122,914	118,493	1.5
6000	Depository institutions	122	120	2.4	1,906	2,078	19,547	21,107	37,627	44,569	2.0
6020	Commercial banks	69	69	2.2	1,109	1,309	21,086	22,121	21,307	25,995	1.5
6030	Savings institutions	26	25	2.7	670	653	18,072	20,080	14,446	16,696	5.3
6100	Nondepository institutions	35	35	2.3	235	225	22,162	25,262	5,890	5,616	1.0
6140	Personal credit institutions	22	24	3.6	194	182	21,546	25,253	4,731	4,512	2.6
6200	Security and commodity brokers	28	27	2.2	224	231	61,393	55,446	10,932	11,894	1.8
6210	Security brokers and dealers	20	20	2.8	215	224	57,991	53,536	10,347	11,513	2.2
6300	Insurance carriers	43	40	2.2	816	667	29,059	32,162	22,974	21,596	1.0
6310	Life insurance	18	13	2.6	355	237	29,262	27,814	9,360	6,919	1.3
6320	Medical service and health insurance	5	6	4.5	281	247	26,890	33,150	7,950	7,670	1.9
6400	Insurance agents, brokers, and service	130	134	2.4	551	558	27,688	28,072	15,940	15,031	1.9
6500	Real estate	158	157	2.1	812	885	20,296	17,537	17,608	16,981	1.6
6510	Real estate operators and lessors	85	79	2.4	454	428	21,930	20,486	11,007	9,065	2.8
6530	Real estate agents and managers	48	51	1.6	209	305	14,833	11,659	3,365	4,340	0.8
6540	Title abstract offices	5	5	2.3	35	33	57,600	42,667	1,476	1,271	2.4
6550	Subdividers and developers	19	19	2.9	114	117	12,351	15,179	1,743	2,255	1.8

Source: County Business Patterns, 1994/95, CBP-94/95, U.S. Department of Commerce, Washington, D.C., November 1997. SIC categories for which data were suppressed or not available for both 1994 and 1995 are *not* displayed. The employment columns represent mid-March employment in the year. Pay per employee is calculated by dividing 1st Quarter payroll, annualized, by mid-March employment. The columns headed "% State" show the county's percentage of the state total for the SIC in 1995; for example, 1.4% for SIC 6000 means that the county had 1.4 percent of the state's total establishments (or payroll) in SIC 6000 in 1995. A dash (-) is used to indicate that data are not available or cannot be calculated; *nec* means not elsewhere classified.

Continued on next page.

SIC	Industry	No. Establishments			Employment		Pay / Employee		Annual Payroll ($ 000)		
		1994	1995	% State	1994	1995	1994	1995	1994	1995	% State
MAHONING, OH - [continued]											
6552	Subdividers and developers, n.e.c.	7	8	2.6	25	37	5,280	9,189	212	756	0.9
6553	Cemetery subdividers and developers	12	11	3.6	89	80	14,337	17,950	1,531	1,499	3.9
6700	Holding and other investment offices	13	13	2.2	399	72	26,627	38,333	11,943	2,806	0.8
MARION, OH											
60 –	**Finance, insurance, and real estate**	123	124	0.5	664	633	21,090	21,498	13,235	13,871	0.2
6000	Depository institutions	34	34	0.7	321	289	15,190	17,536	4,896	5,154	0.2
6020	Commercial banks	20	23	0.7	237	240	13,705	17,350	3,379	4,263	0.2
6300	Insurance carriers	13	10	0.6	113	100	34,726	29,640	2,961	2,926	0.1
6310	Life insurance	3	3	0.6	96	88	35,000	29,227	2,433	2,495	0.5
6400	Insurance agents, brokers, and service	28	28	0.5	77	81	14,597	15,457	1,292	1,370	0.2
6500	Real estate	36	39	0.5	102	113	15,647	16,071	1,866	2,004	0.2
6510	Real estate operators and lessors	19	19	0.6	63	59	8,381	9,559	600	669	0.2
6530	Real estate agents and managers	10	14	0.4	24	41	38,167	26,732	1,071	1,129	0.2
6550	Subdividers and developers	5	5	0.8	15	13	10,133	12,000	186	202	0.2
MEDINA, OH											
60 –	**Finance, insurance, and real estate**	216	233	1.0	2,693	2,823	28,055	31,780	89,458	103,188	1.3
6000	Depository institutions	47	47	1.0	547	522	18,625	19,004	10,082	9,870	0.4
6020	Commercial banks	33	32	1.0	418	385	19,426	20,260	7,931	7,689	0.4
6160	Mortgage bankers and brokers	5	6	1.0	14	28	31,429	13,143	514	732	0.4
6200	Security and commodity brokers	9	10	0.8	281	151	17,238	24,530	5,677	3,628	0.5
6400	Insurance agents, brokers, and service	49	57	1.0	203	302	20,000	24,781	5,088	8,703	1.1
6510	Real estate operators and lessors	23	24	0.7	50	64	10,640	10,563	734	865	0.3
6530	Real estate agents and managers	34	35	1.1	87	98	17,241	16,490	1,899	1,987	0.4
6540	Title abstract offices	10	9	4.2	57	47	18,667	18,298	1,088	998	1.9
6553	Cemetery subdividers and developers	4	5	1.6	14	18	8,571	12,444	163	244	0.6
MEIGS, OH											
60 –	**Finance, insurance, and real estate**	21	21	0.1	133	133	14,857	16,571	2,181	2,351	0.0
6000	Depository institutions	6	6	0.1	92	94	16,000	16,596	1,634	1,689	0.1
6020	Commercial banks	6	6	0.2	92	94	16,000	16,596	1,634	1,689	0.1
6400	Insurance agents, brokers, and service	8	8	0.1	23	22	14,957	14,182	364	351	0.0
6530	Real estate agents and managers	3	3	0.1	4	3	7,000	5,333	32	19	0.0
MERCER, OH											
60 –	**Finance, insurance, and real estate**	76	81	0.3	706	666	22,839	25,526	15,399	15,697	0.2
6000	Depository institutions	27	25	0.5	319	314	22,633	26,064	6,251	6,381	0.3
6020	Commercial banks	22	20	0.6	280	267	23,229	27,446	5,547	5,662	0.3
6400	Insurance agents, brokers, and service	23	22	0.4	79	80	21,570	24,100	1,815	2,004	0.2
6510	Real estate operators and lessors	7	8	0.2	10	11	17,600	19,273	213	234	0.1
MIAMI, OH											
60 –	**Finance, insurance, and real estate**	166	171	0.7	992	1,064	23,254	24,023	23,019	26,612	0.3
6000	Depository institutions	42	41	0.8	506	498	22,980	25,847	11,418	12,464	0.6
6020	Commercial banks	27	26	0.8	306	289	22,131	24,969	6,706	7,123	0.4
6030	Savings institutions	10	10	1.1	187	187	25,112	28,706	4,445	5,019	1.6
6060	Credit unions	5	5	0.7	13	22	12,308	13,091	267	322	0.3
6100	Nondepository institutions	12	10	0.6	49	48	24,571	22,000	1,190	1,307	0.2
6300	Insurance carriers	8	7	0.4	121	123	32,033	29,691	3,760	4,109	0.2
6400	Insurance agents, brokers, and service	40	43	0.8	134	143	25,642	23,944	3,616	3,488	0.4
6500	Real estate	58	63	0.8	166	171	13,831	13,099	2,492	2,720	0.3
6510	Real estate operators and lessors	23	23	0.7	85	91	13,318	12,220	1,105	1,228	0.4
6530	Real estate agents and managers	27	28	0.9	51	51	15,765	13,961	910	895	0.2
6552	Subdividers and developers, n.e.c.	3	4	1.3	6	7	14,000	13,143	148	188	0.2

Source: County Business Patterns, 1994/95, CBP-94/95, U.S. Department of Commerce, Washington, D.C., November 1997. SIC categories for which data were suppressed or not available for both 1994 and 1995 are not displayed. The employment columns represent mid-March employment in the year. Pay per employee is calculated by dividing 1st Quarter payroll, annualized, by mid-March employment. The columns headed "% State" show the county's percentage of the state total for the SIC in 1995; for example, 1.4% for SIC 6000 means that the county had 1.4 percent of the state's total establishments (or payroll) in SIC 6000 in 1995. A dash (-) is used to indicate that data are not available or cannot be calculated; nec means not elsewhere classified.

SIC	Industry	No. Establishments			Employment		Pay / Employee		Annual Payroll ($ 000)		
		1994	1995	% State	1994	1995	1994	1995	1994	1995	% State

MONROE, OH

SIC	Industry	1994	1995	% State	1994	1995	1994	1995	1994	1995	% State
60 –	**Finance, insurance, and real estate**	22	23	0.1	112	99	14,714	17,818	1,801	1,871	0.0
6000	Depository institutions	8	8	0.2	83	74	15,181	18,486	1,361	1,412	0.1
6400	Insurance agents, brokers, and service	8	8	0.1	19	18	14,737	16,667	304	306	0.0

MONTGOMERY, OH

SIC	Industry	1994	1995	% State	1994	1995	1994	1995	1994	1995	% State
60 –	**Finance, insurance, and real estate**	1,230	1,248	5.3	14,967	13,470	28,346	28,887	398,129	393,869	4.9
6000	Depository institutions	235	239	4.9	4,941	4,838	24,096	24,265	112,799	113,195	5.0
6020	Commercial banks	143	139	4.5	3,687	3,492	23,846	24,914	83,016	81,833	4.7
6030	Savings institutions	44	53	5.8	697	744	29,647	24,892	18,902	19,304	6.2
6060	Credit unions	38	37	5.0	512	524	19,500	21,153	10,130	11,140	10.1
6090	Functions closely related to banking	10	10	7.9	45	78	10,933	10,103	751	918	-
6160	Mortgage bankers and brokers	47	50	8.1	385	346	36,592	27,665	11,996	10,264	5.0
6200	Security and commodity brokers	64	64	5.3	849	937	67,180	68,807	54,482	60,079	8.9
6210	Security brokers and dealers	31	32	4.5	539	585	66,798	63,665	33,071	35,178	6.8
6300	Insurance carriers	98	101	5.6	2,412	2,166	26,274	29,481	64,707	64,350	2.8
6310	Life insurance	31	29	5.8	734	664	27,074	29,205	19,507	18,304	3.3
6320	Medical service and health insurance	12	14	10.6	535	482	30,019	35,876	16,915	19,010	4.8
6330	Fire, marine, and casualty insurance	44	48	5.0	908	787	22,736	25,616	21,657	20,154	1.6
6360	Title insurance	3	3	3.6	55	47	36,436	40,085	1,468	1,467	4.3
6370	Pension, health, and welfare funds	8	7	6.7	180	186	26,622	27,570	5,160	5,415	10.4
6400	Insurance agents, brokers, and service	291	302	5.4	1,291	1,245	26,686	28,212	38,676	40,768	5.0
6500	Real estate	427	426	5.6	3,378	2,622	18,326	19,829	65,963	55,674	5.2
6510	Real estate operators and lessors	198	195	5.9	1,361	1,171	14,974	16,079	22,800	21,428	6.7
6530	Real estate agents and managers	190	191	5.8	1,656	1,122	21,210	24,620	36,169	27,912	5.0
6540	Title abstract offices	13	12	5.6	188	133	20,915	22,797	4,190	3,230	6.0
6550	Subdividers and developers	18	18	2.7	164	165	14,293	13,285	2,636	2,672	2.2
6552	Subdividers and developers, n.e.c.	8	8	2.6	23	20	36,870	24,000	759	644	0.8
6553	Cemetery subdividers and developers	9	9	3.0	141	140	10,610	11,657	1,853	2,008	5.2
6700	Holding and other investment offices	25	26	4.3	1,251	901	45,832	34,220	35,228	33,262	8.9
6710	Holding offices	14	14	4.8	1,171	804	47,102	34,313	32,897	27,713	9.9
6790	Miscellaneous investing	7	8	4.7	67	83	17,791	35,663	1,614	5,283	8.1

MORGAN, OH

SIC	Industry	1994	1995	% State	1994	1995	1994	1995	1994	1995	% State
60 –	**Finance, insurance, and real estate**	20	21	0.1	94	95	14,638	16,295	1,438	1,536	0.0
6000	Depository institutions	7	7	0.1	78	74	15,692	17,622	1,275	1,322	0.1

MORROW, OH

SIC	Industry	1994	1995	% State	1994	1995	1994	1995	1994	1995	% State
60 –	**Finance, insurance, and real estate**	26	28	0.1	103	98	13,476	12,898	1,426	1,374	0.0
6000	Depository institutions	7	5	0.1	45	34	14,844	15,176	644	515	0.0
6510	Real estate operators and lessors	6	6	0.2	14	9	6,857	8,000	93	82	0.0
6530	Real estate agents and managers	4	6	0.2	26	30	12,769	10,800	354	362	0.1

MUSKINGUM, OH

SIC	Industry	1994	1995	% State	1994	1995	1994	1995	1994	1995	% State
60 –	**Finance, insurance, and real estate**	144	152	0.7	1,006	1,061	22,855	24,441	22,846	25,489	0.3
6000	Depository institutions	33	32	0.7	529	534	22,261	25,393	11,192	12,645	0.6
6020	Commercial banks	18	17	0.5	342	354	21,497	24,712	6,891	7,626	0.4
6100	Nondepository institutions	12	14	0.9	48	48	22,750	26,667	1,155	1,307	0.2
6160	Mortgage bankers and brokers	3	4	0.6	9	8	19,111	16,000	143	222	0.1
6200	Security and commodity brokers	8	8	0.7	36	36	68,333	56,889	2,181	2,020	0.3
6300	Insurance carriers	13	16	0.9	99	109	27,919	28,294	2,875	3,240	0.1
6310	Life insurance	4	4	0.8	59	56	25,898	26,071	1,569	1,532	0.3
6400	Insurance agents, brokers, and service	36	36	0.6	136	139	19,147	20,058	3,145	3,193	0.4
6500	Real estate	38	41	0.5	142	158	12,789	14,025	1,932	2,123	0.2
6510	Real estate operators and lessors	19	21	0.6	95	108	11,958	11,333	1,160	1,187	0.4

Source: County Business Patterns, 1994/95, CBP-94/95, U.S. Department of Commerce, Washington, D.C., November 1997. SIC categories for which data were suppressed or not available for both 1994 and 1995 are not displayed. The employment columns represent mid-March employment in the year. Pay per employee is calculated by dividing 1st Quarter payroll, annualized, by mid-March employment. The columns headed "% State" show the county's percentage of the state total for the SIC in 1995; for example, 1.4% for SIC 6000 means that the county had 1.4 percent of the state's total establishments (or payroll) in SIC 6000 in 1995. A dash (-) is used to indicate that data are not available or cannot be calculated; nec means not elsewhere classified.

Continued on next page.

SIC	Industry	No. Establishments			Employment		Pay / Employee		Annual Payroll ($ 000)		
		1994	1995	% State	1994	1995	1994	1995	1994	1995	% State
MUSKINGUM, OH - [continued]											
6530	Real estate agents and managers	14	15	0.5	37	37	14,486	20,541	572	650	0.1
6550	Subdividers and developers	5	5	0.8	10	13	14,400	17,846	200	286	0.2
6700	Holding and other investment offices	4	5	0.8	16	37	30,000	25,838	366	961	0.3
NOBLE, OH											
60 –	**Finance, insurance, and real estate**	10	10	0.0	81	83	19,753	21,349	1,790	1,891	0.0
6000	Depository institutions	4	4	0.1	65	70	18,831	19,886	1,362	1,472	0.1
OTTAWA, OH											
60 –	**Finance, insurance, and real estate**	87	91	0.4	553	567	19,125	19,287	11,346	11,563	0.1
6000	Depository institutions	16	18	0.4	273	267	23,282	23,266	6,115	6,085	0.3
6020	Commercial banks	12	13	0.4	223	214	23,067	22,991	5,122	4,898	0.3
6400	Insurance agents, brokers, and service	27	28	0.5	81	90	15,062	16,089	1,443	1,538	0.2
6500	Real estate	37	37	0.5	129	126	14,760	15,937	2,524	2,620	0.2
6510	Real estate operators and lessors	19	18	0.5	63	54	14,222	14,000	1,008	965	0.3
PAULDING, OH											
60 –	**Finance, insurance, and real estate**	22	20	0.1	133	133	15,278	16,211	2,161	2,254	0.0
6000	Depository institutions	7	7	0.1	76	76	17,842	19,053	1,389	1,409	0.1
6500	Real estate	4	3	0.0	23	25	3,652	4,320	103	113	0.0
PERRY, OH											
60 –	**Finance, insurance, and real estate**	29	32	0.1	175	189	18,469	18,963	3,530	3,790	0.0
6000	Depository institutions	10	10	0.2	116	119	19,690	20,000	2,456	2,571	0.1
6400	Insurance agents, brokers, and service	10	9	0.2	35	38	16,914	19,895	677	756	0.1
6510	Real estate operators and lessors	3	4	0.1	4	5	8,000	5,600	33	36	0.0
PICKAWAY, OH											
60 –	**Finance, insurance, and real estate**	76	79	0.3	375	402	18,635	18,587	7,396	9,499	0.1
6000	Depository institutions	15	15	0.3	165	175	17,624	18,651	2,985	3,324	0.1
6100	Nondepository institutions	6	6	0.4	36	33	20,778	26,788	876	938	0.2
6400	Insurance agents, brokers, and service	20	22	0.4	70	71	17,486	18,535	1,426	1,481	0.2
6500	Real estate	28	29	0.4	77	100	19,273	14,320	1,463	3,099	0.3
6510	Real estate operators and lessors	12	14	0.4	35	35	7,543	9,371	316	441	0.1
6530	Real estate agents and managers	10	9	0.3	15	14	17,067	21,143	352	1,766	0.3
6550	Subdividers and developers	5	5	0.8	26	50	36,923	16,000	791	885	0.7
PIKE, OH											
60 –	**Finance, insurance, and real estate**	23	29	0.1	199	195	15,819	17,436	3,360	3,562	0.0
6000	Depository institutions	7	7	0.1	117	117	17,744	18,427	2,164	2,249	0.1
PORTAGE, OH											
60 –	**Finance, insurance, and real estate**	200	194	0.8	1,381	1,766	22,989	25,991	31,693	39,227	0.5
6000	Depository institutions	49	49	1.0	816	1,141	25,672	30,026	20,165	25,629	1.1
6020	Commercial banks	35	34	1.1	697	1,023	26,456	31,011	17,670	22,917	1.3
6030	Savings institutions	10	10	1.1	99	96	22,061	22,542	2,143	2,284	0.7
6060	Credit unions	4	5	0.7	20	22	16,200	16,909	352	428	0.4
6100	Nondepository institutions	11	11	0.7	48	93	24,917	18,237	1,231	2,119	0.4
6140	Personal credit institutions	5	6	0.9	33	70	25,939	18,743	891	1,555	0.9
6200	Security and commodity brokers	8	10	0.8	48	56	24,083	22,643	1,160	1,384	0.2
6400	Insurance agents, brokers, and service	52	46	0.8	151	132	20,371	21,515	3,041	3,121	0.4
6500	Real estate	71	69	0.9	283	298	14,572	13,799	4,002	3,882	0.4
6510	Real estate operators and lessors	43	38	1.1	169	182	16,852	14,527	2,486	2,400	0.7
6530	Real estate agents and managers	20	20	0.6	72	83	10,778	11,807	935	996	0.2
PREBLE, OH											
60 –	**Finance, insurance, and real estate**	52	52	0.2	276	270	20,130	21,511	5,585	5,872	0.1
6000	Depository institutions	19	19	0.4	154	145	23,221	25,407	3,404	3,546	0.2

Source: County Business Patterns, 1994/95, CBP-94/95, U.S. Department of Commerce, Washington, D.C., November 1997. SIC categories for which data were suppressed or not available for both 1994 and 1995 are not displayed. The employment columns represent mid-March employment in the year. Pay per employee is calculated by dividing 1st Quarter payroll, annualized, by mid-March employment. The columns headed "% State" show the county's percentage of the state total for the SIC in 1995; for example, 1.4% for SIC 6000 means that the county had 1.4 percent of the state's total establishments (or payroll) in SIC 6000 in 1995. A dash (-) is used to indicate that data are not available or cannot be calculated; nec means not elsewhere classified.

Continued on next page.

SIC	Industry	No. Establishments			Employment		Pay / Employee		Annual Payroll ($ 000)		
		1994	1995	% State	1994	1995	1994	1995	1994	1995	% State
PREBLE, OH - [continued]											
6020	Commercial banks	16	16	0.5	142	133	23,775	26,466	3,209	3,379	0.2
6400	Insurance agents, brokers, and service	15	14	0.3	49	48	17,714	19,667	1,053	1,080	0.1
6500	Real estate	14	14	0.2	60	62	11,200	10,645	728	803	0.1
6510	Real estate operators and lessors	3	3	0.1	8	10	13,500	11,200	141	150	0.0
6530	Real estate agents and managers	8	8	0.2	42	40	11,524	10,600	497	515	0.1
6550	Subdividers and developers	3	3	0.5	10	12	8,000	10,333	90	138	0.1
6553	Cemetery subdividers and developers	3	3	1.0	10	12	8,000	10,333	90	138	0.4
PUTNAM, OH											
60 –	**Finance, insurance, and real estate**	50	48	0.2	308	316	17,870	17,873	5,479	5,551	0.1
6000	Depository institutions	18	14	0.3	188	180	20,787	20,889	3,700	3,601	0.2
6400	Insurance agents, brokers, and service	15	16	0.3	45	52	17,067	17,000	831	982	0.1
6500	Real estate	11	12	0.2	58	62	8,897	10,645	613	665	0.1
RICHLAND, OH											
60 –	**Finance, insurance, and real estate**	269	264	1.1	2,355	1,988	25,354	26,885	57,846	51,871	0.6
6000	Depository institutions	65	60	1.2	770	719	18,894	20,178	14,398	14,452	0.6
6020	Commercial banks	38	38	1.2	529	508	20,076	21,630	10,315	10,669	0.6
6030	Savings institutions	17	12	1.3	159	127	17,459	18,331	2,891	2,509	0.8
6060	Credit unions	10	10	1.3	82	84	14,049	14,190	1,192	1,274	1.1
6100	Nondepository institutions	18	17	1.1	85	80	22,118	25,250	1,831	2,147	0.4
6140	Personal credit institutions	9	10	1.5	47	52	23,489	25,462	1,082	1,330	0.8
6300	Insurance carriers	25	25	1.4	850	609	34,758	37,537	27,422	20,756	0.9
6330	Fire, marine, and casualty insurance	17	18	1.9	726	506	36,242	39,866	24,608	18,062	1.5
6400	Insurance agents, brokers, and service	68	69	1.2	256	250	24,844	27,648	6,632	6,934	0.9
6500	Real estate	83	81	1.1	347	278	10,571	13,396	4,635	4,459	0.4
6510	Real estate operators and lessors	46	43	1.3	117	98	8,274	9,510	1,252	1,035	0.3
6530	Real estate agents and managers	24	25	0.8	192	140	10,896	15,829	2,631	2,659	0.5
6553	Cemetery subdividers and developers	7	7	2.3	26	26	12,769	13,538	391	391	1.0
ROSS, OH											
60 –	**Finance, insurance, and real estate**	108	109	0.5	522	502	20,314	22,096	10,596	10,981	0.1
6000	Depository institutions	21	21	0.4	167	197	18,036	19,208	3,155	3,747	0.2
6020	Commercial banks	14	16	0.5	145	176	17,821	19,386	2,717	3,404	0.2
6100	Nondepository institutions	10	9	0.6	96	38	16,250	25,158	1,148	872	0.2
6200	Security and commodity brokers	5	6	0.5	12	17	56,000	42,824	586	838	0.1
6210	Security brokers and dealers	5	6	0.8	12	17	56,000	42,824	586	838	0.2
6400	Insurance agents, brokers, and service	29	27	0.5	80	70	18,900	18,857	1,466	1,322	0.2
6500	Real estate	34	38	0.5	103	119	14,680	14,857	1,933	2,003	0.2
6510	Real estate operators and lessors	17	17	0.5	50	48	11,760	13,583	715	729	0.2
SANDUSKY, OH											
60 –	**Finance, insurance, and real estate**	101	111	0.5	614	652	19,407	19,466	12,558	13,785	0.2
6000	Depository institutions	26	25	0.5	381	382	20,189	20,628	7,995	8,469	0.4
6020	Commercial banks	18	17	0.5	290	284	21,062	21,310	6,395	6,667	0.4
6400	Insurance agents, brokers, and service	44	45	0.8	147	156	18,422	18,692	2,909	2,933	0.4
6500	Real estate	21	27	0.4	58	78	11,448	11,128	733	1,229	0.1
6510	Real estate operators and lessors	11	15	0.5	37	42	13,730	15,810	543	951	0.3
6530	Real estate agents and managers	5	7	0.2	7	21	9,143	4,762	70	137	0.0
6550	Subdividers and developers	4	4	0.6	14	15	6,571	6,933	118	133	0.1
6553	Cemetery subdividers and developers	4	4	1.3	14	15	6,571	6,933	118	133	0.3
SCIOTO, OH											
60 –	**Finance, insurance, and real estate**	115	108	0.5	880	866	17,941	20,231	16,990	16,998	0.2
6000	Depository institutions	28	24	0.5	337	316	21,543	25,684	6,957	7,116	0.3
6020	Commercial banks	18	15	0.5	217	196	20,184	22,286	4,132	4,033	0.2
6100	Nondepository institutions	6	6	0.4	22	22	19,636	25,091	460	569	0.1
6300	Insurance carriers	11	10	0.6	207	183	19,304	22,667	4,609	4,301	0.2

Source: County Business Patterns, 1994/95, CBP-94/95, U.S. Department of Commerce, Washington, D.C., November 1997. SIC categories for which data were suppressed or not available for both 1994 and 1995 are *not* displayed. The employment columns represent mid-March employment in the year. Pay per employee is calculated by dividing 1st Quarter payroll, annualized, by mid-March employment. The columns headed "% State" show the county's percentage of the state total for the SIC in 1995; for example, 1.4% for SIC 6000 means that the county had 1.4 percent of the state's total establishments (or payroll) in SIC 6000 in 1995. A dash (-) is used to indicate that data are not available or cannot be calculated; *nec* means not elsewhere classified.

Continued on next page.

SIC	Industry	No. Establishments			Employment		Pay / Employee		Annual Payroll ($ 000)		
		1994	1995	% State	1994	1995	1994	1995	1994	1995	% State
SCIOTO, OH - [continued]											
6400	Insurance agents, brokers, and service	37	34	0.6	120	127	18,367	17,354	2,545	2,504	0.3
6500	Real estate	29	29	0.4	187	210	8,770	10,514	2,191	2,209	0.2
6510	Real estate operators and lessors	17	17	0.5	79	72	8,000	10,944	798	787	0.2
6530	Real estate agents and managers	8	7	0.2	18	22	14,000	13,273	303	314	0.1
6550	Subdividers and developers	4	4	0.6	90	116	8,400	9,724	1,090	1,105	0.9
SENECA, OH											
60 –	**Finance, insurance, and real estate**	118	118	0.5	569	558	18,931	20,738	11,754	12,670	0.2
6000	Depository institutions	33	30	0.6	320	308	17,125	19,558	5,662	6,159	0.3
6020	Commercial banks	23	22	0.7	238	241	17,109	19,934	4,432	4,988	0.3
6300	Insurance carriers	6	9	0.5	38	41	22,316	27,122	953	1,010	0.0
6400	Insurance agents, brokers, and service	35	36	0.6	98	96	22,694	22,667	2,694	2,953	0.4
6500	Real estate	33	32	0.4	62	61	9,677	9,311	721	770	0.1
6510	Real estate operators and lessors	14	14	0.4	25	27	8,640	9,185	267	387	0.1
6530	Real estate agents and managers	15	14	0.4	32	25	11,000	11,680	411	328	0.1
6550	Subdividers and developers	3	3	0.5	4	7	6,000	2,857	34	36	0.0
6553	Cemetery subdividers and developers	3	3	1.0	4	7	6,000	2,857	34	36	0.1
SHELBY, OH											
60 –	**Finance, insurance, and real estate**	76	75	0.3	398	388	21,518	23,165	8,638	8,815	0.1
6000	Depository institutions	23	22	0.4	266	257	21,383	23,891	5,797	5,996	0.3
6020	Commercial banks	19	18	0.6	220	204	22,127	24,882	4,743	4,829	0.3
6100	Nondepository institutions	4	4	0.3	19	18	17,684	16,000	233	273	0.1
6400	Insurance agents, brokers, and service	24	27	0.5	61	58	18,098	20,759	1,293	1,293	0.2
6510	Real estate operators and lessors	9	8	0.2	15	22	8,000	4,545	118	50	0.0
STARK, OH											
60 –	**Finance, insurance, and real estate**	735	755	3.2	6,097	6,021	23,627	24,512	141,810	148,131	1.8
6000	Depository institutions	171	165	3.4	2,112	2,057	21,254	22,579	42,004	45,561	2.0
6020	Commercial banks	101	107	3.4	1,422	1,629	20,765	23,745	27,408	37,463	2.2
6030	Savings institutions	29	19	2.1	486	191	25,218	22,325	11,295	4,238	1.4
6100	Nondepository institutions	55	62	4.0	428	431	27,505	25,067	10,709	10,933	2.0
6140	Personal credit institutions	28	31	4.6	187	173	26,075	27,746	4,515	4,413	2.5
6160	Mortgage bankers and brokers	23	25	4.0	229	234	29,240	23,111	5,856	5,862	2.9
6200	Security and commodity brokers	39	39	3.2	226	245	60,425	52,522	11,340	12,065	1.8
6210	Security brokers and dealers	24	26	3.7	167	186	69,150	57,269	9,249	9,638	1.9
6280	Security and commodity services	15	13	2.6	59	59	35,729	37,559	2,091	2,427	1.6
6300	Insurance carriers	59	61	3.4	1,237	1,150	28,873	31,576	35,200	34,315	1.5
6310	Life insurance	11	11	2.2	165	151	26,545	24,026	3,921	3,391	0.6
6330	Fire, marine, and casualty insurance	36	37	3.8	795	765	30,787	33,788	24,394	24,026	2.0
6370	Pension, health, and welfare funds	5	5	4.8	104	96	20,500	24,167	2,273	2,469	4.7
6400	Insurance agents, brokers, and service	194	207	3.7	717	750	25,724	26,827	19,483	21,509	2.7
6500	Real estate	203	211	2.8	1,338	1,329	13,898	14,679	21,866	22,043	2.1
6510	Real estate operators and lessors	83	84	2.5	350	316	12,960	13,949	4,870	4,615	1.4
6530	Real estate agents and managers	85	89	2.7	757	799	14,114	14,914	12,930	13,230	2.4
6540	Title abstract offices	6	7	3.2	48	41	20,083	18,732	1,013	972	1.8
6550	Subdividers and developers	29	30	4.6	183	173	13,180	13,965	3,053	3,177	2.6
6552	Subdividers and developers, n.e.c.	10	10	3.2	37	42	33,297	29,905	1,573	1,825	2.2
6553	Cemetery subdividers and developers	19	20	6.6	146	131	8,082	8,855	1,480	1,352	3.5
6700	Holding and other investment offices	14	10	1.7	39	59	25,231	25,898	1,208	1,705	0.5
6710	Holding offices	8	6	2.1	14	12	26,571	23,333	413	458	0.2
SUMMIT, OH											
60 –	**Finance, insurance, and real estate**	1,104	1,091	4.7	11,369	12,197	26,684	30,010	305,049	360,054	4.4
6000	Depository institutions	216	206	4.2	4,411	4,434	24,143	25,304	102,186	106,955	4.8
6020	Commercial banks	140	137	4.4	3,531	3,638	24,886	26,025	84,829	91,301	5.3
6030	Savings institutions	35	29	3.2	592	504	23,311	23,802	12,350	10,057	3.2
6160	Mortgage bankers and brokers	35	33	5.3	297	228	31,057	25,526	7,931	7,750	3.8

Source: County Business Patterns, 1994/95, CBP-94/95, U.S. Department of Commerce, Washington, D.C., November 1997. SIC categories for which data were suppressed or not available for both 1994 and 1995 are *not* displayed. The employment columns represent mid-March employment in the year. Pay per employee is calculated by dividing 1st Quarter payroll, annualized, by mid-March employment. The columns headed "% State" show the county's percentage of the state total for the SIC in 1995; for example, 1.4% for SIC 6000 means that the county had 1.4 percent of the state's total establishments (or payroll) in SIC 6000 in 1995. A dash (-) is used to indicate that data are not available or cannot be calculated; *nec* means not elsewhere classified.

Continued on next page.

SIC	Industry	No. Establishments			Employment		Pay / Employee		Annual Payroll ($ 000)		
		1994	1995	% State	1994	1995	1994	1995	1994	1995	% State
SUMMIT, OH - [continued]											
6200	Security and commodity brokers	71	67	5.5	473	477	66,047	55,094	26,513	26,834	4.0
6210	Security brokers and dealers	36	37	5.2	369	386	78,352	62,238	23,733	23,972	4.6
6280	Security and commodity services	35	30	6.0	104	91	22,385	24,791	2,780	2,862	1.9
6300	Insurance carriers	111	98	5.4	2,515	2,104	28,175	34,243	69,948	69,640	3.1
6310	Life insurance	29	26	5.2	626	540	26,773	27,237	16,588	12,934	2.3
6330	Fire, marine, and casualty insurance	55	56	5.8	1,259	1,218	32,994	38,315	42,758	44,188	3.6
6370	Pension, health, and welfare funds	18	6	5.8	447	184	16,886	27,717	5,274	6,807	13.0
6400	Insurance agents, brokers, and service	267	265	4.8	1,108	1,006	25,704	28,171	31,020	30,172	3.7
6500	Real estate	335	357	4.7	2,110	2,587	20,724	20,980	52,030	58,110	5.4
6510	Real estate operators and lessors	123	131	4.0	576	833	14,132	14,170	9,563	12,528	3.9
6530	Real estate agents and managers	148	157	4.8	1,018	1,225	22,063	23,207	28,427	31,934	5.7
6540	Title abstract offices	25	23	10.6	231	215	21,368	22,419	5,786	5,156	9.6
6550	Subdividers and developers	33	36	5.5	277	284	29,184	30,915	8,096	8,075	6.5
6552	Subdividers and developers, n.e.c.	18	19	6.2	145	164	39,559	38,878	5,419	5,402	6.5
6553	Cemetery subdividers and developers	13	14	4.6	132	117	17,788	20,444	2,664	2,634	6.9
6710	Holding offices	14	15	5.2	133	1,074	43,038	55,300	7,153	52,694	18.8
6790	Miscellaneous investing	11	6	3.5	56	29	26,429	40,138	2,127	1,314	2.0
TRUMBULL, OH											
60 –	**Finance, insurance, and real estate**	334	339	1.5	2,406	2,565	19,671	19,855	49,050	52,743	0.7
6000	Depository institutions	89	85	1.7	1,239	1,391	20,210	19,764	24,090	27,208	1.2
6020	Commercial banks	55	51	1.6	682	830	16,669	18,342	11,877	14,872	0.9
6030	Savings institutions	20	20	2.2	382	379	25,602	20,433	8,246	7,791	2.5
6060	Credit unions	14	14	1.9	175	182	22,240	24,857	3,967	4,545	4.1
6100	Nondepository institutions	19	20	1.3	79	78	25,013	34,615	2,085	2,217	0.4
6140	Personal credit institutions	12	13	1.9	51	55	20,627	35,564	1,206	1,427	0.8
6160	Mortgage bankers and brokers	4	3	0.5	18	18	38,444	34,222	731	662	0.3
6280	Security and commodity services	6	6	1.2	18	24	16,889	9,167	336	306	0.2
6300	Insurance carriers	12	14	0.8	78	95	31,333	35,663	2,659	2,840	0.1
6400	Insurance agents, brokers, and service	82	86	1.5	301	312	19,336	18,859	6,755	7,160	0.9
6500	Real estate	112	116	1.5	591	558	13,685	13,312	9,310	8,895	0.8
6510	Real estate operators and lessors	51	51	1.5	191	169	11,518	12,497	2,652	2,422	0.8
6530	Real estate agents and managers	39	42	1.3	337	316	14,231	13,620	5,372	5,132	0.9
6540	Title abstract offices	8	7	3.2	33	34	24,121	17,059	790	725	1.4
6550	Subdividers and developers	12	13	2.0	28	31	10,286	10,839	477	506	0.4
6552	Subdividers and developers, n.e.c.	6	5	1.6	12	9	9,667	11,111	281	203	0.2
6553	Cemetery subdividers and developers	5	5	1.6	16	16	10,750	10,250	192	178	0.5
6700	Holding and other investment offices	7	6	1.0	73	73	34,849	38,411	2,735	3,055	0.8
TUSCARAWAS, OH											
60 –	**Finance, insurance, and real estate**	163	165	0.7	1,051	937	19,174	21,648	20,235	20,373	0.3
6000	Depository institutions	39	39	0.8	529	498	20,507	22,233	10,392	10,599	0.5
6020	Commercial banks	29	29	0.9	429	398	20,942	22,533	8,429	8,466	0.5
6060	Credit unions	4	4	0.5	53	55	15,472	17,236	826	943	0.9
6100	Nondepository institutions	17	16	1.0	66	61	26,727	33,836	1,935	1,809	0.3
6160	Mortgage bankers and brokers	5	6	1.0	17	23	39,294	24,000	541	608	0.3
6200	Security and commodity brokers	7	6	0.5	16	14	44,000	43,429	634	644	0.1
6400	Insurance agents, brokers, and service	45	45	0.8	143	140	22,657	23,457	3,478	3,532	0.4
6500	Real estate	45	53	0.7	217	167	10,378	13,413	2,542	2,682	0.3
6510	Real estate operators and lessors	16	21	0.6	84	50	6,476	10,000	516	707	0.2
6530	Real estate agents and managers	21	22	0.7	114	100	12,877	15,160	1,747	1,705	0.3
6553	Cemetery subdividers and developers	5	5	1.6	8	7	7,500	8,571	77	57	0.1
UNION, OH											
60 –	**Finance, insurance, and real estate**	44	45	0.2	227	202	19,524	20,356	4,629	4,142	0.1
6000	Depository institutions	13	15	0.3	136	122	22,118	22,426	3,166	2,664	0.1
6020	Commercial banks	9	11	0.4	119	104	21,277	21,500	2,712	2,135	0.1
6060	Credit unions	4	4	0.5	17	18	28,000	27,778	454	529	0.5

Source: County Business Patterns, 1994/95, CBP-94/95, U.S. Department of Commerce, Washington, D.C., November 1997. SIC categories for which data were suppressed or not available for both 1994 and 1995 are not displayed. The employment columns represent mid-March employment in the year. Pay per employee is calculated by dividing 1st Quarter payroll, annualized, by mid-March employment. The columns headed "% State" show the county's percentage of the state total for the SIC in 1995; for example, 1.4% for SIC 6000 means that the county had 1.4 percent of the state's total establishments (or payroll) in SIC 6000 in 1995. A dash (-) is used to indicate that data are not available or cannot be calculated; nec means not elsewhere classified.

Continued on next page.

SIC	Industry	No. Establishments			Employment		Pay / Employee		Annual Payroll ($ 000)		
		1994	1995	% State	1994	1995	1994	1995	1994	1995	% State
UNION, OH - [continued]											
6100	Nondepository institutions	3	3	0.2	9	5	35,111	36,000	227	145	0.0
6400	Insurance agents, brokers, and service	14	14	0.3	39	33	16,205	17,576	622	669	0.1
6510	Real estate operators and lessors	5	4	0.1	23	24	7,478	9,333	217	230	0.1
VAN WERT, OH											
60 –	**Finance, insurance, and real estate**	49	49	0.2	670	672	29,015	31,202	20,269	20,989	0.3
6000	Depository institutions	13	12	0.2	114	105	20,526	21,333	2,519	2,384	0.1
6060	Credit unions	3	3	0.4	4	6	4,000	9,333	24	54	0.0
6400	Insurance agents, brokers, and service	17	15	0.3	42	43	15,714	18,140	671	676	0.1
6510	Real estate operators and lessors	3	4	0.1	5	25	9,600	11,520	65	511	0.2
VINTON, OH											
60 –	**Finance, insurance, and real estate**	7	8	0.0	95	88	19,916	22,136	2,303	2,158	0.0
WARREN, OH											
60 –	**Finance, insurance, and real estate**	166	181	0.8	1,207	1,263	22,058	22,046	25,091	28,343	0.3
6000	Depository institutions	55	56	1.1	609	588	17,189	18,075	9,714	10,972	0.5
6020	Commercial banks	43	45	1.4	557	544	16,266	17,029	8,113	9,393	0.5
6100	Nondepository institutions	7	9	0.6	121	131	40,628	42,321	4,212	4,983	0.9
6140	Personal credit institutions	3	5	0.7	55	48	35,127	37,083	1,817	1,869	1.1
6300	Insurance carriers	11	10	0.6	88	67	35,227	33,910	2,460	2,152	0.1
6310	Life insurance	4	4	0.8	74	55	35,730	30,909	1,911	1,562	0.3
6400	Insurance agents, brokers, and service	38	37	0.7	145	143	21,407	24,392	3,330	3,582	0.4
6500	Real estate	51	60	0.8	210	275	11,524	11,898	3,020	4,076	0.4
6510	Real estate operators and lessors	19	23	0.7	119	164	8,504	8,415	1,244	1,494	0.5
6530	Real estate agents and managers	27	30	0.9	82	101	16,146	17,663	1,556	2,287	0.4
6550	Subdividers and developers	5	6	0.9	9	10	9,333	10,800	220	285	0.2
WASHINGTON, OH											
60 –	**Finance, insurance, and real estate**	117	118	0.5	848	961	19,425	20,183	18,193	20,095	0.2
6000	Depository institutions	30	30	0.6	485	603	19,266	19,496	9,278	11,306	0.5
6020	Commercial banks	23	23	0.7	432	548	19,306	19,423	8,214	10,171	0.6
6100	Nondepository institutions	7	8	0.5	47	39	27,745	31,795	1,298	1,296	0.2
6200	Security and commodity brokers	4	4	0.3	17	16	24,000	21,250	415	428	0.1
6400	Insurance agents, brokers, and service	29	29	0.5	106	113	21,434	22,088	3,025	3,218	0.4
6500	Real estate	37	37	0.5	117	96	11,214	13,458	2,268	1,441	0.1
6510	Real estate operators and lessors	21	19	0.6	71	56	7,718	10,071	1,456	674	0.2
WAYNE, OH											
60 –	**Finance, insurance, and real estate**	195	200	0.9	1,700	1,766	22,854	25,373	37,632	42,845	0.5
6000	Depository institutions	56	56	1.1	820	836	19,937	21,756	16,081	17,514	0.8
6020	Commercial banks	37	39	1.3	511	581	19,155	21,955	9,480	12,226	0.7
6030	Savings institutions	11	9	1.0	276	220	22,275	22,527	6,164	4,811	1.5
6060	Credit unions	8	8	1.1	33	35	12,485	13,600	437	477	0.4
6100	Nondepository institutions	9	9	0.6	47	42	17,872	19,238	838	871	0.2
6200	Security and commodity brokers	10	11	0.9	22	32	41,273	37,625	959	1,339	0.2
6210	Security brokers and dealers	10	11	1.6	22	32	41,273	37,625	959	1,339	0.3
6300	Insurance carriers	11	13	0.7	352	355	29,807	31,335	8,806	9,801	0.4
6400	Insurance agents, brokers, and service	50	50	0.9	164	171	21,732	21,684	4,128	4,409	0.5
6500	Real estate	54	55	0.7	275	312	22,982	29,910	6,430	8,526	0.8
6510	Real estate operators and lessors	24	23	0.7	131	188	33,221	37,170	4,093	6,113	1.9
6530	Real estate agents and managers	24	25	0.8	124	104	14,032	20,269	2,057	2,139	0.4
6550	Subdividers and developers	4	4	0.6	12	11	12,667	14,545	172	171	0.1
6700	Holding and other investment offices	5	6	1.0	20	18	19,000	24,667	390	385	0.1
WILLIAMS, OH											
60 –	**Finance, insurance, and real estate**	53	58	0.2	397	406	18,741	20,453	8,177	9,937	0.1
6000	Depository institutions	22	24	0.5	256	295	19,109	19,200	4,826	6,325	0.3

Source: County Business Patterns, 1994/95, CBP-94/95, U.S. Department of Commerce, Washington, D.C., November 1997. SIC categories for which data were suppressed or not available for both 1994 and 1995 are *not* displayed. The employment columns represent mid-March employment in the year. Pay per employee is calculated by dividing 1st Quarter payroll, annualized, by mid-March employment. The columns headed "% State" show the county's percentage of the state total for the SIC in 1995; for example, 1.4% for SIC 6000 means that the county had 1.4 percent of the state's total establishments (or payroll) in SIC 6000 in 1995. A dash (-) is used to indicate that data are not available or cannot be calculated; *nec* means not elsewhere classified.

Continued on next page.

SIC	Industry	No. Establishments			Employment		Pay / Employee		Annual Payroll ($ 000)		
		1994	1995	% State	1994	1995	1994	1995	1994	1995	% State
WILLIAMS, OH - [continued]											
6020	Commercial banks	16	19	0.6	211	256	19,488	19,250	4,012	5,543	0.3
6400	Insurance agents, brokers, and service	11	13	0.2	40	43	26,100	33,581	1,547	1,683	0.2
6510	Real estate operators and lessors	5	5	0.2	25	13	2,880	6,154	78	83	0.0
WOOD, OH											
60–	**Finance, insurance, and real estate**	221	220	0.9	1,537	1,259	22,938	23,015	34,015	29,068	0.4
6000	Depository institutions	63	56	1.1	761	441	20,836	19,429	13,660	8,489	0.4
6020	Commercial banks	41	41	1.3	573	359	20,161	18,830	10,192	6,635	0.4
6030	Savings institutions	12	7	0.8	151	52	24,053	25,154	2,832	1,348	0.4
6200	Security and commodity brokers	16	16	1.3	71	62	31,944	34,065	2,333	1,842	0.3
6300	Insurance carriers	11	13	0.7	147	124	30,231	29,258	4,347	3,811	0.2
6310	Life insurance	3	3	0.6	85	85	27,153	27,765	2,464	2,319	0.4
6400	Insurance agents, brokers, and service	52	52	0.9	179	175	23,151	25,166	4,281	4,488	0.6
6500	Real estate	70	69	0.9	320	349	15,963	15,198	6,205	6,180	0.6
6510	Real estate operators and lessors	38	37	1.1	210	225	15,448	14,791	4,004	4,025	1.3
6530	Real estate agents and managers	25	26	0.8	66	72	15,394	15,722	1,178	1,157	0.2
WYANDOT, OH											
60–	**Finance, insurance, and real estate**	45	43	0.2	350	388	19,166	18,753	6,617	6,722	0.1
6000	Depository institutions	15	15	0.3	289	270	19,751	22,770	5,521	5,492	0.2
6400	Insurance agents, brokers, and service	17	17	0.3	27	28	19,259	18,429	450	497	0.1
6500	Real estate	9	7	0.1	18	13	9,111	14,769	259	229	0.0
6510	Real estate operators and lessors	3	3	0.1	6	6	6,000	11,333	72	73	0.0

Source: County Business Patterns, 1994/95, CBP-94/95, U.S. Department of Commerce, Washington, D.C., November 1997. SIC categories for which data were suppressed or not available for both 1994 and 1995 are not displayed. The employment columns represent mid-March employment in the year. Pay per employee is calculated by dividing 1st Quarter payroll, annualized, by mid-March employment. The columns headed "% State" show the county's percentage of the state total for the SIC in 1995; for example, 1.4% for SIC 6000 means that the county had 1.4 percent of the state's total establishments (or payroll) in SIC 6000 in 1995. A dash (-) is used to indicate that data are not available or cannot be calculated; nec means not elsewhere classified.

OKLAHOMA

SIC	Industry	No. Establishments			Employment		Pay / Employee		Annual Payroll ($ 000)		
		1994	1995	% State	1994	1995	1994	1995	1994	1995	% State
ADAIR, OK											
60 –	**Finance, insurance, and real estate**	18	19	0.2	97	88	16,619	20,000	1,864	2,071	0.1
6000	Depository institutions	4	4	0.3	55	57	18,836	19,860	1,294	1,379	0.3
6020	Commercial banks	4	4	0.5	55	57	18,836	19,860	1,294	1,379	0.3
6100	Nondepository institutions	5	7	0.8	11	11	18,182	25,091	221	317	0.3
6400	Insurance agents, brokers, and service	4	3	0.2	16	6	9,000	16,667	106	96	0.1
6500	Real estate	5	5	0.2	15	14	15,467	18,000	243	279	0.1
ALFALFA, OK											
60 –	**Finance, insurance, and real estate**	16	15	0.2	70	59	16,914	16,814	1,101	1,010	0.1
6000	Depository institutions	7	5	0.4	58	45	17,586	18,133	923	821	0.2
6020	Commercial banks	7	5	0.6	58	45	17,586	18,133	923	821	0.2
6400	Insurance agents, brokers, and service	6	6	0.3	8	8	12,500	14,000	105	114	0.1
6500	Real estate	3	4	0.2	4	6	16,000	10,667	73	75	0.0
ATOKA, OK											
60 –	**Finance, insurance, and real estate**	13	13	0.2	95	101	18,232	16,673	1,770	1,897	0.1
6400	Insurance agents, brokers, and service	5	5	0.3	10	11	9,200	10,545	107	100	0.1
BECKHAM, OK											
60 –	**Finance, insurance, and real estate**	41	42	0.5	206	216	21,029	19,296	3,985	4,082	0.3
6000	Depository institutions	9	8	0.7	110	113	20,909	20,602	2,273	2,420	0.5
6400	Insurance agents, brokers, and service	13	14	0.8	28	31	14,143	15,484	446	481	0.3
6500	Real estate	13	13	0.5	50	55	18,640	14,909	634	632	0.3
BLAINE, OK											
60 –	**Finance, insurance, and real estate**	24	25	0.3	126	128	17,810	18,125	2,439	2,546	0.2
6000	Depository institutions	5	5	0.4	94	95	19,830	20,084	2,013	2,091	0.4
6020	Commercial banks	5	5	0.6	94	95	19,830	20,084	2,013	2,091	0.5
6400	Insurance agents, brokers, and service	9	10	0.5	19	18	11,579	12,000	221	225	0.1
6500	Real estate	7	7	0.3	9	11	10,667	11,636	128	160	0.1
6540	Title abstract offices	4	4	2.6	6	8	14,000	15,000	105	139	0.4
BRYAN, OK											
60 –	**Finance, insurance, and real estate**	46	49	0.6	348	346	17,966	18,324	6,602	7,042	0.4
6000	Depository institutions	10	10	0.9	192	210	20,188	19,562	4,360	4,648	0.9
6100	Nondepository institutions	11	11	1.3	39	42	16,103	17,810	653	695	0.6
CADDO, OK											
60 –	**Finance, insurance, and real estate**	39	39	0.5	279	219	18,538	22,247	5,780	5,163	0.3
6000	Depository institutions	15	14	1.2	168	148	22,786	24,054	4,121	3,766	0.7
6500	Real estate	9	10	0.4	53	23	4,755	13,217	281	319	0.2
6510	Real estate operators and lessors	4	5	0.5	36	11	2,556	12,364	106	138	0.2
CANADIAN, OK											
60 –	**Finance, insurance, and real estate**	109	116	1.5	763	773	18,464	18,013	15,209	14,797	0.9
6000	Depository institutions	21	20	1.7	304	280	21,671	21,343	7,041	6,425	1.2
6020	Commercial banks	14	14	1.8	225	245	21,547	21,927	5,215	5,761	1.3
6400	Insurance agents, brokers, and service	26	28	1.5	74	75	16,216	17,867	1,326	1,380	0.9

Source: County Business Patterns, 1994/95, CBP-94/95, U.S. Department of Commerce, Washington, D.C., November 1997. SIC categories for which data were suppressed or not available for both 1994 and 1995 are *not* displayed. The employment columns represent mid-March employment in the year. Pay per employee is calculated by dividing 1st Quarter payroll, annualized, by mid-March employment. The columns headed "% State" show the county's percentage of the state total for the SIC in 1995; for example, 1.4% for SIC 6000 means that the county had 1.4 percent of the state's total establishments (or payroll) in SIC 6000 in 1995. A dash (-) is used to indicate that data are not available or cannot be calculated; *nec* means not elsewhere classified.

Continued on next page.

SIC	Industry	No. Establishments			Employment		Pay / Employee		Annual Payroll ($ 000)		
		1994	1995	% State	1994	1995	1994	1995	1994	1995	% State
CANADIAN, OK - [continued]											
6500	Real estate	42	44	*1.8*	335	370	11,928	12,573	4,417	4,739	*2.3*
6510	Real estate operators and lessors	20	17	*1.7*	232	218	10,310	11,211	2,426	2,408	*3.6*
6530	Real estate agents and managers	16	18	*1.7*	70	60	12,800	13,200	917	842	*1.0*
CARTER, OK											
60 –	**Finance, insurance, and real estate**	126	118	*1.5*	724	678	19,812	21,221	14,053	14,573	*0.9*
6000	Depository institutions	17	16	*1.4*	346	353	22,590	23,433	7,498	8,050	*1.5*
6020	Commercial banks	13	12	*1.5*	327	333	23,156	24,048	7,245	7,766	*1.8*
6100	Nondepository institutions	25	24	*2.8*	70	69	16,171	17,739	1,284	1,260	*1.0*
6140	Personal credit institutions	20	18	*2.9*	58	59	16,069	17,288	1,047	1,060	*1.9*
6200	Security and commodity brokers	8	7	*1.8*	17	19	27,765	21,474	418	449	*0.4*
6400	Insurance agents, brokers, and service	33	30	*1.6*	137	100	15,533	24,320	2,355	2,522	*1.6*
6500	Real estate	27	28	*1.1*	88	99	13,182	12,242	1,290	1,338	*0.6*
6730	Trusts	5	4	*3.6*	17	10	14,353	18,400	187	114	*1.1*
CHEROKEE, OK											
60 –	**Finance, insurance, and real estate**	53	54	*0.7*	232	257	18,707	21,790	5,127	5,382	*0.3*
6000	Depository institutions	8	9	*0.8*	134	159	20,269	24,730	3,472	3,625	*0.7*
6100	Nondepository institutions	14	12	*1.4*	31	30	12,000	12,400	361	363	*0.3*
6500	Real estate	16	17	*0.7*	34	32	15,294	17,125	562	611	*0.3*
6510	Real estate operators and lessors	6	9	*0.9*	10	13	14,000	12,923	159	229	*0.3*
6530	Real estate agents and managers	6	5	*0.5*	10	10	11,600	12,000	129	124	*0.1*
CHOCTAW, OK											
60 –	**Finance, insurance, and real estate**	25	24	*0.3*	119	122	16,807	17,869	2,040	2,131	*0.1*
6000	Depository institutions	4	4	*0.3*	68	71	20,706	21,972	1,428	1,516	*0.3*
6020	Commercial banks	4	4	*0.5*	68	71	20,706	21,972	1,428	1,516	*0.4*
6100	Nondepository institutions	8	9	*1.1*	24	26	11,833	10,769	298	268	*0.2*
CIMARRON, OK											
60 –	**Finance, insurance, and real estate**	6	6	*0.1*	34	34	16,706	17,176	689	662	*0.0*
CLEVELAND, OK											
60 –	**Finance, insurance, and real estate**	331	339	*4.4*	1,862	1,760	19,499	20,845	38,727	40,609	*2.5*
6000	Depository institutions	34	39	*3.4*	599	571	21,549	21,821	13,060	13,172	*2.5*
6020	Commercial banks	22	26	*3.4*	528	498	22,326	22,345	11,862	11,855	*2.7*
6100	Nondepository institutions	23	31	*3.6*	90	114	27,467	22,877	2,301	3,038	*2.5*
6140	Personal credit institutions	15	18	*2.9*	59	65	21,559	23,262	1,183	1,565	*2.8*
6160	Mortgage bankers and brokers	6	10	*7.1*	27	43	42,519	23,814	1,058	1,388	*3.5*
6200	Security and commodity brokers	15	18	*4.5*	30	46	47,467	38,435	1,551	1,911	*1.8*
6210	Security brokers and dealers	12	14	*5.0*	27	41	50,370	40,976	1,468	1,807	*2.2*
6280	Security and commodity services	3	4	*4.0*	3	5	21,333	17,600	83	104	*0.5*
6300	Insurance carriers	15	17	*3.8*	41	41	40,488	45,951	1,648	1,762	*0.5*
6400	Insurance agents, brokers, and service	68	66	*3.5*	210	199	21,943	21,769	4,923	4,950	*3.1*
6500	Real estate	163	153	*6.1*	796	676	13,427	15,757	11,976	11,624	*5.6*
6510	Real estate operators and lessors	66	59	*5.9*	261	200	10,330	12,680	2,942	2,602	*3.9*
6530	Real estate agents and managers	72	68	*6.3*	271	252	12,546	12,460	3,732	3,388	*3.8*
6540	Title abstract offices	6	6	*3.8*	126	90	21,492	26,222	2,738	2,527	*8.0*
6550	Subdividers and developers	17	16	*9.2*	135	122	13,719	20,820	2,510	2,998	*18.0*
6552	Subdividers and developers, n.e.c.	9	10	*9.9*	122	110	14,361	22,109	2,370	2,890	*34.3*
6700	Holding and other investment offices	13	15	*3.4*	96	113	26,542	26,407	3,268	4,152	*3.3*
COAL, OK											
60 –	**Finance, insurance, and real estate**	4	3	*0.0*	-	-	-	-	-	-	-
COMANCHE, OK											
60 –	**Finance, insurance, and real estate**	271	277	*3.6*	1,625	1,571	17,583	18,062	28,667	28,960	*1.8*
6000	Depository institutions	33	31	*2.7*	695	652	18,164	19,258	12,482	12,549	*2.4*

Source: County Business Patterns, 1994/95, CBP-94/95, U.S. Department of Commerce, Washington, D.C., November 1997. SIC categories for which data were suppressed or not available for both 1994 and 1995 are *not* displayed. The employment columns represent mid-March employment in the year. Pay per employee is calculated by dividing 1st Quarter payroll, annualized, by mid-March employment. The columns headed "% State" show the county's percentage of the state total for the SIC in 1995; for example, 1.4% for SIC 6000 means that the county had 1.4 percent of the state's total establishments (or payroll) in SIC 6000 in 1995. A dash (-) is used to indicate that data are not available or cannot be calculated; *nec* means not elsewhere classified.

Continued on next page.

SIC	Industry	No. Establishments			Employment		Pay / Employee		Annual Payroll ($ 000)		
		1994	1995	% State	1994	1995	1994	1995	1994	1995	% State
COMANCHE, OK - [continued]											
6020	Commercial banks	19	19	2.5	534	490	19,356	20,890	9,986	10,066	2.3
6060	Credit unions	7	7	4.7	120	122	14,267	15,180	1,891	2,012	4.5
6100	Nondepository institutions	56	58	6.8	201	185	19,582	19,719	3,783	3,653	3.0
6140	Personal credit institutions	46	46	7.4	161	149	19,081	19,060	3,024	2,872	5.2
6160	Mortgage bankers and brokers	6	6	4.3	33	28	24,970	26,571	715	727	1.8
6200	Security and commodity brokers	9	9	2.3	41	33	43,317	31,515	1,454	1,269	1.2
6300	Insurance carriers	11	13	2.9	51	62	37,020	39,355	1,885	2,065	0.6
6400	Insurance agents, brokers, and service	52	55	3.0	147	143	15,456	15,888	2,452	2,640	1.6
6500	Real estate	107	106	4.2	456	463	11,772	12,104	6,111	6,006	2.9
6510	Real estate operators and lessors	48	50	5.0	258	265	10,403	11,200	2,932	2,990	4.5
6530	Real estate agents and managers	47	44	4.1	139	146	12,288	12,110	2,118	2,086	2.4
6552	Subdividers and developers, n.e.c.	6	5	5.0	15	7	12,267	18,286	129	52	0.6
6700	Holding and other investment offices	3	5	1.1	34	33	20,824	24,727	500	778	0.6
COTTON, OK											
60 –	**Finance, insurance, and real estate**	7	7	0.1	-	-	-	-	-	-	-
6400	Insurance agents, brokers, and service	3	3	0.2	6	6	14,667	18,667	83	87	0.1
CRAIG, OK											
60 –	**Finance, insurance, and real estate**	31	32	0.4	188	197	20,170	20,670	3,834	4,294	0.3
6000	Depository institutions	7	7	0.6	124	125	20,710	21,248	2,479	2,661	0.5
6510	Real estate operators and lessors	6	7	0.7	13	19	21,538	19,579	442	615	0.9
CREEK, OK											
60 –	**Finance, insurance, and real estate**	83	89	1.2	539	568	19,109	18,190	10,683	10,859	0.7
6000	Depository institutions	14	15	1.3	357	365	19,854	19,090	7,256	7,208	1.4
6100	Nondepository institutions	19	19	2.2	59	61	14,644	13,836	900	926	0.8
6140	Personal credit institutions	16	15	2.4	52	51	15,077	14,039	802	770	1.4
6400	Insurance agents, brokers, and service	23	25	1.3	54	61	15,926	16,197	900	1,113	0.7
6500	Real estate	21	24	1.0	59	72	14,983	12,778	942	972	0.5
6510	Real estate operators and lessors	8	11	1.1	18	20	11,333	10,200	222	273	0.4
6530	Real estate agents and managers	7	7	0.6	14	16	12,571	10,000	177	146	0.2
6540	Title abstract offices	3	3	1.9	18	16	16,889	19,500	341	308	1.0
CUSTER, OK											
60 –	**Finance, insurance, and real estate**	86	81	1.1	427	399	18,792	21,133	8,395	8,417	0.5
6000	Depository institutions	16	14	1.2	205	199	21,678	23,256	4,711	4,692	0.9
6020	Commercial banks	10	10	1.3	180	179	22,533	24,223	4,320	4,394	1.0
6100	Nondepository institutions	11	10	1.2	48	44	20,500	21,091	858	894	0.7
6400	Insurance agents, brokers, and service	25	26	1.4	70	71	13,314	19,380	1,205	1,189	0.7
6500	Real estate	28	26	1.0	59	50	10,305	10,960	703	656	0.3
6510	Real estate operators and lessors	17	15	1.5	36	29	8,889	11,034	390	360	0.5
DELAWARE, OK											
60 –	**Finance, insurance, and real estate**	42	41	0.5	226	259	16,336	18,131	4,122	5,113	0.3
6000	Depository institutions	8	8	0.7	120	145	19,000	20,331	2,437	3,098	0.6
6500	Real estate	23	22	0.9	87	89	12,368	13,528	1,222	1,388	0.7
6510	Real estate operators and lessors	6	5	0.5	8	10	9,000	9,200	75	96	0.1
6530	Real estate agents and managers	12	12	1.1	57	56	9,965	10,929	689	717	0.8
DEWEY, OK											
60 –	**Finance, insurance, and real estate**	10	10	0.1	73	75	20,877	20,107	1,597	1,599	0.1
6000	Depository institutions	5	5	0.4	59	58	23,864	23,586	1,478	1,445	0.3
6020	Commercial banks	5	5	0.6	59	58	23,864	23,586	1,478	1,445	0.3

Source: County Business Patterns, 1994/95, CBP-94/95, U.S. Department of Commerce, Washington, D.C., November 1997. SIC categories for which data were suppressed or not available for both 1994 and 1995 are not displayed. The employment columns represent mid-March employment in the year. Pay per employee is calculated by dividing 1st Quarter payroll, annualized, by mid-March employment. The columns headed "% State" show the county's percentage of the state total for the SIC in 1995; for example, 1.4% for SIC 6000 means that the county had 1.4 percent of the state's total establishments (or payroll) in SIC 6000 in 1995. A dash (-) is used to indicate that data are not available or cannot be calculated; nec means not elsewhere classified.

SIC	Industry	No. Establishments			Employment		Pay / Employee		Annual Payroll ($ 000)		
		1994	1995	% State	1994	1995	1994	1995	1994	1995	% State
ELLIS, OK											
60 –	Finance, insurance, and real estate	9	9	0.1	51	50	18,745	19,760	974	1,046	0.1
6000	Depository institutions	3	3	0.3	39	37	20,923	22,270	818	881	0.2
6020	Commercial banks	3	3	0.4	39	37	20,923	22,270	818	881	0.2
GARFIELD, OK											
60 –	Finance, insurance, and real estate	156	158	2.1	921	951	22,267	21,262	21,231	21,228	1.3
6000	Depository institutions	25	25	2.2	423	416	21,655	22,375	9,697	9,481	1.8
6020	Commercial banks	17	17	2.2	334	323	22,766	22,724	8,070	7,697	1.8
6100	Nondepository institutions	17	17	2.0	75	73	24,800	25,589	1,946	1,901	1.6
6140	Personal credit institutions	14	14	2.3	46	49	19,130	19,265	948	1,014	1.8
6200	Security and commodity brokers	10	10	2.5	30	26	71,600	45,846	1,550	1,236	1.2
6300	Insurance carriers	10	10	2.2	71	61	31,155	37,770	2,185	2,217	0.6
6400	Insurance agents, brokers, and service	35	36	1.9	103	101	17,786	19,168	2,252	2,435	1.5
6500	Real estate	48	51	2.0	203	259	13,675	11,954	3,172	3,572	1.7
6510	Real estate operators and lessors	24	24	2.4	84	92	9,762	9,652	1,043	1,077	1.6
6530	Real estate agents and managers	18	20	1.9	91	139	15,033	11,396	1,511	1,872	2.1
6700	Holding and other investment offices	11	9	2.1	16	15	32,500	34,400	429	386	0.3
GARVIN, OK											
60 –	Finance, insurance, and real estate	55	58	0.8	253	261	19,130	20,736	5,498	6,040	0.4
6000	Depository institutions	13	13	1.1	169	171	19,834	21,099	3,912	4,334	0.8
6100	Nondepository institutions	6	6	0.7	21	22	20,000	25,455	446	446	0.4
6500	Real estate	11	12	0.5	14	20	11,714	11,800	208	254	0.1
GRADY, OK											
60 –	Finance, insurance, and real estate	66	66	0.9	408	396	18,696	19,475	8,084	8,277	0.5
6000	Depository institutions	15	14	1.2	261	256	19,218	19,656	5,298	5,489	1.0
6100	Nondepository institutions	11	10	1.2	28	32	16,286	16,375	504	542	0.4
6300	Insurance carriers	5	6	1.3	24	21	25,667	33,143	639	729	0.2
6400	Insurance agents, brokers, and service	12	13	0.7	37	37	16,541	15,243	606	581	0.4
6500	Real estate	15	17	0.7	41	42	14,146	16,381	766	709	0.3
GRANT, OK											
60 –	Finance, insurance, and real estate	16	14	0.2	81	72	22,864	23,333	1,925	1,830	0.1
6000	Depository institutions	8	6	0.5	70	58	24,057	25,586	1,748	1,629	0.3
GREER, OK											
60 –	Finance, insurance, and real estate	12	11	0.1	72	93	14,944	18,925	1,393	1,845	0.1
6000	Depository institutions	4	4	0.3	47	46	17,106	19,217	849	925	0.2
6020	Commercial banks	4	4	0.5	47	46	17,106	19,217	849	925	0.2
HARMON, OK											
60 –	Finance, insurance, and real estate	8	8	0.1	53	52	14,264	21,692	1,092	1,282	0.1
6400	Insurance agents, brokers, and service	3	4	0.2	7	7	17,714	18,857	153	151	0.1
HASKELL, OK											
60 –	Finance, insurance, and real estate	11	11	0.1	49	51	20,571	20,314	1,223	1,044	0.1
HUGHES, OK											
60 –	Finance, insurance, and real estate	20	17	0.2	116	115	15,379	16,800	2,006	2,053	0.1
6000	Depository institutions	4	4	0.3	86	87	17,023	18,299	1,618	1,705	0.3
6020	Commercial banks	4	4	0.5	86	87	17,023	18,299	1,618	1,705	0.4
6400	Insurance agents, brokers, and service	4	4	0.2	11	12	10,182	13,667	129	155	0.1
JACKSON, OK											
60 –	Finance, insurance, and real estate	55	59	0.8	318	346	16,541	20,069	6,202	6,793	0.4

Source: County Business Patterns, 1994/95, CBP-94/95, U.S. Department of Commerce, Washington, D.C., November 1997. SIC categories for which data were suppressed or not available for both 1994 and 1995 are *not* displayed. The employment columns represent mid-March employment in the year. Pay per employee is calculated by dividing 1st Quarter payroll, annualized, by mid-March employment. The columns headed "% State" show the county's percentage of the state total for the SIC in 1995; for example, 1.4% for SIC 6000 means that the county had 1.4 percent of the state's total establishments (or payroll) in SIC 6000 in 1995. A dash (-) is used to indicate that data are not available or cannot be calculated; *nec* means not elsewhere classified.

Continued on next page.

SIC	Industry	No. Establishments			Employment		Pay / Employee		Annual Payroll ($ 000)		
		1994	1995	% State	1994	1995	1994	1995	1994	1995	% State
JACKSON, OK - [continued]											
6000	Depository institutions	11	11	1.0	195	206	16,533	22,039	3,796	4,252	0.8
6100	Nondepository institutions	12	12	1.4	49	56	17,306	18,357	980	1,022	0.8
6530	Real estate agents and managers	7	7	0.6	7	9	8,000	6,667	61	72	0.1
JEFFERSON, OK											
60 –	**Finance, insurance, and real estate**	13	12	0.2	72	74	17,667	16,919	1,337	1,491	0.1
6000	Depository institutions	4	4	0.3	53	51	19,170	18,510	1,059	1,166	0.2
6020	Commercial banks	4	4	0.5	53	51	19,170	18,510	1,059	1,166	0.3
6500	Real estate	4	4	0.2	6	10	9,333	8,800	71	89	0.0
JOHNSTON, OK											
60 –	**Finance, insurance, and real estate**	7	6	0.1	43	36	13,395	16,444	561	578	0.0
KAY, OK											
60 –	**Finance, insurance, and real estate**	126	122	1.6	690	713	19,832	21,027	14,318	14,808	0.9
6000	Depository institutions	27	26	2.3	401	393	20,858	24,366	8,811	9,229	1.8
6020	Commercial banks	20	19	2.5	370	357	21,265	25,389	8,276	8,644	2.0
6100	Nondepository institutions	18	17	2.0	64	75	16,500	18,933	1,251	1,511	1.2
6140	Personal credit institutions	13	14	2.3	47	65	15,745	17,785	935	1,255	2.3
6400	Insurance agents, brokers, and service	32	29	1.6	94	92	17,191	14,957	1,546	1,361	0.8
6500	Real estate	36	36	1.4	92	111	12,000	10,847	1,158	1,202	0.6
6530	Real estate agents and managers	14	16	1.5	16	31	8,500	9,419	168	257	0.3
KINGFISHER, OK											
60 –	**Finance, insurance, and real estate**	30	30	0.4	290	333	19,641	19,796	6,286	6,767	0.4
6000	Depository institutions	9	8	0.7	210	258	22,514	21,550	5,171	5,605	1.1
6400	Insurance agents, brokers, and service	9	9	0.5	33	31	10,182	11,097	357	378	0.2
KIOWA, OK											
60 –	**Finance, insurance, and real estate**	26	21	0.3	108	106	16,963	17,774	2,040	2,097	0.1
6000	Depository institutions	8	8	0.7	81	82	19,407	19,317	1,734	1,740	0.3
6020	Commercial banks	8	8	1.0	81	82	19,407	19,317	1,734	1,740	0.4
6400	Insurance agents, brokers, and service	11	7	0.4	18	15	7,333	9,333	137	156	0.1
6500	Real estate	3	3	0.1	5	5	14,400	15,200	79	89	0.0
LATIMER, OK											
60 –	**Finance, insurance, and real estate**	14	11	0.1	65	57	15,446	17,404	1,021	1,049	0.1
6100	Nondepository institutions	4	3	0.4	9	9	19,556	11,556	120	101	0.1
6400	Insurance agents, brokers, and service	4	3	0.2	4	5	8,000	7,200	38	35	0.0
LE FLORE, OK											
60 –	**Finance, insurance, and real estate**	66	65	0.8	341	346	18,393	19,503	6,906	7,426	0.5
6000	Depository institutions	11	11	1.0	205	208	20,176	21,692	4,653	5,031	1.0
6100	Nondepository institutions	12	12	1.4	36	36	15,222	16,556	550	542	0.4
6400	Insurance agents, brokers, and service	20	21	1.1	37	43	13,622	13,581	516	684	0.4
6510	Real estate operators and lessors	7	5	0.5	13	7	8,308	6,286	80	48	0.1
6530	Real estate agents and managers	5	5	0.5	5	7	11,200	9,143	65	70	0.1
LINCOLN, OK											
60 –	**Finance, insurance, and real estate**	32	36	0.5	512	540	23,430	27,348	14,201	15,081	0.9
6000	Depository institutions	13	13	1.1	187	187	20,128	21,262	4,035	4,097	0.8
6020	Commercial banks	10	10	1.3	170	168	20,518	21,667	3,738	3,761	0.9
6530	Real estate agents and managers	4	5	0.5	8	8	4,500	7,500	44	54	0.1
LOGAN, OK											
60 –	**Finance, insurance, and real estate**	37	35	0.5	157	165	19,134	19,224	3,350	3,426	0.2
6000	Depository institutions	9	9	0.8	96	101	19,417	20,752	2,078	2,139	0.4

Source: County Business Patterns, 1994/95, CBP-94/95, U.S. Department of Commerce, Washington, D.C., November 1997. SIC categories for which data were suppressed or not available for both 1994 and 1995 are not displayed. The employment columns represent mid-March employment in the year. Pay per employee is calculated by dividing 1st Quarter payroll, annualized, by mid-March employment. The columns headed "% State" show the county's percentage of the state total for the SIC in 1995; for example, 1.4% for SIC 6000 means that the county had 1.4 percent of the state's total establishments (or payroll) in SIC 6000 in 1995. A dash (-) is used to indicate that data are not available or cannot be calculated; nec means not elsewhere classified.

Continued on next page.

SIC	Industry	No. Establishments			Employment		Pay / Employee		Annual Payroll ($ 000)		
		1994	1995	% State	1994	1995	1994	1995	1994	1995	% State
LOGAN, OK - [continued]											
6100	Nondepository institutions	6	6	0.7	10	10	12,400	11,200	130	132	0.1
6140	Personal credit institutions	6	6	1.0	10	10	12,400	11,200	130	132	0.2
6400	Insurance agents, brokers, and service	9	7	0.4	25	24	14,880	15,833	420	420	0.3
LOVE, OK											
60 –	**Finance, insurance, and real estate**	14	13	0.2	95	85	16,716	15,482	1,600	1,364	0.1
6400	Insurance agents, brokers, and service	4	4	0.2	4	4	6,000	9,000	28	33	0.0
MCCLAIN, OK											
60 –	**Finance, insurance, and real estate**	31	34	0.4	209	204	17,837	19,686	3,944	4,452	0.3
6000	Depository institutions	6	6	0.5	148	139	20,135	22,388	3,117	3,246	0.6
6400	Insurance agents, brokers, and service	15	15	0.8	38	39	11,789	12,308	501	498	0.3
6500	Real estate	6	8	0.3	16	19	13,250	13,263	233	526	0.3
MCCURTAIN, OK											
60 –	**Finance, insurance, and real estate**	41	43	0.6	272	270	17,941	19,200	5,512	5,871	0.4
6000	Depository institutions	9	9	0.8	180	180	20,044	19,667	4,215	4,140	0.8
6400	Insurance agents, brokers, and service	14	15	0.8	40	39	12,000	13,641	507	528	0.3
6510	Real estate operators and lessors	5	4	0.4	7	4	10,286	13,000	85	60	0.1
MCINTOSH, OK											
60 –	**Finance, insurance, and real estate**	27	27	0.4	127	131	15,307	16,366	2,793	2,832	0.2
6000	Depository institutions	5	5	0.4	85	83	17,553	18,024	2,254	2,223	0.4
6400	Insurance agents, brokers, and service	8	9	0.5	16	16	11,500	12,750	204	235	0.1
6500	Real estate	10	9	0.4	19	21	8,421	14,286	216	241	0.1
MAJOR, OK											
60 –	**Finance, insurance, and real estate**	16	15	0.2	79	80	21,823	21,950	1,759	1,797	0.1
6000	Depository institutions	5	5	0.4	55	54	26,109	26,000	1,449	1,429	0.3
MARSHALL, OK											
60 –	**Finance, insurance, and real estate**	26	24	0.3	123	121	15,089	16,496	1,999	2,109	0.1
6000	Depository institutions	3	3	0.3	79	79	18,329	20,709	1,533	1,709	0.3
6020	Commercial banks	3	3	0.4	79	79	18,329	20,709	1,533	1,709	0.4
6100	Nondepository institutions	3	3	0.4	7	11	7,429	7,273	68	81	0.1
6140	Personal credit institutions	3	3	0.5	7	11	7,429	7,273	68	81	0.1
6400	Insurance agents, brokers, and service	6	5	0.3	10	9	8,000	8,444	98	76	0.0
6500	Real estate	11	10	0.4	24	16	10,167	9,750	263	183	0.1
6530	Real estate agents and managers	6	7	0.6	6	7	9,333	10,857	111	96	0.1
MAYES, OK											
60 –	**Finance, insurance, and real estate**	41	42	0.5	279	291	19,814	20,784	5,528	5,970	0.4
6000	Depository institutions	11	11	1.0	198	199	20,525	22,050	3,857	4,018	0.8
6100	Nondepository institutions	7	7	0.8	15	15	17,600	18,133	235	270	0.2
6140	Personal credit institutions	7	7	1.1	15	15	17,600	18,133	235	270	0.5
6400	Insurance agents, brokers, and service	9	10	0.5	29	31	17,931	17,935	645	729	0.5
6530	Real estate agents and managers	5	5	0.5	10	15	8,000	10,133	121	161	0.2
MURRAY, OK											
60 –	**Finance, insurance, and real estate**	16	18	0.2	94	107	18,128	18,729	1,857	2,097	0.1
6000	Depository institutions	5	5	0.4	67	69	19,582	20,870	1,431	1,568	0.3
MUSKOGEE, OK											
60 –	**Finance, insurance, and real estate**	144	149	1.9	893	845	20,009	21,856	19,276	18,029	1.1
6000	Depository institutions	25	23	2.0	417	334	20,643	21,760	9,333	7,264	1.4
6020	Commercial banks	15	14	1.8	352	255	20,284	22,525	7,864	5,780	1.3
6100	Nondepository institutions	24	26	3.0	76	79	16,211	16,658	1,350	1,348	1.1
6200	Security and commodity brokers	4	4	1.0	15	11	46,667	37,818	563	425	0.4

Source: County Business Patterns, 1994/95, CBP-94/95, U.S. Department of Commerce, Washington, D.C., November 1997. SIC categories for which data were suppressed or not available for both 1994 and 1995 are not displayed. The employment columns represent mid-March employment in the year. Pay per employee is calculated by dividing 1st Quarter payroll, annualized, by mid-March employment. The columns headed "% State" show the county's percentage of the state total for the SIC in 1995; for example, 1.4% for SIC 6000 means that the county had 1.4 percent of the state's total establishments (or payroll) in SIC 6000 in 1995. A dash (-) is used to indicate that data are not available or cannot be calculated; nec means not elsewhere classified.

Continued on next page.

SIC	Industry	No. Establishments			Employment		Pay / Employee		Annual Payroll ($ 000)		
		1994	1995	% State	1994	1995	1994	1995	1994	1995	% State
MUSKOGEE, OK - [continued]											
6210	Security brokers and dealers	4	4	*1.4*	15	11	46,667	37,818	563	425	*0.5*
6300	Insurance carriers	11	11	*2.5*	56	50	26,000	28,880	1,357	1,448	*0.4*
6400	Insurance agents, brokers, and service	34	34	*1.8*	123	121	20,618	20,727	2,574	2,592	*1.6*
6500	Real estate	34	41	*1.6*	156	164	11,256	11,805	2,055	2,018	*1.0*
6510	Real estate operators and lessors	15	20	*2.0*	104	113	7,538	8,602	1,065	1,071	*1.6*
6530	Real estate agents and managers	14	14	*1.3*	22	22	13,636	15,273	322	327	*0.4*
6700	Holding and other investment offices	12	10	*2.3*	50	86	31,600	41,628	2,044	2,934	*2.4*
6730	Trusts	3	3	*2.7*	5	4	8,800	13,000	44	50	*0.5*
6790	Miscellaneous investing	4	3	*1.6*	10	6	13,600	22,667	159	137	*0.6*
NOBLE, OK											
60 –	**Finance, insurance, and real estate**	23	23	*0.3*	126	128	18,667	17,594	2,539	2,579	*0.2*
6000	Depository institutions	6	6	*0.5*	89	94	21,573	20,213	2,160	2,102	*0.4*
6400	Insurance agents, brokers, and service	10	7	*0.4*	20	18	10,200	9,778	165	193	*0.1*
NOWATA, OK											
60 –	**Finance, insurance, and real estate**	17	19	*0.2*	88	95	23,773	23,116	2,097	2,171	*0.1*
6500	Real estate	6	7	*0.3*	22	26	29,636	25,385	566	606	*0.3*
OKFUSKEE, OK											
60 –	**Finance, insurance, and real estate**	12	11	*0.1*	70	77	26,343	24,623	1,511	1,493	*0.1*
6000	Depository institutions	3	3	*0.3*	50	55	20,160	19,200	1,123	1,081	*0.2*
6020	Commercial banks	3	3	*0.4*	50	55	20,160	19,200	1,123	1,081	*0.3*
OKLAHOMA, OK											
60 –	**Finance, insurance, and real estate**	2,161	2,213	*28.9*	21,603	21,318	26,590	27,908	578,164	606,897	*37.7*
6000	Depository institutions	235	254	*22.2*	5,873	5,898	25,302	27,130	143,881	153,884	*29.3*
6020	Commercial banks	127	130	*16.8*	4,035	3,869	25,603	28,265	99,549	102,351	*23.7*
6030	Savings institutions	31	30	*23.1*	628	613	26,446	24,848	14,493	16,891	*54.3*
6060	Credit unions	47	48	*32.4*	754	899	21,788	24,374	17,710	21,161	*46.8*
6100	Nondepository institutions	181	190	*22.2*	1,942	1,850	25,722	27,648	49,953	56,644	*46.8*
6140	Personal credit institutions	105	109	*17.6*	841	865	22,021	24,472	18,716	22,703	*41.0*
6150	Business credit institutions	11	14	*30.4*	119	156	40,168	46,487	5,619	10,752	*53.5*
6160	Mortgage bankers and brokers	63	63	*44.7*	982	827	27,141	27,424	25,610	23,114	*58.8*
6200	Security and commodity brokers	130	132	*33.3*	825	871	59,927	51,789	48,477	48,636	*46.7*
6210	Security brokers and dealers	83	89	*31.8*	568	613	60,838	54,029	31,189	34,053	*41.3*
6220	Commodity contracts brokers, dealers	7	5	*31.3*	44	20	36,364	67,000	1,712	1,506	*70.7*
6280	Security and commodity services	40	38	*38.4*	213	238	62,366	44,739	15,576	13,077	*66.8*
6300	Insurance carriers	213	205	*45.9*	5,658	5,520	29,776	30,768	164,924	164,581	*45.6*
6310	Life insurance	70	66	*52.8*	2,493	2,475	31,806	30,455	71,248	67,373	*61.0*
6320	Medical service and health insurance	23	18	*41.9*	1,128	1,043	24,794	29,131	30,854	30,900	*44.3*
6330	Fire, marine, and casualty insurance	93	94	*39.8*	1,500	1,484	33,397	35,189	50,575	53,420	*32.8*
6400	Insurance agents, brokers, and service	519	522	*28.0*	2,353	2,208	23,925	26,406	62,387	65,420	*40.4*
6500	Real estate	729	740	*29.6*	3,901	3,931	17,236	17,393	72,061	71,165	*34.4*
6510	Real estate operators and lessors	342	325	*32.3*	1,692	1,762	14,459	15,435	26,411	26,686	*40.1*
6530	Real estate agents and managers	304	318	*29.4*	1,288	1,405	19,379	19,465	27,094	29,018	*32.9*
6540	Title abstract offices	27	27	*17.3*	444	352	23,505	23,352	9,545	8,649	*27.5*
6550	Subdividers and developers	38	39	*22.4*	471	285	15,524	13,221	8,627	4,633	*27.9*
6552	Subdividers and developers, n.e.c.	23	22	*21.8*	255	39	19,216	21,333	5,875	1,276	*15.1*
6553	Cemetery subdividers and developers	11	13	*22.8*	215	242	11,126	11,570	2,662	3,205	*44.7*
6710	Holding offices	21	29	*28.4*	563	489	30,345	48,589	18,477	27,488	*31.1*
6720	Investment offices	8	8	*44.4*	26	46	11,231	10,087	369	476	*63.3*
6730	Trusts	35	38	*34.2*	168	180	28,929	30,911	4,359	4,809	*47.6*
6732	Educational, religious, etc. trusts	9	11	*33.3*	6	41	24,000	18,244	323	794	*24.7*

Source: County Business Patterns, 1994/95, CBP-94/95, U.S. Department of Commerce, Washington, D.C., November 1997. SIC categories for which data were suppressed or not available for both 1994 and 1995 are not displayed. The employment columns represent mid-March employment in the year. Pay per employee is calculated by dividing 1st Quarter payroll, annualized, by mid-March employment. The columns headed "% State" show the county's percentage of the state total for the SIC in 1995; for example, 1.4% for SIC 6000 means that the county had 1.4 percent of the state's total establishments (or payroll) in SIC 6000 in 1995. A dash (-) is used to indicate that data are not available or cannot be calculated; nec means not elsewhere classified.

Continued on next page.

SIC	Industry	No. Establishments			Employment		Pay / Employee		Annual Payroll ($ 000)		
		1994	1995	% State	1994	1995	1994	1995	1994	1995	% State
OKLAHOMA, OK - [continued]											
6733	Trusts, n.e.c.	26	27	34.6	162	139	29,111	34,647	4,036	4,015	58.3
6790	Miscellaneous investing	84	83	43.9	287	266	41,923	40,556	12,876	12,205	50.9
6792	Oil royalty traders	38	41	45.6	143	139	41,846	44,374	6,100	6,129	49.6
OKMULGEE, OK											
60 –	**Finance, insurance, and real estate**	61	62	0.8	346	349	21,006	21,501	7,412	7,423	0.5
6000	Depository institutions	12	11	1.0	224	223	23,714	25,686	5,490	5,611	1.1
6020	Commercial banks	7	7	0.9	188	189	25,149	27,344	4,772	4,976	1.2
6100	Nondepository institutions	12	12	1.4	23	25	17,913	16,000	424	398	0.3
6140	Personal credit institutions	12	12	1.9	23	25	17,913	16,000	424	398	0.7
6400	Insurance agents, brokers, and service	14	16	0.9	42	41	11,810	11,122	537	475	0.3
6500	Real estate	11	12	0.5	33	44	10,545	10,818	384	473	0.2
6510	Real estate operators and lessors	3	3	0.3	10	8	8,400	7,000	82	56	0.1
6700	Holding and other investment offices	6	6	1.4	6	6	10,667	12,000	67	72	0.1
OSAGE, OK											
60 –	**Finance, insurance, and real estate**	29	31	0.4	156	197	23,667	21,827	3,335	4,472	0.3
6000	Depository institutions	9	10	0.9	96	131	28,292	24,611	2,487	3,495	0.7
6500	Real estate	8	10	0.4	25	33	15,680	13,333	421	477	0.2
6510	Real estate operators and lessors	3	3	0.3	6	5	19,333	20,800	110	126	0.2
OTTAWA, OK											
60 –	**Finance, insurance, and real estate**	66	66	0.9	428	412	17,187	18,223	8,003	7,896	0.5
6000	Depository institutions	13	13	1.1	208	216	16,885	18,685	3,943	4,378	0.8
6020	Commercial banks	10	10	1.3	159	162	16,528	17,062	2,925	3,072	0.7
6100	Nondepository institutions	9	9	1.1	32	40	15,250	17,200	552	691	0.6
6140	Personal credit institutions	9	9	1.5	32	40	15,250	17,200	552	691	1.2
6300	Insurance carriers	4	3	0.7	8	8	35,000	33,500	264	239	0.1
6400	Insurance agents, brokers, and service	14	14	0.8	38	38	20,105	22,632	787	840	0.5
6500	Real estate	21	22	0.9	128	97	12,750	11,918	1,878	1,207	0.6
6530	Real estate agents and managers	8	8	0.7	39	53	11,179	13,585	614	639	0.7
PAWNEE, OK											
60 –	**Finance, insurance, and real estate**	18	19	0.2	105	105	20,686	19,429	2,293	2,236	0.1
6000	Depository institutions	6	6	0.5	84	81	23,429	21,284	2,059	1,901	0.4
PAYNE, OK											
60 –	**Finance, insurance, and real estate**	139	140	1.8	808	817	16,866	18,066	14,693	15,635	1.0
6000	Depository institutions	21	21	1.8	404	426	19,782	21,822	8,489	9,558	1.8
6020	Commercial banks	13	15	1.9	341	386	20,305	22,694	7,137	8,966	2.1
6100	Nondepository institutions	11	15	1.8	47	44	17,447	19,000	756	873	0.7
6210	Security brokers and dealers	6	5	1.8	12	11	26,333	24,727	424	420	0.5
6400	Insurance agents, brokers, and service	41	38	2.0	110	109	14,109	13,798	1,784	1,868	1.2
6500	Real estate	51	53	2.1	225	217	11,627	11,834	2,911	2,629	1.3
6510	Real estate operators and lessors	23	23	2.3	83	97	9,590	10,928	944	1,060	1.6
6530	Real estate agents and managers	20	22	2.0	112	95	13,679	13,011	1,488	1,300	1.5
6553	Cemetery subdividers and developers	3	3	5.3	9	6	7,111	8,000	70	46	0.6
6700	Holding and other investment offices	5	4	0.9	4	4	33,000	13,000	80	37	0.0
PITTSBURG, OK											
60 –	**Finance, insurance, and real estate**	81	78	1.0	519	512	17,595	18,953	9,567	9,660	0.6
6000	Depository institutions	10	12	1.0	256	262	17,078	19,160	4,916	5,432	1.0
6020	Commercial banks	7	9	1.2	245	248	17,045	19,355	4,716	5,195	1.2
6100	Nondepository institutions	19	19	2.2	56	60	19,714	21,200	1,181	1,205	1.0
6330	Fire, marine, and casualty insurance	4	4	1.7	12	12	39,333	46,667	510	549	0.3
6400	Insurance agents, brokers, and service	18	18	1.0	63	57	16,762	15,649	1,030	905	0.6

Source: *County Business Patterns, 1994/95*, CBP-94/95, U.S. Department of Commerce, Washington, D.C., November 1997. SIC categories for which data were suppressed or not available for both 1994 and 1995 are *not* displayed. The employment columns represent mid-March employment in the year. Pay per employee is calculated by dividing 1st Quarter payroll, annualized, by mid-March employment. The columns headed "% State" show the county's percentage of the state total for the SIC in 1995; for example, 1.4% for SIC 6000 means that the county had 1.4 percent of the state's total establishments (or payroll) in SIC 6000 in 1995. A dash (-) is used to indicate that data are not available or cannot be calculated; *nec* means not elsewhere classified.

Continued on next page.

SIC	Industry	No. Establishments			Employment		Pay / Employee		Annual Payroll ($ 000)		
		1994	1995	% State	1994	1995	1994	1995	1994	1995	% State
PITTSBURG, OK - [continued]											
6500	Real estate	24	19	*0.8*	109	104	9,651	9,192	1,108	1,049	*0.5*
6510	Real estate operators and lessors	8	4	*0.4*	24	19	5,667	6,105	144	121	*0.2*
6530	Real estate agents and managers	12	12	*1.1*	49	54	11,184	9,407	600	555	*0.6*
PONTOTOC, OK											
60 –	**Finance, insurance, and real estate**	82	71	*0.9*	420	366	19,838	19,257	8,404	7,371	*0.5*
6000	Depository institutions	15	14	*1.2*	258	221	19,597	19,765	5,552	4,791	*0.9*
6020	Commercial banks	8	8	*1.0*	208	210	19,115	20,095	3,977	4,240	*1.0*
6100	Nondepository institutions	15	15	*1.8*	48	50	14,667	15,280	672	714	*0.6*
6140	Personal credit institutions	15	15	*2.4*	48	50	14,667	15,280	672	714	*1.3*
6400	Insurance agents, brokers, and service	21	19	*1.0*	70	57	20,000	21,053	1,258	1,093	*0.7*
6500	Real estate	21	15	*0.6*	27	29	12,889	16,276	400	480	*0.2*
6530	Real estate agents and managers	9	7	*0.6*	13	15	8,000	8,800	94	168	*0.2*
POTTAWATOMIE, OK											
60 –	**Finance, insurance, and real estate**	113	116	*1.5*	684	592	17,187	19,601	11,502	11,547	*0.7*
6000	Depository institutions	19	19	*1.7*	318	301	16,302	21,395	5,114	5,777	*1.1*
6020	Commercial banks	12	11	*1.4*	286	267	15,986	21,738	4,476	5,036	*1.2*
6100	Nondepository institutions	17	18	*2.1*	53	55	16,528	17,818	928	1,126	*0.9*
6280	Security and commodity services	3	3	*3.0*	4	6	10,000	8,667	43	47	*0.2*
6400	Insurance agents, brokers, and service	27	30	*1.6*	74	74	15,297	15,622	1,179	1,151	*0.7*
6500	Real estate	35	34	*1.4*	132	126	13,030	14,095	1,865	1,775	*0.9*
6510	Real estate operators and lessors	18	19	*1.9*	52	55	13,846	14,836	799	758	*1.1*
6530	Real estate agents and managers	13	11	*1.0*	38	37	12,842	12,973	554	518	*0.6*
6700	Holding and other investment offices	5	3	*0.7*	87	13	20,000	44,615	1,578	876	*0.7*
PUSHMATAHA, OK											
60 –	**Finance, insurance, and real estate**	11	11	*0.1*	106	113	17,396	18,124	2,456	2,304	*0.1*
6000	Depository institutions	3	3	*0.3*	56	56	19,786	21,286	1,487	1,473	*0.3*
6020	Commercial banks	3	3	*0.4*	56	56	19,786	21,286	1,487	1,473	*0.3*
ROGERS, OK											
60 –	**Finance, insurance, and real estate**	90	86	*1.1*	544	557	17,779	19,978	10,300	10,630	*0.7*
6000	Depository institutions	12	12	*1.0*	265	265	19,472	22,974	5,451	5,592	*1.1*
6100	Nondepository institutions	7	9	*1.1*	20	19	22,600	31,368	447	451	*0.4*
6400	Insurance agents, brokers, and service	26	23	*1.2*	71	71	13,972	13,915	1,063	1,077	*0.7*
6500	Real estate	37	33	*1.3*	179	187	15,084	16,150	2,931	2,967	*1.4*
6510	Real estate operators and lessors	16	13	*1.3*	87	101	11,080	14,693	1,158	1,423	*2.1*
6530	Real estate agents and managers	15	15	*1.4*	51	44	20,235	20,000	1,006	886	*1.0*
SEMINOLE, OK											
60 –	**Finance, insurance, and real estate**	43	43	*0.6*	196	193	15,673	17,016	3,282	3,332	*0.2*
6000	Depository institutions	8	8	*0.7*	107	107	16,636	17,944	1,963	1,950	*0.4*
6100	Nondepository institutions	8	8	*0.9*	17	17	16,941	19,765	256	304	*0.3*
6140	Personal credit institutions	8	8	*1.3*	17	17	16,941	19,765	256	304	*0.5*
6400	Insurance agents, brokers, and service	14	14	*0.8*	39	36	14,154	15,333	531	534	*0.3*
SEQUOYAH, OK											
60 –	**Finance, insurance, and real estate**	54	57	*0.7*	253	297	16,901	17,764	4,976	5,539	*0.3*
6000	Depository institutions	8	8	*0.7*	123	134	17,691	18,687	2,426	2,653	*0.5*
6100	Nondepository institutions	19	21	*2.5*	56	63	18,929	17,841	1,087	1,097	*0.9*
6140	Personal credit institutions	19	21	*3.4*	56	63	18,929	17,841	1,087	1,097	*2.0*
6400	Insurance agents, brokers, and service	8	10	*0.5*	27	31	16,444	17,935	464	601	*0.4*
6500	Real estate	13	12	*0.5*	39	53	13,641	14,642	827	890	*0.4*
6530	Real estate agents and managers	4	4	*0.4*	11	14	14,182	9,429	244	171	*0.2*
STEPHENS, OK											
60 –	**Finance, insurance, and real estate**	90	87	*1.1*	718	680	20,953	21,782	14,965	13,367	*0.8*

Source: County Business Patterns, 1994/95, CBP-94/95, U.S. Department of Commerce, Washington, D.C., November 1997. SIC categories for which data were suppressed or not available for both 1994 and 1995 are not displayed. The employment columns represent mid-March employment in the year. Pay per employee is calculated by dividing 1st Quarter payroll, annualized, by mid-March employment. The columns headed "% State" show the county's percentage of the state total for the SIC in 1995; for example, 1.4% for SIC 6000 means that the county had 1.4 percent of the state's total establishments (or payroll) in SIC 6000 in 1995. A dash (-) is used to indicate that data are not available or cannot be calculated; nec means not elsewhere classified.

Continued on next page.

SIC	Industry	No. Establishments			Employment		Pay / Employee		Annual Payroll ($ 000)		
		1994	1995	% State	1994	1995	1994	1995	1994	1995	% State
STEPHENS, OK - [continued]											
6000	Depository institutions	23	23	2.0	341	346	23,683	24,416	7,742	7,039	1.3
6020	Commercial banks	15	15	1.9	303	303	24,594	25,743	7,103	6,351	1.5
6100	Nondepository institutions	15	15	1.8	63	70	19,302	21,886	1,437	1,478	1.2
6400	Insurance agents, brokers, and service	22	22	1.2	92	98	18,478	17,714	1,736	1,834	1.1
6500	Real estate	15	14	0.6	136	136	12,000	12,471	1,919	1,854	0.9
6530	Real estate agents and managers	7	8	0.7	63	66	7,746	9,455	557	676	0.8
6700	Holding and other investment offices	8	7	1.6	27	19	41,481	51,158	854	766	0.6
TEXAS, OK											
60 –	**Finance, insurance, and real estate**	37	38	0.5	242	220	23,372	24,873	5,955	6,498	0.4
6000	Depository institutions	6	5	0.4	149	114	21,933	21,860	3,453	3,052	0.6
6200	Security and commodity brokers	4	4	1.0	8	8	47,000	31,500	329	287	0.3
6530	Real estate agents and managers	5	5	0.5	6	5	7,333	11,200	50	54	0.1
TILLMAN, OK											
60 –	**Finance, insurance, and real estate**	19	20	0.3	117	119	18,974	19,529	2,297	2,784	0.2
6000	Depository institutions	5	5	0.4	90	90	21,333	21,600	1,927	1,893	0.4
6020	Commercial banks	5	5	0.6	90	90	21,333	21,600	1,927	1,893	0.4
6400	Insurance agents, brokers, and service	7	7	0.4	12	13	8,667	8,923	123	159	0.1
6500	Real estate	4	5	0.2	7	8	9,143	11,000	77	518	0.3
TULSA, OK											
60 –	**Finance, insurance, and real estate**	1,648	1,702	22.3	18,325	17,562	29,055	29,868	531,773	532,847	33.1
6000	Depository institutions	200	202	17.7	4,184	4,211	27,502	27,857	110,652	112,252	21.3
6020	Commercial banks	105	108	13.9	3,398	3,374	28,950	29,459	93,344	93,451	21.6
6030	Savings institutions	21	18	13.8	111	105	19,856	15,771	1,884	1,956	6.3
6060	Credit unions	44	44	29.7	535	579	21,331	22,556	12,147	13,291	29.4
6090	Functions closely related to banking	30	32	36.4	140	153	22,000	20,863	3,277	3,554	-
6140	Personal credit institutions	81	88	14.2	484	470	20,521	20,511	10,260	9,632	17.4
6150	Business credit institutions	17	19	41.3	135	192	28,711	30,167	4,143	8,761	43.6
6160	Mortgage bankers and brokers	42	43	30.5	540	477	35,348	29,476	15,388	13,411	34.1
6200	Security and commodity brokers	92	97	24.5	689	704	60,813	54,710	35,641	37,875	36.4
6210	Security brokers and dealers	59	63	22.5	584	594	64,699	57,394	31,789	33,524	40.7
6300	Insurance carriers	127	124	27.7	5,546	5,358	30,522	33,424	167,537	172,443	47.8
6310	Life insurance	44	37	29.6	1,641	1,621	24,436	24,975	39,404	38,001	34.4
6320	Medical service and health insurance	17	18	41.9	1,062	1,102	29,202	30,472	34,523	35,557	51.0
6321	Accident and health insurance	8	9	45.0	69	90	32,174	28,622	2,401	2,823	9.4
6324	Hospital and medical service plans	9	9	39.1	993	1,012	28,995	30,636	32,122	32,734	82.1
6330	Fire, marine, and casualty insurance	57	60	25.4	2,761	2,445	34,884	41,091	91,390	94,143	57.8
6400	Insurance agents, brokers, and service	401	389	20.9	1,704	1,741	27,242	27,897	46,931	48,909	30.2
6500	Real estate	569	618	24.7	3,681	3,261	22,410	19,811	87,197	70,880	34.3
6510	Real estate operators and lessors	206	216	21.4	919	931	20,749	19,360	21,331	18,741	28.1
6530	Real estate agents and managers	300	323	29.9	2,251	1,792	22,989	19,924	53,972	39,187	44.4
6540	Title abstract offices	10	13	8.3	320	271	25,125	24,030	7,447	7,080	22.5
6550	Subdividers and developers	33	39	22.4	174	193	19,448	19,295	4,001	4,897	29.5
6552	Subdividers and developers, n.e.c.	27	30	29.7	59	58	23,186	26,690	1,767	2,165	25.7
6553	Cemetery subdividers and developers	6	6	10.5	115	135	17,530	16,119	2,234	2,647	37.0
6710	Holding offices	26	31	30.4	212	697	52,377	44,080	12,199	44,116	50.0
6730	Trusts	27	32	28.8	67	88	26,985	27,318	2,131	2,637	26.1
6732	Educational, religious, etc. trusts	12	11	33.3	40	45	29,800	32,800	1,256	1,603	50.0
6733	Trusts, n.e.c.	15	21	26.9	27	43	22,815	21,581	875	1,034	15.0
6790	Miscellaneous investing	51	43	22.8	246	228	33,659	33,825	9,092	8,685	36.3
6792	Oil royalty traders	20	15	16.7	157	130	34,904	35,200	5,755	4,532	36.7
6799	Investors, n.e.c.	25	22	26.8	70	78	36,571	34,256	2,958	3,472	34.0
WAGONER, OK											
60 –	**Finance, insurance, and real estate**	36	38	0.5	188	186	17,489	19,505	3,680	3,790	0.2
6000	Depository institutions	8	7	0.6	106	100	18,868	22,680	2,292	2,246	0.4

Source: County Business Patterns, 1994/95, CBP-94/95, U.S. Department of Commerce, Washington, D.C., November 1997. SIC categories for which data were suppressed or not available for both 1994 and 1995 are not displayed. The employment columns represent mid-March employment in the year. Pay per employee is calculated by dividing 1st Quarter payroll, annualized, by mid-March employment. The columns headed "% State" show the county's percentage of the state total for the SIC in 1995; for example, 1.4% for SIC 6000 means that the county had 1.4 percent of the state's total establishments (or payroll) in SIC 6000 in 1995. A dash (-) is used to indicate that data are not available or cannot be calculated; nec means not elsewhere classified.

Continued on next page.

SIC	Industry	No. Establishments			Employment		Pay / Employee		Annual Payroll ($ 000)		
		1994	1995	% State	1994	1995	1994	1995	1994	1995	% State
BUTLER, PA - [continued]											
6400	Insurance agents, brokers, and service	72	71	1.4	216	200	21,944	23,100	4,522	4,685	0.4
6500	Real estate	85	97	1.3	284	295	15,394	16,258	5,119	5,605	0.5
6510	Real estate operators and lessors	38	42	1.5	149	144	14,792	16,944	2,529	2,799	0.8
6530	Real estate agents and managers	30	34	1.0	102	111	15,961	16,144	1,873	2,024	0.3
6540	Title abstract offices	3	4	1.8	10	11	21,600	15,636	295	275	1.1
6550	Subdividers and developers	13	15	1.6	23	27	14,087	12,741	417	376	0.3
6553	Cemetery subdividers and developers	13	15	2.4	23	27	14,087	12,741	417	376	0.6
6700	Holding and other investment offices	7	6	0.9	38	47	28,842	26,383	1,107	1,195	0.2
CAMBRIA, PA											
60 –	**Finance, insurance, and real estate**	300	302	1.3	3,384	3,904	21,299	22,471	89,872	89,238	0.8
6000	Depository institutions	101	98	1.8	1,477	1,322	19,583	21,071	30,738	27,605	1.0
6020	Commercial banks	73	72	1.9	1,175	1,123	19,581	21,685	24,157	24,020	1.1
6210	Security brokers and dealers	9	9	1.1	44	48	69,636	50,417	2,758	2,659	0.4
6300	Insurance carriers	24	23	1.2	844	830	21,137	19,966	20,376	18,123	0.6
6310	Life insurance	9	8	1.2	736	681	19,261	20,235	16,290	14,110	1.3
6400	Insurance agents, brokers, and service	70	74	1.4	336	356	22,131	24,820	8,202	8,634	0.8
6500	Real estate	71	72	1.0	415	1,001	15,528	21,483	18,624	21,435	1.9
6510	Real estate operators and lessors	36	34	1.2	289	831	15,488	23,187	16,401	18,527	5.1
6530	Real estate agents and managers	18	21	0.6	64	107	19,875	14,280	1,323	1,996	0.3
6553	Cemetery subdividers and developers	12	12	1.9	48	50	11,500	11,200	697	718	1.2
6700	Holding and other investment offices	8	7	1.0	195	265	35,631	31,321	7,439	8,422	1.2
6710	Holding offices	4	4	1.7	184	259	37,000	31,614	7,306	8,303	2.1
CAMERON, PA											
60 –	**Finance, insurance, and real estate**	5	5	0.0	51	42	14,431	17,048	758	655	0.0
CARBON, PA											
60 –	**Finance, insurance, and real estate**	85	79	0.3	499	503	19,174	19,610	9,877	9,962	0.1
6000	Depository institutions	29	26	0.5	329	333	19,805	21,225	6,649	6,943	0.2
6020	Commercial banks	20	19	0.5	290	308	19,986	21,506	6,142	6,481	0.3
6510	Real estate operators and lessors	3	4	0.1	6	6	12,667	6,667	68	42	0.0
6550	Subdividers and developers	10	10	1.1	20	35	9,600	9,029	226	392	0.3
6552	Subdividers and developers, n.e.c.	3	3	1.1	7	21	18,857	12,952	147	336	0.6
6553	Cemetery subdividers and developers	7	7	1.1	13	14	4,615	3,143	79	56	0.1
CENTRE, PA											
60 –	**Finance, insurance, and real estate**	271	287	1.2	2,224	2,405	21,869	24,694	52,657	58,174	0.5
6000	Depository institutions	66	69	1.2	980	1,041	18,094	20,430	19,217	20,427	0.7
6020	Commercial banks	58	57	1.5	930	953	18,052	20,562	18,205	18,626	0.8
6140	Personal credit institutions	9	9	1.3	36	36	21,778	26,667	874	916	0.5
6160	Mortgage bankers and brokers	7	6	1.1	60	68	25,067	29,118	1,579	1,931	0.8
6200	Security and commodity brokers	27	28	1.9	108	121	50,111	55,306	5,826	6,145	0.6
6210	Security brokers and dealers	16	17	2.0	57	65	57,404	55,385	3,060	3,068	0.4
6280	Security and commodity services	11	11	1.9	51	56	41,961	55,214	2,766	3,077	0.9
6300	Insurance carriers	15	18	0.9	209	263	31,656	29,932	5,974	7,661	0.2
6310	Life insurance	7	7	1.0	118	173	30,136	27,815	3,348	4,808	0.4
6400	Insurance agents, brokers, and service	62	62	1.2	247	293	19,757	25,666	6,358	7,766	0.7
6500	Real estate	79	88	1.2	479	455	17,370	19,349	9,312	9,566	0.8
6510	Real estate operators and lessors	37	41	1.5	215	207	15,256	16,966	3,767	3,807	1.1
6530	Real estate agents and managers	33	34	1.0	245	226	18,596	19,858	5,069	4,925	0.8
CHESTER, PA											
60 –	**Finance, insurance, and real estate**	895	910	3.8	12,155	11,109	35,236	41,656	482,526	487,819	4.6
6000	Depository institutions	159	165	3.0	2,316	2,319	26,437	28,526	61,842	65,657	2.3
6020	Commercial banks	114	113	3.0	1,654	1,550	25,763	28,568	44,191	44,531	2.0
6030	Savings institutions	24	27	3.6	478	535	29,833	30,886	12,518	15,060	6.1
6060	Credit unions	17	18	2.2	143	152	18,965	19,947	3,009	3,418	2.9

Source: County Business Patterns, 1994/95, CBP-94/95, U.S. Department of Commerce, Washington, D.C., November 1997. SIC categories for which data were suppressed or not available for both 1994 and 1995 are not displayed. The employment columns represent mid-March employment in the year. Pay per employee is calculated by dividing 1st Quarter payroll, annualized, by mid-March employment. The columns headed "% State" show the county's percentage of the state total for the SIC in 1995; for example, 1.4% for SIC 6000 means that the county had 1.4 percent of the state's total establishments (or payroll) in SIC 6000 in 1995. A dash (-) is used to indicate that data are not available or cannot be calculated; nec means not elsewhere classified.

Continued on next page.

SIC	Industry	No. Establishments			Employment		Pay / Employee		Annual Payroll ($ 000)		
		1994	1995	% State	1994	1995	1994	1995	1994	1995	% State
CHESTER, PA - [continued]											
6090	Functions closely related to banking	4	7	3.5	41	82	40,098	28,244	2,124	2,648	3.3
6100	Nondepository institutions	68	62	4.3	1,472	1,146	37,035	47,735	49,421	52,089	9.5
6150	Business credit institutions	12	10	8.5	917	739	39,996	54,739	35,158	38,840	36.0
6160	Mortgage bankers and brokers	38	32	5.7	500	327	32,952	31,645	12,818	10,268	4.5
6200	Security and commodity brokers	72	75	5.2	528	580	72,697	75,483	42,625	47,010	4.4
6280	Security and commodity services	44	47	7.9	246	257	86,699	109,401	26,558	28,954	8.8
6300	Insurance carriers	73	82	4.2	3,018	2,693	30,176	42,418	101,373	106,181	3.4
6310	Life insurance	21	21	3.0	2,370	2,082	25,813	35,176	68,762	68,812	6.4
6330	Fire, marine, and casualty insurance	35	43	5.1	482	444	49,162	76,874	26,514	30,905	2.4
6400	Insurance agents, brokers, and service	207	215	4.2	1,939	2,028	43,688	47,600	126,743	126,292	11.3
6500	Real estate	286	283	3.8	2,461	1,989	28,936	32,595	72,656	67,666	5.9
6510	Real estate operators and lessors	90	89	3.2	956	407	23,439	27,135	22,448	11,768	3.3
6530	Real estate agents and managers	144	143	4.3	1,192	1,204	33,554	34,754	39,536	38,143	6.0
6540	Title abstract offices	9	5	2.2	46	26	29,652	21,846	1,248	723	2.8
6550	Subdividers and developers	40	36	3.9	266	310	27,970	33,819	9,261	16,589	13.6
6552	Subdividers and developers, n.e.c.	24	20	7.0	156	175	33,795	46,034	7,154	14,097	23.2
6553	Cemetery subdividers and developers	13	13	2.1	109	132	14,752	15,879	1,851	2,078	3.5
6710	Holding offices	15	11	4.6	314	274	77,299	70,555	24,449	19,726	5.1
CLARION, PA											
60 –	**Finance, insurance, and real estate**	72	70	0.3	454	451	21,128	22,492	9,897	9,799	0.1
6000	Depository institutions	22	22	0.4	242	238	18,165	19,697	4,601	4,786	0.2
6020	Commercial banks	16	16	0.4	209	204	18,660	20,294	4,062	4,213	0.2
6400	Insurance agents, brokers, and service	20	19	0.4	97	96	25,856	26,958	2,175	2,254	0.2
6500	Real estate	21	19	0.3	58	61	16,759	16,525	1,055	1,046	0.1
6530	Real estate agents and managers	4	5	0.2	15	20	16,000	11,400	319	280	0.0
CLEARFIELD, PA											
60 –	**Finance, insurance, and real estate**	119	115	0.5	898	948	20,708	21,852	19,307	20,017	0.2
6000	Depository institutions	38	39	0.7	533	566	19,212	19,484	10,791	11,398	0.4
6020	Commercial banks	34	35	0.9	514	543	19,424	19,720	10,528	11,090	0.5
6300	Insurance carriers	11	9	0.5	109	89	25,358	32,000	2,835	2,465	0.1
6310	Life insurance	4	4	0.6	96	77	24,667	29,143	2,119	1,892	0.2
6400	Insurance agents, brokers, and service	30	30	0.6	128	134	23,719	22,090	3,112	3,093	0.3
6500	Real estate	27	24	0.3	100	124	19,320	26,161	1,919	2,325	0.2
6510	Real estate operators and lessors	10	9	0.3	28	49	11,857	9,633	377	475	0.1
6530	Real estate agents and managers	12	12	0.4	57	64	24,912	40,938	1,317	1,688	0.3
6550	Subdividers and developers	4	3	0.3	11	11	13,091	13,818	166	162	0.1
6553	Cemetery subdividers and developers	4	3	0.5	11	11	13,091	13,818	166	162	0.3
CLINTON, PA											
60 –	**Finance, insurance, and real estate**	53	52	0.2	296	293	16,486	20,287	5,092	5,746	0.1
6000	Depository institutions	18	15	0.3	145	115	16,662	22,991	2,407	2,700	0.1
6020	Commercial banks	12	10	0.3	108	75	16,593	24,960	1,645	1,843	0.1
6300	Insurance carriers	4	3	0.2	30	28	26,000	22,714	730	624	0.0
6400	Insurance agents, brokers, and service	14	14	0.3	36	41	19,333	30,244	775	933	0.1
6500	Real estate	14	17	0.2	79	98	10,127	12,041	996	1,252	0.1
6510	Real estate operators and lessors	6	6	0.2	55	49	9,455	11,755	613	559	0.2
COLUMBIA, PA											
60 –	**Finance, insurance, and real estate**	118	112	0.5	721	708	16,161	17,893	13,080	12,871	0.1
6000	Depository institutions	33	30	0.5	374	382	16,246	17,707	6,977	6,902	0.2
6140	Personal credit institutions	5	5	0.7	16	23	20,000	20,522	396	479	0.3
6300	Insurance carriers	7	8	0.4	73	69	28,877	29,043	2,180	2,027	0.1

Source: County Business Patterns, 1994/95, CBP-94/95, U.S. Department of Commerce, Washington, D.C., November 1997. SIC categories for which data were suppressed or not available for both 1994 and 1995 are *not* displayed. The employment columns represent mid-March employment in the year. Pay per employee is calculated by dividing 1st Quarter payroll, annualized, by mid-March employment. The columns headed "% State" show the county's percentage of the state total for the SIC in 1995; for example, 1.4% for SIC 6000 means that the county had 1.4 percent of the state's total establishments (or payroll) in SIC 6000 in 1995. A dash (-) is used to indicate that data are not available or cannot be calculated; *nec* means not elsewhere classified.

Continued on next page.

SIC	Industry	No. Establishments			Employment		Pay / Employee		Annual Payroll ($ 000)		
		1994	1995	% State	1994	1995	1994	1995	1994	1995	% State
COLUMBIA, PA - [continued]											
6400	Insurance agents, brokers, and service	33	31	0.6	89	86	16,360	17,860	1,629	1,547	0.1
6500	Real estate	34	34	0.5	161	140	9,590	12,143	1,750	1,759	0.2
6510	Real estate operators and lessors	12	12	0.4	106	76	9,396	13,895	1,119	968	0.3
CRAWFORD, PA											
60 –	**Finance, insurance, and real estate**	134	142	0.6	705	688	20,369	21,965	16,484	15,861	0.1
6000	Depository institutions	35	37	0.7	293	301	18,703	19,322	5,765	6,168	0.2
6020	Commercial banks	24	26	0.7	228	234	20,123	20,838	4,803	5,114	0.2
6100	Nondepository institutions	9	10	0.7	39	39	27,077	29,744	966	1,016	0.2
6300	Insurance carriers	10	10	0.5	103	94	29,553	36,128	3,256	3,152	0.1
6400	Insurance agents, brokers, and service	29	31	0.6	104	100	21,769	23,680	2,466	2,552	0.2
6500	Real estate	42	43	0.6	120	106	10,333	10,906	2,687	1,640	0.1
6510	Real estate operators and lessors	17	16	0.6	72	58	11,056	12,828	2,159	1,085	0.3
6530	Real estate agents and managers	16	18	0.5	28	28	8,857	8,000	280	313	0.0
CUMBERLAND, PA											
60 –	**Finance, insurance, and real estate**	540	537	2.3	11,779	11,822	28,522	30,332	328,558	343,478	3.2
6000	Depository institutions	121	116	2.1	1,708	1,685	20,253	22,944	35,740	36,408	1.3
6020	Commercial banks	81	88	2.3	1,284	1,305	20,738	23,105	26,977	28,069	1.2
6030	Savings institutions	18	6	0.8	204	118	16,961	24,542	3,637	2,714	1.1
6060	Credit unions	22	22	2.7	220	262	20,473	21,420	5,126	5,625	4.7
6100	Nondepository institutions	53	49	3.4	390	357	33,703	31,754	12,266	11,742	2.1
6160	Mortgage bankers and brokers	31	28	5.0	268	227	36,731	33,727	8,948	8,171	3.5
6200	Security and commodity brokers	28	30	2.1	209	357	58,679	32,303	10,073	11,079	1.0
6210	Security brokers and dealers	23	21	2.5	193	184	61,679	54,500	9,692	9,679	1.3
6280	Security and commodity services	5	9	1.5	16	173	22,500	8,694	381	1,400	0.4
6300	Insurance carriers	60	66	3.4	7,493	7,699	30,506	32,356	217,619	233,830	7.4
6330	Fire, marine, and casualty insurance	27	28	3.3	1,406	1,408	34,677	36,631	49,719	51,470	3.9
6400	Insurance agents, brokers, and service	122	121	2.4	993	891	29,909	31,511	30,673	29,094	2.6
6500	Real estate	145	143	1.9	887	768	14,616	20,958	17,409	16,429	1.4
6510	Real estate operators and lessors	47	47	1.7	222	221	13,838	14,878	3,665	3,711	1.0
6530	Real estate agents and managers	72	68	2.0	388	388	19,515	22,825	8,995	9,099	1.4
6540	Title abstract offices	4	5	2.2	19	13	23,579	17,231	377	256	1.0
6550	Subdividers and developers	22	20	2.2	258	145	7,256	25,655	4,372	3,343	2.7
6552	Subdividers and developers, n.e.c.	15	13	4.6	200	86	4,480	30,279	3,152	2,232	3.7
6553	Cemetery subdividers and developers	7	7	1.1	58	59	16,828	18,915	1,220	1,111	1.9
6710	Holding offices	5	3	1.3	78	49	55,538	70,122	4,368	3,649	0.9
6790	Miscellaneous investing	3	4	2.4	17	5	14,588	28,000	270	213	0.3
DAUPHIN, PA											
60 –	**Finance, insurance, and real estate**	520	520	2.2	9,567	9,845	27,634	29,897	269,749	294,666	2.8
6000	Depository institutions	126	124	2.2	3,053	2,956	25,484	27,670	77,061	77,554	2.8
6020	Commercial banks	90	96	2.5	2,238	2,287	25,321	27,879	55,395	59,894	2.6
6060	Credit unions	17	17	2.1	477	532	23,816	26,361	12,629	13,957	11.8
6100	Nondepository institutions	29	32	2.2	242	154	31,570	34,857	7,857	4,316	0.8
6200	Security and commodity brokers	23	21	1.4	349	142	27,014	67,549	9,524	8,647	0.8
6210	Security brokers and dealers	14	13	1.6	133	122	60,481	70,590	7,547	7,138	1.0
6280	Security and commodity services	9	8	1.3	216	20	6,407	49,000	1,977	1,509	0.5
6300	Insurance carriers	64	63	3.2	4,100	3,863	31,453	32,855	130,349	132,210	4.2
6310	Life insurance	15	12	1.7	360	231	35,956	38,303	10,662	7,470	0.7
6330	Fire, marine, and casualty insurance	34	34	4.0	2,088	1,921	33,109	34,388	71,297	68,225	5.2
6400	Insurance agents, brokers, and service	125	123	2.4	994	1,868	24,849	28,321	25,905	53,186	4.8
6500	Real estate	143	147	2.0	758	794	18,116	19,824	16,234	16,545	1.4
6510	Real estate operators and lessors	63	63	2.3	395	426	16,759	18,413	7,595	8,214	2.3
6530	Real estate agents and managers	57	61	1.8	263	287	22,236	22,369	6,948	6,834	1.1

Source: County Business Patterns, 1994/95, CBP-94/95, U.S. Department of Commerce, Washington, D.C., November 1997. SIC categories for which data were suppressed or not available for both 1994 and 1995 are not displayed. The employment columns represent mid-March employment in the year. Pay per employee is calculated by dividing 1st Quarter payroll, annualized, by mid-March employment. The columns headed "% State" show the county's percentage of the state total for the SIC in 1995; for example, 1.4% for SIC 6000 means that the county had 1.4 percent of the state's total establishments (or payroll) in SIC 6000 in 1995. A dash (-) is used to indicate that data are not available or cannot be calculated; nec means not elsewhere classified.

Continued on next page.

SIC	Industry	No. Establishments			Employment		Pay / Employee		Annual Payroll ($ 000)		
		1994	1995	% State	1994	1995	1994	1995	1994	1995	% State
DAUPHIN, PA - [continued]											
6540	Title abstract offices	5	4	1.8	19	11	19,158	17,455	390	243	0.9
6550	Subdividers and developers	17	17	1.8	81	70	11,111	18,343	1,300	1,245	1.0
6700	Holding and other investment offices	10	10	1.5	71	68	29,746	29,765	2,819	2,208	0.3
DELAWARE, PA											
60 –	**Finance, insurance, and real estate**	1,235	1,203	5.1	14,916	15,116	35,537	37,167	549,005	606,949	5.7
6000	Depository institutions	216	203	3.6	2,902	2,748	22,518	24,376	69,455	70,760	2.5
6020	Commercial banks	132	126	3.3	2,062	1,902	22,960	24,700	49,665	47,696	2.1
6030	Savings institutions	47	40	5.3	453	448	21,280	23,750	10,954	13,072	5.3
6060	Credit unions	26	24	2.9	315	319	19,390	22,533	6,741	7,937	6.7
6090	Functions closely related to banking	11	13	6.4	72	79	31,333	27,544	2,095	2,055	2.5
6100	Nondepository institutions	66	59	4.1	890	555	32,764	26,674	27,054	15,779	2.9
6140	Personal credit institutions	24	26	3.7	182	183	27,319	26,470	4,876	5,093	3.0
6150	Business credit institutions	9	6	5.1	64	64	37,625	41,625	2,610	2,643	2.5
6160	Mortgage bankers and brokers	33	25	4.4	644	304	33,820	23,816	19,568	7,822	3.4
6200	Security and commodity brokers	102	101	6.9	1,037	1,042	80,679	81,777	96,684	110,480	10.3
6300	Insurance carriers	122	110	5.7	5,306	5,504	38,782	40,378	195,487	217,302	6.9
6310	Life insurance	45	41	5.9	1,327	1,084	37,640	35,919	46,522	35,768	3.3
6330	Fire, marine, and casualty insurance	41	42	4.9	3,648	3,643	39,784	43,137	137,669	149,691	11.4
6400	Insurance agents, brokers, and service	292	293	5.7	1,819	1,876	38,368	43,885	76,018	85,645	7.7
6500	Real estate	385	384	5.2	2,660	2,721	21,373	24,343	65,951	77,957	6.7
6510	Real estate operators and lessors	145	145	5.2	1,191	1,312	20,060	22,043	27,694	31,249	8.7
6530	Real estate agents and managers	184	178	5.4	1,051	970	22,946	27,497	28,083	31,789	5.0
6540	Title abstract offices	13	11	4.9	65	54	28,123	25,481	1,611	1,412	5.4
6550	Subdividers and developers	34	36	3.9	340	338	19,718	22,391	8,102	8,032	6.6
6552	Subdividers and developers, n.e.c.	13	15	5.3	57	69	32,632	28,928	2,488	2,025	3.3
6553	Cemetery subdividers and developers	21	20	3.2	283	269	17,117	20,714	5,614	5,942	9.9
6700	Holding and other investment offices	48	49	7.3	224	588	56,321	26,558	12,947	23,668	3.4
6710	Holding offices	15	18	7.5	86	169	74,233	47,929	5,456	15,856	4.1
6790	Miscellaneous investing	16	15	9.0	77	83	52,260	52,145	4,476	4,689	7.1
6799	Investors, n.e.c.	10	9	10.2	40	32	62,100	70,250	2,736	2,952	9.9
ELK, PA											
60 –	**Finance, insurance, and real estate**	55	58	0.2	302	299	20,225	21,298	6,567	7,046	0.1
6000	Depository institutions	23	23	0.4	170	168	18,212	19,643	3,292	3,579	0.1
6020	Commercial banks	14	14	0.4	118	119	19,831	21,210	2,435	2,656	0.1
6030	Savings institutions	5	5	0.7	39	36	15,077	16,889	693	747	0.3
6060	Credit unions	4	4	0.5	13	13	12,923	12,923	164	176	0.1
6400	Insurance agents, brokers, and service	18	18	0.4	63	61	21,016	21,836	1,433	1,620	0.1
6500	Real estate	8	9	0.1	24	23	15,500	17,739	532	538	0.0
ERIE, PA											
60 –	**Finance, insurance, and real estate**	515	527	2.2	5,371	5,438	25,555	27,463	150,602	156,610	1.5
6000	Depository institutions	149	152	2.7	1,694	1,660	20,314	21,108	34,374	34,886	1.2
6020	Commercial banks	74	76	2.0	1,209	1,156	21,780	22,505	25,828	25,684	1.1
6030	Savings institutions	19	21	2.8	226	226	18,106	20,195	4,368	4,712	1.9
6140	Personal credit institutions	20	23	3.2	126	119	23,714	25,613	2,863	2,896	1.7
6200	Security and commodity brokers	30	36	2.5	168	171	56,310	48,538	7,963	8,844	0.8
6210	Security brokers and dealers	19	23	2.8	140	137	62,029	53,314	7,071	7,568	1.0
6280	Security and commodity services	11	13	2.2	28	34	27,714	29,294	892	1,276	0.4
6300	Insurance carriers	39	41	2.1	2,069	2,148	29,976	30,862	73,266	71,978	2.3
6310	Life insurance	14	12	1.7	281	269	26,804	25,636	7,039	6,666	0.6
6400	Insurance agents, brokers, and service	131	126	2.5	590	697	24,292	30,324	16,726	21,213	1.9
6500	Real estate	126	128	1.7	629	543	14,060	15,381	9,184	9,892	0.9

Source: County Business Patterns, 1994/95, CBP-94/95, U.S. Department of Commerce, Washington, D.C., November 1997. SIC categories for which data were suppressed or not available for both 1994 and 1995 are not displayed. The employment columns represent mid-March employment in the year. Pay per employee is calculated by dividing 1st Quarter payroll, annualized, by mid-March employment. The columns headed "% State" show the county's percentage of the state total for the SIC in 1995; for example, 1.4% for SIC 6000 means that the county had 1.4 percent of the state's total establishments (or payroll) in SIC 6000 in 1995. A dash (-) is used to indicate that data are not available or cannot be calculated; nec means not elsewhere classified.

Continued on next page.

SIC	Industry	No. Establishments			Employment		Pay / Employee		Annual Payroll ($ 000)		
		1994	1995	% State	1994	1995	1994	1995	1994	1995	% State
ERIE, PA - [continued]											
6510	Real estate operators and lessors	54	53	1.9	258	260	12,481	13,077	3,581	3,944	1.1
6530	Real estate agents and managers	53	53	1.6	234	219	14,974	17,059	3,920	4,291	0.7
6550	Subdividers and developers	16	16	1.7	102	59	19,059	19,593	1,567	1,411	1.2
FAYETTE, PA											
60 –	**Finance, insurance, and real estate**	196	198	0.8	1,226	1,188	19,873	19,593	25,897	24,608	0.2
6000	Depository institutions	57	57	1.0	624	613	18,237	19,374	12,162	12,651	0.5
6020	Commercial banks	39	39	1.0	530	519	18,649	19,807	10,520	10,931	0.5
6030	Savings institutions	8	8	1.1	59	61	18,305	18,820	1,203	1,250	0.5
6060	Credit unions	10	10	1.2	35	33	11,886	13,576	439	470	0.4
6100	Nondepository institutions	10	10	0.7	52	52	25,385	25,923	1,240	1,329	0.2
6300	Insurance carriers	14	14	0.7	208	171	23,538	23,579	4,831	3,979	0.1
6310	Life insurance	6	6	0.9	196	159	21,694	21,132	4,130	3,218	0.3
6400	Insurance agents, brokers, and service	46	46	0.9	137	143	16,496	16,280	2,579	2,548	0.2
6500	Real estate	56	59	0.8	166	181	13,398	13,017	2,904	2,953	0.3
6510	Real estate operators and lessors	27	31	1.1	59	72	15,186	14,667	1,339	1,284	0.4
6530	Real estate agents and managers	18	16	0.5	46	54	10,087	10,667	679	718	0.1
6550	Subdividers and developers	11	11	1.2	61	53	14,164	13,509	886	943	0.8
FOREST, PA											
60 –	**Finance, insurance, and real estate**	7	7	0.0	-	-	-	-	-	-	-
FRANKLIN, PA											
60 –	**Finance, insurance, and real estate**	189	197	0.8	1,426	1,371	21,540	24,537	30,781	32,402	0.3
6000	Depository institutions	66	64	1.1	982	893	20,257	23,377	18,945	19,196	0.7
6020	Commercial banks	53	53	1.4	830	770	21,133	24,057	16,700	16,908	0.7
6100	Nondepository institutions	10	11	0.8	41	50	28,098	26,960	1,076	1,293	0.2
6210	Security brokers and dealers	4	4	0.5	31	28	61,935	70,143	1,693	1,715	0.2
6300	Insurance carriers	6	6	0.3	26	26	32,000	39,231	1,025	1,080	0.0
6400	Insurance agents, brokers, and service	37	43	0.8	137	176	27,212	29,364	4,158	5,292	0.5
6500	Real estate	61	62	0.8	199	185	15,377	16,692	3,739	3,645	0.3
6510	Real estate operators and lessors	17	16	0.6	64	58	13,188	11,931	858	841	0.2
6530	Real estate agents and managers	32	34	1.0	100	97	14,640	17,732	1,954	2,065	0.3
6540	Title abstract offices	3	3	1.3	8	6	7,500	12,000	103	121	0.5
6550	Subdividers and developers	8	8	0.9	27	23	25,630	26,087	823	614	0.5
6552	Subdividers and developers, n.e.c.	3	3	1.1	8	7	19,500	19,429	251	156	0.3
6553	Cemetery subdividers and developers	5	5	0.8	19	16	28,211	29,000	572	458	0.8
FULTON, PA											
60 –	**Finance, insurance, and real estate**	11	14	0.1	-	-	-	-	-	-	-
6000	Depository institutions	7	7	0.1	89	93	14,831	15,183	1,435	1,542	0.1
6020	Commercial banks	7	7	0.2	89	93	14,831	15,183	1,435	1,542	0.1
GREENE, PA											
60 –	**Finance, insurance, and real estate**	44	44	0.2	304	297	19,013	23,044	6,206	6,582	0.1
6000	Depository institutions	14	14	0.3	209	207	19,885	23,208	4,388	4,602	0.2
6400	Insurance agents, brokers, and service	14	13	0.3	56	49	18,143	24,490	1,073	1,123	0.1
6510	Real estate operators and lessors	7	8	0.3	15	15	13,333	19,733	241	264	0.1
HUNTINGDON, PA											
60 –	**Finance, insurance, and real estate**	62	61	0.3	578	561	20,021	20,549	11,538	11,466	0.1
6000	Depository institutions	26	24	0.4	260	224	18,431	18,875	4,975	4,301	0.2
6020	Commercial banks	23	21	0.6	253	217	18,530	18,894	4,854	4,169	0.2
6100	Nondepository institutions	4	5	0.3	13	12	26,462	27,333	268	297	0.1
6400	Insurance agents, brokers, and service	12	11	0.2	279	296	21,878	22,324	5,875	6,408	0.6

Source: County Business Patterns, 1994/95, CBP-94/95, U.S. Department of Commerce, Washington, D.C., November 1997. SIC categories for which data were suppressed or not available for both 1994 and 1995 are not displayed. The employment columns represent mid-March employment in the year. Pay per employee is calculated by dividing 1st Quarter payroll, annualized, by mid-March employment. The columns headed "% State" show the county's percentage of the state total for the SIC in 1995; for example, 1.4% for SIC 6000 means that the county had 1.4 percent of the state's total establishments (or payroll) in SIC 6000 in 1995. A dash (-) is used to indicate that data are not available or cannot be calculated; nec means not elsewhere classified.

Continued on next page.

SIC	Industry	No. Establishments			Employment		Pay / Employee		Annual Payroll ($ 000)		
		1994	1995	% State	1994	1995	1994	1995	1994	1995	% State
HUNTINGDON, PA - [continued]											
6500	Real estate	12	13	0.2	15	18	8,000	8,889	160	167	0.0
6550	Subdividers and developers	3	3	0.3	2	2	4,000	4,000	17	15	0.0
6553	Cemetery subdividers and developers	3	3	0.5	2	2	4,000	4,000	17	15	0.0
INDIANA, PA											
60 –	**Finance, insurance, and real estate**	138	139	0.6	1,116	1,144	23,391	25,490	26,167	29,690	0.3
6000	Depository institutions	38	39	0.7	712	698	21,612	23,473	14,934	16,506	0.6
6020	Commercial banks	34	35	0.9	617	606	21,809	23,386	12,922	14,284	0.6
6100	Nondepository institutions	8	8	0.6	30	28	22,000	24,000	630	677	0.1
6400	Insurance agents, brokers, and service	36	34	0.7	155	160	23,897	26,600	4,088	4,520	0.4
6500	Real estate	37	39	0.5	106	103	10,755	12,427	1,278	1,455	0.1
6510	Real estate operators and lessors	17	20	0.7	45	56	11,644	12,714	610	815	0.2
6550	Subdividers and developers	4	5	0.5	14	14	11,143	12,000	193	216	0.2
JEFFERSON, PA											
60 –	**Finance, insurance, and real estate**	72	69	0.3	402	384	18,239	19,958	7,565	7,712	0.1
6000	Depository institutions	21	21	0.4	206	213	21,650	22,216	4,451	4,651	0.2
6020	Commercial banks	18	18	0.5	195	200	21,846	22,080	4,233	4,384	0.2
6400	Insurance agents, brokers, and service	20	19	0.4	65	67	16,677	21,493	1,299	1,467	0.1
6500	Real estate	23	23	0.3	81	65	10,025	10,215	831	750	0.1
6510	Real estate operators and lessors	10	9	0.3	36	28	10,667	10,286	378	327	0.1
6530	Real estate agents and managers	6	6	0.2	26	24	9,385	7,167	246	182	0.0
6550	Subdividers and developers	7	7	0.8	19	13	9,684	15,692	207	231	0.2
6553	Cemetery subdividers and developers	7	7	1.1	19	13	9,684	15,692	207	231	0.4
JUNIATA, PA											
60 –	**Finance, insurance, and real estate**	27	29	0.1	212	212	16,283	17,792	3,736	4,063	0.0
6000	Depository institutions	12	12	0.2	166	164	14,988	16,366	2,717	2,997	0.1
6020	Commercial banks	12	12	0.3	166	164	14,988	16,366	2,717	2,997	0.1
6400	Insurance agents, brokers, and service	7	8	0.2	32	34	21,125	24,118	691	781	0.1
LACKAWANNA, PA											
60 –	**Finance, insurance, and real estate**	383	380	1.6	4,032	5,841	25,038	26,877	117,774	149,749	1.4
6000	Depository institutions	99	98	1.8	1,870	3,693	20,389	24,173	50,506	81,679	2.9
6020	Commercial banks	75	73	1.9	1,684	1,986	20,808	30,455	39,611	52,677	2.3
6100	Nondepository institutions	16	21	1.5	64	101	24,188	33,149	1,756	2,793	0.5
6140	Personal credit institutions	12	13	1.8	55	85	24,000	33,129	1,381	2,273	1.3
6200	Security and commodity brokers	20	19	1.3	123	131	58,862	48,763	7,361	8,088	0.8
6210	Security brokers and dealers	17	16	1.9	117	123	61,402	51,350	7,292	8,024	1.1
6280	Security and commodity services	3	3	0.5	6	8	9,333	9,000	69	64	0.0
6300	Insurance carriers	36	36	1.9	1,033	1,005	35,059	39,403	37,389	37,062	1.2
6310	Life insurance	17	15	2.2	760	706	34,695	39,190	27,038	26,351	2.4
6330	Fire, marine, and casualty insurance	13	12	1.4	209	179	38,603	48,894	8,168	7,581	0.6
6400	Insurance agents, brokers, and service	99	96	1.9	425	438	22,344	23,489	10,979	11,154	1.0
6500	Real estate	100	103	1.4	448	436	15,071	15,706	8,037	7,714	0.7
6510	Real estate operators and lessors	43	42	1.5	297	250	14,209	14,352	4,783	3,906	1.1
6530	Real estate agents and managers	36	38	1.1	104	127	16,000	15,244	2,076	2,307	0.4
6540	Title abstract offices	3	3	1.3	4	5	13,000	12,000	62	63	0.2
6550	Subdividers and developers	16	18	1.9	43	53	18,977	23,774	1,111	1,428	1.2
6552	Subdividers and developers, n.e.c.	4	6	2.1	12	13	30,000	34,769	391	475	0.8
6553	Cemetery subdividers and developers	12	12	1.9	31	40	14,710	20,200	720	953	1.6
LANCASTER, PA											
60 –	**Finance, insurance, and real estate**	819	839	3.5	8,892	8,320	25,945	27,825	230,254	230,163	2.2
6000	Depository institutions	205	217	3.9	3,439	3,225	21,992	26,689	78,283	84,059	3.0
6020	Commercial banks	161	181	4.8	3,205	3,010	22,089	27,015	72,615	79,128	3.5
6030	Savings institutions	19	13	1.7	123	86	15,805	17,302	2,314	1,570	0.6
6100	Nondepository institutions	46	50	3.5	570	396	34,351	30,242	16,805	12,736	2.3

Source: County Business Patterns, 1994/95, CBP-94/95, U.S. Department of Commerce, Washington, D.C., November 1997. SIC categories for which data were suppressed or not available for both 1994 and 1995 are not displayed. The employment columns represent mid-March employment in the year. Pay per employee is calculated by dividing 1st Quarter payroll, annualized, by mid-March employment. The columns headed "% State" show the county's percentage of the state total for the SIC in 1995; for example, 1.4% for SIC 6000 means that the county had 1.4 percent of the state's total establishments (or payroll) in SIC 6000 in 1995. A dash (-) is used to indicate that data are not available or cannot be calculated; nec means not elsewhere classified.

Continued on next page.

SIC	Industry	No. Establishments			Employment		Pay / Employee		Annual Payroll ($ 000)		
		1994	1995	% State	1994	1995	1994	1995	1994	1995	% State
LANCASTER, PA - [continued]											
6140	Personal credit institutions	19	22	*3.1*	120	125	33,800	32,512	4,240	4,387	*2.6*
6160	Mortgage bankers and brokers	23	24	*4.3*	362	178	34,309	26,674	9,695	5,237	*2.3*
6200	Security and commodity brokers	46	52	*3.6*	271	308	48,812	46,805	13,617	14,191	*1.3*
6210	Security brokers and dealers	23	27	*3.2*	207	247	56,870	52,486	12,008	12,483	*1.7*
6280	Security and commodity services	23	25	*4.2*	64	61	22,750	23,803	1,609	1,708	*0.5*
6300	Insurance carriers	70	68	*3.5*	1,510	1,375	35,009	35,808	47,929	46,507	*1.5*
6310	Life insurance	15	12	*1.7*	413	350	34,276	36,926	11,839	11,436	*1.1*
6320	Medical service and health insurance	3	4	*3.6*	85	122	35,247	37,049	2,819	4,237	*0.7*
6330	Fire, marine, and casualty insurance	38	40	*4.7*	920	811	36,030	35,911	30,307	28,045	*2.1*
6360	Title insurance	5	5	*5.9*	43	38	27,628	30,526	1,328	1,125	*2.1*
6370	Pension, health, and welfare funds	6	4	*2.7*	46	48	28,957	29,167	1,553	1,579	*2.6*
6400	Insurance agents, brokers, and service	172	177	*3.5*	855	859	28,150	30,491	24,816	27,505	*2.5*
6500	Real estate	257	253	*3.4*	1,893	1,977	18,536	17,653	37,419	36,767	*3.2*
6510	Real estate operators and lessors	95	98	*3.5*	739	863	15,037	14,795	13,293	14,542	*4.0*
6530	Real estate agents and managers	113	107	*3.2*	943	967	20,759	19,793	20,814	18,699	*3.0*
6540	Title abstract offices	8	7	*3.1*	69	32	21,971	21,250	1,143	693	*2.7*
6550	Subdividers and developers	38	35	*3.8*	129	94	20,341	21,191	1,842	2,323	*1.9*
6552	Subdividers and developers, n.e.c.	16	16	*5.6*	68	50	29,000	26,480	1,037	1,117	*1.8*
6553	Cemetery subdividers and developers	21	18	*2.9*	60	42	10,200	14,476	756	1,106	*1.9*
6710	Holding offices	8	8	*3.3*	119	117	46,050	46,496	5,786	5,720	*1.5*
6790	Miscellaneous investing	10	9	*5.4*	195	29	14,872	34,897	3,824	1,231	*1.9*
LAWRENCE, PA											
60 –	**Finance, insurance, and real estate**	149	143	*0.6*	1,687	1,732	21,740	23,085	37,930	40,232	*0.4*
6000	Depository institutions	53	51	*0.9*	642	622	22,336	24,000	13,342	14,222	*0.5*
6020	Commercial banks	28	28	*0.7*	382	381	22,681	24,157	7,759	8,377	*0.4*
6030	Savings institutions	11	10	*1.3*	199	179	20,201	22,011	4,108	4,392	*1.8*
6300	Insurance carriers	12	11	*0.6*	502	532	19,625	23,571	11,584	11,958	*0.4*
6400	Insurance agents, brokers, and service	39	35	*0.7*	151	157	21,033	21,325	4,206	4,472	*0.4*
6500	Real estate	34	33	*0.4*	119	145	10,387	11,117	1,516	1,758	*0.2*
6510	Real estate operators and lessors	12	12	*0.4*	57	58	9,544	10,069	588	519	*0.1*
6530	Real estate agents and managers	15	14	*0.4*	38	60	12,105	11,200	515	783	*0.1*
6550	Subdividers and developers	6	6	*0.6*	24	22	9,667	11,455	313	334	*0.3*
LEBANON, PA											
60 –	**Finance, insurance, and real estate**	173	173	*0.7*	1,516	1,489	21,847	23,046	34,228	34,569	*0.3*
6000	Depository institutions	49	51	*0.9*	733	697	21,981	24,539	16,502	17,110	*0.6*
6020	Commercial banks	41	44	*1.2*	670	632	22,663	25,722	15,449	16,001	*0.7*
6100	Nondepository institutions	15	15	*1.0*	88	75	17,136	15,307	1,301	1,174	*0.2*
6140	Personal credit institutions	11	10	*1.4*	66	61	14,000	11,672	790	687	*0.4*
6300	Insurance carriers	7	7	*0.4*	149	134	30,148	33,134	4,307	3,763	*0.1*
6400	Insurance agents, brokers, and service	42	38	*0.7*	174	163	22,207	23,288	4,357	4,165	*0.4*
6500	Real estate	50	51	*0.7*	306	349	12,092	13,043	4,460	4,981	*0.4*
6510	Real estate operators and lessors	21	22	*0.8*	219	270	11,562	12,252	3,151	3,635	*1.0*
6530	Real estate agents and managers	15	15	*0.5*	32	39	14,125	14,769	487	661	*0.1*
6540	Title abstract offices	3	3	*1.3*	24	15	13,500	17,067	330	259	*1.0*
6550	Subdividers and developers	11	11	*1.2*	31	25	12,645	16,480	492	426	*0.3*
6552	Subdividers and developers, n.e.c.	3	3	*1.1*	9	5	20,444	35,200	216	172	*0.3*
6553	Cemetery subdividers and developers	7	7	*1.1*	22	19	9,455	11,368	272	240	*0.4*
LEHIGH, PA											
60 –	**Finance, insurance, and real estate**	645	670	*2.8*	10,052	10,674	28,557	28,996	284,455	312,588	*2.9*
6000	Depository institutions	129	132	*2.4*	1,975	1,872	23,236	25,515	50,108	47,753	*1.7*
6020	Commercial banks	97	96	*2.5*	1,596	1,441	23,504	25,593	40,630	36,489	*1.6*
6060	Credit unions	19	19	*2.3*	224	241	18,018	21,046	4,609	5,140	*4.3*
6100	Nondepository institutions	61	77	*5.3*	625	880	34,509	33,423	18,495	30,890	*5.6*
6140	Personal credit institutions	26	33	*4.6*	321	499	36,137	34,766	9,900	17,825	*10.4*
6150	Business credit institutions	8	10	*8.5*	41	176	40,390	38,045	1,879	6,560	*6.1*

Source: County Business Patterns, 1994/95, CBP-94/95, U.S. Department of Commerce, Washington, D.C., November 1997. SIC categories for which data were suppressed or not available for both 1994 and 1995 are not displayed. The employment columns represent mid-March employment in the year. Pay per employee is calculated by dividing 1st Quarter payroll, annualized, by mid-March employment. The columns headed "% State" show the county's percentage of the state total for the SIC in 1995; for example, 1.4% for SIC 6000 means that the county had 1.4 percent of the state's total establishments (or payroll) in SIC 6000 in 1995. A dash (-) is used to indicate that data are not available or cannot be calculated; nec means not elsewhere classified.

Continued on next page.

SIC	Industry	No. Establishments			Employment		Pay / Employee		Annual Payroll ($ 000)		
		1994	1995	% State	1994	1995	1994	1995	1994	1995	% State
LEHIGH, PA - [continued]											
6160	Mortgage bankers and brokers	25	32	5.7	253	186	31,510	25,462	6,244	5,580	2.4
6200	Security and commodity brokers	42	46	3.2	468	441	56,376	62,912	23,487	26,331	2.5
6210	Security brokers and dealers	23	26	3.1	369	373	66,667	68,643	21,310	23,911	3.3
6280	Security and commodity services	19	19	3.2	99	68	18,020	31,471	2,177	2,418	0.7
6300	Insurance carriers	58	60	3.1	5,038	5,518	27,146	26,305	131,586	145,647	4.6
6310	Life insurance	21	24	3.5	3,086	3,170	26,542	26,861	78,629	83,465	7.7
6320	Medical service and health insurance	5	5	4.5	398	402	21,819	23,154	8,991	10,165	1.6
6330	Fire, marine, and casualty insurance	24	24	2.8	1,538	1,909	29,935	26,137	43,798	50,946	3.9
6400	Insurance agents, brokers, and service	125	133	2.6	581	604	32,585	33,669	24,542	24,467	2.2
6500	Real estate	215	203	2.7	964	932	16,888	16,206	16,889	16,547	1.4
6510	Real estate operators and lessors	86	76	2.7	491	423	16,073	16,189	8,412	7,641	2.1
6530	Real estate agents and managers	89	88	2.7	309	348	16,078	15,529	5,354	5,883	0.9
6540	Title abstract offices	7	6	2.7	38	11	24,211	17,091	482	232	0.9
6550	Subdividers and developers	30	28	3.0	104	120	21,962	18,367	2,262	2,245	1.8
6552	Subdividers and developers, n.e.c.	8	8	2.8	38	50	40,947	29,760	1,410	1,395	2.3
6553	Cemetery subdividers and developers	22	19	3.1	66	69	11,030	10,319	852	846	1.4
6790	Miscellaneous investing	3	5	3.0	3	5	13,333	12,000	51	67	0.1
6799	Investors, n.e.c.	3	5	5.7	3	5	13,333	12,000	51	67	0.2
LUZERNE, PA											
60 –	**Finance, insurance, and real estate**	623	599	2.5	7,359	6,288	24,015	28,182	190,996	169,601	1.6
6000	Depository institutions	189	149	2.7	3,033	2,071	21,606	22,905	73,345	46,474	1.7
6020	Commercial banks	129	91	2.4	2,380	1,391	22,608	24,894	60,608	32,683	1.4
6030	Savings institutions	22	21	2.8	509	509	18,900	20,157	10,310	11,184	4.5
6060	Credit unions	38	37	4.5	144	171	14,611	14,901	2,427	2,607	2.2
6100	Nondepository institutions	47	46	3.2	825	831	22,575	23,471	18,494	18,873	3.4
6140	Personal credit institutions	24	26	3.7	120	111	25,233	29,586	3,174	3,383	2.0
6200	Security and commodity brokers	29	38	2.6	274	284	53,971	69,507	15,010	15,719	1.5
6300	Insurance carriers	50	52	2.7	1,595	1,409	24,539	28,324	41,353	40,448	1.3
6310	Life insurance	23	20	2.9	616	318	23,110	29,371	14,281	8,858	0.8
6400	Insurance agents, brokers, and service	130	130	2.5	662	627	23,184	24,791	16,130	16,067	1.4
6500	Real estate	167	171	2.3	827	947	19,831	24,321	18,695	21,973	1.9
6510	Real estate operators and lessors	67	66	2.4	380	420	21,221	32,467	9,291	11,260	3.1
6530	Real estate agents and managers	57	57	1.7	318	375	19,585	18,976	6,662	7,662	1.2
6540	Title abstract offices	7	8	3.5	41	41	21,659	17,268	974	1,045	4.0
6550	Subdividers and developers	34	35	3.8	86	105	13,767	14,438	1,579	1,659	1.4
6552	Subdividers and developers, n.e.c.	8	8	2.8	15	25	12,267	14,400	348	372	0.6
6553	Cemetery subdividers and developers	26	27	4.4	71	80	14,085	14,450	1,231	1,287	2.2
LYCOMING, PA											
60 –	**Finance, insurance, and real estate**	229	239	1.0	2,769	2,224	23,006	24,847	59,201	53,296	0.5
6000	Depository institutions	57	57	1.0	1,154	913	21,588	25,253	22,230	21,848	0.8
6020	Commercial banks	42	42	1.1	1,087	846	21,958	25,858	21,085	20,685	0.9
6140	Personal credit institutions	9	9	1.3	62	41	14,516	25,756	890	1,005	0.6
6200	Security and commodity brokers	8	12	0.8	75	72	73,867	79,556	4,730	5,598	0.5
6300	Insurance carriers	20	23	1.2	749	716	21,031	24,168	15,732	15,697	0.5
6330	Fire, marine, and casualty insurance	9	10	1.2	422	370	21,545	28,086	9,619	9,464	0.7
6400	Insurance agents, brokers, and service	55	58	1.1	177	188	20,181	21,468	4,170	4,509	0.4
6500	Real estate	69	71	1.0	446	268	19,650	12,940	8,373	3,854	0.3
6510	Real estate operators and lessors	24	25	0.9	91	80	15,033	16,100	1,558	1,478	0.4
6530	Real estate agents and managers	33	33	1.0	256	95	25,500	13,600	5,769	1,399	0.2
6550	Subdividers and developers	11	12	1.3	98	90	8,816	9,511	1,012	966	0.8
6552	Subdividers and developers, n.e.c.	4	5	1.8	60	56	6,800	7,000	436	400	0.7
6553	Cemetery subdividers and developers	7	7	1.1	38	34	12,000	13,647	576	566	0.9
MCKEAN, PA											
60 –	**Finance, insurance, and real estate**	87	89	0.4	430	395	18,428	19,676	8,465	8,411	0.1
6000	Depository institutions	31	30	0.5	258	248	17,519	19,113	5,002	5,182	0.2

Source: County Business Patterns, 1994/95, CBP-94/95, U.S. Department of Commerce, Washington, D.C., November 1997. SIC categories for which data were suppressed or not available for both 1994 and 1995 are *not* displayed. The employment columns represent mid-March employment in the year. Pay per employee is calculated by dividing 1st Quarter payroll, annualized, by mid-March employment. The columns headed "% State" show the county's percentage of the state total for the SIC in 1995; for example, 1.4% for SIC 6000 means that the county had 1.4 percent of the state's total establishments (or payroll) in SIC 6000 in 1995. A dash (-) is used to indicate that data are not available or cannot be calculated; *nec* means not elsewhere classified.

Continued on next page.

SIC	Industry	No. Establishments			Employment		Pay / Employee		Annual Payroll ($ 000)		
		1994	1995	% State	1994	1995	1994	1995	1994	1995	% State
MCKEAN, PA - [continued]											
6020	Commercial banks	17	16	0.4	177	174	19,119	20,322	3,721	3,832	0.2
6400	Insurance agents, brokers, and service	28	31	0.6	73	68	20,658	22,353	1,503	1,644	0.1
6500	Real estate	19	19	0.3	39	35	8,821	10,286	382	389	0.0
6510	Real estate operators and lessors	6	6	0.2	19	18	9,684	11,111	184	199	0.1
MERCER, PA											
60 –	**Finance, insurance, and real estate**	196	198	0.8	1,456	1,428	22,363	23,594	33,930	35,298	0.3
6000	Depository institutions	55	55	1.0	827	822	21,582	23,231	18,208	19,656	0.7
6020	Commercial banks	41	42	1.1	731	724	21,806	23,575	16,391	17,741	0.8
6140	Personal credit institutions	9	8	1.1	30	28	19,733	25,429	708	755	0.4
6300	Insurance carriers	14	15	0.8	188	179	28,213	28,782	5,203	4,849	0.2
6310	Life insurance	6	7	1.0	168	156	26,333	25,923	4,224	3,823	0.4
6400	Insurance agents, brokers, and service	45	45	0.9	150	156	21,253	21,513	3,807	4,088	0.4
6500	Real estate	56	58	0.8	177	171	11,209	12,398	2,464	2,495	0.2
6510	Real estate operators and lessors	24	24	0.9	69	76	10,203	10,053	907	889	0.2
6530	Real estate agents and managers	19	19	0.6	56	57	15,357	16,912	954	1,019	0.2
6550	Subdividers and developers	10	11	1.2	52	36	8,077	10,222	510	461	0.4
MIFFLIN, PA											
60 –	**Finance, insurance, and real estate**	64	69	0.3	451	421	20,204	20,466	9,221	8,447	0.1
6000	Depository institutions	23	23	0.4	254	234	19,921	21,128	4,964	4,736	0.2
6020	Commercial banks	17	17	0.5	214	193	20,542	21,741	4,211	3,934	0.2
6400	Insurance agents, brokers, and service	17	18	0.4	57	67	18,105	21,075	1,288	1,436	0.1
6500	Real estate	14	18	0.2	48	46	11,917	15,652	693	750	0.1
6510	Real estate operators and lessors	7	8	0.3	22	23	15,455	20,000	418	439	0.1
6530	Real estate agents and managers	3	6	0.2	3	5	13,333	8,800	40	87	0.0
6550	Subdividers and developers	4	4	0.4	23	18	8,348	12,000	235	224	0.2
6553	Cemetery subdividers and developers	4	4	0.6	23	18	8,348	12,000	235	224	0.4
MONROE, PA											
60 –	**Finance, insurance, and real estate**	264	246	1.0	1,694	1,585	18,028	19,601	33,750	31,432	0.3
6000	Depository institutions	60	46	0.8	501	506	16,375	18,530	9,813	9,481	0.3
6020	Commercial banks	45	32	0.8	365	355	16,088	17,499	7,107	6,449	0.3
6030	Savings institutions	9	9	1.2	111	127	17,946	22,520	2,393	2,724	1.1
6060	Credit unions	6	5	0.6	25	24	13,600	12,667	313	308	0.3
6100	Nondepository institutions	25	23	1.6	77	74	21,558	23,946	1,930	1,988	0.4
6140	Personal credit institutions	7	7	1.0	24	27	25,667	29,630	621	747	0.4
6160	Mortgage bankers and brokers	18	16	2.8	53	47	19,698	20,681	1,309	1,241	0.5
6400	Insurance agents, brokers, and service	42	44	0.9	179	178	22,369	22,427	3,992	3,900	0.3
6500	Real estate	115	118	1.6	842	783	14,679	15,903	13,940	12,936	1.1
6510	Real estate operators and lessors	16	15	0.5	78	81	11,897	12,346	1,173	938	0.3
6530	Real estate agents and managers	65	64	1.9	581	451	15,208	14,998	9,710	7,421	1.2
6540	Title abstract offices	13	15	6.6	69	52	18,203	18,462	1,260	1,081	4.1
6550	Subdividers and developers	17	18	1.9	110	188	11,636	19,064	1,753	3,325	2.7
6552	Subdividers and developers, n.e.c.	14	13	4.6	100	178	11,920	19,596	1,656	3,207	5.3
6553	Cemetery subdividers and developers	3	3	0.5	10	10	8,800	9,600	97	103	0.2
MONTGOMERY, PA											
60 –	**Finance, insurance, and real estate**	2,545	2,564	10.8	44,863	44,797	33,107	35,213	1,543,389	1,643,149	15.4
6000	Depository institutions	375	367	6.6	6,064	5,330	26,759	29,472	167,434	152,138	5.4
6020	Commercial banks	246	232	6.2	4,589	3,805	26,316	29,586	127,025	107,827	4.7
6030	Savings institutions	77	78	10.3	1,031	1,040	24,601	25,892	26,175	27,194	11.0
6090	Functions closely related to banking	9	14	6.9	87	111	77,103	63,712	4,870	6,750	8.3
6100	Nondepository institutions	168	169	11.7	3,166	3,809	36,303	49,107	116,570	187,445	34.0
6140	Personal credit institutions	50	51	7.2	794	835	37,249	90,970	27,527	52,870	30.8
6150	Business credit institutions	23	26	22.0	239	1,014	37,289	38,458	8,523	36,243	33.6
6160	Mortgage bankers and brokers	95	90	16.0	2,133	1,959	35,841	36,798	80,520	98,056	42.5
6200	Security and commodity brokers	196	211	14.5	1,737	2,145	70,508	58,665	121,155	138,682	13.0

Source: County Business Patterns, 1994/95, CBP-94/95, U.S. Department of Commerce, Washington, D.C., November 1997. SIC categories for which data were suppressed or not available for both 1994 and 1995 are not displayed. The employment columns represent mid-March employment in the year. Pay per employee is calculated by dividing 1st Quarter payroll, annualized, by mid-March employment. The columns headed "% State" show the county's percentage of the state total for the SIC in 1995; for example, 1.4% for SIC 6000 means that the county had 1.4 percent of the state's total establishments (or payroll) in SIC 6000 in 1995. A dash (-) is used to indicate that data are not available or cannot be calculated; nec means not elsewhere classified.

Continued on next page.

SIC	Industry	No. Establishments			Employment		Pay / Employee		Annual Payroll ($ 000)		
		1994	1995	% State	1994	1995	1994	1995	1994	1995	% State
MONTGOMERY, PA - [continued]											
6210	Security brokers and dealers	98	103	12.4	1,127	1,415	79,915	62,123	80,095	89,310	12.3
6300	Insurance carriers	265	287	14.8	17,213	17,244	34,993	34,904	589,351	583,810	18.5
6310	Life insurance	111	129	18.7	10,906	10,280	35,569	33,533	363,283	327,692	30.4
6320	Medical service and health insurance	15	15	13.6	975	1,085	29,797	35,174	31,138	40,179	6.2
6321	Accident and health insurance	7	6	14.6	269	233	32,074	39,931	8,713	9,039	13.8
6324	Hospital and medical service plans	8	9	13.0	706	852	28,929	33,873	22,425	31,140	5.4
6330	Fire, marine, and casualty insurance	85	93	10.9	4,596	5,153	36,393	37,696	172,356	188,116	14.4
6360	Title insurance	18	14	16.5	219	225	31,872	30,613	8,599	7,084	13.4
6370	Pension, health, and welfare funds	31	29	19.3	478	466	19,464	32,094	12,113	18,341	30.7
6400	Insurance agents, brokers, and service	582	590	11.5	4,476	4,532	33,387	35,492	162,377	178,627	16.0
6500	Real estate	841	826	11.1	6,561	6,139	20,808	22,634	153,063	148,786	12.9
6510	Real estate operators and lessors	306	296	10.6	2,105	2,127	18,928	20,402	44,957	44,925	12.5
6530	Real estate agents and managers	434	421	12.7	3,720	3,466	21,472	23,481	89,252	88,290	14.0
6540	Title abstract offices	33	25	11.1	214	80	25,402	27,900	5,842	2,715	10.4
6550	Subdividers and developers	55	61	6.6	442	411	22,217	25,061	11,180	10,841	8.9
6552	Subdividers and developers, n.e.c.	30	35	12.3	133	140	28,782	31,857	4,471	4,180	6.9
6553	Cemetery subdividers and developers	24	24	3.9	308	266	19,364	21,519	6,663	6,589	11.0
6700	Holding and other investment offices	111	107	16.0	5,587	5,532	34,754	36,747	230,625	251,015	36.3
6710	Holding offices	47	41	17.1	1,250	1,193	46,310	42,471	56,140	50,318	13.0
6730	Trusts	20	19	9.3	75	71	17,920	18,761	1,305	1,438	3.4
6732	Educational, religious, etc. trusts	8	8	7.3	29	34	10,759	15,765	391	639	2.2
6733	Trusts, n.e.c.	12	11	11.7	46	37	22,435	21,514	914	799	5.8
6794	Patent owners and lessors	10	10	18.2	288	322	42,431	42,087	13,137	14,099	50.6
6799	Investors, n.e.c.	17	15	17.0	265	282	50,868	66,681	16,973	17,458	58.5
MONTOUR, PA											
60 –	**Finance, insurance, and real estate**	31	30	0.1	216	191	20,574	26,304	5,128	5,136	0.0
6000	Depository institutions	11	11	0.2	145	122	16,855	25,049	3,163	3,069	0.1
6020	Commercial banks	8	8	0.2	111	85	17,333	29,365	2,578	2,441	0.1
6060	Credit unions	3	3	0.4	34	37	15,294	15,135	585	628	0.5
NORTHAMPTON, PA											
60 –	**Finance, insurance, and real estate**	397	382	1.6	3,930	3,532	28,959	30,826	115,832	109,561	1.0
6000	Depository institutions	125	123	2.2	1,948	1,779	26,240	27,991	49,529	49,449	1.8
6020	Commercial banks	97	93	2.5	1,737	1,556	26,655	28,602	44,685	43,991	1.9
6030	Savings institutions	14	14	1.8	152	151	24,842	28,265	3,843	4,402	1.8
6100	Nondepository institutions	21	20	1.4	74	74	26,432	26,919	2,608	2,002	0.4
6140	Personal credit institutions	9	10	1.4	34	41	22,588	22,634	868	966	0.6
6200	Security and commodity brokers	14	14	1.0	73	57	72,822	41,053	4,693	2,812	0.3
6210	Security brokers and dealers	10	10	1.2	70	51	75,714	44,627	4,643	2,732	0.4
6280	Security and commodity services	4	4	0.7	3	6	5,333	10,667	50	80	0.0
6300	Insurance carriers	34	30	1.5	970	797	30,936	30,128	30,592	24,901	0.8
6330	Fire, marine, and casualty insurance	19	17	2.0	448	394	36,196	35,421	16,748	13,803	1.1
6400	Insurance agents, brokers, and service	82	78	1.5	362	328	25,746	27,183	9,723	9,215	0.8
6500	Real estate	110	107	1.4	445	440	26,607	35,227	14,228	16,613	1.4
6510	Real estate operators and lessors	36	36	1.3	161	176	21,317	21,273	3,912	4,224	1.2
6530	Real estate agents and managers	50	47	1.4	124	102	14,645	18,314	2,260	2,254	0.4
6550	Subdividers and developers	21	21	2.3	148	154	43,757	63,662	7,876	9,992	8.2
6552	Subdividers and developers, n.e.c.	7	7	2.5	86	90	65,488	96,444	6,699	8,851	14.5
6553	Cemetery subdividers and developers	14	14	2.3	62	64	13,613	17,563	1,177	1,141	1.9
6700	Holding and other investment offices	11	10	1.5	58	57	73,310	110,877	4,459	4,569	0.7
NORTHUMBERLAND, PA											
60 –	**Finance, insurance, and real estate**	123	121	0.5	978	904	21,943	21,381	21,538	20,588	0.2
6000	Depository institutions	41	39	0.7	559	493	21,682	21,753	11,660	10,827	0.4
6020	Commercial banks	32	31	0.8	509	465	22,106	21,884	10,747	10,231	0.4
6300	Insurance carriers	7	7	0.4	126	107	24,857	18,729	3,050	2,522	0.1
6400	Insurance agents, brokers, and service	30	28	0.5	142	140	22,648	22,000	3,592	3,613	0.3

Source: County Business Patterns, 1994/95, CBP-94/95, U.S. Department of Commerce, Washington, D.C., November 1997. SIC categories for which data were suppressed or not available for both 1994 and 1995 are not displayed. The employment columns represent mid-March employment in the year. Pay per employee is calculated by dividing 1st Quarter payroll, annualized, by mid-March employment. The columns headed "% State" show the county's percentage of the state total for the SIC in 1995; for example, 1.4% for SIC 6000 means that the county had 1.4 percent of the state's total establishments (or payroll) in SIC 6000 in 1995. A dash (-) is used to indicate that data are not available or cannot be calculated; nec means not elsewhere classified.

Continued on next page.

SIC	Industry	No. Establishments			Employment		Pay / Employee		Annual Payroll ($ 000)		
		1994	1995	% State	1994	1995	1994	1995	1994	1995	% State
NORTHUMBERLAND, PA - [continued]											
6500	Real estate	37	38	0.5	115	123	13,530	16,325	1,854	2,132	0.2
6510	Real estate operators and lessors	15	15	0.5	41	40	12,000	17,100	628	733	0.2
6530	Real estate agents and managers	14	15	0.5	36	50	16,111	15,440	639	800	0.1
6550	Subdividers and developers	8	8	0.9	38	33	12,737	16,727	587	599	0.5
PERRY, PA											
60 –	**Finance, insurance, and real estate**	52	55	0.2	268	269	15,567	17,814	4,663	5,162	0.0
6000	Depository institutions	19	19	0.3	194	184	16,124	17,174	3,359	3,334	0.1
6400	Insurance agents, brokers, and service	14	16	0.3	36	41	19,333	20,780	695	820	0.1
6500	Real estate	13	12	0.2	28	25	9,143	9,760	371	358	0.0
6530	Real estate agents and managers	4	3	0.1	4	4	10,000	10,000	57	39	0.0
6553	Cemetery subdividers and developers	5	5	0.8	11	9	2,909	3,556	35	35	0.1
PHILADELPHIA, PA											
60 –	**Finance, insurance, and real estate**	2,247	2,269	9.6	71,759	69,313	32,676	36,768	2,299,952	2,393,695	22.5
6000	Depository institutions	613	603	10.8	21,919	19,124	29,605	33,858	651,446	584,569	20.9
6020	Commercial banks	315	301	8.0	17,178	14,348	30,289	35,575	519,592	445,747	19.6
6030	Savings institutions	98	92	12.1	1,144	1,135	25,192	28,307	29,556	31,902	12.9
6090	Functions closely related to banking	109	121	59.9	1,006	1,200	25,996	26,617	26,203	30,908	38.1
6100	Nondepository institutions	71	73	5.1	1,313	808	43,129	53,465	55,414	42,188	7.7
6140	Personal credit institutions	29	34	4.8	418	284	48,967	47,873	20,288	10,609	6.2
6200	Security and commodity brokers	205	216	14.8	4,860	5,024	79,419	88,990	353,861	414,613	38.8
6210	Security brokers and dealers	138	142	17.0	3,316	3,224	83,718	88,974	251,713	278,979	38.6
6280	Security and commodity services	59	64	10.8	1,191	1,440	77,306	101,658	87,175	121,180	36.8
6300	Insurance carriers	178	184	9.5	26,193	26,889	30,633	33,296	783,483	851,869	27.0
6310	Life insurance	61	64	9.3	12,788	14,221	17,692	18,687	220,270	275,060	25.5
6320	Medical service and health insurance	12	13	11.8	3,735	3,823	38,006	43,594	131,492	152,879	23.8
6330	Fire, marine, and casualty insurance	61	64	7.5	8,662	7,638	45,112	53,659	392,594	379,119	29.0
6360	Title insurance	15	14	16.5	497	588	61,899	57,020	26,307	27,410	51.8
6370	Pension, health, and welfare funds	23	25	16.7	470	605	23,702	31,451	11,293	16,924	28.3
6400	Insurance agents, brokers, and service	252	253	4.9	3,259	3,208	43,319	47,320	147,540	156,501	14.0
6500	Real estate	832	838	11.3	12,990	13,235	19,446	21,070	256,619	275,975	23.9
6510	Real estate operators and lessors	358	345	12.4	3,210	3,125	18,358	19,700	61,564	61,458	17.1
6530	Real estate agents and managers	401	406	12.2	9,232	9,536	19,483	20,857	180,507	196,512	31.1
6540	Title abstract offices	23	22	9.7	180	157	23,200	19,261	3,839	3,279	12.6
6550	Subdividers and developers	39	41	4.4	358	386	26,179	37,959	9,753	12,740	10.5
6552	Subdividers and developers, n.e.c.	18	20	7.0	113	124	39,009	71,000	4,029	6,642	10.9
6553	Cemetery subdividers and developers	20	21	3.4	241	262	19,851	22,321	5,553	6,098	10.2
6700	Holding and other investment offices	89	94	14.1	924	848	49,602	88,901	41,319	59,110	8.6
6710	Holding offices	24	23	9.6	507	372	63,890	160,817	26,364	35,427	9.1
6730	Trusts	40	42	20.6	282	333	30,468	29,021	9,523	17,346	40.8
6732	Educational, religious, etc. trusts	28	29	26.4	151	192	40,291	33,750	6,754	13,915	48.5
6733	Trusts, n.e.c.	12	13	13.8	131	141	19,145	22,582	2,769	3,431	24.8
6799	Investors, n.e.c.	11	11	12.5	48	48	48,000	56,750	2,627	2,870	9.6
PIKE, PA											
60 –	**Finance, insurance, and real estate**	58	56	0.2	600	616	16,180	16,565	10,718	11,086	0.1
6000	Depository institutions	14	12	0.2	151	103	23,338	30,291	3,600	3,056	0.1
6020	Commercial banks	14	12	0.3	151	103	23,338	30,291	3,600	3,056	0.1
6500	Real estate	30	31	0.4	414	473	13,169	13,108	6,268	7,039	0.6
6530	Real estate agents and managers	20	23	0.7	303	377	12,475	12,541	4,486	5,546	0.9
6540	Title abstract offices	3	3	1.3	15	12	16,533	18,333	242	210	0.8
POTTER, PA											
60 –	**Finance, insurance, and real estate**	26	26	0.1	136	130	17,294	22,000	2,409	2,874	0.0

Source: County Business Patterns, 1994/95, CBP-94/95, U.S. Department of Commerce, Washington, D.C., November 1997. SIC categories for which data were suppressed or not available for both 1994 and 1995 are not displayed. The employment columns represent mid-March employment in the year. Pay per employee is calculated by dividing 1st Quarter payroll, annualized, by mid-March employment. The columns headed "% State" show the county's percentage of the state total for the SIC in 1995; for example, 1.4% for SIC 6000 means that the county had 1.4 percent of the state's total establishments (or payroll) in SIC 6000 in 1995. A dash (-) is used to indicate that data are not available or cannot be calculated; nec means not elsewhere classified.

Continued on next page.

SIC	Industry	No. Establishments			Employment		Pay / Employee		Annual Payroll ($ 000)		
		1994	1995	% State	1994	1995	1994	1995	1994	1995	% State
POTTER, PA - [continued]											
6000	Depository institutions	8	8	0.1	86	78	15,767	23,179	1,293	1,770	0.1
6020	Commercial banks	8	8	0.2	86	78	15,767	23,179	1,293	1,770	0.1
6400	Insurance agents, brokers, and service	9	8	0.2	16	16	10,750	13,500	203	220	0.0
SCHUYLKILL, PA											
60 –	**Finance, insurance, and real estate**	232	229	1.0	1,803	1,698	20,754	21,894	38,262	37,535	0.4
6000	Depository institutions	85	80	1.4	1,103	967	21,893	23,950	23,587	22,235	0.8
6020	Commercial banks	65	64	1.7	988	903	21,453	24,434	22,067	21,136	0.9
6030	Savings institutions	13	9	1.2	86	34	28,744	17,059	1,023	571	0.2
6060	Credit unions	7	7	0.8	29	30	16,552	17,200	497	528	0.4
6100	Nondepository institutions	10	10	0.7	61	61	21,574	25,377	1,307	1,571	0.3
6300	Insurance carriers	14	15	0.8	208	203	23,135	24,099	4,837	5,304	0.2
6310	Life insurance	7	7	1.0	175	149	22,674	22,658	3,847	3,195	0.3
6400	Insurance agents, brokers, and service	63	63	1.2	237	262	19,089	17,908	5,389	5,464	0.5
6500	Real estate	55	56	0.8	180	195	13,311	13,046	2,740	2,594	0.2
6510	Real estate operators and lessors	17	19	0.7	33	34	11,758	15,882	520	620	0.2
6530	Real estate agents and managers	21	19	0.6	70	73	13,886	13,589	1,118	1,144	0.2
6540	Title abstract offices	3	3	1.3	10	8	15,600	17,500	178	113	0.4
6550	Subdividers and developers	14	15	1.6	67	80	13,134	10,900	924	717	0.6
SNYDER, PA											
60 –	**Finance, insurance, and real estate**	64	66	0.3	393	368	17,069	20,054	7,376	7,896	0.1
6000	Depository institutions	15	15	0.3	262	251	17,191	19,968	4,984	5,490	0.2
6020	Commercial banks	15	15	0.4	262	251	17,191	19,968	4,984	5,490	0.2
6400	Insurance agents, brokers, and service	14	17	0.3	47	49	18,979	18,367	980	950	0.1
6500	Real estate	30	29	0.4	64	53	13,000	15,019	877	936	0.1
6510	Real estate operators and lessors	12	12	0.4	32	31	13,500	13,806	486	512	0.1
6530	Real estate agents and managers	14	13	0.4	28	17	13,571	19,529	352	384	0.1
6550	Subdividers and developers	3	3	0.3	4	4	5,000	6,000	34	30	0.0
6553	Cemetery subdividers and developers	3	3	0.5	4	4	5,000	6,000	34	30	0.1
SOMERSET, PA											
60 –	**Finance, insurance, and real estate**	119	117	0.5	867	1,450	20,429	16,135	18,196	23,252	0.2
6000	Depository institutions	37	34	0.6	477	473	18,113	19,214	8,957	9,349	0.3
6020	Commercial banks	37	34	0.9	477	473	18,113	19,214	8,957	9,349	0.4
6300	Insurance carriers	5	4	0.2	162	136	26,864	29,206	3,996	3,988	0.1
6400	Insurance agents, brokers, and service	35	31	0.6	104	113	16,808	16,460	1,880	1,954	0.2
6500	Real estate	31	36	0.5	84	411	15,333	14,414	1,491	5,117	0.4
6510	Real estate operators and lessors	18	19	0.7	39	50	9,231	9,680	397	477	0.1
6530	Real estate agents and managers	5	6	0.2	36	344	24,000	15,442	967	4,420	0.7
6550	Subdividers and developers	6	8	0.9	8	10	7,000	7,200	91	157	0.1
SUSQUEHANNA, PA											
60 –	**Finance, insurance, and real estate**	52	49	0.2	388	291	18,000	26,186	6,843	8,292	0.1
6000	Depository institutions	21	20	0.4	296	199	16,635	27,678	4,570	6,114	0.2
6020	Commercial banks	21	20	0.5	296	199	16,635	27,678	4,570	6,114	0.3
6510	Real estate operators and lessors	3	3	0.1	9	12	10,222	8,667	84	83	0.0
6530	Real estate agents and managers	5	5	0.2	21	21	8,571	8,952	401	377	0.1
TIOGA, PA											
60 –	**Finance, insurance, and real estate**	54	57	0.2	359	371	22,072	24,108	7,671	8,345	0.1
6000	Depository institutions	16	16	0.3	275	281	22,996	26,093	6,087	6,717	0.2
6020	Commercial banks	13	13	0.3	264	267	23,167	26,697	5,858	6,491	0.3
6400	Insurance agents, brokers, and service	19	20	0.4	48	51	18,333	18,039	926	929	0.1
6530	Real estate agents and managers	6	7	0.2	9	8	8,444	10,500	88	93	0.0
6550	Subdividers and developers	5	5	0.5	5	7	20,000	18,857	148	164	0.1
UNION, PA											
60 –	**Finance, insurance, and real estate**	58	60	0.3	373	358	20,011	23,609	8,084	9,565	0.1

Source: County Business Patterns, 1994/95, CBP-94/95, U.S. Department of Commerce, Washington, D.C., November 1997. SIC categories for which data were suppressed or not available for both 1994 and 1995 are not displayed. The employment columns represent mid-March employment in the year. Pay per employee is calculated by dividing 1st Quarter payroll, annualized, by mid-March employment. The columns headed "% State" show the county's percentage of the state total for the SIC in 1995; for example, 1.4% for SIC 6000 means that the county had 1.4 percent of the state's total establishments (or payroll) in SIC 6000 in 1995. A dash (-) is used to indicate that data are not available or cannot be calculated; nec means not elsewhere classified.

Continued on next page.

SIC	Industry	No. Establishments			Employment		Pay / Employee		Annual Payroll ($ 000)		
		1994	1995	% State	1994	1995	1994	1995	1994	1995	% State
UNION, PA - [continued]											
6000	Depository institutions	17	17	0.3	191	174	19,979	24,299	4,299	4,638	0.2
6200	Security and commodity brokers	4	4	0.3	3	6	17,333	17,333	77	132	0.0
6400	Insurance agents, brokers, and service	12	13	0.3	44	47	17,636	18,213	858	872	0.1
6500	Real estate	21	21	0.3	80	73	7,850	9,370	666	755	0.1
6510	Real estate operators and lessors	8	7	0.3	36	28	5,889	6,714	230	191	0.1
6530	Real estate agents and managers	10	11	0.3	37	38	10,595	12,421	390	516	0.1
6550	Subdividers and developers	3	3	0.3	7	7	3,429	3,429	46	48	0.0
6553	Cemetery subdividers and developers	3	3	0.5	7	7	3,429	3,429	46	48	0.1
VENANGO, PA											
60 –	**Finance, insurance, and real estate**	89	93	0.4	848	884	24,434	26,633	20,841	23,785	0.2
6000	Depository institutions	26	28	0.5	641	650	24,362	27,268	15,398	17,840	0.6
6020	Commercial banks	16	18	0.5	569	582	25,786	28,729	14,299	16,724	0.7
6200	Security and commodity brokers	7	7	0.5	34	38	50,000	48,526	1,565	1,804	0.2
6300	Insurance carriers	7	7	0.4	58	63	28,138	31,937	1,996	2,021	0.1
6400	Insurance agents, brokers, and service	20	21	0.4	54	63	18,370	18,222	1,102	1,224	0.1
6500	Real estate	24	25	0.3	45	57	10,311	9,895	528	605	0.1
6510	Real estate operators and lessors	10	11	0.4	20	26	10,200	8,923	222	247	0.1
6530	Real estate agents and managers	8	9	0.3	12	18	14,000	11,333	202	212	0.0
6550	Subdividers and developers	6	5	0.5	13	13	7,077	9,846	104	146	0.1
WARREN, PA											
60 –	**Finance, insurance, and real estate**	82	87	0.4	519	523	20,532	19,969	12,005	12,612	0.1
6000	Depository institutions	24	24	0.4	317	337	19,495	20,427	7,441	8,505	0.3
6200	Security and commodity brokers	6	7	0.5	17	19	72,235	47,789	1,104	1,109	0.1
6400	Insurance agents, brokers, and service	20	22	0.4	52	60	18,154	16,133	916	993	0.1
6500	Real estate	19	19	0.3	66	62	9,455	10,000	758	744	0.1
6510	Real estate operators and lessors	7	8	0.3	27	25	12,889	13,600	424	416	0.1
6530	Real estate agents and managers	6	5	0.2	26	22	6,615	7,636	189	184	0.0
6550	Subdividers and developers	6	6	0.6	13	15	8,000	7,467	145	144	0.1
6553	Cemetery subdividers and developers	6	6	1.0	13	15	8,000	7,467	145	144	0.2
WASHINGTON, PA											
60 –	**Finance, insurance, and real estate**	315	318	1.3	2,065	2,090	24,674	25,749	51,021	54,590	0.5
6000	Depository institutions	84	82	1.5	908	896	20,590	22,397	18,379	20,257	0.7
6020	Commercial banks	48	48	1.3	577	578	22,329	23,993	12,261	13,757	0.6
6030	Savings institutions	20	17	2.2	270	247	17,674	19,385	4,965	5,013	2.0
6060	Credit unions	16	17	2.1	61	71	17,049	19,887	1,153	1,487	1.3
6100	Nondepository institutions	17	17	1.2	75	89	23,360	20,090	1,800	1,864	0.3
6140	Personal credit institutions	11	9	1.3	56	56	24,571	22,214	1,381	1,242	0.7
6200	Security and commodity brokers	14	17	1.2	58	61	44,690	43,148	2,711	3,047	0.3
6210	Security brokers and dealers	9	11	1.3	36	37	48,556	44,541	1,568	1,873	0.3
6280	Security and commodity services	5	6	1.0	22	24	38,364	41,000	1,143	1,174	0.4
6300	Insurance carriers	20	19	1.0	205	225	26,185	29,209	5,877	6,697	0.2
6310	Life insurance	5	5	0.7	69	84	23,942	20,714	1,526	1,533	0.1
6400	Insurance agents, brokers, and service	82	82	1.6	290	285	20,041	25,502	6,598	7,163	0.6
6500	Real estate	93	97	1.3	469	481	18,311	20,258	9,292	10,009	0.9
6510	Real estate operators and lessors	40	40	1.4	269	265	19,881	22,717	5,510	5,668	1.6
6530	Real estate agents and managers	36	40	1.2	124	149	18,065	18,470	2,482	3,142	0.5
6550	Subdividers and developers	17	16	1.7	76	67	13,158	14,507	1,300	1,174	1.0
6700	Holding and other investment offices	5	4	0.6	60	53	135,733	108,377	6,364	5,553	0.8
WAYNE, PA											
60 –	**Finance, insurance, and real estate**	97	89	0.4	938	980	19,399	19,980	19,991	20,295	0.2
6000	Depository institutions	28	28	0.5	414	403	19,527	21,548	8,709	8,838	0.3
6300	Insurance carriers	3	3	0.2	17	17	32,706	35,765	572	618	0.0
6400	Insurance agents, brokers, and service	22	23	0.4	105	98	19,924	23,265	2,356	2,555	0.2

Source: County Business Patterns, 1994/95, CBP-94/95, U.S. Department of Commerce, Washington, D.C., November 1997. SIC categories for which data were suppressed or not available for both 1994 and 1995 are *not* displayed. The employment columns represent mid-March employment in the year. Pay per employee is calculated by dividing 1st Quarter payroll, annualized, by mid-March employment. The columns headed "% State" show the county's percentage of the state total for the SIC in 1995; for example, 1.4% for SIC 6000 means that the county had 1.4 percent of the state's total establishments (or payroll) in SIC 6000 in 1995. A dash (-) is used to indicate that data are not available or cannot be calculated; *nec* means not elsewhere classified.

Continued on next page.

SIC	Industry	No. Establishments			Employment		Pay / Employee		Annual Payroll ($ 000)		
		1994	1995	% State	1994	1995	1994	1995	1994	1995	% State
WAYNE, PA - [continued]											
6500	Real estate	37	30	0.4	380	436	13,979	12,303	6,431	6,202	0.5
6510	Real estate operators and lessors	7	4	0.1	25	13	6,080	7,385	251	173	0.0
6530	Real estate agents and managers	24	20	0.6	338	407	14,237	11,862	5,863	5,719	0.9
WESTMORELAND, PA											
60 –	**Finance, insurance, and real estate**	674	691	2.9	4,414	4,360	21,547	22,207	97,645	98,117	0.9
6000	Depository institutions	179	182	3.3	1,748	1,738	19,924	22,400	35,319	37,677	1.3
6020	Commercial banks	110	113	3.0	1,426	1,418	20,555	23,323	29,639	31,688	1.4
6030	Savings institutions	15	15	2.0	172	168	17,558	18,976	3,044	3,157	1.3
6060	Credit unions	54	54	6.5	150	152	16,640	17,579	2,636	2,832	2.4
6140	Personal credit institutions	25	31	4.4	134	145	23,582	25,186	3,339	3,445	2.0
6160	Mortgage bankers and brokers	6	6	1.1	56	45	27,357	20,089	1,471	1,198	0.5
6200	Security and commodity brokers	29	30	2.1	173	156	52,902	49,128	8,843	7,263	0.7
6210	Security brokers and dealers	18	19	2.3	95	109	66,316	50,018	5,506	5,822	0.8
6300	Insurance carriers	50	48	2.5	849	797	22,723	23,252	19,446	19,094	0.6
6310	Life insurance	16	15	2.2	454	405	18,097	17,057	7,648	6,646	0.6
6330	Fire, marine, and casualty insurance	24	26	3.1	342	355	29,345	31,110	10,689	11,814	0.9
6400	Insurance agents, brokers, and service	171	176	3.4	563	546	18,728	19,751	12,449	12,712	1.1
6500	Real estate	181	186	2.5	631	606	13,655	15,135	9,862	10,066	0.9
6510	Real estate operators and lessors	84	84	3.0	312	327	13,141	13,615	4,359	4,742	1.3
6530	Real estate agents and managers	64	70	2.1	143	136	13,427	17,206	2,198	2,265	0.4
6540	Title abstract offices	6	6	2.7	49	43	18,776	17,302	1,040	837	3.2
6550	Subdividers and developers	26	24	2.6	119	97	14,017	16,825	2,144	2,087	1.7
6552	Subdividers and developers, n.e.c.	6	4	1.4	12	5	24,000	29,600	384	351	0.6
6553	Cemetery subdividers and developers	19	19	3.1	107	89	12,897	16,180	1,735	1,687	2.8
6710	Holding offices	4	5	2.1	51	59	95,686	64,949	2,903	2,505	0.6
6733	Trusts, n.e.c.	15	13	13.8	117	163	8,923	6,896	1,453	1,533	11.1
WYOMING, PA											
60 –	**Finance, insurance, and real estate**	42	41	0.2	260	264	17,892	18,288	4,633	4,927	0.0
6000	Depository institutions	17	17	0.3	162	176	14,790	14,818	2,559	2,810	0.1
6020	Commercial banks	12	12	0.3	140	151	14,686	14,649	2,207	2,422	0.1
6400	Insurance agents, brokers, and service	13	12	0.2	55	54	28,000	27,481	1,514	1,449	0.1
6500	Real estate	8	7	0.1	14	16	26,286	27,750	271	364	0.0
YORK, PA											
60 –	**Finance, insurance, and real estate**	583	593	2.5	6,148	6,202	26,768	27,986	173,493	179,293	1.7
6000	Depository institutions	163	163	2.9	3,130	3,058	23,456	24,578	76,314	76,126	2.7
6020	Commercial banks	114	123	3.3	2,554	2,556	24,590	25,742	63,280	65,370	2.9
6100	Nondepository institutions	28	35	2.4	170	193	34,494	28,021	5,872	5,226	0.9
6200	Security and commodity brokers	21	21	1.4	171	196	69,474	63,388	10,687	11,675	1.1
6210	Security brokers and dealers	12	12	1.4	138	155	70,174	58,555	8,302	8,618	1.2
6300	Insurance carriers	39	33	1.7	967	1,053	34,771	34,420	35,205	37,943	1.2
6330	Fire, marine, and casualty insurance	21	22	2.6	592	633	38,601	41,991	23,208	26,281	2.0
6400	Insurance agents, brokers, and service	117	121	2.4	831	830	27,143	31,764	26,414	28,558	2.6
6500	Real estate	199	202	2.7	792	786	17,207	18,239	15,263	16,203	1.4
6510	Real estate operators and lessors	57	59	2.1	232	231	16,276	15,030	3,864	3,811	1.1
6530	Real estate agents and managers	100	100	3.0	365	376	18,301	20,840	7,925	9,157	1.4
6540	Title abstract offices	8	8	3.5	75	47	18,187	20,681	1,343	1,070	4.1
6550	Subdividers and developers	30	30	3.2	116	120	15,138	15,567	1,901	1,890	1.6
6552	Subdividers and developers, n.e.c.	6	6	2.1	12	12	34,667	29,000	346	253	0.4
6553	Cemetery subdividers and developers	24	23	3.7	104	108	12,885	14,074	1,555	1,629	2.7
6710	Holding offices	7	8	3.3	57	64	54,947	47,250	3,240	2,854	0.7
6790	Miscellaneous investing	4	4	2.4	24	12	16,500	27,667	399	404	0.6

Source: County Business Patterns, 1994/95, CBP-94/95, U.S. Department of Commerce, Washington, D.C., November 1997. SIC categories for which data were suppressed or not available for both 1994 and 1995 are not displayed. The employment columns represent mid-March employment in the year. Pay per employee is calculated by dividing 1st Quarter payroll, annualized, by mid-March employment. The columns headed "% State" show the county's percentage of the state total for the SIC in 1995; for example, 1.4% for SIC 6000 means that the county had 1.4 percent of the state's total establishments (or payroll) in SIC 6000 in 1995. A dash (-) is used to indicate that data are not available or cannot be calculated; nec means not elsewhere classified.

RHODE ISLAND

SIC	Industry	No. Establishments			Employment		Pay / Employee		Annual Payroll ($ 000)		
		1994	1995	% State	1994	1995	1994	1995	1994	1995	% State
BRISTOL, RI											
60 –	**Finance, insurance, and real estate**	65	66	3.3	298	329	22,631	20,790	7,073	7,332	0.9
6000	Depository institutions	15	13	4.7	135	131	19,822	17,618	2,460	2,326	1.2
6020	Commercial banks	9	9	5.2	89	96	21,888	18,125	1,783	1,784	1.1
6400	Insurance agents, brokers, and service	12	11	2.7	60	65	29,333	32,431	1,954	2,123	3.0
6500	Real estate	26	32	4.0	63	84	17,143	15,714	1,350	1,395	1.7
6530	Real estate agents and managers	11	12	3.0	19	18	22,316	25,111	551	438	1.1
KENT, RI											
60 –	**Finance, insurance, and real estate**	377	358	18.1	5,800	5,322	25,040	26,505	153,142	138,212	17.1
6000	Depository institutions	48	38	13.8	1,021	719	19,632	20,985	18,151	15,652	8.0
6020	Commercial banks	21	20	11.6	292	302	19,658	17,391	5,404	5,434	3.4
6100	Nondepository institutions	51	47	32.9	432	278	32,454	29,468	12,775	8,958	16.0
6200	Security and commodity brokers	17	13	9.8	188	29	54,723	21,793	8,697	753	0.9
6300	Insurance carriers	37	38	27.3	2,991	3,120	24,522	28,453	82,811	82,395	29.9
6310	Life insurance	11	11	26.2	1,753	1,772	18,574	17,540	35,594	30,337	58.6
6330	Fire, marine, and casualty insurance	20	20	28.6	956	1,025	32,611	43,719	35,964	38,673	26.8
6400	Insurance agents, brokers, and service	80	81	19.5	374	388	31,401	32,711	13,026	13,099	18.5
6500	Real estate	134	134	16.8	716	728	19,447	19,852	16,154	16,118	19.3
6510	Real estate operators and lessors	37	33	11.3	373	380	18,777	20,495	8,066	8,283	27.2
6530	Real estate agents and managers	77	78	19.8	294	298	19,306	17,745	6,220	5,616	13.9
6700	Holding and other investment offices	10	7	8.8	78	60	23,949	20,533	1,528	1,237	3.3
NEWPORT, RI											
60 –	**Finance, insurance, and real estate**	183	185	9.3	1,040	1,047	26,819	31,022	27,419	30,768	3.8
6000	Depository institutions	30	30	10.9	451	441	24,071	26,286	9,755	9,888	5.1
6020	Commercial banks	10	10	5.8	105	103	22,819	20,388	2,049	1,889	1.2
6200	Security and commodity brokers	15	16	12.1	60	70	54,667	49,486	3,034	3,202	3.7
6400	Insurance agents, brokers, and service	31	31	7.5	116	121	37,793	41,455	4,561	4,626	6.5
6500	Real estate	88	91	11.4	319	302	17,693	22,477	6,001	7,335	8.8
6510	Real estate operators and lessors	28	33	11.3	80	114	25,800	30,281	2,187	3,513	11.6
6530	Real estate agents and managers	50	49	12.4	221	172	14,063	17,047	3,293	3,273	8.1
PROVIDENCE, RI											
60 –	**Finance, insurance, and real estate**	1,201	1,187	59.9	17,463	17,691	33,847	34,918	576,960	600,187	74.4
6000	Depository institutions	186	166	60.4	5,338	5,310	29,365	29,924	153,512	152,137	78.1
6020	Commercial banks	107	113	65.7	4,385	4,639	30,824	30,797	133,629	136,314	86.3
6060	Credit unions	40	33	51.6	461	460	21,683	23,391	10,750	11,179	54.4
6100	Nondepository institutions	89	88	61.5	1,411	1,207	34,432	36,219	42,149	44,177	79.1
6160	Mortgage bankers and brokers	59	59	59.6	887	714	29,921	29,737	23,033	24,536	71.0
6200	Security and commodity brokers	89	95	72.0	1,676	1,806	47,826	46,173	72,846	81,260	93.5
6210	Security brokers and dealers	42	44	78.6	686	629	62,140	62,715	37,620	39,319	90.5
6300	Insurance carriers	84	84	60.4	5,086	5,280	36,797	36,216	187,626	190,081	69.0
6310	Life insurance	28	27	64.3	784	738	35,985	33,496	24,335	20,554	39.7
6330	Fire, marine, and casualty insurance	39	37	52.9	2,730	2,641	37,234	40,385	100,570	103,821	71.8
6400	Insurance agents, brokers, and service	258	258	62.2	1,450	1,380	28,058	29,899	45,330	44,715	63.1
6500	Real estate	446	440	55.3	2,270	2,423	19,588	21,568	49,189	54,114	64.7
6510	Real estate operators and lessors	185	180	61.9	801	781	18,312	20,896	16,112	16,635	54.7
6530	Real estate agents and managers	212	205	52.0	1,214	1,319	19,018	20,961	25,337	28,389	70.4
6540	Title abstract offices	6	6	54.5	102	84	11,216	13,857	1,224	1,233	92.7
6550	Subdividers and developers	31	34	47.9	135	158	37,511	32,152	5,790	5,568	63.1

Source: County Business Patterns, 1994/95, CBP-94/95, U.S. Department of Commerce, Washington, D.C., November 1997. SIC categories for which data were suppressed or not available for both 1994 and 1995 are *not* displayed. The employment columns represent mid-March employment in the year. Pay per employee is calculated by dividing 1st Quarter payroll, annualized, by mid-March employment. The columns headed "% State" show the county's percentage of the state total for the SIC in 1995; for example, 1.4% for SIC 6000 means that the county had 1.4 percent of the state's total establishments (or payroll) in SIC 6000 in 1995. A dash (-) is used to indicate that data are not available or cannot be calculated; *nec* means not elsewhere classified.

Continued on next page.

SIC	Industry	No. Establishments			Employment		Pay / Employee		Annual Payroll ($ 000)		
		1994	1995	% State	1994	1995	1994	1995	1994	1995	% State
PROVIDENCE, RI - [continued]											
6552	Subdividers and developers, n.e.c.	10	11	36.7	45	50	66,222	54,960	3,285	2,901	59.7
6553	Cemetery subdividers and developers	20	21	56.8	90	108	23,156	21,593	2,493	2,644	71.7
6710	Holding offices	20	22	68.8	138	198	213,797	218,061	22,852	29,780	94.5
WASHINGTON, RI											
60 –	**Finance, insurance, and real estate**	188	187	9.4	1,013	1,016	24,707	26,661	28,075	29,707	3.7
6000	Depository institutions	30	28	10.2	569	564	22,524	24,525	13,530	14,799	7.6
6020	Commercial banks	20	20	11.6	469	488	23,104	24,934	11,509	12,505	7.9
6400	Insurance agents, brokers, and service	31	34	8.2	180	187	28,111	30,310	6,297	6,317	8.9
6500	Real estate	103	99	12.4	186	178	19,613	20,831	4,952	4,712	5.6
6530	Real estate agents and managers	52	50	12.7	92	91	18,087	19,429	2,527	2,581	6.4
6552	Subdividers and developers, n.e.c.	6	6	20.0	8	6	23,500	21,333	364	240	4.9

Source: County Business Patterns, 1994/95, CBP-94/95, U.S. Department of Commerce, Washington, D.C., November 1997. SIC categories for which data were suppressed or not available for both 1994 and 1995 are *not* displayed. The employment columns represent mid-March employment in the year. Pay per employee is calculated by dividing 1st Quarter payroll, annualized, by mid-March employment. The columns headed "% State" show the county's percentage of the state total for the SIC in 1995; for example, 1.4% for SIC 6000 means that the county had 1.4 percent of the state's total establishments (or payroll) in SIC 6000 in 1995. A dash (-) is used to indicate that data are not available or cannot be calculated; *nec* means not elsewhere classified.

SOUTH CAROLINA

SIC	Industry	No. Establishments			Employment		Pay / Employee		Annual Payroll ($ 000)		
		1994	1995	% State	1994	1995	1994	1995	1994	1995	% State
ABBEVILLE, SC											
60 –	**Finance, insurance, and real estate**	29	27	0.3	143	135	17,650	19,052	2,504	2,641	0.1
6000	Depository institutions	12	12	0.8	102	96	17,412	18,833	1,766	1,846	0.4
6020	Commercial banks	7	7	0.7	68	62	16,059	18,129	1,112	1,150	0.3
6100	Nondepository institutions	6	6	0.5	17	16	15,529	18,250	270	312	0.1
6140	Personal credit institutions	6	6	0.7	17	16	15,529	18,250	270	312	0.3
AIKEN, SC											
60 –	**Finance, insurance, and real estate**	224	221	2.8	1,257	1,279	23,564	25,213	30,754	31,762	1.7
6000	Depository institutions	48	52	3.5	679	687	20,837	22,509	14,425	14,568	2.9
6020	Commercial banks	23	24	2.3	237	240	19,241	18,717	4,346	4,032	1.1
6100	Nondepository institutions	31	34	2.8	114	131	25,404	22,382	2,633	2,973	1.3
6140	Personal credit institutions	22	22	2.4	84	96	21,571	20,833	1,638	1,961	1.9
6300	Insurance carriers	17	15	3.0	119	119	37,714	37,714	4,828	4,474	1.1
6400	Insurance agents, brokers, and service	38	36	2.5	130	122	22,831	22,721	3,139	2,842	1.3
6500	Real estate	76	70	2.6	192	185	19,438	23,589	4,393	4,793	1.5
6510	Real estate operators and lessors	18	20	2.5	28	60	11,000	38,267	701	2,869	4.1
6530	Real estate agents and managers	42	39	2.6	88	86	15,636	14,930	1,561	1,228	0.6
6550	Subdividers and developers	12	8	3.0	75	35	27,147	20,914	2,084	657	1.2
ALLENDALE, SC											
60 –	**Finance, insurance, and real estate**	13	14	0.2	-	-	-	-	-	-	-
ANDERSON, SC											
60 –	**Finance, insurance, and real estate**	271	302	3.8	1,504	1,571	22,793	25,385	36,108	39,861	2.1
6000	Depository institutions	52	61	4.1	635	691	22,331	23,757	13,719	15,845	3.2
6020	Commercial banks	31	39	3.8	374	441	22,481	22,739	8,404	10,018	2.7
6030	Savings institutions	14	16	7.8	228	217	23,053	26,654	4,768	5,173	7.0
6060	Credit unions	7	6	3.2	33	33	15,636	18,303	547	654	1.5
6100	Nondepository institutions	57	63	5.1	187	199	22,695	23,618	4,641	4,891	2.1
6140	Personal credit institutions	44	47	5.2	154	166	21,636	23,494	3,551	3,954	3.8
6300	Insurance carriers	13	14	2.8	193	185	33,451	34,984	6,566	6,427	1.6
6310	Life insurance	6	6	2.9	172	164	29,558	28,780	5,131	4,719	3.1
6400	Insurance agents, brokers, and service	52	56	3.8	193	194	20,953	23,340	4,320	4,620	2.1
6500	Real estate	82	90	3.3	232	233	12,034	14,335	3,663	3,660	1.1
6510	Real estate operators and lessors	16	17	2.1	38	40	10,947	13,500	608	559	0.8
6530	Real estate agents and managers	41	46	3.1	117	131	13,060	14,137	1,965	2,009	1.0
6540	Title abstract offices	4	5	12.5	13	14	11,692	14,000	186	187	7.3
6550	Subdividers and developers	15	14	5.3	60	44	11,267	16,182	842	816	1.5
6552	Subdividers and developers, n.e.c.	9	6	4.1	27	15	10,074	14,400	361	259	0.7
6553	Cemetery subdividers and developers	6	6	6.3	33	29	12,242	17,103	481	547	4.7
BAMBERG, SC											
60 –	**Finance, insurance, and real estate**	24	24	0.3	115	118	18,017	18,610	2,182	2,163	0.1
6000	Depository institutions	9	8	0.5	74	73	18,703	19,781	1,438	1,422	0.3
6500	Real estate	3	4	0.1	6	5	13,333	13,600	69	47	0.0
BARNWELL, SC											
60 –	**Finance, insurance, and real estate**	24	24	0.3	108	102	18,000	18,863	1,950	2,059	0.1
6000	Depository institutions	9	9	0.6	68	65	19,706	19,938	1,286	1,313	0.3
6100	Nondepository institutions	5	5	0.4	12	13	19,667	20,000	223	274	0.1
6140	Personal credit institutions	5	5	0.6	12	13	19,667	20,000	223	274	0.3

Source: County Business Patterns, 1994/95, CBP-94/95, U.S. Department of Commerce, Washington, D.C., November 1997. SIC categories for which data were suppressed or not available for both 1994 and 1995 are not displayed. The employment columns represent mid-March employment in the year. Pay per employee is calculated by dividing 1st Quarter payroll, annualized, by mid-March employment. The columns headed "% State" show the county's percentage of the state total for the SIC in 1995; for example, 1.4% for SIC 6000 means that the county had 1.4 percent of the state's total establishments (or payroll) in SIC 6000 in 1995. A dash (-) is used to indicate that data are not available or cannot be calculated; nec means not elsewhere classified.

Continued on next page.

SIC	Industry	No. Establishments			Employment		Pay / Employee		Annual Payroll ($ 000)		
		1994	1995	% State	1994	1995	1994	1995	1994	1995	% State
BARNWELL, SC - [continued]											
6400	Insurance agents, brokers, and service	4	4	0.3	15	10	18,667	27,200	349	375	0.2
6500	Real estate	6	6	0.2	13	14	6,769	6,857	92	97	0.0
6530	Real estate agents and managers	3	3	0.2	6	8	8,667	8,500	66	74	0.0
BEAUFORT, SC											
60 –	**Finance, insurance, and real estate**	383	416	5.3	3,021	3,495	27,870	25,114	82,659	94,692	5.1
6000	Depository institutions	44	44	3.0	540	546	22,904	24,630	12,202	12,930	2.6
6020	Commercial banks	30	29	2.8	402	405	23,184	24,741	9,023	9,461	2.6
6030	Savings institutions	10	10	4.9	95	95	23,874	25,053	2,291	2,314	3.1
6100	Nondepository institutions	33	36	2.9	176	160	20,136	25,750	4,016	5,133	2.2
6200	Security and commodity brokers	15	25	8.1	84	123	102,857	68,585	7,056	9,014	8.1
6210	Security brokers and dealers	11	19	8.3	78	114	107,282	72,070	6,822	8,767	8.4
6300	Insurance carriers	8	6	1.2	48	37	27,917	31,135	1,755	1,542	0.4
6400	Insurance agents, brokers, and service	36	36	2.5	184	187	29,478	27,636	5,296	5,624	2.5
6500	Real estate	237	258	9.5	1,857	2,253	22,020	21,252	44,762	53,621	16.6
6510	Real estate operators and lessors	54	57	7.1	113	213	16,566	12,000	2,314	3,317	4.7
6530	Real estate agents and managers	153	157	10.6	1,212	1,433	22,376	22,493	29,874	35,266	18.4
6540	Title abstract offices	6	6	15.0	18	24	22,444	19,833	596	573	22.4
6550	Subdividers and developers	20	26	9.9	504	511	22,484	22,239	11,777	13,513	25.5
6552	Subdividers and developers, n.e.c.	18	25	16.9	504	511	22,484	22,239	11,758	13,393	33.8
6700	Holding and other investment offices	10	11	7.1	132	189	90,818	40,042	7,572	6,828	13.0
6710	Holding offices	4	4	6.1	119	178	96,370	39,573	6,974	6,203	14.7
BERKELEY, SC											
60 –	**Finance, insurance, and real estate**	94	105	1.3	406	401	18,404	20,070	8,129	8,786	0.5
6000	Depository institutions	18	18	1.2	156	144	18,615	20,778	3,036	3,080	0.6
6020	Commercial banks	10	9	0.9	110	94	19,273	21,489	2,166	2,060	0.6
6100	Nondepository institutions	16	16	1.3	63	56	22,032	21,786	1,443	1,251	0.5
6400	Insurance agents, brokers, and service	19	23	1.6	74	82	18,703	19,512	1,519	1,699	0.8
6500	Real estate	33	40	1.5	91	105	14,813	16,267	1,689	2,155	0.7
6510	Real estate operators and lessors	14	16	2.0	47	53	15,915	17,509	905	1,069	1.5
6530	Real estate agents and managers	16	20	1.3	35	41	13,829	15,805	655	900	0.5
6550	Subdividers and developers	3	3	1.1	9	11	12,889	12,000	129	166	0.3
CALHOUN, SC											
60 –	**Finance, insurance, and real estate**	13	14	0.2	-	-	-	-	-	-	-
6000	Depository institutions	3	4	0.3	19	19	17,263	16,211	335	339	0.1
6020	Commercial banks	3	4	0.4	19	19	17,263	16,211	335	339	0.1
6500	Real estate	3	3	0.1	4	5	15,000	14,400	67	64	0.0
6510	Real estate operators and lessors	3	3	0.4	4	5	15,000	14,400	67	64	0.1
CHARLESTON, SC											
60 –	**Finance, insurance, and real estate**	863	893	11.4	7,236	7,240	24,851	25,826	187,003	194,450	10.4
6000	Depository institutions	146	145	9.7	1,923	1,868	23,027	24,413	44,422	47,667	9.7
6020	Commercial banks	91	92	8.9	1,136	1,091	24,187	25,089	26,110	28,155	7.7
6060	Credit unions	23	22	11.9	371	360	18,728	22,300	7,779	8,088	18.6
6100	Nondepository institutions	104	110	8.9	714	567	32,443	27,845	18,756	15,125	6.6
6140	Personal credit institutions	69	72	8.0	348	343	25,632	26,006	8,960	8,678	8.4
6150	Business credit institutions	4	4	10.8	19	14	13,684	18,857	265	220	-
6160	Mortgage bankers and brokers	31	34	13.4	347	210	40,300	31,448	9,531	6,227	6.2
6200	Security and commodity brokers	36	37	12.0	254	263	59,606	62,844	16,787	17,166	15.5
6210	Security brokers and dealers	22	22	9.6	226	236	60,124	65,424	15,143	15,928	15.3
6280	Security and commodity services	13	12	16.9	27	26	57,185	41,231	1,631	1,210	18.7
6300	Insurance carriers	49	50	10.1	1,615	1,684	28,436	31,202	46,918	50,434	12.5
6310	Life insurance	28	27	13.0	970	966	26,256	26,265	25,038	24,081	15.9
6400	Insurance agents, brokers, and service	147	148	10.1	741	734	22,926	24,033	19,753	20,096	9.0
6500	Real estate	354	371	13.7	1,910	2,011	17,001	18,148	38,239	41,559	12.9
6510	Real estate operators and lessors	114	114	14.1	677	746	15,882	18,692	12,572	15,699	22.4

Source: County Business Patterns, 1994/95, CBP-94/95, U.S. Department of Commerce, Washington, D.C., November 1997. SIC categories for which data were suppressed or not available for both 1994 and 1995 are not displayed. The employment columns represent mid-March employment in the year. Pay per employee is calculated by dividing 1st Quarter payroll, annualized, by mid-March employment. The columns headed "% State" show the county's percentage of the state total for the SIC in 1995; for example, 1.4% for SIC 6000 means that the county had 1.4 percent of the state's total establishments (or payroll) in SIC 6000 in 1995. A dash (-) is used to indicate that data are not available or cannot be calculated; nec means not elsewhere classified.

Continued on next page.

SIC	Industry	No. Establishments			Employment		Pay / Employee		Annual Payroll ($ 000)		
		1994	1995	% State	1994	1995	1994	1995	1994	1995	% State
CHARLESTON, SC - [continued]											
6530	Real estate agents and managers	200	214	*14.4*	973	978	18,450	18,192	21,122	20,318	*10.6*
6540	Title abstract offices	6	5	*12.5*	18	14	16,889	15,714	321	225	*8.8*
6550	Subdividers and developers	23	23	*8.7*	164	165	15,829	17,406	2,963	3,332	*6.3*
6552	Subdividers and developers, n.e.c.	17	17	*11.5*	89	108	20,315	19,667	2,169	2,400	*6.1*
6553	Cemetery subdividers and developers	6	6	*6.3*	75	57	10,507	13,123	794	932	*8.0*
6700	Holding and other investment offices	27	32	*20.8*	79	113	23,443	21,062	2,128	2,403	*4.6*
6710	Holding offices	8	11	*16.7*	33	66	28,121	19,879	1,018	1,148	*2.7*
6730	Trusts	7	6	*31.6*	19	23	14,316	12,348	359	371	*-*
6790	Miscellaneous investing	8	9	*17.6*	16	14	24,000	33,429	399	423	*6.8*
CHEROKEE, SC											
60 –	**Finance, insurance, and real estate**	61	68	*0.9*	302	310	21,205	21,148	6,936	6,755	*0.4*
6000	Depository institutions	11	11	*0.7*	135	139	21,541	20,547	2,849	2,717	*0.6*
6100	Nondepository institutions	14	16	*1.3*	62	59	19,548	19,729	1,241	1,242	*0.5*
6300	Insurance carriers	7	7	*1.4*	28	31	29,857	28,387	809	954	*0.2*
6400	Insurance agents, brokers, and service	10	11	*0.8*	32	31	25,375	26,194	996	992	*0.4*
6500	Real estate	16	19	*0.7*	42	44	11,333	14,364	809	568	*0.2*
6530	Real estate agents and managers	9	11	*0.7*	14	19	18,857	15,579	600	297	*0.2*
CHESTER, SC											
60 –	**Finance, insurance, and real estate**	37	36	*0.5*	193	191	19,876	22,199	3,955	4,289	*0.2*
6000	Depository institutions	10	10	*0.7*	98	102	21,510	23,529	2,048	2,306	*0.5*
6020	Commercial banks	6	6	*0.6*	48	46	19,500	22,087	913	1,057	*0.3*
6300	Insurance carriers	4	4	*0.8*	29	29	21,931	21,793	729	746	*0.2*
6500	Real estate	7	5	*0.2*	11	5	11,636	16,000	103	77	*0.0*
CHESTERFIELD, SC											
60 –	**Finance, insurance, and real estate**	46	45	*0.6*	227	207	19,189	19,807	4,563	4,493	*0.2*
6000	Depository institutions	13	12	*0.8*	131	105	19,237	20,076	2,510	2,230	*0.5*
6500	Real estate	8	8	*0.3*	15	16	10,933	11,500	200	196	*0.1*
6510	Real estate operators and lessors	4	4	*0.5*	7	7	11,429	12,000	102	89	*0.1*
CLARENDON, SC											
60 –	**Finance, insurance, and real estate**	37	38	*0.5*	188	197	21,489	21,096	4,612	4,576	*0.2*
6000	Depository institutions	5	5	*0.3*	79	82	20,354	19,561	1,633	1,691	*0.3*
6020	Commercial banks	5	5	*0.5*	79	82	20,354	19,561	1,633	1,691	*0.5*
6100	Nondepository institutions	15	16	*1.3*	43	44	18,791	19,000	815	950	*0.4*
6550	Subdividers and developers	3	3	*1.1*	6	6	11,333	11,333	68	69	*0.1*
COLLETON, SC											
60 –	**Finance, insurance, and real estate**	73	76	*1.0*	454	471	21,551	22,140	11,749	11,594	*0.6*
6000	Depository institutions	12	13	*0.9*	120	129	19,000	20,155	3,367	2,788	*0.6*
6100	Nondepository institutions	16	16	*1.3*	61	64	22,951	24,938	1,451	1,609	*0.7*
6300	Insurance carriers	5	5	*1.0*	101	105	34,574	34,857	3,949	4,181	*1.0*
6310	Life insurance	5	5	*2.4*	101	105	34,574	34,857	3,949	4,181	*2.8*
6500	Real estate	28	30	*1.1*	135	135	14,519	14,222	2,226	2,216	*0.7*
6510	Real estate operators and lessors	9	10	*1.2*	30	35	10,000	13,486	349	403	*0.6*
6530	Real estate agents and managers	14	13	*0.9*	93	84	16,301	15,238	1,737	1,628	*0.9*
DARLINGTON, SC											
60 –	**Finance, insurance, and real estate**	95	91	*1.2*	434	443	19,217	20,632	8,300	9,041	*0.5*
6000	Depository institutions	28	28	*1.9*	262	270	21,969	23,304	5,558	6,126	*1.2*
6020	Commercial banks	19	19	*1.8*	183	188	20,393	20,596	3,536	3,844	*1.1*
6400	Insurance agents, brokers, and service	24	23	*1.6*	67	74	14,925	16,432	1,109	1,285	*0.6*
6510	Real estate operators and lessors	10	7	*0.9*	19	12	8,632	11,000	151	124	*0.2*
6530	Real estate agents and managers	10	8	*0.5*	19	17	10,737	11,294	214	188	*0.1*
DILLON, SC											
60 –	**Finance, insurance, and real estate**	49	51	*0.6*	263	268	17,293	18,672	4,801	5,336	*0.3*

Source: County Business Patterns, 1994/95, CBP-94/95, U.S. Department of Commerce, Washington, D.C., November 1997. SIC categories for which data were suppressed or not available for both 1994 and 1995 are not displayed. The employment columns represent mid-March employment in the year. Pay per employee is calculated by dividing 1st Quarter payroll, annualized, by mid-March employment. The columns headed "% State" show the county's percentage of the state total for the SIC in 1995; for example, 1.4% for SIC 6000 means that the county had 1.4 percent of the state's total establishments (or payroll) in SIC 6000 in 1995. A dash (-) is used to indicate that data are not available or cannot be calculated; nec means not elsewhere classified.

Continued on next page.

SIC	Industry	No. Establishments			Employment		Pay / Employee		Annual Payroll ($ 000)		
		1994	1995	% State	1994	1995	1994	1995	1994	1995	% State
DILLON, SC - [continued]											
6000	Depository institutions	9	9	0.6	83	76	19,759	22,474	1,606	1,638	0.3
6020	Commercial banks	9	9	0.9	83	76	19,759	22,474	1,606	1,638	0.4
6100	Nondepository institutions	10	12	1.0	38	47	17,368	17,191	686	870	0.4
6400	Insurance agents, brokers, and service	11	11	0.8	44	50	16,818	18,960	963	1,009	0.5
6510	Real estate operators and lessors	9	8	1.0	27	17	6,519	6,118	128	148	0.2
6530	Real estate agents and managers	6	6	0.4	14	20	11,429	10,200	192	197	0.1
DORCHESTER, SC											
60 –	**Finance, insurance, and real estate**	130	132	1.7	634	591	18,505	19,980	12,031	12,039	0.6
6000	Depository institutions	31	30	2.0	282	265	19,617	18,521	5,553	5,014	1.0
6020	Commercial banks	23	23	2.2	227	209	20,282	18,411	4,511	3,902	1.1
6100	Nondepository institutions	18	20	1.6	80	77	25,950	26,234	1,876	1,962	0.9
6140	Personal credit institutions	14	17	1.9	62	68	23,355	25,647	1,512	1,732	1.7
6200	Security and commodity brokers	6	6	1.9	8	10	17,000	20,400	196	224	0.2
6400	Insurance agents, brokers, and service	26	27	1.9	86	85	17,256	17,553	1,486	1,598	0.7
6500	Real estate	43	44	1.6	169	145	10,651	16,276	2,293	2,479	0.8
6510	Real estate operators and lessors	16	15	1.9	88	58	8,227	12,069	691	662	0.9
6530	Real estate agents and managers	20	21	1.4	49	48	11,918	13,500	645	808	0.4
FAIRFIELD, SC											
60 –	**Finance, insurance, and real estate**	26	26	0.3	87	94	21,011	20,383	1,996	2,015	0.1
6000	Depository institutions	7	7	0.5	56	61	21,643	20,197	1,250	1,237	0.3
6100	Nondepository institutions	4	4	0.3	10	10	26,400	30,800	287	309	0.1
6400	Insurance agents, brokers, and service	7	7	0.5	14	13	15,429	14,769	277	257	0.1
6530	Real estate agents and managers	4	4	0.3	4	6	18,000	15,333	91	102	0.1
FLORENCE, SC											
60 –	**Finance, insurance, and real estate**	284	291	3.7	3,772	3,658	18,796	20,667	73,338	77,831	4.2
6000	Depository institutions	47	48	3.2	594	611	21,603	22,920	12,922	16,196	3.3
6020	Commercial banks	31	30	2.9	468	469	21,915	23,633	10,274	13,226	3.6
6100	Nondepository institutions	60	62	5.0	1,094	1,121	19,272	18,212	22,680	21,338	9.3
6140	Personal credit institutions	43	44	4.9	181	185	21,945	22,076	3,935	4,063	3.9
6300	Insurance carriers	21	22	4.5	1,387	1,219	16,660	21,634	23,348	24,155	6.0
6400	Insurance agents, brokers, and service	68	64	4.4	255	249	20,753	23,165	6,024	6,304	2.8
6500	Real estate	73	84	3.1	273	296	16,059	17,743	4,259	5,435	1.7
6510	Real estate operators and lessors	29	32	4.0	91	134	14,549	14,716	1,435	2,029	2.9
6530	Real estate agents and managers	38	42	2.8	153	129	16,601	20,806	2,269	2,785	1.5
6550	Subdividers and developers	6	8	3.0	29	27	17,931	19,556	555	566	1.1
GEORGETOWN, SC											
60 –	**Finance, insurance, and real estate**	105	116	1.5	721	806	21,010	20,824	16,754	17,946	1.0
6000	Depository institutions	25	23	1.5	234	228	21,812	21,070	4,936	4,908	1.0
6020	Commercial banks	16	16	1.5	146	142	20,603	20,704	2,797	2,729	0.7
6100	Nondepository institutions	17	17	1.4	59	64	17,695	19,313	1,052	1,117	0.5
6210	Security brokers and dealers	5	7	3.1	40	40	67,200	59,600	2,165	2,271	2.2
6300	Insurance carriers	5	5	1.0	55	54	23,418	27,481	1,627	1,907	0.5
6400	Insurance agents, brokers, and service	12	11	0.8	41	39	24,976	24,615	1,111	1,068	0.5
6500	Real estate	39	51	1.9	285	377	13,600	15,363	5,728	6,534	2.0
6510	Real estate operators and lessors	11	12	1.5	44	75	10,182	10,400	597	715	1.0
6530	Real estate agents and managers	21	26	1.7	163	203	14,429	15,724	2,900	3,598	1.9
6550	Subdividers and developers	6	8	3.0	78	94	13,795	18,851	2,226	2,124	4.0
GREENVILLE, SC											
60 –	**Finance, insurance, and real estate**	947	977	12.4	10,723	10,080	27,301	33,842	314,623	343,878	18.4
6000	Depository institutions	166	170	11.4	2,827	2,603	25,006	30,571	69,197	83,914	17.0
6020	Commercial banks	122	123	11.8	2,210	1,954	25,471	32,682	54,269	67,776	18.5
6030	Savings institutions	23	23	11.2	492	509	23,504	24,754	12,128	12,984	17.7
6060	Credit unions	17	18	9.7	107	121	23,664	23,273	2,429	2,718	6.2

Source: County Business Patterns, 1994/95, CBP-94/95, U.S. Department of Commerce, Washington, D.C., November 1997. SIC categories for which data were suppressed or not available for both 1994 and 1995 are not displayed. The employment columns represent mid-March employment in the year. Pay per employee is calculated by dividing 1st Quarter payroll, annualized, by mid-March employment. The columns headed "% State" show the county's percentage of the state total for the SIC in 1995; for example, 1.4% for SIC 6000 means that the county had 1.4 percent of the state's total establishments (or payroll) in SIC 6000 in 1995. A dash (-) is used to indicate that data are not available or cannot be calculated; nec means not elsewhere classified.

Continued on next page.

SIC	Industry	No. Establishments			Employment		Pay / Employee		Annual Payroll ($ 000)		
		1994	1995	% State	1994	1995	1994	1995	1994	1995	% State
CAMPBELL, TN - [continued]											
6400	Insurance agents, brokers, and service	9	9	0.4	41	39	17,659	19,692	769	823	0.2
6500	Real estate	14	18	0.5	87	62	7,264	9,935	860	1,036	0.2
6510	Real estate operators and lessors	4	8	0.6	18	18	4,889	8,444	90	408	0.3
6530	Real estate agents and managers	4	4	0.2	4	6	7,000	8,667	43	59	0.0
6550	Subdividers and developers	6	6	2.0	65	38	7,938	10,842	727	569	1.5
CANNON, TN											
60 –	**Finance, insurance, and real estate**	15	13	0.1	110	107	16,836	19,477	2,018	1,778	0.1
CARROLL, TN											
60 –	**Finance, insurance, and real estate**	40	42	0.4	244	262	17,852	18,656	4,796	5,479	0.2
6000	Depository institutions	18	18	0.8	180	196	19,667	19,714	3,876	4,298	0.4
6500	Real estate	11	12	0.3	31	23	8,000	9,043	264	222	0.1
6530	Real estate agents and managers	6	7	0.4	13	11	5,231	6,545	81	81	0.0
CARTER, TN											
60 –	**Finance, insurance, and real estate**	56	58	0.5	351	348	22,906	26,230	8,824	9,436	0.3
6000	Depository institutions	18	18	0.8	228	232	22,596	26,707	5,224	5,502	0.6
6030	Savings institutions	5	5	2.9	49	52	27,592	27,923	1,303	1,356	2.0
6100	Nondepository institutions	6	6	0.6	33	33	24,485	25,818	913	953	0.4
6140	Personal credit institutions	6	6	1.0	33	33	24,485	25,818	913	953	0.7
6500	Real estate	11	12	0.3	35	34	13,600	15,529	540	551	0.1
6530	Real estate agents and managers	5	6	0.4	9	11	11,111	12,727	108	140	0.1
CHEATHAM, TN											
60 –	**Finance, insurance, and real estate**	21	20	0.2	102	106	21,804	25,019	2,157	2,579	0.1
6000	Depository institutions	7	7	0.3	71	78	25,014	24,821	1,678	1,781	0.2
6500	Real estate	8	7	0.2	14	10	10,000	38,000	142	447	0.1
6530	Real estate agents and managers	5	4	0.2	8	4	7,500	16,000	56	62	0.0
CHESTER, TN											
60 –	**Finance, insurance, and real estate**	15	12	0.1	79	74	19,342	20,703	1,860	1,809	0.1
CLAIBORNE, TN											
60 –	**Finance, insurance, and real estate**	30	33	0.3	368	298	11,717	15,758	4,566	4,862	0.1
6000	Depository institutions	10	11	0.5	165	165	17,891	20,630	3,205	3,766	0.4
6400	Insurance agents, brokers, and service	6	5	0.2	16	12	18,250	24,000	332	359	0.1
6500	Real estate	11	14	0.4	16	21	8,750	9,905	194	283	0.1
6510	Real estate operators and lessors	3	4	0.3	3	10	28,000	12,800	97	173	0.1
6530	Real estate agents and managers	3	4	0.2	10	9	4,000	8,000	75	72	0.0
6550	Subdividers and developers	5	5	1.7	3	2	5,333	4,000	22	24	0.1
COCKE, TN											
60 –	**Finance, insurance, and real estate**	37	33	0.3	193	183	17,990	17,989	3,591	3,492	0.1
6000	Depository institutions	12	10	0.4	132	124	19,091	18,742	2,575	2,382	0.2
6400	Insurance agents, brokers, and service	6	5	0.2	21	19	13,905	15,579	312	292	0.1
6500	Real estate	11	10	0.3	14	13	9,429	8,000	154	236	0.1
6510	Real estate operators and lessors	6	5	0.4	7	7	9,714	6,857	73	89	0.1
COFFEE, TN											
60 –	**Finance, insurance, and real estate**	90	87	0.8	672	648	19,857	20,469	13,733	12,410	0.4
6000	Depository institutions	21	21	0.9	437	338	20,183	22,627	9,042	7,713	0.8
6100	Nondepository institutions	13	13	1.2	50	127	23,120	19,024	1,248	1,452	0.6
6140	Personal credit institutions	7	8	1.3	42	37	22,000	28,432	928	955	0.7
6400	Insurance agents, brokers, and service	18	14	0.6	45	60	22,044	16,333	1,171	1,080	0.3

Source: County Business Patterns, 1994/95, CBP-94/95, U.S. Department of Commerce, Washington, D.C., November 1997. SIC categories for which data were suppressed or not available for both 1994 and 1995 are *not* displayed. The employment columns represent mid-March employment in the year. Pay per employee is calculated by dividing 1st Quarter payroll, annualized, by mid-March employment. The columns headed "% State" show the county's percentage of the state total for the SIC in 1995; for example, 1.4% for SIC 6000 means that the county had 1.4 percent of the state's total establishments (or payroll) in SIC 6000 in 1995. A dash (-) is used to indicate that data are not available or cannot be calculated; *nec* means not elsewhere classified.

Continued on next page.

SIC	Industry	No. Establishments			Employment		Pay / Employee		Annual Payroll ($ 000)		
		1994	1995	% State	1994	1995	1994	1995	1994	1995	% State
COFFEE, TN - [continued]											
6500	Real estate	31	31	0.9	84	78	11,143	12,718	953	1,145	0.3
6510	Real estate operators and lessors	10	10	0.7	34	35	9,882	10,743	348	392	0.3
6530	Real estate agents and managers	17	17	1.0	26	27	7,846	10,222	241	376	0.2
CROCKETT, TN											
60 –	**Finance, insurance, and real estate**	19	19	0.2	121	136	19,041	15,706	2,845	2,892	0.1
6000	Depository institutions	10	10	0.4	105	122	19,010	15,508	2,520	2,618	0.3
6020	Commercial banks	10	10	0.6	105	122	19,010	15,508	2,520	2,618	0.3
CUMBERLAND, TN											
60 –	**Finance, insurance, and real estate**	66	72	0.7	580	604	17,276	17,987	9,559	11,013	0.3
6000	Depository institutions	14	16	0.7	174	160	20,184	19,700	2,989	3,244	0.3
6100	Nondepository institutions	5	7	0.7	14	15	17,143	29,067	260	382	0.1
6140	Personal credit institutions	5	7	1.1	14	15	17,143	29,067	260	382	0.3
6400	Insurance agents, brokers, and service	13	13	0.5	31	31	13,032	15,226	474	537	0.1
6500	Real estate	29	28	0.8	281	308	13,466	12,065	4,011	4,169	1.0
6510	Real estate operators and lessors	8	6	0.4	141	167	14,553	11,545	1,858	1,843	1.5
6530	Real estate agents and managers	16	17	1.0	120	123	12,167	12,260	1,815	1,973	0.8
6550	Subdividers and developers	3	3	1.0	15	14	12,800	14,857	245	227	0.6
DAVIDSON, TN											
60 –	**Finance, insurance, and real estate**	1,836	1,872	17.2	28,837	26,790	33,067	35,018	942,127	923,649	27.6
6000	Depository institutions	239	237	10.5	7,515	7,697	30,464	32,461	216,336	227,134	23.3
6020	Commercial banks	161	172	10.6	5,612	6,000	31,679	33,227	165,053	177,098	22.8
6060	Credit unions	48	44	12.2	414	414	23,121	25,411	10,080	10,748	13.7
6100	Nondepository institutions	157	176	16.6	1,441	1,436	38,937	39,429	54,179	59,750	22.7
6140	Personal credit institutions	81	89	14.4	435	558	32,028	39,656	15,621	20,762	15.4
6150	Business credit institutions	17	18	26.1	483	465	48,977	47,673	21,187	23,230	54.3
6160	Mortgage bankers and brokers	58	64	21.3	521	412	35,478	29,825	17,332	15,527	19.7
6200	Security and commodity brokers	101	106	21.7	1,426	1,349	86,942	73,601	89,339	98,259	27.1
6210	Security brokers and dealers	53	52	18.1	1,239	1,147	89,388	75,404	77,312	83,144	28.9
6300	Insurance carriers	201	194	23.6	7,494	6,726	28,964	35,598	227,282	236,991	32.0
6310	Life insurance	69	64	22.8	3,303	3,341	28,160	32,164	96,213	101,233	33.2
6330	Fire, marine, and casualty insurance	97	95	23.6	3,348	2,521	29,278	39,959	104,979	102,695	37.7
6400	Insurance agents, brokers, and service	386	398	16.8	3,008	3,260	39,423	39,599	122,169	130,427	32.8
6500	Real estate	645	666	18.8	4,329	4,851	18,067	20,673	91,191	107,233	25.7
6510	Real estate operators and lessors	291	300	21.1	1,523	1,721	15,480	18,020	25,974	32,119	26.8
6530	Real estate agents and managers	304	308	18.7	2,384	2,661	20,163	22,818	56,746	65,540	27.0
6540	Title abstract offices	14	16	19.3	117	101	25,231	27,921	3,463	3,282	26.8
6550	Subdividers and developers	30	30	10.1	304	345	11,868	15,096	4,954	5,675	15.3
6552	Subdividers and developers, n.e.c.	21	21	13.4	52	59	12,385	20,000	1,379	1,816	9.0
6553	Cemetery subdividers and developers	6	6	4.8	250	284	11,360	13,366	3,459	3,758	22.8
6710	Holding offices	21	25	20.2	216	616	90,704	37,299	20,651	26,366	24.1
6730	Trusts	19	18	26.1	106	87	24,113	27,264	3,520	2,808	35.8
6732	Educational, religious, etc. trusts	10	8	25.8	81	66	25,481	27,879	2,763	1,907	41.1
6733	Trusts, n.e.c.	9	10	27.0	25	21	19,680	25,333	757	901	28.2
6790	Miscellaneous investing	55	41	35.7	446	408	35,247	42,588	17,758	15,271	45.6
6794	Patent owners and lessors	38	21	46.7	369	317	30,038	32,517	12,764	9,543	50.6
DECATUR, TN											
60 –	**Finance, insurance, and real estate**	14	14	0.1	82	103	18,829	20,816	1,771	2,176	0.1
6000	Depository institutions	6	6	0.3	71	67	20,169	22,567	1,510	1,714	0.2
6020	Commercial banks	6	6	0.4	71	67	20,169	22,567	1,510	1,714	0.2
DE KALB, TN											
60 –	**Finance, insurance, and real estate**	26	25	0.2	144	141	20,861	20,794	3,073	2,798	0.1
6000	Depository institutions	9	9	0.4	115	115	22,609	21,878	2,635	2,353	0.2

Source: County Business Patterns, 1994/95, CBP-94/95, U.S. Department of Commerce, Washington, D.C., November 1997. SIC categories for which data were suppressed or not available for both 1994 and 1995 are not displayed. The employment columns represent mid-March employment in the year. Pay per employee is calculated by dividing 1st Quarter payroll, annualized, by mid-March employment. The columns headed "% State" show the county's percentage of the state total for the SIC in 1995; for example, 1.4% for SIC 6000 means that the county had 1.4 percent of the state's total establishments (or payroll) in SIC 6000 in 1995. A dash (-) is used to indicate that data are not available or cannot be calculated; nec means not elsewhere classified.

Continued on next page.

SIC	Industry	No. Establishments			Employment		Pay / Employee		Annual Payroll ($ 000)		
		1994	1995	% State	1994	1995	1994	1995	1994	1995	% State
DE KALB, TN - [continued]											
6020	Commercial banks	9	9	0.6	115	115	22,609	21,878	2,635	2,353	0.3
6400	Insurance agents, brokers, and service	6	6	0.3	15	15	18,667	21,333	291	325	0.1
6500	Real estate	11	10	0.3	14	11	8,857	8,727	147	120	0.0
DICKSON, TN											
60 –	**Finance, insurance, and real estate**	61	65	0.6	364	403	21,121	21,012	9,052	10,160	0.3
6000	Depository institutions	14	14	0.6	203	218	20,631	20,752	4,284	4,821	0.5
6400	Insurance agents, brokers, and service	17	17	0.7	80	85	25,600	23,718	3,103	3,236	0.8
6500	Real estate	20	21	0.6	36	35	9,778	12,000	421	457	0.1
6530	Real estate agents and managers	11	10	0.6	19	24	11,789	12,167	285	341	0.1
DYER, TN											
60 –	**Finance, insurance, and real estate**	81	79	0.7	586	593	23,980	21,949	14,008	12,825	0.4
6000	Depository institutions	18	19	0.8	324	345	21,963	21,287	6,761	6,899	0.7
6100	Nondepository institutions	10	9	0.9	48	46	28,500	26,435	1,227	1,087	0.4
6400	Insurance agents, brokers, and service	20	17	0.7	83	86	20,578	23,256	2,348	2,514	0.6
6500	Real estate	26	27	0.8	45	52	16,178	17,538	895	1,030	0.2
6510	Real estate operators and lessors	16	18	1.3	37	41	16,973	17,854	720	834	0.7
6530	Real estate agents and managers	8	7	0.4	6	7	12,000	13,143	86	106	0.0
FAYETTE, TN											
60 –	**Finance, insurance, and real estate**	19	22	0.2	137	140	16,438	17,571	2,623	2,859	0.1
6000	Depository institutions	5	5	0.2	110	111	17,418	18,234	2,288	2,403	0.2
6020	Commercial banks	5	5	0.3	110	111	17,418	18,234	2,288	2,403	0.3
FENTRESS, TN											
60 –	**Finance, insurance, and real estate**	15	15	0.1	123	119	17,659	19,496	2,449	2,582	0.1
6000	Depository institutions	4	4	0.2	75	77	20,320	20,727	1,583	1,684	0.2
6400	Insurance agents, brokers, and service	4	4	0.2	16	16	16,750	20,250	299	296	0.1
FRANKLIN, TN											
60 –	**Finance, insurance, and real estate**	43	48	0.4	219	261	17,735	17,609	4,038	4,721	0.1
6000	Depository institutions	11	11	0.5	143	172	18,881	17,023	2,746	2,814	0.3
6100	Nondepository institutions	5	7	0.7	18	22	22,667	21,273	405	555	0.2
6500	Real estate	12	13	0.4	22	25	9,455	7,840	224	231	0.1
6530	Real estate agents and managers	7	8	0.5	10	12	8,400	7,333	101	111	0.0
GIBSON, TN											
60 –	**Finance, insurance, and real estate**	78	80	0.7	470	472	19,668	20,686	9,545	10,577	0.3
6000	Depository institutions	29	30	1.3	345	341	19,733	20,762	6,672	7,416	0.8
6100	Nondepository institutions	7	7	0.7	15	20	21,600	21,400	346	422	0.2
6400	Insurance agents, brokers, and service	20	19	0.8	66	67	20,000	19,940	1,379	1,363	0.3
6500	Real estate	16	17	0.5	25	26	10,240	10,615	325	282	0.1
GILES, TN											
60 –	**Finance, insurance, and real estate**	31	33	0.3	268	258	20,955	23,287	5,500	5,550	0.2
6000	Depository institutions	11	10	0.4	204	197	22,706	25,726	4,513	4,586	0.5
6020	Commercial banks	11	10	0.6	204	197	22,706	25,726	4,513	4,586	0.6
6400	Insurance agents, brokers, and service	9	10	0.4	24	22	16,167	19,091	392	415	0.1
6500	Real estate	8	9	0.3	36	31	14,111	13,290	500	415	0.1
6530	Real estate agents and managers	4	5	0.3	12	12	8,000	8,667	110	128	0.1
GRAINGER, TN											
60 –	**Finance, insurance, and real estate**	9	9	0.1	-	-	-	-	-	-	-
GREENE, TN											
60 –	**Finance, insurance, and real estate**	82	86	0.8	463	510	21,443	22,918	10,276	12,470	0.4
6000	Depository institutions	30	29	1.3	286	283	19,986	21,922	5,892	6,455	0.7

Source: County Business Patterns, 1994/95, CBP-94/95, U.S. Department of Commerce, Washington, D.C., November 1997. SIC categories for which data were suppressed or not available for both 1994 and 1995 are *not* displayed. The employment columns represent mid-March employment in the year. Pay per employee is calculated by dividing 1st Quarter payroll, annualized, by mid-March employment. The columns headed "% State" show the county's percentage of the state total for the SIC in 1995; for example, 1.4% for SIC 6000 means that the county had 1.4 percent of the state's total establishments (or payroll) in SIC 6000 in 1995. A dash (-) is used to indicate that data are not available or cannot be calculated; *nec* means not elsewhere classified.

Continued on next page.

SIC	Industry	No. Establishments			Employment		Pay / Employee		Annual Payroll ($ 000)		
		1994	1995	% State	1994	1995	1994	1995	1994	1995	% State
GREENE, TN - [continued]											
6020	Commercial banks	19	19	1.2	226	225	21,062	22,684	4,842	5,317	0.7
6400	Insurance agents, brokers, and service	21	21	0.9	71	74	20,394	17,459	1,366	1,342	0.3
6500	Real estate	14	17	0.5	25	29	11,360	13,793	312	426	0.1
6510	Real estate operators and lessors	6	7	0.5	14	15	8,571	8,267	135	132	0.1
6530	Real estate agents and managers	5	6	0.4	7	8	18,857	26,500	136	228	0.1
6550	Subdividers and developers	3	4	1.4	4	6	8,000	10,667	41	66	0.2
HAMBLEN, TN											
60 –	**Finance, insurance, and real estate**	116	119	1.1	558	589	20,602	20,727	12,363	13,081	0.4
6000	Depository institutions	26	24	1.1	256	223	20,781	22,457	5,431	4,959	0.5
6020	Commercial banks	14	13	0.8	142	141	23,746	24,426	3,260	3,371	0.4
6030	Savings institutions	4	3	1.7	87	53	17,379	19,623	1,690	1,058	1.5
6100	Nondepository institutions	14	15	1.4	72	80	16,611	15,800	1,317	1,327	0.5
6140	Personal credit institutions	10	12	1.9	60	74	17,000	15,784	1,154	1,246	0.9
6400	Insurance agents, brokers, and service	29	29	1.2	111	107	18,054	19,028	2,363	2,433	0.6
6500	Real estate	37	38	1.1	76	103	17,263	16,699	1,652	1,798	0.4
6530	Real estate agents and managers	18	18	1.1	35	35	10,514	12,686	407	476	0.2
6550	Subdividers and developers	4	5	1.7	9	38	60,889	22,737	821	868	2.3
HAMILTON, TN											
60 –	**Finance, insurance, and real estate**	757	779	7.2	11,088	11,025	32,742	33,961	336,651	323,232	9.7
6000	Depository institutions	152	158	7.0	2,044	2,074	28,472	27,088	54,492	54,242	5.6
6020	Commercial banks	100	105	6.5	1,644	1,656	30,131	28,493	45,623	44,909	5.8
6060	Credit unions	44	44	12.2	370	397	21,870	21,401	8,328	8,584	11.0
6100	Nondepository institutions	77	79	7.5	398	417	26,744	25,141	10,037	10,896	4.1
6140	Personal credit institutions	38	40	6.5	243	262	25,909	25,908	5,901	6,503	4.8
6160	Mortgage bankers and brokers	32	32	10.7	131	137	29,069	23,299	3,576	3,778	4.8
6200	Security and commodity brokers	45	45	9.2	295	317	53,315	49,931	16,210	16,279	4.5
6210	Security brokers and dealers	22	23	8.0	229	239	60,489	54,360	13,765	13,304	4.6
6280	Security and commodity services	23	22	12.0	66	78	28,424	36,359	2,445	2,975	4.4
6300	Insurance carriers	74	78	9.5	6,267	5,866	36,340	39,921	199,758	179,890	24.3
6310	Life insurance	31	31	11.0	3,569	3,080	41,272	48,136	126,628	98,353	32.3
6400	Insurance agents, brokers, and service	158	157	6.6	715	810	28,257	28,316	21,562	24,181	6.1
6500	Real estate	223	238	6.7	1,227	1,467	21,816	22,312	30,709	35,262	8.5
6510	Real estate operators and lessors	103	104	7.3	341	298	14,475	18,510	6,189	6,215	5.2
6530	Real estate agents and managers	89	93	5.6	722	774	25,490	27,716	20,343	22,239	9.2
6540	Title abstract offices	6	9	10.8	50	75	27,840	19,947	1,445	2,352	19.2
6550	Subdividers and developers	24	28	9.5	113	313	17,947	13,214	2,669	4,191	11.3
6552	Subdividers and developers, n.e.c.	15	17	10.8	45	139	14,844	14,647	1,115	1,710	8.5
6553	Cemetery subdividers and developers	8	10	8.0	68	173	20,000	12,023	1,515	2,415	14.6
6710	Holding offices	12	9	7.3	51	35	34,510	34,286	1,927	1,482	1.4
6730	Trusts	7	7	10.1	56	20	11,786	24,200	622	513	6.5
HARDEMAN, TN											
60 –	**Finance, insurance, and real estate**	26	26	0.2	220	222	16,273	17,495	3,999	4,330	0.1
6000	Depository institutions	9	9	0.4	167	170	18,347	19,882	3,417	3,702	0.4
6400	Insurance agents, brokers, and service	7	7	0.3	18	15	12,444	15,200	235	210	0.1
6500	Real estate	7	7	0.2	31	30	4,903	4,933	202	216	0.1
HARDIN, TN											
60 –	**Finance, insurance, and real estate**	41	37	0.3	192	234	17,125	16,171	3,875	4,228	0.1
6000	Depository institutions	14	14	0.6	102	121	21,490	21,355	2,325	2,678	0.3
6400	Insurance agents, brokers, and service	8	7	0.3	19	23	16,632	12,696	334	369	0.1
6500	Real estate	12	11	0.3	54	75	6,889	6,880	534	620	0.1
6530	Real estate agents and managers	7	7	0.4	15	16	8,267	9,250	132	200	0.1
HAWKINS, TN											
60 –	**Finance, insurance, and real estate**	44	45	0.4	188	218	18,809	18,716	3,561	4,433	0.1

Source: County Business Patterns, 1994/95, CBP-94/95, U.S. Department of Commerce, Washington, D.C., November 1997. SIC categories for which data were suppressed or not available for both 1994 and 1995 are not displayed. The employment columns represent mid-March employment in the year. Pay per employee is calculated by dividing 1st Quarter payroll, annualized, by mid-March employment. The columns headed "% State" show the county's percentage of the state total for the SIC in 1995; for example, 1.4% for SIC 6000 means that the county had 1.4 percent of the state's total establishments (or payroll) in SIC 6000 in 1995. A dash (-) is used to indicate that data are not available or cannot be calculated; nec means not elsewhere classified.

Continued on next page.

SIC	Industry	No. Establishments			Employment		Pay / Employee		Annual Payroll ($ 000)		
		1994	1995	% State	1994	1995	1994	1995	1994	1995	% State
HAWKINS, TN - [continued]											
6000	Depository institutions	15	14	0.6	129	146	19,380	21,370	2,587	3,343	0.3
6020	Commercial banks	10	10	0.6	85	94	20,235	22,681	1,668	2,280	0.3
6400	Insurance agents, brokers, and service	5	7	0.3	12	12	13,000	15,000	165	170	0.0
6500	Real estate	18	18	0.5	32	46	10,375	9,043	404	535	0.1
6510	Real estate operators and lessors	5	4	0.3	11	12	10,545	11,667	131	151	0.1
6530	Real estate agents and managers	9	10	0.6	18	31	10,889	8,387	236	354	0.1
6550	Subdividers and developers	4	4	1.4	3	3	6,667	5,333	37	30	0.1
HAYWOOD, TN											
60 –	**Finance, insurance, and real estate**	29	29	0.3	258	252	19,566	20,508	5,240	5,283	0.2
6400	Insurance agents, brokers, and service	8	8	0.3	24	22	13,333	18,545	356	411	0.1
6500	Real estate	7	6	0.2	20	20	6,200	8,200	151	166	0.0
HENDERSON, TN											
60 –	**Finance, insurance, and real estate**	33	35	0.3	193	218	19,938	22,954	4,159	4,804	0.1
6000	Depository institutions	16	17	0.8	154	161	20,468	26,012	3,270	3,672	0.4
6400	Insurance agents, brokers, and service	9	9	0.4	24	26	17,000	17,385	567	701	0.2
6500	Real estate	3	4	0.1	7	19	10,286	3,158	60	73	0.0
HENRY, TN											
60 –	**Finance, insurance, and real estate**	46	52	0.5	322	340	19,801	22,576	6,543	7,767	0.2
6000	Depository institutions	17	18	0.8	258	252	20,357	23,095	5,205	5,919	0.6
6400	Insurance agents, brokers, and service	11	11	0.5	27	30	13,778	16,933	420	544	0.1
6500	Real estate	13	13	0.4	25	24	12,480	10,167	267	269	0.1
6530	Real estate agents and managers	7	7	0.4	16	17	15,750	10,118	192	193	0.1
HICKMAN, TN											
60 –	**Finance, insurance, and real estate**	11	13	0.1	99	97	18,909	20,330	1,905	2,003	0.1
6000	Depository institutions	4	5	0.2	80	74	21,000	23,514	1,675	1,764	0.2
HUMPHREYS, TN											
60 –	**Finance, insurance, and real estate**	22	22	0.2	86	149	25,442	36,295	2,241	5,120	0.2
6000	Depository institutions	8	9	0.4	54	82	21,630	28,146	1,187	2,151	0.2
JOHNSON, TN											
60 –	**Finance, insurance, and real estate**	23	23	0.2	103	108	16,699	16,630	1,893	1,900	0.1
6000	Depository institutions	5	6	0.3	64	66	20,438	20,545	1,443	1,446	0.1
6400	Insurance agents, brokers, and service	6	5	0.2	6	8	8,000	11,500	60	73	0.0
6500	Real estate	6	7	0.2	18	21	7,333	6,857	136	154	0.0
KNOX, TN											
60 –	**Finance, insurance, and real estate**	974	1,006	9.2	8,194	8,431	27,804	28,909	237,068	255,090	7.6
6000	Depository institutions	148	155	6.9	2,451	2,410	25,738	29,135	61,948	67,114	6.9
6020	Commercial banks	87	89	5.5	1,699	1,642	27,903	32,231	44,987	48,700	6.3
6030	Savings institutions	20	21	12.2	397	400	20,987	21,200	9,311	9,796	14.1
6140	Personal credit institutions	49	57	9.3	302	347	28,397	28,657	8,444	9,934	7.4
6160	Mortgage bankers and brokers	33	37	12.3	219	191	29,954	32,042	6,345	6,698	8.5
6200	Security and commodity brokers	51	51	10.4	410	407	62,098	53,170	23,473	24,532	6.8
6210	Security brokers and dealers	29	28	9.8	347	338	63,654	57,432	20,731	21,785	7.6
6280	Security and commodity services	22	23	12.5	63	69	53,524	32,290	2,742	2,747	4.0
6300	Insurance carriers	89	93	11.3	1,203	1,255	28,831	31,873	35,588	39,448	5.3
6310	Life insurance	31	33	11.7	848	893	26,656	28,757	23,470	25,057	8.2
6330	Fire, marine, and casualty insurance	43	44	10.9	227	205	36,229	42,439	8,497	9,093	3.3
6400	Insurance agents, brokers, and service	222	219	9.2	1,040	1,124	28,396	29,893	33,581	38,139	9.6
6500	Real estate	349	356	10.1	2,082	2,084	18,006	18,983	45,633	45,418	10.9
6510	Real estate operators and lessors	134	137	9.7	515	527	21,017	20,751	12,018	12,105	10.1
6530	Real estate agents and managers	160	161	9.8	1,254	1,207	16,817	19,112	26,479	26,103	10.8
6540	Title abstract offices	16	16	19.3	94	82	22,043	22,488	2,362	2,169	17.7

Source: County Business Patterns, 1994/95, CBP-94/95, U.S. Department of Commerce, Washington, D.C., November 1997. SIC categories for which data were suppressed or not available for both 1994 and 1995 are *not* displayed. The employment columns represent mid-March employment in the year. Pay per employee is calculated by dividing 1st Quarter payroll, annualized, by mid-March employment. The columns headed "% State" show the county's percentage of the state total for the SIC in 1995; for example, 1.4% for SIC 6000 means that the county had 1.4 percent of the state's total establishments (or payroll) in SIC 6000 in 1995. A dash (-) is used to indicate that data are not available or cannot be calculated; *nec* means not elsewhere classified.

Continued on next page.

SIC	Industry	No. Establishments			Employment		Pay / Employee		Annual Payroll ($ 000)		
		1994	1995	% State	1994	1995	1994	1995	1994	1995	% State
KNOX, TN - [continued]											
6550	Subdividers and developers	33	31	10.5	213	256	16,263	14,172	4,646	4,827	13.0
6552	Subdividers and developers, n.e.c.	17	18	11.5	47	59	25,957	26,102	2,128	2,590	12.8
6553	Cemetery subdividers and developers	13	11	8.8	164	191	12,902	10,387	2,362	2,180	13.2
6700	Holding and other investment offices	22	27	8.1	424	546	47,972	36,784	19,901	21,079	13.4
6710	Holding offices	9	9	7.3	333	420	54,907	39,733	17,720	17,269	15.8
6730	Trusts	5	6	8.7	44	41	27,636	22,537	1,079	858	10.9
LAKE, TN											
60 –	**Finance, insurance, and real estate**	10	9	0.1	-	-	-	-	-	-	-
LAUDERDALE, TN											
60 –	**Finance, insurance, and real estate**	31	32	0.3	223	225	21,453	24,782	4,811	4,915	0.1
6000	Depository institutions	13	13	0.6	169	174	21,231	25,080	3,623	3,507	0.4
6020	Commercial banks	13	13	0.8	169	174	21,231	25,080	3,623	3,507	0.5
6400	Insurance agents, brokers, and service	7	7	0.3	25	23	16,320	17,739	376	440	0.1
LAWRENCE, TN											
60 –	**Finance, insurance, and real estate**	57	60	0.6	282	303	21,262	22,746	5,828	6,384	0.2
6000	Depository institutions	14	16	0.7	153	165	22,431	23,394	3,122	3,660	0.4
6400	Insurance agents, brokers, and service	17	18	0.8	45	52	25,956	29,769	1,186	1,257	0.3
6500	Real estate	15	14	0.4	29	30	6,897	8,267	184	241	0.1
6530	Real estate agents and managers	10	9	0.5	24	21	6,000	8,000	107	151	0.1
LEWIS, TN											
60 –	**Finance, insurance, and real estate**	11	12	0.1	65	66	22,646	22,667	1,321	1,241	0.0
LINCOLN, TN											
60 –	**Finance, insurance, and real estate**	47	46	0.4	279	242	20,989	23,008	5,715	5,495	0.2
6000	Depository institutions	17	14	0.6	200	167	23,400	24,862	4,377	3,992	0.4
6100	Nondepository institutions	5	6	0.6	13	18	22,154	22,222	305	448	0.2
6400	Insurance agents, brokers, and service	10	10	0.4	29	27	19,034	24,444	568	597	0.2
6530	Real estate agents and managers	7	8	0.5	12	10	9,000	15,200	149	203	0.1
LOUDON, TN											
60 –	**Finance, insurance, and real estate**	57	62	0.6	458	494	20,908	23,482	10,373	11,649	0.3
6000	Depository institutions	17	18	0.8	215	239	22,772	24,268	5,421	6,076	0.6
6020	Commercial banks	11	12	0.7	190	214	23,895	25,159	5,028	5,645	0.7
6140	Personal credit institutions	3	3	0.5	9	12	19,111	20,000	205	242	0.2
6400	Insurance agents, brokers, and service	14	14	0.6	32	23	15,125	15,130	425	387	0.1
6500	Real estate	18	22	0.6	187	209	20,257	23,981	4,054	4,665	1.1
6510	Real estate operators and lessors	6	7	0.5	18	19	15,778	24,000	435	414	0.3
6530	Real estate agents and managers	6	6	0.4	105	104	14,629	16,846	1,826	2,014	0.8
6553	Cemetery subdividers and developers	3	3	2.4	2	3	6,000	5,333	16	24	0.1
MCMINN, TN											
60 –	**Finance, insurance, and real estate**	67	68	0.6	424	454	24,774	24,300	9,954	10,832	0.3
6000	Depository institutions	27	27	1.2	288	304	24,222	24,474	6,390	7,173	0.7
6020	Commercial banks	18	18	1.1	214	227	24,636	24,599	4,600	5,382	0.7
6300	Insurance carriers	3	3	0.4	15	7	29,067	30,286	439	212	0.0
6400	Insurance agents, brokers, and service	13	13	0.5	54	58	25,926	25,655	1,348	1,473	0.4
6500	Real estate	18	18	0.5	46	63	23,130	18,730	1,158	1,234	0.3
6530	Real estate agents and managers	8	8	0.5	12	14	22,000	20,571	300	360	0.1
MCNAIRY, TN											
60 –	**Finance, insurance, and real estate**	30	29	0.3	179	164	18,346	19,878	3,677	3,380	0.1

Source: County Business Patterns, 1994/95, CBP-94/95, U.S. Department of Commerce, Washington, D.C., November 1997. SIC categories for which data were suppressed or not available for both 1994 and 1995 are not displayed. The employment columns represent mid-March employment in the year. Pay per employee is calculated by dividing 1st Quarter payroll, annualized, by mid-March employment. The columns headed "% State" show the county's percentage of the state total for the SIC in 1995; for example, 1.4% for SIC 6000 means that the county had 1.4 percent of the state's total establishments (or payroll) in SIC 6000 in 1995. A dash (-) is used to indicate that data are not available or cannot be calculated; nec means not elsewhere classified.

Continued on next page.

SIC	Industry	No. Establishments			Employment		Pay / Employee		Annual Payroll ($ 000)		
		1994	1995	% State	1994	1995	1994	1995	1994	1995	% State
MCNAIRY, TN - [continued]											
6000	Depository institutions	10	11	0.5	140	126	18,714	20,381	2,929	2,627	0.3
6400	Insurance agents, brokers, and service	10	9	0.4	26	20	13,538	15,200	414	387	0.1
6510	Real estate operators and lessors	4	4	0.3	5	7	12,000	9,714	61	66	0.1
MACON, TN											
60 –	**Finance, insurance, and real estate**	20	20	0.2	155	164	20,052	20,073	3,028	3,116	0.1
6000	Depository institutions	8	8	0.4	122	131	21,738	22,076	2,502	2,644	0.3
MADISON, TN											
60 –	**Finance, insurance, and real estate**	208	213	2.0	1,426	1,459	25,088	24,384	34,219	35,854	1.1
6000	Depository institutions	50	52	2.3	553	548	24,347	24,985	13,303	13,999	1.4
6020	Commercial banks	36	38	2.3	456	440	24,588	25,864	10,944	11,536	1.5
6100	Nondepository institutions	20	27	2.6	135	151	30,993	28,742	3,786	4,053	1.5
6140	Personal credit institutions	12	18	2.9	67	77	31,104	28,571	1,981	2,210	1.6
6200	Security and commodity brokers	7	5	1.0	39	39	64,718	39,385	1,743	1,636	0.5
6210	Security brokers and dealers	7	5	1.7	39	39	64,718	39,385	1,743	1,636	0.6
6300	Insurance carriers	29	29	3.5	360	355	27,511	27,899	9,472	9,420	1.3
6310	Life insurance	16	15	5.3	319	319	25,379	26,031	7,916	7,841	2.6
6400	Insurance agents, brokers, and service	41	43	1.8	143	147	20,448	19,837	3,147	3,155	0.8
6500	Real estate	55	49	1.4	161	162	14,758	14,099	2,337	2,683	0.6
6510	Real estate operators and lessors	21	18	1.3	63	66	10,667	11,455	677	700	0.6
6530	Real estate agents and managers	27	26	1.6	78	60	17,590	19,067	1,365	1,540	0.6
6550	Subdividers and developers	5	4	1.4	20	36	16,600	10,667	280	432	1.2
6700	Holding and other investment offices	6	8	2.4	35	57	11,429	15,860	431	908	0.6
6790	Miscellaneous investing	3	3	2.6	7	6	29,143	24,667	171	123	0.4
MARION, TN											
60 –	**Finance, insurance, and real estate**	25	25	0.2	157	145	18,573	33,352	3,005	4,419	0.1
6000	Depository institutions	9	8	0.4	118	104	19,119	40,000	2,317	3,695	0.4
6020	Commercial banks	9	8	0.5	118	104	19,119	40,000	2,317	3,695	0.5
6400	Insurance agents, brokers, and service	8	9	0.4	17	19	18,824	20,211	367	420	0.1
MARSHALL, TN											
60 –	**Finance, insurance, and real estate**	38	36	0.3	200	200	20,400	22,480	4,012	4,661	0.1
6000	Depository institutions	11	10	0.4	140	141	22,971	25,305	3,071	3,684	0.4
6100	Nondepository institutions	3	3	0.3	11	11	16,364	13,455	169	152	0.1
6530	Real estate agents and managers	8	7	0.4	11	10	11,636	15,200	145	156	0.1
MAURY, TN											
60 –	**Finance, insurance, and real estate**	114	122	1.1	1,316	1,386	23,799	24,863	33,528	35,181	1.1
6000	Depository institutions	29	28	1.2	417	429	19,492	20,103	8,844	8,811	0.9
6020	Commercial banks	22	21	1.3	376	392	19,489	20,143	8,045	8,181	1.1
6400	Insurance agents, brokers, and service	24	27	1.1	87	88	20,414	20,000	2,138	2,195	0.6
6500	Real estate	39	43	1.2	151	169	13,801	15,645	2,382	2,843	0.7
6510	Real estate operators and lessors	16	20	1.4	51	65	12,000	11,015	660	759	0.6
6530	Real estate agents and managers	19	18	1.1	72	75	13,667	18,453	1,234	1,480	0.6
MEIGS, TN											
60 –	**Finance, insurance, and real estate**	2	2	0.0	-	-	-	-	-	-	-
MONROE, TN											
60 –	**Finance, insurance, and real estate**	48	49	0.5	257	293	29,743	27,959	6,432	8,131	0.2
6000	Depository institutions	19	20	0.9	187	199	27,936	26,030	4,191	4,600	0.5
6400	Insurance agents, brokers, and service	11	10	0.4	28	27	18,000	18,519	558	584	0.1
6500	Real estate	14	15	0.4	20	42	8,400	6,762	195	422	0.1
6530	Real estate agents and managers	8	9	0.5	7	7	8,000	10,286	78	125	0.1
MONTGOMERY, TN											
60 –	**Finance, insurance, and real estate**	171	189	1.7	1,095	1,187	20,040	20,853	24,269	27,070	0.8

Source: County Business Patterns, 1994/95, CBP-94/95, U.S. Department of Commerce, Washington, D.C., November 1997. SIC categories for which data were suppressed or not available for both 1994 and 1995 are not displayed. The employment columns represent mid-March employment in the year. Pay per employee is calculated by dividing 1st Quarter payroll, annualized, by mid-March employment. The columns headed "% State" show the county's percentage of the state total for the SIC in 1995; for example, 1.4% for SIC 6000 means that the county had 1.4 percent of the state's total establishments (or payroll) in SIC 6000 in 1995. A dash (-) is used to indicate that data are not available or cannot be calculated; nec means not elsewhere classified.

Continued on next page.

SIC	Industry	No. Establishments			Employment		Pay / Employee		Annual Payroll ($ 000)		
		1994	1995	% State	1994	1995	1994	1995	1994	1995	% State
MONTGOMERY, TN - [continued]											
6000	Depository institutions	37	38	*1.7*	453	476	21,413	22,597	10,485	11,405	*1.2*
6020	Commercial banks	22	26	*1.6*	299	346	21,980	23,549	6,701	8,207	*1.1*
6060	Credit unions	5	5	*1.4*	26	27	16,308	16,741	433	455	*0.6*
6100	Nondepository institutions	17	22	*2.1*	72	81	27,000	24,691	2,035	2,247	*0.9*
6140	Personal credit institutions	11	13	*2.1*	45	54	24,978	23,926	1,164	1,371	*1.0*
6300	Insurance carriers	9	9	*1.1*	87	81	28,598	27,852	2,484	2,249	*0.3*
6400	Insurance agents, brokers, and service	35	37	*1.6*	136	122	18,941	21,082	3,056	3,178	*0.8*
6500	Real estate	62	70	*2.0*	274	331	12,964	14,187	4,255	4,796	*1.2*
6510	Real estate operators and lessors	30	35	*2.5*	93	114	10,151	11,404	1,292	1,547	*1.3*
6530	Real estate agents and managers	26	28	*1.7*	150	168	15,280	15,381	2,398	2,436	*1.0*
6550	Subdividers and developers	4	4	*1.4*	31	45	10,194	16,622	445	590	*1.6*
MOORE, TN											
60 –	**Finance, insurance, and real estate**	4	4	*0.0*	-	-	-	-	-	-	-
MORGAN, TN											
60 –	**Finance, insurance, and real estate**	9	9	*0.1*	52	127	18,538	12,787	924	962	*0.0*
6400	Insurance agents, brokers, and service	3	3	*0.1*	6	86	6,000	9,953	52	267	*0.1*
OBION, TN											
60 –	**Finance, insurance, and real estate**	58	62	*0.6*	367	360	20,643	21,967	7,231	7,585	*0.2*
6000	Depository institutions	17	19	*0.8*	223	238	21,399	21,613	4,584	4,757	*0.5*
6400	Insurance agents, brokers, and service	12	15	*0.6*	54	49	22,222	27,265	1,149	1,316	*0.3*
6500	Real estate	18	18	*0.5*	60	52	9,133	11,077	567	574	*0.1*
6510	Real estate operators and lessors	9	8	*0.6*	41	39	9,073	11,077	408	429	*0.4*
6530	Real estate agents and managers	9	10	*0.6*	19	13	9,263	11,077	159	145	*0.1*
OVERTON, TN											
60 –	**Finance, insurance, and real estate**	16	16	*0.1*	115	119	26,122	27,462	2,894	3,149	*0.1*
6000	Depository institutions	6	6	*0.3*	89	96	26,831	26,250	2,183	2,332	*0.2*
6400	Insurance agents, brokers, and service	6	7	*0.3*	21	18	25,333	36,000	609	709	*0.2*
PERRY, TN											
60 –	**Finance, insurance, and real estate**	12	11	*0.1*	50	44	18,720	18,000	1,016	939	*0.0*
6500	Real estate	4	3	*0.1*	9	9	5,778	8,000	82	74	*0.0*
PICKETT, TN											
60 –	**Finance, insurance, and real estate**	5	7	*0.1*	-	-	-	-	-	-	-
POLK, TN											
60 –	**Finance, insurance, and real estate**	14	14	*0.1*	572	558	28,350	28,251	15,948	15,537	*0.5*
6020	Commercial banks	7	7	*0.4*	137	134	18,657	22,448	2,586	2,801	*0.4*
PUTNAM, TN											
60 –	**Finance, insurance, and real estate**	106	124	*1.1*	662	706	23,511	23,513	15,152	17,549	*0.5*
6000	Depository institutions	26	27	*1.2*	348	330	24,931	24,679	7,893	8,218	*0.8*
6020	Commercial banks	21	23	*1.4*	329	320	25,204	24,800	7,463	8,039	*1.0*
6140	Personal credit institutions	5	9	*1.5*	19	20	25,053	26,000	461	640	*0.5*
6300	Insurance carriers	7	6	*0.7*	69	67	27,942	28,000	1,630	1,679	*0.2*
6400	Insurance agents, brokers, and service	23	24	*1.0*	81	89	19,407	23,820	1,994	2,388	*0.6*
6500	Real estate	35	47	*1.3*	119	164	13,277	12,293	2,235	3,107	*0.7*
6530	Real estate agents and managers	18	22	*1.3*	68	101	15,941	13,941	1,475	2,134	*0.9*
6700	Holding and other investment offices	5	4	*1.2*	4	14	19,000	29,429	101	332	*0.2*
RHEA, TN											
60 –	**Finance, insurance, and real estate**	32	29	*0.3*	129	158	20,930	17,215	2,771	2,640	*0.1*
6000	Depository institutions	7	6	*0.3*	83	112	24,434	17,607	1,984	1,863	*0.2*
6100	Nondepository institutions	5	6	*0.6*	15	15	20,800	24,000	341	420	*0.2*

Source: County Business Patterns, 1994/95, CBP-94/95, U.S. Department of Commerce, Washington, D.C., November 1997. SIC categories for which data were suppressed or not available for both 1994 and 1995 are not displayed. The employment columns represent mid-March employment in the year. Pay per employee is calculated by dividing 1st Quarter payroll, annualized, by mid-March employment. The columns headed "% State" show the county's percentage of the state total for the SIC in 1995; for example, 1.4% for SIC 6000 means that the county had 1.4 percent of the state's total establishments (or payroll) in SIC 6000 in 1995. A dash (-) is used to indicate that data are not available or cannot be calculated; nec means not elsewhere classified.

Continued on next page.

SIC	Industry	No. Establishments			Employment		Pay / Employee		Annual Payroll ($ 000)		
		1994	1995	% State	1994	1995	1994	1995	1994	1995	% State
RHEA, TN - [continued]											
6400	Insurance agents, brokers, and service	6	5	0.2	17	17	12,706	15,059	234	230	0.1
6500	Real estate	14	12	0.3	14	14	10,286	9,429	212	127	0.0
6510	Real estate operators and lessors	5	5	0.4	6	7	5,333	7,429	79	36	0.0
6530	Real estate agents and managers	6	4	0.2	6	4	14,667	12,000	101	56	0.0
ROANE, TN											
60 –	**Finance, insurance, and real estate**	48	53	0.5	244	290	18,443	21,186	4,497	5,985	0.2
6000	Depository institutions	17	19	0.8	127	177	19,780	23,797	2,357	3,894	0.4
6020	Commercial banks	10	11	0.7	73	137	22,301	24,584	1,584	3,134	0.4
6030	Savings institutions	3	4	2.3	38	24	16,000	21,833	464	427	0.6
6060	Credit unions	4	4	1.1	16	16	17,250	20,000	309	333	0.4
6400	Insurance agents, brokers, and service	13	12	0.5	38	34	10,737	12,235	479	503	0.1
6500	Real estate	13	15	0.4	25	24	13,280	14,833	457	370	0.1
6510	Real estate operators and lessors	5	7	0.5	5	12	24,800	18,333	145	216	0.2
6530	Real estate agents and managers	4	5	0.3	7	4	6,857	9,000	49	41	0.0
6550	Subdividers and developers	4	3	1.0	13	8	12,308	12,500	263	113	0.3
ROBERTSON, TN											
60 –	**Finance, insurance, and real estate**	69	71	0.7	268	256	20,090	20,500	5,527	5,643	0.2
6000	Depository institutions	16	15	0.7	134	127	21,881	20,945	2,744	2,662	0.3
6100	Nondepository institutions	7	7	0.7	23	21	25,913	30,286	607	607	0.2
6500	Real estate	28	28	0.8	54	51	11,704	12,078	750	734	0.2
6510	Real estate operators and lessors	10	9	0.6	21	19	12,762	11,789	276	218	0.2
6530	Real estate agents and managers	15	17	1.0	27	29	10,963	12,552	427	496	0.2
RUTHERFORD, TN											
60 –	**Finance, insurance, and real estate**	226	235	2.2	3,483	3,310	31,105	33,778	102,949	106,692	3.2
6000	Depository institutions	49	49	2.2	571	586	23,426	24,164	12,155	13,626	1.4
6020	Commercial banks	37	38	2.3	405	442	23,388	24,063	8,291	10,051	1.3
6100	Nondepository institutions	22	26	2.5	114	160	31,439	26,500	3,754	4,029	1.5
6140	Personal credit institutions	14	17	2.8	69	110	25,333	21,818	1,885	2,165	1.6
6400	Insurance agents, brokers, and service	42	46	1.9	142	137	16,028	18,628	2,468	2,655	0.7
6500	Real estate	82	89	2.5	333	334	10,751	14,503	4,469	6,061	1.5
6510	Real estate operators and lessors	30	32	2.3	103	129	11,184	12,341	1,248	1,723	1.4
6530	Real estate agents and managers	49	49	3.0	209	185	9,301	15,005	2,721	3,099	1.3
6700	Holding and other investment offices	3	5	1.5	14	16	14,286	7,500	82	103	0.1
SCOTT, TN											
60 –	**Finance, insurance, and real estate**	12	13	0.1	124	127	15,613	16,850	2,067	2,364	0.1
6400	Insurance agents, brokers, and service	4	4	0.2	8	10	15,500	14,000	137	164	0.0
SEQUATCHIE, TN											
60 –	**Finance, insurance, and real estate**	10	11	0.1	91	100	13,363	13,480	1,326	1,505	0.0
SEVIER, TN											
60 –	**Finance, insurance, and real estate**	178	187	1.7	1,542	1,531	16,911	19,321	29,996	31,689	0.9
6000	Depository institutions	29	31	1.4	425	457	20,772	22,486	9,254	10,539	1.1
6020	Commercial banks	24	25	1.5	402	430	20,856	22,744	8,737	9,905	1.3
6140	Personal credit institutions	3	3	0.5	8	7	24,500	33,143	197	218	0.2
6200	Security and commodity brokers	4	5	1.0	3	9	30,667	16,000	159	167	0.0
6400	Insurance agents, brokers, and service	20	20	0.8	87	93	20,000	20,731	2,101	2,148	0.5
6500	Real estate	110	117	3.3	850	760	14,485	18,353	14,775	15,279	3.7
6510	Real estate operators and lessors	34	36	2.5	304	171	9,592	13,614	3,527	2,835	2.4
6530	Real estate agents and managers	62	64	3.9	514	550	17,479	20,124	10,656	11,656	4.8
6550	Subdividers and developers	10	10	3.4	22	29	12,727	14,483	398	525	1.4
SHELBY, TN											
60 –	**Finance, insurance, and real estate**	1,947	1,992	18.3	24,571	23,982	35,375	34,631	865,307	870,611	26.0

Source: County Business Patterns, 1994/95, CBP-94/95, U.S. Department of Commerce, Washington, D.C., November 1997. SIC categories for which data were suppressed or not available for both 1994 and 1995 are *not* displayed. The employment columns represent mid-March employment in the year. Pay per employee is calculated by dividing 1st Quarter payroll, annualized, by mid-March employment. The columns headed "% State" show the county's percentage of the state total for the SIC in 1995; for example, 1.4% for SIC 6000 means that the county had 1.4 percent of the state's total establishments (or payroll) in SIC 6000 in 1995. A dash (-) is used to indicate that data are not available or cannot be calculated; *nec* means not elsewhere classified.

Continued on next page.

SIC	Industry	No. Establishments			Employment		Pay / Employee		Annual Payroll ($ 000)		
		1994	1995	% State	1994	1995	1994	1995	1994	1995	% State
SHELBY, TN - [continued]											
6000	Depository institutions	337	348	15.5	7,654	7,704	32,496	30,610	236,452	225,002	23.1
6020	Commercial banks	211	216	13.3	5,966	5,966	33,973	30,543	186,935	170,632	22.0
6030	Savings institutions	24	25	14.5	694	696	27,643	31,379	19,790	22,612	32.6
6060	Credit unions	83	82	22.7	775	841	28,444	31,838	24,544	26,426	33.8
6100	Nondepository institutions	178	202	19.1	2,249	1,598	37,992	32,778	71,617	52,178	19.8
6140	Personal credit institutions	94	104	16.9	614	617	25,199	27,929	15,228	16,666	12.4
6150	Business credit institutions	24	22	31.9	121	124	43,967	42,484	4,763	4,967	11.6
6160	Mortgage bankers and brokers	58	67	22.3	1,511	832	42,721	35,260	51,512	29,942	37.9
6200	Security and commodity brokers	116	127	26.0	2,046	2,052	91,949	71,468	192,732	201,930	55.7
6210	Security brokers and dealers	65	66	23.0	1,763	1,735	93,615	70,965	149,447	149,016	51.9
6220	Commodity contracts brokers, dealers	14	13	76.5	79	66	98,278	83,273	7,253	6,952	96.5
6280	Security and commodity services	37	47	25.5	204	251	75,098	71,841	36,032	45,952	67.3
6300	Insurance carriers	190	195	23.8	3,926	3,820	30,153	33,897	119,132	119,785	16.2
6310	Life insurance	72	70	24.9	1,499	1,411	28,899	33,434	41,144	39,410	12.9
6330	Fire, marine, and casualty insurance	83	89	22.1	999	1,076	33,441	35,338	32,481	35,890	13.2
6360	Title insurance	4	6	28.6	120	119	35,633	31,563	3,738	3,404	51.2
6400	Insurance agents, brokers, and service	443	431	18.1	2,456	2,562	33,147	40,303	84,847	99,774	25.1
6500	Real estate	600	607	17.1	5,030	4,916	20,531	22,047	113,730	116,264	27.9
6510	Real estate operators and lessors	263	250	17.6	1,637	1,590	20,924	20,926	33,404	32,575	27.2
6530	Real estate agents and managers	272	283	17.2	3,003	2,942	20,876	23,044	71,530	73,753	30.4
6540	Title abstract offices	5	7	8.4	34	24	31,412	35,333	1,067	934	7.6
6550	Subdividers and developers	52	46	15.5	354	312	14,768	15,808	7,393	6,546	17.6
6552	Subdividers and developers, n.e.c.	39	34	21.7	149	112	19,463	24,179	4,838	4,080	20.2
6553	Cemetery subdividers and developers	12	9	7.2	204	199	11,353	10,975	2,522	2,388	14.5
6710	Holding offices	29	26	21.0	872	677	36,069	47,988	31,999	31,463	28.8
6732	Educational, religious, etc. trusts	6	7	22.6	20	30	21,200	32,000	568	1,063	22.9
6790	Miscellaneous investing	32	32	27.8	205	207	35,200	34,145	7,742	7,167	21.4
6794	Patent owners and lessors	13	12	26.7	166	171	32,747	33,029	5,975	5,202	27.6
6799	Investors, n.e.c.	19	20	31.7	39	36	45,641	39,444	1,767	1,965	16.4
SMITH, TN											
60 –	**Finance, insurance, and real estate**	20	22	0.2	118	150	20,780	18,400	2,769	3,376	0.1
6000	Depository institutions	8	8	0.4	85	107	21,694	19,738	1,967	2,462	0.3
6020	Commercial banks	8	8	0.5	85	107	21,694	19,738	1,967	2,462	0.3
6500	Real estate	6	8	0.2	15	28	9,333	6,714	182	212	0.1
STEWART, TN											
60 –	**Finance, insurance, and real estate**	11	11	0.1	61	77	25,508	22,286	1,532	1,760	0.1
SULLIVAN, TN											
60 –	**Finance, insurance, and real estate**	283	285	2.6	1,841	1,942	23,535	25,806	45,290	51,422	1.5
6000	Depository institutions	66	68	3.0	687	780	23,010	25,559	17,021	23,656	2.4
6020	Commercial banks	39	41	2.5	419	493	25,690	28,949	10,480	13,440	1.7
6030	Savings institutions	12	12	7.0	196	198	19,531	20,343	5,213	8,420	12.1
6100	Nondepository institutions	28	29	2.7	125	133	24,960	25,895	3,591	3,720	1.4
6140	Personal credit institutions	21	23	3.7	103	122	25,631	25,443	3,098	3,310	2.5
6200	Security and commodity brokers	7	7	1.4	36	37	54,111	48,108	1,434	2,042	0.6
6300	Insurance carriers	26	28	3.4	361	358	31,922	37,732	10,517	9,301	1.3
6310	Life insurance	11	11	3.9	302	273	29,417	35,590	7,913	5,561	1.8
6400	Insurance agents, brokers, and service	65	61	2.6	258	267	23,612	23,670	6,915	7,197	1.8
6500	Real estate	82	83	2.3	337	341	12,593	14,123	5,183	5,060	1.2
6510	Real estate operators and lessors	34	36	2.5	139	152	11,424	16,553	1,825	2,671	2.2
6530	Real estate agents and managers	37	35	2.1	102	73	18,588	15,616	2,386	1,229	0.5
6550	Subdividers and developers	9	9	3.0	89	106	7,326	8,943	898	1,009	2.7
6553	Cemetery subdividers and developers	5	5	4.0	83	88	6,988	8,227	740	771	4.7

Source: County Business Patterns, 1994/95, CBP-94/95, U.S. Department of Commerce, Washington, D.C., November 1997. SIC categories for which data were suppressed or not available for both 1994 and 1995 are *not* displayed. The employment columns represent mid-March employment in the year. Pay per employee is calculated by dividing 1st Quarter payroll, annualized, by mid-March employment. The columns headed "% State" show the county's percentage of the state total for the SIC in 1995; for example, 1.4% for SIC 6000 means that the county had 1.4 percent of the state's total establishments (or payroll) in SIC 6000 in 1995. A dash (-) is used to indicate that data are not available or cannot be calculated; *nec* means not elsewhere classified.

Continued on next page.

SIC	Industry	No. Establishments			Employment		Pay / Employee		Annual Payroll ($ 000)		
		1994	1995	% State	1994	1995	1994	1995	1994	1995	% State
SULLIVAN, TN - [continued]											
6700	Holding and other investment offices	9	9	2.7	37	26	16,000	12,000	629	446	0.3
6710	Holding offices	4	4	3.2	15	9	27,467	16,000	426	242	0.2
6730	Trusts	5	3	4.3	22	16	8,182	9,750	203	178	2.3
SUMNER, TN											
60 –	**Finance, insurance, and real estate**	192	200	1.8	944	1,243	24,441	21,413	24,287	27,474	0.8
6000	Depository institutions	41	42	1.9	379	405	24,338	23,723	8,712	9,428	1.0
6020	Commercial banks	35	39	2.4	353	393	24,748	24,010	8,195	9,260	1.2
6100	Nondepository institutions	20	20	1.9	94	79	20,596	24,506	2,128	3,697	1.4
6140	Personal credit institutions	13	12	1.9	76	68	20,684	24,118	1,791	3,282	2.4
6160	Mortgage bankers and brokers	4	6	2.0	14	7	19,143	27,429	240	314	0.4
6200	Security and commodity brokers	4	5	1.0	7	8	33,143	25,500	212	260	0.1
6300	Insurance carriers	14	15	1.8	66	78	31,455	27,538	2,067	2,407	0.3
6400	Insurance agents, brokers, and service	48	48	2.0	137	136	22,248	25,324	3,389	3,916	1.0
6500	Real estate	59	65	1.8	151	193	20,212	21,492	3,590	4,781	1.1
6510	Real estate operators and lessors	18	20	1.4	52	59	16,846	16,881	1,100	1,124	0.9
6530	Real estate agents and managers	30	33	2.0	78	96	22,462	25,042	1,629	2,670	1.1
6550	Subdividers and developers	6	6	2.0	11	13	23,636	20,000	405	549	1.5
6700	Holding and other investment offices	6	5	1.5	110	344	31,855	14,907	4,189	2,985	1.9
TIPTON, TN											
60 –	**Finance, insurance, and real estate**	49	52	0.5	402	458	19,234	17,153	8,002	8,273	0.2
6000	Depository institutions	12	13	0.6	229	220	20,332	20,764	4,432	4,552	0.5
6400	Insurance agents, brokers, and service	14	14	0.6	45	50	31,289	28,720	1,643	1,665	0.4
6500	Real estate	15	17	0.5	38	85	7,474	4,376	350	412	0.1
6530	Real estate agents and managers	9	9	0.5	16	51	5,000	2,118	125	108	0.0
TROUSDALE, TN											
60 –	**Finance, insurance, and real estate**	8	7	0.1	60	79	25,533	21,418	1,502	1,527	0.0
UNICOI, TN											
60 –	**Finance, insurance, and real estate**	15	16	0.1	81	86	18,173	19,488	1,561	1,765	0.1
6000	Depository institutions	5	5	0.2	56	58	20,071	22,276	1,102	1,362	0.1
6400	Insurance agents, brokers, and service	5	5	0.2	17	19	16,000	14,947	304	283	0.1
6500	Real estate	5	6	0.2	8	9	9,500	11,111	155	120	0.0
UNION, TN											
60 –	**Finance, insurance, and real estate**	14	15	0.1	63	69	12,889	20,638	942	1,215	0.0
6500	Real estate	4	5	0.1	3	15	9,333	34,933	32	220	0.1
VAN BUREN, TN											
60 –	**Finance, insurance, and real estate**	4	4	0.0	-	-	-	-	-	-	-
WARREN, TN											
60 –	**Finance, insurance, and real estate**	51	55	0.5	305	325	21,548	21,317	6,645	7,695	0.2
6000	Depository institutions	16	15	0.7	224	211	22,911	24,152	5,048	5,397	0.6
6500	Real estate	15	19	0.5	27	54	9,333	10,889	388	912	0.2
6530	Real estate agents and managers	4	5	0.3	3	4	6,667	11,000	30	52	0.0
WASHINGTON, TN											
60 –	**Finance, insurance, and real estate**	229	238	2.2	1,185	1,273	24,955	26,228	29,148	34,300	1.0
6000	Depository institutions	46	50	2.2	543	539	24,840	28,119	12,330	14,601	1.5
6020	Commercial banks	30	31	1.9	405	394	26,558	29,340	9,315	10,745	1.4
6030	Savings institutions	9	9	5.2	97	105	20,289	24,990	2,140	2,967	4.3
6100	Nondepository institutions	17	23	2.2	74	107	32,973	24,262	2,450	2,780	1.1
6140	Personal credit institutions	12	16	2.6	53	84	25,358	23,667	1,147	2,048	1.5
6200	Security and commodity brokers	13	12	2.5	77	80	50,026	43,500	3,293	3,657	1.0
6210	Security brokers and dealers	10	9	3.1	73	76	52,384	45,316	3,259	3,611	1.3

Source: County Business Patterns, 1994/95, CBP-94/95, U.S. Department of Commerce, Washington, D.C., November 1997. SIC categories for which data were suppressed or not available for both 1994 and 1995 are not displayed. The employment columns represent mid-March employment in the year. Pay per employee is calculated by dividing 1st Quarter payroll, annualized, by mid-March employment. The columns headed "% State" show the county's percentage of the state total for the SIC in 1995; for example, 1.4% for SIC 6000 means that the county had 1.4 percent of the state's total establishments (or payroll) in SIC 6000 in 1995. A dash (-) is used to indicate that data are not available or cannot be calculated; nec means not elsewhere classified.

Continued on next page.

SIC	Industry	No. Establishments			Employment		Pay / Employee		Annual Payroll ($ 000)		
		1994	1995	% State	1994	1995	1994	1995	1994	1995	% State
WASHINGTON, TN - [continued]											
6280	Security and commodity services	3	3	*1.6*	4	4	7,000	9,000	34	46	*0.1*
6300	Insurance carriers	20	19	*2.3*	130	111	32,338	34,631	4,606	4,156	*0.6*
6310	Life insurance	8	8	*2.8*	91	76	31,077	33,579	2,994	2,539	*0.8*
6500	Real estate	80	82	*2.3*	223	255	12,700	13,914	3,531	4,118	*1.0*
6510	Real estate operators and lessors	41	43	*3.0*	129	149	10,109	10,309	1,515	1,761	*1.5*
6530	Real estate agents and managers	29	29	*1.8*	70	77	14,743	18,649	1,418	1,734	*0.7*
6540	Title abstract offices	3	3	*3.6*	6	9	29,333	20,000	199	191	*1.6*
WAYNE, TN											
60 –	**Finance, insurance, and real estate**	15	14	*0.1*	102	108	17,098	17,259	1,844	2,013	*0.1*
6000	Depository institutions	7	7	*0.3*	92	100	17,696	17,800	1,750	1,923	*0.2*
6020	Commercial banks	7	7	*0.4*	92	100	17,696	17,800	1,750	1,923	*0.2*
6400	Insurance agents, brokers, and service	5	4	*0.2*	6	7	10,667	10,857	69	79	*0.0*
WEAKLEY, TN											
60 –	**Finance, insurance, and real estate**	52	53	*0.5*	324	298	13,951	16,470	5,097	5,399	*0.2*
6000	Depository institutions	20	21	*0.9*	207	206	15,961	16,835	3,643	3,853	*0.4*
6020	Commercial banks	17	17	*1.0*	202	200	16,079	17,000	3,580	3,772	*0.5*
6500	Real estate	12	12	*0.3*	33	34	6,182	12,471	379	418	*0.1*
6510	Real estate operators and lessors	5	5	*0.4*	15	17	3,467	14,588	201	246	*0.2*
6530	Real estate agents and managers	7	7	*0.4*	18	17	8,444	10,353	178	172	*0.1*
WHITE, TN											
60 –	**Finance, insurance, and real estate**	28	29	*0.3*	138	123	20,551	18,862	2,703	2,444	*0.1*
6000	Depository institutions	6	6	*0.3*	64	63	18,563	19,302	1,198	1,313	*0.1*
6400	Insurance agents, brokers, and service	8	9	*0.4*	19	18	25,474	18,222	416	431	*0.1*
WILLIAMSON, TN											
60 –	**Finance, insurance, and real estate**	387	391	*3.6*	3,024	4,650	29,786	32,171	98,794	157,272	*4.7*
6000	Depository institutions	44	41	*1.8*	563	588	25,798	27,340	14,594	15,196	*1.6*
6020	Commercial banks	36	35	*2.2*	486	518	25,646	27,390	12,534	13,414	*1.7*
6100	Nondepository institutions	45	47	*4.4*	377	1,735	34,430	34,349	15,603	65,682	*24.9*
6140	Personal credit institutions	11	14	*2.3*	184	1,314	30,304	31,656	5,860	44,504	*33.1*
6200	Security and commodity brokers	23	24	*4.9*	57	83	34,175	32,434	2,283	2,698	*0.7*
6210	Security brokers and dealers	15	16	*5.6*	47	50	34,213	33,840	1,768	2,077	*0.7*
6300	Insurance carriers	40	39	*4.8*	568	562	35,430	39,181	20,062	20,355	*2.7*
6310	Life insurance	11	10	*3.6*	121	128	35,570	28,594	3,975	3,306	*1.1*
6330	Fire, marine, and casualty insurance	19	17	*4.2*	382	349	37,518	46,315	14,481	14,838	*5.4*
6400	Insurance agents, brokers, and service	89	98	*4.1*	533	664	31,565	38,283	19,761	28,866	*7.3*
6500	Real estate	119	120	*3.4*	774	825	20,879	18,415	19,115	16,745	*4.0*
6510	Real estate operators and lessors	31	29	*2.0*	228	240	15,246	14,083	3,896	3,772	*3.2*
6530	Real estate agents and managers	71	69	*4.2*	462	461	22,242	18,490	11,803	8,824	*3.6*
6552	Subdividers and developers, n.e.c.	9	12	*7.6*	51	90	33,333	28,756	2,275	2,923	*14.5*
6700	Holding and other investment offices	27	22	*6.6*	152	193	49,421	44,560	7,376	7,730	*4.9*
6710	Holding offices	8	8	*6.5*	59	66	40,746	41,697	2,295	2,592	*2.4*
6790	Miscellaneous investing	12	7	*6.1*	70	101	49,657	45,426	3,604	3,838	*11.5*
WILSON, TN											
60 –	**Finance, insurance, and real estate**	104	103	*0.9*	544	549	23,066	23,971	13,464	15,489	*0.5*
6000	Depository institutions	29	27	*1.2*	336	365	25,048	24,932	9,198	10,730	*1.1*
6100	Nondepository institutions	9	10	*0.9*	26	36	29,077	25,111	863	1,028	*0.4*
6400	Insurance agents, brokers, and service	17	19	*0.8*	52	52	21,538	21,231	1,125	1,205	*0.3*
6500	Real estate	40	39	*1.1*	107	82	11,664	15,366	1,333	1,864	*0.4*
6510	Real estate operators and lessors	12	9	*0.6*	55	27	10,691	12,000	502	407	*0.3*

Source: County Business Patterns, 1994/95, CBP-94/95, U.S. Department of Commerce, Washington, D.C., November 1997. SIC categories for which data were suppressed or not available for both 1994 and 1995 are not displayed. The employment columns represent mid-March employment in the year. Pay per employee is calculated by dividing 1st Quarter payroll, annualized, by mid-March employment. The columns headed "% State" show the county's percentage of the state total for the SIC in 1995; for example, 1.4% for SIC 6000 means that the county had 1.4 percent of the state's total establishments (or payroll) in SIC 6000 in 1995. A dash (-) is used to indicate that data are not available or cannot be calculated; nec means not elsewhere classified.

TEXAS

SIC	Industry	No. Establishments			Employment		Pay / Employee		Annual Payroll ($ 000)		
		1994	1995	% State	1994	1995	1994	1995	1994	1995	% State
ANDERSON, TX											
60–	**Finance, insurance, and real estate**	56	55	0.1	325	336	25,194	23,869	8,286	8,749	0.1
6000	Depository institutions	11	10	0.2	209	210	25,742	24,838	5,350	5,607	0.2
6020	Commercial banks	6	6	0.2	185	188	26,681	25,383	4,988	5,134	0.2
6400	Insurance agents, brokers, and service	14	14	0.2	44	48	17,545	18,833	905	1,065	0.1
6500	Real estate	16	15	0.1	31	34	11,613	12,471	424	516	0.0
6510	Real estate operators and lessors	8	8	0.1	13	16	12,923	16,250	210	289	0.0
ANGELINA, TX											
60–	**Finance, insurance, and real estate**	150	150	0.4	972	1,082	20,930	22,274	21,613	25,257	0.2
6000	Depository institutions	19	19	0.4	460	506	20,974	20,885	10,310	11,194	0.3
6020	Commercial banks	6	7	0.2	346	396	21,098	21,222	7,848	8,775	0.4
6030	Savings institutions	6	5	0.9	87	81	20,598	19,753	1,874	1,791	0.6
6060	Credit unions	7	7	0.7	27	29	20,593	19,448	588	628	0.2
6100	Nondepository institutions	9	10	0.3	30	34	19,467	19,765	607	729	0.1
6200	Security and commodity brokers	6	5	0.2	12	14	79,667	70,000	836	880	0.1
6210	Security brokers and dealers	6	5	0.3	12	14	79,667	70,000	836	880	0.1
6300	Insurance carriers	8	8	0.3	75	71	27,307	28,394	2,097	2,035	0.1
6310	Life insurance	3	3	0.4	55	52	23,491	23,308	1,333	1,200	0.1
6400	Insurance agents, brokers, and service	48	48	0.5	190	183	20,337	21,661	4,298	4,874	0.3
6500	Real estate	55	54	0.3	197	265	15,959	21,721	3,356	5,380	0.2
6510	Real estate operators and lessors	31	30	0.5	75	75	16,000	18,613	1,229	1,407	0.2
6530	Real estate agents and managers	17	17	0.2	97	160	13,031	22,200	1,476	3,266	0.2
6550	Subdividers and developers	5	5	0.5	16	21	36,000	33,333	520	596	0.3
6700	Holding and other investment offices	5	6	0.3	8	9	12,500	16,000	109	165	0.0
ARANSAS, TX											
60–	**Finance, insurance, and real estate**	41	47	0.1	162	303	14,000	10,904	2,590	3,201	0.0
6000	Depository institutions	4	4	0.1	36	28	18,444	21,286	680	575	0.0
6400	Insurance agents, brokers, and service	7	8	0.1	36	33	18,000	12,364	621	667	0.0
6500	Real estate	23	27	0.2	76	223	8,211	5,291	852	1,089	0.0
6510	Real estate operators and lessors	7	6	0.1	13	13	11,385	11,692	252	149	0.0
6530	Real estate agents and managers	10	18	0.2	54	201	6,444	4,100	431	755	0.1
ARCHER, TX											
60–	**Finance, insurance, and real estate**	12	13	0.0	68	58	18,529	20,759	1,267	942	0.0
6000	Depository institutions	5	5	0.1	41	41	20,878	22,439	907	697	0.0
6400	Insurance agents, brokers, and service	3	4	0.0	7	5	12,571	16,000	69	77	0.0
ARMSTRONG, TX											
60–	**Finance, insurance, and real estate**	5	5	0.0	-	-	-	-	-	-	-
ATASCOSA, TX											
60–	**Finance, insurance, and real estate**	40	43	0.1	243	214	19,193	18,262	4,536	3,856	0.0
6000	Depository institutions	8	8	0.2	116	110	21,793	22,182	2,464	2,422	0.1
6020	Commercial banks	8	8	0.3	116	110	21,793	22,182	2,464	2,422	0.1
6100	Nondepository institutions	8	10	0.3	39	34	30,051	17,412	1,028	518	0.0
6510	Real estate operators and lessors	6	6	0.1	25	22	6,080	6,364	152	150	0.0
6700	Holding and other investment offices	4	4	0.2	8	6	11,500	12,667	87	64	0.0
AUSTIN, TX											
60–	**Finance, insurance, and real estate**	54	53	0.1	365	346	18,838	19,988	7,440	7,487	0.1

Source: County Business Patterns, 1994/95, CBP-94/95, U.S. Department of Commerce, Washington, D.C., November 1997. SIC categories for which data were suppressed or not available for both 1994 and 1995 are *not* displayed. The employment columns represent mid-March employment in the year. Pay per employee is calculated by dividing 1st Quarter payroll, annualized, by mid-March employment. The columns headed "% State" show the county's percentage of the state total for the SIC in 1995; for example, 1.4% for SIC 6000 means that the county had 1.4 percent of the state's total establishments (or payroll) in SIC 6000 in 1995. A dash (-) is used to indicate that data are not available or cannot be calculated; *nec* means not elsewhere classified.

Continued on next page.

SIC	Industry	No. Establishments			Employment		Pay / Employee		Annual Payroll ($ 000)		
		1994	1995	% State	1994	1995	1994	1995	1994	1995	% State
AUSTIN, TX - [continued]											
6000	Depository institutions	11	10	0.2	187	185	20,321	21,449	4,134	4,444	0.1
6400	Insurance agents, brokers, and service	10	12	0.1	45	42	20,889	17,810	916	883	0.1
6500	Real estate	24	21	0.1	117	91	11,624	12,879	1,771	1,194	0.1
BAILEY, TX											
60 –	**Finance, insurance, and real estate**	13	14	0.0	71	74	24,225	22,541	1,636	1,681	0.0
6000	Depository institutions	3	3	0.1	51	49	25,412	24,898	1,228	1,251	0.0
6020	Commercial banks	3	3	0.1	51	49	25,412	24,898	1,228	1,251	0.1
BANDERA, TX											
60 –	**Finance, insurance, and real estate**	23	22	0.1	105	87	21,638	18,575	1,724	1,665	0.0
6400	Insurance agents, brokers, and service	5	4	0.0	40	16	24,900	20,750	420	272	0.0
6530	Real estate agents and managers	7	6	0.1	11	12	12,364	12,000	189	216	0.0
BASTROP, TX											
60 –	**Finance, insurance, and real estate**	40	38	0.1	235	260	18,332	18,508	4,599	5,130	0.0
6000	Depository institutions	8	8	0.2	153	176	20,497	19,341	3,296	3,717	0.1
6400	Insurance agents, brokers, and service	10	10	0.1	33	38	12,970	15,158	509	594	0.0
6500	Real estate	19	17	0.1	44	40	14,364	15,400	661	614	0.0
6550	Subdividers and developers	3	3	0.3	4	4	19,000	23,000	89	94	0.0
BAYLOR, TX											
60 –	**Finance, insurance, and real estate**	11	13	0.0	44	40	17,545	17,900	792	723	0.0
6000	Depository institutions	3	3	0.1	33	29	19,152	19,310	642	551	0.0
6400	Insurance agents, brokers, and service	5	5	0.1	9	7	9,333	10,286	82	76	0.0
BEE, TX											
60 –	**Finance, insurance, and real estate**	48	45	0.1	278	279	19,022	19,097	5,445	5,510	0.0
6000	Depository institutions	9	8	0.2	147	149	20,218	20,134	3,012	3,121	0.1
6100	Nondepository institutions	5	5	0.1	15	14	13,867	14,000	215	191	0.0
6140	Personal credit institutions	5	5	0.3	15	14	13,867	14,000	215	191	0.0
6400	Insurance agents, brokers, and service	11	10	0.1	51	47	17,725	19,234	952	1,008	0.1
6530	Real estate agents and managers	9	9	0.1	10	22	17,600	8,727	186	205	0.0
BELL, TX											
60 –	**Finance, insurance, and real estate**	390	402	1.0	3,364	3,601	17,283	17,440	59,895	65,324	0.5
6000	Depository institutions	43	47	0.9	942	1,010	20,964	20,024	19,438	22,006	0.7
6020	Commercial banks	26	31	1.0	753	821	21,620	20,175	15,874	18,218	0.7
6060	Credit unions	8	8	0.8	133	138	19,218	20,232	2,697	2,959	1.1
6100	Nondepository institutions	35	39	1.2	750	865	19,477	19,491	14,875	16,155	1.2
6140	Personal credit institutions	24	27	1.7	108	126	17,111	18,222	1,939	2,407	0.5
6200	Security and commodity brokers	21	20	0.9	52	74	46,615	32,270	2,371	2,419	0.2
6300	Insurance carriers	25	25	0.8	557	573	9,659	10,883	5,686	6,562	0.2
6330	Fire, marine, and casualty insurance	17	18	1.1	430	430	6,977	7,181	3,217	3,517	0.2
6400	Insurance agents, brokers, and service	77	79	0.9	299	304	18,368	17,803	5,544	5,524	0.4
6500	Real estate	181	185	1.2	730	747	12,844	14,163	10,510	11,117	0.5
6510	Real estate operators and lessors	83	75	1.1	326	308	10,307	11,753	3,752	3,690	0.6
6530	Real estate agents and managers	74	82	1.1	267	310	16,090	16,594	4,749	5,402	0.4
6540	Title abstract offices	5	5	1.3	70	57	17,314	19,158	1,284	1,220	1.6
6550	Subdividers and developers	17	18	1.6	66	69	7,636	10,377	719	734	0.3
6552	Subdividers and developers, n.e.c.	8	9	1.3	25	28	10,880	11,286	316	337	0.2
6553	Cemetery subdividers and developers	7	7	2.1	39	36	5,846	10,111	355	362	0.6
6700	Holding and other investment offices	8	7	0.3	34	28	32,706	39,286	1,471	1,541	0.2
BEXAR, TX											
60 –	**Finance, insurance, and real estate**	2,796	2,826	6.8	38,418	40,265	28,673	30,012	1,126,640	1,285,781	9.0
6000	Depository institutions	320	331	6.4	9,516	9,946	23,854	24,746	232,512	251,527	7.9
6020	Commercial banks	154	160	5.3	5,335	5,466	24,562	25,851	127,960	138,333	5.6

Source: County Business Patterns, 1994/95, CBP-94/95, U.S. Department of Commerce, Washington, D.C., November 1997. SIC categories for which data were suppressed or not available for both 1994 and 1995 are not displayed. The employment columns represent mid-March employment in the year. Pay per employee is calculated by dividing 1st Quarter payroll, annualized, by mid-March employment. The columns headed "% State" show the county's percentage of the state total for the SIC in 1995; for example, 1.4% for SIC 6000 means that the county had 1.4 percent of the state's total establishments (or payroll) in SIC 6000 in 1995. A dash (-) is used to indicate that data are not available or cannot be calculated; nec means not elsewhere classified.

Continued on next page.

SIC	Industry	No. Establishments			Employment		Pay / Employee		Annual Payroll ($ 000)		
		1994	1995	% State	1994	1995	1994	1995	1994	1995	% State
BEXAR, TX - [continued]											
6030	Savings institutions	32	32	5.7	1,844	2,071	28,176	26,918	57,294	63,834	20.7
6060	Credit unions	78	82	8.1	1,884	2,000	19,244	20,306	39,197	40,551	15.4
6100	Nondepository institutions	250	274	8.2	2,712	2,810	30,106	37,507	76,429	90,740	7.0
6140	Personal credit institutions	132	143	9.0	1,448	1,550	19,936	21,778	31,494	36,865	8.2
6160	Mortgage bankers and brokers	82	81	7.1	1,134	1,004	42,176	62,327	39,168	42,677	8.5
6200	Security and commodity brokers	104	115	4.9	1,654	2,101	56,443	43,299	83,280	94,663	6.2
6300	Insurance carriers	252	253	8.3	14,135	14,235	32,898	34,650	485,428	564,164	17.8
6310	Life insurance	74	72	8.5	2,658	2,296	32,144	33,834	76,809	81,107	8.6
6320	Medical service and health insurance	27	26	14.1	1,295	1,251	25,328	30,823	36,247	42,541	11.1
6321	Accident and health insurance	11	7	8.6	331	208	26,888	32,750	8,100	7,214	6.7
6324	Hospital and medical service plans	16	19	18.4	964	1,043	24,793	30,439	28,147	35,327	12.8
6330	Fire, marine, and casualty insurance	124	128	7.7	9,726	10,396	34,200	35,119	360,097	430,225	26.4
6360	Title insurance	11	13	6.9	293	246	38,362	44,081	10,429	9,052	7.5
6400	Insurance agents, brokers, and service	624	622	6.8	2,898	3,060	25,920	27,702	79,835	88,336	6.0
6500	Real estate	1,104	1,077	6.7	6,615	6,763	19,055	20,316	133,649	142,350	6.0
6510	Real estate operators and lessors	466	434	6.6	2,609	2,602	17,550	19,178	46,553	50,265	8.5
6530	Real estate agents and managers	546	548	7.5	3,208	3,447	19,261	20,113	66,852	74,764	5.2
6540	Title abstract offices	13	13	3.5	236	205	27,898	30,829	6,487	4,832	6.3
6550	Subdividers and developers	55	55	5.0	546	469	21,502	23,650	13,442	11,497	5.1
6552	Subdividers and developers, n.e.c.	44	44	6.3	400	325	23,430	25,957	10,710	8,792	5.7
6553	Cemetery subdividers and developers	8	7	2.1	145	136	16,166	17,941	2,585	2,503	3.8
6700	Holding and other investment offices	134	144	6.1	594	1,022	41,448	37,714	26,242	39,999	4.5
6710	Holding offices	32	29	4.8	194	265	67,113	50,777	13,191	14,412	2.6
6720	Investment offices	6	7	11.1	5	11	22,400	24,364	190	268	2.1
6730	Trusts	24	30	7.0	143	458	25,762	29,083	3,917	12,963	16.4
6732	Educational, religious, etc. trusts	8	10	6.7	39	35	11,897	16,229	496	578	2.3
6733	Trusts, n.e.c.	16	20	7.2	104	423	30,962	30,147	3,421	12,385	23.3
6790	Miscellaneous investing	67	62	5.5	250	264	31,152	38,833	8,569	10,870	4.7
6799	Investors, n.e.c.	42	38	5.4	171	178	31,789	39,034	5,667	7,594	5.4
BLANCO, TX											
60 –	**Finance, insurance, and real estate**	14	14	0.0	86	84	19,256	19,857	1,814	1,903	0.0
6000	Depository institutions	5	5	0.1	63	63	20,317	20,698	1,384	1,412	0.0
6400	Insurance agents, brokers, and service	4	4	0.0	16	13	18,000	21,231	328	387	0.0
BOSQUE, TX											
60 –	**Finance, insurance, and real estate**	35	34	0.1	124	119	18,613	20,336	2,461	2,613	0.0
6000	Depository institutions	9	9	0.2	79	76	21,620	23,105	1,814	1,925	0.1
6020	Commercial banks	9	9	0.3	79	76	21,620	23,105	1,814	1,925	0.1
6400	Insurance agents, brokers, and service	10	9	0.1	27	28	12,148	14,714	377	400	0.0
6500	Real estate	7	7	0.0	8	5	12,500	16,800	117	134	0.0
6700	Holding and other investment offices	4	4	0.2	5	5	10,400	9,600	47	52	0.0
BOWIE, TX											
60 –	**Finance, insurance, and real estate**	177	174	0.4	1,100	1,125	24,149	23,989	26,961	28,792	0.2
6000	Depository institutions	33	32	0.6	541	539	22,403	21,477	12,177	12,156	0.4
6020	Commercial banks	18	18	0.6	401	380	22,663	23,168	9,168	9,082	0.4
6100	Nondepository institutions	18	18	0.5	76	73	17,368	18,904	1,388	1,485	0.1
6140	Personal credit institutions	13	13	0.8	55	53	15,345	17,132	858	960	0.2
6300	Insurance carriers	14	13	0.4	84	69	36,619	43,362	2,807	2,779	0.1
6400	Insurance agents, brokers, and service	53	47	0.5	203	220	29,616	31,345	6,957	7,920	0.5
6500	Real estate	53	57	0.4	179	201	15,240	13,174	2,444	2,760	0.1
6510	Real estate operators and lessors	26	27	0.4	97	97	10,392	11,093	1,074	1,234	0.2
6550	Subdividers and developers	6	6	0.5	23	19	9,913	10,105	252	257	0.1
BRAZORIA, TX											
60 –	**Finance, insurance, and real estate**	282	292	0.7	1,689	1,813	21,132	20,225	36,042	36,994	0.3
6000	Depository institutions	45	45	0.9	734	773	21,624	21,728	15,534	17,068	0.5

Source: County Business Patterns, 1994/95, CBP-94/95, U.S. Department of Commerce, Washington, D.C., November 1997. SIC categories for which data were suppressed or not available for both 1994 and 1995 are not displayed. The employment columns represent mid-March employment in the year. Pay per employee is calculated by dividing 1st Quarter payroll, annualized, by mid-March employment. The columns headed "% State" show the county's percentage of the state total for the SIC in 1995; for example, 1.4% for SIC 6000 means that the county had 1.4 percent of the state's total establishments (or payroll) in SIC 6000 in 1995. A dash (-) is used to indicate that data are not available or cannot be calculated; nec means not elsewhere classified.

Continued on next page.

SIC	Industry	No. Establishments			Employment		Pay / Employee		Annual Payroll ($ 000)		
		1994	1995	% State	1994	1995	1994	1995	1994	1995	% State
BRAZORIA, TX - [continued]											
6020	Commercial banks	30	30	1.0	570	582	21,979	22,027	11,998	13,024	0.5
6100	Nondepository institutions	9	11	0.3	20	27	27,200	23,407	498	921	0.1
6140	Personal credit institutions	4	7	0.4	10	14	24,400	18,286	181	385	0.1
6160	Mortgage bankers and brokers	5	4	0.4	10	13	30,000	28,923	317	536	0.1
6300	Insurance carriers	18	19	0.6	60	57	36,933	51,789	2,383	2,442	0.1
6400	Insurance agents, brokers, and service	72	72	0.8	243	237	21,992	21,451	5,077	5,125	0.3
6500	Real estate	125	133	0.8	555	680	15,560	14,153	9,597	9,519	0.4
6510	Real estate operators and lessors	63	68	1.0	218	268	14,587	13,313	3,389	3,614	0.6
6530	Real estate agents and managers	51	54	0.7	196	212	14,714	15,075	3,314	3,352	0.2
6553	Cemetery subdividers and developers	4	4	1.2	80	148	15,450	11,865	1,520	1,528	2.3
BRAZOS, TX											
60 –	**Finance, insurance, and real estate**	254	272	0.7	2,035	2,212	22,502	22,812	51,260	54,571	0.4
6000	Depository institutions	22	24	0.5	673	711	21,872	23,646	17,953	18,776	0.6
6020	Commercial banks	10	9	0.3	267	270	22,037	25,926	6,150	7,202	0.3
6030	Savings institutions	7	9	1.6	366	393	22,634	23,410	11,250	10,979	3.6
6100	Nondepository institutions	21	22	0.7	134	133	26,388	25,474	3,598	3,771	0.3
6140	Personal credit institutions	13	15	0.9	69	70	25,913	25,829	1,708	1,766	0.4
6200	Security and commodity brokers	19	20	0.9	76	90	53,368	41,289	3,941	3,616	0.2
6210	Security brokers and dealers	11	11	0.7	63	69	60,190	49,855	3,547	3,230	0.3
6280	Security and commodity services	8	9	1.2	13	21	20,308	13,143	394	386	0.1
6300	Insurance carriers	13	13	0.4	85	70	30,918	35,829	2,613	1,941	0.1
6400	Insurance agents, brokers, and service	47	51	0.6	416	433	28,865	30,753	12,842	14,503	1.0
6500	Real estate	120	127	0.8	600	675	12,140	12,409	8,086	9,196	0.4
6510	Real estate operators and lessors	58	56	0.9	271	271	10,672	10,804	3,141	3,205	0.5
6530	Real estate agents and managers	50	60	0.8	298	355	13,436	13,904	4,400	5,341	0.4
6552	Subdividers and developers, n.e.c.	4	3	0.4	6	6	6,667	6,000	92	37	0.0
6700	Holding and other investment offices	12	15	0.6	51	100	30,588	23,440	2,227	2,768	0.3
6792	Oil royalty traders	3	3	1.0	10	6	26,400	40,000	290	267	0.6
BREWSTER, TX											
60 –	**Finance, insurance, and real estate**	19	21	0.1	130	127	13,385	13,827	1,884	2,003	0.0
6400	Insurance agents, brokers, and service	3	3	0.0	7	7	12,571	13,143	86	79	0.0
6510	Real estate operators and lessors	3	5	0.1	4	5	5,000	4,000	20	31	0.0
BRISCOE, TX											
60 –	**Finance, insurance, and real estate**	6	6	0.0	-	-	-	-	-	-	-
6500	Real estate	3	3	0.0	3	5	6,667	3,200	24	21	0.0
BROOKS, TX											
60 –	**Finance, insurance, and real estate**	10	11	0.0	74	79	15,568	16,051	1,323	1,413	0.0
6000	Depository institutions	3	3	0.1	57	58	16,421	17,655	1,093	1,166	0.0
BROWN, TX											
60 –	**Finance, insurance, and real estate**	55	58	0.1	286	296	21,888	20,797	6,522	6,628	0.0
6000	Depository institutions	10	11	0.2	139	146	20,921	18,685	3,052	2,938	0.1
6020	Commercial banks	5	5	0.2	114	118	22,421	19,729	2,651	2,461	0.1
6400	Insurance agents, brokers, and service	17	16	0.2	50	51	15,920	16,941	856	900	0.1
6500	Real estate	15	16	0.1	37	39	14,378	13,026	603	656	0.1
6510	Real estate operators and lessors	4	4	0.1	5	5	15,200	15,200	78	79	0.0
6530	Real estate agents and managers	7	7	0.1	6	8	15,333	7,500	99	78	0.0
BURLESON, TX											
60 –	**Finance, insurance, and real estate**	23	19	0.0	141	136	18,326	19,912	2,881	3,079	0.0
6000	Depository institutions	7	7	0.1	103	111	21,437	21,622	2,490	2,767	0.1
6500	Real estate	5	3	0.0	9	7	10,222	13,143	93	92	0.0
BURNET, TX											
60 –	**Finance, insurance, and real estate**	69	70	0.2	246	271	20,976	26,096	5,599	6,487	0.0

Source: County Business Patterns, 1994/95, CBP-94/95, U.S. Department of Commerce, Washington, D.C., November 1997. SIC categories for which data were suppressed or not available for both 1994 and 1995 are not displayed. The employment columns represent mid-March employment in the year. Pay per employee is calculated by dividing 1st Quarter payroll, annualized, by mid-March employment. The columns headed "% State" show the county's percentage of the state total for the SIC in 1995; for example, 1.4% for SIC 6000 means that the county had 1.4 percent of the state's total establishments (or payroll) in SIC 6000 in 1995. A dash (-) is used to indicate that data are not available or cannot be calculated; nec means not elsewhere classified.

Continued on next page.

SIC	Industry	No. Establishments			Employment		Pay / Employee		Annual Payroll ($ 000)		
		1994	1995	% State	1994	1995	1994	1995	1994	1995	% State
BURNET, TX - [continued]											
6000	Depository institutions	9	9	0.2	112	121	20,071	19,669	2,467	2,429	0.1
6400	Insurance agents, brokers, and service	11	11	0.1	35	46	31,086	34,087	1,134	1,821	0.1
6500	Real estate	37	40	0.3	64	77	9,125	9,195	581	729	0.0
6510	Real estate operators and lessors	24	28	0.4	38	54	5,474	6,148	269	370	0.1
6530	Real estate agents and managers	8	6	0.1	11	8	11,273	20,500	101	143	0.0
CALDWELL, TX											
60 –	**Finance, insurance, and real estate**	40	39	0.1	177	184	17,853	18,065	3,341	3,418	0.0
6000	Depository institutions	5	5	0.1	99	100	21,010	20,320	2,006	2,013	0.1
6100	Nondepository institutions	4	4	0.1	12	8	19,333	19,000	229	156	0.0
6400	Insurance agents, brokers, and service	7	6	0.1	22	20	12,545	14,000	279	279	0.0
6500	Real estate	18	20	0.1	38	49	10,842	12,816	613	713	0.0
6510	Real estate operators and lessors	9	10	0.2	22	28	11,273	15,000	366	427	0.1
6530	Real estate agents and managers	4	6	0.1	7	11	8,571	8,364	86	100	0.0
CALHOUN, TX											
60 –	**Finance, insurance, and real estate**	30	29	0.1	208	179	19,923	21,788	3,850	4,074	0.0
6000	Depository institutions	9	9	0.2	163	143	22,405	24,140	3,324	3,600	0.1
6020	Commercial banks	4	4	0.1	135	113	22,696	24,956	2,710	2,899	0.1
6400	Insurance agents, brokers, and service	7	7	0.1	21	18	9,905	10,667	208	196	0.0
6500	Real estate	11	9	0.1	21	14	7,429	6,571	169	90	0.0
6510	Real estate operators and lessors	5	4	0.1	9	7	6,667	5,714	57	42	0.0
CALLAHAN, TX											
60 –	**Finance, insurance, and real estate**	12	13	0.0	79	85	17,570	19,059	1,610	1,859	0.0
6000	Depository institutions	4	4	0.1	62	68	18,903	20,412	1,378	1,622	0.1
6020	Commercial banks	4	4	0.1	62	68	18,903	20,412	1,378	1,622	0.1
6500	Real estate	4	4	0.0	8	8	16,000	17,500	139	138	0.0
CAMERON, TX											
60 –	**Finance, insurance, and real estate**	538	568	1.4	3,604	3,430	18,426	19,964	70,325	66,884	0.5
6000	Depository institutions	67	70	1.3	1,233	1,076	21,622	23,498	28,454	22,906	0.7
6020	Commercial banks	40	41	1.4	1,074	895	22,745	25,345	26,295	20,308	0.8
6060	Credit unions	9	10	1.0	119	130	13,983	13,938	1,603	1,835	0.7
6100	Nondepository institutions	55	60	1.8	276	296	21,246	21,541	5,946	6,398	0.5
6140	Personal credit institutions	46	49	3.1	241	262	21,112	21,557	5,120	5,559	1.2
6200	Security and commodity brokers	12	13	0.6	56	57	59,857	44,772	2,941	2,712	0.2
6210	Security brokers and dealers	8	10	0.7	46	51	71,652	48,157	2,886	2,532	0.2
6300	Insurance carriers	18	19	0.6	188	186	25,383	32,387	5,279	5,713	0.2
6310	Life insurance	7	7	0.8	165	164	21,333	28,049	3,991	4,302	0.5
6400	Insurance agents, brokers, and service	95	100	1.1	421	436	21,131	23,321	8,993	10,349	0.7
6500	Real estate	279	293	1.8	1,358	1,300	10,943	12,080	16,455	16,695	0.7
6510	Real estate operators and lessors	140	147	2.2	469	483	11,497	11,867	5,677	6,053	1.0
6530	Real estate agents and managers	125	118	1.6	827	674	10,515	12,582	9,612	8,440	0.6
6550	Subdividers and developers	12	20	1.8	42	125	12,476	9,856	885	1,858	0.8
6552	Subdividers and developers, n.e.c.	9	9	1.3	30	40	15,333	16,100	824	946	0.6
6730	Trusts	4	3	0.7	8	8	9,500	12,500	83	88	0.1
6733	Trusts, n.e.c.	4	3	1.1	8	8	9,500	12,500	83	88	0.2
6790	Miscellaneous investing	4	4	0.4	8	10	10,500	17,600	105	152	0.1
CAMP, TX											
60 –	**Finance, insurance, and real estate**	18	19	0.0	112	169	23,571	22,225	2,174	3,105	0.0
6000	Depository institutions	4	4	0.1	81	106	27,951	27,660	1,774	2,483	0.1
6400	Insurance agents, brokers, and service	6	6	0.1	20	22	13,800	22,364	308	402	0.0
6500	Real estate	5	6	0.0	8	35	7,000	7,429	50	135	0.0

Source: County Business Patterns, 1994/95, CBP-94/95, U.S. Department of Commerce, Washington, D.C., November 1997. SIC categories for which data were suppressed or not available for both 1994 and 1995 are not displayed. The employment columns represent mid-March employment in the year. Pay per employee is calculated by dividing 1st Quarter payroll, annualized, by mid-March employment. The columns headed "% State" show the county's percentage of the state total for the SIC in 1995; for example, 1.4% for SIC 6000 means that the county had 1.4 percent of the state's total establishments (or payroll) in SIC 6000 in 1995. A dash (-) is used to indicate that data are not available or cannot be calculated; nec means not elsewhere classified.

Continued on next page.

SIC	Industry	No. Establishments			Employment		Pay / Employee		Annual Payroll ($ 000)		
		1994	1995	% State	1994	1995	1994	1995	1994	1995	% State
CARSON, TX - [continued]											
60 –	**Finance, insurance, and real estate**	14	12	0.0	89	86	21,483	24,884	1,940	2,111	0.0
6000	Depository institutions	4	4	0.1	52	57	26,462	27,930	1,326	1,493	0.0
CASS, TX											
60 –	**Finance, insurance, and real estate**	46	49	0.1	257	272	18,381	17,853	5,170	5,429	0.0
6000	Depository institutions	12	12	0.2	136	142	22,235	21,380	3,247	3,214	0.1
6020	Commercial banks	7	7	0.2	106	108	21,132	21,259	2,517	2,469	0.1
6100	Nondepository institutions	5	5	0.1	14	14	13,714	16,857	188	230	0.0
6140	Personal credit institutions	5	5	0.3	14	14	13,714	16,857	188	230	0.1
6400	Insurance agents, brokers, and service	13	16	0.2	45	49	19,556	18,612	915	1,066	0.1
6500	Real estate	13	13	0.1	52	59	8,769	8,881	612	778	0.0
6530	Real estate agents and managers	10	9	0.1	39	44	6,564	7,091	379	327	0.0
CASTRO, TX											
60 –	**Finance, insurance, and real estate**	21	19	0.0	84	102	23,000	24,863	1,780	2,219	0.0
6400	Insurance agents, brokers, and service	6	6	0.1	15	18	9,600	10,222	169	180	0.0
6500	Real estate	6	5	0.0	10	12	9,200	7,333	95	98	0.0
CHAMBERS, TX											
60 –	**Finance, insurance, and real estate**	24	26	0.1	136	139	16,853	18,331	2,473	2,831	0.0
6000	Depository institutions	4	4	0.1	73	75	22,630	23,147	1,785	1,875	0.1
6020	Commercial banks	4	4	0.1	73	75	22,630	23,147	1,785	1,875	0.1
6530	Real estate agents and managers	5	7	0.1	11	15	5,818	8,533	57	118	0.0
CHEROKEE, TX											
60 –	**Finance, insurance, and real estate**	56	60	0.1	314	317	24,497	24,126	7,643	8,211	0.1
6000	Depository institutions	12	12	0.2	198	180	29,192	30,178	5,630	5,980	0.2
6020	Commercial banks	8	8	0.3	137	124	27,679	31,645	3,976	4,272	0.2
6100	Nondepository institutions	10	10	0.3	36	36	17,333	18,778	701	681	0.1
6400	Insurance agents, brokers, and service	10	10	0.1	25	32	13,600	12,625	375	436	0.0
6510	Real estate operators and lessors	8	9	0.1	15	25	10,933	12,160	178	305	0.1
6530	Real estate agents and managers	5	4	0.1	10	6	12,800	11,333	87	79	0.0
6700	Holding and other investment offices	4	4	0.2	6	6	8,667	10,667	71	65	0.0
CHILDRESS, TX											
60 –	**Finance, insurance, and real estate**	18	18	0.0	62	77	18,452	20,260	1,201	1,475	0.0
6400	Insurance agents, brokers, and service	5	4	0.0	8	10	13,500	14,400	136	159	0.0
CLAY, TX											
60 –	**Finance, insurance, and real estate**	12	12	0.0	65	70	20,308	20,229	1,631	1,768	0.0
6000	Depository institutions	3	3	0.1	49	50	23,429	23,520	1,394	1,512	0.0
6020	Commercial banks	3	3	0.1	49	50	23,429	23,520	1,394	1,512	0.1
6400	Insurance agents, brokers, and service	6	6	0.1	8	10	10,000	10,400	98	97	0.0
COCHRAN, TX											
60 –	**Finance, insurance, and real estate**	6	5	0.0	-	-	-	-	-	-	-
COKE, TX											
60 –	**Finance, insurance, and real estate**	7	7	0.0	31	47	14,710	16,255	765	836	0.0
COLEMAN, TX											
60 –	**Finance, insurance, and real estate**	17	17	0.0	96	90	18,667	18,667	2,023	1,917	0.0
6000	Depository institutions	4	4	0.1	73	68	19,726	19,471	1,684	1,554	0.0
6400	Insurance agents, brokers, and service	6	6	0.1	11	10	11,273	13,600	125	138	0.0
6500	Real estate	3	3	0.0	5	5	11,200	12,800	66	71	0.0
COLLIN, TX											
60 –	**Finance, insurance, and real estate**	580	591	1.4	5,313	5,823	30,661	32,363	160,909	181,856	1.3

Source: County Business Patterns, 1994/95, CBP-94/95, U.S. Department of Commerce, Washington, D.C., November 1997. SIC categories for which data were suppressed or not available for both 1994 and 1995 are not displayed. The employment columns represent mid-March employment in the year. Pay per employee is calculated by dividing 1st Quarter payroll, annualized, by mid-March employment. The columns headed "% State" show the county's percentage of the state total for the SIC in 1995; for example, 1.4% for SIC 6000 means that the county had 1.4 percent of the state's total establishments (or payroll) in SIC 6000 in 1995. A dash (-) is used to indicate that data are not available or cannot be calculated; nec means not elsewhere classified.

Continued on next page.

SIC	Industry	No. Establishments			Employment		Pay / Employee		Annual Payroll ($ 000)		
		1994	1995	% State	1994	1995	1994	1995	1994	1995	% State
COLLIN, TX - [continued]											
6000	Depository institutions	58	61	1.2	869	972	25,501	25,354	21,640	24,167	0.8
6020	Commercial banks	42	45	1.5	673	756	25,373	25,360	16,237	18,408	0.7
6100	Nondepository institutions	61	58	1.7	333	338	42,222	43,846	13,092	14,639	1.1
6140	Personal credit institutions	13	13	0.8	56	60	29,714	19,933	1,793	1,682	0.4
6150	Business credit institutions	7	8	2.0	79	112	69,418	72,429	4,304	5,997	2.2
6160	Mortgage bankers and brokers	39	34	3.0	194	162	34,948	33,185	6,745	6,792	1.4
6200	Security and commodity brokers	35	36	1.5	191	215	55,686	44,781	11,467	11,743	0.8
6210	Security brokers and dealers	21	24	1.6	153	170	63,529	51,106	10,171	10,696	1.0
6300	Insurance carriers	44	47	1.5	1,914	2,287	32,339	37,383	56,989	75,019	2.4
6330	Fire, marine, and casualty insurance	31	33	2.0	394	416	40,609	46,894	15,753	17,922	1.1
6400	Insurance agents, brokers, and service	153	146	1.6	590	573	31,092	31,735	16,637	16,758	1.1
6500	Real estate	198	210	1.3	1,154	1,173	25,331	24,685	33,217	31,835	1.3
6510	Real estate operators and lessors	65	74	1.1	704	741	23,097	26,013	20,097	19,109	3.2
6530	Real estate agents and managers	110	106	1.4	343	357	23,055	22,387	8,626	9,002	0.6
6540	Title abstract offices	4	3	0.8	67	20	30,448	27,000	1,472	734	1.0
6550	Subdividers and developers	12	11	1.0	35	40	84,457	21,700	2,913	2,472	1.1
6710	Holding offices	12	10	1.7	54	44	52,296	38,909	3,276	1,810	0.3
6730	Trusts	4	6	1.4	7	21	12,000	24,571	118	444	0.6
6790	Miscellaneous investing	12	12	1.1	27	24	27,704	38,500	831	951	0.4
6799	Investors, n.e.c.	8	8	1.1	19	20	33,474	39,600	663	763	0.5
COLLINGSWORTH, TX											
60 –	**Finance, insurance, and real estate**	4	5	0.0	37	52	19,135	19,000	913	1,073	0.0
COLORADO, TX											
60 –	**Finance, insurance, and real estate**	33	30	0.1	165	161	21,600	21,143	3,894	3,736	0.0
6000	Depository institutions	8	8	0.2	108	112	23,148	21,857	2,801	2,814	0.1
6400	Insurance agents, brokers, and service	11	11	0.1	14	18	15,429	13,556	244	243	0.0
COMAL, TX											
60 –	**Finance, insurance, and real estate**	127	129	0.3	620	609	16,761	18,240	11,667	11,067	0.1
6000	Depository institutions	9	9	0.2	177	174	18,847	21,333	3,523	2,579	0.1
6280	Security and commodity services	4	4	0.5	7	7	33,714	34,857	230	249	0.1
6400	Insurance agents, brokers, and service	30	29	0.3	102	102	17,961	19,255	2,404	2,312	0.2
6500	Real estate	62	63	0.4	259	246	12,556	12,016	3,664	3,425	0.1
6510	Real estate operators and lessors	22	19	0.3	74	68	9,459	10,176	783	666	0.1
6530	Real estate agents and managers	27	30	0.4	103	94	13,243	11,830	1,532	1,465	0.1
COMANCHE, TX											
60 –	**Finance, insurance, and real estate**	20	19	0.0	123	134	18,602	18,716	2,489	2,651	0.0
6000	Depository institutions	7	7	0.1	94	100	20,043	20,520	2,034	2,165	0.1
6400	Insurance agents, brokers, and service	7	6	0.1	22	27	14,364	12,593	336	363	0.0
COOKE, TX											
60 –	**Finance, insurance, and real estate**	49	49	0.1	272	318	20,912	19,220	6,249	6,548	0.0
6000	Depository institutions	10	10	0.2	170	183	22,729	22,142	4,305	4,333	0.1
6020	Commercial banks	6	6	0.2	155	167	23,819	23,162	4,105	4,113	0.2
6400	Insurance agents, brokers, and service	14	13	0.1	28	31	16,429	17,161	527	577	0.0
6530	Real estate agents and managers	8	9	0.1	41	46	14,439	13,739	623	685	0.0
CORYELL, TX											
60 –	**Finance, insurance, and real estate**	75	73	0.2	407	417	16,511	17,928	7,663	8,131	0.1
6000	Depository institutions	10	11	0.2	231	239	17,974	18,795	4,832	4,959	0.2
6100	Nondepository institutions	4	5	0.1	6	9	24,000	16,000	135	163	0.0
6500	Real estate	41	40	0.3	120	121	14,233	14,083	1,738	1,912	0.1

Source: County Business Patterns, 1994/95, CBP-94/95, U.S. Department of Commerce, Washington, D.C., November 1997. SIC categories for which data were suppressed or not available for both 1994 and 1995 are not displayed. The employment columns represent mid-March employment in the year. Pay per employee is calculated by dividing 1st Quarter payroll, annualized, by mid-March employment. The columns headed "% State" show the county's percentage of the state total for the SIC in 1995; for example, 1.4% for SIC 6000 means that the county had 1.4 percent of the state's total establishments (or payroll) in SIC 6000 in 1995. A dash (-) is used to indicate that data are not available or cannot be calculated; nec means not elsewhere classified.

Continued on next page.

SIC	Industry	No. Establishments			Employment		Pay / Employee		Annual Payroll ($ 000)		
		1994	1995	% State	1994	1995	1994	1995	1994	1995	% State
CORYELL, TX - [continued]											
6510	Real estate operators and lessors	9	10	0.2	15	35	8,533	7,429	159	384	0.1
6530	Real estate agents and managers	22	21	0.3	59	56	11,458	14,071	755	832	0.1
6540	Title abstract offices	3	3	0.8	25	19	15,040	18,526	428	445	0.6
COTTLE, TX											
60 –	**Finance, insurance, and real estate**	3	3	0.0	-	-	-	-	-	-	-
CRANE, TX											
60 –	**Finance, insurance, and real estate**	6	6	0.0	29	32	18,483	17,250	571	591	0.0
6000	Depository institutions	3	3	0.1	17	17	21,647	22,353	395	417	0.0
CROCKETT, TX											
60 –	**Finance, insurance, and real estate**	5	5	0.0	54	56	20,889	22,429	1,218	1,369	0.0
CROSBY, TX											
60 –	**Finance, insurance, and real estate**	15	16	0.0	73	76	18,301	18,421	1,322	1,420	0.0
6000	Depository institutions	5	5	0.1	51	53	18,275	18,264	1,014	1,083	0.0
6400	Insurance agents, brokers, and service	4	4	0.0	10	12	19,200	17,333	185	204	0.0
CULBERSON, TX											
60 –	**Finance, insurance, and real estate**	2	3	0.0	-	-	-	-	-	-	-
DALLAM, TX											
60 –	**Finance, insurance, and real estate**	25	32	0.1	148	170	19,351	22,094	2,963	3,068	0.0
6000	Depository institutions	6	6	0.1	96	115	22,208	25,426	2,133	2,163	0.1
6400	Insurance agents, brokers, and service	6	5	0.1	21	16	11,429	16,500	247	278	0.0
6500	Real estate	9	17	0.1	22	32	12,909	11,250	322	404	0.0
6510	Real estate operators and lessors	4	12	0.2	5	14	11,200	7,429	61	100	0.0
6530	Real estate agents and managers	4	4	0.1	17	17	13,412	14,824	260	300	0.0
DALLAS, TX											
60 –	**Finance, insurance, and real estate**	7,098	7,233	17.4	126,249	123,544	36,207	38,878	4,496,377	4,721,015	33.2
6000	Depository institutions	684	687	13.2	22,009	23,230	34,262	35,177	693,327	731,219	22.8
6020	Commercial banks	336	345	11.4	17,222	17,702	34,340	35,435	534,632	546,848	22.1
6030	Savings institutions	91	88	15.5	1,515	2,129	41,426	35,942	58,182	72,643	23.6
6060	Credit unions	132	131	13.0	1,421	1,667	23,355	25,761	34,398	43,203	16.4
6090	Functions closely related to banking	118	115	20.0	642	532	28,318	34,368	17,327	16,493	27.8
6100	Nondepository institutions	613	627	18.7	17,036	17,290	38,749	36,545	641,341	654,608	50.6
6140	Personal credit institutions	150	169	10.7	4,341	5,516	41,887	37,695	182,473	224,539	49.7
6150	Business credit institutions	148	150	37.1	4,431	5,096	34,039	33,965	160,190	177,104	65.3
6160	Mortgage bankers and brokers	307	294	25.8	7,917	6,157	39,104	36,519	279,825	229,250	45.6
6200	Security and commodity brokers	551	564	24.1	7,824	6,949	79,271	86,514	538,435	547,593	36.0
6210	Security brokers and dealers	323	334	21.9	5,341	5,361	88,828	90,042	385,124	424,077	39.3
6280	Security and commodity services	219	216	29.4	2,451	1,549	58,707	75,453	151,223	121,871	29.0
6300	Insurance carriers	688	682	22.3	28,658	27,223	35,316	38,766	1,005,457	1,023,140	32.3
6310	Life insurance	212	206	24.3	7,197	6,415	34,158	38,181	243,956	235,015	24.8
6320	Medical service and health insurance	59	58	31.4	5,538	5,590	32,380	36,016	176,945	197,670	51.5
6321	Accident and health insurance	30	26	32.1	1,536	1,391	30,932	37,464	46,137	46,210	42.8
6324	Hospital and medical service plans	29	31	30.1	4,002	4,198	32,936	35,545	130,808	151,419	54.9
6330	Fire, marine, and casualty insurance	295	308	18.6	13,845	13,219	37,266	40,640	514,852	521,703	32.0
6350	Surety insurance	14	12	31.6	230	208	37,948	46,615	8,843	8,476	47.2
6360	Title insurance	52	52	27.5	1,111	860	42,596	47,674	44,269	35,622	29.6
6370	Pension, health, and welfare funds	51	38	31.9	700	853	19,697	19,798	15,327	17,929	31.3
6400	Insurance agents, brokers, and service	1,383	1,371	15.0	11,258	10,784	35,306	37,541	403,382	412,723	28.1
6500	Real estate	2,645	2,755	17.2	31,582	28,965	25,091	27,967	869,817	849,772	35.7
6510	Real estate operators and lessors	1,066	1,072	16.3	6,944	7,171	22,653	23,082	167,019	165,773	28.1
6530	Real estate agents and managers	1,332	1,386	18.9	21,774	18,361	25,937	30,610	623,529	591,320	40.8
6540	Title abstract offices	39	37	9.9	568	354	30,944	31,740	15,698	12,549	16.4

Source: County Business Patterns, 1994/95, CBP-94/95, U.S. Department of Commerce, Washington, D.C., November 1997. SIC categories for which data were suppressed or not available for both 1994 and 1995 are *not* displayed. The employment columns represent mid-March employment in the year. Pay per employee is calculated by dividing 1st Quarter payroll, annualized, by mid-March employment. The columns headed "% State" show the county's percentage of the state total for the SIC in 1995; for example, 1.4% for SIC 6000 means that the county had 1.4 percent of the state's total establishments (or payroll) in SIC 6000 in 1995. A dash (-) is used to indicate that data are not available or cannot be calculated; *nec* means not elsewhere classified.

Continued on next page.

SIC	Industry	No. Establishments			Employment		Pay / Employee		Annual Payroll ($ 000)		
		1994	1995	% State	1994	1995	1994	1995	1994	1995	% State

DALLAS, TX - [continued]

SIC	Industry	1994	1995	% State	1994	1995	1994	1995	1994	1995	% State
6550	Subdividers and developers	133	138	12.4	2,059	2,748	22,590	22,751	54,421	66,250	29.4
6552	Subdividers and developers, n.e.c.	106	107	15.3	1,460	1,797	23,211	25,300	39,216	45,829	29.9
6553	Cemetery subdividers and developers	21	19	5.7	595	917	21,069	15,939	14,850	17,460	26.6
6700	Holding and other investment offices	498	507	21.6	4,971	6,756	42,716	54,818	230,429	356,283	40.0
6710	Holding offices	118	131	21.8	2,305	4,390	51,648	58,632	131,789	232,137	42.4
6720	Investment offices	20	18	28.6	97	45	94,433	69,244	8,699	3,162	25.3
6730	Trusts	74	73	16.9	415	454	25,455	30,159	12,293	13,747	17.4
6732	Educational, religious, etc. trusts	21	23	15.3	139	164	25,669	24,610	3,917	4,742	18.5
6733	Trusts, n.e.c.	53	49	17.6	276	290	25,348	33,297	8,376	8,917	16.8
6790	Miscellaneous investing	267	253	22.3	1,522	1,581	47,827	54,937	76,487	96,508	41.7
6792	Oil royalty traders	63	57	18.4	333	315	42,763	50,527	15,784	14,613	34.1
6794	Patent owners and lessors	23	18	24.7	298	269	39,570	35,732	13,695	14,373	42.1
6798	Real estate investment trusts	10	12	27.9	119	123	16,807	46,244	2,122	7,530	57.6
6799	Investors, n.e.c.	171	166	23.5	772	874	57,979	63,661	44,886	59,992	42.4

DAWSON, TX

| 60 – | **Finance, insurance, and real estate** | 23 | 24 | 0.1 | 140 | 132 | 19,229 | 20,970 | 3,055 | 3,250 | 0.0 |
| 6400 | Insurance agents, brokers, and service | 10 | 10 | 0.1 | 26 | 26 | 23,692 | 26,769 | 479 | 638 | 0.0 |

DEAF SMITH, TX

60 –	**Finance, insurance, and real estate**	39	36	0.1	177	174	27,571	26,736	4,140	4,232	0.0
6000	Depository institutions	4	4	0.1	90	89	24,800	26,562	2,213	2,490	0.1
6100	Nondepository institutions	3	3	0.1	8	6	31,000	26,000	192	148	0.0
6400	Insurance agents, brokers, and service	13	11	0.1	52	49	34,923	31,020	1,158	993	0.1
6500	Real estate	14	14	0.1	19	24	10,105	11,333	240	268	0.0
6510	Real estate operators and lessors	7	7	0.1	8	11	7,500	9,455	83	95	0.0
6530	Real estate agents and managers	3	3	0.0	3	3	9,333	9,333	28	23	0.0

DELTA, TX

60 –	**Finance, insurance, and real estate**	8	7	0.0	37	37	17,946	15,892	732	718	0.0
6000	Depository institutions	3	3	0.1	32	30	18,875	18,533	662	673	0.0
6020	Commercial banks	3	3	0.1	32	30	18,875	18,533	662	673	0.0

DENTON, TX

60 –	**Finance, insurance, and real estate**	483	522	1.3	2,782	2,895	25,881	27,384	75,791	80,983	0.6
6000	Depository institutions	63	67	1.3	973	1,019	24,181	22,681	23,582	23,960	0.7
6020	Commercial banks	45	49	1.6	806	847	24,839	22,824	19,895	20,629	0.8
6030	Savings institutions	7	6	1.1	63	58	22,921	25,586	1,451	894	0.3
6100	Nondepository institutions	31	33	1.0	260	281	30,292	44,256	10,485	11,888	0.9
6150	Business credit institutions	5	4	1.0	163	189	25,840	51,746	7,157	8,622	3.2
6200	Security and commodity brokers	26	20	0.9	62	66	47,097	31,697	2,759	2,253	0.1
6210	Security brokers and dealers	18	14	0.9	53	60	53,358	34,267	2,681	2,195	0.2
6280	Security and commodity services	8	6	0.8	9	6	10,222	6,000	78	58	0.0
6300	Insurance carriers	47	47	1.5	431	359	36,130	40,758	15,678	12,378	0.4
6330	Fire, marine, and casualty insurance	27	30	1.8	208	147	39,423	49,415	9,033	6,755	0.4
6400	Insurance agents, brokers, and service	117	126	1.4	310	323	21,987	26,365	7,622	8,408	0.6
6500	Real estate	189	216	1.4	733	832	19,640	21,875	14,813	19,257	0.8
6510	Real estate operators and lessors	76	81	1.2	293	334	16,041	19,162	5,160	7,773	1.3
6530	Real estate agents and managers	93	113	1.5	352	421	24,114	24,798	8,223	9,976	0.7
6550	Subdividers and developers	11	13	1.2	58	45	13,034	17,156	791	866	0.4
6552	Subdividers and developers, n.e.c.	5	7	1.0	17	10	22,353	33,600	352	412	0.3
6553	Cemetery subdividers and developers	5	5	1.5	39	33	8,923	11,515	389	413	0.6
6700	Holding and other investment offices	10	13	0.6	13	15	68,615	19,200	852	2,839	0.3
6720	Investment offices	3	4	6.3	4	4	16,000	15,000	140	75	0.6
6730	Trusts	3	3	0.7	2	3	14,000	21,333	47	62	0.1

DE WITT, TX

| 60 – | **Finance, insurance, and real estate** | 30 | 29 | 0.1 | 123 | 125 | 17,756 | 19,808 | 2,234 | 2,568 | 0.0 |

Source: County Business Patterns, 1994/95, CBP-94/95, U.S. Department of Commerce, Washington, D.C., November 1997. SIC categories for which data were suppressed or not available for both 1994 and 1995 are not displayed. The employment columns represent mid-March employment in the year. Pay per employee is calculated by dividing 1st Quarter payroll, annualized, by mid-March employment. The columns headed "% State" show the county's percentage of the state total for the SIC in 1995; for example, 1.4% for SIC 6000 means that the county had 1.4 percent of the state's total establishments (or payroll) in SIC 6000 in 1995. A dash (-) is used to indicate that data are not available or cannot be calculated; nec means not elsewhere classified.

Continued on next page.

SIC	Industry	No. Establishments			Employment		Pay / Employee		Annual Payroll ($ 000)		
		1994	1995	% State	1994	1995	1994	1995	1994	1995	% State
DE WITT, TX - [continued]											
6000	Depository institutions	12	11	0.2	94	85	19,915	21,929	1,928	1,925	0.1
6400	Insurance agents, brokers, and service	8	7	0.1	16	17	7,250	8,706	123	165	0.0
6500	Real estate	7	7	0.0	9	11	12,000	6,545	100	109	0.0
6530	Real estate agents and managers	3	3	0.0	3	5	14,667	8,800	55	78	0.0
DICKENS, TX											
60 –	**Finance, insurance, and real estate**	6	5	0.0	28	27	29,857	27,852	694	666	0.0
DIMMIT, TX											
60 –	**Finance, insurance, and real estate**	15	15	0.0	82	69	17,707	19,246	1,811	1,478	0.0
6400	Insurance agents, brokers, and service	4	4	0.0	14	8	10,286	14,500	130	119	0.0
6500	Real estate	4	5	0.0	11	11	20,727	23,273	408	386	0.0
DONLEY, TX											
60 –	**Finance, insurance, and real estate**	11	10	0.0	51	86	16,784	22,651	1,397	2,140	0.0
6000	Depository institutions	3	3	0.1	18	65	18,222	22,462	875	1,648	0.1
6020	Commercial banks	3	3	0.1	18	65	18,222	22,462	875	1,648	0.1
EASTLAND, TX											
60 –	**Finance, insurance, and real estate**	34	34	0.1	157	158	20,586	20,025	3,655	3,378	0.0
6000	Depository institutions	9	9	0.2	103	105	20,350	21,143	2,340	2,342	0.1
6400	Insurance agents, brokers, and service	11	12	0.1	27	24	14,963	17,167	448	468	0.0
6500	Real estate	6	6	0.0	10	12	19,200	20,000	240	231	0.0
ECTOR, TX											
60 –	**Finance, insurance, and real estate**	212	204	0.5	1,290	1,269	23,228	23,266	30,001	29,909	0.2
6000	Depository institutions	36	33	0.6	460	445	22,278	22,382	10,054	9,837	0.3
6020	Commercial banks	10	11	0.4	301	326	25,276	24,405	7,083	7,576	0.3
6060	Credit unions	10	10	1.0	71	53	21,183	20,453	1,666	1,125	0.4
6100	Nondepository institutions	18	20	0.6	132	151	31,970	33,642	4,377	5,249	0.4
6140	Personal credit institutions	14	16	1.0	92	96	25,348	27,375	2,385	2,613	0.6
6200	Security and commodity brokers	7	8	0.3	38	41	55,895	41,171	1,573	1,629	0.1
6310	Life insurance	3	3	0.4	44	23	22,818	25,565	1,041	549	0.1
6400	Insurance agents, brokers, and service	54	53	0.6	238	229	28,134	25,205	6,671	6,265	0.4
6500	Real estate	77	74	0.5	321	327	14,069	14,239	5,067	4,667	0.2
6790	Miscellaneous investing	5	6	0.5	34	37	18,941	27,027	700	885	0.4
EDWARDS, TX											
60 –	**Finance, insurance, and real estate**	5	7	0.0	13	15	16,923	16,267	285	305	0.0
ELLIS, TX											
60 –	**Finance, insurance, and real estate**	148	155	0.4	812	800	18,650	21,565	15,844	17,742	0.1
6000	Depository institutions	28	28	0.5	366	368	21,082	22,891	7,852	8,406	0.3
6020	Commercial banks	19	19	0.6	331	334	21,740	23,545	7,311	7,778	0.3
6140	Personal credit institutions	5	5	0.3	13	12	16,000	16,333	209	190	0.0
6300	Insurance carriers	14	12	0.4	140	129	20,743	24,775	2,865	2,992	0.1
6400	Insurance agents, brokers, and service	29	32	0.4	72	71	14,833	15,887	1,155	1,203	0.1
6500	Real estate	60	65	0.4	190	184	12,379	18,196	2,782	3,916	0.2
6510	Real estate operators and lessors	22	25	0.4	87	54	7,908	12,296	852	740	0.1
6530	Real estate agents and managers	25	25	0.3	51	58	12,706	12,483	712	906	0.1
6540	Title abstract offices	6	5	1.3	45	48	21,600	23,083	1,125	1,158	1.5
6550	Subdividers and developers	6	7	0.6	7	23	6,286	34,957	61	1,051	0.5
EL PASO, TX											
60 –	**Finance, insurance, and real estate**	1,008	1,052	2.5	7,731	8,033	22,147	22,822	178,322	188,764	1.3
6000	Depository institutions	101	112	2.1	2,819	2,855	20,736	22,124	60,710	65,500	2.0
6020	Commercial banks	39	49	1.6	1,610	1,671	22,137	23,818	36,763	39,501	1.6
6060	Credit unions	36	33	3.3	812	784	18,320	19,439	15,852	18,387	7.0

Source: County Business Patterns, 1994/95, CBP-94/95, U.S. Department of Commerce, Washington, D.C., November 1997. SIC categories for which data were suppressed or not available for both 1994 and 1995 are *not* displayed. The employment columns represent mid-March employment in the year. Pay per employee is calculated by dividing 1st Quarter payroll, annualized, by mid-March employment. The columns headed "% State" show the county's percentage of the state total for the SIC in 1995; for example, 1.4% for SIC 6000 means that the county had 1.4 percent of the state's total establishments (or payroll) in SIC 6000 in 1995. A dash (-) is used to indicate that data are not available or cannot be calculated; *nec* means not elsewhere classified.

Continued on next page.

SIC	Industry	No. Establishments			Employment		Pay / Employee		Annual Payroll ($ 000)		
		1994	1995	% State	1994	1995	1994	1995	1994	1995	% State
EL PASO, TX - [continued]											
6100	Nondepository institutions	126	134	*4.0*	780	755	21,236	21,383	16,980	16,784	*1.3*
6140	Personal credit institutions	87	90	*5.7*	537	558	19,665	19,756	10,946	11,172	*2.5*
6160	Mortgage bankers and brokers	31	32	*2.8*	214	163	25,477	26,528	5,399	4,705	*0.9*
6200	Security and commodity brokers	32	31	*1.3*	196	214	57,612	58,224	9,908	11,353	*0.7*
6210	Security brokers and dealers	16	18	*1.2*	169	191	62,817	60,482	9,209	10,675	*1.0*
6300	Insurance carriers	84	87	*2.8*	740	730	29,481	29,710	21,095	20,781	*0.7*
6310	Life insurance	21	22	*2.6*	287	319	26,230	26,019	7,029	7,658	*0.8*
6330	Fire, marine, and casualty insurance	41	46	*2.8*	216	246	34,111	32,228	7,678	7,949	*0.5*
6360	Title insurance	13	10	*5.3*	179	115	28,067	26,748	4,456	2,826	*2.3*
6400	Insurance agents, brokers, and service	203	208	*2.3*	1,002	1,012	22,044	23,079	23,768	24,317	*1.7*
6500	Real estate	429	443	*2.8*	1,994	2,264	17,625	17,465	39,612	42,543	*1.8*
6510	Real estate operators and lessors	188	188	*2.9*	623	577	14,202	17,470	9,762	10,455	*1.8*
6530	Real estate agents and managers	205	218	*3.0*	1,231	1,448	17,647	17,550	24,899	27,543	*1.9*
6550	Subdividers and developers	26	26	*2.3*	134	172	33,552	16,767	4,576	3,152	*1.4*
6552	Subdividers and developers, n.e.c.	21	19	*2.7*	87	75	45,655	26,507	3,956	2,095	*1.4*
6553	Cemetery subdividers and developers	5	5	*1.5*	47	93	11,149	9,376	620	1,022	*1.6*
6700	Holding and other investment offices	33	37	*1.6*	200	203	29,280	34,384	6,249	7,486	*0.8*
6710	Holding offices	10	11	*1.8*	54	43	46,593	67,349	2,531	3,078	*0.6*
6790	Miscellaneous investing	12	14	*1.2*	57	62	20,491	23,935	1,625	1,631	*0.7*
ERATH, TX											
60 –	**Finance, insurance, and real estate**	46	53	*0.1*	270	264	17,956	19,470	5,324	5,607	*0.0*
6000	Depository institutions	10	11	*0.2*	151	145	20,371	22,207	3,341	3,431	*0.1*
6400	Insurance agents, brokers, and service	13	12	*0.1*	64	62	12,000	12,968	852	858	*0.1*
6500	Real estate	16	21	*0.1*	27	29	8,593	10,069	255	288	*0.0*
6530	Real estate agents and managers	6	8	*0.1*	4	14	11,000	13,143	77	187	*0.0*
FALLS, TX											
60 –	**Finance, insurance, and real estate**	35	35	*0.1*	130	123	13,169	14,959	1,855	1,957	*0.0*
6000	Depository institutions	9	9	*0.2*	71	70	15,549	17,143	1,291	1,351	*0.0*
6020	Commercial banks	6	6	*0.2*	44	43	14,636	15,907	770	811	*0.0*
6400	Insurance agents, brokers, and service	11	11	*0.1*	22	22	7,273	9,818	165	247	*0.0*
6510	Real estate operators and lessors	6	5	*0.1*	16	10	4,500	6,400	71	63	*0.0*
FANNIN, TX											
60 –	**Finance, insurance, and real estate**	47	49	*0.1*	446	414	22,161	23,227	9,602	9,493	*0.1*
6000	Depository institutions	15	14	*0.3*	147	130	22,776	23,785	3,093	3,017	*0.1*
6400	Insurance agents, brokers, and service	13	13	*0.1*	43	47	14,791	16,511	742	852	*0.1*
FAYETTE, TX											
60 –	**Finance, insurance, and real estate**	52	49	*0.1*	285	297	20,281	21,320	6,149	6,360	*0.0*
6000	Depository institutions	15	15	*0.3*	184	196	21,109	22,041	4,316	4,629	*0.1*
6400	Insurance agents, brokers, and service	14	13	*0.1*	44	44	22,909	24,727	824	851	*0.1*
6500	Real estate	13	10	*0.1*	40	38	9,000	9,263	423	376	*0.0*
6510	Real estate operators and lessors	5	5	*0.1*	20	21	8,600	8,381	194	191	*0.0*
FISHER, TX											
60 –	**Finance, insurance, and real estate**	6	6	*0.0*	58	30	20,897	24,267	1,213	851	*0.0*
FLOYD, TX											
60 –	**Finance, insurance, and real estate**	21	22	*0.1*	73	73	16,219	15,945	1,269	1,317	*0.0*
6500	Real estate	8	8	*0.1*	9	12	5,778	4,000	64	68	*0.0*
6550	Subdividers and developers	3	3	*0.3*	2	4	4,000	2,000	21	26	*0.0*
6553	Cemetery subdividers and developers	3	3	*0.9*	2	4	4,000	2,000	21	26	*0.0*
FOARD, TX											
60 –	**Finance, insurance, and real estate**	4	4	*0.0*	-	-	-	-	-	-	-
FORT BEND, TX											
60 –	**Finance, insurance, and real estate**	375	405	*1.0*	3,842	4,575	30,313	27,591	112,273	130,974	*0.9*

Source: County Business Patterns, 1994/95, CBP-94/95, U.S. Department of Commerce, Washington, D.C., November 1997. SIC categories for which data were suppressed or not available for both 1994 and 1995 are not displayed. The employment columns represent mid-March employment in the year. Pay per employee is calculated by dividing 1st Quarter payroll, annualized, by mid-March employment. The columns headed "% State" show the county's percentage of the state total for the SIC in 1995; for example, 1.4% for SIC 6000 means that the county had 1.4 percent of the state's total establishments (or payroll) in SIC 6000 in 1995. A dash (-) is used to indicate that data are not available or cannot be calculated; nec means not elsewhere classified.

Continued on next page.

SIC	Industry	No. Establishments			Employment		Pay / Employee		Annual Payroll ($ 000)		
		1994	1995	% State	1994	1995	1994	1995	1994	1995	% State
FORT BEND, TX - [continued]											
6000	Depository institutions	41	44	0.8	519	570	23,645	22,863	13,092	13,716	0.4
6020	Commercial banks	26	29	1.0	361	402	23,302	22,876	9,100	9,502	0.4
6030	Savings institutions	8	7	1.2	125	124	26,240	24,806	3,334	3,418	1.1
6100	Nondepository institutions	22	21	0.6	110	102	33,527	29,882	3,186	2,869	0.2
6140	Personal credit institutions	7	7	0.4	21	26	23,810	20,769	555	582	0.1
6160	Mortgage bankers and brokers	11	11	1.0	75	62	35,947	32,839	2,163	1,899	0.4
6200	Security and commodity brokers	15	20	0.9	125	147	56,192	59,429	6,590	11,428	0.8
6210	Security brokers and dealers	8	12	0.8	82	98	58,878	63,633	3,849	7,881	0.7
6300	Insurance carriers	40	42	1.4	1,963	2,509	32,255	28,451	60,594	69,231	2.2
6310	Life insurance	9	8	0.9	1,338	1,891	34,284	28,283	43,924	52,006	5.5
6330	Fire, marine, and casualty insurance	24	29	1.8	99	112	52,283	53,786	5,091	5,664	0.3
6400	Insurance agents, brokers, and service	103	107	1.2	555	684	23,928	23,462	12,693	14,390	1.0
6500	Real estate	137	151	0.9	522	509	27,257	24,621	14,112	12,076	0.5
6510	Real estate operators and lessors	48	56	0.9	158	136	9,899	12,059	1,549	1,588	0.3
6530	Real estate agents and managers	69	71	1.0	247	255	24,810	19,325	7,378	5,488	0.4
6540	Title abstract offices	3	3	0.8	27	19	27,111	24,842	731	516	0.7
6550	Subdividers and developers	10	13	1.2	75	90	75,787	58,133	3,102	4,045	1.8
6700	Holding and other investment offices	17	20	0.9	48	54	55,333	26,815	2,006	7,264	0.8
6710	Holding offices	4	5	0.8	33	26	59,879	32,769	1,365	6,533	1.2
6790	Miscellaneous investing	9	12	1.1	13	17	23,385	21,176	357	405	0.2
6799	Investors, n.e.c.	6	9	1.3	6	10	18,667	18,800	157	175	0.1
FRANKLIN, TX											
60 –	**Finance, insurance, and real estate**	13	14	0.0	109	105	14,459	19,200	1,912	2,053	0.0
6000	Depository institutions	4	4	0.1	67	67	18,030	20,955	1,338	1,479	0.0
6500	Real estate	6	6	0.0	23	23	6,783	12,696	251	309	0.0
FREESTONE, TX											
60 –	**Finance, insurance, and real estate**	24	24	0.1	112	127	16,714	16,346	2,032	2,419	0.0
6000	Depository institutions	5	6	0.1	63	85	20,571	17,600	1,392	1,767	0.1
6400	Insurance agents, brokers, and service	7	6	0.1	19	19	12,842	12,842	257	264	0.0
6500	Real estate	8	7	0.0	22	17	9,636	12,941	269	239	0.0
6550	Subdividers and developers	3	3	0.3	9	6	9,778	12,000	95	70	0.0
FRIO, TX											
60 –	**Finance, insurance, and real estate**	17	21	0.1	109	105	19,119	19,962	2,285	2,131	0.0
6000	Depository institutions	4	4	0.1	66	57	22,121	24,000	1,603	1,362	0.0
6400	Insurance agents, brokers, and service	4	4	0.0	10	10	10,800	14,800	143	157	0.0
6500	Real estate	3	6	0.0	6	11	12,000	13,091	82	150	0.0
GAINES, TX											
60 –	**Finance, insurance, and real estate**	21	20	0.0	116	121	16,828	17,818	2,126	2,295	0.0
6000	Depository institutions	4	4	0.1	75	83	18,240	18,602	1,426	1,602	0.1
6400	Insurance agents, brokers, and service	7	6	0.1	17	15	16,706	21,067	390	395	0.0
6500	Real estate	7	7	0.0	16	15	9,500	9,333	151	133	0.0
GALVESTON, TX											
60 –	**Finance, insurance, and real estate**	381	381	0.9	4,349	4,507	32,822	24,807	118,755	115,827	0.8
6000	Depository institutions	67	67	1.3	1,118	1,151	22,190	22,478	25,200	26,151	0.8
6020	Commercial banks	36	36	1.2	845	894	22,452	22,421	19,072	20,104	0.8
6060	Credit unions	17	17	1.7	188	194	22,106	23,588	4,408	4,783	1.8
6100	Nondepository institutions	19	21	0.6	71	76	38,704	26,316	2,371	1,849	0.1
6140	Personal credit institutions	11	13	0.8	36	44	17,222	17,636	607	781	0.2
6200	Security and commodity brokers	16	20	0.9	89	94	45,663	44,128	4,073	4,292	0.3
6300	Insurance carriers	23	25	0.8	1,740	1,839	50,067	28,792	59,929	55,024	1.7
6400	Insurance agents, brokers, and service	88	84	0.9	381	399	23,916	26,095	10,173	11,705	0.8
6500	Real estate	152	150	0.9	873	881	15,171	16,795	15,493	15,187	0.6
6510	Real estate operators and lessors	66	64	1.0	291	360	14,557	14,611	5,198	5,326	0.9

Source: County Business Patterns, 1994/95, CBP-94/95, U.S. Department of Commerce, Washington, D.C., November 1997. SIC categories for which data were suppressed or not available for both 1994 and 1995 are not displayed. The employment columns represent mid-March employment in the year. Pay per employee is calculated by dividing 1st Quarter payroll, annualized, by mid-March employment. The columns headed "% State" show the county's percentage of the state total for the SIC in 1995; for example, 1.4% for SIC 6000 means that the county had 1.4 percent of the state's total establishments (or payroll) in SIC 6000 in 1995. A dash (-) is used to indicate that data are not available or cannot be calculated; nec means not elsewhere classified.

Continued on next page.

SIC	Industry	No. Establishments			Employment		Pay / Employee		Annual Payroll ($ 000)		
		1994	1995	% State	1994	1995	1994	1995	1994	1995	% State
GALVESTON, TX - [continued]											
6530	Real estate agents and managers	70	69	0.9	372	346	13,946	16,301	5,861	5,741	0.4
6550	Subdividers and developers	12	12	1.1	208	165	18,327	22,618	4,344	3,953	1.8
6552	Subdividers and developers, n.e.c.	6	6	0.9	112	82	22,857	29,707	3,031	2,569	1.7
6553	Cemetery subdividers and developers	6	6	1.8	96	83	13,042	15,614	1,313	1,384	2.1
6700	Holding and other investment offices	16	14	0.6	77	67	21,455	24,299	1,516	1,619	0.2
6710	Holding offices	4	4	0.7	21	25	29,143	28,000	523	676	0.1
GARZA, TX											
60 –	**Finance, insurance, and real estate**	8	9	0.0	24	36	18,667	15,222	460	550	0.0
GILLESPIE, TX											
60 –	**Finance, insurance, and real estate**	41	43	0.1	248	272	21,500	19,853	5,252	5,286	0.0
6000	Depository institutions	7	7	0.1	138	147	23,681	25,061	3,272	3,537	0.1
6400	Insurance agents, brokers, and service	8	9	0.1	45	49	14,756	14,776	732	730	0.1
6500	Real estate	16	14	0.1	34	54	12,235	6,519	427	346	0.0
6510	Real estate operators and lessors	8	8	0.1	7	36	10,286	3,778	94	116	0.0
6530	Real estate agents and managers	5	3	0.0	14	4	12,000	5,000	138	28	0.0
GONZALES, TX											
60 –	**Finance, insurance, and real estate**	32	36	0.1	154	611	16,390	21,944	3,050	15,256	0.1
6000	Depository institutions	7	7	0.1	76	80	20,316	23,750	1,806	2,030	0.1
6100	Nondepository institutions	4	4	0.1	8	8	16,500	19,000	133	137	0.0
6530	Real estate agents and managers	3	4	0.1	4	4	8,000	8,000	33	28	0.0
GRAY, TX											
60 –	**Finance, insurance, and real estate**	66	69	0.2	303	633	17,056	22,673	6,125	8,526	0.1
6000	Depository institutions	15	17	0.3	171	196	17,708	22,612	3,434	4,162	0.1
6020	Commercial banks	4	6	0.2	108	151	20,000	24,795	2,489	3,418	0.1
6400	Insurance agents, brokers, and service	18	17	0.2	53	53	16,377	14,642	985	938	0.1
6500	Real estate	17	18	0.1	42	350	11,143	23,829	712	2,648	0.1
6510	Real estate operators and lessors	12	11	0.2	29	34	10,069	11,529	523	452	0.1
6700	Holding and other investment offices	7	8	0.3	4	3	13,000	16,000	153	152	0.0
6790	Miscellaneous investing	7	8	0.7	4	3	13,000	16,000	153	152	0.1
GRAYSON, TX											
60 –	**Finance, insurance, and real estate**	202	201	0.5	1,897	1,867	23,165	22,993	42,132	42,944	0.3
6000	Depository institutions	33	28	0.5	537	518	22,592	22,533	11,729	11,743	0.4
6020	Commercial banks	23	18	0.6	499	472	22,990	23,144	11,055	10,966	0.4
6100	Nondepository institutions	17	20	0.6	79	78	18,633	20,667	1,856	1,833	0.1
6140	Personal credit institutions	14	16	1.0	61	62	15,213	17,032	1,063	1,190	0.3
6200	Security and commodity brokers	9	11	0.5	41	39	124,488	98,564	3,067	2,701	0.2
6300	Insurance carriers	14	13	0.4	880	868	22,195	22,309	19,291	19,823	0.6
6400	Insurance agents, brokers, and service	49	49	0.5	111	111	18,595	22,018	2,268	2,376	0.2
6500	Real estate	73	75	0.5	245	244	14,694	14,623	3,793	4,024	0.2
6510	Real estate operators and lessors	41	40	0.6	78	88	16,308	13,318	1,334	1,387	0.2
6530	Real estate agents and managers	24	26	0.4	105	90	14,514	16,178	1,547	1,592	0.1
6700	Holding and other investment offices	7	5	0.2	4	9	10,000	47,111	128	444	0.0
GREGG, TX											
60 –	**Finance, insurance, and real estate**	294	309	0.7	1,932	2,017	23,627	24,171	45,525	49,141	0.3
6000	Depository institutions	44	42	0.8	946	972	22,892	23,720	21,322	23,339	0.7
6020	Commercial banks	19	19	0.6	736	770	24,201	24,977	17,343	18,477	0.7
6100	Nondepository institutions	26	27	0.8	91	102	20,000	22,745	1,723	2,170	0.2
6140	Personal credit institutions	20	22	1.4	58	83	19,310	24,241	1,171	1,852	0.4
6200	Security and commodity brokers	20	19	0.8	117	118	51,419	46,814	5,112	4,856	0.3
6300	Insurance carriers	22	23	0.8	163	161	32,638	32,894	4,981	5,068	0.2
6400	Insurance agents, brokers, and service	66	65	0.7	248	283	20,081	20,353	5,365	6,252	0.4
6500	Real estate	105	116	0.7	354	361	15,842	17,440	6,743	6,641	0.3

Source: County Business Patterns, 1994/95, CBP-94/95, U.S. Department of Commerce, Washington, D.C., November 1997. SIC categories for which data were suppressed or not available for both 1994 and 1995 are not displayed. The employment columns represent mid-March employment in the year. Pay per employee is calculated by dividing 1st Quarter payroll, annualized, by mid-March employment. The columns headed "% State" show the county's percentage of the state total for the SIC in 1995; for example, 1.4% for SIC 6000 means that the county had 1.4 percent of the state's total establishments (or payroll) in SIC 6000 in 1995. A dash (-) is used to indicate that data are not available or cannot be calculated; nec means not elsewhere classified.

Continued on next page.

SIC	Industry	No. Establishments			Employment		Pay / Employee		Annual Payroll ($ 000)		
		1994	1995	% State	1994	1995	1994	1995	1994	1995	% State
GREGG, TX - [continued]											
6510	Real estate operators and lessors	48	55	0.8	116	127	14,483	16,031	2,132	2,220	0.4
6530	Real estate agents and managers	41	40	0.5	135	114	15,674	18,737	2,576	2,168	0.1
6540	Title abstract offices	5	5	1.3	56	62	21,214	21,355	1,368	1,364	1.8
6550	Subdividers and developers	8	11	1.0	45	53	13,422	14,264	630	789	0.3
6700	Holding and other investment offices	11	17	0.7	13	20	19,077	25,000	279	815	0.1
GRIMES, TX											
60 –	**Finance, insurance, and real estate**	25	29	0.1	155	170	21,135	22,212	3,601	4,064	0.0
6000	Depository institutions	7	7	0.1	84	94	21,619	20,766	1,938	2,155	0.1
6400	Insurance agents, brokers, and service	6	7	0.1	20	18	16,400	20,444	327	384	0.0
6500	Real estate	8	10	0.1	20	26	16,400	13,692	392	435	0.0
6510	Real estate operators and lessors	4	5	0.1	7	10	20,000	14,000	194	212	0.0
GUADALUPE, TX											
60 –	**Finance, insurance, and real estate**	89	98	0.2	447	459	19,821	21,124	9,117	10,075	0.1
6000	Depository institutions	9	9	0.2	210	205	23,829	25,249	4,824	5,101	0.2
6400	Insurance agents, brokers, and service	21	22	0.2	75	76	19,040	21,526	1,600	1,719	0.1
6500	Real estate	38	43	0.3	119	133	13,076	13,805	1,764	1,994	0.1
6510	Real estate operators and lessors	18	18	0.3	36	35	9,667	10,971	373	385	0.1
HALE, TX											
60 –	**Finance, insurance, and real estate**	72	70	0.2	404	408	19,782	21,382	8,613	9,328	0.1
6000	Depository institutions	14	12	0.2	184	175	22,652	24,891	4,536	4,707	0.1
6020	Commercial banks	8	8	0.3	165	158	23,200	25,494	4,205	4,382	0.2
6200	Security and commodity brokers	3	3	0.1	14	15	27,429	24,267	413	381	0.0
6400	Insurance agents, brokers, and service	24	26	0.3	74	88	15,243	15,682	1,257	1,454	0.1
6510	Real estate operators and lessors	12	10	0.2	35	26	9,714	9,846	317	289	0.0
6700	Holding and other investment offices	4	4	0.2	10	10	8,400	8,000	90	112	0.0
HALL, TX											
60 –	**Finance, insurance, and real estate**	8	6	0.0	42	34	15,714	17,529	652	619	0.0
HAMILTON, TX											
60 –	**Finance, insurance, and real estate**	13	14	0.0	69	65	19,130	18,646	1,437	1,317	0.0
6400	Insurance agents, brokers, and service	5	5	0.1	13	15	13,538	12,267	197	228	0.0
6500	Real estate	3	3	0.0	5	3	15,200	18,667	75	78	0.0
HANSFORD, TX											
60 –	**Finance, insurance, and real estate**	17	14	0.0	100	102	23,200	23,647	2,259	2,331	0.0
6000	Depository institutions	4	4	0.1	73	75	27,014	28,000	1,870	1,993	0.1
6400	Insurance agents, brokers, and service	7	6	0.1	18	21	14,889	13,333	293	295	0.0
HARDEMAN, TX											
60 –	**Finance, insurance, and real estate**	8	9	0.0	54	57	20,889	21,684	1,244	1,351	0.0
6000	Depository institutions	3	3	0.1	45	47	22,933	23,319	1,132	1,209	0.0
6020	Commercial banks	3	3	0.1	45	47	22,933	23,319	1,132	1,209	0.0
HARDIN, TX											
60 –	**Finance, insurance, and real estate**	54	53	0.1	247	274	18,364	20,701	4,880	5,796	0.0
6000	Depository institutions	9	8	0.2	146	146	19,890	20,548	3,093	3,246	0.1
6100	Nondepository institutions	6	5	0.1	9	16	18,222	23,500	204	399	0.0
6400	Insurance agents, brokers, and service	18	16	0.2	44	46	16,455	18,348	674	755	0.1
6500	Real estate	15	16	0.1	33	35	13,576	16,686	525	527	0.0
HARRIS, TX											
60 –	**Finance, insurance, and real estate**	7,674	7,856	18.9	94,521	91,242	37,088	39,108	3,380,218	3,453,184	24.2
6000	Depository institutions	946	936	18.0	22,139	22,497	32,990	35,333	697,484	774,547	24.2
6020	Commercial banks	493	492	16.3	17,133	17,873	32,950	35,575	530,064	617,212	24.9

Source: County Business Patterns, 1994/95, CBP-94/95, U.S. Department of Commerce, Washington, D.C., November 1997. SIC categories for which data were suppressed or not available for both 1994 and 1995 are not displayed. The employment columns represent mid-March employment in the year. Pay per employee is calculated by dividing 1st Quarter payroll, annualized, by mid-March employment. The columns headed "% State" show the county's percentage of the state total for the SIC in 1995; for example, 1.4% for SIC 6000 means that the county had 1.4 percent of the state's total establishments (or payroll) in SIC 6000 in 1995. A dash (-) is used to indicate that data are not available or cannot be calculated; nec means not elsewhere classified.

Continued on next page.

SIC	Industry	No. Establishments			Employment		Pay / Employee		Annual Payroll ($ 000)		
		1994	1995	% State	1994	1995	1994	1995	1994	1995	% State
HARRIS, TX - [continued]											
6030	Savings institutions	110	105	18.6	1,922	1,636	41,270	40,555	76,911	64,170	20.8
6060	Credit unions	156	159	15.8	1,399	1,476	22,270	22,442	31,736	34,374	13.0
6080	Foreign bank and branches and agencies	24	22	73.3	439	432	61,913	64,861	29,565	27,316	-
6100	Nondepository institutions	476	486	14.5	5,483	5,276	37,288	36,995	198,220	204,028	15.8
6140	Personal credit institutions	106	106	6.7	893	1,096	29,178	31,529	26,503	34,534	7.6
6150	Business credit institutions	77	82	20.3	488	707	57,648	51,615	29,634	37,684	13.9
6160	Mortgage bankers and brokers	283	277	24.3	4,089	3,419	36,702	35,953	141,663	130,414	26.0
6200	Security and commodity brokers	455	518	22.1	6,611	6,764	92,848	86,976	517,583	546,623	36.0
6210	Security brokers and dealers	273	313	20.5	4,523	4,477	96,864	81,013	363,032	352,324	32.7
6280	Security and commodity services	162	180	24.5	1,934	2,116	83,423	99,609	139,726	177,578	42.3
6300	Insurance carriers	581	604	19.7	14,129	13,914	36,677	41,399	518,868	538,764	17.0
6310	Life insurance	181	174	20.5	7,162	6,846	31,680	40,953	236,672	250,989	26.5
6320	Medical service and health insurance	25	25	13.5	649	853	37,374	33,533	25,266	29,807	7.8
6321	Accident and health insurance	14	11	13.6	239	210	37,490	39,657	8,783	8,390	7.8
6324	Hospital and medical service plans	11	14	13.6	410	643	37,307	31,533	16,483	21,417	7.8
6330	Fire, marine, and casualty insurance	300	330	20.0	4,650	4,565	41,316	41,302	192,889	193,011	11.9
6350	Surety insurance	10	9	23.7	95	110	65,600	54,727	5,916	5,025	28.0
6360	Title insurance	31	36	19.0	1,273	1,201	47,274	50,648	48,980	49,467	41.1
6370	Pension, health, and welfare funds	34	26	21.8	300	291	28,413	34,763	9,145	9,291	16.2
6400	Insurance agents, brokers, and service	1,545	1,569	17.2	10,056	9,609	34,268	36,413	351,764	359,390	24.5
6500	Real estate	3,114	3,169	19.8	28,071	26,254	22,401	23,508	654,464	625,092	26.2
6510	Real estate operators and lessors	1,174	1,202	18.3	7,432	7,024	19,397	18,465	162,832	135,433	22.9
6530	Real estate agents and managers	1,662	1,629	22.2	18,521	16,369	23,154	24,802	435,618	402,229	27.8
6540	Title abstract offices	34	26	7.0	487	325	28,994	30,117	12,721	10,164	13.3
6550	Subdividers and developers	172	168	15.1	1,573	2,163	25,452	28,762	39,016	63,025	28.0
6552	Subdividers and developers, n.e.c.	119	123	17.6	584	1,238	39,555	39,063	22,904	47,690	31.1
6553	Cemetery subdividers and developers	44	33	9.9	978	913	17,096	14,953	15,913	14,295	21.7
6700	Holding and other investment offices	536	551	23.4	5,135	4,906	48,394	54,532	261,887	274,447	30.8
6710	Holding offices	166	179	29.8	2,506	2,524	59,796	70,803	157,083	181,517	33.1
6720	Investment offices	16	12	19.0	124	105	46,613	51,695	6,067	5,429	43.5
6730	Trusts	81	76	17.6	849	883	22,869	27,388	22,283	25,937	32.9
6732	Educational, religious, etc. trusts	27	26	17.3	441	473	22,086	20,448	9,994	9,762	38.2
6733	Trusts, n.e.c.	54	50	17.9	408	410	23,716	35,395	12,289	16,175	30.4
6790	Miscellaneous investing	262	257	22.7	1,637	1,354	44,450	42,372	75,163	59,295	25.6
6792	Oil royalty traders	67	70	22.6	247	260	49,960	52,954	12,765	15,930	37.1
6794	Patent owners and lessors	23	19	26.0	300	264	30,160	27,545	11,717	7,201	21.1
6798	Real estate investment trusts	13	13	30.2	141	146	28,426	27,918	4,530	4,875	37.3
6799	Investors, n.e.c.	159	155	22.0	949	684	49,914	47,158	46,151	31,289	22.1
HARRISON, TX											
60 –	**Finance, insurance, and real estate**	84	85	0.2	657	702	20,420	21,658	14,483	15,348	0.1
6000	Depository institutions	14	14	0.3	252	265	22,349	24,936	5,929	6,585	0.2
6020	Commercial banks	6	6	0.2	227	241	23,031	25,544	5,474	6,047	0.2
6060	Credit unions	4	4	0.4	13	14	18,769	18,571	285	291	0.1
6100	Nondepository institutions	11	12	0.4	23	31	22,609	20,774	556	734	0.1
6140	Personal credit institutions	11	12	0.8	23	31	22,609	20,774	556	734	0.2
6200	Security and commodity brokers	6	7	0.3	19	21	50,947	50,286	920	955	0.1
6300	Insurance carriers	7	7	0.2	67	50	19,045	19,440	1,307	884	0.0
6400	Insurance agents, brokers, and service	18	17	0.2	216	252	15,870	17,111	3,556	3,776	0.3
6500	Real estate	21	20	0.1	60	67	17,733	17,254	1,717	1,917	0.1
6530	Real estate agents and managers	9	8	0.1	24	28	21,167	16,571	1,032	1,167	0.1
6700	Holding and other investment offices	7	8	0.3	20	16	26,400	28,500	498	497	0.1
HASKELL, TX											
60 –	**Finance, insurance, and real estate**	17	16	0.0	88	105	17,955	18,095	1,800	2,167	0.0
6000	Depository institutions	5	5	0.1	69	77	19,362	20,260	1,460	1,702	0.1
6400	Insurance agents, brokers, and service	7	7	0.1	14	13	8,857	12,308	192	277	0.0
HAYS, TX											
60 –	**Finance, insurance, and real estate**	135	142	0.3	623	960	18,510	23,279	12,064	24,097	0.2

Source: County Business Patterns, 1994/95, CBP-94/95, U.S. Department of Commerce, Washington, D.C., November 1997. SIC categories for which data were suppressed or not available for both 1994 and 1995 are not displayed. The employment columns represent mid-March employment in the year. Pay per employee is calculated by dividing 1st Quarter payroll, annualized, by mid-March employment. The columns headed "% State" show the county's percentage of the state total for the SIC in 1995; for example, 1.4% for SIC 6000 means that the county had 1.4 percent of the state's total establishments (or payroll) in SIC 6000 in 1995. A dash (-) is used to indicate that data are not available or cannot be calculated; nec means not elsewhere classified.

Continued on next page.

SIC	Industry	No. Establishments			Employment		Pay / Employee		Annual Payroll ($ 000)		
		1994	1995	% State	1994	1995	1994	1995	1994	1995	% State
HAYS, TX - [continued]											
6000	Depository institutions	17	17	0.3	253	265	18,862	19,668	4,998	5,468	0.2
6020	Commercial banks	9	9	0.3	179	192	20,089	20,479	3,781	4,174	0.2
6100	Nondepository institutions	15	18	0.5	50	148	22,560	17,054	1,227	2,569	0.2
6400	Insurance agents, brokers, and service	23	24	0.3	77	75	16,883	17,600	1,358	1,337	0.1
6500	Real estate	55	58	0.4	160	280	13,175	28,157	2,270	9,760	0.4
6530	Real estate agents and managers	25	27	0.4	97	215	13,649	33,060	1,427	8,880	0.6
6550	Subdividers and developers	4	4	0.4	4	8	10,000	12,000	44	97	0.0
6700	Holding and other investment offices	11	11	0.5	33	139	18,909	25,871	550	3,106	0.3
HEMPHILL, TX											
60 –	**Finance, insurance, and real estate**	14	15	0.0	66	81	27,636	28,198	2,027	2,522	0.0
6400	Insurance agents, brokers, and service	3	3	0.0	10	10	10,800	11,200	115	117	0.0
6700	Holding and other investment offices	5	5	0.2	11	25	36,000	28,480	646	1,078	0.1
HENDERSON, TX											
60 –	**Finance, insurance, and real estate**	93	91	0.2	651	627	16,516	17,033	12,355	12,405	0.1
6000	Depository institutions	18	16	0.3	303	296	20,422	20,243	7,035	7,383	0.2
6020	Commercial banks	15	13	0.4	236	231	23,068	22,788	6,365	6,668	0.3
6100	Nondepository institutions	5	3	0.1	9	10	21,333	16,000	258	147	0.0
6400	Insurance agents, brokers, and service	23	24	0.3	66	75	14,848	16,000	1,046	1,083	0.1
6500	Real estate	40	41	0.3	226	236	11,327	12,407	3,013	3,370	0.1
6510	Real estate operators and lessors	17	18	0.3	106	119	10,302	10,891	1,166	1,362	0.2
6530	Real estate agents and managers	16	15	0.2	62	61	11,548	13,115	915	1,039	0.1
6552	Subdividers and developers, n.e.c.	3	3	0.4	35	30	11,314	13,600	506	545	0.4
HIDALGO, TX											
60 –	**Finance, insurance, and real estate**	671	717	1.7	3,884	4,507	20,117	21,871	79,350	96,370	0.7
6000	Depository institutions	88	88	1.7	1,599	1,932	21,921	23,934	34,979	46,844	1.5
6020	Commercial banks	46	46	1.5	1,251	1,568	23,690	25,602	29,338	40,829	1.6
6060	Credit unions	14	14	1.4	160	162	16,600	17,975	2,725	2,835	1.1
6100	Nondepository institutions	81	85	2.5	346	386	17,850	18,829	6,729	7,307	0.6
6140	Personal credit institutions	69	73	4.6	275	299	16,625	18,181	4,945	5,385	1.2
6200	Security and commodity brokers	18	25	1.1	93	116	67,441	47,345	4,951	6,034	0.4
6210	Security brokers and dealers	11	15	1.0	53	74	108,679	64,865	4,253	5,140	0.5
6300	Insurance carriers	26	30	1.0	179	192	29,810	31,604	5,618	5,952	0.2
6310	Life insurance	5	5	0.6	124	137	21,581	23,299	2,781	2,916	0.3
6400	Insurance agents, brokers, and service	129	135	1.5	536	578	20,627	20,021	11,861	11,180	0.8
6500	Real estate	307	330	2.1	1,035	1,215	12,290	17,086	13,459	17,860	0.7
6510	Real estate operators and lessors	150	153	2.3	571	584	11,692	20,973	6,674	8,645	1.5
6530	Real estate agents and managers	99	102	1.4	268	283	12,910	13,908	3,709	4,376	0.3
6550	Subdividers and developers	50	62	5.6	126	262	13,016	13,053	2,117	3,719	1.6
6552	Subdividers and developers, n.e.c.	41	51	7.3	79	153	11,696	13,935	1,227	2,188	1.4
6553	Cemetery subdividers and developers	8	8	2.4	47	103	15,234	11,417	856	1,438	2.2
6730	Trusts	9	12	2.8	31	33	6,839	6,424	224	243	0.3
6732	Educational, religious, etc. trusts	4	5	3.3	21	24	5,905	6,167	140	181	0.7
6733	Trusts, n.e.c.	5	7	2.5	10	9	8,800	7,111	84	62	0.1
6790	Miscellaneous investing	7	6	0.5	40	39	18,000	12,923	890	491	0.2
HILL, TX											
60 –	**Finance, insurance, and real estate**	51	51	0.1	292	327	20,507	20,245	7,487	6,965	0.0
6000	Depository institutions	9	9	0.2	133	131	25,985	26,046	3,119	3,154	0.1
6300	Insurance carriers	6	6	0.2	27	31	17,037	16,000	489	511	0.0
6400	Insurance agents, brokers, and service	9	8	0.1	19	22	14,947	13,273	300	305	0.0
6500	Real estate	19	19	0.1	100	125	14,360	16,256	3,235	2,574	0.1
HOCKLEY, TX											
60 –	**Finance, insurance, and real estate**	38	42	0.1	212	317	19,849	18,498	4,901	4,971	0.0
6000	Depository institutions	9	9	0.2	125	144	22,336	22,111	2,751	3,236	0.1

Source: County Business Patterns, 1994/95, CBP-94/95, U.S. Department of Commerce, Washington, D.C., November 1997. SIC categories for which data were suppressed or not available for both 1994 and 1995 are *not* displayed. The employment columns represent mid-March employment in the year. Pay per employee is calculated by dividing 1st Quarter payroll, annualized, by mid-March employment. The columns headed "% State" show the county's percentage of the state total for the SIC in 1995; for example, 1.4% for SIC 6000 means that the county had 1.4 percent of the state's total establishments (or payroll) in SIC 6000 in 1995. A dash (-) is used to indicate that data are not available or cannot be calculated; *nec* means not elsewhere classified.

Continued on next page.

SIC	Industry	No. Establishments			Employment		Pay / Employee		Annual Payroll ($ 000)		
		1994	1995	% State	1994	1995	1994	1995	1994	1995	% State
HOCKLEY, TX - [continued]											
6100	Nondepository institutions	5	5	0.1	14	19	26,286	23,789	433	466	0.0
6400	Insurance agents, brokers, and service	11	13	0.1	31	29	17,290	20,552	490	540	0.0
6500	Real estate	9	9	0.1	35	118	10,857	12,644	1,082	578	0.0
6510	Real estate operators and lessors	4	4	0.1	21	14	5,905	8,286	133	108	0.0
HOOD, TX											
60 –	**Finance, insurance, and real estate**	58	63	0.2	407	478	18,280	18,176	8,406	9,811	0.1
6000	Depository institutions	9	9	0.2	179	172	19,575	21,279	3,930	4,121	0.1
6020	Commercial banks	9	9	0.3	179	172	19,575	21,279	3,930	4,121	0.2
6200	Security and commodity brokers	3	4	0.2	7	8	23,429	19,000	179	172	0.0
6400	Insurance agents, brokers, and service	17	16	0.2	65	72	21,662	20,778	1,695	1,859	0.1
6500	Real estate	26	30	0.2	144	214	13,611	13,738	2,257	3,222	0.1
6530	Real estate agents and managers	14	17	0.2	101	129	12,436	15,070	1,404	2,055	0.1
HOPKINS, TX											
60 –	**Finance, insurance, and real estate**	53	54	0.1	489	534	21,096	20,951	10,182	11,450	0.1
6000	Depository institutions	9	9	0.2	307	312	21,016	23,205	6,647	7,333	0.2
6100	Nondepository institutions	7	8	0.2	46	47	18,957	20,170	844	923	0.1
6400	Insurance agents, brokers, and service	16	14	0.2	40	44	14,300	17,727	673	714	0.0
6500	Real estate	16	18	0.1	76	119	13,316	13,345	1,086	1,705	0.1
6530	Real estate agents and managers	7	9	0.1	18	55	9,333	10,764	179	652	0.0
HOUSTON, TX											
60 –	**Finance, insurance, and real estate**	34	32	0.1	191	162	20,754	22,099	4,180	4,038	0.0
6000	Depository institutions	9	8	0.2	116	102	21,862	23,490	2,617	2,729	0.1
6100	Nondepository institutions	3	3	0.1	18	15	24,667	22,933	600	451	0.0
6400	Insurance agents, brokers, and service	7	7	0.1	18	17	15,333	17,176	291	302	0.0
6500	Real estate	12	11	0.1	32	23	11,625	13,739	369	354	0.0
6510	Real estate operators and lessors	4	4	0.1	6	6	8,000	13,333	57	87	0.0
6530	Real estate agents and managers	5	3	0.0	13	4	11,077	11,000	120	48	0.0
HOWARD, TX											
60 –	**Finance, insurance, and real estate**	74	72	0.2	399	392	20,221	20,602	8,364	8,385	0.1
6000	Depository institutions	16	16	0.3	222	208	21,946	23,192	5,381	5,224	0.2
6020	Commercial banks	5	6	0.2	138	136	22,841	24,471	3,476	3,633	0.1
6400	Insurance agents, brokers, and service	24	23	0.3	70	70	15,143	14,400	973	981	0.1
6500	Real estate	22	21	0.1	63	68	13,524	12,471	811	821	0.0
6510	Real estate operators and lessors	12	12	0.2	37	43	9,838	9,674	402	406	0.1
6530	Real estate agents and managers	6	6	0.1	10	10	10,000	8,000	93	85	0.0
HUDSPETH, TX											
60 –	**Finance, insurance, and real estate**	2	2	0.0	-	-	-	-	-	-	-
HUNT, TX											
60 –	**Finance, insurance, and real estate**	106	105	0.3	618	641	18,058	17,997	11,726	12,138	0.1
6000	Depository institutions	15	15	0.3	275	275	20,902	20,975	5,861	5,885	0.2
6200	Security and commodity brokers	7	6	0.3	14	15	32,571	38,667	587	643	0.0
6400	Insurance agents, brokers, and service	31	29	0.3	110	124	12,982	12,129	1,774	1,590	0.1
6500	Real estate	40	40	0.3	152	161	13,395	13,317	1,942	2,382	0.1
6510	Real estate operators and lessors	16	15	0.2	57	57	10,175	9,474	579	595	0.1
6530	Real estate agents and managers	16	19	0.3	44	68	10,000	11,765	446	836	0.1
6540	Title abstract offices	3	3	0.8	31	28	26,581	24,714	762	821	1.1
HUTCHINSON, TX											
60 –	**Finance, insurance, and real estate**	41	36	0.1	188	187	20,553	21,091	3,912	3,929	0.0
6000	Depository institutions	11	10	0.2	125	124	21,408	22,226	2,725	2,756	0.1
6020	Commercial banks	5	5	0.2	88	85	20,500	21,412	1,832	1,842	0.1

Source: County Business Patterns, 1994/95, CBP-94/95, U.S. Department of Commerce, Washington, D.C., November 1997. SIC categories for which data were suppressed or not available for both 1994 and 1995 are *not* displayed. The employment columns represent mid-March employment in the year. Pay per employee is calculated by dividing 1st Quarter payroll, annualized, by mid-March employment. The columns headed "% State" show the county's percentage of the state total for the SIC in 1995; for example, 1.4% for SIC 6000 means that the county had 1.4 percent of the state's total establishments (or payroll) in SIC 6000 in 1995. A dash (-) is used to indicate that data are not available or cannot be calculated; *nec* means not elsewhere classified.

Continued on next page.

SIC	Industry	No. Establishments			Employment		Pay / Employee		Annual Payroll ($ 000)		
		1994	1995	% State	1994	1995	1994	1995	1994	1995	% State
HUTCHINSON, TX - [continued]											
6060	Credit unions	6	5	0.5	37	39	23,568	24,000	893	914	0.3
6400	Insurance agents, brokers, and service	14	13	0.1	32	29	19,750	19,586	610	560	0.0
6500	Real estate	8	9	0.1	21	21	10,857	11,048	246	231	0.0
IRION, TX											
60 –	**Finance, insurance, and real estate**	2	2	0.0	-	-	-	-	-	-	-
JACK, TX											
60 –	**Finance, insurance, and real estate**	11	15	0.0	62	72	23,677	22,444	1,549	1,653	0.0
6000	Depository institutions	4	4	0.1	49	50	27,510	25,840	1,312	1,340	0.0
6400	Insurance agents, brokers, and service	4	6	0.1	11	19	7,636	14,316	110	188	0.0
JASPER, TX											
60 –	**Finance, insurance, and real estate**	48	51	0.1	358	297	18,682	18,343	6,899	5,593	0.0
6000	Depository institutions	10	11	0.2	253	175	20,870	21,097	5,295	3,746	0.1
6400	Insurance agents, brokers, and service	14	15	0.2	41	43	11,220	11,721	528	542	0.0
6500	Real estate	18	17	0.1	48	56	10,417	11,357	608	642	0.0
6510	Real estate operators and lessors	10	10	0.2	31	30	10,839	12,533	398	396	0.1
6530	Real estate agents and managers	5	4	0.1	7	7	8,571	11,429	71	66	0.0
JEFF DAVIS, TX											
60 –	**Finance, insurance, and real estate**	5	5	0.0	26	23	17,385	20,696	449	546	0.0
JEFFERSON, TX											
60 –	**Finance, insurance, and real estate**	485	515	1.2	3,407	3,674	24,527	23,495	89,984	90,372	0.6
6000	Depository institutions	79	79	1.5	1,240	1,432	22,361	22,380	28,213	31,705	1.0
6020	Commercial banks	34	33	1.1	727	906	24,105	23,369	17,792	20,806	0.8
6060	Credit unions	32	32	3.2	415	440	20,752	20,891	8,783	9,229	3.5
6100	Nondepository institutions	30	36	1.1	260	284	23,554	22,028	5,827	7,503	0.6
6140	Personal credit institutions	16	20	1.3	145	174	20,248	20,460	3,002	4,124	0.9
6200	Security and commodity brokers	23	25	1.1	157	171	78,446	56,842	14,638	10,120	0.7
6210	Security brokers and dealers	16	20	1.3	142	160	84,085	59,500	9,803	9,620	0.9
6280	Security and commodity services	7	5	0.7	15	11	25,067	18,182	4,835	500	0.1
6300	Insurance carriers	45	51	1.7	383	337	29,410	32,617	11,455	10,756	0.3
6310	Life insurance	17	17	2.0	258	220	26,946	26,618	6,653	5,474	0.6
6330	Fire, marine, and casualty insurance	18	24	1.5	67	66	45,672	53,455	3,314	3,575	0.2
6400	Insurance agents, brokers, and service	135	140	1.5	488	522	22,975	21,134	12,477	12,683	0.9
6500	Real estate	147	156	1.0	755	804	13,992	14,294	11,650	12,224	0.5
6510	Real estate operators and lessors	80	80	1.2	282	346	12,397	12,578	3,964	4,433	0.8
6530	Real estate agents and managers	50	55	0.8	229	222	16,681	18,144	4,094	4,572	0.3
6540	Title abstract offices	4	4	1.1	63	58	27,556	25,034	1,754	1,465	1.9
6550	Subdividers and developers	10	14	1.3	180	171	8,333	9,216	1,805	1,687	0.7
6710	Holding offices	5	7	1.2	50	61	42,000	47,934	3,136	3,228	0.6
6730	Trusts	6	6	1.4	8	8	15,500	17,500	121	157	0.2
6792	Oil royalty traders	7	7	2.3	12	14	10,333	8,286	123	89	0.2
6799	Investors, n.e.c.	6	6	0.8	9	6	7,111	6,667	68	73	0.1
JIM HOGG, TX											
60 –	**Finance, insurance, and real estate**	9	8	0.0	58	58	16,621	18,414	1,102	1,143	0.0
JIM WELLS, TX											
60 –	**Finance, insurance, and real estate**	54	57	0.1	418	435	18,957	20,561	8,669	9,326	0.1
6000	Depository institutions	9	9	0.2	178	176	22,787	25,500	4,198	4,194	0.1
6100	Nondepository institutions	9	9	0.3	38	35	19,789	24,000	774	807	0.1

Source: County Business Patterns, 1994/95, CBP-94/95, U.S. Department of Commerce, Washington, D.C., November 1997. SIC categories for which data were suppressed or not available for both 1994 and 1995 are not displayed. The employment columns represent mid-March employment in the year. Pay per employee is calculated by dividing 1st Quarter payroll, annualized, by mid-March employment. The columns headed "% State" show the county's percentage of the state total for the SIC in 1995; for example, 1.4% for SIC 6000 means that the county had 1.4 percent of the state's total establishments (or payroll) in SIC 6000 in 1995. A dash (-) is used to indicate that data are not available or cannot be calculated; nec means not elsewhere classified.

Continued on next page.

SIC	Industry	No. Establishments			Employment		Pay / Employee		Annual Payroll ($ 000)		
		1994	1995	% State	1994	1995	1994	1995	1994	1995	% State
JIM WELLS, TX - [continued]											
6400	Insurance agents, brokers, and service	17	17	0.2	68	85	20,882	20,235	1,682	2,349	0.2
6500	Real estate	14	16	0.1	96	105	9,708	9,790	1,165	1,184	0.0
6510	Real estate operators and lessors	7	7	0.1	50	62	8,960	9,097	580	648	0.1
JOHNSON, TX											
60 –	**Finance, insurance, and real estate**	134	134	0.3	822	826	19,392	19,608	17,725	18,273	0.1
6000	Depository institutions	29	29	0.6	516	519	21,310	21,118	11,676	12,444	0.4
6020	Commercial banks	24	24	0.8	485	485	21,666	21,435	11,043	11,756	0.5
6100	Nondepository institutions	5	7	0.2	16	19	23,250	24,211	405	510	0.0
6400	Insurance agents, brokers, and service	37	38	0.4	91	93	14,286	14,624	1,482	1,422	0.1
6500	Real estate	49	46	0.3	140	141	11,543	13,674	2,217	2,418	0.1
6510	Real estate operators and lessors	22	20	0.3	76	67	9,421	9,731	1,179	1,009	0.2
6530	Real estate agents and managers	18	18	0.2	18	22	11,111	10,000	263	240	0.0
6552	Subdividers and developers, n.e.c.	5	3	0.4	17	28	14,118	16,857	300	676	0.4
JONES, TX											
60 –	**Finance, insurance, and real estate**	25	26	0.1	113	129	21,841	21,147	2,769	2,654	0.0
6000	Depository institutions	4	4	0.1	60	66	25,800	26,242	1,776	1,632	0.1
6400	Insurance agents, brokers, and service	10	11	0.1	28	35	12,286	12,114	364	404	0.0
6500	Real estate	6	6	0.0	9	9	9,333	10,222	93	82	0.0
KARNES, TX											
60 –	**Finance, insurance, and real estate**	17	20	0.0	111	120	20,144	21,567	2,354	2,723	0.0
6000	Depository institutions	5	5	0.1	76	75	23,000	24,160	1,827	1,885	0.1
6020	Commercial banks	5	5	0.2	76	75	23,000	24,160	1,827	1,885	0.1
6400	Insurance agents, brokers, and service	6	6	0.1	10	10	14,400	14,400	145	146	0.0
KAUFMAN, TX											
60 –	**Finance, insurance, and real estate**	87	92	0.2	540	568	20,859	20,437	12,396	12,387	0.1
6000	Depository institutions	16	16	0.3	315	348	21,219	21,322	7,280	8,007	0.2
6020	Commercial banks	13	13	0.4	304	336	21,132	21,226	6,985	7,672	0.3
6100	Nondepository institutions	5	6	0.2	9	9	16,000	16,444	133	203	0.0
6400	Insurance agents, brokers, and service	24	22	0.2	59	62	18,237	18,387	1,256	1,405	0.1
6500	Real estate	34	40	0.3	104	125	17,423	15,968	2,131	2,234	0.1
6530	Real estate agents and managers	9	13	0.2	16	37	12,500	12,108	227	455	0.0
6540	Title abstract offices	5	5	1.3	27	25	22,074	23,520	820	712	0.9
KENDALL, TX											
60 –	**Finance, insurance, and real estate**	47	48	0.1	280	223	15,386	17,776	4,604	4,493	0.0
6000	Depository institutions	7	6	0.1	66	49	24,424	22,694	1,667	1,373	0.0
6200	Security and commodity brokers	3	3	0.1	5	5	16,800	16,800	83	105	0.0
6210	Security brokers and dealers	3	3	0.2	5	5	16,800	16,800	83	105	0.0
6400	Insurance agents, brokers, and service	9	11	0.1	34	37	19,647	18,486	690	809	0.1
6500	Real estate	21	21	0.1	98	64	12,122	16,563	1,283	1,131	0.0
6540	Title abstract offices	4	4	1.1	21	19	14,857	18,737	387	343	0.4
KENT, TX											
60 –	**Finance, insurance, and real estate**	1	1	0.0	-	-	-	-	-	-	-
KERR, TX											
60 –	**Finance, insurance, and real estate**	109	121	0.3	492	379	23,024	23,314	11,543	8,772	0.1
6000	Depository institutions	9	7	0.1	200	79	21,680	23,089	4,241	1,744	0.1
6020	Commercial banks	5	3	0.1	187	63	21,840	24,000	3,927	1,432	0.1
6280	Security and commodity services	5	5	0.7	18	16	82,000	55,250	1,425	1,004	0.2
6400	Insurance agents, brokers, and service	17	21	0.2	40	49	16,700	14,449	743	771	0.1
6500	Real estate	55	61	0.4	163	171	16,859	20,421	2,990	3,293	0.1
6510	Real estate operators and lessors	20	26	0.4	54	61	20,222	28,721	1,192	1,406	0.2
6530	Real estate agents and managers	25	25	0.3	67	63	12,418	13,397	923	914	0.1

Source: County Business Patterns, 1994/95, CBP-94/95, U.S. Department of Commerce, Washington, D.C., November 1997. SIC categories for which data were suppressed or not available for both 1994 and 1995 are not displayed. The employment columns represent mid-March employment in the year. Pay per employee is calculated by dividing 1st Quarter payroll, annualized, by mid-March employment. The columns headed "% State" show the county's percentage of the state total for the SIC in 1995; for example, 1.4% for SIC 6000 means that the county had 1.4 percent of the state's total establishments (or payroll) in SIC 6000 in 1995. A dash (-) is used to indicate that data are not available or cannot be calculated; nec means not elsewhere classified.

Continued on next page.

SIC	Industry	No. Establishments			Employment		Pay / Employee		Annual Payroll ($ 000)		
		1994	1995	% State	1994	1995	1994	1995	1994	1995	% State
KERR, TX - [continued]											
6540	Title abstract offices	3	3	0.8	35	37	19,543	18,270	695	765	1.0
6550	Subdividers and developers	5	5	0.5	7	9	20,000	22,667	172	195	0.1
6552	Subdividers and developers, n.e.c.	5	5	0.7	7	9	20,000	22,667	172	195	0.1
6700	Holding and other investment offices	10	11	0.5	31	19	17,290	11,158	594	188	0.0
KIMBLE, TX											
60 –	**Finance, insurance, and real estate**	10	11	0.0	51	53	17,882	17,736	1,089	1,056	0.0
6500	Real estate	5	5	0.0	10	10	8,400	8,800	100	104	0.0
KLEBERG, TX											
60 –	**Finance, insurance, and real estate**	51	55	0.1	296	367	16,811	14,943	5,118	5,429	0.0
6000	Depository institutions	7	7	0.1	180	249	17,511	15,341	3,286	3,497	0.1
6020	Commercial banks	4	4	0.1	161	230	17,516	15,009	2,947	3,105	0.1
6060	Credit unions	3	3	0.3	19	19	17,474	19,368	339	392	0.1
6100	Nondepository institutions	5	7	0.2	20	29	22,000	18,759	446	568	0.0
6140	Personal credit institutions	5	7	0.4	20	29	22,000	18,759	446	568	0.1
6400	Insurance agents, brokers, and service	15	17	0.2	43	45	12,930	12,622	587	611	0.0
6500	Real estate	17	17	0.1	41	33	10,244	9,212	431	338	0.0
6700	Holding and other investment offices	4	4	0.2	6	6	42,000	8,667	204	228	0.0
KNOX, TX											
60 –	**Finance, insurance, and real estate**	9	9	0.0	54	55	18,444	18,327	1,048	1,137	0.0
6400	Insurance agents, brokers, and service	4	5	0.1	9	11	7,111	6,545	67	72	0.0
LAMAR, TX											
60 –	**Finance, insurance, and real estate**	89	91	0.2	595	618	17,257	18,032	11,090	12,290	0.1
6000	Depository institutions	15	15	0.3	262	269	20,702	22,052	5,725	6,497	0.2
6060	Credit unions	3	3	0.3	4	4	10,000	13,000	42	45	0.0
6100	Nondepository institutions	9	9	0.3	30	29	18,533	20,690	559	584	0.0
6400	Insurance agents, brokers, and service	22	22	0.2	163	169	11,043	11,834	2,145	2,341	0.2
6500	Real estate	33	36	0.2	82	97	9,805	10,227	960	1,212	0.1
6510	Real estate operators and lessors	20	22	0.3	49	51	7,673	9,412	475	623	0.1
6530	Real estate agents and managers	9	10	0.1	18	20	9,778	9,400	203	225	0.0
LAMB, TX											
60 –	**Finance, insurance, and real estate**	25	25	0.1	124	139	21,839	20,489	2,772	3,033	0.0
6000	Depository institutions	9	9	0.2	92	106	25,609	23,434	2,406	2,652	0.1
6550	Subdividers and developers	3	3	0.3	6	9	5,333	4,889	48	53	0.0
6553	Cemetery subdividers and developers	3	3	0.9	6	9	5,333	4,889	48	53	0.1
LAMPASAS, TX											
60 –	**Finance, insurance, and real estate**	22	21	0.1	93	95	19,140	19,453	2,004	2,100	0.0
6000	Depository institutions	5	5	0.1	55	58	21,964	22,138	1,353	1,448	0.0
6400	Insurance agents, brokers, and service	4	4	0.0	11	10	13,455	15,200	156	204	0.0
6500	Real estate	7	7	0.0	19	18	9,263	9,111	203	191	0.0
LA SALLE, TX											
60 –	**Finance, insurance, and real estate**	6	6	0.0	29	31	16,276	15,484	523	539	0.0
LAVACA, TX											
60 –	**Finance, insurance, and real estate**	44	46	0.1	293	298	21,925	17,557	5,973	6,302	0.0
6000	Depository institutions	10	10	0.2	150	146	18,373	19,123	3,219	3,706	0.1
6020	Commercial banks	6	6	0.2	134	130	18,597	19,415	2,950	3,470	0.1
6400	Insurance agents, brokers, and service	14	14	0.2	33	33	12,485	12,848	403	439	0.0
6500	Real estate	9	11	0.1	17	28	8,000	7,429	220	283	0.0
6510	Real estate operators and lessors	3	3	0.0	7	15	7,429	7,733	126	133	0.0

Source: County Business Patterns, 1994/95, CBP-94/95, U.S. Department of Commerce, Washington, D.C., November 1997. SIC categories for which data were suppressed or not available for both 1994 and 1995 are not displayed. The employment columns represent mid-March employment in the year. Pay per employee is calculated by dividing 1st Quarter payroll, annualized, by mid-March employment. The columns headed "% State" show the county's percentage of the state total for the SIC in 1995; for example, 1.4% for SIC 6000 means that the county had 1.4 percent of the state's total establishments (or payroll) in SIC 6000 in 1995. A dash (-) is used to indicate that data are not available or cannot be calculated; nec means not elsewhere classified.

SIC	Industry	No. Establishments			Employment		Pay / Employee		Annual Payroll ($ 000)		
		1994	1995	% State	1994	1995	1994	1995	1994	1995	% State
LEE, TX											
60 –	**Finance, insurance, and real estate**	27	23	*0.1*	270	181	17,156	18,829	4,412	3,965	*0.0*
6000	Depository institutions	7	6	*0.1*	92	87	19,174	20,092	1,977	1,731	*0.1*
6400	Insurance agents, brokers, and service	7	7	*0.1*	65	73	18,708	17,151	1,547	1,744	*0.1*
LEON, TX											
60 –	**Finance, insurance, and real estate**	16	18	*0.0*	91	96	17,143	16,500	1,697	1,748	*0.0*
6000	Depository institutions	5	5	*0.1*	57	58	20,982	20,759	1,291	1,308	*0.0*
6400	Insurance agents, brokers, and service	8	8	*0.1*	21	27	10,857	9,333	237	258	*0.0*
LIBERTY, TX											
60 –	**Finance, insurance, and real estate**	71	73	*0.2*	417	472	18,600	17,203	7,901	18,922	*0.1*
6000	Depository institutions	11	11	*0.2*	228	233	20,719	21,425	4,794	5,220	*0.2*
6100	Nondepository institutions	4	5	*0.1*	14	12	27,429	27,000	343	404	*0.0*
6400	Insurance agents, brokers, and service	24	22	*0.2*	73	74	14,685	15,027	1,183	1,207	*0.1*
6500	Real estate	24	25	*0.2*	66	93	17,515	9,591	1,003	1,006	*0.0*
6510	Real estate operators and lessors	12	12	*0.2*	21	22	12,000	9,636	275	242	*0.0*
6530	Real estate agents and managers	9	10	*0.1*	37	58	23,568	11,310	699	731	*0.1*
LIMESTONE, TX											
60 –	**Finance, insurance, and real estate**	34	33	*0.1*	171	160	19,953	20,650	3,155	3,362	*0.0*
6000	Depository institutions	9	10	*0.2*	106	106	22,151	22,906	2,417	2,601	*0.1*
6200	Security and commodity brokers	3	3	*0.1*	5	13	54,400	26,154	160	233	*0.0*
6400	Insurance agents, brokers, and service	11	12	*0.1*	17	28	13,176	12,429	290	337	*0.0*
6530	Real estate agents and managers	3	3	*0.0*	6	4	2,000	3,000	12	12	*0.0*
LIPSCOMB, TX											
60 –	**Finance, insurance, and real estate**	10	10	*0.0*	57	55	19,789	21,745	1,312	1,366	*0.0*
6400	Insurance agents, brokers, and service	4	4	*0.0*	15	14	21,067	22,000	364	300	*0.0*
LIVE OAK, TX											
60 –	**Finance, insurance, and real estate**	11	11	*0.0*	84	89	20,143	20,360	1,903	1,968	*0.0*
6000	Depository institutions	3	3	*0.1*	63	65	22,286	22,831	1,556	1,548	*0.0*
6020	Commercial banks	3	3	*0.1*	63	65	22,286	22,831	1,556	1,548	*0.1*
LLANO, TX											
60 –	**Finance, insurance, and real estate**	42	43	*0.1*	184	185	23,913	27,092	5,275	5,868	*0.0*
6000	Depository institutions	10	9	*0.2*	105	104	20,914	24,615	2,985	3,451	*0.1*
6400	Insurance agents, brokers, and service	9	8	*0.1*	24	21	19,000	19,619	483	475	*0.0*
6500	Real estate	19	22	*0.1*	53	53	31,396	36,679	1,712	1,836	*0.1*
6530	Real estate agents and managers	11	14	*0.2*	19	24	20,842	18,500	491	512	*0.0*
LUBBOCK, TX											
60 –	**Finance, insurance, and real estate**	602	610	*1.5*	4,091	4,401	24,666	24,426	107,965	111,541	*0.8*
6000	Depository institutions	56	57	*1.1*	1,397	1,581	24,395	25,576	38,712	42,951	*1.3*
6020	Commercial banks	36	41	*1.4*	1,251	1,433	25,055	26,381	35,813	40,299	*1.6*
6060	Credit unions	13	12	*1.2*	82	92	19,415	19,478	1,688	1,827	*0.7*
6100	Nondepository institutions	36	42	*1.3*	270	333	25,511	23,784	6,990	8,038	*0.6*
6140	Personal credit institutions	21	22	*1.4*	163	234	24,368	20,325	4,254	4,517	*1.0*
6160	Mortgage bankers and brokers	10	11	*1.0*	83	64	26,602	23,438	1,914	1,718	*0.3*
6200	Security and commodity brokers	45	40	*1.7*	221	207	44,887	44,618	8,705	8,721	*0.6*
6210	Security brokers and dealers	30	29	*1.9*	180	175	50,956	48,937	7,773	7,832	*0.7*
6300	Insurance carriers	53	51	*1.7*	430	396	31,014	34,505	13,819	12,399	*0.4*
6310	Life insurance	16	16	*1.9*	262	246	26,885	28,260	6,826	5,877	*0.6*
6320	Medical service and health insurance	4	4	*2.2*	32	45	39,375	47,911	1,591	2,282	*0.6*
6330	Fire, marine, and casualty insurance	27	28	*1.7*	96	78	42,417	48,718	4,543	3,444	*0.2*
6400	Insurance agents, brokers, and service	195	193	*2.1*	745	752	27,227	23,596	21,746	18,165	*1.2*
6500	Real estate	191	200	*1.3*	959	1,059	14,557	14,980	15,037	18,153	*0.8*
6510	Real estate operators and lessors	110	111	*1.7*	402	395	11,662	13,519	5,298	5,340	*0.9*

Source: County Business Patterns, 1994/95, CBP-94/95, U.S. Department of Commerce, Washington, D.C., November 1997. SIC categories for which data were suppressed or not available for both 1994 and 1995 are not displayed. The employment columns represent mid-March employment in the year. Pay per employee is calculated by dividing 1st Quarter payroll, annualized, by mid-March employment. The columns headed "% State" show the county's percentage of the state total for the SIC in 1995; for example, 1.4% for SIC 6000 means that the county had 1.4 percent of the state's total establishments (or payroll) in SIC 6000 in 1995. A dash (-) is used to indicate that data are not available or cannot be calculated; nec means not elsewhere classified.

Continued on next page.

SIC	Industry	No. Establishments			Employment		Pay / Employee		Annual Payroll ($ 000)		
		1994	1995	% State	1994	1995	1994	1995	1994	1995	% State
LUBBOCK, TX - [continued]											
6530	Real estate agents and managers	62	70	*1.0*	444	498	16,477	17,092	7,588	10,712	*0.7*
6550	Subdividers and developers	10	9	*0.8*	78	124	10,974	9,032	1,011	1,177	*0.5*
6730	Trusts	7	7	*1.6*	8	22	17,500	8,364	156	206	*0.3*
LYNN, TX											
60 –	**Finance, insurance, and real estate**	13	14	*0.0*	75	81	21,173	25,284	2,089	2,224	*0.0*
6000	Depository institutions	4	4	*0.1*	57	57	21,614	27,649	1,455	1,606	*0.1*
6400	Insurance agents, brokers, and service	6	7	*0.1*	13	18	13,231	14,222	402	378	*0.0*
MCCULLOCH, TX											
60 –	**Finance, insurance, and real estate**	14	16	*0.0*	87	88	18,851	19,045	1,805	1,932	*0.0*
6000	Depository institutions	4	4	*0.1*	63	64	20,190	19,438	1,395	1,495	*0.0*
MCLENNAN, TX											
60 –	**Finance, insurance, and real estate**	465	469	*1.1*	4,287	4,462	24,361	26,322	106,741	117,517	*0.8*
6000	Depository institutions	57	59	*1.1*	1,135	1,172	22,509	22,802	25,687	27,354	*0.9*
6020	Commercial banks	27	28	*0.9*	863	885	23,736	24,181	20,506	21,739	*0.9*
6060	Credit unions	20	20	*2.0*	160	171	18,225	19,111	3,102	3,417	*1.3*
6100	Nondepository institutions	48	47	*1.4*	433	411	22,467	24,360	10,244	10,640	*0.8*
6160	Mortgage bankers and brokers	13	9	*0.8*	255	224	21,647	24,054	5,849	5,933	*1.2*
6200	Security and commodity brokers	23	24	*1.0*	123	131	49,171	43,328	5,562	5,905	*0.4*
6210	Security brokers and dealers	15	17	*1.1*	96	103	52,750	46,757	4,451	4,822	*0.4*
6280	Security and commodity services	8	7	*1.0*	27	28	36,444	30,714	1,111	1,083	*0.3*
6300	Insurance carriers	43	42	*1.4*	1,318	1,351	27,062	29,338	34,786	38,718	*1.2*
6310	Life insurance	18	18	*2.1*	718	703	23,432	26,191	16,508	17,544	*1.9*
6400	Insurance agents, brokers, and service	110	109	*1.2*	506	477	26,680	29,342	13,294	13,516	*0.9*
6500	Real estate	149	153	*1.0*	583	689	14,566	16,197	9,112	11,816	*0.5*
6510	Real estate operators and lessors	74	70	*1.1*	271	283	14,627	15,039	4,082	4,411	*0.7*
6530	Real estate agents and managers	60	67	*0.9*	215	270	13,563	14,296	3,454	4,188	*0.3*
6700	Holding and other investment offices	35	35	*1.5*	189	231	28,847	44,346	8,056	9,568	*1.1*
6710	Holding offices	11	13	*2.2*	66	75	35,879	69,440	3,289	3,953	*0.7*
6730	Trusts	6	6	*1.4*	14	20	18,571	25,400	455	476	*0.6*
6790	Miscellaneous investing	12	11	*1.0*	82	105	28,634	35,924	3,432	4,233	*1.8*
6794	Patent owners and lessors	7	7	*9.6*	61	84	30,623	36,429	2,748	3,535	*10.4*
MCMULLEN, TX											
60 –	**Finance, insurance, and real estate**	2	2	*0.0*	-	-	-	-	-	-	*-*
MADISON, TX											
60 –	**Finance, insurance, and real estate**	15	15	*0.0*	114	130	18,947	17,846	2,991	2,814	*0.0*
6000	Depository institutions	5	5	*0.1*	92	107	19,478	18,617	2,267	2,328	*0.1*
6500	Real estate	5	5	*0.0*	12	11	10,333	10,909	135	158	*0.0*
MARION, TX											
60 –	**Finance, insurance, and real estate**	9	10	*0.0*	46	44	18,870	21,909	891	953	*0.0*
6500	Real estate	4	5	*0.0*	6	4	5,333	12,000	51	58	*0.0*
6530	Real estate agents and managers	4	4	*0.1*	6	4	5,333	12,000	51	51	*0.0*
MATAGORDA, TX											
60 –	**Finance, insurance, and real estate**	68	71	*0.2*	303	310	20,950	22,065	6,350	5,791	*0.0*
6000	Depository institutions	9	10	*0.2*	152	156	24,263	27,590	3,743	3,025	*0.1*
6020	Commercial banks	6	6	*0.2*	137	127	24,642	28,724	3,414	2,373	*0.1*
6400	Insurance agents, brokers, and service	14	14	*0.2*	45	50	31,378	21,600	1,261	1,260	*0.1*
6500	Real estate	32	33	*0.2*	89	85	8,899	11,247	843	886	*0.0*
6510	Real estate operators and lessors	10	10	*0.2*	38	35	9,053	10,400	360	377	*0.1*
MAVERICK, TX											
60 –	**Finance, insurance, and real estate**	51	51	*0.1*	329	342	15,805	17,193	5,461	6,064	*0.0*

Source: County Business Patterns, 1994/95, CBP-94/95, U.S. Department of Commerce, Washington, D.C., November 1997. SIC categories for which data were suppressed or not available for both 1994 and 1995 are *not* displayed. The employment columns represent mid-March employment in the year. Pay per employee is calculated by dividing 1st Quarter payroll, annualized, by mid-March employment. The columns headed "% State" show the county's percentage of the state total for the SIC in 1995; for example, 1.4% for SIC 6000 means that the county had 1.4 percent of the state's total establishments (or payroll) in SIC 6000 in 1995. A dash (-) is used to indicate that data are not available or cannot be calculated; *nec* means not elsewhere classified.

Continued on next page.

SIC	Industry	No. Establishments			Employment		Pay / Employee		Annual Payroll ($ 000)		
		1994	1995	% State	1994	1995	1994	1995	1994	1995	% State
MAVERICK, TX - [continued]											
6000	Depository institutions	5	6	0.1	145	141	18,952	20,397	2,629	3,182	0.1
6100	Nondepository institutions	14	14	0.4	44	50	13,636	15,760	712	792	0.1
6140	Personal credit institutions	12	14	0.9	42	50	13,810	15,760	691	792	0.2
6500	Real estate	20	19	0.1	49	50	13,633	12,400	752	692	0.0
6530	Real estate agents and managers	5	4	0.1	5	7	15,200	9,143	104	65	0.0
6550	Subdividers and developers	7	5	0.5	11	7	7,273	8,571	145	62	0.0
6552	Subdividers and developers, n.e.c.	5	3	0.4	9	5	8,000	10,400	134	52	0.0
MEDINA, TX											
60 –	**Finance, insurance, and real estate**	42	40	0.1	198	199	18,990	19,899	3,930	4,221	0.0
6000	Depository institutions	13	13	0.2	126	128	21,079	21,250	2,769	2,897	0.1
6100	Nondepository institutions	5	5	0.1	14	16	31,429	30,750	477	502	0.0
6400	Insurance agents, brokers, and service	9	9	0.1	28	30	14,429	15,333	434	533	0.0
6500	Real estate	11	9	0.1	22	17	5,818	8,706	118	145	0.0
6530	Real estate agents and managers	8	5	0.1	17	7	6,118	6,286	97	44	0.0
MENARD, TX											
60 –	**Finance, insurance, and real estate**	5	5	0.0	23	26	14,261	16,462	384	418	0.0
MIDLAND, TX											
60 –	**Finance, insurance, and real estate**	336	358	0.9	2,060	2,175	25,408	26,266	52,451	60,843	0.4
6000	Depository institutions	37	35	0.7	753	682	26,120	26,282	18,248	17,774	0.6
6020	Commercial banks	17	16	0.5	641	541	27,738	28,089	15,939	14,646	0.6
6160	Mortgage bankers and brokers	5	7	0.6	16	18	43,000	35,333	413	567	0.1
6200	Security and commodity brokers	28	32	1.4	155	178	52,155	48,607	7,655	8,687	0.6
6210	Security brokers and dealers	21	25	1.6	137	163	55,007	50,086	7,226	8,266	0.8
6280	Security and commodity services	7	7	1.0	18	15	30,444	32,533	429	421	0.1
6300	Insurance carriers	20	20	0.7	174	146	29,586	27,589	4,958	5,004	0.2
6310	Life insurance	6	7	0.8	125	106	25,440	20,943	3,120	2,993	0.3
6400	Insurance agents, brokers, and service	59	66	0.7	229	233	24,210	24,979	6,628	6,379	0.4
6500	Real estate	128	133	0.8	595	642	15,919	16,773	10,768	11,321	0.5
6510	Real estate operators and lessors	64	65	1.0	241	296	13,560	14,122	4,271	4,596	0.8
6530	Real estate agents and managers	55	58	0.8	244	236	19,492	21,576	5,058	5,077	0.4
6540	Title abstract offices	4	3	0.8	54	44	16,889	17,727	850	760	1.0
6550	Subdividers and developers	5	5	0.5	56	63	9,571	10,476	589	819	0.4
6700	Holding and other investment offices	48	53	2.3	103	234	27,107	34,786	2,776	9,909	1.1
6710	Holding offices	4	5	0.8	4	124	20,000	40,774	137	5,560	1.0
6730	Trusts	10	9	2.1	28	26	33,571	33,077	995	921	1.2
6790	Miscellaneous investing	33	38	3.4	71	83	24,958	26,506	1,630	3,405	1.5
6799	Investors, n.e.c.	12	13	1.8	32	37	28,375	28,649	708	1,624	1.1
MILAM, TX											
60 –	**Finance, insurance, and real estate**	33	30	0.1	226	215	20,673	21,563	4,981	5,314	0.0
6000	Depository institutions	8	7	0.1	138	138	23,043	23,536	3,481	3,891	0.1
6400	Insurance agents, brokers, and service	12	10	0.1	47	36	12,340	14,556	576	522	0.0
6500	Real estate	6	6	0.0	15	15	11,200	11,733	171	179	0.0
MILLS, TX											
60 –	**Finance, insurance, and real estate**	10	13	0.0	70	74	17,714	18,703	1,352	1,612	0.0
MITCHELL, TX											
60 –	**Finance, insurance, and real estate**	13	14	0.0	67	68	17,433	17,118	1,196	1,122	0.0
6400	Insurance agents, brokers, and service	5	5	0.1	10	8	11,600	14,000	113	98	0.0
6510	Real estate operators and lessors	3	3	0.0	14	14	6,857	5,143	93	47	0.0
MONTAGUE, TX											
60 –	**Finance, insurance, and real estate**	26	29	0.1	162	172	18,864	18,698	3,311	3,491	0.0

Source: County Business Patterns, 1994/95, CBP-94/95, U.S. Department of Commerce, Washington, D.C., November 1997. SIC categories for which data were suppressed or not available for both 1994 and 1995 are not displayed. The employment columns represent mid-March employment in the year. Pay per employee is calculated by dividing 1st Quarter payroll, annualized, by mid-March employment. The columns headed "% State" show the county's percentage of the state total for the SIC in 1995; for example, 1.4% for SIC 6000 means that the county had 1.4 percent of the state's total establishments (or payroll) in SIC 6000 in 1995. A dash (-) is used to indicate that data are not available or cannot be calculated; nec means not elsewhere classified.

Continued on next page.

SIC	Industry	No. Establishments			Employment		Pay / Employee		Annual Payroll ($ 000)		
		1994	1995	% State	1994	1995	1994	1995	1994	1995	% State
MONTAGUE, TX - [continued]											
6000	Depository institutions	7	7	0.1	112	117	18,464	19,077	2,313	2,403	0.1
6400	Insurance agents, brokers, and service	9	10	0.1	30	25	11,333	13,280	364	353	0.0
6500	Real estate	6	7	0.0	13	24	13,538	13,667	263	408	0.0
MONTGOMERY, TX											
60 –	**Finance, insurance, and real estate**	331	361	0.9	2,368	2,593	29,084	27,483	68,508	69,932	0.5
6000	Depository institutions	32	41	0.8	479	546	24,894	23,326	11,274	11,437	0.4
6020	Commercial banks	22	29	1.0	405	475	25,333	23,469	9,657	9,838	0.4
6060	Credit unions	3	3	0.3	38	38	23,474	24,526	924	914	0.3
6100	Nondepository institutions	25	27	0.8	233	233	26,489	25,854	6,273	6,338	0.5
6140	Personal credit institutions	10	13	0.8	46	71	15,391	16,789	1,076	1,653	0.4
6150	Business credit institutions	3	3	0.7	19	24	46,737	40,167	1,252	1,295	0.5
6160	Mortgage bankers and brokers	12	10	0.9	168	137	27,238	28,146	3,945	3,378	0.7
6200	Security and commodity brokers	18	20	0.9	93	105	61,849	52,914	5,344	5,996	0.4
6210	Security brokers and dealers	12	14	0.9	63	70	64,635	52,000	3,564	3,970	0.4
6300	Insurance carriers	23	28	0.9	267	237	46,292	43,308	12,135	10,491	0.3
6400	Insurance agents, brokers, and service	69	76	0.8	195	240	24,041	21,350	4,963	5,166	0.4
6500	Real estate	148	152	1.0	1,011	1,100	23,818	24,207	24,185	25,048	1.1
6510	Real estate operators and lessors	46	43	0.7	411	433	14,511	15,778	6,474	6,331	1.1
6530	Real estate agents and managers	81	82	1.1	343	355	21,959	24,237	7,754	7,977	0.6
6540	Title abstract offices	4	4	1.1	92	77	25,696	26,286	2,342	2,087	2.7
6550	Subdividers and developers	14	16	1.4	162	206	50,568	41,942	7,528	8,018	3.6
6700	Holding and other investment offices	16	17	0.7	90	132	43,289	37,364	4,334	5,456	0.6
MOORE, TX											
60 –	**Finance, insurance, and real estate**	34	33	0.1	156	151	20,795	21,536	3,578	3,514	0.0
6000	Depository institutions	9	8	0.2	110	92	21,200	21,652	2,530	2,190	0.1
6400	Insurance agents, brokers, and service	11	10	0.1	23	32	18,261	14,875	539	567	0.0
6500	Real estate	7	8	0.1	12	12	6,333	6,667	86	94	0.0
MORRIS, TX											
60 –	**Finance, insurance, and real estate**	13	16	0.0	104	116	20,962	21,103	2,288	2,654	0.0
6000	Depository institutions	8	8	0.2	90	95	21,778	21,137	2,035	2,202	0.1
6020	Commercial banks	4	4	0.1	72	77	21,556	20,416	1,609	1,774	0.1
NACOGDOCHES, TX											
60 –	**Finance, insurance, and real estate**	100	104	0.3	655	578	16,525	19,384	12,221	12,810	0.1
6000	Depository institutions	13	18	0.3	386	324	15,130	20,506	7,162	7,973	0.2
6020	Commercial banks	10	13	0.4	374	309	15,144	20,751	6,963	7,696	0.3
6100	Nondepository institutions	8	7	0.2	35	25	25,029	20,800	728	563	0.0
6400	Insurance agents, brokers, and service	24	25	0.3	93	93	20,172	20,215	1,894	1,893	0.1
6500	Real estate	41	42	0.3	106	103	10,679	11,223	1,383	1,297	0.1
6510	Real estate operators and lessors	24	22	0.3	63	57	9,968	9,684	614	604	0.1
6530	Real estate agents and managers	14	17	0.2	34	36	11,412	13,333	592	561	0.0
6700	Holding and other investment offices	6	5	0.2	12	12	8,667	8,000	112	120	0.0
NAVARRO, TX											
60 –	**Finance, insurance, and real estate**	83	91	0.2	596	599	20,060	21,636	12,245	13,150	0.1
6000	Depository institutions	17	17	0.3	246	238	20,016	21,462	4,998	5,252	0.2
6020	Commercial banks	12	12	0.4	235	223	20,068	21,919	4,759	5,070	0.2
6100	Nondepository institutions	9	11	0.3	26	26	30,615	34,308	552	647	0.1
6140	Personal credit institutions	5	7	0.4	17	14	12,941	17,143	268	333	0.1
6200	Security and commodity brokers	4	5	0.2	15	16	21,867	22,250	320	376	0.0
6210	Security brokers and dealers	4	5	0.3	15	16	21,867	22,250	320	376	0.0
6300	Insurance carriers	4	4	0.1	98	94	19,755	24,766	2,035	2,224	0.1
6400	Insurance agents, brokers, and service	18	19	0.2	40	42	12,800	14,571	565	591	0.0

Source: County Business Patterns, 1994/95, CBP-94/95, U.S. Department of Commerce, Washington, D.C., November 1997. SIC categories for which data were suppressed or not available for both 1994 and 1995 are not displayed. The employment columns represent mid-March employment in the year. Pay per employee is calculated by dividing 1st Quarter payroll, annualized, by mid-March employment. The columns headed "% State" show the county's percentage of the state total for the SIC in 1995; for example, 1.4% for SIC 6000 means that the county had 1.4 percent of the state's total establishments (or payroll) in SIC 6000 in 1995. A dash (-) is used to indicate that data are not available or cannot be calculated; nec means not elsewhere classified.

Continued on next page.

SIC	Industry	No. Establishments			Employment		Pay / Employee		Annual Payroll ($ 000)		
		1994	1995	% State	1994	1995	1994	1995	1994	1995	% State
NAVARRO, TX - [continued]											
6500	Real estate	23	27	0.2	154	164	17,351	16,341	2,800	2,932	0.1
6530	Real estate agents and managers	9	10	0.1	27	29	15,704	18,345	466	669	0.0
6700	Holding and other investment offices	8	8	0.3	17	19	46,353	51,789	975	1,128	0.1
NEWTON, TX											
60 –	**Finance, insurance, and real estate**	7	8	0.0	27	45	17,037	19,022	484	961	0.0
6400	Insurance agents, brokers, and service	3	3	0.0	5	4	7,200	7,000	30	28	0.0
NOLAN, TX											
60 –	**Finance, insurance, and real estate**	29	29	0.1	177	157	21,785	21,529	3,940	3,917	0.0
6000	Depository institutions	5	6	0.1	103	84	21,942	22,714	2,287	2,312	0.1
6400	Insurance agents, brokers, and service	10	11	0.1	34	35	15,647	17,600	629	672	0.0
6510	Real estate operators and lessors	4	5	0.1	8	9	21,000	6,667	168	58	0.0
NUECES, TX											
60 –	**Finance, insurance, and real estate**	760	764	1.8	6,459	6,730	22,050	21,311	146,286	153,933	1.1
6000	Depository institutions	93	89	1.7	2,228	2,176	22,889	23,164	49,568	54,339	1.7
6020	Commercial banks	48	47	1.6	1,293	1,169	21,766	22,905	26,234	26,042	1.1
6100	Nondepository institutions	61	61	1.8	377	341	22,281	21,584	8,454	7,936	0.6
6140	Personal credit institutions	42	40	2.5	287	280	21,338	21,629	5,874	6,107	1.4
6200	Security and commodity brokers	27	31	1.3	251	285	64,271	53,249	13,635	15,724	1.0
6210	Security brokers and dealers	21	24	1.6	241	270	64,432	53,911	13,202	15,287	1.4
6300	Insurance carriers	49	47	1.5	650	485	26,978	30,136	18,620	16,572	0.5
6310	Life insurance	13	14	1.7	368	286	23,120	27,860	9,521	8,868	0.9
6330	Fire, marine, and casualty insurance	23	23	1.4	55	52	44,509	49,385	2,641	2,712	0.2
6400	Insurance agents, brokers, and service	170	167	1.8	700	767	22,829	23,186	17,357	18,610	1.3
6500	Real estate	312	323	2.0	2,129	2,557	13,881	13,322	32,882	36,526	1.5
6510	Real estate operators and lessors	141	142	2.2	655	815	14,834	14,748	10,961	12,389	2.1
6530	Real estate agents and managers	150	156	2.1	1,321	1,542	12,948	12,184	18,771	20,800	1.4
6550	Subdividers and developers	15	16	1.4	127	171	17,827	16,211	2,711	2,779	1.2
6552	Subdividers and developers, n.e.c.	6	6	0.9	12	5	18,000	29,600	216	172	0.1
6553	Cemetery subdividers and developers	6	6	1.8	115	154	17,809	15,974	2,367	2,469	3.8
6710	Holding offices	8	7	1.2	27	30	42,222	47,467	1,376	1,566	0.3
6730	Trusts	9	9	2.1	38	27	15,789	14,815	480	429	0.5
6732	Educational, religious, etc. trusts	3	3	2.0	11	9	24,000	26,667	256	222	0.9
6733	Trusts, n.e.c.	6	6	2.2	27	18	12,444	8,889	224	207	0.4
6790	Miscellaneous investing	27	25	2.2	45	46	36,444	38,348	3,441	1,593	0.7
OCHILTREE, TX											
60 –	**Finance, insurance, and real estate**	20	19	0.0	140	136	22,171	23,971	3,379	3,785	0.0
6000	Depository institutions	4	4	0.1	104	99	22,077	24,727	2,424	2,773	0.1
6400	Insurance agents, brokers, and service	5	4	0.0	12	9	19,000	22,222	296	246	0.0
6500	Real estate	6	5	0.0	8	11	10,500	8,364	99	104	0.0
OLDHAM, TX											
60 –	**Finance, insurance, and real estate**	2	3	0.0	-	-	-	-	-	-	-
ORANGE, TX											
60 –	**Finance, insurance, and real estate**	105	107	0.3	660	687	21,364	21,374	14,069	14,826	0.1
6000	Depository institutions	21	22	0.4	305	343	23,567	21,306	6,904	7,091	0.2
6020	Commercial banks	8	9	0.3	211	246	23,109	19,496	4,695	4,597	0.2
6400	Insurance agents, brokers, and service	31	31	0.3	104	113	17,731	21,274	2,085	2,575	0.2
6500	Real estate	32	34	0.2	121	114	15,207	16,035	2,025	2,053	0.1
6510	Real estate operators and lessors	13	13	0.2	41	30	11,707	15,067	546	512	0.1
6530	Real estate agents and managers	10	11	0.2	37	46	21,081	18,957	872	1,011	0.1
6550	Subdividers and developers	8	9	0.8	43	38	13,488	13,263	601	524	0.2

Source: County Business Patterns, 1994/95, CBP-94/95, U.S. Department of Commerce, Washington, D.C., November 1997. SIC categories for which data were suppressed or not available for both 1994 and 1995 are not displayed. The employment columns represent mid-March employment in the year. Pay per employee is calculated by dividing 1st Quarter payroll, annualized, by mid-March employment. The columns headed "% State" show the county's percentage of the state total for the SIC in 1995; for example, 1.4% for SIC 6000 means that the county had 1.4 percent of the state's total establishments (or payroll) in SIC 6000 in 1995. A dash (-) is used to indicate that data are not available or cannot be calculated; nec means not elsewhere classified.

Continued on next page.

SIC	Industry	No. Establishments			Employment		Pay / Employee		Annual Payroll ($ 000)		
		1994	1995	% State	1994	1995	1994	1995	1994	1995	% State
ORANGE, TX - [continued]											
6552	Subdividers and developers, n.e.c.	4	5	0.7	30	26	15,067	14,154	468	382	0.2
6553	Cemetery subdividers and developers	4	4	1.2	13	12	9,846	11,333	133	142	0.2
6700	Holding and other investment offices	6	6	0.3	90	84	24,089	25,905	2,016	2,097	0.2
PALO PINTO, TX											
60 –	**Finance, insurance, and real estate**	41	39	0.1	197	259	18,985	19,722	3,787	5,324	0.0
6000	Depository institutions	12	12	0.2	133	128	21,203	21,625	2,899	2,868	0.1
6020	Commercial banks	9	9	0.3	124	119	21,839	22,185	2,788	2,740	0.1
6500	Real estate	16	14	0.1	38	103	11,684	18,602	443	1,991	0.1
6510	Real estate operators and lessors	6	5	0.1	24	26	7,167	8,923	236	232	0.0
PANOLA, TX											
60 –	**Finance, insurance, and real estate**	30	31	0.1	172	175	20,000	20,960	4,082	3,931	0.0
6000	Depository institutions	8	8	0.2	111	110	22,342	22,909	2,805	2,653	0.1
6400	Insurance agents, brokers, and service	5	5	0.1	17	17	14,118	14,824	382	403	0.0
6500	Real estate	12	10	0.1	33	33	7,879	12,242	521	350	0.0
6510	Real estate operators and lessors	8	7	0.1	13	17	8,923	8,471	314	164	0.0
PARKER, TX											
60 –	**Finance, insurance, and real estate**	83	91	0.2	523	567	20,451	19,097	10,690	12,255	0.1
6000	Depository institutions	12	12	0.2	304	325	22,974	23,040	7,001	7,577	0.2
6020	Commercial banks	9	9	0.3	289	308	23,100	23,182	6,701	7,254	0.3
6400	Insurance agents, brokers, and service	21	20	0.2	68	78	17,059	14,821	1,325	1,378	0.1
6500	Real estate	37	48	0.3	98	94	10,980	11,617	1,147	1,770	0.1
6510	Real estate operators and lessors	18	21	0.3	54	48	10,519	10,500	570	797	0.1
6550	Subdividers and developers	4	7	0.6	7	8	14,286	17,000	125	258	0.1
PECOS, TX											
60 –	**Finance, insurance, and real estate**	19	18	0.0	129	131	17,953	18,992	2,404	2,517	0.0
6000	Depository institutions	4	4	0.1	86	84	19,907	21,667	1,767	1,844	0.1
6400	Insurance agents, brokers, and service	6	6	0.1	16	16	15,500	17,250	245	250	0.1
POLK, TX											
60 –	**Finance, insurance, and real estate**	57	51	0.1	286	279	21,902	19,742	5,367	5,508	0.0
6000	Depository institutions	7	7	0.1	178	166	24,944	22,337	3,585	3,615	0.1
6100	Nondepository institutions	4	4	0.1	6	6	24,000	26,667	145	182	0.0
6400	Insurance agents, brokers, and service	15	14	0.2	32	32	25,375	21,375	606	669	0.0
6500	Real estate	24	20	0.1	59	63	12,542	12,508	797	786	0.0
6530	Real estate agents and managers	8	7	0.1	17	21	10,353	11,429	230	186	0.0
6540	Title abstract offices	3	3	0.8	17	19	18,824	17,895	327	352	0.5
POTTER, TX											
60 –	**Finance, insurance, and real estate**	326	331	0.8	2,749	2,889	26,183	27,736	74,849	79,770	0.6
6000	Depository institutions	36	39	0.7	1,084	1,083	22,369	24,443	25,367	25,201	0.8
6020	Commercial banks	18	21	0.7	871	858	23,146	25,678	20,914	20,534	0.8
6060	Credit unions	12	12	1.2	153	167	20,784	21,222	3,319	3,567	1.4
6100	Nondepository institutions	30	32	1.0	195	183	27,672	28,743	5,449	5,837	0.5
6140	Personal credit institutions	20	23	1.5	150	137	24,667	25,577	3,749	4,022	0.9
6200	Security and commodity brokers	22	23	1.0	140	147	56,171	44,952	7,186	6,900	0.5
6210	Security brokers and dealers	10	14	0.9	105	109	64,724	49,651	5,707	5,726	0.5
6220	Commodity contracts brokers, dealers	3	3	5.5	12	14	65,667	48,286	1,200	717	5.6
6280	Security and commodity services	9	6	0.8	23	24	12,174	21,667	279	457	0.1
6300	Insurance carriers	33	29	0.9	419	438	38,778	39,808	16,290	18,039	0.6
6310	Life insurance	8	8	0.9	260	252	44,415	46,460	11,404	11,467	1.2
6360	Title insurance	5	5	2.6	54	48	27,481	27,000	1,243	1,135	0.9
6400	Insurance agents, brokers, and service	72	73	0.8	410	434	20,917	26,415	9,421	10,885	0.7
6500	Real estate	103	106	0.7	398	492	15,548	15,902	6,914	7,970	0.3
6510	Real estate operators and lessors	56	58	0.9	176	199	15,159	15,618	2,614	2,961	0.5

Source: County Business Patterns, 1994/95, CBP-94/95, U.S. Department of Commerce, Washington, D.C., November 1997. SIC categories for which data were suppressed or not available for both 1994 and 1995 are not displayed. The employment columns represent mid-March employment in the year. Pay per employee is calculated by dividing 1st Quarter payroll, annualized, by mid-March employment. The columns headed "% State" show the county's percentage of the state total for the SIC in 1995; for example, 1.4% for SIC 6000 means that the county had 1.4 percent of the state's total establishments (or payroll) in SIC 6000 in 1995. A dash (-) is used to indicate that data are not available or cannot be calculated; nec means not elsewhere classified.

Continued on next page.

SIC	Industry	No. Establishments			Employment		Pay / Employee		Annual Payroll ($ 000)		
		1994	1995	% State	1994	1995	1994	1995	1994	1995	% State
POTTER, TX - [continued]											
6530	Real estate agents and managers	41	39	0.5	198	235	16,485	16,511	3,974	4,123	0.3
6550	Subdividers and developers	5	6	0.5	24	30	10,667	12,933	318	394	0.2
6710	Holding offices	4	5	0.8	33	33	30,788	32,364	983	1,012	0.2
6799	Investors, n.e.c.	8	7	1.0	14	23	45,143	71,826	723	1,079	0.8
PRESIDIO, TX											
60 –	**Finance, insurance, and real estate**	11	10	0.0	56	95	17,571	10,147	1,150	1,024	0.0
6400	Insurance agents, brokers, and service	3	3	0.0	11	12	18,909	20,000	233	243	0.0
6500	Real estate	4	3	0.0	6	4	6,667	5,000	28	18	0.0
RANDALL, TX											
60 –	**Finance, insurance, and real estate**	187	191	0.5	784	788	19,036	19,706	16,086	17,074	0.1
6000	Depository institutions	13	15	0.3	166	178	20,964	22,944	3,705	4,391	0.1
6100	Nondepository institutions	11	14	0.4	120	119	17,733	17,815	1,958	2,085	0.2
6200	Security and commodity brokers	6	7	0.3	6	12	26,667	20,000	179	366	0.0
6400	Insurance agents, brokers, and service	53	50	0.5	129	136	17,364	17,588	2,542	2,755	0.2
6500	Real estate	83	81	0.5	311	287	14,405	14,063	5,342	4,653	0.2
6510	Real estate operators and lessors	49	48	0.7	157	115	14,752	13,843	2,845	1,925	0.3
6530	Real estate agents and managers	25	25	0.3	89	91	11,416	13,319	1,214	1,369	0.1
6550	Subdividers and developers	7	6	0.5	63	80	17,905	14,600	1,243	1,270	0.6
6790	Miscellaneous investing	7	6	0.5	16	14	44,500	43,429	646	580	0.3
REAGAN, TX											
60 –	**Finance, insurance, and real estate**	5	4	0.0	35	39	16,229	16,000	625	642	0.0
RED RIVER, TX											
60 –	**Finance, insurance, and real estate**	18	20	0.0	90	95	17,422	18,484	1,771	1,916	0.0
6000	Depository institutions	6	6	0.1	54	60	18,593	18,733	1,116	1,255	0.0
6020	Commercial banks	3	3	0.1	40	42	17,100	18,000	756	848	0.0
6100	Nondepository institutions	4	4	0.1	10	10	13,200	14,400	145	147	0.0
REEVES, TX											
60 –	**Finance, insurance, and real estate**	26	23	0.1	122	114	15,443	16,491	2,148	2,081	0.0
6000	Depository institutions	7	5	0.1	73	70	15,562	15,257	1,342	1,255	0.0
6400	Insurance agents, brokers, and service	5	4	0.0	14	13	14,286	16,000	207	210	0.0
6510	Real estate operators and lessors	4	5	0.1	5	5	12,800	12,000	62	84	0.0
REFUGIO, TX											
60 –	**Finance, insurance, and real estate**	15	15	0.0	69	70	20,580	20,629	1,624	1,661	0.0
6000	Depository institutions	5	5	0.1	55	52	21,018	22,538	1,281	1,335	0.0
ROBERTS, TX											
60 –	**Finance, insurance, and real estate**	2	2	0.0	-	-	-	-	-	-	-
ROBERTSON, TX											
60 –	**Finance, insurance, and real estate**	20	20	0.0	120	114	16,933	18,491	2,424	2,560	0.0
6000	Depository institutions	4	4	0.1	86	86	20,419	21,442	2,077	2,179	0.1
6020	Commercial banks	4	4	0.1	86	86	20,419	21,442	2,077	2,179	0.1
6400	Insurance agents, brokers, and service	7	6	0.1	12	9	6,667	8,000	81	79	0.0
ROCKWALL, TX											
60 –	**Finance, insurance, and real estate**	60	60	0.1	391	384	20,082	19,844	8,621	8,657	0.1
6000	Depository institutions	7	7	0.1	97	103	21,278	20,466	2,309	2,276	0.1
6200	Security and commodity brokers	4	4	0.2	12	6	32,000	28,000	383	214	0.0
6400	Insurance agents, brokers, and service	10	13	0.1	67	67	22,687	23,582	1,802	2,382	0.2
6500	Real estate	30	30	0.2	191	181	17,634	17,680	3,527	3,189	0.1

Source: County Business Patterns, 1994/95, CBP-94/95, U.S. Department of Commerce, Washington, D.C., November 1997. SIC categories for which data were suppressed or not available for both 1994 and 1995 are *not* displayed. The employment columns represent mid-March employment in the year. Pay per employee is calculated by dividing 1st Quarter payroll, annualized, by mid-March employment. The columns headed "% State" show the county's percentage of the state total for the SIC in 1995; for example, 1.4% for SIC 6000 means that the county had 1.4 percent of the state's total establishments (or payroll) in SIC 6000 in 1995. A dash (-) is used to indicate that data are not available or cannot be calculated; *nec* means not elsewhere classified.

Continued on next page.

SIC	Industry	No. Establishments			Employment		Pay / Employee		Annual Payroll ($ 000)		
		1994	1995	% State	1994	1995	1994	1995	1994	1995	% State
ROCKWALL, TX - [continued]											
6510	Real estate operators and lessors	12	11	0.2	22	21	17,455	18,286	478	432	0.1
6530	Real estate agents and managers	12	12	0.2	124	119	15,355	17,109	2,047	1,921	0.1
6540	Title abstract offices	3	3	0.8	33	25	29,939	26,400	876	712	0.9
RUNNELS, TX											
60 –	**Finance, insurance, and real estate**	25	23	0.1	134	116	18,119	20,448	2,689	2,575	0.0
6000	Depository institutions	9	8	0.2	99	84	20,929	22,952	2,268	2,118	0.1
6400	Insurance agents, brokers, and service	9	9	0.1	27	24	10,963	14,333	338	353	0.0
RUSK, TX											
60 –	**Finance, insurance, and real estate**	47	54	0.1	348	380	19,885	20,337	7,564	8,570	0.1
6000	Depository institutions	12	12	0.2	236	250	21,169	21,888	5,524	6,076	0.2
6400	Insurance agents, brokers, and service	12	15	0.2	41	41	20,683	19,610	927	926	0.1
6510	Real estate operators and lessors	4	6	0.1	22	21	9,091	9,524	216	236	0.0
6700	Holding and other investment offices	4	4	0.2	11	11	25,455	27,273	289	311	0.0
SABINE, TX											
60 –	**Finance, insurance, and real estate**	9	11	0.0	66	76	19,030	18,368	1,263	1,401	0.0
6000	Depository institutions	4	4	0.1	54	58	21,333	21,862	1,156	1,264	0.0
6020	Commercial banks	4	4	0.1	54	58	21,333	21,862	1,156	1,264	0.1
SAN AUGUSTINE, TX											
60 –	**Finance, insurance, and real estate**	10	11	0.0	61	58	14,361	15,655	1,165	1,068	0.0
6000	Depository institutions	4	4	0.1	47	43	15,915	18,047	924	867	0.0
6020	Commercial banks	4	4	0.1	47	43	15,915	18,047	924	867	0.0
6500	Real estate	3	3	0.0	6	7	8,667	8,571	161	115	0.0
SAN JACINTO, TX											
60 –	**Finance, insurance, and real estate**	11	12	0.0	53	51	17,283	17,490	1,024	752	0.0
6400	Insurance agents, brokers, and service	4	4	0.0	10	9	14,000	13,333	146	118	0.0
SAN PATRICIO, TX											
60 –	**Finance, insurance, and real estate**	88	88	0.2	370	407	16,984	17,464	6,503	7,309	0.1
6000	Depository institutions	18	18	0.3	152	165	19,711	20,000	3,008	3,232	0.1
6020	Commercial banks	12	13	0.4	123	140	20,455	20,086	2,529	2,743	0.1
6400	Insurance agents, brokers, and service	22	20	0.2	75	79	16,587	17,519	1,268	1,455	0.1
6500	Real estate	35	38	0.2	95	120	11,074	11,367	1,111	1,551	0.1
6550	Subdividers and developers	3	4	0.4	4	9	12,000	11,111	59	110	0.0
SCHLEICHER, TX											
60 –	**Finance, insurance, and real estate**	4	4	0.0	-	-	-	-	-	-	-
SCURRY, TX											
60 –	**Finance, insurance, and real estate**	32	30	0.1	182	175	21,099	20,229	4,120	3,959	0.0
6000	Depository institutions	6	6	0.1	115	113	21,635	21,805	2,966	2,918	0.1
6020	Commercial banks	3	3	0.1	97	94	22,392	22,468	2,583	2,505	0.1
6400	Insurance agents, brokers, and service	12	11	0.1	28	30	13,571	11,600	387	373	0.0
6530	Real estate agents and managers	3	3	0.0	3	2	6,667	2,000	21	5	0.0
SHACKELFORD, TX											
60 –	**Finance, insurance, and real estate**	8	8	0.0	40	38	21,400	25,474	889	831	0.0
SHELBY, TX											
60 –	**Finance, insurance, and real estate**	43	40	0.1	243	253	17,630	17,660	4,663	5,115	0.0
6000	Depository institutions	6	6	0.1	158	168	20,354	19,976	3,448	3,850	0.1

Source: County Business Patterns, 1994/95, CBP-94/95, U.S. Department of Commerce, Washington, D.C., November 1997. SIC categories for which data were suppressed or not available for both 1994 and 1995 are *not* displayed. The employment columns represent mid-March employment in the year. Pay per employee is calculated by dividing 1st Quarter payroll, annualized, by mid-March employment. The columns headed "% State" show the county's percentage of the state total for the SIC in 1995; for example, 1.4% for SIC 6000 means that the county had 1.4 percent of the state's total establishments (or payroll) in SIC 6000 in 1995. A dash (-) is used to indicate that data are not available or cannot be calculated; *nec* means not elsewhere classified.

Continued on next page.

SIC	Industry	No. Establishments			Employment		Pay / Employee		Annual Payroll ($ 000)		
		1994	1995	% State	1994	1995	1994	1995	1994	1995	% State
SHELBY, TX - [continued]											
6100	Nondepository institutions	6	7	0.2	15	20	17,867	16,200	297	336	0.0
6400	Insurance agents, brokers, and service	13	13	0.1	36	35	11,000	10,857	478	507	0.0
6510	Real estate operators and lessors	8	6	0.1	11	11	11,273	10,182	121	135	0.0
SMITH, TX											
60 –	**Finance, insurance, and real estate**	422	447	1.1	3,031	3,237	27,403	27,218	83,864	90,621	0.6
6000	Depository institutions	51	50	1.0	874	905	23,968	23,390	21,733	22,139	0.7
6020	Commercial banks	29	28	0.9	748	774	24,754	23,798	19,287	19,301	0.8
6060	Credit unions	13	12	1.2	76	71	17,474	20,563	1,331	1,442	0.5
6100	Nondepository institutions	41	42	1.3	194	198	25,608	26,667	5,372	5,686	0.4
6140	Personal credit institutions	30	33	2.1	166	164	24,313	25,610	4,185	4,563	1.0
6160	Mortgage bankers and brokers	6	6	0.5	14	20	38,857	35,400	534	712	0.1
6200	Security and commodity brokers	22	24	1.0	125	140	67,200	60,029	7,308	8,423	0.6
6210	Security brokers and dealers	15	17	1.1	105	110	74,400	68,691	6,535	7,392	0.7
6280	Security and commodity services	7	7	1.0	20	30	29,400	28,267	773	1,031	0.2
6300	Insurance carriers	39	38	1.2	628	693	29,624	26,609	18,428	18,927	0.6
6310	Life insurance	13	13	1.5	198	197	24,929	24,162	5,348	4,999	0.5
6320	Medical service and health insurance	5	5	2.7	92	108	21,565	19,333	2,102	2,339	0.6
6330	Fire, marine, and casualty insurance	21	20	1.2	338	388	34,568	29,876	10,978	11,589	0.7
6400	Insurance agents, brokers, and service	121	120	1.3	541	562	26,292	28,797	14,052	16,271	1.1
6500	Real estate	118	139	0.9	429	541	17,809	17,353	8,359	10,851	0.5
6510	Real estate operators and lessors	57	62	0.9	200	247	15,700	14,915	3,479	4,077	0.7
6530	Real estate agents and managers	42	54	0.7	183	229	19,169	20,052	3,789	4,573	0.3
6540	Title abstract offices	5	5	1.3	30	33	24,533	21,576	786	706	0.9
6550	Subdividers and developers	12	13	1.2	12	25	20,667	14,400	282	1,310	0.6
6552	Subdividers and developers, n.e.c.	9	10	1.4	10	13	20,800	16,000	234	1,162	0.8
6730	Trusts	8	8	1.9	16	25	15,000	14,720	307	286	0.4
6790	Miscellaneous investing	17	17	1.5	36	44	23,889	24,273	946	860	0.4
6792	Oil royalty traders	12	12	3.9	29	34	25,931	27,529	830	739	1.7
6799	Investors, n.e.c.	5	5	0.7	7	10	15,429	13,200	116	121	0.1
SOMERVELL, TX											
60 –	**Finance, insurance, and real estate**	8	8	0.0	-	-	-	-	-	-	-
STARR, TX											
60 –	**Finance, insurance, and real estate**	31	33	0.1	185	197	13,081	14,883	2,652	3,075	0.0
6000	Depository institutions	5	7	0.1	76	84	18,105	20,000	1,488	1,760	0.1
6400	Insurance agents, brokers, and service	9	9	0.1	25	25	7,200	7,680	214	219	0.0
6550	Subdividers and developers	3	3	0.3	10	17	9,600	12,706	111	286	0.1
6552	Subdividers and developers, n.e.c.	3	3	0.4	10	17	9,600	12,706	111	286	0.2
STEPHENS, TX											
60 –	**Finance, insurance, and real estate**	20	20	0.0	103	99	19,650	18,101	1,940	1,769	0.0
6000	Depository institutions	4	4	0.1	70	65	21,657	20,062	1,403	1,238	0.0
6400	Insurance agents, brokers, and service	6	5	0.1	10	11	12,000	12,000	141	137	0.0
6500	Real estate	6	7	0.0	13	14	12,308	12,286	184	205	0.0
STERLING, TX											
60 –	**Finance, insurance, and real estate**	2	2	0.0	-	-	-	-	-	-	-
SUTTON, TX											
60 –	**Finance, insurance, and real estate**	11	12	0.0	50	53	23,760	23,245	1,121	1,210	0.0
6500	Real estate	5	7	0.0	4	7	12,000	9,714	68	70	0.0
SWISHER, TX											
60 –	**Finance, insurance, and real estate**	16	15	0.0	103	87	19,223	19,172	1,741	1,491	0.0
6000	Depository institutions	5	5	0.1	67	59	21,254	19,797	1,241	967	0.0
TARRANT, TX											
60 –	**Finance, insurance, and real estate**	2,647	2,737	6.6	27,267	26,821	29,653	30,247	815,803	811,814	5.7

Source: County Business Patterns, 1994/95, CBP-94/95, U.S. Department of Commerce, Washington, D.C., November 1997. SIC categories for which data were suppressed or not available for both 1994 and 1995 are not displayed. The employment columns represent mid-March employment in the year. Pay per employee is calculated by dividing 1st Quarter payroll, annualized, by mid-March employment. The columns headed "% State" show the county's percentage of the state total for the SIC in 1995; for example, 1.4% for SIC 6000 means that the county had 1.4 percent of the state's total establishments (or payroll) in SIC 6000 in 1995. A dash (-) is used to indicate that data are not available or cannot be calculated; nec means not elsewhere classified.

Continued on next page.

SIC	Industry	No. Establishments			Employment		Pay / Employee		Annual Payroll ($ 000)		
		1994	1995	% State	1994	1995	1994	1995	1994	1995	% State
UTAH, UT - [continued]											
6540	Title abstract offices	8	7	*13.5*	87	64	22,023	23,875	2,159	1,846	*14.2*
6550	Subdividers and developers	16	32	*18.5*	54	71	13,111	17,859	938	1,974	*12.5*
6700	Holding and other investment offices	14	17	*11.9*	50	78	17,920	25,795	1,299	2,935	*9.5*
WASATCH, UT											
60 –	**Finance, insurance, and real estate**	23	24	*0.5*	98	93	16,653	16,731	1,706	1,506	*0.1*
6000	Depository institutions	4	4	*0.5*	28	28	19,857	20,571	558	585	*0.2*
6400	Insurance agents, brokers, and service	5	6	*0.7*	25	27	19,520	18,963	493	481	*0.3*
6500	Real estate	11	11	*0.6*	23	22	6,957	8,364	163	180	*0.1*
6530	Real estate agents and managers	8	7	*0.8*	21	16	7,048	8,250	138	128	*0.1*
WASHINGTON, UT											
60 –	**Finance, insurance, and real estate**	166	166	*3.7*	843	949	18,762	18,904	18,305	21,479	*1.7*
6000	Depository institutions	19	19	*2.4*	286	291	22,070	23,395	6,625	9,155	*2.4*
6020	Commercial banks	14	14	*2.9*	227	230	22,150	23,496	5,126	5,809	*2.4*
6100	Nondepository institutions	16	12	*2.5*	77	59	25,247	24,136	1,699	1,583	*1.0*
6140	Personal credit institutions	4	3	*2.1*	11	9	16,000	14,667	210	137	*0.3*
6160	Mortgage bankers and brokers	12	9	*3.3*	66	50	26,788	25,840	1,489	1,446	*1.9*
6200	Security and commodity brokers	5	7	*3.5*	16	22	32,750	39,273	657	975	*1.2*
6400	Insurance agents, brokers, and service	24	25	*2.7*	132	138	18,576	19,536	3,289	2,863	*1.9*
6500	Real estate	96	94	*5.5*	321	421	12,822	13,045	5,096	6,072	*3.3*
6510	Real estate operators and lessors	19	20	*3.7*	92	100	12,609	13,360	1,418	1,516	*2.9*
6530	Real estate agents and managers	56	49	*5.7*	148	216	13,189	11,870	2,214	2,939	*2.9*
6550	Subdividers and developers	16	15	*8.7*	65	70	11,262	16,343	1,119	1,010	*6.4*
6552	Subdividers and developers, n.e.c.	13	13	*9.4*	64	69	11,250	16,406	1,072	981	*7.4*
WAYNE, UT											
60 –	**Finance, insurance, and real estate**	2	2	*0.0*	-	-	-	-	-	-	-
WEBER, UT											
60 –	**Finance, insurance, and real estate**	341	351	*7.7*	3,055	2,951	21,198	21,979	64,379	66,631	*5.4*
6000	Depository institutions	65	71	*9.1*	1,280	1,303	23,256	22,487	30,204	30,065	*8.0*
6060	Credit unions	27	27	*11.4*	628	639	18,019	18,191	12,864	13,213	*25.8*
6100	Nondepository institutions	29	30	*6.3*	271	180	27,439	29,778	7,089	5,842	*3.6*
6140	Personal credit institutions	14	14	*9.8*	68	64	22,000	24,250	1,538	1,450	*3.3*
6160	Mortgage bankers and brokers	14	15	*5.6*	201	108	29,493	34,407	5,516	4,314	*5.7*
6200	Security and commodity brokers	14	15	*7.4*	70	89	64,114	74,921	3,785	5,680	*6.8*
6210	Security brokers and dealers	10	10	*11.1*	62	79	66,710	79,241	3,400	5,194	*7.8*
6300	Insurance carriers	20	21	*6.9*	247	273	27,498	27,458	6,946	7,610	*3.9*
6310	Life insurance	4	4	*5.6*	137	119	23,153	25,412	3,000	2,953	*5.8*
6400	Insurance agents, brokers, and service	73	77	*8.4*	249	241	15,727	17,793	3,959	4,069	*2.7*
6500	Real estate	128	126	*7.4*	902	841	12,732	13,436	11,568	12,747	*6.9*
6510	Real estate operators and lessors	45	45	*8.4*	182	186	12,308	11,677	2,006	2,488	*4.7*
6530	Real estate agents and managers	70	62	*7.2*	619	562	11,057	11,915	7,279	7,615	*7.6*
6540	Title abstract offices	5	5	*9.6*	67	58	23,701	24,966	1,335	1,404	*10.8*
6550	Subdividers and developers	5	9	*5.2*	34	27	23,882	34,519	893	1,117	*7.1*
6730	Trusts	4	5	*14.3*	8	8	11,500	14,000	83	277	*10.4*

Source: County Business Patterns, 1994/95, CBP-94/95, U.S. Department of Commerce, Washington, D.C., November 1997. SIC categories for which data were suppressed or not available for both 1994 and 1995 are *not* displayed. The employment columns represent mid-March employment in the year. Pay per employee is calculated by dividing 1st Quarter payroll, annualized, by mid-March employment. The columns headed "% State" show the county's percentage of the state total for the SIC in 1995; for example, 1.4% for SIC 6000 means that the county had 1.4 percent of the state's total establishments (or payroll) in SIC 6000 in 1995. A dash (-) is used to indicate that data are not available or cannot be calculated; *nec* means not elsewhere classified.

VERMONT

SIC	Industry	No. Establishments			Employment		Pay / Employee		Annual Payroll ($ 000)		
		1994	1995	% State	1994	1995	1994	1995	1994	1995	% State
ADDISON, VT											
60 –	**Finance, insurance, and real estate**	58	63	4.2	324	328	22,346	23,354	7,686	8,157	2.1
6000	Depository institutions	17	17	5.6	131	127	19,115	21,764	2,653	2,812	2.5
6400	Insurance agents, brokers, and service	14	15	4.8	59	57	23,119	23,509	1,350	1,354	3.0
BENNINGTON, VT											
60 –	**Finance, insurance, and real estate**	100	96	6.3	537	534	23,166	24,150	12,593	13,373	3.4
6000	Depository institutions	21	21	6.9	255	262	20,376	23,374	5,132	5,563	4.9
6020	Commercial banks	16	16	7.5	216	223	20,519	22,906	4,182	4,505	5.3
6100	Nondepository institutions	4	4	8.7	16	13	28,000	20,615	410	509	-
6160	Mortgage bankers and brokers	4	4	13.8	16	13	28,000	20,615	410	509	8.5
6400	Insurance agents, brokers, and service	11	11	3.5	58	61	37,034	38,230	2,313	2,506	5.6
6500	Real estate	51	47	7.4	175	167	16,960	17,126	3,182	3,433	6.4
6530	Real estate agents and managers	31	28	8.0	101	90	21,109	21,733	2,207	2,424	9.6
CALEDONIA, VT											
60 –	**Finance, insurance, and real estate**	73	75	4.9	466	463	21,468	23,188	9,962	10,703	2.7
6000	Depository institutions	16	18	5.9	211	217	19,128	20,719	4,019	4,739	4.2
6300	Insurance carriers	3	3	3.1	69	84	32,406	32,143	2,157	2,335	2.3
6310	Life insurance	3	3	10.7	69	84	32,406	32,143	2,157	2,335	3.7
6400	Insurance agents, brokers, and service	17	18	5.7	56	58	20,929	23,379	1,319	1,310	2.9
6500	Real estate	30	28	4.4	99	75	13,535	15,840	1,328	1,278	2.4
6550	Subdividers and developers	8	8	8.3	3	4	6,667	6,000	42	43	1.2
6553	Cemetery subdividers and developers	8	8	14.5	3	4	6,667	6,000	42	43	6.4
CHITTENDEN, VT											
60 –	**Finance, insurance, and real estate**	451	458	30.2	4,146	4,476	31,138	32,028	128,394	140,730	36.0
6000	Depository institutions	70	72	23.6	1,597	1,785	26,129	27,704	41,475	46,529	40.8
6020	Commercial banks	48	50	23.5	1,209	1,276	26,859	31,495	31,831	36,692	43.0
6100	Nondepository institutions	18	18	39.1	402	392	33,741	36,398	14,467	14,056	-
6200	Security and commodity brokers	21	20	28.6	223	211	63,516	58,692	12,922	12,519	36.6
6210	Security brokers and dealers	11	12	30.0	195	198	69,723	60,000	12,122	11,874	70.5
6280	Security and commodity services	10	8	29.6	28	13	20,286	38,769	800	645	3.7
6300	Insurance carriers	48	55	57.3	396	500	34,475	35,032	13,486	17,623	17.7
6330	Fire, marine, and casualty insurance	19	23	48.9	118	188	43,797	37,957	5,163	7,257	32.3
6400	Insurance agents, brokers, and service	105	101	32.1	556	574	34,676	35,749	19,479	20,763	46.1
6500	Real estate	171	174	27.6	634	633	22,580	22,673	14,397	14,714	27.3
6510	Real estate operators and lessors	53	53	33.1	217	220	23,945	22,727	4,231	4,342	17.7
6530	Real estate agents and managers	94	93	26.5	357	343	21,647	22,531	8,471	8,581	33.8
6550	Subdividers and developers	21	21	21.9	59	67	23,525	23,582	1,676	1,726	49.4
6552	Subdividers and developers, n.e.c.	16	17	42.5	52	60	25,231	25,200	1,530	1,640	58.1
6553	Cemetery subdividers and developers	4	4	7.3	7	7	10,857	9,714	101	86	12.9
6700	Holding and other investment offices	18	18	34.6	338	381	36,675	39,013	12,168	14,526	59.8
ESSEX, VT											
60 –	**Finance, insurance, and real estate**	3	4	0.3	16	14	18,750	18,000	292	264	0.1
FRANKLIN, VT											
60 –	**Finance, insurance, and real estate**	71	66	4.4	318	666	22,667	31,868	7,146	21,266	5.4
6000	Depository institutions	19	18	5.9	177	167	21,446	23,713	3,708	3,762	3.3
6020	Commercial banks	13	12	5.6	158	149	22,582	25,235	3,455	3,549	4.2
GRAND ISLE, VT											
60 –	**Finance, insurance, and real estate**	7	5	0.3	17	11	21,176	19,273	261	215	0.1

Source: County Business Patterns, 1994/95, CBP-94/95, U.S. Department of Commerce, Washington, D.C., November 1997. SIC categories for which data were suppressed or not available for both 1994 and 1995 are not displayed. The employment columns represent mid-March employment in the year. Pay per employee is calculated by dividing 1st Quarter payroll, annualized, by mid-March employment. The columns headed "% State" show the county's percentage of the state total for the SIC in 1995; for example, 1.4% for SIC 6000 means that the county had 1.4 percent of the state's total establishments (or payroll) in SIC 6000 in 1995. A dash (-) is used to indicate that data are not available or cannot be calculated; nec means not elsewhere classified.

SIC	Industry	No. Establishments			Employment		Pay / Employee		Annual Payroll ($ 000)		
		1994	1995	% State	1994	1995	1994	1995	1994	1995	% State
LAMOILLE, VT											
60 –	**Finance, insurance, and real estate**	48	51	*3.4*	295	265	18,169	21,117	5,710	6,046	*1.5*
6000	Depository institutions	10	11	*3.6*	153	145	19,007	20,828	2,967	3,186	*2.8*
6020	Commercial banks	10	11	*5.2*	153	145	19,007	20,828	2,967	3,186	*3.7*
6400	Insurance agents, brokers, and service	10	9	*2.9*	39	41	28,513	29,561	1,231	1,291	*2.9*
6500	Real estate	25	26	*4.1*	98	71	12,898	17,577	1,448	1,450	*2.7*
6530	Real estate agents and managers	15	14	*4.0*	82	56	11,854	17,357	996	1,034	*4.1*
ORANGE, VT											
60 –	**Finance, insurance, and real estate**	44	47	*3.1*	214	211	18,692	20,246	4,332	4,672	*1.2*
6000	Depository institutions	13	13	*4.3*	133	121	19,669	21,917	2,694	2,689	*2.4*
6020	Commercial banks	8	8	*3.8*	81	63	18,815	21,016	1,497	1,395	*1.6*
6400	Insurance agents, brokers, and service	13	13	*4.1*	57	58	17,404	19,862	1,190	1,354	*3.0*
ORLEANS, VT											
60 –	**Finance, insurance, and real estate**	51	50	*3.3*	248	246	19,903	19,805	4,768	4,886	*1.3*
6000	Depository institutions	14	14	*4.6*	157	164	21,121	19,341	3,062	3,139	*2.8*
6020	Commercial banks	9	9	*4.2*	136	142	21,559	19,408	2,702	2,715	*3.2*
6400	Insurance agents, brokers, and service	14	13	*4.1*	38	40	19,474	26,900	792	973	*2.2*
RUTLAND, VT											
60 –	**Finance, insurance, and real estate**	173	161	*10.6*	1,173	1,181	25,033	27,309	28,805	30,104	*7.7*
6000	Depository institutions	29	26	*8.5*	558	555	24,007	26,991	12,571	13,584	*11.9*
6020	Commercial banks	22	19	*8.9*	325	299	22,880	26,970	7,262	7,439	*8.7*
6100	Nondepository institutions	4	3	*6.5*	15	11	26,667	27,273	216	266	*-*
6200	Security and commodity brokers	5	5	*7.1*	25	30	62,560	51,867	1,521	1,550	*4.5*
6300	Insurance carriers	11	9	*9.4*	58	50	31,517	29,920	1,708	1,145	*1.1*
6400	Insurance agents, brokers, and service	47	43	*13.7*	167	171	22,802	24,000	4,105	4,116	*9.1*
6500	Real estate	72	70	*11.1*	257	265	14,615	16,725	3,994	4,066	*7.5*
6510	Real estate operators and lessors	20	19	*11.9*	83	71	13,349	16,563	1,094	1,054	*4.3*
6530	Real estate agents and managers	36	35	*10.0*	165	179	15,588	17,408	2,702	2,806	*11.1*
6553	Cemetery subdividers and developers	8	8	*14.5*	7	7	8,000	8,000	138	131	*19.6*
6700	Holding and other investment offices	5	5	*9.6*	93	99	49,591	54,384	4,690	5,377	*22.1*
6710	Holding offices	5	5	*17.2*	93	99	49,591	54,384	4,690	5,377	*28.7*
WASHINGTON, VT											
60 –	**Finance, insurance, and real estate**	165	162	*10.7*	2,695	2,725	32,358	41,813	82,504	109,274	*28.0*
6000	Depository institutions	37	34	*11.1*	393	375	22,514	25,483	8,018	8,602	*7.5*
6020	Commercial banks	22	19	*8.9*	184	154	19,565	24,000	3,219	3,354	*3.9*
6200	Security and commodity brokers	9	11	*15.7*	111	221	66,667	96,652	7,593	16,582	*48.5*
6300	Insurance carriers	17	14	*14.6*	1,817	1,696	35,106	43,691	57,702	74,756	*74.9*
6400	Insurance agents, brokers, and service	27	26	*8.3*	141	145	25,191	26,841	3,919	4,031	*8.9*
6500	Real estate	64	65	*10.3*	199	234	13,508	14,444	3,358	3,490	*6.5*
6510	Real estate operators and lessors	13	12	*7.5*	39	46	9,949	11,043	512	535	*2.2*
6530	Real estate agents and managers	42	44	*12.5*	153	181	14,379	15,315	2,688	2,816	*11.1*
6550	Subdividers and developers	9	9	*9.4*	7	7	14,286	14,286	158	139	*4.0*
WINDHAM, VT											
60 –	**Finance, insurance, and real estate**	115	124	*8.2*	1,116	1,049	23,943	25,296	24,622	26,097	*6.7*
6000	Depository institutions	26	27	*8.9*	538	582	25,792	26,900	12,433	14,702	*12.9*
6020	Commercial banks	18	20	*9.4*	474	505	27,038	28,190	11,396	13,446	*15.7*
6100	Nondepository institutions	6	7	*15.2*	79	78	28,911	30,000	2,099	2,175	*-*
6400	Insurance agents, brokers, and service	17	17	*5.4*	113	109	20,283	22,862	2,424	2,620	*5.8*
6500	Real estate	47	50	*7.9*	186	157	15,462	17,478	2,861	2,842	*5.3*
6530	Real estate agents and managers	28	29	*8.3*	153	120	14,850	17,700	2,164	2,087	*8.2*
6700	Holding and other investment offices	6	7	*13.5*	74	54	27,568	26,889	2,022	1,715	*7.1*
WINDSOR, VT											
60 –	**Finance, insurance, and real estate**	154	154	*10.2*	696	725	19,443	19,840	15,022	15,087	*3.9*

Source: County Business Patterns, 1994/95, CBP-94/95, U.S. Department of Commerce, Washington, D.C., November 1997. SIC categories for which data were suppressed or not available for both 1994 and 1995 are not displayed. The employment columns represent mid-March employment in the year. Pay per employee is calculated by dividing 1st Quarter payroll, annualized, by mid-March employment. The columns headed "% State" show the county's percentage of the state total for the SIC in 1995; for example, 1.4% for SIC 6000 means that the county had 1.4 percent of the state's total establishments (or payroll) in SIC 6000 in 1995. A dash (-) is used to indicate that data are not available or cannot be calculated; nec means not elsewhere classified.

Continued on next page.

SIC	Industry	No. Establishments			Employment		Pay / Employee		Annual Payroll ($ 000)		
		1994	1995	% State	1994	1995	1994	1995	1994	1995	% State
WINDSOR, VT - [continued]											
6000	Depository institutions	34	31	*10.2*	227	216	19,471	19,889	4,517	4,458	*3.9*
6020	Commercial banks	24	23	*10.8*	179	172	19,218	19,767	3,491	3,555	*4.2*
6400	Insurance agents, brokers, and service	36	35	*11.1*	146	144	22,658	22,194	3,587	3,382	*7.5*
6500	Real estate	74	81	*12.8*	294	342	16,585	17,158	5,951	6,234	*11.6*
6510	Real estate operators and lessors	15	19	*11.9*	118	118	13,661	15,932	1,655	1,842	*7.5*
6530	Real estate agents and managers	45	49	*14.0*	141	181	19,234	18,762	3,503	3,764	*14.8*
6553	Cemetery subdividers and developers	6	5	*9.1*	7	7	7,429	6,857	151	95	*14.2*

Source: County Business Patterns, 1994/95, CBP-94/95, U.S. Department of Commerce, Washington, D.C., November 1997. SIC categories for which data were suppressed or not available for both 1994 and 1995 are *not* displayed. The employment columns represent mid-March employment in the year. Pay per employee is calculated by dividing 1st Quarter payroll, annualized, by mid-March employment. The columns headed "% State" show the county's percentage of the state total for the SIC in 1995; for example, 1.4% for SIC 6000 means that the county had 1.4 percent of the state's total establishments (or payroll) in SIC 6000 in 1995. A dash (-) is used to indicate that data are not available or cannot be calculated; *nec* means not elsewhere classified.

VIRGINIA

SIC	Industry	No. Establishments			Employment		Pay / Employee		Annual Payroll ($ 000)		
		1994	1995	% State	1994	1995	1994	1995	1994	1995	% State
ACCOMACK, VA											
60 –	**Finance, insurance, and real estate**	63	63	0.4	341	337	21,619	21,662	7,418	6,945	0.1
6000	Depository institutions	19	19	0.6	170	160	26,376	28,525	4,086	3,846	0.3
6400	Insurance agents, brokers, and service	9	10	0.3	52	54	19,154	16,963	1,117	983	0.2
6500	Real estate	29	29	0.5	82	85	11,512	10,729	1,249	1,119	0.1
6530	Real estate agents and managers	19	18	0.6	55	57	11,127	10,316	861	761	0.1
ALBEMARLE, VA											
60 –	**Finance, insurance, and real estate**	75	70	0.5	431	367	19,137	22,311	9,437	9,485	0.2
6000	Depository institutions	9	8	0.3	39	31	17,231	18,839	614	613	0.0
6020	Commercial banks	5	5	0.2	30	24	18,533	20,333	491	514	0.0
6060	Credit unions	4	3	0.8	9	7	12,889	13,714	123	99	0.1
6500	Real estate	44	42	0.7	318	270	17,862	22,415	7,054	7,109	0.9
6510	Real estate operators and lessors	13	13	0.7	49	50	13,633	15,040	716	747	0.4
6530	Real estate agents and managers	24	22	0.7	86	73	21,116	26,082	2,177	1,862	0.4
6550	Subdividers and developers	6	6	1.3	183	145	17,464	23,310	4,146	4,487	5.1
AMELIA, VA											
60 –	**Finance, insurance, and real estate**	5	6	0.0	-	-	-	-	-	-	-
6000	Depository institutions	3	4	0.1	23	25	25,217	24,800	535	520	0.0
6020	Commercial banks	3	4	0.2	23	25	25,217	24,800	535	520	0.0
AMHERST, VA											
60 –	**Finance, insurance, and real estate**	38	41	0.3	215	217	22,791	23,521	4,708	4,837	0.1
6000	Depository institutions	10	10	0.3	118	119	23,898	24,739	2,731	2,901	0.2
6400	Insurance agents, brokers, and service	9	9	0.3	32	29	11,375	12,828	385	391	0.1
6500	Real estate	13	16	0.3	19	27	11,789	12,444	260	361	0.0
6510	Real estate operators and lessors	3	3	0.2	5	6	12,000	10,667	63	66	0.0
6530	Real estate agents and managers	6	8	0.3	10	10	13,600	16,000	173	176	0.0
6550	Subdividers and developers	3	4	0.9	4	5	7,000	4,000	19	48	0.1
6552	Subdividers and developers, n.e.c.	3	3	1.0	4	5	7,000	4,000	19	46	0.1
APPOMATTOX, VA											
60 –	**Finance, insurance, and real estate**	18	20	0.1	138	144	22,029	29,278	3,533	3,552	0.1
6000	Depository institutions	5	6	0.2	63	71	18,730	20,282	1,135	1,257	0.1
6500	Real estate	6	6	0.1	13	12	14,462	16,333	315	278	0.0
ARLINGTON, VA											
60 –	**Finance, insurance, and real estate**	545	529	3.5	6,786	6,069	28,911	27,384	204,496	171,351	3.2
6000	Depository institutions	105	102	3.4	1,313	1,368	24,012	25,439	33,286	32,204	2.2
6020	Commercial banks	72	70	3.2	1,016	1,077	24,350	25,118	26,240	25,569	2.3
6060	Credit unions	19	19	5.0	198	199	21,657	25,769	4,561	4,577	2.8
6100	Nondepository institutions	12	12	1.0	113	132	56,779	54,636	5,431	6,790	0.9
6200	Security and commodity brokers	28	31	3.9	144	265	57,611	55,623	12,238	21,649	4.8
6210	Security brokers and dealers	11	10	2.5	27	26	35,259	47,385	1,080	1,169	0.3
6280	Security and commodity services	17	21	5.5	117	239	62,769	56,519	11,158	20,480	17.4
6300	Insurance carriers	31	31	2.7	947	730	39,295	38,279	36,145	28,244	2.8
6310	Life insurance	10	9	3.1	682	571	38,076	39,117	26,687	23,022	8.5
6400	Insurance agents, brokers, and service	55	55	1.9	223	187	37,848	34,652	8,566	5,854	1.3
6500	Real estate	289	271	4.8	3,390	2,847	23,976	23,705	87,701	67,963	8.2
6510	Real estate operators and lessors	145	136	7.0	1,296	1,030	16,701	19,623	22,360	19,919	10.4
6530	Real estate agents and managers	121	112	3.8	1,998	1,756	28,102	25,952	61,115	46,228	8.8

Source: County Business Patterns, 1994/95, CBP-94/95, U.S. Department of Commerce, Washington, D.C., November 1997. SIC categories for which data were suppressed or not available for both 1994 and 1995 are *not* displayed. The employment columns represent mid-March employment in the year. Pay per employee is calculated by dividing 1st Quarter payroll, annualized, by mid-March employment. The columns headed "% State" show the county's percentage of the state total for the SIC in 1995; for example, 1.4% for SIC 6000 means that the county had 1.4 percent of the state's total establishments (or payroll) in SIC 6000 in 1995. A dash (-) is used to indicate that data are not available or cannot be calculated; *nec* means not elsewhere classified.

Continued on next page.

SIC	Industry	No. Establishments			Employment		Pay / Employee		Annual Payroll ($ 000)		
		1994	1995	% State	1994	1995	1994	1995	1994	1995	% State
ARLINGTON, VA - [continued]											
6550	Subdividers and developers	14	15	3.3	78	49	37,641	27,347	3,451	1,398	1.6
6700	Holding and other investment offices	25	27	5.9	656	540	35,091	13,948	21,129	8,647	3.7
6710	Holding offices	9	8	5.4	67	36	149,015	32,444	7,111	1,429	0.9
6730	Trusts	10	12	9.3	553	488	18,828	12,434	11,368	6,484	22.2
6790	Miscellaneous investing	6	6	4.2	36	12	72,889	20,333	2,650	721	1.7
AUGUSTA, VA											
60 –	**Finance, insurance, and real estate**	83	74	0.5	250	283	16,624	16,961	4,381	4,460	0.1
6000	Depository institutions	19	16	0.5	96	86	17,500	17,535	1,589	1,562	0.1
6020	Commercial banks	16	12	0.5	87	77	17,747	17,299	1,443	1,389	0.1
6500	Real estate	35	35	0.6	96	139	12,208	14,935	1,551	1,679	0.2
BEDFORD, VA											
60 –	**Finance, insurance, and real estate**	43	46	0.3	152	113	16,000	21,345	3,198	2,787	0.1
6000	Depository institutions	7	7	0.2	21	32	15,810	24,375	535	831	0.1
6400	Insurance agents, brokers, and service	7	10	0.3	19	21	21,263	22,095	451	511	0.1
6500	Real estate	25	23	0.4	84	43	15,286	16,279	1,661	842	0.1
6510	Real estate operators and lessors	4	5	0.3	5	8	12,000	10,000	72	96	0.1
6530	Real estate agents and managers	14	13	0.4	28	29	16,286	14,483	491	519	0.1
BOTETOURT, VA											
60 –	**Finance, insurance, and real estate**	35	34	0.2	155	156	18,865	19,051	2,904	2,945	0.1
6000	Depository institutions	10	9	0.3	106	105	18,075	18,819	1,912	1,997	0.1
6500	Real estate	14	13	0.2	25	27	20,640	17,185	501	426	0.1
6510	Real estate operators and lessors	3	3	0.2	7	8	12,571	16,500	112	102	0.1
6530	Real estate agents and managers	6	6	0.2	6	6	46,000	26,000	149	132	0.0
6550	Subdividers and developers	5	4	0.9	12	13	12,667	13,538	240	192	0.2
BUCHANAN, VA											
60 –	**Finance, insurance, and real estate**	29	31	0.2	201	205	19,124	18,829	4,114	4,192	0.1
6000	Depository institutions	11	10	0.3	150	151	20,613	19,656	3,307	3,275	0.2
6020	Commercial banks	11	10	0.5	150	151	20,613	19,656	3,307	3,275	0.3
6510	Real estate operators and lessors	3	3	0.2	8	6	2,500	3,333	20	19	0.0
BUCKINGHAM, VA											
60 –	**Finance, insurance, and real estate**	13	17	0.1	-	-	-	-	-	-	-
6400	Insurance agents, brokers, and service	5	5	0.2	6	6	10,667	11,333	67	71	0.0
CAMPBELL, VA											
60 –	**Finance, insurance, and real estate**	62	58	0.4	233	229	18,558	18,865	4,623	4,616	0.1
6000	Depository institutions	15	15	0.5	127	131	22,425	22,962	3,062	3,153	0.2
6020	Commercial banks	9	9	0.4	103	108	22,680	23,333	2,593	2,654	0.2
6400	Insurance agents, brokers, and service	18	18	0.6	43	39	9,023	11,179	463	490	0.1
6500	Real estate	22	19	0.3	47	44	13,021	12,091	643	574	0.1
6510	Real estate operators and lessors	9	7	0.4	16	15	10,250	10,133	155	172	0.1
CAROLINE, VA											
60 –	**Finance, insurance, and real estate**	27	27	0.2	197	182	17,746	20,505	3,258	3,919	0.1
6000	Depository institutions	6	5	0.2	112	117	19,500	22,632	2,038	2,517	0.2
6400	Insurance agents, brokers, and service	6	6	0.2	17	19	20,471	21,053	342	390	0.1
6500	Real estate	11	11	0.2	56	40	12,286	14,100	670	584	0.1
6530	Real estate agents and managers	8	8	0.3	53	37	12,453	14,595	645	565	0.1
CARROLL, VA											
60 –	**Finance, insurance, and real estate**	23	25	0.2	100	91	17,640	19,560	1,786	1,649	0.0
6400	Insurance agents, brokers, and service	12	10	0.3	31	29	15,226	16,966	489	474	0.1
CHARLES CITY, VA											
60 –	**Finance, insurance, and real estate**	2	1	0.0	-	-	-	-	-	-	-

Source: County Business Patterns, 1994/95, CBP-94/95, U.S. Department of Commerce, Washington, D.C., November 1997. SIC categories for which data were suppressed or not available for both 1994 and 1995 are not displayed. The employment columns represent mid-March employment in the year. Pay per employee is calculated by dividing 1st Quarter payroll, annualized, by mid-March employment. The columns headed "% State" show the county's percentage of the state total for the SIC in 1995; for example, 1.4% for SIC 6000 means that the county had 1.4 percent of the state's total establishments (or payroll) in SIC 6000 in 1995. A dash (-) is used to indicate that data are not available or cannot be calculated; nec means not elsewhere classified.

SIC	Industry	No. Establishments			Employment		Pay / Employee		Annual Payroll ($ 000)		
		1994	1995	% State	1994	1995	1994	1995	1994	1995	% State
CHARLOTTE, VA											
60 –	**Finance, insurance, and real estate**	11	12	*0.1*	65	61	20,800	22,557	1,387	1,624	*0.0*
CHESTERFIELD, VA											
60 –	**Finance, insurance, and real estate**	494	533	*3.5*	4,410	4,433	28,996	31,692	130,871	142,394	*2.7*
6000	Depository institutions	89	90	*3.0*	1,164	1,049	22,072	26,135	26,056	25,760	*1.7*
6020	Commercial banks	64	67	*3.1*	782	864	23,274	27,329	18,896	22,020	*2.0*
6100	Nondepository institutions	42	50	*4.2*	341	263	40,739	41,460	12,020	10,895	*1.5*
6160	Mortgage bankers and brokers	24	24	*3.9*	266	177	45,444	47,955	8,843	7,108	*3.3*
6200	Security and commodity brokers	22	26	*3.3*	57	153	51,789	33,804	6,129	7,347	*1.6*
6210	Security brokers and dealers	10	9	*2.2*	20	98	33,400	13,878	789	1,504	*0.4*
6280	Security and commodity services	12	17	*4.4*	37	55	61,730	69,309	5,340	5,843	*5.0*
6300	Insurance carriers	53	58	*5.0*	1,674	1,759	35,314	40,209	59,454	69,539	*6.9*
6330	Fire, marine, and casualty insurance	28	34	*5.8*	403	433	31,911	34,402	13,226	14,746	*2.8*
6400	Insurance agents, brokers, and service	130	132	*4.5*	501	485	23,737	23,662	11,988	12,270	*2.8*
6500	Real estate	146	165	*2.9*	603	657	19,602	19,056	12,862	14,007	*1.7*
6510	Real estate operators and lessors	37	44	*2.3*	189	150	17,545	19,067	3,231	2,867	*1.5*
6530	Real estate agents and managers	83	94	*3.2*	312	385	20,026	19,003	6,630	8,009	*1.5*
6540	Title abstract offices	5	7	*6.4*	36	32	21,333	20,500	820	713	*5.3*
6550	Subdividers and developers	16	15	*3.3*	64	85	22,875	18,729	2,049	2,254	*2.6*
6552	Subdividers and developers, n.e.c.	9	9	*3.1*	21	30	26,667	23,333	1,002	1,055	*1.6*
6553	Cemetery subdividers and developers	6	5	*3.7*	43	54	21,023	16,296	1,040	1,196	*5.6*
6700	Holding and other investment offices	12	12	*2.6*	70	67	35,829	33,970	2,362	2,576	*1.1*
CLARKE, VA											
60 –	**Finance, insurance, and real estate**	17	19	*0.1*	98	117	17,469	21,299	1,991	2,391	*0.0*
6500	Real estate	7	8	*0.1*	16	29	10,750	20,138	285	483	*0.1*
6530	Real estate agents and managers	4	4	*0.1*	9	13	13,333	32,615	203	273	*0.1*
CULPEPER, VA											
60 –	**Finance, insurance, and real estate**	54	56	*0.4*	502	420	39,952	44,438	20,085	18,942	*0.4*
6000	Depository institutions	10	10	*0.3*	347	265	47,666	46,943	16,426	14,179	*1.0*
6160	Mortgage bankers and brokers	3	4	*0.7*	8	8	49,500	46,000	292	304	*0.1*
6500	Real estate	20	20	*0.4*	46	35	13,043	17,829	692	736	*0.1*
CUMBERLAND, VA											
60 –	**Finance, insurance, and real estate**	6	5	*0.0*	22	22	20,545	19,091	557	481	*0.0*
DICKENSON, VA											
60 –	**Finance, insurance, and real estate**	10	9	*0.1*	83	84	17,157	15,524	1,540	1,317	*0.0*
6000	Depository institutions	5	4	*0.1*	67	61	18,448	17,377	1,334	1,077	*0.1*
6020	Commercial banks	5	4	*0.2*	67	61	18,448	17,377	1,334	1,077	*0.1*
6400	Insurance agents, brokers, and service	5	5	*0.2*	16	23	11,750	10,609	206	240	*0.1*
ESSEX, VA											
60 –	**Finance, insurance, and real estate**	20	20	*0.1*	155	139	20,800	20,863	3,370	3,124	*0.1*
6000	Depository institutions	6	6	*0.2*	80	86	20,050	20,279	1,627	1,782	*0.1*
6020	Commercial banks	6	6	*0.3*	80	86	20,050	20,279	1,627	1,782	*0.2*
6500	Real estate	6	5	*0.1*	8	5	16,000	24,000	143	131	*0.0*
FAIRFAX, VA											
60 –	**Finance, insurance, and real estate**	2,532	2,515	*16.5*	34,742	31,399	42,373	43,230	1,423,612	1,297,838	*24.2*
6000	Depository institutions	348	331	*11.1*	7,544	7,581	28,197	30,851	217,056	224,552	*15.2*
6020	Commercial banks	247	239	*10.9*	4,202	4,243	27,341	31,037	114,007	122,150	*10.9*
6030	Savings institutions	55	43	*14.1*	846	718	31,816	33,794	25,276	16,065	*19.6*
6060	Credit unions	34	33	*8.7*	2,313	2,339	26,423	26,907	68,051	72,262	*43.8*
6100	Nondepository institutions	288	278	*23.2*	8,523	7,201	55,213	60,046	405,415	406,686	*56.9*
6150	Business credit institutions	25	29	*30.9*	565	495	58,202	64,210	41,367	33,220	*22.0*
6160	Mortgage bankers and brokers	215	199	*32.5*	3,414	2,238	43,438	39,101	113,569	93,394	*43.3*

Source: County Business Patterns, 1994/95, CBP-94/95, U.S. Department of Commerce, Washington, D.C., November 1997. SIC categories for which data were suppressed or not available for both 1994 and 1995 are *not* displayed. The employment columns represent mid-March employment in the year. Pay per employee is calculated by dividing 1st Quarter payroll, annualized, by mid-March employment. The columns headed "% State" show the county's percentage of the state total for the SIC in 1995; for example, 1.4% for SIC 6000 means that the county had 1.4 percent of the state's total establishments (or payroll) in SIC 6000 in 1995. A dash (-) is used to indicate that data are not available or cannot be calculated; *nec* means not elsewhere classified.

Continued on next page.

SIC	Industry	No. Establishments			Employment		Pay / Employee		Annual Payroll ($ 000)		
		1994	1995	% State	1994	1995	1994	1995	1994	1995	% State
FAIRFAX, VA - [continued]											
6200	Security and commodity brokers	183	196	*24.5*	1,576	1,185	62,629	52,078	98,003	66,012	*14.5*
6210	Security brokers and dealers	75	78	*19.4*	776	856	64,804	56,603	45,954	48,872	*14.5*
6280	Security and commodity services	105	113	*29.4*	799	321	60,546	40,984	51,959	16,993	*14.5*
6300	Insurance carriers	174	188	*16.4*	2,485	2,421	39,525	42,249	92,317	102,434	*10.1*
6310	Life insurance	38	38	*12.9*	946	852	35,687	38,366	32,844	29,823	*11.0*
6320	Medical service and health insurance	13	15	*21.7*	401	125	33,087	41,792	9,559	6,854	*4.1*
6330	Fire, marine, and casualty insurance	80	89	*15.1*	879	1,201	46,366	44,067	40,012	55,645	*10.7*
6360	Title insurance	23	27	*23.7*	150	118	35,947	46,780	4,799	4,633	*20.3*
6370	Pension, health, and welfare funds	15	10	*17.9*	67	76	37,254	37,474	2,664	2,647	*12.0*
6400	Insurance agents, brokers, and service	400	399	*13.6*	2,718	2,801	33,564	35,296	94,045	97,166	*21.8*
6500	Real estate	1,012	998	*17.6*	7,609	7,973	25,892	29,229	212,953	236,226	*28.4*
6510	Real estate operators and lessors	224	215	*11.1*	1,630	1,446	18,319	21,231	33,318	33,344	*17.4*
6530	Real estate agents and managers	660	629	*21.3*	5,003	4,899	28,419	32,177	151,374	157,594	*29.9*
6540	Title abstract offices	30	31	*28.2*	223	117	30,242	32,513	5,907	4,746	*35.0*
6550	Subdividers and developers	65	66	*14.5*	729	1,394	24,466	26,568	21,075	35,425	*40.4*
6552	Subdividers and developers, n.e.c.	58	55	*18.9*	513	1,183	29,653	27,743	17,627	31,200	*48.6*
6700	Holding and other investment offices	107	107	*23.5*	1,690	714	44,869	55,087	74,675	40,645	*17.2*
6710	Holding offices	35	29	*19.5*	1,376	265	46,648	72,906	61,232	17,860	*11.5*
6730	Trusts	28	30	*23.3*	79	223	29,114	40,502	3,021	9,909	*33.9*
6732	Educational, religious, etc. trusts	18	19	*22.9*	54	87	30,963	38,161	2,225	4,173	*24.2*
6733	Trusts, n.e.c.	10	10	*22.2*	25	135	25,120	42,163	796	5,726	*47.8*
6790	Miscellaneous investing	39	39	*27.5*	230	186	39,948	42,925	9,726	8,548	*19.9*
6794	Patent owners and lessors	9	11	*31.4*	82	104	36,976	46,346	4,019	4,797	*42.7*
6798	Real estate investment trusts	4	4	*11.4*	14	12	10,571	11,667	164	100	*-*
6799	Investors, n.e.c.	26	24	*34.3*	134	70	44,836	43,200	5,543	3,651	*17.1*
FAUQUIER, VA											
60 –	**Finance, insurance, and real estate**	107	113	*0.7*	817	727	22,884	23,703	19,011	18,246	*0.3*
6000	Depository institutions	24	24	*0.8*	459	384	23,773	25,125	11,145	10,120	*0.7*
6020	Commercial banks	19	19	*0.9*	395	344	22,977	24,721	9,618	8,600	*0.8*
6100	Nondepository institutions	5	6	*0.5*	53	29	21,811	36,414	1,160	1,049	*0.1*
6200	Security and commodity brokers	5	5	*0.6*	14	16	123,143	64,500	1,221	1,141	*0.3*
6400	Insurance agents, brokers, and service	21	21	*0.7*	70	62	26,286	28,452	1,844	1,844	*0.4*
6500	Real estate	44	47	*0.8*	200	211	12,720	14,085	3,121	3,359	*0.4*
6510	Real estate operators and lessors	11	13	*0.7*	133	143	8,722	11,217	1,519	1,753	*0.9*
6530	Real estate agents and managers	24	25	*0.8*	53	54	21,283	20,296	1,317	1,289	*0.2*
FLOYD, VA											
60 –	**Finance, insurance, and real estate**	11	11	*0.1*	71	74	19,380	19,243	1,333	1,376	*0.0*
6500	Real estate	4	4	*0.1*	3	2	6,667	8,000	34	24	*0.0*
FLUVANNA, VA											
60 –	**Finance, insurance, and real estate**	12	13	*0.1*	106	96	16,000	16,417	1,777	1,706	*0.0*
6500	Real estate	5	7	*0.1*	79	71	16,861	17,352	1,376	1,386	*0.2*
FRANKLIN, VA											
60 –	**Finance, insurance, and real estate**	55	53	*0.3*	309	283	17,411	20,580	5,888	5,665	*0.1*
6000	Depository institutions	15	15	*0.5*	167	157	18,491	21,605	3,249	3,478	*0.2*
6500	Real estate	18	16	*0.3*	88	71	12,227	15,718	1,467	971	*0.1*
6530	Real estate agents and managers	11	9	*0.3*	56	29	11,000	18,483	810	256	*0.0*
FREDERICK, VA											
60 –	**Finance, insurance, and real estate**	43	63	*0.4*	218	340	21,706	20,659	5,694	7,941	*0.1*
6000	Depository institutions	10	11	*0.4*	73	85	19,671	19,341	1,697	1,944	*0.1*
6020	Commercial banks	10	11	*0.5*	73	85	19,671	19,341	1,697	1,944	*0.2*

Source: County Business Patterns, 1994/95, CBP-94/95, U.S. Department of Commerce, Washington, D.C., November 1997. SIC categories for which data were suppressed or not available for both 1994 and 1995 are *not* displayed. The employment columns represent mid-March employment in the year. Pay per employee is calculated by dividing 1st Quarter payroll, annualized, by mid-March employment. The columns headed "% State" show the county's percentage of the state total for the SIC in 1995; for example, 1.4% for SIC 6000 means that the county had 1.4 percent of the state's total establishments (or payroll) in SIC 6000 in 1995. A dash (-) is used to indicate that data are not available or cannot be calculated; *nec* means not elsewhere classified.

Continued on next page.

SIC	Industry	No. Establishments			Employment		Pay / Employee		Annual Payroll ($ 000)		
		1994	1995	% State	1994	1995	1994	1995	1994	1995	% State
FREDERICK, VA - [continued]											
6400	Insurance agents, brokers, and service	9	12	0.4	41	45	18,634	19,822	991	1,024	0.2
6500	Real estate	21	29	0.5	69	107	19,420	17,757	1,688	2,216	0.3
6510	Real estate operators and lessors	12	15	0.8	54	72	20,296	18,389	1,424	1,619	0.8
GILES, VA											
60 –	**Finance, insurance, and real estate**	20	18	0.1	94	83	16,383	18,410	1,642	1,465	0.0
6000	Depository institutions	9	8	0.3	63	63	19,365	19,937	1,304	1,157	0.1
GLOUCESTER, VA											
60 –	**Finance, insurance, and real estate**	51	60	0.4	222	240	18,901	20,767	4,507	5,390	0.1
6000	Depository institutions	11	11	0.4	121	123	19,537	21,398	2,560	2,955	0.2
6400	Insurance agents, brokers, and service	10	12	0.4	35	37	24,686	25,081	817	862	0.2
6500	Real estate	24	27	0.5	57	62	12,561	13,097	851	847	0.1
6510	Real estate operators and lessors	6	6	0.3	17	16	10,824	15,000	229	270	0.1
6530	Real estate agents and managers	14	15	0.5	34	33	13,647	12,727	504	441	0.1
6550	Subdividers and developers	3	4	0.9	6	11	11,333	12,364	114	105	0.1
GOOCHLAND, VA											
60 –	**Finance, insurance, and real estate**	16	18	0.1	57	92	29,193	48,957	3,315	7,137	0.1
6500	Real estate	9	8	0.1	16	16	19,000	19,500	317	355	0.0
6510	Real estate operators and lessors	3	3	0.2	5	5	12,000	12,800	58	50	0.0
GRAYSON, VA											
60 –	**Finance, insurance, and real estate**	13	14	0.1	75	76	18,240	20,632	1,496	1,650	0.0
HALIFAX, VA											
60 –	**Finance, insurance, and real estate**	13	12	0.1	37	39	23,027	22,154	891	896	0.0
6500	Real estate	4	4	0.1	4	9	22,000	10,667	92	98	0.0
HANOVER, VA											
60 –	**Finance, insurance, and real estate**	151	154	1.0	1,081	1,100	24,470	24,895	27,022	28,225	0.5
6000	Depository institutions	33	34	1.1	470	454	19,277	21,445	9,227	9,650	0.7
6020	Commercial banks	29	30	1.4	446	430	19,363	21,628	8,780	9,175	0.8
6100	Nondepository institutions	13	12	1.0	90	60	43,689	44,933	3,448	2,456	0.3
6300	Insurance carriers	13	14	1.2	65	70	30,585	26,229	2,203	2,271	0.2
6400	Insurance agents, brokers, and service	28	30	1.0	194	193	30,907	32,601	6,570	6,702	1.5
6500	Real estate	57	56	1.0	217	272	14,378	15,044	3,314	4,190	0.5
6510	Real estate operators and lessors	12	12	0.6	25	39	11,040	8,821	338	323	0.2
6530	Real estate agents and managers	39	38	1.3	168	215	14,238	15,833	2,521	3,452	0.7
6550	Subdividers and developers	4	4	0.9	23	16	19,130	19,500	424	384	0.4
HENRICO, VA											
60 –	**Finance, insurance, and real estate**	659	680	4.5	15,251	17,868	30,745	32,614	513,794	556,979	10.4
6000	Depository institutions	124	122	4.1	6,128	6,085	23,701	25,181	157,549	155,207	10.5
6020	Commercial banks	97	95	4.3	5,970	5,916	23,788	25,314	154,221	151,579	13.5
6060	Credit unions	18	18	4.8	118	126	20,983	21,429	2,682	2,942	1.8
6100	Nondepository institutions	56	62	5.2	458	3,723	38,655	31,267	58,871	106,398	14.9
6200	Security and commodity brokers	33	34	4.3	277	269	82,123	79,063	26,794	26,439	5.8
6210	Security brokers and dealers	10	10	2.5	79	67	33,873	26,030	2,209	2,439	0.7
6280	Security and commodity services	23	24	6.3	198	202	101,374	96,653	24,585	24,000	20.4
6300	Insurance carriers	79	78	6.8	4,377	3,852	35,561	40,503	146,378	139,968	13.8
6310	Life insurance	23	21	7.1	1,055	1,106	37,084	36,669	38,792	37,256	13.8
6330	Fire, marine, and casualty insurance	38	38	6.5	1,474	1,327	37,769	34,460	52,944	46,109	8.9
6400	Insurance agents, brokers, and service	156	154	5.3	2,456	2,428	34,953	38,959	83,287	87,493	19.7
6500	Real estate	194	207	3.7	1,238	1,196	22,375	24,562	29,481	29,991	3.6
6510	Real estate operators and lessors	55	56	2.9	379	344	16,887	17,686	6,566	6,335	3.3
6530	Real estate agents and managers	111	118	4.0	643	680	24,572	25,882	17,110	17,722	3.4
6550	Subdividers and developers	25	23	5.0	204	160	25,098	34,075	5,493	5,554	6.3

Source: County Business Patterns, 1994/95, CBP-94/95, U.S. Department of Commerce, Washington, D.C., November 1997. SIC categories for which data were suppressed or not available for both 1994 and 1995 are *not* displayed. The employment columns represent mid-March employment in the year. Pay per employee is calculated by dividing 1st Quarter payroll, annualized, by mid-March employment. The columns headed "% State" show the county's percentage of the state total for the SIC in 1995; for example, 1.4% for SIC 6000 means that the county had 1.4 percent of the state's total establishments (or payroll) in SIC 6000 in 1995. A dash (-) is used to indicate that data are not available or cannot be calculated; *nec* means not elsewhere classified.

Continued on next page.

SIC	Industry	No. Establishments			Employment		Pay / Employee		Annual Payroll ($ 000)		
		1994	1995	% State	1994	1995	1994	1995	1994	1995	% State
HENRICO, VA - [continued]											
6552	Subdividers and developers, n.e.c.	20	18	6.2	152	112	25,921	40,964	4,234	4,410	6.9
6553	Cemetery subdividers and developers	5	5	3.7	52	48	22,692	18,000	1,259	1,144	5.4
6790	Miscellaneous investing	7	8	5.6	88	79	13,409	23,089	1,322	1,554	3.6
HENRY, VA											
60 –	**Finance, insurance, and real estate**	57	58	0.4	316	358	16,962	17,017	5,818	6,396	0.1
6000	Depository institutions	13	13	0.4	197	208	17,401	19,635	3,717	4,267	0.3
6400	Insurance agents, brokers, and service	23	23	0.8	65	61	18,769	20,328	1,287	1,297	0.3
6500	Real estate	16	18	0.3	39	75	11,077	6,133	546	530	0.1
6510	Real estate operators and lessors	8	9	0.5	18	42	11,111	5,619	231	277	0.1
HIGHLAND, VA											
60 –	**Finance, insurance, and real estate**	7	6	0.0	-	-	-	-	-	-	-
ISLE OF WIGHT, VA											
60 –	**Finance, insurance, and real estate**	35	36	0.2	131	189	20,855	18,011	3,032	3,848	0.1
6000	Depository institutions	8	7	0.2	76	81	23,474	23,654	1,823	2,007	0.1
6400	Insurance agents, brokers, and service	8	8	0.3	21	27	19,810	18,519	425	505	0.1
6500	Real estate	14	16	0.3	28	72	13,857	10,444	608	1,078	0.1
6530	Real estate agents and managers	6	7	0.2	17	57	14,588	10,316	385	742	0.1
JAMES CITY, VA											
60 –	**Finance, insurance, and real estate**	59	77	0.5	341	539	24,235	24,267	9,317	11,995	0.2
6200	Security and commodity brokers	5	6	0.8	5	14	33,600	41,143	176	672	0.1
6400	Insurance agents, brokers, and service	9	9	0.3	16	15	13,750	14,667	225	207	0.0
6500	Real estate	34	42	0.7	263	426	25,840	23,962	7,843	9,124	1.1
6510	Real estate operators and lessors	10	14	0.7	57	53	15,228	15,925	987	782	0.4
6530	Real estate agents and managers	19	22	0.7	200	337	29,100	26,659	6,682	7,776	1.5
KING AND QUEEN, VA											
60 –	**Finance, insurance, and real estate**	2	2	0.0	-	-	-	-	-	-	-
KING GEORGE, VA											
60 –	**Finance, insurance, and real estate**	18	18	0.1	102	101	18,627	19,644	2,096	2,055	0.0
6000	Depository institutions	4	4	0.1	77	80	20,156	21,400	1,706	1,736	0.1
6530	Real estate agents and managers	5	6	0.2	11	9	9,455	12,000	117	117	0.0
KING WILLIAM, VA											
60 –	**Finance, insurance, and real estate**	21	23	0.2	147	140	21,469	30,029	3,256	4,000	0.1
6000	Depository institutions	9	9	0.3	105	106	19,200	24,528	2,039	2,489	0.2
6400	Insurance agents, brokers, and service	4	4	0.1	16	14	21,750	25,143	418	369	0.1
LANCASTER, VA											
60 –	**Finance, insurance, and real estate**	44	46	0.3	296	258	27,122	26,651	7,957	6,861	0.1
6000	Depository institutions	12	15	0.5	174	158	21,172	22,152	3,483	3,275	0.2
6400	Insurance agents, brokers, and service	7	7	0.2	24	17	23,667	18,588	589	364	0.1
6500	Real estate	16	17	0.3	39	30	11,692	16,133	632	507	0.1
6530	Real estate agents and managers	12	13	0.4	27	23	10,519	14,435	446	352	0.1
LEE, VA											
60 –	**Finance, insurance, and real estate**	27	29	0.2	188	191	17,915	18,031	3,691	3,773	0.1
6000	Depository institutions	12	12	0.4	150	154	19,920	19,662	3,213	3,296	0.2
6510	Real estate operators and lessors	3	3	0.2	8	6	3,500	3,333	33	27	0.0
LOUDOUN, VA											
60 –	**Finance, insurance, and real estate**	266	274	1.8	1,393	1,505	30,659	30,573	45,681	51,971	1.0
6000	Depository institutions	47	46	1.5	500	497	24,496	24,451	12,233	11,945	0.8
6020	Commercial banks	35	35	1.6	428	410	22,598	22,810	10,174	9,712	0.9

Source: County Business Patterns, 1994/95, CBP-94/95, U.S. Department of Commerce, Washington, D.C., November 1997. SIC categories for which data were suppressed or not available for both 1994 and 1995 are not displayed. The employment columns represent mid-March employment in the year. Pay per employee is calculated by dividing 1st Quarter payroll, annualized, by mid-March employment. The columns headed "% State" show the county's percentage of the state total for the SIC in 1995; for example, 1.4% for SIC 6000 means that the county had 1.4 percent of the state's total establishments (or payroll) in SIC 6000 in 1995. A dash (-) is used to indicate that data are not available or cannot be calculated; nec means not elsewhere classified.

Continued on next page.

SIC	Industry	No. Establishments			Employment		Pay / Employee		Annual Payroll ($ 000)		
		1994	1995	% State	1994	1995	1994	1995	1994	1995	% State
LOUDOUN, VA - [continued]											
6030	Savings institutions	8	7	2.3	58	70	40,414	35,829	1,791	1,914	2.3
6060	Credit unions	4	4	1.1	14	17	16,571	17,176	268	319	0.2
6100	Nondepository institutions	12	14	1.2	76	62	38,000	43,226	2,933	4,652	0.7
6160	Mortgage bankers and brokers	6	5	0.8	41	34	52,878	51,412	2,185	2,551	1.2
6200	Security and commodity brokers	10	14	1.8	19	52	58,737	42,769	1,504	3,062	0.7
6300	Insurance carriers	23	21	1.8	103	92	31,340	38,000	3,308	3,557	0.4
6400	Insurance agents, brokers, and service	50	47	1.6	260	296	39,462	39,054	10,282	12,406	2.8
6500	Real estate	114	121	2.1	332	411	23,145	22,122	9,980	10,617	1.3
6510	Real estate operators and lessors	26	33	1.7	74	89	19,405	15,775	1,497	1,830	1.0
6530	Real estate agents and managers	68	66	2.2	196	228	25,388	26,281	6,750	7,010	1.3
6540	Title abstract offices	4	3	2.7	8	5	34,000	24,800	258	63	0.5
6550	Subdividers and developers	12	11	2.4	54	80	18,519	17,750	1,352	1,492	1.7
6552	Subdividers and developers, n.e.c.	9	8	2.7	45	69	20,711	18,841	1,255	1,358	2.1
6700	Holding and other investment offices	10	11	2.4	103	95	51,301	50,611	5,441	5,732	2.4
MADISON, VA											
60 –	**Finance, insurance, and real estate**	10	13	0.1	-	-	-	-	-	-	-
6500	Real estate	5	7	0.1	14	13	8,857	14,769	164	224	0.0
MECKLENBURG, VA											
60 –	**Finance, insurance, and real estate**	59	62	0.4	-	-	-	-	-	-	-
6000	Depository institutions	15	18	0.6	132	141	22,576	22,894	2,921	3,236	0.2
6400	Insurance agents, brokers, and service	17	18	0.6	55	54	19,636	20,148	1,202	1,250	0.3
6500	Real estate	20	18	0.3	57	56	11,579	13,000	810	764	0.1
6510	Real estate operators and lessors	5	5	0.3	20	22	8,200	8,727	275	241	0.1
6530	Real estate agents and managers	11	9	0.3	12	16	11,333	12,250	206	204	0.0
6550	Subdividers and developers	4	4	0.9	25	18	14,400	18,889	329	319	0.4
MIDDLESEX, VA											
60 –	**Finance, insurance, and real estate**	26	26	0.2	112	103	19,643	19,922	2,241	2,106	0.0
6000	Depository institutions	7	6	0.2	48	45	21,667	23,200	971	979	0.1
6020	Commercial banks	7	6	0.3	48	45	21,667	23,200	971	979	0.1
6400	Insurance agents, brokers, and service	7	8	0.3	28	24	23,714	26,333	721	662	0.1
6500	Real estate	12	12	0.2	36	34	13,778	11,059	549	465	0.1
6510	Real estate operators and lessors	3	3	0.2	10	12	6,800	6,333	82	101	0.1
6530	Real estate agents and managers	9	9	0.3	26	22	16,462	13,636	467	364	0.1
MONTGOMERY, VA											
60 –	**Finance, insurance, and real estate**	130	129	0.8	978	1,039	20,446	20,393	22,562	23,040	0.4
6000	Depository institutions	34	33	1.1	416	431	20,115	19,852	9,292	8,842	0.6
6020	Commercial banks	28	27	1.2	373	371	21,223	21,563	8,794	8,226	0.7
6160	Mortgage bankers and brokers	4	5	0.8	4	9	25,000	19,556	159	415	0.2
6400	Insurance agents, brokers, and service	23	21	0.7	68	69	19,000	19,884	1,528	1,429	0.3
6500	Real estate	47	49	0.9	424	460	17,849	18,052	9,003	10,058	1.2
6530	Real estate agents and managers	24	25	0.8	169	223	24,734	20,753	4,984	5,410	1.0
NELSON, VA											
60 –	**Finance, insurance, and real estate**	16	17	0.1	81	85	40,840	29,694	3,096	2,633	0.0
6000	Depository institutions	5	5	0.2	33	30	16,727	17,733	547	560	0.0
NORTHAMPTON, VA											
60 –	**Finance, insurance, and real estate**	19	17	0.1	67	64	20,716	21,000	1,391	1,332	0.0
6400	Insurance agents, brokers, and service	4	3	0.1	11	8	13,818	12,000	143	95	0.0
NORTHUMBERLAND, VA											
60 –	**Finance, insurance, and real estate**	22	19	0.1	77	82	25,299	23,463	1,756	1,815	0.0

Source: County Business Patterns, 1994/95, CBP-94/95, U.S. Department of Commerce, Washington, D.C., November 1997. SIC categories for which data were suppressed or not available for both 1994 and 1995 are *not* displayed. The employment columns represent mid-March employment in the year. Pay per employee is calculated by dividing 1st Quarter payroll, annualized, by mid-March employment. The columns headed "% State" show the county's percentage of the state total for the SIC in 1995; for example, 1.4% for SIC 6000 means that the county had 1.4 percent of the state's total establishments (or payroll) in SIC 6000 in 1995. A dash (-) is used to indicate that data are not available or cannot be calculated; *nec* means not elsewhere classified.

Continued on next page.

SIC	Industry	No. Establishments			Employment		Pay / Employee		Annual Payroll ($ 000)		
		1994	1995	% State	1994	1995	1994	1995	1994	1995	% State
NORTHUMBERLAND, VA - [continued]											
6000	Depository institutions	6	6	0.2	60	60	27,667	27,000	1,433	1,498	0.1
6020	Commercial banks	6	6	0.3	60	60	27,667	27,000	1,433	1,498	0.1
6400	Insurance agents, brokers, and service	6	6	0.2	10	14	21,600	16,000	245	233	0.1
ORANGE, VA											
60 –	**Finance, insurance, and real estate**	45	51	0.3	245	241	16,718	16,896	4,504	4,394	0.1
6000	Depository institutions	11	11	0.4	70	67	20,171	20,358	1,432	1,415	0.1
6500	Real estate	19	24	0.4	127	122	11,717	13,344	1,776	1,816	0.2
6530	Real estate agents and managers	13	10	0.3	110	97	12,109	14,144	1,602	1,556	0.3
PAGE, VA											
60 –	**Finance, insurance, and real estate**	34	32	0.2	172	168	17,558	18,048	3,128	3,139	0.1
6000	Depository institutions	10	10	0.3	119	118	19,563	19,898	2,437	2,447	0.2
6020	Commercial banks	10	10	0.5	119	118	19,563	19,898	2,437	2,447	0.2
6400	Insurance agents, brokers, and service	9	8	0.3	23	25	16,522	16,160	375	387	0.1
6500	Real estate	12	11	0.2	21	20	4,762	5,400	115	122	0.0
6510	Real estate operators and lessors	4	3	0.2	6	2	3,333	4,000	17	12	0.0
6530	Real estate agents and managers	5	5	0.2	9	12	7,111	7,000	82	94	0.0
PATRICK, VA											
60 –	**Finance, insurance, and real estate**	20	23	0.2	103	100	19,301	25,240	2,630	2,676	0.0
6000	Depository institutions	8	8	0.3	77	68	20,468	30,118	2,192	2,118	0.1
6020	Commercial banks	8	8	0.4	77	68	20,468	30,118	2,192	2,118	0.2
PITTSYLVANIA, VA											
60 –	**Finance, insurance, and real estate**	53	60	0.4	233	248	19,657	19,452	5,300	5,218	0.1
6000	Depository institutions	10	11	0.4	58	58	18,759	18,966	1,043	1,209	0.1
6500	Real estate	16	19	0.3	69	79	14,145	13,722	1,131	1,210	0.1
POWHATAN, VA											
60 –	**Finance, insurance, and real estate**	15	15	0.1	92	86	22,522	25,256	2,478	2,106	0.0
PRINCE EDWARD, VA											
60 –	**Finance, insurance, and real estate**	39	47	0.3	364	394	18,429	18,569	6,792	7,310	0.1
6000	Depository institutions	10	16	0.5	93	103	22,280	20,854	2,075	2,093	0.1
6400	Insurance agents, brokers, and service	11	10	0.3	58	48	17,517	19,667	1,086	1,035	0.2
6500	Real estate	12	13	0.2	35	35	13,600	18,171	559	572	0.1
6530	Real estate agents and managers	4	3	0.1	9	9	14,667	16,444	181	131	0.0
PRINCE GEORGE, VA											
60 –	**Finance, insurance, and real estate**	21	20	0.1	122	133	20,590	20,301	2,793	2,803	0.1
6000	Depository institutions	5	5	0.2	62	60	15,806	16,467	1,088	1,095	0.1
6500	Real estate	8	7	0.1	21	21	16,952	14,476	535	381	0.0
PRINCE WILLIAM, VA											
60 –	**Finance, insurance, and real estate**	277	281	1.8	1,473	1,348	25,219	25,288	35,843	35,024	0.7
6000	Depository institutions	58	53	1.8	617	524	21,854	22,443	13,937	12,669	0.9
6020	Commercial banks	39	39	1.8	397	347	19,980	21,107	8,285	7,491	0.7
6060	Credit unions	6	6	1.6	82	93	20,829	19,140	1,921	2,064	1.3
6100	Nondepository institutions	27	26	2.2	246	163	37,463	35,117	6,714	4,954	0.7
6160	Mortgage bankers and brokers	16	12	2.0	201	108	41,353	39,407	5,729	3,478	1.6
6280	Security and commodity services	3	3	0.8	1	2	24,000	6,000	81	45	0.0
6400	Insurance agents, brokers, and service	51	53	1.8	119	135	21,311	21,244	2,814	2,875	0.6
6500	Real estate	105	115	2.0	381	403	17,690	21,112	6,912	9,014	1.1
6510	Real estate operators and lessors	23	26	1.3	148	175	13,784	18,651	2,197	3,168	1.7
6530	Real estate agents and managers	67	67	2.3	183	174	19,760	20,713	3,731	3,717	0.7
6540	Title abstract offices	6	6	5.5	26	18	22,308	30,889	527	683	5.0

Source: County Business Patterns, 1994/95, CBP-94/95, U.S. Department of Commerce, Washington, D.C., November 1997. SIC categories for which data were suppressed or not available for both 1994 and 1995 are *not* displayed. The employment columns represent mid-March employment in the year. Pay per employee is calculated by dividing 1st Quarter payroll, annualized, by mid-March employment. The columns headed "% State" show the county's percentage of the state total for the SIC in 1995; for example, 1.4% for SIC 6000 means that the county had 1.4 percent of the state's total establishments (or payroll) in SIC 6000 in 1995. A dash (-) is used to indicate that data are not available or cannot be calculated; *nec* means not elsewhere classified.

Continued on next page.

SIC	Industry	No. Establishments			Employment		Pay / Employee		Annual Payroll ($ 000)		
		1994	1995	% State	1994	1995	1994	1995	1994	1995	% State
PRINCE WILLIAM, VA - [continued]											
6550	Subdividers and developers	5	10	2.2	21	27	22,476	32,444	417	1,300	1.5
6700	Holding and other investment offices	12	9	2.0	44	50	33,273	30,720	1,465	1,473	0.6
6790	Miscellaneous investing	5	5	3.5	21	27	28,762	22,963	578	657	1.5
PULASKI, VA											
60 –	**Finance, insurance, and real estate**	47	47	0.3	199	203	18,573	19,034	3,773	3,946	0.1
6000	Depository institutions	13	13	0.4	97	107	16,784	17,720	1,762	1,978	0.1
6020	Commercial banks	9	9	0.4	68	75	17,765	19,093	1,330	1,470	0.1
6400	Insurance agents, brokers, and service	12	11	0.4	43	40	22,326	24,700	889	870	0.2
6510	Real estate operators and lessors	10	11	0.6	28	23	10,714	11,652	353	311	0.2
RICHMOND, VA											
60 –	**Finance, insurance, and real estate**	13	14	0.1	75	74	20,427	23,838	1,528	1,678	0.0
6500	Real estate	6	6	0.1	10	10	8,000	9,200	85	113	0.0
ROANOKE, VA											
60 –	**Finance, insurance, and real estate**	212	215	1.4	2,786	2,855	25,833	26,945	72,875	76,697	1.4
6000	Depository institutions	39	39	1.3	337	350	22,861	22,274	7,442	8,056	0.5
6020	Commercial banks	24	24	1.1	236	249	23,051	22,297	5,197	5,709	0.5
6030	Savings institutions	10	10	3.3	52	49	27,692	27,673	1,407	1,420	1.7
6060	Credit unions	5	5	1.3	49	52	16,816	17,077	838	927	0.6
6100	Nondepository institutions	16	14	1.2	109	90	31,339	30,533	2,857	2,573	0.4
6140	Personal credit institutions	5	5	1.2	36	32	35,000	41,250	1,162	1,037	1.4
6160	Mortgage bankers and brokers	11	9	1.5	73	58	29,534	24,621	1,695	1,536	0.7
6300	Insurance carriers	33	35	3.0	1,902	1,938	27,977	30,083	54,209	57,422	5.7
6310	Life insurance	9	8	2.7	78	103	27,077	29,359	2,206	2,736	1.0
6320	Medical service and health insurance	3	4	5.8	53	70	37,509	37,200	2,081	2,352	1.4
6330	Fire, marine, and casualty insurance	21	22	3.7	1,771	1,764	27,731	29,857	49,922	52,324	10.1
6400	Insurance agents, brokers, and service	59	63	2.2	207	185	21,411	21,557	4,664	4,014	0.9
6500	Real estate	59	59	1.0	221	280	13,665	13,943	3,487	4,352	0.5
6510	Real estate operators and lessors	17	19	1.0	102	139	12,902	13,151	1,405	1,993	1.0
6530	Real estate agents and managers	37	32	1.1	113	125	14,018	13,728	1,844	1,979	0.4
6550	Subdividers and developers	5	6	1.3	6	15	20,000	22,933	238	342	0.4
ROCKBRIDGE, VA											
60 –	**Finance, insurance, and real estate**	13	15	0.1	67	67	15,642	16,597	1,063	1,106	0.0
ROCKINGHAM, VA											
60 –	**Finance, insurance, and real estate**	91	90	0.6	763	808	18,637	22,158	18,840	20,490	0.4
6000	Depository institutions	20	18	0.6	210	179	19,162	18,860	3,906	3,782	0.3
6100	Nondepository institutions	5	6	0.5	23	24	24,870	26,167	574	669	0.1
6400	Insurance agents, brokers, and service	17	18	0.6	98	106	24,163	24,943	3,004	2,769	0.6
6500	Real estate	39	41	0.7	387	488	13,674	22,492	9,096	13,000	1.6
6510	Real estate operators and lessors	16	19	1.0	71	83	13,070	11,036	992	1,001	0.5
6530	Real estate agents and managers	19	18	0.6	313	402	13,879	24,965	8,069	11,964	2.3
6550	Subdividers and developers	4	4	0.9	3	3	6,667	8,000	35	35	0.0
RUSSELL, VA											
60 –	**Finance, insurance, and real estate**	29	32	0.2	192	195	18,333	19,077	3,687	3,854	0.1
6000	Depository institutions	11	11	0.4	137	135	18,774	20,622	2,624	2,799	0.2
6400	Insurance agents, brokers, and service	12	15	0.5	29	31	12,828	13,806	410	477	0.1
SCOTT, VA											
60 –	**Finance, insurance, and real estate**	25	24	0.2	137	147	36,847	30,667	4,160	4,173	0.1

Source: County Business Patterns, 1994/95, CBP-94/95, U.S. Department of Commerce, Washington, D.C., November 1997. SIC categories for which data were suppressed or not available for both 1994 and 1995 are not displayed. The employment columns represent mid-March employment in the year. Pay per employee is calculated by dividing 1st Quarter payroll, annualized, by mid-March employment. The columns headed "% State" show the county's percentage of the state total for the SIC in 1995; for example, 1.4% for SIC 6000 means that the county had 1.4 percent of the state's total establishments (or payroll) in SIC 6000 in 1995. A dash (-) is used to indicate that data are not available or cannot be calculated; nec means not elsewhere classified.

Continued on next page.

SIC	Industry	No. Establishments			Employment		Pay / Employee		Annual Payroll ($ 000)		
		1994	1995	% State	1994	1995	1994	1995	1994	1995	% State
SCOTT, VA - [continued]											
6000	Depository institutions	9	9	0.3	61	58	18,492	18,621	1,113	1,052	0.1
6020	Commercial banks	9	9	0.4	61	58	18,492	18,621	1,113	1,052	0.1
6400	Insurance agents, brokers, and service	6	5	0.2	13	13	10,154	13,231	147	190	0.0
SHENANDOAH, VA											
60 –	**Finance, insurance, and real estate**	82	72	0.5	387	454	23,907	24,167	11,040	13,797	0.3
6000	Depository institutions	25	19	0.6	249	282	22,811	21,603	6,321	6,057	0.4
6020	Commercial banks	22	16	0.7	236	268	23,220	22,000	6,141	5,871	0.5
6500	Real estate	28	24	0.4	58	62	8,138	9,742	637	669	0.1
6530	Real estate agents and managers	14	14	0.5	35	46	8,343	9,652	433	475	0.1
SMYTH, VA											
60 –	**Finance, insurance, and real estate**	42	43	0.3	203	204	19,645	22,020	4,272	5,618	0.1
6000	Depository institutions	11	11	0.4	128	131	21,219	24,733	2,923	3,419	0.2
6400	Insurance agents, brokers, and service	17	17	0.6	34	34	16,706	16,471	605	627	0.1
6500	Real estate	8	8	0.1	27	25	11,852	12,160	362	424	0.1
SOUTHAMPTON, VA											
60 –	**Finance, insurance, and real estate**	26	23	0.2	84	76	15,286	15,947	1,338	1,229	0.0
6000	Depository institutions	6	5	0.2	33	28	17,212	17,571	566	504	0.0
6020	Commercial banks	6	5	0.2	33	28	17,212	17,571	566	504	0.0
6500	Real estate	12	12	0.2	28	28	7,000	8,714	286	243	0.0
6510	Real estate operators and lessors	7	7	0.4	14	11	6,857	8,364	114	92	0.0
6530	Real estate agents and managers	5	5	0.2	14	17	7,143	8,941	172	151	0.0
SPOTSYLVANIA, VA											
60 –	**Finance, insurance, and real estate**	32	33	0.2	246	303	21,382	18,521	5,772	6,248	0.1
6000	Depository institutions	5	5	0.2	35	35	18,743	20,229	668	729	0.0
6500	Real estate	20	19	0.3	192	248	20,188	17,871	4,531	5,054	0.6
6530	Real estate agents and managers	15	14	0.5	143	222	17,427	17,063	3,573	4,538	0.9
STAFFORD, VA											
60 –	**Finance, insurance, and real estate**	143	142	0.9	1,585	2,534	24,300	26,354	46,231	69,697	1.3
6000	Depository institutions	26	27	0.9	297	561	19,556	17,462	5,892	10,159	0.7
6020	Commercial banks	19	20	0.9	235	506	19,779	17,289	4,780	9,369	0.8
6030	Savings institutions	7	7	2.3	62	55	18,710	19,055	1,112	790	1.0
6100	Nondepository institutions	6	7	0.6	54	202	36,444	34,158	7,574	7,229	1.0
6500	Real estate	70	63	1.1	320	279	16,575	19,971	6,091	5,835	0.7
6510	Real estate operators and lessors	15	16	0.8	60	66	15,600	17,455	1,122	1,314	0.7
6530	Real estate agents and managers	41	36	1.2	163	159	18,429	18,717	3,346	2,884	0.5
6540	Title abstract offices	4	3	2.7	65	10	7,877	24,400	487	337	2.5
6550	Subdividers and developers	8	6	1.3	31	42	27,097	27,905	1,113	1,272	1.5
6552	Subdividers and developers, n.e.c.	8	6	2.1	31	42	27,097	27,905	1,113	1,272	2.0
SUSSEX, VA											
60 –	**Finance, insurance, and real estate**	15	17	0.1	86	94	22,512	22,553	1,908	2,260	0.0
6000	Depository institutions	9	9	0.3	65	69	21,108	20,754	1,354	1,456	0.1
6020	Commercial banks	9	9	0.4	65	69	21,108	20,754	1,354	1,456	0.1
TAZEWELL, VA											
60 –	**Finance, insurance, and real estate**	115	119	0.8	677	662	20,798	19,130	14,698	12,740	0.2
6000	Depository institutions	32	31	1.0	320	308	22,050	19,909	7,056	6,072	0.4
6020	Commercial banks	28	27	1.2	305	293	22,597	20,328	6,885	5,883	0.5
6200	Security and commodity brokers	6	6	0.8	12	14	13,000	16,286	210	233	0.1
6210	Security brokers and dealers	6	6	1.5	12	14	13,000	16,286	210	233	0.1
6400	Insurance agents, brokers, and service	21	22	0.8	80	84	15,900	16,143	1,422	1,451	0.3
6500	Real estate	44	44	0.8	194	151	19,278	15,020	4,134	2,519	0.3

Source: County Business Patterns, 1994/95, CBP-94/95, U.S. Department of Commerce, Washington, D.C., November 1997. SIC categories for which data were suppressed or not available for both 1994 and 1995 are not displayed. The employment columns represent mid-March employment in the year. Pay per employee is calculated by dividing 1st Quarter payroll, annualized, by mid-March employment. The columns headed "% State" show the county's percentage of the state total for the SIC in 1995; for example, 1.4% for SIC 6000 means that the county had 1.4 percent of the state's total establishments (or payroll) in SIC 6000 in 1995. A dash (-) is used to indicate that data are not available or cannot be calculated; nec means not elsewhere classified.

Continued on next page.

WASHINGTON

SIC	Industry	No. Establishments			Employment		Pay / Employee		Annual Payroll ($ 000)		
		1994	1995	% State	1994	1995	1994	1995	1994	1995	% State
ADAMS, WA											
60 –	**Finance, insurance, and real estate**	29	31	0.2	119	116	17,748	19,345	2,172	2,269	0.1
6000	Depository institutions	10	10	0.5	66	68	18,667	20,647	1,229	1,310	0.1
6500	Real estate	10	9	0.1	21	17	9,524	8,471	228	150	0.0
6510	Real estate operators and lessors	7	6	0.2	16	13	10,250	8,923	182	120	0.1
ASOTIN, WA											
60 –	**Finance, insurance, and real estate**	30	29	0.2	114	123	20,035	21,854	2,142	2,789	0.1
6000	Depository institutions	5	5	0.2	52	48	21,615	22,833	1,031	1,059	0.1
6500	Real estate	14	12	0.2	39	25	11,795	10,880	412	271	0.0
6530	Real estate agents and managers	4	3	0.1	10	7	14,000	10,286	136	80	0.0
BENTON, WA											
60 –	**Finance, insurance, and real estate**	262	265	1.8	1,684	1,779	22,487	19,750	37,300	36,017	0.9
6000	Depository institutions	34	31	1.4	605	571	19,954	19,587	11,986	11,697	1.1
6020	Commercial banks	16	16	1.2	333	304	17,742	17,868	5,947	5,523	0.8
6030	Savings institutions	12	9	2.1	106	87	24,604	20,874	2,300	2,077	1.1
6060	Credit unions	6	6	1.8	166	180	21,422	21,867	3,739	4,097	3.4
6160	Mortgage bankers and brokers	15	12	1.7	62	42	52,903	40,095	2,074	1,584	0.8
6200	Security and commodity brokers	10	12	1.5	68	70	63,706	55,943	3,595	3,758	1.0
6300	Insurance carriers	16	17	2.1	141	128	32,766	34,125	4,317	4,141	0.5
6400	Insurance agents, brokers, and service	45	50	2.0	180	201	21,444	20,637	4,357	4,429	1.0
6500	Real estate	132	129	2.0	590	571	14,922	14,529	10,000	8,687	1.3
6510	Real estate operators and lessors	73	74	2.6	309	314	12,039	12,395	4,024	4,246	2.1
6530	Real estate agents and managers	44	42	1.4	156	153	17,359	15,843	3,231	2,721	0.7
6553	Cemetery subdividers and developers	4	4	4.1	22	23	18,727	18,609	463	487	2.9
CHELAN, WA											
60 –	**Finance, insurance, and real estate**	198	203	1.4	1,184	1,188	22,959	24,148	27,000	28,860	0.8
6000	Depository institutions	35	35	1.6	457	450	29,444	28,782	11,749	12,295	1.2
6020	Commercial banks	23	23	1.8	378	298	30,931	29,235	10,012	8,667	1.3
6100	Nondepository institutions	13	12	1.1	47	50	29,106	29,520	1,472	1,577	0.6
6160	Mortgage bankers and brokers	7	6	0.9	24	26	28,500	28,923	765	862	0.5
6200	Security and commodity brokers	11	15	1.8	43	50	44,000	45,280	2,087	2,352	0.6
6210	Security brokers and dealers	7	10	2.0	36	37	49,778	56,865	1,950	2,194	0.7
6280	Security and commodity services	4	5	1.6	7	13	14,286	12,308	137	158	0.2
6300	Insurance carriers	10	9	1.1	38	35	33,053	36,114	1,120	1,181	0.1
6330	Fire, marine, and casualty insurance	6	6	1.3	9	8	42,222	59,000	402	439	0.1
6400	Insurance agents, brokers, and service	31	33	1.3	126	136	23,365	23,529	3,207	3,422	0.7
6500	Real estate	95	96	1.5	466	453	12,918	14,260	6,862	7,276	1.1
6510	Real estate operators and lessors	45	43	1.5	162	155	9,580	9,419	1,778	1,756	0.9
6530	Real estate agents and managers	44	46	1.6	274	265	14,555	15,849	4,587	4,719	1.3
6550	Subdividers and developers	4	5	1.0	28	26	15,571	27,385	424	729	1.0
6552	Subdividers and developers, n.e.c.	4	5	1.3	28	26	15,571	27,385	424	729	1.3
6700	Holding and other investment offices	3	3	0.7	7	14	35,429	76,571	503	757	0.6
CLALLAM, WA											
60 –	**Finance, insurance, and real estate**	141	133	0.9	686	666	20,157	21,333	14,227	14,470	0.4
6000	Depository institutions	26	26	1.2	320	331	19,300	20,906	6,783	7,243	0.7
6020	Commercial banks	10	10	0.8	103	105	17,825	19,695	1,981	2,103	0.3
6030	Savings institutions	13	13	3.1	198	206	20,000	21,670	4,405	4,717	2.4
6060	Credit unions	3	3	0.9	19	20	20,000	19,400	397	423	0.3

Source: County Business Patterns, 1994/95, CBP-94/95, U.S. Department of Commerce, Washington, D.C., November 1997. SIC categories for which data were suppressed or not available for both 1994 and 1995 are not displayed. The employment columns represent mid-March employment in the year. Pay per employee is calculated by dividing 1st Quarter payroll, annualized, by mid-March employment. The columns headed "% State" show the county's percentage of the state total for the SIC in 1995; for example, 1.4% for SIC 6000 means that the county had 1.4 percent of the state's total establishments (or payroll) in SIC 6000 in 1995. A dash (-) is used to indicate that data are not available or cannot be calculated; nec means not elsewhere classified.

Continued on next page.

SIC	Industry	No. Establishments			Employment		Pay / Employee		Annual Payroll ($ 000)		
		1994	1995	% State	1994	1995	1994	1995	1994	1995	% State
CLALLAM, WA - [continued]											
6300	Insurance carriers	8	8	*1.0*	45	47	33,600	31,660	1,607	1,513	*0.2*
6400	Insurance agents, brokers, and service	24	24	*1.0*	84	81	22,238	23,210	1,860	1,837	*0.4*
6500	Real estate	72	62	*0.9*	209	182	13,761	13,055	2,798	2,626	*0.4*
6510	Real estate operators and lessors	28	22	*0.8*	76	63	8,737	7,746	611	523	*0.3*
6530	Real estate agents and managers	34	31	*1.1*	81	70	14,025	13,086	1,084	1,033	*0.3*
6552	Subdividers and developers, n.e.c.	4	3	*0.8*	5	3	7,200	8,000	55	41	*0.1*
CLARK, WA											
60 –	**Finance, insurance, and real estate**	656	655	*4.5*	5,127	5,030	23,774	24,954	124,504	127,205	*3.3*
6000	Depository institutions	110	110	*5.1*	1,340	1,412	22,612	24,314	33,012	35,666	*3.4*
6020	Commercial banks	59	57	*4.4*	781	803	21,808	24,872	18,752	19,277	*2.9*
6060	Credit unions	30	30	*9.2*	344	383	23,709	23,436	8,263	9,241	*7.6*
6100	Nondepository institutions	61	55	*5.0*	324	269	41,679	38,662	12,460	11,254	*3.9*
6140	Personal credit institutions	12	12	*4.5*	59	54	38,576	37,259	1,750	1,770	*3.3*
6150	Business credit institutions	5	6	*5.3*	16	8	49,250	38,000	696	452	*1.3*
6160	Mortgage bankers and brokers	44	37	*5.4*	249	207	41,928	39,053	10,014	9,032	*4.8*
6200	Security and commodity brokers	33	34	*4.1*	88	99	34,000	38,626	3,603	4,320	*1.1*
6210	Security brokers and dealers	18	21	*4.2*	67	75	40,239	46,613	3,278	3,996	*1.3*
6280	Security and commodity services	15	13	*4.2*	21	24	14,095	13,667	325	324	*0.5*
6300	Insurance carriers	39	37	*4.5*	1,102	1,023	32,541	33,611	33,217	31,868	*3.7*
6360	Title insurance	6	6	*9.5*	152	105	29,368	27,505	3,695	3,026	*6.6*
6400	Insurance agents, brokers, and service	118	125	*5.0*	454	461	24,458	24,130	10,655	11,425	*2.5*
6500	Real estate	284	277	*4.2*	1,783	1,710	15,215	17,399	29,572	30,416	*4.6*
6510	Real estate operators and lessors	120	118	*4.1*	525	530	13,364	14,174	8,156	8,501	*4.3*
6530	Real estate agents and managers	135	117	*4.0*	1,117	1,032	15,234	18,318	17,637	16,833	*4.6*
6550	Subdividers and developers	22	26	*5.0*	96	108	21,083	22,741	2,700	3,515	*4.7*
6700	Holding and other investment offices	11	17	*4.1*	36	56	27,778	30,429	1,985	2,256	*1.7*
6710	Holding offices	4	6	*5.6*	10	19	24,400	30,947	785	1,065	*1.2*
COLUMBIA, WA											
60 –	**Finance, insurance, and real estate**	8	7	*0.0*	24	18	19,167	24,222	451	391	*0.0*
COWLITZ, WA											
60 –	**Finance, insurance, and real estate**	180	176	*1.2*	1,103	1,054	21,142	21,336	23,020	23,321	*0.6*
6000	Depository institutions	32	30	*1.4*	526	492	22,281	23,341	11,196	11,592	*1.1*
6060	Credit unions	12	12	*3.7*	287	294	21,770	23,238	6,440	7,102	*5.9*
6160	Mortgage bankers and brokers	4	5	*0.7*	22	21	37,455	39,619	600	769	*0.4*
6200	Security and commodity brokers	4	5	*0.6*	9	10	81,333	56,800	639	587	*0.2*
6300	Insurance carriers	10	10	*1.2*	57	39	31,579	45,436	1,789	1,701	*0.2*
6330	Fire, marine, and casualty insurance	6	6	*1.3*	11	11	48,727	54,909	595	637	*0.2*
6400	Insurance agents, brokers, and service	39	37	*1.5*	168	131	21,452	19,389	3,371	2,711	*0.6*
6500	Real estate	83	80	*1.2*	289	320	14,076	13,588	4,717	4,984	*0.8*
6510	Real estate operators and lessors	50	44	*1.5*	150	180	10,373	9,978	1,779	1,902	*1.0*
6530	Real estate agents and managers	25	29	*1.0*	86	84	16,326	18,095	1,548	1,671	*0.5*
DOUGLAS, WA											
60 –	**Finance, insurance, and real estate**	47	46	*0.3*	218	226	18,312	19,363	4,268	4,674	*0.1*
6000	Depository institutions	12	11	*0.5*	106	106	21,434	22,642	2,188	2,353	*0.2*
6500	Real estate	20	19	*0.3*	86	80	13,395	14,100	1,405	1,426	*0.2*
6510	Real estate operators and lessors	10	9	*0.3*	34	30	10,824	10,267	410	403	*0.2*
6530	Real estate agents and managers	6	5	*0.2*	44	42	15,636	16,952	846	822	*0.2*
6550	Subdividers and developers	4	5	*1.0*	8	8	12,000	13,500	149	201	*0.3*
FERRY, WA											
60 –	**Finance, insurance, and real estate**	5	8	*0.1*	20	19	12,800	14,526	303	310	*0.0*
FRANKLIN, WA											
60 –	**Finance, insurance, and real estate**	57	59	*0.4*	280	286	18,729	19,930	5,320	5,736	*0.1*

Source: County Business Patterns, 1994/95, CBP-94/95, U.S. Department of Commerce, Washington, D.C., November 1997. SIC categories for which data were suppressed or not available for both 1994 and 1995 are *not* displayed. The employment columns represent mid-March employment in the year. Pay per employee is calculated by dividing 1st Quarter payroll, annualized, by mid-March employment. The columns headed "% State" show the county's percentage of the state total for the SIC in 1995; for example, 1.4% for SIC 6000 means that the county had 1.4 percent of the state's total establishments (or payroll) in SIC 6000 in 1995. A dash (-) is used to indicate that data are not available or cannot be calculated; *nec* means not elsewhere classified.

Continued on next page.

SIC	Industry	No. Establishments			Employment		Pay / Employee		Annual Payroll ($ 000)		
		1994	1995	% State	1994	1995	1994	1995	1994	1995	% State
FRANKLIN, WA - [continued]											
6000	Depository institutions	14	13	0.6	131	126	15,969	18,190	2,207	2,250	0.2
6020	Commercial banks	9	8	0.6	101	95	15,129	17,937	1,585	1,598	0.2
6100	Nondepository institutions	5	4	0.4	14	14	30,000	37,714	451	605	0.2
6400	Insurance agents, brokers, and service	13	14	0.6	52	63	26,769	25,143	1,522	1,678	0.4
6500	Real estate	21	24	0.4	74	73	15,784	15,452	936	1,030	0.2
6510	Real estate operators and lessors	11	13	0.5	53	59	11,245	10,373	686	823	0.4
6530	Real estate agents and managers	5	5	0.2	12	9	12,000	11,556	125	87	0.0
6550	Subdividers and developers	5	5	1.0	9	5	47,556	82,400	125	117	0.2
GARFIELD, WA											
60 –	**Finance, insurance, and real estate**	7	8	0.1	23	23	18,609	20,348	362	404	0.0
6000	Depository institutions	3	3	0.1	14	14	18,000	20,571	211	242	0.0
GRANT, WA											
60 –	**Finance, insurance, and real estate**	109	116	0.8	467	476	19,289	20,756	9,307	10,225	0.3
6000	Depository institutions	21	21	1.0	199	187	20,141	22,118	4,128	4,055	0.4
6020	Commercial banks	14	14	1.1	141	136	19,660	21,676	2,793	2,738	0.4
6100	Nondepository institutions	4	5	0.5	27	28	34,370	38,143	881	943	0.3
6300	Insurance carriers	3	3	0.4	20	21	28,800	28,762	555	539	0.1
6400	Insurance agents, brokers, and service	28	31	1.2	120	121	20,367	22,182	2,485	2,875	0.6
6500	Real estate	48	50	0.8	93	109	8,301	8,294	970	1,337	0.2
6510	Real estate operators and lessors	28	27	0.9	56	58	5,643	5,862	386	412	0.2
6530	Real estate agents and managers	13	14	0.5	24	27	14,167	14,222	448	426	0.1
6550	Subdividers and developers	6	8	1.5	13	21	8,923	7,429	119	436	0.6
6552	Subdividers and developers, n.e.c.	3	5	1.3	6	13	8,667	6,769	46	357	0.7
6553	Cemetery subdividers and developers	3	3	3.1	7	8	9,143	8,500	73	79	0.5
GRAYS HARBOR, WA											
60 –	**Finance, insurance, and real estate**	133	139	1.0	824	871	18,689	18,792	16,177	17,638	0.5
6000	Depository institutions	37	38	1.8	369	382	21,463	22,262	7,964	8,303	0.8
6020	Commercial banks	16	17	1.3	161	152	20,994	23,579	3,107	3,123	0.5
6030	Savings institutions	10	10	2.3	141	158	23,433	22,228	3,547	3,698	1.9
6400	Insurance agents, brokers, and service	28	28	1.1	114	96	17,614	18,917	1,989	1,875	0.4
6500	Real estate	58	61	0.9	279	326	12,903	12,871	4,282	4,623	0.7
6510	Real estate operators and lessors	21	25	0.9	152	189	9,342	10,857	1,966	2,161	1.1
6530	Real estate agents and managers	28	26	0.9	92	93	16,174	13,634	1,427	1,414	0.4
6552	Subdividers and developers, n.e.c.	3	3	0.8	1	3	12,000	18,667	24	59	0.1
ISLAND, WA											
60 –	**Finance, insurance, and real estate**	118	126	0.9	759	631	21,929	22,789	15,348	17,681	0.5
6000	Depository institutions	25	25	1.2	451	346	22,040	21,965	8,797	10,336	1.0
6030	Savings institutions	8	8	1.9	170	162	24,941	24,296	4,073	6,505	3.4
6400	Insurance agents, brokers, and service	19	20	0.8	112	106	22,321	29,585	2,522	3,399	0.7
6500	Real estate	62	71	1.1	169	160	13,751	15,050	2,588	2,798	0.4
6510	Real estate operators and lessors	22	21	0.7	52	39	7,538	9,744	483	371	0.2
6530	Real estate agents and managers	33	42	1.4	89	97	14,382	15,876	1,425	1,834	0.5
JEFFERSON, WA											
60 –	**Finance, insurance, and real estate**	58	67	0.5	216	240	21,241	19,683	4,963	4,974	0.1
6000	Depository institutions	10	10	0.5	83	80	18,410	18,050	1,652	1,523	0.1
6030	Savings institutions	3	3	0.7	31	28	19,871	17,000	660	586	0.3
6500	Real estate	32	39	0.6	88	104	20,318	18,000	1,994	2,073	0.3
6510	Real estate operators and lessors	10	13	0.5	14	19	7,429	7,579	109	197	0.1
KING, WA											
60 –	**Finance, insurance, and real estate**	5,990	6,050	42.0	72,828	65,987	34,299	36,069	2,370,891	2,328,475	60.5
6000	Depository institutions	759	711	32.9	21,325	17,335	30,289	32,755	627,416	553,462	53.2
6020	Commercial banks	453	438	33.7	12,025	12,062	30,527	32,797	350,127	366,825	55.0

Source: County Business Patterns, 1994/95, CBP-94/95, U.S. Department of Commerce, Washington, D.C., November 1997. SIC categories for which data were suppressed or not available for both 1994 and 1995 are not displayed. The employment columns represent mid-March employment in the year. Pay per employee is calculated by dividing 1st Quarter payroll, annualized, by mid-March employment. The columns headed "% State" show the county's percentage of the state total for the SIC in 1995; for example, 1.4% for SIC 6000 means that the county had 1.4 percent of the state's total establishments (or payroll) in SIC 6000 in 1995. A dash (-) is used to indicate that data are not available or cannot be calculated; nec means not elsewhere classified.

Continued on next page.

SIC	Industry	No. Establishments			Employment		Pay / Employee		Annual Payroll ($ 000)		
		1994	1995	% State	1994	1995	1994	1995	1994	1995	% State
KING, WA - [continued]											
6030	Savings institutions	165	138	32.4	6,801	2,837	29,518	32,436	203,143	106,657	55.2
6060	Credit unions	71	73	22.4	1,331	1,392	23,522	24,974	32,401	36,328	29.9
6080	Foreign bank and branches and agencies	10	10	100.0	178	178	50,022	53,281	9,226	10,508	100.0
6100	Nondepository institutions	555	521	47.3	5,731	3,816	34,908	36,052	166,632	144,918	50.7
6140	Personal credit institutions	92	102	38.1	787	870	32,605	36,818	26,400	32,236	59.8
6150	Business credit institutions	72	66	58.4	455	410	44,396	46,059	19,019	18,489	54.0
6160	Mortgage bankers and brokers	386	345	49.9	4,485	2,521	34,293	34,261	121,017	93,829	49.9
6200	Security and commodity brokers	390	433	52.7	3,795	3,904	69,640	69,736	260,492	278,163	71.9
6210	Security brokers and dealers	220	244	49.2	3,165	3,200	71,521	71,274	215,702	229,727	72.2
6280	Security and commodity services	157	176	57.5	610	678	60,774	63,947	43,737	47,312	70.4
6300	Insurance carriers	385	386	46.8	17,362	16,099	39,696	41,964	597,240	619,383	71.0
6310	Life insurance	105	105	59.7	4,093	4,057	38,725	39,503	143,698	146,408	74.7
6320	Medical service and health insurance	30	27	45.0	2,559	2,824	33,019	37,540	87,282	96,637	51.6
6330	Fire, marine, and casualty insurance	200	199	42.6	8,923	7,689	42,090	45,672	306,867	320,137	78.7
6400	Insurance agents, brokers, and service	922	950	37.8	6,499	6,538	36,698	38,716	241,723	253,525	55.5
6500	Real estate	2,743	2,798	42.7	15,988	16,073	22,050	23,045	376,738	377,968	57.1
6510	Real estate operators and lessors	1,208	1,229	43.2	4,829	5,212	18,090	18,650	97,650	104,387	52.6
6530	Real estate agents and managers	1,279	1,261	43.4	10,092	9,365	23,363	24,313	244,847	232,410	63.8
6540	Title abstract offices	4	5	12.5	6	12	9,333	25,667	71	314	2.4
6550	Subdividers and developers	181	197	37.5	1,003	1,225	27,908	32,023	31,751	35,059	46.7
6552	Subdividers and developers, n.e.c.	153	164	42.4	774	836	28,512	37,589	25,200	26,552	48.4
6553	Cemetery subdividers and developers	19	18	18.4	226	213	26,071	27,793	5,869	6,001	35.9
6700	Holding and other investment offices	218	238	57.9	1,988	2,137	47,861	46,430	89,019	96,867	73.2
6710	Holding offices	63	66	61.1	1,166	1,130	55,238	59,618	55,317	61,564	71.2
6720	Investment offices	13	12	75.0	29	150	26,345	23,520	1,844	3,492	86.4
6730	Trusts	51	63	51.2	383	414	33,399	25,440	11,866	14,727	78.3
6732	Educational, religious, etc. trusts	19	22	64.7	143	141	38,210	24,738	5,333	3,881	89.4
6733	Trusts, n.e.c.	32	41	46.6	240	273	30,533	25,802	6,533	10,846	75.0
6790	Miscellaneous investing	83	82	59.4	409	423	42,005	38,799	19,753	15,461	76.5
6794	Patent owners and lessors	19	19	70.4	221	239	28,760	15,079	9,116	4,214	74.2
6798	Real estate investment trusts	6	6	54.5	24	22	19,167	18,000	394	460	32.7
6799	Investors, n.e.c.	58	57	57.0	164	162	63,195	76,617	10,243	10,787	82.2
KITSAP, WA											
60–	**Finance, insurance, and real estate**	434	441	3.1	2,688	2,613	23,208	23,899	60,589	62,543	1.6
6000	Depository institutions	67	68	3.1	877	891	22,299	22,487	19,883	21,309	2.0
6020	Commercial banks	37	37	2.8	554	553	24,339	24,456	13,017	13,833	2.1
6060	Credit unions	14	15	4.6	236	236	17,983	18,949	4,641	5,112	4.2
6100	Nondepository institutions	36	37	3.4	295	229	32,624	28,541	8,196	7,038	2.5
6160	Mortgage bankers and brokers	27	28	4.1	260	194	34,262	29,711	7,421	6,181	3.3
6200	Security and commodity brokers	28	24	2.9	97	75	46,845	77,333	3,774	3,942	1.0
6210	Security brokers and dealers	16	14	2.8	76	58	53,421	78,552	3,032	3,244	1.0
6280	Security and commodity services	12	10	3.3	21	17	23,048	73,176	742	698	1.0
6300	Insurance carriers	26	26	3.2	279	251	32,115	35,825	8,347	8,584	1.0
6360	Title insurance	5	5	7.9	132	85	32,606	32,612	3,426	2,549	5.5
6400	Insurance agents, brokers, and service	73	76	3.0	274	258	20,321	21,147	5,323	5,683	1.2
6500	Real estate	193	198	3.0	819	838	15,331	16,391	13,206	13,911	2.1
6510	Real estate operators and lessors	78	75	2.6	267	252	9,468	10,873	2,825	2,776	1.4
6530	Real estate agents and managers	102	103	3.5	433	443	19,169	18,573	8,399	8,592	2.4
6550	Subdividers and developers	10	15	2.9	119	142	14,521	19,408	1,963	2,246	3.0
6552	Subdividers and developers, n.e.c.	6	9	2.3	76	66	15,632	28,182	1,376	1,449	2.6
6730	Trusts	4	6	4.9	3	11	16,000	5,455	55	75	0.4
6733	Trusts, n.e.c.	4	5	5.7	3	11	16,000	5,455	55	74	0.5
KITTITAS, WA											
60–	**Finance, insurance, and real estate**	64	65	0.5	245	235	18,596	18,145	4,951	4,574	0.1
6000	Depository institutions	11	11	0.5	108	105	19,481	20,305	2,286	2,278	0.2
6020	Commercial banks	7	7	0.5	88	85	19,682	20,941	1,873	1,894	0.3

Source: County Business Patterns, 1994/95, CBP-94/95, U.S. Department of Commerce, Washington, D.C., November 1997. SIC categories for which data were suppressed or not available for both 1994 and 1995 are not displayed. The employment columns represent mid-March employment in the year. Pay per employee is calculated by dividing 1st Quarter payroll, annualized, by mid-March employment. The columns headed "% State" show the county's percentage of the state total for the SIC in 1995; for example, 1.4% for SIC 6000 means that the county had 1.4 percent of the state's total establishments (or payroll) in SIC 6000 in 1995. A dash (-) is used to indicate that data are not available or cannot be calculated; nec means not elsewhere classified.

Continued on next page.

SIC	Industry	No. Establishments			Employment		Pay / Employee		Annual Payroll ($ 000)		
		1994	1995	% State	1994	1995	1994	1995	1994	1995	% State
KITTITAS, WA - [continued]											
6400	Insurance agents, brokers, and service	13	12	0.5	57	48	19,439	18,583	1,170	902	0.2
6500	Real estate	34	36	0.5	71	73	15,718	13,808	1,229	1,128	0.2
6530	Real estate agents and managers	14	15	0.5	21	25	18,476	11,680	357	356	0.1
KLICKITAT, WA											
60–	**Finance, insurance, and real estate**	26	26	0.2	94	103	18,468	18,214	1,988	2,081	0.1
6000	Depository institutions	4	4	0.2	42	42	21,429	23,143	962	1,004	0.1
6020	Commercial banks	4	4	0.3	42	42	21,429	23,143	962	1,004	0.2
6500	Real estate	12	13	0.2	20	31	12,200	10,839	352	373	0.1
LEWIS, WA											
60–	**Finance, insurance, and real estate**	102	108	0.7	610	646	22,407	23,232	14,336	14,704	0.4
6000	Depository institutions	23	24	1.1	272	270	24,338	25,393	7,210	6,439	0.6
6020	Commercial banks	14	15	1.2	201	198	24,756	26,869	5,447	4,643	0.7
6100	Nondepository institutions	5	5	0.5	24	23	31,333	35,304	741	844	0.3
6300	Insurance carriers	6	7	0.8	52	73	22,615	29,973	1,269	2,123	0.2
6400	Insurance agents, brokers, and service	21	22	0.9	87	89	27,310	25,888	2,043	1,995	0.4
6500	Real estate	41	45	0.7	164	180	14,659	14,244	2,695	2,895	0.4
6510	Real estate operators and lessors	16	15	0.5	61	53	7,934	8,075	578	464	0.2
6530	Real estate agents and managers	18	18	0.6	55	70	14,400	12,457	942	1,034	0.3
LINCOLN, WA											
60–	**Finance, insurance, and real estate**	30	28	0.2	105	101	18,019	21,188	1,940	2,013	0.1
6000	Depository institutions	11	11	0.5	60	60	20,133	24,000	1,189	1,260	0.1
6400	Insurance agents, brokers, and service	9	9	0.4	27	30	18,667	18,933	515	533	0.1
6500	Real estate	10	8	0.1	18	11	10,000	12,000	236	220	0.0
MASON, WA											
60–	**Finance, insurance, and real estate**	78	89	0.6	515	516	18,571	18,550	10,032	10,132	0.3
6000	Depository institutions	14	14	0.6	204	205	19,471	19,980	4,202	4,369	0.4
6020	Commercial banks	8	8	0.6	78	77	21,590	20,260	1,943	1,709	0.3
6400	Insurance agents, brokers, and service	11	11	0.4	38	39	21,158	19,179	860	782	0.2
6500	Real estate	43	53	0.8	233	235	14,884	15,523	3,731	3,770	0.6
6510	Real estate operators and lessors	11	12	0.4	59	67	9,695	9,552	602	681	0.3
6530	Real estate agents and managers	24	30	1.0	111	108	14,198	15,444	1,668	1,536	0.4
6552	Subdividers and developers, n.e.c.	4	4	1.0	10	9	22,000	20,889	223	279	0.5
6700	Holding and other investment offices	3	3	0.7	15	11	10,133	8,000	141	112	0.1
OKANOGAN, WA											
60–	**Finance, insurance, and real estate**	68	63	0.4	259	253	22,826	20,949	5,280	4,782	0.1
6000	Depository institutions	17	16	0.7	147	138	24,816	22,000	2,824	2,631	0.3
6020	Commercial banks	14	9	0.7	129	77	25,767	22,909	2,430	1,532	0.2
6400	Insurance agents, brokers, and service	16	13	0.5	43	41	22,140	18,829	906	739	0.2
6500	Real estate	32	31	0.5	58	64	15,448	17,063	1,158	1,030	0.2
6530	Real estate agents and managers	11	12	0.4	22	24	15,818	20,833	343	325	0.1
PACIFIC, WA											
60–	**Finance, insurance, and real estate**	49	48	0.3	217	221	17,088	18,244	4,142	4,444	0.1
6000	Depository institutions	14	14	0.6	108	113	20,222	20,142	2,499	2,677	0.3
6500	Real estate	22	19	0.3	60	56	10,400	14,643	646	675	0.1
6510	Real estate operators and lessors	6	6	0.2	8	6	8,500	8,000	56	39	0.0
6530	Real estate agents and managers	11	9	0.3	46	41	10,435	12,585	490	484	0.1
6550	Subdividers and developers	4	4	0.8	5	9	12,800	28,444	94	152	0.2
PEND OREILLE, WA											
60–	**Finance, insurance, and real estate**	17	16	0.1	71	66	15,606	19,212	1,404	1,499	0.0
6000	Depository institutions	4	4	0.2	32	31	17,875	21,677	706	786	0.1
6500	Real estate	9	7	0.1	26	23	13,385	15,478	496	423	0.1

Source: County Business Patterns, 1994/95, CBP-94/95, U.S. Department of Commerce, Washington, D.C., November 1997. SIC categories for which data were suppressed or not available for both 1994 and 1995 are not displayed. The employment columns represent mid-March employment in the year. Pay per employee is calculated by dividing 1st Quarter payroll, annualized, by mid-March employment. The columns headed "% State" show the county's percentage of the state total for the SIC in 1995; for example, 1.4% for SIC 6000 means that the county had 1.4 percent of the state's total establishments (or payroll) in SIC 6000 in 1995. A dash (-) is used to indicate that data are not available or cannot be calculated; nec means not elsewhere classified.

SIC	Industry	No. Establishments			Employment		Pay / Employee		Annual Payroll ($ 000)		
		1994	1995	% State	1994	1995	1994	1995	1994	1995	% State
PIERCE, WA											
60 –	**Finance, insurance, and real estate**	1,288	1,338	9.3	9,971	10,949	26,041	28,635	267,227	315,876	8.2
6000	Depository institutions	228	223	10.3	2,811	3,472	25,356	27,047	74,691	94,018	9.0
6020	Commercial banks	151	151	11.6	1,911	2,572	22,987	25,565	47,818	65,793	9.9
6030	Savings institutions	25	23	5.4	186	179	31,634	24,603	5,359	5,161	2.7
6060	Credit unions	37	37	11.3	571	598	26,844	27,639	14,250	15,663	12.9
6090	Functions closely related to banking	15	12	12.6	143	123	42,909	58,732	7,264	7,401	22.7
6100	Nondepository institutions	102	116	10.5	636	1,089	32,176	36,033	19,281	39,028	13.6
6140	Personal credit institutions	34	39	14.6	160	193	29,425	32,166	4,888	5,806	10.8
6150	Business credit institutions	5	5	4.4	57	60	31,439	44,533	2,157	2,384	7.0
6160	Mortgage bankers and brokers	63	70	10.1	419	835	33,327	36,331	12,236	30,762	16.4
6200	Security and commodity brokers	57	60	7.3	433	475	51,686	54,712	22,955	26,142	6.8
6210	Security brokers and dealers	33	35	7.1	261	282	55,295	55,631	13,574	15,453	4.9
6300	Insurance carriers	59	62	7.5	1,244	1,157	26,267	26,672	28,952	29,557	3.4
6310	Life insurance	10	10	5.7	172	160	30,233	32,150	5,246	5,084	2.6
6360	Title insurance	9	10	15.9	302	214	33,470	28,411	7,286	5,496	11.9
6400	Insurance agents, brokers, and service	211	232	9.2	1,469	1,465	41,421	46,567	62,373	65,916	14.4
6500	Real estate	602	617	9.4	3,160	3,105	14,609	15,736	52,271	53,778	8.1
6510	Real estate operators and lessors	274	287	10.1	1,183	1,242	11,408	12,435	16,566	17,333	8.7
6530	Real estate agents and managers	268	265	9.1	1,727	1,581	15,280	17,187	28,718	29,072	8.0
6550	Subdividers and developers	47	44	8.4	223	239	25,525	23,280	6,219	6,431	8.6
6552	Subdividers and developers, n.e.c.	37	34	8.8	95	110	24,000	18,364	2,598	2,631	4.8
6553	Cemetery subdividers and developers	7	7	7.1	128	126	26,656	27,587	3,579	3,683	22.0
6790	Miscellaneous investing	13	12	8.7	25	31	22,240	15,355	777	788	3.9
SAN JUAN, WA											
60 –	**Finance, insurance, and real estate**	59	58	0.4	197	218	23,675	22,899	6,309	5,632	0.1
6000	Depository institutions	8	8	0.4	77	80	20,623	20,350	1,889	1,935	0.2
6400	Insurance agents, brokers, and service	8	8	0.3	35	24	30,629	28,333	1,091	711	0.2
6500	Real estate	38	37	0.6	67	86	11,463	13,581	1,490	1,819	0.3
6530	Real estate agents and managers	19	18	0.6	41	35	11,902	14,857	595	662	0.2
SKAGIT, WA											
60 –	**Finance, insurance, and real estate**	240	238	1.7	1,099	1,104	21,460	22,344	24,815	25,923	0.7
6000	Depository institutions	47	48	2.2	450	459	20,071	21,351	10,214	10,603	1.0
6020	Commercial banks	24	25	1.9	301	319	19,296	20,627	6,755	7,370	1.1
6030	Savings institutions	16	16	3.8	108	102	23,111	23,961	2,733	2,496	1.3
6100	Nondepository institutions	20	21	1.9	77	62	32,571	30,774	2,150	1,991	0.7
6160	Mortgage bankers and brokers	16	17	2.5	61	46	32,066	31,652	1,702	1,512	0.8
6200	Security and commodity brokers	11	12	1.5	29	36	66,897	67,667	1,839	2,123	0.5
6210	Security brokers and dealers	6	7	1.4	23	28	80,696	83,429	1,751	1,982	0.6
6280	Security and commodity services	5	5	1.6	6	8	14,000	12,500	88	141	0.2
6400	Insurance agents, brokers, and service	38	38	1.5	183	171	26,470	28,211	4,784	5,062	1.1
6500	Real estate	115	109	1.7	314	306	14,127	15,307	4,839	4,898	0.7
6510	Real estate operators and lessors	46	39	1.4	125	111	10,112	11,207	1,319	1,129	0.6
6530	Real estate agents and managers	54	55	1.9	146	140	15,753	17,543	2,547	2,543	0.7
6552	Subdividers and developers, n.e.c.	9	8	2.1	11	25	16,364	13,280	248	538	1.0
SKAMANIA, WA											
60 –	**Finance, insurance, and real estate**	9	11	0.1	25	26	11,520	12,000	318	347	0.0
6500	Real estate	5	6	0.1	11	13	6,545	5,231	93	86	0.0
6510	Real estate operators and lessors	3	3	0.1	8	9	4,500	5,778	53	57	0.0
SNOHOMISH, WA											
60 –	**Finance, insurance, and real estate**	1,157	1,158	8.0	8,671	7,950	29,094	27,722	239,474	229,778	6.0
6000	Depository institutions	174	175	8.1	2,169	2,018	25,453	25,364	53,828	52,284	5.0
6020	Commercial banks	96	97	7.5	1,315	1,292	23,090	23,885	29,659	31,493	4.7
6030	Savings institutions	48	49	11.5	623	507	29,618	27,787	18,456	14,746	7.6
6060	Credit unions	18	19	5.8	182	190	30,396	30,126	4,989	5,315	4.4

Source: County Business Patterns, 1994/95, CBP-94/95, U.S. Department of Commerce, Washington, D.C., November 1997. SIC categories for which data were suppressed or not available for both 1994 and 1995 are not displayed. The employment columns represent mid-March employment in the year. Pay per employee is calculated by dividing 1st Quarter payroll, annualized, by mid-March employment. The columns headed "% State" show the county's percentage of the state total for the SIC in 1995; for example, 1.4% for SIC 6000 means that the county had 1.4 percent of the state's total establishments (or payroll) in SIC 6000 in 1995. A dash (-) is used to indicate that data are not available or cannot be calculated; nec means not elsewhere classified.

Continued on next page.

SIC	Industry	No. Establishments			Employment		Pay / Employee		Annual Payroll ($ 000)		
		1994	1995	% State	1994	1995	1994	1995	1994	1995	% State
SNOHOMISH, WA - [continued]											
6090	Functions closely related to banking	12	8	8.4	49	27	17,551	17,185	724	509	1.6
6100	Nondepository institutions	114	108	9.8	1,090	763	35,204	34,941	31,985	27,527	9.6
6140	Personal credit institutions	26	29	10.8	116	123	27,897	28,455	3,322	3,761	7.0
6160	Mortgage bankers and brokers	80	69	10.0	964	624	36,066	35,994	28,229	23,086	12.3
6200	Security and commodity brokers	41	45	5.5	178	194	58,539	50,412	9,023	10,139	2.6
6210	Security brokers and dealers	25	26	5.2	153	174	64,993	53,701	8,527	9,642	3.0
6300	Insurance carriers	73	72	8.7	1,983	1,954	40,240	35,801	75,001	72,550	8.3
6310	Life insurance	12	11	6.3	267	185	33,678	32,476	8,267	5,988	3.1
6330	Fire, marine, and casualty insurance	50	52	11.1	430	439	42,735	45,412	18,472	19,475	4.8
6400	Insurance agents, brokers, and service	196	208	8.3	789	752	25,511	25,372	20,463	19,675	4.3
6500	Real estate	539	529	8.1	2,375	2,200	19,592	19,124	47,118	45,687	6.9
6510	Real estate operators and lessors	222	227	8.0	1,147	1,176	15,582	15,861	20,292	21,897	11.0
6530	Real estate agents and managers	259	242	8.3	1,056	861	20,701	19,902	21,315	19,228	5.3
6550	Subdividers and developers	42	38	7.2	160	131	37,700	35,756	4,595	3,385	4.5
6552	Subdividers and developers, n.e.c.	31	26	6.7	120	90	45,000	43,511	3,764	2,529	4.6
6700	Holding and other investment offices	20	21	5.1	87	69	20,874	24,000	2,056	1,916	1.4
6730	Trusts	9	7	5.7	50	41	15,600	16,683	772	741	3.9
SPOKANE, WA											
60 –	**Finance, insurance, and real estate**	1,107	1,157	8.0	10,679	10,913	27,599	28,868	289,191	311,044	8.1
6000	Depository institutions	188	192	8.9	3,253	3,320	23,477	25,618	79,047	82,570	7.9
6020	Commercial banks	115	116	8.9	2,261	2,335	24,547	26,868	56,431	59,403	8.9
6030	Savings institutions	23	23	5.4	319	339	25,292	25,192	9,435	9,436	4.9
6060	Credit unions	46	46	14.1	659	631	19,041	21,471	12,934	13,451	11.1
6090	Functions closely related to banking	4	7	7.4	14	15	18,286	15,200	247	280	0.9
6100	Nondepository institutions	93	98	8.9	1,065	979	34,595	34,721	33,501	34,800	12.2
6150	Business credit institutions	12	18	15.9	284	326	28,577	32,675	9,055	11,116	32.5
6160	Mortgage bankers and brokers	54	52	7.5	476	388	34,050	33,113	13,986	13,395	7.1
6200	Security and commodity brokers	76	74	9.0	660	625	50,673	56,371	31,396	34,797	9.0
6210	Security brokers and dealers	50	47	9.5	484	462	56,496	63,403	25,554	28,119	8.8
6300	Insurance carriers	87	83	10.1	2,446	2,460	28,775	28,821	65,861	71,183	8.2
6310	Life insurance	26	26	14.8	1,208	1,173	22,579	23,410	26,255	26,685	13.6
6320	Medical service and health insurance	7	6	10.0	425	466	36,508	28,318	12,891	16,476	8.8
6330	Fire, marine, and casualty insurance	41	39	8.4	629	668	36,700	38,395	22,566	23,785	5.8
6360	Title insurance	3	3	4.8	127	94	23,874	30,255	2,581	2,487	5.4
6400	Insurance agents, brokers, and service	215	225	9.0	875	958	28,846	31,261	25,630	29,158	6.4
6500	Real estate	423	453	6.9	2,148	2,223	15,415	14,940	36,932	38,491	5.8
6510	Real estate operators and lessors	174	181	6.4	808	862	13,371	13,615	12,615	13,478	6.8
6530	Real estate agents and managers	200	207	7.1	1,108	1,084	15,379	14,387	18,602	18,534	5.1
6550	Subdividers and developers	33	37	7.0	119	144	25,210	21,361	3,004	3,369	4.5
6552	Subdividers and developers, n.e.c.	22	27	7.0	43	76	28,372	20,632	1,099	1,682	3.1
6553	Cemetery subdividers and developers	8	9	9.2	65	66	23,815	22,545	1,695	1,631	9.8
6710	Holding offices	8	7	6.5	113	121	133,805	160,231	11,982	13,413	15.5
6790	Miscellaneous investing	6	7	5.1	21	105	17,143	9,295	423	1,259	6.2
STEVENS, WA											
60 –	**Finance, insurance, and real estate**	40	43	0.3	217	195	20,074	18,523	4,467	4,240	0.1
6000	Depository institutions	6	6	0.3	71	62	21,972	21,484	1,640	1,309	0.1
6400	Insurance agents, brokers, and service	10	12	0.5	60	59	25,333	20,610	1,376	1,397	0.3
6500	Real estate	19	21	0.3	65	56	13,415	14,500	1,038	923	0.1
6510	Real estate operators and lessors	5	5	0.2	14	13	8,286	10,154	135	175	0.1
6530	Real estate agents and managers	9	12	0.4	35	39	17,486	16,615	671	680	0.2
6550	Subdividers and developers	3	3	0.6	4	4	7,000	8,000	66	48	0.1
THURSTON, WA											
60 –	**Finance, insurance, and real estate**	425	414	2.9	2,920	2,602	23,751	23,931	69,915	63,903	1.7
6000	Depository institutions	78	74	3.4	1,205	1,088	24,299	23,846	29,595	27,168	2.6
6020	Commercial banks	36	35	2.7	476	484	22,378	21,785	12,477	11,164	1.7

Source: County Business Patterns, 1994/95, CBP-94/95, U.S. Department of Commerce, Washington, D.C., November 1997. SIC categories for which data were suppressed or not available for both 1994 and 1995 are not displayed. The employment columns represent mid-March employment in the year. Pay per employee is calculated by dividing 1st Quarter payroll, annualized, by mid-March employment. The columns headed "% State" show the county's percentage of the state total for the SIC in 1995; for example, 1.4% for SIC 6000 means that the county had 1.4 percent of the state's total establishments (or payroll) in SIC 6000 in 1995. A dash (-) is used to indicate that data are not available or cannot be calculated; nec means not elsewhere classified.

Continued on next page.

SIC	Industry	No. Establishments			Employment		Pay / Employee		Annual Payroll ($ 000)		
		1994	1995	% State	1994	1995	1994	1995	1994	1995	% State
THURSTON, WA - [continued]											
6030	Savings institutions	26	22	5.2	371	225	26,059	26,436	8,415	6,614	3.4
6060	Credit unions	13	13	4.0	340	362	24,059	23,713	8,002	8,707	7.2
6090	Functions closely related to banking	3	4	4.2	18	17	43,333	51,059	701	683	2.1
6160	Mortgage bankers and brokers	14	10	1.4	116	50	31,862	34,320	2,539	1,591	0.8
6200	Security and commodity brokers	17	19	2.3	85	90	48,800	53,956	4,066	4,438	1.1
6210	Security brokers and dealers	12	13	2.6	73	79	52,493	59,291	3,830	4,241	1.3
6280	Security and commodity services	5	6	2.0	12	11	26,333	15,636	236	197	0.3
6300	Insurance carriers	27	28	3.4	376	275	32,394	36,887	11,383	10,077	1.2
6310	Life insurance	4	4	2.3	196	181	31,184	32,155	5,592	5,627	2.9
6400	Insurance agents, brokers, and service	71	68	2.7	229	224	23,301	22,250	5,820	5,301	1.2
6500	Real estate	202	200	3.1	838	813	15,236	15,316	14,468	13,220	2.0
6510	Real estate operators and lessors	90	82	2.9	318	294	11,421	12,694	3,973	3,922	2.0
6530	Real estate agents and managers	91	89	3.1	432	416	16,843	16,538	8,164	7,041	1.9
6550	Subdividers and developers	14	20	3.8	35	53	17,943	16,226	1,009	943	1.3
6552	Subdividers and developers, n.e.c.	10	14	3.6	11	26	17,091	13,846	514	306	0.6
6553	Cemetery subdividers and developers	4	5	5.1	24	27	18,333	18,519	495	587	3.5
WAHKIAKUM, WA											
60 –	**Finance, insurance, and real estate**	6	6	0.0	20	15	13,000	18,133	322	305	0.0
6500	Real estate	3	3	0.0	8	6	11,500	16,000	100	106	0.0
WALLA WALLA, WA											
60 –	**Finance, insurance, and real estate**	92	92	0.6	890	727	25,402	26,267	19,375	17,980	0.5
6000	Depository institutions	22	18	0.8	542	473	27,018	27,780	12,079	11,955	1.1
6020	Commercial banks	10	10	0.8	224	249	24,375	24,321	5,582	5,765	0.9
6100	Nondepository institutions	5	5	0.5	114	19	24,421	41,474	2,231	749	0.3
6400	Insurance agents, brokers, and service	19	19	0.8	76	92	29,684	27,478	2,117	2,292	0.5
6500	Real estate	38	41	0.6	129	119	13,829	15,025	1,901	1,960	0.3
6530	Real estate agents and managers	14	15	0.5	36	32	17,000	18,250	580	668	0.2
6550	Subdividers and developers	5	5	1.0	35	25	12,800	16,640	499	410	0.5
WHATCOM, WA											
60 –	**Finance, insurance, and real estate**	402	409	2.8	2,643	2,586	25,000	28,852	67,032	73,261	1.9
6000	Depository institutions	75	74	3.4	1,038	984	22,709	25,833	25,298	26,071	2.5
6020	Commercial banks	43	42	3.2	607	569	21,885	25,525	14,482	14,368	2.2
6030	Savings institutions	21	23	5.4	246	252	26,016	28,286	7,012	7,765	4.0
6100	Nondepository institutions	26	23	2.1	110	92	38,800	42,957	3,076	3,145	1.1
6160	Mortgage bankers and brokers	17	15	2.2	87	63	41,425	51,111	2,454	2,458	1.3
6200	Security and commodity brokers	21	23	2.8	80	84	59,250	58,857	4,720	5,023	1.3
6210	Security brokers and dealers	15	15	3.0	70	71	64,800	66,873	4,503	4,774	1.5
6280	Security and commodity services	6	8	2.6	10	13	20,400	15,077	217	249	0.4
6300	Insurance carriers	18	19	2.3	221	209	31,149	33,531	6,674	6,807	0.8
6330	Fire, marine, and casualty insurance	11	10	2.1	21	20	53,905	62,000	1,211	1,248	0.3
6400	Insurance agents, brokers, and service	61	60	2.4	309	341	27,883	28,997	8,787	8,991	2.0
6500	Real estate	189	192	2.9	847	809	20,118	26,680	17,240	20,446	3.1
6510	Real estate operators and lessors	80	76	2.7	357	289	12,045	13,218	4,323	4,159	2.1
6530	Real estate agents and managers	90	85	2.9	247	259	19,482	19,429	4,712	4,747	1.3
6550	Subdividers and developers	17	22	4.2	238	248	32,924	50,565	8,100	11,205	14.9
6730	Trusts	3	4	3.3	2	3	18,000	18,667	57	78	0.4
6790	Miscellaneous investing	5	6	4.3	15	32	10,667	10,250	291	385	1.9
6799	Investors, n.e.c.	5	6	6.0	15	32	10,667	10,250	291	385	2.9
WHITMAN, WA											
60 –	**Finance, insurance, and real estate**	83	87	0.6	360	382	19,100	18,911	7,159	7,565	0.2
6000	Depository institutions	26	27	1.2	213	217	20,319	20,922	4,442	4,650	0.4
6020	Commercial banks	22	23	1.8	177	181	19,254	20,287	3,508	3,715	0.6

Source: County Business Patterns, 1994/95, CBP-94/95, U.S. Department of Commerce, Washington, D.C., November 1997. SIC categories for which data were suppressed or not available for both 1994 and 1995 are *not* displayed. The employment columns represent mid-March employment in the year. Pay per employee is calculated by dividing 1st Quarter payroll, annualized, by mid-March employment. The columns headed "% State" show the county's percentage of the state total for the SIC in 1995; for example, 1.4% for SIC 6000 means that the county had 1.4 percent of the state's total establishments (or payroll) in SIC 6000 in 1995. A dash (-) is used to indicate that data are not available or cannot be calculated; *nec* means not elsewhere classified.

Continued on next page.

SIC	Industry	No. Establishments			Employment		Pay / Employee		Annual Payroll ($ 000)		
		1994	1995	% State	1994	1995	1994	1995	1994	1995	% State
WHITMAN, WA - [continued]											
6400	Insurance agents, brokers, and service	21	22	0.9	60	60	16,867	18,267	1,067	1,148	0.3
6500	Real estate	31	30	0.5	73	90	13,370	11,822	1,146	1,272	0.2
6530	Real estate agents and managers	8	9	0.3	24	33	13,667	11,636	380	440	0.1
YAKIMA, WA											
60 –	**Finance, insurance, and real estate**	385	392	2.7	2,169	2,188	25,534	27,234	56,401	59,292	1.5
6000	Depository institutions	70	65	3.0	816	809	23,279	24,677	19,132	20,561	2.0
6020	Commercial banks	44	45	3.5	536	571	23,425	25,310	12,731	14,244	2.1
6100	Nondepository institutions	15	17	1.5	80	74	32,600	34,378	2,300	2,523	0.9
6200	Security and commodity brokers	14	13	1.6	79	70	78,481	103,714	6,019	5,296	1.4
6210	Security brokers and dealers	11	9	1.8	75	64	81,920	112,125	5,952	5,154	1.6
6300	Insurance carriers	21	23	2.8	165	158	34,255	37,418	5,780	5,946	0.7
6310	Life insurance	6	5	2.8	123	115	32,390	33,148	4,094	3,787	1.9
6400	Insurance agents, brokers, and service	95	96	3.8	478	492	27,983	27,902	13,748	14,215	3.1
6500	Real estate	162	168	2.6	502	532	13,865	15,805	7,639	8,966	1.4
6510	Real estate operators and lessors	82	88	3.1	226	255	11,876	12,863	2,820	3,597	1.8
6530	Real estate agents and managers	65	62	2.1	191	168	14,429	17,381	2,914	3,069	0.8
6550	Subdividers and developers	10	12	2.3	83	99	17,831	19,030	1,836	2,080	2.8
6552	Subdividers and developers, n.e.c.	4	5	1.3	34	49	23,647	24,408	1,140	1,271	2.3
6553	Cemetery subdividers and developers	6	6	6.1	49	48	13,796	13,917	696	794	4.8
6700	Holding and other investment offices	8	10	2.4	49	53	32,490	33,434	1,783	1,785	1.3

Source: County Business Patterns, 1994/95, CBP-94/95, U.S. Department of Commerce, Washington, D.C., November 1997. SIC categories for which data were suppressed or not available for both 1994 and 1995 are not displayed. The employment columns represent mid-March employment in the year. Pay per employee is calculated by dividing 1st Quarter payroll, annualized, by mid-March employment. The columns headed "% State" show the county's percentage of the state total for the SIC in 1995; for example, 1.4% for SIC 6000 means that the county had 1.4 percent of the state's total establishments (or payroll) in SIC 6000 in 1995. A dash (-) is used to indicate that data are not available or cannot be calculated; nec means not elsewhere classified.

WEST VIRGINIA

SIC	Industry	No. Establishments			Employment		Pay / Employee		Annual Payroll ($ 000)		
		1994	1995	% State	1994	1995	1994	1995	1994	1995	% State
BARBOUR, WV											
60 –	**Finance, insurance, and real estate**	13	12	0.4	104	106	21,269	21,208	2,041	2,030	0.4
6000	Depository institutions	4	4	0.6	87	90	23,724	23,200	1,870	1,872	0.8
6020	Commercial banks	4	4	0.8	87	90	23,724	23,200	1,870	1,872	0.9
6400	Insurance agents, brokers, and service	5	4	0.5	10	9	12,400	14,667	135	129	0.2
6500	Real estate	4	4	0.3	7	7	3,429	4,000	36	29	0.0
BERKELEY, WV											
60 –	**Finance, insurance, and real estate**	121	126	3.9	790	697	19,484	22,129	16,141	16,133	2.8
6000	Depository institutions	26	23	3.5	426	300	18,413	22,253	7,718	6,574	2.7
6020	Commercial banks	18	15	3.1	386	260	18,674	22,908	7,027	5,823	2.7
6400	Insurance agents, brokers, and service	15	18	2.3	77	85	22,649	24,329	2,008	2,125	2.6
6500	Real estate	58	63	5.1	190	194	14,021	15,629	2,982	3,546	5.1
6510	Real estate operators and lessors	18	20	3.0	83	93	11,325	12,258	1,132	1,076	2.9
6530	Real estate agents and managers	28	30	8.0	59	65	17,627	19,262	1,103	1,680	8.9
6550	Subdividers and developers	11	11	6.2	48	34	14,250	18,000	730	731	6.5
BOONE, WV											
60 –	**Finance, insurance, and real estate**	27	27	0.8	409	379	34,210	39,240	14,674	14,683	2.6
6000	Depository institutions	6	5	0.8	116	111	17,379	18,054	2,224	2,222	0.9
6510	Real estate operators and lessors	5	5	0.8	9	8	20,889	24,500	156	198	0.5
BRAXTON, WV											
60 –	**Finance, insurance, and real estate**	14	15	0.5	84	98	17,143	16,245	1,564	1,785	0.3
6500	Real estate	5	6	0.5	4	13	11,000	8,000	73	137	0.2
BROOKE, WV											
60 –	**Finance, insurance, and real estate**	24	26	0.8	131	146	16,641	16,767	2,395	2,739	0.5
6000	Depository institutions	7	8	1.2	73	81	15,781	17,086	1,248	1,473	0.6
6400	Insurance agents, brokers, and service	6	7	0.9	19	20	15,158	14,600	285	313	0.4
6550	Subdividers and developers	4	4	2.2	8	12	9,000	9,000	99	131	1.2
6553	Cemetery subdividers and developers	4	4	3.7	8	12	9,000	9,000	99	131	1.7
CABELL, WV											
60 –	**Finance, insurance, and real estate**	254	255	7.9	1,946	1,881	24,349	25,480	47,307	48,575	8.5
6000	Depository institutions	42	42	6.3	819	780	19,497	20,744	15,236	16,036	6.6
6020	Commercial banks	21	21	4.3	626	586	20,492	21,911	11,931	12,545	5.7
6100	Nondepository institutions	13	13	9.5	92	94	23,565	25,362	2,257	2,529	-
6200	Security and commodity brokers	13	13	13.4	90	88	62,089	63,636	4,995	5,077	17.3
6300	Insurance carriers	19	18	9.0	190	162	30,968	34,642	5,717	5,712	6.3
6310	Life insurance	9	7	9.3	137	108	27,445	28,556	3,530	3,068	10.5
6400	Insurance agents, brokers, and service	65	68	8.8	222	237	23,369	23,055	5,466	5,869	7.1
6500	Real estate	85	87	7.0	302	346	14,450	17,006	4,777	6,117	8.9
6510	Real estate operators and lessors	50	52	7.9	184	211	12,261	15,697	2,358	3,441	9.2
6530	Real estate agents and managers	27	24	6.4	80	81	21,700	24,840	1,966	2,075	11.0
6550	Subdividers and developers	7	8	4.5	38	51	9,789	10,902	452	582	5.2
6700	Holding and other investment offices	17	14	13.6	231	174	35,602	39,103	8,859	7,235	17.1
6730	Trusts	4	3	10.7	2	3	18,000	25,333	57	72	-
CALHOUN, WV											
60 –	**Finance, insurance, and real estate**	6	8	0.2	60	70	12,467	9,486	785	765	0.1
CLAY, WV											
60 –	**Finance, insurance, and real estate**	5	6	0.2	-	-	-	-	-	-	-

Source: *County Business Patterns, 1994/95*, CBP-94/95, U.S. Department of Commerce, Washington, D.C., November 1997. SIC categories for which data were suppressed or not available for both 1994 and 1995 are *not* displayed. The employment columns represent mid-March employment in the year. Pay per employee is calculated by dividing 1st Quarter payroll, annualized, by mid-March employment. The columns headed "% State" show the county's percentage of the state total for the SIC in 1995; for example, 1.4% for SIC 6000 means that the county had 1.4 percent of the state's total establishments (or payroll) in SIC 6000 in 1995. A dash (-) is used to indicate that data are not available or cannot be calculated; *nec* means not elsewhere classified.

988

SIC	Industry	No. Establishments			Employment		Pay / Employee		Annual Payroll ($ 000)		
		1994	1995	% State	1994	1995	1994	1995	1994	1995	% State
FAYETTE, WV											
60 –	**Finance, insurance, and real estate**	59	61	*1.9*	-	-	-	-	-	-	-
6000	Depository institutions	17	17	*2.6*	272	257	18,397	18,848	5,088	4,896	*2.0*
6020	Commercial banks	14	14	*2.9*	257	241	18,630	19,170	4,881	4,679	*2.1*
6400	Insurance agents, brokers, and service	16	17	*2.2*	50	53	16,080	16,377	941	980	*1.2*
6510	Real estate operators and lessors	11	11	*1.7*	23	18	8,000	10,222	203	203	*0.5*
6550	Subdividers and developers	3	3	*1.7*	17	28	14,353	9,857	259	280	*2.5*
6553	Cemetery subdividers and developers	3	3	*2.8*	17	28	14,353	9,857	259	280	*3.5*
GILMER, WV											
60 –	**Finance, insurance, and real estate**	4	6	*0.2*	-	-	-	-	-	-	-
GRANT, WV											
60 –	**Finance, insurance, and real estate**	21	21	*0.7*	114	121	19,333	19,669	2,350	2,483	*0.4*
6000	Depository institutions	4	4	*0.6*	75	77	17,653	19,532	1,440	1,578	*0.6*
6020	Commercial banks	4	4	*0.8*	75	77	17,653	19,532	1,440	1,578	*0.7*
6530	Real estate agents and managers	4	5	*1.3*	8	10	9,000	7,200	90	71	*0.4*
GREENBRIER, WV											
60 –	**Finance, insurance, and real estate**	67	69	*2.1*	392	372	19,643	21,172	7,860	7,690	*1.3*
6000	Depository institutions	12	12	*1.8*	254	228	21,890	24,614	5,558	5,293	*2.2*
6300	Insurance carriers	4	3	*1.5*	18	19	31,111	27,368	572	512	*0.6*
6400	Insurance agents, brokers, and service	18	17	*2.2*	35	37	19,200	20,324	745	756	*0.9*
6500	Real estate	29	31	*2.5*	74	77	8,811	9,818	730	887	*1.3*
6510	Real estate operators and lessors	12	14	*2.1*	23	26	8,000	10,000	217	325	*0.9*
6530	Real estate agents and managers	9	11	*2.9*	21	23	8,762	10,957	178	247	*1.3*
6550	Subdividers and developers	8	5	*2.8*	30	28	9,467	8,714	335	312	*2.8*
HAMPSHIRE, WV											
60 –	**Finance, insurance, and real estate**	27	27	*0.8*	160	162	18,775	18,864	2,868	2,995	*0.5*
6000	Depository institutions	8	8	*1.2*	102	112	18,863	18,607	1,872	2,019	*0.8*
6530	Real estate agents and managers	4	4	*1.1*	7	5	4,571	8,800	56	56	*0.3*
6550	Subdividers and developers	4	5	*2.8*	14	12	4,571	4,667	58	91	*0.8*
HANCOCK, WV											
60 –	**Finance, insurance, and real estate**	57	61	*1.9*	396	428	16,687	17,561	7,071	7,878	*1.4*
6000	Depository institutions	20	20	*3.0*	299	323	17,686	18,601	5,515	6,156	*2.5*
6020	Commercial banks	7	7	*1.4*	135	139	18,519	19,770	2,694	2,859	*1.3*
6400	Insurance agents, brokers, and service	13	13	*1.7*	45	45	14,933	14,311	670	691	*0.8*
6500	Real estate	20	21	*1.7*	45	46	11,111	13,565	720	756	*1.1*
6510	Real estate operators and lessors	11	12	*1.8*	30	34	11,600	14,000	545	596	*1.6*
6530	Real estate agents and managers	6	6	*1.6*	6	6	12,000	13,333	74	83	*0.4*
6550	Subdividers and developers	3	3	*1.7*	9	6	8,889	11,333	101	77	*0.7*
6553	Cemetery subdividers and developers	3	3	*2.8*	9	6	8,889	11,333	101	77	*1.0*
HARDY, WV											
60 –	**Finance, insurance, and real estate**	23	24	*0.7*	139	128	21,755	18,875	2,925	2,352	*0.4*
6000	Depository institutions	6	6	*0.9*	87	94	21,517	21,830	1,783	1,973	*0.8*
6020	Commercial banks	6	6	*1.2*	87	94	21,517	21,830	1,783	1,973	*0.9*
6500	Real estate	8	8	*0.6*	12	13	10,667	10,769	127	130	*0.2*
HARRISON, WV											
60 –	**Finance, insurance, and real estate**	154	156	*4.8*	1,044	1,048	20,575	22,149	22,188	23,286	*4.1*
6000	Depository institutions	37	35	*5.3*	498	469	19,871	22,047	9,757	9,490	*3.9*
6020	Commercial banks	27	25	*5.1*	475	442	20,042	22,371	9,361	9,024	*4.1*
6140	Personal credit institutions	10	10	*9.9*	42	42	18,762	21,238	839	1,105	*8.6*
6300	Insurance carriers	14	12	*6.0*	141	135	31,972	34,637	4,392	4,405	*4.9*
6310	Life insurance	6	5	*6.7*	90	94	27,244	28,340	2,439	2,331	*8.0*
6400	Insurance agents, brokers, and service	41	37	*4.8*	184	189	18,152	18,878	3,814	3,851	*4.7*

Source: County Business Patterns, 1994/95, CBP-94/95, U.S. Department of Commerce, Washington, D.C., November 1997. SIC categories for which data were suppressed or not available for both 1994 and 1995 are *not* displayed. The employment columns represent mid-March employment in the year. Pay per employee is calculated by dividing 1st Quarter payroll, annualized, by mid-March employment. The columns headed "% State" show the county's percentage of the state total for the SIC in 1995; for example, 1.4% for SIC 6000 means that the county had 1.4 percent of the state's total establishments (or payroll) in SIC 6000 in 1995. A dash (-) is used to indicate that data are not available or cannot be calculated; *nec* means not elsewhere classified.

Continued on next page.

SIC	Industry	No. Establishments			Employment		Pay / Employee		Annual Payroll ($ 000)		
		1994	1995	% State	1994	1995	1994	1995	1994	1995	% State
HARRISON, WV - [continued]											
6500	Real estate	42	52	4.2	136	136	10,382	12,294	1,667	2,044	3.0
6510	Real estate operators and lessors	24	25	3.8	82	71	9,854	11,042	870	925	2.5
6530	Real estate agents and managers	12	16	4.2	45	47	11,289	11,319	600	664	3.5
6550	Subdividers and developers	5	9	5.1	8	16	11,500	20,250	176	412	3.7
JEFFERSON, WV											
60−	**Finance, insurance, and real estate**	68	68	2.1	363	361	18,556	20,665	7,352	7,549	1.3
6000	Depository institutions	15	14	2.1	250	243	18,880	19,852	4,943	4,910	2.0
6500	Real estate	37	38	3.0	69	74	12,000	12,432	961	913	1.3
6510	Real estate operators and lessors	14	14	2.1	28	26	10,000	11,077	328	293	0.8
6552	Subdividers and developers, n.e.c.	3	5	8.1	4	6	13,000	10,667	76	75	2.4
KANAWHA, WV											
60−	**Finance, insurance, and real estate**	574	573	17.8	5,975	6,186	28,098	28,127	163,711	167,682	29.2
6000	Depository institutions	77	79	11.9	2,065	2,151	24,335	23,461	45,736	45,947	18.9
6020	Commercial banks	50	52	10.7	1,846	1,921	24,470	23,454	40,700	40,542	18.5
6140	Personal credit institutions	15	16	15.8	107	110	27,776	27,091	2,861	3,106	24.2
6200	Security and commodity brokers	26	24	24.7	264	220	71,152	77,255	15,270	14,414	49.2
6210	Security brokers and dealers	22	19	26.8	257	212	72,669	79,509	15,160	14,219	50.2
6280	Security and commodity services	4	5	19.2	7	8	15,429	17,500	110	195	19.5
6300	Insurance carriers	63	60	30.2	1,496	1,542	25,302	27,245	39,911	41,077	45.4
6310	Life insurance	27	25	33.3	467	501	25,876	26,331	12,646	11,910	40.7
6330	Fire, marine, and casualty insurance	22	21	22.3	233	229	41,511	48,017	10,218	10,333	35.1
6400	Insurance agents, brokers, and service	117	116	15.0	929	975	31,539	34,544	29,374	33,407	40.4
6500	Real estate	238	241	19.3	904	971	20,367	18,723	19,060	20,061	29.1
6510	Real estate operators and lessors	152	149	22.6	511	574	22,521	18,411	11,134	11,901	31.7
6530	Real estate agents and managers	63	69	18.3	294	308	18,231	20,013	6,207	6,414	34.0
6550	Subdividers and developers	21	20	11.2	99	87	15,596	16,598	1,701	1,707	15.2
6552	Subdividers and developers, n.e.c.	5	6	9.7	15	11	10,933	18,545	165	195	6.2
6553	Cemetery subdividers and developers	15	14	13.0	84	76	16,429	16,316	1,521	1,512	19.1
6700	Holding and other investment offices	29	28	27.2	177	182	54,260	47,253	10,588	8,536	20.2
6710	Holding offices	6	6	14.0	149	141	59,087	51,291	9,705	7,193	20.7
6730	Trusts	14	11	39.3	10	17	26,400	16,235	283	287	-
6732	Educational, religious, etc. trusts	7	6	42.9	4	10	18,000	8,400	87	101	44.7
6733	Trusts, n.e.c.	7	5	35.7	6	7	32,000	27,429	196	186	-
6790	Miscellaneous investing	9	11	35.5	18	24	29,778	45,500	600	1,056	-
LEWIS, WV											
60−	**Finance, insurance, and real estate**	24	25	0.8	139	150	14,734	15,920	2,346	2,469	0.4
6000	Depository institutions	4	4	0.6	77	79	16,104	17,063	1,346	1,338	0.5
6020	Commercial banks	4	4	0.8	77	79	16,104	17,063	1,346	1,338	0.6
6500	Real estate	11	12	1.0	14	22	9,429	10,364	172	243	0.4
6510	Real estate operators and lessors	6	6	0.9	7	8	9,143	8,000	67	84	0.2
LINCOLN, WV											
60−	**Finance, insurance, and real estate**	13	13	0.4	69	64	15,942	18,438	1,148	1,209	0.2
6400	Insurance agents, brokers, and service	4	4	0.5	11	11	14,909	14,545	172	166	0.2
LOGAN, WV											
60−	**Finance, insurance, and real estate**	58	56	1.7	337	334	21,579	23,868	7,309	7,580	1.3
6000	Depository institutions	13	13	2.0	203	187	20,276	22,182	3,961	3,896	1.6
6500	Real estate	22	19	1.5	70	71	16,000	16,225	1,304	1,256	1.8
6510	Real estate operators and lessors	12	11	1.7	43	50	16,651	15,600	860	804	2.1
6530	Real estate agents and managers	5	4	1.1	6	8	8,667	11,500	83	99	0.5
MCDOWELL, WV											
60−	**Finance, insurance, and real estate**	28	29	0.9	208	226	19,365	19,858	4,828	5,526	1.0

Source: County Business Patterns, 1994/95, CBP-94/95, U.S. Department of Commerce, Washington, D.C., November 1997. SIC categories for which data were suppressed or not available for both 1994 and 1995 are not displayed. The employment columns represent mid-March employment in the year. Pay per employee is calculated by dividing 1st Quarter payroll, annualized, by mid-March employment. The columns headed "% State" show the county's percentage of the state total for the SIC in 1995; for example, 1.4% for SIC 6000 means that the county had 1.4 percent of the state's total establishments (or payroll) in SIC 6000 in 1995. A dash (-) is used to indicate that data are not available or cannot be calculated; nec means not elsewhere classified.

Continued on next page.

SIC	Industry	No. Establishments			Employment		Pay / Employee		Annual Payroll ($ 000)		
		1994	1995	% State	1994	1995	1994	1995	1994	1995	% State
MCDOWELL, WV - [continued]											
6000	Depository institutions	10	10	1.5	149	156	20,993	21,538	3,852	4,017	1.6
6020	Commercial banks	10	10	2.1	149	156	20,993	21,538	3,852	4,017	1.8
6510	Real estate operators and lessors	5	6	0.9	19	22	13,053	13,273	293	323	0.9
MARION, WV											
60 –	**Finance, insurance, and real estate**	98	102	3.2	1,087	786	17,696	19,282	15,290	15,369	2.7
6000	Depository institutions	24	25	3.8	557	524	14,707	19,313	7,952	9,396	3.9
6020	Commercial banks	17	17	3.5	480	478	16,583	20,226	7,709	8,890	4.0
6060	Credit unions	7	8	5.9	77	46	3,013	9,826	243	506	-
6300	Insurance carriers	7	7	3.5	67	68	31,522	30,353	2,351	2,378	2.6
6400	Insurance agents, brokers, and service	17	21	2.7	68	65	19,294	20,308	1,655	1,741	2.1
6500	Real estate	38	35	2.8	368	100	19,217	9,320	2,644	1,097	1.6
6510	Real estate operators and lessors	15	14	2.1	330	62	20,485	9,290	2,076	647	1.7
6530	Real estate agents and managers	13	11	2.9	21	17	6,095	7,294	271	170	0.9
6550	Subdividers and developers	10	10	5.6	17	21	10,824	11,048	297	280	2.5
6552	Subdividers and developers, n.e.c.	4	4	6.5	5	9	10,400	12,444	105	100	3.2
6553	Cemetery subdividers and developers	6	6	5.6	12	12	11,000	10,000	192	180	2.3
6700	Holding and other investment offices	6	6	5.8	12	11	14,333	19,273	193	214	0.5
MARSHALL, WV											
60 –	**Finance, insurance, and real estate**	28	39	1.2	-	-	-	-	-	-	-
6000	Depository institutions	12	12	1.8	164	175	17,585	17,417	2,757	2,792	1.1
6020	Commercial banks	8	8	1.6	155	164	17,961	17,805	2,650	2,668	1.2
MASON, WV											
60 –	**Finance, insurance, and real estate**	31	32	1.0	203	191	16,118	16,984	3,479	3,664	0.6
6000	Depository institutions	8	8	1.2	141	131	17,532	17,893	2,613	2,660	1.1
6400	Insurance agents, brokers, and service	10	10	1.3	26	26	12,308	13,846	341	417	0.5
MERCER, WV											
60 –	**Finance, insurance, and real estate**	107	112	3.5	810	904	28,198	28,027	22,476	23,009	4.0
6000	Depository institutions	26	26	3.9	407	463	22,054	23,732	8,982	9,279	3.8
6020	Commercial banks	19	19	3.9	396	452	22,444	24,106	8,888	9,190	4.2
6060	Credit unions	7	7	5.2	11	11	8,000	8,364	94	89	-
6300	Insurance carriers	7	7	3.5	69	56	35,768	40,071	2,659	2,215	2.4
6310	Life insurance	3	3	4.0	56	41	31,429	33,561	1,877	1,414	4.8
6330	Fire, marine, and casualty insurance	4	4	4.3	13	15	54,462	57,867	782	801	2.7
6400	Insurance agents, brokers, and service	31	29	3.8	167	170	31,617	33,482	4,637	4,848	5.9
6500	Real estate	28	29	2.3	77	113	26,390	20,071	2,139	2,247	3.3
6530	Real estate agents and managers	7	7	1.9	13	16	17,231	14,500	240	233	1.2
MINERAL, WV											
60 –	**Finance, insurance, and real estate**	28	30	0.9	160	161	15,475	18,236	2,753	2,808	0.5
6000	Depository institutions	11	11	1.7	107	97	17,495	20,041	2,091	1,927	0.8
MINGO, WV											
60 –	**Finance, insurance, and real estate**	36	35	1.1	350	349	17,634	19,862	7,009	7,555	1.3
6000	Depository institutions	12	12	1.8	279	267	17,548	19,940	5,335	5,630	2.3
6020	Commercial banks	12	12	2.5	279	267	17,548	19,940	5,335	5,630	2.6
6400	Insurance agents, brokers, and service	7	7	0.9	24	23	17,667	20,870	521	577	0.7
6500	Real estate	13	13	1.0	33	32	13,455	9,375	437	448	0.7
MONONGALIA, WV											
60 –	**Finance, insurance, and real estate**	184	179	5.6	1,240	1,186	17,816	19,609	25,633	24,341	4.2
6000	Depository institutions	30	29	4.4	619	607	18,397	20,409	13,701	12,745	5.2
6020	Commercial banks	21	20	4.1	575	557	18,810	20,984	13,113	12,023	5.5
6200	Security and commodity brokers	8	7	7.2	14	15	15,143	29,333	289	480	1.6
6300	Insurance carriers	16	12	6.0	103	86	29,165	28,419	3,363	2,803	3.1

Source: County Business Patterns, 1994/95, CBP-94/95, U.S. Department of Commerce, Washington, D.C., November 1997. SIC categories for which data were suppressed or not available for both 1994 and 1995 are not displayed. The employment columns represent mid-March employment in the year. Pay per employee is calculated by dividing 1st Quarter payroll, annualized, by mid-March employment. The columns headed "% State" show the county's percentage of the state total for the SIC in 1995; for example, 1.4% for SIC 6000 means that the county had 1.4 percent of the state's total establishments (or payroll) in SIC 6000 in 1995. A dash (-) is used to indicate that data are not available or cannot be calculated; nec means not elsewhere classified.

Continued on next page.

SIC	Industry	No. Establishments			Employment		Pay / Employee		Annual Payroll ($ 000)		
		1994	1995	% State	1994	1995	1994	1995	1994	1995	% State
MONONGALIA, WV - [continued]											
6400	Insurance agents, brokers, and service	28	30	3.9	100	101	23,680	24,554	2,370	2,535	3.1
6500	Real estate	90	93	7.5	354	341	11,458	13,595	4,827	4,838	7.0
6510	Real estate operators and lessors	60	60	9.1	238	203	10,235	12,039	2,815	2,923	7.8
6530	Real estate agents and managers	22	23	6.1	85	89	13,882	17,079	1,463	1,245	6.6
6550	Subdividers and developers	8	8	4.5	31	37	14,194	12,541	549	483	4.3
MORGAN, WV											
60 –	**Finance, insurance, and real estate**	20	20	0.6	106	108	18,377	17,926	2,071	2,132	0.4
NICHOLAS, WV											
60 –	**Finance, insurance, and real estate**	44	45	1.4	196	197	18,592	21,401	3,841	3,965	0.7
6000	Depository institutions	7	7	1.1	131	121	19,969	25,256	2,582	2,621	1.1
6400	Insurance agents, brokers, and service	12	13	1.7	27	32	15,852	14,250	515	545	0.7
6510	Real estate operators and lessors	11	13	2.0	16	22	14,250	11,818	255	337	0.9
OHIO, WV											
60 –	**Finance, insurance, and real estate**	138	138	4.3	1,668	1,629	21,600	22,075	35,161	36,081	6.3
6000	Depository institutions	30	27	4.1	772	745	20,756	21,621	15,792	16,521	6.8
6020	Commercial banks	16	15	3.1	635	589	21,461	22,112	13,140	13,665	6.2
6140	Personal credit institutions	4	4	4.0	21	20	19,429	24,000	445	453	3.5
6200	Security and commodity brokers	6	8	8.2	72	78	76,889	64,359	4,194	4,458	15.2
6210	Security brokers and dealers	6	8	11.3	72	78	76,889	64,359	4,194	4,458	15.7
6300	Insurance carriers	14	13	6.5	405	385	21,432	22,068	8,980	8,351	9.2
6310	Life insurance	7	6	8.0	146	130	22,740	20,954	3,322	2,647	9.0
6400	Insurance agents, brokers, and service	24	24	3.1	112	114	22,714	23,965	2,541	2,810	3.4
6500	Real estate	56	58	4.7	233	220	9,150	10,091	2,462	2,555	3.7
6510	Real estate operators and lessors	32	35	5.3	143	154	9,846	9,792	1,494	1,628	4.3
6530	Real estate agents and managers	19	18	4.8	43	28	6,884	10,714	360	389	2.1
6550	Subdividers and developers	5	5	2.8	47	38	9,106	10,842	608	538	4.8
6553	Cemetery subdividers and developers	5	5	4.6	47	38	9,106	10,842	608	538	6.8
PENDLETON, WV											
60 –	**Finance, insurance, and real estate**	9	8	0.2	-	-	-	-	-	-	-
PLEASANTS, WV											
60 –	**Finance, insurance, and real estate**	12	11	0.3	76	68	15,474	17,412	1,212	1,226	0.2
6000	Depository institutions	4	4	0.6	61	56	16,459	18,286	1,033	1,061	0.4
POCAHONTAS, WV											
60 –	**Finance, insurance, and real estate**	16	17	0.5	128	118	16,750	16,949	1,959	1,818	0.3
6500	Real estate	8	9	0.7	44	50	11,909	11,840	406	452	0.7
PRESTON, WV											
60 –	**Finance, insurance, and real estate**	47	49	1.5	237	244	22,549	22,525	4,960	4,981	0.9
6000	Depository institutions	12	12	1.8	153	161	17,046	16,820	2,746	2,887	1.2
6510	Real estate operators and lessors	9	10	1.5	13	15	10,769	8,000	113	111	0.3
6550	Subdividers and developers	5	6	3.4	5	7	4,000	2,286	31	27	0.2
6553	Cemetery subdividers and developers	5	6	5.6	5	7	4,000	2,286	31	27	0.3
PUTNAM, WV											
60 –	**Finance, insurance, and real estate**	55	58	1.8	282	267	18,610	21,663	5,825	6,288	1.1
6000	Depository institutions	10	13	2.0	155	129	21,858	24,093	3,538	3,283	1.3
6020	Commercial banks	6	9	1.9	143	117	22,182	24,581	3,319	3,045	1.4
6300	Insurance carriers	3	4	2.0	4	25	48,000	38,080	430	1,062	1.2
6400	Insurance agents, brokers, and service	18	16	2.1	46	46	15,826	16,870	862	941	1.1
6500	Real estate	20	22	1.8	60	53	8,600	10,189	594	608	0.9
6510	Real estate operators and lessors	8	8	1.2	34	26	6,353	9,077	240	244	0.7
6530	Real estate agents and managers	4	5	1.3	4	5	5,000	4,000	17	41	0.2

Source: County Business Patterns, 1994/95, CBP-94/95, U.S. Department of Commerce, Washington, D.C., November 1997. SIC categories for which data were suppressed or not available for both 1994 and 1995 are not displayed. The employment columns represent mid-March employment in the year. Pay per employee is calculated by dividing 1st Quarter payroll, annualized, by mid-March employment. The columns headed "% State" show the county's percentage of the state total for the SIC in 1995; for example, 1.4% for SIC 6000 means that the county had 1.4 percent of the state's total establishments (or payroll) in SIC 6000 in 1995. A dash (-) is used to indicate that data are not available or cannot be calculated; nec means not elsewhere classified.

Continued on next page.

SIC	Industry	No. Establishments			Employment		Pay / Employee		Annual Payroll ($ 000)		
		1994	1995	% State	1994	1995	1994	1995	1994	1995	% State
PUTNAM, WV - [continued]											
6550	Subdividers and developers	8	8	4.5	22	21	12,727	12,952	337	307	2.7
6552	Subdividers and developers, n.e.c.	5	5	8.1	11	8	17,091	20,500	248	224	7.1
6553	Cemetery subdividers and developers	3	3	2.8	11	13	8,364	8,308	89	83	1.1
RALEIGH, WV											
60 –	**Finance, insurance, and real estate**	147	154	4.8	939	953	23,050	24,227	22,346	24,022	4.2
6000	Depository institutions	21	22	3.3	390	397	19,190	19,557	7,716	7,548	3.1
6020	Commercial banks	15	15	3.1	360	362	19,122	19,160	7,071	6,680	3.0
6300	Insurance carriers	11	11	5.5	99	101	33,859	41,030	3,626	3,887	4.3
6400	Insurance agents, brokers, and service	37	39	5.0	143	139	25,986	26,360	3,506	3,713	4.5
6500	Real estate	59	65	5.2	242	253	21,504	22,672	5,592	6,939	10.1
6510	Real estate operators and lessors	37	39	5.9	136	162	23,353	25,136	3,712	5,348	14.3
6530	Real estate agents and managers	13	15	4.0	47	36	10,809	12,222	455	477	2.5
6550	Subdividers and developers	7	6	3.4	59	50	25,763	22,640	1,379	1,026	9.1
RANDOLPH, WV											
60 –	**Finance, insurance, and real estate**	58	57	1.8	391	378	15,274	16,730	6,482	6,831	1.2
6000	Depository institutions	10	10	1.5	215	222	16,707	17,117	3,927	4,102	1.7
6100	Nondepository institutions	5	4	2.9	9	14	26,667	29,714	330	342	-
6500	Real estate	23	21	1.7	104	82	8,308	9,024	776	858	1.2
6510	Real estate operators and lessors	13	12	1.8	89	68	7,775	8,294	606	686	1.8
RITCHIE, WV											
60 –	**Finance, insurance, and real estate**	12	11	0.3	97	81	20,330	24,494	1,759	1,649	0.3
6000	Depository institutions	5	5	0.8	71	56	17,070	21,429	1,106	989	0.4
6020	Commercial banks	5	5	1.0	71	56	17,070	21,429	1,106	989	0.5
ROANE, WV											
60 –	**Finance, insurance, and real estate**	18	16	0.5	124	148	19,516	17,865	2,475	2,670	0.5
6000	Depository institutions	4	4	0.6	106	122	20,830	19,311	2,205	2,369	1.0
6020	Commercial banks	4	4	0.8	106	122	20,830	19,311	2,205	2,369	1.1
6400	Insurance agents, brokers, and service	6	6	0.8	9	13	15,556	14,769	164	188	0.2
6500	Real estate	8	6	0.5	9	13	8,000	7,385	106	113	0.2
SUMMERS, WV											
60 –	**Finance, insurance, and real estate**	16	11	0.3	106	59	20,604	18,441	2,227	1,111	0.2
6500	Real estate	5	4	0.3	5	7	7,200	9,143	42	69	0.1
TAYLOR, WV											
60 –	**Finance, insurance, and real estate**	11	13	0.4	64	59	10,813	16,136	794	848	0.1
TUCKER, WV											
60 –	**Finance, insurance, and real estate**	21	19	0.6	140	122	13,600	14,426	2,091	2,011	0.4
6000	Depository institutions	5	5	0.8	53	56	14,113	13,929	883	919	0.4
6020	Commercial banks	5	5	1.0	53	56	14,113	13,929	883	919	0.4
6500	Real estate	12	9	0.7	76	54	11,053	11,926	843	677	1.0
6530	Real estate agents and managers	7	5	1.3	62	25	9,806	8,000	644	271	1.4
TYLER, WV											
60 –	**Finance, insurance, and real estate**	9	10	0.3	69	68	17,507	18,176	1,135	1,138	0.2
6000	Depository institutions	5	5	0.8	58	56	19,517	20,786	1,047	1,051	0.4
UPSHUR, WV											
60 –	**Finance, insurance, and real estate**	29	27	0.8	171	159	17,474	20,654	3,148	3,146	0.5
6000	Depository institutions	6	5	0.8	117	104	18,564	22,077	2,317	2,202	0.9
6020	Commercial banks	6	5	1.0	117	104	18,564	22,077	2,317	2,202	1.0

Source: County Business Patterns, 1994/95, CBP-94/95, U.S. Department of Commerce, Washington, D.C., November 1997. SIC categories for which data were suppressed or not available for both 1994 and 1995 are not displayed. The employment columns represent mid-March employment in the year. Pay per employee is calculated by dividing 1st Quarter payroll, annualized, by mid-March employment. The columns headed "% State" show the county's percentage of the state total for the SIC in 1995; for example, 1.4% for SIC 6000 means that the county had 1.4 percent of the state's total establishments (or payroll) in SIC 6000 in 1995. A dash (-) is used to indicate that data are not available or cannot be calculated; nec means not elsewhere classified.

Continued on next page.

SIC	Industry	No. Establishments			Employment		Pay / Employee		Annual Payroll ($ 000)		
		1994	1995	% State	1994	1995	1994	1995	1994	1995	% State
UPSHUR, WV - [continued]											
6500	Real estate	10	9	0.7	19	17	10,105	14,118	218	243	0.4
6510	Real estate operators and lessors	3	3	0.5	3	3	13,333	13,333	39	54	0.1
6530	Real estate agents and managers	7	6	1.6	16	14	9,500	14,286	179	189	1.0
WAYNE, WV											
60 –	**Finance, insurance, and real estate**	40	42	1.3	226	234	17,858	19,419	4,383	4,352	0.8
6000	Depository institutions	11	11	1.7	130	121	17,815	20,893	2,442	2,313	0.9
6020	Commercial banks	7	7	1.4	112	103	18,679	21,786	2,201	2,021	0.9
6400	Insurance agents, brokers, and service	11	13	1.7	56	67	23,071	21,731	1,315	1,452	1.8
6510	Real estate operators and lessors	9	8	1.2	26	28	13,692	16,571	528	477	1.3
6530	Real estate agents and managers	5	6	1.6	12	12	5,000	6,333	85	92	0.5
WETZEL, WV											
60 –	**Finance, insurance, and real estate**	39	37	1.1	223	240	15,587	16,200	3,833	4,020	0.7
6000	Depository institutions	15	14	2.1	168	169	16,024	17,325	2,812	2,906	1.2
6020	Commercial banks	10	9	1.9	123	121	15,415	16,562	1,952	1,961	0.9
6500	Real estate	11	12	1.0	18	27	12,444	11,259	293	334	0.5
6530	Real estate agents and managers	3	4	1.1	7	8	14,857	14,000	111	126	0.7
WIRT, WV											
60 –	**Finance, insurance, and real estate**	5	5	0.2	-	-	-	-	-	-	-
WOOD, WV											
60 –	**Finance, insurance, and real estate**	195	200	6.2	1,606	1,583	21,517	24,493	35,814	39,681	6.9
6000	Depository institutions	37	36	5.4	659	581	21,839	24,317	13,106	12,611	5.2
6020	Commercial banks	25	25	5.1	594	522	22,498	25,226	12,069	11,555	5.3
6100	Nondepository institutions	7	8	5.8	27	30	24,741	19,733	689	604	-
6200	Security and commodity brokers	11	11	11.3	31	40	58,323	27,500	1,655	1,575	5.4
6210	Security brokers and dealers	7	7	9.9	26	33	66,615	31,273	1,577	1,519	5.4
6280	Security and commodity services	4	4	15.4	5	7	15,200	9,714	78	56	5.6
6300	Insurance carriers	16	16	8.0	437	437	24,275	25,748	11,789	12,172	13.5
6330	Fire, marine, and casualty insurance	7	7	7.4	88	94	34,545	36,383	3,282	3,581	12.2
6400	Insurance agents, brokers, and service	50	54	7.0	136	143	18,176	18,993	2,909	3,035	3.7
6500	Real estate	68	67	5.4	295	265	13,247	14,355	4,431	4,106	6.0
6510	Real estate operators and lessors	40	39	5.9	162	146	13,136	14,466	2,469	2,263	6.0
6530	Real estate agents and managers	20	19	5.0	89	78	14,427	15,282	1,445	1,272	6.7
6700	Holding and other investment offices	6	8	7.8	21	87	33,333	59,540	1,235	5,578	13.2
WYOMING, WV											
60 –	**Finance, insurance, and real estate**	23	22	0.7	135	131	17,363	20,580	2,424	2,232	0.4

Source: County Business Patterns, 1994/95, CBP-94/95, U.S. Department of Commerce, Washington, D.C., November 1997. SIC categories for which data were suppressed or not available for both 1994 and 1995 are *not* displayed. The employment columns represent mid-March employment in the year. Pay per employee is calculated by dividing 1st Quarter payroll, annualized, by mid-March employment. The columns headed "% State" show the county's percentage of the state total for the SIC in 1995; for example, 1.4% for SIC 6000 means that the county had 1.4 percent of the state's total establishments (or payroll) in SIC 6000 in 1995. A dash (-) is used to indicate that data are not available or cannot be calculated; *nec* means not elsewhere classified.

WISCONSIN

SIC	Industry	No. Establishments			Employment		Pay / Employee		Annual Payroll ($ 000)		
		1994	1995	% State	1994	1995	1994	1995	1994	1995	% State
ASHLAND, WI											
60 –	**Finance, insurance, and real estate**	42	40	0.3	271	218	17,373	17,083	3,883	4,473	0.1
6000	Depository institutions	9	9	0.4	120	116	14,500	16,138	1,865	2,539	0.3
6500	Real estate	9	8	0.2	21	16	10,095	8,250	269	295	0.1
6530	Real estate agents and managers	5	5	0.3	12	10	9,333	6,000	170	225	0.1
BARRON, WI											
60 –	**Finance, insurance, and real estate**	89	91	0.8	484	470	20,975	21,481	10,191	10,522	0.2
6000	Depository institutions	23	23	1.0	260	256	21,708	21,141	5,295	5,428	0.6
6020	Commercial banks	15	15	1.1	204	204	22,667	21,431	4,262	4,356	0.7
6400	Insurance agents, brokers, and service	31	29	0.9	76	76	18,000	18,579	1,765	1,945	0.5
6500	Real estate	28	30	0.8	93	78	16,043	19,026	1,584	1,588	0.5
6510	Real estate operators and lessors	10	11	0.7	14	11	10,571	13,455	134	172	0.2
BAYFIELD, WI											
60 –	**Finance, insurance, and real estate**	20	21	0.2	97	106	17,443	17,962	1,970	2,587	0.1
6000	Depository institutions	10	9	0.4	79	80	18,430	20,650	1,741	2,220	0.2
6530	Real estate agents and managers	6	7	0.4	7	18	11,429	7,556	91	235	0.1
BROWN, WI											
60 –	**Finance, insurance, and real estate**	483	502	4.3	8,201	6,643	25,473	28,330	211,021	196,896	4.5
6000	Depository institutions	91	90	3.8	1,725	1,700	23,362	24,576	40,196	40,559	4.1
6020	Commercial banks	44	43	3.3	1,196	1,160	24,037	25,917	29,267	29,120	4.4
6030	Savings institutions	25	23	4.6	262	267	26,031	23,610	6,213	6,044	3.6
6100	Nondepository institutions	18	23	4.1	170	198	31,694	32,828	5,271	6,690	3.6
6160	Mortgage bankers and brokers	8	12	5.0	90	111	29,600	31,532	2,767	4,169	4.3
6200	Security and commodity brokers	34	30	4.7	250	258	54,544	47,209	9,775	11,760	3.3
6210	Security brokers and dealers	21	19	4.7	225	233	59,413	51,142	9,482	11,501	4.5
6280	Security and commodity services	13	11	4.9	25	25	10,720	10,560	293	259	0.2
6300	Insurance carriers	37	43	5.6	2,838	3,041	27,188	29,684	74,245	95,652	5.0
6330	Fire, marine, and casualty insurance	17	16	4.1	468	419	40,744	29,566	12,268	11,935	2.1
6400	Insurance agents, brokers, and service	145	149	4.7	2,418	592	23,120	31,764	61,876	18,961	5.2
6500	Real estate	146	154	3.9	670	705	15,355	15,881	11,677	14,249	4.1
6510	Real estate operators and lessors	59	60	3.8	336	327	13,536	14,373	4,524	4,952	4.4
6530	Real estate agents and managers	66	69	4.0	196	247	19,918	15,417	4,464	4,847	2.8
6540	Title abstract offices	7	7	5.0	115	101	13,809	13,901	2,259	2,014	8.8
6550	Subdividers and developers	14	16	3.8	23	29	10,783	44,138	430	2,401	6.8
6552	Subdividers and developers, n.e.c.	9	11	7.1	7	13	8,571	81,846	163	2,119	9.1
6553	Cemetery subdividers and developers	5	5	2.0	16	16	11,750	13,500	267	282	2.5
6700	Holding and other investment offices	12	13	4.2	130	149	47,938	50,121	7,981	9,025	5.3
6710	Holding offices	6	9	5.7	118	129	50,881	55,690	7,619	8,740	5.9
BUFFALO, WI											
60 –	**Finance, insurance, and real estate**	28	32	0.3	129	139	19,380	18,043	2,640	2,632	0.1
6000	Depository institutions	9	9	0.4	83	88	20,530	19,182	1,876	1,851	0.2
6500	Real estate	7	10	0.3	8	13	4,500	4,923	71	77	0.0
6530	Real estate agents and managers	3	3	0.2	3	3	5,333	8,000	28	13	0.0
BURNETT, WI											
60 –	**Finance, insurance, and real estate**	21	19	0.2	101	123	18,772	19,675	2,122	2,435	0.1
6000	Depository institutions	6	6	0.3	66	80	21,455	22,750	1,497	1,663	0.2
6530	Real estate agents and managers	6	4	0.2	8	11	9,500	7,273	109	151	0.1

Source: County Business Patterns, 1994/95, CBP-94/95, U.S. Department of Commerce, Washington, D.C., November 1997. SIC categories for which data were suppressed or not available for both 1994 and 1995 are *not* displayed. The employment columns represent mid-March employment in the year. Pay per employee is calculated by dividing 1st Quarter payroll, annualized, by mid-March employment. The columns headed "% State" show the county's percentage of the state total for the SIC in 1995; for example, 1.4% for SIC 6000 means that the county had 1.4 percent of the state's total establishments (or payroll) in SIC 6000 in 1995. A dash (-) is used to indicate that data are not available or cannot be calculated; *nec* means not elsewhere classified.

SIC	Industry	No. Establishments			Employment		Pay / Employee		Annual Payroll ($ 000)		
		1994	1995	% State	1994	1995	1994	1995	1994	1995	% State
CALUMET, WI											
60 –	**Finance, insurance, and real estate**	61	62	0.5	327	324	20,661	21,160	7,494	7,645	0.2
6000	Depository institutions	17	16	0.7	167	144	19,090	19,917	3,227	2,868	0.3
6020	Commercial banks	10	9	0.7	111	85	19,928	21,600	2,244	1,838	0.3
6200	Security and commodity brokers	3	4	0.6	16	17	30,750	22,824	460	425	0.1
6210	Security brokers and dealers	3	4	1.0	16	17	30,750	22,824	460	425	0.2
6400	Insurance agents, brokers, and service	21	20	0.6	50	45	12,160	13,778	740	754	0.2
6500	Real estate	12	13	0.3	65	81	21,292	18,222	1,581	1,640	0.5
CHIPPEWA, WI											
60 –	**Finance, insurance, and real estate**	79	82	0.7	472	513	20,381	19,314	10,273	10,817	0.2
6000	Depository institutions	27	26	1.1	299	322	17,779	18,385	5,547	6,146	0.6
6020	Commercial banks	17	16	1.2	214	243	18,430	18,716	4,279	4,882	0.7
6400	Insurance agents, brokers, and service	26	31	1.0	77	89	17,299	17,888	1,926	2,186	0.6
6500	Real estate	19	18	0.5	36	50	7,778	8,720	407	595	0.2
6510	Real estate operators and lessors	9	8	0.5	17	15	8,941	10,133	167	163	0.1
6530	Real estate agents and managers	3	4	0.2	10	11	7,200	8,364	82	119	0.1
6550	Subdividers and developers	6	5	1.2	9	7	6,222	8,000	84	85	0.2
6553	Cemetery subdividers and developers	6	5	2.0	9	7	6,222	8,000	84	85	0.8
CLARK, WI											
60 –	**Finance, insurance, and real estate**	61	60	0.5	339	325	17,758	19,003	5,661	5,807	0.1
6000	Depository institutions	24	23	1.0	249	240	19,518	20,567	4,369	4,510	0.5
6020	Commercial banks	19	18	1.4	227	216	19,947	21,093	4,004	4,117	0.6
6400	Insurance agents, brokers, and service	19	17	0.5	39	45	12,718	14,400	535	621	0.2
6500	Real estate	13	14	0.4	22	19	10,727	12,211	301	273	0.1
6530	Real estate agents and managers	5	6	0.3	11	9	10,909	12,000	155	139	0.1
6550	Subdividers and developers	3	3	0.7	2	3	4,000	2,667	8	8	0.0
6553	Cemetery subdividers and developers	3	3	1.2	2	3	4,000	2,667	8	8	0.1
COLUMBIA, WI											
60 –	**Finance, insurance, and real estate**	109	101	0.9	706	676	17,847	16,888	12,604	13,096	0.3
6000	Depository institutions	26	25	1.1	308	314	20,091	20,904	6,834	7,286	0.7
6020	Commercial banks	20	19	1.4	275	281	20,887	21,623	6,323	6,764	1.0
6030	Savings institutions	3	3	0.6	28	29	14,714	16,000	483	498	0.3
6060	Credit unions	3	3	0.6	5	4	6,400	6,000	28	24	0.0
6300	Insurance carriers	9	8	1.0	88	29	29,045	19,310	1,085	589	0.0
6400	Insurance agents, brokers, and service	29	27	0.8	69	65	13,391	14,523	1,092	1,057	0.3
6500	Real estate	38	34	0.9	219	245	9,991	10,237	2,894	3,312	0.9
6510	Real estate operators and lessors	11	10	0.6	35	49	6,743	7,918	305	410	0.4
6530	Real estate agents and managers	17	15	0.9	152	172	9,368	10,186	2,025	2,377	1.4
6550	Subdividers and developers	6	5	1.2	15	10	10,933	7,600	177	154	0.4
6553	Cemetery subdividers and developers	3	3	1.2	6	6	3,333	2,667	32	30	0.3
CRAWFORD, WI											
60 –	**Finance, insurance, and real estate**	30	31	0.3	140	146	17,743	18,219	2,643	2,860	0.1
6000	Depository institutions	7	7	0.3	101	105	18,812	19,162	1,984	2,150	0.2
6510	Real estate operators and lessors	3	3	0.2	3	2	4,000	4,000	12	11	0.0
DANE, WI											
60 –	**Finance, insurance, and real estate**	1,118	1,136	9.6	22,154	22,019	29,415	31,452	652,092	668,708	15.4
6000	Depository institutions	162	165	7.0	4,352	4,550	24,305	25,709	108,158	110,918	11.3
6020	Commercial banks	81	79	6.0	2,226	2,314	26,133	26,930	58,667	56,945	8.5
6030	Savings institutions	39	41	8.2	902	957	21,441	20,071	18,756	20,510	12.2
6100	Nondepository institutions	55	62	10.9	1,037	930	29,138	32,684	28,610	27,391	14.7
6140	Personal credit institutions	19	22	9.5	496	528	30,137	33,061	13,855	15,053	26.1
6160	Mortgage bankers and brokers	26	30	12.6	376	245	28,585	34,384	10,623	7,989	8.2
6200	Security and commodity brokers	70	72	11.3	510	565	71,678	74,450	34,823	37,690	10.5
6210	Security brokers and dealers	42	38	9.5	328	329	65,171	62,322	18,985	19,354	7.6

Source: County Business Patterns, 1994/95, CBP-94/95, U.S. Department of Commerce, Washington, D.C., November 1997. SIC categories for which data were suppressed or not available for both 1994 and 1995 are not displayed. The employment columns represent mid-March employment in the year. Pay per employee is calculated by dividing 1st Quarter payroll, annualized, by mid-March employment. The columns headed "% State" show the county's percentage of the state total for the SIC in 1995; for example, 1.4% for SIC 6000 means that the county had 1.4 percent of the state's total establishments (or payroll) in SIC 6000 in 1995. A dash (-) is used to indicate that data are not available or cannot be calculated; nec means not elsewhere classified.

Continued on next page.

SIC	Industry	No. Establishments			Employment		Pay / Employee		Annual Payroll ($ 000)		
		1994	1995	% State	1994	1995	1994	1995	1994	1995	% State
DANE, WI - [continued]											
6300	Insurance carriers	114	113	*14.7*	12,271	11,492	31,551	34,939	379,881	381,339	*19.9*
6310	Life insurance	32	30	*15.3*	3,782	3,781	41,541	45,497	138,944	145,771	*14.8*
6320	Medical service and health insurance	19	19	*19.4*	3,670	3,512	21,799	25,278	84,571	91,994	*31.7*
6321	Accident and health insurance	7	7	*24.1*	324	331	44,321	64,097	13,135	19,344	*16.7*
6324	Hospital and medical service plans	12	12	*17.6*	3,346	3,181	19,619	21,239	71,436	72,650	*41.7*
6330	Fire, marine, and casualty insurance	49	49	*12.4*	4,648	4,013	30,753	33,394	149,562	137,620	*23.7*
6400	Insurance agents, brokers, and service	262	263	*8.3*	1,119	1,165	27,800	28,223	32,736	35,053	*9.7*
6500	Real estate	421	428	*10.9*	2,646	3,045	19,855	18,915	59,146	66,865	*19.2*
6510	Real estate operators and lessors	172	186	*11.9*	862	1,059	14,738	16,427	16,234	22,777	*20.1*
6530	Real estate agents and managers	204	194	*11.3*	1,407	1,529	20,864	20,505	32,296	33,461	*19.2*
6540	Title abstract offices	7	7	*5.0*	205	156	24,839	22,077	4,373	3,481	*15.3*
6550	Subdividers and developers	27	30	*7.2*	156	293	29,590	18,157	5,220	6,766	*19.1*
6552	Subdividers and developers, n.e.c.	20	22	*14.1*	137	254	31,474	18,693	4,785	5,874	*25.2*
6553	Cemetery subdividers and developers	5	6	*2.4*	19	21	16,000	16,952	396	416	*3.7*
6710	Holding offices	10	10	*6.3*	48	44	64,667	59,727	3,010	1,959	*1.3*
6730	Trusts	10	9	*18.0*	21	27	15,048	15,852	392	485	*5.6*
6790	Miscellaneous investing	9	8	*10.4*	82	117	35,024	40,239	3,309	4,330	*34.6*
DODGE, WI											
60 –	**Finance, insurance, and real estate**	136	142	*1.2*	761	758	18,512	19,578	14,349	15,187	*0.3*
6000	Depository institutions	39	38	*1.6*	438	413	19,023	19,002	8,426	7,953	*0.8*
6020	Commercial banks	24	24	*1.8*	380	353	19,853	19,773	7,609	7,044	*1.1*
6030	Savings institutions	6	5	*1.0*	37	36	15,027	17,222	576	629	*0.4*
6060	Credit unions	9	9	*1.8*	21	24	11,048	10,333	241	280	*0.3*
6300	Insurance carriers	7	8	*1.0*	57	58	20,912	22,345	1,307	1,411	*0.1*
6400	Insurance agents, brokers, and service	42	42	*1.3*	128	123	17,406	19,512	2,272	2,483	*0.7*
6500	Real estate	38	40	*1.0*	90	99	9,867	9,455	1,081	1,090	*0.3*
6510	Real estate operators and lessors	12	14	*0.9*	35	40	6,971	7,500	321	365	*0.3*
6530	Real estate agents and managers	14	13	*0.8*	24	28	14,500	13,000	359	356	*0.2*
6550	Subdividers and developers	9	10	*2.4*	20	21	3,800	3,048	161	158	*0.4*
DOOR, WI											
60 –	**Finance, insurance, and real estate**	88	93	*0.8*	430	482	20,205	19,859	8,274	9,035	*0.2*
6000	Depository institutions	17	17	*0.7*	174	233	29,448	23,039	4,355	4,638	*0.5*
6200	Security and commodity brokers	5	5	*0.8*	17	21	44,471	58,476	747	1,067	*0.3*
6210	Security brokers and dealers	5	5	*1.2*	17	21	44,471	58,476	747	1,067	*0.4*
6400	Insurance agents, brokers, and service	17	16	*0.5*	74	44	15,730	24,273	1,130	1,062	*0.3*
6500	Real estate	46	52	*1.3*	161	171	9,391	9,614	1,848	2,073	*0.6*
6510	Real estate operators and lessors	9	9	*0.6*	28	28	8,429	7,571	251	248	*0.2*
6530	Real estate agents and managers	31	33	*1.9*	114	111	9,018	10,126	1,342	1,403	*0.8*
DOUGLAS, WI											
60 –	**Finance, insurance, and real estate**	85	78	*0.7*	481	467	18,578	22,758	9,040	10,220	*0.2*
6000	Depository institutions	22	18	*0.8*	288	294	18,972	19,592	5,460	5,774	*0.6*
6020	Commercial banks	8	7	*0.5*	183	178	21,115	21,640	3,673	3,851	*0.6*
6300	Insurance carriers	5	5	*0.7*	12	16	36,667	39,250	459	506	*0.0*
6400	Insurance agents, brokers, and service	21	19	*0.6*	85	77	20,988	39,948	1,766	2,708	*0.7*
6500	Real estate	33	33	*0.8*	86	71	12,558	14,085	1,207	1,088	*0.3*
6510	Real estate operators and lessors	14	14	*0.9*	21	23	10,095	12,522	259	298	*0.3*
6530	Real estate agents and managers	11	10	*0.6*	43	24	10,791	14,667	519	380	*0.2*
DUNN, WI											
60 –	**Finance, insurance, and real estate**	78	74	*0.6*	391	387	22,435	22,594	8,314	8,058	*0.2*
6000	Depository institutions	25	25	*1.1*	262	264	22,244	22,530	5,682	5,504	*0.6*

Source: County Business Patterns, 1994/95, CBP-94/95, U.S. Department of Commerce, Washington, D.C., November 1997. SIC categories for which data were suppressed or not available for both 1994 and 1995 are *not* displayed. The employment columns represent mid-March employment in the year. Pay per employee is calculated by dividing 1st Quarter payroll, annualized, by mid-March employment. The columns headed "% State" show the county's percentage of the state total for the SIC in 1995; for example, 1.4% for SIC 6000 means that the county had 1.4 percent of the state's total establishments (or payroll) in SIC 6000 in 1995. A dash (-) is used to indicate that data are not available or cannot be calculated; *nec* means not elsewhere classified.

Continued on next page.

SIC	Industry	No. Establishments 1994	1995	% State	Employment 1994	1995	Pay / Employee 1994	1995	Annual Payroll ($ 000) 1994	1995	% State

WALWORTH, WI - [continued]

SIC	Industry	1994	1995	% State	1994	1995	1994	1995	1994	1995	% State
6550	Subdividers and developers	10	14	3.3	25	34	20,480	34,000	596	1,124	3.2
6552	Subdividers and developers, n.e.c.	4	7	4.5	9	20	42,667	51,600	466	987	4.2
6553	Cemetery subdividers and developers	6	7	2.9	16	14	8,000	8,857	130	137	1.2

WASHBURN, WI

60 –	**Finance, insurance, and real estate**	39	43	0.4	228	204	18,877	15,569	3,652	3,427	0.1
6000	Depository institutions	8	7	0.3	141	104	19,489	17,962	2,159	1,999	0.2
6500	Real estate	23	29	0.7	59	72	12,407	11,111	897	859	0.2
6510	Real estate operators and lessors	5	5	0.3	7	7	4,571	5,714	43	40	0.0
6530	Real estate agents and managers	13	19	1.1	48	59	12,000	10,305	685	656	0.4

WASHINGTON, WI

60 –	**Finance, insurance, and real estate**	196	195	1.7	1,984	2,161	25,240	24,557	51,213	55,704	1.3
6000	Depository institutions	36	34	1.4	602	600	20,538	19,640	12,341	12,189	1.2
6020	Commercial banks	26	24	1.8	425	438	20,979	21,187	8,897	9,548	1.4
6200	Security and commodity brokers	9	10	1.6	296	306	45,324	36,261	10,059	10,062	2.8
6300	Insurance carriers	12	12	1.6	605	692	23,802	23,462	15,742	17,764	0.9
6400	Insurance agents, brokers, and service	63	61	1.9	219	226	20,676	23,841	4,828	6,051	1.7
6500	Real estate	66	67	1.7	198	228	20,444	22,263	5,721	6,192	1.8
6510	Real estate operators and lessors	26	23	1.5	101	122	24,950	28,164	3,612	4,167	3.7
6530	Real estate agents and managers	28	31	1.8	61	69	12,262	12,464	882	958	0.6

WAUKESHA, WI

60 –	**Finance, insurance, and real estate**	1,106	1,141	9.7	11,051	11,069	30,390	33,412	348,646	374,879	8.6
6000	Depository institutions	145	144	6.1	2,502	2,408	22,654	24,870	58,047	58,495	6.0
6020	Commercial banks	84	84	6.4	1,645	1,609	21,751	24,495	36,942	37,659	5.6
6030	Savings institutions	37	37	7.4	519	486	24,054	25,457	13,763	13,815	8.2
6100	Nondepository institutions	88	100	17.6	849	835	32,895	31,310	25,388	28,182	15.1
6140	Personal credit institutions	31	29	12.5	265	313	34,143	36,665	9,058	10,329	17.9
6150	Business credit institutions	14	16	28.1	101	99	31,802	36,566	3,290	3,844	23.2
6160	Mortgage bankers and brokers	43	54	22.7	483	422	32,439	26,161	13,040	13,996	14.3
6200	Security and commodity brokers	63	63	9.9	853	782	51,442	75,345	53,665	63,234	17.6
6210	Security brokers and dealers	38	37	9.2	384	335	40,656	49,672	14,900	19,744	7.8
6280	Security and commodity services	25	26	11.6	469	447	60,273	94,586	38,765	43,490	41.3
6300	Insurance carriers	107	115	15.0	3,413	3,390	32,992	36,112	111,866	119,211	6.2
6310	Life insurance	28	30	15.3	445	460	35,461	31,600	14,523	11,601	1.2
6320	Medical service and health insurance	15	14	14.3	570	765	30,625	32,737	18,161	25,674	8.9
6330	Fire, marine, and casualty insurance	50	54	13.7	2,179	1,947	32,909	38,291	72,949	73,908	12.7
6370	Pension, health, and welfare funds	7	8	17.4	52	65	35,154	32,800	2,072	2,547	14.0
6400	Insurance agents, brokers, and service	334	345	10.8	1,532	1,648	31,436	33,500	52,322	55,634	15.3
6500	Real estate	342	347	8.8	1,630	1,724	19,642	20,262	35,497	38,339	11.0
6510	Real estate operators and lessors	112	123	7.8	427	462	15,897	20,234	7,200	9,206	8.1
6530	Real estate agents and managers	189	180	10.5	924	951	21,017	19,937	21,104	21,281	12.2
6550	Subdividers and developers	32	29	6.9	164	202	21,732	24,673	5,288	5,871	16.5
6552	Subdividers and developers, n.e.c.	21	20	12.8	59	106	19,254	25,358	2,718	3,381	14.5
6553	Cemetery subdividers and developers	9	8	3.3	96	94	23,625	23,915	2,443	2,438	21.8
6730	Trusts	4	4	8.0	19	13	4,632	9,231	99	115	1.3
6733	Trusts, n.e.c.	4	4	11.8	19	13	4,632	9,231	99	115	1.6
6790	Miscellaneous investing	13	12	15.6	18	33	56,000	37,091	1,348	1,473	11.8

WAUPACA, WI

60 –	**Finance, insurance, and real estate**	122	116	1.0	657	658	21,364	22,182	14,551	14,490	0.3
6000	Depository institutions	28	26	1.1	386	365	19,472	21,523	7,805	7,766	0.8
6020	Commercial banks	20	19	1.4	320	305	19,563	21,744	6,684	6,738	1.0
6030	Savings institutions	4	4	0.8	34	37	25,294	24,541	748	756	0.4
6060	Credit unions	4	3	0.6	32	23	12,375	13,739	373	272	0.3
6300	Insurance carriers	5	5	0.7	62	63	42,645	41,651	2,492	2,484	0.1
6400	Insurance agents, brokers, and service	38	36	1.1	98	104	21,469	20,538	2,076	2,122	0.6

Source: County Business Patterns, 1994/95, CBP-94/95, U.S. Department of Commerce, Washington, D.C., November 1997. SIC categories for which data were suppressed or not available for both 1994 and 1995 are not displayed. The employment columns represent mid-March employment in the year. Pay per employee is calculated by dividing 1st Quarter payroll, annualized, by mid-March employment. The columns headed "% State" show the county's percentage of the state total for the SIC in 1995; for example, 1.4% for SIC 6000 means that the county had 1.4 percent of the state's total establishments (or payroll) in SIC 6000 in 1995. A dash (-) is used to indicate that data are not available or cannot be calculated; nec means not elsewhere classified.

Continued on next page.

SIC	Industry	No. Establishments			Employment		Pay / Employee		Annual Payroll ($ 000)		
		1994	1995	% State	1994	1995	1994	1995	1994	1995	% State
WAUPACA, WI - [continued]											
6500	Real estate	44	42	1.1	89	104	12,674	11,808	1,579	1,487	0.4
6530	Real estate agents and managers	15	14	0.8	55	63	11,491	11,175	953	952	0.5
6552	Subdividers and developers, n.e.c.	4	4	2.6	2	2	6,000	30,000	63	50	0.2
WAUSHARA, WI											
60 –	**Finance, insurance, and real estate**	39	40	0.3	206	183	14,369	18,885	3,120	3,217	0.1
6000	Depository institutions	8	9	0.4	114	97	14,491	20,289	1,656	1,863	0.2
6020	Commercial banks	8	9	0.7	114	97	14,491	20,289	1,656	1,863	0.3
6500	Real estate	19	18	0.5	59	51	10,508	14,275	772	668	0.2
6530	Real estate agents and managers	6	6	0.3	10	13	8,800	10,769	122	143	0.1
WINNEBAGO, WI											
60 –	**Finance, insurance, and real estate**	338	347	2.9	3,369	3,484	24,289	23,695	76,318	81,345	1.9
6000	Depository institutions	80	79	3.3	1,372	1,455	20,155	21,872	28,915	30,129	3.1
6020	Commercial banks	31	28	2.1	834	845	22,201	24,360	18,911	18,590	2.8
6030	Savings institutions	16	17	3.4	189	202	17,376	17,327	4,001	4,479	2.7
6060	Credit unions	33	34	6.9	349	408	16,768	18,971	6,003	7,060	8.0
6100	Nondepository institutions	14	17	3.0	82	88	27,610	27,045	2,230	2,626	1.4
6140	Personal credit institutions	8	9	3.9	48	56	23,000	25,500	1,290	1,530	2.7
6160	Mortgage bankers and brokers	6	8	3.4	34	32	34,118	29,750	940	1,096	1.1
6200	Security and commodity brokers	18	22	3.4	74	96	47,189	35,458	2,794	3,226	0.9
6210	Security brokers and dealers	10	13	3.2	53	69	60,604	42,493	2,470	2,753	1.1
6280	Security and commodity services	8	9	4.0	21	27	13,333	17,481	324	473	0.4
6300	Insurance carriers	22	23	3.0	784	771	39,031	32,607	23,114	24,111	1.3
6330	Fire, marine, and casualty insurance	14	15	3.8	548	564	40,445	29,234	15,903	16,199	2.8
6400	Insurance agents, brokers, and service	78	74	2.3	335	328	19,976	23,427	6,844	7,803	2.2
6500	Real estate	113	118	3.0	629	644	12,375	13,025	8,936	9,638	2.8
6510	Real estate operators and lessors	47	50	3.2	242	252	10,579	11,698	2,840	3,274	2.9
6530	Real estate agents and managers	53	49	2.9	314	289	13,057	14,616	4,859	4,640	2.7
6550	Subdividers and developers	8	13	3.1	63	81	13,841	10,667	853	1,162	3.3
6552	Subdividers and developers, n.e.c.	4	7	4.5	22	31	32,727	20,645	650	683	2.9
6700	Holding and other investment offices	13	14	4.5	93	102	35,957	36,588	3,485	3,812	2.2
6710	Holding offices	5	5	3.2	77	85	39,377	40,329	3,205	3,452	2.3
WOOD, WI											
60 –	**Finance, insurance, and real estate**	168	169	1.4	965	960	20,298	22,200	19,447	20,729	0.5
6000	Depository institutions	48	50	2.1	644	642	19,839	21,259	12,361	13,187	1.3
6020	Commercial banks	24	24	1.8	396	381	21,040	21,995	7,596	7,913	1.2
6060	Credit unions	15	16	3.3	151	163	14,437	15,730	2,548	2,765	3.1
6200	Security and commodity brokers	8	7	1.1	22	17	41,636	51,529	954	893	0.2
6330	Fire, marine, and casualty insurance	6	6	1.5	14	15	37,714	41,600	544	593	0.1
6400	Insurance agents, brokers, and service	42	39	1.2	141	141	18,638	23,177	2,934	3,218	0.9
6500	Real estate	57	58	1.5	116	117	11,966	11,795	1,541	1,603	0.5
6510	Real estate operators and lessors	27	28	1.8	41	42	10,049	9,524	436	463	0.4
6530	Real estate agents and managers	21	20	1.2	47	46	9,532	10,348	519	530	0.3
6540	Title abstract offices	4	4	2.9	18	18	24,444	22,889	444	454	2.0
6550	Subdividers and developers	5	4	1.0	10	9	8,800	7,556	142	104	0.3

Source: County Business Patterns, 1994/95, CBP-94/95, U.S. Department of Commerce, Washington, D.C., November 1997. SIC categories for which data were suppressed or not available for both 1994 and 1995 are *not* displayed. The employment columns represent mid-March employment in the year. Pay per employee is calculated by dividing 1st Quarter payroll, annualized, by mid-March employment. The columns headed "% State" show the county's percentage of the state total for the SIC in 1995; for example, 1.4% for SIC 6000 means that the county had 1.4 percent of the state's total establishments (or payroll) in SIC 6000 in 1995. A dash (-) is used to indicate that data are not available or cannot be calculated; *nec* means not elsewhere classified.

WYOMING

SIC	Industry	No. Establishments			Employment		Pay / Employee		Annual Payroll ($ 000)		
		1994	1995	% State	1994	1995	1994	1995	1994	1995	% State
ALBANY, WY											
60 –	**Finance, insurance, and real estate**	76	68	5.2	417	379	21,055	24,190	8,701	8,700	5.2
6000	Depository institutions	10	10	5.3	159	155	21,283	25,213	3,614	3,710	5.3
6020	Commercial banks	5	5	4.4	105	102	21,371	24,863	2,486	2,518	4.4
6200	Security and commodity brokers	5	5	6.8	8	8	45,000	40,000	341	289	1.8
6500	Real estate	34	31	5.3	65	69	8,862	9,159	693	767	3.1
6510	Real estate operators and lessors	15	15	5.4	34	35	7,176	6,857	276	302	3.0
6530	Real estate agents and managers	18	15	6.1	31	30	10,710	11,867	408	427	3.8
BIG HORN, WY											
60 –	**Finance, insurance, and real estate**	15	17	1.3	86	88	25,488	23,182	1,805	1,685	1.0
6000	Depository institutions	5	5	2.7	65	67	28,615	26,627	1,496	1,405	2.0
6500	Real estate	5	6	1.0	7	6	4,000	4,667	32	35	0.1
CAMPBELL, WY											
60 –	**Finance, insurance, and real estate**	71	69	5.2	417	435	20,556	20,920	8,443	9,273	5.5
6000	Depository institutions	9	8	4.3	154	164	24,779	25,146	3,747	3,976	5.6
6100	Nondepository institutions	3	3	6.3	36	33	43,333	38,182	1,081	1,211	-
6400	Insurance agents, brokers, and service	14	13	4.3	54	44	17,704	21,818	1,019	1,090	-
6500	Real estate	36	37	6.3	146	149	10,548	12,832	1,810	2,148	8.8
6530	Real estate agents and managers	20	19	7.8	92	93	9,348	11,613	987	1,235	11.0
CARBON, WY											
60 –	**Finance, insurance, and real estate**	34	33	2.5	167	225	18,251	14,738	3,079	3,241	1.9
6000	Depository institutions	7	7	3.7	102	151	20,941	15,735	2,205	2,227	3.2
6400	Insurance agents, brokers, and service	8	8	2.6	25	30	16,640	14,400	305	465	-
6500	Real estate	16	15	2.6	30	33	8,400	8,000	284	283	1.2
6510	Real estate operators and lessors	7	7	2.5	15	19	10,667	8,842	177	163	1.6
CONVERSE, WY											
60 –	**Finance, insurance, and real estate**	27	26	2.0	126	108	18,952	24,519	2,416	2,496	1.5
6500	Real estate	10	10	1.7	33	33	12,485	13,939	434	530	2.2
CROOK, WY											
60 –	**Finance, insurance, and real estate**	7	8	0.6	37	42	20,541	19,429	827	871	0.5
FREMONT, WY											
60 –	**Finance, insurance, and real estate**	81	84	6.4	479	449	15,658	16,909	7,852	7,836	4.7
6000	Depository institutions	12	12	6.4	151	148	19,629	22,351	3,267	3,410	4.8
6020	Commercial banks	6	6	5.3	116	111	19,759	21,514	2,561	2,625	4.6
6400	Insurance agents, brokers, and service	24	24	7.9	75	68	11,573	15,000	953	1,049	-
6500	Real estate	34	35	6.0	131	114	14,290	13,298	1,960	1,663	6.8
6510	Real estate operators and lessors	17	17	6.1	108	83	14,704	13,928	1,590	1,309	13.2
GOSHEN, WY											
60 –	**Finance, insurance, and real estate**	30	29	2.2	109	107	19,229	23,178	2,163	2,361	1.4
6000	Depository institutions	5	5	2.7	67	66	20,836	24,545	1,491	1,613	2.3
6400	Insurance agents, brokers, and service	11	11	3.6	20	19	13,000	16,000	256	291	-
6500	Real estate	10	9	1.5	12	11	8,000	8,727	93	104	0.4
JOHNSON, WY											
60 –	**Finance, insurance, and real estate**	24	22	1.7	94	93	24,340	22,667	2,149	2,095	1.2

Source: County Business Patterns, 1994/95, CBP-94/95, U.S. Department of Commerce, Washington, D.C., November 1997. SIC categories for which data were suppressed or not available for both 1994 and 1995 are *not* displayed. The employment columns represent mid-March employment in the year. Pay per employee is calculated by dividing 1st Quarter payroll, annualized, by mid-March employment. The columns headed "% State" show the county's percentage of the state total for the SIC in 1995; for example, 1.4% for SIC 6000 means that the county had 1.4 percent of the state's total establishments (or payroll) in SIC 6000 in 1995. A dash (-) is used to indicate that data are not available or cannot be calculated; *nec* means not elsewhere classified.

Continued on next page.

SIC	Industry	No. Establishments			Employment		Pay / Employee		Annual Payroll ($ 000)		
		1994	1995	% State	1994	1995	1994	1995	1994	1995	% State
JOHNSON, WY - [continued]											
6000	Depository institutions	4	4	2.1	67	67	23,463	22,687	1,535	1,533	2.2
6500	Real estate	13	11	1.9	10	12	10,000	9,000	140	164	0.7
6530	Real estate agents and managers	7	5	2.0	4	6	13,000	9,333	79	74	0.7
LARAMIE, WY											
60 –	**Finance, insurance, and real estate**	219	213	16.2	1,973	1,527	24,087	25,818	49,690	38,677	23.0
6000	Depository institutions	38	35	18.6	846	573	24,586	26,681	24,568	14,231	20.1
6020	Commercial banks	18	18	15.9	466	364	24,343	28,000	15,005	9,683	16.9
6100	Nondepository institutions	13	14	29.2	134	102	30,209	28,588	3,772	2,936	-
6300	Insurance carriers	16	15	20.5	388	355	24,918	29,375	10,428	10,173	53.0
6310	Life insurance	6	5	41.7	160	131	31,125	32,397	4,921	4,179	84.4
6400	Insurance agents, brokers, and service	56	52	17.2	309	184	21,683	25,674	4,840	4,461	-
6500	Real estate	72	69	11.8	205	223	13,405	14,278	3,213	4,067	16.6
6510	Real estate operators and lessors	33	31	11.1	89	82	10,472	12,829	1,066	1,507	15.2
6530	Real estate agents and managers	33	33	13.5	103	130	16,194	15,785	2,037	2,469	22.0
LINCOLN, WY											
60 –	**Finance, insurance, and real estate**	21	25	1.9	99	98	17,576	18,816	1,904	2,027	1.2
6000	Depository institutions	4	4	2.1	57	60	18,035	18,733	1,187	1,243	1.8
6020	Commercial banks	4	4	3.5	57	60	18,035	18,733	1,187	1,243	2.2
6500	Real estate	6	8	1.4	11	10	9,091	11,200	123	187	0.8
NATRONA, WY											
60 –	**Finance, insurance, and real estate**	201	208	15.8	1,144	1,133	28,385	29,352	29,641	30,365	18.0
6000	Depository institutions	22	23	12.2	404	370	24,505	25,092	9,700	8,736	12.4
6020	Commercial banks	12	12	10.6	355	307	25,206	26,098	8,693	7,531	13.1
6100	Nondepository institutions	8	10	20.8	111	108	41,622	39,407	3,444	3,804	-
6200	Security and commodity brokers	16	16	21.6	102	88	50,549	54,364	4,482	4,337	26.9
6300	Insurance carriers	17	20	27.4	104	123	29,385	33,593	2,672	3,370	17.6
6400	Insurance agents, brokers, and service	51	54	17.9	165	182	24,897	26,066	4,420	4,861	-
6500	Real estate	80	79	13.5	234	236	13,299	15,424	3,546	3,848	15.7
6510	Real estate operators and lessors	33	32	11.4	117	119	11,897	13,513	1,549	1,768	17.8
6530	Real estate agents and managers	39	40	16.3	98	96	13,918	15,292	1,469	1,475	13.1
6540	Title abstract offices	4	3	33.3	12	11	19,667	21,455	418	423	45.0
6700	Holding and other investment offices	7	6	12.2	24	26	105,000	92,923	1,377	1,409	-
NIOBRARA, WY											
60 –	**Finance, insurance, and real estate**	6	7	0.5	-	-	-	-	-	-	-
PARK, WY											
60 –	**Finance, insurance, and real estate**	62	68	5.2	323	325	20,248	21,366	6,848	7,406	4.4
6000	Depository institutions	15	16	8.5	214	216	20,187	21,833	4,482	4,962	7.0
6020	Commercial banks	7	7	6.2	171	172	21,380	23,233	3,849	4,326	7.5
6400	Insurance agents, brokers, and service	15	15	5.0	50	49	15,520	15,755	827	757	-
6500	Real estate	24	29	5.0	35	41	12,000	14,927	571	834	3.4
6530	Real estate agents and managers	11	14	5.7	20	19	10,600	13,053	244	285	2.5
PLATTE, WY											
60 –	**Finance, insurance, and real estate**	17	17	1.3	72	73	19,056	19,452	1,329	1,408	0.8
6000	Depository institutions	5	5	2.7	53	55	19,698	20,582	981	1,062	1.5
SHERIDAN, WY											
60 –	**Finance, insurance, and real estate**	136	138	10.5	570	523	22,905	22,822	11,748	14,274	8.5
6000	Depository institutions	12	11	5.9	202	183	29,109	26,710	5,431	4,539	6.4
6020	Commercial banks	6	5	4.4	158	135	29,696	26,726	4,123	3,167	5.5
6300	Insurance carriers	5	4	5.5	43	5	18,512	39,200	328	181	0.9
6400	Insurance agents, brokers, and service	15	15	5.0	75	85	21,120	18,824	1,539	1,804	-

Source: County Business Patterns, 1994/95, CBP-94/95, U.S. Department of Commerce, Washington, D.C., November 1997. SIC categories for which data were suppressed or not available for both 1994 and 1995 are not displayed. The employment columns represent mid-March employment in the year. Pay per employee is calculated by dividing 1st Quarter payroll, annualized, by mid-March employment. The columns headed "% State" show the county's percentage of the state total for the SIC in 1995; for example, 1.4% for SIC 6000 means that the county had 1.4 percent of the state's total establishments (or payroll) in SIC 6000 in 1995. A dash (-) is used to indicate that data are not available or cannot be calculated; nec means not elsewhere classified.

Continued on next page.

SIC	Industry	No. Establishments			Employment		Pay / Employee		Annual Payroll ($ 000)		
		1994	1995	% State	1994	1995	1994	1995	1994	1995	% State
SHERIDAN, WY - [continued]											
6500	Real estate	91	93	15.9	213	208	8,000	8,500	1,848	1,840	7.5
6510	Real estate operators and lessors	73	73	26.1	149	143	5,530	4,923	850	776	7.8
6530	Real estate agents and managers	14	15	6.1	48	43	14,750	17,116	787	735	6.5
SUBLETTE, WY											
60 –	**Finance, insurance, and real estate**	12	13	1.0	50	63	14,640	14,540	1,014	1,317	0.8
6500	Real estate	6	8	1.4	9	15	6,667	9,867	292	424	1.7
SWEETWATER, WY											
60 –	**Finance, insurance, and real estate**	103	95	7.2	537	475	20,142	20,387	10,221	9,740	5.8
6000	Depository institutions	15	13	6.9	224	209	24,179	27,349	5,953	5,702	8.1
6020	Commercial banks	8	6	5.3	181	164	24,398	26,854	4,935	4,553	7.9
6200	Security and commodity brokers	8	7	9.5	12	11	22,667	45,455	295	322	2.0
6300	Insurance carriers	4	3	4.1	13	10	31,385	35,200	373	373	1.9
6400	Insurance agents, brokers, and service	26	23	7.6	117	60	22,120	16,933	1,438	1,097	-
6500	Real estate	46	44	7.5	161	170	11,826	10,518	1,963	1,923	7.9
6510	Real estate operators and lessors	24	24	8.6	100	104	13,400	11,500	1,363	1,304	13.1
6530	Real estate agents and managers	14	12	4.9	30	33	8,133	7,758	247	275	2.5
6550	Subdividers and developers	5	5	17.2	19	22	9,684	10,000	216	220	13.8
6552	Subdividers and developers, n.e.c.	5	5	21.7	19	22	9,684	10,000	216	220	14.2
TETON, WY											
60 –	**Finance, insurance, and real estate**	97	100	7.6	640	481	22,200	30,902	13,656	16,292	9.7
6000	Depository institutions	4	4	2.1	139	131	24,691	29,221	3,379	3,494	4.9
6020	Commercial banks	4	4	3.5	139	131	24,691	29,221	3,379	3,494	6.1
6500	Real estate	63	63	10.8	415	249	13,677	18,137	5,071	4,821	19.7
6510	Real estate operators and lessors	18	19	6.8	31	37	16,000	17,946	585	692	7.0
6530	Real estate agents and managers	33	33	13.5	182	187	15,780	16,364	3,007	3,075	27.4
6550	Subdividers and developers	8	6	20.7	192	12	11,083	45,000	1,246	607	38.1
6552	Subdividers and developers, n.e.c.	8	6	26.1	192	12	11,083	45,000	1,246	607	39.3
6700	Holding and other investment offices	6	7	14.3	11	18	40,364	32,444	429	568	-
UINTA, WY											
60 –	**Finance, insurance, and real estate**	35	36	2.7	137	137	17,664	21,255	2,832	3,154	1.9
6000	Depository institutions	8	7	3.7	81	79	19,457	24,506	1,875	2,143	3.0
6400	Insurance agents, brokers, and service	9	9	3.0	20	19	12,800	18,105	284	312	-
WASHAKIE, WY											
60 –	**Finance, insurance, and real estate**	21	21	1.6	112	114	22,286	22,561	2,429	2,404	1.4
6000	Depository institutions	5	5	2.7	69	72	23,130	23,000	1,584	1,515	2.1
6400	Insurance agents, brokers, and service	7	7	2.3	20	23	18,800	18,957	388	434	-
6500	Real estate	6	5	0.9	13	10	12,923	12,000	159	133	0.5
WESTON, WY											
60 –	**Finance, insurance, and real estate**	12	12	0.9	77	77	20,260	20,831	1,310	1,389	0.8
6000	Depository institutions	3	3	1.6	59	61	23,254	23,934	1,119	1,232	1.7
6020	Commercial banks	3	3	2.7	59	61	23,254	23,934	1,119	1,232	2.1
6500	Real estate	3	3	0.5	7	5	4,000	7,200	35	30	0.1

Source: County Business Patterns, 1994/95, CBP-94/95, U.S. Department of Commerce, Washington, D.C., November 1997. SIC categories for which data were suppressed or not available for both 1994 and 1995 are not displayed. The employment columns represent mid-March employment in the year. Pay per employee is calculated by dividing 1st Quarter payroll, annualized, by mid-March employment. The columns headed "% State" show the county's percentage of the state total for the SIC in 1995; for example, 1.4% for SIC 6000 means that the county had 1.4 percent of the state's total establishments (or payroll) in SIC 6000 in 1995. A dash (-) is used to indicate that data are not available or cannot be calculated; nec means not elsewhere classified.

SIC INDEX

The SIC Index shows all 4-digit SICs covered in *Finance, Insurance, and Real Estate U.S.A.* in numerical order. A separate section, listing the industries in alphabetical order, follows. Indented names indicate 4-digit SIC categories for which company names are listed separately but for which no other detailed information is provided. In the alphabetical section, each industry name is followed by the SIC number (in parentheses) and then by one or more page numbers. This SIC structure is based on the 1987 definitions published in *Standard Industrial Classification Manual*, 1987, Office of Management and Budget. The abbreviation 'nec' stands for 'not elsewhere classified'.

KEYWORD INDEX

The Keyword Index holds the names of industries, activities, and services that are part of the Finance, Insurance, and Real Estate industries of the U.S. Also included are names of government agencies and institutions. Each keyword is followed by one or more page numbers; these pages refer to the first page of the industry; one or more SIC categories follow in brackets.

Keyword Index

COMPANY INDEX

This index shows, in alphabetical order, more than 2,900 companies in *Finance, Insurance, and Real Estate U.S.A*. Organizations may be public or private companies, subsidiaries or divisions of companies, joint ventures or affiliates, or corporate groups. Each company entry is followed by one or more page numbers. After the page numbers, the SICs under which the company is listed follow in brackets preceded by "SIC" or "SICs". Some company names are abbreviated.

American Bonding Co., p. 259 [SIC 6351]

American Clearing House Association, p. 91 [SIC 6099]

American Credit Indemnity Co., p. 258 [SIC 6351]

American Credit Services Inc., p. 112 [SIC 6141]

American Electric Power Company Inc., p. 384 [SIC 6719]

American Electronic Association Credit Union, p. 61 [SIC 6062]

American Equipment Leasing Company Inc., pp. 126, 324 [SICs 6159, 6519]

American Excess Insurance Association, p. 259 [SIC 6351]

American Express Co., pp. 79, 123, 151 [SICs 6082, 6153, 6211]

American Express Credit Corp., p. 123 [SIC 6153]

American Express Financial Advisors Inc., pp. 151, 184 [SICs 6211, 6282]

American Family Life Assurance Co., p. 198 [SIC 6311]

American Fidelity Group, pp. 221, 359 [SICs 6321, 6552]

American Financial Corp., pp. 198, 245, 385 [SICs 6311, 6331, 6719]

American General Corp., pp. 111, 197, 245 [SICs 6141, 6311, 6331]

American General Finance Corp., p. 111 [SIC 6141]

American General Finance Inc., p. 385 [SIC 6719]

American General Life and Accident Insurance Co., pp. 198, 219 [SICs 6311, 6321]

American General Life Insurance Co., p. 199 [SIC 6311]

American Health and Life Insurance Co., p. 222 [SIC 6321]

American Health Properties Inc., p. 441 [SIC 6798]

American Heritage Life Insurance Co., p. 220 [SIC 6321]

American Home Funding Inc., p. 112 [SIC 6141]

American Income Life Insurance Co., p. 222 [SIC 6321]

American International Group Inc., pp. 197, 245, 383 [SICs 6311, 6331, 6719]

American International Specialty Lines Insurance Co., p. 258 [SIC 6351]

American Life Holding Co., p. 199 [SIC 6311]

American Life Resources Group Inc., p. 114 [SIC 6141]

American Manufacturers Mutual Insurance Co., p. 246 [SIC 6331]

American Medical Security Inc., p. 305 [SIC 6411]

American Mutual Holding Co., p. 200 [SIC 6311]

American Mutual Share Insurance Corp., p. 295 [SIC 6399]

American National Bank and Trust Company of Chicago, p. 21 [SIC 6021]

American National Insurance Co., pp. 199, 219, 246 [SICs 6311, 6321, 6331]

American Re-Insurance Co., p. 246 [SIC 6331]

American Real Estate Partners L.P., p. 335 [SIC 6531]

American Republic Insurance Co., p. 222 [SIC 6321]

American Residential Holding Corp., p. 139 [SIC 6162]

American River Federal Credit Union, p. 60 [SIC 6061]

American Savings Bank, p. 45 [SIC 6036]

American Savings Bank F.S.B., p. 43 [SIC 6035]

American Savings of Florida F.S.B., p. 43 [SIC 6035]

American Securities Transfer Inc., p. 188 [SIC 6289]

American Southern Insurance Co., p. 307 [SIC 6411]

American Southwest Financial Corp., p. 154 [SIC 6211]

American Speedy Printing Centers Inc., p. 430 [SIC 6794]

American States Financial Corp., p. 245 [SIC 6331]

American Stock Exchange Inc., p. 173 [SIC 6231]

American Stock Transfer and Trust Co., pp. 89, 187 [SICs 6091, 6289]

American Stores Co., p. 384 [SIC 6719]

American Title Co., p. 349 [SIC 6541]

American Travellers Corp., p. 221 [SIC 6321]

America's Favorite Chicken Co., p. 428 [SIC 6794]

AmeriCredit Corp., p. 112 [SIC 6141]

Amerin Guaranty Corp., p. 258 [SIC 6351]

Amerinst Insurance Group Inc., p. 259 [SIC 6351]

Ameritech Corp., p. 384 [SIC 6719]

Ameritech Credit Corp., p. 127 [SIC 6159]

AMGRO Inc., pp. 114, 124 [SICs 6141, 6153]

Amica Mutual Insurance Co., p. 247 [SIC 6331]

Amli Residential Properties L.P., p. 336 [SIC 6531]

Amli Residential Properties Trust, p. 443 [SIC 6798]

Amoco Corp., p. 383 [SIC 6719]

Ampal-American Israel Corp., pp. 127, 140 [SICs 6159, 6162]

Ampersand Ventures, p. 453 [SIC 6799]

AMR Corp., p. 384 [SIC 6719]

AMREP Corp., p. 361 [SIC 6552]

AMRESCO Inc., p. 185 [SIC 6282]

AmSouth Bancorp., pp. 20, 381 [SICs 6021, 6712]

AmSouth Bank of Alabama, p. 24 [SIC 6022]

AmSouth Bank of Florida, p. 24 [SIC 6022]

AmSouth Mortgage Co., p. 139 [SIC 6162]

AmTrust Value Fund, p. 394 [SIC 6722]

Amwest Insurance Group Inc., p. 258 [SIC 6351]

Anchor BanCorp Wisconsin Inc., p. 44 [SIC 6036]

Anchor National Life Insurance Co., p. 198 [SIC 6311]

Andover Bancorp Inc., p. 45 [SIC 6036]

Andover Bank, p. 45 [SIC 6036]

Anheuser-Busch Employees Credit Union, p. 61 [SIC 6062]

Anthem Insurance Companies Inc., pp. 246, 305 [SICs 6331, 6411]

Aon Corp., pp. 198, 219 [SICs 6311, 6321]

Aon Group Inc., pp. 305, 384 [SICs 6411, 6719]

AON Re Inc., p. 306 [SIC 6411]

Aon Specialty Group Inc., pp. 258, 306 [SICs 6351, 6411]

Apex Investment Partners, p. 453 [SIC 6799]

Apple South Inc., p. 429 [SIC 6794]

Applebee's International Inc., p. 429 [SIC 6794]

Arbor National Mortgage Inc., p. 140 [SIC 6162]

Arby's Inc., p. 430 [SIC 6794]

Arena Associates Inc., p. 318 [SIC 6512]

Argonaut Group Inc., p. 247 [SIC 6331]

Argonaut Insurance Co., p. 247 [SIC 6331]

Aristar Inc., p. 112 [SIC 6141]

Arizona Central Credit Union, p. 62 [SIC 6062]

Arizona Federal Credit Union, p. 58 [SIC 6061]

Gallatin Mortgage Co., p. 141 [SIC 6163]

Game Financial Corp., p. 91 [SIC 6099]

Gannett Fleming Affiliates Inc., p. 317 [SIC 6512]

Gardner Inc., p. 319 [SIC 6512]

Gasco Credit Union, p. 61 [SIC 6062]

Gates Credit Union, p. 63 [SIC 6062]

Gateway Bank, p. 45 [SIC 6036]

Gateway Title Co., p. 269 [SIC 6361]

GATX Capital Corp., p. 126 [SIC 6159]

Gay and Taylor Inc., p. 306 [SIC 6411]

GE Capital Mortgage Services Inc., p. 257 [SIC 6351]

Geldermann Inc., p. 163 [SIC 6221]

GEMISYS Corp., p. 89 [SIC 6091]

Gencare Health Systems Inc., p. 235 [SIC 6324]

Gene B. Glick Company Inc., pp. 321, 322, 335 [SICs 6513, 6514, 6531]

Genelco Inc., p. 307 [SIC 6411]

General Acceptance Corp., p. 113 [SIC 6141]

General Accident Insurance Company of America, p. 247 [SIC 6331]

General Cocoa Company Inc., p. 163 [SIC 6221]

General Credit Corp., p. 91 [SIC 6099]

General Electric Capital Corp., pp. 111, 123, 125, 257 [SICs 6141, 6153, 6159, 6351]

General Electric Capital Mortgage Services Inc., p. 138 [SIC 6162]

General Electric Capital Services Inc., pp. 151, 245, 383 [SICs 6211, 6331, 6719]

General Electric Mortgage Insurance Corp., p. 257 [SIC 6351]

General Growth Properties Inc., p. 359 [SIC 6552]

General Motors Acceptance Corp., pp. 111, 137, 245 [SICs 6141, 6162, 6331]

General Motors Corp., p. 125 [SIC 6159]

General Nutrition Companies Inc., p. 429 [SIC 6794]

General Re Corp., pp. 245, 383 [SICs 6331, 6719]

General Star Management Co., p. 295 [SIC 6399]

Genevieve Holdings of Arizona Ltd., p. 124 [SIC 6153]

GENEX Services Inc., p. 306 [SIC 6411]

GenFed Federal Credit Union, p. 59 [SIC 6061]

George Mason Bankshares Inc., p. 138 [SIC 6162]

Georgeson and Company Inc., p. 187 [SIC 6289]

Georgia Federal Credit Union, p. 59 [SIC 6061]

Gerald Metals Inc., p. 163 [SIC 6221]

Gertrude Gardner Inc., p. 323 [SIC 6514]

Getty Realty Corp., p. 324 [SIC 6519]

GFS International Inc., p. 334 [SIC 6531]

Gibraltar Trade Center Inc., p. 319 [SIC 6512]

Gillco Inc., p. 127 [SIC 6159]

GK Capital Management Inc., p. 164 [SIC 6221]

Glenborough Realty Trust Inc., p. 441 [SIC 6798]

Glendale Federal Bank F.S.B., p. 41 [SIC 6035]

Glenwood Investment Corp., p. 89 [SIC 6091]

Glimcher Realty Trust, p. 440 [SIC 6798]

Global Assurance L.L.C., p. 124 [SIC 6153]

Globe Life and Accident Insurance Co., p. 222 [SIC 6321]

GNI Inc., p. 270 [SIC 6361]

Gold Company of America, p. 395 [SIC 6726]

Golden 1 Credit Union, p. 61 [SIC 6062]

Golden Bay Federal Credit Union, p. 59 [SIC 6061]

Golden Rule Financial Corp., p. 221 [SIC 6321]

Golden Triangle Industries Inc., p. 420 [SIC 6792]

Golden West Financial Corp., pp. 41, 380 [SICs 6035, 6712]

Golder, Thoma, Cressey, Rauner Inc., p. 452 [SIC 6799]

Goldman Sachs and Co., p. 151 [SIC 6211]

Golodetz Trading Corp., pp. 126, 184 [SICs 6159, 6282]

Good Health Plan of Washington, p. 235 [SIC 6324]

Goodale and Barbieri Cos., pp. 318, 321 [SICs 6512, 6513]

Gould Investors L.P., p. 411 [SIC 6733]

Government Employees Credit Union, p. 59 [SIC 6061]

Government Employees Insurance Co., p. 246 [SIC 6331]

Government National Mortgage Association, p. 101 [SIC 6111]

Government Securities Clearing Corp., p. 187 [SIC 6289]

Granite Financial Inc., p. 128 [SIC 6159]

Granite State Credit Union, p. 61 [SIC 6062]

Great American Insurance Co., p. 247 [SIC 6331]

Great Financial Corp., p. 43 [SIC 6035]

Great Lakes Bancorp, A Federal Savings Bank, p. 43 [SIC 6035]

Great Lakes Higher Education Corp., p. 101 [SIC 6111]

Great Northern Insured Annuity Corp., p. 305 [SIC 6411]

Great Northern Iron Ore Properties, p. 324 [SIC 6519]

Great Northwest Management Company Inc., pp. 321, 322 [SICs 6513, 6514]

Great Southern Bancorp Inc., pp. 46, 139 [SICs 6036, 6162]

Great-West Life and Annuity Insurance Co., p. 198 [SIC 6311]

Great-West Life Assurance Co., p. 219 [SIC 6321]

Great Western Bank F.S.B., p. 41 [SIC 6035]

Great Western Financial Corp., pp. 41, 111, 137, 380 [SICs 6035, 6141, 6162, 6712]

Great Western Life Insurance Co., p. 306 [SIC 6411]

Greater Cleveland Fire Fighters Credit Union Inc., p. 63 [SIC 6062]

Greater Detroit BIDCO Inc., p. 124 [SIC 6153]

Greater Texas Federal Credit Union, p. 59 [SIC 6061]

Green Tree Financial Corp., p. 137 [SIC 6162]

GreenPoint Financial Corp., pp. 44, 381 [SICs 6036, 6712]

Greenspring Fund Inc., p. 395 [SIC 6726]

Greenwich Capital Markets Inc., p. 153 [SIC 6211]

Greenwood Trust Co., p. 24 [SIC 6022]

Greylock Management Corp., p. 454 [SIC 6799]

Grotech Capital Group Inc., p. 453 [SIC 6799]

Ground Round Inc., p. 430 [SIC 6794]

Group Council Mutual Insurance Co., p. 308 [SIC 6411]

Group Financial Partners Inc., p. 317 [SIC 6512]

Group Health Cooperative of Puget Sound, p. 233 [SIC 6324]

Group Health Credit Union, p. 62 [SIC 6062]

Company Index

Landvest Title Associates Inc., p. 270 [SIC 6361]
LaSalle Bank F.S.B., p. 42 [SIC 6035]
LaSalle National Bank, p. 21 [SIC 6021]
LaSalle National Corp., pp. 23, 382 [SICs 6022, 6712]
LaSalle National Trust N.A., p. 89 [SIC 6091]
LaSalle Partners Inc., pp. 140, 186, 334 [SICs 6163, 6282, 6531]
Laub Group Inc., p. 307 [SIC 6411]
Laurentian Capital Corp., p. 221 [SIC 6321]
Lawyers Title Corp., p. 269 [SIC 6361]
Lawyers Title of Arizona Inc., p. 270 [SIC 6361]
Lawyers Title of North Carolina Inc., p. 270 [SIC 6361]
Lazard Freres and Company L.L.C., p. 153 [SIC 6211]
Leader Federal Bank for Savings, p. 43 [SIC 6035]
Leader Financial Corp., p. 43 [SIC 6035]
Leasing Solutions Receivables Inc., p. 124 [SIC 6153]
Lefrak Organization Inc., pp. 320, 359 [SICs 6513, 6552]
Legg Mason Inc., pp. 152, 185 [SICs 6211, 6282]
Lehman Brothers Holdings Inc., pp. 151, 183, 384 [SICs 6211, 6282, 6719]
Leland O'Brien Rubenstein Associates Inc., p. 188 [SIC 6289]
Lennar Corp., pp. 269, 349 [SICs 6361, 6541]
Leucadia National Corp., pp. 199, 219, 246 [SICs 6311, 6321, 6331]
Lexford Properties Inc., p. 336 [SIC 6531]
Lexington Corporate Properties Inc., p. 442 [SIC 6798]
LFC Holdings Inc., pp. 183, 198 [SICs 6282, 6311]
Liberty Corp., p. 359 [SIC 6552]
Liberty Financial Companies Inc., pp. 151, 183, 198, 384 [SICs 6211, 6282, 6311, 6719]
Liberty Mutual Insurance Co., pp. 219, 245 [SICs 6321, 6331]
Liberty National Life Insurance Co., p. 220 [SIC 6321]
Liberty Property Trust, p. 440 [SIC 6798]
Life Insurance Company of Virginia, p. 199 [SIC 6311]
Life Re Corp., p. 220 [SIC 6321]
Life USA Holding Inc., p. 200 [SIC 6311]
Lifeguard HMO Inc., p. 235 [SIC 6324]
Lincoln Insurance Group Inc., p. 307 [SIC 6411]
Lincoln National Corp., pp. 197, 219, 245, 383 [SICs 6311, 6321, 6331, 6719]
Lincoln National Investment Management Co., p. 185 [SIC 6282]
Lincoln National Life Insurance Co., pp. 183, 197 [SICs 6282, 6311]
Lincoln Property Co., p. 359 [SIC 6552]
Linsco/Private Ledger Corp., p. 187 [SIC 6289]
Lipton Realty Inc., p. 318 [SIC 6512]
Listerhill Employees Credit Union, p. 62 [SIC 6062]
Litchfield Financial Corp., p. 112 [SIC 6141]
Little Caesar Enterprises Inc., p. 428 [SIC 6794]
Litton Loan Servicing Inc., p. 91 [SIC 6099]
LJM Realty Advisors Inc., p. 141 [SIC 6163]
Lloyd Center, p. 320 [SIC 6512]

LMSC Federal Credit Union, p. 57 [SIC 6061]
Loan America Financial Corp., p. 139 [SIC 6162]
Loan Pricing Corp., p. 187 [SIC 6289]
LOC Federal Credit Union, p. 59 [SIC 6061]
Local Federal Bank F.S.B., p. 43 [SIC 6035]
Lockheed Martin Corp., p. 383 [SIC 6719]
Lockton Cos., p. 308 [SIC 6411]
Loews Corp., pp. 197, 245 [SICs 6311, 6331]
Lomas and Nettleton Mortgage Investors, p. 442 [SIC 6798]
Lomas Financial Corp., pp. 123, 139, 360 [SICs 6153, 6162, 6552]
Long and Foster Real Estate Inc., p. 335 [SIC 6531]
Long Island Savings Bank F.S.B., p. 42 [SIC 6035]
Long John Silver's Restaurants Inc., p. 429 [SIC 6794]
Longleaf Partners Fund, p. 394 [SIC 6722]
Los Angeles County Employees' Retirement Association, p. 279 [SIC 6371]
Los Angeles Federal Credit Union, p. 58 [SIC 6061]
Los Angeles Police Federal Credit Union, p. 57 [SIC 6061]
Louisiana Cos., p. 307 [SIC 6411]
Louisiana Health Service and Indemnity Co., p. 235 [SIC 6324]
Lovitt and Touche Inc., p. 307 [SIC 6411]
Lowe Enterprises Inc., pp. 333, 359 [SICs 6531, 6552]
LSI Capital L.L.C., p. 124 [SIC 6153]
LTC Properties Inc., p. 442 [SIC 6798]
Lubar and Co., p. 453 [SIC 6799]
Lumbermens Mutual Casualty Co., p. 247 [SIC 6331]
Lynch Corp., p. 185 [SIC 6282]

M and I Capital Markets Group Inc., p. 454 [SIC 6799]
M and I Marshall and Ilsley Trust Company of Arizona, p. 90 [SIC 6091]
M and T Bank, p. 23 [SIC 6022]
MacDill Federal Credit Union, p. 57 [SIC 6061]
Macerich Co., p. 441 [SIC 6798]
Macerich Partnership L.P., p. 395 [SIC 6726]
Madison Dearborn Partners Inc., p. 454 [SIC 6799]
Madison Square Garden Corp., p. 318 [SIC 6512]
Maestro Latin America Inc., p. 91 [SIC 6099]
MAF Bancorp Inc., p. 43 [SIC 6035]
Magna Bank N.A., p. 25 [SIC 6022]
Magna Group Inc., p. 24 [SIC 6022]
Mahoney Group, pp. 259, 335 [SICs 6351, 6531]
MAIC Holdings Inc., p. 257 [SIC 6351]
MainStreet BankGroup Inc., pp. 21, 23, 382 [SICs 6021, 6022, 6712]
Malan Realty Investors Inc., p. 443 [SIC 6798]
Managers Funds L.P., p. 394 [SIC 6722]
Manhattan Mortgage Co., p. 141 [SIC 6163]
Manpower Inc, pp. 386, 428 [SICs 6719, 6794]
Manufacturers Alliance Insurance Co., p. 258 [SIC 6351]
Margaretten and Company Inc., p. 138 [SIC 6162]
Margaretten Financial Corp., p. 138 [SIC 6162]
Marine Midland Bank N.A., p. 20 [SIC 6021]

Company Index

OCCUPATION INDEX

This index lists those occupations in the Finance, Insurance, and Real Estate sector that account for 1 percent or more of employment. This limitation excludes many occupations employed in the sector in small numbers. All told, 68 employment groups are shown, translating into 130 specific occupations or their alphabetical rotation. After the name of each occupation, a value in parentheses shows the number of 3-digit manufacturing industry groups in which the occupation occurs. One or more page numbers follow. After the page numbers, the 3-digit SICs are shown inside brackets. *Please note:* page and SIC references are sorted so that they point to industry groups with descending employment (the first page reference is to the largest employing industry group). Only the top ten industry groups are referenced.

[SIC 641, 633, 631, 632, 635, 636, 637, 639]

Clerks, legal, nec (6) 253, 265, 275, 291, 345, 355 [SIC 635, 636, 637, 639, 654, 655]

Clerks, mail (1) 215 [SIC 632]

Clerks, office (30) 15, 37, 53, 301, 193, 329, 241, 313, 215, 133 [SIC 602, 603, 606, 641, 631, 653, 633, 651, 632, 616]

Clerks, real estate (1) 329 [SIC 653]

Clerks, statement (3) 15, 37, 53 [SIC 602, 603, 606]

Computer operators, ex peripheral equipment (6) 215, 5, 75, 85, 169, 179 [SIC 632, 601, 608, 609, 623, 628]

Computer programmers (20) 193, 241, 215, 147, 159, 169, 179, 5, 75, 85 [SIC 631, 633, 632, 621, 622, 623, 628, 601, 608, 609]

Correspondence clerks (3) 215, 97, 119 [SIC 632, 611, 615]

Credit analysts (7) 133, 97, 119, 107, 5, 75, 85 [SIC 616, 611, 615, 614, 601, 608, 609]

Credit checkers (2) 97, 119 [SIC 611, 615]

Data entry keyers, except composing (13) 215, 241, 169, 179, 5, 75, 85, 97, 119, 253 [SIC 632, 633, 623, 628, 601, 608, 609, 611, 615, 635]

Duplicating, mail, office machine operators (6) 15, 37, 53, 5, 75, 85 [SIC 602, 603, 606, 601, 608, 609]

Examiners, claim (7) 241, 215, 193, 253, 265, 275, 291 [SIC 633, 632, 631, 635, 636, 637, 639]

Examiners, title (6) 253, 265, 275, 291, 345, 355 [SIC 635, 636, 637, 639, 654, 655]

Executives (30) 15, 37, 53, 301, 329, 376, 390, 400, 416, 313 [SIC 602, 603, 606, 641, 653, 671, 672, 673, 679, 651]

Farming, forestry, agriculture supervisors (2) 345, 355 [SIC 654, 655]

File clerks (8) 301, 241, 193, 215, 253, 265, 275, 291 [SIC 641, 633, 631, 632, 635, 636, 637, 639]

Financial managers (27) 15, 37, 53, 107, 329, 376, 390, 400, 416, 301 [SIC 602, 603, 606, 614, 653, 671, 672, 673, 679, 641]

Financial sales workers (18) 147, 159, 15, 37, 53, 169, 179, 376, 390, 400 [SIC 621, 622, 602, 603, 606, 623, 628, 671, 672, 673]

Food preparation workers nec (3) 313, 345, 355 [SIC 651, 654, 655]

Forestry supervisors (2) 345, 355 [SIC 654, 655]

Gardeners, nursery workers (4) 313, 345, 355, 329 [SIC 651, 654, 655, 653]

General managers & top executives (30) 15, 37, 53, 301, 329, 376, 390, 400, 416, 313 [SIC 602, 603, 606, 641, 653, 671, 672, 673, 679, 651]

General office clerks (30) 15, 37, 53, 301, 193, 329, 241, 313, 215, 133 [SIC 602, 603, 606, 641, 631, 653, 633, 651, 632, 616]

Guards (7) 313, 329, 345, 355, 5, 75, 85 [SIC 651, 653, 654, 655, 601, 608, 609]

Health professionals/paraprofessionals nec (1) 215 [SIC 632]

Information clerks (21) 329, 301, 313, 133, 147, 159, 215, 345, 355, 376 [SIC 653, 641, 651, 616, 621, 622, 632, 654, 655, 671]

Insurance adjusters, examiners, investigators (8) 241, 301, 215, 193, 253, 265, 275, 291 [SIC 633, 641, 632, 631, 635, 636, 637, 639]

Insurance claims clerks (8) 215, 193, 241, 301, 253, 265, 275, 291 [SIC 632, 631, 633, 641, 635, 636, 637, 639]

Insurance policy processing clerks (8) 301, 241, 193, 215, 253, 265, 275, 291 [SIC 641, 633, 631, 632, 635, 636, 637, 639]

Insurance sales workers (8) 301, 193, 241, 215, 253, 265, 275, 291 [SIC 641, 631, 633, 632, 635, 636, 637, 639]

Interviewers, loan (1) 133 [SIC 616]

Investigators nec (1) 241 [SIC 633]

Investigators, insurance (8) 241, 301, 215, 193, 253, 265, 275, 291 [SIC 633, 641, 632, 631, 635, 636, 637, 639]

Janitors & cleaners, maids (8) 313, 329, 345, 355, 376, 390, 400, 416 [SIC 651, 653, 654, 655, 671, 672, 673, 679]

Keyers (13) 215, 241, 169, 179, 5, 75, 85, 97, 119, 253 [SIC 632, 633, 623, 628, 601, 608, 609, 611, 615, 635]

Labor relations specialists (4) 376, 390, 400, 416 [SIC 671, 672, 673, 679]

Lawyers (5) 241, 376, 390, 400, 416 [SIC 633, 671, 672, 673, 679]

Legal assistants & clerks nec (6) 253, 265, 275, 291, 345, 355 [SIC 635, 636, 637, 639, 654, 655]

Loan & credit clerks (14) 15, 37, 53, 133, 107, 97, 119, 253, 265, 275 [SIC 602, 603, 606, 616, 614, 611, 615, 635, 636, 637]

Loan interviewers (1) 133 [SIC 616]

Loan officers & counselors (10) 15, 37, 53, 133, 107, 97, 119, 5, 75, 85 [SIC 602, 603, 606, 616, 614, 611, 615, 601, 608, 609]

Maids (8) 313, 329, 345, 355, 376, 390, 400, 416 [SIC 651, 653, 654, 655, 671, 672, 673, 679]

Mail clerks (1) 215 [SIC 632]

Mailing machine operators (6) 15, 37, 53, 5, 75, 85 [SIC 602, 603, 606, 601, 608, 609]

Maintenance repairers, general utility (8) 313, 329, 345, 355, 376, 390, 400, 416 [SIC 651, 653, 654, 655, 671, 672, 673, 679]

Management support workers nec (20) 147, 159, 193, 169, 179, 241, 301, 376, 390, 400 [SIC 621, 622, 631, 623, 628, 633, 641, 671, 672, 673]

Managers & administrators nec (21) 15, 37, 53, 193, 241, 215, 376, 390, 400, 416 [SIC 602, 603, 606, 631, 633, 632, 671, 672, 673, 679]

Occupation Index